HEAD
SCHOOL

C000010730

'EXCELLENT' IN ALL CATEGORIES, ISI INSPECTION, MAY 2015

Successful day and boarding school for girls aged 3-18 set in 23 acres in the heart of Oxford

- Dance and Fitness Centre new for 2015
- 240-seat Theatre, Music School and Art School
- All weather sports pitches and swimming pool
- New Library and class room suite for 2016

Termly Open Days and Meet the Head events

www.headington.org/admissions

Headington School is a leading educational charity.
Registered Charity No. 309678 (1942)

 gsa

THE GOOD SCHOOLS GUIDE

Boarding Schools

"If everyone is thinking alike, then no one is thinking."
Benjamin Franklin

At Frensham Heights, we are proud to think differently. We know every child is an individual and we treat them as such. That's why you'll continue to find Old Frenshamians leading in everything from medicine to opera and from the boardroom to the stage.

Come and see for yourself what makes Frensham so successfully individual. Visit www.frensham.org or call 01252 792561 to order a prospectus or arrange a visit.

Frensham Heights | Think, Create, Explore

Frensham Heights, Rowledge, Farnham, Surrey GU10 4EA Tel. 01252 792561 Charity No. 312052

First Edition published 2016 by Lucas Publishing Ltd
Good Schools Guide, 10 Greycoat Place, London SW1P 1SB
www.goodschoolsguide.co.uk
ISBN 978-1-909963-07-8
Copyright © 2016, Lucas Publications Ltd
Printed by Cambrian Printers Ltd

A CIP catalogue record for this book is available from the British Library.
Every care has been taken to ensure that all information was correct at the time of going to press.
The publishers accept no responsibility for any error in detail, inaccuracy or judgement whatsoever.

Acknowledgments

Writers

Alison Cooper
Anna Colclough
Anne Hadley
Anne Prendergast
Ashley Cavers
Bernadette John
Beth Noakes
Carolyn Murphy
Carolyn Thomas
Catriona Prest
Charles Cowling
Charlotte Obolensky
Charlotte Phillips
Charlotte Simpson
Christine Jefferson
Claire Kingston
Deirdre Shields

Denise Roberts
Elizabeth Moody-Stuart
Emma Lee-Potter
Faye Monserrat
Godfrey Bishop
Jackie Lixenberg
Janet Breeze
Janette Wallis
Janita Clamp
Judith French
Juliet Austin
Kalantha Brewis
Kate Hilpern
Linda Tanner
Lisa Freedman
Lucy Heywood
Mary Bremner

Mary Langford
Mary Pegler
Melanie Bloxham
Melanie Sanderson
Nicky Adams
Patrea More Nisbett
Ralph Lucas
Richard Field
Rosemary Taylor
Sarah Evans
Sandra Hutchinson
Sophie Irwin
Stewart Binns
Sue Fieldman
Susan Hamlyn
Suzanne Everest

Design: David Preston, Harriet Plyler

Typesetting: Theresa Hare, Optima Information Design

Editorial review by Beth Noakes and team: Janita Clamp, Emma Lee-Potter,
Charlotte Phillips, Kathryn Berger and Amanda Perkins

Advertising sales: Charlotte Hollingshead, also Jo Dodds, Publishing Matters

Web manager: Anthony Back

Project management: Katja Lips

Everything held together by: Shari Lord

Photography: Thanks to all the schools who supplied photographs.

Cover photos: Prior Park College, Bedford Preparatory School, Dean Close
School, Harrow School, Queen Mary's School, Sherborne School,
Radley College, Sherborne Preparatory School.

BEDFORD
SCHOOL
HIS FUTURE'S
BRIGHTER
AT BEDFORD
FULL & WEEKLY BOARDING
AND DAY FOR BOYS AGED 7-18
GENEROUS NEW SCHOLARSHIPS
AVAILABLE AT BOTH 13+ & 16+
A-LEVEL & IB
(INTERNATIONAL BACCALAUREATE)
AT SIXTH FORM
TO FIND OUT MORE, PLEASE CONTACT OUR ADMISSIONS TEAM ON 01234 362216
OR VISIT bedfordschool.org.uk/scholarships
Bedford School is part
of The Harpur Trust

Contents

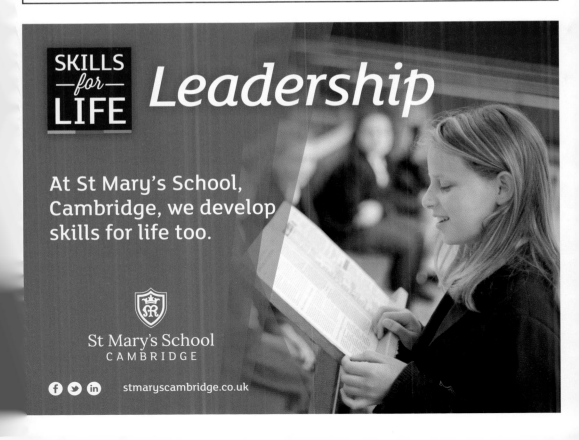

THE Oratory SCHOOL

Boys' Independent Catholic
Day & Boarding School (11-18 years).

EXCELLENCE IN ALL WE DO

OPEN MORNINGS TWICE YEARLY – MARCH AND SEPTEMBER

How to use this book

The colour of the title bar denotes a school's age range:

Junior School

Senior School

Key to symbols:

 Girls' school

 Boys' school

 Co-ed school

 Boys' school with co-ed sixth form

 Girls' school with co-ed sixth form

 Co-ed pre-prep, then boys only

 Co-ed pre-prep, then girls only

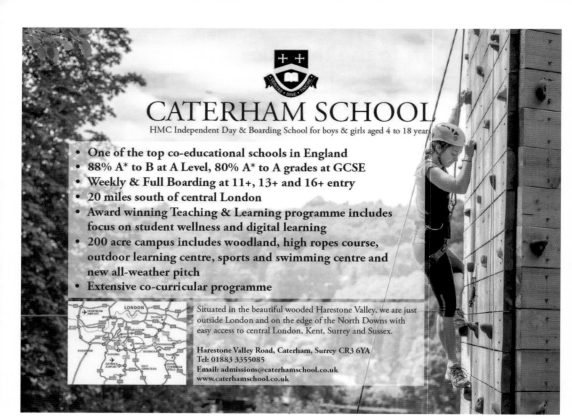
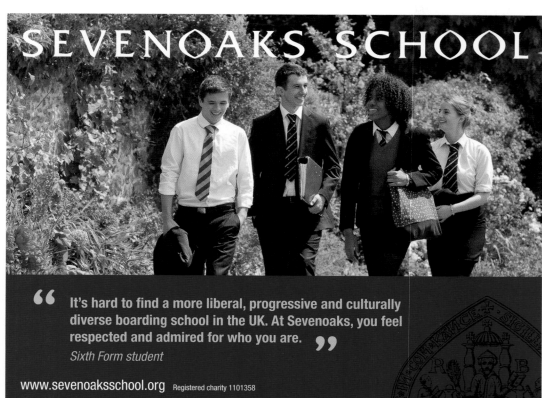

SOUTH WEST 75

City of Bristol
Cornwall
Devon
Dorset
Gloucestershire
Somerset
Wiltshire

HOME COUNTIES WEST 301

Berkshire
Buckinghamshire
Hampshire
Isle of Wight
Oxfordshire

LONDON AND SOUTH EAST 513

City of London
East Sussex
Greater London
Kent
Surrey
West Sussex

EAST OF ENGLAND 795

Bedfordshire
Cambridgeshire
Essex
Hertfordshire
Norfolk
Suffolk

MIDLANDS AND WALES 917

Derbyshire
Herefordshire
Leicestershire
Lincolnshire
Northamptonshire
Nottinghamshire
Rutland
Shropshire
Staffordshire
Warwickshire
West Midlands
Worcestershire
WALES

NORTHERN ENGLAND AND SCOTLAND 1037

Cheshire
Cumbria
Durham
East Riding of Yorkshire
Greater Manchester
Lancashire
Merseyside
North Yorkshire
Northumberland
South Yorkshire
Tyne and Wear
West Yorkshire
SCOTLAND

STATE BOARDING SCHOOLS 1165

UK-wide state boarding schools

Boarding school overview map

For UK-wide map of state boarding schools see p.1165

NORTHERN
ENGLAND AND
SCOTLAND
1037

MIDLANDS AND WALES
917

EAST OF
ENGLAND
795

HOME
COUNTIES
WEST
301

LONDON AND
SOUTH EAST
513

SOUTH WEST
75

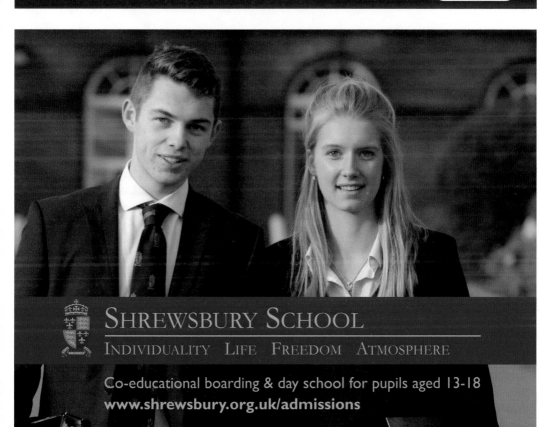

GSG Charter

No school can pay to be included in (or choose to be excluded from) The Good Schools Guide, and we do not charge schools for reviews.

In recent years we have helped to defray our costs by selling advertising space and licensing schools to reprint their own reviews for a fee. We make these offers only to schools that are already in the Guide on merit. Whether or not they choose to advertise has no bearing on their inclusion in the guide nor on the content of their review. Schools we have not chosen for inclusion in the Guide are not allowed to advertise.

The Good Schools Guide Advice Service is a fee paying, personal consultancy service for parents. The Guide and our website also offer other advice on a vast range of education matters, free to subscribers. We receive no commission or any other payment from any school for these services. We provide information on tutor companies on our website, and may charge these companies for carrying out a review, but they are only included after careful vetting.

We take our independence very seriously and the separation of commercial and editorial content is absolute. If you have any questions or concerns about our commercial policy, please write in the first instance to editor@ goodschoolsguide.co.uk.

Why boarding?

Why indeed. It's fair to say that no other educational topic inspires such vehement and polarised opinions. But while the clichés of Dickensian cruelty remain deadlocked against St Trinian's and Hogwarts in the court of public opinion, a quiet revolution has taken place. Boarding schools have changed beyond measure in the last 30 years, not least because all schools, and society, have done so too. Traditional full boarding schools remain, albeit in much reduced number, but for many children today 'boarding' just means staying at school a couple of nights a week.

Boarding school heads tell us that the boarding family profile is much more varied than it used to be. These days it's likely that both parents are working – sometimes abroad or a long commute away. While boarding is still a tradition in some families, others come to it for the first time for a variety of reasons. Maybe your child has a particular aptitude – some boarding schools have the facilities and specialist staff on hand to develop sporting or musical talents. Families with several children may opt for flexi or weekly boarding because it's preferable to hours in the car on multiple school runs. Sixth form boarding is particularly popular and a great preparation for university – although some may find university accommodation less salubrious than their school's. In other circumstances a small, nurturing boarding school can provide stability and a haven for a child with an unhappy home life.

Forces personnel posted abroad have always been a core group for whom boarding schools are essential. The allowances have become considerably less generous in the last few years but many state and independent boarding schools give priority and some financial assistance to children from these families.

One thing that hasn't changed for the better is the cost of sending a child to boarding school, now running at £30,000+ a year. This hasn't discouraged applications from

CASTERTON
SEDBERGH PREPARATORY
SCHOOL

CO-EDUCATIONAL

NURSERY - 13

Boarding at Sedbergh Prep.
More than you ever thought possible...

'Top 10 Best Value Prep School in the UK'

THE TELEGRAPH

www.sedberghprep.org | t: 015242 79200 | facebook.com/SedberghPrep | twitter.com/Sedbergh_Prep

wealthy international families but there are real concerns that the middle class British parents, who for years have just managed to afford private education by scrimping, saving and remortgaging, are being priced out of the market. Places at state boarding schools where parents only pay for the boarding element (usually around £12,000 a year) and tuition is free, are consequently more sought after than ever.

A few years ago, possibly as a result of the economic downturn, the boarding demographic in some schools was not well managed. While this may have secured short-term benefits, bursars quickly realised that parents – whether they come from Beijing or Bognor – want their children to be part of a diverse and well-integrated boarding community. Today you will find that schools take great care to ensure that this is the case.

Boarding, twenty-first century style, is flourishing. The number of families choosing boarding schools for their children is increasing and the decision to board is, as often as not, made by children themselves. This book, our first dedicated to boarding schools, contains over 300 of the Good Schools Guide's highly informative and famously frank reviews. Every single school has been visited by our writers, who check out everything from dorms to food and weekend activities. We also speak to parents and, most important of all, pupils.

Whether you're interested in big names, local treasures, state boarding schools or country preps where your daughter can board along with her pony, this book is your unbiased guide to all that's best in British boarding.

Full, weekly or flexi boarding?

If you're reading this you've probably already decided that boarding might suit your son or daughter. If so the next step is to consider the arrangement that best suits your family. Unlike the old days, when youngsters were packed off to school at the age of 7 or 8 and didn't see home again until the end of term, today's boarding schools offer parents a choice of full boarding, weekly boarding, flexi boarding or even a combination of these. For instance, flexi boarders may wish to weekly board during exam times or become full boarders in the sixth form.

Whichever option you choose, there's no doubt that boarding schools are more skilled than ever at helping their charges settle in and feel at home. They may run taster weekends, get new pupils to start before the rest of the school arrives and appoint buddies and mentors to guide them through the first few weeks and beyond. Pupils are encouraged to keep in regular touch with their parents – and it's not just a handwritten letter hastily scribbled before church on Sunday mornings either. Children can email, Skype and – if mobile phones are allowed – text or phone home when they wish.

Full boarding

Full boarding schools are in the minority these days, but if you're looking for a school where everyone boards and there isn't a mass exodus at weekends, you still have quite a few options.

Boys' full boarding schools

These include many of the most famous names in British education such as Eton, Winchester, Radley and Harrow. Historically, boys from the English upper classes were sent here to be educated as future leaders, public servants, clergymen and military commanders. Today, boys from many different backgrounds compete for places from all over the world. Nor do you necessarily have to come from a wealthy family. The former head of Eton, Anthony Little, believes schools like Eton should be 'needs blind'. He told the Good Schools Guide in 2013, 'We do not want to be a finishing school for the titled and rich.' Noble sentiments that schools such as his are trying to live up to with scholarships and 100 per cent bursaries.

At these schools all pupils (all boys) board and may go home only for exeats, usually two per term, Saturday pm to Sunday pm. However, parents are more involved with school life than formerly; those who live close enough attend matches, concerts and plays.

Schools may run taster weekends or get new pupils to start before the rest of the school arrives

Technology enables contact over long distances too, although boys whose families live abroad must still have guardians, either relatives or else professional guardians (see page 53) to act in loco parentis.

Boys at these senior schools may well have attended full boarding boys' preps such as Cothill House and Horris Hill, or preps where boarding is compulsory for all in the last two years (7 and 8) such as Caldicott and Papplewick.

'I know that full boarding numbers across the country are declining, but I am certain that there will always be a place for schools like Cothill,' says headmaster Duncan Bailey. 'On summer evenings, when the boys are running around in the sunshine, surrounded by their friends, or building camps on the edge of the woods, there are few better places for any active boy to be – whatever their age.'

Girls' full boarding schools

Benenden and Heathfield are among the very few exclusively full boarding schools for girls. Downe House, Wycombe Abbey, Sherborne Girls and Tudor Hall are essentially full boarding (no flexi/weekly) but also take a few local day pupils. Hanford School in Dorset is one of a tiny handful of girls only boarding preps.

The best known girls' boarding schools such as Roedean, Badminton and The Cheltenham Ladies' College were established in the mid- to late-19th century by formidable pioneers of women's education. This makes them relative newcomers compared to the likes of Winchester College, believed to be Britain's oldest school, which was founded in 1382. It also explains why most girls' schools lack the extensive property portfolios and endowments enjoyed by their brothers.

Co-ed full boarding schools

If you want your sons and daughters to attend a full boarding school together there are quite a few co-ed choices including Ampleforth, Milton Abbey, Uppingham and Marlborough College. Because of its proximity to London, Wellington College is de facto weekly boarding since so many pupils go home for Saturday night, nevertheless all boarders must spend two Saturday nights in school per term. All these schools take a small number of day pupils but don't offer weekly or flexi boarding options. Girls and boys live in separate boarding accommodation with clear rules about what is out of bounds to visitors of the opposite sex.

Some schools have co-ed sixth form boarding houses, but appropriate boundaries are in place. See 'Sex and drugs and homesickness', page 32 for more information on this.

Weekly boarding

Weekly boarding is growing in popularity, particularly for children who live too far away to be day pupils or whose parents work long hours and/or frequently travel abroad. Weekly boarders either go home on Friday evenings or Saturday afternoons and return to school on Sunday evenings or Monday mornings. For many children, this offers the best of both worlds: they can enjoy school during the week, work hard and spend lots of time with their friends, then relax at home with their parents on Saturdays and Sundays.

Parents are keen on weekly boarding too. They like the fact that they don't have to nag about homework or getting up on time in the morning and feel that home time is 'quality time.' Many opt for boarding schools within an hour's drive so they can still turn up for sports matches, concerts and drama productions during the term. The mother of a year 7 boarder who drops her son off at Sexey's School (a state boarding school in Somerset) on Monday mornings and picks him up on Friday afternoons says her family gets 'the best of both worlds,' adding that with no Saturday school 'we get a proper family weekend.'

Flexi boarding

Flexi boarding gets a mixed press; parents are generally in favour but for some schools it's a step too far. One prep headmaster describes it as 'a bit of a nightmare, like glorified hotel management.' Unlike full and weekly boarding, one school's definition of 'flexi' may not be the same as another's. It's certainly never going to be bed and breakfast at the drop of a hat. Most schools require parents to book boarding nights at the beginning of each term, with Thursdays and Fridays being the most popular. Not surprising if it means parents can enjoy a night out without having to find a babysitter (and not have to get up for the Saturday morning school run).

While it can be complicated for schools to manage, flexi boarding could be just the ticket if your child has to stay at school late for sport, music or drama one or two nights a week, or if you want to dip a toe in the water and see if boarding suits your family. Schools that offer flexi boarding will inevitably have some spare beds and many tell us that they will always do their best to accommodate a pupil at short notice if there's a family emergency.

At Monkton we look
at schooling differently.
Come and see us and
find out how.

Open Mornings 2016
Saturday 5 March
Saturday 7 May
Saturday 8 October

What will *your* day at *Monkton* be like?

MONKTON

monktoncombeschool.com
01225 721133

Day and Boarding School. 2 to 18

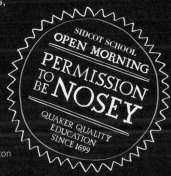

State boarding schools

If you think your child would benefit from a boarding school education but are put off by the high fees and consequent limited social mix of a typical independent boarding school, you may find that a state boarding school is the answer. These have seen a surge of popularity in recent years, partly due to increasing numbers of families with both parents working long hours. 'We all work hard during the week, and get together at weekends,' said one father. 'It's much less stressful than trying to oversee homework and music practice after a long day at work and travelling, and my daughter is happy to spend week nights at school with her friends.' Those schools offering full boarding are popular with families working abroad, in the Forces, the diplomatic service or with international companies.

'It's much less stressful than trying to oversee homework and music practice after a long day at work and travelling'

What do they cost?

State boarding schools are comparatively cheap – mostly somewhere between £10,000-£14,000 a year in boarding fees – because the government foots the bill for tuition. The majority of pupils in most state boarding schools are day pupils, but many stay for after-school activities alongside the boarders – 'a boarding experience minus the bed,' as one school put it. Some of the schools, such as Gordon's in Surrey, levy a compulsory 'day boarding' fee of several thousand pounds to all day pupils to cover after-school activities (though bursaries are available for low income families). Others, such as Hockerill Anglo-European, have free day places for normal school hours attendance, but charge a day boarding fee to those who wish to arrive for breakfast and stay for activities, supper and homework.

The
Good Schools Guide International

Who can apply?

As with other state schools, these are open to British citizens, EU passport holders and anyone with a right of residence in the UK. Some are academically selective, some are single sex, and they are permitted to interview pupils (which other state schools are not) in order to ensure they are suitable candidates for boarding.

How many are there?

There are 38 in England, including one in the Scilly Isles, plus one each in Wales and Scotland – the latter for children from Forces families – with a total of some 5000+ places. Some offer full boarding, others only weekly boarding, some have boarding for sixth formers only and one is a specialist sixth form college run by the Ministry of Defence.

What to consider

As with any other school, read prospectuses, school magazines and newsletters, inspection reports and reviews such as those in this book. We review about half of British state boarding schools, and have extensive data for all of them on our website.

Distance

How far are you prepared to travel for concerts, parents' evenings, matches and weekend pick ups? Many seasoned boarding school parents caution against choosing a school more than about 90 minutes away.

Activities

What happens after school and at weekends? Do activities accord with your child's interests and abilities, whether in sport, music, art or drama? The Games, options, the arts section of our reviews will give a flavour of what goes on.

Here are some extracts:

'The John Muir award for conservation is undertaken by everyone; beyond that the surrounding mountains and lakes create a whole realm of opportunities to get seriously wet and/or muddy with canoeing, raft-building, orienteering, sailing, rock-climbing, fell-running, horse-riding, mountain biking and skiing all on offer.' Extract from the GSG review of Keswick School.

'Sporting whizzes will be right at home here. The head reels off a long list of current and former pupils who are competing at the highest levels. 'We're very good at tennis, we've got the under-14 number two in the country. We've allowed him to reduce his timetable and take time off school. One girl is representing the country in the under-19 MCC ladies' cricket team. Two girls represent England in the ISF World Cross Country Under-18 championship'....' Extract from the GSG review of Sir Roger Manwood's School.

Numbers

How many boarders are there of your child's age? And how many regularly stay in school at weekends? If you are considering full boarding, it's vital that your child doesn't spend weekends rattling around with few friends or activities.

On your visit

Draw up a shortlist and arrange visits. Don't expect state boarding schools to have the extensive grounds and expensive facilities of many independent schools – though some do. A bit of tattiness won't matter, but if you sense neglect, beware. Don't assume single en suite rooms are essential: many younger children in particular like the camaraderie of dormitories. Most important is the atmosphere. Could you imagine your child living here? Does it feel friendly? Are pupils happy and enthusiastic? And most of all – is your child keen to join? The 'Background and atmosphere' and 'Pastoral care, well-being and discipline' sections of our reviews will give a flavour of what goes on. Here are some extracts:

'Parents say it is warm and friendly and has the intimate feel of a small school. Pupils spontaneously want to share not only personal news but also what they have been reading or hearing. There is an informality about the relationships and a sense of mutual respect.' Extract from the GSG review of Adams' Grammar School in Shropshire.

'Not just a place to be – a place where you grow up,' said one remarkably mature young man. Strong sense of mutual respect between teachers and pupils: 'Teachers give a lot. We want the knowledge and they help us to learn'. Extract from the GSG review of Hockerill Anglo-European College.

For reviews of state boarding schools please see page 1165.

What age to start boarding?

Most children start boarding at the age of 11 or 13. At this age children themselves tend to have a say in the matter. Indeed, Good Schools Guide writers report that children often ask their parents to let them board – rather than the other way round. Some prep schools admit boarders under 10 and make special provision for them with bedrooms that look much closer to how things are at home (rather than dorms) and, because numbers will be small, an evening regime that is flexible. At Horris Hill, for example, where they have a few boarders under the age of 10, 'if it's hot they can have a swim, if everyone's exhausted they go to bed early.'

The sixth form is another entry point for first time boarders. We visit many schools where there are more boarders in the sixth form than lower down the school – largely because 16 to 18-year-olds are keen to concentrate on their studies, socialise with friends and get a taste of living away from home prior to university. Sixth form boarders will generally have their own study bedrooms in separate accommodation with well-equipped kitchens (Ocado will deliver to boarding schools!), washing machines, even yoga studios. At Westonbirt school where over three quarters of sixth formers board, one girl told us, 'there aren't so many distractions, it helps us stay focused on our studies.'

Groups of sixth formers take turns to stay for five days in the school flat in the nearby village

Today's boarding schools pride themselves on helping students become more independent before university. At Heathfield, an all-girls' boarding school in Ascot, Berkshire, girls in the upper sixth live in their own bungalow on site while Burford School, a co-ed state boarding school in Oxfordshire, has created a flat within the boarding house for a group of sixth form girls – to get them ready for the university years. At Rendcomb College in Gloucestershire groups of sixth formers take turns to stay for five days in the school flat in the nearby village. They are given housekeeping money and (apart from lunch at school) must manage this and the chores. Apparently sometimes it runs like clockwork, sometimes 'mummies deliver food parcels and help clean up at the end.'

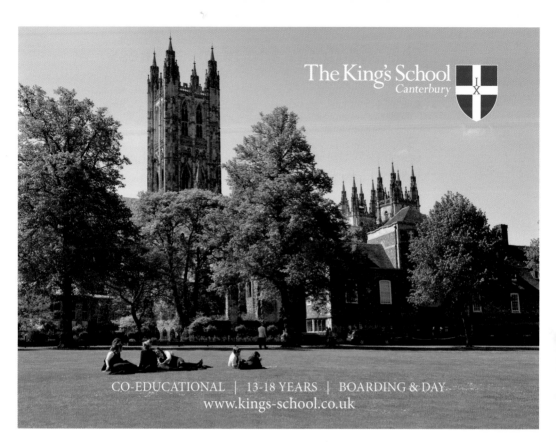

Sex and drugs and homesickness

Given that the majority of boarding school pupils are aged from 13 upwards, some parents might think school fees a price worth paying for letting trained professionals steer their hormonal offspring over the turbulent waters of adolescence. Even so, we all know that risk taking, underage drinking, drugs, sex, self-harm, anorexia and the other ills that teenage flesh is heir to, can occur right under parents' noses. What then should you expect boarding schools to do to keep young people safe?

Not that long ago the term 'pastoral care' was rarely heard. These days it's up there with academic results as a key measure of any school's success and as closely monitored as exam performance. In addition to the normal school inspection visits (Ofsted for state schools, ISI for independent schools), government inspectors visit all boarding schools to check every aspect of provision from fire escapes to mattresses and they also talk to staff, pupils and

Families are encouraged to look round several, if not all, boarding houses and apply in order of preference

parents. All schools should have a link to the latest boarding inspection report (and their response to any issues raised) on their website. But knowing the number of locks on a dormitory window won't tell you if someone will notice your child staring miserably out of it.

All schools provide copious information on how they ensure pupils' safety (usually termed 'safeguarding') and well-being (if they don't, make your excuses and leave). It's up to you to attend the open days, go to the talks, read the literature and then weigh up whether the regime will suit your child. See page 1252 for more details about child protection.

Houseparents

Houseparents, as the name suggests, will be most closely involved in your child's day to day life at school. Houseparents are your first point of contact and you should feel able to ask them anything and expect to get prompt answers to your questions. This is a highly professional and responsible job and to a great extent your child's happiness will depend on their (and your) relationship with these people.

Many, but not all, houseparents are married couples, often with children – and pets – of their own. One (or very often both), is likely to teach at the school. They live in the boarding house along with several other adults such as 'gappies' (young people, often from Australia or S Africa), matrons and/or tutors. The nomenclature and precise arrangement will depend on the school and the number/age of boarders, but there's generally at least one resident adult per corridor/floor in addition to houseparents.

Most schools have 'vertical' (mixed age) boarding 13 – 16, with sixth formers accommodated separately; they may also keep year 7 and 8 boarders in a separate house. Some smaller schools have 'horizontal' (year group) boarding houses. In either case, there will be separate bed times, rules etc that are appropriate to the age of the children.

What house?

Parents often ask us how to get their child into a particular house – maybe they've heard on the grapevine that 'x' is the 'sporty' house or 'y' is the 'best' house. While it's true that the character of the houseparents or housemaster/mistress is inevitably going to have an influence, schools tell us that they work hard to ensure every house has a good mix of types. It's also worth bearing in mind that during your child's years at the school house staff may leave, so it's best not to pin all your hopes on someone you happen to particularly like. Families are encouraged to look round several, if not all, boarding houses and apply in order of preference – but school has the final say.

House or home?

While people are always more important to the ethos of a school than buildings, architecture will also influence your decision. Girls at Westonbirt School sleep under the high ceilings of grade 1 listed state rooms and our reviewer found 'Priceless silk wallpaper, preserved under Perspex, rubbing shoulders with One Direction posters.' Boarders at Cheltenham College live in elegant town houses – one advantage of this is that it puts a little distance between school and 'home'. Modern, purpose built boarding houses, while less characterful, are likely to have better plumbing. All in all, boarding accommodation seems to be improving year on year, no doubt keeping local building trades very busy over the summer holidays.

Wonderful cooked breakfasts, delicious vegetarian options, in-house coffee shops and locally grown produce are almost standard

Pupils with physical disabilities

Historic buildings rarely make for easy disabled access and if your child needs special arrangements you must discuss these with the school well in advance. This won't just apply to boarding houses; classrooms may be up several flights of stairs and there can often be a fair way to walk between lessons. That being said, we know of many schools who have done all they can to accommodate pupils in wheelchairs or with visual or hearing impairments.

Food glorious food

You will be relieved to hear that our reviewers, who always try and eat lunch in the schools they visit, have never been faced with the grim fare endured by the likes of Oliver Twist and Jane Eyre. Nor we hope will today's boarders find themselves afflicted in adult life with 'boarding school eating'. This not entirely polite style of consumption, which stems from parsimonious portion control at schools in the 1960s and 70s, is characterised by rapid scoffing of everything in sight before someone else snaffles it.

Wonderful cooked breakfasts, delicious vegetarian options, salad bars, in-house coffee shops and locally grown produce are almost standard these days. Most schools have a central dining hall, but at some, like Malvern College, boarders eat all meals in their houses. This may be a practical arrangement if houses are a little distance from the main school building, but it also has a beneficial influence on table manners as well as making it easier for staff to spot a child who isn't eating. Boarders will also have access to house kitchens with toasters, microwaves etc and fresh fruit is always available. Nor have tuck boxes been consigned to history; full boarders still use them to keep favourite treats under lock and key.

At Tudor Hall School sixth formers told us they like to buy bacon and eggs from the nearby farm shop and make their own breakfasts at the weekend. Boarders at town schools will find that the local takeaways are more than happy to deliver; this is particularly popular with boarders from overseas who might fancy an (albeit Anglicised) taste of home.

Playing by the rules

Googling a school may lead you to press reports about historic sexual abuse, expulsions for drug use and other stories guaranteed to make a parent's blood run cold. The measure of a school is not so much that these things happened (they do, though thankfully very infrequently) but how such serious and unfortunate incidents are handled. If a school declares, for instance, that possession of drugs will lead to immediate expulsion but fails to expel those who break this rule, you should make your own judgement. (Some schools will allow pupils to return to sit public exams.)

Remember, too, that although occurrences like this are surprisingly rare, just because a school has a squeaky clean record is no guarantee that something won't happen in the future. You will have to take much on trust, just as the school will trust your child not to break the rules.

Even in the sixth form it's unlikely that your son or daughter will enjoy the freedoms they have at home. Parents and children will be expected to agree to and abide by the school's policies on everything from uniform, energy drinks and alcohol to PDAs (public displays of affection – kissing, holding hands etc) and random drugs testing. These policies (all of which will be on the school's website) have been drawn up to ensure the whole boarding community is safe.

Some schools allow 18 year olds to visit 'approved' pubs or restaurants in the nearest town, but such freedoms are a privilege instantly rescinded if abused. Others – perhaps in more rural areas – have a sixth form bar where alcohol is dispensed under supervision and always with parents' consent. At some full boarding schools older pupils may apply for permission to host parties in designated areas. What happens under the radar is, inevitably, another matter – as it often is at home.

Parents should feel able to raise questions and discuss concerns on any matter with the school

Relationships between pupils at boarding schools are a concern for parents and, we imagine, a chronic headache for staff – especially at co-ed full boarding establishments. At most schools 'intimate or explicit sexual relations' are classed as 'misconduct' that can lead to suspension or expulsion. Some schools ban any public display of affection; some don't. However, as with drink and drugs, banning sex doesn't mean it won't happen. Parents of girls in particular may want to get a feeling for the state of gender relations in the school. Is there any suggestion that girls are second class citizens while (say) rugby captains are gods?

Rules about what happens on school premises are fair enough, but it's a much greyer area when full boarders attend private parties at, for instance, a day pupil's house. Parental permission must be obtained to attend this kind of event, but responsibility for policing pupils' behaviour under these circumstances cannot be the school's.

You should feel able to raise questions and discuss concerns about this or any other matter with the school. Talking to parents with older children at the school is also a good idea if you want to see what kind of 'intimate relationship' there is between reality and policy. The 'Pastoral care, well-being and discipline' section of our reviews will cover some of these issues.

If your own domestic regime is more Liberty Hall than Dotheboys Hall you will need to discuss potential schools' disciplinary policies with your child and be realistic if you think the worlds are too far apart.

Homesickness

Homesickness is almost always a short-term problem that the school, the parents and the child can weather by working together. It's not a universal affliction, but many children away from home and family for the first time are likely to have a bout. Schools manage this by keeping their charges busy, busy, busy during the first few weeks and being ultra vigilant. Several have told us that managing parents during this time is equally challenging and that, depending on circumstances, it can be more settling if children aren't chatting to anxious mummy every night. Some children sail through their first term but come down with a nasty case when they return to school after the Christmas holidays. No school will want to keep a child boarding if they are profoundly and persistently unhappy, and in these relatively rare circumstances parents are advised accordingly. Sometimes it's a case of trying again after a few terms, but sometimes a different type of school is the only answer.

The Education Theatre
The big thinkers of British education

ABOVE Professor Mark Bailey, High Master of St Paul's School, speaking at the 2015 Independent Schools Show

Meet the big names of British education

As the UK's largest open day, the Independent Schools Show welcomes 200 of the country's leading schools to Battersea Park, 12–13 November. Join us at this informative and dynamic event to meet key admissions teams; speak with heads; enquire about entry requirements at all stages; explore scholarships and bursaries.

The Education Theatre, the programme of talks and events at the Show, is the UK's leading forum for parents to find information and answers about independent education.

Watch the 2015 Education Theatre talks and register for 2016 tickets at www.SchoolsShow.com

Independent
SCHOOLS
Show
LONDON 2016

Saturday 12 November 10:00 - 17:00
Sunday 13 November 11:00 - 16:30

Battersea Evolution, Battersea Park,
London, SW11 4NJ

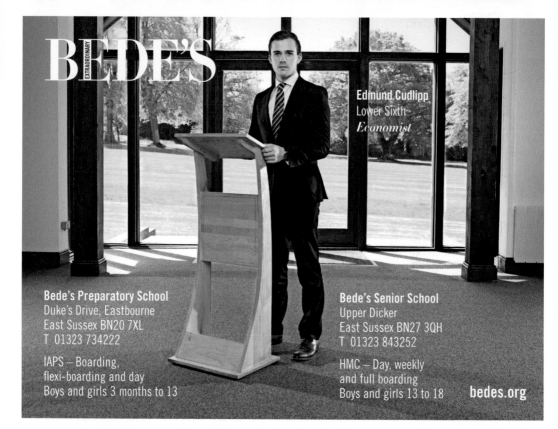

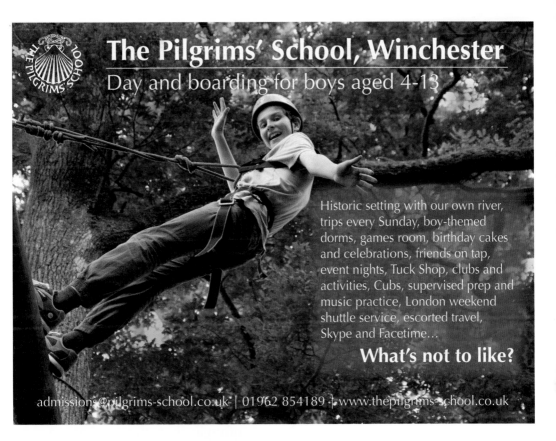

Look before you leap

You've just visited a school and you think it could be the one. The head was inspiring, the facilities top notch, the pupils delightful and the admissions staff ever so helpful. It's easy to be swept along on a wave of relief and enthusiasm when you find exactly the kind of school you've been looking for, but before you hand over the deposit be sure you've done your homework.

School closures are, it's fair to say, reasonably few and far between. When they do happen, however, the resulting stress can be traumatic for parents, pupils and staff, particularly in the case of a boarding school where parents, often on the other side of the world, have to scrabble around to find an alternative, often at short notice, that is a match for courses, facilities and results. If a school fails, it's usually for the same Micawberish reasons as any other struggling business. If annual fee income consistently fails to match expenditure, there's unlikely to be a happy ending.

If a school fails, it's usually for the same Micawberish reasons as any other struggling business

An obvious sign of trouble ahead is falling pupil numbers. The Good Schools Guide regularly trumpets the virtues of low pupil to teacher ratios, but it's as well to check that they're there by design and not because half the families have gone walkabout over the summer hols.

One useful repository of hard data is the Charities Commission website. Not every private school is listed but very many are, all required to fill annual data on their financial state of health. As with any other information, it should be interpreted with a degree of care. Assets, for example, can be look like an impressively chunky sum but may be based almost entirely on the value of the school buildings and land.

Liabilities, too, can appear daunting – frequently running into millions – but for a big school with many hundreds of pupils, substantial borrowing could simply reflect a well thought out, well funded expansion plan.

On its own, no single piece of information can provide the key to a school's survival. Size alone is no key to success, as the registrar of many a tiny but hugely oversubscribed boarding prep will tell you as they politely invite you to add your name to a lengthy waiting list.

A school's financial well-being can't be judged by one report any more than the staff list can tell you how much your child will enjoy her history lessons. But if you're torn between two schools, one living well beyond its means, the other prudently within them, it's worth doing the sums – theirs as well as yours – before you make your final decision.

Advice for international applicants

Boarding schools should be and generally are exceedingly pleased to welcome overseas pupils. Quite apart from bringing the world to Britain, their patronage almost certainly saved a fair few establishments from going under when the financial crisis was at its worst.

British boarding schools have never enjoyed a higher standing abroad. Each year thousands of pupils from all over the world pile in for a taste of the boarding experience, and that experience is much better than it used to be. Major rethinks on how pupils are cared for and substantial investment in facilities (much of it compulsory following the imposition of new regulations) have seen the best bits of tradition retained and some of the less attractive aspects banished for ever.

Newly refurbished accommodation is bordering on luxurious (but don't expect many en-suite bathrooms)

Pastoral care is now given as much prominence as academic standards. Newly refurbished accommodation is bordering on luxurious (but don't expect many en-suite bathrooms) and the transformation of school food is nothing short of miraculous, though fish and chips and custard – separately, of course – remain culinary fixtures.

But before completing your registration form and committing your chunky deposit, it's worth checking that you know what you are buying and whether it will suit your family.

English language support

The vast majority of international pupils follow a mainstream curriculum and work towards standard 16 and 18 plus qualifications. For those whose English isn't yet quite good enough or whose previous education puts them behind others of the same age, extra support from teachers who specialise in EAL (English as an Additional Language) may be needed.

Some schools run separate classes in key subjects, structured to allow more time for the language component so that maths and science students, for example, have sufficient understanding to decode word-based problems.

A growing number of boarding senior schools also run International Study Centres that offer a range of specially structured courses in what is effectively a school within a school. Pupils may board or play sport with their 'mainstream' peers but will follow a largely separate and slimmed down academic programme, working towards a smaller number of GCSEs with a big emphasis on learning English. These are covered in more detail on page 59.

Social life

While the academic side of boarding is undoubtedly important, the social dimension is just as vital. An isolated child is rarely a very successful one. Schools with substantial numbers of international pupils will invariably portray life as multi-cultural heaven, a glorious melting pot where nation speaks unto nation and pupils leave with their ideals intact, their horizons and tolerance vastly expanded and a lifetime of reunions all over the world to look forward to. In many cases, when a school selects a blend of nationalities, such as at UWC Atlantic College, this is exactly what happens. Good Schools Guide reviewers regularly hear of enduring friendships that span religious or cultural divides, or of lessons enriched by pupils on opposite sides of wars, sanctions or economic policy.

You can get a Harrow education in Bangkok, Beijing or Hong Kong, or sign up for Brighton College in Abu Dhabi

It works less well when a school operates a monoculture policy. A large number of pupils from one nation in a single year group may help fend off homesickness but can also reduce the motivation for pupils to immerse themselves in

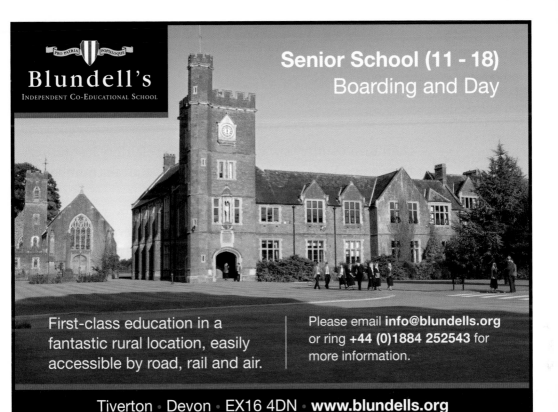

their host country's way of life – an opportunity lost rather than gained. It's okay to ask admissions staff for numbers if you're at all concerned.

Similarly, a school where the number of overseas pupils is so small that they are swamped by the prevailing culture can also lead to a miserable experience – particularly if they are the only full boarders in the place at weekends while everyone else goes home. Immersion is one thing, invisibility quite another – so it's also essential to find out just how many pupils of your child's age are actually around over the weekend. Many schools start off with a packed house for Saturday morning lessons or matches but empty out seconds after the final whistle (or bell) sounds.

Exporting education – big names abroad

Finally, for those happy to ditch some of the trimmings, it's increasingly possible to get the ethos, results and teaching quality of a traditional British education without travelling anywhere near the UK. Over the past few years, some of the most famous names in education have opened offshoots overseas. You can get a Harrow education in Bangkok, Beijing or Hong Kong, become a Haileybury pupil in Kazakhstan and or sign up for Brighton College in Abu Dhabi. Ethos and teaching standards are recognisably the same even if the facilities (sport is often air-conditioned and inside, for example) aren't.

Worth knowing...
- Remember that schools can go down as well as up, and famous isn't always best. A school may be trading on past glories rather than future brilliance, so check whether you're being sold the up to date version.
- Look past fabulous exam results. Top schools do well because they select top pupils. What it proves is that

parents of the brightest children send them here. It doesn't necessarily tell you how well it teaches them.

- Distrust any educational firms offering to find your child a place in a UK school. If free to you, they may well be getting a commission. Similarly, a bill for securing you a 'guaranteed' school place should also sound alarm bells. Speak to the school yourself.

- Do visit any school you are interested in, and bring your child if possible. No prospectus, however glossy, beats experiencing a school in the flesh.

- Check how EAL provision (if required) is organised. Ideally, ask to sit in on some lessons to give you an idea of the standards/commitment and enthusiasm you'll be getting – and try to talk to similar pupils.

- Consider applying for scholarships if your child is outstanding (academic, musical and sporting excellence are the norms) and ensure that your idea of excellence is the same as the school's but...

- Don't be won over by worthless scholarships, sometimes offered as an incentive by schools to seal the deal.

- The key entry points into UK schools are at age 11, 13 or 16. Many schools will look at potential pupils outside these times, but bear in mind that it's often on a one in, one out basis – places become available only if another family leaves.

- Check how often a child won't be boarding. Half terms, bank holidays and occasional weekend exeats all add up to a considerable chunk of time when pupils aren't in school and will need somewhere else to stay. A guardian is essential (see page 53) but you may also want to ensure family visits coincide with these dates.

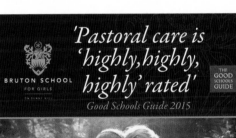

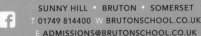

Guardians

If a child is starting school in the UK and their parents can't be with them, it makes sense to have another adult in the frame, someone outside their school who can act as a stand-in parent and become a trusted presence in their lives when they need someone to turn to. The people who take on the job are known as guardians.

While there are usually two fixed points – the airport meet and greet at the start of term and the reverse process when it ends – there's a mixed bag in between that could include just about anything, and frequently does. Possible add-ons can range from form signing and attending parent teacher meetings to sorting out mobile phone contracts and coordinating dentists' appointments. Guardians may also need to step in at very short notice in bad times if a child hits a problem and is excluded, suspended, or needs urgent medical treatment.

For many parents, the most important aspect of guardianship is the knowledge that their child has a part-time home from home, there for them at half term and weekends when they can swap timetabled routine for the friendly, welcoming informality of family life. But when you look for a guardian, what exactly are you getting and what assurances do you have that your child will be safe and well cared for?

Guardians may also need to step in at very short notice in bad times if a child hits a problem

Search online and you could be forgiven for believing that the appointment of a guardian is a legal requirement, as vital a component in a successful overseas applications process as a passport or visa. Many firms cite assorted laws and acts, the implication being that only one of the top-notch, gold-plated guardians on their books will satisfy the British government's safeguarding concerns.

'Following the Children Act (1989), The Care Standards Act 2000 and The National Boarding Standards 2002, boarding schools in England require parents to appoint a guardian who can be available at all times...' isn't un-typical. Even the august FT recently got it wrong.

The reality, however, is that unlike legal guardians who take on full responsibility for every aspect of a child's upbringing, often through the courts, when their parents can't care for them, education guardians have no formal status.

Aegis (The Association for the Education and Guardianship of International Students), which is the closest the industry comes to a trade body, confirmed that it is not a legal requirement for an international student to have an educational guardian whilst studying in the UK. Their name may sound ultra official but it's the only thing that is.

Boarding standards, while sharpening up many of the safeguarding requirements, include minimal direct references to guardians unless, that is, 'external lodgings' as they're described, are organised directly by schools. If that's the case, schools are compelled to visit them, interview all adults on the premises, take up references and ensure that DBS checks have been completed, as well as interviewing pupils at least every term and keeping a written copy of their comments. No wonder schools prefer to outsource so that the contract is between the guardian and the family.

So while failure to appoint an education guardian may tax your relationship with a school and severely impede your chances of being offered a place (it's often made a condition of acceptance), it isn't breaking the law and you won't be in trouble with child protection teams or immigration services.

While one legal firm has produced a report condemning what it describes as incorrect information being circulated by those in the guardianship industry, this aspect of guardianship isn't much mentioned. Given the ever-rising numbers of overseas pupils, their reticence isn't hard to understand. Guardianship fees of £1,000 a term aren't uncommon for basic support that includes round the clock emergency help, at least in term time. Many firms also give families the option of paying more for a premium service marketed variously as gold, platinum and – for the status conscious – VIP and royalty.

Guardianship firms come in every conceivable shape, size and cultural direction. Some specialise in one particular nationality. One website, written almost entirely in Chinese, is garlanded with pictures of top schools and universities, its aspirational messages somewhat less than subliminal. Some companies are cannily expanding into new areas. Additional services include day school packages, where, for a competitive price, children board with a host family in term time.

Guardianship firms should recruit and vet host families, ensuring they lead blameless lives and have squeaky clean records

All guardianship firms should recruit and vet host families, ensuring they lead blameless lives, have squeaky clean records and, importantly, live within easy travelling distance of your child's school. Unfortunately, membership of Aegis, which runs its own inspections, remains optional. The organisation is campaigning for safeguarding to be tightened and inspections made mandatory, but with only 10 per cent of schools currently working with Aegis members, it still has a lot of convincing to do.

In the meantime, there are other ways of finding a guardian. Schools sometimes recruit – very sensibly – through their own parents. Other families prefer to make their own arrangements, turning to friends or relations as stand-in, and stand-by, mums and dads. When you're shelling out a small fortune for a child's school fees, it's not hard to see the appeal of a slightly less formal, less expensive one-to-one arrangement.

Money isn't the only reason. The reassurance of knowing that in an emergency their child will be with somebody they have known all their lives can be priceless, though it's not infallible. Some relations can be too old, sick or far away to be of much practical use. One mother had to step into the breach when her daughter's best friend was suspended and the 100-mile journey was just too much for her frail guardians.

But what it you don't happen to have a ready-made guardian? You can start by asking the school. If they are reluctant to recommend specific firms – their reticence can stem from terror of being held accountable if something goes wrong – they may well be prepared to put you in touch with parents who can help.

It's in their interests, after all. Happy children learn better. For overseas pupils, a compatible guardian who cares about your child's well-being and happiness almost as much as you do can be an essential part of the educational experience.

What to ask:
- What am I paying for – and what will cost extra?
- How close is the host family to my child's school and what are the contact arrangements?
- Will my child's host family have other overseas pupils staying with them?
- What are the house rules (particularly as regards Wifi/alcohol/going out and curfews)?
- What will happen if there is an emergency (particularly relating to finance or health)?

Start here go anywhere

Clifton College is a leading day and boarding school in Bristol for girls and boys aged 2-18. Our inspirational teaching and focused individual care helps our pupils achieve their full potential both in and out of the classroom. This year, our outstanding academic results led to us being named one of the Daily Telegraph's Top 100 independent schools. Seventeen pupils gained places at Oxford and Cambridge, two of those for prestigious organ scholarships.

To find out more visit cliftoncollege.com

Or book a personal visit with our Admissions team on : 0117 405 8417

CLIFTON COLLEGE

ESTABLISHED 1862

Uni in the USA

The British student's guide to great universities
in the USA from Harvard to Hopkins

Tells you how to choose, how to apply and how to pay

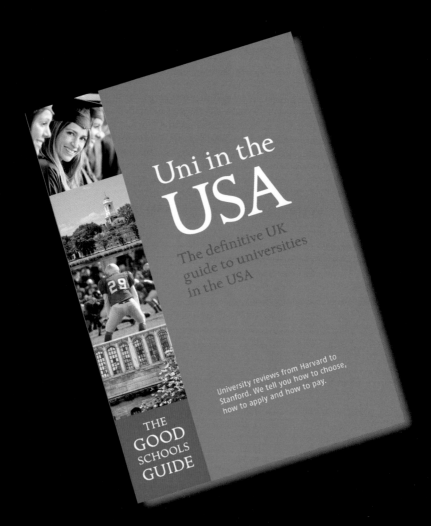

Uni in the
USA

The definitive UK
guide to universities
in the USA

University reviews from Harvard to
Stanford. We tell you how to choose,
how to apply and how to pay.

THE
GOOD
SCHOOLS
GUIDE

International study centres

International study centres are found throughout the UK. They provide the educational support necessary for foreign (non-English-speaking) adolescents to make the transition into life in an English school, most often as boarders. Students not only follow intensive English language programmes, they also learn about English culture and in some cases GCSEs or IGSCEs in 'core' subjects are offered. The study centres prepare students for either A levels or, in some cases, the IB diploma, which then leads to university entry.

Many international study centres are 'stand-alone' and not affiliated to any specific school, but a growing number of independent boarding and day schools have opened their own international study centres as what might be described as adjunct 'feeder schools'.

Whether they choose a stand-alone international study centre or one linked to a school, parents of international pupils need the same information as other parents: inspection reports; pastoral, health and safety (including medical emergencies) and safeguarding policies (including off-site travel privileges and transport); examination results, university destinations. In the case of the latter two it is good to be specific about the international pupils as well as the overall pupil population.

In addition we would advise parents to consider the following points, many of which may also apply to unaffiliated international study centres:

- What are the admissions criteria and how does the school assess non-English speakers and their previous learning?
- Can English language or other assessment tests be done in the home country?
- What are the qualifications of the teachers at the centre? What level of training do they have to teach EAL (English as an Additional Language)?
- How does the school handle the orientation and integration of new international pupils?

- How culturally, linguistically and economically diverse are the pupils who attend the centre? Large numbers of pupils from the same country may tend to talk amongst themselves rather than working on learning English. Wealthy pupils with extravagant spending habits can create a different sort of divide.
- How flexible is the school about dietary or religious practices?
- How much interaction do the international study centre pupils have with those in the main school? Do they share classes, sports, trips or accommodation? If the main school is both day and boarding, what proportion are boarders? Who will be around in the evenings and at weekends?
- If parents do not speak English, is there anyone who can speak the parents' language in the event of an emergency?
- What percentage of the international students are accepted into the school's sixth form after they have finished the international study centre programme? Where do those go who have not gained places, and how does the study centre help with finding a place elsewhere?
- Those who need visas to study in the UK must ensure that the study centre or school has the appropriate authority to issue CAS letters for the pupil.
- Lastly, those working via an educational agent, should make sure any financial arrangements are clear, and ensure that the international study centre is also in agreement with any transactions that are to take place with third party agents. Transparency about such matters is in the interest of all parties.

Scholarships and bursaries

Boarding schools, like all schools, want clever children. Children who will shine in arts and sports, children who will be excellent all-rounders and who will contribute generously to the academic, cultural and social life of the school. To this end they will offer considerable financial help to families with children who meet this description but who would not otherwise be able to attend because of high fees.

Many good boarding schools offer scholarships and bursaries in order to attract able and talented pupils. Scholarships are now usually worth more in glory than in fee reduction but bursaries can be worth up to 100 per cent of fees plus supplementary help for trips and equipment.

But how do you find out what financial assistance could be out there for you? And at which school? And would it cover just the tuition or might it stretch to boarding fees and even instrumental fees or help on school trips?

These are serious and important questions to which it is not always easy to find answers. Often, the information on schools' websites is hazy and unhelpful and you have no option but to call up and, perhaps, tell more about yourselves than you feel ready to with so little information.

The GSGAS Scholarships and Bursaries Service

The Good Schools Guide Advice Service has created a unique central resource for parents. We now hold information on the fee assistance available at more than 500 schools in The Good Schools Guide and, increasingly, at other good schools.

We won't be able to tell you exactly what – in raw financial terms – a school might offer you in terms of bursarial help, as this will depend on many things, such as your income, your financial commitments, the number of children you have etc – but we will be able to tell you the school's criteria for scholarships and bursaries, how they select their recipients, how many awards they have to offer and, most importantly,

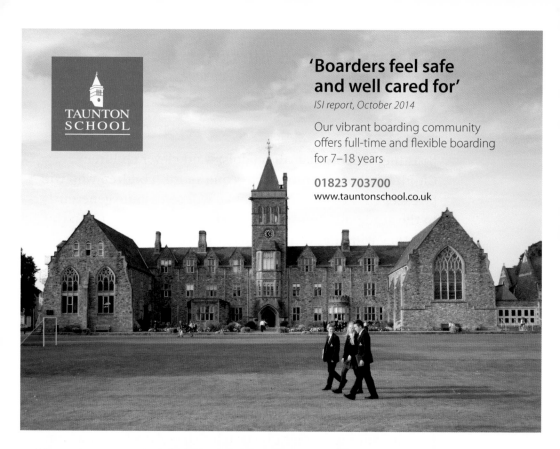

their special awards eg for particular skills or talents – sports, arts, music etc. We also know of odd and unusual awards eg for the children of clergy, sailors or children whose parent has died. We will be able to explain to you how a scholarship might be topped up by a bursary and answer any other questions you may have.

The Good Schools Guide Scholarships and Bursaries Service is a fee-paying service but we keep those fees as low as possible. For example, if you want a list of 10 top senior schools in London which offer, potentially, 100 per cent of fees for a bright child, we would charge around £150. If you want details of fee assistance at Roman Catholic girls' or coeducational boarding schools within a given area, we would charge around £180. This includes all the details we hold of the schools' criteria for awarding the assistance eg exams and interviews/auditions. Our charges depend on the number of schools or the breadth of the area you would like us to research.

NB Our information depends on how much the schools disclose to us so the amount of information we have varies from school to school.

Reality check

We are always honest and realistic with you. Far more parents apply for fee assistance than get it. Schools' resources – even the rich ones – are limited and they disburse money with great care. Your child may be top of everything at his primary school and your family income may be low, but this does not entitle you to a place or help with fees at any school. Informing yourself, getting the timing right and applying realistically is the best approach and – as around one third of all children at fee-paying schools now have some fee remission – it has to be worth a try.

NB All enquiries are treated individually. We will tell you

how much our search would cost before you decide whether to go ahead.

The Scholarships and Bursaries Service is handled by Susan Hamlyn, Director of The Good Schools Guide Advice Service, and arranged by our administrator, Shari Lord. You may be certain of absolute confidentiality. Call 0203 286 6824 or email: advice@goodschoolsguide.co.uk.

The Good Schools Guide Advice Service

www.goodschoolsguide.co.uk

In this new guide you can read reviews and detailed information on over 400 of our best boarding schools – as well as finding facts, statistics and information of all kinds to do with UK boarding education. But reviews – however informative and revealing – and statistics aren't always enough. In recent years, thousands of parents from Britain and all over the world have used our consultancy services – the Good Schools Guide Advice Service (GSGAS) – to give them *individual* help and guidance on finding the right schools for their children according to their own, unique family circumstances.

You can ask us anything

You plan to hand over the care and responsibility for your children, 24 hours a day, five, six or seven days a week to people you haven't even met yet. How are you to know if they will be taught to the highest standards and given every possible opportunity to succeed, thrive and be happy? What are the boarding houses – and staff – like? What will your children do outside lesson time? Who will take care of them if they feel unwell or unhappy? How much communication will there be between the school and you?

These are the kinds of questions to which you need honest and reliable answers and this is where The Good Schools Guide Advice Service comes in. We act as your knowledgeable, experienced and hard-working friend though the whole process of finding the best school for your children.

We have 30 expert advisors and we choose, with great care, the advisor best suited to you and your needs. All our advisors are parents and all have had to make the choices you now face. Many were themselves educated in boarding schools or have taught in them. Many have also worked and lived abroad and know what it's like to move home and country, finding schools with each move, adapting and then

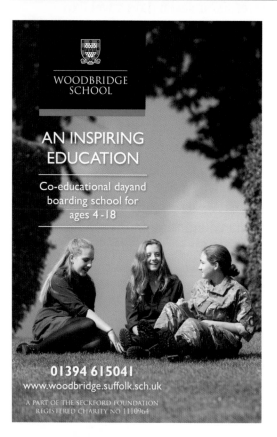
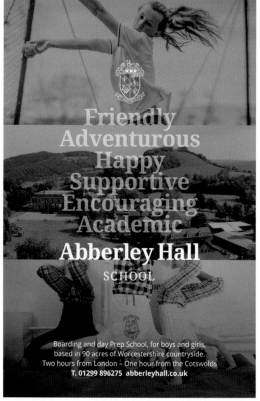

re-adapting. They understand how daunting it can be. Some of our advisors have children of their own with educational special needs. They know how hard it can be to find the best possible schools to give their children the same opportunities to develop their potential as everyone else.

Our advisors are our most experienced writers. Between them, they have visited every school we review. They all know their own locality and its schools inside out. They have specialisms eg boarding, the International Baccalaureate, girls' schools, sporting schools, schools which have excellent provision for overseas pupils, for those whose English is their second language or for children with special needs. Parents considering a boarding education have their own, important, reasons for this big decision. It may be that the schools' academic performance, results and ultimate university placement are the most important thing for you. Or, perhaps, the pastoral care and an informal atmosphere is what you feel is best for your child. It could be outstanding sports facilities that matter to you. Or proximity to an airport? You may want a small, nurturing, single sex school or a school which doesn't have Saturday lessons so that you can have a proper family weekend. You may want a school in which there are no large groups from any one particular country or you may want a truly international school with a lively cosmopolitan atmosphere. Parents ask our expert consultants to help them with concerns such as these every day.

Agents – a word of caution

British boarding schools are world-famous. Families from around the globe dream of sending their children to a high quality, beautiful and prestigious school in the UK. This means that the pressure on places at these schools is ever-increasing. Some of our most over-subscribed and popular schools now refuse to deal with agents and will only talk direct to parents or, of course, to us.

There are, of course, less good schools and unscrupulous agents who survive by exploiting parents' hopes and their lack of information. Sadly, we are contacted every week by parents who have been misled and misinformed by agents overseas – often having been grossly overcharged as well.

The Good Schools Guide Advice Service takes no money from schools for recommending them to you – even if you accept a place there. Your concerns and requirements are always at the top of our list of priorities.

Our service is tailored to you

The Good Schools Guide Advice Service offers you a range of services to suit your needs, whatever they are. We can rush to action if you need a school quickly. We can plan your child's education for years ahead if that's what you want. Our website lists all the many ways in which we can help you, from assessing your child's English, maths and reasoning skills to helping you find a scholarship or a bursary. On our website, you can see pictures and read profiles of all our advisors, our administrators and of Susan Hamlyn, the Director of the *GSGAS*

Call us on +44 203 286 6824 or email us on advice@ goodschoolsguide.co.uk.

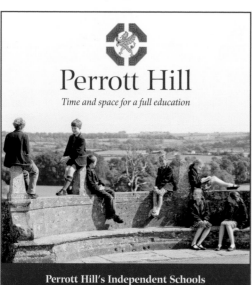
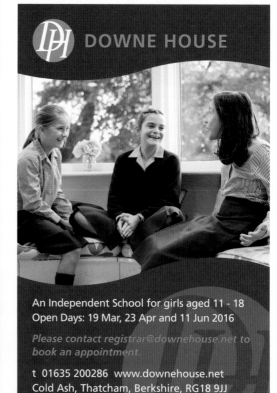

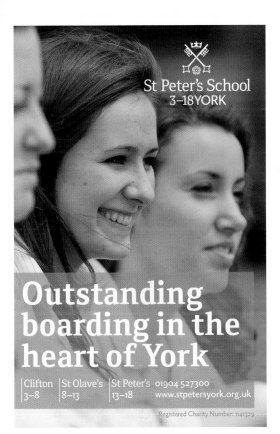

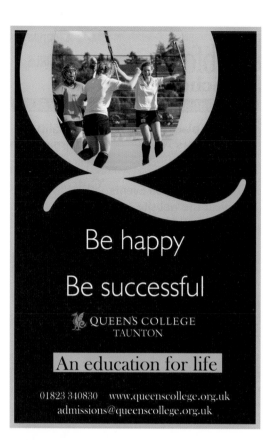

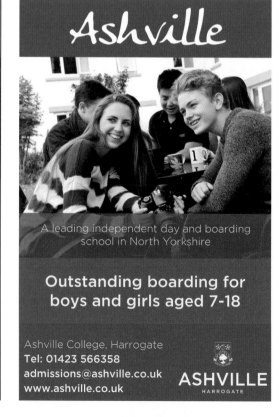

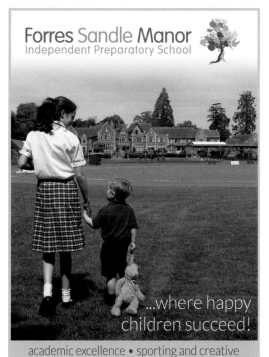
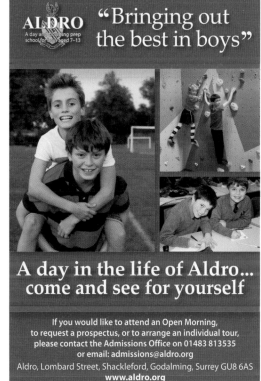

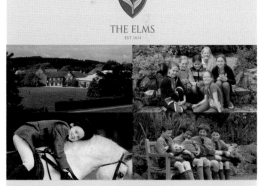

South West

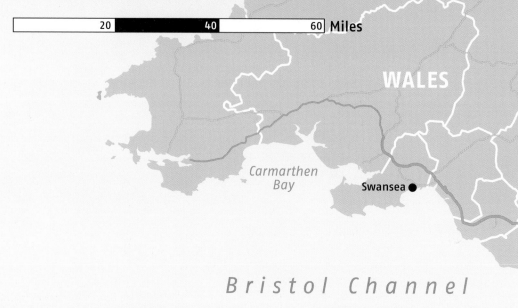
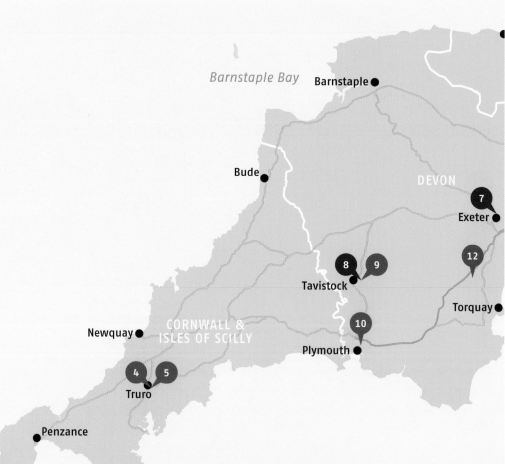

20   40   60 Miles

WALES

Carmarthen
Bay

Swansea ●

Bristol Channel

Barnstaple Bay Barnstaple ●

Bude ●

DEVON

7 Exeter ●

8 **9**

Tavistock ●

12

Torquay ●

Newquay ●

CORNWALL &
ISLES OF SCILLY

10 Plymouth ●

4 **5**

Truro ●

Penzance ●

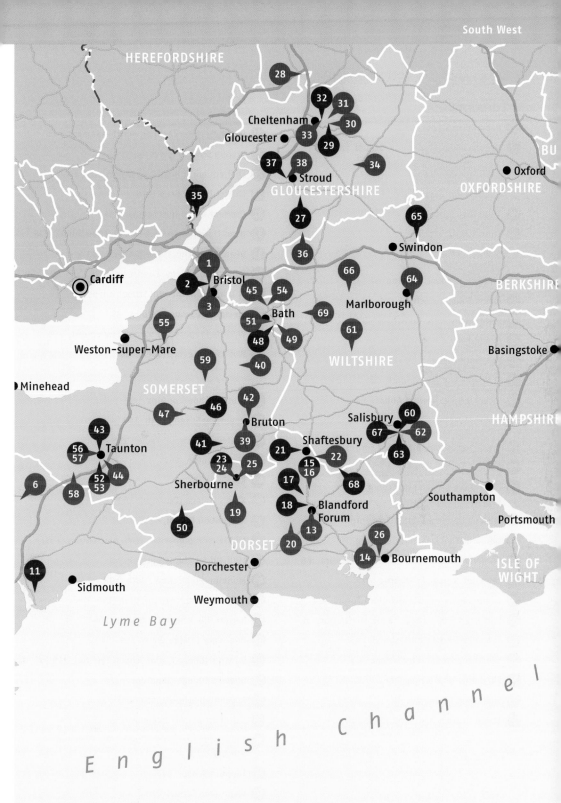

South West

Badminton School

Westbury Road, Bristol, BS9 3BA

01179 055271
admissions@badmintonschool.co.uk
www.badmintonschool.co.uk

Ages: 11–18 (junior boarding from 9)
Pupils: 455; sixth form: 110
Boarders: 175 full, 16 weekly/flexi (plus 8 junior)
Day: £8,490 – £17,880 pa
Boarding: £31,530 – £33,870 pa

Headmistress: Since 2012, Mrs Rebecca Tear (40s), BSc MA PGCE. Her degree in chemistry from Exeter preceded a career in teaching science almost exclusively to girls, and which included other significant responsibilities eg head of sixth form and deputy head at Wycombe Abbey, taking in a masters in leadership in education along the way.

An unequivocal believer in single sex education from her early teaching practice, where she saw how the less confident girls needed bringing out in lessons, she says, 'Teaching girls by themselves breaks down any preconceptions, barriers or stereotyping; when subjects don't acquire masculine or feminine connotations, girls tend to make more realistic personal choices.'

Somewhat jolly hockey sticks in manner – she strode across the drawing room, extending a hand and introducing herself as 'Bex' – we warmed to her no-nonsense and open personality; staff describe her as a real hit with the girls. For her part, Mrs Tear has made strenuous efforts to bring parents and guardians into school more: new ventures like the summer fair and fireworks night have

been welcomed. 'I don't want the first time I meet a parent to be in a bad news situation', she says.

Married to another chemistry teacher, she has two young sons who doubtless counterbalance all those girls. Passions include outdoorsy things like running, ski-ing and cycling with her family, and she is a keen cook – though at home she regrets the lack of a lab technician to wash up for her.

Academic matters: Well, it certainly matters at Badminton. Selection at entry, rigorous exam preparation and small classes (averaging 14 until GCSE) all the way through the school make for stunning results, and a reputation as Bristol's most academic school. A level results in 2015 saw 64 per cent A*/A (87 per cent A*-B) grades, with the majority of girls taking four subjects. At GCSE, 79 per cent A*/A in 2015. Options are (unusually) not blocked, so virtually any subject combination is possible. SAT training also provided for those hoping to go to American universities, plus the first ever opportunities fair, which featured a talk on world class university applications. Girls greatly encouraged to take on all manner of academic challenges outside

81

school; two girls were recently invited to go to a UK Mathematical Trust Olympiad training camp, out of only 22 youngsters in the country, and external essay prizes are frequently awarded. Everyone does English Speaking Board exams, which, for the year 8 class we visited, involved learning, reciting and discussing chunks of poetry – a Shakespeare sonnet in one case. Years 8 and 9 are also offered a 10 week STEM experience with engineering or manufacturing companies with Go4SET. 'They push them, but not in any way too much,' said one mother, who also appreciates the way teachers go over work with individuals when they find it difficult. EPQ added to sixth form enrichment programme.

An innovative range of activities including kick-boxing and water polo means no-one has the chance to be idle. Badminton's riders enjoy considerable success

SEN provision is modest – not much call for it here – and mostly delivered by 'flexible in-house support'. Weekly sessions at Bristol Dyslexia Centre to improve skills in English and maths are laid on for more severe cases: whilst some parents accept this, others resent the extra time expended, and the stigma associated with leaving the school by taxi, and feel that daily intervention would be a darn sight more use. More emphasis is given to extending the gifted and talented – a term the school avoids. EAL is also offered in school to support overseas girls.

Games, options, the arts: Games and sports are well catered for (Astro, tennis courts, netball courts and a 25m pool) on the school's site, unlike so many of Bristol's schools, whose playing fields are a bus ride away across the suspension bridge. Hockey, netball, tennis and swimming are the main sports, but an innovative range of activities including kick-boxing and water polo means that no-one has an excuse to be idle. Badminton's riders enjoy considerable success: one was selected for the Prince Philip cup – the height of mounted athleticism. Hockey and netball players are regularly selected for the county. One parent was unhappy that only top players were ever picked for teams, and that mediocre participants barely got a game; also that the (beautiful) pool was used very little by the girls 'because it was always being hired out'. The absence of swimming teams or even a swimming club is an oddity.

Artistic life flourishes too, with top notch music, drama and art. Much is rightly made of high calibre musicians (one to the Royal College on

Saturdays, two to the National Children's Orchestra, several playing in city orchestras, a recent leaver in training for The Sixteen) and school is fortunate to perform in St George's Bristol, a national concert venue. Most girls learn one instrument if not two, and school is proud of the number and scope of ensembles it lays on for musicians of all standards and persuasions. New music building has enabled school to bring all of its music teaching and practice activities to a single location and created a new focus for the department. The building includes teaching and practice rooms, a new music library and a generous classroom for curricular music lessons. Drama reasonably prominent too, with six productions a year plus a staff pantomime, as well as collaborations with outside initiatives at local innovative theatre the Tobacco Factory and Garden Opera, recently as a chorus of urchins in Carmen. Several notable actresses are OBs: Clare Bloom, Phyllida Law and Rosamunde Pike.

Art is housed in a most appealing setting, where mannequins dressed in creations fit for a Milan catwalk grace the entrance. Textiles, ceramics, painting, digital media (aka photography) and all types of artistic endeavour go on here. Badminton girls gain places at prestigious colleges such as St Martin's.

Boarding: From age 9 although there's only a handful of junior boarders. Boarders accommodated in three houses grouped by age – interestingly, Bartlett houses girls from years 5-8, spanning both junior and senior schools. Sanderson is the newest build for the middle girls; sixth formers are separate. One parent reported a tendency to cliques among the girls, which she felt the school did little to address, and that it 'feels like a boarding school which day girls attend'; another felt that integration was fine.

Weekends fairly relaxed for those who stay in school: girls might be involved in sports or drama, off on a surfing trip, going out for a meal or to the theatre. As elsewhere boarders from abroad are required to have a guardian, but here they do so much more than that rather dry word suggests and are more like surrogate mums – we applaud this.

Background and atmosphere: Founded over 150 years ago, Badminton is older than most girls' schools of its type and was set up to provide the same educational opportunities for girls as their brothers enjoyed. That sense of academic seriousness, courage, confidence and an international outlook still prevail – girls here tackle any academic challenge head-on. Originally sited in Badminton House in nearby Clifton, it moved to its present premises on the edge of the downs in Bristol, arguably the greenest and most desirable part of the city. Main building is Georgian and gracious (we were ushered in to a warm and luxuriously carpeted drawing room, where Classic FM played discreetly); over the years the site has been filled in with all sorts of additions of varying degrees of beauty, making the school compact, rather than crowded.

Groups of girls scurry purposefully about the place in their practical uniform of blue shirts, sweaters and checked skirts. 'Why no trousers?' asked one mum. Sixth form dress is much less restricted than in some schools: torn jeans and strappy tops are out, otherwise more or less anything goes. Overseas girls are welcome here and come in droves, mostly from Hong Kong but a good few from Russia and Nigeria; a sprinkling from the rest of the world. Bristol's own ethnic and religious mix well represented and catered for too: any dish containing pork was firmly labelled at lunch. Old Badmintonians include Indira Ghandi and Princess Haya Bint Al Hussein of Jordan.

Male company is provided mostly by QEH, Bristol's only remaining boys' school – academic and social interactions, we gather, which include a shared minibus from Chepstow.

Pastoral care, well-being and discipline: Discipline, in as much as it is needed in this high-achieving environment, works on girls' general desire to please, and dislike of letting people down, so the head might well say, 'I am rather disappointed that I have to speak to you, Jemima', on the rare occasions that girls come before her. Smoking, alcohol and drugs will lead sinners straight to her study. Achievement of all kinds is recognised, but interestingly there is no honours board, and school's annual open day is as much about displays, demonstrations, music, drama and food than interminable speechifying; the only prize awarded is the Iris Murdoch (another OB) prize for creative writing.

That sense of seriousness, courage, confidence and an international outlook still prevail – girls tackle any academic challenge head-on

---

Pastoral care reads as well as one would expect for a school like this, with a tutor assigned to each girl, a vertical house system and peer mentoring, but one mother told us her daughter's confidence had been undermined by too great an emphasis on academics, and too little on making supportive friendships.

Pupils and parents: Quite mixed socially and ethnically, but united by high academic expectations and aspirations. We found the girls friendly, unpretentious and open-minded – and were pleased to

see some tucking into the sponge pudding we are probably no longer allowed to call spotted dick. 'The school does not turn out a mass product,' said one mother with several years' knowledge

Entrance: Most girls arrive in year 7, but everyone below sixth form is required to sit papers in English (English as a foreign language for those who have been at school in the UK for less than two years) and maths and to do an online reasoning test. The transition from the junior school is not automatic and girls do exactly the same assessments as those coming from elsewhere (in practice, the vast majority are accepted). Sixth form hopefuls must sit papers in two of the subjects they intend studying at A level, plus a general paper. Everyone desirous of a place at Badminton is interviewed, via Skype when necessary.

Exit: Some fall-out after GCSEs (around 20 per cent) from day girls wanting pastures new, and perhaps boys in particular. Those who stay go not only to our most prestigious universities, but also to top notch international ones in Asia and the US (three to USA in 2015). London is the most popular destination, followed by Durham, and a good handful to Oxbridge each year (two in 2015). Wide choice of degree courses, more sciences than arts.

Money matters: Fees are much in line with comparable schools, though boarders from outside the EU pay over £2000 more per year to cover the cost of escorted journeys to UK international airports – and of the boarding travel co-ordinator. Scholarships are awarded to a maximum of 20 per cent of fees; bursaries are means tested. New-ish regional award for girls 'who will bring something special to Badminton'; the school intends this as a way to recognise wider achievement and potential than the range of scholarships currently on offer.

Remarks: Undoubtedly a distinguished Bristol institution, yet its size, compact site, high proportion of boarders and fearsome academic reputation (which frightens some off) mean it enjoys a lower profile than it should in the city. The head describes it as a hidden gem, so her mission, should she choose to accept it, is perhaps to polish up all its facets so it shines a brighter local light.

Beaudesert Park School

Minchinhampton, Gloucestershire GL6 9AF

01453 832072
office@beaudesert.gloucs.sch.uk
www.beaudesert.gloucs.sch.uk

Ages: 4–13 (boarding from 8+ years)
Pupils: 436
Boarders: 72 weekly/flexi
Day: £8,130 – £15,930 pa
Boarding: £20,700 pa

Headmaster: Since 1997, James Womersley (50s). Educated at The Dragon and St Edward's Oxford, studied economics, history 'and rugby' at Durham, PGCE from Oxford. Came to Beaudesert after Eagle House, Emanuel London and nine years at his old prep school. He cites this time at the Dragon, where he became a housemaster, as a formative influence.

Mr W and his wife, Fiona, make a prep school power couple. Parents can be assured that whatever (or whoever) comes their way, the Womersleys have probably seen it before. Mrs W comes from a prep school family, although she claims it was the 'last thing I thought I'd find myself doing'. Nothing daunted she takes care of marketing, catering,

pastoral and safeguarding – and somehow manages to look groomed and elegant at the same time. The Womersleys are a great advert for the youth-enhancing properties of prep school life – fizzing with energy and joie de vivre. Certainly not ready for retirement, 'not while we're still enjoying it'. Their three sons all went to Beaudesert and St Edward's Oxford.

The Womersleys' job satisfaction must be infectious; they've created a school with a strong sense of identity and 'real soul', as one parent put it. The atmosphere is professional and collaborative, everyone we met was relaxed and friendly (well, it was near the end of term...). Mr W speaks of his teaching

And what job would he be doing if he hadn't become a prep school head? He ponders – perhaps he never thought of doing anything else. 'An art historian,' he says

staff with pride – several current heads and deputy heads cut their teeth at Beaudesert.

He describes Beaudesert as 'virtually independent', by which he means that paths to schools such as Marlborough and Cheltenham College are well maintained – after all, it's the reason many families choose this prep. Nonetheless, parents can be confident that advice about senior schools is unbiased by anything apart from their child's best interests.

Although Mr W no longer teaches he does take cover lessons. And what job would he do if he hadn't become a prep school head? He ponders – perhaps he never thought of doing anything else. 'An art historian' he says finally.

You might think that the indefatigable Womersleys spend their leisure time having a well-earned sit down, but you'd be wrong. They play golf and tennis and enjoy skiing. Phew.

Entrance: While not fiercely selective, Mr W says Beaudesert attracts a 'generally high level' and 'families with bright children'. Pupils come from local nurseries or, since 2012, the school's own. Transfer from pre-prep generally straightforward.

Exit: Majority in roughly equal numbers to Cheltenham College and Marlborough, then St Mary's Calne, Cheltenham Ladies' College, Downe House (girls) and Eton, Radley, Winchester, Sherborne (boys). Also Bradfield, Malvern College, Stowe and St Edward's Oxford. Good spread of scholarships every year too (10 in 2015).

Remarks: Beaudesert Park School was founded in Warwickshire in 1908, moving to its mock Tudor Cotswold folly 10 years later. That folly has been joined over the years by buildings in a variety of architectural styles, the latest being a superb performing arts centre. Any deficit in architectural coherence is more than made up for by character – round every corner is a different view, whether it's terraced lawns and playing fields or the free-range cattle on Minchinhampton Common, who look as though they could wander into the car park (they can't, thanks to a grid). Towers, curved walls, covered outside staircases and walkways – it all looks rather like an animated Escher drawing as pupils go busily up and down between lessons.

Although Mr Womersley regrets the dominance of exams in schools today, he's a champion of CE and believes it gives children a worthwhile goal. 'They work hard and get the joy of success', he says. But as several parents told us, at Beaudesert the balance between academic work and the myriad other activities on offer is skilfully maintained. Those who have moved their children from London preps really notice the difference and value the unpressurised environment – even more so when their children go on to gain places at top senior schools. 'They challenge the children academically by keeping them engaged,' said one. Homework is sensible too, certainly not hours every night. Nursery and pre-prep have their own mini-school with all the facilities including a hall and stage.

Pupils setted for maths, English and languages (French, Latin from year 6, optional Greek for scholars). No separate scholarship stream. Well-equipped labs where legendary 'screaming jelly baby' and other spectacular experiments are staged – obviously science is not impervious to Mr W's performing arts campaign. Old-fashioned values do not extend to technology and there's a full complement of whiteboards, iPads and the like. Delightful, bright art studios with separate ceramics room and proper kiln. SEN provision received mixed reviews. Pupils told us the help they'd received was 'brilliant', but parents raised concerns. Several thought that a school with a relatively unselective intake should have wider in-house experience to identify specific learning needs early on.

Towers, curved walls, covered outside staircases and walkways – it all looks rather like an animated Escher drawing

Part of the charm of Beaudesert, according to parents, is that it's a proper 'outdoors' school: 'It's a real country school', 'a proper all-round education', 'the children are connected to their surroundings.' Several made the distinction between country preps that are 'sporty' and Beaudesert, where, in addition to plenty of sport, there's free range tree climbing, den building, night camps, forest school for the little ones and bushcraft ('It's mainly about knives', a Just William character told us).

Main sports arranged along pretty traditional lines, rugby, football and cricket for the chaps, netball and rounders for the girls. Both do hockey (girls very successfully) and there's some overlap with cricket coaching. Athletics for all in the summer, plus tennis and cross-country. We didn't hear any grumbles about teams and matches, most parents thought the arrangements were fair enough and that pupils in the B and C teams enjoyed their games just as much as those in the As. Swimming is a real strength – all Beaudesert pupils learn to swim and indoor and outdoor pools mean year round training. The school regularly qualifies for IAPS national finals and swimmers compete in local and national teams. This being Gloucestershire, there's a fair amount of equestrian activity – school team recently won national junior polo championships. Golf, fly fishing and mountain biking also on offer. Pupils can bring their own bikes and learn cycle safety and maintenance.

Modest proposals included golf buggies to transport pupils to games fields over the common, compelling teachers to sit their own exams, and 'unlimited ice cream'

In defiance of Noel Coward's advice, Mr W believes that everybody's daughter or son benefits from taking to the stage. Even before the opening of the new performing arts centre, music and drama were enthusiastically pursued by the majority. Minutes after the builders left preparations were under way for the inaugural concert, featuring school choirs, orchestra, ensembles and soloists. This glass and Cotswold stone building sits, appropriately enough, at the centre of the school and hosts plays, concerts, assemblies, parents' evenings, music and drama lessons and exhibitions. The exterior features distinctive cedar planks, rather like xylophone keys, positioned to deflect the light.

Pupils can board from year 4 and most will have some experience of boarding by the time they leave. Options are flexi or weekly – everyone goes home after Saturday school (lessons until 12.30pm), or matches. Boarders up to year 6 can work towards bronze, silver and gold 'Beaudesert Badges' – activities include first aid, cookery, gardening, outdoor skills and charity work.

One boarding house with boys' and girls' sections up different staircases. Jolly kitchens and comfortable shared areas for 'TV and talking'. Brightly decorated boys' dorms run into each other (no doors), girls have separate (shared) rooms. Everything clean and homely. 'I love boarding, you get to sleep over with all your friends,' said one of our guides. Houseparents plus matrons, nurses and gappies oversee proceedings. 'There's always someone to talk to,' we were told. Food gets a big thumbs up, especially pulled pork buns and good old treacle sponge.

Year 8 girls informed us proudly of the small privileges of seniority – white shirts in winter, benches in assembly, 'senior snacks' (cereal and squash at 8pm on a Friday) and, best of all, 'senior supper' with the Womersleys – none typical 12 year olds' aspirations. Advocates of the 'real world' undoubtedly educate their children elsewhere and even its biggest fans concede that there is a Beaudesert bubble, but how many parents would wish their children to grow up more quickly?

Houses, we were told, are 'no big deal', thus rather suiting their prosaic names: A, B, C and D. No head boys and girls, instead all year 8s have duties and responsibilities. Newish school council has achieved victories including modifications to the year 8 uniform. 'Boys can choose their own socks, but they mustn't be luminous or white.' What else would improve their school, we asked? Modest proposals included golf buggies to transport pupils to games fields over the common, flattening the bump in the Astro, compelling teachers to sit their own exams, and 'unlimited ice cream'.

According to Mr W, the parent profile has changed in the 19 years he has been at the helm of Beaudesert – these days both parents are probably working, often weekly commuting to London. He welcomes the fact that parents are 'in a lot more' and encourages their involvement. Families all fairly local – few alternatives in the immediate area and weekly boarding only see to that. No PTA but active Friends of Beaudesert who organise fundraisers and socials. No class reps either – they don't really feature in the boarding model – but most parents happy with home-school communications, prompt replies to enquiries and general delightfulness of front of house staff. High praise, too, for pastoral care and teachers' 'genuine concern' for pupils, 'Nothing's too much trouble. You can't fault it', we were told.

Beaudesert and its lucky pupils continue to thrive under the expert custodianship of the Womersleys. Mr W has no need of educational jargon; his philosophy is a simple one: healthy, happy children learn best. Happiness isn't a subject to be taught, it should be the founding principle of any school – it certainly is at Beaudesert.

Blundell's School

Blundell's Road, Tiverton, Devon EX16 4DN

01884 252543
registrars@blundells.org
www.blundells.org
C of E

Ages: 11–18 (boarding from 8)
Pupils: 590 pupils; sixth form: 195
Boarders: 132 full, 238 weekly/flexi
Day: £12,870 – £21,690 pa
Boarding: £14,880 – £31,755 pa

Head: Since 2013, Mrs Nicola Huggett (40s) MA PGCE (Oxon). Educated at St Gabriel's and Marlborough, she read PPE at Oxford before embarking on a brief career in advertising with J Walter Thompson – brief because she soon realised it was not for her. 'Why did no-one tell me about teaching before?' she says of her experience shadowing a teacher in a comprehensive near her home. Since then her career has taken her via Haileybury, ultimately as head of boarding, during a time when the school went fully co-ed and introduced IB, and Downe House as deputy head, before being made the first female head of Blundell's since its inception in 1604. Only moderate harrumphing greeted her appointment, and those foolish enough to do so must now be eating their words, such has been the wave of approval from all quarters. 'A wow appointment,' declared one mother. Mrs Huggett is clearly superwoman – as well as running a school, where she still teaches four lessons a week, she also runs marathons, rides – oh, and raises four children of her own, all at Blundell's. Husband Spencer runs a car dealership in Barnstaple and has always moved around with her. 'Blundell's appealed to me because

there's an honest and unpretentious feel about the place – and I'm a country girl,' she says. 'Though when I saw the sign that said Headmaster's Visitors, I said "That'll be the first thing to go!".'

Academic matters: Traditionally not the brightest star in the firmament of South West schools, but there's a determination on the head's part to make the school as academic as it is sporty. ('She'll have her work cut out for her,' remarked one parent.) To that end she has made some key appointments since she arrived, such as a head of learning support, who is an ed psych, and a switched-on academic deputy from Wycombe Abbey, as well as introducing a proper tutor system, which has gone down well with parents. A level results are sound, with 69 per cent graded A*/B and 41 per cent A*/A in 2015; sciences, geography and maths – good take-up of further maths too – are most popular, languages lamentably not, though it is impressive to note that the school has run Spanish, Russian and Latin for sole takers. Four to Oxbridge in 2015, and parents reckon that student aspirations will be raised under the new regime; many already take

EPQ in sixth form alongside A levels. The brightest sparks are invited to join the scholars' club, which 'offers stimulation for rapid progress' in the dry language beloved of inspectors. At GCSE, 55 per cent graded A*/A in 2015. DT enjoys a big take-up: we would have been happy to give house-room to many of the items of small wooden furniture we saw. Students with a wide range of intellectual gifts are catered for: at GCSE science for example, school offers choice between IGCSE or less demanding boards. Everyone does French and Latin from the start with the choice of German and Spanish in year 9. Just over a fifth of students receive SEN support, including plenty of help for those whose first language is not English.

Games, options, the arts: Make no mistake, this is a very sporty school, and might not be the place for a pale aesthete. That said, there is masses on offer for those with little or no eye for a ball, as well as the usual fare of rugby, hockey (both huge here) netball and cricket (for girls too, plus football, tennis, squash and fives): CCF, D of E, Ten Tors and the Devizes to Westminster canoe race keenly pursued. In the spring, the whole school participates in the (frankly bonkers) Russell – named for the eponymous Jack (of terrier fame and an OB) – a hotly contested cross-country race for which local landowners open their land. We had never seen quite such cheerfully muddy girls as the ones we met just back from a practice. General heartiness extends to an outdoor pool only – 'reassuringly heated,' says school – though an indoor one is on everyone's wish list, and keen swimmers can use the indoor facilities in Tiverton. Riding strong here too – Blundell's riders regularly compete at events in the South West and recently won the National Schools Jumping-with-style contest – but it's not the kind of school where turning up with a horsebox is de rigueur; no equines on site.

Activities range from aerobics to yoga; everyone is expected to sign up for a minimum of two. Boarders are offered an adventure and leadership programme over eight weekends comprising gorge-walking and survival training along with other feats of derring-do. But Blundell's isn't just good at the strenuous stuff: a long tradition of debating both in school and beyond was crowned by winning the ESU national final in 2013. Artists in all media compete and show their work far beyond the school, with success at the Tate, in the Saatchi Art Prize for Schools (online but also, more excitingly, in the Kings Road) and more locally in Tiverton and Exeter. We were gutted that an art scholar's rendition of the Mona Lisa in peanut butter and chocolate spread had (presumably) been eaten before our visit. Music facilities have just been brought bang up to date with an editing suite and composition/technology studio, but there has long been masses of music

> *The whole school participates in the (frankly bonkers) Russell – named for the eponymous Jack – a hotly contested cross-country race*

both sung and played: concerts and recitals, plus recently Grease, Cabaret and open mic night on the lighter side. In the last couple of years groups have been to Prague, Brittany and Venice, as well as prestigious venues nearer home. Drama takes places in the Ondaatje Hall, named for its generous donor, the notable philanthropist, brother of the author and an OB; plenty of backstage and technical experience on offer as well as acting, plus visits and workshops from French and Spanish theatre groups – a great initiative which other schools would do well to emulate. A long tradition of house and year group plays means there are opportunities for all budding thespians.

Boarding: Relationships between staff and students seem extremely good, with house staff coming in for particular praise – some email parents with photos of boarders' activities and high jinks just about the moment they happen. The seven houses accommodate a mix of all kinds of boarders (full, weekly, flexi) and day pupils, divided into two co-ed at the beginning and end of a student's time at Blundell's, two girls' and three boys'; all are known by their initials – NC, SH etc. The latter, School House, for years 7 and 8, was one of the first matters the head tackled on arrival as a result of considerable parental dissatisfaction: all now report huge improvements.

Twice as many boys as girls are full boarders and parents of full boarders rather wish more kids stayed in at weekends, and that the food was, on occasion, more girl-friendly. Some of their accommodation could do with a bit of tlc too. The crowning glory of boarding has to be Westlake, the co-ed sixth form house where students get as close a feeling of university life as possible before they get there, yet where girls and boys respectively can retreat from the hurly-burly to their own part of the house.

Background and atmosphere: Four-square Victorian red-brick buildings face more modern additions across Blundells Road in Tiverton – such is the importance of the school to the town that it has a road named after it – set off by gracious green spaces and a distinctive clock tower; though the school was founded by the generous legacy of one of England's wealthiest cloth merchants, Peter Blundell, over 200 hundred years earlier, it moved to its permanent home only in the 1880s. The values of that time persist in some measure today with the school's emphasis on 'distinguished performance in those games which the Victorians [had] developed to replace the rude sports of earlier centuries'. No more cock-fighting then. Definitely a traditional feel about the place, with a bewildering number of ties, though certainly not fuddy-duddy, with boys below sixth form wearing tawny tweed jackets, the colour of autumn bracken on Dartmoor, and girls red ones. Even the sixth form wear uniform; their jackets are navy blue, striped for those who have been awarded full colours – given not only for sports, but all manner of accomplishment.

What in other schools might be called assembly takes place in Big School and is called Latin prayer, concluding as it does with the Lord's prayer in Latin; chapel on other mornings in the school's own beautiful chapel. The first girls arrived in 1975 and the school went fully co-ed in 1992. We are delighted that the last head girl exercised her right to keep a pig at school for her final term, something conferred on the head boy from the start.

Parents love the friendly and inclusive feel of the place, the lack of arrogance among the students and the resilience the school instils in them. 'Absolutely non-stop programme of extracurricular activities means my children are absolutely exhausted by the time they come home – perhaps they need more soothing down-time at weekends to recover,' observed one mother of boarders. Great affection and loyalty for the school from past and present students and staff – one finally took retirement after 30 years' service; terrific and long-standing network of events for OBs, not just the 'winter lunches' in Devon, but all over the world.

Pastoral care, well-being and discipline: Discipline appears to be kept with a lightish touch – parents of drinkers and smokers can expect 'to be invited in to discuss a way forward', according to the head. Drugs weren't even mentioned, and bullying gets zero tolerance. 'There's a sexting issue every year in year 9,' said one mother phlegmatically, 'but the school just deals with it'.

Pupils and parents: Mostly local but a good handful (about 15 per cent) from abroad, giving the school a more cosmopolitan feel than mid Devon might otherwise manage. Among the farmers, local professionals and the military, there are boarders from Cornwall, where there is little on offer, and of course refugees from London in search of a better life; some first time buyers of independent schooling too, one of whom said, 'My son is having the kind of education that I work for and dream of him having'. Pupils are as grounded and unpretentious as any you will find at a UK boarding school, the kind who will have a go and take a risk; we suspect that the rebellious, the precious and the show-off would not thrive here.

Entrance: Mostly at 11, since Blundell's Prep finishes at year 6, by means of papers in English, maths and non-verbal reasoning in the January preceding entry; at 13+ via common entrance or the school's own entrance test in English and maths in June. At sixth form, hopefuls have to satisfy relatively undemanding entrance requirements of a minimum of five GCSEs at a C or above with at least a B in subjects to be taken to A2, plus interview

Exit: The vast majority to university and traditional ones at that, up and down the country. 'No-one goes to Exeter – too close to home,' sixth formers informed us. Recent Oxbridge successes (four in 2015) may well boost applications in that direction. Popular universities include Durham, Imperial College, Warwick, Reading, Bristol, Leeds and Manchester. Degree choices again tend towards the conventional and/or vocational, such as medicine (three in 2015), geography, economics, biochemistry, law and business management.

After that, Old Blundellians fan out across the globe, to the extent that there are OB gatherings in South Africa, Japan, Germany and Hong Kong. An extremely busy development office ensures strong links with the old school tie. Famous OBs include RD Blackmore, (the hero of whose chef d'oeuvre Lorna Doone was a fictional pupil), 40s actor Gerald Hamer and his director son Robert (Kind Hearts and Coronets), defence correspondent and author Robert Fox, organist Peter Hurford, TV journalist Claire Marshall and the drummer of The Vamps, Tristan Evans.

Money matters: For the first 300 years of its existence, Blundell's was maintained by the profits from its properties in Tiverton and estate in south Devon, but these days fees charged are in line with comparable schools. Decent range of scholarships for sport, music, art, drama, all-round as well as academic; only music and academic at 11+. Peter Blundell Foundation bursaries are awarded in cases of financial need where 'Governors wish to reflect the spirit of Peter Blundell's vision'. The school is innovative in attracting an array of corporate sponsors to fund events.

Remarks: Ancient and distinguished Devon institution preserving traditional values and feel, yet turning out considerate and balanced young people all set for careers across the globe. Not perhaps for those seeking exclusively to scale the heights of academia or social cachet, but deserves far higher prominence than the lowish profile ('Not in the west country!' protests school) it currently assumes. Over to you, Mrs Huggett.

Bredon School

28

Pull Court, Tewkesbury, Gloucestershire GL20 6AH

01684 293156
enquiries@bredonschool.co.uk
www.bredonschool.org

Ages: 4–18 (boarding from 7)
Pupils: 246 (roughly 80 per cent boys); sixth form: 62
Boarders: 60 full, 39 weekly/flexi
Day: £6,615 – £17,985 pa
Boarding: £19,410 – £28,185 pa

Headmaster: Since September 2013, Mr David Ward MA BEd, previously head of St Felix School in Suffolk. Has also headed Skegness Grammar. A former rugby international, he is a qualified canoeing coach and is interested in sailing, swimming and riding. He is vice chair of governors of St David's College in Llandudno, a school that specialises in dyslexia and dyspraxia using outdoor pursuits.

Academic matters: Maximum 15 to a class but the most we saw was a group of 14. Most classes are much smaller (around seven) and often have a teaching or support assistant alongside. The school's academic results are all to do with value added: while this is emphatically not a special school, a very high proportion of the children here use the learning access centre, and of the 230 pupils, around 90 have diagnosed learning difficulties or statements of special educational need (dyslexia, dyspraxia and communication difficulties are most common). Special educational needs are not regarded as a hindrance – 'Nobody's different, because everybody's different'.

All children participate in the school farm – which features a prize-winning bull as well as sheep, poultry, pigs and vegetable-growing

Consequently, children without a learning difficulty are also treated very much as individuals and will, if appropriate, take GCSEs early or pursue particular interests with the support of staff. Lots of kinaesthetic learning resources across the school, with all staff accustomed to dealing with learning difficulties and a dedicated unit of 10 SPLD trained staff working in a purpose built access centre.

In general, children achieve far beyond what they expected – or indeed what was expected of them. All the pupils we spoke to said they were doing things they had thought they couldn't do. In 2015, 7 per cent A*/A grades at GCSE and 62 per cent of pupils got 5+ A*-C GCSE grades including English and maths – mostly down to tiny classes, lots of support, and a carefully tailored programme of subject choices.

As well as the core curriculum of English, maths and sciences, most children take Spanish, art, DT and history or geography. Catering and business studies are also popular. Some will drop a GCSE to use the time in the access centre to improve their learning skills and strategies for other subjects. Others will take entry level qualifications, ASDAN qualifications or foundation level. Individual education plans are built in to lessons with teachers aware of objectives for each pupil.

In the sixth form lots of vocational as well as academic subjects available – level 2 and 3 OCR and BTec courses in business, sport, agriculture, engineering, ICT and health and social care, as well as A level tuition in most of the usual flavours (English, maths, economics, history, drama, Spanish). The A level range isn't huge, partly because the school is small (20-25 per year in sixth form) and partly because the range of vocational courses is so extensive. Pupils can pick and mix a combination that will work for them. In 2015, 22 per cent A*-B grades at A level, 5 per cent A*/A, and 100 per cent pass rate in many vocational courses.

Strong emphasis on outdoor and practical learning, with all children participating in the school farm – which features a prize-winning bull as well as sheep, poultry, pigs and vegetable growing. All junior students spend time on the farm every week, gaining skills and confidence. Many of the senior pupils take advantage of the farm to study agriculture or horticulture, with the opportunity to take animals to major agricultural shows and help out with the lambing.

The school also now has a 13 acre forest school site and a smaller area of quieter woodland, used in cross-curricular teaching of art, maths, science and English. Parents are sent four sets of grades a year, two with full reports.

Games, options, the arts: Lots of options, with the outdoors at the forefront: mountain biking, rugby, hockey, kayaking/canoeing, climbing and swimming. Head expanding outdoor education programme. Regular fixtures against other schools. Numbers taking individual instrumental lessons, though not high, are on the rise – currently drums, guitar and woodwind are the most popular. Passionate art staff, an artist in residence, and good art/creative facilities, including sculpting and impressive metalwork shop. Other options after lessons end include needlework, car maintenance, clay pigeon shooting, sugarcraft and lacrosse. Senior students are encouraged to work for awards such as sports leader, basic education leader, British Canoe Union and D of E.

Boarding: Boarding can be full or weekly – about half the pupils (the vast majority of them boys) board. No Saturday morning school but lots of activities for those who stay including outings, such as paintballing, clay shooting, museum visits, canal boat trips, shopping trips, visits to castles and National Trust sites, Warhammer competitions and so on. There's a new sixth form area, but much of the boarding accommodation, though clean and tidy, is on the basic side.

Background and atmosphere: Founded in 1962 by Lt Col Tony Sharp OBE, whose motto, 'The journey is as important as the destination', remains at the heart of the project here. The school is now owned by the Spanish-British education group Colegios Laude.

Some of the buildings have been built by the children, who are rightly proud of what they have created

It is in a rather tucked-away corner of Gloucestershire, in lovely rolling countryside, very calm and peaceful, and built around Pull Court, a rather grand Victorian pile in which many of the children board. The grounds extend to about 80 acres which encompass the farm, forest school, woodland and playing fields etc. Some of the buildings could do with updating; boarding facilities are spacious but a little tired in places; as with many other schools, there is a rolling programme of updating facilities and accommodation with many recent updates. The buildings are full of displays of the children's artwork, and some of the buildings and grounds (notably a new greenhouse, landscaped area and fountain), have been built by the children, who are rightly proud of what they have created. Lots of whole school charity fundraising, walks/runs and swims, sponsorship too of a school in Zimbabwe with practical input from teaching staff.

Pastoral care, well-being and discipline: Small tutor groups which meet twice a day. Parents say pastoral care is a great strength of the school: 'They are genuinely bothered – if there is a problem they listen – there is always someone to talk to'. Boarding and academic staff are separate – to give a sense of 'really being at home', and not under the maths teacher's eye when lessons are over. There is a school nurse on site.

Pupils say there is no problem with bullying – anything that arises is dealt with quickly: 'you don't get picked on for being different'. Zero tolerance of drugs and alcohol – not encountered often, but pupils immediately expelled if they cross the line.

The food is good: provided by local caterers who are subject to the wrath of the student council if the potatoes aren't up to scratch. Plenty of variety in the menu and a rather stunning view from the lovely light dining room over the surrounding countryside.

Pupils and parents: About 80 per cent boys. Some rather quiet pupils, but all speak sincerely about what the school has done for them: 'The tutors help

you a lot, they're approachable'. 'They help you so much, you feel confident – you get lots of support.' 'I can keep up now.'

The school often has a cohort of Spanish pupils spending a term or two experiencing English culture

Boarders, about a quarter from abroad, come from as far afield as Pakistan and Dubai, and from all over the UK. As part of the Colegios Laude group, the school also often has a cohort of Spanish pupils spending a term or two at the school experiencing English culture and learning the language. Day pupils are bussed in from all over Gloucestershire and Worcestershire – local families keen on the outdoors, a handful of Forces families too. Parents range from celebrities to engineers, professionals and farmers.

Entrance: Via interview with head and assessment. The school is not a special school and statements of SEN etc are examined carefully. No written tests. Prospective pupils are invited to submit current school reports plus any from eg ed psych, and complete three day guest visit. Open mornings throughout the year. For those with SEN, school will consider both current reports and own assessment to ensure needs can be met by the learning support staff.

Exit: A rising number of pupils (about 70 per cent) stay on for sixth form. Of those, nearly all go to college or university. To a variety of places including Leeds, Manchester, Cardiff, Hartpury College. Range of courses including lots of business, quite a lot of agricultural/environmental, as well as art, criminology, sports management etc. The school seems to produce pupils with an entrepreneurial and creative edge.

Money matters: There are bursaries and scholarships (sporting, arts, academic) available up to 20 per cent, plus 20 per cent discount for second siblings and 40 per cent for third siblings.

Remarks: A small school that rebuilds confidence and transforms prospects for many children with learning difficulties, but also offers unique outdoor learning and practical skills teaching for any child not set on the standard academic course. If your child dreams of farming or sculpture or starting her own business, and wants to spend plenty of time getting muddy in the interim, this could be just the place.

Bruton School for Girls

Sunny Hill, Bruton, Somerset BA10 0NT

01749 814400
admissions@brutonschool.co.uk
www.brutonschool.co.uk

Ages: 11–18 (junior boarding from year 4)
Pupils: 216; sixth form: 47
Boarders: 63 full, 9 weekly
Day: £5,430 – £15,135 pa
Boarding: £18,447 – £25,551 pa

Headmistress: Since 2012, Mrs Nicola (Nicky) Botterill BSc MA NPQH FRGS FRSA (late 40s). A geographer by academic discipline, with a first degree from Middlesex Poly and a master's from the Institute of Education, Mrs Botterill has taught in girls' schools for her entire career, except for one stint in a mixed state school, ascending through the hierarchy as far as the deputy headship of St Mary's Calne, from where she was appointed head of BSG.

'I felt immediately at home here and found the girls grounded and unstuffy', she says. Early exposure to travel and living abroad as a child imbued her with a love of adventure and foreign climes; the fact that she took a mid-career gap year has done it no harm at all.

Bruton is small girls' school in a part of South West England that is richly populated with good schools. Mrs Botterill was brought in to increase numbers but has achieved rather more than that since her arrival – her work supporting newly qualified teachers within the Girls' Schools Association was recognised by their award for 'an outstanding contribution from a recently appointed head' in 2014 – and has garnered approval from all quarters.

'She did not grab the reins, but took the time to get to know people'; 'But you know she's in charge,' say parents. In her trademark fuchsia jacket and pashmina, we found her engagingly warm, frank, chatty, approachable – all reiterated by parents and girls. Any free time she might have could be spent doing arts and crafts, such as pottery and stained glass, even DIY on occasion.

Academic matters: Non-selective but scores highly on value-added. Forty-four per cent of GCSEs were graded A*/A in 2015; 42 percent of A levels taken came in at A*/A. Before GCSE, the curriculum includes compulsory classics (including Greek and Latin), DT and 'home technology'. In sixth form, Leith's certificate in food and wine is popular – we would happily have stayed in any ski chalet catered by BSG students, judging by what was being made in the kitchen. Typically, girls take nine or 10 subjects at GCSE, to include separate sciences, but no language, ancient or modern, is compulsory; a choice of French, German, Spanish or Latin is offered. Flexible and enlightened enough to allow girls to take certain GCSEs (eg French and maths) two or three years early, in exceptional cases. Twenty-one subjects to choose from in sixth form.

Small class sizes, averaging under 10, hard work and the 'enthusiastic, effective teachers – the kind you get in a grammar school,' according to one parent, contribute to the school's academic success and high praise is given to SEN diagnosis and support: 'My daughter's in-house plan is tailored to her', said another, whose daughter had fled the local comprehensive. The wide ability range 'has meant my girls have learnt to tolerate all levels of ability, which is much more like real life,' commented one thoughtful mother of clearly bright girls. Stand-out subjects are English, drama, art and biology; some report that maths is currently in flux. Our impression was of interesting subject matter (West Side Story being used to demonstrate the realities of immigration for Hispanics, capital punishment v the safety and protection of prisoners) being delivered with IT as support rather than as a substitute for honest-to-goodness teaching, to a very compliant, quiescent flock – just for our benefit?

Games, options, the arts: Hockey and netball the main games here, with no fewer than 17 netball teams. An impressive fixture list where BSG looks more like David up against local Goliaths Sherborne Girls and King Edwards Bath. Several netball courts doubling up for tennis, a delightfully sunny Astro where strenuous hockey practice was taking place when we visited, plus an athletics track behind the main group of buildings. At present the swimming pool is an outdoors, solar-heated, summer only affair; the five swimming teams use opponents' indoor facilities for matches at less clement times of year. An indoor pool is top of the parental wish list. Although there is a riding team, this is not the kind of place where girls bring their own steeds, and the ability to pilot a horsebox is not a requirement for entry. Sporty activities include quidditch and tchoukball (truly – we wished we'd seen either).

West Side Story was being used to demonstrate the realities of immigration for Hispanics, capital punishment v the safety and protection of prisoners

Music comes in for high praise – deservedly so, judging by the singing practice for the director of music's own composition that we heard, the recital at assembly and admissions to national and county youth choir and orchestra. A school orchestra, smaller ensembles for brass and strings inter alia, a Baroque group, theory classes for those taking

grades and plenty of opportunities to play beyond the school gates make for a rich musical offering: we enjoyed the CD (and cookies) we were given on departure very much.

Drama takes place in the Hobhouse theatre: although it is a popular option, outside the devised and scripted requirements of public exams – when we witnessed genuine belly laughs and dramatic talent in the GCSE piece we saw – the scope seems limited to one musical per year, but 'Please please don't make us play boys again,' beg the girls. The art department is truly vibrant – a crammed creative space where girls seem to be able to pursue any artistic fancy: the series of photographs resulting from one girl persuading an obliging friend to immerse herself in milk in a variety of poses was memorable. Good links with the arty town of Bruton enrich the life of the school – the installation by a local artist of felt poppies suspended on threads to commemorate the First World War was innovative and moving. Plenty of trips to local and not so local theatre, concerts and galleries complement the lively arts scene within school.

Boarding: Three boarding houses, arranged by age, at either end of the site cater for full, weekly and flexi boarders. Accommodation is homely and not obsessively tidy: a couple of sixth form girls had transformed their room into a Christmas grotto, complete with glitter and a snow scene, without attracting the wrath of the domestic staff. Intra-school allegiance, which might attach to houses with full vertical boarding in a bigger school, is created by assigning each girl (day and boarding) to one of four halls named for local stately homes.

Background and atmosphere: One of a disproportionate number schools in Bruton (owing to the beneficence of Hugh Sexey, an auditor of the Exchequer in the early 1600s), a small charming Somerset market town of golden stone, BSG sits on Sunny Hill, certainly so the day we visited, with distant hazy views of Glastonbury Tor. Established in 1900 and known originally as Sunny Hill School, it has mostly been independent but spent 30 years in the maintained sector early in the last century. It is possibly this which gives the school a delightful lack of pretension and snobbery, 'a place where the teachers don't parade like cockerels, but where they get a remarkable amount out of the girls,' in the words of one mother. 'It's slightly Enid Blyton with cocoa and biscuits at break,' said another. We liked the fresh air and heartiness about the place – the gaps between buildings necessarily mean a breather between lessons, through the beautifully tended grounds and eccentric pop-up garden, with its giant chessmen.

Proud and unapologetic to be a girls' school, where both the girls and their parents choose to be: 'My daughter was offered the chance to move at

We felt a genuine sense of community over a delicious lunch of steak pie and fresh veg

sixth form and declined,' one parent told us, another recounted a story of her daughter taking refuge from the local state offering and finding sanctuary at BSG. 'We landed on our feet here', said yet another satisfied customer. The school's size means that girls form friendships across year groups, and we felt a genuine sense of community over a delicious lunch of steak pie and fresh veg. 'Friendly' kept popping up as the most common adjective used to describe the school: 'My daughter took all of two days to settle in,' reported one happy mother.

Pastoral care, well-being and discipline: Highly, highly, highly rated by everyone we spoke to, and hot on friendship issues, a perennial subtext in girls' schools. 'Bruton stood out over other local schools,' in one parent's view, 'and the school is not afraid to tackle issues head on, yet sensitively'. Tutor groups are mixed age until sixth form (these meet daily), and between tutors and heads of halls, no-one appears to fall through the net. Relationships between staff and students and between the students themselves are sound and supportive, 'but we do teach them resilience and that things going wrong isn't necessarily a problem,' adds the head. 'Honourables' are awarded for exceptional work, 'hallmarks' for acts of courtesy and community-mindedness, colours for sporting prowess. Discipline is not a matter which seems to rear its ugly head very often: rudeness, lateness and wilder interpretations of uniform do not go unremarked; smokers and drinkers can expect a sliding scale of punishment, whilst druggies and persistent offenders face exclusion. 'Fluffy and lenient we are not,' states the head.

Pupils and parents: 'Confident without being arrogant' – that overworked phrase to which every school aspires – is echoed by parents. We found the girls, who arrive in anything from helicopters to old bangers, cheerful, unpretentious and very happy to be at this school. 'This isn't the place for hair-flicking city types, but for well-grounded families, wanting the best for their girls', says Mrs Snow, head of the prep. 'Our parents aren't flashy but aren't without aspiration either'. A welcoming parent community helps to reassure first time buyers that they have made a wise choice. About one fifth of girls is from overseas.

Entrance: Non-selective, but via online verbal and non-verbal reasoning tests to assess potential, plus interview. At sixth form the bar is higher, at five GCSEs at grade C or above, with Bs at subjects to be taken at A level. Termly open days and visits by arrangement. Main feeders at year 7 are school's own prep and local primary schools, at year 9 local preps. Several buses serve surrounding area within 20 mile radius.

Exit: To a wide range of universities and an equal variety of courses. Most girls get to their first choice: everything from Cambridge (one off to study biochemistry in 2015) to Russell Group, red-bricks and the 1994 group, studying veterinary science, journalism, project management for construction – you name it. Famous old girls include Clarissa Farr, High Mistress of St Paul's Girls' School and journalists Viv Groskop, Imogen Sellars and Catherine Davies.

Money matters: As independent education goes, good value for money, at about 25 per cent cheaper than its most expensive competitors. 'Bruton offers everything academic and holistic a parent could ask from a 21st century girls' school, without charging the ridiculous fees that most other schools charge', so said one mother. Scholarships, awarded for the usual range of talents, are nominal, but governors' exhibitions are awarded in cases of means-tested need to a maximum value of 40 per cent of fees.

Remarks: 'It's just not very BSG to promote itself,' one father remarked, but if we were expecting an apologetic little school lurking in rural Somerset, we did not find it. Hidden gem is more like it – a place of unpretentious endeavour where girls can be girls and achieve as much as they are capable of. 'Follow the gleam,' may be the school motto, but in our view it could be time for a spotlight.

Bryanston School

Bryanston, Blandford Forum, Dorset DT11 0PX

01258 452411
admissions@bryanston.co.uk
www.bryanston.co.uk
C of E

Ages: 13–18
Pupils: 687; sixth form: 283
Boarders: 603
Day: £27,459 pa
Boarding: £34,407 pa

Head: Since 2005, Ms Sarah Thomas (50s). A GDST girl hailing from Birkenhead and proud of it, Ms Thomas read Lit Hum (classics – the proper kind with Greek) at Oxford, before becoming an articled clerk to a notary public. Both her parents taught, but their entreaties not to follow in their footsteps clearly fell on deaf ears, for she left the law to do her PGCE at King's College London, before longish stints at Sevenoaks and Uppingham. All that formative experience of co-ed boarding has equipped her admirably for Bryanston. 'A female head is just a part of who we are, and the best part of my job is recruiting outstanding staff', she says. We found her a (charming) force to be reckoned with, whom we can imagine causing stuffier members of HMC to choke on their sherry. 'Splendid', say parents, '100 per cent approachable, with fine powers of judgment'. Ms Thomas makes a point of keeping her hand in at the chalk-face – everybody has to do Latin in the first year, and a fair few take it on to GCSE; a brainy minority do Greek as well.

Ms Thomas' husband teaches at nearby Hanford and writes children's books and plays; they have two daughters at university. In her precious time off? 'Reading – for its peaceful aspects and the opportunity to lose myself in other worlds', she says, plus walking her dog and cooking.

Academic matters: Not desperately selective, with an expectation of 50 per cent for each subject at CE – but what marks this school out is the way academic life is structured. The timetable contains assignment periods for each subject alongside lessons, where prep, further study or one-to-one sessions with the subject teacher take place – the latter ominously named 'correction periods'. In the first three years, assignment periods are supervised by the subject teacher, providing access and extra help outside lessons. Academic progress is tracked more tightly here than in any school this editor had seen: weekly assessments are provided by each subject teacher and entered on the e-chart, the online mark-sheet to which parents also have

access. All assignments (prep) are set to be handed in a week later, so being organised and learning to manage a workload is a skill learnt early. 'The tutorial system ensures success,' says the school: each student is allocated a tutor for the duration of his/her time at the school – so far, so conventional – but these individuals do so very much more than that somewhat over-used term suggests. 'We tutors deal with the academic, spiritual, moral and act as a kind of PA', said one. Parents greatly value this and tutors' accessibility both to students and parents. SEN provision supports what goes on in class: each department appoints a staff member to liaise with learning support. One-to-one tuition is available; all help offered is discreet and without stigma. School claims to 'deliver for every child we admit.'

So does it pay off? At GCSE in 2015, 46.2 per cent A*/A grades and in some years, school is on a par with local independents such as the Sherborne schools, where entry requirements are higher. 'My daughter got results beyond our wildest dreams', raved one mother, who also reckoned that Bryanston had been perfect for all three of her children, with differing abilities and interests. Visual arts of all kind very popular and successful, as is Latin and Greek; results suggest as much enthusiasm as aptitude for Latin, but it is heart-warming to see such a resurgence in classical languages. School keeps a Greek theatre tucked away in its extensive grounds, and the JACT summer school in Greek – of formidable repute – for all-comers is held here. At A level, 68.2 per cent graded A*/B and 46.2 per cent A*/A in 2015, but value-added shows up strongly against comparable schools. Business studies and English are the most popular choices, sciences hot on their heels, followed by art and design in its various forms. History and geography have a moderate following; modern languages surprisingly little, along with music and drama. First IB results in 2014, with an average of 35 points and one pupil achieving the maximum of 45.

Games, options, the arts: The scope is amazing – clearly something for the most idle couch potato. All the sports and facilities one would expect in a school of this type feature (rugby, hockey, netball, cricket, tennis, rowing) and both hockey and lacrosse are on offer in consecutive terms. Luscious grounds stretch down to the river Stour, where rowing of increasing seriousness takes place out of a beautiful new boathouse designed by an OB and keen oarsman (sadly we weren't shown this). New arrivals learn navigation skills and how to survive a night in the open – useful for those times when they get lost in the grounds. A carousel of adventurous options takes place in the second year, comprising (amongst other things) falconry, canoeing and rock-climbing. Riding might seem quite mundane; we were bemused not even to be shown

the stabling, indoor and all-weather schools, or cross-country course on our visit. Keen riders can bring their own steeds. Sailing in the school's own fleet of Lasers in Poole harbour. School is notable local and national player in a variety of sports. OBs include Phil de Glanville.

The art at Bryanston hits you between the eyes as you walk in. Enormous canvasses adorn the long walls of each of the central corridors in the main building: the scope of the department and amount of available hanging space, plus the skills and dedication of teachers and students, mean the most ambitious projects can be executed. The art department is divided into 2D and 3D; both aspects enjoy a passionate following and are fabulously resourced. Best work of both past and present pupils has twice been showcased in Cork St (no less). School's reputation for a creative curriculum is well deserved, and fulfils the aspiration for 'the joy of the abundant life' which an early headmaster articulated.

We found her a (charming) force to be reckoned with, whom we can imagine causing stuffier members of HMC to choke on their sherry. 'Splendid,' say parents

Music and drama (both excellent and ambitious in scope) tend to be avidly pursued for the love of them, rather than chasing yet another GCSE. The 600 seat Coade Hall measures up as well as any school theatre facility, indeed visiting theatre companies stage performances here. Usual musicals (Cabaret, Guys and Dolls in recent years) sometimes include a showing for prep schools – canny marketing! Annual play for each year group (eg The Crucible, Pride and Prejudice in a specially adapted version). Much student-led drama, and our guides enthused about house drama, where even the most reluctant performers tread the boards. New Tom Wheare Music School (named after retired head) includes stunning 300 seat concert hall with huge stage designed to hold a large-scale symphony orchestra, plus, inter alia, large numbers of practice rooms, recital rooms, recording studios, soundproofed band rooms and courtyard area for outdoor performances (plans for performances and masterclasses from renowned musicians). Let's hope they are generous with it. Again, any musical whim can probably be accommodated – if not here, then where? Over a fifth of students sing in a group or choir: we heard the first rehearsal of one of mixed age and mixed ability during the lunch hour, and tuneful and enthusiastic it was too. Musicians perform all over the place, including

London and abroad – the dance band to Paris, the chamber choir and orchestra to Florence. All students have to learn a musical instrument in the first year, which may be where the enthusiasm and lung capacity to play the bagpipes starts – there is even a pipe band. 'What the musicians did in the hols' was an interesting little aside in the school's extensive literature; one boy's attendance at a course at Berklee College in Boston helped him gain a place on its coveted degree programme.

Extracurricular activities are taken seriously here in pursuit of the abundant life – there is everything from Accessorise (jewellery) to yoga, and a choice of four out of more than 100 is compulsory in the first two years.

Boarding: Three boarding houses are contained within the main building, the rest scattered over the grounds immediately around the main building. Accommodation is comfortable rather than de luxe. Everybody eats centrally in the delightfully refurbished dining hall, and the food is all it's cracked up to be: we sampled the excellent salad bar but the hot choices and puddings all smelt and looked scrummy too. Rather cool café in lieu of tuck shop sells smoothies, cookies, pizza and other appealing fare; houses also have kitchens for making snacks and drinks. When we asked about the long walk into Blandford, students looked

Bryanston has kept its reputation for blazing a trail – 'Just don't call us progressive,' said the head, with a visible shudder

slightly blank – why would they need to do that when everything is at school?

Background and atmosphere: Exceedingly long drive through woods leads eventually to a baby château perched on a rise overlooking the river Stour. Modelled on Menars in the Loire valley by Norman Shaw, the house had to be sold to meet the death duties of Viscount Portman after the family had lived there for just 30 years. In 1928 a young Australian school master bought it and founded the school on traditional and modern principles – et nova et vetera, as the motto says. Going co-ed in the early 70s was well ahead of the trend, and Bryanston has kept its reputation for blazing a trail – 'Just don't call us progressive,' said the head, with a visible shudder.

Acres (400) of grounds and beautiful bold modern additions surround the house, which aside from the diggers and heavy plant constructing the new music school, make a harmonious whole. Inside, two long parquet-floored corridors dotted with sofas in the main house give the continuing impression of being fortunate residents of a mansion, though everyone looks more purposeful. Even the staff and visitors' loos were contained in a spacious cloakroom with leather armchairs in which to retreat from the fray.. Teaching spaces are high spec, particularly the science labs, with their wet and dry areas in the newish Sanger building, named after a double laureate biochemist and OB.

Pastoral care, well-being and discipline: Exceptionally good care is taken of all students. Newbies meet their tutors on arrival at school, and the team formed between him/her and the housemaster or mistress (known as a hsm, to rhyme with bosom) is a tight one. It seems as though it would be hard for any unhappiness or falling off in performance or morale to go unnoticed. Each house has a distinct character and students are placed in them according to a process 'akin to Hogwarts' sorting hat', according to the head. Boys spend a year in one of two junior houses; girls go straight into the house in which they will spend their whole time at the school.

We liked the understated but definite sense of a spiritual life at Bryanston, led by the chaplain. As well as the church in the grounds, there is a dear little chapel in the vaults of the main house which acts as a calm retreat from the hurly burly of life going on outside its open doors. One parent told us her son had 'quietly gone off and got himself confirmed', slightly to her surprise (but pleasure).

The persistent reputation for unchecked behaviour and general licence, drugs in particular, has been slow to die, but one parent briskly dismissed it as 'quite unmerited'. According to the school and the parents we spoke to, any involvement would result in immediate expulsion – and the kids know it. A civilised and age-appropriate view is taken of alcohol for sixth formers, 'carefully monitored under adult supervision,' says school. Any misdemeanours are 'harshly dealt with,' a mother confirmed. The school rules and regs fit on one side of paper and are unequivocal and up to date, eg 'Computers/iPods/MP3s must not be used to watch films, play games, listen to music in lessons, prep and after lights out'. For a school with a dress code rather than uniform below sixth form, we found the students tidier than at many other schools: the drill is a coloured polo shirt with a sweater with black or navy trousers or skirts; more leeway for sixth form.

Pupils and parents: When asked if she could sum up a Bryanston pupil, the head said no she couldn't, though one hallmark would be 'someone comfortable in their own skin', who would enjoy being a part of things. We were actually allowed to meet very few, just the head boy and girl who showed us around, who were of course charming and very much on-message. As for the parents, quite a range professionally from doctors to financiers to creative types, but they struck us as exceptionally thoughtful about their children's education. The geographical spread, in common with many schools, has contracted so that Bryanston is really a South West school, though with a significant minority coming from London and the south east, and a handful from the furthest reaches of the UK. A few from overseas.

Notable OBs include Lucian Freud, all the Conran boys, Mark Elder, John Eliot Gardiner (who sent his daughter too), Ben Fogle and Emilia Fox.

Entrance: There are 130 places at 13+ via CE (50 per cent expected in all papers) or by Bryanston's own papers from an amazing number of prep schools. Close links forged with preps and prospective parents; instead of open days with a cast of thousands, the school arranges group visits for 12 or so families, as well as individual visits. Registered pupils are also invited to various events in the two years before they arrive. Between 25-30 new students arrive at sixth form for which 50 points at GCSE are required, after a day of tests (maths, English and abilities) and interviews at the school. Existing pupils also have to meet the points requirement, waived only in very exceptional cases.

Exit: Around 15 per cent leave after GCSEs. Nearly half of upper sixth leavers apply to university once they have their results. The head of sixth form is all for this, and has tweaked the school's UCAS process to accommodate it. University strategy starts with tutors early in lower sixth and the vast majority of students do go on, whenever they apply. 'Less formal relationships between staff and students mean they are confident enough to bounce up to them and ask for what they need,' he says of the application process. About half take gap years.

Degree courses, interestingly, tend to be conventional choices (business in various forms, history and English – but classics too – hurrah!) in conventional places: Bristol, Leeds, Oxford Brookes and UWE. A sprinkling of medics, linguist and politicians too, plus around 10 per cent to art foundation courses. In 2015, seven Oxbridge places.

A few gripes about careers and higher education guidance at AS level from parents; while they like the rather unpressured approach to UCAS, they feel alternatives should be more clearly spelt out. Newish head of sixth form appointment is grounds for optimism, however.

Money matters: Fees in line with comparable schools but some items appear on the bill as extras, unusually, such as stationery, art and DT materials. Scholarships across a range of disciplines including

DT and ICT to a maximum of 25 per cent of fees. Bursaries on application.

Remarks: Stunning school with unrivalled facilities and a great deal of latitude and encouragement for students to explore any aspect of academic, sporting and artistic life which takes their fancy. Too much too young? Possibly. A great deal more traditional than its reputation would suggest, but myths can take a long time to break down. We could not find any detractors, try as we might!

Canford School

Wimborne, Dorset BH21 3AD

01202 847207
admissions@canford.com
www.canford.com
C of E

Ages: 13–18
Pupils: 635 (60 per cent boys); sixth form: 260
Boarders: 430 full
Day: £25,008 pa
Boarding: £32,616 pa

Headmaster: Since 2013, Ben Vessey BA MA MBA (40s). Educated at Magdalen College School, Oxford, then read history at Southampton. Intended to join the army but after tearing both knee ligaments playing rugby worked as an oil and gas broker for five years in the City and on placement in Texas. 'But when I came back from the US I realised that it wasn't what I wanted to do,' he says. Applied to Dauntsey's, who snapped him up to teach history. Became head of history and housemaster there, followed by four and a half years as head of history, politics and law at Millfield. Spent six years as senior deputy head at Christ's Hospital – 'it was a great apprenticeship for headship,' he says. Along the way he did an MA in history, a PGCE and an MBA in education management.

Loves teaching and teaches five periods a fortnight to a year 9 history set. 'I write reports and do parents' meetings and it keeps me in touch with the rhythms of teachers' busy routines,' he says. Much in evidence around the school and makes a point of dropping in on lessons to see colleagues in action in the classroom. Has lunch with pupils and staff as often as possible and supper with them twice a week. 'I leave them alone at breakfast,' he jokes.

Energetic, enthusiastic and impressively focused, he lives and breathes the school. He loves Sounds of Canford (the school's informal concert series), watches as many concerts, plays and sports matches as he can and catches up with Year of Genius, an innovative enrichment project launched by the school, as he cycles on his spin bike. Lives in a house on-site with his wife Harriet, their three sons (the eldest of whom started as a day boy at Canford at the same time as his dad) and two black labradors. In his spare time he plays golf, cycles and reads (he's a fan of Bernard Cornwell's Sharpe novels and other historical fiction). Winston Churchill is his hero and a bronze miniature of the legendary PM left to the school by old boy Terrence Cobden Pike has pride of place in his study. Churchill was a relation of the Guest family, who owned Canford before it became a school and apparently spent many summer holidays there.

Academic matters: Results are easily as good as other co-ed schools with illustrious names. In 2015, 51 per cent A*/A at A level and 84 per cent A*-B (figures include Pre-U for art and languages). At GCSE, 69 per cent A*/A. Considering the breadth of intake this speaks volumes for the first-rate teaching. Maths and chemistry are the most popular A level subjects but many pupils do a mix of sciences, arts and humanities subjects. EPQ on offer too. Sixth formers we spoke to were full of praise for the support in the run-up to A levels and the study skills workshops on offer. Study leave is awarded on an individual basis but most sixth formers opt to stay in school, keen to make the most of time-tabled lessons, past papers and one-to-one help. 'Everyone works hard here,' a sixth former told us while another said: 'The teachers want you to do well and they really support you.'

All year 9s do French and Latin, as well as German or Spanish. Most take 10 subjects at GCSE, including at least one language and two sciences. Pupils are set for maths and languages from the word go. Computer science has been introduced throughout the school and is increasingly popular – 16 taking it at GCSE when we visited, 11 at AS and three at A2. 'Prep schools should be trying to embed computer science in the curriculum, rather than just IT,' we were told. Good provision for those with learning difficulties, mostly dyslexia, mild dyspraxia and language attention difficulties. Learning support housed in the Lovell Building, along with the humanities department. Year 9 pupils who need additional support can take extra English instead of Latin, while in years 10 and 11 learning skills are offered for a number of pupils instead of one GCSE subject, with focus on developing study skills. One-to-one tuition available when the need arises. Average class size is 15 in years 9 to 11, nine in the lower sixth and eight in the upper sixth.

Facilities throughout the school are second to none. Glorious library (complete with oak panelling, chandeliers and 18,000 books, DVDs and audio CDs, plus thousands of virtual resources). Excellent science labs. We liked the fact that every classroom

and office has an inspiring and appropriate moniker – Roddick (after Body Shop founder Anita Roddick) for economics and business and Olympus for classics are just two examples. Even the book cupboard in the classics department gets its own name – Hades, of course.

Catches up with Year of Genius, an innovative enrichment project launched by the school, as he cycles on his spin bike

Pro-active careers department organises advice on GCSE and A level subjects, annual careers symposium and interview experience. Work experience isn't compulsory but a growing number of students are applying for internships and work placements. In 2015, sixth formers gained places on two of the UK's top corporate career programmes.

Games, options, the arts: Sport is a big deal here and Canford teams score notable successes at every level. Main sports are rugby, hockey and cricket for boys, hockey, netball and tennis for girls and athletics and rowing for both. Rowing VIII were Henley finalists recently. Acres of pitches, real tennis court (there aren't many of those around), fitness suite and a 25m indoor swimming pool. In years 9 to 11, four teams regularly fielded per year group so everyone gets the chance to represent the school. Other options include cross country, sailing, dance, basketball, golf, squash, badminton, canoeing and fitness. Sports facilities and pool are used by local community at allotted times. When we visited a keep fit class for the elderly was in full swing in the sports hall.

Art is stunning – and in many cases highly original and ambitious. We were particularly taken with a vast oil painting (3.5m x 1.5m) of a turtle family. Canford pupils have achieved the highest Pre-U grades for art for two years running and up to eight students a year go on to do art foundation courses. Music is terrific, with a large number of choirs, orchestras, strings groups and jazz band. Around half of pupils take individual music lessons. Two major concerts a year, one at Canford, the other at the Lighthouse in Poole, home of the Bournemouth Symphony Orchestra. Lots of drama, with opportunities on stage, backstage and in technical roles. Several pupils have won National Youth Theatre places in recent years. Productions, house plays and an annual school musical take place in the Layard Theatre, opened by film and theatre director Sir Richard Eyre in 1999. Theatre used by professional companies too.

CCF isn't compulsory but is very popular. In 2015 nine cadets from the Royal Marine section beat the likes of Harrow, Winchester and Shrewsbury to win the Pringle Trophy, the premier inter-schools' cadet competition. Others opt for D of E, adventure training and/or community service programme. Seniors work in local primary schools and with disabled groups, run drama workshops and coach sport while juniors work as conservation volunteers. School is the lead sponsor of The Bourne Academy, a secondary school in Bournemouth. Canford pupils act as teaching assistants for languages, computing and science and sign up for book clubs and quizzes.

School is full of bright ideas – everything from Radio Canford to Connections, a general studies programme that challenges pupils to think beyond the curriculum and links different academic disciplines. Another innovation that caught our eye was Yellow Hour, an hour set aside twice a term for pupils and staff to perform in front of an informal audience. Recent highlights included the director of studies performing a maths equation and the head reading a short story he'd written. Year 9s do a carousel of activities every Wednesday – sculling, mixed lacrosse, bell ringing, even etiquette. A plethora of academic, sporting and cultural trips abroad as well as community projects in Argentina, Ghana and India. The Canford Partnership was set up following the discovery (and sale) of a £7 million Assyrian Frieze in the school tuck shop in 1994 and supports worthwhile community projects in the UK and Third World.

Boarding: Full boarding only, no weekly boarding. Flexible exeat system means pupils can spend several Saturday nights a term at home if they want but on average two-thirds of boarders stay in

Dining hall, known as the Great Hall, where Edward, Prince of Wales, danced in 1890 following a ritual slaughter of birds at a shooting party, is particularly magnificent

school at weekends. Seven boarding houses – four for boys and three for girls (plus three mixed day houses). Each house has a married houseparent, three tutors and at least one matron (described by one teacher as 'the heart and soul of the boarding house'). Houses are modern and well equipped. In Beaufort, one of the girls' houses, youngest girls are in dorms of four, year 10s and 11s in twos and sixth formers get singles. When pupils arrive at 13 they are assigned a mentor from the year above and are so busy that they settle in quickly – weekend activities programme includes an assault course, pizza nights and trips to the beach. Beaufort housemistress has two cats and two dogs – 'they're brilliant therapy for anyone who feels homesick,' she says.

Most boarding houses are close to the main school buildings but Court and Franklin, two of the boys' houses, are a scenic seven-minute walk from the main school. Boys told us they enjoy the stroll and some bike or skateboard back and forth. Youngest pupils hand their mobile phones in at night but a housemaster we spoke to says pupils are so busy that electronic devices aren't generally a problem. Boys in his house prefer to play Connect Four and chess than stare at screens in their spare time. Very refreshing to hear.

Background and atmosphere: Canford is one of the most beautiful schools in the country. Located in 250 acres of parkland beside the River Stour, it even has its own Victorian arboretum, complete with 350 tree species and one of the largest sweet chestnut trees in the UK. A building of some sort has stood on the Canford site since the Domesday Book. The oldest parts are a pretty Norman church, used for services but too small to take the whole school, and the early 15th century John O'Gaunt's kitchen, used for debates, meetings and receptions. The stunning 19th century main building, originally known as Canford Manor and designed by Edward Blore and later Sir Charles Barry (architect of the Houses of Parliament), is Grade I listed. Lord Wimborne sold the manor in 1923 and the school was founded the same year. It first admitted girls into the sixth form in 1969, went fully co-ed in 1995 and is now 60 per cent boys, 40 per cent girls.

School is a mix of grand, historic buildings and ultra-modern, but stylish additions. Dining hall, known as the Great Hall, where Edward, Prince of

Wales danced in 1890 following a ritual slaughter of birds at a shooting party, is particularly magnificent. These days a modern cafeteria system is in place. Food is cooked in-house and gets the firm thumbs-up from pupils. All meals eaten in the Great Hall but there are kitchens with tea and toast-making facilities in every house, plus a tuck shop known as the Grubber.

The whole place fizzes with activity from dawn till dusk. Youngsters we spoke to said there's so much going on that it can be 'a bit overwhelming' at first but they quickly learn time management skills. Day pupils must be in school by 8.15am and leave at 6pm, although many stay on later. All look smart – blue jumpers and tartan skirts for girls up to year 11, tweed jackets and ties for boys, sixth form girls in navy. Everyone has to be presentable, we were told. No heavy eyeliner for girls – the look is 'healthy and glowing.'

Pastoral care, well-being and discipline: Parents told us that there's plenty of support via the tutor system. Doctors' surgeries held every weekday and confidential counselling services available on site. Pupils describe the chaplain, known as 'Rev Jack,' as 'really charismatic' and praise him for the way 'he involves everyone.' Midweek chapel for all, plus compulsory service for boarders on Sundays.

Zero tolerance on drugs. If pupils are caught smoking outdoors they get detention and parents are informed. If caught smoking indoors they are suspended. School aims to educate pupils about 'sensible, social drinking under controlled conditions' and sixth formers are allowed to have maximum of two drinks (wine and beer) with food at Saturday evening socials in the sixth form centre. 'It is very closely monitored,' we were told by a group of upper sixths.

Pupils and parents: Most pupils live within a 90-minute drive of the school. A sizeable chunk come from Dorset, Hampshire, Sussex, Surrey and Wiltshire and a smattering from London and further afield. Around three per cent of boarders are international students – from places like Hong Kong, Poland and Bulgaria. Quite a few sons and daughters of Old Canfordians and lots of siblings and cousins. Day pupils come from all directions. School puts on 50-seater coach from Bournemouth and Poole, plus minibuses from Dorchester, Blandford and Wool to the west and Christchurch, Ringwood and Fordingbridge to the east.

The pupils we met said personalities of all types thrive at Canford. 'If you are a quiet sort of person the teachers will help you gain confidence,' one girl told us. Those we met were enthusiastic, full of appreciation for the quality of teaching and delightfully unpretentious. Parents (who include lots of medics) praised the place for its academic results, good communication and down-to-earth atmosphere. 'It's not stuffy at all,' one said. Their only criticism was that no building is big enough to hold the whole school for the Remembrance Day service.

Entrance: Pre-assessment in year 7 (literacy, numeracy and reasoning, plus interview, group activities and prep head's report), with offers made to more than 60 per cent for conditional 13+ places. Registrar suggests that parents should register children for pre-assessment by the end of year 6 and says school is looking to identify 'attitude and a have a go mentality as much as raw ability.' If you don't register by then, 'the door isn't closed.' A few places usually come up in year 8. CE benchmark is 55 per cent, although vast majority achieve higher. Candidates who haven't attended prep schools take entrance exam in year 8 (this aims to spot academic potential rather than test knowledge). Around 125 places for year 9 cohort (known as Shells), including 30 to 35 scholarships. Pupils come from around 100 prep schools. Large numbers of boarders from Twyford, Port Regis, Highfield, Chafyn Grove, Walhampton, Westbourne House and Forres Sandle Manor. Day pupils often from nearby Castle Court and Dumpton.

Twenty-five to 30 join in the sixth form – assessment test in November the year before plus minimum of 42 points on students' best seven GCSEs (A* equates to eight, A to seven, B to six etc). A grades expected in subjects to be studied at AS level and at least Bs in English and maths. Highly competitive at this stage – around four applicants (slightly more girls than boys) for every place.

Exit: Around 10 to 15 a year leave after GCSE – for academic or personal reasons or for a change of scene. After A level, more than 95 per cent to university. Bristol, Cardiff, Durham, Exeter and Manchester perennially popular, with courses ranging from biochemical sciences and medicine to history and business. Six to Oxbridge in 2015. Interest in US universities is growing and school has its own international university adviser.

Money matters: A range of 13+ and 16+ scholarships, plus means-tested bursaries worth up to 100 per cent of fees.

Remarks: As we said last time, a very special school and one that can easily hold its own with the most popular in the country. With its first-rate teaching, stunning setting and innovative ideas, Canford is definitely at the top of its game.

Chafyn Grove School

Bourne Avenue, Salisbury, Wiltshire SP1 1LR

01722 333423
office@chafyngrove.co.uk
www.chafyngrove.co.uk
C of E

Ages: 3–13
Pupils: 285
Boarders: 55
Day: £6,585 – £15,885 pa
Boarding: plus £6,060 pa

Interim Headmaster: Mr Jeremy Griffith, BA PGCE (50s) is in charge for 2015/16 academic year. Educated at Winchester College, Bristol University (Hispanic studies) and South Bank University, where he completed an in-service PGCE in modern languages. Began his 35-year teaching career at Horris Hill School, followed by seven years at The Dragon School and another seven at Windlesham House School as housemaster and head of modern languages. After 13 years as head of both Winchester House, Brackley and St Andrew's School, Eastbourne, left to set up his own education and leadership consultancy in 2010. Was tempted

back into headship at Pilgrim's School throughout 2014 (after sudden departure of previous head) before joining Chafyn Grove as interim headmaster.

Acknowledges that he comes across as 'a safe pair of hands' and that his principal role is to 'facilitate the arrival of the new head'. Nevertheless, Mr Griffith has his finger firmly on the school's pulse and has got to grips very quickly with its ethos of 'happy purposefulness and achievement'. Would like to 'reverse the local perception that Chafyn is only for high achieving and competitive pupils and parents' and has put this on record in the press, pointing out breadth of school's exit. Keen to continue fostering kindness and encouragement alongside all that aspiration and achievement. 'Any school which aspires to a lot needs to keep a balance between pride and humility.' Values the staff he has inherited.

'I tone down sport as the children do win a lot – they have to get used to the fact that it isn't all about winning'

Married with two grown-up children, his interests range from architecture to wine and motorcycles. We suspect that he will be missed after the year is up.

Entrance: Children join at all ages and stages and from all over the area. Entry is non-selective. After registration, places are offered two terms before joining and children are invited to spend a day at the school the term before they begin. Scholarships of up to 15 per cent are available in years 2 (academic and all-rounder), 4 (add music and sport) and 6 (add drama and art). Forces discounts of 10 per cent (day) and 15 per cent (boarding) and sibling discounts from 5 to 15 per cent are also offered. Means tested bursaries typically range between 10 and 40 per cent of the combined tuition and boarding fee.

Exit: Canford, Dauntsey's and Millfield top the list of 'next schools', followed by other relatively local choices, eg Bryanston, Claysmore, Marlborough and Winchester. Otherwise pupils disperse to a range of schools, eg Charterhouse, Clifton College, Godolphin, Hampshire Collegiate and Monkton Coombe. Sports and all-rounder awards dominate the scholarship lists, but academic awards are on the up with a scattering of art, DT and music scholarships and exhibitions. Around 10 leave at 11 each year for the Salisbury grammar schools and independents.

Remarks: A 1914 school photograph shows just 17 boys and three members of staff sitting in the grounds of a large Victorian building. Today, that solemn handful of Edwardian scholars would be very surprised to find around 300 pupils at Chafyn Grove, including over 100 girls.

Founded in 1876 as Salisbury School and changed its name in 1916 following an endowment by Lady Chafyn Grove. Although it caters for a wide ability range, there is a work ethic firmly in place. Has taken the unusual step of dropping history, geography and RS from the common entrance syllabus to focus on maths, English, science, French and Latin. This doesn't mean that pupils don't study these subjects, just that teachers can be more flexible in their approach, eg lessons on early history topics such as the Crusades and Medieval Life and geography lessons on South America. French is taught from year 1, Spanish in years 4 and 5 and Latin from year 6. Latin is strong and some pupils get to near GCSE standard. The odd truly hopeless linguist is allowed to drop languages rather than self-destruct in CE. Maths is set for everyone from year 3, top sets are streamed for all subjects from year 5 and lower sets in the last two years. Scholars aiming for the likes of Eton are educated separately, with extra lessons and lots of practice papers. This is certainly a change from times past, when 'Eton, Winchester and Harrow were not Chafyn's remit.' Sessions in thinking, presentation, research and current affairs freshen up the timetable. Year 8 also studies 'Business Skills', involving Dragon's Den-style pitches and advertising campaigns to create and market a product for sale at the end of the year. Teaching body is very stable, with several married couples and long-standing staff members. 'You only realise how well they're being taught when they get to the next school.' At the time of our visit, there were 42 pupils on the SEN register. Taught by 5 members of staff in two dedicated rooms, there is a broad sphere of activity which includes study skills, spelling and learning support alongside help for dyslexia, dyspraxia, EAL etc. One-to-one sessions once or twice a week are free and school is honest about which conditions it can support.

School has the strongest sport in Salisbury and its reputation gives the opposition food for thought before walking out against Chafyn Grove. Everyone plays in a team and with so many – up to 20 on match days – school can send its top teams further afield to other seriously sporty schools, eg Sandroyd

and Port Regis, whilst B and C teams play elsewhere. All the usual sports on offer; boys and girls can also take part in archery, riding, sailing, cross-country and steeplechase. There is an equestrian and a sailing team, both of which compete successfully. Outdoor swimming pool used in summer. In addition to the regular tally of match wins by all teams throughout the year, all four first hockey teams reached the national final in 2015, which school promptly won (champions in 2013 too). Lots of individual success in athletics, eg U13 Hurdles National Prep Schools Champion in 2014. A team of coaches fosters everyone's talent (not just the superstars) on school's pitches and Astroturf, which spread out behind the school up to (distant) railway embankment at edge of school grounds. There's enough space for a gym, squash and tennis courts. Phone app keeps parents abreast of sports fixtures. 'I try to tone down sport a bit as the children do win a lot – they have to get used to the fact that it isn't all about winning,' said a parent. Saturday school (from year 4) is often taken up with matches.

In a nod to childhoods of yesteryear, year 4s go on a Pioneer Camp and learn to put up tents, tie knots and stalk. Bushcraft weekends involve building shelters and campfires

Art department is roomy and light, with plenty of quality work on display including some excellent papier mâché creations. We noticed a good reference library for art and DT. Drama has long been of a high standard and parents rave about the quality of the annual spring production. 'The singing is always very good in these.' Years 3 and 4 put on their own play in the summer term. In music, we'd award a merit. One third of pupils were learning an instrument at the time of our visit and school teaches up to ABRSM grade VI. Some parents feel this isn't enough, although we feel that given the excellent sport and academics, school does a pretty decent job since many serious musicians are likely to head for the Cathedral School. Singing is very popular and there are three choirs, as well as a school orchestra, training orchestra and Jazz Band. Large performance hall has good acoustics, a grand piano and an organ. Practice rooms are small but masses of space for storing instruments and music. Instrumental lessons rotate through the timetable and practice sessions are scheduled for boarders.

Lots of trips, including the usual, eg Normandy, London, the theatre and skiing, and the less usual – a visit to a Sikh temple. Activities during the last two periods on Monday and Thursday are intended to 'give children room to breathe' and include gardening, cookery, golf and Mandarin. In a nod to childhoods of yesteryear, year 4s go on annual Pioneer Camp and learn to put up tents, tie knots and stalk. Bushcraft weekends for seniors involve building shelters and campfires, as well as catching, gutting and cooking their own fish.

Boarding accommodation is comfortable and homely; parents speak very highly of boarding house parents and matrons. 'They are totally on top of who, where, what and why.' Rooms are shared (6-8 per room) and boarding life is well organised, with shower rotas and different items of clothing collected daily for laundering. Year 8 girls have an ensuite shower room which, though clean, is crying out for new tiles. Boarders' sitting room and green room where children can Skype parents. Mobiles are allowed in free time but must be handed in at night. At the time of our visit, there were 26 full boarders, 20 boarding three nights a week and 40 casual boarders, averaging 40 to 50 per night. One third stay in on weekends and there is a full programme of activities, eg bowling, shopping, cycle rides in the woods and trips to London and the beach.

The original Victorian building is still home for the boarders, but most of the teaching takes place in modern buildings which seem to flow into one another on school's compact site. Children were engaged and interested in academic lessons; traditional classroom seating with everyone facing forwards. 'Children like their teachers and don't want to disappoint them.' However, atmosphere is nether old fashioned nor very strict (no standing for visitors). Our two student guides were polite, confident and very honest in their answers to our questions. 'It's a great school if your child is confident and outgoing and knows who they are,' said a parent.

Pupils feel comfortable about reporting any problems to teachers, who do their best to resolve unkind behaviour. 'They name names and know exactly who is doing what.' Likewise parents feel that they can turn to the staff. 'They are very likeable and approachable and they're always in the playground at pick-up times.' Head will summon parents and children and rap heads together if a situation appears to be escalating. There is a seven-point system to discourage bullying and extra mentoring sessions in place for girls in years 5 and 6. Every pupil belongs to an Eight (house) with appealing names – Wasps, Frogs, Birds and Knights. Food is prepared in the school kitchen by the chef and served cafeteria style; meal times are informal and children sit where they like. Lunch was good on the day we visited with plenty of fruit and veg. Day children can arrive at 8am if parents work and stay on for supervised prep until 7pm.

Lovely modern pre-prep with bright, spacious classrooms, own hall and play area. Reception starts small, after which numbers gradually increase. Children in pre-prep can stay until 5:30pm and have their own after-school club and activities including paper craft, football, netball and hockey.

Like most Salisbury schools, there is a mix of local professionals, Forces, business and London commuters. Only a handful from abroad, mostly Spain and a few English with parents working overseas. 'I can't distinguish parents' wealth and professions,' says head. Parents confirm that

atmosphere is 'not snooty or overpowering'. A quick snoop along Bourne Avenue at pick-up time confirms that cars are mostly common or garden.

A busy, happy and academically sound school which still retains a friendly, family atmosphere. Will suit confident children who are happy in their own skin. Needless to say, sporty children are in their element here, although parents of the very talented might need to keep small feet firmly planted on the ground. Is, without a doubt, the go-to school for sport in Salisbury.

Cheltenham College Preparatory School

29

Thirlestaine Road, Cheltenham, GL53 7AB

01242 522697
theprep@cheltenhamcollege.org
www.cheltenhamcollege.org
C of E

Ages: 3–13
Pupils: 395
Boarders: 70
Day: £7,485 – £16,815 pa
Boarding: £16,755 – £21,855 pa

Linked school: Cheltenham College

Headmaster: Since September 2013, Mr Jonathan Whybrow BEd (50s). Educated at St Paul's School and 'loved every minute.' Joined the Royal Marines and then studied for a BEd in physical education and geography at Exeter. Much of his early career was spent at schools in or near London including Latymer Upper, Emanuel School, Devonshire House

Prep (where he was deputy head). Previous headships at City of London Freemen's School, Ashtead and then Beachborough School, Northamptonshire. Married with two daughters, one at the school.

The headship of Cheltenham College Prep has been through a rather uneasy time but, cross everything, Mr W is a keeper. He set his sights on the school as early as 1999 when he attended a conference here and 'fell in love.' He says that he knew there and then that he 'wanted to be part of one of England's great schools.' The stars didn't align in his and the school's favour until 2013, but now he's arrived and does he ever mean business. His mantra comes courtesy of the Royal Marines: Don't be late; don't ask your troops to do what you wouldn't do yourself; concurrent activity (aka multitasking).

Parents we spoke to were very, very happy. Several were in awe not only of his energy but also his mysterious capacity to be all places at once. 'He's everywhere,' said one, 'and he sorts things out straight away. We're so lucky.' Pupils equally impressed, 'He knew everybody's names by the end of the first week,' we were told.

When he's not being omnipresent at school Mr W enjoys golf, skiing, supporting West Ham and holidays in his house in France. He proudly showed us the 'burnt orange' 1977 MG tucked away in a garage – a recent acquisition and one he hadn't quite got round to telling his family about. (He has now.)

Entrance: Taster day for entrance to nursery and up to year 3. For years 4 – 6 it's a taster day and entry assessments in maths, English and non-verbal reasoning. More choosy later on to ensure pupils are up to CE at 13. Discount available for third and subsequent siblings. Generous discounts for Forces families; means-tested bursaries available. A further 20 or so children arrive at 11+ and at this age scholarships of up to 30 per cent of fees in a variety of areas may be awarded. These are valid throughout Cheltenham College.

Exit: 'Four or five' leave at age 11 for local grammars or girls' schools. Majority stay on until 13 and then move over the road to senior school. Those who don't stay go on to (recently) Eton, Harrow, Marlborough, Radley, Wellington and Cheltenham Ladies'.

Remarks: School has been on present site – friendly jumble of Edwardian red-brick and newer additions in extensive grounds just across the road from senior school – since 1908. It was founded in 1863 as the 'College Juvenile Department' and spent a couple of years squashed into a corner of the big school. Parents might be interested to learn that boarding fees in 1865 were 50 guineas (£52.50) a year and it was an extra £1 for a seat in the chapel. Smart rebranding has seen the name change from Cheltenham College Junior School to Preparatory School, with typography emphasising the 'Preparatory School' part of the name. 'It's about trust,' says Mr Whybrow, 'parents must be confident that we will do the same job as a stand-alone prep. If Cheltenham College is not the right senior school for your child then we'll say so.' Understandably, he would prefer pupils to remain until age 13, but the local education market is a competitive one and realpolitik extends to what Mr W calls 'help' for children applying to grammar schools. He's not quite so generous when it comes to the occasional cheeky bit of poaching by a certain nearby girls' school, crisply describing his relationship with The Cheltenham Ladies' College as 'businesslike'.

This has always been a popular prep but parents' loyalty has been tested in recent times by the drift that inevitably results from a rapid turnover of leadership. It's not often that we hear a pupil describe their headmaster as 'the best we've had.' Mr Whybrow is candid about the effect that time of 'uncertainty' had on the morale of pupils, parents and staff. Bringing with him a wealth of experience from leading stand-alone and linked preps, he implemented some changes straight away that were visible on the first day of term – new signage, a general freshening up – small things that make a big difference. In consultation with parents he has re-instated French classes for the youngest children, brought back 'proper' prize-giving (we saw the new trophies in his study), revived the very popular school musical which had 'got lost' and appointed a director of co-curricular activities to beef up this aspect of provision. Longer-term plans involve material improvements to facilities and organisation that will benefit everyone.

High-ceilinged classrooms, old wooden desks and iPads – teaching and learning at Cheltenham College Prep is a creative mix of the best of traditional methods and the latest technology. Small classes, subject specialist teaching and plenty of individual attention enable pupils to progress at their own rate – something parents really

appreciate. 'The teachers are very encouraging, it's made such a difference to my child's confidence' and, 'they make time to follow a child's interest in a subject and take teaching beyond the curriculum.'

During our visit Mr W reduced a class, their ballet mistress and this reviewer to hysterical laughter by his attempts at 'naughty toes'

Pupils learn French as soon as they start in the Kingfishers and between years 6 and 8 pupils can opt for French or Spanish. Most are expected to take Latin – the class we saw looked like so much fun we wanted to stay and decline a verb or two – and there's also the option of 'off timetable' Greek. There are currently lessons on a Saturday morning but Mr W says that this is 'under discussion.'

Learning support has its cheerful offices in the Coach House, there are two full-time members of staff plus a team of part-time assistants. All children are screened and extra support is mostly given in small groups or parent funded one to one sessions. EAL is also based here; Cheltenham may not strike the observer as excessively multicultural but the headquarters of ARRC (NATO Allied Rapid Reaction Corps) is close by.

Pre-prep, known as Kingfishers, occupies low-rise chalet, not an architectural gem but more than compensated for by the fresh air facilities, including forest school. Information boards outside let parents know what their children have been doing each day – great for conversations on the way home. During our visit Mr W reduced a class of 3-year-olds, their elegant ballet mistress and this reviewer to hysterical laughter by his attempts at 'naughty toes' and 'good toes'. I'm sure he wouldn't mind us observing that he is not built for the ballet.

Whether it's sport, music or drama, 'inclusion' is the starting point – there are teams from A to E and bands and choirs 'for all'. Every child has the opportunity to play in a competitive sports team from year 3. Lively house competitions – not just the usual sport but creative stuff too such as poetry, photography and music. Plenty of matches, pupils claimed that the win/lose rate with nearest rivals is pretty even. National winners in schools' rugby recently; finalists in national comps for hockey, netball and also skiing.

Everyone is enjoying the extended range of after-school clubs – 30 or so options including polo, equestrian, archery, chess, street dance and the enticingly named 'Grow your own money.' In addition to termly calendars the school now produces a what's on of events for the whole year – much appreciated by busy parents – with dates for everything from school photos to 'try boarding' nights and theatre visits.

As we walked through the grounds in golden autumnal sunshine, Mr W (who in another life would be a farmer) stops at a muddy pen to scratch the backs of the Gloucester Old Spots, two of which would be attending bonfire night in sausage form. He's keen to extend the forest school provision to include more animals: lambs are next and also chickens who will take up residence on an island in the lake – we hope Gloucestershire foxes can't swim.

Improvements to the school's rather convoluted layout are next on Mr W's to do list – he wants to consolidate teaching into departments. A consequence of this will be a sad farewell to the atmospheric DT room with its parquet floor, wooden cupboards and historic sawdust from 1,000 bird boxes. Outside in the corridor are glass cases displaying beautiful model boats made by a former teacher (they used to be sailed on the lake) and a drop-down model railway track. Art room similarly characterful but will be spared the same fate, not being located in the path of progress. The music department has a rather grand home, Lake House, with baronial fire places and wood-panelled walls. Nearly all pupils learn at least one instrument and there are plenty of opportunities to play or sing – whether it's chapel choir, jazz band, guitar group or, as on our visit, to compose and perform at a polyphone (surprisingly tuneful blue plastic tubes) workshop.

Mr W is a great believer in what he calls 'prep school world', in other words junior pupils should be self-sufficient when it comes to facilities. Fortunately this prep occupies a large site and any sharing is by choice rather than necessity. Full size rugby pitches, Astros and a sports hall that's about to get a £7m makeover are all at the disposal of the juniors. Older children get to use the seniors' new labs for some science lessons.

One parent told us that 'children are encouraged to express their own opinions,' so we put this to the test and asked a few what they thought about their school. 'There are loads of new activities', 'We have a proper roast on Sunday, everyone sits down and is served at the table.' 'Mr Whybrow is amazing.' Yes, yes, but how about some constructive criticism? 'I wish they hadn't stopped us playing football in the car park. There's not enough time at lunch to change into a tracksuit and go out on to the field.'

One central boarding house on two floors (girls below, boys above, shared common room) and dorms divided into rather charming old style curtained cubicles with notice boards and cabin beds – those we saw were not over tidy, just comfortable, with soft toys, photos and the ubiquitous bunting.

All freshly painted and carpeted, new bathrooms too. Lots of staff on hand – house parents, a matron and five gappies. After activities in the evening there's 'properly supervised' prep – overseen by the head or deputy head. School is aware that even very young children are under increased pressure these days and the head and teachers are vigilant to ensure that pupils keep things in perspective. 'School can be pretty full on, we need to be sure there's a good balance', says Mr W.

Boarding reasonably flexible but school can no longer accommodate 'drop of the hat' requests,

especially at the end of the week. At around £35 a night we're not surprised it's so popular – the majority of prep parents are both working (medics, GCHQ, Forces, not so many farming families these days) and this certainly helps.

A few unsteady years would dent the confidence of any school so it's testament to staff and parents' faith in Cheltenham Prep that they've come out of the experience bigger, brighter and bolder. It's heartening to see this historic school under dynamic new leadership facing the future with energy and optimism.

Cheltenham College

Bath Road, Cheltenham, Gloucestershire GL53 7LD

01242 265600
registrar@cheltenhamcollege.org
www.cheltenhamcollege.org
C of E

Ages: 13–18
Pupils: 660; sixth form: 280
Boarders: 534
Day: £25,350 – £26,265 pa
Boarding: £33,795 – £34,710 pa

Linked school: Cheltenham College Preparatory School

Headmaster: Since 2010, Dr Alex Peterken BA MA DEd (30s). Five children, one at the college and two at the prep; he enjoys choral singing (bass) and walking in the Cotswolds. Dr Peterken was educated at The Prebendal School, Chichester where

he was head boy and head chorister, thence to Eton College as a Music Exhibitioner. BA in theology from Durham, MA in educational management from London and a doctorate in education from Surrey. After 11 years at Charterhouse where he was

head of higher education and careers and latterly housemaster of Saunderites, he joined the College in 2008 as deputy head and still teaches religious studies.

Referred to admiringly as 'the man with the plan,' he fearlessly embarked on a programme of significant changes when he took up the headship, building for the future on the school's traditional strengths. Has he succeeded? 'It's the same but better,' we were told over and over again, so that's a yes. Genial, very youthful (one of the youngest HMC heads) and delightfully unstuffy, he teaches half a term of RS to all the first years and sits in on lessons, 'not at the back; I sit next to the pupils and ask questions.' Pupils can visit Dr Peterken, without an appointment, before chapel each morning; he wants to know what's going on, what's exercising his charges. While there may not be queues at his door at 8 in the morning, all the pupils we spoke to said that they 'felt listened to'.

Academic matters: In 2015, 63 per cent A*/A at GCSE. IGCSEs are offered in maths, English literature and science and were recently introduced for history and geography. Maths, English, DT, music, history and science results are particularly impressive. 2015 A levels 45 per cent A*/A grades and 75 per cent A*/B. Dr Peterken has no time for the excuse 'you can't do all things well', and while there are no plans to become more selective or chase league table rankings, there is a strong drive to enrich the academic opportunities for all students via a broader approach to the curriculum and programmes that enable pupils to learn more effectively.

Lessons are 35 minutes long and the new two-week timetable is, apparently, much less confusing than its eight-day predecessor. We saw thoughtful group work (boys and girls at separate tables) in Latin and a biology class where all but one were learning to love leaf mould and get to know its inhabitants. Science dept completely renovated in 2014.

The sixth form has received considerable attention with the introduction of an independent learning project for the lower sixth designed to extend and deepen subject knowledge (offered in addition to the EPQ). The college is also the first UK independent school to run an innovative accredited leadership and life skills course in the sixth form based on Sean Covey's book 'The 7 Habits of Highly Effective Teenagers'. Pupils can choose from 24 A level subjects including textiles, theatre studies, history of art and Latin and Greek. Critical thinking can be taken as an AS.

One of the assurances Dr Peterken and his team gives is that no pupil is allowed to 'slip under the radar'; academic problems are tackled promptly via an 'academic support plan' drawn up with the pupil, parents, housemaster, tutor and subject teachers. The head is also very keen for pupils to learn from each other: disorganised pupils are assigned a buddy to help them on the path to order; older and wiser pupils give talks along the lines of 'Things we wished we'd known ...'

EAL pupils attend an induction programme prior to the start of the academic year and are supported by two EAL specialists. Learning support department caters not only for those with mild dyslexia, dyspraxia, ADHD etc but also ensures the gifted and talented are suitably challenged. The role of this department extends to the whole school, overseeing initiatives to develop the learning potential of all pupils.

Even more enticing than golden silence are the iPads mounted on plinths that pupils can use to search the library catalogue which does not, we are told, extend to Angry Birds

Main school library has just been completely revamped, its wonderful tiers of gothic windows pour light onto new shelves and lounging readers. Banished with the old furniture is conversation; a kind of un-modernisation which, according to our guides, has been welcomed by all. Even more enticing than golden silence are the iPads mounted on black metal plinths that pupils can use to search the library catalogue which does not, we are told, extend to Angry Birds.

Games, options, the arts: Dr Edward Wilson the Antarctic explorer was educated here and no fewer than three intrepid members of staff (one of whom is director of activities) have climbed Everest – surely some kind of a record. While the hills and fields of Gloucestershire offer little to challenge explorers or mountaineers, pretty much everything else is available to fortunate Cheltonians. The first ever inter-school rugby match was played on the school's splendid pitch in 1844, overlooked no doubt by the confection of a pavilion that resembles a miniature Brunel railway station. In the summer this perfect pitch, which won the College's groundsman Groundsman of the Year award, plays host to the venerable Cheltenham cricket festival.

County and national triumphs in rugby, hockey, cricket, tennis, rowing and polo; coaching for all abilities is now 'much more professional' and even third and fourth team matches are keenly contested and enthusiastically supported. Rackets (a forerunner of squash) is one of the more arcane sports on offer and the college has won the national championships three times and is consistently in the top four. Golf, swimming, water polo, dance and fitness are part of the exhaustive (and exhausting) sports programme as is yoga, a surprising hit with the boys; apparently it is very effective for rugby injuries.

CCF, Young Enterprise and D of E are all enthusiastically tackled, the latter being offered in its less common cycling, horseback and ski-touring options in addition to the usual walking challenge. Service activities take place every Wednesday and volunteers give their time locally at schools and residential homes. Longstanding links with Kenya see college pupils working on projects there, often carrying this on into gap years.

Art, music and modern language teaching takes place in the rather grand neo-classical surroundings of Thirlestaine House, a former gentleman's residence. Its original features – huge mirrors, chandeliers, ornate cornices and radiator covers – have survived generations of school children (just) and create a suitably bohemian home for the creative chaos of art and pottery studios. The long gallery is venue for exhibitions, lectures and public events. Two students have recently gained places at RADA for costume design and backstage training courtesy of the outstanding DT department while another gained a place for acting.

Nearly half of pupils learn a musical instrument, a lower uptake than comparable schools but the figure is increasing. Chapel and chamber choirs plus orchestras, bands and ensembles must keep that 40 per cent pretty busy. Performing arts centre complete with dance studio, green room and, less predictably, a plaster frieze of the Parthenon uncovered during refurbishment. School and house plays and reviews are hugely popular, everyone is encouraged to get involved either performing or backstage.

A recent group of upper sixth leavers asked if they could record themselves in the chapel singing favourite hymns as a parting memento

The College also plays its part in Cheltenham's cultural life, participating in the annual festival fest. The combined choirs of the college and Dean Close opened a recent music festival. Harmony with nearby Dean Close and the Ladies' College is described as 'cooperative' with pragmatic sharing of visiting speakers, careers events and collaboration between international students' societies. Pupils are more forthright, acknowledging and enjoying the rivalry.

Boarding: Houses are in residential roads just outside the campus perimeter – separating 'home' and school is considered very important: the head encourages pupils to adopt a professional attitude to school, 'it's a place of work', whereas houses are a home from home, informal and a place for relaxation. Parents are encouraged to join in with weekend or social events and are pretty much in agreement with Ofsted's conclusion that boarding provision at the college is 'outstanding.'

In addition to a matron, each house has a resident tutor who hosts academic 'clinics' outside school hours. Christowe, one of the original Victorian boys' boarding houses, has been beautifully decorated by the current housemaster and his wife (an interior designer) and there's not a whiff of the institutional in the first floor family rooms. As with all the boys' houses, 60 or so boys live here, sharing for the younger and single rooms for sixth formers. The common room and library are full of house memorabilia (house names a constant in the college); fascinating archive photos and a mini museum all foster a sense of continuity and house identity. Wonderful cushions decorated with the piratical house insignia of skull and crossbones were a gift from a parent. Clubby red-painted snooker and games room much admired. Ashmead, one of the girls' houses, was built round a garden quad with secure key pad entry system, lovely light bedrooms and civilised socialising areas. Boys are allowed to visit for film evenings and the like – apparently rom-coms are rather favoured. The housemistress heads off cliques by splitting up prep school groups and changing room-mates each year. All residents meet twice a day – a practical system that also enables staff to observe shifting dynamics. House staff and prefects alert to meal skipping and similar warning signs when 'faddy could tip into eating disorder.'

Background and atmosphere: Beautiful mellow Victorian gothic buildings along Cheltenham's busy Bath Road undergoing final stages of major re-vamp – grade 1 listed status an expensive headache but good news for Gloucestershire's stone masons and other master craftsmen. It's easy to see why visiting Americans (NATO base nearby) get a touch of the vapours; it's every inch the English public school. Public areas certainly getting the five star treatment though classrooms remain workaday and well used (all have requisite IT and smart boards). Stonework not the only area revamped: Dr Peterken has installed a duo of deputies, one pastoral, one academic, a director of learning, a new head of sixth form and 30 new members of teaching staff. Numbers, like results, are rising and a modest increase in places (about 40) is planned, as is another girls' boarding house. Students and parents tell us that much has changed for the better, not change's sake. Singled out for mention were improved home school communication and relations between teachers and pupils. Interestingly, members of staff said that they thought this had always been one of the strengths of the college but our sixth form guides were very certain that things were different and teachers were 'much more involved and friendly'. The staff we met lived up to their billing and were indeed friendly, funny, charmingly young fogeyish in a few cases, and clearly enjoying both the teaching and strong sense of community at the College.

Pastoral care, well-being and discipline: Pupils start each day in the glorious chapel, no doubt energised for study by the famously enthusiastic hymn singing. This is such a feature of college life that a recent group of upper sixth leavers asked if they could record themselves in the chapel singing favourite hymns as a parting memento. The house system is everything here, for boarders and day pupils alike; each is a community within a community and fiercely competitive. Every house has its own character and distinguishing traditions such as prefect blazers and boaters (worn with pride apparently).

Housemasters/mistresses first in line for problems whether academic or social and liaise very closely with teaching staff to ensure 'joined up' care. Older pupils train for peer mentoring responsibilities and can often pick up on wobbles before they become serious. Mobile phones (aka 'the biggest headache') only allowed in houses and, along with laptops, must be handed in before bed. If a housemaster overhears parents being berated or harangued – not uncommon in a school population that is totally teenage – he will challenge (hooray!). The writing of proper thank you letters (to former prep schools, weekend hosts and the like) is another courtesy expected of pupils. While most pupils come from similar backgrounds, staff are alert to potentially insensitive displays of conspicuous consumerism – affording one the unexpected chance to ask a parent to 'take back the mink'.

Some pupils disgruntled about recent tightening up on trips into Cheltenham town centre – now only Sundays unless there's a legitimate need. Head has responded to parents' view that since the school offers so many activities, 'hanging around in town' need not be a supplementary option. Bath Road still in bounds for banks, supermarkets and cafés, not that the last should be necessary – food is plentiful with lots of choice: salad bar, curries, carvery and good puds served in the former chapel and 'legendary' bacon rolls and snacks dispensed by the very friendly ladies in the tuck shop. This is a town school and necessarily takes firm line on drugs, drink and similar misdemeanours. Sixth form privileges are realistic – at 17 pupils can go out for a meal at an 'approved' restaurant; at 18 they may visit a similarly endorsed pub. The sixth form social room in the main school has a café/bar; 'we have to prepare them for life beyond school', one housemaster told us.

Pupils and parents: Good mix of first time buyers, second generation Cheltonians, Forces and international. Around 18 per cent from outside UK – 30 countries represented. Not snobby or excessively label conscious. Many boarders are from local area or within a few hours of Cheltenham. Children don't have to grow up too fast here; they're down-to-earth, polite and confident without being arrogant. 'It's not a London school', one parent said approvingly. Uniform of navy and cerise plus usual complexity of ties generally adhered to, all pupils wear own choice of pastel shirts; boys' individuality expressed mainly via hair.

OCs include Rageh Omar, journalist; Tim Bevan, film producer; General Sir Michael Rose; Nigel and Jack Davenport, actors; James Whitaker, royal correspondent; James Stout, world rackets champion; Sir Alan Haselhurst MP, The Right Hon Lord Anthony Colwyn CB and the Norfolk coroner, William Morris. Several events marked the centenary of Dr Edward Wilson who died with Scott in the Antarctic in 1912.

Entrance: Increasingly competitive. Most via common entrance, 40 per cent from own prep school, others from plethora of localish preps including Beaudesert Park, Abberley Hall, Pinewood, St Hugh's, Hatherop Castle, The Dragon, Bilton Grange, Moor Park and St John's on the Hill. Entrants from state schools take exam (papers in English, maths and, where appropriate, French); sixth form candidates require at least five B grades at GCSE and must sit papers in subjects to be studied.

Exit: Around ten per cent leaves after GCSEs. Almost all sixth formers to higher education. Handful to Oxbridge (four in 2015), most to top universities, huge range from Bath to Manchester to UCL. Most popular subject choices: biological sciences, psychology, economics and management, history, engineering.

Money matters: Scholarships (up to 25 per cent) and exhibitions (10 per cent) offered at 13+ and 16+ in academic, art, DT (13+ only), drama, music and sport. All-round award may be made at college's discretion. Additional means-tested bursaries also available.

Remarks: Radical modernisation does not always fit easily with old traditions, whether architecturally or educationally, but Cheltenham College has emerged refreshed and ready for a new era. This school is a happy, spirited community inspiring real affection and loyalty in its members.

Cheltenham Ladies' College

Bayshill Road, Cheltenham, Gloucestershire GL50 3EP

01242 520691
enquiries@cheltladiescollege.org
www.cheltladiescollege.org

Ages: 11–18
Pupils: 840; sixth form: 325
Boarders: 669
Day: £22,215 – £25,263 pa
Boarding: £33,090 – £37,275 pa

Principal: Since 2011, Eve Jardine-Young MA (30s). Educated in Malawi, won a sixth form scholarship to the school she now leads, a place she credits with 'changing her life profoundly.' After graduating in engineering from Cambridge she worked for Ove Arup (structural engineers) before moving into teaching. Taught economics at Radley, moved to Epsom College where she was housemistress and head of sixth form, thence to Blundell's as director of studies. Married, her husband also works in education. Hobbies include reading, music (she is, apparently, rather a good pianist), gardening and a talkative cockatoo.

Her appointment surprised some, but the CLC Council has a record of selecting left field candidates although they've only had to choose 11 since the school was founded in 1853. Ms Jardine-Young described the protracted recruitment process as: 'Extraordinary, the Council are very involved and take their responsibility extremely seriously.' Ms Jardine-Young lives up to her name and looks scarcely old enough for such a heavy mantle (or

such big shoes, albeit worn with the previous owner's blessing). When asked if she felt the weight of history on her shoulders she said she saw her responsibility as 'stewardship, not of buildings but of tradition and future potential.'

So far Ms Jardine-Young has wisely kept her head down, watching and learning the ropes of the mighty ship CLC and we don't expect her to turn up in the press any time soon banging the drum for girls' schools. Her experience in both single sex and co-ed establishments keeps her diplomatic on this subject, 'at their best, both systems work very well'. The words most often used by parents and girls to describe the principal are 'friendly,' 'approachable' and 'sincere' and indeed she is; talkative she may be but she is not a loose cannon, so we wondered why a marketing person sat in on our interview. Apparently it was for 'training purposes.'

Ms Jardine-Young is her own woman and, in the best possible way, has not yet developed a headish persona. She isn't fixed, she likes exploring ideas and thinking aloud, but don't be fooled, she brings a formidable intellect to her alma mater. Nostalgic talk of a Proustian flashback courtesy of the smell of varnish is followed by discussion of the school's institutional 'meta language'...'while we rightly praise girls who achieve, do we give enough thought to what it means to be a winner? Do we articulate other values frequently enough?' She brims with excitement and vigour and her commitment to and passion for the school shine through. She says she has plans. We can't wait.

Academic matters: League tables may come and go but CLC's academic record remains mighty. In 2015, 87 per cent A*/A at GCSE. At A level an impressive 72 per cent of passes were at A* or A, 92 per cent A*-B. Sciences, maths, economics, history and English by far the most favoured subjects but there are plenty of options and small numbers take Japanese, physical education, theatre studies, classical Greek and history of art. It's early days but so far the IB results are extremely strong: points average of 39.8 (out of 45) in 2015. Recent golds in chemistry and biology Olympiads and finalists in the national maths team challenge. It must be said that, as in similar schools, pupils from the Far East raise the bar considerably in subjects such as maths and music. We have also heard from several sources that for some a popular summer holiday activity is subject extension classes in Hong Kong. The principal says, 'We're not producing clones, the model of exam grades at any cost leads to mental brittleness.' Try telling that to the tiger mothers.

Educated in Malawi, won a sixth form scholarship to the school she now leads

The year 7 music lesson we observed was pretty serious, girls working at a high level, keen to answer questions, otherwise quiet and diligent. IB French – a debate on the uses of philosophy – was a bit livelier. The science labs looked like those in a university, girls in white coats utterly engrossed in their experiments. Parents tell us that while the prevailing mood is indeed serious there are 'inspirational' teachers and the girls enjoy their lessons. Average class size is 16 (seven in the sixth form), progress is monitored closely and girls move up or down through sets as necessary. The brightest may take one or two subjects early but most do 10 or so GCSEs at the normal time and in their stride. Parents impressed by proactive way in which teachers identify any problems and put solutions (extra lessons etc) in place swiftly. Pupils must learn to manage their time from day one – not only do they have to get to and from house to school promptly but they also have free periods for music lessons/practice and homework.

Small numbers with EAL or SpLD, mainly dyslexia. Specialist support for girls who need help with study skills, literacy and mathematics, but clearly CLC is not the place for those with significant problems and the school is frank about this. Most areas of school fully accessible by wheelchair but distance of houses precludes all but a day pupil in these circumstances.

Games, options, the arts: Full programme of music and drama – size of school means there are opportunities for all who wish to perform; impressive results in LAMDA and music exams. Up to 50 music scholars (abandon hope if you're not grade 8 or diploma at 11) must delight the ears at concerts and lunchtime recitals. College's jewel in the crown is the new arts centre, the Parabola (it's in Parabola Road). Just across from main school, it has a 300-seat theatre, dance rehearsal rooms and small gallery primarily for school use but also hosts public shows and exhibitions. It's carving out a niche as a venue for new writing and experimental theatre, the type of thing that attracts a bijou audience, in Cheltenham at least. The town's many festivals also provide plenty of opportunities for cultural enrichment.

Miss Beale wanted her girls to learn in surroundings as beautiful as those boys had been favoured with for hundreds of years

---

Impressive plate glass and metal arts building, school often has artists and writers in residence too, most but not all, women. Super textiles dept (school produced designers Katharine Hamnett and Amanda Wakeley) sadly Marie Celesteish with only three or so girls taking it beyond GCSE. Cornucopia of extracurricular options as one would expect but school is explicit in warning girls that academics must come first. Strong tradition of charitable doings: prefects nominate three UK and three international causes to fundraise for each year. Pupils also volunteer to work at St Hilda's East, the charity established in 1889 by the 'Guild' (alumni association, now 10,000 strong) in London's East End. 'What,' we asked naively, 'is Hilda patron saint of?' Answer came there none but a few red faces and a Google later we discovered that she is saint in charge of learning. Old girls who work at City law firms also do pro bono work for the charity. We doubt Miss Beale would recognise today's East Enders but the area served by the charity is still very deprived and there remains much for the Cheltenham Ladies to do. Closer to home there is a well established community links programme and girls from year 11 upwards are to be found all over the locality helping out at homeless shelters, animal sanctuaries, primary schools and retirement homes.

Sports acreage and facilities (partly open to public) are pretty good and about to get even better when the sports hall extension is completed. This will enable sports such as hockey, tennis and lacrosse to be played all year round. Notable individual achievements in athletics, tennis, skiing, riding; team sport triumphs more frequently at county level although recently CLC has got through to national finals in hockey, tennis and dry slope skiing. Most agree that sport not in premier league with few opportunities for the C,D,E team players to turn out (given size of school there must be a fair number of these). Some physical activity compulsory all the way through with zumba and pilates for the less sporty from year 5, but the sixth formers we saw were hardly rushing to the gymnasium. On the other hand we hear of considerable efforts made to find something for the keen but not so able to participate in. The school is most successful at national level in equestrian sports, with a girl in the GB under 16 team and talented riders competing for India and Australia. Not sure the school can take direct credit for this -Gloucestershire with its links to the European riding scene may have been a deciding factor. There's no stabling at the school but girls may keep their mounts 20 minutes away in Leckhampton. Polo is played at Birdlip.

Boarding: Younger girls' dorms spacious and very jolly with home duvets, under-bed storage and lots of photos and personalisation. At the foot of every bed was a brightly coloured tuck box. Single rooms for older girls are small but characterful, many with inspiring views. A place in one of the old-fashioned 'cubs,' dorms where beds have a curtain around them, highly coveted.

Parents full of praise for pastoral care whether for boarders or day girls – house mistresses in particular singled out for responding to email/

She was a suffragette who pioneered women's education when biology had to be code-named 'human geography' to stop irate fathers taking their girls home

telephone calls by return. Incidents – friendship issues or bullying – nipped in bud equally promptly we hear. Girls bring their own laptops but internet use is heavily monitored. Boarders may use social networking sites from year 3 up out of school hours. The sixth form house we visited was originally the indefatigable Miss Beale's teacher training college. With its elegant library (plus wireless of course), it is intended to be a 'halfway house to university.' Girls may come and go with more freedom but the academic tutors and house mistresses liaise to minimise girls pushing themselves too hard and staff on each floor listen out for late night working.

Background and atmosphere: Miss Dorothea Beale led the school (including a nursery and a teacher training college) from 1858. She was a suffragette who pioneered women's education at a time when biology had to be code-named 'human geography' to stop irate fathers taking their girls home, because to learn about such things would make them unmarriageable. Not content with revolutionising women's school education, the astonishing Miss Beale also founded St Hilda's College, Oxford. What would she make of today's Cheltenham Ladies as they sweep all before them, outperforming most boys and becoming leaders in their chosen careers? Ms Jardine-Young says that the college has become 'more open, less introspective,' since she was a pupil there. Her aim is to take that forward and enable girls to 'become more adventurous learners, prepared to succeed but resilient enough to cope with failure.'

The main entrance to the college is on one of Cheltenham's wide boulevards. If it weren't for girls in PE kit massing on the steps it could be mistaken for a corporate HQ and, with 800+ pupils and over 600 employees, in one sense that's what it is. Behind lies a glorious quad, three parts Victorian gothic creeper-clad grandeur, one part grim 1970s concrete modernism. Miss Beale wanted her girls to learn in surroundings as beautiful as those boys had been favoured with for hundreds of years. The original fabric of the college, with its wonderful chequerboard marble corridor, grand library, mullion windows and arts and crafts frescoes, was thus as much a political statement as a seat of learning. The teaching rooms we saw were in the main functional and surprisingly anonymous. You couldn't

tell you were at such a legendary school unless you happened to be daydreaming and looked out of the window (and we're sure that never happens).

On the day of our visit there had been something of a non-story in the national press about 'draconian guidelines' issued to ensure that 'mufti' (or home clothes) were sufficiently modest. School rather twitchy about this and we never did get the chance to ask girls what their opinion was. Parents say they resented the tone of the letter rather than its content (some outraged by both). Many admitted that they were pleased to deflect responsibility for discouraging tiny shorts etc onto school. Uniform is pretty dreary though – the most enthusiasm we could elicit from parents was that 'it does the job.' The good people of Cheltenham may have nicknamed the girls 'greenflies' but something a little less evolved, 'algae', perhaps, would more precisely describe the shade of the green skirts and jumpers. Sixth formers may wear navy pin-stripe trousers although to this reviewer the effect of these with regulation shirt and jumper is a curious half-bank worker, half-schoolgirl centaur. But away with such frivolous concerns, we feel the disapproving shade of Miss Beale urging us to look at the bigger picture. She's right, of course.

Pastoral care, well-being and discipline: This is a big school and the house system works well by breaking it down into manageable units – roughly 60 girls per house. Whole school meets every day in the Princess Hall for prayers, notices etc. Houses, most substantial and Victorian, but pleasingly not too unsympathetically subdivided, are scattered in nearby leafy residential roads and strings of Ladies' College girls walking to and fro are one of Cheltenham's perennial sights (hence, perhaps, worries about unsuitable attire on mufti days).

Some houses are quite a hike away, conveniently making sensible footwear a must. Fair bit of road crossing necessary and this concerns new parents as girls travel in unaccompanied groups. Girls eat all meals in their house, a buffet lunch is available in the main school for those taking exams or with commitments that use up travelling time. Each house has its own chefs but meals are planned centrally – economies of scale no doubt, also cuts down on lunch envy – girls get to choose favourite menus. Eating environment and food seemed pleasant enough in the houses we visited. Significant boarding refurbishment project planned and to enable this a new junior boarding house has been acquired into which each house will 'decant' in turn; also new sixth form house.

Pupils and parents: So sorry to undermine a popular cliché but we encountered no braying Henriettas or snooty aristos, just normal girls – friendly, unaffected and full of fun. Our year 9 lunch companions were sweetly excited about how much they 'loved going to Waitrose' (store has wisely established itself as the nearest supermarket) and triumphant that they had persuaded the local ice cream van to call at their house. Some observe (as did we) that nationalities tend to stick together both in and out of lessons – inevitable perhaps – and a look at the results lists in the excellent school magazine tells its own, by now familiar, story of the formidable Chinese work ethic.

Whispers on the GSG grapevine that the school is not quite as fashionable with metropolitan parents as once it was but London is still the home city of boarding majority. In the main, parents are the usual spectrum of by no means rich professionals who choose the College because of the opportunities it offers their bright daughters. Several

mentioned that they valued the school's relative conservatism and high expectations in a world of declining standards. All said that the pace is fast; too fast for a few.

Entrance: Entrance exam at 11+ (English, maths, VR). 'Please don't coach,' the school begs parents. 'We can spot the child who has been coached.' We imagine most parents have their hands over their ears and are singing loudly. At 13+ exams in maths, English, science, VR and French (if previously studied). For entry to the sixth form girls must sit exams in the subjects they wish to study.

So what exactly, we quizzed the head of admissions, does CLC look for? All girls take the same exam, thus candidates from outside the UK must have a very high standard of English. Every admission is considered on an individual basis; a girl's extracurricular interests are an important factor. The message from parents is, if you think it will suit your daughter, have a go. One told us, 'my daughter wasn't top in her prep school but she got a place and is loving it.' CLC wants girls who 'accept that they are joining a community.' Families are strongly encouraged to visit several times so that they know 'what they are getting.' Indeed families are under nearly as much scrutiny as girls themselves. Great importance is attached to what the school calls 'generosity of spirit' – interpret that as you wish. Roughly 25 per cent from outside the UK (ex-pats as well as foreign nationals), many from the Far East, and the IB programme attracts strong candidates from Europe and South Africa. The 200 day girls keep school's Gloucestershire roots strong.

Exit: A few leave post-GCSE but most stay on and benefit hugely from the higher education and careers advice provided by the school's Professional Guidance Centre. Support includes subject mentors to aid with further reading and personal statements, interview training and the opportunity to talk with Guild members about university and career choices.

In 2015, 22 gained places at Oxbridge to read eg Spanish and linguistics, biochemistry and natural sciences. Rest to top universities at home (eg Edinburgh, Durham, UCL, Bristol) or abroad. US increasingly popular with 50 offers in 2015 from Stanford, Princeton, MIT and Yale among others. Careers of old girls give a flavour of what Cheltenham ladies do next: heaps of lawyers, MPs, medics and scientists. They include Nicola Horlick (financier), Cheryl Gillan (Conservative MP), Rachel Lomax (first woman Deputy Governor of the Bank of England), Dame Mary Archer (scientist), Lisa Jardine (historian) and Rosie Boycott (journalist).

Money matters: Plenty of 'merit based awards' and scholarships for eg academics, art, sport and music.

'Limited amount' of funding for means-tested bursaries and some help for families of current pupils in financial difficulties. Bursaries intended to widen access to college are 'carefully awarded' to girls who would benefit from a college education. Principal very keen to extend opportunities in this area.

Remarks: A top flight school with strong traditional values and a clear sense of purpose. For the bright and energetic all rounder this school offers an exceptional education that is both broad and deep, with endless opportunities for fun and enrichment along the way.

Claysmore Preparatory School

Iwerne Minster, Blandford Forum, Dorset DT11 8PH

01747 813155
prepadmissions@claysmore.com
www.claysmore.com
C of E

Ages: 2–13
Pupils: 230
Boarders: 64
Day: £7,089 – £17,310 pa
Boarding: £16,290 – £23,310 pa

Linked school: Claysmore School

Head: Since September 2014, William Dunlop, previously head of first year at Kingston Grammar School. He is a former pupil at Claysmore Pre-Prep. English degree from Liverpool, then did officer training at Sandhurst and joined the army. Married to Celia, also a teacher; they have two young children who have joined the school.

Entrance: Taster day, report from previous school and informal assessment (educational psychologist's report sometimes required). Like the senior school, a mainstream school, with a cracking learning support team: 'will take any child we can develop educationally'. Highly praised by CReSTed

for its success with dyslexic children. Admissions ramp up dramatically at year 7 (mainly transfers from local primaries). Nursery takes from rising 3s upwards and majority continue through school.

Exit: More or less seamless transfer to senior school: 90 per cent go on (prep provides half senior school entry). Others to senior schools including Bryanston, Canford, Milton Abbey.

Remarks: Sharing beautiful 62 acre site with senior school, main prep school building forms a two storey cruciform shape. Proximity of dormitories and classrooms seen as a major advantage.

119

Impressive Everett building provides four classrooms for years 3 and 4, a geography room, two science laboratories and residential accommodation on top floor. Previously based in Charlton Marshall, school was founded in 1929 by Dick Everett, succeeded in 1963 by Lt Col Ivor Edwards-Stewart who, when he retired in 1974, 'funded a school of a most modern design' on the senior school campus. Dedicated play area where pupils have 'muck' (drink and snack) at breaks. Adjacent former gym has been refurbished as drama studio plus social area for year 8 pupils. Surprisingly successful blend of the makeshift (eg creative art department flourishing in somewhat dated prefab) and the purpose built. Former stately squash court houses music department for both prep and senior schools with plenty of practice rooms, separate classrooms, joint ensemble room and a music technology suite. New adventure playground and play facilities include improved ball-park. Joint use also made of sports facilities, senior school dining room (three minute trail to meals even on short legs), chapel and leisure centre.

Very popular with local families, sprinkling of ex-pat children, some foreigners, high percentage of boarders from Forces plus siblings of those in the senior school, a number of first-time buyers and London escapees. Boarding full (60 or so) when we visited, day children may stay for a minimum of two nights a week all term if space available. Still predominantly Anglo-Saxon, school has won British Council award for international

Experienced houseparents (husband teaches by day and is on duty five nights a week, wife provides 'lifeline to parents' by phone) live on site

education. Involvement in Comenius programme and global partnerships with Portugal, Gambia and Bangladesh (visiting Bangladeshi teachers were 'bowled over by openness of Clayesmore'). Refugees from state schools and academic hothouses equally at home. Parents emphasise good pastoral care and importance given to individual child. 'School wants children to be happy and settled,' we were told. Elder siblings at senior school can be met regularly and are invited to prep for birthday parties.

Practical everyday uniform, blazers worn on special occasions. Experienced houseparents (husband teaches by day and is on duty five nights a week, wife provides 'lifeline to parents' by phone) live on site and are supported by assistants, matrons and 'the sisters' (qualified nurses who act as 'super mums'); parents are informed if children in sickbay overnight. School chaplain takes Saturday chapel: spiritual life is important but no ramming down throat. Children choose annual charities to benefit from fundraising activities (eg Julia's House – children's hospice in Wimborne). Dormitories kept up to mark with reward system which includes extra muck; children are allowed back after working day. Largest dormitories for youngest and thereafter boarders thin out into smaller units. Mobile phones permitted for boarders (overseas boarders also have access to Skype) but have to be handed back to staff before lights out. Relaxed atmosphere at weekends with 40+ children on site: 'we're never bored,' said pupils: late rise on Sundays and lots of 'amazing' trips (we were told about power boat rides). Boarders' Council involved in selecting next batch of assistants.

Individual needs department is centre of excellence. Pupils have learning support as and when required, from qualified special needs teacher, half hour lessons only – from two to five a week depending on need. SENCo plus fully-trained learning support assistants help in the classroom, in addition to the class or specialist subject teacher. Gym club and OT group to develop gross and fine motor skills, touch-typing, speech and language therapy once a week, sloping desks, special pens – all sorts of tricks brought into play. Multi-sensory and auditory processing used as appropriate. Parents pay extra for one-to-one help according to level of support required. Register of gifted and able: staff aim to stretch them. Library is at centre of school's

reading culture and is somewhere to crash out during breaks; plenty of visiting authors and world book day has become a costumed extravaganza.

High percentage of staff have state and/or overseas experience. Long hours for day pupils who arrive for 8.20am start and leave at 5.30pm, either by school minibus or with parents (many arrange car sharing) from discrete prep school car park. Lots of activities during lunch hour and after lessons save parents the endless ferrying of children to multifarious venues elsewhere. Years 3 and 4 are taught by form teachers (two sets in year 4 with setting in maths and English) and finish at 12.30pm on Saturdays. From year 5 children are taught increasingly by subject specialists with 30 minute single or hour long doubles. Lots of practical work (DT and cookery were obviously favourites), geographers go out and about locally: eg locating source of river Iwerne. French is specialist from year 3 (songs and games in pre-prep), separate sciences are taught from year 7 and also Latin to higher sets. Two pre-university and four postgraduate teaching assistants provide support in classrooms and boarding areas. ICT geared to encouraging individualised learning and games are restricted. Personal tutors hold regular tutor group meetings, are responsible for PSHE and stay in charge for two years at a time. No complaints about homework (older day pupils attend bus prep to clear one assignment at school). Older children stay for matches on Saturdays. Strong parents' association organises social and fundraising activities through year. Informal parental get-togethers indicative of the school's family atmosphere.

Mexican trees of life and Quentin Blake style illustrations competed for wall space in art room where lunchtime and after-school activities include pottery, banner art, model making and photography. Drama brings creative arts together

Sports facilities are superb; school has inclusive approach (over 90 per cent play in six or more matches) which doesn't detract from success. County level representation in cricket, rugby, hockey and football. Cross-country, swimming (boarders get a 45 minute slot after prep), tennis and squash (coaching in both) and athletics also on menu. Autumn term split between soccer and rugby for boys. Wide range of sporting activities includes horse-riding and sailing (pupils compete at prep schools regatta). House system provides basis for keen competition (including music) in many areas of school life culminating in annual sports day. 'It's cool to be a musician,' say pupils, most of whom have individual lessons: best reach grade 6/7 level as well as national children's orchestras. Lots of performance opportunities for budding musicians, chapel choir has toured widely. Recent finalists in Pro-Corda competition. Picnic in park welcomes other preps and is school's annual jazz bash in grounds. Mexican trees of life and Quentin Blake style illustrations competed for wall space in art room where lunchtime and after-school activities include pottery, banner art, model making and photography. Drama brings creative arts together for four major annual productions in senior theatre and 20+ children have LAMDA lessons with good results. Pupils get out and about: whether it is theatre visits, year 5 pupils experiencing living history in period homes or reception class down at the farm to meet the animals. Popular arts/science week runs at the end of the summer term. Other highlights are ski trips, post common entrance visit to France or Spain for rafting, climbing etc and year 7 trip to Normandy. Year 8 prefects, school and boarding councils ensure pupils' opinions are heard. We liked the annual magazine and the pic filled weekly e-letter (one of the better ones we've seen).

Pre-prep of 60+ children housed in purpose-built, timber-clad classrooms: delightful sylvan setting with bird watching and pond dipping in Zen garden. Nursery area interconnects with reception class: bugs theme well in evidence (including mobiles) when we visited. All-in-one waterproofs at the ready to help make most of safe outside play and veggie growing areas. Nursery vouchers are accepted. Phonic approach to reading with liking for Read Write Inc. SENCo gives support from outset (all children are assessed aged 5) and one-to-one help where necessary. One mother we spoke to was thrilled by how regular 'Mr Tongue' activity sessions with his teacher had helped her son's speech problem. Regular 'coffee and catch-up' gatherings after drop-off provide opportunity to explain anything of importance and open door policy allows for daily contact between staff and parents. Much use made of circle time to improve children's social and communication skills. Pre and after-school clubs and wide range of activities (including swimming) are included in fees.

Never a dull moment was the impression we left with. School takes on a wide range of ability and works hard with every child. Not socially divisive: an unpretentious and happy, family atmosphere for local children and boarders alike.

Clayesmore School

Iwerne Minster, Blandford Forum, Dorset DT11 8LL

01747 812122
mmccafferty@clayesmore.com
www.clayesmore.com
C of E

Ages: 13–18
Pupils: 489; sixth form: 184
Boarders: 251 full
Day: £24,180 pa
Boarding: £32,970 pa

Linked school: Clayesmore Preparatory School

Headmaster: Since 2000, Mr Martin Cooke BEd FCollP (50s). A St Paul's chorister before boarding at Monkton Combe, from where he went to Bishop Otter College, Chichester as an organ scholar and graduated with a Sussex degree in music and education. Began career at Bembridge School, Isle of Wight (now closed), where he was director of music for 15 years, 10 of them as deputy head. 'A great leader of people,' confided a teacher. 'Has put Clayesmore on the map,' commented one father. 'Instills a sense of goodness,' added the mother of a boarder. Had a huge input at the prep for six years prior to landing senior school job.

We have rarely met a head who is more hands on. Works closely with lovely wife, Eleanor. Both their children went through school successfully. Describes his hobbies as music in general, playing the organ and information technology: he is an Apple aficionado and seldom far away from his iPod, iPhone or iPad. A human dynamo with an endearing touch of eccentricity, he reckons that running a music department was excellent training for headship. Enjoys playing for whole school

services and will let rip on chapel organ when he feels so inclined. Has certainly lifted school out of its nineties doldrums and stamped his personality on it. His ambitious 2020 vision to provide more state of the art facilities seems achievable in light of school's recent track record.

Retiring in July 2016. his successor will be Joanne Thomson, currently senior deputy head at Christ's Hospital School. Has been head of English and head of girls' games at Foremarke Hall, and held various senior posts at Aiglon College in Switzerland. A keen skier, she and her husband Frank have two teenage children.

Academic matters: 'Not in business of boosting league table positions,' says head, though both GCSE and A level results exceed admission level expectations. In 2015, 22 per cent A*/A at A level; 27 per cent A*/A at GCSE. Year groups of around 100, six sets in core subjects. Interesting variation in English (not met elsewhere) where both top GCSE sets in English are co-ed but lower sets are single sex: 'works really well,' we were told by HOD. Pupils setted in

French, science and maths (some entered for IGCSE). Spinney Centre has classrooms for geography, history, business studies and careers, all bristling with the latest computer technology. Welcome flexibility in A level choices and new subjects being added (psychology the newest arrival). Now also offers EPQ and BTecs in IT, hospitality and sport.

Gracious library is well stocked and boarders can study there until 9pm. Adjacent ICT room gleams with Apple hardware in constant use. Launch of VLE facility will give every pupil own screen on school network. DT facilities are good (large workshop with CAD-CAM router and separate graphics studio). Various examples of recent projects on display including a 'storage tyre on wheels' design used in pre-prep. DT students get to try their hand in real world outside (eg with local craftsman David Bowerman). We saw (and smelled) yummy nosh being prepared in food science area: pupils working towards BTec award. HOD runs valued activity (usually as part of CCF programme) for autistic pupils from nearby Forum School. Good take up for languages (French, Spanish and German all available to A level) and Latin also on menu. Language teaching facilities include a digital lab; foreign visits and exchanges are well established. Geographers go to Iceland for fieldwork, scientists have been to CERN, Geneva.

New business centre replicates a trading environment and gives a further boost to success of business studies and economics. BTec qualifications in ICT, hospitality, sport plus travel and tourism keep less academic on board for sixth. Small classes and switched-on teaching account for upward drift. Sixth form essay society and evening lectures broaden horizons; careers teaching includes HE visits.

By no means a specialist SpLD school but provides outstanding learning support for children with slight to moderate learning difficulties: 14 staff (all fully qualified), superb learning support centre (LSC) atop Jubilee Building which includes a lecture hall and IT hub as well as individual teaching rooms. School proud of getting dyslexics into top universities: 'my son has flown since joining Claysmore and has overcome his dyslexia,' chirped a very satisfied mother. All children are assessed, by an educational psychologist if needed. About 35 per cent of pupils have some form of support, and a 'tiny number' have serious needs. 'Children don't have to have a label,' said SENCo. Progressively more group lessons which are a fraction of cost for one-to-one help. Pupils generally come out of language classes, extra sessions can be timetabled if necessary, everything and anything to help. Good communication between LSC staff and subject teachers: 'have moved to software that supports every teacher in every classroom.' Support for most able too though labels such as 'gifted and talented'

are seen as divisive. CReSTeD specialist unit category: listing essential for Forces children, who will be deprived of 'unlimited help indefinitely' otherwise. Strong EAL too, with up to six hours a week, either individual or in pairs. Extra charge for both based on level of need. Academic staff hold frequent meetings to assess pupils' performance and communicate any steps taken quickly to parents.

Games, options, the arts: All pupils do sport three times a week and have access to great facilities. Year 9 pupils are expected to try out in major sports. As pupils move up through school there is greater flexibility: non team players generally find their niche by year 11. Impressive fixture lists with some notable successes against bigger schools. A sprinkling of county players, some individuals reaching national levels eg in athletics, and cross-country plus nationally successful orienteering team. Locals share impressive leisure complex: indoor pool, gym, squash courts and modern fitness suite. Sixth formers get free membership for out-of-school sessions. Open swimming in evenings is popular. A few élite swimmers train daily from silly o'clock. Floodlit Astroturf for hockey, tennis and netball. Expeditions on Dartmoor and more ambitiously to Everest base camp, Borneo and Malawi. Regular sports tours abroad (one in pipeline to India). CCF facility includes a rifle range, army and RAF sections for pupils in years 10, 11 and sixth form. Many opt for D of E: high medal haul including golds. Sailing at Ringwood and horse-riding also part of sports programme.

Costumes department particularly professional and is overseen by ex-Star Wars wardrobe mistress. Auditioning for Hairspray when we visited

Exciting music happens in purpose-built department run by committed director, assistant and 14 peripatetics. Pupils have scored 100 per cent success in music exams up to diploma level over last 15 years (including 24 at grade 8 in last three years). Concert band has raised staggering £50K for charity over last six years. Regular music tours with singers and instrumentalists: choir has sung at St Mark's, Venice. Next stop for musicians: Helsinki and Tallinn. School welcomes visiting artists: latterly David Owen Norris. Sophisticated electronic keyboards and recording studio useful for A level music technology. Regular representation in national youth choirs and orchestras. Composition master class in Salisbury, loads of internal concerts, ensembles for strings and woodwind, brass group, flute choir. Recent performances have included Marriage of Figaro and Dido and Aeneas.

Four staff currently involved in teaching drama including dynamic HOD whose youthful appearance belies his age. A level theatre studies and three major school productions a year part of varied and inventive menu. Many pupils get involved on technical side; costumes department particularly professional and is overseen by ex-Star Wars wardrobe mistress. Auditioning for Hairspray when we visited and puppets hanging up in green room were for enacting Russian folk tales – quite a skill manipulating puppets. Dance based in social centre and drumming in band room nearby. Masses of tripettes: Bristol, the Old Vic, London. 'Reading plays' give access to more pupils: can perform in costume with script in hand. Mystery plays at Christmas.

Outstanding art department focuses on championing individuality and creative thinking. Separate village location in former primary school increases the counter-cultural feel: pottery, painting and drawing and sculpture all have discrete spaces. Lively HOD and a real sense of bustle and fun. Sixth formers have a dedicated work space. Latest addition is iMac suite for digital art. We liked the displays of art around the school and admired some senior students' work. End of year exhibition gains universal plaudits. Regular trips to galleries in London and Paris.

Good mix socially: unpretentious lot with some brainboxes; mainly honest citizens who work hard

Keen Greenpower group of pupils won prize for best engineered vehicle at Goodwood meet for electric cars. Recyclers aplenty: eco committee run by geography department.

Huge range of extra activities four afternoons a week and all staff expected to run at least one. Pupils can do anything from fencing and yoga to textiles and pottery.

Boarding: No dip in boarding (60 per cent of pupils) over last eight years. Experienced married houseparents lend distinctive flavour to each of the boarding houses (three boys' and three girls') – all on site except for Devine in former village rectory (where sixth form head of house had cooked a roast lunch for 32 boys the Sunday prior to our visit). Five boys live in a separate house nearby known as 'number four' under the supervision of an adjacent tutor. All round boarding facilities for boys and girls warrant inspectors' recent praise. No separate day houses: works well in school which is majority boarding. Medical centre provides 24 hour cover with permanent nursing staff.

Variety of boarding spaces – most year 9 rooms are five or six bedders, older ones get threes and fours and sixth form either share study bedrooms or get their own. The Capital is sixth form social area with a café (open from 10.30am for paninis, milk shakes etc) down in the London underground-themed basement of main house. 'Watching TV after games a favourite form of relaxation,' sixth formers told us. No alcohol served during week though prefects are granted pub leave on Friday nights. Social centre cum tuck shop for years 9-11 is next to music school and opens up after prep; stages open mic nights etc. Great efforts made to have fun weekends for boarders, including discos, talent contests and popular sixth form parties – houses take turns to organise. Saturday shopping trips organised to gentrified Blandford or Shaftesbury. Southampton shopping mall is most popular destination (for staff too). Duty staff organise Sunday excursions after chapel to local places of interest such as Bath.

Background and atmosphere: Vaguely reminiscent of his gothic revivalist Natural History Museum, the main house (completed in 1878) was designed by Alfred Waterhouse and built for 2nd Baron Wolverton as his country seat. Founded in 1896 by Alexander Devine, school moved to 'Clayesmore's promised land' in 1933 after earlier incarnations in Middlesex, Berkshire and Hampshire. Set in idyllic 62 acre site of well-maintained grounds including a lake (complete with kingfishers and swans) in rural Dorset north of Blandford Forum in the lee of ancient Hambledon Hill.

Overriding impression is of a self-contained and happy extended family. Prep children and seniors (often elder siblings) co-exist happily cheek-by-jowl in these beautiful surroundings. Recent additions include Jubilee Building (nine science labs, ICT and learning support) and the even newer Spinney Centre. We were surprised at the lack of a zebra crossing (not for lack of trying on school's part) to get across busy A350 to reach picture post-card village of Iwerne (pronounced Euan) Minster where Devine house (for boys) and the quirky art department can be found. Pleasantly airy dining-hall serves wholesome nosh with copious salad and vegetarian options Good cross-cultural influences include a celebration meal for Chinese New Year. Lovely chapel not quite large enough for increased size of school: one house drops out weekly for Friday service, trad Sunday morning service for boarders. 'School is radically different from five years ago,' claimed deputy head (formerly head of English at Cheltenham Ladies') who pointed to a 'growth mindset' amongst staff.

Pastoral care, well-being and discipline: Head reputedly keeps a tight lid on discipline, supported by his deputies and pastoral staff. Rare suspensions for more serious behaviour problems but general ethos one of carrot rather than stick. Tutors (sixth formers choose their own) meet pupils weekly. Christian tradition important (school has Anglican chaplain) but not overbearing.

Pupils and parents: Has become a serious contender on local circuit: we met pupils who had preferred Clayesmore's more intimate atmosphere to impressive facilities elsewhere. Good mix socially: unpretentious lot with some brainboxes but mainly honest citizens who work hard and tend to outperform expectations. A recent sixth former gained selection for Global Young Leaders Conference in Washington as well as a place at Oxford. School minibus service covers all points of the compass within a 25 mile radius with some parents ferrying to and from pick-up points from further afield. Can sometimes stay over if late night activities, weekly boarding OK (casual boarding if space available). Senior pupils can bring their own cars. About five per cent are London refugees, a good sprinkling of expat children (Forces, diplomatic etc) plus a small number of foreign students – eg Russia and Germany. No great green wellie influence. Staff-parent meetings timed to coincide with start of two-night exeats. Friends of Clayesmore raise funds for all manner of projects and needs. Clayesmore Society promotes 'The Clayesmore Season', a year-round extravaganza of wider social and cultural activities for family and friends. Electronic reports and newsletters keep parents well informed. Interesting list of former pupils includes former Beatles manager, Brian Epstein; Stephen Joseph (pioneer of theatre in the round); TV artist, Tony Hart; Queen's orthopaedic surgeon, Sir Rodney Sweetnam.

Entrance: 'Ring Margaret' (head's words) to arrange initial visit (you'll be assured of a tour with pupils and a chat with head). Common entrance at 13+ (places not conditional once offered) for those from prep schools, interview with the head. Flexibility over admissions: school likes to take whole range of academic ability. Sibling friendly: 'if Frank can come so can Phyllis,' we were told. 'Willing all-rounders' and 'kind and thoughtful people' are particularly welcome. Just under half come from own prep with rest from 20 or so local (and some not so local) prep schools: Forres Sandle Manor, Walhampton, Highfield, Durlston Court, Port Regis, Dumpton, Sherborne Prep and Castle Court figure large plus a few from maintained schools. Academic, music and art scholarships, several species of all-rounder awards made each year. Sixth form entrants (from a variety of state and independent schools) need five A/C passes at GCSE.

Exit: A quarter or so leave after GCSEs for state alternatives. Sixth form leavers head mainly to higher education: a surprisingly steady trickle to Oxbridge, more to Russell Group and then a host of other university destinations eg UCL, Bath, Exeter, Edinburgh, Leeds, Central St Martins, Southampton, Oxford Brookes. Some Forces, some vocational courses. School turns out vets, medics plus strong art, drama and music stream.

Money matters: Not bargain basement but oodles of scholarships to compensate and help shallower pockets – sixth form up to eight, with a minimum of four reserved for those not presently in the school, others for local candidates (means tested), plus internal, and music (string players preferred). Scholarships, exhibitions and bursarial help for academics, music and art for entry into senior school at 13 (continuity awards operate from 11 to A level via the prep school) and more means tested awards. Closed bursaries for serving members of the Forces.

Remarks: Likely to impress from the moment the prospectus (like no other) drops through the letterbox. Lives up to its marketing image surprisingly well and possibly exceeds it in human terms. Head has made all the difference. Probably what a boarding school should be: not oversize, caring, happy and successful across all ability levels. Ten out of 10 for effort.

Clifton College Preparatory School

The Avenue, Clifton, Bristol, BS8 3HE

0117 315 7503
prepadmissions@cliftoncollege.com
www.cliftoncollege.com/prep
C of E

Ages: 3–13
Pupils: 495
Boarders: 50
Day: £15,360 – £16,755 pa
Boarding: £18,360 – £26,700 pa

Linked school: Clifton College

Headmaster: Since 2008, John Milne (40s). Educated at Montrose Academy and Dartmouth College, an Ivy League university in the US, where he studied British history; played professional football for Aberdeen before doing PGCE at Bristol University. Met his wife Helen when he started working at Clifton in 1994 (she was a housemistress). The couple ran the British School in Manila until they were persuaded to return with their family. Has piloted the school through a period of significant change, raising its academic profile and leading a merger of the nursery and pre-prep (Butcombe) with Clifton Prep to create one of England's largest prep schools. Parents welcome his strong personality, direct and approachable nature and visibility around the school, firmly setting ethos and values. Jo Newman, formerly at Yateley Manor School in Hampshire, headmistress of the pre-prep, also said to be 'a breath of fresh air'.

Entrance: Informal assessment in literacy and maths for Y1, Y2, Y3 (none in EYFS). Entrance tests in English, maths and general ability for Y4-8, Minimum requirement usually appropriate national curriculum Sats level for age group.

Exit: Most take scholarship exam and move on to Upper School. Some sit common entrance for other major public schools.

Remarks: Restructured from three separate schools – nursery, pre-prep and prep school (popularly known as the Pre) – to an all-through school, aligned with Clifton College upper school, allows for a more seamless curriculum and learning experience for children and for families. Head admits it has been hard for staff – 'not without its issues' – but everyone realised it was being done for the right reasons. 'Some were initially territorial but are now seeing tangible benefits.' In the transition, seven staff with a total of 198 years' experience left.

Those who remain are 'reinvigorated', enjoying the challenge of being responsible for curriculum progression from Y1-Y8.

Children benefit from being taught by specialists for music, science, technology, languages, and from access to improved facilities for art and IT. 'There can't be many pre-prep schools that have these kind of facilities at their disposal. We have found subtle ways to keep the best bits and give each part of the school its distinct identity. We were braced for a reaction but parents have embraced it. They were confident the merger would work. They now feel part of one college, not a piece of a big jigsaw. They buy into the Clifton lifestyle and ethos.' Term dates and exeats aligned too. One parent confirmed: 'There was a lot of difference academically between Butcombe (the pre-prep) and the Pre – that's not the case now.' Parents are impressed that the school has sought their views and acted upon them. 'There has been a real willingness to listen.' 'It's a sign of a school that wants to move forward.'

Very strong EYFS provision with nursery and reception in own building, fabulously equipped for child-led learning. Messy room was a beach when we visited – one child had insisted on bringing her swimsuit. Children love the smart table, with age-appropriate games and apps, which encourage collaboration. Wonderful early years library. Lovely outdoor area with willow tunnel, fake grass, sandpits, spider frame. Three reception classes. Forest school – every week – an integral part of the curriculum. Lots of feedback for parents – interactive learning diaries, including video and audio, with mums and dads encouraged to add photos and information from home.

Y1 and Y2 follow a topic-based curriculum, with plenty of innovative and imaginative activities to suit all types of learners. Children use iPads increasingly. Four Y3 classes, learning mainly with their class teachers. Y4 has science lessons with specialist teachers; more specialist teaching in various subjects as children move up the school. Scholarship class for high fliers in Y8. Standards and expectations high, but parents and staff adamant that school is not a hothouse. One parent said she specifically chose the school because she felt it would not 'push them to hard too quickly academically' and would develop the whole child. One-to-one support from specialist teachers where needed for children in pre-prep found to have dyslexia, dyscalculia or dyspraxia or other specific learning needs. Prep school has its own specialist learning centre, the Coach House, where short and long term needs are addressed 'as part of the school, not an added extra.' Parents feel that communication has improved. 'Previously reports were a bit vague. A really positive change is that we can access achievement points online through the parent portal. It means I can give my children immediate praise and feedback.'

Music very strong from the start. Every child in Y2 learns violin and in Y3 recorder. Singing, composing, choirs, individual instrumental tuition encouraged. Art is of exceptional quality. Dance and drama are very popular; children relish the opportunity to stage shows in the school hall and in the Redgrave Theatre. Five thousand books in the library. Design technology facilities are better than many a secondary school.

Pupils have swimming lessons in the college pool from reception onwards. A host of other sports both on site and at the college's sports ground at Beggar's Bush, including rugby, hockey and football. 'My boys absolutely love the sport, even though they are not A-team kids,' said one mum. Saturday school from Y4 – lessons followed by matches.

As the head points out, 'it's not every school that has a zoo in its back garden.' A firm link has now been established with Bristol Zoo education centre. Positive relationships with state primaries too, and not just in the middle-class area near the school. Music projects and teacher exchanges have been set up with inner-city schools and those on deprived estates and there are aspirations for more local schools to be able to make use of the Beggar's Bush facilities.

Biggest growth area is western Europeans, some of whom attend for a few years while their parents are working in the aerospace or energy industries

'There is a perception of Clifton as "the toffs on the hill" and I think we have softened that image,' said Mr Milne. He is determined to continue to break down barriers and ensure his pupils realise how fortunate they are and how important it is to care for others. 'We are very much changed, more engaging and more accessible. We can't afford to follow what we did 50 or 70 years ago. The thing I am most proud of is the way social impact has taken off in the prep school,' he said. 'We have always been charity minded but we are taking a step further than cake sales.' As well as working with organisations such as Fairbridge and Prince's Trust, the school runs a unique project called 'Colour My Life' in which staff, parents and some children redecorate and refurbish a home for an underprivileged family, Changing Rooms-style. 'It is one of the most meaningful things we have done. It changes children's outlooks dramatically.'

Another factor that helps pupils realise 'that Britain is not the centre of the universe' is the international nature of the school. Contrary to popular perception, it's not full of rich Russians. Biggest growth area is western Europeans, some of whom attend for a few years while their parents are working in aerospace or energy industries in the West Country. Because they arrive speaking Spanish, French or German, their English is not always good enough to hit Sats level 5, meaning Clifton misses out in league tables, but that's a small price to pay. And, as one pupil said, having native MFL and Mandarin speakers is a great help when it comes to homework and practising for oral exams. 'We have friends from all over the world.' one pupil observed. This is seen as an asset by many Bristol parents, including doctors, lawyers and other professionals. Proportion of girls in the school continues to increase – now around 40 per cent.

There's a day house and a combined day/boarding house each for girls and boys. Children join the houses from Y4; Y3s have a common room where they can start to feel more independent. Families value the pastoral support from matrons, houseparents and their teams. 'I feel like they are surrounded by people who care. There is always someone to talk to.' 'It is a very nurturing environment.' 'So many

people get to know your child, each from a different perspective.' Houses, mostly in Victorian buildings, are well maintained and continually upgraded. A major investment in recent years saw the £3.5 million development of 1 The Avenue, which contains a girls' and boys' day house and a dance studio.

Most full boarders are Y7 and Y8, although some are younger. British boarders largely from Forces families. 'School is 24/7 even for day pupils,' says head. Weekly boarding and flexi-boarding options popular with busy local families, as are early start and late pick-up wraparound care. Sleepovers for day pupils popular. 'Still a critical mass of boarders around at weekends.' Recognition that children (and adults) get tired and possibly tearful from busy school day and need TLC. Emphasis on supporting families – 'one stop shop, we take care of everything'.

Incredible range of clubs and activities for children from dawn until beyond dusk, seven days a week. 'We want everyone to find their niche; discover their passion.' Older children also encouraged to take on responsibilities and to celebrate the achievements of their peers. 'Everybody has a chance to shine here,' one said.

Clifton College

32 College Road, Bristol, BS8 3JH

0117 315 7000
admissions@cliftoncollege.com
www.cliftoncollege.com
C of E

Ages: 13–18
Pupils: 695; sixth form: 315
Boarders: 350
Day: £15,360 – £24,330 pa
Boarding: £21,000 – £35,370 pa

Linked school: Clifton College Preparatory School

Interim Head Master: Since January 2016, Dr Tim Greene MA DPhil (Oxon). He came to Clifton as head of chemistry in 2006, becoming deputy head (academic) in 2013. The early part of his career was in the university sector; various positions at Oxford including senior research fellowship at Jesus College. Took up lectureship in inorganic chemistry at University of Exeter in 2001, moving to Queen's College, Taunton, in 2005 as head of chemistry. Dr Greene is married to Lydia Massiah and has three sons.

Academic matters: Academic profile of the school has sharpened, resulting in dramatic improvements

in GCSE and A level results. 'We have established a new benchmark in terms of expectations,' said head. Record A level outcomes for 2015, with 82 per cent A*-B and 55 per cent A*/A grades. Thirty per cent of entrants achieved straight A*s and As. Maths, classics, sciences, humanities all scored highly. Similar successes at GCSE and IGCSE, where three-quarters of exams taken resulted in A* or A grades. Ninety-six per cent of physics, 97 per cent chemistry and 93 per cent of biology results were A* to A, while the figure was 83 per cent for Latin and ancient Greek. Success attributed to tougher entrance requirements at all levels and recruitment of very high calibre teachers, including an Oxford

don and a research fellow. 'We have some fantastic young subject specialists among our staff. This is a competitive neck of the woods – we have to be on our mettle.' As well as keeping up with Bristol day schools, Clifton now feels it can match many of the top independent schools. Science has always been strong – several Nobel Prizewinners among alumni. Excellent facilities over three floors of the school science building, including the Stone Library, with more than 5,000 science titles. Classics also enjoying a resurgence.

Aim is for it to have a university atmosphere, with seminar rooms and a cafeteria

English has been something of a poor relation, but that is expected to change following the opening in September 2015 of a new centre for the subject and for modern foreign languages. Aim is for it to have a university atmosphere, with seminar rooms and a cafeteria. Broad range of subjects on offer in third form (Y9) and fourth and fifth forms (Y10-11). Thirty A level subjects as well as a range of supplementary subjects (sector E) to further develop strengths and interests. Sixth form growing rapidly – now makes up half the school. EAL lessons are provided where needed and additional classes can be purchased. Individual support for students with dyslexia and other specific learning needs is provided to improve literacy and numeracy and exam skills. Independent learning

department, with its own head, is in a separate building to ease stress.

Games, options, the arts: 'There's a breathless hush in the Close to-night, Ten to make and the match to win' – lines written by Clifton head Master Henry Newbolt in 1881 the beautiful Clifton cricket pitch. Seven years later, AEJ Collins scored 628 not out there in a house match, and WG Grace also played on the turf. No wonder cricket is still a major draw: 'Watching my son play cricket on the Close is just incredible,' said one father. 'He is so proud to wear the kit.' Four ex-county cricketers on the staff, providing high-standard coaching and school has firm links with Gloucestershire CCC. Girls' cricket is also strong. School is the site of the the oldest English inter-school contest in the game of rugby, Clifton College vs Marlborough, the Governor's Cup. Clifton won the 150th anniversary contest in 2014; trophy presented by Old Cliftonian John Inverdale. It was noted that the rules of the game might have changed since the original 20-a-side fixture, but the rivalry had not. Swimming pool, gym and other sporting facilities on site but most of the games provision is over the Clifton suspension bridge at the school's 90-acre Beggar's Bush grounds. These include a water-based hockey pitch, 3G rugby pitch and a netball and tennis dome. Hockey for girls and boys also of high standard; Lily Owsley recently won first full international cap while still at the school. Real tennis, racquets, fives, water polo, chess, fencing ... the list goes on. Lots of outdoor pursuits, CCF, trips, expeditions 'developing the whole child'.

Music is also integral – 'It's in the fabric of the school, embedded, starting in the Pre (prep school).

We have an absolutely brilliant music department. Music is seen as a cool thing to do.' Outstanding facilities for recording and practice in the Joseph Cooper Music School. More than half of pupils take instrumental lessons, and they have a wide range of opportunities to perform – chapel, recital hall, theatre – in classical, jazz, blues and many other styles, both solo and in orchestras and ensembles. Alumnus violinist Julia Hwang, BBC Young Musician of the Year finalist, won a scholarship to Cambridge. In 2015, two students won organ scholarships to Oxford. Singing prominent too; chamber choir one of many opportunities. Links with Bristol Old Vic Theatre School provide opportunities for students, as does the Redgrave Theatre, named after former pupil Sir Michael Redgrave. Annual college musical and Shakespeare play are highlights of the school year. New dance studio with sprung floor. Students have talents in art too; Clifton has won the annual Bristol schools' art competition for six years out of nine. DT has been transformed and is now 'more girl-friendly, linked to art rather than a subset of engineering', including graphic design, CAD-CAM and resistant materials. Photography (school has its own darkroom), sculpture and ceramics also popular.

Boarding: The school offers day, flexi and full boarding, with the latest trend towards full boarding, often even for those whose family homes are nearby.

During our visit there was a wonderful Alice in Wonderland theme, including a curtain of playing cards, but the 21st century is represented too

Clifton has a total of 11 day and boarding houses for the upper school – with more girls' houses now because of increasing demand. There's a continual programme to upgrade the boarding houses, with the girls and boys often given a say over décor and furnishings. Even parents get involved, helping to upgrade a garden area, for example. Spacious communal facilities, with lots of games and activities. House singing competitions and plays keep them all pretty busy. 'It's full on; you never get bored,' a pupil told us. Some pupils complained to inspectors that there were too many evening and weekend activities, but it was judged that there were 'appropriate facilities to be alone or to mix informally with friends should they so wish'. Staff are very sensitive to individual needs and provide a listening ear, and the pupils support one another. 'It's like an extended family, with sisterly relationships.' Houseparents also celebrate personal achievements as well as academic – one has initiated a 'Good Egg' honours board. The dorms are equipped with robust, good quality furniture that can also be used to provide some personal space. Younger pupils are in rooms of up to six, while GCSE students are in threes and sixth-formers in twins or singles. Children swap rooms every term. The houses include kitchen and laundry areas and pupils are encouraged to be increasingly independent.

Background and atmosphere: Describes itself as a traditional British public school with modern teaching values. Founded in 1862 as a 'public school for the people of Bristol' and housed in imposing Victorian buildings. German and Russian families particularly attracted by the 'English boarding school experience package – and we certainly tick the Hogwarts box'. Each day begins in the impressive chapel with a hymn and an assembly led by a different department. Although robustly Anglican, there's also a synagogue as part of the school's Jewish heritage and students of all faiths or none are accommodated. You can wander the cloisters and see team sheets posted on carved wooden boards – though, crucially, the information is also available online. There's a sixth form common room in the Crypt – and how many schools have their own Armoury? The Percival Library is the highlight – 15,000 books on carved wooden shelves, some adorned with fairy lights. A whole wall of titles about or by Old Cliftonians from John Cleese to Earl Haig. During our visit there was a wonderful Alice in Wonderland theme, including a curtain of playing cards, but the 21st century is represented too, with a 3D printer in the library and some excellent DT creations on display in modern cabinets. Dictionaries in many languages are a necessity. Three full-time professional librarians manage physical and digital stock and periodicals and run activities including film clubs, book clubs, creative writing clubs, competitions and events. Lessons still take place on Saturdays, followed by matches. Saturday brunch, a recent innovation, has gone down well with pupils. All food is tasty and ample and the catering operation is impressive.

Pastoral care, well-being and discipline: House masters and mistresses are the lynchpins, leading a team of tutors, matrons and support staff. Pupils of all ages know exactly where to go if they need help or advice and are hugely appreciative of the way they are looked after at school. The school has its own medical centre too. Parents seem happy with the systems in place to let them know what's happening. A comprehensive handbook outlines rules, sanctions and guidelines for so many eventualities. To an outside observer, it's a fascinating mix of ancient and modern: rustication, exeats and removing hands from pockets when passing through the Memorial Arch through to policies on the use of 'legal highs' and dietary supplements. Changes in ICT require all schools to be constantly on the alert; while Skyping mum and dad from the other side of the world is an obvious boon, the use of Wifi enabled devices also presents many challenges.

And, sadly, it's nothing new. Clifton was rocked by the arrest in 2014 of a housemaster who had been downloading indecent images. He was jailed and the school described his actions as an 'unforgivable breach of trust' and an 'affront to our values'. Specialist education lawyers were appointed to ensure best practice over safeguarding and child protection, partly in response to an unannounced ISI inspection in July 2015 that found some written procedures were not up to date, pending a reinspection in January 2016. Parents we spoke to all said they were satisfied with the way college had responded to the matter. 'I think they've handled it well – changes are visible but not obtrusive,' said one.

Pupils and parents: More than 40 nationalities in the school. No one overseas group is dominant. China is the biggest – not Russia, as sometimes perceived. The Russians that do come are from wealthy but not oligarchical backgrounds. Hong Kong has always been strong, these days from both expat Brit and Chinese families. Biggest growth is in children from Western Europe – often with parents working at Airbus in Bristol or EDF in Somerset. Reputation

of Bristol as a lively European city, with a wide mix of entrepreneurs and innovators, is a draw. Proximity of the airport makes the school accessible from around the globe. Very able students from countries such as Ukraine are being drawn to Clifton by word of mouth: 'It's a quality rather than a quantity argument for us,' said head. 'Our brand recognition is higher in some countries than in the UK, maybe because we are not inside the M25.'

Sixth form has mushroomed; big demand for places, especially for girls. Parents see it as a conduit to the top universities. British families love the life-enriching experience of mixing with brilliant young people from around the world and gaining a global address book. 'The education is excellent, but it is the contacts and opportunities the children are getting that make Clifton stand out,' said one father. Students from some countries struggle a bit with cricket, but football proves a lingua franca and there is a multinational team. 'Our international dimension is one of the great strengths of the school.' Diverse, eclectic. Broader mix of social and economic backgrounds than in some similar schools, thanks to 100 per cent bursaries, which enable sons and daughters of taxi drivers to mingle happily with wealthy offspring of Old Cliftonians. Day and boarding is about a 50/50 split. This, coupled with the position within walking distance of the city centre, enables the school and its staff and pupils to be closely linked with the community.

Entrance: Most join from the prep school, after taking an entrance exam of the same standard as common entrance. Some bring scholarships awarded at 11+. Additional scholarships available at 13+. External candidates take common entrance or common scholarship at age 13. Entry to the sixth form usually conditional on achieving three A grades and three B grades at GCSE, plus an English language paper for overseas students.

Exit: Around 10 per cent leave after GCSEs. Eighteen students (more than 10 per cent of leavers) won places at Oxbridge in 2015, including two organ scholarships to Oxford, and two music awards to Cambridge. Other destinations include UCL, Imperial, LSE. But not only academia; high achievers in the arts go to higher education at the London School of Fashion, Central St Martins and the Vienna Conservatoire.

Money matters: Academic, art, music, organ and sport scholarships and awards for up to 25 per cent

of fees are offered on merit at 13+ and for sixth form and means-tested bursaries up to 100 per cent of fees are available.

Remarks: Visiting Clifton on a sunny day, the setting is almost too perfect. Among Bristol residents, the college is often viewed as full of rich, rugby kids with little grasp on the realities of life. But these stereotypes go nowhere near telling the story of the school. Whatever their backgrounds, the students are aware that the privileges they enjoy go way beyond the material. They are courteous and respectful – and modest about their frequently incredible achievements. Many of them are fluent in two or three languages. We met a brilliant young Somali boy from a disadvantaged area of Bristol who loves astronomy, intends to become an inventor and has settled in wonderfully to the school. Excellent prospectus gives a flavour – but explore the extensive website to get the widest perspective on life at Clifton College in the second decade of the 21st century.

Dauntsey's School

West Lavington, Devizes, Wiltshire SN10 4HE

01380 814500
info@dauntseys.org
www.dauntseys.org

Ages: 11–18
Pupils: 825; sixth form: 290
Boarders: 295 full
Day: £17,340 pa
Boarding: £28,980 – £33,450 pa

Head Master: Since September 2012, Mr Mark Lascelles (40s), previously lower master, and temporary acting head of King's School Canterbury – something of a rough ride. He was educated at Shrewsbury School and Durham, where he read geography and was keen and proficient in cricket and football to county level and beyond. Now he only plays social cricket – frustrating, as he is very competitive. Back at Shrewsbury for a further 17 years, he became a housemaster and coached many of the Shrewsbury teams before joining King's School in 2009. He is married to Amber, a teacher and graduate of Durham, who was a national level canoeist. They have three young daughters.

Mr Lascelles is stunned by 'the quality of pupils' at Dauntsey's, not just their academic level but their genuine niceness and the energy injected by having an intake at 11: something he had 'missed out on before'. He sees Dauntsey's as a collegiate school, for families who understand about good education, and are not blinded by fashionable pretension.

So far both the curriculum and the classrooms are quite traditional (he promised not to make changes early) but the stunningly high level of pupil satisfaction registered in the recent ISI inspection bears witness to the excellence of the teaching. Parents like him and say he is accessible, listens and takes a personal interest in all pupils, meeting the school bus every morning and being a friendly presence at most activities. He had a hard act to follow and is very different to his predecessor, 'but has finally mastered the art of feeding biscuits to paddling canoeists as they pass in the Devizes to Westminster race!' Out of school he enjoys travel, skiing, reading and theatre – and is rapidly developing a taste for musicals, which is just as well as at the time of our visit Dauntsey's was about to put on Sondheim's Into the Woods followed by Mamma Mia.

Academic matters: Over the last few years Dauntsey's has come up quite a few pegs in the academic stakes and has a pretty impressive record for a 'not

overly selective' school – though of course success breeds demand which ups the ante. In 2015, 50 per cent A*/A grades at A level and 76 per cent at GCSE – mostly IGCSEs which, pupils say, 'prepare better for A level'. Big Cheeses of the school world locally should look to their laurels or Dauntsey's might pip them at the post. Curriculum includes a four language carousel of French, German, Latin, and Spanish for the first year from which two or three languages may be chosen. Other languages – Mandarin, Russian, Japanese, Greek, Arabic etc – are done in extracurricular time. Native speakers are encouraged to take exams in their own languages.

Is rapidly developing a taste for musicals, which is just as well as Dauntsey's was about to put on Sondheim's Into the Woods followed by Mamma Mia

Three science IGCEs for two-thirds of the year group; the rest do dual award science (three sciences taken as two GCSEs). Spanking new science labs full of GCSE groups practising practicals. A spectacular full-size skeleton monoplane hangs in the hallway and the charming courtyard with super bosky pond has raised beds crammed with Japanese anemones.

No limits on choices at A Level. DT (resistant materials), in a whizzy new class room, with new courses in psychology, history of art and English

language starting. Outstanding in maths and further maths and more than sound across a very wide board including theatre studies, music technology and class civ as well as the mainstream stuff.

Class size around 16 in GCSE years. Busy SEN department with three full-time staff, providing help, within the timetable but at extra cost. Mainly helps mild dyslexia and offers a safety net for the organisationally challenged but, 'If pupils pass the entrance exam,' says the head, 'it is rare for us to say we can't cope with their special needs'. Impressively wheelchair friendly (even disabled wet-room showers) for a school with no current need for it. Thirty or so need and get EFL tuition, which is thrown in as part of the special enhanced international fees. Efficient IT taken for granted, having virtually reached IT saturation point, though pupils are pretty impressed that free standing printers at convenient points access and print from their personal files activated by thumbprint. Pupils register by thumbprint too for afternoon school, but house staff like to lay eyes on everyone in the morning.

Games, options, the arts: Sport is definitely big and timetabled three times a week. Boys' and girls' hockey, rugby and cricket doing pretty well at county and regional level. Football played in senior years, tennis, for all, and netball, for girls, all tackled competitively. A smart-looking rugby pavilion graces the grassy expanse in front of the main school and new sports pavilion is under way.

Girls regularly send a hockey team to South Africa to match the triennial rugby tour of the Australia, and there is no shortage of opportunity. The recently acquired Mercers' field has extensive pitches, 'levelled by computer,' pupils say. Archery happens there but was elusive on our visit, though we spotted the coach's van. A huge range of 'strenuous pursuits' available in the 'long break'.

Situation alone gives Dauntsey's a whiff of bracing contact with the great outdoors, focussed, during our visit, on the whole school cross-county race. The delightful lower school guides, when asked what happened to non-sporty people, didn't think there were any. Some parents feel that the less talented enthusiasts need more chances to play in teams, even against each other. Masses of expeditions like the Brecons Challenge and a long distance canoe race from Devizes to Westminster. Moonrakers, a third year programme, offers all sorts of outdoor adventure challenges (at no extra cost), and the more ambitious Dauntsey's Mountaineering and Expedition Society travels to the orphanage they have adopted in Romania or visits their contacts in Bhutan. Lots do D of E though they skip silver because of exam pressure.

Solid rather than spectacular facilities – indoor swimming pool, two handsome Astros, sports hall, athletics track a hike away – a source of grumbles for a few; macho fitness area with scary weights and levers has had a facelift and a bit more space. Too unusual to omit is the sailing club. No Optimists or Fireflies on a pond for Dauntsey's, instead school has bought a 100 year old tall ship, the Jolie Brise. Pupils have competed in the Fastnet (she actually won the first in 1925); they also cruise more lazily off the Isle of Wight. Everyone gets a go in mixed teams of eight and parents are envious.

What the music department lacks in size it makes up in enthusiasm – multitudinous groups of every genre happily play away, certainly more than 20 groups timetabled – choirs, orchestras bands. It needs a bit more space. A good take up

School has bought a 100 year old tall ship, the Jolie Brise. Pupils have competed in the Fastnet

of instrumental tuition on every instrument ever invented makes for plentiful concerts with some mature and accomplished performance. Practice sessions timetabled for junior boarders.

There is serious drama – King Lear is probably as serious as it gets – when enthusiastic performers can be weaned away from everyone's first love, the many enormous school musicals and 'extraordinary performances' which sometimes even make it to London theatres. Smashing A level results in theatre studies. The multi-function 'memorial' school hall has really good lighting and equipment thanks links with the West End. Plans are a foot to refurbish it with better seating (sinking into the floor) though it would be a pity to end such bizarre juxtapositions as the stately school altar, sanctuary and organ at one end and a stunning full size white puppet cow at the other. Annabel's, the well-equipped drama studio, has everything needed to launch careers via the Edinburgh fringe and such venues. Good and popular dance studios too – it's in the curriculum – with a few boys taking part.

Across the playing field, the chimneyed art block has a deceptively arts and crafts look but is full of all the relevant IT and pottery things. It's about to get an upgrade to make more space and dark room for photography planned for A level. Head of art keen on observational drawing. Bags of school trips – modern languages to Spain and France, geography to Iceland, RS to India, Adventurers to Bhutan, skiing in Italy

There's not much you can't do at Dauntsey's, which is probably just as well for 300 or so boarders residing in a leafy backwater.

Boarding: One advantage of being almost at the back of beyond is that Dauntsey's has plenty of room to spread itself – a seven hole golf course at the Manor House (co-ed boarding for juniors) who undoubtedly get the prettiest building. Some choose to ramble home through a lovely mile of so of woodland path, from which their Victorian mock Tudor mansion welcomes them at 4.30pm into a spacious galleried hall with inviting sofas round blazing fire in winter, to take tea and delicious looking scones and cake. It's a spick and span version of Hogwarts, with its long oak tables and panelled common rooms smelling of furniture polish rather than 60 small boys and girls. Dormitories are functional but spacious with lovely views, weekends full of well planned, child friendly activity, mostly on the spot.

Boarding houses (single sex), both old and new are exceptionally spacious, some with en-suite facilities and all have kitchens, workspace and proper recreation area. A sixth former described it as 'certainly better than adequate but not quite luxury'. Day houses get everything the boarders have except the bedrooms and the juniors have their own similar on-site day centre.

Background and atmosphere: Founded in West Lavington in 1542 on the deathbed largesse of William Dauntsey, master of the Worshipful Company of Mercers, the school opened in 1895. Mercers' Company still provides six governors, occasional generous financial help and annual knees-up for its associated schools which include an unlikely spread from St Paul's Schools in London – both boys' and girls' versions – to Peter Symonds College (state sixth form in Winchester), two new academies and The Royal Ballet School.

Lawns and trees enhance the setting of the handsome main school building, and the recently redesigned reception area is reminiscent of a five star hotel with its glass topped tables, comfortable furniture and well lit pictures changed regularly by the art department – and it is nice to see the artist's names. Other facilities are more functional, but very well maintained. Perhaps a bit countrified for some hardened Londoners – until 1930 the school was known as Dauntsey's Agricultural School.

Dauntsey's has mushroomed, to the extent that buildings jostle haphazardly with an increasing number of lawned and planted milling-about spaces between buildings, so the brightly coloured maps at every corner are necessity not decoration. A young pupil claimed to have taken only a week to find his way about. What impresses is that it has absolutely every facility a school should have but nothing extravagant.

The most spectacular feature is a superb bright and airy new library – which must say something about academic priorities. Some exposed desks/computers down the centre of the building may not be everyone's cup of tea (where do they hide the sweet packet?) but more sheltered study space is available upstairs plus round tables and comfy chairs for a good read. Fooling around can be done in the cyber café or in the tuckshop. Lessons finish at 4pm and it is technically possible for day pupils to creep off then, but most stay on for prep or take part in clubs or sports until the mass bus exodus at 5.30pm. Boarders have two hours of prep in the evenings, one just before and one after supper.

Uniform is as expensive but not more than most. Girls have a rather limp blue check skirt with blue blouse and pullover. Boys in blue shirt and grey-blue jacket. No uniform in sixth form but smart-ish dress required (suits or chinos, tie and jacket for boys and at least a nod towards formality

for girls) – quite widely interpreted. The reversible black and white rugby shirts are just being phased out for smart though less popular mainly white ones which wash better but get smelly very quickly. The busy school shop has an endless supply to lend to those who forget games things. The San is modern and inviting with quiet places to sit and suffer and comfortable looking bedrooms. Pupils definitely value the care given there, including counselling.

Pastoral care, well-being and discipline: Much less privilege orientated than many schools, so apart from the 17 Club, which is the hub of sixth form social life, and biscuits at morning break, sixth form and prefects live and work alongside the upper school and take a full part in house life. Relationships between year groups are definitely flexible. The pastoral system functions through the houses, in which the house staff and at least four assistants act as tutors to about 60 pupils. Parents say problems are handled successfully and with great sensitivity.

Breakfast provided for all-comers in the pleasant dining hall. Boarders have to be there by 8.15am. Buffet service with spectacular and popular 'live cook' every day and all meals in on the fees though not compulsory. Staggered sittings to manage flow of hungry diners but a few choose to use the house kitchens if the dining room is full.

Responsibilities taken seriously by prefects and captains of houses, who are selected by head and staff. Drugs get immediate expulsion and pupils know it. Apart from that, 'rules are', pupils say, 'a matter of common sense', though a new rule book is issued each year. The comments they made on 'how far into the opposite sex house' they are allowed showed they had a pretty shrewd idea of what is and is not acceptable. They also emphasised the trust between pupils and staff.

Pupils and parents: Not toffs on the whole, more local families, farmers and small businesses, with quite a number from state primaries or first time buyers. Lots of professional families with two parents working to earn the fees. Being just over an hour from London, Bristol and Southampton makes boarding pretty accessible from UK or abroad. International intake widening from Hong Kong and Russia to a wide spread of countries: Europe and beyond. Fifteen bus routes from Salisbury (south), Swindon (north), west to Frome and east to Hungerford and Andover, which puts them into competition with a number of good grammar schools as well as some top independents.

Entrance: At 11+, from state schools and a few preps, entry is by Dauntsey's own exam (maths, English, VR and optional music auditions). Selective in that they accept about the same standard of candidates as Salisbury Grammar, according to the head. At 13+ they take mainly boarders from prep school and some from abroad via 13+ CE or scholarship exams, with very few day places at this stage, adding an extra two forms. Feeders include Chafyn Grove, St Francis (Pewsey) and St Margaret's (Calne), All Hallows and Thorngrove plus many local state primaries. Everyone sitting an exam at 11+ is automatically considered for a scholarship and around 15 pupils out of 80 admitted get some sort of award.

Some 50 pupils join the school for sixth form, around a third from abroad – a minimum of three A and three B grades at GCSE is required from UK pupils, plus interview.

Exit: A trickle – some 10 per cent – leave after GCSEs, mainly for local sixth from colleges. Good proportion to solid science, medicine, languages etc courses at uni (Exeter, Bristol, Birmingham and Cardiff popular recently) and a respectable number to Oxbridge (six in 2015).

Money matters: Much more aware than many schools that parents' resources are not infinite. The vibe from parents is that day fees here particularly good value for money. A few nice touches: music lessons cost the full whack for first instrument but less for second and subsequent ones; a 10 per cent reduction for siblings who are boarding at the same time (a very sibling-friendly school). Mercers' connection is a help when it comes to funding building projects but not a bottomless pit.

Remarks: It's in there competing with the heavies but still unpretentious, with feet firmly on the ground. Parents value its special atmosphere, rooted in being reasonably non-selective, both academically and socially. Steadily improving results and facilities are putting Dauntsey's among the front-runners in the area. Its friendliness, breezy campus and outdoorsy image belie a focussed academic purpose, which encompasses arts and sciences, though it doesn't inhibit the pupils from having a pretty good time. Dauntsey's is fab.

Dean Close Preparatory School

Lansdown Road, Cheltenham, Gloucestershire GL51 6QS

01242 258001
dcpsoffice@deanclose.org.uk
www.deanclose.org.uk
C of E

Ages: 2–13
Pupils: 431
Boarders: 75
Day: £10,485 – £15,852 pa
Boarding: £18,405 – £23,310 pa

Linked school: Dean Close School

Head: Since September 2015, Paddy Moss, who was previously head of St Andrew's Prep School, Turi, in Kenya. He attended the school himself in the 1970s and was head of the prep between 2006 and 2015. His wife, Julie, is also a teacher and they have three daughters.

Entrance: Own exam (English, maths, VR) plus interview and school report. Year 3s mostly from own pre-prep, but roughly a third more come into year 7 from local preps and primaries. School makes the test as unthreatening as possible – on our visit we saw one girl enjoying chocolate and having a fuss made of her in the office, having finished her

paper. Choristers (boys only) auditioned between 7-11 years.

Exit: Nearly all to Dean Close School. Some five per cent go on to a mixture of other schools – Shiplake College, Winchester, Marlborough.

Remarks: Pre-prep, fondly known as The Squirrels, headed since 2011 by Dr Carolyn Shelley. Early years' focus on developing children's senses, to prepare them for learning in prep and beyond. Plenty of hands-on activities, positive reinforcement and encouragement for achievement of all kinds, not just academic. These Squirrels are fortunate enough to have their own forest school in the extensive grounds – regular visits allow them to experience the changing seasons, go on expeditions and meet small invertebrates. Back indoors, facilities are just as appealing: great library and ICT suite – all designed for this age group – plus ground floor classrooms linked by creative areas. Sports facilities shared with prep and main school (swimming pool, tennis courts). Plenty of singing and music; all learn recorder with option of lessons in violin, viola, cello (in their reduced sizes) and piano. Dance classes also available. Burgundy sweatshirts with squirrel logo, tartan tunics for girls.

The prep school has opened a newish £4.5 million building which includes a reception area, theatre, music suite, hall for drama, concerts, assemblies and exams, plus IT suite, drama rooms and classrooms. The new classrooms are arranged to aid cross-curricular work. Prep is separated by playing fields from big school but with use of seniors' specialist sports facilities, such as dance studio

and pool, in addition to their own considerable outdoor and indoor provision. At least four sessions of timetabled sport a week plus the option to join clubs and try out shooting, climbing, dance and golf. The floodlit, covered play area is a great asset, a huge space for pupils to race about, kick balls and even roller blade in, no matter what the West Country weather throws at them.

No chance for backsliding in instrument practice – one of the tutors in each boarding house is a musical gappie

The school aims to 'fire the imagination and enthusiasm of every pupil', and children here benefit from subject specialist teachers, increasingly as they move towards common entrance. Setting from year 6 onwards based on individual learning plans. Subject knowledge boosted by frequent trips and plenty of hands-on activities – the emphasis is still on fun and teamwork. Those with mild dyslexia, numeracy or specific curriculum needs are supported in groups or one-to-one by specialist SEN staff; EFL also offered.

Dean Close is the Schola Cantorum for Tewkesbury Abbey, educating the boy choristers who sing there (four evensongs and Sunday services). Several other choirs, orchestras, ensembles and bands give ample opportunities for young players and singers to perform in house and at public events such as the Cheltenham festival of performing arts. Speech and drama thriving, with both timetabled and extracurricular sessions – great for confidence building. The list of clubs, many set up by the children themselves, runs from the predictable Warhammer to the gloriously unexpected Norman Wisdom film club, and takes in Fun with Wool, Start Greek, gymnastics and riding along the way.

In senior prep (years 7 and 8), pupils are given more responsibilities in order to develop independence and leadership skills, ready for senior school. All take part in community action projects and trips are further afield – Snowdon, camping in Devon and fencing in France, for example.

Approximately a third board – the vast majority are full boarders, meaning plenty of company after school and at weekends. In addition a very few places for 'day' boarders, who stay up to three nights a week. Of course many structured activities and outings, but equally important is free time to play outside and explore the extensive grounds, woods and brook. Three boarding houses: one for boys, one for girls and Wilton, a mixed house for the youngest; each is presided over by houseparents – a married couple with children, resident matron,

two tutors and non-resident staff. Common rooms with televisions (weekends only), Wii, games consoles etc, plus table tennis, craft and model making areas, baking, a graffiti wall and milk shake nights are just some of the temptations on offer.

No chance for backsliding in instrument practice – one of the tutors in each boarding house is a musical (grade 8 minimum) gappie whose job is to oversee scales, accompany on the piano and encourage young singers and players. Boarders' rooms are bright and full of home comforts; we liked the customised carrels in the girls' prep room – all feathers and glitter. Children can speak to family via Skype and text, but no personal laptops allowed. Parents receive a Friday evening email from housemaster telling them what's been going on, so they can chat knowledgably with their offspring – a boon for those with uncommunicative young.

Seems to have the balance just right, providing a secure, caring environment in which pupils receive a first class academic grounding and explore their own talents and interests. As one parent put it, 'The school doesn't expect them to grow up too fast – it lets them enjoy just being children.'

Dean Close School

Shelburne Road, Cheltenham, Gloucestershire GL51 6HE

01242 258044
registrar@deanclose.org.uk
www.deanclose.org.uk

Ages: 13–18
Pupils: 480; sixth form: 200
Boarders: 245 full, 40 flexi
Day: £22,731 pa
Boarding: £32,940 pa

Linked school: Dean Close Preparatory School

Headmaster: Since September 2015, Bradley Salisbury MEd PGCE, deputy head at the school since 2009 and a successful acting headmaster. After studying at University of Leeds (completed part time masters at Bristol), taught religious studies at Gordano School before moving first to Bristol Cathedral School as head of department and head of years ten and 11 and then to Wells Cathedral School where he was head of religious studies and a housemaster.

Jonathan Lancashire, former head, now becomes warden, responsible for overseeing senior school, two preps, two pre-preps and three nurseries. Mr Lancashire read maths at Cambridge, taught maths at Radley, then qualified as a chartered accountant. After a spell as bursar at Rishworth

School he moved to Dean Close in 2000. His wife is head of history and politics at Cheltenham Ladies' and they have two children at university.

Mr Lancashire is urbane but approachable; a sharp dresser, he says he is a country boy and pig farmer manqué but, if he is, we're talking Lord Emsworth, not Neil Carter. He enjoys sailing and climbing and surprised pupils by competing in a recent Tough Guy challenge against them. Having previously been a spectator, he decided that he would rather take part than watch, even if it meant floundering in the mud being out-performed by his pupils. Parents impressed by his 'quiet authority' and what seems like an uncanny ability to be everywhere.

Academic matters: Solid results for all at GCSE and A level and though year groups vary, the trend is upwards. The head says that the school looks for 'attitude as well as aptitude', a statement that demonstrates his confidence in the school's proven ability to develop and boost its pupils.

In 2015, GCSE/IGCSE: 56 per cent A*/A. Twenty-two subjects offered, with most taking 10 or 11, smallish numbers for classics, Latin and Greek. Separate sciences, excellent maths and physics results. At A level, 77 per cent A*-B, 49 per cent A*/A. Once again the mathematicians are light years ahead with A*/As – whatever it is they put in the water in the maths department should be bottled.

Classes are small, between 15 and 20 (12 in the sixth form) and teachers, according to one parent 'work with each child's individual abilities', and, according to another, 'achieve miracles'. Mild SEN (dyslexia, dyspraxia) catered for and EAL is taught in individual lessons or groups.

The head is proud of the extension programme for sixth formers designed to help them develop critical thinking skills, engage with different ideas and 'confront non-standard stuff'. A critical essay competition open to the whole school is judged by an external adjudicator and keenly contested.

Games, options, the arts: Hockey is the game here for boys and girls, with seemingly every team vanquishing all comers, including the likes of Millfield, to become county champions and national finalists. One of our guides was a rugby fanatic but realistic about his school's performance against the big names: 'We're probably not near the top'. Emphasis is on everyone getting a game – at least

three and up to five teams for every year group. A pool, gym, rifle range, dance studio and climbing wall and, in addition to acres of playing fields, a large covered pitch so the younger children can play outside whatever the weather.

Having previously been a spectator, he decided that he would rather take part, even if it meant floundering around in the mud being out-performed by his pupils

Equestrian sport is an increasingly popular option – this being Gloucestershire, a handy polo club in nearby Birdlip where riders can learn this sport from scratch. Teams take part in schools show jumping, cross-country, eventing and dressage competitions, with individuals competing at national and international level in all disciplines. No stabling, though, so you'll have to leave the pony at home.

Music here was described by one parent as 'second to none' – all are encouraged to take up an instrument or sing. Practice sessions are not timetabled but schedules are agreed with music tutors, which apparently results in more productive practice. The music school houses teaching and practice rooms and the Prince Michael Hall, used for concerts and public speaking. Hosts of chamber ensembles, rock bands, choirs and orchestras and musicians perform locally and nationally. Regular tours have taken them to Paris, Venice and New York. A strong tradition of Oxbridge organ and choral awards; the boy choristers from Tewkesbury Abbey's Schola Cantorum (stars of many a CD) are educated here. In residence is the new head of strings, the celebrated Carducci Quartet.

Art, too, has its own purpose built 'school' and exhibition space. Results at GCSE and A level are strong, a good proportion go on to continue their artistic education in some of the country's most acclaimed art colleges, including Central St Martin's, Chelsea, Camberwell and The Slade, and further afield such as the Charles Cecil Studios in Florence. Sixth form artists have allocated spaces where they can leave out works in progress. The art school's BonBernard Gallery is used to display both pupils' and professionals' work.

In addition to a studio theatre and a large amphitheatre in the grounds, fortunate thespians can also tread the boards of the Bacon Theatre, a 550 seat venue that wouldn't look out of place in small town. Named after former headmaster, Christopher Bacon, it hosts at least eight school plays a year, a major musical such as Les Misérables or Guys and Dolls every two years, as well as numerous professional productions; lecturing luminaries including Judi Dench, Samuel West and Peter Hall. In addition to GCSE and A level theatre studies, pupils are prepared for the RADA and LAMDA examinations

Wonderful history classroom with a makeshift display of shells (exploding variety) and a tin helmet. Was that chalk dust floating in the shaft of sunlight? Probably not

up to diploma level. The school theatre company, Close Up Theatre, has performed sell-out plays at the Edinburgh Fringe for several years.

Add to the above a huge choice of clubs and societies, CCF training, D of E and a community action programme where pupils work on projects locally and abroad (building a school in Uganda) – it's no wonder boarding (or 'day' boarding, two nights a week) is so popular with local pupils: they don't want to miss out.

Boarding: The girls' boarding house we visited was light and modern with glass brick floors in the corridors. Rooms were reassuringly untidy (inspections on Sundays), customised with posters, photos and plenty of home from home clutter. 'Keep calm and carry on' seems to be the motto de choix on many walls. Sixth formers have single rooms with linked ensuites and plenty of Cath Kidson bunting. Fourth form prep is done in separate study areas and monitored by sixth formers. Downstairs are squashy sofas with bright red cushions, board games, puzzles, a Wii, DVDs and music. Saturday night is film night. Boys' boarding similar standard but less bunting, and sofas evidenced rougher treatment.

Background and atmosphere: One parent described the atmosphere at Dean Close as 'relaxed yet achieving' and that just about sums it up, rather more succinctly in fact than the colour printing fest of promotional literature – considerably more quality photography, paper and gloss than other schools we've visited and needing its own Dean Close carrier bag. School mags, The Decanian and Young Decanian, are similarly shiny and flawless and perhaps just a little corporate. The school is more humane and down to earth than its brochures let on; the pupils we met were charming and grounded – one said that the best thing about school life was being part of a 'community of individuals'.

Occupying 50 green acres just beyond the centre of Cheltenham, it could be quite a daunting place but somehow keeps the protective ethos of a small school on its big site. The main school is a familiar mix of Victorian and later additions – although it is by no means short of the latest smartboards and ICT equipment, we were delighted to see a well-stocked library like an upturned boat and a wonderful high ceilinged history classroom with piles of books, walls covered in posters and a makeshift display of shells (exploding variety) and a tin helmet. And was that chalk dust floating in the shaft of sunlight coming from the tall windows? Probably not. The head has plans for a major redevelopment in the heart of the school, 'a radical approach to teaching space' (plus a new swimming pool) – we hope the history classroom's days aren't numbered.

The dining hall serves hearty home-cooked food with plenty of choice, pupils and staff eat at refectory tables with a fine view of the grounds. Boys and girls we spoke to were generally positive about the meals – several said they thought the food had improved while they had been there. Boarders can supplement with toast, hot chocolate and other snacks they prepare in the kitchenettes.

Pastoral care, well-being and discipline: The principles of Christianity form the moral heart of the school and for some this is a deciding factor, but 'no pressure' to get involved beyond cultural Christianity. One parent, not a churchgoer, was positively evangelical about what he identified as the 'spirit and energy' of the school. Our guide, who was very involved in this aspect of school life, said, 'It's not uncool to be a Christian here.' A whole school evensong in the chapel every Friday and voluntary communion and Bible studies plus a pupil-run Christian Union. The popular female chaplain organises various programmes to develop pupils' spiritual awareness.

The school is more humane and down to earth than its brochures let on; the pupils we met were charming and grounded and liked being part of a 'community of individuals'

No significant behaviour problems – main challenge, according to the head, is day pupils, who very occasionally get into trouble 'off-site' at Cheltenham's seedy dives. (Are there any?) Testing for any suspected of substance abuse; immediate dismissal for dealing. School takes a 'cultural approach' to bullying and staff vigilant for anything, even if it's just chit-chat, that may make a child feel isolated. Head very hot on challenging what he feels is a contemporary fashion for sexist put-downs. Prefects trained to look out for anyone feeling wobbly. Parents we spoke to describe pastoral care as 'fantastic', 'The staff genuinely care about the children'. A few grumbles from parents of day pupils, who wanted more opportunities to discuss their child's progress than the termly meetings with staff, but all agreed teachers were approachable and quick to respond to queries.

Pupils and parents: A good number of boarding parents are first-time buyers – the lack of old boy snobbery is a big draw. Significant numbers of Forces and diplomatic families are delighted to find a school where all their children can be educated together. School keen to stress its 'local' character, but even pupils whose parents live within bus distance elect to board when they get older (both our guides fell into this category). Mix of established families and London defectors has energised population in recent years. Roughly 15 per cent from overseas but no dominant nationality.

Famous Old Decanians include Tom Johnson and Pete Brown, rugby players; Hugh Quarshie, actor; George Adamson, author of Born Free; Francis Bacon, artist; Lord Bernard Ribeiro, former president of Royal College of Surgeons.

Entrance: 'Quite accessible,' according to the head, but two applications for every place; he adds that one of the qualities Dean Close looks for is curiosity, children who will 'have a go' and embrace every opportunity the school offers. Pupils enter at 13 from the school's own prep and after common entrance from others such as Pinewood, Beaudesert Park, Hatherop Castle, Prior Park, St John's-on-the-Hill. Sixth form entrants are accepted on the basis of three subject-based papers with VR or EAL.

Exit: Around half to Russell Group, handful every year to Oxbridge (four in 2015), plus a few to art college and drama school. Popular subjects: engineering, accounting and finance (no surprise there, given calibre of mathematicians) and geography; favoured institutions currently Bristol, Bath, Oxford Brookes and Exeter.

Money matters: Described by more than one parent as 'value for money'. Scholarships and exhibitions for 13+ and 16+ entry awarded for excellence in academics, music, sport, art, drama, DT, plus a few for 'all rounders'. Small number of 100 per cent bursaries for those who 'could benefit from a Dean Close education'.

Remarks: Dean Close is a warm and welcoming school, aspirational without being snobby and secure in its strong moral and social values. As one of our guides said, 'You don't have to be a type to fit in here – you just have to be keen to give everything a try.'

Downside School

Stratton-on-the-Fosse, Bath, Somerset BA3 4RJ

01761 235103
admissions@downside.co.uk
www.downside.co.uk
RC

Ages: 11–18
Pupils: 350; sixth form: 140
Boarders: 285
Day: £14,937 – £17,196 pa
Boarding: £23,559 – £30,687 pa

Head Master: Since April 2014, Dr James Whitehead MA MPhil PhD (40s). Previously second master at Worth. Educated at Stonyhurst and Oxford. After an MA in English at Oxford and MPhil in modern poetry at University of Stirling, he worked in the civil service and as a bookseller in his early 20s, then did his PhD (on Thomas Hardy's poetry) at the University of Manchester. Studying for his doctorate 'ignited my love of teaching' and when he spotted an ad for a post at Radley he decided to apply. He spent four years there, as an English teacher, sub-tutor (assistant housemaster) and rugby coach, before moving to Downside as head of English (and later director of studies). 'It was a time of rapid change and development at Downside,' he says. 'We were the most improved school in the country in the league tables.' During this period he introduced new appraisal, reporting and rewards systems – things that are commonplace in schools now but weren't then.

He spent seven years at Worth before taking up the headship at Downside. 'It was a historic opportunity to become the first lay head here,' he says. Since his arrival he has focused on the school's academic delivery, staff development and looking after pupils' wellbeing, as well as overseeing a substantial development programme. 'I think we're really motoring,' he says. 'There is a very joyful atmosphere here – which is how a school should be.' He's proud of the way Downside nurtures 'a real sense of intellectual enquiry' and does his bit by delivering sixth form lectures on subjects like Dante in half an hour, celebrity worship syndrome and faith and modern poetry. He makes time to referee rugby matches too.

Cerebral, forward-thinking and experienced at getting 'the nuts and bolts' of schools right, he is a fellow of the Royal Society of Arts and is passionate about literature and sport. His actress wife Nicola does some LAMDA teaching at Downside and they have two young daughters, both pupils at All Hallows Prep. In his spare time he enjoys walking the family's two labradors, golf and reading.

Academic matters: Results have come on leaps and bounds in recent years. In 2015, 47 per cent A*/A and 79 per cent A*/B at A level and 50 per cent A*/A at GCSE. Usual subjects at A level, plus business studies, economics, history of art, PE, photography and psychology. History department offers the Pre-U – head of history says the qualification involves 'good, old-fashioned essay writing' and enables youngsters to study topics such as monasticism in the 9th century and the Gregorian reforms of the 11th century as well as more recent fare.

Most pupils take 11 GCSEs. English, maths and RS are compulsory and all are encouraged to take at least one language, a humanity and a creative subject. French, German and Spanish are the main languages, but Italian, Mandarin, Russian, Polish, Chinese, Portuguese and Arabic can be arranged. Most pupils do three separate sciences. Director of studies says the school believes in setting 'ambitious realistic targets' and tracks and monitors pupils' progress throughout. School's intake is 'selective, but broadly mixed ability' and its value added scores are particularly impressive. Maximum class sizes of 20 up to GCSE and 16 in the sixth form but classes are often smaller than this. Pupils are set in maths and science up to GCSE. A variety of academic societies, including the Knowles, where Oxbridge candidates present their own research papers.

Head has brought learning support department into the heart of the school (it used to be housed in a separate block). Support given to 30 pupils, either one-to-one or in small groups, but department also offers drop-in sessions for anyone needing additional help. EAL is also available.

Games, options, the arts: With 500 acres of grounds to run around in, fresh air and exercise are an integral part of Downside life. As well as rugby, hockey, football and cricket for the boys and hockey, netball, tennis and rounders for the girls, there's a wealth of other sports on offer, including aerobics, athletics, badminton, cross-country, fencing, squash and swimming. Pupils have three games sessions during the week, plus matches on Saturday afternoons, but many do far more than this. Sixth formers get just as much sport as their younger counterparts – everything from boxercise to circuit training. When we visited, a group of older girls were in the middle of an energetic zumba class, music blasting across the courtyard. Sports facilities include an indoor pool (donated by a family whose son tragically died in a Naples swimming accident in 1925 and refurbished in 2010), rugby pitches galore, football pitches, cricket squares, Astroturf, a glorious 1930s sports pavilion and a sports centre with a weights room and fitness suite.

Parents report that the music is outstanding. Half the pupils have instrumental lessons and there's a multitude of orchestras, chamber ensembles and choirs (the Schola Cantorum is the oldest Roman Catholic school choir in the UK), along with jazz ensembles, a barbershop ensemble, pipe band, brass band, even an open-mic night. Art department

has been refurbished and is equipped with Macs, photographic studio, 3D printers and glass making facilities. Printmaking, textiles, oil painting, landscapes, portraits, graphic illustration, photography, fused glass – you name it, Downside does it. 'I'm a firm believer that everybody is creative in some shape or form,' the dynamic head of art told us. School has strong links with Hauser & Wirth Somerset, the contemporary art gallery in nearby Bruton. Busy drama department. School puts on a whole school play and musical every year, plus a host of other performances in refurbished 500-seat theatre. New Performing Arts Centre opening in 2016.

All year 9s are expected to do CCF for at least part of the year. Many carry on while others opt for D of E and Ten Tors expeditions across Dartmoor. Action-packed co-curricular programme includes chess, astronomy, Model United Nations, Young Enterprise, sewing, contemporary dance and fly fishing.

Boarding: Most pupils board – boarding is 'part of our USP,' says the head. Four boys' houses and two girls' houses. All junior boys (years 7, 8 and 9) start in Powell, a boarding house located in the main school, with open plan dorms and bunk beds for the youngest and a homely kitchen where boys get to cook (and eat) cookies, crumbles and pizza. A parent said some of the boys' dorms could do with a bit of updating but her children think they are fine as they are. Junior girls go straight into Isabella or Caverel, the two girls' boarding houses.

Head of history says qualification involves 'good, old-fashioned essay writing' and enables youngsters to study topics such as monasticism in the 9th century

House staff are adept at helping children to settle in. 'No one gets lost here,' we were told. A housemother reckons that Ovaltine, warm wheat bags (the modern answer to hot water bottles) and talking helps to stave off homesickness. Pupils are kept occupied at weekends with lots of trips and inter-house competitions. Up until the sixth form pupils hand in their mobile phones at night so they get a good night's sleep and aren't distracted by Facebook, Snapchat and the like. Parents thoroughly approve.

Background and atmosphere: The magnificent Downside Abbey adjoins the school and is visible for miles across the rolling Somerset landscape. The school has been on its present site in the village of Stratton-on-the-Fosse since 1814 but dates back more than 400 years. The Benedictine community of St Gregory the Great was founded in France in 1606 by English and Welsh monks living in exile because of the penal laws in England against Catholics. By 1617 English Catholics were sending their boys across the Channel to be educated there. When it became safe in the early 19th century for Catholics to provide education once more the school moved to England. Downside's monastic community (currently 12 monks, some of whom teach) has been in residence for 200 years. Members of an apostolic community from Chile – the Manquehue Apostolic Movement – have a base at Downside too. The school went co-ed in 2005 and the boy/girl ratio is now 60:40.

Downside has a rich cultural heritage. The abbey's Monastic Library, housed in a 1970s building, is one of the largest private libraries in the UK and has a collection of more than 400,000 books and papers, many of them very rare. 'It's like having an Oxford college library on the campus,' says the head. The school's atmosphere and setting are traditional, with historic corridors (the science corridor is lined with pictures of old boys who died in the First and Second World Wars), parquet floors and pupils hurrying to classes in their eye-catching uniform. Worn by all (including the sixth form), the uniform comprises mid-length kilts and

Over 400,000 books and papers. 'It's like having an Oxford college library on the campus,' says head

red or black jumpers for the girls and black jackets and pinstriped trousers for the boys. The pupils' maroon and gold game kit is particularly jazzy – good for spotting players on the games pitch.

School food much improved following the appointment of new caterers (manager formerly worked for River Cottage Canteen Bristol, part of Hugh Fearnley-Whittingstall's culinary empire). A stylish café serves cappuccinos, cookies and toasties during breaks and evenings. Fifty per cent of teaching staff live onsite or in Stratton-on-the-Fosse.

Pastoral care, well-being and discipline: A strong sense of spirituality pervades the school. Around 80 per cent of pupils are Catholic but children from other Christian denominations are welcome. School has a distinctively Catholic and Benedictine character and incorporates the eight aspects of a Benedictine education – welcome, listening, reverence and humility, teaching and learning, personal discipline, concern for the individual, building communion and stewardship of gifts.

School's most recent inspection report commented that 'pupils of all faiths and none possess an inner confidence, and a strong sense of their own identity.' Everyone is expected to participate in the school's spiritual life. Sunday mass in the abbey is compulsory, as is hymn practice on Friday afternoon. While Downside's monastic community prays formally six times a day, each boarding house has prayers in the morning and evening. School chaplains visit each house at least once a week and the school chapel is always open for those who want to go and pray. A third of the school takes part in voluntary prayer groups but it's very much up to individuals. A father with two children at Downside emphasised that religion isn't forced on the pupils – 'it's a gentle, subtle part of what is there,' he said. A mother we spoke to praised the school's ethos. 'There's an emphasis on the whole person,' she said. 'Everyone is made to feel welcome.'

Excellent pastoral care and tolerance for the individual produces happy children. Each pupil has a tutor to oversee academic matters and there's a raft of people to talk to if they encounter problems – tutors, housemasters and housemistresses, housemothers, the chaplaincy team, health centre staff and a school counsellor who visits twice a week. Pupils generally well behaved. Policies on smoking, alcohol and drugs are very clearly spelled out. Smokers are enrolled on a smoking cessation programme in the health centre. 'Responsible' drinking permitted at the sixth form bar.

Sixth form has its own study centre (very quiet and studious when we visited). UCAS coordinator guides pupils through their university entrance. Pupils are prepared well for life after school via spiritual, moral, social and cultural education (SMSC) – topics covered include how to set up a bank account, relationships, even mortgages. School also runs themed weeks on issues like e-safety, alcohol and drugs.

Pupils and parents: Boarders (28 per cent international students) come from all over. At the beginning and end of term school buses ferry pupils to London, airports and local stations. Day pupils tend to live within a 30-minute drive – places like Shepton Mallet, Frome, Bruton and the Chew Valley.

Head says that while some of the pupils are from very privileged backgrounds no one is materialistic or showy. A parent with three boys at the school concurred. 'A lot of schools are quite flash these days,' she said. 'Downside isn't like that at all. The pupils are very well mannered and the school gives them really good values. They know what is right and what is wrong.' An old boy with two children at the school told us that while his daughter was 'almost surgically attached' to her mobile phone before moving to Downside she hardly uses it these days. 'The school is very good at keeping them busy,' he says. 'In my day Sunday was a quiet day but now there are coaches going off all over the place.'

Alumni (known as Old Gregorians) include writer and journalist Auberon Waugh, hotelier Rocco Forte, scriptwriter Peter Morgan and interior designer David Mlinaric. You can spot an Old Gregorian at a dinner party, we were told, because they will always offer to do the washing up afterwards. 'It's that blend of good manners and service,' explained the director of pastoral care.

Entrance: Pupils must be able to cope with the school's 'traditional academic curriculum.' At 11+ and 12+ entrance is via the Downside Junior Assessment Test (English and maths), plus reports and references from pupil's current school. At 13+ most applicants take CE (required mark of 50 per cent but the average is 65 per cent). At 16+ pupils sit tests in subjects they are planning to take at A level. B grades at GCSE required (As for maths and the sciences if they are planning to study these at A level).

Exit: A handful leave after GCSE, usually for day schools or to study vocational subjects. At 18 the vast majority head to university (gap years not so popular these days). Four to Oxbridge in 2015 (including one to do medicine at Cambridge). Others to places like Bath, Bristol, Leeds, Loughborough, Newcastle, Nottingham and York.

Money matters: A 'substantial number' of scholarships and exhibitions are available (the number and size are at the discretion of the head). Means-tested bursaries, discounts of 2.5 per cent for children of Old Gregorians and 10 per cent for siblings.

Remarks: A boarding school with a strong moral compass. Downside is a great choice for Catholics and those seeking strong spiritual direction in a school. Its unpretentiousness, happy atmosphere and keen academic focus give pupils the chance to concentrate on acquiring their own intellectual and spiritual toolkit and to grow up in their own time.

Exeter Cathedral School

The Chantry, Exeter, EX1 1HX

01392 255298
registrar@exetercs.org
www.exetercs.org

Ages: 3–13 (boarding from age 8)
Pupils: 303
Boarders: 13 full, 31 weekly/flexi
Day: £6,519 – £10,872 pa
Boarding: plus £6,786 – £8,223 pa

Headmaster: Since January 2016, James Featherstone, previously head of lower school at the Perse School in Cambridge. Studied French and Spanish at Durham, then did a PGCE there, and was a choral scholar at Durham Cathedral. He later joined the choir of Jesus College, Cambridge and became part of the professional quintet at St-John-at-Hampstead, London. His wife, Julia, was previously assistant director of music at the Stephen Perse Foundation, and they have two young children.

Entrance: Entry to prep by interview plus taster day. Voice trials for choristers. Help available for those in genuine need. Range of top-up bursaries. Choristerships worth 25 per cent for boys and girls off tuition fee. Full academic range includes mild to moderate SENs.

Exit: Most stay to 13 to maximise on prep as opposed to junior school experience. Good cluster of music and academic scholarships. Leavers to West Country schools, ranging from Badminton to Truro High and from Teignmouth Community College to Sherborne School for Girls, and also further afield.

Remarks: WW2 Baedeker raid on Exeter scored a direct hit on school's previous buildings, killing the then head's daughter and forcing a temporary evacuation to Axminster. Still the huggermugger of a place it was when we last visited. ECS has since been cobbled together out of former archdeaconries and canonries, plus a post-war carbuncle of an auditorium whose days could soon be numbered. Lots of to-ing and fro-ing through security keypads for older pupils and staff alike. One of 35 choral schools in the UK, and the only independent school in Exeter to retain boarding.

Royal blue tartans and sunny sweatshirts complement the happy atmosphere of the early years section in Hall House. Safest of outside spaces includes all-weather, rubber-based and grassed play areas, as well as a hideaway section where children can at least feel unobserved. Echoes of Frances Hodgson Burnett in this lovely 'secret garden'.

Well-worn flagstones lead down to nursery and reception classes, where we watched children in small groups enjoying varied literacy and numeracy activities. Atmosphere in this area 'mirrors the

We had a splendid view from the head's study of Lowryesque figures playing all manner of games in the seemingly Victorian playground

home,' pre-prep head (Queensland-trained) Katie Fisher told us. She prefers to 'pick and choose' best elements of learning schemes available. Careful planning by staff, small groups and top-rate liaison with parents (no escaping pre-reading duties here) get these little ones off to a flying start. We liked the whole feel of the place: obviously warm relationships and free flow between the early years classrooms. Ground floor classrooms (years 1 to 3) have more of a sit up and take notice feel about them. We particularly liked the inviting pre-prep library and the music room. French club, music activities, swimming and PE all get under way from reception upwards. Class and individual music lessons begin from 7 years old, and a junior choir for pre-prep pupils. One year 3 boy talked to us about his recent mechanical invention (as part of a cross-curricular challenge) with the confidence of an 11-year-old. Learning support kicks in from reception if appropriate, and we saw one boy in year 1 receiving one-to-one help. By the time pupils reach year 3 two classes; these pupils spend mornings in their Hall House classroom and afternoons in The Chantry or other areas in the prep itself, which helps make the transfer at year 4 pretty seamless.

'Not a nerdy school,' affirmed over breakfast in the efficiently-managed if unexciting dining area. Girls and boys seemed relaxed and talked unpretentiously about everything and anything: reassuringly bling and mobile phone free whenever we saw them. Parents we met soon afterwards at an FECS (F stands for 'Friends of') coffee morning in the head's lounge purred about their offspring being 'able to take steps here they might not take elsewhere'. FECS does a lot to help the school and staff/parent relationships are genuinely warm.

We had a splendid view from the head's study of Lowryesque figures playing all manner of games in the seemingly Victorian playground (soon to be revamped as part of a pupil initiative). Adjacent Eyre House dates back to Georgian times and accommodates some 20 or so chorister and flexi-boarders. Likeable, energetic houseparents are backed up by a live-in tutor and gappers from Pembroke College, Adelaide. Boarding house provides better than basic accommodation with good recreational facilities which include a 'bistro' and games room. Pianos in the dormitories and some practice rooms allow boarders to squeeze in an after-breakfast run-through on their instruments.

School begins with daily morning worship (whole school on Mondays) in vast cathedral chapter house led by lay chaplain or by clergy (we met an enthusiastic 'missioner canon' cum mum preparing an assembly). Mix of teaching styles mirrors the 'lovely assortment' of characters in the staffroom. Children here seem to adapt themselves to very different learning environments. Food tech, DT, music and the science classes we observed were all very hands-on, whilst an impressively academic year 8 English class was stuck into the poetry of Ted Hughes. French also appears popular, and before they leave ECS pupils get to stay at Château Baudonnière for a week's activity in a French-speaking environment.

Parents we consulted are in no doubt about the high levels of pastoral and academic support children receive. 'My son enjoys doing proper homework set by teachers who actually mark it,' commented one parental escapee from a state primary. A reading culture at ECS – closure of the SPCK bookshop across the Close resulted in an unexpected upgrade for the well-stocked and properly-supervised library.

Music certainly counts for a lot, but pupils and parents insist that non-musicians are not in any way marginalised. Choir school status is icing on a rich musical cake: full orchestra, big band, choirs and ensembles with lots of concerts and performances. 'Children enjoy their music here and no-one is forced to do extra,' said one parent, whose daughter had been turned off elsewhere by too much pressure. Watching the choristers practise in the cathedral before evensong was an uplifting

experience: to be 'so accomplished so young' is a rarity these days. Deputy director of music leads Devon County Junior Choir, and when we visited was away doing outreach work in North Devon primary schools.

Drama is a popular activity: recent production of Treasure Island involved large numbers and scored a hit with parents. Art is also strong, with a recent auction (including pupils' work) helping to raise £14k towards the building of Langalanga School in the Rift Valley of Kenya. Well resourced IT room is sensibly managed as a tool rather than a master – hooray.

ECS is more than a choir school these days. Former pupils include 14th century theologian Boniface

Gifted pupils are stretched – recent top scholarships at 13+ prove the point. About 10 per cent of ECS pupils receive learning support at various levels. Two children on LS register recently obtained places at Exeter School. Range of SpLD includes dyscalculia. Extraction from classes, but children don't miss academic lessons. Well-qualified, experienced LS staff get praise from parents. LSCo also teaches mainstream English. Curriculum and pastoral matters seem to be in capable hands. Welfare of choristers (whose working hours would be deemed anti-social in other places) receives special consideration. Small termly stipend paid directly to warblers goes down well.

Sport is surprisingly strong – pupils get to play plenty of other SW independents and aim is to get everyone involved somewhere. Lack of immediate playing fields has led school to use some top facilities in a traditionally sporty city. All-weather surfaces at the main university campus, other facilities at St Luke's and outside the city at Pinhoe complete the mix. Cricket is played at the county ground whilst judo, squash, swimming are all catered for. Climbing, kayaking, cross-Dartmoor walk and annual expedition add to the excitement. Teams generally punch above their weight and some pupils make regional ones.

Food not an issue, though we would have liked to see rather more imagination and variety. Hospitable houseparents invite boarders to their flat for Saturday supper. Small payment only for reliable after-school arrangements (including 'little tea') for day pupils of all ages.

Big on encouragement: willing hands will thrive here. Tradition of choral singing goes back into mists of time but ECS is much more than a choir school these days. Former pupils include 14th century theologian Boniface; more recently, bass player Orlando le Fleming; Chris Martin – lead singer of Coldplay; Hampshire CCC manager, Giles White. Combination of down-to-earth parents, busy children and sometimes quirky teachers has created something distinctive and endearing.

Godolphin, Salisbury

Milford Hill, Salisbury, Wiltshire SP1 2RA

01722 430511
admissions@godolphin.wilts.sch.uk
www.godolphin.org

Ages: 11–18 (junior boarding from 7)
Pupils: 330; sixth form: 100
Boarders: 68 full, 152 weekly/flexi
Day: £17,133 – £19,038 pa
Boarding: £22,299 – £28,848 pa

Headmistress: Since January 2014, Mrs Emma Hattersley, previously deputy head, pastoral, at Sherborne Girls, before which she was a housemistress at Canford School. Mrs Hattersley trained as an opera singer at the Royal Academy of Music and has a music degree from Durham. Married with three children, she says she took her career break early so that now, in her early 50s, with her children pursuing their own careers, she is able to devote her time entirely to Godolphin. Her actor husband is immensely supportive, to the extent of running 'speakeasy' communications and other workshops in school.

Her calm, unthreatening exterior deceptively understates the determination beneath. Since arriving at Godolphin she says she has identified needs for brightening up areas of the fabric, developing staff and increasing opportunities for charitable activities. In fact she has already started on a programme of new showers, 'nice enough to make the girls feel good', surveyed parents of all leavers, consulted girls and produced her vision document for the future. She has also initiated the Elizabeth Godolphin Award for sixth formers, which gives focus to a programme of self-development and preparedness for work/life demands.

She says she believes in the Godolphin ethos: happiness, warmth, development which is aspirational but 'absolutely not at the expense of well-being'. 'We are not a hothouse' she says, but aim at 'the best we can possibly be in each girl's own style, celebrating diverse talent' and encouraging everyone to 'succeed at the level right for them'. Having taken on a school a little stunned by losing its new head to 'higher things' after three years, she has restored confidence and won parents' and girls' respect with her ability to perceive and develop what is best at Godolphin. A parent commented that 'under Mrs Hattersley staff can really develop their own teaching and pastoral skills.'

Academic matters: Definitely academic, with Latin up to A level and Greek on offer, though not taken up much for exams. Spanish, German and French also on offer though with a few following through to A level. Spectacular results in maths and art at both A level and GCSE. Other results certainly respectable, with 44 per cent A*/A at A level in 2015 and 61 per cent A*/A at GCSE. Results have been slightly less stellar since 2013, when the boards tightened up on top grades, but the 2015 results show that the top tranche of really able girls can achieve a sheaf of four A and A* grades at Godolphin.

French, German, Spanish and Latin taught from first year with Mandarin via a club. All available up to A level except currently Latin, and classical Greek done at GCSE via an 'Academic Society'. Girls do either double award science or three individual subjects. The usual subjects are offered plus PE, design and food technology, economics, business studies and drama. Godolphin will put on an A level course for one or two students if necessary, so there's not much you can't do, and options are designed round each girl's requests every year. There is a real buzz of enthusiasm from girls and teachers with excitement about geology coming on-stream as an A level next year. Parents are enthusiastic about the level of encouragement and individual attention given by teachers. One commented that teachers support girls' particular interests by finding articles and information for them even if it is outside the curriculum. Able girls enjoy events put on by the scholars and 'Alpinists' (Accelerated Learning Programme) activities, though sometimes the compulsory ones are 'a bit groan-worthy'. Girls say most are really interesting and attract lots of non-scholars too.

The REBEL (Recreational Enhancement for Bright Energetic Learners) scheme provides appreciated stimulus for year 9.

No lack of outdoor activities. One girl reported enthusiastically on taking part in the Dartmoor Ten Tors expedition after thorough training through CCF

The few SEN students have plenty of help organised by SENCo/ ed psych much praised by parents. Help is one-to-one, in groups, or takes the form of advice to teachers about learning styles of individuals. EAL is managed by SEN department – up to three lessons a week if necessary. Not many pupils need support, but advice to teachers is available from occupational therapist and maths specialist. Godolphin can cope with mild Asperger's. Healthy, friendly respect and affection between teachers and girls abundantly evident.

Games, options, the arts: Art has a huge and impressive building bursting with stunning work in every medium and hugely talented and enthusiastic staff. Very professional looking fabric design work on display as well as fascinating mixed media landscape work and spectacular studies based on work done in the cathedral. Two spacious studios for drawing/painting, with separate rooms dedicated to textiles, ceramics, photography and 3D; another smaller room full of iMacs for graphic design. This a truly brilliant department, making creative use of visits to and by local artists, who regularly initiate GCSE projects, and welcoming parents and visitors to view two floors of really breathtakingly exciting work – smashing results too. DT is no less impressive, with lots of colourful and innovative constructions in wood and plastic on display. It's not surprising academically gifted girls take up art or history of art here and a record number go on to art related courses at uni.

An attractive rotunda houses the performing arts centre with lovely in-the-round theatre, plenty of entertaining space and good practice rooms. Music is very well served, with the head running a popular junior orchestra of girls from prep and senior schools, a head of music who is as encouraging as he is talented, and the meticulous Mrs Sparkhall, who inspires the girls in a choral tradition that wins them the Bernardo's School Choir of the Year and other accolades. Individual lessons still in the unprepossessing and unreconstructed Rose Villa, but pupils and parents don't seem to mind and there's plenty of chamber music, though not much evidence of pop..

All the creative forces come together in drama, typified by December 2014's Oklahoma – spectacular and full of home-grown music and dance. Girls also perform with Portal Theatre, a small, professionally run theatre group. Masses of LAMDA exams and smaller performances.

Lacrosse dominates amongst a total of 90 different teams covering all the usual girls' winter and summer sports. Netball actually fields 23 teams, and tennis 14 teams as well as teams in all the major girls' school sports – quite a feat for a smallish school. All sports reach a pretty high level considering the school's size, swimming aided by a sleek 25 metre indoor pool. Highly competitive equestrian stars, and lacrosse and netball high fliers get to county and regional teams. Achievements include equestrians getting into top three at Windsor Horse Show, U13 netball team winning county championships and one girl selected for England U18 lacrosse squad. One hockey lover's parent commented that perhaps it came second best to lacrosse, but acknowledged that there is plenty of opportunity, even so. No lack of outdoor and other related activities. One girl reported enthusiastically on taking part in the Dartmoor Ten Tors expedition after thorough training through CCF (quite unusual in a girls' school).

Makes creative use of visits by local artists, who regularly initiate GCSE projects, and welcomes parents and visitors to view two floors of breathtakingly exciting work

Boarding: Girls can start boarding from 7 or 8 in the prep, when they join the junior house. Boarding is about as flexi as it goes, with everything from full time to weekly to flexi (one or more nights per week). One parent commented that though full boarding had been ideal for her daughter because they were not too far away, it tends to focus a bit much on activities for foreign students. Current flexibility is dependent on there being some beds available. Accommodation is simple, modern and not unnaturally tidy, with one junior (7-12), two senior (13-16) houses and a very friendly well organised sixth form centre over the road via a pedestrian bridge. Complete refurbishment of boarding is still in progress; study bedrooms are comfortably spacious with plenty of storage and common areas. Parents commented on a lot of changes, probably referring to the recent restructuring of the separate prep boarding to be part of junior house. Shared dining hall adjoins junior and senior houses. Sixth form house has its own dining room, kitchen, study areas, often with staff at hand, careers advice and leisure space with a proper Café Aroma serving the obligatory coffee shop range of expresso etc. Health provision is supervised by the indomitable Sister Gill, who creates an aura of calm, unfussy friendliness much appreciated by all.

Background and atmosphere: Unusually for a girls' school Godolphin has a long history, dating from a bequest made in 1726 by Elizabeth Godolphin, eventually resulting in the establishment in the cathedral close of a school for 'eight orphaned gentlewomen' who followed a remarkably enlightened curriculum for their day. It moved to its present 16 acre site in Milford Hill in 1891, retaining its links with the cathedral, with the bishop and chapter still represented on the governing body. Skilful use of space and the site still has a gracious feel, generated by the mellow red brick of the original building and the lovely open grass pitches with views of the downs enhanced by banks of lavender at the time of our visit. One has to look quite hard to find the few scruffy corners that Mrs Hattersley is determined to clear. The huge gothic school hall has the dusty feel (it certainly isn't, as the school is exceptionally clean and fresh) which old wood, high ceilings and portraits of ex-heads inevitably evoke. Road access is made awkward by several right-angled bends in the road, but efficient planning of parking helps, though parents report it can still be a bit of a maelstrom at pick up time.

Uniform is unremarkable: pale blue shirt, plaid skirt and navy blazer enhanced by stylish boater with crested red ribbons, known as a 'board'. All, however, is concealed by coverall old fashioned pinafores in royal blue for seniors (except sixth who wear own clothes, plus suits for going to the cathedral), red for preps and gingham for nursery. Oddly, girls seem to like this antiquated touch, while one parent attributed the school's exceptionally friendly and unthreatening atmosphere to the fact that no ultra-trendy girl would be seen dead wearing one. This is certainly a school where those who have been bullied elsewhere find general acceptance and support. An exceptionally happy place with few exclusive 'in groups', where the occasional 'falling out' is sympathetically dealt with by friendly staff, evidently liked and trusted by pupils. With its historic cathedral links, this is an overtly Christian school with a chaplain, using the cathedral for services and confirmation, though one parent regretted that it had to be on a Thursday to ensure parent availability.

Pastoral care, well-being and discipline: Pastoral care is delivered to day girls – known as 'Sarums' – and boarders together through the residential houses, which all have provision for day girls and welcome them to work and relax with the boarders. Lessons end at 4pm, but the myriad of school activities and prep run in three sessions after tea. School houses involve all ages from nursery to sixth form for competitions, fundraising and social events. Personal development is delivered in the PERSIL programme (another quirky Godolphin acronym representing Personal, Ethical, Religious and Social Issues in Life). In the sixth form the Elizabeth Godolphin Award encourages activities aimed at preparation for life after school. Truly all-embracing, it includes Prue Leith cookery (expensive), banking and finance, with car maintenance, emotional literacy, women's boot camp and dawn visits to Stonehenge all part of the bigger picture.

Firm, friendly, no-nonsense discipline leads to an atmosphere in which girls and teachers are at home with each other. The best is expected of everyone. Rules are few but clearly stated, and parents say problems such as drugs, smoking or alcohol are 'simply not part of the culture'. Girls rarely abuse the freedom they have to go into Salisbury attend socials with other schools, or entertain guests in the sixth form. 'Staff seem to care as much as I do', one parent commented.

Pupils and parents: Mostly middle class with a total of about 14 per cent international students, mainly from the Far East. Not a 'toff' school, though pupils are not averse to joining up with Eton and Winchester for social events. Huge day catchment area has bus routes (some shared with Leaden Hall School) from every direction. In an area with ambitious state schools, art and music still attract pupils, as does the excellent pastoral care. Parents are pleased at how open pupils seem, speaking easily to adults and confident in public, but also that younger ones still behave like children.

One parent attributed the school's exceptionally friendly and unthreatening atmosphere to the fact that no ultra-trendy girl would be seen dead in a pinafore

Past pupils (with houses named after them) include the full spectrum of women writers, Jilly Cooper, Minette Walters and Dorothy Sayers as well as prolific novelist Amanda Brookfield. TV personalities include Dragon's Den businesswoman Deborah Meaden, Katie Knapman of Countryfile, presenters Helen Bishop and Louise Beale, sportswoman Ruby Smith, yachtswomen Hannah White and Nicola Rodriguez as well actress Charlotte Longfield.

Entrance: At 11+, 12+, 13+ and sixth form. Registered pupils invited for a preview day and night in the autumn term, before taking entrance exams in the spring term. Now uses its own entrance test – maths, English and verbal reasoning, plus interview and team building exercises.

Exit: Around 30 per cent leave after GCSE, to local state schools and sixth form colleges. Most sixth formers go on to higher education, plenty art related, and a good proportion of Russell Group universities. One to Oxbridge in 2015; lots of bright hopes for the future.

Money matters: Scholarships at 11+ and 13+ for outstanding merit or promise in academic work, music, sport or art. Awards are worth 15 per cent of boarding or day fees. In sixth form, scholarships awarded for all of the above plus drama. Additional bursaries may be awarded to scholars in case of financial hardship. Six Foundation Bursaries (worth 70 per cent) are offered to orphans in need of financial support, when one parent has died or whose parents are separated or divorced. An Old Godolphin Association

Bursary (25 per cent) is occasionally available to the daughter or granddaughter of a former pupil at the school. Entrance bursaries are available to all eligible candidates (including at 14+) in order of registration – so it may pay to get in early.

Remarks: It seems an idyllic school, almost too good to be true, and there is no doubt that it offers the very best of single sex education. For all its gentleness and Railway Children look, teaching is tip-top, especially now a real effort has gone into IT. Art and music are about as good as you can get and drama and games exceptional for a small school. Girls can really be themselves and the eccentric and the sociable are equally accepted. A very special place to grow up in.

Hanford School

Child Okeford, Blandford Forum, Dorset DT11 8HN

01258 860219
office@hanford.dorset.sch.uk
www.hanfordschool.co.uk
C of E

Ages: 7–13
Pupils: 102
Boarders: 96
Day: £17,400 pa
Boarding: £21,150 pa

Headmaster: Since September 2014, Mr Rory Johnston, previously head of classics and housemaster at Horris Hill. Read classics at Cambridge and worked in the City for 20 years before taking up teaching. Married to George, who works with him and oversees pastoral care. They have two children.

Miss Sarah Canning MA (70s), the source of Hanford's spirit and owner of the school, retired from her rôle as headmistress in 2003, handing the school to a charitable trust in 2004. The school remains her home and she still runs the riding, teaches Latin, serves as moral backbone and can be found almost everywhere, like a benevolent ('Not always!' she says) genie.

Entrance: Informal – girls can come at any time, if space available (and lately that's a big if). Some at 7, the largest number come as 8 or 9 year olds, and a few at 10 or 11. Locals, Wessex girls, Londoners (regular coach to Battersea) and numerous families posted abroad (popular with Forces and FCO families). A sea of fair hair, blue eyes and wellies; a sprinkling of Europeans, usually Spanish, tip up for a term or year to boost their English, plus a few genuine overseas exotics. Few first-time buyers. Some bursaries.

Exit: Not associated with any particular senior school – strives to find the right niche for each child. Most girls stay to 13 and then move (many with scholarships) on to Bryanston, Sherborne Girls, St Mary's Calne, Benenden, St Swithun's, St Mary's Shaftesbury, Claysmore, Moreland House, Queen's College, London.

Remarks: As the years go by, this school becomes more and more special. It doesn't change, sailing serenely on, while other preps scramble towards identikit purgatory. Has defied the downward trend of girls-only boarding – we note with sorrow that we can now count the number of free-standing girls' boarding preps in England on one hand. Back on track after a wobbly period while the torch was being handed on to new leadership.

Set in 45 acres of rolling countryside (we drove by it three times before spotting the drive, despite having been there before) on the edge of the Stour Valley and surrounded by iron age barrows and Roman fort remains, Hanford House was built in 1620 for Sir Robert Seymer (later Kerr-Seymer). Basically Jacobean with Victorian overtones, it has been splendidly adapted to scholastic life. The magnificent glazed internal courtyard is now the dining room.

We can continue to say this is one of the nicest, if not the nicest, girls' boarding schools in the country, with a gentle, kind, friendly, enthusiastic, gloriously happy-go-lucky, genuine family atmosphere. A place you can feel absolutely confident leaving your ewe lamb in, with the knowledge that the school will probably do a better job of looking after her than you would yourself and, almost as a side issue, give her a thorough grounding in CE subjects, and a fun time with it. Not a flash school: faded carpets, slip-covered arm chairs, large chilly rooms, dogs wandering down corridors and the bracing smell of rotting manure – the informality can be too much for some parents. No uniform – girls sit happily in class in their riding togs, their (seriously padded) crash helmets on the desk in front of them, working as hard as they can, because the next lesson has four legs. Ponies are important here – the school has 'around' 20 – plus a few privately owned (but used by everyone). Ninety-five per cent of the girls ride, although most didn't when they arrived. Indoor riding school, outdoor arena, jumping paddock. A summer treat is a pre-breakfast ride.

History starts with the Norman invasion and works forward. And the breezily non-PC scripture teacher told us, 'We teach them the Bible because they'll only get comparative religion once they leave.' French from age 8 – pupils are usually way past the standard of their senior school by the time they leave (ditto for Latin). 'Native foreign speakers' plus the daughters of British diplomats based abroad are encouraged to continue with their languages. Specialist teachers in all subjects from year 5 onward. No scholarship set per se, but pupils streamed and potential scholars looked after. Occasionally puts girls up a year. Class sizes tiny throughout the school: nine or 10 in each lesson – makes a huge difference. The lessons we watched were so intimate, they reminded us a children's game – 'Oh, I know, let's play school!'

Watch for the magnificent junior cloakroom, a picture of managed chaos with a towering heap of rollerblades, riding kit, trainers, wellies, more or less in their places

On top of this, 30 girls receive extra help for SEN from a mixture of sources who add up to one full time member of staff. Mostly mild to moderate special needs, but a couple in the 'more severe' category. School introducing new 10-15 minute 'drop in sessions' for quick jolts of extra help. Lots of consistency and stability: average age of staff a youthful 50 and many teachers have been with the school for ages. Classrooms are incredible – some in the converted stables (you go in and out of the window – promise) and some in the most ramshackle collection of what might, in a real world, be temporary buildings.

Music very important – 90 per cent of girls learn an instrument and practice sessions timetabled. Two girls preparing for grade 7 exams when we visited. Girls are auditioned for the chapel choir (only). Also a normal choir, folk group, bands for everything

– woodwinds, strings, recorders – and orchestra. Incredibly ambitious art, with ceramics that would not disgrace any senior school; regular masterclasses for gifted artists, plus weekend art club for all. Drama also prolific and good – do ask to see the famously well-stocked costume cupboard. Games (hockey, rounders, pop-lacrosse etc) played on the lawn, adjacent to the outdoor swimming pool. Tap dancing, ballet, year round tennis coaching, even a bit of pistol shooting in the gym. Watch for the magnificent junior cloakroom, a picture of managed chaos with towering heap of rollerblades, riding kit, trainers, wellies, all more or less in their places.

Vast majority board, but loads of flexibility and the line between boarding and day is blurred. All day girls have their own bed and get 20 nights' boarding for free ('They can decide at 6.30 in the evening that they want to stay and, with a quick phone call, it's sorted'). All prep done at school and day girls leave their clobber there. Hanford never closes for exeats – only half term – so perfect for overseas families. Dormitories tidy and feminine – no posters but lots of cuddly toys. Matching bedspreads instead of duvets – now when was the last time you saw that? Not all singing and dancing at weekends – more like a real home, with Sundays spent mooching around the grounds, playing hide and seek, tree-climbing, berry picking, reading. This is a school where time for play is treasured

Girls sit happily in class in their riding togs, their crash helmets on the desk in front of them, working as hard as they can, because the next lesson has four legs

and children are allowed to be children rather than rushed to the nearest shopping centre or games arcade at the first whiff of free time. No TV on week nights – only on weekend evenings (why do so few schools have the guts to do likewise?).

Time-honoured Hanford extracurriculars include sewing and dressmaking (the cherished 'Hanford skirts' were much in evidence), pottery, current affairs and art appreciation. In the IT department girls can email whenever – but a school where the post is still keenly awaited. Loads of Hanford traditions, like using a briefcase as tuckbox, climbing the massive cedar tree (whose branches are each named), early morning rides in the summer, bonfire night entertainments and the marvellously convoluted – and effective – 'manners system', which includes SYRs (serve you rights) for the naughty. Sweets the occasional bribe. School's enormous walled kitchen garden produces veg for the menu plus fruit and the lovely flowers that decorate the main building.

Old Girls include singer Emma Kirkby and Amanda Foreman, author of Georgiana, Duchess of Devonshire, on which the film The Duchess was based. And what better example to the girls that they can do anything in life than Peggy, the 82-year-old paddock manager, who powered past us driving a tractor, as we toured the school? Having said all that, it isn't for everyone. 'You need a resilient child,' one parent told us. 'And if they are, they will have a fantastic, amazing, wild, brilliant time – but they won't necessarily learn (or be taught) kindness and tolerance and understanding of those weaker than themselves.' But – for the confident and outgoing child – no other school like it and nowhere better.

Hazlegrove School

Hazlegrove, Yeovil, Somerset BA22 7JA

01963 442606
admissions@hazlegrove.co.uk
www.hazlegrove.co.uk

Ages: 2–13 (boarding from 7)
Pupils: 380
Boarders: 101 full; 12 flexi
Day: £8,040 – £16,299 pa
Boarding: £18,726 – £23,892 pa

Linked school: King's Bruton

Headmaster: Since 2002, Mr Richard Fenwick BEd Adv Dip Ed MA (50s). Educated at Bishops Stortford College, bosh shot at London University and now, after gaining a first and subsequent MA at the Open University in education management and shaping a notable career and reputation in prep schools, living proof that education doesn't always work at the same time for everyone. Stints at Bilton Grange (qv) as director of studies and teacher of DT – still a fabulous carpenter, according to his wife – and head of St Andrew's Turi (Kenya) preceded his appointment to Hazlegrove; also Vice Chairman of ISEB since 2011. 'I want Hazlegrove to be a place where children feel safe and loved' he says, 'so that, instead of just surviving at school, they can direct their energies into academic, creative or sporting endeavour'. Tall and lean, Mr Fenwick bounds about the school, taking stairs two at a time; we trotted to keep up. Hobbies include running,

surfing, sea-kayaking, golf, fishing and trekking in remote locations (Nepal a particular favourite) during the hols, we were not surprised to learn. Married to Katie, who is more deeply involved in school life than many heads' wives, (she teaches PHSE and wrote an excellent leaflet for parents of new boarders, for example), they have three grown up children. In some ways rather an unconventional and uncompromising head, attributes which perhaps enabled him to turn Hazlegrove from the rudderless place it was when he arrived to the thriving enterprise it clearly is today.

Entrance: Broadly non-selective. All hopefuls are invited for a trial day at which reading/spelling ages and mathematical ability are assessed, plus any need for additional learning support identified.

Exit: To a panoply of greater and lesser public schools at 13+; the majority in South West England (the Sherborne schools, Bryanston, King's College, Taunton and of course around half to its own senior school, Kings Bruton) but national notables such as Winchester, Eton, Marlborough and Millfield too. The array of awards year after year impresses. A recent parent was delighted by the head's efforts in researching a school where Hazlegrove pupils do not usually go. Former pupils include Peter Wilson (Olympic gold medallist in shooting), Maddie Hinch (GB hockey goalie), sculptor Will Newton and author Tobias Jones.

Remarks: A long drive through glorious parkland – we narrowly avoided cows and 4x4s en route – leads to a fine example of 18th century domestic architecture, enhanced by formal gardens. Less sightly parts of what is undoubtedly a well-resourced and purposeful school are mostly hidden away, but facilities and space abound: super indoor pool, two Astros, tennis courts and acres of pitches satisfy the most sporty. Pigs and chickens enthusiastically looked after by pupils, and there's no ducking their eventual fate either. Full use appears to be made of this bucolic setting (faintly marred by the services visible on the A303), recently enhanced by the planting of a five acre Jubilee Wood.

Socks blown off by impromptu marimba recital the head asked a boy to perform when we happened upon him jamming with a couple of other pupils

We were enthralled and impressed by a scholarship English class of 13-year-olds who were getting to grips with the complex themes in William Blake's poetry. Parents recognise and greatly appreciate the fine teaching that goes on at Hazlegrove, and acknowledge the head's insistence in recruiting staff only of the highest calibre: 'The quality of the discussions at parents' evenings is phenomenal,' said one mother. But Hazlegrove is no hothouse, though the children are 'pushed enough' say parents, and does very well by the breadth of ability it admits. About 15 per cent of pupils receive learning support. All these lucky children benefit from exciting and innovative ways to learn, such as a Skype call with astronaut Nicholas Patrick in which the whole prep school participated, and the millionaires club which encourages children to read 1,000,000 words in the course of a term. The latter is part of the Accelerated Reader programme, where books are carefully graded to eliminate unsuitable choices. The librarian gets rave reviews.

Sport, music and drama ditto. There's an extensive fixture list with other schools and plenty of silverware in the trophy cabinet. One parent articulated the common tension between winning at all costs/sport for all, and wondered if there could be more chances for less skilled players to represent the school at matches. (School defends its record on this.) As for the music, well, our socks were knocked off by the impromptu marimba recital (we had not met one before either) the head asked a boy to perform when we happened upon him jamming with a couple of other pupils in the music department. Masses going on of all standards, from absolute beginners to one already at grade 8, and a clutch taking grade 5 theory. Conventional choices for drama, such as Wind in the Willows and The Wizard of Oz put on in purpose-built theatre and much enjoyed by performers and audience alike; pupils also take LAMDA exams. Mandarin club has proved hugely successful and Mandarin introduced for year 5 pupils.

About a third of pupils board routinely (around 10 per cent of these are international pupils), and there is scope for occasional boarders too. Accommodation is fine (quite big dorms with a strong smell of disinfectant in the boys' quarters), though rules are quaintly old-fashioned: no mobiles, letter-writing on Sundays and proper shoe-cleaning once a week. That said, activities are myriad and sometimes rather trendy: we were shown the film the boarders had devised, scripted and made the previous weekend. The feel of an extended family is palpable, enhanced by the fact that half the staff live on site. In the evenings, seating for meals is rearranged into family-style groups so boarders get to know everyone; a black tie dinner with five sets of cutlery enlivens proceedings from time to time.

Hazlegrove is quite smart and not a typical country prep school. A broad cross-section (says school) of local and not-so-local families drive or bus their kids in from all over the place up and down the A303, and it's the school of choice for many families making the big move out of London. The head defined parents, when asked, as the 'sort of people who don't look in the mirror before they come to pick up'; their occupations include farmer, lawyer, doctor, plumber, cheese-maker, helicopter pilot, entrepreneur, designer, author and chef. There is an active and welcoming social scene and parents, mums in particular, take up the exercise classes and tennis coaching with enthusiasm. Try as we might, we could not find anything to fault about this super one-off school with its quirky head.

King's Bruton

Plox, Bruton, Somerset BA10 0ED

01749 814200
office@kingsbruton.com
www.kingsbruton.com

Ages: 13–18
Pupils: 342; sixth form: 130
Boarders: 226 full (154 boys, 72 girls)
Day: £20,604 pa
Boarding: £29,793 pa

Linked school: Hazlegrove School

Headmaster: Since 2009, Mr Ian Wilmshurst MA PGCE (mid-40s). Educated at The Edinburgh Academy, where he was head boy, then Pembroke, Cambridge, where he read geography. Started career at Highgate as geography master, house tutor and games coach, then back over the border to Merchiston, where he was a housemaster for five years, as well as teaching geography and coaching 1st XV rugby, before promotion to deputy headship at The Royal Hospital School in Suffolk. Wants to breathe more commercial realism into a school which has perhaps sometimes suffered the financial consequences of misplaced priorities. Married to Helen, who helps with the marketing, is a tutor and runs the equestrian activity. Their two daughters are at Hazlegrove.

Head's strong sense of justice has already rattled a few cages, but most parents are behind his disciplinary stand and feel that he 'will raise profile of the school'. Wants to improve academic standards (which head doesn't?) while keeping the school's traditional warmth. He sets all King's pupils the three challenges of 'do your best academically, make most of your talents and look after each other.'

'Not afraid to change things,' reported pupils (who 'really respect him'); parents thought he would 'pull up on any sloppiness.' Claims not to be ambitious personally. Parents say that 'he is a very nice man' and 'much more personable than first impressions might suggest.' Enjoys hill walking, the odd round of golf and time out with his young family.

Academic matters: Consistent if not superlative – school admits a wide spectrum of ability. Thirty-eight per cent A*/A grades at GCSE in 2015 and 22 per cent A*/A at A level (55 per cent A*-B). IGCSE is offered to all pupils in maths and to most able as separate sciences; two out of three languages on offer can be chosen in year 10 – teachers choose courses to play to pupils' strengths with brightest sitting 10 subjects. May not match high flyers in Bath or Bristol but delivers more than King's parents often expect.

Head of teaching and learning – a new post created to focus on stretching the more able and to improve independent learning. Pupils are fast tracked (eg scholars in Latin, which is still offered within timetable for year 9 and at A level but is taught as an activity at GCSE) where appropriate, flexible timetabling to meet individual needs and expanding provision for gifted and talented. Thirteen lower sixth pupils currently involved in Extended Project Qualification; some introduced to this and to philosophy in year 9.

Huge range of subjects (17 or 18) in year 9; small class sizes a great plus point; setting in core subjects. ICT is not taught as a separate subject; lots of computers and smartboards but some subjects have been ICT shy, it seems; good use is made of intranet in some GCSE (eg sports studies) and A level (eg geography) work. Surprising location of food technology (very popular with boys) in science building rather than with DT. School benefits from involvement in Mid-Somerset consortium to bring new blood into teaching from other backgrounds – two trainee teachers currently on this GTP programme.

Valued learning support department (it has a long tradition here) with its inviting base conveniently located alongside the library. Head of learning support is keen that pupils receiving help are 'not seen as different'. She helps organise the annual ISC conference on SEN and is very experienced at managing provision: 20 to 25 per cent of pupils currently receive some measure of support. All entrants are screened for reading comprehension, spelling and processing speed. Numeracy is covered from within maths department and two teachers are employed to work with EAL pupils (currently over 20 of 80+ overseas pupils receive support with English). Insists that Bruton's learning support aims to enable pupils to 'make the most of their talents'.

School also offers level 3 BTec certificate, broadly equivalent to one AS level. Says that 'for students who find the A level examinations challenging, BTec provides the alternative to enable them to achieve bite-size tasks which will lead to larger assignments/assessments.' BTecs available in health and social care, hospitality and sport.

Games, options, the arts: Sport (compulsory three times a week including Saturday) counts for a lot – 10 per cent of pupils have performed at representative level. Tennis players reached girls' and mixed finals nationally; other recent national finalists include biathlon and gymnastics plus top equestrian events. Sports teachers are ex-internationals, including professional hockey coach; loads of teams in major sports; increasingly attracting

girl athletes; universal participation in some events (eg annual cross-country). Opportunity to shine in a team at King's as opposed to being one out of 200 overlooked players elsewhere. Large sports hall with gallery and fitness suite; two squash courts, fives court, acres of playing fields and Astroturf. Swimming at nearby Sexey's or Hazlegrove. Range of sporting activities (from archery to trampolining) offered throughout the week.

Strong art department with good studio spaces (including photographic studio) for exciting range of work and new school and community gallery, thanks partly to success of recent art auction. Sixth form curriculum includes life drawing, and history of art also on offer. Music (includes music technology to A2 level) is very popular; about 150 pupils currently play an instrument and opportunities to perform include big band, chapel choir, string orchestra and military band (which recently took part in Lord Mayor's Show in London). Big band goes down a storm at annual black tie dinner dance, Swing into Spring, for parents and friends. Battle of the bands and open mic evenings for extroverts. We listened to lovely chamber choir, which presents range of modern and traditional music with high level of competence; also barbershop and close harmony groups, all under director of choral studies. Lots of concerts each term. Drama offered to A level with productions put on by pupils at all levels in impressive Fitzjames Theatre.

Long list of worthies going back to Hugh Sexey – auditor to Queen Bess and James I and founder of still extant Sexey's Hospital. Lots of military top brass

CCF very well established: gliding, sailing and camps all feature regularly, with some opting for D of E programme instead. Varied and extensive activities programme covers everything from girls' cricket and rugby to Arabic and Scottish reels. Recent visits include year 9 to the World War I battlefields, language students in Barcelona, lower sixth to Paris, biologists at Nettlecombe Court near Exmoor and historians experiencing Nuremberg and Leipzig.

Pupils raise money for charity and annual sponsored endurance challenge in Morocco (organised by the chaplain) funds gap year students (to the tune of £1k+ each last year) who go out to Salem in India to work at a Christian orphanage. School's rural location makes work experience difficult to organise and all but a few miss out; successful careers convention for year 12 involves former pupils in giving advice and information. Strong local links exist mainly through weekly community service, which involves 65 pupils working with groups ranging from primary pupils to senior citizens. Innovative international committee organises events such as European Languages Day and Chinese New Year.

Boarding: Seven houses – three for girls and four for boys – include boarders and day pupils. Usual competitions giving everyone a chance to represent their house at sport or music or drama. Pupils can cook up own food in houses after prep and are provided with basic rations. 'Outstanding' latest Ofsted report for level of care, praise for boarders' activities and leisure resources, safety, achievement and enjoyment of school. After school might find pupils eg rehearsing for the school play, decorating gingerbread houses, learning to kayak.

Background and atmosphere: Mellow yellow stone wonder located at centre of this unusually scholastic country town, in shadow of landmark Dovecote. Founded in 1519 during reign of Henry VIII, shut its doors after only 20 years and was then re-opened in 1550 under Edward VI – difficult for pupils here not to have a sense of history. Straddles busy road to Castle Cary – no zebra crossing yet to make crossing it safer – and sits conveniently alongside main railway line to South West. Has added buildings (eg impressive Hobhouse science centre and 'badly needed' reception area) without destroying the harmony of older ones. Old House (complete with turret added by a former housemaster) is oldest part of school whilst smallest boarding house of seven is Arion – a girls' house. Neighbouring parish church doubles as school chapel twice a week; assemblies are held in beamed Memorial Hall: recently refurbished, thanks to +£90K raised within King's community in memory of Ben Ross (see below). Adjacent John Davie room (used for small functions, concerts and meetings) could be next on the list. Purpose-built, inviting music 'hub' provides for individual and group lessons.

IT is wireless networked throughout school; separate computer rooms available for classes or study periods. School intranet includes useful lesson notes and reviews for pupils. Excellent, active library works closely with English department (eg accelerated reader scheme) to get even the most reluctant reader involved and lots of literary happenings (eg on national poetry day, world book day etc). All boarding houses now refurbished.

Dynamic and popular chaplain (doubles as a rugby coach) insists he's not tried 'to do anything clever' but has upped the Christian vibes here with 'TGI' – a weekly get together – plus drop-ins at lunch-time. Nothing forced – which goes down well with the neutral majority. Definitely a major

element in building a positive ethos at King's (chaplaincy programme described as 'vigorous and popular' by inspectors). Recent influx of new young staff.

Pastoral care, well-being and discipline: 'Family atmosphere' is what attracts parents and pupils – 'friendly children and good mixing between year groups' praised by one father. 'Fantastic pastoral care', said one mum, whose son is now in fourth year of boarding. Some pupils trained to act as mediators where cases of harassment arise. Well established PSHEE programme includes sessions on stress management to help pupils cope with exam pressures. Medical centre provides for day pupils and boarders; free physio sessions on offer for all those sports injuries and visiting counsellor to provide additional support. Large, airy dining area provides wide range of menus.

Smoking less of a problem these days (we didn't have time to check behind the bushes) but rigorous sanctions for those discovered. Sixth form club serves alcohol on Wednesday, Friday and Saturday evenings for an hour or so; junior common room a great success: we were told that 'friends just click with each other here'. Head 'takes all circumstances into account' before applying sanctions in areas such as drugs or illicit sex.

Pupils and parents: All-round traditional education sought by King's parents is steadily moving towards a more focused academic one. Sophisticated incomers appreciate it as much as locals, who prefer its 'slight scruffiness' to more lah-di-dah alternatives. Pupils appear confident and purposeful – apparently they get ('unfairly,' they say) occasional anti-toff flak at inter-school events (eg annual Bruton's Got Talent). Boarders – many from military families or from overseas – are in vast majority and girls are outnumbered by boys about three to two. Internet savvy parents can enjoy seeing sports and other activities on school's 'gallery' (thanks to input from a local parent employed to provide all the visual media) even if they can't attend functions in person; regular newsletters and 'plus one card' sent to parents via house staff whenever an achievement has been recognised.

Long list of worthies going back to Hugh Sexey – auditor to Queen Bess and James I and founder of still extant Sexey's Hospital in Bruton. Lots of military top brass (including more recently Air Chief Marshal Sir Peter Squire) plus less worthy William Dampier – a 17th century explorer and buccaneer – and author of Lorna Doone, RD Blackmore. Also The Sunday Telegraph's Mandrake, comedian Marcus Brigstocke and Sergeant Ben Ross – killed by a suicide bomber in Helmand, Afghanistan, who became the first Brutonian to be killed in action since the Korean War.

Entrance: About half of Hazlegrove's leavers move to King's. Remainder from Chafyn Grove, Perrot Hill,

All Hallows, Port Regis and a host of others. Wide ability range as parents tend to choose King's for its own sake rather than its league table position.

Exit: Around a quarter leaves after GCSEs. Nearly all sixth formers to higher education eg Bath, King's College London, Sheffield and Exeter. One to Arizona State uni in 2015.

Money matters: Twenty per cent discount for Forces families. Fewer scholarships (still available for academic, sixth form and music) than previously but increased number of means-tested bursaries. Year 9 rugby scholarship programme launched recently.

Remarks: 'Fairly useful,' said one dad clearly not given to hyperbole; another parent stressed how King's 'does very well at catering for a wide range of ability'. Parents like the family feel of King's – its safe setting and sense of traditional values make it a popular choice. Moving forwards in curriculum terms but should guard against losing its warmth in a drive to be more ambitious.

King's Hall School

Kingston Road, Taunton, Somerset TA2 8AA

01823 285920
admissions@kingshalltaunton.co.uk
www.kingshalltaunton.co.uk
C of E

Ages: 2–13
Pupils: 265
Boarders: 40
Day: £7,020 – £15,135 pa
Boarding: £16,845 – £21,900 pa

Linked school: King's College (Taunton)

Headmaster: Since 2009, Mr Justin Chippendale BSc (late 40s). His education and subsequent career have caused him to shuttle between Oxford and Taunton, starting at the Dragon, thence to King's Taunton, back to Oxford Brookes for a degree in biology, exercise and health, a stint as housemaster at the Dragon, a detour to Chafyn Grove as deputy head, then back to Taunton. Affectionately and inevitably known as Mr Chips, he works hard to put the child's experience (of personal development, academic stimulus, physical challenge, artistic exploration and so on) as top priority at King's Hall, closely followed by the quality of relationships: between staff and pupils/parents/each other. 'I work on the invisibles and immeasurables', says he. But that's not to endanger academic expectations: 'It has to be cool to work, and ok to talk

about work here,' he adds, and makes it his business to ensure that his charges (and their parents) make well-informed suitable choices for their next schools, even when the majority go on to King's Taunton.

Mr Chips is a keen sportsman and retains the physique of a rugby player, still occasionally coaching. Married with three children at the school, he enjoys entertaining parents 'in order to understand each family's own context' (though a few grumble about not being on the head's dinner list), and he is generally well-liked by both pupils and parents. 'He knows everyone, takes a real interest in us, and we love the Chips Challenge,' opined pupils, who might be asked to research an arcane matter, solve a puzzle or achieve a physical feat.

Entrance: Many join the pre-prep (school also comprises a nursery from 2), but some come from local primary schools and London at 7+. From years 1-4, new children are informally assessed during a welcome day; from years 5-8 they are tested in maths, English and verbal reasoning for which special preparation is not required, says school. Quite an intake also welcomed into year 7 for the final two years before moving on at 13+.

Exit: The majority to King's College at 13+, but a good sprinkling to other schools in the South West, such as the Sherborne schools; also the likes of Eton, Winchester and Downe House, some with scholarships for various talents; academic scholarship set for final last two years.Every child gets into the school of his/her first choice, apparently; 'We didn't get the hard sell for King's', said one mother with a sigh of relief. Famous ex-pupils include actress Juno Temple, founder of Everyday Sexism project Laura Bates, and mad adventurers Ross and Hugo Turner.

Remarks: Sited in the mellow golden former home of the Yea baronetcy Pyrland Hall, dating from 1760, and surrounded by 50 acres of parkland and woods, this is an idyllic setting just minutes from Taunton. But it's not precious – pupils here make the most of the space, freedom and mud to pursue a terrific range of activities and outdoor pursuits beyond the school day which finishes at 4.30pm, mountain biking and archery being just two. Some 15 acres of pitches, an Astro and a sports hall mean all major sports are well catered for and fulfil all expectations, but an indoor pool is undoubtedly on

the parental wish list; as it is, swimming is an extra-curricular activity until the school's outdoor pool is opened in the summer term. But it all amounts to a slice of gracious enough living for the young.

It's not precious – pupils here make the most of the space, freedom and mud to pursue a terrific range of activities and outdoor pursuits

King's Hall is reckoned to be Taunton's smartest and most academic prep school, partly because it's the only place which prepares children for common entrance (and scholarships) at 13+, still the measure and starting point for the most prestigious public schools. From year 3, children are taught in classes of about 15 by specialist teachers. All begin French in year 1 but there's the opportunity to pick up Spanish from year 5 or Latin from year 6. Science and geography get thumbs up from pupils, but 'We don't go to any lessons and think 'Oh no!', said one. Prep amounts to two half hour subjects per night for the oldest: 'It's ok to make mistakes and they will be explained to you again,' said another. One mother observed that some children are held back until they have learnt some basics by rote, and wondered if there should be more 'aspiration and challenge before they have everything right'. Both prep and pre-prep have own library. Some 49 children are currently on the learning support register; school has policy of not withdrawing children from vital lessons to have their two half hour individual sessions per week.

Pastoral care for the children highly rated; class teachers assume pastoral responsibilities in year 3, tutors with mixed horizontal tutor groups thereafter. The newly formed Friends of King's Hall provides purely social events for parents, and is working on extending its reach to everyone. We liked the enshrining of the school rules into six positive exhortations, such as 'do work hard, and do be honest'.

About 50 children board in a variety of arrangements; school entices children with regular year group boarding nights and film nights for the whole prep school. One busy mum told us her youngest had boarded just for a night at the age of 5 – and loved it. The sole boarding house has separate areas for senior boys, junior boys and girls, each with its own common room and quiet areas. 'It's fun and as homely as possible – I board to relax!' one boy told us, and all reckoned that boarders of all persuasions are well integrated. Parents tell us that facilities have improved, but the school 'doesn't have that horrible bling-tastic feel that the other Taunton schools have'. Well, thank goodness! Day pupils are welcome to join in the weekend activities with boarders, which might include dry ski-ing or making the most of the beautiful Quantock Hills nearby for a 16 mile orienteering exercise; facilities at King's College are also on offer at weekends.

The arts are well catered for too. Pupils' art was displayed everywhere we went and the design side has facilities for 2D and 3D design. Three major productions a year for years 4, 6 and 8 put on in the school's theatre or outside in the rose garden are complemented by prizes for acting and poetry recital at local festivals. About half the children learn a musical instrument, achieving grade 6 or 7 in rare cases, and the new director of music has gone down well.

So what's it really like? A question probably best answered by the pupils: 'I look forward to going back'. 'The weeks pass really quickly'. And to sum up? 'I don't instantly feel like the walking dead when I arrive'.

Job done, Mr Chips.

King's College (Taunton)

South Road, Taunton, Somerset TA1 3LA

01823 328204
admissions@kings-taunton.co.uk
www.kings-taunton.co.uk
C of E

Ages: 13–18
Pupils: 450; sixth form: 180
Boarders: 300 full
Day: £20,400 pa
Boarding: £30,000 pa

Linked school: King's Hall School

Headmaster: Since 2007 Mr Richard Biggs (early 50s) BSc MA, a product both of the UK's and South Africa's finest: his first degree (physics) from University of Cape Town, his masters (maths and philosophy) from Oxford as a Rhodes scholar. Some barely discernible vowels hint at his upbringing in South Africa; his subsequent career has been entirely in the UK, at Magdalen College School as teacher of maths and physics then director of studies, from where he was promoted to deputy head at Lancing, thence to King's. Now into his eighth year of headship, he can look back with justifiable satisfaction at his achievements since he started, mainly an increase in numbers and improvements to facilities. 'We can really concentrate on academics now, without being over-selective – the market in this part of the world wouldn't stand for it', he says.

Much liked by parents and students alike, who find him 'very bright, approachable and friendly', but we imagine he fixes miscreants with the eye of a basilisk when required. 'Runs a good ship,' remarked one mother succinctly, and writes a jolly good blog. A musical challenge to pass grade 1 on an unfamiliar musical instrument spurred him on to grade 8 proficiency on that most recalcitrant of instruments, the French horn ('a bit of a devil to play') and a seat in the school's wind band. He is married to Sarah, who edits the school magazine and oversees boarding house design, and has two sons in the school. When term ends, he escapes to his cottage on the north Cornish coast with his family for some rugged maritime r'n'r.

Academic matters: Academically inclusive, as attested by recent A level results, 30 per cent mark

for grades A/A* in 2015 (59 per cent A*/B) and yet do not quite achieve 100 per cent pass rates in all subjects. A sprinkling of U grades perhaps indicates that students are permitted to pursue their dream subjects, even if they are unlikely to get top marks; several popular and rigorous subjects (eg chemistry, biology, maths) receive grades from superb to dire, via mediocre. At GCSE, it is a similar story, with just five subjects in 2014 and 2015 achieving 100 per cent at grade C or above, almost everything else between 80-90 per cent. In 2015, 47 per cent of grades at A*/A. A modern language is expected at GCSE; many study two, and minority languages (German, Japanese, Latin, Russian, inevitably Chinese) laid on for just one taker on occasion. Sciences can either be taken separately or as a dual award. Good range of SEN catered for, and 70 pupils currently receiving extra support; highly praised by a mother of four very different children whom we spoke to: 'My dyslexic child did as well here as anywhere; he received massive support, which meant he exceeded his predictions'. A BTec in sport in collaboration with Exeter City FC and Exeter Chiefs Rugby Club just introduced.

Games, options, the arts: Make no mistake, this is a sporty school. Masses going on, and no exeat weekends mean a full programme of fixtures against other titans of the west country: Millfield is the one to beat. Football and rugby top sports in the winter terms, cricket the undoubted queen of the May in the summer; school is a centre for cricketing excellence as befits its location in Taunton, home of Somerset county cricket with which the school has close links. Year round facilities (as well as beautiful pitches in the heart of the school) mean this is truly a top school for cricket. Hockey and netball also popular with plenty of

opportunities for matches. We thoroughly applaud girls' football, cricket and hockey being promoted and resourced as well as the boys' games.

Minority sports include tennis, swimming, golf and athletics, whilst riders' lives are made easier by the offer of stabling near school for boarders' mounts, and the possibility of integrating riding into the school day for day students. Again, chances to compete and bring home the silverware are legion. Usual range of outdoor roughy-toughy stuff like D of E, Ten Tors, CCF and its precursor, the Chindit programme for year 9. About half the school learns a musical instrument, brass especially popular and school has notable jazz band. Some grade 8 and diploma level players among senior students. Singers abound, their repertoire from the popular to the highbrow, from rock bands to the chapel and chamber choirs, via the new barbershop quartet, Quartones. Performance of whatever standard is encouraged.

'Very bright, approachable and friendly', but we imagine he fixes miscreants with the eye of a basilisk

Musical talents useful for annual school musical too: recently Guys and Dolls, Les Mis, and The Wizard of Oz. One significant play per year, sometimes Shakespeare, many other less elaborate productions in school's own theatre, black box drama studio, recently built amphitheatre – or, memorably, in a pod of the London Eye.

Four floors of art school mean there is room enough for a gallery as well as studio space, where visiting artists can exhibit; one created a willow sculpture of the school's emblem, a pelican. Fine art is the basis of work here but digital media such as film and photography also laid on. We were especially taken by the newspaper tutu. King's has stand-out DT, which has won Arkwright scholarships and GSG awards on several occasions. A car in varying states of (dis)repair lurks in the DT studio for budding mechanics and designers to get their hands on, but the range of objects emerging from this studio combine beauty and functionality in equal measure: the tree-hung beehive is definitely on our wish list.

Despite the wealth of extracurricular activities on offer, 'the school does not push the kids into doing things, but once they sign up, they are expected to commit', according to one parent. 'Some parents don't like this, but the kids can then take credit for the activities they do, which makes them into secure self-starters'.

Boarding: Nearly two-thirds of students board, and it's the real deal: no flexi or weekly, they either board, or they don't. Busy and obligatory Saturdays mean a short weekend, during which a good range of activities is devised and offered by a designated co-ordinator; some of the students seize the advantage of being near-ish to the coast to surf and sail, some might choose to relax, swot or pop home instead. Around 12 per cent of boarders come from abroad: Chinese and Germans predominate, but the head actively explores different markets and will cap the overseas quota at 15 per cent. Military families now have their own liaison officer. Boarders stay in touch with home by email, Skype or Facetime. Devices belonging to younger students get handed in at night but enforcement varies from house to house, we were told. Boarding houses were, in our view, so-so: the girls' house we

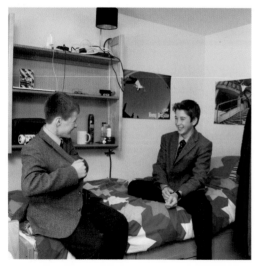

Not surprising to read that 'the art of tying a bow tie has been revived': its reputation as Taunton's smartest school seems entirely deserved

saw had a bitty lay-out separating year groups, but at least some baths still remain for muddy hockey players to soak it all off. Boys' boarding appears to be more integrated between year groups and definitely fewer frills – communal space boasted but some grubby leather sofas ('Eek!' said school 'Not typical') and a huge TV. Day students get one night a week boarding included in the day fee.

Background and atmosphere: A Woodard School, one of about 30 founded by a visionary Victorian cleric, where, these days, Christian values of understanding, diversity and tolerance – 'religious literacy' in the words of the resident chaplain – are inculcated without a whiff of evangelism. The chapel (white, light, beautiful with a decent organ and great acoustic) and collective worship are big parts of school life; all faiths and none are made welcome. But the roots of the school go back to an ancient boys' grammar, founded in the 16th century, but relocated to its current Victorian gothic pile in the 1860s.

It's fair to say that it still feels and looks quite traditional, with conventional uniform with designer tweed jackets and blue shirts, and neatness being identified as a virtue. The dining hall boasts not ancestral coats of arms, but sporting achievements painted on shields all over the walls. We did not have the chance to sample its wares, as we were instead treated to quite the grandest lunch we had ever been offered in the headmaster's dining room: curried monkfish followed by fig beignets washed down with pink bubbly – reader, we succumbed. Not surprising to read that 'the art of tying a bow tie has been revived' at King's: its reputation as being Taunton's smartest school seems entirely deserved, and its parents are disparaging about the others, their attitude on the sports fields in particular. Whilst the façade is impressive, some of the other buildings hit low points of British school architecture – with the exception of the new library whose modern touches integrate wonderfully with the warm reddish Somerset stone.

Pastoral care, well-being and discipline: Highly rated, particularly in the person of the deputy head pastoral, and a sine qua non of Woodard schools. 'Pastoral scaffolding,' as the school explained it, includes tutors, house staff and the school chaplain, who doubles as an additional school counsellor (as well as coaching several sports); parents can raise any concerns they have through the parent portal. Considerate touches include a Facebook page for Chinese non-English speaking parents. 'Any breach of good manners and good sense' will attract censure; punishments range from detention to more community-minded activities like litter-picking, but not in orange jumpsuits. The ultimate sanctions of suspension or exclusion are rarely, if ever, necessary. Commendations are given for all manner of good works and we liked the sound of the Ferrett Prize for 'all round unobtrusive contribution by a member of the 4th Form' – if you can spot it.

Pupils and parents: Unpretentious, happy to be there and grateful for all the opportunities the school offers. A boy from Hong Kong told us that he and his family had 'looked at every school in the country and chosen this one'. Families come from a wider geographical area both in the UK and abroad than the other Taunton schools, and inevitably some parents use the fast railway line to London to commute; the professions, the military, agriculture and the county set are all represented. The school welcomes parents new and existing (but perhaps not vegetarian) with a hog roast at the start of every year.

Entrance: Ninety arrive in year 9 by means of common entrance (passes expected in all subjects but school a bit coy about revealing pass mark), or by school's own papers in maths, English and verbal reasoning. Many, but not all, come from King's Hall, the school's associated prep school; others from prep schools in the South West or from overseas. A handful come into year 10 to start GCSE courses, where space permits. Twenty-five new into the sixth form after 'satisfactory performance at GCSE' or school's own papers for those without GCSEs.

Exit: About a dozen peel off after GCSE, some to the very good and free sixth form college across the road, Richard Huish. Leavers' destinations in recent years include a sprinkling to Oxbridge (four in 2015) and a bunch of conventional destinations up and down the land, 46 per cent to Russell Group, including Bristol and Durham. Some less orthodox choices like the Philip Green Academy for retail and the Academy of Contemporary Music. Several students apply post A level. All become Old Aluredians in any event – surely in the running for the most arcane alumni title. OAs of note include sportsmen/women (cricketers Jos Buttler and Roger Twose, hockey player Maddie Hinch, rugby player Tom Voyce), broadcasters Jonathan Meades and Dominic Wood and actress Juno Temple.

Money matters: The difference between day and boarding fees is closer than at the other Taunton schools but broadly in line. Scholarships for academic, sporting and artistic prowess plus DT, to a maximum value of 20 per cent of the day fee, are awarded at 13+ and sixth form. Academic scholars are expected to contribute to the intellectual life of the school, not just pulling in stonking exam results, but also attending weekly meetings at which papers are presented.

Remarks: Look no further for a traditional public school with distinctly sporty leanings sited in a county town. A Somerset institution housed in a suitably imposing stone monolith and serving its environs.

Kingswood School

Lansdown Road, Bath, Somerset BA1 5RG

01225 734200
admissions@kingswood.bath.sch.uk
www.kingswood.bath.sch.uk

Ages: 11–18
Pupils: 737; sixth form: 210
Boarders: 141 full, 35 weekly
Day: £14,031 pa
Boarding: £22,056 – £31,329 pa

Headmaster: Since 2008, Mr Simon Morris MA (Cantab) modern and medieval languages, especially German (late 40s). Educated at Ipswich School, then a spell in the City after Cambridge – 'But in my heart of hearts, I always knew I'd be a teacher'. Despite exclusively independent school career, has taken pains to cut the mustard by doing his PGCE and NPQH, the latter quite unusual amongst independent school heads. Previously deputy at St John's, Leatherhead, via housemaster and head of modern languages at The Leys and head of German at Warwick School.

First ever non-Methodist head of this Methodist school – openly C of E but embraces Wesleyan philosophy of service. Might seem unassuming but isn't: passionate about instilling high but attainable standards in every individual – in everything they do. Married to Caroline, who teaches modern languages in the school and has lots of state school experience. Three children, all pupils here. Supported by triumvirate of deputies, all good foils to the others. Takes junior PHSE programmes as a chance to stay in touch/get to know the newly arrived. Visible, approachable, welcome and frequent spectator; keen cricketer. Appears to have 'gone down brilliantly' with parents and sixth form, in particular. Firm of handshake and of purpose, a round peg in a round hole.

Academic matters: Strong performance across the board. In 2015, 59 per cent A*/A at GCSE and 61 per cent A*/A grades at A level. Vies for second place in Bath league tables with Prior Park (Kingswood edged ahead last year), behind local academic hothouse, King Edward's. Must do really well on value-added, then, for a school which claims not to be 'narrowly selective'. Masses of choice, with 23 subjects to choose from at GCSE and 26 at A level. Languages lag behind in terms of take-up, despite German being compulsory alongside French in year 7. Two languages too much pressure, some parents think.

Main teaching block (The Ferens) utilitarian and colour coded inside according to subject. OK labs and lots of IT throughout. Unlovely but much loved sixth form block (The Dixon) houses some teaching, the HE and careers department, studies and chill-out space, including a kitchen. Magnificent gothic splendour of a library enough

A super light space boasting a topnotch recording studio and an 'inspirational' head of music who embraces everything from Bach to the Beatles

to make anyone work; sixth form has Perspex platform of privilege at far end. Cosy seminar room at entrance.

Not a huge number of diagnosed SENs but one-to-one help on offer (paid as extra) for those who need it. Head keen to take 'any child who can access the Kingswood curriculum', including those with dyslexia and on the autistic spectrum. Inclusive, non-stigmatised provision. Head's personal experience informs his attitude.

Games, options, the arts: Plenty of pitches/courts/ Astroturf, flattened out on three levels of alarmingly sloping grounds, imaginatively named lower, middle and upper, the latter a short minibus ride up the hill. Usual rugby, hockey, tennis terms for boys, hockey, netball, tennis for girls, but tempting options too for the less sportingly inclined, eg the slow running club(!). Not queuing up to show us the swimming pool.

Strong links with Team Bath at the university – makes good use of its facilities and expertise. Sport taken seriously but no discernible 'jock' culture – in fact current captain of rugby also a musician of note. New pavilion on the Upper, which

also hosts Bath Rugby Club in this rugby-obsessed city. An Olympic swimmer's timetable was pared down to fit training in; a promising young golfer is also in the slips.

The arts generally acknowledged as outstanding and have their own awards ceremony. Charming arts and crafts style studio produces works of exhibition standard in all media; a local gallery has chosen more Kingswood work than from any other Bath school. Sixth formers and staff wear enviable monogrammed smocks.

Music school a super light space boasting a topnotch recording studio and an 'inspirational' head of music who embraces everything from Bach to the Beatles, and whose students recently recorded for Children in Need at Abbey Road. Something for all performers of all styles and standards. Drama right up there too, with proper theatre as well as a studio. Productions for all ages, which neighbouring schools attend, plus a massively popular comedy club for (brave) aspiring stand-ups. Shows are collaborative, with pupils involved with writing, producing, publicising as well as performing. Theatre also twice a venue for BBC Question Time.

Boarding: Has managed to hang on to the feel of a co-ed boarding school with day pupils. A long day for everyone (5.30pm finish after activities or, rarely, prep) and seven mixed day/boarding houses from year 9 right up to upper sixth. New boarding house for senior boys recently completed. No Saturday school but good activity programme for boarders, plus usual sporting fixtures on Sat pms. Littlies spend their first two years in Westwood, a gentler introduction to the big school. Boy and girl boarders occupy separate floors of immaculate dormitories for six to eight, out of bounds to day pupils, who share the slightly dark living space downstairs. Room sizes go down while mess goes up in the six single sex senior houses, where the feel is cosier and autonomous. Space for occasional over-nighters. Around half of the staff live on the school campus.

Background and atmosphere: The only school founded by John Wesley (who believed that education should engage the heart as well as the head) and first ever Methodist one, spawning over 700 across the world since. Moved from Bristol in the early 1850s because of unreliable water supplies and has occupied an imposing pile of purpose-built Victorian gothic on steep northern slopes above Bath ('Satan's throne', according to Wesley) ever since, almost opposite the Royal High School. Other buildings of varying degrees of age and beauty are dotted around its 140 acres of manicured grounds, including the chapel, too small these days to house the whole school, which gathers for religious and

secular assemblies in the theatre. Not at all horribly worthy, as its history might indicate.

A spirit of service (to the school/local/global communities) expounded by the head and lived out in the school, eg by close involvement of sixth form with junior pupils, lots of unglamorous charitable stuff in Bath as well as abroad, eg bricklaying in Malawi – Uruguay at planning stage. Green credentials measure up too: holder of Eco-Schools Green Flag, fluttering proudly from flag pole; in-house (and excellent) catering sources as much food as possible locally or from Fair Trade; sustainable development committee currently looking at ground source heating, reducing food waste and an improved travel plan. Head talks convincingly of 'our responsibilities to the planet'. Right mix of respect and banter between pupils and staff, and pupils at the top and bottom of the school – 'They really look after each other,' said one mother, echoing several others. Central dining in splendid gothic setting helps all 600 pupils get to know each other.

Sees itself as an innovator amongst Bath schools, eg Model UN, and quite keen to show them how it's done. International flavour: pupils come from 15 countries, but an eye is kept to see that no one nationality dominates and all get an essentially British boarding experience. Pupils love it – 'I've got friends all over the world,' declared a sixth former, with an eye to his gap year.

Pastoral care, well-being and discipline: 'Outstanding,' according to parents; 'They're just so nice to each other – and that goes for kids and staff,' said one, whose son fled bullying at another school (it gets zero tolerance here). Touchy-feely stuff not at the expense of academic rigour or general endeavour, however: expectations are laid down early and slacking discouraged. A clear system of sanctions looks good on paper, but we didn't find anyone who would admit to being on the receiving end of it. Emphasis definitely on support and redirection, rather than on chastisement, and all felt help for any problem was very much on hand.

Pupils and parents: Moderately to exceedingly affluent but not especially posh. Wide range of professions amongst parent body, offspring of (more successful) actors, musicians and sportsmen/women amongst pupils. 'Incredibly supportive – and reasonably demanding,' says the head. Pupils are engaging and confident without arrogance, and startlingly uncritical of their school. Most come from north side of Bath – crossing the city at peak-time is hideous and plenty of provision south of the river.

Entrance: Fifty per cent from own prep school, some from other prep schools mostly north of Bath, good few from local (excellent) primary school, St Stephen's, where they have strong links and collaboration. Maths, English and non-verbal reasoning tested at 11+ to try to ensure fairness; coaching not expected and discouraged. Head sees all entrance papers.

Exit: Virtually all go through to sixth form. Handful to Oxbridge and to art and music colleges, others to diverse degree choices all over Britain.

Money matters: Good value for what's on offer: third cheapest in Bath with lots of extras thrown in. Some parents resent those long holidays, which can be a problem for those working so hard to fund it all. Academic and special talent scholarships offered at years 7, 9 and lower sixth. Head keen to increase bursary provision throughout.

Remarks: Super school which has finally gained its place in the competitive galaxy of Bath secondaries. Setting and atmosphere suggest privilege without pretension; particularly good for budding performing or visual artists who require results too. Takes the best of Methodist philanthropy and adapts it for a secular multi-cultural world. Truly global in feel and outlook for an English school.

Knighton House School

Durweston, Blandford Forum, Dorset DT11 0PY

01258 452065
admissions@knightonhouse.co.uk
www.knightonhouse.co.uk

Ages: 3–13 (boarding from age 7)
Pupils: 122
Boarders: 25 full, 27 flexi/weekly
Day: £6,975 – £16,380 pa
Boarding: £21,600 pa

Headmistress: Since September 2014, Mrs Sarah Wicks, previously deputy head. BEd from the University of Hertfordshire; taught at a state primary in Mill Hill and the Royal Masonic School before joining Knighton in 1995 as head of drama and junior class teacher. She's been there ever since, rising through senior mistress to deputy and then head.

Entrance: Any child welcome, more or less at any time so long as space is available. Summer term is a popular time to start and it isn't unusual for girls to come mid-year, sometimes from less happy environments. No entrance exam but the school holds non-compulsory taster days – 'more for the girls to have a look but of course it helps us understand their needs.' There is a scholarship exam, though. Families are mainly local (most from under an hour away), but some from London, plus a handful from Spain or France each term.

Exit: Most stay until 13 when they go to Bryanston (obviously convenient as they're so close), St Mary's, Shaftesbury (parents say that 'it's the same sort of friendly school') and beyond that to anywhere and everywhere, including Marlborough, Canford, St Mary's Calne, Sherborne Girls, Downe House. Good handful of scholarships – for music, art or sport as often as academics. Pre-prep boys mostly go on to Sandroyd, Claysmore or Port Regis.

Remarks: Perched on a windy hillside just by Bryanston's back gate, this happy and quirky little school was founded in 1950 by the parents of Private Eye co-founder Christopher Booker. A rambling rectory-type house with a rather grand staircase (out of bounds), it's thought to have been the dowager home of the Portman family (Dorset worthies) and is surrounded by orchards, stables and paddocks. Mish-mash of old coach-houses, now used for labs and boarding, and stables full

Smashing food, all locally sourced and cooked by popular chef and team. One parent told us: 'Even my super–faddy daughter actually eats it, especially with the new salad bar'

of ponies. Classrooms are serviceable rather than plush and there's a purpose-built multi-use hall and lavish music block. Everything looks a bit haphazard but place is bursting with displays of pupils' work and exceptionally well equipped.

Flexi-boarding is popular, and all weekend boarding is free (a major fun event, sometimes in school, sometimes a trip, is offered every weekend). Almost half the girls in the prep board and everyone gets her own bed, even the two-night-a-weekers.

Refurbished dorms for two to eight (with bunk beds) in the main house for the younger girls, who 'like the bigger dorms'. Plentiful loos, showers and even two end-to-end ancient claw-foot baths. Matron, loved by girls and parents alike, has a four-bedded sick room which girls are busy brightening up. No medical nurse, but extremely kind treatment of minor ailments. All boarding staff have first aid training and there is masses of induction and proper training for gappies (Antipodean and local). Smashing food, all locally sourced and cooked by popular chef and team. One parent told us: 'Even my super-faddy daughter actually eats it, especially with the new salad bar'. Teachers sit at the tables to supervise and teach manners and there is a regular 'French' table. Practical, if eye-catching, scarlet dungarees are worn with apparent relish by all except the top form, on trips or to the village church on Sundays. Then it's the girls' 'best' or, as they put it, 'worst' uniform of box pleated grey skirts, red jerseys, checked blouses and dark grey kilts; grey cloaks for cold weather. Oldest boarders have a flat above the labs and get quite bit more freedom: tuck cupboard, some cooking equipment and a more grown up atmosphere to suit their responsibilities and imminent transition to senior school.

Academically adventurous, with no national testing, though pretty thorough assessment, according to the latest inspection. Curriculum includes Latin (a scholars' parent regretted the recent demise of Greek) French from the second year, three sciences in very well-equipped though old-fashioned-looking labs, enjoyable English and maths. Small classes, maximum 18, with some setting in maths, science, French and English. Parents feel that bright girls are stretched and strugglers supported.

State-of-the-art IT with ambitious animations projects for everyone and masses of computer use within all areas of the curriculum. Very good SEN department with two staff, for girls with mild learning difficulties. DT is mainly cooking and sewing but with a bit of woodwork, ceramics etc thrown in for everyone. Two libraries – reference and fiction. Art is enterprising, with emphasis on cross-curricular uses and fun – lots of innovative 3D work. Junior and senior plays produced every year. Lots of clubs, including German and Spanish. There is a contingent of Spanish pupils and Knighton teachers are busy forging links via the Comenius project with Turkey and Estonia to broaden the school's outlook.

Lots of sport for those who want it, with some outstanding successes in tennis, swimming and running. However an unsporty parent told us: 'There doesn't seem to be too much emphasis on sport, which is a plus for me... but manners are very important, which is great, and all the teachers are very well spoken.' Astroturf, playing fields and a swimming pool in a converted sheep dip/storage tank on the hillside – mainly for recreation as real swimming takes place in nearby Blandford or at Bryanston.

> **'Manners are very important, which is great, and all the teachers are very well spoken'**

But it's the ponies, the music and the friendliness that girls and parents find irresistible. More than half ride and one parent reported that experienced riders are very patient and encouraging with those who start riding at school. Many bring their own ponies and other girls use them too. The stables are close enough for early morning pony visits, (as are the other pet areas and the guinea pig village) and there's an all-weather arena and cross-country course. Friendliness is a defining characteristic. A new parent reported that her daughter, previously anti-school, actually jumped for joy at the end of her first school holidays, while another was delighted to find her two-mornings-a-week toddler was recognised and made a fuss of by older girls. Girls say bullying just doesn't happen 'because we like each other, not because we are told not to,' and a mother told us that a potential incident had been dealt with effectively and kindly for all concerned. The girls we met during our visit were chatty and interested, but not precociously over-confident.

Music has an attractive, dedicated building with a recital room and masses of individual practice rooms. Almost all girls have music lessons, sing and take part in different bands and groups. There's a serious orchestra and small concerts held every Friday to which parents can come. Head of music teaches individual singing and the superb chapel choir sings at the weekly Saturday service, local churches and weddings and has performed grand local venues like Milton Abbey, Lulworth Castle etc. Girls actually get up early for music practice as well as for ponies.

Bright and cosy co-ed pre-prep (The Orchard) and nursery bring in local families, and a weekly toddler group is growing by the hour. ISI inspectors judged it to be outstanding. Children learn at their own pace with masses of careful planned but attractive stimuli. A series of enclosed garden spaces dividing the pre-prep from the main school is evidently much used.

In lots of ways Knighton House seems almost too good to be true. Assessment, checks on new staff, training and above all IT and maths have all been given new rigour recently, without detracting from the essential homeliness of the school. Education and boarding standards are well up to date but the school still has the feeling of one busy, happy and highly motivated family. Parents, who are fed delicious cakes when they come to collect their daughters, wax lyrical, seeing it as a chance for girls to enjoy their childhood in this protected nook. Mooted merger with Hanford in 2014 died amidst parental disquiet and failure of respective boards to agree terms.

As a free-standing girls' boarding prep school, it is one of the last of a dying breed – barely a dozen left in the country. Not smart, glossy or fashionable but a perfect rural idyll in which girls can become confident and well prepared for life.

Leaden Hall School

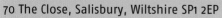

70 The Close, Salisbury, Wiltshire SP1 2EP

01722 334700
admin@leaden-hall.com
www.leaden-hall.com

Ages: 2–11 (boarding from 7)
Pupils: 190
Boarders: 20 full, 20 flexi
Day: £8,010 – £13,785 pa
Boarding: plus £5,520 pa

Headmistress: Since 2010, Mrs Julia Eager BEd (early 50s). Educated at North London Collegiate, with a degree in education and music from Froebel College, London University, and an MSc in educational leadership from Leicester, she's been a thorough-going GDST girl till now, a career primary teacher specialising in music, who has worked in several GDST junior schools such as Howell's in Cardiff and Royal High Bath, before being catapulted in as acting head to Hamlets Prep School,

Liverpool. A term in GDST's education office in London followed, from where she jumped ship to take up her first headship at Leaden Hall. Wife to a professional conductor and mother to three Eton music scholars, now in their late teens or early 20s, she says, 'All my girls are here'.

Parents concur that she had big shoes to fill but that she has done so superbly. Her wish to improve communication between school and home means she is to be found at the gate most mornings greeting girls by name; this accessibility extends to a swift response to any matters raised, and a demeanour so warm and approachable that girls barely knock before walking into her teddy-bear lined office. Can she be scary enough when the occasion demands? We hope so. Her personal mission on taking on Leaden Hall was to improve IT, systems and infrastructure, as well as building closer links with other Salisbury schools, emphatically not to change the feel of the place, which is one of a family where everyone goes happily about her work and is extraordinarily nice to each other. She has not been shy of introducing other improvements either, such as more sporting fixtures and shared transport with other schools, specific 11+ coaching and dealing with some 'staff issues', which have gone down very well with parents. In fact, we could not find even a faintly critical word about her from any quarter.

Hobbies include music, naturally – she is an accomplished oboist and learns the harp (from the royal wedding harpist who also teaches the girls) – and a spot of tennis and reading, when not tackling Kilimanjaro or the Himalayas with her boys.

So warm and approachable that girls barely knock before walking into her teddy-bear lined office. Can she be scary enough when the occasion demands? We hope so

Entrance: Strictly non-selective at reception and below, although further up, the school encourages girls to spend a day there to check it all out. Scholarships on offer for girls of outstanding talent in any area of the curriculum, but fees won't be reduced unless the criteria for bursary help are also met.

Exit: South Wilts Grammar very popular. Other choices include St Mary's Calne, Godolphin School, St Mary's Shaftesbury, Dauntsey's, St Swithun's, Leehurst, Millfield and Hampshire Collegiate. Girls regularly win academic, all-rounder or sports scholarships.

Remarks: Founded at Fareham in 1937, the school moved to its present home in the Close of Salisbury Cathedral in 1948, where it is now charmingly housed in a building of great antiquity, with a fabulous modern timber and glass classroom block at the back, and glorious grounds running down to the river, a view immortalised by Constable. The big red front door opens into a hall where a rocking horse has pride of place – it all feels like a private house, with the head's office in what was

clearly once the drawing room. More classrooms and boarding happen on the upper floors of the old house and dining in a sunny conservatory. Year 6 boarders are five minutes' walk away in a sympathetically converted cottage, where they are two or three to a room.

Although very small boys are accepted in the nursery school, Leaden Hall is very much a female preserve – just one male music teacher, the IT and catering managers and two groundsmen break up the petticoat rule. But one of the most beguiling aspects of the school is that girls can be whatever they want to be. Despite the quaint uniform of a striped dress with sailor collar for summer (and a hat for each season, note), girls can (and do) get dirty, make dens, climb trees and play rugby, without any fear of teasing. Prissy they certainly are not, but the idyllic setting and sheer niceness of the girls and staff and the way they treat each other did make us wonder if it wasn't all a tiny bit precious; however the school's mantra, 'Get real, get right, get going', is an attempt to address any such notion. It's possibly the parents who are inclined to be precious on their daughters' behalf, judging by the ones we spoke to, though one said, 'It might look quaint and eccentric, but it doesn't feel precious once you're inside'.

Despite the quaint uniform, girls can (and do) get dirty, make dens, climb trees and play rugby, without any fear of teasing. Prissy they certainly are not

What really blew us away was the positive experience of boarding every child and parent we spoke to mentioned. Lovely handbooks given out, including one translated into Spanish for the two or three Spanish boarders who come in year 5 and 6. One veteran mum of 14 prep schools said that her daughter 'never cried once' and that the outstanding care taken of the girls extends to the parents, particularly those overseas (some 10 per cent). Top green credentials and recognition – school has double green flag status and is current South West eco champ – come perhaps from this sense of altruism.

Academic pressure is exerted downwards by South Wilts Grammar – see above – and in the minds of some, the spectre of 11+ looms large. Nonetheless, the school appears to succeed at playing down exam stress and to count on its experience in preparing for entrance exams. Year 5 acknowledged as being especially pressured, with 11+ coming up in the September of year 6, so head takes pains to steer the unwary away from unwise choices in plenty of time: 'The head's approach to entrance exams for all schools is absolutely spot-on,' said one mother, though another mentioned the lack of a scholarship stream.

Classes are of mixed ability, but girls are put into sets from year 5 on in English, maths, sciences and languages. Latin compulsory in year 6, German and Spanish available as clubs. No Sats either in year 2 or 6, but school makes use of related material at other stages for internal assessment and tracking, something the most recent ISI report picked it up on. Enjoyment and fun struck us as a feature of the timetable, from the lessons we saw, coupled with genuine affection for teachers. English gets particular thumbs up; proposed French exchange programme; science taught in dedicated lab and dance (big take-up, with lots of adorable little moppets in tutus) and other indoor sports in beautiful light sports hall.

Sport gets good provision, considering the size of the school: hockey, netball, tennis, rounders, football all on offer, with its own tennis/netball courts, playing field and outdoor pool on site, and Cathedral School's Astro and athletics track available for loan. An indoor pool was on everyone's wish list. These days, enough fixtures with other schools to satisfy the sporty, plus some lacrosse and tag rugby from national players, no less.

Music much buoyed up by enthusiastic teacher, but we could see why the head was so excited about the new music room. Everybody sings and many learn musical instruments, top players reaching grade 4 or so. Performance apparently encouraged, with some ambitious and precocious choices like Romeo and Juliet, yet no-one said much about the drama, curiously. Art displayed all over the school with evident pride, but one parent reported that DT had gone off.

Other than that, remarkably few gripes about the school (in fact an overwhelming affection). Food and lack of choice came in for some criticism (head says food is very highly regarded by the majority of parents and girls and school is now providing healthy lunches for a nearby school). Bizarre and unpopular sardine pasta bake the day we visited. Girls eat their lunch in a pinny of their choice and sit in family groups.

All in all, Leaden Hall is a little piece of Eden in Salisbury, where little girls can stay little girls until they have to move on to the real world outside the Close at the secondary school of their choice – in almost all cases. As the inspector said, 'A magical school'.

Leweston School

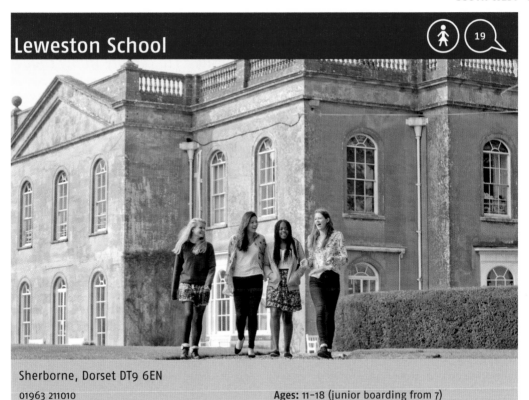

Sherborne, Dorset DT9 6EN

01963 211010
admissions@leweston.dorset.sch.uk
www.leweston.co.uk
RC

Ages: 11–18 (junior boarding from 7)
Pupils: 358; sixth form: 85
Boarders: 100 full, 82 weekly/flexi
Day: £8,376 – £18,495 pa
Boarding: £19,260 – £30,165 pa

Headmaster: Since September 2015, Mrs Kate Reynolds MEd LLB PGCE, previously head of EAL at the school. Law degree from Bristol, and practised until 1994, when she obtained an English PGCE from Bath Spa University. MEd in education leadership from Buckingham. Worked at Gillingham and Sherborne Schools before joining Leweston. Married to Giles, also a teacher; they have four children.

Academic matters: Very much on the up. A level results in 2015 77 per cent A*/B grades and 48 per cent A*/A. Pre-U is offered alongside A levels in music, history, English and history of art, and results are sound, with very few girls getting below a C or equivalent. Twenty-three subjects on offer at A level, with compulsory courses in various things which round out the syllabus, including the global perspectives part of the Pre-U and the extended project. School justifiably proud of the fact that 90 per cent of applications to medical school have met with success in the past five years.

At GCSE, 55 per cent A*/A grades in 2015. Ten subjects out of 20 on offer is the norm; a language

and RS are compulsory. Some subjects can be taken early. The fact that the timetable can be tweaked to accommodate any combination of subjects is a huge plus – and very much to the director of studies' credit. Value-added scores are particularly high for Leweston. Greater numbers being interviewed for Oxbridge and recent success in the British Maths Olympiad all add to the sense of a school whose academic star is in the ascendancy. Parents enthuse about maths, English, Spanish, geography and music in particular.

SEN provision deals with mild end of normal issues, including ADD and ADHD, but can accommodate moderate learning difficulties. All girls tested for SEN on entry and school has CReSTeD status. The gifted-and-talented are not neglected either. EAL also catered for; in fact huge enthusiasm voiced for the school by overseas girls.

Games, options, the arts: Conventional offering of hockey, netball and tennis enlivened by squash and badminton courts and, recently, by the transformation of the gloriously sited outdoor swimming pool into a year-round facility by the construction of a perspex roof with retractable side panels. Over 40 green acres go some way to explaining the school's success in track and field events, particularly cross-country and, interestingly, football. Three sportswomen international standing indicate a school which punches above its weight. Horse-minded boarders can have their mounts at livery: riding lessons can be arranged in either of the two arenas at the school, and teams take on other schools at dressage, show-jumping and eventing. Some kind of sport is compulsory for everyone, including sixth form – all activities are registered. Quite apart from the benefits of exercise (to work off the excellent food), compulsory sport 'gives girls the opportunity to try out different things, and instils a sense of commitment', says the head. All levels of D of E also available.

Music is a key part of school life and the lure of nearby Sherborne, with the abbey (home to the carol service) and its joint Schools Sinfonia Orchestra is enough to make any school raise its game. Three recent top performers achieved diploma-level music. A variety of ensembles provide somewhere for any aspiring or shy musician to play or sing, and the joint forces of music and drama come together to produce a musical, most recently Sweet Charity; also collaborations with Sherborne School, plus other male bastions requiring girls. Good showing in Dorset and beyond, notably at the Mid Somerset Festival in Bath for music, drama and recitation. Art and design strong too; we particularly liked the textiles, whose remarkable creations would (and do) grace any catwalk. In fact there is an increasingly well-trodden path to colleges of fashion from Leweston. Many sixth formers take up the option of Leith's basic certificate in food and wine with gusto – a professional qualification and simply essential for those stints as a chalet girl in one's gap year

No nuns these days, but the tiny, exquisite 17th century Trinity chapel hosts small weekday masses

– while all girls have to do survival nutrition and cookery (new home economics room).

Boarding: Boarders up to year 8 share the Junior House; older girls have increasingly more privacy and greater independence. Saturday morning prep and lectures, with sports matches in the afternoons; the evenings may see joint socials with other local schools, whilst Sundays are spent relaxing, riding, cycling, visiting the beach or local attractions.

Boarding has had a shot in the arm and numbers are rising, particularly at sixth form level, now standing at about 50 per cent. 'There was some lack of clarity about it', says school, 'but putting all the junior boarders in one house has improved matters.' School could still do with more local boarders – 'there needs to be a critical mass', according to one mother, who also remarked that her daughter did not enjoy staying in at weekends – weekly boarding is an undoubted trend. Interestingly, Leweston was one of only 10 schools recently chosen to trial the new BSA Boarding Skills Award, a kind of D of E of boarding (but without the yomping): 'to be used as a currency for employability alongside academic results', according to those who devised it. (Everyone passed.)

Background and atmosphere: Founded originally in Sherborne in 1891 by the fearsomely named Religious of Christian Instruction (a group of nuns hailing from Ghent), the school moved to its current home three miles away in the Palladian manor of Leweston in 1948, which was purchased from the Rose family (of lime juice fame). A palpable sense of Catholicism still prevails, but not the nasty exclusive you-can't-take-communion-here kind; we felt that girls of any faith, and possibly none, would be welcomed. No nuns these days, but the chapel is central to school life, and the tiny exquisite 17th century Trinity chapel in the grounds hosts smaller weekday masses.

Pleasing mansion of golden ham stone sits at the end of a long drive through the park, somewhat marred by later necessary additions, some of which (eg classrooms round the back) are barely fit for purpose, say parents. They are also well aware that the facilities 'don't compare with Sherborne Girls', although a welcome new sixth form den with a café and Wifi has recently been opened. Somehow, though, the relative modesty and make-do-and-mend feel rubs off on the girls, who are appreciative, charming, bright and definitely going places. 'I chose it for my daughter because of the kind of girl who goes there', said one mother, herself an Old Antonian, as former pupils are called. A very accepting culture was also widely praised – of girls from abroad, and of personal quirks, for example – making it a place where girls can truly be themselves, whether that means not growing up too fast, or fleeing bullying at other schools. 'I am thrilled that my daughter has been able to do loads of sport, which she loves, instead of being made to stick just to academics and music, which she's good at', said one happy mother, 'and she's been able to stay younger for longer'.

The social pressures of being right in Sherborne with 600 boys are of course less marked at Leweston, but some parents feel that more use should be made of opportunities for joint productions and sports training, and voiced faint irritation at the fact that there is a 10 per cent sibling discount between Sherborne and Sherborne Girls – but not with Leweston. However, joint trips to Cordoba and New York, as well as musical, dramatic and social endeavours.

Pastoral care, well-being and discipline: Discipline was not mentioned – these girls seem a biddable flock – but pastoral care gets a big thumbs-up. High staff:pupil ratio at 1:7 means no-one feels out of her depth without a life-belt.

Pupils and parents: The majority, nearly 80 per cent, British; a sizeable minority of girls from SE Asia and a good mix of Europeans make for a reasonably cosmopolitan feel to the place (around 30 per cent of boarders are from overseas). Most UK residents are very local; one mother said she felt at a disadvantage coming from Hampshire, as it was hard to get to events during the week. A sprinkling from London. All we met seemed down-to-earth and unpretentious, with realistic expectations of school and life generally

Entrance: At 11, 13 or into sixth form, but at other points by arrangement. School sets own entrance tests at 11 (academic, numerical and perceptual reasoning), relies on common entrance at 13 and on six 'good GSCE passes' at sixth form. Everyone has an interview with the head. Scholarships in art/DT, drama, music and sport offered along with academic ones.

Exit: Up to a third pull stumps after GCSE, possibly in search of boys. Those who stay are glad they did; in fact we were told of one girl who tried a neighbouring school but headed hot-foot back to Leweston after a couple of weeks. University choices span the length and breadth of the land, with a variety of degree courses, from English and history of art to maths and medicine. Spanish most popular as language degree course. In 2015, one to Oxbridge and others to eg UCL, Exeter, Essex and Cardiff. Eminent old girls include Kristin Scott-Thomas, Erin Pizzey and Serena de la Hay (whose Wicker Man can be seen from the M5).

Money matters: Cheaper than many competitors by over £1000 per term for boarding in some cases. Scholarships to the value of 10-30 per cent, 50 per cent for three scholars of exceptional ability across all disciplines at 11+.

Remarks: Gaudere and bene facere, rejoice and do well, so says the school motto: Leweston girls certainly do both. Hidden gem in a sleepy hollow, definitely meriting a look from those seeking to escape the glitzy rat-race that some girls-only education has become.

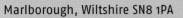

Marlborough College

Marlborough, Wiltshire SN8 1PA

01672 892300
admissions@marlboroughcollege.org
www.marlboroughcollege.org
C of E

Ages: 13–18
Pupils: 923 (558 boys, 365 girls); sixth form: 405
Boarders: nearly all full
Day: £28,830 pa
Boarding: £33,930 pa

Master: Since 2012, Jonathan Leigh (60s), previously head of Ridley College, Canada and before that head of Blundell's School and second master of Cranleigh School. Married to Emma, also a Cambridge history graduate, they have two grown up children and the obligatory black lab. Educated

at St George's Windsor where he was a chorister, thence to Eton. Degree in history from Corpus Christi College, Cambridge, where he was a choral exhibitioner. He still sings (tenor) and on leaving Cambridge thought seriously about going professional, but instead 'drifted' into teaching and consolidated this drift with a PGCE.

Mr Leigh seems to be the go-to chap if you want to do something structural and potentially controversial at a school. He took Blundells co-ed and taught Canada to love the IB at Ridley College. He is a great advocate of the IB but for some reason the qualification (brought in by previous master) failed to 'take root' at Marlborough and, pragmatically, he de-introduced it here. 'It's very hard to run a dual system', he told us, 'especially since A levels have been toughened up. You need a critical mass to make the IB work and it didn't attract the take up at Marlborough that it has elsewhere.' Under 20 candidates is indeed very far from a critical mass – it's a shame though, the results were pretty good (average 36).

Since accepting the post of master, at a time when he might have been contemplating retirement, Mr Leigh and his wife have thrown themselves into Marlborough life and society, much to the admiration of parents (Marlborough parents, we have discovered, don't hold back) who describe him as, 'charming and user-friendly.' He's perhaps a little shy at first,' we were told, 'but he's a modest and gentle man who's terrific with the children.' Mrs Leigh is equally popular: 'she's brilliant at fundraising events' and 'great company'.

Marlborough is a big school but the master is diligently applying himself to meeting all its pupils, having breakfast or lunch with groups of four to six at a time. He also 'teaches a bit' – an upper sixth elective course on his specialist subject, Middle Europe 1400-1715.

Unsurprisingly, Mr Leigh is an opera lover; his favourites are Samson and Delilah and The Magic Flute. Somewhat more surprisingly he's part of a 50 strong flat racing syndicate and has shares in two horses (both winners, apparently). Syndicate is called The Fifty, horses are called, wait for it, Fifty Shades of Grey.

We found Mr Leigh thoughtful, diplomatic, quietly humorous and without the hubris that is sometimes par for the head course. He has provided Marlborough with much more than a 'safe pair of hands' and parents agree that the College is extremely lucky to have him. 'I only wish I could have started here 10 years earlier,' he says.

Academic matters: In our last review we remarked that what with A levels, the pre-U and IB, Marlborough offered something for everyone. But clearly everyone didn't want quite that much choice. IB has quietly expired and 2015 leavers were its last takers. Academic head hadn't turned his IB poster to the wall (maybe he never will) and delivered a touching eulogy about the bountiful legacy of the qualification's brief life. Its general goodness will float around like educational ectoplasm, enriching the remaining qualifications. He didn't actually say that. He did say, 'Marlborough already offers much of what the IB contains, more so now that A levels are returning to the linear format.'

College motto is Deus dat Incrementum ('God gives the increase') but steady advance of exam results may have less divine origin. Admissions criteria are now somewhat more academically demanding (although prep school head's reference is still crucial). CE result mainly used to 'keep them on the boil and help us with setting'. In 2015, 63 per cent A*/A grades at A level and Pre-U equivalent; at GCSE, 75 per cent A*/A grades. Stand out results

in A level art, drama, sciences, geography and maths but good tail of non-vowel grades as well. Astronomers fare well, but then they do have the famous Blackett Observatory to aid their star gazing – local schools also get their turn to view the cosmos from a field in Wiltshire. Parents singled out teaching in philosophy as 'inspirational', and its popularity at Pre-U, not to mention the results, endorse this. We know, we know, it's not all about exams and comparisons are invidious, but just out of interest that puts Marlborough some way ahead of many co-ed rivals.

Mr Leigh seems to be the go-to chap if you want to do something potentially controversial. He took Blundells co-ed and taught Canada to love the IB

Exam syllabi excepted there seems to be an (admirable) ideological aversion to the churning out of standard curriculum fare at Marlborough. Shell (first year)'s first taste of their new school's academic approach is 'Form', a multi-disciplinary enquiry into the 'origins of human civilisation', no less. These lessons take the place of separate English, history and RS lessons. Run in parallel with this is the 'Artemis' PHSE course: new pupils take part in guided discussions within their boarding houses. All do two modern languages and Latin, some may also take ancient Greek. Sixth formers can choose from around 35 'electives', mini courses that teachers – including the master – devise to impart specialist knowledge on subjects from cryptic crosswords (now that's a life skill) to special relativity or conducting – the baton, not electrical, kind. These must be as much fun for the staff who run them as they are for pupils.

Average class size is 15, eight in the sixth form. Approximately 100 students have learning difficulties such as moderate dyslexia, dypraxia and ADHD. School says a great deal of thought goes into assessing pupils with SEN to ensure Marlborough is the 'right learning environment' before places are offered. Learning support department works one-to-one and provides a programme of support appropriate to the individual's needs. School also helps a number of students with planning and organisation.

Games, options, the arts: It's no surprise that we filled an entire notebook and ran out of ink during our visit to Marlborough; there's so much on offer beyond the academic timetable. Lest we also deplete our stock of superlatives, suffice it to say that art, drama, sport music are all very, very good. Generous facilities and 'inspirational' specialist teaching help every pupil, from the most talented to the least coordinated, play, sing, throw or create something to be proud of.

The college may have been co-ed for nearly 50 years, but on the sports field rugby is still king. Four England captains and 38 internationals is indeed a noble heritage. 'The first X1 get clapped onto the pitch at the start of the season,' one parent told us. 'They are the undisputed heroes,' said another. These were observations rather than criticisms and everyone agreed that there are so many fixtures everyone gets the chance of a good match. Besides, the girls are doing just as well: the U14 hockey team recently retained the Wiltshire County Championship and several girls have been picked to represent their county and country in sports such as netball, sailing, lacrosse and athletics. Long tradition of excellence in shooting. Most sports including fly fishing and clay pigeon shooting take place within the college grounds, but there's also a off-site programme that offers beagling, canoeing, caving, coasteering, mountain biking, mountaineering and sub-aqua.

Seemingly universal admiration for 'amazing' drama and music, although the former gets more takers at A level than the latter. Performances and teaching take place in the Bradleian studio theatre and on the flexible stage of the Ellis Theatre that seats up to 400. There are three ambitious audition-only main school productions a year, a musical every two years and a house play festival each summer. Nearly half of pupils take individual music lessons and house music competitions get everyone doing something tuneful. There's a symphony orchestra, choirs, loads of ensembles and plenty of opportunities to perform in the college as well as nationally and internationally. Chapel choir has made several recordings and recently returned from a tour of France. Organ scholars get to learn on the beautiful and recently restored Van Beckwith teaching organ. The department also has an impressive concert programme of visiting professionals and partnerships with the Southbank Sinfonia and individual musicians including Julian Lloyd Webber and Ioan Davies, head of chamber music at the Yehudi Menuhin School.

The college is a founder member of the CCF and has 300 cadets and a 25m indoor range. Those who choose not to join the CCF take part in a variety of service activities, working at primary schools, with younger children in the homes of local families or at a school for children with learning difficulties in Swindon; another group helps with local riding for the disabled. There are also opportunities to work with the elderly or on conservation projects.

There's a real energy and buzz at Marlborough; you can feel it. Pupils are busy, busy, busy. Maybe too busy, sometimes. Sensible advice comes from several parents: don't try and do it all, especially in the sixth form. You can't star in the play, play in the firsts and come first in the tests. 'You can do your academic work and one other thing well,' we were told. School says most do more than one thing well but they are vigilant about possible overload. Girls especially can feel the strain: 'the boys are more laid back but girls put themselves under tremendous pressure,' said one mother.

Boarding: Fifteen boarding houses (six boys, five girls, four mixed) are run by housemasters or housemistresses who live there with their families; they are supported by resident tutors, dames and other members of the pastoral and support staff. Vertical (mixed age) boarding promotes cohesion between year groups and house loyalty is fierce. 'It's really competitive,' several parents told us. Plenty of opportunities to do battle – house shouts (singing), plays, matches and so on.

The master's garden looks down to the River Kennett but alas, the Tennyson tree, a glorious copper beech planted by the poet laureate, is no more

Every house has its own character, dictated as much by its position and architecture as the team running it. In Hermitage, one of the older houses, we admired a wonderful ground floor bedroom with huge marble fireplace. This prize billet is given to the chap (it's a boys' house) the housemaster thinks is the hardest working, and its occupant looked very proud to have been chosen.

While we did spy some distinctly less than fancy corners as we ran behind a very long-legged housemaster, most boarders at Marlborough seem to get a pretty good deal. Some of the recently refurbished accommodation we visited looked fit for an interiors magazine – walls painted in the sort of modish shade that might be called Vole's Whisper – and, in one, a spectacular glass wall in the kitchen/dining area that overlooked playing fields.

Shells (first years) sleep in four or five bed dorms, graduating to twin and then single rooms from Hundreds (fifth year) up. Occupants are moved around every half term or so. Shell have supervised prep (no gappies, house prefects do this job), Removes (second year) have separate shared studies, after that pupils work in their own rooms. Pupils may Skype their parents (or vice versa) any time apart from during prep; 'we are flexible because of time zones'. Sensible rules re mobiles etc. Meals are taken centrally but continental breakfast, snacks and drinks available in houses.

Although we didn't inspect all 15 houses, we very much liked those we saw. Considerable thought and expense is going into boarders' surroundings and we're sure the refurbishment programme will eventually transform even the ugliest corners. We often say that boarding school accommodation is of a higher standard than university rooms, but at Marlborough some would surely outclass many homes.

So we asked, how can parents ensure their son or daughter is in the 'right' house? Short answer is, you can't. 'There is no 'best' or 'right' house', we were told firmly. What, no sporty house? No musical house? No. 'Parents must come to house open days and visit as many as they can – at least four; some end up seeing six or seven.' Applications are then made to three but school is in charge of mix and has final say. And parents, while you are inspecting the houses you can be sure members of staff are giving you a surreptitious once over.

Background and atmosphere: Marlborough has both in spades. Surely there is no other school on earth where one can walk out of a glorious Victorian gothic revival chapel (stained glass by Burne Jones and former pupil William Morris, sculpture by Eric Gill) and come face to face with a neolithic mound. 'Merlin's Mound', as it was dubbed by the 12th century tourist board (with 17th century poetic grotto at its foot), is the second largest man-made mound in Europe. 'Mound' though alliteratively effective, doesn't really describe its stepped shape: it looks more like a fancy Victorian pudding mould. In the 10th century the mound was recycled into the motte of a motte-and-bailey castle – its moat flows beneath the performing arts centre.

Take a few paces more and you will see the Memorial Hall, a neoclassical theatre and assembly hall built in 1925 to honour the 749 men who fell in 1914-1918. Constructed upon a floating 'raft' over the water meadows, the 'Mem' no longer holds the whole school (actually it could, but not if school wants to stay on the right side of health and safety legislation). Apparently the acoustics are excellent and the beautifully preserved interior remains very evocative. The hall is to be restored in time for the centenary of the end of the Great War in 2018. Peeping out from behind the Mem is the 'most architecturally important building in the school', a white painted 1930s concrete science block with ocean liner style aluminium windows and topped with a gourd (head of science at the time was Mr Gourd). It is hoped that this building can be converted into a new design centre.

Forgive all this talk of bricks and mortar – we know schools are about people – but somehow the eclectic mix of ancient and modern across the school estate embodies the breadth and quality of a Marlborough education. We were fortunate enough to be shown around by the head of admissions, an architectural historian. He describes the college site as both 'its greatest asset and a glorious problem' and knows the provenance of every wall and window. If ever a chap was in his happy place...

Marlborough College was established in 1851, the Church of England's response to a shortage of vicars. It wanted to provide a good, affordable education for clergymen's sons from the South West of England on the assumption that these young men would go on to take the cloth. List of clerical OMs testament to success of this operation. School was established in an 18th century mansion and former coaching inn which was gradually joined by Georgian, Victorian and Jacobethan buildings including the former town goal (now converted into a gym). The master's garden looks down to the River Kennet but alas, the Tennyson tree, a glorious copper beech planted by the poet laureate (his son, Hallam, was a pupil), is no more. Its huge canopy of leaves proved too heavy to bear and crashed down during a summer storm.

Marlborough claims to be the first public school to go co-ed (sixth form only, 1968). Surely Bedales, founded in 1893 and fully co-ed in 1898, should get that prize. But let's not quibble, it'll be 50 years in 2018 and even if boys still outnumber girls in the lower years it definitely doesn't feel like a boys' school. Marlborough College Malaysia was established in 2012 and has already doubled in size. This is not a franchise but a 'genuine expansion of the home school', with linked management and governance.

It's impossible to cover everything that goes on at Marlborough in this review. The school is a 24 hour educational, creative and cultural challenge to teenage apathy and we can only stand back in admiration. 'We ask a great deal of our staff,' the master told us; 'during term time there's no such thing as working hours.'

Pastoral care, well-being and discipline: All food is prepared in house and eaten in the large communal dining hall. Lunch is staggered between 12 and 1pm, an arrangement that we hope has improved the lot of Shells who we hear sometimes used to go hungry, elbowed out of the way by older children. Pupils eat with their friends at long wooden tables, there's plenty of choice and what we tried was delicious. Breakfasts and lunches get full marks but (and we heard this from several quarters) supper could do better – not an uncommon complaint at boarding schools, must be something to do with leftovers. Former pupil John Betjeman wasn't a fan of this meal either, although we're sure it's much nicer than what he got in the 1920s.

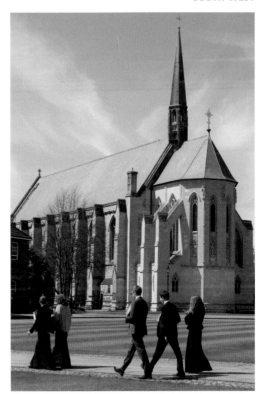

So what about discipline? It hasn't always had a robust reputation at Marlborough, although our impression is that it is now an extremely well run school. A rummage through the college's many 'policies' leads somewhat circuitously to chapter and verse. Suffice it to say that 'explicit or intimate sexual relations' will get you suspended or excluded. Likewise drugs, alcohol, bullying, theft, use of weapons and a whole load of other nasties. Prefects can go to some of the town pubs but on the whole partying is an in-school affair (there's a policy about it on the website) or – and this sounds like more fun – takes place at friends' houses during the holidays or on exeats.

Relations between boys and girls seemed friendly and relaxed, more best mates than Romeo and Juliet. 'There's great banter between the girls and boys,' a father told us. 'There's the odd bit of snogging in the bushes but nothing serious,' said another parent. While we can't comment on the activity we can confirm that the school grounds are well supplied with shrubs of all kinds.

Great praise for housemasters/mistresses, tutors, dames and all others directly involved in pastoral care. Parents like the 'clear' chain of command and felt that anxieties or problems were dealt with swiftly. Good medical care, plenty of joined up thinking and sharing of information (where appropriate) in cases of illness, stress etc.

Medical centre or 'Sanny' looked rather forbidding and was described by one parent as 'grim' (building, not people).

House identity is great for bonding but there are still a few grumbles about pupil hierarchy and the lot of the youngest. Efforts are being made, there's a mentoring system and older children write to new pupils before they start, but maybe there's still room for improvement here.

Pupils and parents: Traditional full boarding families broadly sums up the type you will meet here but school doesn't (and doesn't want to) feel like the 'default outcome of a dinner party conversation.' Yawn. It's sparkier and quirkier than that – fish pie and a decent Muscadet at the kitchen table with slightly naughty friends perhaps, rather than 'faine daining', competitive parenting and house prices. Less country than schools further south but 'not too London' either. Some very local day pupils, six per cent international students.

Important part of the interview is to discover whether a child will be boarding by consent or 'compulsion'

Pupils are a great advert for co-education – self-assured, good company, the sort you could see fitting in anywhere. Many parents get to know their children's friends socially at weekends (exeats, privis) or during holidays. 'They're a great bunch', we heard, 'the sort who always help clear up after a party.'

In addition to ranks of clerical and military worthies, notable former pupils include artists: William Morris, Graham Shepard, Lauren Child; writers: John Betjeman, Louis MacNeice, Siegfried Sassoon, Bruce Chatwin, Frances Osborne; actors: Wilfrid Hyde White, James Robertson Justice, Michael Pennington, Jack Whitehall; politicians (and their spouses): Hallam Tennyson, Rab Butler, Christopher Chope, Mark Reckless, Sally Bercow, Samantha Cameron; plus Sir Francis Chichester, Mark Phillips, Simon Fanshawe, Mark Tully, Frank Gardner, HRH Princess Eugenie of York and HRH Duchess of Cambridge (she was a prefect). Quite some school reunion that would be.

Entrance: Parents are advised to start the process (visiting boarding houses etc) at least three years in advance. According to the director of admissions, 50 per cent of the decision to admit a child rests with the prep school head's reference, 10 per cent on a bespoke test designed by Durham University (to check the academic part of the head's reference) and two interviews in a boarding house by HM and a tutor to verify other aspects of the reference. CE's biggest use, he maintains, is to help with setting once a child joins. Important part of the interview is to discover whether a child will be boarding by consent or 'compulsion'. No one wants the latter. Nor do they want children who have been tutored, 'we're looking for potential for happiness.' Someone will be offering to coach children in that soon.

Consensus from many parents that Marlborough is a great family school. School says it does its best to accommodate siblings, but warns, it's not automatic. 'We can't be a closed shop and sometimes this isn't the right place.' Pupils come from over 100 preps but main suppliers are Beaudesert, Cheam, Cothill The Dragon, Farleigh, Highfield, Lambrook, Ludgrove, Pinewood, Twyford and Windlesham.

We have in the past heard from parents somewhat bruised by Marlborough's 'brusque' response to admissions enquiries. School horrified to learn this: 'we go out of our way to be welcoming and give people time'. Certainly all the front of house staff we met could not have been more charming and less intimidating.

Exit: Very few leave post-GCSE, certainly no kicking out for under par results. Influx of girls in sixth form swells numbers. Big improvements in careers advice, we loved the huge signposts showing all the directions OMs can take. As previously, Edinburgh, Manchester, Bristol, Exeter, Durham and Leeds popular destinations; much the most popular courses are in history, art history, modern languages. Twenty plus applications to USA and Europe. Ten Oxbridge places in 2015.

Money matters: Fees on a par with other similar schools. Still lots of scholarships (more honour than hard cash) but before you bask in the warm glow do check small print and talk to your child about the expectations that go with these.

Means-tested bursaries of up to 100 per cent available and school may assist in individual cases of hardship. Marlborough is one of 'very few schools' who have followed the Charity Commission's advice and transferred all scholarship funds into bursaries. College is currently raising an appeal for substantial additional bursary provision.

Remarks: The college defines its 'triple foundation' as 'rigour, respect and responsibility', an ethos that is at once modern and yet in keeping with its Anglican traditions. Pupils at Marlborough are part of a diverse, creative and academic community – 21st century co-ed boarding at its very best. To paraphrase lines John Betjeman wrote after revisiting his old school in the 1960s, Marlburians 'Live in a world as rich as is a king's. How sweet are tastes to them, how deep their dreams. How hopeful and how possible their schemes.'

Millfield Preparatory School

Edgarley Hall, Glastonbury, Somerset BA6 8LD

01458 832446
office@millfieldprep.com
www.millfieldprep.com

Ages: 2–13 (boarders from 7)
Pupils: 463
Boarders: 120 full, 46 weekly/flexi
Day: £7,995 – £17,550 pa
Boarding: £25,800 pa

Linked school: Millfield School

Headmistress: Since September 2010, Mrs Shirley Shayler MEd BSc PGCE. Educated at Carrickfergus Grammar School, Northern Ireland, degree in biology from the University of Stirling, PGCE from Queen's University, Belfast, masters in educational management. No stranger to Millfield, having taught biology at the senior school 1989-2002 and undertaken an impressive spread of pastoral and extracurricular rôles including coaching first XI girls' hockey and being a houseparent. Deputy head of Taunton School for four years then head of Stonar for another four plus years doing much to expand and improve the sixth form. Lives on site with husband Gary, biology teacher and head of careers at senior school, and daughter, Caragh, who attends Millfield Prep and rides a school pony.

'Delightful' and 'caring' but steely when need arises. Parents we spoke to all thought she was 'a good head who works hard' and commented on how 'she has won respect through not being afraid to stick to her guns.' Loves being back at Millfield: 'a way of life rather than a job,' she commented to us. Really believes in educating 'whole child' and in releasing children's potential. Often seen walking family labrador (she recently delivered seven puppies). Still involved in hockey and also enjoys swimming, cycling, skiing (annual family ski trip is a highlight for Shaylers), reading and the theatre. Vision for future includes providing more enrichment à la Dragon's Den-style enterprise activity, more involvement in the local community and further developing pastoral care.

Entrance: Many admitted via interview and report from previous head (eg from prep schools finishing at 11). Some arrive from pre-preps or local primaries and others from as far away as Venezuela or Hong Kong (we have seldom seen such a varied list

of feeder schools). LDC tutor involved at interview where there are special learning needs. Can be flexible – will always make the effort to take pupils and has been a sanctuary for pupils unhappy or failing to thrive elsewhere: 'IQ not the only arbiter; we need to see the child, not just a collection of data.' Can and will take when space available; means-tested bursaries available in cases of genuine need and a number of scholarships (all the usuals plus chess) for entry into years 6, 7 and 8. The former depend on success in the scholarship exams which can be sat each January.

Exit: Most proceed to senior school. Dozen or more scholarships won annually to senior school: academic, art, music and sport. Transfer automatic subject to good behaviour and satisfactory academic standard. A small number move elsewhere, mostly to other independent schools.

Remarks: Millfield provides a top notch experience in almost every sphere. Lively boarding community which doesn't high tail it home at weekends (apart from exeats) – around 40 per cent of boarders are from overseas – and still includes Sunday chapel. Boy and girl numbers pretty equal throughout. Many sign up for complete (2-18) Millfield experience. Parents underline how school 'instills confidence and maturity' and how it 'has brought a global dimension to rural Somerset.' Prep campus benefits from more acreage than its senior partner. Centrepiece is an elegant Victorian home of former local landowners. Oak-panelled hall leads to head's capacious study (now made-over to suit her taste) overlooking grounds. Internal standard of classrooms, sports and other facilities more than compensates for lack of architectural cohesion on a site that has grown like Topsy. Unusual external

Reception area shouts creativity and fun; classrooms are flexible learning spaces with eye-catching displays, live animals and loads of interest

touches include a huge outdoor chess set and the multi-coloured climbing wall. Children seem quite content, scurrying around like worker bees under the queen's command. Main entrance sits on a bend of A361 on the Pilton side of Glastonbury opposite (and safely accessible via footbridge over main road) school's small chapel, nine-hole golf course and Edgarley Manor (a boys' boarding house) at the foot of the famous Tor.

Show starts with Millfield Minis, a three-day-a-week event for local parents and toddlers using pre-prep hall from 10.00-11.30am. There are even Minis' swimming, tennis and trampolining. Pre-prep department caters for pupils aged 2-7. Safe, ideal location within former walled garden. Reception area shouts creativity and fun; classrooms are flexible learning spaces with eye-catching displays, live animals and loads of interest. Outdoor raised beds for veggie growing, safe play and exploration including Forest School (two teachers trained leaders) nearby. Pond includes underwater camera for pupils to watch submarine activity on linked computer screen. We liked the three little pigs guarding the gazebo and outside quiet area. Cosy library to make reading fun and indoor tumble room for scrapes without scratches. Read Write Inc a favourite phonic approach, number games abound and we saw some beautiful progressions of pupils' cursive handwriting on display. Humanities and science themes run alongside core learning. Music, art and drama all play a big part.

Children coming into pre-prep are automatically assessed for learning support: one-to-one groups and lessons for those who need extra help from two specialist teachers who work closely with school's learning development centre. Parents appreciate the experience of many long-serving teachers and the extent to which it is 'an inclusive environment' rather than pushy.

Most of the prep school buildings are modern (if not of any particular architectural merit) and provide well for a community of around 400 children. The large, refurbished assembly hall serves for school's frequent drama productions and activities such as fencing and gymnastics. The well-stocked library is above the dining complex (probably the best we've seen in a prep school: all shiny service counters and friendly staff). Food is plentiful and varied.

We observed versatile teaching across a broad curriculum in small classes (maximum is normally 16) from an experienced and friendly staff. Years 3-5 are taught by group tutors for most lessons. Setting from year 3 in English, maths and languages with mixed-ability tutor groups. From year 6 all lessons are taught by subject specialists, with tutors continuing to have pastoral oversight. Academic standards are reassuringly high. Despite many children needing extra English, the school's 'language for all' policy ensures that every child can take Spanish as part of their programme. French and Latin are on the main menu with some linguistic side orders also available (eg Mandarin, Russian and Japanese).

The five science labs are still housed in very adequate temporary accommodation close to the main teaching areas, and teachers we spoke to were in no rush to move into a new building. Young number crunchers perform well in competitions such as UK Maths Challenge and we were told that children particularly enjoy using MangaHigh software. Splendid IT suite where we saw some pupils operating robots they had programmed; good use made of smart boards and digital projectors in all subjects. Scholarship group starts in year 7 and we saw some year 8 scholars preparing for Salters chemistry festival at Bath University. Strong eco bias (Green Flag holders) with regular focus on environmental issues (eg switch off fortnight) and annual eco day. Pastoral team overseen by experienced deputy head: each child is watched over by group tutor, responsible for welfare and progress, and first port of call for anxious parents. Reports are termly, with grades for effort as well as attainment. Parents contacted every half-term regarding progress.

Even the chaplain has a sporting seam running through him (he was going off with a golfing group when we met him). Millfield brain does as well as its brawn

Millfield is not a special school, but it attracts pupils with a range of problems from mild literacy difficulties to those with a diagnosis of dyslexia and/or speech and language difficulties. The language development centre (LDC) is a centre of excellence with five full-time and four part-time specialists plus a classroom assistant. Strong liaison throughout between LDC, pastoral and academic staff as well as with senior school. If reading or spelling is more than a year behind chronological age, this is flagged up, 'But data is not the only aspect taken into account when determining a

pupil's current needs.' Speech and language therapist works closely with both the prep and pre-prep. Parents praised how their daughter, previously in a specialist school, was now 'blossoming' at Millfield through the combination of specialist help and 'an emphasis on the positive side of everything.' Group help at both ends of the spectrum included in fees but one-to-one support and recall to therapists are chargeable. Special programme (Potential Academic Curriculum Excellence or PACE) undertaken by super-bright. EAL teacher uses academic lesson time with over 30 international students to immerse them in English before they are progressively fitted into mainstream curriculum.

Sport is a big deal here and a pull for many parents: five PE specialists and a number of ex-international coaches. Sixty pupils in swimming squad alone, partnership with LTA to provide top class tennis coaching, and bubble over one of nine courts on site (pupils go to senior complex if necessary) ensures practice continues through winter. Stonking sports hall (includes large spectator area and four squash courts – two of which are glass backed), equestrian centre with extensive stabling and arenas for dressage and show jumping, a nine-hole golf course just for Millfield prep, a fine 25-metre pool (ditto), new sports pavilion and all sorts of courts, pitches and fields to cater for every conceivable sport and activity (seven county champions in athletics alone).

Rising stars can miss a regular PE lesson to receive individual coaching (eg from ex-first class cricketers). U13 girls had just won national (not just preps) cricket title at Lord's when we visited. A powerful presence across all major sports at county and national levels. School is not invincible and meets some stiff competition on the prep schools circuit. Individuals star in many disciplines: fencing, tennis and golf being recent examples. Even the chaplain has a sporting seam running through him (he was going off with a golfing group when we met him). Millfield brain does as well as its brawn with chess teams defending an enviable reputation in tournaments at all levels.

Good environment in both drawing and painting; innovations downstairs included an ex-government printing press bought for a song and stone carving taught in warmer months by talented working artist in a lean-to adjacent to the art department

Cracking music department under long-serving director: attractive modern recital hall (seats 200), classrooms and practice rooms; wide range of instruments, 350 individual lessons, 29 music ensembles and 18 annual concerts. Junior baroque chamber orchestra plus four choirs and a chapel choir. Pupils selected for national children's choir and orchestra. Annual highlights include home-grown Young Musician of the Year competition and a rock and pop concert. Drama lessons lead to many pupils becoming involved (on stage or behind the scenes) in one of four major productions held annually. Staff sometimes have to write plays to suit Millfield's large casts. Parents have been amazed at positive effect of school drama on their children. Art (including popular after lessons clubs) is strong as evidenced by displays around school, from print-making to ceramics via ICT, with critical discussion an integral part of its teaching. Good environment in both drawing and painting studios; innovations downstairs included an ex-government printing press bought for a song and stone carving taught in warmer months by talented working artist and done under a lean-to adjacent to art department. Picture of the week chosen from pupils' artwork for insertion in school's newsletter. Design facilities are more akin to a senior school and include

CAD design and a laser cutter. Products range from torches to clocks. Textiles aplenty downstairs and food science upstairs encourages innovative cooking which even includes an inter-house competition.

House system is used for internal competitions of all kinds (not just sport). Apart from Edgarley Manor (boys' boarding house) across A361, remaining four boarding houses are on main site: all modern with capacity for 38 boarders each. No large dorms: boarders either in two, four or six bed units (early swimmers kept in rooms together to avoid disturbing others when they get up to train). More of a home from home than an institutional feel and bright colours help keep spirits high. Year 8 allowed to do prep in rooms; otherwise, boarders are supervised in school between 5pm and 6pm. Well-equipped common rooms and cosy kitchens for snacking and chatting. Extra tuck part of house reward system. Boarding houses have outside play areas including tennis court and enclosed field. Medical staff available 24/7.

Minibuses ferry day pupils (early rises for some) from outlying villages in time for 8.25am start. Younger ones can leave at 3.45pm but majority of stay for activities until 5pm. Great choice includes sailing at Durleigh, sub-aqua group aiming at PADI junior qualification and caving on Mendips. Weekday activities include Airfix modelling and touch typing, as well as sports from pop lacrosse and indoor go-karting. Diverse theme days and stimulating educational visits to destinations as distant as Rome or as close as Glastonbury Abbey all add to broad mix. Charity fundraising and activities within the local community are also given importance.

We liked the way that so many year 8 pupils get leadership roles on a rotating basis and how 20 of them trained with Kidscape to become peer mentors. Former pupils include 10 current first class cricketers (including half of Somerset CC first XI), rugby stars: Matt Perry and Chris Robshaw, Olympic hockey brothers: Simon and Richard Mantell, Euan Dale (Scottish swimming medallist), Joey Barrington (squash international), Ruth Kelly MP and Max Milligan (photographer, author and explorer).

Happy school with genuine excitement at every level. Pupils find their niche here (be it academic, sporting or creative) and 'want to do well.' Facilities to take your breath away but school produces well-rounded individuals rather than arrogant know-it-alls. 'My daughter was dancing with the daisies before she joined Millfield,' said one mum, 'and now the change is unbelievable.' Parents testify to extent that 'academic and less academic pupils can flourish alongside each other.' Hard to do better than this if the package suits.

Millfield School

Butleigh Road, Street, Somerset BA16 0YD

01458 442291
admissions@millfieldschool.com
www.millfieldschool.com

Ages: 13–18
Pupils: 1,234; sixth form: 580
Boarders: 924 full
Day: £23,280 pa
Boarding: £34,650 pa

Linked school: Millfield Preparatory School

Head Master: Since 2008, Mr Craig Considine MA (50s). Degree in applied science in human movement (Australian version of sports science) from Royal Melbourne Institute of Technology; diploma and masters in education from Melbourne and Charles Stuart Universities. Was headmaster of Wanganui Collegiate School, New Zealand (Prince Edward worked there for two terms in his gap year). Before that taught at Geelong Grammar School, where he was much involved in the school's five week Timbertop programme in 'Alpine wilderness' (Victorian Alps, in case you're imagining St Bernards and yodelling). Would like to increase this kind of 'experiential education' at Millfield (it's said to develop life skills, values, independence, teamwork, leadership.. Has no one told them about the Duke of Edinburgh Award?).

A large bear of a man – represented Australia in the Commonwealth Games (decathlon) and played professional Aussie rules football. Quieter, less flashy than his predecessors. Thought, by parents and pupils, to be steering the school towards greater emphasis on academics and generally tightening up rules and behaviour – not to everyone's approval. Keen on more structure; would like more staff living on site; wants year 9 pupils tended more carefully; more opportunities for 'middle ability' games players. Aims for nothing less than the school being known as the 'best boarding school in the country'. Some parents (and staff) concerned this means turning Millfield into a run-of-the-mill boarding school by diluting the quirks and sports obsession that make it special, and some resistance.

Married to Penny, who has much experience working in boarding houses (BA in youth work). Four children – twins at Millfield, an older teenager boarding back at Geelong High, and one on a gap year.

Academic matters: Breathtakingly broad ability range – one of the few big, famous public schools that remains proudly non-selective academically. Exam results close to the national average for A levels (25 per cent A*/A and 52 per cent A*-B in 2015). Usually comfortably above average for GCSEs – in 2015, 32 per cent of grades were A*/A, 59 per cent A*-B. The bright end is clever indeed – two to Oxbridge and two to Harvard in 2015 – and

the dimmer end stretches out eternally to the distant horizon. So setting is important here: 'There's setting for everything – even art!' a pupil told us. BTecs in everything from art and design to business, music technology and sport.

Pupils say the head wants to beef up academics and cite as evidence the move to longer lessons (from 35 minutes to 50 – head says it was planned before he arrived; helps the organisationally challenged). But academics will never be the point of Millfield – parents choose the school for the full Monty: the 'Millfield mix'. Enormous range of A level subjects, from Latin to media studies. Has dipped toe into the medicinal baths of the Pre-U by offering it for history instead of A level. Introduced Extended Project Qualification and CISI securities and investment course. Vocational BTecs in art and design and in sport; a double A level award in leisure studies also popular. One girl said to be doing ancient Greek. Well-stocked library open from 8.30am Monday to Saturday.

Millfield is dauntingly large, yet classes are pocket-sized (maximum 15, usually much smaller) and the staff:pupil ratio an extraordinary 1:6.5. With nearly 200 academic and coaching staff, Millfield boasts the largest common room of any school in the UK. Prep in house for an hour and a half each week night. Lots of support and empathy for overstretched sportsmen and women. 'They understand how time-consuming sport is and help you to work around it,' said a cricketer. Busy pupils can take fewer GCSEs.

At Geelong Grammar School he was much involved in the Timbertop programme in 'Alpine wilderness' (Victorian Alps, in case you are imagining St Bernards and yodelling)

There are 400+ pupils with SEN 'from mild to quite severe'. Millfield's expertise in specific learning difficulties goes back a long way: Jack Meyer was summoned to London in 1941 to discuss the possibility of Attlee's 'word blind' son entering Millfield. He passed his exams to enter the School of Navigation at Southampton 18 months later and Millfield's reputation for helping dyslexics was made. Support delivered by school's SEN unit mainly in small groups rather than one-to-one. Bright dyslexics may 'drop in' to work with SEN specialist teacher – no shame in visiting the unit. Others will be timetabled to be there, usually in place of a foreign language – there is an entire English class in each year who are taught English in the SEN dept. 'Language development'

lessons help pupils struggling with writing to structure essays – helps them across the board. Maths dept runs dyscalculia workshop in lunch breaks. Dyslexics, dyspraxics, mild Asperger's, autism, ADHD all assisted – some come with statements of needs and ed psych reports, others are identified during their school career. Five full-time staff and two part-timers, all qualified teachers and either dyslexia qualified or with loads of experience. NB: No extra fee for SEN. Some 100 international pupils take advantage of the very good EAL provision.

Games, options, the arts: Seen by many as a specialist sports school, and it would certainly qualify – if it wasn't so maddeningly good at everything else. Sports teams habitually bring their opposition to its knees, so much so that they have been known to dispatch their B team to play the A team of some quite famous schools. The high standard can be a shock to some pupils who played on their prep school A team and now find themselves demoted to the bottom of the Cs. Rugby, hockey, cricket, swimming top the fixture list. Rugby players won all the levels they entered in recent huge National Schools Sevens Competition (prep, U16 and open).

Fabulous cricket pavilion, the glass walls etched in cricket balls (this editor thought they were coffee beans until put right), 50m swimming pool one of the best in Britain and used for Olympic training, nine-hole golf course with indoor tuition centre (Independent Schools Golf Association winners recently and also recent team and individual boys' and girls' World Schools Golf Challenge champions). Golfers have a winter top-up session in the Desert Springs resort, Almanzora, Spain. Indoor tennis centre (plus lots of all-weather courts), running track, shooting range, three Astro hockey pitches, acres of playing fields, dedicated fencing salle and judo room, high-power ski team. Equestrian centre has indoor and outdoor arenas, X-C schooling fields, Derby course and stabling for 53 horses including facilities for pupils' own horses. Pupils can study for their British Horse Society Preliminary Instructor's Certificate as a timetabled subject. Own polo pitch and has won the National Schools' Polo Championships more than once. Lots of overseas tours.

Minor sports not given as much peer approval, say some pupils. Sports scholars tell us that serious sportsmen and women need to hunker down and concentrate on excellence in their chosen sport – not the place for all rounders if you're playing at the highest levels: 'It's very full time'. Some specialist treatment – sports nutrition, sports psychology and physiotherapy – available to these top athletes. Fifteen Old Millfieldians competed in the 2010 Commonwealth Games (mostly rugby, swimming and hockey) and six took part in the 2012 Olympics, including Helen Glover, who won gold for Team

GB in the women's pair rowing. Well-staffed physiotherapy department and weights rooms. Ten Tors for those wanting a physical challenge that does not involve bat or ball.

Two main school productions each year (in school's 500 seat theatre), with large casts, but still plenty of disappointed would-be thespians in a school of this size. GCSE and A level pupils have smaller coursework shows and years 9 and 10 take part in the house drama competition. Dance – all kinds – big here, especially for a co-ed school. Elite 'Bazique' programme for the school's top nine or 10 dancers. Debate society going strong, with pupils taking part in the European Youth Parliament.

Art extraordinary with fabulous facilities and space, space, space. BTec art pupils mount a fashion show each year. Music surprisingly good and housed in splendid newish building with acoustically perfect concert hall. Awash with pianos, top of the line Macs, beauteous music lockers, recording studio, drum kits and lovely practice rooms – nothing is wanting. 'Tea and music' informal concerts provide lots of performance opportunities. Quality, at the high end, is impressive, with Millfield pupils in the National Youth Orchestra every year and moving on to music conservatoires.

MAP – the school's activities programme – offers a virtually unlimited range, from dissection to chunky knitting to Caterham car club to jewellery making – year 9, 10 and 12 pupils must take part in one each week. D of E involvement strong. Impressive food technology dept under Leith's aegis popular. 'It used to be that sport was everything here,' a pupil told us, 'but not so much now.'

Serious sportsmen and women need to hunker down and concentrate on excellence in their chosen sport

Apart from gymnastics, trampolining and diving it's all here, but be warned – the emphasis is on choosing what you want to be good at and going for it, rather than dabbling across the myriad spheres, 'otherwise you will be left behind'.

Boarding: Fine boarding houses – pupils mainly in double rooms, then singles in sixth form. House identity not the huge deal it can be at other schools (school allocates houses – we hear Orchards is good at cricket, Keen's Elm swimming, the day houses academics). Three boys' boarding houses off campus (boys bussed in and out), all other boarding on site, including 'day centres' for day pupils – two for girls, two for boys – to base themselves. The girls' day house has dedicated areas for prep and relaxation, with Wifi throughout. Newer on-site boarding houses particularly impressive with smashing kitchens, Sky and huge common rooms.

Around 22 per cent of boarding community is from overseas and school keeps going throughout the term with weekend activities (though guardians etc pick up during half term).

Background and atmosphere: If you're seeking ivy-clad spires or comically antiquated uniforms, look away now. Feels exactly like a small American university campus, beautifully tended with walkways, sculpture and a mishmash of building styles. Over 300 acres of grounds: large, non-traditional, and slightly impersonal by UK private school standards – 'You don't know everyone in your year,' a boy told us. Top heavy, numbers-wise, with enormous sixth form somewhat dominating the feel of the place.

Founded in 1935 by Jack Meyer with seven Indian pupils, of whom six were princes, and swiftly adopted the Robin Hood principle – squeezing money from the exceedingly rich to subsidise the needy, talented poor. From day one, in a large, rented Somerset house, he set about promoting individual ability, in whatever sphere. Proud of having been built up from nothing and owing nothing. Used to paying its way – hosts range of Easter revision courses and summer English language courses as well as conferences.

A large dining hall, notable for its finer than average fare, sits at the heart of the campus and is given a universal thumbs up by pupils, even the vegetarians.

Pastoral care, well-being and discipline: Always a challenge at a co-ed school with so many pupils of such diversity. Drugs and alcohol bound to enter the frame, but head maintains that Millfield's policy is 'tight compared to other schools'. Five boys suspended a few years back for use of cannabis. Transgressions always helpfully flagged up by The Daily Mail. Pupils noticeably more streetwise than at many private schools, and not a school you'd choose if you're looking for mollycoddling. Sixth formers given much freedom to come and go on weekends. Girls' skirts shortish, though not horrendous. Chaplaincy centre a haven for exam-stressed pupils, plus other counsellors in the place; dedicated prayer room for Muslims. Strong community service locally.

Pupils and parents: Varied – first school that has ever answered our question about geographical range of intake with 'the world' (63 countries). Some 22 per cent international pupils, six per cent expats – 'We see ourselves as an international school – we want that diversity,' explains the head. Majority of pupils come from Surrey, followed by Glos and Sussex. (Boy/girl ratio is 60/40). Immense range of family backgrounds, from the dyslexic sent by a local authority in north Wales to the one-armed swimmer from Essex to a Middle Eastern prince wallowing in cash – makes for some challenges. 'Not the place to send your son if you want him to learn to speak like a gentleman,' one overseas father murmured. 'My son left Millfield far better prepared to deal with the real world than if he'd been cocooned at one of the traditional public schools,' said a mum.

The school sent us a five page, small font, narrow spaced, alphabetised list of noteworthy former pupils: John Sergeant, Max Mosley, cricketers Ian Ward and Ben Hollioake, British Lions and Wales rugby international Gareth Edwards, DJ Tony Blackburn, Diana's special friend James Hewitt, film producer Jeremy Thomas (The Last Emperor), chief executive of the Royal Aeronautical Society Simon Luxmoore, Nicolette Sheridan (Edie in Desperate Housewives), Sophie Dahl (expelled), Steward Copeland (of The Police) and lots of Olympic swimmers are the tip of an eclectic iceberg.

Entrance: At least 210 enter at year 9, 30+ at year 10 and 130+ at sixth form. Interview and previous head's report the usual route in, with CE used to determine set for core subjects – 'We have 16 maths sets in year 9'. No written test required for overseas applicants – a huge selling point for many. Anything up to 80 feeder schools, but by far the largest day number come from its own prep school (see separate entry). Pupils enter and exit at odd times including mid-year and, at least once, we hear, departing in the middle of the night (money problems; overseas pupil).

Exit: Most to university, the full range with over 60 UK universities and colleges listed and a large slice to overseas universities, especially in the States and including Harvard (two in 2015, plus two to Oxbridge). Bristol, King's College, Loughborough and Cardiff popular.

Money matters: Over £3.5 million worth of 'fee concessions' each year, and the Millfield Foundation (former pupils) is beavering away to swell the pot. Scholarships for all-rounders, sportspeople (was the first school to offer these), academics, musicians (instrumental and choral) artists, actors and even chess players – they're worth no more than 15 per cent of fees, but can be topped up with means-tested bursaries. Also a limited number of Headmaster's Awards of up to 50 per cent. Sixth form scholarships said to be more plentiful than 13+ (fewer years for the school to shell out, and helps cherry-pick 16 year olds).

Around 35 per cent get some form of award, so a couple of pupils mentioned tensions between 'rich kids' and 'scholarship kids'. Famously muddy fee structure has finally shaken the habit of three-quarters of a century and is now 'crystal clear'. No longer a separate fee bracket for 'international' students.

Remarks: One of the few schools that really is all things to all pupils (almost). But less and less a school for all-rounders than for passionate specialists. Undergoing a slight, but seismic, culture shift. SEN still excels.

Milton Abbey School

Blandford Forum, Dorset DT11 oBZ

01258 880484
admissions@miltonabbey.co.uk
www.miltonabbey.co.uk
C of E

Ages: 13–18
Pupils: 235 (175 boys, 60 girls); sixth form: 115
Boarders: 215
Day: £16,650 pa
Boarding: £32,880 pa

Headmaster: Since January 2014, Magnus Bashaarat MA PGCE (40s), previously deputy head of Stowe. Educated at The King's School, Canterbury (he and Stowe head Anthony Wallersteiner were contemporaries there), followed by University of Edinburgh, where he read English. After work experience at the York Evening Press he decided to become a journalist and worked for the Observer and Evening Standard for a while. He changed direction after taking a course in teaching English as a foreign language – found he loved 'standing up in front of a class and helping people to learn.' PGCE at King's College London, followed by two years at Sherborne and a 15-year stint at Eton, where he taught English and drama and was a housemaster for seven years. He also did a year at Sydney Grammar as part of a teaching exchange with Eton. Moved to Stowe in 2009 and spent five years as deputy head. He says Milton Abbey is similar to Stowe – 'just on a different scale' – and that its size means 'everyone is seen as an individual, everyone is valued and pupils have a very good relationship with staff.'

Mr Bashaarat is dynamic, forward-thinking and hit the ground running when he arrived. He didn't teach during his first year at Milton Abbey but now teaches an English GCSE retake set. 'It's lovely to have contact time again,' he told us. He's adamant that a head shouldn't be a remote figure and makes a point of seeing the pupils as much as possible, chatting at lunch, running a school cycling group and popping into the boarding houses in the evenings. 'This place has a very honest, nurturing ethos and pupils are very looked after,' he says.

He cycles (his road bike is propped against the door of his study), rows and likes 'serious drama'

His wife Camilla used to work in communications for the NHS and now runs Milton Abbey's parents' association, or MASPA as it's known (everything from a yoga retreat in Norfolk to a trip to Champagne in France). They have three children – sons at Stowe and Eton and a daughter at Sherborne Girls. In his spare time, he cycles (his road bike is propped against the wall of his study), rows at nearby Canford and goes to the theatre as much as he can. He likes 'serious drama' and if he can't get to London drives to Poole, Salisbury and, a new find, The Tobacco Factory in Bristol.

Academic matters: Milton Abbey's strengths lie in its value-added. School doesn't publish its GCSE and A level results, taking the view that students have such a broad range of ability that their achievements wouldn't be accurately represented by what the head calls the 'crude mechanism' of league tables. 'The value added we get for our pupils wouldn't be represented by the league tables,' he says. Students range from a boy who got three A*s at A level in 2015 and headed to Oxford to read archaeology and anthropology to those who find formal academic learning 'really difficult' and opt for a more vocational route. The school talks a lot about 'parallel learning pathways' and prides itself on tailoring an academic programme to suit individual students. At sixth form, a third of pupils take A levels, a third take a combination of A levels and BTECs and a third take BTECs. In year 11 youngsters attend an options evening, when they discuss individual sixth form choices with tutors and heads of department. Pupils' GCSE profiles are taken into account and subject combinations are based on advice from tutors and teachers (no chance of doing physics A level and a BTEC in hospitality). Pupils are encouraged to pursue their passions and interests and all the usual A levels are on offer, plus economics, politics, history of art and music technology.

The school is ahead of the curve when it comes to vocational learning. Milton Abbey says it offers the broadest range of BTECs in the independent sector and is one of the few schools to offer

You can't fail to be enchanted by the ancient abbey nestling in a wooded Dorset valley. 'It's deeply rural, but not remote,' is the head's description

BTECs at extended diploma level – equivalent to three A levels. BTECs (available in countryside management, performing arts, enterprise and entrepreneurship, equine management, hospitality, creative media production and sport) aren't an easy option though. They are made up of continued assessment, with a small percentage of the course assessed by exam at the end of two years. The school's 2015 ISI report commended its approach, saying that 'pupils, who come with widely different educational backgrounds and needs, often suffering a negative experience of education elsewhere, are enabled to rebuild the foundation of their knowledge and skills, as well as the self-confidence needed to progress.' The assistant head (academic) concurs with this. 'We're all about getting the best out of our pupils,' she says.

Pupils take between seven and nine GCSEs, with everyone doing English, maths and a science. Class sizes are small – average of 12 up to GCSE and six at A level. 'The small class sizes mean that we have much better outcomes for learners,' says the head. Pupils are streamed by ability for the core subjects. Lessons are now one hour long – school says this helps pupils to concentrate better.

Milton Abbey is resolutely mainstream but learning support, with four teachers and six teaching assistants, is the biggest department. Some pupils are screened before they start and around two-thirds access learning support in some way – for a wide range of difficulties, including dyslexia, dyspraxia, dyscalculia, mild Asperger's). Learning support assistants provide additional help in lessons and there's one-to-one or group support outside lessons too (charged on top of the fees). EAL support and study skills support on offer. Some pupils have learning support lessons instead of doing French or Spanish. The department is very welcoming, with its door permanently open to help anyone who wants to drop in for revision tips, essay planning and time management. 'Quite often their self esteem and confidence is low and it's our job to raise that,' says the head of learning support.

School library has 9,000 resources and pupils are encouraged to read books for pleasure as well as for study. Robert Muchamore and Meg Rosoff are two current favourites – 'we like to get the pupils in the habit of reading,' the school librarian told us.

Games, options, the arts: Sport is taken seriously here but the emphasis is on enjoyment and there's loads on offer. Rugby, hockey, cricket and football predominate but golf (there's a course in the grounds), sailing and polo have a strong take-up too. The fixtures list and results show the school punches above its weight on the sports field. Relatively small number of girls means everyone gets the chance to represent the school at hockey, netball and lacrosse during the winter and tennis and rounders during the winter. Facilities include a 25-metre swimming pool, two gyms, squash court, all-weather pitch, sports hall and outdoor pitches galore. Everyone does games on Tuesdays, Thursdays and Saturdays but the sportiest do far more. Wednesdays are given over to CCF or community service (including visiting the elderly, taking dogs for walks and cleaning the local church). There's all manner of country pursuits, like fishing, ferreting (you can bring your own ferret, although none were in residence when we visited), clay pigeon shooting, beagling and mountain biking.

It's possible to combine a burgeoning equestrian career with school life. Pupils can bring their own steeds – many of the keenest riders take a BTEC in equine management and keep their horses at the school stables (each individual stable is labelled with the inhabitant's name – Sparky, Dolly and the like). They manage the day-to-day care of their horses and can choose to ride instead of playing other sports.

Art is a popular subject and we saw artwork that was easily on a par with larger schools. A year 12 boy showed us an astonishing oil painting inspired by renaissance art that he'd worked on over the summer. School puts on a big drama production in its theatre every year and there's a vast array of music. Hymn practice is held in the Abbey every Friday, when the whole school gathers to sing at the tops of their voices. 'The volume creeps up bit by bit and it sounds wonderful,' a sixth-form boy told us.

Milton Abbey runs the innovative Entrepreneurship in Residence competition, aiming to inspire pupils with ambitions to launch their own business. Top-notch designers like Anya Hindmarch and Cath Kidston have fronted the scheme in the past and now Johnnie Boden is leading the next generation of young entrepreneurs. Unlike some boarding schools, students do work experience – usually with school alumni (an Inner Temple barrister and a Coutts banker were among those who volunteered this year). Other activities include D of E, farm club and the Ten Tors expedition across Dartmoor. School is a member of Round Square, a worldwide organisation that encourages young people to broaden their horizons and gain greater understanding of the wider world through exchange trips, community work and themed activities within school.

Boarding: Milton Abbey offers full boarding or day places – 'we don't have anything in between,' says the head. Two three-day exeats a term to allow for longer journeys home. Five boarding houses – four for boys and one for girls. We visited the two newest houses, both wholesome and welcoming, with disabled access and underfloor heating. Each has a housemaster or housemistress, resident tutors and two matrons, who take charge of laundry and cleaning, offer support to pupils and help them to prepare for life beyond school. One matron told us she'd just taught a boy how to iron his shirt – 'it was important he learned how to do it himself.'

Common rooms in the boarding houses are equipped with TVs but these aren't allowed on during the day. There's no mobile phone signal on most of the site so phones are less of a problem here than at other schools. Most use the old-fashioned landlines in the boarding houses to phone home.

Background and atmosphere: Milton Abbey, with 76 acres of rolling countryside, is one of the prettiest schools in the country. You can't fail to be enchanted by the ancient abbey nestling in a wooded Dorset valley, 15 minutes' drive from Blandford. 'It's deeply rural, but not remote,' is the head's description. We visited on a sunny day but were assured that it looks lovely in the rain and mist too. The school was founded in 1954 and occupies the converted monastery buildings. The vast abbey belongs to the Diocese of Salisbury but the school has full use of it, with services four times a week. Milton Abbey also has its own farm (complete with pigs, sheep, goats, turkeys and chickens), makes its own honey and grows flowers, fruit and vegetables.

Pupils eat all their meals in the Abbot's Hall, a grand dining room complete with stags' heads and

a huge mural of the school painted by a parent to commemorate the school's 50th anniversary in 2004. Pasta, salads, wraps and paninis on offer at lunch-time, as well as hot meals, plus snacks at break, fresh fruit and cake in the afternoons. 'No one goes hungry,' grinned one boy. Uniform is smart. Younger girls wear tartan skirts and blazers while sixth form girls are clad in grey skirts and tweed jackets of their choice. Boys wear tweed jackets, grey trousers and ties.

Pastoral care, well-being and discipline: Pupils keep the same tutor from year 9 to year 11, and see them two or three times a week. In the sixth form students get a say in their choice of tutor – often someone who teaches them or whom they have a good relationship with. School operates a system of rewards and sanctions when it comes to behaviour – awards given for good work, sporting achievements and acts of kindness.

Entrepreneurship in Residence competition aims to inspire pupils to launch their own business

Good communication with parents – school has introduced a new parent portal where parents have access to weekly notes on everything from a missed prep to an academic triumph. Pupils told us that 'there aren't hundreds of rules. They give you a degree of trust.' Student voice is considered important. Head boy and head girl (who meet the headmaster every morning), heads of houses and a raft of prefects – called 'pilots' here.

Pupils and parents: Pupils come from 120 or so prep schools and from all over the country – quite a few from London and from as far afield as Northumberland. International students from France, Germany, Italy, Kenya and the US. Day pupils ('our day fees are really competitive,' says the head) tend to live within a 30-minute drive. School minibus service covers Blandford, Wimborne, Poole, Dorchester, Shaftesbury and Salisbury. Day pupils leave at 6pm but there's the option to stay on for activities and prep if they wish.

Despite such privileged surroundings, the pupils we met were outgoing, enthusiastic and delightfully unsnobby. Sixth formers summed the school's appeal up in a nutshell. 'For the people it's right for, this is the best school in the country,' one boy declared. 'I love it. My sister's at Millfield and her year group is as big as this whole school. Here, everybody knows everybody and the support you get is second to none.' A girl said she liked being 'a big fish in a small pond' while parents told us they

love the family atmosphere, plus the fact that their children get loads of country air and aren't glued to their phones, tablets and laptops.

Former pupils include Professor Jonathan Freeman-Attwood, the principal of the Royal Academy of Music, screenwriter and TV director Harry Hook, restaurateur Oliver Gladwin, sculptor Robert Rattray, documentary maker Anthony Geffen and Professor Alastair Bruce, royal, religious and constitutional affairs commentator for Sky News.

Entrance: School is 'inclusive and non-selective.' Around 70 per cent of pupils do CE – pass mark is around 50 per cent but school is flexible on this and says 'there's no hard and fast rule.'

Applicants attend a taster day to see if the school suits them. Usual entry points are 13 and 16 but a handful of pupils – six in 2015 – start in year 10, often because they didn't settle at their original choice of school. Milton Abbey doesn't chuck pupils out if they don't make their GCSE grades either. Head believes that when a school accepts a youngster at 13 it should stick with them for the duration.

Exit: School loses a few pupils after GCSEs – largely due to relocation or for financial reasons – but equal numbers join from other schools. At 18 or 19 pupils choose a plethora of routes. In 2015, one to Oxford, others to Queen Mary University of London, Royal Holloway, Swansea, Royal Agricultural University, Harper Adams, Falmouth School of Art and Guildhall School of Music and Drama. School has strong links with international catering colleges, such as Glion and Les Roches in Switzerland, and several pupils have headed to these in the past.

Head points out that 'a degree isn't a guarantee of a job' these days and is keen on courses that 'will facilitate future employment.' He admits that if he was choosing a degree now he would probably go for vocational journalism and media rather than English. School has forged a close relationship with The Arts University Bournemouth, which specialises in art, design, media and performance across the creative industries.

Money matters: A range of scholarships at 13+ and 16+ – academic, all-rounder, art, DT, drama, music and sport. All worth 10 per cent of the fees, although these may be increased 'where financial need is demonstrated.' School also offers means-tested bursaries, plus scholarships for day pupils living in Dorset.

Remarks: Milton Abbey's setting, countryside expertise and innovative mix of qualifications give pupils, some of whom may not have thrived elsewhere, a host of opportunities to shine – both inside and outside the classroom.

Monkton Prep School

Combe Down, Bath, Somerset BA2 7ET

01225 831202
admin@monktonprep.org.uk
www.monktonprep.com

Ages: 2–13 (boarders from 8)
Pupils: 254 (155 boys, 99 girls)
Boarders: 37 full, 9 weekly/flexi
Day: £8,730 – £15,984 pa
Boarding: £21,378 – £23,040 pa

Linked school: Monkton Senior School

Head: Since September 2014, Andrew Marshall-Taylor, previously deputy at Twickenham Prep. MA from Edinburgh and PGCE from Cambridge. Taught French and German at Rugby School and RGS Guildford. At both schools, he was master in charge of hockey, and has a strong track record of involvement with the Duke of Edinburgh Award Scheme. Has been actively involved in the Christian life of the schools. Married to Rosie, who taught art, photography and history of art at Surbiton High School until recently.

Entrance: Essentially non-selective. Parents pleased that the entry policy allows a wide range of abilities and types, though they're even more pleased that the standards achieved at Monkton Prep rival schools that select. 'The best prep school in England,' one told us. Boarding numbers have doubled over the past few years, so the feel is definitely of a boarding school with day pupils, especially as there is a significant tranche of pupils from abroad (some 35 per cent of boarders). Informal interview for pre-prep. For the prep at age 7, interview plus tests (English, maths and verbal reasoning). Parents are mostly local professionals and business folk, and a few Forces' families too – an easy mix of the churched and the un-churched. New year 7 scholarships for academia, art, music, sport and drama.

Exit: Some 60 per cent to the senior school at 13, but CE scholarships mean significant minority aim at major independents – Cheltenham, Canford, Bryanston, Brymore, Millfield.

Remarks: Fiendishly hard to find down a genteel residential cul de sac, school has a dramatic hilltop setting with great downland views. The stunning

sweep of the cricket pitch and leafy lawns isn't spoilt by the mish-mash of school buildings tacked onto the back of the manor house.

Academically sound and according to our pupil guides offers a stimulating and enjoyable education. Despite its non-selective ethos, a parent told us that there are plenty of 'incredibly able' children about. Two-form entry in years 3, 4 and 5; streaming from year 5 and an extra scholarship stream added in year 6. Saturday morning school for year 4 and above. Smallish classes (16 to 17). Lots of emphasis on finding out what a child has to offer. Masses of reading lays a foundation for this, with a programme of author visits and a library offering books, board games and beanbags. Long established learning support staff – 'a cracking team' – offer in-class support, handwriting and spelling groups.

Children carry journals and too many negative entries result in Saturday detention – but slates are wiped clean every quarter term. The worst sanction, exclusion for disruptive behaviour, is hardly ever needed. Tutors know children well enough to sense when something's wrong so potentially bullying is picked up quickly but 'children do fall out' and need a 'chat.' Enthusiasm for school meals and even more for the three nurses who care for boarders (and day children when needed).

Pre-prep and nursery in a separate converted villa that retains its homely feel. Building work has started on a new pre-prep and nursery building which will from September 2016 link to the prep school and include new play spaces plus upgraded sports centre and swimming pool.

Plenty of sport. Classy pool and new Astroturf hockey pitches (used by senior school too). Great opportunity for competition in top years as the corresponding years in senior school play friendlies against them. Music of every genre – a culture of singing and oodles learn instruments. Some top notch music scholarships to senior schools for the best. Art and drama, with a plethora of expert staff and a chance for everyone to join in. Bags of time for play (not sure how they fit it all in) but even on fine days they are not forced out at break.

Boarders live in Hatton House which overlooks the golf course and has views across the valley. Boarding numbers have increased in recent years as has the number of pupils from abroad. Up to 70 pupils stay during the week with around 30 or so in at the weekends. Plenty going on at weekends including trips to Wales, Dorset Coast, rock climbing, cinema and shopping in Bath. After church on Sunday there's roast dinner and time to relax. Computers rationed for boarders, but with dedicated daily Skype time for keeping in touch with home.

The school's evangelical Christian ethos underlies all aspects of education here. A happy place, where much is expected and much achieved. Staff, and therefore pupils, work to the highest Christian principles of honest work, self-discipline and concern for the needs of others. 'It teaches how to be a good person,' said one firmly non-Christian parent, 'and allows children to be accepted and to make their own minds up.' Pupils come first, education next but never as second best. Though open-minded, and progressive in the ways which matter, this is an unashamedly and all pervasively Christian foundation

Monkton Senior School

Church Lane, Bath, Somerset BA2 7HG

01225 721102
admissions@monkton.org.uk
www.monktoncombeschool.com

Ages: 11 –18
Pupils: 387; sixth form: 145
Boarders: 198
Day: £8,730 – £19,503 pa
Boarding: £21,378 – £31,113 pa

Linked school: Monkton Prep School

Principal: Since January 2016, Christopher Wheeler, previously principal and CEO of Hillcrest International School, Nairobi, Kenya. He has an English and philosophy degree from Durham and a PGCE from Bristol. Taught English at St John's, Leatherhead; then he moved to Peponi School, Kenya, as deputy head, boarding housemaster and head of English and drama. Back in the UK he became a housemaster at Brighton College and then head of St Christopher's, Hove, part of the

Exams still feel on the tough side to them, so those we met were proud of their results and parents gave across-the-board thumbs up – 'the brightest are definitely stretched'

Brighton College family of schools. He is married to Georgie, who teaches English and sport and is a keen rider. They have three young children, who will join the school.

Academic matters: In 2015, 70 per cent of GCSE grades A*/A, and 34 per cent of A levels. For a 'not particularly selective' school which has 'a default position of supporting a pupil's ambitions, even if they are a long shot' this is fairly respectable. Pupils say they enjoy lessons, work hard and get lots of encouragement. Exams still feel on the tough side to them, so those we met were proud of their results and parents gave across-the-board thumbs up – 'the brightest are definitely stretched.' School is currently upping its academic image. Though intake at year 9 'gets a gentle ride' (gives them a chance to settle between CE and the start of GCSE syllabus) bright children are taught 'up to their level.' Class sizes 18 to 20 up to GCSE, smaller thereafter.

Safe curriculum for GCSE, with few soft options. Mandarin now available at KS3. Increasing number of subjects going to IGCSE. One or two languages for all except extra English candidates at GCSE. Latin but no Greek. In science top set do three separate sciences and the rest dual award. A level courses include photography, theatre studies, sports studies, DT, critical thinking and psychology. Some smashing maths results – shiny new £4 million maths and science centre may have helped, plus programme of university links enabling sixth formers to get placements in science research departments. Smartly refurbished arts and crafts library, now renamed learning resource centre.

The learning support unit is sound but the school is no longer registered CreSTed as Monkton provides only for minor difficulties. Nonetheless it is inclusive and copes well with unusual children and physical problems. Students get up to 45 minutes a week one-to-one and teachers are tuned into special needs and work with the learning support unit. Study skills on offer too.

Games, options, the arts: Strong for a smallish school, with the expected trio of rugby, hockey and cricket for boys and hockey, netball and tennis for girls. Male and female tennis players sponsored by LTA via the University of Bath. Rowing's the in thing – perhaps not surprising with a new Olympian rowing coach Matt Wells (won bronze at Beijing). Several former pupils have achieved national and international rowing success, including Steve Williams (who won Olympic golds in 2004 and 2008) and Alex Partridge (who won silver in 2008). Pupils don't have to be sporty – but the surroundings encourage them, as do the facilities – new Astro surfaces, good sports hall, picturesque cricket.

Music has had a huge boost with new £3.2 million music school (opened by Felicity Lott and

Richard Stilgoe) complete with magnificent wood-lined auditorium, multitudinous teaching and practice rooms and larger rehearsal rooms, all the electronic mod cons of recording and manipulating music. Some pretty impressive piano playing doing justice to the brand new Steinway during our visit. List of successful ex-Monkton musicians is growing. Every sort of music, including lively jazz, professional sounding big band and rock bands (always the sign of a truly musical environment).

Art and DT rooms extended and refurbished – exhibition space plus print-making, textiles, photography and CAD areas; A level artists rival mathematicians in the success rates. Lots of exciting stuff – sculpture, photography and first-rate painting. Lashings of drama, with ambitious productions (Shakespeare and Dickens as well as more contemporary shows) and good enough facilities, though they are in the list for development. Visiting artists and workshops, links with local galleries and University of Bath. Art trips abroad every other year, plus exchanges, music trips et al.

CCF is an attractive option. School building up community service. D of E on the up. Other activities include poetry, creative writing and Dearlove Society (focuses on European intellectual life – Camus, St Augustine, the influences of classical Greece – and ends the year with a frisbee competition in Greek robes).

One boarder said it didn't matter if his friends were day boys because he had so little time when they weren't there, and anyway he got on with everyone

Boarding: Flexible boarding available up to year 9, which can include three, four or five nights a week. From year 9 it's full boarding or day. Day pupils can sleep over if necessary, however (they get 10 boarding nights a year free of charge), and most go home so late it hardly seems worth it. One boarder said it didn't matter if his friends were day boys because he had so little time when they weren't there and anyway he got on with everyone. Houses are run like families, with pupils learning to take responsibility. The number of day pupils who come in at weekends is good measure of how much there is to do. Full Saturday programme of morning lessons followed by afternoon sport mean other weekend activities are necessarily fairly low-key – film nights, barbecues, informal concerts. Seven boarding houses – four for boys, two for girls and one junior house.

Background and atmosphere: Campus still has a whiff of the school's clerical foundation. Founded in 1868 by the evangelical Revd Francis Pocock, school started with five pupils. School is still popular with clergymen and missionaries. Since merging in 1992 with girls' school next door it's been fully co-ed, with a prep and a pre-prep. The setting at the bottom of a deep-cleft valley is ravishing – sufficiently isolated to feel safe to parents but handily near Bath for weekend shopping and other forays, say pupils.

The school is centred on its strong Christian tradition. This is embodied in the attitude of staff to children and symbolised by such groups as the International School Society and array of social projects it initiates at home and in far-flung places. Pupils definitely buy into respect for each other's needs and personalities. A parent reports a commendable understanding of the occasional oddball. The vibrant Christian Union is run entirely by the students and around a third attend every week. No Sunday service but a large number go into Bath or to local services (often those aimed at university students) of their choice.

Pastoral care, well-being and discipline: 'Pastorally brilliant,' say parents, many of whom add that this was their reason for choosing Monkton. The house system (mixed ages but single sex) involves boarders and day pupils alike and husband and wife houseparent teams include both in their care. Houseparents are profiled on boarding pages of school website with family photos, lots of background information and homely details about dogs, baking etc. Reassuringly un-corporate.

Academic tutors attached to houses, though in the sixth form pupils choose their own tutors, The system aims to support, inspire and encourage good working habits and is part of the network of personal support which characterises Monkton. Induction for prefects teaches them to be kind, not martinets. Definitely no sense of parading prefect privilege, though they are proud of their level of responsibility

The trust between pupils of all ages and pupils and staff is very evident, for instance in the dining hall where the interchange is informal and considerate. Statistics show no bullying. 'We pick it up before it's a problem,' said one tutor. 'If you know a child you can see when something is wrong.' One might wonder if this is a little too trusting? One parent definitely felt that cooping up large number of teenagers in a small valley brings its own problems and that pastoral staff have sometimes been a bit naïve, though principal is tougher than his charm suggests. Problems are tackled and for teenagers this is a safe place where they can be themselves and there is unfailing support for the troubled.

Pupils and parents: Popular, of course, with evangelical Christians and those who want the values, but plenty of non-subscribers too. Seven-day boarding week is good for the many Forces' families. Wide geographical range, including 10 to 15 per cent international students (20-plus nationalities). International tradition strong and long established. Some need ESL support, but all are tested in English before arrival and many go straight into mainstream English classes. Cultural acclimatisation is thoughtfully addressed too.

Some pretty impressive piano playing doing justice to the brand new Steinway during our visit. List of successful ex-Monkton musicians is growing

School is handy for both ends of the M4, so London and Wales mix harmoniously. Children seem friendly, unpretentious and modestly confident.

School's church connections only account for part of the exalted list of past pupils promoted to glory on earth – former spymaster Sir Richard Dearlove, songwriter and humourist Richard Stilgoe, blockbuster novelist Bernard Cornwell,

Piers Forster (who shared a Nobel prize for climate change). The development department is doing a professional and very enterprising job keeping the school in touch with old Monktonians in the worlds of business and arts.

The setting at the bottom of a deep-cleft valley is ravishing – sufficiently isolated to feel safe to parents but handily near Bath for weekend shopping and other forays

Entrance: Monkton looks for 50 per cent plus at CE. Standard rising. Special needs evaluated to make sure a pupil will cope comfortably with what has become a slightly more academic curriculum. 'Definitely pulling out of their less able image,' a parent commented, but parents of 'strugglers' are delighted with unexpected A*s and As. Pupils come from Monkton Prep, St Andrew's School (Turi, Kenya), Castle Court, Mount House, Rose Hill, All Hallows and Summer Fields.

Exit: About 80 per cent go through to sixth form. Up to 10 Oxbridge applications per year – though only a smidgeon get in (two in 2015). A tranche to good solid courses and good solid unis, Exeter to Edinburgh, and plenty to useful-looking vocational courses including art college, not on the whole the whacky sort. Plus some to US and other countries.

Money matters: Bursaries on offer to children of missionaries and clergy – means-tested. A clutch of academic, art, drama, music and sport scholarships on entry to years 7, 9 and 12. Has secured a £2 million donation for the school and is embarking on a £35 million development programme – seriously confident in straitened times.

Remarks: A school that sees itself as on the up, its image polished by a super-efficient development department busy developing everything in sight. Governors clearly have no fears for the future. Despite the ongoing makeover, its Christian ethos shines out in the unforced friendliness and directness of its pupils and through the disciplined but loving care of its staff. Service to others comes first, but confidence and academic achievement are treasured as the means of achieving it. One parent said, 'I thank my lucky stars every day that I found Monkton.' These boys and girls go on to do well and to do good.

Mount Kelly Prep

Mount Tavy Road, Tavistock, Devon PL19 9JL

01822 813193
admissions@mountkelly.com
www.mountkelly.com
C of E

Ages: 3–13 (boarders from year 3)
Pupils: 245
Boarders: 40 full and flexi
Day: £6,375 – £12,960 pa
Boarding: £14,970 – £21,600 pa

Linked school: Mount Kelly

Head of Prep: Since September 2014, Matthew Foale BEd MSc (early 40s), previously head of Kelly College Prep, which merged with Mount House school to form the new Prep at Mount Kelly as part of the Mount Kelly Foundation. Mr Foale is in charge of the Prep, but he is responsible to Mark Semmence who, since September 2014, has been head master of the senior school and overall head of the Foundation.

Mr Foale, born, bred and educated in the West Country, has a PE degree and achieved his MSc while teaching, sure evidence of determination and organisation. Before joining Kelly Prep as deputy head in 2009, he was director of sport at The Hall School in Hampstead and then deputy head of Orley Farm School in Harrow. Married to Marie-Claire, who trained as an art therapist and is now manager of a care home in Plymouth. Three children. Commutes from Plymouth every day. 'It's an easy journey and gives us a well-balanced life.'

He appears to have enjoyed the challenge of combining two very different prep schools. He is delighted, both that no pupils (presumably from Kelly Prep) have been lost in the transfer and that some of his 13+ candidates are now considering the college. One parent said that Mount parents and Kelly junior parents are essentially different, but form a strong parent body, thanks particularly to the contribution of the head and deputies' wives, who are 'amazing' and go to everything, giving 'modest courageous and warm support'. Pupils who were a little overshadowed in the rarefied Mount House atmosphere have blossomed in the larger context. Thoughtful and calm and with obvious integrity, he clearly has an eye for detail without losing an awareness of the overall picture.

Entrance: Wide ability range – tests in English and maths 'more for benchmarking than selection,'

says head. Most entrants attend a taster day in February prior to admission. Majority join the pre-prep at start of year 3, but growing numbers delay start until year 7, transferring automatically to the college at 13.

A few means-test bursaries available.

Exit: Pupils prepared for 13+ transfer to the College at Mount Kelly or elsewhere. Presumably any pupil wanting to 11+ transfer elsewhere is prepared for this. The hope is for the majority of prep children to move into the main college at 13.

Remarks: In the merger which established the Mount Kelly Foundation in June 2014, Kelly Prep children moved into the sumptuous Mount House facilities, which are conveniently adjacent to the main Mount Kelly College buildings. A bridge over the road (still at planning stage when we visited) will mean that the prep will benefit from the college's impending Olympic size pool and college pupils gain access to the prep's sports hall, extensive grounds and other impressive facilities.

Stunning grounds include a trout stream (ideal for fly fishing) and a beautiful lake (great for science) bordering on Dartmoor National Park. A recent team of inspectors dubbed it 'an inspirational learning environment'. The prep is based in and around an elegantly proportioned, stone-built Georgian manor house with an assortment of additions, some historic and some ultra-modern purpose built. The attractive hall, accessed rather curiously through an office rather than its lovely

Recycling motivates the highly organised CDT department, where self-sufficiency is second nature and everything from day-old chicks to bicycle wheels finds a use

glass doors, fulfils a variety of functions including regular assemblies and church services. The head's oak-panelled study leads off on one side and the school dining hall on the other. Upstairs are all the boys' and girls' dormitories in separate areas plus the sick bay. Dormitories of between four and eight are extremely well designed, with bathrooms etc between each pair of dorms. Boys' rooms are clean, fresh and pretty tidy, while the girls obviously like to express themselves more freely via plenty of pictures, and personal touches.

A plethora of buildings clusters behind the main house, some old and definitely unusual – the original stables have been converted in a variety of ways, including the 'giraffe house', which features

a climbing wall, plus some really impressive purpose built facilities: the modern sports hall (with two squash courts), two large science laboratories and impressive music school. Music had a bit of a hiatus after the merger but seems to have recovered to 'even better than before', partly thanks to the 'best singing teacher in the universe'. 'Proper' church choir contributes to festivals etc and music is definitely 'in'. Full orchestra, jazz band, woodwind, choir, rock band all perform regularly. The school has a record of music and art scholarships, and the inviting art department had work on display which more than explained this.

Prep schools with such an array of enterprising ventures are few and far between, especially in deepest Devon. Recycling motivates the highly organised CDT department, where self-sufficiency and sustainable technology become second nature, and everything from day-old chicks to bicycle wheels finds a use. It is masterminded by an enthusiast who also runs a small farm in the school grounds. All ages contribute and 'truly love it'. Amongst animal and other agricultural activities, pupils are building a sustainable hut which even provides it own electricity (solar micro generators) while the tractor runs on the kitchen's recycled vegetable and the water supply comes from a borehole.

Most of the classrooms are an extension of the main building: attractive internally – some with stunning displays – and all with high level of equipment (smartboard in every classroom). Eighteen PCs in IT suite and staff are mostly IT savvy. 'Some fantastic teachers with a wide variety of styles from formal and well organised to lots of fun' – but all of them kind and good at building confidence. Mount House parents had valued the long term view that a third of all ex-pupils end up at Oxbridge, and this ethos has not disappeared. The recurring theme from parents, however, is that teachers are kind while children enjoy lessons and are happy. 'Mix of old timers and new blood on staff works well,' commented one father. Average class size is about 16. Curriculum is designed to allow pupils to go off piste and generate individual enthusiasms. High quality of written work wherever you look; motivational French lessons was another strong point noted.

Director of studies acts as SENCo with some 35 pupils on special needs register. Pupils are screened for dyslexia and a dedicated education psychologist will develop an IEP if required. Two part-time SpLD staff give one-to-one help where required.

Pre-prep in purpose-built, low level accommodation for 60 children up to end of year 2 with discrete outside area. High level of care and individual attention – most pre-preps transfer seamlessly aged 7. Lots of fun and outdoor experience for this end of the school, as well as developing strong foundations in the classroom basics.

Most pupils spill out into grounds after prep, but there are also lovely hidey-holes in the subterranean library for dedicated bookworms, and a space for quiet relaxation

Boarding ethos is all-important, especially to day pupils. One who begged to do a term's boarding loved it and found it problem free. No cliques or bullying and the occasional loner supported and encouraged. The new régime has relaxed some of the compulsory weekend elements but includes Saturday evening pick-up after activities, then low-key, on-site Sunday programme. Ten couples/families live on site and rotate weekend duties. Early signs are encouraging, with boarding numbers apparently on the increase. All staff stay here until 6pm every day; prep finishes at 7pm for older pupils (younger ones have clubs) and duty team of staff remains until dorm staff take over at 8.30pm. Most pupils spill out into grounds after prep but there are also lovely hidey-holes in the subterranean library for dedicated bookworms, and a lovely

---

The Shackleton Award scheme (junior D of E type project) was in full swing doing splashy things down by the enchantingly beautiful lake during our visit

decked space for quiet relaxation complete with multi lingual telephone box.

Five days a week sport here – facilities include fine pitches, heated outdoor pool (very popular) and full size Astroturf; national/regional successes principally in rugby, cricket and girls' hockey. Boarders love to play in the nets or swim after prep in the summer. Pony-mad pupils get a look in with the local hunt and inter-school equestrian events. The Shackleton Award scheme (junior D of E award type project aimed at building confidence) was in full swing doing splashy things down by the enchantingly beautiful lake during our visit. The exceptionally beautiful grounds with waterfall and sloping lawns are meticulously managed by a groundsman who is endlessly kind to pupils, and even to parents with engine trouble or no petrol.

Pupils are well turned out – variety of dress according to age and season; they come mainly from Devon and Cornwall, professional, farming and Forces families plus a few from London or elsewhere (very few overseas). Twice-termly lectures, alternating between the prep and the college, for parents and pupils across the Foundation, tap parental know-how: recent outside speakers have included explorer Pen Hadow and yachtswoman Tracy Edwards. Lots of local visits for all ages, annual trips to Northern France for the older pupils and regular ski trip to Alps. Former pupils include Phil de Glanville (England rugby captain), Adrian Lukis (actor in Pride and Prejudice), former foreign secretary and SDP co-founder, Lord David Owen, and explorer, long-distance swimmer and environmentalist, Lewis Pugh, to name but a few.

This combination of traditional prep and local junior schooling has given the far west a potentially remarkable school. One parent commented that the last few days of summer term are a triumph and say it all. Pupils leave, whether to take up academic, sporting or artistic scholarships at the college itself, or other schools, able to 'catch a fish, thread a sewing machine and bake a cake', full of the confidence to face the next step eagerly.

Mount Kelly

Parkwood Road, Tavistock, Devon PL19 0HZ

01822 813193
admissions@mountkelly.com
www.mountkelly.com
C of E

Ages: 11–18 (boarders from 7)
Pupils: 540; sixth form: 100
Boarders: 148 full, 20 weekly
Day: £6,375 – £16,440 pa
Boarding: £14,970 – £28,740 pa

Linked school: Mount Kelly Prep

Head Master and Principal of Mount Kelly Foundation: Since September 2014, Mark Semmence, previously assistant head at Rugby School. An economist with degrees from Durham (BA and MBA), London (PGCE) and Warwick (MA), he taught at Ludgrove Prep, then worked in international sports marketing before returning to teaching. Played cricket for England Schools U19 and Durham University; a member of MCC Youth Cricket Committee. Married to Alison; they have two young daughters. Mr Semmence cites architectural history as one of his interests, which is probably just as well as he has inherited a building whose Victorian architect clearly thought that the naval officers it aimed to produce required a medieval monastic training.

He is certainly equal to the challenge, having managed to pull off a universally excellent Independent Schools Inspectorate review within six months of taking the merger of Kelly College and Mount House into the Mount Kelly Foundation.

This has involved a restructuring of both staffing and of the way the prep and the college relate. Parents comment that he has been 'ruthless about upping academic teaching standards'. Masses of 'rebranding' has been done to tempt both local day pupils and traditional 'public school' boarding. He must have done a remarkably thorough and well-planned job, as ISI normally requires 'embedded values': hard to achieve in six months. He has also acquired a swimming pool left over from the London Olympics. Wow!

Academic matters: Mount Kelly is one of those schools brave and sensible enough to eschew the 'league tables'. A level results commendable in 2014 and 15, especially for a school which is not academically selective, with maths definitely impressive at all levels. Mr Semmence's new team is to be congratulated on increasing the percentage A* in 2015, when the exam boards were notoriously stingy. Twelve per cent A*, 36 per cent A*/A and 53 per cent A*-B grades at A level, and 17 per cent A*, 44 per cent A*/A grades at GCSE in 2015.

Class sizes are small – sometimes very small at A level. Currently the school will put on a course for one pupil – sadly necessary since the take up in modern foreign languages, art and music is select but able. Pupils we spoke to were full of praise for the extra help offered by their teachers when necessary. A good range of solid academic subjects on offer, with excellent language and IT areas. Parents spoke of the expert and sensitive advice they had had from staff when trying to help their children choose the most suitable subjects for them. Perhaps fewer now feel the urge to go further afield for a 'real academic education'. Parents and pupils speak very highly of the help given to those with special needs.

Games, options, the arts: Mount Kelly is rapidly becoming synonymous with swimming. Its reputation, built up over 30 years, is currently growing under the tutelage of Robin Brew, ex-pupil and international and Olympic swimmer, who heads a team of coaches of similar calibre running a comprehensive coaching programme for swimmers with competitive ambitions. The programme is built round the academic day and so is considerably less stressful and probably less expensive than the constant travel, early mornings and compromises with school that many young swimmers

Despite its gentle lawns and lush green pitches, a craggy looking place, all gothic arches, dark wood and stone staircases, echoing corridors and lots of pointy bits

have to make. A parent commented that only one or two British schools have anything like comparable swimming and coaching facilities, and that Mount Kelly's pastoral care for such pupils is leagues ahead. To crown it all, a third pool to latest Olympic standards purchased from the London Olympic site is being installed. No wonder the school boasts that, on average, a Mount Kelly swimmer a year has represented the UK either nationally or internationally.

Non-swimmers, however, are far from sidelined. Pupils spoke with enthusiasm of music, debates and outdoor activities, and there are myriads of curriculum supporting events. It's a lively place but also cheerful, friendly and definitely not frenetic, even at exam time. It is old fashioned enough to insist on school blazers with ribbons and badges festooned all over athletic gods and goddesses, but musicians, artists, thespians and prefects can be equally decorated – the school is just good at celebrating and acknowledging. The pitches and grounds in both Prep and College areas are superbly managed and the acquisition of the Mount House School site has brought the one missing element, a fantastic sports hall. It will be a real boon for the seniors once there is a bridge across the A386 into Tavistock. Sport plentiful but traditional – rugby and cricket for boys and hockey and netball for girls. Both girls and boys play hockey and compete in a mixed summer league.

A splendid and most interestingly designed performing arts centre with superb facilities for music, drama and debate – to say nothing of interval entertainment – is close by, as is the art building with evidence of creative painting and pottery. Since the college snuggles into a valley on the edge of Dartmoor, it's hardly surprising that outdoor education, D of E, CCF and all those sort of things are available and popular. Huge numbers of girls as well as boys complete the 125-mile canoe marathon from Devizes to Westminster and the Ten Tors expedition, as well as training as divers, rifle shots and mountaineers.

Boarding: Despite its monastic appearance, the renovated sections of boarding are exceptionally well done. Clever planning means that day pupils and boarders can socialise on the lower floors with plenty of well-equipped work and milling about space, while the bedroom floors above remain private. We were not taken to the 'unreconstructed' areas but, since two out of four houses are already redesigned and the others proceeding apace, most pupils entering now will not see them either. The four houses are divided into girls' sixth form, boys' sixth form and two co-ed houses for years 9-11, each managed by housemasters with a team of tutors drawn from academic staff as well as non-teaching matrons. Full medical service on hand. Boarders spoke enthusiastically of the sixth form centre and the activities arranged at weekends. Flexi boarding is very flexi.

Background and atmosphere: The buildings, tucked under the edge of Dartmoor just outside the pretty little town of Tavistock, have historical connections with the Duke of Bedford, who donated the land for the college, founded in 1877 by an Admiral Kelly. Despite its gentle lawns and lush green pitches, it's a craggy looking place, all gothic arches, dark wood and stone staircases, echoing corridors and lots of pointy bits. Academic mustiness, however, is banished by skilfully placed features of interest, pictures, honours and information about the school's past and the pupils' futures. Handsome library presided over by enthusiastic librarian and dusty looking (actually it isn't) chapel still exuding an odour of past sanctity, used four times a week.

Huge numbers complete the canoe marathon from Devizes to Westminster and the Ten Tors expedition, as well as training as divers, rifle shots and mountaineers

Attractive new buildings higher up the hill behind the Victoriana, one of them the delightful Conway House, where the younger boys and girls live in comfortable harmony before joining the senior houses. Co-ed has been going here for nearly 40 years, so it all feels very relaxed and natural.

Pastoral care, well-being and discipline: Lunch in the dining room (masses of choice – cooked meals, salads and faster-looking stuff – particularly delicious lemon posset) was a good insight into the relationships between staff and pupils. Enough mutual respect and genuine affection to allow friendly banter on occasions. The pupils were forthcoming, friendly and honest in their conversation with us, though we were not shielded from meeting the odd awkward customer – treated with helpful sympathy and understanding. While accepting that bullying was always a possibility,

they felt that the tutorial system in place was a good safety net and protection – always someone to talk to; above all they said they genuinely like the staff. Pretty common sense school rules result in very little indiscipline. Pupils all looked smartish, though lots dressed in mufti or sportswear towards the end of the day.

Pupils and parents: Parents come from a broad spectrum. Mount Kelly is trying to bridge the gap between being a good local option for the West Country and an upmarket public school. Boarding is boosted by swimmers from England and abroad. One parent commented: 'My son can swim but hates it. But he gets stuck into lots of other things and that's the point. I take the view that excellence breeds excellence.' Others praise the community feel among parents, stressing how welcoming they are to families who move to Tavistock for schooling. The pupils we met and observed were open, friendly and trusting, and we noticed how much family-like interaction existed between the different age groups. Though there is definitely a sense that Mount Kelly is on its way to joining the league of 'top schools', it still feels a friendly, relaxed place where children can be children as much as is possible in this day and age.

Entrance: At 13+, about 75 per cent of entries come from the prep. Academically, the emphasis is on literacy and numeracy, with as much attention paid to potential as to knowledge. Entrance at sixth form is based on GCSE results (or equivalent) – normally about 20 new sixth formers joining each year. The important thing is to be alert, bright-eyed and willing to be taught. That applies as much to rugby players as potential Nobel Prize winners.

Exit: Three-quarters go on to the sixth form. Nearly all of these to university. A sensible number to well established ones all over the UK (and occasionally USA) to do old fashioned academic subjects and one or so a year to Oxbridge proves they can do it.

Money matters: Scholarships and bursaries are available. Forces families may receive 10 per cent discount – don't be afraid to ask.

Remarks: Definitely worth watching. The signs are that it may succeed in providing an excellent environment for girls and boys set on local schooling as well as building up a boarding clientèle based on academic success enhanced by the lure of swimming. A sound, progressive place, where effort is rewarded and friendships flourish, unhampered by snobbery or over-sophistication, and on its way to giving the West Country a really fantastic school. Numbers up in the college with more boarders this year, so the signs are positive..

Perrott Hill School

North Perrott, Crewkerne, Somerset TA18 7SL

01460 72051
admissions@perrotthill.com
www.perrotthill.com
C of E

Ages: 3–13 (boarders from 7)
Pupils: 218
Boarders: 9 full, 51 weekly/flexi
Day: £6,105 – £14,910 pa
Boarding: £17,550 – £21,540 pa

Headmaster: Since September 2015, Tim Butcher (30s), previously deputy head at Winchester House School.

Entrance: Pupils may enter aged 3, when they will spend two years on the Montessori foundation course before joining years 1 and 2 and thence the prep school. In fact boys and girls may join at any stage, providing room. We met a girl who had joined aged 11 and found it 'very easy to settle in'. No formal test but taster days, then, 'Providing we feel we can do a good job with them, we'll offer a place'. Staff refer any concerns to the excellent learning support team and the children are given help and encouragement when necessary. Scholarships and bursaries are available – do ask.

Exit: Currently the most popular destinations are the three Taunton schools and other local schools such as Milton Abbey, Canford, Bryanston, Downside, St Mary's Shaftesbury, but that list only tells part of the story. Eton, Marlborough etc have featured, as have many others. Pupils regularly win a good spread of scholarships and the school prides itself on matching children with appropriate senior schools, something appreciated by parents and registrars.

Remarks: Once you reach the pretty village of North Perrott, you need to keep a sharp look out for a small sign to the school. Driving down the lane shuttered with branches, do not cease from exploration nor be deterred by the road sign that informs you are following a dead end: remember this is Eliot country, where 'In my end is my beginning' – but there's nothing dead about Perrott Hill. Through beautifully-kept gardens and past the converted stables, you will then come to what was the manor house, built in 1878 by the architect Thomas Wyatt, described by Mark Girouard as 'tireless and tedious'. The house itself is much of the first and nothing of the latter. It has been adapted marvellously since it became a school during the second world war and the children love it. Wonderful big L-shaped hall which acts as an assembly room/chapel. When we visited a blazing log fire was much enjoyed by children and staff. A superb focal point, where everyone can congregate and chatter. Library now moved to the orangery.

Most boarding schools trumpet their 'family atmosphere' – here it is the real thing. Part of the reason is that 12 members of staff live with the 50 or so boarders (the numbers have just about tripled in the last three years). Excellent head of boarding is responsible overall. He and his wife look after the boys; a junior housemistress and experienced matron look after the girls. The dormitories have recently been painted and there are new showers and loos. Each house has a common room, more like a family room, with inviting chairs for lolling around, television and facilities for making toast and hot chocolate. Staff, including three gappers, and children mingle happily together all under the same roof – that's family atmosphere.

Do not cease from exploration nor be deterred by the road sign that informs you are following a dead end: remember this is Eliot country, where 'In my end is my beginning'

Full, weekly and flexi boarding are all available, but increasing popularity has made flexi-boarding harder to come by. Exeats from Friday pm to Sunday evening every three weeks; in between family Sundays where the boarders eat with the staff and generally behave as they would at home, sometimes going to the nearby beach, local town for shopping or to the cinema. Also massively popular activity Sundays, themed and varied. When we visited they were gearing up for a circus weekend when they were going to learn juggling and other activities. The children are extremely enthusiastic about them and parents talked of the need for booking up well in advance. From year 5 all pupils attend Saturday school: morning lessons and games in the afternoon. Matches take place most Wednesdays and Saturdays.

This ambitious programme would be impossible without a fizzy, dedicated staff. We saw some terrific teaching. No interactive whiteboards – just interactive teaching, supported by projectors and intelligent use of computers. Extracurricular activities with staff seem boundless and the mutual affection and respect between staff and pupils are extraordinary. One youngish teacher in response to a question about moving on replied, 'This school is a graveyard for ambition. Why on earth leave this?' Too much of a comfort zone? Results and attitudes don't support that suspicion. This is an active and positive school, not a sanatorium for professional skivers. The children (and staff) are friendly and forthcoming, wearing their manners like well-worn clothes and not as straitjackets.

Since it is a small school, everyone gets involved in all the main activities. Sport is for all and results are impressive. Traditional games are played on five afternoons a week and the school regularly punches above its weight. A number of pupils go on to represent the county and some regularly win sporting awards to public schools. Drama, too, is enormously popular, as is public speaking, art and music, with over 70 per cent learning musical instruments. Facilities are good without being flashy – indeed some of the teaching buildings are a trifle scruffy. The science lab, for instance, is very basic, but the children and parents we spoke to were enthusiastic about the education offered there. Plans are in place to upgrade the lab, but that won't improve the teaching. Another area which is distinctly cramped is the art and DT department, housed in the old hayloft above the converted stables. Since it is a listed building, expansion is restricted, but no restrictions on the creative energy and ingenuity of the young artists. Everyone has two lessons of art a week; scholarships and prizes at local shows confirm the standard achieved in that cramped but lively place with excellent teaching – ask about Captain Pugwash. Most of the classrooms, however, are bright, airy and congenial for their purpose. The music department at the top of the house is well kitted out with practice rooms and computers – music is clearly important.

Two sports halls – as the school grew, the original one proved too small for its original purpose but has been skilfully converted into a spacious and well-used theatre; a larger one was opened recently with space for indoor hockey, cricket nets, netball, fencing – you name it. Outside, tennis courts (hard and grass), a heated swimming pool and good games pitches – though ideally more – including new Astroturf. The house is surrounded by 25 acres of woodland and scrub where children muck about happily in boilersuits, construct dens, invent games and on occasions in the summer enjoy what the pizza cob offers. On the day we visited, a seal would have longed for shelter, but it's not hard to imagine the fun and laughter ('the children in the apple tree') echoing round the gardens and woodlands in this idyllic spot. No wonder Perrott Hill boys and girls 'retain the wonder of childhood'.

Art and DT housed in an old hayloft above the converted stables. Expansion is restricted, but no restrictions on the creative energy and ingenuity of the young artists

But in order for children to feel really happy and fulfilled, they need to be loved and secure within a clear framework. Each child is assigned a tutor who closely monitors work and morale; a clearly defined Circle of Friendship addresses any unhappiness. Staff and pupils are alert to any evidence of bullying (neither of our guides could remember any) and every week the staff discuss the work and happiness of every pupil. In addition to the resident matrons, another matron comes in every weekday afternoon to help with anyone who is feeling ill or 'just feels like a chat' – all part of the family.

For many the start of the Perrott adventure takes place in the pre-prep, safely and excitingly housed in the cleverly converted stable block close to the big house. There, using the Montessori method, they learn to learn, gaining in confidence and, while safe behind the gates, use the appropriate facilities of the prep school. 'It's lovely having them around,' said a senior girl.

Parents whom we asked spoke appreciatively of the coach service (the school runs three minibuses) not only because of the convenience but also because of the personal service. The three excellent groundsmen, who have been at the school for ages, know the children well and will go out of their way to make special and individual arrangements. One father talked of his amused delight at watching one of the drivers delivering his two young sons with one tucked under each arm, an image which in many ways sums up the joy of Perrott.

We have never come across such universal appreciation of a school. It's hard to find fault with this idyllically placed and excellently run 'traditional prep school', and we failed miserably. One parent told us that at the start of each term he murmurs, 'And all shall be well and all manner of things shall be well.'

Pinewood School

Bourton, Shrivenham, Wiltshire SN6 8HZ

01793 782205
office@pinewoodschool.co.uk
www.pinewoodschool.co.uk
C of E

Ages: 3–13 (boarders from year 5)
Pupils: 403
Boarders: 41 weekly, 83 flexi
Day: £8,049 – £16,425 pa
Boarding: plus boarding supplement £4,008 pa

Head: Since 2002, Mr Philip Hoyland BEd (50s), educated at The Downs, Malvern, followed by Cheltenham College. Read English and education at Exeter; previously housemaster, then deputy head, at The Dragon. Married to the warm, compassionate Henrietta; they met at Ludgrove when she was under-matron and he a rookie teacher (they have three grown-up children). Very much a partnership, her gentle humour a foil for his sense of adventure; both fully involved with the school (she is head of girls' boarding and central to much of school life).

Articulate, charming, a gentleman, Mr Hoyland wants education to be explored, and enjoyed. Seeks to offer 'non-conformist, old-fashioned values, coupled with innovative learning.' More than a sense that his Quaker heritage (his great-grandfather was businessman and philanthropist George Cadbury) shapes his views. Says, 'we work hard to ensure we have happy children here, it is difficult to do anything if they are not; children need to take risks, to be excited'. We watched as gaggles of animated youngsters flocked to his side, eager to tell of their day, show off work, badges, awards. Parents say he is kind, an intellectual and fantastic with the children, 'they adore him', but seemingly he's not always quite so good with parents: 'He's not a gushing head and if you expect your child to always be the star of the show you're probably not going to get on too well here.' Other mutterings that he backs staff over parents, but all unanimous that he really has propelled the school forward.

Entrance: Mainly via nursery and pre-prep; register early. Deliberately takes broad-ish ability range, 'deal with what we get', but always considers what is in child's best interests (occasional one helped to move elsewhere). Assessment for entry into prep. Handful with parents at nearby Defence Academy (nominally for a year or two, but many convert to boarding and stay). Most years full with waiting lists, though movement, especially of day children, and flexibility for additional groups, means places materialise.

Exit: Primarily Marlborough, Cheltenham, Dauntsey's, St Edward's Oxford, Sherborne and Stowe – amongst others. Occasional early departure from parents who believe school isn't pushy enough, yet they annually win a clutch of

scholarships (art, music, academic and all-rounder) to a selection of schools.

Remarks: Founded in 1875, moved to this pretty Victorian Cotswold stone house in 1946. Nursery and pre-prep in former stable block with fantastic play area in old walled garden.

Noughties, and the arrival of the Hoylands, saw shift from a school languishing in the doldrums – 'it really was falling down,' said one parent – to one riding a wave, albeit with choppy interludes. 'There was too much complacency; we had made strides but not leaps', admitted the head. 'Our parents were shocked but it allowed the final clearing of driftwood'. Now vast majority of teachers are head's own appointments; admits he has taken a few risks, going for the fizzy or alternative to encourage excitement and develop a joy of learning. This strategy hasn't been lost on the youngsters; pupils were eager to tell what they had learned, and how: 'Exciting teaching, kind teachers, some a bit mad but the good thing is you remember what they say, it stays with you and they will always help'. We saw super maths model villages (lots of nets and shapes, fashioned into 3D high streets); we even gently teased our charming guides about the designer outlets and Jack Wills stores; they responded with good humour, enthusiasm and grins. We were dragged to the plush changing rooms (complete with under-floor heating) but the boys didn't swallow our tease that we especially loved the girls' sauna and steam room (alas not yet!). They got their own back with tales of 'breaking the ice' in the outdoor pool – not literally, but an annual event that usually sees the head dive in first, followed by a posse of pupils.

Now vast majority of teachers are head's own appointments: admits he has taken a few risks, going for the fizzy or alternative to encourage excitement and joy of learning

Only the caffeine kept us from drifting off as the head recounted the extensive building work but, as we toured, we began to appreciate how fundamental the redevelopment has been to the Pinewood metamorphosis, with library rehoused in renovated Orangery, super performing arts centre, new sports hall etc. Pupils certainly appreciate the changes, possibly nowhere more so than in science where the newish labs have opened a whole world of discovery and experimentation. Indeed, we were hijacked by an endearing chap who insisted on explaining his classification diagram (task carefully differentiated) and cheerfully showed us the errors his partner had made, and how they were putting them right. Refreshingly, this is a school where children are encouraged to make mistakes, take risks, explore their learning and get it right.

French from 4, Latin from 10, Greek and philosophy for scholars, enrichment for anyone who will benefit. Classics, French, science and maths top the popularity bill but, unusually (for a prep school), history and geography under kids' radar: 'They lack the zing of other subjects,' was parental response. ICT important for all, even wee ones are encouraged to Google. Usual plaudits for art, groans that DT had been chopped for older years and applause for drama and music (including ensembles, jazz band, a chorus of choirs and inclusive performing opportunities). Daily sport for all ('cept Thursday which is given over to activities); every child has ample opportunity to represent the school. Lots of motivational messages on notice boards and gentle reminders: 'win with honour, lose with dignity.' Thanks to new sports director, PE back with a bounce, carefully thought out, planned and linked to games programme, health etc. A hardy bunch, practise in all weathers; used to lose at everything but no longer the case, indeed they are recent National Junior Cross-Country Riding Champions and recently became mini schools show jumping, cross-country and eventing champions.

Solid learning support and a genuinely multi-sensory approach mean those with mild dyslexia, dyspraxia, ADD (bluetac et al for fiddlers), high functioning ASD are well served. Access arrangements and laptops if needed. OT, speech and language therapy, play therapy, in-class learning support plus one-to-one or small groups as required (most incur additional fee) but not the place for those with moderate or severe needs who need frequent, or intensive, support.

Quietly Christian (aside of the rousing hymns), emphasises tradition, kindness, fun and adventure. Think greenhouse not hothouse; tender plants (and tough weeds) will be nurtured, watered but not pruned, though delicate darlings might flounder: 'We are about climbing trees and falling out.' Very much preparing children to make choices.

Boarding genuinely popular and on the wish list of many; handful of full boarders (fortnightly exeats mean grannies and guardians essential for boarders from far-flung corners). Comfortable, squidgy, homely accommodation and great food, including imaginative vegetarian choices, continental cuisine and school-dinner stalwarts. Squabbles usually sorted over a mug of hot chocolate in Mrs Hoyland's kitchen. Unpleasantness dealt with promptly, no complaints from anywhere on that score; only slight grumble from parents is that communication dwindles as pupils move through the school. Reading room (much loved by youngsters) and old chapel provide quiet spaces, with games room (table tennis, air hockey, snooker) for the active. German spotlight (risk assessed) a unanimously favourite pastime. 'It's so dangerous,' said one wide-eyed youngster, then quickly added, 'well, only kind of', doubtless concerned that we might be among the spoilsports keen to curtail anything remotely daring.

Think greenhouse not hothouse; tender plants will be nurtured, though delicate darlings might flounder: 'We are about climbing trees and falling out'

Parents proud that it remains steadfastly a local school; majority live within an hour's drive. True country prep, car park more mud-splattered four-by-fours than flashy Ferraris. Concentrates on extending childhood – the pre-pubescent 'up-do, make-up and manicure' brigade would either roll-up their sleeves and regain their innocence – or, likely as not, hate it. Very much for those happy to don a boilersuit, roll down a hill, climb a tree, play hide and seek or chase through a meadow.

Wellies essential, rain or shine, outdoors as important as in. Annual activities week for each year group the icing on a well-filled cake. Pinewood is one of the country's leading outdoor schools (they even have an award to prove it). It's not just the Astro and sports pitches but the tree-tops adventure, outdoor classroom, fairy garden, child-friendly woods, super sensory gardens; colours for the youngest, then scented, smelly, touchy

Suits the worms, germs and stones brigade; aim for children to fall in love with learning (we suspect most tumble head-over-heels). Carefully planned in and outdoor activities

feely and finally a polytunnel of polygons, plants, maths and more.

Pre-prep headed by the energetic, triple-hatted director of learning. Suits the worms, germs and stones brigade; aim for children to fall in love with learning (we suspect most tumble head-over-heels). Children encouraged to explore their learning through carefully planned in and outdoor activities. Parents genuinely welcome to spend time with their child at beginning and end of the day; no classroom barriers here. Learning is multi-purpose and multi-sensory, extending well beyond the regular primary diet. Learning of 'oo' in moon includes the baking of tasty m'oo'n rock cakes and tracing sounds in sand. Parents appreciative – 'they are really good at getting the basics firmly in place' – though another added, 'Lots end up having learning support which costs extra,' adding cynically, 'You wonder if so many really need it or if it is just prevention better than cure mentality.' School disputes this, saying only 18 per cent of pupils have learning support with fewer than two per cent in pre-prep (equating to handful of pupils max) – so seems perception is misplaced. Curriculum 'wow' days have seen youngsters take off on a variety of adventures including transatlantic travel: office converted to aircraft, check-in desk, tickets, airline food, sick bags – an experience so real, one boy cried at the thought of flying without mum.

Good at building confidence; suits the London day school refugee, but not a place for the London set, nor for those into clicking heels and clucking 'Yes sir, no sir.' If you could recreate the secret garden you'd probably do it here; active children fizz with enthusiasm, happily maintaining the innocence of a bygone era but with the benefits of modern technology and teaching. A genuinely wholesome school that emphasises cooperation rather than competitiveness, confidence not arrogance and and team before me. Especially good for the creative boy or girl with boundless energy, sporty or not, and limitless curiosity.

Plymouth College

Ford Park, Plymouth, PL4 6RN

01752 505100
mail@plymouthcollege.com
www.plymouthcollege.com
C of E

Ages: 11–18
Pupils: 512; sixth form: 180
Boarders: 144 full, 11 weekly
Day: £12,645 – £14,970 pa
Boarding: £25,245 – £28,920 pa

Headmaster: Since April 2015, Jonathan Standen, previously head of The Crypt School in Gloucester. He has also been deputy head at St Augustine's Catholic College and Bishop Wordsworth's School and assistant head at Hardenhuish School, all in Wiltshire. Formerly a qualified ski instructor, he has been a rugby and cricket coach and is a keen cyclist and golfer. His partner, Suzie, is an accountant.

Academic matters: Outperforms itself academically given wide range of ability in intake. Increasing number of students doing IGCSE (49 per cent A*/A grades at I/GCSE in 2015). At A level, 60 per cent A*-B and 30 per cent A*/A grades – maths and economics popular and strong. IB cohort averaged an improved 34 points each. Outstanding national success in business competitions spearheaded by head of sixth form and IB co-ordinator, who was a finalist in recent national teaching awards.

Year 7 pupils remain largely in mixed ability groups with setting in core subjects and French from year 8 upwards. RE compulsory to end of year 9 and thereafter optional RS at GCSE and A level. We watched several lessons including a lower English

set in year 10 fairly buzzing with its creative writing task and sixth form geographers making shoreline models out of Play Doh. Sixth form business studies/economics students were thrashing out how to survive a 'fire in the warehouse' of their imagined company in realistic fashion. Students can choose Latin, German, Spanish or classical civilisation in year 8. Small classes: five to 10 students common at AS and A levels, with average of 16 in younger years. Sports and adventure baccalaureate for those wanting a hands-on as opposed to academic route in sixth form.

Staff tend to stay here but we noted how younger staff take initiative when it comes to giving workshops on new approaches to learning. 'Very inspiring,' said one old hand. Excellent library open daily for homework and research until 5.30pm, linked cultural activities such as Andrew Motion poetry workshop and enrichment days.

Effort put into making transition from own prep and other feeders as smooth as possible. Contact with future pupils can start as early as year 4 and parents praised sensitivity of head of year 7 and the 'comfortable feeling in school' for new arrivals.

Comprehensive learning support based in suite of three rooms at top of Victorian turret, with spectacular view over Plymouth Sound. More than 100 students receive help with specialist staff able to tackle SpLD and a variety of other needs. Individual and drop in sessions before school, at lunchtime and after school. SEN co-ordinator worked previously at Plymouth state school and offers counselling alongside learning support. Key information shared securely online with staff. All pupils screened for dyslexia in year 7 and class-room assistants employed with statemented pupils if appropriate. One mother praised how her son's memory had been boosted by use of innovative resources. Separate EAL unit for overseas pupils.

Games, options, the arts: On-site sporting facilities include 25 metre heated indoor pool (low chlorine content helps those who spend hours in it every day), sports hall complex with two squash courts, original school playing field with 1st X1 cricket square and now an adjacent mini all-weather pitch. Delganey is eight-acre site, with own changing facilities for rugby etc including first XV; slightly nearer is new Olympic standard Astroturf (owned and shared with Marjon College). Plymouth Life Centre (on doorstep) is now 'icing on the cake,' providing Olympic standard pool complex.

Captain's house exclusively for elite swimmers has clinched this option for serious minded athletes who rise at 5.30am

---

Sporting reputation on international footing thanks to highly successful partnership with Plymouth Leander swimming club: four swimming scholarship pupils competed in the London 2012 Olympics, including gold medallist Ruta Meilutyte, who powered her way to a shock win in the 100m breaststroke, and bronze medallist diver Tom Daley. Host of accolades for school's top stars who achieve unparalleled national and world class success. Impressive rugby results: Devon Cup champions in each year group and senior player in U18 England rugby team. Representative colours for rugby at U20 level for England, Irish Exiles and the South West. Modern pentathlon and fencing academy with national athletes and full-time coach. One girl is double British fencing champion. Other recent successes include a sixth former making top 10 in world clay pigeon shooting rankings, horse riding and triathlon. County successes in netball, hockey, athletics, cricket and tennis. Squash and basketball academies (latter with Plymouth Raiders).

House system fosters community spirit and inter-house competition: many events held at lunchtime. Activities fair organised in September for younger pupils to choose from extensive lunch-time and after school menu; seniors have Friday afternoon activities programme which includes CCF, D of E, art and junior sports leader award.

Flourishing outdoor education department has specialist vehicle, fleets of mountain bikes and kayaks and makes frequent use of Whiteworks (school's own outdoor residential centre on Dartmoor for up to 20 pupils). CCF had been in decline but has been revived under ex-regular CO. Contingent is made up of both Plymouth College pupils and those from a neighbouring comprehensive: 'a good experience for both lots,' we were told. Shooting range can be modified for either cadets or pentathletes. School enters 35, 45 and 55 mile Ten Tors teams, with serious overnight training on Dartmoor beforehand. Recent sixth form expedition to Annapurna in Nepal involved survival at high altitude. Ecovation (college's young enterprise business) won national honours and even sold one of the company's bird feeders to cabinet minister Vince Cable. Visits pile up on each other and range from scuba diving off Gozo to helping to build accommodation at a Gambian school. Annual activities week for years 7 to 10. Careers programme includes introduction to workaday world in year 8 through 'The Real Game' and work experience in lower sixth.

Plenty of practice and performance rooms for music. Over a quarter of pupils take instrumental or singing lessons; chamber orchestra and wind band brass group both strong. Chamber choir had successful music tour to Prague, lower school and year 7 choirs meet at lunchtimes. Two boys in national youth choir. In-school concerts often fundraisers for charity eg £900 towards educating orphans in Gambia. Annual remembrance service draws congregation of more than 1,000 in St Andrew's, Plymouth. Recording studio and performance hall with professional audio and lighting equipment. Music scholars showcase talents at evening concerts and there's a creative arts week at end of school year.

Separate art house displays fantastic artwork. Recent Good Schools Guide winners in art and design A level categories. More than 40 take art in sixth form (emphasis on fine art) and photography and digital graphics especially popular. We enjoyed seeing a year 9 class making face masks using strips of gummed tissue paper as part of their work on the human body. 'Inspired' drama department. Studio space (in former squash court) for GCSE and A level work plus large stage in main auditorium for major productions.

Introducing a sports baccalaureate, which enables talented athletes to combine their training with IB studies.

Boarding: Experienced married couple run joint boarding house on main site: boys are accommodated in three houses to one side of the houseparents' flat and girls in three on the other. Room for more girls when we visited. Firm, parental-type discipline based on reward and praise. Mainly shared study bedrooms with modern facilities and 'lashings of hot water for showers etc,' say pupils. Common rooms and kitchens are well used. Occasional boarding offered to day pupils (up to 14 nights per term).

Separate sixth form house, plus newly converted accommodation with single rooms for sixth formers opened over past few years. Distinct international flavour in boarding houses – all get along and one English boy told us, 'it's better than being at home.' Captain's house exclusively for élite swimmers has clinched this option for serious minded athletes who rise at 5.30am. Activities at weekends range from bowling to surfing, with more relaxed régime generally. No moans about food: modern cafeteria style dining area and portions to match the consumer. Bacon baguettes in sixth form centre from 8am, with snacks and coffee available through the day.

Background and atmosphere: Founded in 1877, Plymouth College has sprawled towards nearby Mutley Plain (in contrasting architectural styles) from the castellated, granite fortress that formed the original school. Embraces a number of Victorian villas and houses that provide mainly boarding and office accommodation. Reception area lined with photos of medal-bearing Plymothians, leaving no doubt about school's strengths. A myriad of corridors and doors make for a quiet and peaceful atmosphere, though must be somewhat daunting for newcomers.

A Christian foundation, but neither chapel nor daily service. Assemblies held separately for different years in 1970s auditorium. Staff applications are high volume: a dream for any committed teacher. American style yearbook provides a glossy annual overview (we particularly liked the inclusion of cleaners and catering staff).

Sixth form senior prefects adorned with graduate-style gowns when accompanying visitors or on special days. Day pupils from varied social and professional backgrounds. Red piping on blazers for main school and double breasted blazers or charcoal grey suits for sixth form boys and girls respectively. Lessons finish at 3.30pm but most are on site until 5.15pm, when coaches leave. Future Council looks after sustainability and green issues generally whilst active school council voices pupil concerns. Recent charity fundraising included leg waxing for year 11 boys and a staff v pupils swimming gala.

Pastoral care, well-being and discipline: Generally felt to be a happy and caring place, with good relationships between day pupils and boarders, including elite athletes. Buddy system, trained listener and school nurse available for listening ears. Matrons in each boarding house. Imaginative rewards for good behaviour; bullying seems to be rare but well dealt with.

Pupils and parents: Very international: 27 nationalities currently on roll, with some two-thirds of boarders from overseas. Largest contingents of overseas boarders from Germany and Spain, but plenty from China, Africa and Americas as well as Eastern Europe. Introduction of IB and the high profile sports programmes account for the growing international interest. Well-presented and polite mixture though different cultural mores sometimes call for careful management. 'Elite swimmers in top 10 per cent academically,' we were told and staff see these athletes as role models for others. Parents we spoke to had 'no axes to grind' and subscribed to a 'healthy body, healthy mind' philosophy.

Active parents' association organises social events, helps at key functions and raises funds for school's wish list.

Former pupils include David King (developer of the CT scanner), former Labour leader Michael Foot, landscape painter Gerry Hillman, Welsh rugby player William James, comedienne Dawn French and Olympic diver Tom Daley, to name but a few from an impressively long list.

Entrance: Wide range of ability on entry. Some 50 per cent enter from own prep, with remainder from mix of local primaries and some independent. Day catchment area extends from Fowey in Cornwall to Exeter in Devon. Often lower ability than neighbouring grammars on 11+ entry, but GCSE and A level results compare favourably. Six GCSE passes, including maths and English and a minimum of three B grades to enter the sixth form.

Exit: Higher than usual percentage take a gap year. About half head for traditional courses and universities, with remainder covering everything imaginable. Oxbridge entrants few and far between,

but three places in 2015. Increasing number look for sports scholarships at American universities (four off the US in 2015) and IB also opens up wider possibilities, especially for Europeans. Alongside Bristol, Exeter, London, Plymouth and Cardiff, pupils off to Paris, Dusseldorf, Canada and Australia.

Money matters: Year 7 academic scholarships available (up to half tuition fee). Similar year 9 plus awards worth up to one third remission for art, music and sports. Sixth form academic scholarships worth up to one third remission for outstanding candidates including two IB scholarships. Rugby, golf and swimming scholarships plus other sports awards. Also a limited bursary fund. Modern pentathlon and fencing programme with scholarships on offer for this discipline.

Remarks: Plymouth College has bucked the boarding trend and reinvented itself as a thriving international campus – to the benefit of locals. Combines a sense of tradition with an unapologetic commitment to excel at what they do best.

Port Regis Preparatory School

Motcombe Park, Shaftesbury, Dorset SP7 9QA

01747 857800
office@portregis.com
www.portregis.com
C of E

Ages: 3–13 (boarding from year 3)
Pupils: 300
Boarders: around 125
Day: £8,670 – £17,997 pa
Boarding: £20,250 – £24,300 pa

Headmaster: Since January 2016, Stephen Ilett, previously head of Milbourne Lodge in Surrey. History degree from Oxford (where he played rugby for the first XV); spent 18 years at Lloyd's of London before moving into education. Taught for eight years at Caldicott, becoming director of studies and head of year 7. Wife Amanda will play a major role in school life; they have five children, most in their 20s, between them.

Entrance: Main entry points are nursery and year 3, but school adds about 10 pupils in years 4 and 5, a dozen in years 5 and 6 and a handful in year 8 (usually foreign nationals). Children come from own pre-prep, local state primaries and other prep schools, including London preps. Entry is via interview with the head, present school reports and assessment (verbal and non-verbal reasoning tests). School accepts those with mild learning difficulties, but children must be able to cope with CE syllabus.

Exit: With such a wide-ranging intake, pupils scatter to more than 30 different schools. Most popular destinations are Sherborne Boys' and Girls' Schools, Bryanston and Marlborough, then Canford, Claysmore, King's Bruton, Millfield and St Mary's Shaftesbury. A number go to Eton, Cheltenham Ladies', Harrow, Radley, Rugby, Winchester and Wycombe Abbey. Boys and girls regularly win a good clutch of sport and academic awards each year, along with all-rounder, art, design and ICT scholarships and exhibitions. Tally of music awards looks to be rising. Most stay until 13 (a very small number leave at 11) and almost everyone in pre-prep moves up to the main school.

Remarks: Located in 150 acres of sweeping Dorset parkland, it's tempting to reach for more and more superlatives when describing Port Regis. Previous reviews have likened the campus to Disney World and classrooms to Trump Towers in New York

(which of course they aren't) but it's still safe to say that this is a magnificently equipped prep school and could easily be mistaken for a good public senior school. Sense of 'other worldliness' perhaps arises from the exceptional architecture (different for each building), well-equipped classrooms, out-standing facilities, central lake (with fountain) and extensive playing fields and grounds. One might almost expect to be whisked away by monorail from the car park. Main school building is a Victorian mansion built in 1894 by Baron Stalbridge (younger brother of the 2nd Marquis of Westminster) sur-rounded by a collection of modern, purpose-built additions. School was founded in 1881 by Dr Praetorius, a German native, in Weymouth St, London W1 and moved to Motcombe Park in 1947 from previous homes in Folkestone, Broadstairs and Bryanston. Latin for 'Kingsgate', Port Regis was renamed after it moved to premises in Broadstairs (Charles II landed there in 1863).

Although only mildly selective, academic results are good and getting better. Parents con-firm that teachers are enthusiastic and always quick to respond to any queries. 'I couldn't be more impressed with them,' said one. Fabulous school buildings doubtless make teaching and learn-ing more efficient, eg Cunningham Hall (maths, science, art, DT and SEN), which feels especially light and spacious thanks to acres of glass walls. Humanities subjects are housed in an innovative building which self-regulates temperature; 12 bore holes descend 80m into the ground to provide geo-thermal heating and ventilation is controlled via automatic air vents. ICT suites also in this build-ing and in keeping with the 'no expense spared'

nature of the place there are virtual noticeboards everywhere, displaying school diary, running house point totals, match results etc. More tradi-tional classrooms for younger years in the mansion, which makes sense as their dorms are here. School library is located in oldest part of the school too, and is rather charming (elaborate Victorian room makes a change from all the modernity elsewhere).

Up to 20 fixtures are arranged (memories of searching pitch after pitch one Wednesday trying to find the right rounders match)

Maths is set from year 4, humanities by subject groups and everyone is streamed for all subjects by year 6. 'The good ones are pushed quite hard and the less good are helped quite hard.' French is taught from the beginning and Latin from year 6; scholars also learn ancient Greek and one CE set studies Spanish instead of French. Tuition in other languages, including Mandarin and Japanese, is available as an extra. Class sizes average 14 (with a maximum of 20); generally few more boys than girls. Around 20 teachers have been on the staff for more than 10 years, but parents say a host of newer recruits have 'immediately absorbed the energy.' Specialist EAL teacher for small groups of children whose first language is not English (about 25). Spacious SEN department for those with mild learning difficulties (44 on the register when we visited), also tutors scholars to iron out any performance difficulties. Parents report progress in post-CE programme.

Well known locally for its sporting prowess, school has on average a dozen teams for all the usual major sports, including boys' hockey. Up to 20 fixtures are arranged each Wednesday and Saturday (memories of searching pitch after pitch one Wednesday trying to find the right rounders match as a visiting school parent). It is rare that any Port Regis team loses more matches than they win and some are undefeated all season (although school breathed a small sigh of relief when 1st XV rugby team's seven-year winning streak finally came to an end as the pressure was off for a bit). Two squash teams (boys), six girls' tennis teams, golf and swimming teams also have busy fixture lists. Gymnastics is exceptionally strong here and school has a dedicated gymnasium with sunken trampoline which hosts national IAPS championships. Boys and girls win gold medals galore and school has won 'Overall Best School' title for more than a decade. Second sports hall, two squash courts, 25m swimming pool, shooting range and nine-hole golf course are all (except older sports hall) as well-appointed as the gym. Individuals also compete successfully in athletics and riding. The downside of all this sporting talent is that 'Port Regis is the school everybody wants to beat.' Those

Nursery and pre-prep are so delightful that one finds oneself thinking that teaching small children might make a rather agreeable career change. Wonderful rustic forest school

not blessed with all-round sporting talents need not worry too much. 'If children aren't good at a particular sport, it isn't frowned on by the rest of the year.'

Farrington music school, a stone and glass octagon with views over school grounds, would be the envy of many a senior school. Fabulous air-conditioned recital hall (those superlatives again) is at the heart of the building, circled by 14 practice rooms. On the floor below there are extra rooms for ensemble coaching and class music lessons, a recording suite and music technology room. Around 75 per cent learn an instrument and over 400 individual lessons are scheduled each week. All 8-year-olds learn recorder and all 9-year-olds violin, free of charge. School has three orchestras and multiple choirs including boys' close harmony barbershop ensemble. Schola Cantorum has undertaken successful choir tour to Italy and we observed its choirmaster (blessed with seemingly boundless energy and enthusiasm) conducting a very creditable E and F form (year 3 and 4) choir. Ensembles include swing band, samba group and two string quartets.

Three rooms for DT, computers for design and huge art studio with some very good work on show. Pottery teacher apologised profusely that most of her pupils' best work was out on display at local gallery when we visited (what was left behind was still good). Several drama productions each year are staged in Centenary Hall which has tiered seating and a stage. School has links with Shakespeare Birthplace Trust and offers LAMDA coaching. List of over 70 hobbies is of dizzying length (beekeeping, French movies, quilting and web design to name just a few) and activities happen between early evening 'famine queue' and supper. 'Every evening there's something to look forward to.'

Pastoral care is very much at the forefront and school aims to instil five core values in every Port Regian: hospitality, perseverance, reconciliation, generosity and respect (parents say efforts are working). Children choose their own personal tutor from C form (year 6). School is 'quick to sort any bullying and will listen to parents.'

Boarding provision is excellent. Senior girls have the most luxurious surroundings with individual 'cubies' (complete with own wash basin), separated with a bead curtain at every 'door.' As usual, girls' cubies are awash with posters and

cuddly toys, whilst boys' cubicles (though along the same lines) relatively unadorned. Games room in senior boys' boarding house, complete with pool table and table football, is probably envied by all. Everything spick and span, with dorms marked each week for tidiness (prizes for the winners). 'Beds have to be made and children keep themselves clean and tidy.' We noticed rotas for nit checks and boys' haircuts each week. A and B forms and overseas students have limited use of mobile phones; no 3G Kindles, iPods or iPads allowed. Home clothes are limited and girls not too conscious of what label they're wearing. Gap students organise weekend activities. No flexi-boarding, but staged entry to boarding is possible and school caters for individual requirements. School says that 'In practice boarding routine is very flexible.' Most go home on Saturday afternoons after school assembly, lunch (parents welcome to eat in school free of charge) and matches, returning on Sunday evening or Monday morning (often with a friend in tow).

Food is excellent, plentiful and most is locally sourced. Cafeteria is wonderfully spacious with panoramic views; atmosphere is informal and children can sit where they like. 'Children are encouraged to eat sensibly and they discourage fussy eating.'

Nursery and pre-prep are so delightful that one finds oneself thinking that teaching small children might make a rather agreeable career change. Wonderful rustic forest school built in nearby woods with campfire and wooden instruments made and used by the children (unaccountable whiff of the Lord of the Flies in all this rough-hewn woodwork).

Perceived wisdom is that Port Regis is the preserve of the very rich, but in reality children come from a wide variety of backgrounds. Some wealthy families, but others choose the school because 'it offered the most on the boarding front.' Means-tested academic and all-rounder awards – worth up to 50 per cent of school fees – are available for exceptional academic promise or ability in two extracurricular areas (eg drama and sport). Most children are British and live a short hop from the school, some come from London. Around 25 overseas British (including Forces) and about the same from Nigeria; others from Far East, Spain and Russia. No compulsory exeats so overseas pupils can stay in school at weekends. Children are confident, poised and polite. Former pupils include Bo Bruce, Jasper Conran, Ralph Fiennes, Peter Phillips, Zara Phillips, Henry Pyrgos and Bruce Sharman.

As we've said in previous reviews, it's difficult to find fault with Port Regis. Previously we might have singled out an overly competitive and sporty culture, but this looks to be changing. 'The school is trying very hard to make everyone feel included and part of a team.' Parents still feel that 'you have to be good at something [to fit in] here,' but also say 'if anyone is going to bring out what your child is good at, Port Regis will.'

Prior Park College

Ralph Allen Drive, Bath, Somerset BA2 5AH

01225 831000
admissions@thepriorfoundation.com
www.thepriorfoundation.com
RC

Ages: 11–18
Pupils: 590; sixth form: 200
Boarders: 95 full, 64 weekly
Day: £14,055 – £15,510 pa
Boarding: £23,670 – £29,745 pa

Head Master: Since 2009, Mr James Murphy-O'Connor MA PGCE. Educated at St Benedict's, Ealing, before reading history at Greyfriars Hall, Oxford, and then PGCE at Peterhouse, Cambridge. Began career at Stamford where he taught history, thence to Sherborne, where he was a housemaster before appointment to headship of brand new Sherfield in Hampshire. Father, Jim, played rugby for Ireland and was eldest of five brothers who attended Prior Park – most illustrious of them being (Cardinal) Cormac. Previous career experience was commendably outside the Catholic fold.

He is fourth lay head since Christian Brothers left in early 80s. Married to Ali, they have four children (all former or current pupils). 'Has worked really hard to get to know everyone,' say parents, who find him 'extremely easy to communicate with'. Acknowledges pupils' achievements in all areas (writes them personal, handwritten letters) and has won their respect. Parents like the way 'he looks you in the eye' and are impressed by how quickly he learns names. Has built up the boarding side, spearheaded the construction of the new sports centre and moved the school forwards with IT. Makes no excuse for pushing sport, particularly rugby, but is also keen on the arts: fan of F Scott Fitzgerald and Thomas Hardy, plus Picasso's 1920's art. Enjoys mountain climbing and surfing when able to get to family house at Mayo in Ireland. Intuitive understanding of Prior's mission; loads of energy, a firm faith and refreshingly open-minded.

Academic matters: In 2015, 75 per cent A*/B grades and 40 per cent A*/A at A level. Mathematics currently outshines sciences at this level, philosophy is outstanding but humanities and modern languages more than hold their own. Strength in depth and wide choice of subjects on offer are healthy signs. Head keen to consider new sixth form curricula but disinclined to embrace IB. We witnessed a lively A level philosophy session based on Nietzsche's ideas on property. Theology is compulsory throughout. Well-established PSE programme also reflects Catholic thinking and the resident school chaplain ('He's fab,' said one non-Catholic mum) plays a central rôle.

At GCSE in 2015, 51 per cent A*/A. Vast majority take separate sciences. Smartboards commonplace and some innovative teaching: we also watched an interactive year 8 maths class (pupils all had separate white boards to work out their answers) with a teacher (ex-PwC accountant) who was more hip than his pupils, with cool lines such as, 'I'm loving that answer – it's beautiful', to encourage even the most innumerate. Now teaches IGCSE maths. DT suite works well with lively staff: textiles area alongside well-resourced workshop and classroom areas. Good staff balance between experienced long servers and high octane younger blood.

Interactive year 8 maths class with a teacher (ex PwC accountant) who was more hip than his pupils

Highly experienced learning support team (one full-time and two part-time teachers) – heavily oversubscribed area (accounts for around seven per cent of 11+ entry each year). Applicants need psychological report; school now includes non-verbal test in entrance exam; thorough screening of all entrants for SpLD. Learning support situated alongside library and sixth form centre (some seniors help with paired reading). Open door policy; main emphasis on dyslexia and supporting literacy, but copes with range of specific learning difficulties including dyspraxia and mild Asperger's. Sixty-five pupils currently have individual learning plans. EAL is provided by two members of staff to overseas pupils – one of whom won last year's English essay prize: enough said.

Games, options, the arts: Sport, music and drama all impressive. Sport, though strong, doesn't dominate and achievement in the arts is equally recognised. Younger pupils get plenty of exercise (timetabled PE and games) and a good tradition of seniors helping to coach juniors. Recent appointments include top rugby coach from head's alma mater. More flexibility with sports options from year 10 upwards. Extensive playing fields plus Astroturf are all within jogging distance from the main school buildings. Strong fixture lists in

all sports with plenty of local rivalry. Basketball players use military facility at Colerne. Lots of representative athletes from district to national level. Sports tours are affordable – rugby tour to France latest venture. Major sports field 10 teams weekly; host of 'activity sports' plus Ten Tors, ski trips and D of E activities. Dance (offered to A level) has been a great hit: popular annual show features both sexes. Traditional Fisher Road Relay involving staff and pupils winds up Lent term enthusiastically.

New sports hall should plug a gap in sports provision; recently completed Mackintosh dance studio is up to professional standards. Planners prevented extension of indoor pool from its present, quirky 19 metres to 25, but it provides a well-used space. Old fives courts another area ripe for imaginative conversion (planners willing).

We discovered some keen sixth form artists (they enjoyed showing off their eye-catching folders) in suitably bohemian, basement studios, working on a variety of approaches under inspired direction; art and design centre recently refurbished. Not huge numbers for A level but plenty of passion and variety of work on display around the school.

Cracking music department fields three teachers with well-established director, Roland Robertson, whose reputation goes before him. Over half the pupils take instrumental lessons and standards vary from grade 1 to diploma level. Aim is to 'take pupils musically where their interests (and talent) lead them' – seems to bear fruit. Exquisite John Wood chapel provides venue for lots of concerts – we attended an informal ('get up and have a go') lunch-time one, following on from a junior brass practice which belted out a recognisable James Bond theme inter alia. Music to suit all tastes: high level of participation with several choirs, bands and orchestras. Opera every other year, annual musicals and a choral society which includes staff and parents – recent performances include Handel's Messiah and Verdi's Requiem. Many pupils participate in Mid-Somerset Festival. We liked the whole ambience of the music department (once we had panted up seemingly endless flights of stairs to reach it) – recording studio, class and individual practice rooms plus split level area for music technology (limited numbers who take it seriously at AS and A level here) taught by a musical housemaster. African drumming group especially popular with international pupils. Over 50 per cent of chapel choir are day pupils – incredible, given requirement to turn out every Sunday.

The Julian Slade Theatre provides a small but cutting edge theatrical environment. Three drama teachers and one theatre technician all have a professional background and it shows: no end to the number of productions (well, 23 actually in current year) from musicals (head of science directs these) to Ibsen and Beckett. Recent production of The Crucible got rave reviews. Parents 'brilliantly supportive' when it comes to meeting late night returns from theatre trips to Bristol etc.

Has gone overboard when it comes to activities: over 60 on offer each week with main slots on Saturday mornings (140 boarders and day pupils turn up for this) and Tuesday afternoons. Activities range from a Leith's cookery course to PADI scuba diving. Prior Concern for those in sixth wishing to get involved in community service. We saw one sixth former going through a tai chi form as his alternative to the prescribed Tuesday choices – 'Quite acceptable here,' confided an assistant head.

Majority join CCF at start of year 10 in either naval or army sections; well-organised alternative programme caters for the non-combatants. Compulsory residential course early in year 7 and team building day for year 8 pupils make for better relationships from the junior end upwards. Lots of educational visits including history trips, school exchanges with France and Germany, plus study visits to Spain. Recent pupil exploits include participation on polar and Uganda expeditions and national youth choir member.

Boarding: Boarding starts from year 9 and with about a quarter boarding and 30 per cent practising Catholics, it does not feel like yet another largely day school with token boarders or nominal religious affiliation. Seven senior houses (three mix day pupils and boarders and four have day pupils only). Roche and Allen are relatively civilised boarding houses for boys on the upper floors of the mansion, whilst girls are accommodated in enviable surroundings in St Mary's House, which occupies the nearby 'Priory'. Some day pupils opt to be in boarding houses because they prefer the ethos; weekly boarding is popular.

Background and atmosphere: Founded in 1830 and run by the Christian Brothers until 1981, now one of the largest independent co-educational, Catholic day and boarding schools in the UK. This position owes much to the successes of the three previous headmasters, who guided the school into the modern educational age. Unmistakably co-educational, with fairly even numbers of boys and girls throughout. Magnificent Georgian architecture of the 'mansion' provides backdrop for an unsurpassed vista over the grounds (much of which are now National Trust property, including the famous Palladian Bridge) and Bath beyond.

Imposing chapel accommodates whole school for weekly assemblies (impressive level of pupil and staff involvement). mass for whole school roughly once each half term plus particular feast days. Compulsory mass on Sunday mornings for boarders.

New ICT centre and is networked throughout school; well-organised library has 20 laptops which can be signed in and out. Pupils' use of fiction, reference and study areas speaks volumes for the self-regulating approach here. Day pupils have nominal workspaces in their rather crowded house accommodation, where prep is supervised between 4.50 and 5.50pm. Junior pupils split into small vertical

groups, which counters the risk of year 8s dominating within Baines House (recently upgraded) where juniors are registered. New sixth form centre comprises common room, café and study centre.

Former head's performance of Show Me the Way to Amirillo, dressed as Elvis, at the Staff in Your Eyes show, apparently 'brought the house down'

Pastoral care, well-being and discipline: Catholic approach 'looks at whole child,' insists head. Lots of help and advice from all quarters: 'Staff at Prior [compared with her son's previous school in Bath] are superb at following things up,' we were told by one mother, whose son transferred at lower sixth level. Reward system (head's distinctions doled out for all kinds of worthy endeavours) breeds a positive approach. No evidence of a punishment culture. Pupils are generally well turned out without being ostentatious. Strong counter-bullying policy and all sixth forms shoulder some responsibility through a variety of committees; pupil hierarchy survives in terms of a head boy and head girl together with heads of houses. Pupils are 'at ease with the staff,' say parents.

Half-terms are of sensible length (10 days in Michaelmas term) and don't exploit guardianship arrangements. Central but not overly accessible medical centre. Suite of dining areas copes with peak periods and provides good choice of menus to suit most tastes.

Pupils and parents: Most from within an hour's drive. Half of the leavers from own boarding prep school at Cricklade transfer to Prior at 13. Nearby Paragon Junior School provides good co-ed intake at 11. Six daily minibus and coach routes transport day pupils from a 30 mile plus radius. Boarders generally come from further afield, including a mix of overseas boarders. Good environment for language learning, insisted our Chinese guide, who spoke impeccable English. Former pupils and current parents are very supportive, with a range of fundraising and social events and pages on the school website.

Majority of pupils are non-Catholics. Religion is packaged sensitively for all persuasions. Former pupils have gained selection for England and Scotland under 21 rugby teams; others on masters degrees at Royal Academy of Music (choral and composition). Famous Old Boys include Cardinal Cormac Murphy-O'Connor (see above), former Archbishop of Westminster, famous musical producer, Sir Cameron Mackintosh, international rugby player Damian Cronin and television presenter Hugh Scully.

Sense of mutual respect between pupils and staff: 'No horrible teachers,' confided pupils. 'A school you have to immerse yourself in,' explained one new parent. Sixth formers have a particularly open and relaxed manner without being laid back. Pupil mentoring now under way. We liked the idea of information evenings for parents prior to each term's personal development programme (for pupils in years 7-11), which includes topics such as 'sex and responsibility' and 'respect for life'.

Student-run charities committee raise large sums during the school year – former head's performance of Show Me the Way to Amirillo, dressed as Elvis, at the Staff in Your Eyes show apparently 'brought the house down'. Worthy causes range from Searight Hospital to Aid for Albania. Parents join Saturday activities (eg Leith's cookery classes). Active parents' group hosts range of events (eg annual quiz served with curry and pud).

Entrance: Must register interest with the admissions department. January entrance tests for 11+ with majority of entrants coming from own 3-11 prep and about 20 per cent from state primaries. Non-verbal reasoning score used as baseline for assessment. Lists close at least a year in advance for LDP (see above) applicants. About 40 pupils join at 13+, with about half of them from the prep school at Cricklade, Witshire. November interviews

for entrants into lower sixth, who need a satisfactory reference and a minimum of six A*-C grades at GCSE, with higher grades in chosen A level subjects.

Exit: Few leave after year 11, most choosing to continue into the sixth form. Almost all to universities (lots take a gap year) with Cardiff, Exeter and Manchester recent popular choices, plus art and music courses. Regular successes at Oxbridge – one place in 2015.

Money matters: Extensive range of scholarships (academic, art, music, all-rounder and sport) and bursaries, with good academic scholars, typically gaining 30 per cent remission of fees. Services bursaries. Currently around 150 award holders (normal range between 5-50 per cent). Drama awards at 13 and 16. Some continuity scholarships from preparatory school. Discounts for siblings. Bus services charged monthly and quite pricey. Music tuition fees represent excellent value for money.

Remarks: School which suits parents looking for deeper values and an ethos which 'enables rather than prescribes'. Unusually successful at nurturing, encouraging and stimulating its pupils. Gentle Catholicism in the broadest sense within an inspiring setting and atmosphere.

Queen's College Junior School

Trull Rd, Taunton, Somerset TA1 4QP

01823 272990
junior.sec@queenscollege.org.uk
www.queenscollege.org.uk

Ages: 3-11 (boarders from year 3)
Pupils: 205
Boarders: 15
Day: £5,850 – £11,865 pa
Boarding: £12,780 – £22,500 pa

Linked school: Queen's College (Taunton)

Headmistress: Since September 2010, Tracey Khodabandehloo, educated in Wellington, Somerset, trained at Goldsmith's, London University. Started her teaching career in London, then completed her masters in Bristol whilst teaching in the city centre. Has been head of two well-respected Somerset schools and has also raised a family of three, two of whom were educated at Queen's. Hobbies include horse riding and travel. Passion for providing an interesting, challenging and motivating primary curriculum which focuses on the whole child.

Entrance: Many children come into the delightful pre-prep, a hop, skip and jump across the field. Others into the prep come via a day's visit for mutual assessment and a friendly test in maths and English. They are assessed again in year 5, to make sure they are on track for the senior school and to give them that extra confidence.

Exit: More than 90 per cent make the easy stroll across the grounds to the college to continue the great Queen's adventure.

Remarks: Much lively teaching across the board with involvement from the pupils and much interaction. This is where achievement as opposed to attainment come in. It's rare to find philosophy timetabled into a prep school, but here 9, 10 and 11 year olds have one session a week. Cynics may scoff, but the lesson we saw was wonderful – children were sitting around in a circle discussing whether the apple that was in the middle was alive or dead. Sounds cranky? It wasn't: what it did elicit was enquiry, evaluation, questioning what seems obvious (even pointless), which leads, in turn, to a healthy challenging of convention – wonderful assets in a carefully packaged, health and safety, risk-free society. It's around such emotional intelligence that the academic life of the school is run.

Nor are more conventional subjects ignored. The usual subjects are there, taught in bright and airy classrooms, but every class we saw was enlivened by the spirit of enquiry. Good learning support, where children have 40 minutes a week for help in essay planning, study skills and organising their time. Described as 'excellent' by one parent we spoke to; interesting sculpture and painting in the art rooms; good ICT and creative DT. A real feeling of buzz around the place.

The boarding house has recently been completely redecorated. Currently three boys' dorms and two girls': space for 28 with a dedicated couple looking after them, assisted by matron and a resident tutor. Sleepovers are available and increasingly popular. Bags to do in the evenings and boarders may go home at the weekend. On the other hand, weekends are fun: not only is

The lesson we saw was wonderful – children were sitting in a circle discussing whether the apple in the middle was alive or dead

the vast range of the college's facilities available but also frequent expeditions. 'It's brilliant fun,' said one boy, 'and breakfast is later on those days.' (No Saturday school.) Plentiful sport and hobbies: 'They're never bored,' said a delighted mum.

It's good to note the mutual respect and affection between the two halves. Boys and girls in the senior school recall with great fondness the days at their junior school and recognise from where their subsequent happiness stems – it's an essential step to another good school. Scholarships and bursaries are available for talented children in a wide variety of skills. Parents with more than one child in the college may well be assisted – don't be afraid to ask.

Over all, a lovely school where individuality really does seem to be encouraged and happiness abounds. 'One college, four schools' is the advertising slogan for Queen's, and the junior school represents the important foundation for the overall package.

Queen's College (Taunton)

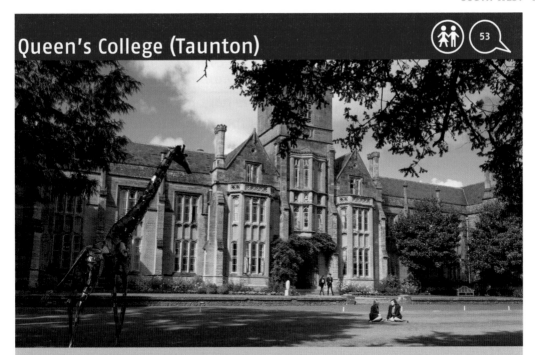

Trull Road, Taunton, Somerset TA1 4QS

01823 340830
admissions@queenscollege.org.uk
www.queenscollege.org.uk

Ages: 11–18
Pupils: 555; sixth form: 195
Boarders: 210
Day: £5,850 – £16,920 pa
Boarding: £12,780 – £31,350 pa

Linked school: Queen's College Junior School

Head Master: Since 2001, Mr Christopher J Alcock BSc FRSG (late 40s). Graduate of Durham University (geography and anthropology). Taught at Stamford School, where he was boarding housemaster and rugby coach, before going on to be deputy head at St Edward's, Witley.

Friendly, approachable, amusing and deeply committed to his charges. Not a pin-striped suited, jargon-spouting managerial head but a get-in-among-the-troops-and-love-them head. Study is full of 'significant' photographs. He singled out one in particular, a boy who had written to thank him for his time at Queen's – 'No one else would take me, but you did and now I'm at university'. 'Lowly grades, but he really fought for them,' added the head. 'That's what I delight in. Literally and metaphorically the winning pass in a fourth XV match is as important as anything in the first XV.' That's not empty rhetoric – he really believes it, always looking out for opportunities to praise and encourage all round efforts. Waxes lyrical about holistic all round education. His monthly letters to parents are

not couched in flowery prose but, for the most part, lists of individual achievements. Parents love that. 'If I had a son of school age,' said a successful prep school head, 'I would send him to Alcock, whatever the distance.' Evidence that others are doing just that – numbers have increased by over 100 during his tenure. Wife, Linda, teaches French in the junior school and they have two sons at Queen's.

Academic matters: 'What I really love about Queen's,' a mother told us, 'is that they go for potential rather than force-feeding. If your child is A grade material, that's what he will achieve; if he's D grade, he won't be made to feel stupid. He'll be congratulated on his achievement and made to feel good about it.' GCSE results are excellent with good performances from the brighter pupils and gutsy performances from the less able. In 2015, 44 per cent A*/A grades. Twenty-three subjects to choose from at A level – 44 per cent A*/A grades and 72 per cent A*/B. But this is not a school overly bothered with statistics – go back to good teaching and potential.

Wonderful support from the SEN department with super-caring staff. The designated area is presided over by a brilliant lady who combines compassion with common sense and expertise. Careful screening and individual follow up for the 10 per cent who are dyslexic, help and encouragement for those with ADHD – 'They often make good rock climbers or swimmers. The important thing is to find something which will engage their interest'. Not just a learning support area – an overall support area: 'My daughter's not bad at maths, but she goes for individual help because it increases her confidence'. 'I love coming here,' said a bright and engaging girl. 'It's a comfort zone'.

Has invested in computers in a big way and pupils are very proud of their proliferation. They are skilfully woven into lessons, much clever use of interactive white boards. Classrooms are functional with a good but not outstanding library – very helpful librarian, though. No lessons on Saturday mornings – not just the inspectors who have noted an improvement in academics since that decision was taken. 'It's a question of charging batteries,' says the head. 'They really do arrive fresher on Monday mornings after a break.' No lessons does not mean that nothing happens – three hour rehearsals for plays, expeditions out into the country, hobbies and activities abound.

Games, options, the arts: Sport is compulsory up to year 10, but most continue beyond that because this is not just a first and second team school. Everyone has a chance to play in a team – up to four in each sport. Beautiful cricket and rugby grounds and masses of floodlit, all-weather pitches and tennis courts. Hockey academy with Olympic coach. Good

Not just a learning support area – an overall support area: 'My daughter's not bad at maths, but she goes for individual help because it increases her confidence'

swimming pool with notable successes (Matt Clay, near Olympic swimmer, is an old boy) and shoals of pupils representing the county and beyond. National and international successes at rugby, cricket, swimming, cycling, athletics and fencing. Talented games players thrive; less talented have a go and love it. 'Everyone finds an activity they can enjoy,' said a charming girl who had experienced six schools. Some 50 per cent of the pupils play a musical instrument and the facilities are encouraging, with bright airy practice rooms in the theatre complex. When we were there, pupils were queuing up to practise. Bags of opportunities for playing in orchestras and ensembles and indulging in various sorts of music.

Large and well-equipped theatre doubles up as an assembly hall and chapel. Drama of all kinds is very popular with pupils and parents and eagerly looked forward to. School reviews have been known to include a memorable performance on the spoons by the head and the four notes he can play on the sax. 'Was it as many as four?' asked a boy. Wonderful and sympathetically designed art school overlooks the cricket pitch (how suitable it should have been opened by Jack Russell) and is full of exciting work. Every year an arts festival where artists visit and exhibit, evidence of which can be found in the beautiful stag and imposing giraffe which guard the buildings to the front. Much emphasis is placed on inculcating leadership (the head does not have a senior management team; instead he has a leadership group – a subtle and genuine difference). Lots of D of E with rock climbing and expeditions, to say nothing of community service. The cross-curricular approach encourages self-esteem and confidence as well as a strong sense of community

Boarding: Boarding houses have been, and are being, refurbished, and are brightly coloured and comfortable. We were interested to see pin ups of handsome RC priests in a girls' house. Lovely, ebullient house staff, including matrons who care.

Background and atmosphere: Founded in 1843, the first independent school in Taunton, one of nine schools owned by the Methodist Church. The main building, fine educational gothic, is impressive without being threatening – as you look at it you're surprised you haven't approached it by a long tree-lined drive. Instead you slip in off a pleasant leafy suburb. New buildings crowd around the back – and they do crowd – before giving way to acres of beautifully mown playing fields. 'This is a Christian name school,' said the head groundsman – groundsmen are always a useful indicator of school's morale. 'It's very, very friendly.'

Indeed that is the overriding atmosphere of the school. The pupils we met were marvellously forthcoming and fun and clearly used to chatting with alleged adults. 'We're suave, sophisticated bachelors,' said one boy. The last word is probably true; the other two, mercifully, not. In more measured tones, the inspectors commented on the pupils as 'open, tolerant, friendly and self-disciplined'.

The sixth form centre is 'a school within a school', housed in its own building with restricted access to ensure greater privacy; it stays open every evening and at weekends. An impressive learning resource centre with banks of computers and shelves of books. Downstairs are good chilling out facilities, including television and music systems, and a snack bar. Boys and girls were very enthusiastic about it and seemed to enjoy the monthly meetings of the sixth form society, when a variety of guest speakers come and entertain and provide opportunity for discussion. It certainly acts as a good bridge between school and university.

Pastoral care, well-being and discipline: Thanks to the excellent parents' handbook, which tells them everything they need to know, and thanks to the very detailed but not overly fussy school rules, clear parameters are laid out within which pupils know where they stand and are the happier for it. Reins are held lightly but never dropped. Prefects are selected through sixth form ballot and consultation with staff – ongoing training

School reviews have included a memorable performance on the spoons by the head and the four notes he can play on the sax. 'Was it as many as four?' asked a boy

with opportunities to discuss their responsibilities and any problems they may encounter. Parents we spoke to described the pastoral care as 'brilliant'.

The house system is the spring of tutoring and sets the tone. Each pupil is assigned a tutor with whom they have regular meetings. Clear guidelines on drugs (zero tolerance), and bullying is swiftly confronted, though 'very little of that'. A calm, peaceful atmosphere permeates the busy bustling, an indication that pupils are happy, know where

they stand and appreciate the genuine interest shown in them. All schools are very fond of trumpeting 'family atmosphere/values and a sense of community'. It isn't always easy to detect that on a visit – here those qualities are obvious.

Boys and girls seemed to enjoy the monthly meetings of the sixth form society, when a variety of guest speakers come and provide opportunity for discussion

Pupils and parents: Parents come from a cross-section of society, a number making considerable financial sacrifices to send their children. Boarders are drawn from the Forces, particularly the navy and the marines; others from abroad. A feature of the school is the loyalty and involvement of parents.

Entrance: Seventy per cent come from the prep school. Others from local preps and a few from state schools. Entrance requirements are broad and generous. Pupils at 11, 12 and 13 sit school's entrance papers in English, maths and verbal reasoning or common entrance. 'I find it very hard to refuse anyone,' said the head, 'though, very occasionally, I am forced to conclude this is not the right school for an applicant.'

Exit: Around 40 per cent move on after GCSEs. Regular one or two to Oxbridge (one in 2015 – deferred entry); otherwise to a wide range of universities. Difficult to detect any pattern in subjects read, but as wide a range as you would expect from such a school.

Money matters: Scholarships for the usual things and discounts offered to Forces parents.

Remarks: Not a swaggering school nor a showing off one. Nor does the apparent happiness disguise anything – it enlivens and invigorates a wholly unpretentious school.

Rendcomb College

Rendcomb, Cirencester, Gloucestershire GL7 7HA

01285 831213
admissions@rendcomb.gloucs.sch.uk
www.rendcombcollege.org.uk

Ages: 11–18
Pupils: 260; sixth form: 75
Boarders: 107
Day: £6,840 – £21,450 pa
Boarding: £22,440 – £29,655 pa

Headmaster: Since September 2015, Robert Jones, previously deputy head at Shiplake College. Educated at Swansea (economics), Worcester (PGCE) and Buckingham (MBA); has also taught economics and business at Canford, Clifton College, King's Worcester and Dauntsey's, coached rugby and rowing and run day and boarding houses. While at Shiplake, he undertook successful major reorganisations of the timetable, pastoral care and teaching systems – so unlikely to rest on his laurels here. Two children.

Academic matters: Pretty sound and the trend is upwards: in 2015, 46 per cent A*/A at GCSE and 36 per cent A*/A at A level (61 per cent A*-B). English, science (double and single), maths and further maths strongest contenders at both levels with history (surprisingly), French and music least popular A level options.

Classes of maximum 18 and smaller in the run up to GCSEs mean lots of individual attention. Good range of A level options including psychology, economics and business studies inevitably means

that there could be just one or two in some of these classes. Compulsory study skills sessions recently introduced. Whether tutorial sized classes are a bijou bonus or a bit of a one man band depends greatly on student teacher relationships. Sixth formers generally seem to enjoy the small groups and getting to know teachers well in a more reciprocal environment. School's emphasis on personal development and independent learning goes up another gear after GCSEs, when in addition to more freedoms and responsibilities, pupils are encouraged to take the Extended Project Qualification and participate in a varied enrichment programme. A new head of sixth form has been appointed.

Perhaps those language and literature results are helped along by the inspiring view over the Churn Valley enjoyed by the English department classrooms. Teaching we observed was an energetic mixture of old school dry wit, lively discussion and subtle encouragement – an admirable combination only found in places where teachers know their pupils really well. Science, maths and ICT departments are housed in the former stables across the (very quiet) lane from the main school site, so commuting between lessons can take time and pupils sometimes 'get a bit soggy' when it rains. Economics gets 'half a stable' – sixth formers think it should 'join up with business studies and become a full size department.'

School takes children with dyslexia, dyspraxia, mild Asperger's and SpLDs. Learning support and EAL sessions arranged around pupils' individual lesson plans, and parents describe the former as 'astonishing' and 'inspirational' (not to mention 'very well organised, switched on and professional'). Another parent praised the way the school accommodates the 'eccentric' child saying that the same amount of effort goes into supporting the highly academic as it does those with SEN.

Rendcomb is highly regarded for its inclusive approach, but such a reputation can sometimes work against a school. It was clear to us (our opinion confirmed by parents and university destinations) that the very bright are equally well served – particularly if the competitive cut and thrust of a large, highly academic school would be likely to stifle, rather than bring out, their best. School seems to have a real knack for building pupils' confidence; one parent told us that she had been 'astonished' by her child's academic progress, 'She used to struggle, now she's flying'.

Games, options, the arts: With just under a third of pupils achieving A*/A for art at GCSE, it's surprising that no more than one or two continue with the subject at A level. Facilities in the purpose built 1960s block are ample with large, light studios and there's a real creative buzz, enhanced by the sound of music drifting down from upstairs practice rooms. Pupil and professional art is on display including, when we visited, a large ceramic hare at the main entrance to the school; pupils have also exhibited at Calcot Manor and The Paragon Gallery in Cheltenham. The beauty of the Gloucestershire countryside, not to mention the school's architectural features such as arts and crafts style stained glass panels and ornate plasterwork, would inspire anyone. Well, nearly anyone. As we cooed over this view or that cornice our sixth form guide admitted that he'd been there since he was 4 and had 'stopped noticing', but knew he'd look back and realise how lucky he'd been.

Masses of music with orchestral and singing groups to suit all inclinations and abilities and excellent GCSE results although, as is often the case, there's minimal take up at A level. The same goes for drama and theatre studies, but even if drama's not first choice as an A level, Rendcomb fosters some dynamic talent, with a student group recently taking a play written and directed by themselves to Edinburgh. Newly introduced music technology A level (with all the kit) may change this; the

proposed performing arts centre certainly will. Current venue, the Dulverton Hall, was originally the house's orangery – hence the cast iron pillars. It's had a rough life, having previously served as a gym – presumably after the glass had been removed – and is crying out for restoration. Beautiful reading room also used for concerts etc.

Good to see such welcoming surroundings in the junior boys' house. With its worn and polished flagstones and jumble of beanbags, it was more home than house

Rendcomb's possibly unique claim is that every pupil will at some stage represent the school at sport. The prevailing attitude to team sport here is very different: the fact that a place in the first team may be open to what in other places would be a third team talent delights pupils and parents alike. 'My daughter would never have got a look in elsewhere', one mother told us, adding that the more able at sport develope leadership skills early on because they 'get to motivate and bring on others in their team'. Facilities include plenty of pitches, tennis and squash courts, a climbing wall, golf course and an open-air pool. There's a packed fixture list and they 'play good schools and learn, whether they win or lose.' Quite a few pupils are county and national level players and school teams have recently competed and won in lacrosse and shooting competitions. All this notwithstanding, Rendcomb is probably not going to be first choice for the highly competitive, sports-mad child. Other sporting options include riding (and polo), mountain biking and even fly-fishing on the River Churn that runs through the grounds. The delightful director of sport (who would certainly have inspired this PE-dodging writer) is keen to make even more use of the college's 230 acres and get students to see fitness as a habit for life. To this end he tries to ensure that all the sixth formers keep doing 'something' in the sporting line – a noble aim and one in which we're sure he'll succeed.

Generous range of co-curricular options including D of E. Big on outdoor education – from forest school for youngest pupils and extending, via bushcraft, all the way to sixth form leadership challenges. School 'sends a powerful message encouraging kids to grab every opportunity,' a parent told us.

Boarding: Boarding was described to us as 'laid back' and we rather agree. Rules is rules, of course – we're not talking about lax discipline – but sometimes school boarding accommodation can be a little sterile. Here it was good to see such characterful and welcoming surroundings in the junior boys' house, The Old Rectory. With its worn and polished flagstone floors, Delft tiled fireplace and jumble of colourful beanbags in the cinema room, it was more home than house. Boys get to name their own dorms – currently Harry Potter characters – and bedside tables were littered with books, mugs and evidence of snack attacks. House parents have decorated the walls with huge photo collages. Day pupils are assigned to a boarding house and have book lockers there.

Sixth formers live in Park House – girls' and boys' wings separated by a common room and kitchen. Park House was built in the 1970s and, predictably, is not a thing of beauty, but study bedrooms are serviceable and the atmosphere convivial and relaxed. All sixth form students get a taste of independent living with their stay in 'the flat', in the village. Groups of four (students don't get to choose) are given housekeeping money and live there from Monday to Friday. They have lunch at school but must manage the rest – buying provisions from the village shop and arranging domestic chores. The results are variable – sometimes it runs like clockwork, sometimes mummies deliver food parcels and help clean up at the end.

Sensible rules about phones and technology in general and the school internet is turned off at 11pm – not popular with older students burning the candle to finish essays. Mobile phone reception was described by one parent as 'dire' (we agree). Discipline, when necessary, is firm but fair; small numbers and strong sense of community mean that unkindness, unhappiness, bullying etc quickly spotted and dealt with.

'There are lots of characters here and we all grow up together. It's good for team spirit'

Background and atmosphere: Rendcomb was founded in 1920 by Noel Wills (of the philanthropist tobacco family) as an idealistic experiment in the 'power of opportunity and environment'. Wills believed that 'the true aristocracy among men is in reality simply an aristocracy of brains and character.' Initially the school provided 40 local boys with a free boarding education and preparation for entry to public schools. Wills was inspired by the ideas of educationalist J H Simpson, persuading him to leave his post at Rugby and become founding head of Rendcomb College. Under Simpson, Rendcomb started taking boys from age 11 and preparing them for university. Contrary to the Spartan regime that then prevailed in most public schools, Simpson and Wills shared the Platonic view that students flourish in beautiful surroundings and should be educated together regardless of class differences. Revolutionary stuff.

While the school has inevitably evolved over time, its founder's influence remains. For instance, there are no house competitions, thus enabling the whole school community to work together rather than dividing tribally. The emphasis on learning to lead, rather than win at all costs, was also well understood by the pupils to whom we spoke. As Noel Wills wrote of his school in The English Review in 1924, 'Work and games are abundantly worthwhile. Neither is the former rewarded by prizes, nor the latter by colours.'

Pretty much equidistant between Cheltenham and Cirencester, Rendcomb is in Cotswolds profond. This is Laurie Lee country – steep wooded valleys, ancient hedgerows, lush pasture and winding streams. School and village are as one – the post office (school played a key role in saving it from closure) is also the tuck shop, there's a surgery and even though the pretty church can't quite accommodate the whole school (carol service is held in Cirencester), it's still used for junior school assemblies and monthly boarders' services.

It may look more like a country house hotel than a school from the outside but on the inside, though clean, Rendcomb is well worn. Heating and maintaining a building like this with its huge windows and stone corridors must be a bursar's worst nightmare. The Wills family remain as trustees and, with the board of governors, are still very much involved in the school's educational and charitable ventures. Parents generally like the fact that it's 'not flash', and one commented, 'It's not about the latest facilities, it's about giving children an appetite for learning.'

Rendcomb's visitors are (or perhaps, were) met, somewhat broodingly, by a huge marble statue of King Saul that 'came with the house'. We got the impression that the poor old chap wasn't entirely popular, and he certainly seemed out of kilter with the school's welcoming atmosphere. We're not sure whether King Saul was beloved of old Rendcombians, but it seems that his days as gate-keeper are numbered. School was rather coy about his fate, but we gathered that he was off to a new home in the USA, having boosted the performing arts centre funds. Let's hope he cheers up.

Pastoral care, well-being and discipline: School says there's 'no hierarchy' at Rendcomb, and along with the school council is keen to see even more collaboration between year groups. A sixth former told us, 'It's a small community but there are lots of characters here and we all grow up together. It's good for team spirit.' Parents hugely appreciative of the individual care their children have received; one mother with two very different children said that 'each got exactly what they needed'. The UK guardian of an international student who had previously disliked school told us that he had 'blossomed' and now 'loved boarding'. She also praised the excellent communication from teachers and house parents.

Pupils and parents: County folk and mostly local families make for an active parents' association. Quite a few had chosen Rendcomb despite their children having gained places at local grammars, 'We wanted a school where the focus wasn't so narrow,' said one. About 65 per cent of boarders

from abroad, a considered mix of European and those from further afield. 'It gives the students a great network after they leave.'

Entrance: At age 11 majority come up from junior school plus others from local primaries; influx from preps such as Airthrie, Beaudesert, Hatherop, Pinewood and Prior Park at age 13. Candidates for sixth form need minimum of GCSE grade B in subjects to be studied, plus reference and interview. School takes pupils with SEN who can cope with the curriculum; all are assessed individually. Nature of site means it's unlikely to be suitable for pupils with more than minor physical disabilities.

Exit: As diverse as one would expect, from politics and international relations to sports and exercise science to speech and language therapy. London colleges, Bristol, Edinburgh, Exeter and Birmingham currently popular. One thespian and three artists in 2015.

Money matters: Very good value, especially boarding, compared to nearby competition. Music lessons, SEN and EAL support are extra. Academic, choral, sport, music and art scholarships on offer. Noel Wills full bursary awarded annually to one local state primary pupil.

Remarks: Rendcomb remains true to its founder's gently progressive vision. This is a genuinely civilised and humane school where chalk and cheese flourish alike in one of Gloucestershire's happiest valleys.

Royal High School, Bath GDST

Lansdown Road, Bath, Somerset BA1 5SZ

01225 313877
royalhigh@rhsb.gdst.net
www.royalhighbath.gdst.net

Ages: 11–18 (junior boarding from year 5)
Pupils: 691; sixth form: 130
Boarders: 141
Day: £12,105 – £12,339 pa
Boarding: £22,149 – £25,836 pa

Head: Since April 2015, Mrs Jo Duncan MA, previously head of Princess Helena College. Educated in N Ireland; studied English/theology at St Andrews and then PGCE at Homerton College, Cambridge. Taught RS at The Latymer, then moved to Benenden, where alongside teaching RS was also deputy housemistress, part of weekend activities team and award officer for D of E. After seven years, appointed head of Princess Helena. Is an ISI boarding inspector. Loves travel and has organised and led trips

to eg India, China, Belarus and Israel. Married to Murray, a lawyer, and they have two children.

Academic matters: In 2015, 64 per cent A*/A grades at GCSE and 45 per cent A*/A at A level. Pupils taking IB achieved average of 37 points. Wide choice of subjects plus IB must make the 35 per cent exodus of girls after GCSE particularly galling, but we imagine that's not really about options. Relatively small classes where active participation is encouraged makes for a happy flock. A level classes run for sole takers, on occasion.

Achievements recognised both inside and outside GDST, with successes in Maths Challenges/Olympiad, Nuffield Bursaries, Nomura Scholarship and Young Science Writer prize recently awarded; one parent, however, had reservations about the quality of advice offered for Oxbridge during UCAS. The school's recent ISI report judged its academic offering to be 'excellent' and its value-added scores are high. That same report also sounded a cautionary note that GCSE pupils should be allowed to lift their nose from the grindstone from time to time..

SEN gets a thumbs-up from parents. Early identification of problems in the junior school means the senior school is well-equipped to deal with their own new intake. Parents cite a supportive culture with no stigma and teachers who employ a variety of techniques to help, not just with the three Rs but also with organisation, presentation and strategies for revision. 'Concentration on their performance skills builds their confidence enormously,' remarked one father, a leadership expert. Extra help is paid for.

Games, options, the arts: Lots on offer from Dance Storm to D of E. All the games and sports you would expect are played on the school's own facilities: Astro, tennis courts and sports hall on campus, larger grass pitches and athletics a short drive to more level but windswept terrain on top of Lansdown. Swimming in the outdoor pool in summer or at the university across the city – the facilities and coaching are worth the drive. Hockey and netball particularly strong and the school puts on a good showing locally and

One girl, whose sister left in seach of springier pastures after GCSE, said she couldn't possibly leave because of the sport

nationally. One girl, whose sister left in search of springier pastures after GCSE, said she couldn't possibly think of leaving because of the sport. Sporting interests which fall outside the curriculum well catered for too, eg judo, fencing and aerobics, and individual talents encouraged, not just amongst the pupils: a teacher is a serious Olympic prospect in archery. A full voluntary activity programme is offered on Saturday mornings, but members of school teams are expected to commit at least some of their weekend to their sport – maybe going on tour to Barbados compensates. It is, however, quite possible to blag your way out of sport completely in the sixth form, it seems.

Wonderful art emanates from the fantastic new art school, where light airy studios with panoramic views give students every opportunity not only to create masterpieces but to exhibit them as well. All you could wish for, including ceramics, textiles, sculpture and photography. RHS has long been known for its music and drama; these remain strengths, though one parent reckons that music has perhaps lost a little of its sheen in an attempt to 'become more democratic', as she put it; 10 ensembles seem to us to be a sign of a healthy musical life and a recent choral scholarship to Cambridge,

soloists in Bath Abbey and the current leader of the county orchestra suggest that music produces the goods. Associated Board results confirm this, with most entrants getting merits or distinctions.

The jewel in the crown is drama: loads of plaudits from the Mid Somerset Festival and LAMDA. Single sex schools do of course demand versatility on the stage on their pupils, though boys are imported from local boys' comp, Beechen Cliff, to form Bathos (!) theatre troupe, and no poverty of dramatic ambition: recent productions include The Crucible and musicals and Gilbert and Sullivan are staged to general acclaim. Strong support given to girls keen on the tech side too with the opening of an new media centre offering activities from sound recording to green screen CGI filming. The centre, which is now known as The Sophie Cameron Performing Arts Centre, named in honour of a former head girl, hosts key cultural events throughout the year.

Boarding: Two or three bedded rooms for 11-16 year olds are on the upper floors of the main school building; some sixth formers have study bedrooms in Level 6 in the main house, others in Gloucester House, a purpose-built sixth form building nearby. Recent refurbishment of common rooms and parts of boarding houses. Usual weekend offerings include eg ice skating, shopping, theatre trips, bowling.

Background and atmosphere: Victorian stone monolith stands back from the road up a drive through an off-puttingly narrow archway. First impressions of austerity are dispelled by the warmth and courtesy of staff and pupils and by more natural light at the back of the main building – the library is lovely, though other parts could use a lick of paint here and there. It all feels rather traditional, despite mod cons, and the girls fit in. Edgy it isn't, despite valiant new initiatives such as the sixth form college (with its brief introduction of boys) and IB. The Royal High has blazed something of a trail within GDST as its only school to offer boarding (a legacy from the amalgamation between Bath High and the Royal School in 1998). The school draws a distinction between the experience of the first five years and the last two, by housing the sixth form college in a separate block with teaching space for small groups, space to chill for larger ones and a café, in a genuine attempt to address the gap between school and university. Each sixth former is issued with a bright red laptop, all wired up to the school intranet and ready to go, a move universally welcomed, coming as it does with full technical support. Further down the school, it feels reassuring – a place where girls can be girls and pursue trad 'male' subjects without distraction or fear of censure: the shortish school day (finishing at 4pm but with an option to stay till 6pm) and

proximity to town mean plenty of opportunity to socialise after school.

Parents report a happy school with an inclusive culture, where results aren't everything, and achievement of all kinds is celebrated. Social awareness is also inculcated and a sense of the world beyond school, with a good current affairs programme, Model UN and a partnership with a Kenyan school, as well as the 20 or so foreign pupils. Most, whose daughters have come up from the junior school, look nowhere else.

Pastoral care, well-being and discipline: Girls are well looked after and look after each other. The detailed PHSE programme ensures they are as savvy as the school can make them about the pitfalls and downsides of teenage life – and sanctions for those who transgress. Anyone caught smoking, drinking or with drugs can expect the heave-ho or suspension for shop-lifting. Sixth formers lead discussions about aspects of contemporary life with the younger ones; sessions have included celebrity culture and Fairtrade. Conduct within school, and occasionally beyond, is governed by a system of merits, commendations and debits – the emphasis, according to the school, very much on praise rather than blame, although we picked up the odd gripe from parents about heavy-handedness over petty things. Support structures and expertise in the problems besetting teenage girls, eg eating disorders, definitely in place, though.

Pupils and parents: 'Hard to generalise,' but school says RHS girls share the values of open-mindedness, respect, courtesy and a sense of their own individuality. We found them polite, articulate – and perhaps a touch inhibited by the presence of a senior teacher over lunch, for reasons of safeguarding, note. A good cross-section of parents – most professions and some media types represented, plus humbler occupations, and of course the 20 or so overseas boarders. Not a snobby school – girls come from anything up to 20 miles away by bus or train; the school runs a minibus from the station and, as well as its own, two buses run in collaboration with King Edward's across the city.

Famous old girls include Mary Berry, Baroness Elspeth Howe and the last head of Queen Anne's Caversham.

Entrance: Seventy-five girls arrive in year 7, having passed examinations in English, maths and verbal reasoning the previous January, plus interviews with the head and year 7 co-ordinator. Academic taster days for year 6 prospective applicants. The main route in is its own junior school, but girls come from local independents and primaries too across Wiltshire, South Gloucestershire, Somerset and Dorset as well as from overseas. More will arrive in year 9 after entrance exams in English, maths and science and the offer of scholarships at this entry level, then another intake in lower sixth, where six GCSEs, with A grades for A level subjects, are required. Transition arrangements come in for particular praise at year 7.

Exit: Some 35 per cent leave after GCSEs to go to local co-eds, state and independent; others join. After A levels or IB, pretty well everyone makes their first choice destinations, embracing a range of courses from the vocational to the theoretical. Bristol, Durham, Exeter, Edinburgh and London universities currently the most popular destinations. Several to Oxbridge most years (five in 2015), despite some caution on the school's part about putting pupils forward. Gap years the exception rather than the norm. GDST girls become members of GDST Alumnae, the Trust-wide network for communication and support amongst former pupils, which offers the inside track on various universities and professions.

Money matters: Remarkably good value for money – unusually, exam fees, books and insurance are included, though most extras and lunch are paid separately. Forces' offspring get a 10 per cent discount. Boarding fees are significantly cheaper than any boarding establishment we know of – how do they do it? Thrift extends to sensible and well priced uniform. Scholarships and bursaries offered for academics, art, music, drama and sport; bursaries for bright girls whose parents could not otherwise afford it also available, as is short term assistance for temporary hardship cases.

Remarks: Consistently good girls' day school, as befits the GDST, with some interesting departures – boarding, a collegiate sixth form offering A levels and the IB. A safe bet which should fulfil almost any girl, but not perhaps for the rebel.

St John's-on-the-Hill School

Castleford Hill, Chepstow, Monmouthshire NP16 7LE

01291 622045
Office@stjohnsonthehill.co.uk
www.stjohnsonthehill.co.uk

Ages: 4–14
Pupils: 179
Boarders: 20
Day: £7,689 – £12,669 pa
Boarding: £17,835 pa

Headmaster: Since September 2015, David Griffiths, previously deputy head, and English and RS teacher. A quick promotion – he joined the school in January 2015 from Monmouth Girls, where he was head of department.

Entrance: Mixed ability entry. Assessment is based on a 'taster day' in English and maths plus report from previous school. Procedure is 'painless,' say parents, who compared it favourably with other schools. Pupils may enter at any point provided spaces are available. Main catchment area is Newport/Cardiff through Monmouthshire to Forest of Dean and west Gloucestershire. Boarders come from all over.

Exit: Has gained reputation for gaining scholarships near and far. Most popular: Dean Close, Monmouth (boys and girls), Kings Gloucester, Christ College Brecon, Marlborough, Rougemont, Clifton College, Cheltenham College, Malvern College.

Remarks: Perched above river Wye, a short stone's throw into England, school overlooks Chepstow in Wales. Founded in 1923 in a rambling Georgian manor (rebuilt in 1805 after a fire). Succession of proprietorial heads until '60s but co-ed and charitable trust (incorporating former Brightlands School) since then. New buildings (and new conservatory entrance area) fit well into overall scheme of things on a pleasant eight-acre site (plus 12 more acres of playing fields across the road).

Our visit on a 'Foodie Friday' coincided with 'wormy pasta salad' on classroom menus

Spectacular growth of nursery education (now provided on three sites, including one in Newport) complete with state-of-the-art baby units. Seventy per cent of pre-prep intake comes from the school's own nurseries. Our visit on a 'Foodie Friday' coincided with 'wormy pasta salad' on classroom menus. Highly professional early years teachers and assistants ensure tinies are happy and cared for. Impressive range of activities for these tots – stimulation in the nursery section includes sensory and soft play rooms plus safe outdoor play areas for all.

'Seamless' progression to reception level on Tutshill site where children 'learn to read without noticing,' say committed staff. Phonic introduction alongside activities such as puppets and story telling. Loads of measuring and counting too. Each day begins with assembly in spacious hall; weekly link-up with nursery from below and to prep (in their hall) once a week. Communication between teachers and pre-prep parents includes 'wow cards' and home-school link books. Wide corridors in this modern, purpose-built building boast frequently changed displays including output of creative arts club and strong evidence of cross-curricular work:

eg 'forces of movement' incorporating art, science and ICT work. Smart boards in each year group and laptops already in use at this level, not to mention school intranet on plasma screen. Huge choice of readers ('fireflies' non-fiction popular with boys). Tea after school for those involved in clubs, activities or post-lessons care.

Pupils leave the swish pre-prep for the cleverly converted coach house which accommodates years 3 to 5 in what a previous head described as 'a bit of a Tardis.' Smallish but cheery classrooms (maximum class size is 16) for these years.

Much better than average prep school facilities for science: junior (in a quaint outpost) and senior (modern) laboratories with well-qualified teachers to match. Lovely dining area combines best of cafeteria and sit down traditions whilst civilised entrance (with memorabilia on show) and meeting room (referred to as the Embassy) add gravitas. Prep is awash with subject specialists (some escapees from state sector, others ex-independent) who can take pupils as far as they want to go. Art teachers (ex-Monmouth senior) explained how they are adapting OCR syllabus for St John's and thereby widening pupils' artistic horizons. We appreciated the ongoing Picasso exhibition whilst annual Arts Week gives pupils a chance to let their creativity run wild. Athletic head of DT (he manages British universities' cross-country team) oversees a well-resourced area which includes 3D model making.

Somewhat dated school hall serves for assemblies as well as concerts and school productions (last one was a full blown Grease.) Music has a large classroom base plus three individual practice rooms. Everyone in year 3 gets a violin and learns to scrape – like it or not. Orchestra and wind band plus choirs (school subs for Newport cathedral choir and also sang at recent IAPS conference) are all well supported

and three ex-pupils have graduated to National Youth Orchestra. Specialist ICT rooms are well used but school maintains a healthy balance between new technologies and more traditional approaches.

Sports facilities include half-size Astroturf and hard tennis/netball courts, attractive 15-metre swimming pool and oodles of playing fields. School more than holds its own against larger preps with an impressive fixture list (includes Millfield and Cheltenham College). Wide choice of sports features rugby, soccer, cricket (boys and girls) as well as netball, rounders, swimming, tennis and golf. All pupils encouraged to participate as best they can.

Refreshingly open, happy pupils – well turned out and polite nonetheless. We observed a school council meeting chaired effectively by a year 8 boy. Plenty of evidence of pupils' ideas bearing fruit eg new homework diary and rewards system not to mention refurb of pupils' loos. Pupils also discussed making a new outdoor classroom interactive – cutting edge stuff for 12-13 year olds. Large number (33 last time) go for a whole month's exchange with host schools in Stirling and Cape Town, South Africa. Led (10 visits so far) by a staff member who hails from those parts. Does wonders for pupil personal development and bonding. Pupils wax eloquent about how they are all 'given a chance' by 'kind teachers' and how 'friendship' is the magical ingredient at St John's. We were shown a wide variety of pupils' work – impressive in its quality and diversity. Alumni include Olympic showjumper, Richard Mead, Welsh rugby player Marc Batten and Rebecca Watts (in first group of ordained women priests).

Fleet of minibuses ('drivers are really kind,' say parents) to ferry day pupils twixt home and school. Boarders get a good deal here with lovely, mixed (not the dorms) accommodation, dedicated and well qualified houseparents who 'go the extra mile' to develop a family, 'home from home' atmosphere. Bathrooms recently upgraded. Houseparents even cook for boarders on Saturdays (take-aways are not unknown) but school roast on Sundays is 'to die for,' they confess. Junior boarders write home (plus ICT and reading) on Saturday mornings whilst their seniors are in lessons. Dorm points add up so that winners get a reward outing. Regular 'Boarders' Bugle' adds to monthly school newsletters to keep boarding parents well informed. Flexi-boarding clearly popular with parents. Active Parents' Association have raised loads of dosh for worthwhile projects plus social and sporting events such as the summer ball and PA Golf Day. Parents help children's fundraising through their four houses to benefit of a wide range of local, national and international good causes.

Great 'family' school for youngsters with 'gunpowder in the barrel' – 'we'll take them as far as they want to go,' insists school. Parents were at a loss to pick out a single outstanding feature – 'excellent teachers'; 'all pupils get involved'; 'a super school in all respects' was the consensus. Recently acquired by Dean Close School (Cheltenham).

St Mary's Calne

Curzon Street, Calne, Wiltshire SN11 0DF

01249 857200
admissions@stmaryscalne.org
www.stmaryscalne.org
C of E

Ages: 11–18
Pupils: 350; sixth form: 110
Boarders: 282
Day: £26,400 pa
Boarding: £35,250 pa

Headmistress: Since 2013, Dr Felicia Kirk MA PhD (early 40s). Born and raised in Maryland, USA, Dr Kirk's distinguished academic career in languages, both ancient and modern, took her to the École Normale Supérieure in Paris, where she met the Brit she would later follow to England and marry, leaving the groves of academe for the real world of teaching children. Her first job was at the Royal Hospital School in Suffolk, followed by a move into girls' education as director of higher education at Wycombe Abbey, then latterly as head of sixth form at Ipswich High School. Of her move to Calne, she says, 'I missed the boarding, and I liked the fact that the school is small, yet ambitious'.

Totally committed to girls' education, she intends to build on breadth of opportunity at Calne 'unencumbered by gender stereotyping'; building both literally and figuratively, that is, with an ambitious 10 year development plan to squeeze every last square inch (OK, centimetre, then) out of this school's compact site, with increased provision for arts, sports, a new library and more science labs. Any faint question marks about an American leading this very British institution are utterly dispelled on meeting her – she's hardly even mid-Atlantic in

accent, and elegantly clad in a tweed jacket with velvet collar the day we visited – and parents appreciate the richness brought by experience from elsewhere, as well as her plans for the place: 'The school needs more than academia to keep it at the top table,' said one mother. Try as we might, it was impossible to break through her professional, though charming, veneer. Her girls describe her as enthusiastic and easy to talk to, are pleased to see her walking her dog in trackies and to receive a birthday card in their first year. 'Plus she's innovative,' said one. What does that mean again? 'It's new stuff like introducing company jumpers,' said a helpful friend.

Dr Kirk is married to an accountant. Her home is in Suffolk, where she also keeps her retired eventer.

Academic matters: Undoubtedly what the school is about, but not all it's about. At A level, 56 per cent A*/A grades in 2015. Stand-out subjects are maths, history, Spanish and Latin. A handful to Oxbridge every year (seven in 2015), the majority of the rest to Russell group. In 2014, nearly half the cohort – an unusually high number – did not go straight to university; online speculation bubbled, yet the school assured us that more girls were taking gap years and that those wishing to apply to university post A level were equally well supported through UCAS even though they were no longer at school.

At GCSE, results have crept up over recent years to the point where 78 per cent were A*/A in 2015. Geography, Latin, art, and music excel here. Results are more exciting than the classrooms which produce them, and teaching does not appear to be

as reliant on IT as is the case in many schools we see; that said, refurbishing the labs cannot come a moment too soon. Library provision too is good but scattered, and will be consolidated under the development plan. Enrichment week – inter alia, gung ho girls in camouflage crawling enthusiastically under netting taking orders from an army officer – was in full swing when we visited, but we were pleased to note an A level history class of about six discussing Mary Tudor's relationship with the clergy, rather than the apparently ceaseless rehash-

---

We were pleased to note an A level history class discussing Mary Tudor's relationship with the clergy, rather than rehashing two world wars

---

ing of the two world wars. Ditto Northanger Abbey read in its entirety in year 9 – none of these bite-sized chunks beloved of modern exam setters. Recent success enjoyed in prestigious maths and German Olympiad competitions too. SEN provision is as expected at a school of this calibre – definitely the mild end of dys- spectra – though everyone is tested on entry. About eight per cent of girls have an identifiable educational need catered for; provision equally is made for EAL and the very brightest sparks too.

Games, options, the arts: An astonishing amount of sporting facilities is crammed into this compact site, with more planned. A full-sized Astro and new netball/tennis courts (all floodlit) opened in the few days before our visit form part of an ambitious upgrade of the sports offer, which has already seen the leasing of pitches plus track and field facilities a short distance away, making the hosting of fixtures with other schools easier. Lacrosse is the winter sport on offer, alongside netball, which is played against schools not offering lax; hockey is played in the spring term. The youngest girls all represent the school early on; later, team practice becomes optional and from year 10, girls can drop ball sports altogether, as long as they do something to get them off the couch and away from the toaster. Tennis, swimming, fencing happen all year round, rowing and sailing in summer. Though no horses reside at school, show-jumping and eventing are a successful part of the sporting calendar. Skiing is prominent too: as well as the usual ski-trip, school also takes part in the quaintly named but deadly serious British Schoolgirls Races in Flaine each year, to some acclaim.

The arts take centre stage. Huge portraits adorn the entrance (colloquially known as the goldfish bowl), and paintings most of the walls. Sculpture is big here too – long before art becomes a GCSE option, junior girls experiment with life-sized figures. A full size war horse and cavalry officer in the early stages of construction out of wood and

chicken wire has to be built in a gazebo outside the art school: 'I can't wait for the new studios,' remarked one member of staff with feeling. Drama a high point too: an inspirational head of drama who retired a few years ago left a legacy of adventurous excellence, which is not limited to an annual musical, Shakespeare (recently an all-female Hamlet), performances at the egg theatre in Bath and at the Edinburgh Fringe. Tess of the d'Urbervilles was on the week we visited – we were charmed by the hay and ancient agricultural machinery strewn throughout the foyer of a somewhat tired theatre. Quite the glossiest programmes we had ever seen. Much of the singing harks back to its roots in the English choral tradition, to be expected in a school where chapel is still central to its life, but its reach extends to the charitable, profitable and glittery: a concert at Chelsea Old Church with a sideshow of celebrities raised £19,000. A symphony orchestra, jazz band, opera, string and flute groups complete the offering, which both brings top performers into school, takes musicians out of school (not only in the UK but abroad to Paris and so on) and music to local venues and primary schools as part of its community outreach. Generously resourced and imaginative in scope, the music department recently commissioned an opera to commemorate the start of WW1.

Boarding: The majority board, housed in year groups and moved into accommodation of increasing luxury each year as they progress up the school; day girls belong to houses along with their boarding counterparts and integration seems seamless. The new lower sixth house with its en-suite bathrooms and groovy décor (not sure about the bilious green chairs, however) will surpass anything likely to be encountered in most freshers' lodging, or even at home. House unity, as generally understood, is generated through companies, five groups of girls of all ages named after former bishops of Salisbury; a coloured band on the regulation navy jumper denotes it, and the company shout (known elsewhere as house music) loudly affirms it.

Background and atmosphere: Founded in 1873 by the then vicar of Calne, as a place where girls would receive an excellent academic grounding and would be able to develop their individuality within an Anglican foundation, the school still delivers on all three fronts. Its compact site right in the small somewhat undistinguished (yes, the last entry said that, but we agree) Wiltshire town means a lack of rolling acres and constant improvement, redevelopment, refurbishment rather than expansion of existing facilities, resulting in a startling mix of architectural styles redolent of the time they were built. No pretty gardens or places to escape to for a quiet cig, that we could detect – maybe that is why vice seems so notably absent. Parents like the fact that the school is not London-y, though there is a posse from London and buses run at the start and end of every term and half-term.

Unquestionably a female preserve or possibly a refuge, but not a nunnery: 'It's easier and less distracting not having boys around,' said one little scrap

It all feels quite cosy and its size is frequently mentioned as a positive by both girls and parents. Uniform is ubiquitous kilted skirt and light blue blouse. Sixth formers' dress code is quite relaxed, and perhaps because there are no boys, make-up is minimal. Unquestionably a female preserve or possibly a refuge, but not a nunnery: 'It's easier and less distracting not having boys around,' said one little scrap, though the junior dorms were full of pictures of boys (and ponies), known or dreamed about. Older girls regret the lack of socials with boys' schools, though the mixed lacrosse match is possibly a less stilted encounter.

It all feels rather traditional, despite the 14 per cent from overseas, partly on account of daily chapel, not always religious, but serious and, when the occasion demands it, reverent.

Pastoral care, well-being and discipline: Highly rated by both girls and parents. Each girl is allocated a tutor (who can be changed in the unusual event of it not working out) and has a weekly individual meeting. Between the housemistress and tutor, 'it's like having a mum and dad at school,' said one. Plenty of avenues to seek help if ever things go wrong, and generous provision for anyone needing medical attention, with a fully equipped, permanently manned medical centre. Not only is good work (both absolute and relative) rewarded by 'blues', but so are other virtues such as kindness, punctuality and tidiness. A 'good egg' prize is awarded each year for the sort of qualities which make a community run joyously. Miscreants who talk after lights might be made to do the house washing up the following day; major sins attract an escalating scale of punishment. Smokers' fines are donated to cancer charities.

Pupils and parents: Well-mannered and forthright with plenty of get-up-and-go. 'If you want something started, ask a Calne girl,' said the head. The ones we met were certainly privileged but not in the slightest bit tiresome. One mother said she chose the school because she wanted confidence not arrogance instilled in her daughters; something the girls in Grosstete company might be particularly mindful of. The school appears to run on old money, rather than new – 'The car park is full of Audis, Volvos and battered old Fords,' one parent observed – with a tangible affection from its former pupils, some of whom send their daughters. Considerable camaraderie on the lacrosse touchline too.

Entrance: Registration is advised three or four years ahead of proposed entry at year 7 (LIV in school parlance). Places conditional on entrance exams (either CE or school's own 11+ exam) are offered after an assessment day held in the September one year before entry. Process for 13+ (year 9, UIV) starts a year earlier; assessment day held almost two years before entry. Bright sparks are invited to apply for scholarships. Girls come from the smarter prep schools in the south and South West, some from London, some from school's own prep, St Margaret's, and a few from local primaries.

Around 15 new into sixth form with good GCSEs, sparkling in subjects to be taken to A level

Exit: A handful – some 15 per cent – after GCSE in search of (in no particular order) boys, brighter lights, wider subject choices, more freedom; the rest to top notch universities up and down the land (seven to Oxbridge in 2015 and one to Hong Kong) or art foundation. School takes great care over the next stage: hosting a higher education conference for GSA, Oxbridge aptitude testing in school and 'Futures', a new half termly publication covering exclusively university applications, developments and more adventurous overseas options, plus alumnae experience. Increasing number of gap years. Famous OGs include Laura Bechtolsheimer, Olympic dressage medallist, and writer Lucy Hughes-Hallett (plus David Cameron's sister).

Money matters: Not a rich school, but one husbanding and developing its resources to ensure its place amongst the UK's top girls' schools. Usual range of scholarships offered, including a choral scholarship at 13+. A nominal five per cent fee reduction is given, but up to 40 per cent depending on means-testing. Two sixth form scholarships to internal candidates and one to external on offer too. A foundation scholarship of up to 100 per cent of day fees at both year 7 and sixth form is aimed exclusively at state school pupils for whom 'reasons of financial restriction' would otherwise preclude going there.

Remarks: A school for clever girls? Certainly, though 'it doesn't matter if they're not – they're usually good at something else.' Quintessential English girls' boarding? Absolutely. Social cachet? Unquestionably.

St Mary's School (Shaftesbury)

Donhead St. Mary, Shaftesbury, Dorset SP7 9LP

01747 857111
registrar@stmarys.eu
www.st-marys-shaftesbury.co.uk
RC

Ages: 11–18
Pupils: 270; sixth form: 80
Boarders: 200 full
Day: £17,220 – £19,335 pa
Boarding: £24,960 – £28,050 pa

Headteacher: Since January 2016, Mrs Mary Arnal MSc, PGCE, FRSA, previously head of Sherborne International School, and before that head of the prep school at St Teresa's, Effingham. She is an applied linguist with a masters from Edinburgh, and has a background in university lecturing and teaching in the UK and overseas, including being senior housemistress at St John's School Leatherhead. Her specialist subjects are English language and philosophy and she has experience teaching the IB in Spain, where she was director of studies at a school in Madrid. She has also taught and lived in Peru. She describes herself as English by birth, Irish by blood and Spanish in spirit.

Mary is married to mathematical analyst, Don Antonio Arnal; they have two children.

Academic matters: Popular A level subjects include English literature, history and history of art, geography, fine art and photography. Steady uptake of science, economics, business studies, maths and modern languages. For a small school with pupils of mixed ability, results are consistently good. In 2015, 55 per cent of A levels graded A*/A. Drama AS level continues to broaden the range of subjects available.

GCSE results also good with 62 per cent A*/A in 2015. Girls do well in English literature, modern languages, science, the humanities and art. Languages department has introduced iGCSE exams throughout and runs a language 'circus' where girls can try Spanish or German for a term; six-week taster sessions in Italian and Portuguese also on offer. French exchanges for those interested.

Thirteen-year-olds don wellies and stride off in small groups over the fields for Saturday afternoon shopping in Shaftesbury

Parents praise 'very experienced teaching staff' for their dedication, openness and lack of pretension. Some have been there for years, but head says the average age is beginning to come down. General consensus is that self-motivated girls are very well supported. 'If you do want to be bothered [with work], the teachers will bend over backwards.' One commented that the school 'hides its academic light under a bushel', although all agreed that 'the teaching shines'.

Those looking for a warm and caring environment where they can achieve and be themselves will feel at home

Three dedicated SEN rooms at the top of humanities block helps those with mild learning difficulties (dyslexia, dyspraxia) as well as running revision sessions and helping girls to improve their grades in maths and English. At the time of our visit, 46 pupils (up to three at a time) were receiving EAL coaching.

Games, options, the arts: 'Sport for all' is school's aim and girls play all the usual sports up to GCSE plus a few less common, eg water polo, yoga, pilates and zumba. School will lay on an activity if there is sufficient interest, eg scuba diving. In years 10 and 11 girls have access to the school's fitness suite and can begin the sports leaders programme which continues in sixth form for those taking A level PE. Circuit training and conditioning machines used for school's elite athlete training programme. Large sports hall and 25m pool sit side by side, surrounded by Astroturf pitch, netball and tennis courts. Swimming and tennis available year round. A few girls play hockey at county level and train at the county netball academy, with some year 10 girls put forward for LTA tennis league each year. Regular match fixtures and swimming galas throughout the year; teams hold their own and win against much larger schools.

Stunning, spacious art block opened in 2014; the creative arts are a real strength here and evidence of this hangs in corridors throughout the main school building. 'Art is outstanding and all visual arts are very good.' Busy textiles room with lots of sewing machines humming; textiles and design taught in six-month blocks, fine art all year. Photography offered at GCSE and A level and textiles at GCSE. Trips abroad to exhibitions in Paris, Florence and Barcelona for sixth formers.

Excellent music block, with 25 individual practice rooms, small concert space, music technology room and dedicated classroom, plus a well-stocked music library with archive material and CD recordings. Some 60 per cent learn a musical instrument, 15 per cent study two and some learn two instruments and singing. Each term, around 40 girls take ABRSM and Trinity Guildhall practical exams.

Instrumental lessons rotate through the school day up to year 9, after which they are fixed; practice is timetabled. Ensembles include school orchestra, percussion and wind bands plus a rock band; others are formed depending on instruments and girls are encouraged to take the initiative. Everyone sings each week, either in class or as a form. Young maths teacher runs a GLEE club. 'The school needs a bit more singing outside the chapel choir.' Two school choirs, one of which is the 'awesome' chapel choir which rehearses three mornings a week for chapel assemblies, Sunday mass and tours abroad. St Cecilia's pupils' concert takes place each year. Regular outreach to primary schools and local choirs, including annual Choral Day.

Extensive range of extracurricular activities, clubs and societies on offer; these include equestrian polo, rock climbing and a young enterprise scheme. French society is very popular and includes a literary circle. Sixth formers can qualify for Leith's Basic Certificate in Food and Wine in well-appointed cookery school. Several drama productions across the age range each year and LAMDA exams are popular. D of E awards are a big part of school life, with two-thirds completing these every year. In keeping with school's Catholic ethos, girls fundraise and lead charitable expeditions to countries such as Rwanda, Chile and Zambia to work with schools and orphanages. The Mary Ward Lecture Series encourages girls to think through listening to speakers on topics such as war theory, bioethics and religious pluralism.

Boarding: Boarding arrangements work well; years 7 and 8 board separately in individual 'cubies'; day girls are welcome to visit the boarding house. After this, girls move into one of four houses where they sleep in single, double or four-person bedrooms. Some bedrooms are small, but each house has a spacious common room and a kitchen. Rooms rotate regularly and day-to-day housekeeping is efficient. 'A brilliant woman runs the laundry and the shift system for washing clothes works.' Parents full of praise for sixth form housemistress. 'She's seen everything and can deal with anything.' Girls in sixth form are given independence, eg preparing their own breakfast and entertaining outside friends to dinner parties.

Two-thirds are full boarders, so school doesn't empty out on weekends, though flexi boarding is available. Day girls can go home after lessons, but many choose to stay on for clubs, homework and supper. Supervised prep sessions on Saturday mornings and plenty to do on weekends. Long, wrap-around green kilts up to year 11 are very popular with the girls; sixth form uniform phased out in favour of smart home clothes.

Boarders are escorted to and from various airport terminals by school minibus on exeat weekends, at half-term and at the beginning and end of term; those going to London on exeats can travel by escorted coach to Richmond. Parents confirm that school is very aware of where girls are.

Background and atmosphere: St Mary's was founded in 1945 and can trace its origins back to Mary Ward, an English Catholic nun who championed the rights of girls to receive an education, despite living in hostile Tudor times. Imprisoned for her beliefs, she succeeded in establishing a school for girls in York before her death in 1645.

With the school set in 55 acres of parkland and approached down a winding, tree-lined drive, there is a sense of leaving the outside world behind as one arrives at an imposing early Victorian mansion. Sensitive efforts have been made to modernise the interior, with glass screens to let in light. Spread around the main house is a collection of buildings ranging from ultra-modern to slightly frayed labs and other older classrooms. New and old nestle side by side and somehow manage not to look incongruous, but the impression is of much brown and green.

In contrast to the school's cooler colours is its warm, family atmosphere. Teachers, parents and girls alike champion it as safe and nurturing. 'It's a very caring school which fosters life-long friendships.' Walking round, we were struck by the genuinely supportive relationships between girls of all ages. 'If you could bottle the atmosphere at St Mary's, it would be invaluable.'

Pastoral care, well-being and discipline: Strongly underpinned by school's Catholic faith, pastoral care is 'brilliant' and 'house assistants are excellent'. 'Somehow the school makes the girls very caring and respectful.' Full-time chaplain lives on campus, with school's own priest in residence from

Thursday to Sunday. Anglican minister visits once a week to lead the Eucharist. 'The school operates more on praise than sanction,' said one parent. Any misdemeanour earns the culprit a lavender ticket, 'lavvies' to the girls. Punishments range from parental meeting to suspension. 'The girls want their community to work – we have to deal with so few sanctions.' Strict on smoking and alcohol, the odd suspension has happened for having one too many at socials with boys' schools.

Despite being 'in the sticks', parents insist their daughters don't feel cut off as school allows enough freedom. Thirteen-year-olds don wellies and stride off in small groups over the fields for Saturday afternoon shopping in Shaftesbury; older girls catch the train to Salisbury. School puts on a bus to Bath if enough girls wish to go.

School meals served in cafeteria with staff on hand to supervise; good food with several choices including a vegetarian option, plenty of fresh fruit, cheese and puddings.

Girls are allowed mobile phones, but no Skype or Facebook until year 11. School Wifi switched off at night. School says that trust between staff and pupils forms the basis of school community; 'older staff are very good at dealing with any minor teasing or bullying'.

Pupils and parents: Girls joining in year 7 come from local primaries, London day schools and boarding preps, eg Leaden Hall. Intake doubles at 13+ from prep schools such as Farleigh, Sandroyd and Port Regis. Some foreign nationals join the school later. Average year group numbers 55, with 70 per cent of families within an hour's drive. Some 15 per cent from abroad, mostly Mexico, Spain and Hong Kong, with a few from Nigeria, Japan and the rest of Europe. There are 25 military families, though no extra bursaries for Forces. Parents are a mixed bunch, some wealthy, some not, whilst girls are natural, unspoilt, polite and articulate. 'The girls like themselves, know themselves and are very confident in their own skins.'

Entrance: Main entry points are at 11 and 13, although girls can join in any year. Entrance examination day takes place in January and includes tests in maths, English and verbal reasoning plus an interview. At 16, girls need a minimum of eight GCSE C grades.

Exit: Most to Russell Group universities throughout the country, eg Bristol, Exeter, UCL, Manchester, Newcastle and Edinburgh. Oxford Brookes also popular. One to Cambridge in 2015 (anthropology). A good handful to art college each year, eg Bournemouth, Falmouth and Plymouth. Most choose arts degrees; good to see that a sprinkling of girls opts for the sciences, eg anatomy, biomedical sciences, physics and nuclear astrophysics. A small number pursues practical courses such as agriculture, publishing and events management. Just a few leave post-GCSE to other sixth forms, mostly co-ed.

Money matters: Usual range of 11+, 13+ and 16+ music, academic and art scholarships on offer together with one 11+ Catholic Local Primary Scholarship. Head's Scholarships 'for excellence' plus means-tested bursaries worth up to 50 per cent of school fees are available at school's discretion.

Remarks: In the past we have described St Mary's as 'a jolly nice girls' Catholic boarding school' but this belies its true character. A reasonably pacey school, St Mary's is performing pretty well on all fronts, albeit with great modesty. 'They don't blow their own trumpet enough,' remarked a parent. With lower fees than many independent schools, this school is quietly delivering excellent value. Girls wanting to be educated with boys and/or dolled up to the nines should look elsewhere, but those looking for a warm and caring environment where they can achieve and be themselves will be right at home.

St Peter's School

Harefield, Exmouth, Devon EX8 5AU

01395 272148
hmoffice@stpetersprepschool.co.uk
www.stpetersprep.co.uk

Ages: 3–13 (boarders from age 7)
Pupils: 299
Boarders: 10 weekly/flexi
Day: £6,870 – £11,790 pa
Boarding: £17,730 pa

Headmaster: Since 2009, Mr Noel Neeson BEd NPQH (late 30s); was educated at Notre Dame High in Glasgow before reading maths at his native city's university. A lifelong supporter of Celtic, he spent two years as a prep school teacher at St Aloysius College in Glasgow before moving south of the border to Crackley Hall, Kenilworth, where he became deputy head. Turned around a failing Catholic primary school in Leamington Spa before being appointed to St Peter's.

'Very, very good,' say parents, who appreciate how he 'takes on board what people say.' 'Distinctly different from his predecessors' and 'communicates his objectives very clearly,' we were told. Man of faith and passionate about his pupils' welfare and progress. Children like the fact that he listens to them first. Energetic, brimming with ideas, he champions assessment for learning and the St Peter's Baccalaureate, which is generating interest in some educational circles.

Married to Juliet (whom he met on the staff at Crackley Hall); they live in centre of school with daughter, Beatrice, who is in the pre-prep. Juliet provides pastoral support for girls and counsels according to need; also teaches RS part-time. Head enjoys watching Exeter Chiefs and playing golf at Aberdovey whilst on holiday in Wales. 'One of the best heads St Peter's has seen,' said one long-term parent.

Moving on in July 2016 to head The Blue Coat School in Birmingham.

Entrance: Non-selective: 'not saturated with tests on taster days,' we were told. Takes rising 3s upwards; staff will decide on admission either into KG or nursery class (voucher system operates but those not aiming at pre-prep go to back of the queue).

Exit: Most remain to 13 and proceed to south-west independent day and boarding schools (Exeter, Blundells, Wellington, King's Taunton, Maynard). Up to two-thirds obtain scholarships; net is being cast wider to include Badminton, Canford and Sherborne. Small number leaves at end of year 6, mainly to Colyton and Torquay grammars.

Remarks: Founded in 1882, St Peter's enjoys a stunning position (a sign near the main entrance invites visitors to 'please enjoy the view') overlooking the Exe estuary. Built for a local notable in late 1820s, Harefield House was in the hands of the Peters family (a portrait of late Admiral Sir Arthur Peters can be seen on the main staircase) for a century until 1949 when the then head, Mr Theophilus Rhys Jones (grandfather of HRH Sophie), moved the school here from Exmouth. Current bursar and a former head are co-proprietors; school is run by an executive management team, assisted by a broad-based committee of reference; estate trustees have considerable say on development issues.

Produces 'aspirational pupils' of all abilities; hugely committed staff are encouraged to 'go with their own ideas.' Head's brainchild is home-grown baccalaureate which encompasses three key learning skills: curiosity, finding and presenting. Core academic areas are balanced by creative and performing arts, plus sport and personal qualities. All children are marked throughout school for effort. Emphasis on personalised learning: children present their understanding using any medium which suits them (which may well not be essay writing). Senior schools have shown considerable interest in this approach. Experienced academic team track children's achievement with emphasis on early intervention.

Co-educational since 1974, balance between sexes fluctuates from year to year; overall numbers close to capacity. Small (14 bed) boarding facility with houseparents in charge; separate dormitories and combined games and common room areas. 'Head makes a fuss of the boarders,' said one boarding mum whose son 'simply loves it.' Flexi-boarding remains a handy option for parents; Friday night provision includes entails sprog collection by 10am on Saturday.

Site includes three main outside areas. Lovely cricket pitch with own pavilion (highlight is annual game against Lympstone village team); adventure playground, separate 10-acre field nearby (used for athletics and rugby) is reached via safe path which snakes its way through much-used forest school woodland area; adjacent smaller field used for pre-prep sports as well as daily activities. New Astroturf for mini hockey and tennis; outside heated swimming pool in use between May and September. Refloored sports hall (squash court also in complex) provides a full size basketball court; doubles up as a venue for assemblies and smaller scale productions.

We saw youngest children measuring paper worms and making numbers with them. Role play areas mutate from fairy castles to butterfly gardens

Discrete early years' section located in somewhat dated timber-clad classrooms: 'we're more interested in what goes on inside,' a mother told us. Carefully zoned outside play areas; new outside performance facility has sound system provided through parental fundraising. Cosy KG classroom boasts highest staff:pupil ratio. Easy transfer to nursery (shell 3) and 90 per cent proceed to reception (shell 4) classes. Forest school and outside learning an important element: we saw tinies enjoying hot chocolate by a camp fire.

Pupils get the 'Swallows and Amazons' treatment and leave knowing they are achievers

We liked the way that planning, monitoring progress and regular information sharing with parents all figure prominently as part of a whole school approach. Goals for youngest broken down into 'stepping stones'. Wide range of reading resources; some nursery children are 'reading ready', we were told. Obvious focus on language development: separate 'time to talk' area promotes confidence; home/school diaries used daily; plenty of imaginative numeracy work: we saw youngest children measuring paper worms and making numbers with them. Lively classroom displays are linked to changing themes. Rôle play areas mutate from fairy castles to butterfly gardens. Regular pre-prep assemblies: classes take turns to present items. Music and French from the start.

Junior years in separate red-brick building. Streaming in English and maths from year 1, and from year 5 upwards teaching is subject-based. Top set all sit CE 11+ exams. Separate scholarship and CE sets in years 7 and 8. German and Spanish introduced in addition to French from year 7 plus Latin for scholars. High proportion of all-round scholarships obtained attributed to breadth of school's curriculum.

Seniors shuttle for lessons between outside classrooms, the main house and modernised science laboratory in wing of the sports hall. Refurbished library on ground floor of main house is focus for research including computers, book related activities throughout year eg for World Book Day. Large music room is used for classroom teaching and rehearsals. New ICT suite on first floor provides for class-based work and is carefully monitored. Large art and DT area in separate hut buzzes with creativity: scholars have own carrels and produce work which impressed us by its range and quality. Every pupil had picture in last art exhibition.

Two formal parents' evenings during year; staff often meet parents after school in flagpole area to sort out small concerns. Email access to all staff and regular newsletters.

Sixty-nine children currently on learning support register; two children are statemented. Strong, switched on remedial help with 'open doors' policy: 'nothing should ever be a shock to parents,' said SENCo, who came to St Peter's with 11 years' experience at Belmont Primary, Chiswick. Range of difficulties includes SpLD and mild Asperger's; to date no child has failed to get a place at a mainstream senior school.

Exceptionally strong sports record maintained over long period with more than a handful making at least county level representative teams. Usual major games for boys and girls; school has really shone at rugby (undefeated 1st XV), netball and squash recently; two boys recently represented English prep school U13 rugby team on tour to France and school also has current England prep schools' U13 squash champions. All children participate at some level; good fixture lists with South West schools, matches on Wednesday afternoons.

Sixty per cent of pupils have individual music tuition; director is supported by 14 peripatetic staff. School hosts Devon Youth Choir/Orchestra and Brass Band. Regular music assemblies, concerts and performances for soloists and groups throughout year. Activities include chamber choir, woodwind groups, brass ensemble and pop cantata. External festivals, competitions and evensong at Wellington School. Most recent tour to Edinburgh. Large scale dramatic productions staged in Exeter's Barnfield theatre.

Jolly lot of pupils with lots to do. No mobile phones allowed during school day. Staff will 'all go the extra mile,' we were told. 'The way everyone joins in to help with school productions speaks volumes,' said deputy head who runs Cross Keys (outdoor adventure) programme. Pupils get the 'Swallows and Amazons' treatment and leave knowing they are achievers. Plenty of after-school activity with full range on Friday afternoons. Options start in year 1 and include drama, yoga and horse riding, not to mention cooking and sailing. Visits start early on and full blown tours feature at upper end and include year 7 stay at Château de la Baudonnière, artists staying in St Ives and ski trip to Andorra.

Pupils come from wide catchment area; many use fleet of liveried minibuses. School day for seniors ends at 5pm. Year 8 pupils take on responsibilities and have own social area. Children meet in tutor groups at start and end of each day. Holiday programme (site closes for only one week in summer) is heavily oversubscribed. Supportive Friends of St Peters run fundraisers and social events such as annual ball and more recently (de rigueur given head's origins) Burns Night celebration. Notable alumni include Olympic yachtsman Ben Rhodes, journalist Anna Tyzack and children's TV entertainer, Dominic Wood.

Bursaries granted on individual basis; substantial number of internal scholarships awarded for years 7 and 8 at head's discretion.

A school with a 'real heart' that may be short on some mod cons but compensates by giving value for money. Unique blend of progressive philosophy and traditional standards in a beautiful setting. Obviously happy children who achieve beyond expectations. A breath of fresh air in every sense.

Salisbury Cathedral School

The Old Bishop's Palace, Salisbury, Wiltshire SP1 2EQ

01722 555300
headsec@salisburycathedralschool.com
www.salisburycathedralschool.com
C of E

Ages: 3–13 (boarders from 7)
Pupils: 208
Boarders: 18 full, 37 weekly/flexi
Day: £7,605 – £14,430 pa
Boarding: plus £6,780 pa

Head Master: Since 2013, Mr Clive Marriott MA BEd (40s). Educated at Queen Elizabeth's School, Crediton and read geography at Winchester. Spent eight years in a large maintained primary school in mid Devon before spending 14 years as deputy head of St Paul's Cathedral School. A very warm, welcoming and genuine man, he is clearly well liked by staff and pupils alike. Began as he means to go on by slimming down the management team, streamlining school process and appointing key stage coordinators to develop the curriculum.

Acknowledges the difficulty of driving some cultural changes, but says, 'What keeps me going is the fact that I'm doing it for the children.' Wants to 'keep raising the bar' of academic standards without losing sight of school's breadth and happy ethos. It's clear that the children are his firm focus as the walls of his study are full of pupils' artwork.

Wears his choir school head's hat with ease in understanding the importance of maintaining good relations with the cathedral and attends nearly every service. Recognises too that the school isn't just about the choristers and is strong on pastoral care for everyone. Would like to banish the term 'non-chorister' for school's other pupils and always appoints head boy and head girl from among year 8 students who are not in the choir.

Has needed his considerable people skills to calm anxious parents, concerned about proposals to move the school from the Bishop's Palace into modern, purpose-built classrooms. At the time of writing, the governors have stated that they do not intend to vacate school's current home. A keen amateur musician, with interests in church music and musical theatre, loves the outdoors and lives by the sea in north Devon. Enjoys cross-Channel sailing and the delights of French culture and cuisine. Fascinated by urban design and especially the architectural landscape of the City of London. "When asked if I have a family, I simply say, 'Just look around you'."

Entrance: Many come up from the pre-prep, otherwise at all stages. Hugely oversubscribed chorister places – uniquely, it has parallel boys' and girls' choirs with entirely equal treatment – are offered as a result of a voice trial, academic assessment and interview; there is an informal test for others. Scholarships are available for music, sport and academic ability at 7 and 11. Day children come predominantly from local primaries and boarders from a wide area: 'choristership knows few boundaries'. A few Forces children and occasional Spanish and South African boarders (none needing extra English), but like most co-ed preps in the area, it could use a few more girls. Leaden Hall and Godolphin Prep are right on the doorstep and claim the lion's share of girls. School's governing body is genuinely endeavouring to keep a lid on fee increases.

Exit: Mainly at 13 to a range of schools eg Eton, Marlborough, Bedales, Cheltenham College, Canford, Bryanston, Warminster, Goldolphin, Kings Bruton, St Swinthun's. most with music

One of the oldest schools in the country; founded in 1091 by St Osmund to educate the choristers of his cathedral at Old Sarum. In the shadow of Salisbury's magnificent spire, its setting is idyllic

awards, but also with sport and all-rounder scholarships or exhibitions. One or two gain specialist music school places. A handful leaves after year 6 to Salisbury's grammar schools or independent schools such as Godolphin and Leehurst Swan (school runs 11+ practice sessions) but only the odd intrepid explorer manages to navigate the choppy waters of the 13+ exam for late entry to the grammar schools (boys' grammar often full). Academic scholarships pop up occasionally – the school says, 'Scholars are being given greater focus and we are proud of the results.'

Remarks: One of the oldest schools in the country; founded in 1091 by St Osmund to educate the choristers of his cathedral at Old Sarum. Moved to its present home, the former 13th century Bishop's Palace centred in 27-acre grounds within the Cathedral Close, in 1947. In the shadow of Salisbury's magnificent spire, its setting is idyllic and appreciated by parents and pupils alike.

School was an early adopter of the Independent Curriculum. Small class sizes (12 on average) are a

big draw for some parents. Strong on science teaching; year 8 pupils regularly do well in chemistry competitions at Southampton University. Geography also good; field trips conducted thoroughly and children encouraged to think independently. French and English teaching much improved. Maths, a long-standing thorn in the school's side, also looks to be on the up. Latin for all from year 6; classical history trips to Italy round out non-linguistic studies (budding classicists don't leave translating Virgil, however). No scholarship set, so able children rely on individual teachers to stretch learning (some do). Regular study-skills workshops introduced for years 7 and 8, plus year 8 maths-skills sessions and English grammar and etiquette lessons for year 5.

Library is very well stocked and organised. All classrooms have whiteboards. Good ICT facilities. Imposing Big School Room, its walls lined with portraits of past Bishops of Salisbury, is an unusual venue for school assemblies and plays. Lovely ancient chapel in main school is used for morning worship twice a week. Welcoming SEN room provides help for 'mainly dyslexic' children.

Music is clearly the school's greatest strength. Some 85 per cent of pupils play at least one instrument; some learn three. 'Music Circus' in years 3 and 4 allows young musicians the chance to try out a wide range of instruments free of charge and determine which they would most like to play. Further up the school, young organists revel in the opportunity to play the cathedral's Father Willis organ. There is a school orchestra, concert band, myriad lunchtime and after-school music ensembles and an annual friendly, non-competitive music festival. 'Everyone' sings and there are three school choirs as well as the two cathedral choirs. Jazbytes, the school jazz band, occasionally performs in public and invariably brings the house down. Weekly, informal Monday lunchtime concerts allow players the chance to perform in front of a kind audience (staff, pupils and parents). Practice sessions are scheduled for boarders and a few day pupils. Music department enters dozens of candidates every term for ABRSM exams and most pass with merit or distinction. A good number pass grade V theory every year. A child doesn't have to be musical to come here, but it would be difficult to leave without a song on the lips and some appreciation of classical and choral music.

Sport continues to improve thanks to new sports teachers. Good Astroturf, three rugby pitches and generous scholarships attract sporty children. All-inclusive approach means nearly everyone gets a chance to represent the school (usual list of prep school sports on offer) and fixture card is healthy. First rounders' team had an unbeaten season recently and all senior teams put in a respectable performance. Wednesday afternoons

devoted to sport. Match teas for parent supporters are 'the best on the local circuit'; the school does these beautifully in summer, complete with home-made cakes and a marquee on the lawn in full view of the cathedral spire. Parking for matches on Wednesdays can be a challenge if lots of parents turn up, as can escaping from school afterwards.

School chaplain promotes a strong Christian ethos in and out of RS lessons; her Friday morning services in the cathedral for the whole school are legendary (balloons have been known to lodge themselves cheerfully in the organ pipes). A good number of parents attend every week and exemplary values are enthusiastically encouraged – Esther Rantzen spoke eloquently about bullying

---

Match teas for parent supporters are 'the best on the local circuit'; the school does these beautifully in summer, complete with home-made cakes and a marquee on the lawn in full view of the cathedral

---

at one year's speech day. As most pupils meet the school's high moral expectations, serious issues are notable by their absence. Upbeat, happy, 'busy bee' school atmosphere possibly explains why the rare case of low-level unkind behaviour lurks below the radar (any concerned parent is always given a prompt hearing) and school staff may need to fine tune their pastoral antennae and ensure that disciplinary procedures remain consistent.

Switched on to the needs of busy parents; day pupils may arrive from 8.00am (to the strains of choristers at morning rehearsal) and stay until 5.30pm at no extra charge. Day prep sessions are easy going; boarder prep is more effectively supervised. No Saturday school, although there is morning music practice for choristers. Other boarders staying in school take part in separate activities. Excellent range of clubs on offer at lunchtimes and before and after school: chess, ukulele, rock band, general knowledge, archery, football, golf, swimming, drama, photography, street dance and sewing are just a few. 'Eco' club tends the lake in Palace grounds (useful for practical science). School musical every year (Guys and Dolls, Oklahoma!, Fiddler on the Roof). Everyone in the prep school can be involved; choristers do not automatically win main singing roles. 'It's the highlight of the school year, and such fun.' Unusual exchange programme with a South African boarding school – two year 7 pupils can spend a term in Graaff-Reinet. Yearly ski trips in Easter holidays. Annual history excursions to France, alternately visiting World War battlefields and Normandy beaches.

Boarding house tucked behind a cream tea shop five minutes' walk away, so boarders (nearly all English) stride off to school for breakfast and do not return until 7 or 8pm. Boarders' bedrooms are wholesome, if rather cosy, with largish dorms for youngsters shrinking to doubles for older children; lots of common areas downstairs. Excursions planned most weekends for those staying in. In term time there are always two choirs in residence and day choristers are required to board twice each term – most regard this as a treat and look forward to 'chori hols' at Christmas, Easter and in July. Boarding house staff works hard to punctuate the choristers' duties with rest and fun (choir parents quip that a closed school kitchen on the final day three times a year isn't so much fun for them).

Music standards consistently good; regular concerts, recordings and live broadcasts in addition to weekly services (duties shared equally between girls' and boys' choirs)

Chorister life runs like clockwork thanks to cathedral's supremely organised director of music and a chorister tutor who puts in hours beyond the call of duty. Musical standards are consistently good and choirs undertake regular concerts, recordings and live broadcasts in addition to their regular weekly services (duties shared equally between girls' and boys' choirs). Choristers play a full part in school life and are treated much the same as other pupils, although they clearly have an extra workload before and after school. Foreign choir tours no longer an annual event, more's the pity.

Boarding house tucked behind a cream tea shop five minutes' walk away, so boarders (nearly all English) stride off to school for breakfast. Excursions planned most weekends

Pre-prep housed in classrooms tucked away in a corner of the Palace grounds, overlooking a pleasant area of lawn. Takes pupils from age 3; these youngest children are charmingly known as Ladybirds, moving up to Dragonflies (year 1) and Busy Bees (year 2). The head – 'a wonderful teacher' – is well supported by committed staff. Approach to early education isn't pushy; nevertheless children thrive and emerge happy, balanced and confident. Red Badges are awarded each Friday for effort, achievement or any other positive contribution and winners are applauded at Monday assemblies. The best class wins the privilege of having Mr Gnome to stay for the week. Has its own sports day and prize giving, an informal lunchtime concert each term, and takes part in the annual music festival. Staff stage a play every summer in addition to the customary nativity. Weekly timetable includes RS, French, games and ballet; pupils use the main school's library, gym and ICT facilities. Year 2 pupils have the chance to experience Music Circus. Own play area and sandpit; teachers are very good at ensuring children play outside every day. Golf coaching sessions, football and gardening clubs, trips to Salisbury Museum and grandparents' tea parties all keep young ones cheerful and interested. No surprise that numbers here are on the up.

Informal atmosphere – cheerful, super-efficient school secretary does much to keep it that way. Head's PA is also a gem, unfailingly helpful and courteous. A tight-knit school where each child is known well, most pupils are very happy and care about one another. 'It's the kind of place where you can go up to some of the teachers and give them a hug.' Former pupils include MPs Robert Key and Michael Mates, actress and singer Amy Carson (Kenneth Branagh, The Magic Flute), organist Bernard Rose, composer Peter Gritton and Sir Anthony Lewis, former president of the Royal College of Music. Judging by the strength of the alumni association and the lasting friendships between former pupils, SCS is a happy and very special place to spend your early school years.

Sandroyd School

Rushmore, Salisbury, Wiltshire SP5 5QD

01725 516264
office@sandroyd.com
www.sandroyd.org
C of E

Ages: 2–13 (boarders from 7)
Pupils: 182 (two-thirds boys)
Boarders: 107 full, 49 weekly/flexi
Day: £8,160 – £19,575 pa
Boarding: £18,750 – £23,700 pa

Headmaster: Since 2003, Mr Martin Harris BSc PGCE (40s). Educated at The Skinners' School and read geography at Loughborough University. Began his teaching career at Ashdown House in East Sussex; after a stint as deputy head at King's School, Rochester, he returned to Ashdown House as deputy head (acting head for one year). A naturally charming, personable man, he is refreshingly honest and has a good sense of humour. Clearly gets on very well with his staff; has overseen much change in his years at the helm and shows no signs of flagging. Ten years ago, Sandroyd was a very traditional all-boys prep school; today it educates girls and boys in what has become 'a more academic, yet also more child-friendly environment.' As if to underline this, Dyllis, the head's small shaggy terrier, nosed her way into his study and trotted across the floor.

Still keen to achieve bigger and better, Mr Harris wants 'Sandroyd to be known nationally for 21st century boarding.' Also preparing the ground to aim for top academic awards to high flying schools, eg Eton, and says teachers are up for the challenge.

Parents praise his tenure. 'During Martin's time, he has made positive changes on all fronts, whilst drama, music and the arts have come on in leaps and bounds,' said one. A keen sportsman, he plays cricket, golf and tennis. Wife Catherine, a chartered physiotherapist, is very involved in all areas except the classroom, eg helping house parents, taking children to appointments, teaching cookery and keeping an eye on staff welfare. They have two young sons, both at the school.

Moving on in July 2016 to head Cheam School. His successor will be Alastair Speers (late 30s), currently senior housemaster at Oakham. Degree in building engineering and management from the University of the West of England; worked for six years in architecture as a consultant engineer, before completing his PGCE at Cambridge in 2005. Has recently completed a master's in education leadership at Buckingham. Keen on rugby, cricket, skiing, sailing, squash and performing arts. Married to Alice, an English teacher; they have two young daughters.

Entrance: Pupils join at all stages, although school policy is to keep numbers below 200, hence there is a waiting list in some year groups. The Walled Garden (pre-prep) takes children from the age of 2. Many join the main school in year 3 from local primary or pre-preps (mostly in Wiltshire and Dorset) and the first full boarders start in year 4, when the school doubles in size. Some come at 10 or 11 from further afield, specifically for senior boarding. Not selective, but all those joining aged 7 and above have an informal interview with the head and are assessed in reading and reasoning. School stresses that tests are not pass/fail exercises.

Means-tested bursaries are available on an annual, case by case basis. Single 100 per cent bursary from year 7 (joint award with Bryanston) is awarded to one child. A further 100 per cent bursary (in conjunction with Radley, St Mary's Calne and Downe House) is available for children of servicemen or women killed or wounded on operational tours.

Exit: Most leave at 13 for eg Eton, Harrow, Radley, Downe House, Marlborough, Winchester, Bryanston, Canford, St Mary's, Sherborne, Dauntsey's, Blundells, Downside, Claysmore; otherwise to schools far and wide. A good handful leave with sport or all-rounder scholarships or

Although it is now less traditional, we were pleased to see that some 'old style' disciplines remain, eg shoe polishing, letter writing and good manners

exhibitions and some win academic, music and art awards.

Remarks: Founded in 1888 by the Rev Wellesley Wesley as a 'small coaching establishment' for aspiring Etonians at his own home, the school quickly flourished. It moved first to Surrey and in 1939 to Rushmore House (the Pitt-Rivers' family home) on the Wiltshire/Dorset borders. School purchased the house and 57 acres within the 400-acre Rushmore estate in 1966. Like most elegant country houses, it sits at the end of a long, winding drive in solitary splendour, surrounded by playing fields, woods and parkland.

Beautiful entrance hall with open fireplace, cosy sofas and lovely wood panelling; head's study is bigger than some studio apartments and has a stunning view of open countryside. Entire school (except pre-prep) is in the original house, although there have obviously been significant additions and alterations, eg theatre, chapel, classrooms and girls' boarding wing. Everything connected by lots of passages (even our pupil guides managed to miss out half the school first time around) but there is an order to the layout once you get the hang of it. Bright, spacious classrooms on the far side of the house are mostly ranged along two main corridors and also have marvellous views. Still feels very much like a country home in the boarders' quarters (sitting rooms and comfy sofas) where house parents have apartments. Although it is now less traditional, we were pleased to see that some 'old style' disciplines remain, eg shoe polishing, letter writing and good manners.

Still true to its original purpose, the school fosters a 'cool to work and achieve' ethos and parents confirm this. 'If you are destined for Eton, you will get there.' Children get lots of support along the way, with each child assigned to a personal tutor who monitors academic progress and keeps an eye on extracurricular activities. 'Tutors always have time to talk to parents and seem to know the children very well.' Strong in most areas of the curriculum thanks to good teaching and positive attitudes, together with small classes of no more than 16. Saturday morning lessons start in year 4. Teachers reward effort and achievement with 'alphas' and discourage slacking with 'omegas'. Pupils collecting enough alphas are treated to an outing and those given omegas have to do penance with a chore.

Maths is set in years 7 and 8; able mathematicians in year 6 join advanced classes. French from year 4 and Latin from year 5. Year 3 also gets a taste of French, German and Spanish, whilst year 8 is introduced to Greek. School has scholarship sets in English, maths, French and Latin. Year 7 pupils go on an annual residential trip to a château in Burgundy. Two very well-appointed ICT suites and an excellent, bright, modern science laboratory. SKULL (skills, knowledge and understanding for lifelong learning) educates beyond the classroom, eg study skills, art appreciation and career skills for older pupils, financial literacy and European culture sessions for younger ones. RATS (reasoning and thinking skills) culminates in a GCSE in year 8 (head took it one year and was out-smarted by some of his pupils). General knowledge questions set for whole prep school every week and tested every Friday. At the time of our visit, there were 32 pupils in the learning support unit and nine pupils with EAL requirements – mostly Spanish pupils at the school for one year. SEN classrooms are welcoming, light and bright (with those brilliant views again).

A very sporty school – games every day and Wednesday and Saturday afternoons devoted to matches and sport. Lots of boys' teams, eg four senior boys' rugby teams with an A and B side at every level, means everyone gets the chance to play for the school. As well as the usual prep school sports for boys and girls, there is tennis and squash coaching, plus archery, shooting and clay pigeon shooting, plus a girls' cricket team. School sur-

We vaulted a stile and strode off across the paddock to watch a lesson. Naturally, the pony promptly morphed into a Thelwellian devil and refused to jump anything

rounded by acres of green space for games and has wide expanses of grass pitches, plus an all-weather pitch, cricket pitch, new netball and tennis courts. Local primary schools invited to enjoy the facilities from time to time. New sports hall. Many individual sporting accolades, eg finalists in IAPS national swimming and athletics championships; some selected for Wessex rugby and U14 and U13 county hockey teams.

A third of the pupils have riding lessons, either on school's ponies or their own (ponies are welcome to board) – eager beginners up to advanced equestrians. In our enthusiasm to see the whole school, we vaulted a stile and strode off across the

paddock to watch a lesson. Naturally, the pony promptly morphed into a Thelwellian devil and refused to jump anything (much to the chagrin of both pupil and instructor, to whom we apologised profusely). Head confessed ruefully that he couldn't see the appeal of riding when his charges fell off! Clearly they don't come off too often, as senior boys' show jumping team has competed in the National Schools Equestrian Association finals.

Head has encouraged the arts and these appear to be in rude health; music is on the up with new head of music. The chapel choir, which now practises several times a week, sings Sunday morning service in the school chapel and has sung evensong in Salisbury Cathedral. There are two further choirs, a school orchestra, string ensembles, brass and saxophone groups, a jazz band and the School of Rock. There are concerts every term and an annual school musical. Eighty per cent play an instrument and music lessons are rotated through the timetable; practice sessions are timetabled and checked. All the usual instruments on offer, plus some less likely, eg tuba, banjo and bagpipes. Music theory and aural training are also available. All pupils in year 4 receive free tuition for one term on an instrument of their choice.

Fantastic theatre, probably the best we've seen outside senior schools, used by all ages from reception upwards. Every year group in the prep school puts on a play and reluctant thespians are encouraged to help out with lighting, scenery and sound. Lovely bright art studio affords plenty of space and light; next door is a small exhibition space for art scholars to display their work. Very well-equipped DT studio, with computers for designing projects (doubles up as a bike repair shop on Wednesday evenings). Lots of activities on offer during designated 'hobby' afternoons, after school and at the weekend, including astronomy, philosophy, scuba diving, pony care, survival skills and den building in woodland belonging to the Rushmore estate. Great climbing wall perches at the back of the main house.

Very well-equipped DT studio, with computers for designing projects (doubles up as a bike repair shop on Wednesday evenings). Lots of activities during 'hobby' afternoons

Boarding provision is very well organised, with a junior house for boys and girls, middle house for boys and senior boys' and girls' wings. Senior girls' wing accommodates those in the top two years. There is flexi or weekly boarding lower down the school, but by year 7 children are expected to board full time and a busy programme at the weekend means most do. As 60 per cent of teachers live on site, every house and wing has its own houseparents as well as a team of matrons. Pastoral care is 'fantastic' and parents praise swift communications between home and school. Any unkind behaviour is stamped on quickly; a parent commented that 'school culture provides very little room for bullying.' Girls' dorms are probably the prettiest we've seen, with lots of pink and attractive lampshades and curtains. Boys' dorms are plainer and slightly more spacious in the senior wing, with three or four to a room. Older pupils have desks in their bedrooms and can choose to do prep here if they wish. They also have their own common rooms and kitchens, where they can make toast and cocoa (and learn to wash and tidy up). We were amazed to learn that school washes day pupils' sports kit as well as all the boarders' clothing. The laundry room resembles a commercial operation – rows of machines and banks of shelves for clean towels, shirts etc.

School lunches are generally good and served in a large bright, airy dining room; snacks of fresh fruit are available throughout the day. Some mothers felt school teas could be healthier, but supper seemed wholesome enough (milk, cereal, bread and fruit). Mobile phones are not permitted in school; overseas boarders are allowed to Skype their parents and others can buy phone cards to call home. There are two obligatory 'weekends in' per term, but on most Sundays children are allowed out for lunch with their parents after chapel. Many choose to remain at school with their friends to join in afternoon activities, eg football, cycling, cookery and hacking across the Downs. 'My only concern about boarding is that my children would rather be at school than at home,' said one mother wistfully.

The Walled Garden (pre-prep) is built on to an original wall surrounding the formal gardens to one side of Rushmore House. A sympathetically designed, unusual curved fibreglass ceiling lets in plenty of light without spoiling the existing aspect. Children are taught in small classes, often by a specialist teacher, with a strong focus on numeracy and literacy. The Walled Garden has its own hall for drama and assemblies (which doubles up as an art studio). A new library has recently been opened. Pre-prep pupils use the main school computers and swimming pool, walk up to the dining room for lunch and can stay on to take part in after-school activities. The playground is packed with activities such as sandpit, musical instruments, bikes, trikes, chickens, wormery and a recently opened Bug Café.

School is 'a happy mix of local and less local folk', with students from all over – a few Spanish there to learn English, with others from Germany, Norway, Japan and Mexico, plus a few expats from Hong Kong, Nigeria etc. School escorts pupils on the train to London on exeat weekends and at half-term, it arranges taxis to airports for overseas pupils. Pupils are uniformly polite, display excellent manners (standing up for the head and visitors to the classroom) and perhaps more important, are utterly unpretentious. A luminary roll call of former students includes Sir Terence Rattigan, Sir Ranulph Fiennes, Lords Carrington, Gladwyn and Wilberforce, Archbishop Ramsey of Canterbury, Rt Revd Roger Wilson, Bishop of Chichester, Professors Hawkes, Godley and Dummett, Randolph Churchill, Ian Gow and many other British and foreign dignitaries.

A very happy school. Full of 'really confident but not arrogant children,' it offers a well-balanced education in spectacular surroundings. Not a hothouse, but prepared to 'push when necessary' to prepare for senior school. There is lots of sport, so those allergic to games might not feel totally at home here. Has retained the best of traditional boarding school values and consigned the outmoded to the dust. We'll watch the top scholarship tally in years to come with interest.

Sherborne Preparatory School

Acreman Street, Sherborne, Dorset DT9 3NY

01935 812097
info@sherborneprep.org
www.sherborneprep.org
C of E

Ages: 2–13
Pupils: 230
Boarders: 40
Day: £8,685 – £16,035 pa
Boarding: £21,960 – £22,980 pa

Headmaster: Since September 2015, Nick Follard, previously head of St John's-on-the-Hill prep in Chepstow. BSc and PGCE from Loughborough; taught young deaf people for three years before moving to Blundell's. He taught A level geography there, and was housemaster for six years, before becoming inaugural head of Blundell's Prep. Used to play first class cricket for Somerset; is also an ISi inspector. His partner, Diane, has a background in speech and language difficulties. He has two children, at senior school and university.

Entrance: Non-selective, non-snooty. Interview with head and school report. Informal assessment when the pupil comes in for a trial day before joining the school. Mainly local families, plus London drift, plus 10 from overseas (boarding from year 3). Scholarships available for academics (papers in maths and English), music, sports and all-rounders. Bursaries awarded on a case by case basis for existing parents. New parents may apply if their child wins a scholarship. Forces discount. A few JET (Joint Educational Trust) children accepted.

Exit: It is independent of the senior schools Sherborne School and Sherborne School for Girls, but has special entry arrangements as a 'preferred prep'; around half of the boys and a quarter of the

---

Now a bustling community hiding behind a mild-mannered Sherborne street-front

girls go on to these schools. Others to eg Winchester, Eton, Canford, Bryanston, Leweston, Cheltenham Ladies', St Mary's Shaftesbury, Marlborough, Rugby, Radley, many with scholarships.

Remarks: Characterful prep marching to the beat of its own drum. Founded in 1885, the school is now

a bustling community hidden behind a mild-mannered Sherborne street-front. Difficult to capture in words – Sherborne Prep looks traditional but thinks outside the box. Open to new ideas; this was the first prep in the area to dump Sats exams. Optional, non-academic Saturday morning programme. Pupils may choose from vast menu of activities and come along – in mufti – for only one hour, or up to three. So families used to their children being occupied on Saturday mornings are happy, teachers enjoy the variety, there is more flexibility for the child who has Saturday commitments outside school etc. Also takes pressure off weekdays – play rehearsals can take place on Saturdays rather than after school or during lunchtimes. Ambitious offerings include extra languages for pupils and/or parents, rock and music tech workshop, bushcraft, forensic detectives, sports coaching, karate, sewing, stage design. Sounds fab, and parents we spoke to were enthusiastic. More than 90 per cent of the children take part and, according to parents, 'it is an outstanding success' with activities supported by Sherborne School and Sherborne Girls. Saturday afternoon matches continue as before.

Keen on international links. Not only is the head from New Zealand but the head of art is Spanish, head of science is French, a senior French teacher is Zimbabwean, the German teacher is Swiss, the Mandarin teacher is Chinese, the EFL teacher is Swiss, gappies come from New Zealand and Australia. Breaking the mould when it comes to languages. In years 1 to 4 pupils learn French, Spanish, German and Mandarin (one each year).

Having glass walls, 'our art room is a place of discovery: pupils learn about themselves while looking at the world, literally'. DT also produces interesting projects

Everyone hunkers down to French in years 5 and 6 plus Latin/classical civilisation. In the final two years, when streaming kicks in, pupils can continue with French or shift to Spanish. Pupils in the CE stream may drop Latin and opt for Spanish alongside French, emerging with two living languages – an option not available to scholars (though the keen can do extra languages on Saturdays).

Thirty-three pupils currently receive help for SEN in big, airy learning support room. Beauteous new library (shoes off before entering) and art room – a wonderful open space, full of light and colour. Having glass walls, 'our art room is a place of discovery; pupils learn about themselves while looking at the world, literally!' DT, also well-housed, produces

Ambitious offerings include rock and tech music workshop, bushcraft, forensic detectives, sports coaching, karate, sewing, stage design. Sounds fab

interesting projects, a notch above standard prep school fare. Main computer room adequate rather than cutting edge. Lots of sport, with girls' sport on a high, says school. Netball best season ever and reached final of Dorset Championships. Girls' hockey is becoming stronger each year as the coaching improves. The U13 girls' hockey team is very strong. Swimming going from strength to strength with new swimming coach in place and pupils competing at the IAPS national finals and winning medals. Boys' hockey is strong, they finished in the top 10 at the nationals last year and boys' cricket had an excellent year, only losing one match. Makes use of some Sherborne School sports facilities eg its Astro (school has its own smaller version). Ninety per cent of pupils play a musical instrument, from beginners up to grade 8; concerts every term. The music centre has now been refurbished to create an even larger teaching space, boasting a new baby grand piano, new (very loud) drum kit, projector, computer with composing software and new musical instruments. Recently appointed first head of drama, indicating the subject's importance within the school.

Lovely children with nice manners. What do they like best? Their 'funny, nice teachers'. Gripes? Would like better match teas ('we get baked beans and sausages instead of cakes'). Retains some of the best prep school traditions like an intricate assortment of lapel badges to indicate accomplishment or responsibility, and teachers dolloping out lunch family-style. Many teachers double up their teaching in weird and wonderful ways eg DT and maths, science and maths, art and basketball. Religion present but inconspicuous. Boarding appealing (especially girls'), flexible and low key. Boarders are mainly children of local working parents, plus a few pupils from overseas and small Forces contingent. Some pop home on weekends, including non-Brits who may enjoy the hospitality of their local friends. A trip is organised on Sundays for those who remain in school. Cheerful pre-prep and nursery, with small classes and much encouragement. Also mother-toddler group. OBs include poet Louis MacNeice and the literary Powys brothers.

Sherborne Girls School

Bradford Road, Sherborne, Dorset DT9 3QN

01935 812245
registrar@sherborne.com
www.sherborne.com
C of E

Ages: 11–18
Pupils: 450; sixth form: 175
Boarders: 410
Day: £18,945 – £23,310 pa
Boarding: £25,890 – £32,085 pa

Headmistress: Since 2006, Mrs Jenny Dwyer BEd (late 40s), formerly head of Prior's Field. Educated at Bradford Girls' Grammar and then read maths at Homerton College, Cambridge. First job at Benenden (teaching/housemistress), then went on to Queen Anne's School, Caversham, where she was deputy head responsible for pastoral care. 'Glad to be back in full boarding', she asserts that 'all girls, not only the very brightest, should have a chance of a seriously good education'. Boarding numbers are up by more that 20 per cent since her arrival and the school is nearing completion of a huge development programme of new buildings and thorough refurbishment of old.

Married to a 'very supportive man', they have two sons (educated at Charterhouse and Milton Abbey). Keen on maths, hockey and dinghy sailing at her home on the Norfolk coast. Pastoral care is her particular passion. Vivacious and easy to talk to, she appears full of creative energy and very stylish. Her most obvious attribute, apart from the ability to negotiate stairs and rough ground at speed on needle thin three-inch heels, is the ability to get people talking freely and confidently. She also listens to what they say.

Academic matters: The number of girls taking IB has grown. Sherborne Girls now offers it as the boys' school dropped it from their curriculum (boys can still do IB with the girls). Mrs Dwyer says girls thrive on its rigour and staff return from IB training courses full of enthusiasm which filters down to everyone. Evidently it's horses for courses, as one girl said she had started it but found she preferred A levels. Results pretty impressive, with average point score of 37 in 2015, including five girls with 40+ points.

At A level greatest uptake is maths with strong results – exceptional in further maths – followed by art and art history (also impressive) and religious studies. Wide range, including Russian, Japanese, theatre studies and DT reflects broad curriculum. In 2015, 60 per cent of A level entries were graded A*/A. IGCSE now used for sciences, maths, and English. These core subjects and modern languages are really star-studded at GCSE, as are art and food

technology. In 2015, 60 per cent of GCSE papers were graded A*/A. One parent commended the school for being hot on picking up and remedying any weakness in the curriculum.

New labs, each with practical and teaching areas, don't even smell of chemicals and announce their purpose to the world via curious sundial on the squat turret. Adjoining is the bright refurbished language department with lots of lovely language IT. When Sherborne refurbishes it's root and branch, not just a lick of paint. French, German, Spanish (plus Latin) on offer and native speakers of other languages can study them to GCSE. New languages, including Russian, introduced in second year – they also get a Prue Leith Cookery School course (the sixth form can brush up on Prue Leith too).

> *Bright, refurbished language dept. When Sherborne refurbishes it's root and branch, not just a lick of paint*

There is flexibility to take subjects jointly with Sherborne Boys' at A level and IB. Theatre studies is genuinely a joint enterprise but has quite a small take-up.

Much setting and streaming from age 13. No form tutors; girls meet individually with personal tutors moving to a new one approximately every two years. The Junior Diploma is an initiative to keep girls consciously reflecting on their own competencies in the foundation areas of knowledge, learning skills, personal attributes and contribution to the curriculum. About 20 per cent of pupils have mild special needs; they may get extra lessons outside hours.

Games, options, the arts: Sport has a high-ish profile now at Sherborne and girls' teams are definitely up with the best in Dorset. They are old hands at the increasingly popular lacrosse and have hosted ELA lacrosse finals for 1st and U15 teams throughout UK. The girls are proud of their record and Sherborne holds pop lacrosse tournaments for prep and primary schools. Even the less sporty get encouragement.

Hockey (county champions and have provided England team members) and netball seriously competitive. All levels of players have access to good coaching. L4 and U4 have sport every day, L5 to U5 have at least three sessions per week, plus activities. The Oxley Sports Centre, with indoor pool, fitness suite, gym, dance studio plus floodlit Astro is getting a facelift, and offers first class facilities to girls and to the town in a smooth-running shared arrangement. Plenty of grass pitches and 27 tennis courts (eight floodlit), mostly artificial.

Bags of other sporty things. Riding team does well in National Schools' Show Jumping at Hickstead, polo, ski trips, various martial arts, dance etc and opportunities via Sherborne Boys' for things like rifle shooting as well as everything (almost) put on for the town in the Oxley Centre.

Art block with libraries, photography and printmaking, has cunning wooden bars across the wide stairwell and entry, allowing for effective display of textiles etc. There are ambitious plans to link this with a new performance centre in the next development phase. Masses of accomplished architectural studies all over the school as well as a few landscapes that might be mistaken for one of the modern masters. Head of art is an inspirational teacher. Good studio space for A level candidates who appear virtually to live here. Weekend workshops offered on juicy topics eg book-binding, stained glass, paper or jewellery making. Overseas trips made jointly with history of art dept. Computer-aided design and manufacture suite.

The undoubted advantage of an all boys' school in the same small market town means the girls can share entertainment and have sensible access to town life

The lovely singing from above when we arrived was Friday choir practice. Several choirs sing in the abbey and even Salisbury Cathedral and benefit from having accessible boys' choirs. Sherborne Choral Society runs jointly with boys' school, one area in which their proximity really enables girls to keep up in an area notoriously hard for girls' schools to build a good tradition. Sherborne Schools' Symphony Orchestra skims off the cream of musicians from Sherborne Girls, Sherborne Boys and nearby Leweston to produce two joint orchestras. Singing, chamber orchestra, jazz band, senior choir, elite madrigal choir etc etc. Girls enjoy music and even take up instruments

when previous experience has been off-putting. Current music building bursting out of its breeze-blocks into huts alongside, so the new performing arts centre is eagerly awaited. Joint musical theatrical productions with Sherborne School and some separate drama.

'A plethora' of societies and clubs for intellectuals (from astronomy to current affairs), the arty crafty (life class – gardening), domestic goddesses (cookery – all sorts) or sporty types (ballet – yoga). D of E gets about 150 and 40+ go on to gold.

Lots of charitable activities including a lovely project for the juniors in the New Aldhelmsted West (just say West) with past pupil Camila Batmanghelidjh CBE, who opened the house. Trip to Nepal exploring and helping in an orphanage – plus all the usual exchanges and field trips such as sea kayaking and trekking in the Spanish Picos. School exchange links with Toronto and Tasmania.

Boarding: Sherborne is one of the few true boarding schools remaining with only about 40 day girls (seven per cent). Day girls are allocated to boarding houses and given their own space (some even their own bed) there. They can stay for the occasional night. No flexi-boarding and there is Saturday school. The majority want to be in on the weekend activities. Ideal for expat parents. Day girls allowed home at 6pm but some stay to do prep until 8pm.

Massive refurbishment of boarding houses means all have pleasant meeting, working, library and dining areas plus 'drawing rooms', for entertaining or watching Downton Abbey. Some girls sleep in cubicles (partitioned compartments in a dormitory – they claim not to make a habit of vaulting the partitions) but most in double or single rooms. Upper sixth girls move into Mulliner with individual study bedrooms and bit of independence. After February of their final year they are allowed into Sherborne pubs.

Background and atmosphere: Founded in 1899 by the Wingfield Digby family – local bigwigs owning Sherborne Castle – the main building is a rambling Victorian warren in the pretty local hamstone. Meticulous planting makes an attractive site with the main boarding houses and teaching facilities forming a crescent round a green expanse of playing fields and lawn on the edge of the town. Still a few 'huts' for drama and music but the five year development plan is already nearing completion after only four years, making way for the next performing arts phase.

Recently completed Aldhelmsted West is a fabulous environment for the first two years with sunny dining room, laid out for birthday tea on our visit, work rooms for homework, lots of comfortable play space and room for music practice. Parents get involved in sports as West positively encourages them to get to know one another. Several live-in staff and a housemistress' house attached with openings onto all three floors. Good big bedrooms, mostly for four, with loo and shower en suite.

The undoubted advantage of an all boys' school in the same small market town means the girls can share entertainment and have sensible and reasonably safe access to town life, a situation envied by similar girls-only schools in the area. Younger girls can go into town at weekends. Lower sixth can go as far as Yeovil, Exeter, Salisbury. Upper sixth girls allowed into the sixth form bar at Sherborne Boys. Common features include coordinated term dates, some A level courses, IB, social events, two joint plays, the Academic society and Epicurean society as well as music.

Pastoral care, well-being and discipline: School rules are straightforward, based on 'keep safe and consider others'. Exclusion for dealing drugs; experimenters can 'expect' to go but 'touch wood no issues' and smoking not really a problem. 'Robust' attitude to alcohol, shared by boys' school, includes possibility of breathalysing. Daily living still done the old school way with all meals in houses with their own separate kitchens and dining rooms. Formal lunches (sixth form do table plans, staff at each table), but cafeteria-style suppers. Hot drinks machines for girls to entertain friends, male and female, in the downstairs areas. Afternoon tea at 5pm and supper at 7.30pm means sensible pre- and post-supper time for supervised prep and activities. Girls say food's pretty ok.

Resident housemistresses, some with families and pets (one house is pet free for allergy sufferers), run the houses like homes with minor medical help and a friendly ear available during the day. Proper school san. The popular school chaplain teaches, offers confirmation etc and keeps an eye that all denominations get spiritual support. Has the right balance of welcome and warmth with respect for girls' views, say parents. Teams of house tutors give personal and academic support on an individual basis. Issues (homesickness, cliques, etc) do crop up but they are very well resolved, said one parent.

Pupils and parents: Still lots of old west country families but also Forces families, diplomats, Londoners with South West connections (Sherborne is on the main line to Waterloo). About 10 per cent come from Hong Kong and elsewhere: Dubai, Nigeria etc plus Europe since IB was introduced. Around 25 need EAL support of one lesson per week. Recently awarded the DfE International School Award in recognition of the international dimension being a key part of school ethos. Sixth form are let out of uniform but have regulation black tailored suit (with a quite skimpy skirt) worn with their own accessories.

Old girls – Camila Batmanghelidjh, soprano Dame Emma Kirkby, violinist Ruth Rogers, writers Sophie Kinsella, Santa Sebag Montefiore, Dames Deirdre Hutton of the Trading Standards Institute and Juliet Wheldon, who was legal advisor to the Bank of England. Sherborne Old Girls are exceptionally efficient: organised into regional circles, they support all sorts of school initiatives, their own charitable causes and a careers information network. Such benevolent networking may lie behind the remarkable collections of speakers who visit Sherborne – AC Grayling on the day of our visit, Germaine Greer, recently, Becky Anderson of CNN, Matthew Pinsent...

Entrance: Visit, registration, 'at work days', taster weekends, deposit paid, then scholarship exams, common entrance papers or own entrance exams in maths, English and reasoning plus an interview. One form enters at 11, a few girls join at 12 but the majority (three forms) enter at 13. Mainly from Hanford, Port Regis, Hazlegrove, Knighton House, Sherborne Prep, Leaden Hall, Perrott Hill, Cheam, Bute House, Newland, Thomas's, Mount House Farleigh, Forres Sandle Manor, Twyford and Sunninghill. About 20 join for sixth form – at least five grade B or above GCSEs required for A level or IB.

Exit: A few leave after GCSEs, mainly to sixth form colleges. After A levels, practically all go on to university to read a wide variety of courses (modern languages, theology, lots of sciency things including medicine). Bristol, Durham, Edinburgh, Exeter, Newcastle, Oxford Brookes and London (LSE, Imperial and UCL) currently leading the pack. A few to Oxbridge most years (three in 2015) and several to art schools or to study academic art history.

Money matters: Boarding fees about what you would expect, on a par with co-ed fees for boarders though less than the boys. Day girls on the expensive side, not really surprising since they are in school nearly twice as long as a day school.

Scholarships generous for a girls' school. Academic, art and music awards pay up to quarter of fees, plus bursaries based on need. Music scholars get up to three lessons per week – more than at most schools. Nearly 100 girls are receiving some sort of award or bursary. Currently appealing for bursary fund. School has also introduced elite swimming programme for which scholarships are offered.

Remarks: No longer the stuffy warhorse of girls' education, though its academic standards are undiminished. Parents appreciate that its good teaching avoids hot housing and encourages a balance of activities. A real gem amongst the girls' only full-boarding schools with all the advantages of its symbiotic proximity to Sherborne boys'.

Sherborne School

Abbey Road, Sherborne, Dorset DT9 3AP

01935 812249
registrar@sherborne.org
www.sherborne.org
C of E

Ages: 13–19
Pupils: 605; sixth form: 230
Boarders: 552
Day: £27,525 pa
Boarding: £34,005 pa

Headmaster: Since January 2016 Dr Dominic Luckett, previously head of Mill Hill School. Educated at the University of Leicester, where he obtained a first class honours degree in history, and at Magdalen College, Oxford, where he completed his doctorate on Henry VII. Taught for 11 years at Harrow School, where he was head of history and an assistant housemaster, before moving to Worth School as deputy head. In 2007 he was appointed headmaster of Mill Hill School and chief executive of the Mill Hill School Foundation comprising the senior, prep, pre-prep and international schools. Mr Luckett, who is married with two children, has published various articles on early Tudor history, is an inspector with the Independent Schools' Inspectorate and a member of the Council of the University of Leicester. His interests include paragliding, skiing and hill-walking.

Academic matters: New academic deputy, David Smith, has gone down well both with boys and parents and is busy ensuring that academic life is 'at the centre of the wheel, with everything else forming the spokes', as he put it. Boys encouraged 'to become much more independent about their learning', and at the same time they are incentivised to do well by the payment of £10 per 10 commendations! Nine or 10 GCSEs is the norm out of the 20 subjects on offer; virtually all do separate sciences (all science is at IGCSE), and at least one language and one humanity, from a list including Latin/Greek, is compulsory. Results are good, rather than stellar, with A*/A grades awarded to 57 per cent of entries in 2015. Individual subject stars tend to be art, all three sciences, history, RS and German. A*-B grades awarded for 72 per cent of A levels taken in 2015; 44 per cent of grades A*/A.

No plans to raise the bar at entry, but those who did not achieve their target GCSE grade in the exams held in the last week of the Michaelmas term were required to come back a day early in January to resit them. Teaching is praised by boys and parents alike: stimulating, with levels of banter which do not overstep the mark (mostly).

'They teach the subject, not just to pass exams,' said one mother, approvingly. Learning support, housed in the top corner of the beautiful science block, was pointed out with the wave of the hand by our guide, whose own needs, hitherto unrealised by him, had been identified and acted upon by its staff. 'Sensationally good, and I still pop in there for extra help', he said, unprompted. All boys are screened on arrival, and sessions on learning styles and study skills are timetabled, as are revision classes as GCSEs loom. Subject teachers work closely with learning support staff in individual cases – all quite unobtrusive, but clearly effective.

Games, options, the arts: Gosh, where to start! Sherborne does everything rather well in the sporting line (except rowing), and it's an important part of life here. Acres of verdant pitches (including the hallowed turf of the Upper, a piece of which went to Rwanda as part of a cricket pitch the boys constructed in 2008), tennis courts, Astro the school has in abundance. Twenty-six sports on offer – including fives, polo and real tennis outside the mainstream; clubs and/or trips cater for minority tastes like surfing, canoeing and skiing. Simply masses of fixtures for all standards and tours (recently Australia and Dubai) for top teams. Main sporting rival is Marlborough. Boys get to try most things out in their first year. Pool and fitness suite on site used by local community, and school has sports physio on the staff. Prominence in the regional or national arena actively promoted by director of sport, who says 'I don't want us to produce good players on an ad hoc basis'. Strong tradition of CCF, Ten Tors and D of E too, actively supported by boys and staff alike.

> *Singing, whether in the sublime setting of the abbey, chanting on the Upper or in the revived house song, matters a lot*

Arts too are tops here. Strong drama emanates from Powell theatre and Victorian Big School Room, neither one ideal performance spaces on grounds of size or original purpose. Lots of productions on school and house level, plus lavish musicals with other schools, Sherborne Girls particularly, but also Leweston and local comprehensive, The Gryphon (all GSG schools). Foreign language plays too, and productions to Edinburgh Fringe. School has produced several notable thespians: John le Mesurier, Jeremy Irons, Hugh Bonneville and rising star Charlie Cox, the two latter (type) cast as posh chaps in Downton Abbey, and Charles Collingwood, landowner and former Lothario, Brian Aldridge in The Archers.

Music has been rehoused in a splendid newish facility, a contemporary yet sympathetic addition to Sherborne's fine buildings. All is state-of-the-art here, so that rock bands (v big here, at least 10 in school) and string quartets can rehearse in neighbouring rooms without conflict. Gorgeous 120 seat recital hall graced with one of several concert grand pianos, all bought new. Technically top notch recording and music tech facilities too; provision, teaching and charismatic head of music, who has returned to teach at his alma mater, all combine to produce some outstanding musicians of all timbres. Practice time protected in an hour after lunch (Q time). Music is a much-loved part of Sherborne for many boys, past and present: 'My son isn't particularly musical, but still plays the piano,' said a parent. Singing, whether in the sublime setting of the abbey twice a week, chanting on the Upper or in the revived house song (banned for a few years for being too rude), matters a lot. Hymns for Sunday services are practised with gusto at Congo and everyone knows the school song, with its rousing chorus of 'Vivat! Vivat! Vivat!' How sad that limited space in the abbey constrains some lower school parents from attending the carol service, an exposition of the finest English choral tradition.

Visual arts have super, dedicated block and permanent exhibition space, where teachers' art is displayed alongside pupils'. Scope for fine art, digital media and DT enormous and very well resourced. Boys love weekend availability, when dabblers seeking light relief are as welcome as fevered public exam candidates hard up against a project deadline. Artworks shown all around the school, which also collaborates with local galleries to put on exhibitions and shows in the town. Impressive results at all levels.

Boarding: Boarding houses all over the town – some in existing buildings (Wallace and the Digby used to be hotels), some purpose-built (Lyon). Accommodation comfortable but certainly not luxurious. Boys in their first year have tended to be housed in one enormous dorm, with individual sleeping compartments for a modicum of privacy, though school tells us they are now mostly in smaller units; thereafter twin rooms and, finally, single rooms at sixth form, sometimes before.

Previous head's mission was to change the culture in boarding houses, where, to an extent, house custom and practice was down to the senior boys; in some, 'chores' (younger boys might nip down to the chippy on behalf of sixth formers, for example) still persisted. No longer. Senior boys are now heavily involved in the pastoral education (not 'care', note) of the younger boys – and assertive, not aggressive or submissive, is what they should all strive to be.

Background and atmosphere: Beautiful school forming a substantial part of a charming and well-heeled Dorset market town, fashioned from gloriously golden ham stone. Founded as a grammar school by Edward VI in 1550 (and still using

> *Atmosphere is one of entitlement – to fabulous surroundings, facilities and opportunities – yet it does not feel horribly posh*

some of those ancient buildings), yet tracing its origins back to the eighth century, it travelled a somewhat rocky road until a period of mass expansion and financial bolstering up in the mid years of the 19th century. School's heart is in the Courts, surrounded by the most historic of its mostly exquisite architecture, boasting two cloistered walls and sharing one with the abbey, and main school facilities, including the dining hall are centrally located. Additions sensitively designed so that they blend well – Pilkington science block an outstanding example. Boys walk through the town on their way to and from lessons. 'I can't believe the freedom, Mum', marvelled one new boy on arrival.

Atmosphere is one of entitlement – to fabulous surroundings, facilities and opportunities – yet it does not feel horribly posh: no anachronistic uniform here, but supremely practical navy blue shirts and jumpers, which don't show the dirt. Suits and ties at sixth form. Definite masculine and work-a-day feel to the place and female staff in an obvious minority. 'Sherborne remains a place where boys will be boys – and girls are welcome,' says the school. Tremendous house loyalty and fierce though good-natured competition between them. Much made of the ideal combination of single sex education provision within the same town, with plenty of opportunities for socialising.

Pastoral care, well-being and discipline: Our previous write-up alluded to the 'occasional Sherborne refugee [from bullying] at other schools', something the previous head was determined to strike out. To that end, he completely overhauled the pastoral guidelines (which have long included an entire section on culture shock for international boys). He was also keen on the idea of value-based leadership promoted by the Bloxham project; school chaplain Lindsay Collins (a senior female appointment which raised a few eyebrows) is a trustee.

A close eye is kept on all boys by their tutors, who meet them at least once a fortnight and who oversee their well-being in and out of the classroom, and by the house staff, particularly matrons, whose status has definitely been raised. It would be difficult for anyone to go on being unhappy for long without someone noticing, according to the pastoral deputy. Bullying swiftly jumped on, school claims, and 'I'd be disappointed if a delicate flower or a quirky chap couldn't survive', the previous head told us. We will see – Sherborne's reputation for a robust environment (robust, mind, not tyrannical) will take some dismantling, even if it no longer reflects the place.

Sanctions have been simplified and far more rigorously enforced too, to some dismay among boys. 'Heavy-handed,' said one, with numerous house gatings on a Saturday evening being handed out for academic shortcomings, as well as the ever-present smoking and drinking offences. 'OTT!' said another, outraged at being gated for being 'one minute late'. 'Clarity of expectations', says school, which, in the previous head's first term, suspended 30 boys for different things; suspensions rarer now boundaries are better defined.

Pupils and parents: Varies from long-established families to first time buyers, but we nearly laughed when the previous head talked about 'a wide economic mix' – with fees over £30k per annum. Catchment tends to be London extending westwards and eastwards from Devon and Cornwall but not much further afield. Members of all professions, the Forces and local gentry send their sons. Turns out confident (perhaps not confident enough, said previous head – but he was an Etonian) and likeable boys, who form many enduring friendships at school. So many people we spoke to remarked that they 'had never met a Shirburnian they didn't like'. Sprinkling of boys from other countries who enhance the place. Limited opportunities to meet parents from other houses socially is a pity, say some; school does put on fantastic events such as Commem (Speech Day), but jollifications are organised within houses, as are refreshments at parents' evenings and the carol service – if you can squeeze in. Parents report improved communications from school, especially by means of the parent portal, where every aspect of their son's school life can be viewed.

Boys walk through the town on their way to and from lessons. 'I can't believe the freedom, Mum,' marvelled one new boy on arrival

Notable old boys include Sir Alastair Pilkington, John le Carré, Chris Martin (Coldplay), Gulf War commander Major General Sir Patrick Cordingley DSO, political commentators Peter Oborne, Tom Bradby, newsreaders Chris Vacher, Simon McCoy, in addition to many others who have reached the top of the tree in the diplomatic service, academia, the church or the sporting arena.

Entrance: At 13, by entrance exam – either CE, scholarship papers or school's own papers. Average of 55 per cent expected at CE. Process starts a minimum of three years in advance by registering and paying a non-refundable fee, currently £100; pre-test in year 7 with guaranteed places for successful applicants, who sit CE as normal. Parents wanting a particular house advised to say so and register early. They may not then know who will be housemaster when little Johnny goes – housemasters remain in post for 10 years, with a further two by mutual agreement. Boys spend a day at school two years before they start. Final confirmation (subject to meeting entrance requirements) plus hefty but refundable deposit 18 months before entry. At sixth form, entry requirements are five GCSEs at grade C or above, with AS subjects at grade B or higher. School not shy to suggest to weaker candidates that they look elsewhere for sixth form. Handful of newcomers (some from abroad) join at this point.

Exit: Around 90 per cent stay on after GCSEs. Almost all to higher education and university of first choice. Inordinate care taken over UCAS advice and applications. Exceptionally well researched and well resourced programme, which extends to boys who defer or redo UCAS after they have left. Surprisingly small numbers to Oxbridge (four in 2015). Top choices are Newcastle, Durham and other northern universities, old and new. A dozen or so to London; Bristol, Cardiff and Oxford Brookes also popular; increasing interest in US universities. Some to medical school or music college, others to land-based careers. Wide range of degree courses taken.

Money matters: Six scholarships of up to 20 per cent and six exhibitions of up to 10 per cent of fees offered at 13+, on basis of 'academic potential and proficiency'. One closed exhibition to 10 per cent of fees offered to sons of the military. Academic scholarships also offered at sixth form, plus awards for artistic, sporting, musical and practical abilities at both entry points. A third of boys receive some financial assistance. Sherborne Foundation supports occasional exceptionally deserving cases, as well as helping the school's wish list to become reality. Expect extras on the bill for trips, all learning support, plus of course the siren call of the school shop.

Remarks: First class boys' boarding in spectacular golden setting, which succeeds in combining the best of ancient and modern without diminishing either. Sharpening up of the academics will secure its place in the galaxy of the greatest English public schools. Stat of flux caused by sudden dismissal of previous head should stabilise as new head makes his mark.

Sidcot School

Oakridge Lane, Winscombe, North Somerset BS25 1PD

01934 843102
admissions@sidcot.org.uk
www.sidcot.org.uk

Ages: 11–18
Pupils: 583; sixth form: 150
Boarders: 170
Day: £14,580 – £16,029 pa
Boarding: £24,045 – £30,333 pa

Head: Since 2012, Mr Iain Kilpatrick BA Med FRSA PGCE, a former RBS banker who saw the light and turned to schoolmastering in the mid-90s, by way of a degree in English from Stirling and a PGCE from Edinburgh. Though English-born, Mr Kilpatrick's upbringing, education and career until Sidcot has been north of the border, but 'Much as I love Scotland, there's not a huge diversity of schools. IB was quite a draw, plus the mix of day and boarding, the area and the size and atmosphere at Sidcot'. Having thrown himself wholeheartedly into the holistic life of Strathallan and during his first headship of Beaconhurst, an all-through day school, he has shown himself ready to do the same at Sidcot, and is often to be seen around school, at its performances and indeed away matches.

Parents reckon he has smartened up the place and the people in it, made it 'more corporate' (for good or ill), and on occasion let technology obfuscate the message – some parents would be perfectly happy with good old-fashioned letters or emails, rather than having to download an app to check what's going on. Some also suspect that he is eyeing the academic performance of the Bristol independents with which Sidcot competes for Bristol families – with a view to upping Sidcot's game. Personally, he is dapper and articulate – 'Not to be messed with,' said one mother – and possessed of a good firm handshake. His students find him 'Scottish, smiley, interested in everything you do, with the power to make things happen'. Married to Katrina (a pharmacist), he has a son and a daughter in the school, and is very family-minded: 'children are an endless source of optimism, humour and entertainment'. Though he admits to being that kind of annoying person who always enjoys their job, he takes much pleasure in the countryside (walking and golf), as well as theatre.

Academic matters: Results are solid if not stellar, with nearly 36 per cent of GCSEs graded A*/A and 38 per cent at A level in 2015. That said, maths is acknowledged as being exceptionally well taught. Year 11 Pathway (up to seven GCSEs taken in a year) scoops up students who need GCSEs, and fast – perhaps because they have bombed elsewhere, perhaps

because they plan to do A levels or IB and need the ground work, or because their English requires a shot in the arm. IB (taken up by about one in five) average score was 32 in 2015. Resolutely not an academic hothouse, which is a large part of its appeal – 'Being force-fed academically just because she is bright would not suit my daughter,' remarked one mother – yet parents are confident that bright children will be sufficiently inspired and well enough taught to achieve all of which they are capable.

'Everyone who needs support, gets it,' according to one parent. 'The teachers will help you hundreds of times till you get it right,' affirmed one child

Mr Kilpatrick is keen on breadth, and has introduced the Sixth Form Passport, comprising the CAS elements (creativity, action and service) of the IB syllabus for all sixth formers, plus 'post-school survival skills'; EPQ is also encouraged. SEN students with mild to moderate learning difficulties, as well as social and emotional issues like anxiety and (a lack of) social skills, are well provided for by well regarded and qualified staff in a light and colourful room; school has CReSTeD status, and staff work closely with English and maths depts. Integration and acceptance are total here – everyone is screened on entry, and periodic assemblies on dyslexia to raise awareness mean it's just part of school life. The undiagnosed are also welcome to ask for support, for example at exam time, and 'Everyone who needs support, gets it,' according to one parent. 'The teachers will help you hundreds of times till you get it right,' affirmed one child.

Games, options, the arts: Twenty acres of pitches, including new all-weather pitch, and a multi-purpose sports hall with the nicest school pool we have ever seen – life-guarding and kayak tuition also happen in it – mean there is plenty on offer at Sidcot. The size of the school causes some parents to bemoan the strength and depth of rugby talent – but naked aggression is possibly not the Quaker way. Sidcot is not, perhaps, the place for an élite sportsperson – more serious players often belong to local clubs – although a pair of sisters have achieved considerable regional and national success at swimming, both in the pool and open water. The equestrian centre opened to the public for livery, Pony Club and equestrian studies in 2010. Its purpose for the school seems to be more to provide qualifications (BTec, BHS) and opportunities for students to ride (some boarders bring their own steeds) than to identify and kick on young, promising riders. All benefit from an indoor and outdoor school (floodlit) and 160 acres of glorious country to hack in. Plenty else for those unmoved by ball games or horses, such as trampolining, archery, TV production, debating and so on. New sports development director giving increased focus on life skills acquired through sport.

Arts are housed in a new light, airy centre which accommodates visual arts, drama and music. Visual arts astound in particular. We witnessed the most controversial A level art exhibit we had ever seen, depicting the conflicting duality of Muslim women, the siren beneath the burqa. Ceramics and textiles also noteworthy. All manner of artistic media are on offer, and those not studying art are welcome to scratch any creative itches at a club or society. DT and product design stand out too: from a man-powered bushfire extinguisher to an iPhone-powered record player – a range of practical, aesthetic and downright eccentric projects are realised. Seven drama productions a year; recent ones include Into the Woods and A Midsummer Night's Dream (directed by students) performed in the grounds; facilities exist to make film and radio also. International students are encouraged to take part, partly to improve their English – but Struwwelpeter in Chinese was surely not to be missed. School takes a show to Edinburgh every other year. Sidcot's music, the school readily admits, would appeal more to fans of One Direction than the Endellion Quartet, resulting in some of the school's most talented classical musicians choosing to take their lessons in Bristol, rather than at school – but they don't half sound impressive at concerts. The auditioned choir (all girls, necessarily limiting the repertoire) tends towards 'the Gareth Malone end of the spectrum', quite possibly because there has never been a tradition of church music. Facilities and tuition designed rather for music tech, creativity and composition.

Outdoor stuff on offer such as D of E, and good use is made of the extensive grounds for gardening, bee-keeping and the construction of a nature trail, inter alia. Trips include a French exchange, Tanzania, Vienna for culture/art/language. PASS – Programme of Activities for Sidcot School – 'a co-curricular initiative based on our key values of integrity, stewardship, self-reflection, adventure and community'.

Boarding: Majority full but a few flexi boarders; around half from overseas. The five boarding houses are sprinkled through the grounds, facilities are clean, tidy yet homely; we were struck by the warmth and knowledge of each boarder displayed by the house staff. Three or four share a room in the younger years; sixth formers in ones or twos. Usual range of sporting and artistic activities after school and at weekends, plus trips to eg cinema, ice skating rink, local festivals.

Background and atmosphere: Sidcot's USP: everyone, nay everyone, we spoke to singled out the atmosphere at the school as being the reason for being there. The school's proud Quaker origins (dating from its founding in 1699), history and traditions are lived out every day, giving it a curiously contemporary feel which is so much more than lip service. The school's first ever founding director of peace and global studies has recently been appointed, with a brief to 'bring 21st century Quakerism to life' right through the curriculum, weaving in themes such as social justice, conflict resolution and global responsibility. Sidcot is now a 'change-maker school', as a member of the Ashoka movement, which aims to 'empower the next generation to lead social, environmental and economic development'. Specifically, the atmosphere is one of respect and tolerance – for those of all faiths and none, for different nationalities, for different gifts, skills or shortcomings, for each individual. Quaker half hour is held every week and presided over by sixth form elders, at which teachers and students have equal rights to speak and to be listened to.

The school's proud Quaker origins, history and traditions are lived out every day, giving it a curiously comtemporary feel

We had never met a more thoughtful bunch of young people. 'The children look out for each other, and the school does its best to bring out well-rounded young adults'; 'a home from home for your child, with similar principles as the ones we have brought them up with at home'; 'the teachers are accountable to the children' were just some of the views we heard. One mother described her daughter as a 'bruised and tender plant when she arrived at Sidcot', but who 'had turned into a strong, forthright and confident young woman, which is moving to see'. We heard about several instances of parents choosing Sidcot for its ethos (dread word) over other schools whose academic, sporting or musical prowess was more notable. Learning is conducted in a calm and conducive environment, where 'punishment is not a word we use,' said one member of staff; some parents though feel on occasion that the benign Quaker view of children needs to be tempered with a dose of realism when it comes to high jinks in class.

There are some charming gardens, covered in brightly coloured gazebos on the scorching summer day we visited, to represent each of four virtual houses

Conveniently situated just beside the A38 running south from Bristol (thankfully with a bridge over it to get to the sports fields), the school's main façade is a pleasing white stucco building, with the inevitable less sightly additions behind it. The main complex of buildings is compact and extremely well signed, but there are some charming gardens in among them, covered in brightly coloured gazebos on the scorching summer day we visited, to represent each of four virtual houses. Sidcot has no physical house system, though there are (of course) five separate boarding houses sprinkled through the grounds, plus the meeting house: a little oasis of calm and quiet just metres from the main building. We were enchanted by the ponies grazing beyond the fence bordering the garden to one of the girls' boarding houses, with a tantalising glimpse of the Mendips behind.

Pastoral care, well-being and discipline: Respectively, exceptionally good and deploying the lightest of touches. We did not uncover any rebels, tearaways, lads or ladettes, and when quizzed, students listed acts likely to attract reproof as 'not listening, disobedience, laziness, doing what you want'. Hardly hanging offences. Censure from one's peers would be a greater deterrent, we sense. According to parents, the head is adamant about drink and drugs in school – one strike and you're out. Sidcot has no bar, unlike most boarding schools with a vibrant sixth form.

Pupils and parents: An intriguing mix of individuals conforming to shared expectations and outlook, but card-carrying Quakers a small minority. Though the students look conventional enough, with uniform on the posh side (striped shirts, blazers), we suspect that Sidcot families conform to fewer than usual independent school stereotypes. When asked what sort of parent would send a child to Sidcot, the head replied, 'Guardian readers indifferent to sipping sherry on the lawn on speech day, whose children see diversity as a strength, who are prepared to stand up for what they believe in'. Also a few locals, refugees from Bristol schools and nearly 20 per cent from overseas thrown into the mix. Notable alumni include Sir George Trevelyan (dubbed the hippies' champion), geologist Robert Shackleton, founder of Macmillan Cancer Support, Douglas Macmillan, Zoe Wanamaker, Justin Webb, and Deborah Warner.

Entrance: Sidcot is academically non-selective so transfer is automatic (and highly praised) from the junior school; otherwise applications are taken at any stage except into years 11 and 13, and places offered on the basis of previous school reports and interviews at the school to 'children who will benefit from an academic education and activities at Sidcot and who will contribute to and benefit from the ethos of our school community', to quote the admissions policy.

Exit: A few after GCSE for a change if they have been there since nursery, some to a greater range of courses and subjects post 16, and quite possibly the brighter lights of Bristol. Destinations comprise old and new universities up and down the land to do an array of courses, with a leaning towards art and design; some gap years. One to Hong Kong, one to Vienna and one to London College of Fashion in 2015.

Money matters: Fees are stepped according to year group, and a loyalty discount (about 12 per cent for boarders, seven per cent for day) applies to anyone staying on to sixth form. In general, fees are noticeably lower than local boarding competition in Bristol, but more expensive than the Bristol day schools which have no boarding infrastructure to fund. Ten per cent sibling discount. Quaker families on occasion receive 100 per cent remission of fees. Scholarships awarded for academics or talent; level of funding is discretionary.

Remarks: A school more likely to produce the head of an NGO than a merchant bank. For those untroubled by notions of social pretension or academic snobbery, yet for whom a considerate altruistic atmosphere really matters, this is just the place

Stonar

Cottles Park, Atworth, Wiltshire SN12 8NT

01225 701741
admissions@stonarschool.com
www.stonarschool.com

Ages: 11 –18 (junior boarding from 8)
Pupils: 181; sixth form: 50
Boarders: 75 full and weekly
Day: £14,625 – £15,795 pa
Boarding: £28,500 pa

Head: Since April 2015, Dr Sally Divall MA PhD PGCE, previously deputy head academic. Following a BSc and PhD in natural sciences at Cambridge, Dr Divall has worked variously at BP, the Bristol Exploratory, as a visiting lecturer at UWE and as a research fellow at Bath University before joining Stonar in 1999. She has two grown up daughters and is a qualified mountain leader. Away from work she enjoys off-road running and mountain trekking.

Sadly, our wish that previous head 'Mr Nutt will stay in the saddle longer than his two predecessors' proved vain, and he left very suddenly in March 2015 after just two years 'to pursue other options', according to the school's new owners, the Spanish consortium, NACE, who are playing this mighty close to their pecho. Nothing unsavoury attaches to Mr Nutt, and some parents are up in arms at the abrupt ending of what had been a popular appointment. The school seems in good heart, despite recent shenanigans, and is doubtless looking forward to a period of stability under a respected successor.

Academic matters: Completely non-selective, and does well by its pupils. Sound teaching, a staff to pupil ratio of 1:6 and rigorous tracking using all the gismos at the school's disposal (CAT, ALIS,

YELLIS) have been put in place to squeeze every drop of potential out of them. 'We want the best academic development for every child – but not at the expense of everything else'; we should think so too.

Vocational options up for grabs in the sixth form such as the British Horse Society qualification

School's results shine more brightly when looked at in relative rather than absolute terms: value-added scores compare well with competitors (38 per cent A*/A grades at GCSE in 2015 and 27 per cent at A level). That said, clever girls also get results which stand up anywhere, but 'Not the school to choose if you want your daughter to go to Oxbridge,' opined one mother. Good single science results at GCSE, but more effort perhaps needed for weaker scientists, where not everyone manages a C even in core and additional syllabuses. Spanish far and away the most popular modern language at GCSE; a two year certificated classics course including basic Latin in years 8 and 9.

Twenty-six subjects on offer at GCSE but a mere 15 at A level (18 on demand, says school); mention must be made, though, of the vocational options up for grabs in sixth form such as the British Horse Society Assistant Instructor qualification, Leith's Basic Certificate in Food and Wine and ECDL. Parents appreciate these alternatives and the clear indication given by the school when their daughters are not A level material. Pupils are now benefitting from a lively programme of cultural, academic and inter-school exchanges and events between schools in the NACE group.

SEN well catered for: about a third of girls have some kind of identified need, mainly dyslexia, but visual and hearing impairments as well as ASD also accommodated.

Games, options, the arts: None can hold a candle to Stonar's equestrian education. The celebrated cross-country courses and show-jumping arena border the drive and lift any rider's heart (this editor's included) and provide a permanent home for the Inter-Schools One Day Event, ISODE. The equestrian facilities (an indoor and outdoor flood-lit school, stabling and grazing for 70 horses) and resources thrown at it deserve their reputation. This is further burnished by recent arrival of a new director of riding, Darrell Scaife, an international event rider of some repute in his first role of this sort. His aim is to produce horsewomen, rather than solely competition riders, and he starts with the building blocks to successful riding: position, anatomy and movement. He's also much interested in learning styles and in equipping his riders to bring on young horses; in fact he has persuaded the school to purchase, with help from sixth form fundraisers, a youngster for his riders to develop. It may all sound rather high-flown, but Mr Scaife has

Challenge Romania, where girls build a home for a destitute family in one formative week, preceded by raising the funds for the opportunity to go

come from Brixton where he is still involved with Ebony Horse Club, which gives inner-city troubled youngsters the chance to ride, and has arranged a highly successful exchange – an eye-opener for all concerned. 'No glamour and plenty of muck', he says and the busy pupils, who do everything for their steeds, whether owned or loaned, bear this out. Clinics from visiting luminaries like Tina Cooke, competitions and trips to national shows and events, plus an exchange with an equestrian overseas boarding school, give riders lots to aim for. New rider development programmes give individual equestrian and academic timetables.

But the riding is prominent, not dominant. About a third of the pupils ride, but those who don't are in no sense second class citizens – and they don't have to get up early to muck out. All usual sports on offer for them (hockey, netball etc but also full contact rugby coached by a Welsh rugby international, no less) and parents like the fact that small numbers mean players of modest ability get to represent the school. Tennis courts grace the front of the main house, and usual independent school provision of floodlit Astro, sports hall, fitness suite and squash courts, 'but the swimming pool is tired', said one parent. Recently upgraded, says school. D of E and lots of trips – to Cornwall for the artists, to Le Touquet as a combined offering for the modern languages and food tech departments, plus skiing and Challenge Romania, where girls build a home for a destitute family in the course of one formative week, preceded by raising the funds for the opportunity to go. Back at school, there are allotments and chickens to be tended – and their produce to be enjoyed. Goats and pigs to follow.

Better known for its drama than its music, perhaps. Vibrant drama dept puts on (amongst other things) a Shakespeare play every year to great acclaim – and not just the easy ones either: Othello was a recent choice. Tons of silverware comes home from the Mid-Somerset Festival and is displayed in the front hall. Small class sizes mean all hopefuls get to star – in a performance space which is functional rather than flashy. About a third of girls take music lessons up to grade 8, but lots of scope too for the more technically inclined, with a well-equipped recording and music tech studio. Concerts at notable Wiltshire Music Centre in nearby Bradford-on-Avon as well as local venues and in school. No singing in assembly, though, when we visited, but a certain amount of bopping and lip-synch-ing in seats, as Aretha Franklin's Respect launched the (entirely secular) topic for the day.

Visual arts housed up stairs in a series of studios; we were lucky enough to see the end of year exhibition hung the height of an airy staircase. The huge dark-room, kilns and Macs ensure all types of artists are well provided for.

Boarding: Sixth form, senior and junior boarding houses have recently received major refurbishment. Upper sixth boarding offers individual study bedrooms and lots of communal space in purpose-built York House.

'Definitely not for metropolitan types,' say parents, which is perhaps why they chose it, and for the fact that girls can be girls without having to keep up appearances

Super homely feel, particularly from house staff and nursing sister; tasty food also an important morale-booster with such limited opportunities for shopping. Parents and girls love the sense of family, and house staff seem nothing short of cuddly. Communication between home and school on the boarding side is reported as good; issues raised are dealt with. 'We've found the school open and accommodating,' one mother confirmed, and girls have opportunities to ask for help with any aspect of their school lives.

Background and atmosphere: Looks and feels like a slightly run-down country house. The school moved to its present home in 1939: it was evacuated from Sandwich and never returned from the Grade 2 listed Cottles Park, a very pretty Strawberry Hill gothic mansion sitting elegantly in acres of rural Wiltshire about eight miles from Bath. 'No muddy boots!' on every outside door – we'd never seen so any pairs of Hunters and Du Barrys gathered in one place. Gracious panelled hall and head's office soon give way to unfortunate, though doubtless durable, red lino corridors, along which purposeful girls scurry, sometimes in regulation navy jodhpurs and fleeces. Again, functional but not flashy.

Less pretty additions hidden behind the main house, as are all the stabling and manèges, and all that green space and lack of traffic – barring a few Landrovers and horseboxes – is beguiling. But it is very rural, with intermittent mobile signal – 'definitely not for metropolitan types,' say parents, which is perhaps why they chose it, and for the fact that

girls can be girls without having to keep up appearances (we saw no make-up, jewellery, tattoos or short skirts) or grow up too fast. The girls like that too.

'At least they're not hanging about on street corners,' said one mother. Super homely feel, particularly from house staff and nursing sister; tasty food also an important morale-booster with such limited opportunities for shopping. Enough male staff – around a third – ensure it does not feel like a nunnery, though some parents feel there could be more.

Bought in 2013 by NACE, a European education group with 21 schools in Europe, India and the US, with development prospects both in academic and bricks-and-mortar terms. Investment in boarding and sports facilities has been swift and evident.

Pastoral care, well-being and discipline: Highly praised. Discipline was hardly mentioned, but sins listed include lateness, untidiness and lack of co-operation. Drink and drugs in school will usually result in suspension, or the boot, depending on the severity of the incident, as will persistent smoking. School anxious to stress that such issues are extremely rare: 'but we've got the policies'. Sanctions start with a green slip progressing to detentions, 'internal exclusion' before sending hard-core miscreants off site on a temporary or permanent basis (not many of those). What did impress, though, was the self-discipline of riders, who need to be up at 7am and to fit all the care and exercise of their mounts in and around the school day.

Pupils and parents: Day girls come from about a 35 mile radius, but boarders from much further eg London and home counties; around 70 per cent from overseas, predominantly SE Asia. 'I was so shy when I came here', said one charming, bright, Hong Kong Chinese girl, misty-eyed at the thought of leaving but destined for Imperial. Parents refreshingly down-to-earth, and free from the hoof-mark of arrogance and pretension which sometimes brands the horse world. Girls seemingly more than content with their rural lot, and unencumbered by pressures from boys/mobiles/social media, none of which function reliably at Stonar. 'Sparky, energetic, quirky but not cliquey,' according to the head. Parents speak well of school events, such as firework night and the end-of-year ball, a splendid affair, judging by the billowing expanse of marquee we saw when we visited.

Friendly integration between nationalities and year groups appears to be standard, but more between day girls and boarders would be welcome; particularly marked at sixth form, where day girls are allowed into the upper sixth boarding house only by invitation. 'But they can all use the sixth form centre', says school, with justification.

Entrance: Non-selective, but girls do sit an entrance exam in January, preceded by a taster day in November, for setting purposes once they arrive in year 7. Scholarships are offered for academic ability, drama, music, sport and riding. From September 2016 boys will be admitted into year 7 and coeducation will be gradually extended throughout the senior school.

For sixth form, admission depends on an interview and report from current school; same range of scholarships on offer, plus all-rounder. Figures from the school suggest quite a few comings-and-goings in most years.

Exit: Quite a few – some 45 per cent – peel off after GCSEs, in search of brighter lights, boys and wider A level choices in Bath or Chippenham; some parents reckon it's all a bit sheltered and quiet for sixth form, and not a realistic preparation for life beyond Stonar's Cotswold stone walls. Of those who stay, the majority head straight off to further education, in many – but not all (eg Sandhurst) – cases to university. Degree courses include medicine and veterinary science at institutions all over the country

and beyond – one to Hong Kong University and one to New York University in 2015. Distinguished old girls include big names in riding such as Junior and Young Rider gold medallist, Georgie Spence and twice Olympic short-lister Lucy Weigersma; actor Romola Garai and controversial author Gitta Sereny.

Money matters: Fees cheaper than many competitors, which is commendable, given the high staff:pupil ratio. Extras on the bill, as expected, but riding good value at about £300 a term. Scholarships to a maximum of 15 per cent of fees, even if more than one awarded; Forces and sibling discounts. Bursaries means-tested, generally to a maximum of 20 per cent off day fees.

Remarks: Stonar's reputation as being a place for the dim and horsy is undeserved and out of date. Not a hothouse, but the distinction made between exhorting girls to do their best and exerting too much pressure is well made. Hunter wellies essential, ability to drive or at least negotiate an oncoming horse-box highly desirable.

Stover School

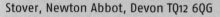

Stover, Newton Abbot, Devon TQ12 6QG

01626 354505
registrar@stover.co.uk
www.stover.co.uk

Ages: 11–18 (junior boarding from year 5)
Pupils: 205; sixth form: 60
Boarders: 90
Day: £7,560 – £12,240 pa
Boarding: £18,570 – £25,050 pa

Head: Since 2014, Richard Notman BSc. Studied finance and stats at Birmingham University but soon discovered he was not made to be an auditor. After taking his PGCE in Manchester, he spent the next eight years in inner-city comps before teaching maths at Withington Girls School and then becoming head of maths at Alderley Edge School for Girls. From there he went to Longridge Towers, Northumberland as deputy head, and finally Cundall Manor School, Yorkshire as head teacher before he swapped the moors for the Devon hills.

'A breath of fresh air', said one parent. He is more than up for the challenge and is excited to be at Stover. He says he 'can cherry pick the best of state and independent practice' and feels he now has the experience, knowledge and confidence to take the school forward. Plus it's rural, small, non-selective, 3 to 18, and co-ed; everything he wants in a school. It's not just a new life for him though; his wife and young family have moved to live in the

school grounds, and his two children are settled in the prep school. He's keen to make this a family venture, and one parent told us, 'Both Mr Notman and his wife Helen have done everything they can to integrate their family into the school and make themselves known and accessible to all. They are a tremendously friendly family, and have placed emphasis on getting to the root of what the parents and children of Stover want changed and improved.'

Some major changes (or 'tweaking' as he calls it) are already under way and parents have been impressed so far. 'Communication from the school has been excellent in this matter,' they say. Research-based learning has been introduced and teachers have all taken it on board enthusiastically. Parents said, 'He has focused the staff on the bigger picture and has given a renewed energy across the school.' Pupils are 'very inspired by his assemblies and messages he is getting across.' His to-do list includes major makeovers for the sixth form

Some impressive work including a John Lennon mural, and large fish sculptures inspired by a recent trip to the aquarium. We were particularly impressed by the photography

and boarding; getting parents more involved; and making as much use as possible of the extensive grounds. One parent told us, 'The new head has been fantastic at attracting new children, as Stover was good but too small.' In his first four months numbers through the whole school rose from 285 to 315. Not a bad start at all.

Academic matters: At GCSE in 2015, 22 per cent A*/A grades. At A level, 14 per cent A*/A and 40 per cent A*-B. Newly introduced vocational qualifications: BTecs in home economics, sport, ICT and performing arts. Maths is a strong subject with top grades at both levels. Stover won the Regional Maths Challenge in 2012 and came third in 2015. Chemistry another strong subject with three students recently winning places at the prestigious Salters Chemistry camps. Photography very popular at A level.

Stover welcomes pupils of all abilities. One parent said, 'It's a non-selective school and does very well in terms of exam results given its mixed ability (and after the grammar schools cream the top academics off).' A boarding school with 15 per cent of overseas students, English is not everyone's first language and this is sometimes reflected in the grades. Parents speak highly of the learning support department, and a whole range of learning difficulties are well looked after here. One said, 'When extra help is required they have the staff to support your child and our daughter was given her own "adult" in maths to sit with her and help her on a one-to-one basis, which helped hugely.'

Along with the introduction of research-based learning, Stover is setting up 'bring-your-own-device'. It is planning to invest heavily in a new (and safe) server instead of upgrading equipment. This will give teachers a new teaching aid, encouraging pupils to research online and become more tech savvy on their own computers. The ISI inspectors reported that 'teaching was excellent,' but we heard some concerns from parents about its quality. One said, 'I think there should be a review of the current teaching staff to ensure any weaker members of the team receive up-to-date training to help them improve their methods.'

Games, options, the arts: Extensive grounds and good sports facilities. Pupils 'relish the 60+ acres at Stover.' There are six all-weather floodlit tennis courts, netball courts, a gym, plus football, rugby, hockey and cricket pitches. The only drawback is that Stover is a small school and there aren't always enough players of the same standard to make winning teams. One parent said, 'They seem to punch above their weight and have won hockey and netball leagues recently against much bigger schools.' However, other parents agreed that there's room for improvement: they would like to see 'a bit more sport and a few more fixtures in the senior school,'

as well as 'investment in a school swimming pool.' Extracurricular activities include table tennis (big here), judo, fencing, clay shooting and more recently a Stover riding team. With the school on the edge of the moors, D of E and Ten Tors are very popular and are a part of life here. The head has linked up with Devon Schools Sports Partnership so that other local schools can make use of the grounds too. They hosted the Devon Schools' Area Athletics Cross-Country Championships 2015 with over 350 competing athletes.

Good music department. One parent said her daughter 'has been inspired by the head of music.... they have nurtured her talent; she was very disengaged with it when she first joined.' Most pupils learn an instrument, there's plenty of concerts and groups to join: the orchestra, brass and jazz bands and choirs. Another parent said, 'Stover has several choirs and is very good at singing and music. They win almost everything in local and regional competitions. My son's year even went to Bruges Cathedral after winning one competition.' Productions, assemblies and concerts all take place in the dome-shaped Jubilee Hall which also houses a recording studio and practice rooms.

As well as music, performing arts and public speaking are strong themes throughout the prep and senior school. Regular productions and plays. 'The ones I have seen are very well produced. I went

We saw the Ukulele Club doing karaoke, and the Ready Steady Fry club had just finished making dough in the well-designed home economics room

to Bugsy Malone the other year and the Match Girls last year. So, very different ones,' said one parent. Stover also offers LAMDA speech and drama lessons with Stagecentre plus performance exams.

The art department has a building to itself. It's well set out with art downstairs, a separate sixth form area at the back, and photography upstairs. Pupils 'love being able to go outdoors to learn – in science and art they will often make use of the natural world around them.' Great displays and some impressive work including a John Lennon mural, and large fish sculptures inspired by a recent trip to the aquarium. We were particularly impressed by the photography upstairs, including some portraits taken on a trip to Brick Lane. More than 10 students taking A level, a high number for such a small school.

The Millennium building is modern and bright with science labs downstairs, and maths upstairs. Floor to ceiling windows, new equipment and colourful murals by a teacher make the labs cheerful and inviting. Small class sizes also mean that there is always enough equipment. Fish, gerbils and even an adopted stray ginger cat add to the happy vibe here. Recent trips include The Big Bang and the Eden Project. Upstairs are two bright and sunny (when we were there) maths rooms, linked by a large balcony, also used as form rooms.

Separate wooden buildings or cabins are used for English, humanities and modern languages. All freshly painted – we could still smell the paint – something else the new head has done to freshen up the school. French is compulsory, then pupils can choose to take either Spanish or German too. There have been group language trips abroad but no home stays due to safety concerns, a teacher told us.

The last wooden building in this cluster is for sixth formers. It has a pool table, the obligatory tatty sofas and a small outside area to sit, chat and play cards. Sixth formers complained to the head that they didn't feel private here and that they felt they 'hadn't moved on'. So, this summer, they will be rehoused in the art building and a new art space will be created. Lucky sixth formers.

Clubs or daily activity sessions take place at lunchtime, with a late-ish school finishing time of 4.30pm. Mixed messages from parents on this. It suits some, but not all. When we were there we saw the Ukulele Club doing karaoke, and the Ready

Steady Fry club had just finished making dough in the well-designed home economics room. Other activities, apart from the usual offerings, include bush-craft, astronomy, Dragons Den, the Raving Reporters, Knitting Club and Man Choir. There's also plans to make more use of the grounds and set up horticultural and farming activity clubs.

As well as language trips abroad, there are regular theatre trips, art trips to galleries locally and in London, field trips to Dartmoor, history trips to Flanders, and a recent sixth form expedition to Tanzania.

Boarding: Boarders make up around 40 per cent of the school (90 pupils). The head sees Stover as different, not as 'regimented' as other boarding schools; he says it's ultimately 'a school, that has boarding provision.' Admissions criteria have been changed and there is now much more focus on language (interviews by Skype). There is also a more varied mix of nationalities, with pupils coming from Bulgaria, Serbia, Russia as well as China, Vietnam, Spain, Germany and Cuba. The plan is to recruit mainly full boarders and offer the flexi option in a very limited and controlled fashion – they don't want it to 'feel like a motel.' Short stays will still be offered during the summer as these serve as good tasters, and day pupils will still be able to take advantage of the wrap-around care.

The boys are lucky to be in the original part of the building with high ceilings, ornate cornices, huge bay windows with shutters, original fireplaces and great views

Girls board on the opposite side of the main school building to the boys. Both areas have been recently refurbished. The boys are lucky to be in the original part of the building with high ceilings, ornate cornices, huge bay windows with shutters, original fireplaces, domed ceilings, arched hallways and great views. It's very tidy; the military background of their houseparent keeps them in check, apparently. He's also well known for getting the boys together for regular evening chats round the dining table. Cheerful rules boards dotted around – live, laugh, love etc – make it feel homely. The large dorms feel light and spacious.

The girls' side, without the original features, is less impressive. The common room felt stuffy, and although it was equipped with PCs, a Wii, a drinks area and dining table, it didn't have the same inviting feel as the boys' room. On the plus side, the girls do have single, double and treble rooms as well as dorms. When we were there the girls were obviously getting ready for the prom, dresses proudly displayed on most wardrobes. Good-sized showers and bath facilities. In fact all the facilities are good – kitchen areas, drinks area and laundry facilities all promote independent living as much as possible.

Usual rules for mobile phones and such, but all seemed pretty relaxed. The boarders here really get to know each other, and the staff, well. Parents say it has a 'friendly, family atmosphere.' Some students even come back for more. Gap year students help out with admin duties, evening activities like football or tennis, and weekend trips to the cinema, the beach, shopping and just recently Stonehenge and Thorpe Park.

Background and atmosphere: Stover School is set in beautiful grounds, 64 acres of parkland located between Dartmoor and the sea. Founded in 1932 by two sisters on the Stover Estate, the object was to help pupils lead independent lives. Boys and girls have been in the prep school since it started in 1996, and boys in the senior school since 2005. The main house, built of granite ashlar, is an impressive sight as you drive in. With its double flight of portico steps it wouldn't look out of place on a film set. Inside, the grand entrance hall continues to impress with high ceilings, beautiful plasterwork and ornate fireplaces. The school is proud of its heritage and cups, plaques and photos adorn the corridors. The rest of the school is housed in various well-designed buildings and wooden outbuildings in the perfectly manicured grounds.

All pupils agree full-heartedly on two things at Stover. Firstly, it's friendly. And secondly, the food is excellent. We saw long queues of hungry pupils looking forward to the curry of the day. One said, 'I love Roastie Wednesday and Fishy Friday!' and apparently lots of pupils happily get dropped off early in time for the boarders' breakfast.

Pastoral care, well-being and discipline: Well-behaved, well spoken and polite. Good behaviour is part of life here and is instilled at a young age – walk into any prep class and they will all stand. The pupils we spoke to seemed happy and proud of their school. Due to its small size, problems are spotted quickly and dealt with swiftly. Everybody knows everybody, but there is a solid support network of house parents, tutors, the school nurse, the school counsellor and the school chaplain if needed. The chaplain takes an active role in school life as well as regular collective worship and running the Christian Union Group.

'One parent per class keeps a database so that round-emails can be distributed with details of coffee mornings and birthday parties – you soon feel part of the furniture'

The house system runs all the way through the prep and senior school and helps to give the pupils a sense of belonging. It's also great to bring out the competitive streaks. There are three houses, but strangely they are then split into boys and girls, making it six houses in all. The pupils we spoke to had no idea why it was like this as the only aspect they are separated for is sport. Presumably this is just a hangover from days gone by when boys and girls didn't mix. Strange that it hasn't changed with the times.

Pupils and parents: Day pupils from Newton Abbot, Exeter, South Hams, Torbay, Bovey Tracey, Plymouth. Boarders mainly from overseas. Parents mostly in professional occupations. Good bus service, or parents can take advantage of the wraparound service from 7.30am to 6.30pm.

Communication is good, there's even a parents' app for news, events and photos. Plus Soundcloud to access all the latest music. Friends of Stover are always busy fundraising, and the upcoming Summer Ball was causing a bit of a buzz. 'There is also a monthly Friend's of Stover coffee morning where parents meet with the headmaster, Mr Notman, and his wife Helen, and can exchange information, chat and generally catch up, which is lovely,' said one mother.

Entrance: Interview with the head, school reports, and a compulsory taster day where they are assessed on academic ability and attitude. One parent told us, 'We all found the entrance process very good. The older two started half way through the year but, they didn't seem to have any problems fitting in and finding their feet. The staff were welcoming, helpful and informative and communication with us was good. Since starting we have not had one single morning that they haven't wanted to go to school.' The school also has a system of parent class reps to help the new parents settle in – 'one parent per class keeps a database of details so that round-emails can be distributed with details of coffee mornings, birthday parties and play-dates – you soon feel like part of the furniture even when you've only been at the school for a matter of months!'

Exit: Around 70 per cent leave after GCSEs, mostly to non fee-paying alternatives. Popular university choices are Plymouth, Exeter, Bristol, Cardiff and Falmouth. One leaver worth a mention is Debra Newbury, awarded the MBE for her services to transatlantic rowing.

Money matters: Academic, music, art and sport scholarships available at most ages up to 20 per cent of day fees. Two means-tested scholarships at year 10 and sixth form, the Maurice Key and Laurus scholarships offering up to 100 per cent of day fees. There's a maths scholarship available to international sixth form students covering 25 per cent of fees at Stover and 10 per cent of fees at Plymouth University. Armed forces and the police force are offered a 10 per cent discount.

Remarks: Stover is a small, friendly school. It's for mixed abilities, and for those that wouldn't suit a larger mainstream setting. It's undergoing some major changes. For the better. Everyone agrees there are 'exciting times ahead'. As one parent put it, 'It was a good school in many ways, but now I think it has the chance to be really outstanding.' And having met the head, we think this is just the beginning. One to watch.

Talbot Heath School

Rothesay Road, Bournemouth, BH4 9NJ

01202 761881
office@talbotheath.org
www.talbotheath.org
C of E

Ages: 11–18
Pupils: 350; sixth form: 120
Boarders: 40
Day: £5,880 – £12,825 pa
Boarding: plus £8,829 – £9,894 pa

Head: Since 2010, Mrs Angharad Holloway, previously head of MFL and IB at Royal High School, Bath. Married, with two girls at the junior school. Mrs Holloway has made some 'fantastic changes,' said a parent, who described the the previous head as somewhat old fashioned. Not so Mrs Holloway, who is gently updating school, curriculum and thinking with a largely conservative constituency of parents. Lively energy – 'enthusiastic all the time,' said one mum. Not goaded by Jeremy Paxman on his visit, so unlikely to be shaken by much.

Keen her girls should have coping strategies for life, and teaches women and leadership to her 12 year olds, who end the course understanding not just about leadership, but also work/life balance and the right to flexible working. Teaches international politics to 11 year olds to broaden their horizons. Most desired quality for her girls on leaving school – resilience. Quite.

Academic matters: 'A first class education for girls,' say parents, who expect results – '[the] priority's always academic,' said one. And they achieve good results. In 2015, 78 per cent of A levels were A*-B (55 per cent of these A*/A). GCSEs – nearly 60 per cent A*-A. 'We do it well,' says the head. 'We are not a hothouse, but [we] do wish each girl to give of her best.' This is strongly felt in the atmosphere of this school. It's not a school where it is cool to muck around. Girls are very aware of why they are there and the importance of exams – 'all the girls want to achieve,' said a parent – but there are light touches. One mum described how her daughter had the school webcam – situated in a nesting box in the woods – on while she revised, so she could keep an eye on the babies.

A great school for value added. Entry requirements not stringent, so the high standards achieved in exams are all the more remarkable. At least in part due (says the head) to being an all-girl environment where girls can flourish – there is not that

'second's hesitation' before a hand goes up. Attracts a number who didn't make the grammars, who do very well – 'I think it's because...the staff genuinely care that the girls do well. Parents' evenings are very businesslike – this is what we need to do for your daughter, and this is how we will do it.'

'Subjects are traditional,' said a parent, 'nothing weird.' It is a conventional and fairly short list (classical civilisation finds a natural home here), but with Mrs Holloway at the helm, with her aim of holistic education, parents can be confident the girls are not being limited. Good take up (around 40 per cent) for A level chemistry and biology – the girls say the teaching of biology is outstanding. Physics is not so popular (just 10 per cent), and the results are less stellar. The head has set up a number of projects with local universities: music, drama – even forensic science; and of course there are her own pet subjects – international politics and women and leadership. Extended Project is also available. Languages are limited to French, Spanish and Latin, and some would like to see German back on the curriculum (it was dropped due to low uptake). But extracurricular Italian was implemented to assist a girl who wanted to study modern languages at university, and attracted a number of other takers, all enthusiastic about achieving GCSE Italian in a year. 'They provide extra if they can,' said a parent.

Sixth formers spoke with great enthusiasm of coming into school with extracurricular questions about favourite subjects and discussing them with teachers during lunchtime – 'It's like we're exploring and learning about it together.' Lunchtime lectures are very popular with sixth formers – one spoke eagerly about listening to Professor Frances Ashcroft talking about ion channels – 'they suddenly fitted in to life.'

Not goaded by Jeremy Paxman on his visit, so unlikely to be shaken by much

Good computer provision: science block has dedicated space for computers, CAT block has a computer room for younger seniors, and lower and upper sixth each have a computer room.

Learning support gets a thumbs up from the girls – apparently no stigma here. 'They help a friend with her spelling every week,' said one matter of factly. Unusually, extra sessions from learning support are free here. Around 10 per cent have support for a range of mild learning disabilities, and they can drop a subject to make life easier. Girls have the highest opinion of teachers, who apparently go out of their way to help those who are struggling. One pupil, who had what she described as a 'maths crisis', spoke with enormous praise and affection about the maths teacher who devoted so much time to helping her regain skills and confidence. Lunchtime maths and science clinics available for those who are struggling.

Girls who speak English as a second language are welcome, providing they pass the entrance exam. Specialist in-house EAL lessons, and will be supported by staff in class. Children from many countries, including Russia, Spain, Germany and Jordan.

Lots of change in the staff in the senior school – around 50 per cent in the last four years (but largely due to retirement). Three classes in each year. Small class sizes (maximum of 20) please parents, who believe they promote good relationships between staff and pupils – and of course get those results.

Games, options, the arts: Dedication to sporting excellence described by parents as 'second to none'. Special tennis programme designed with the nearby West Hants tennis club. About 10 girls are enrolled on the programme, and it is pricey, although the school awards a scholarship to tennis players, so that they are not paying overall more than a regular full fee payer. There is no wish to expand numbers of elite tennis players, so competition to get a place is fierce.

Specialist programmes are not limited to tennis: Talbot Heath has 20 girls at national level in 14 sports, including tennis, netball, rowing and badminton, and there are Youth Olympians among the pupils. This school is small enough to tailor-make education for individual girls, and flexible teaching accommodates the need for elite athletes to train and travel around the country to tournaments, whilst still providing a rigorous education.

But although there are the elite – and yes, they are cool – genuine efforts are made to encourage all: there are some 56 rowers and 70 netball players of all abilities who turn up to training sessions. One parent said they are always coming up with weird and wonderful sports to keep the girls engaged.

'[Sporting] facilities are not as good as at more expensive schools,' said a parent, 'things need to be bigger and better.' In particular, a new pool to replace the 'tired' existing outdoor pool, or at least a cover so year round swimming would be possible, said another. The pavilion on the sports field is a bit ropey (and match teas 'could be a bit nicer' too), but although facilities are not as 'fantastic as they could be...it doesn't really matter,' said one. 'The staff are the thing, and they're amazing, and they work really long hours.' The level of sporting excellence at this school suggest their facilities are indeed secondary to success.

Excellence here is not limited to sports: there are members of the National Youth Ballet, the National Youth Choir, the National Children's Orchestra, the National Youth Orchestra and Wessex Youth Orchestra. Those outstanding in certain areas can drop a subject and have a reduced timetable to accommodate their specialist subject. Many win classes at the Bournemouth Music Festival, and there are monthly informal concerts for parents and friends, as well as more formal affairs.

Drama is popular: and although the drama block is a bit scruffy, it is clearly well loved, with an effective (if claustrophobic) curtained black box space. There are five productions a year, using the black box or the decent sized stage in the school hall. Girls often write their own adaptions – The Lion, The Witch and The Wardrobe was in dress rehearsal when we visited, written by 14 GCSE drama pupils. At another recent production, a parent described things as being '... stuck together...Heath Robinson style,' but the parents we spoke to appreciated the team spirit and the 'all hands on deck' feel, and pupils certainly have a wonderful time.

There's a well-attended debating society, very popular with girls after their stint with the heat in international politics. Art is a strong department, say parents, although conditions are rather cramped. The CAT block includes a room with a battalion of sewing machines – certainly the warmest in the school (everywhere else kept at a fairly brisk temperature; no falling asleep in muggy classrooms here); there are old but well-preserved cookers in the food technology room, where lower sixth is taught a range of low cost dishes in preparation for university.

Boarding: Glossy new facilities in St Mary's boarding house (after a mediocre report from Ofsted). Spacious shared dormitories for those in years 6, 7, 8 and 9, with a cubicle effect (giving semi privacy)

created by desks and cupboards, all in crisp new pale wood. No bunk beds. Own rooms from year 10, which increase in size considerably for those in upper and lower sixth. The boarding house has a rather clinical feel at the moment (it has only recently been finished), but the art department is going to provide some pieces to make it feel a bit more homely.

Sixth formers spoke of coming in with extracurricular questions and discussing them with teachers during lunchtime – 'It's like we're exploring and learning together'

Bathroom facilities clean and new – 'the shower's better than home,' said one girl feelingly. Food varies from average to good, depending on the chef that day, say boarders. Practice room with a piano, and comfy lounges with TV and Wifi. Boarders can have laptops, Kindles and phones – although latter removed at night.

The 40 or so boarders mix across age groups – which creates a family feel, says the housemistress. Boarders seem very happy and well cared for. Most stay at school for the weekend, and are kept busy with a variety of activities, from ice cream making and adventure days to archery and shooting, evena pamper afternoon with homemade facial scrubs (inspired by a trip to Lush).

Background and atmosphere: School formed in 1886 by Mary Broad to provide a first class liberal education for girls. She shocked the locals by exercising her girls on the local common and taking them on trips around Europe.

'Traditional' is a word which comes up a lot when speaking to parents (although the current head is certainly blowing away any remaining dusty elements). Curriculum, staff, behavioural expectations – all traditional, and parents like it. Attractive to one parent for being 'well structured, organised and friendly, [with a] structured discipline.' It is a disciplined environment – although it didn't feel stifling. But rebellious and disruptive girls would certainly stand out; and if their behaviour continued, would need to find a home elsewhere.

Founder Mary Broad shocked the locals by exercising her girls on the local common and taking them on trips around Europe

C of E school, but focus primarily on fundamental values, so those of all faiths fit comfortably. Don't have to attend faith assemblies, but most choose to.

Rather foreboding buildings in the pine woods (but what a lovely smell). Some 30s charm, particularly a gorgeous gym which looks as though it has been perfectly preserved since the building's inception (there's a modern sports hall too). Even has original WW2 bunker classroom, complete with toilet buckets bearing TH emblems. Flags festoon the ceiling of the language corridor. There is art, and it's very good, but it's not spread lavishly around the place (apart from a few entrance displays: a sleepy china pig in bed with many covers, pop art shoes, and the school birthday quilt which all pupils embroidered). School is extremely well ordered, with tidy notice boards.

Chosen by one parent who moved to the area for the selective grammars, but fell for Talbot Heath. She 'loved the calmness...the silence during lessons, and the sense of purpose [in the school]'. One pupil, who chose the school after looking at three in the area, did so on the basis that it was the most welcoming, and said they 'focused on me as an individual.' The individual point is one frequently mentioned by parents, particularly in the context of the local school options: the grammars are big and impersonal, you're just one of the crowd; here teachers treat girls as individuals and want them to succeed. The grammars expect 14 GCSEs. Only nine or 10 taken at Talbot Heath, to make time for the rest of life – for sport, music and drama. One sixth former said she felt she had learnt that you need to spend time doing things just because you enjoy them.

Navy uniform, with a super blue cloak for the juniors (or coat alternative for the self-conscious). No uniform for sixth formers, and although there is the standard no-denim rule, girls succeed in looking very relaxed in skirts and leggings. More comfortable than smart, but these girls have a tremendous sense of purpose. Sixth form common rooms with kitchen facilities, with which they are tremendously pleased. The girls appreciate being treated more like adults in the sixth form, and like the tutorial feel of some of the lessons – cosy further maths lessons for two at the moment. The sixth formers we met were friendly and articulate, but didn't have that public school confidence bordering on arrogance.

Communication good – they do take notice of feedback, said a parent who had protested about the large amount of homework expected of year 9 compared to other independent schools. Another said 'food...is the biggest moan,' but she thought the school was trying to address the issue (on the day of our visit it varied from average pasta to excellent sticky toffee pudding). Parent Staff Society (PSS) meets every three months and responds to every point raised: apparently the PSS works hard to try and keep parents involved after the increase in independence expected of the girls after the move to senior school. Parent portal has got better recently, and the school is proud of its new website.

Pastoral care, well-being and discipline: This is a strong community, and there is a great feeling of vigilance here. Teachers will go out of their way to support pupils, and parents had high praise for their efforts. It's a very supportive environment, and several parents commented on the girls' tendency to encourage and care for each other – 'they positively want each other to succeed'.

Head says there is a strong ethos of respect and care, so those who don't follow this stand out a mile, fitting with school motto – 'honour before honours' (one does feel a hint of Malory Towers here). The school aims to resolve any issues rapidly, and through discussion: 'this is a talking school,' says the head. Differences of opinion are usually sorted by consultation. One parent described how a personality clash between her daughter and another child was sorted out amicably and quickly by coming in to discuss it. Staff are very approachable, say parents, and it's easy to come in and talk.

Usual system of sanctions for unsatisfactory work or behaviour. No one we spoke to had come across drug taking of any sort – of course they experiment at some point, said one parent, but the strong school culture militates against it, at least on school premises.

Pupils and parents: Pupils both from the immediate area and further afield, by bike, train and school buses. About three-quarters of boarders from overseas, and Forces parents – also the tennis whizz kids, who work long days and find it helpful to be on site.

Some comfortably affluent parents, but most feel it's a big decision to pay for education, and those who fork out have academic results as their main priority. Wouldn't suit one-dimensional girls, suggested one parent; nor, with its academic emphasis, those looking for a more vocational education.

Former pupils include Judge Cosgrave, Lady Faithful (social worker and reformer), Charlie Lee-Potter (journalist), Pat Smythe (show jumper), Natalie Clein (cellist), Dame Shirley Williams (politician), Kate Royal (opera singer), Nicole Faraday (actress), Caroline Gledhill (engineer) and Frances Ashcroft (geneticist).

Entrance: Own exam – maths, English and verbal reasoning. Waiting lists for some years, currently 10-12. Most juniors pass the exam to progress to the senior school.

Exit: Lose some to the grammar, mostly for financial reasons, although around 30 per cent depart before sixth form to study something more unusual. They depart after sixth form to universities all over eg London, Exeter and Southampton. Subjects range from veterinary medicine and law to animal behaviour.

Money matters: Parents say the school is cheaper than many independent schools in the area, and very good value for money. 'Prices could go up, and we would still go,' said one parent with enthusiasm. 'Bargain,' said another. Around a quarter of pupils are on scholarships or bursaries of around 10-20 per cent.

Remarks: Does what it says on the packet: a first class education for girls, provided with a great sense of purpose and vigour. Though academic, sport also strong, and excels in accommodating sporting and other extracurricular specialists. Feels like a very safe and caring environment. Better introduce boys yourself along the way though, suggested one parent, or some girls could go a bit crazy at university.

Taunton Preparatory School & Pre Prep and Nursery

Staplegrove Road, Taunton, Somerset TA2 6AE

01823 703307
admissions@tauntonschool.co.uk
www.tauntonschool.co.uk

Ages: 0–13 (boarders from 7)
Pupils: 506
Boarders: 37 full, 41 flexi
Day: £6,660 – £14,430 pa
Boarding: £12,990 – £23,550 pa

Linked school: Taunton School

Headmaster: Since September 2013, Mr Duncan Sinclair MA HDE. Born in Zimbabwe, Mr Sinclair moved to South Africa at the age of 7 and was educated at The Ridge Preparatory School in Johannesburg, and then St Alban's College in Pretoria. Read English and environmental science at the University of Cape Town before completing a higher diploma in education. Began his teaching career in Cape Town at Diocesan College Prep School (Bishops) in Cape Town, also coaching cricket, rugby and athletics. At the same time, he enjoyed a secondary career as a semi-professional rugby player representing Western Province as a second row forward. Moved to St Michael's Preparatory School, Kent, in 2002 where he was year 4 teacher, head of

geography and PSHE and deputy head and completed his MA in educational leadership and management. In addition to taking part in competitive cricket and hockey, Mr Sinclair plays the clarinet, trombone and tuba and is a keen chorister. Married to Georgina, a primary teacher with a PE specialisation. Their son Hamish attends the TPPS Nursery.

Entrance: There are three rungs to the school's ladder. Entry into the nursery classes; then the pre-prep; and finally at 7+ the prep school itself. The first two rungs involve no formal assessment, but rather familiarisation sessions to ensure all parties are happy. Entry into the prep school in year 3 is when those moving up from the pre-prep are joined by some half dozen or so new pupils. Since the prep school year groups grow in size from 36 in year 3 to 72 in year 7, entry is usually possible at all ages. Potential prep school pupils spend a day in the school individually or in pairs, joining their peers for lessons, before sitting papers in maths, English and non-verbal reasoning.

Scholarships available at 11+ for internal and external candidates, academic, music, sport or all-rounder. The all-rounder involves the academic papers plus two of sport, music, drama, art and technology.

Exit: Not surprisingly, the majority go on to the senior school, which is bang next door and offers a gentle and friendly way of moving on with little cultural and social shock. The prospect of spending so many years together doesn't seem to faze the pupils. 'They make friends for life,' said a parent with a child in both schools. No CE but children are setted according to the prep school exams and detailed reports. The headmasters of the prep and senior schools have regular meetings, anyway. Entry to the senior school is almost, but not quite, automatic. Occasionally pupils are recognised as not being up to it and are 'diverted to somewhere else where they can succeed.' The school aims to help the parents select a suitable alternative and to avoid sudden hatchet jobs. Occasionally parents do choose to send their children elsewhere; in the last few years pupils have won scholarships to Winchester, Millfield and Sherborne School for Girls. 'Staff love the challenge and it's healthy to have some variety.'

Remarks: Very good teaching facilities – new, brightly coloured and functional – with an atmosphere of busy purpose, which some of the tattier buildings do nothing to disperse. Indeed, one boy

showed us with justifiable pride a hole in a prefab-looking building where he had driven a cricket ball ('It was an off drive, you see'). Games are taken very seriously, excellent indoor swimming pool.

The dormitory arrangements (girls' named after hills and boys' after rivers) were very popular with our guides, as were the (segregated) common rooms with televisions, presided over by a splendid matron who said she enjoyed being at 'the hub of things'. Tasters are available.

Conducted by a flaming haired Celt who could charm sweet music out of a buffalo

The most stunning aspect of the school is its music. Lessons are offered on an astonishing variety of instruments. There is an orchestra, a jazz band, a clarinet ensemble and a percussion group amongst other formal and informal groups. Some 60 per cent of pupils learn at least one instrument and there are over 100 in the (voluntary) choir. A smaller and selected singing group, coached and conducted by a flaming-haired Celt who could charm sweet music out of a buffalo, has recently sung in Venice. Previous destinations have included Rome, Barcelona and Prague. A vast range of out-of-school activities. Weekend activities for the 40 or so boarders are well organised and popular.

Strong special needs ('learning success') department. All pupils are assessed on entry and provision is put in place, if appropriate. The department consists of a full-time head of department and five part-time teachers and is housed in its own area, which is bright and homely. There is also a 'gifted and talented' extension programme.

The matter of bullying is tackled thoroughly. 'Buddy Groups' – vertical rather than horizontal – meet regularly, as do form captains. In groups and assemblies all are constantly reminded that 'different people have different sensibilities.' Leavers' questionnaires deal with the topic and regular self-assessment reports provide opportunities for airing anxieties. There is even, rather touchingly, a Friendship Bench overlooking the playground. The story is told of an exhausted member of staff plonking himself on the bench only to be approached by a young child asking if he had no friends.

This is a school for children with stamina. It's an action-packed day, and given that some of the children set off early on school buses from as far afield as Bristol and Exeter, Glastonbury and Sidmouth, it's a long one. Just as well the food – eaten separately from the main school but sharing the same kitchen – is so delicious.

Taunton School

57

Staplegrove Road, Taunton, Somerset TA2 6AD

01823 703700
registrar@tauntonschool.co.uk
www.tauntonschool.co.uk

Ages: 11–18
Pupils: 990; sixth form: 280
Boarders: 348 full/flexi
Day: £6,660 – £17,700 pa
Boarding: £12,990 – £33,000 pa

Linked school: Taunton Preparatory School & Pre Prep and Nursery

Headmaster: Since January 2015, Lee Glaser, previously deputy head for five years. Read maths at Liverpool University before qualifying as a chartered accountant with Coopers and Lybrand, and then teaching at Millfield School as senior master and director of sport.

Academic matters: Results are sound considering the non-selective intake: 57 per cent A*-B and 27 per cent A*/A at A level in 2015. Forty-nine per cent A*/A at GCSE. IB Diploma average score was 32.

Alongside the IB, Taunton maintains a broad curriculum culminating in 23 subjects at A level, including photography, music technology and critical thinking (a school passion and something of a hallmark). Mandarin and Chinese literature are offered as part of the IB syllabus.

Taunton's goal seems to be to produce young people that are highly motivated, fully developed and ready to meet the challenges of the 21st century. Taunton may not be a strongly religious school, but there is whiff of Victorian 'muscular Christianity' in its ether: 'We believe we should prepare pupils for the next 50 years of their lives, not just for the next five. Our job is to equip them with values and experiences for a future anywhere in the world. We are not interested in producing children who are clones of their parents; we want them to be themselves.'

In keeping with its commitment to being prepared for change, Taunton is planning a radical overhaul of teaching in science and technology. New facilities for departments of engineering and life sciences will be created to make the academic structure more relevant to new technology and contemporary employment prospects. New courses will include robotics, electronics and computer programming plus co-curricular projects like biochemistry and green power.

Games, options, the arts: The heads of art, music and drama are role models for their pupils. They spoke with passion about the importance of their departments and the value of their subjects to the youngsters. We were treated to Bach on the chapel organ (a spontaneous moment, not a pre-arranged performance) and a drama rehearsal by a group of boys who all seemed to be in touch with their inner Kenneth Branagh, and witnessed myriad examples of paintings, sculptures, installations and photography.

The head of classics, when he's not describing the deeds of the heroes of the Trojan War, can be found pumping iron in the school's new fitness centre

The design technology department is a delight, with tools and machines from modern digital gizmos to old fashioned benches, vices and even a huge anvil a traditional blacksmith would be proud of. It is also the proud manufacturer of a 'Greenpower' car. When we asked about the teaching of craft skills, the answer was short and sweet, 'The pupils confront the task, work out what skills they need to meet it and then acquire them; they could involve a laser or a carpenter's mallet and chisel.'

Sport and exercise are high priority for staff as well as pupils: the registrar is an ultra-runner and the head of classics, in addition to a PhD in classical literature, has the muscles of a body-builder. When he's not describing the deeds of the heroes of the Trojan War, he can be found pumping iron in the school's new fitness centre, an amazing facility that looks like a private members' gym and which earns outside revenue for the school.

There is an abundance of more traditional fields of play, including 20 tennis courts, three gymnasiums, two swimming pools and a pair of Astroturf pitches. Competitive sport thrives at all levels and county-level participation is given precedence over school fixtures. As a consequence, results are excellent and individual achievements impressive.

The range of extracurricular options at Taunton is fascinating. Radio astronomy, green power, rifle shooting, Warhammer and vocal funk are just a few of the more unusual on offer. There's also healthy uptake for D of E and CCF, and we were assured that the senior wind band was an ensemble of musicians, not a nickname for the staff common room.

Boarding: Just under half of pupils board and around 60 per cent of boarders are from overseas. Most stay at weekends, when there is a rota of activities which includes conservation projects, clay pigeon shooting, cycle trips along the local canal, house cookery, fishing, house outings to theme parks and castle visits and picnics. All very jolly.

Background and atmosphere: Taunton's grand neo-gothic Victorian exterior conforms to the popular image of a traditional independent school. The tall clock tower and spire overlooking immaculate lawns and flowerbeds is archetypal, likewise the long corridor of gothic arches and wood panelling. But don't be fooled, this school is far from being educationally conservative, declaring, '…we have little time for social pretence,' and is proud that it has 'no snobs and no yobs'. Typically, a recent trip to China was subsidised at a fixed price of £200 per head to ensure that as many children as possible had the chance to go.

Established in 1847 as an inter-denominational foundation for the sons of nonconformists, and co-ed since 1973, Taunton still has a radical feel. Overtly non-selective, the banner headline for its very glossy, highly professional marketing literature (also emblazoned on its huge fleet of buses) is 'Offering More'. For that, read 'more' than a narrow commitment to academic success; 'more' than sport; 'more' than a single focus on a particular kind of education. Taunton's goal seems to be to produce young people from John Newton's mould: highly motivated, fully developed people ready to meet the challenges of the 21st century.

Staff, parents and pupils alike claimed that, despite its strong work ethic and drive to succeed, Taunton is a very friendly and relaxed place to live and work. Our experience, from two nourishing visits to the dining hall and a parents' evening, where we were left to roam and natter to our hearts' content, suggests that Taunton has got the balance exactly right. The staff mingled jovially, the parents smiled appreciatively and the youngsters behaved like responsible young adults.

Our charming 'minder' was a model English gentleman, except that he was Bulgarian, a product of the school's strong international perspective. Taunton International School, a 9 to 17 adjunct to the main school, serves as a proving ground for foreign students preparing to join the English system, and runs a programme for Taunton youngsters hoping to go to university in America.

Pastoral care, well-being and discipline: The core of the pastoral system at Taunton is the five boarding houses and six day houses. Each housemaster/mistress is responsible for each pupil's well-being and progress and is the first point of contact for parents. They are supported by a house assistant and a team of house tutors. There is a chaplain, a health centre and school prefects. Peer monitoring is encouraged and an 'independent listener' is available by phone.

Our charming 'minder' was a model English gentleman, except that he was Bulgarian, a product of the school's strong international perspective

School is savvy enough to realise that society's ills lurk everywhere and that to keep them at the gates takes constant vigilance. School believes that experienced house staff are vital. They must be able to 'read the tea leaves' and sniff and smell for problems when they are brewing, not when it is too late. Reassuringly, school does not pretend that Taunton is free of the problems that afflict us all, but is confident that most are nipped in the bud, or, on the occasions when they become more serious, are dealt with quickly and appropriately. Parents concurred with this: 'The school is relaxed, but the children know where the boundaries are'. The young people we spoke to agreed. 'The senior staff set a good example, they're easy to talk to, but you respect them because we all know how much they do for us'. 'Most problems are dealt with in our houses, even if they've come in from outside. It's very unusual for anyone to be unhappy here'.

Pupils and parents: Taunton is a modern school for modern times. We met confident, articulate young people and grateful and contented parents. The staff were evangelists for their subjects and it was easy to imagine the positive impact they have on their students.

Parents are a cross-section of society from a huge catchment area; bus routes run from as far away as Bristol, Exeter, Yeovil and Minehead. We met farmers, teachers, nurses, small business owners, civil servants and military personnel; all were gushing in their praise: 'lovely school', 'good kids', 'the staff are great'. Several parents praised the school's inclusivity. 'Even though we live on Exmoor, we thought it was worth the effort. Both our boys have flourished, especially one of them who had dyslexia, he's flying now.'

Entrance: Seventy per cent of Taunton's intake comes from its own preparatory school at 13. External entrants take common entrance, but school insists that the interview is more critical, as is the report from the child's previous head.

Entry at 16+ normally conditional on a minimum of five GCSEs at grade A* to C, but, again, the interview is also important.

Exit: Up to a quarter of students leave after GCSE. Taunton does not offer vocational courses so it believes most leavers at this stage have reached their academic ceiling and need to go elsewhere to continue their education or vocation. Post A level, 96 per cent of leavers go to universities or colleges (UK and abroad). Three to Cambridge in 2015.

Money matters: There are scholarships at 11, 13 and 16 for academic, music, art, sport and all-rounders.

Remarks: Prospective parents can be confident that whatever the future holds, the Taunton School team will give your children the best possible chance of meeting its challenges.

Truro High School

Falmouth Road, Truro, Cornwall TR1 2HU

01872 272830
registrar@trurohigh.co.uk
www.trurohigh.co.uk

Ages: 11–19
Pupils: 299; sixth form: 40
Boarders: 42
Day: £12,003 pa
Boarding: £22,746 – £23,004 pa

Headmaster: Since 2014, Dr Glenn Moodie, early 40s. Originally from New Zealand, he studied classics and ancient Greek at university before coming to the UK to study a PhD in classics at Bristol, and a PGCE at Leicester. This is his first headship, previously at Wycombe Abbey as director of studies, and prior to that, teaching roles at Uppingham School and Clifton College. Currently teaches Latin and history of art to sixth formers. Married to Vanessa, a primary school teacher, their daughter attends the prep. They are still adjusting to life in Cornwall, but he says the drive to school often evokes nostalgic memories of New Zealand, which makes him smile. What he loves about Cornwall is that many people are there because they have made a choice; they want a better work/life balance and their perspective on life is different – health and well-being are paramount.

Truro High School is the only single-sex school in Cornwall. The school says, 'An all-girls education is liberating with students able to be themselves and take on challenges without fear of censure.' However, the co-ed idea was thrown into the ring just as Glenn started and it definitely stirred up

the parents, many of whom are 'more wedded to the idea of single-sex education.' One parent sympathised, saying, 'Dr Moodie had a tricky start with the whole co-ed question – which we believe was essentially down to the governors. Everything has settled now.' In the end, the governors decided to stay all-girls, as they have been for 135 years. Another parent told us, 'The co-ed idea was very badly handled, but communication has been much better since. I would like the head to be much more visible, especially at events where parents are in school. It is his school, he should be there "pressing the flesh".'

In years gone by, there was a co-ed sixth form at Truro High, and although this could be suggested in the distant future, the whole co-ed matter has now been parked indefinitely. Things have without doubt settled down now, and confidence is improving, 'We feel the head teacher is extremely diligent, approachable and non judgmental and that he puts the interests of the school first and foremost.'

Academic matters: In 2015, 30 per cent A*/A grades and 64 per cent A*-B at A level, slightly down from last year; 57 per cent A*/A at GCSE, slight increase on last year's results. The school is regularly top of the county league for A level and GCSE. Twenty-one subjects on offer at A level. Maths and physics are strong, and all girls take separate sciences at GCSE. English is consistently good at both A level and GCSE. Latin holds up very well at GCSE and is still there at A level. MFLs include Spanish, French and German, as well as EAL and a Japanese club. RP is compulsory.

He says the drive to school often evokes nostalgic memories of New Zealand, which makes him smile

With just 253 pupils, all classes are small, and at A level, some are even one-to-one. Very low turnover of staff but a few recent retirements have made way for some welcome new blood. Parents told us, 'We are impressed by and have every confidence in the head teacher and all the other teachers who have been involved in our child's education.' One was a bit more critical: 'I think the teachers are pretty good, but listening to the girls talk about them, I think covering illness etc could be better handled. I still feel there is a lot of stuff which goes unchecked, spelling errors in work displayed on the wall etc, errors in reports.'

According to the ISI inspection report, the school 'provides a good education....the curriculum is good, successfully providing for the needs of all pupils including those with EAL and SEND.' All staff are trained in assessment techniques and the school provides extra study support for those pupils with dyslexia or dyspraxia. Pupils benefit from the small classes which enables regular monitoring and support.

Games, options, the arts: Facilities are pretty good. There's a 25 metre heated indoor swimming pool, full sized Astroturf, a playing field, two netball/tennis courts, and an athletics area for long/high jump, javelin, discus etc. There's also a separate dance studio building, historically only used for ballet, now packed with yoga classes, and street and lyrical dance ensembles.

Netball and hockey fixtures are weekly and the school has won 37 county team sport titles over the past five years. Twenty-five girls represent the county and nine play either hockey or netball for West of England. Girls' football and tag rugby are now included in the curriculum and the new rugby club on Mondays was hot news of the day. Proper rugby, not tag, we were informed. They even had the Cornish Pirates in for a session. Swimming is popular, as is horse riding; they have their own team. Outdoor pursuits like D of E and Ten Tors

are a part of life here. Third fastest all-girl team in Ten Tors challenge on Dartmoor recently.

Most girls learn an instrument and there's a 120-strong choir and a 60-strong orchestra. The new music building has six individual practice rooms and a large main room set up with instruments aplenty and 10 iMacs. Groups include a jazz band, samba band, flute choir, chamber choir and a ukulele club. Recent choir trips and tours include Belgium and Hong Kong.

The performing arts centre has a small theatre used for presentations, as well as larger productions. This year rehearsals are under way for Into The Woods. Last year it was The Importance of Being Earnest. Girls are keen on debating and participate in competitions organised by the ESU and the Cambridge Union. Large numbers doing LAMDA qualifications and Rotary public speaking competitions. One parent told us, 'I think Truro Hugh ultimately gave my daughters self belief. My youngest became the member of the youth parliament for mid Cornwall; she had been taking extracurricular lessons in speech & drama, and debating society. These little extras can make a huge difference to one's future.'

Art is set in yet another outbuilding; rooms are a good size and sixth formers have their own area. Plenty of girls go on to do the prestigious Falmouth foundation course. Textiles also popular and former pupils have gone on to get firsts in design courses, and land jobs at Mulberry or Karen Millen. Head of department once worked for Laura Ashley and knows not just the creative side, but also the logistics of production and manufacture. On our visit there was a lot of excitement for the fashion show that night. Proceeds going towards The Mermaid Centre at Royal Cornwall hospital and purchase of a laser cutter for the department.

Up until GCSEs, girls alternate terms of textiles and food & nutrition. The latter includes food science and is popular, with some even taking it at degree level. One sixth former told us she's signed up for a 'Cooking for Uni' course as one of her enrichment options on Wednesday afternoons. Other options include ceramics, life drawing and photography.

Football, rugby and engineering are also available and enthusiastically taken on board. The school is adamant that there is no pressure, and girls are given the space and confidence to choose. There has been a big drive towards engineering with guest speakers and events on Women In Engineering. The school also has its own racing car team with five cars. With help from the local community, the girls are raring to go and compete in national racing events.

Boarding: 'The fact that both girls loved weekly boarding had a huge bearing on their success at school.' Majority of full boarders are from abroad but the school promote their flexi facilities so families can use them whenever necessary. No plans to change the boarding; the head says it provides the school with some essential cultural diversity, something Cornwall rather lacks. The German students tend to come just for a term to improve their English, but other boarders from Russia, China and Australia and the local islanders from the Scillies are more permanent.

The new rugby club on Mondays was the hot news of the day. Proper rugby, not tag, we were informed. They even had the Cornish Pirates in for a session

Two boarding houses – Dalvenie (years 8 – 10, Rashleigh, (years 11 – 13). Trips for all boarders on Saturdays and Sundays. Treasure hunts in town for the new girls, beach trips, horse-riding, shopping in Exeter and visits to the Tate in St Ives and the Eden Project. For nights in, there's swimming, plus pool parties with inflatables, barbeques, baking and movie nights. Boarders all participate in after-school clubs, and the older girls are allowed into town in pairs – back for supper at 6pm.

The younger girls are four to a room with communal showers and toilets. The older girls can opt for either two in room, or individual rooms, all with ensuites – very much like university rooms (actually a little better). In Dalvenie the common room has a TV, Wii, a pool table, piano, PCs, a dining table and a comfy sofa area. Rashleigh was refurbished a few years ago and the lounge is really rather grown up, set out like a large apartment with sofa/TV area and a fully fitted kitchen. Next door is a quiet room with pianos, a room for the girls to be able 'to get away from it all'. Girls do their own laundry and have a council and regular meetings. Houseparents live on site with their families (and cat). Their daughters also attend the school, so it really is a family affair here.

Background and atmosphere: Founded in 1880 by Bishop (later Archbishop) Benson (first Master of Wellington College) who built Truro cathedral and gave Henry James the idea for The Turn of the Screw. Situated close to the centre of Truro, the school has been on the same site since 1896. The aim was to provide an academic education for girls within a Christian community. The school retains its founding links with Truro Cathedral and commitment to a Christian ethos but welcomes girls of all faiths or none. Hymns are sung in assembly once a week, girls attend services at the cathedral threes times a year, plus twice-termly church services at the local parish church have just been introduced.

The main building is partly castellated and made of Cornish granite, not a grand entrance but a welcoming one. Inside, it's an old building; narrow corridors, wooden staircases, plaques dating back to 1800s, fairly antique toilet facilities, in need of a lick of paint here and there. Outside, the site is very well-maintained, the gardens are lovely, but overall it feels a little disconnected as outbuilding after outbuilding appears, as do seemingly ad-hoc extensions. Shining stars are obviously the most recently built language centre, music block and performing arts building.

The library seems well-used and well-resourced, with a separate sixth form area. School is definitely not overrun with computers, but given its size maybe this is reasonable. Best IT resources appeared to be suite of iMacs in the music room. Wireless internet is available in certain areas of the school and to sixth formers. All social media is blocked until 4pm, when the boarders can log on.

'The sixth form building is fantastic,' say parents. Both floors have work-station rooms with individual carrels – the girls call these 'caroles' and personalise them as much as possible. Most amusing was the fact that the girls were using wine glasses for water (it was definitely water); young ladies at work. Shared common room opens out onto garden. Kitchen with dishwasher, toaster and coffee machine. Girls seemed happy and relaxed, chatting away over a mountain of toast. Lunchtimes in town are allowed but they rarely go, occasionally on birthdays.

Pastoral care, well-being and discipline: Discipline problems are rare and pastoral care is lead by the form tutors and house parents. There is also a nurse on site. Good mentoring and prefect system means that girls of all ages get to know each other – lots of impromptu hugging on our tour as our guide saw her younger friends. This is a small, friendly and unintimidating school. One girl told us how she was bullied in her last school and that she couldn't have felt more welcome when she started Truro High. She made friends easily and says she has never looked back: 'Coming to Truro High was the best thing I've ever done.'

One parent of a boarder told us, 'Only last week my youngest, now in upper sixth, was not feeling very well, but a quick call to the boarding house reassured me. One of the senior members of staff has been there many years and I have formed a good relationship with her. Boarding in Truro High really worked for my girls, it's fun, friendly, relaxed.'

Pupils and parents: Parents are professionals, company directors and the like; many have relocated and now commute by plane or train to London. One told us, 'We are not particularly enamoured of the attitude which is common amongst some of the children and parents of the top tier private schools so were looking for a "third way" of excellent schooling without some of the arrogance, stress levels etc found elsewhere.' They went onto to say, 'We wouldn't have moved to Cornwall if it wasn't for Truro High.'

Others said, 'We were delighted by the atmosphere of the place. The wit and dynamism between children and teachers, the warmth between the girls – the spark was exactly what we were looking for (and what was lacking at the other schools).' Communication from the school to parents is good. 'There is a huge amount of information to share and parentmail does the job well. Teachers are approachable and helpful when required. Communication regarding the general management of the school has improved.'

Uniform up to year 11 is a Balmoral tartan skirt and green pullover. Sixth formers could easily be mistaken for staff – very mature, not a rebel in sight. Parents enthused, 'Can't speak highly enough of the culture of Truro High. Our girls come home at the end of the day with a smile on their faces. They look forward during the holidays to going back to school.'

The school has recently had a publicity makeover thanks to the new director of marketing, Sarah Lillicrap, a former ITV Cornwall news presenter. Amart promo packs, new-look magazines, local news articles, radio plugs and a Facebook page that is updated several times a day. Sarah, an old girl herself, has two daughters at the school and continues to fly its flag by setting up events like the fashion show in conjunction with local businesses, and letting parents use the grounds – one recently put on a refugee in crisis event.

The school is also strengthening its relationship with local community and parents with events such as 'family swim days' at weekends. Anyone is welcome for a small token that is then used to pay the (qualified) sixth formers to lifeguard.

Entrance: Mainly from own prep plus Polwhele House, Roselyon, St Piran's, Bolitho and Truro prep. A decent number are from local state primaries. Boarding numbers are mainly from the UK and Scillies, biggest overseas market currently is Hong Kong, others from Russia, Germany, Spain and Australia.

Girls of all ages get to know each other – lots of impromptu hugging on our tour as our guide saw her younger friends. This is a small and unintimidating school

Applicants for the senior school are invited to a taster day (boarders have a trial night), then sit an exam and interview before admission. For sixth form entry, GCSE grade A*/A in proposed A level choices, plus interviews for UK candidates and test papers/school assessments for overseas students.

Exit: One girl to Oxford in 2015 to study classics/languages; another is studying medicine at Cambridge. Popular choices include Bath, London, York, Leeds and UWE.

On average half leave at 16 to go to (free) Truro College up the road, Truro School or co-ed boarding elsewhere. Old girls include Dame Lynne Brindley (master of Pembroke College, Oxford), TV presenter Hannah Sandling and mezzo soprano Anna Burford.

Money matters: Academic, music, drama, sports and art scholarships available, plus means-tested bursaries at year 7 entry, and into sixth form.

Remarks: Truro High School is unique in Cornwall. It's a small, all-girls school that delivers on qualifications, but nurtures and cares. One parent said, 'We wanted all-girls, so it was a no-brainer.' But most have been overwhelmed by the 'spark' and 'atmosphere' of the school. A few minor grumbles about teachers' spelling and communication, but all we saw were happy, well-behaved girls. One parent said, 'I thoroughly recommend Truro High, for sciences and humanities, for quieter children and more vocal – I have one of each!' It's the type of school that needs to be visited; parents will know immediately if it's right for them or not.

Truro School

Trennick Lane, Truro, Cornwall TR1 1TH

01872 272763
jeg@truroschool.com
www.truroschool.com

Ages: 11–18
Pupils: 760; sixth form: 205
Boarders: 80
Day: £8,550 – £12,945 pa
Boarding: £21,585 – £24,885 pa

Headmaster: Since 2013, Andrew Gordon-Brown BCom MSc QTS (40s). Educated at Hyde Park High School in Johannesburg, read commerce at University of Cape Town and then qualified as a chartered accountant. He rowed for South Africa in the 1992 Olympic Games (team came a creditable eighth) and set his heart on rowing for Oxford or Cambridge. He achieved his dream when he completed an MSc in agricultural economics at Keble College, Oxford and picked up a rowing blue along the way (he rowed for Oxford in the 1994 Boat Race). After 12 years in banking and financial services, working for blue chip companies such as Deloitte, UBS and JPMorgan Chase, he had a 'Damascene conversion' and decided to become a teacher. 'I turned my back on the big bucks,' he told us with a smile. Achieved his QTS via the University of Gloucestershire, taught economics and rowing at Radley for four years and then spent five years as deputy head at Stonyhurst College in Lancashire.

Dedicated, energetic and charming, he has always loved Cornwall (his family owns an old farmhouse on The Lizard) so jumped at the chance to take the reins at Truro School. Keen to use his business background to help pupils, he teaches careers guidance to year 11s and runs financial literacy classes as part of the sixth form's enrichment programme. Has a very global outlook and tells students they should see the world 'as their labour market.' He holds regular lunches for year groups and describes pupils as 'wonderfully unpretentious.' 'Unlike in bigger conurbations, they don't have an edge to them,' he says. Discipline isn't a problem either. As he puts it: 'The teachers teach, the pupils learn and the parents are very supportive.'

His wife Harriet (who was on the same MSc course as him at Oxford) is very involved in school life and they have three children, the eldest at the senior school, the younger two at the prep. They live in a house on the school site.

Still a keen sportsman, he enjoys running, cycling and going to the gym. His family has just bought a boat – 'but I'm a novice sailor' – and he

sings whenever he can (most recently in the Truro School Choral Society performance of Faure's Requiem at Truro Cathedral).

Academic matters: It's cool to work hard here – and the pupils do. Fifty-one per cent of GCSEs were A*/A in 2015, with English lit, maths and physics all strong performers. At A level, 50 per cent A*/A, with maths leading the field. The sciences and maths are particularly strong and many go on to be medics, dentists, engineers and, perhaps not surprisingly given the location, geologists. The school is one of only 230 in the country to offer geology – 'we've got a department that isn't far off a small university department.' School runs more than 20 subjects at A level, including business studies, economics, PE and psychology. Thanks to a bit of timetabling wizardry, students can take any combination (for options submitted in the preceding spring term). EPQ on offer too.

Everyone does at least one language at GCSE and some take up to three (students can study a third language from year 9 in extra twilight sessions first thing, at lunchtime and after school). Mainly French, German and Spanish but the school will do its best to accommodate requests for others (students have taken Chinese, Dutch and Russian in recent years). Exchange trips for younger pupils and work experience in France and Germany for older ones, with CVs written in French and German of course. Music is offered to talented musicians off-timetable as an extra GCSE.

Learning support department with full-time head and two part-time staff. School caters for students with moderate learning difficulties – dyslexia, dyspraxia, dyscalculia, dysgraphia and Asperger's. All students are tested during their first year at the school – extra support given individually or in small groups (no extra cost).

He rowed for South Africa in the 1992 Olympic Games (team came a creditable eighth) and set his heart on rowing for Oxford or Cambridge. He achieved his dream

All pupils are encouraged to be the best they can (school motto is 'To be rather than to seem to be') and they get regular progress reviews, on attitude in lessons, ability to study independently and organisation skills, as well as academic achievement.

Games, options, the arts: A very sporty school, with county champions in rugby, hockey and netball. First XV regularly gets into the last 16 of the NatWest Schools Cup and a sixth former was recently selected for the England U18 XV. Teams often have to travel long distances to compete but pupils don't seem to mind. The school has 40 acres of playing fields, Astroturf, eight tennis courts, cricket pavilion and grounds, climbing wall and a 25m pool, but the jewel in the crown is the new Sir Ben Ainslie Sports Centre, opened by the man himself, which boasts an eight-court sports hall, two squash courts, fitness suite and dance studio. It's used by the local community too – 400 members signed up in a flash when it opened. The days of the school being regarded as 'the rich kids on the hill' have long gone. The school also excels at fencing and runs an elite academy programme. Several youngsters fence at national and international level and are aiming for the 2020 Olympics. A girl in the upper sixth is currently ranked fifth at senior level in the GB. As the head reminded us, 80 per cent of Cornwall's county border is sea, so the school makes the most of the plethora of water pursuits on the doorstep – like sailing, surfing and snorkelling.

The music department buzzes with activity from dawn till dusk. A third of pupils takes instrumental lessons and there are orchestras, choirs, bands and jazz bands to join. Pupils frequently selected for National Youth Orchestra and National Youth Choirs. Around three or four a year take music at A level. School has a strong relationship with Truro Cathedral – it recently announced a new partnership whereby girl choristers aged 13 to 18 will join the cathedral choir and get a 25 per cent scholarship from the school.

Drama is top notch. When we visited, the school was gearing up for a production of Sweeney Todd, complete with an ambitious two-storey revolving stage. Theatre was opened by Sir Tim Rice, and as well as school productions and Friday lectures for the sixth form, it opens its doors to touring companies. Art is superb – everything from oil paintings and life drawing to sculpture and ceramics. The head's study, corridors, boarding houses and art department are lined with stunning artwork. School has strong links with nearby Falmouth University and with local artists (some of their work is exhibited at school's new Heseltine Gallery). We loved the graffiti-style mural painted up the side of the gallery steps – pupils came up with ideas and street artist Cosmic spent five days on a cherry picker creating it. Theatre studies and art are popular at A level. So is DT, which is taught in a proper workshop. Many of the pupils' creations are inspired by the sea. We spotted model yachts, a gadget for cleaning boat chains and a rocking hammock.

Just like their children, they are genial, unpushy and appreciative of the school. As we said last time, there's 'nothing lah-di-dah here'

Wednesday afternoons are given over to extra-curricular activities – everything from sport and music to surfing and war games. Truro pupils certainly don't lack fresh air, that's for sure. D of E is huge here (over 100 take part each year) and there are always school teams in the gruelling Ten Tors Challenge across the wilds of Dartmoor. World Challenge on offer, plus a raft of expeditions at home and abroad.

Boarding: Small number of boarders but head says that he has 'given boarding a bit of a push', and recently opened an additional boarding house for girls. There are now four boarding houses (two for girls, two for boys), all small and homely and each with a resident housemistress or housemaster. Boarders do 90 minutes prep a night in the library, overseen by staff and sixth formers. Lots of activities organised for them at weekends, particularly for the youngest – kayaking, coasteering, surfing, barbecues etc. Older pupils get time to socialise with their friends – 'it's important not to timetable every part of their day,' said a housemistress. Some flexi-boarding available.

Background and atmosphere: Gloriously situated on a hill overlooking the River Truro and the cathedral (you get tantalising glimpses of it as you walk between the buildings). A Methodist school founded in 1880, it opened with 35 boys and two teachers in a schoolroom in the centre of the city and moved to its current site in 1882. Original gothic building in local stone has been much added to – it's 'a bit of a warren,' said a parent – but it adds to the charm. School went co-ed in 1990 and these days 40 per cent of the pupils are girls. Buildings include a lovely 1920s chapel (year 7 and 8 pupils attend twice a week and year 9s and above once a week) and library with 18,000 resources. Whole school assembly every Tuesday. Library staff are dynamic – they produce own reading for pleasure guide, say John Green (The Fault in Our Stars) is the most requested author right now and invite the likes of Meg Rosoff and Patrick Gale to do author events.

Food gets the thumbs-up – 800 lunches served up every day, payment by lunch cards and lots of choice. Boarders eat in the main school, although they can make toast, pasta, hot drinks etc in boarding house kitchens. Sixth formers have to be in school every morning but if they haven't got lessons, they are allowed out after 12 noon. They also have their own café and sixth form centre, complete with common room, study area and thumping music at break time.

Pastoral care, well-being and discipline: School has clear expectations of pupils but everyone we spoke to reckoned it's a fair, equitable place. Prefects are trained to play a big brother/sister role to younger counterparts – all adding to the friendly atmosphere. Most lower sixth pupils do a 16-week peer counselling programme led by the chaplain (who's known as The Rev). When we asked if the school is strict, a year 7 pupil told us: 'There are lots of rules but they are reasonable ones.' Homework is pretty sensible too – starting at 20 minutes a night per subject (up to three subjects a night) and rising as youngsters get older. Good support for new pupils – sixth form prefects look after younger pupils and maps doled out to help them navigate their way round the site. The only improvements year 7s and 8s could think of would be a mini-buggy or ski lift to transport them around the campus. We can't see it happening any time soon.

Deputy head is responsible for pupil progress and welfare. Tutor groups organised by year and tutors are pupils' first port of call if there are any problems (they can also go to their head of year, chaplain, medical centre, school counsellor and sixth form peer counsellors). Head boy and head girl, plus deputies and a raft of senior prefects, and a house system in place. New head is said to be stricter on uniform than his predecessor and pupils are well turned out. Sixth formers wear business dress – 'we have our own fashion sense but we have to look smart,' said one. No jeans and trousers must have a crease.

Pupils and parents: The youngsters we met were down-to-earth, motivated and refreshingly modest about their individual achievements. Our guides included a talented 800m England schools champion and a jazz singer who's in the National Youth Choir, but we had to drag the information out of them. 'Anyone can fit in here – even if they are quite shy,' we were told. Pupils come from all over Cornwall – around half from Truro itself, but others from up to an hour away and as far afield as St Austell, Bodmin, St Ives and Penzance. Many travel long distances by train (a fleet of double-decker buses ferry them from the station) and parents have organised minibuses from places like Helston.

The boarders include weekly boarders who live in the Scilly Isles, children of expats and a small number of international students from countries like Germany, Spain, Italy, Hong Kong, China, Nigeria, Georgia and Ukraine (around 40 with EAL requirements). Everyone mixes in together – 'it's a really friendly place,' a sixth former told us.

Parents are an eclectic group – lots of doctors, accountants and lawyers plus farmers, holiday park owners and entrepreneurs. Just like their children, they are genial, unpushy and appreciative of the school. As we said last time, there's 'nothing flash or lah-di-dah here.' A mother who'd moved from Surrey told us: 'The teachers are incredibly supportive and down-to-earth – questions and queries always get dealt with, and unlike my son's old school, I never come home grumbling.' Parents also said they approve of the way the school treats youngsters as individuals and seeks to discover everyone's talents.

Distinguished former pupils include former M&S chairman Lord Myners, actors Robert Shaw, John Rhys Davies and Nigel Terry, baritones Benjamin Luxon and Alan Opie, sopranos Lynette Carveth and Saffron Jones, quadruple Olympic gold medallist sailor Ben Ainslie, chess grandmaster Michael Adams and Queen drummer Roger Taylor.

Entrance: Around 40 per cent of the pupils come from the school's own prep, the rest from a host of state and prep schools. School is moderately selective (around 110 applications for 85 year 7 places) and main entry points are at 11, 13 and 16. Admission before sixth form is by entrance exam, school report and interview. For pupils joining sixth form, predicted GCSE grades, school report and interview.

Exit: Around a third leave after GCSEs, either because they want a change or to do subjects not offered by Truro School (many head off to the mighty Truro and Penwith College four miles away, although new head says he is determined to increase retention). After the sixth form most go to university (80 per cent straight from school), including a handful to Oxbridge (five in 2015). Maths, sciences and geology are the most popular subjects and Cardiff, Exeter and Bristol the most popular destinations over the last five years, with a few off to Europe or the US. The school offers a specialised careers programme for budding medics, dentists and vets.

Money matters: Academic, art, music, drama, fencing and sport scholarships worth five to 10 per cent of the fees offered. Not a rich school – no endowments – so relies on prudent husbandry and strives to be as inclusive as it can afford to be. Some means-tested bursaries and headmaster's boarding awards (fee discount of 25 per cent) for boarders.

Remarks: A friendly, high achieving school with a real sense of purpose. It combines the best of old and new, makes the most of the bracing Cornish sea air and encourages pupils to find their own niche, whatever it may be.

Wellington School

South Street, Wellington, Somerset TA21 8NT

01823 668800
enquiries@wellingtonschool.org.uk
www.wellington-school.org.uk
C of E

Ages: 11–18 (boys board from 11, girls from 13)
Pupils: 752; sixth form: 150;
Boarders: 105 full, 17 weekly
Day: £5,850 – £14,070 pa
Boarding: £21,174 – £29,028 pa

Headmaster: Since September 2014, Henry Price MA (40s), previously senior housemaster at Rugby. After reading classics at Oxford, started teaching career at Sydney Grammar School (Oxford Classics Fellow), before moving to Sherborne. At Rugby for 13 years; was head of classics, housemaster, coached rugby, cricket and netball, and was involved in 'trips, debating and much more'. He is a governor of Skinner's Academy in Hackney. Married to Mary, whom he met at Oxford, and who is training for her first triathlon; they have four young children. Holidays are spent on the beaches of Anglesey and walking in Snowdonia.

Academic matters: Wellington sits comfortably between its local Taunton independent rivals in academic achievement and considerably higher than the nearest sixth form college. Over the past 10 or so years it has had pretty consistent sound results at GCSE and A level. It is rightly proud of 72 per cent A*-B and 40 per cent A*/A grades at A level in 2015, which is above local competitors. While it's not right at the top of the national league tables, recent scores in maths and science, both IGCSEs, are impressive. (In 2015, 43 per cent A*/A grades overall.) Classes average 22, but not larger than 25. All study French in the first three years and pick up either German or Spanish and Latin. All do RS, Eng lang and lit, maths (IGCSE), either three separate sciences (IGCSE) or dual award, and at least one language (if two taken one has to be French ie can't do Spanish and German). State of art language IT, in use on our visit. Outstanding classics department gives Latin an exceptionally high take up. Music and drama on offer in a basically standard selection, except for Greek, which has grown from a club started 10 years ago, and is taught in spare time. A level offers a free choice and generally manages to timetable it. Economics and classical subjects get a small take up as do all mod langs, with maths (plus further maths) and physics topping the bill, both with very good record of A/A*s. Plenty of options for less academic students, whose results are more than adequate. High fliers – quite

Aristotle the axoltl (Mexican amphibian with external gills) is lovingly looked after by the physics technician, typifying the enterprising flexibility of the school

a few of them – with some fast track arrangements when parents request it.

Extensive new labs are well designed (by teachers) with separate areas for study and practical work. Aristotle the axolotl (Mexican amphibian with external gills) is lovingly looked after by the physics technician, typifying the enterprising flexibility of the school. Though large and exceptionally well-equipped, the labs are functional rather than spectacular, with lots of bare breezeblock – reflecting the common sense economy which has allowed the school to undertake massive developments over the years. Spacious but understated new English teaching block also houses a comprehensive SEN department (SEN help offered at need on individual or group basis by qualified staff of three, though charges for extra English for foreign students) and an enormous exam hall. It means other spaces don't get blocked at exam time and gives assembly and function space. One year GCSE programme for students from abroad allows them to get up to five basic subject passes in order to do A levels in sixth form or IB elsewhere.

Games, options, the arts: Even those reluctant to exercise seem to get a look in. A parent commented that boys and girls alike are encouraged but not forced, and the truly non-sporty get support, a few concessions but enough exercise. Lots of teams for everything with girls' hockey and boys' cricket getting players to county level, while girls' netball is making a splash locally. There's definitely a rugby set, parents say, with 10 teams posting enthusiastic reports of results in the school mag. Most of the usual summer and winter sports (no soccer?) with athletics outstanding. Elite cricket and athletics programme. Fantastic pale blue Princess Royal Sports Centre (she opened it) with its own department of sports medicine, huge adaptable sports hall with viewing and teaching spaces and fitness suite. Lovely dance studio is also home to fencing with a small but very distinguished take up reaching national level.

New music block is rather small, which belies the emphasis on music (an 'all Steinway school'). Regular chapel sung services, lots of orchestras and small groups orchestral, choral, classic and pop, include 'Girlforce9', a self-generated a capella choir. 'Cushion concerts' in lunch hours for lower school as well as the usual full school ones and masses of encouragement for all types of music, such as the summer 'fretted strings' celebrations for guitarists.

> *Air force cadets get a flight before they leave sixth form, navy actually get to sea plus plenty of free sail training etc, and army cadets were handling some alarmingly real guns*

Drama uses the main school hall converted to a blacked-out all-singing-and-dancing venue, opened by past pupil David Suchet. A bit of a desecration of what must have been a gracious, light-filled school hall (not a permanent one, says school – curtains frequently drawn back for events), one of the few original buildings, but allowing frequent huge musical productions which pupils clearly adore. There's serious stuff as well: The Crucible, Odysseus, Tristan and Isolde. Brilliant posters and some outstanding theatre photography attest to the quality achieved. Smashing photography in lots of the school's promotional bumf must emanate from the influence of the art department. Its policy is 'to encourage self expression', but the work on show in the cramped department bursts with exceptional observation and drawing as well as tremendous imaginative use of material, extending to 3D and photography. Some of the best school art around.

Prominent CCF means that school is full of service (all three) uniform every Friday and drilling seemed to occupy most of the afternoon we visited. Year 11 was embarking in huge numbers on a weekend camp. Air force cadets get a flight before they leave sixth form, navy actually get to sea plus plenty of free sail training etc and army cadets were handling some alarmingly real guns.

'Almost too much to do,' a parent commented. Twenty or so activities on offer, from semi-academic to energetic, as well as all the sport/music/drama/CCF programmes. The usual exchanges and visits abound. A sample school mag reported 15, 10 of which were abroad – New York, South Africa, Greece and Alps for skiing etc (not counting CCF and D of E) and Barbados, the Arctic Circle and Tunisia are in the pipeline. Occasional financial support for trips central to curriculum.

The recently devised 'Aces' scheme encourages pupils to take responsibility for their own development and learning. Pupils have a termly tutor interview to reflect on their underlying skills, based round competence in action, communication, exploration and self-development.

Boarding: Boys can board from 11, girls from 13. Top juniors and first two years of senior have mixed boarding in Overside. Senior boarding boys have two houses, and one for senior girls. The vast majority of day pupils are split into three boys' and three girls' houses. Fairly basic accommodation in comparison with the five star rooms of some schools, but boarders seem contented, and there are all the trimmings of common rooms, kitchens, showers etc and the odd bath for easing the rugby stiffness.

Background and atmosphere: Founded in 1837 as Benjamin Frost's Classical Mathematical and

Commercial Academy, occupying the great hall, where all teaching took place, Wellington morphed into the West Somerset County School. In 1945, as Wellington School, it became the first direct grant school and became fully independent in the 1970s. Girls infiltrated it from 1972, and in 1997 it added Wellington Junior School, now called Wellington Prep. The current site straggles across a busy-ish road (no over- or underpass) in the little town of Wellington, birthplace of the Iron Duke. A mixture of Georgian-type houses converted into sixth form centre, head's house and san, and facilities purpose built or acquired over its 175 years rejoice in styles of these various times. A huge tree-lined green expanse edged by new labs, pool etc creates central campus. It softens the red-brick neoclassical great hall and gothic spikes of the chapel, built to commemorate the fallen of WW1, with a stunning blue star-studded ceiling, carved oak pews and angel decked organ. Used for daily assembly and masses of music it is, physically, the central point of Wellington.

It softens the gothic spikes of the chapel, built to commemorate the fallen of WW1, with a stunning blue star-studded ceiling, carved oak pews and angel decked organ

Smart, refurbished reception and head master's offices – definitely welcoming; comfortable library with terrific AV, friendly round tables for clean cafeteria style dining, serving a choice of Friday fish, on our visit, including popular but rather small portions of moules marinières. Lunch is extra but very few opt out.

Pastoral care, well-being and discipline: Pastoral care is delivered via the houses, with each pupil allocated a tutor who takes pupils right through the school and is first point of call for parents. Problems are dealt with sensitively, say parents, and children given every support in settling and studying. No recent incidents calling for ultimate sanction of permanent exclusion. Parents agree that neither drugs nor drink are rife, and say pupils know where they stand on this (urine tests for suspects) and other matters of discipline. Plenty of responsibility for house and school captains, and for lower school prefects.

Pupils and parents: Definitely not a toff school, but lots of Somerset families – inevitably farmers and businesses relating to farming. Professionals and families where both parents work to cover the

fees. A few expats and a tranche of international boarders (about 65 per cent), some of whom come in via the school's one year GCSE programme. Huge majority of day pupils come in by bus from Exeter and Chard to the south, Minehead and Dulverton to the north west and beyond Bridgewater to the east.

Despite the usual reservations of some parents and pupils that kilted skirts don't suit all shapes, and regulations are not always enforced, Wellington uniform of blue crested blazer (quite expensive), white shirt and grey trousers/skirt is worn with evident pride by pupils. Not a half-mast tie or dipping hemline in sight. Second hand shop.

Past pupils include David Suchet, Jeffrey Archer, the late Keith Floyd, actress Carly Bawden, ex Black Rod Sir Freddie Viggers, mathematician and author Simon Singh and marine biologist, Dr Jon Copley.

Entrance: Main entry at 11, with 30 per cent from junior school, then at 13 and to lower sixth. Pupils can enter for any year, but if it is half way through an exam course and the syllabus does not match, they may be advised to repeat a year. Broadly selective, tending to discourage potential non-copers. At 11 all, including juniors, take the school's own exam in January. At 13 from prep schools, it is common entrance, or, as in all other years, by interview in maths, science and mod langs.

International pupils can enter via one year GCSE programme and pay a higher fee to cover any extra tuition needed.

Exit: Vast majority from upper sixth to uni, about half in mainstream subjects to established courses. Two to Oxbridge in 2015, not many doctors but lots of mathematicians, linguists and classicists. Tiny trickle straight to Forces or training. Almost 20 per cent leave after GCSE, often to Taunton's Robert Huish College, which has a good reputation. The head points out that some parents make a strategic decision to fund years 7–11.

Money matters: Both boarding and day are pretty good value in comparison with similar schools. Scholarships, both academic and talent related (music, drama, sport), between 10 and 50 per cent of fees awarded at years 7, 9 and 12 by examination, audition etc. Scholarship holders can apply for means-tested bursaries of up to 100 per cent. The school spends cautiously, avoiding the flashily expensive, but has nevertheless achieved tremendously improved facilities over the last six or seven years.

Remarks: Can't think why Wellington hasn't featured in Good Schools' Guide until recently. Friendly, purposeful and busy, it is a solid, well-managed school, neat but not glossy, giving its pupils a sound education and masses of high points in developmental experience. Its flexible and approachable style means happy pupils and happy parents.

Wells Cathedral School

The Liberty, Wells, Somerset BA5 2ST

01749 834200
main-office@wells-cathedral-school.com
www.wells-cathedral-school.com
C of E

Ages: 11–18 (junior boarding from year 5)
Pupils: 520; sixth form: 200
Boarders: 245
Day: £6,999 – £17,223 pa
Boarding: £20,379 – £28,824 pa

Head: Since 2000, Mrs Elizabeth Cairncross, 60s, married with three grown up children. Educated at a girls' grammar school in Reigate (now a sixth form college), then read English at London University (Bedford College, now joined with Royal Holloway College). Formerly deputy head of Christ's Hospital, Horsham, where she had been a teacher since 1986. A passionate believer in co-education, and radiates calm confidence in the school. Not an elite musician herself – a useful asset here, she believes – but came to Wells because 'the Wells way is to look at what's the best way and it was that creativity that attracted me.'

Impresses as a true scholar, who thinks hard about life, the universe and everything; and as a modernizer who is nonetheless at home with tradition. Hugely popular with parents, who queued up to give praise: 'An inspirational leader, who doesn't take any flannel, is very focused, and manages to juggle the many facets of the school with skill and aplomb'; 'Clearly not a head who rests on her laurels, and there is a definite sense of a school wishing to explore new ways of working and not being satisfied with the status quo'; 'An excellent role model with high academic standards'; 'What I love is that the children absolutely and 100 percent come first for her' – etc.

Academic matters: Wells's unique selling point is flexibility. The school goes out of its way to address individual needs and preferences, and the results are highly creditable. In 2015, 64 per cent of GCSEs and 45 per cent of A levels were graded at A*A. Compared with the other specialist music schools, offers a broad and challenging curriculum, with a good range of languages on offer: French, German, Spanish, Italian, Mandarin and Latin. Really excellent maths provision, owing to the innovative Specialist Maths Scheme, which allows able students an extra three hours of maths per week and aims to turn out creative mathematicians who can think beyond the syllabus. Why

maths in particular? School says, 'It grew out of the music – we already knew how to specialize and be flexible.' Science labs endearingly shabby, but science teaching is 'very good, one of the strengths of the school,' according to a parent, and the pupils we spoke to – one of whom was off to Edinburgh to read medicine – agreed. Humanities also popular: one mother wrote, 'The school is now providing some really exciting and interesting history, philosophy, etc.' No IB – head dislikes the amount of assessment involved, and prefers the depth of A levels (Cambridge Pre-U also offered in history).

We heard a stunning young violinist rehearsing Korngold's violin concerto with the school's equally stunning symphony orchestra

---

Everyone praised the teaching staff's willingness to give students the support they needed and to work constructively with all pupils, including those for whom music came first.

SEN well catered for, with specialists in both the junior and senior schools ('second to none,' according to the mother of a dyslexic pupil), and school excels at adapting its provision to the individual student, an approach head clearly relishes: 'In 10 years' time, all schools will have to offer bespoke programmes for everybody.' One mother ran out of superlatives when describing the way the staff had worked with her to draw up a care plan for managing her child's epilepsy. At the other end of the scale, parents rated the way their bright children had been stretched and challenged: 'The teaching is really good for an able child, and the maths has been wonderful.'

Given that Wells isn't overly selective in terms of academic ability, we were much struck with the school's achievements in this area and asked the head how it was done. 'By tailoring, by playing to people's strengths, by being can-do, and by having staff prepared to put the grounding in place,' was the answer. Parents agree: 'The children do incredibly well there, but it comes without the hothousing stress that other nearby schools create,' said one. 'They're really, really good at getting the best out of their pupils, no matter what their level is,' wrote another.

Games, options, the arts: Wells is one of five UK schools accorded specialist music school status by the government's Music and Dance Scheme and, as you'd expect, the music here is very special indeed. We heard a stunning young violinist rehearsing Korngold's violin concerto with the school's equally stunning symphony orchestra, which pretty much set us up for the day. For those who love music, there's a pulse-racingly good range of ensembles and other opportunities offered by the nine performance faculties: brass, composition, choristers, jazz, keyboard, percussion, strings, vocals and woodwind. The new Cedars Hall, due to open in the summer of 2016, will offer a world class concert venue within the school grounds, adding to the school's already-top-notch music facilities. Quirkier aspects of music also catered for: the percussion suite includes a World Percussion room, complete with its own Indonesian gamelan – other specialist music schools, please take note. Parents and students alike praised the inclusivity of the music provision at Wells, saying that all pupils had the opportunity to take part and to excel if they wished, and many felt that the music benefited pupils in

ways beyond the music itself: 'I think that being in a place where musical excellence is encouraged has inspired excellence in other areas,' wrote one mother, and others said similar. May not suit young musicians seeking the hardcore, all-or-nothing ethos of the other specialist music schools, but the parents we spoke to felt this was a strength: 'That's the real and very special feature of Wells,' wrote a father. 'It makes highly skilled musicians feel normal and grounds them in real life.'

Better sports than at any of the other specialist music schools, and pretty good for any school. Lovely new sports pavilion, all blond wood and glass, fronts the tree-dotted cricket pitch that boasts 'one of the best wickets in Somerset' according to proud students. Teams are fielded in cricket, rugby, hockey (boys and girls), netball, rounders, tennis, swimming, soccer and basketball, and everyone who wants to participate will get the chance. Again, inclusivity is the watchword. 'I love that the emphasis is not on winning at all costs,' wrote one parent. 'Sometimes the order will be changed to ensure that the lower order players get to play the key positions, even if that means we are likely to lose the match. I think this is brilliant, although not all parents agree!' It's not all losses, either: remembering a recent victory against Millfield clearly raised our tour guides' testosterone levels. Excellent covered swimming pool used all the year round. Dance studio is home to compulsory dance for both boys and girls up to year 9.

Flourishing drama with at least two productions per year, and remarkably good art and photography, reflecting the very creative ethos. A

huge programme of clubs and societies, everything from jewellery making to CCF.

Boarding: The boarding provision was given the thumbs up by everyone we spoke to, with all boarders confirming that they enjoyed their time here ('It's really nice! Lots of activities at the weekends,' said a sixth former who joined in year 12). Boarding houses are frankly dilapidated – the ones we saw, at any rate – and numbers to a room rather high for this modern age, with four or five being fairly normal. Living in one of the country's prettiest and oldest towns has its flip-side, perhaps. But the students seemed cheerful enough about it, and although we dug hard, we couldn't unearth any complaints. Appraisals of the food were mixed. 'Like the food I had to endure when I boarded 25 years ago!' said one parent, while another countered loyally, 'I'm told it's amazing!' But again the students, all of whom seem to radiate good health, seemed happy with it. We ourselves were served a pleasant and wholesome lunch, so can't comment on this further.

Background and atmosphere: Tracing its roots back to 909, Wells is one of the world's oldest schools, and wears its age beautifully; there surely can't be a lovelier place of learning anywhere. Whether picking our way down the cobbled Vicar's Close, where we heard mellifluous treble recorder playing drifting out of the mullioned windows, or wandering about the many elegant Georgian buildings cocooned in greenery, we thought that growing up here must be a gift. 'I am not sure our children yet realise just how lucky they are,' agreed one parent, 'and when I visit I do have to pinch myself sometimes.'

Lovely new sports pavilion, all blond wood and glass, fronts the tree-dotted cricket pitch that boasts 'one of the best wickets in Somerset' according to proud students

Co-educational since 1969, and a specialist music school since 1970, and remains the only such within the setting of a normal school, something which parents clearly value. Music department housed in gorgeous – if rather cluttered – medieval building directly opposite the cathedral. We liked the library with its stock of 2000 vinyl records plus turntable, although it did seem too small for quiet study, and one parent said that this was a problem throughout the school, describing the boarding houses as noisy.

This is undoubtedly a very happy community; everywhere we looked we saw a kind of upbeat tranquility blended with lively creativity. One mother spoke for everyone when she wrote, 'What I love about Wells is the happy and welcoming atmosphere. Everyone has a smile – and it is really infectious!'

Pastoral care, well-being and discipline: Highly praised by everyone. The school motto is 'Be what you are' ('Esto quod es'), and all parents commented how confident and happy their children had become since starting at the school, and on the good friends they'd made there. Indeed, we spoke to parents whose children had previously been miserable – in one case at a top academic school, in another at a different specialist music school – but were now simply loving life after transferring to Wells. School communications on pastoral issues rated by parents as prompt, efficient and helpful. (Exception to this appeared to be some of the music teaching staff, who, some said, were reluctant to keep parents in the loop and clung to an outdated 'what goes on in my lessons is my business' attitude.) One parent wrote, 'We love this school. It expects high standards of behaviour and achievement but allows children good levels of independence and autonomy in reaching these. The children learn to motivate themselves. They are supported and nurtured and helped with strategies and tools, but they are not micro-managed.'

Focus is on 'mutual consideration, respect and courtesy,' and discipline problems are few. Children are charmingly polite, but very much themselves: 'Hullo, Mrs Cairncross!' exclaimed a 6-year-old lad with grave propriety as we walked by, 'I looked away and when I looked back again you'd popped up!' Older students showed the same style of courteous assurance, duly matured.

Pupils and parents: Day pupils drawn from large local radius – school operates bus routes to bring children in from Bristol, Bath, Taunton, Yeovil and comparable. Boarders come from all over, but a significant proportion still from the South West, perhaps because Wells remains off the beaten track: the nearest train station is Castle Cary, some 13 miles away. International students bring cultural diversity: they are welcomed into the purpose-built International Centre and offered very good EAL support. Parents mostly hardworking professionals, keen for their children to turn out right on all fronts – many families choose to send all their children to Wells for their entire education. Pupils are well-mannered, well-spoken, well-adjusted, well-turned-out, and very likeable.

Entrance: A broad church academically and, as always with Wells, flexibility is key. Children can join the school at any point in their school career, even year 13 – the school works to make it a success. At the usual entry points of age 11 and 13, however, a formal entrance assessment is held in maths and reasoning, and satisfactory report from previous school is required. Entry to sixth form is subject to interview and at least six grade C passes at GCSE, with grade B or above in subjects to be taken for A level. Auditions for music places currently held in November (sixth form) and January (all age groups) after a pre-audition meeting.

Exit: Some 10 per cent after GCSEs. At 18, almost all to higher education, with a high proportion to Russell group universities, or to music conservatoires in the UK or abroad. Six Oxbridge places in 2015: English, history, political science, music and natural sciences.

Money matters: Historically, not a wealthy school, but Wells has made what it's got go a very long way. An unusually wide variety of scholarships on offer: maths, music, sports, creative arts, academic and all-round. Most of these worth no more than 10 per cent, but a sliding scale of means-tested bursary assistance is also available, and school is working overtime to build up its endowment and reach a 'needs-blind' point of admissions. Funding of up to 100 per cent available for some 'elite' specialist musicians via the government's Music and Dance Scheme. Special provision pupils – children who are musically gifted but want to follow the full academic curriculum and keep their options open – often receive financial support for their music tuition.

Remarks: As one parent summed it up, 'We really love this school, and believe that by sending our children here we are giving them the best possible start in life.' A magical place, where children grow into kind, confident and accomplished young adults.

Westonbirt School

Westonbirt, Tetbury, Gloucestershire GL8 8QG

01666 881301
admissions@westonbirt.org
www.westonbirt.org
C of E

Ages: 11–18 (boarders from year 5)
Pupils: 217; sixth form: 70
Boarders: 117 full
Day: £17,295 – £21,300 pa
Boarding: £25,815 – £32,985 pa

Head: Since 2013, Mrs Natasha Dangerfield BA (40s), previously deputy head and head of boarding at Harrogate Ladies' College. Also taught at North Foreland Lodge and Downe House and was director of pastoral care at Gordonstoun School. Mrs Dangerfield studied physical education and English at the University of Brighton and thought she wanted to be a physiotherapist, but while working in sports camps she met teachers who inspired her to change direction. Parents describe her as 'dynamic', and 'approachable' and a great role model for the girls, 'she speaks their language.'

Westonbirt inspires fierce loyalty and we got the impression that any head who messed with

the school's fundamental character would do so at their peril. Most agree that her changes so far have been the right ones – modernisation of some material aspects, gentle 're-booting' in other areas. The fact that she is a parent herself (she has three young children, two boys and a girl, who attend the prep) must be a good ice-breaker. Her husband works in the fire service.

The combination of over 200 lively girls and a grade 1 listed building must be a little worrying, we suggested to Mrs Dangerfield. 'This house is built so well that everything is in pretty good order,' she told us. Fortunately, the Westonbirt Trust takes care of historic preservation; 'To put Venetian silk back on the walls is not our responsibility.'

Lacrosse is Mrs Dangerfield's sport (back in the day she played for England) and she continues to coach – even taking pre-season training for her school team. 'I'm not very good at standing on the sidelines,' she confessed.

Academic matters: In 2015, a disappointing 17 per cent A*/A (44 per cent A*-B) at A level. At GCSE, a more encouraging 52 per cent A*/A (81 per cent A*-B). Highs and lows in all subjects reflect the relatively non-selective intake. While there has certainly been a tightening up of standards and a review of the subjects on offer, head has no plans to change entrance requirements. Focus here is on helping girls reach their potential, whether that's 10 A*s at GCSE, or three 'good' A levels.

Parents have told us how well their daughters are doing and the University of Durham has put a number on it: Westonbirt is in the top five per cent of schools in the UK for value added. This objectively assessed measure calculates pupils' academic improvement between the ages of 11 and 16. Analysis by the University of Durham shows that girls here achieve almost a grade higher in each subject at GCSE than expected.

French from year 7, Spanish, Mandarin and Latin 'tasters' in year 8 and all learn touch typing. In addition to academic subjects, girls in all years follow a 'skills for life' programme that focuses on practical (communication and study skills) as well as personal and social development. With an average class size of 10 (maximum 15), girls here receive what is practically customised teaching; the

parents of several girls who had joined from large preps were astonished at their daughters' progress. 'She thought she was bad at maths and science but now she's so confident and doing really well.' Subject teachers set targets and academic progress is closely monitored by tutors. In a year 7 maths class the atmosphere was collaborative rather than competitive, girls attempting questions confidently, undaunted if they were wrong. Even we wouldn't have been scared to hazard an answer.

Choice of 25 A level subjects – all the usuals plus history of art, classical civilisation and business studies. School says that it is able to accommodate most combinations. Enrichment for sixth formers includes a lecture programme and weekly personal finance lessons.

We would not have been surprised to see Hugh Bonneville and his labrador taking a constitutional

Technology was somewhat prehistoric but is now much improved and used in lessons 'appropriately and with relevance,' although Mrs Dangerfield's announcement of the 'death of the handout' might be a bit previous. iPads now on kit list although school will lend if necessary. Great boon for dyslexic girls who can use the speech facility for essays. Apps etc stored in the 'Westonbirt cloud' and controlled by school. As we were visiting the science, art, design and technology block, we spied a classroom of very overgrown schoolgirls

and boys, concentrating hard. 'Oh, that's the teachers,' our guide said. 'They're having an IT lesson.

'Outstanding' learning support department caters for wide range of SpLDs including dyslexia, dyspraxia, dyscalculia and mild speech and language impairments. Gifted and talented programme also in place.

Games, options, the arts: 'There's so much drama at Westonbirt!' we heard. Ditto singing, dancing and playing of instruments. Emphasis is on enabling everyone to perform, whether it's in the intimate setting of the Camellia House – a charming venue, used for recitals, 'little plays' and socials – or in the 450 seat Orangery Theatre. Fresh air fiends can also tread the grass of the amphitheatre in the grounds. Music practice block suffers somewhat by comparison with the smart Marriott Centre, home to brand new recording and music tech kit. Three choirs and weekly whole school hymn practice keep everyone in good voice. Huge art studios looking out onto peaceful pastures, DT workshops with laser cutters and CAD equipment.

Mrs Dangerfield is applying her expertise to school sport. Local opposition is formidable, and while no one expects Westonbirt to carry home the silverware at every match, there was room for improvement. Sensible trend in this and other girls' schools is a shift from privileging team sports

to an equal emphasis on health and fitness – that way you can keep everyone doing something.

No shortage of running around space here and opportunities to play for the school abound, whether it's lacrosse, netball, tennis, golf (there's a nine hole course), riding or polo. In the £3m sports centre, opened by near neighbours the Prince of Wales and Duchess of Cornwall, there's a 25m pool, dance studio and fitness suite. Or you could just take a book and find a secluded spot in the gardens.

As befits the alma mater of Baden Powell's daughter, the school has a girl guide troop – 1st Westonbirt Guides, although members tend to be from local villages rather than the school itself. D of E to gold level offered plus clubs and activities from app design, through gardening and poultry, to zumba.

Sixth formers have the opportunity to enrol on the very popular Leith's certificate in food and wine. Westonbirt was one of the first two schools to run this course, and to have Leith's on your CV is great for holiday and gap year jobs such as a spot of chalet girling. For those whose ambitions go beyond holiday jobs, there's the Young Enterprise scheme and a separate business school with office space and classrooms – A level business studies is taught here.

Boarding: Years 7 and 8, day girls and boarders, live together in Beaufort House. This junior house is a stepping stone between prep and senior school. There are three senior houses for years 9, 10 and 11 – Badminton, Dorchester and Holford – plus the sixth form. Girls in Holford sleep in what were the family state rooms on the first floor, little beds dwarfed by grand proportions (grade 1 listing is not at home to subdivision). Priceless silk wallpaper, preserved under Perspex, rubbing shoulders with One Direction posters. Beautiful painted panels on the wardrobes and tall wooden shutters instead of curtains. All day girls get one free night of boarding per term and sleepovers are very popular. Wonderful views over the park from common room 'perfect for moon watching'. We asked girls what they thought of the food and the general consensus was breakfast fab, lunch pretty good (we can vouch for that) but catering seemed to run out of steam by supper time. We hope this is on Mrs Dangerfield's to do list.

In the sixth form house every girl has her own study bedroom so day girls can decide at the last minute to stay overnight. There's a dining room, kitchen, laundry facilities, yoga room and bar/café. Not surprisingly, over three-quarters of sixth formers board. Many like to remain in school over the weekend, because it 'helps them stay focused on their studies'. An international student (around 20+ girls are from abroad) told us how much she appreciated learning in such 'serene and calm surroundings.' We loved the spacious common room,

Priceless silk wallpaper, preserved under Perspex, rubbing shoulders with One Direction posters. Beautiful painted panels on the wardrobes and tall wooden shutters

newly decorated in a modish putty colour ('seagull'), a simple vase of marguerites on the coffee table.

Background and atmosphere: Westonbirt is one of the 'Allied Schools', an umbrella body for eight Martyrs' Memorial Trust schools including Canford, Stowe and Harrogate Ladies' College. It was founded in 1927, acquiring Westonbirt House and 210 acres of park and garden from the Holford family who had lived on the estate since the 17th century. The house itself, built in Jacobethan style (later than, though not dissimilar to, Highclere Castle), was completed in 1871 and used by Lord Holford as a country retreat (his main residence was Dorchester House, Park Lane, now site of The Dorchester Hotel). Just over the road is the world famous Westonbirt Arboretum, another of Lord Holford's enduring projects. When the head told us the house was 'well built' she meant it – constructed around a steel frame, it had all the mod cons of its day (gas lighting, central heating), not to mention fire-proof cavities between each wall and floor. Interior décor was in the distinctly un-modern classical style, with splendid marble halls and corridors on the ground floor, richly gilded wood and plasterwork and intriguing architectural details wherever you look. Friday notices and vespers are held in the galleried great hall, and year 11s dine under a ceiling festooned with plasterwork goat skulls.

As we sighed over the refurbished Gentleman's Library, enjoying the irony, we wondered what the girls thought about studying in such sumptuous surroundings. 'It is a bit like Downton Abbey', one confided, and we would not have been surprised to see Hugh Bonneville and his arthritic labrador taking a constitutional in the Italianate garden. What a place.

Pastoral care, well-being and discipline: Pastoral care has always been one of Westonbirt's strengths. In a small community with a high staff to student ratio, problems become visible sooner. Parents say that friendship troubles and the like are dealt with fairly and swiftly. 'Everybody has to get along,' we were told, and 'the older girls look out for you.' Not really the place for 'tricky' personalities, observed one mother. We agree; Westonbirt girls are more likely to ride the horses than frighten them.

Girls are encouraged to take responsibilities such as organising social events – planning for a charity ball was under way when we visited. There's a 'much improved' programme of socials with boys from Abingdon, Radley and even co-ed Cheltenham College. A less welcome visitor is the school's lone peacock, Westy, who frequently has to be escorted off the premises. We hear that the class of 2014 bought him a friend, christened (you guessed it) Birty.

Pupils and parents: From all over the UK, although majority of families live relatively locally. Easy to reach from Bristol and Bath and handy for M4, Heathrow and London. Parents tell us it's 'not posh.' Hmmm. It is, but in a quiet way. Nearest places to spend pocket money are Cheltenham and Bath, although you could do some damage in Tetbury. Smallish cohort (some 25 per cent) of international students from all corners of the globe – as elsewhere, more attention being paid to the mix.

Former pupils include the Hon Mrs Betty Clay (Lord Baden-Powell's youngest daughter), Mercia MacDermott (historian); Anna Hornby (painter); Salma Sobhan (academic and human rights activist); Patsy Toh (pianist); Georgia Byng (author of the Molly Moon series of children's books); Lady Natasha Rufus-Isaacs (designer, founder of Beulah London); TV presenter Ruth Watson; TV producer Patricia Llewellyn; Lady Jenny Bland; Jenefer Greenwood, OBE.

Entrance: Many from Westonbirt Prep, rest from wide range of preps and local primaries. Non-CE candidates sit school's own entrance exams in maths and English plus an online adaptive test. Head likes to interview everyone in person (or via Skype). For entry to the sixth form girls need at least five A*-C grades at GCSE (including maths and English), with A or B in subjects to be taken at A level.

Exit: A few girls leave for pastures new after GCSEs but are replaced by others from elsewhere doing the same thing. After A levels more than half depart for Russell Group universities to study everything from aeronautics to zoology. Business and management popular choices. Occasional one or two to medical school (two in 2015), likewise Oxbridge.

Money matters: Fees broadly in line with similar schools in this part of the country. Academic, art, drama, music, sport, performing arts, organ and choral scholarships up to a maximum of 50 per cent of day fees. Means-tested bursaries may be available – applications considered on an individual basis. Fee reductions for siblings, Forces and clergy families. Girls transferring from prep also get a five per cent discount throughout their senior career. Sixth form bursaries offered to girls from local state schools.

Remarks: Westonbirt has always been highly regarded for inclusivity and exemplary pastoral care, but perhaps its other strengths have been overlooked. Until now. Parents told us that 'there's a new energy, a real buzz' about the place; one described it as 'added sparkle', and they're right.

Inside this solid Victorian stately home we found a vibrant and forward thinking community of young women, hugely appreciative of their beautiful surroundings but very well prepared to take on the world beyond Gloucestershire.

Wycliffe Preparatory School

Ryeford Hall, Stonehouse, Gloucestershire GL10 2LD

01453 820470
prep@wycliffe.co.uk
www.wycliffe.co.uk

Ages: 2–13 (boarders from 7)
Pupils: 323
Boarders: 61 full, 25 flexi
Day: £6,225 – £12,900 pa
Boarding: £17,400 – £24,525 pa

Linked school: Wycliffe College

Headmaster: Since 2003, Mr Adrian Palmer BA (50s). An ex-maths and PE teacher with a range of bright and almost horrific ties, he has been a head for 16 years. After a spell as head at Warminster Preparatory School, he moved to Rendcomb, where he started the junior school and built up numbers rapidly before moving to Wycliffe, 'because I didn't want to get stale'. Works in close tandem with the senior school head and 'we get on very well.' The feeling is mutual. Married to the delightful Julie,

who is deeply involved in the running of the place, and with a son and daughter in the school.

Experience has not brought pomposity to this head. Much of what he achieves is through lightness of touch, a sense of humour and a palpable love for the children. 'They must feel they're having fun. If they are happy, they'll work hard; if they work hard, they'll feel fulfilled.' A simple philosophy but one which seems to work. He is a hands-on leader (we saw him tidying away plates in the dining room after the first sitting for lunch)

and is on easy terms with the boys and girls, joking his way around the place with a cheerful and individual remark for everyone. The children from the nursery and pre-prep, in particular, seem very excited to see him, swarming around shouting out his name and chattering about their recent experiences. A whale amongst minnows. He is clearly approachable, something confirmed by the parents we spoke to. 'He knows the children well and nothing is too much trouble,' said one very satisfied mum. No plans for leaving.

Entrance: Over 60 per cent from the nursery situated across the road from the main prep school, via a charming bridge built in the 1930s to make it safe from the volume of traffic; some, 'an increasing amount', join from other schools via relaxed interview and a good report. Fleets of buses from all over the place. Parents may apply at any time of the year and pupils may join whenever there is room. Scholarships available at 11+ and there are awards in music, drama, dance, sport and art.

Exit: About 95 per cent move on to the senior school. Transition is very nearly automatic (examinations are for setting purposes) and the school aims to give plenty of warning to parents if it is felt that the senior school would not be appropriate.

Remarks: Initially the campus feels rather compact, the main house bears the unmistakeable stamp of an institution, but is essentially handsome and spacious within. A conservatory through which parents enter is welcoming and functional, designed to show off children's art and make you feel happy to be there. The spacious Etheridge Hall, a stunning learning centre for years 7 and 8 offers the very latest high-tech facilities and large common room for year 8 pupils (tea and toast making facilities).

Much of what he achieves is through lightness of touch, sense of humour and a palpable love for the children. 'They must feel they're having fun. If they're happy, they'll work hard'

As with the senior school, computers and interactive whiteboards are everywhere. ICT is taught as 'a discreet subject' and from the age of 7 each pupil has two lessons a week. But these are not budding geeks: computers and their uses seem as natural as telephones. We saw some lively and imaginative teaching: a history lesson involving The Peasants' Revolt, which culminated in the head being decapitated amidst yells of approval, and Latin irregular verbs brought to life. Super computer room. Even the bright and airy library employs computer power and pupils were happy to demonstrate how you could remove and return books using thumb prints. Good fun and, presumably, effective.

Gifted and talented pupils benefit from the school's accreditation with NAGC. Good work with dyslexics. The school is CReSTed. Debating is popular as are court room trials, conducted locally under the supervision of legal beavers. Excellent-looking drama in the charming little theatre, complete with happy mum painting flats. 'Even mums can discover a talent here.' Good art in dedicated building.

'I like it like this,' said a happy girl. 'It's a bit like walking home. Weekends are fun and sometimes we have feasts'

Delightful head of pastoral care organising PHSE programme; regular tutorial meetings with tutees who retain the same tutor for their last two years. There is a zero tolerance of bullying and the head can 'be very frightening about that sort of thing,' said an older pupil. 'He takes it very seriously.' Trouble taken to recognise the difference between good-natured banter and persistent bullying. 'That takes constant alertness,' says the head.

Most of the boarders are Forces children and each house – one for boys, one for girls – is presided over by a house mistress who is not a teacher, which gives them a different perspective on their charges. Super bright accommodation where the décor is unashamedly girly for the girls and boyish for the boys. No problem if you were asked to close your eyes and guess which house you are in. Imaginatively designed common rooms, welcoming bedrooms – some with very daring colours – plenty of games available. Tea and toast-making facilities. The boarding accommodation is across the road from the main buildings and up a gentle slope past the all-weather pitches and next door to the nursery. 'I like it like this,' said an obviously happy girl. 'It's good to get away from the school. It's a bit like walking home. Weekends are fun with lots of activities arranged and sometimes we have special feasts.' The food in the main dining room is very good with the ladies serving behind the cafeteria counters noticeably kind and motherly. Staff sit with pupils. Healthy amount of noise. Optional Saturday morning school for years 3 and 4; thereafter it is compulsory with a mixture of formal and informal.

No consideration of the prep school is complete without visiting the nursery. Behind carefully locked doors and gateways are the classrooms built in the style of log cabins. These are the pioneers of the Wycliffe experience and from their exalted position on the hill they can look down at the prep school, the goal for most of them. Masses of toys – 'learning toys' – everywhere with attentive and experienced staff. Good library – 'the nursery eats books,' said one teacher. Other meals are taken nursery dining room. A very happy set up, well-equipped

and imaginatively run. Good after-school care. Beds are even available for children exhausted by it all.

The Wycliffe empire, incorporating as it does children from 2-18, is a homogeneous package, closely-knit both geographically and in ethos. For those embarking on the Wycliffe adventure, the prep school is an ideal launching pad. Well-equipped and well run, it is a happy school with sensible, worthwhile standards.

Wycliffe College

Bath Road, Stonehouse, Gloucestershire GL10 2JQ

01453 822432
senior@wycliffe.co.uk
www.wycliffe.co.uk

Ages: 13–19
Pupils: 400; sixth form: 195
Boarders: 227
Day: £6,225 – £18,600 pa
Boarding: £17,400 – £32,850 pa

Linked school: Wycliffe Preparatory School

Head: Since September 2015, Nick Gregory, previously deputy head (pastoral) at Mill Hill School in London. Studied French and Spanish at Nottingham; spent eight years at Barclay's before becoming a teacher. Taught modern languages at Barnard Castle School, County Durham and Merchant Taylors' School, Northwood before becoming a boarding housemaster at Old Swinford Hospital, Stourbridge. He and his wife, Helen, have three sons. His aim is for pupils to enjoy and appreciate their time at Wycliffe for its own value and

as a preparation for life, as well as a route to a set of exam passes.

Academic matters: Not a demanding school in terms of entrance requirements, 'though absolutely not a dumping ground,' says school. GCSE and A level results are very respectable. In 2015, 34 per cent A*/A grades at GCSE. At A level, 27 of grades A*/A and 52 per cent A*-B. What the school really prides itself on is value-added. There is a range of nearly 30 subjects at A level with seemingly no limit on the various permutations available. Plenty of guidance and advice on choosing the best options. 'We aim to find the right subjects for individuals, rather than shoehorn them into rigid blocks.' Japanese, for instance, is very popular and the school enjoys excellent relations with its sister school in Japan. Exchanges and visits abound. This school travels.

Supporting and encouraging individual and community progress is the compulsory life skills programme, a wider-ranging version of PHSE. Each year group is involved, the aim being to develop skills beyond the merely academic: thus there are courses on working as a team, problem solving, creativity and 'learning how to learn'. The pupils we asked were very appreciative of the programme. The school offers a Development (third) Year in the sixth form. Primarily designed for pupils from abroad (see Pupils and parents) to get their English up to scratch for A levels but also used for pupils who will benefit from building deeper foundations. Pupils will only sit GCSEs and A levels when they are ready for them, not because they're the right age.

The arrival of two musical whiz kids heading the department has seen a deepening of musical opportunities

Very good remedial and special needs programme with lively, sensitive and fully qualified teachers who help and support. Pupils are automatically assessed on entry to the school. This is as much to identify gifted and talented (the school is the only independent school with an accreditation with NACE) as well as those with learning difficulties (the school is much praised by CReSTed).

Classrooms have been revamped, repainted and in some cases redesigned. There is a light and spacious feel about it all. The science laboratories have been recently renovated and modernised and offer first-class facilities. Computers are everywhere. They appear and disappear on the desks in the excellently laid out library which is also a fabulous multimedia resource centre, very popular with the pupils. In the delightful music department computers aid composition and musical appreciation; they appear alongside work benches in the DT department. Everywhere. Interactive whiteboards are in all the classrooms and are used to engage involvement and interest in ways which seem imaginative and effective. ICT is clearly very important at Wycliffe – now offers computer science at GCSE and A level – and the school has invested nearly a million pounds over the last few years.

Games, options, the arts: We hear mixed opinions on the standard of games at Wycliffe though clearly squash is excellent (Wycliffe are the national squash champions for U19 boys and girls and U15 boys) with frequent tours to Europe and even as far as Peru. But there can be no doubting the excellent facilities. Floodlit Astroturf hockey pitch, an attractive cricket square, masses of squash courts with people queuing to play when we visited, an excellent sports hall: it's all here. Rowing, particularly sculling, is popular and successful as is girls' hockey and basketball.

Not a hearty school but one where pupils are encouraged to participate and expected to take part in Saturday afternoon sporting commitments. Plenty of scope for outdoor activities with D of E and CCF along with plenty of opportunities for caving, climbing and adventure. An active, doing place.

Music has always been important and the arrival of two musical whiz kids heading the department has seen a deepening and broadening of musical possibilities. A huge number learns instruments and both the house singing and drama competitions contests are tremendously popular. Interesting theatre. Theatre studies is very popular. Judging by the pupils' work on display all over the school, art flourishes. Indeed we had the feeling that this is a creative community. We heard much enthusiastic talk from pupils about debating and the Model UN with students going as far afield as Istanbul, Dublin and Chicago, where there's another sister school.

Boarding: Flexi-boarding is a possibility. Three girls' and three boys' houses, all for boarding and day pupils, plus one mixed day house. The co-ed modern sixth form boarding house built round three sides of a quadrangle is miles better than much student accommodation. All rooms en suite and, we were assured, they have a sauna and spa bath.

Background and atmosphere: A busy campus with friendly staff and pupils strolling purposefully around. Some interesting buildings, particularly the original listed building which now houses the head, admin staff and the advanced learning centre. Since the school's foundation in 1882 the powers that govern have chosen their architects with sensitivity and good sense, combining aesthetics with practicality and blending old and new into a pleasing and interesting whole. A feature of the overall layout of the place is the number of sofas and benches dotted around the buildings and grounds, inviting conversation with a sense of reasonable privacy. The dining room is delightfully airy – there's a lot of glass about at Wycliffe – and serves delicious food with a tantalising variety. Sunday brunches 'are to die for.' It's good to witness the easy relationships between cookers and eaters.

Accommodation has much improved. The mixed day house with generously broad corridors, brightly painted studies and common rooms with balconies overlooking the green sward is very pleasant and clearly much appreciated. 'We're like boarders who don't have bed and breakfast,' one told us. The school has been fully co-educational for more than 30 years and feels absolutely right. There's a lovely atmosphere.

Pastoral care, well-being and discipline: The school revolves around the house system for day pupils and boarders, each presided over by a house master/mistress, supported by a matron, house staff and a team of house tutors. Prefects and responsible sixth formers provide invaluable back up and conduits. Those to whom we spoke impressed us with the seriousness of their approach and delighted us by their lack of pomposity. One told us that consideration for others is deeply ingrained. The pupils' handbook is admirably clear about the school's zero tolerance of bullying and via two splendid pieces of writing, from the founder and a later headmaster, establishes clearly the expectations and ethos of the school, while demonstrating that decency is timeless. There are clear guidelines to follow if any pupil feels aggrieved or threatened in any way. Pupils praised the chaplain and appreciated the introduction of the school council. The school approves of pranks and high spirits (providing they are not unkind or thoughtless) and acknowledges that pupils will take risks and make mistakes. 'That's what they learn from.' All very civilised. Assemblies and church services in the delightful chapel, built in the 1950s by pupils and staff incorporating wood from a pier on the Isle of Wight and stone from a bombed church. All faiths are catered for, though many assemblies are forums for discussion rather than 'exclusively religious'.

Pupils and parents: Friendly, open, relaxed pupils who seem healthily proud of Wycliffe and grateful for the experience. We didn't encounter a whiff of arrogance or affectation: the pupils seemed secure in what they were doing and were uniformly and naturally polite. Instinctively. Parents to whom we spoke were pleased to feel included, and though there were some wrinkled brows over the question of extras, expressed satisfaction bordering on affection for the school. A number told us that they enjoy the opportunities for involvement and appreciate the parents' council.

A lot of pupils come from abroad, some 30 per cent from 30 different countries, so it's something of an international experience. That needs to be taken into consideration. As many from Europe as from the far east. Also a number of Forces children.

Entrance: The majority of pupils joining in year 9 come from the school's own prep school, though recently increasing numbers come from other prep schools as well. Pupils from the prep sit scholarship exams or the CE; pupils from outlying schools sit either CE, scholarships or tailor-made exams. Fifty per cent at common entrance is acceptable – or less, if there is clear evidence of specific strengths. (Remember their pride in value added). Entry into the sixth form usually requires at least five GCSEs at grade C or above but they do consider, more carefully than many, the question of potential.

Exit: Just over one-third leave post-GCSEs to vocational courses and sixth form colleges. Over 97 per cent of the sixth form go on to university with a few Oxbridge places; six to the US in 2015 – school runs as American university preparation programme. Some art foundation courses and drama school, otherwise business related subjects and law are favourites.

Money matters: In terms of endowments, the school is not particularly wealthy though stresses that it is 'strong financially.' Scholarships are available at 13 and 16 for academic excellence, art, music, DT, ICT, drama and sport. Maximum value up to 50 per cent but in exceptional circumstances the school may make up the difference. Much depends on school reports and financial circumstances.

Remarks: Strong on breadth and individual tailoring. 'I have three very different children: very bright, very sporty and very dyslexic. Wycliffe was the only school which could cope with them all. It's been wonderful for all three,' said a mum. An Old Boy told us that a few years ago he had the impression that Wycliffe had become a bit dull and dry and 'lost its way. Now it's established its own identity again.' Fair comment.

Home Counties West

Berkshire
Buckinghamshire
Hampshire
Isle of Wight
Oxfordshire

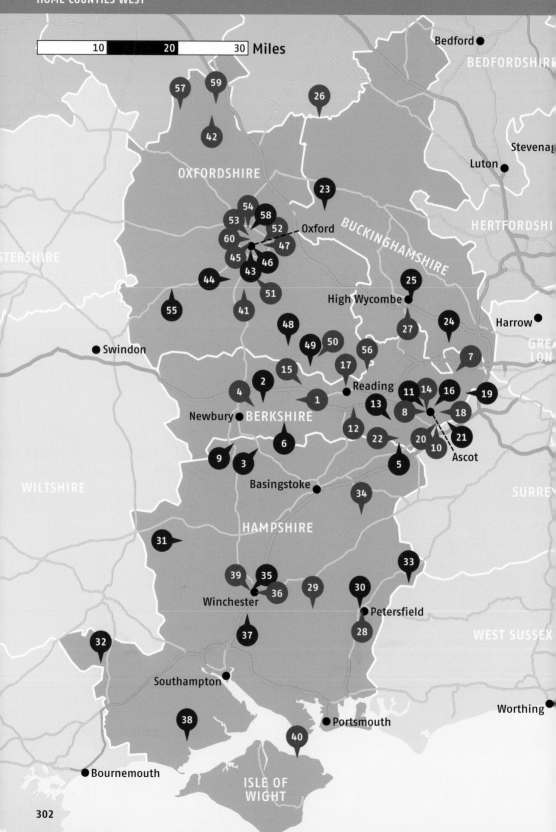

HOME COUNTIES WEST

Abingdon School

Park Road, Abingdon, Oxfordshire OX14 1DE

01235 849041
admissions@abingdon.org.uk
www.abingdon.org.uk
C of E

Ages: 11–18 (boarding from 13)
Pupils: 961; sixth form: 300
Boarders: 100 full, 34 weekly
Day: £17,775 pa
Boarding: £30,870 – £36,960 pa

Head: Since 2010, Miss Felicity Lusk (age: cannot wither her). An organist; director of music in New Zealand schools, moving to Hasmonean High in 1990, rising to deputy head and head of the girls' school. Became head of Oxford High in 1997, where we described her as 'stylish, confident and extremely articulate' – she still is. That colourful and impeccably tailored style (think Mad Men via Buckingham Palace) certainly diverts at least the distaff side of any audience at school functions – much more fun than a sea of suits. Boys predictably noncommittal about what was considered a pretty radical move to appoint a female head. A few mentioned that her assemblies were 'quite short' (we assume this is a positive); one said that she was 'a bit like the Queen', showing her face at most activities but not 'getting really involved' – whether she is expected to dive into a tackle during the rugby or grab a cello during a concert we're not sure.

In her love of music, and her insistence upon the highest possible standards, a perfect match for Abingdon. In her opposition to complacency – 'I constantly want us to evolve and not stand still', as she said of Oxford High – she has found work to do,

not without some ruffled feathers and a number of birds migrating permanently. The timetable has been revamped, football introduced and Saturday school abolished (though Saturdays still full of matches and 'other half' activities). At a guess, two-thirds of parents and 100 per cent of boys are delighted.

Her very readable weekly blog at www.abingdon.org.uk/heads_blog, now also featuring terrier, Dudley, wears no make-up: character shines truthfully through.

Retiring in July 2016. Her successor will be Michael Windsor, currently head of Reading Blue Coat School. First in French and German from Durham; worked briefly in publishing before heading for Bologna to teach English as a foreign language. On his return, did a PGCE at the Institute of Education and then joined King's College Wimbledon to teach foreign languages and take charge of the IB; also deputy head at RGS Guildford for five years. Coached rugby, hockey and athletics, involved in CCF and World Challenge expeditions. Also has an MA in modern German studies from Birkbeck and is an ISI inspector. Keen musician, playing the double bass in classical and jazz ensembles. Married to Shanti, who works at Reading University; they have two daughters.

Academic matters: A top rank academic school, but one with a tradition of breadth: in 2015, 62 per cent A*/A at A level (90 per cent A*-B); 86 per cent A*/A at GCSE, slim but comforting tail of lower grades (no properly human community is ever perfect).

Sciences/maths the most popular subjects at A level, with geography (unusually popular and notably successful), history and economics not far behind. For a boys' school, art, drama and languages (Mandarin, Spanish) fare pretty well, as does classics (a department which receives great praise from parents). Latin for first two years, thereafter optional. Classical civilisation popular GCSE choice for those enthusiastic about the history but less so the languages. RS no longer compulsory for GCSE but English literature has been added (used to be considered 'too narrow') – certain amount of reshuffling in these departments may or may not be connected.

Oarsmen running the mile down to the beautifully designed wooden boathouse in their pink and white strip pass through one of the more lively residential areas

Traditional academic focus: an emphasis on the more rigorous IGCSEs, few of the lightweight 'studies' on offer; previous head allergic to 'ologies', but psychology has recently crept in for AS/A level. Some sixth form subjects (eg theatre studies, politics) taught jointly with nearby St Helen's, as is the new general studies course. Practical activities (DT, computer programming) relatively underdeveloped as academic subjects – but then 'the other half'.

Setting when CE boys come in at 13 based on exam performance in core subjects, but reassessed at the end of the first year – with maths and MFL reset during year 9 as well. School would say only a small difference in ability and final outcome between upper and lower strata – but these competitive boys perceive it more keenly. Some comment that potential Oxbridge candidates not so subtly identified and polished up quite early on, but one is assured that all is not lost for the late bloomers. General rule is 10 GCSEs taken in year 11, though native speakers of foreign languages may take them earlier.

The quality of teaching and learning by best practice is very much a focus for Miss Lusk, who brings with her a strong culture of peer lesson observation. Boys say that teaching is 'generally good, some inspiring', and that they get on well with their teachers, but they did not seem to be as critical as those in some other schools, given that they are well behaved and work very, very hard. Teaching 'well beyond the syllabus, made interesting and relevant'. Room too for the robustly eccentric teacher and here, as elsewhere, those who are not standard issue are usually the most popular.

Classroom learning supplemented by plenty of imaginative day trips, many included in the fees if within UK. Annual classics trip particularly praised – 'way beyond what parents could organise for themselves, well prepared, serious, in the style of the Grand Tour'. Advanced level ancient historians encouraged to write talks about sites and deliver them in situ to the younger boys.

Good learning support – all boys screened, will deal with dyslexia/dyspraxia in children who are fundamentally bright enough to keep up.

The usual methods of regular prep and tests keep boys on their toes and most know how they are faring in relation to others, even if they don't let on at home. Detailed termly reports and regular parents' evenings reveal all. Individual teachers respond quickly to specific enquiries by phone or email.

Games, options, the arts: 'The Other Half', Abingdon's credo for learning beyond the classroom, is an emphatic commitment to breadth in education. Forty pages of stylish brochure lay out the opportunities available and the philosophy behind them. Breadth within breadth: boys cannot do just one sport, or all sport, or indeed all anything, and must 'undertake a period of service-type activity' – classroom assistant in a primary school, charity shop, chatting to grannies among a wide range that is praised by parents for getting the boys really involved.

Sport for all, not just the gifted, though you can just about get away with not taking it seriously after the first few years. The top teams are top notch and the Bs, Cs and Ds are pretty good too. Rugby, hockey and cricket all strong, but come the summer it's the rowers who rule. Oarsmen running the mile down to the beautifully designed wooden boathouse in their pink and white strip pass through one of the more lively residential areas of Abingdon, an educative experience, improving knowledge of the vernacular and self-control. It's all character building and, who knows, may contribute to the Boat Club's string of records and successes at national level (first VIII won the Princess Elizabeth cup at Henley for the third year running recently). Splendid sports centre with eight lane, 25 metre swimming pool. Four pitches by school, others further away. A good range of other sports, no looking down on those who prefer solo to team play, and Real Tennis (at Radley) a rare delight. Regular foreign tours and training trips for

The film unit is extraordinary – an organisation staffed by professional documentary makers and animators, with industry standard kit

the committed can be effectively compulsory – and often expensive.

Though sport is seriously good, it is by no means everything. Music is fine and widespread, with ring-fenced time to avoid encroachment, lots of bands, orchestras and choirs, with a composer-in-residence too, though it is not much studied as an academic subject. Despite the extended lunch time, parents tell us that it can still be a problem for the sporty and musical all rounder (a type Abingdon favours) to fit everything in. Art and design technology well taught to all up to the age of 14, and those who continue with art achieve strong results at A level.

Drama is enjoyed, not least because of joint productions with St Helen's and St Katharine's, but is not part of the life-blood of the school. The film unit, though, is something extraordinary – a semi-autonomous organisation staffed by professional documentary makers and animators, with industry standard kit. Over 100 adventurous, inspirational and award-winning short films have been created there since its foundation.

Boarding: Boarding, full and weekly, mostly located in the rather grand houses that form the crescent adjacent to the school. Small dormitories that are remarkably impersonal – each bed with a large, completely unused pin board above it. We have observed this in some other boys' boarding schools – a certain reluctance to provide hostages to fortune or signs of finer feelings perhaps. Well-organised weekend activities for the full-boarders. Food very good – 'great,' said our guides – but everyone seems to rush lunch to get on to whatever else they are doing. The Asian boarding contingent tends to make or order in their own of an evening, local takeaways no doubt grateful for the regular custom.

Background and atmosphere: A serene place, even on a gloomy day. Parks and playing fields surround a harmonious assembly of Victorian red-bricks. An old foundation (1256), long associated with the Mercers Company. Fine chapel: weekly attendance compulsory, at the inter-denominational end of the Church of England.

With a couple of girls' schools nearby, those pupils who want female company do not have to look far; sixth formers have joint lessons, plenty of musical and dramatic co-productions and a shared bus system. Mothers say their sons do better without a lot of girls at the front of the class with their hands up, and generally cluttering up their lives (but then they would, wouldn't they?).

Undramatic uniform of blue blazer, grey trousers and plain blue or white shirt plus any one of at least 30 ties showing allegiance to house, sport or Other Half activity; suits in sixth form. So far, so economic, but watch out if your boy is a team player – anything with the griffin on it hurts. Parent-run second-hand uniform shop can really help here.

Pastoral care, well-being and discipline: Houses and long, weekly tutorials are the backbone of the system, supplemented by professional counsellor. Pastoral care 'not cuddly, but helpful' – staff are vigilant, and we hear that bullying is stamped on pretty fast; reports too of unusual boys being well supported, the best brought out of them. Not all relish the rough and tumble of the house rooms at lunch time (prefects and CCTV still on the losing side against youthful exuberance), but havens for those who prefer to work quietly. Parents full of praise for lower school (ages 11 and 12); boys are kept at a slight remove from the main school to help them ease into the system.

Good behaviour expected at all times but discipline is kept in perspective, perception amongst boys is that things (especially with regard to hair and uniform) are a little less draconian than of

yore. Straightforward sin treated seriously – this is a boarding school in the centre of a town so it needs to be – and it's out for drugs.

Pupils and parents: Most day pupils from within the 20-mile radius of the ('unreasonably' say parents) expensive bus network. Parents usual Oxfordshire mix of academics, medics, IT professionals, many working long hours to afford the fees. About half the school's full boarders from overseas – a wide range of countries, and well integrated; those we talked to reported close foreign friends. All in all, they're collected and courteous boys.

Correspondence nearly all electronic and weekly email system works a lot better than letters at the bottom of sports' bags. Active parents' association organises all sorts of social events.

Old boys include MP Francis Maude, actor Tom Hollander, comedian David Mitchell, all five members of Radiohead, and countless others who have proper jobs.

Entrance: A good flow at 11 from surrounding primaries (mostly with the help of the local tutorial network, if only to get used to the exams: seek out a good one via the parents of pupils who made the grade) and preps like Chandlings that teach for the Abingdon School exam. A larger number at 13 from prep schools including Abingdon's own, via a mix of exams.

A dozen or two join at sixth form – Miss Lusk has raised the bar somewhat and it's now generally A grade GCSEs for subjects to be studied at A level. Interview and school recommendation important at all ages.

Exit: Very few leave after GCSE (plenty of warning to parents, if needed). Almost all to university – currently popular are Durham, Exeter, Imperial, King's College London, Cardiff and Manchester. Good numbers to Oxbridge, 14 in 2015. Wide range of courses, with engineering and economics prominent; above average numbers choose languages, history and medicine.

Money matters: A range of decorative scholarships, but the money is (as ever these days) in the means-tested bursaries.

Remarks: A premier league boys' school, with a strong commitment to a broad education and academic success. Best suits those robust boys who will knuckle down and do 'a hell of a lot of hard work', but understands that boys need to be amused and not just fed facts.

Ashfold School

Dorton House, Aylesbury, Buckinghamshire HP18 9NG

01844 238237
katrina.hartley@ashfoldschool.co.uk
www.ashfoldschool.co.uk

Ages: 3–13 (boarding from 9)
Pupils: 270
Boarders: 74 weekly/flexi
Day: £3,900 – £15,630 pa
Boarding: Weekly £17,030 – £18,780 pa

Headmaster: Since 1997, Mr Michael Chitty (50s). Educated at Clifton College, Bristol then Exeter University where he read economics before following generations of forefathers to Sandhurst. First bitten by the teaching bug on his gap year in Kenya, where he was a student teacher at The Banda School and later, following an army career that saw him rise to the rank of Captain in the Queen's Royal Irish Hussars via Equerry to HRH Prince Philip, when he returned to Sandhurst as officer instructor.

Landed squarely on his feet in his first teaching position at Stowe School, where he taught economics, politics and European studies, always with an eye to his main ambition of becoming a prep school head. Given role of 'adjutant' to ease communications between the head's office, bursary and staff common room before being appointed housemaster of Grenville House (after which he later named one of his two black labradors). Headhunted after six years to become head of Ashfold, which he transformed with his energy, enthusiasm and clear vision. No longer teaches, although he does share boarding duties, but parents say he is 'very hands on' and he still coaches rugby, hockey and cricket teams, as well as clay pigeon and .22 rifle shooting teams, sits with children at lunch times and is always visible at matches and other school events.

Prospective parents unlikely to meet many heads whose former jobs include 'deployment of the British army worldwide' and Chitty does not disappoint, with his overwhelmingly positive, driven – and some might say military – approach

Prospective parents unlikely to meet many heads whose former jobs include 'deployment of the British army worldwide' and Chitty does not disappoint

to managing his school. An animated and dynamic communicator, he likes to keep up to date with car park chit chat via parents. Says he is running a 'very together school,' and is now 'in a position to do some very exciting stuff.' Recent appointment of a female deputy aims to boost girls' numbers and bring fresh ideas, although head is realistic that the female intake will most likely remain mostly siblings and peak at about 45 per cent.

Lives in a house on site – as do around 15 staff – with wife Louise, a barrister. Two grown up children, now working, come back for regular visits and often join their parents at their second home near Cirencester, where they enjoy spending weekends sailing, walking dogs and occasionally indulging a passion for cricket.

Entrance: Non-selective, with the majority joining reception from the nursery. Prospective pupils for all year groups invited to spend a day in school for assessment only. Head likes children from state primaries to join by year 2 and will hold places for them to this point. From year 3, places are harder to come by, with waiting lists for most year groups.

Exit: Leavers to a wide variety of schools, with about 50 per cent heading off to board most years. Popular co-ed choices include St Edward's Oxford, Rugby and Stowe with Headington popular for girls and the most able boys opting for Abingdon or Magdalen College. Impressive scholarship record – 14 in 2015, from Akeley Wood, Bloxham, Bradfield, Headington, Rugby and Stowe. These can range from art or DT to sport and academic. Head takes care to place less academic children in next schools where they can shine. Very few to state maintained grammars (just a couple each year), with head discouraging 11 plus unless for financial reasons.

Remarks: The cross country drive through rolling hills and farmland and rising fear that the satnav is playing tricks on you is well worth it for the first sight of Ashfold's stunning Jacobean mansion set in 33 acres of fields and woodland. Rugby pitches in the foreground give the impression of a traditional boys' prep but behind the magnificent building are three hard tennis courts, a well maintained, heated outdoor pool, full size Astroturf, netball courts and a lovely adventure playground, proving that that the girls who make up roughly 35 per cent of the school population are well catered for and becoming more integral to the culture of the school.

Wood panelling, winding staircases and cobbled stable blocks bring Hogwarts to mind, and rosy cheeked, windswept and slightly dishevelled children litter the grassy play areas, giving an overall impression of an idyllic country school – worlds apart from the urban London schools many of its commuter families have left behind. Lacks some of the dazzling showcase facilities boasted by many

preps, but every part of the campus is put to excellent use (and in the words of one parent: 'you're a bit restricted with a grade I listing') and the overall effect is of an inspiring, functional and nurturing environment, which, in the head's words, 'celebrates children.'

Purpose-built pre-prep building houses nursery to year 2 in a light, spacious and colourful setting with its own well-equipped playground and large field, complete with bug hotel. Pre-prep children well integrated into the main school, sharing its assembly space (often the village church, situated on site), sports hall and playing fields. Junior department housed in main wing of house, while most senior lessons take place in recently renovated courtyard classrooms.

Largely rural catchment from surrounding villages, with majority of children from hard-working middle class families ('hardly any old money,' said one parent), who travel up to 30 minutes to school. Very few from non-Caucasian families. School keen to prove its country credentials with a flourishing veg patch tended by pupils and weekend challenges set for families, resulting in the presentation of the school's 'countryside certificate' on completion of all 30. Small number of scholarships, with the Stowe-Ashfold scholarship covering 100 per cent of fees and other awards up to 30 per cent, available for pupils 'who show outstanding academic, artistic, sporting, musical or all-round ability' for the last two years at the school.

Girls have been part of the furniture at Ashfold since the 1980s but are almost exclusively siblings of boys. Although they make up 35 per cent of the total cohort, numbers vary between year groups and are very small in some (as low as three in a class), which is 'a bit of a downside,' according to parents. In some year groups, however, girls actually outnumber boys and parents add that all

Head says he won't have any arrogance in the school, on occasion passing over obvious macho choices for head boy for 'a lovely gentleman with outstanding manners'

children get the same opportunities, regardless of gender. School addressing gender balance with increased girl-focused activities such as dance, equestrian and girls' clubs, but head is realistic in his ambition to significantly grow numbers.

Whether arty, sporty, or musical, there's something for every child here ('they look at the child as an individual,' say parents) and academics are solid all round too. Class sizes average around 14 and are capped at 16 in the pre-prep and 18 in the prep. French with a specialist teacher from 7 and Latin from 9. Some mutterings from parents that they would like an earlier introduction to languages. No setting until last two years 'to allow for the genders' different rates of development,' according to head. Pupils entirely specialist taught from year 4 and move around the school for different subjects from thereon. All children screened for dyslexia aged 7 or whenever they join the school. Currently around 12 per cent of pupils under the SENCo for mild needs (SpLD, dyslexia or dyspraxia). In class support and small group work with a learning support assistant covered by fees. One-to-one lessons with the school's SEN specialist charged as extra.

Parents find channels of communication excellent and are able to email class teachers – who they describe as 'a really talented bunch' – directly with queries or issues. Recent introduction of e-learning online assessments for all children from year 3 up have 'really freed up teachers to focus on creative lesson planning,' says head.

High standard of art on show in and around a lovely bright art room; 'you can't usually see the ceiling for work,' said the head of department when we visited (it was the first week in September), although it would be nice to see a bit more of the pupils' work festooning the walls around the rest of the school. New £1m classroom block including new art rooms and a food technology lab should further bolster this strength.

Almost 60 per cent of pupils learn a musical instrument peripatetically, inspired by the head of music (described by parents as 'magnificent'), a surprisingly young addition to the Ashfold team who doubles as a rugby coach and has 'changed the kids' perceptions of music,' say parents, by injecting the school with lively doses of musical theatre. He even had head singing Greased Lightning (actions and all) in a staff and parents' choir recital. Waiting lists for all choirs underscore the school's renewed collective passion in this area and all pre-prep children learn the violin and recorder from year 1. Lots going on in the drama department too, with recent productions including Animal Farm and Charlie and the Chocolate Factory, and plans in the pipeline for more musical productions.

Once children reach the prep school they have an extended day, ending at either 5 or 6pm, depending on age. This enables the curriculum to include daily sport for all, which although adored by most is 'a struggle' for some of the less sporty ones, according to parents. All the usual suspects played to a good level but head exceptionally proud of his U13 girls' hockey team which won the IAPS championship recently and the clay shooting team, also national champions after a few years as runners up. He puts this and other sporting successes down to a 'real focus on coaching' with specialist talent brought in to coach rugby, hockey, netball and football (with an ex-Oxford United coach). Gymnastics and indoor games take place in a good sized sports hall incorporating wonderful changing facilities – 'with hot showers,' the head assures. From year 6, those demonstrating talent in other areas are selected to join scholars' groups (academic, art, drama et al) in place of time allocated to games.

Boarding allowed from year 5, where children can stay for supper after games, then take part in one of a multitude of activities on offer (from rifle shooting or fishing to chess and cookery). Given that this takes them up to 8pm it's a bit of a no brainer for parents of children keen to sample boarding life, and up to 30 children board on any given night. Dorms of up to seven beds have been recently revamped and provide spacious, comfortable accommodation in the mansion, girls at one end of the building, boys at the other. Head says, 'it's proper boarding, not a sleepover,' and boarders sleep in the same bed on their chosen boarding nights. Newly refurbished boarders' common rooms, complete with pool table, two flat screen TVs and comfy sofas, provide a home from home feel and open onto the houseparents' accommodation. No mobile phones, iPods or other gadgets allowed with the exception of Kindles – a very popular move with parents. Lights out at 9.30pm and cooked breakfasts are a hit.

School has a Christian ethos but accepts other denominations. Rightfully proud of its pastoral care with parents reporting 'very clear lines of escalation' should things ever go wrong. Three houses (Gryphons, Lions and Dragons) compete in lots of eagerly contested competitions (parents describe the standard of work in the inter-house art competition as 'unbelievable') with the each term culminating in a house cup. Pre-prep pupils presented with star of the week awards for effort and attainment in weekly assemblies. Prefects appointed in year 8 with the head taking a steer from last year's crew on who should be considered then consulting with staff before making his new appointments. Head boy and girl chosen after October half term amid great excitement. Head clear that 'leadership is about serving others,' and says he won't have any arrogance in the school, on occasion passing over obvious macho choices for head boy for 'a lovely gentleman with outstanding manners.'

No school buses as head wants parents to bring children into school to keep lines of communication open: 'If a child has had a sleepless night, for example, we want to know about it,' he says.

Bedales School

👫 💬28

Church Road, Petersfield, Hampshire GU32 2DG

01730 300100
admissions@bedales.org.uk
www.bedales.org.uk

Ages: 13–18
Pupils: 473; sixth form: 175
Boarders: 315 full, 14 flexi
Day: £17,995 – £26,475 pa
Boarding: £23,145 – £33,690 pa

Linked school: Dunannie and Dunhurst, Bedales' Junior Schools

Headmaster: Since 2001, Mr Keith Budge MA PGCE (50s). Read English at Oxford. Rugby blue. Previously a housemaster at Marlborough and head of Loretto. Married with three children. Not your typical head – but then this isn't your typical school, not by a long way. In open-necked shirt, discreetly striped jacket and subtly – though differently – striped trousers and unsubtle candy-striped socks, Mr Budge – Keith to everyone – has slowly, quietly and resolutely established his authority in this school and its diverse, vociferous constituency. He is relaxed, though serious, in conversation. While his commitment to the school and its ethos is measured in expression, it is genuine and profound. Parents criticise him both ways – 'The school isn't achieving academically as it should'; 'Bedales has become more ordinary and interested in academic results at the expense of its traditional ethos'. You pays your money.

Mr Budge treads a narrow – but clear – line between maintaining and improving academics and maintaining and enhancing what Bedales is about. And he is doing it effectively. Witness the appointment of a 'managing head' of Bedales to allow Mr Budge to oversee all three Bedales schools with a view to 'working on the schools' distinctiveness and performance. I am in charge of which staff and students come into the school – ie appointments and admissions. I also come in when disciplinary matters get to a certain point, whether with a student or member of staff – I have crucial oversight of who comes and who goes and I lead on all areas of policy'. Mr Budge is guiding Bedales with the necessary firm grip but light touch.

Academic matters: Students tailor their studies by a combination of GCSEs, the more challenging IGCSEs and the school's unique GCSE alternative, Bedales Assessed Courses (BACs). All three qualifications use the same A*-G grading system. In 2015, 56 per cent of I/GCSE/BAC grades were A*/A (mostly IGCSEs and BACs).

It gets more unusual as you go further up the school. In Block 3 (year 9) you study a pretty trad curriculum plus one of classical civilisation, German,

Latin or Spanish and, crucially 'outdoor work' – one of the unique Bedalian features. From year 10, you take IGCSE courses in English, maths and dual or triple award science; a GCSE in a modern language plus up to two more GCSEs in either history, ICT, music, computing, ancient Greek, Latin or a second modern language. Students also take up to five BACs from a choice of ancient civilisations, art, classical music, dance, design, English literature, geography, outdoor work, philosophy, religion & ethics and theatre.

We saw home-made coracles, wood being carded and spun, smithing and, unaccountably, a trap that was used in The King and I being lovingly renovated

The approach is cross-curricular and broadening in all respects. 'We had inspirational teachers who were doomed to teach dull and crass curricula,' explains Mr Budge – yes. And parents concur – 'Most teachers are exceptionally dedicated and enthusiastic – they live on site and love engaging with young people'; 'My daughter did the BAC philosophy – she had to produce a massive journal full of her ideas on moral and ethical issues: wonderful'. Some of those who believe that education should be about education, rather than processing and assessment, feel they can't really send their children anywhere much else. 'And UCAS is hugely supportive,' says Mr Budge. That's all right, then!

A levels persist, though, and nothing too revolutionary makes its way onto the timetable, apart from Pre-U music and an option to complete an assessed piece of independent learning – the extended project. Eng lit, at this and at lower levels, has long and famously been outstanding and the uptake at A level outstrips all else. Art (see below) is also outstanding and popular. Likewise, history attracts the many and with good results. Smaller numbers for languages and the sciences, though those who take maths and drama do well. In 2015, 44 per cent A*/A grades and 73 per cent A*-B.

SENs here mostly consist of mild dyslexia/dyspraxia and affect around 25 per cent. One weekly support lesson – occasionally two – is offered and pupils are not withdrawn from classes. More than that needed and you may want to look elsewhere. Wheelchairs are no problem and school also takes those with hearing/visual impairments and integrates them well. Now has EAL teacher because of increase in overseas students.

'Outdoor work' is key at all levels. Has its own farm – over the five years everyone has a chance to herd sheep, keep bees, learn the skills of fencing, coppicing, gardening, hedging, renovating paths, barns and stone walls, draining and maintaining ponds and all kinds of construction, land management and conservation techniques. We saw home-made coracles, wool being carded and spun, smithing and, unaccountably, a trap that was used in The King and I being lovingly renovated.

Everywhere is green – gardens, orchards and meadows surround and abut the school buildings; we loved the historic timber-frame barns and workshops – turned to all kinds of uses – which one discovers on a ramble around the extensive farm village of the school.

Games, options, the arts: Here one cannot detach the outdoor life from the rest. Nonetheless, extensive playing fields and an Astroturf, massive sports hall plus super pool, courts, pitches – everything: sport no longer a bit of a blush and smirk. All have a weekly double PE lesson and all the major sports are offered – even rugby.

Art is uniquely well-resourced and, perhaps, uniquely proficient. Studios and gallery space create a mini art school-within-a-school. The quality of work would do credit to a degree show and we hugely admired the imagination, technical skills, mix of media and the confident handling evident in the work we saw. Life drawing, portraiture, photography, metalwork, pottery, stonework and sculpture, colour and texture experimentation – all impress, along with an informed and liberating grasp of tradition and classical precedents. This is exceptional provision delivered with exceptional dedication and producing exciting results.

Music and drama flourish likewise. Lovely drama studio in adapted workshop, excellent flexible theatre. Productions attract the masses and most enthuse about the last show they were in. They learn production techniques, eg sound and light, too. Music block unappealing on the outside but truly warm and inspirational inside – baby grands everywhere and deep painted walls and dark wood doors. Most learn at least one instrument and lessons are timetabled. Music tech is well-resourced but does not seem here, as in so many other places, to have become what music is all about. Own arts programme coordinator and runs an impressive and inspiring programme of events which brings in top professionals to perform and run workshops – the posters around the place for upcoming and recent events made us feel we were attending a permanent arts festival.

Boarding: Unique mixed-age dorms. All in first four years have a lower sixth in the dorm and dorms are for one to five students. Rooms comfortable and friendly – girls' more than boys': 'twas ever thus. Boys' flat (boarding) 'was designed by a prison architect,' one inmate confided, but it didn't look bad to us and no bars on the windows, for sure. Jolly nice garden, bird tables and bbq. Steephurst, the girls' house, is lovely – the original farmhouse which began the school. Really nice, comfy common rooms – someone here understands about sofas. Bizarre bathrooms in Steephurst – three abutting baths per room: 'You can have a bath with your friends – it gets slightly noisy,' one girl bubbled. 'Pastoral care is really good – they try terribly hard,' a parent said. Good food eaten by everyone together. Upper sixth in own floors in main building – 'Quad' – with kitchens, study rooms (shared with day pupils) and common rooms – inviting and very much a separate world.

Very few stay in at weekends and little is laid on – but they have the run of the place and expeditions and outings organised on request. Also 'cosy teas' and 'fireside games'.

Background and atmosphere: Started by visionary John Haden Badley and his wife in a house called Bedales, near Haywards Heath, in 1893. In 1898 – having begun to admit girls to counteract any undesirable masculine boorishness – they acquired a country estate in Steep and constructed a school – including state-of-the-art electric light – which opened in 1900. Dunhurst – a prep to feed Bedales – was started in 1902 on Montessori principles, and a pre-prep school, Dunannie, was added in the 1950s. No chapel – Badley's approach was strictly non-denominational – hence its attractiveness in its early days to liberals, intellectuals and non-conformists of all descriptions – both British and European. This was contributed to by the coterie of writers, musicians and artists who settled around Steep from the 1920s onwards.

Grew rapidly in the 1960s – the heyday of its à-la-modishness – and became the school of choice for the children of the super-cool. Lawrence

> **'It's a brilliant school if you're responsible,' a 14-year-old asserted, 'but if you need rules and boundaries it's not the school for you'**

Durrell, Simon Raven, Robert Graves, Cecil Day-Lewis, Peggy Guggenheim, Ted Hughes, Edna O'Brien, John Mortimer, Frederick Raphael, Joseph Losey, Peter Hall, Peter Brook, Laurence Olivier, Susan Hampshire, Mick Jagger, Pete Townshend, Sandie Shaw, Trevor Nunn, AA Gill, Roger Waters, Twiggy, Hayley Mills and Kirsty MacColl have all been Bedales parents.

Few eyesores – boasts two grade 1 listed Gimson designed arts and crafts buildings (the delicious Lupton Hall, 1911, and the Memorial Library, 1921) and two contemporary, award-winning buildings: the Olivier Theatre (1997) and the Orchard Building (2005). Fabuloso library – would grace an ancient Oxbridge college and makes you want to immerse yourself in the cerebral.

The ethos has survived but have had to be concessions – has long since taken day pupils, who now make up 30 plus per cent of its population; academic results do count – even committed Bedalians want something on paper – and the informality of its core values have needed strengthening with some more recent rigour. Some worried in Mr Budge's early days that he would dispel the relaxed ethos, but no-one fusses much now. 'Greening Bedales' involves laudable initiatives on many environmental fronts, which other schools would do well to study. Also informs school's policies on trips and exchanges – not just extravagant junkets for the super-spoiled as elsewhere.

Pastoral care, well-being and discipline: Most really love and conform to the 'take responsibility for yourself and get on with it' ethos, though 'Some people get distracted by all the opportunities and don't work – others don't make enough of the opportunities and doss around,' one wise youngster confided. Own clothes means exactly that – though uniform seems to consist of lots of mini-shorts 'n' tights, track suit bottoms and trainers.

Sanctions for, eg, smoking/drinking/lateness/lying usually means gating. 'It's a brilliant school if you're responsible,' a 14-year-old asserted, 'but if you need rules and boundaries, it's not the school for you.' Not many find they can't hack it here. So we were saddened to learn, a few years ago, about expulsions for drug abuse and as the result of a ghastly end of term fracas. Perhaps this is the price to pay for being famously 'liberal', but it seems an awful pity.

Pupils and parents: Money counts now – one of the top 10 most expensive schools in the UK. But Bedales parents understand what the place is about and choose it in preference to the more conventional routes to wisdom and fulfilment, which includes many London families. Pupils are open, friendly and articulate – we met many on our visit and all were thoughtful and eager to explain their school to us. They are genuinely appreciative of what they have and the differences between their school and those their friends elsewhere attend. Very few overseas nationals – perhaps the ethos of no uniform and 'outdoor work' is not what most people abroad associate with a British boarding education. However, always a sprinkling of the well-connected, minor royal and generally savvy and liberal from all over the country.

Entrance: Around 55 come up from Bedales' own on-site junior school, Dunhurst; the rest of the 90-strong year group from outside. Many from Windlesham, Highfield, the Thomases, The Dragon, Amesbury, Newton and West Hill Park. Those who want to are pre-assessed 18 months before entry; most thereafter come for a two-day residential in January before entry, plus tests in maths, English and reasoning. Around 75 per cent of these will gain places. As in everything, Bedales is unconventional – 'We back our hunches – we disregard scores when we know someone is right for us'. Many more girls apply for places at sixth form than

boys. Assessment via interview – 50 points at GCSE expected (taking A* as 8, A as 7 and so on, based on a nine-subject programme), plus A*/B in A level subjects but, as ever, flexible if they like you.

Exit: About a quarter leave after GCSEs. Lots of artists to Central St Martins, Camberwell etc. Rest to every kind of course – many do science, but few linguists – at unis ranging from Edinburgh to Exeter to LSE. Seven to Oxbridge in 2015, plus one to Berklee College of Music in the US and one to Parsons Paris. However recent Old Bedalian mused, 'I wish the school had been more ambitious for me – they didn't push me.' Another regretted that no-one had told her that her choice of A levels would be seen as 'soft' by universities. Mr Budge now setting 'where they go on to' as one of his missions.

Money matters: Scholarships at 13+ – all means-tested – for outstanding ability in almost anything, plus a separate category for music. At 16, scholarships for academics, art and music and, occasionally, science. Some awards for drama and design at the end of lower sixth.

Remarks: 'If you want an exam factory go somewhere else,' a parent advised. If you want a relaxed, happy and wholesome school with good teaching, real values and a rich outdoor life, look no further. Few Bedalians regret their school days.

Bloxham School

Banbury Road, Near Banbury, Oxfordshire OX15 4PE

01295 720222
admissions@bloxhamschool.com
www.bloxhamschool.com

Ages: 11–18
Pupils: 405; sixth form: 145
Boarders: 190 full, weekly and flexi
Day: £24,150 pa
Boarding: £22,560 – £31,815 pa

Headmaster: Since September 2013, Mr Paul Sanderson (40s) previously a deputy head and director of curriculum at Gordonstoun. Originally from Northern Ireland, he was educated at Banbridge Academy before studying evolutionary biology and genetics at St Andrews University. Postgrad qualifications from Oxford (PGCE) and Cambridge (MPhil). Taught at Lancaster Royal Grammar, Oundle and Carr Hill High before joining Gordonstoun as housemaster.

Drawn to the school's modest size (around 430 pupils), where children are 'less likely to disappear', he describes his first year as a 'rollercoaster', and

has made great strides in raising the academic profile of the school. Ambitious and determined, with a refreshing heart-on-his-sleeve honesty (a few watery-eyed moments when recounting the achievements of his pupils), Mr Sanderson's mission is to re-define what makes a Bloxham education.

A rugby enthusiast, with a passion for ice climbing and skiing. Runs a climbing wall class and recently took a group of students alpine climbing. Married with three young children.

Academic matters: In 2015, 54 per cent A*-B at A level (27 per cent A*/A); small numbers taking most subjects but business studies and maths top the popularity polls. Nearly half A*/A at GCSE in 2015. No plans to introduce the IB. IGCSEs currently offered in English, geography and sciences.

Ambitious and determined, with a refreshing heart-on-his sleeve honesty (a few watery-eyed moments when recounting the achievements of his pupils)

Management restructure has introduced new deputy and five new heads of department and there's a definite sense that the bar has been raised when it comes to teaching standards although it's too early for increased academic rigour to be reflected in examination grades. Staff pupil ratio average is 8:1 and progress is measured across the year through a challenge grade system. Length of lessons has recently been increased from 35 minutes to an hour and music and drama have been shifted to the afternoon in response to latest research that children become more creative as the day goes on.

While Bloxham is quick to point out that it is not a special needs school it does have a good reputation for nurturing able pupils with mild to moderate dyslexia who have become demoralised in more competitive arenas. A specialist dyslexia course is offered for up to six pupils a year in the third, fourth and fifth forms, focused on improving their reading speed and accuracy, spelling and study skills.

The Eunoia Society (ancient Greek for 'beautiful learning') provides an intellectual 'stretching' beyond the academic curriculum. As well as offering prep for Oxbridge entrance, it boasts an impressive programme of events, with trips to exhibitions, opera and ballet and recent visiting speakers have included an art historian, a US diplomat, a professor of biophysics and a senior civil servant.

Games, options, the arts: While there's been some rebalancing of an historic bias towards sport, the school still takes great pride in its achievements. Rugby and hockey are particular strengths (girls reigning county hockey champions at time of visit). Regular rivals include Stowe, Warwick, Marlborough and Wellington and competition is taken seriously. Coaches use iPads to record games for post-match analysis.

Facilities are excellent. In addition to two all-weather pitches, the school boasts extensive playing fields, two squash courts, two fives courts, six outdoor netball courts (doubling up as tennis courts during the summer) and a 23m indoor swimming pool. The Dewey Sports Hall has a well-equipped fitness suite with yoga and an assortment of classes also on offer. Sailing takes place on a nearby reservoir. Recent national successes in both clay pigeon shooting and equestrian competitions (twice national schools eventing champions). No stabling at school but pupils may arrange to bring their own mounts for twice-weekly tuition. Those who don't own their own horses can arrange to hire from local stables.

Bloxham is fast gaining a reputation for its drama programme. Since his appointment in 2013, the director of drama has increased the number of productions from one to eight a year and all pupils are expected to take part, either front of stage or behind the scenes. The school recently staged its first original production (about Bloxham boys who fought and perished in the Great War), selling out all four performances to rave reviews: 'as good as the West End', commented one enthusiastic parent. The Great Hall stages the major productions, with the rest at the Wesley Theatre (a former Wesleyan Chapel).

The music department is housed in the Sam Kahn Music School and there's a new orchestra – quite an achievement given the size of the school's population. Fifty per cent split across music and music tech subjects. We dropped in on a lesson about film scores and learned of an impending visit from an old boy who now works as a film composer in Hollywood – such 'value-added' is much in evidence. Lots of rehearsal rooms support a busy performance schedule and there's the added bonus of a school radio station, run by pupils. Art provision is equally impressive. Sixth form students benefit from dedicated personal workspaces in a charming room that resembles an artists' garret, complete with sloping eaves.

'We want kids who are hungry and ambitious inside and outside the classroom', says Mr Sanderson and Bloxham's enrichment programme is extensive. As well as the Eunoia Soc (see above), pupils can choose from clubs ranging from astronomy to knitting as well as a wine society for sixth formers. Animal club is offered once a week for pupils keen to help look after the school's resident lizards, snakes, hermit crabs and beetles.

Boarding: First and foremost a boarding school; day pupils (known as day boarders) make up half the population and can stay until 10pm. There's also the option of flexi-boarding (pay per night). One local parent said her son doesn't want to come home for fear of 'missing out on the fun'. This flexibility was a big draw for a number of the parents to whom we spoke.

Seven boarding houses are clean and bright with large communal areas – a bit dated in places but a rolling programme of refurbishment is under way. Weekly and flexi boarding in years 7 and 8, with own lower school boarding house. Full boarding from year 9. Thirteen per cent of boarders from overseas. Maximum of three beds to a room, full boarders have their own room from year 10.

Background and atmosphere: With its picture-book cluster of buildings in honey-coloured Horton stone, manicured lawns and homely atmosphere the school blends harmoniously with beautiful

Bloxham village. The lower school (Exham House) is actually situated in the former village pub.

Originally known as All Saints School, Bloxham was founded in 1860 by The Reverend Philip Reginald Egerton who wanted to establish a school that embodied the high church values of the Oxford Movement. In 1897 it joined the Woodard Foundation, the group of schools founded by Canon Woodard to promote education in an actively Christian environment.

Food excellent (we took full advantage of visiting on 'Curry Thursday'). Great choice and emphasis on healthy eating. Sociable lunchtimes with teachers sitting happily alongside pupils.

Pastoral care, well-being and discipline: Self-proclaimed 'gold standard' of pastoral care is justified. Multiple systems in place to ensure children's emotional welfare, including a team of 'peer listeners' – sixth form student volunteers with formal counselling training. Small size of school promotes healthy mixing and solid friendships between girls/boys and different year groups. Head meets daily with head boy and girl, helping to keep abreast of any grumbles or issues. School refreshingly honest about (infrequent) incidents of bullying; intervention swift and effective, according to parents. Keen sensitivity about emotional needs of pupils: 'let's face it, the teenage years are difficult', says head.

Holy communion for all once a week. School doesn't shy away from talking about the importance of spiritual development in education but head recognises need for religion to 'translate into the 21st century'. It's less about doctrine and more about getting children to think about their place in the world, 'To be a giver, rather than a taker'.

This ethos is reflected in service initiatives such as Reading Club, where older pupils help children from local primary schools with reading difficulties. According to head this has inspired at least one student to go on and train as a primary teacher.

Pupils and parents: Bloxham has long been a popular local option and is now increasingly so for London refugees looking for a smaller, more 'gentle' boarding school. Recent push to improve parent-school communications has been warmly welcomed. Very informative parents' handbook published annually; newly established parents association. Saturday matches are well attended and there are plenty of opportunities for parents to get involved if desired. Former pupils include impressive numbers of high ranks from all three forces plus novelist Tom Sharpe and journalist John Sergeant.

Entrance: Candidates for lower school (age 11) via school's own exam (maths, English and verbal reasoning) and interview; CE for 13+ entry. Sixth form requires minimum six GCSEs at grades A*- C, with at least a B in chosen A level subjects (A grade required

for maths and physics). Lower school intake is from state primaries or independents such as Carrdus; at 13+ pupils from preps including Ashfold School, Beachborough, Bilton Grange, Swanbourne House and Winchester House.

Exit: Small leakage (around 10 per cent) after GCSEs. Post-A level, varied subjects and destinations, including Russell Group, ranging from veterinary science at Cambridge to land management at Cirencester. Two Cambridge places in 2015.

Money matters: Parents say flexi-boarding option and late stay for day pupils represent value for money. Scholarships (20 per cent fee reduction) for academics, sport, DT music and drama. Means-tested bursaries can be combined with scholarships; limited number of full-fee bursaries.

Remarks: Successfully combines academic challenge with plenty of sport, service and practical life skills. A perfect environment for happy all-rounders.

Bradfield College

Bradfield, Berkshire RG7 6AU

01189 644516
admissions@bradfieldcollege.org.uk
www.bradfieldcollege.org.uk
C of E

Ages: 13–18
Pupils: 775 (471 boys, 283 girls); sixth form: 325
Boarders: 670
Day: £27,420 pa
Boarding: £34,275 pa

Headmaster: Since September 2015, Dr Chris Stevens, previously second master at Marlborough College. Read modern and medieval languages at Cambridge; began his teaching career as a college lecturer while researching for a DPhil in Italian literature at Oxford. He then established a school in France for Ashdown House prep. He joined Uppingham in 1997, where he was master-in-charge of cricket and a housemaster for nine years; he had been at Marlborough since 2011. He is a keen sportsman, playing cricket, hockey, fives and golf. His wife, Helen, is associate professor of English at Corpus Christi, Oxford and they have three young daughters.

Academic matters: Where has the old Bradfield gone and what have you done with it? A level results have shot up over the past decade. Sixth form value added scores very good (bearing in mind the school scoops up a nice, fresh sixth form intake

including girls arriving from high flying single sex schools). In 2015, 41 per cent A*/A grades and 74 per cent A*-B (a dip on 2014). Second IB cohort got an average of 35 points. School now keen to give a similar boost to GCSEs (60 per cent A*/A grades in 2015). Vast majority of pupils now do three separate sciences at GCSE, with impressive results. Arty GCSEs on offer including dance, textiles and photography (the latter two also available at A level; A level students can also choose film studies or the unfathomable 'science in society'). History, the sciences and maths all achieving well, as are modern languages – the latter a bit surprising in this virile school. Newish modern languages block offers French, Spanish, German (quite a few native speakers who come over for the upper sixth year), plus a smattering of Arabic and Mandarin. Latin and Greek both taught. Recent state-of-the-art science centre uses the very latest in sustainable design technology – 13 sophisticated laboratories plus

groovy roof garden used for field studies. Around 40 ambitious sixth formers pursue an Extended Project Qualification.

Still, no danger of Bradfield becoming a hothouse, and geeks remain thin on the ground. A few parents feel the school does not always squeeze the best out of its most academic pupils. Has gone a bit Anthony Seldon, with all pupils now taking emotional literacy and well-being lessons in years 9, 10 and 11. All take a course in study skills in their first year. The Athena Programme, a lecture-based enrichment programme, broadens sixth form minds. Some 155 pupils receive learning support, most for mild dyslexia.

Games, options, the arts: 'The perfect school for a child who is a jack of all trades, master of none,' one parent told us. The exception to this may be sport, which remains outstanding. Bradfield's football (21 teams!) is the stuff of legend and can be played for two terms, by both boys and girls – some families choose the school for its football alone. Hockey, golf, cricket and even polo also doing very well. Boys won the Micklem Trophy (golf) recently, beating Rugby School, Eton and Wellington. The boys' 1st tennis team were runners up in LTA Aegon National Schools' Senior Students Finals. Cricket coaching runs all year via the Julian Wood Academy and several boys play for counties. The 1st XI skipper won man of the series this summer for England U19 and has won a pro contract with Middlesex. Tennis the main sport for girls in the summer and we hear good things about the netball. Lowish numbers of girls means that a talented sportswoman may be playing in three matches a

week – good, or not so good, depending on how you look at it. Sports facilities glorious: pristine playing fields, vast sports hall, indoor tennis centre, two floodlit Astros, nine hole golf course, fab indoor pool, dance studio – you get the picture. Masses of minor sports offered including squash, fives, fencing, riding, polo, sailing, shooting, water polo and 'fishing'.

Good to see music riding high. The department is well housed and humming with activity – pupils can practise during activity times and evening prep. Choral music particularly strong and the chamber choir travels abroad every year, most recently to Toronto. Instrumental players have taken part in the Music Junction project run by the London Chamber Orchestra aimed at bringing together children from 'diverse backgrounds'. Legendary outdoor jazz evening takes place each June, organised by the energetic head of modern languages – spotlights the jazz band, swing band and individual performances, including by teachers.

Enormous range of art media, taught in a cluster of studios and rooms by a highly enthusiastic and creative team – most practising artists themselves. Pupils here can paint and draw, sew, print, photograph, model, carve and sculpt. No proper theatre, but school productions take place in the Big School or the Studio Theatre. Greek theatre under reconstruction but we look forward to the return of classical productions – in Greek – a tradition that goes back the 19th century. The punishing Interhouse Steeplechase was recently revived, last run in 1948, and in full swing on the day we visited.

Humongous list of co-curricular activities from Shakespeare society to ice skating. The message that overseas trips are less in fashion in these days of austerity chic has not permeated into rural Berkshire so Bradfield sportsmen and women, geographers, musicians, economists.. you name it really.. can be found globetrotting. Tennis training? In the Algarve! Film studies? We're off to Hollywood! Even CCF (compulsory in year 10) and D of E teams can be found scaling the rainy heights of Norway and Bavaria.

Boarding: Vast majority of pupils board.. but you could shoot a cannon through the boarding houses on a Saturday evening without much danger of injury, especially in G House and Stanley House, half of whose inhabitants are day pupils. Still, there are usually over 100 pupils in school on Sundays and the numbers staying in over the weekend climb steadily in the summer term. New social club includes a coffee shop and JCR Bar.

Background and atmosphere: Bradfield is a village.. and the village is the school. It is cosy – a 18th/19th century hamlet abounding with cute red-brickery, sloping roofs, chapel, leafy lanes and hillside walks. But it is also isolated – no shops, pubs or post office. Founded as a school by the combined local rector and lord of the manor for the education of sons of the clergy in the 1850s. Bit by bit the school took over the village so it includes, in addition to the old school, the old mill which now houses the art department – the stream and mill race still rushing away – and, gloriously, a fabulous arts and crafts manor house with stunning quadrangle and beautiful gardens. The grounds are among the best-kept we know – immaculate; the National Trust would do well to come and learn.

It's a big site stretching across a minor road and, although most teaching happens pretty centrally,

> *The old mill now houses the art department – the stream and mill race still rushing away – and a fabulous arts and crafts manor house*

fast walking and stout shoes are needed to get from one end to the other. A few privately-owned houses still in the village but most is school-owned and almost 90 per cent of staff live on site. Relatively little turnover in senior staff brings continuity, but also some resistance to change. Average age of staff is 40; 38 teachers have been at the college for more than 10 years.

Relations between pupils are 'mellow', say the kids. None of the pupils we talked to reported bullying. Teachers 'not too pushy' and 'very good at tailoring things to the individual'. Mr Gove would have applauded its community-mindedness: Bradfield now sponsors Theale Green, a nearby comprehensive which has been rated as requires improvement by Ofsted. Continues to nurture a 100 year old association with the Bradfield Club – a youth centre in Peckham, London.

Pastoral care, well-being and discipline: All year 9 pupils – boys and girls, boarding and day – start in Faulkner's House, a modern, custom built boarding house with its own dining hall and separate wings for girls and boys. Very popular with the kids, with most parents seeing it as a good transition between prep and senior school and an easy way for 150 new children to get to know each other. A few sceptics less keen and worried about scope for bullying or discipline issues with no older kids there to rule the roost. All agree, though, that the accommodation is superb, with en suite bedsits, and usually two or three pupils to a room.

Year 10s move into houses spread far and wide over the wooded site, in which they remain for the next four years – no sixth form house. H House is flavour of the month at the minute (en suite AND under floor heating!) while D House currently shines at football. Most day pupils stay for supper, prep and socialising, leaving around 9pm – though they are free to leave after lessons at 6pm.

A friendly place. 'We're basically pro-pupil. We try to separate the behaviour from the individual and give people a second chance.. but sometimes that needs to be somewhere else.' Doesn't believe in zero tolerance. 'Every case has its own context – there's always a shade of grey'. But no pushovers; five pupils out because of drugs a few years ago. Social media sites 'turned off' during lesson times. Alcohol less of a problem here than at some similar schools because most Bradfield pupils go home on Saturday nights instead of into town.

Pupils and parents: Five minutes from junction 12 on the M4 and from Theale railway station; helpful for the chunk of school families that live in London. Also popular with local families and the vast majority of pupils live within an hour and a half of the school. Has not yet been discovered by Chinese and Russians: around 11 per cent of pupils have homes abroad – a mixture of British overseas families and international pupils (from 33 different countries). Boys still far outnumber girls, almost two to one, but school has admitted an extra 50 girls. Top feeders include Cheam, Lambrook, Northcote Lodge, St Andrew's, Broomwood Hall, Thorngrove, Thomas's Clapham, Elstree, Feltonfleet and Eagle House. Former pupils include authors Louis de Bernières and Richard Adams, explorer Benedict Allen, MP Richard Benyon, comedian Tony Hancock (who left school at age 15), actor Claudia Harrison, cricketer and broadcaster Mark Nicholas, Lord David Owen, astronomer Sir Martin Ryle.

Entrance: Tours every Saturday morning – no open days. School says demand for places has 'gone through the roof' in recent years – and our Advice Service can confirm this is so. Now faced with the novel problem of having to select 150 year 9 pupils from an oversubscribed pool. Has resisted raising the CE bar of 55 per cent: 'It would change the inclusive nature of the school – we genuinely believe in things beyond only academic excellence.' Looking for pupils who will take full advantage of opportunities and add 'positive energy', so all candidates are now interviewed. Twice. Children bring a piece of academic work to discuss. No pre-testing, but borderline CE candidates are 'screened' and we have known parents of 12 year olds to be warned in advance that their children are teetering on the borderline. A few children enter year 10 and, unusually, Bradfield admits around 15 pupils into year 11 to do a foundation year before starting A levels or IB.

Some 50-60 new pupils are admitted into the lower sixth. Candidates must be interviewed, submit GCSE predictions (or actual grades) and take a 'General Ability' test in November before year of entry, with possibility for scholarship or award. Places are conditional on attaining a minimum of six B grades, with at least Cs in English and maths.

Exit: Around 10 per cent leave post-GCSE. Then mostly to Russell Group – particularly hot on Exeter, Leeds, Oxford Brookes, Manchester, Bath and Bristol recently. Four to Oxbridge in 2015.

Money matters: Not cheap. The prospectus sets the tone when describing 'The Bradfield Experience': 'It's the fun of House Dinners or a netball tour to Barbados; it's the challenge of an expedition to the High Atlas Mountains..' Provides £2m annually in means tested bursaries up to 100 per cent of fees available at 13+ and sixth form. Scholarships awarded for academics, music, art, performing arts (dance and/or drama), sport and all-round ability.

Remarks: An all rounder's paradise.

Brockhurst and Marlston House Schools

Marlston Road, Thatcham, Newbury Berkshire RG18 9UL

01635 200293
registrar@brockmarl.org.uk
www.brockmarl.org.uk
C of E

Ages: 3-13 (boys at Brockhurst, girls at Marlston House; pre-prep and years 7 and 8 mixed)
Pupils: 320
Boarders: 20 full, 90 flexi
Day: £9,549 – £15,990 pa
Boarding: £21,474 pa

Heads: Brockhurst head since 2000, Mr David Fleming MA MSc (50s); himself educated at Brockhurst, then Radley College followed by natural sciences at Trinity College, Oxford. A member of the family which owns the school, he projects an air of relaxed authority. Clearly in a very secure position, but doesn't rest on his laurels. Parents like the fact that they are 'talking to the decision-maker.' Aims to 'preserve schools' family feel' whilst maintaining high academic standards and improving existing facilities. Married with two daughters; wife has high flying job outside the school. 'She's the clever one!'

Marlston House operates in tandem with Brockhurst and has own head. Appointed 1999, Caroline Riley MA BEd Cert Ed (50s) works alongside Mr Fleming and has free rein to run the girls' school as she sees fit. Educated at a West Country girls' school and Southampton University, she is former head of a mixed school in Hazelgrove and has taught in both single sex and mixed schools. Allows headmaster to do most of the talking, but they make a good double act: her contributions are quietly efficient, focused and informed. Teaches RS and history in upper school (headmaster teaches geography). Husband is retired and they have two grown-up children.

Entrance: Children join Ridge House (pre-prep) following their third birthday. Youngest children get used to school by attending swimming lessons on Wednesday mornings and free toddler and parent sessions. Boys and girls educated together up to the age of 6, after which they join Brockhurst (boys) or Marlston House (girls). Occasional vacancies for older children after age 9; school says, 'Special help can be given [to boys and girls] to catch up where necessary.' There is an informal interview and assessment for anyone seeking a scholarship or bursary.

Exit: An impressive array of scholarships to some of the most competitive senior schools, eg sports at Millfield and academic scholarships to Downe House, Abingdon and St Helen and St Katharine. Other leavers choose Radley, Marlborough, Wellington, Bradfield and Pangbourne, often with academic, sport, music, art and all-rounder awards. Some go further afield, eg Cheltenham Ladies' College, Charterhouse, Eton and St Swithun's.

Remarks: Founded in 1884 in Shropshire as a boys' prep school, Brockhurst moved to its present home – a mock-Jacobean listed mansion set in 60 acres

History is clearly good fun; walls of history room festooned with pictures of students getting into the spirit of ancient times on Celtic Day

just outside Newbury – in 1945. Marlston House opened its doors to girls in 1995 and is located in a separate (also listed) building on the same site. Main building boasts imposing façade of deep red brick and stone, with baronial windows, turrets and heavy oak main door opening into wood-panelled passages and spacious Great Hall. Heads gave their interviews in a large room with impressive views over school's extensive grounds – would make a good backdrop for filming period drama. The rest of the school's buildings, although modern, sit comfortably alongside older ones and blend in thanks to clever architecture and landscaping.

Two schools join forces to marry the best of co-ed with single-sex education; boys and girls are educated separately between the ages of 6 and 11, only coming together for art, music and drama. Classes merge in the final two years of 'senior school', in order to prepare pupils for academic scholarships and common entrance exams on an equal footing. Quirky 'back-to-front' year groups mean those leaving reception begin in year 8 and finish in year 1.

Lots of evidence of modern, quality teaching and good effort from pupils is everywhere to be seen. Able children streamed into scholarship sets as soon

as they are ready, usually in year 5. Maths tuition caters for a wide range of ability and pupils take common entrance at all three levels. Scholars take level 3 maths in year 7 and then focus on scholarship papers. English teaching excellent; pupils are encouraged to read widely and develop critical skills. CE syllabus completed by year 7 and scholarship set extends pupils' knowledge in final year. Good provision for languages, especially French, which is taught from age 4. Château Robert near Biarritz is school property and all 11 and 12-year-olds spend two weeks every year studying the language intensively and exploring the area. Latin from year 4 to both CE and scholarship levels; those taking scholarship Latin also learn Greek. Pupils begin German in the last two years and have taster sessions in Russian and Spanish once exams are over.

Usual range of subjects elsewhere on the timetable; we observed a lively practical science lesson in which pupils spoke confidently about extracting chlorophyll. History is clearly good fun; walls of history room festooned with pictures of students getting into the spirit of ancient times on Celtic Day (ably assisted by those 60 acres). Knights of the Sealed Knot have visited to perform re-enactments of medieval battles. Plenty of school trips, eg to Hampton Court. Good ICT facilities and library. Parents praise school communications and particularly news section of website. 'They get it right 90 per cent of the time.' Progress reports issued two or three times every half term. 'Children are treated as individuals, with stars, effort points and lots of praise for good work ... the sheer scope of opportunities seem boundless.' Saturday school from year 2 up, so schools run clubs in the morning for younger siblings.

Everyone takes part – children hold torches and process with their parents to the bonfire, which is traditionally lit by the youngest child in the school

Learning development centre (LDC) goes well beyond usual remit of dyslexia, eg developing comprehension and study skills and exam revision techniques. LDC helps gifted and talented to extend knowledge, supports EAL students and even adults from the local community with dyslexia. Also helps pre-prep pupils who don't pick up on phonics first time around.

Music is clearly in good health, with around 80 per cent receiving individual tuition on one or more instruments. There are senior and junior orchestras and choirs, plus a chamber choir and string quartet. Swing and R+B bands, guitar, flute and recorder groups provide other opportunities to make music. Class music includes use of composition suite. Heads keen to point out that schools are very flexible and 'will adjust timetable to suit individual talents such as music.' Art and DT block ranges over two floors which provide plenty of space for painting, drawing and pottery; not as well-equipped for practical DT as some other preps we've seen, although facilities for art and pottery are excellent. Standard of work on display is high and the most talented pupils are coached for art awards. Trips to galleries and museums organised post CE.

Schools' extensive grounds are a boon to sports staff; all major sports are on offer in addition to minor sports such as golf, judo, shooting and fishing in school's lake. Soccer, rugby, cross-country running and cricket for boys; hockey, netball, rounders and tennis for girls – all do athletics and swimming in 25m indoor pool and boys can play hockey too. Sport is timetabled every day and there are A, B and C teams for major sports. A big draw for girls is the equestrian centre, where pupils can stable their own pony or learn to ride on schools' horses. Heads are proud of sporting record of their pupils, which have included winning national judo championships, IAPS swimming gold and athletics at county level. Keen to build more tennis courts; at present there is one indoor and three all-weather courts. Joint drama productions take place in new performing arts centre.

Family ethos encourages good pastoral care; we met a very dedicated housemaster who clearly poured heart and soul into the job. There is zero tolerance for bullying and parents report that issues are sorted immediately. One parent commented, 'The headmaster took time out from a school inspection [to deal with my concerns].' All pupils belong to a house and school council meets once a month.

Full-time boarding is encouraged, but flexi-boarders must spend a minimum of two nights a week in school. Boys' dorms are much less pretty than girls' dorms, as is the norm. Corridors kept tidy and routines well organised. Lots of posters on walls to reinforce anti-bullying ethos; full boarders can have mobile phones and iPads and their use is managed by boarding house staff. Overseas boarders have access to Skype in a specially designated room.

Multiple evening clubs and activities on offer (day pupils can join in) and all staff give up one or two evenings a week to run these. Lots of sporting activities but a couple of unusual options include geo-caching and barbeque club. School fireworks display is an annual highlight. Everyone takes part – children hold torches and process with their parents to the bonfire, which is lit traditionally by the youngest child in the school. Three sittings for lunch ensure that all pupils sit on a 'family table' with a member of staff present. Food a bit plain on the day we visited, but not in short supply and plenty of fresh fruit, cheese and other choices for pudding. School runs daily bus services to local towns and there is good after-school care for working families.

Children come from a wide variety of backgrounds, eg South Africa and the US, but are polite, articulate and unassuming without hiding their light under a bushel; they state (honestly) that there is nothing about the schools that they would change. Centenary and Foundation Scholarships are worth up to one third of fees, but headmistress keen to point out that 'a talented child can come here on a full scholarship.'

Twin schools offer a unique blend of co-ed and single-sex education. Blessed with a rich endowment, they are free to indulge mild idiosyncrasies such as different holiday and half-term dates. Clear moral steer and family values keep students, staff and parents on side. Obviously hard working – the school motto is 'no reward without effort' – but a happy place as well.

Brockwood Park School

Brockwood Park, Bramdean, Hampshire SO24 0LQ

01962 771744
enquiry@brockwood.org.uk
www.brockwood.org.uk

Ages: 14 –19
Pupils: 66; sixth form: 46
Boarders: all full
Boarding: £20,790 pa

Co-principals: Since 2013, Dr Gopal Krishnamurthy and since September 2015, Mr Antonio Autor. Dr Gopal has spent most of his life, since the age of 4, as a student and teacher at Krishnamurti's schools in India, the UK and the USA. He was a student, mature student and staff member at Brockwood and teaches physics and maths as well as being co-principal. He has a PhD in education, MAs in education and philosophy and a BA in physics.

Antonio Autor has a degree from the Bilbao School of Business Studies and was a professional footballer for nearly 10 years. After that, he studied English in Cardiff, Brighton and London, and joined Brockwood Park in 1987. He has been head gardener here, sports organiser, pastoral coordinator, business studies teacher and adult study centre coordinator. He lives with his partner and daughter.

Why two principals? 'We'd like to avoid the notion of the heroic head.' They both, in common with all residential staff, are committed to the teachings of Jiddu Krishnamurti, inspirational writer and speaker on philosophical and spiritual subjects.

Academic matters: Exams 'are not our main thrust', says school, with understatement, 'but are seen in perspective alongside things like yoga, working in the garden, and care of rooms' (all compulsory). Now offers IGCSEs (50 per cent A*/A grades in 2015, but NB 'we offer only maths as a taught subject'). The school uses Cambridge International Exams for A levels, and mixed results are achieved – in 2015, 25 per cent A*/A and 49 per cent A*/B grades (hard to draw out any trends from such a tiny number of students). Some retakes taken at local sixth form college and many pupils will be returning to their home countries for higher education, so British exams not the be all and end all but do need to be recognized in Europe.

No fixed academic timetables into which pupils must slot – each programme is created afresh for each child with plenty of scope to concentrate on a single passion. An 18-year-old musician we met had secured two free days a week to spend on intensive piano work. Another had dropped all academic subjects to study only art, yoga and pottery. Others were focused on more traditional subjects.

Lots of sitting on floors here. 'Inquiry time', when the whole school gets together to discuss a theme – eg why are we vegetarians?; why do we value silence? – a core part of education

No pressure; no punishments if homework is not done; lots of one-on-one teaching. SEN support offered on individual basis – one weekly session is partially covered by the fees, further help is charged for. ESL for overseas students who need it. Computers discouraged but permitted. 'K Class' compulsory once a week to study Krishnamurti, held in soothing white carpeted room with scatter cushions. Lots of sitting on floors here. 'Inquiry time', when the whole school gets together to discuss a theme – eg why are we vegetarians?; why do we value silence? – a core part of education.

Staff comprised of renaissance men and women, most teaching two or three subjects at any given time. So some teaching inspired, while some a bit patchy, 'and teachers can suddenly head off on sabbatical or stop offering a subject,' said a parent. Non-residential specialist teachers are brought in to fill gaps.

Games, options, the arts: Health and fitness, yes – games, no. Some sort of exercise is scheduled twice a week (gym with fitness equipment). Not keen on competition, no prizes. Has been known to play football against another school, but never in anger.

Music inspiring and given space to flourish, with two concerts a year and a variety of instrumental lessons offered. 'It's not about excelling,' a teacher told us. 'It's about a feeling of enjoyment.' Five pianos, a drum kit and a recording studio on hand – pupils can record their own albums. Art barn, designed by Keith Critchlow in the arts and crafts Cottage style, is the fine art centre. Dance, drama, photography, pottery – all the arts – thriving.

Boarding: Boys' rooms, 'the Cloisters', surrounding small pond – exceptionally nice, like a boutique hotel (though boys speak of noise reverberating through the thin partition walls and single glazing). Seven new and beautiful interconnected boarding pavilions now provide extra accommodation.

Originally set up to be international, fully boarding (no day pupils, and pupils may stay over half terms) and small, and has remained so to this day, 'But we could get a bit larger,' says school. Has softened its early ascetic, socialistic ethos, when staff were discouraged from having children of their own, yet remains curiously spartan – no TV, 'except news and football' on one aged set 'that receives three channels'! No cleaning or kitchen staff – all members of the community, including teachers, do their own laundry and help clean/clear tables/wash up meals.

Background and atmosphere: Founded by Krishnamurti in 1969 with a gift of £40,000. This was meant to be his retirement fund – instead he bought Brockwood Park and 40 acres of inspiring, serene grounds within South Downs National Park. Still has the same gentle feel he would have liked,

with the main building housing admin, classrooms and girls' dorms. Beautiful octagonal assembly hall used for silent meditation before breakfast, whole school meetings (twice a week) and concerts. A huge rambling and impressive library with interesting selection of books, eg on alternative medicine.

Garden and greenhouse lovingly tended by all, produces everything from pumpkins to sweetcorn – all eaten at the school. Seeds are gathered for the following year. Twenty chickens provide eggs

Kitchen fully vegetarian and mainly organic. Smaller 'eco-kitchen' available to the students. Garden and greenhouses lovingly tended by all, produces everything from pumpkins to sweetcorn – all eaten at the school. Seeds are gathered for the following year. Twenty chickens provide eggs. Care for the environment a priority and recycling given its own room. Roughly 10 'mature students' (early 20s) an important cog in the Brockwood wheel – they do the cooking and some other work within the community in exchange for room, board and the opportunity to study and bask in Brockwoodian tranquility.

Pastoral care, well-being and discipline: No school rules – instead pupils and parents sign an 'open letter', a group of agreements including meat-free diet, attending morning meeting, staying in rooms after 10pm and no smoking, alcohol or drugs. No automatic punishments for anything – everything open for discussion. 'Fear is a destructive force in education. Take away fear and authority and pupils can be creative, willing to try things. It's important to discover what they love to do.' Relationships, getting along in a community, solving problems are key. Drinking a big no-no, whatever a pupil's age: this may be the first school we have visited where drinking and smoking are highly uncool. All that said, does have to expel the odd pupil, for the usual reasons, and can be tension between providing structure for younger pupils and freedom for the 18 and 19 year olds.

Some 30 members of staff, plus the mature students, live on the campus and students work and live alongside them, the school's greatest strength – or a weakness, depending on how you look at it. Telephone numbers of school's 'independent listener' and Childline prominently displayed around the school.

Pupils and parents: International – around 15 out of 78 from the UK, none local. Others Spanish, French, German, Dutch, Danish, and then from literally everywhere. Everyone looks quite normal – not much inclined to purple hair or facial piercings – and impressively verbal, eloquent and softly spoken. Most pupils come from families with an interest in Krishnamurti. Others find it on the web (key words vegetarian, holistic or alternative). Some parents consider Brockwood Park alongside other alternative schools, eg Bedales, Frensham Heights, St Christopher's, the Steiners (especially Michael Hall), Summerhill (A S Neill got some of his educational ideas from Krishnamurti). A few come from Inwoods, the 'small school' within Brockwood Park grounds educating 30 children age 4-11 (started as a school for staff children). Estimates that around 1,400 men and women have now been educated at Brockwood Park and keen to involve them more in the school through workshops, fundraising etc.

Entrance: Same process for prospective pupils and for staff – a trial week followed by a meeting of the school community to share impressions of the visitor. Up to a third of applicants are turned away. Maturity is the essential qualification according to the pupils – 'We won't take someone who ruins the community'. Despite unorthodox ethos, most definitely not a magnet for alienated teenagers. 'We're low profile, and don't want to be a sink school for problem kids.'

Exit: Students leave equipped for life, though not necessarily for higher education in the UK. However most students will go to university, either straight away or eventually – frequently overseas, especially the USA.

Money matters: Fees kept low. All residential staff are paid the same (frugal) salary so are, in effect, subsidising the running of the school. One third of pupils receive some level of bursary.

Remarks: Uplifting and unique school with the modest aim of completely transforming consciousness and creating a new human being. 'The bar is set high,' said one member of staff. 'Feels a bit like an academic retreat,' said a student trying to sum up the school's ethos. Or a kibbutz. The sort of school that changes lives. Intellectual curiosity will flourish here – but exam results may be elusive.

Caldicott School

Crown Lane, Slough SL2 3SL

01753 649300
registrar@caldicott.com
www.caldicott.com

Ages: 7–13
Pupils: 289
Boarders: 114
Day: £15,255 – £16,695 pa
Boarding: £24,615 pa

Headmaster: Since 1998, Mr Simon Doggart BA (50s), educated at Winchester and read history at Cambridge. School-mastering is in his blood – his father was a legendary figure at Winchester for many years – and he previously taught history at Eton, where he also ran the cricket. Friendly, relaxed even, he is nevertheless utterly professional and we doubt he's ever off duty. Parents describe him as 'charismatic' and 'very genuine, not corporate' and, 'best head ever.' He knows every inch of his school, is proud of its thoughtful developments and is greeted cheerfully by the boys as we pass by. 'He's outside the school every morning at 8, welcoming the boys in, he's an amazing figurehead,' said one very impressed mother. Maximum praise and affection also for his wife, Antonia. She hosts 'girlie' lunches for mothers, birthday teas (complete with parlour games) for the boys and, we are sure, attends to the innumerable duties that a head's spouse is heir to. 'Food, pastoral, I notice things,' she says, with classic understatement. The Doggarts have three children, two at university and one at Wellington, and a working cocker spaniel.

The last few years must have been very difficult as historic abuse made headlines (with the unrelated juice of Caldicott being Nick Clegg's old school). Mr Doggart's remedy has been 'light and windows', both metaphorically and literally. Every parent we spoke to wanted to put on record how well the school handled the court case and attendant revelations. They say that the head kept them informed in advance at every stage and that he was always available to answer questions.

> *Schoolmastering is in his blood – his father was a legendary figure at Winchester for many years*

Glancing round his comfortable study, it was hardly necessary to ask Mr Doggart about his interests; the Wisdens and history books did the talking. He remembers being inspired by Gary Sobers' autobiography as a child and these days enjoys reading

Robert Harris. School holidays find the Doggarts beside the seaside in the Witterings.

Entrance: Two form entry in year 3 is joined by another two form entry in year 4 (legacy of Bucks middle school system). There is a short formal academic assessment plus an opportunity to meet other pupils and teachers. Mr Doggart likes to show prospective parents round (several said they felt they were under as much scrutiny as their sons) and there is an open day in June.

Exit: Nearly all at 13, mainly to trad boys' boarding. Harrow gets the lion's share followed by Eton, Radley, Wellington, St Edward's, Winchester and Stowe. Good clutch of scholarships most years (six in 2015), mostly sport, art and all-rounders. Definitely not a school for those with eyes on the Bucks grammars at 11.

Remarks: Caldicott sits on top of a wooded escarpment with views down to Windsor; 40 acres of prime Bucks real estate adjoining beautiful Burnham Beeches. The school was founded in 1904 by Heald Jenkins who named it after his new bride, a Miss Theodora Caldicott Ingram. The school and its wonderful Harrison Harrison organ (recently restored and residing in the chapel) moved from Hitchin to Farnham Royal in 1938.

Do the H team's duckers and triers really get the same standard of coaching as the Olympians in the As? Certainly, says Mr D. 'We want everyone to take part, the coaches aren't baby-minding'

Perfect pitches extend as far as the eye can see, busy with grounds staff rolling and mowing grass that already looks like a billiard table. We defer to one of our guides who observed, 'I can't think of a prep school with better pitches.' Cricket and rugby are a big deal here with up to eight teams (is there really an 'H' team?) ready to take on all comers at all levels. Oxford's Dragon School, as its name suggests, is their fiercest opponent. And what about that H team? Do its duckers and triers really get the same standard of coaching as the Olympians in the As? Certainly, says Mr D. 'We want everybody to take part, the coaches aren't baby-minding. The challenge can be finding other schools ready to field as many opposing teams.' When it comes to sport for all, noble aims such as these are often at odds with the grass roots actualities. Not so at Caldicott. Parents of unsporty boys do not find them swinging round the corner posts while the A team triumphs on a distant pitch. 'If the A team is playing then so are the Bs, Cs and Ds.' And it's the same with other things, drama for instance, lots of groups (teams) at all levels to 'keep everyone improving'.

A jarring note in the song of praise for Caldicott seems to be the standard of its music. Memorably described to us as 'joyless', music seems to occupy a lower profile than in similar schools so this may not be the place for your mini Mozart. No shortage of practice rooms and lots of music tech equipment, but something's missing. There are a few chamber groups but no orchestra, the chapel choir is, well, just that and the repertoire of the junior and senior choirs has been, to paraphrase several parents politely, 'underwhelming.' However, things may be on the up. A recent whole school performance of Captain Noah at St Paul's Knightsbridge was a triumph, joyfully received by boys and parents.

Half the pupils are local, the other half come in from the capital on the 7.30am Caldicott express. Mr D says school 'invented' busing in from west London – we hope the other busing Bucks preps pay a copyright fee. 'The service is incredibly efficient, the buses run like clockwork, they're travelling against the traffic,' we were told. Youngest go home at 4.30pm but rest stay until 6pm – it's a long, active day, but at least there's no homework 'apart from a few spellings or a bit of reading,' until the last two years (and the boys are all boarding then). Saturday school is 'proper' with lessons until 12.30 for all and matches in the afternoon for the older boys. London parents just as visible on sidelines as locals. Is there a divide between the local and London boys, we asked? 'Not at all, the boys don't even notice,' said one mother, although she conceded that the London chaps seemed 'a bit more polished and prepared' when they joined.

All boys in years 7 and 8 board; it's an integral part of their preparation for senior schools such as Harrow, Eton, Radley and Winchester. Dorms are upstairs in the main school building – clean, bright with home duvets, photos and posters. Evenings and weekends are busy with dedicated clubs including fly tying and model making, and competitions and activities such as fondue nights (boys have to go and buy the cheese as well as cook it) and a Caldicott Bake-off. New boarders are given an 'uncle', an experienced boarder in the same dorm who will help him settle in. Senior houseparents live on site with their family and all full-time staff do boarding duty. Our sixth form (year 8) guides, almost ready to leave for senior school, were waxing nostalgic, 'There's so many people around, it's a community,' said one. What would they remember, we asked? 'Summer evening cross-country runs through Burnham Beeches; after-school swims in the outdoor pool; the boarders' Christmas party with carol singing around the huge tree.' Sigh.

Well-equipped labs. Mr D was not in his happy place when we asked him about programming and mighty relieved to bump into a physics teacher who could tell Raspberry Pi from Python

Teachers are called 'sir' and 'ma'am' but that apart, education is firmly in the 21st century with bright classrooms, smartboards, well-equipped labs and lots of techy stuff. We loved the screens outside the DT studio flashing up individual photos of every boy proudly holding his finished work. Mr D was not in his happy place when we asked him about programming and mighty relieved to bump into a physics teacher who could tell Raspberry Pi from Python. Back in his comfort zone, the head proudly showed us the new wedge-shaped ('cheesy') library, built on the site of a 'horrendous 60s pre-fab' that the 'whole school watched being demolished'.

One way in which Caldicott is untraditional is its neatness – it's the tidiest prep we've ever visited. In fact it was a relief to see some naughty geranium cuttings sprawled muddily beneath a windowsill in the biology lab. Even the art room, usually reliable as a haven of creative chaos, was ship-shape. Parents describe the Doggarts as 'incredibly well organised' and it really does seem that no corner of the school escapes their attention to detail. Very reassuring.

Boys are 'loosely' set in maths from the start and in other subjects later on. According to the head there's 'much less setting than of yore', but several parents commented that the system wasn't clear and didn't seem that flexible. Average class size is 16, there's a good mix of staff – old and new – and about a third of teachers are women. The lessons we peeped into were lively and interactive, boys bursting with ideas and eager to contribute. Some grumbles in the recent past that school was slow to pick up SEN but this no longer seems to be the case; several new parents said teachers had been very quick to act on potential problems.

Monitoring is generally regarded as good and communication as excellent, 'Teachers are all contactable by email and usually reply within a couple of hours.' Pastoral care and school counsellor came in for high praise; wobbly new boarders are ably helped through those tricky first few weeks. Several parents remarked how thoughtfully boys in different year groups (so often tribal) related to each other.

Boys say food is 'so much better'. Chicken Kiev is top choice, closely followed by the Thursday roast and cooked breakfast. We were, however, told to 'avoid Saturday lunch at all costs.' We couldn't find out exactly why, but you have been warned. On the wall of the school dining room we were shown the honours boards and there he was, Nicholas Clegg, the only head boy in the school's history to hold the post jointly. The Caldicott coalition – you couldn't make it up.

The word we keep reaching for is 'traditional', but in its best, unstuffy, sense. Parents who choose Caldicott told us they do so because it has secure values: courtesy, fair play, loyalty, regard for others. 'When the boys leave they are young gentlemen,' one said. All in all, this is a cracking prep that will play more than fair by any boy lucky enough to get a place.

Cheam School

Headley, Newbury, Berkshire RG19 8LD

01635 268242
office@cheamschool.co.uk
www.cheamschool.com
C of E

Ages: 3–13
Pupils: 425
Boarders: 41 weekly, 140 flexi
Day: £11,085 – £19,395 pa
Boarding: £26,250 pa

Head: Since 1998, Mr Mark R Johnson BEd (50s). Charismatic, enthusiastic, 'preppy' (his own word). Passionate about boarding, having done so himself from a young age and loved it. Educated in the West Country, went straight to Summer Fields post-university and stayed for 17 years. Taught maths, German and rugby. Rose to housemaster and deputy headmaster for five years before moving to Cheam and transforming it. Known by all as Mr J, much loved by parents and children alike. Abounds with energy. Full of ideas for the school, now and in the future. Driven by the constant need for a new project: the latest was the transformation of the old sports hall into an up-to-date design and technology centre. No longer teaches – 'there simply isn't time'. Mad about sport, played cricket to minor county standard while at university and is still a playing member of the MCC.

Lists golf, fishing, shooting, racing, opera and ballet as other enthusiasms. Goodness knows when he finds time for them all. Has been governor of three other prep schools, represents IAPS on Boarding Schools' Association executive committee and was recently invited to sit on council of IAPS as boarding representative. Elected Tatler's 'Best Prep School Headmaster of the Year' a few years ago. Definitely believes in keeping busy, and his school has the feel of a very busy place. Married to Jane, a bouncy, bubbly, energetic classicist who teaches both Latin and Greek to scholarship and common entrance level and designed the tartan seen round the school and worn as part of the girls' uniform. Two daughters, now at Manchester University.

Retiring in July 2016. His successor will be Mr Martin Harris BSc PGCE (40s), currently head of Sandroyd School. Educated at The Skinners' School and read geography at Loughborough University. Began his teaching career at Ashdown House in East Sussex; after a stint as deputy head at King's School, Rochester, he returned to Ashdown House as deputy head (acting head for one year). A keen sportsman, he plays cricket, golf and tennis. Wife, Catherine, is a chartered physiotherapist. They have two young sons.

Entrance: Non-selective into the nursery and pre-prep. Higher up, the headmaster sees all children for a familiarisation day to ascertain their suitability for entry. This is not just based on academic data but rather an assessment of the whole child, games, musical ability, character etc.

Exit: A main feeder to Marlborough but also regularly sends pupils to eg Bradfield, Eton, Radley, Wellington, St Edward's Oxford, Sherborne, Downe House, St Mary's Ascot and St Mary's Calne. The transition to mainly boarding public schools appears to be reasonably easy, according to one parent of girls who loved the place so much she returned to work in the bursar's office when her children moved on. However, we were told by others that some boys seem to find it hard moving into a less protected environment.

Remarks: A school for active, busy children. As one parent said, 'it's incredibly beautiful'. Set in 100 acres of glorious countryside, it is the perfect place for sporty, outdoor loving, energetic types to spend their early school days. Anybody who remembers it, as we do, as the rather stuffy, unexciting royal school of the early '90s, would be amazed to walk round it today. One current father, ex-Cheamite, who refused to even look at it until his children went there, is now one of its greatest fans. The focus here is not totally on academia and they get so much more than just lessons. The outcome is a band of happy, confident, well-balanced children who generally get into their chosen school, often with scholarships.

A broad curriculum from the start in preparation for common entrance to top schools. All children setted for maths and French. Scholarship forms for two top years with Greek introduced to the brightest. Young teachers (average age 35 to 40) have easy, relaxed relationship with pupils. Parents feel Mr J selects staff well. Some bachelor staff accommodation in grounds, 'Cheamville', so fewer geographical restrictions. Small classes, max 18, often fewer. Books regarded as an essential part of their lives. Silent reading, or 'digest', is timetabled in for half an hour after lunch each day and, for boarders, every evening. Weekly general knowledge quiz encourages them to look things up.

Light, bright classrooms with interactive white boards throughout. Good IT, art, science facilities. New art and design centre. Parents say 'music and drama very strong' and they put on 'excellent productions'. One major play or musical each year. Lots of choirs and several orchestras including a jazz band. Most learn an instrument with lessons timetabled differently each week and practice sessions set up for boarders. Anything from beginners to grade 6. Masses of art and photographs on display everywhere. Internal news and information

computer screens in main halls. Loads of field trips, expeditions and excursions, home and overseas. These really are privileged children.

Perhaps it's sport that's the most impressive and they all love it. Everything is on offer from football, rugby, tennis, hockey and cricket to polo, judo, fencing and golf on their own course. Games every afternoon with matches on Wednesdays and Saturdays. National polo champions, national cross-country champions and cricket and rounders teams reached the National Jet finals in Oxford. Lots of matches against other schools and overseas cricket and hockey tours. The trophy cabinet is proof of their achievements. Despite this, one parent told us 'even non-sporty children are well catered for. One boy even got a scholarship to the Royal Ballet School'.

A long list of extracurricular activities. There is even a climbing place called 'Cheam Tops' in the grounds. Indoor sports hall ingeniously provides courts for different games as well as all necessary gymnastic equipment and great changing rooms. Everything has been well thought out. Only parental complaint: 'Why do they have to be sexist? Why can't girls play football?'

She replied, 'I love it. It's so great to be at home with my brothers on Sundays and to see my horse, but it's also good to be at school with my friends'

Excellent pastoral care and learning support where needed. This will be one or two sessions a week with a specialist teacher on a rotating basis if in lesson time. About 10 per cent have processing problems, there is the occasional statement but nothing seriously major. Gap year students help with games when needed. Gentle counsellor is always there to listen. Believes very much in the importance of building self-esteem, which she feels is definitely one of the school's assets. Specialist EFL help given, often one-to-one in class. Believe it's absolutely essential to keep parents involved. 'Our children do not have difficulties, they have differences'. G&T register currently being reformed. PSHE is strong, each child has a tutor and anything verging on bullying (probably not the right word) is quickly and sensitively dealt with. 'We want everyone to be happy'! Timetables rigorously watched, so the whereabouts of any child at any time is always known.

Parents have nothing but praise. 'A very happy school', 'the head really has his finger on the pulse', 'sussed out our daughter very fast and gave us excellent advice on her next school', 'children are easy-going, sensitive and supportive of each other', 'very good at involving parents', 'the kids have such fun'. One even told us, 'we brought our children over from South Africa where they were a good year behind academically and the system was totally different. Nevertheless, our 11-year-old was quickly assimilated into the system, booked himself into boarding after one term and achieved an all-rounder scholarship to Radley'. A happy parent indeed.

Boarding is either weekly or flexi. Children can do just two nights a week if they like. We were assured that this is not at all unsettling and that they seem to love it, opting in and out as and when. The majority of the top year weekly board in preparation for their next school. They go home after games on Saturday afternoon and return in time for lessons on Monday morning. Most come from within a 15 mile radius of the school although there is a largish London contingent. Dorms are upstairs in the main building, boys on one floor and girls on another. Homely, welcoming rooms with a variety of duvet covers and lots of teddies. Always one or two older pupils in with the younger ones. Smart modern bathrooms, not at all as we used to know them. Great pile of bags on the landings waiting to be collected by flexis at the end of the day. Recent 'outstanding' boarding certificate from Ofsted. We asked a pupil what she felt about weekly boarding. She replied 'I love it. It's so great to be at home with my brothers on Sundays and to see my horse but it's also good to be at school with my friends'. Bedtime routine pretty regimented with time for reading and talking before lights out but after that, silence reigns.

Quite a large amount of charitable stuff going on. Support for a school in Zambia, a rural school in Johannesburg, the Red Cross children's hospital in Cape Town and the children's wards in the Royal Hampshire Hospital. Hands-on partnership with local primary schools who can apply for funding and use their facilities for free. Some scholarships and bursaries and a fund for suddenly needy children.

Perhaps the oldest prep school in the country, with its origins in the 17th century, there is an interesting archive room containing mementos of past headmasters and pupils. Apart from HRH the Duke of Edinburgh and HRH the Prince of Wales, William Pitt the Younger, Lord Randolph Churchill, Ivo Bligh, 8th Earl of Darnley and Jake Meyer also spent their formative years at Cheam.

A school full of happy, open, confident, polite, exceptionally busy children who are used to living to a rigid timetable and to keeping their shoes done up and their shirts tucked in. One slightly wonders how they will manage to cope with the rebellious, disorganised world outside.

Christ Church Cathedral School

3 Brewer Street, Oxford OX1 1QW

01865 242561
registrar@cccs.org.uk
www.cccs.org.uk
C of E

Ages: 3–13 (chorister boarding from year 4)
Pupils: 135
Boarders: 20 choristers
Day: £6,795 – £14,580 pa
Boarding: choristers £9,183 – £10,158 pa

Headmaster: Since January 2014, Richard Murray BA MA (Durham), previously a housemaster and English teacher at St Edward's School in Oxford.

Entrance: Most day boys are from the Oxford or Bucks area, and enter at nursery or reception; the single class grows as more boys join in year 3 and the majority stays until common entrance. A few girls in nursery only. Assessment is by participation in class for the younger boys and informal academic tests for the older boys. Four chorister places are available each year from year 4, selected by voice trial. Choristers come from further afield, board and receive a two-thirds fee reduction in a bursary established by royal appointment in 16th century.

School benefits from recommendations by old boys, siblings and music teachers. The Cardinal's Scholarship is a new introduction, for up to three year 3s, who are expected to achieve well academically throughout the school. Parents of choristers are a particularly music-focused sub-set; others are local professionals, medics and academics

Exit: To a range of schools: Abingdon, Bedales, Bloxham, Charterhouse, Eton, Fettes, Harrow, Leckford Place, Magdalen College, Our Lady's Abingdon, Purcell. Plenty of music scholarships and exhibitions, as one would expect.

Remarks: Described by one parent as 'the secret of Oxford', it is hidden in a historic corner of the town in the shadow of Christ Church Cathedral. Every available inch has been transformed, embracing the original Tudor residence of Cardinal Wolsey, a Victorian parsonage-type house commissioned by Dean Liddell, father of Alice in Wonderland, and a bright new block to commemorate old boy William Walton. The net effect is a warren of classrooms, labs and play areas combining traditional and modern. Henry VIII's charter of 1546 established the education of eight boy choristers and a master for Christ Church Cathedral. Shame it didn't stipulate a few parking spaces too, as staff parking on the playground is an issue, according to one parent.

Music permeates through the school, from music-stands among the pyjamas to treble clef murals in the corridors. The cathedral choristers' day kicks off at 7.30am to fit in their three hours of choir practice and daily services. In addition they all learn the piano and one other instrument. There are celebratory services throughout the year, including Easter and Christmas Day, as well as singing tours, recently as far afield as China, performing in the world's largest concert hall. The rest of the school has caught the bug too: with pianos in every corner and 140 individual music lessons per week, there are informal concerts which start with the smallest to encourage confidence, 'even if it's a recorder and they play the same note 10 times,' laughs one parent. However, having heard the choir sing like angels at evensong, we were struck by the skill and professionalism of even the youngest. Parents are welcome to watch the weekly service in

the cathedral and some day boys are chosen for Worcester College choir. 'They see that older boys are doing it and it's fun'.

We witnessed a vibrant Latin class and were invited to help judge a Roman legionary cut–out doll competition – it was a tough decision, but the joy of learning was infectious

These are not just pretty voices: under the surplices there is an academic rigour to the school, starting with the tiny tots in the Montessori nursery. The historic cardinal's house now holds a climbing frame and zoo animal frescoes in the garden. Small class sizes in the pre-prep, approximately 16, rising to a maximum of 20 when choristers join in year 4. The pre-prep enjoys recently refurbished classrooms with play areas, music corners and piano. French classes in year 2. There is a conscious promotion to the prep, a separate building, a more formal uniform, and a more exacting curriculum, in which subjects are taught by specialists from year 5 and maths is set in year 6. We witnessed a vibrant Latin class and were invited to help judge the Roman legionary cut-out doll competition – it was a tough decision, but the joy of learning in the classroom was infectious. IT resources have multiplied and are used, among other things, for workshops on Sibelius (musicians' software, not the chap). Head sees all parents in year 6 to discuss future schools and makes prefects of all the final year boys. Teachers include alumnae of the college.

The school makes good provision for a surprising variety of SEN children, with one full-time and two part-time staff. 'Some schools attract a uniform product and this is a school which attracts eccentrics'. One parent reported that a boy who was severely dyslexic won a top place in the annual poetry competition. 'That's part of the school's draw: it treats everyone with a lot of respect'. Oxford's fluid population means that there is often a handful of EAL children, which our guide appeared to relish as contributing to the school's rich tapestry.

Picture the most idyllic cricket field you can imagine – these boys play on it, overlooked by the dreaming spires of Magdalen and Christ Church, the sound of rare breed cows lowing by the river; a timber cabin of a cricket pavilion, now with modern additions, electricity and a loo. One parent criticised the school's outdoor areas – 'Boys don't have far to run in the playground' – but Merton field over the road more than makes up for it. No wonder the fixtures in rugby, football, cricket and athletics are successful and many boys make the renowned A teams in their next schools. Parents enjoy a summer fair here on sports day, a scene which is eagerly photographed by tourists, looking

The choristers' common room is in cardinal red, like their cassocks, and houses a computer to email home and, of course, ivories to tinkle on

for a snap of old England. 'I've never seen so many cakes,' gasped a parent. The school is conscientious about all boys representing the school in sport at some stage. Inflatable sharks and papier mâché snakes in the art room testify that the creative child is catered for. Art and poetry are celebrated on Arts Day, by visiting professionals who run workshops in photography, fine art, music and poetry. This year's cartoonist helped produce some lively portraits of composers, one of whom looked suspiciously like the bursar.

Named after the cathedral's organists, including John Taverner, the boarders' rooms in the main building are decked with photos and teddies from home; the largest dorm sleeps eight cosily. The bright and tidy shower room confirmed our suspicions that these are no ordinary boys. 'We try to make it their home,' said our guide. The choristers' common room is in cardinal red, like their cassocks, and houses a computer to email home, TV and, of course, ivories to tinkle upon. Our noses led us enticingly to the dining room, lined with scholars' and house point boards – houses are named after dignitaries associated with the school: (Lewis) Carroll; (Cardinal) Wolsey and (Dorothy L) Sayers, who lived next door and whose father was headmaster. There's a traditional tie for the winners of the merit awards to wear each term; another system for poor behaviour culminates in a mild punishment of sitting outside the staff room. Good discipline is inherent in a musical training: 'It's not external discipline we're after, it's a means to self-discipline'. Lots of clubs after school, from knitting to furniture-making to amuse the boys, while parents fight with the city traffic: 'Bit of a pain to get to at 5.30 at night,' said a parent. Free after-school prep club until 6pm pleases working parents. However, not really set up as a boarding school; reports of choristers at school at weekends kicking their heels with no organised activities, and sometimes missing meals.

The school is proud of its reputation for good manners, and rightly so. Boys stand when visitors enter the classrooms, address teachers as 'sir' and learn to hold the door open at an early age. It is a conscious emphasis on courtesy which comes across as old-fashioned. As one parent remarked, 'I think we are paying for the education I received'. Parents are happy with the contact from teachers: 'They speak to you, and really listen to what you say';

office staff got particular praise, 'even with difficult parents they are very diplomatic'. It is no coincidence that in premises seeped in history the school play should be Old Father Time. He has certainly instilled character and sound traditional values here, from the daily Latin quotation in the head's study to the boys' charming Thomas More-style hats. The honest traditions are summed up by the bursar: 'Snowballing? Of course we allow it. I think being a boy nowadays is not as exciting as it should be'.

Cothill House

Cothill, Abingdon, Oxfordshire OX13 6JL

01865 390800
jane@cothill.net
www.cothill.net
C of E

Ages: 8–13
Pupils: 220
Boarders: all full
Boarding: £26,220 pa

Headmaster: Since 2011, Mr Duncan Bailey (30s). Educated at Cothill, followed by Eton and a gap year in West Africa, then Manchester University (French) and Vienna University (German). Bitten by teaching bug during his year abroad but harboured ambitions to nurture his passion for sport, particularly tennis (he was a contemporary of Tim Henman) and moved into sports management. 'Fell into teaching' after being asked to stand in for the head of modern languages at Eton, where he spent two years. Prior to taking headship at Cothill ran Sauveterre, the Cothill Trust's French outpost, for eight years.

Married to Maria (his 'secret weapon' according to parents), lives at heart of school with his two young daughters, currently schooled at nearby Chandlings. A hands-on head couple, the Baileys are in true loco parentis – head says he is 'a parent above all things' – taking full responsibility for the four year groups housed in the main school building. Maria 'does everything,' from rolling up her sleeves to help with cooking, cleaning, teaching and running the school if required, right down to marching boys back to the salad bar if they don't have enough veggies on their plates.

Relaxed and approachable, with the chameleonic ability to switch between the persona of favourite uncle and respected leader, and not adverse to taking pupils on at table tennis or joining in with an after-hours skateboarding session, head says he 'likes boys to be happy, expects them to be busy and insists they are polite.' Parents consider him 'very dynamic, involved and committed to the school' and the few that were 'worried he might be a bit green' when appointed have climbed firmly back into their boxes.

Entrance: Recruits about 20 boys with a 'fairly broad brush' into year 4, with intakes in both September and April and numbers swelling to between 25 and 30 by end of year. Parents and boys interviewed together ('we choose the whole family') to establish fit rather academic ability. Boys assessed rather than tested, in English and maths. Majority at this point from London prep schools with just a few local boys in the mix. Good number of Forces children and between 10 and 15 per cent international (mainly Spanish and Russian with a few Chinese and Thai) although head insists on fluent English and no EAL on offer ('they have to be able to survive in the boarding environment').

Relaxed and approachable, with the chameleonic ability to switch between favourite uncle and respected leader

Oversubscribed from year 5, with head looking for 'boys who are prepared to roll up their sleeves and get stuck in' above all else. Drop-out rate of less than one a year. A number join in summer term of year 5 to settle in before real focus on destination schools starts in year 6.

Exit: As in previous years, 20 to 25 per cent each to Eton, Radley and Harrow in 2015. Smaller numbers to Winchester, Marlborough and Wellington, plus Sherborne, Stowe, St Edward's and Malvern for less starry academic achievers. No fall-out to day schools. Huge focus on 'negotiating' places with destination schools with evidence of heart and soul going into making sure boys land in the best places. 'A good handful' of scholarships most years, most notably in art and music.

Remarks: Steadfastly traditional, Cothill is so discreet you could almost miss it altogether in its picturesque village setting. No grand buildings or flashy reception. Visitors arrive directly into the heart of the school (the dining room) – giving the first clue to school's substance over style ethos. Main building is a large country house with several later additions nestled in 26 acres of grounds, playing fields and woodland. Sports and leisure facilities include a super 15 metre indoor pool, six all weather tennis courts, a nine-hole golf course, a somewhat shabby, albeit well used squash court cum table tennis room and a fleet of shiny BMXs for tearing around the woods. Equally appreciated by pupils is the wealth of retreats where they can spend as much free time as they like indulging creative passions such as woodwork (a real favourite with boys, guided by former police officer known as 'PC'), pottery and art. There's also a large, modern library and gleaming ICT suite for, amongst other things, Skyping home, although a handwritten letter once a week is compulsory.

It's a school where boys can 'have a childhood,' say parents. Boys can build dens or bird boxes, go pond dipping or interpret Notre Dame Cathedral in clay

No common rooms to speak of, bar a pool room, and no significant evidence of televisions (junior movie nights and major sporting events only are hosted in head's sitting room) or other passive distractions. Parents report boys roaring around on scooters in their pyjamas before bedtime rather than gluing themselves to screens. And therein lies the magic of the place. Macs and iPads do have a home here but what Cothill really offers is a Swallows and Amazons approach to education. It's a school where boys can 'have a childhood,' say parents. Boys can build dens or bird boxes, go pond dipping or interpret Notre Dame Cathedral in clay to their hearts' content. Parents and boys also firmly supportive of full boarding ethos (two exeats per term), which makes for fun-filled weekends jam packed with activities for all, not just those who live too far from school to make a weekly journey home. Broad geographical spread, from Scottish Highlands to Norfolk as well as overseas, makes for a collegiate bunch.

Majority of parents from upper echelons, most of whom have gone 'through the system' (read Eton, Harrow etc), with titles aplenty. Car park generally occupied by ancient mud splattered 4x4s rather than gleaming Maseratis on match days and supporters, who are encouraged and welcomed to visit twice a week, tend to be of the green welly variety, with the odd royal godparent thrown in for good measure. In the words of one mother, 'definitely not the facelift and white Range Rover crowd.' That said, head reports increasing numbers of professional, middle class London parents, keen to escape the hothouse London day school scene and allow their boys the space and roundedness offered by a country prep. One such parent reported that without exception the children are just from 'incredibly nice families who want the very best education.' Boys confident, smiley and polite with no sign of entitlement or arrogance and, with shirts untucked and ties askew, the slightest hint of Just William.

Strong artsy feel around the place with examples of boys' excellent work festooning every spare wall and surface. Music, art and DT highly praised by parents and boys alike and head's bet with us that 'about 70 per cent' of boys would say their favourite subject was history appeared to be bang on the money. A visit to the history room demonstrated what teaching at Cothill is all about – getting boys out of their seats and experiencing things firsthand. A mini Battle of Trafalgar was laid out across pushed together tables, complete with tablecloth sea and stacks of wide, slim drawers opened to reveal other famous (mostly French) battlefields to enable boys to visualise and act out events. Another recent highlight for history department was the re-enactment of the Dambusters raid on the school field. No wonder it's top dog, although this kind of thing is apparently all in a day's work for most departments here, with teachers across the board described as 'inspiring' and often 'quirky – in a good way.'

The star draw though, has to be Sauveterre, Cothill's unique French chateau outpost near Toulouse where all year 7 boys spend a whole term immersing themselves in French language, culture, food and sunshine. Parents evangelise about the benefits of this, not only where tipping the balance at CE is concerned but in terms of an unforgettable life experience.

Boys 'loosely set' from the outset for all subjects with maths more tightly so, but flexible according to exam results. Class sizes between 10 and 15 at the bottom of the school, gradually shrinking to seven or eight from year 7 onwards, consistent with head's belief that 'success at common entrance comes from small classes at the top of the school.' Each subject teacher reports to head on every boy on a weekly basis, resulting in a score out of 10 read out in Friday's assembly. High running totals at the end of term lead to treats and trips. Although school not equipped to deal with serious SEN, superb support in place for those who need a bit of extra help with a highly experienced,

Another recent highlight was the re-enactment of the Dambusters raid on the school field. This kind of thing is apparently all in a day's work

passionate SENCo who spends time with every boy before they join the school.

'Spectacular' drama, with frequent plays and shows, including My Fair Lady, Mary Poppins and original works written by Cothill teachers. And yes, boys do take on the female roles ('mainly with enthusiasm,' they told us). Around 80 per cent of cohort plays a musical instrument and there are bands and choirs galore for them to showcase their talents. Sport every day, with a focus on health, fitness and everyone getting a go at representing the school. Lower teams celebrated as vigorously as superstars – a recent fixture saw the bottom football team allowed to wear the first team strip as a reward for thrashing the opposition in their previous match.

Parents moving 'overeducated' children out of London preps shouldn't be surprised if boys cruise a bit academically initially. Year 4 is all about getting to grips with boarding to set the foundations for future success and happiness. Tidy, basic dorms for about eight boys, adorned with all the usual football paraphanalia, house years 4, 6 and 7 in the main school and year 5s are split between here and 'the bungalow' – a cosy outpost across the games field where according to parents boys feel

'terribly grown up.' Action packed weekends mean boys eventually become wistful when they are at home, missing the mix of organised activities – an optional trip out every week and free time on their rollerblades, Ripsticks or exploring the woods.

All year 8s minibussed out after supper each evening to sleep at nearby Chandlings School, which looks disastrous on paper but in reality 'works brilliantly' according to parents and boys we spoke to and gives boys 'the space to be pre-teenagers.' Weekends also spent there, in the care of an 'extraordinary' house couple, with boys given their own activities and free run of Chandlings' facilities. Formerly sceptical parents now evangelise and are insistent that this part of Cothill life should 'never change.'

Unsurprisingly top notch pastoral care with parents reporting that school 'celebrates high spirits' and 'really understands each boy's potential and how to get him to reach it,' with more than one parent telling us their son had been 'turned around.' Very impressive, albeit informal, daily staff meeting where issues or concerns are raised (from which boys need to be reminded to wear their spectacles to who is struggling with the pressure of scholarship exams) leads to holistic care for every pupil. Boys know they can confide in whomever they wish, whether it's their tutor or junior matrons (usually gap year girls). Parents report boys returning to school 'without a backward glance' – and our guides themselves encapsulated the spirit of the school by telling us that the only kind of boy they could imagine not liking Cothill would be 'an iPad lover.'

d'Overbroeck's

The Swan Building, Oxford OX2 6JX

01865 310000
mail@doverbroecks.com
www.doverbroecks.com

Ages: 11–18 (boarding in sixth form)
Pupils: 485, plus 38 in international study centre
sixth form: 272
Boarders: 160 full
Day: £15,375 – £21,600 pa
Boarding: plus £6,900 – £12,300 pa

Principal: Since 1996, Mr Sami Cohen BSc (50s). Educated in Baghdad, then moved to London at the age of 17 to do his A levels. Read chemistry and French at Leeds University – the course was created for him and sparked a lifelong passion for 'breadth' in education. Followed in the footsteps of his mother and aunt, who were both teachers, and began his own teaching career at d'Overbroeck's in 1979 – two years after sixth form was founded.

Moved to Paris in 1992 before being invited to return to d'Overbroeck's as principal four years later.

Charismatic, focused and approachable, he is particularly proud of opening the college's 11-16 arm in 2005, transforming d'Overbroeck's from a sixth form college into an all-through 11-18 school. 'We are able to offer each age group an environment that suits that particular age group,' he explains. 'We are open to a reasonably wide range of abilities and we value people with interests and enthusiasms. We want everyone to have a well-rounded, lively education, to be able to laugh a lot, to make great friendships and to feel that they have personally grown, developed and flourished.'

A keen linguist (he speaks French, Italian and Arabic), he no longer has time to teach these days – 'which saddens me.' Knows all the students well and is a familiar presence around the school's two sites, constantly stopping to chat. Pupils address teachers by their first names at d'Overbroeck's so he is 'Sami' to all. 'I'm totally immersed in the life of this place,' he says. 'There's a lot more I feel I can contribute.' Wife Emily is an EFL specialist and they have three daughters. The elder two both attended d'Overbroeck's before going on to undergraduate degrees at Oxford and UCL.

Academic matters: Sixth form offers 31 subjects at A level (all the usual, plus others like film studies, history of art, philosophy, sociology and photography). Unlike some schools (and thanks to nifty timetabling) students can choose virtually any mix of A levels. 'The key to students' success is getting the subjects right,' says the principal, who encourages students to choose the subjects they'll enjoy and do well at. 'There is no subject combination that we rule out,' says the head of sixth form. Alongside their A levels some sixth formers do an Extended Project Qualification (EPQ). Lower sixth students must get a minimum of CCCD grades at AS level to continue into the upper sixth – the school reckons that if youngsters don't achieve this they're unlikely to cope with the rigours of A2. Good support for the tiny handful who don't manage this

Read chemistry and French – the course was created for him and sparked a lifelong passion for 'breadth' in education

hurdle, though, and in some cases students retake the year. In 2015, 85 per cent A*-B and 57 per cent A*/A grades.

The principal says the school appoints teachers 'who know their subjects inside out,' are enthusiastic and care deeply about teaching. Lessons are relatively informal, while being highly engaging and interactive, with teachers constantly checking that everyone has 'got it' before moving on. The students we met were unanimous in singing their teachers' praises. 'You won't find better teaching anywhere,' one girl told us appreciatively. 'I switched to economics quite late and my teacher stayed behind for an hour every week to help me catch up, from the day I started till the week my AS exams began. I've never found teachers who care this much.' Another said: 'The teachers want the best for you and it makes you want the best for yourself.'

GCSE results are good too. Fifty-six per cent A*-A grades in 2015, with maths, biology, chemistry, physics and drama particularly notable. Most pupils take 10 GCSEs, including three separate sciences and at least one language. French, Spanish, Latin and classical civilisation are on offer but school can organise German, Japanese, Mandarin

and Russian if required (the benefits of having the dreaming spires of Oxford close by).

Academic ethos is the same in both sections of the school. 'We are an academic school,' Mark Olejnik, the genial head of years 7-11, told us, 'but we want children to enjoy their learning. Happiness is the very essence of what we do here.' Learning support offered for mild dyslexia and dyspraxia at no additional charge. Sixth form teachers have been known to spot issues that have been missed by previous schools and target appropriate help for students. Class sizes are small – no more than 15 up to GCSE and up to 10 at A level. There's an emphasis on discussion and confidence-building throughout, with pupils encouraged to offer their views.

Games, options, the arts: The school has worked hard to offer a broad range of sports and activities. Sport isn't compulsory for sixth formers but students are expected to do at least one extracurricular activity in the lower sixth – everything from hockey, rugby and netball to film club, yoga and first aid, plus Young Enterprise and D of E. Lower sixth students also have a compulsory enrichment programme – a variety of outside speakers, from university professors and admissions tutors to writers, scientists and entrepreneurs.

d'Overbroeck's doesn't have its own playing fields but makes the most of the extensive facilities across Oxford. This seems to work well, with students being ferried by minibus to a number of excellent sporting venues including Oxford Brookes (which has an Astroturf, fully equipped sports hall, fitness gym, squash, badminton and basketball courts, climbing wall and more). Year 7 and 8 pupils get three hours of games a week while those in years 9, 10 and 11 have two hours and 20 minutes of timetabled sport.

Drama is a delight, with younger pupils teaming up with sixth formers to stage major productions like Les Misérables and Peter Pan. In years 7, 8 and 9 pupils have a double lesson of art and a double lesson of music each week. When we visited, a group of year 8s were studying 'impossible architecture,' designing fantastical creations that would give our most eminent architects a run for their money. Many go on to study art in the sixth form and one parent told us: 'I am an artist myself and can say that my daughter has been brilliantly taught.' Eighty students take individual music lessons – all levels (beginners to grade 8) and everything from the violin to electric guitar. Recitals by pupils are often held at the Jacqueline du Pré auditorium at St Hilda's College, as well as regular concerts for students of all ages in the school hall. Music and music tech are popular at A level too.

Debating and public speaking are hugely popular. A couple of years ago, a team of year 9 pupils reached the national final of the Youth Speaks

public speaking event. 'Opportunities are thrust on you here,' one of the team told us. 'It really makes you want to participate.' Loads of school trips, including recent summer expeditions to Namibia, Iceland and China for year 10 to 13 youngsters, annual ski trips and visits to theatre productions in London and Stratford-upon-Avon, science visits to the Rutherford Appleton Laboratory, one of the UK's national scientific research centres, and much else besides.

> **'You won't find better teaching anywhere,' one girl told us. 'I switched to economics quite late and my teacher stayed behind for an hour every week to help me'**

Boarding: Most lower sixth boarders live in one of two co-ed boarding houses close by (20 places at 106 Banbury Road and 18 places at Hayfield House). Double rooms with en-suite bathrooms at '106', singles with shared bathrooms at Hayfield. Girls and boys live in separate 'zones', but meet up in communal areas for meals and socialising. Houseparents cook supper, lend a friendly ear to boarders, oversee the 7pm to 9pm study periods and make sure everyone is in by the 10.30pm curfew (11.30pm on Fridays and Saturdays). Upper sixth boarders live with host families, all carefully vetted and regularly inspected. There's also a small girls' boarding house – Benson's.

Background and atmosphere: d'Overbroeck's is 'a mushroom-shaped school' – the place gets bigger as it progresses up the age range. It started out as a sixth form college, founded in 1977 by French and Spanish teacher Malcolm van Biervliet, who was head of languages till he retired in 2007. Invited to speak about the school's ethos he said: 'Friendship is a cornerstone in the d'Overbroeck's structure, contributing to the happiness of staff and students alike, and thus making the process of teaching and learning a more enjoyable and symbiotic experience.' Staff and students agree that his vision still holds true today.

Sixth form is housed in two large Victorian villas in leafy north Oxford, complete with stained glass windows, tessellated floors, classrooms, library, student common room, admin offices and a large garden at the back. Students doing science A levels walk up to Ewert Place in Summertown while the performing arts department is based round the corner in Leckford Place. Lessons are 65 minutes long and sixth formers get 15 minutes in between to get to their next class.

There's a real buzz everywhere you turn – lots of lively chatter, teachers and pupils on first name terms and an informal and energetic atmosphere throughout. No dining room but a local caterer, Taylors, sets up shop in the common room to sell sandwiches, paninis and drinks at lunchtime. Lots of students stroll up to M&S or Taylors in Summertown to buy lunch – they're spoiled for choice. 'This is a relatively informal environment,' says the principal. 'We don't stand on ceremony but there are clear boundaries and we have high expectations of the students.' Youngsters heartily approve. 'It's not stuffy here at all,' a girl told us.

d'Overbroeck's opened its lower school in 2005, snapping up a Victorian building in nearby Leckford Road previously occupied by Phil and Jim's, a local state primary. A 10-minute walk from

The lower school now boasts a galleried library resembling the upper deck of a ship, light and airy classrooms and a social area with a vivid pink wall, café tables and glossy blue lockers

the sixth form, the years 7-11 site is compact but makes the most of every inch of space. The lower school now boasts an ingeniously designed main building, with a galleried library resembling the upper deck of a ship, light and airy classrooms and a social area with a vivid pink wall, café tables and glossy blue lockers. The original school hall next door is used for lunch (wholesome meals dished up by nearby St Hugh's College), assemblies and theatrical productions. Numbers in years 7-11 are now pretty much on capacity at around 175, with two forms in years 7 and 8 and three from year 9.

No uniform for sixth form but year 7 to 11 pupils wear smart navy polo shirt or jumper with school logo. 'Apart from that they can wear their own clothes,' says the head of years 7-11. 'As long as they are reasonable. No purple hair, hoodies, hats or nose piercings.' He admits that being called by his first name took a bit of getting used to though the principal and students reckon it enables everyone to be themselves.

Pastoral care, well-being and discipline: Pastoral care is widely praised. Sixth form students are assigned their own director of studies (universally known as a DoS) – usually one of their subject teachers. Youngsters talk to them about academic and pastoral matters, with academic progress, attendance, punctuality, work rate and general well-being closely monitored. 'I see my DoS every day,' one boy told us. Parents get a progress report by email every six weeks. Pupils can also talk to a trained school counsellor if they prefer and many turn to the school's dynamic young social organiser – a huge asset to the school, who organises everything from film nights to barbecues. 'We are strict about the things that we need to be strict on,' says the principal, and students and parents concur with his words.

Firm rules on alcohol, drugs and smoking. No drugs tolerated – offenders asked to leave immediately. Students say bullying 'just doesn't happen here' and that unlike many other schools 'there is no sense of being considered cool or not cool.' 'Everyone is included,' a sixth former told us. 'It's a really friendly place.'

Sixth formers say that d'Overbroeck's has got its priorities right and appreciate the fact that it doesn't impose pointless rules and regulations. 'If you want a school that makes you go to chapel and has an army of prefects this probably isn't the right school for you,' one boy remarked. The school is firm about pupils being prompt for lessons and handing work in on time. Students who are 10 minutes late aren't allowed into the class at all and an email is immediately sent to their parents. The only gripe we heard from sixth formers was the lack of lockers – a perennial whinge.

Form teachers are the first port of call in years 7-11, with tutor groups meeting every day and staff holding a meeting every week to discuss pastoral issues. The head of years 7-11 stands at the school gate every morning to greet pupils – 'even in the pouring rain,' said one girl. 'It makes you feel really welcome.' Younger pupils we spoke to praised everything about the school, from the small class sizes, 'fair' rules and chocolate cake ('it's not overcooked') to being able to email teachers for help and getting answers back in double-quick time. 'You rarely have anyone in a bad mood here,' said another pupil. 'And I'm not just saying that.' The school has its own car-themed house system – Cooper, Morris and Austin – but unlike more traditional establishments, these focus on environmental matters and fundraising for charity as well as competitions and sport.

The head of years 7 – 11 stands at the school gate every morning to greet pupils – 'even in the pouring rain,' said one girl. 'It makes you feel really welcome'

Pupils and parents: Pupils are an eclectic mix of high achievers and grafters. Year 7 pupils generally arrive from local primary schools while year 9 entrants tend to come from Oxford preps like Christ Church, the Dragon and New College. No boarding at 11-16 – most live in Oxford and surrounding villages, but some travel from as far afield as Wantage, Faringdon, Swindon and even Warwick. More boys than girls in lower years, but a few more girls than boys in the sixth form. Post-16, equal numbers of day pupils and boarders. UK students come from a vast range of schools (both state and independent) while international students fly in from more than 30 different countries, including Italy, Spain, Russia and China. A handful of very clever Thai government scholars every year too.

The school makes a big effort to keep parents in the loop. Parents we spoke to appreciated its 'modern, unstuffy approach,' 'family atmosphere' and 'emphasis on the important things.' 'My son never enjoyed school until he came to d'Overbroeck's,' one mother told us. 'But he has thrived and been happy here right from the start. He'll be very sad to leave.'

Entrance: The school is selective but its principal emphasises that pupils should have 'a reasonably wide range of abilities.' Alongside the academic requirements staff are looking for students 'who will enjoy the environment and make the most of it.'

Main entry points are year 7, year 9 and sixth form. At 11 and 13 applicants take internal assessment tests in English, maths and non-verbal reasoning, plus a short interview and reference from current school. 'We are looking for potential,' says the head.

At 16 prospective students have an informal interview (they can also sit in on a few lessons if they wish) and need eight A*-C grades at GCSE, including maths and English. the school also stipulates that pupils need at least a B in subjects being taken at A level while those doing maths need at least an A at GCSE (further maths needs an A*). International students sit written English language test (and maths test, where appropriate) and their level of English must be strong enough for the courses they want to do.

Exit: At 16, two-thirds of year 11 pupils progress through to the sixth form (a few head to local state schools like Cherwell and Cheney and in recent years a few girls have moved to Magdalen College School's co-ed sixth form). At 18, virtually all go to university – six to Oxbridge in 2015; others to eg King's College London, University College London, Bristol, Birmingham, Bath, Queen Mary's London, Edinburgh, Durham, Royal Holloway and LSE.

Money matters: A range of academic, art and performing arts scholarships for pupils entering years 7 and 9 (up to 20 per cent of tuition fees). Academic, art, performing arts and environmental awareness scholarships available at sixth form level (up to 50 per cent of fees).

Remarks: d'Overbroeck's has made its mark in Oxford as an exciting and forward-thinking place to be, with a lively, happy environment that fizzes with energy and ideas. Along with top-notch teaching and rigorous academic standards the school helps students to achieve impressive results and make lifelong friends along the way.

Downe House School

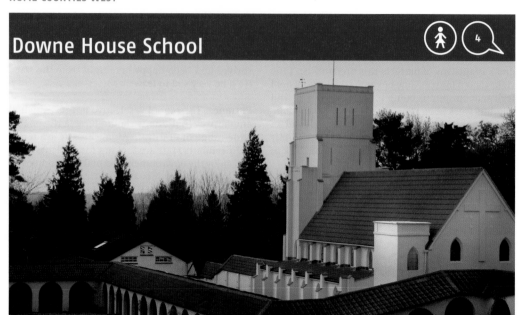

Cold Ash, Thatcham, Berkshire RG18 9JJ

01635 200286
registry@downehouse.net
www.downehouse.net

Ages: 11–18
Pupils: 579; sixth form: 179
Boarders: 569 full
Day: £24,570 pa
Boarding: £33,960 pa

Headmistress: Since 1997, Mrs Emma McKendrick BA PGCE FRSA (40s). Educated at Bedford High and at the universities of Liverpool and Birmingham (German and Dutch). Previously at The Royal School, Bath, where she had been i/c careers and sixth form, a housemistress and deputy head before becoming head in 1994. Remarkably young when appointed to her first headship – that this was so is to the credit of the school's governors. She is soft-spoken, stylish, somehow very grown up, calm and relaxed. Her office and the room in which she receives visitors is a joy – windows on three sides so she can 'see everything', bright, light and taste-ful. Parents – who tend to be deeply passionate about the school and many of whom are old girls – sigh with pleasure: 'She is excellent, on top of everything'; 'She is miraculous – I can say nothing against her. She is so professional, warm, and has a sense of humour. One cannot but be in awe of her, but you love her too'.

Academic matters: Has opted for Pre-U in prefer-ence to A levels in all but a few arts subjects. The reasons are admirable – more teaching time with no AS exams getting in the way and the capacity to focus on real teaching and learning. 'It really has made a difference to my upper sixth,' says the head. 'They are forced to be more independent. They are far better served by the Pre-U in terms of coping with what they will get at university.'

In 2015, 81 per cent A*-B grades and 74 per cent A*/A at A level, and 85 per cent A*-B equivalent (grades D1 – M2) and 61 per cent A*/A equivalent (grades D1 – M1) at Pre-U. Maths very popular, with biology and English close behind. Good numbers for Latin and the odd taker for Greek. Politics, pho-tography and economics offered along with history of art, plus all the trad subjects. Wide range of lan-guages including support for home ones. Eighty per cent A*/A at GCSE in 2015. Blissfully small classes – this is nurturing indeed.

Most teachers highly praised, many seen as 'inspiring'. Learning skills support given to those with mild dys-strata plus those who need extra help with organising themselves or time management. Also stretching help for the most able. Hopeless site for anyone in a wheelchair – the buildings are too scattered and the site is too up and down for this to be possible. EAL support given where needed – 35 in receipt of individual help when we visited.

Games, options, the arts: That the extracurricular life of the school is run from its own sizeable woodland cabin in the heart of the site with designated staff tells you everything. Every kind of opportunity is offered here – from trips to The Royal Opera House to playing lacrosse for Berkshire, to preparing soup for hungry people in South Africa from sackfuls of bones fresh from a slaughterhouse during a trip to a link school there. Lots of visits from outside speakers, who clearly inspire and motivate. Much lively and imaginative charitable activity – often with the boys from Radley. Excellent drama – again, often with Radley – generously supported by Old Girl, Geraldine James, who opened the performing arts centre and has been known to take aspiring actresses under her wing. Two recent successful auditions for the National Youth Theatre. Successful and popular debating.

Sports are many and varied and include, for older girls, pilates, fencing and golf. Several girls are England lacrosse players – lax taken more seriously here than other sports. Internal competition between houses seemingly counting more than fixtures against other schools. Art is lively, though housed in the least attractive building on site – great range of activities: we loved the individuality of work in textiles, ceramics and woodwork, along with truly impressive painting. Ballet, modern dance, tap and hip hop on offer and around half the girls take speech and drama. Practically all of them learn at least one instrument. 'They all do so much extra,' a parent told us, half-admiring, half-concerned. 'They do whack on the pressure – the girls themselves, that is.'

Arched walkway linking most of the classrooms which – with its white walls, arches and terracotta pantiles – is incongruously Moorish in the heart of Berkshire

Houses clearly of immense importance here – friendly but significant rivalry in all areas of school life. Lots of trips at home and abroad – all with sound educational or charitable purposes. Most exciting, memorable and generally aaaahed over is the term spent during year 8 at the school's own converted farm in the heart of Perigord. Those who join the school in year 9 seem to spend the next five years biting their lip at having missed an unforgettable experience. A seasoned sixth former told us – as if it were obvious – 'Oh, we never stop talking

about it.' It's about French and French life, cuisine, charity work, community and living ensemble.

Boarding: All but a handful of local day girls are full boarders. One boarding school veteran told us that the boarding staff were much the best she'd ever come across. The boarding houses themselves are much loved. We relished the dressing up boxes in the junior houses.

Most exciting, memorable and generally aaaahed over is the term spent during year 8 at the school's own converted farm in the heart of Perigord

New lower school house for all year 7 and 8 girls, providing a sheltered introduction to boarding life. Older girls are in mixed age houses – dorms are mostly spacious; singles and doubles for the older girls are homely and attractive. Everywhere is properly carpeted and curtained. Fresh flowers abound – no sense here that 'nice' areas are just for show – this is home and it feels like it. All houses either wireless or with network points.

Sixth form houses are exceptionally well designed and furnished. Pigeonholes for girls' post and newspapers; sofas, careers areas, meeting rooms, kitchens. Girls can be independent here, if they wish – no wonder so few leave after GCSEs. All have a personal safe in their rooms. Further extension to and enhancement of the boarding facilities planned.

Lessons until 12pm on Saturdays are followed by sports, so everyone signs up to the full boarding life. Saturday evenings are spent in rehearsal, at concerts, trips to theatres, cinemas etc. Sundays include trips, D of E activities and chillin'.

Background and atmosphere: Founded in 1907 by Olive Willis, its first headmistress, as an all-girls' boarding school. Its first home was Down House in the village of Downe, Kent – formerly the home of Charles Darwin. The school outgrew the house so Miss Willis bought The Cloisters in Berkshire – its present home – on a high ridge which provides occasional views over distant downs. The Cloisters – still at the heart of the school – comes as a surprise. Built by Maclaren Ross for an order of Spanish nuns, who named it The School of Silence, it has an arched walkway linking most of the classrooms which – with its white walls, arches and terracotta pantiles – is incongruously Moorish in the heart of Berkshire.

However, the school has grown many newer buildings – boarding houses, specialist blocks etc – around the main building and the site is now extensive – many buildings nestling amongst trees, woody areas and neatly planted beds. All maintained by 'little green men' who hover around the site on electric car-lets. No architectural gems here – nor any monsters – though a few blocks lack charm. The whole has a sense of modest purposefulness – described by one mother as 'almost spiritual'.

The uniform is standard school green skirt, shirt and jumper, though the sixth form still cling to their floor length black skirts – 'They wear them so they can keep their pyjamas on underneath,' one mum told us.

Pastoral care, well-being and discipline: 'Completely faultless,' a mother said of the pastoral care. 'The house staff are very responsive and email you back at once.' 'When people complain, things do get done,' another vouchsafed. 'We've been bowled over by the pastoral care,' said yet another. 'The attention to detail is extraordinary – almost obsessive. Nothing is too much trouble.'

The loveliest school dining room we have seen in over 100 schools – proper tablecloths on round tables seating six to encourage time over meals. Food – 'We make all our own bread and sausages and buy in the absolute minimum' – which occasions rhapsodies in the girls.

Some sense that the sixth form centre separates older from younger girls and work still to be done on integrating those who arrive after the first year, but this is tricky in girls' schools everywhere. Very few discipline problems – smoking sighed over as 'an occasional safe rebellion which one wishes they wouldn't do', and illicit drinking looked upon as a threat to a girl's personal safety – 'You need to

Food – 'We make all our own bread and sausages and buy in the absolute minimum' – which occasions rhapsodies in the girls

be safe, to look after yourself and to preserve your dignity,' the head reminds them. No drugs incidents within memory and the very rare girl who 'cannot stop being unkind has to go'.

Pupils and parents: Girls from all over the UK and beyond; increasing numbers of daughters of alumnae. Seven per cent from overseas – mostly from the Far East but also the US, Nigeria, Kazakhstan. Parents solid middle class, usually with boarding backgrounds.

Exceptionally impressive list of notable alumnae includes: chemist and educator Rosemary Murray, Geraldine James, Clare Balding, Mary Midgley, Elizabeth Bowen, Priscilla Napier, Anne Ridler, Audrey Richards, Sophie Conran, Lulu Guinness, Fru Hazlitt, wildly different comics Miranda Hart and Laura Solon, Hannah Wright – pioneering barrister, Jenifer Hart – pioneering civil servant and Oxford don and Aileen Fox – pioneering archaeologist. Oh – and Kate Middleton. A rare degree of loyalty amongst alumnae – few schools excite more affection, it seems, and many keep in touch. Mrs McKendrick fosters this in imaginative ways, enlisting old girls to support newbies in their professions, eg an established barrister mentoring a recent alumna in her pupillage. A considerable attraction to potential parents.

Entrance: Lists close at 110 applicants and head interviews all those over four days, during which all are tested in maths, English and reasoning. They also participate in drama and sports activities et al to see whether they're happy and likely to fit in with boarding life. Eighty then invited to sit CE for the 60 available places. At 13, around 65 are assessed similarly for the 35-odd places. Girls from 180+ preps/primaries have joined Downe in recent years – from all over the UK.

At 16, it depends on how many are leaving but usually around 8-10 places for the 'huge' number who apply. Applicants sit the school's own papers and the strongest are then interviewed, the best offered conditional places. Seven I/GCSEs at B or above expected including A*/As in sixth form subject choices.

Exit: Some 10 per cent leave after GCSEs, often for co-ed sixth forms. Most to top universities, eg Bristol, London, Warwick, Exeter, Leeds, Edinburgh;

12 to Oxbridge in 2015. Some to universities in the US. Popular subjects include science/medicine, psychology, history of art, MFL, economics, politics, RS, business related degrees plus music and creative arts.

Money matters: Scholarships for sports, arts and academics more of an honour than a significant contribution to fees. Bursaries up to 100 per cent of fees plus additional help available for the right applicant.

Remarks: Archetypal traditional girls' full boarding school turning out delightful, principled, courteous and able girls who go on to make a significant contribution to the world. As one parent said, 'We couldn't be more thrilled.'

Dragon School

Bardwell Road, Oxford, Oxfordshire OX2 6SS

01865 315405
admissions@dragonschool.org
www.dragonschool.org

Ages: 4–13 (boarding from 8)
Pupils: 845 (510 boys, 335 girls)
Boarders: 240
Day: £10,920 – £19,440 pa
Boarding: £28,020 pa

Headmaster: Since 2002, Mr John Baugh (50s), BEd. Born in Uganda, educated at Aldenham School and St Luke's, Exeter. Previously head at Solefield School, Sevenoaks and Edge Grove, Hertfordshire. Believes in breadth of education and being child-centric – the relationship between staff and pupils is paramount. Teaches RS occasionally, observes each and every teacher once a year in the classroom and would not appoint a member of staff who was not willing to adapt to the needs of the child. His mantra to the children is 'be kind, be kind, be kind'. 'This is a school that never stops,' he says, 'it hums like an ocean liner'. Parents comment that he plays a straight bat and is good for PR.

Married to Wendy who teaches at the school and has two grown-up daughters, one of whom also teaches at the school – 'not appointed by me,' he is quick to point out. Says the school is his passion but enjoys escaping to his house in France in the holidays. A former sportsman, he once played for Exeter City, and continues to enjoy sports, especially cycling.

Entrance: Register early – as early as you like post-conception. The school is full and there are waiting lists at all stages but head is keen not to put off potential pupils as spaces can occur at any time. Backed up by parents who confirm places appear all the time despite horror stories to the contrary. Potentially easier to get in as a boarder but it depends on the year group. Non-selective entry although the school does assess maths and English to check that a child will be able to cope. Five 100 per cent bursaries at year 4 for five years – means-tested and not based on academic merit – head maintains they 'start with need', but the school has to be sure the family is able and willing to commit to the Dragon way of life – Saturday morning school, extracurricular commitments etc. Scholarships up to 50 per cent fees based on academic merit and non-means-tested. Weathering current economic climate.

Exit: Frequent destinations include Abingdon School, Cheltenham Ladies' College, Eton College, Harrow School, Magdalen College School, Marlborough College, Radley College, Rugby School, Stowe School, St Edward's School, Wellington College, Winchester College and Wycombe Abbey. No favourite school, but 'we have the greatest number of matches with St Edward's', as the two schools have similar ethos and are co-ed day and boarding. Pupils are not prepped for pre-test at 11 or entrance exams at 11 – no hothousing for local academic day schools. Head would not want a child to get into a school on the basis of excessive prepping. Deputy agrees that schools take note of the Dragon's reports and trusts their judgement but this isn't a school whose priority is to get children into the most academic local seniors. Bucket-loads of scholarships won – 35 to 40 per year. Famous Old Dragons include Sir John Betjeman, Leonard Cheshire VC, John Mortimer, Antonia Fraser, Alain de Botton, Rageh Omaar, Hugh Laurie and Tim Henman to name but a few.

Happy, free-range children roaming around, unrestricted by petty rules and health and safety, having a jolly time; play by the river still possible

Remarks: The Dragon, so named after an early school football team called 'dragons', is as sought-after as ever. Originally founded as the Oxford Preparatory School by a group of dons who wanted a progressive, liberal school for their sons where learning would be fun. Once avant-garde, education and society have caught up with these principles so that today the Dragon can only aspire to unconventionality. It has resisted formality and retains the ethos of ordered disorderliness – a charmingly unpretentious, relaxed atmosphere. The head confesses they are relaxed about petty issues – untucked shirts, scruffy uniform and clutter – while concentrating on the things that matter, such as learning. He likens the school to an upturned swan – feet paddling busily on the surface whilst the underlying systems of the school are serene and quiet. Unconventionality, or 'colouring outside the lines', has always been and still is encouraged, although head admits it is 'a balancing act' between risk-taking in schoolwork, striving for imagination and curiosity on one side, and discipline and toeing the line on the other. The Dragon aims for and encourages both.

Broad curriculum with a huge extracurricular programme including languages such as Mandarin, Japanese, Arabic and bilingual French as well as 'toast and translation' (a Latin club), music and drama etc. Most subjects are setted with scholarship classes at the top of the ability range. Learning support needs are screened in year 2 or on intake and help is available at extra cost. Dedicated learning support unit with five full- and three part-time members of staff who advise and update colleagues and draw up IEPs. Additional groups provided at no extra cost for handwriting, reading comprehension and social skills.

Breadth is key at the Dragon with excellence across the board – outstanding sport with fantastic facilities and accolades too numerous to mention. Non-sporty children can find refuge in music – equally successful and receiving high praise from parents. Over two-thirds of pupils take individual music lessons. Fantastic art work in light airy art rooms and space in the Forum for the annual art exhibition – check out the school magazine – worthy of any secondary school. Facilities in general match those at many senior schools with science labs, impressive library (look out for dragons etched on the glass fronted mezzanine), 25m swimming pool and playing fields stretching down to the river and boat house. A mini-campus with happy free-range children roaming around, unrestricted by petty rules and health and safety, having a jolly time; play by the river still possible as long as a child can swim two lengths of the pool fully clothed. Traditions such as this survive along with others – female teachers are called Ma, Bun Break at mid-morning and tea in the afternoon. The blue cords of yesteryear have stood the test of time – shorts in summer, longs in winter plus polo shirt and jumper; for girls, a kilt and bright yellow shirt, summer plaid dresses.

The Dragon is large (640) plus pre-prep Lynams, a mile or so up the road. Boys outnumber girls two to one. Some grumbles about middle of the road children lost in the masses and unable to find a niche if not sporty or musical. Head says that the children are separated into smaller units within the school so that they operate within age-related spheres at any one time without being overwhelmed. Good pastoral care – children are discussed weekly and communication is paramount. The school takes its privileges with responsibility and is committed to raising money for charity through entrepreneurship which starts with the concept of the 'little society' and the teaching of philanthropy to children, and extends to ventures such as the locally renowned Dragon Sale which raises tens of thousands of pounds. School is lead sponsor of a new multi-academy trust which includes three Blackbird Leys primary schools, The primaries can use the school's science, art, music and sporting facilities, while Dragon teaching staff are developing initiatives within the new academies. The Café Dragón brand of ethically-sourced coffee is sold at school events.

Boarding houses, separated by sex and age, run by married couples with a homely atmosphere and individuality. Bun breaks and tea in the houses with supper in the dining hall. Children can pop in and out of their house during the day. Day pupils often invited back. Full boarding means that the boarders are 'the heartbeat of the school', says the head. Weekends are packed with activities and many day pupils opt to board – one boarder walked from his boarding house past his family home every day. Day pupils easily fielded until 6pm, playing with boarders or participating in the huge number of extracurricular activities.

Once established for dons, they have largely been priced out of the market (in line with all independent schools, points out head). Lots of London money and business parents buying up north Oxford but professions also in evidence – many medics, lawyers, as well as a few academics (wealthy ones or few children). Lots of OD children. The Dragon remains the choice for the social elite of Oxford – if you want to be invited to the smartest dinner parties, this is your school. Head says there is still plenty of mix and parents agree that everyone can find their level and this is not necessarily a school full of nannies in the playground. Boarders local and international, with no particular country in predominance. Currently 30 pupils have EAL lessons.

The Dragon is still the prep school in Oxford, in sound heart as ever, chosen by parents for breadth of education, good old-fashioned freedom and encouraging a 'can do' attitude. Lifelong friends and contacts start here.

Dunannie and Dunhurst, Bedales' Junior Schools

Alton Road, Petersfield, Hampshire GU32 2DR

01730 711733
jjarman@bedales.org.uk
www.bedales.org.uk

Ages: Dunannie 3-8 Dunhurst 8-13
Pupils: 173
Boarders: 30 full, 22 flexi
Day: £8,205 – £18,345 pa
Boarding: £23,145 pa

Linked school: Bedales School

Headmistress: Since September 2011, Mrs Jane Grubb BA MA (Ed) PGCE, previously academic deputy head at Hurstpierpoint College prep school, where she worked for many years, starting as head of art, having also taught at Brockenhurst College. She is an Independent Schools Inspectorate (ISI) inspector and – we approve – a practising artist. She likes fishing, hiking, surfing and wild camping in remote places. Also plays the piano, saxophone, flute and acoustic guitar.

Head of Dunannie: Since May 2010, Ms Jo Webbern, Froebel CertEd, (50s), previously class teacher and then head of kindergarten at Ibstock Place for 26 years. Full of enthusiasm and excitement – 'I feel these are my roots. One can deliver that special ethos and creativity here while teaching children all the important skills of life'. Keen on the outside classroom.

Entrance: No selection in nursery – and the school has a crèche which takes staff babies and others – except to try and balance boys/girls. Healthy waiting list. Otherwise, applicants to Dunannie – 15-20 places – and to Dunhurst – 45 places for applicants from outside – spend a day in school before having a more formal assessment. Twenty odd places at 11+ – very over-subscribed. Much depends on whether the school and families like each other – understanding of and sympathy with the ethos is all-important.

Exit: Some 95 per cent from Duannie to Dunhurst (others to Highfield and Twyford); 95 per cent Dunhurst pupils to Bedales, but also to Bryanston, Canford, Marlborough, Winchester and Seaford.

Remarks: Nursery, for the 2+-4 year olds, is in a fabulous old barn nesting in trees, full of activities worth getting on your knees for. We liked the owl's tree-top house and the Brio train. Thence to Dunannie, the purpose-built and super school for the tots, cunningly housed under six overlapping and interlocking colourful roofs with big windows and home to the pre-prep years. 'It's a nice school,' an 8-year-old told us. 'It's very comfortable – you

They make textiles too and pottery (witty stuff) – observant pieces on parts of animals: a crocodile's jaw, a turkey's eye, an elephant's trunk. Other lessons are likewise creative

feel more free than in most schools. People don't mess about because the teachers are very calm and don't say, "Do this, do that!"' Much to enjoy here: the super wall-hanging – 'We weaved it and felted it with Steve-the-Weave, one of those workshoppy people'; the year 3 enchanted forest illustrating A Midsummer Night's Dream; the super seasons project with outsize drawings of pomegranate seeds. Every inch is covered with displays, book boxes and hangings – creativity drips off the walls. Outside is garden and space, space, space. We loved the 'Celtic hut' in the orchard, the 'sound garden' and the musical fort. Children everywhere, in tiny classes, are absorbed, relaxed and happily occupied.

Up to Dunhurst when you are 8. Boarding begins at this stage (boys' boarding house recently renovated) and most children spend some nights each week in school, though hardly anyone is in over the weekend. Outdoor work also features importantly now – masses of woodwork, gardening and animal care. Woodwork – in yet another old barn (see Bedales entry) – uses lots of different materials and techniques – soldering, circuitry – and the children make toys, automata, bird boxes, lamps, guitars, chairs and library steps. We loved

the sound-operated cars and toys. They design on paper using pencils – hooray. They make textiles too and pottery (witty stuff) – observant pieces on parts of animals: a crocodile's jaw, a turkey's eye, an elephant's trunk. Other lessons are likewise creative and collaborative – in art they study colour, while in science they cover primary colours and the spectrum. Not rocket science – why can't other schools do this? 'We like our science room,' we were told. 'We have to invent or discover something which would make a difference to us or to the world.'

Subject areas are traditional but informed by the Bedales ethos and a consistency between the three schools, as well as a welcome cross-curricular approach (see the Bedales entry for a fuller description of this). SEN teacher supports those who need it. 'She's a miracle worker,' one bright little button told us. A family therapist works with parents and children when appropriate.

Saturday school until 1.00pm. Many staff and some facilities shared with Bedales. All eat (toothsomely) together in dining room decorated with African mural and wall-hangings. The older children are very teen-y – floppy fringes, low-slung jeans and mini minis or shorts over tights, the Bedales uniform. All are relaxed and chatty – this is a school where people smile spontaneously. Relations between staff and pupils are open, friendly and mutually respectful – the first-name business doesn't seem odd after you've been here five minutes. The three heads are clearly in harmony and share values and goals. This informs continuity in academic, ethical and pastoral matters. The school feels in good heart.

Eagle House School

Sandhurst, Berkshire GU47 8PH

01344 772134
info@eaglehouseschool.com
www.eaglehouseschool.com
C of E

Ages: 3–13 (boarding from year 3)
Pupils: 390
Boarders: 10 full, 90 weekly/flexi
Day: £10,590 – £16,575 pa
Boarding: £22,245 pa

Linked school: Wellington College

Headmaster: Since 2006, Mr Andrew Barnard BA (40s). Educated at Christ's Hospital, thence to Sheffield for a degree in archaeology (claims he 'still gets excited by a pile of earth'). 'Dabbled' in the restaurant business but was diverted to a PGCE via a stint helping out in various prep schools. Started at Eagle House as head of history and English teacher, then housemaster and head of English and drama at Heath Mount School, deputy head at Winchester House and then back to Eagle House as head. He loves poetry, especially the Liverpool poets. Favourite author? Julian Barnes. Married to Sarah, who comes from a dynasty of teachers – no doubt it is from them that she has learned to embody grace under pressure: serving lunch to the nursery children, shepherding excited girls as they mass to play a rounders match against her old school, teaching French and EAL, taking care of front of house. They have three children, all at Wellington.

The Barnards have steered Eagle House successfully though some big changes. Their initial challenge was the move to co-ed and they admit that increasing the number of girls at the top end was, initially, 'hard to crack'. Intake is now 'robust' at about 40 per cent, with the few who leave at age 11 replaced and then some by girls joining for the last two years. Next item on the list? Building. The Golden Eagle Centre, a splendid sport and performing arts centre, opened in 2013 and there's yet more construction under way: new homes for DT and art, another science lab and a food tech room.

Current rather daunting project is bidding to run a new primary academy, a younger sibling to Wellington's. Why, we wondered, does Mr Barnard want to take this on? He says he has, 'already learnt from the process', which has, 'opened his eyes'. The mutual benefits he cites are professional development for staff and 'enrichment of diversity' for pupils at both establishments. There's a gleam in his eye when he talks of these plans; he recently returned to his alma mater, Christ's Hospital, and this has further strengthened his faith in the positive impact of bridging social and educational divides.

Living on site means the boundaries between home and work are pretty porous though the

Barnards say that they and their children love every minute. This notwithstanding, sanctuary is a house in the Loire and all things French.

Entrance: Parents are advised to visit and register 12 months before their child is due to start. Pre-prep: trial day and usually automatic progression to prep. Prep: trial day, copies of reports and a reference from current head. Prep is relatively non-selective but pupils are 'expected to be able to cope with the school's academic course'. Year 7 entrants are tested in English, maths and reasoning.

Exit: Up to 80 per cent to Wellington – this is, after all, part of the deal. Bradfield scoops up most of the rest; singles to eg Marlborough, Cranleigh, Millfield.

Remarks: Set in woods and heathland between Crowthorne and Sandhurst, Eagle House was founded in Hammersmith in 1820 and has been on its current 30-acre site since 1886. Owned by near neighbour Wellington College (the two schools share a boundary) and head says that these days, 'links are much better defined'. Being part of 'brand Wellington' includes teaching exchanges (each member of Eagle House staff is twinned with one from Wellington) as well as a definite trickle down (or up) of innovative approaches to education. For the past two years staff have attended life coaching courses at Wellington, there is a life skills club for prep pupils and now parents are snapping up taster sessions. We were particularly struck by how teachers of all ages were fired up by new ideas,

History comes to life in the Tudor House, a thatched replica where children dress up and learn about the past through workshops

welcoming change and educational debate – Eagle House clearly no place for moss gatherers.

Lessons are an hour long and those we saw were well-paced and active, pupils using hands as well as heads. Although Eagle House is not an official forest school, increasing use is being made of the grounds with lessons from science to English taking place outside. History comes to life in the Tudor House, a thatched replica where children dress up and learn about the past through workshops and activity days. Creativity is boosted by evening writing workshops and there are plans for another school literary festival after the success of the first one. Setting from year 3 in English and maths, and then for French and Latin in year 6. Latin for all from year 5, Greek for scholars. Four SEN staff support pupils individually with dyslexia, dyspraxia, mild ADHD (extra charge). EAL also offered.

We hear that as pressure to gain coveted places at Wellington builds a few parents are paying for extra tuition in years 5 and 6 to prepare for pre-testing in year 7, though when exactly their children fit this in is unclear. Not a reflection on the prep's teaching, rather more indicative of the holy grail a Wellington education has become. School is alert

to this, saying that a few parents have unrealistic expectations, wanting their children to be 'brilliant at everything'. Some grumbles that the scholarship class (years 7 and 8) is 'divisive', citing detrimental effects on friendships. Scholarship exams are in February and March so the children in this class are 'off on trips' while the rest are studying for CE until June.

Eagle House differs with Wellington on one thing at least: books. The clean lines of big brother's splendid new library may not be spoilt by shelves and their dusty contents but for now at least, eaglets are still encouraged to curl up on squashy sofas with a good book. 'Over my dead body' were the young librarian's words when we asked if there were plans to defect to e-readers. Long may she reign.

In keeping with the school's 'learning for life' ethos, the Golden Eagle programme of activities introduces pupils to a rich mix of experiences intended to challenge and develop interests. Clubs such as golf, orienteering and Scalextrics run in the extended lunch break – a good example of making a virtue out of a necessity since limited size of the otherwise charming wood-panelled dining room means that it takes two hours to feed everyone. A conservatory-style extension is on head's list but the courtyard memorial garden will have to relocate. Years 3 and 4 can do optional Saturday morning activities and older children also have timetabled Golden Eagle session once a week.

The trophy cabinets show that boys do well at county level hockey and cricket but it's the girls' silverware that fills the shelves. The under 13s were national champions in hockey

The Eagle House journey starts, naturally enough, in The Nest. Here in the nursery little ones (many of whom have older siblings in the prep) begin to learn through play. They are introduced to the big school and its curriculum via weekly sessions of swimming dance, music and IT. Delightful inside and outside spaces full of tempting toys, sand and water.

Pre-prep pupils gradually begin to explore the subjects that they will be taught once they move up, with specialist teachers for French, music, art and drama. Head of the pre-prep wants her pupils to have a 'happy start to school life, develop confidence and a love of learning' – we thought the kinaesthetic approach to numbers via 'maths stories' looked like a great idea. Literacy is taught using Read Write Inc phonics and the pre-prep is a

model school for this scheme. No male class teachers, but music and football are taught by chaps borrowed from the prep. Dance is a popular activity and we enjoyed watching 5-year-olds' imaginative evocations of tarantulas – all part of the term's rain forest topic. Apparently playing medieval games in the Tudor house and visits from a 'real, live knight' are highlights.

A trio of energetic eaglets treated us to an access all areas tour. The dorms are on the first floor of the original mock Tudor house, rooms have large windows and high ceilings. The boys' (blue) rooms were predictably unadorned but the girls' (pink) rooms were as homely and sparkly as anyone could wish. Isn't this blue/pink cliché rather at odds with the progressive educational ethos of brand Wellington, we wondered? The eaglets told us gleefully that the showers and changing rooms in the new sports centre were similarly gendered, right down to the colour of the soap. Bathrooms, corridors and common room are clean and fresh, if towards the make do and mend end of the homely spectrum. The 15 or so pupils in over the weekend (or rather Saturday evening to Sunday evening) amount to, as Mrs Barnard pointed out, a 'minibus full'. Each member of staff does a Sunday stint so we imagine that minibus must go on a very interesting range of trips.

According to our guides, hockey and football are the main sports and nearby Cranleigh is the arch rival. The trophy cabinets show that boys do well at county level hockey and cricket but it's the girls' silverware that fills the shelves. Most recently the under 13s were national champions in hockey and the under 12s in netball. Such success is certainly celebrated but the Eagle House philosophy is not 'win at all costs' and the children we spoke to got huge enjoyment from their daily sport

– whatever the result. Facilities are pretty good, with standard issue multi-purpose gym and an indoor swimming pool. Outside there's Astroturf and all-weather pitches for hockey, netball and tennis, though boys told us they would like separate cricket and athletic fields. There's a lot of beautiful green space around the school but much of it belongs to venerable trees bearing preservation orders so, in the absence of a hurricane, cricketers and athletes will be sharing for many summers to come.

Music department resides in a deceptively spacious Portakabin though once inside listening to a superb impromptu performance of a Schumann Polonaise we wouldn't have cared if we were in a coal bunker. 'Brilliant' was the adjective most often used by parents to describe music at the school. Trial lessons and plenty of opportunities to develop talents great and small; lunchtime concerts allow new players to have their first experience of performing in a 'non-judgemental' environment. As we admired the beautifully decorated small organ in the charming chapel, choirmaster told us that organ lessons were just being established.

School may not have its own theatre (major productions are staged in Bracknell) but drama is big here. In the new performing arts studio we saw year 3 and 4 pupils belting out a song for their forthcoming show, not a single reluctant soul mouthing the words. On the walls of the foyer are larger than life photo canvases of past theatrical triumphs. So much for the stars, what about the tremblers in the wings? Everyone gets a chance to shine, school said; parents, while praising the 'wonderful' productions, weren't quite so sure.

Art and DT departments may be eagerly anticipating move to their new premises but no sign of a reduction in creativity. In art pupils were busy

In the new performing arts studio we saw pupils belting out a song for their forthcoming show, not a single reluctant soul mouthing the words. On the walls of the foyer are larger than life photo canvases

learning the patient craft of stop motion animation using 'indestructible' iPads and in DT they were dreaming up designs for boats. Work of a very high standard was on display everywhere.

Pastoral care generally praised and children we spoke to had a clear understanding of anti-bullying policies and what to do if they had a problem. Every child now has their own tutor from year 5 (prior to this form teachers are first point of contact) and the new system is intended to be more 'open and flexible', involving all members of staff in pastoral roles.

Most pupils are from 15-20 mile radius but increasing numbers from London. Handful from abroad, no dominant country. Small contingent of Spanish children come for a year or two – it's not an organised thing, more 'word of mouth', according to the head. Parents, the usual Thames valley mix of management and high-tech industry professionals, like the boarding ethos even if their children are day pupils. We're not surprised, pupils can stay until 6pm and by then prep has usually been done (older children may have to finish theirs at home). For most though it's the Wellington connection that makes this a first choice school and leavers' destinations over the last few years bear this out. Several parents told us they thought the school had changed, describing it as much more 'under Wellington's thumb'. However another said, 'We initially chose Eagle House because of its links with Wellington but now realise that's only one aspect. It's a great start, wherever your child goes on to'.

Eagle House is a happy, creative school. The atmosphere is eager and unstuffy – honouring the best of prep school tradition; nimbly assimilating 21st century educational thinking. Eaglets headed for Wellington and other eyries will find this a great place to learn to fly.

Elstree School

Woolhampton, Reading, Berkshire RG7 5TD

01189 713302
registrar@elstreeschool.org.uk
www.elstreeschool.org.uk
C of E

Ages: 3–13
Pupils: 260
Boarders: 15 full, 85 weekly/flexi
Day: £10,590 – £19,035 pa
Boarding: £24,339 – £24,420 pa

Headmaster: Since 2013, Mr Sid Inglis BA (40s), previously headmaster at Ludgrove. Uncertain as to career until taught English in Chile (where met wife Olivia) and realised that as professions go 'there is no finer job.' Appointed at exciting if nerve-wracking time following wobbles in leadership, parent confidence and pupil numbers. It's now all go again, with school at capacity, no need even to contemplate going fully co-ed (girls leave at 8), scholarships back to full honours-board levels – and all right in world.

Mr Inglis's first name is unusual and, even more unusually, shared with last head but two. Would be karma except that real name is Andrew. All the other more predictable essentials are also in place: labrador ('though had her before we arrived,' says equally charming Mrs Inglis), three cherubic offspring (two still at the school) and website must-have – photograph capturing whole shebang smilingly disporting themselves on well-positioned, sunlight-drenched bench if human (and beside it if not).

Would take a mean-spirited reviewer to deny that Mr Inglis exudes winning headmasterly qualities of authority and personability. Out and about like nobody's business. 'Very much a figurehead,' said parent. 'I don't know how he can be in so many different places all the time. He and his wife go around like a pair and are very supportive of one another.'

Even slots in weekly story-reading session to different pre-prep class each week (we encountered him en route with book, wondering if would require 'funny voices'). While parent approval can reach adoration levels, pupils' response more down to earth. 'Lets us get on with life as long as we're sensible,' said one. 'Doesn't feel special – acts just like a normal teacher.'

Relaxed, too – when this reviewer turned up at the very last minute for an open day visit, he (and all colleagues) were genuinely welcoming (if there were any less positive feelings, were fathoms deep).

He thinks it's part and parcel of the ethos that made this a dream job. Does a spot of teaching (RS, his degree subject, has yielded to classics here) and loves it. Aim, as laid out in prospectus, is to discover 'how a child is intelligent rather than how intelligent a child is' – while still preparing them for range of senior schools.

Translated, means that 'don't want academic success at the expense of muddy knees,' he says. 'If a child is confident and happy in their own little shell, academics will follow.' School, he says, isn't for chest-beating alpha males, jostling for position (or females, either). Will have a few who struggle academically but exude sense of purpose elsewhere, shining on sports field or stage. Combination of variety, straight-talking pupils and enjoyable challenge of (successfully) giving school boost it needed makes this a role he relishes. 'Love being busy.'

He is passionate about sport, particularly rugby and cricket, and enjoys playing golf and fishing. He took over after the school spent a year under an acting head, after the abrupt and unexplained resignation of the previous head, and brought with him parental hopes for stability after troubled times.

Head of Home Farm School (the pre-prep), Mrs Kay Markides, arrived from St Gabriel's in September 2009. Graduated in science, married with a family (including a son who attended Elstree) before deciding to train for teaching young ones. Taught for a while at another school nearby. Thrilled to be involved with Elstree, and it shows. Warm and at ease with the children ('I love them') she is clearly not only very competent but also exudes calm dependability. Presides over a talented young staff who clearly relish the company of their young charges, patiently explaining things and then rushing around with them in the grounds of the prep school.

Entrance: Non-selective in Home Farm, the pre-prep (nursery to year 2), whose 60 pupils are accommodated in next door farmhouse and converted outbuildings, with own separate entrance and playgrounds but overlapping grounds. Co-ed but boy-dominated as 'people are signing up for the whole school,' points out amiable pre-prep head

> **'Don't want academic success at the expense of muddy knees,' he says. 'If a child is confident and happy academics will follow'**

and former parent Mrs Kay Markides. No girls in current year 2 and a cheerful minority over in the prep for year 3.

Open to learning needs including ADHD. Key is ability to keep up academically and impress with right attitude: prospectus stresses that 'effort is king'. Growth of waiting lists (in almost every year group) means that while ability range is wide, 'we have become gently selective,' says Mr Inglis.

While teachers sometimes sorely tried, rare that won't make a go of it, helped by much-praised learning needs department. Will, though, review progress in years 4 and 6 when long-term compatibility of child and school will be weighed up, says headmaster. Thus far, nobody has been asked to leave.

Exit: Good links with Bradfield (former head, now at Eton, sent all his brood here), most of first rank southern staples represented. Eton, Harrow, Winchester, Radley, Bradfield, Stowe have all featured recently. Record scholarships in 2015.

Year 3 girls to St Andrew's Pangbourne, Cheam, St Gabriel's, Marlston House and the Manor, Abingdon.

Remarks: School that likes life in duplicate. Pre-prep's 60 pupils have large magical woodland area (annexed from prep), paths canopied with intertwined branches or bordered with wild grasses (there's even a troll bridge) – and a second mini wilderness for everyday, star attraction a palatial roofed sandpit big enough for whole class to enjoy. Even Mrs Markides shares year 2 teaching duties with colleague (though second best rule undoubtedly doesn't apply).

Appearance, in pairs or otherwise, is winningly green and traditional. School's 150 acres include two lakes, one used for Elstree Award activities (like D of E but bespoke), croquet lawn with wire sculpture of (Lewis Carroll inspired?) flamingo, courts and pitches, dog-walking parents and staff adding homely touch.

Though vibe is venerable (pre-prep uniform list specifies named napkin ring), mood is progressive. 'Lots of tradition and trust, but we're well aware it's a modern world,' says Mrs Inglis. Mr I stresses importance of charitable activities that open pupils' eyes 'to the wide world away from idyllic leafy confines.' Perhaps accounts for staff list hedging its bets – some male teachers are Esq, some are

Mr, while headmaster, straddling both worlds, is bereft of any salutation at all.

'Pushes children hard but pleasantly so,' thought prospective parent. 'It's not "you will learn 10 verses by Tuesday".' By way of proof, there's combined staff and pupil YouTube version of 'Happy' to mark departure of recent batch of girl leavers, treat for dad dancing (or teacher equivalent) connoisseurs and anyone needing lesson in chutzpah.

Full boarding the only traditional element that isn't faring so well, hanging on but only just. Now a minority occupation for 15 out of the 100 or so boarders, mainly overseas (Russians, sprinkling of Spanish) plus odd Londoner. They 'get used to it,' thought pupil. Not most ringing of endorsements, even backed by run of grounds at weekend.

However when it comes to flexi or weekly stays, 'boys are clamouring to board,' the head told us firmly, reeling off vast list of evening activities on offer when they do – from bridge to fantasy football, debating and improvisation. School now so 'full to bursting' from Monday to Friday that it's a case of joining the queue with waiting list in operation. No quibbles with boarding logistics, which work a treat, year 4 to 6 dorms to the side – we liked their emergency cuddly toy cubby hole to keep homesickness at bay – while years 7 and year 8 have separate quarters in main building.

Greta Garbo tendencies no doubt forgotten in excitement of hotly contested corridor cricket

Dorms on large side – eight to 10 not uncommon- but with spacious, pleasant rooms and friendly, uncrowded feel. Décor variable, one room a shrine to Shoot! magazine, plastered floor to ceiling with pictures of footballers, another, the former ballroom, featuring stucco storks looking down from ceiling in gentle amazement at year 8 pupils' beds in formation on parquet floor. Possible setting for new reality TV show, 'Come boarding,' perhaps?

If full boarding continues to decline and parent vibe suggests it will – 'strong majority who like the day aspect,' thought one – Big Weekends could be the future, with 40 or so other pupils piling in for fun and games including Laser Tag and exciting Indoor Lions, inside version of Stuck in the Mud played in the dark for added thrills.

Extremely popular (currently free of charge, so no wonder) and means 'full boarders have more company,' says school. Also an organisational cinch as Saturday school – a full day with lessons and afternoon games – is in full force from year 4. Can be shock to the system (as is late weekday finish) for those coming from state sector, though 'only do easy subjects then,' said tour guide. Well, maybe – if you consider French and maths a bit of light weekend banter, though heavy-duty exercises are interspersed with the odd quiz, which helps. And without Saturday school, 'weekends are too long,' thought pupil.

Best teaching (and there's lots of it) combines humour and memorability. One English teacher (a school favourite) known for quick draw funny pictures – enthusiastic year 7 boys (like all other pupils smilingly standing up for adults) praising memorable stick person imagery that instantly conjured up poetic protagonist 'swimming against tide with heart sinking…'.

Impressively inclusive, say parents, with children's confidence boosted by lessons cannily pitched at challenging rather than daunting. 'My son thinks he's brilliant because they've given him the work that's appropriate,' said mother. Even less inspirational teachers – maths felt to be slightly variable – usually get the results in the end. 'If you get something right, you get a point. Didn't like it but it does work,' thought one pupil.

Heroic efforts elsewhere, with year 7 pupil in DT class who had elected to make sundial out of seasoned oak and, equipped with bow saw, was two-thirds of way through chunky tree trunk. 'Has taken an hour already,' was weary comment.

Pre-prep pupils similarly keen on lessons and given undiluted praise from parents – staff 'can't do enough, there morning, noon and night, so happy and 100 per cent involved with the children' – no wonder. One small maths fan was full of praise for 'hard sums', another extolled virtues of recent pirate topic because 'they kill people' – before being gently shepherded into more wholesome approach by teacher. 'Our pirates wouldn't do things like that.' (He didn't look totally convinced).

Music 'absolutely thriving,' says head, with 200 individual lessons timetabled each week, top performers reaching grade 8, two recent scholarships (Radley and Charterhouse) and department 'always full of boys.' Prep choir (one of three) is 30-deep, recent delights including Choral Evensong at Bath Abbey.

Encouraged by many means, including piano located somewhat unusually on first bend of main staircase in prep school for impromptu concerts – one boy at a time, ban on James Bond theme tune (popularity led to aural repetitive strain injury risk for admin staff nearby).

Drama similarly successful with boys happy to take female roles and lack of self-consciousness that comes with single-sex environment. Parents thrilled with gentle encouragement that sees the formerly un-keen blossoming into performers. Talent search starts early with violin (free lessons for all in year 1) and recorder (year 2) – parents apparently thrilled with results, performers shining in end of year concert.

Sport equally strong and inclusive (goes down to E teams and sixth XIs). Fine summer evenings an enthusiast's delight, with croquet on front lawn. Lots more – from swimming to shooting, golf and judo, as well as school staples – athletics, football, rugby, hockey, cricket (coach, current Berkshire captain, also teaches pre-prep pupils, one mightily impressed to find his teacher known to Lord's).

Plenty of informal activities, too; one tree full of roosting boys, like giant navy blue rooks. Though staff presence seemed to us to be relatively hands-off, some parents and pupils feel free time can be over-supervised. 'Always a teacher walking round.' Reasons for adult presence well understood – 'it's so someone doesn't get hurt,' and by year 8, said pupil, things improve. 'They accept you need some time alone.'

Greta Garbo tendencies no doubt forgotten in excitement of table football matches and hotly contested corridor cricket. Boys very keen, though one thought teachers possibly less so when caught in path of on-coming cricket ball during evening rounds.

Gentle pace gets up speed through the school, senior school entrance exam pressure an inevitable fact of life for year 8 pupils, though teachers do best to defuse the tension, felt boys. Weekly form time used to air difficulties; friendly gap students a more informal source of support, comfort food – evening bowls of cereal – provided for boarders.

Pastoral care generally felt to be good, from daily staff briefings to half hour catch up sessions at lunchtime. Pupils urged to use common sense if someone is feeling left out of activities – 'they expect us to find something that fits,' said pupil. Bullying clearly well managed. 'Issues dealt with very quickly with children pulled in. If you overstep the mark there's a punishment and everyone knows that,' said parent. Pre-prep opts for circle time and golden rules. Staff had slight struggle to remember them but do appear to work, parents full of praise at absence of problems in any age group.

Highly organised parents notable for efficiency and ability sweep up newcomers – 'integration' events include lunches for the mums and curry nights for dads (or vice versa one progressive day?). Praise, bar mutterings about over influential queen bees from former parent, was universal, school community the icing on the cake. Attracts London exiles as well as locals, drawn by welcoming culture and lots to keep sporty and arty happy.

'Son has been pushed where would like to be pushed and pushed along where needed to be. An amazingly efficient school that continues to surprise me,' said mother.

Eton College

Eton, Windsor, Berkshire SL4 6DW

01753 370611
admissions@etoncollege.org.uk
www.etoncollege.com
C of E

Ages: 13–18
Pupils: 1,320; sixth form: 520
Boarders: all full
Boarding: £35,724 pa

Head Master: Since September 2015, Mr Simon Henderson MA PGCE (an extremely youthful looking late 30s; possibly Eton's youngest ever head), previously head of Bradfield College. Educated at Winchester College, followed by Brasenose College, Oxford, where he read history. Teaching career started at Windsor Boys' School, moving to Eton College in 2001, where he was a deputy housemaster and head of history, and on to Sherborne School in 2009 as deputy head (academic). Straight-talking,

unpretentious – more technocrat than autocrat, Merkel than Berlusconi, Bill Gates than Donald Trump. Married to Ali (a civil servant) with four children under the age of 5.

Academic matters: First class all round. Tutor for admissions told us that it's seen as 'cool' to be academically successful at Eton. Majority of boys take A levels, but Pre-U offered in a growing number of subjects too. Maths is most popular subject at A level, followed by history, RS, physics and economics. Seventy-nine per cent A*/A grades at A level in 2015. School doesn't have plans to offer IB – 'The advantage of the IB is breadth,' a master told us, 'but we feel that the boys get that breadth anyway through the options on offer.' As well as their main subjects, sixth formers choose two additional options – a wealth of choice, from philosophy to Portuguese.

At GCSE, most boys take 11 subjects, including at least two of the three sciences. Ninety-six per cent A*/A grades in 2015. IGSCEs taken in sciences, languages, maths, history, music and DT. Fabulous languages department – nine languages taught, including Arabic, Japanese, Mandarin and Russian (department will soon move to new £20 million quadrangle, complete with 22 classrooms, two language labs and a library). Younger boys in classes of 20 to 22 (setted from ability from their first year and up to 14 sets per year group), with smaller class sizes as they get older. Total of 35 lessons (called schools at Eton) a week, but most boys have some free periods. Pupils have internal school exams in Michaelmas and summer terms. Youngest

boys get an hour of prep a night, and two to two and a half hours as they progress up the school.

Full-time teaching staff numbers 150 – a good mix of old and new, and more women teachers than before. School is keen to encourage boys to be independent learners and boys get sessions on time management, study skills and exam technique. Rather than instructing pupils, 'You must do it like this,' school asks boys, 'How do you think we could do this better?' All pupils have a tutor and they meet once a week in small groups (maximum of six) at their tutor's house. Same tutor for first three years, then boys choose their own sixth form tutor.

When we visited, eclectic forthcoming productions ranged from Cyrano de Bergerac to Flames over New Jersey, a play co-written by a pupil and a member of staff

Has invested heavily in SEN support – an educational psychologist spent a year setting up and coordinating the SEN unit and training staff. Around 50 to 60 boys receive regular learning support for mild to moderate dyslexia, dyspraxia, dysgraphia – either one-to-one or in small groups. All boys assessed during their first term and any whose results give cause for concern get extra help.

School reports are meticulous. All subject masters write reports for every boy they teach. These are sent to tutors, who add their own reports, then to housemasters and finally to parents. 'You get a pretty good idea of how your child is doing,' says one appreciative mother.

Games, options, the arts: Excellent – every extracurricular activity on offer, including cookery lessons from top chef (and provost's wife) Caroline Waldegrave. 'The opportunities are phenomenal,' a father told us wistfully. 'I only wish I'd gone there.' Sport remains superb, with facilities (and results) second to none. Boys must commit to a main sport every term – football or rugby in Michaelmas term, hockey, rowing or the Field Game in the Lent term and athletics, cricket, rowing or tennis in the summer. A raft of minor sports on offer – from Eton's own Wall Game to beagling. Unlike some schools, boys encouraged to continue with sports through exam terms.

Dazzling art department (the Drawing Schools), with marvellous open aspect over playing fields – one of the best we've seen. Remarkable and challenging work, beautifully executed and displayed. When we visited, eight boys were off to do art foundation courses after A levels. Paintings by the likes of Anthony Frost and Patrick Heron hanging on walls, collection of ceramics donated by an old boy, art library, CAD suite, two 3D printers – the place definitely has the wow factor. Music is brilliant too. Department attracts the brightest and best in the country via its music scholarships. Around 1,300 instrumental lessons a week and regular and very polished concerts held in concert hall.

Not surprisingly, with starry alumnae like Hugh Laurie, Damian Lewis, Dominic West, Eddie Redmayne and Tom Hiddleston, takes drama very seriously indeed. The drama department has its own full-time designer, carpenter and manager, plus a part-time wardrobe mistress, and puts on

a plethora of school and house plays, some led by teachers, some by boys. When we visited, eclectic forthcoming productions ranged from Cyrano de Bergerac to Flames over New Jersey, a play co-written by a pupil and member of staff.

Buildings of mellow old brick, medieval courtyards, grounds running down to the Thames, boys in tailcoats and white bow ties hurrying to lessons

Huge number of outings, visits and field trips, and good provision for pupils post exams. CCF very popular – army is the biggest single employer of Old Etonians (including ex-soldier Prince Harry, of course). Vast number of clubs and societies, with top-notch speakers, often launched and run by the boys themselves. 'We give boys confidence in themselves,' says one beak. 'We treat them as adults and they get a lot of responsibility quite young.' Recent activities range from a charity cycle ride to raise money in memory of Horatio Chapple, the Eton pupil who died in tragic circumstances in Norway, to a spectacular fashion show (attended by Dame Vivienne Westwood, no less) staged by a boy with ambitions to be a fashion designer. 'I would have worn one of his ballgowns,' an impressed mother told us.

Boarding: Twenty-five boarding houses, including College (for King's Scholars). Single study bedsits for all from day one. Huge variety of rooms and décor. The rooms we saw were pretty salubrious – one housemaster we met drew the line at 'floordrobes'. Sanctions imposed for messy rooms range from laundry duty to black-bagging, where boys' possessions get stuffed in a bin bag and the culprit must pay a fine to get them back. All rooms networked and school endeavours to teach boys about responsible computer use. Boarding houses scattered either side of the High Street and beyond. Houses are known by the names of the housemasters in charge. They are in post for 13 years, so the names of the houses change with them.

In the boarding houses dames keep a weather eye on the boys, stay in contact with parents and run domestic matters. 'They are the co-runners of the houses,' a housemaster told us. 'They're not emergency first aid SWAT teams.' Older pupils volunteer to mentor new boys and answer questions like how to cope with the volume of work or what to do on Sunday mornings. House common rooms equipped with table football, pool table and TV. Lots of inter-house competitions.

Half the houses offer in-house catering while boys in the others eat breakfast, lunch and supper in a large central dining hall. Lunch is a formal, if speedy, affair, with grace said at the start and finish. 'The houses are like little schools within a house,' a father told us. 'Everyone says their own house is the best.'

Background and atmosphere: Founded in 1440 by Henry VI (sister college of King's College, Cambridge, which was founded a year later). Seventy King's Scholars still live in the original buildings (most elegant dining hall and ancient classroom with original benches and graffiti). Buildings of mellow old red brick, medieval court-yards, grounds running down to the Thames, boys in tailcoats and white bow ties hurrying to lessons – the whole place looks like a film set. Magnificent chapel built by Henry VI and a second chapel for Lower Boys. Has appointed an imam and RC chaplain, Jewish and Hindu tutors on the staff too.

Boys wear tailcoats and stiff collars – apart from office bearers, who wear proper wing collars and white ties. Brilliant for posture, as boys stuff pockets in their tailcoats with essential school kit, pulling even the most round-shouldered teenagers straight. School uniform not as expensive as you might think – good second-hand trade, both boy-inspired and via the school tailors in the High Street. Fancy waistcoats worn by the school prefects, or to give them their proper title, the Eton Society ('Pop'). Pupils don't wear tails across the bridge to Windsor any longer – much informal changing and half-changing (putting on a jacket rather than tails) after lessons. Teaching staff mostly live within 600 yards of the school, which creates a 'good sense of community'.

Lively atmosphere. Every day is structured and active, with boys and beaks constantly on the go. Beaks wear gowns for their three-line whip coffee break – Chambers – when one beak will attract the attention of another by tugging at his gown. Has its own traditional (and ever-evolving) school language: terms are 'halves', weekly tutor sessions are 'private business' and boys who aren't King's Scholars are Oppidans – luckily, a helpful glossary on the school website to explain all. Excellent school mags (The Chronicle, The Junior Chronicle) which are sold on high days and holidays for commission. All boys now have mobile phones and discount-available laptops.

Pastoral care, well-being and discipline: Still the traditional school it always was, but broad-minded, outward-looking and liberal in principle. Boys who get into trouble are given lots of support. Clear policies on drugs, alcohol and cigarettes. Any boy caught using, selling or possessing drugs 'will go,' says school firmly. But if a suspicion that a

pupil may be dabbling with drugs and is prepared to talk about it, school takes 'a different route' – parents are informed and both they and the boy are asked to sign a contract, offered counselling and subjected to lectures and random drugs testing. Alcohol less of a problem now ('tiny numbers,' says school) but smoking is still there – though less than in co-ed schools, apparently. For first offences, smokers pay fines to cancer charity and will 'go on the bill' – Eton-speak for when a boy misbehaves and is sent to the headmaster or lower master. Boys have limited (but increasing with age) rights to go into Windsor and further afield – but only with their parents' permission.

Pupils and parents: 'There isn't a typical Etonian,' the tutor for admissions told us. 'It's a very big school but it isn't one homogenous block. It's a school that is vastly more socially and culturally diverse than it's ever been.' He reckons that the boys who thrive are those who are 'curious, prepared to try out new things, have a love of learning and a deep-seated desire to get on'. Around 20 boys a year from state schools and 12 per cent from overseas – Hong Kong, China, Russia, Germany, France, Italy, Nigeria and the US.

The boys we met were a sparky bunch who cited the sports facilities and the friendly atmosphere as the best things about the place. Boys say they aren't bothered by being at a single-sex school – girls from St Mary's Ascot, Wycombe Abbey and St George's Ascot team up for some drama productions and, as one chirpy pupil told us, 'We can meet girls in the holidays'. Asked whether you have to be a boffin, gifted sportsman or one of the lads to get the most out of the school, Eton insists not. 'A boy who wouldn't say boo to a goose when he arrived got really involved in theatre lighting and sound while he was here,' a master said. 'By the time he got to 17 he was so respected that he was cheered admiringly every time his name came up at the end of performances.' A mother said that even though boys need to be 'self-starters and able to keep up with the work', the school suits different types – super-bright, sporty, quirky, you name it – and boys don't have to be utterly brilliant. 'My three sons are all quite different,' she told us. 'But they have all been very happy there and done well.' Another parent described it as 'an extraordinary school, with amazing opportunities', though, given its size, 'perhaps not the place for wilting violets'.

The fourth of June (aka school speech day) is as buzzy as ever, but the mass of royal watchers have gone. A huge mix of families – 'We have boys whose families live in castles and boys whose families live on inner-city estates,' says school. Lots of first-time buyers, along with sons of Old Etonians.

Notable old boys listed on school website – illustrious roll includes Hubert Parry, David Cameron and 18 previous prime ministers, loads of politicians (Eton provost William Waldegrave, Nicholas Soames, Douglas Hurd, Boris Johnson), Captain Oates, the poets Gray and Shelley, Princes William and Harry, a clutch of journalists (Charles Moore, Nicholas Coleridge, Craig Brown), plus chef Hugh Fearnley-Whittingstall, rower Matthew Pinsent, counter-tenor Michael Chance and Edward Gardner, musical director of the English National Opera.

Entrance: Around 1,000 candidates for 250 places – from more than 100 different schools. Entry procedure appears to be working well (the traditional 'put his name down at birth' regime was abolished in 2001) and the parents we spoke to expressed firm approval of its thoroughness. Pupils must be bright enough to cope with the academic demands of the school, but Eton is also looking for boys with spark, flair and potential who will thrive in a boarding environment.

All prospective applicants assessed in year 6 – ultra-detailed assessment includes verbal reasoning, numeracy, perceptual potential, interview and school report. Five-strong committee spends two days assessing the candidates, and out of 1,000 boys assessed at the age of 11, 250 will be offered places (conditional on passing CE or, for boys at state schools, Eton's own exam in year 8). Another 80 are placed on the waiting list. School recognises that by assessing in year 6, system may penalise late developers, so stays in touch with school heads and gets feedback on near-miss candidates. Successful candidates visit four boarding houses and list their choices – 80 per cent get one of their top two preferences.

Scholarships are a central part of the school – around 20 per cent of boys receive some form of financial support. Scholarship boys include 14 King's Scholars (decided on academic merit alone), plus New Foundation scholars (boys joining Eton from state schools) and many more.

To progress into the sixth form boys need a minimum of six A grades at GCSE, although in reality this is easily exceeded by all of them. Twelve sixth form scholarships offered a year – only for boys from state sector or independent schools lacking sixth form provision.

Exit: Sometimes loses one or two after GCSE – mainly those who opt for co-ed or day schools. At 18, virtually all progress to higher education. PPE, PPS, philosophy and theology the most popular subjects, followed by history/history of art, science and engineering. School says between 60-80 a year to Oxbridge, but refuses to give numbers for 2015; others to Russell Group and increasing numbers to American universities, the majority Ivy League.

Money matters: Pots of money and assets. Stunning setting means school has a popular sideline from films (The Madness of King George etc). Can afford to (and does) have everything of the best. Pays its staff very well indeed. Aim is that finances shouldn't be an obstacle to any boy who is offered a scholarship and a large number of bursaries for parents who can't afford the fees or have fallen on hard times. Regular subsidised summer schools – rowing a popular option for prep school wannabes.

Masses of public activity – the rowing lake at Dorney is used nationally for training international rowers (and for the London 2012 Olympic rowing and kayak events), and the athletics hall and swimming pools (indoor and outdoor) are much in demand by locals out of term time. Currently on a mission to raise £50 million to fund further bursaries – has raised more than half so far.

Remarks: Still the number one boys' public school. With teaching and facilities that are second to none, Eton produces bright, purposeful, articulate young men with a sense of ambition and self-worth. School is far more forward-thinking and outward-looking than many realise and really does encourage boys to make the most of the dazzling array of opportunities on offer.

Farleigh School

Red Rice, Andover, Hampshire SP11 7PW

01264 710766
office@farleighschool.co.uk
www.farleighschool.com
RC

Ages: 3–13 (boarding from year 3)
Pupils: 430
Boarders: 75 full/weekly, 33 flexi
Day: £4,905 – £17,865 pa
Boarding: £20,955 – £23,250 pa
(HMF Boarding £19,764 pa)

Headmaster: Since 2004, Father Simon Everson BA Cert in theology (50s). Educated at Caterham School, studied theology at Leeds Collegiate and Ripon College, followed by three year certificate in theology awarded by Oxford University. An Anglican curate and vicar in London for 14 years, he moved to Hurstpierpoint College as senior chaplain in 1996. Following his conversion to Catholicism, he was appointed as chaplain and teacher at Farleigh in 1999, then head five years later.

A modest, softly spoken and self-effacing man, he doesn't engage his inner salesman straight away – prospective parents take note and beware of making snap judgements. Current parents and pupils were falling over themselves to tell us how highly they rate him (one mother phoned three times) and that he is an outstanding head. Whilst watching over every aspect of his charges' development – spiritual, social, moral and academic – he endeavours to dispatch children to their senior schools as educated, fair, kind and generous human beings. Still teaches half the school each week and leads by example, setting high expectations for

manners and behaviour. Positively lights up around his pupils. Firmly believes that the school is there for the whole family and encourages wholesale parental and sibling participation.

Head's wife, Gail, is involved at all levels – a qualified nurse, she works as a learning support teacher in the pre-prep, helps in the nursery, teaches swimming and organises school flowers. They have two daughters, both at senior school.

Entrance: Not selective, pupils join at all stages. In pre-prep, the majority join aged 3; a few more at 5 (mostly from local nurseries), leaving occasional places in years 1 and 2. No formal assessment in pre-prep. Most transfer to the prep, but entry is not automatic (parents are kept well informed). From year 3, pupils come from local primaries or London schools, eg Broomwood Hall, Thomas's, Newton Prep, Fulham Prep and Finton House. One-to-one assessments in reading, writing, spelling, vocabulary and maths ('get to know the child' sessions) and report from current school required.

Numbers capped at 425, therefore priority given to practising Catholics, boarders and siblings, plus children of past pupils. Usually oversubscribed. Means-tested bursaries at head's discretion, 15 per cent discount to boarding children of Forces families.

Exit: Most at 13 – more than a third leave with scholarships and exhibitions: a good tally across the board, with sport and art featuring strongly, plus a healthy scattering of academic, all-rounder and music awards. Catholic schools are obviously popular, eg Downside, Ampleforth, St Mary's Ascot and St Mary's Shaftesbury, although a good number opt for local choices, eg Sherborne, Sherborne Girls', Marlborough College, King Edward VI, Winchester College and Cheltenham Ladies'. A few boys go to Eton, Radley and Harrow each year. A small number (fewer than five) leave at 11, mostly to senior girls' boarding schools, eg Downe House, St Swithun's and Godolphin.

Remarks: Founded in 1953 by Jocelyn Trappes-Lomax as a prep school for Catholic boys, initially based at Farleigh House, residence of the Earl of Portsmouth. Moved to its present home in 1982, a magnificent 19th century Georgian house built by General Webb. Set in 60 tranquil acres of sweeping parkland and has a landscaped arboretum (for history buffs, trees were planted in the troop formation of the Battle of Malplaquet in 1709). It's hard to believe that the A303 threads its way past just five minutes' drive from the school gates (handy for London parents).

The house has been sympathetically adapted to school life and some of its original charm remains in the elegant drawing room, used by the whole school as a common room in the evenings.

Elsewhere the focus is on the modern and practical, both within the main house and without. All new buildings – including new science and food tech building – have been added to one side of the school, thereby preserving swathes of parkland on the other side and woodland to the rear.

Whilst watching over every aspect of his charges' development – spiritual, social, moral and academic – he endeavours to dispatch them as fair, kind and generous human beings

Parents are full of praise for academic approach and achievement. One told us, 'Farleigh fulfils parents' ambitions and then some.' Children are taught by subject specialists from year 5 (French from year 2). Small class sizes – average 15. We observed plenty of sound teaching in core subjects. Maths is set from year 4 (for all other academic subjects from year 6) and parents say teaching is 'exceptional'. Able mathematicians given extra work and compete against other schools (a pupil in year 8 was current maths champion at Dauntsey's). English is also good – 'The teacher is wonderful, really old school' – and clearly effective, as a year 7 pupil won Marlborough's poetry competition. French good and looked like huge fun. Latin taught from year 6 and plenty of it, so those needing higher levels in CE can get there. Whole school follows a course known as The Way, The Truth, The Life in RS (not limited to Catholicism).

Exam preparation for scholarships is excellent. We noticed lots of extra coaching sessions squeezed in for individual year 8 pupils in most subjects (some voluntary). Scholars also have taster sessions in Spanish and Greek. Gifted and talented group meets several times a week for extra activities, eg debating (school has won Marlborough's prep school debating competition several times). All are helped to discover how they learn best. 'Teachers go the extra mile for the children – if a child expresses an interest in something they'll use breaks to teach it,' said one parent. Another told us: 'A work ethic is instilled in year 7 and there are grades every four weeks, so any problems are picked up early.' ICT provision is quirkily good, with a room full of computers and iPads for classroom use. Well-stocked library is run by hugely enthusiastic librarian and pupils can borrow Kindles as well as books, newspapers and magazines.

Exceptional, free SEN provision provided by four members of staff with impressive qualifications (69 pupils on the register when we visited). A few Spanish nationals receive EAL tuition. No surprise that more than a dozen teachers have stayed at Farleigh for more than 10 years – 'Father Simon has created a very happy stable ...The school has a satisfied customer feel'.

Sport takes place on wide expanse of playing fields bordering the front drive of the main house. Games on four afternoons a week and matches on Wednesday and Saturday afternoons. All the usual prep school sports on offer and staff put together three or four teams at the top of the school for boys' rugby, football and cricket and girls' hockey and rounders, with many more lower down the school. 'Everyone gets a chance at sport,' says the school. Annual rugby tour to France for boys in years 7 and 8; senior girls go on hockey and netball tours. Pre-season training is free of charge. Consistently good athletics results, with around 10 children each year representing the school at the National Athletics Championships. Unusual amount of competitive tennis on the calendar, eg house tennis, internal tournaments and matches against other schools. Pupils play tennis all year, with 80 per cent having coaching in the prep school. LTA Mini Tennis Awards scheme followed to year 6 and colours also awarded.

A good range of minor extracurricular sport played on two afternoons a week, eg girls' football, golf, squash, badminton, riding and fishing. Boys who don't enjoy rugby matches can choose to play hockey. School has a large gym and full size indoor swimming pool – boarders have access all week for free swimming. The best are invited to join swim squad; also weekly aqua fit and water polo sessions. Outdoor pool amongst the trees is used in summer.

The arts are thriving – modern, bright art block (two large rooms with high ceilings for painting, ceramics etc) doubtless contributes to the healthy number of art scholarships gained by pupils, who can use it whenever they like in free time. Well-equipped DT room next door.

Music block is somewhat less spacious – rooms for individual tuition and practice either side of a single corridor, with space for ensemble rehearsals on entry. Some 300 pupils have private music lessons, with over 60 learning more than one instrument. Singing is a popular choice and nearly 80 have voice lessons (we noticed good exam results here, with half the total number of distinctions awarded for voice). Lots of singing on the timetable, eg daily in chapel, weekly hymn practice and in class music lessons. Chapel choir is auditioned and occasionally tours abroad. Individual music lessons rotate through the timetable (year 8 pupils don't miss academic lessons) and practice timetabled for all. All the usual instruments on offer, as well as harp and bagpipes. Two further choirs, a school orchestra and rock academy, plus around 20 ensembles which rehearse weekly and perform music from jazz to chamber repertoire. Senior jazz band, The Thundering Herd, has played twice

at the Edinburgh Festival. School musicians give seven big annual concerts, including a jazz dinner night. Music theory is offered as an extracurricular activity. Father Simon even makes music part of his morning assemblies, eg listening to Maria Callas.

School theatre is well equipped, with semi-professional lighting and sound and tiered seating (a good view of the stage at last). Two annual school productions include a year 8 musical (The Sound of Music, Bugsy Malone) and alternate productions by years 3 and 4 (Alice in Wonderland) or years 5 and 6 (Annie). LAMDA speech and drama lessons available and pupils can take exams if they wish. Optional creative activities include ballroom dancing, pottery and toy making.

Approximately one-third of the school boards, with flexi boarding available from year 3 up to the summer term of year 7, when families choose between day and full boarding. The majority choose to board in preparation for senior school. About 30 children stay in school every weekend and the full complement on the four 'all in' weekends every year.

Boarding provision is well organised (junior and senior dorms for boys and girls) and the house parents are 'brilliant at instilling spiritual values and manners'. Bigger rooms with more beds for the younger ones, shrinking to doubles for older children, and quite the cleanest and most orderly bathrooms we've yet to see, with a place for everything and everything in its place (possibly for our benefit, but suspect probably not). A really lovely touch is that some single rooms available for exam candidates, so they get a good night's sleep before a big day. Not a lot of room for storing personal possessions in dorms, so most clothing is stored in communal (and very tidy) cupboards and drawers, which lead into large senior common rooms with lots of home comforts, eg computers, TV, squashy sofas and toasters (healthy bowls of fruit here too).

School food is excellent, served cafeteria style in a bright, welcoming dining room. Even though we were slightly late for lunch, still plenty of choice and the food was very good, with fresh fruit on offer for pudding daily. School chef is a bit of a local hero, we gather, not least because he treats boarders to Dinner Night twice a term – pupils dress up and sit down to a themed dinner, which can be anything from Indian to Spanish. Junior boarders get the chance to cook every Friday, when they become kitchen sous chefs and prepare supper for the whole school.

Everyone is encouraged to 'look beyond themselves' by helping others eg hosting children with severe learning difficulties in school each week

Masses to do during evenings and weekends (including for day children staying late), from cub scouts, zumba and tennis to band practice and street dance. Acres of space to play in outside, either at Fortress Farleigh (traditional play area on the edge of the woods) or deeper into the trees, where pupils are free to roam, build dens etc.

Pastoral care praised time and time again by parents, as was inclusive ethos – 'The school includes my family in their big family,' a parent said. Staff too are welcomed into the fold – all staff members (not just teachers) belong to a house. As well as fostering community spirit, head cares passionately about behaviour and standards – 'Father Simon instils good moral values..The children become self-regulating'. Pupils confirmed zero tolerance of bullying and that kindness to others is prized above intellectual prowess. Everyone is encouraged to 'look beyond themselves' by helping others, eg hosting children with severe learning difficulties in school each week, helping at a local food bank and actively supporting a charity for street children in Colombia – 'It keeps hearts large,' said a parent.

The Catholic faith is at the school's core and Sunday mass is open to all. As well as preparing for first communion and confirmation, children can

go on (short) religious retreats; an annual gathering for Patronal Feast Day. Head aims to keep faith both enjoyable and contemporary, eg interpreting the book of Genesis through Holst's The Planets. Members of other churches stress they 'never feel discriminated against for not being Catholic' and 'there is no default setting to send children to Catholic schools'. Perhaps most important is that the school's caring side ensures 'every child will leave with the sense that they have a strength ... not always the usual – it could be something unusual'.

Pre-prep housed in a super building on the fringes of the main campus and is 'beautifully run and thoughtfully managed'. Kindergarten off to one side, away from the hurly-burly. Children looked happy and engaged. Head of pre-prep made us smile by wishing aloud for more room – in fact the building is positively spacious, with four classrooms for years 1 and 2, another for reception, its own library and four separate play areas, not to mention masses of storage space for wellies, bookbags, coats and trainers.

Children in pre-prep walk to the main school for lunch and use other facilities, including the swimming pool and tennis courts. Swimming lessons and ballet timetabled for everyone all year; tennis coaching and football from year 1. After-school clubs include football, cricket, hockey, rounders and woodland games. A free violin taster group each term. French taught from year 2. Staff put on an annual summer concert, spring term production and Christmas show. Father Simon takes assembly one day a week to present children with 'good worker' certificates.

Parents are a harmonious mix of Londoners, locals and some Forces – 'There is a real mixture of people, some Sloaney and some not so; the Forces families are taken very seriously'. Lots of siblings, a few Spanish nationals and overseas British complete the mix. School escorts London-based pupils on the train to and from town on exeats and at half-term. Overseas boarders often stay with local families on exeat weekends (matrons help to coordinate arrangements). Pupils are open, honest, thoroughly genuine young people who clearly love their school and have respect and regard for each other. The fact that the Farleigh Society (old boys and girls) publishes a 25-page newsletter every year is proof that strong bonds are forged here; these often continue on through senior school and beyond.

Former pupils include Lord Stafford, Marquis of Bute, journalist Craig Brown, actor Rupert Everett, rugby player Hugh Vyvyan, TV presenter Hugh Cordey and climber Tarka l'Herpinière.

Every so often, we visit a school which is enjoying a real purple patch and getting most things right. Parental plaudits say it more succinctly than we could – 'It hasn't sacrificed values for academic successes,' and 'They are unwavering in their advice, honest and direct.' When it comes to the head, parents can verge on the evangelical, such as, 'Father Simon is absolutely extraordinary ... on a pedestal with so many parents'. We'll let them off – were we parents here, we rather think we would say the same. Not perhaps for anyone unwilling to buy into school's ethos, but clearly most see the light, and we suspect that this outstanding prep school will become even more sought after than it already is.

Forres Sandle Manor School

Sandle Manor, Fordingbridge, Hampshire SP6 1NS

01425 653181
office@fsmschool.com
www.fsmschool.com
C of E

Ages: 3–13 (boarding from 7)
Pupils: 220
Boarders: 75 full, 25 weekly
Day: £8,010 – £16,410 pa
Boarding: £18,390 – £22,410 pa

Headmaster: Since 2010, Mr Mark Hartley (40s), previously deputy head at Winchester House, Brackley, and before that housemaster at Mount House School, Tavistock. Studied biological sciences, now teaches PSHE to older ones and maths tutors those who struggle. Started his working life as an insurance underwriter, met wife Beth at a 21st birthday party and shortly afterwards discovered his true vocation – teaching. Three children later, Beth has returned to her former stomping ground with responsibility for marketing and promoting FSM – though we hear bottles of champagne, sent to parents, for recruiting newbies, are a thing of the past. Described as fresh, fun and funny by youngsters, Mr Hartley is something of an action man, enjoying hockey, cycling, kayaking and climbing. Inheriting a school that required fine tuning rather than wholesale overhaul, he has tinkered at the edges: tightening up reporting procedures, smartening the kids, introducing a parent portal and encouraging more competition via house events. So far so good on the parental front, 'He's livened things up, smartened up the children but not pushed things too far'.

Entrance: Most at age 3 or 8, boarders from 7. Non-selective but works from premise of 'Will a child be happy here?' Stomping grounds include New Forest, Avon Valley and environs of Cranborne. Predominantly white British with a handful of short-stay pupils from Norway and Spain. Boarders a 50-50 mix of expats, mostly Forces, and locals. Around half are first time buyers. Start when you like, if room (pressure on boarding places – must pay for full even if weekly board). Means-tested bursaries and discount for Forces.

Exit: Over 25 different schools in the last four years, including Canford, Bryanston, Clayesmore, King's College Taunton, the Sherborne schools, Eton, Winchester, Marlborough, Stowe and Uppingham. Over half won scholarships in 2015. Eminent old boys: Michael Foot (Forres), Alec Guinness (Sandle Manor).

Remarks: Set in child-friendly grounds, centred around an elegant Jacobean manor, a stone's throw from the New Forest. It's hard to imagine a more captivating environment for the tweenager. Delightful pre-prep with inspirational head who ensures learning is child-led, fun but pacey. Super pirate ship playground and forest school ensure year round fresh air and plenty of boisterous play.

We especially liked the 'naughty bus' that hides on a daily basis and had been found encased in ice

All 6 year olds screened for reading delay – those found in need are given booster sessions till back on track. 'We never guarantee a child will improve but are yet to have one that doesn't.' Fans of Ruth Miskin's Read Write Inc, which promises every child a reader by age 6. Imaginative teaching and learning captivates the spellbound youngsters. We especially liked the 'naughty bus' that hides on a daily basis and had been found encased in ice on our visit. Even an errant bus can't compete with the excitement of making stinky, brown poo – a simulated investigation which begins with crushing of digestive biscuits (to mirror crunching of teeth), mixed with water (replacing saliva), washing up liquid and vinegar added (enzyme and stomach acid), then squeezed through grandma's stocking, simulating the intestine and final movement: learning at its gory, imaginative, and experiential best.

Fairly relaxed approach to learning in the prep school – not a soft option, but perhaps uniquely, youngsters say they'd like more prep sooner, 'The year 8 workload is a shock and we could be better prepared for it'. Gifted children pepped up via PACE activities; some, such as Green Giant, an eco project examining biodiversity and recycling with hands-on fun – chopping bamboo, mixing smoothies and making wool – open to all.

Ennui not an option – daily sport and afternoon activities as diverse as scuba diving, golf and banana boating, alongside trips to everywhere from Iceland to Africa

Learning support encompasses wide range of cognitive ability. 'We have children who cannot read/decode but are L4 and L5 national curriculum in some subjects, so we have to help and support'. Parents enthuse, 'My child struggled at his previous school, but since he came to FSM and got the support he needed, he has never stopped smiling.' Another added, 'It's a long day yet my child is never tired. Somehow they work it just right.'

Most teachers deliver multi-sensory lessons geared to active learning. English, drama and science top the popularity polls; 'Our science teacher respects us – he's not patronising, we do lots of experiments, it's fun and there is practically no writing,' cooed one boy. History, geography and RE depart from confines of CE, a conscious decision to develop skills of enquiry and investigation. Testing topics include Smuggling in Fordingbridge. Senior schools approve and see some seriously good work – not that fun doesn't come into it: we spotted a wall of history jokes, our favourite, 'Who built the Ark? I have Noah idea!' Post CE youngsters hone their practical and problem-solving skills – changing a tyre, wiring a plug, ironing shirts or finding the scariest ride at Thorpe Park.

Most lessons take place in The Barn with scattering of specialist buildings for art (we loved the bronze Olympian action sculpture), DT and music. Sports hall and climbing wall on wish list, but grounds contain heated outdoor swimming pool, courts for netball and tennis plus myriad of pitches. Ennui not an option – daily sport and afternoon activities as diverse as scuba diving, golf (even for the tinies) and banana boating, alongside annual trips and tours to everywhere from Iceland to Africa. Project week and cub-camp, with Boy's Own firelighting, knife-skills, cooking and camp craft, perennially popular. All lower school do ballet (a good way to spot potential dancers and dyspraxics) – optional classes for seniors. We listened to the fledgling Exterminators jamming and spotted imaginatively named groups, eg Flute Pastilles, and fabulous fiddlers. School has a competitive edge: thrice finalists in the Junior Memory Championships and recent debut as finalists in Kids Lit.

Seemingly parents equally competitive when it comes to teams, with boarder parents saying, 'Local parents seem to have everything sewn up – it can be difficult for the boarding fraternity to get a look in, especially for parent fixtures,' adding, 'Communication could be better – they're great at reporting on the kids but not on activities: we need time to schedule and plan'. Parents kept busy with quiz nights, football, hockey, plus 'maths for mums and dads', courtesy of Friends of FSM – hardly surprising they jest that an in-school Costa Coffee concession is on their wish list.

Meals are table served in one of two dining rooms, the mantra to always try a little, including experimental offerings such as beetroot brownies and soup concoctions dreamt up by the youngsters. Sports teas are legendary and, as we flicked the last melt-in-the-mouth crumbs from our lips, could only nod in heartfelt agreement as our trusty guide declared them 'outstanding!'

A boarding school that welcomes day children – 'It's a family-friendly community, flexible when we need it'. Fairly healthy weekend boarding numbers though parents of full boarders (75, compared with some 25 weekly) say to check the age and gender of those who stay, if this is important to you. Cheery boarding accommodation with ongoing renovations – though we were a tad overwhelmed by the swathes of bubble-gum pink adorning the girls' dorms. We loved the 'getting better bay' with healthy doses of TLC for the homesick and panaceas for the poorly. Seemingly all want to try boarding, so expect up to 11 per dorm and the odd grumble that it can be difficult to escape, 'Sometimes you need time or space but they can be hard to find'. Nothing too heavy-handed on discipline front: naughty boarders are red-carded and miss the coveted Wednesday special boarding night or put on dreaded laundry duty, sorting socks, folding shirts. Matrons praised, 'You can tell them things because they have seen it all before and know what to do', ground-staff lauded as cheery and fun, 'They have a nickname for everyone'.

Focuses on developing happy, confident children. Takes a broad range, delivers the goods, 'One minute you are watching a really talented child, the next someone who is just keen to join in'. Children are respected and 'feel part of the gang,' say parents. Children candid, 'It can be a bit difficult for those who are naturally loners or need quiet space.' Not posh or pushy. A happy, homely school with a sunny disposition, going from strength to strength. Turns out friendly, confident, quietly ambitious youngsters.

Godstowe Preparatory School

Shrubbery Road, High Wycombe, Buckinghamshire HP13 6PR

01494 529273
registrar@godstowe.org
www.godstowe.org

Ages: 3–13 (boarding from 7)
Pupils: 440 (320 girls in prep, co-ed pre-prep)
Boarders: 100 full and flexi
Day: £9,690 – £14,895 pa
Boarding: plus £6,990 pa

Headmaster: Since 2006, Mr David Gainer (50s). Educated at Claires Court, Maidenhead and Belmont Abbey in Herefordshire, followed by St Mary's University College, Twickenham, where he studied maths and drama. Began career at Llanarth Court Prep in South Wales then returned to alma mater Belmont Abbey as housemaster, followed by three years at Forest Grange Prep in Horsham as deputy head, before taking up first headship at Belmont Prep near Dorking in 1991.

Lives in the thick of it in the main school building with wife Cathy, the school registrar. According to one parent, 'if you could choose a headmaster for your son or daughter, it would be Mr Gainer.' Girls and parents alike comment on his energy, enthusiasm and hands-on presence around the school (he attends all sports matches and eats dinner with the boarders every night) – and they're not the only ones: he was recently named best head of a prep school by Tatler. Praise indeed. Commands respect yet obvious affection from pupils – appears truly in loco parentis. Parents are 'hooked' as soon as they meet him – and no wonder: he lets them have his home telephone number.

Passionate about the benefits of years 7 and 8, the head describes these years as 'dynamic bubble wrap' – keeping the girls in a nurturing environment while they mature, yet allowing them genuine responsibility, freedom and leadership opportunities at the top of the school. Highly focused on personal development and believes that academic success depends on it. According to the head, Godstowe encourages 'everyone to aim high, whatever their ability and potential.'

Pioneered a system of deferred senior school places, 'brokering deals' to secure girls' places at 11 to transfer at 13. Strong relationships with senior schools borne out by the fact that 25 schools choose to send their head as representative to Godstowe's biannual senior school fair.

Entrance: Despite Godstowe's growing popularity, head is adamant that it will remain a 'first come first served', non-selective school. Majority intake

(about 80 per cent) at 7 from its own pre-prep, The Lodge, with girls joining all the way through to year 6 from a variety of local prep and state schools, and boarders joining from further afield in the upper years. Boarding can be full time or flexible with many day girls choosing to try it in years 7 and 8 as a taster for senior school.

Exit: Not a specific feeder, with alumni most years heading off to some 20 different secondaries. Several each year to Wycombe Abbey, Cheltenham Ladies, Queen Anne's and Downe House; others to eg St George's Ascot, Rugby, Wellington, Stowe, Haileybury, Tudor Hall, Oundle, Uppingham, Pipers Corner, St Edward's, Bradfield.

Remarks: England's first girls' boarding prep school and Enid Blyton's inspiration (though not the only contender) for Malory Towers, purpose built in 1900. The grounds make excellent use of a hilly, if a little blustery, site overlooking High Wycombe, with the original pretty Virginia creeper-clad buildings now housing years 3 to 8, plus The Lodge and nursery buildings. The few boys in pre-prep, mostly siblings, move on at the age of 7.

The airy new double height reception building (buzzing at pick-up and drop-off times) is a modern addition to the more rustic Victorian buildings and has a gallery-like atmosphere, setting the tone for the rather artsy feel of the whole school. Other recent revamps include the dining room (we highly recommend the lasagne), early years centre, art room and food technology centre, opened in 2007 by Raymond Blanc. There's also a new £2m sports hall for eg indoor tennis, hockey and lacrosse plus dance and gymnastics to compensate for the antiquated and somewhat uninviting swimming pool building, chilly water and all. The school says it has

made significant investments in this in recent years but it is far from being its star attraction.

Definitely not a school placing importance on hushed tones, although good manners are notably present. Girls dash about chatting noisily between lessons, picking up considerable speed when heading to the dining room for lunch. Posters all over the school that indoctrinate pupils to be happy, confident and successful are clearly doing the trick.

Dedicated sewing room where girls knock up the odd wedding gown for the year 8 fashion show

Non-selective it may be, but success is in the air here. Minority (about 15 per cent) peel off at 11 to local schools (parents have to 'opt in' to 11+), but unlike many prep schools in the area which hothouse pupils for the sought-after Bucks grammars, this is a true 3-13 establishment, feeding its post-CE alumni into a heady mix of top day and boarding indies, many with scholarships. Which are pretty abundant, by the way, with the current record for one year standing at 26, to 17 different schools. Head puts this down to 'quality teaching' and the fact that girls are 'led rather than pushed through the curriculum'. He is proud not to share the pushy reputation of some of his competition.

French is taught from reception, Latin and Spanish from year 5 in creatively themed classrooms. Classes in pre-prep school 'subtly' streamed, with a maximum class size of 18. Formal streaming from year 6 for English, maths and French. Girls stay in form rooms for lessons in years 3 and 4, after which they start to move around the school for individual subjects.

General acceptance that everyone learns differently and SEN is all in a day's work rather than marginalised. Two dedicated SEN staff in place and an excellent EAL programme – mostly for those boarders from the Far East, Spain and Nigeria, with girls' needs assessed upon entry to the school and timetabled to meet their specific requirements. Boarders' prep takes place from 4.30pm to 6.30pm, although an hour of this is often taken up with an enrichment activity. Day girls report homework levels to be acceptable.

Creative pursuits are well catered for, with a dedicated sewing room in CDT where girls knock up the odd wedding gown for the year 8 fashion show. Some 300 girls learn musical instruments and practise daily in bright, well-equipped studios. Pupils' artistic endeavours are displayed throughout the school – and with good reason. They look more like GSCE work, thanks to the inspirational head of art, who specialises in 3D work.

The art department, with its gleaming new extension, has the wow factor in terms of space and light, as does the work on show there, from glazed pottery meals on plates to life-size papier mâché humans – not a still life fruit bowl in sight. Taught by specialists from the word go, senior girls win art scholarships every year, but importantly parents report that a passion for creativity has been bred into the core of the school and latent talent is eeked out of those who didn't know they had it.

Parents say the standard of music is 'incredible', with one slipping in that the girls' achievements and public performances by far outstrip those at their brothers' schools. All pupils are encouraged to participate from the age of 3 in regular recitals and choir is compulsory in years 3 to 6. Revamped JK Theatre is used for music concerts, after-school clubs, art exhibitions, assemblies and parents' evenings.

Sports lessons are four times a week, with the usual suspects (netball, lacrosse and hockey) taking centre pitch – all to a high competitive standard. Athletics, rounders and swimming are also on offer, as are ballet, gymnastics and dance. Parents of children in larger year groups occasionally grumble that the A and B teams are a bit exclusive, with not everyone getting a go, but the head is keen to introduce more teams and by and large most girls are able to compete at some level, often with winning results.

Boarding facilities have a real home from home feel, with bedrooms (sleeping between four and eight) rather than dorms, cosy sitting rooms and homely kitchens. All have their own large gardens, with swings and other outdoor equipment.

Housemistresses are non-teaching staff, leaving them free to focus on girls' pastoral care. Pupils are charming and poised without a hint of precociousness and describe their typical peer as 'kind and happy'. Early drop-off plus breakfast (7.30am) and late pick-up plus supper (6.30pm) is available for day girls at low cost.

The mobile phone arms race was stopped by the clever acquisition of 100 bog standard phones (yes, these do still exist) into which girls can insert their own SIM cards to call home. Thursdays are 'no go gadget' evenings in the boarding houses to further encourage those old fashioned skills, reading, conversation and game playing. Girls say the best thing about Godstowe is 'everyone is happy all the time' – future careers in PR await.

The 'enrichment curriculum' – that's afterschool clubs in old money – offers up to 50 free options for two hours a day from 4.30pm. These range from the traditional sports, LAMDA and wind band to the more diverse knitting, prop-making and cross-stitch, with up to 100 girls staying for these. Boarders benefit from a buzzing spectrum of activities at weekends too (rarely fewer than 50 girls in), many of which take place off site (bowling, skating, theatre, cinema etc).

Post CE, year 8s are given a lifestyle crash course to prepare them for a less cosseted existence. Includes classes in self-defence, internet safety and relationships, charitable works, trips out, visiting lecturers and, in a surprisingly retro twist, a hair and beauty day, which seems a little old fashioned but, hey ho, girls will be girls.

Headington School

Headington Road, Oxford, Oxfordshire OX3 7TD

01865 759113
admissions@headington.org
www.headington.org
C of E

Ages: 11–18
Pupils: 812; sixth form: 270
Boarders: 218 full and weekly
Day: £15,900 – £17,385 pa
Boarding: £26,235 – £33,945 pa

Head: Since 2011, Mrs Caroline Jordan (50s). A local girl, she was educated at St Helen and St Katharine in Abingdon, read geology at Oxford and did her PGCE (science) at Manchester. Previously head of St George's Ascot and before that spent 10 years at Wycombe Abbey where she was head of sixth form and deputy senior housemistress. Lives on site; married to Richard, a company director, one adult son, two border collies. Currently chair of the Girls' Schools Association Education Committee, in

2016 (after extremely busy centenary year in 2015) she becomes president of the whole GSA.

Before going into teaching Mrs Jordan ran her own business. She says that heads 'need those skills'; they do, and indeed we could imagine her as one of the dragons on Dragons' Den – not that she's scary, but she is direct and, well, businesslike. As one parent said, 'definitely not fluffy'. She's forward thinking and ambitious, hyper alert to social and educational change and ready for whatever the future holds in these areas. Parents describe her as 'really on the ball' and 'ahead of the game' and are mostly in favour of the changes she's making. 'She's mad about rowing,' we were told; 'you should hear her shouting from the riverbank when her crew are racing!' Another was impressed by Mrs J's energetic networking when she accompanied crews to a competition in the US. 'She took the girls round as many universities as she could, making contacts.' We anticipate US college scholarship offers rolling in for Headington rowers.

Parts of the school are being seriously revamped – not just bricks and mortar but also Headington's Achilles' heel (rowing excepted): sport. Mrs Jordan is frank about this; historically lack of opportunities and support meant that girls had to join outside clubs to progress in team games such as hockey. A complete overhaul of facilities and teaching will see the 'inspirational' head of rowing become director of sport, no doubt expected to do his magic in other departments.

Favourite childhood reads were Dorothy Dunnett's Scottish historical novels but these days Mrs J enjoys quick crime thrillers on her Kindle. Down time is spent 'mixing concrete' – she and her husband are restoring a 500-year-old house in France.

Academic matters: In 2015, 86 per cent A*/A at GCSE. At A level, 64 per cent A*/A. Maths, economics, sciences, fine art and English literature notably successful. Languages don't seem to attract many (as is so often the case).

At recent Student Robotics Competition, the Headington team designed, built and programmed an autonomous robot from scratch to become champions

More than respectable IB average of 38 in 2015. Take-up for IB roughly 20 per cent and growing – Mrs J certainly thinks it is a more secure option at a time when 'A levels are up in the air.' She's particularly keen on the IB theory of knowledge course and this is now being offered lower down the school. We're sure the girls benefit but it's also a canny and not so subliminal bit of IB marketing.

Gone are the days when girls ploughed through up to 13 GCSEs; it's 10 now with increasing number of IGCSEs. Choice of one language from French, Spanish and German; surprisingly there's no Mandarin GCSE although it's offered as an after-school club, as is ancient Greek. All do Latin in first two years.

We could imagine her as one of the dragons on Dragons' Den – not that she's scary, but she is direct and, well, businesslike

Twenty-nine subjects to chose from at A level including fine art, photography, computing, law, psychology and government and politics. EPQ encouraged but there's 'not much time' in term and research and writing during the summer holidays post-AS exams can be a big ask. Oxbridge, medicine and veterinary hopefuls get application support and so do girls applying for architecture. The latter receive specialist lectures and help with portfolio preparation – must account for the unusually high number of Headington girls accepted to study this over-subscribed subject.

Special mention here for ICT – girls learn to code in Python and apply this and other skills to robotics. Not content with winning 'best rookies' and 'first moves' prizes at recent Student Robotics Competition, the Headington team (one of just two all girl teams) designed, built and programmed an autonomous robot from scratch to become champions. 'It sent a real buzz through the whole school,' the head girl told us proudly.

School says it makes 'reasonable adjustments' for girls with mild SEN including one-to-one weekly support for girls in the lower school and drop-in sessions for the middle school and sixth form. EAL tuition also provided.

Games, options, the arts: The 'inspirational' leadership of Headington's South African head of rowing has brought the school national and international success on the water (most recently the J8 crew won the Henley women's regatta). Girls start training in the summer term of year 7 and some parents think this is too young (boys generally don't begin until age 13); school says the programme is run in conjunction with Oxford Brookes and everything is very carefully monitored. Compared to the riverside facilities enjoyed by other notable Oxfordshire rowing schools such as Abingdon, Headington has it tough – they row out of a couple of portakabins shared with St Edward's School. 'Our success is all down to inspiration,' says Mrs Jordan.

School boasts over 30 different sporting activities (many are lunchtime or after-school clubs) including fencing, synchronised swimming, dance and cheerleading. It's also pretty horsey, despite the urban setting. 'It's a side branch of the Pony Club,' we were told. What if you don't have a horse? We asked. 'Oh, someone will lend you one,' came the airy reply. Girls compete in blue Headington silks and bring back plenty of rosettes.

Mrs J acknowledges that there's still work to do when it comes to 'sport for all'. 'Every girl should have her own regime to stay fit and healthy, whether or not that includes competitive sport. We should expect these things from a school.' She wants team sport to be 'for everybody', not just the chosen few. With this determination and the new facilities taking shape in the grounds, Mrs Jordan's ideal of 'scholar athletes' may soon be realised.

Budding artists, actors and musicians are spoilt for choice – facilities include a 240 seat theatre complete with box office and professional back-stage team. The seriously well-equipped music school, opened by Brian Eno, a former parent, pro-vides ample teaching, practice and recording space. Girls must participate in some musical activity during their first two years – the emphasis is on taking part and most choirs, orchestras and ensem-bles are audition free. Music for all is the message with break and lunchtime concerts and, recently, a Garsington opera workshop. Pupils' paintings of a very high standard are proudly displayed all over the school, including the head's office. A level results for fine art should also be put in a frame – almost every candidate is awarded A*. As we marvelled at the work in the splendid double height art building our guide confessed that it was 'a bit overwhelming for those who can't draw.'

CCF (from year 10 upwards) is 'huge' and girls love the camps – whether in Dartmoor, Scotland or the school grounds. D of E attracts good numbers too. Tempting range of trips from geography in the Alps and diving in the Red Sea to expeditions and charity work in Ethiopia, Kenya and Zanzibar.

Boarding: About a third of pupils board, either full time or weekly. Head is not a fan of flexi board-ing (describes it as 'bed blocking') but school may accommodate pupils for one offs (plays, trips) or family emergencies. Year group boarding houses are cheerful with plenty of home comforts. Most have double study bedrooms with good storage and room mates are swapped around each term (sixth form can choose). For those who don't go home on Fridays there seems to be plenty on offer – we saw sign up sheets for strawberry picking, a day trip to Brighton and a make up workshop. Sixth form boarders have kitchens and may cook for them-selves as long as they ask in advance – enables house parents to be sure girls aren't missing meals. They can also go to parties and stay over with school friends – parents are emailed for permission.

Background and atmosphere: Founded in 1915 by a group of evangelical Christians to provide a 'sound education for girls to fit them for the demands and opportunities likely to arise after the war.'

Occupied various houses in the area, trading up as it grew from 18 to today's 1,000 (including 280 in prep school). Present main school was built in the 1930s in a sharp-edged, no frills style described (rather kindly) as neo-Georgian. Set in 23 acres just off Oxford's busy London Road, it's right next to the hospitals and ambulance sirens lend it an extra urban edge. Despite its town site there's a sense of space, and plenty of greenery remains undevel-oped. Newer buildings are very well appointed, especially the Diamond Jubilee Building – home to large, modern teaching rooms, ICT and that award-winning robot.

A brief introduction to the principles of critical theory and they were off, producing Marxist and feminist readings of Where the Wild Things Are

Lessons we observed were challenging but not intimidating, girls were contributing enthusias-tically and seemed keen to have a go and share opinions. In an A level English 'taster' class we were impressed by how quickly students got to grips with new ideas. A brief introduction to the principles of critical theory and they were off, pro-ducing Marxist and feminist readings of Where the Wild Things Are. The library is all you could ask for and dedicated librarians also provide a cut-tings service – filing cabinets hold the latest journal or newspaper material for over 250 subjects. This resource, hand in hand with Google, introduces girls – particularly sixth formers tackling the EPQ – to university style research techniques. 'They know everything here', said our guides.

Pastoral care, well-being and discipline: Parents and girls we spoke to were generally very posi-tive about pastoral care, but this is a large, busy school and we did wonder how quickly a quiet or unhappy child would be noticed. This is where the sixth form prefects come in. Each class of around 20 is allocated two prefects, whose job is not only to be a friendly non-teacher face, but also to get to know the girls and alert staff if they suspect a girl is struggling socially or in any other way. There is also a drop-in counsellor. Prefects are elected by peers and candidates for head girl and deputies have to make speeches at hustings before those on the chosen short list go before senior staff for final interviews. Win or lose, it's all very good experi-ence. Sixth form common room was looking rather forlorn when we visited, but it's since had a make over and is now, apparently, much more inviting.

Some concerns expressed about the lunch arrangements – feeding 800 girls in an hour and a half must be quite a challenge. Sittings are by year group, but with only five minutes in between, one pupil acknowledged that lunch break was 'a bit of a mosh.' Staff 'bouncers' are positioned outside for crowd control and 'when it's raining you push.' All good fun when you're used to it but 'quite intimidating' for newbies. Once you're in, though, food is seriously good, varied and plentiful. We enjoyed a delicious meal in the large, modern dining hall decorated with huge canvases of old school photos – all the food is serve yourself and girls help themselves to as much as they like of everything.

Pupils and parents: 'Not too posh' – nice, swishy-haired girls who don't seem to kick too hard against uniform, skirt length and make up regulations. Most families from Oxford's private and public sector employers – medics, lawyers, academics, IT professionals. Head says, 'girls understand that parents are making an investment'. Growing cohort of weekly boarders commute from London on the Oxford tube (stops outside). International students from 47 countries – IB and rowing reputation are attracting more Europeans. Zealous overseas recruitment in the past led to large groups of one nationality (evident when we visited the sixth form Costa café). Parents say that this has been 'a big issue' and they would like to see better integration. Head acknowledges these concerns and says things are now being managed. OGs include Baroness Young, Julia Somerville, Lady Longford, Christina Onassis, Emma Watson and Lily van den Broecke

Entrance: Several applicants for every place (but bear in mind that girls will be sitting for other schools too). For entry at 11+ girls sit papers in English, maths and non-verbal reasoning and have an interview. Prep school candidates (13+ entry) come for an interview and taster day after the pre-test. Sixth form entrants sit exams at Headington in the November before their proposed entry.

Exit: Inevitably some girls depart post-GCSE, lured to local co-ed sixth forms, although we hear that it's not uncommon for there to be a return to the fold after a few weeks. Nearly all sixth form leavers go on to university, including usually several to Oxbridge (none in 2015); LSE, UCL, Durham, Bristol, Bath, Brimingham trending currently. Surprisingly few to US colleges, though rowing scholarships to Duke and Yale in 2015, one off to study musical theatre at the Urdang Academy, three to art foundation courses and one to Leith's Cookery School. Occasional one to prestigious work based training such as the Ernst and Young school leaver programme.

Money matters: Academic, music, art, drama and sports scholarships (£300 per year). Means-tested bursaries of up to 100 per cent of fees plus help for Forces and clergy. Of course there are extras but parents told us that these weren't unreasonable; they also said that they approved of the sensible and inexpensive uniform.

Remarks: This dynamic school is going from strength to strength. True to its founders' aims, nearly a century on it is still sending out girls ready and able to tackle whatever the future has to hold.

Heathfield School

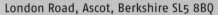

London Road, Ascot, Berkshire SL5 8BQ

01344 898343
registrar@heathfieldschool.net
www.heathfieldschool.net
C of E

Ages: 11–18
Pupils: 200; sixth form: 60
Boarders: nearly all full
Day: £22,680 – £23,310 pa
Boarding: £32,400 – £33,300 pa

Headmistress: Since 2009, Mrs Jo Heywood BSc PGCE (40s); a chemist. Began her teaching career in a large comprehensive in Surrey, thence to St Mary's, Ascot – a shuttlecock's flight away. She stayed there for eight happy years as teacher of chemistry and head of house. Concerned that she should not become 'complacent', she moved down the road to Heathfield in 2005 to become deputy head (pastoral). When her predecessor became ill,

Mrs Heywood became acting head, and the subsequent decision of the school's governors to appoint her to the headship was a popular one with, it seems, the entire school community. 'She's so Heathfield,' one girl enthused – 'she understands the homeliness and the traditions.'

And it is not hard to see why they wanted her. She is the fourth head in 10 years and is in it for the long run. She 'knew everyone' and was ideally

placed to bring ambitious aspirations in terms of academic attainment, stability and personal commitment to a school she already loved. She provided, however, more than much-needed continuity. She is a warm, commonsensical head with youthful enthusiasm, generosity of spirit and a firm belief in what Heathfield is all about, which are just what's needed here. 'She's lovely,' said a parent. And she has taste – her refurbished room is peachy and beautiful: hits exactly the right note. Heathfield survived the previous difficult decade in remarkably good shape. A good long spell of steady renewal and growth is already proving successful in restoring this unique school back to full health and stability.

Academic matters: Warm, friendly and positive atmosphere, striving for every girl to be the best she can be. Small class sizes enable girls to thrive. Offers a wide range of subjects at GCSE, including accounting, further mathematics, classical civilisation and Latin. Mathematics popular and successful. Creative talent is encouraged with art and design, textiles, photography. Single sciences, geography, religious studies, art and design and drama stand out; also strong English and mathematics. In 2015, 40 per cent A*/A grades at GCSE; at A level, 40 per cent A*/A and 70 per cent A*-B.

New STEM (science, technology, engineering and maths) building opened in 2015.

Games, options, the arts: Everything done with energy, enthusiasm and friendly collaboration. Core sports are netball, lacrosse, tennis and athletics but loads else on offer, in particular the school's equestrian strength. 'Around 15-20 now play polo,

we have some fantastic show jumpers and around 15 per cent now ride,' says Mrs Heywood. Team successes in several sports and notable individual stars include an international skier, national skating and lacrosse players. 'We will always help if they need to go away to play their sport,' says the head, as if it were quite the most normal thing in the world.

Excellent support with no rigidity – 'If the dog or the horse has died, we're not so Dickensian that we won't let them out for pastoral reasons'

Many school trips and tours to exotic places. The inviting cookery room encourages girls to roll up their sleeves. Everyone learns cookery in the first three years, no-one does in years 10 and 11 (except for leisure) but very popular Leith's course available in the sixth. The cookery room is also used imaginatively – we observed a biology class learning about micro-organisms in food. Yum!

The school's theatre (opened by Mother Winsome, late of St Mary's Wantage and diplomatically named St Mary's) seats 300 and includes drama room, music rooms (including music technology) and attractive conference room. Drama is adventurous and strong, considering the small forces available. Theatre balcony cleverly overlooks sports field – rather like the grandstand at Lord's. Textiles and photography are exceptional and art in general is varied, imaginative and surely outstanding, again, for so small a school. Heathfield is the only school in the country to have a partnership with University of the Arts London.

Masses to do at weekends, though, according to parents; 'this is when good friendships become great'.

Boarding: Heathfield now the only small full boarding school for girls in the UK. Rightly proud of this unique status and all that it offers to the right family. Numbers are on the rise – though not too much. Boarding is good – everyone who wants to has a single room from year 10 upwards and dorms for those below. In the year 10, you get a trial week in the upper sixth bungalow – such fun and sense of independence engendered by this canny move that very few leave after GCSEs: they can't wait to experience the freedom and fun the top year enjoys. They are allowed to cook their own meals and do their own washing – quelle joie!

Excellent pastoral support within the full boarding system but no rigidity – 'If the dog or the horse has died, we're not so Dickensian that we won't let them out for pastoral reasons'. Girls enthuse – 'Our house mothers are so lovely!' Friendships lauded – 'We all get on – you have to in such a small community'; 'It's so nice knowing everyone'; 'You can't afford to be cliquey here'. 'The teachers are on the side of the girls and get the best out of them.' Proper support for boarding families includes transport help and luggage storage.

Background and atmosphere: Founded in 1899 by Eleanor Beatrice Wyatt, who began by starting small schools for girls in London but, on deciding that out of London would provide a healthier environment, acquired this 18th century house, built

Such fun and sense of independence engendered by this canny move that very few leave after GCSEs: they can't wait to experience the freedom

in the style of a restrained Italian villa for the Paravacini family. Off the main road out of Ascot – very discreet sign: you need to know.

The white-painted, modest exterior belies the pleasures of the interior – most notably the splendid drawing room now given over to the lower sixth as its privileged common room. Elsewhere, the interior of the main house provides unremarkable but pleasant accommodation with some distinctive attributes – the classrooms are huge for these small numbers and most now boast areas with comfortable chairs and sofas as well as the usual desks and tables. The common-rooms are exceptionally well-appointed – every year has one – though girls would always like more, of course. The upper sixth kitchen looks more like a real family kitchen than any school kitchen we can remember.

Beautiful and rather special chapel of which the girls are clearly proud, and in which they spend 10 minutes each morning. Dining room now less formal – no more top table, thank goodness. Food definitely good. The grounds are charming – lots of huge trees and plenty of space everywhere. Virginia creeper and other sensitive planting around its buildings old and new (newer ones are low and attractive) make these real gardens. In a unique and privileged location just outside Ascot (which has a station), six miles from Windsor and Eton (Windsor bus stops at school gate), 20 minutes from Heathrow, 30 minutes from London, this school has a relaxed and country house feel and everything is on an inviting human scale.

Merged with St Mary's Wantage in 2005. Lots gained in terms of dosh from sale of Wantage plus a few migrants and some excellent staff. Mrs Heywood always keen to invite St Mary's old girls, in the hope they may come to feel at home in their land of adoption.

Pastoral care, well-being and discipline: A successful four-house system – Austen, de Valois, Seacole, Somerville – felt by girls to have improved inter-year relationships in general. All but the upper sixth wear uniform – trad navy with blue tie; upper sixth wear their own clothes. Quaint system of 'bows and bearings' – badges for conduct and manners, kindness, deportment etc – apparently much prized: girls wear these and other honours in long chains down the front of their jerseys. Very few disciplinary concerns. Focus always on the individual. 'The school could not have been more helpful when my daughter joined at an odd time,' a parent told us. 'Instead of disciplining people,' said a sixth former, 'Mrs Heywood tries to help them.' 'The head of boarding has been here for ever,' said another. 'She knows every trick in the book. She can read your mind.'

Pupils and parents: Lots of daughters, nieces and granddaughters of old girls. But newcomers too – all drawn by the palpable sense of tradition and, now, a sense of a school firmly in the 21st century – in many ways – while weird, anachronistic things like writing real letters still encouraged. Not falling into elephant traps into which so many others have been lured – 'We've been through a bit of a time and we could fill the school with overseas pupils, but we're not going down that road,' says wise Mrs Heywood. Fifty per cent from London, 20 per cent from home counties, 15 per cent from overseas – everywhere: no dominant nationality. Up-market clientèle – this school has lost none of its cachet, though parents claim, 'It's not for snobby show-offs – the girls are lovely and natural: they have no "London edge".' Lots of social stuff with Eton, Wellington, Radley and Harrow.

Entrance: Around two applicants for each of the 18 places at age 11. The usual academic tests but much emphasis put on the head's report from current school. Strong intake at 13. At 16, around 10 or so join to replace those who have left.

Now takes a handful of day pupils.

Exit: Around 10 per cent leave after GCSEs. A lively list of sixth form destinations includes Bristol, Exeter, Reading, Edinburgh, Newcastle and the University of the Arts, London, plus the University of British Columbia in Canada.

Money matters: A few bursaries available to means-tested applicants; the Old Girls' Association also offers financial assistance to deserving cases. Academic scholarships awarded, though these dish out prestige rather than dosh.

Remarks: Unique now in offering traditional, full boarding for lucky girls in a close, happy, small community with all mod cons and opportunities. Sensible, sound and super.

Highfield School

Highfield Lane, Liphook, Hampshire GU30 7LQ

01428 728000	**Ages:** 8–13
admissions@highfieldschool.org.uk	**Pupils:** 265
www.highfieldschool.org.uk	**Boarders:** 120 full, 45 weekly
C of E	**Day:** £17,025 – £19,575 pa
	Boarding: £21,450 – £23,550 pa

Head: Since 1999, Mr Phillip Evitt, MA (Cambridge) and previously head of history at Dulwich College (50s). Brainy, articulate and a dead ringer for Tony Blair in his glory days, reckon a fair few parents (particularly the mums), some staff and probably pupils too, if able to connect with dim and distant political past.

Personable (head, that is – we can't comment on T Blair) with smile, voice, animation and epic hand gestures to the fore, but very much his own man. Attractively self-deprecating – 'It's very sweet of you,' he says when complimented. Emphatically not a spin doctor, he's 'totally genuine' thought a parent (coal-effect gas fire in his study was only non-authentic accessory).

He's good with the 'pushy, intelligent, success-ful parents,' says a dad and even better at cultivating highly effective relationships with senior school heads, securing places through 'amazing contacts to enable you to get what you want. If school's oper-ating well, that's really what you need at the end.'

Leads a happy band of teachers who have 'a strong sense of unity – they're all good mates,' thought one, though it's taking a few turns of the wheel to secure uniform quality across the subject range. Maths and sciences 'excellent' but 'weaker in languages,' reckoned one parent, though 'not borne out in the sets the children are placed in at senior school,' says school.

Lyrical about post, for which he was head(master)hunted despite having no plans to go to the country and prepare for government. 'I never aspired to headship.'

Drove down 'on a profoundly unpromising late April day' battling new baby sleeplessness (last of four children, all – impressively – home births, now aged from teens to their twenties, who came through the school), and was instantly captivated by pupil élan as future charges played in the rain with evident enjoyment. 'I thought "how intriguing." These were children who felt comfortable being children, they didn't have that world weariness of the south London streetwise 13 or 14 year old.'

Modestly assumed he wouldn't suit. Of course, he did, and still does. Now well into his second decade, he's sixth head since school's foundation in Southampton in 1892, though far from being its longest serving (number two, member of family that still owns the school and responsible for move to purpose-built accommodation in 1907, clocked up a staggering 49 years).

Not much given to imposing his own world view, he lets school success (and its originators) speak for itself (we particularly liked school's weekly parish-style newsletters, featuring ads from local business amidst the reports of sporting and musical successes).

Relishes all that school has to offer in the way of tradition but is careful to keep the pace of innovation ticking over. Years 7 and 8 pupils have iPads which talk to school whiteboards and can store and file homework. May sound fancy but well in keeping with school's reputation for doing things earlier than most (it's been co-ed, and taken day pupils, since the 1970s).

He's taken difficult decisions from the off, starting by axing the 'madness' of compulsory boarding which was putting off many a parent who loved everything else about the school. To traditionalists, 'I was the hunter who'd shot Bambi's mother.' Many others approved and ultimately it proved a vote-winner. Now it's boarding because you want to, not because you have to – and, combined with sterling exam success, school is packing in the numbers, helped by increasingly popular pre-prep incubating the next generation.

Feels it's vital to listen to parents. Schools were 'conceited and arrogant' for too long, the experts in education who kept their customers at arms' length. These days, with successful, highly educated parents, 'you ignore what people have to say at your peril'.

Picturesque brickwork casts early morning shadows on a sea of green, pitches everywhere, side order of bluebell-carpeted woodland (home for achingly on trend forest class)

Suiting action to the word may make him 'possibly too accessible,' thought a parent. 'Does well to keep himself slightly aloof because otherwise, he'd end up having to get involved in every single micro issue that every parent had.'

Radiates clearly heartfelt belief in role of schools in providing not just rigour but also 'joy and wonder, enchantment, delight, challenge, excitement, fun.' Collect the set and learning becomes 'something you get out of bed to do, like turning a page in a book and wanting to move on to the next page.'

Despite rumours that he was considering his options as he approached his 10th anniversary, we weren't picking up any sense that he was off to scribe his memoirs (or indeed, set up a Peace Foundation). Just as well, then, that there's no Gordon Brown figure lurking on the premises.

Best bit about the top slot? 'Genuinely, I want to make things better.' We feel a song coming on. Could it be D:Ream circa 1997? We think it could.

Entrance: Non-selective-ish, most from Brookham, school's in-house pre-prep, though parents think number told they may not make the cut is rising (there's also no automatic rite of passage for siblings.) 'Definitely raising the standards,' reckoned one parent. 'When we first started, you had to have a severe problem not to get in.'

Families, broadly local, are augmented with influx of well-heeled Londoners, offspring increasingly the products of Thomas's and similar ultra-smart establishments.

Atmosphere is changing too. Once 'a bit chaotic and very friendly', it's now 'much slicker' – bemoaned by some though 'not necessarily a bad thing,' thought one mother. Though on the rise, the pushy, assertive contingent ('mums who wear hats at matches,' according to a local – we're keeping a watching brief on this one) is small enough 'to be squashed' by fellow parents. Tutoring, so far at least, remains a minority out of hours occupation 'and only if your child is really struggling.'

Though parent felt that SEN support could be even better, it's generally still felt, however, that full time SENCo, five other therapists and positive attitude from owner, a brilliant and dyslexic businessman (sister was a highly-rated teacher here until recently) creates haven for those with mainly mild learning needs. Children are 'never made to feel persecuted' and '...one of the great glories of the place in that we are a very broad church,' says head. Especially good with late developers, giving them the confidence to bloom in senior school – and many do.

Exit: School has opted for laissez-faire approach to departure age, loosening the ties by offering preparation for 11 plus (and even 12 plus) as well as common entrance. It's proved a smart move, parental freedom of choice coming down strongly in favour of staying the course, with what head describes as 'a small attrition rate' – as few as four leaving at end of year 6 and senior boarding for most. Widespread destinations, from Eton and Winchester, to Bradfield and Cranleigh, reflects ability range, Canford, Wellington and Marlborough amongst the perennial favourites. Scholarships, being pushed hard, thought parents, are going great guns.

Other local schools, wrestling the will they, won't they stay on beyond year 6 conundrum, must envy top years stability here. Though a few do leave early (some, reluctantly, because of financial pressures) seniors-only delights lure vast majority, headed by wonderful trips – voluntary year 7 trip to remote Scottish island to build own camp (look, no adults) one of the most memorable.

Parents feel breadth of talent and characters in top years something to celebrate. 'You've got people who are going to Eton, people who are struggling ...but who might be the best at sport or the best at music, and they can accommodate that,' says parent.

Remarks: Approached through prosperous Liphook, school looks a treat on a sunny spring day. Picturesque brickwork casts early morning shadows on a sea of green, pitches everywhere, side order of bluebell-carpeted woodland (provides fuel for new biomass boiler as well as home for achingly on-trend forest classroom), all 175 acres well-used by mothers who 'turn up in their lycra and go running with their labradors,' says former parent who also bemoaned the fact that 'it's easy to start feeling a bit smug.'

Top-up scenery fix every Wednesday when there's post-match 'car park time', families enjoying picnics together (courtesy of Messrs J Sainsbury – branch a short 4x4 schlep away), invitations to international boarders from local families ensuring nobody is left out.

Interiors are corridor heavy, twists and turns best tackled with an expert guide – star turns include attractive, solemn (but not sombre) chapel (nearby plaque commemorating school's founder must be touched if passed – brings luck, say older girls), nice, bright main music room (with a second for composition); excellent library, walls stuffed with reading lists, each personalised with jacket illustrations as effective aide-memoires – a time-consuming but worthwhile labour of love that ensures everyone broadens literacy horizons, say staff – and one of the small details that shows just why, academically, the school shines.

'What we do – I'm sure all schools say this – is absolutely aim to add value,' says head, disarmingly. Boasts 'unbroken record in getting everyone to first choice senior school'. Trickier these days because of the rise of pre-assessments, think parents, which has pushed up academic standards, and a tribute to what one described as 'fantastic' teaching across the ability range.

Houseparent's cosy office becomes an informal meeting place for 'tea and gossip' and has custody of special huggable piggy loaned to ward off homesickness

So far, no sense of pressures feeding through to pupils, let alone creating the 'pale, wan' types that one parent reported seeing at other, more academically-focused hothouses closer to the capital. Indeed, this bunch were notable for good cheer (and delightful manners, too) though some parents felt that a few families have increasingly to be restrained from ramping up the anxiety levels at home.

Pupils, though reassuringly relaxed, have no doubts as to expectations, though lead-in is gentle, usually (though not invariably) mixed ability teaching for everything in year 4, maths set in year 5, when there's across the board specialist teaching,

academics ramped up several notches in year 6 with three sets for everything, strengths in English, maths and science determining who you're with for everything else, including music and sport.

Fourth set is added in year 7, and scholars identified. 'They try to give them other names,' say pupils 'but we know exactly which group we're in.' (School, which sticks to 'obvious' one to four numbering, was slightly baffled by this).

Staff, reckons one of their number, are 'lifers, not bolters' who '...all like children, and that's not always the case with some teachers,' says head (laughing, but we don't think he's joking).

This lot include many clearly in love with their subject – head of maths was happy to deliver short tutorial on iPad geometry apps, their habits and haunts to this reviewer (only flaw the occasional unintentional transmission of scrawled notes to mothership whiteboard in classroom, visible to all).

Year 8 pupils, with impressive maturity, were quick to acknowledge that though some teachers were clearly more down with the kids than others (sports teachers and witty head of music particular favourites) even those with a less obviously child-pleasing style 'could turn a good pupil into an excellent one,' said one – and had the scholarship to prove it.

With increasing numbers testimony to school's appeal there's the inevitable fraying at the edges. It's all change, however, with new sports hall planned, together with major surgery to senior teaching block including two additional science labs.

Parents, while praising efforts, keen to see replacement of 'old fashioned' kitchens which, though good for terrific range of break time snacks and 'lovely' lunchtime fajitas as well as recently introduced salad bar, can be slightly over-reliant on stodge for afters. May improve when attractive dining hall refurb, allowing whole-school reunion for meals (older pupils currently have meals separately) is completed.

Boarding has also had a fairly substantial shake up following period when lack of feedback made parents feel uncertain about pastoral care. New houseparents have 'definitely breathed new life and energy into our boarding.' Parents agree. Now 'hand on heart I'd say boarding is excellent whereas before I wouldn't have been able to recommend it,' thinks one.

Stalwart adult presence reassures – you're never more than two dorms away from a houseparent – as does good communication including separate boarding email updates and mobiles 'strapped to us' says houseparent, whose cosy office becomes an informal meeting place for 'tea and gossip' and who has custody of special huggable piggy which 'slots round stomach' and is loaned out to ward off homesickness blues. Approachable matron, meanwhile, full-on mending session under way when

Who can blame them when evening cricket calls, and lures include guinea pigs and climbing frame in juniors' cosy cottage garden, as well as dress down Sunday morning breakfasts and cook your own supper sessions

we visited, is 'always here at breaktime for chats and spare clothes.'

There's considerable smartening up (showers in reds and pinks, girls' dorms very fetching – Tom Daley pin ups adding final touch) with more to come. Loss of linen room, imminent, will be mourned by the heat-starved Spanish boarders who 'go in to soak up the warmth,' says houseparent. Biggest casualty, though, will be boys' shower golf, fondly imagined to be a secret from staff, ball propelled round vast, old-fashioned, Carry on Camping style washroom course, bonus points awarded for sinking hole in one into tooth mug.

Has all made boarding wildly popular. Pupils plead to start – 'mine were supposed to be day,' says one mother, resignedly – and is almost universal in top years. Who can blame them when evening cricket calls (there's always a summer term surge in numbers) and lures include guinea pigs and climbing frame in juniors' cosy cottage garden, as well as dress down Sunday morning breakfasts and highly rated cook your own supper sessions for years 7 and 8, run by Mrs Evitt who, though a vegetarian, gamely tackles hard core red meat dishes including 'delicious' burgers stuffed with mozzarella.

Day pupils, however, get fair share of the action, staff interests swiftly channelled by head into delightful range of clubs. School boasts of 'enough to experience something different every day of the week' – probably an understatement, given range extending from recently introduced 'Hyperdrive' after school talks (history of flight the ambitious inaugural topic) to the remote control club which races model boats across smart swimming pool), as well as Bushcraft group (one for the Bear Grylls wannabees, if ways with newly defunct wild rabbits anything to judge by).

Bonds are further strengthened by compulsory Saturday school, well tolerated by all (marginally later starting time sweetens the pill – just – for sleep-starved parents), as allows five clear afternoons of sport a week, Thursdays reserved for Highfield Keys – school's own D of E equivalent with 'spectrum' of activities ranging from 'charity outreach to outdoor pursuits.'

House on house whomping is a big thing (not for nothing do their names commemorate famous English victories). Ranges from the big set piece pomp and ceremony of sports day, where knights set forth from separate marquees to do battle, to Bonfire Night guy contest, Lady Gaga a recent winner (Bradley Wiggins would have been a strong contender but 'his head fell off' – rarely a recommended tactic). If there's no house to duff up, 'we can turn anything into a competition,' says year 8 pupil, citing tidiest dorm, cleanest teeth and best veg plot by way of proof.

Matches are, naturally, played to win with staff who are proud that their own teams regularly trounce those of other schools setting high class example. School says that it's emphatically not out 'to win at all costs' and stresses that all pupils shall have team games and represent the school in matches, whether endowed with athletic superpowers or not. Good sportsmanship comes with the territory and 'full respect is given to other teams in defeat and in victory. It's not personal.'

Parents agree that victory never comes shorn of good manners, which are emphasised throughout the school, year 8 monitors supervising younger pupils at break and lunchtime.

Ranges from the big set piece pomp and ceremony of sports day, where knights set forth from separate marquees to do battle, to Bonfire Night guy contest

School, as a result, is a breeding ground for 'amiable killers,' says one parent, with netball stars known for pausing as they streak to victory to voice tender concern for opponents after collision. 'My daughter stops to say, "are you OK?" if she treads on someone's feet,' said mother. Boys' sport is 'excellent – I would say they win three-quarters of their matches,' reckoned dad. One parent felt girls' sport was a bit undernourished compared with boys'. Absolutely not so, says school, which puts it down to perceptions that girls currently 'don't win as many of their hockey matches because they are less experienced on Astroturf than other schools' teams,' though will all change when they get their own.

All in all, a super school that radiates enthusiasm and good cheer. Head says it's the happiest place he's ever worked in, felt previous GSG description 'tradition with a twist' summed it up to a tee. Aim is for greater cultural variety in the future, particularly in the top years, 'because it's good and healthy for the children.' Track record of all round success makes it a safe bet that it will add extra flavour to the mix.

Horris Hill School

Newtown, Newbury, Berkshire RG20 9DJ

01635 40594
enquiries@horrishill.com
www.horrishill.com
C of E

Ages: 7-13
Pupils: 115
Boarders: 98 full
Day: £18,525 pa
Boarding: £24,960 pa

Headmaster: Since 2011, Mr Giles Tollit BA (40s). Tall and lean, reminded us a little of Bryan Ferry in his salad days. Seems reserved at first but soon unbends and shows a nice, dry sense of humour. Educated at Holmewood House in Kent and then Sevenoaks, where he was an academic scholar. Initially destined for a career in the military, he studied classics at Bristol on an army bursary. Took gap year job at a prep where he was expecting to teach Latin in a fairly junior capacity, but before term started found himself head of classics. Such a fiery baptism would have been enough to turn a lesser chap off teaching, but it had the opposite effect on Mr Tollit, and Sandhurst's loss turned out to be preps' gain. Ten years at Caldicott and thence to Bilton Grange as deputy head. He's 'delighted to be back in an all boys boarding school' (he loved his own time at prep) and certain about the positive benefits of a sector he believes suffers from outdated stereotypes. Not that he has to sell boarding to the parents he meets; they've all done it themselves. Describes school, memorably, as being 'not dissimilar to a cruise ship; doors close at the start of each term and off we go.'

Mr Tollit teaches Latin and Greek and helps the scholars polish their skills in debating, logic and philosophy, he 'mucks in' as necessary and takes year 8 camping at his house in North Wales after exams. Describes HH as a 'seven day a week' school and is unconvinced by flexi-boarding, which he feels is sometimes the worst of both worlds. A former UK shot, he has introduced clay pigeon shooting and a rifle range is planned. He's also a keen photographer and, because 26 miles just isn't enough of a challenge, an ultramarathon runner.

> *Describes school as being 'not dissimilar to a cruise ship; doors close at the start of each term and off we go'*

Married to Molly, also a classicist, whom he met at university. It seems that three young sons aren't enough of a challenge for Molly who has turned her energies to transforming part of a field in the school grounds into a thriving kitchen garden. Establishing one at their former school, Bilton Grange, taught her 'what works and what doesn't' and HH is reaping the rewards. Chickens, an orchard and a dog (standard issue black lab?) are next on the list.

Parents think the Tollits have brought new energy to the school and like the fact they have their own young family. They have total faith in Mr Tollit, think he knows their boys incredibly well and praise his (and rest of staff's) swift response to calls and emails. Boys think head needs to be 'a bit more relaxed' but like the fact he's introduced clay pigeon shooting.

You'll need your satnav so as not to miss the quaint wooden signpost directing you down an unpromisingly narrow lane: it's as though only those who need to will find their way

Entrance: From age 7. No exam 'as such'. Head meets all prospective parents. Boys have informal interview, simple academic assessment and spend a day. Mr Tollit says he's 'not looking for superstars'; boys are observed to see how they interact and whether they are comfortable being 'in the academic spotlight' of such small classes.

Exit: Nearly all to senior boarding schools. Recently: Winchester, Radley, Eton, Harrow, Sherborne, Marlborough.

Remarks: Founded in 1888 to prepare boys for entry to Winchester, Horris Hill is set in 80 acres of wooded heathland on the borders of Berkshire and Hampshire. You'll need your satnav first time round so as not to miss the quaint wooden signpost directing you down an unpromisingly narrow lane; it's almost as though only those who need to will find their way here.

One of Horris Hill's idiosyncrasies is that it doesn't do year groups, it does 'termly remove'. Boys are placed in small classes (average 12) according to the progress they are making and remain there until they have mastered all their subjects to the requisite level. It might sound like a nightmare to organise but head says the maximum discrepancy between similar age boys is 'a couple of terms either way'. A boy's performance is reviewed via 'form order' (mark, position and effort grade) every three weeks, and at the end of term he stays or moves up accordingly. It's an unusual (possibly unique) system and only feasible in a school of this size (max 130) and age group. Besides accommodating summer birthdays, advantages are no B stream, no individual subject setting and ongoing challenges for both brightest and less able. According to Mr Tollit, it's as close as you can get to an education that is customised to each boy's needs. Arrangement is only for academic work; boys are grouped by age for sport, dorms etc. Parents all in favour, say it's great both for confidence and humility as boys are usually towards the lower end during first term and nearer the top in the second. The consensus is that the system works, even if one or two parents admitted they didn't entirely understand it.

Lessons we observed were fun, inclusive and challenging – a hard trio to achieve but less so with a class of 10, perhaps. Subject classrooms are named after senior schools: Winchester, Harrow, Eton, Radley etc. It took a bit of getting used to seeing such an age range, but the boys' enthusiasm and rapport with teachers was inspiring. In geography, impressive answers to quick fire questions were rewarded with chocolate; in the next classroom we thought we'd come across boys being punished but discovered that immersion in French pop music is a great way to practice listening and vocab. In the DT workshop, small boys in enormous aprons were busy sanding and drilling – some with more finesse than others. Was there anything, we asked, that they would like to change at their school? Extra free time was one suggestion, as was getting rid of second prep (senior boys do this after supper). Most popular idea was being able to bring small pets to school, something we mentioned to Mr Tollit, who promised to consider the proposal. Few boys with SEN – dyslexia, dyspraxia – receive support but this isn't the place for those with more than mild problems.

The no mobiles, laptops, iPads (basically, no screens) rule is, as far as we could tell, no big deal

and so much easier than trying to control limited access. Boys write weekly letters and may email/Skype from the house computer. As a teacher observed, if the no screens policy were to change, 'it would mean more rules.' Boys accept the policy and parents love it. They're not quite so keen when, for instance, CE results come out and they can't talk to their sons because the boarding house telephone is engaged – surely room for a little more 21st century communication technology here? This is a school where 'live' notice boards mean that someone changes the pictures and display on the wall in the dining hall corridor several times a day. There aren't smartboards in every classroom, although those we saw were being creatively employed; boys treasure the one or two teachers who spurn their use. Science labs, art and DT rooms have all the necessaries in a charmingly scruffy, no-frills style. By contrast, a high-tech rooftop weather station relays the prevailing conditions to a screen outside the geography room.

Sensible uniform features navy blue cords – either trousers or shorts, boys can decide. Apparently 'some boys wear shorts even when it snows.' Sartorial democracy extends to choice of tie as well. Long morning and lunch breaks allow plenty of time to work in the kitchen garden, ride bikes (boys can bring own), play outside in the meadows, make dens and have adventures in their own bosky dominion (known as 'Spain' because it's roughly the same shape). Nowhere is out of bounds but pupils mustn't go off alone. Camping out and cooking in the woods is one of the ultimate post-CE treats. Juniors have their own wood, 'too tame for us,' said our super-confident year 8 guides. One of the characteristics of HH is the amount of personal freedom pupils enjoy, finely balanced by the equivalent expectation of personal responsibility. Boys

One of the school's 'quite old fashioned secret things' is the modelling and train room, a glue and paint besmattered garret

organise their own activities (or Sign Up), recording where they are on a notice board so that everybody knows.

Youngest boarders (age 7-9) have lovely rooms in the 'Private Side' above the head's family quarters, with teddies on beds and lots of posters. Evening activities include silent reading, film nights with popcorn, board games and even shoe polishing (try suggesting that at home...). Numbers are small so things are flexible; if it's hot they can have a swim, if everyone's exhausted they go to bed early. Gappies 'bridge the gap' between boys and staff and are, as always, very popular. What about the homesick, we ask? Of course it happens, but staff are vigilant and boys support each other, telling tutors if they're worried about someone. 'You feel awkward at first,' our guides said, 'but it only lasts a week.'

Lots of younger teachers with families live on site, married couples head up the boarding houses, but after the junior forms most of the teaching staff are men. This notwithstanding, the traditional boys' own atmosphere prevails and is what many, especially army families, treasure. There are a few local day boys who are 'building up to boarding', rest may go home after matches on Saturday until Sunday evening (except first and last weekend of term) but most stay, 'or you miss too much fun.' That fun includes cross-country cycling, tree running, kite flying and ghost stories round the campfire. A parent praised the 'pater' system that pairs new boys with older boys and said that these cross-age friendships are kept up throughout school. Older boys move on to one of two Edwardian houses a short walk across the playing fields. Four-bed rooms are very comfortably furnished with home duvets, posters, beanbags and lovely soft carpet. Fruit bowl and toaster fill the gaps between meals, all of which are eaten in school dining room. Everyone, staff and pupils, sits down together at large tables, boys serve the food. Head v keen on benefits of 'interaction across a table'.

Spacious and well-designed music school can accommodate all for studio theatre or concert performances. Twenty-six practice rooms means there's no excuse for not getting down to scales and arpeggios after breakfast. Parts for all in 'fantastic' music and plays. Main venue for drama, assemblies etc is rather tired windowless sports hall, not enhanced by pervasive whiffy trainer smell, but

never fear, Mr Tollit is on the case and this part of the school is undergoing complete refurbishment. As he says, 'HH is not a flash school', but a shooting range, climbing wall and upgraded squash courts are on the way. Interestingly, it seemed to us that there was less of an obsession with organised sport and winning here than at other similar schools. Plenty of options: usuals plus hockey, squash, tennis, sailing, golf, fencing. Boys think cricket and football are what they're best at and all get to represent school in something. Parents come and watch matches, although it's a long round trip if you live in London. Swimming pool is outdoors (very) with wooden changing huts – all a bit basic but doubtless character building. One of the school's 'quite old fashioned secret things' is the modelling and train room, a glue and paint besmattered garret where Warhammer enthusiasts create their miniature worlds and model railway buffs of all ages can operate trains and signals.

With a maximum of 130 pupils, quite a few who are siblings, the parent body is small, self-selecting and fiercely supportive. Although it's in a wealthy part of the country, HH is definitely not (outwardly at least), a smart school. Parents are welcomed to plays, concerts, matches and Sunday evening chapel and there are social events such as fathers' and sons' cricket matches and mothers' and sons' tennis, but there's no PTA, sports day or speech day. One father, who had considered London day schools for his sons, spoke of the way in which HH 'preserves innocence' – not just by absence of personal technology but also because full boarding means boys develop a camaraderie that is not influenced by each others' possessions or houses. On a more practical level, parents love the fact that all sports kit is provided, washed and maintained by the school.

Horris Hill is such a distinctive school it's unlikely you could choose it by mistake; proud to be different, it epitomises the very best prep school traditions without being pompous or rigid. HH boys are confident but not precocious; they think for themselves but aren't arrogant. There's room for big characters but a shy child won't be trampled underfoot; academic success is important but not to the exclusion of other talents. As another happy parent told us, 'it's a hidden gem.'

Hurst Lodge School

Bagshot Road, Ascot, Berkshire SL5 9JU

01344 622154
admissions@hurstlodgesch.co.uk
www.hurstlodge.co.uk

Ages: 3–18 (boarding from 9)
Pupils: 267; sixth form: 20
Boarders: 34 weekly and flexi
Day: £9,330 – £15,030 pa
Boarding: plus £8,805 pa

Principal: Since 2013, Miss Victoria (Vicky) Smit BSc (40s). Had an earlier stint as head between 1998 and 2011. But, concerned about the propriety of being both co-owner and head (her brother, Sir Tim Smit, started the Eden Project and the school belonged to their mother), she appointed another head in her place for a brief period. It didn't work and Miss Smit is once again head.

This former Hurst Lodge girl, who 'has been 23 years in the place,' bounced into our meeting in rather fetching wellies, waterproof trousers and trackie top. She had been helping out at Hurst Lodge's forest school and was clutching a wet teddy – which she handed to her assistant with the comment that 'he needs to have his bum dried.'

Previously worked with the army and a team of agricultural management consultants but helped her mother move the school in 1999 and never left. A forest school leader (younger Hurst Lodge pupils learn how to take risks in the real world), she has undertaken 'multi-discipline training' (which sounds a bit like being qualified in common sense). A joy – rather like the best possible Girl Guide, favourite aunt or big sister. She bubbled with enthusiasm, giggled and waxed lyrical and we positively skipped round the school, hopping up the odd staircase to avoid being mown down by busy children. (Our notes actually say: 'bubbly, bouncy, loving'.)

Academic matters: Not a Russell Group route. School is non-selective and mixed ability. One third are on the SEN register – the majority are on the dys-spectrum: dyslexia, dyspraxia, dyscalculia, plus Asperger's, high functioning autism, ADD, ADHD, epilepsy, diabetes. Mild Tourette's, but no pupil who 'would disrupt the balance of the class' is accepted. All children with SEN are assessed prior to entry. Taster for all, sometimes two or three tasters (and usually after the third, the answer is no).

Two SENCos, eight staff with 'SEN commitment,' tiny caring classes (10 the norm for GCSE, max 18).

Children are withdrawn for support from mainstream classes – between one and five lessons per week (charged as extra, same as individual music lessons). Some statemented children have learning support assistants in class and a number of students attend sessions with the speech therapist. Timetables are adaptable, nothing is written in stone. Gifted children either work with the class above or attend special extension classes. EFL support on tap. The odd GCSE module taken early. Parents and guardians invited along to relevant assessment meetings with ed psychs and SENs, co-training sessions and open discussion with and by all concerned with any particular pupil's problems. Regular reports home and school hopes that parents will be upfront about concerns and vice versa. School both small enough to care and big enough to pull punches.

Spanish from 2+; French from 12. Baby science room and tremendous playroom and studio theatre.

At GCSE a full range of subjects on offer. Double science, triple science, interactive white boards, computers, everything you might expect from a mainstream school. Students take an average of 11 GCSEs each, 'as in 10.5 GCSEs each, of which seven are academic and three and a half arty.' Wide range of traditional academic subjects alongside more vocational stuff – dance and performing arts. BTec in childcare, in-house nursery and placements available (next step perhaps to follow Norland into self-defence?)

We loved the idea that the principal would happily cancel all lessons to have a gigantic snowball fight. Or get the entire school to make kites and fly them one windy day

In 2015, 18 per cent A*/A GCSE grades. Difficult to quantify results from such a tiny cohort. Some subjects offered as IGCSE or BTec, which school says gears 'subject delivery to individual need.' For most, each exam passed, at whatever level, is the result of a massive joint pupil/parent/teacher input and a huge boost to self esteem and morale.

Academic change is in the air and new enhanced sixth form programme began in September 2014. This has 'a slightly different focus' and subjects offered include business studies, English, history of art, Spanish, French, environmental studies, art, textiles, photography, drama, and music.

A joy – rather like the best possible Girl Guide, favourite aunt or big sister. She bubbled with enthusiasm, giggled and waxed lyrical

Pupils say that teachers go out of their way to explain things and really take time. 'We get lots of attention; our teachers are amazing,' we were told. School practises a total immersion approach – if, for instance, the history project is the Tudors, then it is Tudor in the art room, Tudor exploration in geography, Shakespeare, Marlowe and probably lampreys for all at lunch time.

The most recent ISI inspection found the school to be 'excellent.' So did we, and we loved the idea that the principal would happily cancel all lessons to have a gigantic snowball fight. Or get the entire school to make kites and fly them one windy day, while the music department blasted 'Let's go fly a kite' on mega-megaphones.

Games, options, the arts: Terrific. Halfway to a stage school, with all students studying performing art (including ballet and modern tap) until the age of 14 – boys too. Hair workshop (dancers' buns – natch) and make-up lessons. Some pupils combine school with performing in the West End, while others take part for the hell of it. Two amazing (odd floor surface – slightly bungey) dance studios which link up to provide the most impressive performance space. Huge LAMDA take-up. Large numbers go on to further dance, ballet, modern, tap and jazz, ditto drama. Southern circuit national drama heats held here. Principal is the Independent Schools' Association National Arts Co-ordinator and in charge of national drama, art and essay competitions. Eighty per cent of pupils learn a musical instrument and most take voice lessons. Recording studio on site.

Mind-blowing creative arts, undoubtedly amongst the best fabric/art portfolios we have seen in any school. Outstanding. We were seriously impressed by a quilted memory box with fabric detail of professional standard. Artwork round the school wasn't that bad either and sewing machines and cookers vied for space in the art/craft room. Life class, computer aided art, Photoshop. Practical cookery lessons preferred to the more theoretical food tech – optional at 15 and compulsory for sixth formers. Ceramics, sculpture and animation (there's also a wowser YouTube video online of Buff Orpington eggs hatching as part of school's eco project).

International sportsmen/women (and an Olympian or two) are allowed two weeks off for competitions during the year. Swimming important – school has open air 25m pool, surrounded by child-inspired gardens. Lifesaving, tennis, footie with the local village club on Saturday, riding Tuesdays, polo Thursdays, netball, hockey, rounders, karate and athletics, judo.

Pupils grow veggies in a polytunnel, and a nearby pen is full of weird and wonderful ducks and chooks (their eggs currently off the agenda until six weeks after worming). This is a hands-on smallholding and we were constantly interrupted during our tour by little people asking 'if they could help feed the hens.' The head replied: 'tomorrow we have to put cream on them. Do you think you could hold them?' Bees – and school makes own honey. For many pupils, this hands-on approach to life beyond the classroom or their (sub)urban roots is their first taste of how the other half lives.

Forest school is important at Hurst Lodge, with younger pupils (kindergarten to 11 year olds) all enjoying role play and exploration. In the real Hurst Lodge world (a bit like Enid Blyton's if that's not a dirty word), pupils learn how to take risks and set their own boundaries. They may not wave sticks about but they climb trees ('they mustn't climb higher than they can get down from,' says the head), build shelters, light fires and make their own seesaws with real saws, branches and logs. They fabric besoms, build forts from wood and burn them down – 'a practical lesson in why wood gave way to stone in ancient times as a building material.' This is idyllic childhood stuff. The young learn to work as a team and have survival days in all weathers. Parents occasionally complain about the lack of homework and are assured that their young have learned how to negotiate, use their imagination and identify various trees by bark and by leaf. This is grown up stuff – serious companies call it bonding and charge heaps.

They may not wave sticks about but they climb trees, build shelters, light fires and make their own seesaws with real saws. They build forts from wood and burn them down

Learning for life classes important throughout, but particularly at the top end where pupils are prepared for the world outside. Strong links with the Eden Project started by Tim Smit, and work experience there, as well as on the school's own smallholding. This is sustainability education at its best.

Pupils are taught interview techniques (and what to wear), public speaking, sex education, first aid, flower arranging (well, you never know), deportment, proper etiquette, how to lay a table, which glasses to use for what wine and how to reply to formal invitations (might be quite clever to offer a level 2 food hygiene certificate so the little darlings could get proper paid holiday jobs). Staff brainstormed to come up with a list of skills that proved most useful in later life and this programme is the result.

Mega collection of after-school clubs. School estimates that only about 20 per cent of pupils go straight home after school – all the others (usually fortified with a cake and drink from the canteen) stay to do extra activities. Dance of all descriptions, ballet, tap, jazz, modern. Pupils can take a GCSE after hours, if they can't fit it into their timetable, plus all the usual sport, arts and crafts, gardening, electronics, public speaking, and polo. Staff stay on too; mathematical challenge popular plus knitting, touch typing...

Boarding: Small boarding house upstairs in school proper, max 38. Students can board from the age of 9. Weekly or flexi boarding or odd night. Small size means the students have friends of all ages and it's run like a large family, with students and staff sitting down to breakfast and supper together. Ofsted reckoned the boarding provision to be 'outstanding.'

Three/four to a room (the most recent conversion still smelled of paint during our visit, having been subdivided the previous week) and a third boy joined the other couple of boarders three weeks into term. Pupils can start at any time assuming there's space available and with the taster caveat previously mentioned. We much enjoyed a short chat with the (married) housemistress who tries to make life as homelike as possible, organising trips to the cinema, board games, bread making, barbies and 'going off-site.' In-house wickedness equals discussion, followed by 'house chores.' Buddy system of the same age for new boarders. Girls have a splendid dolls' house and Wendy house and boys their own common room. Waiting list for boarders at some ages.

Background and atmosphere: Founded as a dance school in London in 1942 by Doris Stainer, a formidable woman with a cane. The school has grown and moved several times since then – to its current 22-acre site on the outskirts of Ascot in 1997. Main school building is nostalgically Victorian with extensive add-ons, including kindergarten, classrooms and studio block. Jolly modern nursery for tinies from the age of 3 to 6. Roughly 50/50 boys (who are wriggling their way up the school). The tiny chapel – now used for choir practice – has rather fun stained glass and a very low door to ensure that one slightly bolshy incumbent actually made obeisance to the altar.

Children deeply involved in the food they eat and catering staff happily join them at mealtimes to discuss future menus and their respective nutritive values. This is an all-embracing outlook on education, celebrating every achievement and keen to boost self confidence. Supervised homework, limited access to the internet and constant advice regarding social media and cyber-bullying.

The recent addition of boys is gradually having an effect. It started when one boy – a sibling – was taken on to help a family in need and snowballed from there. A third of pupils are boys, most of whom, to be honest, are in the junior school. But as co-ed credentials fairly recent, numbers growing. Three boy boarders as we write. School ain't for all boys though. Unsurprisingly, it's the fathers who have the biggest problem with hearing their sons may be dancing (optional for boys as they may choose an alternative such as sport or technical lighting), but could suit some gentler souls who might flounder in a large, male-dominated environment.

Pastoral care, well-being and discipline: Ofsted found pastoral care to be 'exceptional.' Not many rules – they are summed up as 'accept everyone.' Pupils have a good relationship with staff – friendly but respectful. One of the worst sanctions is apparently that head is 'disappointed.' Polite pupils stand up when teachers and visitors enter a room.

A happy mainstream school that's not afraid of a special need or two. And it doesn't have to be anything major – also good for helping pupils who just need a little bit extra

Non-denom, 'global mix'; church for Christmas, synagogues visited, comparative religion taught (though veggie not kosher). Proper wrap-around care, from brekky at 7.45am to supper at 5.45pm. Assembly for all on Tuesdays, plus the odd parent. Neat tartan pinafores and tweed hacking jackets for all.

Pupils and parents: Locals from a 30-mile radius. Boarders from Birmingham, Cornwall, plus a fair sprinkling from overseas, Korea, Japan, Africa. Working parents appreciate the good before and after-school care provided. Boon for all: 'There's so much laid on here that I don't need to run myself ragged taking them to activities outside,' one told us. 'They can even have some tea here and then do their homework. It's a real help.' Number of

first time buyers, plus old girls' children. Notable old girls include Duchess of York, actresses Juliet Stevenson and Claudie Blakley and TV presenter Emma Forbes.

Entrance: More or less at any time into any age group. Non-selective, but 'pupils need to fit in to the class without altering its dynamic significantly,' says principal. Twelve-year-old would-be pupils spend a day here, with papers in English, maths and reasoning – more of a placement test than entrance exam. At all other times, they spend a taster day (or two or three: ditto those with SEN hiccups) at the school, during which they will be assessed 'to ensure that they can access the school's curriculum.' Special needs children are assessed by the learning support team who need a copy of their last ed psych report or EHC plan. No place offered if the school reckons they can't offer the right kind of support.

New pupils welcome at any time throughout the year assuming there's space available (often from the state sector in the run-up to Christmas or in instances where 8/9-year-olds are overwhelmed by transition to independent preps).

Exit: Chaps sometimes leave at 11 for trad preps, including Woodcote House, Hall Grove and Papplewick. Nearly all junior girls move up to senior school. Over half leave after GCSEs, many for art college or performing arts courses, leaving a tiny sixth form. No 2015 leavers, but current year 13s are considering engineering at Keele, medicine, dentistry, pharmacy, dance and theatre school.

Money matters: Academic, dance, drama, music and art scholarships on offer. Be warned that there are extras to pay – LAMDA exams, special needs support, after-school care etc. Discounts for siblings and Forces families. 'Lost a few' in the recent recession, but numbers are stable, with rather more refugees from the state system.

Remarks: It is not often that this long-time Good Schools Guide editor comes out of a school with a happy buzz that lasted all the way back to London, and even now, when faced with the computer, still feels that all can be right with the world. A happy mainstream school that's not afraid of a special need or two. And it doesn't have to be anything major – also good for helping pupils who just need a little bit extra individual attention to help them succeed, whatever their talents. Unusually strong performing arts programme. No amazing sparkly facilities, just spoonfuls of common sense and human kindness.

Lambrook School

Winkfield Row, Nr Ascot, Berkshire RG42 6LU

01344 882717
info@lambrookschool.co.uk
www.lambrookschool.co.uk
C of E

Ages: 3–13
Pupils: 510: 315 boys/195 girls
Boarders: 30 – 40 flexi
Day: £10,680 – £17,862 pa
Boarding: £19,998 – £21,417 pa

Headmaster: Since 2010, Mr Jonathan Perry, previously head of Kingsmead School in Hoylake. Wife Jenny is a clinical pharmacist who works part-time at a nearby hospital but also has a pastoral role at the school. She has an eye for interior decoration too: the fresh flowers front of house and general spruced up air are thanks to her. The Perrys' son and daughter attended the school (have since progressed to Wellington and Downe House) and were described by one parent as 'a perfect fit'. Mr Perry is the son of a bishop, his degree is in religious studies and history, but there are teachers in his family as well as members of the clergy – certainly a strong tradition of public service. Although he teaches no timetabled lessons, he runs current affairs sessions in his study for the older pupils. He told us modestly that he 'helps out' with sport, but parents love the fact he's so visible – greeting children every morning, present at all the matches – and is always available. He has revitalised Saturdays and added a lecture programme (parents welcome to attend these) to the extended learning sessions. Saturday school compulsory for years 6 and above. Another thing we learned about Mr Perry during our visit is that he really does seem to know every pupil, and not just by name either.

School is increasingly popular but headmaster has no plans to expand; he is 'happy with the size' and concentrating instead on improving facilities. The Performing Arts Centre was opened by HRH the Earl of Wessex and has stimulated and inspired a love of the arts across the school. It would be fair to say that not all parents saw this project as a necessity, but they have now been very much won over. There is no doubt Lambrook's many musicians and performers have enjoyed treading its boards providing an excellent space for rehearsing for drama performances at the Edinburgh Fringe and choral performances in Notre Dame. A new cedar clad 25 metre indoor swimming pool came to fruition in February 2015. Also in the pipeline is a plan to build new art and tech studios. Managing these projects must be taking up a fair bit of Mr Perry's time, but he is determined to ensure that the results will

respect the school's tradition and surroundings and has changed architectural details to this end. 'Parents like to see things happen in their time,' he says. The coffee table in the head's study is made from the trunk of an oak from the grounds, its rings marked with events from the school's 150 year history – must help put things in perspective. A keen sportsman, Mr Perry enjoys golf, tennis and cricket, but more often these days from the sidelines. Favourite book? Sebastian Faulks' Birdsong. Cornwall is where the family go to get away from it all – sea being practically the only thing lacking in Winkfield Row.

Entrance: Mostly at 3, 4 and 7 years. The school meets with all prospective pre-prep families to ensure they can best meet the family's needs. There is a formal assessment day for entrance to the prep, which takes place up to a year before prospective entry. Children are assessed against a number of criteria including their academic ability, wider interests, character and the behaviour of each child to ensure that they would thrive in such an environment here.

Increasingly favoured by West London parents, word-of-mouth is also attracting families from beyond Ascot, Windsor and Maidenhead to villages across Berkshire, Buckinghamshire and Surrey. Some girls join in year 7, mainly those aiming for Wellington or Downe House. Parents a mix of traditional and first time buyers.

Exit: All, many with scholarships, to first choice senior schools including Wellington, Bradfield, Eton, St Mary's Ascot, Downe House, Harrow, Marlborough, Charterhouse, Radley and Stowe.

Remarks: On the glorious early summer day of our visit Lambrook could not have looked finer. The school's 52 acres of Berkshire's lushest prime estate were at their peak of green and pleasantness; children played under venerable trees, the cricket pitch was like velvet as was the nine hole golf course – and birdsong was nearly winning against the noise coming from the construction site (now the performing arts centre). Inside the main building the newly extended library, with its gothic wood panels and shelves, seems timelessly bookish but was originally the dining room. Here, as elsewhere, are historic photographs of past pupils – teams, plays etc – part of the fabric rather than separated into an archive. Founded in 1860, Lambrook is alma mater of, among others, Lord Alfred Douglas (Oscar Wilde's downfall), Queen Victoria's grandsons Prince Christian Victor and Prince Albert, W C Sellar and R J Yeatman, authors of 1066 and all that. More recent alumni include actor Alex Petyffer and rugby internationals Max and Thom Evans.

The choir had recently sung evensong at St George's Chapel and had obviously been given the royal seal of approval

The fine chapel with its gleaming brass and polished pews can no longer accommodate everyone, so whole school assemblies and inter-house competitions (singing etc) take place in the the performing arts auditorium. The boy:girl ratio is 60:40 overall but despite this the feel is thoroughly inclusive and co-ed. Children with SEN and/or physical disabilities 'welcome' so long as the school can meet their specific needs.

In addition to the aforementioned birdsong and building, another noise we heard as we toured the school was laughter. Lambrook lessons seem to be good fun, with relaxed but respectful relations between pupils and staff, many of whom live on site. Parents told us they like the balance of male and female teachers and the mix of quirky 'old school' and new blood teaching styles. Thumbs up too for the enthusiastic gappies from pupils and parents alike. We saw heads in books in English and quick fire questions and answers in science too – it was just a few weeks before CE, after all. Our year 8 guides (scholarships in the bag) already sounded nostalgic about their Lambrook years. Music is exceptional; over 80 per cent of children learn at least one instrument up to and including grade 8 and play in school bands and ensembles, not to mention a full symphony orchestra. The choir had recently sung evensong at St George's Chapel, Windsor and had obviously been given the royal seal of approval because they've been asked to return. Newish performing arts centre with

Choice of clubs described as 'ridiculously diverse' and so it is – from creative writing to diving, sailing and polo (well, this is Ascot)

theatre, peripatetic teaching rooms, green room and dance studio. In recent years Lambrook has provided actors and singers for professional productions including The Sound of Music, Oliver! and Matilda and has even performed at the Edinburgh Fringe. In the wonderful, creatively messy art room, pupils were singing along to music and screen-printing their own designs onto sports day t-shirts.

It must be tough to do justice to the perfection of the pitches (or, apparently, the match teas) but boys' and girls' teams are bringing home gold and silverware in rugby, hockey, trampolining, tennis, skiing and basketball, played at county and national levels. Plenty of joint activities, but girls get separate PE, hockey, and netball. Everybody loves winners, but we were encouraged to hear of children who were never going to make the team being included and given important non-playing roles. Choice of clubs and after-school options described by one parent as 'ridiculously diverse' and so it is – from creative writing to diving, sailing and polo (well, this is Ascot).

We visited the nursery, separate from but close to the main school, just before lunch (meals on wheels from main school kitchen). Tinies sitting on the floor were engrossed in a story. At age 4 children move on to the pre-prep, not a huge step geographically but parents praised the way the staff prepare children for this transition. This is the time when educational needs may show themselves, and the pre-prep SENCo observes and identifies any potential learning, speech and language problems. For those who need a little more time to consolidate the basics there is extra phonics and 'maths crew', activity-based small group work to reinforce knowledge. Pre-prep has its own hall, used for before (from 8.15am) and after (until 6pm) school care – a bonus for parents, especially if they have older children at the main school. Lively notice boards give parents all they need to know about what's going on, lesson topics and other key information. Expansion of nursery provision has not been without collateral damage – in this case the pre-prep library. Wider than average though it may be, a corridor doth not a library make. Something else for Mr Perry to add to his grand plans.

The girls' dorms are up three flights of stairs in the eaves of the main house, charming rooms looking out over the grounds painted in contemporary colours and full of homely touches such as beanbags. The boarders' kitchen was large and sunny with gingham oilcloth on the table and fresh flowers. Every effort has been made to keep things as uninstitutional as possible. Flexi-boarding is particularly popular at the end of the week – parents certainly appreciate it – and most of the older day pupils have tried (and, apparently, enjoyed) it at one time or another.

Lambrook is a lively and unstuffy prep school in an idyllic pastoral setting where boys and girls are educated to the best of their potential without excessive pressure. Several parents said to us that although they rather liked the fact it was a 'well-kept secret', the school deserved to be better known. We agree. To quote from old boys Sellar and Yeatman's classic, 1066 and all that, Lambrook is 'a Good Thing'.

Leighton Park School

Shinfield Road, Reading RG2 7EE

01189 879600
admissions@leightonpark.com
www.leightonpark.com

Ages: 11–18
Pupils: 470; sixth form: 150
Boarders: 97 full, 50 weekly/flexi (roughly two-thirds boys)
Day: £16,524 – £20,313 pa
Boarding: £22,524 – £32,382 pa

Head: Since January 2013, Mr Nigel Williams BA MA PGCE (known here – as are all staff – by his first name). Educated at Monmouth School, Nigel read history at Bristol and then a masters in Victorian Studies at University of London. Began career at St Albans, where he became head of general studies. Joined Leighton Park in 1994 as head of history and became, successively, housemaster, director of studies, deputy head: academic, deputy head: pastoral and then, with nowhere else to go – head. An unusual trajectory and represents a terrific vote of confidence from the school governors and community. Plus a recourse to stability and continuity. His tenure followed the lengthy reign of a highly-regarded predecessor with a brief hiccup in between when another appointee rapidly came and went. No scandal but a mismatch and no hard feelings thereafter, in a way that is characteristic of the school as a community.

> *He embodies his school and its values but is more than a safe pair of hands, having learned the place all through and having sound and sensible ideas of his own*

Nigel – whose delight and surprise at his assumption of the headship is touching and genuine – is larger than life, colourful, smiley, warm and an easy man to talk to. He embodies his school and its values but is more than a safe pair of hands, having learned the place all through and having sound and sensible ideas of his own. This was a wise appointment. Leighton Park, already in stout heart, will be the better for it.

Academic matters: Academic work is taken seriously and pupils strive for success – as they should – although not, thankfully, a results-driven school. in 2015, 73 per cent A*/A at GCSE. A level and IB offered though IB numbers not yet on a par with A level takers. In 2015, 35 per cent of A levels gained A*/A. Overall IB average 34. IB retained partly because 'its values are so much those of the school,' explains Nigel. Useful cross-fertilisation – IB and A level languages often taught together in year 12 and all take an Extended Project Qualification for its educational value. Good languages. Very good teacher:pupil ratio at 7.5 pupils to one full-time teacher and some sixth form classes with only one or two students. Small but well-stocked library and much praise for the range of visiting outside speakers. Interesting displays of work – we were moved by the WW1 montage of Old LPs fallen in battle which made it all pathetically real.

Parents, for the most part, praise the teaching – 'my son is enthused by everything – especially the Mandarin', while there is some sense that a little more rigour, vigour and initiative might not come amiss here and there. Probably not a school for workaholics, but then, they probably wouldn't come. Very much a school for joiners-in and those with breadth and brain.

EAL classes for small number of students who need them and school prepares them for FCE and IELTS exams. They don't take an additional language and use one of the class English lessons to boost their language skills. Some 15 per cent on the SEND register – surprisingly few for a school with such a good reputation for supporting those with an educational special need. Individual learning centre and all staff involved in support. No in-class assistants unless provided by the pupil's LA. Helpful and flexible approach, as parents attest, and 'they are quite relaxed about Ritalin, they take it in their stride'. A sense that the large and highly-regarded

SEN team are there to make themselves less and less needed.

Games, options, the arts: Large and beautiful site, with fields, pitches, courts and tracks which positively set your muscles aquiver. 'My son is not sporty but they have really got him to love it,' a mother marvelled. Music is big here and no other house activity compares with the annual House Music, which is taken very seriously – 'almost too seriously,' we were told, 'as everyone gets really into it and the noise is louder than at a football match'. Good number learn an instrument in school and remarkable cohort of fine musicians – ie beyond grade 8 – practise here. Art exceptionally varied and imaginative. We loved the year 10 work on 'Surfaces, facades and veneers' and the sixth form studio was full of mind-stretching, clever creativity, alongside examples of the crucial skills of drawing and painting. Pottery, photography, textiles and DT work provide evidence of novel, individual ideas being fostered. DT provision newly enhanced by laser cutter, CNC router and 3D printer. Drama also lively – big productions, mostly musicals, in attractive, flexible theatre, its regular seating arranged, interestingly, in the guise of a Meeting. Also small drama studio in stand-alone brick building, formerly a squash court.

Nor is it 'alternative'. The Quaker philosophy is central and, although it is never pushed at you, its calm wisdom steals gently into one's consciousness

Lots to do. And lots of encouragement to try things out. Huge range of clubs and activities and masses of space for them all. Young Enterprise, D of E, trips of all kinds but no CCF, of course.

Boarding: School would not claim that boarding accommodation is up-to-the minute. Rooms are spacious enough. Most younger years share in 3s and 4s. Sixth formers in singles but not an en-suite or even a bedroom with basin anywhere on site – yet. All houses well-provided with table games, TVs and sofas – they feel like home only with more fun. Meals now eaten in Oakview rather than in houses and pyjamas – to the regret of some. Many day pupils stay until 7.00pm or even 9.00pm, thus getting the best of two worlds.

Many staff live on site and have boarding duties. Head's modest house, also on site, all adds to the sense of community and pupils love that 'our tutors are in the boarding houses after school and we can just chat to them'.

Background and atmosphere: Situated in the centre of 'the park' – an apt name for this spacious, meadowed site with hundreds of mature trees, garden areas, large reedy pond, generous planting and low-rise blocks – is the main building, an elegant 1850s white house. It was bought by an earlier incarnation of the school in the 1880s and more land was donated by the Reckitt family – the aim being to educate Quaker children for Oxbridge. It remains a Quaker-run school as the majority of governors are Quakers and, although no member of the Friends remains on the staff and only penny numbers of pupils are Quakers, the school lives by and exudes those gentle, civilised and socially responsible values. Few who leave here take nothing of those with them, and many see them as a guide for a healthy life. A palpable sense of calm pervades the place – you feel it as you drive in and your shoulders drop as you step out of your car and breathe out.

This is not just another school and it is best not to approach it as such. Nor is it 'alternative', though the pupils and teachers being on first name terms can deceive you into thinking so. The Quaker philosophy is central and, although it is never pushed at you, its calm wisdom steals gently into one's consciousness. 'When you're in year 9, you don't really get the meaning of it,' one soon-to-be-leaver told us, 'but, by the end, especially when life is hectic, you really appreciate it. It helps you find quiet time to clear your thoughts.' Weekly Meeting for Worship and monthly Meeting are the overt Quaker practices but, in the diverse mix of today's population, no particular faith dominates and everyone brings to the sessions what they wish.

In practice, this approach changes relationships. 'Calling teachers by their first names makes you treat them as people – you don't have to be on your best behaviour and it makes you more inclined to learn,' we were advised. And, of pupil:pupil dynamics – 'If we fall out we tend just to fix it and hug it out.' The 2015 Peace Pole – an extraordinary carved wooden column visible from most parts of the school – enshrines these principles, as do the many examples of pupil creativity – benches, tables etc carved from fallen trees on the site – around the place. Very much a school for joiners-in and those with breadth and brain.

Lots of buildings of all eras, little of startling architectural merit though the recent Oakview restaurant is cleverly designed and a popular addition. We were very impressed by the food – its freshness and variety – and deeply regretted not being able to stay to sample it. 'Theatre Special is when they cook it in front of you – like a performance; pork baguette is a thing of beauty,' apparently!

Some splendid individual rooms, especially in the main building. We were repeatedly struck by the good order of the site – not an instance of peeling paint, a shabby carpet or a stained wall met our eye and, over an extensive tour, we saw not a shred of litter. Signing is useful and not municipal in style.

'Calling teachers by their first names makes you treat them as people – you don't have to be on your best behaviour and it makes you more inclined to learn'

Houses, named after notable Quakers, matter but not too much – except at House Music. But the traditions and values of the place inspire spontaneous, unaffected loyalty.

Pastoral care, well-being and discipline: Discipline maintained with a light touch and some incomers given refuge after mishaps elsewhere become model citizens here. A great place for deserving second-chancers – 'The only people to get kicked out are complete idiots as they'll have had several warnings'. So – very occasional permanent exclusions, usually of those with more money than sense. A parent told us that 'they encourage them to become self-reliant and independent' and 'unlike at other schools, they can pick up their own clothes and make their own supper'. 'They are good at integrating kids who've been fish-out-of-water at their previous schools.' More rules than you might expect – no eating while walking around,

no use of mobiles during the school day – but all designed to consider others and to maintain the peace. And Nigel is subtly stiffening the teacher-pupil dynamic to remind all that, in the classroom, work is what matters and discipline is there to protect that principle.

Pupils and parents: Day pupils outnumber boarders 3:1. Full boarders outnumber flexis by 4:1. And boys outnumber girls – as in most co-ed schools – by more than 2:1. Some 72 per cent are UK nationals, the rest from everywhere – 29 nationalities at time of our visit, so no cliques and enclaves. Vast majority of UK students are local or local-ish. Healthy 75 per cent of boarders in school at weekends. Old Leightonians: Sir David Lean, Sir Richard Rodney Bennett, Jim Broadbent, Laura Marling, Eliza Bennett, Michael Foot, Lord Caradon, Lord Frederick Seebohm and a fair clutch of MPs plus Rowntrees, Cadburys, Clarks, Reckitts, Morlands and Frys.

Entrance: Entrance tests in English, maths and non-verbal reasoning in the January preceding entry for years 7-10, plus interview. Entry to sixth form conditional on GCSE or equivalent results, plus interview. At 11+, 95 apply for 40 places; at 13+, 35 apply for 15-20 places. At year 10, 20 apply for 10-15 places. Year 11 is a 'pre-sixth' year for overseas students. There are six applicants for each of the 20-30 places in the sixth form. Second language speakers sit an EAL test.

Exit: Around 25 leave after year 11 but most stay on. Most who leave after sixth form go to a range of courses at respectable universities but, as one parent enthused, 'we liked the fact that alongside the leavers who read medicine at Oxford they celebrate those who go and learn circus skills'. Most, however, to eg Sheffield or Exeter to read eg engineering or philosophy. Sometimes one or two a year to Oxbridge.

Money matters: Not an immensely rich school but a decent amount of money available for bursaries. Emphasis on enabling those whose financial situation would not allow them to attend, to do so, so most recipients on awards of 50 per cent or more. Robust mean-testing and assessment of income/commitments/assets etc. Six on 100 per cent bursaries at time of our visit. Scholarships mostly worth 10 per cent.

Remarks: A school in which to grow. Not for hustlers, bustlers and takers but great for thinkers, makers, givers, be-ers.

Lord Wandsworth College

Long Sutton, Hook, Hampshire RG29 1TB

01256 862201
admissions@lordwandsworth.org
www.lordwandsworth.org

Ages: 11–18
Pupils: 540; sixth form: 160
Boarders: 85 full, 223 weekly/flexi (roughly two-thirds boys)
Day: £19,110 – £20,940 pa
Boarding: £21,480 – £29,700 pa

Headmaster: Since September 2015, Adam Williams, previously senior deputy head at The Glasgow Academy. Geography degree from Durham, where he also won national honours in cricket and golf. Has been head of geography at both Bradfield College and Oakham School, before becoming a housemaster for nine years at the latter. A keen sportsman, singer and cricket coach, he has also been an officer in the CCF.

Married to Karen, a consultant histopathologist; they have three children.

Academic matters: A good, broad, mid-range school, and a good place to be a bright kid – they are well rewarded for working hard, half a dozen Oxbridge candidates each year. 'He is being well stretched, and has taken to classics to our great surprise', a parent told us. Lots of setting – from the start, five sets for maths – but not a pressurised place: 'he's pushed enough, but not too much'. Plenty of homework, but can be done before you go home. 'Do the basics beautifully' is the mantra here.

Fifty-three per cent A*/A at GCSE in 2015. About half take all three sciences – twice the proportion of boys than girls, which shows up at A level too, sadly, especially in physics. Sixty-six per cent A*/B at A level in 2015 and 38 per cent A*/A; art, geography, English and languages relatively popular, compared to similar schools, with business studies, economics and psychology on the rise.

Chirpy, well thought out, involving teaching much appreciated by pupils. Parents say teachers are engaging and effective, know their pupils well – 'staff put so much into the school'. All live on site, several miles from the nearest village (though there is a pub just outside the gates), so quite a community.

Very keen on the AQA extended project: feel that it develops breadth and intellect, can be dropped if it proves all too much, plays to LWC pupils' strengths, and shows them up beautifully at Oxbridge.

Screening for learning difficulties in the first and third years, and in the lower sixth. Dyslexia the commonest, followed by information processing problems. All teachers briefed on the particular needs of each child, and generally this works well.

Games, options, the arts: Takes sport seriously and keenly. One parent we talked to remembered, and who would not, their son's yomp in the Welsh mountains in filthy weather. Nonetheless, you won't be sidelined if sport is not your thing. Not large enough to be sure of beating all-comers, and is just as interested in the C team as the A. Rugby (but no football), cricket (a close relationship with the MCC, tour to Sri Lanka, and match teas to sigh for on glorious summer evenings). Determined that girls' sport should be great too – hockey coach in the GB Olympic team. Netball and, in the summer, rounders and cricket (hurrah!).

Minor sports include swimming (25m pool and you can do scuba training here), squash, badminton, tennis, horse riding. Will support pupils whose performance takes them out to county competitions and above – swimmer, fencer and showjumper included currently.

A strong push under way to improve and extend all arts provision. 'Focus on the co-curriculum' is another school motto and there's a clear intention to add substantially to the quality and quantity of an already decent provision.

Art itself is already a most inspiring department, popular and with excellent exam results (almost all A* or A), aiming to help pupils explore

Main campus pleasingly higgledy-piggledy. Glorious feeling of surrounding space, though no unsupervised access to wilder bits

their talent rather than corral them into standard styles. Pupils participate in teaching – discussing how to approach new topic areas. Short on computing support, more said to be on the way. Art and sport a common mix of enthusiasms.

Drama clearly much enjoyed, the centre of school life for some pupils and an enjoyable part of it for most. An ambitious list of productions – Ayckbourn, Pinter, Shakespeare. English teachers involved in drama activities – encourage scriptwriting. Lots of have-a-go and 10 took it at GCSE in 2015. Few take A level though – none in 2015 – the result of a staff hiatus of a few years ago, but good cohorts now coming through. A new dance studio being used to effect, boys being drawn in by house dance competitions etc.

Music provided in fine quantity and improving quality: two-thirds of juniors take lessons in school, half that number in the senior school, but not notably important to the life of the school.

Strong CCF, linked to RAF Odiham with aerial results. D of E – an accredited awarding centre so not reliant on external assessors. Expeditions to all corners of the country.

Computer programming just getting going. DT keen and reasonably well provided for. No science club. As our school reports often said, 'could do better', but in LWC's case there are improvements afoot.

Pupils encouraged to do a lot – and 'those who do, do better academically too,' say parents. Pupils set frequent 'challenges': anything from cooking to karate – to broaden their experience. 'There do not appear to be waiting lists – they seem to get into an activity as soon as they want to'.

Boarding: Boarding in comfortable houses: nice study/recreation areas (mostly), restrained decoration, comfortable dormitories with engaging personalities – but too many blank pinboards and animal-free beds. No nasties, a certain amount of mess and tubs of Promax and Diet Fuel for the sports-mad boys. Mixed-sex house (but separate dormitories) for the first two years, separate houses thereafter.

Weekends properly provided for, with trips and films. The film 300 is a favourite with the boys: 'an inspiring story about duty and loyalty, courage and honour' or, according to A O Scott's review, 'about as violent as Apocalypto and twice as stupid'.

Background and atmosphere: Created in 1912 under the will of Sydney James Stern, Lord Wandsworth. Twelve hundred acres of Hampshire chalk down were bought as a refuge for agricultural orphans, the occupations provided drifting gradually away from manual to academic toil, taking fee-paying pupils soon after the last world war. Well spread out in these rather bare uplands, looking much like a 20th century Hampshire village, never inspiring in its architecture but not offensive either. Main campus pleasingly higgledy-piggledy. Glorious feeling of surrounding space, though children not allowed unsupervised access to the wilder bits, or the working farm.

The care of orphans remains central to the school's identity and ethos, though with the current dearth of gruesome agricultural accidents the school no longer asks for a farming background. Foundationers, as they are known, make up 10 per cent of the school population, are heavily supported financially (about eight per cent of fee income is used, with the full support of those paying, for this purpose), and fit seamlessly into this unpretentious school. As long as Foundation candidates are up to the school's entrance standards they are chosen on the basis of need, not performance: the objective is to do well by the children, not flatter the school's exam and sporting performance with imported superstars.

The care of orphans remains central, though with the current dearth of gruesome agricultural accidents the school no longer asks for a farming background

Parents speak of an immensely friendly school. And, with the inevitable exception of the boys' changing rooms, it smells good too. 'The school understands parents, opens its arms to them, says "how can we help – how can you help".'Lots of parental involvement with the school as a result. 'I am as much a part of LWC as my son is'.

School runs from 8.15am to 4.15pm, but it rarely works out that way. What with activities (so many, so well run, so enthusiastically enjoyed), and friendships, and homework, and boarders to set the pace, parents report days that run till 8 or even 9.30pm – and then there's the flexi-boarding: occasional nights at any time and at short notice, but if you contract for three nights a week you get 'your own bed' (we think this means a dedicated bed, rather than not having to sleep top to tail) and competitive rates.

Pastoral care, well-being and discipline: School sets out to help children mix – senior pupils lead junior activities, for instance. Has worked, we are told: parents and pupils say there are no cliques and school friends span academic, sporty, arty, their own houses and others, as well as across years. 'Everyone just gets on with each other'. Parents speak of the real attachment between houseparents and their charges and praise tutors too. Staff also involved and helpful – pupils and parents email them at all times of day and evening and get quick answers. Staff know immediately (systems, not memory) who else is involved with each child, and so can pass on news, views and worries quickly.

Not a school where sin flourishes in any obvious way – pupils are trusted, and act accordingly. Not a boozy school – the boys asked that the 1st XV tour to South Africa was dry, as they didn't want to get dehydrated! Smoking is not tolerated. A pupil who persisted would be asked to leave.

House life is important. 'Once pupils touch base there they are left to their own devices', parents say. Form strong friendships. Girl/boy relationships respectful and civilised. They don't tend to couple up. Sex is forbidden.

Very occasional soft drug issues have been dealt with sensibly. Food raved about by pupils, but by no means gourmet.

Pupils and parents: Parents mainly middle class, many new to independent education. 'I chose LWC because I work hard and could not fit in with the state school day, but I had not realised what I was getting. My son comes home from school asking "can I do this can I do that?" There is so much more going on that it seems to generate another culture'.

Pupils are 'well rounded, decent people who understand themselves and have a social conscience'. Confident. Not dreamers. Grounded. 'Well balanced, confident, level-headed, quite polite'; 'comfortable in their own skins', 'ready for life', 'can manage their day, talk to people', 'have a broader toolkit than just the academic,' say parents. The ones who showed us round were a real pleasure to be with. Lots of hearty folk, but you don't need to be robust to flourish: we heard several parental stories of shy kids, or loners even, the ones who 'always end up at the bottom of the rugby scrum', who have been picked up by the school, set challenges, helped to make friends and generally brought out of themselves.

Old Sternians, as they are known, include Jonny Wilkinson (as you will not fail to notice if you tour the school).

Entrance: From Amesbury, Eagle House, Yateley Manor and a wide range of prep and state primary schools. Bus services from as far as Winchester,

Bagshot, Churt, Crookham, Hindhead, North Waltham and Yateley.

Likes all rounders. Entrance exams 'not horrific, but neither are they a doddle,' say parents. In the centre of the local independent school academic scale, taking children who are average and above. If you are coming from a state school, use a tutor to familiarise your child with the style of the exam questions.

Exit: No hoofing out at 16 unless you do so badly at GCSE that A levels are not a realistic option, but nonetheless up to a third leave then, mostly for one or other of the excellent local state (and hence free) sixth form colleges.

Barring accidents, all who remain here for the sixth form go on to university – popular destinations include Cardiff, Exeter, Oxford Brookes and York. One Oxbridge place in 2015 (innovative and effective support from the school). One fifth take a gap year.

Money matters: Ten per cent of pupils supported by The Foundation. Means-tested awards restricted to British children who have lost the support of one or both parents through death, divorce or separation, and whose surviving parent (if there is one) has not formed a new relationship. The order of priority is: 'children who have an identifiable boarding need, the need for pastoral care and support, the need for stability and security in a structured environment, the candidate's home and family situation, the ability to cope academically, integrate socially and contribute to the college community, the family's financial circumstances'.

Remarks: Long known to us, never before thought worth a place in the Guide, Lord Wandsworth was an Ugly Duckling whose spring has arrived. Well on the way to Swan-dom.

Ludgrove

Wokingham, Berkshire RG40 3AB

01189 789881
registrar@ludgroveschool.co.uk
www.ludgrove.net

Ages: 8–13
Pupils: 190
Boarders: all full
Boarding: £25,350 pa

Headmaster: Since 2008 Mr Simon Barber BA (40s) following six years as a teacher here and, before that, at Ashdown House.

Mr Barber, who grew up here (and has fond memories of watching cows being milked in what is now the art and carpentry block), completed teacher training at robust state school Cranford Community College with aplomb, tweed jacket and Eton education no barrier to pupil acceptance – when asked where he was at school 'I said, "down the road, just south of Slough".' Spell teaching geography at LVS Ascot was followed by short digression 'as junior squit' in corporate finance – quickly realised not for him.

Headship shared until 2013 when joint incumbent moved on to school of his own. After initial parental nerviness, Barbers now universally reckoned to be bit of all right, having grown into role. Mr Barber teaches Latin, PSHE and Greek myths – 'so important, you can see their little minds buzz.' He's nice but strict if necessary, thought pupil – 'if people are talking after lights out.'

Mrs Barber ('Sophie' to all) sorts domestics – 'kitchens, matrons, nurse, cleaners' – as well as being first point of contact 'for mothers' worries' and prepping boys for first phone calls home.

'[Mr Barber] likes children, enjoys their company and knows how to make them feel good about themselves,' said one parent. 'As a team, they are superb,' agreed another.

Barbers' immersion in school life is almost total (though Mrs Barber does get short daily break to collect youngest child – they have two daughters and a son – from local school). Instead of separate house have own (though separate) quarters in the main building, but appear miraculously claustrophobia-free. Mr Barber, in particular, can go for days without leaving the building. 'I love walking round the school and thinking about creating an environment that is fun, safe and full of opportunities,' he says.

Entrance: Takes 30 in year 4 when it's completely non-selective – unless you count speed of registration as competitive sport. 'Don't believe in testing

boys at 8,' says school. After initial enquiry (at birth) parents receive letter from head (handwritten) with registration form (printed). Two years before joining, there's a fun day for boys with confirmed places, followed by final make-your-mind-up time.

For occasional places (around eight in year 5, four in year 6 and even a couple in year 7 – generous bursary scheme helps bright boys fill gap between state primary and common entrance), hopefuls sit English and maths tests 'to be sure they can slot in easily.' Duvet changing and tie-knotting practice before start of first term also urged.

School trips return having learned that 'a sense of humour can see you through most tricky situations'

No official feeders, but road here well trodden by families moulded in traditional cast (plenty of second generation pupils or better). Around 40 per cent from well-connected pre-preps (Finton House, Thomas's Fulham, Eaton House, Knightsbridge and Broomwood Hall in London, Pinewood and Farleigh outside), many escaping competitive inferno of London school entrance.

Around half of places to country dwellers, most within two-hour commute (Wiltshire, Hampshire, Berkshire, Northants). A few from further away (East Anglia, Scotland). Remaining 10 per cent overseas, split about equally between expats (FO, MOD) and international pupils from all over – India, Thailand, Ukraine, Russia, Spain, China, Nigeria,

Korea. A few arrive for year's immersion in penultimate year then head for home. DBS-cleared drivers (ideally same one both ways) on tap to do the airport run.

Exit: Given diverse input, rightly proud of output – reckon to get around three-quarters, sometimes more, into Eton, Harrow and Radley (12, nine and six places respectively in 2015, with two scholarships). Mr Barber's expert knowledge of all three won't mean special treatment at CE, though word dropped in admission tutor's shell-like can't go amiss if results an unexpected disaster.

Best-known OBs are Prince William, Prince Harry and Bear Grylls (who recently waxed lyrical about his experiences in print). Very occasionally head may suggest specialist school. One dyslexic pupil has recently gone to Bruern Abbey, though 'welcome back at any time,' says Mr Barber.

Remarks: Mood is determinedly upbeat...'a belief that one should always look on the bright side of life,' says prospectus and reflection of Mr Barber's philosophy. May not sing the Monty Python song but lives it. 'The eternal optimist,' says Mrs Barber.

So at their best, teams 'are a match for anyone.' School trips – a range, from Devon (leavers and geographers) to Sauze D'Oulx (skiers) – return having learned that 'a sense of humour can see you through most tricky situations'. Torrential rain makes sports day 'a memorable occasion.' Breakages in Roman-themed pottery session 'added to the authenticity.' Boys ward off looming homesickness by 'thinking of funny things and looking forward to the next lunch,' said one.

Upbeat approach translates into academics. Teachers are 'amazing,' say parents, talking round subjects and knowing their pupils. 'They work you hard but within your ability,' thought pupil. 'I wasn't clever when I arrived – now I am.' 'Never gave up on my son...and he flew,' said parent.

Small classes (average 12, maximum 15, minimum eight) undoubtedly help. So does overall staff to pupil ratio of just under one to seven (and that's not including the nurse and six matrons; all live-in). Streaming in English and maths from the beginning, lessons lively – new boys attacking Venn diagram in geography with enthusiasm; ditto 11 year olds discussing perils of 16th century religious affiliation. (Can read on in cheerful, traditional library, popular titles enticingly face up in long rows, pupils trained in old-fashioned referencing using real encyclopaedias).

Boys go through order papers with division master (form tutor) so clear on how to improve. Ups and downs caused by small class sizes and narrow range of marks (can shoot from second to eighth place) can cause occasional jitters among success-focused parents who need lots of reassurance. 'Boys pick up on their hopes and fears,' says Mr Barber. While coming top is well and good, the message that endeavour counts is received loud and clear. 'Trying hard is better,' said top year boy firmly. Workload in and out of lessons bearable,

'Support without throttling,' said a parent. 'Nurtured from the start but guided towards independence as they get older'

adjusted if necessary. No shame in saying you're struggling – teachers will set less and help with catch up, thought boys.

Individual excellence (good work) commended by head and rewarded with sweets. Plus marks also awarded, best performing house rewarded with special (and, needless to say, 'delicious') tea. The naughty get minus marks – occasional detentions. Boarding runs its own rewards system, giving angels, however dirty their downstairs wings, a second chance at redemption

Parents get emails summarising life in and out of the classroom and can phone child's class during a 40 minute slot at lunchtime to speak to son. Resulting free-for-all generally works (a bit of muttering about parents who go beyond allotted five minutes) though substantial redialling sometimes required. Alternative – giving boys mobile phones – felt by all to be far worse. Some – 'particularly sweet boys who want to make sure their parents are all right,' said mother – also send emails.

Daily staff meetings, attended by boarding nurse, ensure whole-school awareness of any issues. Wobbles impressively dealt with. 'Support without throttling,' said parent. 'Nurtured from the start but guided towards independence as they get older.'

Solid assistance for pupils with learning needs – around 30 or so in the school – includes academic support (booster groups for spelling, maths, reading) as well as help with handwriting, one-to-one EAL lessons and esteem and confidence-building sessions – we liked King of the Shelves award for better organisation skills. Four specialist teachers develop programmes for pupils with more complex needs – speech and language or specific learning difficulties – and ensure that subject teachers know how to implement it. 'Have been called a Rottweiler,' says jolly but firm head of learning support. Younger pupils have support sessions during art, drama and music while older pupils can opt to miss occasional rest period or break so don't lose out on favourite subject.

Merely mastering school's year group numbering system must be considerable source of pride. 'Sixes are year 4; fours year 5, threes year 6, twos year 7 and top year is year 8,' says school handbook. And those missing fives? 'Not a year group but a game with a small ball and leather gloves,' it adds, helpfully.

Uniform options similarly quirky. In addition to giddy whirl of jacket choices (a tweed spotter's dream), school jumpers offered not just in navy, but rather more exotic pink and green, adding welcome flash of colour to massed gatherings.

Great outdoors spread over 130 acres includes usual playing fields as well as nine-hole golf course and plenty of space for building camps. Every parent commented approvingly on boys being out in all weathers. 'All is underlined and bold and caps,' said one. Sports rampant and not just for current pupils, either. Most recent alumni calendar featured five matches and just one drinks party.

However, quantity doled out can be varied to taste. Everyone, talented or otherwise, gets shot at glory of minibus trip and match tea. How much glory is a tad confusing to decipher, what with online match reports dating back to 2013 with tendency to linger on the glories of game well played rather than the score.

Deadline for posting team lists is 7.00pm the night before, seemed a bit tight in giving parents sufficient time to change all arrangements and rush up to watch their son score the winning try/goal/run – but felt largely to work as most teams, once settled, there for the duration. Parents in broad agreement, biggest issue we encountered relating to yawning gap between the keen and talented – who get lion's share of training and interest – and keen but less so, who don't and can be completely overlooked. More matches on the cards for every shade of ability, says school, while swimming notable for squad training that's open to all.

Not a job for the boys, though perhaps it should be, joining list of well-organised activities carefully balanced to ensure that everyone is just busy enough

The less athletic joyfully opt for extra art, pottery or, top favourite, carpentry/DT, where Portuguese fishing dinghy, owl nesting box as well as enough chairs and tables to equip several classrooms are among impressive projects to have helped school to several DT scholarships in recent years.

Music busy, with choirs, open access music block, numerous ensembles and vast majority (85 per cent) playing at least one instrument (bagpipes, tuba and bassoon adding interesting new timbre to conventional choices). Not as busy as drama, however, now in impressive new theatre (none of that 'performing arts centre' nonsense here...) where according to prospectus, boys 'have been on stage non-stop...' Crumbs. Our visit clearly took place during one of brief periods of non-occupancy. (Drama teacher was having lunch at the time, explained school later, keen to ensure nobody got the wrong end of the stick). No wonder exeats billed as a time to relax. Happen every fortnight, so not too punishing for the youngest recruits.

Attractive 19th century building was purpose-built as school and it shows. Dorms, all south-facing with attractive big windows and same gorgeous view over greenery as from head's study but a floor up, hold four to 10 pupils from single year group, some in bunk beds, each with top year monitor, honoured with different coloured laundry basket (vibrant pink in one case). Every pillow adorned with loved, often dilapidated soft toy, resident seamstress ('crucially important,' says Mrs Barber) on hand to work miracles when teddies' arms come adrift or eyes go missing – 'upsetting but it's the smell they like...' Matrons much praised. 'Never shout if you do something wrong,' said pupil. 'Say it doesn't matter, don't worry.' Occasional accidents sensitively sorted – boys squeeze matron's arm when woken up, signal for sheets to be unobtrusively washed and replaced.

Dedicated maintenance posse roams school, killing at least 99.9 per cent of all known germs dead and rounding up errant possessions. Basins, loos, baths in communal washroom all radiant; boys' clothes and towels a tribute to precision folding, cloakroom a thing of wonder, coats and shoes lined up as if on parade – a daily, 90 minute task undertaken with pride.

Not a job for the boys, though perhaps it should be, joining list of well-organised activities carefully balanced to ensure that everyone is just busy enough and thus avoiding too much time for introspection, particularly for newbies (who have dedicated matron and allocated 'shadow' to help them settle in), but ensuring 'can flop if they want to,' says school.

Saturday is the faster-paced weekend day, with lessons till lunch, matches afterwards followed by free time, film screenings and a spot of X-Factor if in season. Sunday has fixed slots: chapel and assembly to announce the day's happenings. Otherwise less structure, with activity staples (swimming, art, films) and specials (visiting climbing wall, circus workshop and – occasionally – ice cream van) but also potential for spontaneity – boys will organise own games of cricket, five-a-side football or make camps. Less official dorm raids and stair run (down one, up the other at night without being caught) also happen but 'I know nothing about it...' says Mr Barber.

For youngest, there's comfort zone story time with Mrs Barber, 'special half hour when they're piled like puppies on the sofas and all over the floor.' Tuck, in the form of sweets, isn't allowed. Instead, school suggests packing 'useful and fun' – but inedible – items such as bluetac, string, stickers and playing cards.

School-supplied treats appeared attractive replacements for missing goodies, particularly birthday ice cream cake with choice of five flavours, multi-coloured remnants being solemnly enjoyed by small break time group on day of visit. Similarly colourful foodfests celebrate pupil nationalities (Ireland with mandarin, whipped cream and lime jelly...). Match teas a more restrained mix of sandwiches and cakes (parents) with doughnuts, crisps and juice for boys. Pupil committee gets unpopular dishes pulled and replaced (fish pie with scampi).

Other trad preps can feel as if saturated in own past. Here, though pride in history is evident, it's not overwhelming, with few pictures of ancient OBs. Instead, names of new boys are added to the honours board within a few weeks of start of first term – simple but effective way of generating pride and self-confidence and looking ahead.

'You've got to look at what you're doing – and how to do it better,' says Mr Barber. 'It's amazing,' said one parent. 'The camaraderie amongst the boys is one of the key things and they leave with lifelong friends. I couldn't fault it at all.'

LVS Ascot (Licensed Victuallers' School)

London Road, Ascot, Berkshire SL5 8DR

01344 882770
registrar@lvs.ascot.sch.uk
www.lvs.ascot.sch.uk

Ages: 4–18 (boarding from 7)
Pupils: 868 (two-thirds boys); sixth form: 195
Boarders: 195
Day: £9,255 – £16,590 pa
Boarding: £23,685 – £31,167 pa

Headmistress: Since 2010, Christine Cunniffe BA MMus MBA. Three children, all at the school (husband goes to the parents' evenings). Personable, open, quietly assured and one of what seems like growing number (or should that be band?) of musicians to forsake lieder for leadership. Other careers have beckoned. After university, had close brush with the law (professionally speaking, that is) securing postgraduate traineeship with Slough-based legal practice only to succumb to alternative role as pianist to fashionistas and London high society (think white baby grands and late nights in plush hotels). Four years in, realised that though 'loved life, not what I wanted to do when I was getting older'. Putting aside renewed yearnings for law when husband-to-be pointed out years of study ahead, she tried her hand at teaching and loved it from the off, going straight in as head of music, first at a Stevenage school, then St Bernard's, a selective co-ed grammar school in Slough. Joined LVS Ascot as ambitious director of music in 2003

(school, which had no choir when she arrived, was performing Vivaldi's Gloria at Eton College Chapel just two terms later).

Overcame crisis of confidence in first year as head when numbers dipped (they're now on the rise again), confessing all in school magazine – unusual if not unprecedented openness for a head – which, she feels, sends useful message to pupils. 'You have self-doubt. I thought, the children are going to face problems in life, so why pretend it doesn't happen?'

Is considered by parents to be doing a good job though some would like a greater presence and more speechifying at major school events. 'She needs to be seen and heard a bit more...you've got to be the front runner, Ursain Bolt-ish and get up there if you're a head with over 1,000 pupils and fee-paying parents,' said one. Pretty visible during the school day though, the more so as job comes with house in grounds (she also has west London bolthole for change of scene). 'I'm not one of those

people who hides behind a closed door; there's no point.' Doesn't teach but asks boarders to choose lessons for her to observe every week, and on day of visit was in gym encouraging sixth formers flagging half way through 56-mile sponsored row for charity. 'I said, "I'll be your Mrs Motivator".'

All parents have her email address, a useful barometer as 'they'll only bring something to me directly if they are really upset,' and doesn't shy away from taking criticism on the chin. 'I don't want people to tell me what they think I want to hear but to be honest.' Pleased, she insists, to get lots of 'forthright' comments when recently invited parent group in for dinner and presentation on proposed introduction of heads of year to help raise academic bar through better tracking and target setting.

Own experiences make her sympathetic to late developers. 'I experienced problems at about 13 and it's made me passionate about not giving up on a child until we have exhausted all areas,' though firm when line has to be drawn – handful of children have been asked to leave during headship. 'The boundaries are like an elastic band – you have to know when it's going to break.'

Like Mary Poppins, will go when mission is accomplished. 'I'm a realist. If, after five years, I think my job's done, I'm not going to stay around.' Not necessarily to another headship, either. 'I might just become a lawyer after all,' she says.

Academic matters: Though tolerant, school isn't the place for skivers. 'The school's a hard runner... and they want the exams. Non-selective doesn't mean an easy ride,' said a parent.

Mission in junior school is to ensure that no child is left to languish in educational no man's land; regular meetings picking out those 'falling below or zooming ahead'. Children give a high rating to all subjects, particular favourites being literacy (popular library-based reading scheme, which carries on into main school, tests comprehension rather than merely rewarding headlong dash for the last page) and science in year 6 – where, joy of joys, 'you get to light the Bunsen burner'. They're also unexpectedly appreciative of small teaching groups (average is about 12). 'In state schools you have 60 in a class,' says one horror-struck year 6 guide.

Secured traineeship with legal practice only to succumb to alternative role as pianist to fashionistas and London high society (think white baby grands)

There's minimal setting (maths from year 3) and a pick and mix approach to national curriculum – used or modified where it works, ditched if it doesn't (children's progress well ahead of national averages). Everything is seasoned with welcome dash of carpe diem flexibility so teachers can go off piste if not-to-be-missed educational opportunities present themselves; recent stick collection and den-building exercise for reception was a case in point. Lots of popular outings, too, including the inevitable trip to Swanage.

Exam results compare well with local competition – GCSEs in 2015 26 per cent A*/A, reasonable for non-selective school, let alone one so large. Ten the norm though whittled down to nine for some students with learning difficulties who fill the time with extra English and maths support. Choice of around 20 subjects, nothing showy (there's no Latin or classics, for example). English, maths, French or Spanish and science/environmental science all compulsory with options including German, humanities, all the sciences, media/business studies, art and PE.

Sixth form options broad and getting broader, with law and psychology recently added to the roster of around 30 courses. Students will need GCSE B grades or better in chosen subjects though vocational courses such as ICT and sport also available for those of a more practical mindset. In 2015, 42 per cent A*-B and 16 per cent A*/A grades at A level.

Head on mission to ensure that ability is unearthed and nurtured earlier through advanced data crunching and addition of heads of year to management team. 'We haven't even scratched the surface with gifted and talented children,' she says (something also picked up in recent inspection). School's strength thus far has centred on bringing low achievers up to snuff (several heart-warming stories of pupils helped up the academic ladder to top exam grades) and parents like the approach, big on encouragement, small on class sizes – average teacher to pupil ratio of 12 to one – and low on hothouse forcing (definitely not the school's style).

Games, options, the arts: School's philosophy is that there's something for everyone and brave attempts are made (with help of extensive range of activities, all bar four included in the fees) to keep participation rates high all the way through the school. A dip in current year 10 and 11 girls' teams reflects lack of numbers rather than interest.

Two games halls, the large with climbing wall and cricket nets, the smaller with cushioned floor for happier landings in judo and high impact sports

Approach, strong on inclusion and optimism – sports honours board runs to 2023 – is recognised by award of Sportsmark Gold and helped by cracking facilities including two games halls, the larger with climbing wall and cricket nets, the smaller with cushioned floor for happier landings in judo and high impact sports. Enticing heated pool is well used, offering all-ability training at 6.30am three times a week, while thumping pop music from upstairs broadcasts presence of well-equipped fitness suite, predictably popular with older boys. Has recently set up elite golf academy for sixth formers which combines coaching at a nearby club with a BTec in sports science.

Huge, ambitious productions with 100-strong cast (all 'proper' parts: 'People don't want to be a third tree') and special effects including ultraviolet bubbles

With recent wins in judo, swimming and rugby, achievement counts but so does nurturing, for B as much as A teams so not seen as also rans. Felt by some parents to handicap the single-minded. 'Everyone gets a game which is to be encouraged but [can be] a drawback if you really want to excel at one sport,' said one.

Head would like greater take up of outdoor activities and has appointed ex-marine who 'doesn't sleep and likes to live in tents' to make it so. With re-jigged timetable incorporating two additional sessions a week for all (year 9 upwards can do as part of D of E, open to as many as are interested) expect substantial increase in fresh air intake.

Vibrant artistic life is similarly wide ranging (though indoor-based) with ringing endorsement from award of Artsmark Gold to prove it and enthusiastic support from (literally) all-singing, all-dancing staff who aren't averse to taking to the boards as hoofers in zingy, highly regarded productions like Hairspray and Bugsy Malone. (By all accounts do a mean version of 'Teacher, leave them kids alone' too).

Year 3 teachers (and their classes) break into spontaneous song about Mothers' Day. 'It happens a lot here,' says one, who's also, as it turns out, responsible for junior school's huge, ambitious productions with 100-strong cast (all 'proper' parts: 'People don't want to be a third tree') and special effects including ultraviolet bubbles and even an exploding shark – 'every gizmo I can get into it'. Every other summer there's a Dance for Fitness workshop instead – fun and worthy, no doubt (and considered sufficiently cool for embarrassment-free participation by older boys) though you sense teacher's regret that it can't be waterfalls of lights and smoke effects every year.

With five choirs, numerous ensembles including rock school, and around a third of pupils learning instruments, some to diploma standard, performance is shifting from niche activity to sizeable minority occupation. Possible that numerous pianos lurking in school nooks and crannies (some boarding houses have several) are conveying subliminal positive message; whizzy music tech studio probably better recruitment ad. Admittedly, boys in years 10 and 11 remain somewhat shy and retiring – 'Music's not a cool thing to do,' says pupil – but some at least are drawn in again to at sixth form (though the need to pep up UCAS forms with wholesome balance of activities is, they confess, also a factor).

Boarding: Four boarding houses – co-ed junior house, one each for senior boys and girls and co-ed sixth form house – are now plushness personified with full-size beds and colour-matched walls, carpets and curtains chosen by pupils. Palettes err towards predictable blues in boys' boarding house though biggest difference is in communal areas where girls arrange smart leather sofas close together to maximise eye contact and conviviality, boys in contrast opting for side by side seating for maximum cheering-on potential during pool matches.

Boarding house staff, particularly those with experience of compromise Victorian conversions, are enthusiastic. 'A breeze to run,' comments one. Experienced houseparents are experts at sidestepping homesickness and ditching superfluities like complex laundry rules – 'I'd much rather you were clean than worried about what day you need to put your washing in,' says one.

It's all about fine-tuning to achieve delicate balance between homely family feel (thoughtful inclusion of year 8 boarders with juniors for extra cosseting) and early detection of transgressions. Morning lethargy beyond normal teen parameters can signal OTT late night laptop/mobile use (enormous phone bills arriving at parental home the other tell-tale sign). Controlled independence, such as giving year 11s separate kitchen and TV 'so they don't have to watch the same thing as year 8s,' explains teacher, is carefully cultivated.

Keeping idle hands (and brains) busy is the priority. 'We don't want boarders sitting around, twiddling their thumbs,' says pastoral head. Steady but not relentless stream of activities from house talent shows to relaxed Saturday breakfasts in pjs. Weekend minibuses, booked by the hour, swap returning sports teams for boarders off on assorted excursions (shopping, films and bowling all popular) with departures and arrivals as precisely coordinated as flight control at Heathrow.

Background and atmosphere: Site was formerly home to Heatherdown, an ultra-traditional prep school for chaps and David Cameron's pre-Eton alma mater, with own miniature steam railway. It was demolished in 1982 after Licensed Trade Charity (LTC) – which runs school, founded 200 years ago to support drinks trade employees – made such an advantageous sale of previous premises in Slough to well-known supermarket chain that could fund construction of what prospectus claims is the 'most modern boarding school in the UK'.

It comes complete with LVS branded drainpipes and school houses named, delightfully, after major drinks brands, leading to such pleasing sentences as 'this year saw the introduction of many new staff and students to Guinness,' in school magazine.

And yes, lovers of mellow brickwork may need to recalibrate their aesthetic sensibilities when it comes to the exterior (think sheltered housing designer meets Etch a Sketch addict – prospectus sensibly avoids any full-on shots of the facade). However, it's well worth the effort as school lacks neither charm nor character and is stuffed with quirky touches from the formal (two back-to-back reception desks, one glitzy for corporate visitors to charity HQ, the other, smart but workmanlike, for school traffic) to the relaxed (skeleton of dolphin in science lab, Garfield soft toy clasped lovingly between jaws). There's tradition, too – the 25 acres of grounds with rustic bridge spanning small but perfectly formed lake prove the point – but exists primarily to serve a purpose (lesson bell all but abolished after it broke five years ago, ending mid-sentence rush for the door and making teachers so happy that was never re-introduced).

Thoughtful layout now past 30th birthday may no longer be at cutting edge of school design but fundamentals still apply, noticeably the way space-intensive subjects like performing arts get the room they need in central location rather than being consigned to outer reaches of site, while related subjects are housed together making navigation a breeze – at least if you're a pupil. 'It's the adults who struggle,' says passing teacher.

It's all well cared for, too – maths display board with cracked plastic cover is rare exception ('Children pick at it without realising they're doing it,' explains staff member) and nicely spruced up where required.

Add lively art room with wall-to-wall high quality work (intriguing bronze-effect sculpture floats above plinth), busy, popular DT department with more saws than you could shake a freshly trimmed stick at and fabulous learning resource centre; light, airy and staffed by team of affable universal aunt and uncle types who always have a giant jigsaw on the go and live for research – 'You need a bit up here and to love finding things out,' says one – and easy to see why purpose-built practicality gets parental thumbs up. 'Some private schools try to make the best of the [space] they happen to have, such as a former chambermaid's room being used as a biology class room, [whereas] LVS have great class rooms built to deliver good lessons,' said a father.

Junior school has good-sized infants' play area with buddy bench (hardly used, though, insist pupils 'because there's a bare minimum of people who feel sad') and lots of sturdy wooden equipment to climb and balance on. Year 3s and up enjoy scaled up versions in adjoining area, separated by unmarked but universally recognised boundary line. Reception also has smart new outdoor classroom and cheerful playhouse, starting point for innumerable let's pretend games. Eagerly awaited musical train complete with three carriages and bells (if no whistles) currently being built by senior school sixth former as part of DT A level is arriving soon.

Pastoral care, well-being and discipline: Highly regarded focus of pastoral care is the tutor group system with same teacher responsible for child's well-being throughout school career. Works well given high percentage of old-timers (figuratively speaking) on staff – 40 out of 340 have been there over 10 years – and is liked by parents and pupils. 'They have a vested interest in you as a person, you're more than just a pupil,' said 17-year old.

Eagerly awaited musical train complete with three carriages and bells currently being built by sixth former

In contrast, tribal Yin to sensitive tutor group Yang is a house system that's far more than convenient administrative format. Pitting combined boarders – normally four houses strong – against teams of day pupils, it's a focal point of school life, with fiercely contested matches generating 'as much rivalry amongst the [teachers] as pupils,' says member of staff.

Not as daunting as it sounds, however, given universal insistence that loyalties do not cross into lessons nor escalate beyond friendly rivalry ('It's just banter,' confirmed sixth former). Day pupils can also cross to other side by signing up for occasional one-off boarding sessions and there's added flexibility with extended day, including meal and the run of learning resource centre, popular with working parents.

School works hard to raise aspirations without upping the pressure, particularly at junior school level. Parental feedback – 'not sure what a hothouse is,' said parent, when questioned – suggests it's working.

Pupils and parents: A nice, un-showy and straightforward bunch, pupils are thoughtful rather than introspective, articulate but not glib, and fond of school (in touch with emotions, too – one burley and soon to be ex-sixth former has admitted to welling up when contemplating imminent departure). Start of term, said one, 'feels like you're going home rather than just going back.' There's affectionate tolerance for teachers who, they say with preternatural (but approving) gravitas, 'want to have fun but in a sensible way'.

As in other schools, pupils on show to visitors usually the top dogs. Here, cheeringly, they may only recently have had greatness thrust on them and reformed Horrid Henries stand as much chance as card-carrying Perfect Peters of getting their day in the sun. 'Prefects aren't just the "right" people,' explained one of the current glorious band of brothers (and sisters).

Families cover socially and economically broad spectrum from royalty to socially deprived (borne out by range of parental cars at drop off – five and

six figure off-roaders rubbing fenders with elderly mid-range saloons). Mix of working parents/career mothers, but either way are generally friendly and polite, though won't hesitate to come forward if there's a problem, though occasional hothouse impulses 'are squashed quite quickly by the school,' said approving mother.

Entrance: Most children arrive at junior school in reception (single form to year 2) or year 3 (two forms to year 5). At 11+ majority from school's own junior department with assorted state and private schools supplying the rest. Also small but significant international component, with 30 overseas students from as far afield as China, Russia and Korea and 40 or so from expat families, many in Forces.

Once settled, pupils tend to stick around. 'We were never going to take the boys out unless we needed to,' says mother. Locals form large proportion of the clientèle and, while job mobility means some degree of coming and going each year, there's not as much as you might suppose. Around 50 per cent of pupils stay on into sixth form ('places will only be offered where deemed appropriate by the head of sixth form, director of studies and head,' says admissions policy) with incomers, including first time boarders from local day schools, plugging the gaps. 'In my [elder] son's year, I'd say that 80 per cent went all the way through,' said parent.

Catchment area extends 15-20 mile radius or so to Reading in west and Maidenhead up north, compass points ably covered by seven school bus routes (some over-subscribed, so worth checking). Head is on a mission to spread the word elsewhere so expect increasing numbers of refuseniks from super-selective London fringes, deepest Berks and Bucks

Exit: As you'd expect given breadth of intake, pupils take corresponding range of university courses from the solidly academic – medicine, law, economics – to the more vocational, including photography and journalism. Many secure first rank uni places including one or two to Oxbridge some years. In 2015, Bath, Birmingham, Bristol, Exeter, Imperial College, Southampton, Manchester as well as Bournemouth, Brighton, Cardiff, Chester, Kingston, Loughborough, Royal Holloway, Westminster and Winchester. Old boys and girls end up as community stalwarts, many as successful entrepreneurs or 'something in the City'. Few facts and figures to back this up though with-it marketing manager is making good the omission with 'where are they now?' campaign.

Money matters: Ten per cent discount for siblings (but only third onwards and then only while all three attend school), 15 per cent off for MOD and diplomatic service employees, including five per cent early payment discount and a 20 per cent reduction for anyone who has worked in the licensed drinks trade for five years or more.

Families are attracted by all-through co-education, cracking facilities, local reputation and complete absence of entrance exams unless you're after a scholarship, academic worth a not-to-be-sniffed-at 50 per cent off fees; music, art, drama and sport a slightly less headline-grabbing £1,000 a year, in which case standard hurdles apply.

School tries to keep budgeting simple with many senior school clubs and activities included in the fees – rowing, riding, sailing and ballet plus individual instrumental lessons and one-to-one language or learning support are the main extras. Means headline fees are just that, with minimum of extras buried in the frequently expensive small print.

Remarks: All-comers welcomed in this well-equipped, friendly and unpretentious school that combines non-traditional exterior with timeless values and makes non-selectivity the starting point for success rather than a justification for its absence.

Moulsford Preparatory School

Moulsford, Wallingford, Oxfordshire OX10 9HR

01491 651 438
pa.registrar@moulsford.com
www.moulsford.com

Ages: 4–13 (boarding from 10)
Pupils: 336
Boarders: up to 50 weekly or flexi
Day: £10,185 – £15,225 pa
Boarding: weekly £19,095 pa

Headmaster: Since 2014, Mr Ben Beardmore-Gray (40s). Educated at Ludgrove (where his father taught) and Ampleforth. After history degree at Newcastle he trained as a lawyer and worked in the City, but the lure of the family business was too much for him and he succumbed to teaching. Back he went to Ludgrove where he gained his QTS, thence to Farleigh Prep as deputy head followed by seven years as head of Mowden Hall School in Northumberland.

Mr B-G is a huge fan of boarding. He and his wife, Sarah, have done a stint as house parents and he also ran boarding at Farleigh. While the majority of pupils at Moulsford may be day boys, the small Monday to Friday boarding community is 'key to the school's ethos,' he says. He sees weekly boarding as 'dynamic' and 'forward thinking' and believes it could well be the future for schools like his.

Boarding also 'draws staff' who are enabled, courtesy of the school's staff flats and houses, to live in what could otherwise be a prohibitively expensive part of the country.

By all accounts Mr B-G had a job of work to do in his first headship at Mowden Hall, so he must have been glad to find his next school in such rude health. He pays tribute to his predecessor (who retired after 20 years) and says, with some relief, that he inherited a 'cracking school' that was 'running very nicely' and 'fantastic' staff. He also seems to have been bowled over by the support and dynamism of the parent community.

Having 'spent his first year observing' and consulting parents, Mr B-G has exciting plans for Moulsford's future. The school already has a deservedly strong reputation for sport; Mr B-G wants to raise its profile in other areas, particularly the performing arts. Hence forthcoming redevelopment of the theatre and music school – cue more plays, ensembles and concerts. He wants Moulsford boys to enjoy breadth of opportunity in as many different areas as possible. All this, we were assured, will not come at the expense of sporting excellence. Some parents we spoke to hoped that leadership

Popular with locals; distinctive red blazers and caps give chaps a retro Just William charm and make for great free PR in Waitrose

change would also herald ethos change in this area. While no one wanted the school to be less successful on the sports field, quite a few wanted more opportunities for chaps who are never going to make the A teams.

Mr and Mrs Beardmore-Gray, who met at university, both hail from this part of the world. Sarah has taken on the unenviable task of revamping the school's utterly dire website, which seems to have been designed expressly to repel interest or enquiry. We wish her well. The couple have three children – one at Radley, one at Cheam and one at Moulsford – plus the standard issue black lab. Down time is for cricket, golf, tennis and cycling.

Entrance: Main entry points are reception (for pre-prep) and year 3 (for prep). One pre-prep class; expands to three in year 3 when boys join from schools such as Rupert House (Henley), Cranford House (just across the road), The Manor (Abingdon) and Harriet House (Frilsham), which all kick boys out after year 2.

Entry to reception is first come, first served. Assessment day in October for following September's year 3 applicants. School says it's not 'overtly

academically selective' but paucity of boys' prep options in Henley area means a scramble for places.

Exit: Abingdon takes the lion's share of day boys followed by Pangbourne, Bradfield, Shiplake, The Oratory and Magdalen College School. Boarders to Radley, St Edward's Oxford, Marlborough, Wellington, Stowe, Harrow and Eton. In 2015 one third of year 8 leavers awarded scholarships.

Remarks: Moulsford and its eponymous village sit on the banks of the Thames just outside Wallingford in South Oxfordshire. Fast rail links to the capital make this picturesque area attractive to London escapees with young families (and deep pockets). The school has always been popular with locals; its distinctive red blazers and caps give chaps a retro Just William charm and make for great free PR in Waitrose (just as well given the dreadful website). The strange dearth of boys' preps in and around Henley is Moulsford's gain – about a third of the school's pupils come in from there by coach (about half an hour each way).

Before Moulsford took up residence in 1961 the Victorian red-brick building at its centre was a private house and subsequently the boarding accommodation for Cranford, the girls' school across the road. It sits, high and dry, on top of a steep bank overlooking the Thames. Lush water-meadows at the foot of the bank do their job if the river floods and the rest of the time accommodate a fire-pit, camps and the school's fleet of river craft.

– mattresses especially came in for a slating. School confirms that full refurbishment of boarding house is imminent.

The boarders themselves seemed oblivious to such details. As we looked through the windows we wondered if they were also inured by familiarity to the priceless view of river and water meadows so charmingly framed by Virginia creeper. We hope these lucky boys remain blithely ignorant for as long as possible of the hours they would have to slave in order to open the curtains onto such a vista as adults.

About 35 boys board at any one time and those we met were keen to tell us how much they enjoyed the experience. 'There's so much freedom. After prep and supper you can kayak or go in the pool and in winter there's movies'. Food – especially fish and chips – got the thumbs up apart from 'something like couscous'. We certainly enjoyed sharing the boys' riverside barbecue lunch.

General consensus from parents is that teaching is 'brilliant'. First on our tour was an inter-house maths challenge in the multipurpose hall with stage, retractable seating and very impressive lighting gantry. Small groups of boys, the 'top two or three from each house', were tackling maths problems in a relay. Later on the whole school (including staff) gets involved. Apparently it's very entertaining although we remain to be convinced by the dramatic potential of equations.

Next stop was a year 6 class in the rather swish ICT suite. Boys were learning how to select and export images for use in the picture books they were designing for young children. By way of contrast we also saw little year 2s who were learning to tell the time in a reassuringly hands on and low tech style.

No 12-year-old boy should be without the ability to say 'There is a stain on the pillow' or 'The mini bar is empty' and these chaps could bandy phrases with Gallic gusto

Head's study and front of house admin are downstairs and boarding accommodation is upstairs. The library occupies what must have been a delightful drawing room with bay windows overlooking the river. Room and contents have just been refurbished and there's a new librarian to go with the new reading material.

No Saturday lessons but extensive programme of matches demands attendance. Boarding starts at age 10 and is Monday to Friday only. Flexi boarding parents must commit termly in advance to minimum of two nights a week. 'Day boarders' can stay until 8pm. Dorms sleep up to 13 and were, we thought, rather dark and just over the tipping point between comfortably scruffy and down at heel. Parents we spoke to were of the same opinion

Top set French was a hoot. An inspiring teacher, a bag of props and imaginative use of the interactive whiteboard kept everyone on their toes. No 12-year-old boy should be without the ability to say 'There is a stain on the pillow' or 'The mini bar is empty' and these chaps (according to our notes they were all called Henry or Monty) could bandy such useful phrases with Gallic gusto.

Science labs and art rooms are in good shape and we loved the new stand-alone classroom, all cedar and glass, topped by a living roof – it's been commandeered by geography, which considering the riparian views, seems fair enough. Music and drama are tackled with typical enthusiasm. There are currently two choirs and an orchestra; parents said that music had improved in recent years and all supported head's plans to raise the status of the performing arts.

Currently after-school clubs are limited to optional 'Hobbies', twice a week. This is something parents felt needed addressing, pointing out that compared to other preps the day is relatively short and they'd like a much wider range of after-school activities. Mr B-G says the 'structure of the whole school day is under review, including activities and the range on offer.'

We mostly heard praise for Moulsford's approach to SEN though there were one or two grumbles about cost and how out of class support timings didn't always fit in sensibly with lessons. 'Little and often' is the mantra and whether it's help with motor skills, speech and language or handwriting the school will provide support from in-house or external experts. 'Come and talk to us' if you're worried, the head of SEN tells parents.

> *Canoes, kayaks and dinghies are launched from the school's own creek for expeditions upriver to 'Goose Poo Island'. Camping in the teepee, bows and arrows*

And so to sport – acknowledged by everyone to be Moulsford's forté. Cricket, rugby, football, hockey, tennis – courts and pitches are tip-top. 'Rugby is our best sport,' boys told us, but added that the school isn't 'just about rugby'. School says all teams get expert coaching and plenty of matches against rivals such as the Oratory Prep, The Dragon and Caldicott. Some parents say this isn't the case for the boys in teams C-F and felt boys who weren't natural athletes not encouraged enough to try different sports such as hockey or tennis. Moulsford is also a top judo school (came joint first in 2015 IAPS championships) and offers trampolining, fencing, gymnastics, a climbing wall and 'wonderful match teas'.

> *Now boys can enjoy multiple goes at hurling themselves down a huge water slide while parents drink champagne and try not to watch. We imagine most are secretly relieved*

Canoes, kayaks and dinghies are launched from the school's own creek for expeditions upriver to 'Goose Poo Island'. Forest school, camping in the tepee, bows and arrows, fire building and whittling – plenty of opportunities to make the most of school's dampest asset. Not quite Swallows and Amazons though – participation is limited by the number of craft so not everyone gets a go. Nevertheless, by the time they leave boys should be pretty handy around boats of all kinds – great for those heading to rowing schools such as Abingdon, Eton or Harrow.

The legendary post-CE tradition of throwing each other in the river, beloved by former pupils (known as Old Moles), was retired with the last head. Now boys can enjoy multiple goes at hurling themselves down a huge water slide while parents drink champagne and try not to watch. We imagine most are secretly relieved that their sons are in no danger of a ritual ducking in the Thames

What did they think of the new head, we asked a group of boys enjoying their riverside barbecue? 'He's lively,' we were told. And what should he do for the school? 'Make it more famous, not enough people have heard of it.' Other boys were keen to add to Mr B-G's to-do list with requests for a retractable roof for the outdoor pool (parents echo this one) and loos on the far pitches. The cricket nets are, apparently, fine for fast bowlers but too low for spinners. Several boys were very keen to see fishing re-introduced as a hobby. Greatest consensus was over the inverse relation between the expense and quality of the special school socks. 'Six pounds a pair and look!' (They fall down.)

With a loyal crew and new captain at the helm the good ship Moulsford is steaming ahead. Yes, things will change but from what we heard the head's plans are in harmony with parental consensus. Mr B-G told us his favourite book is The Great Gatsby but parents can be confident that under his leadership Moulsford will most definitely not be 'borne back ceaselessly into the past.'

Oratory Preparatory School

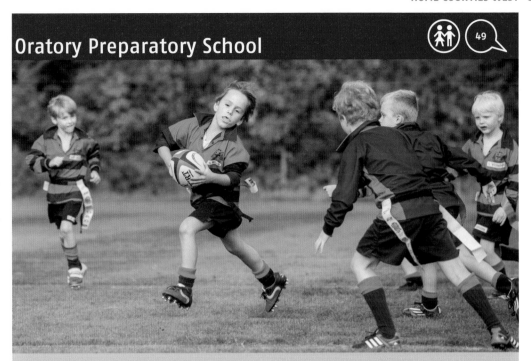

Goring Heath, Reading, Oxfordshire RG8 7SF

01189 844511
registrar@oratoryprep.co.uk
www.oratoryprep.co.uk
RC

Ages: 2–13 (flexi boarding from year 3, full and weekly from year 6)
Pupils: 417
Boarders: 19 full, 7 weekly
Day: £8,895 – £14,550 pa
Boarding: £18,750 – £21,750 pa

Linked school: The Oratory School

Headmaster: Since 2010, Mr Joseph Smith BA PGCE (40s). Son of a farmer, educated at Catholic primary school and then the local comp in King's Lynn where he says he 'achieved despite the poor education he received'. Admits he was 'rather lazy' and believes that sometimes children 'need to be compelled' to learn. (Parents say, approvingly, that he won't let pupils coast, even post CE.) He 'didn't start working until university' (studied English at Liverpool) but then something clicked and he graduated with a first. After PGCE at Brunel his first post was at Colfe's School in London, then 12 years at Monkton Combe, Bath where he was head of English and housemaster. Currently studying for MEd in educational leadership at Buckingham.

This is Mr Smith's first headship; his mission is to maintain high academic standards without compromising the school's non-selective ethos. While reassuring parents that their daughters will be fully prepared for 11+ entrance exams he also wants to encourage more girls to stay until 13.

A 21st century interpretation of Cardinal Newman's motto, 'heart speaking to heart', perhaps

Although a third or so boys go on to The Oratory (the 'big O') at 13, Mr Smith is under no internal pressure to promote this route. 'The governors and I believe it is the head's job to send boys to whichever school is right, not just automatically to the senior school'. Parents we spoke to confirm that advice is unbiased and 'all about their child'.

Genial and decidedly unstuffy, Mr Smith is full of praise for the school's 'outstanding' teachers, many of who are a few years older than he is.

Says his appointment has initiated some 'gentle evolution'. Likes to communicate face to face with colleagues and parents, not 'hide behind emails' – a 21st century interpretation of Cardinal Newman's motto, 'heart speaking to heart', perhaps. Parents give him the thumbs up – they say he's very visible and 'understands children'. He also seems to understand parents and endeared himself to many a father by introducing beer to match teas.

Since moving to Oxfordshire he says he is returning to the country pursuits he was brought up with. When time allows he enjoys shooting and cooking the results. Loves dogs, has just acquired a black lab (wry smile, he knows it's a headmaster cliché) and plays cricket for the village. His wife, Debbie, is the registrar and they have three children at the school. Favourite books? Sir Gawain and the Green Knight and Byron's Don Juan (well, he is an English graduate…).

Entrance: No academic selection for prep, assessment morning and report from previous school. Observed visit for pre-prep entrants or else head of pre-prep visits them at current nursery.

Exit: At age 11 – handful of girls plus one or two boys. Rest leave at age 13. Around a third of boys to The Oratory, girls to Queen Anne's School, Caversham, St Mary's Ascot, St Helen and St Katharine. Others to Abingdon, Bradfield, Canford, Marlborough, Uppingham. Good number of scholarships to The Oratory, Bradfield, Wellington, Headington and Abingdon.

Remarks: Approach is down a quiet lane and through a riot of rhododendrons. The 65 acres of grounds are a real feature of this school with beautifully kempt topiary, sunken lawns ideal

for croquet or a marquee (recently hosted 300 for dinner and ball) and, when we visited, sculpture by a visiting artist. One parent commented that it's by no means a 'ritzy' school; this may be true but it's certainly easy on the eye. Looking out over another perfect view one couldn't help wondering whether the imperfections of the real world come as a shock to departing pupils.

Stand out memory for one was 'all the hands-on science stuff and experiments'; for the other it was performing in the annual Shakespeare festival. A special mention for fish and chips and chocolate cake and custard

Our year 8 guides (who were remarkably composed considering they received their CE results during our visit) started the tour in the chapel. Although neither was Catholic, both knelt respectfully and spoke warmly of the school's inclusive and welcoming attitude to non-Catholics. When we asked what their stand-out memories of prep school were, for one it was 'all the hands-on science stuff and experiments'; for the other it was performing in the annual Shakespeare festival. The learning support department got a special mention, as did fish and chips and chocolate cake and custard.

Average class size 16. Latin from year 6, no Greek. We sat in on a year 7 maths class, impressed by the pupils' teamwork as they explored different methods of solving what seemed to us pretty challenging algebra. In history we enjoyed an enthusiastic and knowledgeable debate on arms escalation in the First World War – serious stuff enlivened by role playing and hammy French and German accents. Parents were full of praise for staff, from dinner ladies to teachers, particularly 'old hands' who might seem a bit old fashioned but were 'loved by children' and 'brilliant'. Smallish library is welcoming and well stocked, there's a library lesson once a week and, according to our guides, 'always lots of new books'. Around 30 pupils with SEN, mainly mild to moderate dyslexia, dyspraxia etc. School approach focuses on developing necessary skills and self-confidence via one-to-one lessons with specialist staff (extra charge).

Extensive games fields plus one Astroturf for hockey and three tennis/hockey pitches. As at 'the big O', sport, above all rugby, is central with local and national successes. More than one parent commented to the effect that a non-sporty child would

not get the most out of the place. Creditably, we heard no grumbles that girls' sport comes second, nor that the keen but less good were overlooked. The rather swish 25m swimming pool plus separate learners' pool is a real bonus. Decent sports hall but boys' locker rooms must be bit of a bear garden at peak times – our guides thought they ought to go on head's improvement list. Seven music practice rooms plus a recording studio; large numbers of singers and instrumentalists have gained grade 5 or above by the time they depart. Serious choir (for mass) plus orchestras, ensembles etc – we were treated to a blast from the excellent jazz band as they rehearsed for forthcoming annual trip to Torquay.

The children we met were polite and sociable. Mr Smith is as keen on good manners as the next head but would prefer children to learn by example rather than being made to feel awkward. Four houses, named after the school's previous locations, compete for the usual glory and silverware. What about bullying, we asked, in front of a notice board showing work done during recent anti-bullying week. Our guides were confident: 'You can tell any teacher and if you tell them it will stop.' School's extremely useful parents' handbook covers policies about this and pretty much everything else.

Our visit coincided with CE results day and was punctuated by relieved, happy year 8s clutching mark sheets and being warmly congratulated by their teachers. Some concerns expressed that smaller numbers of girls in years 7 and 8 meant that fallings out were harder to weather, but on the plus side there are plentiful opportunities for positions of leadership and responsibility. And, as a parent observed, girls who stay on don't seem to grow up quite as fast.

Majority of pre-prep staff female, balance redressed somewhat by gap chaps who looked as enthusiastic about the games set up for a pretend fête as the excited children

Boarding described by one parent as 'fantastic'. Lovely quirky dorms at top of main building, various size rooms with maximum 10 beds. Boarding most popular in the last year with pupils keen to gain experience for senior school. Regular influx of Spanish boarders who stay for a few terms.

Jolly common rooms with properly comfortable sofas and cushions for film nights, quizzes and meetings. Four bed san with nurse on site. Matron, houseparents and family live in, staff augmented by gappies. Flexi and occasional boarding possible if there's room and school will always 'scoop up anyone' in emergency. Working parents praise 'huge support' from matrons who will, for instance, review and acquire necessary uniform items and kit on their behalf. Likewise weekly newsletter that keeps all informed about what's going on.

Day pupils come from within a 30 minute drive: Henley, Reading, Watlington, Didcot and closer villages, vast majority are white British. Families, 60 per cent of whom are not practising Catholics, choose school for its strong faith-based values. Overseas boarders (about two-thirds of total) mainly from Spain. Active parents' association (FOPS) organises coffee mornings, fundraisers and class reps.

Pre-prep housed in delightful chalet-style wooden buildings (were old stables) with verandas and bright hanging baskets. Top of the range outdoor facilities include a good size kitchen garden, 'jungle' (wooded) and covered play areas and athletics track. Majority of staff female, balance redressed somewhat by gap chaps who looked as enthusiastic about the games set up for a pretend fête as the excited children. Yellow curtained classrooms are plastered in colourful posters and children's work. Multi-sensory approach to learning includes lots of work outdoors and exploring in adjoining fields and ponds. Weekly baking, art and all other messy stuff happen in a stand-alone room so no need to clear up ongoing projects. In core subjects (maths and English at this stage), a teacher plus a TA cover one topic but pupils (max 18) divided according to learning style and ability to tackle the work in different ways. RE (Catholic syllabus) once a week, pre-prep mass once a term. Lovely old barn for assemblies and after-school clubs (include Mandarin, music, dance, Lego) that run from 4-6pm starting with tea. Small charge for activities goes towards buying new equipment – head of pre-prep ensures after school toys and equipment are 'not the same as those used during lessons'.

New Little Oaks nursery now open. One or two parents commented that they hoped there would also be investment at the top end.

The Oratory Prep is a vibrant, welcoming community, just the place for your sporty all rounder – boy or girl – and now the 'little O' experience is available to their younger siblings. Head said that someone described his school as a 'sleeping giant', and while we're not sure about the slightly scary part of that simile, we agree that it has been a little under the radar – undeservedly so in our opinion.

The Oratory School

Woodcote, Nr Reading, South Oxfordshire RG8 0PJ

01491 683500	**Ages:** 11–18
enquiries@oratory.co.uk	**Pupils:** 380; sixth form: 125
www.oratory.co.uk	**Boarders:** 210
RC	**Day:** £16,050 – £23,250 pa
	Boarding: £21,540 – £31,950 pa

Linked school: Oratory Preparatory School

Head Master: Since September 2015, Adrian Wyles, previously academic deputy head at Sutton Valence School in Kent. Has also spent six years at Hurstpierpoint College. Geography degree from Royal Holloway and master's in educational leadership. A runner, cricket umpire and football coach, he is also an accomplished musician. Married to Dee, also a teacher; they have one grown up son.

Academic matters: School describes academic results as, 'inching up' although this is perhaps a little too incremental for some parents. Relatively non-selective intake yields solid results at GCSE (IGCSEs now in English language and literature, French, Spanish, three sciences). In 2015, 35 per cent A*/A grades at I/GCSE. Wide choice of subjects at A level and school will accommodate single students who wish to study, for instance, Dutch, Latin, Italian. All take RI GCSE (Catholic syllabus) and subject remains compulsory in the sixth form, although it is not a public examination subject. As for A level results, leaving aside art (see below), majority achieve A to C but there's clearly still work to do on the A* front (41 per cent A*/A grades in 2015; 60 per cent A*/B). Time spent talking to the director of studies about the school's 'value added' results will add some colour and detail to the statistics. Academic high flyers certainly not held back as Russell Group and Oxbridge success attests. Sixth formers are encouraged to do the extended project qualification and have tackled subjects as diverse as military law, hotel management and Greek tragedy. There's a new head of SEN and for boys who need it there is the option of taking nine, rather than 10, GCSEs, the remaining timetable being reserved for curriculum support – thus improving final outcomes. A system of mini reports ('fortnightlies') means that any academic problems/homework issues are not allowed to slide too far. Parents we spoke to were on the whole pretty positive about this provision and felt that it would be hard for a boy to fall down any cracks. 'Our son feels secure, that the school is on his side.'

Lessons we observed were in good order: challenging, information-rich chalk and talk in A2 classical civilisation, sparky and good humoured quick-fire thinking challenges in first year English. Science labs have been refurbed but we were delighted to find boys and Bunsen burners at the original wooden benches with old burns and battle scars still visible beneath the new varnish. Usual technology seemed to be present but not dominant in labs and classrooms; library peacefully free from such modern menaces but is, apparently, soon to be networked into the 21st century.

The area is hardly undersupplied with high-achieving academic schools but these are not for everyone. Parents we spoke to had chosen The Oratory because it offered their boys an academic environment that is individually challenging without being overly competitive – along with lashings of unashamedly competitive sport. School acknowledges that the timetable might seem a little old fashioned and some parents observed that there is a certain amount of 'wasted time' post games that could be put to more profitable use. Dr GSG tentatively wonders if shaving just one or two hours a week from the time spent on corpore sano might not improve the mens sana still further.

Games, options, the arts: Let there be no mistake, this is not a school for boys who don't enjoy running around or those who raise a cynical eyebrow at competitive sport (such boys do exist). Sport is big here, pitches seemingly endless and there's nowhere to hide. Cricket is played on a glorious sward with views over the Chilterns and Thames valley and, apparently, 'the best match teas.' New £4m sports centre with pool. Morning lessons and lunch are followed by two and a half hours of rugby, football, cricket, rowing, real tennis, shooting, swimming, golf, polo and the rest (delete as appropriate according to preference/season). Sport happens every day, apart from Thursdays when it's CCF, compulsory until fifth year after which the less military minded can take part in conservation work or community service. No wonder The Oratory was crowned Sports School of the Year in recent Education Business Awards (this in addition to similar accolades in previous years). The yellow and black-hooped Oratorian rugby players are formidable foes for many opposing teams drawn from larger schools. Celebrations for the school's 150th anniversary were heightened by the 1st XV declaring an unbeaten season, as did the junior colts A and B teams. No sloping off for sixth formers either. Sport may be big, but it's also inclusive and everyone gets to play in matches whether representing school or house. We asked a number of boys what they thought about this during our visit but were met with rather blank responses. 'If you don't like rugby you can do shooting.' And boys who don't want to do rugby or shooting? 'It's probably not the right school for them,' we were told but got the impression that such boys were beyond the imagination of Oratory chaps.

Let there be no mistake: this is not a school for boys who don't enjoy running around or those who raise a cynical eyebrow at competitive sport (such boys do exist)

And so to art. Some schools have art rooms, others may boast art departments; the Oratory says it has an art department but what it really has is a kingdom. Results in art and design subjects, both at GCSE, A level, Pre-U and foundation (yes, foundation) are in a league of their own. School has won GSG top boys' school for A level art award an unprecedented six times in the last eight years. The head of art (who lives on site in the cottage where J R R Tolkein wrote several of his books) may look the part with his paint spattered tie and avuncular twinkle but while one hand urges the boys forward to explore their own and others' creativity, the other has a death grip on the specification details of the syllabus. It's clearly a winning combination. Wonderful facilities (printmaking, etching, ceramics, DT, sculpture) arranged around a gallery corridor with tomes on plinths open at pertinent pages. A professional painter gives drawing lessons or, as he describes it, 'lessons in how to look,' and boys work standing (no chairs allowed) at easels. There's a dark room too; in these days of ubiquitous cameras and instant images, all boys learn the ancient art of developing photographic prints.

Culture more than holds its own alongside sport. Plenty of music, Schola Cantorum sings at masses, vespers and school functions and there's a variety of bands, orchestras and ensembles. Popular programme of visiting speakers. The Hopkins society (named after poet Gerard Manley Hopkins who was a master at The Oratory School under Cardinal Newman in the 1860s) oversees cultural activities such as trips to the theatre and also runs a bookshop. Sixth formers debate and deliver papers on a range of topics at Windhover Society meetings (named after Hopkins' poem – nice to see the old chap getting a double look in). Drama is a popular after school option, girls are borrowed from nearby Our Lady's Abingdon or St Anne's Caversham, but as an academic subject it is perhaps more Cinderella than Fame. The new 200 seat theatre complete with the latest sound and lighting technology may inspire future thespians.

Boarding: Boarding houses we saw were in pretty good nick; there are two brand new and three refurbished. Seniors have single study bedrooms, younger boys are four to a room and occupants are mixed up every half term. Just under 10 per cent of boarders are from overseas.

St Philip house is for junior boys (11-13) and they have separate recreation, social and teaching areas as well as their own sports teams and clubs. Day boys have a locker room (and we do mean just lockers, nary a chair or poster) in each house, but perhaps they are not intended to linger here. Resident house parents, live-in tutors plus a day housemother and gappies oversee proceedings. In senior houses boys are responsible for washing and ironing their own clothes – with some assistance at first; great training for future domestic harmony we thought, but limited evidence of ironing

(although the Spanish boys are apparently exemplary at this task).

Background and atmosphere: The Oratory School was founded in 1859 by Cardinal John Henry Newman. Newman, who was beatified in 2010, was a Christian thinker and educational pioneer and the school was intended as a boarding school along the lines of the English public schools ('Eton minus its wickedness') serving England's Catholic community. Newman's personal motto is also the school's: 'Cor ad cor loquitur' (Heart speaking to heart). While it remains a proudly Catholic institution the school welcomes boys of all faiths and none; the doctrine of valuing the special gifts of every individual makes The Oratory an accepting and welcoming community.

The school may be only 20 minutes' drive from Reading but enjoys, to quote Hopkins out of context (but not out of county), a 'sweet especial rural scene.' Visitors ascend a drive flanked by red maples and velvety playing fields leading to the Queen Anne style manor house, home to the school since its move from Birmingham in 1942. Grounds, all 400 acres of them, are immaculately maintained. Front of house is impressive with echoing marble foyer and arresting 'black room' (black and gold are Papal colours) used for concerts and teas. Business areas the usual confusion of scuffed corridors and unremarkable teaching rooms. Pace art department, school not lavishly decorated with boys' efforts, rather restrained, formal atmosphere prevails – but our visit was at the start of term.

Pastoral care, well-being and discipline: Sensible rules re use of laptops, mobiles, social networking sites. Junior chapel is in a rather charming former tithe barn, senior chapel is a slightly less inspiring modernish building. Daily prayers in houses, weekly assembly for all; Sunday evening mass for all boarders, optional for day boys. Non-Catholic parents we spoke to seemed to have different perceptions of the religion's role in school life. One thought it was a dominant (dominating) feature; another didn't think it impinged too much on their boy's school day. All participate in the spiritual life of the school and Catholic and non-Catholic boys serve at mass.

Not much in the way of transgression: one imagines exhaustion may be a contributory factor (the school's mantra is 'a busy boy is a happy boy'); three hours of games every day plus weekend matches and evening activities such as circuit training must take the edge off boyish over-exuberance. In those cases where it doesn't, standard regime of detentions is called into play. Exonerated in a recent case where a housemistress sued the school for unfair dismissal – though the case did reveal some extremely unsavoury behaviour amongst one or

Sixth formers debate and deliver papers at Windhover Society meetings (named after Hopkins' poem – nice to see the old chap getting a double look in)

two boys. After matches on Saturday boarders can go into Reading; some parents felt older boys left a little too much to their own devices on these trips. Houses have cinema and steak nights, pool competitions etc and there are socials with girls from Queen Anne's Caversham and St George's Ascot as well as ballroom dancing for the lower sixth – culminating in a ball held at Queen Anne's.

Our guides thought the food was 'excellent'. 'There's loads of it. It's boy food,' they said. So, anyone for seconds of slugs, snails and puppy dogs' tails? Breakfasts came in for especial praise: 'you can have cereal and then the works, every day'. Boarders can supplement with toast, pot noodles etc from the kitchens on each floor. Newly formed food council has managed to get Cocoa Pops onto the breakfast menu but on the whole one feels that the school is closer to benign dictatorship than democracy. The school day officially ends at 7pm after prep but day boys may question the logic of going home; some live up to an hour's drive away and there's no bus service. Parents advise packing provisions for pick up at 7pm because supper is not provided for day boys (although those staying on for other activities get supper and it's not billed). Boys can stay overnight if they are involved in evening activities but we have also heard that some GCSE options necessitate staying in school until 9pm. Boarding numbers

certainly increase in the upper years, pragmatism triumphing over home comforts perhaps.

Pupils and parents: The old fashioned certainties are all present and correct here. Boys are confident, smart, polite and look you in the eye. RC and non-RC – all religions welcome. Day and flexi-boarding pupils come from Reading and South Oxfordshire villages. Boarding is a cosmopolitan mix of UK boys, those from European Catholic families (Spain in particular, some for just one year) and Russians; fewer Chinese boys than at other places. No parents' association but plenty of opportunities for fraternisation at matches etc.

Entrance: At 11 by English, maths and non-verbal reasoning exams plus informal interview; at 13, CE pass at around 55 per cent required plus head's report from previous school and interview. Numbers from nearly Oratory Prep. Special consideration will be given to brothers of boys already in school and the sons of old boys. Five C grades at GCSE minimum entry to sixth form.

Exit: In 2015, destinations ranged from biochemistry at Imperial to classics at Durham. A few embark on military careers.

Money matters: Scholarships and exhibitions up to half fees available: academic, art, music, sport and all-rounder. Generous bursaries. Extra charges for specialist sports coaching eg golf, real tennis, books, trips, laundry and haircuts.

Remarks: One of a kind. Go and explore, meet the head, chat to the boys – we doubt you will be undecided by the end of your visit. If you have an exuberant energetic boy with an artistic bent this could be the perfect match.

Pangbourne College

Pangbourne, Reading, Berkshire RG8 8LA

01189 842101
registrar@pangbourne.com
www.pangbourne.com

Ages: 11–18
Pupils: 421 (two-thirds boys); sixth form: 135
Boarders: 102 full, 123 weekly/flexi
Day: £15,999 – £22,548 pa
Boarding: £20,082 – £31,890 pa

Headmaster: Since 2005, Mr Thomas Garnier BSc PGCE (40s). Educated at Sandroyd and Radley, read physics at Bristol and was a seaman officer in the Royal Navy for seven years. He left the Navy 'for love' after meeting his wife Alexandra and trained

as a teacher. Did PGCE at Oxford, followed by first teaching job at King Alfred's, high performing state school in Wantage, Oxfordshire. Spent 10 years at Abingdon School, where he progressed to housemaster and then head of boarding.

Dedicated, energetic and keen to listen to pupils' views, he still manages to fit in some physics teaching and runs the naval section of Pangbourne's CCF. He describes Pangbourne pupils as 'good, solid citizens who are prepared to work hard and willing to participate.' Makes a point of being out and about in school and meets the two chief cadet captains (head boy and head girl) for 10 minutes every morning. 'We suit active children who like being busy,' he says.

Head's wife is very involved in school life and they have two sons. They live in a house attached to the main school building, with panoramic views stretching 20 miles across the Berkshire countryside. In his spare time (not that there's much of it) he enjoys rowing, running and music. A firm believer in 'lifelong learning,' he recently took up the flute again after a 25 year gap, passed his grade 8 with ease and plays in the school orchestra. He is keen to start piano lessons too. 'Someone said to me "you can always find 15 minutes a day and if you do that it adds up to 90 hours a year".'

Academic matters: School takes children across a broad range of ability. Head agrees that Pangbourne is sometimes perceived as being 'for the less able' but says they do a very good job for academic children (there's a gifted and talented programme for the most able). In 2015, 51 per cent of A level grades were A*/B and 22 per cent A*/A. The school told us: 'While the top students gained their straight A grades, some of the most heartening performances were to be found in the middle ground, among those who worked tremendously hard to secure Bs and Cs. We take real pride in these.' Some sixth formers, particularly those considering careers in the Forces, take public service BTec as well as their A levels.

Dynamic housemaster of Dunbar ('he's strict but great fun') also teaches DT and memorably described his subject as 'making a noise and making a mess'

Most pupils take 11 GCSEs, including IGSE English and maths. French, German and Spanish taught and music, art, DT, drama, business studies and PE on offer at GCSE. In 2015, 38 per cent A*/A grades. New timetable has introduced one-hour lessons. Pupils are setted for maths, English, science and languages – four sets in years 9 and 10 and five sets in year 11.

Teaching staff (two-thirds male and a third female) are a healthy mix of experienced and

A firm believer in 'lifelong learning', he recently took up the flute again, passed his grade 8 with ease and plays in the school orchestra

newly qualified teachers (school has links with teacher training departments at universities of Buckingham, Reading and Oxford Brookes). Half the teachers live on site. Staff hold regular academic clinics for youngsters who need help (pupils can also email their teachers). Learning support available for pupils with minor learning difficulties – individual lessons on offer at extra cost. Tutor system – in senior school pupils stay with same tutor for year 9, then change for years 10 and 11 and again for the sixth form.

Games, options, the arts: A very sporty school. Teachers and pupils alike told us that 'Pangbourne punches above its weight' when it comes to sport, and its impressive results bear this out. School regularly beats far larger schools, particularly at rugby and rowing. Pangbourne boathouse is a mile from the school, on the scenic banks of the Thames, and school has won the Princess Elizabeth Challenge Cup at Henley four times.

Unlike some schools, where pupils drop sport in the sixth form, everyone does sport here. School's size means that virtually all get the chance to represent Pangbourne. Main boys' sports are rugby, hockey, rowing and cricket while girls do netball, hockey, rugby, rowing and tennis. Open-air pool (keen swimmers get bussed to indoor pools at Bradfield, Reading and Newbury). Lots of equestrian enthusiasts – riding and polo are popular.

Stunning new music school houses recital hall, recording suite and 10 practice and teaching rooms, as well as four prized Steinway grand pianos. Around a third of pupils take individual music lessons, with brass, drums, guitar and singing leading the pack. Loads of musical groups to join, including orchestra, jazz band, choirs and a marching band. Art and DT departments thriving, with healthy numbers taking subjects at GCSE and A level. Performing arts are on the up with a variety of college productions, theatre trips and drama workshops. Three drama studios and pupils encouraged to take LAMDA exams. Everyone does CCF for at least a year and D of E is compulsory in year 9.

Boarding: Four boys' houses and two (ultra-modern) girls' houses. Just over half of the pupils board – more than 100 are full boarders while the others ('part boarders') board four nights a week (Monday, Tuesday, Thursday and Friday). Boarding grows in popularity as the pupils move up the school – by sixth form 75 per cent are boarders. 'We don't actively push boarding,' one teacher told us. 'It's a natural phenomenon.' No flexi-boarding, although school offers parents chance to buy 15 extra boarding nights a year per pupil. Girls' houses are stylish and bright – 'I want to make it like home from home,' a housemistress told us. Pupils eat breakfast, lunch and supper in the central mess hall.

The youngest pupils (years 7 and 8) are housed in Dunbar, a detached red-brick house with its own garden (loads of space to play football, jump about on the trampoline and catch up with friends). Lower school lessons take place in the main school but the rest of the time pupils trot back to the cosy environs of Dunbar. Dynamic housemaster of Dunbar ('he's strict, but huge fun,' one parent told us) also teaches DT and memorably described his subject as 'making a noise and making a mess.' Dunbar pupils have their own head boy and head girl and all pupils are divided into four 'watches,' (Port, Starboard, Forward and Aft), each with their own 'watch captains.' Currently more boys than girls in this age group, but numbers vary from year to year.

Background and atmosphere: School is set in 230 acres, in an area of outstanding natural beauty. Founded in 1917, Pangbourne's aim was to prepare boys for service in the Merchant Navy and Royal Navy. In 1969, however, the school was established as a charity, with a similar curriculum to other schools, and these days only two or three leavers a year join the Forces. Even so, Pangbourne prides itself on maintaining many of its original traditions and is the only school in the UK where pupils wear Royal Navy officer cadet uniform every day.

Pupils parade in their number one (ceremonial) uniforms every third Sunday. Uniforms have to be immaculate and shoes polished. A guest of honour inspects the whole school on the vast parade ground and takes the salute as pupils march past. Head says Pangbourne's parades are an integral part of school life and help to develop self-discipline (pupils have to stand still for 15 to 20 minutes, often with a biting wind whistling across the parade ground), confidence, teamwork, leadership and a community spirit as well as attention to detail. When we visited pupils told us that the parades 'bring us together' as a school, while parents are hugely supportive (many turn up to watch every parade). 'It is very impressive,' a mother told us. 'It seems to give them great pride in what they do.' But despite the emphasis on teamwork, the school encourages youngsters to be individuals. 'We certainly aren't trying to put everyone in a mould,' one teacher told us.

Pangbourne has its own distinctive vocabulary, much of it nautical. Study bedrooms are cabins, house common rooms are gunrooms, the dining hall is the mess hall and casual clothes are always referred to as scruff. When the head arrived he introduced 'flag values' – kindness, integrity, industry, moral courage, selflessness, resilience and initiative. He sees these as the school's core values and pupils are urged to display them throughout their time at the school. Firm Christian ethos. Chapel is a key part of Pangbourne life, from 'congers' (congregational practice) to Saturday evensong for boarders. Many services are held in the Falkland Islands Memorial Chapel, opened by the Queen.

School has been fully co-ed since 1996 (it's now two-thirds boys and a third girls).

Pangbourne prides itself on maintaining many of its original traditions and is the only school in the UK where pupils wear Royal Navy officer cadet uniform every day

School is keen on student voice and pupils sit on food committee and pastoral welfare committee. Very inclusive 'Team Pangbourne' feel to the place and pupils are fiercely loyal to their school. Sixth formers can apply to train as peer mentors, helping others to cope with everything from time management and exam preparation to friendship issues and internet safety. Raft of prefects – called cadet captains – chosen by head and senior staff. Lower sixth pupils take leadership course in readiness for their responsibilities in the upper sixth and head reckons this has reaped dividends.

Pastoral care, well-being and discipline: Head says school's policies on drugs, alcohol, cigarettes and knives are 'crystal clear.' Any pupil caught using, selling or possessing drugs 'can expect to be expelled,' he says, though 'every case is treated on its merits.' School devotes a lot of time to PHSCE and is strict about boy-girl relationships – PDAs banned. Sixth formers have their own bar (Medway), which is open for soft drinks on Thursday evenings and pizzas and beer/lager (strictly limited) on Saturday nights. Pupils are allowed mobile phones but firm rules on when they can be used. If phones go off in lessons, for instance, they get confiscated for 24 hours.

Staff believe that the school's strict uniform policy is a 'great leveller.' Pupils must need hefty trunks to pack all their kit though – list includes number one uniform (jacket, trousers/shirt and cap with badge for Sundays and ceremonies), number two uniform for every day (trousers/skirt, navy jersey, epaulettes, beret and Dr Martens shoes), and recreational rig (known as 'rec rig') for social occasions and away matches. And that's before they even think of throwing in games kit and weekend clothes.

Pupils say that Pangbourne is 'a caring, friendly school' and that it's easy to settle in. One boy told us that wearing the distinctive uniform had given him 'a sense of discipline' and that most pupils see it as 'really cool.' Asked whether it's a snooty school, sixth formers said 'definitely not.' Other pupil comments during our visit included 'people come out of their shells here,' 'it makes you really independent' and 'it prepares you for life outside.'

Pupils and parents: Fleet of minibuses brings day pupils in from as far afield as Basingstoke, Newbury and Highclere. Majority of boarders live within an hour's drive. Around eight per cent from overseas (including the Far East, Kenya and Germany). Despite school's naval associations, only 20 youngsters from Forces families. Former pupils include the late film director Ken Russell, Olympic gold and silver medallist sailor Andrew (Bart) Simpson (a sailing foundation was set up in his name after he drowned whilst training for the America's Cup), motorcycle racer Mike Hailwood, hedge fund founder David Harding, former Second Sea Lord Admiral Sir Michael Layard and Dazed & Confused founder and journalist Jefferson Hack.

Pangbourne prides itself on taking pupils 'from a broad spectrum of ability.' A parent told us: 'Pangbourne isn't known for being an academic school but the opportunities are there for academic children and they do really well. At the same time the school brings out the best in those for whom studying isn't so easy. Every child seems to have their chance in the sun.' School says it selects as much on character and suitability as academic criteria and is looking for youngsters who will throw themselves into Pangbourne life and make a difference. The only children the school might turn away, says the head, are those whose learning

difficulties are 'too profound for us to cope with' or youngsters with 'behaviour issues.'

Entrance: Pupils come from a host of state and prep schools, including Brockhurst, Moulsford, Thorngrove, St Andrew's, Pangbourne and many more. Main entry points are at 11, 13 and 16. At 11 and 13, admission is by school's own entrance exam or CE (interview and head's report taken into account too). Pupils joining sixth form (up to 20 a year) must have at least five GCSE passes, including English and maths.

Exit: About a quarter leave after GCSEs, mainly to do subjects not offered by Pangbourne, or as one pupil told us wryly, 'because they want more free time.' Around 90 per cent to university and sometimes one or two a year to Oxbridge. Destinations in 2015: Angela Ruskin, Bath, Bath Spa, Birmingham, Brighton, Cardiff, Coventry, Edinburgh, Exeter, Kent, Leeds, Manchester, Newcastle, Norland College, Nottingham, Portsmouth, Reading, Royal Holloway, Sheffield, Southampton, Swansea, University of West England, Winchester. The rest start full-time work (one boy recently went straight to aviation college to do his commercial pilot's training), with a handful going into the Forces.

Money matters: 'We're not a rich school,' the bursar told us, although with its centenary coming up in 2017 the school is busy upgrading many buildings. Means-tested bursaries available (from 10 per cent to 100 per cent) and a variety of scholarships (including academic, music and sport) at each entry point.

Remarks: A small and distinctive school that puts huge emphasis on self-discipline, teamwork and leadership. Caring and supportive, Pangbourne buzzes with activity and encourages every pupil to have a go and get involved.

Papplewick School

Windsor Road, Ascot, Berkshire SL5 7LH

01344 621488
registrar@papplewick.org.uk
www.papplewick.org.uk
C of E

Ages: 6–13 (boarders from 8)
Pupils: 216
Boarders: 128 full and flexi
Day: £14,925 – £20,715 pa
Boarding: £26,985 pa

Headmaster: Since 2004, Mr Tom Bunbury BA PGCE, (40s). Educated at nearby Woodcote Prep and then Millfield, read law at Durham but turned his back

on the legal profession to return first to Woodcote, then Homerton College Cambridge for a PGCE followed by Papplewick, where he has remained since

1993. He was head of maths, a housemaster and then deputy before taking over as head. It was, he says, a chance to lead a great team and make it stronger. He is modest and quietly confident, with a charming absence of ego. Parents appreciate the fact that he has guarded the traditions of Papplewick while moving with the times on issues such as demand for flexi-boarding.

Many have families; the boys enjoy playing with the younger children, teaching them to ride bikes and explore

He lives on site with his wife, Sallie, and four children. Sallie oversees the matrons and catering – each week she organises a 'tasty table' at which 12 boys picked at random on their way in to the dining room get to try a new meal and give it the thumbs up. Or down. The head places great emphasis on the school's 'real family atmosphere', two-thirds of staff live on site and many have families; the boys enjoy playing with the younger children, teaching them to ride bikes and explore. Parents endorsed this, seeing it as a real strength of the school. Living at one's place of work may be convenient but you need an escape route, and whenever time allows the Bunburys pack buckets and spades and head off to their bolt-hole on the Isle of Wight.

Entrance: Entry from age 6, first come, first served. Day boys from local preps in Berks, Bucks and Surrey but increasing numbers now coming in from west London. Parents have cottoned on to the fact that just 40 minutes on the Papplewick express will enable their boys to escape the capital's overheated prep rat-race. Several we spoke to described Papplewick as 'a blessed relief' from the intense competitiveness of the capital's schools, adding that their boys still got to the senior schools of their choice but at their own pace. According to the head, there's no 'Papplewick type', families have 'broad horizons' and the atmosphere is tolerant and uncliquey; parents say much the same. About 10 per cent from outside UK, no dominant country, some expats, EFL available. Handful of academic and all-rounder awards available annually, can be worth up to 50 per cent of fees.

Exit: Most popular choices are Eton, Harrow, Wellington and Charterhouse. Impressive scholarship record, including to eg Eton, Harrow, Wellington and Winchester.

Remarks: Papplewick may be across the road from Ascot racecourse but it's not going to give the new grandstand (or indeed the old one) a run for its money in the architectural stakes. Parents say a few may be disappointed by the absence of grandeur but 'the boys don't notice'. Recent building works have transformed what was a rather jumbled site; the new entrance hall is particularly impressive – it seems to pull everything together as well providing a light and modern space for exhibitions and receptions. Plans have been drawn up for an art, DT and ICT block as well as a pipe dream of a stand-alone year 8 boarding house – both in the pipeline. As for the inside, take a boy of your acquaintance, multiply him by 200, imagine the toll this cohort might take on the interior of any building and you will be ready for Papplewick. There is a Just William charm about this place and its delightful pupils – unaffected, exuberant boys in their element. Uniform is blue shorts and blue shirts, open necked in the summer or fastened with one of the huge number of ties that declare an individual's allegiance to house, sporting or other pursuits.

Our year 8 guides were quite the best PR team we've had the pleasure to be escorted by. When we ventured that the absence of poolside changing might make winter bathing a little frosty we were told that it was 'very character building.' Asked whether they thought other schools were better equipped, they conceded that this might possibly be the case but claimed that they just 'deviated around any lack of facilities.' To be fair, all the pre-requisites of 21st century schooling are present and correct – plenty of computers including a suite of Macs in the music tech room, smartboards and such like. Chapel is a dog-leg off the main hall, demarcated on our visit by a truly impressive display of art – some by boys who had just won scholarships. Two imperious (if slightly moth-eaten) stags' heads,

whence the school emblem, oversee proceedings – if only they could talk! Electronic screen in the hall shows live feed of house points, great for motivation; weekly winners get to choose Friday night supper – usually chicken and chips.

Average class size is 12. Flexible setting and streaming – boys moved up and down as necessary. Cambridge Latin course for all, Greek for scholars. In the classes we observed there was a palpable rapport between staff and pupils; one felt that boys knew exactly how far they could go with their sparky banter and wouldn't push it any further. Likewise, the teachers responded to the boys as individual characters, enjoying their company. And all the time minds were developing, being guided and challenged.

Snake Club is for all ages – boys buy their reptiles, now all bred in house, for a modest £10 and learn about the creature's habitat and how to care for it

There are some younger boarders, 'I was a bit shy to start with but I soon got used to it,' and some flexi boarders (around 15), but most start when it becomes compulsory in the summer term of year 6. As one boy told us, 'You can have fun with your friends all day, you don't have to worry about rushing because mum wants to go somewhere.' The year 6 French class we chatted to were very keen to tell us about their favourite activities – extra DT where you can 'make what you like', drama, clay pigeon and rifle shooting three times a week, golf and polo. All games (apart from polo) played on site; football, rugby and cricket are tackled with gusto and everybody gets a game. Most unusual and tremendously popular is Herpetology or Snake Club; this is the first time a Good Schools Guide reviewer has conducted interviews with a bearded lizard on her shoulder. As with many of the activities, including a game of football we saw, Snake Club is for all ages – boys buy their reptiles, now all bred in house, for a modest £10 and learn about the creature's habitat and how to care for it. Any offspring are sold back to the club for the same price. The club was founded by the charismatic science master who joined from a school in South Africa, having 'discovered' Papplewick via a visiting rugby team. Some 10 years on and he's still 'loving' it; his wife is in charge of life upstairs in the dorms.

Each year group has its own den (common room) with friezes painted by a member of the art department (these also adorn the dorms), and a mixture of pool tables and tiered benches for watching films.

Dorms are no-frills but they're tidy and boys expected to change their own sheets; pin boards were fairly empty when we visited but there is, we were told, a hotly contested prize for the best decorated. There are televisions and beanbags in the dorms and boys can watch after 4pm; mobile phones are allowed but for talking only – no moving images. Parents are mainly contacted via Skype or mobile. Year 8 can use Facebook under supervision. The boys we met were very clear about the rules and seemed to take them in good part, understanding the necessity. Posters visible in strategic places detailing where to go for help; boys can take problems to their tutor or, if preferred, can phone and speak confidentially to the 'private listener' who will give advice.

Head keen to point out that while the idea of a boarding prep may strike some as old fashioned,

Papplewick has evolved along with modern family life. Parents are welcome to drop in whenever they like; Saturdays are particularly popular – those who come to watch matches stay and listen to the sublime four-part choir ('full of first XV rugby players') at a short chapel service and then eat lunch with staff and boys. The 40 or so boys who are in school for the weekend enjoy camp outs, trips to local restaurants and socials (bit of a Lynx fest apparently) with Wycombe Abbey, Heathfield and St Mary's.

According to the head, relocation to a larger site was considered a few years ago but decided against – would it have broken the spell? Who knows. There's certainly a whiff of magic about Papplewick that seems to inspire fierce loyalty in staff, parents and boys. We think perhaps Mr Bunbury should bottle it and build that new boarding house.

The Pilgrims' School

3 The Close, Winchester, Hampshire SO23 9LT

01962 854189
admissions@pilgrims-school.co.uk
www.thepilgrims-school.co.uk
C of E

Ages: 4–13 (boarders from year 4)
Pupils: 237
Boarders: 87 full
Day: £10,170 – £17,685 pa
Boarding: £22,335 pa

Head: Since January 2015, Tom Burden (40s), previously head of Hereward House School in London. He grew up on the Isle of Wight, where he was educated at local schools before proceeding to Oxford (with a scholarship) to study theology. After

graduating, he started teaching as a bit of fresh air before settling down to something earnest, but was soon gripped. Five years at Alleyn Court School, Southend, then a further five at boarding prep Lockers Park, Hertfordshire, where he headed the

English department and ran the scholarship set, while still managing plenty of sports coaching. 'I loved every minute and took away the idea that boys should be boyish, enjoy their childhood and be trusted to have responsibilities.' A sports fan and regular at Lords, he relaxes by playing football, bowls and cricket. His boy's own enthusiasms include Bletchley Park, the Underground, the gothic Revival and the London sewer system. He's also 'hugely interested' in politics, philosophy and religion.

Entrance: Boys are assessed at all main entry stages and tests vary depending on age. Reception entry via 'fun activity morning'. School offers around 10 extra places at 7+ and 8+ – assessment during individual taster day. Around six more join the school in year 7 to prepare for 13+ entry to senior schools. Those interested can get a taste of boarding life (from age 8) by spending a few nights in school. Places in other years are occasionally available. School states that it is 'selective in the broadest sense' but clearly has an academic focus.

Auditions for the two choral foundations are in November, with most new choristers (who sing in Winchester Cathedral) and quiristers (who sing in Winchester College Chapel) joining in year 4 and 5. Voice trials include singing a prepared piece, aural tests and an academic assessment.

Boys come from all over to be a Pilgrim, moving from local nurseries, state primaries, independent pre-preps and London schools. Overseas parents choose the school as a route into Winchester College.

Exit: Around 40 per cent of leavers to Winchester College in any given year, many with music scholarships and exhibitions and a few with academic or double awards. Steady trickle to Eton, Harrow, Radley, Charterhouse, Canford, Sherborne, Bryanston, King Edward VI, many with music, academic and all-rounder awards. One or two may leave at 11+ for independent day schools.

Remarks: School can probably trace its origins back to the early song schools associated with Winchester Cathedral in Saxon times. Current school was founded in 1931 in former priory (thought to have been redesigned by Sir Christopher Wren) when non-singing 'commoners' joined the choristers for their education. Quiristers, boys who have sung Winchester College chapel services since 1382, moved from the college to Pilgrims' in 1966. Cathedral and remains of Wolvesey Castle form an imposing backdrop to main school building, which sits in a far corner of The Close. Once inside, there's more space than the outer façade suggests; two inner quadrangles flanked by octagonal concert hall and modern classrooms rub shoulders with

Cathedral and remains of Wolvesey Castle form an imposing backdrop to the main school building, which sits in the far corner of The Close

ancient medieval hall and converted Priory stable block. School escapes feeling cramped thanks to extensive playing fields in front of Bishop's Palace and design of newer buildings.

We got the feeling that this school does lots of things well, and parents confirm that academic standards are good. Form tutors and academic tutors (years 6-8) keep tabs on individual study via daily meetings with their charges and are 'very honest about progress.' Director of studies 'seems to know the capabilities of all the boys and school reports are extremely thorough, accurate and personal.' Maths set from year 4, English from year 5 and there is further division from year 7 into Winchester entry, scholarship and CE sets (depending on destination schools). Separate sciences taught from year 5, Latin from year 6 and French from year 3 (senior French classroom had piles of shiny new textbooks and posters of complex tenses on walls). Enthusiastic head of English encourages creative writing at every opportunity; clearly has a love for poetry, and boys produce some really imaginative work inspired by anything from Pilgrim's Progress to a letter from the Queen. Rest of curriculum is as expected and music is clearly strong. The three groups – choristers, quiristers and commoners (non-scholars, the majority) – are all mixed together in lessons and socially. 'The school is geared up for boys and there are lots of good male teachers.' At the time of our visit, 15 students had SEN reports (dyslexia, dyspraxia) and two learning support specialists were giving individual and group lessons to around 30 pupils. Class numbers are capped throughout at 20; numbers in year 7 and 8 classes are smaller and determined by 'next schools.'

Housed in converted medieval stables, music department is very accomplished, active and busy, with around 235 individual music lessons taught each week by 27 visiting music teachers. 'Almost everyone plays an instrument,' noted a parent; singers usually learn two. Every boy is assessed for musical potential on entry to the school. Children in year 2 have strings and woodwind taster sessions and usually begin formal instrumental lessons in year 3. Bands, orchestras and choirs abound. Main prep school orchestra tackles repertoire such as finale of Beethoven 5 and Mahler 1 (arranged by director of music) with weekly sectional rehearsals. Big band, woodwind and baroque ensembles also practise weekly; music staff 'team boys up into [chamber music] groups that work.' Junior strings and band sometimes join seniors for concerts. Four other choirs besides the two professional choirs give everyone a chance to sing. Music lessons rotate through the timetable and aim to miss the same subject no more than once every six weeks. Practice sessions for boarders (four per instrument per week) are timetabled and supervised; 25 pupils can practise simultaneously, including a few day boys. Music theory lessons for all and acres of space for music technology and composition suites. School organises two full days of ABRSM music exams every term, routinely passed with distinctions and merits. Music department has access to Winchester College for larger concerts and uses hall and the Octagon for smaller affairs. Cathedral (chorister) and College Chapel (quirister) choirs sing to professional standards and parents say there is no difference in kudos between the two. Parents (and boys) can choose at audition whether they wish to be considered for one or both. Daily singing for all, although quiristers sing fewer services, practise more secular repertoire and have no holiday commitments (a bonus for some families). Both choirs make recordings and go on tours. 'It's fantastic to go to a school where there is music going on, it's just part of life ... even if you don't know you're learning, you are.'

Although the two choirs spend a lot of time together, close bonds are also formed in the football field. Parents of commoners say their sons couldn't care less about the name

Despite being renowned for music, Pilgrims' manages to field an impressive 11 teams for football, 12 for rugby, nine for cricket and a first hockey team. Parents say results are respectable, even though one laughed, 'The boys are so polite that they're more likely to say "after you" on the football pitch.' Usual range of sports and games timetabled daily; less mainstream activities include fives, golf, fencing, rounders, judo, martial arts, squash, water polo and sailing. All-weather court floodlit for use on darker evenings. Sporting successes include U13 1500m national prep schools champion and cricket at Hampshire county level. Heated outdoor pool – affectionately dubbed 'the puddle' – for swimming in warmer months, although boys use 25m indoor pool at the college next door for serious swimming, eg lessons, swim squad and galas. Large art room, smaller DT room, ICT suite and library dotted around the quads. Parents say that drama

is very good lower down the school, with a 'fantastic junior production each year,' but add that they would like to see more for older pupils. School says, 'We have a senior production every year, the last was an outdoor Shakespeare.' Productions staged in atmospheric, medieval Pilgrims' Hall, in purpose-built Octagon theatre, outdoors in the Quad or in the cathedral.

Two boarding houses have space for 82 beds, all fully occupied when we visited. Lovely couple in charge stress that all boarders are treated equally and there is a clear division between the school day and boarding. Senior quiristers board in Q-school, a few minutes' walk away. Dorms homely and comfortable; each has a year 8 dorm monitor in charge of waking boys up etc. Breakfast served on family tables, after which boys go off to choir, instrumental practice or have free time. Extracurricular activities (known as 'Commoners' as singers have choir practice) happen after school on four afternoons a week. These include lots of sport, but unusual pursuits like fishing, bell ringing and Mandarin caught our eye. Boarders come back to the house after evening prep; houseparents keep a close eye on any missed homework and help singers cope at busy times. Laundry done in-house and parents say belongings are checked regularly. No flexi boarding, but commoners can go home at weekends and choristers occasionally; around a dozen boys are in school regularly on Sundays. Lots of trips and activities arranged on weekends and during 'choir time', when choristers board over Christmas, Easter and a week in summer.

Parents are happy with pastoral care and school's attitude towards misdemeanours, bullying etc. 'Issues are dealt with proactively and nobody brushes anything under the carpet.' In spite of the fact that boys wear distinctive sweaters depending on whether they are choristers (red), quiristers (blue) or commoners (green), we didn't sense any social divisions. Boys are mixed up when allocated to one of five 'Sets' (houses) on entry to the school, and we observed different coloured jumpers dotted all over at lunch tables. Although the two choirs spend a lot of time together, close bonds are also formed on the football field. Parents of commoners say their sons couldn't care less about the name and feel 'just as important as anyone in a red jumper or a blue jumper.' The only quibble was that there are too few phones in the boarding house, although any urgent messages are unfailingly delivered by staff on duty. School says, 'Several mobile phones are handed out each evening and there are ample landlines to use.'

Super little pre-prep has its own hall for assemblies (youngest children have lunch here) and plenty of outdoor space. Outdoor learning in forest school every Monday and there is an outdoor play area and garden. Pre-prep holds special assembly in the cathedral every fortnight and parents are welcome. Has its own choir and music teacher (director of music also takes lessons) and there are two clubs just for the under-7s. Lots of non-fiction in library encourages boys to enjoy reading.

Pilgrims' attracts a broad mix of families – overseas nationals hail from Hong Kong and China; a few others come from Russia and Switzerland. Some overseas British based in Brazil, France and Russia. Boys are lively, but generally well-behaved, courteous and very natural. Not a Sloane Ranger in sight. Choral foundation provides scholarships worth 40 per cent to all choristers and quiristers and free music tuition on one instrument. Means-tested bursaries worth up to 100 per cent are available for all. Over 20 boys had additional funding when we visited. Any boy awarded a bursary also receives his first set of uniform free. Former pupils include Jon Snow, Jack Dee, Patrick Gale, Ollie Baines and Jules Knight (members of Blake), Nick Glennie-Smith (film composer) and Anthony Smith (sculptor).

A fine school in which the musical, the sporty and the clever boy will positively flourish. Atmosphere is now less formal and the school has a good work/life balance.

Queen Anne's School

6 Henley Road, Reading, Berkshire RG4 6DX

01189 187300
admissions@qas.org.uk
www.qas.org.uk
C of E

Ages: 11–18
Pupils: 440; sixth form: 120
Boarders: 220
Day: £21,075 pa
Boarding: £31,050 pa

Headmistress: Since 2006, Julia Harrington BA, NPQH (50s), previously deputy head at Prior's Field School. Mrs H comes from a family of teachers, was educated at a grammar school in Lydney and studied history and politics at Exeter. Worked in the media and then decided to train as a teacher and psychodynamic counsellor. As a child she 'wanted to be a vet' but was told that 'girls didn't do jobs like that'. You don't need a qualification in counselling to see that this experience might have shaped her as an adult.

Mrs Harrington is a head who doesn't just sit back and let the same old tried and trusted methods do their best. She keeps up with the latest neuroscience research into how people learn, working with university psychology departments at Reading and Oxford. It's certainly heady stuff; never before have we heard the word 'amygdala' used so many times in one conversation. She stresses the importance of environment and mindset, 'Instead of saying, "I

can't do this", we want girls to say, "Why not me?"' To this end she is working with preps so that girls don't come into senior school already thinking, for instance, that they're 'rubbish at maths.'

Let us say with admiration that the teenage brain is, apparently, not a mystery to this head. 'I tell the girls, the reason you want to keep checking your phones or Facebook is for the dopamine hit. If you understand the brain then you can give a reason for behaviour. Girls on the social front are hardwired to conform and it's this that can lead to behaviour like saving seats or being unkind. We challenge this by making girls aware of what they're doing and why.' Mrs H has the zeal of the convert and her enthusiasm is infectious, but before we got too carried away on the crest of a cortex we wanted to know whether she was in danger of treating her school like a laboratory. 'Not at all. I always ask, so what? How can this research help our girls?'

Mrs Harrington enjoys running but 'doesn't find it easy', and is learning Mandarin at Saturday morning classes alongside QA parents. Lives on site with her husband, who works in IT for a cancer research charity, and has three adult children (doctor, barrister, nuclear scientist. Yes, really). Favourite book would be, we assumed, some weighty work of neuroscience. It's not, well not quite. The Little Book of Thunks is a compendium of brain challenging questions that she likes to use in assembly. Favourite childhood read is good old Enid B's Five at Finneston Farm.

Academic matters: In 2015, 63 per cent A*/A at GCSE. Very good results in individual sciences and IGCSE maths but languages are trailing a bit. Three per cent A* in French last year? Zut alors! At A level, 50 per cent A*/A in 2015 (a great improvement) and again the sciences and maths are strongest with French still in dernier place. New head of modern foreign languages appointed.

Teaching methods are developed through the school's 'Life and Learning' programme and staff are encouraged to apply their knowledge of the teenage brain to develop 'brain friendly lessons'. Such educational initiatives notwithstanding, teaching we observed was reassuringly similar to what we see in good schools everywhere – small classes, attentive pupils, smartboards, plenty of Q and A. The World Cup based maths lesson we witnessed was described by the teacher as 'light relief' after summer exams and looked like a lot of fun. As Mrs Harrington explained, 'by providing a complex real world mathematical challenge but framing it

as an ethical conundrum,' girls are 'encouraged to take risks suggesting competing solutions to find the most ethical outcome.' In the smart and very well equipped biology lab we were impressed by the lack of squeamish squeaking as scalpel wielding as pupils prepared to dissect hearts. Girls are set in core subjects following the first half term in year 7. Lessons are 40 minutes long, doubles for eg languages maths and science.

She keeps up with the latest neuroscience research into how people learn. It's heady stuff; never before have we heard 'amygdala' used so many times

Our year 9 guides had obviously been paying attention to the head and were keen to tell us that 'striving' was very important at their school. 'We're not put under pressure but teachers help us strive to achieve our very best.' One or two parents mutter that they would like their daughters to be pushed to strive a bit harder, but general consensus is that school has balance about right.

Heaps of praise for excellent individual attention, subject support and UCAS advice in the sixth form but we hear that girls who don't want to go to university feel rather sidelined. School says that recent pupils who haven't gone on to university have taken up places at RADA, Central St

Martins and the Deliotte Undergraduate Training Programme.

SEN support mostly provided in class; individual sessions also available if necessary. EAL taught in place of modern foreign languages or Latin; all international pupils take English language and literature GCSE.

Games, options, the arts: At the time of our visit, the performing arts centre was being fitted out for the lower school production of Peter Pan (flying scenes to be done with puppets) and we enjoyed chatting to some very excited cast members. What would they do with a million pounds to spend on their school, we asked? 'We'd build a theatre like the one in Glee!' they cried. These young actors felt the school would benefit from bigger, better performing arts facilities but, though smallish, their current theatre lacked for nothing as far as we could see.

Plenty of options for the musical – choirs, ensembles, swing band and orchestras plus an exciting programme of visiting professionals, not only from the world of the arts but also science and business, all part of a programme called 'World Class in Class'. The head is keen for girls to 'see and know excellence' and also to demystify it. 'They meet these talented people and discover that they are also ordinary human beings who work very hard.'

Sloping games field is apparently a bit of an uphill struggle in lacrosse matches (it's the C team that gets to play on the steepest bit) but such hardships are obviously character building since QA lax is pretty fierce and successful. Main rival is Downe House. Excellent sports facilities, including 25m pool, fitness suite, dance studio, climbing wall plus loads of tennis and netball courts mean that there's something for everyone – even ballroom dancing

International students love to cook up a taste of home, and Ocado delivers any esoteric ingredient not to be had in Caversham

with The Oratory boys. Plenty of horsey stuff, too, including riding and polo clubs and the annual Queen Anne's Grass Roots and Inter-Schools' Show Jumping Competition.

Boarding: All seven boarding houses are tip top – these are the bases for day girls as well – and quite the smartest we've seen. Purpose built, modern and (very) brightly furnished (pink and blue chenille sofas and bucket chairs) and carpeted in house colours. Student artworks decorate the walls and common rooms, as does an abundance of bunting. No poky kitchenettes here; huge kitchens with all the kit are a great social hub. The large fridges are filled with Waitrose bags – older girls may go down the road to this and other local emporia in groups. International students love to cook up a taste of home, and luckily Ocado delivers any esoteric ingredients not to be had for ready money in Caversham. Girls are challenged to produce meals on a budget, they bake cakes for charity sales and teach each other favourite dishes. They also host dinner parties and invite chaps from nearby schools.

Upper sixth day and boarding girls are based in Michell, a house that is separate from the main cluster of buildings, affording privacy and a degree of independence. Many older day girls drive in and can park on site. Swish new sixth form centre is next building project.

Background and atmosphere: Built on 34 acres of primest Caversham (or 'Caversham actually,' as it's known by residents. It may be just over the bridge from Reading but mix the two up at your peril). Handsome Victorian brick pile set in immaculate lawns with, at the time of our visit, groups of girls dotted decoratively about, reading in the sunshine. Reception hall and offices are elegant, rather in the smart country hotel style; vibrant contemporary stained glass panels in the front door are the first hint that this school may be traditional, but with a modern twist.

Queen Anne's is part of the Grey Coat Hospital Foundation (other schools include Grey Coat Hospital, Emanuel, Sutton Valence and Westminster City School) and was established on its current site in 1894. Historic links with Westminster and the Abbey remain.

Website and marketing material are big on warm and fuzzy but rather low on boring old facts such as exam results by subject. We don't want to come over all Gradgrind but sometimes facts are necessary. Especially when parents or grandparents are making expensive decisions. The prospectus declares that the school is 'full of bubbly, smiley and enthusiastic people'. While we can't argue with that (actually, we might pick a fight with 'bubbly': it's usually an adjective of last resort and rarely applied to an intellectual equal), one can't help pondering whether all the buzz words – resilience; empowerment; brain plasticity; synthesis – might put off those who just want to know exactly what you get for boarding fees of close on 10 grand a term. Stick with it, we say, it's all here and a bit more too.

Pastoral care, well-being and discipline: Atmospheric galleried chapel now only accommodates everyone when upper years are on study leave. Chapel services for lower and upper school several times a week and regular hymn practice; female chaplain recently appointed. The original dining room looks charming, with gothic stone fireplaces at either end, but is rather small for current needs, so the next building project includes new dining facilities. Meal times are staggered and those who need to be at clubs and activities get packed lunches or can collect a deli-style lunchbox. Staff and students eat together and the food got a moderate thumbs up. Apparently breakfasts are fantastic and fish and chips on Friday is top lunch. Sixth formers have their own rather cool café in an old hall (former gymnasium); other years can get lunch there on Saturdays – much friendlier than having to eat in a half empty dining room. Regular socials with nearby schools – mainly The Oratory and Shiplake. Parents say that there's not much to persuade older girls to stay at the weekend and most prefer to head for home.

Day girls have a desk and often a bed and can stay over at short notice – flexi and weekly boarding options much appreciated by parents. It's a long day (home at 6.30pm) but prep is done under supervision in houses and tea is provided. After 4.30pm it's clubs and, if necessary, subject clinics; girls choose a minimum of three clubs from an enticing range of sporting and cultural options.

Parents told us that pastoral care is excellent, and our guides loved the strong inter-year group relations; the older girls 'are like big sisters'. Girls told us that there are no cliques and that everybody gets a chance to shine in drama, sport and music. Sixth formers have smart single en-suite study bedrooms. As we observed and several parents confirmed, university accommodation is sometimes a let down after this.

Recent drive to spruce up uniform not entirely popular with older pupils but has gone down well with younger pupils and parents. Sleeveless red V

neck pullovers, white shirts, blazers and, according to our guides, socks, not tights, even in winter, 'In the snow!' Perhaps there was a bit of dramatic licence here, since school says it isn't the case. Staff are 'very' vigilant about skirt lengths, apparently. Sixth formers wear the dreaded 'smart business' mufti. Distinctive red hooded cloaks are no longer mandatory but still used at biennial service of thanksgiving at Westminster Abbey, carol services and other special occasions. They're also rather photogenic, especially in the snow, and as a result are more frequently seen in marketing material than in real life. Girls we spoke to thought the school rules were 'strict but fair. Apart from the socks.'

Pupils and parents: Generally rather well-heeled. Majority local, boarders mostly live around an hour away. Increasing numbers from London who see it as a positive and also convenient (only 25 mins to Paddington) alternative to metropolitan school rat race. International students from over 15 countries seem to integrate well and UK girls get invitations to plenty of exotic sleepovers. Famous Old Girls include Posy Simmonds, Jenny Seagrove and the real Joan Hunter Dunn, immortalised by John Betjeman.

Entrance: Prospective pupils (from wide range of local preps and state primaries) are encouraged to

attend a taster day and overnight stay. Assessment for entry at 11+ consists of tests in maths, English, verbal and non-verbal reasoning and a group interview. For entry to the sixth form students sit an exam and will need a minimum of six GCSEs at grade C or above (including English and maths) and B in subjects to be studied at A level

Exit: Some depart after GCSEs to local colleges or co-ed sixth forms. Those who stay for A levels go on to respectable universities including Imperial, Edinburgh, Durham, Manchester. Wide range of subjects (law, medicine, engineering, art and drama) testament to strengths in all areas. Two to Oxbridge in 2015 and a couple to the US.

Money matters: Boarding fees broadly in line with home counties compatriots. Day fees are good value considering girls get extended school day and thus some of the boarding perks. Art, music, drama, sports and all-rounder scholarships at 11+ and 13+. Will help in cases of hardship.

Remarks: A welcoming, dynamic and forward-thinking school. Delivers academically but there's much more than that to an education at Queen Anne's. Who would it suit? We leave the answer to Mrs Harrington: 'When parents ask what kind of girl is a Queen Anne's girl, I answer that I hope there never is one, they are all individuals.'

Radley College

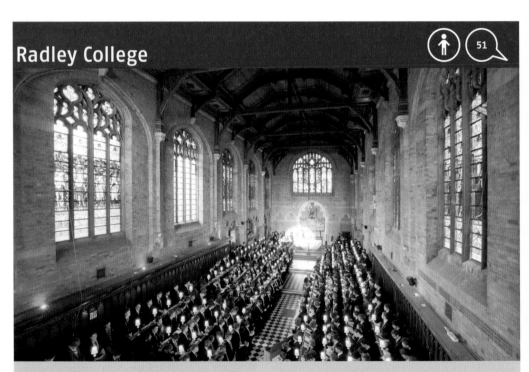

Radley, Abingdon, Oxfordshire OX14 2HR

01235 543000
admissions@radley.org.uk
www.radley.org.uk
C of E

Ages: 13–18
Pupils: 691 sixth form: 285
Boarders: all full
Boarding: £34,000 pa

Warden: Since 2014, John Moule MA (40s), previously head of Bedford School. Educated at a Telford comprehensive and sixth form college, he won a history scholarship to Lady Margaret Hall, Oxford and left with a first. Refreshingly atypical background for a post like this. Taught history and politics at Dean Close, Cheltenham, moved to Stowe as head of history and became housemaster, then senior housemaster. Perhaps it's Radley's proximity to Oxford but we thought Mr Moule had a little of Laurence Fox's (aka Sgt Hathaway in Lewis) lean, pale intensity. This impression only somewhat dampened when we learnt that pallor was a result of his 'feeling under the weather'.

He seems to have made a very favourable impression and was described to us as a 'brilliant' speaker, able to hold an audience of parents and boys simultaneously. 'He's very visible and really involved' one mother told us, 'He drops into Socials (Radley-speak for boarding house) and plays chess with the boys.'

Married with three children, his eldest daughter is a veterinary student, his son is finishing A levels at Bedford School and the youngest is at a girls' day school nearby. Having worked in medical research his wife completed a second degree in maths and now divides her time between the many and varied duties of a head's spouse and teaching at a school in Oxford.

Like so many heads Mr Moule claims to have 'fallen' into teaching. (Watch out, there must be a huge and cunningly disguised hole somewhere designed for just this purpose.) It goes like this. He was all set to study for a PhD in 16th century English theological history but the grant awarding bodies had other plans and chose this moment to withdraw the financial support that had hitherto been awarded to arts students with first class degrees, 'You could say that I was saved by lack of funds'. At a loose end in Oxford someone inevitably suggested he try teaching. 'I'd never set foot in an independent school but after two weeks I knew it was right.'

Of course Mr Moule is convinced of the benefits of a full boarding school. 'It fosters strength of character and independence'. He goes on, 'the 24 hour culture is hugely creative, it allows teachers to develop boys' genuine interests beyond the classroom.' He describes the 'powerful' triangle formed by the school, the parents and the boy, 'all have to buy into it', he says. For fee paying parents that is both metaphorically and literally the case.

Since becoming warden Mr Moule has done a great deal of observing. Not only has he dropped unannounced into lessons and watched every don (Radley-speak) teach, he also shadowed pupils throughout their day (including late afternoon and evening) to learn more about their experience as well as the school's 'flow'. And what were his conclusions? He was seriously impressed by the variety he found but felt some lessons were rather too teacher led. We imagine it can be hard to avoid in a school full of bright boys who for the most part will arrive having had eight or more years' listening and learning in prep school. We saw some young hopefuls during our visit, serious little chaps wearing polished brogues and tweed jackets – just like the fathers accompanying them.

He wants to do more to raise boys' awareness of the world beyond Radley's 800 prime Oxfordshire acres and has also told parents, and boys, that he intends to 'wage war on teenage apathy'. While acknowledging that every day should still contain a little time for creative boredom, he says boys have a tendency to do 'just enough' and feels this should be challenged. When he's sorted that one out perhaps he could let us know.

Of course it's important to the 'sincerely spiritual', but it's also valued by chaps who just want a bit of peace and quiet, or 'separated space' as the warden puts it

His plans for the school itself are well underway. The website has already been improved beyond recognition – it's now (fanfare) welcoming and informative – and the College's famously esoteric ('mystical' was how the warden described it) entry procedure has been revised. It used to be the case that if you had to ask Radley how to apply then you were probably too late. The process is now more open, in line with other, similar schools, though the 'List' remains and is an advantage for those who want to sign up early. Increased bursarial support is another target, as is 'careful' recruitment of applicants from beyond (even far beyond) the home counties.

Mr Moule's strong Christian faith means Radley's timeless tradition of whole school chapel four times a week is in safe hands. Boys 'love' chapel he told us, 'especially as they get older', and indeed this was borne out by those we spoke to. Of course it's important to the 'sincerely spiritual' but it's also valued by chaps who just want a bit of peace and quiet, or 'separated space' as the warden puts it. It may not be as fashionable, but perhaps this is mindfulness, Radley style.

When not wardening Mr Moule says he is an 'avid' armchair sportsman and enjoys a spot of golf or real tennis. Reading is, naturally, another recreation and favourite books include Wilkie Collins' The Woman in White and P G Wodehouse's classic, The Mating Season. Box sets are also high up on this warden's list, especially The West Wing and the US version of The Office. And if he hadn't so carelessly 'fallen' into teaching? Journalism, the law and the church are all the poorer for his stumble.

Academic matters: Even with the recent changes to its entrance procedure Radley is not a school that selects solely on academic ability; excellent GCSE and A level results stem from fine teaching and staff who don't think their job is done when the lesson finishes. Recent reintroduction of the linear, two year A level has proved that Radley wasn't so maverick after all when it held out against AS levels being taken at the end of the first year sixth. We did detect a certain quiet satisfaction that the rest of the country has finally come into line. Sixth formers sit three or four A levels, a fourth subject is generally one that contrasts with the other three. All will also do an extended project.

In 2015 81 per cent A*/A at IGCSE/GCSE; particularly strong results in, well everything, but also some Cs, Ds, even a few Es. At A level just under 64 per cent A*/A, most popular subjects history, maths and English literature followed by sciences. Notable proportion of A* in art and English lit. Nice to see decent numbers taking classics, languages and geology too. While maths and further maths are very popular, Radley has always stood apart from the overwhelming science/maths dominance so commonly found in boys' schools and we're glad to see this remains the case.

Teaching in the lessons we observed was of the tried and tested sort – a fast pace and lots of quick fire questions kept everyone on their toes. Very clearly exam focused. However, despite adding a distinctly scholarly air, gowns didn't seem to make Radleians any more elevated or less prone to muttering at the back than their non-gowned counterparts at other schools.

Latest ISI report called learning support 'exceptional' and parents are in agreement. All boys have to meet the entrance criteria to get into the school but once there SEN support is extensive and

We met some really amusing and inspiring dons who just seemed to love their jobs (less jobs, more way of life, we thought)

lacks stigma. Individual and small group sessions are arranged according to need. Some take place during what is known as 'central hour' (1.30 – 2.30 daily), time set aside for relaxing, working, music lessons, extracurricular activities etc.

We met some really amusing and inspiring dons who just seemed to love their jobs (less jobs, more way of life we thought) and the very stones of the place. Good mix of ages and lots of women among teaching staff. Dogs seemed to be part of the package too – that explained the water bowls we'd wondered about in some of the classrooms. All dons and their families live on site.

Much talk of efforts to 'learn from other schools and widen diversity'. Strong links with local primaries and a Maidenhead secondary school; some exchange of teaching staff but latter a little too far away for frequent activities. Closer to home the Warden hopes to further develop joint academic extension activities for A level subjects such as music, English and geography with Headington School. There are links for the scholars with St Helen and St Katharine's and plans for 'ambitious extension days' with Oxford High School. Lest we get too carried away by all this talk of diversity, at Radley take your dog to work day is unlikely to be joined by enrol your daughter day any time soon.

Games, options, the arts: All rather civilised. Manages to maintain a creditable sporting reputation without the ruthlessly competitive atmosphere than can prevail at boys' schools. We got the impression that the disinclined to run are not regarded as also rans. Rugby is main game of Michaelmas term – around 20 separate teams do battle every Saturday.

When it warms up the 'wet bobs' row; 'dry bobs' play hockey, fives, cricket or tennis in the summer term. Boat house on the Thames is ten minutes away and those wet bobs are usually up there with near neighbours Abingdon and rivals Eton and St Edwards during the Henley Regatta and head of the river competitions.

Twice weekly so-called 'minor sports' include swimming, golf (there's a course on site), fives, squash, real tennis, cross-country, rackets, tennis, badminton. Those who wish to can do a spot of beagling. Alternative sports programme (ASP), is a circus of different sports for boys (remove upwards) who don't take to rugby. Sixth formers can choose which sport they want to play.

Art school, complete with rather cool gallery space, is in Clocktower Court. Pupils' work, paintings, ceramics and photography, not confined to here, it's all over the school – eerily lifelike papier mâché boys peer down from beams in the library. Ambitious projects undertaken in DT include surfboards and a rather spectacular trebuchet. Once again, facilities lack for nothing and are open late into the evening and at weekends. Nine or ten boys take art or DT at A2 with creditable results.

Large chapel choir with trebles from local primary schools and preps sings at services and evensong in chapel and elsewhere, including Oxford colleges. Weekly concerts in the school coffee shop, house and college concerts give boys as many solo and ensemble performing opportunities as possible. The music school is open until 10.15pm and boys are expected to organise their own practice although a member of staff is on hand to help. Just one or two doing music at A level despite high profile of music in the school – theatre studies more popular option.

Indeed, Radley still has that slightly separate feel of an Oxford college, enhanced by the sight of boys rushing to and fro, gowns billowing behind

---

Inter-house competitions and endowed prizes are great motivators and boys take to the stage for such keenly fought contests as the part song competition, debating, declaiming, battle of the bands, piano and percussion trophies. The legendary Piano Extravaganza featured, most recently, 91 players from age 6 upwards (under 13s are dons' children) playing on eight pianos. The Silk Hall is school's premier music venue and next door is the theatre where college and year group plays are performed as well as A2 drama devised pieces. Parents rave about the drama at Radley, even shy boys take to the stage. No reluctance from boys to take on female roles but every so often school puts a 'Girls wanted' advert in the local paper if the production requires the genuine article. Warden told us he directed several plays at his former school and might be tempted again.

CCF compulsory for removes, fifth form do community service and sixth formers can choose enrichment activities such as opera, film or cooking. Couple of parents thought a few more 'life skills' wouldn't go amiss at this stage. Seriously impressive calendar of visiting speakers including

WW2 RAF hero, Auschwitz survivor, scientists, authors, journalists, MPs and members of the clergy. Vast array of trips – theatre in London, art in Florence and music tours (singers and instrumentalists) to America. Energetic fundraising for variety of good causes including partner school in Tanzania and Christian Aid.

Boarding: Boarding houses at Radley are known as 'Socials' and Socials are distinguished by letters of the alphabet (A Social, B Social and so on). First years ('shell') have curtained 'cubs' or cubicles with a sink and cabin bed. Apparently Radley was the instigator of this arrangement that affords pupils some degree of privacy within a dormitory. It caught on and can still be seen in many prep and senior boarding schools. From removes (second year) on it's single study bedrooms. In typical boarding boy fashion these were all rather tidy, noticeboards generally unadorned by photos, posters and the like. Our guides told us they liked the busy, structured days at school and appreciated the relative freedom of home life all the more for it. 'We probably take Radley for granted' one added.

Boys may buy uniform, stationery, tuck etc in school's shop (known, wait for it, as 'Shop'). Card system for purchases in Shop or coffee shop; 'jam account' (upper limit of £60 per term) for tuck. One parent thought it was a shame there was no opportunity to buy second hand uniform, sports kit etc.

'Oxford leave' allows boys (mostly sixth formers) to travel into Oxford (by bus or taxi). Upper sixth chaps may spend Saturday night there as long as they're back in Social by 10.30. Quite a restricted regime for boys of this age, although exeats and privis allow a few slightly longer Saturday nights out elsewhere.

Background and atmosphere: In the quartet of boys' full boarding schools (first violin Eton, second violin Winchester, cello Harrow), Radley would be the viola – less frequently played ('mystical' entrance requirements), smallish solo repertoire (690 boys), confident, necessary, but unflashy (low profile) and so on. It's also the newcomer, having been founded by Oxford movement devotees, The Revs Sewell and Singleton in 1847 to 'provide a public school education on the principles of the Church of England.'

The founding Revs organised their school along the lines of colleges at the University of Oxford, hence some of the nomenclature: warden, dons etc. Indeed, Radley still has that slightly separate feel of an Oxford college, enhanced by the sight of boys rushing to and fro, gowns billowing behind. Last vote saw proposal to do away with gowns defeated by 95 per cent. Daily choral services were, and remain, a key aspect of the school.

It was believed boys' minds and souls would be improved by learning in a beautiful rural setting and well-designed environment. Shades of William Morris perhaps. School motto is the succinct, 'Sicut Serpentes, Sicut Columbae' (Be ye wise as serpents, and harmless as doves') and these creatures appear on the coat of arms – with the cross keys of St Peter to whom the college is dedicated – safely between them.

Radley College is neither overwhelmingly grand nor intimidating. Reception is small and unpretentious, seating would indicate that they do not expect more than three people to arrive at any one time. Reception staff friendly but appeared to be fighting a losing battle to stop the office becoming overwhelmed by on-line delivery packages. 'Radley boys keep Amazon in business' said a long-suffering voice from behind a pile of boxes.

School originally occupied the Mansion, an 18th century house that belonged to the Stonehouse, then Bowyer families. This rather elegant building with grand panelled reception rooms is now home to admin and the warden's offices. Other parts are usual mix of charming and slightly less charming additions. Wide vistas, generous lawns and paths are another great advantage of a large, rural site. The grounds were by laid out by Capability Brown and some features of his design remain visible. Many trees, looking especially lovely on the golden autumn day of our visit. Immaculate pitches (delightful cricket pavilion) stretch into the distance.

Queen's Court (aka the Doughnut), opened by Her Majesty in 1997, may dominate aerial views of the College but we were rather taken with the inside, which seems to have stood the test of time. It's home to maths, economics, biology, geography and geology and the communal space outside the classrooms is full of fascinating natural history specimens and large tanks containing turtles, scorpions and cockroaches. Members of the animal society come here to get up close with reptiles and snakes, if not doves.

Pastoral care, well-being and discipline: The tutor (housemaster) is the key figure in a boy's life at Radley. He oversees the boys in his Social along with sub-tutors and pastoral housemistresses (PHMs) – the latter come in for particular praise from mothers of younger boys. Form masters monitor academic progress. Boys in the first two years also have a lower sixth mentor. Cocoa at 9pm every night is a chance for all the boys in a Social to meet up and chat about the day; this and other activities help blur year group hierarchies. Boys are expected to help with the running of their Social: shell do chores such as collecting post; sixth form house prefects supervise prep and bedtimes. Parents all praise dedication of Social staff and say that any enquiries are dealt with 'by return', they also like the regular progress reports.

Two exeat weekends per term and boys earn 'privis' or privilege weekends for good behaviour, work etc. On 'Sunday outs' boys can go out with parents or a friend after chapel for the day. One mother lamented, 'My son doesn't take his privis, there's too much going on at school to miss.' Rather sweet little handbook sent to boys before they join includes useful advice such as, 'Bring more tuck. Most don't bring enough,' and, 'If you are lost, confused or unhappy don't be afraid to ask for help.' Information about who to ask (both in and outside College) and how to do this is also included.

Cocoa at 9pm every night is a chance for all the boys in a Social to meet up and chat about the day; this and other activities help to blur year group hierarchies

School places great emphasis on tolerance, kindness and manners. Biggest crime, according to new boys' handbook is, 'to be rude to a cleaner, a member of catering staff, the ladies who help you in Shop or any other member of the College staff.' This is not intended in a de haut en bas way – as the Warden says, 'we discourage any sense of entitlement or arrogance.'

School is keen to enhance the quality of social activities with girls' schools. Shell still get the chance to disco with the likes of Wycombe Abbey, but older boys now join girls from St Mary's Calne, Tudor Hall, Headington and St Helen and Katharine for dinner and discussion or joint theatre trips.

Pupils and parents: The warden describes a Radleian as 'civilised, friendly and engaging, in short, good company' and all the boys we met lived up to his definition. He also debunks a commonly held myth (that may stem from former entrance procedure) that most boys are sons of former pupils. 'It's 15 per cent', he told us. Seems that the lower sixth drama group we had spoken to where all but a couple were second or third generation Radleians was just a blip. 'Most people find out about us through word of mouth,' continued the warden, 'they've met and liked a Radleian at work or university and think of us as a possible school for their own son.'

Even so the hour has arrived to tweak what school describes carefully as its 'cultural variety'. Don't expect a revolution, or a rainbow nation – it'll be a while before the grain of truth packs its bags and departs from school's nickname, 'Ra Ra' Radley. Change will happen, carefully, in Radley's own time, and it will most certainly be for the (even) better.

Former pupils (ORs) include Andrew Motion, poet; Sir Clive Stafford Smith, human rights lawyer; Lord Wilson of Dinton, former cabinet secretary; Peter Cook, comedian; Sandy Nairne, former director of the National Portrait Gallery; Christopher Hibbert, Historian; Ted Dexter, Andrew Strauss and Jamie Dalrymple, England cricketers; Sir Charlie Mayfield, chairman of John Lewis; Lord Wolfson, CEO of Next. And many other actors, writers, lawyers, engineers, sportsmen, clergymen and public servants of all kinds.

Entrance: Still the forward planner's choice. Radley remains loyal to those who register early and 'conditional' offers (subject to performance in entrance exam and head's report) are made three years in advance to boys on 'Provisional' and waiting lists. No open days, individually arranged visits all through the year. Friendly and approachable admissions staff will explain system.

Admissions procedure is changing but up until 2018 boys not already registered may apply for one of around 40 'Warden's List' places. Radley puts 'much emphasis' on candidate's performance at interview and head's report when assessing applicants for these. From 2019 onwards, after conditional offers are made to boys on the 'Provisional' list, there is an open entry system whereby all interested candidates are first asked to sit the ISEB Common pre-test in year 6 and send a school report; interviews will be offered to shortlisted candidates.

Few (around 8) places at 16 + but on the whole this is a settled community and there's not much movement.

Exit: Bristol, Durham, Edinburgh, Exeter, Leeds, Manchester, Newcastle and UCL hoover up most of Radley's leavers. Regular 15–20 boys to Oxbridge every year (16 in 2015) – mock interview exchange scheme with nearby Abingdon School seems to benefit both sides. School's university entrance team recently expanded to integrate expertise in applying to universities in North America, Europe and beyond.

Money matters: Cheapest of the quartet (no viola jokes please) but there's barely a gnat's crotchet between them. Uniform requirements less painful on the purse – parents told us that suits, shirts etc can be bought from high street. Gowns aren't expensive and, look on the bright side, might save on jacket dry cleaning bills (and they cover books if it's raining, boys told us). Sports kit will cost you but then it does everywhere. Lack of coffee shops (or indeed any shops) in immediate vicinity looks promising but remember the Amazon overwhelmed reception desk ...

Scholarships of up to ten per cent off fees awarded annually at 13+ and can be topped up to 100 per cent with means tested bursaries. Foundation awards enable boys from state system to attend a prep school for two years before admission. Armed Forces Fund provides assistance to boys from Forces families. All very clearly explained on school website.

Remarks: In our last review we said that Radley was the connoisseurs' choice; this remains the case. Yes, it's traditional, but it's utterly unstuffy. Like the serpent and the dove in the coat of arms, respect for tradition lives harmoniously with tolerance, intellectual curiosity, humour and humanity. Radley provides boys with an immersive education of the highest quality and a strong moral and spiritual core.

Ryde School with Upper Chine

Queen's Road, Ryde, Isle of Wight PO33 3BE

01983 562229
school.office@rydeschool.net
www.rydeschool.org.uk
C of E

Ages: 11–18
Pupils: 507; sixth form: 140
Boarders: 55 full, 3 weekly/flexi
Day: £6,900 – £11,955 pa
Boarding: plus £3,850 – £4,410 pa

Headmaster: Since September 2013, Mark Waldron. Previously head of the English College in Prague, deputy head of Sherborne, and taught at The Leys School and Radley College. Eager for a new challenge, returned from Prague to run Ryde – and for the joys of Waitrose. Mr Waldron's experience in Prague has given him a different perspective and he feels well placed to make a difference at Ryde: he emphasises the importance of preparing pupils to compete internationally, and has shaken up language provision to support this. Parents find the head approachable, are impressed by his change in priorities, and say the school is friendlier now he's in residence.

The head encourages his teachers to think about the potential for creative and independent thought when planning their lessons: could the lesson take place without the pupils? Mr Waldron teaches maths – always the bottom set, so he knows the lowest common denominator. Regularly turns cakes into fractions; and what are the chances of getting that elusive blue in a tube of smarties?

He is learning to sail, and currently classes himself as incompetent crew; is a politics junkie and devotee of the races. Just finished reading Solar by Ian McEwan, and is about to embark on a book about Gordon Brown's spin doctor – feels a bit guilty when reading fiction. Likes pub quizzes. You can see how he might.

Academic matters: Good solid academic results for a non-selective school. In 2015, 66 per cent A*-B at A level, 41 per cent A*/A. At GCSE, 43 per cent A*/A. IGCSE also available, and the head has introduced the vocational IB (IBCP). Ryde is chosen by some parents for its consistently good results, which give a 'degree of assurance': it is in the privileged position of being virtually the only independent mainstream school on the Island (the other is very small), and it is fair to say that Island state secondary schools do not rank highly in the league tables. One parent said that he feels his children 'have the chance to excel and achieve their full potential'.

Class sizes at A level 8-14, a maximum of 22 at GCSE. Lessons are now 55 mins instead of 35 mins – an improvement, pupils and parents agree. There's a five min break between lesson times to ensure that no one is late – or 'that's the intention,' said one pupil, cautiously. There is a strong work ethic

at Ryde – the classes we saw were almost universally heads down, working hard, the concentrated effort almost palpable. Pupils who have come from other schools comment on the fact that it is ok to work hard at Ryde – 'It's not something that you get teased for: it's actually cool to be clever.'

Maths and science are popular – due in part, says the head, to the large number of doctor parents; and illustrated by year 10 turning the whole periodic table into cupcakes in the school bake off. Victoria sponge...or periodic table...They must like it.

The head has come from a school where students were studying in their third or fourth language, and firmly subscribes to the saying 'if you only speak one language then you can only live one life': he is determined that everyone shall learn at least one other language. Spanish is the new second language at Ryde – it's also easier for dyslexics to learn. Mandarin and Latin are also finding a place in the curriculum.

With Mr Waldron has come a new emphasis on the sixth form, which will soon blossom in a new sixth form block on the main campus: it may house sixth form boarders, and will be a micro university experience. The sixth are pleased that the previous nod towards career planning, apparently only really useful if you wanted to be an engineer, has been replaced by something really helpful; and lifelong learning has been introduced in a personal development lesson every Monday. It's about destinations, says Mr Waldron: pupils needs to understand where they want to go, and how to get there. IB students know what they are doing and why; not always the case for those studying A levels. So at Ryde even A level pupils will do the

Maths and science are popular and illustrated by year 10 turning the whole periodic table into cupcakes in the school bake off

theory of knowledge core of the IB, so they 'get an idea of what it means to think.'

The sixth formers we met were polite and articulate, although they didn't quite have the spit and polish you might encounter in some mainland independent schools: perhaps this is because the Island and school constitute a secure and rather more laid back environment. Mr Waldron is well aware that his domestic pupils might lack some of the edge which is evident in his international students, particularly those from the eastern block, who are well aware of the privilege of attending Ryde and of the international stage on which they will be competing. This is something he is clearly determined to address.

Parents receive mini monthly report cards detailing effort and progress, until GCSE, when this turns into attainment, and predicted and target grades – to flag up any problems with work. Focus on praising effort: merit badges worn on blazers, like awards for courage under fire, are awarded entirely for effort. When the school as a whole has achieved 2000 efforts there's a mufti day.

Strong SEN provision: around 15 per cent of pupils here have special needs, and the school makes provision for up to moderate dyslexia. Aim for SEN pupils: to make all capable of independent learning.

Games, options, the arts: Music is super here – our tour guides, neither of whom were taking music A level, said their happiest hours at school were spent in the music block. The teaching inspires a real love of music, and as well as junior, chamber and concert orchestras, there is a student-led ukulele orchestra. Pupils relish the joys of the annual Global Rock – an international dance competition. Students put together routines and costumes themselves: parents describe the results as 'incredible'. The summer musical and winter production are popular with parents and locals alike, and lots of pupils are keen to take part.

Not a school, says the head, for a top sportsman or woman: two pupils left at 16 to attend schools with more focus on hockey and rugby. The provision is decent; but a parent commented that it's difficult to get good mainland schools to come and play on the Island because of the travel expenses involved; another said that although sports teaching and facilities are good, Ryde is a small school,

so there's a limited choice of pupils for teams. But the compensation is that those good at sport get to be a big fish in a small pond and can become team captains – positions they might not occupy at larger schools.

Senior pupils say there is not sufficient emphasis on sport: because their standard is much higher than that of the other schools on the Island, they easily win local matches, but can struggle with matches against schools on the mainland, who tend to play at a higher level – 'we don't lose all our matches,' said one sixth former (actually, this is a bit harsh – most sports have a respectable showing). But sailing, recently started at the school, is thriving (as might be expected at an island school where so many children sail regularly with their parents). More alternative options for sixth formers include yoga and mindfulness.

Grand DT room in the predominantly glass block built three years ago to house art and DT. 'If I get them in year 7, they stay,' said the DT teacher with a smile; and indeed both our guides expressed huge enthusiasm for the subject, and remembered with affection their first task of designing an insect in year 7. Roof terrace with lovely view out over the sea – it's made full use of for parties – and a few beds of weeds which apparently have an eco purpose. The art rooms have the hushed atmosphere of a cathedral: any talking is done in whispers, pupils concentrate hard. Here, clearly, there is no sense that art is a light option: it is afforded proper respect. Pupils commented on the dedication of those taking art A level; and GCSE students are apparently rarely out of the art department, spending all their lunch times perfecting work. The new building contains a large IT suite just for DT and art – apparently the other IT space can get crowded, and it isn't quiet enough for the artists here. Lower sixth reached the regional finals of a young enterprise competition last year selling luxury gift items, cards and gift wrap and such, and won a Kenko competition for designing a logo. Design is clearly a thriving area.

Both CCF and D of E are popular here; a parent commented that it is the good provision for music, arts and extracurricular that give children here such a good level of confidence.

Boarding: The boarding campus is some 10 miles from the school, but there's a daily bus service and the school pass can also be used to obtain free travel on public transport on the Island. The boarding houses are beautiful arts and crafts buildings, sensitively restored and converted. Admiring the lower gallery, a long elegant sitting room with squashy sofas, packed bookshelves and piano, you might think you are being shown around a rather lovely National Trust property. Then you would spot the drum kit and TV and know you're not. The upper gallery above has been turned into double bedrooms surrounding a living area for year 10 girls – an idyllic set up, flooded with light from the long windows. Sixth formers get single rooms, unless they request to share. Others are usually in rooms for two. Two house parents resident overnight so pupils have someone who they can contact if ill.

Ryde chosen by one parent for the strong sense of family in the boarding houses, compared to other schools where boarding provision seemed like 'housing for battery chickens.' His children are happy; any minor issues arising have been dealt with successfully, and he has 'absolute confidence in the boarding set up'. Some boarders' parents fall in love with the Island when they visit their children here: one Tunisian mum even decided she would rather retire to the Island than to the south of France.

The large site is shared with an activity centre, so there are plenty of outdoor facilities for boarders to enjoy – anyone for after-school caving? Indoors there's a room with pool, table tennis and table football. Pupils say the boarding experience is sold on the basis of lots of activities, but really some of them rarely happen: quad biking, for instance, only happens during the first week of term. (There is, perhaps, a particular push on special activities at the beginning of terms to help new kids to bond.)

Boarders can roam the 100 acre grounds more or less as they please, providing they sign out first. Must keep in sight of the drive on dark winter days, and need to seek permission to go the beach, which is off campus. The youngest boarder is currently year 6 – there isn't an age restriction, but the head of boarding likes there to be boarders of a similar age to keep each other company.

Pupils comment that the food in the boarding house is 'awful' (in comparison, food at the school

is 'gourmet'). School is well aware of the problem, which is tricky to rectify since the catering facilities at the boarding house are shared with the activity centre. But there is a gorgeous mural in the dining room of animals waiting to board Noah's ark, a pair of black cats, tails held jauntily high, leading the way. The mural remains unfinished: the painter pupil didn't return from the First World War to finish it off; but it must be lovely to look at while wading through the substandard grub.

The head is keen for pupils to look beyond the Solent – pupils must not be limited by the stretch of water: they will need to compete nationally and internationally

Boarders set up their own clubs – cheesy Tuesdays (the cheese on toast club) and the Coco Pops club – foodie clubs popular for obvious reasons. They make good use of the kitchen facilities, and can cook as they please – there's plenty of fruit and cereal available at all times, and a Tesco run every Friday night (no Red Bull allowed).

Boarders have plenty of opportunities to make their views heard, with a suggestion box, weekly house meetings and an open door policy for the head of boarding (and yes, they have mentioned the food).

Background and atmosphere: A school surrounded by stunning scenery – how lovely to sit in the library and stare out at the picture postcard view over the sea. Venerable main building with nondescript (but well cared for) adjuncts; swish new glass DT and art centre.

The advantages of attending school on the Island are clear: it is safe, secure and beautiful. The counter to this is perhaps an element of complacency born of isolation: the head is keen for pupils to look beyond the Solent – pupils must not be limited by the stretch of water: they will need to be able to compete nationally and internationally. Mr Waldron intends to ensure they can.

Pupils are friendly and polite (although this is not a leap to your feet place) and pupils clearly enjoy being at school – a pupil who transferred to Ryde from a local school commented how good it is to be at a school where he actually wants to stay and do activities; just because it's nice to be there. One parent said the best thing about Ryde are its pupils: 'grounded, mature; and nice kids to be around.'

Feels like a traditional environment – although surprisingly pupils are allowed to use mobile

phones in class for task-related research: one parent commented that he is not happy with a rule so open to abuse. C of E but with a light touch – prayers at the end of assembly, because that's just what happens; much like a full stop at the end of a sentence. But Mr Waldron is keen for religion to play a larger part, and has introduced compulsory church as a fortnightly event. Sixth formers are unimpressed: they've been told that this is reflection time, but don't quite see why it should have to take place in church.

Parents are happy with communication levels, and reaction to complaints (which are rare): when one did have a problem and raised the issue with the head, it was dealt with swiftly and well.

School council of pupil representatives who have been feeling a bit disenchanted with the slow reaction to their views and requests: for instance, the school council requested a shelter outside the canteen, so that pupils waiting in the lunch queue on rainy days didn't get wet. A sensible request – but it took a couple of years to happen. The head says this has been addressed: democracy has come to Ryde, and the school council is operating under a new pupil-run system.

End of year trip to somewhere theme parkish has been replaced by an activity week focusing on life skills. This has not been uniformly welcomed by pupils, the majority lingering on the side of 'not fair.' Lower sixth, in particular, felt they might have had more fun on a roller coaster than learning to tidy and clean – although there must have been a number of grateful parents, and those changing a tyre skills may well come in handy. Year 7 spent their week building a secret garden, which some love; another year group were camping on the games field with team building exercises – apparently a bit too local to be considered fun.

Uniform is the usual fare, but some parents, apparently, are obsessed with wanting a 'trendy exclusive uniform' – think black blazers with yellow trim; although one parent we spoke to observed dryly that 'Ryde kids don't actually want to stand out on the bus.' Quite.

Pastoral care, well-being and discipline: Parents view the pastoral care at Ryde as exceptional – 'they do a terrific job' – and describe the advantages of a small school where staff know all the pupils and their families. Parents like the strong community atmosphere at school, and comment on the extraordinary level of support and counselling from the school following the tragic death of a pupil, both to the immediate family, and to other pupils; another parent was similarly appreciative of how supportive the school were after a family death: 'wonderful' and 'very caring'.

The head is keen for his pupils to achieve a balance in life, and there is new emphasis on life skills and mindfulness to emphasis the importance of enjoying and experiencing the present (involves controlled breathing – even those who were sceptical beforehand were happy to admit that this was super – one admitted to taking relaxation as far as sleep). This does not feel like the sort of school where grades will be achieved at the expense of well-being; indeed the head muses on whether the Norland nanny in last year's batch of sixth formers, who worked hard to achieve her two A levels, will be happier than the Cambridge mathematician.

Disciplinary system of minus points and detentions run on Friday and Saturday mornings (Saturdays are relatively rare). Drug taking can and has led to expulsion.

Pupils confident that there would be a teacher or form tutor they could talk to if they had a problem. There is a move to involve sixth formers more with younger years, and prefects now wear listener badges, so kids have an obvious person to go to if they want to talk to someone other than a teacher. Any bullying occurs is dealt with properly – 'sensitively and appropriately' said a parent.

Pupils and parents: Large number of parents scrimp and save to get their kids to Ryde – the state schools on the Island are famously poor. Around 80 per cent of boarders are international; also pupils from all over the Island, DFLs, and those from Portsmouth who commute over on the ferry. More pupils arriving across years 9/10/11 since Island middle school closure. Parents range from fish and chip shop owners to medics. Not a snobby school, although one parent commented that 'a few parents are'.

Former pupils include: Seb Clover (sailor), Donald Gordon (cricketer), Philip Norman (author), Lucy Emmerson (academic) and Arthur Venables (cyclist).

Entrance: Non-selective, tests for placing purposes only. Interview with head for all prospective pupils. Most pupils stay through to the sixth form.

Exit: The majority to a range of universities, particularly King's College London, Southampton and Loughborough. Three to Oxbridge in 2015 and three medics.

Money matters: Wants to keep fees affordable for Islanders. Three IB scholarships of 50 per cent which are advertised on the island. Bursaries of up to 90 per cent of fees, available on a needs basis, the number available depending on the amount of the bursaries already paid. A number of small scholarships of around 10 per cent, which may soon be combined into fewer more meaningful scholarships, possibly in sailing. Pupils feel current absence of scholarships in sports or music suggests that these subjects are perceived by the school as less important, and this is something the head is keen to address. Around 30 per cent of pupils have discounted fees. Four 100 per cent HMC scholars from eastern Europe.

Remarks: A school distinguished by its strong community, set in beautiful surroundings with solid academic provision. Not somewhere you are likely to encounter much unscheduled exuberance, but vitality is likely to increase with Mr Waldron at the helm. Clearly the best option for many Islanders.

Rye St Antony School

Pullen's Lane, Oxford OX3 0BY

01865 762802
info@ryestantony.co.uk
www.ryestantony.co.uk
RC

Ages: boys 3-8, girls 3-18 (boarding from year 5)
Pupils: 450; sixth form: 55
Boarders: 90 full/weekly/flexi
Day: £9,360 – £14,175 pa
Boarding: £18,930 – £23,400 pa

Headmistress: Since 1990, Miss Alison Jones BA. Miss Jones studied English literature at York University and did her PGCE at Oxford. She spent 14 years at St Mary's School, Cambridge as an English teacher, head of English and head of sixth form. Only the fourth headmistress since Rye's foundation in 1930, she is poised, calm and immaculate, self-possessed but not aloof and utterly dedicated to her school. 'My heart is here', she says. Apparently she was 'born wanting to be a headmistress' and never considered any other path. Miss Jones knows all the pupils and their families by name and, although she no longer teaches regular lessons, she works with girls at lunchtime and visits classes. She is herself taking lessons in how to use her Blackberry – from a first year. She lives on site, as did her predecessors, and shares their belief that her work is 'faith in action'. Does she get lonely in the school holidays? Not at all. Her four nephews love coming to stay and old girls are in the habit of dropping in unannounced; they are always made welcome. She loves the poetry of Eliot and Hopkins, both wrestlers with faith, and her desert island novel is Middlemarch. Indeed, perhaps Miss Jones shares some of Dorothea Brooke's more admirable qualities – a sense of higher purpose, the desire to serve.

Rye's junior and nursery departments are presided over by Miss Jo Reed, who joined the school in 2008 from nearby Headington Prep. Miss Reed is proud of Rye's inclusive philosophy: 'we don't label children here, we accept them for who they are regardless of ability.'

Academic matters: Rye is not a league table school, nor does it seek to be. In a city like Oxford you have to be pretty steadfast not to be sucked into the slipstream of academic competition, to steer a different course. Miss Jones is indeed steadfast; she is concerned about the pressure to win that comes from society and girls themselves; 'They can become like racehorses,' she warns. Rye is an inclusive school with a 'wide focus'; the school's aim is for every girl to achieve her full potential. The school's public exam results endorse the soundness of the Rye approach; in 2015, 40 per cent A*/A grades at GCSE. At A level, 52 per cent A*/B grades and 25 per cent A*/A. Rye may be a small school but this in no way limits the subject choices available at GCSE and A level. The school can support individuals who wish to take GCSEs in subjects such as classical Greek, Chinese and Russian and also offers the additional maths and science. Girls may choose from 22 subjects at AS/A level including theatre studies, textiles, Latin, Japanese and Spanish.

The average class size is 16 and the pupil to teacher ratio is 1.5, so no chance for a pupil who may be struggling to slip under the radar. EAL specialist teachers support up to 25 pupils and learning support tuition is available to any pupil, whether for help in a specific area or with wider study skills needs. The curriculum is extended with, for example, a science fair when girls present research projects. Recently Rye fielded the only all girls' team in the Annual International Space Settlement Design Competition and won through to the finals of this prestigious and demanding event held at Imperial College.

Recently judged as 'outstanding' by Ofsted, the junior school and nursery are on the same site as the senior school with delightfully quirky accommodation in a Victorian house. The nursery is up in the eaves of King House with gabled classrooms full of tactile equipment, books, paints and dressing up. Working parents are grateful for extended flexible opening hours (7.30am to 6.30pm); children can come for morning, afternoon or all day sessions.

In a city like Oxford you have to be pretty steadfast not to be sucked into the slipstream of academic competition. Miss Jones is indeed steadfast

Juniors are taught in Langley Lodge, another Victorian gem that retains its original charm with wonderful windows, fireplaces and high ceilings, so much more inspiring for young imaginations than standard issue classroom boxes (requisite technology and smart boards also present). Classes are small and children benefit from an extended broad curriculum with subject specialist teaching in music, food technology, French, ICT (in the new technology building), art, science, maths PE and DT. Plenty of time allowed for sport, music and creative stuff. Formality increases gradually as children move towards senior school but no decrease in fun quotient – we saw a class of year 5 girls in a junior science lab excitedly acting out the behaviour of molecules. At the school's annual science fair mixed age teams compete against each other, developing research and presentational skills.

Games, options, the arts: The director of studies referred tellingly to the 'arms race' to provide bigger and better facilities in independent schools. This is a race Rye doesn't need to enter, partly because its residential location limits expansion and further building but also because Rye pupils are already well catered for.

Staff and pupils run a large programme of more than 30 lunch time and after-school clubs from photography to juggling, pottery, dance and debating. Service and charitable activities are enthusiastically undertaken and girls volunteer and fundraise for local and international causes, including on-going support for street children in Calcutta.

The library is large and very well stocked; displays change frequently as the librarian guides and challenges readers to try books from outside their comfort zones. The librarian also organises creative writing workshops led by authors, literary quizzes and book groups. Sixth formers have a separate study area and loans are made using a fingerprint system. The art facilities are generous and AS/A level artists have spaces to leave work out; the displays of pupils' work all over the school were inspiring – wonderful textiles, paintings, still life drawings and collages with all year groups and abilities represented. According to the head, 'all girls participate in the musical life of the school'; this must be so with five choirs, an orchestra, two jazz bands, chamber groups and various instrumental and voice ensembles. Choral groups compete in local and national competitions and recent choir tours have performed in Paris, Spain and Italy. Plenty of practice rooms and a full range of instrumental tuition including the harp. The acquisition of a set of Jamaican steel pans and an Indonesian gamelan reflect the head of department's enthusiasm for world music.

Beyond the tennis courts a curving path winds through trees to the sports centre – its wooded exterior blends perfectly with the surroundings. Inside is a very large multi-purpose space with a well-equipped gym on the first floor. On the day we visited it was hosting an inter-form debating competition; subjects under discussion included 'This house believes that Barbie is a positive role-model for young girls' and 'This house believes that vampires are cooler than werewolves'. The motions were extremely well argued and backed up with creditable research including the possible medical origins of vampires and werewolves and references to their first cinematic appearances. The audience

listened intently and asked challenging questions, but we left before the vote so cannot reveal which mythical creatures won.

Sports teams participate in fixtures against much larger schools with success across the board, notably in netball, tennis, hockey and cross-country. Sports options and clubs include all the usual ones plus volleyball, football, rowing, sailing, boxercise and a rock climbing course at Oxford Brookes for sixth formers. An outdoor heated swimming pool for summer term use.

Subjects under discussion included 'This house believes that vampires are cooler than werewolves'

Junior Walls and notice boards covered with creativity and evidence of enthusiastic fundraising – the juniors choose their own charity each term. We were introduced to the Rye bear and baby bear who spend each holiday with a different child; the guardians report back with a presentation and photos. Equally popular is the duo of dwarf rabbits who are lavished with exemplary care.

Boarding: No more than 65 girls boarding at any one time and the school is flexible, able to offer accommodation for a single night or short-term response to a family crisis. An Australian gappie showed us round The Croft, a large late Victorian house where younger boarders (years 5–10) live, its former grandeur somewhat compromised by the necessity of fire doors and generations of feet and bags. Notice boards and walls rather bare, but then our visit was near the end of term; shared bedrooms full of photos and stuff from home. Older girls have lovely rooms in the eaves, endless stairs more than made up for by character and privacy. Saturdays are for organised activities with trips to London, street dance workshops, ice-skating in Oxford and the like. Also organised socials with Magdalen and Abingdon boys' schools. Year 10 girls can go into Oxford in groups on Sunday afternoons. Years 11–13 live in The Cottage, a low-rise building arranged around a peaceful courtyard garden. Each boarder has her own small study bedroom, good preparation for university. The sixth form centre is here also, beautifully designed in wood and glass with a cafe (hot food and salad bar) and socialising area on the ground floor and IT, study and teaching rooms above.

Background and atmosphere: More than one parent described Rye as 'a hidden gem' and never is this truer than on one's first visit. The entrance is via electric gates in a quiet residential cul-de-sac just off Headington Road in central Oxford; a small car park and cluster of modernish additions give a less than imposing first impression, but don't rush to judgement. The extremely helpful staff in the school office must have one of the best views in town, pace nearby dreaming spires – beautifully tended gardens, rolling lawns, huge ancient trees and, instead of traffic, birdsong. Pretty much everything is on a charming domestic scale, but we are talking wealthy late-Victorian domestic. New buildings such as the sports hall, sixth form centre and library have been skilfully designed to provide ample modern space without jarring or dominating the original architecture. Can't be many city schools where children can run off at break time and play in a 'jungle' of trees rather than concrete. Juniors enjoy joint academic and extracurricular activities with the seniors and there's no demarcation of outside space, all of which contributes to the strong sense of community commented on by so many parents and visitors.

It's hard to describe the very special atmosphere at Rye without making it seem like an anachronism (it's not at all), but something of the pioneering spirit of its founders, Elizabeth Rendall and Ivy King, lives on. On the wall in Miss Jones' bay-fronted study is the most wonderfully evocative black and white photo of Miss Rendall, the school's first headmistress, sitting thoughtfully at her desk, cigarette in hand. Miss Rendall and Miss King started the school in a house on the Woodstock Road in 1930; rising pupil numbers prompted a move to the current site, a house formerly owned by Arthur Balfour, curator of the Pitt Rivers, in 1939. (The beautiful Japanese screen in the dining room

> *The extremely helpful staff in the school office must have one of the best views in town – beautifully tended gardens, rolling lawns, huge ancient trees, and birdsong*

was bought for £5 with the house.) King's mother and sister, Gwen, moved into the new school and adults and children saw out the war here – growing vegetables and fruit in the gardens and taking fire warden duties at night. Girls learnt to scull on the Cherwell and swimming lessons were at Dame's Delight (ladies' counterpart to Parson's Pleasure). On Miss Rendall's retirement, Miss King became headmistress. Her successor was Miss Sumpter, from whom Miss Jones took over in 1990. What inspiring role models are these redoubtable women, who were as capable of fixing the electrics as teaching Latin; who did the maintenance and

the gardening as well as persuading parents to allow their daughters go to university. No wonder the school has such a devoted band of 'Old Ryes'.

Pastoral care, well-being and discipline: Rye is a lay Catholic school. What this means in practice is that while Catholicism is integral to its ethos, the school is inclusive and outward looking, welcoming girls of all faiths and none. Where other schools have rules, Rye requires its pupils to understand and observe principles – these are intended to develop habits of tolerance, consideration and service that characterise the school community and will benefit the wider world.

Each new pupil is allocated a housemother (a year 6 pupil in the junior school; a sixth former in the senior school); her role is to help with adapting to school life, someone to turn to for all those questions or worries that a new girl might not feel able to ask an adult. Responsibility for organising this system lies with the Patricians, senior prefects who also help staff and governors and are involved in management and policy making. Girls are expected to participate at all levels of school governance, not just the school council, and are represented on all committees. They are appointed to roles such as prep, ICT and library supervisors, minute secretaries, food committee and care of the environment. This is not tokenism, nor is it a crafty way of getting jobs done (although this must be a side-benefit!). Miss Jones calls it 'learning to lead'; positions have proper job descriptions and are intended to develop workplace skills such as negotiation, organisation, problem solving, planning, public speaking and communication.

We chatted with a group of girls who thought that the school has the balance between freedom and supervision just right in the sixth form – 'Staff have lots of time for you, but they also chase up work if it's late'. They loved the fact that they knew practically everyone in the school by name and they felt that their opinions counted – ' If you aren't happy, they listen to you and try to change things'.

Takes a whole-school preventative approach to bullying – tolerance and respect for others are central to the school's principles and these values are integrated into the curriculum. Housemistresses, form tutors, the school nurses and chaplain are the foundation of pastoral care and pupils may be referred to external counsellors if necessary. Senior pupils are trained as peer counsellors and anti-cyber bullying mentors. Distinctive red uniform until year 11, thereafter own clothes.

Pupils and parents: Cosmopolitan mix of local and international pupils. Only around a third of the school population is Catholic, others are attracted by Rye's principles and inclusivity. Parents include medics from the nearby John Radcliffe hospital, resident and visiting academics. Longstanding links with families in France, Spain, Italy and Germany bring visiting pupils for the last half of the summer term.

Entrance: Nursery places (age 3-5) offered after visit. Separate application must be made for place in junior school. Candidates for junior school spend a day and are informally interviewed and assessed. Report from previous school required. No examination for progression to senior school.

Prior to examination, 11+ entrants spend an 'ordinary' year 6 day at the school and meet the headmistress. The school sets its own examination papers in English and maths. Boarding applicants combine the day visit with an overnight stay. Girls wishing to enter the sixth form are interviewed and must have a minimum of five GCSE passes with grade B or above in subjects to be studied.

Exit: Junior boys mostly to local preps aged 8; nearly all junior girls go through to the senior school. Some 15 per cent leave after GCSEs. One sixth former told us that she had left, only to return a short time later, having found that the grass wasn't greener. With such a small cohort of leavers each year no significant subject bias or trend in university destinations. Destinations in 2015 included a few to Birmingham and Cardiff, one to study Japanese at SOAS and one to the Royal Academy of Dance.

Money matters: Up to five scholarships at 11+, 13+ and 16+ and some means-tested bursaries. Girls can apply for a King Award while at the school, a sum of money (usually between £100 and £300) that enables them to further an interest or learn a skill, for instance music lessons, scuba diving, riding, dancing, or fees for a short course.

Remarks: Miss Rendall and Miss King founded Rye as a school where 'academic potential' would not be the sole deciding factor for entry. They believed that both sides of the personality should be allowed to 'grow together'. Eighty-five years later this principle still holds true. While Richard Dawkins might not approve, Rye's inclusive and humane approach to education has an appeal that is catholic as well as Catholic.

St Clare's, Oxford

139 Banbury Road, Oxford, Oxfordshire OX2 7AL

01865 552031
admissions@stclares.ac.uk
www.stclares.ac.uk/ib

Ages: 15–19
Pupils: 280
Boarders: 250 full, 2 weekly
Day: £17,280 pa
Boarding: £35,630 pa

Principal: Since 2005, Ms Paula Holloway MSc PGCE. Educated at Cowbridge High School for Girls in Glamorgan and the LSE, where she read geography. She began her career in banking but started teaching when she moved to Hong Kong and has never looked back; 'I just knew I had found what I wanted to do for the rest of my life', she recalls. On her return to the UK did an MSc in educational studies by research at Jesus College, Oxford, and became deputy and then head of Latifa School for Girls in Dubai. Head of Ashford School in Kent from 2000 to 2004. Married to management consultant and lives close to college. Astute and professional but friendly with it, described herself as 'not a soft touch but not unapproachable'. Efficiently runs an international staff with no clerical tier; slightly surprised at the school's continued success – 'I don't know quite how we do it' – though it is apparent

she and her 'wonderful senior management team' set the standards high; 'we are very good at modelling what we expect'.

Academic matters: They come from the four corners of the globe to study here for the two-year IB diploma. The school was a proud pioneer in offering the IB, now has over 35 years' experience, and achieves consistently high results. IB is no walk in the park, six subjects: three at standard level, three at higher, including home language and English, a humanities subject, science, and maths, not forgetting the compulsory theory of knowledge course; extended essay and community, action and service (CAS) programme. Principal describes it as an 'outstanding qualification in terms of the breadth and depth it offers'. Parents happy with the diversity of subjects: 'My daughter had no clear idea of what to do, therefore keeping it broad in range of topics rather than specialising too early was one of the things that attracted us to the IB'. Others with children who had attended a range of different schools abroad felt the IB was the only option: 'It would have been difficult for him to settle into a traditional English school, with uniform and rules'. St Clare's has the edge over other IB schools, claims the principal, in that it doesn't attempt to teach A levels at the same time. Recent leavers' results put St Clare's regularly top of the Oxfordshire sixth form tables. Average score of 36 in 2015.

Students too young to sit the IB course, or whose English needs practice, take the Pre-IB course. This is flexible in length (up to one year) and can be joined at any time, to prepare English and core subjects for diploma level.

All tuition is in English and class sizes average nine, some even smaller. All students study the literature of their home language so individual tutors are often recruited from the university for more exotic tongues, anything from Ukrainian to Farsi. Classrooms, in a number of nearby houses, are abuzz with IT equipment – students encouraged to bring their own laptops. Informal teaching style from a multi-lingual staff; 'if you can't enjoy teaching at St Clare's, I don't know where you will enjoy teaching', says the principal. Parents impressed by calibre of staff: 'They simply ooze experience' said one. 'None of this fluffy "your son is such a nice boy" stuff'. A new teaching block, with four new science labs and classrooms, co-ordinates with local architecture. Cosmopolitan lab technicians and librarians can juggle Dostoyevsky in English or Harry Potter in Cyrillic. Art takes place in a charming converted chapel, where the high ceilings and gallery provide a serene light for painting. There's a dark room, complete with leering skeleton, for photography.

Cosmopolitan lab technicians and librarians can juggle Dostoyevsky in English or Harry Potter in Cyrillic

Apart from the display of retro propaganda posters from various nations, the classroom was more like a modern boardroom, throbbing with discussion about European current affairs; 'It brings history and economics to life,' said a student. Watching these 16 year olds unpick global economics certainly gave us hope for the Euro crisis.

There is no SEN department. Profound learning difficulties are not provided for, but the college has had students with dyslexia, ADHD and hearing impairment.

Games, options, the arts: As a mandatory part of the IB programme, students take CAS (Creativity, Action and Service) over the two years to develop personal skills of planning, team work and conscientious thinking. A minimum number of points is needed in these areas, preventing any of the students becoming too bookish. In reality, the plethora of activities from art to zumba make up the social life of the school and run into the weekends and evenings. A mass of notices about clubs, classes and overseas projects draws students to the 'covered way', a busy corridor between classes and café. One family chose the school for the efforts it made to accommodate their son's ice hockey talents; 'I didn't want to go to a school where everybody rowed or played rugby'. The creative part involves a wide range of arts, music, writing, debating, Model United Nations, dance and drama. Behind the guitars, drums and piano in the music room is a full-time music teacher, and Sibelius music software is available for the budding composer. Concerts take place throughout the year, but the hot ticket is the international day concert in which students and some staff stage their own gig, with singing, dancing and jokes. Theatre productions by each year group were remembered fondly by senior staff, even if they had a senior moment remembering the titles.

The school has no playing fields. All students are given membership of the local sports centre and swimming pool; other facilities are a short minibus ride away at local schools or at Oxford Brookes University. Football and rugby teams use Astroturf pitches at Oxford City grounds. Parents forgive the lack of facilities: 'St Clare's does a great deal with very little'. Girls' volleyball is a particular strength. The CAS programme also involves community service (not the punitive kind), which takes the form of charity work in local shops, visiting the elderly or helping at local schools. A personal tutor is on hand every week to monitor progress and offer advice. The programme is open to Pre-IB and IB students and changes every term.

Concerts take place throughout the year, but the hot ticket is the international day concert in which students and staff stage their own gig, with singing, dancing and jokes

Students make full use of the cultural life of Oxford University, as well as the local shops and cafés of nearby Summerstown. There are organised excursions to places of interest in half terms, plus D of E field trips. Students are encouraged to go home in the holidays to recharge, but foreign excursions and tours to more remote parts of the British Isles are arranged for those who want them. Each year's leavers celebrate by cruising on the Thames in a party boat.

Boarding: St Clare's boarding houses are all within a five-minute stroll. First years share rooms with someone of a different nationality; 'arguments are rare,' we are told, and language learning rapid. 'Suddenly she had a massive range of friends from other backgrounds,' chimed a dad. Second years can have a single room or join with a friend in a double. All are comfortably furnished, most with own shower, hairdryer, strongbox and Wifi. Fraternising takes place in the common room, over the TV and kitchen area. A warden, in loco parentis, handles general well-being of the youngsters and counts them all in before the strict curfew. Day students are allocated a house and can stop over one night a week. Our impression when stepping out into the raked gravel drive was less of having visited a typical teenager's bedroom and more of a comfortable hotel.

Background and atmosphere: The school motto, 'To advance international education and understanding', stems from the principles of the visionary founder, Anne Dreydel, who despite being confined to a wheelchair by a bomb during the blitz, established exchange programmes for German students in her drawing room. Rightly recognised with an OBE and the German equivalent, her cultural olive branch towards international peace has grown into a thriving sixth form for 260 students. A collection of fine Victorian villas (27 buildings in total) along the cherry blossomed streets of genteel north Oxford provides boarding accommodation

and classrooms. 'The buildings do not look as smart and luxurious as those of most boarding schools', commented one parent. To the rear, gardens dotted with the quirky addition of red telephone boxes have been joined and landscaped to allow the students some green space to eat, work or chill, but no loud music, smoking or ball games allowed.

Students can take three meals a day in the canteen, which serves up a suitably international menu. Predictably, none of the students rated the dish from their own country but were positive about the others. Stylish refectory tables encourage mingling and English chat out of the classroom. The Sugar House (refreshingly un PC name) offering a continuous temptation of snacks, pizzas and lattes, was doing good business when we visited.

Pastoral care, well-being and discipline: With so many youngsters far away from home discipline could be a problem, but isn't, thanks to the school's clear code of actions and 'consequences' – a portentous term that is famously effective at deflecting trouble, we are told. A strict curfew is respected, 11pm during the week, midnight at weekends. Alcohol is not tolerated, drugs result in an immediate suspension and we couldn't see any bike sheds for the usual teenage experiments: smoking and sex. The system works on trust; 'It's a very powerful glue,' says the principal. The students are given a reasonable degree of freedom in return for responsible behaviour. 'When my son transgressed (in a very minor fashion), they were immediately on to him', said a parent. Lateness or poor behaviour results in loss of free time, confinement to the library or the house for varying spells, at worst for a term. 'It's rare someone will transgress twice', smiles the vice principal, eloquently.

A weekly session with a personal tutor, on first name terms, covers pastoral and academic issues. Rather than homesickness, the students complained that home life now seemed quiet; 'I miss people around me'. Student council, elected democratically, is first experience of democracy for some of these youngsters. Councillors hold office from January to December so as not to interfere with serious study, and meet with senior staff once a week to pow-wow: coffee machines, laundry problems and swivel chairs were the order of the day when we visited. 'It's easier to deal with a small problem than let it grow', says the principal pragmatically. Parents have email addresses of teachers and tutors as well as official parents' days at the beginning and end of terms. 'There isn't the tradition of parents' evenings as in a normal school', said a parent, but in practice, there is an open invitation to visit whenever in the UK. Reports and test results can be viewed electronically via the parent portal, explained a parent, and 'we can see when he's been late!'

The students grow noticeably in confidence over the first term, and parents report that after seven weeks a different person has come home – 'the levels of motivation are astonishing' – confident in English and more self-reliant. 'At the start of the year people looked for comfort in their own national group, but not now', chorused a bunch of students. 'The more you get to know about each other, the more relaxed you are'. Despite the school's name, there was no sight of any religious bias, rather an emphasis on internationalism, learning about culture and diversity from each other. 'People think differently here...you learn a lot of stuff about the world. It's eye-opening', said one student. 'Awesome,' said another.

Pupils and parents: Forty-six different nationalities with almost as many different languages; biggest groups are German and Italian, but Russian is also common. Some 85 per cent of boarders are from overseas. Students criticised the size of some of the national groups. Eight per cent are British, who join from international schools abroad or are UK youngsters with an interest in the IB. Ten per cent are day children, with parents working in Oxford at the university, BMW or similar businesses. Round a table, they are an impressively mature, articulate and dynamic bunch, redolent of a UN delegation. Principal says, 'students bring each other on'. Perhaps they were hiding the mumbling, moody teenagers, but we didn't meet any. Instead, the break time discussion was open-minded and lively, peppered with a dose of multi-cultural joshing. Hugely purposeful about the work; 'Studying in the UK gives international prestige and broadens your interests', said one girl. The standard of English was astounding – rivalling many native schools – and the dress sense a positive improvement.

Entrance: Students are drawn to St Clare's by word of mouth or siblings' experience. No entrance test (except for scholarships), but highly dependent on two years of reports and references from previous school. The 'personal and intense' selection process won over one family who had initially looked for a public school. Interview in UK is compulsory, at which students are sized up for their enthusiasm for the IB programme. 'This is not a place for people to try to escape from their existing school', said the principal. Her instincts must be good, as St Clare's is full to capacity. Test for maths at interview determines which IB maths course students can tackle. There is a four day induction programme for newcomers, supported by senior students.

Exit: Majority go to university, 75 per cent to UK (LSE, Bath, Exeter and UCL are recurring choices) some to US or European universities and business schools. One to Cambridge in 2015. Popular courses are engineering, medicine, law, economics and, not surprisingly, international relations. Principal is proud that St Clare's has equipped them well for it; 'our students do not drop out of university'. An award–winning careers adviser offers one-to-one advice on applications and CV with seminars to prepare for UK and USA applications in the final year. 'Within a month...he was suddenly seriously

considering his future and deciding what he should do', revealed a shocked mum. An education day of visiting speakers from business was under way when we visited, with groups of students carrying out Alan Sugar-style challenges, the kind of thing most of us first experienced at job interviews. These global citizens are ahead of the game; 'they are more willing to look abroad for opportunities in education and for work', says the careers adviser.

Money matters: Fifteen students each year receive scholarships or means-tested bursaries based on previous academic performance and scholarship exam; February deadline. Registrar called the fees 'reassuringly expensive, good value for Oxford'.

Remarks: Academically and pastorally mid way between school and university or, as principal said, 'University life with safety nets'. St Clare's attracts ambitious students from around the world, with an eye to a global career via a UK, US or European university. 'In some ways St Clare's is not a boarding school', said one mum, 'but rather a pre-university college'. The diverse student population is savvy; already aware that the world is a shrinking place and that the motivation to do well comes from within. Restores your faith in world peace.

St Edward's Oxford

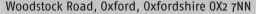

Woodstock Road, Oxford, Oxfordshire OX2 7NN

01865 319200
registrar@stedwardsoxford.org
www.stedwardsoxford.org
C of E

Ages: 13–18
Pupils: 661; sixth form: 290
Boarders: 553 full
Day: £27,714 pa
Boarding: £34,632 pa

Warden: Since September 2011, Mr Stephen Jones MSc MLitt (50s), previously head of Dover College. Educated at both Hurstpierpoint and Lord Wandsworth Colleges. Erudite, a man of many degrees, went to Durham to read maths and physics but graduated with a rare first in philosophy, then read maths before embarking on research in philosophy of maths. Was an assistant housemaster at Cheltenham College, head of maths at Berkhamsted School and a social tutor at Radley before his appointment at Dover. Married to the delightful Katie, who has her own successful career in the church – no mean feat alongside being a headmaster's wife. They have three children, two of whom have flown the nest.

We're told he is a good sportsman, keen on staying in shape, enjoys fives and sailing and has a keen sense of humour, 'His student house was dubbed Front, so he could talk about going back to Front'. An accomplished mathematician, he loves poring over the figures and has a brain that specialises in pure logic, in whatever discipline. Parents say, 'Youngsters respect him, he is easy to talk to.' When we meet he is chatty, relaxed, enthusiastic – 'I don't have all the answers, what head does?' – but stresses that 'I want to engender a culture of academic excitement, sharpen things, raise expectations tempered with understanding of what the world is really like'. He is realistic too and under no illusion that keeping St Edward's on top of its

game and rubbing shoulders with competitors will demand toughness and vision.

Academic matters: Most take nine or 10 subjects at IGCSE/GCSE, all the usual plus Latin or classical civilisation and Greek alongside PE, DT and drama. In 2015, 66 per cent of GCSE papers were graded A*/A. Philosophy/ethics/political literacy courses for lower school pupils and all sixth formers study for an EPQ or equivalent: 'Great preparation for independent study at university and beyond,' says warden. In 2015, 68 per cent of A level grades were A*/B (41 per cent A*/A) and the IB average was a creditable 36. Scholars' societies – OX2 for lower school and The Woodstock Group for seniors – stretch the able. Parents say science teaching is variable: 'Joint offering of IB and A level has resulted in good teachers being stretched too thinly' – school aware and say they are working hard to redress. At A level biology and art & design popular and successful.

Good for self-esteem: those who can, will, those who can't will be helped to. Currently 15 per cent of pupils receive learning support, mainly for mild dyslexia – timetabled and free: 'We are an inclusive school so subject support is offered'. Learning support concentrates on strategies, including use of smartphone and ICT. 'If they are disaffected we look closely at what is going on. They can't hide here.'

Has a reputation for being gentler on the old grey matter – both entry and exit – than many of its near competitors yet, in these league table propelled days, parents may seek a school that is 'forgiving' on entry but don't want an apology on exit – nor do they get one. Teddies (as it

is affectionately known) has been shimmying up the league tables: not via hothousing – 'There are enough schools in the locality doing that,' says school – nor by upping the entry ante (though scholarships have been expanded and a new girls' house, Jubilee, helpfully nudges boy-girl ratio close to 3-2); rather the main thrust has been to eke more out of everyone, think good breezy airing, rather than squeezed through the wringer. Pupils write A* and keep in their pockets; IGCSEs introduced; IB has been extended ('Oversold,' say parents, school says not the case, adding, 'Pupils are choosing it in increasing numbers'). A levels remain, though no Pre-U, the tougher alternative to A levels; 'Not really the thing for our cohort', said warden.

Indoors there is a superbly equipped, sparkly leisure centre – the hub of middle class Oxford mummies working off their lunches – shared with the school

However the biggest buzz (and buzz-word) is meta cognition ('know about knowing,' said our young informant). Warden wanted children to develop intellect, to reason, question and enquire. 'Some children arrive browbeaten through CE; we have to rebuild their confidence, inspire and invigorate them'. Working on the youngsters meant developing staff. 'I appointed a new academic director who encourages staff to share good practice, go off-piste, explore and enjoy their subject,' says warden. A move that appears to be working: 'Teachers love the curve ball question but some had lost their nerve, teaching only to pass an exam rather than exploring their subject,' says academic director. 'That is changing'. Dead Poets Society this isn't, there is still a generous nod to the syllabus and ticking boxes – plenty of routine revision, past papers, chalk and talk during our spring visit, but our guides said they're treated to discussion-based, interactive, active lessons. Parents approve: 'It's a happy, friendly common room with a great vibe that rubs off on kids'. Academic push still a work in progress but generally all things learned are looking up and bucking up.

Games, options, the arts: Fabulous facilities – 100 acres of prime north Oxford; outdoor courts, cricket pitches, a new cricket pavilion (Gloucestershire Cricket Club runs a satellite academy at the school for pupils and local juniors), a nine hole golf course, boathouse. Indoors there is a superbly equipped, sparkly leisure centre – the hub of middle class Oxford mummies working off their lunches – shared with, and leased from, the school, providing a fantastic gym, indoor and outdoor pools, indoor tennis courts and fitness and dance studios. Pupils win accolades – cricket team undefeated, have their fastest first eight ever, runners up at National Schools' and Henley; several GB junior oarsmen and county cricketers; girls' senior hockey team have been county champions seven years in a row – currently county champions at U14, U16 and U18. Rugby less robust: 'We take a few hits,' confess boys, though school hopeful tide turning. New director of sport is working hard to tempt talent of tomorrow to Teddies – with an array of special events. Not that those who wince at the thought of catching a ball should worry: 'They will find a sport you can not only do but do so proficiently; it's all about building confidence. Staff get involved too – it's lovely to see their commitment – it rubs off on the youngsters.' Only moan is expense of sports kit: 'Always something else on the bill; they must be in-league with the supplier,' joked one parent.

Art good with results to match, especially at A level with facilities for jewellery making, ceramics, sculpture and large fine art displays. The North Wall Arts Centre (enjoyed by the local community – hosts visiting artists and theatre groups) boasts exhibition galleries, drama studios and a cosy 250 seat theatre. Parents say dance has come on in 'leaps and bounds' and music is on the up (new music school in the offing), with something for everyone regardless of where you sit in the talent pool. 'Kids try hard, there's a huge number of bands, plus excellent choirs including one for parents and the community.' Excellent extracurricular provision including ever popular Duke of Edinburgh and CCF.

Boarding: Boarding houses have own identity – Quad or Field side – choose quad for a disorganised child, field for those who relish open space. New girls' house, Jubilee, is, according to warden, 'more like an upmarket hotel than a traditional school house'. For most of the rest, including odd Cinderella house ('about to improve,' say school) it is standard, homely rooms – shared save for the older years, with an assortment of communal facilities.

Cohesive boarding houses provide welcome support and foster inter-year friendships. Good food, all dine centrally, pupils say it's fun to mix with friends from other houses, parents rue table manners: 'They're noticeably very much "bolt-food" variety.' Safari suppers, ice-skating and discos are a sample of the many weekend jollies.

'Lots of boarders go home on Sunday after chapel, leaving school feeling somewhat empty and unloved for those forced to stay in,' said one parent, but another added, 'I like that they can come home on Sundays; we relish the family time.'

Ideal for the late bloomer, the all-rounder and the high-flyer who doesn't wish to be a mere pebble, fighting for survival, in the tidal wave of Oxford's academic powerhouses

Background and atmosphere: Situated in leafy north Oxford, the setting is privileged indeed. Much akin to an Oxford college, the main buildings surround a lawned quad. Recent additions include an eco-inspired life sciences building – solar powered with 'more technology than you could wish for'. School isn't the grandest we've seen, it may lack the edge of some of its established upper-crusty rivals, but it has enough of everything, is polished and looks good. Simple peaceful chapel, compulsory on Sundays for boarders, C of E but all faiths welcome. Day pupils stay until 9pm (ad hoc early finish at 6pm on request), all can have a bed in the boarding houses and sleep over if they're too spent to go home.

Pastoral care, well-being and discipline: Parents say pastoral care is excellent, only caveat, 'We'd love our child to have the same tutor throughout, someone who can help and support when pressure builds or child overloaded, overwhelmed or overwrought'; school counters 'structured tutor system for continuity of tutoring in lower school and in sixth form is ideal for a boarding school'. Still has its fair share of rich kids, some with arguably too much pocket money at their disposal.

Tough on drugs; warden says, 'If we suspect, we test; if positive, save the most exceptional circumstances and I can't think of any of those, they're out.' Punishments for smoking, parents say booze handled brilliantly for the child. 'Quite a number drink and smoke in younger years (same everywhere?), they push boundaries but school pushes back.' Local pubs policed, those aged 18 get a pub pass but other savvy sixth formers sneak off to Summertown for their Saturday night tipple. 'If they get caught they get bust but it doesn't stop them,' said our mole, adding, 'You must be able to say a lucid goodnight to your HM, otherwise it's a night in the san and the ignominy of being woken every 30 minutes.' School adds, 'All have cheese and biscuits and spend an hour with HM when they return; it's great fun for HM and means we get to keep a friendly eye.' Despite tolerance, some parents feel school needs to be more trusting, offer more privileges to older ones, with a long rein tugged hard for those who rail against.

Pupils and parents: Parents a mix of academics, professionals and business. Twenty per cent of boarders from overseas, from a huge variety of countries. Most of rest from Oxford or the home counties. Has a local reputation of privilege and at times pushing the boundaries – Teddies' girls in particular – yet the pupils we met were grounded, down to earth and friendly, a view shared by others we spoke to. 'They're clubbable, they've had to live with people in close confinement, they learn how to get the most out of others,' says warden, with a student adding, 'My parents gave me The Good Schools Guide and I chose Teddies; it has lived up to all in the review but especially on the friendship and friendliness front.' Notable former pupils include Kenneth Grahame, Laurence Olivier, Douglas Bader, Guy Gibson, Jon Snow, Emilia Clarke and Sam Waley-Cohen.

Entrance: From a range of prep schools, majority of day from Dragon. Skype interviews possible for those based overseas. Gently academic 55 per cent at CE, non CE candidates take the school's own exam. A handful sit an exam at 11+ to guarantee a place. Runs an academic challenge day for local year 6 pupils, with diet of philosophy, Arabic, economics, architecture and politics, to spot scholarship potential and encourage applications.

Exit: Handful (some 10 per cent) leave post 16 to pursue courses not offered here or to save on fees. Six to Oxbridge in 2015, rest to eg London, Exeter, Bristol, Edinburgh, Newcastle, the US (Columbia, Berkeley, Chicago), Europe and Australia. Three medics in 2015; other popular subjects include geography, biomedical sciences, engineering, maths, modern languages and history. Inspiringly, St Edward's doesn't view the path to university as job well done: 'We look to the bigger picture, the young employable 25-year-old making strides in business, commerce, enterprise and academia. Understanding the cut and thrust of the world beyond university is paramount.'

Money matters: New scholarships introduced – academic, music, sport and all-rounder can be means-tested to a maximum of 100 per cent. Sizeable number on bursaries: 'Often the most able,' says warden. 'Attracting bright pupils is good for the school, good for the teachers and good for results.' All are considered annually for an honorary scholarship. Minor scholarships available for drama, art and dance.

Remarks: For those uncomfortable with ultra prestige, the trappings of the old and bold, or the sheen of highly-polished academia, St Edward's offers an established, acceptable, dependable alternative. Those who seek out Teddies will either be judging it against day school rivals or other co-ed boarding schools; it doesn't sit at the top of either pile but it holds its own, taps on elbows and keeps them on their toes. All-round broad education with plenty of nurturing, perceptibly raising expectations and results while maintaining its discernible cheer and friendliness. A busy school with a rosy outlook, ideal for the average to above average child, the late bloomer, the all-rounder and the high-flyer who doesn't wish to be a mere pebble, fighting for survival, in the tidal wave of Oxford's academic powerhouses.

St George's School (Ascot)

Wells Lane, Ascot, Berkshire SL5 7DZ

01344 629900
admissions@stgeorges-ascot.org.uk
www.stgeorges-ascot.org.uk
C of E

Ages: 11–18
Pupils: 277; sixth form: 85
Boarders: 86 full, 30 weekly
Day: £20,700 pa
Boarding: £30,180 – £32,025 pa

Headmistress: Since 2011, Mrs Rachel Owens MA PGCE NPQH (40s). Previously vice principal at New Hall School and, before that, head of history at Prior Park College, Bath, following spell in career-nourishing environment of North London Collegiate School. Married to Tom, who teaches at RGS.

State educated (former grammar turned comp), Oxford history graduate who started reading for the bar, realised wasn't for her and instantly got teaching job near home town of Bolton, in part to alleviate guilt towards perennially-supportive parents. Hasn't looked back since, appointment one in the eye for pessimists predicting failure owing to lack of poshness. Eating words now (silver service, we trust) as she approaches half decade there, seemingly with near universal backing of the entire school community.

Adores the job – would keep going even with a lottery win, her only desire, says website, a 'car with windscreen wipers that worked' (can't somebody organise a whip round?).

Poised and super bright, radiates quintessential head qualities, say parents. Highly energetic and, as mother of primary age twin sons, undoubtedly

needs to be. Needle-sharp efficiency, too – completed Open University PGCE while teaching full time and impresses parents with presence at majority of sports events, home and away.

'Puts a dress on every day and looks smart and fashionable but really cares about the girls and the school. She'll walk into daughter's dorm and say "wow, nice duvet cover," or put on her running kit and do the Georgian Gallop [timed St George's Day circuit of school],' says approving mother.

No sign of being taken over by the zombie corporate message machine. Speaks her mind, stresses role as major family breadwinner and is at pains to point out that life to date has had fair share of grit (cites 'Ask' by The Smiths as fave song – 'I like a bit of northern angst,' she says). Proof by way of early teaching experiences in salt of the earth state schools in the North West (would southern softies would have weathered the experience? We get the strong impression they wouldn't).

Wants girls to at least consider those less fortunate than themselves (a big job: round here, it's about 99.9 per cent of the rest of the population). A willing role model, says that 'girls know I'm a feminist.' Sort of, though message distortion seems to be happening en route to teenage brains – long pause before sixth former, when asked, ventured that, 'she has a strong working woman thing.' Well, it's a start.

No such doubt attaches to community vibe. Before her arrival, school, though popular, not best version of itself, with housemaster at big name local school flinching, according to pupil, when joint social was suggested. Atmosphere casual, uniform and manners ditto. 'If you turned up to a lesson late, it didn't matter,' says pupil. Now? 'Just wouldn't happen.'

With smartly turned out girls snapping to attention when visitor enters classroom, guides for whom nothing is too much trouble ('use my back to rest your notebook on,' urged one) we believe her.

New senior leadership team, small, tight-knit and fun to be around (and we don't say that lightly), is busy plugging small-ish academic holes (fillings rather than root canal work), with regular reviews of pupil performance and curriculum (business and communications studies GCSE in, computing out) and greater parent involvement. 'Recruiting in her own image,' thought parent.

Mrs Owens has also given pupils more of a say in everything, from decisions on uniform and sanctions to staff appointments – sixth formers interview candidates. Huge pride that their views are considered, fearless in putting points across – even petitioned Mrs Owens direct when felt best woman for job of sixth form was in danger of being overlooked.

Expect slow burn realisation of other goals as new head's temptation 'to think I have to do it now' is resisted, courtesy of hero Robert Peel, who knew a thing or two about delayed gratification. 'He was going to repeal the Corn Laws years before he did it,' she says.

Some incredulity at maths team's uncanny knack of inspiring the previously un-keen

First on list is demolition of the Terrapin, learning support centre whose army surplus exterior (not a green you warm to) belies the inspirational teaching, courtesy of Helen Arkell dyslexia centre staff, that goes on inside. 'Be as rude about it as you like,' says Mrs Owens, who would be happy to 'tie a rope round it and pull it down myself.'

It's awfully easy to think of school as cotton wool construction, outside world and its realities pushed away. Might be tiny wee school, but under Mrs Owen's leadership, unlikely to be surrendering to too many Dresden china moments.

Relishes headship, even though there's nowhere to hide. 'All the things you think should be in a school you have an opportunity to do. And if you don't do it, then you only have yourself to blame,' she says.

Speaks her mind, stresses role as major family breadwinner and points out that life has had fair share of grit

Moving on summer 2016 to become head of St George's College, Weybridge.

Academic matters: School is 'deliberately small' says the blurb. Titchy, really, with just 35 pupils per year in years 7 and 8, another 14 added in year 9, class sizes pre-GCSE capped at 20 though average 14 in first three years, 10 for GCSE studies and just eight in sixth form (and often rather smaller).

Teachers jolly, chatty and exude contentment with their lot (we got the impression that those who didn't had been encouraged to find temperamental niche elsewhere), average age 40 and a quarter or so around for 10 years or over. Bar (rare) worries from minority of parents about some favouritism, imperfectly concealed, there's nothing but praise for staff, with some incredulity at maths team's uncanny knack of inspiring the previously un-keen – one unwell child insisting on attending lesson. 'Asked if they'd got the right girl,' said stunned father.

However, 'not a hothouse' says school, though parental perception is that temperature, under Mrs Owens, likely to rise to at least balmy levels. As it is, school ladles on the added value (GCSEs average a grade higher than entry levels would suggest), impressive given mixed entry, with 41 per cent of A levels and 51 per cent of GCSEs graded A*/A in 2015.

Lots of stress on growth as individual, being best you can be – if not, won't be for want of trying, with staff on call during study leave, pep talks blended with reassurance, changes frequently rung – 20-questions-style quiz, past papers and spider diagram creation simultaneously under way in one notably calm GCSE history class. Lower down the school, there's help of a more basic nature. 'Don't use "of" as a verb' is tip in first year pupil's English folder.

With nine lessons a day (extra pre-lunch bonus session for sixth form), 8.15am start and 6.15pm or later finish ('terrific value for money,' Mrs Owens points out) no shortage of opportunities to be inspired and, in case of most able, sufficiently challenged. 'Could give them textbook, tell them to learn it and would still get an A* – it's about giving them something extra that goes beyond confines of syllabus,' says deputy head.

Hence AQA Baccalaureate, a calorie controlled version of IB diploma, encompassing AS in critical thinking, assorted sports and community service related add-ons as well as extended essay projects, one top-graded effort exploring finer points of depleted uranium 'at least undergraduate level,' reckons school.

Pre-16, 10 GCSEs the norm for most, business and communication systems the only deviation from the norm, though curriculum has been expanding, Spanish now on offer as a second language from year 9 together with more 'exotic' options such as Chinese and Japanese (agreed) and ... German (who knew?).

Learning needs similarly well planned, around 50 girls receiving support, overwhelmingly for specific learning difficulties (teachers from Helen Arkell Institute, one of UK's top dyslexia centres, visit regularly) similar numbers speaking English as an additional language. Sensible aids to diagnosis – those struggling in exams swap to different coloured ink when into extra time. 'Sister's grades have improved so much,' says year 10 pupil. 'Dyslexic girls do as well or better than those who aren't because they get fantastic study skills,' says school insider.

Support, not spoon feeding, self-discipline encouraged, freedom doled out in ever increasing amounts as girls go up the school (trips to high street

Head of art is 'just fantastic at getting the most out of everybody', art room filled with quality produce including delightful silk snakes threading their way through ceramic hoops and exuding (just resisted) strokeability

allowed from year 3 – though one parent queried wisdom of arranging GCSE geography field trip there during Ascot Week to ask harassed shopkeepers if they were busier than usual...) tempered with emphasis on cultivation of desirable learning habits via timetabled study skills sessions for first years, regular subject clinics and even sessions with subject tutors as one of the Saturday morning activity options.

Thoughtful touches make it easy to get the work and play balance right, prep setting making home a largely work free zone. Study areas in communal rooms, though generous, often off to one side. 'Work but not to excess,' seems to be the message, underpinned by separate fiction library, tiniest of three (all pending major redevelopment elsewhere) stuffed with sofas and smelling (mysteriously) of roses, urging the prep-weary to tarry awhile, an antidote to the pleasant but business-like atmosphere of non-fiction section on the other side of the wall.

Games, options, the arts: The works, website giving equal prominence to lively productions as well as range of sports (U14 championship success) and economics (serious talk from think tank expert) by way of proof.

Arts, performing and otherwise, very strong, ranging from seriously good acting talent (judging by mesmerising final rehearsal of A level drama monologue) to audition-only chapel choir (occasional HRH in audience no doubt adds to appeal) and head of art who is 'just fantastic at getting the most out of everybody,' says parent, art room filled with natural light and quality produce including delightful silk snakes threading their way through ceramic hoops and exuding (just resisted) strokability. Some parents harder to win over when comes to carrying on to A level. 'Want daughters to do subjects leading to a good job,' says member of staff.

Outside world also fully embraced. If Australian exchange scheme for two year 9 pupils doesn't bring home sense of good fortune, plentiful additional reminders driven home via community service both near (help for Slough homeless and socially excluded) plus carol singing and visits to the elderly, and far (fundraising for READS Indo International School in Rajasthan).

Energetic equally well catered for indoors (vast fitness suite, soon-to-be replaced swimming pool and good sized sports hall) and out, with lots of convertible spaces (netball to tennis; lacrosse to athletics). Something for everyone, polo amongst team sports on offer, paid add-ons including tennis, zumba and..polo again (well, Ascot race course is but an anvil's throw away).

While not the most seriously sporty school, manages steady supply of county lacrosse players, work sometimes trouncing play, mainly timetabled after 4.00pm and on Saturdays when replaced by compulsory prep for anyone not selected for matches. Tone, running from rugged to dauntless, set by head of sport, former women's army champion, with timetabled events running through exam season, enabling welcome sublimation of nervous tension through exercise, pupils 'staying on to unwind,' said one, sixth former grimly tackling treadmill by way of demonstration. Plenty for also-rans, felt do best in junior years when A to D teams and a bit of dedication can take you a long way. 'Turn up to training and you'll be in a match,' said pupil.

Some good results, though a bit of parental grumbling about occasional stonking defeats by lesser schools. Later on, when team options smaller (As and Bs only) it's less about taking part, more about winning, with girls who 'care so much that cry when they lose,' said parent. Sensitive souls pulled in several different directions at once can find it all too much (some parental niggles about early morning detentions handed out for missing practice sessions). Confident, multi-talented high flyers lap it up, however. Will be tired but, 'it's a good tired,' said mother.

Boarding: Well thought-out boarding houses. Larger scale to start with – up to eight to a room, daily tidiness vetting (termly winners treated to pizza). Sensibly, say older girls, as 'you want to be with as many people as possible,' particularly when homesickness strikes. 'Helps as there's so much going on.'

Looks range from the jolly for younger pupils (bright pink patches above beds for personalisation, custom made centralised storage) to cleaner feel later on, single Hokaido-style plants straining sinuously round corners for year 4 sophisticates, who also enjoy sombre shades of common room. 'Not one for bright colours,' said one. Bar the odd slightly dim and grey-ish corridor – school does its best to add natural light where architecture permits – boarding is thoroughly welcoming with clear demarcation between work and relaxation that's appreciated by girls. 'Really homely,' says one. 'Makes you feel the day is done.'

Terrific activities sandwiching army assault course between film nights and ice skating. Spontaneous family treat times also encouraged. 'Really smart about how boarders need to have a hot chocolate with their mums sometimes, whereas with other schools, absolutely not,' said parent.

Unsurprising that boarding is highly popular, day girls enticed in with free trial sessions (space availability permitting) that let them experience the joys of home cooking (most go no further than popcorn and toast), though experiment with separate penthouse enabling sixth formers to try out independent living wasn't a hit with girls and has since been abandoned.

Background and atmosphere: Approached off high street down side road, tranquillity temporarily duffed up into submission by roar of builders' lorries (this is prime mansionville), parking a perennial problem. Winding lane opens up, unexpectedly, into vista of open spaces and tree tops, school perched attractively on hilltop. Steep descent to car park apparently irresistible in snowy weather – 'we go down it on tea trays – and so do the staff,' say pupils.

School's motto 'Vincent Qui Se Vincunt' or 'They Will Conquer Who Overcome Themselves' could usefully have been adopted by original founders, who went bust in 1904. School, which had up till then been a boys' prep attended by the very young Winston Churchill, and was lavishly equipped with the very latest in educational fixtures and fittings including electric light, was also notable for flogging-mad head.

Tone, from rugged to dauntless, set by head of sport, former women's army champion, with timetabled events running through exam season, enabling sublimation of tension

Reincarnated as a girls' finishing school in 1904, school took off in 1920s with arrival of new owner rich in academic as well as social aspirations for pupils. Stayed put through Second World War (courtesy of air raid shelters in the grounds). Further 'structural metamorphosis' aka major building splurge added chapel, labs, music and sixth form space and assorted classrooms in 1980s, art and technology block and sports complex in 90s, performing arts block in 2002. Small footprint should, and mainly does, make navigation easy despite moments when split level construction and multiple entrances would make Escher feel right at home.

Pioneering spirit much in evidence from the start with girls prepared for college entrance from the 1920s. Has continued unabated – school had first wireless network up and running in early noughties, while nimby-ism certainly not an issue, with some original buildings and land sacrificed to make way for the new, though we admired grotto-like construction, once key decorative feature that formed part of extravagant water course.

Excellence of food could well damp down culinary aspirations. Food outstanding – menu, in conspicuous contrast to many others we've seen, was as delicious in reality as on paper (first time drooling has ever threatened effective note-taking).

Domestic bursar's Mafia-like tentacles (probably marinated, though he's ex-Forces rather than Sealife) extend to nationwide quayside contacts, fish 'caught yesterday,' everything cooked fresh in six at a time batches. 'Always enough of the nice things,' said pupil, approvingly. Only complaint – a minute steak that was 30 seconds late – was something we could probably learn to live with.

Pastoral care, well-being and discipline: Framework as sturdy as they come, school endeavouring to set girls' own moral compasses pointing in right direction for life. Friendships wide-ranging, helped by shake-up when new intake starts in year 9 (or 3, in school parlance) ensuring absence of them v us as new and old faces are thoroughly mixed in class and dorms.

Helped by house system that promotes togetherness without overdoing the aggressive loyalty, together with pervasive sense of encouragement – we liked big screen and website beaming messages of support for GCSE students about to embark on exam performances, like cheering on-lookers at a regatta.

> *Domestic bursar's Mafia-like tentacles (probably marinated, though he's ex-Forces rather than Sealife) extend to nationwide quayside contacts*

A bit of soul-searching appears to have taken place when it comes to behaviour, initiation rites banned (not that they happened anyway, says Mrs Owens, who puts presence in policy down to excessive 't' crossing and 'i' dotting by conscientious back office team, ditto on-line posting of 'incorrect, inappropriate or inflammatory material' verboten 'without permission' – rarely granted, we'd suspect!).

> *Though accurate, website pictures of girls seated on balustrades dreamily overlooking tons of top-quality Berkshire countryside tell only part of the story*

Requirement for bullies and victims to 'understand each other's feelings and points of view' (victims often understand bullies' perspective all too well in our experience...) appears to work, remaining an occasional blight, largely dying out when GCSE preparation becomes uniting factor, say pupils, bar very occasional unhappy story of social isolation (not the experience of the vast majority, however).

Overall, however, Mrs Owens 'knows which battles to pick,' said approving parent, who with others praised quick, decisive action on rare occasions when girls have been asked to leave. Down in part to sensible rules – pupils in year 9 and above can hang on to phones and tablets overnight, though excessive tiredness can lead to privilege being withdrawn – together with top down nurturing, prefects watching out for younger girls, sympatico gap students (one highly skilled at plaiting hair) and highly effective form tutor system.

We heard lavish compliments for, amongst others, head of music – 'the heart of the school' and 'big teddy bear' from pupils and 'heaven, has made being in a choir cool,' from parent – together with head of sixth form who 'really listens and explains, takes our side,' says pupil, gist is that for each girl, there's a kindred spirit to talk to on the staff. Styles vary, though brisk member of pastoral team who 'believes in school of hard knocks,' thought parent, is countered by wonder matron, on hand for tea (or hot chocolate) and sympathy, running popular sessions on everything from skin care to pre-exam stress busting. 'A really nice woman,' says one pupil.

Pupils and parents: Haven for the blue blooded with Princess Beatrice of York, Lady Davina Lewis and Lady Rose Gilman amongst the OGs, together with assorted actors and assorted presenters, DJs and the occasional personality.

Somewhere between 10 and 20 per cent per cent are international boarders, China (mainland and Hong Kong) and Russia by far biggest nationalities represented (plus, currently, a couple of Ukrainians).

While locals are well represented, numbers of weekly boarders from London are also healthy, meanwhile (handy bus service collects Chiswick/South Ken Sunday, drops Friday), though locals still rule OK (literally so, given proximity to Windsor Castle).

Inclusive, active Parents' Association – 'like meeting up with friends,' said mother – with annual meet and greet event for new parents and decent array of suitably social/fundraising events of a reassuringly trad nature, recently including get together at – where else? – Guards Polo Club.

Entrance: Popular and getting more so (candidate numbers up 60 per cent in a year), most desirable entrants those capable of bringing something unique to school which, in practice (and excluding own one of a kind DNA), means nothing too outré. 'I'm looking for a girl whose eyes sparkle,' says Mrs Owens. Around 20 feeders, many local (Coworth-Flexlands, Upton House School and St George's, Windsor Castle) others in London (Garden House).

Following appetite-whetting taster sessions for 8 to 10 year olds, consisting of lessons plus overnight stay, would-be year 7 pupils sit English, maths, VR papers plus interview, no Sats equivalent – pass rate around the 65 per cent mark. Not as academic as some but 'still need to be able to work towards 10 or 11 GCSEs,' says Mrs O.

Second smaller intake at 13, successful candidates spending day with class to be and invited to school events. Occasional vacancies in other years (though won't accept pupils once GCSEs under way). For (large) sixth form, not desperately demanding – minimum six A*-C GCSEs with at least B grades in A level subjects.

Exit: Used to lose fair few post-GCSE. Only five or so leave now, single sex blues and desire for larger-scale environment almost universal reason. While some seepage inevitable as 'we're not getting bigger and we're not providing boys,' says realistic Mrs Owens, sixth formers extol benefits.

Higher education advisors help sixth formers whittle down higher education options, leavers heading to broad spread of unis and courses, everywhere from Durham to Southampton to Central St Martins, subjects ranging from molecular biology to social policy and criminology, creative arts well represented. Two or three to Oxbridge or Ivy League each year (four to Oxbridge in 2015), school good at securing interviews, less good at closing the deal – Mrs Owens is on the case, reckon parents.

Money matters: Range of 11 + scholarships available. Standard range (academic, music, art, sport) gratefully received – though one parent felt varying levels of participation by scholars (music scholars, for example, not obliged to join choir) meant their gain was sometimes school's loss. Same again, plus drama, at 13, open also to internal candidates, as are sixth form scholarships. Maximum reduction 10 per cent but means-tested bursaries available.

Though not HMC school, part of their scholarship programme, offering 100 per cent funded boarding place each year to super bright East European whose family has income of £25,000 or under.

Remarks: Though accurate, website pictures of girls seated on balustrades dreamily overlooking tons of top-quality swathes of Berkshire countryside tell only part of the story. Change in style, from quirky 'traditionally English school' to ambitious and aspirational pleases almost all, though parent who joined pre-Mrs Owens felt had 'bought into one thing and you're existing in another.'

The many who approve feel children are offered not a retreat from life but a well planned introduction to its realities. Princesses on board? Though they can come (sometimes literally) with the territory, if Mrs Owens gets her message across, they should – together with other pupils – end up as princesses with attitude. 'Am still waiting for the bubble to burst but each year is as good as the last,' said one mother.

St Hugh's School, Oxfordshire

Carswell Manor, Faringdon, Oxfordshire SN7 8PT

01367 870700
registrar@st-hughs.co.uk
www.st-hughs.co.uk
C of E

Ages: 3–13 (boarders from 7)
Pupils: 340
Boarders: 19 weekly, 96 flexi
Day: £10,530 – £17,880 pa
Boarding: Weekly plus £1,175 per term

Headmaster: Since 2006, Mr Andrew Nott BA (early 50s). Son of a bishop, educated at The Beacon Prep and King's, Taunton. Studied history at the University of Wales, PGCE Westminster College, Oxford. Worked for the Church Commissioners where he met his wife, Sarah. First teaching post at St Andrew's School, Eastbourne, rose to deputy head. Thence to Davenies for his first headship prior to St Hugh's. Parents describe him as 'amazing' (adjective also frequently applied to Sarah) on a personal level; one or two said they found him a little shy on more public occasions.

Mr Nott is proud of his scholars' achievements but he is also a true champion of the strugglers and late bloomers who are inevitably part of the cohort of a non-selective school. He told us that he had thoroughly enjoyed his time at prep and it is this 'carefree' existence that he wants children at St Hugh's to experience. He loves sport, especially cricket (he is a member of MCC and had a bookcase dedicated to copies of Wisden) and is

determined that all the children at St Hugh's get a match, including the E and F teams. He vividly remembers 'the boys who weren't in the A team picking daisies on the boundary' during his prep school cricket matches, and though St Hugh's may be a traditional school in many ways, this is one bit of history Mr Nott does not want to repeat. His mantra is 'excellence and inclusion' and he's also a big champion of kindness, a 'hugely important virtue' that he believes is undervalued these days.

School has acquired five acres of adjoining land for additional games fields, but although the roll is full there are no plans to increase numbers of pupils significantly. Mr Nott says, 'We could be a lot bigger but I want to keep the character of the school, to know every child.' Sounds pretty definite to us but a few parents expressed worries about the school getting bigger. Development on this beautiful rural site is no doubt a planning nightmare, but the newish Cannon Building – named like other parts of the school after a former head – is

a superb facility housing science, art and DT. The heads of these departments worked with architects to design their ideal rooms and are still purring contentedly.

Mr Nott and his wife Sarah have five children; four attended St Hugh's and the two youngest are still there. Sarah is responsible, among many other things, for the tastefully low-key marketing and excellent newsletter. The Notts live just over the lane from school; it's not much of a boundary but just far enough to allow time to switch off and enable the head to enjoy planning the family's next trip abroad and practising creative cookery. Though usually pretty competent, he admits to a recent disaster courtesy of Heston Blumenthal (who doesn't?). He's also fascinated by the academic side of leadership. Favourite childhood reads? Tintin and the Willard Price series of adventure stories.

Entrance: Non-selective, non-competitive, it's first come, first served. Mr Nott likes to meet parents as well as children. Prospective pupils spend a day; those entering year 3 or above have assessments in English and maths. Main entry is into reception (up to 26 places), year 3 (up to six places), year 5 (up to six places). Nursery takes up to 25 a year.

Exit: To schools all over home counties. Many to board eg Cheltenham College, Cheltenham Ladies', Radley, Eton, Marlborough, St Edward's Oxford, St Mary's Calne. Rest to local day schools including Abingdon, Headington, Magdalen College School and St Helen's and St Katharine's. Over ninety-five per cent of girls stay on until age 13; apparently this is increasingly popular with parents – perhaps because their girls stay children for that little bit longer.

Remarks: We arrived on a perfect English summer's day and Carswell Manor, which looks like a bijou country house hotel, seemed to glow with the golden warmth of Cotswold stone. On closer inspection much of façade is pebbledashed but somehow still pretty classy. The Manor was once home to the Niven family and it seems fitting that David Niven, the quintessential English gentleman, was born here – the old place even gets a mention in his autobiography. St Hugh's is without doubt the tidiest school we've ever visited and it's not just the buildings and grounds that are polished and groomed, the teachers too were quite remarkably elegant – not a baggy cardigan or tatty sandal in sight.

Founded 1906 in Chislehurst with three pupils and co-ed since 1977, St Hugh's is now very much a family school – nursery was established in response to parent demand and the minute it opened was 'immediately full with younger siblings.' Mothers walk their dogs in the grounds after morning

drop off. Indeed dogs are a bit of a feature: they kept trotting by or popping out from under tables during our visit – all glossy coated and impeccably behaved, of course. Though we saw no ponies we hear that they also loom large here – jodhpurs (very much not pyjamas) are what the busy St Hugh's mother wears first thing in the morning.

It's not just the buildings and grounds that are polished and groomed, the teachers too were quite remarkably elegant – not a baggy cardigan in sight

Small classes (average 13), spacious modern facilities and glorious surroundings are enough to inspire any child to reach their full potential, and while not all will be scholars and high flyers, everyone is encouraged to find their talent. Much is expected of these children and sometimes Mr Nott's role is to manage expectations; by their second or third child old hands know they can relax and put their trust in the school. Parents we spoke to felt that Mr Nott's advice about senior schools was excellent and absolutely right for their child; the broad spectrum of schools St Hugh's sends to bears this out.

Maths and English set from year 3, French from year 6; rest of subjects taught in mixed ability groups but this can and does vary from year to year according to cohort. French and Latin for all, optional extracurricular Spanish and Mandarin. Greek for scholars. One or two grumbles about Sigma group (potential scholars) being creamed off in year 6, but this is a perennial source of low level muttering at many preps. Middle school pupils (years 3 and 4) have their own teaching block and activities such as drama, choir, sports day etc – a nice way to let the youngest take centre stage. Low turnover of staff apart from gappies (usually old boys and girls) who stay for a year. In lessons we observed pupils were quiet, engaged, working hard individually and in pairs. Small class sizes mean teacher can tailor tasks according to ability; they also make it hard to mess around at the back (not that there seemed to be any such tendency). Parents describe SEN support as 'brilliant'; the head of the service told us that the aim is for it to be 'flexible and fluid', to give pupils a boost when needed and then 'launch them back, even if they need to be picked up again later.' Support is either individual or in booster groups and is not charged as an extra. Pastoral care also came in for high praise – merest whiff of bullying is dealt with at lightning speed.

A school tradition and one of the highlights of year 8 is a week's post-exam adventure trip to Wales, during which Mr Nott gives the children their CE results over fish and chips on the beach. Once back in Oxfordshire as part of an extensive leavers' programme, pupils are initiated into important life skills such as how to tie a bow tie, polish shoes and iron shirts; they also create and stage a fashion show for a local children's charity.

One of the highlights is a week's trip to Wales, during which Mr Nott gives the children their CE results over fish and chips on the beach

Excellent sporting facilities both inside and out host sport for all, every day. All main ones plus squash, basketball, tennis and introduction to lacrosse. Head confirms that every child gets to represent the school in matches. Notable recent success in tennis (and real tennis) and cross-country. Large number of sports scholarships awarded to St Hugh's pupils every year. Music and drama are also inclusive with enough plays, choirs, bands and ensembles to accommodate the full range of abilities and a new music block. Outdoor production of A Midsummer Night's Dream staged around atmospheric ivy-clad 'temple' in the grounds. St Hugh's seems to produce thinkers and listeners (as opposed to shouters) and recognition for this comes in the form of a clutch of top awards for debating and public speaking. Art and DT thriving in their new building – art room boasts a large walk-in kiln, ready to receive the most ambitious ceramic creations and electric windows that can be controlled to provide optimum natural light conditions.

Pre-prep is housed in the old stable block with classrooms round a flexible central space that can be divided up and used for small group work. Rooms are carefully decorated with colourful posters and children's work and, as in the main school, the atmosphere seemed to be one of gently restrained exuberance. Or so we thought until we came across a monsieur from the big school delighting the pre-prep pupils with his all-singing and dancing weekly French lesson. Literacy taught via Read Write Inc phonics programme and for this children are grouped by their stage of development, not age. Official forest school: pupils from nursery to year 6 get to do lots of messy learning in the woods (last two years have bushcraft). As one member of staff remarked, 'Some children come to life outside, and it's not just the boys.' Parents promised us that pupils really are allowed to get muddy.

Youngest (age 3 upwards) start in The Cottage nursery, a charming house that originally belonged to the groundsman (he is happily accommodated elsewhere). On our visit we saw determined excavation in the large sandpit that is, fortunately, six feet deep. Children sign in for their sessions on the interactive whiteboard and there is an ICT suite upstairs along with a rest room for pupils who still need a nap. Same phonics programme as pre-prep used to introduce letter sounds etc. Specialist teaching for music, dance, ICT. Introduction to French is via croissants and chocolat chaud.

Flexi and weekly boarding – parents pre-select boarding options at the start of term. Those wanting a full week get priority, those who want a couple of days are most likely to get them if they are consecutive. As a rule can't do sleepover style occasional boarding but will work something out in an emergency. Boarding is very often 'children driven', it's the parents who need persuading. Comfortable, characterful dorms up in the eaves, all very civilised – common room with original John Piper on wall (sigh). Matrons inspect every morning to ensure that boarders live up to the St Hugh's standard of tidiness. Day pupils can stay until 7.30pm for prep and supper (no extra charge) and about a third do. Saturday school for years 6-8 only. Wednesday evenings are reserved for 'fun' things and there's no prep. Parents pre-select home time but emergencies and late changes accommodated. Sensible uniform and termly bill low on the dreaded 'extras'. Fees include all trips (including trips abroad) and SEN support. Means-tested bursaries of up to full fees available.

So, what's the demographic? Put on your deerstalker and consider these clues: nearly all the pupils are children of privately-educated parents; a school bus scheme was discontinued after a couple of terms because no one used it (private lift sharing arrangements more popular); mussels are a favourite on the scrumptious lunch menu. So far, so county, but though the social profile be small, parents say it's neither snobbish nor exclusive and the children we met were down to earth, funny, normal kids.

St Hugh's is seemingly a school with nothing to prove. It doesn't advertise and prospective parents are not bombarded with glossy anythings. For a flavour of the place, ask to see a copy of the beautifully produced half-termly magazine, St Hugh's News. Such understatement, coupled with fees that are higher than local average (but are all-inclusive and considered 'good value' by the parents we spoke to), might seem counter-intuitive in an area that is not under-served with preps, but St Hugh's is always full courtesy of the low-tech marketing marvel money can't buy: word of mouth. Happy parents, happy children, happy dogs – what could be better?

St John's Beaumont School

Priest Hill, Old Windsor, Berkshire SL4 2JN

01784 432428
admissions@sjb.email
www.sjb.community
RC

Ages: 3-13 (boarders from age 7)
Pupils: 310
Boarders: 30 full, 30 weekly
Day: £8,670 – £16,590 pa
Boarding: £16,230 – £25,170 pa

Headmaster: Since 2006, Mr Giles Delaney (40s). Educated at Hereford Cathedral School, studied music and psychology at Cardiff (instruments are the not-at-all-easy French horn and organ). PGCE at Cambridge and thence to St John's Beaumont. Became deputy head three years later before being catapulted at a very young age to headship on sudden death of his predecessor. He seems so at one with the school, staff and boys that we wonder if it was always his plan to stay at the old place for so long; his answer is a wry smile.

St John's Beaumont, like other RC schools, has a reputation for being pretty disciplined, although Mr Delaney is anything but a martinet. He sees no reason why boys can't be expected to give their very best in a caring and nurturing environment. He's extremely interested in research on how boys learn, especially the importance of pupils' relations with staff: 'boys don't learn subjects, they learn teachers.' In a boys' school 'everyone will have a go at

orchestra, choir, dance. They will give everything a shot and smile if it doesn't work.' Certainly when it comes to the importance of context, relating academic subjects to the real world, it seems that Jesuit schools were there long before the educationalists.

Mr Delaney, who looks a bit like a young Colin Firth, is modest and charming. He told us that he had taught 'most stuff', still teaches year 5 ('getting them ready for pre-tests surreptitiously') and is looking forward to a new challenge: introducing the pre-prep boys to music. We weren't taken in by his self-deprecating answers. Boys and parents say his teaching is 'absolutely brilliant', 'fantastic', 'the best'. Loves preparing assemblies and shares a keen interest in medieval history with his wife, Katie, who teaches in a school in North London. He is currently studying for an MSc in education at Oxford. They have four daughters – must be something of an antidote to life at SJB. And if he hadn't gone into teaching? A conductor, he thinks, or a graphic designer, 'something not in an office.' Favourite book? Solzhenitsyn's One day in the life of Ivan Denisovich: 'It's about endurance, valuing the smallest things.'

Entrance: There's a waiting list so plan ahead. Most boys enter at age 4 after attending a taster session to assess suitability. Parents and children interviewed. Further small intake at year 3 (dependent on performance in school's own assessment and reference from current head). Priority given to practising Roman Catholic families, siblings and applicants with connections to St John's or a Jesuit education

Exit: To all the big beasts and all the more impressive given non-selective intake: Eton, Harrow, Tonbridge, Winchester, Wellington, Charterhouse, Ampleforth, Downside, Stonyhurst, Hampton. Notable record of academic, sport and all-rounder scholarships.

Remarks: St John's Beaumont sits in red-brick gothic grandeur on a hill overlooking Old Windsor, surrounded by 70 acres of grounds and playing fields next door to Windsor Great Park. Designed by John Francis Bentley (also responsible for Westminster Cathedral) and opened in 1888, it was the first purpose-built prep school in England. Tucked behind the Victorian edifice are recent additions: a fine sports centre with vertigo-inducing climbing wall, music, science and art departments, a theatre and the pre-prep block, all on a rather more human scale. The huge reception hall, hung with portraits of old boys and next door neighbour

Her Majesty the Queen, sets a rather formal tone. Classical music playing discreetly in the background only just takes the edge off what could be an intimidating first impression for some prospective parents and their boys.

We asked what would improve the school. The answer was unanimous: girls! Apparently girls would 'make the place tidier' and 'help with questions'. Dream on, chaps

Our visit started in one of the original high ceilinged classrooms with a year 8 maths lesson. Considering it was nearly the end of term and these boys had done CE (many had won scholarships), their quiet concentration was remarkable. Working in pairs, they applied themselves to bisecting a line so that they would 'impress maths teachers at their next schools'. In accordance with the principles of Jesuit education, they then discussed context, suggesting where this technique could be applied in real life. Maths is a particular strength of SJB and the best take part in national competitions and maths challenges, winning medals at all levels. Three finalists recently gained distinctions in Junior Maths Olympiad. Science very hands-on; boys told us that a highlight was 'setting custard powder on fire' and went on to explain the theory behind the conflagration. Latin from year 6, Greek for scholars.

Having learnt (and swiftly forgotten) how to bisect a line it was off to year 6 history in a slightly less lofty Portakabin. After the maturity of the mathematicians we were relieved to find a sparky class tackling the causes of the First World War. Their presentation skills may have been a work in progress but there was no doubting their enthusiasm and depth of knowledge. Here, context was relating 1914 alliances to the current situation in Afghanistan. Distracting them from the task in hand, we asked what one thing would improve their school. The answer was unanimous: girls! Apparently girls would 'make the place tidier' and 'help with questions'. Dream on, chaps.

Golf, cycling, climbing, sailing, skiing – SJB boys pursue and excel at all kinds of sport, but rugby rules. They regularly field 16 teams and successfully play David to some much bigger Goliaths. Most recently the 1st XV was undefeated in all but one match. Usual parental grumbles that it's not much fun in the lesser teams who don't get any of the specialist coaching. Football gets a proper look in, too. There's an impressive swimming pool and a climbing wall in addition to all the usual facilities. Proximity to the Thames doesn't always guarantee a commitment to rowing but in this case it does and there are 50 boys in the squad netting a haul of medals in regional and national championships. For years 6, 7 and 8 it's sport every day plus matches on Saturday. It's a long day too: years 4 and 5 finish at 5pm, for older boys it's 6pm or later if they're doing extra activities. One of our guides said he thought parents should know that 'it's quite tiring'. Music, art and drama don't seem to be overshadowed by the sports behemoth; that long day means there's time for both.

Sixty or so boys board (one junior and one senior dorm) and according to one parent, it's 'proper boarding, not flexi.' Full weekend programme of activities, many chosen by boys on the boarding committee, includes paintballing, tank driving and trips to Windsor Castle and the Science Museum. Weekly boarding also an option. Interesting animal themed house system engenders keen rivalry for 'TYE' points (Tiger, Yak and Emu). Junior uniform (navy blue Bermudas and year 6) looks smart but several parents still reeling from eye-watering cost of anything crested, including jumpers and shirts.

Approximately 60 per cent of boys come from RC families but don't imagine this leads to monoculture – a peek into any classroom will dispel doubts on that score. Parents unanimously praised the pastoral care and the way the school welcomed diversity. One who was not Catholic said that religion was 'not an issue' but described the RE curriculum as 'very truly Catholic, up to and including creationism', so SJB unlikely to be destination of choice for Dawkins minor. School's view is that

they welcome boys of any faith or none but those who join, 'join a community', and must play their part, including attendance at mass. Admissions process wise to parents who are only interested in the school for its CE results. The scholarship boards provide a record of the school's evolution. Thirty years ago practically all went on to Catholic schools such as Stonyhurst, The Oratory, Ampleforth; today's scholars are just as likely to be bound for Eton, Winchester and Wellington.

At Christmas there are several services so that all parents can enjoy the special atmosphere and 'magical music'

Mr Bentley the architect obviously believed in giving boys lots of space and air, hence the wide corridors and high ceilinged classrooms, and the generosity of his design, while unmistakably Victorian, stands up pretty well to the demands of the 21st century. His intimate and beautifully decorated chapel, bearing the scars of wartime bombs, only seats 60, and at Christmas there are several services so that all parents can enjoy the special atmosphere and 'magical music'. Whole school events take place in the somewhat less atmospheric sports hall. Part of the Jesuit educational ethos is that a child should be 'well rounded and worldly wise' and to that end SJB boys go far and wide; not only history and sports trips to France and Italy but also swimming the Midmar Mile in South Africa to raise money for charity. They're also stretched by the school's impressive Magis programme; senior boys

461

have weekly lectures from visiting speakers, parents and members of staff and are also encouraged to present talks themselves. Recent subjects include deafness and language acquisition, Battersea Dogs' Home and space exploration. Lots of fundraising to support a sister school, St Rupert's, in Zimbawe.

Day boys come in from a 10 mile radius (bus service operates from Chiswick and Maidenhead). Parents a mix of trad Windsor and glossy Middletonshire (or as someone put it, those who have Wentworth membership and those who

don't). Their sons are commendably oblivious to such pigeonholing and there's a great sense of camaraderie; boys are proud of their school and its traditions. Mr Delaney describes St John's Beaumont as a community that asks its members, 'What can you give?' It expects the very best but also give boys the confidence to try new things and learn from mistakes. As a parent remarked, 'It can appear prescriptive but the boys don't see it like that, they thrive on structure and clear rules. My son loves going to school.'

St Mary's School Ascot

St Mary's Road, Ascot, Berkshire SL5 9JF

01344 296600
admissions@st-marys-ascot.co.uk
www.st-marys-ascot.co.uk
RC

Ages: 11–18
Pupils: 386; sixth form: 120
Boarders: 375
Day: £24,330 pa
Boarding: £34,170 pa

Headmistress: Since 1999, Mrs Mary Breen BSc MSc (40s). Married, no children. Previously spent seven-year stint at Eton, where she ended up as head of physics. Before that, taught science at The Abbey School Reading.

Her career was kick-started by head at Wellington who, having appointed her husband to a teaching post, saw Mrs Breen's useful physics degree lying fallow and suggested putting it to practical use. 'A few months later, my first class was 22 Wellingtonians. I discovered I could do it and loved

it,' she says. The rest, as they say, is history or, in her case, science.

The school's first lay head, she has commendably piloted St Mary's through the choppy waters of changing educational fashions without once changing course. The result is a school that has remained totally true to itself – and unapologetically so. 'We're not trying to be all things to all people', she says, 'but we've got a coherence that works'.

Smart, with a hint of va va voom (and no doubt requiring every ounce of it at times), she relishes the job and is reassuringly in control without anything of the martinet about her. Her genuine and purposeful charm is particularly effective when directed at parents. 'I say "we're Catholic. We're all girls. We're full boarding. We're a good medium size, with just under 400 and no plans to get any bigger or smaller. And we're very proud of our academic reputation. If that's a match for your daughters, let's take it further."' Most do.

Transformation of geese to high-flying swans isn't lost on parents, who talk of being 'staggered' by GCSE top grades. It's something the head doesn't care to overstress

Head is no slouch when it comes to heading off potential defection higher up the school. 'Having seen them grow up as teenagers, you want them as your gorgeous sixth form', she says. Plenty of official endorsement too. School recently breezed through visits from Ofsted and ISI (who decided to pop in at the same time) and scored glowing reviews from both.

Parents are universally full of praise, highlighting head's professionalism and nous. One father told us she should have a 'sainthood'. 'All you could ask for in a head', said another parent. 'She's the right person at the top to build the right team round her'. Admiration extends to 'excellent' communication following a one-off resignation of a member of staff found with inappropriate images on computer in an incident which was, the head is at pains to point out, 'unrelated to school'. Equal enthusiasm from pupils. 'She knows everyone's name and is personable, efficient and approachable', said one. Felt to be particularly good with family-related issues requiring delicate handling.

Wears regular questions about whether she's thinking of moving on with slight (and understandable) weariness. Her answer? Until she wakes up thinking she doesn't want to do this job, she has no intention of moving on, though she wouldn't be averse to a bit of industry-spokesperson duties on the side were the opportunities to come her way. Our advice to suitable bodies? Snap her up while stocks last. A natural in front of a crowd, she'd be jolly good at it too.

Academic matters: All round excellence, helped by well-stocked staff room (overall pupil-teacher ratio of six to one). Class sizes average 16 up to year 9, 15 for GCSE years and seven at A level. Three in a class

not uncommon for more rarefied subjects such as further maths.

At A level, 76 per cent A*/A grades and 95 per cent A*/B in 2015. GCSE results similarly classy – 89 per cent A*/A grades in 2015. Head is keen to dispel the suggestion that results are easily come by or a foregone conclusion. While they may suggest highly academic intake at 11+, with the vast majority at the top end of spectrum, behind the scenes number crunching (school uses MIDYIS) tells a very different story. Pupils span just about everything from the mid-range and below to the giddy super-bright heights.

A well-managed process steers a careful line between encouragement and pressure. The universally cheerful and confident demeanour of sixth formers about to enter final preparation for A2 exams indicated that it was working. Pupils rated supportive ethos – 'It's cool to work', said one – and extensive out of hours access to staff. 'So many of the teachers stay late that it's easy to meet up with them', confirmed another. Well-structured lessons where peers, as well as staff, assist with problem areas are a boon, too, say pupils.

Transformation of geese to high-flying swans isn't lost on parents, who talk of being 'staggered' by strings of GCSE top grades achieved. It's something that the head, to her credit, doesn't care to over-stress, given that it's unlikely to do much in the way of improving pupil confidence.

Subject range, though not vast, is well chosen and augmented only after considerable deliberation. Religious studies a non-negotiable core subject at GCSE. Latin (taught like French from year 7) taken by around half the year group at GCSE, well ahead of Spanish, German, Italian (added year 8) and Greek (year 9).

Three cheers for science, a particular strength, with five well equipped labs and surging physics numbers post-16 (head takes some classes) on a par with biology and chemistry. Around 10 (not far short of 20 per cent) take it to A level and the numbers are about to double as a particularly science-oriented group works its way through the school.

Maths also has consistent numbers of fans, though broad sweep of subject popularity (English literature, politics and French all make an appearance in the top five most years) means most tastes are well catered for. 'There's no subject that's a no-go area. When people ask me, I'm really proud to say what I'm doing,' said a further maths and science star.

Games, options, the arts: 'We're academic but with lots of extracurricular activities', a pupil told us. 'The school encourages you to thrive'. And how. Being not just good but 'brilliant' at everything, including sport, drama and music, is the goal, though not easy in such a small school stresses the head. If anything holds them back, it won't be resources, with sports facilities positively glistening with new honed and toned additions. In addition to swimming pool, the Orchard Centre has a big sports hall, two squash courts and a dance studio. Will soon be one of few girls' schools to have own 400-metre running track, green instead of customary red. Polo available, courtesy of local stables.

Staples include mass pizza ordering, as well as rare forays into deepest girly territory (nail decoration a favourite) and specials like St Patrick's Day marked with cookery

While there's a steady crop of outstanding individuals and teams at county level and above (tennis a particular strength), any lingering perception that the keen but hopeless are left to languish is out of date, says the head. All shall have matches (if not prizes). Team sport ceases to be compulsory post 16 but there's enough to inspire even the most sedentary-minded to stay happily active. Body conditioning, universally (though to official disapproval) known by girls as LBT (legs, bums and tums) particularly popular.

As with sport, the arts boast range of spaces that would be outstanding in a school with double the numbers. With its studio, full-size theatre, enormous green room (partitioned for girl/boy casts), bar and extensive costume room, the Rose Theatre is a budding thespian's dream. Many work towards

LAMDA exams, gaining the full set by the time they leave. Productions every term, some girls-only, others involving other schools. Production of The History Boys featured an all-girl cast, apart from the French mistress, who was played by an Etonian. A sixth form group took its own play to Edinburgh Festival, gaining good reviews into the bargain.

Art, housed with textiles (DT, though not a GCSE option, is taught as a carousel subject in years 8 and 9) is terrific. In some schools, head of department's hand often all too visible in strikingly similar interpretations of GCSE/A level coursework theme: here, variety (including burqa-clad, slogan adorned figures in entrance) suggests pupils really do think for themselves. Quality is so impressive that you almost forget where you are and start peering for red spots. Portraiture wonderful – not surprising as school, in one of many go-ahead moments, offers life drawing. Here as elsewhere, school's decision to go its own way has left it ahead of the game. 'We stick to traditions worth sticking to', a senior teacher told us.

Music is a high-profile affair. Well-equipped recital room, numerous practice rooms (including one, doubly soundproofed, for drums), concerts also in the chapel to capitalise on 'wonderful' acoustics. New head of music who grows her own compositions is now inundated with requests for new works following première of spine-tingling Easter Story and also plans to up numbers taking subject at GCSE and A level (scant handful currently).

Activities provide outlet for girl power in every form. For younger pupils, few delights trump pet club housed in mish-mash of cages and runs. Hamsters and rabbits dominate. with talent shows featuring animals in natty little homemade outfits. Animal friendliness is a big thing generally and mercy dashes aren't unknown. 'Only this school would put a damaged pigeon in a taxi and send it to the only vet open on a Sunday,' said a member of staff.

Wide range of clubs and societies, from the mind-expanding (human rights, music appreciation, current affairs) to D of E, London theatre trips and upscale wine-tasting (upper sixth only). Born movers and shakers (and there are many) can hone their organising skills in assorted forums, from influential school council ('what we recommend gets done', say girls) to range of committees. Old girls regularly pop up to widen careers horizons as part of a programme that kicks in from year 9.

Boarding: Modernising elsewhere in the school has seen large-scale abolition of big dorms (mostly no more than five to a room). Top favourite, however, was blast from the past curtain-partitioned 'cubies' in year 8 dorm, voted the best fun, with last night of term midnight feasts.

Sixth form privileges include no uniform (pupils were delighted by this, some parents less so), permission to queue barge at meal times and annual ball. Biggest perk is separate living quarters, away from main school hurly burly, circle of little homes corralled around own courtyard. Decent kitchens are well used (fruit and veg high on request list, adding to menu staples of toast, pasta – and chocolate crispie cakes). Entertaining is encouraged, with guests treated to more elaborate fare (visiting Etonians haven't thus far reciprocated in kind. 'They don't have the same facilities,' say the girls).

Production of The History Boys featured an all–girl cast, apart from the French mistress, who was played by an Etonian

Multitude of house-organised weekend activities helps to dispel any boarding blues. Staples include mass pizza ordering as well as rare forays into deepest girly territory (nail decoration a favourite) and specials like St Patrick's Day marked with cookery (Irish potato scones) and crafts (shamrock felt jewellery).

Background and atmosphere: School was founded in 1885 by the Institute of the Blessed Virgin Mary (IBVM), a religious order begun by Mary Ward (1585-1645). Her dreams of founding a Jesuit-inspired apostolic women's order (she even crossed the Alps on foot to put her case to the Pope) came to nothing in her lifetime. Undaunted, followers continued to plead her cause, though it was 2009 before her 'heroic virtue' was recognised by Rome.

Catholicism defines the school, sweeping in the committed and the less so. Morning chapel compulsory for all while regular weekday masses are optional, attracting anything from a dozen to 60 just before exams. Houses take it in turns to organise mass and pick the hymns, the more rousing the better. Recent election of Pontiff greeted with huge excitement. 'Someone started screaming "white smoke!" – I had coursework to do but the Pope comes first', a sixth former told us.

School makes the most of its 55-acre site. Main buildings, some on gothic revival lines, go up rather than out, with long but not unfriendly corridors, helped by warm terracotta and mosaic tiles and a riot of gleaming staircases (some now adorned with essential if unattractive anti-slip edging).

We were the first outsiders to experience the gorgeousness of school's former concert hall, now transformed into a terrific new senior library (juniors separately and snazzily catered for). Nicer than many universities, say pupils. No wonder, with its curvy window seats, acres of bookcases and wonderful first floor curved ceiling. Café, complete with morning papers, coming soon. No learning resource centre faffage here. Pupils can take in iPads and laptops but the printed word is definitely the star of the show. 'Books betoken silence', says head firmly.

Pastoral care, well-being and discipline: A little light rule-bending aside, few serious offences on this head's watch. Sanctions, when they do occur, are now consistent from house to house (just about the only minor imperfection found after recent inspections). Internet misuse would lead to merit-cancelling red ticket. Drink and smoking, almost unheard of, would result in suspension and 'you'd be out' for drugs.

Day to day, six heads of house have the biggest pastoral responsibility. They're considered mainly excellent. Praise too, for boarding. Inevitable beginner homesickness well handled with the help of older buddies and kindly boarding staff, vast majority of whom don't teach. 'They're lovely and very sympathetic if you say you have too much work,' said sixth former. Residential chaplain is mentioned by almost everyone as inspirational force for good and a multi-tasker to boot.

There's a fair bit of moving around which stems from a sensible desire to head off anything that could lead to cliques forming. Sleeping arrangements changed at least once a term and occasionally twice to mix and match the personalities. As a result, happiness tends to rule, and on the rare occasions it doesn't, there's a swift resolution of problems. Sixth form exceptionally strong, with friendships that often endure for life.

Pupils and parents: Around a third from London, a third within an hour's travel, a fifth from overseas (half non British) and the remainder from elsewhere in the UK.

Before head's arrival, vibe was a bit 'Frost in May', with slight sense that the very grandest of old Catholic families had a more exalted cachet than others. Now, though they're still represented, and anyone paying full fees needs to be 'mega rich' to afford them, there's a more egalitarian spirit abroad.

Increasing numbers are funded by bursaries, and though there's lots of emphasis on socialising with other top notch schools (Eton the top favourite) there's careful control of the trappings of excess. Nickames, amongst them Biggles, Squeaky and Booey, are plentiful and once bestowed are generally there for life.

Parents are a happy bunch. Not hard to see why, given the St Mary's effect, resulting in girls who emerge ready to subdue the world with charm, intelligence, confidence and poise. 'I think anyone in my year could stand up quite happily in front of 500 people and speak,' one former pupil told us.

Entrance: Selective but not awesomely so. Siblings, while favourably viewed, need good dose of what it takes to secure a place. School gives preference to girls who are Roman Catholic (nearly all pupils are). Many from bilingual backgrounds, though no formal support offered. Learning support geared towards those with 'generally mild' dyslexia and dyspraxia, with weekly, external support from Dyslexia Action.

Main entrance points are 11 (English, maths and general knowledge/intelligence tests) and 13 (English, maths, science, religious studies, history or geography, MFL, Latin). Feeder schools many and various (300 preps and maintained primaries); so oversubscribed that process can be 'an exercise in disappointment' says head.

For the unsuccessful, there's another chance in the sixth form (test in proposed A level subjects plus general paper). Chances of success are diminutive though. The maximum new intake is just five, though in reality often fewer.

Exit: Thirteen to Oxbridge in 2015, plus seven off to the US. Bristol and Edinburgh also popular. Subjects range from sciences to languages, law to art. Numbers going into performing arts are increasing – one old girl is currently working with Steven Spielberg.

Money matters: Standard range of scholarships at 11, 13 and 16 on offer (five per cent reduction on the fees). Music scholarships include free tuition on up to two instruments.

Remarks: Catholic education at its best. So popular that when it comes to getting a place, faith may not be enough.

St Swithun's School

Alresford Road, Winchester, Hampshire SO21 1HA

01962 835700
admissions@stswithuns.com
www.stswithuns.com
C of E

Ages: 11–18
Pupils: 509; sixth form: 155
Boarders: 109 full, 118 weekly
Day: £19,005 pa
Boarding: £30,453 pa

Headmistress: Since 2010, the contained and cogent Ms Jane Gandee MA (40s). Read French and Spanish at Girton College, Cambridge, then a local government accountant until she went into teaching (OU PGSE) at Lord Wandsworth College, Oakham, Queenswood and finally director of studies at City of London School for Girls. The stamina and thoughtful tactics that make her a successful athlete (represented Cambridge at athletics and cross-country, captained the women's football team) are combined with a rigorous passion in her stewardship of the girls here.

Her retired husband manages the logistics of shuttling their three kids to school (St Swithun's Junior and Kings' School Winchester) enabling her to teach Spanish in the lead up to GCSEs and speak at two out of the five assemblies each week, finding raw material in books ranging from Freakanomics to Daphne du Maurier novels.

Proud of the expanded co-curricular and sport options ('she's got the place buzzing'), determined to open the pupils' eyes to a real range of issues via external speakers (John Humphries, Germaine Greer, Polly Toynbee) so they can make their own decisions. Committed to developing girls' resilience and confidence – they once took the mickey out of her for her frequent championing of feminism, but now they join in.

Academic matters: Brilliant exam results, up in the dizzying thin air at the top of the league tables. How a relatively unselective school like this one manages it is mysterious and must drive the London hothouses – with their exacting entry testing of pupils from the age of 4 – around the bend. Parents say 'they don't cream off the top of their applicants; they help girls reach their potential'. Famed for its hotshot sciences (three floors of dedicated labs) and maths – English is just as impressive, even if pursued by fewer girls – pupils say teachers are great, 'no duffs'.

Food tech, psychology and art history offered at A level (though take-up is low for food – cookery not seen as a golden ticket into Oxbridge). Compulsory GCSE subjects are English, maths, PE plus a foreign language and at least two sciences. Setting in maths and modern languages – with support (one full-time SENCO, part time assistants and outside support if necessary) an SEN child can still access the curriculum. French and German both studied to the end of year 9 when Spanish enters as an option. Most take (only) 10 GCSEs, and just French taken early – a strategy that produces few results below a B. In 2015, 83 per cent A*/A grades at GCSE. At A level, 94 per cent A*-B, 69 per cent A*/A.

Parents report that teachers expect a lot and the girls push themselves, which means that confidence must be built elsewhere if not academically strong. The whole of the lower school enters the Maths Challenge, which encourages different ways of thinking. The Stretch programme helps put academia in perspective – a compulsory hour per week of a loosely cerebral activity for every pupil eg film clubs, music composition, chess, Amnesty international.

The timetable is in half hour units but most lessons are an hour; each A level choice has an hour of each subject per day for balance and to mitigate risk when missing a day. The light and warm library is used for study periods mostly by the sixth form, although whole classes can book out the IT area. In the upper sixth both day and boarding girls can return to their one dedicated house to study and hang out.

The Stretch programme helps put academia in perspective – a compulsory hour per week of a loosely cerebral activity for every pupil eg film clubs, chess

Careers fair annually in Harvey Hall with parents and old girls and speakers ranging from architects to philosophy teachers. Families report that careers advice strong on well-trodden paths such as medicine and Russell Group universities, yet quirky directions need more research initiative from home.

Games, options, the arts: Lacrosse is the strongest sport with a fixture every Saturday in both the two terms it is played, attendance at the nationals and amazing international tour (Niagara Falls is on one itinerary) a highlight. Conscious effort to broaden the range of sports – netball and tennis are on the up in terms of competition; also swimming, archery, golf, fencing, squash, scuba diving, badminton, cheerleading, football, polo, skiing, pilates. Some of these are only on offer as one of the 30 or so co-curricular choices, others have emerged into the fixture list. The pool is 25m with an Olympic standard diving board (Winchester residents use it too), stables are 10 minutes away and the sailing squad heads off most Sundays. Location in South Downs National Park means limited permanent floodlighting for sports pitches but play continues regardless through temporary arrangements. Gym cards track over- or under-zealous exercisers (early morning swimming popular until studying gets really serious in sixth form) and equipment has been recently updated so apparently girls watch The Big Bang Theory while running.

In the lower years there is an hour of art, drama and food tech each week, all housed in the same block. Very enthusiastic art team with a regular life model, Rosa Verloop inspired sculptures (stuffed tights), nominated desks and eventually cubby holes for A level students – DT floor just as sparky with electronics, laser cutter and Green Power car (has to be fast, green and involve good team) racing every year at Goodwood, but no A level take up at present. Amazing aromas sandwiched on the floor between the other choices, cooked up in the professional tech kitchen. Textiles popular too with A level newly on offer.

Performing arts centre provides a lively hub for music and drama in the school (and doubles as the venue for morning assembly). Drama studio backs on to the main stage and is used for lessons (no A level at present). Girls do plays on their own initiative too, inviting Winchester boys in for male parts (and vice versa) eg Alan Ayckbourn's Bedroom Farce. Parents would like more academic links to Winchester College, but it plays quite hard to get; lots of local girls' schools would like to be partnered with it more closely.

Head girl team instigates a school wide and term long game of tag. This has everyone searching for targets, who in turn dye their hair, even hide in cupboards

Great range of orchestras, bands, ensembles and choirs – chamber, gospel and a capella – some open to all, others more selective. Music school houses practice rooms and an IT suite with Sibelius for composition, basic Cubase skills for recording performances. Around 55 per cent of pupils learn a musical instrument and some 145 candidates are entered for external music exams each year. Senior choir sings evensong each term in the cathedral and tours overseas every other year.

Boarding: Separate boarding and day houses until a single combined one for upper sixth; the latter are the only ones allowed to go back to their house to work during the day. The seniors do prep duty for the younger ones and there are clusters with a 'mother' in the sixth form and younger 'sisters' or 'cousins' in other years, a 'family' that looks out for each other. A race back to day houses for a hot chocolate made for the girls at break – and letter delivery for the boarding girls; day and boarding girls become less separate as they move up the school. Different nationalities are more likely to hang out with their own at the weekend – the balance is well set between cultural comfort and integration.

Initially Toblerone shaped dorms with equal sections under Velux windows, flexible boarding and school bed linen for the youngest, privacy growing through curtains to a single room at GCSE with a hand basin, useful essay quotes and posters on the wall. Each house has thoughtful inclusive touches that soften the necessary (safeguarding) communality – word of the week board for little ones, movie night, pool table, Wii, piano – as well as the vital drudge of learning to do laundry. Everyone sits around the breakfast bar at the weekend in their pyjamas and the houseparents make sure that full boarders keep busy with three activities during week nights and three at weekends eg a trip to the zoo, decorating your mobile phone cover, making gingerbread men, skating or music practice.

Background and atmosphere: Founded as Winchester High School in 1884 by Anna Bramston, daughter of the Dean of Winchester, who remained as school secretary for over 40 years – the dean, the headmaster of Winchester College and the mayor are still part of the governing body. Changed its name to St Swithun's in 1927 and moved to the present 45 acre site in 1931. Vast, intimidating, red-brick, Queen Anne style building with blonde parquet flooring, large windows and long corridors – girls learn to look up and smile as they pass each other rather than hold/avoid gaze as they approach from either end.

Tight community of supportive girls with a culture of 'go for it' rather than 'too cool' to join in eg minority of girls remain in normal clothes on dress up days. Flip side of this is the pressure for good results that they can exert on each other. Boarders and day pupils retreat to different houses for break but all eat together at lunch, and head girl team blogs, runs the school forum and instigates a school wide and term long game of tag. This has everyone searching for their targets, who in turn dye their hair, swap uniforms and even hide in cupboards – all for glory, chocolate and side effect of integration. Pupils give regular assemblies and topics range from Beyoncé to the Khmer Rouge, while the school forum has input to subjects as disparate as the air con in the gym and more tenor timbre in the hymns. Fundraising Friday is another equaliser, as money is raised for the voted annual charities, and some girls do EdClub, a worldwide initiative that uses Skype to encourage disadvantaged children (many in slums) to learn using broadband.

Winchester the town is important for the freedom it offers only 15 minutes' walk away – and usually a cab ride back up hill. Provides an opportunity to meet up with Winchester boys; the seniors can eat out or go to a play. The outgoing ones say it is very relaxed, no-one puts on make-up, they are all just a group of friends with about 20 per cent in relationships and many of the day girls knowing the boys from local life; the less confident ones mention a pressure to add the boys as friends on Facebook as soon as they return – yet all monitored (some girls reckon too closely) by the housemistresses and house assistants. The latter have a non-teaching role so that they can concentrate on the emotional temperature in each house – there is a health centre staffed 24 hours on site and a clinical psychologist offers discrete appointments in the old chapel; the whole school benefits from her years of experience of the lives and issues of teenage girls. The leavers' ball is usually just for the girls alone (their choice, no Winchester boys); that, and the singing of Jerusalem, is guaranteed to cause some tears to be shed.

Pastoral care, well-being and discipline: Houseparents are first point of contact for issues from homesickness through bullying to A level choices – although a form tutor is vital for the latter too. Parents feel everything is dealt with swiftly and sensibly; avoiding a before bed phone call can give both parent and child a less weepy night. Phones are used for email nowadays, particularly useful for older girls looking at timetables and emailing essays, restricted for the younger ones.

An art project of smiles photographed around the school has found a permanent home on the wall of the modern (2013) chapel – all full boarders and staff attend every Sunday, optional for the upper sixth. Over-indulging in alcohol the most common serious disciplinary issue – and that not very, if girls' shock at relaxed attitude observed in their visits to boys or co-ed schools is anything to go by.

Pupils and parents: Down to earth parents who value education; armed forces, business people, diplomats, lawyers, doctors and bright children with parents working in less lucrative professions; four wheel drives rather than Bentleys. Over half are day pupils – school bus services are getting better after unflattering comparison with King Edward. Twenty (and rising) per cent of boarders from London, often with more local weekend houses – weekly boarders make up 15 per cent of the school. Heathrow is less than an hour away and Southampton airport only 20 minutes, so 15 per cent of boarders from overseas, range of 20 countries. Occasional international guest pupils come for a term from France, Germany, Spain, Czechoslovakia – must be fluent in English. Alumni range from actor Emma Chambers (Alice in the Vicar of Dibley) to journalist and radio presenter Fi Glover.

Entrance: Main intake at 11 with pre-test, January 11+ and CE. Places offered on pre-test and reference from current head – no longer in order of registration. Everyone must pass CE, whether from state, private, or school's own junior school. The latter provides about a third of the intake, others from London day schools and local preps. About 20 more enter at age 13 with a pre-test 18 months before (can be taken overseas) and then a firm offer; if there is a crisis and they don't make the necessary 60 per cent at common entrance then there is leeway – occasional places further up the school. About 20 join the sixth form with own entry and test in November; a summer year 10 report is necessary before registration – very competitive.

Exit: Around 20 per cent leave after GCSEs, bound for the local sixth form college or for other co-ed sixth forms. Almost all the others go on to university, mostly the old-established ones, with Oxbridge (seven in 2015), London, Edinburgh, York and Durham being favourite destinations, sciences unsurprisingly popular. A couple off to study art, one to Berlin and one to Australia in 2015.

Money matters: One in six pupils have a means-tested bursary, an academic scholarship, sports scholarship or a music award (available at 11, 13 and 16). All scholarships are for up to 20 per cent of fees and based on the calibre of the applicant, rather than need. Bursaries are means-tested and available for 50 to 100 per cent of the fees. Music awards include free music lessons.

Remarks: Academic powerhouse with bluestocking reputation now widened into great co-curricular and sports options; pupil assemblies range from the Beyoncé to the Khmer Rouge. Girls egg each other on to great results and fun too.

Shiplake College

Shiplake Court, Henley-on-Thames, Oxfordshire RG9 4BW

01189 402455
registrar@shiplake.org.uk
www.shiplake.org.uk
C of E

Ages: 11–18 (boarding from 13)
Pupils: 439; sixth form: 175 co-ed
Boarders: 177 full and weekly
Day: £16,200 – £20,220 pa
Boarding: £28,680 pa

Headmaster: Since 2004, Mr Gregg Davies BSc Cert Mgmt (40s), an ISI inspector, married to Alison (teaches in the learning development department); one teenage daughter. Tall, athletic, follicly challenged, he has something of the tri-nations about him – Welsh birth, Scottish heritage, English country life and a northern lilt that blends the three. He greeted us in his trademark, Davies-tartan trews but later switched to his second uniform, smart sports kit. Describes his hobbies as loud singing (runs head's choir for non-singers) and log-chopping; he harbours a desire to branch-out, climb to the top of the tree and claim the crown – as a tree surgeon.

A talented sportsman, equally at home kicking or running with the ball, his own Shrewsbury school days were spent on field, not river. That changed when, aged 18, he discovered his sea legs, and crossed the Pond to Connecticut. In a country where football is characterised by shoulder pads

and 'Giants', he wisely swapped balls for oars, garnering gold in the Stotesbury Cup and New England Championships. St Andrews student life saw him switch sculls for scrums, a move that eventually paved the way to international honours (as a referee).

Began his career at Haberdashers' but disliked the dearth of teaching challenge, 'They didn't need me, just my university notes.' Next stop Fettes. At a time when rot had set in, he not only learned about school as a business but spent glorious days in various remits. His favourite being housemaster, which he says is 'the best job in the world, so long as your wife agrees and those who inspect understand the job, its demands and the decisions you take.' Talks not of potential but of targets and stretching – finger-tip stuff, climbing mountains, appreciating the journey – recognising that sometimes it's not a higher peak but new direction and challenge that are needed.

Described by the boys as approachable, caring, funny, inspirational and charismatic, they say he sets very clear boundaries but does help you when you get things wrong. Praised by parents too, who say he is pivotal to the character and strength of the school. Mr Davies says he's not a typical head, we disagree: he may not be stereotypical but headly characteristics such as tradition, stature, moral code, strong leadership skills and a love of learning are evident. Passionate about (good) teaching, learning, biology and statistics. Not afraid to upset the apple-cart: on arrival head fired strutting-peacocks, expelled the errant and swept dead wood from the staff. The result is a school that has recently crossed the divide (just) from recruiting to selecting.

Academic matters: Beefed-up academics, including monitoring and expectations. Introduced IGCSE maths for most able and single sciences for all; Y9 have learning to learn (study skills, organisation, planning, revision techniques etc) but no happiness lessons – that's a given here. School channels youngsters towards courses and colleges that will work; as much about stretching ambition as curtailing misplaced enthusiasm. Good post-16 choice of A levels (including further maths and recent addition of economics) for the erudite, plus generous smattering of 'studies' (PE, media, drama) and, for those with a practical bias, BTecs in music, business, travel and tourism – hands-on, modular, 100 per cent coursework. Politics and photography on pupil wish list, no guarantees of the former, photography currently offered as an art module.

Nine GCSEs the max here, allowing time to concentrate on English, maths, sciences. Twenty-one per cent of GCSE grades A*/A in 2015; at A level, 21 per cent A*/A and 58 per cent A*-B. Headline results seem pretty ordinary until you dig out the value-added (very positive for almost all) and see that kids perform beyond predictions. Director of studies moved from reactive pursuit of academic rigour to proactive; differentiated work and low-key scholars' programme aims to stretch the able. Still some grumblings from parents, who feel talented children aren't as challenged as they might be elsewhere – others say 'shouldn't mistake kindness for weakness, standards are high, school very on the ball and incredibly quick to get in touch if child appears to even think about slipping.'

Talks not of potential but of targets and stretching – finger-tip stuff, climbing mountains, appreciating the journey – recognising that sometimes it's a new challenge that's needed

Pupils say they enjoy most lessons (though harrumphed about hour long sessions) and appreciate continual help and support of staff. Art and design, history and geography front-runners in the popularity (and performance) stakes (with good showing for girls taking biology); physics and French less so, English on the up. Teaching good and improving; lots of young blood with imagination, ideas and energy, honing their craft alongside the experienced and in some cases, inspirational. We saw traditional, teacher led-sessions but alas didn't witness any of the pizazz that head recounted: biology lessons exploring pond life and the yelps of delight when pupils realised the muddy water houses whole colonies of creatures; or the history lesson where boys not only built trenches, complete with sandbags and duck-boards but spent a miserable 15 minutes up to their knees in cold, damp and dank conditions. A fleeting glimpse of trench life but a life-long appreciation of the horrors of WW1 and the need to 'remember them.'

Lots of support for the 25+ per cent identified with SEN and a deservedly excellent reputation for learning development. There isn't a pill for dyslexia et al but the recommended strategies – small classes, careful monitoring, addressing dominant learning styles and a whole school approach are among the viable antidotes offered here. However individual learning support doesn't kick in until year 9, from when boys can have three hours per week of dedicated learning support in place of a language/GCSE option. The school will accept bright boys with dyslexia/similar in years 7/8, but they need to be able to cope without learning support.

Still no proper library (a big black mark in our book), only small, under-utilised department libraries. Even the paltry shelves in the lower school were

Pièce de résistance is a wonderful bend in the river, below the school's terrace, with boathouse and island for adventure/rafting/camping

too high for most boys to peruse. We left our guides with the task of finding somewhere to position Horowitz, Shan, Ransom et al; hopefully they'll be well-thumbed, scanned, and savoured when we return.

Games, options, the arts: A school for doers; dirty knees okay, wellies obligatory, though we are less sure about the rainy day 'smell like wet dogs' description of the boys that staff shared. Rugby, rowing, hockey, cricket, athletics and netball plus good smattering of minor sports and house fixtures, important, improving, inclusive and competitive (notable successes against much bigger rivals). In line with school spirit, fixture boards welcome the opposition and wish them luck. Good facilities, plenty of pitches, Astroturf, tennis, gym (with squash courts), sports hall, heated outdoor pool used by hardy souls well into the bowels of November. Pièce de resistance is a wonderful bend in the river, below school's terrace and grassy slope, with boathouse and island for adventure/rafting/ camping exercises. Enthusiastic and popular D of E, community service and CCF.

Art much improved and displayed school-wide. Drama edgy, believe in pushing boundaries (ask about the camel, sand and theatre in the round). Lovely studio theatre in old tithe barn, scented with woody smells. Music something of an unfinished symphony; working towards music for all – sixth form girls must join school choir – no sing, no entry and all in lower school play either brass or strings. We listened to the whole (lower) school orchestra rendition of Fanfare; more cacophony than flourish but we'd blow a raspberry at anyone who knocked their heart, hale and effort; a sound all the sweeter when you realise that just two months prior many couldn't even name their instrument, let alone play it.

Boarding: Flexible – a boon to busy parents, though some full-boarders rue increasing numbers of part-timers. Accommodation varies – some younger boys in rooms of up to five, older pupils in singles, mainly functional and reassuringly untidy. Good provision of games rooms, kitchens, common rooms etc plus tuck and endless bread supplies. Activity programme for full boarders.

Background and atmosphere: Stunning middle-England setting, overlooking the Thames;

manicured, groomed, Wind In The Willows idyll. Just five minutes from Henley, Shiplake Court was built in 1895 as a family home and farm; today, characterful, adapted red-brick barns and buildings dot the site along with (mainly) attractive newer buildings, subject blocks and boarding houses. Houses allocated according to boarding status (day, full or weekly boarder).

School-home communication, covering everyone (from receptionists to head) and everything from drug awareness, through disciplinary matters and very regular academic feedback with associated praise, rewards and merits, is outstanding, frequent, inclusive and inescapable. Not a school for a fire-and-forget parent.

Saturday morning lessons now abolished, with sports fixtures taking their place, thus 'allowing more family time at the weekend for day pupils and weekly boarders,' says school.

Pastoral care, well-being and discipline: Available, alert and approachable, the support team, from nurses and the Rev through caterers, cleaners, matrons, masters and mentors make it their business to look out for problems; eating, depression, self-harm just some of the sensitively handled issues. Parents love the fact that girls will always be picked up for high-heels, tight skirts or a blush too far on the make-up front. Food tasty: fruit and salad offered alongside hot; dietary needs catered for, all served in gothic Great Hall.

Whole school assemblies important – indeed this is one of the few schools where pupils (and parents) have spoken about the inspirational assemblies led by the head: not only do they not nod off but it seems they duly act on the pearls cast. Head speaks oft to boys about 'choice, risk and consequences'; so we were most impressed when one of our guides cited this – but slightly less so, when head admitted candidly that this probably had more to do with a recent 'scrape' involving sibling of said guide.

Big on building confidence, esteem and self-belief, work to generate a can-do attitude but with consideration and respect for others. Said one parent, 'My son is able but a complete softie; he's beginning to toughen up though, and school always keeps in touch and deals with sensitive issues speedily.' Kids are genuinely caring and nice (in the best, not boring, sense of the word). Indeed when we asked a group of strapping 16-year-olds what they would change if they were head, the second most popular answer (after abolish Saturday lessons – which has now happened) was 'make more of the mentoring'. Every Y9 boy is allocated a sixth-former who befriends and advises. Those who benefitted from its introduction are keen to expand the remit, with a desire to add socials and structure, to maximise benefit.

Older pupils feel they should be given more slack – allowed out at weekends (or perhaps a student bar/dining club, now drink alone is verboten). Somehow we doubt they'll get the town pass – shenanigans of Shiplake boys (in mid noughties) not totally erased from long-memories of locals. Cleaned its act on the drugs front – a zero-tolerance approach sent shock-waves then, but appears to be paying dividends now (though never say never, whatever the school) – smoking still a burning issue.

Pupils and parents: Parents pretty grounded for this part of the world but demanding and discerning nevertheless. Not a smart or fashionable school, with parents citing manners, etiquette and old-fashioned courtesy as some of the things they love about the school. Few Forces children, fewer yet (some five per cent) from overseas; majority from local schools, some relieved no longer to be in pressure-pot environment of local preps that push hard for places at nearby grammars.

Very much a school for children who enjoy challenges and stretch. 'Kids are privileged yet earnest; no tribes, no real cliques,' said one parent, another added, 'My son has a dimmer switch; sometimes it's turned down low, but since he's been at Shiplake the bulb is burning brighter for longer.' Notable former pupils (aka Old Vikings for most implausible reasons) include Sydney gold medallist Ben Hunt-Davies and Starbucks UK CEO Phil Broad.

Entrance: Getting more picky but not academically so. At 11 and 13 selection takes place during taster day which includes an interview, discussion groups, outdoor activities and short tests in English and maths, not as a pass/fail exercise but to inform. Girls from 16. Incomers require 5+ GCSEs (with

English and maths at C or higher) 'though they make exceptions' for those they feel will fit in. 'We will let our own boys stay on if we can find something useful and enjoyable for them to do.' Rescue those burnt-out from (or shot-out of) Thames Valley swot-houses.

Some 25 per cent have a learning difficulty or difference. The dys-strata and ADD account for most, plus a sprinkle of ADHD and Asperger's and a handful with EAL needs. Trying to attract more scholars and all-rounders.

Exit: Around 20 per cent leave after GCSEs. Outcomes divergent; everything from the occasional Oxbridge/ Harvard student (one to Cambridge and one to Dartmouth College in 2015) to those who pursue art and the vocational. Around 80 per cent to degree courses with new universities – Bournemouth, Southampton Solent etc – outweighing trad – Leeds, Newcastle et al. Handful to vocational further education courses, rest into interesting gap year activities or employment.

Money matters: Art, music and sports scholarships awarded but more for prestige than pounds. Sixth form schls depend on general aptitude test, plus test results in two subjects to be studied at A level. Means-tested bursaries awarded at the school's discretion with small pot to assist existing pupils, should financial hiccups occur.

Remarks: A good school on an upward curve, with a charismatic, no-nonsense, forward looking head (complete with iPad and tweets) plus dedicated team in an enchanting location; especially suited to the reserved or those with bruised esteem. IQs cross many centiles but Shiplake is unlikely to suit the struggling child with little to offer, nor the multi-talented, über-confident, high-flying know-it-all. For everyone else, including abler, gentle souls, sporty or not, there may well be a fit. Send for the prospectus (we love the student one), visit and see if life by the river will float your child's boat.

Sibford School

Sibford Ferris, Banbury, Oxfordshire OX15 5QL

01295 781200
admissions@sibfordschool.co.uk
www.sibford.oxon.sch.uk

Ages: 11–18
Pupils: 430; sixth form: 90
Boarders: 40 full, 26 weekly/flexi
Day: £13,317 – £13,584 pa
Boarding: £24,096 – £26,391 pa

Head: Since 2004, Michael Goodwin BA PGCE. Educated at Bury Grammar School, read history at the University of Nottingham. Previously head of Sheringham High School, Norfolk. Married to Veronika; they have four grown up children. Spends spare time with family, walking the dogs, going to theatre or travelling overseas; used to live in Spain and likes to return whenever possible.

Chatty, confident, open, with a good sense of humour, parents say he is energetic, personable and friendly. 'I'd only ever encountered formal heads before so it was a shock to call him Michael but that is the Quaker way'. 'The more I get to know him, the more I think he is superb. He interviews all potential pupils and is excellent at putting them at their ease and making them feel special. Importantly the children respect him, he listens.' Liked and respected by pupils, but praise from some peppered with criticism – 'He can drone on in morning meetings, he talks a lot about his family and tries to be funny and tell jokes but doesn't always succeed' – though they unanimously add,

'He really cares about us, wants us to do well. We know if we have a problem we can always talk to him and is genuinely interested in us.'
Retiring in July 2016.

Academic matters: Generally good facilities, including a smart, bright, well-stocked senior school library with plans afoot to upgrade those few areas in need of TLC. Classes are small and set independently, so it's possible to be in high group for maths, middle for science, low set for English etc – whatever works for the child. A third take triple science, usually those thinking of studying science at A level, with rest taking 21st century science. 'The course applies science, to everyday life which stimulates interest in a subject when otherwise it might not have been there,' say science staff. Enlightened approach to English setting, look at the whole child and at their ability to understand, analyse and interpret English. 'We have children in top sets who use Dragon software. Sometimes the mechanics of reading or spelling may not be there but they may be incredibly insightful with a high verbal IQ. We have to stretch them, not constantly criticise every spelling mistake or punctuation error.' In 2015, 26 per cent of GCSE grades A*/A.

Wonderful collegiate approach means if a child hasn't understood something with one teacher, it is fine to seek extra help later from a different one

Range of activities for those identified as gifted, talented or able (which includes some 40 per cent also identified as dyslexic). Sixth form pupils make guided subject choices. 'I like the freedom within subjects, the support from teachers when you need it and small classes mean lots of attention'. For the 20 per cent or so who need additional support, learning is tailored to the individual. 'We wanted a school where our son mattered as a person. He slipped under the radar in his previous school. He deserved more, so we looked for a school that would make him feel special and found that in abundance at Sibford.' Full support consists of five 35 minute lessons per week plus in-class support if needed, and consists of any combination of literacy, numeracy, fine motor and speech and language input. Super revision library display board sets the tone, with handy hints such as 'use a timetable', 'record questions and quotations onto your iPod' etc. Lunch

time activities include popular trampoline and swim sessions for those with gross motor difficulties. Regular internal audit process includes pupil interviews to ensure staff are supporting youngsters in a helpful and constructive way so they can learn to articulate their difficulties and accept that it is permissible to be dyslexic. Parents say support is impressive. 'There is no stigma, my child's self-esteem has rocketed; I cannot believe how chatty and confident he is; Sibford has transformed him.' Not a school that worries about league tables; it stands by and encourages pupils.

Music/music technology and textiles currently in vogue, with girls generally performing better than boys, especially in the sciences and maths. Good value added, though typically fewer than 50 per cent A*-B grades at A level (41 per cent in 2015, with 19 per cent A*/A grades); grades must be seen in context of intake and school's policy of allowing pupils to pursue subjects that interest them, not what shows the school in the best light. As pleased with a child who struggles and achieves four or five GCSEs at grade C as they are with the most able who achieve their fistfuls of A stars. 'We take great store by the journey to get there and the effort a child makes'. Wonderful collegiate approach means if a child hasn't understood something with one teacher, it is fine to seek extra help later, either from their teacher or from a different one. If a strength is identified, or child has a passion, staff will do all they can to encourage that. Working to embed independent learning, allows youngsters to fail then succeed. Striving for excellence, candid about where they are, 'We've climbed

the mountain and can see the summit, but like a diet, it's the last push that is the hardest to achieve.'

Games, options, the arts: Something for everyone: proud of music facilities, practice rooms, recording studio, music tech and bright, light ensemble room. Plenty of bands, orchestras and ensembles – with opportunity to perform publicly, regardless of grade. Super art with atmospheric lessons; we dropped in on an introduction to pop art via the psychedelia of Sgt Pepper tracks – fun, and saw impressive displays of pottery, textiles and sculpture. All usual sports: rugby, football, cricket, hockey, netball, rounders plus squash (own courts), riding at local stables and swimming in own swish, 25-metre pool with rowing and a multi-gym on wish list. Clubs galore with youngest expected to participate in at least three lunch offerings; huge variety: knitting, science awards, board games, origami and more. Range of inter-house challenges include musicals for the creative, quiz nights for the cerebral and construction challenges for the practical.

Pièce de résistance, guided by enterprising head of environmental science and horticulture, is outdoor education; whether through science, history, gardening club or just as a hobby. Lessons stretch beyond those of ecology, horticulture and the environment, to the economic, with plants marketed and sold to fund future ventures. The fantastic themed beds, ranging from sensory and historical (world war 2 utility garden and rotating allotment) to a sprinkling of the whacky and experimental, sit alongside a sturdy reconstruction of a Celtic roundhouse and wattle fence. We admired the student-designed prototype greenhouse built from recycled plastic bottles; very much epitomises the school's approach to learning: expect pupils to

think up ideas, create designs, lay foundations, construct, kit-out, appraise, refine and improve. Has embarked on BTec countryside management and animal husbandry: expect to see pigs, sheep and cows among the throng.

Boarding: Only around 40 full boarders (do check age and gender mix) so weekends operate on a cosy, home from home basis with brunch rather than breakfast, a trip out – 'Trips are great fun, they encourage you to mix across the years' – and emphasis on relaxation and rest: no Saturday school or matches. Food much improved but not yet cordon bleu (school says 'excellent' – 'the local council's Eat Well in Cherwell scheme graded us as Platinum') and surprisingly, no-one objects to technology/gadget free lunchtimes. Houseparents mainly get huge thumbs up: 'They listen, are fun and there for us'. Around 60 per cent of boarding community is from overseas.

A school where tomorrow's doctor will be helped and encouraged, not just to gain a place at medical school but to think fully about career paths – surgery, Africa, professorship

Three boarding houses – one each for 11-16 year old boys and girls, plus co-ed sixth form house – all refurbed over recent years and include laundry, games rooms and quiet areas. Praise for the atmosphere, camaraderie and care.

Most recent ISI inspection report described boarding provision and houseparents as 'excellent'.

Background and atmosphere: Sibford Ferris isn't a manicured Cotswold weekend retreat for city slickers playing at country life but a pretty, homely, much-loved village and community, with the school central to that. Sibford was founded as a co-ed boarding school by the Quakers in 1842. Originally housed in a splendid Cotswold stone manor house, in the 1930s it expanded into a hotchpotch of buildings known as The Hill. In recent times, the manor was sold and the proceeds astutely ploughed back into purpose-built music and art blocks, with new sixth form centre following a couple of years later. Extensive, idyllic, 50-acre grounds, include an orchard, woodland, pond and even picnic benches for students. All new year 7 pupils (and new staff) mark their arrival at the school by planting either a tree or bush.

A school with a family feel, attention to detail and few places to hide, it was a heartbeat from failing when Michael arrived. 'I could see the potential but lots had to change. The location is wonderful, I pinch myself that I am here, but the school was looking unloved and uncared for.' He wasted no time appointing a financial director and together they worked out an investment/development plan. Resuscitation was needed, but recognising it is all too easy to pour money into schools, then watch them haemorrhage, they went for the full face lift, rather than sticking plaster approach. Tough decisions were taken. School changed from boarding to a day school with boarding; a sustained and sustainable refurbishment programme began in earnest and some staff departed, not all wholly voluntarily. 'We had become the school of second choice, but thanks to our development programme and marketing initiatives we are now a conscious first choice. People understand what we are about; we focus on the child, take them as our starting point, and that is what our families buy into. The school has a wonderful local feel so we consciously restrict international boarding to 10 per cent. We'd like a few more boarders but not at any cost'.

Pastoral care, well-being and discipline: Excellent pastoral care is a given. 'It is crucial we consider long term mental health, so we start with values and relationships, not academic excellence.' Aim to develop emotional fortitude so pupils leave with emotional robustness. 'We help them balance social life and work so they don't burn out.' Daily staff briefing ensures all aware of potential pupil issues. Parents say pastoral staff never leave problems until the following day, 'They spend an inordinate amount of time dealing with issues, nip things in the bud, give time to parents, explore avenues and work out how to proceed; with child's interests at heart.' Has a deserved reputation for being nurturing and is very much the place where 'you go if dyslexic', but the perception that it is just for dyslexics no longer holds. 'They really do find the best in every single child,' say parents, adding, 'to feel special and to be good at something is incredibly important for self-esteem; our children go from strength to strength. It isn't an easy or soft option, they just have the knack of getting all children to really want to do well.'

Pupils and parents: Not a 'stand aside, call me Sir' school; equitable outlook extends beyond the classroom, so expect to find staff queuing and eating with children. 'Can do, will do' attitude means there's never a lack of volunteers, even if they're not quite sure what they are volunteering for. Happy to get their hands dirty and rise to any challenge. Emphasis on team work. Lack of overt competitive edge means some parents feel it isn't a great place for those aiming for top tier sport, but conversely believe it is ideal for the bright boffin who may either struggle to fit in elsewhere or who

finds the social aspects of school life a challenge. Huge praise from parents. 'It's a fantastic school. If I had known how good it was I would have sent all my children here, safe in the knowledge that all would have done extremely well. Teachers have time for individual pupils so different characters can grow and flourish.' No typical pupils but tolerance is in the blood. 'My child has a huge variety of amazing friends, some slightly weird, some terribly normal.' Few families (or staff) are practising Quakers but all buy into the ethos, with tolerance to the fore. 'My child is geeky but he fits in and is accepted.' Goes beyond the bounds to support and encourage ambition; expect to find budding artists, thespians, entrepreneurs, eco-warriors et al. A school where tomorrow's doctor will be helped and encouraged, not just to gain a place at medical school but to think fully about career paths – surgery, Africa, professorship, though always with emphasis on the importance of all team contributors, whether cleaner, technician or top-dog.

Parents from a wide range of backgrounds and income brackets, including a number of first time buyers; many very involved in school. Not a school for the pushy brigade; most choose Sibford precisely because they do want their children to achieve and do well, but that means prioritising mental health and well-being above exams and grades. Notable old Sibfordians include the late Paul Eddington, Guy Ritchie and Charlie Boorman.

Entrance: Into senior school at 11 and 13 with entry at other times if places are available. Pretty broad brush intake: 10 per cent gifted, 10 per cent who might struggle at hotter-houses. Look for youngsters who want to be at the school and will benefit from their time there. Good at second chances and helping those who have struggled elsewhere; Sibford picks up the pieces, stands by its brood, when other schools surrender. Often second choice school but not second best; it isn't unusual for parents to visit just to tick the boxes, then become enamoured. 'They think they want fancy facilities, labels or names but end up buying into the Quaker values and ethos; those of respect, nurturing, care and quiet ambition.'

Exit: Up to 25 leave after GCSE, mostly for further education colleges, independent schools offering different subjects at A level, apprenticeships or training. Majority to university but school conscious that uni is not right for everyone. One off with a scholarship to study jazz at the Birmingham Conservatoire in 2015; Southampton Solent, Cardiff, Warwick and Oxford Brookes also popular.

Money matters: Not a rich school but offers a number of academic, music and art scholarships, plus means-tested bursaries to both Quaker and non-Quaker families. Sound financial management means the school continues to improve buildings and facilities.

Remarks: In the words of one youngster, 'It just gels; they make you feel important, believe in yourself and want to do well.' No boxes or moulds. A school with a comprehensive intake, universal outlook and concentration on the individual; not fine or fanciful but fun and fair with a flair for finding, and focusing on, talents.

Stowe School

Stowe, Buckingham MK18 5EH

01280 818323
admissions@stowe.co.uk
www.stowe.co.uk
C of E

Ages: 13–18
Pupils: 766: (483 boys, 283 girls); sixth form: 315
Boarders: 653
Day: £23,940 pa
Boarding: £33,300 pa

Headmaster: Since 2003, Dr Anthony Wallersteiner MA PhD (late 40s), Cambridge history scholar and art historian, married to Valerie, three children. Previous two posts were at the academic powerhouses of St Paul's and Tonbridge, but in Stowe he has discovered his nirvana. Charming, impressive, a maverick with a keen sense of fun; on arrival we said, 'Think sired by Stephen Fry out of Nelson's Column with a trace of HRH the P of W and Boris Johnson somewhere under the blanket. He is frank, relaxed, confident, charming and unstoppably chatty.' Plus ça change plus c'est la même chose. 'He is inspirational, lacks ego, delegates,' say staff; pupils add, 'Dr Wallersteiner is friendly, funny and fun; he gets involved, chats to us, knows our results and how we are doing but doesn't pigeonhole.' Parents equally enamoured: 'Simply magnificent. Not an intellectual snob: he just gets the best out of all in the most charming way.'

Dr Wallersteiner's appointment was no accident. Stowe was in the doldrums, needed lifeblood and direction but, with a dictum of academic excellence, nervous onlookers twitched; would this erudite polymath try to morph Stowe into another A* and Oxbridge hothouse with selection limited to the bright and bookish? Or, would his vision be the panacea? 'I wanted to return Stowe to the glory days, to its founding principles, but with a 21st century twist. We used to stand shoulder to shoulder with the great public schools: Eton, Rugby, Harrow; Stowe was renowned for being idiosyncratic, for looking after the individual, encouraging them to pursue interests with enthusiasm, allowing characters to emerge – Leonard Cheshire, David Niven – Stoics with an innate sense of confidence. Branson in the 60s probably typifies what it is to be a Stoic and that's what I wanted to inject into the place. Old Stoics have set the world alight; I want that to continue'.

A perfect fit for the school, precisely because he didn't always fit at school: a boy whose prep school reports tell only of a time waster, a lazy boy who would never amount to anything. Yet his final school report dazzled; a cerebral scholar heading for Cambridge. Inspirational teachers unlocked both talent and a desire to learn; masters lit the flame, he uncovered a universe. 'You can't

Charming, impressive, a maverick with a keen sense of fun; 'Think sired by Stephen Fry out of Nelson's Column with a trace of HRH the P of W and Boris Johnson'

underestimate the power of a teacher in transforming lives. I want the pupils to find their passion and drive, to be inspired and to inspire, to love learning, to appreciate the beauty of life, to be creative, to find their Utopia. You have to be so careful with children: they remember the time they were told they were thick or stupid, it sticks. If you say they will never amount to anything that one line can define their experiences, motivation and determination. A teacher should stand up, perform and remember that the hundredth time for them is still the first time for a child.'

Academic matters: Buildings have had massive numbers of facelifts, so few blots remain. We were in awe of the library with its magnificent ceiling (part of an £8.8m restoration) but less enamoured by the 1960s science block and so keen to view from the inside. In one lesson children were eagerly examining the effects of emulsifiers on oil and water and in another teams were collectively working out how to construct model DNA.

Dr Wallersteiner has moved academic rigour centre stage: 'I didn't want people to apologise for coming to Stowe'. Pupils are motivated to achieve, some aiming for traditional paths, medicine, economics, others for courses we had never heard of – lots keen on the environment with study to

match. Head passionately believes if one path is blocked others should be tried, so good teaching and openness to new ideas, delivered in a supportive environment, are the priority. 'I watch some staff teach and feel so humble: many are masters of their craft, they are inspiring and motivating.' He pleads the fifth amendment when we quiz him about weaker departments and staff, but concedes not all are centres of excellence, though says the pockets are getting bigger. Drive to improve teaching and learning has included time spent looking at how all individuals learn, not just those with a recognised need. Teaching has new blood, greater monitoring and evening clinics for everything; if you don't get it first time round, there is always a second chance: 'A child's brain has to be unblocked with sympathy and care'. We met dyslexics who enthused about help not just from support staff but across the board.

Value added is excellent and confidence high; results fine given the comprehensive intake. A level results on the up (35 per cent A*/A in 2015), and nearly 50 per cent A*/A at GCSE in 2015. Latin and Greek remain, chemistry and religious studies popular options, DT – the Cinderella when it comes to provision – as favoured and successful as ever. Head wants the school to embrace the estate and hopes to offer farm-orientated courses in the future.

Games, options, the arts: Heart and soul spring to mind – whether trout fishing or trotting, beagling or bugling, singing or shooting, running or reading. All do CCF or D of E with push towards community work. Sport strong, with national representation in rowing, cricket, rugby, lacrosse, golf, fencing and equestrian events. Teams draped in accolades too – top the National Schools' League Table for cricket, first division lacrosse champions,

with similar levels of success for polo, hockey and rugby. Superb facilities: playing fields, assault course, a new golf course, courts, sports hall, climbing wall, fencing salle, fives courts, and pool. Latest offerings include a scrambling track (shiny motor bikes) and brand new equestrian centre with 20 stables. Bring your own horse or ride one of the rescue ones. Key winter sports of rugby, hockey and lacrosse cede to summer offerings of leather on willow, athletics and tennis, with polo, rowing, sailing, clay pigeon shooting and golf just some of the country-club offerings.

Strong art and arts – several to art school – annual arts festival encompasses science, sport, dance, music, art, drama. Music popular, plentiful, oft polished with weekly, summer al-fresco performances the perfect backdrop for picnicking parents. New music school. Stowe also boasts its own radio station with resident DJs plus weekend nightclub (kitted out from the remnants of Crazy Larry's in London) hosting high-octane party nights, ranging from themed skiing to bungee runs and magic.

Boarding: Twelve boarding houses in total, all comfortable with kitchens and communal rooms. Boys envious of newish, purpose-built accommodation for the girls (en-suite rooms) which boasts in-house gym, pool room etc. Care is delivered in abundance with everyone from cleaners and caretakers, housemistresses and academic staff on hand to help, plus close liaison with parents, as befits a proper full boarding school.

Background and atmosphere: Breathtaking, such stuff as dreams are made on; so resplendent that romance, not tragedy, be inspired; imagine Isolde sailing into the sunset with Tristan, Anthony falling not on his sword but into the arms of Cleopatra, Romeo

Breathtaking, such stuff as dreams are made on; so resplendent that romance, not tragedy, be inspired; imagine Isolde sailing into the sunset with Tristan, Romeo living happily ever after with Juliet

living happily ever after with Juliet. Youngsters adore the place: 'Once you get here you never want to leave; when it snows, it looks more magical than Narnia.' The 750 acres of parkland and sublime landscape gardens are widely regarded as most significant in Europe and the embodiment of 18th century enlightenment. They include exquisite woods and waters, temples and gardens. The school campus is surprisingly compact with boarding houses, courts and other facilities nestled cosily in sylvan wilderness. The main building – 'the mansion' – is a splendid, neo-classical palace, largely modelled by Robert Adam in the mid-18th century and benefiting from the respective geniuses of Sir Johns Vanbrugh and Soane, William Kent and Capability Brown among others, and became a school only in 1923. In 1989 house and gardens passed to the National Trust and opened to visitors – much restored, Plug Street, named after the village of Ploegsteert south of Ypres, at the southern end of a famous series of long tunnels, is home to the school's nerve centre. This stone-flagged, below-stairs administrative centre includes the head's breathtaking study – 'Sir John Soane in gothic fantasy mode' – a mini replica of Henry VII's chapel in Westminster Abbey with fabulous fan vaulting, lead canopies, brass screens and tracery. Grandeur yes, but if London and the bustle of the city set your child's heart racing or, when visiting, they see fields not dreams, Stowe may be a county too far. 'It is a tight-knit place, but can be too claustrophobic for some,' say pupils.

Pastoral care, well-being and discipline: All eat together in super dining hall overlooked by three Knellers. 'Food is simple but tasty with plenty of variety,' say pupils. Head sees every child on their birthday. 'It's a good opportunity to chat to them, find out what works, what doesn't.' We quizzed the pupils on vices and sins: drink and drugs? 'Compulsory and random testing. Second chances may be possible but never a given'. Bar for sixth form but random breathalyser catches those who transgress. Eating disorders? 'Careful monitoring and being there for friends,' with a comforting 'putting friend before confidentiality and informing staff', if things look serious. Cyber bullying? 'Fairly recent exclusions, discussed openly and frankly in both assemblies and pastoral time so all informed and understood.' Not that there are many transgressions these days, but the press hounds round at the merest whiff of a wrongdoing. Google the craft knife incident if you must but remember virtually all schools have skeletons somewhere; Stowe's are in the open not the closet.

Pupils and parents: Eclectic accepting place where cultures and languages mix. Attracts the solid and the decent plus odd balls and those who might be overlooked elsewhere. Blend of high flyers and spiky IQs: 'We like those', confided the head. Pupils, formal in approach, are polite, grounded and know how to behave and interact. 'They are confident and entertaining, the sort of person you want to sit next to at a dinner party,' say staff. Parents a mix of entrepreneurs, academics, old money (lots), new money (handful), country, creative and celebrity. 'Stowe may look posh but most of us aren't,' say pupils; parents add, 'A few are from wealthy backgrounds but equally some live in modest semis with parents who struggle to find the fees'.

Entrance: Handful from state schools, rest from a range of preps, including Winchester House, The Dragon, Summer Fields, Ashdown House, Papplewick, Sunningdale and Windlesham. School is no longer the 'back-up plan' but a conscious first choice. Looking for 50 per cent plus at CE and happy to take a chrysalis and nurture until a butterfly emerges. 'When I interview prospective pupils it is not high grades that are important, though they are welcome, but there must be a spark, something we can ignite. I look for success – however small.

Plane spotters, stamp collectors, ferreters, budding astronauts, entrepreneurs, the imagined destination less important than the drive and journey.'

Exit: Majority to a broad spread of universities – usually a couple to Oxbridge (four in 2015) and others to the Courtauld, SOAS, Warwick, Manchester, York and UCL. One or two to US. Business-related courses popular. A considerable number to good art schools, with some going to highly-acclaimed music or drama schools.

Money matters: Range of means-tested scholarships (more about honour than finance). Means-tested bursaries available, a small number of fully-funded places for exceptional candidates with proven financial need. Additionally, Roxburgh schols (named after Stowe's revered founding headmaster) awarded to outstanding all-rounders nominated by the heads of their previous schools. Stephan schols available for bright day pupils from the state sector – worth up to 25 per cent of fees, with further support from bursaries as with other scholarships.

Remarks: 'My son loves it, there is so much to do, he is flourishing, has great friends – boys and girls – like a huge extended family.' Captivating from first glimpse to last breath, something for everyone. Mixes the erudite with the sporty and studious, with space reserved for the eclectic and maverick. Ideal for those keen to learn within, and beyond, the bounds of the classroom; but if your sights are firmly set on bright lights, league tables and brags about academia, Stowe is ready for you but you're probably not yet ready for Stowe.

Summer Fields

Mayfield Road, Oxford, Oxfordshire OX2 7EN

01865 454433
office@summerfields.com
www.summerfields.com
C of E

Ages: 8–13
Pupils: 237
Boarders: 204 full
Day: £20,901 pa
Boarding: £26,991 pa

Headmaster: Since 2010, Mr David Faber MA Oxon (50s); came to Summer Fields as old boy; former parent and governor, as well as grandson of illustrious alumnus, Harold Macmillan PM. After Eton and Balliol, became a Conservative MP from 1992-2001, including Opposition spokesman foreign affairs (recently secured schools minister as a speaker for a meeting of prep and public school heads). A keen cricketer (sits on MCC committee) and has

introduced new cricket nets to the fields; also referees boys' football matches.

Interesting appointment as not originally from a teaching background. Urbane and reserved in manner until on the subject of the boys' achievements – fond collector of past medals; 'sporting caps' and historical mementoes of the school. Uses his experience as a historian and author (two books on modern history) in teaching history to the older years and lecturing on 'Appeasement and the Munich Crisis' to public school history societies. Popular with parents ('dream headmaster'), who have seen him institute 'a lot of changes for the better, one thing at a time'. Makes himself available to the parents and appears to know the boys by name and character. Married to Sophie, not on school staff, with two school-aged daughters and a son at Oxford University.

Entrance: Boys are selected by assessment day, which includes written tasks (English, maths and reasoning) and team activities, along with an all-important report from current school. Early registration necessary, but occasional late entry places and mid-year starters also accepted. Special assessment day for the Maclaren Scholarship – up to 100 per cent bursary for a year 6/7 boarder given to a high-flyer, usually from a state primary. Music scholarships from age 8 for gifted musicians. Head refers to it as a 'national' prep school, with most coming from within an hour's drive of Oxford; some overseas and regular group of Old Summerfieldian sons. Previously thought of as upper-crust, and hasn't entirely shaken off the image. Head disagrees, but one parent regretted the narrow social compass. No plans to take girls or to increase much in size – emphasis on keeping a tight-knit community, especially in chapel and dining room.

A recent class of day-only pupils at age 7 ('The Mynors') has now been discontinued to focus on boarding from 8 years upwards.

Exit: Strong links with Eton; up to 40 per cent accepted there each year; and increasing number going to Winchester; also to Harrow; Radley; Charterhouse; Stowe and a few to local public day schools. In 2015, five scholarships: Eton, Harrow (two), Repton and Magdalen College School. Head maintains, 'Proof of the pudding is that the less academically able boys still get into public schools'. Parents like the fact that it doesn't feel like a 'feeder' but still gets great results.

Remarks: Set in over 70 acres of stunning grounds in the heart of North Oxford, the school is unremarkable from the front, but boasts a stately bow-fronted building with fields, woods and river at the rear. Founded by Victorian educationalist husband and wife team, Maclarens, in 1864 and still conscious of its Christian traditions with Victorian chapel and oak-panelled hall. However, there are more modern additions of several smaller houses along adjoining road; two pools (indoor and outdoor); a sports complex, Eton fives courts, a climbing wall, new all-weather tennis and Astroturf courts, as well as golf course and cricket nets and new very large sports pavilion.

Very long day for both boarders and day boys, starts with whole school convening for chapel or assembly. Lessons in small classes (10-17) and early setting promote strong academic results at CE. Scholarship class in last two years given Greek, and Latin and French learnt by all. New DT and ICT suite and science labs, where boys encouraged to 'design your own experiments and make things pop', as well as large, busy library. Boys genuinely motivated by trips to Oxford museums and field trips, including to France. Teaching staff visible round school, as most live in, some of long-standing (30+ years); 'most staff leave to become a headmaster somewhere else'. Academic success earns boys personal and house points which can be enjoyed by tangible rewards in the school shop ('Buzzer') and a House Feast. A staff of six for learning support, with some experience in EP support and statements. One

parent felt that it was particularly good for boys who aren't particularly socially confident and so may experience difficulties elsewhere.

Lodges (boarding houses) for boys of same year group; run by husband and wife team and kept apart from the teaching rooms (no homework or dining in lodge). Remarkably neat dorms, sleep 4-6, with effective in-house incentives for boys to change own sheets, polish shoes and tidy up. One parent commented, 'What I like is that Summer Fields doesn't smell like a school'. Generous but confusing system of 'credits' allows boarders extra weekends out above normal exeats. Pastoral care is managed with a three-tier 'belt and braces' approach. Lodge parent claims, 'Homesickness is more of a problem for the mums' than the boys, who are kept busy in the evenings with board games, computers and giant chess sets. Parent of a young boarder was hugely relieved how easily the youngest were settled in. Discipline maintained by healthy competition and withdrawing privileges rather than anything more gruelling. Boys appear to appreciate this.

Music is a strength, with a dedicated music block and theatre. Three choirs, one with adult voices, sing in Oxford colleges and on tour (Rome recently). Specialist music staff allow boys to take up to three instruments (we heard of a 10 year old playing four), ranging from conventional to electric guitar, even quirky. They recently hunted down a Marimba (Eastern xylophone) teacher in Oxford for a lad from the Far East. Drama productions for different year groups from Twelve Angry Men to We Will Rock You, open to all those who risk taking time from their scholarship clubs. Sport is plentiful and all-inclusive; parents like the fact that all boys make the teams, which play twice a week. Football has recently had its best season since 1937; rugby and hockey also strong, with some players in county cricket and rugby teams.

Prolific art and ceramics studio, obviously not pc – fantasy coats of arms and big game trophies made from papier mâché adorn the walls.

Boys emerge from lessons brightly but quietly. They are articulate and confident, although suspiciously neat and clean in brightly coloured shirts and sweaters. Parental niggle that boys were 'a bit too polished'. However, children appear kind and supportive – 'when you are in the third year you know everyone's names' – and a nice touch that both staff and children refer to the school as 'We...'. Boys don't seem fazed by formality or overt competition – academic progress bulletins are posted on the board every two weeks for all to read – but seem to enjoy it as 'healthy rivalry'. There is a wealth of extra-mural activities, spanning spiritual (Time for God group), sporting (fencing, shooting, polo) and more earthy interests (cookery and Adventure Quest – bushcraft-style camps – for handy skills in lighting the campfire and skinning a rabbit).

An appreciation of the school's history is encouraged with scholars' boards lining the walls of the hall; and a moving remembrance day service, when choral speakers read out names of the fallen alumnae. Boys follow this up with a trip to the Somme. Old Summerfieldians include generous helpings of baronets, colonial civil servants and military leaders as well as Dick Francis, who set one of his detective novels at the school. Active Old Boy links suggest happy memories.

A small and cosy school, in a serene and beautiful setting, successfully eases a boy in to a boarding career. It provides a breathtaking array of sports and music facilities as well as being reliable in placing boys in top public schools. Sense that boys work hard/play hard and turn out to be happy, considerate and polite, if slightly formal. Not for Just Williams.

Sunningdale School

Dry Arch Road, Ascot, Berkshire SL5 9PY

01344 620159
headmaster@sunningdaleschool.co.uk
www.sunningdaleschool.co.uk

Ages: 7–13
Pupils: 114
Boarders: 104 nearly all full
Day: £17,370 pa
Boarding: £22,350 pa

Headmaster: Since 2005, Mr Tom Dawson MA PGCE – and recent distinction in grade 1 piano (40s). Previously taught at Harrow before taking over the shop (school is fully owned by the Dawson family) inheriting headship 'because I'm the boy' he jokes (slightly).

Family-run is understatement and a half. Wife Elisabeth, fellow modern languages graduate, is highly organised director of studies, garnering almost as much praise as husband. 'Lovely' 'kind' and their ilk crop up in conversation with parents with Swiss railway regularity.

Amy, a jolly Dawson sister, one of three (others educationally occupied elsewhere) runs high quality art department and masterminds school productions, more fulfilling than previous career as mural painter (only so many David Beckhams you can glorify on child's bedroom wall without spot of existentialist angst).

Also living and working on site are Mr Dawson's own parents and uncle, who acquired school as going concern in 1960s and are a genial background presence, mother putting final touch to colossal flower arrangements, father waving from ride-on roller. 'Keeps them going,' says their son.

We wondered about sotto voce presence of school parents, who don't, currently, have own association. 'Don't need one,' says Mr Dawson, who points to numerous 'meet the Dawsons' opportunities at well-attended matches, concerts and exhibitions. Parents, professing ardent faith in his leadership, fall over themselves to deliver several carillons' worth of ringing endorsement apiece. 'Exudes incredible values,' 'outstanding personality' two among many.

A genial background presence, mother putting final touch to colossal flower arrangements, father waving from ride-on roller. 'Keeps them going,' says their son

Mr Dawson, while amiable, is reckoned to miss nothing and parents felt that wouldn't shirk from tough decisions. 'If there's one super naughty boy in the school then I guess somebody has to be expelled, as in all schools,' thought one. Impressive networking skills don't go amiss either. 'I know a lot of people,' he says, and what a useful crowd they are. Barnaby Lenon, former Harrow head, extols virtues of pupils and school at length on school website. Mr D cultivates contacts through cricket – a predictable passion. Another – repairing pre-digital Roberts radios (impressive range neatly arranged in his study) – possibly less of an obvious social asset.

Entrance: Register at birth for one of 22 places, waiting list if full (as, increasingly, it is). Mr Dawson understandably hates putting up 'no vacancies' sign – 'don't want to be known for it,' – but is currently 'turning down a lot. It's a cosy, happy place and I don't want to get any bigger.'

While has plenty of high flyers, entrance requirements aren't stratospheric. School expects fluent reading and writing and grasp of basic arithmetic. May ask for report from current school and very occasional pupil is directed elsewhere.

Prospective pupils spend day at the school year before they join when sit short papers in maths, English and VR. Also attend music, art and sport workshops. Main purpose is to work out forms ('we don't really operate in year groups,' says school). Some scholarships available as well as means-tested bursaries. Also takes maximum of 10 day boys through the school, all locals, inherited by Mr Dawson who has 'just stuck with them.'

If you miss the boat, there's a diminutive chance of place or two in year 7 – 'incredibly rare for anyone to leave,' says Mr Dawson – offered after cognitive ability tests (though non-academic strengths also taken into account).

No linked feeders; elite London mob – Garden House, Thomas's, Eaton House – increasingly feature, as do old boys' offspring – at 10 per cent and rising, says school, which stresses that fees 'are kept as low as possible.'

Gaps increasingly filled by international families – one boy we met saw family only three times a year – though school has recently started live feeds for concerts. Otherwise, pupils come from all over the country 'except Cornwall'. We were hoping for some ancient West Country vs home counties blood feud. Disappointingly, down merely to poor transport links.

Exit: Mr Dawson not a fan of serial entrance exams and suggests maximum of three senior schools, two aspirational, one 'a safer bet'. To most of major, trad names in south-east. Harrow often features prominently, with two places and three awards in 2015 including first for DT – but not the last, judging by covetable director's chair, frame wonderfully welded from lengths of old copper tubing. Other usual (and desirable) suspects include Winchester (academic scholarship in 2015), Eton, Charterhouse, Uppingham, Radley and Marlborough.

Remarks: Long the place where old money arrived as small change. Cricket commentator Henry Blofeld, Duke of Westminster, horse trainer Sir Henry Cecil – list of old boys says it all. All it takes is names of first two heads – Girdlestone and Crabtree – to know you're in the presence of Tradition, with capital (and gold-embossed, gothic-lettered) T. Would make a fine detective series title as well. Additional helpful pointers come by way of slightly fly-blown pictures of Victorian worthies in visitors' loos – OBs Duke of Marlborough 1893; Lieutenant the Honorable FHS Roberts VC, killed Colence SA 1899.

Scratch the surface and you'll find...more tradition, bookcase packed with Biggles, Worrals and even a Henty or two (remnants of old library) adorning the morning room – or, more prosaically to those of less gentle birth, the school office. Makes

'Two?' asked Mr Dawson, experiencing a mild Beadle–like moment. 'Why would anyone want to read more than one at a time?'

statement architecture of curved library – first building visitors see and the newest – the more startling by comparison. Accoutrements – refectory table and two sternly positioned sofas – are set off by glow-in-the-dark bright blue carpet (also a dormitory feature), bare walls crying out for some splendiferously mustachioed OBs, picture windows giving vistas not of bosky woods or slumbrous streams but cars approaching up the drive.

Shelves reassuringly weighted in favour of fiction, wooden blocks with school number marking borrowings, one per boy. And if you want to borrow two books? 'Two?' asked Mr Dawson, experiencing mild Beadle-like moment. 'Why would anyone want to read more than one at a time?' It's the hallmark of a school with a strong sense of its own place in the world, conventional yet not in thrall to crowd mentality. Summer half term, for example, happens a week later than normal. Trade off, with school taking strain of final revision for CE exams, worth hassle of arranging two sets of holiday activities for offspring elsewhere, reckoned parents.

Class structure, average size 12, also takes a bit of getting used to. Ability rather than age-based, so while nobody is ever moved down, brighter boys will go up a year, sometimes two, never more. In top years, carefully planned scholarship work ensures there's no 'here's one I made earlier' duplication.

From animated debate on how to stop extinction of coral reef in science – 'tries to make it as visual as possible,' said star pupil – to year 6 pupils reading (beautifully) extracts from end of year English exam, a 'do-able' past CE paper, impression was of willing learners enthusiastically taught. Bright, super-engaged staff, majority male and with average age of 39, includes several of distinctly young fogey-ish disposition and bouffant charm – Boris Johnston recast with auburn and brunette tresses.

Impressive commitment to pupils with SEN. One, with ASD, initially reluctant to attend lessons, supported with one-to-one help, funded by parents, 'fully integrated,' says Mr Dawson. More usual needs (mild dyslexia) respond – miraculously so, thought one parent – to small classes and skilled teaching without intervention. Head 'isn't a big believer in throwing tons of time and money at extra tuition,' said one parent. 'Because the classes are so small, and teaching so good, you don't really need it.'

Staff praised not just for ability to inspire love of learning – 'never did we expect such commitment,' said mother – but for reinforcing universally wonderful manners and behaviour. One parent thrilled when master told son to 'stand up and show the way for your mother.' Compliments, convertible to house points, awarded for the dutiful, complaints doled out for the untidy or overly chatty lead to writing out code of conduct.

Had been very slight relaxation in discipline, now checked, thought one pupil (like peers, a charming lunchtime host) and all to the corporate benefit. 'Wasn't working so well before – now good for the school but bad for the individual.'

Minor transgressors write out school code of conduct; serial offenders lose 'privs' for a week, part of plentiful school jargon that includes 'going across' – signals need for comfort break rather than deepening interest in spiritualism – 'grub' (sweets) – and 'lemonade', a generic term covering hot chocolate, juice and even cake.

Parents universally thrilled by restricted presence of i-anythings out of lessons, and tactical use within. Rather than mass breaktime retreat into solitary cyber universe, pupils here whizz energetically about in real time with friends. 'Really important because children become so addicted to these games that they don't interact with their peers,' said relieved mother.

Plenty for them to enjoy, from lovingly tended plots with courgette flowers and tomatoes to three Gloucester Old Spots, sensibly not named, bees ditto – though for logistical rather than emotional reasons. Other tucked away treats include shaded mini-adventure playground for first years and personable wood-paneled and about to be extended colonial-style chapel, consecrated 1880 after arriving in kit form (so many identical labradors on site that you start to wonder if assembled in similar way).

While academic success is all well and good (and often very well and very good), school also does best to find ubiquitous spark. Music a strength, with 80 boys learning at least one instrument, variety of ensembles to play them. Many cheering examples of mild reprobates transformed by gift for singing (there's a queue to join the choir, say parents).

But whichever formerly dark area of the curriculum light of budding talent might illuminate, helps to have at least nascent interest in sport. Not for everyone, one OB recently describing it as 'an acquired taste', but for most, it's a way of inculcating right values, particularly as school size ensures participation by all. 'Perfect because even the boys who are mediocre at sports all get to make the teams – nobody gets left out,' said parent. Year to year results vary considerably – inevitable consequence of small size. One cricket and rugby team had been undefeated all season; others with less enthusiastic cohort won't do half as well.

In addition to big three (football, rugby, cricket), tennis, Eton fives (since 1892), golf and swimming are all provided on site. Five pitches (four multi-use) appear to stretch away into far distance, courtesy of clever landscaping that makes the most of stand out planting, including massed rhododendrons (Mr Dawson has sole pruning rights over favourite). Provides effective masking of more functional buildings including vast sports hall (for basketball, fencing, air rifle shooting and much more) and gives 25-acre grounds feel of something much bigger.

Sport, inevitably, dominates the summer term after school activities list, replaced in winter by idiosyncratic range that currently includes Warhammer and fly-tying (teachers, all required to take at least one sport or activity, encouraged to indulge own enthusiasms). All adds to the fun, as do the 'endless' activities (now that's what we call organisation). Being on the go essential (particularly for new boys) in helping to acclimatise to full boarding lifestyle – weekly an option in the first two years, though 'half full board from the word go,' says school.

In addition to two long weekends (Friday to Monday evening), a couple of bonus Sundays and half term, there's much anticipated treat of year group excursions to school/family-owned house in France. Icing on the cake (almost literally) is first class food prepared by Mrs Dawson Snr. One boy 'asked why I can't cook like that,' said mother.

School points out that boarding for all hurts parents far more than the boys – 'always rather sad for the mother,' agreed one, 'but we just knew they'd be so happy.' Also ensures a full house at weekends for Saturday film nights (no lonely minority waiting for life to start again on Sunday evenings) when all but first years, who have own small scale version, pile into theatre with pillows and duvets.

All happens within or next to main building, dorms six to eight-bedders, comfortable rather than haut couture ('they're nice, cute, small, humble,' said parent), possessions neatly arranged, pinboards sometimes rather sparsely filled. Bathrooms and loos clean, fragrant and hygienic – bar single cracked tile surround in need of repair. Most pupils in top two years enjoy additional privacy of individual cubicles (new arrivals will start off in dorm). Buddies take settling in duties seriously – 'boys were all waiting and had his bed made,' said parent, leaving son for taster weekend.

For the very youngest there are separate quarters with common room (reassuringly compact) and playroom (ditto – Hide and Seek games a non-starter) and own live-in matron, one of five, three full time, notable for reassuring names (Miss Turnball and Miss Foynes – yet another detective team, surely?) and a guaranteed presence on the touchline at matches.

Education here is all about bestowing resilience, self-awareness, realism and courage (fairy godmothers might blench). 'Finally and most importantly, pupils must learn to love life…' says website. If they don't while they're here, won't be for want of trying.

Parents are in no doubt they succeed. 'We put our trust in Mr Dawson,' says mother. 'We've been so incredibly impressed with the results.'

Tudor Hall School

(59)

Wykham Park, Banbury, Oxfordshire OX16 9UR

01295 263434
admissions@tudorhallschool.com
www.tudorhallschool.com

Ages: 11–18
Pupils: 334; sixth form: 85
Boarders: 256 full
Day: £19,845 pa
Boarding: £31,110 pa

Headmistress: Since 2004, Miss Wendy Griffiths, BSc PGCE (50s). Educated at Queen Elizabeth Grammar School, Carmarthen, read zoology at University of Wales – still a trace of her Welsh accent. Previously head of sixth form at Tormead School, then director of studies at St Catherine's, Bramley.

Before our meeting we'd already been entertained by the sight of Miss Griffiths dancing and lip synching to Chic's 'We are family' in a film made by the girls of Todd (year 7 house). There aren't many heads we can call to mind who would even consider doing this, let alone be able to pull it off with such groovy aplomb. The video was playing on a wall-mounted screen, somewhat at odds with the restrained décor of the entrance hall. It's also on the school website, along with others – they like making films at Tudor Hall.

As a student she had plans to become a doctor, but while teaching in a Portsmouth comprehensive Miss Griffiths had an epiphany. After seeing how excited her class became during an 'ambitious' practical lesson she succumbed to pedagogy and has never looked back.

With her sleek bob and leather skirt, Miss G is poised and highly professional (albeit with a twinkle). She was described to us as someone who 'never slows down', which may account for the fact that in addition to the responsibilities of headship she is also just coming to the end of a stint as chair of the Boarding Schools Association in its 50th anniversary year. What about boarding schools then, we asked, are they still necessary? 'Almost more than ever', was the not unexpected reply. A boarding school is able to inculcate so much more than narrow academics: 'instead of sitting at home glued to social media, at boarding school children have to be be social, they learn how to get on with everyone'.

Miss Griffiths still interviews prospective pupils and teaches a GCSE biology class – that's four lessons a week, very unusual for a senior school head. She lives on site with her husband, who teaches history at Sibford School; they have one daughter. Spare time, should there be such a thing, is for dog walking – plenty of Cotswolds on the doorstep for that

To conclude, here's a little list of the the words parents used to describe Miss Griffiths: 'Outstanding', 'astonishing', 'highly professional', 'diplomatic', 'inspiring' and (we heard this one repeatedly), 'a great role model'. 'She just gets it', said one.

Academic matters: Gradual upward trajectory of academic results is testament to small classes (average 15), plenty of individual attention and by all accounts, dedicated and inspirational teaching. In 2015, 69 per cent A*/A at GCSE and 83 per cent A*-B at A level (42 per cent A*/A). Top performers at A level are geography, economics and maths. That maths is one of the most popular A levels speaks volumes for the teaching – head told us with regret how girls continue to arrive from prep schools saying they 'can't do' it.

No sense that sixth formers are all expected to board the non-stop university express – one told us how much support she'd had for her decision to go into interior design

Innovative work to inspire girls to stay engaged not just with maths but also science subjects. Super new labs for exploding jelly babies as well as more serious experiments. We saw girls in smart red lab coats investigating their own cheek cells under the microscope. Lively programme of extracurricular science clubs, visits to science fairs and National Space Centre etc.

We shared a delicious lunch with girls who had very different and exciting plans for their future – lots of gap years followed by courses from criminology to drama. No sense that sixth formers are all expected to board the non-stop university express

487

– one told us how much support she'd had for her decision to go straight into interior design rather than take a degree in the subject.

Visiting speakers widen horizons as does head's initiative, 'Tudor in three continents', which includes travel scholarships for girls to participate in projects in India, Bolivia and South Africa; has recently become 'Tudor in four continents'. School has added a project that doesn't involve epic amounts of air travel: mentoring children at the Bolton Lads and Girls (sic) Club. Meeting less fortunate children in their own country, rather than thousands of miles away, has been a very profound experience.

Parents told us staff keep an eagle eye on each girl's progress and are quick to intervene if she appears to be lagging. 'Teachers work so hard to get the right results; if there's a problem they really drill down to find the root cause'. Girls love the fact that teachers are so accessible: 'there's always a subject teacher who can help if you're stuck on homework or revision'. What parents love is the individual attention given to their daughters' academic progress; all those we spoke to said they were confident no child would be allowed to struggle or fall behind.

SEN or EAL support provided individually or in classes but head says this is not the place for a girl with serious needs; 'we want all pupils to be able to participate fully in the curriculum'. Dynamic learning support team uses variety of approaches including latest educational technology such as iPad apps.

Games, options, the arts: School has put considerable efforts into improving sports provision and parents say that it's much better. Facilities are all present and correct including glass roofed outdoor

Perhaps he would have penned something a little jollier if he had visited a few years later when the Tudor Hall girls were in residence

swimming pool (not used in the winter) and plenty of pitches. Girls told us that a 'bigger gym' and a 'pavilion on the top pitch' would be great. Larger schools' A teams are likely to have the advantage so notable and sustained recent successes at county level in hockey and cross country are all the more creditable. Individual talents in tennis (lovely courts in former walled garden), skiing and riding are well supported and a wider range of non-competitive options such as swim fit and zumba are offered in the sixth form. Girls also work with Carrdus School (Oxfordshire prep owned by Tudor Hall) and local primary schools to provide pupils with coaching and taster sessions in eg lacrosse.

Drama is offered at GCSE and A level but TH girls love to perform, whether or not they are pursing it as a subject option. Great results in LAMDA speech and drama exams too. Regular participation in Shakespeare Schools' Festival, plenty of theatre trips and a choice of stages – new (2015) studio theatre has eye-catching neon sign. Dance is accorded greater status here than at other schools and can be taken as a GCSE. Reaction, the audition only school dance group, has been going for over 20 years; the house dance title is as keenly fought as house singing and drama competitions. Music, too, offers girls of all abilities the chance to perform – whether at school concerts, carol singing at care homes or carrying off trophies at Banbury Young Musician of the Year competitions.

The quality of the art, both in the studios and (perhaps a little infrequently) displayed throughout the school, fair took our breath away. Quite the best we can remember seeing anywhere. Likewise textiles and photography. Style and subject matter went from traditional to unexpectedly edgy and challenging. The textile and art rooms stay open into the evening and at weekends and girls love the freedom this gives them to work on their projects outside lessons. Textiles currently housed in Portakabin but purpose built studios are in the offing. Leavers regularly go on to art foundation and fashion design courses.

Extracurricular options encompass just about everything from Model United Nations to the very popular dissection club. It seems not only can a Tudor Hall girl address a crowd and whip up a soufflé (if she's done the Leith's course), she can also eviscerate a frog. Parents approve of the way girls are kept very busy lower down the school, gradually developing independent study skills as they approach the relative freedom of the sixth form.

Boarding: The full Monty – two exeats per term and no flexi or weekly. Saturday school with lessons until 1pm and games in the afternoon, trips, activities and down time thereafter. Boarding is arranged horizontally – ie by year group – meaning that everything (activities, bed times etc) can be tailored to the age group. Works especially well at exam times – much easier if everyone around you is revising.

Year 7 boarders and day girls are based in Todd (named after the school's founders), a charming house with a large peaceful garden on the edge of the school grounds. It's as uninstitutional as possible with a large family kitchen, colourful soft furnishings and lots of toys and games. And, when we visited, a body on the sitting room floor. 'Just step over it, we're doing first aid,' the housemistress told us. Todd girls love putting on plays and concerts for their captive audience, they also enjoy 'special breakfasts', baking and Sunday excursions (day girls can go too). Todd girls have lower sixth buddies, described to us as a 'big sister support system'.

Dorms vary from two to six cabin beds; bathrooms are clean but on the functional side. Apparently they're 'due for a refurb'. Personal technology at this end of the school limited to mobile phones for 10 minutes a day. Skype etc always available, 'we never stop a child speaking to their parents'. Glad to hear it. Housemistress has set up a Facebook page for Todd parents who get daily photos and updates on their girls' activities.

Other houses (known as The 11s, The 111s and so on) are spacious and well equipped. Girls need no encouragement to personalise their space; walls were papered with photos, letters, bunting and many, many rosettes – plenty of keen horsewomen here.

Each boarding house has its own character and traditions so there's a real sense of progression through the school. Sixth form accommodation is designed as a halfway house to prepare girls for living independently. They can cook, are responsible for their own laundry and organise trips and activities. One such is the Christmas shopping trip to Paris (plus Disneyland Paris); no shortage of teachers signing up to chaperone that one, we imagine.

Background and atmosphere: One of the oldest girls' boarding schools in England, Tudor Hall was founded in 1850 by Rev T W Todd and his wife. In 1908 the school moved from London to rural Kent and on the outbreak of the Second World War it decamped to Burnt Norton, a small Cotswold manor house, to escape the air raids. Pupils, teachers and parents stayed here, even during the

holidays, and old girls remember those times with great affection. It was a visit to the gardens at Burnt Norton that inspired T S Eliot to write his eponymous poem, a meditation on time, memory and original sin. Perhaps he would have penned something a little jollier than 'Garlic and sapphires in the mud clot the bedded axle-tree' if he'd visited a few years later when the Tudor Hall girls were in residence.

Surrounding area predominantly rural – grazing cows more common than passing traffic – but access to Oxford, London, Stratford etc pretty easy. Nearest town is Banbury. A great summer treat for the older girls is, we were told, to walk to the nearby farm shop, buy a picnic and eat it in a field. Wouldn't suit a committed urbanite, but that's not really the demographic which is, we suspect, one that is accustomed to town and country living and has the right shoes for both.

It seems not only can a Tudor Hall girl address a crowd and whip up a soufflé (if she's done the Leith's course), she can also eviscerate a frog

First time visitors may be surprised to find no busy reception desk; the entrance hall, with its bergere furniture, beautiful flowers and polished wood, is rather reminiscent of an exclusive hotel – but the welcome is warm and personal. Usual mix of buildings – not everywhere is country house gracious – but all well tended. School magazine and publicity material are similar – high production values but nothing boasty or brash. Come to think of it, that probably sums up the Tudor Hall pupil.

Pastoral care, well-being and discipline: Tudor Hall has long had a reputation for the highest standards of pastoral care, but don't confuse caring with soft. Yes, it's a nurturing environment, as all the best small schools are, but within that environment girls are encouraged and tested; challenged to overreach their own boundaries and try new things.

All the parents we spoke to felt that their daughters were in the safest of hands and cited many examples of occasions when tutors or other members of staff had gone above and beyond to help or advise them. Day and boarding parents get a weekly update from tutors about what's been going on and home school communication in general receives nothing but praise.

A couple of people we spoke to thought the downside of year group boarding was that it contributed to a somewhat stratified hierarchical atmosphere, but we didn't feel this was the case. Vertical house system, not to mention the mix of different clubs and sporting activities, must go a long way to defuse this.

Day girls are very well integrated and can join their boarding friends for trips and weekend activities, but it's a long day and, with Saturday school, a long week. Even year 7 day pupils don't finish until 6.45pm or later, although they will have had an hour or so's break, a snack and done their homework.

Regular socials with chaps from Radley, Eton and Harrow. The young gentlemen from Harrow are current favourites, but apparently this changes from year to year.

What do you gain from boarding, we asked a group of sixth formers? They all cited strong and lasting friendships; others valued the 'accessibility' of teaching staff and the fact that there's always someone around to help with academic work. 'It helps you become responsible and independent – and it stops you taking home for granted.' We like that last one but doubt it survives the summer holidays.

Pupils and parents: Most recent ISI report described Tudor Hall pupils as 'overwhelmingly positive in outlook' which sounds rather alarming – a posse of Pollyannas, perhaps. It would be so easy to fall back on the old stereotype of Tudor Hall girls as darling daughters of the home counties, what with Leith's, polo, doing the ski season, etc – but that wouldn't be fair or accurate.

The girls we met were friendly, thoughtful, comfortable in their own skins and definitely not the identikit result of an educational production line. There's no arrogance or sense of entitlement and definitely no hair flicking. Girls know they are fortunate and are very aware that the world beyond Banbury is considerably less shiny; it certainly won't be any the worse for having Tudor Hall alumnae in it.

Pride in one's school is not usually compatible with the teenage psyche, but Tudor Hall girls aren't too cool for that. Lots of daughters of old girls – always a good sign. Other old Tudorians include Katherine Hooker, tailor to Duchess of Cambridge; Cleo Barbour, shoe designer; Julia Peyton-Jones, director of Serpentine Gallery.

Entrance: Candidates for 11+ and 13+ invited for 'taster day' (or day and night for prospective 11+ boarders) and assessment days with tests in maths, English and verbal reasoning. The tests are to 'ensure girls are compatible with academic pace' of school. Girls applying for entry at 13+ offered conditional places dependent on outcome of CE. All candidates are interviewed by the head who told us she is looking for 'character.' She believes that girls who are 'sparky about something' succeed because the school can channel their enthusiasm into other areas.

Exit: Art foundation seems to be most popular post A level choice and Oxford Brookes attracts quite a few. Bristol, Edinburgh, Newcastle and Exeter are current Russell Group favourites. Occasional one or two to Oxbridge (none in 2015).

Money matters: Fees at the slightly less eye watering end of the boarding range; day fees look like good value considering time spent in school. Academic, music, art, drama and sport scholarships (up to £1,000 pa) available at 11+, 13+ and 16+. Also textiles and dance at 16+. Means-tested bursaries to support new and current parents in financial need.

Remarks: Leave your preconceptions at the door and prepare to be bowled over. Whether your daughter is headed for fashion design or Oxbridge, under Miss Griffiths' dynamic stewardship Tudor Hall deserves a place on everyone's short list.

Twyford School

High Street, Winchester, Hampshire SO21 1NW

01962 712269
registrar@twyfordschool.com
www.twyfordschool.com
C of E

Ages: 3–13 (boarding from 9)
Pupils: 482
Boarders: 116 weekly/flexi
Day: £10,170 – £18,117 pa
Boarding: £22,800 pa

Head: Since 2010, Dr Steve Bailey BEd PhD FRSA; educated at Kent College, Canterbury, Southampton University and St Paul's College of Education (50s). Born and raised bilingually in Hong Kong before

teaching history (all levels) at Winchester College for 30 years; housemaster for the last 12. A Fellow of the Royal Society for the Arts, Research Fellow of the International Olympic Committee, author

of six books and with an international reputation as an historian of sport and the Olympic Games, it's no surprise that he has shaken things up a bit at Twyford.

Dr Bailey began by curtailing lessons to 45 minutes and encouraged teachers to deliver lessons beyond 'narrow' CE requirements. Regularly observes teaching and makes no secret of his ambition for more creativity in the classroom; is keen to avoid 'death by worksheet.' Banished formal exams in the first two years of prep school and introduced extension lessons, known as Apprenticeships, in the timetable. 'Children are capable of far more than we sometimes offer.' Intellectual and erudite, is also a keen sportsman. Played hockey at county and regional levels and enjoys tennis, water polo and surfing. Wife Paula MSc (health psychology) has taught ICT as well as tutoring children with specific learning difficulties. They have three children, all in full-time education.

Entrance: Main entry points are nursery and year 3, although places are occasionally available in other years. Nursery places allocated according to date of registration; siblings have priority on waiting lists at other times. Short half-day assessment in November for those joining prep school the following academic year, which school says is 'not a rigorous hurdle.' Most pupils live within 30 mile radius, some weekly boarders further afield. Numbers have risen by 30 since Dr Bailey's arrival.

Exit: Nearly one third of boys leave for Winchester College, a steady few with music and academic awards. Other boys and girls scatter far and wide, but most popular destinations are Bradfield, Bryanston, Canford, Charterhouse, Cheltenham Ladies', Downe House, Eton, Godolphin, King Edward VI, Marlborough, St Swithun's, and Sherborne boys' and girls' Schools. Tally of scholarships is on the up under Dr Bailey's stewardship; boys and girls gain a more diverse range of awards including academic, music, sport, all-rounder, art and DT scholarships and exhibitions.

Remarks: Main school building, a beautiful Queen Anne house, is set in over six acres of playing fields and surrounded by the South Downs. Moved to its present location in 1809 from premises in nearby Twyford and can probably trace its origins back to the mid-17th century. (A Latin grammar book has turned up bearing the inscription 'Twyford School, 1775'.) Boarders still live in original house, which has a pretty Victorian chapel, oak-panelled library, atmospheric old school hall and large modernised refectory. Teaching takes place in a collection of modern buildings dotted around quadrangles.

Lots of hard work going on for CE when we visited; most pupils aim to sit level 3 in subjects across the board (some level 2 if appropriate). 'Dr Bailey has increased the aims and aspirations of the children.' Maths set from year 4 and all subjects by year 6. French from reception, Latin from year 5 and study skills as a separate subject from year 7, otherwise all subjects taught as usual. 'Learning qualities programme' encourages children to think more independently and take responsibility for their own learning (praised in latest ISI school

491

inspection). Classrooms are modern, bright and spacious; science labs are immaculate (including snakes!). Class sizes average 16-18. Children are divided up into three sets in the last two years, depending on their 'next school'. Boys aiming for Winchester and all other scholarship candidates join 'W set' in year 7, the rest are divided into two common entrance sets. ICT provision is well planned, with fixed terminals for younger ones and laptops for year 5. Year 6 up have tablets to enable independent research in geography, history and science lessons. Five SEN specialists help with (mild) learning difficulties and around 70 one-to-one sessions (including pre-prep) were timetabled when we visited. These are free, but school doesn't take children who need more than one session a week.

Traditional prep school sports for boys and girls, with matches on Wednesday and Saturday afternoons. First and second teams have an excellent sporting record in fixtures against other schools. Parents tell us that school 'is starting to address girls' sport' by drawing up C and D teams and organising more fixtures, but even so 'not everyone gets on a team.' Pupils also compete in swimming, water polo, athletics, tennis, lacrosse and girls' tag rugby. School is a 'centre of excellence' for girls' cricket in Hampshire. Large gym and indoor 25m swimming pool sit side-by-side, with 25m traversing wall outside. Has several all-weather courts for tennis and netball, plus Astroturf for hockey and football. 'Sports day is fabulous.' Netball teams have had success at regional IAPS tournaments and individual footballers at national schools' level. Other pupils perform at county level in cricket, cross-country running, hockey, rugby and swimming. 'Court Cricket', invented at Twyford and played here for at least a century, is still in robust health at break times.

Outstanding art and DT departments, probably the best we've seen for quality of work. Small, permanent gallery at the side of two storey art block displays pupils' work throughout the year; standard of painting and ceramics is excellent. 'Artist in residence' paints school scenes on site so children can observe brushwork – no surprise that number of art scholars is on the rise. DT is also very good with some really imaginative work (high level of design) on show, eg insect 'hotel'.

Regularly observes teaching and makes no secret of his ambition for more creativity in the classroom; is keen to avoid 'death by worksheet'. Introduced extension lessons

Music block sits in unusual amphitheatre setting overlooking tennis courts. Bright, airy performance space upstairs with several practice rooms on lower floor; more pianos are dotted around elsewhere in the school. More than 80 per cent of children learn at least one instrument, including the less usual, eg harp, drums and bagpipes. Lessons are fixed for older children and rotate for younger ones. School is a centre for ABRSM and Trinity College music exams and many pupils pass these at higher grades. Three school choirs, including a show choir, school orchestra and various ensembles give occasional concerts. Drama is improving, with a weekly lesson for all taught by specialist teachers and more performance space in Mulberry Pavilion, but 'dramatic aspirations could be higher ... we need a whole-school musical once a year.' Dance (ballet, modern and tap) is on offer as a lunch time club. Regular Shakespeare workshop for year 8 takes place after CE.

'Apprenticeships' (Saturday activities) are compulsory for all children from year 4. Activities become increasingly academic further up the school, and include ancient Greek, Arabic, critical thinking, debating, fencing, Mandarin, music theory, philosophy and photography. Everyone chooses a different apprenticeship each term, although 'quite often children don't get their first choice.' Staff run weekday clubs after school, eg art, cookery, judo, water polo and yoga. Outdoor education programme, eg navigation, orienteering, shelter building and survival techniques, 'encourages children to solve practical and physical problems.' One residential course away for each year group every year; in school there is a tree house complex with outdoor classroom and advanced adventure playground.

No longer offers full boarding, but can arrange for long-distance boarders to stay with local guardians on Saturday and Sunday nights (currently, there are seven weekly boarders). Otherwise, most children board a few nights per week (68 stay one night a week, 38 for two nights and just three for three nights) from year 6 in preparation for going away to senior school and around 20 from Monday to Friday. Dorms for younger children; cosy two-man (or girl) cubicles for year 8s allow more privacy and the chance to room with a friend. We noted clean, well-appointed bathrooms, a comfortable common room and plenty of storage space for belongings. Boarders have limited use of mobile phones (matron keeps phones at all other times). Parents full of praise for boarding houseparent, also head of sport.

Excellent meals are served cafeteria-style and atmosphere is informal; children can sit where they like (we didn't notice staff on each table). Perhaps (enviably) this isn't needed, as school works hard to instill a broad set of values in its pupils. Regular services in chapel throughout the term are reinforced by anti-bullying PSHE lessons and constant vigilance by boarding and teaching staff (often around in the evenings running clubs or supervising prep). Everyone belongs to one of four houses and is assigned a house tutor from year 6. End-of-term Team Feast for house with the highest house point scores; individual high scorers are 'sent up good' on Fridays for lemon sherbet from the head (a Twyford tradition). Still has a friendly atmosphere, although parents say times are now more formal. Nevertheless they add, 'It still feels like you're part of a big family and [that] requires family involvement.'

Pre-prep going from strength to strength with over 120 on the register when we visited. 'The nursery is outstanding.' Two classes in reception and year 1 grow to three in year 2, which

has been rehomed from Portakabins to a permanent building – windows at child height is a nice touch. Children grouped for phonics and spelling ability; reading is taught both individually and in groups. French and music learned from an early age. Homework is limited to spelling, reading and topic work, eg Knights and Castles. 'It's a really full-on day.' Has small SEN room and ICT suite. Lots of outdoor play; children spend an entire afternoon outside every three weeks and have access to forest lodge in small woodland area. All attend chapel services and use the pool and library. Puts on annual show for 'grandparents' week', where little ones can show off their music, ballet and ESB exam preparation. Clubs include gardening, hand bells, ukulele and recorder ensemble. Most go on to join prep school in year 3, causing prep school numbers to rise. Universal feeling from parents is that school is at capacity; would like to see new pupil numbers capped.

A relatively wide mix of families, but it's safe to assume that most are comfortably off. Two 100 per cent bursaries (means tested) for new children joining as weekly boarders in year 7; sibling discounts are limited to five per cent for third and subsequent children. Boys and girls are polite, confident and increasingly aspire to top schools. Old Twyfordians include Alexander Pope, Douglas Hurd, Hubert Parry, Mark Tully, Thomas Hughes and, more recently, The Apprentice winner Tom Pellereau. Very active Twyford Society keeps ex-pupils in touch.

Although well into the process of changing from 'a slightly scruffy, not very ambitious place' to one with a much greater focus on academic success, Twyford is still a friendly school where parents enjoy being part of the 'family'. Will continue to send a good number of boys to Winchester College, but is clearly aiming just as high for girls and boys going on to other schools.

Walhampton School

Walhampton, Lymington, Hampshire SO41 5ZG

01590 613300
registrar@walhampton.com
www.walhampton.com
C of E

Ages: 2–13 (boarders from 7)
Pupils: 430
Boarders: 30 full, 30 flexi
Day: £8,295 – £16,095 pa
Boarding: plus £5,535 pa

Headmaster: Since 2012, Mr Titus Mills (Eton, University of East Anglia and Oxford). Has taught across the spectrum, latterly as head of The Paragon, an independent school in Bath, and prior

to that as head of St George's International Junior school in Rome and deputy head of St Mark's C of E school in Lambeth. Named Titus after the family donkey. The kids from St Mark's sang 'Oh Happy

Day' at his wedding to Jemima, who is involved in many aspects of school life, from meeting parents to arts and crafts. They have three young sons at the school.

Head is charming, his ease of manner no doubt stemming from his Eton roots; he is also warm, penetrating, and very enthusiastic. Mr Mills relishes a challenge: he has turned around schools in the past, and has a remit to do something similar for Walhampton. Not that it was failing, but he is there to make it fly – 'he's brimming with positivity,' said a parent.

Since taking up his post, head has swept through the school like a brisk wind, removing all dusty elements and making significant changes to staff, uniform, even the school emblem (the sticking out tongue has been lopped off the stag). There was 'lots of debris,' commented a parent. Another enthusiastic parent said that the head works 'at the speed of light' and will respond to an email request within half an hour with an action plan. Happy constituents indeed.

Entrance: Non selective. Tests for placing purposes.

Exit: To more than 20 senior schools. Clayesmore and Canford most popular, followed by Winchester, Marlborough, Radley, Ballard and Bryanston.

Remarks: Walhampton is exceptionally lovely, with glorious buildings and grounds. But there's something more than that: a feeling that your favourite childhood fiction might come to life in this place. The prospectus dust jacket (no, we've never seen a dust jacket on one before either) is just like the map in the front of Swallows and Amazons – there's Portmere pond for sailing, Sandwalk pond for fishing; even a Curly Wurly mountain. For Enid Blyton lovers there's the Faraway tree and a Wishing Seat. Beehives sit in a wildflower meadow and there are stables, camps and bluebell woods.

Thoughtfully arranged library – books reserved for years 7 and 8 on one side, so the librarian can see if a crafty year 3 nips across to pick a book that is not age appropriate, although 'We don't really do [books full of teenage] angst here.' Library sessions each week, but library evidently used at all times: a jigsaw is always on the go – a child stressed out by a lesson calms down after five minutes with a jigsaw, the librarian told us.

Learning comes alive here: the Battle of Trafalgar takes place on one of the ponds, and ditches are currently doubling as trenches for WW2 enactments

This place's stately past is not completely diluted by its school present. Standing on the terrace during break, watching the children at play, it is extraordinary to think this is a school and not a home. The family feel is underscored by the fact that many teachers live on site with their families.

Children are a lively, happy bunch and properly young: they all play at break time, including the enormous 13 year old boys, who looked as though they should already be at a senior school, but raced around, twisting each other on a tree swing. There are the usual number of screens here, but children are equally likely to enthuse about an outside activity – riding, flags or the tremendously popular 'escape from Colditz': children have to escape

from an area of the grounds, in the dark, and get up to the headmaster's study and ring the bell. Staff, equipped with miner's lamps as headgear, try to spot and stop them. 'Wet, windy and wild,' says the school mag, The Mercury. This is a school where they are not afraid to get dirty; or take risks.

Manners well to the fore: children leapt to their feet as we went around and held open doors, one small child moved out of our way, saying decidedly 'good evening,' (just after lunch). With much fanfare, Mr Mills introduced new comprehensible school rules and a merits/sanctions so kids understand what they've done right and wrong. Beach huts in house colours collect stag tokens, handed out for behaviour, effort and achievement – very popular with kids who love posting their tokens. Each half term the school, pupils and teachers alike, aims to develop a particular learning characteristic – perseverance at the time of our visit: clearly taken very much to heart by the children, and the determined cross-country runner who came in last, but persevered to the end.

Children feel that their views are listened to: school council got the water fountains it requested and also managed to secure something more yummy than banana chips at break. Food much improved since regime chance – it was certainly delicious on the day of our visit.

Head's main focus has been on increasing academic standards, and for the first time in the school's history two boys were awarded academic scholarships to Winchester recently. Subjects are traditional (Latin is compulsory), but learning comes alive here: the Battle of Trafalgar takes place on one of the ponds, and ditches are currently doubling as trenches for WW2 enactments. History, understandably, is a tremendously popular subject. The head is keen to take learning outside as much as possible and as a result this was one of the most deserted schools we have ever toured. 'Mud is part of the curriculum,' said one member of staff. Class sizes range from 15-20.

In the pre-prep the little ones have wet weather red dungarees, coats and wellies and recently enjoyed operations in a mud kitchen with wok and watering can. Ella and Daisy, the pre-prep hens, potter around happily. There's a new outside area, Owl corner, with bushes to hide in, a wooden stag to climb on, and a rope to pull yourself up a steep slope.

Learning support provided across the spectrum. Although most fit mild to moderate categories, there are a few children here with severe dyslexia. Whether or not children with severe learning difficulties are accepted depends partly on assessment and the balance of children in that year. Support charged as an extra, but 'not expensive,' said a parent. LSU provides 'exceptional support,' said parent of a child with dyslexia. 'No stigma,' and kids likely to help each other with difficulties.

Mixed age tutor groups for years 6 to 8. Pupils have some say in which tutor group they wish to be in and good relationships develop across the age groups, with pupils often helping each other out with academic or other difficulties.

Pupils know who to go to with problems and bullying is dealt with promptly. Parents feel that pastoral care here is very strong. 'The time and energy which goes into each child is remarkable,' said one. Most parents attend chapel on Friday nights – 'a lovely way to round off the week.' Kids say what they want to pray for – there's usually a rabbit or a finger shut in a car door (although the school is 'not deeply religious,' the mum added).

Head of sports sees those who claim they don't enjoy sport as a challenge and does his best to find an activity that a child will take to, archery or golf for instance. Great to see the girls learning rugby. Good sports hall and Astroturf, and funding for two new netball courts. Six Oppies (sailing boats to the rest of us) recently purchased. Riding is extremely popular and many boys ride although they tend to prefer games – anyone for buzkashi? (a Mongolian game played with the stuffed hide of a goat). Even if it's not your turn to ride, you can always go down to the stable and fling your arms around a pony.

Well-equipped music rooms and over half of pupils learn an instrument. Pop bands – The Stags and The Does – as well as a selection of choirs and orchestra. Joseph was in its final rehearsals, and sounded good – a hefty show for a prep school.

There are around 30 full boarders, with numbers increasing to 60 during the week with lots of flexi boarding arrangements, the latter very popular with busy parents. For those who suddenly find themselves stuck in a late meeting, emergency boarding is a bargain at £35 a night. The Walhampton express runs weekly from London down to the school, one of the house parents travelling backwards and forwards to escort weekly boarders. Accommodation has been renovated and redecoration has been sensitive, younger girls having pink and frills, the older girls a more restrained version. Things are kept very neat – posters are carefully framed – no bluetac and tatty edges. Nice little kitchens with cereals for any time (Dorset muesli included, naturally), and tempting hampers of healthy snacks. All kids come into school on Saturday for activities and boarders have special trips out on Sundays.

Parents are well heeled, lots of professionals and business people. Apparently it used to be a school where grandparents paid the fees but this is no longer the case. Most pupils are from the surrounding area, including the Isle of Wight, but some also from London and overseas. Academic scholarships awarded to internal or external applicants from year 2 upward; sports scholarships of up to half fees from year 3 upwards aimed at those talented in a range of sporting disciplines who would not otherwise be able to afford to come to Walhampton.

Wellington College

Duke's Ride, Crowthorne, Berkshire RG45 7PU

01344 444013
admissions@wellingtoncollege.org.uk
www.wellingtoncollege.org.uk
C of E

Ages: 13–18
Pupils: 1,045; sixth form: 470
Boarders:835 full
Day: £26,130 – £30,030 pa
Boarding: £35,775 pa

Linked school: Eagle House

Master: Since September 2015, Julian Thomas (40s), previously head of Caterham School. Degree in computer science from King's College London and MBA in educational leadership (international). Taught maths at Forest School and St Dunstan's College, co-authoring several maths text books. Then director of studies at Portsmouth Grammar and second master at Hampton before joining Caterham. He was a junior county cricketer, won a rugby league half-blue while completing his PGCE at Cambridge and has climbed Mont Blanc and Gran Paradiso, as well as trekking the Chemin de la Liberté across the

Pyrenees, which commemorates one of the WW2 escape routes into northern Spain. He is married to Julia and they have two sons.

Academic matters: Has leapt from genteel backwater to heavyweight. Seventy-two per cent of A level results were A*/A in 2015, 93 per cent A*-B. Maths the most popular A level with biology not far behind. Almost a third of pupils now opting for IB diploma instead of A levels, with an impressive average point score of 39 in 2015. Some overlap between the two programmes: unusually, the IB's Theory of Knowledge is taught to both. The impact of selection is unmistakable in GCSE results: 89 per cent were at A*/A in 2015. Boutique offerings include textiles, either via art or DT departments, and music technology (rarely offered as a GCSE). A lot of attention is given to languages in the impressive Modern Languages Institute (swish languages block). It is here that one of the school's signature offerings – Mandarin – is taught, along with the usual range of languages.. and Hebrew! New Mandarin Centre now open – the country's first. Many do Greek, most Latin too. All sixth formers attend a series of lectures on astronomy, history of art and philosophy. 'Well-being' taught in years 10 and 11 – much rolling of eyes among the children on this one, but parents think it will serve them in years to come.

'The Eight Aptitudes' philosophy stands as the cornerstone of the school's 21st century reinvention – a reworking of Howard Gardner's theory of multiple intelligences. Staff encouraged to think across the aptitudes in order to develop the whole child. Hour long lessons; children kept busy. Their only real gripe to us was that they had too little time for lunch – a tiger parent's dream! 'Not a place to come if you don't have aspirations,' warned a parent, 'though the selection process helps to weed out those who don't tend to work.' 'You're in a bit of hot water if your effort grades slip', said another, 'but there's a good tutoring system to help bring you back up.'

SEN provision not given the prominence it has at some similar schools (not mentioned in the school's prospectus) but around 90 pupils receive some learning support – department, and its head, commended by the children ('flamboyant' and 'enthusiastic'). The pupils' homespun advice was for children with learning needs to aim for one of the central boarding houses: 'they're very good if you're disorganised!'

Games, options, the arts: Sport 'diversifying away from rugby' – though all boys still start with a term of the game and the 1st VII won the National Schools 7s at Rosslyn Park recently after reaching the final for the fifth year in a row. Range of sports is vast, facilities impress eg two floodlit Astros, indoor and outdoor pool, dance studios, squash courts, shooting range, new sports pavilion.

Nine-hole golf course still lovely (one of the top 18 courses every golfer should play before they die according to Country Life). Polo, skiing, shooting and rackets have had notable success of late. Football now firmly on the fixtures list. Chess going strong – another sign of the school's volte face since the days of Jonty Driver. Games seen as a reservoir of moral, social and creative aptitudes, not just physical. Nice to see the mad tradition of the 'Field Gun Run' (once described as trying to achieve an almost impossible task in a ridiculously short time with too few men on an unsuitable track) still going strong alongside the yoga and tree-hugging. And for the first time ever in the history of the country, there are girls in the field gun team. Girls' teams moving up the inter-schools ladder; hockey and netball well embedded with some girls competing at county and national level. Unusually for a co-ed school, lacrosse is played.

> *Nice to see the mad tradition of the 'Field Gun Run' (once described as trying to achieve an almost impossible task in a ridiculously short time with too few men) still going*

Art fizzing, housed in two spacious and airy buildings. School hosts a summer arts festival, most recently featuring an exhibition of Matisse lithographs in the student café. Textiles and ceramics both a strength – the quality of the textiles eloquent testimony to the authenticity of co-education here. Inroads being made into film and animation and there is student TV company. Drama offerings rich and varied in the school's newly refurbished theatre. Dance a thriving GCSE and A level subject and soon to be offered as an IB option (popular outside the classroom as well). Music is becoming a major feature of the college – the a capella group are national champions and standards – particularly in the college orchestra and chapel choir – are high. An astonishing 40 pupils at grade 8 or beyond (scholars perform twice a year at St Martin-in-the-Fields), masterclasses, full range of ensembles including drum corp, jazz and two chapel choirs, weekly prize for the most diligent practiser. Impressive, student edited magazine; recent editions have featured interviews with Sebastian Faulks and Sir Michael Howard. A university style 'college carnival' at the start of each academic year allows clubs and societies to set out their wares. D of E. All fourth formers take part in CCF and some carry on throughout their time at school.

Boarding: The developments have resulted in 17 houses, each with 50-65 girls or boys, all of a good standard (in many houses only the youngest boarders share a room). Day pupils base themselves in one of the two day houses (the cheaper option) or are attached to a boarding house (an extra £1000 per term). Day pupils can leave at 6pm, though many stay much later.

Vast number live quite close, spending most Saturday nights at home. Edging towards de facto weekly boarding, though boarders are required to stay in school with their year group one or two Saturday nights per term, so never an empty boarding house.

Background and atmosphere: In 1852, when the Duke died, plans were in place to erect his statue in every town in England. Cooler heads prevailed and a school was reckoned to be a more fitting monument to Britain's most distinguished military leader. HM remains the school's official Visitor. So much has been written about the school, and all is in such fine fettle, that an arriving visitor feels as if he or she is entering the Emerald City wearing green-lensed spectacles. Immaculate, formal grounds reached via imposing avenue of oaks, Wellingtonias and Andean pines. Five lakes, endless lawns and abundant green space; three gardeners have been spotted simultaneously raking the gravel outside the Lodge. Beautiful chapel, tranches of memorials to the fallen now updated. With the opening of the £2.5m new e-learning centre, a temple to iPads, Kindles and educational apps, the five year building cycle coming to a pause.

Splendid V&A social centre – feels like a cross between a hotel lobby and a Starbucks – is a pupil meeting place serving vaguely health conscious snacks, sandwiches, smoothies, coffee. Parent run charity tuck shop dishes up the pure refined stuff. The school raises loads for charity, presumably not

all through the penny sweets priced, admirably, from 5p and up. A nice sideline in educational conferences – Wellington's are the best in the business.

Pastoral care, well-being and discipline: We're thrilled to bits to see the 'Basic Courtesies,' still published in school diaries – sets the high standard for behaviour (how many schools still have rules like, 'If you are wearing any kind of head-gear, you should raise it – or at least touch the brim – to all adults'? And, our favourite, 'In our culture, it is considered discourteous – and probably a sign of weak character – not to look directly into the eyes of the person who is talking to you'). Surprisingly fierce about drugs for such a caring, sharing place: one whiff and you're out. 'Other schools say it, but here the pupils know they mean it', said a mum. Many new, mainly youngish, houseparents, deeply beady eyed. Pupils can also be expelled for bullying, 'serious alcohol', theft, cheating or sex. Bullying carefully monitored via anonymous surveys which show that the school has fewer problems on this score than most, though it's never plain sailing. Facebook enabled on school filter 7-8am and 9-10pm. More than 60 Twitter accounts now operating out of the school.

The arriving visitor feels as if he or she is entering the Emerald City wearing green-lensed spectacles

Member of the Round Square since 1995 (international family of schools, associated in this country with Gordonstoun, Kurt Hahn and bracing fresh air and exercise). The organisation provides endless opportunities for fundraising for impoverished schools in the southern hemisphere and ready-made destinations for school trips. Recently hosted the organisation's final conference ('it's grown too big for us all to meet'). A service learning coordinator has recently been appointed to bring service into the heart of lessons via a 'connected curriculum'. Twenty minute chapel service once a week and a termly communion service on a Sunday evening; morality may be high on the agenda here, but this is not a churchy school. Girls wear rather shouty blue and lemon kilts in the lower years; all sixth formers in their own dark suits.

Pupils and parents: Some 15 per cent foreign – 32 nationalities (no ESL tuition; the school requires very good English for entry). Still some Forces children, though numbers dwindling, and now only 2-3 per cent are from British families overseas. OBs include Sir Harold Nicolson, Robert Morley, Sebastian Faulks, Rory Bremner, Peter Snow, Sir

Nicholas Grimshaw (architect of Eden Project), Christopher Lee, Pop Idol winner Will Young and 15 winners of the VC.

How many schools still have rules like, 'If you are wearing any kind of head-gear, you should raise it – or at least touch the brim – to all adults'?

Parents much involved at every turn. The school offers them outings, visiting speakers, concerts, happiness lessons, A level English and maths lessons, a book club – all reflecting the view that schools work best when families are involved. Has cemented what was already 'a strong and loyal community', a parent told us, with OWs also integral as visiting speakers and sources of work experience or first jobs. Most parents cited 'innovation' as a reason they had chosen Wellington, particularly for sixth form. In a bizarre twist of fate the most traditional of public schools now finds itself the 'alternative' school of choice – viewed by some parents as an academically supercharged version of Bedales.

Entrance: Three applicants for every place: 'We're inundated,' the registrar told us. For 13+, register by December 31 of year 6. Children then sit ISEB common pre-test around Easter time, either at their prep school or at Wellington; references requested from current school. Strongest 300 or so are invited to assessment days during the first term of year 7. These assessment days are based on Wellington's 'eight aptitudes' and getting to know the whole child, rather than narrow academic criteria. Those

offered places still required to sit CE (around 65 per cent mark). Late assessment in year 8 possible via Master's List – need recent school report and recommendation from current head. Main feeders: Broomwood Hall, Caldicott, Cheam, Crosfields, Danes Hill, Dragon, Eagle House (a mile away and owned by Wellington), Feltonfleet, Hall Grove, Highfield, Lambrook, Northcote Lodge, Papplewick, Shrewsbury House, St John's Beaumont, Thomas's schools, Twyford, Westbourne House and Yateley Manor. A handful join at 14+. Forty enter at sixth form: 'academic bar rising' – most candidates have straight A*/As at GCSE unless they are a star artist, musician or sportsperson.

Exit: Very few leave after GCSEs. Largest numbers to Exeter, Bristol, Edinburgh, Leeds and Durham. Twenty-four to Oxbridge in 2015. Many go on to art foundation and conservatoires. Up to 60 per cent to gap years. Others to US, Canadian, Australasian and European universities: 'Oxbridge is looking for ego-driven monsters,' a member of staff said dryly. 'Some very bright kids just don't fit the mould.'

Money matters: Scholarships for academics, sports, music, arts at 13+ and 16+. Scholarships do not carry fee remission in themselves but can be complemented by a means-tested bursary worth up to 95 per cent of the fees. Foundation awards (up to full fees) are available for children of members of the Forces, or other services eg the police, or for the children of civilians who 'have died in acts of selfless bravery'. Do pursue if you qualify and meet the school's academic requirements.

Remarks: Ignore the spin and the hype: this really is one of the most exciting and successful independent schools in the country.

Winchester College

College Street, Winchester, Hampshire SO23 9NA

01962 621247
admissions@wincoll.ac.uk
www.winchestercollege.org
C of E

Ages: 13–18
Pupils: 682; sixth form: 262
Boarders: all full
Boarding: £35,610 pa

Headman: Since 2005, Dr Ralph Townsend MA DPhil, an Australian with no trace of it in his voice (early 60s). Dr Townsend taught briefly at Dover College and Abingdon before proceeding to Oxford, where he was first a senior scholar at Keble then a junior research fellow, tutor and dean of

degrees at Lincoln, teaching theology. In 1985, he became head of English at Eton, leaving in 1989 to head Sydney Grammar School. Ten years later he returned to England to become head of Oundle – thus 16 years headmasterly experience before his arrival in Winchester. He is cerebral, direct, a bit intimidating, and the possessor of a very cool pair of circular tortoiseshell spectacles. Married to Cathy, a musicologist, who helps with visitors, staff and boys, and assists the music department during music scholarship awards and other periods of pandemonium. They have two adult children.

Intentionally avoids the media spotlight, oft frequented by the heads of similar schools. Mentioned 'league tables' with distaste. His commitment to the school's fundamental ethos, its unique traditions of scholarship and teaching through dialogue, is manifest and resolute. Described Winchester as the 'least conventional' of schools where the 'intellectual life' of pupils comes above all else. Some parents find him 'aloof', and certainly he has little to do with most boys' daily experience of the school which will be largely influenced by his housemaster and Div don.

Retiring in July 2016. His successor will be Dr Timothy Hands, currently master of Magdalen College School. A state school pupil turned down by Cambridge ('I was told by the careers adviser at my grammar school that I wouldn't get to university at all'), he read English at King's College, London, then went on to St Catherine's, Oxford, followed by Oriel, where he ended up as a lecturer. He became housemaster at King's Canterbury, then second master at Whitgift School, then head of Portsmouth Grammar. He comes from a long line of teachers, including both parents and an ancestor who was schoolmaster on HMS Victory. Likes sport and music – was co-leader of the London Schools Symphony Orchestra and conductor of the Oxford University chamber choir, Schola Cantorum. The author of several books about Victorian literature and teaches English A level.

Married to Jane, a solicitor; two sons.

Music very important, very strong and very classical. James Blunt and Genesis may have attended public schools, but they would not have been Wykehamists

Academic matters: Winchester offers Cambridge Pre-U examinations as a replacement for A levels in most subjects. The head takes a dim view of the latter, especially in modern languages which have been 'vandalised' ('you can now take an A level in French without reading a book!'). The Cambridge Pre-U has no coursework and opens up sixth form study as a serious two-year programme, studying three subjects in depth, with examinations at the end, much as A levels were before successive reforms of the last 25 years. Some mathematicians

It aims to instil a knowledge and understanding of British, European and world history and culture, and as such is a true, liberal education

take four (or even five) Pre-U exams, sitting maths at the end of the lower sixth and further maths the following year.

Results always outstanding (75 per cent D1-3 – A*/A equivalent – at pre-U in 2015), and the school continues to offer the shortest list of exam subjects of any reputable sixth form in England. Forget film studies and froth – here you will not find examined drama, classical civilisation, politics, business studies, PE or psychology. Chemistry and physics the most popular Pre-U subjects, followed robustly by history and English lit. Philosophy and theology on a roll at the minute. No great cornucopia of GCSE choices either: all boys sit IGCSEs in three sciences, maths, English, Latin, and any modern language so long as it's French, plus usually three other subjects which can include more languages. In 2015, 60 per cent A* grades at I/GCSE.

'Div' is the unique and highly-prized complementary programme at the heart of the Winchester ethos. It aims to instil a knowledge and understanding of British, European and world history and culture and, as such, is a true, liberal education. 'The boys and dons love it,' says Dr Townsend. 'It's the one bit of this over-structured world in which they can pursue their own intellectual interests.' It's a holistic approach that we expect to find in Montessori education and schools on the alternative end of the spectrum. 'It means the staff have to be of the highest calibre so that they can lead this cross-subject, cross-cultural tutorial,' a parent explained. Average age of teachers has come down significantly in recent years, and is now a youthful 38.

IT not cutting any edges, reflecting an institutional reserve about the digital world. Little, if any, work done on computers in a boy's first year (or two) here. Offers learning support for around 100 boys, mainly for mild dyslexia, dyspraxia and information processing. One boy registered blind, one deaf.

Games, options, the arts: The sport is 'brilliantly flexible', a parent told us. Enthusiasts can play as much as they want. 'My son went from the 4th team at his prep school to the A team here', chuckled one mum. 'There's a great spirit in the school sport', another told us, 'very unpressurised.' 'If you are determined to do no games, it's possible', concedes the head (refreshing, and probably unique, to hear this said in a British public school). But some sort of physical exercise ('ekker') is compulsory. Main sports are soccer, Winchester College football (read the rules) and cricket (huge here – the cricket coach also runs the Hampshire U16s) but these are supplemented by everything from aikido to water polo. Fabulous playing fields and sports facilities of all kinds. Recent national competition wins in rackets, fives, fencing and cross-country running.

Music very important, very strong and very classical. James Blunt, Genesis and Mumford and Sons may have attended public schools but they would not have been Wykehamists. Two-thirds of boys learn a musical instrument; many learn two or three, taught by a long list of specialist teachers. Pipe organ very strong here (one Winchester boy we know was making a tidy sum playing weddings while still in sixth form). Music school includes 50(!) practice rooms, a music tech classroom, recording studio and editing suite. Vast range of musical ensembles and performance opportunities – weekly Tuesday concert and many more throughout the year – many open to the public.

Art and drama lively and of quality, though they do not quite enjoy the accolade of music. CCF compulsory in year 10, after which it can be replaced with community service.

Boarding: All boys board. First year boys are generally in rooms of four. By IGCSEs they're in doubles. All sixth formers have single rooms, except the scholars. A boy's life here begins and ends with his house. Houses, while still more autonomous than at any other school in the UK, have been brought some distance into dreary conformity in this era of Health and Safety, school inspections and the like. There is now a lot more consistency of discipline, food (all meals are eaten in house) and day to day routine and less competition between houses (and housemasters). Current crop of housemasters praised by the parents we spoke to. Accommodation and food improving but still seen as of secondary importance, both to the school and to (British) parents.

Saturdays consist of lessons until lunch, then sport, then reading, then prep. Most boys go out after chapel on Sundays – younger boys to lunch at home, older ones into town. The school's inflexible attitude towards Sunday boarding is a source of contention for a few boys who have to pass up outside sports fixtures.

Background and atmosphere: Founded in the 14th century by William of Wykeham, Bishop of Winchester, Chancellor to Richard II, and the sage behind the school's motto: Manners makyth man. Began in 1387 with a Warden, 10 fellows, two schoolmasters three chaplains, 70 scholars and 16 quiristers – the Winchester version of choristers. The bishop also founded New College, Oxford,

with which the college maintains strong links. The quiristers are now educated down the road at the Pilgrims' School but continue to board at Winchester College and sing in chapel. So this is a quiet land of flinty walls, leafy quads, a venerable chapel, many other buildings of ancient date and visible history (the school was used as Cosette's Paris convent in the film version of Les Mis). Later foundations, eg Eton College, seem like modern upstarts by comparison. Not that the college hasn't kept building and acquiring. There are 10 boarding houses in adjacent streets, and buildings for all major disciplines. The college is now building a new museum in a converted stable to display its trove of treasures – paintings, porcelain, silver, scientific instruments, books etc.

The atmosphere is donnish – the masters are called dons here and the college has a language of its own (called Notions) for almost every aspect of daily life. The lack of girls, together with the school's academically elitist ethos, gives the boys the gift of unselfconsciousness rarely seen elsewhere. The school considered admitting girls when Dr Townsend became head – 'I started off thinking we'd do it', he remembers. In the end, they decided against: 'Girls dominate academically, especially in the lower years. To introduce that here would change the intellectual ethos of the school. What we do is distinctive – we do not have a wide ability range. It is the high quality of the boys' ability at the 'bottom' that is key here.'

So this is a quiet land of flinty walls, leafy quads, a venerable chapel, many other buildings of ancient date and visible history (the school was used in the film version of Les Mis)

Surprisingly, the school has no formal relationship with Winchester Cathedral – who needs it when you've got such a superb school chapel (built 1392)? The cathedral is used for school choir concerts. 'It casts an ecclesiastical aura', noted Dr Townsend. Has a 5+ year relationship with Midhurst Rother College (academy) and some pupils from the academy come to Winchester for a Saturday morning programme of classes.

Pastoral care, well-being and discipline: School rules cover 10 tightly spaced typed pages and make a terrifically good read. You will find a complex list of warnings about alcohol (depending whether wine, beer or spirits and where purchased) and learn that the possession of firearms or explosives is forbidden (with the exception of 'shotguns brought into school with parent permission'). Boys are also reminded not to wear 'T-shirts bearing slogans which are anagrammatical' (what harm is an anagram, we ask?). No hats. And before you ask, no earrings.

Mobiles allowed so long as they are 'inaudible and invisible'. School takes a hard line on drugs, but they remain a recurring nuisance. Unusually, for a school of this vintage, there is no sixth form bar. Housemasters run most aspects of a boy's life – pastoral and academic – but serious matters end up with the head.

Pupils and parents: Some 87 per cent of boys come from the UK. All pupils speak English as it if were their first language; around 20 pupils are bilingual. Quite a lot of Hong Kong Chinese families – who tend to coalesce at the academic hothouses of this land. 'Russians haven't found us yet,' commented one of the admissions staff (more likely, they shun it because it's single sex). Boys come from a large assortment of preps mostly in the southern half of the UK, with Pilgrims' School, Horris Hill, Twyford, The Dragon, Summer Fields and Sussex House leading the field. The school does not break its back to court parents – neither current nor prospective: there is one rather sober open day each year.

Boys are reminded not to wear 'T-shirts bearing slogans which are anagrammatical' (what harm is an anagram, we ask?). No hats. And before you ask, no earrings

Parents we spoke to were keen to emphasise that though boys must be clever and academic to be happy here, they need not be geeks: 'There's a view that Winchester boys are anaemic swots. There are some very studious individuals here – yes, but there are also normal, clever but lazy boys who like their sport and are not averse to sunshine.' Not the place for hovering parents – signing on here takes a leap of faith and the school is set in its ways ('clear about what it wants and expects,' says the school). List of well-known old boys is long, but curiously unexciting. Lots of politicians, academics, cricketers, journalists, pillars of The Establishment.. and Tim Brooke-Taylor.

Entrance: You'll need to be on your toes. The school asks parents to register their sons after they've turned 8 but 'well before the end of year 5'. No need for early registration for those attempting scholarships – winning an award carries with it the automatic right to a place. Admissions for 'Commoners' are via the housemasters who see 25 to 30 sets of parents when the boys are 10-11, interview and test them (a short verbal and numerical reasoning test), get reports from existing schools and offer places to around half. A deposit is then requested and the place is firm, barring (rare) failure of the college's entrance exam which is taken two years later in May of the year of entry in all usual CE subjects (with Greek and German as additional options, but not Spanish). It helps to have an idea of which houses you are interested in – parents may arrange meetings with up to three housemasters. 'If parents are still unsettled after seeing three houses, this may not be the school for them', said the admissions department with customary directness.

Scholars and exhibitioners selected by exams in English, maths, science and a multiple choice 'general reasoning' test. Candidates must also choose three optional papers from among: Latin, French, Classical Greek/German/Spanish, history, geography, maths II or general paper II. Scholars live in 'College' – a separate house pulsating with hyperactive brain cells. The life of a scholar here is not for all, and we know of families turning down an academic scholarship (especially now that they bring no automatic fee remission). A half dozen boys come fresh into the sixth form via exam and a minimum of six GCSE A*/A grades (ie mainly A*s but the odd A won't rule you out).

Exit: In 2015, 35 to Oxbridge. The rest to a predictable spread of the best redbricks. Increasing numbers (around 20 lately) to a distinguished list of top North American universities. Six As required at IGCSE to proceed to sixth form and, thought this is a low hurdle for most boys here, the college is said to be 'ruthless' (school says 'firm') about enforcing this rule. A handful of unfortunate boys receive 'the letter' each year.

Money matters: Since 2011, all scholarships – given for academic and musical ability; no sports, art or drama frippery here (though candidates with those talents may bring along a portfolio of their work) – bring zero fee remittance. However means-tested bursaries can be awarded up to 100 per cent of the fee where necessary. Music scholars, of which there are 10 (usually grade 8 by age 13), receive free tuition on up to two instruments and singing; music exhibitioners (closer to grade 6) get free tuition on one instrument. NB Charges an inexplicable £500 'entrance fee' (in addition to a registration fee and deposit).

Remarks: A very special place for intellectually curious boys and their teachers. Unique.

Wychwood School

74 Banbury Road, Oxford, Oxfordshire OX2 6JR

01865 557976
admissions@wychwoodschool.org
www.wychwoodschool.org

Ages: 11–18
Pupils: 110; sixth form: 46
Boarders: 41 full/weekly
Day: £14,400 pa
Boarding: £21,690 – £22,950 pa

Headmistress: Since 2012, Mrs Andrea Johnson BSc (50s). Comes from a family of teachers and doctors and intended 'never to do either'. She read chemistry at Durham, did a PGCE 'because it might be useful' and unexpectedly fell in love with teaching. Formerly assistant head at Tudor Hall where she worked for 20 years, she is the first head of Wychwood not to be an old girl. Teaches chemistry to year 7 and 11. Married to a retired scientist, two adult children, at least one intends to continue the family tradition and is training to be a teacher.

Mrs Johnson is energetic, genuine and very friendly – her presence is reassuring, rather like a wise owl, and one feels she could cope with anything (parents tell us that she does). Just as well really, since that's what you need to be able to do when you run a small school. And as far as Mrs J is concerned, when it comes to education, small really is beautiful. She sees Wychwood as a place that can be responsive to the needs of the individual, to educate girls who 'want to think and achieve but would sink in the hurly burly of a bigger school.' The school gets its fair share of 'burn out' refugees from some of Oxfordshire's super-heated

girls' independents, but is equally a positive choice for many families from the word go. 'We enable any child who comes here to get the best possible exam results.'

Parents we spoke to were extremely supportive of Mrs J and tell us that they welcome her sensitive moves towards modernisation and determination to raise the school's profile.

Academic matters: With only 110 pupils in total, results would benefit from micro, rather than macro analysis, but they're pretty respectable: in 2015, 59 per cent A*/A at GCSE – the vast majority of pupils getting A*-B in all subjects – and 73 per cent A*-B, 33 per cent A*/A at A level. Small class sizes mean teaching staff can give every girl individual attention and customise their approach. We watched year 8s getting to grips with evaluating historical sources and you could almost touch the intense concentration in the room. In fact quiet and studious pretty much sums up the atmosphere of Wychwood. A display of beautifully produced project work showed Jane Eyre's end of term report, as well as prospectuses and other material from

Lowood (somewhere that definitely wouldn't make it into the Good Schools Guide).

In a smart and well-equipped lab we came across the head teaching year 7 chemistry and yet more rapt attention and eager answers. The biology lab was festooned with a long, pink papier maché tube, 'That's a life-size model of the large intestine,' we were told. Length, not girth, we hope.

One thing we kept hearing about Wychwood was that 'teachers have time for you' and that 'they encourage us to follow our own interests'. The school will ('within reason') run a course for just one student; for instance, GCSE astronomy was taught for the benefit of a single star-gazing girl. In the sixth form, some A level classes might just be two or three strong – more like the tutorial teaching that goes on at the university down the road. Individual tuition in particular subjects can also be arranged and in some cases girls may repeat a year.

Girls take maximum of nine-and-a-half GCSEs and different strengths and interests are accommodated: double or triple science; both Englishes or just English language; psychology; art, textiles and, unusually, photography. Most do French and Spanish, German offered privately, as are GCSEs in, for example, Chinese, Japanese, Persian, for native speakers. Exchange trips to Spain and France in alternate years. All do short courses in RS and ECDL in ICT. At A level most popular subjects are maths, the sciences, photography and history of art.

Games, options, the arts: Textiles, art and photography each enjoy their own light and modern studios in a converted stable block decorated with impressive examples of students' work. As one pupil commented, 'for our size we have so many resources.' It was in the textile studio that we had a sneak preview of the new uniform 'unshortenable'

In fact quiet and studious pretty much sums up the atmosphere at Wychwood. A display of beautifully produced project work showed Jane Eyre's end of term report

skirt, designed by the textiles teacher. If it's successful she should patent it and make her fortune, but since it doesn't feature something that padlocks it to below the knee we fear that girls will always find a way. New uniform design has not been received joyfully, but is it ever? In fact, as far as we could see, Wychwood pupils seemed rather modest in their skirt minimising aspirations, compared to other schools we've visited.

Few mutters that Mrs Johnson isn't as supportive of the arts as former heads have been. School says that girls may opt for more than one GCSE out of art, textiles and photography but since they only take nine-and-a-half in total they often only choose one. At AS/A2 girls can do all three if they so choose.

There's a school orchestra and choir, a chamber choir and music lessons are offered in any instrument – harp seems to be a favourite. House plays, written, designed and directed by the girls, are performed competitively; LAMDA exams popular. D of E up to gold offered and Model UN.

If your daughter is sports mad and keen to play for the winning side then, with heavy heart, we suggest you look elsewhere. On the plus side, as a parent pointed out, 'you always get picked for the team.' Not that Wychwood is a complete stranger to victory: our guide was still buzzing from a recent and unexpected rounders success. As the head says, 'Girls learn to lose with grace, but when they win ...' On-site facilities include tennis, basketball and badminton courts, and fitness suite (in a rather gloomy basement room). Nearby off-site are an athletics field, Astro, and more tennis courts. Main opponents are Oxford High and St Helen's; years 7 and 8 play against The Dragon. School does all it can to support girls competing at high levels (county and national) in particular sports by adapting individual timetables etc. Rather surprisingly we discovered that there is a Wychwood equestrian team. No sign of horses trotting down the Banbury Road, rather girls with their own steeds compete on behalf of the school. Recent 'uproar' when timetabled sport was reduced to an hour a week during GCSEs. Schools say that this was to accommodate girls doing 12 GCSEs at the time. Timetabled sport will increase once option choices are rationalised. Quite right too.

Until the 1960s swimming took place in the nearby River Cherwell. Girls used to cycle down to a muddy pool called (for reasons lost in history) the Rhea where non-swimmers were initiated by being dragged through the water on the end of a pole. Punting was also on the curriculum. There are delightfully nostalgic accounts of the Rhea and its rather whiffy mud in the school's centenary history book. Today's Wychwood swimmers use the Kidlington pool, undoubtedly safer but much less to reminisce about in future years.

Boarding: About a third of pupils board, a fairly even split between full and weekly or flexi. Parents book flexi boarding (usually 1-3 nights per week) at the start of term but school can, and does, accommodate pupils at short notice. Day girls can stay after evening activities such as trips to London or the theatre – bunk beds (only for occasional boarders) add to the sleepover excitement. We were told that news of major road works caused a spike in boarding applications – even fairly local parents appreciate the benefits when gridlock threatens Oxford's already notorious traffic.

When we describe the boarding as 'homely' it's a compliment as well as a reality check. Years 7-9 have large first floor rooms – sash windows and high ceilings – with three to four beds in each. School says mixing the age group helps foster sisterly ethos; colourful curtains and duvets, bedside clutter and lots of family photos and posters add to the family feel. There's wardrobe and under bed storage but no desks – homework takes place elsewhere under supervision.

Sixth formers have characterful single study bedrooms, mostly up in the eaves. Rooms have names such as North Pole, Elysium and Valhalla – harking back to earlier and less centrally heated times. What would their former occupants think about today's duvets and power showers?

The original brass plaque on the door modestly announces its presence in an area where a Latin primer, carefully launched, is bound to hit an educational establishment

During the week there's a table plan for supper – another way of making sure everyone knows each other – but things are more relaxed at weekends. Girls can make themselves snacks – they just go down to the kitchen and ask for supplies. Activities include film nights, Oxford-based bowling, ice skating and trips to Port Meadow along with regular forays to Camden and Bicester Village for shopping. Boarders also take part in community activities – most recently litter picking for Oxclean (voluntary but apparently rather popular). There's a big trip once a year to somewhere like Thorpe Park that's funded by old girls – day pupils can go too but they have to pay.

Background and atmosphere: The school was founded by a Miss Lee and Miss Batty in 1897 and has always been on Oxford's busy Banbury Road. Miss Lee, the younger of the two, was a pioneer, obtaining a first-class degree in English at St Hugh's and going on to lecture and become vice-principal. She funded the school from her earnings and continued to lecture in both Oxford and London. The school was named after Oxfordshire's Wychwood forest in 1918, having formerly been known unofficially as the Battery or Battery Lees, and a uniform of forest green was adopted. One of the early teachers, the redoubtable Miss Rendall, went on to found another Oxford school, Rye St Antony.

Today's Wychwood is still domestic in scale, the original brass plaque on the door (featured heavily in promotional literature) modestly announcing its presence in an area where a Latin primer, carefully launched, is bound to hit a venerable educational establishment. There's nothing flash here, no plate glass or modern architecture, but everything is well loved and cared for. Head of boarding is from the hotel industry – what a good idea – and facilities have been upgraded accordingly, although The

Randolph it isn't. This was Mrs Johnson's first undertaking on arrival, strongly backed by the 'brilliant' governors, the chair of whom is a former pupil.

Pastoral care, well-being and discipline: Mrs Johnson says, 'a child can't learn if she is unhappy.' Parents say that pastoral care is outstanding: girls who need it are given time and space but this doesn't mean that the school can't be tough when called for. In a small community one person's actions can significantly affect all and Mrs Johnson will ask a girl to leave if she feels that the school can't accommodate her needs. As one parent put it, 'Yes, your daughter is an individual but she is also part of a respectful community.' Some grumbles that pupils arriving at odd times eg half way through a term can make things a little disjointed.

Majority of local parents are Oxford professionals – lawyers, doctors etc. Girls we met were thoughtful, independent-minded – lacking the swagger of nearby sisters, perhaps

Famously democratic, girls are genuinely involved in decision making – much to the horror of the Daily Mail in the 1960s (plus ça change ...). The founders' original forward-thinking structure of councillors and 'citizens' with voting rights, responsibilities and privileges still operates today (albeit with a few modern tweaks). As Mrs Johnson says, 'We're so small that everybody can be involved.'

Lower ground canteen is as nice as a lower ground canteen can be. Girls mostly complimentary about the food – favourites are the breakfasts and Friday fish and chips. There are, and have been since the school's foundation, buns at break time. Cook deserves honourable mention for skilfully adapting meals so that girls with eg dairy or gluten intolerance can eat the same as everyone else.

Some might discount a school such as Wychwood because of its small size, but consider the benefits: it's responsive, girls notice there's a play or event on down the road (this being Oxford it's more than likely) and arrangements can be made to go double quick. Parents are very involved, professionals including medics from the John Radcliffe come in to talk to pupils – this happens in other schools but it's more likely to be a lecture than a conversation. Parents told us that Wychwood was uncliquey and that foreign students integrated very well. One commented that it was very good preparation for work because you 'had to get along with everyone'.

All schools say that they nurture every child as an individual, but common sense tells us that this is easier to achieve in a school of 120 rather than an academic super tanker of 800 or more.

Pupils and parents: Used to be known as the 'Dons' school' but draws from a wider pool these days. Majority of local parents are Oxford professionals – lawyers, doctors etc. Girls we met were thoughtful, independent-minded – lacking the swagger of nearby sisters perhaps – and fiercely loyal to their school and its ways. Lots of summer-born girls, fair few refugees from schools that were too big and girls going through upheaval eg parents' divorce. And then there are girls who visited on an open day and 'fell in love' with Wychwood.

Former pupils include Margaret Casson, architect, designer and photographer; Joan Aiken, writer; Vicky Jewson, film maker; Rebecca Stockland, opera singer; Matilda Leyser, actress and aerialist; Izzie Lawrence, comedian; Honor Fell, microbiologist.

Entrance: Girls join at age 11 from local primaries/preps and there's another influx from preps at age 13. Prospective year 7s spend a day at the school and are tested in maths and English. External candidates for sixth form need minimum of six GCSEs at grades A*-C and A*/A in A level subjects. Places may be available in other years, subject to interview and assessment.

Exit: Around 30 per cent leaver after GCSEs. This isn't a school that unthinkingly crams sixth formers onto the non-stop university express, although most girls do go on to further study. Art and design at Oxford Brookes and elsewhere popular; other courses range from law at Reading to animal behaviour at Anglia Ruskin. Girls have also gone on to be Norland Nannies, Montessori educators, farriers and business entrepreneurs.

Money matters: Day fees on a par with local equivalents – OK, you're not getting the sports facilities but you are getting something pretty close to a customised education. Boarding comparatively good value. Academic, music and creative arts scholarships of approximately £1,200 pa available, as are means-tested bursaries.

Remarks: Charming pint-sized power house. Much-needed alternative to the academic overdrive of some other Oxford girls' independents (if it didn't exist someone would certainly have to invent it). A positive choice for many relieved families, one of whom described it as 'a jewel, we wouldn't want our daughter to be anywhere else.'

Wycombe Abbey School

Abbey Way, High Wycombe, Buckinghamshire HP11 1PE

01494 520381
registrar@wycombeabbey.com
www.wycombeabbey.com
C of E

Ages: 11–18
Pupils: 560; sixth form: 170
Boarders: 527 full
Day: £26,775 pa
Boarding: £35,700 pa

Headmistress: Since 2013, Mrs Rhiannon Wilkinson MA MEd (50s). Previously principal at Harrogate Ladies' College, one of many curves in perfectly rounded career that includes five years at Haileybury as director of studies and two at Cheadle Hume School where was director of pastoral system. Married with children – husband, Donald is headmaster of Bearwood College.

Choice of profession early and unwavering, thanks to family clan of fulfilled teachers (has happy memories of washing out paint pots in mother's classroom). Started in large comprehensives in Devon and south Manchester, then (sensibly ignoring relative's confident predictions of 'career suicide') spent 11 years in Hong Kong and Brunei schools where managing international and affluent families honed parent-whispering skills. Only career downside – has lived in school accommodation since age of 27. 'Probably makes me a sad person'. (Not on evidence so far.)

Far more to the post than simply ensuring all that excellence in terms of popularity and superb results carries on ad infinitum, from righting genuine wrongs – 'would always be first to admit if we make a mistake' – to curbing 'me, me, me' excesses,

nicely. 'You can't run any school for an individual,' she says.

Key is transparent admissions process, ensuring name and glittering prizes don't blind families to school values. 'Want parents to choose us because truly know us, not based on the name.' Spends every Tuesday with prospective parents – 45 minutes apiece – to get message across.

Expert knowledge extends to on-site wildlife, from red kites to badgers and Stumpy the Canada goose

Staff love her and she's getting there with parents. 'A true educationalist who is clearly passionate about the school – maybe too passionate,' commented one. 'I don't think you can be too passionate because if you weren't you would lose your enthusiasm when you face some challenging times,' counters Mrs W.

Weekend 'meet the head' lunch programme under way to increase exposure, linked to match

fixtures for maximum efficiency. Has also put in the time with pupils, from individual meetings in top years to throwing jolly party at house in grounds for all 65 first years. 'By end of first half term, knew everyone by name,' says parent.

Expert knowledge extends to on-site wildlife, from nesting red kites to badgers, deer and – her favourite – Stumpy the Canada goose, named for deformed wings, tenderly cared for by school with occasional Jammy Dodger as a treat.

Girls like what they've seen of her: has achieved finely judged balance that hovers somewhere between friendliness and formality, thought parent. 'She's super, so there for them, doesn't go round being all huggy or anything – they're scared of her in a nice way and the staff are also very behind her,' says mother.

Unlike predecessor, doesn't teach – yet – and is eyeing up the timetable (shame to waste that Oxford history degree). May have work cut out with building programme – two new boarding houses on site of disused swimming pool. Also starting, in a quiet way, to build public profile – was quoted in The Times talking about the ability of boarding to rescue children from otherwise pressurised existence. Looking at results with jaundiced eye this might seem a tad kettle and pot-like but no, she insists, school does amazingly well with all-embracing support rather than 'trot on Smudgy' crack of the whip. Pupils might feel cocooned; they won't feel driven.

Academic matters: Easy to see results as inevitable consequence of admissions process – bright in, gleaming out. Results impeccable – 85 per cent of A levels and 98 per cent of GCSEs graded A*-A in 2015. 'Results are amazing,' said parent. 'Feels as if no barriers to what the girls could achieve.'

> 'She's super, so there for them, doesn't go round being all huggy or anything – they're scared of her in a nice way and staff are very behind her'

However, not quite the effort-free equation it might appear. Smaller numbers applying to come here means school has to spread admissions net just that bit wider than equivalent boys' school – and it's how they manage the talent that's their forte. Whisper it softly, but sexism is still rife in education, thought parent. Boys get the very best, but for 'the girl it doesn't matter quite as much, so a school like [this] has not got such a huge pool of clever children to draw from.'

There's also the darling daughter factor, thinks Mrs Wilkinson, where doting parents can't quite bear to part from their girls. 'They are very precious, daddy's little princess, the friends of mothers and hard to let go.'

Everyone here is bright – with compulsory Latin and attempt at classical Greek for all, wouldn't cope here if they weren't, though don't overdose on GCSEs, with 10 or 11 the goal for most, one girl insistent on 13 talked down to more manageable 12. 'Great achievement is bringing up girls who are competent but don't shine and getting them to get the really top grades,' said parent.

Not a place where learning support is rushed off feet: though 54 (around 10 per cent) are identified as having special needs, for most this translates into academic support – aka learning enhancement – to plug previous curriculum gaps, particularly for overseas pupils. Just five have help with SpLD, a further five working with EAL specialist – and every pupil in the school needs to enjoy the challenge. 'My daughter's somewhere in the middle [which means] she has a lot to strive for and works harder,' thought mother.

Key is micro monitoring. No slightly below par result is given the benefit of the doubt, no progress chart left unplotted, communication between staff of the instant message variety. Parents, pupils and staff know exactly where every girl is in every subject (pre-GCSE tracking grades include three for A* – high, secure and low – alone). If anticipated trajectory shows any signs of premature wilting, the SWAT team is ready and waiting. 'The ones that would struggle, they just spend more time with them. Literally, the teacher's all over them,' said mother. 'Nobody's going to fail their grades by accident,' agreed another. Timetable underpins the message – Saturday kicks off with breakfast at 8.00am with lessons until 11.50am (detention, scheduled for 8.20am, isn't compulsory, we were pleased to hear).

Tests, predictably, are frequent but well managed and not done 'in a kind of heartrendingly tedious way,' thought parent. Inevitably, some girls find relentlessness of approach harder to bear than others, but transmogrified into gratitude when desired grades came in. 'There are times when you think "wish you would stop hounding me and accept standard" but it's worth it in the end,' said sixth former.

Parental comments acted on. Issue with one teacher relating to lesson pace 'sorted out instantly and school kept us informed on an almost daily basis [until] problem solved,' said parent. One teacher, total convert to boarding, felt it enabled tiny changes where girl 'not quite herself' to be picked up and sorted before could escalate. 'It's that swift response to a change in demeanour – remarkable, rewarding and very satisfying.'

Staff fabness is the norm, best teachers trending at top of charisma settings and 'adored' by pupils for effortless ability to take scenic route through the curriculum and 'teach round the subject, which I think is really important,' said mother. (Latest inspection report gushes agreement.)

Among many favourite subjects history teaching gets rave reviews, sharing joint honours with maths. 'School encourages you to do the subjects you love,' says pupil. 'Very foolish to take on two years in sixth form to study subjects you're not committed to,' agrees teacher.

Fairly brisk staff turnover inevitable consequence of recruiting top talent – no weights are going to hold back rise to greater things for long. Recent departure of fab director of studies to become head elsewhere par for the course. 'If you're recruiting at the top level, it's going to happen,' said parent, one of many who perceive this as price worth paying for quality teaching, while long stay figures (average age 46 with 76 staff members here for 10 years plus) do send reassuring message of stability. Only niggle is that some departures could occasionally be better timed, thought one. More quality staff accommodation – school lags behind others in this respect – would also help, feel staff and parents.

While care and attention that goes into creating the finished pupil hugely appreciated by parents, we heard more than once that aspects of culture had been a tad joy-free. 'There's a sense that growing up is a serious business,' said parent. 'We don't laugh at ourselves, we don't question ourselves that much. We know what we do, we're good at it, deal with it.'

Similarly, when rules are broken 'there's no knowing smiles, no "I've got to give you this penalty, please don't do it again but we're still friends,"' said parent. 'It's "we really expect girls of your age

to behave much better than this and it's not funny at all."' Occasionally po-faced? Possibly, thought staff. 'I think staff felt needed permission to let hair down,' says head.

Staff confirm that fun, once the three letter word that dare not say its name, is now out and proud – mostly. Immediate muting of clearly very jolly (and refreshingly noisy) Latin lesson heard when this reviewer hove into view suggests not all teachers have got the message that head is, as one put it, 'in favour of jollity.'

Girls, though, stress noses are removed from grindstones on regular basis. Everyone works hard but there's 'lots of laughing and joking in the kitchen,' stressed sixth former. 'Not so serious that you shouldn't be scared to come here. We know how to have fun.'

Games, options, the arts: As with other high-achieving schools, everything you'd expect in the way of stunning stuff to play, perform or create is on show on a nearby pitch, platform or podium. Bashful won't get you places though, thought parent. 'If you're not going to do grab the opportunities, probably wouldn't suit.'

Caters for all sorts in innumerable venues, sweet-toothed first years to Cadbury's World, skiers to Whistler, budding sixth form medics to West Herts Hospital and female highflyers past and present regularly celebrated with events and talks – subsequent pupil write-ups, even by youngest, are little gems of well-observed journalism.

If anticipated trajectory shows any signs of premature wilting, the SWAT team is ready and waiting. 'The ones that would struggle, they just spend more time with them'

The 550 plus weekly instrumental lessons are also somehow fitted in, handful most years reaching diploma standard, substantial numbers hitting grades 7 and 8. Drama, equally ambitious, includes day of Shakespeare miniatures – Titus Andronicus (and others) each done and dusted in just 30 minutes.

Games widely enjoyed and lots of them, team sports 'formidable' with even tiniest slivers of talent encouraged to flourish. Teams don't straddle the alphabet – size means lacrosse, for example, only reaches C after the first year when 'have more teams so as not to make the girls feel left out.' Sure footed pretty much across the board, football, netball, tennis and squash teams among those whizzing up to quarter final stage and above in national tournaments, sailors recently taking part in world championships.

Not so sporty thrive, happy to trade games for other interests, school good at helping find inner something ('funazise' weekend activity option sounds fun, bootcamp possibly less so). Music, drama, or art, 'they'll find a way of making that come to you,' said parent.

Marvel of timetabling helps to avoid overloads – one third year had opted for piano, violin, ballet, riding and extra lacrosse. 'Very tailored. I don't know how they do it,' said parent. Sheer willpower and not letting sun set on unfinished work was pupil tip though can lead to lateish finish (10pm rare but not unheard of).

Only small bone of contention was desire to embrace the new rather than stick to tried, tested and trophy-ed – one parent thought rowing, recently introduced, could be made more of. Another, however, had nothing but praise for polo, also new to the school and thus far a galloping success.

Boarding: It's all or nothing full boarding (unless you're one of the very few day pupils). School operates non-negotiable 'closed' weekends (following hols, half terms and exeats). No choice over houses either – decision is made by school and that's that, though with posh lighting, carpet and paint upgrade programme under way, will be few complaints wherever you end up – fabbed-up bits of Daws Hill, for example, well worth a visit.

Oldest and youngest pupils have own houses. First years get chickens for extra homeliness, upper sixth ditch poultry for first taste of independence – wear own clothes, too (sensibly point out that as universities don't insist on work wear, why should they?). Can be heady experience – school occasionally has to coax those briefly high on prospect of unlimited toast making and TV watching back into more humdrum aspects of school life.

In between (years 2 to lower sixth) girls join one of nine mixed-age houses, each with around 45 pupils. Older girls are enlisted as mother and granny substitutes, brilliant at 'been there, done that' advice, many issues resolved without recourse to adult intervention. Also compels older girls to keep conversation within age-appropriate limits, pointed out parent. It's rounded off with formality of timetabled slots with housemistresses and elected house prefect system (one housemistress uses two vote system, one for loyalty candidate, the other 'for one they'd really like to win – they're never wrong').

Add packed programme of evening and weekend activities, from shopping trips to ice skating and even, according to website, 'vegging out' (inverted commas – theirs – probably say it all) and parental approval pretty much universal.

Background and atmosphere: Entrance via one of High Wycombe's statement roundabouts makes countrified setting a particular pleasure. 'Abbey' is a misnomer (it's a nun-free zone, name for status purposes only) but from ecclesiastic trimmings in main building – an 18th century former mansion – to performing arts centre overlooking lake, with incredible number of performance areas (one handily combining grand piano and chaise longue for artistic swooning to music), school is very easy on the eye.

Founded 1896, school was 'new experiment' by pioneering Miss – later Dame – Frances Dove. One of Girton College's test batch of girl students and school's first headmistress, was every ounce a character, on-line portrait notable for fabulous, gravity-defying hair probably held up by principles alone.

Arts centre overlooking lake, with incredible number of performance areas (one handily combining grand piano and chaise longue, for artistic swooning to music)

Her aim – girls' education every bit as good as boys' through pursuit of excellence, development of talents, godliness and an understanding of the needs of others – remains top of the checklist. School's view is that even if her reaction to chicken nugget-making or 'baking with Mr Whiteley' sessions might be harder to call, Dame Frances would feel right at home with current ethos and achievements.

All happens on suitably inspirational site, originally belonging to Carringtons (current Lord Carrington is school enthusiast and regular visitor), enlarged by 1929 purchase of next door estate, Daws Hill, big enough to house a school all on its own, used for weddings and a good five minutes from main school by car (staff often drive, girls in its three boarding houses take compulsory scenic route). Has just got back World War II underground bunker, annexed after school was requisitioned as HQ for US Eighth Air Force – history department no doubt licking lips at potential for truly authentic lessons.

Little sign of world-weary London – and on and on – vibe here. Instead, children remain children – against the odds. Delightful 'Fairies' event (you'll have to ask for details – we're sworn to secrecy) where magical beings turn every house into (tinsel) town one night in Christmas term, appears proof against teen cynicism.

Was it really healthy to put so much distance between pupils and real life, wondered one older girl, worried for health of contemporaries' souls. Definitely, think parents, who appear simply relieved that school's imposition of rules, including bans on make up and travelling unaccompanied on public transport until reach 16, keeps them off the hook. 'Might be a bit ridiculous but means girls feel safe and can be scruffy and dirty when it's appropriate,' says parent.

They also love their jargon. Prefects, unofficially, are 'mons' (once monitors); booters the temporary lockers where pre-lunch gubbins is stowed. (And, oh, the relief of seeing a bit of learning sprawl, with books, calculators and even the odd sock in contrast to pristine conditions elsewhere.)

There's Big School (actually the school hall – smell, instantly recognisable, of 'dust, old wood and overworked brains,' thought staff member) overlooked by bust of Frances Dove, grim as death, a martinet in marble, exiled from classrooms where was scaring the teachers (a joke, they said – though we wonder..)

Add Gym Courtyard (gym went years ago), four boarding Out Houses, inside the school grounds but 'you have to go out to them' – well, of course – and Long Corridor – the through route that thinks it's a communal room – and no wonder that even long-serving staff freely own up to being occasionally surprised by unfamiliar nooks and crannies.

Pastoral care, well-being and discipline: Housemistress as personality cult may be dead but continue to exert considerable beneficial influence, experts in even-handedness and clued-upness, matron and tutor completing house triumvirate. 'You get this impression, if something's happened in the morning, housemistress will know about it by lunchtime,' said parent.

Not always a breeze. Some girls won't get on with others in their house – and sophisticated urbanites vs the rest can make for occasional trouble. Staff antennae don't miss much, however, and one parent was pragmatic. Daughter has 'realised that she's just going to have to get on with it,' she said.

Pupils and parents: With school seen as nearest you'll get to girls' Eton equivalent in terms of ethos, location and facilities (impressive list of joint social events adds to sibling feel), it's often purchased as part of matching pair. Old girls are solidly brilliant type you'd expect (reality TV slebs aren't their thing, so far) and include Rt Hon Lady Justice Butler-Sloss, Baroness Howe, plus star journalist India Knight and actress Rachel Stirling.

You won't find idle rich featuring in the parental mix: hard-working, high-flying, well connected and dual income professionals dominate – as

indeed they must to stump up hefty fees, though still find time to attend matches.

Some reservations about amounts of money sloshing about. 'Do worry that when many of her friends have their own Addison Lee account daughter might have a warped view of what is "normal",' said one mother. School asks for birthday celebrations to be limited to pizza or noodle bar excursions to avoid escalation of party politics.

'Don't want them to be in a privileged little bubble,' agrees head, while pointing out that anyone who can afford the fees unlikely to be on breadline. Fast growing bursary programme will help those who can't – new boarding houses will lead to gradual increase in numbers to 600. 'Thirty extra girls over seven years won't dilute product,' says head.

Girls may cover the gamut of characters, outer appearance occasionally au naturel as regards make up but sharing hefty degree of inner self-confidence (it's the quality most commented on by parents elsewhere) and appetite for success. 'Good with strong, silent type,' said one parent. Won't be squashed and there's 'healthy situation where girls help each other [but] if you're not the type that is striving to do well, you'll soon be left behind.'

Entrance: Potential pupils will 'like their notebooks and fluorescent pens – busy little bees who love finding out the way things fit together,' says head – which might help when it comes to working way through complex entrance procedures and deadlines. Register 18 months to two years in advance for 11+ and 13+ entry and at least 15 months ahead for sixth form hopefuls – minimum nine A and A* GCSEs required. Pre-tests for all candidates.

Feeders include high profile preps in London and South East: Maltman's Green, Bute House,

Francis Holland, Pembridge Hall, Glendower, Ken Prep and Garden House in year 7 (65 places – around 180 applicants). Godstowe and The Dragon at 13 (more competitive with 100 applicants for 25 places), separate exams for UK prep and overseas/ senior school candidates). Around 25 per cent international pupils, Hong Kong, Malaysia and Nigeria most strongly represented. Thirty day places awarded to top performing locals.

Exit: Head's lightbulb moment was to stop post-16 exodus by giving fifth formers Through the Keyhole invite to previously, and pointlessly, top secret delights of upper sixth boarding house. While Westminster remains most desirable of alternative destinations (for some, lessons with b**s just too much of a lure) vast majority now stay on. With 28 Oxbridge places in 2015 as well as Browns, Harvard, Dartmouth and NYU, why risk chances elsewhere, argues head?

Money matters: At five per cent off the fees, scholarships more gloss than dosh (hopefuls also need to invest six pounds in past papers); exhibitions worth £600 a year. Help for those in need via expanding bursary fund, donor generosity permitting.

Remarks: A classy, focused school, true to high-minded educational objectives of pioneering founder. Knows what it's about and makes year in, year out results look easy. Appreciative parents accept school for what it is and don't expect much in the way of radical change – except, that is, at Christmas, when the Fairies come to call. 'Encourages girls to dream big and shows them what is possible,' said one. 'We'd do it again in a heartbeat.'

London and South East

City of London
East Sussex
Greater London
Kent
Surrey
West Sussex

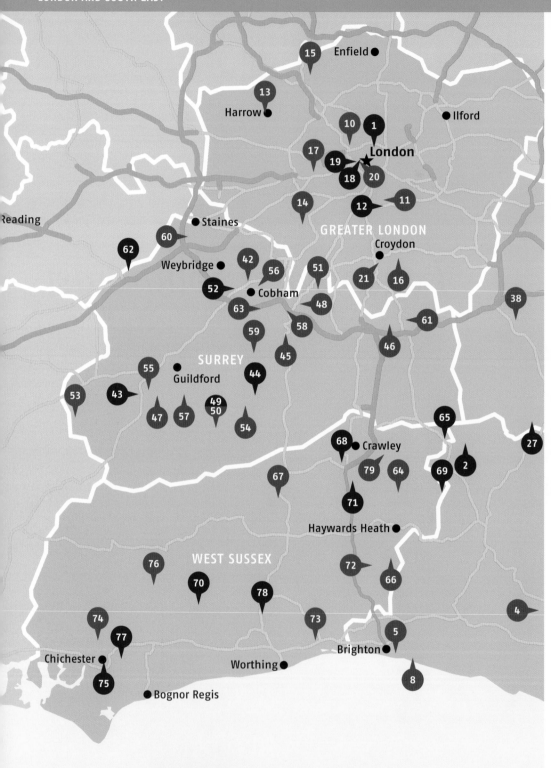

Basildon

Southend-on-Sea

Gravesend
24
30
Gillingham

41
Ramsgate
36

34

35
28
33
Canterbury

Maidstone
31

39

KENT
25
Dover
22
40

29
26
Folkestone
Cranbrook
32
23

7
37

9

EAST SUSSEX

Strait of Dover

Hastings
Bexhill

6
Eastbourne

3

LONDON AND SOUTH EAST

ACS Cobham International School

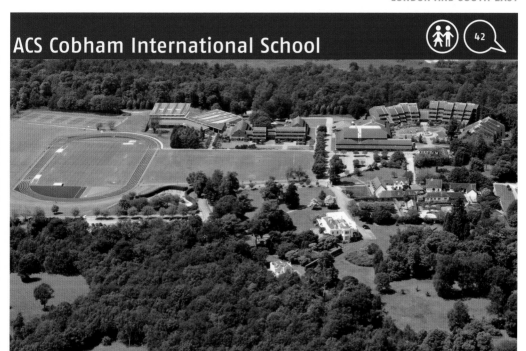

Heywood, Cobham, Surrey KT11 1BL

01932 867251
cobhamadmissions@acs-schools.com
www.acs-schools.com

Ages: 2 – 18 (boarding from 12)
Pupils: 1,480; sixth form: 435
Boarders: 81 full, 25 weekly
Day: £7,340 – £25,050 pa
Boarding: £36,240 – £43,730 pa

Headmaster: Since 2011, Tony Eysele (50s) BSc Natal University, HDE Edgewood College of Education, organisational behaviour degree Heriot Watt University. After two years in the army, started his teaching career in a South African state school before moving into, and progressing upwards in, the independent sector. Headships in Johannesburg and Harare until, in 2004, moved to the UK with his wife and sons and became foundation director at Lord Wandsworth College, Hampshire. One of his sons is now a teacher, the other is a professional athlete. His wife is admissions director at Marymount International School in Kingston-on-Thames.

Enthusiastic, approachable and popular, he says, 'Children in our school are all incredibly happy', and from what we saw as we walked round, we tend to agree with him. Parents say 'very approachable', 'quick to react to good suggestions for change' and 'really does seem to be listening to us'. Has increased the number of staff where needed. It's hard to take over from a long-standing predecessor (who spent nearly 20 years at the helm) but Tony Eysele seems to have handled the challenge well and parents, staff and pupils are all equally happy.

Academic matters: Non-selective so a real mix of ability throughout. A truly international school – 72 different nationalities represented and a multitude of different languages spoken.

In the early childhood years pre-schoolers are prepared gently for the future. They build their social skills and interact with each other, developing their language and communication abilities through play. With such a large range of backgrounds, we were delighted to see them chattering away together and enjoying participating in group discussion and activity.

The lower school contains grades 1-4 and the majority of core lessons are classroom-based. They largely follow the American curriculum, but elements of the International Primary Years programme are also included. These are the preparatory years, when teachers discover strengths and weaknesses and begin to unearth any particular talents. All classes are mixed-ability. No formal exams or tests at this stage, though parents say general testing is continuous – presumably because MAP (Measure of Academic Progress) begins in grade 2.

519

At around 10 they move into the middle school for four years. This is when their futures begin to be mapped out. Timetables are based on the individual needs of the children, who are grouped by ability within their own age groups. Each child begins to follow a curriculum based on his known strengths and weaknesses. Classrooms are now subject-based, and it's the pupils not the teachers that move. The school is determined to provide a solid grounding and ensure that pupils can work together in teams, sharing their ideas and listening to each other. Exceptionally able children will sometimes be transferred to work with older pupils for particular subjects, thus assuring that they are being properly stimulated and working at their correct levels. Middle school children can be found studying their native language several grades higher than their ages.

At 14 it's high school, still in the same building as the middle school. They are separated by a large marble hall where these older pupils have Wifi access and the use of computers. The curriculum is wide and mixed, with 17 languages currently available. Timetables are based on each child's needs, exams are coming into the picture – decisions will soon have to be made. Some opt to study iGCSEs for a year, though they don't sit external exams in all subjects. For their final program(me), some decide to follow the International Baccalaureate, others take a variety of AP courses (18 available), and the rest work for the American High School diploma and SATs. Much depends on whether they

The early childhood village cossets the very young, giving them a sense of security before they move on. Light, bright and welcoming

are heading for university in the UK, the USA or continental Europe. This school prepares them for all, thus really meriting the international label. Generally around 80 per cent get 3+ AP scores; IB average 35 points in 2015. Not bad for a non-selective school.

Games, options, the arts: At a school sitting in 128 acres of country, with plenty of playing fields and its own a six-hole golf course, you'd expect the sports to be good. And they are. Not only outdoors, but in the all-singing, all-dancing sports centre as well. We were fascinated by the swimming pool with its computerised touch pads, enabling the raising of the pool bottom or adjustment of water temperature, at will, depending on activities of users. And as for the dance studio/gym with a professional sound system and sprung wood flooring; the fitness suite for older exercisers where the equipment is card controlled; the international-sized basket/volleyball show court and the café for spectators and participators alike – these children have no excuse for being unfit. PE is compulsory for all the whole way through the school.

From middle school up, all take part in a good mix of indoor and outdoor sports, competing against other schools and, once in high school, in the ISST (International Schools Sports Tournaments) programme Europe-wide. A varied selection of different sports each season, something for everybody. A parent said, 'Sport is a big deal. Even the less sporty children find something they enjoy doing.'

Theatre, drama and music are also 'a big deal'. The amazing new performing arts centre provides everything budding thespians and musicians need. Several drama studios and music practice rooms; a music technology suite and an amazing high tech theatre which some drama schools would die for – even has an automated fly-tower. Instrumental and choral groups to suit all tastes. For those who want it, it's all there. No wonder the middle school singers have won their category in the Godalming Music Festival at least twice and drama students have been selected to participate in the National Theatre Connections project. Plenty of opportunities for students studying theatre for the IB. And for the musicians, it's all there for them as well – there is even a large lift so that a grand piano can take its place on the stage for a special recital. Good artist in

residence programme when, for instance, a visiting band spends time with all instrumentalists, working with them and introducing them to new concepts.

Art on display all round, certainly appears to be plenty of talent. Imaginations run riot. Well-equipped studios enable experimentation, self-expression and developing talents to thrive.

Plenty of expeditions and field trips within UK, Europe or worldwide – exploratory, educational or languages involved. Around 100 working for the Duke of Edinburgh Award, at all levels. Recently two current students got their golds – a significant achievement given that most don't complete this till university.

Boarding: About 100 boarders aged 12-18, most full, with equal numbers of boys and girls, and 25 weekly (more boys). About 80 per cent from overseas. Boys and girls in separate wings, but plenty of chance for social mixing. A banner in the entrance hall reads: 'Because we are all different, we are all the same'. Jolly, caring, head of boarding says, 'We are a home from home and, with children representing so many nationalities, this is a great opportunity to understand and embrace different cultures. All are well integrated, no cliques.' Trips organised every Saturday. Supervised prep every evening between 7.00pm and 9.00pm; the younger ones in a study room, the older ones in their rooms with the door open. Rooms look clean and comfortable. Seniors given personal privacy and do their own washing.

Background and atmosphere: Originally built in the 13th century, the main house at Cobham went through a variety of owners, from the aristocracy to businessmen, until it was acquired by ACS in 1975 in order to create their first American school in England. They now have two others in Surrey and Middlesex, and one overseas in Doha. Originally aiming to provide an American education for families living and working here, they have now become 'international' and the curriculum has been broadened to include the IB programme and enable pupils to attend universities worldwide. Looking round at the huge mix of nationalities represented, 72 at present, the change is merited. And you certainly notice it as you walk round this ultra-modern, high tech school where classroom and studios are fully equipped with every possible learning aid. This is the 21st century.

No uniform, but a code, for both pupils and staff, and those not sticking to it are in trouble. Some parents told us they would prefer to have one, and felt staff should perhaps be stricter on the boundaries, but they also agreed that their children are perfectly happy with the way it is. We noticed no extremes: most pupils we saw looked neat, tidy and relaxed. The head says having no uniform 'means focusing on the child'.

A closed campus, surrounded by its own land, no entry without a pass; this is a safe place for children of all ages. The early childhood village cossets the very young, giving them a sense of security before they move on to the lower school building. Here floors and classrooms are colour coded, all mixed ability, light, bright and welcoming; they only move for specialist classes. Great library, where language books are plentiful and some are colour coded to lend variety to different reading levels. For the first two years children are each lent an iPad for class use; from grade 3 onwards, they are given their own to take home. Both lower school and early childhood have their own playgrounds, while the middle school has its own playing fields, and the high school pupils have their own designated areas during break times.

The technology is blinding in the middle/high school building. From the interactive learning centre in the basement where they appear to be able to reach out all over the world, to the science labs where they can work together with their iPads, to huge divisional libraries again filled with books in a multitude of different languages, you could say the atmosphere buzzes.

And as for fuelling the inner child – the new dining area is high tech. Canteen style, children collect their food, from a range of options, in coded containers, which are then scanned and a thumb scan identifies the child – no money changes hands, and parents are digitally informed what their children are eating. Or, at least, what they are taking to their tables. Big Brother is definitely watching over these children. Selections are such that no-one can get away with eating unhealthy food, and staff are watching carefully for any secret non-eaters.

Pastoral care, well-being and discipline: With such a large range of nationalities, there is a huge need for EAL support, particularly in the lower and middle schools. So, EAL numbers are capped. Children are initially assessed by EAL teachers and given as much support as they feel necessary. Depending on need, this can be in class or out of class, either in small groups or individually. IPads are used for translation and general help.

About 250 pupils have some form of mild to moderate learning difficulty or EAL need. Each one is looked at individually, 'one-to-one case management', and a programme devised for them. Learning support numbers are capped each year and children are only accepted if the school feels it can support their particular needs.

Parents report some communication problems over learning support, as teachers are not always ready to listen but, on the whole, happy with the situation. The holistic approach adds extra dimension, treating the whole child. Excellent occupational therapy room, and imaginative ways of helping. Enthusiastic, sympathetic teachers with specialists at even the youngest age groups.

From the interactive learning centre where they appear to reach out all over the world, to libraries filled with books in different languages, you could say the atmosphere buzzes

Head said substance abuse problems rare and dealt with quickly and efficiently on a case by case basis. Can't realistically control what happens outside the school grounds, but does not believe anything serious. As school in own guarded grounds, cases of bringing forbidden items rare. No toleration of antisocial or unkind behaviour. Rules are there to be obeyed.

Pupils and parents: A multi-national, multi-cultural school. Around a third are American and about a third of the rest are from the UK and other English speaking countries – the remainder cover Europe and the rest of the world. Inevitably, turnover quite large in the early years. Lots of expats from various different walks of life, some in transit, some who have decided to settle here – at least

while their children are at school. Truly representative of today's mobile world. Excellent bus service, covering a huge area from Godalming to Hyde Park Corner, before and after school, means that quite a few travel from London. Beware the fleet of buses at arrival and departure times.

Parental involvement huge, as you would expect from a largely American school. Also makes relocation and transition easier. Plenty of charity support, organised social gatherings and career advice given.

Students appeared relaxed and happy. We asked one what he would change about the school: 'Nothing, really but maybe lessons could be shorter?'

Entrance: Inevitably, because of the transitary national side of the school, places can crop up at different stages. So it is always worth trying. Academic records examined and references required, but no testing until 13+, when English is assessed. However, school adds the caveat: 'We will take any child at any stage providing we have space and can meet their needs academically and socially'. In the last two years, they will only take IB pupils if they are already following the programme and their courses can be matched. Any child can join the American Programme, even, occasionally, for their last year. But they do have to stay for at least one semester.

Exit: Typically 40 per cent of graduates to UK universities, 40 per cent to American universities and the remaining 20 per cent worldwide. Every student assigned a college counsellor at high school level. For the first two years they may just consult them, but at 11th grade it is compulsory for each student to work with them. A huge and varied exit list definitely featuring Ivy leagues in the US plus Oxbridge and top London colleges in the UK.

Money matters: Well, it's certainly not the cheapest. But just a look around will tell you why. That said, fees cover pretty well everything, including curriculum related field trips, all books and those iPads. Private corporate owners of all four ACS schools. No scholarships and limited bursaries but some financial aid occasionally available.

Remarks: If you are looking for a large, lively, international school with a multitude of opportunities and facilities to die for, or if you are in transition round the world, then this could be perfect for your child. Shy, retiring children might just get a bit lost, but then again the holistic approach could also help them. Anyone looking for a traditional, structured, English establishment, however, should probably look elsewhere. That said, this school has a huge amount to offer any child prepared to think outside the box.

Aldro

Lombard Street, Godalming, Surrey GU8 6AS

01483 409020
hmsec@aldro.org
www.aldro.org
C of E

Ages: 7-13 (boarding from 8)
Pupils: 220
Boarders: 7 full, 55 weekly/flexi
Day: £15,510 – £17,235 pa
Boarding: £20,520 – £22,245 pa

Headmaster: Since September 2015, Mr James Hanson, previously head of the boys's senior school at the Royal School, Haslemere. Studied maths and zoology at Oxford; MPhil in maths education from Brunel. Ten years at Harrow, where he was senior maths master, head of the G&T programme and of rowing, and deputy housemaster. He is married to Jenny, and they have two daughters.

Entrance: At 7+ a largely local intake. School is full and with a waiting list – boarding numbers are up since introduction of more flexible system but generally more competition for day places than boarding. Two form entry. Exam, assessment and reports in January for the following September. Boys come from many different feeder schools – over 30 at the last count, but always a chunk from St Hilary's. A few substantial bursaries available through the Royal National Children's Foundation.

Exit: Expert and practised at feeding the public school system. Aldro boys hoover up scholarships and head off in their 10s to Charterhouse (five minutes away – Aldro seen as a feeder, but isn't officially) in handfuls to Eton and Wellington and ones and twos elsewhere – typically to around a dozen different destinations, including Sherborne, Radley, Winchester and recently the more local Royal Grammar School, Guildford and St John's Leatherhead.

Prep is done at the end of the day, so no homework; 'wonderful,' chorus mothers, who don't have to chivvy

Remarks: An old-fashioned, traditional school which sees itself as very much part of the 'establishment' of leading public schools. With academics at its core, be aware that the thrust of the place is to get the boys to major public boarding schools. 'It's an unspoken thing, but I very much got the feeling the school wondered why I would want to go anywhere other than those schools – that's the culture,' a parent told us.

Long school days with the youngest boys finishing at 5pm, older pupils going on past 6pm. Boys here are all of above average ability, but still divided on academic lines in year 7 into 'scholars' and 'others' (or 'brainy and thick,' as one son told his mother). School happy to support boys who may struggle in one area and will take those with mild dyslexia or dyspraxia. Around 10 per cent of pupils have some extra help from specialist SEN teachers. But it's probably not for a boy who may struggle across the board – he simply wouldn't get the best out of the place.

Each school day begins with short service in the beautiful chapel – whole school, two hymns and a reading and a few words from the head or senior staff. Then it's straight into lessons. Prep is done at the end of the day, so no homework needs to go home with the day boys; 'wonderful,' chorus mothers, who don't have to chivvy.

It's a fairly challenging academic environment; Aldro boys are undoubtedly hard working, well monitored and generally encouraged to develop high levels of independence, self-motivation and organisation skills. Quite a few longstanding teachers doing what they've always done, with some young blood to leaven the mix. Higher than average numbers of husband and wife teaching combos. Particular parental mention for 'stand-out' science and 'superb' French. Although long-serving head of department has retired, two native French speaking staff are much praised – we spotted Monsieur teaching pétanque during break and school has its own bouledrome. Pupils keen on history teacher operating out of distinctive classroom with mood-setting, old-fashioned fixtures and fittings, who organises chances to dress up and act out characters and events. Seventy per cent of full time teachers are male – great role models for the boys

– 'lots of nice teachers,' they told us. Good manners abound – boys will sometimes say 'thank you' after a lesson and staff sometimes say it too, if boys have been particularly productive and engaged.

Blessed with seemingly boundless bosky grounds, bordered by woods where they make dens and play in the treehouse, on the rope bridge and in the rowing lake

A pleasingly broad curriculum: boys say the best thing about this school is the variety of things they get to do – drama (in new studio), plenty of art and DT, including pottery, music (two-thirds of boys have an individual lesson every week and masses of practice rooms) and, of course, sport galore. Past feeling that less sporty boys get overlooked has changed as staff work hard to achieve 'sport for all'. 'I like the fact they go back to basics, including working on fitness levels that can be overlooked,' said one parent. Main sports are rugby, football, hockey, tennis, cricket and athletics. Aldro's 1st XV rugby team have been national under-13 champions. New sports centre completed 2015. Boys can also hunt (for fossils), shoot (pistol and rifle) and fish. This place is also tremendously strong on chess and even a model railway – basically, if your son has an interest, this school will ensure he develops it.

Boys really can be boys here – blessed with seemingly boundless bosky grounds, bordered by woods where they make dens and play in the tree house, on the rope bridge and in the rowing lake. 'They have a lot of freedom outdoors and it can be quite a shock after their usually sheltered pre-prep experiences, where they are marshalled from pillar to post,' said one mother. 'It's simply idyllic,' said another. 'And because the boys are free to roam in the great outdoors they get great self-confidence, which has benefits in all sorts of areas.'

Indoors, the main building is arts and crafts, centred around an imported Jacobean staircase. Most of the classrooms are in a much newer 1990s block including the flashy IT stuff and a tip-top library. But generally the school is selected for its reputation, rather than swanky facilities. A glance around the car park on match days will confirm Aldro parents are generally a very well-heeled bunch; the majority are the married upper-middle classes.

Aldro has a distinct boarding school ethos, even though on bald numbers it has many more day pupils. While the school has the occasional boarder at 7 or 8 (these tend to be Forces families), more typically pupils board by 9 or 10 in readiness

for their move to a senior boarding school. 'The whole boarding set up is brilliant and was just what we needed by year 7,' said one mother. 'The boys have supper and some time to relax and have fun, but are then brought back to task with prep and revision sessions – fantastic; I couldn't have done as well at home.'

'The boarding is great and be warned, your son will want to try it before he leaves,' counselled another mother. 'We live too close to make it viable, but my son would leave home for school tomorrow if I said the word.' Just seven boys board full time, 20 are weekly and the rest flexi, with an average of about 50 sleeping at school on any one night. In reality 'flexible' means 'pre-arranged part time', though of course the school will try to facilitate the odd night when required. But it takes its responsibility to the regular boarders seriously. 'A boy needs to feel settled and to know who'll be in the next bed on any given night,' says boarding master. Certainly the current arrangements must work well, because since introducing this more flexible approach (in the past it was all or nothing) boarding has flourished here.

Boarders and hanger-on day boys have supper at 6pm, after which the day boys leave and it's 'Mars time' for boarders – from the old advert 'work, rest and play'. But for 'work' school means 'do some', for a rest 'read your book' and 'play' means 'play your instrument'. At 7.15pm an activity, then 20 minutes or so access to phones/iPods before showers and bed (year 6 at 8.30pm). We spotted a Wii gathering dust in the corner of the common room – apparently it comes out in terrible weather – and a (thankfully more popular) pet hamster. Accommodation is typical of modern boarding facilities, functional and homely rather than luxurious, all supervised by young matrons in the 'big sister/concerned aunt' mould.

Parents find the school nicely sociable, usual set up of 'Friends', class reps and so on. Mothers enjoying a tennis morning when we were there. Not tons of extras to find. It's expensive, but that's it – you won't pay for much else. Lunch and books included in fees and not many outings or fancy trips. Thriving and established market in second-hand blazers, so check that out before you buy a new one.

Overall a successful school with a real Christian ethos – no lip service here – and lots of traditional elements: high standards of work, play and simple manners. Good for active, go-getty characters. Not for the faint-hearted – academically or personality-wise. If your son needs brow-mopping and spoon-feeding, think again.

Ardingly College

College Road, Haywards Heath, West Sussex RH17 6SQ

01444 893000
registrar@ardingly.com
www.ardingly.com
C of E

Ages: 13–18
Pupils: 550; sixth form: 249
Boarders: 257 full/weekly
Day: £21,960 – £23,160 pa
Boarding: £24,585 – £31,425 pa

Headmaster: Since September 2014, Ben Figgis MA (Cantab). Previously deputy head at Oakham, where he also taught sixth form history and theory of knowledge. Has also been history teacher, housemaster and head of boarding at Abingdon. Before taking up teaching had a life in media, which he left after concerns about the ethical compromises involved in news gathering. Keen to provide pupils with a modern education, and a world view. Enrichment is a word which comes up a lot – an interest and excitement in subjects is as important as achieving a particular grade.

Pupils are very enthusiastic about the head and say he's 'balanced' (in comparison to his predecessor who was apparently more hard line). Described by a parent as 'approachable', though still finding his feet; but she said her children all really like him.

Loves theatre, and enjoys fly fishing. Just finished Paradise Postponed by John Mortimer. Married to Joanna.

Academic matters: Excellent GCSE results, mostly climbing steadily each year. In 2015, 62 per cent of GCSEs A*/A. Subjects are almost uniformly excellent, with sciences and maths being popular high performers, and humanities also doing very well. Only performance in classical civilisation is comparatively underwhelming, though the few opting for Latin get mostly A*s and As.

IB points a very good 38 per pupil. A levels not quite so startling: 38 per cent A*-A, 73 per cent A*-B, though maths, chemistry (National Chemistry champions – won the RSC's Top of the Bench competition), and physics remain high achieving subjects, as does English literature. The international nature of the sixth form also means a good showing in MFLs such as Chinese, Russian and German; but performance is less strong in other areas. A reasonable list of subjects on offer, although one parent said she would like to see the inclusion of some less purely academic subjects, such as sociology.

High take up of IB in this internationally minded school (40 per cent): they're in the top 10 IB schools in the UK, and very enthusiastic about it. The IB results at Ardingly are consistently higher than the A level results – so whereas most pupils get Bs in A level history, most pupils get a 6 in IB history (roughly equivalent to an A). Bright and well-motivated students are more likely to take the IB, says the head, accounting for the much more impressive IB results.

The IB way of learning and thinking is here viewed as so beneficial that it has been adopted for A level pupils, who also study the IB core of extended essay, theory of knowledge, and action and service. A parent described her daughter as 'a bit miffed' at the extra work, but can see the benefits of the community service and mindfulness elements. She was rather more dubious about the extra written work, feeling that A levels on their own are quite enough for some stressed teens to cope with.

There are plans to develop science and technology to enhance pupils' preparation for undergraduate study – computer science is on the way in 2016, and the head is particularly keen to make sure science options, usually dominated by boys, are appealing to girls.

The head relishes the fact that footballers about to compete opted to spend the morning at the Ardingly Shakespeare conference

Ardingly is keen to promote independent learning and one of the parents we spoke to said this was one of her favourite things about the school: she praised their promotion of independent research, thinking outside the box and examining information with a critical eye. 'It sparks their interest', she said. The skills for independent learning start in year 9 with iMind – not, as you might think, a new app, but how the brain functions, mindfulness and a personal project on any chosen subject (from what makes the perfect curry to what makes people interested in the paranormal). In an eye-catching project which illustrates their innovative thinking, pupils built a solar car which was entered for 3,000 km World Solar Challenge across Australia in 2015. Didn't complete the course but was a first for a school in Europe.

Pupils here are lively and interested in what they're doing. We joined an English lesson on The Importance of Being Ernest, and were impressed by an energetic teacher, and pupils' interested and thoughtful approach. A parent commented that she loves the 'relaxed open relationship with teachers', and this was evidently the case.

Learning support good for those with mild disorders. We spoke to a parent whose daughter has

mild dyslexia, and whose LS with maths and English helped her get the grades she needed at GCSE. But pupils need to be able to cope on their own at A level.

Games, options, the arts: Grounds are extensive and gorgeous – it is succulently green all around. One of our guides glanced with familiar affection across the fields: one of them, the scene of a recent victory, had become his favourite place at school.

Strong sports department with county and national winners in hockey, football, fencing and golf, and plenty of individual winners too. Pupils were keen to point out that the glory is not exclusively for high performers: pupils in first XI all the way down to the sixth XI go on school tours, and receive school awards, although a parent said she felt that the greatest focus was on the senior A and B teams.

A bit boy-heavy in emphasis, said a mum (the girls are probably delighted, she added dryly), with the girls only really excelling in hockey; but the head points out the same resources are put into girls' and boys' sports.

A minimum two games sessions a week for all, and day pupils' kit often ends up being laundered at school.

Monday activities include minor sports such as horse riding, and sailing or rowing on the reservoir; and an ever-changing variety of other activities, from bee keeping and book binding to the interestingly named Ardinglay (it's a chicken club). DofE: lots do silver, and a few gold – in canoes and on horseback in recent years. It's not cliquey – the head relishes the fact that footballers about to play in the Boodles cup opted to spend the morning at the Ardingly national Shakespeare conference. You can choose to be very busy indeed; but pupils assured us that not everyone does, and that's fine too.

CCF is not popular here, to the chagrin of one of our guides, who clearly has a wonderful time. 'I think the parades put people off,' she said wistfully, 'but it's so much fun. There's a section attack on the headmaster's field this afternoon,' she added enthusiastically, as a canon was wheeled into the quad. 'It just shoots blanks,' she said cheerfully, 'but it makes lots of noise.' It's difficult to argue with the evident joys of shooting a canon. Almost worth the parades, one might think...

Large number of instrumental lessons and ensembles; in particular the 70-strong flourishing chapel choir which sings at cathedrals at home and abroad – and is a good outlet for exam stress. A vocal ensemble and the London Philharmonic visit to coach and inspire, and Ardingly hosts a concert series which stars national and international musicians.

Drama is popular, particularly with boys, to the delight of the head, who feels that creative art is too often the preserve of girls. They haven't got the posh modern theatre many independent schools boast, and one of the parents commented that the infrastructure could do with a bit of investment, but a gradual programme of modernisation is under way. Pupils perform at the Edinburgh fringe and home grown ArtsFest each year (a post-exam joy here), fun even for those not into drama, who do half day workshops on anything from making short films to mask mimes.

Superb art department with a gallery packed with amazing work – we could happily have spent hours here appreciating the extraordinary creative work on view, showing that art students at Ardingly see life from all sorts of interesting angles, from butterfly dresses to a view inside a body which almost seemed to pulsate. There's a free range element to the GCSE, A level and IB art curricula, with students choosing which areas they wish to pursue; and you can see how much this freedom is appreciated by the quality of the work. Pupils can even have lessons from the sculptor in residence.

Boarding: Feels a bit like a university campus, with boarding houses reached by a path through a tranquil bluebell-lined woodland glade. Boarding houses are modern purpose-built blocks, decorated in house colours. Corridor walls covered in photos chosen by boarders, organised by year, up to lower sixth on the top floor. Very strong house feeling – all must compete in cross-country run, and apparently even reluctant runners are happy to compete for their house. A map of the world decorated with flags and photos shows where each boarder comes from in this truly cosmopolitan school; and there's a list of names of older students from whom youngsters can seek academic help. There's a teacher on duty every night too, but one boy said that older pupils can often help better – they explain things in a different way.

Parents of boarders were full of praise: one said all her children wanted to board, and really enjoy it. The boarding master responds promptly to emails, and she likes the easy mix between boarders and day pupils.

Rooms for two to four younger boarders, with singles for older pupils. A housemaster admitted rooms are on the spartan side, being limited to bunks, desks and wardrobes; but said he doesn't want pupils lingering in bedrooms: they are for sleeping and studying, and the rest of time should be spent in the common room: spacious, squashy leather sofas, TV, pool, table football, the Times and Telegraph. Brew rooms (kitchens) on each corridor, and one equipped with oven for more serious culinary matters (used under supervision). Lower sixth supervise youngsters' studying and bedtime rituals, studying supervision being much preferable, said one of our guides with small shudder at the thought of bedtime duty (they are given advice about how to manage this).

Parents liked the weekly service, one saying she felt it was important for children to develop the ability to sit still, be silent and respectful: 'you can hear a pin drop'

Activities and sports on Saturday – recently a night of cowboy fun complete with hired rodeo bull; the head of boarding was moving with due care for bruises. Sundays for relaxation (gym and pool are open), with a trip out every three weeks. There's a tremendously popular Sunday shuttle to Sainsburys, with each year group getting £50 for ingredients: serious cooking follows. No making their own breakfast though: kitchens are locked to ensure pupils go to the dining hall for a proper breakfast –'no surviving on just toast until lunchtime.' Each floor has a disabled loo and lift access.

Around half of boarders are overseas students, including expats, so there's no dominant country and no general exodus at weekends. Every Wednesday the blog is updated to communicate boarders' latest doings to parents. Pupils use own laptops to keep in touch – letter writing is largely a thing of the past here.

In the latest edition of Logo there are articles on the Bible and feminism, and whether the Christian tradition ever treated women with respect

Upper sixth have their own boarding house – like Premier Inn, suggested a member of staff; there is some similarity, though we've never seen a Premier Inn in such a lovely setting; or with such a nice gym. Super en suite study bedrooms, kitchens, huge common room, which is divided at 10pm between boys and girls, and opens at 7am. There's even a bar (two beers or two wines limit) but not many choose to drink. Encouraged to do own laundry– some actually do.

Background and atmosphere: Not as stiff and traditional as the cream paper in the guide for parents would suggest. One parent chose the school because the children who go there seem so 'normal', and for the strong sense of community. There's no held breath tension in the corridors here: pupils are relaxed and happy, with an outward looking politeness (pupils enquired after reviewer's journey etc – it doesn't often happen). It's not a leap to your feet school, but there was a genuine friendliness in the courtesy and smiles we encountered on our tour.

Charming red-brick buildings form the older parts of the school, whose atmosphere lacks the rarefied feel which often goes with the presence of quads. Modern and rather nondescript buildings house the music and boarding houses; but the green surrounds offer ample distracting beauty. One of the favourite places of our guides was the terrace, with its stunning views over the Sussex countryside; just below lies the head's garden, viewed longingly by both pupils and the head of prep – it's clearly Eden here.

This Woodard school was originally for the children of clergy; and it is no surprise that there is a clear religious structure here, with a weekly communion service in the chapel for all (including non-believers and other faiths). High church with bells and smells, and what one parent called 'some obscure hymns'. The parents we spoke to liked the weekly service, one saying she felt it was important for children to develop the ability to sit still, be silent and respectful: 'you can hear a pin drop,' said approvingly. Another, while liking it herself, admitted her children thought it was boring, and said the new head is revisiting the ethos of chapel with pupils. The head believes there's a value in exposing pupils to chapel, but there is no expectation of them adopting Christianity –'pupils need to feel comfortable and welcome.' Notably, divinity is joined by philosophy in the curriculum, and in the latest edition of Logos, the school magazine, there are articles on the Bible and feminism, and whether the Christian tradition ever treated women with respect. The Sophos philosophical debating club regularly debates pupil chosen topics such as life after death. This is not a school for unquestioning acceptance, and this critical eye extends to its founding Christian ethos.

Pastoral care, well-being and discipline: Pastoral care is 'outstanding,' said one parent; 'paramount,' said another, who said the ability to cater well for each child's individual needs is the best thing about the school. What's more, 'they take on difficult kids from other schools and bring them into line.'

Eudaimonia, not a rare disease, but 'human flourishing' al la Aristotle (PHSE to the rest of us) is part of the curriculum throughout senior school. Encompasses the usual sex, drugs and internet warnings; but also friendship, positive thinking and the wonder of every individual.

Firm line on bullying: pupils are encouraged to whistleblow, and expulsions will follow if the situation's unresolvable, say pupils, who also commented on some expulsions a few years ago for smoking dope, which they completely supported – 'we wouldn't have wanted them here,' they said in shocked voices.

The new head is clearly just as principled as his predecessor, and has expelled a pupil for being rude and disrespectful to a member of the catering staff. But he seems more likely to understand that children experiment and less likely to damn them for doing so: those who come clean about offences and promise not to reoffend are likely to have a second chance.

Pupils choose their own tutor, whom they meet fortnightly to ensure individual needs are being met – for example in timetables or teaching methods. However, the head also has a strong belief in the values of service and community, and is wary of growing expectations from customer parents to have school life flexed to suit their children. Some requests are reasonable, but there is some danger that children who always having things adjusted to their needs feel everything will always revolve around them: the values of living in and adapting to a community need to be understood.

There's an on campus chaplain and independent listener for those who need to talk through problems confidentially.

The community here is very strong, say parents, which is reflected in the reward structure: the usual system for effort and attainment, but with extra emphasis on becoming a good citizen: ACES (Ardingly Citizenship Exemplary Student award) is given to pupils whose good behaviour models

the justice and compassion desired for all pupils at Ardingly. Good citizenship is the avenue for year 8 pupils to achieve monitor and prefect status.

Pupils and parents: Thirty different nationalities in the school, with 28 per cent of pupils coming from overseas. The head deliberately manages the numbers of overseas students, from around 18 per cent in Shell (year 9), up to a third in upper sixth, increasing diversity and international thought as students get stuck into the IB.

Parents include many London professionals, expats, and foreign office. 'There is wealth in the school, but it has a down to earth quality.' There's someone topping up fees by working in Sainsburys; and then there's a few more who buy their new four wheel drive every February when it's bonus time.

Half termly assessments and reports. The new head's introduced a weekly email telling parents what's going on, which is much appreciated. Parents are confident they could approach a form tutor or head of house with a problem.

Old Ardinians include racing driver Mike Hawthorn, Ian Hislop, composer Stephen Oliver, actors Terry-Thomas and Alan Howard.

Entrance: Need 55 per cent at CE, 110 CAT test. Written assessments in English, maths and verbal reasoning, and interview with the head. Overseas

students need to have fluent English, and pass the same assessments as English counterparts.

Entrance to the sixth requires six or more grade B passes at GCSE, including at least a C in English and maths.

Exit: Some 30 per cent leave after GCSEs, mostly for local sixth form colleges, Lots of sixth form leavers to Russell group universities eg UCL, Exeter, Manchester; three to Cambridge in 2015, plus universities in the US, Hong Kong, China and Germany.

Money matters: Over a third of pupils on some sort of support or bursary. Once a prospective pupil gets a scholarship, the level of support depends on need, and is not restricted by the numbers already in receipt of scholarships.

Remarks: A strong and caring community which finds a balance between excellent pastoral care and academic achievement. This modern school with its focus on independent thought would suit those with a broad outlook and interests.

Ashdown House School

Forest Row, East Sussex RH18 5JY

01342 822574
secretary@ashdownhouse.com
www.ashdownhouse.co.uk
C of E

Ages: 4–13
Pupils: 125
Boarders: 102 full/flexi
Day: £8,010 – £17,400 pa
Boarding: £25,680 pa

Headmaster: Since January 2013, Haydon Moore BTh, previously deputy and acting head. A popular appointment: he 'understands the ethos of the school', say parents. Has worked in prep schools for most of his career; married to Annie.

Entrance: By informal assessment and a maths and writing test plus a report from the child's current school – the key criterion being that the child is going to be happy and won't struggle. The ultimate test is common entrance and they need to be up to

this. Children can join at any time if there are spaces, – now has a pre-prep for 4-7 year olds – but most start in years 3 and 4 (many as day children to start with) and a number of boarders join in the 3s (year 6) – just gives enough time for children to prepare for common entrance. About 30 per cent of children come from London day schools, some from local private and state schools and a number of expats, many from Hong Kong, Singapore and the Caribbean.

A few start aged 7 as day children but are soon begging their parents to become boarders as feel they are missing out on all the fun. About 25 day children altogether; they have to attend Saturday school and afternoon matches.

Exit: To the major national public schools: Benenden, Eton, Marlborough, Downe House, Harrow, Wycombe Abbey, Rugby, Radley, King's Canterbury, Bryanston, Stowe et al. Leaving at 11+ is not encouraged and virtually all stay on to 13. Good scholarship record.

Remarks: The school was founded in Brighton in 1843 and moved to its present site in 1886. The main house, neoclassical in style, was designed in 1793 by Benjamin Henry Latrobe, who later moved to the USA, where he was responsible for the building of the Capitol and the White House. The original Tudor manor house, dating from 1575, forms one wing of the school. It is set in 40 acres of land, half a mile from the nearest road – many former pupils say that one of their lasting memories of Ashdown is the glorious setting.

Children streamed for the last three years but setted in maths from the 4s (year 5). Scholarship class for the last year. Average class size about 12, max 15. Latin for last three years and Greek for most for the last one or two years.

Ashdown recently became part of the Cothill Educational Trust and one of the many benefits is the use of Château de Sauveterre in the South of France. It is run as a separate French prep school with all lessons in French and the children learn French history, geography etc; trip includes a week's skiing in the Pyrenees for those going at the right time of year. All children in the 2s (year 7) spend one term here – a high point in their Ashdown careers and a real confidence builder. The younger children can spend a week at La Chaumière, a farm on the estate.

Three well-equipped science labs in the Jungle Block and there is a large pond for fishing for creepy crawlies. The Old Malt House, also part of the Cothill Educational Trust, is an ex-prep school on the Dorset coast which has been developed as a natural history centre staffed by experts from the Natural History Museum – the 2s (year 7) spend five days here studying real life science and geography and doing outdoor pursuits.

About 20 per cent of children need some sort of SEN support, mainly for mild dyslexia. One full time and two part time teachers based in the purpose-built log cabin in the garden – individual or group tutoring for which parents are charged. Annual cognitive tests to ensure no one slips through the net. One EFL teacher for about 12 children – the school is careful that no one nationality dominates.

Sport every day – a huge part of school life. The usual sports and enough teams for everyone to play in a match if they want to – give other local preps a run for their money but all played with a balance of competitiveness and good humour. Particularly strong netball and recent SE England U13 football goalie. Cricket nets and football in the old barn – perfect for letting off steam on wet days.

One cosy and happy home from home where everyone feels part of the family and the headmaster's door is always open. Family dogs wandering round the house

Fab art and DT – pictures all over the dining room which doubles as an art gallery and the ultimate honour is to have a piece picked to hang in the headmaster's study. Art scholarships most years and brightly coloured totem poles dotted around the grounds. Chess also a big thing at Ashdown, on the curriculum for the juniors and many develop a lifelong love of the game here – lots of competitions and one girl recently picked for the U14 GB chess squad.

Lots of music – concerts, bands, etc under the direction of inspirational head of music and a dedicated team of visiting music staff – huge range of instruments played including the harp and electric guitar. Ten children performed in the children's chorus in Hansel & Gretel at Glyndebourne recently. Everyone is involved in the annual Choral Day – it is all about taking part, you don't have to be particularly good at singing. Music scholarships most years.

Series of lectures on Wednesday evenings teaches children to listen and ask spontaneous questions. Speakers have included cricketer Henry Olonga, mountaineers and adventurers, a magician from the Magic Circle and the artist and conservationist David Shepherd.

Activities every Friday afternoon, anything from riding at the local riding school, martial arts, squash, water colours, gardening – the younger children love to grow their own vegetables – photography and ceramics. A huge range of clubs on Saturdays: nature watch, pottery, debating, cooking, film making. Staff do things they are passionate about and thus fire up the children's enthusiasm. Popular modelling area in the cellar and, of course, the Scalextric room where the headmaster still holds the record for the fastest lap.

Lots of plays – one for each age group every year and three for the top year. Super theatre with a big screen – useful for lectures. Lots of outdoor activities and trips all over the place, Dale Fort in Wales, Swallows and Amazons trip to the Lake District and the very popular three day bushcraft survival course when the children build their own shelters to sleep in and cook their meals over open fires.

Staff do things they are passionate about. Popular modelling area in the cellar and, of course, the Scalextric room where the headmaster still holds the record for the fastest lap

Very much a full boarding school with day children and some flexi boarders in the lower years – older ones nearly all full boarders. Apart from the set exeats, children allowed out after chapel on four Sundays a term (although some seem to bend the rules a bit here). Everyone has to write a letter home on Sunday mornings – something particularly appreciated by the parents: a phone call is just not the same. Five landings divided between year groups, two for girls and three for boys, each with a houseparent, an assistant housemaster and gap student. Top year children act as dorm captains. School also vertically divided into four patrols: Hippos, Rhinos, Elephants and Kangs, with two members of staff in charge of each patrol and with seniors looking out for the younger children. Church of England school but with an ecumenical

A dedicated team of teachers; they run clubs at weekends and often build bonfires so the children can toast marshmallows and bake potatoes in the embers

approach. Chapel every Sunday, prayers in some assemblies and grace after lunch.

Warm and welcoming atmosphere. Top of the range facilities for the things that matter like science labs, ICT, interactive whiteboards (some masters still prefer chalk), art and music. Other areas, like the dorms, reassuringly scruffy but that is the spirit of Ashdown – one cosy and happy home from home where everyone feels part of the family and the headmaster's door is always open. Family dogs wandering round the house – in fact one of them has its own blog – plus chickens, rabbits and guinea pigs in the garden. Golf clubs piled up in the front porch – the school has its own golf course. No one feels pushed or pressurised here but school still gets fantastic results and there is a spontaneous celebration in each other's achievements. Children are natural and confident and are happy to strike up a conversation with adults but can remain children for longer in these idyllic surroundings with lots of space and time to be free. They are allowed to climb trees and make dens in the jungle and there is plenty of time for just mucking about. An extraordinarily dedicated team of teachers, many of whom live on site; they run clubs at weekends and often build bonfires so the children can toast marshmallows and bake potatoes in the embers. Staff eat with children at lunchtimes – good food and plenty of choice and lots of barbecues during the summer.

Emphasis on kindness and consideration. Guidelines laid out at the back of the termly calendar: Be polite and smile, 'do not feel shy about using really good manners'. Stress on common courtesy and awareness of other people in the community. The school reinforces the simple message at the start of every term – Be Kind. Be Kind. Be Kind. Parents generally down to earth and unpretentious, some aspirational and a few first time buyers. About 30 per cent from London, others local or expats. No parents' group but open house for matches, plays, concerts etc and always made to feel welcome.

Ex pupils include Boris Johnson, Rachel Johnson (former editor of The Lady), Damian Lewis, Nicholas Coleridge and Viscount Linley.

Ashford School

East Hill, Ashford, Kent TN24 8PB

01233 625171
registrar@ashfordschool.co.uk
www.ashfordschool.co.uk

Ages: 11–18 (junior boarding from year 6)
Pupils: 480; sixth form: 175
Boarders: 155
Day: £8,400 – £16,200 pa
Boarding: £28,500 – £32,400 pa

Headmaster: Since 2005, Mr Michael Buchanan (50s) BSc PGCE NPQH. Educated at Downside and King's College London, where he read physics and trained as a teacher. Previously spent 10 years at Highgate School in north London, where he left as principal deputy head. Part of his brief there was to bring in co-education, and he has done a similar job at Ashford with great success. Previously head of sixth form at Royal Grammar School, Guildford. Businesslike and charming, he has a passion for physics, sport and choral music – he is a highly experienced, lead ISI inspector. 'Very approachable and a good communicator and you know who is in charge', according to one parent. Still teaches and referees sport when he can. Married with two daughters who attended the school; his wife works for a bank in London. He says the whole family felt welcomed from the moment they arrived at Ashford.

He is a 'very good motivator', according to one former pupil, and has introduced the Adventurous Learning programme that is all about taking people – staff and children alike – out of their comfort zone and challenging in all areas, personal as well as academic. It might be trying something new like speaking in front of the whole class and then the whole school. He 'wants children to develop as self reliant all-rounders who have a sense of responsibility, compassion and teamwork and the resilience to cope with adversity'. He also wants pupils to take responsibility for their own learning and to feel able to make mistakes. Likes every sort of success to be rewarded and feels that learning should be fun. Head and staff lead by example: Mr Buchanan has taken up the euphonium and 40 teachers have taken up other musical instruments to remind themselves what it feels like to be a pupil.

The school has grown by over 150 since he arrived, helped by the massive building boom in Ashford and the fast rail link to St Pancras. He is gradually replacing the ageing school buildings at the same time as driving the rise in academic standards.

Academic matters: Broad intake, results improving year on year. In 2015, 74 per cent A*/B and 50 per cent A*/A at A level; at GCSE, 33 per cent A*/A. Particularly good results in science and maths. Everyone takes separate sciences from Year 7. All students learn two languages chosen from Spanish, German and French; German most popular. Pupils from abroad also encouraged to take GCSE in their first language eg Chinese or Dutch. Good range of subjects at A level including Chinese, business studies, psychology, textiles, sports studies and drama. In sixth form Russian, German and Spanish offered as a business language (basic language skills, mostly conversation). Very accommodating timetable and school willing to offer a subject to only a handful of students. Digital literacy programme for year 7. A very tech savvy school – radio voting handsets have proved popular and effective – children text answers to the screen anonymously, useful for shy children but also means there is no chance of a snooze at the back of the class as everyone has to participate. Pupils set by ability in core subjects but there is plenty of flexibility and children can be moved up or down mid term if appropriate. No plans to introduce the IB.

Loyal team of teachers who love the challenge and freedom to innovate and are encouraged to use their initiative. Headmaster likes to recruit those with outside experience who can offer something

A group of pupils recently designed a stained glass window for a church in the Holy Land and were then invited to install their work in situ

different. Good mix of old hands and NQTs – school runs a leading and innovative graduate teacher training programme. Biology teacher won a UK top teacher award and also organises the school's rock festival, AshBash. A new higher education advisor has recently joined the team to help with UCAS forms and beyond – he was previously a university admissions tutor. The Oxbridge Club provides extra coaching in problem solving and analytical and critical thinking. Lots of language exchanges and trips that help bring learning to life and 'take school work into the real world,' according to one happy father. A level physicists visit CERN.

Some 35 pupils with SEN ranging from organisation skills to severe dyslexia, dyspraxia, dyscalculia and school can support children with physical disabilities, 'The teachers really go the extra mile for a child who struggles – nothing is too much trouble'.

New International Centre for 21 11-16 year olds offers a one-year intensive English language course.

Games, options, the arts: Good sports facilities with two gyms and a floodlit Astroturf as well as a fitness centre and dance suite, indoor swimming pool and all weather basketball court. Cricket played at the local club a few minutes' walk away and a new sports centre opened in 2013 with Sport England specification. Boys' sport now fully developed and there are senior first teams in rugby, hockey and cricket, but fixtures still a bit sparse as other schools are a 'bit slow to twig that Ashford boys are actually rather good at games'. Teams maintained into sixth form and everyone has to take part in a physical activity at least once a week. Yoga and exercise classes popular, especially with the senior girls, along with street and jazz dance and personal survival. Strong house loyalty and everyone expected to take part in house events.

Lots going on in the drama department from house plays and speech and drama recitals, lower school productions and the spectacular whole school summer musical. Active junior drama club as well as technical drama club for those who prefer to keep out of the spotlight. Drama a popular option at GCSE and also offered at A level and school prepares pupils for speech and drama and LAMDA exams. Vibrant music and art departments: head of music is a colourful character who has transformed the musical life of the school;

numbers participating have shot up, as has the standard. Tuition on most instruments available from the bassoon to the organ and school has two Steinway pianos as part of the Steinway schools programme. Lots going on: concert band, chamber music groups, string quartet, rock bands, string ensembles, community orchestra. Concerts every three to four weeks. Head wants music to be 'about performance and enjoyment' with plenty of opportunities for showmanship from 'teatime tootles' in the atrium to singing in Westminster Abbey.

Fabulous textiles and 'big and bold' approach to art; several go on to art foundation courses each year. A group of pupils recently designed a stained glass window for a church in the Holy Land and were then invited to install their work in situ. Another group made some wall hangings for the local hospice. 'We do random and different things and let it all come out', says one pupil.

Head wants music to be 'about performance and enjoyment' with plenty of opportunities for showmanship from 'teatime tootles' to singing in Westminster Abbey

Huge range of clubs and activities, from Lego robotics to cooking and debating – something for everyone and all have to take part until sixth form. Strong debating team has represented the school at the Oxford and Cambridge Unions' competitions and taken part in the European Youth Parliament at the Foreign Office. Amnesty group won an award for 'Best Fundraising Event in UK Schools' with their 'Dare to be Different Day'. CCF popular and about 12 pupils complete their D of E Gold each year.

Boarding: Boarding from year 6 (bussed over to junior school) but very few in this age group. Boarders well supported and cared for; they are also allocated a house and are not allowed back into their boarding houses during the day, which means plenty of interaction with day children. Lots of boarders' activities and birthdays always celebrated. Houses recently refurbished; sixth formers have en suite bathrooms. Six houses, each led by a head of house, a teacher who oversees academic progress and personal development of each child. Children from abroad spend the first weekend of term with a day pupil – helps integration. Close liaison with parents and tutor and regular progress reviews. Lots of leadership opportunities running house events and activities, from community work to the house play. No lessons on Saturday mornings

but time devoted to sport, rehearsals and activities – day children always happy to come in and it means the boarders are kept busy.

Background and atmosphere: Founded in 1898 with the aim that the pupils should play an active role in the life of the town and with an emphasis on 'training and development of character', the school moved to its present site in 1913 and became part of United Learning in 1999 (a group of 31 schools). This brought a welcome injection of cash resulting in new buildings springing up all over the place. Senior school is at the foot of the High Street, approached by a narrow lane and enclosed by high red-brick walls with lawns and greenery stretching down the hill. It's a green oasis in the middle of busy Ashford and quite difficult to find if you don't know where to look. Extensive rugby and cricket pitches are a short walk away. It's an international and friendly community – pupils are expected to engage with school life, and head says he 'does not want passengers on board and expects everyone to take part'. Good food, cafeteria style, lots of choice and healthy salad options. Brightly painted Atrium café a popular meeting place, also open to parents at pick up and drop off time.

Pastoral care, well-being and discipline: Strong pastoral care via house system; everyone is allocated a house on arrival as well as a specialist tutor; new joiners in year 7 also have a sixth form mentor.

Pupils and parents: About 70 per cent day children from as far afield as Maidstone, Sittingbourne and Cranbrook (minibus service). Very few weekly boarders so room for growth here. Families from a broad social spectrum; parents have high expectations and are encouraged to get involved and be part of the community. Twenty per cent foreign nationals, over 24 nationalities and particularly popular with Chinese, Germans, Eastern Europeans and Nigerians – school takes care that no nationality dominates. 'Ashford is very good at taking kids of any type and getting the best out of them', says a parent, 'and I like the way the school takes trouble to develop the kids' characters as well as the academic side.'

Entrance: About 60 per cent come up from the prep school, others from local primaries and prep schools eg Sutton Valence, Dulwich and Spring Grove. Wide ability range – some very bright, others who struggle, but all must have the ability to pass at least six GCSEs. Almost automatic entry from prep school but must be within the academic range. Children joining from other schools sit assessment tests in English, maths, science and non-verbal reasoning and take part in a team building exercise. Preference given to siblings where possible. A further 15 or so join at 13+ via school's own tests. Sixth form entry tested in proposed AS subjects and must have six GCSEs A*-B or equivalent, plus English proficiency test if appropriate. Lots of foreign nationals come for sixth form as well as several each year from local state schools.

Exit: To a huge range of different institutions from Russell Group (two-thirds) to modern, including a smattering to Oxbridge over the last few years – broad minded higher education and careers advisor takes huge trouble to guide right student to right course. A few leave at 13+ – no coaching for CE but good relationships with other local schools; around a third depart after GCSEs.

Money matters: Academic, music, art, drama and sports scholarships offered – usually 10-30 per

cent of day fee. Means-tested bursaries for children of clergy, mostly Anglican but will consider other Christian denominations. Twenty per cent discount for Forces families, discounts for siblings. Church Schools Foundation Assisted Places assessed on a combination of academic ability and financial need, worth up to 85 per cent of fees – offered to those entering in year 7, 9 or sixth form. Short-term emergency bursaries available.

Remarks: A forward-looking school with a strong international contingent which is going from strength to strength, benefitting in part from the huge growth of Ashford town. The school has 'changed beyond belief in the last eight years' and appeals to a wide range of families with its strong pastoral care and adventurous learning programme.

Bede's Preparatory School

Duke's Drive, Eastbourne, East Sussex BN20 7XL

01323 734222
prep.admissions@bedes.org
www.bedes.org

Ages: 3 months–13 years (boarding from year 4)
Pupils: 377
Boarders: 11 full, 7 weekly
Day: £9,435 – £16,050 pa
Boarding: plus £7,455 pa

Linked school: Bede's Senior School

Headmaster: Since 2013, Mr Giles Entwisle BA (French, politics and economics at Loughborough) PGCE (late 40s). He came from a deputy headship at Highfield, prior to which he was head of year, housemaster and head of MFL at Holmewood House, near Tunbridge Wells. An enthusiastic, ambitious and engaging, career prep school man, he and senior school head Dr Maloney are a mutually appreciative team, sharing a vision of Bede's and its shining potential. Mr Entwisle, a keen skier – so, clearsighted, focussed and energetic – has a palpable commitment to getting the best out of everyone – pupils and staff alike. Married to a Spaniard and school fosters many links with Spain. Oh – and he is an expert juggler, always useful for a headmaster.

Parents are delighted: 'He's lovely with the children – he knows everyone by name and is getting an excellent new team around him.' 'His door is always open.'

Entrance: Not yet oversubscribed by much but this is likely to change so get in early. Around twice as many boys as girls – as elsewhere.

Exit: Vast majority to the senior school (you need to see it and feel it to understand why) though a few to other local and less local senior schools.

Remarks: You can't beat it for location. At the upmarket end of the grassy Eastbourne seafront where the land curves and rises to the great cliff of Beachy Head, perches an attractive five storey, mock-Tudorbethan pile, its long windows facing the sea. Surrounded by fields on all but its southern aspect, with a cluster of smaller buildings round about, it sits like a benign hen comfortably supervising its offspring, assured that all can run about safely in a healthy, beautiful, open space.

Space is a key asset and to anyone used to, for example, an urban prep or primary, Bede's is a revelation. There are more fields five minutes up the hill and another five minutes inland – all facilitate the range of sports available to these lucky children, who have the look of relaxed freedom that inhabiting such openness gives. Space also in eg the dining hall, one wall of which is just large windows fully open on warm, sunny days, so that the outside and the inside blend.

Two main buildings. Holywell Mount – a large Edwardian house to the right of the main building if you face the sea – houses the pre-prep and nursery. We visited at the end of a long day and were astonished by the bright-eyed vitality of the teachers. They told us of the new topic with which each term is launched in each classroom: 'It's so exciting – they can't wait to come in and see what we're going to do!' And on offer in just some rooms were: Under the Sea World, Ice World, Out of the Egg (and you should have seen the egg!) and Knock Knock – imaginative stuff, inviting exploration and discovery of all kinds.

Almost surrounded by fields, it sits like a benign hen comfortably supervising its offspring, assured that all can run about safely in a healthy, beautiful, open space

Sports are exceptional – and not just because of facilities – at both ends of the spectrum. Says Mr Entwisle: 'We're the best cricketing prep in the country' and, as parents told us,'even the non-sporty get enthused – and they have elite schemes for the really talented'. 'They do wonderful trips, especially for sports and languages.' Children concur: 'We went to Portugal and got trained by Benfica.' Senior school fields etc also used. Several

teams in most sports for all years so that all but the child with thumbs glued to his iPad get a look-in, though some sense that more could be done for the less than athletic. Dance is serious – remember that Bede's is home to The Legat Dance School – so all do dance up to year 5 and many continue. Teachers seen as 'brill!'. Music has a new director and is set to sparkle; art and drama well on the way.

Parents enthuse: 'The teachers are wonderful – so imaginative and approachable!' – and especially about individual needs and pastoral care: 'superb – any problems or hint of bullying are dealt with at speed' and 'they answer emails practically before you've sent them'. Weekly staff meeting to discuss and act on academic or pastoral concerns with head of learning support on hand if needed. Pupil praise too – 'They push you to your potential and we are only 10 in some groups so they can really help you'. Small group specialist work in eg fine motor skills, writing, reading, phonics for tots who seem to be falling behind. All lower classes have a TA to support individuals but some feel this should continue into upper years, 'where they need it just as much if they are struggling with a subject'. As a pupil told us, 'When I'm stuck, if they take time to explain it to me, I really get it!' Individual support – and around 25 per cent on the SEND register here – described as 'good but pricey'.

'Health and safety are taken very seriously,' parents tell us, as are efforts to integrate newcomers, especially into year 7 when there is a fairly substantial intake. And there is masses to do. 'My daughter was very shy but there are so many performances and so on – her confidence has grown unbelievably.' No shortage of facilities, inside and

out – big sports hall, 18m pool, climbing walls, decent library – 'they'll get books you want if you ask' – good theatre and lovely, light rooms with the downside that 'if I'm facing the sea I just go into a daydream,' as one youngster confessed.

Most are local, though word is spreading and pupils now bus or car in from a wider range of villages. School runs its own bus service on eight routes. Boarding – small but growing here, unlike elsewhere, with 11 full and seven weekly boarders – currently starts at year 5 (nearly half of boarders from overseas) and is found in two attractive houses

over the road from the main buildings, staffed by warm and cheery houseparents with their own children on site and lively Aussie gappies. Plans afoot to develop this provision and school set to become a significant player in prep boarding on the south coast.

A happy school – 'It's good at turning out all-rounders,' said several. 'It's pretty unsophisticated and relaxed – you don't get awful pushy parents there – they trust the school to know what it's doing.' And, in the words of a pupil, 'My parents wish they could have come here.'

Bede's Senior School

The Dicker, Hailsham, East Sussex BN27 3QH

01323 843252
admissions@bedes.org
www.bedes.org

Ages: 13–19
Pupils: 724; sixth form: 349
Boarders: 237 full, 70 weekly
Day: £20,415 pa
Boarding: £29,100 – £30,930 pa

Linked school: Bede's Preparatory School

Headmaster: Since 2009, Dr Richard Maloney MA (theology at St Andrew's) PGCE (Cantab), early 40s. An alumnus of Latymer Upper School, Dr Maloney began his career in West Yorkshire. In 1997, he became head of RS and, later, head of sixth, at Chigwell School, during which period he completed an MA at King's College, London. In 2006, he

was appointed deputy headmaster of Sutton Valence. During his tenure there he became a PhD but left after three years to take up this headship – whilst still in his 30s. An impressive start.

Remember 'impressive' and 'start'. A man of palpable energy – physical and intellectual – complemented by equal measures of compassion,

'Bede's learning support finds what they're good at – the teaching is multi-sensory, the classes are alive, the teachers are passionate'

dedication, ambition and vision. A very attractive, very modern head. Modern in that he understands the potential of the virtual, business and academic worlds and is busy threading this through Bede's educational provision, but also modern in that his focus is less on what is provided and more on maximising the potential of every pupil and of every member of his staff. His philosophy is for all to be the best they can, in whatever sphere is right for them. So elite academics, while central, are not elevated above eg elite art, cricket, dance, ceramics. And, increasingly, the staff is composed of his own, outstanding, appointees.

Pupils somewhat in awe but not intimidated. 'He knows more than he shows. He is a real presence when he walks in the room,' we were told. 'His assemblies are brilliant – he's the best speaker I have ever heard.' His colleagues tell us, 'He's very demanding. He always expects to move things up a gear and the staff are up for it.' 'Amazing foresight – he is always thinking ahead so that he can leave a brilliant legacy for future generations.' And parents trust him – 'He celebrates the individual'. Yes, he talks the talk and does so eloquently, persuasively, lucidly. But it's not just buzz – he means it. He has turned around this school, and anyone who visits cannot fail to be both impressed and moved. Of course there is still plenty to do, and he clearly loves the school, its situation and its community. But, by any standards, he is hot property, and is off in July 2016 to head Uppingham. A real coup for them but a sad loss to Bede's, and we await with more than a little interest to see who they will find to build on his substantial legacy.

Academic matters: Unusually large range of GCSE options includes two popular business courses, Mandarin, dance and PE alongside all the more predictable options. Also popular are art, history and geography. Impressive results in art and the sciences in particular. BTecs on offer in nine subjects – including animal management, music performance and business studies. Similarly impressive list of A level subjects includes accounting and computer science. Pre-U rather than A levels offered now in English and music – wise choices. Art, again, the stand-out subject in terms of results, but this is not – thankfully – a results-driven school. The point here is to be 'better' – a word Dr Maloney uses all the time. He is unfussed about league

tables save those which measure value added – and Bede's scores very highly here. 'We prove you can have great results with inspired, holistic teaching.' Parents agree. One – a parent of three – told us: 'It's ridiculous to say it's not academic. My exceptionally bright son is brilliantly taught and is flying. And my other two, who are very different, are well-supported and are equally happy and successful.' In 2015, 80 per cent A*/A at GCSE, and 78 per cent A*-B, 49 per cent A*/A at A level.

Learning enhancement in its own block and central to the ethos of the school. Lots of screening. Years 9-11 have effective revision technique classes, and 'anyone can have learning support in individual subjects or just help with learning in general' – a useful approach. Year 9s also have 'prep project' to learn study techniques. Some 25 per cent of entrants to the earlier years and 12-15 per cent of sixth form entrants come with some kind of, usually mild, SEN. So, additional help is normal here and, as several grateful parents told us, with 'absolutely no stigma'. One parent typified the rest. 'My son has mild SEN problems – I looked at 25 schools and then made a shortlist. They all promised everything but there were cracks in what they said. Bede's learning support finds what they're good at – the teaching is multi-sensory, the classes are alive, the teachers are passionate. My son has grown in independence. He doesn't need support any more.' Others agree: 'They find ways to ensure you don't fail though, on occasions, some more constructive criticism wouldn't be bad,' we heard. Separate EAL dept.

Many a young sports star in the making stays on here rather than joining some club programme 'because it's just as good and I can do my academics too'

Library not the most impressive aspect of school's provision, though modern fiction stock is good. But why a whole set of Hugh Walpole and no Thackeray? Or were Barry Lyndon and The Newcomes etc out on loan?

Games, options, the arts: Dance is big. Bede's is home to the Legat School of Dance and dance attracts much young talent to the school. One large and two smaller studios – the large one is light and lined with photos from the school's history. For some, dance increases in importance and they leave to pursue careers in this area. For others, academics or other pursuits take over and dance becomes a passionate hobby. Teaching is dedicated and inspirational. Dancers work. 'It has been hard at times but it's so convenient having everything in the same place,' one young hopeful explained. 'Dance can be stressful but the pastoral care here is amazing.' Very good drama, led by lively staff in excellent theatre and studio, encompasses the conventional to the experimental. And not just musicals. Technicians from Glyndebourne help and guide, and major productions shown in Eastbourne theatres.

Let us know if you find more inspired, better equipped or more varied ceramics anywhere. It's a real feature of the school, led by veteran potter in the Old Kennels, with three kilns, a spray glazer, electric wheels and a kick wheel dating from 1945 which he found on eBay. Graduates of this A level go on to product design, architecture, fashion, photography, interior design and textiles – a fabulous hand and eye education. Good music, super art – as good as anywhere we know. Photography, mixed media – all impress. No strait-jacketing here but evidence everywhere of imaginations encouraged to flow and flourish. Endless other activities from bee-keeping to the breeding of small animals in the unique Animal Management Centre, where we met some of the 500 inhabitants including a common plec, a sun beetle and a lesser hedgehog tenrec. Links with several zoos. All go to support pupils' studies in the practicalities of animal care.

And then there's the sport. Cricket on glorious pitches – now embellished by the Martin-Jenkins Pavilion celebrating the family's links with the school. Elite sportsmen and women on the staff; many a young sports star in the making stays on

Unique Animal Management Centre; we met some of the 500 inhabitants including a common plec, sun beetle and lesser hedgehog tenrec

here rather than joining some club programme or other, 'because it's just as good and I can do my academics too'. They do anything from athletics to water polo – huge range and super facilities. They don't necessarily win everything but some sports, eg boys' U18 tennis and football, are hard to beat. Everything done with verve and energy.

Boarding: Just under half board of whom 18 per cent are from overseas. Majority are full boarders, about 70 weekly. The five boarding houses, are, of course, mostly recent and cleverly designed with large, light and airy atria which act as common rooms and off which rooms radiate. This system 'produces community right away – no long corridors in which people can get lost or hide away.' No mixed houses. Younger years in rooms with four beds, later in twos or singles. Good shared bathrooms, no en-suites. Houses staffed mostly by couples/families, their cats and dogs being house pets adored by all but asthmatics. Everyone 'patriotic' about their houses.

Background and atmosphere: Unusually, Bede's Senior grew out of a prep. The prep, founded in 1895, was thriving and, in the 1970s, its then head was urged by parents to provide continuation and the search for premises was on. Could they have done better? They found a house – The Dicker – around 12 miles inland – which had belonged to the extraordinary Horatio Bottomley (well worth looking up if you don't know) – a splendid, early 20th century, arts and crafts-cum-mock-medieval-Tudor extravaganza with a splendid landscaped park surrounded by stunning countryside. Dr Maloney's own 'salon' is an exquisite blend of the Victorian at its best and the ultra modern. Gorgeous 'old' dining room.

The school opened in 1979 and has, since then, spawned around 40 lesser buildings – everything from pre-fabs to what Dr Maloney described as a Kenyan Safari Lodge, atop which, in an improbable eyrie, sits the school library. Huge 'MPH' houses gym, pool, vast assembly space etc. Sussex flint, free-standing chapel used for talks by chaplain but no heavy-duty religion practised here. Bio-mass boilers and solar panels – school runs almost entirely on sustainable energy. Plans to lose several lesser buildings and construct a major, multi-flexible, classroom block – pupils are involved in the planning of the project and Dr Maloney pays tribute to their insights and ideas. All nestles in the park – extensive fields, meadows, gardens, plus a large, lilied lake and all, seemingly, in terrific nick. All this and train connections to London are close and quick.

Pastoral care, well-being and discipline: Transition from preps and primaries handled well. Integration of new pupils from different cultures, likewise. Integration of day pupils and boarders to be supported by new system of mixing up the houses. Day pupils able to stay until late and each house will have boarding, day and late-staying pupils.

Pupils consulted at each stage. 'I'm a real believer in pupil leadership,' says Dr Maloney. 'They make real decisions and decide on their legacy to the school.' Tartan skirt and blouse for girls, who wear suits in the sixth; boys wear dark suits but can move into chinos in the sixth. Most enthuse about the food and all like the range of choice.

Parents testify to the absence of bullying and say that anything more than light banter between pupils is handled sensitively. 'And they don't force you to do things you're uncomfortable with,' a parent averred. 'They allow you to be who you are without mortifying you as other schools do.' Tutors, houseparents and a thoroughly understood system of rules and sanctions maintain the school's tangible peace. Few serious misdemeanours – those few handled 'both formally and personally', according to pupils. Permanent exclusions a rarity. Dr Maloney well up on 'safe' internet use and says, wisely, 'We have a group of kids advising us on what we need to know.'

Pupils and parents: From an ever-widening arc – Bognor to Hastings. The vast majority are local or local-ish. Boarders from hither and yon and likely to grow in number. Everyone from wealthy Sussex farmers to London refusniks, to looked-after children in care of the LA – seamlessly and sensitively integrated. United in being smiley, fulfilled and grateful.

Entrance: Over-subscribed at all points but not by much. This is set to change and far-sighted parents need to get down and register. Currently, for sixth form, five B grades at GCSE are required with As in key subjects. Five Cs needed for entry to BTec courses

Exit: Far fewer now leave after GCSE and most who do go locally to sixth form colleges. Post-sixth leavers to a great range of places and courses. Lots to vocational courses eg sports management, advertising, accounting but also maths, medicine, English at Russell group universities and a few each year to Oxbridge (two in 2015). Alumni of either the prep and/or the senior branch include Eddie Izzard, Nicky Henson, Jamie Lloyd, footballers Dan Harding and Soloman March and a growing stream of cricketers including Ollie Rayner, Luke Wells and, newbie, Shai Hope.

Money matters: Scholarships of up to 25 per cent and a good and growing bursary fund. But – being a newish school – without massive endowments etc, of course.

Remarks: Head says, 'What I want parents to know is that their children will be bloody well taught and we are doing great things with them.' Parent says, 'Look at it seriously – whoever your child is'. Pupil says, 'I am so lucky to be here.'

Belmont Preparatory School (Dorking)

Feldemore, Dorking, Surrey RH5 6LQ

01306 730852	**Ages:** 2-13
schooloffice@belmont-school.org	**Pupils:** 211
www.belmont-school.org	**Boarders:** 21 weekly/flexi
C of E	**Day:** £8,310 – £13,950 pa
	Boarding: plus £2,940 – £6,240 pa

Headmistress: Since 2006, Mrs Helen Skrine BA. Following a music degree at Exeter, she took up posts teaching music, English and Latin at Wrekin College, Greenacre School, and Chinthurst Prep and was deputy head at Highfield School, Liphook.

A sound business head comes across when she describes how she has steered the school through the challenges of the recession, but there's also a strong maternal streak. On our tour we came across a boy with a bloodied knee being helped in by his friends. 'Oh my darling boy,' she exclaimed. 'Let's get that knee up. Matron is coming with her blue light on.'

Described by parents as 'very hands on and responsive' and 'a strong but caring leader.' Much praised for pastoral care. 'She has even offered support to our son whilst he struggles to adjust to secondary school,' said one mother. Another said: 'She is completely honest and open when it comes to issues with bullying. We were approached by her regarding our daughter being upset in school, something we found most refreshing.'

Two sons now at university. Her home is next door to the school building, not even a stone's throw away. She's not remotely tempted to move off site for a more private off-duty life, as some heads are. 'Last evening the children were all outside here playing,' she said. 'Some boys came to borrow the dog. I love it. It's a life, not a job.'

Entrance: 'First and foremost I look at the parents,' says the head. Yikes. No need to brush up on algebra though – she means she wants to be sure that they are buying into the school's ethos, which is not of the all-stations-to-Oxbridge variety. 'We want parents who understand what the ethos of this school is,' she says. 'We do a really good job academically but we are also interested in developing the co-curriculum areas and developing the children as people. I really believe school should be fun, not weighed down in endless testing, stress and strain.'

Who wouldn't it suit? 'Some of the tiger mums I met in my daughter's previous school,' says one mother. Another parent concurs, telling us: 'I haven't met any overly pushy parents at Belmont but I imagine that they would struggle to fit in.'

Next on the head's selection list is: 'Does the child have a spring in his/her step, will they throw themselves into everything and will they fit academically in the range of the year group?' Assessment is through reasoning tests and classroom observation. 'We won't take children outside the average range, but we will take low average pupils – sometimes it's just that they're not thriving in their current school,' the head says. Once in, the children are guaranteed a place until 13, unless any serious learning difficulties arise.

The school never sets time-consuming projects for the children where the parents end up spending endless hours making models of Egyptian vases. 'It's such a relief'

Key points of entry are at 2, reception, year 3 – and some come from other preps at 11. Entrance mid-school is well catered for. A mother told us: 'The parents in my daughter's year have been extremely welcoming. A barbecue and trip to Legoland were organised by the class rep before the start of the academic year so the new children could meet everyone before their first day. Mothers were quick to give me tips and advice about matters such as games kit.'

There's a two form entry per year, and that's the limit. 'I won't go to more than 32 to a year group,' says the head. 'I don't believe big is beautiful.'

Exit: Most parents are buying into private education for the duration – it's rare for a child to leave at 11 for local state secondaries. The head is a big fan of boarding and the children spread their wings far and wide. Box Hill the most popular recently, followed by Lancing, Farlington and Seaford. Others to Charterhouse, Reigate Grammar, Hurstpierpoint and Cranleigh.

Remarks: The campus is a glorious 65 acres, with children's playtime roaming through nooks and glades – only constrained by dots on the trees, which indicate when they are out of hearing range of the bell. The main school building is based around the one-time home of Edwin Waterhouse (of the Price Waterhouse Cooper accountancy firm), and although the original 1880 house was rebuilt after a fire, it retains its grandeur, with high corniced ceilings, lots of wood panelling and deep window seats. Classrooms for the older children are based here, while years 2 to 4 are accommodated in a modern building, and early years children – two reception and two year 1 classes – have their own buildings arranged around a courtyard, patrolled by three cats.

Specialist subject teaching kicks in from year 5, and children are split into two sets for all CE or scholarship subjects in years 5 to 8. This is flexible, with lots of movement between the sets, and pupils feel it's no big deal to be in a lower set. 'It's exactly the same work – they just slow it down to your speed,' they explained to us.

Parents are overjoyed by the fact there is no homework until year 7 (even then it's not an arduous load, with two preps of half an hour each). Up until then prep is timetabled in a daytime session. 'This is where Belmont differs from most prep schools,' a parent told us. 'They actively keep the pressure off the children and parents right up until year 7. The work handed in is theirs alone, and not the parents'. In addition, the school never sets time-consuming projects for the children where the parents end up spending endless hours making models of Egyptian vases or the like. 'It's such a relief, as a working parent.'

Feedback to parents comes in the form of half termly grades, full written reports twice a year and parents' evenings. There's lots of informal reporting. 'Every parent has the email address of every teacher,' says the head. 'I encourage email and we have a policy of getting back within 24 hours.' There's also afternoon tea with the head on a Friday afternoon, which parents say is a great way to meet other parents and have an informal chat with the head and teachers.

The head is passionate about ensuring that it's not just academic achievement that carries kudos here. 'We get lots of awards for things such as work of the week, good manners, boarder of the week,' said the children. During our visit the head's table was strewn with rosettes and certificates – all being sorted ready for prize-giving at the weekly assembly. 'Winning a commendation certificate from the headmistress is a most sought after prize,' said one parent.

An array of clubs. These can be mixed and matched, most having no requirement to commit for a term – no battles then to haul a recalcitrant child along to a club which he didn't like by week two. Invitation clubs for the most talented run alongside general access clubs.

Sport is very much an all-inclusive affair. The commitment to involve everyone, combined with small year groups, mean that if a prestigious A team is high on your list, it may not be the place for you. 'Some may feel it does not have enough children to pick teams of excellence,' said one parent. 'We feel our daughter plays her major sports externally, at county level, so for us she is learning to be a team player, to lose sometimes, and to enjoy sport.'

Another told us: 'Small class sizes and year group numbers do limit sports team ability levels at times since the teams often have to mix in different year groups. The benefit of this however, is that every child, however good or bad at sport, gets to play sport for the school.'

Head points out that the school fields U13, U11 and U9 teams that are selected on ability, and says they 'win many more games than they lose.' Parents praise the school's willingness to embrace individual needs – timetabling cricket and tennis sessions with the boys' teams for a very sporty girl, for example.

On the arts side, the head says 'every child is on stage in front of the parents at least once a year.' Bands, choirs and string groups, with teaching from a professional opera singer and a director of drama. The school has its own biannual festival, Bel Artis, where visiting professionals lead workshops for children, culminating with an evening of performance.

The school shares the site with Moon Hall, a specialist school for dyslexia. The two have separate governing bodies and are separate companies, but there's much crossover outside academic lessons. The Moon Hall children wear Belmont uniform and join Belmont for playtime, assembly, lunches and extracurricular activities. They can be in a school play and board alongside the Belmont pupils. Superb option if you have a dyslexic in the family.

Children can be dropped for breakfast from 7.30am and parents have a broad range of pick up times to choose from – at the end of the school day at 4.30pm, after clubs at 5.45pm, after supper at 6.30pm, after prep at 7.45pm, or children can board for an occasional night or any number up to five nights per week. All of this can be done on an ad hoc basis, so there is great flexibility for the working parent. Nearly 100 pupils board in some form – currently three boys and one girl weekly, 17 boys, and seven girls on flexi basis. 'Our daughter begs to board as often as we will let her,' a mother told us. 'It is a wonderfully warm and friendly environment with the boarders doing lots of interesting activities and going on trips.

Benenden School

Cranbrook Road, Cranbrook, Kent TN17 4AA

01580 240592
registry@benenden.kent.sch.uk
www.benenden.kent.sch.uk
C of E

Ages: 11–18
Pupils: 551; sixth form: 186
Boarders: all full
Boarding: £34,455 pa

Headmistress: Since January 2014, Mrs Samantha Price, 40s. Attended Malvern Girls' College (now Malvern St James), so knows about life at a girls' boarding school from both sides. Read history of art at Edinburgh University and began her career in the Tate Britain marketing department, but soon felt office-bound and switched to teaching. Worked at Reading Blue Coat School, King's Canterbury and Hereford Cathedral School before taking up her first headship at Godolphin School in Salisbury, from whence she was headhunted for her present post. Leaving was a very difficult decision, she says, but she has no regrets: 'Benenden is my dream school, and full boarding is in my DNA.' Married to Iori, an army chaplain, with a young daughter and son.

A passionate devotee of girls' education, and a powerhouse of ideas and energy underneath a warm and civilised exterior. 'I'm very proud of this school. It's a wonderful place to be.'

Academic matters: Impressive: in 2015, 78 per cent A*/A at GCSE and 66 per cent A*/A at A level. Pretty much always in the top 50 independent schools nationally. Everything you'd expect on offer, with breadth prized as much as depth: girls study a good range of languages, both modern and classical, and DT, art, music and drama are compulsory throughout the lower school. Science very popular, and is taught in truly amazing brand new science block, all glass and blond wood, opened in 2012: a floor per science, and at least three laboratories per floor, plus designated experiment rooms just for sixth formers, and a 150-seater lecture theatre which hosts a rolling programme of visiting speakers. 'My daughter's teachers have inspired her to be really passionate about science,' wrote one happy father, 'and she has really enjoyed science club.' Classrooms are large, modern and well-equipped, and superb library offers space and quiet.

'I don't think we'll do a food technology A level, but we might run Cordon Bleu courses, and I'd like to run Leith's Diploma. Being realistic and practical gets you ahead'

No plans to introduce the IB: A levels are taught as part of a refreshingly commonsense yet innovative approach which makes any such change unnecessary. Girls can almost always study the combination of subjects they want, and the EPQ is offered to all girls to provide additional academic challenge. Lots of skills and vocational courses on offer which sound genuinely appealing rather than drearily functional. For instance, 'I don't think we'll do a food technology A level,' says head, 'but we might run Cordon Bleu courses, and I'd like to run the Leith's Diploma. Being realistic and practical will be increasingly what gets you ahead.' No danger of gender bias in this forward-looking school, however: DT is one of the most popular options, taught in an excellently-resourced technology block which even sports its own ICT suite. The school is currently introducing a Professional Skills Programme for the sixth form, which will enable girls to work alongside professionals in a variety of fields and develop real-life experience of eg reading balance sheets, developing ideas into business proposals, etc.

The tutor system allows for a lot of contact time, and parents and students alike praise the caring and friendly approach. SEN department supports those girls diagnosed with dyslexia and dyspraxia, and students can have weekly individual lessons if needed (as with most independent schools, these are chargeable). That said, the school acknowledges that this probably isn't the school for those with more than mild difficulties. Extension programme for gifted and talented throughout the school.

Wherever we looked we saw girls relishing the curricular opportunities on offer. As one put it, 'At a school like this, you get to try everything!' A parent added, 'Academically, my daughter has come on amazingly since she joined the school.'

Games, options, the arts: 'You've got to involve yourself,' observed our tour guide, and there's so much to do here that it really would be crazy not to. Loads of traditional girls' sports, with lacrosse, netball and tennis topping the list; but more niche activities such as scuba diving and pool also popular. Dance is big here: there's a lovely dance studio where girls can learn tap, ballet and contemporary dance, plus a rather ace fitness suite for those wishing to acquire the body beautiful (or just keep fit).

Fabulous theatre was opened by Helena Bonham Carter, staffed by two full-time technicians from whom the girls can learn lighting, sound and set construction. Professionals would kill to have facilities this good. Drama is concomitantly lively with at least two major productions a year and lots of student-led performances. LAMDA also flourishing. Music block was built in the 1960s and in another school would be something to boast about, but here looks down-at-heel and in fact is due to be rebuilt soon. Masses of music going on notwithstanding – instrumental lessons, ensembles, orchestra, choir, the works. Art and design is particularly impressive, with wonderful work on display: etching, lino printing and some whacky sculpture rubbed shoulders with really beautiful embroidery. How refreshing to find a school where girls can still learn such things if they wish to.

Lots of trips both home and abroad. Good range of weekend activities appreciated by students and parents alike. 'My daughter has thoroughly enjoyed the weekend programme,' said one grateful mother.

Boarding: All students here are full boarders. School is relaxed about letting girls go home at weekends. Boarding rooms are colourful, light and homely – perhaps a little crowded for some tastes, with up to five girls in a room for the lower school, but all the girls we spoke to insisted they liked it that way. Older girls can choose to have smaller rooms and fewer room-mates, and all sixth formers have their own room in a deluxe modern block built especially for them, designed to be a halfway house between school and university. Fully equipped and spotlessly clean, we couldn't help thinking that most university accommodation would be a bit of a come-down afterwards.

Background and atmosphere: Started in 1923 by Miss Sheldon, Miss Hindle and Miss Bird, three teachers from Wycombe Abbey, the school moved to its present site in 1924 and has flourished ever since. Held in immensely high esteem by its alumna, many of whom had gathered to pay it affectionate respect when we happened to visit. Many girls here whose mothers – even grandmothers – attended the school.

The original house, Hemsted, still serves as the school's main building, and must be everyone's idea of what an English boarding school looks like. The magnificent wood-panelled entrance hall and staircase are hung with portraits of the Earl of Cranbrook's family, and coats of arms are etched upon the stained glass. It was actually built in the 19th century, but was designed to look much older, and the effect is frankly gorgeous. We found ourselves thinking of Daisy Pulls It Off, and apparently most newcomers cry 'Hogwarts!' as soon as they get through the front door. It's still possible to board in Hemsted, and the girls that do told us they absolutely love it.

However, a massive programme of refurbishment over the past 20 years has ensured that Benenden can more than hold its own in the 21st

century. All the facilities here are stunningly good, and the whole is set in 240 acres of exquisitely landscaped grounds: beyond the playing fields, where we saw girls desporting themselves at lacrosse, are lawns, roses, woods, water features, flower beds, a walled garden, lime tree avenue, all overlooking miles of hills and greenery beyond. 'I love it!' confirmed a cheerful sixth former, adding in proper Benenden patois, 'and you can walk into vill whenever you like.'

Built in the 19th century but designed to look much older, and the effect is frankly gorgeous. Apparently most newcomers cry 'Hogwarts!'

Excellent school shop, where students can buy everything needful from shampoo to study aids, and an air of unfussy practicality throughout. Food universally praised (we can confirm the chocolate brownies were to die for), and girls say that their suggestions for the menu are listened to. We were also impressed to learn that a building programme of staff housing was about to get under way, because local property prices were deterring many good teachers from applying. This is a school that takes people's everyday comfort seriously, and puts its money where its mouth is.

Pastoral care, well-being and discipline: No real behaviour issues – this is a happy ship, and the care and support given to the girls were praised everywhere. 'It was a big move to the UK for my daughter,' wrote an overseas mother, 'and the house staff looked after her as if she were their own, giving cuddles and love whenever she needed it. They still do so now.' And everyone we contacted said something similar. In addition to her tutor and housemistress, each girl is allocated an older girl or 'big sister' to look after her, and girls spoke to us with fondness about the friends they'd made across the different year groups.

Rules are enforced with a light touch. One mother commented, 'I like the fact that they teach the girls the right thing to do rather than impose really strict rules, eg they don't ban access to the internet – even for the younger girls; they spend time teaching them about internet safety instead.' Girls said again and again that they felt able to be themselves, and mothers frequently commented that their daughters hadn't felt pressured into growing up too quickly.

Considerable privileges and latitude given to sixth formers, who really value the increased independence and are consequently less likely to switch to co-ed at this stage. All the girls wear uniform, even the sixth, but it's an unfussy uniform and the girls honestly didn't seem to mind – it's a community that fosters a sensible and pragmatic attitude to life's challenges. As one parent enthused, 'Everything at Benenden is done so smoothly and efficiently. Our daughter loves it and so do we. We are struggling to find a school as good as this for our son!' Another wrote, 'My daughter speaks of being school-sick during the holidays, the opposite of homesick, because she loves everything about the school so much – she is very, very happy at Benenden.'

Pupils and parents: Fees are high, and Princess Anne may be Benenden's most famous alumnae, but this is not a school for snobs. About 20 per cent from abroad, many of them expats. Otherwise, families are solid professional London and home counties people who want the best for their children and 'work their socks off to send their girls here,' according to head. Bursary assistance ensures at least some social diversity: one girl on a 110 per cent bursary spoke movingly to us about her own experience: 'The school has helped in every possible way. I've never felt out of place, and I owe them so much.'

Entrance: Forty girls join at 11 and 50 girls at 13. Both intakes oversubscribed, but not dauntingly so. Plan ahead, though: the lists can close a year or more in advance. Girls have to achieve at least 55 per cent at common entrance, but in practice

many applicants will, so the school also uses pre-tests and interviews and works closely with local prep schools to be sure they're getting it right. 'We're looking for sound academic competence and potential. We're a broad church.' Occasional places for other years – the school operates a waiting list. Entry to sixth form dependent on exam, interview and current head's report, but fantastic sixth form opportunities mean that very few existing students leave, so not many additional places available.

Exit: At 16, hardly anyone: occasionally girls may opt for a co-ed experience at schools such as Charterhouse. At 18, about 10 per cent to Oxbridge (ten in 2015), the rest mostly to Russell group universities to read a broad range of subjects – engineering and physics currently enjoying a surge in popularity. An increasing number to US and Ivy League colleges.

Money matters: Scholarships of up to 10 per cent for academics, music, art, DT, sports and drama. Those who've been awarded a scholarship can apply to the generous bursary fund: a number of girls here benefit from means-tested assistance of up to 80 per cent. The Benenden School Trust also offers up to three 110 per cent bursaries each year to girls coming from local state schools.

Remarks: Traditional girls' boarding brought radiantly up to date, jettisoning what was bad, retaining everything good and adding a huge amount more. An exciting and appealing place: if we were young again, we'd be clamouring to go there.

Box Hill School

Mickleham, Dorking, Surrey RH5 6EA

01372 373382
enquiries@boxhillschool.com
www.boxhillschool.com

Ages: 11–19
Pupils: 415; sixth form: 120
Boarders: 130 full, 25 weekly
Day: £16,140 – £17,700 pa
Boarding: £24,600 – £35,850 pa

Headmaster: Since April 2014, Mr Corydon Lowde BSc, MEd, NPQH (40s), previously school's deputy head who took over following sudden departure of predecessor. Before that, nearly three years' handy overseas experience in similar role at British International School of Boston, preceded by seven-year stint at Hampshire Collegiate School, starting career at large state comprehensive.

'Has a vision he wants to share' and 'never tires of talking about what we're doing.' Hours

he's putting in (lots of them) paying off, thought insider. 'School is going up.' Was 'gutted' that had to speak on the phone (in hospital having wonky knee put right on day of visit) as meeting best way of 'understanding where all that energy is coming from and where the school is going.'

Felt to be doing as good a job as anyone could manage in difficult circumstances, style reserved but friendly, reviews cautious but generally positive. 'It's new thing but I feel that Cory is on the right track,' thought one parent, speaking for pretty much everyone. Overwhelming desire is that he keeps school atmosphere just the way it is. Nobody is hungry for change.

A teacher from the off (management, part of his degree, was the career that got away), he comes across as quiet, mild-mannered and slightly quirky with self-deprecating Brit humour (honed, no doubt, during own schooldays at Dragon and Frensham Heights) that must make international parents want to take him home gift-wrapped in a Burberry bag. (Should really be Duchamp, says Mr Lowde, a loyal fan of their ties, socks and, indeed, 'pochettes'.)

Goal is school that reflects the world when it comes to nationalities (they have around 30 but no monocultures) and ability range. Would like more Brits – 'who wouldn't?' he says – and is hoping rising tide of Londoners is high enough to lap against admissions desk.

When not headmastering, follows sport. Was British Karate Champion in the 1990s (not an Olympic sport – down to international wrangling). We had visions of desk being reduced to matchwood after one emphatic gesture too many but, no, it's all neat and splinter-free.

Karate, he says firmly, is all about 'turning search for perfection into your own personal journey – not about aggressive confrontation,' – a nothing-to-prove message that's not million miles away from how would like school to see itself.

Academic matters: That increasingly rare sighting in them thar Surrey hills – senior school that has continued to welcome the all and sundries who,

these hard-nosed, results-driven days, wouldn't necessarily gain a place elsewhere. In circumstances, IB diploma average of 32 in 2015; and 76 per cent of pupils getting 5+ A*-C GCSE grades (22.7 per cent A*-A grades) a tribute to quality of teaching.

While near neighbours have sought solid A grade glory, here they've carried on with broader ability range (many are around the national average). But school's frequent self-referencing as 'non-selective' needs grain of salt. Minimally selective, yes, but everyone accepted as 'greenies' (blazer colour worn to year 11) needs to be capable of passing eight or nine GCSEs.

Able pupils who do deliver top grades (parents pinching themselves at children's better than predicted results aren't hard to come by) won't, however, be held up as only aspirational model worth pursuing. 'Am great believer that competition crushes one's self-esteem,' says head (though not when it comes to sport, where all-out drive to win is 'about character'...).

Academically, it's about 'my growth, learning and success [being] made greater by your learning,' sentiments that do him credit, as does desire for kind, empathetic colleagues. They're well up to the job, say pupils, and palpably keen to get everyone involved. Maths department gets X Factor squared award for pupil recruitment, department head 'a genius.'

Similar stories elsewhere. Even visitors may find themselves dredging up rusty French and Spanish greetings, courtesy of bustling, friendly language teachers who won't take non for an answer, while we assume whiteboard spelling of 'clergimen' [sic]

Cobble-paved stables give atmospheric home for DT, every tool's home marked by pencilled outline – very Patrick Caulfield

in otherwise pacey English lesson was designed to test pupils' eye for detail.

Ethos derives in part from membership of Round Square group of schools, linked to ideals of eccentric but hugely influential educationalist Kurt Hahn, who stressed compassion coupled with 'just do it' mentality. (We quizzed tour guides who, impressively, were able to cite every one of key principles – and swore they hadn't mugged up in advance...).

Extreme cleverness catered for but also support 150 pupils with SEN, from mild dyslexia to school refusers – 'though we're not special school,' says head and pupils must be able to access curriculum. Helped by lowish pupil to teacher ratio (nine to one) and small class sizes (average 15 to 18 up to year 11, as few as two pupils in EAL and ISC lessons). Support includes one-to-one specialist help (normal maximum of an hour a week, mostly maths or literacy focused) and multi-sensory teaching. Will also try to help those (often with high functioning Asperger's) struggling with social communication.

About 70 of 110 EAL pupils follow mainstream syllabus, 50 in sixth form, English studied at range of levels, from IB diploma level to IGCSE, ESOL and IELTS. Others are found among 40 plus pupils at International Study Centre who can chose from four courses aimed at 14-16ish age range, most popular the one-year intensive GCSE programme (also marketed as pre-IB).

Some ISC pupils start a year or so behind peers, about half eventually joining 'mainstream' pupils (school's words, not ours). All 'fully integrated into school life...' says glossy literature (repeated several times for added emphasis) though some national groups stick together and school pupils can feel onus is on them to make first contact and bridge the cultural gap.

School's best recent curriculum decision has been reintroduction of A levels in Sept 2014, reducing at a stroke post-16 departures of the IB-averse who 'want to stay but don't want to take six subjects,' says head, though they're encouraged to opt for extras such as IB Theory of Knowledge, extra maths and creativity, action and service – and some do (one keen A level student was even doing IB Spanish module out of love for the subject, though skipping the exam). Staff, insouciant about extra workload involved, see dual system as best

way of boosting numbers studying top subjects at top unis, particularly maths and straight sciences.

Games, options, the arts: With practice rooms open all hours (7 in the morning till 9 at night) and free instrumental taster lessons, no shortage of opportunities for 100 or so budding musicians who hone skills, some to diploma level – one so impressive that visiting top musician offered tuition on the spot.

Other hands-on subjects housed in range of (mainly original) buildings including small, cobble-paved stables minimally converted to create atmospheric and fitting home for DT, every tool's home marked by pencilled outline on wall behind – very Patrick Caulfield.

Visual arts headed by practising artist, who, paintbrush in hand, was adding final touches to own masterpiece as pupils worked around him, inspiring similarly accomplished work (our favourite among many featuring off-duty angels enjoying an off-duty cig).

Sport key to 'holistic' approach, though girls enjoy pinker-shaded version – holassism, perhaps? – and do netball and rounders (rugby and cricket for boys) with hockey and football in common, though pupils confident that if school would happily accommodate changes if demand was there. Frank acknowledgement that team sports 'not for all'. Room to improve, thought parent, as not viewed as top priority, perceptions rubbing off on potential staff recruits (lure not yet sufficiently great to attract top talent). Results, which tend to align with levels of each intake's innate talent, can fluctuate fairly widely from year to year. That said, manifest advantages for the keen who, with minimal numbers of school teams, can get their fill of matches, though accepted that anyone requiring high quality sporting fix and nothing but will probably end up elsewhere.

Sensible decision to offer individual fitness from year 10 when 'almost anything is possible,' says school, the more so as sport happens twice a week, Tuesdays and Thursdays being reserved for school activities including magic club, sign language and – a rare treat – corsetry and dressmaking class which teaches traditional panelling and boning skills and is run by passionate devotee, enthusiasm largely responsible, as with fashion and textiles GCSE, for bringing in impressive numbers of boys.

Boarding: With large numbers of full boarders (76 boys, 54 girls, with 19 boys, 6 girls weekly) spending priority is six boarding houses, four in the grounds, two across the (quiet) village road. House names, though full of meaning to school, have certain random quality for outsiders, Constantine named after eponymous Greek king – school patron; Ralph apparently commemorating past VIP (though sounds like rakish English take on IKEA furniture policy).

Plenty to help boarders take mind off décor difficulties. After prep on Saturdays, seniors can travel into London. Must be back by '2230' [sic] (time rather than century, we assume), shopping trumping culture every time. Excellent range of trips including 'experiences' (Jamie Oliver and Harry Potter). One houseparent (male) runs regular pizza making sessions ('leave dough to rise during the day, cook in the evening.') 'Never a dull moment' insists school, firmly. Boarders agree. 'Can be almost too much going on,' said one.

Background and atmosphere: Word du jour, judged to pack a punch in terms of punter appeal, is 'inspiring', writ large throughout new school video, overlaying jolly images of suitably fired up pupils fencing on the school lawn (a summer term reality, not just camera-friendly set up) or putting up tents at summit of Box Hill, buffeted by gale force winds.

There's also much talk of holistic approach, though 'mindfulness', other all-purpose buzz word of choice, appears to be the meme that got away – so far. 'Not sure why aren't using it,' says member of staff.

'Stunning' is other obvious candidate, given village setting in Mickleham, between Dorking and Leatherhead and about 20 miles from London. As pretty as they come, main building once private gothic revival Victorian house with aspirations to grandeur, full of delightful stained glass biblical scenes and window seat epidemic (even modern boarding houses are rotten with them). Newer wings tacked on at the back sufficiently sympathetic to keep the charm intact though some more elderly stand-alones have their work cut out. 'Has

the smell of an experienced building,' says one of tour guides of modern languages block.

Original grandeur belies school's relative youth, founded only in 1959 by Gordonstoun housemaster on principles inspired by inspirational educationalist Kurt Hahn, with much emphasis on whole pupil development (and plenty of non-Hahn inspired beatings for those failing to progress along right lines, according to one rueful 1970s-vintage OB). Now, pupils 'will all excel at something,' reckons school, while extending talent range to include high profile qualities such as friendship and general good egg-dom, which are 'acknowledged though not in OTT way,' says member of staff.

And when Titus Andronicus palls, there's always the fun of watching vast tame rodents (gerbils not rats, despite unnerving tails) rolling around in exercise balls

---

In any case, it's Hahn-lite (don't set them loose in all weathers on high seas: land-locked setting on Surrey Downs is against them) but ticks off must-dos: democracy, environment, adventure, leadership and service – with whole school activity week in September with camping, canoeing and rock climbing for all in Wales or New Forest. D of E – closely linked in ethos – from year 9 and just about everyone takes bronze. 'No reason not to,' says school, though silver and gold recruited on opt-in basis. Star attraction is trip to Philippolis, South Africa, where pupils have helped add new buildings including crèche and classrooms. 'Proof of faith in school,' said mother, whose son, just turned 13, had spent a month there.

Luxury goods on offer to counteract struggle with elements – 90 inch TV in new sixth form common room used for films and for pupils to 'enjoy live streams from the Royal Shakespeare Company,' trumpets prospectus. We're sure they do little else (sotto voce giggling when we asked undoubtedly down to recollection of Bard's many bon mots...). And when Titus Andronicus palls, there's always fun of watching vast tame rodents (gerbils not rats, despite unnerving tails) rolling around in exercise balls.

Overall impression is of well-tended school with little evidence of slight messiness reported by a couple of visiting parents – nothing to do, we're sure, with sign reading 'GSG visit [today]. Rooms have to be very tidy...' And so what if it's not immaculate? 'Don't send son to school for the décor,' commented mother.

Grounds undiluted gorgeousness (impressive mown stripes of grass that continued either side of small pond on back lawn giving unnerving impression that Jerry – the groundsman, and noted duck whisperer; pupils say he's followed by family of mallards each year – can walk, or at least ride, on water).

Golden glow set to spread as governor-sanctioned spending spree continues, aided by canny bursar who 'always has six months of staff salaries in the bank,' and is clearly a dab hand at curbing any headmasterly dash over cash tendencies. 'We're strong and robust – though hate that word, makes me sound like politician,' says head.

Now well on the way to transforming slightly dismal befores to far nicer afters. Rooms where clutter of tables and beds currently fight yellowing paint for supremacy slowly but surely transformed by attractive furniture, much of it custom created 'by our own maintenance team' and essential as most non-standard alcoves aren't compatible with off the peg designs.

'Work in progress,' says head. Will be followed by new sports hall (biggest current absence) – local council currently dragging heels – and more space for creative arts ('absolutely not forgotten,' says head). Some Portakabins – some exteriors slightly shabby, interiors as well as can be expected and could be far worse – will remain.

Pastoral care, well-being and discipline: 'Willing to cherish the children for what they are – don't treat them as a commodity,' thought feeder school registrar. 'Very open and honest, don't sweep things under the carpet,' agreed parent. Example is alcohol policy. If over 18, boarders can purchase but 'carefully monitored' – to ensure any headaches are admin, not consumption, related.

Quality of communications only widespread complaint, described with single-word pithiness by several parents fed up with night-before notifications of matches and recent music event. (Though full marks to music staff for re-running one child's performance so late arriving mother didn't miss out).

Other parents, however, reckoned that greater attention to termly calendars and school website would iron out most of the difficulties. New fortnightly newsletter from head also generally going down well, while more text alerts and email updates should take uncertainty out of nitty grittyness of who is doing what and when.

Nurturing element otherwise practically perfect, attended to with care and sensitivity. One pupil, bullied elsewhere and finding settling in hard, was cajoled out of foyer into class by head of year, now thriving. 'Helped him become accustomed to school until he was able to let go of that helping hand for a day or two.' Unpleasantness does happen but quickly and effectively dealt with, think parents whose children have been on receiving end.

School's 'expose and eradicate,' approach includes ambassadors – 'our eyes and ears,' says head – who report any hint of transgression, backed up by anonymous on-line whistleblowing.

Boarders send two reps from each of the six houses to discuss issues – often food related, with school headed by 13-strong syndicate who supervise breaks, administer tellings off for minor uniform infringements and are led by head boy and girl, known as Guardians, superhero connotations a highly successful recruitment tool. Handover speech to successors an annual tear jerker, with one post-holder 'talking to her parents through the speech and saying how grateful she was,' said mother, welling up all over again at the memory.

Unlike other top dogs we've encountered, not shy about using superpowers and will impose detentions, though not often and mainly for repeated rudeness. 'Know when someone's just being cheeky.' Given incumbents' nicknames (President Nice and Madame Fuhrer) we thought they showed commendable forbearance, though all pupil behaviour witnessed, in and out of lessons, was universally immaculate.

Pupils and parents: Parents range from diverse international community to ecstatic locals, often first time buyers, thrilled about what school has done for their children. All aware that school still seen as second choice. 'Wrong postcode for some Reigate mums,' says one. General sense that won't last, though nobody's in a hurry to add more competitive feel to a place felt to run on happiness. Boy numbers (outnumber girls two to one) and international element (around 84 per cent of boarders) also put others off, though seeing real life consequences of world events played out – one parent cited falling out of former best friends from different war zones – provides 'amazing' insights.

Monthly Friday teas for parents when school provides the cakes but 'doesn't overpower with teachers,' says mum. Later life reunions all over the place – Hong Kong the latest when checked bustling Facebook page (as well-tended as the grounds) though plenty of alumni stay don't move far away, careers covering eclectic range from surveyors to musicians and authors.

Entrance: Officially take into years 7 (40 places), 9 (20 places) and 12 (variable) but if there's space, will take at other times.

Majority of pupils from 10-mile radius though extending, Kingston and Horsham (as well as thriving metropolis of Nork) all now within reach thanks to extensive bus network (6.45am start for furthest flung locations). Micklefield, Downsend, Reigate St Mary's, Chinthurst, Aberdour, Priory Prep and Kingswood House among preps sending pupils, though no official feeders. Local primaries also well represented.

Exit: Many schools have much-trumpeted cohort who leave post-16, recognise error of ways and stage tearful prodigal son (and daughter) return, accepted with nary a 'we told you so'. Here, parent confirms it's the real McCoy with mother phoning Mr Lowde to ask if could have place back. 'Missed it so much.'

Other post-16 losses, often to local sixth form colleges, partially staunched but trickle will continue, think parents, as pupils cast off 360 degree care for grittier experiences elsewhere. 'Not a criticism of the school but tribute to confidence-building,' pointed out mother.

University entrance for most, over 80 per cent to first choice, no Oxbridge currently but aiming for one or two a year – no special department as 'we're small enough to personalise timetable where needed.'

Unis of Kent, Northumbria, Sussex popular destinations, ditto Exeter. Subjects include business, management and economics, regular contingent each year to art and music colleges including Central St Martins and Northern Royal College.

Money matters: Generous support for deserving families whose income range isn't cosily clustered at top end of £ dial. Warmth of welcome and matter-of-fact help with bursary application process felt to speak volumes about school's ethos.

Remarks: Warm-hearted, encouraging school that's easily overlooked in favour of guarantees of undiluted top grades elsewhere. 'Not right for families who want everything in neat and tidy boxes,' thought mother. 'It's not draconian here. You're doing it because it's what you need to succeed.'

Brambletye School

Lewes Road, East Grinstead, West Sussex RH19 3PD

01342 321004
registrar@brambletye.com
www.brambletye.co.uk
C of E

Ages: 2½ –13 (boarding from 7)
Pupils: 340
Boarders: 64 full, 17 flexi
Day: £6,960 – £18,990 pa
Boarding: £22,200 – £23,400 pa

Headmaster: Since September 2015, William Brooks, previously deputy head at Port Regis school. Studied combined arts at Durham; also has a PGCE and an MBA in educational leadership. Has also been deputy head at Bruern Abbey and Sunningdale. At Port Regis, he taught maths and coached sport – he is a keen sportsman and plays cricket and golf in his spare time. Wife Amelia plays a leading role at Brambletye; their three children have joined the school.

Entrance: No assessment for pre-prep but likes to see previous school reports. Consciously broad intake, but has introduced an assessment morning and reasoning tests and a chat for the prep school. About half come up from pre-prep and the rest from elsewhere. Will only turn a child away if it is felt they would not be able to cope with common entrance. A handful join for the last two years.

Exit: To a huge range of schools – Tonbridge, Benenden, Brighton College, Charterhouse,

Lancing, Ardingly, Stowe, Eton, Millfield and Winchester among the more popular. Not a feeder to anywhere in particular and three children going to the same school in one year is considered a lot. In 2015, 22 scholarships – academic, art, music, DT, all-rounder and sport. Virtually all stay on until 13, but girls occasionally leave at 11. No specific preparation for 11+ but children well prepared in verbal and non-verbal reasoning and current affairs for pre-tests.

Remarks: Founded at Sidcup Place, Kent in 1919, it moved to its current site in 1933 along with the chapel which was moved brick by brick from Sidcup. The original building is an old hunting lodge set in 140 acres up a long drive a mile from East Grinstead and 20 minutes from Gatwick Airport. Glorious views in all directions, and children can look out of their dormitory windows across the terrace and playing fields to the reservoir in the distance with not another house in sight, yet only 30 miles from London. Everything you could wish for here: sports hall, purpose-built theatre, indoor swimming pool and award-winning classroom block complete with its own weather station, and even a red letter box outside the front door; not to mention dens, zip wires and an assault course. Wonderful panelled hall and rambling passages adorned with sports trophies and portraits of previous headmasters. Brambletye's signature pink and grey colours everywhere from the uniform to the rugby posts, and even the ponies in the show jumping team have pink saddle cloths.

The 1960s prospectus stated that 'our main aim is for our boys to do what is right because they choose and not because they have been told to do so'. Although so much else has changed about the school in the intervening years (including girls since 1999), these core aims still hold true. Children are encouraged to develop a set of values and to appreciate what they have got and what they can do for others – 'community, co-operation and team spirit'. They are expected to 'do the right thing and hold a conversation with confidence'.

Brambletye's signature pink and grey colours everywhere from the uniform to the rugby posts, and even the ponies in the show jumping team have pink saddle cloths

Specialist subject teachers for older children – good balance of youth and experience, with several recently appointed heads of department. 'It's the teachers who make the difference' – all are very supportive and committed and about 80 per cent live on site. Setting in maths, English and science from year 4 and in other subjects where possible, and all learn Latin from year 5. Scholarship stream for the last three years.

Good learning support with a specialist teacher, mainly for mild to moderate dyslexia. Each child has an individual education plan with appropriate targets and is given one-to-one and in-class support and allowed to use a laptop in exams. Everyone subtly tested for learning difficulties via reading and spelling age tests and CAT tests. 'Teachers' instincts are crucial'.

Boys play football, rugby and cricket and girls netball, hockey and rounders. Athletics for all in the summer. A myriad of other sports also offered: canoeing, taekwondo, fencing, judo, golf, squash, riding and clay pigeon shooting to name a few – and has recently introduced sailing on the local reservoir. 'Great emphasis is placed on good sportsmanship, on winning in a sporting manner and losing with grace'. Football and netball trips to Madrid and cricket to Kenya as well as mini tours in the UK. Inspired heads of art and DT – you can feel the buzz as you walk in the door, and school gets about 10 art and DT scholarships a year. Artist in residence and local sculptor, and art students come in at weekends and work alongside the children – many children spend a lot of their free time here. Annual exhibition of pupils' work at local Arts Centre in East Grinstead.

Music increasingly vibrant and you hear the sound of music all round the school. About 85 per cent learn at least one instrument, some to grade 8. Newish director of music and team of peripatetic teachers have 'made music fun and everyone wants to be in a band'. Orchestra, chamber group and other instrumental groups, kettle and African drum ensembles and three choirs. Production each term in 250 seat theatre as well as drama in form assemblies. Big musical for top two years like Oliver! and South Pacific with professional musicians and microphones and often hired stage sets.

'Whenever I call in the place is always filled with laughter, and I love to see the children just mucking around in the garden'

Children help choose a different charity each year and have raised over £100,000 in last 10 years – some recently visited a school in Kenya for which they had raised £14,000.

Most children board for the last two years – about 60 boarders in on Saturday nights; weekly boarding not an option at this stage but exeats every two weeks. Boarders in year 6 and below can go home every weekend after matches. Recently introduced fixed-night boarding has proved popular and most beds now full. Bright, light dorms gradually being refurbished and beds laden with teddy bears and walls covered in posters – Harry Stiles and One Direction much in evidence in the girls' dorms. Visiting speakers on Saturday nights and for chapel on Sunday mornings. Some trips and treats on Sundays but most activities on site – the banning of hand-held games consoles has been surprisingly well received by the children: 'Now I have more people to play with,' said one. Good food – homemade cookies for break and plenty of choice at lunch and supper, and even Weetabix before bed for anyone who is still hungry. Staff eat at tables with children and much emphasis placed on manners and good behaviour.

Parents involved and welcomed. Mainly London commuters, many of whom have boarded themselves – very few first time buyers. About 17 international children from a wide range of countries; strong links with Spain and Thailand – no EAL offered but do offer curriculum support. No parents' group as such but lots of events involve parents – focus on charitable fundraising and the 4x4 challenge a major feature of the social calendar. Doesn't have to be a Range Rover, the old farm Land Rover will do just fine. 'The school produces lovely, all round, grounded children, well prepared for the next stage,' said one mother. 'Whenever I call in during free time the place is always filled with laughter, and I love to see the children just mucking around in the garden,' said another. The most famous old boy is probably Benedict Cumberbatch.

Pre-prep and nursery run by the much-loved 'progressive and welcoming' Dawn Atkinson; 'She sold me the school,' said one happy mother. The 85 children aged 3-7 housed in purpose-built octagonal building adjacent to the prep school with its own entrance and car park. Central hall and lots of space indoors and out, with two playgrounds and fencing made to look like brightly coloured pencils decorated with wellington boots planted with flowers. Big focus on rewards, and children earn crystals and gems for good work and behaviour. They learn music from year 2 and have own practice room. Big on drama and dance, and children encouraged to take part in assemblies, concerts and the Christmas production. Use the prep school's theatre, sports

hall, swimming pool and games pitches,and come over to the dining room for lunch. Teachers from the prep come over to teach ICT, and netbooks and iPads used in lessons. Children allowed to go at their own pace, and booster groups offered for the very bright and those who struggle.

New weekly baby and toddler group gives families a glimpse of what Brambletye has to offer.

Brighton College

Eastern Rd, Brighton, East Sussex BN2 0AL

01273 704200
registrar@brightoncollege.net
www.brightoncollege.net
C of E

Ages: 11–18
Pupils: 1,000; sixth form: 360
Boarders: 365
Day: £15,300– £22,110 pa
Boarding: £30,360 – £38,640 pa

Linked school: Handcross Park School

Head Master: Since 2006, Mr Richard Cairns MA (40s). Left Oxford with a first in history; his path to Brighton led him through a law firm in Australia, a Palestinian refugee camp, Stewart's Melville in Edinburgh, The Oratory in Reading and the deputy headship of Magdalen College School, Oxford. The list of achievements/accolades in his tenure is staggering – it includes the opening of Brighton College Abu Dhabi; a rise from 147th to top 20 in the UK academic rankings; a doubling in boarding numbers; a trebling in applications; a huge new building programme; the acquisition of Roedean Junior School and Handcross Park Prep School; an ISI inspection report with outstanding in every category; The Sunday Times Independent School of the Year.

Keen not to take the credit for this all by himself but has built a teaching and management structure that ensures that ideas and initiatives can be sparked and grown – whether inside or outside the student body. That type of attitude is magnetic – for pupils, parents and staff. He sees himself and the college as a mix of tradition and modern – that was the design brief for the decorating team that were part of the recent revamp but it goes much deeper than the furnishings. 'I want every pupil to be who they want to be – as I say to them in assembly [pupils agree he does, and they remember it ...] "If I try to be him, who will be me?".'

Plenty of other schools trying to tempt him away – the governors recently agreed to a 10 week international trip, he says, 'to give me thinking time for the next seven years'. It was a global

reconnaissance mission, visiting universities in the US and Canada as well as potential twin schools in Finland, Sweden, Singapore, Ontario and Hungary. Such symbiotic connections are characteristic of this head – and they appear to stem from a dedication to improving education wherever he can use his influence or initiative. He kicked off his tenure with compulsory Mandarin lessons – but in doing so also connected with Kingsford, an East London school that was doing the same. Out of this link grew the London Academy of Excellence (LAE) in Stratford, East London, the first new sixth form free school academy in the country, helping kids from disadvantaged backgrounds to get into university by making sure they pass the right A levels – with a powerful independent school sponsoring one of each of the major subjects eg Brighton College sponsors economics, Eton does English, Highgate does maths etc.

Has high expectations for his pupils, wanting them to be excited in the classroom for the 200 days a year that they come to 'this place of learning' and is keen for them to leave to begin careers rather than just enter a profession (no matter how elevated). He teaches history to all of the fourth form – meeting every child, marking their work. They report creative punishments from him for inattention eg writing a whole story about a turtle, or a poem about the girl the note was being passed to. Less formally, he has breakfast with the prefects and invites sixth formers to dinner. The pupils love getting to know the head in this way (one of seven children, he certainly knows how to cope with a large dinner table) and relevant issues, ranging from divorce to cricket, often emerge casually. Refreshingly and realistically, he's not shy of stating financial figures to his pupils either – from how much the new boarding developments cost to how much he would need to be sponsored to run the Big Balls relay for charity.

Academic matters: Shining results, and they keep getting better: In 2015, 93 per cent A*/A at GCSE, 99 per cent A*-B and 85 per cent A*/A at A level; this is up with the best in London too – years of consistent improvement in results (and counting). One of top value-added schools. Twenty-six subjects offered at A level. A 60/40 split arts/science at A level; biology, chemistry, economics and maths are particularly popular (the latter taken by about two-thirds of the pupils). About a quarter do four A levels all the way through. Advice given to A level students is integral to their choices: a year group assembly on careers and outside speakers (John Major, Boris Johnson, Viv Richards, David Dimbleby, David Starkey, Jeremy Paxman, Michael Gove, Matt Prior..) visit in a Wednesday afternoon slot. Each department runs both a course-specific and a general Oxbridge activity, which obviously pays off, with a record number of pupils heading up to Oxford or Cambridge.

Quirky and effective teaching is respected by the pupils – whether it is their Mandarin teacher throat singing on YouTube, or a video of a worked through past maths paper

Staff are sparky and motivated – attracted by the charms of 'London by the sea' and being part of a school that's going up and up. An appraisal system is at the heart of the classroom: the kids fill in an online questionnaire on each teacher which gets fed back to the head of department, who in turn gives a summary to the director of studies. So sub-standard teaching should not slip under the radar and many teachers turn down career progressing jobs elsewhere to remain. Quirky and effective teaching is respected by the pupils – whether it is their Mandarin teacher throat singing on YouTube, or a video of a worked through past paper available for maths A level revision. The Story of Our Land course combines history, geography, philosophy and religion for the third form – when talking about an invasion force coming over the cliff, study the geography of that cliff, or debate the merits of the Muslim or Christian standpoint while looking at the Crusades. This is in line with Michael Gove's draft national curriculum – and has surprising parallels with a Steiner main lesson.

Languages are popular, not just through the Mandarin innovation – compulsory in the pre-prep since 2007 and now a GCSE option (mostly A* grades so far), with graduate students from Chinese universities to assist – but also Latin, French, Spanish, Russian, Italian, German and Greek. The burgeoning Mandarin option is now confirmed as a USP, with the school being awarded Confucius Institute status by the Chinese Government as a centre of excellence for the teaching of the language – the first such honour for a UK school. The school-wide recommendation of only nine academic GCSEs (with at least one other being artistic or creative) encourages a good balance between academic and extracurricular – as does lesson time between 8.30am and 4pm being sacrosanct, enabling an extra five hours a week for music, sport or dance.

All new pupils attend a literacy class and the dyslexia centre is nationally famous, specifically helping around five per cent of pupils. English is taught within the centre (instead of a second modern language) for years 7-11 in small groups, individual help available in sixth form. Taking complete control of English makes a huge difference, removing embarrassment and stress. School actively seeks out and welcomes the bright child with dyslexia, dyspraxia or dyscalculia. Entry based on recent education plan report, CE assessment morning (observed in groups) and interviews by head and excellent head of centre. Approximately 50 taught in centre, also supports the prep school students. Group work means that children become fantastically supportive of one another, concentration on remediation with younger ones and study skills with older. Time to finish tasks is not an issue – a good end product motivates students.

The bright library has a mezzanine level and is used to provide quiet working space for the sixth form frees. The dedicated sixth form centre also has computers but is generally more social. There's a comprehensive intranet with update alerts sent by email and text. Saturday morning revision classes on offer in the holidays, mostly to boost confidence before exams. Class sizes average 18 up to GCSE; after GCSE, the average is eight.

Games, options, the arts: Year groups of 150 mean that someone will always be into the same thing as your child. Everyone has to do dance, PE and drama. House drama, house song and up to 15 different productions a year (including visiting companies, A level and GCSE performances and Commedia dell'Arte). Dance boasts nearly 100 per cent A*/A at A level and at GCSE in performing arts studio completed in 2000 (outside classes offered to the community). Six-strong faculty teaches over 72 dance classes a week. Examinations taken in ballet,

Cricket for both sexes is a great strength – three former pupils have gone on to play for England women's team

modern, tap and jazz, and the school boasts boys' street dance, modern and tap groups from junior to senior level. The Montague studio is two minutes' walk away.

The new music school can only improve an impressively productive performing arts department. Half the pupils have one individual music lesson per week from more than 40 visiting music teachers and 22 music groups rehearse weekly: choirs, orchestra, rock groups, concert band and various chamber groups, with participation in the National Chamber Music Competition as well as tours to Prague and Moscow. Ex-parents miss going to the performances.

Two hugely popular and innovative sixth form house competitions stem from the entrepreneurship programme and Strictly Come Dancing. The former gets academics and creatives developing a business plan together, each team competing to win £3,000 to commercialise their idea – previous winners have been a parking app and a device to stop babies knocking hot tea over. Strictly ensures boys are valued for more than just sport – the biggest applause in Monday morning assemblies is drawn by the most unconventional achievements.

Purpose-built spaces for art, photography and DT mean all is in place for the making of beautiful art and design – there are still some lessons when the pupils get to watch a video for low maintenance inspiration, but the proof of the art is hanging on walls around the campus.

Sport is enormously important here, all pupils taking part in games twice a week – rounders, netball, tennis, cricket, swimming and rugby possible on campus, otherwise it's a minibus to the college's Jubilee Ground, with six rugby pitches or two cricket grounds, further floodlit netball courts, a pavilion and three hockey Astroturfs nearby. Withdean's athletics stadium also hosts fixtures; each weekend sees some 300-400 children involved in competitive matches. National trophies in rugby (1st XV have particularly strong record of victories in Sussex) and netball (Sussex champions and national finalists), and leads the county in athletics. Cricket for both sexes is a great strength – three former pupils play have gone on to play for England women's team.

Community service is a vital part of school life: every week, pupils visit elderly people and help disabled children, or teach pensioners how to use a computer; Make a Difference Day (MADD) sees every single member of the college out serving in the community in more than 100 different activities, from cleaning beaches and clearing scrub to sorting clothes for charity. Throughout the year the school raises money for local charities (including Whitehawk Inn, Rockinghorse, Chestnut Tree House) and those further afield (Romania, Kenya, Sri Lanka, India).

Boarding: Weekly boarding is extremely popular because there is no Saturday school; many go straight home after Saturday morning matches. Full-time boarders can avoid the school curfew at the weekend if they stay with local families who take responsibility. Pupils can return from home by 9.30pm on a Sunday night or on a Monday morning – there are buses to outlying towns.

Five boarding houses for years 9-13 – two for girls and three for boys – plus a junior boarding house for 11-13 year olds at Handcross Prep. Plenty of inter-house competitions, plus lectures, debates, music evenings, quizzes etc, and the after-school use of all facilities eg swimming pool and art department.

Background and atmosphere: Compact campus in Kemp Town, just four blocks from the sea front. Imposing buildings purpose-built in 1840s by Gilbert Scott (designer of St Pancras Station and the Albert Memorial). The school has spent £35 million in the past five years on an award-winning School of Design and Technology and teaching block for English, language suites, two boarding houses, two sports pavilions and an award winning Smith Café, where boarders can meet in the evening, health centre and staff common room. The most popular part of this are the places where the boys and girls get to hang out casually together instead of signing in and out of each other's boarding houses.

Entrepreneurship programme sees teams competing to win £3,000 to commercialise their idea – previous winner has been a device to stop babies knocking hot tea over

Sited to the east of the landmark pier and pavilion, the school succeeds in being fashionable, practical and innovative – the lack of Saturday morning school means that everyone can have a full weekend and the chance to be part of the town instead of just being educated within it. This could put some parents off, since Brighton and Hove, like many seaside cities, has its fair share of addicts, drunks and loons. However, we've heard no reports of pupils happening on any of these and most sensible local parents realise that their children are going to come to Brighton at the weekend anyway, and it is far better that they feel comfortable in their favourite cafés, bars and shops rather than loitering round Churchill Square.. Officially, there is a square patch of Kemptown streets where pupils can stroll for 20 minutes of an afternoon, in a group, as long as they sign out. However some definitely sneak a walk to the beach – they feel it's their right considering the prospectus proudly features pupils enjoying this out of bounds place.

This gives the pastoral staff a heads-up on what house might suit a newbie. The little ones arrive three days before the rest of the school and go on a treasure hunt

The children are thoughtful and articulate – we visited on the day of Thatcher's funeral and got into a discussion with a group of 13 year olds about whether people would dislike her so much if she had been a man who had implemented the same policies. The head picks an individual each Monday to share a random act of kindness in assembly – this type of awareness is at root of the school's ethos which goes a fair way to balancing the social mix here. As in all schools, cliques could be described if you were looking for them, but the most popular are not necessarily the richest or prettiest; difference is respected and often admired. The pupils are aware that they are privileged. The sixth form wear smart business-like clothes with some restrictions that are flouted when girls fancy tottering on high heels. They can drive themselves into school but must use street parking – high council charges are unpopular, with parents driving to attend chapel as well.

The whole school benefits from a good sense of the outside world, whether it is through exchanges with schools in Russia, Africa, America and Australia, the perspective offered by pupils from an inner-city school or the opportunity to twist their tongues round a year's worth of Mandarin Chinese. A link with Kingsford Community School in Newham, East London, beginning with heads' shared desire to make Mandarin mandatory has grown into an HSBC sponsorship of three Newham pupils' education in Brighton for a year. Sixth formers buddy up with pupils at the London Academy of Excellence and share study tips via Facebook (boarders allowed 10 minute slots) and email.

The chapel, just big enough for the whole school, is used three or four times a week for secular and multi-faith assemblies as well as Christian ones. Tradition still holds firm here (the oldest public school in Sussex) with the heads of school taking it in turns to sit alone in a pew, yet the chaplain is entertaining and eccentric – a new hymnal was an opportunity to get each house to prepare a song and belt it out in competition.

Pastoral care, well-being and discipline: As the head comments, this is 'a town school that is part of the real world, not apart from it'. At the beginning of every term he reiterates the ground rules on theft, bullying and beyond: expulsion and no second chances is the line on drugs and the security at the school gates is tight, yet cheery.

A report is emailed home every three weeks and there are parent meetings – although some parents report not much time for parent feedback. Those needing the most help definitely get it – those who are motivated enough to dance between options will attract it too.

The head of the lower school and the headmaster meet every single registered pupil in their own school before they enter Brighton College. This reduces the fear about attending a new school and gives the pastoral staff a heads-up on what house and friendship group might suit a newbie. The little ones arrive three days before the rest of school and go on a treasure hunt to help them get their bearings. The transition to the upper school is another focus point for the empathetic head of lower school – moving from being one of 40 to one of 150 under the shared care of tutors and houseparents.

One lower school house and 13 others when the post common entrance cohort enter, 325 boarding and 650 day – about 70 children in each so a good chance to develop cross year relationships. All of the youngest year in each senior school house share a tutor – as pupils grow they are matched with another for GCSEs and then A levels. Majority of housemasters and housemistresses are married and parents report incredible empathy for the fallout from tricky family and financial situations. Pupils learn how to iron a shirt, sew on a button and hold their own at a dinner party through house activities – really useful preparation for university admission and beyond.

Any bullying is dealt with speedily and with emotional intelligence – no homophobia or racism, some teasing but real respect for individuality. Two options at meals and dishes containing wheat are labelled, the school is nut free. Food is also available in the Smith Café and Café de Paris below the dance studio – and the houses all have kitchens for an emergency stack of toast for a starving teenage boy.

Pupils and parents: A great social mix from the children of butchers to highbrow TV presenters, successful entrepreneurs and a smattering of Conservative MPs; 33 per cent boarding, most weekly, but seven per cent overseas (five per cent Asian). Less than one per cent black pupils (reflects demographic of Brighton). Lower school just under 50 per cent from Brighton state schools, also many from London schools that stop at 11. Head ensures that useful parent contacts are wound into life of school in way that benefits both– from Leon providing soup recipes for sidelines at matches to a stylist helping with a fashion show. No Saturday school (weekly boarders can leave Friday 4pm, return Monday am) is popular with parents. School buses from towns ranging from Crowborough to Eastbourne with express services for weekly boarders Friday evening and Monday morning from Tunbridge Wells and Chichester. Pupils are cheerful, enthusiastic, friendly and polite and have an easy, relaxed relationship with teachers – at the top end of the school they feel part of a wider community, again, good preparation for life outside.

Entrance: Eleven plus entry via maths, English and verbal reasoning tests. Dynamic head of lower school has worked hard to build brilliant enrichment days for Gifted and Talented at local primaries – practical lessons in science labs, language work and unique experience of a senior school. All of this very attractive alternative to Brighton state school ballots.

Head ensures that useful parent contacts are wound into the life of the school – from Leon providing soup recipes for sidelines to a stylist helping with a fashion show

Pre-test assessment for 13+ entry; CE pass mark now 60 per cent – whether from coming from prep school or externally – with a minimum of 55 per cent in English and maths. Emotional intelligence used in assessment of intake for Brighton College Prep so a maximum of five out of 60 each year do not go through to the college – they must be the bright side of average or they will not be happy here – and those who disrupt the learning of others won't fit in either. Around 45 from the prep join 40 already in the lower school. Seventy more from 54 other preps including St Christopher's, Hove and Handcross (now run by Brighton College).

Around 70 new pupils at sixth form (B+ grades at GCSE are essential), mostly from Burgess Hill, Brighton and Hove High School, Eastbourne, Hurst and Lancing.

Exit: A handful after GCSEs to local sixth form colleges, almost always for financial reasons. One hundred per cent of A level leavers to university. Twenty-seven to Oxbridge in 2015; others to eg UCL, KCL, Bristol, Imperial, Durham, Manchester, Exeter and Leeds. Famous Old Brightonians, including Peter Mayle (writer), Lord Alexander of Weedon (lawyer and banker), Lord Skidelsky (historian and politician), Laurie Penny (writer), David Nash (sculptor), Matt Prior and Holly Colvin (cricketers), Sir John Chilcot (chairman of the Iraq Inquiry), Sir Michael Hordern (actor) and Jonathan Palmer (racing driver), testify to range of successful careers which may ensue.

Money matters: At a recent open morning, parents were wondering about what extras Brighton College might offer to justify its fees being higher than rival local schools' despite its limited campus space – half an hour later they were totally sold, having been treated to a Commedia dell'Arte take on the drama, a taste of Strictly Come Dancing by sixth formers and the heads of schools speaking about the high quality lessons. Many parents struggle to pay the fees but bursaries and up to 20 academic awards (5-50 per cent off basic fees), five music scholarships (up to 30 per cent off), art, drama, dance, sport, chess and all-rounder awards (up to 25 per cent off) and a DT scholarship (up to 15 per cent off) are available.

Registration fee of £110, then hefty deposits for accepting an offered place from £1,750 (day) to £13,750 (overseas boarders). Only refundable if pupils don't pass the entrance exam. Deposits retained to cover extras charged in arrears, balance refunded on exit from the school.

Extras include £270 per term per musical instrument, £260-£1,125 per term for the use of the dyslexia support centre, £1,325 per term for English as an additional language.

Remarks: Happy, broad-minded town school for children and families who are keen on learning – producing fantastic results and sparkling individual success stories. Pupils are encouraged to achieve as much as they can, so you'd never be bored, but you could end up with too much on. Bold ideas fostered in student, staff and parent body, all the while anchoring the opportunities enabled by the fees in real world experience. Detractors of the school (often parents of ex-pupils at the prep or pre-prep) see it as too results focused, with some families turning to outside tutoring to enable their children to get into the College. Raising of CE pass mark to 60 per cent fuel for the fire of those who judge the school to be top-slicing to climb the results ladder, explained transparently by the school as a tool to manage the high volume of applications.

Burgess Hill Girls

Keymer Road, Burgess Hill, West Sussex RH15 0EG

01444 241050
registrar@burgesshillgirls.com
www.burgesshillgirls.com

Ages: 11–18
Pupils: 535; sixth form: 92
Boarders: 52 full, 3 weekly
Day: £7,200 – £16,200 pa
Boarding: £25,500 – £28,200 pa

Head: Since 2014, Kathryn Bell. Vigorous, friendly and energetic – would be the last woman standing against battalions of establishment men; and in fact was the only female head ever appointed at her last post at Ackworth school. Previously second deputy head at Ardingly, and earlier teaching posts at Burgess Hill Girls, Brighton and Hove High, Hazelwick and St Michael's Burton Park. Has four grown up children, one of whom has had some educational and health problems, which means she has particular empathy with parents struggling with SEN.

Determined to dispel the myth of girls' schools being fluffy and pink, and Burgess Hill Girls has undergone a recent rebrand to stamp out all traces. Girls need 'to punch above weight in all disciplines', says the head, who has no time for female quotas. 'If you were shipwrecked, Burgess Hill girls would be those helping others to survive'. Wants her girls 'not to apologise for being who they are. They are not pretentious; but can stand up boldly and show what they have achieved and what they can offer'. Enjoys a 'good meaty discussion'.

Both pupils and parents approve; described by parents as 'amazing','proactive and approachable' and 'frequently with the children'; and on one occasion 'covered in mud', added a pleased mum. Pupils like the fact she spends time with them, and is 'really interested'.

Academic matters: Consistently excellent results – over 80 per cent A*-B grades at A level for last 13 years (81 per cent in 2015, with 47 per cent A*-A). Parents are very satisfied with their children's progress. Similar consistent achievement at GCSE, with 70 per cent A*/A in 2015.

GCSE maths and IGCSE science are high performers, alongside success in English, humanities and the arts. A good variety of mostly traditional subjects, with plenty of languages, both ancient and modern. Lovely language suite built in 2013, with laptops which rise from the desk lid when required. A pupil was awarded a gold medal at the International Linguistics Olympiad, which included a four hour challenge translating the

Universal Declaration of Human Rights from Armenian into English.

Small class sizes in sixth form (3-12) mean the girls have plenty of attention in class. Around 40 per cent of entries at A level are in science, maths and technology, and girls achieve excellent results in these subjects, with plenty of experience in using them: 'engineering experience day made me realise that engineering is not just about fixing things but about being creative and making a difference'. There's also an engineering education scheme, in which lower sixth pupils have a seven month project working alongside a company.

Very good results in many other areas, including PE, media studies and textiles, and although one parent commented that the range of subjects on offer at A level is not extensive, she was satisfied that the it was best for her daughter to concentrate on 'bread and butter' subjects now: she could always specialise at university. 'Traditional values and methods here,' she added. Traditional values clearly do matter here; but this school comes across as modern and engaged. Value added is carefully monitored using CEM, which shows that GCSE performance is on average one grade higher than of children of a similar ability: girls certainly thrive academically here.

There's a good mix of male and female staff, and the dedication of these teachers is, parents say, extraordinary. Extra clinics and one-on-one support means no one falls behind – one parent described how her daughter received extra help in science, running over things whilst others were at registration. Pupils say it's easy to ask for help.

There's a new focus on SEND, until recently ad hoc in different rooms, but now in a dedicated room. Parents who have used the SEND provision say it very good, and are pleased that the support in small group sessions (in English, maths and science) is free of charge. (One-one is charged as an extra, as it uses outside support.)

A beguilingly named head of futures advises on A levels, university and careers, and will go over personal statements umpteen times until just right. There's lots of careers advice, and parents are encouraged to participate in 'take your daughter to work day' – all part of the head's drive to get the girls out there.

Decent size library, open 8.30am-18.05pm. Super computers sunk into the desks, screens visible through transparent desk top, key boards pulled out for use as required.

Games, options, the arts: Both curriculum sports and clubs available to all, regardless of ability, with fixtures at all levels. There's one field on site for athletics and rounders, lovely pavilion, five floodlit hard netball courts, also used for tennis, and floodlit Astroturf. The gym is old, but light and well

kept. Facilities are not quite as extensive as parents might like, but on site expansion limited by site. Size of facilitates is no predictor of success: teams here do very well, girls saying being a small school means that they get more time from coaches. The girls excel at netball, hockey, athletics, rounders and horse riding.

Girls need 'to punch above their weight,' says the head, who has no time for female quotas. 'If you were shipwrecked, Burgess Hill girls would be helping others to survive'

Girls enthuse about extracurricular sports for all ethos at lunchtime, with clubs in badminton, ultimate frisbee, and fitness and dance. If there's demand of an activity, the school will do its best to provide: polo club started recently. School buses pupils to Ardingly reservoir for water sports and uses excellent local facilities for swimming and hockey.

Rare weekend fixtures means girls have the time to join local clubs, and girls like the fact that those busy with competitions have ring-fenced time to catch up with their academic work.

Creative arts events for all to enjoy – 'they don't chose the in your face confident girls to do everything here', said a parent approvingly. Busy drama and music departments, with regular productions ranging from Euripedes to Playhouse Creatures (a play about the struggles of actresses in a men's world). A big musical every year, last year The Shot Heard Round the World – written, composed and directed by three girls in upper sixth (one of the girls is now at Berkeley USA studying music and song writing). Croft II Drama was built onto the hall in 2013, a circular soundproof room with good acoustics which serves as a drama studio, recital room and place for parents to mingle during the interval of events held in the hall. The hall was refurbished at the same time, the (underused) stage removed and replaced with removal flooring, and stadium seating for 300 installed, which can fold back into a huge wooden wall.

Art is housed in a prefab block with a flat roof (bane of the bursar's life), surprisingly light around the edges, with a dedicated room for sixth formers, who can leave work undisturbed. The darker, but well lit space towards the centre of the building houses the exhibition of excellent A level and GCSE work.

Textiles are taken seriously here, and it's a very successful department. Material here is used for anything and everything, from the practical making of device cases for laptops, to a hand-bag styled like a pocket watch, with an opening clock face (the maker winning national handbag designer of the year 2014 aged just 15).

Plenty of extracurricular, from law society and public speaking to D of E and Young Enterprise. But, the girls say, if don't want to be busy, that's fine. OMG here (not the expletive – Only Motivated Girls), but 'in our own particular little ways'.

Boarding: Boarders live in one of the two elegant Edwardian boarding houses, which house girls of mixed ages. Alongside full and weekly boarding, there are two flexi boarding spaces (£45 a night). Boarding available from year 7 upwards, occasionally year 6 depending on the maturity of the child.

Most boarders are from overseas (Hong Kong and China), with around eight nationalities in total (no wish to increase overseas numbers, says the head). One parent told us he would prefer boarding to be less of an overseas service; but it has meant his daughter has a best friend from Madrid and a desire to learn Mandarin.

Describes as a day school with boarding, and this felt like the case. The boarding house we visited felt quiet: the girls don't return to houses during the day, so there's not the busy to and through evident in many big boarding schools. But boarders are very happy here, and call the houses home. One parent told us, 'The care and attention from the staff is exemplary. I feel my daughter is extremely well looked after'; another, that 'boarding has had a huge and positive effect'.

Inviting trellis covers the entrance to a boarding house; inside, a comfortable common room with TV, table football, books and games; kitchen with fruit and cereal always available. Games room, with a church pew to perch on – makes lingering games seem unlikely – and large screen in front, also used for dancing with the Wii. One of the messiest rooms we have ever seen, but we are told this is unusual, and a reward scheme is in place to encourage tidiness. Fresh decoration, with bathrooms recently redecorated and deep cleaned.

If parents are late picking up day girls, they simply go over to the boarding house. Burgess Hill Girls is well situated in town, so if boarders haven't got a club, they may go into town in small groups after school. Supervised prep, then down time in the boarding house until bedtime, with years 7-9 handing in electronic devices before lights out at 10pm. Wifi is turned off at midnight and comes back on at 6am. Boarders contact home via Skype or internet phone, with the office phone or computer available as back up.

Activities organised for each weekend, both trips and on site activities, compulsory for year 7-10. Ideas for activities come from the girls. There is a suggestion box, a weekly discussion between

One was chatting to a teacher about her daughter's anxiety, and the next day received a handwritten card suggesting websites that might help

pupils and catering; and although parents told us the quality of evening meals is not the same as lunches, the school say suggestions for changes to food are acted on immediately.

Background and atmosphere: Set back from the road in a leafy suburb of large houses and big old trees; we had to peer up driveway to be sure it was the right place – planning permission is being sought for an 'illuminated totem' (a bright sign you can see from the road) and new entrance railing.

Buildings are a mixture of old Victorian villas and modern, with a slightly colonial feel; beautifully kept grounds, encircled by trees gives an immediate sense of safety and seclusion. But the girls here are not cosseted; Mrs Bell feels the most important thing is to 'get the girls out there' –and they are out there a lot.

Entry through glass doors, a large navy sign fronted with gold chairs, and a vertical radiator. Everything about the entrance says up to date. Parents describe the buildings as 'clean, crisp and fresh.' Decor inside varies from swish purpose built to elderly, with recently refurbished areas in blue and gold; a blue stripy carpet that makes you feel as if you are in a mathematical game with lines which sway and lift your path. Traditional moments though: portraits of heads decorate an old staircase, much like 10 Downing St.

The food is tasty, agree the girls, and the chef takes on board suggestions from the box in the dining hall. There are old fashioned school desks filled with fruit (described in several languages), a spoon and fork clock, and a good selection of food, to which soup is added midway through the autumn term. In the annual poverty lunch, pupils lunch on soup, with one piece of bread and a piece of fruit: a reminder of how fortunate they are.

Most of the parents we spoke to were not specifically looking for a single sex school, but chose Burgess Hill Girls because it was school they liked most –'it felt the most authentic', said one; 'plain speaking', said another. The head believes being away from boys allows girls room to develop, to be themselves – and the necessary strength, resilience and broad shoulders to cope and be the best in a male dominated world. The girls we spoke to agreed; one girl who came from a mixed sex school said she was not afraid to shine here – 'boys interrupt,' she added. Parents feel girls here don't get shouted down or belittled by boys; and although one admitted her daughter did find life at university a bit of a shock, she added that the sixth formers are well prepared, and have workshops on everything...including boys.

Girls here are encouraged to step out of their comfort zones: on Roche days, twice a year, pupils spend a day pushing their boundaries – we saw a group learning to plaster, patiently working their way up four columns planted in the lawn (no chance of contamination, with hooded plastic space suits and plastic goggles). Roche day ends listening to motivational businesswomen, encouraging the girls to take risks to succeed.

Other activities are designed to practise business rapport, and networking breakfasts are organised by the girls. There are plenty of trips out, from Greece to the Old Bailey; and the lower sixth annual challenge to race the sun, setting off at sunset to walk across the downs to reach Beachy Head by sunrise, dressed up for the occasion as nuns, football players and pirates; the nuns, appropriately, treating everyone to highlights from the Sound of Music on the way.

The navy and stripe uniform is about to change, with pupil and parent views being sought; although it might have been less controversial to move the school to the Bahamas, says the head wryly. Sixth formers currently wear their own clothes, with the requirement to be smart (although jeans are allowed). Teachers apparently have different views of what's smart, and what's acceptable to some isn't smart enough for others, say the girls. Suits are being considered.

Lower sixth challenge to race the sun, setting off at sunset to walk across the downs to reach Beachy Head by sunrise, dressed as nuns, football players and pirates

I am, I can, I ought, I will are the words of the school motto, and they pop up all over the place. There is a strong moral tone about this non-denominational school, with a focused time to reflect on moral messages during a period of silence on arrival and departure from assembly, and healthy links with the local community. This is one of the few schools we have visited which views community service as an essential part of life balance, alongside academic work and play, rather than an optional extra, and it appears in many areas of life at Burgess Hill: from raising money for local charities, to holding an annual pamper day for local carers, and helping children with their reading at a local primary school. Sixth formers raised money for a local nursery and helped set up its Facebook page, while year 10 held a workshop to make bags for hospice patients to hold medication. The whole school take part in the Sports Relief Mile, and on an international level, the school supports Plan – a charity to raise the profile of girls across the world who do not have access to education.

Pastoral care, well-being and discipline: Parents say the staff work 24/7 for the girls 'above and beyond the call of duty'. 'If you send an email saying you're worried about something, you'll be at school at 8am the next morning chatting about it'. The school is excellent at keeping in touch, and parents emphasis the all round care – one described how she was chatting to a teacher about her worries about her daughter's anxiety, and the next day received a handwritten card through the post suggesting websites that might help. Girls agreed that they all knew who they would go to with a problem, from the head to favourite teachers, or the nurse (much loved by all). Sixth form mentors help younger girls, and all girls meet their teacher mentor every fortnight, to discuss work and anything else.

Bullying is dealt with straight on, and rapidly, said a parent. Both parties received counselling, and, most importantly to the parent, her daughter was taught strategies for dealing with bullies.

The honesty of this school is much appreciated by parents, who feel that problems here are dealt with head on: they are very engaged with the problems that can assail girls, and often make their appearance in years 9 and 10 – for example, obsession with image and being skinny, and rare instances of self harm. 'They are right on it', said a parent. A comprehensive drugs policy exists, with every girl treated as an individual and every situation independently assessed before decisions are made.

This feels like a place where a high standard of behaviour is expected, and by and large adhered to by the girls. Parents felt that poor conduct is very unlikely and would be much more of an issue here than poor performance.

A lively house system; though a little strange, you might think, for a modern girls' school to name its houses after dead male poets. A little bit of left over tradition, says the head. Lots of inter-house competition throughout the year, from public speaking, chess and sports, to performing arts day.

Pupils and parents: Parents are a mix of wealthy and not: city professionals, businesspeople, and working several jobs to keep their girls at Burgess Hill. Some are competitive – 'keen to ensure their daughters are achieving and being seen to achieve'.

Parents receive a grade sheet for attainment and attitude to learning every half term. Year 10s upwards receive working at and working towards grades as well. Two parents' evenings and one full report per year.

The school bus service is popular – a year 6 girl described her bus driver as one of the nicest things about school. It covers eight routes around Sussex every morning, children coming from as far afield as Horsham, Crawley and Uckfield. Season ticket is £400 a term, each route being offered in the morning and twice after school, with an early bus at 4.00pm and a late bus at 6.15pm. Drop off is a bit tricky; cars can drive in, through, and out, but it gets congested, and many parents drop off at the road outside. School is three minutes walk from Burgess Hill station, and just 45 minutes by train from London.

Communication with parents is excellent, and there's no prolonged email back and forth with parents: the head encourages teachers to invite parents with a concern or issue to come in, or pick up the phone.

Notable former pupils include Holly Willoughby, television presenter, Kim Sears (Mrs Andy Murray) and Caroline Atkins, former international cricketer.

Entrance: Most (80 per cent last year) come from the junior school. A good number also from local state primaries and preps in the south east and London.

Exit: One to Oxford (French) and one to Cambridge (medicine) in 2015, with the majority going to Russell Group, and others to art schools. Vast majority gain places at first choice universities, for mostly traditional subjects.

No one has had to leave in the last few years due to poor GCSE results. This school emphasises personalised education, and will create a programme to suit the needs of a pupil who got weak grades at GCSE, to include re-sitting key GCSEs, and close monitoring of progress.

Money matters: No charge for pre and after-school care, from 8am-6pm, including breakfast. Academic, music, art, sport and drama scholarships, up to 40 per cent of fees, awarded at 11+,13+ and 16+. A number of significant bursaries (which do not take account of academic standard). Great value for money, say parents. 'The John Lewis of education,' says the head.

Remarks: This nurturing school puts time and thought into finding the best in each girl. Its excellent academic standards do not make it intellectually exclusive – parents felt it would suit all sorts, one saying that it suited both her very academic daughter, and the one whose talents were more middle of the road.

Caterham School

Harestone Valley Road, Caterham, Surrey CR3 6YA

01883 343028
admissions@caterhamschool.co.uk
www.caterhamschool.co.uk

Ages: 11–18
Pupils: 878; sixth form: 304
Boarders: 164
Day: £16,056 – £16,806 pa
Boarding: £27,345 – £31,359 pa

Headmaster: Since September 2015, Mr Ceri Jones, previously second master at Tonbridge School. Read history at Fitzwilliam College Cambridge and is completing an MEd in educational leadership. He is a former head of history at Caterham and returns after 10 years at Tonbridge. In 2012, in collaboration with The Sutton Trust, Fitzwilliam College and a number of Kent independent schools, he launched an access programme for disadvantaged but academically bright year 9 students at state comprehensives in Kent. In 2013 he was seconded as executive principal to the Marsh Academy in New Romney, which is a state school that Tonbridge School co-sponsors. He is married to Kay Moxon and they have two daughters.

Academic matters: Now among the UK's top independent schools, outperforming many of its more famous rivals, yet strangely still just under the radar. At GCSE in 2015, 80 per cent A*/A. At A level, one of the top 50 independent schools in the country – 88 per cent A*-B and 65 per cent A*/A.

Maths and science are stand out subjects here (triple science the norm). The biology and physics departments have received a several GSG awards for A level results over the past few years. French, German, Spanish, Latin and Greek offered to GCSE and A level. The school has introduced iPads so that, eventually, each pupil will have their own mobile device. There are 800 computers throughout the school, all networked and with email and internet access.

However, school quick to stress that academic success must not be the pupils' only achievement – watchwords are 'An education for life'. Parents agree that the school gets the best out of all the children – not just the super-academic. Also on the curriculum are study skills such as speed-reading, research techniques, typing, all designed to give students the edge out in the real world. The first independent school to be awarded Thinking School status by Dr Edward de Bono – too detailed to explain here, but it involves planning thinking processes using coloured hats. Children we met understood it perfectly; school offers courses to enlighten confused parents. No plans to introduce IB, but IGCSE offered in English, maths, sciences.

First class teaching team works hard to engender a passion for learning. Parents describe it as dynamic, dedicated and (again) youthful. Lessons are enjoyable and lively, not all chalk and talk. Great head of science, wearing a bright pink overall when we saw him, and pupil guides proudly announced he had new labs designed to his specification. Lots of on-going staff training and opportunities mean turnover is low. Class sizes in first three years average 20-24, dropping to 15-20 for GCSE teaching and usually eight to 12 for sixth form. All the facilities, resources, bells and whistles you would expect for the money. Oozes prestige.

Not huge call for SEN provision (a handful) but around 90 pupils have learning difficulties and disabilities. A TA for the visually impaired and some one-to-one teaching. A dyslexia specialist is available. Inclusive system of study buddies sees older students passing on their experience to the younger years – anything from straightforward

subject help to other issues like time-management. Eighty or so pupils receive EAL support.

Games, options, the arts: All strong, in keeping with school's aims to develop all-rounders. Sparkling achievements on the sports field are just as impressive as the academic results. Priority sports are rugby, hockey, cricket, lacrosse and netball, with many teams winning regional awards, but lots of others on offer, from athletics to taekwondo. Sport is taken seriously but not just for the elite – everyone encouraged to have a go.

Inclusive system of study buddies sees older students passing on their experience to the younger years – anything from subject help to issues like time-management

Drama has a fairly high profile and is improving. Impressive performance space but no dedicated studio. Music next on list for development. Up to 30 per cent of pupils currently learn a musical instrument (exams can be taken) and plenty of opportunities to perform. But although lots get involved in high standard school and house productions and concerts, only handfuls take music and drama at GCSE and A level. Better take-up of art and design, with pottery, textiles and photography offered.

Both the Duke of Edinburgh Award Scheme and the Combined Cadet Force are thriving – pupils regularly win armed forces scholarships. All told, around 35 clubs and societies, from chess to debating, kit car challenge popular. 'Put us up against any school and we'd win for sheer range of activities on offer.'

Boarding: Boarding facilities recently upgraded. Years 7-9 in good sized, four-bed rooms, thinning out as they rise through the ranks to qualify for single, ensuite accommodation by upper sixth. Ofsted pronounced the boarding offering as 'outstanding' – in fact some university halls may be a come-down. Homely atmosphere – lots of staff live in and build up good relationships with their charges. Growing requirement for flexi-boarding acknowledged and accommodated wherever possible. More space from September 2016 for rising numbers of weekly boarders. Boarders (100 boys, 64 girls and around a fifth overseas) do really well here where their life is fun, but well-structured. Prep every night under controlled conditions and then checked – boarders get great results. Staff delighted as TVs and computer games gather dust – too much else on offer: loads of sport and special events.

Background and atmosphere: Situated in 200 acres of loveliness in a wooded valley of the North Downs, south of London, just inside the M25. Approach is via a quiet residential road of substantial houses. Main school building is an attractive, Victorian, red-brick building looking out onto its own impressive playing fields, hills beyond. Inside a preponderance of tiling and brick – looks nicer than that might sound. Modern science block and sixth from centre.

Staff delighted as TVs and computer games gather dust – too much else on offer: loads of sport and special events

All the pupils smartly turned out, business suits for sixth formers. A happy, vibrant place, where students are enjoying, rather than enduring, their days. Nice easy atmosphere – always visitors around, parents welcome, teachers used to having their classroom doors opened mid-lesson.

Pastoral care, well-being and discipline: Standards of behaviour are high ('exemplary,' says ISI) and pastoral care is top-notch, based on the principle of mutual respect. Any problems dealt with quick time and would never punish a significant misdemeanour without getting to the root cause – a holistic approach. School conscious that young people get a maelstrom of mixed messages in today's media and can get caught up in a 'cool to be cruel' culture. School sees itself as the counterbalance to that – 'we want to show the pupils that kindness and courtesy matter'. Staff set the tone, aiming to turn out 'nice people that parents and school can be proud of'. Need we add zero-tolerance of bullying, drugs and drink – all non-starters? Minor demeanours dealt with by way of warnings and gating – practical things like litter duty, rising to detention. Suspension and expulsion obviously the end game – but both are rare events. Pupils generally have good relationships with teachers and other staff. School linked to URC, but it's a light touch, no Christian exertion, all welcome.

Pupils and parents: Parents are really supportive of this place – it's not unusual for 500 spectators to support Saturday fixtures. Largely a local school – 70 per cent travel less than five miles to school – but other day pupils from up to 30 miles away (plenty of school buses and good transport links with mainline BR just a 15 minute walk). Boarders from 25 different countries, including UK, but significant numbers from East Asia and Eastern European countries.

Parents from a wide mix of professions and businesses. Successful and productive parents' association has a good time raising significant sums for the school. Old Cats (boys so far, as school only fully co-ed since 1995) include Geraint Jones (organist, conductor); Angus Deayton (television presenter); Sir Alan Moncrieff (first Nuffield professor of child health); Sir Arthur James (Court of Appeal) and recently cricketers Ali Brown, David Sales and James Benning. Old Cats a big feature

– turn up at all the events, plays, fixtures, magazine launches, giving the current pupils a real sense of their school's history and traditions.

Entrance: Academically selective, mainly at 11, 13 and 16. Own exam used (English, maths and verbal and numerical reasoning) plus interview and report from current school (common entrance for setting at age 13). For sixth form entry, six GCSEs at grade A (grade B for existing pupils moving up).

No special skills or religious requirements; school has URC affiliation but pupils of many faiths within it. Thirty per cent of intake from state schools (plus 10 per cent to sixth form).

School's main feeder is Caterham Preparatory School, which provides around 40 pupils in year 7. Others are The Hawthorns, Hazelwood, Oakhyrst Grange, St Mary's C of E Junior School, Sevenoaks Preparatory School, New Beacon School and Copthorne School.

Exit: Around 10 per cent leave after GCSE, generally because eg drama or art specialists, or for financial reasons. All sixth form leavers to university, 15 to Oxbridge in 2015, most of rest to other top tier destinations. Exeter, Southampton, Birmingham, York and Bath all popular in 2015.

Money matters: About a third of pupils receive either scholarships or bursaries. Scholarships and exhibitions awarded at 11 and 13 (academic, art, music, performing arts, sports and all-rounder). At 16 academic, art, music, sport, science and drama are available. Most represent 25 per cent of fees with academic scholarships of up to 50 per cent. Boarding/international scholarships are also available. All 11+ and 13+ day pupil candidates are automatically considered for academic scholarships, but specific application forms are required for other scholarships. The number offered varies each year, but essentially funds are available equivalent to 10 school places.

School also has a bursaries scheme for children of United Reformed Church clergy, for families in the Forces or those on a low income. There is a new, fully funded sixth form bursary named in honour of slavery abolitionist William Wilberforce, who was a friend of the school's founder and a subscriber to the school, giving Caterham 10 guineas a year.

Remarks: A classic independent school – great results, large, leafy grounds, good facilities, strict discipline, polite, charming and well-informed pupils. You can see what you are paying for here. It's on the up and pulling ahead of the pack now.

Charterhouse

Admissions Office, Godalming, Surrey GU7 2DX

01483 291501
admissions@charterhouse.org.uk
www.charterhouse.org.uk
C of E

Ages: 13–18
Pupils: 800; sixth form: 412 (275 boys, 137 girls)
Boarders: 770 full, 30 day boarders
Day: £29,361 pa
Boarding: £35,529 pa

Head Master: Since January 2014, Mr Richard Pleming MA (early 50s). First a chorister at Canterbury Cathedral, thence to King's School, Canterbury (became captain of school) thereafter to Pembroke, Cambridge where he took a first in English. After a year as marketing officer for Scottish Opera, he spent five at Schroders and 3i. Saw the light (and a massive salary drop) in 1990 and began teaching at St Paul's, London, then at Eton. Housemaster and head of English at St Edward's, Oxford and, finally, became head of Wrekin College for two and a half years. Married to Rachel Crowther, a doctor and novelist; they have five children.

We took to him at once. Soft-spoken, donnish, clear-sighted and canny, he is a man of understated but palpable principle. 'Social responsibility' is a phrase we heard more than once and the idea that a start in life as privileged as the one provided by Charterhouse demands a sense of duty to society at large underpins Mr Pleming's educational vision. Not merely for the purpose of box-ticking or to fulfil statutory obligations is his commitment to inculcate in Carthusians a sense of their place in and responsibility to a truly global society. A head who combines traditional educational values and standards with a sound grasp of the modern world, he also has ambition. When asked why the school was, perhaps, less well-known in some quarters than you might expect – 'If they don't know us, they're going to know us.'

Charterhouse parents enthuse. 'He's very good at getting onto problems,' one veteran told us. 'He's what was needed,' another claimed. 'He's good at consulting parents and is very hot on the pastoral side.' Pupils talk of how much he is seen around the school – an innovation they like. 'He is very hot on bullying,' they told us. Seen as tough and even 'ruthless' by some, his attention to pastoral care is also praised by many. He sees it as his first priority and talks feelingly about the ever more complex pressures on today's young. Consensus is that he will do what is needful. 'He gets stuff done.' A clever, insightful appointment.

Academic matters: Most take either the Cambridge Pre-U or the IB diploma. A levels survive in four subjects, the most popular of which is government & politics. The Pre-U still seen as controversial among parents, who worry unnecessarily that universities are bemused by it. IGCSEs taken in preference to GCSEs in most subjects. But Mr Pleming – who was new to the Pre-U – is a convert and has no plans to change the current arrangements while, as he says, A levels are 'in flux' and, in fact, now teaches Pre-U English.

The mix of curricula here make judgements about exceptional performance in specific subjects difficult. Maths, history and economics are the stand-outs in terms of sixth form popularity. Art does well and many minority subjects shine. IGCSEs sparkle and demonstrate the value added by good teaching and individual attention. 2015 results saw 82 per cent of IGCSEs A*/A; 93 per cent of Pre-U exams achieved distinction or merit (A*-B equivalent) and 56 per cent distinction (A*/A equivalent). Average IB point score 37. This has to be impressive for a school which requires only 60 per cent at CE.

Home for 80 pensioners (gentlemen in poverty, soldiers that have borne arms by sea or land, merchants decayed by piracy or shipwreck)

'Not frighteningly academic if you've come from a pushy London day school,' we were told by one parent, while another said, 'It's far more academically rigorous than we'd expected.' A third felt that, 'A lot of the seriously bright chaps are the international students.' However, 'There's a culture of trying hard and achieving,' another observed. Mr Pleming has introduced an 'academic tie' ('It's a rather attractive apple green,' he avers) for under school boys, to match the one for senior school boys and girls. We deeply approve of the first year's geography and history syllabus being largely focused on the rich history of the school. Not here do you meet pupils with no idea of the key figures and moments in the story of their alma mater. Careers provision and university preparation, having been described as 'needing a kick' by several parents, now rapidly improving, and school is building on Old Carthusian networks and willingness to support current leavers.

System of 'Calling Over' – boys get praised for effort or pulled up for lack of it publicly in class four times a term – is controversial. 'It's brutal,' complained one parent while acknowledging that 'it does mean they are doing something if a boy isn't pulling his weight.' Mr Pleming admits he

was uncertain about it at first but now sees it as a useful tool to help monitor progress, and assures us that 'the more difficult conversations are held one-to-one'.

Very few with recognised or serious SEN of any kind. No withdrawal from classes for individual support. 'We subscribe to the idea enshrined in current legislation that all teachers must be teachers of special educational needs. The best person to support a pupil's needs is his or her subject teacher. All teachers receive regular training in supporting pupils' individual needs.' Head says, 'We individualise learning as much as we can.'

Games, options, the arts: Everything done with vigour, dedication and enthusiasm. Ben Travers Theatre – opened by the great farceur himself in 1980 (at 93) – now looking a little tired, but still an excellent performing space with a cosy foyer. Lots of productions. Surprisingly small proportion learn an instrument – only 280 of the 800 pupils – but the standard of those who do, and the intensity of participation in multiple performance opportunities of all kinds, is exemplary. Very lively and creative art and DT ('someone made a motorbike') – each sixth form artist has their own space and we admired the flair and scope of work. Super ceramics, collage and painting, especially. Two new 3D printers.

Enormous sports complex with everything you'd expect and used, out of lesson time, by the general public. All-weather pitches, courts, fields and tracks in all directions plus a nine hole golf course. A famous football school – Spurs 'Legend' directs the game – with seven teams in each year and masses of matches for all. Sporting opportunities and achievements here of all kinds and hard to better. 'And if there's something you want to do which they don't offer they will try and set it up for you,' we were told. Also a famous CCF and formidable pioneering expeditions to all kinds of high up and far away places.

Boarding: Old houses and new houses and everyone has an opinion on each and on the system as a whole. The new houses – 'architecturally weird and further away from everything' – are preferred by some as more functional, better resourced and nearer to sports facilities. Eating in the new houses is communal, so 'You can't go down in your pyjamas – such a shame,' thought one parent. Four girls' 'hostels' but they study in the boys' houses until 10pm when they trot demurely home. Boys not allowed anywhere near girls' hostels – ever. Sixth form facilities being extended at time of our visit to add a further 30 or so boarding places.

Girls' hostels felt to be better – all rooms have en-suite bathrooms, are very cosy and their rooms are only for sleeping. Accommodation in the older houses is not up to that offered in many top schools

these days. En suites are scarce, some rooms are tiny, though no-one shares a room with more than one other. Arcane systems of swapping rooms and girls changing hostels every term – we won't try to explain here; you need to ask – but all is aimed at integrating people and fostering community.

Background and atmosphere: Lincolnshire man, Thomas Sutton (1532–1611), discovered coal on two estates he had leased near Newcastle-on-Tyne and made his fortune. He endowed a hospital on the site of the London Charterhouse and left a legacy to maintain a chapel, almshouse and school. After much legal wrangling, a foundation was set up to run a home for 80 pensioners (gentlemen by descent and in poverty, soldiers that have borne arms by sea or land, merchants decayed by piracy or shipwreck, or servants in household to the King or Queens Majesty), and to educate 40 boys.

The school moved to its present home in stockbroker-Surrey in 1872. The main school building, a substantial gothic statement of purpose, cannot fail to awe. Its post-WW1 chapel – the largest war memorial in the country – is vast, stark and sombre; no mistaking the genuine horror and grief at the nearly 700 lost Carthusians which inspired it. Many more buildings – some of less obvious architectural merit – have since accrued, some having been opened by impressive visitors eg HM the Queen and – the MFL building – by Javier Perez de Cuellar in 2007. Super library – subdued lighting, comfortable sofas, tables with laptop points and exemplary stock; a library that has been nurtured and loved.

The site has grown to 250 acres with fields and pitches stretching away into the landscape. Trees, little gardens and courtyards humanise it and pathways meander about to give the impression of a sizeable and complex school 'village'. And some people definitely drive too fast down the main thoroughfares!

The advent of sixth form girls into what many still feel is a very male establishment is a source of joy for most. 'The boys love it when the girls arrive,' one seasoned father of boys told us. 'It gives them the best of both worlds.' One sixth form lad told us the only thing that would make the school better would be more girls. Others concur, though stress, 'it takes a certain type of girl – they have to be confident and not stand any nonsense.' Sporty girls go down particularly well, it seems. And, inevitably, 'They do rank us on prettiness so you have to be robust'. School getting better at integrating the girls. A two-day get-to-know-you pre-term event introduced in head's first year has done much.

A Christian school and a school in which this is still overt – for all its inclusiveness. A school with its own argot – yes, teachers are 'beaks' here. Parents comment on that old-fashioned thing, the school 'spirit'. 'There's a strong sense of loyalty. They engender it very quickly. Loyalty to both house and school.' A seriousness about the place reflected in its publications, its sending of expert teachers to support the teaching of individual subjects in local state schools and in Mr Pleming's new appointment of a 'director of social responsibility'. We like this.

'The boys love it when the girls arrive,' one seasoned father of boys told us. 'It gives them the best of both worlds.' 'It takes a certain type of girl – they have to be confident'

Most weekends, pupils may go home after sports fixtures on Saturday afternoons and return for chapel on Sunday evening. For those pupils who remain in school overnight on Saturday (around 20 per cent), a full programme of weekend activities. This a welcome Pleming innovation – 'There used to be absolutely nothing to do at weekends,' a sixth former told us. 'Now there's loads.' So not, as some parents fear, a lure to keep boys from going home – though it might work that way with some. Most staff live on site – many in a strange tower, nine floors of a highly eccentric 1970s folly – and all live within a mile of school. Some school officers allowed bikes to get around. We wonder whether this privilege could, without imperilling safety or hierarchy, be extended to others on such a large campus?

Pastoral care, well-being and discipline: Vertical tutor system described as 'brilliant!' – one tutor for two boys from each year. Tutor sees each tutee at least once weekly and parents feel 'My son's tutor is on his side – we can't fault the system'. Very much a school for joiners-in. 'They do their best to make them try out everything. So even lazy boys get really pushed to try things.' Pupils are polite and charming and discipline is good, though parents tell us of the odd drink smuggling escapade. 'It's really not a problem here' though, affirm sixth formers. Junior boys wear tweedy jackets, older boys wear blue blazers and girls seem uniformly to have long hair and short black skirts. No pushing at boundaries to be seen anywhere.

Most housemasters accorded warm praise, though one or two houses described by parents as 'out of control'. Head assures us this is being tackled – and we gather there have been several recent changes in the pastoral team. Boarders are 'very well supervised,' in their leisure time and 'the school is very sensible about absences and so on,' assert parents. Matron is especially highly praised. Most teachers described as 'incredibly kind' and as being a good mix of 'nice young ones – sharp-witted and impressive – and safer, older pairs of hands'. 'Kindness' was a word we heard a lot from parents – this being valued highly in the school community as a whole. School seen by almost all as collaborative and encouraging mutual respect between staff and pupils. A sense that Mr Pleming will stand for no nonsense from anyone. 'A good school is one in good order, where everyone understands the boundaries and one with proportionate use of sanctions – a school in which school, pupils and parents work together.' Yes.

Pupils and parents: About 80 per cent from London or the home counties, and currently many go home after Saturday sports at weekends. Vast majority boards and all boarders have to be back for Sunday night chapel. Twenty per cent made up of around 37 nationalities – a few have some EAL support but this is not the norm. Presence of overseas pupils is not new: Charterhouse has a relationship with Hong Kong going back 200 years and has long valued its international reach and reputation. The IB 'reflects our international perspective,' says head. Some sense that being sporty is valued more highly than being arty, and some creative but left-footed types take a while to feel at home. However, the Pleming enthusiasm for music and art becoming increasingly influential and may well shift this slight imbalance.

Immense list of notable Old Carthusians includes poets Richards Crashaw and Lovelace, writers Joseph Addison, Richard Steele, WM Thackeray, Max Beerbohm, Ben Travers, Robert Graves, Simon Raven, Frederick Raphael, publisher John Murray, classicist Henry Liddell, actor-manager Johnston Forbes-Robertson, founder of the scouts, Robert Baden-Powell, cartoonist and wit

Osbert Lancaster, composer Ralph Vaughan-Williams, historian Hugh Trevor-Roper, sculptor Anthony Caro, politicos and journalists James Prior, William Rees-Mogg, Dick Taverne, the Dimblebys, Jeremy Hunt, Duncan Carswell, philosopher Don Cupitt, pop impresario Jonathan King, the rock group Genesis, composer Rachel Portman and innumerable venerable ecclesiasts (among them, John Wesley) and redoubtable military men of high renown.

Entrance: Register early. School very popular and lists can close three years before entry, so don't hang about. Year 6 interview and prep school reports – which carry much weight. Houses matter here. Parents and boys visit two or three houses, meet housemaster and staff and boys and have a good poke about. All are interviewed in the first house they visit – a record is kept for other housemasters to see if necessary. Parents then choose their preferred house – but they don't always get it.

For those entering from September 2018, entrance arrangements will change. Candidates will sit the ISEB common pre-test in year 6 at their current school. School assures parents that boys will still be invited for interview and close contact will be maintained with prep schools. Some consternation among parents who wish that the school had 'stuck to its guns'. School insists it will continue to take note of any major discrepancies between the pre-test results and the picture created of an individual by the interview and school report and consult prep heads where necessary. A few places not dependent on pre-testing will remain for late applicants and exceptional cases.

Pleming says, wisely, 'We don't want to disappoint children at 13 because it's bad for them'.

At sixth form, 75 girls and 30 boys come, most as boarders and a few as day pupils. Admission by competitive examination, school reports and interview. Offers of places are unconditional but high proportion of GCSE A*s and As are expected. Little choice of houses.

A few places reserved in years 9 and 12 for overseas candidates. Quite diverse admissions systems, depending on where you are from. 'It doesn't suffer from being too fashionable,' one wise parent ventured. 'It is good at choosing the boys who will suit it.'

Exit: Thirteen to Oxbridge in 2015. Large numbers to Bristol, Durham, Exeter, Manchester, Nottingham, Newcastle and, increasingly, to prestigious colleges in the US – Chicago, NYU, California, Berkeley. No narrow range of subjects studied but a bent towards economics, politics, business and management perhaps. No silly subjects pursued by anyone.

> *Very much a school for joiners-in. 'They do their best to make them try out everything. So even lazy boys get really pushed to try things.' Pupils are polite and charming*

Most are offered conditional places plus places in their first or second choice house. Parents pay an initial deposit to confirm place and are asked whether Charterhouse is their first choice. Boys not offered house places are placed on the general list, as are those who are accepted after general list interviews. They are invited to choose a house after meeting housemasters during the spring of year 8. In the autumn of year 8, preps send updated reports – this can result in some boys being asked to withdraw.

About 125 places in year 9. CE pass mark of 60 per cent expected. They don't over-offer. Mr

Money matters: Not a rich school. Most fee assistance now in the form of bursarial help rather than scholarships. Scholarships – whether at 13+ or 16+, exhibitions, academic, art and music scholarships, more for glory than dosh. However, can be topped up by mean-tested bursaries up to the value of full fees in cases of proven need.

Remarks: An all-round impressive school – confident of what it does and doing it well. New head is giving it the spur into the future it needs. 'We are delighted,' parents enthused. Pupils genuinely value what they are given here. As one, thoughtfully, expressed it, 'You feel you're part of something that should continue'.

Christ's Hospital

Horsham, West Sussex RH13 0YP

01403 211293
enquiries@christs-hospital.org.uk
www.christs-hospital.org.uk
C of E

Ages: 11–18
Pupils: 882; sixth form: 290
Boarders: 814
Day: £15,750 – £19,800 pa
Boarding: £30,450 pa

Head Master: Since 2007, Mr John Franklin BA Dip Teaching MEd admin (60s), came from nine years of headship at Ardingly. Born in Australia and is quietly-spoken yet firm. His experience is spread across both hemispheres – six years as a deputy at St Peter's Adelaide, the oldest continuous school in mainland Australia, prior to that an English teacher and acting housemaster at Marlborough for three and a half years. Wife, Kim, teaches English part-time. He is all set to teach again, an ambition that has been leapfrogged in the past seven years by his role in the modernisation of the school and foundation's joint governance structure.

Likes to tinker with cars and compares Christ's Hospital on his arrival to an E-type Jaguar that was terminally rusty and had two drivers fighting for the wheel – the clerk of the foundation and the headmaster. Now the vintage car has been lovingly restored, is running soundly and the head is comfortable in the driving seat; a whimsical metaphor for what has been a gargantuan and sometimes Machiavellian struggle from a £4.5 million deficit

to more than half a million net profit from holiday lettings, and an ISI inspection giving the school an excellent across the board rating. The division of governance is now clear and functional and the school is being marketed for the first time in its life – 'a school like no other.'

Sets clear expectations and they are firmly applied, so pupils respect him. Temperature testing of the school is done via the Senior Grecians (head boy/girl and prefects) and by walking the school and sports pitches (with or without his dogs). Understated in his pride of 'the bright and talented pupils who otherwise would not have had these opportunities; and what they achieve, year on year.' Thoughtful and perceptive, it'll be 2017 before he retires to his cottage in Storrington. Aware that the archaic uniform erases all trappings of family circumstances and passionate about diversifying the pupil population with fee-paying families without eroding the school's unique ethos.

Academic matters: Junior class sizes up to 25, 20 in core subjects at GCSE and fewer in option groups, 10 or 11 for A level or IB. Latin compulsory for first two years, second foreign language for one. GCSE subjects chosen at end of year 8 – one modern language and one humanities subject must be included in the four options outside the core curriculum. Pupils say staff try exceptionally hard to incorporate exams in unusual first languages. The first cohort of IB diploma finished in 2013. Take up was slow initially (28 in first year but now rising), partly because pupils are very concerned about getting it right (most have no family money to fall back on if exams don't work out). In 2015, 70 per cent A*/A grades at GCSE, 42 per cent at A level; IB average 37 points.

Campus arranged by subject blocks, all with high ceilings and plenty of space and equipment, including science and language labs. The ugly sister IT department (was known as Grange Hill by the students), replaced 2015 with a new classroom block and resource centre. One main library, with a 16th century painting (cut to size in the move from Newgate a century ago; unfortunately the signature was a casualty) and a mezzanine level with extra computers. Scheduled to be redone as a sixth form centre with a focus on careers and vocations – the thinking is that Old Blues can provide enough mentoring and connections for some pupils to enter a profession in the City without going to university. Art and humanities have their own specialised libraries (open for evening work, as are all academic departments, providing support).

The SEN unit has one part-time and two full-time SENCos – support ranges from mild to a tailored IEP if SEN is profound. Everyone with SEND gets a laptop. The whole campus has Wifi and all the IB pupils and upper sixth are offered a laptop too – these can be taken home. Parents appreciate 'equality of provision and equality of access to provision.'

Weekly chapel and tutorial periods; upper sixth get weekly lectures on topics ranging from photo-journalism, through medicine, dentistry and accountancy to Tom Avery's experience as a polar explorer. There is a huge amount on offer here and as pupils grow older they tend towards the management of their own studies, as they would at university, an enormously important piece of preparation for life after CH. Houseparents and staff who supervise prep periods play a great role in advising children on study choices as well as pastoral issues.

Games, options, the arts: Main sports are hockey, netball, football, rugby, cricket and tennis, with a decent fixture list against local co-ed schools, winning about 60 per cent. Blue Coats sports centre – 25m pool, double-sized sports hall, six squash courts, spin bikes, split-level fitness suite, vending machines and a café – is used by the public 60 per cent of the time, although the school has its own changing rooms. More esoteric sports such as fives also on offer. D of E and CCF very popular. Scout hut now converted to a multifunction theatre seating 200.

Likes to tinker with cars and compares Christ's Hospital on his arrival to an E-type Jaguar that was terminally rusty. Now the vintage car has been lovingly restored

A 500-seat theatre, modelled on Shakespeare's Globe, with padded red benches instead of the standing yard, is used by travelling drama companies too (contemporary dance as well as curriculum-relevant plays). Open access attitude for these performances endears the school still more to Horsham residents. The debating society and the Model United Nations give student speakers more confidence in competition in and outside school.

The music department is a popular target for donations such as harps, bassoons, French horns. Listen to, play or sing in any one of the 43 ensembles, inside or outside the school, and the joyful noise is gorgeous. Chapel choir is now restricted to a maximum of 150, the gospel choir has around 80 members as does the Big (jazz) Band, the junior choir 50, 150 in the symphony. Most pupils love to sing and the cathartic feeling of their voices joined together, soaring past the frescoes in the chapel is one of the moments they squirrel away in their hearts – the BBC was hugely impressed that it could record them in just one take. Lots of Macs enable bedroom producers to hone their skills with music technology at A level.

Energetic art department, successful and focused on working on pupils' own ideas, which produces an enormous range of work – exhibiting at the train station and a theatre in Horsham grants a wider audience. Three floors of bright and naturally-lit space, an artist in residence, art historian, two full-time staff, sewing room, computer suite (although the primary source of each project is drawing, digital images are always involved) and a library full of glossy books – all open from 7.15am to 10pm. DT department occupies almost as large a space and is just as well equipped with computers, AutoCAD, laser cutter, graphics area etc. and admirable focus on SMART objectives for each project. Two D1 grades at Pre-U in 2015; one pupil not only achieved the top Pre-U Art mark nationally recently, but also won the sculpture category of the new HMC Schools' Art competition with his remarkable recreation of a Brazilian favela.

Boarding: Eighteen boarding houses – 16 single sex ones along The Avenue and two upper sixth co-eds built in 2000. Nearly all are looked after by a married couple (most of the 110 staff live on site, often with their own families), so every child gets a taste of parental and sibling relationships that may well be lacking in their own home. A recent revamp has left these boarding facilities sparkling – no junior shares a room with more than three others, big common rooms with ping-pong and snooker, bright kitchens, a phone room (for the first two years everyone hands in their mobile until 2pm). Every new arrival gets a nursemaid in the year above – they write letters to the new students the summer before they arrive – and this relationship produces a family tree stretching across year groups. Ingenious support where need arises – matrons giving hugs, cleaning staff joshing the dedicated student and the head of learning support teaching a tai chi course, an innovative balance to the busyness of student days.

The two Senior Grecian houses (the nomenclature comes from the sixth form historically having to study classics) would be the envy of any university student. Often more space than the children might have to themselves at home – big windows, a sink in each (senior's) room, double-height communal spaces, bowls of fruit, kitchens shared between eight, a BBQ on the deck, a little library area with a piano and students' art displayed. A quarter of the Grecians might be in long-term (more than a year) relationships with each other but no peer pressure to do this. The proximity of co-ed living space means that sex could be a problem, but the co-ed nature of the full school normalises boy/girl

relationships. Lovely story of a Valentine's Day charity fundraiser, pay a penny for a snuggle – really inclusive.

Matches on Saturday afternoons while Saturday evenings feel good with discos, theme nights or just a fun time in each house – watching football, a film or playing a game devised by the seniors with a slapstick pie in the face for those who mess up.

The co-ed nature of the school normalises boy/girl relationships. Lovely story of a Valentine's Day charity fundraiser, pay a penny for a snuggle – really inclusive

CH runs in three-week blocks before a leave weekend – some children don't want to or can't go home; they can stay in or get matched with a friend and spend the weekend with their family. 'There's no one way to be a CH pupil,' we were told. This diversity is the school's strength – whatever obstacles or advantages your home life might present, everyone is equal as soon as they tie on the bands of their uniform. The new 'deps' (deputy Grecians, lower sixth) probably find the acclimatisation most difficult. Pupils learn within the first year to live with a huge range of personalities, which stands them in good stead in later life.

Background and atmosphere: School was given its Royal Charter by Edward VI in 1553 to help orphan children of London. In 1902 the boys moved to the current purpose-built campus in Horsham (designed by Sir Aston Webb, also responsible for the façade of Buckingham Palace and King's College, Cambridge). The girls, who had stayed at a site in Hertford, joined in 1985 to make it co-ed once again. Nowadays the demographic is much more mixed, but the uniform is still resolutely Tudor – mustard coloured socks and long blue coats. The pupils love the warm 'Houseys' and although the younger ones choose their 'civvies' carefully after lessons are over, the older ones default to school tracksuits – a refreshing lack of emphasis on trainers as a signifier of social tribe.

Progress supports the heritage showcased by the plaque-studded cloisters – from the plasma screen with BBC news and current school photos in the reception to the skylight-lit food hall. Six days a week, barring rain, the entire school marches to lunch from the quadrangle, house by house, to the accompaniment of the parade band. Parents and pupils say 'butterflies in the tummy' are caused by this sharing of 'music, ambience, exhilaration, aesthetic, ceremony, tradition and spirit' on a daily basis.

The food (delicious and varied) is cooked by team headed by a chef who has turned down offers from Michelin starred restaurants, and is eaten under the longest oil on canvas in Christendom. This mingling of tradition and technology is characteristic of the school. It may appear incongruous yet, in truth, it is inspirational.

The pupils are proud of their uniform, don't mind being taunted as Harry Potter lookalikes on trains (they prefer references to The Matrix), are delighted to be recognised by Old Blues on the tube and smile wryly when confessing to smelling like wet dogs after marching in a rainy Lord Mayor's Show. They pour through the cloisters between their lessons, some holding the lead of a master's dog for a treat. One of the best bits of the school is reported to be the spread at breakfast. They need that as fuel to get them around the huge campus – by the upper sixth you earn the privilege of a bike.

The whole school meets in the chapel on Sunday morning – seats 1,000, 140 in the gallery. Stained glass windows (some Victorian and a couple of 14th century Flemish) came from the earlier campuses, but the Sir Frank Brangwyn frescos were commissioned for the Horsham site. Whole school assembly is conducted every three weeks by the head in Big School, under the largest unsupported wooden ceiling in the country.

Pastoral care, well-being and discipline: Chapel services are important, not least because it is a space big enough for all the pupils to gather on Tuesdays and Sundays. The school was founded partly in response to a sermon preached by the Bishop of London and sermons are still powerful today; even if every pupil is not touched, they definitely pay attention. Lots of children here whose parents or carers are ill or struggling, so faith can be a real touchstone. School council is very thoughtful, student-run although spearheaded by an English teacher. Recent topics include racism, considering the effect close groups of international students (Hong Kong Chinese) can have in a community – empathetic research came up with how tiring it was to speak in your second language all day long, therefore what a retreat your own culture could be.

Minor misdemeanours mean getting up for 7.15am and a dress parade. Mini-detentions on Sunday am, the big one is on Saturday night, and a card system which restricts free time by having to sign in (for smoking, bullying, drinking alcohol.)

Internet access is not restricted very much (you often can't get onto useful sites with blanket bans) but it is monitored – a 14-year-old looking at porn will lose his/her laptop and school email account. 'Swearing at the staff is unacceptable' (suspension) and continued difficulties will result in a behaviour contract between the pupil, parents and school – a line drawn in the sand. Drugs – class A

or supplying – mean immediate expulsion with the involvement of the police; for cannabis there will be one chance, after which the ongoing drug testing policy is implemented. Family circumstances are always taken into account. Parents really appreciate consistent and accessible staff. Email conversations may continue long after they have been sparked during parents' evenings.

Pupils and parents: The pupils know they're lucky to be here. For every student who gets in, four or five are turned away. Accepts pupils from all over the UK, in reality about 30 per cent from London (Hackney, Tower Hamlets, Islington, Acton), 30 per cent from Sussex, 30 per cent south west and home counties, rest from Scotland, Wales, north of England (most from further afield enter at sixth form, but only if they have some extended family in the south east). Historical links with Richmond, Newbury, Reading and Twickenham – the towns on the route of John and Francis West (17th-century scriveners) to Christ's Hospital.

Eleven per cent international pupils – mostly Europe (three and a half per cent) or the Far East (five per cent). Lots of second and third generation Nigerians and Gambians, Hong Kong Chinese are particularly attracted by CH's status as The Royal Mathematical School and German anglophiles love the school's excellence and tradition while valuing the fact that it is not an enclave of privilege. Since 2011, five per cent each from the UK, Europe and the rest of the world pay full fees – these are families who have made a conscious choice to pay for an egalitarian ethos. It has not been easy to change the pupil profile. A small number of international pupils were admitted initially with great care taken to see what they and their families needed. Now students appreciate the still wider diversity. It's easier to chat in German with a friend who is a

native speaker or swipe some Asian cooking tips in the house kitchen.

Only 42 per cent of pupils have both parents resident at home and lots of aspiring middle class and freelancers. Houseparents encourage communication between parents when new pupils arrive (forums and blogs online help this). Pupils are drawn from all walks of life and the majority enjoy some form of means-tested bursary. If CH does its job, then former pupils will be ineligible to send their children to their alma mater, unless they pay the full fees.

Notable Old Blues (the dead ones have boarding houses named after them) include Coleridge, Middleton, Peele, Barnes Wallis, the cricketer John Snow, comedians Mark Thomas and Holly Walsh, the academic Alan Ryan, conductor Sir Colin Davis, Martin Linton MP, England Rugby Union second row Joe Launchbury, Baroness Ruth Deech, Lord Simon, former Chairman of BP, and General Sir Garry Johnson MC, strategic adviser to the MOD.

Entrance: Most at 11+, 25 to 30 at 13+ and 45 to 50 after GCSE. No feeder schools, but a very good relationship with south of England primaries and preps. Fifty heads came to a recent open day so they can see what type of child will thrive at CH.

Not on the public school radar, so not much cachet on the dinner party circuit. The initial application form elicits lots of information about family circumstances and finances – from previous school, local church, social services. The staff in the admissions office are at the end of the phone to answer questions and baffled or swamped parents really value this.

Exit: Some 10 per cent leave after GCSE for vocational courses. More than 90 per cent of sixth formers to university – the Upper Grecian houses are a real stepping-stone to life there. In 2015, six to Oxbridge. UCL, Durham, Bristol, York, Manchester, Leeds, Birmingham and KCL popular; medicine, engineering, archaeology, classics, law, music, maths degrees. Artists (six in 2015) seem to take it in turns to go in posses to Camberwell, Falmouth and Central St Martins.

Money matters: Currently 14 per cent pay nothing, 40 per cent pay less than 10 per cent of full fees, 80 per cent less than half the fees and less than 18 per cent pay the full fees. Of the £301 million allocated to means-tested bursaries by ISC schools last year, £16 million of that was at Christ's Hospital alone.

Parental contributions are assessed on the total family income of the home in which the child resides, interest and dividend payments plus a percentage of any financial and other assets above £25,000. Most DSS benefits are included, but not housing benefit, disability allowance and carer's allowance. Reviewed each year. Discounts for siblings within school. Tudor-style uniform is free. Extras include £20 pocket money per term, music contributions (means-tested again), a dictionary and a bible. CH has a big endowment but, like every other school, lives beyond its means.

Curriculum-based trips are partially funded by the foundation (means testing applies). Old Blues provide travel grants for gap years etc.

Remarks: Well-adjusted, confident and accepting children who look forward to coming to school. This is the only independent school that escapes the state school prejudice when attracting principled teachers. The Old Blues are incredibly loyal and you can see why – with 75 per cent of them in the top quartile of income in their later life, CH turns many lives around in an unpretentious and joyful manner. Admirable work.

City of London Freemen's School

Ashtead Park, Ashtead, Surrey KT21 1ET

01372 277933
admissions@clfs.surrey.sch.uk
www.clfs.surrey.sch.uk

Ages: 13–18
Pupils: 505; sixth form: 210
Boarders: 50
Day: £12,984 – £16,224 pa
Boarding: £23,049 – £26,289 pa

Headmaster: Since September 2015, Mr Roland Martin, previously head of Rendcomb College in Gloucestershire. Read English at York; Newcastle-under-Lyme School for six years followed by 13 at Eton, where he taught English and drama, was head of year 11 and a housemaster. Friendly, but not effusive, he has a rather charming, understated intensity. Married to Kerri, also an English teacher; they have two children. He loves 18th century novels, particularly Tristram Shandy and, in no

The stunning facilities are not aged or beautiful but very much contribute to an environment which cannot fail to impress a pupil (or their parents)

particular order, is a huge fan of Simon Armitage, cricket and Italy – above all Venice.

Academic matters: Very good results year on year at both GCSE and A level – in 2015, 82 per cent A*/A at the former, with 70 per cent A*/A, for the latter.

Not a pressured academic hothouse. Parents are universally complimentary about the teaching, singling out physics, English, politics and business studies – 'Teachers fabulous, with lots of them there a long time'; 'Teaching is excellent and without high pressure'. Superb teaching facilities housed in the Haywood Centre (named after the previous, long-serving and very popular head). This hub of the senior school is an airy and attractive, well-equipped block of classrooms, IT and multimedia rooms plus a large library open until 6pm for individual study.

Not a first choice school for a pupil with significant SEN, and ask lots of questions for a child with mild SEN just to make sure the school can help. SEN support is limited – very few pupils with statements. School would ask parents to consider whether this is the right academic environment for their child – it 'may not be suitable for pupils with formal SEN statements'. A parent of a mildly dyslexic pupil reinforces this view saying, 'There is little specialist help, but teachers are kind and supportive and do the necessary such as extra time in exams; maybe it wouldn't be suitable for a child who is quite dyslexic.' A head of learning support provides help within the curriculum for mild needs, such as a slow reader, and support classes are available for children who are struggling in English. A parent of a pupil accessing this help praised it, saying, 'The kids call it the remedial class, but they have a very positive attitude towards it.' They have had hearing impaired children and wheelchair users and the issue is, 'Can we enable a youngster with special needs to access the curriculum?'

Games, options, the arts: The stunning facilities are not aged and beautiful but very much contribute to an environment which cannot fail to impress a pupil (or perhaps even more their parents). Sports facilities are outstanding and would compete easily with the best of the public school fraternity. Glorious and extensive grass pitches, huge Astro pitch for tennis, football and hockey, a vast sports hall, an enviable 25-metre indoor swimming pool,

two squash courts and a multi-activity room for table tennis and aerobics. Sport is well and truly part of life here – parents report a 'massively active programme but it's not forced' and sport is 'made fun not a chore'. Very much a 'come and try' atmosphere, rather than a 'team place or else' school. For the seriously sporty, A and B teams are fielded in the more popular sports. Most fixtures are scheduled on Saturday mornings and squad members are required to attend.

Drama occupies as central a position as sport, both within the curriculum and in extracurricular clubs. A hugely enthusiastic head of drama (who maintains a dedicated drama website for the school), plus more terrific facilities including a professionally equipped theatre, mean plenty of productions. Good GCSE and A level results and some impressive acting alumni. Music is encouraged, with plenty of choirs, ensembles and an orchestra putting on about 30 performances and concerts; new music school. Musical theatre productions performed to sell-out audiences in a nearby 800-seater public venue are described as 'great' and 'the highlight of the musical year'. Students' artwork of a high standard is displayed around the school and the art and design technology facilities, like others, really are top class.

He has a rather charming, understated intensity. He loves 18th century novels, particularly Tristram Shandy and, in no particular order, Simon Armitage, cricket and Italy

A huge range of lunchtime and after-school clubs cater for all tastes and interests. Senior pupils run some and can even start them on their own initiative. Trips out of school include an annual whole school visit to the City of London to celebrate the school's close ties with the City, plus many regular field trips both locally, within the UK and abroad – the list of destinations is long.

Boarding: Boarding is part of the school's statute and must be provided. (To this day a small number of 'foundationer' places – they have their fees, be it boarding or day, met in full.) However, boarders are almost exclusively pupils from abroad (vast majority are sixth form entrants). The boy boarders are from Hong Kong and Russia, apart from seven English pupils. All the girl boarders are from Hong Kong or the Far East. The girls' housemistress said she had to make them 'stop working sometimes and go out for a walk' – they are under immense personal and family pressure to succeed. With their very strong work ethic and extremely high standards, the boarders are often culturally different from the local day students.

The girls' accommodation in the main house is by no means trendy and high tech – in fact, quite the opposite: rather old fashioned and fusty. Boys' boarding house is a rather uninspiring building due to be completely renewed; new co-ed boarding house. Potential for boarding numbers to increase to 80.

Background and atmosphere: Founded to educate orphaned children of the Freemen of the City of London and owned by the Corporation of London. Support staff are employed by the City of London and governors are largely from the Court of Common Council (ie City officialdom). The Corporation provides financial support for capital projects, which helps to keep fees to a minimum. HR, planning and management all operated by the City, which leaves the head and school free to run and manage the education – the Corporation was described as 'forward looking with a long term view, also traditional and a little bureaucratic'. 'A little bureaucratic' may be something of an understatement – all our interaction with the school was slow and slightly difficult. The admin side worked like an old fashioned office, hierarchical and by the book – one gets the impression the whole school probably works like that, as everyone ultimately refers to a more senior authority.

Ashtead Park's 57 acres are owned by the City of London Corporation and the grounds are subject to open spaces regulations. Expansive, formal and well kept, with zebra crossings and double yellow lines, the City of London coat of arms on railings and bins really do make it feel like a London park. The feel is of a campus with pupils moving between various buildings. Parents particularly appreciate the 'beautiful setting' and 'great atmosphere to work in'. The 'mansion house', in grand country house style, houses music practice rooms and the dining room (rather small and old fashioned) plus reception rooms, offices and girls' boarding.

All pupils and staff are in one of the three houses – good opportunities for positive relationships between age groups. Each house holds a weekly assembly and accumulates merits through music, sporting and other achievements and good work to win the annual house competition. The sixth form has its own centre and is run 'almost like a separate school'.

Pastoral care, well-being and discipline: Parents are positive, describing pastoral care as 'excellent' and 'second to none'. Pupils have a daily tutor group and parents are encouraged to get in touch if they have any issues – they feel 'It's made clear who is responsible' and they 'always have somewhere to go – staff have an open door policy'. The spirit of

Some parents we spoke to were positively anti 'the four wheel drives and mothers dressed for tennis one upmanship' of some other local schools. 'Everyone is friendly'

the school is respectful and listening and pupils are encouraged to be kind and helpful. Parents and staff describe it as 'a family school with lots of siblings across it', the environment is 'caring and very friendly', 'Boys and girls mix well' and 'They grow up to be rounded on gender issues'. Pupils report that 'staff treat them with respect', which sets a good example and gives them self-confidence. Senior pupils mentor juniors and volunteer as class prefects and to run extracurricular clubs.

Discipline is laid down in clear policy and stuck to firmly; bullying is not tolerated. Incoming pupils sometimes find the regime initially rigorous as they learn the rules, but it is seen as fair. Parents say 'no bolt out of the blue – problems are flagged up early' and it's the 'right balance'.

Pupils and parents: Pupils neither scruffy nor especially tidy – just nicely ordinary. Despite our request to be shown round by a pupil, we were, unlike at most schools, put firmly in the hands of the marketing manager. Both boys and girls we met en passant were communicative and pleasant when asked questions. Pupils predominantly from surrounding Surrey towns of Ashtead, Epsom, Banstead, Leatherhead, Esher and Cobham, but some travel down from south west London and even a couple from north London. School transport from most of these local areas plus a shuttle bus to Ashtead Station help parents avoid the school run.

Families from a wide range of backgrounds – plenty with both parents working. Parents say this 'adds to the rounded normal feel of the school'. Many find the variety comfortable, with lots of ordinary families. Definitely not posh, does not even try to compete with its neighbour Epsom College. Some parents we spoke to were positively anti 'the four wheel drives and mothers dressed for tennis one upmanship' of some other local schools. 'Everyone is friendly', parents can get involved if they want and regular parent and family socials.

Entrance: Many directly from junior school at 13+ with no entry tests – seen as a major advantage by parents. A further 25-30 are added from local preps including Downsend, Danes Hill, Cranmore and Lanesborough. Entry is competitive with screening tests at 11 and 12 confirmed by entrance exam or common entrance at 13. Head is pleased to add a little variety from other schools to 'leaven the mix'. Sixth form entry on predicted GCSE grades, school report and interview – about 20 join, including overseas boarders.

Exit: About 20 per cent leave after GCSE to taste life in a sixth form college or another school. Those who stay expect to go to university and do, mostly to Russell Group; 13 to Oxbridge in 2015, plus four medics and one vet, and two to the US; other current favourites Exeter, Warwick, LSE, Imperial, Birmingham and Newcastle.

Money matters: Generally perceived by parents to be excellent value for money and cheaper than

other comparable schools in the area. Academic and music awards at 13 and sixth form available to current pupils and incomers. Means-tested bursary awards, sponsored by the City Livery Companies and often tied to certain professions. A very small number of children of Freemen who have lost one 'family breadwinner' parent attend completely free as Foundationers.

Remarks: A good, solid school, not quirky or elitist, in fact quite the opposite. It does what it says on the tin: genuinely providing pupils with wide opportunities and an all-round education including consistently good academic results, without a hothouse atmosphere.

Cobham Hall

Cobham, Gravesend, Kent DA12 3BL

01474 823371
enquiries@cobhamhall.com
www.cobhamhall.com

Ages: 11–18
Pupils: 180; sixth form: 70
Boarders: 89 full, 7 weekly
Day: £16,086 – £20,361 pa
Boarding: £24,300 – £30,627 pa

Headmaster: Since 2008, Mr Paul Mitchell BSc in maths and PGCE from University of Newcastle (50s). Previously deputy head at St Mary's School, Cambridge, and before that taught at Royal High Bath, Godolphin in Salisbury, Radley College and in the state sector.

Early on, a keen interest in sport a factor in his career choice, granting him the flexibility to keep at the top of his field as an international pentathlete – he represented Britain for 10 years. Now often to be found out of hours at the stables with his two horses, but brought his enthusiasm for sport to the school. Not someone to put too much emphasis on this or that standard, far more on the individual and how each can find their niche and come to life at the school. Keeps tabs on them all. He speaks with disarming candour and while evidently fiercely loyal to the school and conscious of economic realities, you feel his genuine openness and his appreciation of openness in others. 'I'd approach him about anything, but he'd probably know and have done something about it already,' we were told. Unmarried.

Academic matters: IB introduced in 2009, in keeping with the traditional internationalism and Round Square ethos of the school. (A Levels phased out at the same time and are now no longer offered.) Since then, sixth form intake has increased slightly, suggesting that both IB and the one-year pre-IB course may be a draw for overseas parents. UK parents prize the broad, values-based education that the IB promotes, but so far Cobham's average IB points score has been underwhelming, with an average of just under 29 in 2015. At GCSE, 69 per cent of pupils got 5+ A*-C grades including English and maths and 31 per cent of grades were A*/A in 2015. However, parents don't seem overly concerned and are quick to mention cases of teachers generating interest and unexpectedly good results in particular subjects. The school's mantra and Round Square motto is 'There's more in you than you think', and with small class sizes (12-15 in the lower school, middle 10-12 and a small sixth form) enabling a high degree of individual attention, parents are confident that staff bring out the best in them, in and outside the classroom. Students were warm in their praise of staff: 'They care about us so much.' 'They're really encouraging and they go out of their way to help you.' 'My grades have got much better since I came here,' were typical comments. Over half awarded a bi-lingual diploma.

Scattered about with wonderful nonchalance are portraits of past owners, framed historical documents, and even a horse-drawn carriage resting idly

The Susan Hampshire Centre (student support department) caters for pupils requiring learning support. Predominantly, pupils using the centre have dyslexic/dyspraxic tendencies or Irlen Syndrome (a condition which affects the way the brain processes visual information). For each, an IEP drawn up covering literacy, maths and study skills, according to their needs. Two specialist EFL teachers.

Little touches like putting a teddy in a flexi-boarder's bed, the big sister system to look after newcomers and peer mentoring

Games, options, the arts: The Head says that the school was somewhat at the 'egg and spoon race' stage a few years back, but this is changing. The girls enjoy their sport and relish a more competitive approach and the greater focus on field and track. Notable recent successes in the biathlon, high jump and 1500m. Some new specialist sports coaches; enthusiasts enabled to go to county netball and local hockey club training. Rounders also popular, and if that doesn't tickle their fancy, always badminton, dance, zumba, aerobics and swimming.

Just under half the pupils study a musical instrument or sing and have the opportunity to join instrumental groups and one of four choirs. Regular lunchtime concerts and a major performance each term in the fabulous Gilt Hall. Drama is evidently innovative and fun – inter-house drama and music festivals every other year in which all have to participate. Being an extra during the filming of Wild Child at the school must also have been a real thrill for some.

Good sporting and other facilities include an indoor heated pool, indoor and outdoor tennis courts, dance studio and fitness suite. Bikes encourage the girls to be more active. Well-equipped theatre and, judging by the art and sculptures on display, artistic talents well catered for. Programme of lunchtime and after-school clubs and, at the weekend, film, culture and shopping trips keep boarders occupied.

In truth, none of these activities nor the D of E is out of the ordinary. What excites most is the school's membership of the Round Square and the opportunities for adventure that it creates. It's obviously a subject of much discussion and anticipation amongst the girls, who come up with varied fundraising ideas – fashion shows, bake sales and sponsored cycle rides – to enable them to travel to and support community projects in far-flung places. School exchanges and international conferences also a regular feature. Parents love all this character-building and eye-opening stuff plus the sense of security which comes with the school's 40 year Round Square association and vast international network.

Boarding: Sixth form boarders live in dedicated houses, with cooking and other facilities to reflect their greater independence. Younger full-time and flexi-boarders have bedrooms in the main school building which are comfy and spacious. Little touches like putting a teddy in a flexi-boarder's bed, the big sister system to look after newcomers and peer mentoring are examples of how the girls look out and care for each other. Day pupils are encouraged to try out boarding as part of the induction and get five free nights per term – part, perhaps, of the school's current strategy to tip the balance more in favour of boarding. This, and the fact that many day pupils stay late, means no great day/boarder divide. Some parents comment that it would be good if boarders were invited out more regularly but, with 80 per cent or so staying in at the weekends, it is rare for anyone to be at a loose end. Day girls can flexi board at any time.

Background and atmosphere: Cobham Hall is only a short distance from Ebbsfleet International railway station (London, St Pancras 17 minutes) and major motorway links, but passing through the gates is like entering a time warp away from the noise and bustle of modern life. A Grade II listed Elizabethan building comes into view, all more modern classrooms and boarding houses discreetly tucked away out of sight so as not to detract from the 150 acres of beautiful parkland. The buildings are made accessible for various events during the year and, in the spring, the grounds are open to the public, who can gaze in awe at the carpet of flowers. Inside, many rooms are beautifully preserved with the help of English Heritage, and scattered about with wonderful nonchalance are portraits of past owners, framed historical documents, and even a horse-drawn carriage resting idly at the end of the Independent Learning centre.

Since its establishment in 1962, has had internationalism at its core, and cultural integration and enrichment are still very much a part of life here. On Friday nights pupils tell stories from around the world, and assemblies feature explanations of different religious beliefs and traditions. Nonetheless, as one pupil put it, it does feel a bit of a 'bubble community', a small world of its own. No bad thing, say parents of, in particular, younger pupils, as it allows, indeed encourages, them to develop a strong values-base on which to build their future lives.

Pupils are proud of the community and individuals' achievements and, through the various student committees and leadership structures, play an ongoing and important role in promoting them. If they didn't like the head – and most do – arguably they would have themselves to blame: after all, they interviewed him before he got the job.

Pastoral care, well-being and discipline: 'We're a close community. We all know each other and everyone has the freedom to be who they want to be.'

Quiet, outgoing, musical, academic, sporty, the school accommodates all, bar perhaps those who want to break away and form their own group. It has a gentle and friendly atmosphere with real thought and care taken to ensure that, whatever your background, you settle in well. In this nurturing atmosphere even the shyest gain confidence.

Discipline is 'tough but fair'. Incidents of a serious nature are rare, as is bullying, problems mostly limited to minor fall-outs, perceived as inevitable amongst teenage girls. Where parents have had concerns of this nature or in relation to academics, they find staff accessible and responsive.

Pupils and parents: 'Outside, they think we're all posh but we're not,' says one girl. This is backed up by a parent's observation: 'There's anything from old bangers to Rollses coming up the drive each morning'. Around 75 per cent international boarders. Living in a small community while acquiring a good level of English is clearly a strong draw amongst the 32 nationalities represented.

Parents say pupils are polite and chat quite happily with them in a relaxed and mature way. They are supportive of each other in work and play and tend to just get on with whatever they are tasked to do. In the all-girl environment, parents celebrate that little pressure to grow up too fast. Sixth

formers wear suits; few uniform infringements lower down school.

The Unicorn (parents) Association is very active and welcoming – 'You almost have to beat them off'. Regular teas before exeat weekends, coffee mornings, school events, art exhibitions, salsa and jazz evenings provide ample opportunities to meet other parents. The wide catchment area can otherwise make this and sharing transport difficult.

Former pupils include BBC newsreader/journalist Mishal Husain, Alex Crawford, foreign correspondent/journalist, and Kate French, who represented Britain in the 2012 Olympics pentathlon.

Entrance: At 11+ and 13+ applicants sit mathematics and English assessments, provide a report of recommendation from their current school, attend an interview and take part in group activities. Those wishing to enter the sixth form (both internal and external applicants) sit the IB entrance examination. A further 15 or so girls every year come from various countries for a term or two specifically to improve their English.

Exit: Approx 45 per cent move on after GCSEs, mostly to larger mixed schools or sixth form colleges. The introduction of the IB has had little impact on sixth form numbers. Of those staying on until 18, a small minority take a gap year. Most pursue further studies in their countries of origin or in the UK at a variety of universities and colleges, including Hult International Business School, Exeter, Bristol, Nottingham Trent and University for the Creative Arts

Money matters: Discounts are available for daughters/granddaughters of old girls (Elders). Reductions for those staying on in the sixth form and discounts for Forces families, diplomats and families working for UK charitable trusts overseas. Bursaries and scholarships available. Fees for extras are considered reasonable and no extra charge for day pupils on boarder taster weeks or for breakfast and supper when they are involved in clubs.

Remarks: A friendly and caring environment with strong international links and the premise that everyone achieves, given belief and support.

Cottesmore School

Buchan Hill, Pease Pottage, West Sussex RH11 9AU

01293 520648
office@cottesmoreschool.com
www.cottesmoreschool.com
C of E

Ages: 4–13
Pupils: 150: (100 boys, 50 girls)
Boarders: 120 full
Day: £8,620 – £11,505 pa
Boarding: £16,155 – £22,080 pa

Headmaster: Since 2008, Tom Rogerson, married to Lottie, and small son Wilf. Cottesmore runs in the family (grandad and dad were heads before him) – 'I've been quietly planning to take over since I was 17', said the head. Routed via other schools (Ludgrove, Eaton House and Broomwood); his dad wouldn't let him take the headship too early. Quite right, dad.

Articulate and thoughtful, focuses on each pupil and knows them all – they chatter away happily with him. A strong team with Lottie, who provides ballast for the head's lively energy.

Parents like him – 'He's a warm guy, easy to talk to, and always there when I pick up and drop off from exeats'. Another: 'A school derives its culture from the head – and I like its culture. It places emphasis on traditional Christian values: kindness, courtesy, honour and fair play.'

Entrance: Pre-prep: taster day, during which prospective pupils will do a piece of work assessing English and maths. Prep: English and maths tests, interview (children need to be 'interested and interesting') and head's report from previous school.

Exit: To many of the more magnificent public schools: Eton, Harrow, Cheltenham Ladies College, and other varieties too. Thirteen academic scholarships in recent round – nearly half the year.

Remarks: Approach the school past towering rhododendrons, lawns mowed to velvety smoothness, golf flags, the fragrance of flowers and hedges. Cottesmore is a stately Victorian pile – enter through the heavy wooden door carved with mischievous sprites. Wood panelled walls, stately hall with minstrels' gallery; fishing rods leaning casually against the wall in a corridor. Things here are orderly, but it's not an institutional tidiness:

there's a feeling of a home, where places for things arise organically and become established through habit.

Grounds which beg to be played in: climbable trees everywhere, from the monkeys – a cave of under rhododendron/under tree branches – to the hollow oak: climb its ancient trunk in a circular direction (teacher present, and only up to a certain height). Bamboo for forts and den making – so popular here that it occasionally has official activity status. A parent described his son, who had fallen out of a tree, limping towards his wife on the last exeat – 'he's having a childhood and that's wonderful.'

Children here are bubbling, confident and eager, so keen to tell us about their school that we hardly needed to ask questions. They happily fill their own skin: we've rarely met a group of children so content to be themselves. Some bounced up to say hello and give their views; easily said, in front of their head, what they didn't like about school (the chairs are too low and they want new showers).

We met too, quieter introverts, busy with the library and their model railway in the basement. They've started their own after-supper library lecture series ('tea' was exceedingly popular). Not so likely to bubble eagerly about the things they love; but no hesitation in expressing their views, and total confidence in their value. Geekiness is certainly not frowned upon – 'they're slightly lauded for loving the library', said Lottie.

The head said, 'we're a family school', then chuckled: whether this is a good thing clearly depends on how dysfunctional the family. Certainly the warmth and care seen here must exceed what many families experience at Christmas. Home to 150 pupils ('beautifully small', said a mum).

Broad church here – which means chapel isn't optional. Cultural Christianity, whose values informally underpin the community, but 'we go about it quietly'.

An academically rigorous school – 'rigour balanced with fun', said the head. A flamboyant fashion designer to be is celebrated; but 'he has to be good at maths by the time he leaves'. Lack of endeavour here would be a problem – 'that's not an option'.

'Not a pressure cooker', said a parent who has experienced the hothouse of London preps, '[and] notches up in balanced and useful lives'. Relative to other preps in the area, it's doing extremely well: another parent we spoke to was very happy with the academic side, describing it as 'pretty strong and rigorous', with parents getting regular feedback – every three weeks. (His son had just got a place at Harrow – he was an extremely happy dad.)

Small classes, no bigger than 14. Single form entry until year 4, then double form entry, finally splitting in three in the final year. Pupils are streamed (but not labelled) and set within those streams. Academic subjects take place around the quad, the fountain in the middle providing restful accompaniment to those getting their heads down. Lively walls showing work, but order and method evident – displays are exceedingly neat. This school does extremely well at enthusing its pupils: they showed a keen interest in Latin, eagerly pointing out Latin in the roots of words, and telling us their favourite myths.

Maths lessons have been transformed by new IT (iPads, chrome books and a Raspberry Pi). Pupils were whizzing through tables on iPads – less time marking means more time teaching; or 'connecting', as the head likes to say. Excelling at maths is something this school particularly prides itself on: the head has increased the number of maths teachers and seen CE scores soar.

A geography teacher was enthusiastically making geography pertinent to the real world: 'What are the pros and cons of building a Tesco in the Cottesmore grounds?' (The head's smile became a little fixed at this point...) Making ant homes was cited by one excited little girl as the best geography lesson ever. Parents are happy that the computer room is well policed: no chatrooms or other elicit Youtube pleasures; no own devices in school.

Achievement is celebrated through stars (house points), show ups and stay ups. Show ups for extremely good work or behaviour; stay up for a jolly if you come top in an assessment or effort, or when teams have an unbeaten day – popcorn, movie and games. A popular treat.

Learning support helps students who have mild dyslexia, dyspraxia and dyscalculia, also those with speech and language difficulties. Ten to 20 per cent of pupils receive one-to-one help, and in-class

assistance (charged as an extra). The fact a child has SEN doesn't make any difference to attainment here, says the head.

A parent described his son, who had fallen out of a tree, limping towards his wife on the last exeat – 'he's having a childhood and that's wonderful'

Behind a glass panelled door is pre-prep, the colour and liveliness evident through the glass panels. Coloured cellophane hung from the ceiling in strips – 'we're doing under the sea at the moment'. Single form entry, around 10 per class, children seated at round tables, doors in each class opening onto the lawn: a much more relaxed, crazy colour atmosphere than on the other side of the door, but a similarly high standard evident from the written work in displays. The rather extraordinary cubed times tables produced by a boy in year 1 caused adults in the area to look at each other blankly, each hoping one of the others might know if he'd got them right. A parent told us that Cottesmore was the only school they visited who were more interested in the child than the parents: Lottie got right down to her daughter's level – 'so, do you like spiders?' And off they went to find one.

A large array of games on offer: 33, including all the usual major sports, as well as the less usual: archery, shooting and billiards. Pupils of all abilities play in matches, and even the C and D teams play a good number of fixtures. They win plenty of matches (the Colts As and Bs recently unbeaten in any sport for seven months) and get plenty of support – Danish housekeeping team take great joy in waving their pompoms in support of the third X1.'It is competitive – they care a lot for sport, but they know they have all types, and encourage and get the best out of everyone.'

Houses here are called sets, and there's plenty of friendly inter-set competition. A parent, commenting on the set dash, said 'The whole school cheer each other, particularly the useless ones...To be very kind, is to be very Cottesmore', he added.

Indoor heated pool and Astroturf large enough for three tennis courts; three grass courts too, with some boys racing in from playing tennis at break. The 'gravel' – an open sided, covered Astroturf – is so popular that ripping it down was out of the question – the tattered roof is being replaced.

Plenty of clubs, from real tennis to fishing for carp in the pond – 'the film club is just the best', said one girl. Chess compulsory for two years – it's taken very seriously here (under 11 girls champs).

Music is strong, with 80-90 per cent learning instruments; there are three choirs, including the chapel choir, which often tours abroad. The head of music is also head of drama, so every play tends to be a musical, said a parent: Oliver! the last, described by another parent as 'excellent – my quite shy son volunteered for it...'

Everyone in the prep has a bed and boards to some extent: 75 per cent full time, everyone else up to four nights a week (must stick to chosen nights). In this small school, there are no separate boarding houses: everyone just troops upstairs to bed, the head's flat situated between the boys' and girls' dorms. Parents love the feeling of intimacy – a truly family school.

Large dormitories for 10, three per room for older pupils, the usual is six. Pupils wake to music – the latest charts.

'Palatial since my day', said a parent; but actually they're mid renovation – decoration of some rooms is a bit tired, and a few of the original Victorian window panes are cracked (they're gradually being replaced). Some new loos, one landing with a squidgy new carpet, and couple of lovely lampshades, one in white feathers, another rose shape (both in response to pupil request). Pine bunk beds, well used. Showers and basins clean, but a bit elderly – nice old taps though; 'it's all going', said the head briskly; although the parents we spoke to were happy with it as it is.

Matrons and nurse (who is an angel, we were repeatedly told) reside in nearby rooms on every corridor: if pupils are poorly in the night, they wake the dormitory monitor who gets matron. Lovely bright sick bay, complete with bears and TV.

Year groups take it in turn to occupy the drawing room in evenings (music, piano, chess, Wi dance), other year groups spilling out into hall, library and ICT room, playing ping pong or snooker. Children here flow everywhere – no feeling of being penned into a particular area.

Lots of activities at the weekends: Saturday morning school, then matches; trips on Sundays – children talked with great joy of a trip to Brighton Pier, when older pupils were allowed to go off in groups of four, and told us how much they love the independence – 'at my last school they never stopped watching us', said one, impatiently. 'Here, they trust us'.

Children keep in touch by email 'asking for things', Sunday letter writing, Skype and can phone if they want to.

Each class sends a rep to the school council and food committee – a food committee board in a class room simply stated 'BETTER BURGER'; but they don't have much to complain about: they've won awards for their food, which a parent described as 'brilliant' – the custard (with stewed apple) was clearly not just tipped from a tin of Ambrosia.

The children's happiness is testament to how well they are cared for – and indeed the school Happiness Charter is on the wall of every room. A parent described the school as 'gentle'; they chose Cottesmore for its rounded, happy pupils, and nurturing environment. Easy for pupils to speak to staff here – they're all out in the hall at break time, accompanied by their coffee trolley.

Certainly the best mannered children we've met at a prep, leaping to their feet if we so much as glanced over, opening doors, shaking hands. Watching the children, it seemed evident that the respectful environment influences how they treat each other.

Time out area on a wooden chest in front of the study – pupils who've been a bit rowdy perch there until they've calmed down. A clear bullying policy: pupils and staff are expected to bring forward if they see it. The one incident a parent described to us was 'clamped down on quickly'.

Pupils from London, home counties, and abroad, including expats and diplomats. Lots of London parents, but not the competitive ones. A parent from London told us he looked at 20 prep schools, and Cottesmore had the best combination of options one could get: 'A* in all the things that really matter in life'.

Cranleigh Preparatory School

Horseshoe Lane, Cranleigh GU6 8QH

01483 542058
fmjb@cranprep.org
www.cranprep.org

Ages: 7–13
Pupils: 329
Boarders: 46 weekly/flexi
Day: £13,950 – £18,105 pa
Boarding: £22,425 pa

Linked school: Cranleigh School

Headmaster: Since 2008, Mr Michael Wilson BSc (50s). Raised in Africa, educated in Kenya and at Sherborne then Keele University. He started his teaching career in the early '80s at Cranleigh as a chemistry teacher and sports coach in the senior school. After a few years he returned to Africa, held teaching posts at a couple of schools in Nairobi and was a national and Davis Cup team tennis coach. The draw of Cranleigh pulled him back and over the next seven years he worked through deputy house master, head of sixth form girls and girls' housemaster. After short-lived posts in Thailand and at Bradfield he was back at Cranleigh as housemaster in the senior school again, 'brought back to help sort out boarding,' he tells us. Then in 2002 he became head at Edge Grove Prep and finally moved back to Cranleigh Prep as head in 2008; he assures us he's here for the long run.

His own 'uncluttered' Kenyan childhood forms the core of his beliefs about how childhood is best conducted and is a recurring theme in his conversation. He likes old-fashioned values, letter writing, good manners and the freedom to play unfettered outdoors; he doesn't like materialism, selfishness and moaning. He believes daily chapel is important for reflecting on shared values and the Christian ethos of the school.

The school has a family theme for the Wilsons; Mrs Wilson heads up the prep's learning support department and their three children have all been educated at least in part at Cranleigh. Mr Wilson's long-term on-off career here means he has taught the parents of many of his current pupils.

Mr Wilson tells us that he sees all parents at school social events or parent briefings and reminds them to 'buy into the whole school', meaning they should celebrate and support all the teams whether their children are in them or not. 'They may get their chance in the future but not everyone can play for the firsts and it's a lesson in life'.

Entrance: The main entry point is at 7+, with another chunk of pupils wanting to join at 11+, enough to add one or two more classes. During the assessment day for entry at 7, children complete comprehension, maths, spelling and reasoning on computer, plus a handwritten piece of creative writing; they also take part in art and PE sessions. Quite a day for a 6-year-old, although the school does 'try to make it as relaxed as possible'. For entry at 11 children come to an 'activity morning' for an interview plus art, sports, problem solving and team building sessions. They then return a few months later for computer based maths, reasoning, spelling and reading plus handwritten comprehension and creative writing. At this stage children are being assessed on whether or not they would thrive academically and socially at the Cranleigh School across the road. However, this is not a pre-test for the senior school; pupils still need to take common entrance and go through the formal admissions process at Cranleigh School. Crucially, Mr Wilson ensures he meets the parents, usually twice, and talks to feeder heads. He tells us he uses his 'gut feeling' about which children will cope with and contribute to Cranleigh.

Exit: Three-quarters move 'across the road' (an oft used phrase here) to Cranleigh School. The links between prep and senior schools are increasingly strong and up to a third win Cranleigh scholarships. However, it is quite accepted that others will want to move elsewhere and they are given equal support and advice. Those who do move go on to a wide range of public schools including Charterhouse, Millfield, Wellington, Eton, Winchester, Tonbridge, Sherborne, RGS Guildford, Marlborough, Prior's Field and St Catherine's, a handful each year with scholarships.

Remarks: A traditional prep school with an outdoorsy, sporty feel. Whilst it's co-ed, the boyish culture seems to dominate somewhat. Parents describe it as 'busy, robust and challenging' and those children who enjoy life here are energetic, sporty and have a sense of humour about 'banter' from other pupils and younger staff. Families are generally well-heeled, some extremely so, mostly from the surrounding countryside and villages. They pitch up to school events and matches, often more dads making an appearance than at other schools, and describe themselves as a pretty vocal and often demanding lot. Mr Wilson tells us he spends plenty of time seeing parents one to one, managing expectations.

Academically inclusive with the range of abilities catered for by extensive setting within classes and, in the top two years, streaming into one scholarship and three or four common entrance forms depending on numbers. 'Academics have been upped, which is no bad thing,' reports a parent

of long standing; another tells us her scholarship form daughter gains confidence from being at the top here academically. Learning support, co-ordinated by Mrs Wilson and her specialist team, is 'at the centre rather than a satellite' with dyscalculia, dyspraxia and dyslexia all catered for and just under a fifth of pupils receiving some level of support. Needs are spotted early on and thoroughly addressed with classroom assistants and interventions in small groups or one-to-one. All pupils' progress is closely monitored via a thorough record system with inputs from all staff.

He likes old-fashioned values, letter writing, good manners and freedom to play unfettered outdoors

Art is of an amazingly high standard. The head of art is confident and enthusiastic about children's abilities and she seems to get fantastic work out of everyone. The art room is stuffed full of current projects by pupils of all ages, including some really unusual ceramics, textiles and sculptures alongside more expected drawing and painting. Talented artists could find the perfect niche here.

Drama and music are also well covered; both are part of the curriculum for all ages with numerous performances each year. Individual instrumental or singing lessons are held in the music school, recently enlarged with the addition of a practice room for ensembles and choirs. Talented musicians benefit from a programme called 'Cranleigh Music 7-18' in which music teachers work at both Cranleigh Prep and Cranleigh School and the most able musicians play in ensembles across the age range.

Sport is a major focus of school life, whether you ask pupils, parents or staff; it's timetabled every day with matches mid-week and on alternate Saturdays. Rugby and hockey are big, but there are less usual options including riding over at the senior school's on-site stables. The 'Cranleigh Sport 7-18' programme brings sports staff over from the senior school to spot talent and coach at all levels. Parents expect their children to be able to represent the school in matches and teams are fielded from A to D to give everyone a good chance. Of course pupils know who will be in the As but they say, 'it's possible to get places in other teams'. Non-sporty or quiet bookish children may well find this whole active vibe just too much; as one parent says, 'it's horses for courses'.

Pastoral care is the remit of the deputy head; she has been at Cranleigh Prep for 21 years and is familiar with the ups and downs of life here. Incidents are tracked and dealt with pragmatically, parents are phoned, high jinks are recognised, punishments are taken and pupils move on. An annual anti-bullying questionnaire identifies any new issues – such as the ever-present Facebook, which has been addressed using a visiting outside agency to talk to children and parents. A few parents have told us about persistent unkindness from other children which has left their own feeling upset and unsupported; the deputy head responds that bullying and unkindness are taken seriously, efforts are focused on changing unsociable behaviour and pupils have been suspended in the past. She points out that she recently asked staff to send her any notes from parents praising their children's care and her file of these is much thicker than her file of dissatisfied and problematic correspondence.

The great outdoors is what defines Cranleigh: acres of grassy pitches, an Astro pitch, tennis courts and netball courts. The senior school across the road dominates the views, keeping that future option ever in mind. The buildings are a mix of Edwardian and a hotch-potch of newer, including a new one providing three more classrooms and a common room. Some are a bit disappointing inside, a few rather poky classrooms and a sports and performance hall which felt like a cavernous shed; others are good, the well-stocked library, a couple of IT suites with brand new desks and integral computers and the welcoming, very comfortable reception area. Boarding houses are traditional, or somewhat old-fashioned depending on your view. The girls' boarding house we visited (18 girls board compared with 28 boys) had dorms for four or six boarders, high windows, firm mattresses and lots of Justin Bieber and 1-Direction posters. In the bathroom, rows of wash basins, four or five showers and a bath. Two matrons are always on hand to keep an eye on things for boarders and day pupils; they offer TLC in their cosy room or the next door sick bay or in the brightly furnished sitting room cheerfully labelled the 'Ikea Room'. Boarding is weekly or flexi with a minimum of two nights a week; there are no weekend boarders. Although day pupils hugely outnumber boarders, the daily routine of late finishing, prep at school and Saturday school on alternate weeks feels rather more like a boarding school.

A few scholarship awards are given to exceptional candidates at 11, nothing earlier. Sibling discounts are available for third and subsequent siblings at any stage in Cranleigh Prep or senior school.

In short, a sporty co-ed school run on traditional lines in a glorious rural setting with strong links to its senior school. A good choice for a broad education, less academically pressured than many others and with plenty of learning support for those who need it. Robust and energetic pupils preferred.

Cranleigh School

Horseshoe Lane, Cranleigh, Surrey GU6 8QQ

01483 273666
admissions@cranleigh.org
www.cranleigh.org
C of E

Ages: 13–18
Pupils: 625; sixth form: 212
Boarders: 470 (285 boys, 185 girls)
Day: £27,855 pa
Boarding: £34,170 pa

Linked school: Cranleigh Preparatory School

Headmaster: Since September 2014, Mr Martin Reader (40s), previously head of Wellington School in Somerset. He was educated at St Olave's, Orpington and read English language and literature with Middle English and Old Norse at Oxford, and played rugby for the university. Deciding that he maybe hadn't the academic edge for a university career, he went to teach at St Edward's Oxford and from thence to Oundle, before becoming deputy at Reigate Grammar. His wife is also a teacher, and

they have two children. He loves sport and is an avid birdwatcher as well as a loyal supporter of his local church.

Academic matters: Results have improved greatly of late, not least because of the introduction of girls throughout the school. At GCSE in 2015, 63 per cent A*/A grades. At A level, individual strengths vary from year to year, but drama, economics, English, history, languages, maths and the sciences usually up there with good grades. In 2015, 79 per cent A*-B, 48 A*/A. School says that pupils 'don't have to be superstars,' but one parent commented that the academic side is definitely hotting up and 'B and C students may struggle'. A SENCo who screens all entrants, support offered for those who need it – one-to-one sessions which cost extra.

Games, options, the arts: 'Sport is a very important part of just about every Cranleighan's life.' The sheer range of sports available is staggering – really something for everyone. Facilities extremely impressive – 100 of the 200 acres of the school land given over to playing fields – and include the Trevor Abbott sports centre, four all-weather pitches, one of which converts to 12 tennis courts in summer, to add to the other 12 courts (all packed with Wimbledon wannabes when we visited), indoor and outdoor swimming pools, cricket and rugby pitches stretching as far as the eye can see, championship standard squash courts, six Eton fives courts, nine hole golf course, stables with own horses (pupils can bring their own horse(s) if desired), and so on. Key sports include rugby, cricket, hockey, lacrosse, netball,

tennis and athletics. Football nowhere near the same emphasis as rugby – might put off a soccer-mad boy. Opportunities for all levels of talent – parents with non-sporty but enthusiastic children say that they really enjoy what they do. But certainly don't bother applying if your child absolutely loathes sport.

If you are looking for a school where the kids are home at 4.00pm lounging around and chatting to parents, forget it – this is not the school for you

Art generally praised, but one informed parental critic 'wasn't that impressed'. Drama particularly strong with fantastic theatre facilities (very professional tiered auditorium) and a new technical studio, and lots of chances to perform throughout the year in a variety of different shows. Musically, opportunities vast, with choirs, orchestras, individual instrument tuition, concerts throughout the year. Interestingly, though, music not hugely popular at either GCSE or A level.

Other than sport, the options are wide-ranging and children have lots of opportunities to fill their day.

Boarding: Six houses: four boys', two girls'. Boarding houses seem well designed – the newer ones obviously more swish with bright and airy feel; dorms (generally sleep four) for younger pupils (individual rooms for older ones) on the whole seem like the typical teenage bedroom – posters on wall, clothes strewn everywhere, but a homely atmosphere. Dining hall atmospheric, pupils help themselves from a choice of food – 'Rather like motorway services.'

Boarding actively encouraged – majority do board, not out of necessity but desire to engage in all the school has to offer. If you are looking for a school where the kids are home at 4.00pm lounging around and chatting to parents, forget it – this is not the school for you. Absolutely key at Cranleigh are the sporting/extracurricular opportunities and a long school day – whether boarding or not. A parent of a day pupil commented, 'She loves the social whirl and doesn't want to come straight home.'

Background and atmosphere: Founded in 1865 for farmers' sons, going through something of a renaissance and currently wildly fashionable. One parent described how it was her daughter's 'dream come true' to get in. Set in stunning grounds, it certainly fulfils every expectation of an English boarding school. Beautiful, impressive façade – breathtaking architecture which continues inside to the chapel, library, quad.

Pupils encouraged to eat, sleep and breathe Cranleigh and are busy from dawn till dusk – school day is from 7.30am until potentially 9.00pm at night. 'If they really want to go home after that, they can.' Everyone expected to participate in the school fully and the school is very pro boarding.

Everyone has Saturday school virtually every week, and over a third of boarders stay at the weekend – although one boarding pupil said, 'We all go home at the weekend,' so it depends what a particular peer group does. A number of parents we talked to felt there should be more weekend exeats. 'My children aren't usually home till 6.30pm on a Saturday, which makes going away for the weekend or seeing friends very difficult,' said one parent of day pupils. Boarders need to be back by 7.00pm on a Sunday, so an even shorter weekend for them.

Pastoral care, well-being and discipline: Christian values underpin school society. Huge crackdown in recent years on sloppy discipline – drugs definitely not tolerated in any way; two boys expelled recently for possession, although 'those expulsions surprised nobody,' says a not particularly shocked parent. Personal possession of alcohol and smoking also big no-nos leading to a variety of sanctions, including gating and detentions. Persistent offenders suspended. Sex education, not surprisingly, quite high up the agenda here and romantic attachments between pupils definitely discouraged. 'Inappropriate' sexual behaviour leads to suspension or expulsion.

Christian values underpin school society. Huge crackdown in recent years on sloppy discipline – drugs definitely not tolerated in any way

Staff say whole feel of school is 'more like a university' and that pupils will need self-reliance. Pupils' daily pastoral care managed within each of the six houses and weekly meeting between head and tutors allows specific problems to be discussed. Bullying tackled via the tutorial/house system where pupils can talk in confidence. Individual housemasters and housemistresses have their own views on mobile phones, going out etc – it's the luck of the draw ('Nonsense!' says school. 'The only variation is whether the house actually collects phones overnight/during prep').

Surprisingly, considering tough line on transgression, school not a pageant of well-turned-out pupils – lots of customised uniform in evidence and funky hairstyles. Sixth formers wear suits – but for some the word 'suit' is ambiguous. All this trendy dishevelment and urban cool seem a bit incongruous in such glorious surroundings.

Pupils and parents: Interestingly, for a predominantly boarding school, parents tend to be from quite a small, local radius (certainly no more than 30 miles the norm) – and it's not unusual for parents to actually live in Cranleigh. Parents are 'a mix of backgrounds,' says school – although as it is hardly cheap, presumably most are well-heeled (though school keen to stress that a significant number have bursarial assistance). One parent said that school is 'like a movie set – full of beautiful people,' and certainly pupils are particularly cool souls who come across as mature, self-possessed individuals.

Entrance: Entrance list opens in May, two and a half years before September entry. Candidates and parents interviewed for interests/values/aspirations – conditional offers based on these and prep school reports, pending CE results. Very oversubscribed so can afford to be choosy about who gets in. Looking for pupils who 'enjoy being at school and have the capability to be interested in a wide range of things'.

For entrance to the sixth form (about 15-20 come in at this stage) the expectation is to have gained six points at GCSE, with two points for an A* or A grade and one for a B grade. Also at least a C grade at GCSE for maths and English language. Candidates will also be interviewed and reports sought from previous head.

Exit: Up to 10 per cent leave post GCSEs, for 'places offering more diverse AS/A2 courses than us', but the vast majority stay and go on to a wide range of universities. Eight to Oxbridge in 2015; Bath, Bristol, Nottingham, Exeter, Loughborough, Durham and Oxford Brookes all popular.

Money matters: Fees by no means cheap, but most parents seem to feel that 'you get what you pay for' with the huge amount on offer. Scholarships available – academic, music, art and the Eric Abbott for candidates of 'strong academic ability and at least one other area of excellence', eg sport/drama etc – up to a maximum of 10 per cent of fees for the top awards. Other than that you'll need to remortgage.

Remarks: Hugely popular school with lots on offer, strong academia and mega street cred. Ideal for the sporty, energetic, sociable and independent child.

Cumnor House School (Haywards Heath)

Danehill, Haywards Heath, West Sussex RH17 7HT

01825 790347
registrar@cumnor.co.uk
www.cumnor.co.uk
C of E

Ages: 4–13 (boarding from 7)
Pupils: 390
Boarders: 70 full and flexi
Day: £9,750 – £18,435 pa
Boarding: £21,945 pa

Headmaster: Since 2001, Christian Heinrich BA PGCE (40s). Degrees from Kent and Oxford. Previously housemaster, then deputy head, at Summer Fields. ISI Inspector, IAPS appraiser of fellow heads, and chairman of the Boarding Schools Association in 2013, so plenty of insight into schools at all levels. Confident, and very sure of his approach to childhood and education: 'If a child is happy, education takes care of itself.' Described by pupils as fair, fun and someone who 'doesn't get unreasonably cross.' Most important quality for pupils to achieve in their time at Cumnor House: consideration. Loves films, skiing and wine: takes great joy in picking the bottles for post-parents' evening jollies.

Parents are very enthusiastic about him: 'Incredibly kind and supportive of kids – particularly those who struggle'; 'Easy to see when you want to'. 'Radical and brave...in that he works for the kids and not the parents,' added one parent thoughtfully, giving the example of his support for strong story lines in year 8 film making: a recent film told of a child desperate to win a swimming gala who practises all night and drowns. It was felt parents might not be able to stomach this ending, and a parent version was filmed in which the child comes up for a breath. Parents might find it difficult to accept the extraordinary level of pressure to succeed that can be absorbed by children – but the head and pupils here are fully cognisant, and the head does what he can to relieve the pressure.

Married to Belinda, who teaches French in the pre-prep; they have four children.

Entrance: Non-selective in early years; thereafter selection of those most likely to be fully involved in school life. Prospective pupils join in for a day to be observed for fit, with interviews for the occasional candidate for year 6 or above. Most join in nursery or year 3, but there's a healthy smattering in other years up to year 5. No waiting list as such; but they'll only show you around if there's a space.

Exit: To a large variety of senior schools (30+), including Benenden, Brighton College, Bryanston, Cranbrook, Cranleigh, Eton, Harrow, Hurstpierpoint, King's Canterbury, Radley, Sevenoaks, Tonbridge, Wellington, Winchester, Worth. In directing children towards schools, considers not just whether they can meet the academic requirements, but also whether they're sufficiently emotionally robust to cope with life at the school in question.

Remarks: Beautiful setting in the Sussex countryside overlooking the downs. Buildings range from the charming to the unremarkable, in a village-like cluster. The core of the school was once a farmhouse, and some feel of this remains, with the carcass of a barn, formerly a splendid all-weather outdoor area, recently revamped into 'music HQ'. Lush green grounds, and large pond to row over in the Cumnor boat, or swing over on a rope (it's

drained and cleaned and carefully tested for any virulent bacteria first, assured the head's wife).

Main entrance is slightly scuffed country house hotel – parquet floor and log fire, and a few Famous Five books on a window sill by a sofa. Lego table and 70s sweets jigsaw on the go. 'Another genius from Cumnor' cushions – to reassure existing parents, or perhaps tempt prospective ones?

In-house custard creams and jammy dodgers bulge with cream and jam and were startlingly yummy to those of us used to the pedestrian version (they've got an award winning chef)

Common room with a log fire, couple of pool tables and newspapers (including Times and Independent) – not read at the time of our tour, but perhaps flicking through the papers comes later in the day. Award-winning art work on the walls, and a long piece of paper where pupils had drawn self-portraits in the style of Quentin Blake to celebrate World Book Day. Library is on the small side ('shocking,' said one parent), but is due to be rehoused in the new block.

Pre prep is a cosy separate entity that particularly attracted one mum, who remembers fondly the special mothers' day celebration in reception, children presenting mums with handpicked flowers wrapped in foil, then escorting them into school for special cakes and poems – 'very simple and lovely.'

'Academic, but not pushy academic,' says the head. Certainly a school which achieves a goodly number of scholarships, but not, in atmosphere or method, like a prep with an eye on the prize for the duration. Many parents fresh from pressurised London preps may struggle initially with the comparatively relaxed Cumnor environment – 'you don't know at what level everyone else's child is reading,' said one startled mum. Take a deep breath, parents: your kids are not going to be constantly tested, so you won't receive that reassuring stream of test results as evidence that they are progressing nicely towards the senior school of choice. I have to tell them to trust us, says the head – 'children are meant to be enjoying themselves and having fun.'

So things don't get really serious until years 7 and 8, when a scholarship set comes into being. The focus shifts somewhat towards achieving the desirable scholarships, and others start preparing for common entrance.

Usual range of subjects, with children being put into sets from year 5. Just French and Latin on the languages front – Latin is the basis of European

languages, says the head, and teaches logic which can apply to other subjects, giving a derisive snort in passing to other schools' cosmetic glance at Mandarin. Careful consideration of the timetable, which is broken up so kids are not using their brains in the same way for long periods of time – pre-prep dance outside before each maths lesson. No one model fits all – so if there is good reason for the usual school curriculum not to apply to a child, then an exception will be made.

Not much prep until year 7: just vocab and spelling, which could be learnt in the bath or around the dinner table, and reading, occasionally left undone – 'I don't read on Friday nights as mummy and daddy have gin and tonic,' said a child in year 1.

Year 7 and 8s all have iPads for use during lessons, purchased by parents in an optional scheme ('you didn't have to sign up, but if everyone else was going to have one...'). No social media or unsuitable apps.

Learning support is excellent, and not only provides support to (around 30) pupils with special needs, but also to those who just need a bit of extra help now and then. There's an educational psychologist on the staff, who observes classes, and deals with any emotional problems suffered by pupils which may be exacerbated by school, from separation anxiety to bereavement. No extra charge for counselling or one-to-one learning support. Additional charges for extras such as speech therapy.

Saturday school on alternate weekends, which children seem happy with (though some parents would prefer a lie in, and more family time).

School motto – 'be kind' permeates everything, said one parent: apparently the head boy's job is to make sure everyone is happy at break time, and no one is being left out; so it comes as no surprise that the pastoral care is very thorough: regular full staff pastoral care meetings where every child's name is read out, and their welfare considered. Form teachers are the first port of call for difficulties until year 5, after which each child has a tutor whom they meet twice once a week to talk about everything and anything. School policy on bullying is to make sure children understand what bullying behaviour is, and ask them to blow the whistle: senior children attend the ABC committee (Anti-Bullying Committee) every week to report on anyone they are worried about. One parent whose child experienced bullying behaviour said it was dealt with quickly and efficiently, and also praised the presence of 'gappers' (gap year students), who she said could pick up on things teachers might not get to hear.

C of E, but not evangelically so. Exposure to the most valuable tenets of faith with a bohemian touch: daily prayers described by head as also a school silence – a time for a loud school to be silent and consider things (there is a cheery noise as kids move around here, but children are friendly and well mannered).

The school shares facilities in the local community, and links with a local primary each year. The head is setting up the Cumnor certificate (own brand D of E), which will involve years 7 and 8 working in the local community, and being part of drama workshops with younger pupils from local primaries.

Food is 'amazing' say kids – apparently there are no adjectives which can do justice to the wraps. In-house custard creams and jammy dodgers bulge with cream and jam and were startlingly yummy to those of us used to the pedestrian version (they've got an award winning pastry chef). Well, if the cushions didn't do it for you...

Occupations, as clubs are called at Cumnor, range from boules to calligraphy, and vary each term. Cinematography described in detail by enthusiastic kids – 'it makes you look at films in a completely different way.' There's a waiting list for cooking, but everyone gets a turn eventually. Year 8 learn to cook a three course meal as a post-exam treat.

The 'co-curriculum' (sports and arts) is given equal rather than ornamental value here ('they find out what every child has going for them,' said a parent).

Sport is for awareness, commitment and health – and everyone: a poor enthusiastic player will be in teams all the way through, playing matches most weeks. 'It's nice to win,' said a pupil; but it's not the only or main purpose of sport here. No A, B or C teams until year 7: teams change from week to week, and the make-up of teams depends on whom they are playing. Lots of it – up to seven sessions a week, including swimming. Ample playing fields and courts with views over the rolling downs, and a new Olympic size Astroturf. Swish indoor swimming pool, old chilly outdoor version.

Art is 'exceptional,' said one parent. Housed in a barn-like room with high beams, glass doors and space to hang strange colourful objects. Secured the two top prizes in the Royal College of Art Young Art Exhibition last year.

All learn a musical instrument –- it can be dropped in year 7 to make way for the demands of common entrance and scholarships, though many continue. Eight instrumental groups, from orchestra to the sort-of-samba group.

Each year from year 3 upwards does an annual production, Shakespeare being the year 8 remit (one heavyweight, one adapted comedy for those with less Olivier inclinations) to be performed in the mossy green outdoor theatre. Everything from Snow White to Oh! What a Lovely War in the years below.

The uniform and sports kit is good quality but expensive – one parent complained indignantly at the cost of school sweatshirts; but there's some second hand provision in the uniform shop. Sports kit is laundered by the school, much to the joy of parents.

Boarding is possible from year 7: 30+ full timers (although all go home every other weekend), and up to 50 flexi boarders, who spend a few nights every week at school. 'They are completely flexible,' said one grateful parent. Tremendously popular with pupils, several of whom commented on their difficulty persuading their mums they were old enough – 'but it's so fun.' Lots of activities: preparations for Dragons' Den were under way, not to mention Marlborough Murders, Friday night is magic night and day trips at the weekends. So much going on that on just one night in the summer term did boarders watch anything on TV. Gappers help make the boarding experience really fun, said one

parent: they're always there to play a game and provide an injection of energy and enthusiasm.

Rooms are for five, and cosy: four beds at ground level, and one bunk. Bathrooms are clean and up to date. Parents like the proximity of houseparents (described by parents as 'warm and welcoming' and 'extremely efficient'), and the easy access pupils have to gappers, who have rooms on each corridor, and are the first point of call in the night.

Current common room is the one used during the day, transformed for boarders with an additional rug and sofa (the new block will free up space for boarders to have a dedicated room). Fruit is always available, and there's a pantry where boarders can make tea, toast and hot drinks (with gappers' help). Obligatory weekly letter writing, and phones available for making calls in the evening or at break time – parents and pupils were happy this was sufficient. No Skype, iPads or mobiles allowed ('they get technology soon enough,' said one parent). Useful experience for those who move onto boarding senior schools. Currently no overseas boarders.

Parents around 30 per cent London, the rest local, mostly professionals or city types. Not cliquey, said one parent, outgoing and sociable, inclusive of newcomers, with an imminent buddy system to match new parents with old. Parents are encouraged to use the swimming pool and join the zumba class –- 'not a drop and go school.' Indeed coffee and croissants are available every morning in the dining room after drop off. 'Parents should certainly not worry about being lonely in the country.'

One full bursary at the moment, but the Cumnor Foundation is about to be launched, with the aim of providing two assisted places in every year by 2020.

DLD College London

199 Westminster Bridge Road, London SE1 7FX

020 7935 8411
dld@dld.org
www.dldcollege.co.uk

Ages: 14–20
Pupils: 500; sixth form: 400
Boarders: 195 full
Day: £19,990 pa
Boarding: plus £15,000 – £21,000 pa

Principal: Since September 2013, Rachel Borland BEd MA. Originally principal of both DLD and Abbey College in London, until they integrated on a single, purpose-built site with student accommodation on Westminster Bridge Road in September 2015. Previously principal of Abbey College in

Birmingham, as well as principal of the largest private boarding school in Nigeria. In addition, she's been assistant director of studies at the British Council in both Hong Kong and Jordan, and she also worked at Bath University.

A self-acclaimed workaholic, she is both amenable and easy-going – with no hint of the stereotypical authority of more traditional head-teachers. Known among colleagues as being inspirational and collaborative. 'No decision is taken alone by me, although I'm inevitably the finisher,' she says. Typical day involves arriving at 6.30am, checking in with boarding staff, breakfasting with students, having quiet time in her office, then juggling the usual meetings and paperwork with meeting students and finally leaving early evening. 'I'm not a person who can sit still for very long,' she laughs. Travels a lot. The term we visited, she had gone to Nigeria, Dubai and St Petersburg, visiting schools and spreading the word about DLD. Students very much at ease chatting with her. 'We see her every day,' said one, although they add that they rarely have to bother her in her office due to the tight pastoral and academic support, which means other staff members are generally a first port-of-call.

Lives alone in Haywards Heath, Sussex. 'I love London, but I also love fields and space.' Her daughter is a houseparent at DLD and her son was educated through the Alpha Plus Group.

Academic matters: College offers a two-year GCSE programme, whilst a minority (usually those who are older or who have transferred from other schools where they started their GSCEs) do a one-year GCSE course. Most take seven subjects, from a list of 12 options including the basics, plus French, religious studies, art, graphics and drama. Russian, Chinese, Spanish, Italian, German and Arabic are available via individual tuition. Commendable results from a mixed ability intake. In 2015, 16 per cent A*/A grades and 59 per cent A*/C.

A level students get a choice of 33 subjects, including music technology, photography, film and media studies, sociology, psychology and languages, in more or less any combination. Art, economics, religious studies and philosophy are consistently popular, alongside English and maths. In 2015, 81 per cent A*-C grades and 34 per cent A*/A. BTecs also available in media production and business.

Typical day involves arriving at 6.30am, checking in with boarding staff, breakfasting with students, jugging the usual meetings and paperwork and leaving early evening

Some students are disaffected when they arrive, but it's rare for them to be anti-education after a few weeks. 'Because of the small class sizes – on average, 12 – they get lots of individual feedback and huge amounts of encouragement, and most start making progress very quickly,' says the principal, who also attributes their academic success to their focus on fitting the right course to the right student.

Parents can't praise the system enough. 'The small class sizes, and the extra attention that provides each child with, have been the absolute making of my daughter,' one parent told us. Another, who has had two children at DLD, says, 'DLD has a record of helping children who felt they weren't going to achieve anything in a regular school to really do well. There's something about the small class sizes, easy-going environment and quality of teaching that gives them a chance to break out of set patterns of underachieving and underperforming. It really shows, more than anywhere I've seen.'

The college can cope with a wide range of special needs, generally picking up several previously undiagnosed cases each year, including dyslexia, ADHD and autism. Thirty-four per cent SEN when we visited and those benefit from support with study and essay writing skills; individual help is also available at extra cost. 'Our SEN students get more or less the same level of results as the others, due to the amount of input from SEN department, which is run by a two-strong team. This extra help is critical,' says head. Accredited by CReSTeD, whose most recent report speaks of it as a unique school.

Very bright students also well catered for, with parents confirming that their children feel stretched and challenged in a positive way. Others point to the personalised approach of monitoring, feedback and target setting ensuring that students continue maximising their full potential at all times.

Indeed, educational expectations are high for all, with patchy work not accepted by staff. 'We believe in helping students believe they can move up to the next level,' says head. Many staff are from Oxbridge and some come from non-teaching backgrounds – the theatre, the City, the BBC. 'This means our tutors know exactly what employers really want from graduates and it also means they have great connections,' says one student. 'My music teacher, for instance, has invited in songwriters, a music lawyer and others to talk to us, as well as sending out our coursework from people in the industry to get feedback.'

> 'My music teacher has invited in songwriters and a music lawyer to talk to us, as well as sending out our coursework to get feedback'

Teachers only employed if they are accessible to students outside classes, with many not only being available on email, but on a live chat system. Students say they are treated as adults and for many of them, it's that mutual respect that gets them back on track with their education. The most recent ISI report states that students like being at the college and are very happy with the personal support that they receive.

Extended Project Qualification increasingly popular, with 12 students doing it when we visited, although head admits some drop off in first few weeks. 'It's a tough programme,' she says.

Games, options, the arts: A level art and photography are two of the most popular and successful subjects here, and the artwork we saw on display in the large and well-equipped art rooms was striking, with a notable creative energy among the students while they were working. 'I can honestly say every photography lesson is fun,' said one student. LAMDA examinations on offer and the DLD youth theatre puts on two performances a year.

All GCSE students play curricular sport at local centres on Wednesday afternoons, including football, basketball, tennis, netball, dance, rock-climbing and aerobics. Sports clubs and matches after school too, including cricket and yoga. On-site sporting facilities include a swimming pool and gym in the basement. 'But although sport is accessible and enjoyed by many students, DLD is probably not the best place for your child if they're really, really sporty,' one parent told us.

Music popular, with facilities including a recording studio and various practice areas, all of which are soundproofed. There's a vocal group, ukulele group, recording studio club and 59 students do private music lessons, including classical and jazz piano tuition, rock guitar, pop singing, singing and drum kit.

Extracurricular offering has improved in recent years, including Duke of Edinburgh Award, EPQ, debating and art clubs. Located in the heart of Westminster, it's no wonder the school takes full advantage of the galleries, museums and theatres practically on its doorstep, with overseas trips to the likes of Barcelona and Paris.

Boarding: The new site includes over 214 student beds (195 of which were being used when we visited) over 15 floors, with views over the Thames. More to be converted in the future. The areas are gender split, with younger ones on the lower floors. Strict curfews in the week from 9.30-10.30pm and, which are extended on Fridays and Saturdays until 10.30-11.30pm (depending on age). All full boarders, although some do visit home during weekends and half term and the school is very flexible when it comes to students wanting to visit friends and families. Boarders will often arrange their own activities for the weekend, but there are always free activities going on in the boarding house, including movie nights, quiz nights, zumba, birthday parties etc, along with visits to local museums, galleries and places like Harry Potter World.

Mostly single rooms, of different shapes and sizes, all ensuite. Some twin rooms share a bathroom. These rooms have a partition between beds that can be extended along the whole length of the room if required. 'It's the twin ones that are the most popular,' a staff member told us. Rooms are hi-spec, contemporary and minimalist, with a clear wow factor. 'I love my room,' one student told us. 'And because it's soundproofed, I can be as loud as I want and study in peace regardless of how loud anyone else is.' Weekly inspections mean they are kept reasonably tidy, although lots of unmade beds when we visited. Light, airy and spacious communal kitchen on each floor, complete with comfortable seating areas, fridge, freezer, microwave, kettle and toaster, but no hob or oven, with students expected to eat main meals in the refectory. 'It's a really sociable area,' one student told us.

Pastoral care for boarders includes a strong team of house parents, who are fully residential, run by a director of boarding and his assistant – who in turn is overseen by the vice president of principal welfare.

Background and atmosphere: Now one of 16 schools and five colleges owned by the Alpha Plus Group, founded in 1931 to provide tutoring for Oxbridge and Colonial Service entrance exams. After World War II it began to specialise in A and O level teaching. In 2004 it moved from Notting Hill to light, airy, refurbished premises in Marylebone; in August 2015 moved again, amalgamating with Abbey College in a new, purpose built site on Westminster Bridge Road.

On first sight, this shiny new building looks more like swanky corporate offices than any school, both outside and in, but a closer look reveals that education is very much at the heart of the design. A large open space – with huge projector screens on the wall, and which doubles up as a 350-seat performance area when required – forms the central atrium. Then the teaching and study areas – all arranged in colour co-ordinated zones so students can't get lost – sit around the edges. These facilities include six high-spec labs, a creative arts and media faculty, 40 tutorial rooms and an open plan library, study and ICT facilities.

Informal atmosphere, more akin to a college than a school, with staff and students on a first name basis and no uniform. But there's no room for slacking, with students engaged, inquisitive and busy both in the classes when we visited. 'Academically, it's tough, but people want to learn,' said one student. Helping students keep up is a vast array of break-out areas dotted around the different floors – some with individual booths for private study, whilst others have small or large tables for group study.

Active student council, which meets twice a month and organises plenty of charity events (breast cancer awareness day when we visited), as well as bringing about changes such the reintroduction of table football, although one parent told us she'd like to see 'more of a student voice overall.'

'My son kicked back about things like strict uniform at his last school, and he's much happier here'

Fresh food available in the cashless refectory, which is reviewed by a food committee comprised of students and staff. Starbucks also on site. The day begins for students at 8.50am and finishes at 4.40pm, with enrichment extending that until around 6.30pm.

Pastoral care, well-being and discipline: Very strong pastoral system, which had recently been restructured when we visited, so that there are separate staff for pastoral and academic care. 'This is important because we do attract some needy students, including school phobics and SEN,' says head. 'There's no stigma if you need help,' said one student. 'Staff really care about you here,' said another. Parents we spoke to were very moved by what the school had achieved for their children pastorally. 'Staff are so kind and supportive that I'm welling up thinking about what they've done for my daughter,' one told us.

Electronic register is taken in every lesson and parents are texted or emailed if attendance becomes a problem. Each student has a weekly meeting with their personal tutor to talk about progress and future plans; three directors of studies and three directors of welfare work closely with the personal tutors. Expectations, rather than rules, are the norm here. 'My son kicked back about things like strict uniform and not being allowed to go out at lunchtime at his last school, and he's much happier here, where you're expected to turn up and do your work and be respectful, but without lots of petty rules and an authoritarian environment.'

Significant proportion of pupils smoke (nurse runs a stop smoking programme), but there's tough penalties for misusing drink and drugs – those under suspicion are sent for drugs tests, to general parental approval. Most students, even the most troubled ones, buckle down eventually, although head says occasionally things don't go to plan, with around two exclusions every academic year.

Sanctions include supervised study; also a system of verbal and written warnings based on employment law. Bullying is taken very seriously, although students told us the atmosphere is so relaxed and accepting that it's exceptionally rare. 'Nobody judges you here,' said one student.

Peer mentoring introduced in 2011, with around 60 students involved when we visited. 'It's improving my interpersonal skills,' said one student.

Pupils and parents: Students aged between 14-18 (with the odd exception up to 20), most of whom have come from private schools. Some have been ill; some have had mental health or other problems; some have found their previous school too rigid or too stressful. Others come from peripatetic diplomatic families. Some lack confidence and need to learn good working habits. Most thrive in the informal but structured atmosphere. Around 30 per cent from UK, with others mostly from Germany, Latvia, Ukraine, Malaysia, China, Burma, Vietnam, Italy, Kazakhstan and Russia. Little, if any, sense of community among parents, which one said is 'disappointing, but hardly surprising.'

Entrance: Everyone is interviewed and previous schools are asked for references and reports. Those going into the sixth form need a minimum of five grade Cs at GCSE; if they haven't passed maths or English they will need to retake these, alongside their A levels. No student who has been disruptive elsewhere is accepted without a discussion about the need for a change in behaviour. School

is registered for 725 students, although only 500 when we visited. 'Our vision was always to open the new facility with 500 and build it up,' says head.

Exit: A few GCSE students move on elsewhere – perhaps to state sixth form colleges – but most go through to the sixth form. Those aiming at Oxbridge are given an intensive course including lectures, seminars, mock interviews and individual tuition – one to Oxbridge 2015 (and three the year before that). Popular destinations include UCL, Goldsmith's, King's College, LSE, Imperial and Bristol. Wide range of degree courses, with business studies, economics and specialist art areas being the most popular. Extra help also for potential vets, doctors and dentists, via a bespoke medical programme, with three or four a year going onto study these at university.

Money matters: Several scholarships available, worth 10-100 per cent of fees, on the basis on academic attainment, plus means-tested bursaries. 'I'm fortunate to have free rein to be sympathetic to the individual,' says head, who adds that she's keen to support the local community. Indeed, one local boy supported 100 per cent financially when we visited.

Remarks: This unique educational environment seems to capture all the best things about a college environment, combining them with the pastoral care and motivational structures that are more typical of school provision. All this takes place in small classes, with one-to-one help when required, in a state-of-the-art, purpose-built building in the heart of London, where students have the option to board on-site. The result is an informal atmosphere with an underlying structured regime where everyone is kept up to scratch. A fantastic place for the very bright, as well as re-motivating the disaffected, although not for young people who want a more traditional boarding school experience.

Dorset House School

The Manor, Pulborough, West Sussex RH20 1PB

01798 831456
info@dorsethouseschool.com
www.dorsethouseschool.com

Ages: 4–13 (boarding from 9)
Pupils: 130: 75 boys/55 girls
Boarders: 45 flexi/weekly
Day: £7,680 – £16,155 pa
Boarding: £85 per week

Headmaster: Since 2008, Mr Richard Brown MA PGCE (40s). Educated at Magdalen College School, Oxford and at Oxford Brookes, where he read

English and law. After five and a half years as an officer in the Royal Dragoon Guards, he took an MA in English and education at Reading University and

a PGCE at Roehampton. Then spent three years teaching English at the Edinburgh Academy, where he was also a boarding tutor and games teacher. This was followed by eight years as a housemaster and English teacher at Pangbourne. Lives on the school site and teaches the top three years.

'No-one minds about mud – you just fling on your wellies.' Children spend as much time as possible outside

On his arrival the governors gave him the task of introducing girls into the school and phasing out Saturday school. This caused a certain amount of angst and unrest amongst some parents and some took their children away. However, things have settled down and numbers have been rising (girls now constitute over 40 per cent and a couple of year groups have waiting lists). Head feels that school is about 'preparing children for today's challenges – not wrapping them in cotton wool' and that 'small prep schools provide an antidote to a world where children grow up too quickly'. His aim is to 'make learning fun and challenge children to think about the world around them'. Divorced with two sons. In his spare time loves mountaineering and trekking in remote places.

Entrance: Children can join at any time so long as spaces, subject to informal tests in English and maths, a report from their current school and, ideally, a taster day. Parents are made aware of what the school is able to offer and that the ultimate goal is CE.

Exit: To a wide range of senior schools, including Hurst, Brighton College, Lancing, Ardingly, Christ's Hospital, Winchester, Marlborough. Most children stay until CE at 13+, but will prepare for 11+ entry to senior schools and also for pre-selection tests. Scholarships won every year for the past few years – mixture of academic, music, sport and all-rounder.

Remarks: Founded in 1784 as Totteridge Park School in Hertfordshire. After various incarnations it became Dorset House in 1905 and moved to its present site in 1964. Housed in a 12th century manor house, with medieval great barn, modern teaching blocks and separate junior school building. Set in 16 acres of grounds at the end of a quiet country lane, next door to the church and with magnificent views in all directions. Children allowed to build camps and dens in the woods and play in the adventure playground. 'No one minds about mud – you just fling on your wellies,' said one boy. Children spend as much time as possible outside – pre-prep has two hour forest school session each week – and some of the younger children often drink their break-time hot chocolate on a log in the woods. Small amphitheatre in the garden used for speech day and house drama competition.

One-form entry, with a maximum of 20 per year group – nearly full in years 4 to 8 and waiting lists further down. Numbers have now reached 130 (maximum capacity of 160). The 45 boarding places for flexi and weekly boarders are now over-subscribed on some nights – often suits families who live in London and have a weekend cottage nearby. Warren of dorms under the eaves reached by a spiral stone staircase are warm and cosy, with old fashioned iron bedsteads and lots of teddies. Only a few girl boarders so far, but they are accommodated in great style. Real family atmosphere – feels more like someone's elegant country house than a school – the children take their breakfast and tea on the terrace during the summer. Everything immaculate with not a weed in sight and fresh paint everywhere. Head describes the school as 'traditional but forward looking.'

He would like to adopt Anthony Seldon's 'catch a tiger by the tongue' initiative to foster links with China and encourage the children to learn about the likely cultural and economic impact of the rise of China. He has recently visited a number of Chinese schools and a group of 20 Chinese children came to visit Dorset House for five weeks. This made for lots of interesting discussions and the English children were amazed at how hard Chinese parents expect their children to work.

Streaming for maths, English and science from year 5, depending on the class size and the ability range within the group. Scholarship children kept within their year group and offered extension classes at break and lunchtimes.

A dynamic team of staff with a good mix of age and experience. Charismatic science teacher

Bright, light and airy science lab where 'we love blowing up jelly babies in the fume cupboard,' says one budding young scientist

who brings the subject to life – he teaches through experimentation and investigation like testing the efficacy of indigestion remedies. Bright, light and airy science lab where 'we love blowing up jelly babies in the fume cupboard,' says one budding young scientist. Recently won Green Link award which funded the boardwalk around the pond. Children do particularly well in science at CE, often achieving top grades, and many go on to study it at university. Very enthusiastic young geography teacher is also the director of sport – geography trips to the Isle of Wight and the Jurassic Coast; the flood plain of the river Arun just beyond the garden makes a wonderful outdoor classroom. French taught by a native speaker. Latin or classical civilisation introduced in year 5; local vicar teaches RE and Greek (the latter to bright year 8s).

Light, cosy library with comfortable sofas where children can curl up with a book. Prep done at school and supervised by members of staff. Three full-time SEN teachers, mainly for mild dyslexia and dyspraxia. Bright yellow room for the junior SENCo where the motto is 'learning with laughter.' Children not routinely tested but any problems picked up quickly in such a small environment.

Magnificent medieval barn acts as the school hall and is big enough to fit everyone in – also doubles up as the sports hall and is hired out for weddings. Inner barn is used for plays and assemblies. New head of art has revitalised the art department. Art and DT are linked and the kit car club built a car and raced it at Goodwood as part of the Greenpower project. Photography very popular – each child is given their own memory card from year 3 to take photographs around the school and taught to use Photoshop. Photographs of the children displayed around the school and dining room doubles as an art gallery. Brightly coloured totem poles made from recycled materials dotted around the garden.

Young director of music (Dorset House old boy) also acts as a houseparent with his wife (who also teaches reception) and dog Mylo – has made music 'cool and fun' and now lots of informal concerts, ensembles and whole school concerts. The choir sings at services in the church next door and at the Christmas carol service at Arundel. Music timetabled from the early years and every child learns to read music through learning the recorder – about 60 per cent learn a musical instrument. Is apparently the first prep school in the country to have

JamClassHD system which is linked by JamPod technology (no, we don't know what that means either). Senior play each year, plus one or two for juniors as well as the house drama competition. Annual poetry reciting competition and children have to read out match reports and prayers – all great for building self-confidence.

Heavyweight sporting success: under-9 rugby team recently unbeaten in Sussex. Almost all the boys and girls in a year group are required to make up a team and often children who did not consider themselves sporty step up to the plate. All children in years 3 to 8 play in at least three matches a term – everyone has a go. Now enough girls to put together netball and hockey teams to play other schools. Ballet and gymnastics particularly popular and girls can take exams in these. Riding a popular extra and team takes part in regional competitions.

Other extras include drama, pottery, Mandarin, cookery and football coaching (with pros from Chelsea). Chess taught by outside specialists. Recently formed cub group with children from local primaries and some from Dorset House meets in the barn every week during term time.

Leadership and taking responsibility promoted from a young age through leadership programme – 'Children learn how to work together as a team and to listen to one another.' Leadership training once a week before school for year 8s – they take part in the decision making of the school as elected representatives of the school council and act as positive role models. More opportunities to take a position of responsibility in a small school – children start as lunch helpers and book monitors and progress through outdoor adventures and camping trip (including one to the top of Mount Snowdon). Grand finale is an adventure training week in north Devon after CE.

Small nurturing school with a family atmosphere produces open, chatty children where everyone knows everyone and each child is given the chance to find their niche. 'It's a lovely, friendly school where children have a proper country childhood and don't grow up before their time,' one happy mother told us. School is run on Christian principles and the parish church next door is central to the life of the school – Monday morning assembles in the church and parents often come to the special Friday service. The vicar is a part time member of staff and teaches RE. New pre-school for 2+ on site.

Recently introduced house system means lots of crossover between year groups and as one parent said, 'The older children are sweet to the younger ones'. Firm policy on bullying. Many young members of staff live on site and in the manor house, which contributes to the family feel. Board games round the library fire in the evenings for boarders and a dedicated games room.

Most children live within a 20-mile radius and the school is increasingly popular with families moving out of London – 'a good antidote to the pushy London day schools,' according to one new arrival. Active parents' association raised £25,000 at the summer ball for an Astroturf (in a school with 140 pupils). Also organises bonfire night party, quiz and welcomes new parents to the school. A fathers' cricket team meets regularly. Famous Old Boys include former Gordonstoun head Mark Pyper, comedian Harry Enfield and actor Ed Speleers (of Eragon fame).

If you are looking for an all-singing, all-dancing school with facilities galore, this school might not be for you, but if you are looking for somewhere that achieves good academic results, is small and nurturing and where every child gets a chance and is expected to do their bit – take a closer look.

Dover College

Effingham Crescent, Dover, Kent CT17 9RH

01304 205969
admin@dovercollege.org.uk
www.dovercollege.org.uk
C of E

Ages: 11–18
Pupils: 295 pupils; sixth form: 90
Boarders: 86 full, 7 weekly/flexi (around two thirds boys)
Day: £11,880 – £14,925 pa
Boarding: £19,200 – £28,350 pa

Headmaster: Since January 2015, Gareth Doodes, previously (briefly) head of George Heriot's School in Edinburgh, and before that head of Milton Abbey School in Dorset.

Read history at St Andrews; PGCE from Cambridge; worked at Taunton school then at Oakham for seven years, two as master of scholars and five as a housemaster, before joining Milton Abbey.

Academic matters: A broad ability range – 51 per cent A*/B and 36 per cent A*/A grades at A level and 70 per cent of pupils got 5+ A*/C including English and maths at GCSE (23 per cent A*/A grades) in 2015. Sciences taught separately for the dual award. Good range of subjects offered in sixth form. The introduction of BTecs in sport and PE, travel and tourism and health and social care has meant that more are staying on for sixth form. Apart from the usual subjects, GCSEs offered in health and social care, PE and business studies.

About 12 per cent need some sort of SEN – lots of help available, from help with study skills to more intensive one-to-one help. A very dedicated team of teachers who 'go the extra mile' for the children and focus on individual learning styles. 'I could not believe how much trouble the teachers took with my son,' said one mother. Small classes – 12 to 14 for GCSE and sometimes only six for A level.

Has welcomed international students since 1957 and the International Study Centre opened in 2001 – total immersion in English plus lessons with peer group in maths, ICT, DT and sport. Depending on the level of English, pupils prepared for Cambridge Preliminary English Test (PET), IGCSE or IELTS. All international pupils are integrated into the main school. Some start in International Study Centre and move over when ready. Others join the main school on arrival. About 50 pupils need some sort of EAL support.

Games, options, the arts: The usual sports – football, hockey, netball etc. Cross-country popular and successful (Dover College hosts a big inter-school event each year). Aerobics, basketball, sailing with Dover Sailing Club, swimming at a local pool. Everyone given a chance to shine and 'teachers are always trying out new people for sports and giving people a chance to showcase their talents'.

Sport compulsory up to sixth form and most carry on after that. Most girls continue with sport but fitness classes, dance and yoga also popular. Not a school with acres of rolling fields but has its own pitches as well as an Astroturf, sports hall, dance and fitness suites and a basketball court. 'Some of the sports facilities could do with a bit of a makeover,' say some parents. Link with Canterbury Christ Church University's sports department ensures a steady supply of recently qualified sports teachers who 'refresh the department and bring new ideas'.

School likes to bring together students and non-teaching staff. The chef is linesman for the first XI, a minibus driver is the referee and the estates manager runs D of E

Lots of music, including chamber orchestra and ensembles. Members of the local community often play in the orchestra and the choir sometimes sings evensong in Canterbury Cathedral. Tallis Music School has been relocated and refurbished and now provides soundproof pods, a recital room and teaching rooms.

Strong arts. Textiles, art and photography offered at A level. Particularly good photography – annual photographic competition also open to parents and fabulous photos displayed around the school.

Huge range of activities – from belly dancing and debating to madrigals and horse-riding. Leadership activities, including D of E Award (up to eight gold awards a year) and Young Enterprise, all designed to build self-confidence. Strong emphasis

on community and charity work. Senior pupils can get involved in the Ukraine project. A group raises money for the charity and then spends two weeks in the Ukraine refurbishing an old people's home, running a sports camp for disadvantaged children and chopping logs for the elderly. One parent described it as 'a life changing experience for my son, who realised for the first time what true hardship is'.

Boarding: Vast majority (86) are full boarders, with just five weekly and two flexi. Roughly two-thirds are boys. Year 7 and 8 day pupils are housed separately in Priory House, which ensures a gentle introduction to the senior school. All the other houses mix day and boarding so everyone gets to know everyone. 'It's nice to mix with different years because then you get to make more friends', a pupil told us, although another said 'some nationalities still stick together and keep themselves to themselves'. There is 'major house loyalty' and lots of inter-house events – music, sport, drama and the keenly fought house conker competition. All boarders have supper together at the weekends. Entertainment, theatre and shopping trips organised although many are happy 'just chilling with their friends' and catching up with schoolwork.

Background and atmosphere: Founded in 1871 by a group of local businessmen who wanted Dover to have its own public school. Housed in the grounds of the 12th century Benedictine St Martin's Priory, an oasis of green in the middle of Dover with wonderful views of Dover Castle and nestling behind the famous white cliffs. Went co-ed in 1974 (one of the first boys' schools to do so) and now almost 50:50. Although much of the original priory was destroyed by Henry VIII, there is still a feeling of history. This is despite the hotchpotch of buildings added over the years, from late Victorian houses to the uninspiring modern. The school has the only Norman refectory in Britain – still used for its original purpose and doubles as a concert hall and theatre too.

Dover College is a small local school with an international dimension and a strong sense of community 'where everyone knows everyone'. We heard comments like 'it's not overly posh but perfect for where it is' and 'it's a local school with a kind and caring environment which understands the kids' needs and gets the best out of each pupil'.

Christian foundation. Chapel is physically and spiritually at the heart of the college but all faiths and none are made to feel welcome. Three services a week, including Friday afternoon chapel.

Pastoral care, well-being and discipline: 'Because confidence matters' is the motto of the school and huge emphasis is placed on personal development

and building pupils' confidence. 'I am confident that the school has the control of my children's well-being and promotes good social skills and ethics,' a parent told us. 'I am very proud when people comment on how well-mannered my children are'. Well-developed tutorial system, and house staff and prefects have finely tuned antennae for drugs and alcohol. School likes to bring together the students and the non-teaching staff. For example, the kitchen chef is also linesman for the first XI football team, a minibus driver is the referee and the estates manager runs D of E.

Pupils and parents: Day children tend to be fairly local and many are ferried to school via a network of minibuses. About 30 per cent from abroad (30 nationalities), 10 per cent service families (including a number of Nepalese families who serve locally with the Gurkhas). About 10 per cent of local children choose to board 'because it's fun'.

Huge range of abilities – some children very bright whilst others struggle to get five good GCSEs. 'A lot of the kids are not that academic but the school brings out the best in them', said a parent. The emphasis on building confidence produces comfortable, well-adjusted children who are happy to strike up a conversation with anyone. Life is full on here and as one pupil said, 'sometimes we are just too busy as every teacher wants you to do their thing'. Even so, they seem to love every minute of it.

Prefects given lots of responsibility and say that 'it is important to act as role models to the rest of the school'. They apply in writing and are then interviewed by a panel chaired by the head. Lower sixth enrichment week takes the pupils well out of their comfort zone and often a few previously hidden talents come to the fore. Pupils have to stage a senior management meeting, role play a crisis, take part in an Apprentice-style marketing project and film a debate – all in one day. Parents like to feel involved. One mother told us that her children 'are treated in a caring and understanding way and I can talk to the teachers whenever I want'. School has worked hard to develop lines of communication with parents and sees the relationship as a partnership overseeing the children's education. Parents kept up to date with events via parent portal and social media sites.

No typical Old Doverian, although many are entrepreneurs who have made their own way in the world. They tend to keep in touch. Former pupils include composer Dai Fujikura, choreographer Sir Frederick Ashton, X Factor supremo Simon Cowell, film producer Guy East and various ambassadors and military figures.

Entrance: Almost non-selective. School has its own 11+ test in November before entry for setting purposes only and everyone interviewed. Will take children who might fail elsewhere and give them the confidence to succeed. Only turns children away if they won't be able to cope. Most join at 11+ from the junior school and local primaries. A few come in at 13+ from prep schools like Northbourne Park, Spring Grove and Wellesley House. About 25 students join the sixth form – mainly from abroad. Pupils can join at any time if there are spaces, except into year 11.

Exit: About 25 per cent leave after GCSEs, mostly to the state system. Sixth formers head to a range of universities for a wide variety of courses – recent choices include business at City University, sports science at Canterbury Christ Church, pharmacology at Bristol, business at Surrey, engineering at Nottingham, computer technology at Portsmouth. Lots of help with UCAS – careers adviser knows pupils well and 'keeps expectations realistic'. Not many take a gap year.

Money matters: Range of awards offered, including11+ scholarships in English and maths, 13+ scholarship awarded on strength of CE and 16+ scholarship on strength of GCSEs. Academic, art, music, sport and all rounder scholarships on offer. About a third of local pupils on some sort of scholarship or bursary. Not a rich school and bursaries come from fee income but school does what it can for those who encounter unexpected financial difficulties whilst at the school.

Remarks: Not hugely academic and nor does it pretend to be, but this is a happy, relaxed place where the building of self confidence underpins everything the school does. It's high praise indeed when a sixth form pupil said, 'I have been very happy here and can't fault it'.

Dulwich College

Dulwich Common, London SE21 7LD

020 8693 3601
info@dulwich.org.uk
www.dulwich.org.uk

Ages: 11–18
Pupils: 1,525; sixth form: 450
Boarders: 130 full and weekly
Day: £18,231 pa
Boarding: £35,679 – £38,052 pa

Master: Since 2009, Dr Joseph (Joe) Spence BA PhD (mid-50s), a graduate in modern history and politics; the Irish histories and literature of his postgrad line his study walls. Previously headmaster of Oakham School and for 10 years until 2002 held the prestigious position of master in college at Eton, housemaster to the King's scholars, 'surrounded by the brightest'; it was here he found his vocation. His first decade at Dulwich College will coincide with the college's 400th anniversary, entwining their legacies.

Grammar school educated, he describes his career path as the 'story of accident', a happy one. The turning point was a friend's encouragement

that one 'no longer has to be behind a desk as headmaster'. Immensely warm and charming, putting one at ease, the embodiment of the oft repeated 'Dulwich boys can talk to anyone'. He brings a sense of fun to those around him, appearing to wear his responsibilities lightly, preparing to ad lib a speech to a grand assembly as he says goodbye.

He is married to a lawyer, with two sons and daughter. He still finds time to write, recently penning a new libretto for a concert at King's College Cambridge, turning a poem written by PG Wodehouse's brother into a song. He wants these sustaining passions for the boys: 'My duty is to make sure that every Alleynian leaves with something intellectual... a passion which will be with him for the rest of his life'.

Parents, seeming to have adopted the Ofsted phraseology, unanimously declare him to be outstanding. They enthuse: 'a good orator, a great listener'; 'as fiercely passionate about the arts as academics'; 'a great presence and a motivational leader'; 'excellent, effective and innovative'.

You don't have to be a scientist or an artist here – 'learning that is free from the syllabus' allows boys to take risks in a dazzling programme of challenges

His vision for the transformations in progress – physical and philosophical – start with 'get the classroom right, then everything else', but quickly go beyond with the desire to create a generation of original thinkers. You don't have to be a scientist or an artist here – 'learning that is free from the syllabus' allows boys to take risks in a dazzling (we've rarely seen such a weighty catalogue of riches) programme of challenges, national and international competitions, symposia, external prizes, performances and physical adventures.

Academic matters: It's well known that improving the academics was top of the agenda. The college is now in the top eight per cent for value added nationally and the master is confident that the best

is still to come, just around the corner, given the way the current GCSE cohort is flourishing.

In 2015, 85 per cent of I/GCSE grades were A*/A. Plenty of A*s in sciences, English literature, maths, French and Spanish. At A level/Pre-U, 62 per cent A*/A, and (again including Pre-U) 89 per cent A*-B. Maths is most popular by far, followed by physics, history, economics and chemistry. High percentage of A*/As in physics, plus history of art, English, further maths, history and art. A levels remain as the core upper school offer but individual heads of subject have the flexibility to offer Pre-U.

Academic teaching is described by parents as solid lower down the college but inspirational higher up. Thirty-five per cent of teachers in residence for over 10 years. The master says candidly that now only a handful are perhaps not on message, and he won't see boys stuck with them, which chimes with parents, who say, 'very good standard of teaching, noticeable improvement' and 'incompetence would not be tolerated'. They also describe staff as 'hugely committed'; 'they understand a boy's potential'; 'they set the bar high academically' and 'the daily report system is excellent'.

The master drives innovation. A key appointment is the director of science, formerly at lauded Brighton College. Turning things on their head, 'flip' lessons might give boys homework first, then the boys come in and discuss how they found it, or mini-whiteboards may enable a teacher to see at a glance whether boys have 'got it'. Boys were initially consulted on their view of assessments, and came back saying they actually felt there was grade inflation – pupil voice has been used in every key decision

since. Staff share with each other a 'speciality dish' ie what is working for them in the classroom.

Curriculum is largely as one might expect; choosing options is quite complex. Languages have a particularly strong focus throughout. French, Spanish, Chinese and Latin are taught in the lower school, later on there is the addition of German, Italian and Greek. Appealing language trips: year 9s to Salamanca, year 11s to Florence. The boys describe them as holistic, taking in both language and culture, raising their passion for the subject up a notch. Exchanges take place too, but with boys considerably settled in host families in pairs.

The only setting is for maths. All pupils study separate sciences up to IGCSE and the college doesn't necessarily encourage the collection of an excessive number. Intellectual boys wishing to stretch themselves further between years 7 and 11 can enrol on the scholars' programme, described by one as 'the highlight of my week'.

Quirkier A level options include critical and contextual studies and ancient history. Liberal studies in the upper sixth in conjunction with the girls at JAGS allows boys to try something new: modern poetry, yoga, book-binding, Italian cinema and even ballroom dancing.

Also for sixth formers, the Dulwich Diploma, which looks to offer the depth of A level with the breadth of the IB: the three components comprise academic study, at least four AS levels and three A2s, an extended essay or research topic of their choice – recent examples Who Killed Sylvia Plath? and Is Medical Research the New Imperialism? – engagement beyond the classroom and preparation for life after Dulwich.

The boys we had lunch with laughingly said the only thing they didn't like was swimming as there was no point trying to keep up with the Olympic water polo players

Whilst all of this adds up to a very full plate, parents say there are 'high expectations with excellent support through study skills sessions' and 'it's pretty intensive in terms of workload but not too high pressure'.

A team of four well-qualified learning support teachers are shared with the junior school, and provide support to individual boys with a diagnosed learning difficulty – 20 per cent. Eight per cent of middle and upper school boys receive EAL support.

Games, options, the arts: In year 7, whilst skills are built and some sports tried for the first time, rugby,

football, hockey and cricket are all compulsory. By year 8 choices emerge, one being dropping rugby for fencing. Tennis currently squeezed for space with only three courts. No single sport is compulsory in the middle school but a plethora of teams make it tempting to get involved – skiing, rowing, fives, squash, cross-country and basketball, to name but a few. Years 10 and 11 may try golf, rock-climbing, self-defence, taekwondo and rugby 7s, whilst upper school choices aim to involve boys in sport however that may be, perhaps officiating or coaching as well as trying gentlemanly pursuits such as croquet, horse-riding and sailing. The school has responded to the national appetite for competitive cycling and boys are able to use the superb facilities at nearby Herne Hill velodrome.

Seventy acres of playing fields recently re-seeded, and rugby is the triumphant sport with 1st XV recently winning the NatWest Schools cup for the third consecutive year. Success, too, for the under 14s rowers, who are national champions, and the school supplies four members of the under 15 GB water-polo team. Boys we had lunch with laughingly said the only thing they didn't like was swimming as there was no point trying to keep up with the Olympic swimmers and water-polo players.

Dr Spence continues to ponder how one achieves balance amidst such rich opportunities: '50 boys will have played at Twickenham, that's a once in a lifetime experience', but are there 'boys who might have done better academically if they had not done so much?'

'Arts, music and co-curricular are outstanding'. We arrived just in time to be treated to a sensitive rendition of W H Auden's Stop All of The Clocks as part of that day's house poetry competition. The school has a rich theatrical tradition, a flexible theatre space, Chewetel Ejiofor and Rupert Penry-Jones are OAs, makes the very most of the London theatre scene, and each year produces three drama festivals and 24 performance pieces.

A parent said, 'What I really like is the drive to go beyond the curriculum and inspire'. This term's Dulwich Creative week was produced with all of the finesse and confidence of a national arts organisation gone guerrillan and saw art hijacks where every pupil – astonishingly even the babies in the kindergarten – produce a clay self-portrait, which then came together into one installation. A surreal note remains overlooking the cricket pitches, giant polyurethane mushrooms by international street artist Christian Nagel. A new 'found' space, The Store, chills to the bone, but provides an edgy, white-washed, informal rehearsal space which boys can call their own, which also houses art exhibits.

Art and DT facilities are light and bright, and where we found some of the most exuberant classes in full flow. We admired Grayson Perry-ish vases

World class performances from a debating team, who recently trounced the competition. Where next for the boy ranked number one?

produced in ceramics classes, and groovy dog kennels in DT.

Numbers learning instruments peak in the lower school at 45 per cent of boys, falling naturally enough to 25 per cent by the upper school. Standard of musicianship varies from enthusiastic beginners to boys who are leaders of section in the National Youth Orchestra or principals at Glyndebourne and the ENO. The music department is in the process of upgrading: there is a shiny new Mac suite for music technology, a new acoustic percussion suite, and small and large practice areas. Another funky new facility is the electric 'shed', fully sound-insulated, a great place to let rip with the electric guitar.

World class performances from a formidable debating team, who recently trounced the competition at the Oxford and Cambridge Unions. Where next for the boy currently ranked number one in the world?

Long lunch hours ensure even the senior boys feel they have time for clubs and societies, which continue after school. For the lower school these might include fencing, card games, woodwork and Scouts. For the middle and upper school a sophisticated list offers Japanese culture, alternative thinking, finance, Norse and Germanic, ultimate frisbee and rocketry. Poultry society boasts its own hens; whether they are ever eaten is set to be a college myth. Our curiosity was piqued as to what goes on at the Gentlemen's Club (no-one seemed to know); presumably no cigars.

The careers office has a 2,000 strong network of former parents and corporate contacts: a recent event invited 40 such to the Dulwich Picture Gallery. Boys were instructed to read up on everyone's biographies then were sent off to network fiercely.

Boarding: There are 130 boarders, two-thirds in the sixth form, majority from China and Hong Kong but also Eastern Europe. The boarding houses are on the campus, modernised period houses decorated with OA sporting team photos: quite basic in our view, small-ish rooms with less than luxurious en suite bathrooms, but unlikely to worry most boys intent on studying and playing hard surrounded by friends. Common rooms with large screen for movie nights, table football and all-important toasters.

Background and atmosphere: Founded in 1619 by the wealthy actor and businessman, Edward Alleyn. He set up and endowed the Foundation, which distributes its surplus profits to a group of schools including Dulwich College, JAGS and Alleyn's. The college moved to its present site in the 1870s. The main buildings are stunning Italianate red brick designed by the son of the architect of the Houses of Parliament. Inside, the panelled Great Hall lined with the names of Oxford and Cambridge scholars – up until the wall space ran out in the 1960s – has featured in a Hollywood film or two, more often the site of Old Alleynian dinners, the master's library and the Wodehouse library (PG is an Old Alleynian), with a significant theatrical archive including a Shakespeare First Folio.

Sitting amidst vast manicured pitches, the college is a gracious and intriguing south London landmark. Closer up, the collection of modern buildings forming a large part of the teaching spaces, particularly in the lower school, are plain and nothing more than functional, quite possibly a bit depressing. The buildings housing the upper school feel fresher – Ed's place looks like a commercial café, and there is a huge common room, whilst a second one was sacrificed to create a popular 'work room' with banks of computers. Ironically for a school that appears so stunning to the passer-by, it's the fabric of the school which could currently disappoint parents if not boys.

However, much of that is set to change – we donned hard hat and work boots to inspect the almost complete Laboratory, costing over £21m, which will put the college's science offer ever more firmly on the map. The first phase opened in April 2015, the second is due to be completed for summer 2016. Led by prestigious Grimshaw Architects – Cutty Sark, The Eden Project – It literally removes

the divide between arts and sciences, including a 240 seat auditorium, as well as five IT suites and 18 glassy labs looking over the beautiful trees of Dulwich.

At its centre is displayed Shackleton's boat, a treasured college possession previously residing appropriately enough with a stuffed penguin in a chilly cloister. Conrad Shawcross RA, with a committed team of 10 boys, worked on an installation. Naturally it leads the way environmentally too. The finishing touch, which may transform the feel of the college as much as anything, is the bright idea of removing the central car park, replacing it with landscaped recreational and thinking spaces.

The Dulwich College partnership schools overseas thrive, the latest in Singapore, but the master is clear that Dulwich is his absolute focus: he has delegated all but top level sign-off. Similarly, although he has championed outreach and partnership with a London academy group, a pie-chart of time devoted would see this account for only 10 per cent.

Sartorial traditions define the college – 'colours' blazers are boldly striped affairs awarded in recognition of achievement. 'Buy a big size,' advises the school captain – they will be de rigueur come OA reunions. You need a spotters' guide to identify old school ties, there are so many for every society and event. The master sees the Christmas fair attracting 3,000 local residents as a way to prove that the school isn't 'stuck up'. He is aware that the uniform gives off mixed messages, but wants the boys to wear it with pride. Believes the school is and should be 'class, creed and colour-blind'.

School lunches seem due for a make-over, but boys won't starve. Students we spoke to in the lower school were amusing, boisterous; those higher up articulate, but not at all arrogant, and

all with different interests. A regular visitor to the school said, 'The boys appear relaxed and happy, there's always plenty of banter and camaraderie in evidence'.

Far more inclusive than one might imagine, the new bursary scheme needs to be trumpeted far and wide to ensure the school is on the radar of the brightest from all backgrounds

Pastoral care, well-being and discipline: A senior prefect told us he's a rarity, having been at the school all the way from year 1, but has relished meeting new boys – 'each intake year interests and friends shift' – and although the school is large, boys feel they know each other within their year. The transition points are handled thoughtfully, ensuring boys get to bond with each other, for instance on a Welsh adventure when joining the lower school.

Houses are named after great Englishmen, and wooden boards throughout the school see Drake, Spenser et al jostling for position – house competitions facilitate new friendships as well as much rivalry.

We were on the look-out for indifferent pastoral care, but found no evidence for it whatsoever, instead much praise. A parent – 'Boys know where they stand with the master, and whilst he's friendly and approachable, boys know he won't tolerate certain misdemeanours...hard line on bullying'. Another, 'He strikes the right note on being nurturing but also seeing that the boys get on with being independent'. 'A caring atmosphere which celebrates the individual,' said a parent of a child diagnosed with ASD. One noted realistically that 'pastoral care is good, but the biggest problem is to get the boys to overcome male pride and admit they need help.' Gross misconducts such as possession of drugs or bullying would result in consideration for exclusion, whether fixed term or permanent, rather than an automatic exclusion.

Pupils and parents: The college is academically selective and socially inclusive, with a very culturally and ethnically diverse population, augmented by the boarders. Lots of multi-lingual children who might speak Chinese, Russian, Spanish or French at home. Boys mentioned pupil-led assemblies: recent topics include homosexuality and discrimination. The school captain said: 'There is no Dulwich way. You don't have to conform.'

A parent: 'It takes boys who are sporty, academic, musical, artistic and a mixture of all those things. If your child is gifted in one area, they will soar here. If they are a good all-rounder they will be encouraged to be a great all-rounder.' And it may come as a surprise to find that parents describe each other typically as 'a good bunch of mixed, non-stuffy parents', 'un-snobbish and not cliquey.'

Entrance: Not the ultra-elite intake of a few London schools, but still a top 15 per cent ability profile. At 11+, half of the 75 boys arrive from Dulwich College Junior School and half from a variety of local primary and prep schools including Hornsby House, Blackheath Prep, Rosemead, Dolphin School, Oakfield, Honeywell, Belleville, Corpus Christi, Dulwich Hamlet, St John's and St Clements. Parents are asked to send a letter from a registered professional regarding SEN needs to ensure appropriate assistance with the entrance exam. At 13 + the main feeders are Dulwich Prep London, Northcote Lodge and Fulham Prep. Non-refundable registration fee of £100 for Brits and £200 for overseas candidates.

A good number come from the immediate vicinity of Dulwich, but Foundation coaches brings pupils from as far away as Notting Hill, Canary Wharf, Wimbledon and Chislehurst.

Exit: Pupils recently exited to over 47 universities, a list headed this year by Warwick, but closely followed by UCL, Durham, Bristol, Exeter and Manchester. Oxbridge places are consistently around 10 per cent (17 in 2015). There is an increasing focus on global destinations, particularly Ivy League. Currently around a dozen each year exit to overseas universities – often the Chinese University of Hong Kong, a couple to Harvard,

Dutch universities in the slip-stream but the list has also included MIT and UCLA.

Money matters: Currently 411 boys in receipt of financial assistance of various kinds – 145 have means-tested bursaries ranging in value from five to 100 per cent and 266 have scholarships, ranging in value from 10 per cent to one-third of tuition fees. 'Superb value for money,' said one parent of three privately educated children. 'Quite simply, Dulwich College far outstrips the rest in terms of communication, professionalism and results'.

Perhaps most exciting of all in terms of evolution is the college returning to its early 20th century past in launching a New Dulwich Experiment, championed by the master, which will see up to 50 per cent of pupils coming from families who cannot afford to pay full fees, opening up admissions to some of the brightest pupils from all backgrounds. In some ways it is a protective measure against becoming a school for the global super-rich, and the master freely admits it is 'enlightened self-interest', but partly funded by OAs keen to give something back, it sits very well in this already socially enlightened place.

Remarks: A school with a long tradition, with all of the prestige that comes with it, but now with a thrilling new dynamism which is raising the academic ante in every way, creating glittering new learning spaces and delivering a stunning co-curricular vision. Far more inclusive than one might imagine, the new bursary scheme needs to be trumpeted far and wide to ensure the school is on the radar of the brightest from all backgrounds.

Dulwich Prep London

42 Alleyn Park, London SE21 8AT

020 8670 3217
registrar@dulwichpreplondon.org
www.dulwichpreplondon.org
C of E

Ages: Boys 3–13, girls 3–4
Pupils: 850
Boarders: 20 weekly
Day: £10,830 – £16,845 pa
Boarding: plus £4,455 to £4,950 pa

Headmaster: Since 2009, Michael Roulston MBE MEd (50s). Married with three children, educated in Ulster, he is warm and friendly, zipping about and offering to 'play mother' with the Darjeeling on our visit. First impressions aside, one senses his combination of vision, drive and no nonsense was forged during his first headship in the 1980s at The Model School – an informally religiously integrated school in Northern Ireland. His contribution to conflict

resolution in the field of education was recognised by the BP Gulbenkian Citizenship Award in 1994.

After a stint in Japan as headmaster of The British School in Tokyo, earning him an MBE for services to education, he returned to the UK as head of Cranleigh Prep in Surrey. This is a man who clearly thrives on challenge and change, with his eye on the prizes – his and the boys'. We see him as a definite moderniser, sprucing up the old traditions, delivering a slickly presented school with a few fashionable nods – boules, allotments – without straying from his brief of happy parents and pupils at common entrance. Prior to our visit we had heard him described by parents as being 'rather like a successful CEO'. We found him to be business-like certainly, but not stiffly corporate. Yes, very 'on message', but sincere too.

He says of the school, 'It's fun, full of energy from the earliest years all the way though...every day you cannot but be inspired by what the boys do. They are valued, recognised and well-loved'.

Head of the pre-prep since 2011, Mrs Ruth Burtonshaw BSc Phd PGCE Dip dyslexia and learning, is an early years specialist.

Entrance: Admission is selective. Multiple points of entry but majority start in the nursery at 3+ (girls and boys), at 4+ (boys only) or at 7+ (boys only). Limited number of means-tested bursaries to new applicants in years 3 and 4, determined by academic assessment.

Exit: Don't think that entrance to DPL is a do-not-pass-go ticket straight to Dulwich College, but a large proportion of pupils do gain entrance – with others heading in a variety of directions, foremost Westminster, Alleyn's and Tonbridge. Recent leavers exited to 28 different schools. Conversation regarding choice of senior school starts as early as year 4, and headmaster claims that every boy achieves his first (guided) choice of destination. Good tally of academic, sport, art and all-rounder scholarships or exhibitions, with many scholarships offered to Dulwich College. Only two or three boys a year choose to leave at 11+.

Remarks: The main curriculum is fairly traditional. French from year 1 and everyone tries their hand at Latin. Spanish offered as alternative to French. We found the lack of fashionable forward-thinking options such as Chinese or Russian surprising when even the local state primaries are giving them a go. The Head says Mandarin has been offered as a club in the past, but there was little interest.

We were wowed by the boys' 3D acrylic sculpture after Jackson Pollock, and the excitement in the room as the boys made sophisticated digital animations

Setting in maths from year 4, extended to all examined subjects by year 7. This really works, with parents confirming there is sufficient flexibility for boys to move within the year to find the right level for them, and to be encouraged by their ability in different subjects. In each of the classes we visited, young male teachers were particularly noticeable, in amongst the boys or sitting on desks, easily relating to the boys in lessons ranging from European history, via maths to music technology. Energy fairly resounds and parents of pupils at the lower school, particularly, describe it as 'buzzing'.

Almost 20 per cent of boys are identified with a learning difference, mainly mild to moderate dyslexia. The head says that the school will do its best by all, but any with significant difficulties may find themselves guided to a more specialist school such as Fairley House. Highly-trained specialists lead a good number of staff in the learning support department. We saw great learning integration in the older years with dyslexic boys using laptops alongside their peers; parents confirm that boys don't feel singled out in any way if they need extra help. Nonetheless, some comment with feeling on just how tough it can be and wish for a little more two-way communication with teachers.

Sport is well resourced, with fixtures both after school and on Saturdays. Seven full-time PE teachers, specialist coaching from year 4, more than 70 teams, and achievements at national level, particularly in rugby and swimming. Every boy has an opportunity to play. Parents say coaching is less good at the lower levels, and whilst clubs offer exciting opportunities from rock-climbing to kayaking, 'alternatives to the obvious sporting options are very limited in the younger years'.

Homework is as ever controversial. One mother comments that whilst the boys love the varied topic work, parents find it 'never-ending' at weekends.

Drama varies from year to year. There is a year 6 play and an upper school play each year. Year 7 classes have drama and each year 8 class is off time-table for two weeks to produce an original production. Art continues to year 8 with clearly inspiring teaching, new facilities and technologies. We were wowed by the boys' 3D acrylic sculpture after Jackson Pollock, and the excitement in the room as the boys made sophisticated digital animations.

Music is rich, appealing and widely pursued, with over 20 ensembles and choirs, concerts of every type at venues in and out of the school, such as the Royal Hospital, Chelsea and Southwark Cathedral. Ninety per cent of the boys from year 2 upwards study an instrument, many achieving grade 8 before they leave.

Clubs (only a few additional charges) and activities run at lunch-time for boys from years 1-4, but also 4-5 pm from year 5. Current options include Lego, Warhammer, movie-making, bee-keeping, street dance, juggling, Greek, golf and gymnastics. Wide array of trips – no stone unturned on the London museum circuit; further afield during school holidays (often built into the fees) eg Pompeii and Normandy. All this plus a thought-provoking lecture series – featuring recently a holocaust survivor, notable writers, broadcasters and adventurers.

The school was founded as Dulwich College Prep School (DCPS) in 1885. Despite the confusion arising from its name, the school is completely independent from Dulwich College and is an educational trust with its own governing body. This has recently been clarified with the school now styled as Dulwich Prep London (DPL). Situated in a wide, quiet West Dulwich street a few minutes from the train station, the buildings, mostly fairly modern, crowd around the playground.

With just over 800 pupils the school is large, but we saw how the division of the school into four distinct sections, each with its own library and classrooms, really works – 'the boys are quite protected from feeling lost in a huge place, and they're fully prepared for moving on,' says a parent.

Parents from the nursery year to higher up the school all comment on the benefit of a single sex school where teachers are free to focus on knights, dinosaurs, bloody battles etc. If there's one thing this school seems to do brilliantly it's the ability to really 'get' boys and how they learn and put this into practice. There is wiggle time (dancing around between lessons), marble parties or even a pool table as a whole class reward – 'the motivation and excitement are huge'.

The school motto is 'one for all and all for one' and the houses are named after North American Indian tribes from Chippeway to Objiwas. The winning tribe raises their flag weekly up the pole in the playground and if this is all sounds incredibly macho, we hear the boys sometimes choose to sing ABBA as their victory song! Meanwhile others, who choose the calmer activities from book club to weaving and needlework, do so without fear of ridicule. Some parents transfer from a co-ed environment for exactly this reason.

While the head's emphasis on character and kindness rings true – right on cue we witnessed children relating the story of the Good Samaritan to their day – a couple of parents commented that it can take a good while to find your niche. 'If you're not good at sport, you're not popular in the playground.' This is a school which aims to develop 'resilience'. When asked which kinds of boys would be happiest here, parents suggest: 'the bright and the best', 'a self-starter, bright and athletic', 'you've got to be robust'.

No surprises that the majority of parents are highly affluent, most living within an expanding 10 mile radius of the school. However, we hear that there is a healthy mix from the scarily ambitious to the more laid back, so there is a good chance of finding like-minded souls.

School has one boarding house called (not so aptly in our opinion) Brightlands; this can accommodate 25 weekly or flexi-boarders from year 4. Rather a sombre looking house with a garden next to the pre-prep, it's been recently redecorated, and though the housemaster and his family are young and welcoming and boys rush around busily, we spied scary paint colours downstairs and 1950s style curtains in the dining hall. We wondered how this rated as a home from home compared to the boys' weekend surroundings. Definite fun, though,

is one week a year when years 5, 6 and 7 stay from Sunday to Thursday; they experiment with life away from home and gain the Tomahawk Award for life skills such as button-sewing and bed-making.

The pre-prep early years department is a stunningly designed new-build – all wide open flowing spaces, blending indoor/outdoor, the classrooms give way to a huge covered sandpit for wet days. It has a delightfully green outlook surrounded only by playing fields, woodland and the grounds of Dulwich Picture Gallery. Nothing locally compares to the rural feel of this setting, a great comfort for any parent who didn't expect to raise their children in one of the world's biggest cities.

Girls are the minority but are carefully selected and more than hold their own. Parents of girls have little need for concern – except getting them in: applications are over-subscribed. Rainbow Club, staffed by regular teaching staff, offers care and activities pre and post school, from 8am to 4.45pm.

The head assists in girls' applications to local private and state schools. Almost all the boys move up to the prep.

Dulwich Preparatory School Cranbrook

Coursehorn, Cranbrook, Kent TN17 3NP

01580 712179
registrar@dcpskent.org
www.dcpskent.org

Ages: 3–13 (boarding from 9)
Pupils: 570
Boarders: 57 flexi
Day: £5,445 – £16,125 pa
Boarding: £42.50 per night

Headmaster: Since September 2010, Mr Paul David BEd (40s). Married, with two children at the school. Grew up in Cornwall and read maths and education at St Luke's, Exeter University, where he played rugby. Started his career at the City of London Freemen's School, where he taught maths and games, was head of cricket and became a housemaster aged 28. Moved on to Colet Court, where he spent four years as deputy head and taught rugby across all ages and maths to the senior boys at St Paul's School. He then spent eight years as headmaster of Eaton Square School, a mixed ability London prep.

Energetic and dapper, and requires his surroundings to be dapper too – everywhere is immaculate with not a weed or piece of litter in sight (pounces on any he spots). Spiders with any sense of self-preservation have long since picked up their webs and gone elsewhere. Lots of fresh paint on the walls and vases of flowers all over the place. A very visible presence around the school,

attends assemblies at Nash House and Little Stream each week and teaches maths and games in Upper School.

Came into the school after a period of disorganisation had rather unsettled parents. Tightened everything up from manners and pastoral care to redesigning the uniform. Each class now has a weekly greeter who will welcome any visitors and engage them in conversation – head very keen that children should know how to talk to adults and look them in the eye. Parents delighted, teachers too, as far as we can judge (they clearly were made to feel part of the process). Children seem at ease with him. This editor was struck, above all, by how this big, beautiful but soulless school had at long last a feeling of character and style about it.

Not everybody's cup of tea – the Guide and Mr David never hit it off in his previous incarnation – but appears perfectly suited to Dulwich Prep, and vice versa.

Entrance: Priority for siblings, but otherwise on a first come, first served basis. Non-competitive assessment tests from age 7+ – very rare for a child to fail but school doesn't want to take someone who can't cope. Intakes in nursery, reception, years 3 and 5 (and in between, if space). Another intake in year 7, when some children leave for the grammar schools and others come from local primary schools to prepare for Cranbrook entrance at 13+.

Exit: The raison d'être for many for going to Dulwich Prep is to get into Cranbrook at 13, and about half do just that. Fifteen per cent leave for the grammars at 11 – the school takes a positive attitude and is happy to help, but this is not grammar school country (the good ones are quite distant). Otherwise the most popular schools are Tonbridge, King's Canterbury, Kent College, Claremont, Ashford, Benenden, Sutton Valence, Eastbourne, St Leonard's Mayfield, Sevenoaks and Bethany, with a few going further afield to, eg, Charterhouse, Bedales and Winchester. Good selection of academic, art, music, sports and drama scholarships, particularly to Sutton Valence.

Remarks: Established as a war evacuation camp for Dulwich College Preparatory School (now Dulwich Prep London) in the orchard of the then headmaster's father-in-law's land at Coursehorn, and allowed to survive as an independent, unconnected entity when the war was over. Set in 50 acres of grounds, it has a campus-like feel.

The school is divided into three self-contained sections: Nash House (3-5 year olds), Little Stream (5-9 year olds) and Upper School (9-13 year olds). Children from the age of 6 are split into four Tribes: Chippeways, Deerfeet, Mohicans and Ojibwas – lots of inter-tribe competitions and activities.

Nash House and Little Stream (both recently rebuilt; all classrooms opening onto the garden and outdoor retractable roof – light and airy with lots of space) are set away from the main school in interconnecting buildings. Lots of computers and interactive stuff – Mr David a fan, but school has been well stocked for years. Own swimming pool. Superb library, IT and facilities generally in Upper School.

Every class now has a weekly greeter who will welcome visitors and engage them in conversation – head very keen that children should know how to talk to adults

Structured but relaxed atmosphere in Little Stream with lots of theme days. Children are awarded brightly coloured ribbons for good work. Great emphasis on building children's social confidence and they are encouraged to stand up in front of an audience on a regular basis, whether it be relating their news in assembly, taking part in form plays or participating in class 'showing times'. Structured mornings and child initiated afternoons; children spend as much time as possible outside. Outings, talks and workshop days a major part of the curriculum, particularly in history and geography. Specialist teachers for PE, French, science (taught in a lab) and music.

Gets more serious in upper school. Children setted (where possible) for academic subjects, apart from a separate scholarship form in the final year. Average class size 18, maximum 20. Latin for all from year 6 and about 50 per cent take it at common entrance. Authors visit every term, also library competitions and twice yearly book fairs. Educational outings a major feature of school life.

Learning support for maths and English offered as part of the package – either in class, withdrawn in small groups or one-to-one, or as instruction for parents in how to help at home. 'Special needs department on hand to give extra help where necessary.' What this all amounts to is unstinting and unshaming help for (about 20 per cent of) children to get into Cranbrook etc.

Music strong – fab Little Stream music suite decorated with semiquavers; all learn the recorder from year 2 (we feel a wave of sympathy for tortured parents whenever we read this, but violins would be worse) and can learn other instruments from year 3. All children can read music by the time they leave Little Stream; Upper School has a music director and three full-time music specialists. All children have two or three class music lessons a week, and almost all learn an instrument with one of the 19 peripatetic teachers. Lots of extracurricular groups including an orchestra, two wind bands, six choirs, a jazz band, pop groups plus a number of smaller chamber groups. Music tours in Italy, Germany, Holland, Paris and Austria.

Separate Stream House art room with an artist in residence – very creative team – with children's artwork everywhere (ditto upper school). Art clubs

Food praised by all with some quite adventurous choices – pigeon pie, monkfish wrapped in prosciutto – and proper puddings

after school, plus extra tuition for those taking art scholarships (usually wins a couple of these each year). When we visited the children were designing beautiful play houses which were going to be made up in India (no crumbling shelves for those parents). Art room open every lunchtime – jewellery to Scalextric model making. Jewellery making so popular that an evening class was laid on for the parents.

Upper school drama timetabled, with clubs and ESB exams for the enthusiasts. Wonderful John Leakey Hall.

Good sports facilities – well-equipped sports hall for upper school. Large outdoor swimming pool, tennis courts/all weather hockey pitches, eight-lane athletics track etc. Strong tradition of cross-country running for boys and girls. All the usual sports with teams in most: as many children as possible are included – up to four teams per year group and the school tries to have regular inter-school or 'tribe' fixtures. Opportunities to have trials and play for Kent teams.

Parent friendly. Nursery is very flexible and children can build up attendance sessions during the year. Parents welcome at any time to come in and see how their children are learning, and in particular to the Friday morning assembly, when the headmaster celebrates children's achievements and offers coffee afterwards. Even homework clubs and drop in clinics for parents.

Very strong pastoral care and children encouraged to be aware of each others' feelings and friendships issues. They can enter their own and each other's acts of kindness on the good deeds chart. Older pupils choose a member of staff to keep an eye on their academic progress and general well-being. No prefects or head boy or girl, but every year 8 pupil is a 'senior' with a specific area of responsibility.

Food praised by all with some quite adventurous choices – pigeon pie, monkfish wrapped in prosciutto – and proper puddings still on the menu. Children encouraged to try new foods – not British, you may feel.

Flexi boarding (36 boys, 21 girls) popular, with boys at The Lodge and girls at The Manor. School very accommodating (when they have room) if parents need to go away for a few days or on holiday. School day for boarders ends at the same time as for day children, and the boarding houses are very much 'homes from home'.

Most children live within about 15 miles of the school. No Saturday school, but optional Saturday morning academic clinics three or four mornings each term for pupils in year 8 preparing for exams. Lots of parents new to independent education, but great loyalty amongst old boys and girls (Old Coursehornians, after the original house on the site) and many children in the school are second or third generation.

Big. Superb facilities. Produces confident children who are happy and do well, and particularly suits those who are up front, determined and capable – quite a competitive environment. School has high expectations of everyone, but gives them a huge breadth of opportunity to succeed.

Eastbourne College

Headmaster's House, Eastbourne, East Sussex BN21 4JX

01323 452323
admissions@eastbourne-college.co.uk
www.eastbourne-college.co.uk
C of E

Ages: 13–18
Pupils: 635; sixth form: 275
Boarders: 292
Day: £20,940 – £21,300 pa
Boarding: £31,965 – £32,325 pa

Head: Since 2005, the affable yet astute Mr Simon Davies (50s). He broke out of the City in the early 90s when he decided that teaching the workings of futures and options to young bankers was more fun than his broker day job. After a PGCE, a progression through Oxfordshire preps where his roles included head of department, housemaster, the recipient of a transplanted kidney, father of three, deputy head at Bedford School – partnered through all by his wife Robina, who runs a literary charity and speaks at least three languages.

Big man leading a great team backed up by fantastic reporting and intelligent marketing communications, sometimes he bumbles, dissembling his acuity, since he says, 'it is very easy to forget your bulk and that your countenance is foreboding'. Knows everyone through teaching the college values to all year 9, biology to year 11, sixth form revision, and through 'an almost avaricious need' to remember details of pupils' lives.

Describes the college as Wisley Gardens (developing for the long term) rather than Chelsea Flower Show (exhibitionist) and the pastoral system as a lot of weeding, pruning and keeping the edges tidy – although his wife does the gardening nowadays; he's on Twitter instead. Relates to parents who take joy in what their kids become rather than pride in what they've made of them. Parents

615

feel he genuinely likes teenagers and has a sense of perspective – also an insightful metaphor about girls being penguins, huddling for warmth with a danger of ruthlessly excluding those on the edges, while boys growl and bristle like dogs on meeting, then run in a pack.

Passionate about finding the balance between challenging and reassuring pupils, managing (rather than interfering in) the process of their teenage years while ensuring they realise how good life is at an independent school. Excited about the 150th anniversary and site development which aims to concentrate the college resources and strengthen links with the town still further.

Academic matters: Everyone starts with a wide sweep of subjects, tasting everything until they settle down to GCSE choices; can take a selection of French, German, Spanish, Latin and Greek. Parents say not the place for the brightest of the bright but meets the needs of the very smart ones (and stretches – one ex-London prep pupil went up a set in most subjects after first year) while the value added in the classroom and out is excellent – as the head says, 'what really counts is how you work with people'. Lovely large science labs, six ICT suites, fibre optic network, three theatres, library with silent, chatty and headphone screen-watching areas – also an amazing three floor design technology centre.

Insightful metaphor about girls being penguins, huddling for warmth with a danger of excluding those on the edges, whilst boys growl and bristle like dogs on meeting

Four assistant heads, one dedicated solely to the curriculum, mean that each pupil can have a bespoke timetable according to their choices. Mind boggling yet liberating, since 'you only get children achieving their best if they are doing what they want to do'. And they do – whether sciences and languages or textiles, woodwork and product design: in 2015, 56 per cent of GCSE grades were A*/A. School day from 8am to 8pm means that parents have their day children home with no homework when they finally arrive – there is a 6pm bus for those who have nailed all their commitments for the day and commute from further afield (Rye or Tunbridge Wells). Houseparents and the co-curricular assistant head juggling sports, clubs and preps help synchronise multi-talented kids and single-minded staff and ensure 'whatever happens, the kids don't feel the pressure'.

Informative 'white book' provides a structure that the new pupils follow, empowering them to such an effect that a parent recently just sat back and observed as the parents' evening went on between the pupil and their tutor. School aims to include all SEN pupils where possible, but specific provision for mild dyslexia, G&T and EAL. One full-time and one busy part-time teacher. All children are screened on entry. Individual SEN lessons are charged for. No separate cost for the G&T provision, however, which is department specific.

Not a huge breadth of A level subjects – no psychology, sociology, politics. If demand is timely then senior management team will make it happen – RS has become an examination subject with intelligent wide-ranging debate. Maths, science and humanities most popular. In 2015, 49 per cent A*/A grades overall.

Entire jigsaw is monitored with the slick electronic report card which culminates in the tutor sitting down with the pupil and focusing on the past, present and what needs to be done. Input far more supportive than reflective as the houseparent adds their comments before a pdf report is emailed home at least twice a term. Parents are relieved by challenge grades rather than predictive ones (much more motivational). Continuous opportunities for parent or staff to monitor and add input when the issues arise and overseas parents particularly enjoy this access (10 per cent of pupil body). Ramps up staff's accountability to parents and Duke of Edinburgh, Oxbridge or scholar reports can be added for those interested. This transparent system was created by a full-time software developer, who continues to mine the data and present it to the staff via web-based platform, winding in pastoral incidents and academic progress, enabling a holistic view of the pupil when considering discipline or going up or down a set. Parents appreciate standardised teaching that makes it easy for a pupil to move between sets even mid-term.

Games, options, the arts: Activities and sport sandwiched between morning and afternoon of classroom learning suits the youngest ones especially. Myriad teams so that 95 per cent of the pupils take their turn to win or lose together against another school, and with elite talent emerging, there are Olympic or international professionals coaching in tennis, hockey, netball, rugby and cricket; major sports tours for these too. The manicured rugby pitch dominates the front of the school but the main sports fields are a five minute drive away – the girls in particular enjoy the walk for the warm up and catch up it provides. The range of sports currently on offer stretches from basketball to equestrian events (a bit more parental input) and there's zumba classes if team sport really doesn't appeal, or space to chat and

A recent charity bike-a-thon had girls and tutors staying up and eating pizza and supporting the 24 hours of pedalling

listen to music. All full-time sports staff teach academic subjects and are tutors as well, meaning that badminton, table tennis and jujitsu have emerged from clubs to potential fixtures by encouraging children's initiatives.

Development (to be completed 2017, one and a half acres in the centre of the site) will revolutionise the on site facilities, with a small hiatus for swimmers while they splash in other local facilities. This sharing of resources and experiences with the wider Eastbourne community is a pattern that is demonstrated by the architecture of the Birley Centre (public entrance on Carlisle Road) and the school values. The school's creative arts centre (next to the Towner Art Gallery and Congress Theatre) is a part of the town's artistic centre, with musicians from the school busking to raise money for St Wilfred's Hospice, professional artists coming in to run masterclasses in creative barter for the foyer exhibition space and a resident from the Rambert Dance company running courses for local state and private schools and the rugby team. Pupils are involved in all of these initiatives, as well as working with adults with learning needs and teaching pensioners to surf the internet.

Interlocking array of different sized lockers and muted practice rooms is testament to the orchestral music tuition (three choirs, a concert band and two orchestras) while Battle of the Bands is a highlight of the musical year, with a recording studio enabling music technology as an A level option. The art studios are light and bright with examples of excellent student work dotted around the school (routinely 100 per cent A*/A at A level and over 92 per cent at GCSE), plenty of Macs for digital editing and two kilns for firing experimentally glazed ceramics – all anchored by visits from artists making a living in the outside world. Paths to the commercial acting world also well trodden, a whole school production annually, while all year 9 put on a play in their first term and house concerts are really enjoyed – sometimes end up on YouTube.

Boarding: Separate day and boarding houses, so no day pupils feel they miss out on dorm time horsing about, and 6pm and 8pm buses give them the chance to 'organise their work, co-curricular activities and family life most effectively for them and their families'. All pupils are registered in the common room of their house, assemblies,

announcements here too; good facilities, each with their own garden; junior boarders share three to five to a dorm, reducing up to the sixth form, where they have large single rooms – the more modern girls' ones with en suite bathrooms. Real retreats, managed by the houseparents and matrons, with touches that appeal, whether a pupil-run tuck shop with entrepreneurial offers or a mirrored dance studio, girls plaiting each other's hair and boys kicking about on floodlit Astroturf. New development promises more open social space for boys and girls to mix (now mostly the atmospheric cloisters), with no dark corners and the staff common room next door. Majority of sixth form don't have boy or girlfriends at school; boarders get town leave on Saturday night; they hang out with each other in the holidays too. Younger boarders explore restaurants in Eastbourne too and petition their parents to come and take them (and all their friends) out for lunch.

Background and atmosphere: Founded in 1867 with the seventh Duke of Devonshire allotting 12 acres to the new enterprise, the current Duke is president of the Eastbourne College council along with influential Eastbourne residents. Main school is an imposing red-brick building, amid an aesthetically pleasing mix of others, old and sympathetically new and ensconced in the heart of Eastbourne, with five-storey Victorian houses, retirement homes and boarding and day houses all cheek by jowl. Parents see three main communities in this part of Eastbourne, the old people, the young people and those who serve those two communities – many staff live on site or very near; 'kids walk around old people with respect and the old people are safe in the knowledge they won't be mugged!'

Close to the railway and next to Devonshire Park, home to the pre-Wimbledon men's and ladies' tennis tournament; constant traffic of hearty pupils hurrying to lessons; friendly, happy and confident teenagers, who all belong to a single sex day or boarding house. This is their home from home, but they can invite others to come and knock about between preps. In the lower years this means mostly single sex hanging out when not in lessons or activities (whether on comfy sofas or around a pool table). Everyone eats as a school (new dining hall on the horizon); good food with an excellent range of choices.

New sixth formers are welcomed, those from local state schools make new friends and keep their old ones too, broadening the sixth form across all backgrounds and outside the college. Some drive themselves in from more rural homes, others keep younger ones company on the train commute. Chapel every Sunday for boarders and visitors, otherwise one weekly service – with alternative arrangements possible for other faiths – a spiritual basis but nowadays more about a collective act, with thoughts about the wider community.

Pastoral care, well-being and discipline: Very, very strong indeed, with excellent and insightful communication; the first thing all happy parents say is 'they really know our kids'. Probably why it is so successful at reaching all abilities and improving the confidence of many. Housemasters and housemistresses are first point of contact, for day pupil parents on drop off or pick up, for those further afield on email and phone. Often issues have a plan to sort or are sorted before a parent even learns about them, within a school day. 'Families' in girls' houses, with a mother in the sixth form, a cousin in year 10 and peer listeners. Support in boys' houses is organised less metaphorically but the same relationships develop – older ones sit in on prep; not a chore to help with studies, this opens conduit for buddy support and cross-year friendships. A recent charity bike-a-thon had girls and tutors staying up and eating pizza and supporting the 24 hours of pedalling.

We heard concrete examples of issues dealt with empathetically, tactfully and effectively, whether they stemmed from a staff or a pupil incident, with the children's welfare held at the centre. House and school prefects are in the upper sixth; head says, 'not a position for privilege but for service'. Drinking and drugs stamped on hard (although supportive testing if drug use happens out of term), deputy and assistant head of pastoral are fully aware of the range of misdemeanours, from shaving a head, roughing up playing football, through to sexting – and the electronic system enables rapid staff communication on spotting patterns or a change of routine.

Pupils and parents: Varied social mix, with children that are spread across all four quartiles. On one side you have the Sussex Downs and the rolling Sussex countryside, the other side the deep blue sea. Fifty-fifty day to (no flexible or weekly) boarding, farming families who have been coming for generations, more recent locals who also have horses, London boarders and the international contingent (10 per cent) of Chinese, German, Russian, Italian, Spanish and Nigerian. Only 90 minutes by train from London; boarders have exeats every three weeks but Saturday school does cut the weekend short. Parents don't mix much away from the touchline or horse events, unless they know each other from prep schools, although more social functions are being organised.

Entrance: Overseas pupils are accepted provided their level of English is proficient. Candidates for year 9 entry sit CE or the college's scholarship papers. The hurdle for sixth form is B grades or better at GCSE. About 35 pupils enter for sixth form from surrounding state or private schools.

Exit: Very small number leave post-GCSE (15 per cent or so). At 18, mainly to a mix of redbrick, Russell group and vocational colleges; four to Oxbridge in 2015; some 25 per cent take a gap year; Durham, Exeter, Leeds, Manchester, Newcastle and Nottingham popular over the last few years. Old Eastbournians come back to talk about being a pilot, farmer, doctor or graphic designer at the careers fair, just one of over 50 events organised by The Eastbournian Society for alumni, parents, staff and current pupils.

Money matters: Scholarships available for most subject areas (five to 20 per cent) and means-tested bursaries for up to 60 per cent of the fees. The registrar is very switched on, candid and efficient – his practical approach much appreciated by parents, especially if their financial circumstances change. Foundation director oversees the fundraising and bursary fund. He is aiming to build a pot by contributions from parents and staff to allow financial help to the struggling. The headmaster introduced the idea of all staff contributing the price of a pint per week to the fund. This equates to approx £250 a week and thus £15,000 a year. This philanthropic pint fund consequently translates to a) a full bursary for a fortunate and worthy pupil and b) a thirsty staffroom!

Remarks: A school for families who take joy in what their kids become rather than pride in what they've made of them. Bespoke timetables backed up by outstanding pastoral care make for happy and stimulated kids who work and play hard.

Epsom College

College Road, Epsom, Surrey KT17 4JQ

01372 821234
admissions@epsomcollege.org.uk
www.epsomcollege.org.uk
C of E

Ages: 13–18 (11–18 from 2016)
Pupils: 749; sixth form: 333
Boarders: 185 full, 198 weekly
Day: £22,590 pa
Boarding: £30,267 – £33,318 pa

Headmaster: Since September 2012, Mr Jay Piggot, BA MA PGCE (50s). Previously headmaster at alma mater Campbell College, Belfast between 2006 and 2012, and, before that, put in 17 years at Eton (clearly a hard place to leave) starting as assistant master in 1989 and becoming house master 10 years later. Not bad going given that it was only his second teaching job: his first, immediately after completing his MA in English Renaissance literature at Liverpool, was at Millfield, where he taught A level/Oxbridge English.

Career success undoubtedly assisted by personality and appearance – quietly dashing, though doesn't overdo the leading man business. Gimlet vision, too – noticed and swiftly dealt with errant piece of rubbish – a very small plastic wrapper, only one in otherwise immaculate grounds.

Lordy, lordy, what a popular man he is. Pupils – 'a joy,' he says – say he makes an effort to know names, comes to matches and makes with the social chit chat. Biggest vote winner, however, are the birthday cards – otherwise sophisticated international pupil clearly thrilled with his, particularly handwritten signature – cynic had

checked authenticity with damp finger just to be sure.

Parents also like what they see. Innovations all welcomed. 'Very proactive behind the scenes and has pushed through some sensible changes,' says one. Definitely a step up from predecessor. 'School ran well but didn't have the personality.'

Lordy, lordy, what a popular man he is. He makes an effort to know names, makes with the social chat

College was already known to him before the headhunters came a-callling, and found vision, ethos and commitment very much to his taste. Younger son, a keen golfer, moved with him (older brother is going great guns at Eton).

'Would love' to teach again and might when has got through current to-do list, which is lengthy. Getting shorter by the minute, though. 'Some heads would take a while to work out what they were going to do,' says teacher. 'He's made lots of changes already.' Popular changes include axing of seasonal timetables, originally to make most of winter light, but cause of mega all-round confusion to all.

High profile reintroduction of matrons into the houses was an Eton-inspired development that's brought a caring, maternal touch (thus far, all women) to details such as tracking down missing shirts and sewing as well as control of rowdy element. Of even greater significance has been academic shake up, still on-going, starting with observation of every member of staff since he arrived, followed with ISI-style feedback. 'A privilege,' he says. (We're sure they feel the same). Many stay for years. No wonder, with perks headed (for many, though not all) by housing either on-site or within a few minutes' walk. 'My wife told me we're not going to move,' said one. Given Epsom property prices, you can't blame her.

Expect more pupil-organised activities sparking impassioned discussions that ramp up the intellectual temperature from tepid to mercury-busting

In addition to the introduction of heads of year, designed to add missing link identified in recent inspection, he's also not going to stand in path of old-timers who could be moving on to greater things elsewhere, while rejigging weak spots including A level languages and biology and GCSE English literature. Dynamic incomers, including former Uppingham head of modern foreign languages – similar developments in science – are being brought in together with fledgling new generation of bright young things adding oomph to lessons (occasional dullness one of few inferred criticisms in last inspection report).

Still more shaking up to come, however, essential given school's previous sleepiness and 'red-hot' competition – Wellington, Cranleigh and Charterhouse as well as St John's Leatherhead and Reed's School. Bumping up interior life of school is part of the process, with Eton's dawn to dusk (and beyond) intellect-boosting programme the inspiration for mind-expanding programme – expect more pupil-organised drama, musical and debating activities (medical, history and politics societies are already on the go) sparking impassioned discussions that ramp up the intellectual temperature from tepid to mercury-busting.

Mark of success? Would like popularity of places to increase to the point where competition for boarding places as strong as for day hopefuls.

Academic matters: One of formerly mid-ranking schools to have substantially upped game in recent years. Fun lessons got pupils on the go, literally so, with movement minus the music, A level students standing up for miracles (theology) and marginal cost (economics) – everything, in fact, but their rights.

Parents, while agreeing with head that some teachers are 'past their best', think generally offset by vast majority who are 'engaging, personable and, most importantly, able to motivate. They appear to love their subjects and to enjoy teaching and the company of the children – none of these are a given, in my experience.' Megawatt enthusiasm often a game-changer, especially at sixth form level. Sciences score particularly high conversion rates. 'Was my dream to be a translator – now it's chemistry,' said pupil.

Ability to devote time to all (an impressive 55 hours contact time a week) means that 'there are no lost causes,' says head. Plentiful tracking and feedback means pupils know where they are and how they can improve, feedback seamlessly integrated in lessons. 'We put down our comments when we've had a test and it gives teachers a good idea of where we are,' said sixth former.

Though class sizes aren't teeny tiny – average 20 for GCSE (maximum 23) and between 10 and 12 at A level (15 max), with pupil to full time teacher ratio of 8.4 – school is consistently good when it comes to added value, setting in maths, banding in languages and sciences (where small group of less able students might do GCSE dual sciences rather than IGCSE triple). No-one takes 'silly' numbers of GCSEs, says senior teacher – aim is to ensure good grades in manageable quantities.

Currently, results generally very good given relatively mixed intake, with 71 per cent A*/A grades at GCSE; 81 per cent of A level entries graded A*/B and 51 per cent A*/A in 2015.

Good, largely traditional subject range, almost ology-free – 'nothing against psychology but it just isn't us,' says teacher – though language options now include GCSE Mandarin, originally for overseas students but now open to all. However, MFLs not the strongest suit, with few takers at A level – maths and economics much the most popular.

Hugely dynamic head of DT is also bumping up recruitment, particularly amongst girls, by ensuring that environment, full of technological marvels – though it's pupils' superb mortice and tenon joints and chamfering skills that help pull in the A* grades – is also tidy ('was grubby and fragmented') with plenty of wood-turning (apparently the secret of cross-gender appeal).

Big feature is Extended Project Qualification (EPQ), a mini-dissertation that, at best, combines originality and staying power (recent topics include carcinogens in food and madness in Henry Vlll's court – separately). Worth the effort. One pupil, down an A level grade and out of university course, called department head and used hers to talk her way back in again. No doubt that attracts the very able – one pupil, exile from leading girls' school, delighted to be somewhere that praised good work rather than training spotlight on pupils only when failed to deliver top grades – though one parent queried its suitability for the truly brilliant. 'Might be a bit too comfortable,' she thought. 'It's a broad church and some kids are too bright [and] shouldn't be there.'

Extra scaffolding where needed, with clinics all the way through the school in all key subjects and teachers not just present (many live in) but in many cases 'always available.' That said, school isn't geared up to cope with anyone with more than mild learning difficulties. Of the 100 or so pupils with SEN, none is currently statemented, SpLD the overwhelmingly dominant need, though have coped with (mild) ADHD as well.

Plenty of emails home and 'progress reports every three weeks,' ensure that everyone knows what's going on, while lengthy school day (finishing 6.00pm) incorporates sufficient free periods for the organised to sock it to the homework.

And though initially gentle pace startling to alumni of non-stop pushy preps, school gets praise for stress-appropriate levels of pushing tailored to each child. 'They know which way to push,' says mum of recent leaver. 'The teacher told my child that she "might get an A in biology GCSE, but I don't think so".' Nettled, daughter was spurred on to do just that.

Games, options, the arts: Sport success plentiful – boys' and girls' rugby VIIs regular regional winners, lots of post-school success, too (five OEs play for Harlequins), ditto hockey (mixed seniors won Surrey U18 competition), as do minors with 2012 Captain of Golf driving his way to Stanford Golf Scholarship (first European for over 10 years, says school) and shooting. Facilities generous – including swimming pool – and, in case of one of two sports halls, close to giant-size (even better when new sports pavilion up and running), two cracking sports halls, one giant sized, six squash courts, a swimming pool and a fencing salle, No partridge in pear tree (but would undoubtedly be doing a few press ups if there were).

Outside, timetable pushes variety – first years will have both outdoor and inside sports in an afternoon and, further up the school, non-standard sports can be done off site – riding, for example and climbing, until school got its own climbing wall.

Range ensures that 'you're not penalised if you're not sporty,' thinks a mother, with matches for all. 'Sport is very important, whether you're A team or D/E/F team material,' agrees another parent. Sports captains, rated by the rank and file – 'positions are well earned,' thought one – have a real say in team structure. 'You can discuss team composition with the coach and that's good,' thought pupils. Termly activity sheet encourages pupils to experiences shock of the new. One boy, initially dreading jive dance, discovered instead that he was 'that sort of person' – and loved it.

Plenty head for D of E, room for all (can add more staff if demand is high). CCF feather in school cap – one of oldest and biggest in country, teeming with facilities, (we liked esteem-heavy 'confidence' rather than assault course). Wears success lightly – numerous impressive sports cups casually behind bars with the guns).

Arts also attacked with relish. Music felt to be 'on the ascendant,' thought teacher, with lots of instrumental lessons – drums, singing, electric guitar and piano the biggest sellers, some reaching diploma level; challenging, performance opportunities ranging from low stress impromptu recitals to high quality productions including The Cunning Little Vixen and excellent chapel choir, masses lining up to audition – a macho-free area, reckoned year 9 and 10 pupils. Those not making the grade can 'let voices develop' in non-selective Glee Club instead.

Visual arts, recently upgraded, feature confident, instantly recognisable year 9 pictures of Kew Gardens – one of many trips. Everybody gets out a lot, DT excursions to real factories (Brompton bikes to Henry vacuum cleaners) so popular that school staff sign their Sundays away, too, school chef enjoying outing to Cadbury's as much as pupils.

Boarding: Similar numbers for full boarding (102 boys, 83 girls) and weekly (143 boys, 55 girls). Boarding houses, dotted round the site, now all done up to the nines – matching up to head's aspirations to equal best in Britain – with decking and glass snazzy-ness. Sensible trouble-preventing measures include half-termly dorm swaps and plenty of weekend activities for full boarders, from trips to Thorpe Park to house evenings and bowling. 'Never lonely because lots going on,' said sixth former.

Buddy system helps combat homesickness (most reckoned that worst was over within first week), one house even creating own surrogate family, one year group per generation and organising popular old fashioned sports day as an ice-breaker. Here, too, matrons, add much appreciated extra tea and sympathy layer (housemistresses – always academic staff – can 'sometimes be more of figure of authority,' thought sixth formers).

Background and atmosphere: Altogether a civilised place to be, starting with laid-back parking regime, permitted along one side of the one way road that winds round the lush green campus (new upper sixth drivers are vetted by the head), imposing chapel at its heart. Though patron is HM the Queen, not a high-society institution. Started life as the Royal Medical Benevolent College, a charitable

Boarding houses now all done up to the nines – matching head's aspirations to equal best in Britain – with decking and glass snazzy-ness

Good Thing, helping the relics of deceased impoverished medics. Strongly Victorian in spirit and execution – most buildings completed between 1850s and 1920s. School wasn't welcomed by all, overt charitable status 'distasteful' to recipients, reckoned contemporary letter to Lancet.

Took only boys for the first 120 years or so (sisters presumably expected to marry their way to economic success); girls added 1996 largely as emergency recession-busting tactic (local area had suffered heavily and pupil numbers had plummeted). Now, of course, school wouldn't be without them and they're on almost equal terms in the sixth form, though minority partners in other years. Desired ratio is 60:40 is, thinks head, about right, ensuring girls have the same options as boys, particularly when it comes to games. 'All get the chance to contribute,' he adds, firmly. No complaints from girls themselves, or parents, so seems to be working.

Though it's all 19th and early 20th century authenticity from the front with 'real wow factor,' thought parent, sold on first visit, tasteful modern extensions stretch back a considerable distance to the rear (current bursar, a woman, was a former architect, and it shows). Behind public face is 'pupil world', the second sweep of buildings where most of the teaching takes place. Modern additions – humanities building particularly palatable – don't jar (though some areas, like maths and theology blocks, could be nicer, and almost certainly will be when funds permit).

When it comes to décor, different departments exhibit endearing idiosyncrasies – from pot plants in chemistry lab (and sign announcing 'nudisme interdite au delà de cette limite') to blue-painted English rooms (also notable for friendly clutter of framed posters and attractive display boards already filling up nicely in second week of term) while modern languages is all-purple (even down to lampshades). Black wall in one of physics labs, however, is for sensitive experiments and 'not because we're pandering to goths,' explains larger than life department head.

Technology warmly embraced with Wifi throughout (and 'extreme' internet safety settings triggered by word 'Middlesex') and the Hub, new high tech room where lessons can be recorded for posterity. Tradition equally enjoyed but not pointlessly so – most of original medical artefacts

and stuffed animals that once dominated science rooms have gone. 'Antiques dealer took the rest,' says teacher, cheerfully.

Pastoral care, well-being and discipline: Seniors a strong force (and will be even more so once head succeeds in replacing current sixth form block with something altogether spiffier). Take turns to lead assemblies that are so far removed from commonplace fare that we had to double check that searingly articulate reflections on 9/11 were being delivered by sixth form girls. It appears effortless. No wonder – it's been in rehearsal since June, points out the friendly chaplain. Older pupils keen to stress that 'hierarchical system associated with traditional English boarding school, pitting year group against year group' is 'a terrible idea' and will pitch in to take sides if older boys show signs of picking on younger ones. 'It's part of our role and it works.'

Little in the way of serious misbehaviour, however, with just two pupils 'withdrawn by parents' (expulsion by face-saving euphemism) in senior teacher's 15 years. Drugs issues in both cases, though it's very rarely the end, behind the scenes second chances often possible. Day to day, class silliness and late homework the main issues, reckoned pupils, with escalating sanctions – lines, notification of tutors, warnings, departmental then school detentions – rattled off by all.

Lots of rewards, too – from pizza or chocolate for work-related merits and distinctions to privileges of seniority – sixth form day girls cited joy of leaving sports kit on shelves in study rooms instead of trekking, when younger, to go to separate storage area.

And though house system (separate for day and boarding pupils) engenders ferocious sense of competition (choir contest in particular), it isn't carried over into lessons, 'which stops it becoming tribal,' reckoned parent.

Pupils and parents: Predominantly local intake with vast majority of pupils, including 95 per cent of UK boarders, living within 10 to 15 miles. School keen to expand the range but, meantimes, results in happy fusion of streetwise Londoner with leafy Surrey-ite, reckoned teacher – cool without the ennui.

Many staff have own children here (has peaked at 40 or so). One parent we spoke to who'd opted for local alternative thought numbers were excessive – though appeared to be a lone voice. Working mums – far more these days – were something of a feature to the point where socialising tends to feature nights out to ensure 'you don't feel out of the loop,' thought career-driven mother.

Cosmopolitan feel added by international component (largeish at 20 per cent) drawn from Hong Kong, Malaysia, Russia and Korea, though many more from western Europe. For the 10 per cent who are non-native English speakers there is a structured EAL programme in place, but they're fully integrated into the curriculum says the school, 'right from day one'.

Malaysian numbers probably not affected by opening of sister school in Kuala Lumpur in 2014 – first foray into pastures new, as 'there will always be pupils who want a UK education,' reckons school.

Entrance: School is after all-rounders with several strings to their bow and 'fair share of the bright pupils'. Once a second choice regular, increasingly a bill-topper, recruiting from over 40 preps and state schools, likely to increase as it extends reach (Danes Hill and Downsend, Shrewsbury House, Aberdour and Feltonfleet feature prominently though no official feeders). Full-on charm offensive attracting south west London schools.

Different departments exhibit endearing idiosyncrasies – pot plants in chemistry lab (and sign announcing 'nudisme interdite au delà de cette limite')

Main intake (around 130 candidates) in year 9, with January pre-test in year 6 (VR – scores of around 118-120 the norm – NVR, English and numerical skill plus interview), same again (minus NVR) for non-prep candidates in January of year 8. Lots of scholarships on offer, over 230 currently, 43 (sport, art, drama, music and all-rounder) at 13+, value between £500 and £1500 pa.

Boys' day slots normally full by the end of year 6, boarding fills up last, best hope for last-minute applicants though gap closing. Once 'day pupils were brighter and more studious' than boarding pupils, thought one insider. No longer the case.

If no joy at 13+, small number of places at 14+ (three to five only, English, maths and NVR tests). Second biggest influx is post-GCSE with 45 to 50 joining the sixth form, following VR, NVR and numerical skills tests plus interview. Push to up state school numbers (currently around 20 per cent of the total) as a way of 'supplementing the ratios'. Some haggling after AS results with handful of pupils whose D and E grades give cause for concern. Repeating year not an option, dropping a subject can be the solution.

Will open a Lower School (years 7 and 8) in September 2016. Entry via maths, English and VR tests plus interview in January of year 6.

Exit: No shortage of ambition, most achieving first choice unis; Exeter, Bristol, LSE, Loughborough, Nottingham, Warwick, Durham, Edinburgh, SOAS, Manchester, Oxford Brookes and Queen's Belfast are top 10 university destinations; three to Oxbridge in 2015. Economics and finance followed by business, geography and sociology popular though, despite high quality art as A level option – and photography just added – it's currently not being pursued as a degree option.

Money matters: Annual bursary spend close to £750,000 on up to 100 per cent of fees. Possible additional financial support for families with medical connections through the Royal Medical Foundation, based at the school, though since 2000 a separate legal entity.

Remarks: With demographics and parent power going his way, head's boarding aspirations could well be realised. 'A brilliant school for my son,' said mother. Another commented that school had got 'everything there was to get' out of her child. 'You really can't ask much more than that'.

Feltonfleet School

Byfleet Road, Cobham, Surrey KT11 1DR

01932 862264
office@feltonfleet.co.uk
www.feltonfleet.co.uk
C of E

Ages: 3–13 (boarding from 7)
Pupils: 400
Boarders: 48 weekly and flexi
Day: £10,890 – £16,020 pa
Boarding: Weekly £22,020 pa

Headmaster: Since 2012, Mr Alastair G Morrison BA PGCE (40s). Follows 12 years as deputy head and director of sport at Fettes College Preparatory School. Before that, three years as class teacher of Edinburgh Academy Junior School.

Bitten by education bug when shared a house with two teachers at Durham, saw them in action and was won over by variety and fulfilment.

Instant appeal of school took trauma out of first foray south. 'Love being here,' he says on the website. Family immersion is total, what with smiley wife Lizzie, arts and ICT whizz, now 'fully supportive HM's wife' and three daughters all attending the school. Even dog gets own portrait on the 'Who we are' notice board. (Bursar, not an animal lover, isn't keen but as 'doesn't like humans either,' jokes school insider, it's staying.)

Zest, opportunity and confidence, 'the benefit that boys and girls reap from learning' (always good in a school) are some of fab reasons that, says head, puts this establishment 'in the front rank.'

Slightly stiff-sounding formality in print is in marked contrast to relaxed affability in the flesh. Parents unanimously keen. 'Approachable and friendly, cheerful and bubbly,' says one. 'You just want to eat him and take him home,' drooled another.

Officially 'doesn't take himself at all seriously,' proof provided by skills with the dressing up box. Has delighted all by appearing as the Pink Panther. 'Took everyone by surprise,' says parent. More conventionally, donned kilt for Foreign Countries day (in suit and tie during morning of visit, but we're sure he has suitably patriotic knees).

We'd lay odds, however, on necessary layer of igneous rock lying just underneath charm and soft accent, essential when there's law to be laid down and assertive parents to be tackled. 'Definitely strong enough to deal with that – no pushover,' thought mother.

Considered a breath of fresh air to point where parents wonder if hasn't got some of local schools running scared. A little over-stated, reckons Mr Morrison, though is unquestionably ambitious, sights set on making school first choice all the way through rather than acceptable reserve.

Mr Morrison is also charged by governors with bumping up boarding, turning it from current niche add-on – despite considerable perks including extra subject tuition as well as, says school, 'super' choice of fun stuff – to over-subscribed wanna do (expect heavy duty puns round theme of Feltonfleet Knights). With Sir William Wallace, St Joan of Arc and St George all likely to feature, could make for entertaining Saints vs Sirs tournaments...

Though extensive transport links suggest bit of own goal (why board if you can bus daily from Wimbledon?) school won't go the day-only cop-out route. Irreplaceable depth and richness added by boarding makes it a non-negotiable.

What won't change is school-wide emphasis on importance of treating others as you wish to be

Plentiful wildlife, some real (popular guinea pigs, available for cuddles, and tadpoles, who aren't), others artistic creations

treated. Signs promoting head's motto: 'Be kind, be kind, be kind,' started by predecessor and dotted round the school, show every sign of going strong, from refusal by pre-prep staff to hand out party invitations unless whole class invited (we wish it happened everywhere) to prompt quelling of pitchside bad behaviour, parental support now so low key that Mr Morrison is having to put out message that small, selective outbreaks of cheering are perfectly OK. Useful particularly when, as referee, is on business end of choice abuse from opposing teams.

Anxious parents should feel reassured. 'Sounds corny but there's something intangible here which is very warm and special,' says Mr Morrison. 'My predecessor has handed me a lovely school and we're not going to change in too much of a hurry but keep pushing in the same direction.'

Entrance: Though no longer as non-selective as it used to be, exam success still 'not the be all and end all,' thought one mother.

First come, first served nursery entry means, says Mr Morrison, that 'broad range of ability inevitably comes through.' Parents well advised to be fleet of foot, successful bagging one of just 20 places achieved by registering at (or possibly during) birth.

Competition for 35 external year 3 places less of an extreme sport, though popularity growing so fast that border controls in form of maths and English assessment plus interview 'to search out character and enthusiasm for learning' are now in place. (Own year 2 children aren't tested). No official feeders, though The Rowans, Wimbledon College Prep, Lion House, The Merlin, Weston Green and Glenesk all feature on suppliers' list.

Lots of behind the scenes liaison to ensure smooth transition to prep, extra support formalised in year 5 (English and maths), setting introduced for most subjects in year 7 – in class and one-to-one support for 11 EAL and 80 or so SEN pupils a fixture on the menu, head's desire to ensure barriers posed by learning difficulties are surmounted tempered with realities of what can be achieved. While classroom disruption, if severe, point at which school says no, parents praise thoroughness of approach. 'They did assessments and have been all over it – definitely worth it,' said one whose child has mild difficulties.

Occasional places also crop up, year 7 next biggest entry point following some post 11+ departures at end of year 6.

Judging by children we met, school's character-judging abilities are first rate, pupils to a boy or girl displaying a maturity, vivacity and sense of fun that made them outstanding tour guides (and some of the hottest – blazer-clad, through choice, on boiling June day).

Exit: Good guidance on future schools. St John's, Epsom and Reed's remain the obvious destinations in 2015 (and prominent fixtures on scholarship list) though most of big names (Eton, Wellington, King's Wimbledon, Hampton, Brighton College) put in occasional appearances.

School has right connections, reckon parents, head cultivating contacts, scholarships hovering round 16 mark (around two academic, very successful for sport).

Some year 6 departures inevitable, says Mr Morrison, 'mainly those who parents perceive would struggle with CE.' Makes equal boy/girl split in each year group commendable, though with year 7 places easily filled, virtue pays off.

Remarks: 'Really lovely,' say parents, who warn against being over-influenced by either location (side turn off fast road makes for 'hairy' arrivals and departures, says one mother) or building work (new performing arts centre, now open, was under construction on date of visit).

Occasional cement mixing aside, charm is order of day. Calvi, the separate building for nursery to year 2 pupils, winningly equipped, from own hall to shaded play areas (trees a feature everywhere) with big sandpit and marked out scooter track, library that doubles as ICT room (now re-christened Digital Learning Facility – good tinies' tongue-twister, we'd have thought), double-banked computers forming orderly row down the middle.

Sensible child and parent-friendly touches, from box packed with named bottles of sun cream by door on sunny days to big, smiley puppets adding comforting touch to office. Plentiful wildlife, too, some real (popular guinea pigs, available for cuddles, and tadpoles, who aren't) others artistic creations (we liked jellyfish hung at optimum viewing height for the under-7s; adults compelled to peer through forest of dangling paper fronds, Sir David Attenborough-fashion).

Homely domesticity extends to main prep building (mid-19th century Victorian gothic), which opens out into sweep of green, stretching away down gentle slope towards grass pitch, idyllically bounded by woods, dipping pond much used by all year groups, boarders given exclusive romping rights once day children have gone home. 'Wouldn't even guess space was there,' says parent. 'Like a little hidden pocket.' Weekly and flexi plus day boarding options – latter can include a full boarding day without the sleepover.

Here, as elsewhere, essential to shut ears to competing clamour of A3 that borders one side of site, though pupils oblivious, head ditto, despite home so close to slow lane that recently extending kitchen has brought them within number plate spotting distance (governors are considering acoustic barrier – we hope they get it).

Head's study, essay in dignified blues, gets best of panoramic views, where life 'is all happening in front of you,' says parent, from matches to pleasant end of day tradition of biscuit distribution, children flocking in from all over grounds in response to telepathic signal beamed out by biggest box of bourbons we've ever seen, like navy-clad pigeons.

Something of a sanctuary for those arriving from nearby little prince (and princess) establishments, often breathing big sigh of relief at low tiara factor

Plenty of idiosyncratic charm throughout, from recently revamped junior block (years 3 and 4) classrooms with winning cosiness, colour and light to seniors' French classroom with miniature shop and restaurant, complete with groceries and chalk 'specials' board, much used for role play.

We'd also recommend viewing astonishing Latin room, folders block-banked by colour like giant Rubik cube, walls ringed with sturdy supermarket bags – one per child – for instant decluttering before tests, and even back-office, Perspex towers of meticulously labelled stationary boxes soaring to the ceiling, the whole like prayer to Roman god of organisation (if one existed).

Teaching styles similarly varied, shock and awe a science speciality, with prospectus (helpfully written in nice big typeface – boon for older first time parents) featuring open-mouthed wonder as Bunsen burner shoots impressive flames across lab. Most staff are 'lovely', says pupil. 'My son randomly said, "Mummy, I've got the best teacher in the whole world, because she's really kind",' confirms pre-prep parent.

Best, judging by quick-fire exchange with prep pupils in English lesson to tease out clues in short story, are also brilliant, though zeal not yet universal, thought parents. 'Some are not as motivated as I think they should be,' reckoned a mum.

Years 1 and 2 stick broadly to national curriculum (as was) with specialist teaching for French, PE, swimming and music and get shot at DT, too – as well as input from grand-sounding and popular director of digital learning who sweeps in to 'enhance use of computer' – visits nursery and reception, too. Options grow with age, array of tempting additions bulked up in prep, judo to trampolining all good, food tech so sought after that canniest book up in winter, the longest term.

Surprise subject addition all way through from year 1 is positive living, new(ish) big hitter on PSHE timetable, stopping in year 7 (when perhaps pupils are so positive expectations need to be hoicked down slightly).'Love it,' says pupil. 'It's about living a happy and good life.'

Useful antidote to emphasis on emotional resilience made much of elsewhere. 'Saddens me that it's seen as necessary,' says Mr Morrison.

Maximum class sizes of 18, optimum size for lively classroom atmosphere, reckons Mr Morrison, and overall teacher ratio is around half that (one to just over nine) ensuring help for any waifs and strays (almost universally true, save for one child whiling away whole class reading session by reconfiguring contents of pencil case, apparently unobserved).

Parents generally delighted with academic running, bar desire for a little more in the way of help both with exam preparation – 'Child didn't even know how to revise,' thought one – and additional feedback outside formal parent teacher meetings. 'Have to assume no news is good news,' says prep parent. Mr Morrison is on the case with 'eye on the reporting structure,' he says, also stressing staff responsiveness to parental concerns whenever and however expressed.

A few will relate to sport. Strong range on offer (netball, hockey, rounders and lacrosse basic range for girls, football, rugby, hockey and cricket for boys, swimming, cross-country and athletics for both). Fab facilities, too, indoor swimming pool, all-weather Astroturf and 'suite' of cricket nets most recent to be added to 25-acre site which already accommodates yodelling-quality sports hall, hard surface tennis courts and two rifle ranges (air and .22) on top of scenic sports fields. All tucked in neatly, consistency of design making additions easy on the eye.

School recognises not just talent but wholesome attitudes by awarding internal sports scholarships to year 7 pupils (does same with drama and music). Strategy is to seek out challenge, everyone representing the school regardless of talent, plenty of tolerance for the rugby-averse – not the case elsewhere. 'Often the nicest boys who do hockey,' said year 7 pupil.

Mega results in shooting – teams beat everyone everywhere, including older siblings in senior schools (Wellington and Epsom College). Coach, who travels here from Wales 'because he likes us' secret weapon. Success not always replicated elsewhere, felt parent. Enviably good sportsmanship comes at a price – teams losing when, says Mr Morrison 'I know that if they had wanted it a bit more, they could have done it.' Delicate balancing act, thinks parent, who reckons top layer of loveliness needs to be scraped away and long-buried competitive instincts excavated so sport can take off. 'Winning matters, that's how life is, you get the job or you don't get the job. School needs to teach pupils that should love to win but that it's OK to lose.'

Performing arts popular and wide-ranging, one year 3 boy renowned for tap dancing, budding actor in year 6 making West End début. Drama high in pupil approval ratings for raising serious issues (bullying, gender wars) but not neglecting humour. 'Emotional but funny – what you'd find in everyday life,' said year 7 pupil of recent production.

Music draws in many, courtesy of good peripatetics ('nicest school I work in,' said one) almost half learning instruments, talented hitting grade 5 and up, occasional prodigy whistling through to diploma stage, orchestra supplemented by different single-instrument ensembles (flute and wind) as well as choirs (junior and senior), rotating timetables made easy with yellow badge reminders distributed daily. 'You're not going to forget with this hanging off you,' says pupil.

Something of a sanctuary for those arriving from nearby little prince (and princess) establishments, often breathing big sigh of relief at low tiara factor (or gender neutral equivalent). That said, parental attitudes, though NFS (Normal For Surrey) can prove unwelcoming for incomers. Fine for those in at the start – 'joined in nursery and our friends will be friends for life,' said one mother – but can translate to 'cliques and Queen Bees,' according to parent who joined further up the school and felt Mr Morrison might usefully beam 'be kind' message into minds of some adults, too. 'Am hoping [his] influence will trickle down.'

Ditto consideration. Some irritation over parking habits of minority who cope with what one parent describes as 'wholly inadequate' spaces by routinely usurping slots reserved for minibus. 'Seem to feel that so special or busy those normal rules don't apply,' says another parent. Other (minor) niggles include lost property black hole which can suck in objects for months, then mysteriously spit them out again – whereabouts in the meantime a mystery. Recruitment of year 8 prefects to scan changing rooms reducing the problem, reckoned pupils, though excessive spoon feeding should be curbed, thought mother. 'Kids have to learn the responsibility for keeping their own things in check.'

Amongst all parents we spoke to, biggest gripe was reserved for uniform. Tons of it, some sensible or suitably traditional (woolly blazers, nice looking and sufficiently robust to stand repeated use as ad hoc goalposts, a case in point), others tending towards overkill/slightly bonkers, headed by summer only fleece. And don't get parents started on the ankle socks, dark blue with – go faster? – stripes. Justifiable in summer, with khaki shorts, less so in winter with long trousers 'when can't see them anyway.' 'Needs a cull, or at least a rethink,' thought parent. Good news, courtesy of Mrs Morrison, who feels exactly the same way, is that it's getting one.

With the Morrisons running the show, atmospheric school seems set for still better things to come in years ahead. As long as the kindness that really does emanate from delightful pupils remains, it's a gem heading for disco ball sparkle (but without corresponding tackiness). Expect more bullseyes – and not just in shooting.

Frensham Heights

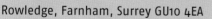

Rowledge, Farnham, Surrey GU10 4EA

01252 792561
admissions@frensham-heights.org.uk
www.frensham-heights.org.uk

Ages: 11–18
Pupils: 519; sixth form: 85
Boarders: 54, 45 weekly/flexi
Day: £16,950 – £18,795 pa
Boarding: £23,775 – £27,810 pa

Headmaster: Since 2004, Mr Andrew Fisher BA MA DipEd (50s). A relaxed, breezy and natural educator. It's in the genes – his grandfather headed Repton and became a bishop, his father was head of Geelong Grammar, a brother heads an international school in Belgium and other relations have run schools both here and in Australia. Mr Fisher – 'Andrew' (everyone is on first name terms at Frensham) – still sounds Aussie, despite 20 years in the UK – the first 10 spent at Wrekin College, where he became head of English and, finally, deputy head (pastoral), and you can immediately see why – the pastoral aspect, that is.

This is a practical, hands-on head and one of the roundest pegs in the most circular hole we've met. He's a motivator and a believer in people. Parents pay tribute to, especially, his skills as a communicator: 'He is a complete star and inspiring,' 'he can speak equally well to parents and children,' 'extremely human and talks to everyone as individuals,' 'he keeps you in touch, even on minor matters' and so on. Wife, Catherine, is deputy head at one of the local large sixth form colleges attended by one of his daughters, the other a pupil at a local comprehensive at time of our visit. A likeable, unpretentious head – we queued for lunch along with everyone else – no way he'd jump to the head of the queue – and he clearly values highly his relationships with the pupils: 'They treat me with great respect but it's not based on traditional school values. I can laugh at myself.'

Academic matters: Not 'selective' as normally understood – this school is more concerned that you join them for the right reasons than because you will help them soar to league-table-topping prominence. A smallish school, so not the hugest range of subject options at GCSE or A level. Very high pupil:teacher ratio makes for lots of small group and one-one support. Impressive results in Eng Lit; the three sciences, when taken separately, also impress though most take IGCSE double award. Blissfully small classes for eg RE, ICT. No Latin, no Greek. Photography taken – spectacularly – as an extracurricular GCSE with huge numbers and great success – see below. All A level subjects taught in small groups – much appreciated by students. English, maths, geography, history, art most popular and most achieve A*-C with around 40 per cent of subjects getting A*/A. Only a few take langs, including some native speakers. Sixth form seen by some as being less rigorous academically than it might but the newish head of sixth is 'driving up standards,' we were assured. And 'we are upping our game in stretching the gifted and talented'. Parents concur. 'Not hothousing doesn't mean they can't achieve highly,' affirmed one. In 2015, 42 per cent A*/A at GCSE and 40 per cent A*/A grades at A level. Disappointing library which doubles as café and place to sprawl in breaks with little evidence of its books being used.

Newer buildings nestle in trees and witty sculptures sprawl on the lawns and in foyers – we loved the slumbrous wire rabbit ('the little kids curl up its ears')

Loads of support – eg maths clinic each lunchtime. Not great for wheelchair users as the site is huge, bumpy and has steps. Main House not wheelchair-friendly at all. But school will try to take anyone they feel will benefit – mild SEN are catered for with enthusiasm and dedication and some families shared between Frensham and nearby More House for those with greater needs. 'My daughter had one-to-one for her reading and her reading age

jumped two years in a term.' SEN support is careful and threaded through the school.

Games, options, the arts: Think, Create, Explore is inscribed around the school and the vast menu of extracurricular options should tempt the most sluggish teenager to do just that. Bike maintenance, American football, boules, tap dancing, barbershop and various dance forms – before, during and after school and at weekends. Excellent new music block; around half learn at least one musical instrument in school – 'Frensham bends over backwards to find teachers if you want to learn some different instrument,' a budding soloist enthused. Masses of bands, orchestras, ensembles, choirs and performance courses through the veins of the school. Dance much praised and popular. Drama is well-provided for and central to the school. The theatre is a wonderful asset – it has everything and does everything – and is well used, as are the two drama studios and the little wooden outdoor theatre on the front lawn. Performance values are high with a healthy, pervasive culture of it being OK to perform. Creative drama team under innovative long-serving head of dept. Outstanding photography under even longer-serving, inspirational leadership and now with unique facilities for techniques old and new. Brilliant, diverse and poly-faceted artwork – we were truly struck by the rigour and values underpinning the skills and the freedom pupils were given to develop as they needed. Witty ceramics, clever textiles, wood and resistant materials productions with mind-opening themes explored with structure and solidity. 'Art and drama must challenge me,' says Andrew. Arguably, the most impressively led art dept in the country.

Sports are enthusiastic, various and 'improving', according to parents, though some feel they could and should be better. School points out that they are now competing against much bigger schools and taking part in various national cup competitions. 'Outdoor education' is important – there is forest school, the outdoor Terrace Theatre, the swimming pool in the walled garden and loads of activities to develop outdoor skills – D of E gold award taken here and the whole school breathes in its own glorious 'outdoors'. Facilities – indoor and out – are certainly conducive to performance but one senses that real energies go into creativity rather than goalscoring.

Boarding: Boarding arrangements changed in 2014 to become co-ed throughout the school. Hamilton House accommodates the 11-13 year-old boarders – boys and girls housed on different floors. They share a breakfast room/kitchen and a large garden. Main House houses the older boarders – girls and boys in opposite wings and with entry codes. Roberts House, the sixth form centre – co-educational from

its inception – is unchanged and is everyone's base all day: day pupils share studies and workspace. We knocked at a random door and found two lads in hoodies actually working and blinking at the disturbance. Whole school on fibre-optic broadband and Facebook etc blocked till tea-time. Boarding is good – decent sized rooms in the main though some singles are tightish; nice bright shower rooms and good kitchens. Exceptionally welcoming sitting rooms – especially 'The Sit', which looks like home. Food – very good, we tried it – served in big dining room with tables and banquettes and everyone eats ensemble. Full boarders in the majority (21 boys, 33 girls). Also 36 weekly and 9 flexi boarders. Around a third stay in at weekend and are busy – see note about extracurricular above. Powerful cleaning fluid smells almost knocked us over in several buildings.

Background and atmosphere: Charles Charrington, the brewer, acquired Fir Grove House on the edge of Rowledge village, overlooking a panorama of Surrey woods and hills and transformed it into Frensham Heights – an imposing gothic red-brick residence with turrets, leaded lights and stained glass, splendid Georgian-style interiors, cornices, architraves, fireplaces – the lot – in 1902, as a would-be ancestral pile. Alas, the first world war intervened and the house became a military hospital and, as the old order changed, was reinvented as a school by three redoubtable women – Edith Douglas-Hamilton and joint headmistresses, Beatrice Ensor and Isabel King. Ensor, an early proponent of Montessori education, was a theosophist, a vegetarian and an anti-vivisectionist. Fascinatingly, one of the teachers at the school in those early years was Krishna Menon. But the school's progressive credentials, being coeducational and liberal, were integral to its ethos from the first. Strangely, every head since its pioneers has been male.

Set in extensive woodlands and the older children trail 10 minutes through the woods to the village with its supermarket and sweetshop. Immense and meticulously kept grounds – Andrew pays tribute to the excellence of the financial management and, indeed, it is admirable that the place is so well maintained with so small a population of fee-payers. Newer buildings nestle in trees and witty sculptures sprawl on the lawns and in foyers – we loved the slumbrous wire rabbit ('the little kids curl up in its ears') and the jokey wax mushrooms, as well as the huge black panther.

No uniform – so everyone bar a few in uniform of hoody, leggings/jeans, sweatshirts, boots/trainers. It looks relaxed and sane – enhanced by the amount of linked arms and hugging we saw – more like a bunch of French children, we thought. Central to the ethos is personal maturity: 'They are given real responsibility,' one parent told us, 'and can take the initiative – the school's approach to that is excellent.' This extends to falling in and out of love, which, of course, they do, but we were impressed by the compassion and mutual respect with which this is handled. 'It does happen but anything more than a hug or kiss in public is frowned on and people are respectful of what others want to see.. if people break up, we look after each other,' a wise mid-teen averred. 'It's not for everyone,' said another. 'If you need real structure and routine it's not for you.' 'Conventional parents need to look beyond the informality and recognise that the pupils respect the teachers because of the way they treat them rather than because of the rules,' a less conventional parent asserted.

Pastoral care, well-being and discipline: Everyone agrees about the staff: 'It's almost personal tutoring – they know how I learn so they explain it to me how they know I can understand,' a bright sixth former told us. 'They encourage pupils to excel in music, art, sport – whatever they're good at,' said a parent. Also a sense of a recent tightening of discipline – especially on illicit fags and booze. 'Some people were getting cocky – they've cracked down on it now,' we were advised. But pastoral care universally praised: 'They're not heavy-handed over minor transgressions – they see them in a learning context but if you cross a line you'll be suspended.' And another parent: 'If you've got that much freedom you need the support to go with it.' A strong sense that mutual respect and mutual support is central to the ethos of the place.

Pupils and parents: Around 75 per cent day pupils who come from a radius of about 40 miles – Petersfield, Goldalming, Farnham. Boarders are weekly eg from London or from overseas and school

> 'Outdoor education' is important and the whole school breathes in its own glorious 'outdoors'. Facilities certainly conducive to performance but one senses that real energies go into creativity rather than goalscoring

has wise policy of not taking more than four pupils who speak any one language into any senior year. So penny nos from eg Russia, Germany, Croatia, Spain. Intensive EAL available though needed by very few. Notable Old Frenshamians include performers Bill and Jon Pertwee, Jamie Glover, David Berglas, Rufus Hound, Hattie Morahan; also Sir Claus Moser, Noah Bulkin (Merrill Lynch, Lazard, now entrepreneur) and Uber-fraudster, Edward Davenport.

Entrance: All candidates for years 7-9 are interviewed. Exams a week or so later – 11+ take tests in reading, writing, spelling, maths and non-verbal reasoning. Same plus a science test for 13+ candidates. Similar for occasional places which do occur. Sixth form places require six GCSEs at A*-C, ideally with Bs in A level subjects, 'but we're flexible,' says Andrew. School also sets its own papers for sixth form entry. Oversubscribed by 4:1 at this stage.

Exit: Around 40 per cent leave at 16 – mostly to the several large state (free) sixth form colleges round about, some few for the IB or for subjects not on offer here. All who stay get to their first choice university which suggests good guidance and realistic applications. To one of the widest range of tertiary education establishments we have seen. Many to creative courses – arts, design, music – but also the odd Cambridge entrant and others to study everything from architecture at Nottingham to geography at King's, London. Different, diverse, distinctive.

Money matters: Sibling discounts for third and subsequent children of 10 per cent. Scholarships and exhibitions in academics, performing arts, creative arts and sport up to £750 pa – so glory rather than gold. Means-tested bursaries in case of need but school has no endowments so not plentiful.

Remarks: A place to grow up in. Every kind of opportunity to become the person you are meant to be and to learn about others while you're at it. Civilised, liberal values with wraparound care and support. We loved it.

Handcross Park School

Handcross, Haywards Heath, West Sussex RH17 6HF

01444 400526
registrar@handxpark.com
www.handcrossparkschool.co.uk
C of E

Ages: 2–13 (boarding from 7)
Pupils: 320
Boarders: 20 full, 25 weekly
Day: £8,910 – £17,580 pa
Boarding: weekly £14,820 – £20,640 pa

Linked school: Brighton College

Headmaster: Since April 2011, Mr Graeme Owton BA (40s). Very approachable, energetic, enthusiastic and hailed as a good thing by staff, parents and pupils. Previously boarding housemaster at Feltonfleet Prep, assistant housemaster and English teacher at Wells Cathedral School, housemaster and English teacher at Wellington and short spell as head of Bodiam Manor (which fell victim to the recession). He has not always been in education – after leaving university (Brunel, English and education) he coached rugby in Sydney and returned a year later to do the same for the London Irish U21s. Eventually he had to decide between education and rugby; fortunately for Handcross he chose education.

Brought in mid-academic year after what some parents describe as 'a few years of coasting' that preceded previous head's retirement. He has implemented many changes with vigour, not least the merger with Brighton College, a timely union that is not only quelling rumblings of parent dissatisfaction and low numbers but also benefitting both schools. Brighton College has gained a country boarding prep with acres of playing fields just 10 minutes from Gatwick; Handcross Park has gained from joining the hugely successful Brighton College family of schools with strong leadership, sound financial backing and support from experienced governors and staff.

His new broom has swept clean where necessary, letting some staff go and appointing many new teachers. He has introduced philosophy for children to foster independent thinking and, rather more bravely, a parents' forum. Apparently he welcomes honesty, but with the caveat, 'Don't come to me with a problem if you can't think of a solution'. 'He says good morning to the children and stops them to repeat it if they do not make eye contact with him,' says one parent. His aim is to build a community of like-minded pupils, parents and staff and educate for the 21st century. He is obviously a strong leader and communicator, as the staff we spoke to echoed these values.

Married with two children, one of whom has started at the school, but the family do not yet live on site. Some might observe that if he wants to champion a family school and has expansion plans for the boarding element, a family move on site should be swiftly considered.

Entrance: Currently non-selective: assessment day plus reports and references from previous school. Pupils come from local nurseries and preps, but with expansion of boarding the catchment area is widening to Brighton, Crawley, Haywards Heath and London. Boarders (30 per cent) mainly from London, Forces families, a few from Europe.

The visitor is treated to a breathtaking approach down a long, roped track through extensive parkland

Exit: Pupils move to a variety of schools, including Brighton College, Wellington, Hurst College, Ardingly, Charterhouse, Worth, Stowe, Epsom College, Sevenoaks, Bedes, Eastbourne College, Christ's Hospital and Lancing. A number gain scholarships – academic, sport, drama, art, music and dance.

Remarks: School founded in 1887 as a boys' boarding establishment and after various changes of name and identity moved to Handcross Park in 1968, became co-educational and took day pupils. The visitor is treated to a breathtaking approach down a long, roped track through extensive parkland and pitches before coming face to face with redbrick mix of Tudor and Elizabethan.

Claims to be one of the first prep schools in the country where all pupils learn the world's top three languages: English, Spanish from age 2 and Mandarin from age 4. The aim is fluency in at least one major European language. 'The workplace is becoming increasingly global and competitive; it will give them the edge in the job market,' says the head. The director of studies explains they work on the philosophy of 'anti pressure but pro challenge', and some new parents commented how motivated their children had become since joining the school. 'The staff are a happy bunch and passionate about teaching,' said a head of maths who, like other staff, sings the praises of the newish head and the fizz he has brought to the school.

Progress in English and maths monitored via verbal and non-verbal reasoning tests, spelling ages, NFER assessments etc. Active tracking procedures considered rigorous enough to avoid any pupil slipping through the net. The school identifies and caters well for special needs from the outset – 'My child was seen to be struggling in nursery, received informal extra help and progressed to more formal support in the main school'. Learning support takes place in the 'dairy rooms' and staff are, apparently, 'great communicators... parents are kept in the loop throughout'. Others speak of the academic and social advances their children have made within this unit and how confidence building it has proved to be. 'We are never complacent and have been to other good schools to view similar departments, but concluded that none could be offering anything better,' said another parent. A high ability programme – some attend master classes at Brighton University. The English department is exceptional, say the pupils, and geography, maths, sport and art also got the popular vote.

Masses of art of all standards on display and pupils have the chance to extend interests via clubs (textiles, sketching, crafts). Music lively with junior choir for all and voluntary senior choir, plus orchestra, jazz, rock and recorder groups. Head of music and performing arts favours a balance of traditional and contemporary music. A drama production held each term with every child taking part in at least one production a year. Plans are afoot for a new theatre in time.

Everything from the usual hockey, netball, rugby and cricket to ballet, riding, street dance and cross country on offer, supported by a team of young and energetic sports staff. Glorious pitches, huge sports hall and Scandinavian design swimming pool. Head believes kindness should be the underlying ethos of the school, but what about on the games field, we asked? Sports staff on message, 'It is not just about winning (although that's nice sometimes) but about sportsmanship.' Parents and visiting teams are greeted by courteous pupils who hand out programmes with a map and a sporting 'code of conduct' just in case...

The pre-prep department is surrounded by high walls enclosing an enchanting 'secret garden' – its head told us that days there were 'all about exploring, challenging, listening, before they go on to learning more formally. We love to take the curriculum outdoors, offering anything but a sedentary education'. Music plays a big part in curriculum and pupils do Spanish every week, an early start to foster the Handcross drive for language learning. Lots of clubs on offer, some at extra cost, eg cookery, swimming, multisport, choir. Weekly 'wow' moments celebrate effort and achievements and a buddy system eases transition to main school.

Boarding house has had a makeover and been extended, but no prospect of flexi option, considered 'bad for continuity'. The rooms, fresh and light with views over the grounds, are almost hotel spic and span – not many personal touches. Are children really that tidy? Food considered excellent and boarders have input into choices and themed menus.

Handcross Park may once have been described as 'coasting' but it is now sailing full steam ahead. With the commitment, vision and energy of the head and Brighton College supporting the climb from good to outstanding, the school's future is set fair on all fronts.

Harrow School

5 High Street, Harrow on the Hill, Middlesex HA1 3HP

020 8872 8007
admissions@harrowschool.org.uk
www.harrowschool.org.uk

Ages: 13–18
Pupils: 830; sixth form: 350
Boarders: all full
Boarding: £34,590 pa

Head Master: Since 2011, Mr Jim Hawkins MA (40s). Educated at King Edward VI Camp Hill School for Boys in Birmingham and read maths at Brasenose College, Oxford (he was a year above David Cameron and knew the PM slightly). Did PGCE at Oxford

before first teaching job at Radley – perfect combination of teaching maths and coaching rugby and rowing. Head of maths at Forest School in Walthamstow, then deputy head at Chigwell School. Prior to Harrow he was head of Norwich School for

nine years – 'a fantastic school in a beautiful city.' Norwich went co-ed during during his headship but there are 'no plans' whatsoever to follow suit at Harrow. 'We are very happy as we are,' he says firmly.

Proud of the fact that Harrow enables boys to enjoy being boys. With a plethora of activities from dawn till dusk, he reckons the school suits 'the kind of boy who wants to take the opportunities we offer and throw himself into things.' He says education at Harrow goes 'way beyond the exam syllabus' and that there's 'no better place for the really bright boy with a strong attitude towards life and learning, the sort of boy who is going to contribute and soak everything up.' School sends loads of boys to Oxbridge but head is equally proud of those who 'work jolly hard to get their As and Bs. They are some of our great successes.' When we asked who the school wouldn't suit he was unequivocal. 'It wouldn't suit someone who wanted a sixth form college sort of experience. Harrow is a highly organised, very busy school and it's very clear what the demands are.'

Dynamic, focused and urbane, with dashing good looks. Still keeps his hand in at the chalkface by teaching 'a bit of maths' to the youngest boys at the start of the academic year. 'It's really nice to have 40 minutes when you are focusing on something entirely educational,' he says. 'The key thing as a head is to find ways of interacting with the boys. Without that you lose touch with reality.' He makes a point of having lunch with boys and in the 'beaks' dining room' when he can. Very sporty – he rowed for Oxford's lightweight crew and was captain of Brasenose rowing. Ran the 10-mile Long Ducker, school's annual charity race from Hyde Park to Harrow, in 90 minutes, though laughingly admits that the director of studies did a faster time.

They live right in the heart of the school (along with their cocker spaniel) and regularly invite boys to breakfast – 'bacon butties and croissants'

Loves his job, although he admits 'the highs are very high and the lows are quite challenging'. Says there are three main educational areas he wants to develop. First is the 'super curriculum' to encourage academic scholarship above and beyond the timetabled curriculum, research, independent thinking and university-style learning. Second is to look at preparing boys even better for university – he's already appointed a five-strong universities team with specific knowledge of Oxbridge, medicine and the US universities – and third is to concentrate on 'leadership and service'. School is already very active in local community (links with primary schools, tea parties for elderly, projects with Mothers Against Gangs charity etc) but head would like to do more. 'We want the boys to understand that leadership and service go hand in hand,' he says.

Wife Zoe is an artist and they have a young daughter. They live right in the heart of the school (along with their cocker spaniel) and regularly invite boys for breakfast – 'bacon butties and croissants.' Enjoys music, sport, reading and the theatre.

Academic matters: Teachers, parents and the boys themselves describe Harrow as an 'academic' school. Harrow's results don't appear in league tables – head says he's fed up with the 'one-dimensional snapshot' they deliver – but results are impressive. At A level in 2015, 67 per cent A*/A grades and 83 per cent A*/A at IGCSE. IGCSEs taken in English, French, German, Spanish, history, geography, maths, as well as biology, chemistry and physics. Drama and PE introduced at GCSE this year. Thirty-one subjects on offer at A level – all the usual, plus business studies, government and politics, history of art, music technology, photography and theatre studies, with a range of languages. Maths is the most popular subject at A level, with nearly two-thirds taking it. Half the boys do four subjects at A level rather than the usual three (one boy recently did nine). Sixth form electives are a recent innovation for sixth form pupils – a chance for boys to experience university-style teaching in specialist areas. Cerebral subjects on offer include programming, the history of western art, the greats of European philosophy, psychoanalysis and its impact on European culture, and financial mathematics.

Dazzling array of languages on offer – French, German, Spanish, Italian, Russian, Turkish, Polish, Japanese, Arabic and Chinese. All three sciences are compulsory at IGCSE. School has its own observatory with three telescopes and astronomy offered as a GCSE. At GCSE classes range between 14 and 20 pupils while at A level the average is 8.5 and none are greater than 12. School caters for mild dyspraxia and dyslexia. One-to-one help given off-timetable, at no additional cost. Dedicated band of teachers (or 'beaks' as they are known at Harrow)

It's where Professor Flitwick's charm classes were shot in the first Harry Potter film (lots of tourists gazing admiringly when we visited)

includes many writers of scholarly books. Women make up 19 per cent of staff.

Games, options, the arts: There's no doubt about it, Harrow is a very sporty school, with hordes of teams regularly trouncing their opponents. Sport played five afternoons a week, 32 sports on offer and director of sport encourages even the less enthusiastic to 'have a go' at something. Main sports are rugby, soccer, cricket and Harrow football. The latter is played with a pork-pie shaped ball which absorbs the wet and can be propelled by any part of the body. Even though it's played in the depths of winter and is a very muddy affair the boys love it and only wish more schools played it (Harrow is the only one). When we visited pupils were counting the days till their Harrow football match against an OH team. Last year lots of their fathers had played and there was even one grandfather in the side – 'but we were very careful with him.'

Vast expanse of playing fields, sports centre with indoor climbing wall, weights room, 25m pool and sports hall, courts for tennis, rackets and squash, nine-hole golf course and Olympic-sized running track. School boasts national champions in rackets, fencing, fives and judo, two boys playing rugby for England and number of cricketers playing at national and county level. The mother of a gifted sportsman was full of admiration for the way the school nurtured her son's sporting talent whilst keeping him focused on his academic studies and helping him achieve stellar grades. 'The school sees each boy as an individual and were very supportive and flexible,' she told us.

Head of music admits that when he arrived there was a perception among rival directors of music that Harrow was 'an old-fashioned school where little value was placed on music and the arts.' To his delight he found the reverse was true and there's a 'wealth of musical talent.' Half the boys learn musical instruments and 50 per cent of these achieve grade 8 or better by the time they leave. Practice sessions timetabled for younger boys. Loads of orchestras, choirs and strong tradition of singing. More than 100 concerts a year, with recent performances at the Royal Albert Hall and Royal Festival Hall. Steady stream of boys to top universities and conservatoires to read music too.

Excellent Ryan Theatre seats 400 and is used for school and professional productions but annual

Shakespeare productions take place in the beautiful arts and crafts Speech Room. A huge, wood-panelled half-moon, it boasts authentic Globe-style staging and seats the entire school. Wonderful art and, befittingly for a school where photography pioneer William Fox Talbot was a pupil, photography. There's no lounging around with nothing to do at weekends either – scores of extracurricular activities to choose from, everything from the Alexander Society for boys interested in military history to the Turf Club for horse racing fans.

Boarding: All pupils board at Harrow. We visited two very different houses – Druries, which dates back to the 1790s and is a maze of charming nooks and crannies, and the ultra-modern Lyon's, or the Holiday Inn, as a few wags have nicknamed it. 'It's the best piece of real estate around here,' joked one boy, hugely appreciative of its light, airy, five-star rooms. 'There's room for us to move around and not cause too much havoc.'

Each house has common rooms, games rooms (kitted out with plasma TV, pool and table tennis tables), garden and 'yarder,' an area where boys can run off steam and kick a ball about. Two boys sharing is the norm in the first year but by year 11 (or even earlier) they get their own room, complete with desk, shelving, computer and, occasionally, en-suite shower. All pupils' names etched on wooden house boards, with head of house's name picked out in gold. Boys can make toast and heat up soup in their houses – 'and the more ambitious make Pot Noodles,' said one boy. We trust he was joking. Meals are eaten centrally and food gets a firm thumbs-up – from us too, if the lunch we had with sixth formers was anything to go by. Boys are allowed to go out for a meal with their parents on Sundays but there's no weekly or flexi-boarding. Two weekend exeats in the autumn and spring terms and one in the summer.

Boys can make toast and heat up soup in their houses – 'and the more ambitious make Pot Noodles'

Background and atmosphere: Harrow is one of only three all-boys, full-boarding schools left in the UK (along with Eton and Radley). Boys have been educated here since the 13th century, but the school was founded in 1572 under a royal charter granted to local farmer John Lyon by Elizabeth I (Lyon's, the newest boarding house, is named after him). The aim was for the school to provide free education for 30 local scholars, a number later increased to 40 by the governors. School sits in picturesque Harrow on the Hill, surrounded by 400 acres and

with panoramic views across London – of it, yet remote from it, as we said last time. On a clear day you can see Canary Wharf from the head's study and it's just 25 minutes by tube to Green Park. Visitors to the undulating school site take note – flat shoes are a must.

School is steeped in tradition and history. The 17th century Old Schools contain the beautiful Fourth Form room, with names carved into every inch of panelling, from Byron to Robert Peel. It's also where Professor Flitwick's charm classes were shot in the first Harry Potter film (lots of tourists gazing admiringly when we visited). The stunning Vaughan Library, designed by architect Gilbert Scott (he also created London's St Pancras Station) has chess sets on tables and stays open late during exam periods. War Memorial Building commemorates the 633 OHs who died in the First World War. You can't help but be profoundly moved by the Alex Fitch Room, an Elizabethan wood panelled room with stained glass windows and a Cromwellian table, given by a grieving mother in honour of her 19-year-old son after he died in the First World War. She asked that it should be used for the purpose of boys meeting their mothers and that a light should always be left on over her son's portrait. Plaques and memorials commemorating quirky events are everywhere. Charles I rested here while preparing to surrender and little inclines have memorable names like Obadiah Slope, wittily named after Trollope's unctuous Barchester Towers character.

Harrow Songs are legendary. No Harrovian, either past or present, fails to mention the strength of feeling they engender and the lump in the throat they provoke. Songs have been an important part of the school since 1864, when the head of music wrote the first song, and they are considered to be 'a unifying force.' In November each year the whole school assembles in Speech Room in honour of its most famous alumni, Sir Winston Churchill, for the Churchill Songs. Like rival Eton, school has its own jargon. 'Skew' is a punishment, 'tosh' is a shower, 'tolley up' is permission to work late and so on.

Pastoral care, well-being and discipline: Pastoral care is meticulous, with highly structured system of resident housemasters, assistant housemasters and matrons. Harrow's 12 houses are integral to the school and boys are fiercely loyal to their own house. Some houses are regarded as stricter than others and parents we spoke to said it's important 'to pick and choose carefully.' One of the houses – West Acre – was recently the subject of an ITN documentary series, following the life of the school for a whole year. Housemasters in post for 12 years and as well as doing most of the admissions assessments each gives their house its character and reputation. They also work round the clock – 'at the beginning of every term I say to my wife "see you at the end of term",' one housemaster told us with a grin.

Harrow takes a pragmatic approach to technology and social media but the boys are so busy there isn't much time to sit around and play computer games. Pupils understand that bullying is 'completely unacceptable' and head says that it has plummeted, 'not down to zero, but pretty close.' School does a bullying survey every winter and housemasters, year group tutors, matrons, two school chaplains, health education tutors and school psychologist pick up on most things. Discipline is clear and firm but the place feels pretty relaxed, with boys knowing exactly where they stand. 'You are given freedom but if you abuse the freedom you would be punished,' one boy told us. Zero tolerance on drugs and use or supply in term-time or holidays means expulsion. Anyone found with spirits suspended and warned while smoking is handled through 'escalating sequence of sanctions imposed by housemasters.'

Smart uniform of dark blue jackets (bluers), grey flannels (greyers), white shirts and ties, plus, of course, Harrow's infamous boaters. Boys wear them or carry them and either love them or loathe them. They're allowed to write their names and draw pictures on the inner rim and spray them with varnish to protect them. Members of Philathletic Club (school's top sportsmen) get to wear bow ties. Sunday wear is black tailcoat and the whole kit and caboodle.

Pupils and parents: Pupils come from all over and school is proud of its 'broad and varied intake.' We said last time that it's the sort of place where a Yorkshire farmer's son will be sharing a room with the offspring of a City banker – and it still holds true. Between 10 and 15 per cent are progeny of OHs, while 20 per cent are from overseas (some expat, others from vast range of countries – 40 at last count). Twenty-five with EAL requirements. Most boys are C of E but there's a 'significant' RC community. Small numbers of all other main faiths or none.

School is proud of its 'broad and varied intake'. We said last time it's the sort of place where a Yorkshire farmer's son will be sharing a room with the offspring of a City banker

The boys we met were engaging, appreciative of the fine education they get and very proud of their school. 'It doesn't give you a sense of entitlement, just a great responsibility to give something back,' one boy told us, while a sixth former who'd joined from a state school at 16 said that he'd been 'pushed and challenged' and that there was 'a lot more opportunity for debate' than at his previous school.

Parents reckon the school suits all-rounders who work hard and like sport. 'It's very disciplined and the boys are busy all the time so they have to be organised,' one mother said. 'There isn't any time to get up to any mischief and the boys are really tired by the end of term. There's a real camaraderie about the place and the boys make life-long friends. I can't fault it.' Another reckoned that even though it's 'strict,' any boy would thrive at Harrow, as long as they can cope with being in a large school where they won't necessarily be 'king pin.'

Long and distinguished list of former pupils – seven former prime ministers (including Sir Robert Peel, Lord Palmerston, Stanley Baldwin and Sir Winston Churchill), 19th century philanthropist Lord Shaftesbury ('a towering figure – we refer to him a lot,' says the head), Jawaharlal Nehru, King Hussein of Jordon, Lord Cardigan (who led the Charge of the Light Brigade), General Sir Peter de la Billière, plus countless other men of military renown (20 holders of the Victoria Cross and one George Cross holder). The arts and sciences are equally well represented, with a dazzling list of luminaries including Lord Byron, Richard Brinsley Sheridan, Anthony Trollope, Terence Rattigan, John Galsworthy, Cecil Beaton, Edward and William Fox, Richard Curtis, Benedict Cumberbatch and James Blunt, plus Crispin Odey (one of the UK's most successful hedge fund managers), Julian Metcalfe (founder of Pret à Manger), cricketer Nick Compton and Tim Bentinck (better known as David Archer).

Entrance: Very competitive. Around 600 apply for the 160 places on offer at 13. Prospective pupils for entry from 2018 onwards supply school reference and sit pre-test in year 6; most are expected to be invited for assessment at the start of year 7, through tests and interviews. Offers are made – subject to CE or scholarship exams 18 months later. Sixty-five per cent expected at CE. 'Some weight' given to sons of OHs and boys' siblings – 'but brothers don't automatically get in,' said a parent. Boys arrive from more than 100 regular feeder schools. All-boys' boarding preps like Caldicott and Cothill top the pack but others from a myriad of co-ed and day schools.

Total of 24 new pupils a year into the 340-strong sixth form. Candidates need at least seven or eight A*/A at GCSE but many will have straight A*s. Candidates write a CV, plus letter to the head explaining why they want to come to Harrow, and take tests in their proposed A level subjects. The best attend a day of interviews and assessments.

Exit: Ninety-nine per cent to university – 18 to Oxbridge in 2015 and most of the rest to Russell Group. Significant number opting for Ivy League universities in the US, including two to Harvard, and other top international institutions – 23 in all heading off overseas.

Money matters: School has given franchises to Harrow Beijing, Harrow Bangkok and Harrow Hong Kong, with a fourth likely to follow in the next few years. These are all successful enterprises carefully monitored by Harrow and also fund generous bursary schemes at home.

Wide range of scholarships and bursaries at 13 or 16. School offers means-tested bursaries of up to 100 per cent of fees to pupils who win a scholarship of any sort. Up to 30 scholarships a year for academic excellence, music, art or talent in a particular area (normally worth five per cent of fees). There are also Peter Beckwith scholarships for gifted and talented boys whose parents can't afford to send them to Harrow. Two awarded each year to boys aged between 10 and 13 – these can cover fees at a private school from the age of 11 and Harrow fees from 13.

Remarks: Parents looking for a top notch, blue chip, full boarding, all boys' school will be hard-pressed to beat Harrow. This is a school on top of its game.

Holmewood House School

Barrow Lane, Tunbridge Wells, Kent TN3 0EB

01892 860006
registrar@holmewoodhouse.co.uk
www.holmewoodhouse.co.uk

Ages: 3–13 (boarding from 6)
Pupils: 465
Boarders: 40 weekly/flexi
Day: £9,900 – £17,460 pa
Boarding: £20,640 pa

Headmaster: Since 2010, Mr James Marjoribanks (pronounced Marchbanks). Education is in the blood, as his father was head at Sandle Manor, although he's made it his business to be less remote in the role. 'Children won't freeze if I walk down the corridor,' he says. Nevertheless he believes they should be respectful to adults. 'Eyes up, heads up, hands out of pockets, move aside for adults,' is the expectation.

His specialism is French (Exeter University), and the interest in languages is clear in the school – even the nursery has a specialist French teacher. Better brush up – he's been known to deliver addresses to parents in French. Career has included spells as head of French at Forres and head of modern languages at Cothill, followed by leadership posts as deputy head of Terra Nova School in Cheshire and head of Chesham Prep School in Buckinghamshire.

He has aimed to make the school more relaxed and family oriented. But his management of pupils, staff and parents alike is robust. 'I'm a benevolent dictator, a school is not a democracy, I consult with colleagues but I have to be firm,' he says.

Our moles told us that he has a tough gig with a particularly forceful parent body, and he is unafraid of holding his ground, which inevitably ruffles some feathers. 'I give the parents what they need, not what they want. We are the education professionals, we know best. A couple of parents didn't agree with a decision last year, but if it is right for school, it has to happen,' he says.

He has his fans too, with one parent saying: 'I really like Mr Marjoribanks. He is very charismatic and approachable. He is a visible character at the school and the children love him. My son had Mr

Marjoribanks for French one year and found him a very good teacher too.'

Entrance: For nursery and reception it's first come first served, and entry into the pre-prep is non-selective, although informal assessments will ensure the child can keep up. Around 15 children join at year 3, and for this stage onwards prospective pupils take tests in maths, reading and spelling, plus there's an interview, and reports from the previous school are considered. Academic scholarships, which can be topped up with bursaries, are available from year 3.

Exit: It has previously had a reputation for not supporting children aiming to take the 11+, and for frowning on departures before 13. However that was a thorny issue indeed in the grammar school hotbed of Tunbridge Wells, and has changed with a new policy in 2015. School now says it welcomes children intending to leave at 11, and although it does not provide bespoke 11+ tuition, the preparation all children receive for secondary school entrance and common entrance pre-tests will be relevant. It's likely to take a while for this change of heart to filter through both in local reputation, and through a cohort which entered before this policy was in place. Not that it was ever impossible to move to a grammar – parents have previously organised their own tuition, and the last few years have seen many pupils move on to grammars.

At 13+ the school has a reputation for harvesting a good crop of scholarships. In 2015, a record 28 scholarships and awards were gained by 22 year 8 pupils (academic, music, drama and sport). Mr

We like the fact that the non-sporty don't get it rammed down their throats as much as in some other prep schools

Marjoribanks has been instrumental in broadening the range of schools children go on to – it used to be Tonbridge for boys, Sevenoaks for girls, but there are now also good numbers going to Brighton College, Eastbourne, Benenden and others. A roadshow with 20 senior schools is held every two years to help families decide.

Remarks: No doubt about it, the facilities are fantastic. It's one of very few prep schools with its own 20 metre rifle range – and the pupils are champion shooters among English schools. There's also a 25m indoor pool, squash courts, a climbing wall, and a snazzy sports hall. Lots of sporting success at county and national level. But we like the fact that the non-sporty don't get it rammed down their throats as much as in some other prep schools – there are two afternoons of compulsory team games, but on the other three they can choose drama, music or craft activities, or individual sports instead.

There's a 350 seat theatre and lots of big productions – and treading these boards launched the careers of old boys actors Dan Stevens of Downton Abbey and actor Tristan Gemmell (Casualty and Coronation Street). More remarkably, perhaps, Shane McGowan of The Pogues was also here.

The already large campus is being extended by a building project in 2015/16 which will create eight classrooms, a learning hub, learning support centre, and new IT centre.

This offering, alongside what the head claims is a high staff to pupil ratio (1:9), and the number of specialist teachers, comes at a cost. You know what you're in for when one of the FAQs on the website is 'Why are your fees relatively high?' Mr Marjoribanks says he has deliberately narrowed the fee gap between the school and neighbouring preps, but it's still about £1,000 a term higher than others in the locality. We heard talk of school gate grumbles about fees funding large numbers of bursaries; whether you applaud that or not will be a matter of personal conviction.

They do a great deal to ease the way for working parents. There are minibuses at 4.30pm and 6pm to accommodate different finishing times through the school, and children can be looked after until 7pm. There is also a health centre staffed by nurses between 8am and 7pm every day. It means they can manage complicated medical regimes, but also look after a child who just needs to rest for half an hour before bouncing back, rather than having to call parents to collect them.

Saturday morning school and afternoon matches means that parents don't have to take off a working day to watch a fixture, and can often schedule school meetings at the weekend. But this is another bone of contention. From year 5 the children are required to attend lessons on Saturdays from 8.50am to 12.50pm, and often also games until teatime. On top of a school day of 8am to 6pm by year 6, it means the children get exhausted, some parents say.

The head says Saturdays account for 125 lessons per year, and 'we would have to dilute our offering if we didn't have it'. He believes parents dislike it more than children do. But he has recently introduced exeats and a two week half term holiday in October to provide some breathing space.

The full-on timetable is part of Mr Marjoribanks' aim to be the top academic prep school, and to ensure that children in common entrance forms (year 6 to 8 have two of these and one scholarship form) are well prepared enough to get into their chosen school without any doubt. 'The last thing we want is them sitting the common entrance exam with everything crossed,' he says.

He has put back creating the scholarship class to the start of year 6, believing they can better identify the children suited to this class after they have had a year working with subject specialist teachers, which begins in year 5. 'It's not a designer accessory. It's hard work and the last thing I want is a child in there who is struggling. Parents perceived that they got the best teachers, but I have deconstructed the idea that you get a better deal in the scholarship class. Now I get children or parents who turn it down because they don't want to be put under increased pressure, and scholarships are not worth much financially these days.'

From year 5 there are two periods a week of Latin, and scholars can also do ancient Greek. There's also Mandarin philosophy in year 8, a Spanish option from year 6, and French from nursery.

The seniors get Christmas and summer term exams in every subject, although for year 5 this has now been cut down to just English, maths and science exams in the Christmas term. Teaching is generally very good; the children learn a lot and are pushed quite hard, parents told us.

There are two full-time specialists and three part-time learning support assistants, and parents reported being very impressed with this input. It was highly visible on our visit, when a number of children were receiving individual or small group tuition.

In the junior school, years 3 and 4 are classroom-based with a form teacher, although they go to music, art, DT and science in dedicated classrooms. There are three proper science labs, complete with a skeleton, and the art department has specialist equipment for etching and a kiln for pottery work. Interesting work on display included flint knapping and cave art.

The pre-prep has a new head – Jacquie Scott joined in September 2014 from the British School in Amsterdam. She is bright eyed at the challenge, and looking first at working on improving comprehension skills and reading. The curriculum includes timetabled IT, and everyone starts an instrument in year 1. This, along with a specialist music teacher just for the pre-prep, enables them amazingly to have a pre-prep orchestra. Reception,

year 1 and year 2 have a separate block with their own dining room. Posters around the building ask: 'Do you have good manners?' They're big here, even illness isn't an excuse, as another poster in the health centre asks children whether they have said please and thank you.

Boarding is available to children from the age of 6, either weekly or on a flexi basis. There are currently seven weekly and 34 flexi boarders, but Mr Marjoribanks aims to bring the weekly ratio up to half. Boarding accommodation has just undergone refurbishment, and there is scope to increase the places to 50. Dorms are six-bedded and there's a combined games room. It's loved by the children – the two houseparents are 'really kind', they say, and they enjoy activities such as playing It, having a pizza party, or playing outside on skateboards.

There's a new energy about the place as Mr Marjoribanks' reforms are working their way through. 'I have deconstructed the atmosphere of elitism generated by a very competitive scholarship stream and attitude to sport; it is wholly inclusive and there is no-one outside looking in,' he says. Whether your child is a scholar or needs extra support, a sporting whizz or an arty type, they'll find their place here.

Hurstpierpoint College

College Lane, Hurstpierpoint, West Sussex BN6 9JS

01273 833636
registrar@hppc.co.uk
www.hppc.co.uk
C of E

Ages: 13–18
Pupils: 775; sixth form: 323
Boarders: 374 majority flexi
Day: £21,540 pa
Boarding: £25,485 – £32,040 pa

Headmaster: Since 2005, Mr Tim Manly BA MSc (40s). Educated at St Edward's Oxford followed by Oriel College, Oxford, where he read classics. He had always wanted to go into the teaching profession and after six years as a headhunter in the City and an MSc in industrial relations from the LSE, he went to Cambridge to do his PGCE at the age of 30. Says it was the best decision he every made and has never looked back. Spent six years at Sevenoaks, where he became head of classics and housemaster, before moving to Oakham as deputy head. Married to Henny; they have four children in the school.

He arrived when Hurst was treading water and has taken it from strength to strength and increased the numbers from 630 to 1,030 (for all three schools). He has raised the intellectual atmosphere, but 'feels that academic achievement is not an end in itself but a key to future success – life is about personal bests and engaging with opportunities'. Manners, civility and courtesy are his personal crusades, and pupils are strongly encouraged to write thank you letters and reply to invitations. He is a man of extraordinary energy who does not believe in down time, apart from the odd brief escape to his cottage in Wales. Feels there is no room for complacency as things can slip very quickly. The staff room has been revitalised, and about 70 per cent of teaching staff have joined since he took over. One pupil said, 'The headmaster makes people want to do well for him'. His door is always open and he knows children and parents by name.

Academic matters: In 2015, nearly 50 per cent A*/A at A level, 77.8 per cent A*/B. At GCSE, 66.5 per cent A*/A. Strong sciences and maths at A level. Pupils can do A level in their native language eg Dutch and Polish. IB offered since September 2011 – average point score 37 in 2014. The school offers the A1 language paper in German. The head would like to see the IB embedded as a viable alternative to A levels and would like about 40 to choose IB each year whilst 100 do A levels. About 30 per cent of A level students take the extended project qualification. Need to get an A or A* in GCSE in subjects to be studied at A Level or IB.

Challenge grades are particularly popular with parents. Based on IQ tests, an ambitious but, with hard work, achievable grade is set at the beginning of each academic year. Children are assessed through challenge grade reviews every three to four weeks and these, accompanied by teacher comments and a graph to plot progress, are emailed directly to parents. 'Problems are picked up as soon as they arise and there are no nasty surprises,' says one happy parent. Children meet their tutors each week to discuss academic progress. There is a strong work ethic throughout the school; children are set extra work during the holidays and half term and are encouraged to take initiative and responsibility in all aspects of their lives.

Good SEN department with three full-time and four part-time teachers – about 15 per cent of pupils need some support, mainly for mild dyslexia and dyspraxia; this is charged for.

Foreign nationals who want to join the sixth form are screened for English before arrival. EAL compulsory for anyone who needs it and is included in full boarding fee for international students. Although there is a well-stocked library, the use of text books is diminishing in favour of electronic media; increasingly, work is done on subsidised iPads, and the academic block bristles with Apple Macs. Plenty of careers guidance – sixth formers are given interview skills coaching and help with writing cvs. Parents and pupils can attend presentations on UCAS and there are gap year fairs and seminars. All are encouraged to take part in Young Enterprise initiative where pupils have the opportunity to create and run their own business – they were the local prize winners for best company in 2011 and 2012. OJ Club of former pupils very supportive of the careers programme and many come back to make careers presentations and offer executive shadowing schemes.

Manners, civility and courtesy are his personal crusades, and pupils are strongly encouraged to write thank you letters and reply to invitations

Games, options, the arts: Games are compulsory in the first year but after that, those who hate team sports can do something else eg outdoor pursuits or health-related fitness programme monitored by the school. Lots of enthusiastic teachers mean that most people find something they enjoy – biking, surfing, kayaking, sailing etc. Everyone has to do at least three exercise sessions a week, reducing to two in the sixth form, and most girls keep going with sport. Minor sports include fencing golf, shooting, triathlon, power-walking and riding – Hurst sponsors the annual schools' competition at Hickstead. House and inter-school competitions in the major sports and many minor sports eg water polo and cross-country running. 'Everyone has a chance to play in a team if they want to – the school will put together a team and find a fixture.' Everyone encouraged to have a go and 'you don't have to be good but just have fun' – it is hoped pupils will

find a sport they want to continue after they leave. Lots of sport played at county level and occasionally pupils are selected to represent their country.

Vibrant music department with orchestra, jazz band and wind band as well as various ensembles and quartets; some 140 in the choir and about half learn a musical instrument. Class music compulsory in Shell (year 9) and the whole school is involved in some way in the annual house music competition.

Huge range of activities from car racing to rock climbing and all Remove (year 10) do silver Duke of Edinburgh award through the CCF. The school has set up a farming project in conjunction with Plumpton College with pigs (one of the pigs is used for the Boar's Head Feast), chickens, fruit trees and a conservation group where children can learn countryside skills like hedge-laying. The aim is that they discover what they enjoy and develop life-long hobbies and interests.

Art room open to all – not just those studying for public exams. Photography, textiles, ceramics, sculpture, graphics as well as drawing and painting. Drama is offered at GCSE and A level as well as an extracurricular activity. There is a Shakespeare play each year and a musical most years as well as lots of small productions in the drama studio – often student directed. There is a playwright in

Has set up a conservation group where children can learn countryside skills like hedge-laying. The aim is that they develop life-long interests

residence with weekly workshops for those who want to write for theatre.

Dance compulsory for Shell (year 9) and is also offered at GCSE and A level. Increasingly popular with boys and girls – contemporary dance, breakdancing, hip hop, street dance all offered. Trips all over the world – community expedition to Malawi, cultural exchange to China, plus subject trips to eg Italy, Barcelona, Iceland.

Boarding: Just under half board to some degree – mostly flexi (equal numbers of girls and boys), often three nights a week, but nearly 90 weekly boarders. Full boarding not offered until sixth form and tends to be for foreign nationals. There are 10 houses up to lower sixth divided into day and flexi-boarding – with a strong system of pastoral care and communal responsibility and a tradition of inter-house competition.

Background and atmosphere: Founded in Shoreham in 1849 by the educational pioneer Nathaniel Woodard. It moved to its present purpose-built site in 1853 and the chapel was finished in 1865 – a beacon of Victorian muscular Christianity. Set in 140 acres, with views to the South Downs and surrounded by playing fields. From a distance it could be mistaken for a monastic community, but this first impression belies a vibrant and forward-looking school. Constant updating and refurbishment – the science and DT blocks were refurbished, the new academic quad was unveiled, second Astroturf completed all in 2011 and new digital library underway

The mantra 'achieving your personal best' permeates all aspects of school life, not just academic but also participation in sport and clubs, activities and social relationships. When the school was founded in the 19th century, 'ancient' ceremonies were introduced to give it a feeling of tradition and history. There are banner ceremonies and on Ascension Day, everyone climbs the nearby Wolstonbury Hill for a special service, and the headmaster distributes 'Lowe's Dole', money left by the first headmaster for the choir. The Boar's Head procession and Feast at the end of the Michaelmas term, when a boar's head is carried through the cloisters accompanied by the choir singing a 16th century hymn, is one of the highlights of the school year.

Pastoral care, well-being and discipline: There is a robust anti-bullying policy, a representative from each year group in each house sits on the school council, and house guardians are chosen for their approachability to discuss any social issues within the house. The lower sixth act as prefects, mentor the younger children, are responsible for the day-to-day running of the houses and supervise prep and lights out. Sniffer dogs and random drugs testing from time to time – all sounds a bit alarming but Hurst does not have a drugs problem.

Upper sixth has its own house, St John's, which is set apart from the main school buildings and is more like a hall of residence where everyone has their own study bedroom. Co-ed, with girls and boys in separate wings, which are alarmed at night. Students have their own common room, kitchen, computer room and laundry room. They run their own lives, but are not cut off from the rest of the school, and organise school functions and charity events; all the sixth form have to do some form of community service.

The Boar's Head Feast, when a boar's head is carried through the cloisters accompanied by the choir singing a 16th century hymn, is one of the highlights

Hurst is a Christian school and the chaplain plays a major part in school life, but Christianity is not imposed on anyone. Pupils encouraged to recognise spiritual dimension and to develop a strong moral compass and sense of duty. Compulsory Friday evening chapel marks the end of the school week. No Saturday school, just sport, activities and play rehearsals.

Pupils and parents: Around 95 per cent live within about 45-50 minute drive. Head wants to keep the school local with an international dimension. Tweeded landed gentry, city commuters, medics and local farmers and businesspeople. Good network of school minibuses run morning and evening from as far away as Hove, Copthorne, Lewes, Seaford, Forest Row and Horsham. 'Very parent friendly, and school bends over backwards to make life easy for parents,' says one working mother – the weekly and flexi-boarding option and no Saturday school particularly popular. Parents particularly praise the very good communication via emails and newsletters and the regular parent-teacher meetings Active parents' association runs social events – coffee mornings, barbecues, inter-house quizzes and the Christmas fair.

Famous former pupils include Admiral Sir Michael Boyce, chief of the defence staff in the Gulf War, various MPs and ambassadors, former general secretary of the National Association of Head Teachers, Sir David Hart, actor Michael York and film director Ronald Neame.

Entrance: Not hugely selective, with 55 per cent pass rate at common entrance. Keeping a fairly broad church becomes increasingly difficult as the waiting list grows. School's own exams in English, science and maths for those coming from schools which do not prepare for CE. Doesn't cull after GCSEs. Many come up from Hurst's own prep school; others come from local prep schools, eg Windlesham House, Great Ballard, Dorset House, Great Walstead, Pennthorpe, St Aubyns, Westbourne House and Handcross Park. Some from local primaries and a few from London day schools. Some 40-50 join in sixth form. Need an A* or A in subjects to be studied plus a minimum of a C in maths and English or the equivalent in home country. Occasionally spaces in year 10 at start of GCSE course – entry by school's own tests. Almost at capacity, with waiting lists in some years – does not want to get much bigger as will grow out of the chapel – already building a gallery.

Exit: About 20 per cent leave after GCSEs, often to go to sixth form colleges – do not lose any to competitor schools. Send to a wide range of universities (most to Russell Group and 1994 Group), including several to Oxbridge each year (eight in 2015, plus two to Royal Veterinary College). Others to a good range of universities – Loughborough, Birmingham, Exeter and Bristol popular this year. About half take a gap year.

Money matters: Means-tested bursaries, sibling discounts and special bursaries to help children of former pupils. Range of awards at 13+ and for the sixth form – academic, art, sport, drama and IT worth up to £1,600 per term – can be topped up by means-tested bursaries. Also means-tested bursaries to take a child to the next stage if parents experience financial hardship.

Remarks: A school which is going from strength to strength under the strong leadership of its dynamic headmaster. It is now the first choice for many parents who would traditionally have sent their children further afield. We tried hard to elicit negatives from parents, but everyone was universal in their praise. Fantastic value added, where each child is tracked and challenged to reach their full potential in all areas of their lives, and where they are encouraged to push themselves beyond their comfort zone.

Hurtwood House School

Holmbury St Mary, Dorking, Surrey RH5 6NU

01483 279000
info@hurtwood.net
www.hurtwoodhouse.com

Ages: 15–18
Pupils: 340
Boarders: most board
Day: £26,370 pa
Boarding: £39,555 pa

Joint Headmasters: Mr Richard Jackson MA (70s), originally an English teacher, is the founding head. Richard's (we are all on first name terms here) soft-spoken and understated manner belies the weighty and imposing presence of a man who has lived and is still living a remarkable dream, a dream he and his team bring about daily for their privileged students.

Mr Cosmo Jackson BEd (40s) and son of Richard was appointed 2004 to do the main day-to-day running of the school. An alumnus of Charterhouse, Cosmo spent two years at Bristol University not enjoying economics and thence to the University of the West of England to do his – perhaps inevitable – BEd. He was, in all senses, to the manner born, as were the majority of his siblings, their spouses and, quite possibly, ultimately, their offspring as Hurtwood is, triumphantly, a family concern and four other Jacksons are on the staff. Parents seem a little bemused. 'He's very charming but the students don't see much of him once they're in. He doesn't teach anyone.' A pity as he is easy to talk to, smilingly enthusiastic and loves his job.

Academic matters: Contrary to popular opinion, this is not just a school for arty/media types. Sciences are strong and the results across the whole range of subjects are uniformly starry. A levels offered include all three sciences, economics and sociology. Some students yearn for more eg philosophy. Most popular are, unsurprisingly, drama, media, English, maths and psychology. Fine art and textiles an astonishing stand-out success. Photography results less strong. In 2015, 63 per cent of A levels were graded A*/A (88 per cent A*-B).

Average class size is between eight and 12, often smaller. Teaching is, according to parents, 'pretty excellent' and the students we spoke to were extravagant in their praise, admiration and, in some cases, hero-worship of teachers. The Jackson philosophy is all about bringing in the best and assiduously monitoring both staff and students to ensure that no slacking, laurel-resting or coasting occur. Parents know what they are paying for: 'They're spoon-fed to a terrible degree,' said one, 'but that's why the fees are so enormous.'

According to the Jacksons, success depends on kindness and monitoring. 'Socially and pastorally we are the friendliest school in the world but we're strict when it comes to work.' Cosmo says, 'We have the cosy feel and intimacy of a prep with the academic rigour and maturity of a university.' Weekly staff meetings to check on anyone whose performance causes concern. Everyone graded A1-U5 and staff swift to pick up on anyone not meeting expectations.

Hurtwood is, triumphantly, a family concern and four other Jacksons are on the staff

No SEN dept – Richard talks of 'enthusiastic amateur support' and acknowledges that among such creative people, the 'dyses' are bound to be common. But, he feels, 'they should, by now, have learned the strategies and techniques to manage their difficulties'.

Games, options, the arts: The glory of Hurtwood and at the heart of its ethos. Arts and media all to professional standards – largely because the teachers are West End/media pros absolutely on top of their game and all the latest in production. And this is the great attraction. We spoke to numerous academically-minded students who had come to Hurtwood because their previous schools offered the chance of one or two productions each year in which they might, or might not, get a part. Here, productions, films, videos of all kinds and sizes roll off the blocks constantly and, if you are of a mind to, you can be constantly engaged in them. Acting 'company', a film 'academy' and a dance 'company' are elite groups restricted to a dozen or so devotees.

No glitzy performing arts centre such as are now routinely found in 'top' schools. The theatre is good, of professional quality and seats 180 though with little backstage or flyroom/wing space. The students learn the design and building of sets not by doing, but by seeing it done by the pros, very expensively, brought in. This a positive policy decision of the Jacksons. They do learn lighting though, again, lighting pros brought in to do the actual biz in the 'jaw-droppingly good' concerts and shows, as parents concur. 'They walk out of here and could manage a BBC studio,' one thought, 'and those who go on to media courses find they know pretty much everything they do in the first year, at least.' New TV studio complex and edit suite the envy of many strapped production companies.

Around a quarter learn an instrument. A further quarter take singing lessons and a sixth take dance. Music tech is, inevitably, a big deal here

with two tech rooms plus recording studio. Art is rich and varied – impressive and imaginative portfolios emerge from the small studio down the track through the woods. Costume design makes practical use of textiles skills and the results are stunning. Monthly newsletter produced in-house and largely by students is a slick, cool number.

Games an also-ran. It's just not why you come. 'If you want to do a sport, you're pretty much in the team,' we were told by an enthusiast who gave up his place in his elite's school's elite first XI to come here. There's a football pitch, all weather-hockey/basket ball pitches, two tennis courts, a new sports pavilion, so it's there if you want it. Pool and table tennis around the place as well.

Boarding: Around 50 boarders live in the upper floors of the main building. Not over-roomy or over-appointed but perfectly adequate and with inspiring views. The rest in houses within a short bus ride – school keeps a fleet of buses which shuttle to and fro. All boarding houses are attractive and interesting architecturally though the loveliness of the interiors varies according, as much as anything, to taste. But most parents agree, 'it doesn't worry the pupils,' and 'the house staff are lovely.' Assuredly, here are not the dinky study bedrooms with en suites and all mod cons found elsewhere. As one parent opined, 'They haven't chucked money at the accommodation, but I'd rather have good teaching than smart bedrooms.'

Background and atmosphere: Richard Jackson conceived his school way back in the late 1960s and it bears the stamp of those idealistic, anything-is-possible, heady and experimental days. Hurtwood's first incarnation was in a building rented from the National Trust and he looked for three years until

he lighted on this lovely house in its perfect spot. It was always to be a 16-19 school, GCSEs being, for Richard, 'the absolute natural breaking point.' And so it has proved.

Set in 25 acres of stunning Surrey rural idyll, the house is a 1900s late Arts and Crafts, genteel mock Tudor fantasy, beautifully sited on the hills overlooking the North Downs. Getting here is a challenge as the road darkens and narrows, winding though and over the wooded hillsides – reminding one just how rural Surrey can still be, though each bend has a gated entrance with entryphone – this ain't your hill-farming sticks! The place is beautifully kept and the car park must have one of the most privileged views in the country. Downstairs is lovely – a huge and inviting drawing room with coffered ceiling, grand fireplace, sink-into sofas and lots of warm limed oak. Similarly, the library has a wondrous ceiling and, when you look down, a jolly good stock of books, periodicals etc. Dead posh loos too. Less artistically pleasing outbuildings house various subjects and classes, common rooms etc.

Food is 'out of this world'. One parent marvelled at 'the amount they must invest in the kitchen. It's all cooked there – nothing is brought in.' Another enthused, 'I turned up one day out of the blue and there was a dressed salmon!' Breakfasts apparently so good, superlatives fail. Much-loved ice cream machine and barbeque bar.

Pastoral care, well-being and discipline: Pupils and staff on first name terms – works fine although those who come from stiff public schools never quite get used to not saying, 'Sir'. Parents praise the 'very secure environment'. Residential 24/7 but students are free to go home at the weekends with permission and around 75 per cent do. No rich programme of activities over the weekends as elsewhere because those who do remain – or come in especially – have rehearsals, projects etc they just can't put down. Occasional weekend activities include hiking, camping in Snowdonia, paragliding, powerboating, high ropes courses and paintballing. School runs buses into Guildford and Cranleigh for shopping etc.

Very strict regs on smoking, drink and drugs. On our trail down to the arts block we met the 'smoking teacher' ready to ambush those having a sneaky drag but, although some parents sighed over these perennial problems, most felt it happened at weekends out of school and school is absolutely resolute against all such folly. Lots of counselling given when needed; random testing for drugs. Mixed boarding houses though sexes on separate floors or wings and 'very-strict no-go areas'. Girls wear black leggings, ankle boots and hoodies and boys wear skinny jeans, trainers and hoodies. Very little self-expression via 'see-me' garb. Sensible

The students learn the design and building of sets not by doing, but by seeing it done by the pros, very expensively, brought in

attitudes seemed pervasive. If there are any worried parents, we did not find them.

Pupils and parents: Approximately two-thirds are British, mostly from London and the home counties. Rest from, well, everywhere – nationals from 33 countries at the time of our visit. Sixty with EAL needs supported by specialist department. We did hear knots of students talking Chinese but mixing is better than at many schools – largely because productions bring people together. No distinction made or felt between day and boarding students, those who drip wealth and those on scholarships. 'There is,' a clear-eyed student told us, 'an ever-present sense of being part of an elite, but most people are very grounded and it's only with some of those from overseas where you really sense loadsamoney.' Everyone says how well everyone mixes.

Parents also a good mix – many in the arts. School/home links not touchy-feely. One parent said, 'They don't do parents' evenings – such a relief as we're not hands-on parents.' On the other hand, another said that they'd like the teachers to be around when they pick up on Friday evenings and a third echoed the feeling that she didn't get a chance to know her son's teachers.

Notable former pupils include Nikki Amuka-Bird, Emily Beecham, Phoebe Boswell, Emily Blunt, Amelia Brightman, Ben Chaplin, Amelia Curtis, William El-Gardi, Edward Fox, Aidan Gillen, Sam Harrison, Jack Huston, Tom Mison, Leah Wood, Hans Zimmer, Hannah Herzsprung.

Entrance: There are 150 vacancies each year (75 boys and 75 girls). No open days, it's much more personal here. School says, 'We are looking for students who are going to make a positive contribution to our community. Character, personality, willingness, cheerfulness, liveliness, helpfulness, maturity, a sense of responsibility and a strong sense of purpose are all qualities that we are looking for.' Admissions criteria like these – in all their triumphantly civilised vagueness – are not found everywhere.

Parents and prospective pupil are seen by the head and the interview usually lasts over an hour. Then, if you are still keen, you register and apply. What matters is whether you will fit in and make the most of the opportunities on offer. Some turned down at that point, a few, obviously outstanding, applicants are offered an immediate place, subject to reference, at that stage; the rest are put in a 'pool' for selection later in the year. Oversubscribed and currently a waiting list of around 50-60, entirely acceptable, hopeful would-bes. Places not dependent on GCSE results (except for eg the sciences and maths).

Exit: To a surprisingly mixed bunch of courses at a very wide range of unis from Cambridge to California eg LSE, Durham, Bristol, King's College London, Warwick, Imperial. Music, art, drama and film courses, as you'd expect but maybe fewer than you'd expect. Quite a few engineering and business management degrees. School runs its own agency, now headed by Emily Blunt.

Money matters: Famously and unashamedly expensive. Until you get here and sense the quality it's hard to gauge quite why. Two performing arts scholarships on offer annually worth 50 per cent of fees; two more at 25 per cent. Jacksons use their discretion to support those who deserve it and need it. Definitely worth trying, especially if you are local and utterly determined to succeed.

Remarks: Unique and impossible to label or compare. If you're talented, hard-working, collaborative, appreciative of opportunities and in love with performance and production, you'll have a stunning time.

The Junior King's School

Milner Court, Canterbury, Kent CT2 0AY

01227 714000
registrar@junior-kings.co.uk
www.junior-kings.co.uk
C of E

Ages: 3-13 (boarding mainly years 6-8)
Pupils: 387
Boarders: 86 full
Day: £10,235 – £17,235 pa
Boarding: £23,655 pa

Linked school: The King's School Canterbury

Headmaster: Since 2000, Mr Peter Wells BEd. Educated at Eltham College and Exeter University where he studied art and design. Before coming to Junior King's he was headmaster of Liverpool College Prep and St Hugh's School in Lincolnshire and previously a housemaster at Dulwich College and head of art and design at Cheltenham College Junior School. Teaches art when he can and likes to get involved with clubs and activities. He is an ISI inspector and a member of the IAPS education committee, as well as being a member of the King's senior management team. A headmaster 'at the top of his game', he is married to Vivienne, who is the registrar and an ISI boarding inspector, and together they make an effective and dynamic team. They live in a cottage in the grounds and escape to Cornwall during the holidays. They have three adult children. Peter is passionate about the school and has a keen eye for detail and is always looking for ways to make improvements. Has recruited 'top notch' senior management and teachers. Respected by children and parents alike and knows all the children by name.

Entrance: Most join in nursery and reception but major intakes into year 5 and year 7 when extra classes are added and occasionally into year 8 for Common Entrance if going on to King's. Younger children have a taster day and informal assessments and from year 5 children tested in English, maths and non-verbal reasoning.

Lady Milner gave Sturry Court, an Elizabethan manor house, and the Tithe Barn, in memory of her husband. It was opened by their friend Rudyard Kipling

Means-tested bursaries available from year 7 for up to 100 per cent of the boarding fee. Academic scholarships offered at 11+ for new joiners and children already in the school – worth a max of five per cent of fees. Additional bursary support available.

Exit: About 75 per cent go on to King's Canterbury. Others to Tonbridge, Eastbourne College, Benenden, Eton, Milton Abbas, St Edmund's. A few leave for the grammar schools at 11+ – some after-school coaching provided but parents usually get their own as well. Scholarships to King's Canterbury every year plus recent academic scholarships to Sevenoaks, Wycombe Abbey and Tonbridge and art and sports scholarships to Tonbridge and music and sport to Benenden. Two recent sports scholarships to Millfield. Those considered borderline for King's required to sit a pre-test and parents are given plenty of advice if it is thought a child might not pass Common Entrance to their chosen school.

Remarks: Founded in 1879 as the prep school for The King's School, Canterbury and spent its first 50 years in the precincts of the cathedral. Boys were known as 'parrots' because of the noise they made and houses are still named after parrots. Moved to current site in 1929 when Lady Milner gave Sturry

Court, an Elizabethan manor house, together with the Tithe Barn, in memory of her husband. It was opened by their friend Rudyard Kipling. Two miles from the centre of Canterbury, it is set in 80 acres of grounds and playing fields with the River Stour running through the middle. Along with King's, it is part of the Canterbury Cathedral Foundation, shares a governing body with King's and has a committee of four governors closely linked to the junior school.

School has a reputation for being quite competitive and according to the prospectus 'endeavour and success are held in the highest regard'; however, the number one Golden Rule is 'Do be kind, gentle, helpful, respectful and polite' and there is great emphasis on good manners, tolerance and friendliness. Parents full of praise for the school: 'My children are all very different and have all been happy – you don't have to be very sporty to have fun here'. 'The competitive environment has brought my daughter out of herself and given her confidence.' All agree that this school is 'best for children who are good at something' and that 'there is a very nice balance between academia and other things so children can build confidence in different areas'.

Strong Christian tradition with weekday and Sunday services at the village church and confirmation and carol services in the cathedral but all faiths made to feel welcome. Full-time and weekly boarders (mainly from year 6+) cared for in two immaculate houses: Kipling (boys) and Juckes (girls). Local children often ask to board for the last year and one mother commented slightly wistfully, 'my daughter wants to be at school more than she wants to be at home'. Lots of evening and weekend activities plus Saturday school with lessons in the morning and sport in the afternoon means there is no time to get bored or homesick. Around 45 per cent boarders are overseas.

Relationships with staff relaxed but respectful and there is always someone to talk to – year 5 onwards have two class teachers, one male, one female. 'The teachers seem interested in developing my child as a human being not just on an academic level,' said one happy parent. Bullying rare and dealt with swiftly via detailed anti-bullying policy. Good healthy food with lots of choice and staff make sure children eat a balanced meal.

School supports a variety of charitable causes and all children expected to be involved at some stage during the year – sponsored walks, donations to Salvation Army, the school fête, visiting old peoples' homes etc. They share their sports facilities and theatre with local groups and the headmaster feels strongly that the school should be part of the local community. Junior King's provides funds for a school in Malawi and children are encouraged to take an interest.

Forest school in the grounds where they learn about nature – they were making nettle pancakes over a campfire on the day we visited

Average class size 15-16, max 18. Three parallel forms with setting in maths from year 5, English, maths and languages from year 6 and science in year 8 – very flexible and all about challenge and support. Separate scholarship class in year 8. Children start learning French in reception and Spanish and Latin taught from year 5. Greek offered to scholars. Special provision for French, Spanish and Chinese bilingual children. Separate sciences taught in specialist laboratories from year 7. ICT incorporated into most subjects and also taught as a specialist subject from year 1 and children learn programming skills eg making computer games as well as spread sheets, presentations and website design. 'Everyone is expected to participate in class and it is a fast-paced academic school which does not suit everyone'. Very occasionally, it is suggested tactfully that a child might do better elsewhere.

Bright, sunny library central to main school with 14,000 books and run by a part-time librarian – the most widely-read children are appointed to 'The Most Honourable Order of the Book'. Pre-prep and year 3 have their own libraries. Experienced staff of 'inspiring and dedicated teachers' as well as talented young graduate assistants who come to work for a year before going to train as teachers. Much more attention given to SEN in recent years, about 10 per cent with some sort of learning support, either withdrawal or in-class help – system of monitoring and referrals means problems picked up early. Two dyslexia teachers, one full-time, one part-time plus a graphologist. EAL support if required.

Sport taken seriously and the school likes to win; pupils consistently encouraged to make the most of everything. Superb facilities and children can go to King's for anything not available at Junior King's. Rowing an option from year 7 in conjunction with senior King's plus a cricket pro and winter coaching and squash offered at King's. Floodlit Astro (funded by a parent) opened in 2013 means hockey now a major sport for boys and girls. Girls have been IAPS champions three times in recent years. Huge galleried sports hall and 14 tennis courts. LTA tennis coach recently appointed and school usually sends a team to the national IAPS tournament at Queenswood. Heated outdoor pool for fun but serious swimming taught at the King's recreation centre. Fencing particularly strong and a number of international fencers started at Junior King's. Few parental grumbles about children not getting picked for teams or getting into school plays but school aware of this and tries to address it. Inter-house competitions give everyone a chance to take part and new talents often emerge at the summer sports day when a huge variety of sports are contested.

Performing arts take place in the Tithe Barn, recently insulated and refurbished thanks to another very generous parent. Music is central to the life of the school with class music from reception upwards, over 60 per cent learn at least one instrument and the choir is a special part of school life. New purpose-built music school opened in January 2016. Range of bands, choirs and ensembles cater for every age and ability and with at least one big concert each term, 'music is never far from your ears.' Advent carol service and sung evensong at the end of the summer term are held in the cathedral and there are music scholarships to King's Senior most years. Drama part of the curriculum from year 3 and just about everyone has a chance to get up on stage at least once a year.

Busy art department – photography, film making, art history, graphic design, pottery, textiles – the sort of opportunities you would expect to find at a senior school and children can use the facilities at King's as well. DT from year 3 includes racing car design when children build and race a car in the Kent championships, jewellery making and T shirt design and a Dragons' Den type competition when children form teams to solve problems.

Annual Spanish exchange, skiing, weekend in Normandy, post-scholarship trip to Greece, the much looked forward to post-CE jaunt to Cornwall, rugby to Paris, hockey to Holland, cricket and choir tours to Brussels – European destinations which do not put too much strain on parental pockets.

Activities most afternoons and evenings, dozens to choose from (some charged for), everything from animation, circus skills and bushcraft to debating, gardening, jazz dance, riding and photography (digital and dark room).

Day children from a radius of about 40 minutes via mini-bus service plus accompanied train from Ashford. Most from professional families – doctors, medics, lawyers and City and creative types. About 45 per cent of boarders are foreign nationals from a variety of countries; strong links with Brussels and the Foreign Office – many parents choose the school for its global outlook. Active Friends Association has weekly breakfasts and organises social events such as hog roast and Christmas bazaar to raise money eg funded the new adventure playground.

Alumni include: former Olympics minister Hugh Robertson, actor Orlando Bloom, Commonwealth Games president Tunku Imran Ja'affar, ceramicist Edmund de Waal and cricketer Freddie Kemp.

Pre-prep housed in the Oast House with own hall and library. Seven classrooms with up-to-date ICT provide a colourful and stimulating environment. Children learn PE, French, dance and music from reception onwards and use the prep school facilities – sports hall, Tithe Barn, sports fields and dining hall. Accredited forest school in the grounds where children learn about nature and risk-taking in a safe environment – they were making nettle pancakes over a camp fire on the day we visited. Nursery now housed in newly built Swiss-style chalet known as Little Barn with all the mod cons and under floor heating – a busy happy place with guinea pigs and fish tanks.

Kent College

Old Church Road, Tunbridge Wells, Kent TN2 4AX

01892 822006
admissions@kentcollege.kent.sch.uk
www.kent-college.co.uk

Ages: 11–18 (junior boarding from 10)
Pupils: 440; sixth form: 130
Boarders: 70
Day: £18,642 – £20,325 pa
Boarding: £28,899 pa

Headmistress: Since January 2016, Julie Lodrick, previously head of The Mount School in York. (40s), BA music and related arts (University College, Chichester), PGCE (Kingston University), MA education, leadership and management (OU), professional practice certificate in boarding (BSA), national professional qualification for headship (NCSL). Wide experience in educational management; deputy head of Farlington School, West Sussex for four years. Also a tutor and lecturer for the Boarding Schools Association. Five years as housemistress at Queenswood School, and as head of music at St Margaret's Senior School, West Sussex before that. Talented singer and pianist, performing when opportunity (has classical music softly playing in study). Believes in healthy lifestyle, runs and swims in school pool daily, completed York marathon in 2013, raising funds for school charity.

Academic matters: Apart from the usual subjects, film studies, product design (textiles), food technology, drama and theatre studies, psychology and PE are offered at A level. In 2015, 76 per cent A*/B grades and 50 per cent A*/A grades. GCSEs: 52 per cent A*/A grades. Option to take all three sciences separately or as a dual award. Inspirational textiles teacher has taken the subject to new heights. Science is strong and a pupil recently won bronze in the International Chemistry Olympiad.

RE taught to all up to the sixth form and all younger girls take food technology. Healthy eating is covered in PSHE. The careers department is proactive and helpful and sixth form attend a higher education preparation programme with weekly sessions on interview technique, gap year planning, money management etc. Due to the recent increase in pupil numbers, several new teachers have joined, so a healthy mix of new younger teachers and others who have been in the school for many years. Plenty of male teachers and housemasters. Good support for minor learning difficulties and good communication between learning support and mainstream teachers.

Games, options, the arts: All the usual sports – girls have competed at national level at swimming, hockey and gymnastics and are recent U13 south east area cross-country champions. A gymnastics academy is also open to outsiders on Saturdays. A fitness suite with gym equipment was added in 2012 and planning has been granted for a new all-weather pitch and extension to existing sports hall.

Outdoor activities seen as important and the school has appointed a head of outdoor education who oversees the Duke of Edinburgh programme and various adventure trips at home and abroad. A 'confidence course' has been built in the grounds which includes a scramble net, a 12 ft wall and a 30 ft abseil tree – school officers in sixth form have a team-building weekend using the course. Sixth formers are required to take part in sport for one double period a week but this could be trampolining, aerobics, aquarobics, Salsa or more mainstream team sports. Everyone encouraged to get involved.

They do have a great zest for life and want to try everything, are encouraged to surpass their expectations and believe they can be anything they want to be

Lots of clubs before and after school and at lunchtime, from tae kwon-do to public speaking lessons and clay pigeon shooting, and girls are encouraged to initiate activities and start clubs, eg a street dance club and gospel choir. Astonishing that they can fit so much into a day. They are even good at beekeeping – the school's honey was commended at the National Honey Show.

Top two years have enrichment programme where they work in a small team on a project of their choice to gain a Record of Achievement by the Open College of the North West. This could be producing the school magazine or a cooking course leading to Leith's certificate in food and wine, an extended essay and community service. Young Enterprise scheme where they can run their own business for six months, working in mixed groups with other local schools. Charity Committee organises fundraising events. Plenty of opportunities to hone public speaking skills and look at the bigger picture in World AIMS (Action in Methodist Schools) Weekend, where such issues as the arms trade, climate change and development are debated, and at the Global Students Forum and model United Nations events in Tunbridge Wells and Bath. Women in Leadership conferences are held annually with outside inspirational speakers; girls also debate subjects such as 'Are women taking over the world?' – lots of thought-provoking and challenging stuff. Dan Snow, Sandi Toksvig and Miriam Margolyes were recent visitors. Drama impressive with whole school productions in the purpose-built Countess of Wessex theatre – 'The school has very high expectations of the girls and they always seem to step up to the plate'. Their highly acclaimed theatrical productions, musicals and operas are very ambitious and rival the West End. Music on the up with a modern music centre and Apple Mac computer suite where girls can compose. LAMDA and English Speaking Board exams and every girl will speak in at least one assembly a year.

Boarding: Small boarding community, 20 per cent from overseas, eg Nigeria, China, Russia, Thailand and mainland Europe, but nationalities carefully balanced and trouble taken to prevent cliques forming. Another 20 per cent of boarders from Forces families. Modern and well-designed junior and senior boarding houses cluster around original baronial style Victorian house and everywhere has a light and airy feel. Usual evening and weekend activities such as shopping trips, skating, cinema and sport. Day girls are allowed in the social areas of boarding houses and encouraged to try flexi-boarding, and older girls help supervise younger ones at bed time.

Background and atmosphere: Founded in 1886 in Folkestone and moved to its present site in Pembury, just outside Tunbridge Wells, during World War II. Managed by the Methodist Independent Education Trust's board – but with a very light touch. Also has its own governing body, half of whom are members of the Methodist Church or members of a Christian church. Methodists state that their schools aim to be 'caring, family communities committed to the development and full potential of each individual, having regard for their personal attributes as well as their academic aspirations'. Kent College certainly does this and caring for the individual is central to the ethos of the school – each girl's well-being is paramount.

Huge amount of refurbishment and number of building projects with fitness suite, science labs and IT suites completed, plus expansion of sixth form centre. £4 million art and library centre, including café, studios and exhibition space, opened in 2013.

Pastoral care, well-being and discipline: The school has a warm and welcoming atmosphere and girls are happy and relaxed while leading incredibly busy lives. A strong Christian ethos is a subtle part of the routine – girls are expected to take part in assemblies but the celebration of other religious festivals is an integral part of school life. A spirit of

Women in Leadership conferences held annually; girls debate subjects such as 'Are women taking over the world?' – thought-provoking stuff

tolerance and respect is part of the ethos. Relaxed and comfortable girl/staff relationships. The tutor system ensures any problems are picked up early – mentors are allocated to girls who struggle; also a school counsellor. Girls are supportive of each other across the year groups and the house system means that different year groups pull together in sporting competitions and charity work. New girls are integrated quickly and attend an induction programme which includes an overnight camp in the school's orchard. Discos, socials and joint productions with local boys' schools are popular.

Pupils and parents: The school seems to breed great enthusiasm and loyalty, seeing itself as a small global community. No typical Kent College girl, but they do have a great zest for life and want to try everything, are extraordinarily confident with a 'can do' attitude and are encouraged to surpass their expectations and believe that they can be anything they want to be – yet no hint of arrogance. They come from as far as Bromley and Tenterden – good network of school buses. Wide variety of parents from all walks of life – great tolerance of difference – but mostly from business and professional families. Famous old girls include the Countess of Wessex and Sarah Sands, editor of the London Evening Standard. Good links with parents, who feel involved at every step. Active parents' association who organise social events throughout the year – a ball, coffee mornings, new parents' social evenings and a pamper evening. Also a thriving old girls' association and active Friends of Kent College Association, which includes ex staff, parents and governors.

Entrance: Not overly competitive – broad intake and can cope with a wide range of abilities as lots of individualised care. Most enter at 11+ and attend the entrance day in the November before entry, when they are interviewed and sit the school's own exams in English, maths and verbal reasoning. The school also requires a letter from the girl's current head. Entry at 12+ and 13+ with exams in the January before, when they are also tested in science and French. A taster day and overnight stay are strongly encouraged. Those who come up from the prep school also have to take the test. Sixth form entrants need six GCSEs at C or above and A*, A or B grades in the subjects they wish to study at

A level. Children come from a wide range of local prep schools and primaries including Holmewood House, Rose Hill, Sevenoaks and St Michael's, Otford.

Exit: Up to 20 per cent leave after GCSEs, usually for co-ed independents or grammars. Sometimes girls come back and have been known to repeat the lower sixth year rather than stay somewhere else. Most go on to some form of higher education at a huge range of destinations, UK and international. In 2015, scholarships to UBC Vancouver and Amsterdam University, one student to Oxbridge

(medicine at Oxford). Eight students received bilingual diplomas. Lots of help with UCAS forms and personal statements. Oxbridge preparation lessons include interview practice with a local boys' school.

Money matters: Academic, music, drama, music, art and sport scholarships offered at up to ten per cent of fees. Means-tested bursaries also available.

Remarks: Has improved hugely over past few years – numbers up, recent glowing report from the Independent Inspectorate. Girls leave with great self-confidence and strong sense of purpose.

King's Rochester

Satis House, Rochester, Kent ME1 1TE

01634 888590
admissions@kings-rochester.co.uk
www.kings-rochester.co.uk
C of E

Ages: 13–18
Pupils: 300; sixth form: 130
Boarders: 33 boys/19 girls full, 6 boys weekly
Day: £17,640 pa
Boarding: £19,950 – £28,650 pa

Principal of King's Rochester and head of the senior school: Since September 2012, Mr Jeremy Walker MA (Oxon) (40s). Previously head of sixth form and senior manager at Berkhamsted School, Hertfordshire. Educated at Sherborne School and read theology at Oxford before taking an MA in educational leadership and management at the Institute of Education, University of London.

Started his career at Bishop Stopford School, a state secondary in Kettering, and became head of department after a year. Then moved to Ardingly, where he was head of religious studies and of theory of knowledge, and housemaster. He does not have time to teach here but is involved with Oxbridge preparation and interview technique and lateral thinking skills. His main objectives have been to improve academic performance, sports and careers and he has already negotiated the acquisition of a local sports centre and had it refurbished, introduced sports scholarships and been involved in setting up an effective careers network.

He says that he has 'built on the strengths of the school but has not shied away from areas which needed attention'. He is proud of the wide ability intake and believes in a broad curriculum and personalised education and, most importantly, that school should be fun. 'You get the best of both worlds here – a day school with a boarding school ethos.' He is 'sticking with King's traditions but making them relevant' and encourages parents to come to services in the cathedral. Parents full of praise: 'He is very disciplined and hard working, and that is the message he gives to the pupils'; 'A very efficient, caring man who knows the kids well and drops into lessons and chats to them; 'Very enthusiastic and has brought new vigour to the school'; 'Kids love him'. He is tightening up on everything including the uniform and has introduced zero tolerance on alcohol.

Met his wife, Harriet, when they were both at Sherborne; they have two children in the school and she teaches in the nursery and is involved with the Friends' Committee (parents' association). The school is their home and family life is very important to them, and they are keen to put down roots in the area. Mr Walker sits on the Cathedral Business Guild and a local cultural partnership to promote Rochester, and has strong links with the local military – the Royal Engineers.

Academic matters: Caters for a wide range of academic ability from 'Oxbridge to average'. In 2015, 44 per cent A*/A at GCSE and 33 per cent at A level (63 per cent A*-B). Pretty impressive for an almost

On site netball means the girls now get match teas – has made the 'netball mums' very happy. Rowing from the school's own boathouse

non-selective school in grammar school country – in fact they often outperform grammars in exam results. Offers double and triple award science and all do RS and ICT at GCSE. PE, music, classical Greek, Russian and German are among other subjects offered. Business studies, government and politics and history of art amongst 24 A level offerings. Will run an A level class for as few as three pupils and 'will go to great lengths to tailor the timetable to suit the children'. Extended Project Qualification also offered alongside A levels – another feather in your cap for university entrance.

An extraordinarily dedicated team of teachers – a good combination of some who have been in the school for many years and bright, young, newly qualified staff, and Mr Walker has brought in some new blood since his arrival, including a dynamic new head of ICT. 'The levels of devotion are extraordinary – they even ran revision classes on Easter Monday,' said one parent. 'The teachers really seem to care how we do,' said a pupil. Dedicated careers department – 'school has beefed up advice for university and beyond,' said a parent. An old boy has set up Jobs Network to provide advice and work experience to current and former pupils and help with interview practice and technique. Current and former parents encouraged to offer help with work experience or as a mentor. All upper sixth have mock job interviews with feedback and lower sixth have cv writing clinics.

Team of qualified SEN teachers – mainly for mild dyslexia, although school happily accommodates those with greater needs where possible. Pupils assisted in class, through withdrawals and with IEPs.

Games, options, the arts: Sport on the up helped by the introduction of sports scholarships and the new facilities. School has recently taken over the Stirling Sports Centre and adjoining Holcombe Hockey Club from Medway Council, now refurbished and renamed the King's Rochester Sports Centre, a 10 minute walk or short minibus ride from the school. Olympic standard Astroturfs and new outdoor tennis and netball courts plus indoor hockey, badminton and cricket nets and a fitness suite. Free membership for King's parents and open to the general public too. Some team sports still played on the pitches within the school grounds. On site netball means the girls now get match teas

– has made the 'netball mums' very happy. Rowing from the school's own boathouse on the Medway near Maidstone – 18 rowing boats and five large canoes. School very supportive of outside achievements eg national level pentathlon plus sailing and skating, and several pupils play cricket, rugby or hockey at county level. Strong tradition of fencing – fencing master was involved with organising Olympic competition. Duke of Edinburgh popular and 10-15 do gold each year. CCF offered in all three services – compulsory for the first two years and many keep going. Our guide had learnt how to fly a plane with the RAF division.

Impressive music – the prep is a cathedral school so the choristers (boys only 8-13) are part of the school and the chapel is Rochester Cathedral. Several choirs, orchestras and ensembles, a wind and jazz group and inspirational and 'brilliant' director of music. About 50 per cent learn at least one instrument with several reaching grade 8 each year, and a number go on to study music, often with organ or choral scholarships; pupils recently won scholarships to the Royal College and Royal Academy of Music. On a lighter note, the annual house music competition and popular termly 'Open Mic' night gives pupils an opportunity to perform in public.

He is proud of the wide ability intake and believes in a broad curriculum and personalised education and, most importantly, that school should be fun. Parents full of praise

Busy art department with photography, sculpture and fine art offered – product design particularly popular and pupils often go on to art college. Three major drama productions a year, numerous theatre and opera trips to London, and visiting theatre groups organise drama workshop within the school.

Numerous after-school clubs and societies with 'something for everyone' including bell ringing, debating, ICT and chess. Ballet popular throughout the school: some up to grade 8, and a handful keep going into sixth form. Lots of trips and outings – choir to Vatican and China, Physics to CERN, maths to NASA and World Challenge to Northern India.

Boarding: Up to 70 boarders, about half from overseas – 14 different nationalities and school works hard on integration. Boys' boarding house for 43 and girls' for 25. Start off in small dorms, and sixth form and most of fifth form have their own room with ensuite bathroom. Always something organised at weekends and children are expected to take part.

Background and atmosphere: Part of the Foundation of Rochester Cathedral, the school was founded in 606AD at the same time as the cathedral and re-founded under Henry VIII in 1541 when the monastery at Rochester was dissolved. It is the second oldest school in the UK after King's Canterbury. Prefects wear a gown and carry a cane but the school is certainly not old fashioned and inward-looking. A great sense of history here with the buildings clustered round the cathedral and next to the Norman castle; Charles II spent his first night in England at Restoration House on his return in 1660 and Queen Elizabeth I is rumoured to have stayed at Satis House (now the school administration building). A range of buildings from the medieval cathedral to Georgian, Victorian and 21st century, with Watling Street running down the high street. An unexpected and peaceful oasis in the middle of the bustling Medway towns. One of the few co-ed independent schools in Kent which offers a seamless education from 3-18 years.

Pastoral care, well-being and discipline: Strong Christian ethos; the cathedral is the centre of school life and the service held four mornings a week is a period of quiet reflection before the day begins. All faiths and backgrounds welcomed. All are expected to come to the services in the cathedral but do not have to participate. A tangible sense of community where everyone knows each other well and it is 'a very family oriented school where there are genuine friendships across year groups and kids look after each other,' said one happy mother. 'It is a close knit community that produces confident, self-reliant children who are not cocky,' said another, and 'It really does try to cater for all, and they are very personal in the way they deal with the kids'. 'My son has at last found a school where he is happy – it offers the best pastoral care I have come across. Most schools say they treat every child as an individual but King's Rochester really does,' said a father. School takes a firm line on drugs and runs a programme of drug awareness through PHSE but has not had any issues.

Pupils and parents: Big range from traditional to first time buyers and some who make genuine sacrifices to send their children here. Some come from the Medway towns and villages, some from 25 miles away and some come down on the train from SE London, Bromley and Blackheath. Extensive minibus service from as far away as Tonbridge and Sevenoaks. Children generally 'down to earth and engaging – they exude confidence and are compassionate, sociable and great fun to be with'.

Former pupils known as Old Roffensians and are hugely supportive with a great sense of loyalty to the school, and tend to keep in touch. They go on to follow a variety of careers and include surgeons, musicians, authors, artists and poets. Alumni include Prof Sir Derek Barton, who won the Nobel Prize for Chemistry, John Gummer, former Conservative cabinet minister, Pete Tong, Radio 1 DJ and Matthew Walker, professional cricketer.

Good communication with parents who say they feel involved. Moodle, a virtual learning environment where children can access classwork, homework and notes is proving popular with parents, who can keep an eye on what is going on.

Entrance: Broad ability intake but children are expected to be able to take 9/10 GCSEs and 3/4 A levels. They can join at 11+ via tests in English, maths and non-verbal reasoning and spend two years in the prep school before sitting entrance exams to the senior school at 13+. These are used for setting purposes and very few fail; and school will give plenty of warning if this is likely to happen. Entry from other schools at 13+ via Common Entrance or school's own tests. Occasionally spaces in year 10. Very few leave after GCSEs. Another 20 per cent join in sixth form and are expected to get at least five GCSEs at grade C or above and As or Bs in subjects to be studied at A level.

Exit: One to Oxford in 2015 (music), one to Michigan and one to British Columbia, plus two medics and two to art foundation courses. Exeter, Royal Holloway and Southampton popular destinations.

Money matters: Offers sports, academic, all-rounder and music (including organ) scholarships worth up to 30 per cent of fees which can be topped up with means-tested bursaries up to 75 per cent of fees. Choral scholarships offered in the prep school. Discounts for clergy, Forces families and siblings.

Remarks: A warm and caring family school with some of the best pastoral care around where children can grow up in the shadow of the cathedral. A wide ability range but all made to feel valued and the brightest get into the best universities. Going from strength to strength under the dynamic newish head.

The King's School Canterbury

31

25 The Precincts, Canterbury, Kent CT1 2ES

01227 595579
admissions@kings-school.co.uk
www.kings-school.co.uk

Ages: 13–18
Pupils: 826; sixth form: 380
Boarders: 636 full
Day: £26,055 pa
Boarding: £34,440 pa

Linked school: The Junior King's School

Headmaster: Since 2011, Mr Peter Roberts MA PGCE (50s), previously head of Bradfield College for eight years. He was educated at Tiffin Boys and read history at Merton College, Oxford where he got a first, followed by a PGCE at London Institute of Education. Started teaching career at Winchester as head of history, then also as master in college. Always immaculately dressed – 'sometimes a vision in tweed and sometimes besuited'. He is super brainy and regarded as 'quirky and eccentric but with a good sense of humour and perfect for the job – we would not want anyone who was run of the mill,' said a happy parent. A thoughtful academic 'who works unbelievably hard and is always out and about with his dog.' He attends every play, recital and concert and even attends the matrons' meeting; describing his job as 'vastly enjoyable.' Teaches the Shells (year 9), 'when he can'. Says he was struck by everyone's enthusiasm about the school when he first arrived and 'listened to the constituent parts'; he has now set out his vision for the future and what he considers to be the 'essence' of King's. Major projects include the acquisition of the Malthouse, which will be converted into a performing and visual arts centre, and a Victorian primary school, which will house the new science centre.

The headmaster describes the ethos of the school as 'interactive osmosis'. 'It is the richness, the diversity and range of our lives here that makes it distinct and special.' He feels the school 'gives a strong sense of belonging, a realisation that King's helped to make them (the pupils) what they are' and 'this creates the wish to give something back in return' and sees the atmosphere of the school as 'like a massive confidence-building machine'.

Expects very high standards from the children at every level and has tightened up on discipline, manners and presentation. Each week the Robertses invite 15 different pupils, one from each house, to lunch in their private dining room. Much expected too from staff and light being shed on the few pockets of less than good teaching.

Married to Marie, an elegant and accomplished Frenchwoman who was head of department at two large state schools and, in addition to teaching French and German, is also a harpist. They have three daughters. Enjoys spending time in France where he sails, practises calligraphy and paints watercolours

Academic matters: The pursuit of academic excellence is at the heart of everything the school does but co-curricular activities given equal weight and pupils have a 'rich' day. The brightest take some GCSEs early, allowing a head start on AS subjects; the less academic may drop a subject at GCSE. Pupils encouraged to take a creative subject like art, drama IT or music alongside academic subjects. In 2015, 59 per cent A*/A at A level (83.5 per cent at A*/B). Seventy-eight per cent A*/A at GCSE (IGCSEs for most subjects). Strong across the board and languages particularly good – mainly taught by native speakers and housed in the Old Palace. Sciences popular – female head of science and five out of the seven physics teachers are women. Most subject combinations can be accommodated even if some have to be taught outside the timetable. School always looking at ways to stretch the most able and curriculum constantly adapted. Currently

27 subjects to chose from at A level (including geology) and advanced extension awards in most. Astronomy offered as a GCSE along with Italian, Russian and Mandarin GCSE ab initio in sixth form. Strong work ethic and 'Children do not seem to realise how much they cram into the day, it is just normal for them,' said one mother.

Always immaculately dressed – 'sometimes a vision in tweed and sometimes besuited'

Pupils encouraged to think about their broader academic profile and alongside AS levels there are enrichment subjects such as critical thinking, perspectives on aesthetics, globalisation and science and the extended project. Careers advice starts in the first year on a drop-in basis and fifth form have timetabled careers periods to help with A level choices and beyond.

Stunning William Butterfield designed library (1848) is centre of academic life with a hushed and studious atmosphere and combining the best of the old and new with 30,000 books and a range of periodicals and European newspapers as well as DVDs and online reference sources. It is a great source of pride and always staffed and open every day until 10pm and at weekends. Somerset Maugham and Sir Hugh Walpole both left their personal libraries to King's.

About six per cent need extra help, mainly for mild dyslexia, and any pupil can ask for help with study skills. Probably would not suit anyone with bigger difficulties and some parental concerns that children do not get as much support as they need. EAL for a handful of pupils but all must be fluent on arrival. No plans to introduce the IB.

Games, options, the arts: Acres of playing fields about 15 minutes' walk away as well as a modern sports centre incorporating pool, indoor courts, climbing wall, café and gym – more akin to the smartest private leisure centre than the school sports department. Huge choice of sports – girls' hockey thriving with 15 girls in the English hockey training system. Cricket and rugby going from strength to strength and several boys have been selected to play for Kent U18s; school has also produced several international fencers. Rowing on the up for boys and girls after a period in the doldrums and old boy Tom Ransley won bronze at London 2012. Sports coaches include England cricketer Mark Ealham and Olympic hockey player Jennifer Wilson. Not everyone represents the school in matches but still play sport for 'fitness, health and fun' and most people find something they enjoy. Everyone is expected to get involved and participation is everything – 'you don't have to be brilliant but just give it a go and have fun.' Sporting trips

Parents and friends come bearing picnics, and it is a major social event culminating in Commem Day and the leavers' ball

all over the world – rugby in Argentina, cricket in Grenada and netball in South Africa.

Long tradition of excellent drama and music and anyone involved is definitely awarded 'cool status.' Fab new junior music school opening early 2016 – over half the pupils learn at least one instrument. Symphony orchestra plus numerous bands and ensembles; the pupil-run jazz club is particularly popular. Plenty of choral groups, from the Crypt Choir which tours annually, most recently to China, to the choral society which is open to anyone who enjoys singing, including parents and staff. 'Wherever you go around the school there is always music coming from somewhere'. Masses of drama both on and off the curriculum – house plays, GCSE and A level productions, drama competitions, fashion shows, full school plays – 'Wherever there is a quiet corner, you will find a rehearsal going on,' as well as regular theatre trips to London. Busy art department housed in 12th-century priory has a different artist in residence each year. New photographic studio and pottery centre opened by old boy Edmund de Waal.

Huge range of activities continues into sixth form – anything from academic societies with visiting speakers to mountain biking, cryptic crosswords, debating and the Model United Nations. CCF once again a popular option. Community work and volunteering are central to school life and are often part of Duke of Edinburgh Award and include teaching science in local primary schools, riding for the disabled and help with swimming for handicapped children.

The famous King's week at the end of the summer term is the highlight of the year for pupils and parents alike and is a festival of music, drama and dance with events being staged in all corners of the school every day for a week – parents and friends come bearing picnics and it is a major social event culminating in Commem Day and the leavers' ball. 'The quality and variety are phenomenal' and there is everything from Shakespeare, classical concerts and jazz as well as a lighter touch provided by the house harmonies. Those not involved do not feel excluded and have as much fun as those taking part.

Boarding: Six boys' and five girls' boarding houses (latest, Kingsdown House, for girls, opened September 2015). Half the houses clustered round the cathedral and the other half across the road on the St Augustine site where they have their own dining hall. Pupils equally happy to be in houses in either location, most popular houses booked up years in advance. Boarding houses friendly and welcoming with areas where pupils can make their own snacks and relax. Small dormitories for younger children and individual study bedrooms for sixth form. Large and popular social centre open for the whole school during the day and for sixth formers in the evening.

Background and atmosphere: Set in the shadow of Canterbury Cathedral and part of a World Heritage Site, this has to be one of the most inspiring settings for a school. Founded in 597 when St Augustine arrived in Canterbury and then re-founded as The King's School during the reign of Henry VIII after the dissolution of the monasteries – not many schools can produce a list of headmasters going back to 1259. Beautiful ancient buildings and cloisters and immaculate gardens with the busy city life going on just beyond the gates. Pupils enjoy the contrast and the fact that the city with its shops and cafés is on the doorstep and say, 'it makes us feel part of the real world'. The headmaster says the combination of the cathedral and a vibrant student city 'grounds the children in a wider reality'. The school sponsors the Folkestone Academy and lends its facilities to the wider community.

Took girls into sixth form in 1970s and went fully co-ed in 1990. Boarding houses plus thee day houses and a smaller sixth form girls' house in a variety of architectural styles from the 13th century Meister Omers to 21st century Grange. A close knit community, 'it's got everything, the spiritual dimension from the cathedral and a sense of beauty and history'. Former pupil Michael Morpurgo said, 'King's is like a university designed for younger people.'

Pastoral care, well-being and discipline: Smart uniform worn throughout the school, pinstripes, wing collars and a jacket – and a brooch for the girls. All look very professional and businesslike; monitors wear purple gowns and are, unsurprisingly, known as 'Purples'. Astonishingly busy day – one of the first lessons the children learn is how to plan their time – but there is still room for lots of fun. Strict rules and punishments regarding drugs, alcohol and parties and children know where they stand. Strong Christian tradition and moral values. The main school services held in the cathedral but different religious and cultural backgrounds recognised and valued.

Children have a healthy respect for each other and are generally self-regulating regarding bullying and other misdemeanours, and honesty and

integrity are highly valued. Pastoral care comes in for particular praise from the inspectors. Big effort to address everyone's happiness with several staff/ pupil committees to ensure all have their say.

Regular communication with parents especially through housemasters and house mistresses. Good interaction between year groups facilitated by mixed age tutor groups and mentoring from older pupils. New 'Shells' have a top year mentor. Day children and boarders mix well and 'you can't tell the difference,' according to one pupil.

Pupils and parents: A good mix socially and culturally with a wide catchment area – popular with locals, London and county sets and Foreign Office families and increasing numbers from abroad. About 20 per cent foreign nationals. Doesn't really produce a type but pupils are articulate, well rounded and very supportive of each other, appearing genuinely to celebrate each other's achievements. 'The finished product is amazing,' according to one mother. 'The boys and girls are charming, personable, not shy or arrogant and have a great sense of fun but are still ambitious'.

The recently formed King's Society, a cultural, social and educational society for parents and friends, now comprises over 300 families. Members organise lectures, music recitals, tours of the cathedral with the dean and social events. Old boys and girls include potter and writer Edmund de Waal, astronaut Michael Foale, Patrick Leigh-Fermor, Christopher Marlowe and William Somerset Maugham, supermodel Jacquetta Wheeler, Olympic silver medallist and world champion rower Frances Houghton and Anthony Worrall-Thompson.

Entrance: At 13+ by common entrance. School's own exam and an interview for those who have not been prepared for CE. Occasionally spaces in year 10. About a third come from Junior King's but they still have to take the same exams as everyone else rest from a range of Kent and Sussex prep schools and London day schools. Pass mark has recently been raised to 60 per cent but school likes to keep families together and takes an enlightened view if someone is borderline. It is also possible for pupils to take an entrance exam to Junior King's at 11+ which would guarantee entry to the senior school – they would still have to take CE for setting purposes. About 30 join in the sixth form with entrance by competitive exam and interview in Nov before entry with minimum of 7 Bs or equivalent at GCSE. Seven Bs required to move into sixth form and three Cs at AS required to stay on for A levels.

Exit: Those who leave after GCSEs (four per cent in 2015), usually go to local schools or London day

schools. Vast majority of sixth formers depart to top universities – 13 to Oxbridge in 2015, with Bristol, Exeter, Edinburgh, Durham, UCL, Manchester, Leeds, Bath and KCL all popular. Increasing numbers to American universities (nine in 2015). Languages, sciences and economics/business management most popular degree subjects recently. Between 10 and 15 to medical school each year.

Money matters: Up to 20 King's Scholarships and exhibitions as well as music and sports and art scholarships, all with a rigorous selection process and worth up to 10 per cent of fees. Three or four sixth form scholarships awarded for outstanding performance in the sixth form entrance exam. Greater emphasis on bursaries – the King's foundation has been set up to fund both scholarships and bursaries and allocated over £1 million a year. Parents means-tested annually and can receive up to 100 per cent of full boarding fee.

Remarks: Thriving academic school with highly motivated pupils. 'The children never stop – I do not know they fit everything into their day and still have time for a busy social life,' said one parent. Not a heavily religious school but the Benedictine tradition of care for body, mind and spirit is very much in evidence.

Lancing College

Lancing, West Sussex BN15 0RW

01273 452213
admissions@lancing.org.uk
www.lancingcollege.co.uk
C of E

Ages: 13–18
Pupils: 550 pupils; sixth form: 260
Boarders: 205 boys/127 girls full, 59 boys/11 girls flexi
Day: £23,130 pa
Boarding: £32,910 pa

Head Master: Since September 2014, Dominic Oliver MPhil, who left an academic career at Oxford to teach in schools, starting out at the Royal Grammar in Worcester, then moving to head of English at Malvern College, before becoming deputy head of Bedales schools. Married to Lydia, with a child at Lancing College and another at Lancing Prep.

Clearly feels comfortably at home at Lancing, which he describes as 'recognisable public schooling with a unique combination of warmth and vigour'; more subtle than Bedales 'self consciously liberal' approach, but perhaps no less radical under its new leader. As a head who enjoys the work of old boy David Hare and other establishment rebels, he wants to hear his pupils' voices: school council

will soon come into being and Mr Oliver teaches the third form debating – he enjoys provoking argument. It takes a certainty and confidence in both self and school to allow dissent and a bit of cheekiness; and quite some nerve to put a big wheel and carousel outside that grimly beautiful sinners and hellfire chapel on founder's day.

Mr Oliver brings a new culture of reflective education, with a greater emphasis on enrichment, and more students than ever doing the EPQ. They're tightening up on entrance standards – there must be evident sparks of intellect, and the very best grades will be needed for entrance and expected as outcomes (although they should be a natural outcome of the new intellectual regime).

Mr Oliver's most desirable quality for pupils is to be illuminated (a word which suggests a glowing sort of enlightenment).

Academic matters: Very good, consistent performance at GCSE and A level: 55 per cent A*/A grades at GCSE in 2015; at A level, 55 per cent A*/A grades, 76 per cent A*/B: great results from a virtually mixed ability school. Not top grades at all costs: pupils are set a target appropriate to them, and there is celebration if the target is met; whether that target be a C or A*. 'Not an exam factory, so doesn't attract those sort of parents', and one parent commented that they opted for Lancing over a more academically pressurising competitor. Tremendous value added at Lancing – pupils achieve exam grades they wouldn't have dreamed of.

Core subjects are always streamed, others usually so (where numbers allow). Class sizes around 18 in years 9-11, down to a maximum of 15 in the sixth form. Maths is outstanding, popular with pupils and excellent results – a triple maths A level student enthused about the teaching, and useful weekly drop in sessions. Pupils give good reports of history too. Super science labs, remodelled in last few years, although science results not outstanding. Great well-stocked library with mezzanine level of computers. There are plenty of languages on offer: French, German, Spanish, Italian, Greek, Latin – pupils start with two languages in year 9, and must continue with one until GCSE. German and Chinese strong. A jolly year 9 German class showed off their iPads (now standard issue), which come into their own when teaching languages: teachers can set oral homework, and iPads will

correct pronunciation; no more lost homework since pupils are emailed assignments.

Two reports during each term with grades for each subject, and a full written report at the end of term. Early remedial action if someone is falling behind – 'no one falls through the net'. A learning support department supports around 80 pupils with mild to moderate learning difficulties (mostly mild dyslexia), of whom 35 require continuous one-to-one support (at extra cost). Recent significant increase of in-class support via two full time and one part time learning support teachers who assist small groups within curriculum areas.

It takes a certainty and confidence in both self and school to allow dissent and a bit of cheekiness; and quite some nerve to put a big wheel outside that hellfire chapel

Games, options, the arts: School week covers six days, so four afternoon sessions for options – pupils here like to keep very busy. One afternoon a week students choose between CCF or community service. Drama is popular, even with non-actors – some of the academic hard core work backstage for light relief. Theatre seats 180, retractable seating means it's possible to play in the round, and make an orchestra pit in part of the old swimming pool on which the theatre was built. Drama GCSE, but not enough takers for A level, though LAMDA available.

About 15 productions a year – recently full-scale musical Oliver! and risque 'Tis Pity She's a Whore. Also an open air theatre.

Plenty of games sessions (down to twice a week for sixth formers), with lots of choice – focus on football, hockey, netball, cricket and tennis, but lots of other options, even for the not keen – 'I get by on yoga,' said one. One boy said he came to Lancing because it's a football school – other public schools generally favour rugby. Extensive playing fields, tennis courts, Astroturf pitch and swimming pool. And for those who love animals, farm is a sports/activities option – a sport hater/animal lover could exist blissfully at Lancing. The farm has really developed in recent years, particularly on the conservation front, and includes rare pigs, alpacas, lamas, turkeys, chickens, geese and goats, and lots of cuddly smalls and sheep – kids can get permission to stay out late and help with lambing. Meat and eggs from the farm have started feeding the school this year, and they are experimenting with a market garden with the aim of supplying veg too. Opportunities for five years' worth of vet experience as well as links with local agricultural colleges and primary schools and, via the school's Young Enterprise programme, for the marketing of college produce and wood supplies.

The music department is housed in standard 60s fare, but is staffed by teachers full of love for their subject and incredibly enthusiastic about sharing that love with pupils. Their scruffy studies overflow with sheet music; one, curiously, with a child's layout mat on the floor and a dog in the corner – who has apparently won over many recruits to music. 'They are mad,' said one pupil kindly, 'but we have a great time.' Plenty of practice rooms, which only get too busy at Associated Board exam times. Drum kit handy for those who want to pop in for a jam. Glorious choir (lovely CD – Surrexit), and numerous orchestras and bands. Lunchtime concerts most weeks, and a big concert every half term. Many continue to patronise the music block even if they don't take the subject, and around 300 learn instruments, some multiple instruments. A fine tradition of composition and of producing organ scholars to Oxbridge colleges.'It's all about joy in music making,' said one teacher – there is certainly much delight taken in music here. One parent, who encouraged her reluctant son to join the choir, says he enjoys it more than he ever (as a teenager) would admit – 'It's a very special thing to be part of.'

Art is a strong area: housed in a contemporary purpose-built centre, full of light, with eager students keen to show off their amazing work: everything from oils to an installation of hanging clingfilm, called 'Urban' – clay room and kiln, printing, etching, photography and fine art – 'Waterfront was our first topic this term, so we went to Venice' – where else? Older pupils have their own areas, so don't have to clear up paintings under way – the spacious rooms feel full of many little studios. Weekly drop-in art sessions for those who have never lifted a brush, or keen artists who just haven't got enough time to follow an art course. Art at every turn throughout the school – one house has turned the curve at the bottom of a stairwell into Venice.

Great DT centre, with examples of GCSE and A level work which wouldn't look out of place in a designer furniture store, along with a few quirky ideas – for dog owners who feel all that bend and throw is just a bit too energetic, how about an automatic dog ball launcher? Again, those who don't continue with this option can nevertheless return to pursue DT as a hobby.

Boarding: Over two-thirds of pupils at Lancing are boarders, around 330 full and 70 flexi (more boys than girls). Certainly boarders seem very happy and enjoy having a wealth of activity available on their doorsteps. Modern, comfortable accommodation, with a rolling programme of refurbishment, although you won't find the gold taps one parent was hoping for. Years 9 and 10, two to four in a room, from year 11, single study bedrooms. Shared rooms are filled to capacity with beds and desks, but the pupils don't object to cosy conditions: one sixth former told me how much she missed sharing a room with friends – 'I've been with them since I was 13 – they are like my

sisters.' Day pupils can board for a night free if they are at school after 9 pm on school business, such as play rehearsals, which pleases parents.

Friends can visit house communal areas – although pupils often go and chat out on the quads after dinner. Houses have common rooms (with Sky +), squashy sofas and views over rolling countryside, and kitchens with daily deliveries of bread, spreads, and fruit for any time consumption. Each house has Wifi throughout; one house has a sweet shop open in the evenings. Sixth formers have their own common room and houses have a number of kitchens for different year groups – 'It's the best thing about the house.' School café opens at break, in the afternoons and evening for hungry pupils after prep.

Flexible boarding structure, with no differentiation between full and weekly boarders, who pay the same fees and can stay at weekends if they wish. Day pupils can pay by the night for flexi-boarding if they have evening activities.

Background and atmosphere: Grand old buildings of Sussex flint, dating from 1848, with elegant quads and huge chapel standing on the hill overlooking the rolling Downs. In this beautiful setting, it feels distinctly public school, but it's not as cut glass as all that. Clearly impresses parents – 'They're experiencing things to do with heritage and a sense of history which seep into their experience and become something they value.'

Purpose-built centre full of light, with eager students keen to show off their amazing work: everything from oils to an installation of hanging clingfilm, called 'Urban'

A Woodard school, it has a strong Christian tradition, still very much in evidence. No skipping weekly chapel here, for conscientious objectors or other faiths – 'It might not be something they carry on with later in life, but at least they have been exposed to it – like maths,' said a teacher. Although a Christian school, they are not out to convert you – pupils of all faiths or no faith are welcome here. It's more about the values of Christianity, and in particular caring for each other. The service is a wonderful thing to experience – inside, the chapel is glorious and the voices of the choir soar – only St Paul's Cathedral has a higher ceiling. High church with plenty of bells and smells and the accompanying pageantry. Pupils seem to attend quite happily though, girls wrapped in 19th century style cloaks of house colours; boys just cold. Most troop up for communion or a blessing. Pupils assure us that a

fair number attend voluntary chapel – held in the crypt daily before breakfast or in the evenings in houses. One parent said she felt doing the communal thing is very important – apparently leavers most miss their time in chapel. New television screens mean that, on high days and holidays, when the place is packed with parents and former pupils, all can see and be involved in the services.

There is a rather splendid dining hall – could almost be a back up chapel should something happen to the other one, with long wooden tables and new wooden chairs. Wide range of food available, nice, but not remarkable on the day of our visit – one pupil said it 'goes up and down a bit.' Sixth formers can skip breakfast in the dining hall and cook their own.

The sixth form is not for those who want to scruff around in jeans and tee shirts for a couple of years – smart business wear is expected here, with more responsibility as prefects or house captains, and more independence, in organising time in and out of school: year 11 and sixth formers can go into Brighton, and they're considering allowing the sixth up to London. In common with the rest of the school, some fabulous trips on offer: the travel section of the school magazine resembles a highly desirable travel brochure.

Pastoral care, well-being and discipline: Parents say it is 'like being part of a community with a strong family atmosphere.' Well-defined house system with a network of people taking care of pupils. As well as housemasters/mistresses (the first point of call for parents), there is a matron on hand, year 10 'uncles' and 'aunts' for new year 9s, and the peer support system provided by sixth formers. If all this fails, 'there is always a teacher you get on with particularly well'. Pupils admit to feeling a bit homesick for a few weeks, but say it quickly wears off. At break time, kids troop back to their house common room for squash and biscuits: some kids pop in and straight out again, others sit and chat to matron and other house staff. It is a moment away from work – like having a break with your mum. Matron – 'We are their family here.'

Parents feel discipline is 'not in your face'. Seems to work, but quite gently done. Approach 'firm but fair'. One mum says the balance must be right, because the kids are so relaxed about going to school. Bullying, drug and alcohol abuse not generally a problem, but will be dealt with severely. The one pupil who could recall an episode of bullying was clearly startled by how strictly it had been dealt with.

Communication is good where a parent has a concern – email or telephone contact will lead to a rapid and thorough response; new Parent Portal. Parents say school is very welcoming and encourages parents to feel involved; plenty of social events – plays, concerts, matches, lectures, informative talks, dinners and a healthy Parents' Association. There is some small tension between the parent who felt that parents of day pupils require more communication (than those of boarders), and the staff feeling that 'occasionally helicopter parents need to be told to buzz off in the interests of their child.' This does feel like a school where parents should be prepared to step back a bit, and let their child develop responsibility for themselves.

Pupils and parents: Fits oddballs – we met some pupils who were strongly individual but seemed very happy at Lancing. 'Not for the inert,' said one teacher, 'nor for one-dimensional academic types,' said another. Pupils from Lancing's two preps and other prep schools in the area. Parents generally middle class professionals, city types, and around 25 per cent of boarders from overseas. School runs its own buses, routes to suit need from the surrounding area, and shuttle between Lancing College and the preps.

Former pupils include playwrights Sir David Hare, Christopher Hampton and Giles Cooper, lyricist Sir Tim Rice, novelists Tom Sharpe and Evelyn Waugh, Shakespeare scholar and writer John Dover Wilson, singer Sir Peter Pears, Archbishop Trevor Huddleston, TV presenter Jamie Theakston, Sir Christopher Meyer, Charles Anson, Dr Rana Mitter, Sir Roy Calne, Stephen Green (Baron Green of Hurstpierpoint) and Alex Horne.

Entrance: Gently selective – mid 50 per cent pass rate at CE, with separate assessment for those from the state sector. For the sixth form, need good GCSEs and school reference, interviews and tests.

A few places in year 10; some 30-35 places for girls at sixth form, 10-15 for boys.

Exit: Around 15 per cent leave after GCSEs. Four to Oxbridge in 2015, several to North American universities. UCL, LSE and other London colleges popular alongside Exeter, Warwick and Bristol. Broad mix of subjects ranging from engineering and economics to zoology and theology.

Money matters: At 13, academic, music, art, drama, sports and all-rounder scholarships, up to half of fees, which can be augmented depending on family circumstances. Sixth form awards – academic, music and art, up to a third of fees.

Remarks: A friendly and beautiful place to grow up. Pupils are happy, and unselfconsciously themselves. This is a place where individuals will flourish, and there is evidently great care and attention to ensure this is so. Not for those who like to take things easy – a culture of keeping busy.

Lavant House

West Lavant, Chichester, West Sussex PO18 9AB

01243 527211	**Ages:** 11–18 (junior boarding from 8)
office@lavanthouse.org.uk	**Pupils:** 85; sixth form: 11
www.lavanthouse.org.uk	**Boarders:** 50 full, weekly and flexi
C of E	**Day:** £6,945 – £13,950 pa
	Boarding: £18,225 – £21,945 pa

Headmistress: Since September 2015, Mrs Nicola Walker, previously head of Ffynone House School in Wales and before that deputy head of Haberdasher's Monmouth School for Girls. Maths degree from Lancaster, PGCE from Oxford, MBA in educational management from Leicester and and MEd in education leadership from Buckingham. Has also been a Welsh schools peer inspector. Married with one grown up daughter.

Academic matters: This is such a small school that statistics are almost meaningless, especially at A level: in 2015, upper sixth between them took 15 A levels, of which 20 per cent were A*/As and 27 per cent A*/B – bright girls do well here and get the top grades, but most are Bs and Cs. Nineteen subjects are offered at A level, including psychology, Chinese and further maths. Maths and science are as popular at A level as media studies and art. The school is very flexible with the curriculum and individual timetables are designed around girls' subject choices – the pupils who showed us round were both receiving one-to-one tuition in one of their A level subjects.

There was an impressive green man exhibition and a particularly beautiful picture of a leopard

In 2015, 81 per cent of pupils achieved 5 A* – C grades at GCSE, 33 per cent of grades were A*/A.

Girls do well in sciences, which are offered as a dual award and individually. Art, music, drama, ICT, Spanish and German, are all offered alongside the core subjects; everyone takes up Spanish in year 8. Lots of participation in outside events – school sends a team to the UK mathematical challenge and other team maths challenges and takes part in the chemistry festival at Brighton University, and girls encouraged to take an active interest in current affairs. Sixth form offered help with time management, study skills and UCAS forms as well as interview practice, and have the option to attend a careers conference in London. Setting in core subjects from year 10, and small classes mean girls can go at their own pace.

Thirteen full time and 19 part time staff (no male teachers currently). 'It's more like a family here,' said our guides. 'We get on well with our teachers and lessons are fun; teachers give us extra help in free time or even in the holidays'. About 25 per cent have mild to moderate dyslexia and either have one-to-one help or in class support. Maths, science and English clinics offered to those who need them and a handful receive one-to-one EAL support.

Games, options, the arts: Thriving music department – chamber orchestra, flute choir, wind band and strings groups give performances and concerts in the ballroom, and also perform at local musical events like the Chichester Cathedral Flower Festival – 'We make real music,' said one enthusiastic girl. Over 50 per cent learn at least one instrument – flute and singing are particularly popular – and music is offered as a GCSE. One girl is doing grade 8 flute and has guitar lessons at the Royal College of Music. They do a whole school production every other year and almost everyone gets involved; girls can also take part in the Chichester Youth Theatre. Good take up of speech and drama lessons, with some pupils reaching grade 8 in LAMDA exams; drama offered at GCSE.

They do surprisingly well at sport for such a small school, and many who might get overlooked in a bigger school can take part – U15 netball regional champions for the last four years, and teams can train at Chichester netball club. Girls encouraged to play for local clubs. School has its own netball and tennis courts and a grass hockey pitch as well as an old fashioned gym and an outdoor pool, and most keep going with team sports – volleyball popular with the older girls. 'You don't have to be very sporty to have fun'. Riding offered at the riding school next door, where girls can keep their ponies.

Art is one of the great strengths of the school: the inspirational art teacher 'encourages the spectacular' and artwork displayed all over the place. When we visited there was an impressive green man exhibition and a particularly beautiful painting of a leopard was on display – huge variety offered, and girls can work on their own skills. Offers the unendorsed GCSE course, so girls can do fine art, textiles, photography, ceramics and 3D design. Works exhibited at Pallant House in Chichester and at the District Fine Arts Society. Local outings to Fishbourne Roman Villa and the Downland Museum and trips to France and Spain open to the whole school. Food technology lab recently opened, where cake making is particularly popular and sixth formers learn cooking for university. Good range of lunch time and after-school activities, including various musical and sports clubs, Duke of Edinburgh, creative writing, debating and public speaking, and the Raspberry Pi computer club where girls learn product and software design, Python coding and testing.

'It's like a family here. We get on well with our teachers and lessons are fun; teachers give us extra help in free time or even in the holidays'

Boarding: The younger boarders are housed in immaculate dorms, all recently repainted, up in the eaves, named after saints and under the beady eye of the excellent and caring senior housemistress. Very flexible casual boarding if there are beds to spare. Year 11 and lower sixth have single rooms and upper sixth have their own cottage complete with a courtyard in the converted stable block, where they can live fairly independently but with the housemistress living nearby.

Background and atmosphere: A very small school with less than 100 girls in the senior school and about 20 in the junior school. It was founded in 1952 by Dora Green, originally for her own children, one of whom is still on the board of governors. Grade II listed 18th century brick and flint house set in 50 acres of gardens and playing fields, it is surrounded by the rolling countryside of the South Downs National Park, but only a few miles north of Chichester. Definitely feels like someone's country house, it is only the netball trophies and photos in the hall which give the game away. It is very elegant and civilized, and although you might feel you have stepped back in time, this is an outward-looking and modern school. The inspectors commented that 'pupils are quietly confident and courteous, in keeping with the graciousness which surrounds them'. Only sixth formers and staff are allowed to walk down the sweeping red-carpeted staircase. Grand dining room which leads out on to the verandah where girls can eat in the summer – with good food and plenty of choice and salads.

Pastoral care, well-being and discipline: Strong Christian ethos with assemblies every morning, and the parish church is used for special occasions. Operates like a large family with great care and concern for individual well-being. Any problems dealt with quickly – 'a quiet word usually does the trick'. 'I cannot fault the school,' said one mother whose daughter had not thrived elsewhere. 'Everyone comes out of the school smiling and no one is in a rush to leave.' In such a small school everyone has to take part, and there are badges for everything and stars for kindness, and in the sixth form everyone gets leadership experience, unlike in larger schools.

Pupils and parents: Mostly local businesspeople, farmers and commuters, all of whom are looking for a small school which focuses on an individual approach to learning. Particularly appeals to those whose children are not reaching their potential elsewhere and who need nurturing. Up to five per cent foreign nationals, with around a third of boarders from overseas – not enough to form cliques, so integrate well. Other international students sometimes come for short periods – anything from a few weeks to a couple of terms. Strong friendships are made with the French and Spanish children who come for the summer term. Good mixing between year groups; 'a real family feel,' says one girl. 'I can talk to anyone and sit and have lunch with different people'; ' Teachers are part of the family and very helpful and nothing is too much trouble'. The ethos is to be 'kind, compassionate and work together as a team', and everyone has to get involved. 'They build your confidence and teach you so many life lessons.' No Saturday school and boarders often go to stay with local girls. Breakfast club for children of working parents who can also stay on for prep at school until 6pm.

Entrance: Most girls join at 11+ but some come at 12+ or 13+, or any other time if there are spaces. Eleven plus assessment day in January with tests in English, maths and non-verbal reasoning, and girls join some lessons and have an interview. Those joining at other times are tested in English and maths and also join some lessons. About 50 per cent come up from the junior school and others from local primaries and prep schools eg Great Ballard, Prebendal and Oakwood. The head of the lower senior school visits all those coming into year 7 at their current school in the term before they join. Sixth form entry on a case by case basis but dependent on GCSE results.

Exit: Large fall out after GCSEs (up to 80 per cent), either into the state system or to co-eds; most sixth formers go on to university or art college. Some to read academic subjects at Russell Group universities, others to more vocational courses like early childhood studies at Norland College or equine management at Hadlow.

Money matters: Academic, art, music and sports scholarships awarded at 11+, 13+ and sixth form, and one riding scholarship. Some funds for bursaries, usually up to a maximum of 50 per cent of the day fee.

Remarks: A charming small school where everyone knows everyone, which brings out the best in its girls with its individual approach to learning, and particularly suits those who need some extra nurturing. Very small classes mean that girls can go at their own speed with the brightest being challenged.

Marlborough House School

Hawkhurst, Cranbrook, Kent TN18 4PY

01580 753555
registrar@marlboroughhouseschool.co.uk
www.marlboroughhouseschool.co.uk
C of E

Ages: 3 – 13
Pupils: 320
Boarders: 40 flexi
Day: £7,875 – £16,290 pa
Boarding: plus £30 per night

Headmaster: Since 2013, Mr Martyn Ward BEd. Educated at Repton and Colston's School, Bristol, then Westminster College, Oxford. Previously deputy head of St Andrew's School, Eastbourne. Before that, taught English and history at The Hall in Hampstead and English at Cothill. A keen musician and sportsman, he's married to Rachel and they have two young daughters.

Entrance: It is worth registering as soon as possible as oversubscribed, but most people who really want a place usually get one. Informal assessment day plus school report and interview with the head. No formal tests – important that the school is right for the child. Those with mild learning difficulties assessed to make sure the school can cater for their needs. Majority of children arrive in the nursery and stay right through until 13, although children can join at any age if spaces. Some children come in from the primaries for the last two years to sit Cranbrook entrance exam. A few move on to boarding preps at 8+. Two form entry throughout the school.

Exit: Mainly to fairly local schools. Around 40 per cent to Cranbrook Grammar, plus Tonbridge, King's Canterbury, Sevenoaks, Eastbourne College,

Brighton College, Benenden, Sutton Valence and Mayfield. Occasionally further afield to, eg, Harrow, Winchester, Rugby, Eton. Good range of scholarships most years. In the past few years pupils have been awarded academic scholarships to Harrow, Sevenoaks, Claremont, Sutton Valence and Mayfield and an academic exhibition to King's Canterbury, a music scholarship to King's Canterbury, art scholarships to Tonbridge and Eastbourne, an art and music scholarship to Ardingly and sports scholarships to Eastbourne, Kent College, Sutton Valence and Mayfield. Three to four a year leave at 11+ for the grammars – the school prepares children for the Kent Test.

Remarks: Founded in 1874, the school moved in 1930 to a Georgian house set in 34 acres of landscaped grounds on the edge of Hawkhurst. Wonderful setting where everything looks beautiful and is kept immaculately. Purpose-built pre-prep and a large sports hall used by all age groups. The nursery is in its own house next to the main school with its own garden and play equipment.

No streaming but children are setted in some subjects from 7. Spanish or Latin introduced as a second language from year 5. Touch typing taught from year 3. No special scholarship class – gifted children are given individually tailored programmes within their year group in the form of one-to-one tuition, discussion forums and small extension groups. Good back-up for mild dyslexia – three full-time learning support staff for individual or group sessions. Teachers always on the look out for problems.

Billed by the school as 'an informal introduction to boarding', it's both a great way to familiarise children who may be going on to boarding senior schools and great fun

An exceptionally friendly school where everyone is quickly made to feel part of the community. The Friends of Marlborough House, a parents' group, is very active in welcoming new parents and making them feel part of the school. They also organise social events throughout the year – quiz nights, various parent/teacher friendlies and the biennial summer ball. Own in-house catering – excellent food with everything prepared on site, justifiably proud of their reputation.

No full or weekly boarding but flexi-boarding (year 8 onwards) is a popular option and most children do a bit of this. Four nights is the maximum with majority staying for one or two per week.

No special scholarship class – gifted children are given individually tailored programmes in the form of one-to-one tuition, discussion forums

Billed by school as 'an informal introduction to boarding', it's both a great way to familiarise children who may be going on to boarding senior schools and huge fun. Described as a 'sleepover with your friends but with enforced lights out'. School produces a booklet that explains boarding to pupils and includes thoughtful information such as 'What happens if I'm ill?' and 'Where can I go if I want to be alone?'

About two-thirds of prep school pupils learn a musical instrument up to and including grade 8 – a good record of music scholarships. A number of informal concerts throughout the year. Lots of opportunities to get involved with music-making. Thriving art department with scholarships most years. Creative pottery workshops for year 8. Annual art exhibition featuring work from every pupil. Strong IT department. All have a chance to get involved in drama productions during the year – one big school play annually and smaller plays for most year groups during the year, plus the very popular Marlborough House X Factor. Everyone given the opportunity to take part in the annual poetry reading competition. Plenty of trips and outings both locally and further afield – geography trips to Montreuil and Isle of Wight. French and classics trip to Aix-en-Provence and annual winter skiing trip.

Produces confident children who are generally tolerant and respectful of each other. School keen to ensure that children are aware of a world beyond the school gates – emphasis on fundraising and charity work, eg the whole school did the Sports Relief mile. Pupils visit the elderly at Bowles Lodge Residential Centre in Hawkhurst to chat to them and the younger pupils visit to entertain the residents with songs and poems. Values for Living Code displayed around the school: be honest, be kind, be helpful, be polite, listen, do your best. Calm, ordered school where everything seems to run smoothly.

Famous old boys include cricketer David Gower, screen writer and director Stephen Poliakoff and his brother, the chemist Professor Martyn Poliakoff CBE.

A very happy, caring and gentle school where every child is treated as an individual and reaches their full potential, academically and in sport, art, drama and music – always looking for hidden talents.

Marymount International School

George Road, Kingston upon Thames, Surrey KT2 7PE

020 8949 0571
admissions@marymountlondon.com
www.marymountlondon.com
RC

Ages: 11–18
Pupils: 260; sixth form: 100
Boarders: 85 full, 14 weekly
Day £18,680 – £21,340 pa
Boarding: plus £13,230 – £14,770 pa

Headmistress: Since 2010, Sarah Gallagher MA (40s). Educated at a convent school, she studied for her degrees at University College Galway. Previous teaching and leadership posts at boarding and day schools including Queen's Gate, Lord Wandsworth College, most recently St Leonards-Mayfield School, taught in Rome. Dips in to teach Latin at Marymount from time to time.

Attractive, stylish and poised, she is articulate and empathetic in her interactions with others, strategic in her approach. The girls say she is 'busy and important' but also approachable. 'Ms Gallagher is so intelligent that you just think to yourself you could not possibly have a conversation with her, but when you do she is lovely.' Can picture this head on Mastermind or in the finals of a schools' edition of 'Strictly'. Husband also a teacher, two daughters at university. 'I want to build on the strength already here, a tremendous appreciation for learning and its significance in the school and its application outside school. The

girls are learning for life; building character and community is integral to this. It's an exciting place to work, parents and students are committed, the philosophy of the IB and RHSM [Religious of the Sacred Heart of Mary] and Marymount London are all compatible.'

Academic matters: Marymount is a Catholic secondary girls school offering the IB Middle Years (MYP) and IB to an international community. The first (1979) girls' school in the UK to take up the IB in Britain, Marymount's grade 6-10 curriculum is built on solid institutional foundations. In 2015 pupils scored an average of 36, with 25 per cent earning 40+ points; one candidate achieved a perfect score (45), a result attained by fewer than 0.2 per cent of students worldwide and several other Marymount girls have achieved similar in previous years.

No resting on laurels, they've been reviewing the MYP to align it with IGCSE content, ensuring

all topics are covered in the IBMYP context by end of grade 9. Head wants parents to be assured of MYP rigour, the priority is to be learning-driven, not taught to the test. Range of IB subjects and results is excellent. Lots of sciences, 'and we do lots of field trips', say the girls. The school is offering a relatively new IB course, environmental systems and societies, which satisfies either the IB science or IB humanities requirement. 'My sister likes geography and science so it's perfect for her.' Marymount's MYP covers the broad spectrum of disciplines, with the interesting addition of philosophy to introduce the girls to 'the language of philosophy' before they embark on theory of knowledge at diploma level. As would be expected, religious education is also a key part of the programme.

School prides itself on the wide range of languages offered. Extra mother tongue support in German and French in grades 6-8 dependent on enrolment. Parents warn that languages are sometimes subject to demand and in a small school it's not always possible to satisfy all requests for second language. It seems that there are mixed messages here and prospective parents are advised to discuss this at the early stages to clarify. The school does its best to support girls in working out alternative options – as one pupil explained, 'a friend who speaks Thai is taking IB Thai mother tongue; she's self-taught with the help of a tutor'.

The school is wireless throughout; iPads now in grades 6-9 and will move up the grades as pupils progress; girls were excited to show off the first new Mac TVs, there are more to come. The library has undergone a complete refurbishment – it has 9,000 volumes and membership of London Library enhances the collection.

Classes never more than 16 and many, particularly at diploma level, only four to six, fewer still

for languages. Some classrooms are designed with small seminar-style groups in mind.

The teaching faculty is an international bunch, average age 40s. Pupil-teacher ratio is six to one and staff seem to know most of the girls, affirming parent comments about supportive and nurturing environment with a caring individualised approach. Low turnover and enough long-termers to provide a cohesive core. Plenty of support staff and school nurse on site.

Remaining nuns live in a wing off the hall. Sisters no longer teach but are part of the fabric of the school, occasionally sharing cocoa and study evenings with the girls

Mild/moderate learning difficulties and other issues managed collaboratively by the learning resource coordinator, teachers, parents and students themselves. Lots of individualised support throughout the school and the girls themselves were quick to talk about peer tutoring offered during free periods or after school.

The enrichment programme for able students has about 40 on the register. These students are invited to apply to programmes sponsored by Ivy Leagues (Stanford, Yale, Princeton, Johns Hopkins) and top tier UK universities. Additional provision includes extracurricular activities as well as resources which are made available to students for independent study and wider reading.

Games, options, the arts: Mix of competitive and non-competitive sporting activities available for all grades on and off site. If the school does not offer a particular sport they will help connect with local teams. Marymount is part of the International School Sports Association and they have produced an impressive record of results in soccer, badminton and tennis at championship tournaments hosted by member schools in different parts of Europe. One pupil training with the Chelsea Ladies' development squad and several play with the Richmond Volleyball Club. When girls were asked why they chose Marymount, one replied that she came for the sport and when you hear that one of their football trainers is with Chelsea, no prizes for guessing which team Marymount girls support.

Musicians have plenty of opportunities to play in ensembles and chamber groups. About 20 per cent take private instrumental or singing lessons; school boasts a 100 per cent pass rate in grade exams. Entry to the choir is by audition and choristers participate in school concerts and annual tours to European cities, performing in major churches and cathedrals. Teachers encourage girls to perform in local festivals and competitions.

Drama is inclusive and the entire community builds up to a major production each year; in true girls' school tradition male roles are played by the girls. Keen thespians can participate in ISTA (International School Theatre Association) festivals and when we visited girls were buzzing about their weekend ISTA trip to Stratford upon Avon. LAMDA examinations offered. Visual arts seem focused on painting and photography – the girls tell us that the art teacher is an inspiring photographer. Framed art by generations of pupils displayed throughout the school.

Consensus is that the most fun of all is the 'international day', when everyone shares their culture and cuisine.'The Japanese do the best, and the [boarding] girls are already planning even though it's still months away'. Zumbathon – a fundraising activity involving the whole community beeping and bopping, swinging and swaying to music – was also highly popular and yielded no casualties.

As a Catholic IB school, community service involves everyone at Marymount. Middle schoolers do environmental projects that include cleaning along the bank of the Thames. Older girls volunteer in local activities including soup kitchens and schools and further afield join other RHSM students in projects working with children in places such as Zambia. All students take part in the spiritual life of the school and attend an annual retreat. Girls of all faiths come to Marymount and this provides opportunities for students to learn about other beliefs and traditions; care is taken to ensure that everyone feels comfortable at mass and prayer. We visited on a Hindu feast day and the girls said they had started the day with a Hindu prayer; Muslim girls wear their headscarves with confidence.

Boarding: Almost half the pupils board and there are four halls, each with its own duo of house parents. Boarding rooms (some bunk beds) and facilities are clean and pretty tidy. Boarding areas are kept locked during the school day unless a girl has a reason to be back in her room. Oldest boarders have the spacious shared bedrooms above and the remaining nuns living in a wing just off their hall. Sisters no longer teach but are very much part of the fabric of the school, occasionally eating or sharing cocoa and study evenings with the girls.

The school's proximity to Heathrow is an attraction for boarding parents; the girls say that the school's proximity to London is the attraction for them. The lure of London aside, boarders enjoy theatre and music trips as well as days out to the seaside (Brighton) and theme parks such as Longleat. There's plenty going on inside school too, including dance and music workshops and

opportunities to explore and develop one's faith. Worth mentioning here that the school also takes weekly boarders from local (ie London) families and it is sometimes possible to arrange short-term boarding for day girls whose parents travel.

Clear procedures allow boarders off-campus freedoms to visit friends and family while ensuring their safety. One guardian who has long looked after boarders during half-term breaks told us that some older girls feel the school is too strict. She helps them, and their far-off parents who hear the grumbles, appreciate that the school is being cautious and not unreasonable. Two exclusions in the last three years of boarders who, after several warnings, broke the rules about leaving campus.

Background and atmosphere: Established in Kingston in 1955 by 10 nuns from the Religious of the Sacred Heart of Mary (RSHM), sent by the Eastern American Province. Mid-19th century French founder of RSHM aspired to provide charity for all classes through schools, homes and orphanages that worked interactively across socioeconomic barriers. Schools opened in France, Ireland, Portugal, England, the US and later Latin America and the rest of the world. The first sisters who came to Kingston started a 'year abroad' programme for US university women, then a school offering the US secondary school curriculum. Early 70s saw the arrival of Sister Anne Marie Hill, a determined Irish mover-and-shaker, well known in international education circles and now executive director of the network of schools. She introduced the IB, making the school more relevant to its growing international student body and reflecting RSHM's original ethos. During the noughties Marymount had a series of heads as RSHM grappled with transition to lay leadership and during that time the board of governors was created.

In Ms Gallagher the sisters seem to have found the ideal head who brings continuity at the top, leading the school from strength to strength thanks to the partnership forged with the RSHM sisters and the board she describes as 'independent and experienced'. Enrolments are at an all-time high and it's all-systems-go for development plans aimed at enhancing programmes and facilities. School works closely with the other Marymount partners under Sister Anne Marie's guidance, meeting every six to eight weeks to discuss areas such as strategic planning and communication. Increasingly involvement with the international network of RSHM schools – 19 worldwide – is now bringing more opportunities to the pupils.

Elegant grounds with lawns and sculptured hedges. 'The teddy bear topiary sold me,' says one dad. 'How can you not love a school that has a teddy bear topiary?'

The school is based in an affluent part of Surrey occupying a large Edwardian house plus various more recent additions connected by walkways. Elegant grounds with lawns, manicured flower-beds and sculpted hedges. 'The teddy bear topiary sold me', says one dad, 'How can you not love a school that has teddy bear topiary?' (We presume he had already consulted the GSG about minor details such as teaching and pastoral care.) Main house, with original wood panelling and stained glass, is head office and reception. The nuns are loved by the girls and parents appreciate their presence. Small school chapel is used by boarders and local community alike and plans to re-develop and open the ceiling to the rafters and heavens above are under way.

Modern blocks house multi-purpose classrooms, the library and university and careers counselling rooms. Another block has the gym (floor replaced recently), music rooms and auditorium for assemblies, all-school mass, drama. Yet another has more dorms, cafeteria (food is 'so-so', particularly at weekends), classrooms, infirmary, student lounges. A new quasi-Scandinavian wooden structure houses more small tutorial rooms just right for the many language classes and designed with IB language examination conditions in mind. Most of the buildings surround the garden and have big windows that bring the outdoors in and give a refreshing sense of space and light.

Pastoral care, well-being and discipline: Spiritual values underpin the ethos of Marymount, rooted in the mission of the RSHM, 'that all may have life'. These values are made explicit on the website: even the most casual browser will see them on every page, running alongside photos. School welcomes girls from all faiths but we think it might not be a comfortable environment for the girl who has none.

Plenty of support available at the school: academic, social, emotional and personal; more expertise called upon if necessary. The headmistress is well briefed and aware of anyone who may be feeling overwhelmed, unhappy, unsettled. Girls say she shows genuine interest.

Parents' Association hosts a welcome back family barbecue during the first weekend of the school year when boarding parents are there dropping off daughters so they are able to meet day families. One parent said the school went out of its way, allowing their daughter to board temporarily so she could start at the beginning of the year, before the family transfer to London took place. Another described how the teachers made an effort to encourage her daughter to join the orchestra for a big performance, even though her late arrival meant she had missed several rehearsals.

Pupils and parents: Marymount girls are internationally diverse, cheerful, articulate, academically motivated, quietly confident and as a bunch, quite enchanting. More aspirational then ambitious, they love their school and really enjoy having peers from all over the world. They look out for each other, especially new ones, and although one day girl says she wishes there were more ways to get closer to the boarders, everyone, including day parents, feels that the day girls and boarders are pretty integrated.

The girls are reflective about the realities of being in a single-sex environment. They feel they are able to focus more on learning, but they would like to find a 'partner' boys' school and the student council have made some moves in this direction. Trouble is that 'all the boys' (schools) seem to be taken', but they have not given up. Head is a big advocate of the girls' school advantage, having also worked in mixed schools. 'When adolescent girls become interested in boys, it can be frustrating to see how much they measure themselves against the approval of the boys in the group. Without that distraction they can develop as intellectually rigorous learners, they are their own people.'

The families that choose the school value the ethos of school, its Catholicism and internationalism, but are equally attracted to the IB. There are 40 nationalities in the school, British representing just over half. Other significant groups are German, Spanish, Japanese, Chinese, US, Australian, Korean and Italian. The numbers within these groups are balanced very carefully to facilitate integration. The school bus service extends into London to Sloane Square and more routes are under consideration.

Parents' Association organises events including outings for parents which are appreciated by newly-arrived expats.

Entrance: Local families are urged to attend one of the open days. Inbound expats on 'look-see' trips to London may book appointments. Girls' admissions based on availability and a review of school reports and teacher references. The headmistress interviews all girls prior to offering a place. English language fluency is required with exceptions made for younger students for whom English is a second language. Most classes have waiting lists so best to apply a year in advance though there is some turnover so you could be lucky.

Local feeder schools include Holy Cross, The Study, Fulham Prep, St Agatha's, The Grove, The Old Vicarage, The German School (Deutsche Schule London), Putney Park, Garden House, Unicorn School, Cameron House, Ursuline School. Day girls come from most SW London postcodes including Richmond, Wimbledon, Putney, Chelsea, South Kensington.

Exit: Small number leave to do A levels elsewhere. Most head to university and the chart we saw on the college counsellor's wall listing every 12th grader's destinations confirms that they are applying

to many countries. Counsellor stays in close contact with parents, especially boarder parents, about each girl's plan and the process they must follow depending on the country of their destination. PSAT and SATs also offered.

Two to Oxbridge in 2015; the rest go to eg Bristol, Durham, Exeter, Imperial, King's, Queen Mary, UCL, Warwick, York, Bath, St Andrews, Royal Northern College of Music as well as universities in the USA, Japan, Hong Kong, Spain and Germany.

Money matters: School has no endowment so financial stability is maintained by tuition and fundraising initiatives. 'Being an international school and in the current economic climate, we need to be sure we are guarded and forward looking – we can't rest on our laurels.' The PA also fundraises for activities that support the school and pupils.

Scholarships (academic, art, music, drama, sport, community service) for grade 6 and 8 students. Some offered for grades 10, 11 and 12. Some financial aid available for means-tested students. About 20 per cent of the pupils benefit from this.

Remarks: Successfully serves a niche market of internationally-minded families seeking a girls' school with a Catholic ethos. In the words of one parent, 'We've been over-the-top-happy. The school provides excellent support and people from all over the world fit in and are welcome there.'

Mayfield School

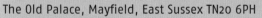

The Old Palace, Mayfield, East Sussex TN20 6PH

01435 874600
admissions@mayfieldgirls.org
www.mayfieldgirls.org
RC

Ages: 11–18
Pupils: 354; sixth form: 120
Boarders: 191
Day: £19,125 pa
Boarding: £30,900 pa

Headmistress: Since 2008, Miss Antonia Beary (30s). Read English at Trinity College, Cambridge, and has an MPhil in Catholic education. Two years at The Leys, Cambridge where she became assistant housemistress of the sixth form house, followed by six years at Ampleforth where she started as an English teacher and ended up in charge of the first girls' sixth form house. Two years as head of sixth form at New Hall before joining Mayfield in 2006 as pastoral deputy. Thoughtful, approachable, charming. Likes to help girls develop a sense of perspective and the confidence to make the right decisions. Humphrey the spaniel, always by her side, offers a

comforting paw to any nervous juniors who need a cuddle.

Academic matters: A level results good – 52 per cent A*/A grades in 2015, and at GCSE 68 per cent A*/A grades. Average class size 14 for GCSE and about 10 for A level. Good mix of teaching staff: some NQTs, some more venerable. Everyone has a laptop connected to school intranet – some financial assistance where necessary. Twenty-four girls currently doing City & Guilds GCSE in cooking, a practical, hands-on course taught in a big, light, airy kitchen – leads to diploma. A level home economics available. Cooking clubs and Saturday workshops well attended. Library a bit dated but a popular, quiet place to work. Plenty of help with personal statements and UCAS forms.

Learning support department very much in the centre of the school, where girls can go for help and reassurance: 'a real haven,' as one dyslexic girl put it. One full-time and two part-time teachers. Some 10-15 per cent need extra help, mainly for mild dyslexia – girls given coping strategies and learning support closely linked with teaching (first six 35 min lessons free; subsequently charged). All girls do baseline tests on arrival and staff quick to pick up any problems. Good ESOL department – eight periods a week – girls taken out of English and PE. Generally high scores on IELTS (average of 7.5 over the past four years) very good reputation with universities.

Games, options, the arts: Spectacular ceramics department. We were there when the GCSE and A level exhibits were on show in the cloister and it was like walking through a museum – we would have happily bought the lot. Enthusiastic and inspired art and textiles teacher. Lots of flexibility for girls to do what they want at after-school workshops four nights a week. Life drawing studio, jewellery, silversmith plus resins and plastics.

The usual sports but no lacrosse. Plenty of sporting opportunities for those who want. Riding a major feature – have won the National Schools Championships for four consecutive years and have a current show jumping hopeful. Recent leaver is a Badminton regular. Girls can keep their own ponies at the school's own equestrian centre within the

grounds, including indoor and outdoor sand schools and a cross-country course. Strong fencing; many girls represent their county and some have represented England at rounders. About 10 girls do Duke of Edinburgh gold each year. School very supportive of what the girls do outside school. Sport seems to tail off a bit in sixth from with a focus on top teams but school is trying to engage other girls in different sports eg sailing. PE offered at GCSE and A level.

Stunning medieval chapel which is central to school life and can seat every pupil, and where the Live Crib is performed each Christmas with a real donkey and real baby

Strong and very experienced music department. Singing particularly good – school's premier choir, the Schola Cantorum, recently performed evening mass in the Basilica di San Marco in Venice. Chapel choir often asked to sing at weddings. Good orchestra plus classical, musical theatre and rock band. Supervised practice after school. GCSE and A levels offered in music. Two or three drama productions per year – girls get involved in all aspects of production, direction, lighting and textiles department make the costumes in-house. A group of girls took a production up to the Edinburgh Fringe Festival. All performed in wonderful concert hall as are fashion shows and various musical events. Theatre studies taught at A level and drama at

GCSE. Annual inter-house performing arts festival – sixth form write, choreograph and produce a range of pieces and hone their people management skills. Dance is compulsory for years 7-9 and is a popular option further up the school, with ballet and salsa being taught by qualified visiting teachers.

Boarding: Majority full boarders of whom 20 per cent are from abroad; 50 or so weekly/flexi boarders. There are three boarding houses split by age. Middle years have dorms with anything up to eight cubicles in each, girls in years 12-13 have study bedrooms and can opt for single rooms. Weekend activities for boarders range from surfing to theatre trips.

Background and atmosphere: Founded in 1846 by Cornelia Connelly, foundress of the religious congregation for the education of Catholic girls, the Society of the Holy Child Jesus; a woman ahead of her time. In 1872 it moved into the The Old Palace of the Archbishop of Canterbury. Previously known as St Leonards-Mayfield, after sister schools joined up in 1953, but dropped the St Leonards prefix in 2015.

Stunning medieval chapel which is central to school life and can seat every pupil and where the Live Crib is performed each Christmas with a real donkey and real baby. All classrooms and facilities on one site. Lower school has its own separate building and own dining room in the main school. Three separate dining rooms – sixth form eat with staff. New sixth form centre with lecture and seminar rooms, ICT suite and independent study chambers. Strong Catholic ethos but over half now non-Catholic. Chapel is very important and central to school life. Everyone has to go and girls organise some of the liturgies. Encouraged to question everything and not take anything for granted.

Pastoral care, well-being and discipline: The first lay head was appointed in 2000. Nuns are still involved in pastoral care and are active in school community. Very supportive school – both girls and staff. 'Be yourself but be aware that you are part of a community.' Actions not Words programme takes girls outside the classroom to serve others and raise their awareness both of the needs of others and of ways in which they can all make a difference. A school of individuals – girls are encouraged to think independently and develop a strong moral awareness and sense of perspective. Not a hothouse. Compulsory mass on Sunday mornings and compulsory liturgy during the week for all year groups as well as occasional whole school masses throughout the term. Christianity rather than Catholicism at the centre of school. A female chaplain recently joined the school and has livened up the weekly liturgies.

Pupils and parents: Mostly local, London and south east. Eclectic bunch from a wide range of prep and

primary schools – currently working on building relationships with local and London primary schools. Holds masterclasses to bring in prep and primary school children for art and music taster days. Up to 10 per cent foreign nationals: a number of Hong Kong Chinese, Spanish and Mexicans but no one group dominates. School maintains good links with parents. Strong old girl network – Holy Child link helps. Old girls include dress designer Lindka Cierach, journalist Dame Ann Leslie, author Maeve Haran, French actress Anouk Aimee, screenplay writer Olivia Hetreed and immeasurable numbers of barristers, physicians, etc.

Entrance: Two-thirds take school's own exam at 11+ and one third take 13+ common entrance. Entrance exams double as academic scholarship exams at 11+ and 16+; at 13+ there is a separate academic scholarship route. Entrance in other years by school's own exam. Not highly selective but does not want someone to struggle academically, as they would not have time to join in other things and have fun. Looks for potential. Some 10-12 per year come in sixth form, often from schools which finish at 16. Tend to settle in well – tutor groups mixed at this stage which helps. Looking for girls who will be open to opportunities and engaged with the ethos of the school.

Exit: A few leave after GCSEs to go to co-ed schools. Many find this quite a culture shock and some even come back – the door is always left open for anyone who changes their mind. Most girls go on to a wide range of universities to read a huge variety of subjects – several to read medicine. A few to Oxbridge each year (six in 2015). One girl recently had to choose between Trinity College, Cambridge and Harvard – poor love! Some gap years – school 'works with students to ensure their gap year is used effectively'.

Money matters: Means-tested bursaries for up to full fees. Awards made at three stages – for year 7, year 9 and year 12 and means-tested every year. Academic and gifted and talented scholarships (creative art, drama and physical theatre, music and sport) – max award is 20 per cent of day or boarding fees.

Remarks: A cosy, happy, caring school with something for everyone. Some can find this cosiness a bit limiting and leave for the co-eds after GCSE. Produces well-rounded girls who are expected to roll up their sleeves, get on with it: 'sew on a button, bake a cake and change a fuse', as one mother put it.

Mill Hill School

The Ridgeway, London NW7 1QS

020 8959 1176
registrations@millhill.org.uk
www.millhill.org.uk

Ages: 13–18
Pupils: 669 (455 boys, 214 girls); sixth form: 240
Boarders: 105
Day: £18,885 pa
Boarding: £25,362 – £29,835 pa

Head: Since January 2016, Mrs Frances King (50s), who is also chief executive of the Mill Hill Foundation and the first woman to lead the school. She was previously principal of Collège Alpin Beau Soleil, a coeducational school in Switzerland. BA in theology from Oxford, PGCE from the Institute of Education, MA in philosophy and religion from Heythrop College, London and MBA in school management from Hull. She became deputy head of St Mary's School, Ascot in 2000, head of Heathfield School in 2003 and head of Roedean School in 2008. She is married to Tim.

Academic matters: In 2015, 47 per cent A*/A and 75 per cent A*-B grades at A level. School's aim is to

achieve each child's full potential while working in a way that makes them feel comfortable – 'for some, three Bs at A level is a real achievement, but others here get three, four or five As.' Some children, too, require a lot of pressure to achieve and others buckle under pressure.

Twenty-four subjects on offer at A level, including Chinese, business studies and government and politics. One parent criticised the subjects on offer as limiting compared to other schools. 'My friend removed her child from the school to go to another sixth form as they didn't offer psychology as an A level,' she told us. Good spread of languages offered at GCSE: French, Spanish, German, Greek

'I came over from Africa when I was 13 without anyone to look after me. My housemaster and my teachers made me feel so welcome'

and Latin, plus Portuguese and Chinese as extras. In 2015, 54 per cent A*/A grades overall.

Two of the learning resources on the campus are worth noting. The library (an 'innovative conversion' of the school squash courts) is a two-tiered, large, bright space, incredibly well stocked with books and a gallery for magnificent artwork by students. The stunning and contemporary Favell building has a glass atrium – providing a light and airy home for seven departments, including modern languages, history and geography. Also used for exhibitions and entertainment. Startlingly quiet classrooms (we had to check to see if there were students inside) surround the atrium on three floors. Well presented but scant student displays and artwork adorn the walls, encased in glass frames.

New science block is under way to replace the rather old-fashioned labs where Nobel-winning scientist Francis Crick once studied. (This doesn't seem to hold pupils back since Imperial College is a popular university destination).

Mill Hill takes in a reasonably broad spread of academic ability and aims to get the best out of each child by helping them to learn effectively. 'We're not a hothouse,' says the head. 'We're never going to be the top academic school in the country, but we want to make teaching accessible and enjoyable and give children high expectations. That said, we have some very bright children. It's a question of identifying what each child is capable of and providing what each child needs.'

The school has limited facilities for SEN. Head is sympathetic but pragmatic. 'We have facilities in place to deal with mild to moderate dyslexia, but for anything more severe, we just don't have the resources in place.' All new entrants are screened for dyslexia and dyspraxia and are given extra time in the CE exam. One parent whose child is moderately dyslexic said the school was 'helpful to a point,' but she had to fight for most things.

Games, options, the arts: Sport, sport, sport. A clincher for pupils and parents alike when choosing this school over others. Competitive and recreational sport has always played a big role at Mill Hill and with its expansive site it's easy to see why. Rugby and cricket are the two biggies here. As one parent told us: 'My son only agreed to come here because of the rugby.' The school established a reputation as a rugby playing school from the

outset, and has produced a large number of international rugby players. Great facilities in which to play.

The school's cricket arena has been called 'one of the most beautiful grounds to play cricket in the London area.' To add to this, they have the services of a professional coach. Players (boys and girls) are regularly selected to represent Middlesex and Hertfordshire and occasionally England.

Golf is another major sport here and is even incorporated into the timetable. This is the only school in London to boast a golf academy (although ironically no golf course – pupils play at nearby Hendon). One girl has been selected for the England U16 girls' golf team. Tennis is very strong – one of the strongest schools in the south east.

Soccer, netball, hockey, cross-country and swimming (the school boasts a beautiful, new 25m pool) on offer. More adventurous pupils can try their hand at sailing, skiing/snowboarding, riding, clay pigeon shooting and taekwondo (these incur extra cost). Mill Hill is also one of the few remaining independent schools to have an Eton fives court. The shape of the court is modelled on the chapel at Eton (we thought it looked like a Roman gladiator chamber).

For non-sporty types (and they are seemingly few and far between), drama is very popular and taken by many at both GCSE and A level. With

drama studio, theatre and large school stage, it is rare for a production not to be in rehearsal. House arts festival takes place every two years (alternating with a house music competition), with 10 plays performed over three nights. Many ex-students have become thesps of stage and screen. Art is strong and some of the art displayed around the school is amongst the best we've seen. This year saw the first inflatable sculpture floating around the studios. Good music facilities (specialised equipment for composition and recording) and in addition to curricular music, lots of opportunities to participate in a wide range of musical activities (chapel choir, string orchestra, jazz band and chamber music). Well-equipped on the DT side with 30 top-end computers and industry standard 3D printers.

A series of monthly lectures on a variety of topics – from classical history to journalism and politics (presenters include Jonathan Dimbleby and Terry Jones) are a popular and successful addition to the already crammed Mill Hill diary.

Thriving charitable work and partnership trips every summer; lower sixth form pupils have the opportunity to work for two to three weeks in a variety of educational projects with partners in Zambia, India and Nicaragua. Those taking part often talk about them being a 'life-changing experience.' As one parent told us: 'The school does exactly what it says on the box – there's something there for everyone.'

Boarding: Boarders are allowed out after lessons to the local (limited) high street. No Saturday lessons. Those who opt for full boarding (and many board weekly) are offered a Saturday morning programme of academic workshops and other activities; weekly boarders and day pupils may join in too. One boarder told us: 'I have been offered so

Indeed the walk to the furthest boarding house is so far we were going to suggest adding Nordic walking to the syllabus

much help with filling out my UCAS form, which is something those with parents around may take for granted.' Boarding house we saw was slightly tired looking – in need of updating.

Housemasters and housesmistresses are the first point of contact for students or parents with concerns. A full-time boarder told us: 'They have become like a surrogate family to me. I came over from Africa when I was 13 without anyone to look after me. My housemaster and my teachers made me feel so welcome and went step by step through everything. The pastoral care is great.' Another said: 'It can be quite a daunting school to come to and I kept getting lost, but I had an excellent mentor and settled in quickly.'

Background and atmosphere: Founded in 1807 by a group of non-conformist Christian ministers and city merchants, who placed their school outside London because of the 'dangers, both physical and moral, awaiting youth while passing through the streets of a large, crowded city.' Once peaceful and rural, The Ridgeway, where the school is situated, has become a busy and frustrating road (to be avoided like the plague at school pick-up). Nonetheless, it is still a very pretty part of the old Mill Hill village, laced with ponds and rambling cottages.

The school itself doesn't disappoint, with its handsome, neoclassical, pillared façade (BBC News website often uses a picture of Mill Hill School for articles about boarding schools). This is more like a stately home than a school, with pale yellow walls, marbled floors, pillars, plaques and elaborately framed portraits (most notably that of Mill Hill's former member of staff, James Murray, the third editor of the Oxford English Dictionary).

Our tour began at the top terrace, with sweeping views across parkland (undoubtedly the school's selling point) and 120 acres of green belt. The panorama is one of immaculately kept lawns, gravelled walkways, ponds and a smorgasbord of varying architecture which marry beautifully from arts and crafts buildings to the glass exterior of the new Favell building. The previous head, we are told, wanted to 'massively transform' the school for its bicentenary. We poked our heads into the beautiful, basilica-style chapel, designed by architect Basil Champney (best known for his work at Oxford and Winchester College). For students it means a compulsory weekly chapel visit, although the school is officially a non-conformist foundation.

Very much a campus school with little access to urban reality, some distance from the gates. It's a vast space for seemingly few pupils and indeed the walk to the furthest boarding house is so far that we were going to suggest adding Nordic walking to the syllabus. Lack of Saturday morning school 'the best thing the school could have done,' a parent told us, and a major factor in her deciding to send her son there. Another parent disagreed and says it gave her son structure and all he'll do now is just 'watch TV.' Day pupils stay on site during the academic day and are members of one of seven day houses. Pupils can hang out in their houses between classes.

Although a fully co-ed school since 1997, it is still very male-centric – around two-thirds boys. This has put some prospective parents off sending their daughters there. One parent told us: 'Any school which is not balanced worries me slightly. You wonder if it is as well geared around girls as it so clearly is for boys.' However, a girl we spoke to disagreed. 'The diversity here makes it a really unique place where everyone is accepted,' she said. Indeed the girls we met on our tour didn't appear to be the shy, retiring types who would worry about being outnumbered. Pupils generally seemed a happy and spirited bunch.

We poked our heads into the beautiful, basilica–style chapel, designed by architect Basil Champney (best known for his work at Oxford and Winchester College)

Has now merged with The Mount School, and opened an international school on that site, offering courses with a focus on English for overseas students who are not ready to join mainstream schools. Pupils have their own boarding house on the Mill Hill site.

Pastoral care, well-being and discipline: Uniform is their thing – 'extremely strict,' one parent told us, and the deputy head is often seen reprimanding students for this reason outside the school gates. The result is an extremely well turned out (and good-looking) bunch of teenagers in traditional dark blazers adorned with the school motto and a myriad of ties denoting their houses. Sixth formers wear their own suits.

Considered to be a kind and gentle school, consistently praised by parents and officials for its outstanding pastoral care – 'very good at

giving children their freedom,' one parent told us. Another parent said you can spot a Mill Hill child in a crowd. 'They always seem to be the most social and well rounded.' One pupil told us: 'It's like being part of a big family.' His only criticism was that 'you can't do an extra year.' This 'freedom' has led some parents to feel that the school is fairly slack in some areas, though. One criticised the fact that pupils get the same detention for smoking behind the bike shed as for chewing gum. She added that the head has improved the standard of the school greatly and praises him for not having double standards or being swayed by money or influence. She said: 'It seems to have been a problem with heads before, that it was one rule for one, and another if you had money.'

Formal exclusions are few and far between. Unlike some other schools, with their zero policy on drugs, this head is realistic, but not lax. 'If you are found with drugs once, it's a suspension, twice, you're out.' He says it nearly 'broke his heart' to permanently exclude a very bright and promising student for bringing drugs onto the premises. But 'you can't start making exceptions,' he told us. 'It blurs the line.'

Pupils and parents: No typical Mill Hill pupil. Quite a lot live locally, even boarders, though in the sixth form there's a significant influx from China, Africa, Germany, France and Russia. Diverse ethnic and religious mix – Catholic, Jewish and Greek possibly the most prominent. Strong entrepreneurial element and urban professionals among the parents, together with 'the seriously rich.' The odd celebrity parent has also been known to grace the hallowed halls. Former pupils include Richard Dimbleby, Francis Crick, Simon Jenkins, Timothy Mo, Denis Thatcher, Katharine Whitehorn and Norman Hartnell.

Entrance: Total of 140 places in year 9, with about 70 or 80 going to pupils from the junior school (Belmont) and a handful of other feeder schools. No place is guaranteed, though – 'the school will politely tell you if they don't think your child is up to it.' Approx 20 places reserved for boarders. Sets its own exams in January before entrance in English, maths, French and science and uses the CE pass mark for setting. Oversubscribed, so 'we want to know what a child will bring. It's partly personality, and partly other factors like sport, music or drama.'

Entry to the sixth form requires two As and three Bs at GCSE, a requirement that applies both externally and internally. These requirements have not always been strictly adhered to, but one of the head's first acts was to enforce it, involving about 15 pupils leaving. 'We've always had a minimum grade requirement, now we're insisting it's met,' he said. One parent grumbled: 'The school is always moving the bar. It used to be automatic entrance into the sixth form.'

Exit: Around a third leave after GCSEs. Most leavers to good universities: one to Oxford in 2015, others to eg Sussex, Bristol, Leeds, Edinburgh, LSE. Business and economics popular, otherwise a great range of subjects including medics, linguists and thespians.

Money matters: Middle to higher end of fee-paying schools in London. A selection of scholarships

in academic subjects, the arts and sports. Fully-funded bursaries awarded each year and a range of other bursaries up to 90 per cent of the fees, on a carefully graded system of finance. The head's intention is that by 2020, 20 students a year will be offered full bursaries.

Remarks: Suits a busy, engaged child happy to try out a wide range of activities and use all the facilities and range of opportunities. A well-balanced school, determined to put the academic underpinning firmly in place.

Northbourne Park School

Betteshanger, Deal, Kent CT14 0NW

01304 611215
office@northbournepark.com
www.northbournepark.com
C of E

Ages: 3–13 (boarders from age 7)
Pupils: 136
Boarders: 45 full
Day: £8,430 to £15,660 pa
Boarding: £19,440 – £24,750 pa

Headmaster: Since September 2015, Sebastian Rees, previously head of Seaford College Prep in Sussex. He has also been assistant head at neighbouring Northbourne Primary School and director of studies at Junior King's School, Canterbury. Studied French at UCL; is also fluent in Spanish and worked in two Spanish schools earlier in his career. Coaches football, cricket and rugby.

Entrance: Taster day and tests in English and maths. The head likes to meet the whole family where possible. Almost non-selective – can adapt the curriculum to suit a child with learning difficulties as long as they are not too severe. They look for children who will be happy at Northbourne and most children are of at least average ability. Usually spaces in most year groups.

Exit: Most children go on to King's Canterbury and St Edmund's in Canterbury. One or two a year to Benenden and Kent College and one or two to Sevenoaks, Tonbridge, Dover College, Cranbrook. Occasionally a couple go further afield. Three or four each year leave at 11 to go to the grammars – the school will prepare children for the Kent Test but doesn't offer one-to-one coaching. Good range and number of scholarships each year – academic, music and sport.

Remarks: Set in 100 acres of parkland and woods on the Betteshanger Estate near Deal, formerly the home of the Northbourne family. Large, rambling Victorian house – a much-loved, happy place. Traditional values, a strong work ethic and a belief in and encouragement of service to the community. Not a grand school – great sense of informality and freedom with a cosy, family feel. Children are encouraged to climb trees, and each year group has a designated area of woodland where they are allowed to play. Some classrooms housed in very well-appointed outdoor classrooms in the garden erected by the Canadians during the war, which somehow got listed along with the rest of the house. Lord Northbourne, whose family used to live in the house, is still involved with the school and likes to take the top year to tea in the House of Lords.

Not a grand school – great sense of informality and freedom with a cosy, family feel

A broadly Christian foundation, with great emphasis on instilling a sense of care and respect for the needs of others both within and outside the school. Boarders attend the local church in the grounds on Sundays. One class per year of about 15 children with a maximum of 19. The brighter children are extended and the less able are nurtured and encouraged. Some setting in the last two years; the scholarship children are taught within the class. Well-equipped new computer room and increasing use of ICT in curriculum. New girls' boarding house with bright airy dormitories; boys' dormitories all recently refurbished.

The French and Spanish programme is unique among prep schools. Two full-time classes of French and French-speaking Spanish children – the equivalent of an extra year 7 and 8, known as the Sixième and Cinquième. This programme is not actively marketed but is spread by word of mouth amongst families in France and Spain whose children come to learn English for one or two years. The smart French children are often from top Parisian schools. The Spanish children tend to be already attending

a Lycées in France and might then opt for British or American schools abroad – tend to be very European-minded. The French and Spanish children are taught separately by French staff and follow the French national curriculum in history, geography, French and maths – the exams are ratified by the Lycée in London and monitored by the CNED in France. The deputy head is French. Children come together outside lessons for all other activities and sport (including cricket), art etc. Charming to hear echoes of French and Spanish voices along the corridors. Inevitable benefits to English children who also spend a few days with an exchange school in Lille and with families in Spain. The children interact well, lots of close friendships are forged here and there is 'much to-ing and fro-ing across the Channel during the holidays,' said one happy mother, whose daughter has been invited to France several times. 'What makes Northbourne really special is the interaction between the English, French and Spanish children. It gave my son a real head start in languages,' said another.

Excellent pastoral care – 'Happiness is at the core of everything they do,' said one mother – and much emphasis on children becoming good citizens. Active school forum for children to develop their own ideas on eg break-time rules and expectations around manners, and an increasing emphasis on the role of the prefects. Girls sometimes have special 'girls' nights in' when matron administers 'beauty treatments' and does their hair. Currently 45 full boarders in the school (mainly the French and Spanish) with some flexi and weekly boarding. Wednesday and Saturday film nights in the old drawing room.

Good food prepared on site and served on a cafeteria system. The school regularly gains the National Heartbeat Food Award – two sittings for lunch and staff sit amongst children to supervise table manners and encourage conversation.

Dynamic director of sport, a Kent county cricket coach, has re-energised sport and breathed new life into the game, and there are now increasing fixtures against other schools – although some parents feel that there could be still more. Quite a small pool to choose from which means everyone has a chance to play in a team, and often children who might be overlooked in a bigger school find they have a sporting bent. Usual range of sports including rugby, plus cross-country, triathlon, tennis, badminton, fencing, clay pigeon shooting and archery – something for everyone. Outdoor heated pool – they go to Duke of York's School or Dover Leisure Centre for triathlon training during the winter.

Head of art produces vast three-dimensional pieces so likes big projects, and won the prize for best giant scarecrow at Hampton Court Flower Show

Gets at least two or three music scholarships each year – recently to Benenden, King's Canterbury, Kent College and St Edmund's. About 70 per cent of children learn at least one instrument, some up to grade 8. Music tech also taught and iMacs used for composition. Lots of collaboration with the local community, and a number of children play in the Betteshanger band and join the Saturday music club. The director of music is an old girl of the school. Lots of encouragement and music lessons from pre-prep upwards. Several opportunities to play in informal concerts – children are encouraged to have a go. Plenty of opportunities to stand up in public too. One junior and one senior play each year – usually a musical. Public speaking competition and occasional debates. In-school clubs include electronics, art, pottery, computers, cookery and the popular and productive gardening club in the old walled garden. After-school academic societies include The Sophists, a literary discussion group open to all and held in the head's study, bilingual society, Greek, Latin, new science, maths, geography and history societies. Senior children and especially scholars are encouraged to attend.

Busy art department – head of art works for the Canterbury Festival and produces vast three-dimensional pieces so likes big projects eg remarkable (authorised!) graffiti in the changing rooms, and won the prize for the best giant scarecrow at the Hampton Court Flower Show. The children love

getting involved even if they are not very artistic. Lots of art competitions, Christmas card competition, pavement art on MDF. Local artists invited to workshops. Pottery housed in the dairy, which still has the Victorian tiles and marble slabs intact.

Good learning support – one full-time and two part-time teachers – mainly dyslexia, dyspraxia and ADHD. Problems identified early and support given either individually or in small groups, in or out of the classroom, each with an individual education plan reviewed by teachers and parents each term (extra charge for the support programmes). The few children in the school with mild Asperger's are carefully selected and assessed. School will take statemented children but not more than one per class. Wants to attract bright dyslexics.

The school day finishes at 5pm, but about half the children stay on for prep until 6pm. The pre-prep children can be looked after until their older siblings are ready to go home. School every other Saturday from year 4 – as well as lessons and games, a leadership course which has been going for years and is a particular feature of the school – like a mini Duke of Edinburgh scheme with lots of den-building and campfires in the woods. Very popular with the children – gives confidence and fosters team-building and leadership skills. Lots of gutsy stuff; children are encouraged but not made to take part. They are put into teams and challenged to build camps in groups – they learn how to make a camp fire and are allowed to use penknives. They then spend the night in their camps, are given luxury ration packs and can turn rabbit and pheasant into a stew if they choose. This often develops a life-long love of the outdoors. Year 8 children go on an adventure holiday to the Ardêche as part of their leadership programme.

The recently-introduced Lord Northbourne Award Scheme also recognises life beyond academia – sport, music, expeditions, drama; children complete this at different levels in their own time. They have to visit the Mountain of Sport, the River of Adventure, The Temple of Learning and the Forest of Beauty and complete challenges in these areas. It culminates in a overseas expedition.

Close links with the French Lycée in London, which sends a group down for a weekend each summer – sleeping outside in the camps can be a bit of a revelation for some of them. Northbourne children do a return day trip to London.

The pre-prep school is housed in the recently-refurbished Old Rectory about 10 minutes walk away, and caters for 3 to 7 year olds. They eat separately – food prepared in main school. The head takes assembly once a week and gets to know the children, who are taught French by French nationals every day from nursery upwards. Hall for assemblies and PE. Directors of music and sport come over from the prep; lots of team sports.

Seamless transition to prep school with year 2 going over once per week for science, games lessons and swimming.

Parents mainly local farmers and businessmen as well as a few from London. Lots of first time buyers and working mothers – quite a cross-section of parents, many of whom have made great sacrifices to send their children here. Loyal and enthusiastic team of staff – some old hands and new young teachers including new heads of maths, science and English. Governing body reinvigorated by new chairman with a clear sense of purpose and direction. Friends of Northbourne Park a welcoming and sociable group. Lots of social and fundraising events – wine tasting, quiz, Christmas fair, a major summer event and a ball every other year.

Old boys include writer Giles Brandreth, composer Sir Richard Rodney Bennett, concert pianist Freddie Kempf and reporter Giles Dilnot.

The Prebendal School

52–55 West Street, Chichester, West Sussex PO19 1RP

01243 772220
office@prebendalschool.org.uk
www.prebendalschool.org.uk
C of E

Ages: 3–13 (boarders from 7)
Pupils: 191
Boarders: 17 boys full, 5 boys/2 girls weekly
Day: £7,500 – £14,250 pa
Boarding: £17,400 – £19,350 pa;
Choristers £9,675 pa

Head Master: Since 2005, Mr Tim Cannell, MA BEd (50s). Educated at Chigwell School and Davies College, followed by Winchester (formerly known as King Alfred's College). Read theology and has a masters degree in education management. Taught maths and RS in several prep schools – Bialla International School, Papua New Guinea, and Eagle House and Moor Park in the UK – where he was variously day master, housemaster and director of studies. A friendly, approachable man who knows his school, pupils (and probably parents!) very well and has thought carefully about how to achieve the best educational balance for both choristers and other students, he was clearly in the throes of planning the amalgamation of the whole school on one site at the time of our visit. A keen cricketer, he also enjoys playing squash and listening to music. Member of IAPS and CSA; has two grown-up children, one a Cambridge graduate and another still studying there.

Entrance: Parents can register for entry to the nursery at 3, but otherwise at any stage; those entering up to year 2 are informally assessed, while those in year 3 up may be tested in English, reading and maths. Current school report is required from year 1. Voice trials for chorister places – boys only – take place in November and February each year, usually for entry the following September, but sometimes sooner. Choir hopefuls are also assessed in verbal reasoning, English and maths to ensure that they can cope with the extra demands of chorister life. Choral scholarships (at least 50 per cent, sometimes more) are awarded by the cathedral chapter and include free piano tuition. Bursaries and academic scholarships (both means-tested) worth up to 50 per cent of school fees are awarded at head's discretion; sibling bursaries offered in increments of five per cent (10 per cent for a third child). Music scholarships (also up to 50 per cent) include free tuition on one instrument. All candidates going into year 7 may apply for two awards in three areas (sport, art, academic) worth up to 15 per cent of day fees. There's also a Forces bursary (maximum award is 15 per cent fees remission).

Exit: Most leave at 13 to a range of senior schools, many with music, academic, all-round, sport or art scholarships. Music scholarships abound here naturally, but there is a healthy scattering of academic awards too and art scholarships are on the up. More than half of year 8 leavers have gained a scholarship since 2006 and the tally is rising. Parents full of praise for head's ability to steer children in the right direction. Portsmouth Grammar School and Lancing College are the most popular destinations but others include Ardingly College, Bedales, Brighton College, Canford, Charterhouse, Cranleigh, Eton, Harrow, King's Canterbury,

Slazenger

As expected, music is at the heart of school life, although it is by no means the sole preserve of the cathedral choristers

Portsmouth High School, Radley, Seaford College, St Swithun's, Uppingham and Worth School. Few leave at end of year 6.

Remarks: Dating back to the foundation of Chichester Cathedral in the 11th century, when it would have been a 'song school' to educate the choristers, the school is the oldest in Sussex. Re-founded as a grammar school in 1497 by the then Bishop of Chichester, it was attached to the Prebend of Highleigh, hence its name. School now occupies a range of buildings dating from the original 14th century song school to the modern Highleigh building.

Separated from the beautiful edifice that is Chichester Cathedral by a stone wall and an iron gate, there is little physical division between the two buildings and this is reflected in the spiritual ties that link church and school. The cathedral is the venue for major concerts and services, eg Founder's Day, and school assemblies take place in the nave twice a week. Next to the splendour of the cathedral, some parents remark that interior of main school building is 'dated and needs modernising ... a bit like a rabbit warren with lots of staircases', but school's expansion into the building next door in 2012 provided more space for classrooms and a more user-friendly layout. The children probably don't mind their surroundings and doubtless learn their way around quickly.

Classwork is based on the national curriculum up to year 6, followed by a focus on CE and independent school scholarships in years 7 and 8. Pupils are taught as a class up to year 4 and then by subject specialist teachers from year 5. Average class size is 13, rising to a maximum of 16 (14 in pre-prep). Head has adjusted the academic timetable, increasing lesson length to 45 minutes, 'so less time is wasted between lessons.' We observed sound teaching in year 5 maths (regular revision throughout the year) and a lively French lesson, which is taught from the age of three. CE syllabus in core subjects is completed by the summer of year 7 to allow for scholarship preparation and exam practice. Maths is set in years 7 and 8 to stretch the able. 'Prebendal really gears up for the scholars,' commented one mother, adding that leavers are usually ahead of their peers in year 9. Latin for all from year 5 is taught by a member of the cathedral clergy and set from years 6 to 8; as a result Latin scholars gain a very good grounding. School monitors the gifted and talented as well as the less able. Academic clubs support classwork after school and on Saturday mornings, eg science revision, maths and French at CE and scholarship levels, geography, history and homework clubs. 'Brilliant' learning support teacher coaches around 20 children; others with special needs are supervised by teachers and a learning support assistant.

Good-sized art and DT studio at the top of the building (up the inevitable long flight of stairs) gets plenty of light; artists enter local school competitions (and win) and gain scholarships to senior schools. There is a well-equipped ICT suite and modern science laboratory. Classrooms opening off narrow corridors aren't especially spacious, but are not overcrowded. Assembly hall doubles up as a performance space for drama and music – year 6s were reading poetry to the whole school on the day of our visit. Another large, if rather cold and damp, older room used for orchestra and ensemble rehearsals; head says a new music block is part of the current expansion plans and will house music technology facilities and a small performance space. Modern Highleigh building, home to the nursery plus all of pre-prep, has light, airy, spacious classrooms and a small separate playground. Charming walled garden provides a quiet outdoor area close to the cathedral gate.

As expected, music is at the heart of school life, although it is by no means the sole preserve of the cathedral choristers. 'Music for all' is the school's philosophy and most parents and pupils buy in with enthusiasm (only six were not learning an instrument at the time of our visit). Peripatetic musicians teach some 280 instrumental lessons each week; there are also two orchestras, two concert bands and five choirs in which over 200 children sing. School choir sings evensong in the cathedral once a term. In addition to the big concerts twice each year, there are regular informal concerts, a house singing competition and a week-long music festival. At the two weekly cathedral assemblies, junior and senior pupils take turns to perform solo, one of the school choirs sings the anthem and a pupil from year 8 does the bible reading. A parent commented that she 'cannot put a price on how much the children gain from performing music and reading in the cathedral.' The pre-prep sings the last anthem of term and has its own music coordinator, orchestra, choir and recorder ensembles. Every chorister receives free piano tuition and usually plays a second instrument; many other students also learn more than one. Although some music lessons are fixed, most rotate through the timetable and parents say the system works well and appears to have little impact on academic work (there is an edict not to miss games). One parent said, 'Music exams make all other aspects of life

easy, like French aurals,' and results support this. A child doesn't have to be musical to thrive here, however, as 'the school is good enough at other things, like sport and academic work.'

Although head has sacrificed one weekly games session, there are still three afternoons largely devoted to games – soccer, rugby, hockey and netball in the winter terms and cricket, athletics, rounders and tennis in the summer. School has its own outdoor, heated pool for swimming lessons in the summer term. As well as the usual grass pitches and courts, there is an all-weather cricket pitch and all-weather cricket nets; the school also has access to Chichester College Astroturf. Everyone is encouraged to represent the school in sport; the less sporty are rotated through the B teams so that they are able to play a match at least once a term. First hockey, cricket and netball teams regularly do well as does the girls' soccer team. Fencing and gymnastics clubs, plus cross-country running, offer alternatives to main school sports.

Everyone is encouraged to represent the school in sport; the less sporty are rotated through the B teams so that they are able to play a match at least once a term

School has a friendly feel and children lining up for lunch looked happy (meals are provided by outside caterers and appeared reasonable). Literature states that individual happiness is important, and this was certainly evident during our visit when one young man seemed distressed during a lesson changeover. Whilst we talked to the (hugely enthusiastic) children about their work, head immediately took the time to speak with the teacher. Two heads of pastoral care (years 3 to 5 and years 6 to 8) lead a regular weekly assembly and are responsible for any serious issues. Parents confirm that discipline is fair and that school is 'very good at dealing with energetic young boys; what happens in school, stays in school' commented one. The chorister tutor sees the 18 choristers and probationers every day to sort out any issues, check prep and manage their busy lives.

The cathedral choir is the mainstay of the boarding community as boys remain in school to sing weekend services. They are joined by a small number of weekly and flexi-boarders and occasionally by children attending Wednesday or Friday 'theme nights', eg LAMDA performance evening, Canadian evening – even water fights! All pupils are English speaking; a few of the school's pupils speak other languages (Romanian, Polish, Chinese,

Japanese). Many of the local medics choose to send their children here. Main dorm has an unusual vaulted ceiling and comparisons with Hogwarts are irresistible – the likeness ends there, however, as boarder parents speak very highly of the matrons. In practice, the choristers are the only boarders in school after lunchtime on Saturday, although they have the opportunity to go home on most Wednesday and Saturday evenings (chorister parents are welcome for Sunday brunch). One mother felt that lunchtime supervision could be better to ensure that younger children are eating well; there are also no mid-morning snacks provided beyond pre-prep for day children.

Extracurricular activities take place every day after school and on Saturday mornings (no Saturday school) and are open to all. Activities range from ICT and music theory to rugby, knitting and stamp clubs. Choristers can join Saturday morning clubs after music practice, eg tennis, rugby and cricket.

There are also supervised prep and revision sessions and voluntary maths coaching on Saturdays. Day pupils can come in if they wish; some clubs incur a charge (eg fencing) but most are free. School trips have included residential trips to Normandy, France, youth hostelling in North Wales and a week in Rome. Very active PTA raises funds for anything from loos on the sports field to whiteboards and car park resurfacing. 'There is a good social network here if parents want it.'

Actively sought out by local parents for its strong Christian ethos, this is a friendly, 'softer round the edges' place than some cathedral schools. It is agile enough to meet the academic, social and spiritual needs of the whole student body without sacrificing the particular requirements of a small number of choristers. The unification of the entire school on one site can only benefit pupils, improve internal communications and continue to foster a family atmosphere.

Prior's Field

Priorsfield Road, Godalming, Surrey GU7 2RH

01483 810551
admissions@priorsfieldschool.com
priorsfieldschool.com

Ages: 11–18
Pupils: 451; sixth form: 85
Boarders: 107 full/weekly/flexi
Day: £16,665 pa
Boarding: £26,850 – £28,065 pa

Head: Since September 2015, Mrs Tracy Kirnig MA PGCE, previously deputy (and for one term acting) head of Caterham School. She has taught religious studies in co-educational and girls' boarding and day schools in the maintained and independent sectors. She studied religious studies and philosophy at UCW Aberystwyth, followed by an MA in education at King's College, London and a PGCE at St Martin's, Lancaster.

Academic matters: Not the top academic school in the county but possibly the most rounded and least competitive. The school does not totally agree with this, saying it's more that 'Prior's Field girls are not unhealthily competitive. They can be when they need to be, as in sport and when winning the Surrey Schools' Problem Solving Competition in 2013'. School says they are now attracting more girls at the top end of the ability range and parents are confident that they are capable of dealing with all sorts. Certainly their results are more than acceptable, and the fact that it 'does not feel like a pressure cooker' enables girls to learn and develop at their own speed. Set in maths, English,

languages and the sciences from day one, but this is flexible and not definitive. In 2015, 37 per cent A*/A grades at A level and 55 per cent A*/A at GCSE

High quality teaching with average age of staff at 42, around a quarter of whom have been at the school for over 10 years. Average class size 15, never more than 22. Pupil:teacher ratio approximately 8:1. A parent said 'their main strength is that they focus on an all round education'. That is certainly born out by the range of subjects they can study, plenty of extras and a huge variety of clubs and activities. Just reading the possibilities is mind boggling – especially in such a relatively small school.

Each girl is treated as an individual and, because the school is not overly selective, the focus is not solely on her intellectual achievement but also on finding the best path for her to follow to develop her personality and confidence. This also encourages most of them to stay on for sixth form, where a girl can pursue pretty well any course or combination of courses that she likes. We met one, on her own, doing AS level food technology, thrilled at the individual help she was being given.

Flexible and inclusive approach to SEN. Anything beyond mild unlikely to be catered for. Prefers to do as much as possible within the classroom situation; anything more may involve individual or group support lessons, charged for as an extra. G and T also treated within the classroom, with an extension programme for scholars. EAL tuition also available.

Games, options, the arts: Good space within the school grounds and sports hall for all the usual activities, especially since recent addition of large all weather pitch. Only small covered swimming pool, so girls taken to Surrey Sports Park for lessons. About 45 per cent take part in some type of competitive sport during the year – either extracurricular or inter-house matches. Some 35 winter and 21 summer teams compete locally and regionally against other schools. Several pupils also reach national level, or higher – one of their tennis players reached number 90 in the under 14 English ranking and others have represented their country in riding, kayaking and skiing. The seniors can choose their own sports, whether they be competitively physical or more along the yoga/pilates line.

Wonderful art on display, the standard appearing exceptionally high. Plenty of opportunities to follow various courses and techniques. Talent abounds; several go on to do degree courses using their well nurtured creative ability. When we visited the textiles department, some sixth form girls were creating extraordinarily complicated designs for an A level millinery project. It really would seem that this school is able to cater for anything anyone wants to learn.

Music also important. Around half of the girls play, ranging from grade 1 to diploma level, on a variety of instruments. They can try orchestral, pop and rock music and learn music theory. Singing also important, with several choirs.

And, of course, there is drama: a whole school production – usually a musical – each year and a lower school play. Everyone is involved in something – on or off stage. Other smaller plays and productions as time and curriculum dictate. Several girls follow the LAMDA courses, and RADA lessons are also offered. Some even go on to drama school and a stage career.

Several go on to do degree courses using their well nurtured creative ability. Sixth form girls were creating extraordinarily complicated designs for an A level project

Plenty of outings and expeditions, and afterschool clubs cover a wide range of interests. D of E programme which included a trip to Norway for the gold recently, and some girls also follow the national Sports Leaders programme. Then there are trips to France, Spain and further afield. Lucky were those who went to Malaysia as part of the World Challenge.

Boarding: Sixth form building is very grown up with own café and common room, and self-decorated, individual bedrooms for all. The overseas pupils get slightly bigger quarters – 'they have more stuff to store'. All looked great fun. Good boarding facilities for 11-15s. The younger children share double rooms, the older ones have single rooms but can choose to share if they prefer. Lighter supervision as girls go through the school – older pupils complete prep in bedrooms to help foster independent learning skills. Bathrooms look a bit shabby but, we gathered, there are refurbishment plans. A couple of common rooms for them to relax in after school is over. Happiness is paramount.

Plenty of flexibility with weekly boarders (most popular option) leaving school Friday night or Saturday morning and returning Sunday or Monday morning – though welcome to join weekend activities. Will also do best to fit in day girls wanting one off stays at school. Each year group has different activities – boarders also meet for themed suppers. Trips include ice-skating, bowling, theme parks, London museums and galleries, theatre visits, meals out, concerts and (naturally) shopping.

Background and atmosphere: Founded in 1902 by Julia Huxley, the granddaughter of Thomas Arnold of Rugby and mother of Aldous, the only boy ever to have attended the school. The main school building was designed by Charles Voysey and, externally, provides an interesting contrast to the extremely modern facilities that have been created inside over the last 10 years. All very well done, his oak hall and staircase remain, as well as his quirky motifs, and the Gertrude Jekyll rose garden is still there for the girls to run round.

The first stop on our tour of the school was the main hall, where all the juniors were seated on the ground in circles drawing small falcons perched amongst them. We had arrived on a cross-curricular day involving problem-solving in mathematics,

feathers, flying and sketching, encouraging enthusiasm and the desire to find out and discover. This appeared to typify the general adventurousness of the school, the imagination brought to engaging the pupils and the importance they put on cross-curricular learning.

Sympathetic, positive head of sixth has been there for many years and never had a problem with drugs, drink or smokers. Says girls give each other lots of support

No uniform; supposedly some limitations but looked pretty relaxed to us. Black suits and jackets for formal occasions. Open, relaxed pupils perfectly happy with the all girls' situation. They said they have 'good relationship with teachers'. Small classes, average eight, some just two to four pupils.

Same buzzy atmosphere throughout the rest of the school. State-of-the-art facilities everywhere. High tech science wing housing six laboratories. New creative arts section, everything to stretch imaginations. Music corridor including composition room full of computers. Everything bright and airy. Incredible DT room, where one pupil was working on her GCSE project – a very modern-looking circular rocking chair. Some other wonderful small creations, and the beginning of an idea for a hovercraft – 'that will take at least two years to put together'. Their last such major engineering project, a solar powered car, has qualified for the national final at Goodwood each year since. Here was a teacher positively brimming with enthusiasm. The old biology lab, now relocated to the science wing, has become a food technology room suitable for MasterChef. And the library, possibly the lightest one we've seen in many trips round schools, is well equipped and resourced. School is acceptably proud of it.

Pastoral care, well-being and discipline: Sympathetic, positive head of sixth has been there for many years and never had a problem with drugs, drink or smokers. Says girls give each other lots of support and the vibrant PSHE programme really does seem to work. Appears to be true throughout the whole school, where it is incorporated into daily routine. Sixth form have one-to-one sessions with their tutor each week, and form tutors meet all girls regularly. We were told 'there is a real yes culture', 'staff do seem to care about their students'. Small school, so really does become 'one big community' where every one cares for everyone else. Nobody should slip through the net.

Pupils and parents: Wide range, local and further afield; day girls, weekly, flexi and full time boarders. Not so much social Surrey, more those looking for value, but not a hothouse. All wanting an all-round education and an unthreatening atmosphere for their daughters, that, even so, pushes them to their full potential. Generally a friendly, relaxed lot.

Approximately 10 per cent from overseas, four per cent Oriental, the rest from all over. Good bus service for day girls. Interesting former pupils: Sam Cam's great grandmother, author of National Velvet, Enid Bagnold; Baroness Mary Warnock, educationalist and philosopher; Lily James, actress; and prominent editor and stylist Grace Lamb.

Entrance: Now this is different: all those registered for 11+ are assessed in the November prior to entry. They sit maths, English and verbal reasoning papers, have a group interview with a member of staff followed by lunch and an afternoon trying their hands at circus skills. Parents get feedback from the school and girls return in January to take more maths and English exams. Places then offered to approximately one in three.

Exit: All over. Some leave at 16+ on the hunt for mixed sixth forms but the majority stay on and leave after A level for an exceptionally wide range of higher education establishments – including Central Saint Martins, Southampton and Exeter – to study courses as varied as structural engineering, architecture and adult nursing.

Money matters: Several scholarships available at all entry points, worth up to 20 per cent of fees; exhibitions worth 10 per cent. Quite a few bursaries which could be worth 100 per cent. Some means-tested sixth form bursaries for locals who will need top GCSE grades in chosen subjects. Forces children eligible for 20 per cent discount and daughters of old girls get 10 per cent. A school, ready and willing to help.

Remarks: If you are looking for a school that will provide a broad education, excellent facilities and get the best out of your daughter in an unpressurised environment, then this could be it. In this high flying, girls'-school-rich corner of Surrey, it provides a refreshing change, nurturing rather than hothousing, unearthing each girl's strengths and teaching her to use them.

Reeds School

Sandy Lane, Cobham, Surrey KT11 2ES

01932 869001
admissions@reeds.surrey.sch.uk
www.reeds.surrey.sch.uk
C of E

Ages: 11–18
Pupils: 695; sixth form: 235 (including 60 girls)
Boarders: 97 full/weekly
Day: £18,165 – £22,710 pa
Boarding: £24,210 – £29,970 pa

Head: Since September 2014, Mark Hoskins, previously senior deputy head of RGS Guildford. Economics degree from Nottingham and PGCE from Institute of Education, plus masters in economics and management and applied economics. Has also been head of middle school and of economics and business studies at Whitgift, and taught at Rosebery School and Wilson's School. Still teaches economics. Married to Sharon; they have two children.

Academic matters: The once gentle, nurturing Reed's that welcomed all-comers, fed, watered and nourished them, fortified their self-esteem but languished near the foot of league tables, has galloped into the first division. In 2015, 57 per cent A*/A at A level and 66 per cent at GCSE; though parents caution that not all leave with glittering grades. Maths, English, economics, biology and geography top the

A level popularity polls. No consistently weak subjects, variation in numbers achieving good grades, in minority subjects, probably a reflection of pupil aptitude rather than teaching quality. School hasn't shied away from challenging and stretch. 'We've just sweated them a bit more'. IGCSE sciences introduced to help bridge gulf between GCSE and A level. Latin offered, Greek an extra, good range of MFL with plethora of trips and activities to bring lingo to life.

A welcoming place for youngsters with mild to moderate specific learning differences. They keep a watchful eye on assessment grades of all pupils to nab those who may have slipped through the net. Some 140+ 'on the list' with 50 per cent of those receiving additional support; 'We are keenly aware that a dyslexic pupil is dyslexic in every lesson. Fortunately we have very good relations with teachers and support staff and all work to best support the child.' Has a fully-equipped English language support centre which uses a structured, individualised, multi-sensory approach – otherwise minimal withdrawal.

Bright, modern classrooms but numbers can creep beyond the 20s and we sense there is little room for further expansion. Good facilities including wondrous new DT building with gadgets, gizmos, CAD/CAM and Lego-technic. We watched in awe at the ease with which plastics were moulded and were lucidly educated on the differences between injection and vacuum moulding but, just as we were about to roll up our sleeves and get stuck in, we were dispatched to science. Chemistry did not disappoint; smells, smoke and spectrum colours galore, tickled our senses, as a range of substances were toasted in bunsen burner heaven.

Games, options, the arts: Premier league sport: tennis takes centre court, golf up to scratch, skiing traverses the two with wild cards of swimming and hockey completing the elite. Twice won the world school championships for tennis (new indoor tennis centre), currently a top five UK school for golf and Britain's number one ski school. Some 90 pupils play at county level or above with 15 internationals among their number including Junior Wimbledon and Junior Davies Cup competitors. Timetable flexes for elite squad members. School has a charismatic, full-time strength and conditioning coach who works with a range of children, not just the elite. Does a lot to help children with dyspraxia or other physical difficulties and parents are free to refer their tubby teens: 'We don't make a distinction so some kids think they are being honed for bigger

things rather than a smaller self.' All usual sports and many additions offered. Play as many squads as they have boys willing to give it a go.

Timetable flexes for elite squad members. School has a charismatic, full-time strength and conditioning coach who works with a range of children, not just the elite

Parents of sporty boys think non-sporty struggle, but parents of non-sporty boys insist their children get a good deal and have fun. 'My son is quite able and very into drama. He loves anything cerebral or dramatic and Reeds offers him a multitude of opportunities in a friendly, non-judgmental environment.' Superb facilities: tennis academy, lots of indoor and outdoor tennis courts, squash courts, 25 metre indoor pool, shooting range, fencing salle, climbing wall – and just for good measure 100 per cent A*/A pass rate for A level PE. Music a strength, more than a third learn an instrument; we listened to the tuneful orchestra marching through tunes with flourish and flair. Termly concerts plus musicals play to critical acclaim and enthusiastic audiences. Consort Choir sings annually at St Paul's Cathedral. Director of drama ensures delivery of innovative productions such as 'Socialism is Great'. Fine art adorns corridors, walls and any unsuspecting space. Great range of extras including LAMDA, cooking, environmental club, photography,

car maintenance and film-making. Outdoor pursuits scheme for third form a precursor to fourth form D of E or CCF; can join the Coldstream Guard cadets or reach for the sky with the RAF.

Boarding: From 11, vast majority boys (predictably) plus 12 sixth form girls, 14 per cent overseas boarders. Three well-kept boarding houses for years 7-8, 9-11 and sixth formers, all clean, tidy, spacious and inviting. Dorms sleep up to six in younger years, with single man rooms from fifth form. Youngest have super social centre/games room with pool tables, table football machines and more. Older ones have computer suite, seminar room, common rooms with sofas and TVs but tend to gravitate to their 'party kitchen', a super-sized room with cookers and toasters. Weekend trips take in local delights (Mercedes Benz World, Chessington World of Adventures) with plenty for action men (and women) to enjoy – stock car racing, paintball, bowling and ice skating plus outings to the Cutty Sark, Gunwharf Quays and naval dockyards for the historically minded. Inspection confirmed all round happiness for the most part – only widespread niggle was quality of internet and phone connections.

Background and atmosphere: A warm, family friendly school with great spirit and a history of caring for, and nurturing, those who need help. Founded in 1813 to educate children whose fathers had died, the school still takes pupils on foundation awards – if they have lost one or both parents, if their parents are separated or divorced, if they come from a single parent family, or, if for some special reason, their home life has been unhappy or unsatisfactory. Approximately 10 per cent are Foundationers, benefiting from up to 100 per cent fees remission; seeks out those who will benefit from their time at Reeds.

Set on a sprawling 40-acre site, the main Edwardian building sits adjacent to the brand new purpose-built elegant design technology building. An assortment of other additions date back to the 60s. Most corners, nooks and crannies now full.

Tasty food, excellent variety: salad bar, veggie meals, pasta – with food clearly marked with nutritional and dietary information. Thursday coffee mornings very much a middle school highlight: 'We gather for hot chocolate, cakes and chat. It is something we all really look forward to,' say pupils. Smart uniform, strictly enforced. Sixth formers dress in 'office wear'. House system with range of competitive activities – arts, chess, music, singing – engenders fierce loyalty. Much support from housemasters and tutors, prep in house, with buses leaving at 5.30pm for day children, ensuring sufficient after-school time for activities or work.

Pastoral care, well-being and discipline: Pupils expect to get Gs and Bs for good work and behaviour with Ms and Ws for misbehaviour and unacceptable work. Rewards for the former, sanctions for the latter, though pupils assure us, 'We get lots of help and support with our work, teachers will explain something in different ways until you understand it.' Parents commend good, structured discipline. Few expulsions in recent years but odd one 'asked to leave', though school does give second chances and will support a child even after they have shown them the door. Pupils say stealing and bullying are no-nos. Will test for drugs if suspicions raised, no problem in school but can't counter what happens outside. School outgrown chapel so visits are limited to three or four times a week and by year groups.

Pupils and parents: 'We admit a range, some are solid all-rounders, others mono-focused'; this includes 10 per cent Foundationers and 10 per cent sporting supremos. Attracts a number of Dutch children – historically a separate Dutch school shared the campus but closed some years ago – a dozen come for half a term to improve their English. 'Our child floundered at prep school but has shone at Reeds; we don't understand how they do it but they really do get the best out of them.' Fee-paying parents perceive that youngsters from poorer backgrounds 'bring down school averages', but school adamant this is completely untrue, saying Foundationers generally outperform the rest (a need for better parental PR perhaps?). Foundationers ensure pupils have a balanced outlook, and staff say drive, determination and diligence of the very sporty rubs off on other students.

Sixty girls in sixth form – tend to be skewed towards the more able, reflecting the gentle competition for places. Many girls come because of reputation for sports, the great facilities and the friendly ambiance. 'My previous school was very pressured, I felt the focus was on the academic with everything else a poor second. Here you are encouraged to play sport, be in the orchestra and have interests. I don't do any less work here, I just have a better outlook, and attitude.' Parents find the lack of cliques among the girls refreshing: 'There isn't the same angst, or bitchiness; the girls all seem to get on.' Parents from all walks of life, the very wealthy, celebs, professional and entrepreneurial families, where typically both parents work, plus a chunk of Foundationers on up to 100 per cent fees. School buses serve a wide area of Surrey.

Entrance: At 11+ tests in English, maths, VR and NVR in January, interview and report from current school. 13+ via pre-test, CE and prep school report. Sixth-form admits 30 girls and a dozen or so boys (depends how many places freed by those who flee at 16). Gets odd state school refugee at other times. From a range of schools, at 11, Surbiton Prep, Donhead, Westward and local state schools; at 13, Parkside, Feltonfleet, Danes Hill, Shrewsbury House, Ripley Court, Cranmore, Hoe Bridge, St Andrew's, Rokeby and Lanesboroughz

A first choice school for tennis and skiing – a good option for golfers and swimmers (though school insists it won't be pitching up poolside to fish winners from the water or stand, flag aloft, on the 18th). Has a wealth of experience in flexing to meet the training/ performing demands of sportsmen, music maestros and other prodigies and tailor the academic programme accordingly. Official CE passmark is 55 per cent but may flex for spiky IQs. Has introduced pre-testing at 11; some harrumphing from local parents who feel this is contrary to the

school's ethos of taking a broad church rather than creaming off the top, but unlikely to change as school insists it is no longer one that will consider taking those pupils who might struggle to get in elsewhere.

Exit: Some 20 per cent leave after GCSEs but twice that proportion (mostly girls) join. Most to university including a number (mainly the sporty) to unis in the USA. In 2015, two to Oxbridge, most of rest to a range of universities; popular destinations include Exeter, Nottingham, Bath, Loughborough, Durham and Royal Academy of Music. Many to art college or design-based courses; some take gap year to consider their options.

Money matters: Have held an annual appeal for funds (to support needy children) since 1815 and about to raise the stakes. Expect between 20 and 50 per cent for an academic scholarship (based on how well your child performs, not how thin your wallet) with additional awards for music, sports, drama, art and DT.

Remarks: A school where once upon a time pupils rattled around, with more slips and slides than Bambi, is now something of a gazelle, still smaller than some rivals but with a speed and grace many can only dream of emulating. While the trophy cabinet overfloweth with sporting regalia, we suspect academic awards are in sight. 'A rounded school,' say pupils. 'Not for the posh or cliquey but where if you have dreams the school will do all they can to help you achieve them'. In a populous and popular area of Surrey, Reeds is riding on a tide; we just hope that it keeps its balance and vision and remains true to its soul.

Rochester Independent College

Star Hill, Rochester, Kent ME1 1XF

01634 828115
admissions@rochester-college.org
www.rochester-college.org

Ages: 11–19 (boarding from 16)
Pupils: 290
Boarders: 60
Day: £12,000 – £16,500 pa
Boarding: plus £10,800 – £12,600 pa

Co-principals: There are three co-principals: Brian (Pain), Alistair (Brownlow), and Pauline (Bailey) – it's all first names here. The three heads say they work in a collegiate way, sharing responsibilities. The kids tell you Brian is the big chief, and the one they're a bit scared of. Brian is as far from a typical public school head as you can imagine. He has a

passion for sailing barges, and he walks into the meeting as if he has just stepped off one – clad in a T-shirt, hair looking like it's been in a force eight, and hands he needs to wash before shaking as he's just been scrubbing blackboards. He tells it like it is, including telling kids who aren't putting in any effort that they are not staying to waste their

parents' money. Alistair's the great communicator, bouncing with enthusiasm like Tigger, and expressing the school's beliefs and methods with an articulacy which backs up his reputation as an ace English teacher. Pauline has a background in management and is the one who ensures they are meeting regulations and dotting the 'I's. She oversees all boarders and the year 7-10s.

It's a stable ship – Brian set up the school with a co-founder in 1984; Alistair joined as a new graduate in 1997, while Pauline was once a pupil here, joined the staff in 1989, and has sent her own two children here. All three still teach, 'so we don't lose sight of what we're here for'. There's no board of governors – the three run it as a plc, and are the only shareholders. It started as an A level college, and extended to take pupils from year 7 in 2007.

Academic matters: There's no uniform or dress code, and the teachers are just as likely as pupils to be wearing a hoody. Everyone goes by their first name. So far so hippy – until you walk around the building during lessons. Hush has descended, and opening a classroom door reveals silent pupils, and desks in rows. Alistair says: 'People try to place us in the progressive/alternative mould, but we're not. It's common sense; small classes, good teaching, and an informal but ordered and respectful atmosphere.'

The next surprise comes in the teaching methods. 'We teach-test-teach-test,' says Alistair. The idea that testing thwarts children gets short shrift here. 'A lot of schools don't do enough regular testing. At A level we do a test every week in each subject. If we're going to put something right we need a rigorous diagnosis of what is wrong,' Alistair says. There's no objection to this degree of testing from pupils – in fact the students seem to welcome it. 'Testing means you can't get delusions, you really know where you are at any point,' said one. Another, who was told by her grammar school that she needed to 'lower her sights', said: 'The teaching style is completely different, we are tested all the time and my grades have gone up consistently.'

Brian is as far from a typical public school head as you can imagine. He has a passion for sailing barges, and he walks into the meeting as if he has just stepped off one

There is a firm concentration on exam technique, but still the school isn't seen as an exam factory. One sixth form pupil said: 'The focus is on exams, but it is still enriching. We get a two hour lesson for everything which means the teachers can drift off topic which helps a lot with general knowledge and essay subjects.'

Teachers are 'very passionate about their subjects,' say parents, and another pupil, comparing the teaching to that at his former grammar school, said: 'The teaching is of a better quality and the teachers know their subject to a greater depth.' And a pupil at the lower end of the school said: 'You don't get to the end of one lesson without doing something fun.'

Many students transfer here after poor progress at AS or A level and the effect can be dramatic. One pupil told us he was predicted to get Ds and Es at AS; he moved from his grammar to the college in February, and in July he achieved three As at AS and an A at A level. Another student moved after getting a U at AS, and she said, 'In my first two weeks here I learned more than I had in the whole previous year.'

There are three pathways through the sixth form, mainly set in different teaching groups. There are those doing a two year A level course through the school; students who have transferred here for year 13 after disappointing AS grades; and those who have done two years elsewhere and are doing retakes. The A level programme is flexible with no option blocks, and students can do speed courses in a new subject to complement retakes. Results for 2015 A levels show 28 per cent of entries achieving A*/A. Maths is the biggest A level subject. English Literature and film studies are also strong departments, both having received Good Schools Guide awards in recent years.

At GCSE, biology, chemistry and physics are taught at International GCSE level for those aiming to study sciences at A level, and students also take the IGCSE in English and English literature. Languages on offer include German, French and Spanish, but it is not compulsory to take a language. Pupils can also take subjects such as astronomy, film studies and photography at GCSE.

And it would be hard to find better provision for an artist. GCSEs are offered in six disciplines – fine art, graphics, photography, textiles, ceramics and 3D. Some students take three of these to A level, which enables them to bypass a foundation year. There is terrific work on display. Two students have won places on the prestigious fine art degree course at UCL's The Slade School. Dominik Klimowski, former BBC online picture editor, teaches photography, and local artist Billy Childish is a visiting lecturer.

School was awaiting delivery of some sculptural musical gates – an art installation created by Henry Dagg, who has transformed his garden fence into a glockenspiel

Parents especially appreciate the efforts made to ensure each pupil gains the best possible grade. One said: 'There are a lot of extra lessons before exams, in the holidays and so on. They will do as much as they can if they think you can improve your grade.'

Another praised the fact that they don't charge for extra tuition in the evenings and holidays, adding: 'I was concerned about my son's maths and suggested getting him some tuition. They said it was their responsibility, and I should not be looking for tutors. They did some extra work with him and he got an A, so I was ecstatic.'

But there is some dissent among parents about the college's policy of sitting AS levels alongside A levels in year 13, as one parent said: 'I would prefer them to be done in year 12, I think it puts too much pressure on to revise two years' worth in one go.' The principals' view is that students inevitably perform better at the end of a two year course, and that this policy in no way prejudices students' chances of receiving offers. Students are only likely to sit them in year 12 if they are expected to get an A, and the pupils say it is an advantage to go to university interviews talking about your predicted grades, rather than possibly some poorer grades from the year before.

Classrooms are named after Brian's beloved Thames sailing barges; 2014 saw this interest taken a step further, with the introduction of an apprenticeship course in boatbuilding, enabling students to gain City and Guilds qualifications up to NVQ level 3.

Games, options, the arts: Sport is growing, but the school doesn't have the infrastructure to provide serious provision. There's a newly created rugby team for year 11 to 13s, which uses the facilities of a local rugby club and is coached by a player from England's women's team. It also supports those playing at higher levels – one sixth former is training with a London football club, and the school enables him to fit lessons around his sporting commitments. Another sixth former is hoping to compete as a sprinter in the next Paralympics. But as one student points out, it is not the type of school which tends to attract the sporty, and so PE provision tends to be more activity based, like ice skating, sailing, self-defence and climbing.

Lower down the school the students play in mixed teams, so boys say games have to be less rough.

There's a rich cultural programme – a drama theatre hosts visiting theatre companies and art shows, and the school's on-site cinema regularly hosts the National Schools' Film week.

Boarding: Boarding is only available to students of 16+. Virtually all students have single rooms. Some have a very small 'pod' ensuite, otherwise it's shared bathrooms. Furnishings are basic but the Georgian high ceilings and big windows add light and space, and all rooms have a phone and internet point. There's a big common room with a pool table and comfy chairs, and a study for quiet work.

Currently 60 out of 280 students are boarders – 40 per cent of these are from the UK, 11 per cent from Europe, and the remainder from countries including Canada, USA, Thailand, China, Russia, Nigeria, and South Africa.

Background and atmosphere: The campus is as unique as the school. It started as one terraced house, but as the school expanded, it gradually bought up 13 properties in adjoining roads, including a Georgian terrace which houses the boarding accommodation. What would once have been the back gardens to these houses now form the grounds with ancient apple trees and wild garden areas, paths to secret nooks and crannies, a viewing platform to climb – and an oversized garden shed where Brian likes to hold his maths classes. Students work on garden projects such as the allotment as part of their D of E award, and the gardens have won a Kent Wildlife Trust Gold Award.

Mid-career, Brian took time out of teaching to become an architect, and the campus reflects this interest. The theatre in the grounds is known as the Womble building – the theatre space is under ground, whilst over the top there's an outdoor seating area which can be used as an open-air auditorium.

An igloo-like structure in the garden is used as an outdoor classroom, shelter, and quiet space. Intended to inspire and motivate, it has a central roof opening for cloud watching.

When we visited the school was awaiting delivery of some steel sculptural musical gates – an art installation created by Henry Dagg, who plays with Icelandic pop star Bjork, and has transformed his garden fence into a glockenspiel. You will be able to play three octaves on these gates, sufficient to pass your music A level, according to Brian. Reflecting on the £100,000 price tag of these gates, Brian says, 'I'm committed to culture'.

Pastoral care, well-being and discipline: A level students have one-to-one meetings with a personal tutor every couple of weeks, more frequently if they wish, and pupils lower down the school have individual meetings every half term.

Parents receive formal reports once a month, which are 'meaningful, not full of euphemisms, and not from a software package'. Younger pupils have a parents' evening, but in the sixth form tutors deal directly with the students as young adults, and reports only go home which they have seen first. 'We promise there will be no surprises through that feedback,' says Alistair.

A number of the pupils have been labelled as bad apples or having limited prospects in previous settings, but have quickly turned things around at the college, where they are free from discipline based on minutiae. One such pupil, previously at a girls' independent, says: 'I was constantly getting picked on by teachers and getting detentions for stupid things, like going to the toilet'.

The principals say they are strict about homework and behaviour, but removing petty rules means the rapport between pupils and teachers is

much better. Or, as one pupil put it, 'The only thing to rebel against here is education itself'.

Other pupils have come from grammars where they felt under too much pressure, or from large schools where they felt overwhelmed, and all say they are learning better and enjoying school more here. 'I worried a lot at my old school, here it's a better environment,' said one. 'At my old school if you improved, they didn't notice,' said another.

Parents all speak highly of the pastoral care, and the growth in confidence they have witnessed in their children. One has three children at the school and she says: 'They are all very different but they are spot on about all of their weaknesses and strengths.'

Pupils and parents: Local pupils form 70 per cent of the cohort and come from a wide catchment – there are minibuses from towns including Tonbridge, Tunbridge Wells, Maidstone, Ashford and Sevenoaks, and the train station opposite brings pupils from Bromley and London. A further 15 per cent come from elsewhere in the UK, and 15 per cent from overseas, including Thai government scholars (who tend to be very high performers, often ending up at Oxbridge).

Numbers lower down the school are small. It starts with around 10 pupils in year 7, who have deliberately opted for a small and different type of school. These are added to over the years, generally by pupils who have been disaffected or haven't thrived in other schools, to numbers in the mid-20s for GCSE years. By sixth form it grows to 50 in year 12, and 130 in year 13/14. This is something to consider in the younger year groups, especially as

---

Those whose strengths lie outside the alpha areas of academic or sporting have their own kudos

---

currently two girls are each the only girl in their years. The flipside is it makes for more natural relationships between the boys and girls and less of the gender division that you see in big schools – they are clearly relaxed in each other's company. None of the pupils or parents we spoke to saw the small year groups as a problem – there's much more mixing between years, and pupils keep up with their friends in their neighbourhood – and many see this as a plus.

The students are a strikingly nice bunch. It's a place for individuals, and there's a lovely air of tolerance and warmth between the pupils – many of whom seem relieved to have found a home among other square pegs. 'They look after each other, and if someone does well they are pleased about this,'

A lovely air of tolerance and warmth between pupils – many of whom seem relieved to have found a home among other square pegs

---

says a parent. Those whose strengths lie outside the traditionally alpha areas of academic or sporting have their own kudos. 'There is a lot more respect for art and creativity,' said one pupil.

Students say it is not competitive, and that there's a huge range in academic ability and ambition. 'If you work your hardest and get an E that's fine,' said one. 'Stronger people help the weaker people; no-one's struggling because everyone helps each other,' said another.

Parents love the lack of school gate competitiveness: 'That playground talk, everyone wanting their child to be in the top set, you don't have that here,' said one relieved mother.

About 50 per cent of pupils have been previously in the independent sector, but a lot of pupils come from families with no tradition of private education.

Entrance: It's non-selective in that there's no entrance exam for children joining at 11 or 13, and there's no minimum GCSE grade requirements for sixth form entry. But every prospective student is interviewed, and the principals say they do turn some away.

Direct entry into any year group at any point in the academic year is possible, and places can be secured in the short gap between exam results and the start of a new term. Around 60 students join each year, either to retake their A levels having completed two years of A levels elsewhere, or directly into year 13 after disappointing AS results in year 12 elsewhere.

Exit: One to Oxford in 2015 and four medics; others to eg Bath, Leeds, Royal Holloway, UCL, Plymouth, Loughborough, Warwick.

The courses students go on to reflect the broad range of abilities and interests catered for: some go on to read law, maths, medicine or classics; others have taken up courses in animal behaviour, film studies, marketing, photography or midwifery.

Money matters: Around £100,000 per year goes into means-tested bursaries, which are awarded not on academic ability, but 'if we think they'll make a good contribution'. Scholarships include the Ralph Steadman Art Scholarship, which offers a two year full scholarship for A levels.

The school has a policy to keep extras to the minimum – music lessons, buses and exam fees are extra, but extracurricular trips are kept deliberately modest. 'We don't take for granted that parents have bottomless pits of money,' says Alistair.

Remarks: This won't be one that sits on your short-list and you can't make up your mind about. You'll either love or hate this place. Your money won't buy the trappings of a public school – no mahogany-rich headmaster's study, certainly no suave head in a handmade suit. No pupils with collars and lips firmly buttoned. No PTA committees or fundraising balls. For some that will be a blessed relief.

You'll get that warm buzz in your heart when you recognise your kid in the personalities here – or not. That might be one of several types we saw – the quirky one, condemned to be picked on in an average school; the fiercely intelligent, who has rubbed teachers up the wrong way by being too smart for his own good in other settings; the kid whose education got derailed by too much focus on petty rules and discipline.

It won't suit sporting jocks – facilities are meagre, and there are rarely enough pupils of the right age and inclination to make a team.

But it's a great option for the cash-strapped; many parents with only enough gold in the pot to fund a couple of years in the independent sector buy in for the last year of GCSEs, for the A level course, or for retakes. And it's a sound investment – most improve considerably on expectations at their previous school.

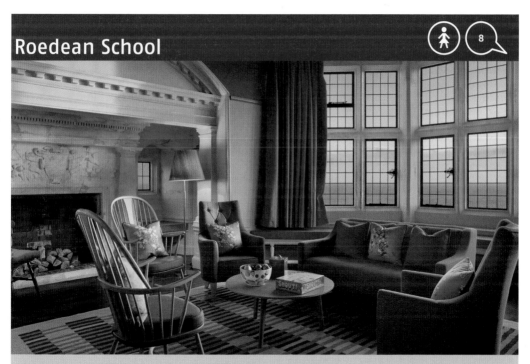

Roedean School

Roedean Way, Brighton, East Sussex BN2 5RQ

01273 667500
enquiries@roedean.co.uk
www.roedean.co.uk
C of E

Ages: 11–18
Pupils: 448; sixth form: 170
Boarders: 230 full, 33 weekly/flexi
Day: £14,970 – £19,470 pa
Boarding: £21,420 – £34,950 pa

Headmaster: Since 2013, Mr Oliver Blond (40s). Previously head at Henrietta Barnett School, one of top selective state girls' schools in the UK, for seven year stint – perfect for seeing through generation of pupils without starting to repeat himself, he says.

Before that, deputy head, North London Collegiate, so something of an expert in all-girls education. Not certain post here was natural fit until visited, when was instantly won over by school's charisma.

So far, the feeling seems to be mutual. 'Aspirational, sweet and delightful,' says Old Girl.

Busy, busy, busy – as well as teaching (English, drama, philosophy) also academic director of the Princes' Teaching Institute charity, as well as raising two young children with wife Helen, teacher turned successful children's author. Highly articulate (goes with the headship territory), he's also soft-voiced and a great listener (both rarer commodities). Forthright mothers, Old Girls and especially pupils who 'know everything that I took six months to learn': he listens to the lot.

Formerly forbidding mood amongst tight-knit school community, including a few who were a tad suspicious to find bloke in charge, now one of almost palpable relief, with rave reviews for speed with which Mr Blond has tackled perma-complacency that dominated teaching and attitudes. School is going back to roots – academic, all-round school for British girls with a smaller percentage of international students, though with many more day students and total numbers increasing to around 500, building on an already healthy surplus.

While working on amplifying siren call to Londoners, even contemplating lowering weekly boarding prices so a closer match for day school fees in the Capital, he's also ensuring locals start to see school not as impenetrable posh fortress but accessible Sussex place offering warm welcome on

He's ensuring locals start to see school not as impenetrable posh fortress but accessible place offering warm welcome on the cliff tops

the cliff tops. They're coming round, brand starting to feature on trendy Brighton ravers' educational wish lists, with admissions team fielding 300 per cent increase in enquiries from locals and over 170 families attending recent open day (one of three).

Integration by stealth should help. Girls and boys from local schools now involved in co-ed go-karting to hip-hop curriculum enrichment, while sixth form Wednesday afternoon community service includes sessions in local primaries. School is also pushing bursaries for state schools in the area. And, yes, though previous attempts have been made to bring in bright but financially challenged, with slightly sporadic results, we'd back Mr Blond to make it happen.

Longer term, would like a third of places offered to UK pupils on needs-blind basis (school already offers some support to similar proportion of existing pupils). Will only work, though, if pupils and families, with or without scholarships, have evidence of change. 'A school that's waiting to be different just isn't enough,' he says. 'That's why we've gone at it really quite quickly.'

Presciently, Mr Blond's first choice career was, apparently, Spiderman. Scaling the heights and accomplishing the impossible? No wonder he's proving so successful.

Academic matters: Formidable competition from other local independents including Brighton College and Lancing, and any number of London options has made school necessarily self-critical about results. Things now very definitely on the up, with 68 per cent of GCSE grades coming in at A* and A in 2015.

At A level, English, humanities (with exception of history) and languages currently minority interests, and of the star subjects, maths is outstanding year in, year out. Further maths also highly successful. Almost the cue for spot of subtle back-patting, A*-B grade percentage at A level rising slightly to 76 per cent in 2015, with 54 per cent A*/A.

Parents are hugely relieved that school's previous shortcomings have been addressed. The fear had been that essence and iconic status as landmark British girls' boarding school were in danger of ebbing away, with rise in international pupils and non-negotiable format – full boarding or nothing – putting off many potential customers. And while nothing wrong with cultural diversity

– 'you get a huge level of tolerance for other people and ideas,' thought insider – proportion of international pupils had caused sense of alienation, numbers of OGs sending own children dropping like a stone.

One of Mr Blond's first acts was to undertake wholesale lesson observation. Though he 'didn't wave a big stick,' thought school insider, a third of staff and half the heads of department left during his first year, many taking arrival as cue to retire. Parents' perspective distinctly un-nuanced. 'About time somebody put a bomb up them,' said mother. 'If I'm paying £35,000 a year, I don't want my daughter to be told to read page 46 if she doesn't understand.'

Focus since has been to seek out 'dynamic, inspirational and energetic staff with new ideas and teaching methods,' he says. The ones we saw in action certainly lived up to their star billing, with head of drama scoring bonus marks from pupils for wearing 'Vans with a suit' (must play well in Brighton). Parents approve of youth and energy. Girls agree. 'They make you feel you can do anything,' says one.

School is also recruiting master teachers, heroic role and a half involving mentoring, studying for extra qualifications and doing a spot of original research on top of normal teaching duties – and quite possibly summoned by shining silhouette of MA gown into night sky.

More is accomplished with less, school day finishing earlier (and no longer at different time each day), some assemblies moved from afternoon to morning slots, lunch break increased and lessons shortened by five minutes. Parents approve, especially day families – under older regime many pupils were simply 'too tired,' thought one, to take advantage of the benefits of plugging into 24/7 boarding school culture.

Rethink of mixed ability teaching also under way following parental concerns about sluggish pace in English lessons. Those needing additional English help in sixth form able to take pre-A level course to bring them up to scratch, parallel streams operating in earlier years.

School also offers strong support for pupils with learning difficulties, staffing recently bumped up with appointment of new head of English with extensive experience of dyslexia. 'They push the message that dyslexic children are taken on the same basis as everybody else,' said parent. Engagement in lessons the only line that must be toed, says Mr Blond. Otherwise, school will do best to help, working with parents to put extra support – as needed – in place.

Million dollar question is how much can be achieved without recruiting more able pupils. Parents like current mix. 'Varied – not just full of professionals' kids who all want to go to Oxbridge,'

says one. Mr Blond adamant that most important point is that 'girls at all levels will thrive here, though standard of entry is rising already with increased interest in the school.' Aspirational, yes, but 'won't become some hothouse and wasn't the case in last school.' Get encouragement and self-confidence right, with school 'a platform for women to go out and feel that anything is possible,' and good exam results will be the by-product with no need to go out and trawl for straight A-grade students.

Key to success, he believes, is ensuring that pupils are listened to – he's very hot on fatalistic tendency of girls to see low grade as final judgment. Wants teachers to say less, listen more and help pupils articulate sometimes hidden ambitions so can be helped to achieve them.

Pupils full of praise for school's desire to cater for budding polymaths, from rescheduling some after–school events to offering subsidised or free overnight stays

Creation of more shared meeting areas – teachers' own dining hall has been sacrificed to the cause; common room with outstanding sea views is on its way out – will mean better communication. School, though, already good at 'finding people's strengths and helping them patch the weaknesses,' reckoned insider. 'Their drive is to make bring out the best in everybody, no matter what it is.' Girls all – unconsciously – smile when asked about life at school. Endorsement doesn't come much more authentic.

Games, options, the arts: A place that allows unforced blossoming amongst kindred spirits. 'Whether you're a singer, guitar player or sports player, it's very good to have social identity around the stuff you're interested in,' says mother.

No them and us divisions between sport and arts, and 'not too binary,' reckoned parent. Pupils full of praise for school's desire to cater for budding polymaths, from rescheduling some after-school events, to offering subsidised or free overnight stays to ensure music or sports enthusiasts have the after-school opportunities they need, to new co-curricular programme for pupils in years 7 to 9, which offers two afternoons a week physical and intellectual stretch (car mechanics to Russian literature). Can result in unexpected blooming – only girls' team to reach national finals of programming competition, for example. Head's push for more community involvement is also building Brighton connection. 'The girls want to pitch in and go and visit old ladies in the sixth form, so there's very much a sense of community,' says OG.

Sports increasingly busy and competitive – 'come back in three years and we'll be winning everything,' reckoned girls, grounds at the front pitch-perfect with all the trimmings and added sea views, fixtures lists, previously on the empty side, busily being filled (and such a priority that features in new sports teacher's title), teams running to D in some sports. As elsewhere, nothing appears too much trouble for highly motivated staff, from developing tempting options for the less enthusiastic (zumba, synchronized swimming) to encouraging links with outside clubs, planning training programmes with external coaches for some of the sports scholars, even finding assessor for pupil working towards umpiring qualification.

Creativity, arts and music consistently good, even through leaner academic times. Art winds way into much of life there, with works on display as beautiful as design of original art room, partially glassed roof letting in northern light – 'the best' says teacher – tiles with scenes of 1930s school life and, our favourite, a stove featuring heaven (gates and kettle stand), purgatory (oven) and hell (fiery flames), which broke in 1960s and hasn't (sadly) been used since.

Sports increasingly busy and competitive – 'come back in three years and we'll be winning everything,' reckoned girls, grounds at the front pitch-perfect

Performing arts a particular strength, vibrant new drama team shaking things up, replacing previous worthy performance choices, all bang on syllabus but distinctly lacking in clapalong appeal, with a few more popular options. 'Was Chekhov before,' thought distinctly envious sixth form tour guides, watching infectiously toe-tapping rehearsal for open day, featuring selection from Hairspray.

Encouragement a feature of the process, with talented instrumentalists working with others who can't read music, for example. 'The degree to which they are supportive of one another is very striking. Has nice moral effect,' thought parent. Latent talent encouraged by trumpet, clarinet or violin lessons for all in first two years and around half the pupils have individual music lessons in school.

School trips extensive, masses abroad.

Boarding: Boarding – four houses each named for a colour and decorated to match – is wonderfully homely, rooms prettily proportioned and furnished, teapot lights hanging cosily down over breakfast bar to add domesticity to giant-height ceilings.

Boarders enjoy busy weekend activities such as visits to Buckingham Palace and local animal sanctuary, which day pupils can also sign up for. That said, with tunnel down to the sea (much enjoyed) and stile onto the South Downs (blank looks when mentioned to pupils, despite mention in school literature), staying put isn't half an attractive option.

Background and atmosphere: Founded by pioneering Lawrence sisters in 1885, heavy financial lifting courtesy of bunch of Midlands industrialists and friends, brilliant connections including artist Sir George Watts. Apart from brief reincarnation as HMS Vernon during the war, when was filled with Royal Navy electrical specialists while school was evacuated to Keswick, has been making stand for girls' education here for well over 100 years.

Like Eton, name has entered national consciousness as shorthand for certain type of education (school is commonly – though not uniquely – thought to be inspiration for Enid Blyton's Malory Towers series). Reality is 'consistent' finished product, thought parent: 'Articulate people who think for themselves and are conscious of the community.'

School now reacquiring spring in step, as increasing numbers of parents discount siren call of nearby co-eds whose idea of success is founded on 'noisy alpha male over-achiever,' said parent. Like others, finds this a less stressful enclave for her 'un-pushy' child. 'My daughter's not one who'll walk in and want to take over socially, but she's managed to have very strong identity here.'

Ditto school itself. 'Looking outward, aiming high,' says sixth form prospectus, with literal accuracy, dainty Oxbridge-style mini cloisters conveying – perhaps – subtle message about founders' higher education aspirations for pupils. Cosy-looking it ain't, at least from the front, with cliff top, slab-like buildings (think turreted Kendal mint cake) menacing coast road to Brighton, 45-acre site on permanent collision course with the elements, salt spray countered by special rations for plants, bracing winds the stuff of nostalgia for past pupils and, we were told by pupils, sea breezes, on one occasion, so strong that minibuses had to be used on-site to prevent accidental Mary Poppins-style departures. (Slightly overstated, thinks school, pointing out that 'we are a sunny seaside location, too.')

Odd Portakabin aside (wall of one is top party joint for local daddy long legs population), much to enjoy, including cheery dining halls (youngest two years have small scale version of their own, formerly staff area, table cloths in cupcake pinks and reds) while Horizons café, small box of lettuce aside, concentrates on essential sugar-rich snacks.

Inside, makeovers are transforming the place. Pupils have also been refurbished, with eccentric uniform policy (comfy in the week, smart only on Sundays) now reversed. Most now reconciled to house tie (initially a sticking point for a few) but all like smart, tailored blazers, badges crammed onto lapels recording sunny hours of school lives.

Pastoral care, well-being and discipline: You want it, they've got it, from excellent health centre taking range of difficulties such as diabetes in its stride to happy relationships between pupils and staff, hot chocolate and chats available for as long as needed to help boarders settle in.

Much to enjoy, including cheery dining halls (youngest two years have small scale version of their own, table cloths in cupcake pinks and reds), while Horizons café concentrates on essential sugar–rich snacks

School listens and responds to problems. 'Has been really easy to get help,' says parent. Bullying isn't tolerated – will expel – while effective peer listening programme, backed with proper training so sixth formers know when adult assistance should be sought, stops anyone suffering in silence. 'If someone is sitting alone in the dining hall, you'll tell them "you're going to sit with me – you're not going to be on your own",' says sixth former.

Big feature of success is open door policy that sees day girls on the premises, with school's blessing, well past advertised hours every evening and welcomed back at weekends.

'They are very clear that you are part of the school whether a day girl or boarder,' says mother. Integration something school has always done well. 'In my day, we were from very different backgrounds and just mulched along together and I'd be very surprised if there was a huge amount of perceived difference between day and boarding pupils now,' agrees OG.

Pupils and parents: 'Sweet, polite girls,' was one comment, though OG pointed out that niceness often comes with 'let's have a pop at it' attitude. 'Makes you more robust so perhaps you do a few more things you wouldn't have done.' Certainly borne out by career choice dilemmas faced by pupils, one agonising over whether to opt for being a barrister or singer, a second torn between primatology and acting...

Pupils feel liberated by school's approach. 'When I came here I was quite a pessimistic, glass half empty person. Here, you feel you've got another chance to get things right if they go wrong, without feeling judged,' thought one.

Once part of the place, it doesn't let go easily, Old Girls busily spreading the word, enthusiasts one and all – and 'a mighty source of strength,' according to school literature. Old Roedeanians see school days as 'catalyst' for happiness and success in later life and very special part of lives. 'Felt I should be at the back giggling with my mates,' said one OG, who'd been back for recent visit.

While 'it's always been quite an international school,' points out one (ample proof in OGs' website, with thriving communities all over the place), increasing recruitment of London and local families is creating a balance everyone is happy with. Mix and match in every sense 'and I like that.'

Entrance: Numbers rising, with additional year 7 form introduced from 2014 and intake now likely to be around 60. Majority from local schools, state and independent. Further 20 to 25 pupils join year 9, up to 60 admitted in sixth form.

Exit: Post-GCSE exodus now substantially slowed after massive confidence-boosting exercise to reassure pupils that school can deliver the results. 'Retentions will improve as soon as our A levels improve.'

Turns out girls with 'a bit of purpose in life,' thought OG. 'We're very good at being able to slightly reinvent ourselves and get on with just about anybody.' Strong on medicine (reflected in pupil base), two to Oxbridge in 2015 and good showing in all the best places, UCL heading list of destinations, closely followed by Bristol, King's College, Loughborough – and Hong Kong. Medicine, maths, engineering, and science-related degrees mop up around a third of degrees. History, economics, politics and business also popular.

Money matters: With £10 million foundation endowment, able to offer considerable help and scholarships worth up to 40 per cent of the fees, bright locals, in particular, should be making a beeline for the place. Brighthelm awards at 11+ and sixth form of up to 100 per cent for extremely bright girls from local state schools, who must be nominated by their current head.

Remarks: No danger of sun setting gently on past glories. This is a school that's going places. Sixth formers leaving as the tide turns would gladly do it all over again. 'Wish my daughter was starting there now,' says mother. 'It's a fabulous place.'

Royal Russell School

Coombe Lane, Croydon, Surrey CR9 5BX

020 8657 4433
admissions@royalrussell.co.uk
www.royalrussell.co.uk

Ages: 11–18
Pupils: 605; sixth form: 180
Boarders: 135
Day: £16,560 pa
Boarding: £24,240 – £32,745 pa

Headmaster: Since September 2011, Mr Christopher Hutchinson BMet Sheffield, PGCE Cambridge FRSA (40s). He started his teaching career at Clifton College in Bristol, where he was head of physics and a housemaster. Thence to Wellington College as head of science and assistant director of studies, before taking over the headship of Newcastle School for Boys. Married to Alex, a fellow science teacher, he enjoys singing, squash, tennis and gardening. Committed to providing a stimulating classroom education alongside a robust co-curricular programme. He has been officer commanding the CCF and also master in charge of rowing.

Academic matters: Exam pass rates generally improving – 42 per cent A*/A grades at A level and 38 per cent A*/A at GCSE in 2015. Mathematics is one of the school's strengths with a number of pupils taking GCSE a year early and AS in year 11, carrying on to A level and further mathematics and the sixth form. A flexible approach is taken to setting; most classes are mixed ability and pupils move into sets for maths, English, science, and modern languages for GCSE. Good choice of GCSEs

offered. Pupils can study dual award or three separate sciences, although only two languages – French and Spanish – available.

Theatre history taught and pupils can become involved in helping to make costumes and set designing

Recently upgraded ICT – everything is interactive with a parent/pupil portal which enables school computer system to be accessed from home. According to parents, good team of male and female teachers from the more mature to young sporty and artistic types. Healthy turnover sees new blood and new ideas coming in each year. Refreshingly unfazed by the league tables, staff are committed to ensuring every pupil reaches their potential. Whilst the school is academically rigorous, a focus on producing broad, well rounded young people.

ESOL tuition is included in the fees and is available for pupils whose first language is not English. Strong learning support department, a charge is made for one-to-one lessons. All departments run lunchtime and after school clinics offering additional support to those who require it. Beautiful library and sixth form centre with small classes and individual attention. Added value is outstanding; sixth formers feed back very positively.

Games, options, the arts: Arts strong all round. Flourishing music department has earned an international reputation, orchestras and choirs travel far and wide to perform. Over 200 ABRSM exams taken by pupils each year – needless to say, pass rate is 100 per cent. Musical experiences are enhanced by workshops, excursions and working with professional musicians. Enviable suite of rooms, including a recording studio, lovely light practice rooms and a 200 seat concert venue.

Lively drama department teaches all age groups, giving pupils the opportunity to try their hand at acting, directing and being light and sound technicians, whilst developing public speaking skills and learning to work cooperatively. Theatre history is also taught and pupils can become involved in helping to make costumes and set designing. Theatre groups visit the school to perform and run workshops, also after-school drama classes and trips to local and West End performances. Pupils benefitting from the recently opened superb performing arts centre. Martin Clunes and Naoko Mori are former pupils. Inspiring light airy art studios where students benefit from expert teaching and a great range of resources.

Just about everything is on offer from traditional sports to archery and windsurfing. Eager representatives at local, regional and national level sports teams and events, school and house matches – being physically active and enjoying sport considered part of pupil well-being. Lots of fun and successes. Teams are coached by outside specialists as well as in-house PE teachers. Extensive playing fields and courts of every shape and size, cross-country course through their own woodland, indoor swimming pool and sports complex, where £2m refurbishment was recently completed. All sporting facilities are well utilised and operate as a local sports centre for the public, parents and local clubs, adding to the community feel of the school. Community link with Coloma Convent for CCF. The range of clubs, societies and activities is almost unlimited. Large number of senior pupils participate in the Modern United Nations programme and the school hosts one of the biggest UK conferences.

Boarding: Boarding houses – one for girls and two for boys – have been refurbished and a full programme of activities runs at weekends. Everyone encouraged to join in house competitions. Most boarders from overseas, so strong multi-cultural dimension. Each boarding house has day pupils attached too; they can arrive for breakfast and stay for supper.

Background and atmosphere: Hidden from the public eye beyond a long driveway lies a great school for the 21st century offering a remarkable number of opportunities for all tastes and talents. Once thought rather down in the doldrums, now offers stiff competition to other south London and Surrey schools. Open-minded and flexible in its general approach, the atmosphere is vibrant and purposeful, a very busy place. The senior management are thought to be caring and in touch with the requirements of today's parents and pupils. An optional extended school day.

Extensive playing fields and courts of every shape and size, cross-country course through their own woodland, indoor swimming pool and sports complex

Established in 1853 at New Cross for the sons and daughters of textile workers – one of the earliest co-ed schools. In 1924 purchased the Ballard's estate, an extensive, wooded, 110-acre site, which now houses both the junior and senior schools. Long history of royal patronage – the present queen has visited the school four times since the 1950s and the Earl of Wessex opened the performing arts centre. Lots of new buildings have popped up recently: a rolling rebuilding programme to upgrade and redevelop is under way and some rather unattractive 1960s buildings have been pulled down and replaced. Christian based, now multi-faith and boasts its own recently restored chapel – much of the original stonework carved by Eric Gill in the 1920s.

Pastoral care, well-being and discipline: House system, nine houses, three of which are boarding houses, which all include some day pupils. Other day pupils have their own houses, with sitting rooms for each year group to relax and socialise in during breaktimes and after school. Supervised homework sessions run each evening and day pupils can stay at school until 9pm (evening meals are included in the fees). Prefect system with head and deputy head boy and girl; each house has its own head of house and sports captains, so a large number of pupils are involved with aiding the day to day running and school functions.

Pastoral staff pride themselves on their knowledge of the needs of young people and understanding the whole child. Housemasters and mistresses together with the chaplain are always available to talk, pupils are treated as individuals and staff go out of their way to help sort out any problems. Small tutor groups also ensure parents and pupils are kept well informed about academic and personal development. School rules regularly reviewed, predominantly in place for everybody's security and safety. Quite strict uniform code and tip top behaviour expected at all times. Pupils tell us the food is delicious, plenty of choices and everybody eats together – the sizable dining hall provides the perfect place to enjoy the company of others.

Pupils and parents: From around 20-mile radius between Clapham Junction and the M25, Bromley, Dulwich, Wimbledon and Croydon. Fortuitously, the tramstop is opposite the entrance, making it an easy journey for many. Folk from all walks of life – many different types and characters, first-time buyers to children of old Russellians. Interesting mix of nationalities, the sixth form being particularly popular with foreign students. Very active PTA helps to organise the numerous social activities, car boot sales and fundraising for charity.

Entrance: At 11+ exam (English, maths and computer-based verbal reasoning or cognitive abilities test), interview and reference from previous school. Small number of places are usually available at 13+ and 16+ for sixth form.

Exit: At 16+, a few to local colleges to study vocational courses. At 18+, all to university or art colleges, an increasing number of students choosing law, economics and veterinary sciences; Exeter, Imperial, Durham, Birmingham and Southampton all popular.

Money matters: All applicants for year 7 and year 9 are considered for academic scholarships via their performance in the entrance exam. Further scholarships are available for year 12 on the basis of GCSE results. Also junior, senior and sixth form art, music and drama scholarships. A limited number of means-tested bursaries. Five per cent discount for siblings.

Remarks: Confident and socially accomplished pupils, proud of their increasing successes across the curriculum. Solid reputation for producing cheerful young people, well-prepared for successful futures at university and in the workplace.

St Catherine's School

Station Road, Guildford, Surrey GU5 0DF

01483 899609
admissions@stcatherines.info
www.stcatherines.info
C of E

Ages: 11–18
Pupils: 714; sixth form: 168
Boarders: 217 full/weekly/flexi
Day: £8,460 – £17,205 pa
Boarding: £28,355 pa

Headmistress: Since 2000, Mrs Alice Phillips MA Cantab (50s). First teaching post was at the Royal Masonic School, Rickmansworth, where she rose to being head of English. Thence to deputy headship at Tormead in 1993. Mrs Philips is president of the Girls' Schools' Association. She impresses at once as being full of brisk common sense, good humour and get-up-and go. But she is also super-bright, super-articulate and super-focused on the highest of standards for her staff, her charges and herself. 'She is utterly determined for her girls,' one mother told us. And this blazes forth in her dedication to the job of equipping girls for the future – 'girls need to be in an environment which demonstrates that there's nothing you can't do'.

Mrs Phillips relishes the process of turning her 'rough-cut GCSE diamonds into highly polished gems' – and the process needs the St Cat's sixth form to be complete. 'We hit the wall of hormones together,' she says, 'I love the wall of hormones,' which she sees as an essential stage in becoming an adult. And she is not interested in turning out demure young ladies. 'We teach them to challenge every darn thing.' Neither is she a petty disciplinarian; 'you pick your fights with teenage girls. If you pick on something trivial and make a fuss about it they will hate you forever.' Parents are universally impressed – 'Her speeches are very entertaining and she devotes her whole life to the school.' 'She is very fair and very good at sorting things out.' A few parents – and girls – can find the intensity of

her commitment 'scary', but one's impression is that her uncompromising concern is for the 'whole' of each girl. When her pastoral care is praised, she responds, 'but we do also seek to get the girls into the best possible universities and to do that you have to get them to aim high and target improvements all the time'. One awe-struck mother summed her up: 'She is amazing.'

Academic matters: IGCSEs in almost all subjects now. No plans to move to the Pre-U or IB – Mrs Phillips is that rare thing, a fan of the AS year (now an endangered species). Success relies on traditional good teaching alongside the best that modern IT can offer – so keen to keep abreast of all that is innovative and helpful. 'The apps for learning languages are fantastic,' enthuses Mrs Phillips, who tells us that her classics department has always led the way when it comes to embracing good new IT. So iPods/iPads allowed in class with an emphasis on 'learning to discriminate' between reliable web info and the rest – we applaud; in fact all girls up to year 10 now required to have iPads. We saw nothing but quiet and attentive classes and teachers who kept order by being interesting rather than via sanctions. Results excellent across the board – no weak areas. Ninety-one per cent of subjects taken at A level in 2015 were graded A*-B, 67 per cent A*/A. Good to see Greek and German surviving alongside business, economics, history of art and photography. At IGCSE in 2015, 90 per cent A*/A grades. It cometh not much better than this. Lots of options, lots of opportunities – real education takes place here.

Disquiet among some parents and girls on the subject of 'SCAGS' (St Catherine's Assessment Grades) – the St Cat's method of assessing and tracking progress. It's designed to support girls in the pursuit of improvement in their different subjects but some are confused or unconvinced. Mrs Phillips – an ardent believer – concedes, 'we are mindful that it is complex and try to inform parents as best we can.' She is lightning quick to react when we report concerns raised with us – 'it is not the St Catherine's way not to listen to parents – we will expand the explanation and make it more user friendly.' And recent results support school's contention that the scheme works – the first group of girls brought up this way achieved 17 per cent more A* grades than their predecessors.

She is not interested in turning out demure young ladies. 'We teach them to challenge every darn thing'

Library open all hours and well-stocked – the only one we have so far seen with a section on 'feminism'. Sensible system of sixth form subject mentors: you're 12 and struggling with physics? – find the sixth former who understands! Overall, the best of trad with the slickest of innovative in matters academic.

Girls with only mild dyses likely to be able to stand the heat. 'We pride ourselves on our tracking system,' says head, 'and on spotting any late-emerging problems' and monitoring, academic mentoring and clinics are more the way here than a busy special needs set-up.

Games, options, the arts: Lively art in many media – photography especially strong but ceramics, DT, life-drawing – all thrive and all run clubs for those who aren't taking them as curricular subjects. A sense of vibrant life and colour about the studios. 'The drama in the senior school is really good,' we were told and the new building has given drama and the technical side of production an immense boost. Music also lively and productive – just as you'd expect with this calibre of girls and encouragement.

Excellent sports facilities and sport now seen as more inclusive – lots of opportunities for those less than Olympian in their prowess. 'My daughter is in C and D teams', said one mother, 'and she has lots of matches.' The Olympians regularly reach the heights – county and national finals places in several sports and stellar showings in swimming, lacrosse and tennis. Range of sports on offer. Riding club run by parents. D of E thrives and everyone is productively busy all the time. Excellent outside speaker programme, sixth form lectures – and PTA lectures – and lots of stimulating trips.

Boarding: Fifty per cent of boarders from overseas. Bedrooms and dorms are spacious enough, welcoming and homely. Most in two-bedders, often with a third bed for flexi-boarders. Even sixth formers mostly share: they in their own separate and much-appreciated block with common rooms – possibly the messiest we have seen – most refreshing! Most full boarders – normally between 50 and 70 girls – remain in school each weekend and are offered a 'full and varied programme of activities'.

Background and atmosphere: Established in 1885, this is a school with a proud tradition and, unusually, has grown and developed all on the one site. Located 10 minutes south of Guildford in a quiet leafy village, it is unremarkable architecturally apart from its striking conference room plus Arts 'n' Crafts fireplace, its memorable gothic style chapel – splendid stained glass windows celebrating notable female saints, fabulous rose window and Willis organ. Boarding and most of the school areas are functional, a little tired in places (upgrading in process), with the emphasis on practicality rather than opulence. Useful 'chat-rooms' for one to-one sessions – a good idea but the one we nosed into was freezing!

House system underpins school activities. Strong ethical dimension to energetic charity work – extends to water vending machine which supports pumping system in Africa

Now boasts a 'fantastic' £15 million complex – the '125th Anniversary Halls' arts and sports building with an unrivalled auditorium (seats 300 and has 'better acoustics than the Barbican') plus other studios and backed by the sports hall, gyms, dance studios etc. All carefully, thoughtfully and skilfully integrated and an exceptional new resource with which the girls are clearly thrilled. School buildings mostly abut big central area used for car parking though pitches and courts stretch away on the perimeter. Latest addition is 'university style' sixth form study centre, designed with input from the girls, plus refurbished lecture theatre that now hosts chamber music recitals, talks, presentations etc.

Immensely strong house system – everything done in the six houses to which loyalty is unflinching – underpins virtually all school activities. Strong ethical dimension to energetic charity work – extends to water vending machine which supports pumping system in Africa. Food seen as improved – salads particularly praised – though 'it can get a bit monotonous for boarders,' we were told. The day we visited the choices included 'deep fried battered pangasius' and 'oven roasted pangasius'. (We had to look it up too – it's a type of catfish.)

Pastoral care, well-being and discipline: 'Lovely dedicated staff,' universally praised. A sense that all girls can fit in and do well here – whatever their aptitudes, enthusiasms, personality – something to which all parents we spoke to attested. 'It can be a bit full-on for some of them,' one parent admitted

– and others agreed: 'the girls themselves push themselves to the limit – the atmosphere makes them want to be the best of the best.' 'They do the best they can,' another said, 'but they do it while looking after each other.' 'They are very supportive of each other's differences,' another agreed. School divides the girls into houses, sets, classes – lots of mixing up to encourage friendship and to discourage cliqueyness – and it works.

Serious misdemeanours off the radar. Preventative and common sense approach. 'We do some very robust woman-to-woman talking with the girls about our expectations and what is and is not acceptable,' says Mrs Phillips and a sense of friendliness, mutual support is tangible. Some of the most approachable staff we know.

Pupils and parents: St Cat's 'Association' founded in 2004 – now a 3000 strong membership of alumnae, parents, former staff – makes a real community of the school, past and present. Head's PA one of around a dozen alumnae now on the staff. Lots of parental involvement and unquenchable enthusiasm. Mostly local-ish families. Lots of Old Girls' daughters. Middle class and comfortable backgrounds, in the main. Notable Old Girls include Francine Stock, Juliet Stevenson, Elizabeth Beresford, Zena Skinner, Davina McCall, Fay Maschler, Joan Greenwood, UA Fanthorpe, Dorothy Tutin, Elinor Goodman, two ambassadors and legions of academics and other high flyers.

Entrance: Entry by academic selection, using St Catherine's own assessment. Eleven plus candidates take papers in English, maths, science and verbal reasoning. Few places at 12+, 13+ or 14+ – papers in English, maths and reasoning. Reports from existing schools. Sixth form general paper, verbal reasoning and predicted GCSE grades – As expected in A level subjects. Interview for potential sixth formers. Roughly 1.3 applicants for each 11+ place – so not too daunting for a bright girl; for those who try for places in higher years, date of registration is important so register as early as you can. Around 70 apply for the 10 or so annual places in the sixth – they can afford to be very choosy. School flexible and helpful – happy to interview via Skype if you're abroad. Locals come from everywhere but mostly the school's own prep and from Haslemere, Midhurst, Farnham, Guildford, Godalming, Cranleigh, Woking, Esher, Oxshott, SW London. Overseas pupils predominantly English with some EU nationals. Full boarders from Turkey, Moldova, Nigeria, Japan, Hong Kong, Russia, Ukraine, Malaysia, Korea and Singapore. Not a school for anyone with less than fluent English.

Exit: Around a quarter leaves after GCSEs – mostly to co-ed sixths or to have a change. Sixth form leavers to top unis – six to Oxbridge in 2015. Exeter, Bath, Durham, Birmingham and Edinburgh popular – aeronautical engineering and chemical engineering two choices. Unusual number of geographers. Good number of medics. All do proper subjects.

Money matters: Small number of scholarships – some open and some internal – most worth up to 20 per cent of fees. Music and art awards. Bursaries for the bright broke at 11+ and sixth. Usual means-testing and disclosures required but up to 100 per cent of fees on offer.

Remarks: If you want convincing that girls only education is the right and modern way for your bright and motivated daughter, go and look. This is as good as it gets.

St Edmund's School

St Thomas Hill, Canterbury, Kent CT2 8HU

01227 475601
admissions@stedmunds.org.uk
www.stedmunds.org.uk
C of E

Ages: Ages: 3–18 (boarders from 11)
Pupils: 557; sixth form: 115
Boarders: 143
Day: £8,772 – £19,116 pa
Boarding: £19,443 – £30,525 pa, choristers £20,451 pa

Head of school: Since 2011, Mrs Louise Moelwyn-Hughes (40s). Previously senior deputy head of The Perse in Cambridge, and spent 13 years in various roles from year head to housemistress at Marlborough College, following a degree in classics at Cambridge. Now immediately dismiss the picture you've formed, because she's far from the Cambridge to Perse public school head you're imagining. Still has the accent from her humble but bookish Belfast background, and says she didn't really know what Cambridge was when a teacher suggested that her schoolgirl love of ancient Greek could be a ticket there.

Utterly comfortable in her own skin, seems to enjoy being different to the pack. 'I do things my own way, I call a spade a spade,' she says. No airs, no grandstanding, just that type of quiet authority which can bring a room to silence just by sitting still. 'A quiet powerhouse,' says a parent. 'She attends many events, but never seeks to take glory from those who organise – so at a chapel service, she may be sitting in the back pew while the lovely chaplain does his bit; same at junior school concerts, there to show support and cheer them on, but lets the master give the thanks and praise. Very respectful, but she watches everything, and seems to know everything.'

She's been responsible for some record-breaking results, and a 20 per cent increase in pupil numbers in the last three years. Parents describe the school as 'better in every element', and the transformation as 'quite extreme'. 'I can't speak highly enough of her,' said one. 'She has turned the school around, and changed the whole ethos, and it's clear teachers have a lot of respect for her.'

Another said: 'It is always quite obvious to me that she knows the students individually, as is the tremendous respect both students and staff members all have for her. I have met very few people in life who display such grace and level of consciousness in their dealings with others.'

Remarkably she has also transformed her home life, with two children produced during her time in post, and these toddlers are now curbing her hobbies of squash, running, walking and reading.

Academic matters: There is now an ex-Perse triumvirate at the top. Deputy head Ed O'Connor joined in September 2013 from head of sixth form at Perse, and September 2015 saw Matthew Jelley, previously deputy head of Perse's Prep school, becoming head of St Edmund's junior school.

Still has the accent from her Belfast background, and says she didn't really know what Cambridge was when a teacher suggested her love of ancient Greek could be a ticket

Three leaders from this academic heavyweight is bound to have an impact, and the head makes no bones about the fact that she is stepping up expectations. 'Perse is in the top 10 academically, St Edmund's will never be that, but I am looking to raise the bar so that people feel tested,' she says. Rebranding means the school is no longer marketing itself as a music and drama school, and no longer describing itself as non-selective.

But while all the families we spoke to were aware of the change, none felt that a more academic bent was at the expense of less able pupils, or non-academic activities. 'I think this is an additional benefit to the school. The music and drama department is just as excellent as it was,' says one parent. 'It's a great turn around, without losing the school's comprehensive ethos,' said another. 'There is no feeling that you can settle for what

you get – if you are predicted a C you have to try to get a B or higher.'

Sixth formers told us that they would be heartily congratulated for a C grade if that was the best of their ability. 'Everyone has their own target grade which they are pushed to exceed,' said one.

We heard particularly strong praise from parents of dyslexic children. 'They are very good at identifying but not labelling,' said one. Another described a child who was struggling with the GCSE curriculum, but through what was described as 'learning tailor-made to him' went on to win a place at Cambridge. Moelwyn Hughes says she expects higher academic standards to result in more pupils with special needs, as it will encompass more students with Asperger's, many of whom are in the highest academic band nationally.

Should your child fall behind, it won't be seen as your problem. In this instance, the head says they find out what is behind it and put in a lot of pastoral and academic support. 'We don't say to parents you are going to have to supervise this, we make it our business to turn things around,' she says.

When some pupils were struggling in French, her response was 'Let's throw Arabic at it'. These pupils took a Cambridge Certificate in Arabic and Middle East studies instead. 'Four kids got distinctions. It's a Perse way to take something which looks higher end and give it to kids who are struggling, it builds confidence,' she says. It might also be testament to her teaching, as the children studied with her. She dismisses her own mastery of Arabic with an 'oh that' wave of the hand.

As well as Arabic other new subjects the head has introduced are economics, politics and Greek. At A level there are 26 subjects to choose from, the EPQ and an option to do the AQA Baccalaureate. The most popular A levels are biology, history and photography. Maths and theatre studies are also strong departments. In 2015, 66 per cent of A level entries achieved A*-B grades and 36 per cent A*/A. At GCSE, 30 per cent of entries were A*/A.

There's no hiding place for teachers. 'If a parent complains about staff performance, I call the teacher in immediately and tell them and I deal with it,' the head says.

Teachers are left to their own styles, as long as it works. Music teaching is said to be 'inspirational' and the head of junior school music was running a lively class investigating scores from Bond films when we visited. A sixth form economics class was studying the cement market, and the teacher was relaxed about some having earphones plugged in as they worked, as he said they were all turning in A*/B grade work.

'There are some fabulous teachers, and there have been some teachers whose tenure has been short because they just weren't up to the job. That's what we call progress. They use different

techniques for different children – above all it's not a one size fits all school,' said a parent.

The pre-prep is also under a new broom – Julia Exley joined as head in 2013 from Northbourne Park School. It has its own bright and cosy classrooms, and the curriculum includes swimming, music, dance and French. In years 3 to 5 subjects are extended to include geography, history, IT and Latin. There is some streaming – we saw year 5 maths groups tackling number problems on paper in one set, while another was learning weights and ratios through making biscuits. The artwork on display in a variety of media is notably good.

In the upper half of the junior school – years 6, 7 and 8 – lessons are taught in a separate block in the upper school, where they can use the senior's science, art and design technology rooms, and all lessons are taught by subject specialists.

Games, options, the arts: Go in with your eyes open. It's a small school so you can't expect to have top flight teams. Some parents mourn the lack of rugby – the school plays football and hockey instead, which works better in a mixed year group of just 65. 'There's lots of sport there if you want to do it, but you have to be realistic, they are not going to beat the massive teams,' says one parent. For the top level players it can be frustrating, but a parent of one of these is pragmatic about it, saying, 'Even in big schools they are only going to get one or two county level players. And they are doing a lot to improve, such as getting in professional coaches.'

Music is strong, as you might expect in the school which educates the choristers of Canterbury Cathedral. There's a purpose-built music school with a recording studio. It's big on theatre too, with theatre studies well subscribed, and a full size theatre with five wings and a green room to perform in.

Some parents would like to see more trips, though one reeled off an impressive list her children had taken part in – skiing in Italy, drama trip to New York, music/language trip and watersports to Spain, Rua Fiola survival adventure, Christmas trip to Lille, language trip to Switzerland, and history trips to Portsmouth.

Saturday morning school is now optional. It's not charged for, pupils don't have to wear uniform, and the activities are the likes of international cuisine, technology, art, film making, sport, and music. One-third of day pupils come in for it.

Boarding: There are 130 boarders, over half of whom are from overseas. There are flexi, weekly, and full boarding options. After optional morning school on a Saturday, afternoons are free, and Sundays see outings to London museums, Bluewater, ice skating and so on. Boys' dormitories have views over the fields to the cathedral, through arched mullioned windows. Girls overlook the changing rooms. Boys have ensuites, girls don't. The boarding rooms are fairly cramped, but there's a big common room/ kitchen and sixth formers have separate studies shared between three or four people. The 26 choristers live separately in Choir House within the cathedral precincts, with a timetable which includes 20 hours singing, attending evensong six days a week, and recordings.

It's a school with a smile on its face, a great sense of ease and happiness pervades. 'It's as friendly and warm as a prep school'

Background and atmosphere: The school is centred around a High Victorian building with its own chapel. The exterior is grand, and there are commanding views across the fields to Canterbury Cathedral. But the senior school interior has stained carpets, holes gouged out of plaster, some cramped classrooms shoved into unlikely parts of the old building, and is frankly scruffy. If you're doing the circuit its shabbiness will be evident among the more glitzy schools; but current parents don't notice it and see it as all part of the warm, family atmosphere. The head has made staffing and small class sizes a priority, and says increased pupil numbers in the last two years will now fund refurbishment.

It's a school with a smile on its face, a great sense of ease and happiness pervades. 'It's as friendly and warm as a prep school. Every single teacher knows me and you just feel welcome,' said one parent.

Will you fit in? One parent describes it thus: 'It's not a competitive school. If you want to be told that your child is number one at everything, don't come here. If you get your kicks from being told you're better than everyone else, it's not for you. If you are a show off, don't come here. There's no pride in being better than someone else here – it's about being better than your own expectations and about being part of the school.'

Pastoral care, well-being and discipline: Praise for the pastoral care from parents was overwhelming. One child missed several months of school owing to health problems in his GCSE year, and he was given one-to-one teaching on his return to enable him to catch up. We also heard about a teenager who had derailed; the response, as the parent describes, 'Spending days after talking, planning, resetting goals and wiping the slate clean for a new start. At all times protecting his dignity and his self-esteem. Within days all teaching staff adopted a completely different set of rules for him, and never mentioned earlier failings.' Moelwyn Hughes says: 'I'm a big fan of meeting with parents and the pupil and deciding what we're going to do.'

Another family had to deal with bereavement, and the parent says: 'I can categorically say that had it not been for the pastoral care and time and attention Louise Moelwyn-Hughes and her housemaster provided to him, and what he gets out of the school community, his world would be a far worse place than it is today. I am eternally indebted to Louise Moelwyn-Hughes and St Edmund's School.'

And lots of parents told us that the head will always seek out children and congratulate them individually on a big achievement in their own sphere. 'It's the little touches you don't normally get in a senior school,' said a parent.

Pupils and parents: People tend to stick with the school. At transition last year, 52 out of 54 came up from the junior to senior school last year, and around 10 new pupils join at this point.

International students represent 28 nationalities – there are larger groups from China and Germany, but kept no bigger than 15 students – and also students from Thailand, The Congo, Kazakhstan, Russia, Nigeria, Poland, Belgium and France.

It's not a school where you need designer clobber for the school run. One parent described the parent body as 'trying to do the best for their children. Very mixed finances, not all necessarily finding the school fees that easy, and not doing it for the social cachet of being an Old Boy. Very few pushy parents, certainly not seeking advance for their own child at the expense of another.'

Another described the school gate as 'friendly, warm, no parents whinging in your ear "my child wasn't the shining star ..."'

Entrance: There's the rub. For day pupils there are currently only places in the junior school and in the sixth form, although the school is hoping to create more places within two years. Best therefore to aim for the key intake points. Junior school entry is based on assessments on a taster day to gauge academic levels. At 11+ entry there are formal entrance tests (verbal and non-verbal reasoning)

and consideration is given to Kent Test results. Year 9 entry involves tests in maths and English, and a guideline requirement would be common entrance marks of around 60 per cent or above (although you don't have to pass common entrance). Sixth formers need A*/B at GCSE in the subjects they wish to study. On top of that, head says personality and character is part of it. 'It matters the mix you have. I take the opportunity to meet every kid so they recognise that I chose them,' she says.

Exit: All go to higher education including conservatoires and drama schools, and popular university destinations are Manchester, Reading, Exeter, King's College, Royal Holloway, UCL, Durham, Bristol and Canterbury. One to Cambridge in 2015.

Money matters: Scholarships from 10 per cent to 50 per cent of the tuition fees for both day and boarding pupils are awarded in academic, music, sport, art and drama categories, and occasionally to all-rounders. These can be topped up by means-tested bursaries for those currently at the school. Discounts offered to children of clergy, members of the armed forces, and third and subsequent children.

Remarks: Which of the effusive quotes to use? We've seldom seen such overwhelming praise for a head, and for pastoral care, from parents. Nor such a sense of a cohesive parent body without factions. Not for you if you want a school high on social cachet and entry to society by school tie, or smart teas after thrilling wins against top flight teams. But if you want a school which is going to take great care of your child, and get the best out of him/her, whether s/he's a Cambridge or C grade student, definitely one for the shortlist.

St John's School (Leatherhead) 58

Epsom Road, Leatherhead, Surrey KT22 8SP

01372 373000
admissions@stjohns.surrey.sch.uk
www.stjohnsleatherhead.co.uk

Ages: 13–18 (11+ from 2016)
Pupils: 660 (425 boys, 235 girls); sixth form: 255
Boarders: 235 all weekly/flexi
Day: £22,275 pa
Boarding: £28,125 pa

Headmaster: Since September 2011, Martin Collier MA, married with three older children. He read modern history at St John's College Oxford, followed by PGCE from London University. His first 10 years of teaching were in the maintained sector, at the 'fantastic' Thomas Tallis in south London and

the 'tough' Weavers School in Wellingborough. He then moved into the independent sector and Oundle School, where he worked through roles of head of history, director of studies and second master. He also has many years' experience as an examiner with different boards, has been involved with the Qualifications and Curriculum Development Agency and has appeared as an examinations expert before the House of Commons select committee on education. In short, he has a broad experience and detailed knowledge of all things educational. We found him to be a quiet, almost unassuming man, a strategic thinker who is looking five years ahead in planning for St John's and has launched some very major changes at the school.

In addition to his responsibilities for the school's strategic management and teaching standards, Mr Collier also covers the outward facing aspects of St John's, which includes meeting all prospective parents and visiting local prep schools. Mr Collier is still rather an unknown to some parents, although they are aware that he has been hard at work behind the scenes developing the significant and progressive changes now taking shape at St John's. We hope his softly, softly approach works.

Academic matters: St John's has been gradually on the up academically over the last few years and is aiming still higher. Exam results in 2015 were 60 per cent A*/A grades at GCSE, and nearly 38 per cent A*/A at A level. It has been considered as a school which provides a good education but not a high pressure one – a suitable place for a child who would not be happy or comfortable in an academically high-flying school. Parents here certainly want their children to do as well as they can academically, but are also looking for an all-round education including social values and leadership.

Mr Collier believes improving academic results goes hand in hand with improving pastoral care and, unsurprisingly, higher levels of academic selection at entry. It's not rocket science, and the effects of changes taking place now should be seen over the next few years. There has been somewhat of a range of teaching styles and standards at the school including one or two described by parents as 'rather unimpressive', but they are reassured by the new broom and improving exam results. The head tells us he has made important new appointments to improve the quality of teaching, introduced new staff performance assessment and a new management structure with a focus on academia – he's obviously on the case and wants to 'increase fizz in the classroom'.

Rugby is at the top of the sports pecking order; the girls' housemistress is a top player and she referees matches – much to the surprise of visiting teams

This big academic push has still to filter through to all pupils; parents tell us that hard work and academic success is not universally seen as cool. Although pupils do work hard and want success, sometimes they keep it rather quiet. Mr Collier notes that girls' academic work and success helps to pull the boys along, although by the sixth form they are equal. In his extensive experience, he has found that boys and girls have different needs and pace at different ages, their operation and processing is different, girls gain confidence and

maturity earlier than boys. The range of academic ability is catered for by setting in all subjects based on the pace at which pupils learn.

All pupils are tested on entry to identify their 'learning profile', which also identifies any SEN. School tells us that learning support is available to all pupils at all ages, ranging from study skills and time management to specialist tuition for specific learning difficulties. Around 10 per cent of pupils currently have SEN and they are catered for by staff in the classroom, by extra small group sessions and, where necessary, by individual one-to-one support. Parents praise the 'excellent' SENCo. The small number of pupils with EAL have flexible, small group provision alongside support from tutors.

Games, options, the arts: All extras and additions to the academic curriculum are taken very seriously at St John's. They are well taught and valued by pupils and their families; school is very keen on leadership development and believes that sport, drama and music are of equal value to academics in developing a rounded and balanced individual.

Sport is pretty well at the centre of life at St John's and is compulsory, daily and at all ages. There are lots of options and the facilities are very good, with spacious pitches and sports centre. Essentially boys play rugby and football, girls play netball and rounders and both boys and girls play hockey, cricket, tennis and do athletics, cross-country and swimming. There's also a whole array of less usual sports and activities available. Saturdays are match days and older pupils tell us they watch and support their school teams. Rugby is at the top of the sports pecking order; the girls' housemistress is a top women's player and she referees matches – much to the surprise of visiting teams.

> Care in the boarding houses is practical and pragmatic, although the nail polish remover had obviously been ignored by one young lady we spotted sporting fushia nails

All this sporting activity brings a deal of success: in rugby St John's boys recently Surrey U16 county VIIs champions and in football won the national independent schools league. The girls have recently won an U16 county hockey trophy and, over the last two years, have been runners up in the county netball championships.

Music is another big part of St John's life, a third of pupils learn an instrument (up to diploma standard) and choral singing is also very strong – pupils win choral awards to universities and are involved in the National Youth Choir and other top external choral groups.

Drama is well represented with lots of opportunities for aspiring actors in many and varied school productions. St John's recently won a number of awards at the local Leatherhead Drama Festival.

Art and DT facilities are superb, housed in a gleaming new classroom block and equipped with everything the most dedicated artists and design technology students could want. The standard of work is correspondingly high, with displays of impressive and inspiring art and functional DT projects. The brainy (and charming) sixth former who showed us round was combining maths, physics and DT at A level and heading confidently towards an engineering degree.

Other activities include CCF (compulsory for four terms), community service and D of E, all involving challenging activities and trips. There are also lots of school activities going on in the evenings: concerts, plays, rehearsals and talks, all of which pupils are routinely involved in. It can be very demanding of pupils' time, particularly if they are not boarders, but it suits families who are busy and those who like their children to be fully occupied with school activities.

Boarding: Although the majority are day pupils, boarding is flourishing. Parents say flexi-boarding, two or three nights a week, has been a real winner and many pupils love it. Mr Collier has further long term plans for boarding he describes it as 'currently in the foothills of change; it needs to lose its old-fashioned connotations and become fluid, social and involve parents in order to thrive'.

Care in the boarding houses is practical and pragmatic, although the nail polish remover in the entrance hall of a girl's house had obviously been ignored by one young lady we spotted unashamedly sporting fushia nails. The accommodation itself varies from neat, modern twin rooms with small en suite loo and shower to somewhat institutional six or eight person dorms with loos down a chilly corridor.

Background and atmosphere: St John's is very much a local school – most pupils come from within a 15 mile radius – with a strong sense of its own community. Essentially it's a traditional environment providing a 'values based education'; school says that parents here are interested in much more than academics, they want a well rounded, emotionally intelligent education for their children so they leave school able to interact well with others.

However, there is no doubt at all that St John's is currently going through some major changes, as previously mentioned regarding academic matters. These changes are also apparent in other areas and are leading to something of a culture shift, from an ultra-trad boys' boarding school into something much more 21st century, while still holding on to the values of an all-round schooling which are popular with parents. Since 2012, girls in every year throughout the school, albeit in the minority, Saturday lessons disappeared a few years ago with the arrival of the younger girls, though St John's is very definitely a six day a week school. Lower school for years 7 and 8 opens in 2016. Boarding is 'family-friendly' and flexible; no full time, seven days a week any more. New buildings have popped up to accommodate the 50 per cent-ish increase in pupil numbers over the last few years, entry requirements have just been hiked to a new high, lesson lengths and timetable arrangements have all been changed and a new tutor system introduced. It's not exactly a case of being dragged kicking and

Most girls here are 'outgoing and get stuck in,' and it's all about 'a values-based education, for privileged children who learn the responsibility of service'. Families here are well-heeled, middle class professionals

screaming but there's a lot happening and there may well be die-hards who need to be convinced. All this change has been brought about by a consultative process, Mr Collier reassures that 'everyone has had their say' – but it's early days and, like everyone else, we can only wait and see.

Some things remain the same – notably the school's structure around houses, 'important in engendering loyalty and belonging in pupils'. School life revolves around pupils' houses, the day starts and ends there, their tutor is to be found there, studying and socialising takes place there. The culture of each house differs depending on the master, but they are not quirky.

The look of the place reflects its character. It comprises a splendid Victorian building with cloisters running around a central quad and an imposing panelled dining room used by everyone for all meals (and once rumoured to be a potential set for Hogwarts). Just beyond the quad are other newer buildings including the terrific classroom, art and DT block and a very attractive modern new boys' house plus a new boarding house for girls.

On one side of the quad is the modern chapel which is a crucially important part of the school. St John's has a Christian foundation which forms the basis of daily life. Pupils are required to attend daily chapel as well as Sunday evening services with their house around once a month. Parents also attend these house services and go on to drinks in the houses.

Pastoral care, well-being and discipline: Pastoral care is yet another aspect undergoing a revamp at St John's. The tutor system has been reorganised so that every staff member is a tutor to a small group of pupils and every pupil has their own tutor for support and monitoring. Mr Collier describes the tutor as 'the pupil's champion and mentor'; tutor's role is as the point of reference for those pupils under their care and the individual who oversees all aspects of a pupil's school life.

Discipline is much in evidence; bad behaviour in class is not tolerated with detentions for minor infringements. There are clear punishments for drinking and smoking, fines and detentions – it does happen; the housemistress pointed out that

pupils are easy to spot around town and do get pulled up. Mr Collier expressed his zero tolerance policy towards drugs – any offence and a pupil would be 'straight out'; he feels education of pupils and parents is the key and more is on the cards.

Pupils and parents: Currently the gender mix is around two-thirds boys to one third girls, but the school is aiming for a 50:50 mix. School says the differing styles of boys and girls are beginning to rub off on each other; most girls here are 'outgoing and get stuck in,' and it's all about 'a values-based education, for privileged children who learn the responsibility of service'. Families here are well-heeled, middle class professionals but less flashy and more down to earth than many other parents at Surrey boarding schools.

Pupils who enjoy St John's are those who can cope with the pace – academic plus everything else, who want to get involved in school life and enjoy the long day. This all-encompassing style of full-on days, Saturday sport and Sunday chapel would be a godsend for families with two working parents who need their children to be kept busy. However, pupils wanting to run a social or sporting life outside school may find the time commitments of school demanding.

It can be very demanding of pupils' time, particularly if they are not boarders, but it suits families who are busy and those who like their children to be fully occupied

We found the pupils to be sparky, friendly, chatty and well-mannered. On the sports field boys are competitive but very decent; rugby is their number one sport and many display its characteristic discipline alongside fun laddishness. Girls are mostly boisterous, sporty, outgoing and comfortable with the boys' banter. On our visit a group of girls were snuggled up chatting on the sofas in their house, while another group in a different house were catching up on work together. Much time is spent in pupils' single sex houses, whether day or boarding, and pupils mainly socialise with others in their own house, so boys and girls tend to socialise separately; a recently opened mixed common room may help them all normalise a bit more in each other's company.

Notable OJs include the architect Lord Richard Rogers and the senior BBC broadcaster Gavin Hewitt.

Entrance: St John's is a popular local option and has around three applicants for each place. Opening a lower school (year 7 and 8) in 2016: entry to year 7 by maths, English and abilities assessment plus informal interview. Selection at 13+ is on the basis of pupil's current head's recommendation and a pre-assessment taken in the January of year 6; parents report that lately some applicants are being turned away at this stage. The common entrance entry standard is now 55 per cent across the board and Mr Collier feels 'maths is the key to selection'. St John's has its own entrance assessment in maths and English for any applicants who are not taking CE. Consideration of the pupil's strengths in sport, music or drama is also important. At 13 most pupils come from a range of local preps, particularly Danes Hill and Downsend.

For entry to the sixth form, applicants sit an assessment and interview in November of year 11, plus report from current school; places are confirmed by GCSE results. 'Co-curricular strengths are taken into account.' At 16, lots of girls come from nearby Manor House, and a few boys wanting a change from local state schools or other independents.

Exit: Pupils exit to a huge range of universities, no clear favourites due to the broad academic range here. Two to Cambridge in 2015; others to eg Birmingham, Nottingham, Loughborough and Exeter. Parental and pupil expectation is certainly for university and hopes are pinned on Russell Group places.

Careers and university guidance is built into the curriculum from the lower fifth (year 10) onwards and there is regular contact with army, navy and RAF careers officers.

Money matters: Scholarships available in music, drama, art, design and technology, sport, academic and all-rounder, at 11+, 13+ and sixth form entry, worth 5-10 per cent. Means-tested bursaries and grants available, including up to 100 per cent of fees for children of Anglican clergy – Foundationers, reflecting the school's foundation. Also two free places available per year – Albany Awards for children from disadvantaged backgrounds. Discounts for siblings are 10 per cent and for children of Old Johnians are five per cent.

Remarks: A local, newly fully co-ed school currently undergoing quite a lot of change and expansion. Excellent facilities and a well-deserved reputation for an all-round education. Straightforward middle class pupils and parents enjoying a busy school with days full of activity.

St Lawrence College

College Road, Ramsgate, Kent CT11 7AE

01843 572931
admissions@slcuk.com
www.slcuk.com

Ages: 11–18 (junior boarding from 7)
Pupils: 400; sixth form: 155
Boarders: 180
Day: £7,047 – £17,436 pa
Boarding: £23,640 – £31,452 pa

Principal: Since April 2013 Mr Antony Spencer MA (Oxon) ACA (early 40s). Educated at Chesterfield Boys' School and Oxford, where he read PPE. Previously spent five years as academic deputy head at Clifton College and before that director of studies at Denstone College in Staffordshire. Offered numerous jobs when he left Oxford, including a place on the police graduate scheme, a place at Sandhurst and the civil service fast stream but chose to train as an accountant at Ernst and Young. The draw of teaching was always there, and after seven years in the City he answered an ad for a job at Eastbourne and has never looked back.

Enthusiastic, energetic and very chatty and easy to talk to, he 'lives and breathes the education system'. He has 'added a bit of contemporary oomph and is just what the school needed,' according to one parent, and is looking at new ways of doing things. He says he has arrived at an exciting time when the school is poised for growth, and it has grown by 10 per cent in his first year and is now nearing capacity. He is raising the profile of the school, has upped the marketing locally and

internationally and redesigned the website. He feels the 'great strength of the school is its size – the optimum size for a close community', small enough to have strong links between year groups but large enough to be able to afford good facilities.

They are pleased that he has moved chapel to the evening, which means they can have brunch and a lie-in

A number of recent retirements – something he knew about before he took the job – has meant that he has been able to appoint his own team, including two deputy heads and various heads of department. Well-liked by the children, who say 'he is friendly and makes us feel comfortable, and understands what we are talking about and listens to what we say'. They are particularly pleased that he has moved boarders' Sunday chapel to the evening, which means they can have brunch and a lie-in on

Sunday mornings. Married to Suzanne, who he met at Oxford, they have four children who have all settled happily into the school. She previously taught history but is now training to be an EAL teacher. They live in a house in the grounds and spend much of the holidays at their house in France.

Academic matters: In 2015, 17 per cent A*/A and 40 per cent A*-B grades at A level, and 63 per cent achieved 5+ A*-C grades including English and maths at GCSE (31 per cent A*/A) – not bad for a non-selective school with quite a few EAL pupils, and good value added. As well as the usual subjects, psychology, music and music technology, PE, ICT and theatre studies offered at A level – 24 subjects in all. AS photography proving very popular. German A level available for native speakers. Pupils do particularly well in history, maths, economics and psychology. No plans to introduce the IB. Science offered as dual or triple award at GCSE and taught by young and enthusiastic team in old-fashioned but redecorated science labs across the road, complete with small science lecture theatre. Popular science and engineering week and science lecture in conjunction with the Royal Society of Chemistry. Maths and science clinics for anyone who is struggling. Non examined RS course for all. A number of foreign trips including geographers to Iceland and physicists to CERN.

About 10 per cent need some SEN help, one-to-one coaching as well as support alongside lessons and some small group teaching with focus on inclusion to make sure pupils do not feel pigeonholed. Head of department a mainstream teacher who has specialised in SEN plus two part-timers. School has CReSTeD status. About 60 pupils receive some EAL support with a determined focus upon integration; now offers intensive EAL course for lower sixth entry. Lots of support tailored to individual needs, most take English GCSE and a few do ESOL. IELTS offered for university entrance.

Careers centre open every afternoon; careers programmes for years 9 and 11 and sixth form – seminars, lectures and group sessions and one-to-one advice about higher education.

Saturday lessons and afternoon sport from year 9 upwards, with years 7 and 8 doing activities on Saturday mornings. Years 7 and 8 taught separately in Kirby House but by senior school teachers, and can use the other specialist facilities. One lesson a week of thinking and study skills and ICT incorporated into core lessons.

Games, options, the arts: Wide range of sports offered and both boys' and girls' hockey particularly strong. Cliftonville hockey club has its home at St Lawrence and a number of old Lawrentians are in the team. The principal is a keen player and trains with the local side when possible. School brings in additional outside coaches and runs a cricket and netball academy during the winter, and several pupils train with the Kent squad – 'sports coaching is exceptional,' said a parent. The school is now the shirt sponsor for the local rugby club and the main sponsor for Kent girls' cricket. Growing sporting reputation is attracting more local families. No-one made to take part in team sports, but everyone has to do some sort of exercise – the mirrored dance studio is popular with the less sportily inclined. Keen to encourage an ethos of sporting achievement and a healthy lifestyle beyond school. 'They like to keep you fit and active,' says one boy, and many day children stay on to exercise in the evenings. Duke of Edinburgh popular and several gain gold each year. CCF compulsory for boys and girls in year 9 and many carry on.

Music part of the curriculum for years 7 and 8 and also offered at GCSE and A level. A number of bands and ensembles including rock, jazz, samba and concert band as well as various sixth form bands outside school, and school has its own recording studio. Regular music trips at home and abroad and school has invested in instruments for children to borrow.

Has a 500 seat multi-purpose theatre with specialist lighting and sound equipment, with seats that can be covered so it doubles as the examination hall; everyone has a chance to take part in

major productions, either on stage or behind the scenes. Drama part of curriculum until year 9 and also offered at GCSE and at A level. Enthusiastic head of drama gets everyone involved.

DT taught by inspired teacher and pupils undertake projects for real clients – we saw a fine chair which had been designed and made for the local council. A number go on to study product design at university. The school has recently bought a 3D printer.

Good range of activities including maths and science club, chess, musical theatre, various minor sports and debating society.

Boarding: Two boys' and one girls' boarding house all with common room, kitchen and tuck shop. House kitchens closed at lunchtimes to make sure pupils eat a proper meal. Year 7 and 8 boarders and day children live and learn in Kirby House, a light, modernist building with a glass atrium and a library which is housed in what looks like a large blue pottery chimney – inspired. Large bright common room area with sofas, table tennis, a piano and a large television and 10 five-bed dorms with en-suite bathrooms and two flats for resident staff. Pupils allowed into Ramsgate at the weekends and some activities organised.

The Virginia creeper clad main building, complete with towers and turrets, is a monument to muscular Christianity. Inside it is all panelled corridors and sweeping staircases

Background and atmosphere: Founded in 1879 as a boys' boarding school with the purpose of combining 'careful religious training with a sound, liberal education'. The college was incorporated as a public school in 1892 and went fully co-ed in 1983. It is set in 45 acres of walled grounds in the middle of Ramsgate and within walking distance of the sea. The Virginia creeper clad main building, complete with towers and turrets, is a monument to muscular Christianity. Inside it is all panelled corridors and sweeping staircases. The chapel, with its beautiful stained glass windows and fine organ, was built to commemorate the lives of over 130 Old Lawrentians who died in the First World War. Impressive 19th century dining hall decorated with portraits, shields and silverware. Major investment in building projects in recent years including the theatre and a new girls' house, Bellerby, which is light and bright with comfy sitting area, galleried atrium and en-suite bathrooms. Sports hall with

School takes a firm line on bullying – principal believes in restorative justice and likes to get to the root of a problem

fitness centre and dance studio, squash courts and climbing wall and a floodlit Astroturf.

Pastoral care, well-being and discipline: The strong Christian ethos of the school underpins its religious and spiritual life. Chapel services three or four times a week and on Sundays for boarders help maintain an ethos of consideration for others and moral values – one of the stated aims of the school is to encourage 'a sense of serving others as a source of personal satisfaction'. The popular chaplain, often with iPad in hand, 'makes the services interesting', according to the children. All major world faiths are represented within the school; Jewish pupils can attend the synagogue in Ramsgate and Muslims can observe Ramadan.

Strong house loyalty and plenty of friendly inter-house rivalry – plays, matches and singing competitions. All houses have live-in house parents and a resident tutor. School takes firm line on bullying – principal believes in restorative justice and likes to get to the root of the problem. Instant expulsion for the supply of drugs – children know where they stand.

Good food with plenty of choice including a salad bar and can cater for special diets and allergies. Food committee made up of pupils and staff and meets regularly to make recommendations. Coffee shop open at break time, evenings and weekends – also popular with parents at drop-off time. Lots of interaction with the local community – children from nearby schools invited to watch plays and the Chemical Magic show and take part in the annual science and engineering challenge.

Pupils and parents: A big range: traditional families from local prep and primary schools, a number of first time buyers and first generation immigrants who are aspirational and ambitious for their children. Popular with the arty crowd moving down from London – new high speed railway means it is just over an hour to St Pancras. School prides itself on its internationalism and 30 per cent of pupils are foreign nationals from 27 countries including a sizeable contingent of Nepalis from the Gurkha barracks in Folkestone. Strong Nigerian connection and particularly popular with the Germans in sixth form. Children generally integrate well, although some say there could be more interaction between boarders and day pupils.

'Relaxed yet respectful' relationships between pupils and teachers. 'I love the way the children are treated like young adults,' says one parent. 'Everyone is respectful of everyone else, it is a very caring and supportive school.' 'My son joined for the sixth form and felt welcome from the start – sending him there was the best thing we ever did'. A very loyal team of former pupils – successful businesspeople and entrepreneurs who help with work experience. Pupils are 'natural and friendly and unpretentious' and very supportive of each other. Lots of mixing between year groups, helped by the house system. Parents encouraged to get involved, and are pleased with principal's improvements in communication, particularly the parent portal where they can view their children's marks, teachers' notes and homework.

Entrance: Just about non-selective but need to ascertain that a child would be able to cope with the curriculum, and international students tested in English and maths. Very few take common entrance – usually just reports from a child's current school and an interview. Will take children at any stage including occasionally into year 11. About 50 per cent come up from the junior school, otherwise from a range of state and independent schools – they have a big primary school engagement programme. Some transfers from local grammars. Around 15-20 join in sixth form – assessed on GCSE performance (normally five passes) and must have adequate English.

Exit: Around a quarter leave after GCSEs, either for financial reasons or to take vocational courses. Most go on to university, with London universities particularly popular. Others to a wide range of careers: one recently went on to train as a yacht-master and another to join the band of the Royal Marines.

School looking into ways of getting those not interested in university onto apprenticeships. Some parents say they would like a bit more information and be more involved in their children's university choices

Money matters: All rounder, academic, sporting and music scholarships offered at 11+ and 13+ – worth up to 50 per cent of fees. Sixth form scholarships for up to 50 per cent of fees for academic, arts, music and sport. Also means-tested bursaries, and special bursaries for Forces families who qualify for the Continuity of Education Allowance. Generous sibling discounts.

Remarks: A school on the up with a new energy and buzz since our last visit, all helped by the raising of standards in all areas, especially sport, and the influx of London commuters taking advantage of property bargains. 'The school has so much potential and is just beginning to realise this,' says one parent.

St Paul's Cathedral School

2 New Change, London EC4M 9AD

020 7248 5156
admissions@spcs.london.sch.uk
www.spcslondon.com

Ages: 4–13 (boarding from 7)
Pupils: 250
Boarders: 35 (boy choristers)
Day: £12,939 – £13,932 pa
Boarding: choristers £8,057 pa, tuition free

Headmaster: Since 2009, Mr Neil Chippington MA (Cantab) FRCO (40s). Music scholar at Cranleigh, organ scholar at Cambridge, Fellow of the Royal College of Organists; music is certainly in his blood. Came from Winchester College where he was a housemaster for eight years and, having himself been a quirister (chorister) at Winchester Cathedral, seems to be the ideal person to have taken the responsibility for 35 boarding choristers and a school bursting with music. Says he wants to make sure that all children reach their academic potential and are stretched to the limit of their abilities without the school becoming a hothouse. Feels it is crucial to get the balance right so that both choristers and day children get a wide breadth of educational experience and benefit from each other's talents.

Currently reviewing the curriculum, looking at different ways of approaching CE. Open minded and not afraid of change. Says 'the bottom line is to instil a love of learning'. Has introduced a more significant staff appraisal system. Communication apparently an issue when he arrived but believes he has opened up the lines. Responds quickly to emails and maintains an open door policy. Parents acknowledge this improvement. Married with two small sons, the elder of whom is at the school.

Entrance: Seventy on list for 20 available places at 4+, so best to put children down early. Informal assessment in November before year of entry. More places at 7+ when boarding choristers also start. January assessment and short test for day children (also taken by those in pre-prep); informal audition with director of music for choristers, followed by formal audition and same academic test as day children. More places for choristers at 8+ and occasionally 9+. Choristers' fees paid by Dean and Chapter of St Paul's Cathedral with parents paying boarding fee. This will carry on even if a boy's voice breaks early. If in need, bursaries available for day children also. Head is keen to build up a fund and expand this.

Exit: At 11+ and 13+ to a mixture of London day schools and top boarding schools. Majority of girls at 11+ though head eager to keep girls and maintain balance. Choristers mostly to boarding schools at 13+. An impressive number of music and the occasional academic scholarships. Westminster appears high among day schools, with Alleyn's, City of London (girls and boys), Dulwich College, Highgate, Forest School and JAGS also featuring. King's Canterbury popular amongst a wide selection of good boarding schools. Recently, Eton, Stowe, Uppingham and Oundle have all offered academic and music scholarships. Famous ex pupils include Alastair Cooke (England cricket captain) and Simon Russell Beale (actor).

Remarks: A small school, nestling in the precincts of St Paul's Cathedral, providing an excellent all round education in a traditional setting with a formal, spiritual context to everything it does. In amongst the hustle and bustle of the City of London, an oasis of orderliness and calm. Boy choristers have been around since 1123, originally linked to a grammar school which became St Paul's School, London, about 400 years later. Only tenuous links remain. In 1989, the Dean and Chapter decided to expand the tiny choristers-only school to include day boys as well. Girls arrived in 1998 and the school grew to the size it is today.

In amongst the hustle and bustle of the City of London, an oasis of orderliness and calm. Boy choristers have been around since 1123. Girls arrived in 1998

Two low concrete towers house the classrooms and are linked by the school hall, the gym, the library and various other communal activity areas. We seemed to wander up and down and across as enthusiastic pupils showed us their school but 'once you know the two towers it's easy,' they assured us. Three lovely bright classrooms for the pre-prep years, two each for years 3 and 4, then subject-based doubling up as home rooms from year 5 onwards.

Broad-based curriculum with all subjects well taught. Parents praise 'inspirational teachers' who are 'passionate about everything they do'. Average age 39 seems about right. Our guides also spoke enthusiastically about their teachers, singling out science and Latin/Greek as exceptional. Certainly pupils did look happy and absorbed in the excellent science lab; however, the French class we looked in on appeared chaotic. Mixed ability classes throughout with some discreet setting, particularly in years 7 and 8. Previously some complaints about lack of preparation for 11+ entrance exams, but head is driving this forward and has made important changes, revamping part of the curriculum and timetabling non-verbal reasoning, study skills etc into earlier years. Parents very happy about this. Creative writing, apparently, a great strength. Latin compulsory from year 5. Modern languages not the strongest point, though French taught from the beginning and Spanish available as an extra. Head's wife a linguist, so change could be in the air. Interactive whiteboards in classrooms and new IT suite. All special needs problems dealt with by head of learning support. Teachers flag up concerns and he is immediately involved. Any necessary help is provided, mostly free of charge. Additional staff available for one-to-one and in-class support when necessary. Parents kept fully in the picture and involved from the beginning.

Reasonable art. Studio also contains a printing press (given by the Stationers' Company) and a kiln for firing imaginative clay models. Location excellent for visiting Tate Modern as part of extended art lesson. Drama strongish and everyone gets a chance to take part in a production. As one of our guides said, 'If you're not particularly musical, you can still do drama and have fun'. LAMDA exam course available.

Inevitably the greatest strength is music, huge both instrumentally and vocally. Virtually every child in the school learns an instrument of his or her choice (no bagpipes!). Choristers learn two, piano being compulsory. Over 300 music lessons given each week, beginners all the way to grade 8. At least six different choirs plus 15 orchestras and ensembles from classic to rock band. Something for everyone, you might say. For musical, creative children it is a great place to be. Opportunities abound. Choristers are in the minority but it is their talent that is the backbone of the school. Head feels that one of the most crucial things he needs to do is clarify the way they are perceived. The day school exists because of them and they are getting a wider breadth of education because of the day school. Thus both sides are gaining a huge amount and it is important to maintain the balance. Choristers are acquiring an excellent academic education and day pupils are seeing, hearing and being involved in music of an exceptionally high standard. All of

them are equally at home in the cathedral, which they treat as an extension of the school. Assemblies and occasional special services held and the majority get the chance to sing there. A parent told us, 'The Christmas service was something to behold.. about six or seven different choirs were fielded, including a combined one which seemed to involve most of the school'.

Choristers are acquiring an excellent academic education and day pupils are seeing, hearing and being involved in music of an exceptionally high standard

Choristers have a pretty heavy schedule with singing practice before school every morning, evensong on Tuesdays, Wednesdays, Fridays and Saturdays plus Saturday morning rehearsals and Sunday services – alongside a multitude of other occasions when they have to perform. One of the first things the head did for them was to negotiate Monday evenings off as well as Thursdays. Seems only fair after an action-packed weekend. He also stresses the importance of watching the development of their voices and becoming more aware of change – necessary with the earlier physical growth that now occurs. Thirteen-year-old trebles are rarer. Both the cathedral's director of music and organist are also committed to their personal development and nurture.

Separate boarding house with two resident qualified nurses; common room with snooker, table football etc. Many choristers live relatively close by and are allowed out with their families during free time in between services at weekends, including Sunday evenings (though they must be back in time for before-school Monday rehearsals).

Those without nearby families are taken out by staff on duty at weekends.

A father said, 'Sport at the school is active, fun and inclusive'. Despite its inner city site, it is well catered for. Pupils are bused to Coram's Fields and Regent's Park for seasonal activities. Matches fielded against other schools in hockey, football, cricket, rounders, fencing and netball. Have been runners up in U12 London Schools' Cricket Association Cup, winners of the Girls' Football South London Tournament and pupils have been selected for the U10 National Fencing Squad and the U11 Surrey County Cricket squad. Also swim at local baths recreationally and competitively. Prep has rubber surfaced playground, marked up for ball games, where teachers also arrange impromptu games and sports practice. Brand new, larger, grass and woodchip playground with climbing equipment for the pre-prep. Older children allowed to play quiet games here but not allowed to climb.

A variety of after-school clubs, mainly on Thursdays to enable choristers to join in, but on other days too. Range from cookery to dance to computing etc. Bound to be something for everyone. Also children may stay to do supervised prep at school, charged as an extra but useful for working parents. Plenty of outings and expeditions, academic, cultural and sporty. Home and occasionally abroad. A lot to see within walking distance as well.

Parents stress the happy atmosphere – 'it has been the making of our little boy' – (of a chorister) and 'our unsettled, troublemaker has been transformed' – (of a day boy). 'Very good discipline, they don't tolerate bad behaviour'. General feeling that children are treated as individuals, academically stretched and made to work to their own levels; that the school is 'well managed and well ordered'. Much of this appears to lie in the vertical tutor system. Pupils are assigned to a tutor from day one and, in normal circumstances, remain with him/her until they leave the school. Thus tutor groups mixed in both ability and age and there is easy rapport between all children across the school. The older ones love helping the younger ones.

According to parents, excellent pastoral care, particularly for the boarders. 'They get well cared for, individual treatment and feel they are part of a family'. Several raved about the deputy head (pastoral) who, they say, really carried the school through recent difficult times. Definitely feel there's a good team in place now.

Effective and active PTA. General feeling is that head is in tune with all pupils and ideal person to be running the boarding section as well. Watch this spot for further developments.

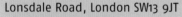

St Paul's School

Lonsdale Road, London SW13 9JT

020 8748 9162
admissions@stpaulsschool.org.uk
www.stpaulsschool.org.uk

Ages: 13–18
Pupils: 1,378; sixth form: 370
Boarders: 33
Day: £22,644 pa
Boarding: £33,915 pa

High Master: Since 2011, Professor Mark Bailey (50s). Career has included both academia and education: former head of The Grammar School at Leeds, he has also been a fellow at Cambridge and at All Souls, and professor of late medieval history at the University of East Anglia, with whom he continues to be involved. Found time to be a rugby international (1984 to 1990) and is now president of the Cambridge University Rugby Club. A thoroughly engaging, astute, relaxed and kindly man, the complete reverse of what one might expect of the high master of such a venerable institution as St Paul's. We meet many head teachers who are fonder of their school than of the pupils in it. Professor Bailey, extremely clever himself, still cherishes the achievements of others. A people-person through and through, who likes 'reading, walking and the wines of the Rhone Valley'. Talks with a refreshing lack of jargon. Married to an HR consultant, and with a teenage son and daughter.

Self-imposed mandate, on coming to St Paul's, was, 'Not to meddle with what this school does outstandingly well; leadership of exceptional institutions is as much about stewardship as change.' That said, he is skilfully overseeing a vast programme of refurbishment that is transforming the 1960s site into a school for the 21st century, and steering both school and students towards greater meritocracy and social responsibility.

Academic matters: The St Paul's recipe for academic stardom remains the same: cream off the very brightest, recruit the very best, light the blue touch paper and stand clear. The resulting sparks illuminate the sky. As one boy put it, 'The real pleasure about being here is going off-piste academically.' Another said, 'The quality of the teaching is beyond compare. It really pushes you further.' Parents agree. 'The teachers are brilliant at their subjects'; 'They're highly skilled at imparting their knowledge'; 'The teaching is simply superb'. A recent inspection report summed it up: 'The effectiveness of questioning in lessons, both from pupils and teachers, is outstanding.'

A thoroughly engaging, astute, relaxed and kindly man, the complete reverse of what one might expect of a high master of such a venerable institution as St Paul's

Broad and challenging curriculum includes ancient history, engineering and technology, and an excellent range of languages, Italian, Russian and Greek among them. Exam success is seen as a by-product of the boys' broader intellectual development, but it ain't a bad by-product: 97 per cent A*/A at GCSE in 2015 and 80 A*/A at A level. Amazing science building offers 18 laboratories, but such is the subject's popularity that, according to staff, 'space

is still tight'. Beautiful library, silent and inviting, and facilities everywhere are excellent, although we were amused to see far fewer interactive whiteboards in the classrooms than we'd seen in a state primary school the week before. Interactivity here is still verbal and cerebral perhaps, rather than fibre-optical. Huzza! But we applauded the really intelligent decision to install air-conditioning in all teaching rooms, ensuring that minds stay alert in the muggiest of weather. (How many times have we seen pupils wilting in the heat of south-facing temporary classrooms?) Specialist support is given to those few students identified as having special needs, but this isn't the place for anything more than mild cases.

There are no plans to introduce the IB, which the high master describes as 'enforced breadth', adding that the Cambridge Pre-U is 'chunky and prescriptive'. A levels are preferred here, because 'they're the easiest of the post-16 qualifications; they enable the boys to matriculate, and this then leaves time to pursue other areas.'

You can feel the thinking going on here. Academically, a very special place.

Games, options, the arts: Superb facilities include six rugby pitches, six football pitches, five cricket pitches, swimming pool, courts for rackets, squash and fives, and its own boathouse stuffed with sophisticated rowing craft. The students wax lyrical about the sport on offer here – 'Sport for me has been the highlight here'; 'There is so much!'; 'It's a big part of my life at St Paul's'; 'Most of my friends have been the ones I play sport with' – and we saw dozens of boys throwing themselves about the playing fields in organised and impromptu games of just about everything.

Music and drama are both extremely strong; concerts are held in the world-class Wathen Hall, and new Samuel Pepys Theatre was recently opened. Art is taught in a magnificent suite of rooms, and the engineering and technology room is surely every young boy's dream. Clubs cater for every taste, although oddly enough we didn't see any, despite having arrived at lunchtime; even the four lads we finally came across in the 3D art room turned out to be revising their French ('I don't know why they're doing it here,' mused the art teacher). But the student-produced magazines we read were testament to the vibrancy of this community of thinkers: page after page of exceptionally mature, sparkily written articles on cinema, sport, current events, modern architecture; a real treasure trove of ideas.

Boarding: St Paul's is a day school – one of only two to be included in the Clarendon Commission's 'nine great public schools of England' – but it does have a very small community of boarders as well, a quarter of them from overseas, who seem to exist to justify the superb round-the-clock catering which all the boys, day and boarding alike, can access if they need to. Boarding facilities have been recently upgraded, and the boarding provision was praised in a recent ISI report. Study bedrooms, common room and TV room, music practice rooms and computer suite. At least two hours' prep a night followed by supervised activities eg music or sport keep boys busy during the week. Many boarders go home at weekends, often after Saturday morning sports matches.

There are 'no plans whatsoever to admit girls at any stage of the school'. Which, if they want to go all Rubens–y about the stairwells, may be a good thing

Background and atmosphere: Founded in 1509 by Dean John Colet, and moved four times before arriving in 1968 at its present riverside home in leafy (and very wealthy) suburbia. A £77 million redevelopment has transformed much of the site. Visitors now are presented with an exceptionally elegant, blond, modern school campus; an architectural version of the Paulines we met, really, and with the same air of informality and purpose.

Having survived the Great Plague, the Fire of London, the Civil War and the 20th century, St Paul's can afford to relax and enjoy its own success. 'Academic rigour and loose ties' was how one parent described St Paul's today, and this was echoed by the high master: 'It has the feel of an über-grammar school. It's more like a university than any other school I've known.'

'The bottom of this particular pile still represents an extremely high level of achievement'

It's cool to be clever here, and so, inevitably, there is peer pressure to do well. This is mostly positive, say boys and parents, and drives everyone on, although one parent added, 'If you were at the bottom of the class, SPS would be a horrible place.' But high master denies this emphatically: 'More time than ever has been put into teaching underachieving boys and providing better support.' And another parent observed, 'The bottom of this particular pile still represents an extremely high level of achievement.' We saw boys working with good humoured focus for an eccentric and witty geographer who was padding around in Muppet-motif socks, interspersing teaching points with cheerful insults which the boys lapped up and batted back, in time-honoured boys' school way. (But there was a detailed scheme of work on the board that accorded with modern practice, demonstrating that old and new styles of education can be blended successfully.)

Indeed, SPS remains an extremely masculine community, where the testosterone coming out of the circuit-gym knocks you over at 20 paces; and perhaps this shows most in the school's being unaware of just how masculine it is. The sur master insisted that there was much 'mutuality' between the Boys' School and the Girls' School, but this was flatly contradicted by the Paulines we spoke to, and by one mother who felt that the school could do much more in this regard. We were ourselves surprised to find a large-scale female nude looking breastily down on us as we ascended the art department stairs, and more surprised to find another one as we went down a different way. There were no male nudes on display, and we couldn't help wondering why, out of all the subject matter that might have been on show, the school had chosen these particular canvases. There are 'no plans whatsoever to admit girls at any stage of the school; no parents, boys or staff have ever suggested it' (high master). Which, if they want to go all Rubens-y about the stairwells, may be a good thing. But the Paulines we met were very personable young men, and the same mother who wanted more contact with SPGS also affirmed, 'Paulines are lovely, decent boys, really articulate, fun, clever and very nice.'

Pastoral care, well-being and discipline: Vertical tutoring system, ie mixing the ages of form groups so that younger and older boys are together. The concept is simple: boys will listen to their peers sooner than their parents, so utilise the more experienced boys for pastoral care and to lead extra-curricular activities. It's been in place for over 10 years, and is clearly popular. As one parent commented, 'From the moment they arrive, the 13 year olds meet boys in every other year and get a sense of what they might do.' Tutors stay with the boys throughout their time at the school, and, says school, often become family friends – the advisability of which the school may be reviewing, in the light of recent events (see below). The nature of this hand-picked community means that bad behaviour is rare: 'There's an intuitive understanding of where the boundaries are,' says high master. 'I've never seen any evidence of bullying here,' was a typical student comment, and sur master concurs: 'We have very, very few boys that would do what could be called bullying more than once, and if they do, we apply school sanctions quickly.'

The school, along with Colet Court, is currently under investigation following allegations of child abuse between the 1960s and 80s.

Pupils and parents: One of the most expensive day schools in the UK, and compared with similar institutions, financial support for poorer families is small – see Money matters. The result is a community which is highly diverse religiously and culturally, but not socially. Parents mostly ambitious and successful professionals with sons to match, hard-working and free-thinking. Old boys list reads like a Who's Who of Influential Britons: a sample includes John Milton, Samuel Pepys, Field Marshal Montgomery, Isaiah Berlin, Oliver Sacks, George Osborne, Rory Kinnear – and Nicholas Parsons.

Entrance: State-educated parents who are starry-eyed for their children but don't know the entrance procedure should start reading it now. SPS takes about 180 13-year-old boys each year, but it's impossible to go there directly from a state school. The 13+ candidates apply either from Colet Court, whose 80-90 boys nearly all go on to the senior school, or from any other prep school – usually those in the London area. Colet Court has its own admission procedures at 7+, 8+ and 11+; see our separate entry, and don't leave it any later than September of your child's year 6 (be grateful: it used to be year 5). Prospective Paulines sit an online common entrance pre-test at their prep school, on the strength of which about 350 are invited for interview. The school then makes conditional offers: boys have to get at least 70 per cent at common entrance. The school is looking for

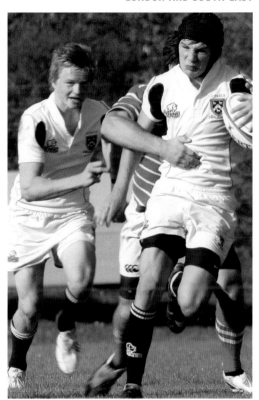

'intellectual curiosity and embracing of novelty'. About 20 more boys also join in the sixth form, which at SPS is called the Eighth.

Exit: In 2015, 56 Oxbridge places, the rest to Bristol, Durham, Imperial, Edinburgh, UCL and other top universities. An increasing number (24 in 2015) leave for USA or Canada unis such as Harvard, Yale and Princeton. Most popular courses economics, history and medicine.

Money matters: Only five per cent of students receive any form of means-tested bursary assistance (although for those few the assistance can be up to 100 per cent of the fees) and scholarships are honorifics only – £60 pa and a silver fish in memory of John Colet. Some remission for families who send three or more children to the school. High master's vision is to increase the amount of bursaries available, so that the school can become genuinely needs-blind.

Remarks: For very bright, confident, motivated boys who like to think for themselves, St Paul's provides a truly unrivalled education. A unique start in life.

Saint Ronan's School

Water Lane, Hawkhurst, Kent TN18 5DJ

01580 752271
info@saintronans.co.uk
www.saintronans.co.uk
C of E

Ages: 3–13 (boarders from year 4)
Pupils: 269
Boarders: 78
Day: £9,585 – £16,431 pa
Boarding: plus £35 per night

Headmaster: Since 2003, Mr William Trelawny-Vernon (40s). Very much a joint enterprise with wife Emma (she's the Trelawny, he's the Vernon) – who is both registrar and head of history. Known as Mr and Mrs TV to pupils and parents alike. The couple met at Exeter, where Mr TV read biology. Previously at Stowe School for 12 years, including posts as a biology teacher and seven years as housemaster of Chatham House. 'Universally loved', according to parents.

The business is in the blood – his father was head of Hordle House (now Walhampton) in Hampshire. Four children – the youngest at the prep, the other three have moved on to King's Canterbury. The family left the head's accommodation to move off site in 2005 and they eschew the parental dinner party circuit, believing it's important to maintain a distance. Parents think they get it right, as one commented: 'One of the areas in which the school excels is in managing very successfully the line between parental involvement and keeping parents distanced when necessary.'

Both grew up in a four-child family, and with their own gang of four have that deep respect for fairness and equality of treatment which comes from big families. 'Neither of us likes the concept of the alpha child,' says Mr TV.

School and family is everything to Mr TV – time off finds him socialising with the wider family, and stress relief comes by sitting on his tractor and mowing the grass, or researching the history of the two families. Both are content with home and hearth, or as Emma puts it, 'We're like labradors sitting in front of the fire'. Holidays take them to the West Country, home of Emma's ancestral seat (her brother John inherited the Salusbury-Trelawny Baronetcy).

Entrance: All children attend a taster day, and children seeking places in year 3 and above are assessed by the class teacher and take verbal and non-verbal reasoning tests. Intake covers wide-ranging abilities, but all are expected to pass common entrance or the Cranbrook grammar tests, so 'There will be a couple of children where we will have an honest dialogue with the parents and tell them that their child's needs are not going to be met here,' says Mr TV.

Scholarships are available for academic, music, art and sporting talents, and there are strictly monitored means-tested bursaries. Minibuses bring children in from Staplehurst, High Halden, Burwash, Wittersham, and the villages en route.

Exit: It's not the place to come if you have your sights on the West Kent grammars – despite these being within travelling distance, the school doesn't encourage exit at 11. Only one or two children per year sit the Kent 11+, so it'll be a lonely experience and you'll have to find a tutor.

> *The emphasis is on old-fashioned, wholesome fun, making every use of this natural playground. 'It's idyllic, they get to dam streams and play with pigs and chickens'*

The majority of parents are buying into private education for the duration, although around 30 per cent of pupils go to Cranbrook grammar at 13. Key destinations include Benenden, Eastbourne, King's Canterbury, Sevenoaks, Sutton Valence and Tonbridge. Others go further afield – recently to Stowe. 'Since I've been head we have fed into 52 different schools,' says Mr TV. Parents say they are very good at helping you choose the next school – the TVs visit a clutch of senior schools together each term so they are well informed, and were freshly back from visits to Sherborne, Bryanston and Milton Abbey when we visited.

Generally a good number of scholarships, and one or two parents admit to feeling some playground one-upmanship from other parents about places and scholarships secured. 'There is competition from some of the parents, which can make you feel uncomfortable if you let it, though not between the children,' said one.

Its quirkiness ensures there is no Saint Ronan's product – and the roll of past pupils is stuffed with the great and good. 'Just look at the alumni to see how successful it is in producing movers and shakers and Boy's Own heroes,' said one parent. Indeed the list reads like a fantasy dinner party guest list; BBC security correspondent Frank Gardner, spy Donald Maclean, MP Airey Neave, Olympic rower Matthew Parrish, and the late Mark Shand, travel writer (and brother of Camilla, Duchess of Cornwall) are just a few.

Remarks: It's a what's-not-to-love campus. Gorgeous grounds with ancient, spreading trees, inspiring

views, a fishing lake, and its own 100 acre wood. And there's even a farm with pigs, alpacas, and chickens – newborn piglets greeted our visit. The emphasis is on old-fashioned, wholesome fun, making every use of this natural playground. 'It's idyllic, they get to dam streams and play with pigs and chickens,' said one parent. Everything is named for Boy's Own adventures – there's the Gulch, an area around a stream ideal for making mud pies, the Saltmines, an overgrown area with secret pathways, and even the pitches have names, such as Timbuktoo (because it's a long journey to reach it). A new classroom on the edge of the woods is the Hobbit House. As one parent put it, 'If Enid Blyton was still around, Saint Ronan's would be exactly the sort of school she would be writing about. We are buying a truly magical childhood experience, not just a superb all-round education.'

All this romping is made easier by probably the most relaxed and colourful uniform we've seen – corduroy trousers, skirts or pinafores in sensible colours, topped with school sweatshirts in a choice of colours – pink, green, red, purple, light blue and navy. There's a formal uniform which is worn on Fridays, key days and for trips out.

The pre-prep is in a separate bright and modern building (where a corridor poster advises on 20 things to do before leaving pre-prep, such as dam a stream, make a mud pie, and hold an animal). There's also a cosy kindergarten in the former headmaster's house.

Moving up to prep brings the grandeur of Tongswood House, a Victorian mansion built by an Oxo magnate. The original features are well-maintained – including a sprung floor ballroom, now used for performances and gatherings, where frescoes of semi-naked nymphs on the ceiling liven up assembly for the older boys.

There's wood panelling and grand staircases aplenty, and classrooms are eccentrically named, such as Old Bailey, 10 Downing Street, Lombard Street (because that's where the safe was), and Windsor Castle (once a lavatory). Children scrape to their feet as you enter – standing up for grown-ups is something the teachers are strictest about, say the pupils, along with manners, being kind, and being honest.

Kindness is the rule for staff too. 'If we heard a teacher shouting at a child, they would have to come into the office and explain why,' says Mrs TV. 'We like to treat them in the same way as our own children. I don't want to be head monster,' says Mr TV. Prefects are elected by the children in a secret ballot 'which means they go for someone who is kind and gentle, not necessarily just one of the first XV,' says Mr TV.

In reception you're greeted by a wood fire burning in the hearth – where parents come to warm up for post-match teas – and a basket of free range eggs for sale. You can also pick up school produced pork and apple juice. The head's secretary is Mrs TV's sister, known as Aunty Amanda. Parents love the reportedly eccentric ways of school admin. They talk of things being done in a Saint Ronan's way, one of 'happy chaos', which 'wouldn't suit parents who want everything done in a completely perfect planned-out way'. It looks disorganised, but it works, they say. 'We do slightly chaotic and quirky with great aplomb,' says one mother proudly.

Prefects are elected by the children in a secret ballot 'which means they go for someone who is kind and gentle, not necessarily one of the first XV'

Whilst it delivers on results (100 per cent success rate in the Cranbrook Grammar and the common entrance exam many years) it does so in a thoroughly gentle way. Prizes are given for contribution as well as achievement, and one parent said, 'although they are encouraged to achieve, this is not done in an over-competitive manner'. And pupils say that the teachers discourage any jostling for position. 'When we get exam results the teachers encourage us not to ask each other what we got, but if you get a bad mark people still always say you've done really well, or tell you what to do to improve. I once got 27 per cent but the others just said I was unlucky,' said one boy. Setting for subjects begins in year 4, with streaming in year 8. Latin is taught from year 6.

Parents praise the efforts made to find and develop talents, which may not be academic. There

It looks disorganised, but it works, they say. 'We do slightly chaotic and quirky with great aplomb,' says one mother proudly

are 16 peripatetic music teachers, and a DT building which develops practical skills – it's equipped with laser cutters and scroll saws, and children take woodwork from year 3, making everything from working pens to cars for drag racing. 'We are so impressed that every child has something they will achieve in. For my kids it has been music for my daughter and sport for my boys,' says a mother.

Sport has developed as the school has doubled in size in the last 10 years, 'so we can now play decent schools,' says Mr TV. There's an impressive new sports hall, an Astroturf and an outdoor pool, and a great range of sports on offer – an extras programme one afternoon per week offers archery, fencing, golf, sailing and lacrosse. The school's sailing team have been prep school champions, and one girl has made the GB under-15 team for fencing. There's other options on extras afternoon for the non-sporty, such as farming, funky dance, fishing, bee-keeping and touch typing.

Much is made by the head and parents about keeping the pupils children as long as possible, and they are clearly successful at cocooning them. The year 8s seem younger than their peers we meet in secondary schools – no less articulate, but definitely less worldly. Parents report no divide between age groups, saying: 'You constantly see older children encouraging and playing with the younger ones, and children in year 3 aren't scared of the year 8s.'

Parents predominantly work in the City of London; others are doctors at the nearby hospital, or farmers. 'It is very inclusive and friendly with no social divides, and parents are always ready to help one another out,' said a mother. There are fitness groups for parents to join including zumba, Nordic walking, and joggy-doggy.

The only gripe you'll hear from parents – and that's a mild one – is that they find it a long day for the prep school children (8.30am to 5.15pm, with prep afterwards at home or at school from year 5 until 6.30pm). A lot of children take up the flexible boarding option – 'really fun,' the pupils agree; around one-third of children stay for up to four nights per week. Rooms are up in the eaves, and again you wouldn't be surprised to find the Famous Five up there having lashings of hot chocolate. Boarders do supervised prep for one hour, then after supper, the options include swimming, singing, and playing outside. Matron Julie is reportedly 'nice to cuddle with'.

St Teresa's Effingham Senior School

Effingham, Surrey RH5 6ST

01372 452037
a.charles@st-teresas.com
www.st-teresas.com
RC

Ages: 11–18 (junior boarding from year 6)
Pupils: 370; sixth form: 90
Boarders: 80
Day: £15,435 – £16,035 pa
Boarding: £25,185 – £27,585 pa

Headmaster: Since 2012, Mr Mike Farmer (50s). First teaching job was as a sailing instructor, spending three years post-graduation in Greece and Turkey. He met his future wife Mary-Ann in Greece and looming marriage and family took him to a job in the real world at Godolphin School, Salisbury, where he taught economics, business and ICT. The head there, Hilary Fender, took him with her to be assistant head at Headington, Oxford in 1997. First headship was at Kilgraston in Perthshire (2003), where he achieved the gong of UK Independent School of the Year in 2011 and turned around a school that had been dubbed 'the Marie Celeste' to achieve the highest growth rate in its sector.

He has a sound business head, the confidence of his governors and a clear sight of what he needs to do to ensure the school flourishes in a wealthy and highly competitive area for independent schools. Comes across as self-effacing and unassuming but what lies beneath is steel. Has taken bold risks to finance capital projects in order to boost the roll and scythed staff where necessary. Educated at a large comprehensive himself and not at all stuffy. 'He's a very humble man – he doesn't have that ego you see in some heads,' a parent told us.

Career paths of his children show that he pays more than lip service to developing individual talents – one is a theoretical physicist, one a theatrical agent.

Academic matters: School is non-selective – head's aim is to boost its academic reputation, but not make it a hothouse. 'We have got to make sure we can stretch the top end,' he says. To this end, he has brought in a new assistant head (academic) who runs the Oxbridge enrichment society and the gifted and talented programme. She is like a glamorous Miss Jean Brodie, brainy and geeky but with spiky heels and stylish clothes. Just the job to have teenage girls hanging on her every word and parents love her weekly 'All geek to me' emails, with their suggestions of enriching books, radio programmes, exhibitions etc. She also runs academic seminar evenings, where girls present findings in front of their peers, and brings in visiting speakers

– recently a talk from the Nuffield Foundation on the ethics of treating dementia.

Most popular A level subjects are English, maths and science. Head has overseen the introduction of new A levels, including classics, classical civilisation, Latin, government and politics and music technology. In 2015, 61 per cent of entries achieved A*/B and 37 per cent A*/A at A level; at GCSE, 46 per cent A*/A.

Languages include French, German, Spanish and Latin, with Mandarin and Russian as after-school options. Double and triple award science on offer and there are visiting speakers of the calibre of Sir Robert Winston. The school is considered a specialist for art, especially in the overseas market, and each year pupils progress to fashion design and art foundation courses. We saw some fantastic textiles work and sixth formers deeply engrossed in their work in the art room.

Just the job to have teenage girls hanging on her every word and parents love her weekly 'All geek to me' emails, with their suggestions for enriching books, exhibitions etc

Pupils talk of the individualism of teaching, so there is not one particular style. We saw a key stage 4 class dissecting a poem and noted the pupils' confidence in voicing their individual interpretation; nearly all had something to say and they were unabashed in front of visitor. Loads of praise for the English department from parents – indeed, for most of the teaching –although one told us: 'There are still a couple of old retainers who some of us feel should be sent down the hill but generally Mr Farmer has got a grip on what he expects from his staff.'

Games, options, the arts: Lots to appeal to tennis players or riders. Newly formed St Teresa's Tennis Academy is headed by former Wimbledon player

Lee Childs. Four hard courts and nine artificial grass courts. Recently opened equestrian centre stables around a dozen horses and riding is offered as an after-school option. Head says it's an unashamed way to draw in new pupils and differentiate the school from the competition.

Sports hall has been redeveloped and a coach brought in to run a swimming academy. Negotiations are under way to become the Surrey hub for Pentathlon GB, which will give the school access to Olympic coaches. 'We will become a very sporty school,' says the head. Meanwhile a parent told us: 'Negative comments have been made about sport (or lack of it) by many parents but this has been addressed by Mr Farmer and a much more efficient PE timetable is now in place.'

Director of music effused enthusiasm as he showed us round the music department. A professional French horn player, he has performed with the most prestigious orchestras but is just as keen on bringing in local rock bands for the girls to produce in their own sound recording studio, or using digital technology. We saw one class composing on computers using serialism, a method often used to produce discordant film music. His contacts enable him to bring in professionals as peripatetic music teachers – cello teacher works at the Royal Opera House, flute teacher is in the BBC orchestra. Noticeboards are crammed with flyers for music events and pictures from overseas choir tours (girls have had the opportunity to perform in venues like Notre Dame Cathedral). School also hosts the Surrey Hills Music Festival, as well as numerous recitals.

A professional French horn player, he has performed with the most prestigious orchestras, but is just as keen on bringing in local rock bands for the girls to produce

Thesps can take LAMDA courses in public speaking, musical theatre and acting. Three achieved gold medals last year and some have gained up to 200 UCAS points from these qualifications. New arts centre on the way – old art rooms will be converted into an new sixth form study facility.

Week night activities for boarders range from pudding club to ice skating to picnics, with Saturday afternoon outings to theme parks, theatre, paintballing, bowling. On site activities include falconry and circus skills. Plus tennis, riding and other sports.

Boarding: Boarding numbers are just under 100 – 60 per cent of boarders are international students though school has set maximum of 10 per cent in school as a whole. Boarding accommodation recently refurbished, decorated in light neutral colours and homely touches. Rooms range from singles for the sixth form to dorms for three to six girls for the younger pupils.

Background and atmosphere: St Teresa's was founded in 1928 by the Religious Order of Christian Instruction, and the main house now forms the centre of the senior school. Other buildings have been tacked on over the years, and the former nuns' accommodation has been converted to classrooms. The prep school was newly built in 2009 (it moved here from another site) – new prep classrooms being added. There's nothing to set an architecture fan's pulse racing, but the classrooms are bright and functional. The campus is a lovely 48-acre parkland with ancient trees, set in an area of outstanding natural beauty. Very secluded – it would be nigh on impossible for girls to sneak out for a night on the town.

When the head arrived he made wide-ranging changes straight away in order to turn around the school's fortunes. Rebranding meant changing the school's name, modernising the school's newsletter and bringing in a new uniform. It was out with the old and in with the new in key staff appointments – 'there was some staff movement,' he told us diplomatically. In September 2013 he brought in a new head of prep, head of science, head of boarding and assistant head (academic).

It's been well received by parents. As one told us: 'I have yet to hear a negative comment about Mr Farmer. I think we are all astonished at how he has managed to turn the school around and increase the numbers in such a short time.' Another said: 'He has transformed it from a good to an amazing school. The children's view of the school and their pride in it has changed a lot.'

There's a buzz about the staff – they are clearly rejuvenated by the changes. And word is spreading. 'I was at a coffee morning for new parents and the vibe was amazing. People were saying it was their number one choice and were queuing up to get in – well, that's new,' said one mother. Year 7 intake went from a two-form entry in September 2012 to four forms in September 2013.

School's Catholicism comes in the gentlest form – as an ethos of kindness, supporting the weaker, and strong pastoral care. Around a quarter of the pupils are Catholic and there's no requirement for staff other than the head to be Catholic. Although certain feast days are celebrated, the school recently celebrated Diwali, led by an Indian member of staff. mass on Sundays is compulsory for Catholics and all boarders attend twice a term. The chapel is modern, with some stained glass and soothing music throughout the day – a place to wander into for peaceful repose. The priest is reportedly young and trendy. There's nothing to frighten off those not of the faith, said one parent. 'The school isn't overly Catholic but it has a Christian way about it, which is a good thing. I know people are put off by it, which is a shame because it makes the school a more nurturing place to be.'

Pastoral care, well-being and discipline: In school, younger girls' well-being is monitored through a buddy system – sixth formers meet their charges once a week. Girls feel able to raise issues and know they will be listened to. "We can make suggestions and we will be heard and acknowledged,' said one girl. 'We weren't happy with the school food so we surveyed pupils and presented the findings and it has improved a lot since.' Head plans to introduce Big Brother style video diaries (which he previously ran at Kilgraston), where girls can raise any concerns.

Pupils and parents: Girls are wholesome looking – all pony-tails and make up-free faces. Wide range of nationalities – 15 per cent of students are international boarders from countries like China, Hong Kong, Mexico, Spain, Russia and Nigeria. Locals bus in from a radius extending to Guildford, Reigate and south London.

Most parents who choose the school haven't put academic reputation as their top priority. This means there's a blessed lack of competitive parent syndrome, we're told. Some very wealthy parents, but a mix of economic backgrounds. 'Those with limited funds will certainly not feel intimidated, although the arrival of the tennis academy and equestrian centre could change this,' said one mother. 'One prospective parent did ask me if a horse was going to be an option on the kit list.'

Entrance: Tougher than it used to be. Senior school currently has a waiting list for the first time in many years. More top end girls have been applying,

which means the academic standard for entry at 11 is now similar to an 11+ pass or level 5 in national curriculum tests. Canny parents who think their child may miss this mark are putting girls in the prep in year 5 or 6 as this gives automatic entry. However other talents can tip it. 'A girl may be very good at sport, art or music – we won't go just on the exam,' says the head. There's a big influx at senior entry – year 7 currently has 25 pupils from the prep and 35 newcomers. Virtually all year 6s progress to the senior school, many with scholarships.

When it comes to the sixth form, all current pupils are accepted 'as long as we can offer them a programme,' while incomers need six Bs and an A at GCSE.

Although the school is Catholic, there is no requirement to be Catholic. Children raised in the faith do not get priority, although it may be a deciding factor.

Exit: Recent higher education destinations include medicine at Leeds, human sciences at Oxford, accounting at Durham and Manchester, art foundation at Central St Martin's and youth and community studies at Winchester. One to Cambridge in 2015 to read natural sciences.

Money matters: Scholarships are awarded for academic excellence, art, drama, music and sport.

Remarks: Moves afoot to ramp up school's educational attainment by pushing the brightest, but not at the expense of the middling. We reckon that this is a school that truly can cater for wide ranging abilities. There's a lovely, gentle atmosphere – we saw no cliques of glossy haired alpha girls. A good fit for girls who want to take their time to grow up or those who need to know it's OK to be geeky.

Seaford College

Lavington Park, Petworth, West Sussex GU28 0NB

01798 867392
jmackay@seaford.org
www.seaford.org

Ages: 13–18 (boarders from 11)
Pupils: 516; sixth form: 160
Boarders: 46 full, 98 weekly, 22 flexi
Day: £9,930– £19,380 pa
Boarding: £19,320 – £29,985 pa

Headmaster: Since 2013, John Green. Background in professional rugby – he teaches the first team, donning wellies with suit. Taught previously at Barry Boys' School, Ardingly College and Hurstpierpoint, before becoming deputy at Seaford. Married to

Sîan with three children, two of whom are still at Seaford.

Tiggerish energy, staunch and unapologetic supporter of the underdog, with a clear vision of how he wants Seaford to be. Works hard to install a sense of value and self worth in all his pupils: A* pupils at Seaford now consider Oxford; BTec pupils are told 'you could be employing those A* pupils in a few years time'. Quality he most desires for his pupils: pride in self.

Academic matters: In 2015, good solid results: 56 per cent A*-B, 30 per cent A*-A, at GCSE; 43 per cent A*-B, 20 per cent A*-A at A level. Judged on its place in a league table – unremarkable. But the remarkable exists within these figures at this non-selective school. The most able are achieving the high grades you would expect; but so are a good number of those of more average abilities, and as an overall picture, they are generally adding at least one grade to pupils' attainment.

New pupils at Seaford all have a data interview: a detailed meeting showing parents and the pupil their CAT scores and the national picture of attainment for someone of their abilities. 'Children in the middle can achieve highly and shouldn't put a ceiling on expectations'. For some, it makes top grades suddenly seem like something attainable: one parent told us about her son, told by his previous school that he was a no hoper. His confidence has soared at Seaford: he's predicted good grades at A level, and led Young Enterprise last year. When he went up on speech day for an academic prize, 'it was worth every penny'.

'Seaford was seen as a school for dunces,' said a parent who was initially dubious about the school, thinking it was a 'too relaxed environment.' On meeting the head, the parent quickly felt that things had changed. Rigour is now a word which could apply to Seaford. One parent described how her son did a mock paper which went wrong: 'they were all over it and him, in a supportive, but thorough way'.

There's a new focus on high flyers here: a head of enrichment now guides the Oxford application process, gently steering candidates away from inserting an academic joke into every sentence at interview. An enrichment programme is under way (in its infancy at present) which aims to select high performers in each subject and add a layer on top of syllabus stuff – masterclasses in maths this term with lectures on chaos and infinity. The aim is to develop the most able, but in true Seaford style, lecture doors will be open to anyone truly interested, while trying to exclude crafty prep dodgers.

The head has made several staff changes, to the relief of parents: 'The dead wood's gone', said one briskly. There was a lot of praise for the effort put in by teachers: 'what makes this school special is its staff'; 'the commitment of staff is extraordinary'; 'teachers go above and beyond to help failing pupils... three extra sessions a week to help my son get a pass'; 'she [a maths teacher] turns her life over to help them'.

An extremely active tutor system, with a weekly meeting of an hour, and daily catch up of five to 10 minutes every morning. Pupils are also part of vertical tutor groups spanning year groups.

Homework is marked with comments, not grades – 'if pupils get a grade, they immediately want to know what their friend got'. Grades are only communicated to pupils in conversation with teachers. Effort grades have been abandoned – 'only pupils really know how much effort they've put in', says

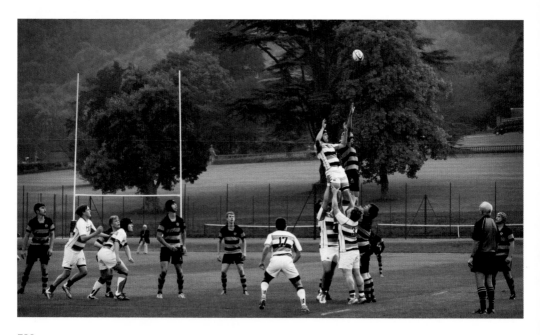

the head. Instead, effort and attainment have been absorbed into the Challenge Grade system: grades set are a indication of potential – what a pupil could achieve if they work hard. Different colours indicate how well they are progressing towards their challenge grades, from significantly underachieving red, through amber, green and gold to extremely high-achieving platinum. Challenge grades are set with tutors and can be upped by pupils if they feel the challenge is not sufficient (hollow laughs from the students seated next to me).

Another described how her dyslexic son 'changed overnight' here. Having been told at his prep that he wouldn't be able to sit GCSEs, he is now at a school of architecture

A good array of subjects on offer at both GCSE and A level, plus BTecs. Pre-university courses, as well as EPQ. A minimum of 45 points is required to go on to sixth form for A levels (A* = 8 points, A = 7 points and so on). Most subjects have a spread of attainment in grade terms, English, history and maths with clusters towards the top end.

Learning support here is done extremely well by a staff of nine specialist teachers, five full-time, four part-time. Seaford proudly locates learning support in the centre of the campus, 'not the usual broom cupboard under the stairs', said a parent wryly. 'There's always a correlation to where the learning support department is, and how much the school embrace it', she added.

Nearly half the pupils at the school use the unit at some point, by teacher or self-referral. Parents like its size and focus, and the fact that the unit is part of a school which excels in many ways – 'you don't have to feel [your child is] attending a second rate school because they support dyslexic children'.

'I've been to a lot of schools who say they are good at SEN', said a weary mum, 'but here it isn't just a soundbite'. The unit describes an approach that involves nurturing and developing individual potential, working hard to increase confidence, by not pointing out what's wrong, but what's right, and how to improve. Even mindfulness is included for some pupils, to support a positive approach to school. High degree of joined-up thinking to enable dyslexics to access the curriculum: the unit meets with teachers monthly, and some departments regularly: someone from learning support attends the weekly English department meetings.

And their approach yields results. A parent spoke of her son's confidence soaring; another described how her severely dyslexic son 'changed

overnight' here. Having been told at his prep that he wouldn't be able to sit GCSEs, he is now at the school of architecture in Oxford, having left Seaford with three A levels and an EPQ. If things weren't working, Seaford always looked for alternatives which fitted him better, she explained.

Mild to moderate dyslexic pupils in general, though the door is not closed to those at the severe end of the spectrum if they have a high IQ or good underlying ability; but they need to be able to access the mainstream curriculum with the help available. Some 220 of unit users are dyslexic, 15 of these severe, 190 moderate and 20 mild. The unit assists 44 pupils with dyspraxia and 13 with speech and language problems. Others using the unit might have slow processing speeds or memory problems which mean they would not perform up to their ability level without help. Would consider mild Asperger's, but not the place for autism. Help also given for ADHD (experienced but not specialists in this).

There is one guaranteed one-to-one session a week (which is charged as an extra). Some end up with more than one session: we spoke to a parent whose son has three sessions a week. She believes he couldn't manage with less and that the level of help is an important factor in his success. Extra sessions are offered to pupils if they become available, on the basis of need. There is a little in-class support.

Challenge grades for those with dyslexia are set according to a pupil's ability, as with any other pupil. They're expected to achieve as well as anybody else, but 'it might just take them longer to get there, and they might get there in a different way', said the head of the unit diplomatically. They have had a number of high-achieving dyslexics, one achieving his eight As and one B at GCSE with the help of a scribe; another part of the current small group of high flyers trying for Oxford.

Games, options, the arts: A new focus on games with the rugby-playing head: hockey's always been strong here (county winners); now rugby's just as good. Girls were languishing behind the boys a year or so ago, but head has given girls' sport a new emphasis: more matches, and they're working hard to get them as good as the boys: hockey and netball are flourishing.

Pupils have six lessons a week (in two triple sessions). Teams for all, the best playing every week, less able around six times a term. Specialist coaching for all ability levels here; and it's not just the top performers who get the accolades: recent team of the term was the under 14 hockey C team.

Cricket and tennis for both girls and boys are taking off. There's a full golf course and lots of other sports on offer, from polo to clay pigeon shooting. New sports centre includes a gym and dance studio. Swimming not currently competitive, but with a glass retractable roof soon to be built over the outside pool, this is an area about to develop.

Some notable individual success, including a national triathlete, national paddle board champion, and a player for the national first XI hockey under 18s.

Music at Seaford is glorious. At a year 9 lunchtime concert, treats included spine-tingling singing of a Mozart aria. Singing is outstanding here – the head of voice is also head of voice at junior Royal Academy in London. The head soloist describes 'music coming up through my toes' – it's no surprise that she and the choir were selected to support Gary Barlow on the last night of his tour. The music block is all white paint and new wood – smooth, calm surroundings to complement the mellifluous sounds. Kids enjoy the 'incredible vibes' at Seafordstock every summer, and the head was keen to ensure that every year has a rock band.

Not as great an emphasis on drama as music ('not enough,' said one parent bluntly) – the arts calendar is dominated by music events. But drama is now part of the year 9 carousel, some pupils do LAMDA, and there's a main school production and senior production each year: Dr Faustus the last, a dyslexic pupil taking the lead part, learning his lines by drawing pictures. They don't shirk the big stuff here.

Compulsory CCF in year 10 – pupils think the parades are rather dull, but 'once you get past standing and marching for half an hour, you get to the woods and the fun stuff'. Both our guides said CCF camp was a favourite memory. D of E also available.

Art here is superb, with a big range on offer, from fine art to creative media production. Exam work was on display in room after room of glories: dresses of balloons and feathers; curvy wooden

Kids enjoy the 'incredible vibes' at Seafordstock every summer, and the head was keen to ensure that every year has a rock band

speakers and fabric stags' heads (they look so much better in tartan). Ghoulish sci-fi heads in the animation area; a fabric prawn (Shaun), life-like and eerily huge, hung casually from the ceiling. Sixth form art students almost live in the block – there's even a kitchen so they can brew – 'we look after them', said the head of art, comfortably. Students depart for art colleges across the country, including Central St Martins, Kingston and the London College of Fashion.

Boarding: It's really particularly nice here, and one of the nicest things is its lack of uniformity. The boarding houses are all different, but each with a strong sense of home. Around 180 boarders spread between four houses: most are weekly, with the greater number of full timers being international (10 per cent of boarders are from overseas). Flexi-boarding is also available, and it's usually possible to get a room at the last minute (£42), by emailing houseparents. Prep school boarders have rooms for seven or eight in the Mansion.

Boys (years 9-12) are in a crisp new building (which parents love), run by houseparents with fluent ease. Basket drawers for shoes as soon as boys come through the door – they generally remember: it's nice to walk around in socks with underfloor heating. If they don't – hoover duty that night. Rooms for two, with temperature gauges in each room and a sofa which can turn into another bed. New wood furniture, built in above bed lights. Rooms compact, but not tight. Worth getting the big jobs – head of house gets a comfy chair and ensuite, TV and fridge (wow).

Wifi throughout (indeed, throughout the campus), and a system so house parents can see if pupils are online when they shouldn't be (after 11.30pm); younger pupils hand in tech at bedtime. Comfortable common room, kitchen for snacks, fruit and toaster. Homework is supervised, house parents pleased that their only niggle ('haven't got any homework sir') has been resolved by internet site which makes it clear what everyone's got. A house mum bakes pancakes and fudge crumpets for movie night. Houseparent dogs bounce into the common room in the evening. The kids love it.

Girls in years 9-12 are housed in the Mansion: rooms of all shapes and sizes for one or two, some extremely spacious – elegant windows, dreamy views. Graceful spiral staircase up to the boarding floor. In various states of paint, just done and needs doing ('needs to be modern and fresher', said a parent). Good quality wood furniture, comfortable furniture, the usual kitchen provision.

Sixth form boys housed in what parent and pupils refer to as 'the youth hostel' (aka Hedon Hall); 'but the boys are all happy in there and love the housemaster'. The fabric is old, and inside it is painted lime green (gulp); but the furniture in bedrooms and common room is smart and new, bathrooms are clean, and the common room is decorated with sports paraphernalia, donated by past and present sixth formers. Residents have a fierce affection for the house and apparently feel no deficiencies.

The pupil who randomly assumed the job of showing us around, was polite, articulate and engagingly straightforward. The usual kitchen, and not just for brews: they competed in Hedon masterchef –'felt sorry for the people who had to try it', said our guide. Head of house is popular with the boys, and from his side, a staunch supporter of them. He enforces an hour's leisure reading every afternoon in the winter term (proper books, not magazines), having found out that dyslexic commuters do better because they read on the train.

Scottish giant of a house dad, casually consuming his Magnum, showed us a bright pink sitting room

Sixth form girls live in a bungalow, well-mown lawn with gnomes and assorted companions in front, patio with BBQ around the back. Some feeling of arriving in antipodean suburbia. Scottish giant of a house dad, casually consuming his Magnum, showed us a bright pink sitting room, golden buddha in the fire place: hippy girl power – felt like a teenage heaven. Kitchen and seated area – they can go to the dining hall for breakfast, but most prefer to eat 'healthy girly breakfasts' in house. Cosy rooms, with the usual high quality fittings. A warm friendly relationship between pupils and houseparents.

Plenty going on for boarders at weekends, with the Sainsbury's trip on Friday evening, sports and shopping trips on Saturday, and trips to places of interest on Sunday.

Background and atmosphere: A long driveway, past golf flags waving the in the breeze and ancient trees with improbably massive trunks up to the mansion house: stately home turned school. Seaford College sits at the foot of the downs, wooded hills rising immediately behind it, mists caught in the trees on the drizzly day of our visit – brewers' dubbin, said the head of English dreamily, clearly finding considerably more satisfaction in the rainy day than most of his fellows. A beautiful flint chapel nestles in the grass behind the school. Compulsory weekly service, but all beliefs welcome.

Stately elegance mixes with old cottages and swish new build. A few tatty Portakabins, due to be ripped down soon. Most parents we spoke to would like things to be a bit smarter –'there shouldn't be peeling paintwork – it needs a bit more polish'; but the head is working hard to spruce up buildings as well as pupils. Some pupils have been less than keen to polish their shoes, but most look smart: just a few shirt tails still hanging out. Manners are of the old-fashioned variety, and include standing up for visitors and handwritten letters of thanks. A taxi driver described pupils as very polite; then added, 'but they could do with mending the drive'.

There's an emphasis here on giving something back: community service activities every week, and community action day once a year, which includes activity programmes with local primary school children, or clearing beaches.

It would not suit a child who was full on academic with no other interests, said a parent. 'Very intelligent children will thrive there if they do other things…it could be a very lonely place for those just absorbed by maths and physics. Everyone's outside at the end of the day – you need to be able to mix and be a bit independent'.

Pastoral care, well-being and discipline: Pastoral care at Seaford is 'unbelievable,' said a parent, as she described the extraordinary level of kindness and understanding from the school when facing family tragedy. And they're very aware of the pressures of growing up. Staff in the Pink House provide a listening ear at any time – pupils can even ask

to be excused in a lesson, and staff will email the Pink House to say a pupil is on the way. It's staffed by one full-time director of care and welfare, a part-time safeguarding officer, the rev, a counsellor and Poppy the dog (who is particularly busy in September helping homesick pupils). At least 10 pupils turn up at the Pink House every day, but problems can be also be picked up by phone, tutors or peer mentors. Any bullying is dealt with promptly, confirm parents. One described how her daughter would pop in to the Pink House to get some perspective on school squabbles – so and so's being a bit nasty, I'll go the Pink House and see what they think.

In discipline terms, rules are firmly based on traditional good manners and strict enforcement of standards. No more easy-going Seaford: the new head is ensuring the school is up to the mark, from looking smart to the top 10 rules: break them and you risk exclusion (interestingly, dishonesty is ranked outside the top 10 as a less serious offence, alongside chewing gum...). No second chances for sex or drugs (although first time joint users might get a managed reprieve, depending on the circumstances). And to make sure no one flouts the rules, sniffer dogs (a crazy spaniel and a labrador) check the lunch queue. They're much loved by kids – and have never actually found anything. Two exclusions in the last year: for persistent disruption, and bullying. No surprise, in this caring school, that those suspended or excluded can go the Pink House for a chat with support workers 'to feel the love.'

Delicious lunch served for us in the head's study – is it always this nice? 'It doesn't look quite like this', said the head boy carefully, regarding a swirl of purée, 'but it tastes good'.

Pupils and parents: Posh, and not, here – 'I know someone with a jet, and others working three jobs to get their kids through'. Lots of weekly boarders from London, and school buses serve the surrounding area.

Fewer girls than boys (around a third), but the head is keen to attract more, and ran an everywoman conference to provide aspirational role models for girls.

Parents are happy with a good level of communication, with frequent emails from school, and teachers letting parents know if there's a problem – 'in the past we'd have had to work this out for ourselves'.

Notable former pupils include: Hugh Bentall, pioneer of open-heart surgery; Sir Louis Blom-Cooper, lawyer; Anthony Buckeridge, children's author; Val Guest, film director; David Purley, Formula One driver; Matthew Rose, opera singer; Toby Stephens, actor and Tom Odell, musician.

Entrance: Fifty per cent of year 9 from Seaford Prep, the rest from a range of preps and local primaries. Non-selective until GCSE; thereafter need 45 points to enter sixth form. Screening for SEN on entry.

Exit: Around 35 per cent leave to go to local sixth form colleges, usually for financial reasons.

After sixth form, a good number head off to Russell group universities; Plymouth and Oxford Brookes are also popular, and a handful have made it to Oxbridge in the last few years (none in 2015).

Money matters: Fees good value for money, said a parent; but she wouldn't want them to be any more. Extra for SEN and counselling. Means-tested bursaries.

Remarks: A happy, exceptionally caring school, which strive to do well by all who cross the threshold, whatever their ability.

Sevenoaks School

High Street, Sevenoaks, Kent TN13 1HU

01732 455133
admin@sevenoaksschool.org
www.sevenoaksschool.org

Ages: 11–18
Pupils: 1,050; sixth form: 420
Boarders: 350 full
Day: £20,763 – £23,571 pa
Boarding: £33,156 – £35,964 pa

Head: Since 2002, Dr Katy Ricks MA DPhil (50s). Educated at Camden School for Girls (to which she attributes her feistiness) and Balliol, where she took a first in English. Educated even more since then and provided a shining example to her pupils – and staff – by being awarded a DPhil in 2014 for her thesis on Dryden's translations of Virgil. Taught at Latymer Upper, King Edward's Birmingham and St Paul's Girls, was head of English at St Edward's Oxford and deputy head of Highgate. An

impeccable, co-educational, academic and quality school cv and one which made her, possibly, uniquely qualified for this job.

And that's just what's on paper. Vivacious, articulate, deliciously enthusiastic and hugely appreciative of her luck in having charge of such a school, her pleasure in it all is palpable and infectious. We canvassed masses of parents and heard not a word against her. 'My children think she is wonderful'...'she comes to everything'...'she speaks brilliantly'...'she's a brilliant ambassador for the school'... 'she's very thoughtful'. 'She's an outstanding head,' an old hand claimed, 'and in a different league.' She, likewise, pays tribute to her staff and her pupils. 'People here think all the time about what they are doing. I have an incredibly clever staff – both in their intellectual expertise and passion for their subject and in their relationship skills. They talk to pupils and parents like proper people – which, of course, they are!' We know what she means. Wisely, she sees the recruitment of top-notch staff as her main responsibility and she pays great attention to the 'feel' of the school. 'I do really believe very strongly that environment shapes character.' The school feels smiley – and she is a very smiley head. Her pride and excitement in the school permeates the place. We felt it in everyone we met.

Academic matters: Sevenoaks is best known for pioneering the IB and for being a strongly international school – not just in its intake but in its outlook. All take IGCSEs in many subjects though GCSE survives in ancient Greek, Russian and some arts subjects. Everyone does a MFL, everyone takes

all three separate sciences. And, in the sixth form, when everyone takes the IB, the language options are exceptional – seven are on offer as part of the IB curriculum and tuition is available in at least eight more for native speakers and others. Greek and Latin thrive, economics, psychology, philosophy, history – med and mod – it's all here. The results are terrific – in 2015, the average point score per student was more than 39. At I/GCSE in 2015, 94 per cent of exams taken got A*/A. That is pretty amazing. You won't find Sevenoaks in league tables – the IB/IGCSE combination make them meaningless.

Impressive library – good blend, here as everywhere, of old and new – the august portraits of Edwardian and Victorian headmasters overlooking the gallery of PCs

Virtually all teaching praised, virtually universally. Staff seen as assiduous – 'they're concerned, caring, tough'. A seriously impressive library – would grace an Oxford college: 30,000 books and 70+ periodicals – good blend, here as everywhere, of old and new – the august portraits of Edwardian and Victorian headmasters overlooking the gallery of PCs. Up to 10 per cent on learning support register with, mostly mild, dyslexia/dyspraxia/dysgraphia. Some with ADHD and visual impairment. Wheelchairs not a problem. Everyone has to have excellent English though school will support EAL if necessary but with no more than one weekly lesson.

Games, options, the arts: Huge amounts of space, all the impressive facilities you'd expect including sports hall, pool, dance studio, indoor climbing wall et al. The usual sports are compulsory but range of super options includes trampolining, judo, yoga and fencing. Regarded as the top sailing school in the country and outstanding success in both tennis and shooting. And both sexes play football. Sport no longer the Sevenoaks Cinderella – impressive wins in athletics, hockey and rugby and numerous individual successes and county colours.

Performing arts centre surely unrivalled in its Pamoja (Swahili for 'togetherness') Hall which seats 450. Built according to sustainable principles from locally sourced wood, matched by the pale gold fabric seats and heated via solar panels, with water from a borehole, it is vast, light and provides a venue of international quality. The stage can accommodate a full orchestra and the two grand pianos we spotted there looked, from the back of the auditorium, like dolls' house instruments. Building also full of practice rooms, a recital room, recording studios, theatre – you name it – and it feels good. And productions to match – arts, visual arts, theatre and musical events to high standards. Virtually all involved in something arty – a large number learn

at least one instrument and ensembles for everything. Not too much pupil art on display as you go round – could do with more, perhaps, though head's extraordinary minimalist study has a vast, meticulous, charcoal representation of the huge tree outside her vast window. Stunning range of awards and prizes in arts, public speaking and representation in National Youth Orch/Theatre etc. A year 10 pupil was a recent finalist in the BBC Young Musician of the Year. They pop up everywhere there's a competition in which to shine and it's their intellectual and expressive skills which most impress. 'Fantastic' outside speakers who are 'really inspiring – especially when they are Old Sennockians'. Internationalism translates into trips abroad – less of the glam skiing and snorkeling and more of the DT trip to Toyota's assembly line in Japan and Model United Nations in The Hague.

Boarding: Boarding provision is good everywhere and exceptional in the sixth. The international students are housed in separate buildings – the boys in a state-of-the-art building (a stunning design with views and provision to match) and the girls in a Queen Anne period house with comparable facilities. We were struck by the zest with which pupils from everywhere share information about their homes and countries – a true global community, literally in the making. Years 7 and 8 housed in Lambardes – much-loved, as is the current housemaster – 'he's ex-army – excellent fun but he knows how to keep discipline,' a parent enthused. 'Even at this stage, there are enough boarders for you to find a friend. We have a battle to get our children to come home at weekends, though; sometimes it's so full-on at school they like to just flop.' Much praise, too, for the way younger and older pupils mix and collaborate. Some houses eg Park Grange a delight and with a big and enviable, communal kitchen in which 'everyone gets to know everyone'. This school understands about sofas, carpets and big TVs. Huge dining room with vast choice of truly tempting food. One pupil who vouchsafed little in answer to our questions, broke out with, 'I'm so pleased I came here – the food is so good!'

Boarders may go home on Saturdays after school commitments are finished, but many stay for weekend trips which might be climbing or mountain biking, cinema, camping or theatre.

Background and atmosphere: You'd pass it without noticing as you drive out of sleepy Sevenoaks on the road to Tonbridge. You might notice the sign to Knole (think Sackvilles, Sackville-West and sofas) on your left but you wouldn't realise that the path to Knole bisects the 70 acre site of Sevenoaks School and that the glories of that Jacobean pile and park abut the playing fields and are a considerable resource to the school. The school's foundation is

The international students are housed in separate buildings. We were struck by the zest with which pupils from everywhere share information about their homes and countries – a true global community

almost as old as that of its illustrious neighbour. And in some respects it eclipses it. Sevenoaks (1432) is the oldest lay school in the UK and this liberal, unallied ethos underpins the exuberance of its intellectual and social life today. There is no one imposing main school house but a collection of 33 buildings from the last 250-odd years – the old and new all generously conceived, stylish and attractive in their own ways and somehow blending to make a welcoming gesamtwerk. The ambience is much assisted by the ubiquitous greenery – gardens, imaginative planting and the disposition of the houses hither and yon. The head's house – perhaps the least inspired architecturally – is plumb centre and reflects the current incumbent's involvement in everything.

Pastoral care, well-being and discipline: Few problems here. No house system. Sound and well-established pastoral system in years and boarding houses. You stay in the same boarding house from 13-18. Misdemeanours mostly sorted by detentions or suspensions. No-one wants to be kicked out of this place. No drinking allowed anywhere and boarders under 16 not allowed to go to day pupils' parties if alcohol is offered. Press had attack of the vapours in autumn 2014 over reports of mass sixth form suspensions following a midnight exodus on a school trip to Prague. Reports were, as ever, sensationalised, though there had been a foolish breaking of bounds after lights out and the temptation of cheap Czech beer was clearly too much for some of the pupils. Head wisely suspended the lot of them for two days – a course much praised by embarrassed parents.

Lots of integration of day and boarding pupils and those who can bear to forgo all the weekend activities often invited home by locals. Universal feeling among parents that you are expected to be independent, take responsibility for yourself and if you forget something or don't do your homework, no-one will cosset, prompt or mollycoddle you. 'It's a very grown-up school – it expects you to be grown-up,' we were told. 'Sometimes,' another parent felt, 'the boarders are just left to get on with it.' But this seen, again, as part of the self-reliance the school builds and not as a deterrent. 'Strongly secular'

ethos, as one parent described it, 'very hands-off, no spoon-feeding.' However, one international sixth former, clearly ecstatic at his good fortune, breathed, 'it's the support – it's flawless – after two years I still haven't found anything wrong'.

Pupils and parents: A proper co-educational school with a truly – and uniquely – global clientele. Possibly nowhere other than our elite universities accommodates such an international crème de la intellectual crème, blending them so successfully, and creating such a rich and enriching mix of cultures. Around a third of boarders, and half of sixth formers, from overseas – but from a bigger range of home countries than any other school – 35 or so – no cliques or sects here, though Germans and Italians are relatively numerous. The majority of overseas students join for the sixth form and are given an unbeatable education in the roundest and broadest sense. The rest from the UK – and two-thirds are day pupils, reflecting the strong local commitment to the school, despite strong competition from Kent grammars. And local can mean right up into London and into Surrey. Pupils are open, unpretentious, clever, thoughtful and hugely appreciative of their luck in being here. Parents describe them as independent, confident but not arrogant. Also as individuals, 'they don't go into tweed jackets and stay in them for the rest of their lives'. Parents likewise, and mostly just grateful for their children's chances here. Some feel that home-school communication could be better but this, as everywhere, varies from house to house and teacher to teacher.

You are expected to be independent, take responsibility for yourself, and if you forget something or don't do your homework, no-one will cosset, prompt or mollycoddle you

Entrance: Around 190 apply for the 65 places in year 7. Candidates sit the school's own exam, are interviewed and prep/primary reports are considered. The odds against getting a place are not as high as they look as there is strong competition at this stage from the Kent grammars, and many who get places here will opt for the state sector. At 13+, around 180 apply for 80 places – again exam (or CE), interview and report. Asks for £750 deposit about six months before entrance assessment – refunded if it doesn't offer a place but not if you opt for another school. Lots of feeders including Holmewood House, New Beacon, Hazelwood, Windlesham, Dulwich Prep. Stronger competition for the sixth form which really is an elite institution. Some 400 apply for 80 places. Required with the application are a personal statement, three exams in their likely 'higher' level subjects and school references. All must have taken the school's pre-test/interview – this can, if needed, in some cases, be conducted in the applicant's home country or on Skype. 'We want people with above average academic ability, strong co-curricular interests and an enquiring spirit,' says head, 'who will enjoy their time here.'

Exit: A trickle leave after GCSEs, mostly for overseas schools or those offering A levels. Truly impressive in the quality and diversity of the post-A level courses and institutions. 2015 saw 31 Oxbridge places. Others to UCL, Durham, Exeter, Imperial, Bath, KCL, LSE, Nottingham, Warwick, Edinburgh, Bristol, US, Canada, continental Europe and Hong Kong. And studying everything from aeronautics to zoology. Notable alumni include musicians Emma Johnson, Mathew Best; journos and writers Plum Sykes, Olivia Cole; academics Francis Everitt, Jonathan Bate, Oliver Taplin; sportsmen Chris Tavare, Anthony Roques, Dan Caprice; and in the arts Daniel Day Lewis, Charlie Higson, Simon Starling, Paul Greengrass, Geoffrey Streatfeild, Emma Hope; also spook Jonathan Evans (DG of M15). To say nothing of William Caxton.

Money matters: Not a rich school but offers bursaries up to 100 per cent of the day fee following means-testing. Scholarships worth up to 20 per cent of day fee awarded for excellence in academics, sport, music, art and drama. One big sports scholarship on offer.

Remarks: Tough for any university not to be an anti-climax after Sevenoaks. Hard to imagine a Sennockian not being an asset to any uni they grace. 'It feels,' one sixth former confided, 'as if I'm an apprentice and the whole school is one big teacher.'

Sutton Valence School

North Street, Sutton Valence, Kent ME17 3HL

01622 845200
enquiries@svs.org.uk
www.svs.org.uk
C of E

Ages: 11–18
Pupils: 480; sixth form: 160
Boarders: 50 full, 111 weekly/flexi
Day: £17,130 – £19,800 pa
Boarding: £25,860 – £30,930 pa

Headmaster: Since 2009, Mr Bruce Grindlay MA Cantab (organ scholar) MusB FRCO (mid-40s). Came from Christ's Hospital School, Horsham where he was director of music for eight years. Previously boarding housemaster and head of chapel music at Bedford School. Came in with desire to up the ante on discipline and academics and has succeeded in taking pupils and parents with him. Parents find him calm, personable and articulate, with his nose to the ground and swift to take action when needed. Pupils frequently pop by his office for advice or to tell of an achievement. Expectations are set high and all are challenged to do their best. 'I'm not slow to remind pupils, or staff for that matter, that termly fees are the cost of a small Caribbean holiday.' His wife teaches English in the sixth form and is completing a PhD. Two children, one here, the other a chorister at Westminster Abbey Choir School.

Academic matters: Parents bridle slightly at the notion that it's a school for the less academic. 'The strong ethos that there's a lot more to school life than exam results in no way means the bright aren't stretched.' The head highlights solid value-added scores; school moved into the top 15 per cent nationally for adding value at A level last year, equating to half to one grade better for each child than initial predictions, per subject. He emphasises that a pupil moving a D to a C is every bit as significant as another getting an A* and that its main focus is on producing confident all-rounders. Small class sizes and a caring, individual approach draw many. ESL and other learning support staff commended for their kindness, patience and dedication with highly-rated SEN support in lessons and, by arrangement, during extra sessions, at times in place of non-core subjects. 'Staff always happy to go the extra mile to help my son and, with such a broad intake, he's never felt different or out of place.' Popular subjects include geography, maths, business studies, art and design. In 2015, 85 per cent gained five A*-C grades including English and maths at GCSE, 33 per cent A*/A grades. At A level 70 per cent A*/B and 41 per cent A*/A. A few grumbles that problem areas, either in relation to particular subjects or pupils, come to light slowly, but once issues are identified, most agree action is swift and effective. The e-newsletter, information evenings and other recent initiatives are welcomed. 'More of the same please. It's great to now know when and what homework is being set and to be able to get more involved.'

Games, options, the arts: It's easy to see why sport forms a major part of life at Sutton Valence. Playing fields stretch as far as the eye can see, there's a track used by Olympic athletes, Astroturf hockey pitch, sports hall and hugely inviting indoor pool. The socialising that goes on around regular after-school practices and fixtures also tempts even the least sporty to have a go. The school fields several teams in hockey, cricket, netball and rugby. Some parents comment that inclusion comes at the expense of developing real excellence and that pupils would benefit from more specialist coaches, but several pupils play at county level and above in hockey, rugby and cricket and the website is brimming with team sport successes. Pupils excel in more unusual endeavours too – roller dance, small bore shooting, ballroom dancing, fly fishing and race walking being just some examples.

So much part of life here are CCF and D of E that there's no great fanfare when pupils routinely go onto the higher levels, though their contribution to individual development and community spirit is emphasised. With his musical background, the head was always sure to encourage that side of things, though music has long been considered strong. Noticeboards are crammed with news of rehearsals and performances and the schedule of clubs and, along with, we're told, truly excellent drama productions in the plush Baughan Theatre, you're left wondering how pupils, parents and staff fit everything in. Little wonder flexi-boarding is such a popular option.

Boarding: Around 50 full boarders with twice as many weekly or flexi boarders; around nine per cent from overseas. Lots of space, friendly faces and homely touches. 'Often think my children would prefer to live there, and on the various occasions when it suits us too the school has always done its best to accommodate,' said one parent.

Expectations are set high and all are challenged to do their best. 'I'm not slow to remind pupils, or staff for that matter, that termly fees are the cost of a small Caribbean holiday'

One of the boarding house matrons in no way resembles the dragon poster she pins on boys' dorms to remind them to tidy up. Not sure that a dragon would have such a keen interest in every child's welfare either. Day, full, flexi or occasional boarders, it's clear staff keep tabs on pupils and do their best to develop a joint approach to overcome homesickness or other issues, most of which are minor. Visits to local preps to put future pupils' fears at bay are also not unknown.

Background and atmosphere: At the core of a small village in Kent, in beautifully kept grounds, gracious old buildings house pleasant and at times grand communal areas and well-equipped classrooms. On a clear day, though, there's a danger it's all overshadowed by the breathtaking view of the Weald to the south. Main site separated by a short distance from the prep school (and junior mixed boarding house). Most staff live on site or nearby. 'A happy and relaxed local community – what better place for my child to learn and grow?'

Perhaps that accounts for its longevity. It's one of the country's oldest established schools, founded by William Lambe in 1576. In 2010 over 1000 attended a ceremony in Westminster Abbey, a fitting location given the school's strong Christian ethos, to mark the centenary of becoming part of the United Westminster Schools Foundation.

Pastoral care, well-being and discipline: Head has impressive recall of pupil names and goings-on and has got the prefects, parents and pupils almost universally on side in introducing somewhat tougher discipline. Nothing too draconian, 'tough love' is its basis. Correct uniform, orderly lunchtime queuing/clearing up and, at the prefects' initiative, the use of pleases and thank yous are all in hand. Head also sweetened pupils up with a fresh system of rewards to acknowledge even small individual contributions and achievements.

Lots of space, friendly faces and homely touches. 'Often think my children would prefer to live there, and when it suits us too the school has done its best to accommodate'

Pupils and parents: Other than real non-conformists, most likely to feel at home here. 'No one thing defines you. I'm not a bit like my siblings but we've all found things to get our teeth into here.' Pupils are described as nice, normal and confident without arrogance. Many parents both work and are a mix of local businessmen/entrepreneurs, farmers and city workers. Foreign students – mostly from Germany and Asia – do not exceed nine per cent of the total and on the whole settle in well, though for some life in rural England is somewhat of a culture shock. Head would like to see a more vibrant PA but, even though most UK families are based in the south east, he may face an uphill battle as many travel quite a distance to get to the school. This can be an issue, especially in bad weather, and makes flexi and occasional boarding popular options (which younger full-time boarders can find

---

Playing fields stretch as far as the eye can see. The socialising that goes on around regular after-school practices and fixtures also tempts the least sporty to have a go

unsettling). The school runs buses and a few sixth formers drive – some in rather flash cars.

Alumni include journalists Robert Fisk and Ben Brown, Ashley Jackson, GB hockey player, opera performer Kathryn Choonara and Sir Rustam Feroze, gynaecologist.

Entrance: Most come up from the prep school and an assortment of other local preps and primary schools. At 11 the school sets its own entrance exam. There's usually a waiting list but a number drop off having secured places at local grammars. Smaller intake at 13 when a CE mark of approximately 55 per cent is required. State school applicants must pass the school's exam. The 25 or so students entering sixth form from outside need at least five GCSE passes at B grade or above. Most international students come in the sixth form and also sit a language exam.

Exit: About 10 per cent leave after GCSEs, most going to local grammars. Almost all sixth formers go on to higher education – popular destinations include Loughborough, Exeter, Bournemouth, Nottingham, Reading and Bath. One medic and one lawyer in 2015, plus four off to study physics.

Money matters: Academic (11+ and 13+), art, DT, music, sports and drama (at 11+, 13+ and 16+) scholarships and the Westminster scholarship (to those obtaining five GCSEs at A*) available. Worth up to a maximum of 20 per cent of either boarding or day fees. Also offers bursaries and reductions for Forces families.

Remarks: Friendly and relaxed atmosphere and solid all-round confidence-building credentials. Its idyllic setting and enviable sports and other facilities make it a popular alternative to more academically demanding senior schools in the south east. Can suffer perhaps from being labelled the non-academic alternative. 'That old chestnut,' says one parent. 'Obviously needs to market itself better. Put all your kids there. It's got lots to offer any child.'

TASIS – The American School in England

Coldharbour Lane, Thorpe, Surrey TW20 8TE

01932 582316
ukadmissions@tasisengland.org
www.tasisengland.org

Ages: 3–19 (boarding from 14)
Pupils: 720; sixth form: 225
Boarders: 200 full
Day: £6,810 – £22,070 pa
Boarding: £38,350 pa

Head of School: Since July 2015, Dr Mindy Hong, previously assistant head at Baldwin School in Bryn Mawr, Pennysylvania. BA in English from Columbia University, MA in English lit from New York University, MEd from Harvard and a DEd in educational leadership from Pennsylvania University. Got a Mellon Fellowship at Harvard for graduate work on neuro-cognitive research and its relation to academic achievement. Has worked in both state and independent schools and been an adjunct professor at two universities.

Married with two daughters, one of whom has joined TASIS.

Academic matters: The primary programme (ages 3-9) is based on a Core Knowledge curriculum – with specialist teachers for music, art, PE, and lessons in technology and library skills. Parents like the approach to homework, saying TASIS teachers are 'very forgiving and highly supportive' teaching children in a 'more academic' learning environment. The littlest ones from nursery (half day) through pre-K have a gentle introduction to school described by one enthusiastic parent as the 'best kept secret, with its multicultural aspect; lots of learning taking place and investigation through play providing an unbelievable foundation year'.

Middle school (ages 10-13) emphasises independent study using the house system, peer leaders, and advisory system. Besides the usual subjects, middle school electives include Latin, photography, yearbook, journalism and broadcast journalism. One parent, a zealous convert from British key stage 1, describes the primary programme as 'holistic and inter-disciplinary', nice foreign language element, comprehensive content yet fun and flexible that inspires a love of learning and promotes 'self-learning' versus 'memorisation rote teaching'.

Upper school is designed to prepare students for university entry and features US Advanced Placement or IB diploma courses (taught separately, with the exception of a few language classes). The

TASIS High School Diploma follows the US curriculum, but is designed to accommodate second language English speakers, or may suit short-term students who come for a semester.

Spanish introduced in primary, and while parents like this, some (non-English speakers or from bilingual families) feel the language provision could be stronger for the international children and lament the discontinuation of a native-Spanish programme, apparently a result of a drop in mother tongue speakers in the lower school. Students choose between French or Spanish in middle school with an optional school language trip to Spain and France. IB diploma Italian, Russian, English, Spanish, and German are offered as mother tongue, another dozen are available as self-taught, and Spanish and French are offered as a second language. EAL is in place throughout the school.

Mostly good and some outstanding exam scores. IB average point score was 34 in 2015. Average class size is 15, maximum about 18; teacher to student ratio is 1:6 Average age of teachers is upper 40s, over half at TASIS for over 10 years, with retirement of long termers contributing to recent staff turnover.

For an additional charge, learning support available up to three lessons per week for children with diagnosed mild learning differences. Some language requirements may be deferred for students with special educational needs.

Games, options, the arts: Varsity sports include basketball, cross-country, dance, golf, lacrosse, soccer, tennis, and volleyball as well as boys' teams in rugby and baseball and girls' teams in cheerleading and softball.

TASIS is known for its strong music, art and drama programmes, but school feels this needs a fresh look to see if there are any tweaks that can be made to upper school academic workloads and timetables to make it easier for all students to take advantage of these great activities.

TASIS sprawls over two adjoinng estates, each with its own Georgian manor houses and listed centuries old buildings – like something from a National Trust calendar

Loads of school trips have always been a part of TASIS: all boarders go somewhere during the October half term for a week (meaning they don't have to travel home), mostly to European destinations. These trips are optional for day students but many choose to take part. The humanities trip, related to ancient civilisations, to places like Greece or Florence and Rome, is recommended for all seniors and IB students.

Big emphasis on community service. Students travel regularly to volunteer for Romania-based projects; raise money for a charity helping children born with cleft palate; volunteer to help local elderly and disabled children.

Plenty of after-school activities daily but also on Saturdays with a range of team sports organised by the school with lots of parent involvement. Parents say that there are so many older day students on campus doing this, and that it's hard to distinguish which ones are boarding and which are not.

Boarding: The boarding programme is supervised by a long-serving teacher. Live-in teachers (some couples) serve as boarding house parents, with other teachers living on campus or locally doing their bit during evenings and weekends. Students who speak different languages are well mixed in to speed up their English acquisition and confidence. Boarders are well-supervised, and say 'it's becoming more strict, but it's open-minded'; parents say 'it's more carrot than stick'. Boarders are required to stay on campus Friday nights, no one is allowed to go off to visit people who are under 25 (no overnights with cousins or older siblings in uni). Day families invite boarders for dinner, to work on school projects or to stay overnight, which makes for a nice change, and there is a good system in place to keep track of the comings and goings.

Boarders who arrive with lower-level English may find the first weeks are challenging and it's hard to assimilate, but once they adjust they are happy. A new scheme to assign freshman (9th grade) boarders to a buddy family has started to address this.

A TPA boarding coordinator liaises with boarding parents by sending regular emails so they know what's going on, helping to explain college counselling, fundraising initiatives. New families' picnics coincide with boarder drop off weekend.

Background and atmosphere: TASIS England was founded in 1976, a sister school to TASIS in Switzerland, by Mary Crist Fleming, and is controlled by the TASIS Foundation, a Swiss, independent, not-for-profit foundation. The school's board of directors oversees governance, policies and strategies, and finances.

The campus is located in the village of Thorpe, close to Virginia Water and Ascot and handy for Heathrow and Gatwick. TASIS sprawls over two adjoining estates, each with its own Georgian manor houses and assorted listed centuries old outbuildings – looking like something from a National Trust calendar. TASIS seems pretty connected to the village, not always the case with international schools.

Thorpe Place, the main building, looks out over an expansive lawn and lake with sports fields and a baseball diamond beyond, and contains the large dining room, a smaller canteen with Starbucks coffee bar, offices and beautiful rooms for high school seminars or parent coffees. Upper floors have newly-refurbished dorm rooms, many overlooking the lake. Other cottages contain student rooms, lounges with microwaves, fridges, and laundry.

The library is in the former splendidly converted chapel with leather sofas creating a comfortable reading nook at one end. A project is the labour of love of a recently-retired history teacher – the restoration of a hidden walled garden and greenhouse, shared by villagers who have allotments there. Students grow fruit and veg which they harvest, cook and eat in the dining hall, or use to make jams for fundraising projects. The wildlife pond is used to learn about creepy crawlies, the beehive produces honey. The star attraction is the Beatrix Potter garden complete with play house and Peter Rabbit for the youngest children who regularly visit.

The other side of the campus centres around Thorpe House, where the primary school is located with its own library; a modern addition accommodates classrooms, lunch room and offices, with more classrooms in the converted coach house.

Pretty incredible facilities generally, in fact, including new buildings with science and technology labs, purpose-designed music and practice rooms, a great theatre that gets lots of use, an art gallery, studios, dark room etc, all full of students' work. There's also a large gym with dance studio, exercise rooms, and changing rooms conveniently located for the additional sports fields beyond.

The youngest children are in a self-contained chalet, Frog Hollow, on the edge of a grove of trees, with access to their own playground.

With boarders, food service is 24/7, and compulsory unless there are dietary restrictions. Upper school eats in the dining room overlooking the grounds, tables spill out onto the terrace for al fresco eating in the nicer weather. Middle school uses the primary lunch room. Food is healthy, balanced, and varied, but not much to rave about and a bit too 'English school meal' for international tastes ('You can always order pizza delivery!'). An advantage to the boarding dimension is that day students staying late or coming to study can have breakfast or dinner there.

Pastoral care, well-being and discipline: Tutor groups meet daily for 30 minutes for problem solving, brainstorming and relaxed chat with peers and teacher or doing homework. Tutors serve as advisors, the first port of call for families with concerns, and the student stays with the same tutor through to graduation. Parents like the simplicity of this, knowing that there is someone on the inside who really knows their kids. Boarding and day student prefects provide peer support for students.

> 'We Skyped before we arrived, shared some family pub lunches after we got here.' There's a group for 'non-working accompanying dads' called 'Trophy Husbands' Club'

'Safe Hands' is a life-skills programme designed with boarders in mind. The school will try to make things work, but if students repeatedly offend, they're out. A parent saw even during the first visit that 'Students were presentable, polite and respectful yet friendly. The school culture was tangible and appealing.' The only co-ed international school in London with uniforms, parents appreciate that 'there is no thought to the fashion stakes and who's wearing what label this week.'

Pupils and parents: Two-thirds are American but community includes numerous other nationalities of expat families – German, Spanish, Canadian,

Russian, Italian, Japanese, Chinese, and Brazilian – on assignment in the UK. Some 70 per cent of boarders are from overseas.

Parents love the PIRC (Parents Information Resource Committee) with its own library and speakers who advise on successfully raising a globe-trotting expat family and which even maintains a list of babysitters. The TPA (TASIS Parent Association) always has something on the go; during the summer they work with admissions to match new families through the Buddy Family Program. 'They connected and we Skyped before we arrived; shared some family pub lunches after we got here'. TASIS parents have plenty to do... there's even a group for 'non-working accompanying dads' called 'Trophy Husbands' Club'.

The bus service extends to Camberley in the south west, Beaconsfield in the north west, into Richmond and Kingston in the east, and Woking and Weybridge in the south... which lets you know the social network is spread across the map. Parents, be ready to drive.

Entrance: Early application recommended; students must be reinvited yearly. Admissions based on previous reports, references, student questionnaire, parent statement. English testing if deemed necessary. The school tries to be sensitive to the sibling issue.

Exit: Lots to North America: popular destinations for the Class of 2015 were Northeastern, University of Wisconsin-Madison, New York University, and Northwestern. In the UK, King's College London most popular followed by City and University College London. IE university in Spain another popular choice, but also the Netherlands, Italy, and Switzerland as well as further afield to Russia and Australia.

The Class of 2015 had one student accept a place at Oxford, and another student went to Harvard. In recent years TASIS students have also accepted Ivy League school places at Columbia, Cornell, U of Pennsylvania, and Princeton.

Money matters: No endowment; financial aid available on the basis of merit, need, and available funds (approximately £150,000-£200,000 given annually in financial aid).

Some fundraising initiatives by the Parents' Association and the school, but parents say they are not 'bombarded'.

Remarks: Parents say it's a fantastic school; the ethos and the character values it develops are what make it special. A critical mass of international boarders add an interesting flavour to this sound American school in the Surrey countryside.

Tonbridge School

High Street, Tonbridge, Kent TN9 1JP

01732 365555
hmsec@tonbridge-school.org
www.tonbridge-school.co.uk

Ages: 13–18
Pupils: 789; sixth form: 340
Boarders: 460 full
Day: £27,216 pa
Boarding: £36,288 pa

Headmaster: Since 2005, Mr Tim Haynes BA PGCE (50s). Educated at Shrewsbury, where he is now a governor, he read history at Reading University and after a couple of years as a stockbroker in the City, he took his PGCE at Pembroke College, Cambridge and began his teaching career at Hampton School where he taught history. He then spent 13 years at St Paul's in London leaving as surmaster (deputy head) and 10 years as headmaster of Monmouth School before taking over the post at Tonbridge. He lives in a house on the edge of the grounds and has two sons.

He is a great enthusiast and is considered very approachable. 'You can always see him in an emergency, and he is measured and helpful.' 'He talks to everyone and is not a headmaster in a gilded tower.' 'The sort of person you would like to sit next to at a dinner party.' He can always be seen bicycling round the pitches during matches on Saturdays. Highly regarded by the boys, he knows all the novi's (new boys) names within the first few weeks. He describes Tonbridge as a 'high octane, high achieving school on so many levels. There is real ambition amongst the boys and a co-curricular breadth and a special quality of relations between boys and their teachers – informal, relaxed, respectful and purposeful'. He describes Tonbridge as a school where 'respect for tradition and an openness to innovation are equally valued'. He meets all prospective families – 300-400 per year.

Academic matters: Very impressive. In 2015, 78 per cent A*/A at A level plus a handful of surprising Ds and Es. Twenty-four subjects offered at A level and, apart from the usual, include Mandarin, PE, theatre studies, business studies and government and politics. Most popular A levels are maths, economics and history, followed by physics and English – particularly good results in maths, English and economics. Boys still find time for further academic work – three presented their scientific research to an international conference in China and another has published a GCSE French text book.

Most take 10 GCSEs (mostly the more rigorous IGCSEs). In 2015, 91 per cent A*/A – among the best results in the country. Science offered as dual award or individually – particularly good showing in individual sciences. All have to take a language at GCSE and a good range offered including French, Spanish, Chinese, Italian and German. Our guide singled out history and French for being especially well taught – 'the head of French is inspired'. Art GCSE offered as fine art or photography. All do non-examined course in divinity, which is largely discussion based and includes critical thinking. Everyone takes digital creativity (ICT) in three fab digital creativity labs. Voluntary Extended Project offered in upper sixth year.

Good liaison between teaching departments – very dedicated team of teachers 'who really seem to care and will go the extra mile for us,' say the boys. 'Bright young teachers [mostly male although there are now 15 female teachers] who are great role models for the boys.' Academic staff also involved with coaching sport and are 'passionate about opportunities available to the boys'.

Boys need to be organised and there is an emphasis on independence from the start, and all encouraged to find their own learning style. All boys screened for learning difficulties on arrival (mainly mild dyslexia and dyspraxia) and all are offered help with study and revision skills and note taking, essay writing, memory and organisational skills – boys often self-refer for drop in sessions or targeted help. Learning mentor training programme so boys can help each other. Year 9 dyslexic pupils trained as dyslexic specialist mentors and can help in partner primary schools. Two part-time EAL teachers mainly offer help with technical and scientific language.

'Not a headmaster in a gilded tower.' 'The sort of person you would like to sit next to at a dinner party.' He can always be seen cycling round the pitches during matches

Games, options, the arts: Huge range of opportunities help develop self-reliance and leadership skills. Long tradition of sporting excellence but ethos of participation by all, and everyone has the chance to play in a team. Truly superb sports facilities, and was a training venue for the London 2012 Olympics. A hundred acres of playing fields, all immaculately groomed, three Astroturfs, clay tennis courts and an all-weather athletics pitch. Sports centre with cricket nets, 25 metre swimming pool and climbing wall and a fitness suite to rival the swankiest of London health clubs. Membership open to general public. School has hockey, rugby and cricket academies, has produced county and international cricketers and has one of the best rugby sides in south east; recent leavers play for Harlequins and Saracens. Every imaginable sport including fives, ultimate frisbee, fencing and water polo and sailing – novi (first year) encouraged to try lots of sports so every boy should find something he enjoys. Weekly house leagues sports for those not in the top teams.

Increasing numbers involved in music, with about five boys taking music A level each year and over 50 per cent of all boys learning one of a huge range of instruments, including the Marcussen chapel organ, one of the best in the country. All Steinway status means top quality pianos in every practice room. Director of music a professional conductor. Wide range of orchestras, bands and ensemble groups for all musical styles including flourishing jazz and pop groups and thriving choral music. Numerous concerts and recitals, including the Octagon concerts, which feature a different instrument each week. Excellent facilities include two recital halls, a suite of teaching practice rooms, music library, soundproof room for jazz and percussion, and a state of the art recording studio. Often team up with musicians outside school eg a concert with Benenden at St Martin in the Fields and South Bank Sinfonia at the Royal Festival Hall; and choir has sung at St George's Chapel, Windsor and Chichester Cathedral, and deputised at St Paul's when the cathedral choir was away.

Drama also thriving, with about eight major productions a year in 400 seat EM Forster theatre (complete with orchestra pit and studio theatre), including three major school plays, with girls from local schools taking part in most productions. Boys get involved with all aspects of production including set design, stage management and lighting. Regular drama competitions and house plays, which are put together by the boys with drama staff acting as mentors, as well as other small scale productions and plays in Spanish, French and German.

The Vere Lodge Centre for DT and art, with its spiral staircase and light-filled space for private views and exhibitions, is particularly impressive

Arts workshops by visiting professionals include street dance, masks, puppetry and film making and upper sixth boys invited to take a play to Edinburgh Fringe via the Hogshead Theatre Company. Boys also take part in the National Theatre's play writing competition. Varied programme of lectures by visiting speakers, and boys can choose from a huge range of societies: cultural, political, scientific and sporting, anything from bee-keeping, astronomy and wine appreciation to sub aqua and robotics.

Seminar programme in GCSE and lower sixth years encourages boys to questions their assumptions and see things from a different perspective – eg sustainability in business or organ transplants. About 200 boys take part in CCF across all three services. Duke of Edinburgh Award also popular with about 20 achieving gold each year. Not forgetting numerous foreign visits and exchange trips during the holidays.

Boarding: There are seven boarding houses and younger boys start in small dorms of up to six. Older boys have their own rooms. Strong system of pastoral care. Housemasters seen as 'father figures' who get to know boys and their families very well. Aided by assistant housemaster and five tutors per house – boys have regular meetings with their tutors. During the week all boys eat in their houses but at weekends boarders eat together in the Orchard Centre. Most boys go home after games on Saturday, but have to be back in time for Sunday evening chapel. Although trips and outings are organised, it can be quite lonely for those who stay in.

Background and atmosphere: Founded by Sir Andrew Judde in 1553, the school still has close links with the Worshipful Company of Skinners, and Skinners' Day is celebrated each year at the end of the summer term. The school grew rapidly in the 19th century and has been rebuilt twice on the

original site. Dominated by the fine rebuilt Edwardian chapel (it was gutted by fire in 1988) the school is set in 150 acres of immaculately kept grounds behind the not-so-glamorous Tonbridge High Street on the northern edge of the town, stretching down to the river and the railway line. The imposing Victorian buildings with tasteful, modern additions manage to combine a respect for tradition with the most up-to-date facilities. The Vere Lodge Centre for DT and art, with its spiral staircase and light-filled space for private views and exhibitions, is particularly impressive. Well-used library built in 1962 with 23,000 books, a number of which date from the 17th century, as well as the 1479 Jensen Bible – although boys seem to get most of their information online.

Pastoral care, well-being and discipline: Seven boarding and five day houses situated on the edge of the playing fields and along the high street (most recently refurbished) each with about 60 boys. Strong sense of belonging in houses helped by range of inter-house competitions in art, music, film, sport plus house plays and concerts, and close friendships are formed. School aims for as wide a mix as possible in each house and tries to split up boys from the same prep school to stop cliques forming. Good food – all eat in their houses, with grace before lunch.

Boys 'very driven – it's cool to work and there are not many problems on the behaviour front – the boys know they are there to work and are expected to work hard – the pace can be quite challenging for some,' said a parent. Mindfulness meditation is taught as part of PSHE to all boys in year 10 and is increasingly popular as an activity. Boys are taught to focus on the present and not worry about the past or the future – a skill for life which helps them cope with stress. There is an emotional literacy programme for senior boys and an on-site school counsellor.

Each house twinned with a house at Benenden for socials, restaurant outings and quizzes

All boys are expected to attend weekday chapel services four mornings a week, and other faiths encouraged to attend their own places of worship for special religious festivals. School is increasingly connected with the local community and there is a growing sense of social responsibility, with large numbers of boys involved with Tonbridge Community Action – boys help in local primary schools and hospitals and develop the skills and confidence to do things which make a difference.

Local primary school children come to use the labs on Wednesday afternoons and hold inter-school sports days at Tonbridge. Recently, 150 boys spent the night under cardboard boxes and raised £5,000 for a homeless charity. Tonbridge has close links with The Marsh Academy at New Romney and is one of its sponsors – Tonbridge boys act as e-mentors and provide help and support to Marsh students, and Marsh students come to Tonbridge for practical science work in the labs. Gap year boys can also work at Marsh Academy for a term.

Pupils and parents: Most boys live within about an hour and a half of the school and it is becoming increasingly popular with London families. The headmaster describes the typical Tonbridge parent as 'understated and low-key' and the boys as having a quiet self-assurance – 'great team players who get on in all settings'. Alpha males thrive here and sport still dominant, but boys also admired for other things and music and culture increasingly important; it is 'a much more tolerant and a kinder place than it was some years ago'.

About 10 per cent foreign nationals from 33 countries, who are generally well integrated. Each house twinned with a house at Benenden for socials, restaurant outings and quizzes. Parents encouraged to get involved, and there is always strong support for Saturday matches. Most parents are members of the Parents' Arts Society, which organises cultural and social events each term, everything from private views at art galleries, theatre trips, wine tastings and lectures to weekend trips to Europe. 'It is such a fun way to get to know the other parents,' said one mother. There doesn't seem to be a typical Tonbridgian – some sporty, some less so, some musical, some not – but all seem to enjoy themselves, and the key seems to be to take part in everything. They have a keen sense of fun, demonstrated at the annual Pink Day when all boys dress up in pink in support of Breast Cancer with some very imaginative and outrageous outfits.

A long list of famous old boys includes EM Forster, Frederick Forsyth, all members of the band Keane, Vikram Seth, Patrick Mayhew, several generations of the Cowdrey cricketing dynasty, Dan Stevens of Downton Abbey fame, Tim Waterstone and Kit Hesketh-Harvey.

Entrance: Most join at 13+ from 50-60 prep schools. Computer based pre-assessment and interview in year 6 followed by common entrance (pass mark about 65 per cent) or the school's own exams in English and maths. School operates a reserve list and keeps in close contact with prep schools. A handful joins in year 10 and about 20 join in lower sixth. Sixth form entry via tests in subjects to be studied at A level.

Exit: In 2015, 37 to Oxbridge. Other popular destinations are the usual suspects: Durham, Bristol, Exeter, Bath, London unis and Nottingham, mostly to read hard academic subjects, but not all follow the herd – other destinations include film production at Bournemouth, golf management at Birmingham, land management at Cirencester and popular music performance at the Royal Northern College of Music. Full-time university and careers advisor widely praised, plus guidance and support from housemasters and other specialist staff. University and careers offices open all day – careers and higher education programme starts at end of first year. Good relationships with European and American universities and provide on-site training for SAT exams. Boys have recently gone to Harvard, Berkeley, New York, Queen's University Canada, Trinity College Dublin and Maastricht.

Money matters: A well-endowed school which offers numerous awards. Up to 45 scholarships offered at 13+ – academic, music, art, drama, technology and sport. Academic and music scholarships offered in sixth form. Top academic scholarship worth 50 per cent and all others 10 per cent, which can be topped up with a means-tested bursary. About 15 boys on full fee remission and a further 15 on 80 per cent fee remission. Means-tested foundation awards given to boys to help fund years 7 and 8 at prep school followed by a guaranteed place at Tonbridge.

Remarks: The prospectus says that 'Tonbridge seeks to excel in everything it does' and it certainly lives up to its aim. 'We have been delighted with the school and our boys have been happy and done well here, but you sometimes wonder if the next stage of their lives can live up to this amazing start', said one parent.

Vinehall School

Robertsbridge, East Sussex TN32 5JL

01580 880413
admissions@vinehallschool.com
www.vinehallschool.com

Ages: 2-13 (boarders from 7)
Pupils: 252
Boarders: 24 full, 28 weekly/flexi
Day: £8,913 – £16,620 pa
Boarding: £19,545 – £21,675 pa

Headmaster: Since 2011, Mr Richard Follett (40s). Married to Jo, who is head of juniors. The pair met as undergraduates at Liverpool University, and have two daughters – one in the prep, the other has moved on to secondary school. Educated at Latymer Upper School and grew up on the river in Hammersmith, West London, where he developed an interest in rowing which took him to international levels, until he was stalled by back injuries. He now coaches and selects for the Great Britain junior team.

Previous post was further along the Thames at Pangbourne College, where he was head of the junior school, housemaster of the junior boarding house and director of rowing. His career has also meandered through another waterside post, 10 years at Bedford Modern School, where he taught geography and headed up rowing; and through a comprehensive in inner-city Walsall, where his duties included tracking down and removing a boy who was dealing drugs to pupils.

As we toured classrooms, children clamoured to show him their work: 'Look at my Jungle Book story,' one beseeched him proudly

While he's a self-confessed snob about coffee (you can be sure it's filter) his career path has taken him through all walks of life and delivered a man who parents describe as 'down to earth', 'very normal' and 'the perfect balance of tradition and innovation'. There's no cosying up to particular families or pupils – parents point out that the current head boy joined in year 7 from the state sector, and was appointed purely on merit.

Nowadays Follett's sports are golf, and cycling – because he can do that before his family gets up, and because it provides him with thinking time. 'I've planned some of my best lessons cycling to Rye,' he says. And he's a keen photographer – the walls of the school are lined with his action shots from home matches and school performances.

Entrance: There's an element of selection because all students are expected to take common entrance or the Cranbrook Grammar exam. Prospective pupils attend a taster day, and not all will be accepted. Those seeking places in year 3 upwards do a maths, English and verbal reasoning test. There are a small number of pupils with dyslexia and dyspraxia, but none with autism. This is more to do with geography than the school's attitude – the specialist Frewen College which caters for these conditions is just five miles away.

Exit: Most popular destinations in the independent sector are Eastbourne College, Tonbridge, Sevenoaks, Mayfield, Benenden, Battle Abbey and Winchester, but pupils go on to about 16 senior schools. Around 15 per cent go to Cranbrook Grammar at 13 each year, but it's rare for a child to leave at 11 for the other Kent grammars.

Remarks: If a pig could talk, should you eat it? Does a dog know it's a dog? These are lessons that children here wrestle with. Philosophy is big on the curriculum at Vinehall as a way of broadening education. 'Common entrance is quite prescriptive, it's rigorous and there's a great volume of knowledge required, but I'm concerned that we teach children to jump through hoops. But do they think for themselves?' says Follett. With concerns about this he started a lunchtime philosophy club, which has now extended to lessons in critical thinking in years 7 and 8, and Puzzle it Out sessions for the pre-prep. It's highly popular with parents and 'sold the school

to me,' according to one. Others mention 'a lot of self-directed learning, which really lights the fire'.

Follett is also working hard on turning around the school's previous reputation as academically elitist – one mother admits that local talk almost put her off viewing the school. 'If they are a potential scholar they will get a scholarship, but we want every child to be happy,' says Follett. 'Not every child is going to get a scholarship, it's the minority, not the norm. Some schools put huge pressure on the children, they are driven by fear of not getting into the next school. We want to be academically excellent, but not for children to feel a failure if they find certain aspects difficult.'

It's clear he's no ogre; children walking past invariably talk to him, including a pre-prep child who announced fiercely, 'I've got a sore tummy'. As we toured classrooms, children clamoured to show him their work: 'Look at my Jungle Book story,' one beseeched him proudly.

The pre-prep comprises a nursery (from age 2) and kindergarten (from age 3) all housed under the same roof as reception to year 2 to enable easy transition. It's a modern, bright building with its own hall and library and a woodland play area.

Nowadays Follett's sports are golf and cycling – because he can do that before his family gets up and for thinking time. 'I've planned some of my best lessons cycling to Rye'

One parent with children in both parts of the school feels that the pre-prep is more traditional. 'The two environments are very different, pre-prep is very formal and structured, and I'd like to see more freedom,' she said. But the school says that the last year has seen a continuation of new innovations in pre-prep teaching, including the use of iPads, a Mandarin club, and higher-order thinking skills sessions.

The prep is situated in a Victorian mansion built by banker Tilden Smith as his family home – the head's study has glorious views over 47 acres of school grounds and miles beyond. Corridors and staircases are lined with shields, each one representing a past pupil and his or her achievements.

There's a separate Millennium building – with subject classrooms arranged around a hub with a library at its centre; also a computer suite, science block, music building, and art, design and technology centre. Subject specific classrooms are used from year 5. Years 7 and 8 have a scholarship form and two mixed ability common entrance forms, with setting for maths.

Reporting back to parents is thorough. There's an Industry Card each half-term, which reports on how hard a child is working only, with full reports at the end of term. A system called Classroom Monitor breaks subjects into component parts so that parents and teachers can be better informed about specifics to work on – in maths it might say, for example, that a child is good at co-ordinates, but finds algebra difficult.

One-third of the pupils receive some form of learning support, which can range from work on posture using Swiss balls, because it can help concentration, to one-to-one support in lessons.

Mr Follett has appointed new heads of maths, science, music and art. 'The calibre of staff in the prep is outstanding,' says a parent. And all the parents praise the prompt attention to any worries. 'I had an issue this morning, they emailed back half an hour later, and it was done and dusted in an hour,' says one.

Everyone studies drama, and productions are staged in a theatre which could grace a small town – it has all the professional equipment and a 250 seat auditorium.

Sports facilities include an indoor swimming pool and a nine hole golf course. Follett has brought a sportsman's zeal to the school, and it's now 'very sporty', say parents. The school is going on its first rugby tour this year, and teams will be taking part in the National Schools Indoor Rowing League. Girls' provision has been revitalised. Follett says: 'Girls' sport now has a culture of competitiveness. I'm all for good sportsmanship, but I want them to win. Before they lost many of the matches, now they win more and show a determination which I'm told wasn't there before.'

No more Saturday morning school for year 7 and 8s – a previous bugbear for some children and parents. Instead, there is an optional enrichment programme for years 3 to 8 – including sports, crafts, and subjects such as astronomy, media and philosophy.

School day now shortened – lessons finish at 4.30pm with optional activity programme including supervised prep (whoopee! say parents) until the school buses leave at 5.25pm.

Boarding is popular, with around 60 boarders on any given night – half of whom will be regular boarders, and half taking up flexi-boarding. The school attracts a number of international boarders (around 25 per cent): currently seven Europeans, three Russians and one South Korean pupil. Full boarding is available from year 3, but junior boarders (years 3 to 6) have the option to board for four nights a week, while year 7 and 8 can opt for full or weekly boarding. There's also temporary boarding for occasional nights. 'I like it that they don't push boarding too much and you aren't deemed second class if you're not a boarder,' one mother commented.

Minibuses bring local children in from all points of the compass including Hastings, Eastbourne, Lamberhurst, Mayfield, Heathfield and Cranbrook. Some parents work in the City but there are also families who find it more of a financial struggle, and they say there is no snobbery. Those who have transferred from the state sector say it's been seamless and they've felt welcome.

Wellesley House School

114 Ramsgate Road, Broadstairs, Kent CT10 2DG

01843 862991
hmsec@wellesleyhouse.net
www.wellesleyhouse.org
C of E

Ages: 7–13
Pupils: 144 (88 boys, 56 girls)
Boarders: 45 full, 54 weekly/flexi
Day: £11,385 – £18,450 pa
Boarding: £21,750 – £24,510 pa

Headmaster: Since 2006, Mr Simon O'Malley MA PGCE (late 40s). Educated at the Oratory School, Reading and at Aberdeen University. Previously a housemaster and later deputy head at Beaudesert Park in Gloucestershire. Ambitious and enthusiastic; has generated an energy and buzz about the school and is justifiably proud of all that it is achieving. Much liked and respected by parents. A keen sportsman, he still plays cricket and teaches English. Met his wife, Katy, while they were both teaching at the Banda School in Nairobi. Says managing parental expectations is an integral part of his job. Encourages parents and children alike to aim high but to be realistic, and on the whole the parents are a pretty happy bunch. He sees the school as 'kind, thoughtful and unique with traditional values but not old fashioned'. He does not rest on his laurels and is constantly striving to 'do things better'.

Katy used to teach art, and following the sudden departure of the art teacher not long before common entrance, brought her skills out of mothballs and got back into the art room. Five children won art scholarships under her watch (the current art teacher is also doing well, with three more scholarships in 2014 and one in 2015). Katy keeps a close eye on pastoral and domestic matters too. They have a son at Uppingham and a daughter at university.

Katy used to teach art, and following the sudden departure of the art teacher not long before common entrance, brought her skills out of mothballs

Entrance: Children can join at any time from 7 upwards – many from local day schools join at this age, with major intakes in years 5 and 6 particularly for boarders. Very occasionally children join for the last year but it can be difficult getting up to speed for common entrance. Girls' places always oversubscribed. Non-selective but entry via interview and reports and examples of work from the child's current school. Would only test if there were concerns about learning support or that a child might not thrive.

Surprisingly large catchment area with many coming from west Kent and East Sussex. About 15-20 from London with an accompanied minibus to Battersea at half term and exeats – headmaster keeps in close touch with London pre-prep heads. Scholarships and bursaries of up to 100 per cent. Discounts for army families.

Exit: To a huge range of senior schools all over the country with King's Canterbury the most popular, followed by Harrow, Eton, Benenden, Stowe and Tonbridge. Others to eg Gordonstoun, Ampleforth and Teddies. Great trouble is taken to pick the right school for each child and the headmaster tries to visit at least two public schools a term. Over a third have won scholarships in recent years – academic, art, music, drama and sports (six in 2015 including art, sport and all rounder). Children hardly ever leave at 11+ and the school does not offer coaching for the Kent Test.

Remarks: Wellesley was founded in 1869 in Ramsgate and moved to its current purpose-built site in 1898, a light and airy red-brick building which has been added to over the years and which is surrounded by flower beds and playing fields. It merged with St Peter's Court in 1969 and went co-ed in 1977. It does not have the rolling acres of some prep schools but everything is immaculate and every inch of the grounds is used – there is plenty of room for den-making, a pond, vegetable plots and even some igloos when it snows. The playing fields are divided by an elegant avenue of trees which has been colonised by a group of noisy, bright green parrots. Lots of refurbishment recently and the squash courts, shooting range and the sunny indoor heated swimming pool and barbecue area are all looking like new. The walls of the new

games room were decorated by the children. The headmaster and his wife like to come back during the summer holidays to take a fresh look at the school and see what needs to be done. Sunny, comfortable, well-used library with lots of space to sit and read and where children can curl up with a book. Each year group has its own common room – recently redecorated thanks to the fundraising efforts of the Friends of Wellesley. Photographs of children past and present line the corridors and there are four rolling news boards around the school showing BBC headlines, birthday announcements, notices and photos of recent events.

Avert your eyes as you drive through the cabbage patches and retail parks of Thanet – it is worth it. Many parents drive miles to send their children here, passing other good prep schools en route. It is a school which embraces the whole family and where friends are made for life: 'My daughter's best friends are still the ones she made at Wellesley,' says one mother. Parents, too, make great friends here – many a mother has been known to weep copiously during the leavers' chapel service. Old Welleslians often end up sharing flats together and there are usually a couple of Wellesley weddings announced in the school magazine. It is a busy, happy school where there is great emphasis on fairness and giving everyone a chance. Academic success is highly valued but good manners, tolerance and consideration for others are equally important. At the annual prize giving each summer, there are not only prizes for academic and sporting achievements but also the headmaster's prize which can be for anything from attitude and effort to just being a thoroughly nice person.

Younger boys live in the junior house which is joined on to the main school and where they do most of their lessons and are cared for by a housemaster and a team of matrons, which gives them a very gentle introduction to boarding. They move over to the main school aged 10 where they are equally well cared for in large, light, airy and extremely tidy dormitories.

Friends are made for life. Old Welleslians often end up sharing flats together and there are usually a couple of Wellesley weddings announced in the school magazine

The girls live at the Orchard, set in its own grounds and surrounded by apple trees on the far side of the playing fields. The Orchard is run by Mr Nichol, who teaches geography and is in charge of the Thanet weather station, and his very elegant and bubbly Spanish wife, Elena, and it is very much a home from home. The Nichols have been in charge here for over 20 years and give the girls an exceptional start in life. There is only space for 43 girls so it feels like a large happy family and is always oversubscribed. Bright, light dorms, all named after Kentish apples, with an abundance of pink and teddy bears on all the beds. One mother who was reluctant to let her daughter board said, 'I cannot deprive my daughter of the Orchard experience, it's truly unique'.

The school motto is 'Open up a world of possibilities' and this is exactly what Wellesley does. There is great emphasis on the individual and 'children get noticed in a smaller school and get opportunities they would not get elsewhere', says the headmaster. Everyone has 'a chance to shine' and with so many activities on offer virtually everyone finds something they are good at. Everything from photography and art, board games and chess, boys' hockey and girls' football, judo, fencing, riding at the local riding school, archery, cooking, needlework for boys and girls, ICT where children can create their own computer programmes and even scuba diving, with the 'shrimp' course taking place in the school swimming pool – the list goes on. Golf is popular – there is a putting green in the grounds and the lucky few are allowed to play at Royal St George's nearby – this can lead to a certain amount of envy amongst the parents. The school is always open to new ideas and the girls have recently set up their own cricket club. Rifle shooting is a popular activity culminating in the annual parents v children shooting match – not just fathers and sons but mothers and daughters as well.

The average class size of 12 means that the school can support children at both ends of the

learning spectrum. Children streamed from year 5 and setted in maths and languages – French (taught by a native speaker) and Latin are taught as part of the curriculum and Spanish can be taught by private arrangement. Very bright children can be stretched and academic scholars are either taught in a separate, accelerated class for the last two years or within the top stream – depends on the number of scholars from year to year.

A good team of teachers, with a healthy balance of age and experience. The children are 'pushed and stretched with full support, and the school has pushed our son to be the best that he can be,' says one happy mother. New computers, and two lessons of touch-typing a week as well programming and website design. High praise from the inspectors who judged that 'The curriculum is excellent, well balanced, stimulating and structured', lessons are 'challenging and interesting' and 'effective anti-bullying procedures include development of awareness of cyber-bullying through PSHE and ICT lessons'.

The school is quick to spot problems and about 20 per cent have some sort of learning support. The department is run by 'the wonderful Mrs Wallace' and there are specialist English, maths and language teachers – some children taught within the class and some withdrawn but lessons rotated so they do not fall behind in any subject; close liaison between learning support and class teachers. Will go the extra mile for children with bigger difficulties. An occupational therapist has designed a programme for dyspraxics. A small number of children work with laptops. In class EAL support available for those who need it.

They are frequent winners of the JET cricket and rounders national competitions, much to the envy and astonishment of much larger and apparently sportier schools

The school has recently been awarded International School status by the British Council which means that all lessons must have an international dimension to encourage children to have a more global outlook – it recently took part in a European day of languages and is already twinned with a school in India.

'The school achieves things it shouldn't for its size,' says the headmaster and it certainly punches above its weight on the sports fields. He puts this down partly to the close bonds that develop in a small boarding community and partly to the support and encouragement from staff. They are frequent winners of the JET cricket and rounders national competitions, much to the envy and astonishment of much larger and apparently sportier schools, and are always represented at the annual national athletics championships in Birmingham. One girl has recently been selected for the England athletics squad and a boy for England cricket training. There is a long tradition of cricketing excellence and alumni include England captains Mann and Cowdrey as well as the Loudon brothers and Sam Northeast, plus three day eventers and Olympic medal winners William Fox-Pitt and Georgina Harland.

Music is part of the curriculum throughout the school with all year 3 learning the recorder and all year 4 the violin, and about 70 per cent continue with at least one instrument; they will find a teacher for any instrument – one child is currently learning the harp. There are instrumental groups and an orchestra and the choir sings in local churches and at weddings; a recent highlight was a trip to Venice to sing in St Mark's on Palm Sunday. Two school plays a year as well as smaller form productions at Christmas mean everyone has a chance to get up on stage. There are also poetry and musical recitals and children are prepared for the LAMDA exams.

Vibrant colourful artwork displayed all over the school with 'six of the best' selected to hang in the head's study. Masses of outings and trips; most year groups visit France and year 7 has an outdoor pursuits trip to the Lake District for an 'educational adventure'. Various charity fundraising events throughout the year from cake sales to sponsored swims and fancy dress days – when children can put their sewing skills to good use. Burns Night is celebrated each year with haggis and reeling and there is a programme of lectures from parents and visiting speakers.

Lots of traditional boarding school parents as well as local professional families and about 20 per cent foreign nationals – from Russia, China, Nigeria and Hong Kong, and also popular with Spanish who often come for a year. Arrangements can be made for children of other faiths, but most are happy to attend chapel twice a week and the full choral service on Sundays. Children not overly sophisticated and do not grow up too quickly but they are still self-assured and confident and are very comfortable talking to adults. The head and his wife invite the top year to dinner parties in their house where the children can dress up and hone their conversational skills. Usually about 60 children in at weekends with plenty going on and outings

planned – ice skating, clay pigeon shooting, bowling or just going to play on the beach. The top year is allowed 'down town' into Broadstairs on Sundays where they can spend their pocket money – a much looked forward to privilege, and many opt to stay in for the weekends just for this.

The Friends of Wellesley House organises social events and fundraising activities including lunches for new parents, quiz nights, the bonfire night and other parties including the recent Wellesley Fest.

A small and extraordinarily caring prep school with traditional values which produces self-assured and considerate children who go on to schools all over the country.

Westbourne House School

Shopwyke, Chichester, West Sussex PO20 2BH

01243 782739
office@westbournehouse.org
www.westbournehouse.org
C of E

Ages: 3–13 (boarders from year 3)
Pupils: 432
Boarders: 59
Day: £9,750 – £16,485 pa
Boarding: £20,205 pa

Headmaster: Since April 2011, Mr Martin Barker BEd Exeter (40s), four years as deputy before – previously at Papplewick in Ascot. Married to Helen – she also teaches, masterminds special projects for the scholarship forms and organises charitable initiatives and donations. They met at university where she concentrated on primary, he on science and PE. Daughter and a son both at Westbourne

and a place near the Everglades for what little non-Westbourne time they have. He's tall and approachable (kids agree), passionate about good teaching having been burnt by the opposite at a grammar school (in the 80s...). His initial brief was on the academic side (brought a database for recording marks to the school) and an impressive scholarship rate backs up the governors'

appointment. So far he's also applied this talent for rationalising systems to the school day, delegation within the teaching staff and boarding options – the result is a more formal structure but parents say a more relaxed atmosphere, 'fewer meetings, the ones that happen count'. Reassuringly, he is most proud of the pastoral improvement – 'reduction in unkindness with the shorter break in the afternoon' – and that the kids are 'rounded and grounded – and so in demand for senior schools'. Still teaches year 8 chemistry and coaches rugby and cricket.

Entrance: Very local school – biggest commute 40 minutes away, 50 per cent of families London migrants. Also local farmers, entrepreneurs (some semi-retired), medics (St Richards Chichester nearby) and Rolls Royce. Diverse lot – double incomes, single parents and the wealthy. Reputation locally for pushy parents. Best entry point at reception/year 1 – 75 per cent – unfiltered for nursery and pre-prep, ability assessment for entry to year 3. SEN would have to be seriously limiting to be turned away – support both in class or with a small group extracted. Composition of intake dictated by composition of new families – waiting lists for years 2,3 and 5 – very hard to keep spaces open later in school if siblings arrive en masse eg from London. Fifty per cent scholarships available for music and some for academic excellence. Means-tested bursaries available for current families, five per cent off for siblings. Continuation scholarships with links to Radley and Cranleigh – entry point year 7 at present, could be changed to year 5 to ensure they have the best chance in senior schools.

Exit: Boarders, from year three (though this is rare) must board a minimum of two nights in years 3 to 6, building up to minimum three nights in year 7 and full week (five nights) in year 8 – vital preparation for the 60 per cent who go on to boarding schools. Top three destinations are Brighton, Canford and Wellington. Portsmouth Grammar is the only popular day school but the train journey puts some parents off. Aims for half a dozen each year to eg Seaford, Lancing, Eton, Benenden, Hurstpierpoint, Cranleigh, Radley, Marlborough, Downe House, St Mary's Ascot, Bryanston, Sherborne. Scholarship hit rate an arrestingly high 35 per cent of all leavers. Eminent outgoers include R4's Marcus Brigstocke (funny) and the late Nick Clarke (news); Monarch of the Glen, Alastair McKenzie; England women's cricketer Holly Colvin

Remarks: Founded as a family school and the atmosphere remains – the original owners, now in their 80s, still live on site (just beyond some wire lions as you enter the beautiful grounds) and continue to be part of school life. Early Victorian main house, sandwiched between beach and the Downs, pupils here stay kids for longer than those in more urban schools and staff make sure they are ready for entry to secondary schools by the time they leave. Complete refurbishment of pre-prep in 2015 following roof fire.

School ethos grew out of scouting – the fleur-de-lys logo is sprinkled about and patrol leaders are voted in (panther, tiger, otter and owl) each term. In the summer the mothers of troop leaders (heads of school) present the prizes – this family involvement is characteristic, whether it is houseparents with children at the school, the parental barometer on teaching standards, support on the games pitches or siblings in different years. A parent could pick up at three different times each day – from nursery, pre-prep and prep – the hanging around can be frustrating but also means relationships are built

---

School ethos grew out of scouting – the fleur-de-lys logo is sprinkled about and patrol leaders are voted in each term. Mothers of troop leaders present the prizes

and social events are surprisingly well-attended.

Children love it here – their favourite parts are the communal ones – form rooms, chapel, the millennium hall, picnics after Saturday morning lessons, BBQ night in the summer – the astounding attraction of a sausage in a bun! They respond to the humanity of teachers and understand the thinking behind structures in the school eg how cleaning works in dining room; that playing in bases (dens) in the boundaries (woods) is organised by rota now – to avoid any tussles or rivalries between age groups. Boarding is popular (one of houses was doubled in size in 2014). Six boarding houses in total, presided over by houseparents, caring matrons and fun gappers. Most boarders go home at weekends, often after Saturday matches.

ICT is omnipresent to free up staff and pupil time for learning and playing – ideally, as in the world outside. Four trolleys of Apple Macs, Wifi – no issues with gaming, kids say they save that for home if they are into it. Older boarders can use iPods before bed. Smartboards in every classroom – yet, as ever, only some teachers use them to the pupils' best advantage. Landlines on wall for calling home – no need or time for mobile phones or Angry Birds apparently. Newspapers as well as screens in the library (due to be revamped).

Breadth in the curriculum, backed up by good facilities. New food tech and science labs, French vocab on doors in main school, ceramics studio a popular retreat (sometimes there's hot chocolate and often CDs playing), stunning art, sparky technology projects, drama opportunities both on, back and above stage, a lake for kayaking (sailing soon), indoor pool and Astroturf. The purpose-built music school fosters a full range – harpists to advert theme tune composers, 80 per cent of children learn an instrument. Peripatetic music teachers mean a catch up period is vital for missed academic lessons.

The risk with such a range of well-supported subjects (and the results to match them) is choice and activity overload, no space left for aimless mucking around (the risk assessed alternative to climbing trees?). Shorter lessons, no time between them, a longer break in the morning, scholarship sets – the long prep at the end of the day is a crowd-pleaser since no homework – the disadvantage is that parents don't see books when they come home. The proof is in the pudding though – really happy families.

Westminster Abbey Choir School

Dean's Yard, London SW1P 3NY

020 7222 6151
headmaster@westminster-abbey.org
www.westminster-abbey.org/choir-school
C of E

Ages: 8–13
Pupils: 34
Boarders: all full
Boarding: (after subsidy) £7,848 pa

Headmaster: Since 2002, Mr Jonathan Milton BEd (50s), married, formerly head of The Abbey School in Tewkesbury. Bred, if not born, into the choir school tradition – he was a choral scholar at York. Music was his degree subject, though he now teaches geography. A gentle man, whose quiet, friendly manner betrays a profound love of his unique school, the tradition it enshrines and the community of boys and staff which gives it ever-fresh life. Clearly, an inspired appointment. Mr Milton is, at once, a traditionalist and a moderniser – exactly the right balance for the place. 'When I came, there were no carpets or curtains and it felt tense – that's now completely gone. It was dark too. We've tried to make it gentler.' He showed us the little IT room next to the dormitories: 'a marvellous way for boys to stay in touch – much simpler than writing a letter. And the staff communicate with parents every week electronically.' Gentler the school may well be but he has also tightened the academics, keeping step with the outside world in which senior school places are no longer assigned in little chats between heads of 'big' schools and trusted prep heads. Mr Milton's openness, thoughtfulness and warmth are mirrored in his boys. Those we talked to were similarly relaxed, candid and friendly. Head and boys share their view of life here, 'it's tough, you get very tired but.. it's fabulous.'

Entrance: No formal entrance test day or the like. Over the year, school will see around 25 boys for voice trials – usually in ones and twos – and usually in year 3. The master of the choristers will hear

them and the head will chat to the boy and parents and, if the lad looks promising, he will be invited back to spend a day in the school. This will include a more formal voice trial, a chance to play their instruments and testing in maths and English. What is looked for is not grade 8 in six instruments but musical aptitude and the kind of attitude to music, community and learning that make for a happy and successful Westminster Abbey chorister. 'They have to enjoy being part of a close-knit team and they must have personality and character,' says Mr Milton. Academic brilliance is less important though, clearly, the boy must enjoy learning. Of the 25 they see, places may be offered to between four and six, on average, though one or two may be invited to come back some months later.

We were terrified by the huge multi-tusked cardboard beast which 'would be tamed by listening to Palestrina'

These days, more than half come from state primaries and can be caught up and supported where necessary. 'With year groups of six or seven, we can tailor-make classes,' says head. School fees are subsidised by the Abbey and no-one, however impecunious, should be put off applying if their boy is a natural chorister. Funds will be found. 'Some pay nothing at all,' says Mr Milton. Boys now come from further afield – Yorkshire and even overseas. Quite tough for an 8-year-old, you might think. 'And,' says Mr Milton, 'few of our parents would have chosen a boarding school – when they see it, they realise it's a way of life.' Yes. This represents the most amazing opportunity for the right child and a peerless preparation for life.

Exit: An astonishing list of leavers' destinations over the last three years. Many win music scholarships to prestigious schools and many win academic and/ or art scholarships too. Most popular senior schools are King's Canterbury, Eton and Winchester with the rest hither and yon, and doing very well wherever they end up.

Remarks: This is the only choir school in the country which is only a choir school – no day pupils, no girls, no non-choristers. Average class size six, maximum is nine. In a way, that says it all. The place hums with quiet activity – mental, physical and musical. It all happens in a tall, unobtrusive building in Dean's Yard – right under Big Ben, the Houses of Parliament and Westminster Abbey. Dean's Yard is a grassy square lined by augustly solid houses. Opposite is the modest arch which leads to Westminster School – no connection with the choir school except that the large pupils and the little choristers see each other passing all day which makes the business of scholarship and growing up in this – the heart of the great centre of London – seem quite the normal thing.

Five floors accommodate all learning, admin and living space. All is freshly-painted and feels light, comfortable and well-cared for. There's a super ground floor 'music room' used for assemblies and the like – a splendid stained glass window commemorating Purcell and the other masters of the choristers who between them make up a history of English choral music – Gibbons, Blow, Simon Preston et al. Classrooms are small with conventional desks, whiteboards and it all looks a bit dolls' house in scale – enhanced, when we visited (during exam week) by the very cuddly teddies (for good luck) sitting reassuringly on desks. More teddies in the dorms which – it is a boys' school – are, if not Spartan, certainly not prettified. Bunk beds with integral cupboards in airy rooms. Good shower rooms, good ICT provision and a very nice sitting room with sofas, piano, TV, books and games and feeling really snug.

Everyone does standard prep school curriculum but flexibility can be built into the system with such small classes and so small a school. Individual help is the norm. No boys with SENs, we are told, though the odd mild dyslexic may creep in. A boy with dyslexia would find chorister-life tough, says Mr Milton – what with having to read music and a foreign language at speed and so on. 'It wouldn't be fair.' Yes.

Sports take place via buses to Battersea Park, The Queen Mother Sports centre in Victoria and water sports in Docklands – Mr Milton is a keen sailor. They kayak, rock climb and sail and Mr Milton sees this – and the opportunity to get away from the closed chorister world – as essential for good relations.

What is looked for is not grade 8 in six instruments but musical aptitude and the kind of attitudes to music, community and learning that make for a happy and successful chorister

Evidence of boy-life and wit abounds. 'WACS Lyrical' – the boys' own noticeboard – details competitions, initiatives, jokes and notices – full of fun and ideas. The art room, open in the evenings, similarly lively – we were terrified by the huge multi-tusked cardboard, paper and paint beast which 'would be tamed by listening to Palestrina'. Boys enjoy textile work, DT – they make fan-powered vehicles for racing – and knitting: 'very popular', we were told. Obviously, music is central to life. Singing practice in the song school happens each morning and each afternoon before evensong – except on Weds and alternate Mons. Instrumental practice is timetabled and very much a normal part of everyday life. Musical guests and ensembles visit, there is a composer in residence – a real privilege for such boys – and school takes full advantage of the concert halls and galleries roundabout. Likewise, the school goes into local primaries – boys take their instruments – to inspire others, 'just to give music a boost'.

What do the boys say – and their parents? 'You have to be very independent and organised,' a seasoned 12-year-old told us. 'You can't rely on your parents to pack your bag and find your pencil case – you have to do it all yourself. You have to manage your own revision and music practice.' (Sounds like a course in choristership might be handy all round.) 'It is very tiring – I'd like to have more of a rest after concerts.' On the other hand – 'singing all the special services we do is brilliant. We did a special service for the spies! [100 years of MI5]. They just looked normal. They don't wear T-shirts saying "I'm a spy".' And 'We're on TV, we go on tours and make CDs.' 'It can be exhausting,' said a parent, 'but they bounce back. It's unbelievably rewarding.' And they clearly enjoy the abbey community with whom they share Christmas and Easter meals and so on. A choristership here is a treasure. A huge commitment for boys and family while it lasts, but a gift for life.

Westminster Cathedral Choir School

Ambrosden Avenue, London SW1P 1QH

020 7798 9081
office@choirschool.com
www.choirschool.com
RC

Ages: 7–13
Pupils: 172
Boarders: 25 (choristers)
Day: £16,854 pa
Boarding: Choristers £8,841 pa

Headmaster: Since 2007, Mr Neil McLaughlan (40s). Married with a young son and daughter, and a man who radiates humour, decency and charm in equal measure. Read philosophy and politics at Durham and spent a few years with Andersen Consulting in London before embarking on a teaching career in 1997. After spells at Stonyhurst and Worth, he took up a post as head of English and director of development at Downside School, before joining WCCS as headmaster. He hopes to be there 'for the duration.' Parents hope so too. 'Lovely guy!' said one. 'So easy to approach!' said another. 'An extremely dedicated head and a great promoter of the school,' said a third. Typically modest, he hopes to do 'lots and lots of small things right.' We think he's doing lots of big things right too. Under his visionary yet kindly leadership, this has become an inspiring school that is going from strength to strength.

Entrance: Main entry points for day boys are at 7+, where 14-15 places are available, and 8+ (a further eight or so places – mostly for choristers). Applicants sit tests in English, maths and non-verbal reasoning in January of the year before entry. Occasional places in other year groups, notably at

11+. The school is always oversubscribed, and, once boys have met the required academic standard, will give preference where possible to practising Roman Catholics and to boys with a brother at the school.

Choristers, who must be Catholic and boarders, join at 8+. Would-be probationers have to pass informal and formal tests with the cathedral's master of music, as well as succeeding at the academic assessment; and if they manage all that, they spend two nights at the school to see whether chorister life will suit them. Only then will they be offered one of the six available places. As the school's popularity grows, so inevitably does the competition; there are now half a dozen serious candidates for each choristership, and for the first time in over a decade, the school has not had to go recruiting for them.

Up to full fees assistance for choristers; none for day pupils, whose families just have to fork out. As a result, there is more cultural than social diversity here. Boys come from a wide range of nationalities, among them France, Spain, Italy, Russia, Ghana and Korea, making this a truly international school. With some 80 per cent of the boys now from Catholic families, the school is less religiously diverse than it was, but remains open to day

boys of all faiths provided their families are happy to support the school's Catholic ethos.

Exit: The head has worked tirelessly to raise the school's profile, and WCCS's exit record is superb. Boys regularly leave for boarding schools like Eton, Harrow, Winchester, Uppingham, Stonyhurst and Ampleforth, and for a raft of top London schools, including Westminster, St Paul's, City of London, KCS Wimbledon, Latymer Upper, Dulwich College and the new Wetherby senior school, often with music scholarships. Others to Cardinal Vaughan and the London Oratory. 'The school is much more linked into the senior schools than it was a few years ago,' reported one satisfied parent. 'Oh yes, the head's always going on about schools,' confirmed one of the boys, equally.

Remarks: The school was endearingly shabby once, but not any more. A five-year programme of refurbishment has just finished, and everything is now bang up to date. Visitors are welcomed in the beautiful glass-fronted foyer, where handwritten Music for mass schedules from 1905 are hung beside huge photos of current pupils radiating health and cheeriness. Throughout the building, ceilings, floors and lighting are all new, and all the classrooms are gleaming and well-resourced, with interactive whiteboards in each one. Large and much-loved playground, covered with Astroturf, where boys play 'crazy games' on the climbing apparatus. 'That was a real selling point for me,' said one parent. 'The boys have a chance to be boys.'

'The key thing,' says the head, 'is to have good, kind people around the boys, good accommodation and excellent food. An army marches on its stomach'

'The way to the heart of little boys is good food and football at playtime, and WCCS excels in both,' confirmed another. We didn't try the football, but we can confirm that the food is splendid, a delicious combination of tasty and healthy. Boarding facilities have also been upgraded. We can't comment on the refurbished boarders' common room, because a curmudgeonly old trumpet teacher therein told us we were interrupting his lesson and to get out, but we did manage to see the sleeping accommodation, which was cheerful, light and airy. The rigours of chorister life notwithstanding, feedback on the boarding experience from both parents and boys was uniformly positive. 'The key thing,' says head, 'is to have good, kind people around the boys, good accommodation and excellent food. An army marches on its stomach.'

Years ago, parents had disquiets about aspects of WCCS. Nowadays, they cannot find enough superlatives with which to express their delight. 'We have been thrilled by both the teaching and pastoral care provided by the school.' 'The staff generate a wonderfully positive energy.' 'It's an amazing school, the teachers are so kind!' 'You couldn't choose a better school, I recommend it to everyone.' 'A wonderful warmth and care is present everywhere.'

A father of a new chorister told us, 'My son absolutely loves it. He's thrilled to pieces. The first weekend they were eligible to go home, he didn't want to come.' (Poor mum!) And a mother of two day pupils wrote, 'Happiness is guaranteed at this school; it is such a nurturing, caring and stimulating environment. I can honestly say that the only problem I have ever had is to find a way to drag my boys out of the playground and back home at the end of the day.' What's behind this remarkable success? 'The one ingredient a Catholic school should have is joy,' said the head, simply and without any side, when we asked him,.

There is joy in the teaching here, that's for sure. A quiet revolution is taking place in the WCCS curriculum that made this reviewer go all excited and wobbly at the knees. Schemes of work have been painstakingly redesigned, with scholarship and a genuine love of learning at their heart. 'The idea is to present knowledge as a unified whole,' explained the head, 'so for instance, whilst they're studying Adam and Eve in RS, they'll be doing CS Lewis's The Magician's Nephew in English. Likewise, we use geometry and graph-plotting in maths to support map skills in geography, and they'll draw antique maps in art at the same time. If the boys are doing the human body in science, they'll look at what the Greeks and Romans discovered about it in history.' The boys we spoke to praised the lessons as 'really good fun,' adding, 'The work's challenging, but in a good way'.

Much emphasis on poetry, with poems studied every week, as well as learnt by heart and declaimed. 'We want them to know the great poets of the English language,' said the deputy head, and to further this, the school has produced its own wonderful anthologies, where the selection is 'unashamedly classic.' In addition to regular English lessons, boys receive two lessons a week on formal grammar and punctuation, and Latin is compulsory from the off – 'Latin is crucial for grammar, it's not an academic luxury,' insisted the deputy head. 'As an international school, the story of the world's great civilisations interests us. But children of this age also need connections, and they need the basics.' All those who have wrung their hands at the disjointed, shallow content of so many modern lessons, lift up your hearts and hope.

Large and much-loved playground, covered with Astroturf, where boys play 'crazy games' on the climbing apparatus. 'That was a real selling point for me,' said one parent. 'The boys have a chance to be boys'

This is clearly a scholarly yet joyful environment, and the quality of student work we saw reflected that. We read, misty-eyed, a set of poems by the year 7s about Westminster Bridge (inspired by Wordsworth's sonnet) that were outstandingly creative and well-written; likewise, a history essay on Thomas Becket was not only mature and insightful, but skilful and lucid in its use of language. But mightn't this approach favour only the brightest? WCCS's SENCo emphatically denied it, asserting that boys at the school with SEN benefited from understanding how language works. We were impressed with the support the school gives to those with dyslexia and dyspraxia, as well as to ESL students, such as the two grave and courteous

Russian boys we saw having extra English tutorials. And all the staff we met were purposeful, well-bred (curmudgeon excepted), cultivated, devoted to what they do, and, according to parents, 'incredibly dedicated.'

'My son is neither Catholic nor musical, but has been recognised for other things he has to contribute to the school. They're grounded children with good values. It's a perfect place for my son to grow into a confident young man'

As you'd expect, the standard of music here is outstanding. The choristers are completely immersed in music-making at the highest level (listen to the downloads on the website, and marvel), and the day boys, swimming in the same element, also achieve great things. We saw year 8 boys composing their entries for the school's Christmas carol competition, and heard much excellent instrumental playing as we went round the school. 'The music programme is amazing,' enthused one parent. 'My son's piano playing has come on by leaps and bounds in just a few weeks.' Many pupils achieve grades 7 or 8 in their chosen instrument(s) by the time they leave.

Football, rugby and cricket are the main sports here, played at local pitches, and swimming and PE are held at the nearby Queen Mother Sports Centre. Lots of extracurricular activities, including debating, philosophy, chess, scrabble, code-breaking, the Airfix model club, current affairs, and cross-country running. 'But where do you run?' we asked, glancing with some surprise at the surrounding streets. 'Oh!' said our tour guide, 'Green Park, Hyde Park, St James's..'

Lucky lads, you might think. And they are, of course. But what struck us most about this lovely little school was how considerate, well-mannered and sanguine about life its pupils seemed to be. They are achieving great things, while remaining likeable and happy boys. As one mother wrote, 'My son is neither Catholic nor musical, but has been recognised for other things he has to contribute to the school. They're grounded children with good values. It's a perfect place for my son to grow into a confident young man.' We agree with her. For boys fortunate enough to come here, this is as near perfect as it gets.

Westminster School

17 Dean's Yard, London SW1P 3PB

020 7963 1003
registrar@westminster.org.uk
www.westminster.org.uk
C of E

Ages: 13–18
Pupils: 741; sixth form: 385 (257 boys, 128 girls)
Boarders: 144 boys/42 girls
Day: £24,276 – £26,322 pa
Boarding: £35,058 pa; Queen's Scholars £17,529 pa

Head Master: Since September 2014, Patrick Derham MA (50s), previously head of Rugby School. At 12, he was sent to live and study on the naval training ship Arethusa, run by the children's charity Shaftesbury Homes to prepare young men for the navy. Two years later the ship was abruptly sold due to financial difficulties and, with a day's notice and little idea what a public school was, he arrived at Pangbourne College on a bursary. He eventually became head of school and read history at Cambridge (first class degree), and feels 'my life was transformed by education.'

Taught at Cheam School and then Radley, where he was head of history and a housemaster for '12 very happy years' before being advised by the warden there to go straight for a headship. Five years as head of Solihull were followed by 13 at Rugby, before landing the headship of 'the home of liberal education – the perfect culmination of my career.'

His background ('my mum still lives in a council house in Scotland') has clearly been a powerful motivating force in his commitment to widening access to a good education – as he points out, 'all the great schools were founded with that intention.' At Rugby, he set up the Arnold Foundation to provide bursaries for children who need the stability of a boarding education ('we didn't just cream off the brightest middle class kids'). He is a trustee of the SpringBoard Bursary Foundation, a national charity modelled on the same lines, and vice chair of IntoUniversity, which gives disadvantaged children academic support and mentoring to raise their aspirations.

'He did an amazing job here and will be brilliant at Westminster,' said a Rugby insider. Very down to earth, personable, fantastic speaker, say Westminster parents. 'You feel like you can trust him'... 'He really cares about getting to know everyone'... 'I like it that he already knows who I am and who my children are'... 'Very responsive to comments'... 'My daughter thinks he's great'.

Clearly no ivory tower head, he loves interaction with pupils and teaches A level history. Parents watching their sons compete in the recent National Schools Rowing Regatta were delighted to see Derham there cheering on the teams (they won the championship eights' title for the first time in the school's history).

Married to Alison, a teacher, with two grown up children. Westminster seems to be in very steady, to say nothing of inspiring, hands.

Academic matters: With these very bright pupils, 'you can teach for the love of the subject and focus on the exam when need be,' says the head. 'It's a breath of fresh air,' said a parent. 'Intellectual risk taking is encouraged. They're never not challenged.' 'It's incredibly inspiring,' said another. Many of the teachers are experts in their fields, encouraged to follow their interests. 'I cannot believe there is a more stimulating place to teach in the country,' said a teacher. 'It is so much more liberal than at my previous school,' said a sixth form student. 'It's not constrained by the syllabus – it's learning for the sake of learning. It really allows you to get a proper understanding outside the exam baselines.' Pupils tend to internalise that love of learning. 'They read and they question and they challenge,' says the head. 'In my first lesson one asked me, "Where is the evidence?" I'd never been asked that before.'

Everyone encouraged to include a practical subject, eg art, electronics, drama, music, at GCSE. Huge range of languages includes Dutch, Arabic and Portuguese. Several parents commented that inspirational teachers had sparked their sons' interest in subjects they had previously hated. 'He'd always been a bit of a maths boy but now he is flying at English and languages too. They've understood how to teach in a way that suits him and developed all these new interests.'

> *'They read and they question and they challenge,' says the head. 'In my first lesson one asked, "Where is the evidence?" I'd never been asked that before'*

Top exam results are, nonetheless, part of the package, with 84 per cent A* and 96 per cent A*/A at GCSE in 2015. At A level/Pre-U, 55 per cent of subjects were graded A* or the Pre-U equivalent (D1/D2) and 86 per cent A*/A. New thinking skills course – designed as a more challenging alternative to critical thinking A level – introduces sixth formers to the elements of informal logic, and helps prepare for university entrance skills tests such as the Oxbridge Thinking Skills Assessment.

High academic ability is obviously a pre-requisite, but study skills coordinator works with all those who need support for eg mild dyslexia,

> *His background ('my mum still lives in a council house in Scotland') has clearly been a motivating force in his commitment to widening access*

dyspraxia or Asperger's, or just lack of organisation, helping them with the skills needed to cope with learning at different levels as they move up the school.

Links with local state schools Grey Coat Hospital and Harris Westminster Sixth Form – the latter sponsored by Westminster School – see sixth formers from these schools joining in German, Latin, music, art history and drama lessons with Westminster students. 'They've done a really good job at integrating us,' said a Westminster sixth former. 'I'm as good friends with students from outside as anyone else in the class.' Joint senior management meetings with Harris Westminster staff: 'We are going to learn from each other.'

Games, options, the arts: An almost overwhelming range of extracurricular opportunities. Societies often stem from the particular passions of both staff and students, ranging from feminist to secular to geography. English society may see Simon Russell Beale answering questions on playing King Lear at the National, whilst Piyush Goyal, national treasurer of the Indian Bharatiya Janata Party (BJP) party tells the political society about Indian public affairs. 'I set up a society and had an ambassador from Panama come to talk,' said one student. 'Staff are really supportive when you want to set up new things.' Huge range of journalists and politicians, scientists and thinkers drop in to give talks; poet in residence inspires creativity. Trips everywhere: climbing in Cataluña, Beijing exchange, art history in Venice. Years 9-11 go off for a week's climbing, sailing, hill walking or camping at home or abroad.

'Phenomenal' music, with professional standard orchestral concerts at St John's Smith Square and the Barbican, carol service in Westminster Abbey, masterclasses, eminent musicians from Nicola Benedetti to Ian Bostridge giving evening concerts. One parent felt that 'unless you are excellent you won't get a look in,' whilst staff point out there are house concerts and ensembles for the less stratospherically talented. 'We like to think there is room for everyone.' Drama equally high performing – Guys and Dolls a recent sell-out but much cerebral fare too, plus house drama and GCSE/A level pieces – and again huge talent required to bag a role in the large scale school productions.

Art, too, 'wonderful', with much emphasis on traditional drawing and painting skills, life classes, film making facilities and a darkroom. Plus, of course, easy access to all of London's galleries and museums. 'My son had no artistic ambition when he arrived, but is now doing art A level. They have totally inspired him,' said one parent, whilst another commented: 'They let these academic boys be so creative – they feel free to explore.'

Sports – known as 'Station' – take place on Tuesday and Thursday afternoons, mostly on the enviably large playing fields in nearby St Vincent Square plus adjacent sports centre (in a previous life one of the Royal Horticultural Halls). In Westminster liberal fashion, no particular sport is compulsory, with a huge range of choices from sailing to judo to golf to girls' football. 'You wouldn't send a very sporty boy to Westminster,' thought a parent, who was grateful that her keen but not-particularly-athletic son had been in teams which he would have been unlikely to make at a more overtly sporty school. However, particularly successful at rowing (and was basking in the glow of recent success at National Schools' Regatta when we visited), fields nine football teams with 'at least respectable' results, and 'we do very well at niche sports such as rock climbing [third in the Independent Schools' Championships] and fencing [bronze medal in U15 Foil]'. Often dominates the London School Cross-Country Championships and the Westminster Secondary Schools Swimming Gala, with pupils representing Westminster in the London Youth Games, and is successful at fives and real tennis. 'You are encouraged to try lots of things and find something you are passionate about,' said a student.

Volunteering taking on increasing importance with new head's passion for outreach, with nearly all Westminsters teaching music or setting up debating societies in local primary schools, working on Hampstead Heath or learning sign language to communicate with deaf children. 'People are really involved and really making a difference,' said a student. 'Staff have the time, passion and faith in us to let us get on with things.' Phab week – where year 12 Westminster students host young people with physical and/or mental challenges, taking part in creative activities and seeing London together – is a 'life changing experience'. 'With privilege comes enormous responsibility to give back,' says the head.

Boarding: The last Anglican monastery in London now houses Purcell's, a girls' boarding and boys' day house with attached chapel. Five other boarding houses, all in or near Little Dean's Yard and all of which include some day pupils. Many rooms surprisingly spacious; younger boys in College, scholars' house, in dorms of up to eight, whilst upper years have their own rooms and those in between may share with one other. 'Because these are all old buildings, the room arrangements can be random, and sometimes we have to improvise.' All boarders are cared for in relaxed fashion by housemaster (male or female), some with own family; resident tutor and matron also on site. Breakfast and supper in College Hall, the medieval dining room of Westminster Abbey, which day pupils may also join.

The only full boarders are sixth formers, and Saturday evenings tend to be quiet, though school is increasing organised weekend activities, particularly for the 10 per cent or so of overseas sixth form boarders.

Boarders have supervised prep sessions, and there are evening activities in the sports and music centres after prep, but those after a full-on boarding experience jammed full of organised activities may want to look elsewhere. 'He likes it for the independence and to be with his mates,' said a boarder parent, whilst another said, 'It feels like a convenient b&b. Much better than having to pick him up at late after a rehearsal or lecture.' However, a sixth form boarder commented on the 'serious sense of community you can only get from living with others. The people in your own house become quite special to you.'

Background and atmosphere: Whilst some other great public schools overshadow their environs,

Westminster is an integral but discreet part of central London, largely located in the walled precincts of the former medieval monastery of Westminster Abbey. Its main buildings surround the square of Little Dean's Yard, known as Yard, where pupils spill out after lessons to chat or kick a football or practise basketball. The Abbey, next door and with its own private entrance, serves as the school chapel, used for twice weekly services plus carol and other concerts.

Westminster had become a school by 1179, with pupils taught by monks of the Abbey at Westminster. It survived Henry VIII's dissolution of the monasteries in 1540 and has been in continuous existence since the 14th century, with Elizabeth I celebrated as the school's official foundress.

'It is an incredibly tolerant and civilised atmosphere,' said a parent. 'Unlike other schools, they don't try to mould pupils into a particular product. They are quite laissez-faire.' Parents of quirky students are relieved to find a school that is very kind and accepting of eccentricities. 'If he was at any other school he'd be toast,' said one. 'Some schools can be so unforgiving: Westminster is the complete opposite.' Another reported that it has 'catered brilliantly' for each of her very different children. 'It's so wonderful to see these kids spark off each other.'

Pastoral care, well-being and discipline: Tutors attached to each house oversee the academic side, whilst housemasters look after all else. One parent felt that both have too many charges to know her son well. 'I feel his well-being is my responsibility, not the school's. I don't think anyone there knows him well in the round.' Others, however, described the pastoral care as 'exceptional', and a student said, 'I have always found the school really responsive. Your housemaster is always there and will take

Particularly successful at rowing (was basking in the glow of recent success at the National Schools' Regatta when we visited)

care of everything from not feeling well to having too much work.'

Pupils expected to be proactive, motivated and organised, with very full timetables but no compulsion to take part in organised activities. 'But anything you want to try, there's some way of doing it,' said a student.

Pupils and parents: 'Lots of people said I wouldn't like Westminster,' reports the head. 'They told me the pupils were arrogant, staff unmanageable, parents difficult. None of this is true.' Westminster families undoubtedly tend to be wealthy, intellectual, metropolitan, cosmopolitan and no doubt demanding, but most parents are extremely supportive of the school. 'It is very hard to withstand this full on praise and delight.' 'I am a real believer.' 'Fantastic on every front.' And from an initial sceptic: 'I am increasingly fond of it.'

Girls entering the sixth form report a much easier ride than they might have expected. 'I had heard rumours about the boys being awful and arrogant – but they weren't,' said one. 'Some would show off in lessons to begin with, but they calmed down pretty quickly.' 'I suspect they look for a certain confidence,' said another. 'If you were insecure you might find it intimidating.' 'It was quite a shock to the system at first,' said a third, 'but we can hold our own.'

'Westminster imbues in you a sense that it is fine to talk to anyone on equal terms,' said an ex-student. 'You have a real feeling of being special.'

Parents – nearly all are Londoners, with even boarders mostly coming from within the M25 – offered a cornucopia of outings to Dulwich Picture Gallery, tours of Westminster Abbey and the Houses of Parliament, plus quiz nights, drinks parties, concerts in the Abbey, and the opportunity to attend expert lectures with their children. 'Parents very friendly and there's a good sense of community and involvement,' said one.

Old Westminsters span the centuries and the professions: the massive list ranges from Ben Jonson, John Dryden, Robert Hooke, Lord Lucan, Kim Philby, AA Milne, John Gielgud, Tony Benn, Corin Redgrave, Helena Bonham-Carter and Imogen Stubbs to Dido and Mika.

Entrance: Register by the end of year 5 for 13+ entry (boys at state primary and other schools that finish at 11 may apply to Westminster Under School). Computer pre-tests in English, maths and reasoning in year 6; high performers who also have a good report from current school called for interview, which includes short maths and English tests. Those with conditional places sit either the Challenge scholarship exam or CE (pass mark 70 per cent) in year 8.

For 16+ places, register between summer and October of the year before entry. Applicants – boys and girls – take exams in their four most likely A level subjects, and are interviewed.

Exit: Excellent and detailed preparation not only for Oxbridge but for American university entrance, with school trips to visit east coast universities. 'The school has been very supportive from an early age,' said a student, 'keeping us up to date with when to take subject tests and when to visit colleges.' Good preparation too for medicine, which is amongst the most popular degree subjects alongside liberal arts.

Up to half of sixth formers do, indeed, go to Oxbridge (68 in 2015, with 14 off to leading American universities), most of the rest to London universities, Edinburgh, Durham and Bristol.

Money matters: A number of means-tested bursaries of up to 100 per cent of fees available at 13+ and 16+; applicants must live in London. Bursaries also available at 11+; boys spend two years at the Under School before moving on automatically to the Great School. Eight Queen's Scholarships awarded at 13+; recipients must board, and the scholarship covers half the boarding fee. This can be topped up by a bursary in case of need. Five exhibitions at this level. Up to six music scholarships at 13+ worth 25 per cent of day or boarding fee, plus free instrumental tuition. No 16+ scholarships.

Remarks: One ex-student commented that Old Westminsters of her acquaintance have gone into a far wider range of careers than those from other schools. 'They seem to be following their passion. Westminster instils a belief that you can do whatever you want to do.'

Whitgift School

Haling Park, South Croydon, Surrey CR2 6YT

020 8688 9222
admissions@whitgift.co.uk
www.whitgift.co.uk
C of E

Ages: 10–18
Pupils: 1,455; sixth form: 339
Boarders: 58 full, 54 weekly/flexi
Day: £17,988 pa
Boarding: £28,980 – £34,656 pa

Head: Since 1991, Christopher A Barnett BA MA DPhil (60s). Previously second master, Dauntsey's School and before that head of history at Bradfield. Married to Laura, psychotherapist and author, four grown up children, one daughter, three sons who all came here, all scaling assorted dizzying career heights from bloodstock agent to Twitter supremo.

First post was in higher education as economics lecturer at Brunel in the 70s, combined with political research for MP. Logical, given impressive string of qualifications to his name, Oxford and history-based for the initial bunch, including doctorate; extras from – amongst others – Downing, Cambridge where he's a fellow commoner (more important than a college lecturer; less than a bye-fellow, apparently) and French government (who wouldn't want luscious-sounding Chevalier dans L'Ordre des Palmes Académiques?).

Switched from higher to secondary education because of power of education to 'impact on the whole child'. Also, you suspect, to provide suitable canvas for his innovations. 'A minefield of ideas,' as colleague put it.

Supremely confident (quality shared by pupils). Rather than endure months of time-sapping debate on funding decent grand piano when first arrived here, simply went out and bought one. Can even stop rain and replace with sunshine – we saw; we believe. Performed similar trick when Patron Duke of York visited. Father shared knack, so 'everyone booked their holiday when he did.'

Unsurprisingly, shuns dead hand of risk-averse culture, leading decisively from the front and exuding vim and vigour, even more energised now, he says, in contrast to other heads who 'fade away' in final years.

'Building a country,' reckoned one parent. Thinks massive, from annual replacement of framed photographs of school achievements lining corridors to big-canvas projects, borrowing £8 million at commercial interest rates to fund sports facilities paid for by rising pupil numbers – now

1,400+ from 875 when arrived – and greater economies of scale.

Probably best known for love of natural world, from dog inclusion policy, horses ditto – school racing syndicate is about to be reinstated, equine visitors not unknown – to assorted wildlife, particularly exotic birds. 'A bit like Dr Doolittle,' thought mother. 'He feels that it gives boys a sense of calmness', reckoned another (boys say they quickly get used to peacocks' shrieks at exam time).

Though pushmi-pullyu yet to make an appearance, other treats include wallabies, turacos and, our favourite, photogenic cranes waiting (unsuccessfully) by back door to be let in (backstage team 'specially trained' in deep-cleaning the mats).

With so much on the go, Dr Barnett delegates 'hugely. If I can engage every one of my 200 staff, then that's 200 times the power of me.' Unsurprising that for some parents he is a slightly distant figure 'pulled out for public occasions,' though agreed that deputy heads and heads of year are able day-to-day managers.

Supporters praised individual take on the role. 'I suppose you've got to have someone a little bit off centre, not toeing the academic line too much,' thought mother. 'A lovely man, very approachable – not completely aloof,' said another. One member of staff expressed fervent hope that, paraphrasing Ramsbottoms, she would have many sons to her name so could send them there.

Emphatically not a timeserver, Dr Barnett is a man who relishes ability to make things happen, sparking like a Catherine wheel (favourite description of his hero, Disraeli). Style may not please all

– but then, nor did Disraeli's. Has announced that he will be retiring in July 2017.

Academic matters: The full English but with continental option – A levels, IB (bilingual option for most advanced French speakers), BTecs and even the occasional Pre-U (occasional top ups for those requiring extra stretch). Extended essay qualifications and the like just about the only no-goes – IB covers the ground, feels head.

Results consistently good. In 2015, 92 per cent of A levels graded A*-B, 71 per cent A*/A. IB marks healthy at average 38. Maths leads subject popularity by a mile, sciences follow, English and humanities put in good showing. Rest – PE, computing and music among them – lag in single figures at the rear.

GCSEs (IGCSEs in English, maths, science, languages) similarly healthy with 87 per cent graded A*/A in 2015. Ten sat by most. Options chosen from relatively compact range bar terrific languages (three rather than two studied) with Japanese and Mandarin already on offer and Arabic and Sanskrit possible future additions. DT hugely popular (we were shown wide range of delightful projects ranging from solar-powered beeswax storage unit to hockey stick unit).

One outsider wondered how staff can cover the range effectively, especially with same teachers for A levels and IB. Their idea, says head. Teachers, a level-headed bunch, averaging late 30s with a quarter into second decade, agree. Benefits of pupil choice outweigh double preparation time, said dedicated scientist, while some subjects with low A level numbers (such as DT) positively gagging to

have a second go at IB now previously dreary syllabus is getting a makeover.

No shortage of teacher talent – former senior bods have gone on to headships everywhere from Magdalen College School to RGS Worcester. School has been academic non pareil in the area and 'the crème de la crème in every respect,' says local and could 'be in the top 10 [nationally] again,' says head, though not a fan of league table glory however.

Supremely confident (quality shared by pupils). Rather than endure months of time–sapping debate on funding decent grand piano, simply went out and bought one

Classrooms have trad feel (admittedly hard to compete with new build excitement elsewhere), pupil numbers around 18 per class, 10 in sixth form. Behaviour immaculate – all rise for adults. Fun year 7 maths class working out probability by throwing dice, sixth form biologists fighting coursework deadline (easy listening music in background to counter tension).

Well on the way to building an education that ensures those focused on academic excellence get their fill, but will customise for those with exceptional sports, musical or other talents – fistful of scholars desirable but making A*s the priority for exceptionally gifted violinist headed for music college is pointless, thinks head.

Good reports for most subjects. More experienced teachers tend to be kept for best, thought a parent, focused on GCSE years and above, though any problems raised (including those with individual teachers) are quickly sorted at whatever stage. Increasing provision for the 10 per cent of pupils with SEN (largely dyslexia though also ADHD, ASD, three statemented), team about to increase to six, including two full time teachers. Currently around 30 EAL pupils from 20 different nationalities.

Homework sensibly organised and, though workload is ramped up from around year 8, staff stick to allocated days and good at helping absentees catch up on missed sessions while 'emails fly back all the time for boys who can't quite manage it.' Felt that would be useful to have drop in clinics and clubs in key subjects focusing more on lesson content exam technique – and we heard of parent being 'actively encouraged' to seek private tuition when child fell behind. Summer school opened for first time in 2015.

Head librarian in senior library (cosier separate version for juniors – some subjects also have their own areas) talked enthusiastically of ways and means to boost reading interest, from book clubs to brunch events. With many boys glued to laptops at break, blind to lure of enticingly packed shelves, looked like an heroic endeavour.

While the academically capable flourish, parents warn that while school 'does what it says on the tin,' pays to be on the ball, proactive parents getting in touch the second a report shows unexpected (downwards) grade movement. Former coasters are in for a shock. 'They do expect you to work to your optimum and you always need to be performing.'

Practical teacher input praised – one boy, struggling with twin demands of homework and role in musical, had rehearsal time halved so able to catch up. 'We can't speak highly enough [of the school],' said mother. 'Their expectations of the boys really surprised us, that everything was possible.'

Games, options, the arts: 'We allow pupils to follow their passion,' feels head. 'I'm only really interested on what we can do for the individual child.' Means pupils don't have to go to university to find out who they are, he reckons (though we worry about all that existential angst forced to find other outlets...). Finding niche can require strong-mindedness, however. One up-and-coming rugby star – Harlequins hopeful – had given it all up for love of singing.

For the natural joiner, undoubtedly paradise, and starts early with all new pupils getting free golf and instrumental lessons (though not simultaneously). Much of massive co-curricular programme included in the fees (100 or so options, from animal to Islamic club). 'So many activities that by the time you leave, you'll have other interests,' thought sixth former.

*Will customise for those with exceptional talents. Fistful of scholars desirable but making A*s the priority for gifted violinist headed for music college is pointless*

One mother felt that sporty, academic or artistic groups of boys tend to follow separate paths. Once, perhaps, said pupils, but no longer the case. 'Have friends with very different interests,' said one.

Sports facilities terrific, luring in outsiders from Surrey cricketers to Olympic hopefuls – approving quotes dot prospectus. Goodies include assorted pitches where seriously rugged hone skills to sports centre with squash courts, fencing salle and fitness suite, as well as swimming pool (different depths fit all, from armband armies to water polo teams). There's even a Transformers-style sports hall (now you see it, now it's a 1800-seat conference centre).

While talent levels mean pupils who would have made top teams elsewhere may not do so here, even C and D teams often win against other schools' As and Bs, while starry coaches including Colin Pates (Chelsea) and Steve Kember (Crystal Palace) are doing for football what is already the norm for rugby, hockey and the rest. Almost easier, in fact, to list sports that don't feature amongst over 100 national titles secured in past five years.

Performing arts also getting substantial injection of resources with International Music Competition for string players, inaugurated 2013, soloist opportunities and fees the prize, and attracting talent from Eastern Europe. Six full scholarship boarders now in residence with more to follow; all potential soloists, reckons head.

With sell-out musicals, some outstanding actors (one has already written and starred in own play) and 380 learning an instrument, some to diploma level, performing arts already in good shape, spaces indoors and out, from Founder's Garden to old swimming pool, all imaginatively used for everything from Shakespeare to sell-out musicals (West Side Story was in rehearsal when we visited), concerts ranging from beginner strings to Mahler at Royal Festival Hall.

If there's a corporate refrain, it's 'best anywhere'. Only parental niggle would be more access to facilities. Pool, for example, is 'amazing' but opportunities to use it outside the timetabled six weeks a year would be appreciated – tricky, admittedly, given extensive use by outside groups. Bottom line, though, is that 'if you're good at something, they've got all the facilities in the world,' thought mother.

Boarding: They've upped ante with boarding (new house catering for 100 13-18 year olds opened 2013). Bright and beautiful, partially powered by solar (though water 'too grey' to recycle, says new boarding housemaster – one of the many staff with rugby-fuelled handshake).

Ancient name, lovely and unusual site – cross between wildlife park and landscaped RHS outpost. Whipsley, perhaps? Don't expect acres of Tudor panelling, however

Features super common rooms, welcoming but airy, uncluttered feel, upmarketing furnishing (new Yamaha piano) and Subbuteo for juniors, snooker (and superior view over greenery) for seniors next door. Beds specially ordered for seven footers and, amazingly, every fragile-looking wall-mounted loo so far intact (must be made from same makers as indestructible cushions).

Highly successful, it's reckoned and, with 40 full boarders at weekends, no forlorn few testing the echoes. While activities generally good they sounded a little low-key when majority are off on voluntary exeats. Actively not trying to create traditions (can be where problems begin, is view of school, which numbers consecutive year groups 1, 3 and 5...).

Background and atmosphere: Ancient name, lovely and unusual site – cross between wildlife park and landscaped RHS outpost. Whipsley, perhaps? Don't expect acres of Tudor panelling, however. Though school was founded in 1600 and current site was owned by Henry VIII (and home to Lord Howard of Effingham, son a very early old boy), most is vintage 20th rather than 17th century (well worth seeing fascinating archive) and pleasant rather than grand in feel, despite commanding hilltop view over south Croydon.

Deep community roots, however, not only endure but extend each year, involvement ranging from extensive financial help for families of pupils in need to vast year-round outreach programme costing around £100,000 and involving 55 local schools, each spending a week at the school with dedicated classrooms and seconded staff with sessions covering sport, arts, science and languages.

Audition-entry weekend arts academy, for local children as well as school's pupils, runs wildly popular courses incorporating drama, dance and musical theatre.

Numbers standing up well to scrutiny and, as the biggest leading independent boys only in the area, as well as highly academically successful, so you'd hope. Theoretically a matching pair with Old Palace, the girls only school also in the Whitgift Foundation, though not an exclusive relationship – joint drama and music productions with Croydon High and St Andrew's C of E High School, too.

Trinity the big rival – 'You have to say 'T' word,' counsels pupil, though others would like more contact. Head says tricky logistically and for now, schools likely to keep dancing to individual tunes.

In unlikely event that new buildings don't deliver wow factor, outside loveliness certainly will, from Founder's Garden, created for 400th anniversary and graced with very own new rose, to Whitgift water gardens, tape cut by Sir David Attenborough, who was bowled over by visions of loveliness before him, rare emerald starling adding final touch of enchantment.

'We were blown away when we saw it,' says mother. Doesn't stop, either, planned science bio-domes each featuring slice of life (flora and fauna) from round the world. Like the Eden Project, says head, only better (from educational perspective at least – though does win on location). Butterflies soon on order. Giant tortoise being debated.

Pastoral care, well-being and discipline: Big on nurturing from day one with older boys mentoring younger ones (a few blank looks from mentorees-in-waiting) on top of formal tutor system. Older pupils often turn to subject teachers for 'excellent' ad hoc support.

Fab induction trip to Lake Garda for year 6s (heavily subsidised) within first few weeks works wonders even for the very shy. Great care taken to create school within a school, 10+ and 11+ intake in own very pleasant building and, with the obvious exceptions such as art, music and games, form-based for lessons, and even a separate house system.

Only question mark was over slightly bleak asphalt-covered junior playground, bins the only ornament. When quizzed, pupils and head unanimous in stressing year-round use for ball games (surrounding windows correspondingly battle-weary), rendering any embellishment undesirable.

Masses of boys can mean occasional testosterone overload, though any low level disruptive behaviour is effectively sorted out as pupils move up through the school. Fisticuffs rare but not unheard of, though parents tend to take this calmly. 'Typical of boys' schools,' said a mother. Ditto pupils. 'It happens. It's better just to deal with it,' said pupil.

Though corridor supervision appeared low key, boys reckoned teachers were never far away – even super sixth form common room has head of year's office in corner, though clearly gaze is benign, judging by relaxed crowd sprawled on easy chairs, one minus shoes. Hot on effective sanctions, too, reckoned a parent, with school services – times spent doing something useful, such as lunchtime litter clearance or cloakroom tidying, cordially loathed and thus highly effective deterrents.

Head plans mass pupil engagement programme – will see around 700 over next year in small groups for elevenses, lunch and tea. Though mainly for success stories, is also asking for teachers to refer boys who may need little extra pepping up to join them. May answer plea by one parent for more sugar to help medicine go down. 'I think I'd like it to be a little less pressurised and use more carrots rather than sticks.'

Pupils and parents: Many Croydon-based, or close; nearby grammars and Trinity the main alternative senior schools, with around 60 per cent of intake from state primaries (preps were in majority when head first joined school, but feels that links with community have boosted appeal to first time buyers). Increasingly attracts those from further afield – into deeper Surrey and even north London with boarding opening it up to the world (Taiwan the latest country expressing desire to forge links).

With old boys numbering TV illusionist Derren Brown, actor Martin Jarvis and Premier League star Victor Moses amongst ranks, average career hard to define, though being a reasonably tough personality to make a success of life here and later on probably helps. 'I think if you can't hold your own then you're going to sink,' felt mum.

For the right child, however, approach works wonders. 'If he'd gone to one of the state schools I don't think he'd be the confident young man he is now,' reckoned mother. 'He's much more able to walk into a room full of strangers and hold a conversation.'

Easy-going parents can come as a relief to new-comers. 'Thought they would be very highbrow and

stuffy but not at all.' Terrific socialising, too. 'We have the best time...we went to a quiz night, there's a summer ball, it's everyone mucking in,' says one.

Entrance: Entrance exam early Jan, day at school. Majority sit 10+, 11+ or 13+ exams (maths, English, VR). Fewer at 12+ and 14+ (maths, English and science). Likelies invited back to interview. Sixth form candidates need seven GCSE passes with A*/As in A level subjects (similar for IB), though possible to enter to take BTec sport, in which case five A*/C passes will suffice. Interesting advent of dual sixth form streams, second for less academic but highly sporty. Head talks with winning enthusiasm for need to educate nation's footballers post-16...

Exit: Little fall-out – 20 per cent left after GCSEs in 2015; those with below par AS results often redoing a year or retaking modules. Occasionally pupils 'advised' to look elsewhere. 'Nobody is ever directly asked to leave,' said senior pupil. Vast majority who sail on reach splendid destinations. Offers from all the big beasts (Warwick, Southampton, Bristol, UCL, Edinburgh etc) and pupils clearly well thought of – one had received Oxford IB offer of 38, high but not stratospheric. Big range of subjects from geography to performing arts and professional sport. Twenty-four to Oxbridge in 2015 – 'What you're paying for,' said parent.

Money matters: Scholarships are one of Whitgift's huge strengths; the number of bursaries and amount of financial help makes school a possibility for those from most deprived of backgrounds. Sensitively handled, too, with those in need of extra funding for school trips given subtle means of applying so need never miss out. Aim is for one in three boarders (mainly music but possibly sports as well) to be on full scholarships.

Remarks: 'Happy and high achieving,' thought a parent, with traditional virtues pushed but never, under sparky headship of Dr Barnett, a dull place to be, even though Zoological Society of London has declined request for elephant. Natural home for academically inclined, sportsmen and performers and ideal not just for wallabies and flamingos but also for confident joiners who may not yet have settled on their passion in life but relish process of discovery.

Windlesham House School

Washington, Pulborough, West Sussex RH20 4AY

01903 874700
whsadmissions@windlesham.com
www.windlesham.com
C of E

Ages: 4–13 (boarding from 8)
Pupils: 380
Boarders: 230 full
Day: £15,600 – £24,450 pa
Boarding: £24,240 – £27,960 pa

Headmaster: Since 2007, Mr Richard Foster, Head at Pembroke House School in Kenya, then at St Anselm's in Derbyshire for 14 years. Thoughtful, warm, much liked by parents and pupils. Incredibly busy wife Rachel is in charge of everything pastoral – parents give Rachel a ring and she races around the school to find the relevant child and tend to it. Three grown up children. Both Fosters refer slightly wistfully to Kenya as home and enthuse pupils with love for the region. Windlesham is the most child centred school Mr Foster has ever taught at – though he is careful to point out (perhaps with the more conservative parents in mind) that 'children [here are] liberated – not liberal.' In his 50s and will stay at Windlesham until retirement. Still teaches, and randomly covers all classes over the course of the year.

Entrance: Non selective. Academic assessment from year 1 upwards for setting purposes plus night's stay from year 3 upwards. Houses have different personalities, and tester night helps school decide in which house the potential pupils would flourish. Waiting list for many years. No scholarships, but means-tested bursaries available.

Exit: Pupils move on to over 30 different schools, including Eton, Marlborough, Lancing, Hurst, Brighton College, Bedales and Oundle.

Remarks: Gorgeous grounds, movingly beautiful even on the miserable day of our visit, with the elegant Queen Anne house standing at the end of a long drive past a mixture of woods, playing fields and golf course. Game rambling around (they don't shoot it here – just clay pigeons). Beautiful entrance hall with roaring fire adds to the impression of

arriving at a country house hotel; one specialising in modern art – it's everywhere, and extremely good.

Feels happy and free – described by one parent as a 'tree climbing education centre.' There is a distinct feel of Famous Five here. The amazing grounds are fully used by the children; one parent described how the matrons have to drag them in to bed during the summer months, and how kids are out playing golf and cricket before breakfast – 'kids have the freedom to be children' (children with a nine hole golf course).

Parents and children all comment on the strong community at Windlesham –'it's an incredibly kind place', which aims to be a family home away from home. No uniform promotes the homey feel, although the strict dress code prevents a grungy look. There's no label competition here – 'they ruin clothes at school, so don't send them in anything good,' said one parent wryly. Birthday parties for boarders in the Fosters' flat – cake, treat food and all. Huge amount of energy devoted to pastoral care. Many staff live on site: one parent said 'they never clock off'. Another: 'teachers go over and beyond what they need to do; nothing is too much effort.' One parent described the 'brilliant support' from the learning centre and houseparents after a family death – they have a 'genuine love of children [here].'

High level of responsibility and support shown between children. Peer listeners appointed from the top class, peer mediators in each year- described lavishly by one of our guides as 'unpaid spies', but a peer mediator calmly countered with an example of a love/hate triangle successfully resolved by her and her counterpart. Any help from adults? 'No, of course not – confidentiality,' she said in a shocked tones. For prep age children, they are astonishingly responsible and outward-looking. This is one of the school's aims, with the head's mantra firmly in mind – be kind, be kind, be kind. Any bullying nipped it in the bud early. 'There's not a great deal of it,' said a parent, whose daughter experienced bullying which was dealt very efficiently.

Kids love the autonomy of deciding what to do every evening: tag rugby, fencing, art, just hanging out with friends – and can always get help if there's a problem with prep

No prefect or monitor system. All pupils in the top year sign up for responsibilities, and at the end of the year it is announced who will have been head girl and boy on the basis of performance.

Huge emphasis on good manners here: children pay good heed to the head's warning – 'get your greeting in before I do.' Good evidence of this on our tour: all pupils held open doors, flattened themselves against walls as we passed and leapt up in classrooms. Children are very aware of rules set down in the code of conduct, and there's open discussion of rules in school council (top year). 'Fatigues if you're really bad' – jobs such as cleaning the dining room.

Pupils can board from the age of 8 and there are 230 full boarders, 18 per cent from overseas. 'Boarding provision is exceptionally good,' said a mum, whose kids started as day pupils, and all ended up boarding at their request. Pupils agree – 'it's a sleepover that doesn't stop.' Homely girls' dorms, with posters, cushions, bears; spartan boys' fare, with coloured duvets the most cosy touch (despite the school's best efforts). 'It's the girls who need One Direction posters,' said one of our guides loftily. Girls also get bedside tables and lights – boys don't because of their tendency to play cricket in the dorms. At the end of the term, children give in a list of people they like, and are guaranteed to find at least one in their dorm the next term. Twelve is the biggest boys' dorm, six the smallest, nine-three for the girls. A little unfortunate that the girls' dorms are named after colours – 'azure,' 'saffron' etc – to suit their delicate natures? – whereas boys' dorms are sturdily named after senior schools -'Wellington' et al. Unfortunate indeed, but no other whiff of sex discrimination here.

There are two boarding houses, each of which has a male and female houseparent, a permanent matron, and a battalion of evening matrons who come in from the surrounding community to assist at bedtime, and make sure kids are clean with clothes sorted for tomorrow. Nightly showers, although boarders can relax in a birthday bath. Bathroom facilities extremely clean, but not all that new. Each year has a comfy room, reduced to cheerful bedlam for the boys, ordered comfort for the girls. No mobile phones or own computers, but phones all over the place for speaking to parents, Skype phones in the comfy rooms for those with parents abroad, and dormitory phones for good night calls to parents (time restricted to give everyone a chance).

Parents say school is just not the same for day pupils, who don't have the same access to activities or teachers as boarders. Kids love the autonomy of deciding what to do every evening: tag rugby, fencing, art, just hanging out with friends – and can always get help if there's problem with prep. Boarding is particularly useful as work steps up in preparation for common entrance, parents say – early bird lessons start at 7.15am, and work ends at 6.30pm, so it's a long day for commuters.

Feels happy and free – described by one parent as a 'tree climbing education centre.' There is a distinct feel of Famous Five here. The amazing grounds are fully used

No pocket money. On school trips pupils are given a set amount to spend, which goes on the school bill as an extra. Boarders get tuck at weekend – not enough to rot their teeth (a chocolate bar, a can and packet of crisps). Can earn various treats, which are usually of an edible nature. Kids talk a lot about grub, one way or another. One pupil earnestly reported that someone actually stopped boarding for lack of crisps (although it should be pointed out that the food here is plenteous and good). Academically, parents and pupils are happy with most subjects, exceptionally so in some areas though French is 'not that popular,' say the kids and parents agree, citing a reliance on work sheets. School says it has taken on new teachers since our visit.

Another parent suggested maths is also a key subject that could be taught better, although the children we spoke to gave maths teachers a glowing report – 'if you listen carefully they're really funny – very sarcastic.' One teacher apparently tells stories of his life in mathematical fantasy (difficult to imagine how this might go...). Those fiddling with their calculator may find it deposited on the outside of the window sill, so that if someone opens the window it would smash – 'really cool,' says a pupil. The head says they are about to appoint an additional maths specialist – an acknowledgement this is an area with which some children struggle.

Head says English and science are exceptionally strong. Pupils agree about science -'one of the finest lessons.' The kids enjoy the interactive classes – 'we always do an experiment, and if you work hard, you can fit in two or three. We are doing chemical reactions, so I'm seeing things explode,' said one of our guides with relish. One science room just updated, others to be done soon.

Set for core common entrance subjects from year 5. French and Spanish to all, Latin from year 6 (can be dropped by those with learning difficulties to concentrate on more core subjects). Provision for Greek, Mandarin, Italian, Russian, Norwegian and Dutch. Basically if a child arrives speaking a language, they will be encouraged to keep it up, whatever it is. Equally if a child has a burning desire to learn a particular language, school will attempt to accommodate the urge.

Forms usually no more than 18, occasionally up to 20. Starts spotting potential scholars in year 6, and a formal academic scholars' group is established in year 7. Two academic scholarship groups at the moment containing 40 children. Some strong feelings about the scholars' group (where offspring have been both included and excluded from the elite), with the suggestion that scholars are more profiled and get more support than others – and have more chances to go on the fabulous biannual charity trips. 'Opportunities should be more evenly spread,' said a parent (although the forthcoming trip to Nairobi is open to anyone in year 8).

Year 8s do have some preparation for independent learning, but one parent thought kids are hand held a bit too long, and could do with a little more independence in personal care, and organising prep.

Rigorous reporting for parents: progress report monthly with attainment and effort, both child and parents get a copy, and a full report at the end of each term. Annual parents' evening (termly for juniors). 'Amazing level of communication,' say parents: written letters from kids every week, emails and phone calls. 'School responds promptly to any query, over and above what you would expect.' Another parent commented how welcome she felt at weekends – you can attend Saturday chapel, watch a play rehearsal or recital. '[You] never feel excluded as a parent – always welcomed.' Parental portal has live stream of events, also available for catch up, ideal for parents who aren't local.

Three computer rooms, one reserved specially for junior use. Dell laptops and iPads to book out, also available to assist those with mild learning difficulties (about 15 per cent of children here). Learning development unit with head and team of assistants. Bright, well-stocked library, open from before breakfast until bedtime, news with a Tory bent – Telegraph and Times, with the honourable exception of the i.

Feels quite hunting, shooting, fishing, but manages not to feel exclusive. Sports are the usual public school fare. Parents are delighted that sports kit left hanging around at school is returned washed and pristine. Some criticism of sports facilities by parents, who feel that the swimming pool and equipment is rather tired – pupils too are keen for a new pool, and complain the Astroturf is rather worn. Changing rooms on the scruffy side. One parent felt that sports could be improved, and

those in teams in the lower echelons should be playing more matches.

Most boarders are around at weekends (though it's possible to go home four weekends a term). Everyone's around on Saturdays: morning school, matches in the afternoon. Plenty of activities available – Capture the Flag is extremely popular at the moment; but also debates, mountain biking, gardening in the walled garden, shows and games – pupils can keep extremely busy if they want to (though some kids just want to live in the woods, and that's ok too.) Chess club is thriving, though the outdoor chess set is largely unused – 'but we do use a couple of the pieces for goalposts.' All love cooking club – you have to run fast if you want to sign up.

All have drama lessons, three productions each year, everyone who auditions is included in some way. Own theatre – the Malden Family Theatre – with visiting productions every term. Some rumblings from parents who are a bit tired of seeing the super-duper children starring again. Music compulsory all the way, but popular even with those who are not musical because of the inspirational director. Over 80 per cent play an instrument. Vast array of music groups of all complexions, from Miremba to rock choir.

Early years housed separately at Little Windlesham (reception – year 2). Relaxed setting,

emphasis on flow and play. Tapestry method of contacting parents, who receive a video stream of their children in class directly to their email at work, which parents love. Described by a parent as being 'part of [the] big school – but very gentle, with a lot of time [spent] in their special oasis.'

The head says Windlesham would suit most types of kids, providing they join in and have a go at things. One parent suggested it would not suit a child who needs to be totally organised by others; nor is it a place for shrinking violets; although conversations with shy pupils suggested they could find their feet and flourish here. One parent emphasised that those who want their children to be day pupils should avoid Windlesham – all kids here will want to board eventually.

Parents from the foreign office, business, Forces, professions, and lots of expats. Some 20 different nationalities in the school, around 12 per cent non British. Assesses language skills on entry, but will give special assistance to learn English as a foreign language. Some 50 per cent of kids local, 50 per cent from abroad or other parts of the country. Parents like the mix of children from different countries, and to a degree, backgrounds – a few means-tested bursaries and no judgement, say parents; although four wheel drive likely to be parent vehicle of choice.

Several parents of leavers said their children are homesick for Windlesham: the move from this caring environment to senior school can be quite tough; but as a parent said, no one would want Windlesham to be less fabulous.

Woldingham School

Marden Park, Woldingham, Surrey CR3 7YA

01883 349431
registrar@woldinghamschool.co.uk
www.woldinghamschool.co.uk
RC

Ages: 11–18
Pupils: 540; sixth form: 175
Boarders: 150 full, 150 weekly
Day: £19,035 – £20,745 pa
Boarding: £30,435 pa – £33,135 pa

Headmistress: Since 2007, Mrs Jayne Triffitt MA, mid 50s. Divorced with two children, daughter educated at the school, son studying physics at Durham. Her second headship, following six highly successful years at St Mary's Cambridge. Before

that, three years as head of sixth form at thoroughly desirable St Mary's Ascot preceded by longest job so far – a decade at La Sainte Union as head of science.

Comparisons with Mrs Thatcher (both had grocer fathers, studied chemistry at Oxford – even worked in the same lab) entirely deliberate

May sound like education at the sheltered end of the spectrum, but while the only grit you'd encounter in any of her former schools would tend to be under construction as a pearl, Mrs Triffitt herself is as down to earth as they come. Calm and bright with a well-tempered dry wit (and a habit of delivering punchlines sotto voce), she's Cornwall born and bred, own mother raising her single-handed after early widowhood, stress on value of training and a career the mantra that drove the young Jayne to get on in life.

Comparisons with Mrs Thatcher (both had grocer fathers, studied chemistry at Oxford – even worked in same lab) entirely deliberate. Even leadership aspirations (school vs nation) differ only by degree, while under that pleasant west country lilt, this Mrs T is a similarly no-nonsense operator. 'You have to have humour and warmth but the steel has to be there, otherwise things will crumble underneath,' she says.

Misses nothing good or bad, from a spot of over-exuberant jumper throwing on lawn outside study window – 'Wouldn't do that if they knew I had a visitor,' she says – to rounding up lost sheep. 'On my first day, I was meant to be in the sports department but was in maths and she directed me,' says year 8 pupil.

Similar protection for staff under pressure if tricky conversation with parent looms. 'Send them straight to me,' is the dictum. We know who we'd back in a fair fight. Parents, none the less, adore her. 'Not that old but she's like your granny,' says mum. 'You want to hug her.'

With reputation as a turn round head (we didn't hear any 'Triffic Triffitt' puns but feel sure they must be out there somewhere) she has made school, once underrated also-ran in an area stuffed with higher profile alternatives including Sevenoaks, Caterham and Charterhouse, credible first choice option, even amongst London preps' head girls (celebrity endorsement or what?).

Need for rock solid finances hasn't deterred Mrs Triffitt from turning away those who wouldn't stay the course academically. Balancing act of 'maintaining ethos, improving academic performance and being more things to more people,' has been achieved with scarcely a wobble, school now just 10 short of capacity which won't be exceeded, despite rising tide of place-hungry Londoners.

Living on site (house also home to adorable but high maintenance sheltie) in idyllic surroundings, Mrs Triffitt satisfied with lot. Staff team the way she wants it. Teachers who might have failed to thrive under her leadership have tended to 'take the hint' and move on. As teacher, changed lives. Now, as centre of community, 'makes a difference to the whole place.'

'I don't have much to prove,' she says. No plans for another headship. Twice, she says, is enough. Others keen to harness talents might disagree.

Academic matters: Long-standing reputation for creative excellence now matched by burgeoning academics. Wannabe Carey Mulligans (school's best known Old Girl) might be applying in greater numbers but artistic temperament without solid academic performance these days no longer enough to secure a place, says head. 'We're not St Paul's but we expect every girl to be capable of achieving 10 or 11 good GCSEs.'

Pupils' ability is above national average and progress made is one of sources of school pride – pupils move up about a grade based on entry level performance, helped by small(ish) classes, average 15 or so to sixth form, nine or 10 thereafter, together with bigger, earlier focus on setting (in maths and science) and banding (humanities) and lots of inspiration along the way, from thought bubbles surrounding topical articles (diligently completed by teachers and a couple of pupils, including head girl) to large type motivational quotes in English corridor: 'Only positive attitudes allowed beyond this point.'

'I love everything,' said several, science hands–on fun making it a list topper. 'We've set fire to a lot of things,' exulted year 8. Perhaps as well not all labs yet refurbished

While 100 or so speak English as a second or additional language, only half need support. Similarly, while all are screened for learning difficulties on entry, needs mainly mild to moderate, though school goes the distance with support, staffing recently ramped up to offer everything from in-class support to separate one-to-one and small group sessions. Though inspection report quibbled, pupils are in no doubt as to value. 'Wanted a school that didn't make me stupid,' says one. 'Here they knew I had difficulties but still felt I could be in the top set.'

Combination of setting in maths and sciences and banding (same group for humanities) allows strengths – and difficulties – to be recognised – though not currently offered in languages, potentially disadvantaging those starting ab initio in year 9. Overall, however, 'not about who's smarter than who but who learns differently,' says year 10 pupil.

With specific learning difficulties by far the biggest need, main form of help given is with organisation – watches, jewellery and memory sticks top lost property lists – and study skills, clearly a school-wide preoccupation, with emergency furniture stuffed into every spare nook and cranny, ensuring no one struck with urgent revision needs is ever more than a few feet from a desk.

More made of most able in recent years, now offered assorted intellect-stretching activities ranging from summer schools at prestigious US unis to encouragement to enter essay writing and maths competitions, plus law, philosophy or creative writing clubs and societies. Also encouraged to take EPQ, where jury currently out. Though results impressive, horribly time-consuming and thus may be destined for early bath.

None of that early exams for the brightest nonsense, however. 'What's the point?' thought director of studies (appropriately aka Mr Clever, according to Mr Men picture 'from wife' in study). Able mathematicians instead enticed with chance to do stand-alone additional maths qualification. (Replaces further maths, an off-putting IGCSE, which attracted few takers).

Suits actions to words with improved results both at GCSE and A level, gap closing between the two, with 58 per cent of A levels graded A*/A in 2015 and 85 per cent A*-B. At GCSE, 76 per cent A*/A grades.

Few trouble spots dim otherwise healthy glow, though, points out Mrs Triffitt, mixed intake does

Enthusiasm and attitude are first class, pluckiness unswerving in the face of disappointment – 'close to coming second,' was a typically upbeat report. Feistiness also an essential attribute

mean that success in toughest subjects may always be uphill struggle for tiny minority of weakest pupils.

Subjects have been overhauled – nothing radical (will always be A levels rather than IB, for example), just gently progressive (pupils we spoke to felt food tech and business studies would be icing on curriculum cake). Cat's cradle complexities of GCSE option choices usually managed with aplomb (timetable room, floor piled high with discarded paper, presumably bears witness to the effort required to pull it off).Everyone now takes European Computer Driving Licence in first two years, budding techies now able to essay HGV version in form of GCSE computing as alternative to ICT.

Art outstanding, work including transformation series with delicately drawn human heart gradually metamorphosing into tree, one of a long row of eye-catching GCSE exam entries forming orderly queue like so many talent show entrants.

At A level, little to complain about, choice impressive and growing (slowly) with PE and media studies recently added and lavish sugar coatings courtesy of delicious-sounding subject-related excursions (sixth form physicists' chance to air surf in a wind tunnel surely top of wish lists).

Translates into broad base of interests reflected in roughly equal numbers taking arts and sciences at A level, maths and economics the single biggest subjects but followed by theatre studies, English about as popular as chemistry. Creative types particularly well catered for with three-way choice of art (textiles and history on top of fine) as well as music and musical technology. Even get bonus of own staff shirt code, smartly suited for conventional subjects, art and music signalled by occasional shift into denim.

Teaching generally excellent, staff putting in as much of own time as necessary to ensure pupils really understand a topic and help the unconfident to blossom. 'Started off as middle of the road and really came out of myself,' enthuses sixth former destined for high ranking university. 'Turn shyness into quiet confidence,' says a parent of year 9 pupil who is now 'relished for who she is – this isn't just a conveyor belt for A and B grades.'

Traditional lesson formats rule though plenty of interaction – year 9 pupils deftly stretched during demanding poetry analysis by encouraging English teacher. Pupils enthusiastic. 'I love everything,' said several, science hands-on fun making it a list topper. 'We've set fire to a lot of things,' exulted year 8. Perhaps just as well not all eight labs have yet been refurbished.

Only handicap the considerable to-ing and fro-ing between lessons, noted by inspectors with some mild accompanying tut-tutting. Given that distance between buildings – it's a fair old trot from science, say, to humanities – remains a fact of life, school does its best with longer 55 minute lessons and five minute travel allowance time. Hard to see how gorgeousness of commute can be anything but a bonus.

Games, options, the arts: Pupils 'need to be robust just to take advantage of all the opportunities,' thinks teacher. Must be, too, what with 300 tough nuts studying drama or instruments (to diploma level), 200 having tennis coaching, remainder able to select from 80 activities so tempting that droves of day girls stay on to take advantage of extended day that runs to 6.30pm; Saturday activities, compulsory for years 8 to 10 (and a popular voluntary extra in year 7) provide another bite of the cherry.

Currently having a bit of a moment are fencing and riding, cookery course, run by Leith-trained school staff, another favourite together with debating – whither EU membership typically (and topically) meaty subject tackled by sixth formers and no doubt packing in the crowds.

Emergency furniture stuffed into every spare nook and cranny, ensuring that no-one struck with urgent revision needs is ever more than a few feet from a desk

Range of entertaining external speakers are additionally wheeled in to galvanise the troops, 'Vampires' the (blood-soaked) cherry on cake for year 7s in National Science and Engineering Week speech. Trips, equally abundant, range from art in St Ives and science in Peru, to music, excitingly 'TBA'...

Acres of space well used inside and out. Parent-pleasing eye candy provided by flight of stone steps rising up to outside swimming pool through series of lush grass terraces. More prosaic, though well used, is floodlit, sand, all-weather pitch and umpteen others for tennis/netball.

Sports rather less monochrome than recent match reports, netball accounting for seven out of the 10, would suggest, hockey faring well, appeal boosted no end by fab weekend tours to major European cities (Lisbon and Rome love the game, apparently).

School works hard to avoid sports and arts activities clashes by rotating priorities so all-rounders aren't torn between the two. While the championship fixated might not thrive, there's enough local success to keep competitive instincts honed, as well as sprinkling of individual county and national success (hockey, netball, British diving team), while enthusiasm and attitude are first class, pluckiness unswerving in the face of disappointment – 'close to coming second,' was typically upbeat report. Feistiness also an essential attribute (one girl was taking A levels as timetabled, despite breaking arm just before first exam).

Though same names tend to crop up in first teams, 'less good do get matches,' reckoned year 8 pupil, and commitment will do the trick every time. 'As long as they turn up for the training sessions then they get a go,' confirms a mother, though further up the school it's a slightly different story, have-a-go mentality giving way to realities of tougher competition, so that keen but hopeless may be side-lined, says school. 'People say it's not sporty – but it's sporty enough,' felt mother.

Arts 'amazing,' thought parents, and similarly busy with much impressive showcasing for top talent, from what pupil review describes as 'raucous' production of Midsummer Night's Dream to local music festivals and energetic house music competition. Focus the knock-out Millennium Arts Centre packed with pupil-friendly extras including concealed high level walkways allowing safe access to lighting rig. Would-be Dorothys can even skip there along yellow brick road linking with main building. More beige, we reckoned, but what's a pantone shade or two between friends?

Boarding: Accommodation for boarders never less than clean and bright with smart, purpose-built storage in companiable shared rooms (maximum five, mostly two to four) with single rooms from year 10, en-suites the perk for upper sixth. Friendly feel that makes boarding feel 'more like home than home', said one pupil.

While thoughtful range of activities and outings filling the Saturday afternoon gaps for full boarders when others head home, top of pops is procession of supermarket delivery vans 'to sixth form houses' stresses school (Ben & Jerry's soothing the exam nerves no official school meal can reach, apparently). Highlight, pizza Tuesdays, when 'it's BOGOF night,' explained senior pupil.

Background and atmosphere: Ticks all the right boxes. Promotional literature, some daintily served in tiny beribboned boxes, is so appetising that you're hard pressed to know whether to read it or serve it with after dinner coffee. Posh and Catholic? 'Yes,' says OG, without even a millisecond's pause for thought. But that was then. Much more inclusive now, says head, down in part to her own far from privileged background, practical results including new-look, entirely washable uniform (smart blazer and tartan skirt all hers, deputy head responsible for sports kit featuring natty pink stripe on trackies.)

School is set ('nestled', says school) – downy image somewhat countered by reality of weighty-looking main building in best Victorian red-brick – in 700 acres, home to cattle, ponies, occasional Muntjac deer and assorted topiary, and extending to local station, drive alone a mile and a half and with enough land to spare for every pupil to have own smallholding (none of this 'you in your small corner and I in mine' nonsense here).

Moved here in 1940s, 100 or so years after foundation of Convent of the Sacred Heart in South West London, stopped being nun-run in 1980s when first lay head appointed, though still part of the Sacred Heart School worldwide movement.

Buildings vary in appeal, original stable block augmented with inoffensive modern additions including agreeable chapel with striking stained glass windows (original is now the art room).

Appearances frequently deceptive. Archetypal 1970s block of apparently little promise big on enchantment within, from extensively revamped classrooms – most neutrally nice, pockmarked notice boards last hurrah of long vanished posters – to highlight of delightful dining room, done up to the nines and even into double figures. Food (once 'awful', said pupil) improved out of all recognition

Ticks all the right boxes. Promotional literature, some daintily served in tiny beribboned boxes, is so appetising that you're hard pressed to know whether to read it or serve it with after dinner coffee

and now as nice as the décor, everything freshly cooked or chopped – none fresher than pedal-powered smoothie maker – sittings abolished as room for all (though sixth formers don't queue up). Thumb print log in ensures anyone missing a meal swiftly picked up – pupils' weight and height regularly checked, too. 'Phenomenal,' said a pupil.

With breakfast served in separate dining room (has own below stairs, slightly weather-beaten entrance below imposing main reception) and regular deliveries of cereal and bread to boarding houses, supplies are plentiful and good, we're assured, even if common room cupboards seemed rather bare by mid-afternoon.

Spotless everywhere but not clinical, occasional sprawl of bags, one hanging off handle of table football game in year 9 common room, circular seating in one of boarding houses another favoured dumping spot.

Common rooms vary, some with stronger institutional whiff than others, lower sixth version particularly nice, with big windows and convivial seating with sofas positively crying out for company.

Pastoral care, well-being and discipline: Spontaneous hug and outpouring of exam worries by sixth former to teacher during tour of school said everything you need to know about quality of relationships between staff and pupils, icing on cake the good cop/great cop relationship between head and deputy, latter, like head he complements, wreathed in parental praise. 'Always smiling, really involved with the girls,' said one.

That said, pays to mind not just your Ps – preparation, punctuality, presentation, politeness, personal responsibility (the five classroom-based expectations) – but your Rs as well. Respect for others, ourselves and the environment plus 'responsibility for our actions' all feature in the behaviour code, on top of faith, hope and social justice (we paraphrase).

Transgressions lead to (and almost always end with) detentions, escalated to withdrawal of privileges, assistance with domestic tasks and – rarely – suspension, removal or expulsion.

Peer-selected prefects, known as ribbons (after sashes they wear) help maintain status quo. With low key burgeoning jollity in revision session instantly quelled by look from supervising teacher, probably not too much of an uphill struggle.

Pupils and parents: Good spread of bus routes packs 'em in from Croydon hinterlands to Sevenoaks, while delicate balancing act with international pupils (make up around a third of boarders) from countries including Hong Kong, China, West Africa, Spain and Mexico (around a quarter of total) ensures no monocultures dominate. Blend creates 'lovely' atmosphere, thought former pupil, a current parent praising (rare) lack of fuss over appearance. 'Even sixth formers will have hair pulled back in a knot because there's nobody to impress.'

Somewhat changed from the days when, with parental permission, older pupils had leave to smoke, midnight feasts also tacitly accepted. Still unchanged, however, is the end product – pleasant, principled girls who, in keeping with best of Catholic educational principles, aren't just doing it for themselves but giving back to the world as well. Unwanted tuck goes to local food bank, these days (what would Bessie Bunter say?).

OGs often span the generations – one in, all in. 'Grandmother, great aunts, aunts and endless cousins attended. Bond that was formed so long is very strong and special,' says OG. Though heirloom education suffered bit of a blip in recent years, school now doing far more to woo alumni, courtesy of assorted publications – kudos to 'The Wold' for pun-free environment: 'Wold news' or 'Wold-wide community' all successfully avoided – and events. Judging by numbers of pupils who mention family links, seems to be working.

Pleasant, principled girls who, in keeping with the best of Catholic educational principles, aren't just doing it for themselves but giving back to the world as well

Entrance: Most enter at year 7 (60 places – school's own exam, looking for Sats level 5, with the occasional 4), further 20 join in year 9 and sixth form, occasionally also in years 8 and 10. Reaches out to those in need. One pupil, disoriented after previous school closed and initially reluctant and last minute newcomer in year 10, now wouldn't be anywhere else.

Popular sleepover event for year 5s also helps school sweep for those with behaviour or social communication issues (may be better served elsewhere) though, if able to cope with the pace, 'we won't rule out the rather unusual,' says head.

Approximately two candidates to each place. We like their requirement for well-rounded pupils with 'a genuine interest in education in the broadest sense of the word' (no laser focus on exam results alone, thanks very much).

Six formers will need minimum four Bs, two C grades at GCSE (though in practice will need to set sights rather higher, with As in desired A level choices). Current school reports also count.

Exit: Not everyone will make it to sixth form, hazard signs appearing early, year 10 exams now held in March so stragglers can be helped and alternatives researched in case results don't come good in year 11.

Post-GCSE brain drain to Charterhouse, once the big temptation ('was only the ones whose parents refused to let them go who stayed,' says OG), now halted. Many of top performers now staying on, though will 'inevitably' lose a few to rival attractions of the IB (Sevenoaks) and boys (almost everywhere).

Leads to broad spread of degrees at (mainly) quality destinations – as likely to head for anthropology at Manchester as economics at Durham, with nine to Oxbridge in 2015 and Hong Kong and US unis (Ivy League and others) also exerting growing appeal. Bulked up careers department stresses gamut of future options, policemen and soldiers attending annual careers fair as a satisfying counter influence to lure of cookery school and fashion journalism.

Typical year group can produce teachers – 'two of naughtiest friends ended up in schools,' says one OG – designers and a 'something in the city' or so. 'An all-rounder type of place,' reckoned former pupil.

Money matters: Not prodigiously endowed, reliant on bank loans and donations (we liked website urging former pupils, euphemistically, to connect or re-connect with the development office). New award to support OG's daughter at the school and £500 post-school scholarships, though less than eager beavers unlikely to be successful, what with requirement to 'consider their contribution to Woldingham during their time at the school' before applying.

Remarks: Delightful school with pupils to match, benefiting from first class leadership and a realistic day school option for anyone within striking distance of Clapham Junction. While not a place for academic no-hopers, ideal for above average (and often well beyond) who prefer teaching adorned with dollops of TLC.

Woodcote House School

62

Snows Ride, Windlesham, Surrey GU20 6PF

01276 472115
info@woodcotehouseschool.co.uk
www.woodcotehouseschool.co.uk
C of E

Ages: 7–13
Pupils: 99
Boarders: 38 full, 28 flexi
Day: £16,350 pa
Boarding: £21,750 pa

Headmaster: Since 2009, Mr Henry Knight BA in classical civilization PGCE MEd (40s). This is the first and only school he has worked in. Joined as an English teacher in 2003, a complete career change after running corporate hospitality for Berry Bros. 'As part of that I set up a wine school and found I enjoyed imparting information and became sure education was what I wanted to do,' he says. He saw an ad for a junior English teacher and house master at WH and the rest is history. Paid his dues as head of department, then joined the senior management team and took on several greater responsibilities before eventually replacing proprietor Nick Paterson when he retired as headmaster.

Mr Knight is the first head from outside the owning, and still very involved, Paterson family, but because he has been entirely home grown and nurtured by his predecessor, he is so imbued with Paterson culture that you could believe he was actually a family member. The transition has been, by all accounts, painless. Doubtless helped by his time at family firms Berry Bros and before that Fortnum and Mason, Henry is entirely au fait and comfortable with the dynamics of such businesses. Also, he

has not made, nor is looking to make, any major changes. 'It is vital that the ethos remains as it is,' he says.

'Mr Nick' Paterson is now on the teaching staff and always on hand to advise when asked. There is no board of governors, instead an advisory board which sanctions any capital spending or change to the feel of the place. So great continuity prevails, and parents pleased about this. 'He's basically a chip off the Paterson block', said one mother. And we'd be remiss not to mention his right hand men, deputy heads David Paterson and Andrew Monk. Generally parents feel he and this new senior management team have brought a fresh impetus to the place, making improvements here and there, rather than instigating a wholesale overhaul of things. Quietly spoken, commands respect, he's no-nonsense, but 'caring' and 'genuine', say parents. He still fits in some English teaching here and there, where he is known as 'inspiring and funny,' and clearly loves what he does.

In common with several staff families, HK and his family all live on site, actually about 10 yards away from the main school building, so he is basically permanently on duty and always on the go. Wife Susannah deals with all matters domestic, including running a team of (very young-looking) matrons, as well as looking after the couple's three children. 'We might as well live in a goldfish bowl,' says HK cheerfully. So quite sensibly they head for the hills during school holidays, actually Cornwall, for a complete restorative getaway. Has evidently made time for some keep fit of late as he looks nothing like his website pic.

Unapologetically focused on doing its own thing – even the unusual brown and yellow school uniform seems a manifestation of a school confident in its own skin

Entrance: No linked schools or significant feeders. ('Wish there was a pre-prep,' said one mother). All quite laid back. Non-selective, but will want to meet you and your son to ensure school and boy will suit each other. Some boys will have been on a list since birth, others rock up mid-term somewhere along the line. Most families are from London and Home Counties. In essence, the school is looking for boys who will put something into the school. Will take the odd hard luck story, a boy who has been bullied elsewhere or got lost in a larger set up. Head has a 'conversation' with prospective pupils and their parents, and will suggest a chat with the SENCo if it seems appropriate – nothing more formal than that. 'We are not going to say, in effect, "you are not clever enough for our school", but you have to be robust enough to cope,' explains HK. 'We want boys who don't mind getting their knees dirty. I wouldn't say we don't want sissies or prissies, but we want boys who want to be boys.'

There is a scholarship morning each March prior to September entry for boys joining the school as day pupils or boarders between years 3 -7. The owning Paterson family put up the equivalent of two sets of boarding fees (introduced to mark school's 150th anniversary) and divide as they deem fit – five boys could get 20 per cent of the available cash, or two boys get the lot, or sometimes nobody gets anything – school does not give them away for the sake of it. Must spot a spark or talent, academic, musical or sporting.

Exit: At 13 to all the top-notch public schools, from Ampleforth to Winchester, with clutches of academic, music and all round scholarships won. Lots to Sherborne of late, plus of course Eton, Harrow, Wellington. Parents given lots of guidance on future schools – evidently a strength of this place.

WH parents are not always chasing Eton and down the list schools. It's all about what is best for the child, and plenty of other factors are considered. 'So the list of schools WH boys go on to does not always reflect the actual academic achievement,' said one parent. And any leaver will not have heard the last of Woodcote. Legend has it that popular long-serving master Colin Holman – a modern day Mr Chips – has been known to drop a note to many of the boy's new senior school housemasters when he remembers a nugget of useful information about them, to the effect of 'If he's like this, try this'.

Remarks: Superb example of that dying breed – the thriving family-owned school. Idiosyncratic – you will either 'get' this school or you won't. Sceptics ask where the owls are kept, but its parents and boys are so glowing in their praise it's unreal. Feels like a proper country prep, although it's just 40 minutes from London. Combines top notch teaching with tons of outside activities so that the boys are both mentally and physically challenged every day. But also makes time for them to do their own thing, so they are happy and flourish. Nice balance of nurture and push.

Unapologetically focused on doing its own thing – even the unusual brown and yellow school uniform seems a manifestation of a school

confident in its own skin. Several parents mentioned how their sons had blossomed at this school, developing their personalities and interests. 'We aim to turn out a young man with good manners who is well-rounded, honest, trustworthy and friendly,' agrees HK.

You will see at a glance that this school isn't splashing your cash on fancy facilities, though new theatre is due for completion in 2016 – the place is delightfully worn at the edges. It really does look as if 100 boys have the run of the place. There's a relaxed feel, plenty of rough and tumble, all part of its charm. Not precious, but quite a cocooned existence. Known to sort out an odd bod or two.

Set in its own 30 acres, including some attractive woods, the main building is Regency and hits you with a real sense of tradition and history – ask about 18th century highwayman, Captain Snow, when you visit. But school has been in its present incarnation since 1931 when it was bought by the Paterson family. Old boys would definitely recognise the place – and that's the idea. 'The Paterson family is very strong and not swayed by fashion. They know what they want to provide and are very good at doing it,' explained one parent. Healthy sprinkling of old boys have their sons here.

Pictures of former pupils line the walls, and many of them were clearly recalled by Paterson matriarch Angela (Nick's mother) when we bumped into her during our visit. And the main thoroughfare, 'Red Lane', is a literally well-trodden path of black and red tiling, pitted and undulated from the patter of boys' feet over the years. Then the dining hall, where whole school, pupils, staff, visitors, all eat together, is decorated by the honours board and pictures of school founders. As they sit chatting together boys are clearly in a stable, traditional environment and confident about talking to adults.

Lessons are relaxed, but industrious. None of the staff 'just teach', they all wear a number of other hats so the boys see their teachers all the time, as much outside the classroom as inside it. Hence no forced formality about the classroom setting, but all is most respectful – staff exude an air of relaxed authority. Still boys scramble to their feet when visitors enter the classroom and to walk through the grounds with a staff member is to be met with a cacophony of 'Morning sir, morning sir'. Very small class sizes, average 10, never more than 14 and just four in the scholarship class we visited – having fun with the Kubla Khan. Fairly holistic approach to teaching as staff tie in topics across subject areas, so that talk of battlefields in history will link to their locations in geography. Staff more like synchronised swimmers, rather than everyone ploughing up and down their own subject lane. Parents full of praise for an enthusiastic staff always pushing for excellence.

None of the staff 'just teach', they all wear a number of other hats so the boys see them all the time, as much outside the classroom as inside it

Long day (8.20am to 6.10pm) for day boys, furthest of whom travel around 20 miles to school. First thing every morning is prep – sensible move as boys are nice and fresh and aren't able to get help from parents. Not a whiff of an interactive whiteboard around the place and HK says he is currently rather conflicted about the role of ICT – never a huge deal here, where teachers largely prefer projectors and coloured pens. 'Many schools will find their fancy ICT suites defunct as everyone clutches hand-held devices like iPads now', he says. (Not that school has those either.) 'ICT is certainly a subject in transition and I need to decide what stance we will take'.

Nothing state-of-the-art about other facilities either, though the boys we met described them as 'good' – 'we've got everything', said one. It's a bit scruffy and ramshackle in places, but not because nobody cares, rather it's just rather battered in places as a result of hundreds of boys kicking around the place – it's clearly a home from home for them.

Woodcote is able to accommodate some special needs and has a dedicated SENCo to handle boys on the autistic spectrum, dyslexia and EFL. About 20 boys (but a fifth of the school, remember) have some type of learning support, for which their parents pay extra. Languages taught are French and Spanish – a significant Spanish entourage among the pupils and Nick Paterson is a fluent Spanish speaker. A few boys from Thailand and Russia and some 15 per cent of Forces families, who particularly appreciate that the place is properly focused on boarding (38 full and 22 flexi boarders), so that weekends are busy and boys are far more than simply 'minded'. School keen to get the UK/overseas balance right. Very good relationships between the boys themselves and then between themselves and their teachers. The overseas boys tend to spend exeats with their more local friends, leading to an informal exchange programme.

Years 3 and 4 are housed in a separate Juniors building to facilitate a slow integration into main school life. Lots of praise for junior head Mrs Woodall; 'She is so very kind to my sons,' said one mother. Similarly, year 8s are given a taste of teenage life when they spend a term during their final year living in Dominies House – within the grounds, but away from the main school and set up to give year 8s some preparation for their life to come at public school – not least a taste of going to and from school each day.

Parents struggle to put their finger on a stand-out subject – 'It's all fantastic', said one mother. 'Whatever the talent, they will bring it out' – but music and art mentioned several times. A Woodcote boy beat 13,000 entries to come second in The Sunday Telegraph/Saatchi Gallery prize. And if your son plays an instrument, however badly, he will perform – this place is big on performance opportunities. 'My heart was in my mouth as I saw my son approach the piano, knowing that he'd only been learning for a couple of weeks,' recalled one parent. Not much timetabled drama, but usually a production per term. Staff write the plays – they seem to enjoy it, though it's probably also a neces-sity to find parts for so many small boys.

The philosophy here is that it is good to be a big fish in this small pool. One mother with several boys at the school felt strongly that each of her sons had found an inner confidence at Woodcote. 'I don't mean they are cocky, in fact they are more polite now, but simply that they've all formed quite distinct personalities and developed a love of study that definitely wasn't there before'.

While things are rather cosy inside, outside the school the boys are spoiled for space, with 35 acres of grounds to run about in, and are encouraged to try out a huge range of outdoor activities. Boys are even kicking about on Rip Stiks during break. From the usual cricket, football and rugby, to the more unusual CCF, bushcraft and even clay pigeon shoot-ing (for older boys) there is masses on offer. School takes its sport seriously and reckons to punch above its weight when taking on other (almost always larger) schools – has only lost 20 per cent of its fix-tures over the last five years.

The philosophy here is that it is good to be a big fish in this small pool. One mother with several boys at the school felt that each had found an inner confidence

Keen on outdoor education, Mr Knight is considering a 'very small' smallholding, and an outdoor pizza oven is also on his wish list. Shame more use not made of on-site swimming pool – but boys seem too busy with other things to be very bothered about this.

And fears that a non-sporty boy might flounder in this place are apparently unfounded as more indoor types can make the teas and help the par-ents park their cars on match days. 'In fact my incredibly non-sporty son even got a few games

with the B team – all the rubbish players do,' said one mother. Other activities for the less physically inclined include archery and golf and plenty of indoor pursuits, even a turf club.

School has a refreshing 'let children be chil-dren' attitude and is happy for them to cook outdoors sitting around a campfire – not in a cav-alier way, but just acknowledging that they will enjoy a few safe risks. Think Just William updated for 21st century. So not surprising to hear that these happy, busy boys sleep like logs. And of course with 75 per cent of pupils boarding, they sleep at school in clean and cheerful accommodation – small dorms with sea blue walls, punchy primary-coloured duvet covers. Largely settled for the night by 8pm (9pm for older ones), older boys three to a room, more as you go down the year groups, but even larger dorms divided into little 'pods' to give a homelier feel. All tidy. A fairly basic common room full of bean bags for when they want to collapse.

Sky Sports available along with controlled access to TV, phones, play stations and associ-ated electrical detritus of modern life, but school would far rather they were outside or generally more gainfully employed – and they usually are. Lovely old-fashioned insistence that, Skype and emails notwithstanding, boys will write a proper letter home once a week. Weekends (starting after Saturday morning school) typically include sports matches against other schools, an outing and a service in the school's own chapel (a charming building – apparently an early flat-pack of the type originally destined to be shipped out to missionar-ies in the 1800s).

Parents are welcome to attend matches and chapel and lots do. In fact we were surprised to see quite a number of parents at a predominantly boarding school – even though several of them were actually parents of day boys dropping books in or sorting out for their sons to stay on for some or other evening activity. There's a full programme of popular Friday night entertainments including visiting speakers – recently a sports commentator and a seven peaks climber. Many day boys do ask to board in the end, so that there are more day boys in the lower school and only one or two by year 8. 'My son doesn't even always want to come home for exeats, he is so happy at school,' said a parent. School offers a graduated approach to boarding, three nights as well as seven, but this is aimed to be an introduction to boarding rather than a babysit-ting service, although it would be flexible about the odd night here and there.

Staff all casually dressed when we visited, including the head as he showed prospective par-ents around – no airs and graces here. You won't get a fresh paint-type royal tour, but will see the place warts and all – the showers, the worst dorm (the last awaiting refurbishment) and maybe even the popular Warhammer dungeon.

Very accessible and welcoming of parents – none of this waving them off at Waterloo in September and not seeing them till Christmas. Parents swing by if they are in the area and teachers happy to respond to 'Can I have a quick word' during a match afternoon in favour of any formally structured pastoral system. 'Pastoral care is fabulous', said one parent. 'You drop the boys off without a worry'.

Not flash or fancy; old fashioned in the best sense of the world; 'Traditional with a modern twist?' offered one mother. Warm and inclusive, quite a gem. A school with a heart and soul where boys will definitely be boys.

Worth School

Paddockhurst Road, Crawley, West Sussex RH10 4SD

01342 710200
information@worth.org.uk
www.worthschool.org.uk
RC

Ages: 11–18 (boarding from 11 for boys, 13 for girls)
Pupils: 591; sixth form: 235
Boarders: 229 boys/73 girls full, 4 flexi
Day: £14,820 – £21,825 pa
Boarding: £18,780 – £30,825 pa

Head Master: Since September 2015, Mr Stuart McPherson, previously a housemaster at Eton College and teacher of English. He took his bachelors degree at the University of Western Australia before completing an MA in literature and religion at Newcastle. He has also taught at Sydney Grammar School. He is married to Johneen, who is the director of studies at St Mary's Ascot, and they have four children.

Academic matters: All about 'academic worth' says the relevant section on school's website and you really can't blame them for indulging in the occasional pun. School has fair share of bright buttons. However, not all are 'are desperate high flyers,' thinks parent. More are having to gain altitude though, what with school upping the ante with six GCSE B grades or better required to make the cut for sixth form. Essential 'to stand realistic prospect of university success,' reckons school. 'Definitely becoming more academic,' agreed one mother, with slight regret.

Offers fully formed dual systems post-16, taught in class sizes averaging around nine (18 in the school as a whole). IB, currently taken by around a third of sixth form, pulls in some locals each year, drawn by rarity value and has strong European appeal (though formerly strong contingent from Germany has waned following changes to education system there). IB results averaged 35.5 points in 2015, ahead of world average. Popularity may increase further now IB subject choices are a closer match with A level options (psychology is the latest to be added).

In 2015, 30.8 per cent A*/A at A level and 64.7 per cent A*-B. A levels continue to be exam of choice for the majority and a non-negotiable for some international students with specialisation already in their sights (maths and science for Chinese pupils, for example).

Sciences have been experiencing distinct off season, biology in particular, psychology broadly similar, with physics and chemistry probably not the best version of themselves, either. It's accounted for by status as third choice subject for many pupils, says the school, which stresses this is no longer the case and is also at pains to point out decent sprinkling of top grades. Also speaks of a 'renaissance' with sciences the choice of a third of current year 12 cohort.

However, plenty of strong subjects including history, art and religious studies, languages in general starting to pack in the boys 'like you wouldn't believe,' comments staff member.

School doesn't shirk from shock of the new, or newish, with economics flourishing (felt to be good route to a crisis-defying well paid job) and government and politics A level on the way in. Unusually no DT, though with design element absorbed into art and successfully so, helping to spawn at least one budding architect in the process, doesn't need to be, thinks head. Ditto engineering which 'we incorporate into science and mathematics.' Lines on the sand are media and film studies. No snob factor involved. 'Just wouldn't be popular.'

GCSE results also very respectable with 50.4 per cent A*/A in 2015. Pedagogues span the age range, some so unnervingly youthful you want whatever they have sprinkled on their bedtime cocoa, others long haul troupers, including one who has featured 'in every school photograph for the last 40 years, even the faded ones,' said pupil.

Have fair share of idiosyncrasies, presentation-focused English teacher responsible for high density notice-board achieving concours standard symmetry (writing quite literally on the wall), language specialist much admired for proselytising Spanish by highlighting party culture rather than demographics (yawn) as well as ways with vocab, word for 'potion' indelibly printed on IB student's memory following mime involving coffee granules and juice.

Overall, broadish palette of ability shades well catered for from the Oxbridge gang (about three or so a year) to the minority who don't have higher education in their sights, in line with one of the plentifully quoted St Benedict's dictums that the strong should have 'something to strive for,' the weak 'not be overburdened.'

School doesn't shirk from shock of the new, or newish, with economics flourishing (felt to be good route to a crisis-defying well paid job) and government and politics A level on the way in

Something school is definitely up for when it comes to support. International contingent are well served by EAL department which concentrates on weighting lessons towards nuance decoding – vital in science and maths exams where word games are all part of the fun (or perhaps not, judging by levels of concentration in EAL science class, ears almost audibly straining to grasp finer points of examiners' habits).

Learning support department doesn't venture much beyond 'dyses' in mild form, Asperger's ditto, as 'we don't have learning assistants in the classroom,' (screening for all in year 9). Individual or small group support by withdrawal (often replacing language).What it does do, it does well, though: parents speak of children 'transformed' by support.

Day to day helping hands plentifully outstretched, felt pupils, sixth form learning prefects who run sessions in range of subjects, including Latin are popular with younger gang as can have edge over teachers who 'don't have the experience of teaching themselves,' thought one.

More formally, anyone falling seriously behind will be supported through GCSEs with involvement of house tutors, learning support and addition of extra lessons in the hope, rarely unfulfilled, that galvanising effect will be sufficient to propel them into the sixth form. On rare occasions it doesn't, school will suggest search for suitable plan B school post 16.

Usually does the trick, think parents. 'Takes all comers, gets the best out of most children and they achieve their potential,' reckons one.

Games, options, the arts: Idleness, said St Benedict, is hostile to the soul, a message taken to heart here, particularly when it comes to sport. Website oozes Catholic take on muscular Christianity (a six pack, at least) featuring video that cuts away to reveal rugby team pitting strength against giant grass roller (and winning, naturally: it'll be a jumbo from nearby Gatwick Airport next). Deceptive, however, as you don't have to be terrifically sporty to enjoy it here, say pupils. Though football is finally acquiring the kudos supporters feel it deserves, rugby (which also musters six senior teams) continues to loom large on the sporting calendar.

School, thought one parent, is 'astute' at picking its opponents, middle rather than top rung, success consistent – with several unbeaten teams – if not always earth shattering, a few 'mixed' and 'disappointings' sprinkled through the end of school reviews (particularly good at quarter finals...). However, 'we're still really bad,' agreed group of pupils, cheerfully. On the plus side, there's no in or out crowd, change from days when rugby heroes were school idols (and life wasn't altogether plain sailing for less hearty). 'Completely gone, now,' says school. Pupils and parents agree. 'Friends can share emotional similarities even if interests are completely different,' thought articulate sixth former. Low stress environment allows sport and arts lovers to have their fill, others preferring not to do either with tolerance for all.

Midweek afternoons given over to colossal range of activities which range from chess, very successful with substantial input from keen father, to community service

Attitudes haven't softened at the expense of choice. Plenty for die hard fanatics to get up to in the way of must-have team sports that tick all the participation boxes. While it's non-negotiable sport for all two afternoons each week and for Saturday fixtures 'not always popular with day pupils and weekly boarders,' most esprit de corps stuff is largely optional beyond year 9, 'though they like us to be in teams,' thought girl. Aerobics, fencing, golf and riding mop up those seeking a personal challenge, the perhaps slightly euphemistically entitled multi-sports catering for those who may not be. 'There's a lot of sport on offer but if you don't want to do it I don't think you have to,' thought parent.

Some sporty girls feel slightly short-changed as they're in a minority and therefore not stretched enough, thought a mum. Something school 'could do little about ... but will be rectified in the natural course of events as more girls come up through the school,' and benefit from 'excellent teaching.'

Gourmet facilities include assorted courts (smart Astroturf firmly padlocked, presumably against ovine marauders) as well as eight hole golf course. Nearby sports centre offers athletics tracks and 50m pool (would be even better if school had its own, thought a parent). Access to pitches the other side of busy 'B' road is via new bridge, following tragic death of a pupil there in 2011.

Two sports halls, smaller very slightly dingy; larger, approached through front door so heavy that even spectators could end up with a decent six

pack, kitted out with decent fitness suite. Somewhat off-message vending machine in foyer, stacked to the gunnels with confectionary and drinks and thoughtfully putting back the empty calories that exercise has taken out, is being restocked with healthier options. (A second, in sixth form house, will retain sugar as principal ingredient).

If sports don't trigger necessary inspiration, terrific array elsewhere (billed as – wait for it – 'Worth extra' – groan) should do the trick. Drama includes three plays for different age groups in the summer term with lots of Shakespeare (added treat is array of beautiful costumes, many borrowed from the National Theatre). Music also strong, helped by super recording studio and Mac-rich room to hone technical and composition skills as well as sensibly soundproofed rock room for band rehearsals. Forty per cent of pupils have individual instrumental or singing lessons, orchestra (quite audibly not an earsore) particularly praiseworthy for size and boy participation. Abbey Choir, which sings weekly mass (website features a nice bit of plainsong) ditto.

Midweek afternoon given over to colossal range of activities which range from chess, very successful with substantial input from keen father, to community service: 'pupils are taken to charity shops....' (to serve, not for sale) as well as 'invasion games' (you have been warned).

Some, such as choir and jazz club, are vetted with auditions; most are entrée libre, many designed for IB compatibility. D of E-worthy, too, driving lessons apparently counting as a credit-earning skill – who knew? – and school, as a licensed centre, able to run and approve awards, popular trips (South America a favourite haunt) adding an edge of glamour.

Creations, some selected for display at the Saatchi Gallery, include orchid-like shapes along wires and a sculpture with the precarious delicacy of a scaled up Jenga game

Sparky individual achievements, too: sixth form are 'influential role models', says prospectus. Not half, with posts including public relations prefects (surely a first) whose duties include scouting for pupils able to take visitors on guided tours. Further down the school, one year 9 pupil has self-published own fiction, originally prep that outgrew the exercise book/took on a life of its own.

Creativity a-plenty elsewhere, too, with two wonderfully big art rooms, generosity of seniors' space influencing scale of artwork – few miniatures here. 'Means you aren't compressed,' says pupil. By way of demonstration, there's vast, decorated tree trunk, donated to the school and apparently taking root in art room. Pupil creations, some selected for display at the Saatchi Gallery, include orchid-like shapes strung along wires, while floor level delights include a sculpture with the precarious delicacy of a scaled up Jenga game and meticulous, technically brilliant paper and wood confections with concertina folds at crazy angles, like Escher on hallucinogens. Like pupils' poetry, seem to plumb otherwise hidden emotional depths.

Boarding: Boarders (vast majority full, 230 boys to just over 70 girls) have well designed bedrooms, tidy but not unspeakably so – boys' gloriously free of après-trainer whiff – fours and fives to a room, dropping to two in year 13; star of the show the solo accommodation for year 13 boys in smart, self-contained Gervase House, the only one to blend day and boarding pupils, and amply conveying undergraduate feel (more upmarket than many a uni) complete with tiny but perfect en-suites.

St Mary's, sole girls' boarding house, is a delight with well thought out bedrooms, duvets adding flashes of pink to light wood sea, and a common room you actually want to spend time in, best feature 'the pit' – lowered hearth area used for house mass and picnic style meals but, alas, never warmed by roaring fire, vetoed by health and safety.

Parents hope houseparent, just leaving, will have successor equally rich in humour and discretion, from curtains ('you'd be surprised how many don't close them') to conversations (office, just off quiet room 'isn't very quiet' so hears 'everything – and amazing what you pick up.')

Thoughtful touches include washing machines for 'emergencies, delicates and underwear,' says school. Girls only, however, as no boys so far have expressed urge to do own washing.

Background and atmosphere: De haut en bas, literally so, with two main groups of buildings taking up 25 of the site's 500 acres and separated by hill steep enough for twice daily ascents to form basis of daily fitness routine.

At the foot, approached by grand entrance (ornate electric gates, gryphon-topped portico, though you have to nip round the corner for commanding views over Downs) there's the stately pile originally built for Cowdray family and acquired by Benedictines, school's founding order, in the 1930s to mop up pupil overspill from Downside, becoming a separate school in the 1960s.

Teaching, meanwhile, goes on at the summit, school's very own mini Parnassus, with standalone main teaching block (a solid 1980s construction shortly to be extended) housing maths, humanities and languages together with serious looking learning resources centre (solid shelves and workaday

displays suggest books as study essentials first, imagination firers second).

It's next to tranche of buildings, home to performing arts, science and the Pitstop, a small café-style eaterie (main low-ceilinged refectory – slightly apologised for; 'it is what it is,' says member of staff; much improved by paint job, mint green replacing previous appetite suppressing mustard yellow – is down the hill). They're clustered in loose extended courtyard arrangement, centrepiece a clock tower so wantonly Disneyesque you half expect it to sprout features and break into song.

Dotted through the site are the school houses, all nine of them, which come at you from every direction. Seen as hugely important centres of r and r for day as well as boarding pupils, they enable everyone to let off steam, enhancing sense of camaraderie as 'you spend a lot of time with your houses even if you're not boarding,' says pupil.

Communal rooms (too many to count – we did try) are swankiest for oldest, who also have study rooms, mainly shared if day, some solo if boarding, while younger day pupils stash stuff in lockers, tops cunningly (and frustratingly) sloped to prevent leaning towers of casually dumped textbooks.

While they take the same newspapers (in assorted shades of blue: Grauniad fans may pine) houses vary enormously in style, ranging from Rutherford House's touch of the Bridesheads (parquet and imposing marble fireplaces no whit disturbed by table football machine and mini bank of computers) to St Bedes's, the newest house, so far away from the main drag that only rooftop is visible on location map, which comes complete with soft furnishings co-ordinated in browns and greens (nicer than it sounds) and eco focus, much lauded though little understood. 'Didn't realise we even collected rainwater,' said pupil.

Pastoral care, well-being and discipline: Insulating tranquillity radiates both from surroundings and what one mother described as 'gentle, smiley' monks, though not a place to come for those with real issues with Catholicism or deep-rooted opposition to introspection.

Spiritual side is 'the heart of the school,' says one of many delightful pupils, impact felt most strongly in tolerance for others with soul-searching high up the agenda and a feature of student magazine which, like a thought for the day compilation, is jam-packed with worthy thoughts about happiness and love and, pick of the bunch, what nuns do all day (pray, apparently).

School temperament is accordingly mild. Even traditional post-exams photograph eschews standard shrieking, certicate-grasping, mid-air riot in favour of a nice, quiet group of girls and boys standing in semi-formal pose, looking slightly embarrassed at being singled out for glory.

Reflects notion of competition as being 'based on the idea of sharing excellence'. Though a possible handicap if opponents' idea of competition is to slaughter the opposition (school team recently lost debating competition because it was 'too politically correct' says magazine report) seems to damp down house on house aggression despite ferocious-looking face paint applied, warrior fashion, before girls' matches. House music competition is the only event capable of triggering anything approaching blood lust 'because we organise it and it involves everyone,' felt pupil.

Pupils and staff spoke highly of events that blend spiritual with social rather than adversorial dimension in keeping with admirable Benedictine tradition of hospitality. 'Food is a very good reason to mix,' says housemistress. Civilised, too, with wine allowed for sixth formers on Feast of St Benedict 'but only with food,' and over 18s allowed to nip down to the local pub with permission (though hadn't been a single request when this reviewer arrived at the start of the summer term – unusual, thought member of staff). Many house parties, too, (not in the format most parents know and dread, we're assured) as well as 'young ladies' lunches' (young gents' versions, too) where pupils from same house or year group foregather in delightful panelled room to swap news and views in civilised surroundings.

Results in easy going, clique-free contact

Parents and staff spoke highly of events that blend spiritual with social rather than adversorial dimension in keeping with admirable Benedictine tradition of hospitality

between year groups, think pupils. 'So refreshing compared with my previous school where the year 11s wouldn't talk to the year 10s. Here, everyone does,' says one recent arrival, who also praised unofficial problem sharing – girls' friendship issues the unsurprisingly regular hot topic.

Tutor groups, house linked except in sixth form, meet regularly; chaplains, one per house, are also useful listening ears. Pupils also felt that lectio devina – Benedictine tradition of reading sacred texts aloud and discussing themes raised – can be effective route in to problem sharing, akin to grown up circle time. 'You can raise worries – it's a personal thing,' felt one.

School recently reported that behaviour had hit an all-time high, and pupils we talked to felt there was little in the way of badness beyond missed home-work deadlines, with normal sanctions consisting of warnings and a series of ever-lengthening detentions or, in the case of 'rude or inappropriate' use of phones (a worry as 'can access everything' unlike computers where school Wifi blocks undesirable sites, including Facebook) minimum 24-hour confiscation.

Not much obvious kicking over the traces in pupils we saw, who seemed born to walk rather than run (though sloping terrain is admittedly a fabulous natural deterrent), although some current models of decorum were, we were assured by pupils, former wild cards who have been 'subdued' as they come up through the school, ending up 'unrecognisably well-behaved.' Schools stays on top of things, confirmed parent. 'I don't get the impression that children drift off the radar. They're not allowed to misbehave or become lost sheep.'

Pupils and parents: Fair few Worthians wanting to spread educational joy to second generation, substantial overseas contingent, some from hyper-Catholic parts of the world. One Brit parent, while accepting school's need to get bums on seats, felt that 'you need to make sure that that percentage doesn't get out of hand.'

Riches represented amongst parents, rags less so, though neither end of the spectrum dominates. 'You'll see the odd Rolls Royce as well as the odd beaten-up car,' thought one mother.

Lots of parent socialising, from informal curry nights to large scale events including masked ball fab summer fair complete with fairground rides, jazz band and a profusion of strawberries. 'A very jolly scene,' thought one.

If all goes according to plan, pupils will emerge from the Worth experience 'wise [and] intellectually astute,' (according to prospectus, size defiantly non-standard and so glossy you could skate on it). They are, as well (so much so that it was a relief to hear off-duty younger girls described as 'very screamy' by sixth former). One parent, with ultra-serious child, felt distinctly frivolous in comparison.

Pupils take great pride in individuality and proclaim absence of a particular school type, backed by staff who thinks school should 'allow people to grow into themselves – a pupil's inner talent could mean that you haven't mastered any one thing but are good at lots. We're 600 weird and wonderful individuals and we've got to learn to get on with each other.' We admired fighting talk, though couldn't help but notice girls' near identical hairdos, most tumbling manes of mermaid-length tresses, varying in colour, finish as high gloss as prospectus.

Star former pupils include actor Robert Bathurst and publisher Sir David Bell, though sports dominated, from Tim Hutchings (athletics) to Tom Symonds (racing) and rugby (Nick Walshe). All admirable stuff. However, as Old Girls start to make their mark on the world aided by slickly run alumni society (which includes a 'Worthians in Property' group), we'd hope for more variety and quirkiness in years to come.

Entrance: Oversubscribed, says school, which advises registration two years in advance. Around 120 places a year, 40 in year 7, 60 in year 9 and 20 in year 12, occasionally in other years. Feeder schools many and various, majority independent, fair few Catholic (though not all) and also include local state primaries and secondaries, though with school bus network puts Tunbridge Wells, Haywards Heath and Horsham within reach.

Just shy of 20 per cent from overseas (Gatwick a 10 minute taxi ride away), some non-native English speakers, support offered though must be sufficiently fluency to cope with normal lessons.

We admired fighting talk, though couldn't help but notice girls' near identical hairdos, most tumbling manes of mermaid–length tresses, finish as high gloss as prospectus

Currently pushing convincing case for 11 plus entry by citing early leadership opportunities on offer to the brightest and best in years 7 and 8 when academic effort plus helpfulness and embodiment of Benedictine ethos can land a handful a place on school council or as prefects. Fine for boys, who can board from year 7 (with three nights a week flexi option), though it's day places only until year 9 for girls (might account for very low representation in current year 7 – just six out of 25-strong year group).

Exit: Up to a fifth leave after GCSE. Around three or so to Oxbridge most years (one musician in 2015), wide range elsewhere recently. Lots to Russell Group and, in recent years, Harvard, Trinity College Dublin, University of Amsterdam, Bocconi (Italy) and Central School of Speech and Drama. Economics, maths, business and management all popular, interesting combinations (history and theology, maths and philosophy) also a big feature.

Sixth formers praised careers advice, helpful email updates arriving at least twice a week, approach informative but low pressure. Many (more than average, it seemed) were postponing university applications with official blessing, gap years viewed as logical make your mind up time.

Money matters: Fees about on a par with nearest competitors. Good scholarships (music, academic and all-rounder) offering up to 40 per cent of fees (music also includes free instrumental tuition). Means tested bursaries are also available though total fees remission generally capped at 50 per cent. Local, bright Catholic children can also apply for St Benedict's Scholarships – fully funded day places, one in year 7, two in year 12.

Remarks: 'At some schools, it's all about how clever or hearty and sporty you are – not here,' thought one parent. Another, with experience of several other leading Catholic schools, had no doubts. 'It's the pick of the bunch.' Encourages reflection, not out to dazzle, producing thoughtful pupils, distinctly themselves and quite definitely Worth it.

Yehudi Menuhin School

Stoke d'Abernon, Cobham, Surrey KT11 3QQ

01932 864739
admin@yehudimenuhinschool.co.uk
www.yehudimenuhinschool.co.uk

Ages: 8–19
Pupils: 80; sixth form: 30
Boarders: 71
Boarding: £41,928 pa for those not on music and dance scheme

Headmaster: Since 2010, Dr Richard Hillier MA PhD (50s). Previously headmaster of The Oratory Preparatory School, in Oxfordshire and, before that, head of classics and housemaster at Repton. Not the obvious choice for the rôle, following Nicholas Chisholm's 22 years at the helm. Has taken quite a leap from head of a rural RC prep school to headmaster of an internationally renowned musical centre of excellence. A former chorister (at King's School Peterborough, then the only state cathedral school), he read classics at St John's Cambridge, where he sang in the choir, then teacher training and doctorate (on Arator: an obscure late Christian-Latin author) at Durham, where he was also a lay clerk in the cathedral choir. Still sings as a freelance baritone soloist (when asked!) and is involved in academic research. Married to Elaine: exams officer, school archivist and alumni contact. They have two grown-up sons – both attended Repton and went on to Cambridge – and a parson russell terrier. Day-to-day musical management in the hands of the school's head of music, Malcolm Singer.

Academic matters: The most specialised of the country's specialist music schools, the Yehudi Menuhin School provides tuition on strings (violin, viola, cello, double bass, and guitar) and piano. 'We operate on a plane above the other music schools,' said one proud pupil. Half the school day is taken up by music (with practice on top) leaving a small but reasonable window for academic subjects. Most pupils take seven GCSEs (sometimes five if they come from abroad), three AS levels and two A2s. The range of subjects is small – English, modern languages, maths, science, music and history – as are class sizes: mixed age groups of between six and 12 pupils. Children in years 3-6 have all lessons with one teacher.

We sensed more emphasis on academics than on previous visits, when academic success was considered largely a matter of luck given the miniature year groups. Exam results certainly impressive when you consider that academic ability is not part of the admissions process. In 2015, 76 per cent A*/A grades at GCSE and 71 per cent at A level. Chinese and maths (and of course music) GCSE results particularly stand out; one student from Hong Kong, one from mainland China and one from Taiwan. Small computer suite with Sibelius software for composition and other computers dotted around. Many pupils have own laptops. Music library stacked floor to ceiling with sheet music and CDs. Also traditional library for other subjects and fiction. Extra English tuition for 15 of the overseas pupils; three pupils with mild dyslexia.

Games, options, the arts: Music dominates both scheduled and free time, starting with a civilised hour of post-breakfast practice (rather than the dawn call we've seen at other music schools). Three or four more hours fitted in during the day (less for the younger children; more for the eldest). Two hour-long instrumental lessons a week on one's main instrument. All string players also learn the piano. Pianists may also learn a string instrument or harpsichord (no organ, but a new chamber organ delivered in 2013 has opened up new possibilities). Lunch time concerts twice every week in the school's fabulous concert venue, The Menuhin Hall. Orchestra, soloists and chamber groups perform regularly in school, around the country and even abroad (school provided half the orchestra for a recent Menuhin violin competition in Beijing). Double bass players attend Royal College of Music junior department on Saturday mornings: 'It's important for group playing experience as they don't get as much as the other string players from chamber music here.'

Swimming now compulsory once a week in newish indoor pool. Table tennis, football, running, badminton, dance, yoga and tennis available, though not played against other schools. Sports that can cause hand injuries (eg basketball, volleyball) are abjured. A bit of Alexander Technique for all. Art part of the curriculum and of high quality; popular for evening relaxation after all that music. Drama also big here – these are not kids who shun the limelight. Growing take-up of D of E – from bronze to gold.

Boarding: Nearly everyone boards. The youngest can go home at 4pm on Fridays; other locals can nip home after Saturday morning school. Fab boarding house for 11-19 year olds with a piano in every room (most are doubles). Pupils live in 'pods' rather than along corridors. The oldest girls live in a small sixth form block. Live in houseparents, and house tutors who cover evenings and weekends.

Background and atmosphere: Yehudi Menuhin founded the school in 1963, 'to create the ideal conditions in which musically gifted children might develop their potential to the full on stringed instruments and piano.' Five decades later, little has changed. While numbers have grown, the ethos remains the same, and the great man's posthumous presence seems to have grown. Buried in the leafy grounds of the Victorian gothic Music House (once owned by a member of the Hansard family), the school's music library contains much of Yehudi Menuhin's own collection. Pupils and some staff have started quoting Menuhin, in the manner of a spiritual guru, prefacing comments with 'Yehudi Menuhin believed..' or 'As Menuhin said..'

The effete world of classical music can be more brutally cut-throat than heavyweight boxing. School tempers this by eg rotating positions in the school orchestra

Dining room enlarged and refurbished since our last visit – offers good, healthy eating – and school continues to grow. No noisy huddles of gossipy school-kids – even lunch was a relatively sober affair. Basically, they know why they're here, they want to be here, and if that means an amount of isolation to get in their two to six hours' practice, then so be it.

Pastoral care, well-being and discipline: Caring but relaxed. For a school that requires such rigorous self-discipline, YM gives its charges an unexpectedly loose rein. Teachers on first name basis. 'We're not a sanction-based school,' said the head. School day finishes at 6:30pm. Saturday morning school for all, except the 8-11 year olds. Behaviour not a big problem, though adolescence throws up the usual issues and the occasional pupil has been suspended. Teachers take pains to keep competition in check. It may come as a surprise to some that the effete world of classical music can be more brutally cut-throat than heavyweight boxing. School tempers this by eg rotating positions in the school orchestra (there is no one leader and even hotshots

may have a turn at the back of the second violins). The pupils support one another and provide an enthusiastic audience. Still, for children who have been used to being big fish in less august ponds, the adjustment to a school where everyone is outstanding cannot always be easy.

Age is not the boundary that it is at most schools and YM prides itself on functioning like a family, with older pupils looking after the younger ones and all working and playing together. That said, uneven year groups can make boarding awkward in younger years. When we visited there were two children in year 5, two in year 6 and six in year 7. 'We take the children who NEED to be here', our guide told us. More mundane criteria, like keeping a balance of instruments and number of available boarding spaces, also come into the play. Increasing trend for 18 year olds to stay a further year to make the most of continued government funding (which carries on to 19). With no pesky national exams or academic lessons, this extra year can be fully devoted to music.

Pupils and parents: Totally non-denom, very broad mix of backgrounds (no parents pay full fees) and countries of origin. Roughly equal mix of boys and girls. About half are UK residents (though many of these were born abroad – overseas families often move to the UK lock, stock and barrel so their children can attend the school). Above all, this is a tiny school. Numbers in most year groups far too small to be true cohorts. Esteemed alumni include Tasmin Little (violin), Nigel Kennedy (violin), Nicola Benedetti (violin) and Paul Watkins (cello).

Entrance: Pupils can join at any age from 8 to 16. Three stage application process ('long and drawn out,' said a pupil). Candidates first send a DVD to see if they 'are even in the ballpark'. If yes, they're then invited for an audition and interviews. The last hurdle involves spending three days living at the school. NB The middle stage is often omitted for overseas applicants. School says it is looking for potential rather than achievement but we suspect both come into play. 'We have applications from lots of well-drilled kids from the Far East but they're not always right for this school. Sometimes we suggest they come back to us in a couple of years. We're not just looking for ability, but something extra.' Also strives for a cultural and international mix. Lack of academic aptitude not an obstacle to entrance. Nor is eccentricity.

Exit: Vast majority to conservatories, either in the UK or abroad. Very few fail to make the grade and regular termly assessment quickly identifies pupils who are 'unsuitable or not interested'. Some pursue music courses at university if they plan to compose rather than perform. Destinations in 2015 range from the Royal College of Music and the Guildhall School of Music and Drama to Mozarteum, Salzburg, Hochschule für Musik, Theater und Medien, Hannover and the National University of Singapore.

Money matters: Fifty-two pupils qualify for an aided place under DfE Music and Dance Scheme (sliding scale according to parental income). School aims to provide bursary support for the rest on a means-tested basis until they qualify for the DfE scheme. Very few paying full whack. Fundraising campaign launched in 2013 in concert (!) with the school's 50th anniversary. The aim is to be truly needs-blind (funds will also help build new music studios). Non-British EU pupils are eligible for sixth form funding only. 'Postgraduates' are funded in addition to the 52 government scholars – so staying on is a good deal for both them and the school.

Remarks: This is no environment for the faint-hearted child or the over-ambitious parent. Don't be tempted unless this is something your child desperately wants – and then wait a year or two. Having said that, it's lovely, refined and nurturing within a harmonious conservatoire setting with a large dollop of eccentricity thrown into the mix.

East of England

Bedfordshire
Cambridgeshire
Essex
Hertfordshire
Norfolk
Suffolk

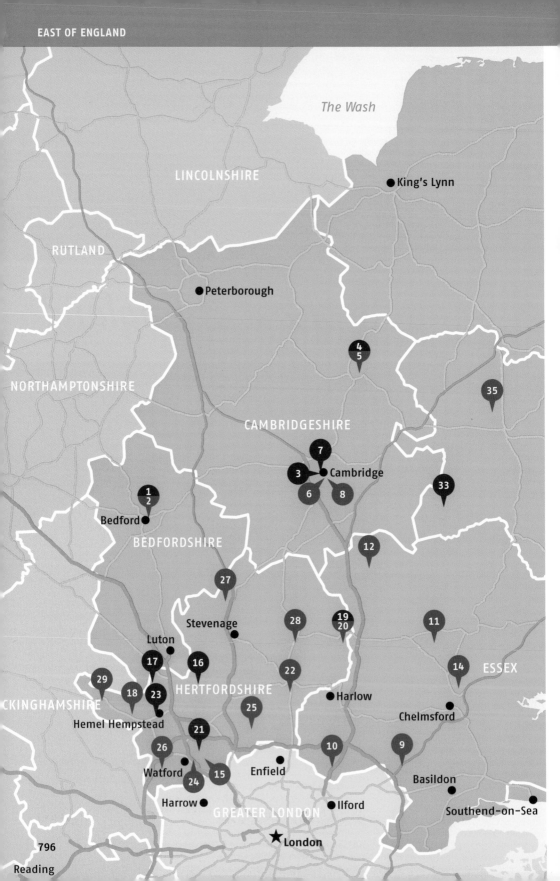

The Wash

LINCOLNSHIRE

● King's Lynn

RUTLAND

● Peterborough

NORTHAMPTONSHIRE

CAMBRIDGESHIRE

4
5

35

7

3 ● Cambridge

6 **8**

1
2

Bedford ●

BEDFORDSHIRE

33

12

27

Stevenage ●

28

19
20

11

Luton ●

17 **16**

22

14 ESSEX

29

18 **23**

HERTFORDSHIRE

● Harlow

Chelmsford ●

CKINGHAMSHIRE

Hemel Hempstead

25

21

26

Watford ●

10

9

24 **15**

Enfield ●

Basildon ●

Harrow ●

GREATER LONDON

● Ilford

Southend-on-Sea ●

Reading

★ London

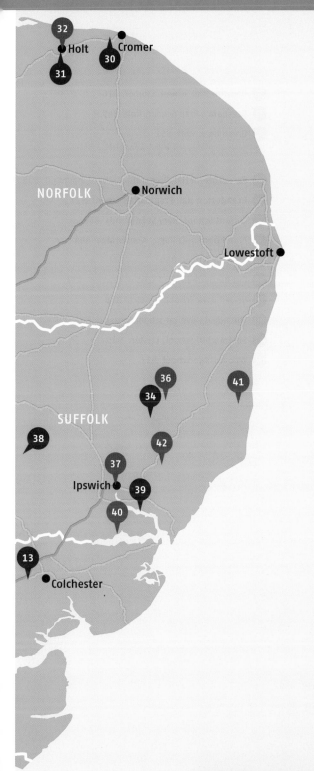

32
Holt
Cromer
30
31

NORFOLK
Norwich

Lowestoft

36
34
41

SUFFOLK

38

42

37
Ipswich
39

40

13
Colchester

| 20 | 40 | 60 | Miles |

EAST OF ENGLAND

Aldenham School

Elstree, Borehamwood, Hertfordshire WD6 3AJ

01923 858122
admissions@aldenham.com
www.aldenham.com
C of E

Ages: 11–18
Pupils: 548; sixth form: 170
Boarders: 43 full, 106 flexi
Day: £14,847 – £20,790 pa
Boarding: £20,481 – £30,471 pa

Headmaster: Since 2006, Mr James Fowler MA PGCE (50s). Educated at Merchant Taylors' School, Northwood and New College, Oxford where he was a choral scholar. Previously head of sixth form at Brentwood School and deputy head at Highgate. Permeates every facet of school with his relaxed charisma and understanding of what makes parents and pupils tick. Unusually, interviews every candidate with their parents before admission. Is he interviewing the parents as well as the child, we asked? 'Of course,' he says. 'I spend a lot of time helping people understand what we are and are not.' And it's to this level of mutual soul searching that he attributes the happy, enthusiastic nature of his cohort in evidence all over the school, almost all of whom he knows by name and who claim that their voice is 'genuinely heard' by him. It's not just the children who are happy with their leader, either. Parents describe head as 'always available', and 'very good at resolving issues in the right way,' adding that 'his attitude filters down to all the staff.'

Definitely not a head chasing glory in the league tables – and one totally at ease with this status; a breath of fresh air in the ferociously competitive North London landscape. Keen to provide a totally different experience to his urban competitors as applications from London families increase, and determined that his charges feel 'secure and safe'. Single-mindedly focused on school providing 'the best possible pathways' for each student, regardless of academic prowess. 'We celebrate successful entry to art school in the same way as entry to Oxbridge,' he says.

Lives on site with wife and two sons.

Academic matters: Situated in the heart of UK's spiritual home of secondary academia (Habs, Merchant Taylors', North London Collegiate et al), Aldenham stands apart with its unpressurised vibe and mixed ability cohort. Perhaps not a destination for the single minded scholar, although pupils say they are strongly encouraged to hit their own personal best; 'the natural spread of ability makes for breadth and roundedness,' according to head. Although those bright enough to get to Russell Group universities – and occasionally Oxbridge – will do, it's immediately evident that it's the journey that defines Aldenham rather than the destination.

A respectable 23 per cent of A*/A grades at A level in 2015 with 48 per cent A*-B, and 36 per cent of GCSE

799

examinations at A*/A grades. Many subjects have now moved to IGCSE to stretch brighter students, who are also recruited into small study and discussion groups such as 'Les Philosophes' with visiting speakers including Anthony Grayling enabling them to exchange ideas and broaden horizons. 'Parents trust us with children of all abilities,' says head.

Small class sizes of maximum 22 and often down to 10 in sixth form, with setting from year 7 in maths and science. Eleven GCSEs the norm with a broad range of subjects available, from the traditional ('the brighter students tend to gravitate towards sciences,' says head) to dance, textiles and DT. French, German, Spanish and Latin on offer in the languages department. Non-traditional subjects on offer at A level include psychology, media studies, government and politics and computing. Parents and pupils appreciate extra revision lessons at lunch times, after school and even on Saturdays laid on in the run up to public exams. University conversations start in year 12, with a series of events including visiting professionals brought in to 'give insights' into the world of work. Pupils feel well supported and guided through uni application process, although one or two parents felt that school could secure more top level places for the brightest if things were slightly slicker.

Good provision for SEN run in dedicated area by full time SENCo, with around 10 per cent on

University conversations start in year 12, with events including visiting professionals who 'give insights' into the world of work

the register – mainly catering for mild dyslexia or dyscalculia although can deal with mild Asperger's and recently sent one such child to Cambridge. One-to-one teaching rooms well used by overseas pupils requiring EAL support.

Games, options, the arts: In a setting that needs to be seen to be believed – over 110 acres encompassing woodland, playing fields plus full-sized Astro hockey pitch, tennis courts, dance studio, well-utilised weights room and an enormous sports hall (recently resurfaced) plus manicured cricket pitch that lies literally at the heart of the school ('the pavilion is one of my favourite spots,' says head) – sport is integral to life at Aldenham and thrives at all levels, from the most elite to the 'just for fun'. It's football, hockey and cricket for the boys, no rugby, while girls focus on netball, hockey and rounders. School known for its footie prowess, with a handful of boys training with top academies, and also embryonic links with Southgate Hockey Club, but parents say it suits students less inclined towards team pursuits well too. Options include zumba, archery, sailing, tennis, athletics, Eton fives, judo and climbing on its climbing wall – in the words of one parent: 'all that's missing is a swimming pool.'

Two compulsory activities a week, ranging from bell ringing, horse riding and film club to a very popular CCF, make for a long school day which for most ends at 5.30pm. This gives school a unique boarding atmosphere, even for those who do not take advantage of the marvellously flexible boarding on offer. Aldenham is 'synonymous with trips' according to pupils, who enthuse about the 'amazing experiences' they have had on CCF trips to Holland, language trips including a Spanish trip to Cuba, geography to Iceland, choir to Rome and a three week charity volunteering trip to Malawi.

Outstanding art department, unanimously acclaimed by everyone from head to parents and pupils, and so popular that school recently built a superb new art cabin to accommodate the large numbers electing to pursue art A level. Fabulous work on display: huge canvasses, three dimensional installations and sculpture with as much rigorous preparation and development of concepts on show as final works. Pupils say that head of art won't accept anything less than excellence and parents report offspring joining school 'unable to draw' and emerging with A grades. Dedicated textiles room also displays high quality fashion design and DT labs are hives of industry, complete with 3D printers in motion.

Music thrives, with bands, orchestras and choirs galore, run by 'fantastic' and 'passionate' musicians, according to pupils. As with sport, there are opportunities for musicians of all levels to participate, with pupils enthusing that the fiercely competitive annual house music event (compulsory participation for all) is one of the highlights of the year. All year 7s offered opportunity of one term's free music lessons on the orchestral instrument of their choice, leading to many taking it up more seriously. Futuristic music technology equipment puts department very much in the 21st century.

'Really strong' drama on and off curriculum, headed by 'inspirational' head of department who clearly drives excellence and pushes boundaries. 'We're into serious drama,' she says – school refreshingly veers away from the usual hackneyed shows and rarely produces musicals, mainly delivering productions of the Sophocles and Brechtian variety, oft performed in the purpose built 150 seat theatre, but sometimes out in the grounds or as a promenade, which are 'just fantastic,' according to parents. A handful of students are members of the National Youth Theatre and it's not unusual for one or two each year to head off to destinations including Central School of Speech and Drama or LAMDA, and these applications are taken seriously – head says that in the year school sent three students off to drama school and three to med school, both were supported and celebrated in equal measure.

Boarding: Around 30 per cent of the school community participates in boarding life at some level – enough to lend it a 'proper' boarding ethos without any trace of 'them and us' between boarders and day pupils. Boarding starts in year 7 in a small co-educational junior boarding house with 25 beds. No full boarding at this stage, meaning that cohort tends to be exclusively UK based with vast majority never having boarded before. Pupils enjoy a 'home from home' environment here – but still relish having a 'lot more freedom' when they move into one of the four main single sex boarding houses (three for boys and one for girls), each with its own strong identity, that shape the school.

Head keen that students 'experience boarding as part of their overall education,' hence provides excellent flexibility with boarders able to stay from just one night to, for a minority of mainly older, overseas students (some 25 per cent of boarders), full time. Up to sixth form, majority are reasonably local though, with boarders heading home at weekends to homes in north London, Herts and Bucks. 'Terrific' live-in house parents supervise their charges in spacious houses – not the most luxurious

we've seen, but functional (well-equipped kitchens and study spaces) and welcoming with plenty of nooks and crannies for down time and socialising. Boys dorm in fours until year 11 when they double up, with girls mostly in twos and threes then single rooms in sixth form. An ongoing programme of renovations is brightening things up.

Evenings see boarders participate in the clubs or activities of their choice, or gather in the art block, library, media suite or gym. Most popular nights to board in sixth form are Tuesdays and Thursdays when the bar opens and pizza is served in the wonderful sixth form centre. Sunday brunch is 'the best meal of the week', attended by most staff who live on site, plus their families as well as weekend boarders, and whilst there are weekend outings, trips and activities on offer, quite often students, having had a long week and sports fixtures on Saturdays, just 'want to chill.'

Background and atmosphere: Founded by brewer, Richard Platt, in 1597 after Queen Elizabeth I granted him letters patent to build 'the Free Grammar School and Almshouses' at Aldenham for elementary children. The Brewers' Company then had a controlling interest in the school and links remain strong. Original Tudor buildings demolished in the 19th century to make place for two new schools – one providing an elementary education for the local population, the second a grammar school for fee-paying boarders. School now occupies a prime position in protected green belt, attracting pupils from affluent local villages like Radlett and Sarratt, London suburbs such as Edgware and Stanmore and increasingly north London, with parents attracted by the fabulous country campus, handy coach services and inclusive ethos.

Main school building is Hogwarts-esque Victorian gothic with gables, tower and turrets, with additions – some more appealing than others – from subsequent decades. Most notable new facility is fabulous sixth form centre – all white walls, squidgy sofas and sliding glass doors offering panoramic view of cricket pitch – complete with its own coffee shop and bar where years 12 and 13 can socialise, study and generally commune outside of school hours. A few tatty corners in other areas, but plenty of up to date Mac technology and a luxurious feeling of abundant space that more than compensates for grubby paintwork.

There's an annual run on the last day of term for those brave enough, from Eros in Piccadilly to the school's statue

An extraordinary chapel (the largest consecrated building in Hertfordshire after St Albans Abbey) which can host entire school – and frequently does – lies across the road that bisects the school. Surprisingly welcoming, the Stanley Spencer altar pieces of yesteryear are but a part of school history now (sold to raise funds during the desperate 1990s) and an attractive ironwork cross and dove now dominates the altar. Despite the diverse religions of the school community (about 60 per cent Christian, 20 per cent Jewish and all other main religions represented) all attend chapel twice weekly to underscore the 'feeling of one community' that's so integral to the school. Beautiful panelled library complete with mezzanine level, spiral staircase and view of cricket pitch and miniature replica statue of old boy Alfred Gilbert's Eros. There's an annual run on the last day of term for those brave enough, from Eros in Piccadilly to the school's statue, just one of the many traditions that pupils say are 'a huge part of the school'.

Break times see pupils congregate en masse on the field with cross year group socialising in evidence everywhere ('we're like a family – everyone knows everyone,' said one happy pupil). Although not the most polished cohort we've ever seen, pupils without exception seem totally at ease with the school and are arguably one of the most sociable and understatedly confident bunches we've met. Quite possibly one of the happiest too. Girls now make up around one-third of the school – many join in sixth form – and school is content with this balance – 'we'd ideally like 35 to 40 per cent,' says head. Second girls' house planned for 2017.

Pastoral care, well-being and discipline: Parents report excellent pastoral care, thanks mainly to the system that places all children in a boarding house, even if they don't board, so staff have a close eye on everyone's well-being. Good sign that many boarders we spoke to live locally and board 'because we love it.' Food has been a small bone of contention although pupils say it is 'getting better'.

The usual disciplinary issues but in the main very few incidents. Suspensions for major breaches of rules (eg boarders driving off campus) but in the main little need to transgress as students given sufficient freedom to spread their wings.

Pupils and parents: Majority of pupils from a 20 mile radius. Lots of busy, professional commuters and London parents attracted by the flexible boarding uniquely on offer here – as well as the atmosphere that they say gives their children 'space to breathe', both literally and metaphorically. Mixed financial demographic – plenty of first time buyers and parents stretching themselves to afford Aldenham – with these children fitting comfortably in with those who can easily cover the fees.

Overseas boarders tend to be in higher year groups. Of these, around 30 per cent from Germany, then handfuls from China, Hong Kong and ones and twos from elsewhere. All are well respected and well integrated – boarding pupils embrace and relish the diversity of their peers. Around 40 boarders stay in school at weekends.

Entrance: Around 60 places in year 7 with between 15 and 20 of these taken by children coming up from on-site prep school and the rest made up of children joining from the state sector (40 per cent) and local 11+ preps. About 30 per cent of year 7 are girls. Another 25 to 30 join in year 9 from a vast array of preps, notably Lochinver House, Orley Farm, Northwood Prep, St Martin's and St John's and further afield The Beacon, The Hall and Davenies. Applicants at 11+ take papers in maths, English and reasoning with the addition of science and a language at 13+. Scholars are interviewed away from their parents.

Late arrivals come from other, more pressured, local schools – not always because they can't cut the mustard but mainly because they are looking for a school that's about more than exam results. And that, here, is what they find. Around 30 places available in sixth form.

Exit: Approximately 20 leave after GCSE to follow vocational courses or A levels elsewhere (mainly state schools or colleges) or to employment. A broad spectrum of destination universities reflects mixed academic intake, with about 20 per cent to Russell Group, a couple each year to art schools (often St Martins) and regular success with applications to top drama schools. Other degree courses tend to veer towards the vocational, many with a business/management focus. One or two to Oxbridge most years.

Money matters: Scholarships at 11+ and 13+ in music, art, sport, DT as well as academic, with a maximum of 15 per cent off fees awarded. Means-tested bursaries available.

Remarks: Head describes Aldenham as 'an extraordinary school for ordinary children' and we concur. An unpressurised environment such as this makes for some of the most contented pupils we have met, and self-motivated children can fare well academically too. Tread carefully if scholarly accolades are top of your wish list or if your offspring need stick rather than carrot, but if it's a rounded and happy child you're after, then Aldenham's definitely one to consider.

Aldwickbury School

16

Wheathampstead Road, Harpenden, Hertfordshire AL5 1AD

01582 713022
registrar@aldwickbury.org.uk
www.aldwickbury.org.uk
C of E

Ages: 4–13 (boarding from 10)
Pupils: 369
Boarders: 50 plus flexi
Day: £11,805 – £14,595 pa
Boarding: plus £28.80 – £35 per night

Headmaster: Since 2003 Mr Vernon Hales BEd (50s). Educated at Langley Park Grammar School and Exeter University, where his education degree majored in PE. After a year in the state system, he started his prep school career at Papplewick ('great fun') before heading off to New Zealand, becoming deputy head in its then largest boarding prep school. Returned as deputy head and boarding housemaster at Elstree School, then joined Aldwickbury as the school's fourth head. Partnered through entire professional journey by wife Claire, also a trained teacher and now head of marketing at school and 'traditional head's spouse'. Educated his two sons, now late teens, at Aldwickbury and The Leys, where they are full boarders.

Relaxed, warm and jovial with the boys, and 'very visible around the school', according to parents, he recently 'came out of retirement' to resurrect his passion for club cricket and harbours personal ambitions to become a good golfer (must be the stunning course surrounding the school grounds calling). Lives in the main school building and is proud of its unique local offering as a boys' (mainly) day school, based on a boarding school model. Recognises that although sport is very important to boys, he wants Aldwickbury to be an 'all round' school. He speaks with conviction about understanding the distinctive needs of boys in their formative years, describing Aldwickbury as 'philosophically a boys school.' Would like to increase school numbers very slightly 'without losing our small school feel'.

Entrance: Non-selective at 4, the school works with local feeder nurseries to ensure smooth transition for its youngest pupils as they join reception. Recently became three-form entry at the bottom of the school, with 15 to a class, due to increased demand for places. Maximum class size in pre-prep fixed at 18. Boys joining higher up the school are invited in for an informal session with their relevant year group head, where they are encouraged to talk about themselves and take tests in reading, maths and spelling to ensure they can access the curriculum. Means-tested bursaries available.

Exit: Vast majority stay at Aldwickbury until the end of year 8. School loses just a few each year at the end of year 6, 'for either financial or academic reasons', according to head. Feeds about half its boys into year 9 at St Albans School, 'a handful' each year with scholarships. Remainder to schools including St Columba's, Bedford and Haileybury. One or two recently to Eton, Harrow and Shrewsbury. 'The key is getting parents to choose the right school for the boy', says head. Parents confirm that he gives them a strong steer in the right direction.

Remarks: Situated a stone's throw up the hill from Harpenden's second (less chi-chi) high street in Southdown, Aldwickbury Mansion, which dates back to 1871 and is full of Victorian character (albeit with a few tired corners), became home to the school in 1948. It makes excellent use of its leafy 20-acre site and has sympathetically incorporated a number of modern buildings to create an appealing and well-functioning school campus. Main school building sits atop grassy terraces and playing fields, affording the head and his boarders a panoramic view of the school grounds. A separate purpose-built pre-prep department was built in 2001, providing the school's youngest pupils with a bright and cheerful base, where they can ease their way into school life without the rough and tumble of bigger boys.

Reception has its own safe haven outside with a small adventure playground area, plus trikes, bikes and a sand table – 'very therapeutic if they've had a tricky morning in the classroom', says head of pre-prep. School places a large emphasis on outside learning at this stage – 'we're not a forest school but we do take on elements of that ethos'. On our visit, reception boys were enthusiastically doing Victorian-style laundry outside. The pre-prep building is festooned with topic-related art and written work and has its own hall for assemblies, activities and performances.

Junior department houses years 3 and 4, when the school starts to 'encourage independence in a gentle way', including the introduction of a more formal uniform. Even maths classrooms are creatively themed and staff overall exude energy and enthusiasm, reinforcing the school's ethos of 'really getting boys'. One year 1 teacher quietly plays classical music CDs when she wants her class to concentrate, and – try it at home – it seems to work. Boys in years 5 to 8 move around classrooms for specialist teaching to prepare them for senior school life.

Lovely heated indoor swimming pool – well used, with weekly lessons for all from reception, plus early morning and after-school swim clubs. The ever-popular DT workshop ('we really look forward to coming in here', say boys) has the shed-like feel of a real man space and industrious pupils turn out quality projects from wind chimes to fruit bowls. Art room on the basic side but a broad spectrum of work on display showcases the boys' enthusiasm. The gym is in dire need of some TLC, but school now has an 'all singing, all dancing' £3.2m hall and music department, plus several new classrooms, 'to provide flexibility and accommodate growth'. Also boasts a gleaming modernised dining hall (food to be recommended) and library.

Ever-popular DT workshop has the shed-like feel of a real man space and industrious pupils turn out quality projects

Parents and pupils alike describe Aldwickbury as 'very friendly and welcoming', and the nurturing feel pervades the fabric of the school. 'Definitely not pushy', say parents uniformly, suggesting that league table watchers may want to look elsewhere. Boys have the knack of knowing when to be quiet (quite a feat in a dining hall of rumbling tummies waiting for someone to say grace) and when to let off steam. Confidence and manners, without arrogance, in evidence in all age groups.

A true 4 to 13 school. 'All year 8 boys have jobs' and are given responsibilities around the school, such as helping teachers get younger boys organised in the mornings and listening to year 5 boys read at lunchtimes. With around half the teachers male, the overall vibe is of a school where boys really can be boys. Year groups encouraged to mix at meal times, with lunch taken as 'sections' (that's houses to the rest of us). Boys compete throughout the year for the section cup, not just in their academic lives and on the sports fields, but also with competitions and challenges, including section Scrabble and top autumn favourite, the 'conker-tition'.

Majority of pupils from the immediate environs, with 50 per cent 'sharing the AL5 postcode,' according to head. Remainder from surrounding towns and villages. Very few from further afield. Overwhelmingly Caucasian majority reflects the local community. Most parents in the professions, many dual income, but a by all accounts a pretty grounded bunch and a number 'stretching themselves' to pay school fees. A parents' association set up recently to bring together parents, staff and boys and foster the school/community relationship. Events so far have included discos with local girls' school, monthly tuck shops with home-baked cakes and a dads vs masters cricket match.

French with a specialist teacher from year 1, with Spanish and German added to the mix in year 5 and Latin from year 6. Specialist teaching from year 3 for ICT, art, music and drama. Mixed ability classes 'by ethos' to end of year 5, although head admits to some 'subtle setting' from year 3 and parents of able children report extra work being given to ensure the brightest are stretched. Classes mixed at end of years 2 and 4 which some parents grumble they find 'stressful', although they admit the school 'normally gets it right'. Streaming introduced from year 6, with two or three classes and a scholarship class in year 8. This, however, is not always uniform in its structure – head is determined to 'start from the point of what's best for the boys'. SEN all in a day's work and good provision in place to deal with minor blips rather than more serious problems.

Music taught by male teachers from pre-prep onwards, which really 'turns boys on to learning an instrument', according to head. Around 160 boys from year 1 upwards take music lessons in a wide range of instruments. Abundance of musical groups to join, from choir to guitar groups, including the popular Aldwickbury Strings group, a collaborative effort between staff (including the bursar, a talented violinist) and boys. Drama is 'really important', says head, with participation in plays compulsory up to year 5 to 'build confidence'. Main school play, most recently A Christmas Carol, performed in the round, is optional in years 7 and 8 but most choose to take part, if not on stage, then in lighting or costume, with the occasional rugby player taking charge of make-up.

Sport is the lifeblood of the school, with specialist teaching twice weekly from year 1 and boys from year 3 up having a daily games lesson. Competitive football, swimming and skiing are 'excellent', says head, and boys regularly compete at national level. Team fixtures for all from A-E teams, so everyone gets a ride on the school minibus and a shot at sporting glory. Colours awards on offer for stars of rugby, football cricket et al, but also for drama, music and citizenship, proving that heroes are not only found on the sports fields here. In the words of one boy, 'all things here are valued the same'.

Football, swimming and skiing are 'excellent', says head, and boys regularly compete at national level

Boarding almost exclusively flexi, with the occasional weekly boarder, but no provision for boys at weekends. The majority of those who board from year 6 are at their 'second home' (as they call it) two or three nights a week, with provision for 33 boarders at any one time. Once the plethora of after-school clubs has finished, there's more fun, with 'non-stop activities,' say boys, followed by weekly film nights in the cosy boarders' lounge and occasional events such as the popular 'chippy night' (one benefit of being so close to the high street). Functional dormitories sleep up to nine year 6 boys, with numbers dropping to four or five in the upper years. No phones with SIMs are allowed but, with all that's on offer, boys have got better things to do than phone home. With the majority of boys living so locally, most are here purely for the fun of it and speak wisely of their new found 'independence' and how boarding has changed them.

Day boys able to join boarders for breakfast from 7.40am and supper for a small cost – handy for commuting parents. All boys from year 5 up stay for prep until between 5.10pm and 5.45pm and there is an after-school club which can take pupils of any age up to supper time at 5.50pm.

Broad range of extracurricular activities to cater for all tastes, from chess, Lego or general knowledge club for the cerebral crowd to skiing, fencing or martial arts for those wanting to try their hand at something more physical. Loads of opportunities to get out and about, with trips aplenty. School makes full use of being on the capital's doorstep, with trips to art galleries and theatres and also ventures further afield (expeditions to France, Iceland and the much anticipated leavers' trip to Dartmoor). A schedule of evening seminars on topics such as 'the history of the Ashes' ('much more interesting than it sounds', says head) is in place for older boys and their parents, and a number of external learning sources are brought in throughout the year. When we visited, boys were buzzing after a visit from a 'mathemagician,' part of the maths week itinerary.

Barnardiston Hall Preparatory School

Barnardiston Hall, Nr Haverhill, Suffolk CB9 7TG

01440 786316
registrar@barnardiston-hall.co.uk
www.barnardiston-hall.co.uk

Ages: 6m–13y (boarding from 7)
Pupils: 220
Boarders: 24 full
Day: £7,635 – £12,735 pa
Boarding: £17,610 – £19,155 pa

Headmaster: Since September 2012 Tim Dodgson BA (history – London) PGCE (Durham). Forties. First joined the school as newly qualified teacher in 1992. Moved to Bedford Prep, returning married and with a young family to Barnardiston as head of history and pastoral care. After a brief sojourn as deputy head at Sedbergh, he returned again to Barnardiston as deputy, before stepping into the position of headmaster. His wife, Emma, also teaches at the school and both of their children attended before moving on to senior schools. The family live in the main school building. Has an easy-going manner, calm and a good listener – something of a foil for the principal's more extrovert style. Has no plans to move.

Principal and owner is Colonel Keith Boulter, Cambridge theology graduate and hockey blue (60s). Barnardiston is one of several schools and institutions run as a family business. Was headmaster from 1990, and despite passing the reins of day to day management to Mr Dodgson in 2012, he remains a force in the school, teaching mathematics, helping with games and choir work and followed everywhere by children, like the Pied Piper. Retains a certain bluff, military manner with great geniality and is greeted with wild

enthusiasm and respect wherever he goes in the school. 'Who has camped in the garden with their teacher?' he asks. A forest of hands goes up. 'Who acted in the play? ' – hands up again (slightly different lot). 'Who wants more homework?' groans and shouts of 'Not me!' His early career in the Royal Army Educational Corps and, later, administering Gurkha schools, has helped shape the school's philosophy. Married, with a grown-up family, and lives in the grounds of Barnardiston. His daughter is head of the pre-prep department and his three grandchildren all attend the school.

Entrance: Non-selective. Pupils accepted at all stages through the school. A number come up from the nursery (6 months-3 years) to pre-prep. No formal exam but previous school reports are looked at and the children meet the head. Taster days are arranged for older children who attend classes, whilst particular needs are noted, and referrals/advice given to parents. The school has provision for educational support and few children are not accepted. Limited bursarial help for overseas pupils and siblings.

Exit: Most go on to a range of local independents at 13 – the Leys, the Perse, King's Ely, Felsted, Framlingham, Rugby, a sprinkling further afield (Gordonstoun recently). One or two leave at 11 for local state schools. Good guidance is given to parents. 'We suggest they visit three schools, two likely ones plus a wild card,' says the head. Pupils all get to where they want to go – a few scholarships each year.

Remarks: A country prep with a strong, slightly quirky character, very much the creation of its owner, Colonel Boulter. With a rural setting, agricultural rather than chocolate box picturesque, it has a splendid indifference to the customary marketing gloss. Boarders live in the main building, an Edwardian villa, alongside the headmaster and his family.

Subject teaching takes place in the converted stables which surround the courtyard, and the purpose built pre-prep department. A series of Portakabins are still in use, though no one appears bothered; in fact, the pupils see the strengths; as one pointed out in the 'temporary' science lab, 'We never have to worry about dropping liquids on the benches – they are so old!' The decorative theme throughout is inspired by the Colonel's travels including elephants and giraffes, displays from Tutankhamen's tomb, wooden carvings, ornamental ponds and, unexpectedly, two full suits of armour standing guard at the end of a passage.

Indoor sports and ballet take place in a marquee (heated), supposedly temporary but no plans to change this. School has a small theatre with raked seating and facilities for sound and lighting – 'We all learn to do it as well as act' – and

productions are all-out efforts of the whole school rather than an elite group. Music, a particular interest of the Colonel, is well taught and popular; around 50 per cent learn an instrument.

> *The decorative theme is inspired by the Colonel's travels including displays from Tutankhamen's tomb, wooden carvings and two full suits of armour*

No formal gardens or prefects' lawns here; the grounds resemble an adventure playground. Approached by a drive full of potholes ('We know the fees aren't wasted on tarmac,' said a parent, approvingly), skateboarding is allowed, as are tree climbing and den building, there is a miniature railway, a bouncy castle – all tastes catered for. Announcements are made over a PA system, known as the 'bing-bong', that operates all over the school; slightly disconcerting at first, rather like a tube station, but pupils like it and think it is sensible.

A lot of parents are commuters and chose the school 'because the pupils seem so happy and relaxed, very different from London schools,' said one. 'Mine have all made tons of friends and have a crack at anything going,' said another, though also warning that 'it's not a place for namby-pambys.' (We think that remark is directed more at parents than pupils.) Adventure and independence encouraged from the outset with form sleepovers.

'We camped with our teacher in the garden when I was 6!' said one pupil, and this spirit continues up the school. Orienteering very popular (Prep National Champions), camping expeditions, and all team sports played with gusto. Long-awaited Astroturf is now installed. Parents welcome the unfussy attitude but warn: 'If you like things Just So and organised months in advance then it might not suit'.

Classes are small, average 14, and setting begins early in the key subjects. Latin and French from early on, though Latin is dropped in the top three years by some. Those who might struggle in other schools find areas where they can shine. 'The staff are brilliant at building confidence,' say parents, who approve of the less stressful approach. Educational learning support is provided in the special needs department (known as The Bridge). Needs range from an extra boost to cases at the mild end of the autism spectrum, dyslexia and dyspraxia. There is also EFL and support for gifted children. A few children have statements and are LEA funded but the school won't take pupils they cannot help.

Boarding facilities are on the top two floors of the main building. Though approached by a slightly depressing staircase, the facilities themselves are comfortable and homelike. Boys and girls occupy separate floors. Bedrooms, mostly four bedded, are light, well-decorated and some have en suite bathrooms. Rather posh bathrooms in fact – think department store loos – good lighting, warm and clean. Friendly matrons, who remain on duty until the younger boarders, at least, are in bed and asleep. Boys, who form some two-thirds of the boarders, also have a common room on their boarding floor with an enormous screen for weekend viewing. The girls have one in their bedroom but, I was assured, there is no signal so can only be used for DVD watching. Mobiles, for all pupils, are looked after by the school during the day and boarders are allowed to use them for only limited periods. 'Can be hard for some, at first, especially those from abroad, but we want them to join in real life here,' said the headmaster. Weekend outings to local towns/places of interest are arranged for those, largely from overseas, who stay in school. With notice, it is possible to remain through the half term holidays also. Occasional boarding is popular and encouraged towards the top end of the school, especially for those moving on to board at senior schools.

This is a tremendously jolly school where a sense of adventure is encouraged. Most pupils thrive and go on to do well at senior schools. 'We often hear of former pupils becoming prefects or house heads,' we were told. Perhaps not suitable for those with hearts set on scholarships to the top flight schools, but definitely worth looking at for those who appreciate a less stressful, unstuffy, purposeful atmosphere and a staff dedicated to the needs of its pupils.

Bedford Preparatory School

De Parys Avenue, Bedford, Bedfordshire MK40 2TU

01234 362216
prepadmissions@bedfordschool.org.uk
www.bedfordschool.org.uk
C of E

Ages: 7–13
Pupils: 387
Boarders: 18 full, 10 weekly/flexi
Day: £11,397 – £14, 934 pa
Boarding: £19,332 – £24,087 pa

Linked school: Bedford School

Headmaster: Since September 2013, Ian Silk (40s), previously deputy head of Bishops Stortford Junior School and former housemaster at Ardingly College. An English and drama specialist, brims with enthusiasm about all aspects of the school – most particularly the spectacular new theatre (2015) shared with the upper school and the town. Married to Sarah, with two sons both at the school – 'they are chalk and cheese,' he told us, 'but the school is brilliant for both of them.' Knows most boys by name – lots of heads do but this is a large prep – and has lunch with all new joiners in small groups.

Entrance: Mainly at 7+, 8+ and 11+. Not heavily oversubscribed but looking for the right fit, ability to keep up and fully participate in school life. 'At 7 some boys might not be there yet,' says head, 'but we encourage them to try again later.' Assessments in English, maths, NVR, creative writing, an inschool day – and that all-important report from

current head. Large contingent from nearby pre-prep and fellow Harpur Trust member Pilgrims and around 30 per cent from local state schools. Buses from Luton, Milton Keynes and Hitchin broaden catchment.

Exit: Almost all transfer to Bedford School with the odd exception departing for the state sector or, for international boarders, their mother country. No prep for CE or formal advice on other destination schools, but existing pupils sit the same test as external candidates for setting purposes. Parents report a seamless transition to upper school, with boys better prepared for workload than those joining from other preps.

Remarks: A boys' own paradise which simultaneously feels separate from and integral to the upper school and offers everything young boys could hope for, whatever their interests. In the space of one lunch time we watched boys hunting for creepy crawlies in bug hotels, singing with gusto in the junior choir, planing chess boards in the DT suite, creating games in the ICT suite, building sets for the school play, having a good old fashioned kick about – and of course, in time honoured tradition for a Friday, tucking into fish and chips in the school dining hall ('really good,' we were assured). Never a dull moment.

'Nicely contained' in a corner of the vast Bedford School campus, one of the main benefits of prep is that it enjoys unfettered access to the wealth of facilities of the upper school – as well as a fair few of its own. Classrooms ranging from the antiquated 'Inky' (incubator for fledgling Bedfordians)

to more modern purpose-built additions sit around a central Astro play area where boys let off steam at break times. A separate adventure playground adds to the fun – although there's so much else going on, we're not sure when pupils would get the chance to use it. Classrooms feel cosy in comparison to the overwhelming sense of space elsewhere. Science labs are well-equipped and art and DT outstanding. Super work of exceptional quality, themed to ignite passionate creativity amongst the all-male cohort by their inspiring male head of art (who doubles up as games teacher), festoons the interiors. We loved the Viking shields crafted in DT and the fabulous gargoyle masks produced in year 8 art. Not a still life in sight.

Outings include go karting, high ropes, bowling and cinema, often followed by a takeaway or one of the housemaster's legendary barbecues

It's rugby, hockey and cricket ('huge' according to head) on the sporting agenda, with a fully inclusive approach and school putting out as many as 18 competitive teams for fixtures, so everyone gets a ride on the bus and a post-match tea at least once a term, whatever their ability. Tons of music and drama to temper the testosterone. Hugely popular (and, crucially, non-selective) junior choir, plus chapel choir for years 5 and up, as well as instrumental lessons on curriculum for years 3 and 4. Great excitement on the dramatic front too, as all major performances now take place in what must be the most stunning school theatre in England – a brand new £7 million structure built (thanks to a legacy donation) on the grounds of a neighbouring Moravian church – altar, stained glass and tablets sympathetically incorporated.

Dedicated SENCo with two supporting specialists and strong emphasis on training whole staff to support individual needs (mild dyslexia and dyspraxia; a few with mild Asperger's). Around 20 boys receiving support. Close communication with upper school a great strength: 'we hand parents and children over individually so nothing falls between the gaps,' SENCo assured. Strong ESOL team caters for overseas students.

Boarding in purpose-built Eagle House for up to 32 boys from year 3 and up, although most start after year 5 as either flexi, full or weekly boarders. A real home from home feel, thanks in no small part to super houseparent couple, as well as plenty of nicely furnished, comfy spaces with lots of personal touches for boys to hang out after school hours. Spacious dorms sleep between four and eight boys, who make them their own with pictures, posters and duvet covers from home. When prep's finished (supervised, in dedicated room for all bar the year 8s), there's a homely common room equipped with computers, a kitchen for snacking and a basement games room with table football and pool on offer. Where boys find the time to use these facilities, though, is anyone's guess, as there's also a full programme of after-school activities each day to take advantage of. Mobiles and other gadgets allowed but must be put on charge in the prep room overnight.

Around half the boarders are either Forces or overseas (from mainly Russia, China and Spain), so there are plenty around at weekends once Saturday school (compulsory for all from year 6) and Sunday chapel are out of the way, to enjoy outings ranging from go karting or high ropes to bowling or the cinema, often followed by a takeaway or one of the housemaster's legendary barbecues.

'Zero tolerance' anti-bullying policy with clear protocol in place for inevitable – albeit rare – lapses. 'We show as much understanding to both sides as possible,' says housemaster. School counsellor available for boys to use for anything from home sickness to help with social skills.

All in all, a really super option for those looking for top notch day or boarding – as long as your sights are firmly set on an all-through education at Bedford. A kind, happy and successful school with the added bonus of a smooth transition to the thriving and successful upper school without the weighty stress of the 11+ or CE.

Bedford School

De Parys Avenue, Bedford, Bedfordshire MK40 2TU

01234 362216
admissions@bedfordschool.org.uk
www.bedfordschool.org.uk
C of E

Ages: 13–18
Pupils: 689; sixth form: 290
Boarders: 235 full and weekly
Day: £17,586 pa
Boarding: £28,761 – £29,745 pa

Linked school: Bedford Preparatory School

Head Master: Since September 2014, Mr James Hodgson (40s), educated at Wellington College and Durham (classics) before being scooped up on the milk round by Ernst and Young and spending a couple of years as a trainee accountant. In his 20s a cricketer hovering around the fringes of the professional game – and uninspired by the world of finance – wrote to Cambridge on the off-chance of a late place on its PGCE course and turned up trumps, meaning he could pursue his long term ambition of running a boarding house as well as playing regular top class cricket, ultimately earning a blue.

Spent six years teaching in Sydney before joining Tonbridge School as boarding housemaster and director of admissions. Latterly senior deputy head of Magdalen College School, Oxford. Impressed on joining Bedford by the boys 'completely at ease' with the staff and each other – 'presenting awards in my first assembly, every single boy shook my hand, looked me in the eye, smiled and said thank you – quite something for a large group of teenagers,' he says. At peace with Bedford not quite hitting

the dizzy academic heights of Magdalen but plans to up the ante a little 'for pastoral reasons – results are just a passport to the next level'. Passionate about boarding ('it develops the whole person') and ready to take on the challenge of keeping it thriving at Bedford. Parents feeling the effect of this already with the recent introduction of a full schedule of celebrations for leavers, including their own speech day followed by house events and a leavers' ball – 'a fitting end to a super education,' in the words of one.

PPE an interesting offer in year 10; parents praise 'inspirational' RS teaching. Outstanding work on show in art and DT

Youthful, energetic and 'really personable,' according to parents – not just a safe pair of hands for parents to hand their sons to, but dynamic, likeable and inspiring. Accessible to pupils – has open door for a period each morning where pupils can come to discuss anything. Presence at matches and performances (with the occasional personal note of congratulations to performers afterwards) noted and appreciated by all. Married to Rachel, with four teenage children.

Academic matters: Solid academics, especially given broad church intake and large proportion swept through from prep having joined at 7+. 2015

saw 61 per cent of GCSEs graded A*/A; 48 per cent A*/A at A level and 77 per cent A*-B, with an average IB score of 35 out of a possible 45 – testament to a focused and dynamic teaching staff ('second to none,' said one happy parent).

One hundred and forty boys join year 9 with about 60 per cent of these moving up from the prep. English and maths set from outset but rejigged along the way. Class sizes capped at 24, shrinking to a pleasing eight or nine for many A level subjects. All take 10 GCSEs, with around 30 per cent taking four full A levels in year 13 (mostly including further maths). Boys opt for either A levels or IB in sixth form. IB numbers 'a bit low' according to head with just over 15 per cent currently opting to take this route. School aims to boost numbers to around a third of the cohort.

Well thought out curriculum with separate sciences and all boys learning at least two languages. Maths and sciences extremely popular options at A level as well as good take up in geography ('a very good department,' says head) and economics. German, Spanish, French and Latin on offer in the languages department, with Mandarin available as a twilight option, but rather low take up of these at A level. PPE an interesting offer in year 10 and parents praised standard of 'inspirational' RS teaching. Outstanding work on show in the art and DT departments, with some mind-blowing projects on display in the year 13 workshop – no wonder so many move on to study engineering at university.

Overseas children in need of ESL offered extra language sessions in place of another language and about half of them take IGCSE ESL instead of English. Boys with SEN (mainly mild dyslexia or dyscalculia) given bespoke care with the department tailoring help according to each boy's individual needs. Seamless transition from prep school with boys and parents benefiting from a one-to-one handover with SENCo to ensure consistency.

Head acknowledges lack of strong articulation of sixth form – super facilities abound at Bedford yet no dedicated centre for years 12 and 13. Parents identified career support as an area in need of improvement – 'so much more that they could do' – and recent appointment of dedicated UCAS and careers specialist hopes to raise school's game in this area. UCAS application process highly praised, with parents barely needing to get involved in the process: 'exactly as it should be', although head hopes to up future Oxbridge numbers.

Games, options, the arts: Sport is the lifeblood of Bedford and although the list of recent accolades is too long to list (in all sports from rugby and cricket to swimming and golf), school maintains it's not just for the elite and says it offers all boys 'the same time on task' when it comes to training – the input and expertise from the directors of all major sports filtering down to even the lowliest of teams. Are less gifted boys afforded the same kudos as the macho sporty crowd, we asked one sixth former? Apparently yes, since the introduction in recent years of colours for art, drama and academia in addition to sport – a welcome addition signified by a colourful array of scarves – and special striped blazers for those awarded cricket colours. Parents, too, concur that school 'absolutely allows boys to be all-rounders'. It's a rugby, hockey, cricket school – with strong rowing too (how many schools have their own boat house on a beautiful stretch of the river Ouse?) but plenty of other options to choose from: you name it and Bedford

offers it, from archery or rifle shooting to pilates and fencing. National and international honours in all main sports plus golf and fencing, and boys have gone on to play for their universities and even their country in most sports played at Bedford, where the main challenge for staff is finding competitor schools strong enough to give them a good game.

Many boarders are former day boys fed up with the daily commute – parents love the fact that boys can 'grow with the school'

Music of a 'fantastic calibre' according to parents, with a state of the art, super modern music centre – designed by award-winning architect Eric Parry and apparently positioned opposite the pavilion so that the director of music can keep one eye on the cricket scoreboard whilst conducting the school orchestra. Choirs, orchestras and bands a-plenty, a brand new music technology suite, gleaming new fleet of iMacs (2014), a recording studio (Desert Island Disks with the head a recent highlight), rock room and inspirational recital hall – used for weekly performances by pupils and recitals from visiting professionals. Something for everyone and parents say even the most reluctant musician is inspired to join in. School's enthusiasm for making music illustrated by wild enthusiasm (parents and boys) for the annual house music, 'the best competition of the year,' by all accounts, which sounds like a cross between 20/20 cricket with boys, faces painted and fancy dressed, raucously chanting and cheering on their housemates, and young musician of the year ('as soon as the singing starts, everyone is silent,' explained our guide).

Opened in 2015, possibly the most stunning theatre we've seen in any school, built on the site of a former Moravian Church, with original features sympathetically included to complement the modern architecture – all exposed brick and floor to ceiling glass. Shared with the town, and able to seat over 280, the theatre not only hosts school productions (recently Shakespeare's The Comedy of Errors by the prep and Henry V by the upper), often in conjunction with Bedford Girls' School, but also productions by visiting companies. A full-time technical director takes care of special effects and shows boys the ropes with lighting and scenery.

A non-stop merry-go-round of extracurricular activities keeps boys busy outside of the classroom. Options range from public speaking to a very popular CCF in all three branches, run in conjunction with Bedford Girls'. Trips and tours galore for all manner of interests from sports tours to choir trips, academic excursions and – occasionally – just for fun.

Boarding: Six boarding houses – four on site and two just a short walk away – offer intimate and cosy homes from home for the 40 per cent of boys who board here. Charming in that none are purpose built, the houses are adapted Victorian villas, each with its own character – all with a fraternity house feel. Described as 'an extension of the housemaster's home', the houses are bright and spacious, with reassuringly untidy dorms (we secretly approve – boys must feel at home to be quite so slovenly) and the kinds of communal spaces day boys would probably die for (Xboxes, pinball machines, pool tables, chess tables – you name it). In keeping with rest of the school, modern facilities are juxtaposed with traditional artefacts (shiny fleets of computers beneath panelled honours boards) and boys have the freedom to come and go during the course of the day. Masters describe the boys as 'like brothers', one commenting that 'there's nothing better than seeing a huge sixth former strolling to breakfast chatting to one of the year 9s'. Many boarders are former day boys fed up with the daily commute – parents love the fact that boys can 'grow with the school'. Over 65 per cent of boarders are there full time so plenty of buzz at weekends, with regular trips and outings as well as free run of sports facilities and time for valuable R&R. Compulsory Saturday school for all.

Background and atmosphere: Don't be put off if you approach Bedford from the M1 via a somewhat grotty suburban high street, at the end of which you catch first glimpse of the school like an oasis in the architectural desert. School takes great pains to remind us of 'the other half' of Bedford which lies behind it – smart rows of Victorian villas (two boarding houses among them) leading down to a beautiful river bank. The school itself has the feel of a university campus about it – the buildings, a delightful mix of old and new, surround the manicured playing fields. The main building is all turrets, spires and a bell tower, with a magnificent hall as the central point and classrooms on four levels.

A Bedfordian has the ability to mix with all age groups and an easy, understated confidence

Impossible to choose a stand-out feature or department as each and every addition to the school has been made with care and deliberation to fuse function and form effectively. From the professional-looking cricket pavilion to the super modern glazed music school (who could fail to be inspired in here?), stunning library full of gleaming new books – but with the antique ones carefully displayed – and the cottage-like art building, set in its own sculpture garden, the whole campus gives the aura of a school offering roundedness in the purest sense of the word. The word chapel doesn't quite do justice to the glorious building where weekly services are held – the school accommodated amongst panelled walls inscribed with war memorials of fallen OBs.

Sports facilities unsurprisingly top notch. Super weights room would give most private gyms a run for their money and there's a 25 metre swimming pool (reportedly 'rather chilly but nobody minds,' according to our guide). Recent refurb and renovation of tennis courts and cricket pavilion (2014) – opened by England captain and Old Bedfordian, Alastair Cook.

Pastoral care, well-being and discipline: Brotherly atmosphere helped twofold by small houses with a family feel and vertical tutor groups where boys can get to know others from all year groups, with the tutor being the first port of call in the event of a problem. Head describes school as 'a fantastic community,' with everyone pitching in to help with greater problems relating to mental health or general well-being should the need arise, and parents describe the way boys support each other through the inevitable occasional difficulty as 'magic to watch'. Teachers available to parents via email, with responses to queries and concerns flying back through the ether at great speed.

'Strong discipline makes a place happier', says head, and major transgressions are dealt with by the amusingly – and aptly – named vice master.

Strict protocols followed in relation to serious misdemeanours with repeated conduct warnings leading to detentions. 'Absolutely no leniency' when it comes to dealing with drugs, either inside or out of school, says head. Timetable collapsed five times each year to focus on PSHCE with age appropriate focus on drugs, internet safety etc.

Pupils and parents: Parents say they have never met a Bedfordian they didn't like – their trademark being an ability to mix with all age groups with an easy, understated confidence. Many OBs in parent cohort, which is healthy mix of traditional types and first time buyers – lots of professionals commuting into London. Buses from Luton, Milton Keynes and Hitchin and easy access from Harpenden by train makes for a broad catchment, with the majority living within 40 miles of school and commuting for up to an hour. Just over 15 per cent overseas boys from 24 countries across Europe, Asia and Russia.

Entrance: Majority into year 9 from on-site prep, with about 50 additional places for those coming from other preps (Aldwickbury, Beechwood Park, Kingshott, Lockers Park major feeders) and state maintained schools. School sets own online entrance examination at 13+. A few extra places at 14+ then about 25 more into sixth form, when hopefuls will need six good GCSEs to go on to do A levels (at least Bs in the subjects to be studied; A grades in maths and sciences). Not ferociously competitive for day boys but boarding places are at more of a premium.

Overseas pupils often offered places conditional to taking ESL, billed as an extra.

Exit: About 10 per cent head to pastures new post-GCSE. Good range of destination universities for those that stay on, with a handful to Oxbridge most years (four in 2015) and around 75 per cent to Russell Group – Birmingham, Bristol, Durham, Imperial and Nottingham feature heavily, with majority going on to study heavyweight academic subjects – lots of sciences and a few to medicine each year. Small numbers opt for creative options or languages.

Money matters: At a shade under the £30K mark for full boarding, relative value for a school of this calibre in comparison with the competition. Good clutch of scholarships and bursaries for entry into years 7, 9 and 12, with art recently added to the list and golf scholarships in conjunction with nearby Woburn Golf Club. Generous – up to 35 per cent of fees, non-means tested, up for grabs 'for boys with exceptional talent' – and buoyant reserves in the hardship fund. Just under 200 boys across the school currently hold awards, with around 10 per cent of these on 100 per cent.

Part of the Harpur Trust but financially independent and benefiting from an extremely active and benevolent OB network.

Remarks: A rare beast – an uncompromisingly single sex school offering flexible day and boarding options without losing its traditional public school appeal. Thriving and successful, with happy pupils and happy parents – a place where all boys can hit their personal best, whether it's on the sports field, in academia or in the arts. Understated confidence and purposefulness abounds. A school of established excellence ready to be taken to the next level by dynamic new head.

Beechwood Park School

Markyate, St Albans, Hertfordshire AL3 8AW

01582 840333
admissions@beechwoodpark.herts.sch.uk
www.beechwoodpark.herts.sch.uk

Ages: 2.5 –13 (boarding from year 5)
Pupils: 484
Boarders: 40 boys/20 girls, all flexi
Day: £9,600 – £14,079 pa
Boarding: £18,120 pa

Headmaster: Since September 2015, Edward Balfour, previously head of Northbourne Park School in Kent. Studied education at Homerton College Cambridge; has taught English and drama at RGS Worcester and English at Whitgift, and been head of drama and housemaster at Bradfield College. Married with three young children.

Entrance: The school has a Montessori nursery on a separate site. All children above nursery age are assessed before entry. For reception children, expect informal assessment (school stresses this isn't about ability but behaviour). Some year groups have waiting lists, so best to get in early.

Exit: The school is praised by parents for 'knowing the children', and parents and pupils alike are carefully navigated through the decision process. St Albans High School and Haberdashers' Aske's (Boys and Girls) are popular choices. Other contenders include local grammars, Berkhamsted and Haileybury. Respectable numbers of bursaries.

Remarks: Rural setting in west Hertfordshire, with far-reaching views over farms and woodland. That is, if you can find it. Our GPS took us down a muddy single track lane where we had to do a U-turn at a field entrance. According to school staff, this isn't uncommon, though they told us signage has now been greatly improved. The Grade 1 listed building and beautiful parkland have a rich history, playing home to barons, nuns and visits from royalty through the years. One effusive parent remarked it reminded him of Swallows and Amazons. We couldn't see any lakes, but we see what he means.

School caters for children up to year 8, with a separate (off-site) Montessori pre-school. Class sizes hover around 20. Setting begins in year 3, with a scholarship set in year 8. Pupils are prepared for 11+ and 13+ entry to senior schools. Parents we spoke to were happy with academics. 'The results speak for themselves', we were told. Boy to girl ratio is 60:40 up to the age of 11, when the majority of girls leave. A brave few stay on – 'I like to be different', said one. It is worth checking expected intakes for individual years as these ratios are not for everyone. Ethnic mix reflects the local demographic. Pupils commute from a 30-mile radius, many catching one of the school buses. There is a strong Christian ethos and assembly is held daily. Senior choirs sing at local churches once a term.

Around 10 per cent of pupils receive SEN support in school (principally for dyslexia, dyspraxia and Asperger's). No extra charge for this (three cheers), unless foreign language assistance is also required. Plenty of help offered in early years; children are weaned off one-to-one support by key stage 2. Staff promise the door is always open for children to return, although one mother has found this transition hard. 'It feels like my son gets less support now', she told us.

Pupils who don't make school teams are encouraged to develop as athletes with the aim that 'everyone can find something they are good at'

Classrooms vary from bright and modern in the junior school to more formal learning spaces for older children. Regency library was advertised as a wow factor by our young guides. Perhaps a little over-hyped (though we admired their enthusiasm) but it is well-stocked with antique books as well as a broad selection of children's literature. In the generous music block, we were treated to a recorder recital in one of the 15 practice rooms.

As you would expect with generous grounds, sport is important and the school has many successful teams, particularly in rugby and cross-country, though we noticed that pictures of boys holding trophies dominated the news pages of the website. Pupils who don't make school teams are encouraged to develop as athletes with the aim that 'everyone can find something they are good at'. The 'sports for all' programme claims breadth, with sailing (for a select few), climbing and golf on offer alongside the more obvious, although this only truly kicks in from middle school.

Huge numbers of after-school activities – outdoor adventures to touch-typing to Brazilian soccer – are a boon for working parents. Children are actively encouraged to take up an instrument and there are concerts and workshops. Five choirs, orchestra, drama, language clubs – 'my friend has really got into Greek this term' – and cookery are all on offer. Parents applaud the breadth. 'My 7-year-old does cello, football, cricket, drama and papercraft', said one. 'It is a well-rounded school'.

Pupils we spoke to were generally happy, apart from usual minor grumbles like 'too much homework' and 'food could be better'. We can't vouch for homework, but the lunch we sampled was adequate, if a little stodgy (school says there are at least eight salads on the menu at each meal, sometimes more, food is generally considered excellent and menus are well-balanced). Parents are enthusiastic about the school too. We heard comments like 'the teachers know the kids well and have their eyes on the ball', 'it has met our expectations' and 'I wouldn't change a thing'.

Pastoral care is seen as a priority. Pupils 'are aware of values' and enjoy a credit system awarded for good behaviour (our guide proudly showed us

Clean and modern dorms run by married houseparents. Roughly a third of all children in years 5 to 8 board

her badges and values booklet). School encourages good behaviour by 'supporting and challenging children so there is no time to be naughty'; the bad behaviour that does exist is managed with a debit system. Pupils we spoke to see it as a fair system. We heard no reports of bullying and while it was acknowledged that disagreements can break out, we were assured that teachers can be relied on to 'help them sort it out'. One parent (a former pupil himself) said that 'pastoral care was the key driver in choosing this school for my son', while another told us, 'I do have a few concerns sometimes, but I suppose it's hard to supervise that many children on the playground'.

Flexi-boarding is offered during the week (no boarding at weekends) in clean and modern dorms run by married houseparents. Roughly a third of all children in years 5 to 8 board, many staying a couple of nights each week: 'I'm not ready to board full time yet, so this is perfect for me,' said one pupil. Boys and girls have separate dormitories, but share common rooms kitted out with air hockey, darts and Xbox. No mobile browsing allowed, but pupils can call home whenever they want.

Beeston Hall School

West Runton, Cromer, Norfolk NR27 9NQ

01263 837324
office@beestonhall.co.uk
www.beestonhall.co.uk

Ages: 7–13
Pupils: 120
Boarders: 50 full, weekly/flexi
Day: £11,265 – £16,440 pa
Boarding: £18,015 – £22,200 pa

Headmaster: Since September 2009, Mr Robin Gainher BSc (mid 40s). Read government at LSE. Previously deputy head at Cranleigh Prep. Married to Ali, who assists in the learning support department, runs a popular cookery club and hosts a weekly 'come dine with us' competition with year 8 boarders. Two of their three daughters are at the school.

Breezy and affable. Parents view him as an 'educationalist' who is bringing the school up to date and is looking at things with a fresh eye. He says, 'We don't need more gadgets,' so the focus is on

teaching and an open approach towards staff development – 'Teachers need to have time to think'. Enjoys being in the classroom whenever possible. Also clearly sensitive to pupils' emotional well-being and keen that boarders should feel Beeston is home from home – dorms have been tastefully homeified and rules re mufti relaxed: an astute move.

Several new appointments as the old brigade retire and a 'few formal edges knocked off' – but a traditional approach is still maintained when it comes to manners, meals, shoe cleaning and no to

computers during break times (how sensible). Plays golf when he can and is passionate about family, food – and Leeds United football club.

Moving on in July 2016.

Entrance: Informal assessment day. Relatively unselective but not a forgone conclusion. Mild to moderate dyslexia and dyspraxia can be accommodated – occasionally severe needs. 'Fun day' before entry with potential boarders getting a chance 'to try it out'.

Means-tested bursaries (general, academic, art, music, sport) plus in-house help for parents who fall on hard times. Sibling discounts if three or more children are at the school at the same time. Ten per cent discount for Forces families. Academic, music, art and sports scholarships now available for year 3 and year 7 entry.

Exit: 'Super deputy who knows the ropes' and gives good advice. All get to where they want. Wide spread of schools and respectable clutch of scholarships (generally around one third of leavers). High proportion board out of county. In the last two years, pupils to Ampleforth, Eton, Gresham's, Harrow, Langley, Norwich School, Oakham, Oundle, Queen Margaret's, Repton, Stowe, Shrewsbury, Tudor Hall and Uppingham.

Remarks: Most children become boarders before they leave – can now be weekly or flexi as well as full – although the school says that day children play an important part in after-school life. High proportion of children come from county, boarding families so those who board are well primed and,

with the help of 'brilliant' matrons, settle quickly. Everything about the place says boarding. Homely, well-ordered atmosphere with parents making positive noises about the level of pastoral care.

Children 'create a good impression' and seem happy, relatively unsophisticated and tremendously polite – door holding and standing up when adults enter a room are de rigueur. No PTA but parents kept in touch through email contact with their child's tutor, frequent newsletters and informal parent forums. Recently introduced clarion call texting service has seen the demise of days when parents forlornly appeared for a just cancelled match.

Rural setting – National Trust woodland, heathland and the North Norfolk coast a stone's throw away. Plenty of space to run around

Teaching is traditional with children 'encouraged to succeed' by cheery staff, but new independent learning strategies and wider curriculum initiatives introduced. Sets from year 6 upwards: scholars, sets 1 and 2 (the latter for the less able). French from year 3 and Latin from year 5. Head says the breadth of the school 'suits a wide spectrum of abilities and, whilst it isn't an academic hothouse, kids do very well'. Some parents thought the super bright might not be stretched enough, but now a master of scholars has introduced a more defined and expanded scholars' programme. Learning support also given a boost with the appointment of an experienced, enthusiastic head of department (SpLD). She works with two part-timers and five teaching assistants, with support mainly in class – removal from lessons only when absolutely necessary. 'Link books' keep lines of communication open and parents can pop in for an informal chat after midweek matches.

Low-key Sheringham is close by (older ones are allowed to venture out) and the setting is rural – National Trust woodland, heathland and the North Norfolk coast a stone's throw away. Plenty of space to run around and everything, everywhere immaculately maintained with the original core, a Regency house, carefully adapted and extended. Facilities, whilst not super glossy, are 'good for a country prep' – upgraded labs, library with sofas, spacious but acoustically challenging dining hall, Astro pitches, tennis courts and a recently completed large, heated outdoor pool.

Good, airy art department plus balcony for potential art scholars – achieves consistently scholarship-wise. Three drama productions a year – drama teacher from the Theatre Royal, Norwich. Cherry on the pie is the music school – more than generous, given the number of pupils. 'Music is a cut above – one of the school's great strengths,' according to parents. Over 80 per cent learn an instrument, including the harp and bagpipes. Plethora of music groups, choirs, ensembles and exam successes. Recently created ukulele band

All the usuals plus sailing on the Broads (school owns a fleet of Toppers) and shooting – they won the prep school league for seven years

is brainchild of the infectiously bubbly head of department, who raves about the inclusivity of the instrument.

Parents feel that, for a small school, sport does well. All the usuals plus sailing on the Broads (school owns a fleet of Toppers which can be used in the hols) and shooting – extra special, as they've won the prep school league for seven consecutive years. Plenty to do out of hours – eclectic range of clubs: Japanese, origami, veg growing, 'shaking up Shakespeare', fencing, and numerous excursions and theme days, including Beeston's Got Talent. It's a Knockout on the beach plus twice-weekly visits from the ice cream van are firm favourites, whilst outside speakers, including a woman who rowed across the Indian Ocean, broaden minds.

Traditional boarding prep with a young at heart, ambitious head. Quietly confident, well-disciplined children who are 'expected to have a go'. It does well by its pupils and turns out friendly, eager, purposeful and confident children. Good foundation, particularly for those who move on to public school.

Berkhamsted School

Overton House, Berkhamsted, Hertfordshire HP4 2DJ

01442 358001
admissions@berkhamstedschool.org
www.berkhamstedschool.org

Ages: 11–18 (weekly boarding from 13 and full boarding from 16)
Pupils: 1,202; sixth form: 353
Boarders: 50
Day: £16,275 – £19,095 pa
Boarding: plus £6,470 – £11,320 pa

Principal: Since January 2016, Richard Backhouse, previously head of Monkton Senior School. Economics degree from Cambridge, where he was vice captain of boat and ran the college Christian Union; has also worked at Oundle and Bradfield. Married to Debbie; two children.

Mr Richard Petty is head of the sixth form – he was previous head of history, politics and year 11 at Notting Hill and Ealing. Mrs Liz Richardson is head of the girls' section and Mr Richard Thompson is head of the boys' section.

Academic matters: Adheres to a traditional philosophy of education in seeking to provide opportunities for broad development. The wide choice of subjects at A level – 27, not to mention the enrichment studies undertaken in year 12, are consistent with this approach. Quantity does not compromise quality, however. In 2015, 47 per cent A*/A grades and 80 per cent A*/B grades at A level. A level art and photography students in the top five nationally for the AQA exam board in recent years. Maths, politics, geography and English are other areas of strength. Care is

taken to steer particularly able pupils towards the more academic subjects while others are nudged towards less demanding curricula. The head of sixth form encourages sharp academic focus and pupils to aim high. Staff praised for being readily accessible and other assistance comes in the form of drop-in maths workshops and lectures from leading experts, organised through the local chapter of the Geographical Association, to which the school is host.

While some enter the school lower down having been denied grammar school entry, parents feel that the non-academic would probably not be happy here. Single sex teaching for key stages 3-4 (co-ed in sixth form). As with A levels, results at GCSE have seen improvement over the past few years – around one in three achieve at least 10 A*/A grades; in 2015, 69 per cent A*/A grades overall. Again, good performance in most subjects – modern languages said by school to be on the up with newish head of department. All are required to take GCSE in RS (full course or short course) and many go on to A level. IGCSEs in English, maths, sciences and RS (full course) to ensure they remain challenged, but the school is apparently not, and will not become, a 'sweatshop'. The learning support department will conduct assessments if requested and supplementary lessons are organised as necessary. Two ESL teachers.

Games, options, the arts: Receives just recognition for its sporting achievements. It recently won the regional lacrosse championships and former and present pupils regularly represent the country and compete at regional and county level across a range of other sports. Emphasis placed on teaching sport well and ensuring that everyone has fun and is able to benefit. Netball and boys' hockey given new emphasis of late. Rugby, hockey, lacrosse, cricket, football, swimming and tennis compulsory, depending on age and gender. The new sports pavilion has opened up wider possibilities both to pupils and the wider community, including squash, aerobics, yoga, badminton and weight-training.

> 'My son's speech at our wedding anniversary was faultless. They even found time to teach him public speaking. May also have honed his dance floor skills at the Strictly-style fundraiser'

Over 50 per cent opt to study singing or an instrument of some kind. A talent competition to raise money for charity and Young Musician of the Year are relatively recent additions to the calendar and audiences are overwhelmed by the diversity of talent. The Friends provide Pimms, soft drinks and strawberries for Proms in the Quad, and all leave with fond memories of rousing and moving performances from solo vocalists and musicians – the ever-popular swing songs from the mixed pupil and staff big band ring in their ears. Drama is a popular option at GCSE and beyond and inter-house competitions to encourage all to take to the stage. Some grumbles from parents that staff compete fiercely for pupil time when schedules conflict, but generally a much appreciated aspect of the school – 'My son's speech at our wedding anniversary was faultless. They even found time to teach him public speaking'. May well have honed his dance floor skills too, at the Strictly Come Dancing fundraiser, one of many community events at which the girls and boys come together.

A tour of the school may well take in the historic armoury. CCF is well established and attracts large numbers of recruits each year. The choice between this and D of E is often a hard one, but few can keep up with the demands of both. In addition to special visits, cadets are offered at least one training weekend a month and the D of E expeditions take candidates anywhere from the wet and windswept Lake District to the altogether more clement foothills of the Dolomites. High level of commitment found with a large proportion completing the award.

Boarding: Boarding houses are within easy walk of the school and indistinguishable from surrounding privately owned flats. Recently refurbished bedrooms, many en-suite, are comfortable, and tasteful pictures, vases of flowers and modern furnishings give a lovely homely feel to communal

A community school. Many enter the prep and stay all the way through. A great feeling of pulling together and mutual support pervades throughout. Vertical house system facilitates friendships across and in between year groups

areas, with quiet and noisier common rooms to suit your mood.

Concentration of overseas students in the boarding house doesn't seem to create a divide between them and the six weekly or 20 or so flexi-boarders (equal girl/boy split). Boarders participate in wider weekend school activities and also organise activities and outings tailored to their interests. ESL lessons are offered; visits to London's Chinatown and markets to buy African foodstuffs reportedly very successful.

Background and atmosphere: Christian foundation school which dates from 1541 and amalgamated with the 1888 girls' school in 1997 and the mixed prep the following year. Boys and girls still have their own campuses but some facilities shared. 'Little school feel, big school infrastructure', and indeed a general feeling that all parts of the school come together and meld peaceably with the pretty and historic town.

The Castle Campus, which mostly houses the boys, plus the sixth form, has some slightly scruffy houses and common rooms but these are more than compensated for by the neat grass quad, well-preserved exteriors and assembly rooms, including the grade 1 listed Tutor hall and 19th century Venetian-style chapel. Some modern classrooms and labs and an ultra-swish new dining hall – little wonder parents queue up for those tasty charity breakfasts. Games on the Eton fives courts provide a popular spectacle and seats under mature trees a traditional girls' meeting place – perhaps not surprisingly, lots of boys milling about nearby.

No-one now suggests the girls, in King's Campus, are hard done by comparatively, enjoying the traditional ('Our art room is more authentic, a Parisian atelier') and the modern – new sports centre and a 500-seat theatre are right on their doorstep, and a more spacious dining hall, chapel and classroom block to the tune of £8 million has now been completed.

Smart suit dress code and sanctioning of moderate make-up help prepare sixth form pupils for life after school. Work experience after AS with targeted placements. Good decision making support in the form of advice from teachers, careers fairs and lunches with parents and others to open their eyes to the world of work – in fact introduction to career choices starts much lower down the school, with research, profiling and guidance interviews in years 8, 10 and 11.

Pastoral care, well-being and discipline: A community school. Many enter the prep early and stay the course. Up until GCSEs, the separation of boys and girls allows them to be themselves and be less inhibited, while extracurricular activities ensure they are not cut off completely from the other sex. Sixth form very much run along the lines of a college, geared towards preparing pupils for the outside world – many choose the school for all these reasons. A great feeling of pulling together and mutual support pervades throughout. A vertical house system facilitates friendships across and in between year groups – 'This is where we meet to do

---

Parents are a mix of first time buyers and more comfortably affluent. Suits those that are willing to try everything out and contribute across the board. Pupils friendly, open and fun – 'Well-mannered and a pleasure to have in your house'

---

our prep'; 'We come here to do presentations, sharing our knowledge of specialist subjects'. Spiritual teaching in the chapel, with all faiths welcome.

Pupils wearing smiley badges gather up lost souls and answer questions. On more serious or personal issues, pupils and parents are encouraged to communicate directly with house tutors. Is there bullying? Well, yes, some, but the caring attitude of staff and fellow pupils usually keeps it to a minimum – 'The kids are pretty sensible on the whole'. No real worries about drink or drugs, though recently a discussion forum has been established – 'Schools should provide a moral lead beyond the school boundaries'.

Pupils and parents: Generally families live within 40 minutes or so of the school. Small number of MOD and expat families. Number of first time buyers along with the more comfortably affluent. The boarding community largely made up of upper school overseas nationals, mostly from Far East and Africa. Overall mix and town location prevents any feeling that they are living in a rarefied environment. Suits those that are willing to try everything out and contribute across the board. Pupils friendly, open and fun – 'Well-mannered and a pleasure to have in your house'. The Friends organise regular social events, including coffee mornings. Good chance to meet other parents and put views across to the principal who attends when he can.

Very vibrant OB association with regular sporting fixtures against the school, meetings with fellow professionals, reunion dinners and regular charitable donations to support school activities. Most famous OB Graham Greene, whose father was the school's head. Others include explorer Robin Knox-Johnston, composer Sir Alexander Goehr, Sir Kenneth Cork (former Lord Major of London), Michael Meacher MP, musician Antony Hopkins and actress Emma Fielding.

Entrance: Seventy or so move up from the prep each year. Wide range of feeder schools in Hertfordshire, Buckinghamshire and Bedfordshire, including Abbot's Hill, Beacon School, Gateways, Lockers Park and Maltman's Green School. Home-grown thought to have an advantage but all have to take an entry exam. This comprises verbal reasoning, English and maths testing at 11+ and additional non-verbal reasoning test at 13+. Can enter in years 8 or 10, when testing also takes place. Push to raise the number of girls and even out numbers.

Approximately 40 apply for sixth form from outside. One in two turned away, based largely on GCSE results. Minimum requirement of at least five B and two C grades, which may possibly include a short course (usually RS) with A or B in the four subjects chosen for AS level. A grade required if choices include English literature, maths, modern languages or science. Prospective students meet the head of sixth form and are required to provide a reference from their current school.

Exit: Most go on to further education, many after a gap year. Nine to Oxbridge in 2015; 64 per cent to Russell Group universities with popular destinations including Birmingham, Durham, Loughborough, Sheffield, Leeds, Bristol, Exeter, Nottingham, UCL.

Money matters: Fees for extras considered reasonable and fair. Limited number of academic, music, drama, art and sports scholarships available, awarded on merit. Also bursaries in case of need.

Remarks: Combines the best of a single sex and co-ed school. Study with strong spiritual basis and community ethos produces confident all-round achievers.

Bishop's Stortford College Prep School

Maze Green Road, Bishop's Stortford, Hertfordshire CM23 2PH

01279 838607
psadmissions@bishopsstortfordcollege.org
www.bishopsstortfordcollege.org

Ages: 4–13 (boarding from 9)
Pupils: 453
Boarders: 11 full, 50 weekly/flexi
Day: £8,088 – £13,998 pa
Boarding: £18,114 – £20,691 pa

Linked school: Bishop's Stortford College

Headmaster: Since September 2013, Bill Toleman BA MSc, FRGS, (40s), previously head of Yarm Prep School. Before that, deputy head at King's Worcester. Read geography at Nottingham University and has since added an MSc in educational management and leadership and fellowship of the Royal Geographical Society. Affable and so unassuming that when we ask him to describe his leadership style he calls in his PA, settles her in an armchair and closes the door on his way out. 'Approachable and informal,' she smiles, as soon as the latch clicks; adjectives bandied about by parents include 'child-centred', 'fair' and 'proactive'. Certainly in his short tenure to date he has systematically swept away all signs of stuffiness – entrance exams are now sat in a multiplicity of cosy classrooms rather than in serried rows in one huge daunting sports hall, for example, and parents and pupils alike pop in at all hours, keen for a chat. 'If people want to come and see me I'm very happy to see them,' he says, although when the queue becomes too long or other matters are too pressing his PA honours visitors with an appointment in the head's diary. 'The children love that,' she laughs. To his regret, no longer has time to teach his beloved geography, although helps out with fieldwork (most recently accompanying lower third to Walton-on-the-Naze). Enjoys surfing in North Devon and still plays occasional cricket and Sunday rugby. Married, with three grown-up sons.

Entrance: Entrance to the pre-prep is by an informal group assessment session and there is a long lead-in for tinies registered to start reception ('messy play' session in progress when we visited). External candidates for the additional 20 places made available at 7+ must sit the entrance exam to the prep school (English, maths and reading), spend a morning in

school and are encouraged to meet the head with parents; no assessment required of existing pupils. A further 20 places offered at 10+ and 20 more at 11+ (academic and music scholarships available) to give a total of 100 pupils per year group by lower third (year 7). No sibling discount or preference given.

Exit: Some 97 per cent plus straight to senior school, Bishop's Stortford College. Remaining handful to other, further-flung boarding schools (in recent years Harrow, Stowe, Millfield, Uppingham, Shrewsbury, Benenden) and a few to state at 11+. As Bishop's Stortford College is selective, prep parents are given plenty of advance warning if their child's ability to keep up after transfer is in question. Other, suitable schools, recommended. Fairly rare occurrence as school prefers to tackle underachievement to keep pupils under its wing.

Remarks: Stunning green and leafy setting right on the edge of town extending in all to 130 acres of rolling Hertfordshire. Accessed via a lane of warm, red-brick Victorian houses and school buildings, some sensitively modernised, others waiting. Nearly all with privet hedges and ancient roses. Prep and senior pupils co-exist harmoniously on the site. Main prep building now all sparkling glass and purple carpet, thanks to £3m extension and refurb. Super reception area, hall with stage and roomy classrooms. Art rooms, including kiln, plus science labs across the attractive brick courtyard (complete with happy preppies chatting on steps, idyllically). Wonderful new library with floor-to-ceiling vistas. Shares with seniors music facilities, super 50-metre indoor pool in own timber-clad edifice, sports hall and hard courts, plus pitches as far as the eye can see. No wonder prep children look relaxed, contented – and well-exercised.

'This is a purposeful, happy place to come to school – it has to be,' says head, 'because we're here for a long time.' Pre-prep for age 4 to 7, prep for 7 to 13s. While pre-prep makes use of national curriculum year group terminology, traditional names still charmingly in use in the prep – so lower and upper shell are followed by forms 1 and 2, then lower and upper third (continuing into the senior). Although less than 20 per cent of prep pupils board, school operates a boarding school week for its pupils aged over 7, with long weekdays until 5pm for the eldest and Saturday morning school for all, afternoons for form 1 and above.

'Children work hard here because they want to, not because we make them,' says head; says a parent, 'My son has been coaxed, encouraged and inspired to push himself and achieve the best he could.' Academic streaming begins in year 4, plus setting for maths. Classical civ for years 5 and 6, Latin to add to Spanish, German and French for years 7 and 8. DT and drama on the curriculum

from year 3 up. Lots of visits and trips, as well as speakers in – curricular activities included in fees. Bring Your Own Device recently introduced for top two years – prep pupils say they use iPads and equivalent in 80 per cent of lessons and that they really help with self-organisation. Wifi all over.

Sport serious here and all involved. National finalists in pretty much everything – rugby, hockey, cricket, netball, even football, although only an after-school club. Standout individuals too, notably swimming and tennis. Lots of music – choirs, groups and tours.

'Have-a-go' culture is alive and well. One afternoon each week devoted to a 'wheel' of activities which changes with the term (street dance and yoga to survival skills). All pupils allocated to a house (either at random or according to family connection) – fierce competition through all manner of contests and quizzes. Highest achieving house wins supper with the headmaster. Fundraising through teddy bears' picnics, film nights, doughnut sales and auctions in aid of the annual chosen charity – £10,000 plus donated every year. Head meets prefects for 'biscuits and a chat' half-termly, and drops into lessons and activities unannounced.

National finalists in pretty much everything – rugby, hockey, cricket, netball, even football, although only an after-school club. Standout individuals too, notably swimming and tennis. 'Have-a-go' culture is alive and well and weekly activities change every term

Strong pastoral care network begins with form tutor as first port of call for parents, then heads of year. Pyramid above of senior teacher (pastoral), director of studies, operations, then deputy head and head. 'Compassionate' teaching and learning support for those with mild SEN much praised by parents of children who have benefited – IEPS, one-to-ones, additional time in exams.

Own comfortable boarding house for prep pupils. Few full boarders but 50+ stay a minimum of two nights a week – most popular Wednesdays (sport after school) and Friday (Saturday morning lie-in for mum and dad). Vast majority of pupils throughout school very local and only half a dozen international students in the prep – EAL support offered.

Parents in the main professionals or city, some farmers – same as in senior as pupils grow up through the school with few additions. 'There really is not a type of child or parent,' said a parent. 'Plenty of commuters as London is so close, but there are farmers and scientists and just about all professions going.'

Prep head's relationship with college head 'mutually supportive' and clearly on the same page.

Bishop's Stortford College

10 Maze Green Road, Bishop's Stortford, Hertfordshire CM23 2PJ

01279 838575
admissions@bishopsstortfordcollege.org
www.bishopsstortfordcollege.org

Ages: 13–18
Pupils: 570; sixth form: 230
Boarders: 48 full, 104 weekly/flexi (about two thirds boys)
Day: £17,496 – £17,655 pa
Boarding: £25,950 – £27,405 pa

Linked school: Bishop's Stortford College Prep School

Headmaster: Since 2011, Mr Jeremy Gladwin BSc MEd. Educated at The King's School, Worcester (chorister) and Whitgift School in south Croydon. Graduated from Durham in geography, taught at Shrewsbury School for 15 years, rising to become head of geography and housemaster, then deputy headmaster at the Royal Hospital School, and headmaster of St Edmund's, Canterbury. Decided to apply for second headship as 'the opportunity to lead Bishop's Stortford College was too good to miss'. Recently took a masters in education at Cambridge, focusing on 'educational leadership and school improvement', the completion of which has prompted his appointment to HMC committee for professional development. 'Heads are lonely,' he says; 'they need more support. That way we might be able to tackle the current high rate of attrition.' Also an inspector for both ISI and Ofsted (boarding). Married with grown-up son and daughter. A keen walker, enjoys watching rugby and plays tennis at club level. Loves music, especially sacred choral (weekly attendance at evensong at St John's College, Cambridge is his de-stresser) and classical. A fine pianist. Mild-mannered, considered, down-to-earth type. 'Runs a tight ship; proactive and forward-thinking,' say parents.

Academic matters: Academic results have soared in recent years – unrecognisable in comparison to the college of 10 to 15 years ago. Head attributes this to the arrival of girls when the college went fully co-ed in 1995 – not only did they bring self-motivation but they raised the academic bar. A concerted effort to improve results through academic rigour, targeting and 'working smarter' has paid off – now among top 20 UK co-ed independent schools. The 68 per cent A*/B A level grades of a few years ago have given way to 82 per cent in 2015 (57 per cent A*/A). Maths, history, English literature, psychology and physics are most popular subjects, with strongest showing in theatre studies, art, and geography. Out of the running for GCSE league tables due to iGCSEs, which parents gladly accept, but a commendable 70 per cent of passes A*/A in 2015. Prestigious '10 club' – tie for at least 10 A*/A grades at GCSE. Language provision has broadened – on joining senior school, pupils choose two modern foreign languages (most having been introduced to French, German and Spanish in the prep, not to mention Latin). Pre-empts the changes to GCSEs which head fears will discourage language take-up.

> *'A really positive environment,'*
> *suggested a parent. Certainly*
> *the all-pervading ethos is one of*
> *kindness, caring and humanity*

Streams and sets for most subjects meet needs of all, including the gifted. A dedicated learning support team of three sensitively supports 30 students with specific learning needs (charged as an extra), including dyslexia and Asperger's. All international students are offered one or two EAL lessons a week and reach iGCSE level (required for university admission). However, this is not solely an academic day school – head recoils at the suggestion of a hothouse. 'We won't sacrifice the breadth that comes with a boarding school curriculum – we just want to do everything well and keep some balance.' Broad-based academic intake – 'results are due to the quality of teaching and learning,' emphasises head.

Bring Your Own Device recently introduced – Wifi all over. Pioneering use of Geographical Information System technology. Interactive Science Action Centre. Solid traditional teaching facilities too.

Games, options, the arts: Successful sports: unbeaten seasons in rugby and hockey now the norm – several ex-international players offer top level coaching and inspiring role models. County hockey and district netball and swimming champions – swimming a major sport in fabulous pool; tennis and water-polo also popular.

Music important – around 10 per cent of pupils perform to grade 8 or beyond. Pianos in most boarding houses, plenty of airy practice rooms. Much-appreciated resident college musician supports in readiness for exams and accompanies. Orchestra and all manner of ensembles large and small. Twenty concerts a year, including choral work for pupils, parents and staff, plus a couple of ventures into the world of opera. Well-equipped theatre provides venue for some stunning musical and dramatic performances (set for recent production of Cabaret still in evidence, though slowly transforming into Scottish heathland for next epic – Macbeth). New art centre with stunningly mature GCSE and A level work on display in spacious ateliers.

Trips and tours across the globe including India, New York, Malawi, South Africa, Barbados, and a fair few closer to home too. Wide choice of extracurricular activities including D of E (the college is the leading school in east Hertfordshire) debating (standing room only for some hot topics) and community work.

Boarding: Three senior boarding houses – two for boys and one for girls. Full, weekly and flexi boarding, the latter most popular. Saturday lessons and sport mean everyone is at school till Saturday afternoon. Most go home on Saturday nights, but eg paintballing and visits to theme parks organised for those still in school.

Background and atmosphere: Founded in 1868 as a non-conformist boarding school, with aspirations of securing an effective and Christian education on terms that should not be beyond the reach of the middle class generally, originally sited on the outskirts of Bishop's Stortford. Once boys only, now 45 per cent girls. Full-on Saturday school for all from 8.20am until 3.40pm has its detractors, but most accept it's necessary if children are to make the most of all that's on offer.

Despite recent new developments and proximity to town, the 130 acre campus still has a rural feel. Governors canny through the economic downturn and fees have remained relatively low. Indeed, an ambitious programme of facilities upgrade ongoing and due for completion to coincide with the school's 150th anniversary in 2018. New addition to existing pretty Edwardian building under way when we visited, which when completed will provide a new girls' day house (to replace the existing one). A brand new boys' day and boarding house is next on the agenda – much more economical to design from scratch than to bring the existing original School House building up to modern living standards; instead it will be repurposed as offices for the head and administrative teams, plus 11 classrooms. By the

end of the project, head predicts the college 'won't just be beautiful, it will be magnificent!'

Despite these physical changes, 'We are a large school, but we retain the small-school feel,' says head, and unabashedly goes on to describe Bishop's Stortford College as 'cuddly'. 'A really positive environment,' suggested a parent. Certainly the all-pervading ethos is one of kindness, caring and humanity – a quality the head has discovered is neatly defined by the Zulu word 'ubuntu' (which we went home and looked up – perfect). 'Pupils here are mutually supportive,' says head. 'They work hard. When asked why, they simply reply "why not?"' Head is keen to resist the spoon-feeding culture in favour of promoting independent learning in preparation for life. EPQ is popular in the sixth form as is the college's own research project programme – no UCAS points but an academic challenge and something to talk about at university interviews and mention on personal statement.

Superb library with two-storey bow windows, well stocked with books, DVDs (multi-lingual) and CDs. Ferguson Lecture Theatre is a cosy additional space, where assemblies can be relayed from Mem(orial) Hall, the original, atmospheric school hall. Sixth form Stars in their Eyes a sell-out. Sports hall with fitness suite in the gallery. Five all weather netball/tennis courts. Two floodlit Astro pitches.

Dining hall large and functional; food plentiful and tasty, on a three-week menu rotation (our sixth form guides tell us the pupils' request for 'chicken zinger' through the school council was provided by the catering manager and it was very tasty).

Pastoral care, well-being and discipline: Few discipline problems – head likes 'to give pupils a chance to get it right'. Strong house system offers support.

Set for recent production of Cabaret still in evidence, through slowly transforming into Scottish heathland for next epic – Macbeth

'The school expects a lot from the children and as a parent that is exactly what I want,' said one parent.

Pupils and parents: Pupils 'normal, not arrogant,' says head. 'I'm not keen on elitism.' Most from within daily travelling distance; about 65 per cent of boarders from overseas, including Europe and the Far East. Parents – 'all professions going' – described by one of their number as 'friendly, sociable, aspirational, encouraging of their children'. Appreciate weekly contact by e-newsletter and the twice yearly news magazine.

Long list of distinguished former pupils includes presenter Andy Peebles, rugby player Ben Clarke, writer Dick Clement and educationalist Professor John Ferguson. The world of espionage features prominently via former heads of MI5, Sir Stephen Lander and Sir Dick White, and Peter Wright, author of Spycatcher.

Entrance: Pupils are selected via interviews, entrance tests and school references; takes a range of abilities, not just academic high-fliers. At 13 majority come from the prep school but also takes some 12-15 external entrants annually; small number join at 14, in time for GCSEs. Some 30-40 join in the sixth form – entrance is by interview and written tests; need at least five B grades at GCSE with A*-B in A level subject choices.

Exit: A handful leaves after GCSEs to study A levels elsewhere. Nearly all sixth formers head to university. Ten to Oxbridge in 2015; Nottingham most popular destination followed by Birmingham, Exeter, East Anglia and Loughborough; others to a range from photography at Falmouth to actuarial science at East Anglia to early years development at Norland College.

Money matters: Assistance for those in financial need. Academic, music, art and sport scholarships offered. 'A considerable proportion of our income goes on bursaries and scholarships,' says the head. 'If a child is talented but his or her parents can't afford us, we will do what we can to help.'

Remarks: Without five centuries of history to draw on, Bishop's Stortford College isn't widely known, but is among the generation of schools founded in the Victorian era that are quietly succeeding. Local word-of-mouth is enough to keep it oversubscribed – without needing to worry about recruiting for tomorrow, the head and governors can look further into securing the college's position well into the future.

Brandeston Hall Preparatory School

Brandeston Hall, Brandeston, Suffolk IP13 7AH

01728 685331
office@brandestonhall.co.uk
www.brandestonhall.co.uk
C of E

Ages: 2–13 (boarding from year 3)
Pupils: 260
Boarders: 25 full, up to 50 flexi
Day: £8,027 – £13,967 pa
Boarding: plus £35 – £38 per day

Linked school: Framlingham College

Headmaster: Since 2007, Mr Martin Myers-Allen BSc PGCE (universities of Newcastle and Bath). A degree in marine biology. After a successful career in stockbroking and IT, Martin became a science teacher at Framlingham College and was enthusiastically involved with sport, D of E and CCF. A 'pied piper', constantly in the thick of activities with pupils, who say he is fun to be with and respected. He feels he 'understands the soul of the school,' and his knowledge of both Brandeston and its senior school, Framlingham College, has obvious advantages. A straightforward, sympathetic person who believes in, and fosters, the pupils' self-confidence by discovering their individual interests and talents, in huge variety of areas, 'not necessarily just in sport or music.' He is married to Helen, who teaches at Framlingham and they have three children, two of whom are now grown up.

Entrance: For entry to the nursery and pre-prep, pupils are invited to spend a day (or morning) for an informal assessment; same for year 3 upwards but their day includes an entrance test. Scholarships at 11+ for entrants to the senior school (Framlingham College) – academic, music and sport.

Exit: Everyone is prepared for common entrance. All but a handful transfer to Framlingham College (results help decide setting in year 9).

Remarks: Idyllic setting down the Suffolk lanes. The original manor house has been rebuilt and remodelled as a memorial to former pupils killed both world wars. Remembrance is taken seriously and VC citations are proudly displayed in the panelled hall. This is a school for exploring and enjoying; massive oak staircases, terraces on which to play games or take off into the ravishing grounds. The country house atmosphere of the main building is complemented by a modern, multi-purpose hall used for concerts, assemblies and plays and well-designed buildings for DT and art, science and technology. Newish classroom block is reached via a covered passageway; spanking new dance and drama studio.

A school for exploring and enjoying; massive oak staircases, terraces on which to play games, ravishing grounds

Nursery and pre-prep occupy their own purpose built accommodation and play areas, but are very much part of the same site. Notice boards with details of after-school clubs, sport and music cover the walls including, one headed Celebration, and pupils proudly point out their names and faces. Boarding is on the top two floors of the original building with spectacular views from every window, redecorated dormitories (mostly four to six beds) and common rooms – no twangy old sofas. Flexi-boarding very popular; 'The whole of year 7 and 8 seem to stay on Wednesday and Friday nights,' say pupils, partly no doubt, because there is Saturday morning school for these years.

Setting begins early for English and maths, and higher up for other subjects. French in pre-prep and Latin from year 7. Help for mild difficulties, notably dyslexia, but the curriculum is not geared for those who seriously struggle. Extension programmes are developed for 'exceptional students' (head prefers this to 'gifted and talented'). Pupils well-mannered and friendly, very at-ease in their school, 'Not precocious, but not scared of adults either,' is how the head puts it. This is a well-run, happy school with no problems recruiting. Would suit a wide range of keen, curious and enthusiastic pupils and is deservedly popular.

Brentwood School

Middleton Hall Lane, Brentwood, Essex CM15 8EE

01277 243243
headmaster@brentwood.essex.sch.uk
www.brentwoodschool.co.uk

Ages: 11–18
Pupils: 1,137; sixth form: 360
Boarders: 41 boys/23 girls
Day: £16,635 pa
Boarding: £32,649 pa

Headmaster: Since September 2004, Mr Ian Davies PGCE MA (50s), theology degrees from Oxford and Cambridge. Previously head of St Dunstan's College. Taught religious studies at Sackville School and became head of year and head of RE at The Latymer, Edmonton. An ISI inspector, member of D of E National Advisory Council, and helped select naval officers for training at Dartmouth for the Admiralty Interview Board. Very approachable – once volunteered as a guinea pig for a nitrogen experiment during science lesson where his hands were set alight. 'It didn't hurt at all, as it burnt above my hand, and the children loved it.' He sees the school as 'educationally... more sophisticated than most' thanks to its diamond structure, educating boys and girls in separate gender classes from age 11 to 16, but together at other ages. 'We all learn in different ways and I think there are gender differences and also gender stereotypes which need to be cracked.' So the school employs all 'the benefits of single sex education' while enabling pupils to 'also get the social benefits of choir, orchestra, combined cadets' and more 'as part of a co-educational environment'. He adds, 'Nothing pleases me more than having a girl who is great at maths and physics go off to university to do engineering.' Considers himself 'very lucky' in his career, having 'worked with great people all the way through' and being mentored by some 'great heads' in the past.

Academic matters: GCSE results in 2015 were slightly down on the previous year's: 59 per cent graded A*/A. Alongside critical and creative thinking and the core subjects, they study French and Latin in year 7, and choose from German, ancient Greek or Spanish in year 8. IGCSE in several subjects; head sees it as 'a stepping stone to the IB'.

At A level in 2015, 44 per cent A*/A grades, with particularly good results in maths, further maths and the three sciences. School offers 26 curriculum subjects, plus other activities such as law, cooking at university, Italian, peer mentoring training and sports leadership. IB scores averaged 35 points.

School encourages creative and critical thinking across all subjects, whether improving goal-scoring in sport, performing West Side Story in German, or applying maths in the composition of music. The school 'teaches you to think for yourself and how it is up to you to determine whether you succeed or not,' said a pupil. The syllabus is 'flexibly adapted to suit all pupils' needs' and 'able pupils do not get bored here', says the school. Parents agree with this, saying that although children are set early in year 7 in French and maths, these groups are not set in concrete and support is available if needed. 'I think it really is important that the children are not stuck with a label of being really clever or really daft,' said a parent. 'That doesn't happen at all. It is very, very flexible.' A 13-year-old with an A* in A level maths currently studies with older pupils, including some sixth form maths lessons.

EAL support provided to 35 pupils, largely through teachers that have lived and worked abroad. The learning and development team also provides support to around 50 students with special educational needs. This includes an Independent Education Plan, one-to-one tuition, subject support and lunchtime drop in sessions. The department is very successful – some who receive additional support make such 'good and exceptional progress' that they 'sometimes outperform their peers', noted the ISI.

Games, options, the arts: There is a long sporting tradition here. This was one of three independent schools selected as an official Olympic training venue and it made world headlines when it opened up its doors to rescue an African Paralympic team left stranded at the airport with neither host nor facilities after a funding promise failed to materialise.

Sport is one of the scholarships offered; football, cricket, hockey, rugby and netball coaches

Boarding houses are situated off campus, 'so you don't feel that you're there all day'. They are run like a 'well-oiled machine', with regular routines for homework, bedtime and activities

often successful sportspeople. Pupils have played at national and international level in fencing, water polo, cricket, football, squash, tennis and netball. School has won the Public Schools Fencing Competition 'more than 30 times since 1962'. Both girls' athletics teams have made it to the English schools' track and field national finals. One England Under-19 cricketer has been offered a contract with Essex. At any one time around 400 pupils are out representing the school in a whole variety of sports. Alongside sports hall, pool, gym and dance studio, there are glass-backed squash courts, fitness suite and a fencing sale, plus extensive playing fields and a full-size running track.

Art, music and drama are also well catered for. Many pupils' works are exhibited at the annual art exhibition and school also tries to instil appreciation for art whether pupils 'consider themselves to be "arty" or not'. Various competitions include the popular water colour competition and the head's sculpting competition. DT and ICT are taught with art and food tech in the Hardy Amies Design Centre, equipped with its own library and computers. Recently a group of students scooped the top prize in an international design award with their life-saving 'glow' glove. The six, led by a student who 'a year ago wouldn't have said boo to a goose', took first prize in the annual Virtual Ventura competition against opposition from 300 teams. 'We thought about different things and narrowed it down to safety as during the dark people don't see cyclists very well.' Their winning design went on display at the Design Museum in London.

Music and drama are taught in a separate building equipped with rehearsal studios and 14 practice rooms. We witnessed one group using Sibelius to compose 'an answer in response to a melody' in preparation for their GCSE creative task: 'We have to pick the right melody chords to make it work. The answer must relate to it but not repeat it'. Many students get involved in the school symphony orchestra, big band (which creates its own CDs), choir or choral society, and the regular musicals and house music concerts. A number of ex-pupils are exhibitioners at London music colleges or hold organ scholarships at university; there are two organs in the school, one in the music hall and another in the chapel.

Similar story with drama: three major annual productions covering every genre from musicals to comedy to classics. Examples include Macbeth featuring video clips showing the war in the Middle East; Antigone performed with modern ballet choreographed by a student; a third year production of Arabian Nights; and West Side Story in German, all performed in the school's 400-seat auditorium. Mainly girls, but a few boys too, take part in dance showcases including tap, jazz and street.

Too many extracurricular activities to name: Trivial Pursuits, cross-country, table tennis, chess, Duke of Edinburgh Award, Cine & Literatura, a Spanish film club, public speaking. 'You have to choose at least three; it's compulsory now,' we heard a year 7 pupil tell a sixth former. The Sir Antony Browne Society invites guest speakers on a wide range of current political, financial and medical topics. One of the most popular activities at the school is the 152-year-old Combined Cadet Force (CCF), one of the largest in the country, which has been enlisted by the DfE to help set up branches at other schools. It really creates a buzz in the atmosphere on Fridays when its 500-odd members come to school dressed in combat gear, ready for the afternoon and weekend activities. These include map reading, camp craft, basic first aid, hill walking, canoeing, flying and skydiving. 'CCF is a big thing here,' said one pupil. 'It opens you up to a lot of things you might not have been able to do', and at very low cost. Other pupils join the Community Service Unit and help raise thousands for charities in the local area and abroad. With so many competitions there is no excuse for not finding something you like, although one student did complain about the lack of a house dance competition.

Boarding: The two boarding houses are a 'home from home' for the small boarding community of some 23 girls and 41 boys, 60 per cent of whom are from overseas. Both are situated off campus, 'so you don't feel that you're there all day'. They are run like a 'well-oiled machine,' say the husband and wife houseparents, with regular routines (for homework, bedtimes and activities) and good links between houseparents, teachers and parents. As well as email, the 'children are Skyping every single night and we are Skyping with parents almost on

Notable former pupils include Douglas Adams, author of the Hitchhiker's Guide to the Galaxy and Sir Hardy Amies, couturier (he designed school's uniform)

a daily basis. I go into the rooms and they say, "Say hello to my mum".'

Background and atmosphere: The story behind the school's foundation is a history lesson in itself. During the English reformation a 19-year-old Protestant was burnt on order of Sir Antony Browne, then acting as a magistrate on behalf of Queen Mary. He purchased Weald Hall and land for the school in 1557 as an act of penance. The school received its motto in 1622 from the pen of John Donne, Dean of St Paul's. It also has its own prayer and song. Was a boys' grammar school, principally boarding, for many years. Admitted girls into the sixth form in the mid 1970s and into the main school in 1988.

Set in the heart of the Essex town of Brentwood, across the road from the cathedral, it stands on a 72-acre site. Not much is left of the Weald Hall save a few ruins. The Old Big School, built in 1568, still has the original front door and is used for lectures, meetings and discussions. There is a beautiful Victorian chapel built in 1868, with arches, beams and stained glass windows detailing the narratives of Moses, Elijah and other biblical prophets, as well as patron saints of the Great War. It seats 320, so cannot contain the whole school at once, but the six year groups take it in turn to have a fortnightly service there.

More recent buildings include the science block, opened by the Queen in 1957, the 1986 Courage Hall sports centre, and the 1999 Hardy Amies design building. The refurbished sixth form block which houses the 400 seat auditorium has distinctively Victorian style arched roofs. Two-storey learning resource centre has open spaces for traditional books and digital media, a lecture theatre, an additional assembly hall, a café and after-school social hub. The main grounds resemble a university campus quadrangle and seem to run as far as the eye can see: beyond the rugby posts is Mill House, the girls' boarding house, Hough House, the boys' boarding house, the prep school and then the running tracks and fields.

Pastoral care, well-being and discipline: Parents say 'pastoral care here is excellent' and that 'the older pupils help the younger pupils'. They value the peer mentoring room where sixth formers make hot chocolate for younger pupils, who can sit and talk if they have a problem. Bullying is rare, and the few 'misunderstandings' that do arise are 'nipped in the bud by the school very quickly,' say parents. One, whose daughter had been home educated and found the first few weeks a little daunting, commented on how well she had been helped to settle in.

Pupils have good relationships with their form tutors and teachers – 'everyone is helpful here', said a year 7 pupil. 'The teachers do tend to treat the children as adults,' said a parent. 'They communicate openly with them, so the children are not frightened to say, "I want to speak to you about something".'

The house system fosters a sense of belonging and there is good support from a careers service, with an annual careers convention. Parents report that initial concerns are likely to involve ensuring children can cope with homework alongside the large numbers of extracurricular opportunities. 'One of the things we were told at a meeting before starting is that you've got to be organised. My son comes into school early to get homework done because he wants to do swimming and football after school.'

Plenty of contact with parents through subject, house and tutor reports and parents' evenings, but parents also appreciate in particular the introductory meeting held for parents of new year 7s. The school is 'really on the ball like that,' said a parent who has two daughters in the school, one in the sixth form and another in year 9. 'Whatever topic it might be, you get the information in time to talk about it.'

Pupils and parents: Parents are mostly professional. There is a mix of backgrounds, races and religions here, with the majority being white English. 'Although we are a Christian school we welcome pupils of all faiths,' says the school. Many pupils come from the linked preparatory school, others from local independent and state schools. The school also has a number of international students (about 60 per cent of boarders, plus a few day pupils) from the Ukraine, Russia and other Eastern European countries, Central Europe and the Far East including China.

A number of notable former pupils including Douglas Adams, author of the Hitchhiker's Guide to the Galaxy, Sir Hardy Amies, couturier and dressmaker (he designed the school uniform), Lord Black of Brentwood, executive director of The Telegraph, Frank Lampard, footballer, Jack Straw, former Lord Chancellor and Secretary of State for Justice, and many more.

Entrance: Year 7 entry by maths, English and verbal reasoning exams examination and an interview to 'assess a pupil's intellectual curiosity, potential and

flair for learning'. Sixth form entrance is by interview and successful GCSE results (generally at least six B grades).

Exit: Most – about 80 per cent – stay on to sixth form and most proceed to university. In 2015, four to Oxbridge and over half to other top 20 universities such as Bristol and Edinburgh, or further afield to Harvard. Record number of medics, dentists and vetc. The school also helps those students who want to go straight into work through the alumni association and network of ex-pupils.

Money matters: A good variety of scholarships, of up to 50 per cent, on offer to top academic scorers in the entrance exam or those with specialist talents in art, drama, music, choral and sport. There are also means-tested bursaries of up to 100 per cent. Sixth form scholarships valued at between £500 and £1000, offered via a two-hour critical thinking paper.

Remarks: Strong on values and has all the facilities and opportunities needed to provide a child with a rounded education. Very impressive.

Chigwell School

High Road, Chigwell, Essex IG7 6QF

020 8501 5700
hm@chigwell-school.org
www.chigwell-school.org
C of E

Ages: 13–18
Pupils: 415; sixth form: 160
Boarders: 30 in the sixth form
Day: £10,200 – £16,020 pa
Boarding: £26,730 pa

Headmaster: Since 2007, Mr Michael Punt MA MSc PGCE (40s), a physicist who lives on site with his wife Gill and their three sons, all of whom attend the school – a fact that many parents say 'keeps him in tune with pupils' and parents' experiences of Chigwell.' His calm and positive influence is palpable throughout the school, with parents describing him as 'approachable,' 'well-liked' and 'respected.' In fact, many were swayed against the local competition purely on the basis of meeting him. 'He doesn't just talk at you in some grand hall – he chats with you in a relaxed way and seems to know exactly what you want to know,' said one.

Pupils also speak enthusiastically about him. 'He knows every one of us, as well as taking an interest in us,' one pupil told us. Not for him a chief executive type headship, but rather a personal touch that's helped by the size of the school and the fact that he and colleagues interview every child that comes here. Mainly, though, it seems to be down to his hands-on approach – he teaches pupils, does a lot of mock interviews and is often

seen around the school. The week before our visit, he'd had all the prefects round for a meal and he eats regularly with the boarders.

Having grown up in nearby Brentwood, he did his degree at Oxford and his masters at Imperial, then worked at St Dunstan's College as a physics teacher, working his way up to head of year and head of physics, after which he did a stint at The Perse School, Cambridge, as deputy head (academic) where he continued to climb the ranks until moving to Chigwell.

Academic matters: Excellent results, which have risen steadily since 2007 – 73 per cent of GCSE grades were A*/A in 2015. Head puts this down to pupils' positive and conscientious attitude to learning and an excellent relationship with teachers, both points which the latest ISI inspection praised. 'Teachers are dedicated, both in and out of the classroom, and they very rarely shout,' one pupil told us. 'I was amazed when my son emailed teachers about his essay during half term and got

detailed feedback the same day, but that's how it is here,' said a parent. The tone of the communication seems to be spot on, too. 'In many schools, it's either too matey or terribly stand-offish, but they seem to have got the balance just right here,' said one parent. Lessons interactive and busy, with plenty of IT embedded across all subjects – and a pilot of tablet-embedded learning going on in years 9 and 12 when we visited. 'We'll see how it goes and may well expand it in future,' the head told us.

Low turnover of around 6-7 per cent a year for teaching staff, with applicants for replacements of a high calibre, and they must be willing to teach beyond their subject, with the school following the somewhat old-fashioned model of all teachers getting involved in an extracurricular activity. 'It's not unusual to see maths staff getting stuck into games or English teachers helping to run chess clubs here,' says the head. 'It's the Chigwell way, this family-type approach.' Head regularly observes all teaching staff and has implemented a rigorous structure that ensures constant reflection, whilst the Teaching Skills Group means staff regularly share good practice. Tracking is big here – both pastorally and academically, with the aim of the two working closely together.

On entry, four classes of 22 maximum, although class sizes drop considerably for at GCSE level and to around a dozen at A level. Latin and French taught to all year 7s, and all try German and Spanish in year 8. In year 9, all pupils continue French and select one or more of the other three languages, with all pupils doing at least one modern language for GCSE. Mandarin also taught as extracurricular from junior school upwards. Setting in French and maths from year 7 and some in German from year 9. English and sciences setted from year 10. Regular testing means there can be movement between sets to start with, although this is uncommon later on. Homework taken seriously, although it's never set for the following day.

At GCSE, all students take maths, both English subjects, one modern language and the vast majority do the three sciences. Other popular options include geography, history, RE, with a strong interest also seen in other languages, drama, DT and music. 'We don't have option blocks – we make the timetable work around the pupils' choices,' says head, who adds that there are no early GCSEs taken here, although the top maths set in year 11 take additional maths.

Wide choice of subjects at A levels. Economics, maths, sciences, geography and English are strong, but psychology, drama and DT are on the rise too, enforcing Chigwell's reputation as a place for the all-rounder. In 2015, 85 per cent A*-B and 61 per cent A*/A at A level.

Plenty of extension opportunities, including EPQ and HPQ (latter at GCSE level), essay competitions and Olympiads. Enrichment programme impressive and includes subject-specific groups, such as law groups, medics' groups, social sciences groups etc. University preparation stunningly good, with guidance for UCAS applications starting in the February of the lower sixth, with plenty of targeted guidance and support, and mock interviews aplenty.

Boarders almost all international and no two boarders who share a language share a room. Everyone agrees they bring a lot to school life. 'The boarders give the school a homely feel'

Junior school pupils screened on entry for SEN, with further testing in the senior school. Learning support provided throughout the school as necessary either inside or outside the classroom. Not a school for severe learning disabilities, however, with only one statemented when we visited.

Games, options, the arts: mass participation in sport does what it says on the tin here, with the possible exception of football, which one parent told us is all about the A team. Core boys' sports include football (first term), hockey (second term) and cricket and athletics (third term). For girls, it's hockey (first term), netball (send term) and rounders and athletics (third term), along with some football and cricket also in the summer term. Other sports include golf (played at nearby club), swimming, basketball and badminton. School punches above its weight in competitions, regularly getting through to regional finals, along with national finals for football and hockey.

Outdoor facilities are vast, with 100 acres of playing fields, including Astroturf, surrounding this small school, and indoor facilities are being steadily improved through an ambitious development plan. Pupils particularly keen to have an indoor pool, rather than just the small outdoor pool they currently have, and many want to see the unfancy sports centre updated – both projects under consideration.

The drama centre is an eye-catching red-brick building with impressively professional facilities – foyer big enough for pre-theatre drinks receptions; 170-seat theatre designed for use by the whole school community; green room; rehearsal and teaching spaces; and dressing rooms. All children use it for weekly drama up until the end of year 9 and it's also a popular GSCE option, with around a dozen taking drama at A level with great success. Related subject areas, such as theatre make-up and costume design, also taken seriously here, and the centre is used for public speaking, debating and LAMDA too. Numerous productions take place throughout the year. 'It would be rare to find a child who isn't somehow involved in drama,' says the head.

Music very inclusive, with every other pupil learning an instrument (over 300 lessons per week from 23 visiting music teachers), some of whom play to incredibly high standards (usually one a year to Oxbridge as a choral music scholar). Plenty of opportunities to perform in ensembles, with a wide range of musical tastes catered from swing bands to string bands, as well as rock and pop. The chapel choir, an elite choir for 40 odd students, performs regularly in the likes of Westminster Abbey, Canterbury Cathedral and Yorkminster, and there are plenty of other choirs too. 'Every aspect of music is amazing here, from the singing right through to every instrument you can think of, along with many you didn't even know existed,' said one parent.

Art and DT work closely together in the spacious and hi-tech facilities, with graphics offered as a GCSE option and many pupils going onto study architecture and fine art when they leave. Phenomenally good artwork displayed throughout the school, much of it in 3D.

Huge choice of extracurricular activities, from D of E and scouts to art exhibitions and the inspiring and thought-provoking talks on everything from evolution to restorative justice for schools, which are run as part of the Williams Project, named after philosopher and Chigwell alumnus, Bernard Williams. 'The amount of opportunities here is immense and you'd frankly be seen as a bit daft if you didn't utilise it,' said one student. 'I

Playing fields stretch towards Epping Forest giving a rural aspect to the school and some lovely views from the classroom windows

haven't had a free afternoon in the last three years – but in a good way,' laughed another. A seemingly infinite amount of trips available too, including French and Spanish homestays, hockey tour to South Africa, scout trip to Switzerland, annual ski trip to France, along with smaller scale trips including activity weekends in the likes of Wales and the Lake District. 'We are conscious that there is a broad mix of wealth and make sure we do not offer all five star trips,' says head.

Boarding: Sixth-form only boarders, of whom there are 30 living across four equal-sized boarding houses, either on the school site or just across the road. Hailing from around 16 countries – mostly central and Eastern Europe and China – the boarders are almost all international, and no two boarders who share a language share a room. Everyone agrees they bring a lot to school life, in terms of the insights they provide into other cultures and a more worldly ethos overall – all helped by the fact that they are encouraged to give talks on the issues affecting their homelands. 'The boarders help give the school a homely feel,' added one student.

Boarding houses are inviting and not the least bit institutional. Rooms mostly twin, although the odd one has three beds, and boarders told us 'there's a good balance between houseparents letting you get on with it, and providing clear boundaries.' Each houseparent, who lives in with their family, is a big part of daily life and seen as a major figure in boarders' lives. 'In our house, the parents have children aged 4 and 6 and we always love hanging out with them,' said one pupil. Curfews are 10.30pm on weekdays; 11.30pm at weekends. Daily study time between 7-9pm during weekdays – 'Even if you don't have work to do, you have to respect that others have and be quiet,' one boarder told us.

No shortage of events – the week we visited, they'd just had Divali weekend celebrations and a film night – which day pupils also join in, but boarders welcome the opportunity to be allowed to be self-reliant too. Boarders told us they'd formed close friendships with both other boarders and day pupils and already felt sad about the prospect of leaving the school.

Background and atmosphere: Founded in 1629 by the Reverend Samuel Harsnett, the local vicar, who became Archbishop of York and Chancellor of

Cambridge University. Today the original red-brick schoolhouse, which is located on the approach road to the historic high street, forms the centrepiece to this pretty village of neat buildings, punctuated by gardens, blooms and trees. The surrounding playing fields stretch towards Epping Forest and give a rural aspect to the school and some lovely views from the windows of the attractive, low-rise teaching blocks. None of the facilities are more than an easy and pleasant stroll apart, with the junior and senior schools just steps away from one another and the stunning new pre-prep a few minutes' walk away. Buildings all kept up to date, with a nice combination of traditional and contemporary, and new building works always in the pipeline. In 2010, for instance, there were two new boarding houses and catering facilities, along with a sixth form coffee shop, whilst 2013 saw the new pre-prep and science labs. The sixth form centre will be ready for 2016 entry, with a dining hall extension, new sports hall and indoor swimming pool next on the agenda.

Of particular note is the 1920s chapel, which was built in tribute to fallen alumni and is a mainstay of life here. Pupils usually attend at least once a week for a service (and another weekly service at the local church), but there's plenty of room for all the beliefs represented at this multicultural school, with speech day services including a passage from each of the six major world faiths.

All have lunch in the Harry Potter-esque dining hall (where teachers eat on the stage) and students can have tea at 4pm for no extra cost, as well as breakfast, for which they can bring parents and siblings. 'Every Thursday, our whole family has breakfast here – we love it,' said one parent. Food is plentiful and very good (we tried it ourselves), with healthy options and popular themed days. The uniform is smart and sober – kilts or plain trousers with a navy blazer, though the sixth formers wear office attire.

No need for intrusive bells here to mark the change of lessons, with pupils making their way around the school in an ordered fashion, and newbies of any age wear a plain tie so they can be spotted and helped when in need. 'This is a harmonious school, with really lovely young people who, in the majority of cases, you'd be proud to have as your own children,' says the head. Indeed, 'happy' was a word used a lot by the pupils we talked to, with several referring to it as one big family. Life really does seem to just flow very smoothly, with laughter never far from earshot. Even communication systems – homework submitted electronically and an electronic noticeboard system, among them – seem to work effortlessly. No wonder old Chigwellians feel such a sense of loyalty, with growing numbers willing to come into do talks, mock interviews and offer work experience.

The school council doesn't seem to have achieved a great deal more than the usual increase in number of water fountains, although they do meet regularly. There's a strong charitable culture, with a committee consisting of staff and pupils who choose the charities to support and raise in excess of £30,000 a year. 'We want to understand the charities we support, we do a lot of promotion around that part too,' says the head, who adds that the school is very much part of the local community, which often joins in with fundraising events.

Pastoral care, well-being and discipline: The transition from junior to senior school is gentle, with parents praising the 'seamless process.' A strong four-house system, and staff who 'really know their pupils', according to the head, mean students are comfortable in the knowledge that they are being 'looked out for'. 'There are lots of personalities among the teachers here, but we all have someone we know we could speak to – a teacher that really stands out for us,' said one pupil, with many of the younger pupils talking about how friendly the older ones are. The school counsellor, employed for two days a week, is also on hand, and works with families where necessary. School promotes a society in which everyone takes responsibility for each other and the wider environment.

'Pupils here aren't saintly, they've got a twinkle in their eye, but they're also very hard working and really nice'

Discipline system highly structured, with detentions the most common sanctions, typically for late homework, missing chapel and being late. 'They're not given out willy nilly, so you take it seriously when you get one,' said one pupil. 'The pupils aren't saintly, and they've got a twinkle in their eye, but they're also hard working and really nice. We don't have many behavioural problems,' says the head. Indeed, current head has only made one permanent exclusion, although occasionally there are temporary ones, for instances such as smoking and repeated misbehaviour. Bullying rare, with pupils pointing out the 'confide' button on every school computer, where you can report issues anonymously at any time, or talk to a staff member confidentially.

Pupils and parents: This leafy suburb is spoilt for choice education-wise, with several good fee-paying schools on the doorstep and some of the best grammars in the country a short hop on the train away. Even Old Chigwellians admit to investigating the competition before signing up their offspring, but the school still wins people over with its ability to develop not just academic success, but confident, well-rounded people. 'One of the things that swung it for me was the way pupils talk to adults in a sophisticated way, but not without respect,' said one.

The parents – around two-thirds of whom are middle-class white British, with the remaining third mostly British Asian – seem to love the sense of community that the school has. 'My children have always said they felt they belong to something here – so much so that my daughter felt a real sense of loss when she left, and the same can be said for many parents,' said one. Most live within a five mile radius, although there's a growth in the number coming in from East London. Mainly affluent parents, although not exclusively. 'I was worried it would be full of rich kids and Landrover-driving parents, but although you do get that, there's a reassuring number of hard-working professional couples who make sacrifices to send their kids here,' said one parent.

There's a good 50:50 split of boys and girls, who we found to be relaxed, confident, articulate and helpful, as well as having a great sense of humour. Parents, meanwhile, particularly welcome the many opportunities to speak informally with staff about their children's progress and well-being at breakfast get-togethers and afternoon teas, as well as the programme of social events put on by the 'Friends of Chigwell' PA which also raises significant funds for things like new canoes and stage lighting. Five school minibuses available for pupils, with others using public transport, notably the tube or bus, whilst many get dropped off by car.

The list of distinguished alumni includes William Penn, Sir Arthur Grimble, Sir Austin Bradford Hill, Sir Richard Dales, Col Bob Stewart and Sir Bernard Williams.

Entrance: Most junior school pupils move up here, forming about half of the year 7 entry, with the other half from a wide variety of local prep and primaries. 'It's very welcoming, so my children took to it like a duck to water, despite not coming from the junior school,' said one parent. Around 300 apply for these 40-odd places; assessment by interview (separate ones for pupils and parents), and English, maths and verbal reasoning papers. Small number of vacancies at 13 (English, maths and a modern foreign language exam). At 16, those moving up within the school are joined by around 10 local entrants as well as around 14 overseas boarders. Entrants to the sixth form are expected to have achieved at least four As and two Bs or in six GCSE subjects and A*/A in their A level choices.

Exit: Hardly any post-16 leavers and 95 per cent of those who leave after sixth form move on to a degree course at university, or music and other specialist colleges. In 2015, four to Oxbridge; some 80 per cent to Russell Group universities, notably Exeter, Nottingham, Bristol, Leeds and LSE. Popular degree subjects include economics, English and humanities.

Money matters: Academic scholarships available at 11 and 13 years; scholarships for art, drama and music offered at 16. Increasing number of means-tested bursaries available. 'I visit every family we are considering for bursaries,' says the head.

Remarks: A happy, nurturing and busy school with a genuinely family feel and an emphasis on creating caring all-rounders. Academically, pupils are put through their paces, but it all seems to be done in such a civilised and pleasant manner that you're far more likely to hear pupils talk about opportunities and prospects than pressure and stress. 'Anyone that wants to do well will do well here,' said one student, 'and I can't think of a nicer place to succeed.'

Culford School

Culford, Bury St Edmunds, Suffolk IP28 6TX

01284 385308
admissions@culford.co.uk
www.culford.co.uk

Ages: 13–18 (boarding from age 7 in prep)
Pupils: 607; sixth form: 150
Boarders: 265, majority full
Day: £10,800 – £17,985 pa
Boarding: £20,880 – £29,085 pa

Headmaster: Since 2004, Mr Julian Johnson-Munday (late 40s). Educated at Norwich School and Leicester University, where he read English. Previously housemaster at Cranleigh and deputy head of Mill Hill (during his tenure he studied for an MBA at Durham). Unpompous, affable manner but makes no bones about the clear direction of the school and the setting of targets for staff and pupils. Is intent on raising the school's profile and has overseen a busy programme of building.

Seeks to maintain and support the school's boarding provision (currently nearly 50 per cent) and is not enamoured with flexi boarding options, as he believes this could compromise a vital spark of the school. His wife, Jo, is the school's marketing and foundation director and they have one son.

Academic matters: Strong performance at GCSE (51 per cent A*/A grades in 2015) and A level (26 per cent A*/A, 56 per cent A*/B) – impressive considering school is not ultra-selective. Head remains calm about occasional downward blips in results, saying with disarming frankness that 'year groups do vary in ability'. Average class size is 17 (seven in sixth form) with setting in the core subjects of mathematics, English, sciences and languages. All pupils study at least one modern language (French, German and Spanish on offer) with Latin available as a GCSE option too. In mathematics, high ability pupils take IGCSE in year 10 (all gain A*/A) and additional maths in year 11. Science is very strong and has superb facilities; roughly half do separate sciences at GCSE. Learning support has its own department and is well resourced.

Pupil support across the curriculum is arranged either on a withdrawal basis or outside the timetabled day. A popular programme of seminars and tutorials with high level speakers for the gifted and talented and potential Oxbridge punters.

The school day includes eight periods (four on Saturday), plus after-school activities. Day pupils don't leave until 5.30pm.

Games, options, the arts: Outstanding sports provision includes a 25 metre indoor pool, floodlit Astroturf, games pitches galore, fitness suite and squash courts. The indoor tennis school attracts students from all over with its elite training programme run by professional coaches. Similar regimes are now available for rugby, hockey and swimming. Many pupils train for and take part in athletics events at county and national level and the whole school does two 80 minute periods of sport each week.

Lord Cadogan's morning room is the head's study – complete with distracting vistas of the park. The grand visitors' lavatory installed for a visit by Edward VII is still in situ

New theatre and dance studio are well used, with two major productions each year (some taken to the Edinburgh fringe) and plenty of choirs, orchestras and ensembles. Large numbers take instrumental or singing lessons and a pupil recently won a choral scholarship to St John's College, Oxford. Art and design are strong subjects in the school with good results at GCSE and A level. Plans are afoot to improve the present facilities.

CCF and D of E popular; CATS – Culford Adventure, Training and Service – is designed for fourth years who don't want to do CCF, and

837

includes first aid, life saving, fair trade and outdoor pursuits. Links with schools in Malawi and India; as well as raising funds, pupils visit to help with general maintenance.

Boarding: Just under 200 full senior boarders and 15 or so flexi, accommodated in five boarding houses, including one co-ed house for the prep school boarders (35 full and 20 weekly and flexi). Good range of evening activities; weekends may include eg a trip to the beach or to Norwich, quad biking, white water rafting, a movie or magic night.

Background and atmosphere: Sublime setting in 480 acres of landscaped parkland, complete with Grade I listed bridge and gardens designed by Humphrey Repton. The main building, originally owned variously by the Cadogan and Cornwallis families, is 18th century. The school moved to its present site in 1935 and has maintained the original fabric to a high standard and made full use of its assets. Lord Cadogan's morning room is the head's study – complete with distracting vistas of the park. The grand visitors' lavatory installed for a visit by Edward VII is still in situ, together with a photograph of the royal visitor. In the grounds, a series of newer and, for the most part, well-designed buildings house classrooms, science laboratories, sports and boarding facilities. High standards of maintenance throughout are helped by generous bequests from old pupils – a notable feature.

Unpompous, affable manner but makes no bones about the clear direction of the school and the setting of targets for staff and pupils. Not enamoured with flexi boarding

Unhurried, almost relaxed air about the school. Excellent staff/ pupil relationships, plenty of banter, easy but respectful. Headmaster greets pupils by name. Girls' uniform, featuring an ankle-length pleated skirt, could be a turn-off for some, though we were told by pupils that it is 'comfortable and cool in summer'. Parents describe the school as a 'hidden gem.'

Pastoral care, well-being and discipline: One of the school's great strengths, and the one most frequently mentioned by parents, is the care of pupils. Tutors and house staff deal with everyday matters but the headmaster keeps himself very well informed and can be the key figure at a moment of

The indoor tennis school attracts students from all over with its elite training programme run by professional coaches

crisis. 'My son was confused about his future,' one father told us. 'The headmaster took him out for a walk with the dog and that seemed to sort everything out.' Emphasis is on consideration for others – kindness and politeness towards staff as well as to other pupils, and few discipline problems.

Pupils and parents: Majority of pupils are drawn from professional and business families from within a radius of 50 miles. They include a fair sprinkling looking for a different pace from that offered by some of the other local schools. About 20 per cent of boarders are Forces children and just over 10 per cent from overseas, including a cohort of 10 from Germany, who attend for a year. Families are tremendously loyal and many pupils are the children of Old Culfordians.

Entrance: At 13, admission is by examination, school report and interview. Around three-quarters join year 9 straight from Culford Prep, with the remainder coming from local state and prep schools. The school report and interview are as important as the exam result – the head knows what he is looking for. Sixth form entrants need seven good GCSEs, with at least Bs in the subjects to be studied at A level.

Exit: Just under quarter left after GCSEs in 2015, just over 10 per cent to return overseas. Almost all go on to university, wide range of destinations including Russell Group institutions. Though no Oxbridge in 2015, increasingly on the radar.

Money matters: A complex web of scholarships and exhibitions available at main entry points (normally worth between 10 and 20 per cent of the fees). Academic, music, art and sports awards are on offer, together with bursaries for the financially hard-pressed, including new foundation academic scholarship at 13+ and 16+ for candidates with Oxbridge potential. Reductions for Forces children and siblings. Overseas pupils charged at a slightly higher rate.

Remarks: A thriving, happy school with excellent foundations and confident leadership. It deserves to be better known than it is.

Edge Grove Preparatory School

Edge Grove School, Aldenham Village, Hertfordshire WD25 8NL

01923 855724
admissions@edgegrove.com
www.edgegrove.com

Ages: 3–13 (boarding from 7)
Pupils: 416
Boarders: 25 full/weekly, about 35 flexi
Day: £11,535 – £15,420 pa
Boarding: plus £4,065 – £5,820 pa

Headmaster: Since 2012, Ben Evans (40s). A Devon lad (mother still breeds Dartmoor ponies there) with a love of all things country. Head boy at Bramdean School before heading to Exeter University to read history and archaeology. Returned, armed with his degree and PGCE, to Bramdean where he 'learned to teach,' before taking up the post of head of history at Brighton College, later returning as deputy head to his alma mater.

Had a 'now or never' moment before hot footing it to Sri Lanka to teach at the junior school of the British School in Colombo, Sri Lanka, where he served a total of six years, the final four as head. Returned to the UK following the birth of his first child and found love at first sight with Edge Grove – 'exactly what I wanted,' he says. Laughingly says wealthy Sri Lankan parents provided good grounding for dealing with those of the ambitious north London variety, although parents say it is clear he is not trying to turn school into 'a typical north London hothouse.'

Lives in head's house at school with wife Alex – 'an absolute gem,' according to parents. Described as dynamic, likeable and no nonsense, she regularly rolls up her sleeves and gets stuck in in the boarding house, sorting things out 'with a deft hand,' says one mother.

Huge sighs of relief breathed by staff and parents alike at the end of Evans' first year in tenure as he appears to be there to stay, having scrapped Saturday lessons, made dramatic changes to the school day and really 'upped the ante' on the academic front. One parent said Evans had achieved more over the summer holidays (new adventure playground, gleaming home economics room and upgrades to textiles facilities) than they'd seen over the last three years. Just what Edge Grove needed after an unsettled patch with a revolving door of head teachers.

Entrance: Gently selective, with relaxed assessments and parental interview – 'we want parents to have chosen us for the right reasons,' says head. Little ones at 3+ and 4+ come for a short session where staff engage them in an activity and observe their skills in, for example, sharing and socialising. Currently oversubscribed for nursery and reception. Entrants at 7+ attend an assessment day and take verbal/non-verbal reasoning tests before spending a day in class to see how they fit in. 'We want the kind of children who will take advantage of all the things we have to offer,' says head.

No bursaries in the lower part of the school apart from those offered to military families. New scholarships introduced for existing pupils in years 7 and 8 to 'acknowledge their contribution to the school.'

Campus feels as if it could accommodate twice the number, with a huge open space for the nursery and separate science and art buildings for older ones

Exit: Exodus of some girls at 11; others and most boys peel off at 13. Girls to St Albans High School for Girls, Abbot's Hill and Downe House, with St Albans Boys most popular for boys; plus both to a range of co-ed schools including Rugby, Haileybury, Berkhamsted and Aldenham. A good handful of scholarships achieved annually, ranging from academic to sport and music. Conversations about next schools start with parents in years 5 and 6.

Remarks: When you arrive at this idyllic country prep it's hard to believe that it's just a stone's throw from north London and that the background hum is the M25. Set in grassy parkland with the requisite cows grazing next to the drive, Edge Grove – formerly the home of JP Morgan – is a world apart from many of its concrete-clad urban rivals.

Smiling boys and girls (school is now 50/50 and 'firmly co-educational,' according to head) in woolly red sweaters cheerfully and proactively greet you as you walk around, giving the impression of a happy, down to earth and confident cohort. Not surprising when you see the space they have to occupy – campus feels as if it could accommodate twice the number, with a huge open space for the nursery alone and separate science and art school buildings for older ones. Lovely manners abound, with classroom doors hardly opened before children leap to their feet.

Pupils and parents 'a really good mix,' according to head. About 20 per cent London based with the rest from around Radlett, St Albans, Elstree and Borehamwood and some Forces, based at Northwood. Ethnically diverse, reflecting the local area: 'wonderful,' say parents. Some discreet old money, others more flash and plenty of hard-working dual income first time buyers.

New school day structure popular with parents who say 'it just makes sense' to teach core subjects in the mornings when the children are most receptive. Activities take place either between 4 and 5pm or 5 and 6pm depending on year group and children can also stay for prep and supper, helping working parents or those further afield manage the pick-up. Saturday school abolished by current head in 2012 and replaced with voluntary Saturday attendance to take part in fun activities like music and drama or the Edge Grove Award (like a mini D of E) and stay for lunch if they wish – 'the quality of what we offer is much better now,' he says. Fleet of new iPads introduced for year 3 and up in 2013, kicking the school firmly into the 'progressive' bracket as far as technology is concerned. Class sizes capped at 20 in the pre-prep and 18 in the prep school.

Head 'aiming for excellence in all subjects.' International Primary Curriculum taught in pre-prep, which also has a forest school curriculum. French taught from reception and classics from year 5 with setting starting in year 3 for English

Parents are able to email class teachers direct and receive prompt, useful replies. Even throw-away comments in the car park are taken seriously and actioned, said one

and maths, then for French and science from year 5. New virtual language lab. Years 7 and 8 see pupils split into a scholarship set and two other common entrance sets. Parents talk about the 'academic rigour' being teased out of pupils on current head's watch and report a welcome increase in homework for younger ones. Mandarin, Spanish and Italian offered as after-school clubs for budding linguists.

Parents praise staff mix: 'some really old school, some young and dynamic,' although concede that 'some are better than others.' Communication between parents and teaching staff is reportedly 'excellent' in the main: parents are able to email class teachers direct and, with occasional exceptions, receive prompt, useful replies. Even throw-away comments in the car park are taken seriously and actioned, said one. Whole school communication 'getting better,' according to parents, with recent introduction of weekly email letting parents know of all forthcoming fixtures and trips to help pupils be better prepared. Head, keen to iron out any bad habits inherited from predecessors, has introduced weekly staff training sessions to ensure consistent quality across the board. SEN and EAL limited to offering

learning support to children with mild difficulties and no plans to increase provision.

Outstanding art taught in inspirational atelier style space with first class work in genres ranging from cubism to pupils' favourite, street art, on display. Host of shiny new sewing machines will no doubt add to pupils' textiles capabilities; home economics also on the curriculum. Classrooms alive with sound of music: head wants 'music to be happening all the time,' and is getting his wish with over 180 peripatetic lessons each week ('brilliantly timetabled,' say parents) and a new director of music (ex Haileybury) driving musical excellence in all its forms. Choral music is 'very strong,' says head and a lucky few get to try their hand in the school rock band – recently kitted out with four electric guitars, a drum kit and, most importantly, a soundproofed practice room. Plenty for budding thespians too – year 5 recently performed A Midsummer Night's Dream in the school's grounds, with a production of Bugsy Malone another success.

Brightly decorated dorms sleep up to eight pupils. Head, determined to avoid 'sleepover culture,' insists that boarders stay for minimum of three nights a week from year 5

Sport taken seriously for both genders with a total of around 800 fixtures a year and specialist teaching from reception. Girls benefit from the guidance of an ex-England netball coach and the school has strong links with Radlett Cricket Club. U13 six-a-side football team current national IAPS champions, with other pupils reaching county standard for cricket, archery and squash and recent introduction of international tours for top teams. For less starry types, there are plenty of inter-house matches and tournaments which are fiercely contested, so everyone gets a go. Weekly swimming lessons and galas take place in the immaculate heated outdoor pool on the site of a former beautifully walled garden, mirrored on the other side by impressively sized, albeit slightly tired, tennis courts.

Around 25 full and weekly boarders, just under 10 per cent international, many Forces children, with a total of 50 beds to accommodate flexi-boarding. Newly appointed non-teaching head of boarding has made a 'huge difference,' to what was formerly a fairly chaotic boarding function according to parents, although many agreed that there is still some way to go in terms of organisation: very little wardrobe space (one wardrobe for seven girls) and no lockers lead to lost clothes, with one parent reporting having lost up to 20 pairs of socks and others on-going problems with lost sports kit. Occasional issues with bullying and bad behaviour are 'not dealt with badly,' for the most part but parents have high hopes the 'new broom' will step up discipline and eliminate these issues altogether, to create a calmer and more nurturing boarding environment.

Bright, newly decorated dorms sleep up to eight pupils, with seniors (years 7 and 8) having their lounging and TV area incorporated into the dorm. There's also a games room in an annexe with snooker, table tennis and table football. Head, determined to avoid 'sleepover culture,' insists that boarders stay for a minimum of three nights a week from year 5, although they can stay for one in years 3 and 4, and all year 3 pupils are expected to board for at least one night during expedition week when years 4 to 8 head off site. Popular fun themed weekends twice yearly give all pupils a chance to taste boarding on a first come, first served basis.

Clubs galore – many of which are included in fees – from gardening and chess to taekwondo and war gaming. These are integrated well into the long school day and parents happily describe their children as 'very busy.' Two minibus services ferry years 3 to 8 to school if they choose, along routes covering Hemel Hempstead, St Albans, How Wood, Totteridge, Whetstone, Barnet, Brookmans Park and Shenley.

Felsted School

Felsted, Great Dunmow, Essex CM6 3LL

01371 822605
ado@felsted.org
www.felsted.org
C of E

Ages: 13–18 (boarding from 9)
Pupils: 542; sixth form: 246
Boarders: 254 full/weekly, 237 flexi (plus 82 in prep)
Day: £21,585 pa
Boarding: £26,985 – £31,785 pa

Headmaster: Since September 2015, Chris Townsend, previously deputy head. Classics degree from Oxford, where he was an exhibitioner and won three cricket blues. First teaching post at alma mater Dean Close, then housemaster and head of boarding at Stowe, then to Felstead in 2010 as deputy head. Married to Melanie; they have two children and, judging by their photo, a couple of red setters.

Academic matters: Not overly selective, but each year a solid cohort achieves top grades across the board in both A levels and GCSEs. In 2015, 50 per cent A*/A grades at GCSE; 58 per cent A*-B, 27 per cent A*/A at A level. Known for its success in psychology, but pupils do well in other subjects – Latin and modern languages, history, maths, science and art, to name but a few. More generally it has the reputation of bringing out the best in all. IB now taking off amongst quite conservative local families – currently about a third of the sixth form opts for it: 34 average point score in 2015.

Parents recoil at the thought of increased pressure and support greater focus on individual educational plans, with the aim of ensuring maximum academic success – but not at the expense of other activities. Recent increase in number of classroom assistants to support the process. SEN pupils, of whom about 45, often take one fewer GCSE, to allow time for more personalised support. EAL teachers also on hand.

Streaming in the lower years and class sizes are kept small – between 15-20 up to GCSE – and often considerably smaller in the sixth form. Staff development encouraged. Recently staff and pupils were asked to suggest what constituted a good or outstanding lesson and the findings have been discussed openly with all – can but add to the pressure to deliver.

Games, options, the arts: Traditionally sporty. It has produced some outstanding cricketers and Olympic athletes. Games fields and facilities stretch as far as the eye can see. Currently has a tennis player in the top 10 nationally. Hockey, cricket, rugby and netball all strong with regular success at regional and national championships. If you don't make the teams, no shame with lots else on offer to keep you fit and occupied. Emphasis very much on participation, be it in sports, regular music events featuring individual talent, the many choirs and orchestras (30 per cent are involved in music of some kind), drama or in the wealth of extracurricular options which make for very full days and busy weekends. Not perhaps for the retiring, ill-organised or easily-wearied type. Huge take up of D of E – at the last count no fewer than 26 gold awards in the upper sixth – and 220 enrolled in CCF.

Very much accords with Round Square school promoting IDEALS – internationalism, democracy, care for the environment, adventurous pursuits, leadership and service. Felsted has been a global member since 2010. In addition to much-appreciated local community activities and links to disadvantaged communities in East London where pupils have been busy promoting cheerleading, the school is reinforcing developing world links. Students queue up for opportunities to break the 'Felsted bubble'. They include visits to the partner school in Ethiopia and jumping aboard a former pupil's Magic Bus which supports children in the slums of Mumbai.

Boarding: Standardising flexi-boarding arrangements has overcome some earlier problems concerning integration of full and part-time boarders and there are robust measures in place to help new and international students settle in. Although many local boarders disappear at the weekends, the stayers-in are rarely short of invitations to stay with local families, outings or on-site activities to fill their time.

Two day and eight boarding houses, five for boys and five for girls, plus co-ed boarding in the prep school from 9 years upwards. Separate upper sixth form boarding houses. Year 9 board in pleasant shared accommodation – all other years have single rooms though some choice of double rooms if pupils prefer it. Homely common room areas and studies.

Background and atmosphere: Traditional, yet progressive, it feeds off its history but is not hidebound by it. Founded in 1564 by Richard, Lord Riche, Lord Chancellor of England, the school's original Guild Hall is still in use with other, later, attractive Grade I and II listed buildings scattered throughout the village, interspersed with well-tended lawns and sports fields and cut through by the quiet Dunmow to Braintree road. Most recent additions include the music school and the sixth form centre – a great space to access the net and meet informally or at regular social events where the odd glass of wine is permitted. Overall impression of being a happy, happening place with parents content to be swept along for the ride.

Pastoral care, well-being and discipline: Recent tightening up on uniform and behaviour welcomed by parents and local businesses alike. Swift and decisive action when bullying and other misdemeanours uncovered, although, in truth, such incidents are relatively rare. Good relations between parents, pupils and staff enhanced by the introduction of clearer reporting systems and a new atmosphere of openness and purpose.

Pupils and parents: We hear that Essex is proud of producing self-starting, entrepreneurial and independent spirits. Parents value the fact that 'they're not sausage making' and champion these qualities at the school. Pupils range from the highly-driven and academically-orientated to the more fun-loving and easy-going, but all pretty down to earth. Characteristics of the typical Felstedian recently assessed, based on feedback from various parties, include being ambitious, motivated, accepting challenge and being self-aware.

Characteristics of the typical Felstedian based on feedback from various parties, include being ambitious, motivated, accepting challenge and being self-aware

Long list of notable OFs includes English test cricketer John Stephenson and General Sir Richard Dannatt, until recently Chief of the General Staff. Huge diversity of talent is reflected in the senior positions and success OFs have achieved in science and medicine, the military, politics and public service, academia, business, sports and the media.

While most live within a couple of hours of the school, it is increasingly attracting London-based families. Taking advantage of its proximity to Stansted Airport, international students make up some 20 per cent of pupils – getting towards the high end amongst schools in this guide. Lots of Germans do IB and a similar number of students from China, Hong Kong and all round the world.

Entrance: Many come up from the prep. Other popular feeder schools are Holmwood House, Heathmount, Orwell Park and Edge Grove. Those taking CE are required to obtain 50 per cent in each paper. Others take a verbal reasoning test, interview and submit a confidential report from their current school. They may take tests in maths, French and English for setting purposes. The same is true at 14+ entry. At 16+ there is a similar entry procedure and pupils are required to obtain six GCSEs at grade B or better including B grades in the subjects being pursued. Pupils who do not have English as their first language will be assessed by the head of EAL.

Exit: Around 90 per cent stay on to the sixth form. After A level most to good universities such as Exeter, Brighton, Leeds and Birmingham, plus a sprinkling to Oxbridge (two in 2015). Business-related subjects, medicine, humanities and the sciences popular.

Money matters: Academic, music, sport, art, design and technology or drama and all-rounder

scholarships offering up to 20 per cent or £1,000 off the fees are available at 13+ and 16+. There are some assisted places up to 100 per cent on a means-tested basis.

Remarks: Real sense of excitement as school aims at becoming 'a leading independent boarding and day school, regionally, nationally and internationally'. Well on its way, from what we hear, with parents welcoming a renewed focus on academic performance but not at the expense of individualism and quirkiness. All agree – it's one to watch.

Framlingham College

College Road, Woodbridge, Suffolk IP13 9EY

01728 723789
admissions@framcollege.co.uk
www.framcollege.co.uk
C of E

Ages: 13–18
Pupils: 450 pupils; sixth form: 200
Boarders: 240, most weekly
Day: £18,305 pa
Boarding: £28,470 pa

Linked school: Brandeston Hall Preparatory School

Headmaster: Since 2009, Mr Paul Taylor BA. Read history and politics at Exeter University. Formerly lower master (deputy head) at King's School, Canterbury, and before that director of sport at Tonbridge School. Very friendly, charming without overdoing it and a good listener. Aims to 'produce a decent, rounded human being who looks you in the eye' and believes the school's good performance should be better known outside East Anglia. Wife, Amanda, is secretary of the Framlingham Society and they have four children – two at university and two at Framlingham.

Academic matters: Performs well at both GCSE and A level, though not highly selective – strong commitment to pupils of varying ability. In 2015, 55 per cent of A levels were A*-B. At GCSE, 39 per cent A*/A grades. Some sixth formers take EPQ

SEN provision well established. Emphasis on supporting the pupils' needs – a register (updated termly) is kept to inform staff across the curriculum of any difficulties. Timetabled access to small group and individual tuition avoids pupil withdrawal from mainstream classes. All pupils must be capable of following the academic programmes at GCSE and A level. Provision for ESL also excellent – separate classes as well as individual tuition. Facilities well thought out, well designed and

un-flashy. Exceptional library and design and technology building. Classes kept small, average size 12.

Games, options, the arts: Excellent provision for all sports. Artificial surfaces, new indoor pool and fitness centre (well used, especially by girls) – hosts many tournaments. Sport is important – all pupils take part competitively, whatever their level of ability. Music and drama popular too. Brand new theatre/performance studio and many pupils take drama options at GCSE and A level. Well attended regular public performances – pupils recently took The Importance of Being Earnest to the Edinburgh Fringe. Concerts held in local churches – Framlingham and Orford, as well as Ely Cathedral. Big takeup for D of E, with numbers reaching gold awards. Curriculum also supported by extraordinary plethora of clubs and activities.

Boarding: Boarding houses well planned and comfortable enough, though girls' quarters, unsurprisingly perhaps, are more home-like and with better decoration. Three houses for girls and four for boys. House competitions range from cross-country to crabbing. Pupils come and go with their own swipe card; most go home at weekends, unless from abroad.

Background and atmosphere: Founded in 1864 in memory of Prince Albert, Queen Victoria's husband (his statue takes pride of place at the front of the school). Imposing Victorian main building in stunning setting, perched on a hillside with a gorgeous view across the valley to 12th century Framlingham Castle. A variety of buildings added over time, none of them particularly distinguished, but well planned to make good use of beautiful and extensive grounds. Stupendous view of the castle from many perspectives (head has bagged dress circle view from his first floor study).

Incorporating day pupils into boarding houses is well established and a great success. Many pupils do 'occasional' boarding

A tone of respectful informality throughout. Pupils well-mannered and noticeably calm, even at lesson changes and in the dining hall at lunchtime.

Pastoral care, well-being and discipline: Policy of incorporating day pupils into boarding houses is now well established and a great success. Many pupils do 'occasional' boarding. A parent told us: 'I can email the housemaster directly if my daughter wants to board at short notice – on the same day, on occasion.' Anti-bullying posters dotted around school and any incidents picked up on quickly. 'The housemaster got to the bottom of the matter on the

same day,' said one parent, 'and the boys are still together in the same house.'

Keeping sixth formers in the house system creates opportunities for leadership. As a relief from house responsibilities, sixth formers have their own common room and social areas – plans afoot to create a technologically sophisticated sixth form centre. The school's 150th anniversary in 2014 was a launch pad for this and other initiatives. The head rightly lauds excellent pastoral track record but emphasises that 'the family is more important. Schools can over-claim for themselves'.

Pupils and parents: Pupils are mainly drawn from middle class East Anglian families. In some cases, several generations have attended the school. A strong body from abroad, notably Germany and the Far East. Head sees the school as poised to appeal as much to the Oundle and Uppingham market as to its Norfolk and Suffolk constituency. Excellent reputation locally and no problems recruiting.

Entrance: At 13, pupils from Brandeston Hall, Framlingham's linked preparatory, accepted 'on the nod' – assuming they can cope with the academic rigour of the college. CE and interview for everyone else, though tests in core subjects (English, maths and non-verbal reasoning) can be arranged for pupils from schools that don't do CE. The interview is key and head also takes prospective pupils' school reports seriously.

Significant numbers enter after GCSE, with places offered conditionally on the basis of an interview, school report and a minimum achievement of seven A*-C passes at GCSE/IGCSE or equivalent.

Overseas candidates also sit tests in English and maths.

Exit: Almost all go to university, with traditional universities well represented. Head is aware of need to identify and support Oxbridge potential early – one off there in 2015. The place of careers advice is stressed – he believes it should be seen as separate from the university application process. Parents rely on the school as an expert resource.

Money matters: A range of scholarships awarded for outstanding academic, musical, artistic and sporting excellence at 13+ and 16+. Further means-tested bursarial help is available as needed. Reductions for siblings and Forces families.

Remarks: A well run, unstressful school, with happy pupils and high levels of achievement in all areas.

Friends' School

Mount Pleasant Road, Saffron Walden, Essex CB11 3EB

01799 525351
admissions@friends.org.uk
www.friends.org.uk

Ages: 11–18
Pupils: 226; sixth form: 52
Boarders: 35 full, 12 weekly
Day: £15,720 – £16,395 pa
Boarding: £20,055 – £26,745 pa

Head: Since September 2013, Anna Chaudhri MA Cantab, PGCE, 50s. Scholar of Robinson College, Cambridge, she attained BA 1st class Oriental Tripos and an MA. Research Fellow of Clare Hall, Cambridge, specialising in Caucasian literature, before taking her PGCE. Began her teaching career as a German teacher and examiner for Cambridge Arts and Sciences, then taught German at St Paul's Girls' School, before moving to Chelmsford County High School for eight years as head of German and careers. Deputy head at Friends' School from 2009 before being appointed head. Her husband is emeritus reader in physics, Cambridge University, and they enjoy music, walking and travel. She is a published author of several research articles on Ossetic literature and editor of two books on related subjects.

Says that Friends' strength lies in its size – 'Many schools in this area are tending to expand and form consortia, and provision at sixth form

is often in large colleges, offering a multitude of courses but to very large classes. Friends' is a small but strong community, where all efforts are directed towards getting the best out of each pupil'. She is described by parents as 'fair, calm and very approachable' and is known – and celebrated – for her high expectations of the children in terms of behaviour and learning. 'She also has a freshness, which is unexpected,' says one parent. 'She says things like, "we'll just have to think flexibly about this one, but I'm sure it's possible".'

Academic matters: 'We offer a standard range of academic subjects, which allow successful progression to higher education and employment,' says head. 'Our education is, however, inclusive and supportive, so that our pupils leave us as well-rounded young adults, with a good moral compass, ready to contribute to society.' For a school whose policy is to select as wide a range of pupils as will fit into its relatively small yearly cohort and will benefit from its curriculum, Friends' does extraordinarily well. There is a rejection of the tyranny of league tables and no policy of withdrawing borderline candidates in order to improve statistics. Small classes – two form teachers per form, and the intake of 30 in year 7 is divided into three forms of 10; three sets in maths and science by year 9.

Value-added is above average (more than a whole grade across the board for many students) and maintained year on year, though achievement fluctuates according to who is in the year group. In 2015, 63 per cent A*-B and 32 per cent A*/A grades. There's a free choice of GCSE subjects and no Ebacc obligation – 'our pupils are individuals and we want them to achieve the best they can without shoe-horning them,' explains head. Cosy sixth form (most tutor groups only six) attracts those who can't face 'factory farm' sixth form colleges nearby. Groups vary in size for A levels (sometimes as few as six, though 18 in the biology class when we visited) and several new subjects recently added, though the weightier subjects such as further maths and science remain as popular as art and photography. In 2015, 50 per cent A*-B and 28 per cent A*/A grades.

Member of the National Association for Gifted Children – caters for the more able as well as special needs. Three specialists in a separate study centre with six assistants for class-based work. Dyslexics predominate but mild Asperger's, impaired hearing and occasionally a statemented pupil can be accommodated. School bumf suggests now a cap on the number with needs in each year group and head won't admit anyone she feels the school can't support well. Established ESOL department.

Games, options, the arts: Friends' regularly slays the local giants on the sports field. Cricket, rugby,

hockey, trampolining... 'There's a real percentage opportunity,' says head. 'In a small school with a lot going on, children get more of a chance to try everything.' At least half of pupils represent their school at some sport or other. Sports hall with sparklingly refurbished swimming pool in which each year group has a term of lessons. Two or three gappies help out. Spacious campus has acres of playing

---

Friends' regularly slays local giants on the sports field. Cricket, rugby, hockey, trampolining... 'There's a real percentage opportunity,' says head

---

fields, hard tennis courts and a 25-metre swimming pool. D of Eers travel further afield.

Music is taught at least once a week all through the school and is a popular choice at GCSE and A level. Around 70 per cent learn an instrument but practice sessions aren't timetabled. The many instrumentalists make use of a large rehearsal space and there's a concert every term involving a rotation of the school orchestra, choirs and ensembles. Annual house music competition is a lively affair by all accounts.

Drama studio was full of seniors rehearsing Daisy Pulls It Off with gusto when we visited, on stage as well as behind the scenes. Annual plays for years 3 and 4, 5 and 6 too and the keenest thesps join drama club.

Workmanlike art studios with some impressive pieces – notably a display of teachers' faces interpreted bravely by their students; a couple every year get into art college. Artist in residence. DT room has a laser cutter as well as the usual CAD/CAM equipment.

Extracurricular programme has been re-energised of late and was praised by recent ISI inspectors for its breadth – from fashion and textiles club to industry days. A recent bank holiday weekend prompted a boarders' trip to Paris. Clubs and activities go on at lunchtimes and after school and there are residential trips and more elaborate journeys – geographers to Iceland, for example. 'They get to do lots of things that we did as children and still fit in the academic work,' says a parent, gleefully citing Easter bonnets, maypole dancing, yoga days, forest school and a long list of trips.

Boarding: Truly flexible boarding with full boarders catered for as well as those who pitch up for the odd night, and around 60 pupils taking up the option. Some nine per cent are international students from around the globe – Asia, US, Eastern and Western Europe (a 35 year tie with German schools) – and are fully integrated into the English boarding school way of life. Separate boys' and girls' boarding houses (up to four in a room) in the main building. Location is a plus – 80 minutes from Heathrow, 30 from Stansted – along with the attention to pastoral care and no Saturday school, so plenty of trips out at the weekends.

Background and atmosphere: One of only seven Quaker schools in the country. Founded in 1702, this well-travelled school began life attached to a workhouse in Clerkenwell. Lifted off to Croydon and, when typhoid threatened, settled on the present site donated by two Friends. Wide barren drive curves up to an imposing Victorian edifice supplemented by several additions of various vintages. Last summer, paths around the campus were upgraded and grass tennis courts nurtured. Land on the school's perimeter was recently sold off for housing development but this hardly impinges on the school's feeling of space, with open areas right in the middle and dotted with picnic benches. Proceeds from the land sale contributed to the new junior and early years building. Sixth formers congregate in a civilized double height space and appreciate the annual Ikea budget – helps build a sense of shared responsibility.

Generally, the atmosphere of an unpretentious grammar combined with a small county school with tight community ties. With its well-worn, old-fashioned feel, a place where individuality is cherished, catered for and celebrated. 'My child said joining Friends' felt like "getting into a warm bath" after his previous, enormous rather impersonal school,' says a parent. Certainly an impressive modern application of the traditional Quaker values, which are kept alive on a daily basis, though

'They get to do lots of things that we did as children and still fit in the academic work,' says a parent, gleefully citing Easter bonnets, maypole dancing and yoga

some sense among wider school community that the inclusive and charitable Quaker ethos might be being somewhat diluted under new regime. Year 7s visit Bourneville, where they learn more about the Quakers (as well as visiting Cadbury World). Parents admit to being slightly irked by the modesty of the place – 'they don't like to trumpet their successes as is not Quakerly, but I guess that the product is more important than the PR,' says one.

The Quaker commitment to 'stewardship' is also driving a refurbishment of the tattier parts of the school's buildings. Now the paths have been spruced up and hedges lowered to create a more open and spacious feel outdoors, there are plans to tackle the heating system and windows and to increase the school's use of renewable energies and its general sustainability. There's also a move towards new technology – the ICT room is a veritable orchard of Apples and a new VLE is up and running.

Pastoral care, well-being and discipline: 'Quakers have been educating the individual since 1702 – it's only now that everyone else is catching up!' points out head. Indeed this is where the Quaker ethos comes up trumps. Pupils truly feel that their school values them and they in turn value it, and each other. Certainly the fact that the emotional and personal well-being of the children is paramount is palpable. Support and encouragement abounds. There's also a welcome sense of stillness in an increasingly frenetic world – school meetings and assemblies begin with a moment of quiet reflection (which the head admits she misses at out-of-school engagements) and it's easy to see why this is a school that suits school-phobics or those bullied elsewhere. A mentoring scheme for year 11s – who select a teacher who'll be there for them if things get a bit much – is a safety net much appreciated by some in particular. No uniform for sixth form nor, in line with Quaker principles, any prefects – a quartet of senior scholars represent their peers.

Just three houses – Merell, Tuke, Lister – but lots of competitions and an easy way for all ages to mix. 'Year 7s can talk to year 11s here,' confirmed our guide. Relatively short day with a 4pm finish, after an 8.30am start. Lunch is a choice of the hot meal of the day, pasta or sandwiches, and at break-time pupils pay for their own sausages rolls and paninis.

Banned substances aren't 'condoned'. Where illegal drugs are concerned, cases are considered individually, but expulsion or suspension plus future random testing are likely outcomes.

Pupils and parents: 'I am not a Quaker but I love the idea of Silent Assembly and the emphasis on looking for the good/God in everyone, which runs counter to some of 21st century popular culture,' says a parent. Indeed Friends' pupils are candidly chatty youngsters who do recognise strengths in themselves (and others) and don't see areas of difficulty as weakness. Only a sprinkle of teachers and pupils from a Quaker background, though the governing body is still essentially Quaker. Day pupils come from a 30 mile radius – Cambridge is 20 minutes away – and boarders from London and the Eastern counties as well as abroad. Parents mainly professional and entrepreneurial.

Old scholars include BBC Blue Planet producer Martha Holmes, rock star Tom Robinson, Lord Newton of Braintree, educator extraordinaire Naomi Sargant and quite a few of the Rowntree clan. Alumni organisation now numbers more than 3,000 and they're kept in touch with a termly newsletter and invitations to school events.

Entrance: Thirty come in at year 7 (60 per cent from Friends' Junior, the rest from Dame Bs, Howe Green House, Heath Mount, St John's, St Faith's et al, as well as local village primaries), swelled by another 10 in year 9 (from St Faith's, St John's and overseas). Entry is by interview and – not desperately difficult – assessment (evidence of intellectual potential to achieve C or above at GCSE). A third of pupils stay on to A level and any new sixth formers are generally from overseas.

Exit: Post-16 exodus to sixth form colleges beginning to slow as A level curriculum broadens. About a quarter tend to take a gap year or go straight into employment, and the rest make it to their chosen universities, including eg Durham, Bristol, Sheffield, Exeter, Birmingham, London universities and art schools.

Money matters: Nobody who could benefit from a Friends' education should be discouraged from applying on the grounds of finance, says head. Fifteen per cent of pupils receive means-tested bursaries, and scholarships are dished out to those arriving in years 7 and 9 for academic excellence, art, drama, music and sport. Sixth form scholarships are at head's discretion (maximum £2000) for those who contribute substantially to school life. Quaker bursaries for Quaker families.

Remarks: Calm, caring place for individuals who benefit from bespoke push, stretch and support.

Gresham's Prep School

Cromer Road, Holt, Norfolk NR25 6EY

01263 714600
prep@greshams.com
www.greshams.com
C of E

Ages: 3-13 (boarding from 8)
Pupils: 220
Boarders: 23 full, 30 flexi
Day: £9,045 – £16,845 pa
Boarding: £23,265 pa

Linked school: Gresham's

Headmaster: Since 2003, Mr James Quick (50s) BA in economic history, PGCE (Durham); began teaching at The Dragon School, then St Edward's, Oxford, where he was housemaster. Did teacher exchange at Geelong College, Australia before coming here. His wife, Kim, teaches English, history and Latin and their four daughters, all but one at university stage or beyond, were at Gresham's. Sparkling-eyed with a youthful appearance and manner, he is clearly at ease with both staff and pupils, but does not overdo the bonhomie in chance encounters.

Has a modest manner and the attractive quality of being quick to praise colleagues. Says, 'Everyone can chip in ideas and rely on each other'. Continues to teach his subjects, history and classical studies, 'doing what everyone else does here'. Says there is no defined Gresham's 'product' as such, but believes hallmarks of pupils are 'the confidence to be themselves (we have room here for the odd squeaky wheel), kindness, a sense of humour, and being prepared to Have a Go.' Sees family in spare time and is a dedicated runner. He recently took part in the Round Norfolk Relay, volunteering for the Thetford – Diss leg at one o'clock in the morning. He is a happy head and in the right job.

Entrance: At all ages and stages from 3 (nursery and pre-prep), 7 and 11 in the prep school, although they will try to accommodate when possible at other times. Some year groups fill quickly, so first come first served. Accepts a fairly wide spectrum of ability, but admission is not a foregone conclusion. Informal assessment in the early forms, the same plus maths, English and verbal and non-verbal reasoning tests at 11. Pupils from the maintained sector often join for years 7 and 8 in preparation for the senior school.

Exit: Great majority, 80 per cent at least, go through the school to year 8 and move up to the seniors. All take the 'exit' exam, those not likely to make the grade are warned in good time. Those wishing to go elsewhere at 13, and there are a few most years, are prepared individually for the necessary entrance exams – Stowe, the Leys and Rugby are common choices.

Remarks: On its own site, though only a brisk walk from the senior school, on the edge of Holt, North Norfolk's stylish market town. Certain facilities such as sport, swimming pool and the theatre are used at the senior school, but in the main, it operates autonomously. Parents queue up to praise this relaxed and happy school where 'childhood still seems to last the right length of time'. One parent thought, 'My son came out of his shell here, he became a different boy'. A number of families

The performing arts, particularly music and drama, have status, and are very well taught within the curriculum and as extra activities ('one of the reasons we chose the school'). Everyone sings in a choir in the lower forms

have both Norfolk and London bases, but choose Gresham's for its 'less pressured atmosphere' over the more hothoused approach found elsewhere.

Without the restriction of teaching for the common entrance (abandoned recently), there can be greater flexibility in the curriculum. Excellent languages: the younger years (2-5) learn a number of languages with the focus on fun and communication. French is taught from year 6 with Spanish and Latin options from year 7. Other languages (eg German, Mandarin) can usually be accommodated on request. Science taught in designated labs, sometimes using the more sophisticated facilities of the senior school. There is mixed ability teaching up until year 4, then setting in most subjects, though 'these are flexible and pupils move up and down'. Pupils have their ability stretched by differentiated targets, rather than being 'pushed'.

Educational support well-resourced, with five specially trained staff (two full-time) who are also class teachers. Caters for mild difficulties such as dyslexia, Asperger's, and other emotional

problems, for example, low self-esteem. About a quarter of pupils receive help, either in one-to-one tuition, small groups, or support in the classroom. Brilliant library, bursting with delectable titles, displays, opportunities to enter competitions and with an enthusiastic, full time librarian, who is doing everything to encourage reading as an enjoyable habit. Open all day long (boarders can use it in the evening for project work), the atmosphere is quiet: 'we don't insist on a deathly silence, but purposeful reading does need peace and quiet'.

The performing arts, particularly music and drama, have status, and are very well taught within the curriculum and as extra activities ('one of the reasons we chose the school'). Everyone sings in a choir in the lower forms, with auditions higher up for the senior and chapel choirs (runners up in the National Barnardo's Contest recently). Over two-thirds of pupils learn an instrument, some at the top grades, and there are many bands, ensemble groups and orchestras with frequent performances. Dance is on the curriculum in the lower forms and an extra activity later on. Drama is timetabled throughout the school; performances take place in the hall with larger productions in the Auden Theatre at the main school. Art and design have their own rather eye-catching building, with spectacular displays of pupils' work (including designs on backs of chairs) and every inducement for creativity. 'We do textiles, mosaics, woodwork, mess generally'. Loads of sport, all the usual team games, and though 'we understand not everyone is mad keen, but it's also important to have to keep going with something you wouldn't necessarily choose'. In addition, pupils can choose shooting or kayaking in years 7 and 8. A large number of fixtures, with parents often on the sidelines in support.

Mostly new buildings of one or two storeys, of varying design, set in the midst of extensive grounds, adventure play areas and piazzas; 'pupils have to play in sight of the gazebo'. Separate boys' and girls' houses, each with capacity for 40 or 50, in bedrooms of two to four. Exceptionally attractive and homelike decoration (strong Cath Kidston influence) and furnishings. Photographs of children enjoying themselves on every wall, bunting, posters; a mock-up of Giles Gilbert-Scott's classic telephone box houses the real telephone – no mobiles during the day or after bedtime. House parents and matrons always around, and pupils return to house at break and lunch.

Careful attention is paid to ensuring pupils' well-being and happiness. As well as the usual offers of counselling well displayed, there is a 'worry box' to post in 'anything they want to discuss, however small it may seem'. Staff keep a weather eye, particularly in changing room areas, which are always supervised. In the un-canteeny dining room, pupils are helped to make good food choices, picking from colour coded categories, green (vegetables), red (protein) and yellow (carbs). Early supper ('children are all starving by 5:30pm') which day pupils often stay for if doing activities, and cereal/toast and hot drinks in the houses before bed.

This is a happy, well run prep that benefits from its connection to the senior school, but is definitely separate. Would suit most types but is not specially geared to preparation for common entrance or other highly competitive school entrance exams.

Gresham's

Cromer Road, Holt, Norfolk NR25 6EA

01263 714500
admissions@greshams.com
www.greshams.com
C of E

Ages: 13–18
Pupils: 475; sixth form: 220
Boarders: 279 full
Day: £23,280 pa
Boarding: £31,950 pa

Linked school: Gresham's Prep School

Headmaster: Since September 2014, Douglas Robb, previously head of Oswestry School in Shropshire. MA in Politics from Edinburgh and MEd from Homerton College Cambridge. Was a housemaster at Oundle and before that taught politics and economics at Loughborough Grammar School. Completed his PGCE at Fettes College, Edinburgh. Once a semi-professional rugby union player, he is married to Lucinda, and they have three children.

Academic matters: Setting in various subjects and on the whole small classes where children 'don't get lost in a crowd'. Parents speak of a generally unpressured approach where pupils are allowed to go at their own pace – 'The focused kid who wants to learn is thrust forward'. The days of 'the lazy happily meandering' seem to be numbered. Ten to 11 GCSEs for the majority; in 2015, 47 per cent of grades A*/A.

For the sixth, A levels or the IB – latter is gaining in popularity amongst the home grown cohort (when introduced, nearly half the entrants were from abroad) even though, as one sixther mused, 'You have to be pretty bright to hack it'. IB subject list is expanding but school will continue to offer A levels too for the foreseeable future. Good results in most areas – 40 per cent A*/A grades at A level; IB: average point score of 34 (max is 45). Relatively low interest in languages – however, compulsory for all as part of IB. Standard facilities spacious and perfectly okay.

Good noises re learning support, given instead of language lessons (three languages compulsory until year 10 – some in the centre do one, two or none). Parents feel the school doesn't want to advertise just how good they are – that's our impression too. Cap imposed by the number who can be accommodated in the cosy unit. Sympathetic, well qualified staff (two full-time, four part-time, plus one who delivers ESL) provide a 'sounding board for all sorts of needs' – dyslexia, dyscalculia, dyspraxia, mild Asperger's and ADD. 'It's a pyramid – there's a big drop in numbers after years 9 and 11 and pupils only need an occasional visit once they are in the sixth.' Strong links with the junior school, screening for new entrants, IEPs for each child, offer of scribes, readers and voice-activated computers. Charges according to the number of

sessions in the unit with a cap of £500 at term. Also applies to ESL.

Games, options, the arts: Outdoorsy lot who appreciate the inclusive ethos and huge number of teams. Hockey (girls' and boys') and cricket particularly strong – rugby still to find consistent form. Ample number of pitches and tennis courts, well used Astroturfs and swimming pool, four refurbished squash courts and a rifle range (justifiably trumpets awards gained by members of the rifle club and the achievements of two pupils who, between them, have been British Junior Ladies champion four years running). Weights room, gym and rowing machines for extra exercise and sailing for those who feel the call of the water.

Flourishing D of E with healthy number of gold and silver awards. Other options include BASC course (British Association for Shooting and Conservation) and the CCF. Drama is big here – 'Outstanding – it blows me away,' gushed a parent. The Auden theatre (the real thing with dressing rooms, professional lighting and sound systems) hosts a tremendous variety of performances given by touring companies – well attended by locals and free to pupils. Also a venue for numerous school productions – we enjoyed an impressive offering produced and played with great brio. Music also valued. Wide choice of instrumental tuition (approx 40 per cent have lessons) plus various orchestral, band and choral activities. Rather crusty music facilities upgraded in time for the 2013 Britten centenary.

Grown-up art block with decent studio space. Oil paints from the start and life drawing on a regular basis. Large canvases all over the place – strong, confidently-realised representational images. Some

The Auden theatre (real thing with dressing rooms, professional lighting and sound systems) hosts a tremendous variety of performances by touring companies

3D work and a new kiln recently installed. Regular artists in residence and exhibitions in the foyer – all very positive.

Boarding: There are seven boarding houses – three girls' and four boys'. Day and boarding pupils are integrated, with the former having a base and or bed in boarders' rooms. Full and weekly boarding with over 40 per cent day pupils – working hard to promote full boarding and parents say weekend activities have improved. Some houses can empty if nothing going on, so worth checking which have a higher proportion of full boarders. Flexi-boarding isn't encouraged ('We're not a baby sitting service') but when activities are full on, pupils can stay the night.

Boarding houses on a rolling revamp programme – some more homely and cared for than others.

Background and atmosphere: Although founded in 1555 as a free grammar school, it wasn't until the 1890s that it became something more. Somewhat random development of the 170 acre site (including 90 acres of woodland) makes for a fair amount of walking – all but the upper sixth have to use a bridge which straddles a road into town. Structures vary from listed to unattractive. Solid Edwardian classroom blocks, a sizeable chapel and The Big School, a rather fine hall with polished wood floors, rub shoulders with the thoroughly modern Auden theatre and now listed 'temporary' '20s thatched huts (scruff shacks). Everywhere spotlessly clean. Comfortable atmosphere. Friendly, relaxed relationships between pupils and staff despite some predictably unpopular tightening up (sixth have to wear suits and girls are meant to tie their hair back – one or two still manage the tousled look).

Inter-house competition important but doesn't hinder cheerful social interaction (most have known each other since they were tinies in the junior school) – sixth whizz off to congregate at the BOP (bar on premises) with the rest flocking to Dave's Diner for a burger and fizzy drink. All allowed into Holt three times a week – charmingly sedate country town.

Pastoral care, well-being and discipline: A small school where everyone knows everyone. Positive interaction between year groups and approachable staff (tutors, house parents, school counsellor and multi-denominational school chaplain) – parents say issues are dealt with promptly. Some pupils find going from junior to senior a big leap, but others relish greater independence and a chance to take responsibility for what they do – new bods are 'buddied'. Polite (lovely to find door holding is de rigueur), biddable lot.

Large dining hall where pupils eat at house tables – staff have a table of their own. Adequate buffet fare with vegetarian option – for hungry moments packets of squadgy white bread can be toasted and buttered in the house kitchens.

Sixth formers have sessions on stress; a clear anti-bullying policy. Zero tolerance re illegal drugs. Pretty tough on boozers (although over 18s are allowed to visit The Feathers with permission) and pupils found in their company can expect to be punished. Same applies to smoking.

Pupils and parents: Fresh-faced, friendly girls and boys – their 'confidence comfortably worn': more upturned collar and bleached rugby shirt than Vivienne Westwood. Most come from East Anglia, Lincolnshire etc – getting that all-important driving licence makes getting home for the odd night or two a breeze. Twenty per cent foreign nationals in the sixth (strong German contingent). In the main parents involved in farming, law, accountancy etc.

Old Boys include Sir Stephen Spender, W H Auden, Benjamin Britten, Ben Nicholson, Sir Christopher Cockerell (inventor of the hovercraft), James Dyson, Lord Reith, Prof Alan Hodgkin and Stephen Frears.

Entrance: School's own entrance exam and interview. Eighty per cent come in from own prep school (parents wonder if its popularity means that cherrypicking will make the school more academic). Rest from local preps or maintained sector. For the sixth form six GCSE A*-B grades with a minimum of C grades in English and maths.

Exit: Around 25 per cent leave after GCSEs. Trickle to Oxbridge (one in 2015), otherwise all over the place with heavyweights well represented – UCL, King's College, Exeter, Edinburgh and Bristol popular this year. Also University of Amsterdam and École Hôtelière de Lausanne, Switzerland.

Money matters: Worshipful Company of Fishmongers, with whom has close links, gives generous scholarships – recent launch of Gresham's Foundation will help fund new builds and bursaries. Academic awards (up to 50 per cent) available, in addition to art, drama, music and sport. Sixth form scholarships (academic, art, music etc) also offered. For pupils whose parents have fallen on hard times school does its best to help them through until next public exam.

Remarks: Has been known as an unsophisticated public school where parents have valued a broad education without an over-pressured, hothouse atmosphere. Introduction of the IB is making its mark – should broaden the school's attractiveness to a wider, out of county audience. An interesting time ahead.

Haileybury

Hertford, Hertfordshire SG13 7NU

01992 706353
registrar@haileybury.com
www.haileybury.com
C of E

Ages: 11–18
Pupils: 770; sixth form: 310
Boarders: 493
Day: £15,435 – £23,220 pa
Boarding: £19,605 – £30,900 pa

Master: Since 2009, Joe Davies MA (Cantab) PGCE (50s). Educated at Christ College, Brecon, then St John's College, Cambridge, where he read history. After graduating, he worked in the City for a year but 'hated every second,' so returned to Cardiff (where his father was an academic) to do a PGCE. 'I'd wanted to be a teacher from the age of 14, but thought it was too drippy to go straight back to school.' Teaching clearly in the blood, since two brothers and three of his four grown children are also in the profession.

Taught at Tonbridge, where he became a housemaster, then deputy head of St John's School, Leatherhead, before taking on his first headship at Sutton Valence. Stills teaches history to the higher level IB. He feels his achievement at Haileybury has been to increase the emphasis on academic performance, while placing ever more significance on the extracurricular. Sets a good example. A keen cyclist and marathon runner (who has recently completed the Venice marathon with his wife and two of his children), he also enjoys cryptic crosswords and reading history.

Academic matters: A famous name in public school education, Haileybury has in recent years become equally well known for its enthusiastic participation in the IB. 'We began in 1998 because it promised a broader curriculum and a boost to boarding, but we're now totally idealist,' says the

head. Today about 110 sixth formers follow the diploma programme, with about 40 arriving each year specifically to do so. A levels, however, are still very much on offer and the school does very well in both sets of exams, with 36 average IB points in 2015, and very pleasing results at A level (54 per cent A*/A in 2015). Biology, chemistry and history notably strong. Though not the easiest thing to run a school with a dual set of qualifications, this is managed by highly-qualified staff (including a hefty sprinkling of doctorates), who generally teach across both systems. The ISI commended the 'often outstanding' teaching.

Lower down, IGCSEs in just about everything, with 63 per cent A*/As in 2015. Here, all do a compulsory core of maths, English language, science and RS ('because of its philosophical and ethical bent'). Languages include Italian, French, Spanish, Latin and classical Greek, with German also taught to the 15 or 20 native speakers taking the IB. Pupils are set in maths and languages from year 7, science and English from year 9. Reasonable numbers who require some type of learning support (typically 50-80), with two teachers to address their needs, one a specialist in language, the other in maths. A small number, too, have extra help with English as a second language. Overall high aspirations, with sane expectations. 'They work hard, but it's very unpressured,' said a parent. 'They expect you to try your very, very best.' Relationships with staff particularly good, both in and outside of the classroom.

Games, options, the arts: Co-curricular activities are very much part of Haileybury's raison d'etre and the school has an outstanding reputation for both sport and choral music. Sport compulsory for all throughout, with games afternoons twice a week and matches on Saturday. Plenty of teams too, often from A-D, so everyone gets a chance to show their mettle. Those who aren't fans of the playing field can do 'something less taxing,' with options including aerobics, badminton, trampolining, rowing, rackets, golf and sailing (which currently boasts one girl who sails for Great Britain). Though boys triumph in hockey and football (where the school play in the Boodles Cup) and girls in tennis and lacrosse (competing at county and national level), rugby (boys only) and cricket (mostly boys) remain the 'communal sports.' 'Boys' rugby is the main thing,' said a girl, and the whole school turns out to cheer on rugby matches played on the front field. Facilities can only be described as superb, with a bright, modern pool, two Astroturf pitches and a professionally operated tennis club in the grounds. The rackets court is also considered one of the finest in the world and plays host to the world rackets championship.

The school has a 30-year tradition of exceptional choral singing and won the BBC Songs of

Praise School Choir of the Year in 2005 (it has reached the semifinal twice since then too). 'One of the things I enjoy most about the school,' said one parent, 'is the Christmas concert. It's just magnificent.' Chamber choir of about 30 ('very intense,' said one member) plus larger chapel choir of about 90. Wide range of other musical opportunities, from jazz bands to concerts and musical theatre. Twenty peripatetic music staff. 'You potentially can do any instrument,' said a teacher. 'We currently have pupils studying the steelpans, jazz piano and the organ.' The stand-alone music building, which already enjoys a charming beamed concert hall, is undergoing a £1m refurbishment.

Facilities can only be described as superb, with a bright, modern pool, two Astroturf pitches and a professionally operated tennis club in the grounds

Art taught in its own large, light, purpose-built building, which not only caters for those doing GCSE or A level, but for leisure enthusiasts, seven days a week and in the evenings. Offers 2D and 3D, print, ceramics, photography and textiles, with exams tailored to individual interests. Dance lessons on offer for about 100 keen participants in jazz, ballet, street and tap, plus an annual dance show. 'Fantastic drama,' said a pupil, listing an energetic range from house drama to full-school musicals, which take place in the well-equipped studio theatre.

An abundance of trips. Sport (South Africa) and music (Slovenia, Prague and Venice), plus charity and subject specific (Uganda, Tanzania, Vietnam, and Sinai), as well as more modest outings to battlefields and cultural events.

Wednesday afternoons are devoted to community service, D of E and CCF for years 9 to 11, broadening out in the sixth form to take in activities like photography and web design. One extended weekend each term devoted exclusively to D of E and CCF (which flourish in equal numbers). Plenty of societies and lectures. Model United Nations particularly popular and the school recently played host to a world conference with 800 delegates. The head, who feels strongly that co-curricular activities build up life skills, has devised a specific year 9 programme which includes such fundamentals as outdoor pursuits skills and life saving.

Certainly you wouldn't enjoy the school if you weren't happy with a busy life. 'Everyone encourages everyone else and invites them to get involved. It's very full on,' said one pupil. 'You do have to learn to plan your time to fit in all your commitments, but you go to bed feeling fulfilled.'

Boarding: From year 9, about 70 per cent of pupils board, with a sizeable chunk of weekly boarders who leave late on Saturday and return on Sunday evening (except for five or six weekends annually, when all remain). Boarding ethos even for day pupils, who stay till 6.30pm and have their own beds at school. Seven boys' houses, five girls'. Four recently built, with light, bright rooms, the rest older but updated. All sit amongst pleasant greenery and house 55 boarders, overseen by a housemaster or mistress, plus a resident tutor. In the early years, eight to 10 pupils share a large, subdivided space; from year 11, single or shared rooms.

'One of the things I enjoy most about the school,' said a parent, 'is the Christmas concert. It's just magnificent.' Chamber choir of about 30 ('very intense,' said one member) plus larger chapel choir

---

Girls do their own laundry, boys have theirs done for them. 'They think girls prefer that arrangement,' justified one pupil. Active inter-house social life and plenty of weekend activities for full-time boarders, with Saturday film nights and Sunday trips. Plus 'a lot of people have flats in London' or visit local pupils (with beneficent parents). Parents ('my son's housemaster is just wonderful – warm, jolly, intelligent, everything you could hope for in a male role model')

'It's cosy and terribly, terribly happy,' says one parent. 'You could not think of a better place to have your teenager running around.' Food comes highly commended

---

and pupils ('my housemistress is the most reasonable woman') praise the boarding care.

Background and atmosphere: The school was designed in 1806 for the East India Company by William Wilkins (also responsible for the National Gallery and Downing College, Cambridge) as a training college for civil servants bound for India. In 1862, after the closure of the college, it was taken over by Haileybury, to be transformed into a public school for families in the professions and services, amalgamating, in 1942, with the Imperial Service College. The first girls were admitted in 1973. Today the school continues to occupy an impressive 550 acres of rural Hertfordshire, complete with magnificent neo-classical university-like buildings constructed round a traditional quadrangle. Later additions are sympathetic and well designed, with most subjects benefiting from purpose-built space. Beautiful, well-stocked and well-used library. 'If they don't have a book, they will get it for you.'

The school remains a Christian foundation with an Anglican chaplain who officiates in a domed chapel of cathedral-like proportions. Though Haileybury is ethnically and religiously diverse (with a fair number of Muslims, Jews and Hindus) everyone must attend services four or five times a week. 'It's here they learn the values that hold the school together,' says the head.

Charity work is taken seriously and the Haileybury Youth Trust, first set up in the East End in 1890 by Old Boy Clement Attlee, has been working with impoverished Ugandans since 2006. It has been commended by the UN as a model of a small-scale charity, patenting a brick now used for buildings schools, kitchens and water towers.

Two further Haileybury branches now operate in Kazakhstan, the first British public schools to be opened in Central Asia. These help underwrite bursaries for UK-based students.

Pastoral care, well-being and discipline: The school essentially operates as two schools, a more-or-less self-contained lower school, running as a day prep from 11 to 13; and an upper school, from 13 to 18, which is very much a boarding school, with a full day of lessons and sport on Saturday.

Not a grand school in atmosphere. 'It's cosy and terribly, terribly happy,' says one parent. 'You could not think of a better place to have your teenager running around.' Food comes highly commended. 'It's one of the things people rave about,' said a sixth former. Three compulsory meals a day (plus an optional snack on games days), but with plenty of choice. The new Costa Coffee, a latter-day tuck shop, is 'the' place to congregate. Manners are formal (new pupils jump to attention, teachers are addressed as Sir) but not stiff. All pupils wear uniform, tartan skirts and blazers in the junior school, plain navy suits in the sixth form.

Discipline runs the usual gamut from detention to permanent exclusion. Drugs dealt with firmly. First offenders are suspended for a week, and regularly drugs tested thereafter, second-time offenders are expelled – though the head 'can't remember excluding someone.' Strong prefect system, with 30 to 40 college prefects given additional responsibilities and privileges (more flexibility in uniform, better rooms, pub visits).

Pupils and parents: Largely from the surrounding counties – Hertfordshire, Essex, Buckinghamshire, Cambridgeshire. In general parents are 'City folk, business people, successful professionals' and as most live reasonably nearby, more involved than usual at boarding schools. Large numbers from Europe for the sixth form, particularly Germans and Italians; a trickle from Haileybury's sister schools in Kazakhstan. Pupils seem happy, confident, friendly and balanced.

Entrance: Fifty in year 7, a further 60 in year 9. Unusually, also a healthy intake (10 to 20) in year 10. Typically 50 new pupils enter the sixth form, including about 40 from overseas. At this juncture the school is heavily over-subscribed, with about three applicants for every place. Entrance tests at all levels in maths, English, verbal and non-verbal reasoning. Year 9 entry pre-tested by negotiation with the prep school 12 or 24 months in advance and CE used for setting. 'We are looking for somebody who wants to do their best, is B+ to A* academically and will throw themselves into the co-curricular,' says the head. Wide range of feeders includes Heath Mount, Edge Grove, Lochinver House and Keble.

Exit: About 10 to 20 leave after GCSEs, often for local day schools. Post A Levels and IB, it's mainly to Russell Group universities (most popular choices include UCL, Warwick, Durham, Nottingham, Leeds, Bristol and King's College London), and increasingly, to Europe and the US. Ten to Oxbridge in 2015. Good range of specialist advisers, for Oxbridge, medical school and North American universities. Three or four to art college.

Money matters: Music, sport, art, and all-rounder scholarships of up to 30 per cent of fees, plus a range of (generous) means-tested bursaries.

Remarks: A dynamic and energetic school, with a long established, successful IB diploma programme. Haileybury actually achieves what many boast about, a well-rounded education. Great fun for those who want to be involved in everything it has to offer.

Holmwood House School

Chitts Hill, Colchester, Essex CO3 9ST

01206 574305
headmaster@holmwood.essex.sch.uk
www.holmwood.essex.sch.uk

Ages: 3–13 (flexi-boarding from 9)
Pupils: 350
Boarders: 60 flexi
Day: £9,150 – £16,125 pa
Boarding: £31.50 per night

Headmaster: Alexander Mitchell, 40s. Originally from Perthshire, though he worries the burr is fading, having spent more of his life down south than north of the border (not to Essex ears, it isn't). Educated at Napier in Edinburgh, with a degree in music from Colchester and PGCE from Reading. Has taught in the state and public, single-sex and co-ed, day and boarding sectors, most recently for three years as head of the music school at Loughborough Endowed Schools and 10 years as director of music at Haberdashers' Aske's School for Girls. ISI inspector for 10 years. He's only the fifth Holmwood head in its 90-year history and the first ever not to have any past association with the school. 'Underneath his friendly, easy-going exterior there is a respected, efficient, deep-thinking workaholic,' notes a perceptive parent. Lives on-site ('handy for fire drills' approves a pupil) with his wife Helen – head of PSHCE – and their three children, all in the school and ranging from reception to year 5. Conducting was his love, but he says he doesn't miss the music – 'I have plenty to be getting on with here as head-master and our head of music and drama is outstanding; I'm very lucky to be doing what I feel I was meant to be doing, it's the best job in the world.' Still finds time to play bass guitar in the school's jazz band. 'Happiness is the key to progress,' he says. 'I can't promise a perfect school but I can promise a happy one.' Chimes with Holmwood's Latin motto, which translates as 'I was glad'.

Entrance: A third from the school's own nursery, which takes 53 children from 6 months and is set in an attractive rural building a few miles from the main school. The rest go off to good local primaries. Usual entry point to the main school is at age 4, straight into the dedicated reception, which takes two classes of 18 in each year. A handful more pupils arrive at throughout each year. Boys in the majority.

Exit: Year 8 children largely depart for Felsted, Framlingham, Ipswich and Oundle. One or two to Uppingham and Rugby and a similar number to Royal Hospital School, Culford, New Hall and Greshams. School proud of range of scholarships won. Occasional places at Eton, Harrow, King's Canterbury, Benenden.

Remarks: The principles of the school have remained the same since it was founded on this very site, two miles from Colchester, in 1922 by a Mr and Mrs Duggan, whose aim was 'to develop the individuality and abilities of each child, to make him self-reliant and adaptable and to help him

Art room described (accurately) as 'humongous' by our guide, and full of unusual projects including animation installations by year 8s

face reality.' A collection of semi-rural buildings punctuated by courtyards and outside spaces that cleverly maximise the opportunities for outdoor education (we've never seen so many woodland classrooms, play areas and nature trails in one prep school). Garden Block arranged around a tranquil garden in memory of a former pupil and treated by all with respect.

The Holmwood day is divided into lessons until tea at 4pm and then prep and activities until supper for boarders and more activities until lights-out. Flexi-boarding – minimum one night – is popular and most take advantage by year 8 ('I tell parents their children will let them know when they want to board,' says head). Houses are named after the elements and there are competitions and challenges all year round. Intriguing range of reward systems – golden leaves, superstars, as well as 'showups' and 'showdowns' for older pupils with the requisite number of showdowns leading to a detention ('I had one once,' confessed our guide. 'I'm not getting another one'). There's 'a week for everything' – recent Citizenship Week brought in speakers from the Red Cross and local charities, and when we visited a celebrated scientist was setting up ready to give a demonstration as part of Science Week.

Reception children have their own little world, across a path from the main school. Cavernous for the two classes of 18 in the early years department – with airy classrooms and intriguing corners tailored to computer play and dress-up – it also has a lovely outside play area with a patch of age-appropriate, safe woodland to explore. The main pre-prep department houses years 1, 2 and 3 in spacious, modern, purpose-built accommodation. Moving into the prep, pupils are arranged by ability in English, maths, French and science and in years 7 and 8 into a scholarship and three further sets. A few new arrivals, but the head points out 'as the year group gets larger, the sets get smaller'. The scholarship set is made up not just of the brightest but those who have the 'emotional maturity to cope with the stretch and challenge'. Pupils from year 4 begin to move to specialist classrooms – 'you're exhausted for the first few days but you soon get used to it,' reassured our guides. Year 6s learn Latin, or study skills for those not suited. French from reception. A few drift off into the strong local state selective system at 11+ but the vast majority press on to CE at 13.

Music and drama is 'about to explode' under the direction of the new head of department, predicts Mr Mitchell. Matilda being rehearsed with years 6 and 7 throughout our visit and, recently Pirates of the Curry Bean! Art room described (accurately) as 'humongous' by our guide, and full of unusual projects including animation installations by year 8s, who all received a still turned into a souvenir picture. DT is offered as an activity in a fully-equipped studio. Sport every day for those who want it. Rugby, hockey and cricket are major for boys, while girls play netball, hockey and rounders. Some 20 acres of the 34 are given over to sport, plus a vast newish sports hall and indoor swimming pool. On-site Lexden Rackets Club – financed by compulsory purchase of school land for the A12

decades ago – is heaving with fit young retirees on a dreary Wednesday morning, but also a superb resource for the school at other times. School has its own tennis and squash coaches.

Library with 12,000 books and an intriguing colour-coded filing system, presided over by the school librarian. Red sofas for the exclusive use of year 8 are as close as they come to a common room. Science labs in converted stables. Jubilee Hall with tiered seating for nearly 200, backed by professional-looking exhibition space – self-portraits when we visited. Dyslexia unit recently renamed learning support (although the sign-maker hasn't yet caught up). Excellent provision for SEN. 'We make progress here,' says the head. 'That might be a scholarship for one child, or an improvement in reading for another. We nurture strengths and support weaknesses and develop young people who are confident, and above all comfortable with whom they are.'

Boarding house open from Monday evenings to Saturday mornings – no full boarding. As well as using school sports, art, music and cooking facilities, boarders have a games room with pool, table football, table tennis etc in the main building cellar for evening recreation.

Courtesy and respect are still ingrained at an early age and children here are at ease with anyone (the head swears by the 'train to Norwich test' – in a parallel universe as the proprietor of his own company, he would be sufficiently confident to put any Holmwood pupil on a two-hour train journey with his best client). 'Every child is well mannered and friendly,' agrees a parent. 'Even on the sporting field – win or lose, the children are always gracious.'

Surrounded by its own playing fields, Holmwood has the feel of a much larger school, but at its heart it's a small community of some 300 pupils which extends to embrace their families too.

Ipswich School

Henley Road, Ipswich, Suffolk IP1 3SG

01473 408300
admissions@ipswich.suffolk.sch.uk
www.ipswich.suffolk.sch.uk
C of E

Ages: 11–18
Pupils: 756; sixth form: 238
Boarders: 45 full/weekly (roughly two-thirds boys)
Day: £12,495 – £13,701 pa
Boarding: £20,424 – £25,359 pa

Headmaster: Since September 2010, Mr Nicholas Weaver BA (late 30s). Read engineering at Jesus College, Cambridge. Previously deputy head (academic) at Portsmouth Grammar, and before that taught physics at the Leys School, Cambridge,

the Royal Grammar School, Guilford, and Radley College. Tall, elegant, with an approachable, unruffled manner. He is keen to develop what he calls the 'growth mind-set' – a strategy for developing the potential of all pupils, with a particular eye on those identified as academically able. The Academic Excellence Programme is designed for this 'elite' group, although open to all comers. Changes to senior management structure have resulted in a more streamlined, collegiate approach; all posts are now advertised externally. He is married and has three children, all at Ipswich Prep.

Academic matters: Pupils are encouraged, even pushed, to work hard. Whilst not an academic forcing house, there is no place for coasting. The brightest of the bright will be fast tracked – lessons before school for some and there is a programme of enrichment, including lectures and seminars, geared specifically at these pupils – 'We are hoping the head doesn't over-do all the elitism and Oxbridge stuff,' commented a parent. Homework is now called PSC, which stands for Preparation, Stretch and Consolidation – 'No one remembers,' said several. Though selective, the school has quite a wide ability range, but despite the head saying, 'we recognise the hard-won B grade', there are not many of these in evidence. In 2015, 64 per cent A*/A grades at GCSE. A level results saw 54 per cent A*/A grades. The head has made clear his priority to raise all teaching in the school to exceptional standard and school expects pupils to have the solid achievement of an A grade at GCSE for subjects studied at A level. Sixth form is no place for slacking, with compulsory enrichment programme alongside ASs. No demand here for IB, as curriculum seems to be diverse enough.

All year 7 entrants are tested for SEN, but as this is a selective school, the needs identified will often be to do with organisation, mild dyslexia, or for ESL, for which support is offered outside the timetabled day. Head has introduced drop in clinics at lunchtime so any pupil can seek help informally.

Games, options, the arts: A recent shift in emphasis in referring to the 'co-curricular' rather than the 'extracurricular', with a designated assistant head in overall charge (formerly head of sixth form). First division player in all the team sports – frequently area and national finalists, most recently in hockey. Sport is for all, and the school often fields teams from A-D. Other sports on offer, and played highly competitively, include karate, sailing and equestrianism. Also entered a winning pair in the national finals of Eton fives. School recently bought nearby sports centre, complete with sports hall, fitness gym and floodlit Astroturf hockey pitch.

Music is taken seriously, with a third of pupils taking individual instrumental lessons and a variety of orchestras, choirs and ensemble groups which perform throughout the year. The Chapel Choir, besides a regular slot singing evensong at St Paul's Cathedral, tours both at home and abroad. The Annual Ipswich School Festival of Music brings internationally-renowned musicians to perform at the school in masterclasses and workshops. Drama GCSE is also offered as an enrichment sixth form option (no theatre studies A level) and several productions are staged throughout the year. The sixth form recently performed Seussical-the-Musical, based on the works of Dr Seuss. Thursday afternoon activities include CCF and Duke of Edinburgh plus a long list of clubs and societies including photography, journalism and robotics. If the club isn't already there, it can be started.

Chapel Choir tours both at home and abroad. Annual Ipswich School Festival of Music brings internationally-renowned musicians to perform at the school in masterclasses and workshops

Boarding: The boarding house is a short walk away, occupying its own grounds – which include the school Astroturf – in a suburban road. Common room and boarders' kitchen; breakfast, dinner and weekend meals eaten in the boarding house. No Saturday school but EFL lessons available on Saturday mornings.

Background and atmosphere: The school has occupied its present site since 1852, but it has a medieval foundation (Cardinal Wolsey is an illustrious Old Boy) and the school's history is well-recorded and treasured. In addition to the original, rather gloomy Victorian structure, there are some fine and functional 20th century buildings which adjoin each other by a series of passages, steps and covered ways. Later additions include the sports facilities and sixth form building, which overlook the playing fields – a focus for relaxation as well as sport. There is a school chapel and a library of exceptional quality and design with windows by John Piper depicting the seasons. Everything is well cared for and maintained. Odd fusty corners in the older part of the school offset by displays of pupils' work, posters and subject information. Pupils by and large polite rather than courtly but clearly intent on their pursuits. Straightforward uniform policy, with sixth formers allowed the latitude of wearing their own clothes. Conformity seems natural here though 'slight oddballs have been successfully integrated'; especially if they are clever.

Pastoral care, well-being and discipline: Usual house and year group tutorial system with a separate identity for years 7 and 8, each form keeping the same tutor. The school chaplain, a full-time member of the teaching staff, plays a key part in the pastoral set up. The matron has her room strategically placed near the hard play area, a reassuring presence at break and lunchtimes. There is a strong expectation that pupils are well-organised and can cope with the pressure, though all know where to turn if in difficulties. Despite the city location, little flouting of rules, and a system of merits and detentions seems to keep the odd backslider on track. Occasional serious offenders dealt with firmly.

Pupils and parents: Mix of farming, professional and business families from the rural reaches of East Anglia together with those from Ipswich itself or other towns, mostly in Essex. Quite a lot of parents are London commuters. Extensive network of bus routes bring many pupils to school, and of the 40 or so boarders, over half come from overseas, mostly Europe and the Far East. Boys continue to outnumber girls by about 2:1 in years 7 to 11; the influx of girls to the sixth form – often from the nearby GDST school – gives a better balance, though girls remain in a minority. Pupils appear to be well able to cope with the rigours of the school; perhaps not ideal for those lacking in confidence or who thrive on pushing the boundaries.

In addition to Cardinal Wolsey, notable Old Boys include the author and illustrator Edward Ardizzone, physicist Sir Charles Frank and the writer Rider Haggard (King Solomon's Mines).

Entrance: The majority join at 11 (year 7) with many coming up from the prep. All take the same entrance exam (results are used to organise setting in year 7). A report from the pupil's present school and a chat with the head are also required. At 13 (year 9), another 30 or so are also admitted via common entrance or school's own exam. Pupils do need to have above average ability to pass and to flourish. Entry to the sixth form requires six GCSEs with at least Bs, preferably As in chosen A level subjects.

For overseas admissions school will now consider UKiset applications (online testing system) rather than paper-based tests.

Exit: Around 30 per cent leave after GCSEs. Majority leave for university with a leaning towards the Russell Group, particularly Exeter, Birmingham, Nottingham and London universities. Six to Oxbridge in 2015, and the head is keen to push up numbers.

Money matters: Queen's (academic) Scholarships equivalent to 50 per cent offered at 11 and 13, based on pupil's performance in the entrance examination plus interview. Means-tested bursaries can cover the full fees if necessary. Scholarships are also available in music, art and sport at 11 and an all-rounder at 13. A full range are offered at sixth form, together with a number of means-tested bursaries.

Remarks: A well run, urban school, with many opportunities for bright, motivated pupils to excel.

King's College School (Cambridge)

West Road, Cambridge, Cambridgeshire CB3 9DN

01223 365814
office@kcs.cambs.sch.uk
www.kcs.cambs.sch.uk
C of E

Ages: 4–13 (boarding from 8)
Pupils: 425
Boarders: 34
Day: £11,163 – £14,199 pa
Boarding: Weekly £22,110; Choristers £7,443 pa

Headmaster: Since 1998, Nicholas Robinson (50s). Studied English at Anglia Ruskin; PGCE in maths at Goldsmiths. Always knew he wanted to teach after spending a gap year at a Suffolk prep school and getting the bug. Five years at Eltham College where he set up an orchestra; headhunted by Worth School in Sussex as a housemaster at 29. Came to King's as head. A bachelor, immaculately turned out with a quiet wit. Sings with the chapel choir twice a year when large choruses needed. Has been known to conduct orchestras. A keen skier.

Well liked by parents. 'I have a great deal of time for him; he's very friendly and approachable.' 'He is why we chose King's,' was another comment. Another parent not quite so sure. 'He is doing a great job but I would like to see him more engaged with the parents and children. I was disappointed he didn't speak to us about where my son should go next, but, to be fair, his deputy offered great advice.' He has increased numbers at the school from 290 to 425. Lots of building work and refurbishment. They're running out of space but have plans to squeeze in a much-needed sports centre in 2016. 'He's a good thing for the school.'

Entrance: Some children registered at birth, or before. All 4 year olds spend over an hour with the pre-prep department, so 'we can get the feel of the child.' Be warned, they're looking for bright bunnies. Siblings, past pupils and fellows of King's given priority. Parents also have a chat with the head. Entry at 7 after assessment. Chorister scholarships for up to five boys in year 4. Open to any boy in the world if he passes the audition, and many try. All choristers (boys only) offered scholarships of up to two-thirds of fees or more, plus free piano lessons. Means-tested bursaries of up to 100 per cent at age 7, available for all. Children come from a wide commutable area, many from Suffolk and Hertfordshire, some boarders further afield. Many parents ex-Oxbridge, academics, medics, City people. Generally a good cross-section. All very ambitious and the driving force behind their offspring.

Exit: The occasional one at 11, but very unusual. No 'evictions'; they work hard, with the help of learning support, to keep them going, and then guide parents to make a 'sensible choice' for the next step. Only one has been 'moved on' in the last 18 years before age 11. Virtually all leave at 13. Over half to local independent schools in Cambridge, particularly The Perse and Leys. Eton, Uppingham and Oundle all popular too. Every chorister offered a music scholarship. About a third of all leavers get scholarships, many music, some academic.

> *Although the choristers are famous throughout the world, they are treated like any other pupils within lessons. But their life is different*

Remarks: Founded in the 15th century to educate the choristers, now housed on one site off a leafy road a brisk walk from King's College. The choristers are an iconic sight walking through the streets in a croc in their Etons and top hats heading for chapel. Primarily a day school with 34 boarders, all boys, 24 of whom are choristers, the rest – some of whom flexi board – in the upper years. The choristers are an important part of the school, famous throughout the world, but are treated like any other pupils within lessons. But their life is different. Compulsory boarders from the age of 8 when they become full choristers, they attend six services a week at the chapel during the university term time, practice for an hour and half before school (in a purpose built acoustic room) and again in the evenings. Weekends during the university term means three more services. They travel the world touring and, of course, there is that carol service every Christmas Eve and the service on Christmas Day. The head plays Father Christmas every year. It's a big commitment with many sacrifices made by the families, but very rewarding, and the boys thrive on it. Every care is taken to make sure they don't suffer academically or personally. 'My son, a chorister, has struggled at times with his work,

but the support from the staff is excellent.' They still get to play in the teams but practice is out; there just isn't time. If a boy's voice breaks before he leaves he is still included and part of the set up.

These children are bright and teaching is excellent, with some well-loved, gregarious characters amongst the staff. The special needs department, one of the first to be set up in the country, is very pro-active. 'The school contacted me very quickly when my daughter started to struggle with her maths. She was offered extra help immediately, which was excellent.' Lots of support available if needed. All parents commented on how well the staff knew their children. 'We like the school for its "ballsy" attitude,' was said by one parent, with many commenting on the relaxed, but focused atmosphere. Lots of new computers available. Plenty of artwork about, modern science labs and a very well equipped DT room. A large, stuffed library attended by a librarian who appears to be a school stalwart. Knows every child, loved by all. Every parent was happy with their child's progress and had confidence in the school. Pace increases further up the school with a scholarship class in year 8. 'They are realising my child's potential,' came up more than once.

Lots of after-school clubs, chess highly recommended, but music dominates. A fabulous music department, and that's excluding the angelic-looking choristers. Virtually every child plays an instrument, many two or more. Lots and lots of chamber groups, choirs, orchestras and quartets. If you can think of it, they've got it. A new organ in situ, played by many, and lots of acoustic rooms for practice, including the church-like room for the choristers.

Music aside, sport is playing an increasingly big part in school life. Many more top-notch staff employed, with more teams available and better results. A new sports centre in the offing. 'Team selection can be a political minefield,' said one parent. 'I don't envy the staff but they handle it well.' The playing fields are at the front of the school, giving the impression of lots of open space – a bit of an illusion: every spare inch of the site is utilised.

A friendly, happy school, pastorally excellent. Bullying usually nipped in the bud very quickly. One father mentioned that an incident had been allowed to escalate before being 'handled excellently.' A mother praised the handling of manipulative children by the male form teacher. 'He was sensitive, calm and firm.' 'The school's policy of keeping parents at arm's length and bringing the children together is the right one,' said one wise mother. A school counsellor available for all and the children are happy to consult. Older pupils mentor younger ones with a buddy system.

The boarding house is also on site. Functional, but immaculate with modern facilities. Bright, airy dorms, duvet covers brought from home, sheets changed by the boys. Housemaster (a woman) praised

and loved by all. An open door policy for the parents and homesickness dealt with kindly. Misdemeanours dealt with quickly. 'Punishment comprises chores, just like I would at home.' Tuck boxes brought out once a week with matron providing more on Saturday evenings. Dog walks on Sunday morning. Very much a family atmosphere, with parents included, as they often pop in mid week and, if local, walk the choristers back from chapel.

Bright purple blazers and sweatshirts make the children stand out. 'My son hates his sweatshirt so gets through a blazer a year.' Girls' summer dresses not popular with parents or pupils. Do note the purple carpet throughout the modernised buildings. Sartorial whimsy, perhaps?

All parents seem happy that the school is on one site and many spoke of the 'family atmosphere.' Every parent we spoke to was delighted with the school and would strongly recommend it. We can see why; you can't help but feel the relaxed ambience. The children are bright and friendly, completely stress free and at ease with their teachers. But don't let that fool you. There is a rarefied atmosphere of intense learning – and you may get to hear some excellent singing as well.

King's Ely Junior

Barton Road, Ely, Cambridgeshire CB7 4DB

01353 660730
dawnburton@kingsely.org
www.kingsely.org
C of E

Ages: 7–13
Pupils: 348
Boarders: 32 full (including boy choristers)
Day: £12,765 – £13,929 pa
KEJ International £19,986 pa
Boarding: £20,352 – £21,483 pa
KEJ International £27,540 pa

Linked school: King's Ely Senior

Headmaster: Since 2008, Mr Richard Whymark BA (Ed) (40s). Previously head of Stonar Junior and before that head of boarding and deputy head of Salisbury Cathedral School. Has an engaging manner and a natural flair for communication – with pupils and parents alike. 'He is usually around at drop-off time', commented one parent.

Firmly believes a good head needs 'a strong voice and a reflective personality – no room for big egos'. Has an easy rapport with students and is clearly a respected presence – on hand to sort out spats. Art, travel and gardening are all interests but, clearly something of a romantic, his passion is for restoring Morris Minors. Has two children at King's and wife Joanna also teaches at the school.

Entrance: Assessment for entrance at 7 consists of diagnostic tests and informal interview. Entry to King's Ely Acremont for ages 2 to 7 (pre-prep, though this term is not used by the school) is by informal assessment and most progress up to the junior department. Screening for dyslexia and dyspraxia at entrance. Moderate difficulties can be accommodated but all pupils must be able to benefit from the full curriculum, with minimal extra support. Those applying as choristers (boys only) must also pass the necessary voice trials.

Exit: Virtually all make the transition to the senior school at 13. The exam also decides setting for year 9. The occasional pupil not suited to the senior school is identified early and support given in

Music is, if anything, even more exceptional. Cathedral choristers apart, the school has choirs, ensembles and bands galore

finding another school in good time, but leaving is generally due to relocation.

Remarks: Occupies a site on the edge of the main school campus. Slightly bleak approach around the back of the senior school but the buildings themselves are well planned and designed. Attention is paid to the grouping of different classes, so years 3 and 4 (and so on up the school) are accommodated together, with their own suite of classrooms and play area. Youngest pupils cluster round a courtyard with a Tarzan trail for play time; years 7 and 8 slightly apart in their own building.

Children are cheerful, friendly and polite (all doors held without reminder), though unstarchy. Setting in maths and English from year 3. Languages introduced early, with taster lessons in Japanese, Mandarin and Arabic. French, and Latin from year 7.

Drama is very strong, with several major productions staged annually. Music is, if anything, even more exceptional. Cathedral choristers apart,

the school has choirs, ensembles and bands galore, and more than 200 pupils have individual instrumental lessons. Stunning exam results – more than 50 distinctions in the ABRSM exams this year.

Parents praise the emphasis on effort and progress; certificates and prizes are awarded for these as much as for attainment. Both ends of ability spectrum well served, with support and extension classes available. 'Confidence is encouraged, but not cockiness', commented a mother. Tutor groups are reshuffled each year, to break up cliques and expand friendship groups. A buddy scheme operates throughout the school and problems are quickly dealt with. The top year groups use some of the senior school's facilities and are taught by specialist staff as a way of managing the transition from junior to senior. Outstanding pastoral care is the underpinning of the school's success.

Choristers live in the Choir House during term time, Christmas and Easter holidays, with the housemaster and his family. They have instrumental practice before school (all are expected to learn at least one instrument), rehearsals before and after school plus services in the cathedral. They are encouraged to play outside during free time and the housemaster takes them on excursions during stayovers.

King's Ely Junior International offers 11-12 year olds intensive English language tuition alongside a wider range of subjects in preparation for 13+ senior school entry.

King's Ely Senior

Barton Road, Ely, Cambridgeshire CB7 4DB

01353 660700
enquiries@kingsely.org
www.kingsely.org
C of E

Ages: 13–18
Pupils: 499 (including King's Ely International); sixth form: 171
Boarders: 169 (inc KEI)
Day: £19,245 pa; KE International Day £26,757 pa
Boarding: £27,858 pa; KE International £35,370 pa

Linked school: King's Ely Junior

Principal: Mrs Sue Freestone GRSM Med LRAM ARCM (60s), who joined the school as head in 2004, and became principal in 2013. She is again in charge of the senior school, after the brief tenure of Alex McGrath as head. Trained at the Royal Academy of Music and Bristol University. Was formerly head of Sibford School, and before that conductor and director of music at Colston Girls. Very energetic, approachable and unstuffy, with strongly held

convictions and an expectation of high standards for herself, the staff and pupils.

Academic matters: Though increasingly selective at 11 and 13, the bar is not quite so high as for certain of the Cambridge schools close by. Considering the reasonably wide ability range, the school is achieving very respectable and frequently glowing results. Pupils are setted for most of the core subjects; close attention is paid to individual progress, and though not an overly pushy school, 'drifting along with little effort will be spotted', a mother remarked. Twenty-four subjects offered at GCSE (57 per cent A*/A in 2015) including single sciences, Latin and Greek. Religious and moral philosophy is compulsory. Twenty-seven subjects offered at A level with economics, mathematics and psychology all popular, and 47 per cent A*/A grades overall in 2015. Those with specific educational needs, such as dyslexia, are well accommodated. There is individual support available, together with a drop-in clinic, and a close eye is kept on subjects chosen at GCSE, with a flexible approach to certain subject choices allowed.

King's Ely International prepares 14-16 year olds with sufficiently good English to take IGCSEs and be able to enter UK independent schools, including this one. The classrooms and boarding accommodation are separate, but the head is encouraging greater fraternisation with the main school: 'It can only benefit all pupils'.

Games, options, the arts: A strength of the school is what happens outside the mainstream academic timetable. Tremendous range of opportunities, from rowing at 6:30am to singing in cathedral services. Music predominates, with more than 50 per cent learning an instrument, and ensembles, choirs and orchestras galore. The girls' cathedral choir recruits from the senior school, for which there is a 33 per cent reduction in the fees, with bursaries available if needed, as the girls all board. This is the first scheme of its kind in England, and is the inspiration of the present head, herself a

Glimpses of the cathedral, the Ship of the Fens, tantalise from many windows, notably from the head's office, in the Old Palace

professional musician. It will be interesting to see if the idea is taken up by other co-educational schools connected with cathedrals. The choir sings regular cathedral services, as well as touring and performing elsewhere. The musical training given to these girls will prepare them for advanced study and choral scholarships at university. A new initiative is sixth form male choral scholarships.

Sport remains central and important, though perhaps 'not the be all and end all as at some schools,' said a parent. Besides regular hockey, rugby and so forth, there is an emphasis on the more recondite sports, especially rowing, which is taken very seriously. The school has its own boathouse, pupils keen enough to be up with the lark and even some Olympic potential.

The Ely Scheme (outdoor pursuits programme) runs compulsorily in year 9 and 10, and many continue. It includes kayaking, rock climbing and navigation, and pupils are encouraged to join either the climbing or kayaking club. The culmination is a major expedition, which could be traversing the Cuillin Ridge or the Picos de Europa, or climbing in the Alps or the Himalayas. Teaches self-reliance, responsibility and leadership skills. Many join D of E too.

The teaching facilities for art and design are impressive – as is the teaching. Eye-catching displays of recent work are quite outstanding and several pupils, thus encouraged, go on to study at prestige institutions, notably in fashion and design.

Boarding: Boarding houses are clean and comfortable, rather than deluxe. Girl choristers have their own boarding house, complete with grand piano in the common room. The Old Palace (former residence of the Bishops of Ely) is now a sixth form centre, with boarding space for 26 girls.

Background and atmosphere: Occupies a sublime position adjacent to the cathedral, partly within the close itself, but largely in a sprawl of buildings (some medieval, others purpose-built) nearby. Glimpses of the cathedral, the Ship of the Fens, tantalise from many windows, notably from the head's office, in the Old Palace; hard for conversation to compete with the Romanesque masterpiece behind. The cathedral's presence is both seen and felt, but the school also has a close relationship with the town through a variety of initiatives with other schools and local organisations. Frequent road-crossing is managed by pupils safely and with aplomb – it is just part of school life. Other buildings include The Monks' Barn, which houses the dining room (think National Trust restaurant – food, if anything, even better), jolly atmosphere, staff eating with pupils. The library has been re-ordered, also within the ancient fabric, but retains a monastic feel.

A strength of the school is what happens outside the mainstream academic timetable. Tremendous range of opportunities, from rowing at 6:30am to singing in cathedral services

Pupils and parents feel they are listened to, and heard. The school council, a forum to discuss new ideas, is taken notice of by the powers-that-be.

Pastoral care, well-being and discipline: The Christian foundation of the school has a strong influence on the community. Rules are few, though strictly enforced, particularly for those boarding, but there is an atmosphere of trust. The head is very aware of the pressures on pupils and feels 'peer perception' can be 'the hardest nut to crack'. Emphasis on enjoyment as well as achieving.

Pupils and parents: Largely professional, business and farming families, drawn from surrounding Eastern counties; Kings Lynn and Cambridge both send cohorts (quick, easy train services). School believes 'it is in no-one's interest for pupils to travel more than half an hour each way'. Overseas contingent (about 12 per cent) including those in the King's International Study Centre. Past pupils include Alan Yentob, the tenor James Bowman and Olympian Goldie Sayers.

Rules are few, though strictly enforced, particularly for those boarding, but there is an atmosphere of trust. The head is very aware of the pressures

Entrance: Own exam at 11 (to prep school) and at 13+, through a common entrance style exam (or common entrance itself). About 75 per cent come up from the King's prep and the remainder from a mixture of local-ish schools, Barnardiston, South Lee and the Cambridge prep schools. Numbers well up and competition for places is increasing. Entry for the sixth form – minimum of six grade A*-C passes at GCSE with at least Bs in chosen A level subjects.

Exit: Up to 50 per cent of students leave after GCSEs, often for Hills Road or other sixth form colleges. Post A level, the majority leave for Russell Group universities to study a wide range of subjects, with a number going to colleges of art and design and performing arts courses; six to Oxbridge in 2015.

Money matters: Variety of scholarships awarded at 11 and 13+. Choral scholarships of 33 per cent of fees for ex-boy choristers who remain in the school choir and senior girl choristers. The new male sixth form choral scholarships offer a 50 per cent fee reduction. Other reductions for clergy and Forces families and top-up bursaries for those in financial need.

Remarks: The school has an atmosphere of purposeful learning, and provides plenty of opportunities for all types to shine. A strong, happy school where the Christian ethos is taken seriously.

The Leys School

Trumpington Road, Cambridge, Cambridgeshire CB2 7AD

01223 508904
admissions@theleys.net
www.theleys.net

Ages: 11–18
Pupils: 571; sixth form: 200
Boarders: 250 full, 120 home boarders
Day: £14,550 – £20,145 pa
Boarding: £21,945 – £30,135 pa

Headmaster: Since January 2014, Mr Martin Priestley, previously head of Warminster School for eight years and teacher and housemaster at Uppingham for 12 years. Studied PPE at Oxford; interests include singing, writing and playing squash.

Academic matters: Traditionally middling but in recent years results have been shooting up. In 2015, 73 per cent A*/A at GCSE – vast majority take separate sciences, physical ed (pupils see it as a big plus that it can be taken regardless of other options) and religious studies (compulsory) taken in year 10. At A level, 45 per cent A*/A in 2015 – strong results from maths, physics, geography and history. Sets for maths, languages and sciences. Parents appreciate the breadth of talents and ages in the staff room and agree that teachers are very 'clued up'.

Indeed a much sharper focus on the academic in recent years, most notably 'learning beyond the curriculum' through a greater use of extension work, often making the most of the talents of Cambridge University postgraduate students who inspire the most able Leysians. Pupils are encouraged to take personal responsibility for their learning – only one hour a night designated prep time, for example, but an expectation that free time will be managed effectively to get it done. 'It's a balance between ensuring good exam results and developing the skills for future learning and responsibility.'

School doesn't flaunt its SEN credentials (dedicated department with three staff, one full-time) but garden variety learning difficulties well supported. A realistic view taken on entry as to 'which children will prosper here and which will not.'

Games, options, the arts: It would be an understatement to say that games are important here. Some real high-flyers – currently numbering national rugby and hockey players (girls and boys), plus a champion equestrian team and keen rowers. School participates in the Cambridge University leagues for some sports and gifted athletes are assured of top level competition. Swimming and rowing are strong.

Top-notch facilities are an attraction – first-class sports hall (shared with local sports clubs), floodlit Astroturf hockey pitch (converts into 12 tennis courts in the summer), recently extended fitness suite, newish pavilion, developing new boathouse in conjunction with three Cambridge colleges. Sport sessions three afternoons a week and after school too for the enthusiastic; however, a more flexible approach now being taken to talents, with those whose are not most in evidence on the field of play being allowed to spend a portion of games time in the music practice room, drama studio, art room or wherever their star shines brightest. Many other activities too – 'our son is taking cookery very seriously,' said one proud parent.

Bikes are welcomed (this is Cambridge, after all) and some houses have communal bikes to borrow. Sixth formers pop in and out of the city as they please

The bright Rugg Centre is the hub of all things artistic – studios, DT, photography and ceramics. Art goes from strength to strength – two finalists in as many years in the Daily Telegraph/Saatchi Gallery art competition and some stunning exhibitions in Cambridge. Serious musicians are now being attracted – many joining from the Cambridge college schools with a strong musical tradition – and there's a large and high quality orchestra, string and wind groups, choir and even a parents' singing group. Distinctions aplenty in LAMDA exams and regular school plays and performances. Heaps of school trips, including scientists to Canada, geographers to Iceland, classicists to Pompeii and Naples, linguists to France, Spain Germany… Also many visitors in, notably authors to inspire the literature group to get reading.

Boarding: The majority of pupils are boarders – girls in a modern block with balconies (for sunbathing) and potted plants. Home boarders, 13 and up, have all the advantages of boarding but with breakfast and sleep at home – the best of both worlds, according to many pupils and their parents – and travel outside of the infamous Cambridge rush hour (it's longer than an hour). Day pupils can be off home by 4.30pm but many stay till 6pm.

A robust community for a small school. Approachable house staff (some with babes and buggies) add to the family feel and students are trusted to go off into the city centre from an early age – repaid by invariably returning when stipulated. Bikes are welcomed (this is Cambridge, after all) and some houses have communal bikes to borrow. Sixth formers pop in and out of the city as they please and have their own club at school, open for an hour or so every evening after 9pm and serving beer and wine (with a strict limit).

Background and atmosphere: Opened in central Cambridge in 1875 with 16 Methodist boys. Redbrick gothic buildings, modern additions, sporting facilities and a dotty miniature railway (with several halts) ring central playing fields. £9.5m Great Hall recently completed – science and performing arts centre comprising assembly hall, theatre, drama and dance studios, science labs, art exhibition space and a café – its architecture bridges the gap between old and new buildings either side. With additional games fields nearby the school has an ample 50 acres. Went co-ed in 1994 and maintains a roughly 60:40 boy:girl split.

Girls' uniform, pre-sixth, recalls the school's wartime evacuation to Pitlochry – Mackenzie tartan kilts – but there's no rigid dress code for either gender in the sixth form and the school tracksuit (attractive dark and light blue) seems most favoured attire.

Pastoral care, well-being and discipline: Parents and pupils are impressed by the pastoral care – the key to its success is the system of one-to-one timetabled tutorials with informal top-ups whenever needed. Housemasters and prefects unearth any problems before they have a chance to take root. Parents report that they often see teachers in general discussion with pupils. Chaplain is popular and much in evidence – parents as well as pupils appreciate his support. Christian ethos is strong and chapel two or three times a week in various permutations of pupil groups (day pupils less keen on the occasional Sunday attendance).

Training for prefects focuses on 'developing antennae for any difficulties' and is all about student welfare. 'There's a real consensus here about what matters in education. If we can get the pastoral care right, then all else will fall into place.'

Discipline is seen more as an opportunity to guide than to punish. No problems with substance abuse for quite a while. Pragmatic approach to bullies but most misdemeanours seen as issues for pastoral care.

Pupils and parents: Mostly UK residents – just 15 per cent from foreign shores, mainly in sixth, though good ESL on offer – and the vast majority live within an easy two-hour commute of Cambridge. 'No PR disasters' in recent memory and boarding is now more popular than ever among UK students – any day boy or girl who leaves before the sixth (local state super-sixths are the alternative) is usually swiftly replaced by a boarder.

Parents are 'not exclusively green wellies' – in fact a good mix of local academics, scientists, medics and many escapees from the capital. Good effort on the part of the school to draw in the parents – parent rep per house and a PTA that is extremely active for a boarding school.

Their children are in the main self-assured and overwhelmingly relaxed and comfortable in their skins. The Leys is appreciated locally as the 'rounded' option (speaks volumes about the perception of the alternatives) and certainly burgeoning personalities are given free rein – the school is small enough to cater to the individual and does it well. There's no 'Leysian type,' says head. Old boys include Martin Bell, Sir Alastair Burnet, Richard Heffer, mathematician Sir Andrew Wiles, J G Ballard.

Entrance: At 11 and 13. Half the intake crosses the road from St Faith's (same foundation), and the rest is made up of arrivals from preps such as Cambridge's King's and St John's, as well as Dame Bradbury's, Orwell Park, Barnardiston Hall, Aldwickbury and a steady recent trickle from Heath Mount. Own entrance exam in English, maths, verbal and non-verbal reasoning and a report from the previous school at 11+ and 13+, but no interviews apart from for scholarship candidates. UKIset tests for year 9 and sixth form overseas applicants. Personal qualities are rated as highly as academic attainment and many considerations. Entry for the sixth is usually a bare minimum of five Bs at GCSE, but most external applicants are armed with a mix of A*, A and Bs. Around 80 per cent of sixth form boards.

Exit: Around 20 local pupils switch to excellent, local sixth form colleges at the end of the fifth (any boomerangers are graciously re-accommodated, usually with a day place). Majority of sixth formers head to university, with a fair number taking gap years. Russell Group most popular of course, especially Edinburgh, Leeds, Nottingham, London; eight to Oxbridge in 2015.

Money matters: Scholarships slashed to five per cent of fees and only for two or three great brains at 11, with talents in music, drama, sport, DT and all-round considered at 13 and sixth form entry. Fee concessions for those who need them and special bursaries available for Forces families, Old Leysians and Methodists. Each year a bursary is made to one Methodist boarder from the City of London through a link with the Wesley's Chapel community.

Remarks: Comfortable school where young people are given the support and space to stretch out and grow into their personalities.

Lockers Park School

Lockers Park Lane, Hemel Hempstead, Hertfordshire HP1 1TL

01442 251712
secretary@lockerspark.herts.sch.uk
www.lockerspark.herts.sch.uk
C of E

Ages: 4-13 (boys), 4-7 (girls) (boarding from 7)
Pupils: 150
Boarders: 20 full, 55 flexi
Day: £9,600 – £16,170 pa
Boarding: £22,350 pa

Headmaster: Since 2013, Chris Wilson BSc, PGCE Cantab (30s). Educated at Winchester House in Northamptonshire, where he boarded from the age of 6, and Oundle. Read rural economics at Newcastle before moving to Cambridge to take a conversion course to enable him to teach maths to A level, followed by his PGCE at Homerton College. Returned to alma mater Winchester House for first teaching role, where he spent 11 years teaching maths and running first XI cricket and colts rugby, heading the boarding house for 10 of them. Moved to Lockers in 2012 as deputy head, drawn by its rigorous sporting culture, boarding heritage ('boarding is infused through the school,' he says) and pastoral approach, as well as its superb musical offering (although he cheerfully describes himself as 'woefully inadequate' in this respect). Headship came after a period which was, according to parents 'turbulent', with three heads of school in six years. He has reportedly 'steadied the ship brilliantly' and restored confidence to staff, with parents describing the change in mood after his appointment as 'palpable'.

Still teaches years 7 and 8 maths and revels in being able to 'physically see the path of the boys' development' in a prep school and having 'involvement in all spheres' of their lives. Parents describe him as a 'fantastic communicator' and say that he has returned a focus on academic achievement which had formerly been 'slightly lost'. A cricket

Everything is focused on bringing out the best in boys, including 40 minute morning break when they tear around fields and woodland

fanatic, he likens the patience and thoughtfulness required for the game to his role as head. Intent that his charges will remember the fun side of school, believes in 'freedom within boundaries' and aims to 'fly in the face' of pushy parents to 'ensure Lockers boys have a childhood'.

Engaging and likeable with a relaxed persona, and ably supported by wife, Hayley, who fulfils a traditional head's spouse role as well as caring for their two young daughters.

Entrance: New pre-prep school housed in a purpose designed building welcomes girls as well as boys. From here, most girls likely to move to local girls' school, Abbot's Hill School, whilst boys move into the 'steadfastly single sex' year 3.

Not currently oversubscribed, although at highest ever numbers. Main intake into year 3 with a 'low key' assessment day including tests in verbal reasoning and maths. Scholarship day in February with applicants also observed in music, sport and a fun activity such as a treasure hunt. Head says they are 'not only looking for academic strength' but for children who can bring 'that certain something' to the school.

Pupils join mainly from state primaries, occasionally other preps (a large influx recently from Berkhamsted Prep), within a 20 to 30 minute radius of the school. Approximately half the cohort are day boys, with the rest doing 'some form' of boarding (two nights minimum). Twenty full time boarders with about 50 per cent of these overseas pupils (typically Russian or Chinese) and some Forces plus some 55 flexi boarders.

Exit: The small number of pupils means they tend to leave in ones and twos to a broad variety of schools. In recent years, good numbers to Harrow plus Bedford, Stowe and Bradfield. Day boys to Merchant Taylors', St Albans or Berkhamsted, with the occasional one to state maintained grammars at 11+, although this is 'definitely not encouraged,' says head. Three or four scholarships achieved each year – six scholarships in 2015. Head deliberates carefully over choosing of senior schools 'on a very individual basis.'

Remarks: Adamantly traditional in its fabric but with a subtly modern feel (thanks to a rolling programme of improvements), Lockers was purpose-built in 1874, based on Mitchell House at Rugby School, and sits atop 25 glorious acres of woodland – a Boys' Own oasis in a drab Hemel suburb. The heart of the school is undoubtedly the stunning, light-flooded panelled dining hall, which typifies Lockers' success in juxtaposing the modern with the school's rich history, the names of alumni etched on its walls. Everything about the school is focused on bringing out the best in boys – from the 40 minute morning break where they can tear around fields and

woodlands with just enough time for a bit of den-building before the bell calls them to lessons, to the pristine well-structured classrooms (if there was a GSG award for the cleanest prep, Lockers would be in with a good chance) and predominantly male staff. Staff know all the boys and are '100 per cent accessible,' say parents – 'clearly visible and just a phone call or an email away.'

The spacious, well-stocked library has a cosy feel, with armchairs and banks of computers, and the chapel can house the whole school at a squeeze. Art room large and airy with its own kiln, although feels suspiciously tidy – and whole school could benefit from more artwork on display, especially as standards are high enough to win a senior school art scholarship most years. DT recently rehomed into a modern block with two super rooms – one for design and one for work. A comfortable board-ers' common room is supplemented by the 'boys' hall' and the old gym, home to table tennis and pool tables for boys to use in their free time. Engine enthusiasts will adore the 'train room' – a dedi-cated space for a huge model railway for boys to tinker with. Pianists practise on a baby grand situ-ated in a very public space rather than tucked away in a practice room – 'great for getting them used to performing,' says head.

Tousled boys bomb happily around between classes with plenty of cheery greetings for staff and visitors. The uniform – or lack thereof – com-prising a check shirt of the boys' choice and a pair of navy cords, sums up the collegiate learn-ing environment where boys can be boys and the endgame is reached via a path punctuated with a lot of good, wholesome fun as well as academic rigour. 'Best' is when the jackets and ties come out – again the boys' own choice of jacket – reserved for school outings, concerts and away matches. School

> *'Best' is when the jackets and ties come out – again the boys' own choice of jacket – reserved for school outings, concerts and away matches*

committed to small class sizes with between 10 and 15 in most forms – parents feel that school's bijoux size is its 'true strength'.

Long days – sometimes up to 11 hours for older boys – with all allowed to arrive in school from 7am and stay for breakfast and supper at no extra charge and with no prior arrangement, all of which helps to cement the seamless boarding vibe – parents say it's like 'one big family.' Boarding house is part of main school, with boys split over two floors accord-ing to age and presided over by a housemaster who is supported by a team of live-in matrons.

Bright, functional dorms housing four to six boarders slightly lack the personal touch, although boys can bring their own duvet covers. Clothes kept in the laundry room and matrons lay out boy's out-fits each day. Exeats every third weekend, unusually from Friday lunch time until Monday evening, with Saturday morning school still going strong on non-exeat weekends, optional for pre-prep.

Setting from year 7 in preparation for CE with specialist teaching across all subjects from year 5. Modern languages exceptionally strong, with head describing French as school's 'stand out' sub-ject and parents adding history and geography to the list. A brief audience with the head of modern languages certainly confirmed his passion for lan-guage and inspirational teaching techniques. Latin and ancient Greek also on the menu, although not considered by parents to be school's strongest suit. Maths and English 'on the up,' says head, due to recent staff changes.

Music 'firing on all cylinders', according to head, led by the 'most dynamic, committed' head of music who secures a music scholarship for at least one boy each year. Violin for all from year 3 and at least 96 per cent of boys continue with an instrument, some playing two or three. Choirs, ensembles and bands galore with an invitation to join the 'intensely serious' main choir considered a real accolade (dare we say cool?) and with parents saying it's 'totally normal for boys to be singing' at Lockers. Drama on curriculum from years 3 to 5 (replaced by Latin in year 6), with opportunities galore for budding thespians to perform in plays, poetry competitions, debating etc.

Sport not the school's raison d'être but a good ethos in place – head laments the demise at some fixtures of the traditional post-match tea in other schools ('a bag of crisps and box of juice – just not the same') – and places huge emphasis on fair play and sportsmanship, fielding A-E teams whenever possible so everyone gets a trip on the bus whatever their ability. Sports department has taken a hit in recent years, tragically losing its two sports coaches to cancer in a short space of time, but is striding on and making the most of its not inconsiderable facilities, including cricket nets, a renovated outdoor pool, tennis courts, and putting green. Sport every afternoon for all boys, with the timetable adjusted seasonally to allow for more light for outdoor fun. Occasional parental grumbles that less sporty boys are 'labelled' in the early years and don't get the same coaching opportunities as their more able peers. Tons of extracurricular from chess club to year-round skiing at the nearby snow dome. Lockers' own cub and scout packs thrive, and boys who take part generally stay the night afterwards.

Chapel every morning takes a 'general studies' approach and acts as a 'reflective, calming exercise' to start the day. Boarders' fun nights well attended by day boys and the anti-health and safety 'Dark Tower' night, an unlit night time treasure hunt

around the school, hugely popular. In summer, day boys stay over after evening barbecues and are 'swept along' with boarding activities throughout the year, some parents saying their boys never want to come home. Action-packed weekends for full-timers with activities split three ways between the cultural, educational and purely fun. All prep done in school – a popular move with boys and parents. School even has its own vernacular – with quirks so numerous that newcomers are issued with a handbook to decipher it all. Parents report that any incidents of bullying or upset are dealt with effectively in a 'supportive and understanding' way.

In all, a small but perfectly formed school which gives boys all the tools they need to continue on to top public schools. Lockers offers the best of both worlds – boarding for those who want it, with all the benefits plus their own beds at home for those who don't. In the words of one happy parent who moved two boys from another prep: 'boys are known and valued at Lockers, rather than unknown and undervalued'. Newish head has much to build on.

New Hall School

The Avenue, Chelmsford, Essex CM3 3HS

01245 467 588
registrar@newhallschool.co.uk
www.newhallschool.co.uk
RC

Ages: 11–18 (junior boarding from 7)
Pupils: 1,157
Boarders: 119 full, 118 weekly/flexi
Day: £8,742 – £18,042 pa
Boarding: £17,690 – £27,702 pa

Principal: Since 2001, Mrs Katherine Jeffrey MA PGCE MA (EdMg) NPQH. Previously an RE teacher at St Mary's School, Shaftesbury, head of RE at Woldingham School, deputy head at The Marist School, Ascot before coming to New Hall as its first ever lay principal and teacher of theology. Awarded the Institute of Directors' East of England Businesswoman of the Year Award, followed by a national Independent Schools Award for Outstanding Strategic Initiative. Since 2010 she has been a committee member of the Catholic Independent Schools' Conference. Mrs Jeffrey is married with four daughters – all educated at New Hall School.

Making the change from dyed-in-the-wool Catholic convent girls' boarding school of variable academic results to one of the UK's foremost successful pioneers of the 'diamond model' (co-educational prep school, single-sex teaching for ages 11 to 16, returning to co-education for the sixth form) took Mrs Jeffrey a speedy five years. Presumably also

nerves of steel, which we don't doubt pulse beneath her polished exterior. 'She oozes confidence and enthusiasm,' swooned one impressed parent, and many laud her 'efficiency'. Indeed, the school comfortably met all the targets it had set itself when adopting the 'diamond model', notably a student body of exactly half girls and half boys. When we visited, New Hall had recently trounced Harrow at rugby and Eton at tennis – to the transparent delight of Mrs Jeffrey. However, amid all this blatant success, at its heart – and its principal's – New Hall remains a Catholic foundation Christian community with core moral values to impart. 'My aim is to shape the adults of the future, form their characters as people of integrity and kindness,' says Mrs Jeffrey. 'We are a community – no-one is here in isolation.'

Academic matters: In 2015, 50 per cent of A level grades were A*/A and 80 per cent A*-B. Similarly impressive results at GCSE – in 2015, 52 per cent

A*-A. Interestingly, the genders at New Hall are on a par results-wise at GCSE, bucking the national trend for boys to fall behind by 10 per cent. More grist to the mill of the 'diamond model', allowing the teaching between 11 and 16 to be tailored to gender-specific learning styles.

French and Spanish are taught from year 7. Theology is compulsory up to year 11. In year 9, classics, Latin and critical thinking are introduced. GCSE students have timetabled religious studies, English, maths, science and a choice of modern language. Head of science has the final say in who takes separate sciences and head of languages gives the 'oui or non' or 'si or no', to students opting for two languages. Most students take 10 or 11 subjects, a few more or a few less according to ability. Each student in years 10 and 11 follows a tutorial programme including 'life skills' and careers education. Games afternoon once a week, with team sports and individual options. Staff reputedly bend over backwards to make sure students shoehorn in their favourite subjects – one parent reported the head of PE giving up his lunch for individual lessons with her son whose GCSE timetable was already full to bursting.

Gifted and talented is taken seriously with accelerated and differentiated learning in lessons and encouragement to take part in enrichment opportunities. The DELTA club promotes scholarly habits (including 'challenge', 'persistence and big picture thinking', 'intellectual courage' and 'meta-thinking'), and the OMEGA club is for the several each year with sights set on Oxbridge.

When we visited, New Hall had recently trounced Harrow at rugby and Eton at tennis – to the transparent delight of Mrs Jeffrey

Games, options, the arts: 'Our co-curricular programme is not an add-on,' emphasises principal. Sport in particular is taken very seriously. Income has been ploughed into facilities – sleek, purpose-built gymnasium block stuffed with cardio machines and weights overlooks a sweep of sports pitches, 10 courts for netball or tennis (full-time tennis pro nurtures future stars), 400-metre cinder running track and chlorine-free pool in its own block with changing room facilities (also used by the Essex swim squad). A former equestrian arena is now an indoor sports hall with state-of-the-art flooring, while the many horse-related activities take place off-site. County and national athletes in many disciplines, including UK independent school golf and equestrian champions, not to mention star swimmers, cricketers, tennis, hockey and rugby players. A New Hallian athlete competed in the Commonwealth Games in 2014.

The first time we've come across a choir that's compulsory – year 7 boys and girls enjoy or endure a year before being given the option to remain. 'We have discovered some great voices that way – people who wouldn't have put themselves forward,' says head of music. Choice of choirs for those inclined, including 'Voces' for the broken-voiced,

plus instrumental ensembles of all kinds and the occasional rock and pop band. Organ lessons on the restored Norman & Beard organ in the school chapel. Many informal as well as the formal performances. Despite a good take-up at GCSE, a small handful study A level music and the odd one or two each year progress to conservatoires.

There are regular – and by all accounts, spectacular – drama productions all year round and involving all ages, and the Walkfares Centre is the venue for all performing arts. Annual dance show is a highlight and dance A level popular. Own dance company takes students from year 10 upwards and crosses over with the local community. ESB and LAMDA thrive. Around 30 a year take art A level – working away in a warren of atelier-style studios – and about a third continue beyond, though architecture tends to win out over fine art.

In keeping with the school's focus on community and charity, all pupils are heavily involved with the New Hall Voluntary Service, which for many becomes a way of life. One pupil recently received the Princess Diana award – for swimming the Channel to benefit Great Ormond Street Hospital – but all make a contribution of some kind.

Eight houses – unrelated to the boarding houses – contest in competitions of all hues.

Boarding: Cream sofas? Cushions? Can this be a boys' boarding house? For 7-13 year olds? Indeed it is at New Hall. Quite apart from Earle House's jaw-droppingly ornate cornicing and mouldings worthy of a royal palace, the place is spotless in the face of a most unforgiving neutrally toned décor – not a muddy rugby sock nor a mouldering trainer to be seen. Either the staff deserve a medal or this is a new breed of boy. The usual entertainment – large-screen TV, Xbox etc – but arranged in such civilised, convivial surroundings that one could happily invite one's grandmother for a spot of GTA. The dorms too are a revelation – again tidy beyond belief with all belongings stowed neatly into storage compartments hiding behind the ladder treads of ingenious high-sleeper beds, designed by the former New Hallian director of boarding and incorporating a study space underneath. Magdalen House, for girls in years 3-8, is more the usual fayre – though rooms for ones and twos rather than the multiples for boys (full boarders usually roomed with the flexi-boarders) – and a comfortable lived-in look with cheery décor chosen by the girls themselves. Four other houses – two for boys and two for girls as they progress through the year groups – accommodating the 33 per cent who board on a flexi, weekly or full-time basis.

Background and atmosphere: The original Palace of Beaulieu, ancestral home of the Boleyn family and thought to represent much of the attraction

to King Henry VIII of his second wife (beheaded), perhaps with good reason. Henry expanded the existing building to create a most imposing and gargantuan edifice, with eight courtyards behind a 550-foot wide red-brick frontage and two enormous gatehouse towers. Channel 4's Time Team dug up evidence of the foundations of what appears to have been a nursery for Henry's first-born, Princess Mary. Having passed through a few hands (including those of Oliver Cromwell) after Henry's demise, in 1799 the palace became occupied by the Canonesses of the Holy Sepulchre, one of the most ancient orders in the Catholic church, established in Europe long before the English Religious Community was founded in 1642. Forced out of their home in the Low Countries by the French Revolutionary Wars, the Canonesses brought their school to the Palace of Beaulieu with the intention of offering a Catholic education to girls denied this in England in the Post-Reformation period. Thus, New Hall is the oldest Catholic girls' school in England.

Today's New Hall is (in terms of footprint at least) but a fraction of Henry's pile, but breathtaking nonetheless and approached via a mile-long avenue at the end of which one fully expects a National Trust ticket booth to appear. Perhaps one of the most impressive interiors is the chapel, with its original solid wood door and Henry VIII's coat of arms over the main entrance.

Behind the long façade of the main building, which houses an impressive entrance hall with waiting room, the chapel, classrooms and a boarding house, there is a dedicated arts block incorporating two large studio spaces (which host the school's popular Saturday dance and drama schools as well as lessons throughout the week). The Eaton Theatre seats 210 and is used for productions as well as lectures and year meetings. Large library with study area for all-comers and hanging with Apple Macs. Eight science labs. Spacious refectory reminiscent of the restaurant in an upmarket London department store with a choice of three hot options (the traditional fish and chips on the Friday we visited), plus a salad bar and other cold choices.

Sixth form is a tight-knit community of 250, presided over by staff other than those that continuing pupils will have met in their junior years. Sixth formers have their own wing of the arts block, with study space and chill-out zone including snack kitchen.

The place is spotless in the face of a most unforgiving neutrally toned décor – not a muddy rugby sock nor a mouldering trainer to be seen

New Hall hit the education sector headlines when it became the first independent school in the country to enter a partnership with a struggling state primary school. The school now lends its expertise and guidance to Messing Primary School, 15 miles away – management input, plus New Hall pupil-run events, such as an international day and community carol service.

On Mrs Jeffrey's wishlist is a new science centre and a large auditorium with the capacity to seat the whole school together, but these she admits have fallen victim to the more pressing need to keep fees 'reasonable' for parents (minimal increases and none at all in one recent year; flexi-boarding rates have actually been reduced).

Pastoral care, well-being and discipline: 'Parents remark on the smiles here – on the faces of pupils and staff alike,' says Mrs Jeffrey and this does appear to be a rather serene community. Personal qualities, kindness in particular, are recognised and drawn out, and pupils we met were certainly happy in their own skin.

Parents too are comfortable in the fold. 'The school has always encouraged parents to give feedback and support the development of the site, by running parent forums and questionnaires,' says one satisfied parent.

Pupils and parents: One clearly in touch with her target market, Mrs Jeffrey appreciates the fact that her school is surrounded by a changing profile of local parents – from the traditional farmers and professionals to city commuters and the grammar school educated. 'Some have attended the historic Catholic schools such as Stonyhurst and Worth themselves and are now looking to us for their children,' she says. Being Catholic is not a prerequisite, but engagement with the religious life of the school very much is. 'If you come here you sign up to the whole package,' says Mrs Jeffrey. 'I would hope that our pupils would leave here well-informed on matters of faith, and that they would have absorbed our core moral and spiritual values.'

Buses zero in on the school from a myriad directions daily and boarders come from all over the south east, many from London thanks to the fast and frequent commuter train service – 35 minutes from Liverpool Street to Chelmsford, four miles away. The rumour is of a proposed new mainline station right at the end of the New Hall drive (no prizes for guessing Mrs Jeffrey's preferred name for it). Long a favourite with overseas pupils, about 45 per cent of boarders, who represent more than 30 countries.

Entrance: Year 7 has 120 places – usually three times over-subscribed. Around 40 pupils come up from New Hall's own year 6, although they too must go through the same entry procedure as external applicants – papers in English, maths and verbal reasoning plus a three-minute presentation to members of the senior school SLT. Lengthy admissions preamble – families have usually visited for at least one open day as well as a group tour including the opportunity to ask questions of the senior leadership team before beginning the formal application. Lower sixth has 150 places, with new entrants needing two As and four Bs at GCSE to be in with a whiff. 'Our A level classes are very fast-paced,' says principal, 'with pupils aiming for A* to B grades.'

Exit: Some 40 per cent leave after GCSEs. Four to Oxbridge in 2015 (medicine, history and classics), others mostly to their first choice of a range of universities to study subjects in all realms, including theology. Former pupils are automatic members of the Old Fishes' Association (being rebranded as New Hallians) and this association numbers many notables, including international fashion designer Anya Hindmarch, CNN international correspondent Christiane Amanpour, artist and novelist Leonora Carrington, opera singer Stefanie Kemball-Read and Horrid Henry actor Theo Stevenson.

Money matters: Scholarships for Catholics, academic, music, all rounder, sport (general) and tennis, plus means-tested bursaries.

Remarks: There is the feeling that New Hall is much more than the sum of its parts, with personal qualities and integrity as central to the ethos as an application to study and success.

Old Buckenham Hall School

Brettenham Park, Ipswich, Suffolk IP7 7PH

01449 740252
admissions@obh.co.uk
www.obh.co.uk
C of E

Ages: 3–13 (boarders from 7)
Pupils: 208: 138 boys/70 girls
Boarders: 48 full, 47 weekly/flexi
Day: £8,652 – £17,550 pa
Boarding: £16,191 – £22,866 pa

Headmaster: Since January 2015, Tom O'Sullivan, previously deputy head and head of science at Mowden Hall School. Law degree from Durham; worked in retail and pharmaceutical industry before seeing the light and getting a PGCE from Cambridge. Keen sportsman; has also taught at Beaudesert School in Gloucs.

Entrance: Pupils enter at nursery, reception and all years up to 7 and 8. No linked feeders, though the majority of pupils come from within a two hour drive. Non-competitive entry through interview and formal assessment plus reports from previous school. Pupils can enter the school on a daily basis and, if they wish, become a boarder at a later stage. A small, but constant, group of pupils come from abroad.

Exit: The school believes that the process of selecting the right choice of school at 13+ can't begin too early and certainly by years 5/6. Popular destinations are those schools fairly close, eg Uppingham, Oakham, Oundle, Stowe and Framlingham, but a clutch to Eton, Harrow, Wycombe Abbey, Cheltenham College, Winchester. Encourages

parents to cast a wide net at senior school stage rather than staying within the safe and familiar choices. A significant number of pupils receive awards and scholarships.

Remarks: Alert, friendly and naturally courteous children – standing up for adults, holding doors etc. Classes are small (fewer than 16 generally) and with setting in the higher forms in preparation for exams/scholarships. The tone throughout is purposeful and light-hearted – one example is the use of Spanish and French in labelling, eg 'le bureau du Directeur'. Music and drama enjoy excellent facilities and highly motivated staff ensure that children make the most of what's available. The full ability range is catered for and SEN is undergoing a full review. The school feels that the withdrawal of pupils with specific difficulties 'does not, in itself, necessarily address their needs – a highly competent teacher plus in-class support may often be the answer'.

One of the school's great strengths is its framework of pastoral support for each pupil. Arrangements for tutor groups and boarding houses constantly appraised and changes are sometimes necessary as staff come and go. The school is looking particularly at the needs of the older pupils. Well-organised and attractive boarding houses, careful thought having been given to the facilities and decoration. The slightly dismal air that can prevail in dormitories and common rooms has been completely avoided – no sagging sofas and ancient cast-off furniture. In years 7 and 8 pupils can decide whether to be a dorm leader or sleep in their year group bedrooms. Boarding is so popular that many board full time despite living close by – 'My friend boards even though she lives less than a mile away!'

Full boarding is run on an 11 day model described by the school as 'unique' – essentially it means that pupils spend every other weekend in school. Weekend activities are certainly appealing: clay pigeon shooting, night orienteering, trips to the Suffolk ski centre and local point to point. If that's not exciting enough, there's even the chance to go shopping in Bury St Edmunds.

Old Buckenham Hall is set to expand from its traditional county boarding base, keen to reach parents who might not naturally consider a prep or boarding option for their child. Positions itself as

Boarding is so popular that many board full time despite living close by – 'My friend boards even though she lives less than a mile away!'

a largely non-selective family school, the majority boarding in the higher years. The pre-prep school runs on a day basis with boarding (weekly and full) becoming available in year 3. School aware that the decision to board needs careful thought and transitional boarding of two or three nights a week is available together with taster weeks.

The school has been quick to respond to the need for flexibility and operates a variety of collection times for pupils both in the prep and pre-prep. The majority of pupils come from within a radius of 40 miles, but quite a number come from further afield and the school operates a taxi service to the airport for those who need to travel abroad.

Orwell Park School

39

Nacton, Ipswich, Suffolk IP10 0ER

01473 659225
headmaster@orwellpark.co.uk
www.orwellpark.co.uk

Ages: 2–13 (boarders from 7)
Pupils: 282
Boarders: two-thirds board
Day: £6,930 – £17,376 pa
Boarding: £20,070 – £22,290 pa

Headmaster: Since 2011, Mr Adrian Brown. Arrived at Orwell Park from Ipswich School, a former professional Essex cricketer and Cambridge Blue. Affable and down-to-earth, much like the pupils in his charge, he lives in the headmaster's house at Orwell Park with his wife Nicole; three children at university.

Entrance: Entry points at 2+ and 4+ (by taster morning in class and a home visit), 7+ and 11+ (tests in maths, English and reasoning, plus a report from the previous school and interview).

Exit: Post-CE, Orwell Park's pupils spread across the UK to top-drawer boarding schools – Eton, Harrow, Winchester, Gordonstoun, Ampleforth, Rugby, Oundle, Uppingham and the like – and local day schools, with no more than four or five per cohort heading in the same direction. Some 15-20 scholarships every year, covering the full range of subjects.

Remarks: One of the most jaw-droppingly gorgeous schools we've ever seen – and it's a prep. Visitors are defied to supress a sharp intake of breath as an idyllic Suffolk leafy lane gives way to impressive wrought iron gates and a sweeping drive heralding a handsome Georgian mansion with late-Victorian additions. Built by a local philanthropist as a venue for royal house parties, it's complete with its own observatory and clock tower, but has been a school since 1937. A combination of effortless elegance (chandeliers and oak panelling in the dining room, ornate tiles and floor-to-ceiling windows in the orangery assembly hall) and down-to-earth, workaday practicality (music practice rooms in the basement) is an appropriate reflection of its clientele – 'the children here are quietly confident,' says head. Indeed the pupils, aged 2+ to 13, who have a 'number one' uniform for best and sweatshirts for every day, are very at home in such grand surroundings. Undoubtedly this is helped by the fact that head knows them all by name (a tour of the school has him checking on this week's second team rugby score with one of its stars, and congratulating a self-effacing young man on the outdoor skills shown on a recent camping expedition).

Every day at Orwell Park begins with a tutor period or an assembly. The timetable also includes a quiet reading slot and there's a serious emphasis on academic attainment, with streaming throughout the juniors. Latin is taught from year 6 – 'they love it' reports head – and includes translation from English to Latin, virtually unheard of even in senior schools these days. Ancient Greek is taught to year 8 scholars, but French is the main MFL, with Spanish and German options at year 6.

Stunning playing fields run down to the river. Junior girls love to make dens and shops in the trunks of the thickets and there's a genuine army–built assault course in the woods

Learning support is for all – welcoming drop-in centre is open all day until late evening with an impressive mind-mapping approach ordering thoughts for any task or project. A SENCo oversees a team of five or six who support dyslexia, dyspraxia, dyscalculia, mild Asperger's and ADHD, but only those who are able to manage in the mainstream. Children are assessed on entry and advised on whether or not the curriculum will suit. After that, any difficulties are dealt with as and when with particular help for spelling, handwriting, reading, maths. Real focus on study skills in the run-up to CE with one-to-one and small group sessions as well as dual teaching in class. Outside agencies are co-opted as necessary – OTs, SALT and physios. Each junior class has a qualified teacher plus assistant and there are six gap helpers, mainly young Aussies.

This is a Mac school and they're everywhere – in the music room for composition, throughout the classrooms and in two dedicated ICT rooms, not to mention the iPads currently being trialled by the heads of department with a view to introducing mobile learning in the near future.

A performance culture – you name it, there's a competition for it (verse, singing, public speaking), usually house clashes or routing the local independent school league opponents on the 110 acres of stunning playing fields, which reach from the French doors of the most impressive salons right down to the shores of the Orwell. Growing bodies are encouraged to run free (though no further than the ha-ha for safety reasons). Junior girls love to make dens and shops in the trunks of the thickets and there's a genuine army-built assault course in the woods. Courts for tennis, squash and netball as well as an Astro, cricket nets, nine-hole golf course, sizeable indoor gym and the most inviting outdoor pool, set in a walled garden complete with barbecue area and reached by means of a wisteria walk. Idyllic.

Art has an inviting airy space and work is of an impressive standard. Prospective senior school scholars have their own area and may work on their portfolios independently. DT is generously equipped and a popular class. Heaps of extracurricular clubs, including clay pigeon shooting, and a stargazing club run by local astronomers in the school's own observatory.

Impressive £1m pre-prep building opened in 2013, making space for 80 under-4s with a large hall

and teaching rooms as well as outdoor learning areas under the curve of an undulating contemporary roof.

Leadership is key here with the recent introduction of the OPS challenge – a mini D of E with long hikes and camp-outs – and outdoor pursuits holidays to Normandy for year 6s and the Ardèche post-CE. Positions of authority bring with them real obligations – head boys and girls are relied on to help run the school and there are dorm captains, house captains and prefects. 'Everyone has the chance to prove themselves if they want to,' says head, 'just by putting their names down.' The Alston lecture series inspires nascent vocations by inviting parents to come in and speak about their careers.

Increase in boarding numbers recently, locals as well as international students, and options are flexi (min two nights), weekly and full. Dorms are spacious with spectacular views and populated by pupils of the same year group plus a year 8 dorm monitor to keep them in order. Evening and weekend activities range from sailing to crochet to trips to the zoo.

The Purcell School

Aldenham Road, Bushey, Hertfordshire WD23 2TS

01923 331100
info@purcell-school.org
www.purcell-school.org

Ages: 8–18
Pupils: 182; sixth form: 79
Boarders: 143
Day: £25,452 pa
Boarding: £32,499 pa

Headmaster: Since January 2016, Stephen Yeo BMus LTCL NPQH (50s), previously head of Exeter Cathedral School. A chorister at The Cathedral School, Llandaff prior to music scholarship at King's College, Taunton. Studied music at Sheffield, then at Trinity College, London. Unusual career path took him first to top-notch senior schools in Ireland. Later became head of music and creative arts at selective King Edward VI, Handsworth, followed by three years at Bedales as director of studies. Joined Exeter Cathedral School after five years as head of Lyndhurst School in Camberley, Surrey. Married to Catherine, a languages graduate, registered nurse and midwife; they have four grown up sons. They both enjoy walking and cycling in Ireland and Wales, where they have a home.

Academic matters: Academic results, having collapsed in recent years, are showing some improvement. In 2015, 42 per cent of A level results A*/A and 72 per cent A*-B. However, music, music tech, art and English lit the only subjects with candidates in double figures; history next in line with eight takers (seven taking maths plus two further maths – both got A*). Negligible numbers studying sciences or languages. Good crop of A*s for music, but hardly any elsewhere. All of this is a sharp change from the fairly recent past when the school routinely featured high in the independent school A level league tables. The school is working hard to 'sort out the academic side', and green shoots are already appearing. In 2015, 61 per cent of GCSE grades were A*/A and 83 per cent A*-B.

Years 5 and 6 taught as one group; thereafter pupils taught within their year groups. Setting for maths starts in year 9. Everyone in the GCSE years takes music, maths, English lang and science but generally take no more than seven or eight subjects. Small classes for everything. New music library and IT has been upgraded throughout. Much individual help and support, especially for musical prodigies who arrive playing perfect Paganini but with little English. SEN well supported.

Games, options, the arts: Sport surprisingly good for a school that doesn't really offer any. 'My son never liked sport until he came here,' enthused one mum who reeled off the games he was now involved in: badminton, volleyball, football. One competitive football match each year against fellow music geeks at the Yehudi Menuhin School. Currently one PE lesson per week; plans perpetually afoot to offer more physical activity. Lots of ad hoc activity, from kicking a ball about the enormous playing fields to a bit of netball and off-site swimming. Art and drama enthusiastically pursued, and drama has recently been formally added to the curriculum (art already there).

Music provision is, of course, superb. The musical day begins at 7.20am with pre-breakfast morning practice and continues, interspersed through the day, until bedtime. Practice supervisors support the under-13s. Choir compulsory for

Music provision is, of course, superb. The musical day begins at 7.20am with pre-breakfast morning practice and continues until bedtime

all – though resented by some as an intrusion into their practice time. That said, the senior chamber choir was described by a parent as 'simply the finest and most exciting youth choir I have EVER heard'. Most of the staff teach at the RCM or RAM and all are of that professional standard – they have to be. Professional accompanists work with the pupils – a real and special privilege. No shortage of performing opportunities. Last year there were 71 public concerts, 15 'outreach' concerts and upwards of 150 lunchtime concerts. Composing very strong and one girl was one of five winners of the BBC Young Composers' Competition recently.

The mint green music centre features a stunning recital room, teaching rooms, a recording studio, dozens of practice rooms, from which concert quality playing seeps, and nice little architectural touches everywhere. Music tech covers all aspects of creative studio work including multi-track recording, electro-acoustic music, arranging, studio engineering, producing and composition for film. A large new percussion suite. The multi-purpose school hall is still used for most concerts.

Boarding: Boarding accommodation, formerly poor, now tickety-boo. Sunley House, upstairs in the main school building, provides accommodation for 50 girls plus resident staff. New co-ed boarding house very popular – with a boys' wing and a, larger, girls' wing. The recently refurbished junior boarding house makes a cheerful home to around 20 (mostly) girls and (a few) boys ages 8-12, all in double rooms (a few singles), though with such small numbers friendships can be hard to form. Sixth form pianists have a piano in their rooms.

Pupils enthuse about their fantastic camaraderie – 'We all encourage each other – everyone is so supportive of everyone else,' and you feel this as you see them greet each other in the corridors. A few girls mentioned feeling (geographically) divided by the current split of girl boarders between Sunley, in the main school, and the new co-ed boarding house. Would make more sense to put all the girls in the new house and whack the boys into Sunley. Most boarders go home on Friday nights and return 48 hours later, but there are always around 50 in on weekends, many from abroad.

Background and atmosphere: An interesting history. Founded as recently as 1962 by Rosemary Rapaport and Irene Forster – but nonetheless the UK's oldest specialist music school. It began life as The Central Tutorial School for Young Musicians, at Conway Hall, then resided for a while in Morley College, from where it moved to Hampstead. In 1973, it was renamed The Purcell School – perhaps reflecting the new enthusiasm for 'earlyish' British music – and, in 1998, relocated to the site of the former Royal Caledonian School in fairly dismal Bushey, Hertfordshire. The main building is an attractive low-rise Edwardian pile with wide corridors, good-sized concert hall, assorted classrooms, smartened up canteen (food now provided by outside caterers and has improved no end) and new girls' boarding accommodation.

Staff and pupil morale knocked in the spring of 2013 by the redundancy of the school's well-liked head of music who conducted the school orchestra. Redundancy, after 25 years at the school, left bad feeling, with pupils melodramatically taking to wearing green ribbons to protest his removal. 'It makes us feel like music is less important now,' said one pupil. 'It's like the nerve centre has been ripped from the school', said another. School governors have had a much-needed shake-out and the average age of staff has plummeted by around 20 years. Rapid through-put of heads does not help stability. All the specialist music schools are going through a period of introspection and Purcell is no exception.

Most pupils receive some kind of financial support – under the government's music and dance assisted places scheme, school bursary or scholarship. Amazing opportunity for the brilliant but broke

Pastoral care, well-being and discipline: Pupils given more leeway than at most schools and chafe when their freedoms are reigned in. Much friction over rules eg about when children are allowed out to visit shops and which shops they may visit. A few expulsions for use of alcohol or cannabis.

Pupils and parents: All sorts, from every economic, academic, national and social background, all united by a love of music. Some 17 per cent of boarders from overseas: nine per cent Korean, five per cent Singaporean and rest from all over. No quotas or limits on nationalities joining. A healthy slab of local children make up the day contingent who lead a very different existence to the boarders. Children can attend from age 8, though numbers are so low at that end of the school that we can't recommend boarding here quite that young. Big intake of (mainly) boarders at sixth form. Former pupils include Oliver Knussen (composer and conductor), Nicholas Daniel (oboist and first winner of the BBC Young Musician competition), Catrin Finch (former harpist to the Prince of Wales), Lara Melda (winner of 2010 BBC Young Musician), Janice Graham (leader, ENO Orchestra), and Yiruma (Korean pianist and composer).

Entrance: Pupils are selected by musical audition, supported by interviews and reasoning test. Auditions take place every week from September to March. Children come for a preliminary audition and then a majority return for a more thorough going over. Musical standard for admission is very high but not ridiculous. No academic threshold, but school must be 'able to cater for them'. No set numbers for entry at any particular age, and more coming and going here than at most schools. About 20 musicians enter at sixth form.

Exit: Mostly to The Royal Academy of Music, The Royal College of Music or The Guildhall, many with scholarships – 23 in 2015. The rest mostly to other music courses hither and yon; a few to university to read other subjects. Four to Oxbridge in 2015, all on scholarships – three to study music and one physics. Most pupils end up with careers in music – whether teaching, production, business or performing.

Money matters: Fees have been frozen for four years. Which cannot be said of any other independent school in the United Kingdom. Indeed, fees now significantly less than many public schools, if you factor in the cost of music lessons which are included here. Meanwhile, most pupils receive some kind of financial support – under the government's music and dance assisted places scheme, school bursary or scholarship. An amazing opportunity for the brilliant but broke – many pay nothing.

Remarks: Buffeted, but not bowed – still providing a unique education to some of the world's most talented youngsters.

Queenswood

Shepherd's Way, Hatfield, Hertfordshire AL9 6NS

01707 602500
admissions@queenswood.org
www.queenswood.org

Ages: 11–18
Pupils: 432; sixth form: 120
Boarders: 184 full/weekly
Day: £20,700 – £24,600 pa
Boarding: £29,550 – £32,700 pa

Principal: Since 2006, Mrs Pauline Edgar BA PGCE (50s). Educated at Dudley Girls' High School, then read history at London University. Previously head of sixth form, teaching and learning co-ordinator and head of history and politics at Francis Holland School. Married to Hamish, a maritime lawyer, with two sons and a daughter.

Only the seventh head in the history of Q, as it is affectionately known. A petite, elegant, well-spoken, cheerful principal. Passionate about history, politics and music, enjoys running, swimming and sailing holidays, but acknowledges she hardly has a life outside Queenswood. 'This is not just another school,' she explains. Has added even greater depth at Queenswood in recent years with innovations in the curriculum and organisational structure and opportunities for girls to be 'open-hearted.' Has an easy way with pupils and they appreciate her 'genuine interest.'

Retiring in July 2016. Her successor will be Joanna Cameron, currently deputy head of Ipswich High. Degree in environmental science from Surrey; she has taught science at St Mary's Wantage and was a member of the senior leadership team at St Gabriel's in Newbury. A keen sportswoman, with a passion for running, hockey and equestrianism, she is married to David and they have two sons.

Academic matters: A level/Pre-U results strong. In 2015, 77 per cent A*/B grades and 48 per cent A*/A. At GCSE, 79 per cent A*/A grades. Broad intake, coupled with commendable performance, places school at pinnacle of Hertfordshire's value-added tables. Languages are hot here, with most girls taking two at GCSE and one to A level. Japanese really gaining momentum from year 8 up, thanks to enthusiastic teaching and a cultural visit to Japan (alternative for those staying at home is a

week of Japanese visitors and activities). Latin from year 7 and the recommendation is that pupils either continue with it or switch to classical civilisation from year 8. Italian and Spanish also on the menu and girls encouraged to continue studies in their own native languages.

A school for budding international sports stars – 'I love watching sports and it's a joy to be part of a school that wins,' says principal

No one is refused a go at a GCSE – 'they're keen to push the academic students as much as possible, but are also prepared to coach and encourage those who are less academic and need a different approach,' notes a parent. Teaching is mainly traditional with ICT increasingly used by all – every girl has a laptop. Sets for maths, French, English and science; class sizes not larger than 24, many smaller (DT scheduled against ICT in year 7 and textiles in year 8 to allow for smaller groups, for example). Pre-U English and history of art going great guns and EPQ alongside A levels (no IB here and no plans). RE growing in popularity with a dozen taking A level and one or two per year to study theology or philosophy at uni (often Cambridge). Government and politics a popular newcomer. Academic scholars have a staff mentor.

About 15 per cent have EAL needs. Support available for those with moderate dyslexia or other, mild SEN. Some 90 on register, many monitored and some receive one-to-one (max two lessons a week) from helpful and enthusiastic learning support co-ordinator. Most have SpLD type difficulties but a few with mild ADD, ADHD or ASD. School earnestly insists that parents matter. 'They're the ones who know the girls, what makes them tick, what causes them to crumble, so we're always keen to discuss issues, strategies and ways forward.'

Games, options, the arts: A school for budding international sports stars – 'I love watching sports and it's a joy to be part of a school that wins,' says principal. Lots of successes at regional and national finals. National hockey players include members of the England junior squad and one recent leaver is now a promising player on the international tennis circuit, another a world-class rower. School is a national LTA clay court centre and hosts the annual national schools' championships. School's tennis team were silver medallists at the 2013 World Schools Tennis Championships and the Lawn Tennis Association recommends it for would-be tennis stars. With 27 courts in all – 12 clay, 13 all-weather and two indoors – 'you can play tennis at any level,' and at almost any time. One pupil is a national and international wheelchair tennis star. Budding stars in all disciplines are carefully mentored – help given with diet, fitness (fitness coach onsite who devises individual programmes), training, fixtures etc. Masses of inter-school competitions ensure sport for all. Facilities include large, modern indoor swimming pool, Astroturf hockey pitch, fully equipped fitness suite, aerobics room, professional dance studio and huge sports hall.

More than half learn a musical instrument and many at least two. Ensembles for everything and very enthusiastic teaching – a lively percussion session was in full swing when we visited. School rock band. One pupil a BBC Young Chorister of the Year finalist in 2014. Meanwhile drama thrives, with half taking LAMDA lessons and awards for actors and public speakers. Lower and upper school productions every year, plus one for GCSE and A level students and scholar plays in between. Rehearsals for Sweeney Todd in the rehearsal space when we visited – great gusto on display. Dramatists visit Edinburgh Fringe. Celebrated its 120th anniversary in style with a music, drama and dance extravaganza at the Barbican Hall in London.

Thriving 3D art department with its own kiln. Around 10 a year continue to A level (upper sixth students have individual atelier workspaces) and a few move on to art school, while architecture is also popular. Artists are inspired on trips to Milan and Florence.

One of only 20 schools to run the elite Leith's cookery course in preference to food tech – taught right from the beginning (even including lessons on choosing the right wine to accompany). When we visited girls were whipping up macaroni cheese or rack of lamb with a herb crust, depending on ability. Timetabled lessons for years 7 and 8 and a club thereafter. Each student issued with her own

set of Sabatier knives, uniform and Leith's 'bible' to keep. Leith's teacher was formerly a chef in the school's own kitchens.

> *When we visited, girls on the elite Leith's course were whipping up macaroni cheese or rack of lamb with a herb crust. Each student issued with her own set of Sabatier knives to keep*

Dance unsurprisingly popular and the school has its own dance team (puts on an annual spectacular and contributes to other school shows too). Model United Nations, Young Enterprise, debating society, plus charity works. Thriving D of E – 25 working on gold, 45 recently achieved bronze. School awarded silver level eco-school status.

Trips galore, especially with London on the doorstep (museums, galleries, Wimbledon etc). Year 9 girls have the opportunity to study for a term overseas, usually Australia or New Zealand. Language visits to Spain and Japan. Sports teams tour all over the world – all 'help the girls to develop independence, work as a team and cope when things don't go right,' says principal. Acknowledgement of the global community though exchange schools in Australia, New Zealand, South Africa, Canada, Japan. Girls work on education projects with schools in Malawi and Zambia. Closer to home, community work in local primary schools and with the elderly – developing 'generosity of spirit and the importance of giving, to counteract the materialism communicated by the media,' principal explains.

Boarding: Cosy houses with contemporary interior design to please even the pickiest of teenage girls integrate day and boarding pupils – one for years 7 and 8, four for years 9, 10 and 11, plus sixth form houses. Day girls have the flexibility to board when they wish if a bed is free and this is encouraged. Some fixed 'in school' and 'home weekends,' otherwise boarders can spend full weekend at home with choice of Sunday evening or Monday morning return. A few traditionalists would prefer a return to full boarding, but most appreciate this is a move to meet 21st century family needs and preserve the boarding ethos.

Background and atmosphere: Founded in Clapham Park in 1894 and moved to purpose-built neo-Tudor building in 1925 (masses of later additions). Splendid grounds – glorious gardens open to the public at end of May and 120 acres of sports fields and woodland. Two miles from the M25, a 'commutable hour' from London. First-rate Audrey Butler Centre (aka the ABC) houses lecture theatre, language labs and masses of classrooms. Impressive new theatre and associated facilities a jewel in the crown. Science labs recently refurbed. Principal is leading the school in 'quietly fundraising' for a Queenswood Hall to seat the school as an alternative to chapel.

Sixth formers have their own comfortable pad – known as the Pizza Hut, originally thanks to its reminiscent shape and roof, but latterly more for the number of Domino's orders. Beautifully decorated common room – very girl suitable, with squishy leather sofas, large flat-screen TV, chic bar tables and stools and pool tables. Quiet area equipped with computers for studiers, plus kitchen corner for break-time snacks.

Girls are smart in grey and purple – 'unfussy and not ridiculously expensive,' approves a parent – with sixth formers in office-style apparel.

Pastoral care, well-being and discipline: There is a Queenswood way of doing things, which begins with the principal and 'permeates its way through the rest of the school,' comments a perspicacious parent. Certainly the school day reflects the levelheadedness that typifies the school's approach to everything. The day starts with boarders' breakfast at 7.30am, then chapel (school is Methodist foundation but services are non-denom) twice a week at 8.15am and lessons from 8.45am until lunch, with a mid-morning break. Year 7s have a study hour incorporated in their day and all girls participate in their chosen activities – crafts, sport and other clubs – after formal lessons finish at 4.20pm. 'Balance is key,' says the school.

Very much a 'sleeves rolled up' school for community-minded doers who are happy to get stuck in. Refreshing to find pre-teen girls still excited by camping out and playing hide and seek. Sixth formers are articulate, poised, feisty but sensible

School's approach is to encourage girls to adapt and assimilate change – 'we applaud having a go,' says the principal. 'We tell them that failure is a part of learning and challenging themselves.' A secure support and pastoral network through housemistresses, tutors and friendly faces. The

overwhelmed or anxious are free to confide in any member of staff with whom they feel comfortable. All keep an eye out in particular for girls who are stretching themselves thinly to take advantage of all Queenswood has to offer.

Houses are run by teaching housemistresses, with assistants and a team of academic tutors (around 10 tutees each). Pupil-teacher and parent-teacher relationships relaxed but respectful – 'we work in partnership with parents; we want them to take an active interest in the school and their daughter's education.' Now a large prefect team with specialist responsibilities. Girls who put themselves forward for head girl must present on stage to the whole school and everyone votes for the speech they found most compelling. Principal's choice from then on.

Range of visiting speakers use personal experiences to raise awareness of hard-hitting issues such as drugs, sex, HIV and alcoholism. Girls taking drugs 'lose their right to be a member of the school.' Rewards and sanctions system aims to reward girls for contributions to school life and help them overcome any problems they may have with that. Postcards of praise, gold badges and stars reward pupils; demerits and detentions aim to deter miscreants. Parents involved at early stages.

Food is 'delicious,' enthuses a self-confessed foodie year 8. Serving area a top hotel would crow about, even with its own showcase area where food is cooked to order. Option of outdoor eating in new picnic/BBQ area when weather permits.

Perhaps acknowledging the reason some girls opt to leave for sixth form, school now hosts joint projects with Bedford and Radley but principal says Q girls never have a problem integrating in a mixed environment when they go to university – 'that's just a myth.'

Pupils and parents: 'The girls are self-confident and very resourceful,' says principal, though adds that there's no particular type. 'They're real individuals, not moulded.' Nearly 50 per cent boarders. Twenty per cent from abroad – fair proportion from Hong Kong and mainland China, with some expats. All continents represented. EAL taken seriously. Scholars are well recognised around the school – 'there's no envy,' said our eloquent sixth former guide. 'Everyone is inspired by them and shares in their success.'

Very much a 'sleeves rolled up' school for community-minded doers who are happy to get stuck in. Refreshing to find pre-teen girls as excited by camping out and playing hide and seek as they are by beauty and make-up sessions. Sixth formers articulate, poised, feisty but sensible.

Lots of first-time buyers, with both partners working. Masses from London. Drawn by Q's 'warmth and positive energy,' explains one. Strong parents' association much involved with social activities throughout the year and generous contributions to school development projects.

Old Queenswoodians' Association is arguably one of the largest, with more than 4,000 members and branches around the world, ready to befriend and advance Queenswood girls in all sorts of careers and all sorts of places. OQs include Sky Sports presenter Georgie Thompson, actress Helen McCrory, Professor Dame Alison Richard (former vice-chancellor of Cambridge University), journalist Carol Thatcher, tennis player Naomi Cavaday and GB athlete Jodie Williams.

Entrance: Early registration advised, but entry into most years if vacancies permit, either by CE or own entrance exam. Visits welcome by appointment, pupils act as tour guides. Broad ability intake but should be capable of gaining good grades at GCSE. Strong sixth form intake – candidates must get six GCSEs at B or above, with As in the subjects they want to study at A level. Pupils join from a number of schools, including Stormont, St Mary's (NW3), Lyonsdown, Beechwood Park, St Hilda's (Harpenden), Heath Mount, Maltman's Green, Duncombe, Edge Grove and Palmers Green High.

Exit: Up to 20 per cent leave at 16, usually lured by co-ed. Some come back. At 18 majority to wide range of universities eg London unis, Birmingham, Bristol, Loughborough, Warwick, York. Many gap years – school offers support with planning.

Money matters: Majority of scholarships are honorary, bringing glory and support rather than cash, though bursaries available in cases of need. Very much looking at what they can offer that will foster girls' talents rather than offering financial sweetener. Music (including organ scholarship), drama, art, tennis and sport scholarships. Occasional bursaries – means-tested. Discount for Forces families.

Remarks: A modern girls' school to which others should aspire. A winning combination of traditional values with a broad, forward-looking education to equip bright young women with the integrity and self-belief to make a difference in the world of the future.

The Royal Hospital School

Holbrook, Ipswich, Suffolk IP9 2RX

01473 326200
admissions@royalhospitalschool.org
www.royalhospitalschool.org
C of E

Ages: 11–18
Pupils: 736; sixth form: 210
Boarders: 484 full/weekly
Day: £13,458 – £19,020 pa
Boarding: £21,624 – £28,845 pa

Headmaster: Since January 2016, Simon Lockyer, previously second master at Portsmouth Grammar. Has also been housemaster and head of department at Wellington College. The son of a naval officer, Simon was educated at Blundell's School, Devon, on a military bursary after which he went on to gain a BSc in microbiology at Newcastle, a PGCE at Cambridge and a masters at Buckingham. His first teaching appointment was at Bishop's Stortford High School in Hertfordshire. He is married to

Abigail, who grew up in Suffolk, and they have three young children.

Academic matters: Sits comfortably between the highly selective Ipswich schools and the maintained grammar schools over the county border. The introduction of day pupils and their increasing numbers mean that academic achievement is rising across the curriculum. In 2015, 40 per cent of GCSE grades were A*/A, 70 per cent A*-B. Pupils have noticed the increased rigour of the timetable, bemoaning that 'he stopped games on two afternoons and we have to do science and languages instead'; not strictly the case, though games have been moved to an after-school slot one afternoon a week to make way for lessons. A modern language is compulsory up to GCSE. All year 7s now have taster lessons in German, Spanish and Latin before selecting one, in addition to French.

Over 25 subjects offered at A level; maths and the sciences very popular. Sixth form purely academic; in addition to A levels, students follow the sixth form enrichment programme, which provides an opportunity to teach useful skills and gain extra qualifications; popular topics include ancient Greek, law, sports leadership training and a handy-sounding course, the seven habits of highly effective people. In 2015, 31 per cent A*/A grades, 58 per cent A*-B.

School has very creditable results considering wide ability range, which includes some 80 overseas pupils for whom English is a second language (also responsible for stunning results in Chinese and Russian). Overseas centre can help them gain a good grasp of English. Over 100 have identified specific educational needs, but the majority of these are mild, and require only class-based support. More serious problems with literacy and numeracy, often a result of Forces families having a disrupted education, are given extra help from the start. Timetabled support can take the place of learning a second language. Mobile learning programme is seeing pupils issued with tablet computers.

Over 100 are on the water three or four times a week in one of a fleet including 48 dinghies, four Cornish shrimpers and four powerboats

Games, options, the arts: A big part of the school's attraction is the exceptional range of sports and activities. Games on three afternoons; all the seasonal team sports, and though not an elite sporting school, the variety is a big plus: rock climbing, squash, shooting and kick-boxing a glimpse of the 70 plus activities. 'We never have nothing to do,' said one pupil, and it is definitely not for lazybones. Gigantic sports hall (or gymnasium), a separate enormous, indoor pool in another vast building and, if you've any energy left, 96 acres of playing fields.

But sailing remains key activity, with undreamed of opportunities for learning the craft and progressing in a sport that is often ruled out for many on grounds of cost. All year 7s receive a full week's instruction: 'We want to find ability among those who are not "dynastic" sailors,' says the RYA (Royal Yachting Association) instructor. Over 100 take to sailing seriously, on the water three or four times a week in one of a fleet including 48 dinghies, four Cornish shrimpers and four power-boats – all replaced every three years. The beauty of the school is the location, overlooking the river Stour and near the Alton reservoir – no trek in a minibus, and 'nothing but the extremes of cold stop us sailing'. Many gain RYA qualifications, enter sailing competitions and have a recreation for life.

Mouth-watering new music school opened by John Rutter, who is patron of the school's annual concert programme, performed by home-grown and professional performers. Recitals hall with spectacular acoustics complete with two grand pianos, 10 others in practice rooms, all brand new and all Bechsteins and Faziolis (Rolls Royce in pianos). Composition suites bursting with equipment. Some 50 per cent learn an instrument; a plethora of orchestras, bands, choirs and ensembles to join. Pupils in the marching band that accompanies Divisions, the regular pupil parades, receive free music tuition.

Art, photography, graphics and product design all housed in separate building with large permanent display area with gallery for pupils' work. A separate print room (formerly manual training centre) harks back to earlier times, and there is serious encouragement for all craft and design skills, with many pupils working on projects outside class time.

Every spare moment filled with activities. Four sections of CCF: royal marines, navy, army, air force compulsory in years 9 and 10, but many continue: 'It encourages leadership and responsibility,' we heard from pupils as well as parents. D of E popular

About a third have a naval background (grandfathers count) and it is unsnobbish. Day pupil numbers likely to increase as naval boarding subsidy is withdrawn

at all stages up to gold. Car maintenance, medieval society, Scottish dancing – choices for all tastes.

Boarding: Boarding houses are comfortable, with well-planned central areas for table tennis, pool and computers, huge kitchens for making snacks (all pupils have tuck lockers) and bedrooms, single or shared, are en suite. TV room stuffed with leather sofas said to be the least used space (though it was the housemaster saying so). The infirmary is a 26 bedded medical centre with full time staff including a dentist (NHS) and counsellor who can be seen confidentially.

Background and atmosphere: Long, proud association with Royal Navy and seafarers gives a distinctive feel to this large co-educational boarding and day school, and many material benefits. The Royal Hospital School was founded in the early 18th century at Greenwich to educate boys for service in the navy. Moved to its present site in the 1930s, when school received a bequest from the estate at Holbrook together with a generous endowment. The old school building is now the National Maritime Museum. The current buildings and layout, on a grand scale, are inspired by the original work by Christopher Wren at Greenwich. The pillared entrance, a massive hall with columns, marble floors and oil paintings, is awe-inspiring and regarded by pupils with affection and pride. The grounds, with wide promenades and parade ground, have the well-kept air of a military establishment, but pupils revel in the space, the vista of the river Stour and the tangible connection to naval history.

Became co-educational in 1991. The phased withdrawal of naval funding, begun in 2005, came with a parting present of £18 million for building projects and a general sprucing up. Day pupils were introduced to broaden the intake and make up the financial shortfall, but school retains the naval connection. Pupils all use navy speak, such as Stations, Mess, and Civvies, and regular parades or Divisions are a regular part of school life. Saturday morning hymn singing in school chapel is a feature and not seen as an imposition. 'It's fun, who doesn't enjoy singing?' say pupils. 'They sometimes grumble, but generally enjoy the parades,' we were told by a parent. 'It is one of those bonding experiences looked back on with affection'.

Pastoral care, well-being and discipline: Friendly house system counteracts the (possibly) daunting size and scale of the school, and we heard nothing but praise. 'Excellent support in the house, matron was key in helping my child over a bout of home-sickness'; 'Matron does a lot more than simply dole out medicine'; 'Staff seem extraordinarily available.' Cries of approval (pupils as well as parents) for disciplined atmosphere and several parents spoke of lives being transformed by all that's on offer. 'Motivation is more likely in school work if they are interested and busy out of the classroom.' Food neither praised or criticised; we saw hearty fare, perhaps not enough in the salad line. Day pupils are increasing in number and fit in to the house system, with many remaining well into the evening to take advantage of everything going on.

Older pupils allowed out at weekends, but taxi fare and trek to Ipswich douse enthusiasm, especially as school operates The Nelson Arm (supervised bar) discos and other events. By the end, a few chafe at restrictions but most think the way things work is fair, and they all know what the position is on banned substances (expulsion) and relationships (courting allowed but strictly outside lesson time). For many there is never a dull moment – 'I can't imagine having more fun at university' – but quieter types fit in just as well.

Pupils and parents: At present the majority of pupils are boarders, of which 15 per cent are foreign nationals, mostly Chinese and German, with a sprinkling of other Europeans. Day pupils largely drawn from Suffolk/north Essex. About a third have a naval background (grandfathers count) and it is unsnobbish. Day pupil numbers likely to increase as naval boarding subsidy is withdrawn. Parents speak highly of school's social mix: 'He rubs shoulders with pupils from all backgrounds and this experience will be useful all his life'; 'There is no arrogance or sense of entitlement.' Great sense of ease and camaraderie between staff and pupils but courtesy insisted on. Pupils appear confident, open and friendly.

Entrance: The majority enter at 11 via entrance tests in maths, English and verbal reasoning. At 13 plus another 30-40, respectable common entrance performance needed, and there is another influx in the sixth form. A reference from the current school is essential and all prospective pupils have an interview with the head.

Exit: Around 20 per cent leave after GCSEs, mostly to sixth form colleges, the majority after A level for higher education. A wide choice of subjects and institutions chosen; not an Oxbridge factory – though three places in 2015 – but heavyweight universities well represented. Significant numbers take a gap year, often for travel and following courses abroad.

Money matters: Complex range of awards and bursaries. School offers a limited number of academic, sporting, drama, music, art and sailing scholarships each year. The value of the award is at the discretion of the headmaster and can be topped up with a bursary. Bursaries of up to 100 per cent of fees, depending on parental means, and siblings get a 15 per cent discount. Forces families claiming the continuity of education allowance (CEA) are also eligible for discounted fees. Greenwich hospital bursaries for the children of seafarers also available, depending on family income.

Remarks: Long association with Royal Navy brings privilege and a sense of service. Would suit the socially outgoing, give-it-a-go types, especially sailors. Excellent full boarding provision.

Royal Masonic School for Girls

Rickmansworth Park, Rickmansworth, Hertfordshire WD3 4HF

01923 773168
enquiries@royalmasonic.herts.sch.uk
www.royalmasonic.herts.sch.uk

Ages: 11–19 (junior boarding from 7)
Pupils: 903; sixth form: 195
Boarders: 105 full/weekly
Day: £15,375 pa
Boarding: £25,050 – £27,180 pa

Headmistress: Since 2002, Mrs Diana Rose MA (50s). Educated at Channing School, London before becoming one of the first women to attend King's College, Cambridge, where she read history and social and political sciences. Knows her market inside out, having spent over a decade in Buckinghamshire grammar schools and six years as head of sixth at St Helen's Northwood, before becoming deputy head at Oxford High. Also a governor at Wycombe Abbey school, and has been on the education panel of the Wolfson Foundation for 20 years. One half of a local educational super-couple, she is married to Stephen Nokes, head of John Hampden Grammar, High Wycombe. Her two sons, schooled at Berkhamsted and the Royal Grammar School, High Wycombe, have flown the nest, freeing her up to study for GCSE Italian and indulge passions for cookery, theatre and the ballet.

Proud of the school offering, 'a unique ethos in the area.' Wedged between academic hothouses on the edge of London and uber-competitive South Bucks and Herts grammar schools (says school is not a 'tough environment' like they are), she is clear that, 'no RMS girl is ever told she's not good enough to continue with us', as illustrated by the fact that there is no entry requirement for sixth form for existing pupils. Expects girls to form good work habits but says she does not nurture 'a perfectionist culture', understanding the harm that such pressure can do to young minds. The antithesis to local grammars striving for A grades at any cost, she takes her girls on a 'calm and broad journey' where they are not pressured to give up extras in favour of academic cramming, even in exam years.

Walks her dogs (as do many parents) around the school grounds daily and keeps fit by cycling which, coupled with a natty wardrobe and stylish shoe collection, all contributes to the fact that she looks a good 10 years younger than she actually is. Has an easy smile and sharp sense of humour. Girls say she is 'very approachable' and love the fact that she knows them all well – not just by name but what they are studying and all their interests too. Passionate about educating pupils to be independent learners and claims that despite the idyllic

Girls enthuse over chess and Chinese clubs as much as astronomy (in school's own planetarium) and taekwondo. Plenty of charitable works too

cosseted campus feel of the school, 'they all thrive at uni'.

Academic matters: Turning formerly dismissive heads and winning more and more parental votes with persistently improving results. In 2015, 42 per cent A*/A grades at A level and 60 per cent at GCSE. Small class sizes (maximum 20) across the board and setting from year 7 in maths and French, with fewer than 10 in some lower sets. More setting (English, science) from year 9 but these are totally flexible, with one parent delighted that her child moved from the bottom to top of six sets for maths in the space of a year. Must be the 'outstanding teaching' that the head is so proud of. Teachers 'go the extra mile', say parents and pupils, and are happy to tutor any stragglers in their free time. Enrichment programmes and extra work for the gifted and lots of clinics to make sure nobody slips through the gaps.

Parents say it's a 'good all round school' where their children can have a go at 'absolutely anything'. They like the fact that the brightest children are made to feel so in this mixed ability environment rather than bumping along feeling average in a class packed with boffins, as they might in

more selective schools. Geography and history most popular subjects at GCSE with sciences and maths coming to the fore at A level.

Both highly academic parents with children to match and those with less intellectual offspring feel that the school has the 'right balance' regarding achievement. Girls can choose to do between nine and 11 GCSEs depending on ability and those staying on in the sixth form to take two A levels in photography or art are treated with as much care as mathematicians and scientists taking four. To keep everyone happy, academic girls wishing to take arty subjects can take A2 exams in these in year 12, freeing them up to concentrate on their academic subjects thereafter. EPQ results are also impressive, with 25 per cent choosing to enter and all of these achieving grades A*-B. Strong languages on offer, with girls able to choose two plus Latin at GCSE; Mandarin on offer for the most gifted linguists from year 8.

Girls put on a 'carousel' of arty subjects in years 8 and 9, dipping into subjects from ceramics and 3D design to home economics and DT. All taught by specialists in purpose designed (albeit a bit tired) facilities.

Good SEN, with individual lessons on offer to girls needing support. All pupils screened to detect literacy or numeracy difficulties on entry. Specialist EAL teaching for overseas pupils, charged as extra.

Games, options, the arts: Impressive sports facilities. Gymnastics, trampolining, dance et al take place in a jawdropping double sports hall that would give most public sports centres a run for their money. Four squash courts and a multi-gym, available for the girls' use whenever they wish, also housed in the complex. Swimming pool is poor relation to the rest, functional at best. Acres of playing fields, great for cross-country and adventure training, and new all-weather pitch.

All meals apart from weekend breakfast, when girls can pad downstairs in their pyjamas, are taken in the senior school. Food is 'outstanding'

Lots of competitive sport with trophies galore of late – the school recently claimed the independent girls' schools golf championship title and the gymnastics team has just been placed nationally. Occasional grumbles from parents, however, that the school needs to work harder to engage more of the less obviously sporty girls in physical activities that are in tune with their lifestyles, claiming

that some older girls get away with doing, 'hardly any or no sport at all', although head disagrees: 'They have all sorts of options from year 10 including zumba, pilates and yoga.' Recent injection of young sports teachers has opened up more opportunities, including football and rugby.

School has strong artsy feel, offering a well-used photography studio and dark room, drama studio and 'loads and loads' of musical and theatrical productions throughout the year, according to girls. Music 'improving all the time', say parents, with 300 girls learning an instrument and plenty of opportunities to show their skills in concerts and shows.

Trips and tours of all sorts, for sports teams, choirs, curriculum and just for the fun of it. Vast array of extracurricular activities including very popular D of E and cadets means the school continues to buzz after lessons are over. Girls enthuse over chess and Chinese clubs as much as astronomy (in school's own planetarium) and taekwondo. Plenty of charitable works too, with prefects nominating a charity for the school to support each year. Others such as the Royal Hospital in Chelsea and schools in far flung places (Ghana, Japan) also benefit from visits and performances.

Boarding: Around 100 boarders in the senior school live in three boarding houses. Boarding most popular in years 10 to 12 with a mix of weekly, flexi and full time. Around 40 per cent from overseas – Europe, the Far East and, increasingly, Russia. Traditionally very popular with Forces families but this is in decline due to MOD cuts. Boarders are treated to an outing every Saturday (bowling, cinema, theatre, London attractions). Older girls allowed to London in groups for shopping and lunch and in years 12 and 13 to the cinema in the evenings. A renovation programme of boarding houses is under way. We visited the most newly refurbished which, like the rest of the school, was extremely spacious, clean and well-equipped with a pool table, DVDs and Wii in its large common room. Not as cosy and homely as many boarding houses we've seen but certainly not lacking in mod cons. Light, bright and modern dining room, where boarders and day girls take all their meals, feels like a hub of chatter at lunch time, with girls seated at sociably round tables, enjoying freshly cooked meals which are, by all accounts, 'outstanding'.

Ten or so full-time boarders among over 200 junior school children, with a handful more taking advantage of flexi- or ad hoc boarding. About a third of full-timers are international (from Asia and Russia) with a handful of Forces families in the mix. Junior boarding house is home from home to girls from years 3 to 7 and has good facilities and plenty of space, although parents are hoping for a refurb soon. All meals apart from weekend breakfast, when girls can pad downstairs in their pyjamas, are taken in the senior school. Food is reportedly 'outstanding'. Boarders take advantage of the full array of after-school activities, plus games, in-house events and an extensive DVD collection. Weekends see them participate in creative activities (tie-dying was named a top recent favourite) and head off on outings such as local bowling, shows and roller-blading or further afield to the seaside.

Background and atmosphere: Founded in 1788 to educate the children of masons who had fallen on hard times, the current 150 acre site, built in the 1930s, is the school's fourth home. A vast campus (NB visiting parents – wear flat shoes, if not trainers, for your tour), more akin to a redbrick university than a suburban girls' school, with smart, identikit buildings surrounding two quadrangles ('teeming with girls chatting in the summer term,' said one), and the longest teaching corridor in Britain. Became an independent school, open to all, in 1978 while continuing to fulfil its charitable obligation and still offering full bursaries to some 50 children in need of financial support at any time, although most staff don't know who they are.

New sixth form centre where all year 12 and 13 girls take the majority of their lessons. Fabulous common room, interior designed by pupils, complete with hot pink walls and matching sofas. All whistles and bells, with girls able to borrow laptops from the library, or bring their own, and log onto the centre's Wifi network. A senior team of 20 drawn from year 13, plus a head girl and eight deputies, elected by girls and teachers. Girls describe guidance at this stage of their education as 'excellent', with teachers giving up free time to help with personal statements and a dedicated Oxbridge co-ordinator on hand for brainboxes. Lovely rotunda library, one of the nicest we've seen: fingerprint withdrawal technology and plenty of space for quiet study.

Parents say the school is 'very into tradition' and this feeling permeates its very fabric. RMS is the only school in the country still to do 'drill': a spectacle of pinafored girls with pinned back hair performing something akin to synchronised swimming but without the water. Places in the squad are highly sought after, with dozens volunteering even for the reserves.

Pastoral care, well-being and discipline: Head is 'anti-clique' and works hard to minimise the inevitable girly issues. Sixth formers are trained as peer mentors by the school counsellor, with year 9 girls taking on 'big sister' roles to new year 7s when they join the school.

Serious disciplinary problems are few but parents say head has never been afraid to 'take a hard line' when necessary and has even been known to call in police to educate girls on the outcomes of certain scenarios if they rear their ugly heads – as in a recent inappropriate staff/pupil relationship. Head claims alcohol is 'not an issue' and persistent bullying is dealt with by permanent exclusion. In a recent Ofsted boarding inspection, 92 per cent of girls interviewed said they had never seen or experienced bullying; 'an exceptional figure', says head, compared to most boarding environments. Year 13 girls are well prepared for the real world with a range of seminars offering advice on subjects from

Pupils love the fact that she has frequent 'birthday parties' in her office with lashings of chocolate cake for the month's birthday girls

budgeting at uni and car maintenance, to getting the most out of gap years.

Parents can email head direct with issues or queries. Boarders know that she works with her office door open on Sunday mornings and often pop in to share news or discuss problems. Year 7 pupils love the fact that she has frequent 'birthday parties' in her office with lashings of chocolate cake for the month's birthday girls. Often takes refugees from high pressure schools and is proud to welcome them into her community where there is a 'real tolerance of difference'.

Chapel once a week, plus Sundays for boarders, taken by the school's full time chaplain. Boarders of other faiths do not have to attend Sunday communion, although many choose to. The whole school crams into this impressive space at Christmas for the traditional carol service.

Pupils and parents: Unlock your sons. RMS girls seem much younger and fresher than their more streetwise grammar peers and are just the kind you would love your boys to bring home for dinner. Confident and articulate without arrogance, they seem a genuinely grounded bunch. Good ethnic mix, reflecting the school's position on the London borders, with the vast majority taking full advantage of all the extras the school has to offer. 'Lots of bat mitzvahs to go to at weekends', said one parent.

Parents from all walks of life from the well-heeled to hard working, dual income, first time buyers. Some expats and international parents, largely of overseas boarders. Many from across the Chilterns and Hertfordshire, with an increasing North London crowd. The school provides an excellent coach service from all these areas, with the London brigade able to take advantage of the shuttle bus from the tube station. Parents of girls at smaller prep schools reported a bit of a culture shock when their daughters joined this vast establishment, but added that they felt totally at home 'after just a few weeks'.

Entrance: Increasingly selective, now parents are seeing RMS as a desirable option in an area of excellent independent and maintained schools. Majority join at 11+ but some places are also available for girls to join up to 14+. Candidates spend a full day during which they take the University of Durham online test to assess skills in English, maths and reasoning. The test is designed to accurately gauge girls' natural

ability and – pushy parents be warned – cannot be tutored for. There's also a creative writing exercise, group activity and group interview. Head is keen to find space for girls with 'something else to offer' and looks closely at report from current school as well as test results. Candidates for entry in later years sit tests in English, maths and non-verbal reasoning.

Around 170 girls compete for approximately 40 places with successful ones, about half from state primaries, guaranteed a place in all future stages. Good sibling policy too, a relief if younger ones aren't as starry as big sister. Approximately 50 per cent join from the school's own prep, Cadogan House (these girls are guaranteed entry, making for a mixed bag academically). Around 25 new places are available in year 12, with girls being selected on GCSE results and extracurricular achievements.

In line with its charitable ethos, school has an ongoing social mission to offer a limited number of assisted boarding places to disadvantaged children from London boroughs of Hillingdon and Tower Hamlets, and Norfolk. Head says that integration of these girls, and that of the mainly international boarders, is 'fantastic'.

Exit: Majority to Russell Group universities, Birmingham, Nottingham, Leeds and Exeter all popular and two to Oxford in 2015. Worth bearing in mind that as school's academic reputation continues to improve, this is likely to increase as fresh talent filters through. A small exodus – around 20 per cent – at 16, recently to local grammar schools; perhaps girls wanting a somewhat more worldly environment, although head says all were for financial reasons.

Money matters: Capital expenditure is underpinned by an endowment set up by the masons and the school is a tenant of the site. Multitude of scholarships and exhibitions available at 11+ (academic, all-rounder, art, music and sport), and sixth form (adding performing arts to the list) offering a maximum 25 per cent discount on fees. Five per cent discount for siblings and 10 per cent for Forces families. Means-tested bursaries available.

Remarks: A school where girls can be girls and sing, act and run their way to well-roundedness in a safe and nurturing environment. Steadily improving academics over a number of years mean RMS has now secured its position as a serious contender in the competitive local market, and first class facilities help turn out real all-rounders.

A school that aims to draw the best out of everyone, whatever their abilities and turns out confident, rounded young ladies. Parents 'never mind writing the cheque to RMS', according to one. Eggheads and pushy parents might prefer some of the surrounding competition, though.

St Christopher School

Barrington Road, Letchworth Garden City, Hertfordshire SG6 3JZ

01462 650850
admissions@stchris.co.uk
www.stchris.co.uk

Ages: 2–18 (boarders from age 11)
Pupils: 493; sixth form: 80
Boarders: 32
Day: £10,470 – £17,355 pa
Boarding: £18,960 – £30,705 pa

Head: Since 2006, Mr Richard Palmer BEd (Nottingham Trent) FRSA. Has deep rooted history with St Chris – he first came here in his gap year aged 18 as the protégé of his then mentor and DT teacher. 'Blown away' by the school and its ethos, he later requested a placement at St Chris to do his teaching practice. Although he has sampled life at other schools, namely St Hugh's Prep in Woodhall Spa and St John's College School, Cambridge, where he spent seven years, rising to deputy head, his heart was always at St Chris and he returned as head of junior school in 2004.

Took over as acting head during a turbulent period ('I just wanted the school to thrive') and was then asked to step into the role on a permanent basis. Ever popular with parents, children and staff, Richard (it's all first names at St Chris) knows the name of even the tiniest nursery child and makes it his business to know all the families in the school community – 'accessible' was a word used by many a parent we spoke to. Clear that his role is to ensure that the school's ethos, part Quaker, part Montessori, translates to modern times. Contrary to local folklore (no, there are not sofas in the classrooms and yes, lessons are compulsory), good academics and strong results are a focus, albeit via a slightly more relaxed route than more traditional schools. 'The endgame is absolutely the same,' he says. Lives on site with his wife who runs the pupil support; two adult children.

Academic matters: Admits broad church academically but absolutely not a school for all comers (entry testing from year 4 demands minimum standardised score of 100) and head is clear: 'it's not for everyone.' Around 25 per cent receive help with what head calls 'individual needs', although not necessarily recognised SEN. School offers excellent support to pupils with mild dyslexia, dyspraxia, dyscalculia and some on the lower end of the autistic spectrum (two head boys in recent years with Asperger's) but this is not the place for children with greater needs, despite the fact that many are attracted by the informal vibe. Five hour-long lessons each day with a break between each makes

for a calm cohort with not a panicked late-comer in sight, despite the lack of bells.

Classes form taught in junior school in groups of 12-20 up to GCSE; A level classes much smaller (some with just one pupil). No testing in junior school although parents say children are 'constantly evaluated'. Setting in maths takes place after October half term in year 7, then in year 9 for English and languages and at GCSE for science. French offered in junior school then Spanish from year 7. Pupils can take two languages at GCSE although neither is compulsory: 'We don't fix our pupils' GCSE options in blocks,' says head. 'And we feel that if a child wants to do all arts or all sciences at A level it's fine.' All the usual suspects on curriculum plus media studies at GCSE and A level, astronomy GCSE and psychology, photography and government and politics on offer at A level. All take 10 GCSEs and sixth formers take four subjects at AS level with around 20 per cent taking four full A levels. In 2015, 45 per cent A grades at GCSE and 43 per cent at A level, with 75 per cent A*-B grades.

> *Contrary to local folklore (no, there are not sofas in the classrooms and yes, lessons are compulsory), good academics and strong results are a focus*

A school for those of all faiths and none and no RE on curriculum. 'Morning talk' is a secular assembly with a silent period for reflection, live music and food for thought, often with a topical twist. After the Charlie Hebdo attacks, a local imam was invited to speak about Islam.

Games, options, the arts: Perhaps not an obvious choice for children who live and breathe sport, but it's all here. Pupils and parents alike rank sport way below the arts in terms of what defines St Chris, but head says that there is a competitive element, although not an exclusive one. Parents relish the inclusivity fostered by a less competitive and generally more artsy cohort. 'Not much rugby' but football, basketball, rounders and netball on offer with frequent fixtures against local state and independent schools. 'Masses' of other sporty options for those looking for something a bit different: kayaking, scuba diving and water polo take place in the school's super 25 metre indoor pool and there's a skate park (pupils bring their own skateboards and scooters for use during break times). The cherry on top is one of the best outdoor climbing walls we've ever seen.

Plenty of chill out spaces, cosy common rooms and a boys' heaven gaming room with bespoke chairs wired for sound

Plenty of opportunities for pupils to get their creative juices flowing in music and drama with productions that involve the whole school – not just as actors, musicians and stage hands but also in advertising and running the social media campaigns to publicise their shows. A viral marketing campaign to publicise the forthcoming production of Les Mis, comprising stickers of rats appearing randomly all over the school, was under way when we visited – brilliant. Around 75 per cent of the cohort takes peripatetic music lessons and all year 3s participate in 'strings project,' learning cello or violin as part of curriculum. Abundant opportunities on offer to perform in any kind of band, choir or group imaginable from jazz bands to 'Boys Aloud' – the all-boys singing ensemble.

Artistic expression forms the lifeblood of St Chris with wonderful spaces for pupils to flex their creative muscles in a huge art block. Bright and spacious art rooms, DT labs, ceramics studio and photography lab are linked together under one roof to form a cohesive (and reassuringly untidy) department which buzzes with creative energy and feels more like an art college than part of a school – thanks in no small part to the quality of work on display. Curriculum follows art college format with pupils 'able to follow their own passions', resulting in a unique diversity in subject and media – and outstanding results at both GCSE and A level: 'our pupils are frequently able to bypass foundation stage and go straight to degree courses,' says head.

Thursday afternoons dedicated to enrichment activities which encompass sporting, creative and community focused pursuits ranging from philosophy or yoga to golf and cycling. D of E not compulsory but 'literally everybody does it'. Weekend trips, open to all and with a 'massive take up' are run most weeks and see the director of activities taking mixed age groups of day pupils as well as boarders off surfing, caving, cycling and climbing or to performances by the English National Ballet. Sounds expensive. 'No, not all of them. We usually just ask parents to help us cover travel costs,' says head.

Boarding: Small boarding community of around 30 pupils, the majority of these in the upper years of the school. About a quarter are full boarders, the rest weekly, with day pupils able to benefit from occasional boarding if they need to. Sixth formers have their own boarding house with 'amazing' house parents, single rooms, a games room with Xbox for down time and a kitchen where they (by choice) cook most of their own meals. Years 7 to 9 housed in the main school building in characterful (again, mainly single) rooms. Plenty of chill out spaces with cosy common rooms and a boys' heaven gaming room with bespoke chairs wired for sound. 'There's huge respect between teachers and pupils,' according to one happy boarder.' Abundant activities at evenings and weekends, and pupils allowed into Letchworth in groups from year 7. New day boarding offer, with senior school pupils able to stay at school from 7.30am until 7.30pm – excellent for busy professional parents.

Background and atmosphere: Set up by Theosophists in the middle of WW1, St Chris, with its lack of uniform, co-ed boarders and staff known by first names, was at the far end of the radical spectrum. Nowadays, firmly rooted in the 21st century, the school retains its New Age forward thinking vibe and wears its liberal, family-based credentials as a badge of honour. Most striking about the school is the mutual respect with which all pupils and teachers treat one another and on which parents uniformly comment. The school is effectively run by an elected student council which is able to facilitate changes by passing a motion which must, if passed by a majority vote, be allowed by the school. Head has power of veto but 'very rarely has to use it – the children wouldn't put me in a position where I had to,' he says. Pupils 'love the freedom and trust' given to them at St Chris and are 'not herded like sheep,' according to one refugee from a traditional boarding school.

Unexpectedly nestled in middle class suburbia, the school's Tardis-like campus is a treat to explore. The compact main building, purpose built in the Arts and Crafts style of the surrounding homes, belies what lies behind – a spacious utopia of light-flooded buildings surrounding a village-like piazza; pristine gardens, pitches and meadows. The Early Years Centre, with its own well-equipped playground leading onto a forest school and seemingly endless fields, is the charmingly adapted former home of Sir Lawrence Olivier. The main part of the junior school, home to 150 of the school's youngest pupils, was designed by a former pupil and built in 2003. Spacious classrooms surround a stunning glass atrium which feels almost like a gallery, adorned with bookcases, open plan computer spaces and pupils' artwork. Super theatre, used by all, seats up to 240, and a discrete music school is equipped with drum kits, electric guitars and plenty of practice rooms. Well-equipped kitchen hosts cookery lessons (sixth formers are coached in university cooking by head) and sixth formers have their own cosy spaces and run the senior school coffee shop – from ordering stock to manning the till.

Wormeries, veggie patches and a special bee garden, complete with solar powered 'babbling brook', plus an enthusiastically consumed vegetarian menu

Strong sense of social responsibility in evidence wherever you look. Music staff overheard talking about sixth formers organising a charity busking event in aid of a recent natural disaster and posters around the school advertise societies – all run by pupils themselves – ranging from human rights and 'be green' to current affairs discussion groups. Wormeries, veggie patches and a special bee garden, complete with solar powered 'babbling brook', plus the enthusiastically consumed vegetarian menu (meat options recently introduced for boarders' breakfasts and suppers) make for a cohort of thoughtful, ethically minded young people. 'The only thing I'd change would be the way other people perceive the school,' said one.

Pastoral care, well-being and discipline: Director of pastoral care oversees pupils' well-being and meets with heads of year each morning to discuss individual issues. Form groups are called companies and form teachers are 'advisors', with pupils having the same advisor from year 8 to year 11. Sixth formers have a personal tutor and higher education advisor. Head describes pupils as 'the most respectful group of kids' and there seems to be a strong sense of discipline amongst them. A single bell is struck during lunch and the room is immediately silent. Fair and democratic when things do go wrong and individually tailored punishment. Pupils excluded for damaging the school, supplying drugs or persistently disrupting lessons.

Plenty of opportunities to rise to the challenge of responsibility, with an elected head boy and girl plus eight other senior pupil posts. Well-being at

heart of school – there's even a 'massage in schools' programme, with pupils encouraged to administer head and shoulder massages (with permission) to classmates from nursery onwards. 'Incredibly successful,' says head.

Pupils and parents: Unsurprisingly, parents tend to be of the modern, forward thinking variety, many choosing the school through personal recommendation. A down to earth bunch of liberal media and professional types, 'they would be just as happy with a barn dance as a ball,' according to head. School mainly attracts families from Letchworth and the surrounding area but also Cambridge and North London, with older pupils taking advantage of the school buses on offer. Americans relocating to the area with large multinationals also identify strongly with the informality and strong student voice. About 15 per cent of the small boarding community is from overseas with no more than three of any single nationality at any one time.

With its casual dress code (clean, mended and non-offensive is the order of the day) St Chris pupils aren't going to win any sartorial neatness awards, but they still present as a highly driven and purposeful cohort – a bit like a bunch of junior ad execs. Bright eyed junior school pupils look like they are having the time of their lives, without stuffy restrictions of uniform and formality to hamper their creativity. From the idyllic setting of the separate early years centre to the oldest children in the senior school, easy smiles abound and the whole place has a slightly surreal air of calm about it with none of the frenetic rushing or high noise levels present in so many schools. Despite the relaxed atmosphere, however, 'nothing could be further from the truth than kids doing whatever they want,' according to head. Are they pushed? 'Absolutely. It would be criminal not to'.

Entrance: Many children come up from the Montessori nursery, others join reception and more join year 3 or 4, though entry at any age is considered. Will take a broad range of ability, 'but our community exists on self-discipline and they must be able to cope.' Two classes move up from the junior school into year 7 and are joined by an extra class of children, half of whom join from the state maintained sector and half from local preps. Applicants tested in English and maths; cognitive ability tests from year 4 onwards. It's expected that pupils move seamlessly from junior to senior school and children are not prepared for entry into any other school. Siblings guaranteed a place and all can stay until the end of their school career regardless of academic prowess – as long as school believes this route is best for the child in question: 'something I feel very strongly about,' says head.

Exit: Around 30 per cent move on after GCSE – mainly those from North London who are fed up with the commute and want to take advantage of good local state maintained sixth form provision. 'We encourage pupils to make an active choice on whether to stay here,' says head. Of those who remain, almost all head off to higher education – a good mix of Russell Group and new universities, art schools and one or two some years to Oxbridge or to read medicine. A special extension group prepares sixth formers for entry into the most demanding courses. Largish numbers to study the arts, including photography, graphic design, theatre design and fine art, and plenty of vocational business focused choices with fewer opting for pure academia. The vast majority of these go on to read maths, sciences and engineering.

Money matters: Academic and art scholarships in years 7, 9 and 12 out of school income. Means-tested bursaries available, with two in sixth form offering up to 100 per cent of boarding fees. Ten per cent discount for siblings. Six per cent of fees ring fenced as hardship fund. A 'very active' parents' circle focuses mainly on charitable fundraising.

Remarks: An unconventional, kind and caring school with solid academics and outstanding arts and science provision at its core.

St Edmund's College

Old Hall Green, Ware, Hertfordshire SG11 1DS

01920 824247
admissions@stedmundscollege.org
www.stedmundscollege.org
RC

Ages: 11–19
Pupils: 642; sixth form: 160
Boarders: 128
Day: £10,020 – £16,185 pa
Boarding: £21,357 – £27,303 pa

Headmaster: Since 2012, Mr Paulo Durán BA MA (London). Educated at the London Oratory, King's College London, and Heythrop College. Married to Alice, a teacher, with one daughter at St Edmund's. After spells at South Hampstead and Alleyn's, he took up a post as head of modern languages at Mill Hill School where he stayed for six years, before moving to St Edmund's as deputy head in 2009. After three years he was offered the headship, and, he says, would like to stop here. Parents hope so too. 'A very warm, very charismatic man and a very strong leader,' said one mother. 'Please don't leave!'

Academic matters: Generally a sound performance with top grades consistently accounting for around a third of results. 2015 figures, for instance were 34 per cent A*-A at I/GCSE and 42 per cent A*-A at A level, which percentages are broadly on a par with the previous two years. 'Results are very good, and I want them to improve,' says head, but aims to achieve same 'without changing the children or the school. It's about moving up those league tables the hard way.' One big change has come, however. Since September 2014, the school has offered the IB alongside A levels. This is in response to parental demand, says school, as well as to a growing awareness that, as an international school, it's the right route to take. 'Catholic means universal, so we're already part of an international network.'

Broad curriculum comprises all the usual arts, humanities and sciences, with maths being a particular favourite. 'I like maths, purely for the fact that the teachers are so willing to help you,' said one boy, and his friends agreed. French, Spanish, German, Latin and Italian are on offer. All students learn French in year 7 and study an additional language throughout year 8 and 9. As you'd expect in a school of this ethos, religious education has a high profile, and RE is compulsory up to and including GCSE. The pupils aren't bothered by this, because 'the RE teachers are really good!' Bang-up-to-date ICT suites, and well-resourced classrooms and science labs. Food tech a popular option, and the children were proud of their achievements in the school bake-off. Lots of good quality work on the wall displays, and we were pleased with the standard of writing and spelling. The handsome library is surprisingly small for a school this size, but was lively and welcoming and regularly hosts visits from the likes of Kevin Crossley-Holland and Dave Cousins.

Our young tour guides were upbeat about lessons and about the amount of individual attention they got from teachers; the average class size is 21 (14 in sixth form). Parents described the teaching staff as 'really fantastic' and 'always there for the pupils', and praised the unwearying help given, in any subject, to students who needed it. 'If you're in the top set, you're pushed just as hard as you would be in a top academic school,' commented one sixth former. But a broad range of abilities is catered for here. The school currently has 105 children on its Learning Difficulties and Disabilities register, and pupils with SEN requirements are well-supported, both in class and at homework club, which happens four afternoons a week. EAL is also important here, because of the school's international intake. IGCSE second language English is offered to overseas students where appropriate.

The intake is only gently selective, which may account for the odd unexpected hiccup in student knowledge here and there. Talking to us about the school's history, a year 9 pupil told me, 'France wasn't Catholic back then, which is why the school moved here.' But the school's history is quite long and involved, and we were impressed by the pride with which the children talked about it. Everyone we spoke to was adamant that the school fostered a strong work ethic and helped all students to achieve their best.

Games, options, the arts: One happy parent, a musician herself, described the music as 'fantastic', and we certainly liked what we saw. The school's top choir, Schola Cantorum, regularly gigs at the likes of Canterbury and Westminster Cathedrals; chapel choir sings on Sundays during term time, and the chamber choir is much in demand for more secular school functions, such as weddings and dances. Lots of ensembles including an orchestra and jazz band, ably supported by a 21-strong team of peripatetic music teachers who get the children up to scratch on voice, strings, brass, woodwind, percussion, piano, guitar, harpsichord and organ (there's a magnificent organ in the school chapel). The school is particularly keen to build on choral scholarships 'and to see where that takes us.' There's a musical production every year; Our House by Madness is a recent example, and the curtain will shortly rise on Half A Sixpence at the nearby Broxbourne Civic Hall. 'They're a lot of work and a big commitment but they're absolutely wonderful!' enthused one student. Drama is also popular, with lots taking LAMDA exams, and student-directed productions such as – amazingly – One Man, Two Guvnors.

The last period of every school day (which finishes at 4.30pm) is given over to extracurricular activities, so all pupils participate in something. An extremely wide range of arts, crafts and other interests are offered, including CCF, D of E and Model United Nations. There are also some pretty special opportunities for travel. 'The trip to Thailand was one of the most amazing things I've ever done,' said one girl, and other pupils were starry-eyed about their experiences in India, America and Barcelona.

Wonderfully spacious campus means lots of playing fields plus tennis courts and Astro. Girls' sport is strong and includes hockey, netball and football. The boys' provision for traditional team games appears to be something of an issue. 'I'd like to see more organised compulsory training for the top teams,' said one boy, diplomatically. Parents (eager in their praise of all other areas of the school) were more forthright, criticising what they claimed was a 'lazy' lack of coaching for school teams who then had to 'go out and get slaughtered every week against better-trained sides.' Students confirmed that rugby/football practices were sometimes scheduled after the school buses had left, so that pupils, who travel in from an unusually wide geographical area, had no choice but to miss the sessions if they wanted to get home. The school counters by saying that the after-school clubs, targeted at mass participation, were scheduled at the request of parents, who had seemed happy to collect their children themselves. A sports academy focusses on the development of elite players in years 7 and 8. The less traditional sports – table tennis, golf, badminton, aerobics – are all flourishing, and there can't be many schools which can offer their students fishing (in the school pond) as an option.

'The atmosphere is lovely,' a typical comment. Prayers are said before every lesson, 'And some of the prayers are really nice! You don't have to join in, but everyone respects it'

Boarding: Boarders (full, weekly and flexi) are very well looked-after, with lots of staff living on site, and the school counsellor is always on hand. 'Bullying here is mercifully rare, and we set the bar low,' said head, firmly. One boys' and one girls' boarding house (twin or single rooms), with a communal common room where they can socialise together after prep. The usual weekend theatre, cinema and shopping trips for boarders, who include pupils from 20 different countries; activities include themed cultural evenings.

Background and atmosphere: Founded in France in 1568 as a seminary for English Catholics when the Reformation's prohibition of Catholic education forced Cardinal William Allen to decamp to Douai in Flanders. A couple of hundred years later in 1793, the French Revolution had professors and scholars packing their bags once again and moving to the village of Old Hall Green just north of Ware, where a small (and very secret) Catholic school had formerly acted as a 'feeder' for the Douai seminary.

On 16 November 1793 – the feast of St Edmund – the school was created. It weathered various changes of fortune during the 19th century, but celebrated its quarter centenary in 1968, admitted girls to the sixth form in 1974 and has been fully co-educational since 1986. The school lists 20 canonised saints and 133 martyrs amongst its alumni, and is proud of its history, which it commemorates throughout the building in drawings, paintings and artefacts. Now occupying the whole of the village of Old Hall Green, the site is spacious (440 acres), wooded, and stunningly beautiful.

If Catholic iconography makes you uneasy, this ain't the place for you. Pictures of popes, archbishops, cardinals and saints are everywhere, along with statues, shrines, relics, holy paintings, and even a graveyard, containing, said an earnest pupil, 'people who died for the school'. It was something to see students lining up, in their own free time at their own volition, to use the Scofield Chantry for a few moments of candle-lit private prayer. The prevailing mood throughout the school, even at its liveliest times, was one of calm benevolence and order. 'We pride ourselves on the way we talk to our students and the way they talk to each other,' said the head, and all the young people we spoke to were in agreement. 'Everybody is nice, everybody respects each other,' 'I love it here, all my friends are nice,' 'The atmosphere is lovely,' were typical comments. Prayers are said before every lesson, 'And some of the prayers are really nice!' cried a pupil, who then recited one for me with great affection, adding 'You don't have to join in, but everyone respects it.' The school's Pugin chapel is lofty and awe-inspiring, and is used for weddings, funerals and baptisms as well as for school services. It's flanked by the smaller shrine chapel, built to hold St Edmund's left fibula that was presented by Cardinal Wiseman in 1863.

The college is overseen not by a specific order but by the Archdiocese of Westminster, and the Roman Catholic ethos is completely central to the life of the school. Even the year groups are named after Catholic principles: Elements, Rudiments, Grammar, Syntax, Poetry, Rhetoric I and Rhetoric II. 'We're proudly and unashamedly Catholic,' as the head put it, but added, 'We're also proud of being inclusive.'

Pastoral care, well-being and discipline: Everyone we spoke to was especially warm in their praise of this aspect of the school. 'It's really good, very strong,' 'The school is very nurturing,' 'A very, very welcoming place, my child settled in straight away,' were some of the comments, and the last ISI inspection report praised the pupils' spiritual and personal development as outstanding. The house system is the main source of pastoral care with each pupil having a tutor and head of house.

A number of pupils and parents commented on the lunch queues, which, they alleged, were not always well-managed. Some children spoke of having to miss lunch if they needed to attend clubs, or even if the queue just was too long. 'She loves the meals, but doesn't always get to eat them!' said one mother, 'I can't understand why they haven't nailed that problem.' (School admits that the situation needs addressing, and says it is working on ways to improve things.) On the plus side, the boarding means that all pupils can stay for supper at the school when they need to – when there are concerts or parents' evenings, for instance – and generally students seemed cared for and contented, moving with calm purpose about the school; uniform was worn tidily and behaviour everywhere was good. The spacious, well-kept and eye-pleasing buildings themselves seemed to help create a relaxed and happy community of individuals, quirky and otherwise, with a refreshing range of life-aspirations: one student hopes to set up a museum dedicated to vacuum cleaner parts.

Pupils and parents: Day pupils make up the majority of students, and are bused in from all over Hertfordshire and beyond via a network of 17 different routes. Excellent scholarships and bursaries ensure wide social diversity. Significant community of international students, many of them from eastern Europe, Africa and Asia. About 40 per cent of pupils are from Catholic families. The rest are from other Christian denominations, and from 'all other faiths and from none'. ('We have a fantastic Diwali celebration every year,' the head told me.) Notable alumni include William Scholl the sandal designer, perfumiers James and Robert Floris, and Ralph Richardson.

Entrance: About 20 a year from St Edmund's Prep, for whom entry to the senior school is automatic, provided they joined in year 4 or below. The rest, who come from a wide range of preps and primaries, sit entrance exams in maths, English and non-verbal reasoning. However, the report from the child's previous school is just as important, along with the St Edmund's interview. 'We interview everyone for at least 30 minutes, and for as long as it takes, really,' says head, who puts great emphasis on getting to know what the children are like. The school's popularity continues to rise and they are now oversubscribed, with around 220 applicants for the 80 available places. Small additional intake at 13+. Some join the school at 16+, for which they need five A*-B grades at GCSE with at least B in their chosen A level subjects.

Exit: At 16+, around 30 per cent to state sixth form colleges, or, very occasionally, to other independents (one boy found he'd grown away from the

Catholic ethos and wanted a change). The rest stay on for sixth form here. At 18+ mostly to university: Manchester current front runner, with Hertfordshire Uni another favourite, alongside several London universities. Three to Cambridge in 2015.

Money matters: Academic scholarships at 11+ and 13+, awarded on performance in the entrance exam. Music, art, sport and all-rounder scholarships also available, often in combination with academic awards. Total awards can be extremely generous – we heard from one parent whose child's scholarship was worth 90 per cent of the annual fees. A few sixth form scholarships. Limited number of means-tested bursaries, covering up to full fees.

Remarks: A successful, flourishing, dependable school with real spiritual heart. Well worth considering.

St John's College School

75 Grange Road, Cambridge, Cambridgeshire CB3 9AB

01223 353532
admissions@sjcs.co.uk
www.sjcs.co.uk
C of E

Ages: 4–13 (boarders from 8)
Pupils: 448
Boarders: 38
Day: £10,692 – £14,100 pa
Boarding: £22,269 pa; Choristers £7,422 pa

Headmaster: Since 1990, Kevin Jones (late 50s). Father in the navy, attended state boarding school in Suffolk, degree and (unfinished) postgraduate research in English at Caius College Cambridge: 'rather pleased that it was eaten by mice; at least it was made use of.' Taught Cambridge undergraduates before deputy headship at Yehudi Menuhin School. Came to St John's as deputy head, offered headship within six months. A very short CV for such a successful head. Interesting that he started with the eldest age group and worked his way down. A busy man, founding chair of Children's University, a charity bringing out-of-school learning to children in deprived areas. On the national steering group of the Cultural Learning Alliance and many more educational charities. Sensible that he is musical but not a musician; he sees the broader picture.

Loved by all, parents, children and staff. 'He's godlike,' said one mother. 'He knows all of the

children and the parents.' 'Enormously approachable and always offers advice if asked,' said another. 'Quite eccentric,' was a third parent's view, 'dreamy and romantic but magnificent, he loves children.' This was apparent. Every time we entered a classroom he was greeted with hugs and chatter; they love him and are not in awe. Great respect, though. 'What better way to spend a dreary Monday morning than to go down to the kindergarten to be greeted by sunny smiles and cheerfulness and lots of chatter? It gives me a great lift,' he says. Quite.

An interesting character, not at all what you might expect. Looks like a hard-nosed businessman, talks like a laid back dreamer with a great love of children. Full of fun. But don't be fooled: he runs a very tight ship, albeit an extremely happy one. Major refurbishments over the last five years throughout the school with updated labs, lots of IT and bright airy classrooms. Junior department the most recent to benefit.

Married with two sons who attended the school.

They are very proud of the choristers, rightly so. They travel the world and are very talented. But once in the school they are just normal pupils

Entrance: Oversubscribed but not overly so. For entry at 4 the children are 'assessed', using sequencing and other methods which even at such a young age shows their potential – as are the parents. 'We want parents to have a feel for the place and we see what they want for their child. If we agree, we can work together.' Don't be complacent; children here are bright. At 7, assessments in English and maths and child is observed during half a day at the school. 'It's all about the child fitting in and coping.' Chorister bursaries for up to five scholars, all boys, at 8, of at least two-thirds of the fees. Means-tested bursaries for those who would particularly benefit. At 11+, potential music scholars welcomed as boarders, with scholarships available. Siblings take priority and then boy:girl ratio to keep the numbers even. Children come from a wide commutable area around Cambridge, or further afield for boarders. The majority of parents are academics, medics from Addenbrooke's or employed on the Silicon Fen,with a Newmarket contingent as well. Many work in the City. All parents very ambitious for their offspring, but nicely so and welcoming to newcomers.

Exit: The odd leaver at 11 but very unusual, usually heading to the state sector. No 'evictions', but occasionally, after much discussion and agreement, the occasional one will be moved on to 'somewhere they will be happier at.' Virtually all leave at 13. Lots of help from the head with future schooling. 'He guides us away from making the wrong choice.' Over half of the year get scholarships/awards, academic as well as music. At least 50 per cent go to local private Cambridge schools, many to The Perse. Eton, Oundle, Uppingham and Rugby all popular.

Remarks: The school is owned by St John's College and was originally set up in the 17th century to educate the choristers. Now housed on a leafy road in Cambridge opposite the college's playing fields, which they share, in three adjacent houses. On entering the main building the first thing you see are the choristers' gowns hanging in the hallway. They are very proud of the choristers, rightly so. They travel the world and are very talented. But once in the school they are just normal pupils. There are no 'stars' in this school so no cabinets full of trophies on display. They have them, but discreetly hidden in the dining room. The life of the chorister is slightly different to other pupils as they start practice at 7.30am, running through to the start of school at 9am, and again after school for a couple of hours. It's a massive commitment but handled well. The school ensures they don't suffer academically or personally.

A very tactile school. 'If a child needs a hug it gets one,' says the head. Many parents spoke of their children 'being allowed to be children and not to grow up too quickly.' 'They are imaginative and modern about learning,' said one parent. 'We are told very firmly to leave the education of our child to them and not to stress about exams. It works, the children are pushed, achieve highly but don't feel under pressure.' No exams until the penultimate year. Children taught to have enquiring minds and embrace learning. Mindfulness is taught to all, even the little ones, and stands them in good stead for future years. Hugely supported by parents. 'All of the teachers are of a similar mindset and embrace the concept and love the children. They wouldn't be here if that wasn't the case,' says the head.

Lots of after-school clubs, but not until year 3. As expected, loads of music, not just for the choristers. The majority of the children learn an instrument, many two or more. Bands, choirs, quartets galore. All the usual sports teams, well supported. Drama very popular. Very impressive artwork framed and displayed throughout the school. A large, airy, newly refurbished art room where the older children can pop in and set to. 'All children can draw by the time they leave St John's,' the very enthusiastic art teacher told us. Timetables are flexible. Extra tuition offered, some at no extra cost, very quickly if needed. Individual needs department proactive. They are on top of the children academically and extra time allocated towards subjects for those aiming for certain scholarships.

A small contingent – including all choristers – board. 'It means we can manage their time well rather than it being wasted travelling.' Larger numbers boarding higher up the school, many weekly, some flexi. Clean, bright, mixed boarding house. Lots of comfy sofas, snooker and table football. A large kitchen with huge table. 'Our parents can come and see us and have a cup of tea with us after services,' said one chorister. Very much an open door policy for parents. Strict rules within the house. No child can enter another dorm. No mobile phones in the boarding house and, very contentiously for our chatty guides, no tuck. 'They decided the choristers were getting too much sugar so cut tuck to twice a week and have now cut it out completely,' was the outraged comment. 'So when we go home we beg our parents for sweets.'

There used to be accompanied visits to town with the older ones going in threes, 'as long as one of us was wearing a watch,' but these have now been stopped. 'They said all we did was buy sweets, but we only had £2 so what can they expect?' from our opinionated guide, 'and how do they expect us to manage money if they won't let us out to spend it?' All said with very good humour and a big smile. We feel our guides have a bright future ahead of them. Homesickness handled well. One pupil allowed to bring her rabbit last term. Lots of contact with parents, though not before bed, in private phone booths. 'Please note the phone number for Childline is listed on our contact lists pinned to the door.' This guide will go far. Dormitories clean and tidy. Bunk beds, six to a room max. Boarders change their own bed linen. Duvet covers brought from home. House parents loved by all, children and parents. 'I couldn't ask for more from them and the receptionist is magnificent.'

Uniform stands out with bright red blazers. 'The uniform is too expensive,' said one rather disgruntled parent, 'particularly the blazers.' The girls wear a rather dowdy summer dress, far too dull for the bright, exuberant characters donning them. 'Pastorally excellent,' was said by every parent. 'There are issues, usually girls and their friendships, but the school handles them sensitively and effectively.' The year 8s mentor the incoming year 5s.

Nearly every parent we spoke to felt 'we are very lucky to have our children at St John's.' We can see why. Certain schools have 'that feel', and this one does. It's a joyous place that's buzzing. Lessons are alive, the children are working hard, utterly engaged. And they are happy, exuberant, confident little people, from the youngest up. Children being children, nurtured through some tough, turbulent times, meeting adolescence with equilibrium and well set for future schooling. Long may it continue.

St Mary's School, Cambridge

Bateman Street, Cambridge, Cambridgeshire CB2 1LY

01223 353253
admissions@stmaryscambridge.co.uk
www.stmaryscambridge.co.uk
RC

Ages: 11–18
Pupils: 663; sixth form: 105
Boarders: 100
Day: £8,943 – £14,457 pa
Boarding: £26,571 – £30,867 pa

Headmistress: Since 2007, Ms Charlotte Avery (late 30s) BA MA PGCE. Read English at St Anne's Oxford. Began teaching in South Africa at a politically tense time when some of the older boys carried AK-47s to school. Back in the UK and several professional moves later – two via GDST schools – became deputy head at Highgate, where she met her French husband, now a teacher at The Perse. (Pupils may address her as Madame Pillet as long as their pronunciation is correct.)

A determined bundle of energy and breathless, almost unstoppable, advocate of her school, Ms Avery has ambitious plans to squeeze more space out of a cramped site. Equally passionate about Lourdes – where 'our girls rose to the challenge in true St Mary's spirit' – and food. 'Dining is an important experience and I'm enjoying eating my way socially through each year group.' Everyone's pleased she's taken on board requests to learn cookery and that a perfectly formed, albeit compact, cookery suite has been installed.

Pupils appreciate her up-to-date approach and, as a committed communicant member of the C of E, she wholeheartedly supports the ethos and values of St Mary's. Enjoys opera and visiting art galleries and is a member of the Ministry of Defence Ethics Committee where she relishes the 'chance to inject some common sense into proceedings.'

Academic matters: Not fantastically pushy but competitive in a 'nice way'. Considering the broad intake, good results at GCSE – 61 per cent A*/A in 2015. Abundant encouragement plus drop-in surgeries for girls who need help – school says there's value-added across the board in spadefuls. Relaxed dialogue and mutually respectful relationships between staff and pupils. Parents are full of praise for the teachers and are convinced the bright do as well here as they would at the stratospherically academic institution round the corner. Recently introduced two-week timetable seems to be working well – head has her finger on the pulse in case tweaks are needed. French plus Latin in year 7 with German and Spanish in years 8 and 9. At GCSE, option of dual award or individual sciences but full

RE course for all – the RE teachers are an 'incredibly sane and dynamic lot', according to the sixth, who love the discussions on every sort of issue.

Strong support network in the sixth. Reasonable spread of A level subjects has been maintained because school offers subjects to groups as small as one or two. A*/A rate – 45 per cent in 2015 – gets a big boost from impressive performances in maths and the proportionally high number of Chinese nationals, not surprisingly, getting top marks in their own language.

Relaxed dialogue and mutually respectful relationships between staff and pupils. Parents are full of praise for the teachers

All year 7 pupils are assessed on entry in English, maths and reasoning. Needs, including those of the gifted and talented, are monitored and sensibly handled – ethos that all have something to offer isn't just prospectus speak. School reckons it's 'dyslexia friendly' but not CReSTed or likely to be despite appointment of experienced head of individual needs/language/learning who has an MA in specific learning difficulties. Three part-timers to hand, access to ed psych and EFL teaching for international students. Differentiated activities enable most to stay in class but, if necessary, withdrawal during a second foreign language lesson. Usually groups of four. One-to-one tuition outside the normal timetable incurs an additional charge. Small teaching space, laptops as teaching aids.

Games, options, the arts: No practices at dawn but the sporty aren't held back – a number of girls play for the county. Enthusiastic staff and older girls happy with the range of options including rowing, touch rugby, yoga and kali – a seemingly ache-making series of movements with long sticks. Limited space so only two netball/tennis courts and smallish first floor gym on site. Hockey pitches a short minibus ride away. Hired pool and Astro nearby.

Drama and music (just over a third learn an instrument) are in fine fettle – conventional orchestras for instrumentalists and samba band for those who fancy something more lively. In the art and photography centre students' 2D and 3D work is liberally displayed and sixth formers have their own space. For the creation of something more practical there's DT textiles with its large bright classroom filled with sewing machines.

School is hot on events for charity and, amazingly, given the number of pupils, raises around £25,000 every year. In the summer hols sixth formers join the popular pilgrimage to Lourdes, where they help the needy.

Two-weekly timetable has freed more time for extracurricular activities, and an Arts Council sponsored award scheme (includes journalism, dance, digital film work, music and drama) is taking root with awards beginning to roll in. D of E is hugely popular and an impressive percentage every year get gold.

Boarding: Virtually all from overseas. Handful of weekly/flexi boarders. Ordered, typically personalised accommodation (recently refurbed) is neatly housed on the upper floors floors and in terraced

An Arts Council sponsored award scheme (includes journalism, dance, digital film work, music and drama) is taking root with awards beginning to roll in

houses on Bateman Street for new sixth form boarders – single rooms for all the sixth and some GCSE students, otherwise up to four to a room. Common rooms are welcoming, with the slightly quirky junior one being especially homely. Likeable and eminently sensible house-staff set great store on trust – sixth are allowed out by arrangement until 10pm on Fridays and Saturdays as long as they let the school know where they are – which, by all accounts, gets the hoped-for response from the girls.

Trips most weekends to eg Harry Potter World, British Library, theatres, castles, German Christmas market in Birmingham, plus use of all school sports and other facilities. Students encouraged to take part in eg Chinese New Year and international language day celebrations, plus school plays and concerts and after-school clubs.

Background and atmosphere: This former convent – the nuns moved out in 1989 – is sandwiched between terraced houses and an edge of the Botanic Gardens. Although there's nothing remarkable, apart from the maze of corridors and staircases, in the diverse collection of dull buildings from the 60s, 70s and 90s which have been tacked on to an early Victorian structure, a sense of safety and warmth pervades this well-loved, tidy place. Sizeable classrooms; new Science Hub includes five new labs – one for sixth form science. Standard gadgetry. Full library plus good range of newspapers and magazines (sixth former appointed as newspaper scanner posts interesting articles on a corridor noticeboard). Sixth have a separate house where they can browse in the careers library or escape to a somewhat lacklustre common room – as one of the girls put it, 'not the tidiest in tidyville.. but it's ours.' Noisy bonhomie in the spacious dining room, which doubles as part of the hall. Consultant has transformed the lunches and, much to everyone's relief, there's a wide choice of tasty dishes and tropical rainforest of a fruit bar.

Pastoral care, well-being and discipline: Catholicism with a small c but charitable Christian Ethos in capitals – there's an understanding that all belong to a wider community and behaviour is expected to be, and is, supportive. At the heart of the school is the universally popular chaplain, who's often found sitting on the radiator at the foot of the main stairs.

Parents say she's a gem, having taught herself at the school for many years she knows everybody and is a source of comfort and solace.

Open, unspoilt girls at ease in this secure environment. They're allowed to develop at their own pace and 'aren't pushed or shoved into a box.' New pupils settle quickly – parents appreciate promptly established lines of communication by phone or email and the way staff are on the ball with problems including difficulties at home.

Pretty well behaved lot – the pragmatic policy re banned substances is rarely implemented. 'We need to think about the wider community so out for dealing. In cases of possession we look at circumstances.'

Pupils and parents: Day pupils are very local whilst others commute by car (absolutely no parking in the vicinity) or train (station is a healthy 10 minute walk away). All sorts – about a third are Catholic – make up the loyal and supportive parent body. Vast majority of boarders are from overseas – international spread with a fair number from the Pacific rim.

Entrance: Mostly at 11 from own prep or local schools. Small number after GCSE. Informal chat with the headmistress then an application when she ascertains whether child is of 'sufficient calibre to benefit from a St Mary's education' – not hugely difficult as school draws from '60 per cent of the ability range' – bit ambiguous but we think we know what they mean. 'Bottom line is girls need to be enthusiastic about learning and committed to the wider community.' No surprise policy and

basic expectation that those from the prep will join the seniors. Any not up to the mark can repeat year 6 (fine if the child stays in the private sector but problematic if, pre-16, there's a transfer to state education where child must be in the correct age banding and may have to 'jump' a year).

Exit: After GCSE many of the locals to Hills Road. As a strand to its career guidance, school has produced a collation of career stories from alumnae – oodles of advice and thoughts including the balance between work and family. The school also has a dedicated head of careers and work experience who can offer impartial advice and beneficial work experience links to students. Good stuff. Sixth move on to a broad range of courses – from computer science to midwifery to business management – and universities – from SOAS to Manchester Met to Leeds College of Music. One to Oxford in 2015 (chemistry).

Money matters: Academic, music, art, textiles, drama, performing arts and sports scholarships at 11, 13 and 16. Mary Ward scholarships for those in years 8 and 10 who make a positive contribution to the school and wider community. Small number of 100 per cent bursaries for year 7 and sixth form entry. Possibility of help, usually to the next public exam, for those who fall on hard times.

Remarks: Energetic head and loyal staff with a positive outlook. Level of pastoral care and awareness of social responsibility give this place something extra special.

Summerhill School

Westward Ho, Leiston, Suffolk IP16 4HY

01728 830540
office@summerhillschool.co.uk
www.summerhillschool.co.uk

Ages: 5–17
Pupils: 75
Boarders: nearly all full
Day: £4,725 – £10,741 pa
Boarding: £10,625 – £17,946 pa

Principal: Since 1985, Zoe Readhead (a very youthful late-ish 60s) – proprietor, keeper of the ethos and daughter of school's founder AS Neill. Literally born, bred and educated at Summerhill. Has been a staunch guardian of school's core values when lesser mortals would have wavered. Inspiring, uncompromising, down to earth rather than airy-fairy (is a qualified riding instructor), does not mince words. Married to Tony, a farmer, with four grown-up children all educated at Summerhill.

In many ways a traditional family business: son Henry presides over the music studio; son William is deputy head and expected to take over running the school whenever Zoe retires.

Academic matters: Of secondary importance here. Summerhill is a 'free' school (NB in no way related to government-approved 'free' state schools) run on the principle that children have the same rights as adults and should be able to choose their own educational goals unfettered by the interference of anxious parents. Lessons are optional – some children will not attend a single lesson for a number of years, if ever. As the parents' handbook emphasises, 'remember, at Summerhill your kid could theoretically NEVER go to a lesson – they have that right. Staff members are not going to persuade, cajole or bully your child about lessons.' Play is considered as valid a part of a child's development as formal teaching: 'Many kids just need to play until they are ready to learn.'

That said, most pupils end up taking at least a few GCSEs, some take five or more. Results all over the shop from A* to G. 'My daughter might have got better exam marks at a different school,' a parent told us, 'but she got the grades she needed for the next step she was planning to take which is what mattered.' Prime emphasis is put on reading and writing, much of it delivered via one-to-one teaching. We observed a physics lesson which consisted of one seated pupil soberly facing a whiteboard where the teacher was instructing – curiously alternative and traditional all at once. A great environment for independent learners – the school brings this out in many of its pupils – but less ideal for those who thrive on a collegiate buzz and constructive competition from like-minded pupils. Nine full-time, live-in teachers, plus peripatetics, offer normal range of subjects plus environmental management, specialist music lessons, sound recording, drama, catering, psychology, French, German, Chinese and Japanese – staff try to accommodate kids' interests. Pupils are entered for Cambridge International O levels for some subjects rather than GCSEs.

One senses kid gloves in Ofsted's almost comically gushing most recent report (how times have changed from 1999 when it recommended the school be shut down): 'An outstanding feature is the way in which learning is closely tailored to match individual pupil's needs, including those with special educational needs and/or disabilities. A fundamental aspect of the school's curriculum is that learning takes place out of lessons as well as in them.'

Far from being a place where you can do anything you like, Summerhill has more rules than any school we have ever visited, however there are few fixed rules

'Special needs' not recognised here. Pupils labelled ADHD elsewhere are taken off the Ritalin and dispatched to play in the woods until they feel ready to learn. 'We take a rather old fashioned attitude to things like ADHD,' says Zoe. 'You've got to get on with it. Everyone is treated an individual here and there's so much one-to-one teaching.' However, school does apply for pupils to be given extra time in exams if they're eligible.

Games, options, the arts: Sports not high on the agenda and, despite its rather windswept tennis court, Summerhill is not likely to produce the next

Andy Murray. Various games played, including Summerhill's own 'tork'. Swimming for the bold in unheated outdoor pool and for the meek at the Leiston Leisure Centre. Dance is an option and performance of all kinds is valued here. Music important with some excellent teaching and good facilities for music technology and studio recording. Similarly, drama is big among these arty kids and the school has a small theatre. Woodwork taken seriously, operating on same footing as English or maths – except it is probably more popular. Other activities include metalwork, Japanese, Chinese, gardening, photography, calligraphy, film-making, crafts, riding, cooking in the café, camping in the grounds, making tree forts etc. But no one is coaxed into any of this: at Summerhill boredom is considered an important ingredient of education. Children become practical, hands on – can light a fire, cook, run a meeting.

Boarding: Not a hippy wilderness – TVs and Xboxes in some of the dorms. Girls' rooms generally nicer than the boys' and fewer girls to a room. Pupils allowed out to Leiston town – a quiet backwater roughly 10 minutes' walk away. No Saturday activities or lessons – 'we just live' – but kids can ask for a lesson if desired.

Background and atmosphere: Founded in 1921 by AS Neill near Dresden, Germany; settled in Leiston in 1927, where it became one of the most famous and controversial schools in the world. The school has been threatened with closure on several occasions, most recently in 1999 after a damning Ofsted report that called the pupils 'foulmouthed' and accused the school of failing the children educationally. Summerhill contested the notice of closure in court and four days into the hearing – in the face of enormous protest from current and former parents and pupils – the government's case collapsed.

Rough and tumble 11-acre setting includes large Victorian house, many single-storey additions, staff accommodation (one basic, hippy-style caravan left, treasured by its occupant – you've got to see it to believe it), wooded grounds. Spectacular beech tree for climbing, rope-swings and general play – a 'Summerhill thing', the pupils told us. Felt less full than on our last visit but school says its numbers wax and wane over the course of the year. Long holidays – five weeks at Christmas, five weeks in the spring and nine weeks each summer, but no half-terms or bank holidays – works well for overseas pupils. Annual festival-style camp for parents and former teachers over a summer term weekend.

Pastoral care, well-being and discipline: Far from being a place where you can do anything you like, Summerhill has more rules than any school we have ever visited. However, there are few fixed rules (other than the laws of the land). Everything is voted on at the Meeting, held twice a week. All children, from age 5 upward, have an equal vote, as do the teachers. No special authority invested in adults, indeed quite the contrary as they are vastly outnumbered. The Meeting is chaired by pupils and will sometimes make outlandish decisions eg to banish bed-times (sooner or later a glassy-eyed pupil will suggest they be reinstated). Misdemeanours are 'brought up' at the Meeting and an appropriate 'fine' is decided upon. Meeting proceedings surprisingly formal, with older pupils chairing on a rotating basis after first attending training sessions – lots of juicy educational stuff going on here. Pupils not afraid to voice complaints about their peers; bullying usually dealt with calmly and swiftly. As a former pupil told us, 'what Summerhill does give you is an ability to communicate with people, and it teaches you to just be nice.'

Large Victorian house, many single-storey additions, staff accommodation (one basic, hippy-style caravan left, treasured by its occupant – you've got to see it to believe it), wooded grounds. Spectacular beech tree for climbing

The school makes much of its claim that it allows kids to be kids. To us, however, at times it felt that it allows kids to be adults. Summerhill's freedom and democracy can extend into unsettling areas. The Meeting decides how to filter internet access and DVD restrictions. Sex is not officially sanctioned, but boys and girls allowed in each others' rooms and there is no effort made to discourage it. The school will assist pupils with contraception 'when it is thought necessary' and parents will not be informed unless the child requests it. Smoking allowed over age 14 but pupils must announce that they are smokers at the Meeting and sit through an anti-smoking information DVD. Smoking rather more prevalent than last time we visited. Drug taking or drinking will get a pupil sent home for four to eight weeks, but a child would only be asked to leave if they consistently made clear they could not fit in eg for extremely disturbed behaviour or consistently failing to follow the community's rules. A young boy we saw walking through the school with an open evil-looking folding knife was chastised by an older pupil.

Everyone up by 8am on weekdays. At lesson times teachers await pupils for 10 minutes, then depart if no-show. Student investigation committee deals with any reported thefts. Food a bit basic, portions smallish, vegetarian option – can be a challenge for hearty or picky eaters, but toast and fruit always available. 'Poc' – weekly pocket money – handed out by age. The school recommends children not bring in extra money (though some do).

Pupils and parents: An international community. The school is well known abroad and around 65 per cent of children come from overseas: Japan, Korea, Holland, China, Germany, France, Poland, Russia.. the nationalities wax and wane over the years. Around half of pupils are receiving some sort of EFL help (if they choose to turn up). Recent drop in Japanese pupils (recession) made up for by upsurge in Chinese. Hodge-podge of languages can be heard as one meanders through the school.

Like home schoolers, parents at Summerhill tend to be ardent advocates of the school, born, no doubt, of having continually to justify their choice of this kind of education. 'A profound place,' said a parent. 'Love creeps up through the floorboards'. Parents here have taken the decision to 'let go' for the benefit of their children; keeping parents at arm's length so that the children can develop free of parental anxiety and interference is a key tenet. There are no school reports and parents will not be informed if their child transgresses. The school's literature says, 'what happens at school is usually considered to be the kid's own business, not necessarily to be shared by parents. Accepting this is part of learning to accept your new independent, free child.' Some children were previously home schooled or attended other alternative schools, though lots come straight from mainstream education. 'Many of us didn't get on in normal schools,' a pupil told us.

You know tiger parenting? Well, this is the opposite. Thank goodness something like this still exists in 21st century Britain where exams and paper qualifications are almost a religion

Entrance: 'Selection is based on whether we feel the child is suitable for Summerhill and vice-versa – the parents also need to understand and support the ethos of the school.' Takes children on up to age 11 – over 12s rarely enrolled. There are day places, but it is basically a boarding school with children going home twice a term for weekends (although they can ask at the Meeting and usually get away more frequently if they want to). Weekly boarding is an option for the youngest children or

---

Like home schoolers, parents at Summerhill tend to be ardent advocates, born, no doubt, of having continually to justify their choice

as a settling stage for pupils who will become full boarders later. Pupils may enter the school at the start of any term and, as they seldom start with a cohort, it is common for them to take several terms to fully integrate. Interested parents are encouraged to read about the school, and then to visit.

Exit: A few leave at 14 to attend a more traditional GCSE course elsewhere; most leave at 16/17; a small number stay on until 18. Majority go on to some kind of further education. Many proceed to sixth form colleges (and then university) although entering a normal school can be a jolt. Some end up working in skilled craft jobs. Children's writer John Burningham (The Snowman) attended the school, as did several successful actors, musicians, dancers, artists and scientists – others are off making tepees in the Welsh hills.

Money matters: Mega-cheap, but then they do not have the overheads of keeping up historical buildings, state-of-the-art sports centres, interactive whiteboards etc etc. Whole place runs on a shoestring with an air of frugality. Teachers' salaries lowish. Ten per cent fee discount, or more, for children of ex-Summerhillians. Some subjects – like Chinese, riding, dancing and music lessons – charged as extras. School squirreling away funds for the AS Neill Summerhill Trust, which will eventually be able to provide limited bursaries for existing pupils.

Remarks: You know tiger parenting? Well, this is the opposite. A living, breathing St Trinians of a school, and we mean that in the best possible way (indeed, its 1999 battle with Ofsted was made into a CBBC TV series). Other schools seek to incorporate watered-down elements of the Summerhill philosophy, but none provides such an uncompromising, full-on, 'free' education – accepting the good (enlightenment) and the bad (illiteracy) that may result. Thank goodness something like this still exists in 21st century Britain where exams and paper qualifications are almost a religion. Educational philosophies and government initiatives may come and go, but Summerhill glides serenely on.

Tring Park School for the Performing Arts

Tring Park, Tring, Hertfordshire HP23 5LX

01442 824255
info@tringpark.com
www.tringpark.com

Ages: 8-19 (optional 3rd year in sixth form for dancers)
Pupils: 326; sixth form: 145
Boarders: 64 boys/145 girls, full
Day: £13,785 – £21,960 pa
Boarding: £23,250 – £32,880 pa

Principal: Since 2002, Mr Stefan Anderson MA BMus ARCM ARCT. Fifties, single, no children. A highly personable man whose Boris Karloff-like photo on the school's website in no way reflects his immense charm and humour. A classically trained musician, he grew up in Canada and attended Carleton University, Ottawa; then moved to the UK and studied at the Royal College of Music and Emmanuel College, Cambridge, where he was an organ scholar. He spent 12 years at Wellington as assistant director of music, then seven years as director of music at King's Canterbury, before taking up the principal's post at Tring in 2002. Very much involved in education nationally: an executive director of the Boarding Schools Association, and a trustee of the National Schools Symphony Orchestra. Universally liked and admired by parents and pupils. 'I think he's wonderful. He's absolutely spot on with the kids,' said one mother. 'They all respect him, but they can have a laugh with him,' said another. 'Kind and courteous and very professional,' pronounced

a third. 'Makes time for you, easy to deal with, very helpful and very fair,' added a fourth. 'He's brilliant, a character,' said a father, 'There's a great fun side to him.' The feeling is clearly mutual. 'I love it here!' Mr Anderson affirmed. 'The students can be high-maintenance, but it's never dull.'

Academic matters: Tring's results are proof that for the right children, the chance to do what they love actually enhances their academic performance. Only half the school day is given over to academic lessons, and the students here are selected solely on their performing abilities (if they pass the audition, applicants sit academic tests for diagnostic purposes), yet results just keep getting better. In 2015, 39 per cent of GCSE passes were A*/A. You could be forgiven for wondering if these results were made up of non-academic subjects such as drama and dance, but no: 84 per cent of pupils got 5+ A*-C grades including maths and English. In 2015, A level results were 64 per cent at A*/B and 31

per cent A*/A. Solid spread of academic subjects offered includes English lit, French, German, RS, history, geography, IT, and all the sciences. 'We push the academic side hard,' confirmed the head, who was brought in to improve Tring's profile in that area. Active and successful learning support department caters for wide variety of SEN, and roughly a quarter of students have either one-to-one or small group support. Parents report themselves very happy with the provision. One mother whose child has dyscalculia reported, 'She really struggles with maths, but she's had excellent support.' A boy with dyslexia told us, 'I've never had so much help as I've had here.' 'The support for dyslexia is brilliant,' said a father.

Those of us who remember the days when stage school was more often than not a byword for poor education can only marvel. But then Tring isn't a stage school in the old-fashioned sense, as the pupils were eager to point out, but a heady mix of high-level vocational and academic education, where the two strands rub together to produce very bright sparks. The head boy will be applying to Imperial to read physics as well as to RADA, and one Tring alumna, also a physicist, has just started her doctorate. As the director of studies, herself a Cantabrigian, put it: 'It's very exciting working with students who are engaged and passionate with their lives. There's a joie de vivre here that

'It's very exciting working with students who are engaged and passionate with their lives. There's a joie de vivre here that spills into academic lessons'

spills into academic lessons.' That said, it's important to remember that this is a vocational school, one of only eight such in the UK funded by the DfE as centres of excellence for exceptionally talented young dancers and musicians. Tring's remit is to produce highly-trained performers who've received a rounded education; not lawyers and doctors who like hoofing.

Games, options, the arts: Believe it or not, Tring had actually played a football fixture shortly before we visited. They lost 11-0. 'But,' assured the head, 'we played with great passion.' Students do get together for an informal kickabout, or walk down the High Street to the local swimming pool, but there are no organised games on Tring's timetable, because there isn't time for them. Instead, half of every weekday is given over to vocational training, and, say parents and students alike, it's amazing. 'Equal to the very best available in this country,' said one parent. 'Inspirational!' said another. 'Second to none, absolutely fabulous,' said a third. 'My son's physical fitness has improved dramatically,' said a fourth. And everyone else said something similar.

Children in the prep (years 4-6) receive training in acting, singing and dancing. Thereafter, students specialise in either dance or theatre arts. Dance training covers ballet, contemporary, tap and jazz; drama training does pretty much the same, but less intensively and also covers voice, improvisation, and other aspects of theatre technique. And of course there's musical theatre and singing too. Tring isn't a specialist music school – aspiring concert pianists would feel frustrated at having to break off and jeté every time they'd sat down to practice – but the music department is strong, with several excellent choirs and all students given the chance to learn instruments and play in ensembles.

Packed programme of shows, plays, musicals and other performances throughout the year, all of them done to an astonishingly high standard. Sometimes students have a chance to do external work – ballet dancers regularly join English National Ballet for productions of The Nutcracker, for instance – but not that often. The school doesn't encourage students to be absent, and children wanting a school that will act as their agent and find them regular professional work should look elsewhere.

Boarding: With limited space and funds, the boarding provision was only rated 'satisfactory' by Ofsted in 2011, and we have to say we thought it pretty basic; we saw seven girls to a room, for instance. On the other hand, the 9-12 year old girls in question didn't seem bothered. 'It's fun! Like we're one big family! And if we're having a row, the houseparents sort it out and then we're all best friends again!' Pupils are encouraged to do what they think will make their quarters nice: thus the girls' accommodation was a profusion of heart-shaped pink fluffiness, whilst the boys' was as fresh and tidy as you'd expect rooms shared by multiple boys to be. Feedback about the food was very mixed, with a number of parents expressing anxiety about how much and how healthily their children were eating, and several stories of boarders needing to pop into town to fortify themselves at McDonald's (a behaviour not confined to Tring students, of course). We ourselves were given a pleasant and nutritionally-balanced meal in the canteen, so it's impossible to comment on this further.

Background and atmosphere: Today's Tring grew out of the Cone Ripman School, founded in 1939 and itself the result of a merger between two previous dance schools. Originally located in London, the outbreak of war forced a move to Tring where the school shared premises with the Rothschild Bank at Tring Park Mansion House (strange bedfellows they must have been). In 1941, the school was able to move back to London but kept its Tring premises as a second school where boarders could be accommodated, and in 1947 both places were re-named the Arts Educational School, to reflect Grace Cone's and Olive Ripman's commitment to a proper academic education for their stage-struck charges. Gradually the two schools diverged, with London becoming more focused on post-18 training, while Tring continued to develop as a vocational boarding school. Eventually they became completely independent and in 2009 the Tring school changed its name to Tring Park School for the Performing Arts, in order to avoid confusion with its former partner. Originally for girls only, one boy was admitted in 1993, 'and that opened the floodgates'.

Still housed in the gorgeously flamboyant mansion in which it took refuge over 70 years ago, Tring Park School literally sings with activity and joy. Half the stunning wood-panelled entrance hall is glazed off as a dance studio, and we arrived amidst cries of 'Five, six, seven, eight, and right! Two, three, four, and left!', while Guys and Dolls mingled jauntily with a more demure strain from the ballet class next door. Everywhere we looked, we saw children enjoying themselves and eager to tell us so. 'Life here is amazing!' 'You get here and everyone has something to give!' 'Everyone's

really welcoming!' 'It's so creative!' 'It just makes you want to dance more, being here. You get to see everyone's talent!' 'You have more time here for what you love, you're more connected!' twittered a group of frankly adorable young things. Parents agree. 'If you have a non-academic child, as we have, the enthusiasm and the passion motivates them to do better at everything. Our son loves it, he absolutely thrives on it,' said one mother. Another commented, 'The children are lovely, all so dedicated, and it really is like a family,' adding, 'When my husband and I are walking round the school, we wish we were there!' 'Every child comes out with poise and confidence from that place, they all know how to present themselves.'

School literally sings with activity and joy. Half the stunning wood-panelled entrance hall is glazed off as a dance studio

The mansion's Grade II listed status has hampered some necessary modernisation – it took years to get planning permission for Wifi to be installed – but the school boasts an impressive array of newly-built dance studios. It has also received funding for an even bigger and better theatre to supplement the existing 176-seat Markova Theatre, while the new art centre will move from the site of Baron Rothschild's zebra cage to a new home next to the theatre. The surrounding tree-studded gardens provide a tranquil and soothing backdrop to all the artistic fervour.

Feathers do get ruffled occasionally. 'Inevitably at a school like this, there is competition, and I think there should be,' said one level-headed student. But everyone we spoke to insisted that the school also fostered care and affection amongst its students. 'We've always been taught not to compare ourselves to others, but to where we were last term,' said one sixth-former. 'If their best friend gets the part, the others still give her a hug,' said one mother. Another said, 'There is no real jealousy or one-upmanship over talent, and good performances are widely praised and discussed between pupils.'

Parents were less starry-eyed about school-parent communication, and everyone we spoke to agreed that it needed improving. 'Communications are not all they should be,' was a very typical criticism, 'they could be more regular and more informative.' Another said bluntly, 'We pay a hell of a lot of money for our child to go to Tring, and if I send an email I expect an answer.' The head acknowledged these criticisms with candour. 'I would absolutely agree. We need to upgrade our facilities so that we can have a parent portal. We email things weekly, but we don't have a newsletter as such. We have plans – our aim is to get a new iSAMs system (school information software). Staff are extremely busy here, but that doesn't excuse it, and I take it on board.' A new appointment, head of careers, was made recently to address concerns that families weren't getting enough information and help with students' UCAS applications.

> **'If their best friend gets the part, the others still give her a hug,' said one mother. 'There is no real jealousy or one-upmanship'**

We also heard disquiet from parents whose children hadn't been allowed to take the course of their choice at 14+ or 16+ after having already spent two or more years at the school. Specifics weren't forthcoming, but we gathered that this particularly applied to those with aspirations to a career in dance. 'This can be a more difficult adjustment than the school acknowledges, and it's you the parent who has to deal with your child's disappointment,' wrote one worried mother. But as other parents observed, a career in the performing arts is tough, and the head was adamant that the school always put the child's best interests first. 'I would dispute very strongly that we block anyone, but we try to get the child onto the course where we feel they'll succeed. If someone has unrealistic expectations, we speak to the child and to the parents. But 95 per cent of the time, parental, child and

> **Children for whom the performing arts are central will feel they've come home the moment they walk through the door**

school expectations match up.' The great majority of parents we spoke to agreed. As one mother wrote, 'Tring provides a very supportive network for students who are struggling or who change their minds about whether vocational training is for them.' Another said simply, 'The support given by Tring's staff is exceptional. Our son is very happy there, and flourishing beyond our imagination.'

Pastoral care, well-being and discipline: To a person, parents praised Tring's pastoral care, with the boarding staff particularly singled out. 'The housemother was wonderful, and my son settled in really quickly,' 'A houseparent in a million' 'The houseparents are so switched on,' ''The houseparents comfort you if you're homesick!' 'They're amazing! They do SO MUCH for us!' were typical comments. The medical unit was also very highly rated: 'Informs you immediately if there are any problems,' 'The medical staff were exceptional,' 'Both pastoral and medical care have always been exemplary.'

Behaviour at Tring is exuberant but respectful. There are the usual sanctions for infringements, but the students want to be here and are generally keen not to mess up. Many parents commented on the children's excellent work ethic, and one boy added, 'My time management has become fantastic since starting here. You really do become reliable, hard working, responsible. You have to work hard.'

Pupils and parents: From a very broad range of backgrounds, and from all over the UK. Some from overseas (around 10 per cent of boarders), and EAL help is there for those who need it. Many of them new to boarding, or to independent schools, or to the world of performing arts, but all of them united by a common ardour. Inevitably, there are more girls than boys, with the current ratio being more than 2:1. Do the boys mind? 'No, because I'm friends with all the boys in my year,' said one young lad, 'and my confidence with girls has increased!'

Entrance: Children can join the school from age 8 to 16, but the commonest entry points are at ages 11-13, 14 and 16. Applications are increasing, particularly at 16+, and overall the school receives seven applications for every place. One-day audition process at which children show what they can do in dance, drama and singing. They aren't expected to excel in all three of these – although many do – but the school is looking for great talent and potential in the candidate's chosen specialism, 'and they have to show a real desire to learn,' says head. If they're successful in gaining a place but need funding to take it up, they're called to a second audition.

Exit: The majority of students continue on into the performing arts in one way or another. A few dance stars progress straight to major companies such as English National Ballet and Scottish Ballet; others might join the school's own dance company, Encore, for a rigorous third year of touring and performing, or take up places at dance schools such as The Place. Drama schools are also a popular destination: Laine Theatre Arts, Bristol Old Vic, etc. 'And we regularly turn out some good classical musicians,' adds head, although invariably these are singers – one recent alumna went on to train at The Royal Academy of Music and has already appeared with Garsington Opera and Opera North. Some go straight into professional work (Downton Abbey has mopped up several Tring alumni). And a number decide to go to university instead: one sixth former we spoke to was waiting to hear back from Trinity Hall, Cambridge, where she'd applied to read history.

Much praise from parents and pupils alike for the way Tring supports and guides students' career aspirations. 'I'd love to get a job in a ballet company,' said one young male dancer, 'but my body doesn't work that way, I'm not flat-turned-out. But the teachers work with you to find other ways you can do things, and they're brilliant.' A parent whose son was now at college told us, 'He knows he can still call on Tring for help and advice, a relationship he really values.'

Money matters: Stonkingly high fees, as you'd expect with all this specialist tuition, but around one third of students are on some kind of support. Dancers who join the school at age 11, 12 or 13 can apply for funding from the government's means-tested Music and Dance Scheme. Dance students joining at 16+ may be eligible for DaDA scholarships (Dance and Drama Awards, another source of government funding). And Tring has its own scholarship fund for musical theatre and drama pupils, to which families can apply. Many Tring students come from families on modest or low incomes. Up to 100 per cent assistance available for those who need it.

Remarks: An extremely impressive vocational school that gives its students an excellent and well-balanced education. Children for whom the performing arts are central to their existence will feel they've come home the moment they walk through the door. As one mother whose daughter had been there eight years said, 'We cannot fault it. She's had a wonderful time, and the training has been amazing. Her work ethic is fantastic, she's very well-prepared for auditions, she's made friends for life, and she's grown into a wonderful young lady.'

Woodbridge School

Burkitt Road, Woodbridge, Suffolk IP12 4JH

01394 615000
office@woodbridge.suffolk.sch.uk
www.woodbridge.suffolk.sch.uk
C of E

Ages: 11–18 (boarders from 13)
Pupils: 599; sixth form: 195
Boarders: 58 full
Day: £14,091 – £15,249 pa
Boarding: £28,266 pa

Headmaster: Since September 2014, Neil Tetley, previously deputy head of Sevenoaks School. History degree and PGCE from Cambridge, then spent a year in Japan before taking up teaching. Ten years at King's College Wimbledon, becoming housemaster and then assistant head, with an interim year at the International School of Brussels. He has a great passion for Russian history, enjoys all things Italian and is an enthusiastic sportsman, particularly enjoying squash and cricket. He is married to Laura, a foreign languages teacher, and they have two young sons.

Academic matters: Despite a keen eye for results, the school is not enamoured with league tables believing, as do many, that too much of a focus on the school's overall performance can lead to individual pupil's needs being ignored. Academically the right buttons are being pressed, with 73 per cent A*-B and 46 per cent A*/A grades at A level in 2015; maths, the sciences and performing arts are the strong suits. At GCSE, 55 per cent A*/A grades; again maths, sciences and languages performing particularly well. Though less eye-catching, the middle range ability pupils' results reflect their solid achievement and success. Pupils are banded from year 7 and setted in certain subjects eg maths. Classes around 20. Everyone takes French in year 7, adding Latin and Spanish or German in year 8; at least one modern language to GCSE, with Mandarin and Japanese optional extras and Greek and Italian available in the sixth form. Around 60 pupils have mild learning difficulties; several full-time teachers offer support individually and in groups. The emphasis is on keeping pupils fully integrated into the mainstream classes. Strong EAL provision for overseas pupils. This is a school that works for all abilities.

Games, options, the arts: Impressive pitches and courts with the sports hall housed in the Eden project-style Dome, which provides room for several classes at a time. Sport is for all and everyone has the opportunity to play competitively in the school teams, often trouncing the opposition. The Sports Development Programme is devised to encourage the most talented pupils, many of whom catch the selector's eye at county and international levels. Swimming is for the hardy in an outdoor pool. Friday afternoon is time tabled for the Seckford Scheme, an extraordinary range of non-academic activities in which the whole school (staff included) joins. All interests and tastes are encouraged: eg sailing, cookery, chess (school has its own Grand Master), and CCF is a top draw for many. D of E is also popular. Music regarded as mainstream – no 'sporty' or 'aesthete', labels and half the school learns one or more instruments. It is 'cool to sing'. School has a close association with Aldeburgh and Snape with masterclasses, courses and recitals

Timewasting is frowned on and most pupils spin from lessons to sport to activities non stop. 'Pupils can have a crack at everything going – there is a niche for everyone'

taking place regularly. Proliferation of choirs, ensembles, orchestras and bands. Drama also wildly popular with eight plays and shows performed annually in the impressive Seckford Theatre. Dance is increasingly popular. The school's international programme provides visits and exchanges throughout Europe, India, Australia, S Africa, China and the Oman. Pupils spend periods of up to 10 weeks at linked schools.

Boarding: Boarders, virtually all from overseas, are fully integrated into the school, and as there are only 58 of them – all sixth formers – they have a close relationship with the boarding houseparents. They are free to visit the town after school and at weekends; some weekend excursions further afield organised to eg London or Cambridge, plus parties, paintballing etc. Help with language issues available.

Background and atmosphere: Founded in the 17th century, the school is part of the Seckford Foundation and has occupied its present site in the

town since the 19th century. It has been fully co-educational for 40 years. School stands on extensive grounds on a hilly plot with the various buildings dotted around, giving a campus atmosphere. The immediate approach to the school passes the slightly unprepossessing boarding house. However, the school buildings are a mix of styles from the Victorian to the contemporary, including the recently-built Seckford Theatre and sixth form centre. Atmosphere in classes, library and areas for independent working is palpably studious. Time-wasting is frowned on and most pupils spin from lessons to sport to activities non stop. One mother commented, 'Pupils can have a crack at everything going – there is a niche for everyone'. Pupils themselves are friendly and polite; teachers, if anything, even more so. Unstuffy relations all round, and the staff give praiseworthy loyal service; most have been there 10 years or more.

Pastoral care, well-being and discipline: Enthusiastic endorsement by parents for vertical tutoring system, which operates from year 10 to 13. Younger pupils have the benefit of knowing older pupils well, and it provides leadership opportunities for sixth formers; 'most pupils know whom they would go to'. Few discipline problems.

Pupils and parents: Pupils drawn largely from professional East Anglian families, many with a media background (Aldeburgh, BT close by). A fleet of buses brings pupils from as far afield as Norfolk, Felixstowe and Colchester. The school is very popular in the town and many parents have moved out from London to take advantage. Foreign students, many from the Far East, are encouraged to come for long or short periods, partly to ginger up what would otherwise be a very English school; about a third of sixth form boarders are from the Far East, others from mainland Europe.

Entrance: Common entrance or test, together with a report from present school, and interview at 11 or 13. Two-thirds of intake at 11 transfer from the Abbey School, the prep department for Woodbridge, the rest from local state and private schools. About three-quarters of those tested are accepted. Entry to the sixth form is based on an interview and GCSE predicted grades.

Exit: Around a quarter leave after GCSEs. Great majority leave sixth form for university. York, Nottingham, Loughborough and UCL current favourites. Sciences, English, business, geography and engineering most popular. Seven to Oxbridge in 2015.

Money matters: Academic scholarships worth up to 50 per cent of fees can be topped-up with means-tested bursaries. Music, sport and art scholarships are also available. Some sibling reductions.

Remarks: A good all-round 'country school in the town'. Lively, and although selective, would suit quite a wide ability range. Exceptional extracurricular provision for what is, largely, a day school.

Midlands and Wales

Derbyshire
Herefordshire
Leicestershire
Lincolnshire
Northamptonshire
Nottinghamshire
Rutland
Shropshire
Staffordshire
Warwickshire
West Midlands
Worcestershire
WALES

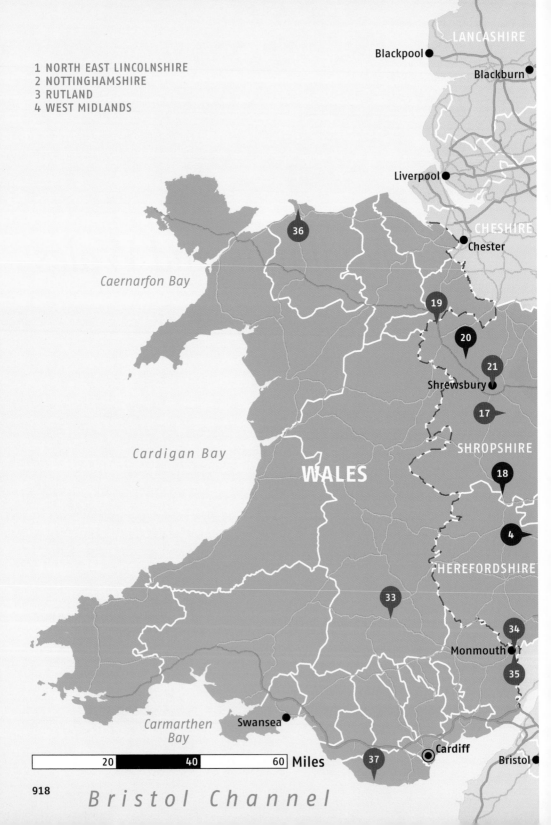

1 NORTH EAST LINCOLNSHIRE
2 NOTTINGHAMSHIRE
3 RUTLAND
4 WEST MIDLANDS

LANCASHIRE

Blackpool ●

Blackburn ●

Liverpool ●

CHESHIRE
● Chester

Caernarfon Bay

Cardigan Bay

WALES

Shrewsbury ●

SHROPSHIRE

HEREFORDSHIRE

Monmouth

Carmarthen
Bay

Swansea ●

◉ Cardiff

Bristol ●

20   40   60 Miles

Bristol Channel

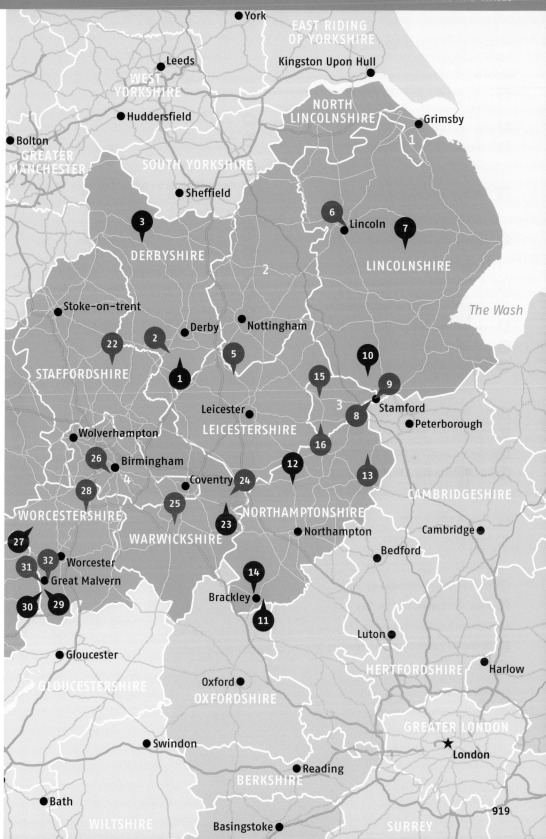

MIDLANDS AND WALES

DERBYSHIRE

1 Foremarke Hall (Repton Preparatory School), Derby 949

2 Repton School, Derby 988

3 S. Anselm's School, Bakewell 995

HEREFORDSHIRE

4 St Richard's School, Bromyard 1003

LEICESTERSHIRE

5 Loughborough Grammar School 959

LINCOLNSHIRE

6 Lincoln Minster School 955

7 St Hugh's School (Woodhall Spa) 1001

8 Stamford High School 1009

9 Stamford School 1013

10 Witham Hall Preparatory School, Bourne 1034

NORTHAMPTONSHIRE

11 Beachborough School, Brackley 926

12 Maidwell Hall, Northampton 962

13 Oundle School, Peterborough 983

14 Winchester House School, Brackley 1031

RUTLAND

15 Oakham School 979

16 Uppingham School 1017

SHROPSHIRE

17 Concord College, Shrewsbury 937

18 Moor Park School, Ludlow 974

19 Moreton Hall School, Oswestry 976

20 Packwood Haugh School, Shrewsbury 986

21 Shrewsbury School 1005

STAFFORDSHIRE

22 Abbots Bromley School, Rugeley 923

WARWICKSHIRE

23 Bilton Grange School, Rugby 929

24 Rugby School 991

25 Warwick School 1027

WEST MIDLANDS

26 Elmhurst School for Dance, Edgbaston 943

WORCESTERSHIRE

27 Abberley Hall, Worcester 921

28 Bromsgrove School 931

29 The Downs Malvern 941

30 The Elms School, Malvern 947

31 Malvern College 964

32 Malvern St James Girls' School 968

WALES

33 Christ College, Brecon 933

34 Haberdashers' Monmouth School For Girls 952

35 Monmouth School 971

36 St David's College, Llandudno 998

37 UWC Atlantic College, Llantwit Major 1020

Abberley Hall

Worcester WR6 6DD

01299 896275
gill.portsmouth@abberleyhall.co.uk
www.abberleyhall.co.uk
C of E

Ages: 2–13 (boarding from year 3)
Pupils: 298
Boarders: 99 full, 40 flexi (two-thirds boys)
Day: £5,085 – £17,340 pa
Boarding: £18,915 – £21,765 pa

Headmaster: Since September 2014, William Lockett, previously classics teacher, housemaster and school beekeeper at Bryanston. An Abberley old boy, who went on to Winchester College and then studied classics at Manchester, he spent several years in industry before becoming a teacher. He has also taught at Dauntsey's and Bryanston. He is married to Beth, a teacher, artist and fiddle player, and they have three children.

Entrance: Entrance is non-selective and some financial assistance is available to those who might benefit from it – not based on scholastic potential but on need and as a partial reflection of the fact that 'we are an educational charity'. This is not a scholarship award and, as often as not, will go to a single parent. Main entry in September but can and will take at any time. Informal interview, no exam as such, but children are tested before their interview to give the school some idea of their strengths and weaknesses.

Exit: Popular schools include Cheltenham College, Gordonstoun, Malvern College, Marlborough,

Millfield, Oundle, RGS (Worcester), St Edward's Oxford, Shrewsbury, Stowe and Uppingham. Boys also to Eton, Harrow, Old Swinford Hospital, Radley, Sherborne and Winchester; girls to Badminton, Cheltenham Ladies' College, Moreton Hall, Malvern St James, St Mary's Ascot, Tudor Hall and Westonbirt.

Remarks: Situated in verdant countryside just north of Worcester, in a rather impressive, listed Victorian pile, the school has a good range of modern blocks attached – a new classroom building, the Rhoddy Swire 'Palace', the renovated girls' boarding house and a very good sized school theatre/hall, the basement of which houses the music department.

The pupil body is almost exclusively English – with boarders from Warwickshire, Shropshire, Herefordshire, Gloucestershire, Staffordshire and Derbyshire. A number of Forces families and some very local children who come up from the nursery and pre-prep to board at the prep. A handful of Spanish pupils and one or two others from further afield. Well integrated with the local community, the grounds provide a venue for local church events, and local schools and pre-school groups are also invited to make use of Abberley's facilities.

Considering its non-selective entry, the school has a strong academic focus and very high standards. Termly competitions improve fluency and confidence in prose, poetry and speech. IT well used – though not as extensively as it might be for private study, 'as the abuse of it is difficult to prevent'. Lots of whiteboards used in class and plenty of access to computers in different parts of the school. Genuinely interactive learning – 'We have a troop of Viking re-enactors coming to camp in the grounds next week' – permeated by a sense of adventure.

All children learn French, Latin and Spanish, with those trying for scholarships at common entrance also learning Greek. The school owns a chalet in the French Alps and all pupils are shipped off for two three-week stints in years 5 and 7, both to learn French and taste a different culture. The school day is demanding but plenty of help for those who need or want it – about 40 per cent of pupils have some additional help with everything from dyslexia to study skills (at an additional charge).

Great labs full of interest and set up on a semi-tutorial type plan, so that the most is made of the very small class sizes (10-12). A very good and well organized DT room open well into the evenings in which the children build everything and anything – including coracles – as well as a textiles room and ceramics studio where they learn enamelling.

Genuinely interactive learning – 'We have a troop of Viking re-enactors coming to camp in the grounds next week' – permeated by a sense of adventure

Light, inviting and well-stocked library and study areas (being upgraded when we visited) where individual pupils have their own little cubbyholes – which they keep in slightly Molesworth-esque style. Dorms are well kept, welcoming, homely and cheerful, and lovely use made of the beautiful buildings which house many of the children.

Sport is central with an hour of games every day and all children from year 4 upwards given the opportunity to represent the school in matches if they wish. A tour of South Africa every two years with boys playing rugby and girls playing hockey. Tennis courts, cricket nets, Astroturf, a 25m indoor swimming pool, a climbing wall and a manège. Also a fishing lake and plenty of room

to train up the cross-country team. Set as it is in about 90 acres of parkland, room for everything and a tree house 'to sleep 25' under construction when we came by.

Tour of South Africa every two years with boys playing rugby and girls playing hockey. Tennis courts, climbing wall, 25m indoor swimming pool and a manège

Most children also have individual music lessons – over 20 practice rooms (generous for a school with these pupil numbers) and a good range of peripatetic instrumental teachers as well as a gifted and enthusiastic head of music. The school concert we attended was awash with children clearly enjoying themselves and performing to a very high standard, all cheered on warmly by peers and parents.

A truly happy place – the children are confident, polite and enthusiastic, with just the convivial combination of opinions and manners you would hope for. Although plenty of pastoral support, with an overall staff:pupil ratio of about 1:7, 'you can go to any of the teachers if you have a problem' – pupils are expected to organise and discipline themselves to a considerable extent by the time they reach the upper years. When asked what the school has taught them they say, 'Honesty, co-operation with others, learning to be trusted, independence'.

Staff turnover is very low, with an emphasis on a good number of live-in staff and settled families providing the mainstay of pastoral support – it has a genuine family feel. Termly reports to parents – still handwritten to avoid them becoming formulaic – and children are free to call their parents as often as they like once lessons are over for the day.

Far from culturally and socially diverse (although the pupil body does include a handful of Catholics and one or two Muslims) – unsurprising considering its catchment area. It is, however, certainly a place where any child would be made to feel welcome.

Happy, confident school in beautiful surroundings, a really nurturing place where your child will find their own voice. Impressive academic results tell their own story.

Abbots Bromley School

High Street, Nr Rugeley, Staffordshire WS15 3BW

01283 840232
enquiries@abbotsbromleyschool.com
www.abbotsbromleyschool.com
C of E

Ages: 11–18 (junior boarding from 8)
Pupils: 176; sixth form: 37 (32 girls, 5 boys)
Boarders: 56 (51 girls, 5 boys)
Day: £10,143 – £13,842 pa
Boarding: £15,021 – £22,860 pa

Executive head: Since May 2013, Mrs Victoria Musgrave MEd FRSA, following the departure of the previous head and a nasty ISI Inspection report criticising senior management and some of the governors, but praising the pupils and, indeed, the curriculum. The school has been extremely fortunate to obtain the services of the vastly experienced and charismatic Mrs Musgrave, whose cv would fill an entertaining booklet. She is senior professional fellow in educational leadership at Liverpool Hope University, a consultant trainer for the Association of School and College Leaders and visiting lecturer at the universities of East Anglia and Manchester. Over the last 20 years, she has been principal of four state secondary schools in London, Manchester and East Anglia, including Britain's largest state boarding school. In 2006, she gained the title Super Head, resulting in visits to 10 Downing Street. Before being parachuted into Abbots Bromley, she was head of Wymondham High School, Norfolk. While there we wrote of her, 'she is one of the best in the business...they are lucky to have her and should perform increasingly well with her at the helm.' They did, and the Abbots Bromley community will be hoping she has retained her magic. She's also a very experienced teacher, an enthusiastic practitioner of that noble art.

If you think this sounds too good to be true, think again. Mrs Musgrave is impressive and has been very successful in training new heads, improving and developing schools, getting them back on track, boosting morale and self-esteem. She's obviously tough when necessary, is a tireless worker, a straight and practical thinker, confident without pomposity or smugness, and an excellent listener with a good sense of humour. She brushes aside awards like Super Head because she is totally focused on Abbots Bromley and genuinely believes in the school: 'I didn't need to take the job at my age [she has four adult children and three grandchildren] but it's well worth doing. This is a very special school. It just needs a bit more academic rigour and some new appointments.'

She admires the school sufficiently to want to get it back on track. After all, to quote from that critical inspection report, 'Pupils of all ages are

highly articulate and confident with good social skills. They show a strong sense of right and wrong and demonstrate excellent behaviour.' So it wasn't all bad by any means, and Mrs Musgrave is determined to work on that. She's a problem solver and staff, pupils and parents rave about her. She has already addressed the issues raised by the report, which would now read very differently. 'It's amazing what she's done in the short time she's been here,' is the rollicking chorus.

Academic matters: This not a results or league table driven school. Abbots Bromley, referred to affectionately as AB, will not kick a pupil out if her GCSE performance suggests that her A level results will damage the school's ranking. When we asked some girls if that happened at AB they looked amazed and replied with tough logic, 'Of course not, you'd be offered more help and guidance.' There is plenty of advice and help given at AB but one of the advantages of being a small school – there are about 30 in the sixth form – is that it is possible to tailor girls' needs and aspirations to suit them. The recent inspection noted and applauded that. Instead of shoehorning pupils into subject blocks, the school, where possible, builds the curriculum around pupils' choices. At best this approach is seen as inspirational and encouraging and not an opportunity for copping out.

The 19th century builders were generous with the size of their windows. They are a delightful feature and contribute much to the rooms, which are airy and spacious

Exam results are commendable for a school which is non-selective; 33 per cent A*/A at GCSE in 2015 and 58 per cent a A level. Girls and teachers seem immensely happy with the opportunities they have to pursue the sciences. In a mixed school these are frequently seen as 'boys' subjects' but here they are pursued enthusiastically. Small classes are greatly appreciated, too. There is a mass of information about subject choices in the excellent booklets that come with the prospectus.

Maths and English are setted for ability but sets are not rigidly static: movement up and down is in response to progress and confidence. Good dyslexia help is available as well as EFL tuition for those 10 per cent who need it. Those we talked to from abroad spoke with genuine fondness of the school, the way in which they had been welcomed and their involvement with dance and other activities. One mother told us of her dyslexic daughter who had struggled agonisingly at her previous school, but once at AB had 'taken off. There's such a wonderful mixture of love and expertise at the school. She's blossomed.' Sixth formers help younger girls with maths and other subjects as a genuine extension of that 'family feeling' as well as points towards their Duke of Edinburgh Award.

Games, options, the arts: Two unique features of AB are the Alkins School of Ballet and the Equestrian Centre, adding depth and variety to a school experience which is genuinely broad and challenging. Ballet may be fun but, be under no illusion, it requires dedication, with a mixture of sensitive response, physical control and courage. Outstanding results for performing arts and dance BTecs. Vocational dance, by audition, involves about eight hours a week; the alternative is dancing for fun, for a sense of release, for 'enrichment'. Both involve commitment. Several students have gone on to perform professionally via the Royal Academy of Dance and other prestigious schools. The excellent director of ballet, a former examiner with the Royal Ballet, and his wife, a former international ballerina, know that the career of a dancer can be cut short and does not last as long as many professions. For that reason they encourage students to do three A levels along with preparing for their BTec and beyond. 'We want them to have the widest possible choice.' Marvellous equipment – lots of barres and mirrors – but more importantly, fabulous teaching in spacious studios.

The superbly equipped Equestrian Centre is reached via a beautiful tree lined avenue and clearly has everything a budding rider needs to move on to Olympic honours. Indoor, floodlit outdoor, bring your own horse or hire one of the school's – you name it. Girls may learn to ride from 6 years old and there have been a number of startling successes both at horse shows and with BHS examinations, the top one of which counts for over 100 UCAS points as well as a teaching qualification.

These two activities are more than hobbies: they really do contribute to the well-rounded character of the school. AB is not an academic hothouse nor a school for trendy air heads aspiring to have their pictures in Country Life: it is a school which

Unique features of AB are the Alkins School of Ballet and the Equestrian Centre. They add depth and variety to the whole school experience

offers education at its broadest and most stimulating. It challenges and nurtures the brain as well as plugging into a lively, creative life of spiritual freedom and energy, artistic expression involving movement in response to music, what the school calls 'enrichment'. The Renaissance was right to combine horsemanship with learning.

Art is exciting and popular with examples of girls' work all over the place, helping to make the passageways of the original 19th century building less formal and intimidating. Plenty of drama, with plays being written and performed by the pupils themselves in house competitions. One wing of the school is dedicated to music, with over 20 individual practice rooms where girls who are now grandmothers practised scales in the morning after cold showers. Now there are computers for composing on after warm baths, as well as a keyboard studio. Music and singing are very popular, with most girls learning at least one instrument and a much travelled chapel choir – Italy, New York, Paris, San Francisco, Lichfield – and a Cantoria Choir that sings regularly on Radio 4.

Matches against bigger schools (and most are) are played with much zest and skill, with county players in many fields. Another school commented to us, 'Abbots Bromley girls always play with tremendous determination'. 'That's part of the ethos of making the most of our abilities and opportunities,' a pupil told us without a whiff of self-consciousness. Hockey, netball, football, cross-country, tennis, swimming, rounders and athletics are all on offer.

Boarding: Boarding is increasing in popularity. Younger girls share with three or four others, sixth formers have individual bedsits of a rather higher standard than they are likely to find at university. Girls we spoke to were most enthusiastic about boarding, 'but I can't get my mum to agree,' said one frustrated girl who is stepping up her nights of flexi-boarding. 'Perhaps then she won't notice I'm not at home.'

Boys' boarding house opened in September 2015 to accommodate male sixth formers and students from new AB International College, which 'provides a variety of courses for overseas students'.

Background and atmosphere: The village of Abbots Bromley has a population of fewer than 2000 and was recently cited in the Sunday Times as an outstandingly good place to live. Most of the pupils and teachers at the eponymous school would agree. There are so many listed buildings in the High Street that the village is preserved at its best: handsome, understated and welcoming. The school itself has two sides: in fanciful terms the mind and the spirit. The academic and intellectual side is what you encounter when you enter from the street and thread your way past the large 1960s building, through narrow alleyways separating the 19th century buildings of the original foundation to the visitors' car park and thence to reception and the head. If you drive towards the equine block, however, you come to the sports fields, the huge Astroturf and the stunning view of Cannock Chase. Here, too, is the grass running track where the school recently had to buy new loudspeakers to make announcements heard above the sound of the girls cheering on their housemates and friends.

Originally two schools (St Mary's and St Anne's), AB was the first girls' school in the Woodard Foundation and is one of the oldest girls' public schools in the country. Woodard was unwilling initially to found a girls' school: he couldn't see the point of girls' boarding schools. Various friends, sensing Woodard's blinkered vision, persuaded him to accept the idea and ultimately he allowed Abbots Bromley into the Woodard Foundation. Six years later, on the other side of the street, St Mary's was founded as a less expensive sister school. The Woodard Schools are religious foundations, but Victorian Anglicanism was very class conscious and St Mary's was for the daughters of less wealthy parents. Later ages were more squeamish about such distinctions and in 1921 the two schools on either side of the road became as one. Later they were linked by name as Abbots Bromley School for Girls.

There are so many listed buildings in the High Street that the village is preserved at its best: handsome, understated and welcoming. Pupils and teachers would agree

On the St Mary's side of the road there is a splendid injunction to motorists from a bygone age: 'Please do not stand your Motors on This Side of the Road'; on the other side of the entrance is a fiercer notice: 'Private property: no trespassing.' This is the home to the swimming pool, sports hall and medical centre (and previously the prep school, which has now moved across the road to join its big sister). The mixture of senior and junior parts of the school contributes to that sense of affectionate unity that pervades the whole place.

The 19th century builders were generous with the size of their windows. Whatever the original motives for such huge windows – wide open at night, no doubt – they are a delightful addition to the facilities and contribute much to the rooms, which are airy and spacious. The lovely and inviting library is in the process of being made even more attractive, science labs have been improved, IT is efficient and attractively laid out and the boarding facilities are homely and inviting.

AB was the first girls' school in the Woodard Foundation and is one of the oldest girls' public schools

The school chapel is, in keeping with Woodard's principles, the most obvious and memorable building. It has height, majesty and atmosphere and will be even more impressive when the lighting is improved. It is clearly central to the atmosphere of the school and though there is no longer daily chapel for all, one or two girls we spoke to told us that they sometimes went to sit there and think. On Fridays the whole senior school attends eucharist and 'it's a wonderful place to sing in.'

The sixth form wing, with its delightful common room, cooking areas and comfortable bedsits, offers an induction into university. As part of the practical preparation for leaving home and school, sixth form girls do some cooking and are responsible for their own laundry.

Girls we spoke to, and how happy they were to talk, expressed huge happiness and delight in their school. 'If I have children,' said one sparky girl, 'I would definitely send them here.' Others nodded in agreement before she added, 'if I could afford it.'

Pastoral care, well-being and discipline: The old adage about family warmth and trust in each other is as true and apparent in AB as any school we have visited. It's partly the size. 'I know every girl in the school,' one happy inmate told us. 'That helps a lot.' Girls and staff greet each other with warmth and interest as they move about. We saw some inspirational teaching born of mutual respect and genuine interest. Classes were lively, active and worthwhile, and outside the classroom the willingness of staff to spend time with the girls and listen, advise or help is much appreciated.

There is much scope for interaction across the age range in the houses, whether it is in the dining room where houses eat together, playing and watching inter-house sport, performing together in plays and concerts, going on outings and trips. Clear anti-bullying policy and girls we spoke to said they felt happy and safe. As far as adults are concerned, girls can turn to their housemistress/master, form tutor, sixth form mentor 'anyone whom they trust.' Some parents have moved to be nearer the school. That's always revealing.

Pupils and parents: There is a genuine elegance and style about the girls but they are not remotely pretentious or posh. Those we met were forthcoming without being arrogant and were innately courteous and good fun. Many spoke of the joy of being at AB because 'you don't have to pretend to be anything other than yourself'; they didn't feel they would be happier at a school that was co-ed throughout. They love the village and the village seems to love them; dads spoke approvingly of visits, 'do you know of any other school which is bang next door to a jolly good pub?' Mums spoke of the love and support given by the school and the fact that the girls are happily busy and involved. Those parents who were disenchanted by the previous regime are now coming back on board. The Commemoration Day, when the whole school walks down the centre of the High Street in costume and singing hymns, continues. 'We like the tradition: it's slightly mad but great fun.'

Entrance: Most of the girls at the prep school come on to the senior school, for which they are well prepared. Others come from abroad, locally and further afield. Entry is, by and large, non-selective: the school is looking for potential, for girls who will contribute and stretch their potential, for girls who will appreciate the variety of activities on offer.

Sixth form entrants – including boys – are assessed in English, maths and by interview.

Exit: Some 20 per cent leave after GCSEs. A mix of sixth form destinations from Oxbridge to art school to Royal Ballet. Courses range from dentistry to accounting and finance. There is no cloning these girls.

Money matters: The school offers scholarships into year 7, year 9, year 10 and year 12 (academic, dance, riding, music, art, sport and children living in the village). Riding and ballet are extras: expect some £800 a term for ballet and stabling around £90 a week. Bursaries may be available. Don't be afraid to ask the bursar.

Remarks: The current head is surely right to see AB as a special school, a school with delightful idiosyncrasies and unique possibilities; a school which really does nurture individuality, offering unrivalled opportunities to pursue dance, the performing arts, music and riding as well as good academic teaching. In 2014 the school celebrated its 140th anniversary and it is now poised to leap into the next decade with 'courage braced and faith rekindled.' There is a new skipper at the helm and a reinvigorated crew. These are exciting times for an exciting school.

Beachborough School

Westbury, Brackley, Northamptonshire NN13 5LB

01280 700071
office@beachborough.com
www.beachborough.com

Ages: 2½ –13 (boarding from 7)
Pupils: 340
Boarders: 90 weekly
Day: £10,035 – £15,759 pa
Boarding: plus £28 – £30 per night

Headmaster: Since September 2013, Mr Jeremy Banks BA MA (40s), previously deputy head for seven years. Prior to Beachborough, he taught at Dulwich Prep London, where he was director of studies and housemaster. His own mother was a headteacher, and having realised relatively young that he too had a way with children, he subsequently did a degree in education studies and geography at Warwick University and a masters in educational leadership (distinction) at Buckingham. A very visible presence throughout the school, he is smiley, energetic and enthusiastic.

Married to Sophie, who is head of Beachborough's junior department, The Boardman. Also a Warwick graduate (education studies and music) and considered a strong female role model in the school. They have three daughters, all at the school.

Entrance: Main entry (non-selective) in September, but can and will take from any time, with the school having grown by 100 pupils since the start of the recession. An informal 'taster' day, with teacher-led assessments, gives the school some idea of a child's strengths and weaknesses. Every year group has two or three classes with a maximum of

School has its own farm and sells its own sausages, and there are plenty of gardens including the nursery sound garden

18 per class (three sets for English, French, maths and science from year 3 upwards). Some financial assistance is available for parents in difficulty via means-tested bursary provision.

Exit: Around half of year 8s leave with scholarships and all reach the pass rate for their chosen schools, the most popular of which are nearby Stowe and Bloxham, with others including Oxford High, Akeley Wood, Warwick, Oundle, Millfield and Headington. A few leave at 11 for schools like Royal Latin, nearby grammar.

Remarks: Set in an impressive rambling country mansion, once owned by MP Sir Samuel Scott, the school has a good range of modern blocks surrounding it, the newest of which is a huge sports hall that many senior schools would be proud of. Others include a very good sized school theatre, science block that usually has Bunsen burners in full swing, and a smart Boardroom Building, where children from nursery up to year 4 are based. There's also staff digs, where many of the 40-strong teaching staff live, including head, two deputies and the head of boarding. All the classrooms are light, airy and inviting. The school hasn't always been based here, however, having originally been founded in Folkestone in 1910, after which it moved to Ewell, Purley and then Stockbridge, finally settling three miles from Brackley in 1942.

The fact that the children use the same school entrance as visitors says it all – this school is all about inclusivity. So whilst the reception areas still have the typical 'smart hotel' look of many rural private schools, there's a refreshing emphasis on displaying children's artwork and there are practical touches like the fridge (albeit hidden behind tasteful built-in cupboards) by the front door so pupils can collect anything they've made in cookery lessons on their way home.

Total of 30 acres of lush countryside for pupils to enjoy – and they really do. We happened to visit on a sunny April day and at break-time, children were running and jumping all over the front lawn, but on rainy days they simply don boiler suits and wellies. School has its own farm and sells its own sausages, and there are plenty of dedicated gardens dotted around, including the nursery sound garden and early years vegetable garden. Forest school means you'll often see pupils taking classes

outside, and when we visited there was even a replica of a trench in one field. This formed part of the school's 'enrichment week', where the timetable is regularly collapsed so that teachers can focus all subjects on a single topic, in this case World War I.

'Enrichment week' and a few other examples aside, lessons up to year 6 are based on the national curriculum. In addition to core subjects of English, maths and science, all children learn history, geography, French (from age of 5), Latin, religious studies, art, DT, music, computing, drama, PE and games. Years 7 and 8 geared towards CE and scholarship exams. Subject specialists teach children from year 5 upwards. Average class sizes of 14 to 18.

In the past, Beachborough wasn't regarded as very academic. But whilst the previous head referred to it as a 'gentle' school, the current head now prefers the description of 'happy, ambitious and challenging' – a combination that pupils and parents agree pretty much sum up the changes he's brought in, ie encouraging a greater academic focus which stretches pupils, although never aggressively. So whilst year 1's computing lesson might focus on coding and older children can expect lectures from the likes of Professor Matt Jarvis from Oxford University on black holes, you'll also find display walls throughout the school celebrating the efforts of the less academically inclined.

Girls play football and cricket too, which reflects 'how Beachborough isn't a boys' prep with girls, but a proper co-ed school' There is pretty much a 50/50 gender split in every year

Good provision for those requiring learning support (dyslexia, dyspraxia), via the learning support department. No charge is made for this – nor, incidentally, for tea and prep time after school; before- and after-school care; or most residential school trips, which include a year 2 trip to Amersham, whilst older year groups go to PGL, HMS Belfast, Spain, Paris and the Lake District. There's also a focus on gifted and talented via the school's able child programme. Self-assessment and peer-assessment are priorities and there's a big push for children (especially the gifted and talented) to be encouraged to allow themselves to take intellectual risks with a view to learning from them, rather than getting stuck in the notion that they must achieve the best marks first time.

Sport is central, with some pupils at regional or national level in sports such as trampolining and cricket. But this isn't a school where only top athletes are celebrated. Every child is involved in team games and team photos displayed around the school are not just of the A and B teams, but also the Cs, Ds and Es. Moreover, whatever their level of sports prowess, children get to compete against other schools, enjoying match teas and hearing their names read out in assembly. The school regularly puts out four or five sports teams to play against other schools. Girls play football and cricket too, which one parent says reflects 'how Beachborough isn't a boys' prep school with girls, but a proper, genuine co-ed school,' where incidentally there is pretty much a 50/50 gender split in every year. Swimming club every week at Stowe School's pool, four miles away, and the newest sport in the school is triathlon, in which 30 children take part every Saturday.

'I've done things I'd never have thought of – like archery,' said one pupil. 'I love the fact that we're always celebrating people. I've learned that everyone is good at something,' said another

Music is big here, with around two-thirds playing an instrument ranging from piano to bassoon, and all year groups have weekly class music in a charming music department at the top of the school. Year 1s and 2s get to try out the violin, recorder and percussion keyboard for 20 weeks before deciding if they want individual lessons. Two choirs, chamber choir and junior choir, for all year 3 and 4 children. Music tours include places like Bruges.

Weekly drama and art classes for all year groups too. Year 8s perform a Shakespeare play every year, while years 7/8, 5/6 and 3/4 also perform annually, with recent examples including Treasure Island and Pirates of the Caribbean Curry Bean. Years 2 and under do a Christmas play. Art – which is overseen by not just a head of art but professional artist – is imaginatively displayed throughout the school, and other activities include Young Enterprise, golf, Mad Science, tennis, archery, craft clubs and dance.

USPs include no Saturday school and a flexible approach to boarding. This includes up to four nights a week, and nearly half the children aged 7+ stay over at least once a week. This is no sleepover, though, with organised activities for boarders, a clear boarding school culture and all the strict rules you might expect, such as bedtime for oldest pupils at 9.15pm and silent reading before lights

out. Dorms, which are located on top floor of main school building and which have girls' rooms on one side and boys' on the other, are well kept, welcoming and cheerful, with stunning wall art (Narnia for girls; war planes for boys). Long-serving school matron is based here. As one pupil, said, 'Some of us have never boarded and you don't feel left out because of it.'

Food is popular, with one pudding known as 'bird seed' (Rice Krispies coated in custard) easily the best loved course. Children eat calmly at long wooden tables, with teachers sitting at each end, and grace is said before and after each meal.

The code of conduct is clear, including 'being friendly is easy and it can make the world of difference' and 'always do your best, whatever the challenge.' By and large, the children seem to live by them, with pupils (and indeed parents) saying the school feels like one big family. Bad behaviour taken seriously, with a naughty bench for the younger children (although it's not called that), but the focus is on prevention. Head says that whilst it's natural for children to fall out from time to time, they don't allow this to descend to bullying, which he puts down to an anti-bullying policy, great pastoral care, a focus on rewards for friendly behaviour and the fact that little problems don't grow due to positive interventions. Parents and pupils agree. Active school council, which had just voted in increased choice in school meals when we visited.

The pupil body is almost exclusively white and, besides the 10-15 per cent Americans, almost all English. But this is unsurprising, given that the majority of children are local, with some coming from Towcester, Bicester, Banbury and Milton Keynes. Parents mainly from farming industries, motor racing employees (Silverstone is round the corner) and hedge-fund managers. Lots of family events, with the Beachborough Association putting on things like murder mystery evenings, coffee stops, quiz nights and an annual camp-out on the front lawn, for which tents were starting to appear when we visited.

This is a happy, nurturing school, set in beautiful surroundings that are truly utilised, and run by a dynamic husband and wife team. We found the children to be confident, polite and animated and completely lacking in arrogance. 'I've done things I'd never have thought of – like archery,' said one pupil. 'I love the fact that we're always celebrating people. I've learned that everyone is good at something,' said another.

Parents talk about the 'special atmosphere' and 'emphasis on inclusivity', as well as the 'individual attention that each child gets.' 'This place is a hidden jewel,' says one parent. 'The children are encouraged in whatever direction they want to go and the staff have a way of getting the best out of them.'

Bilton Grange School

Rugby Road, Rugby, Warwickshire CV22 6QU

01788 810217
admissions@biltongrange.co.uk
www.biltongrange.co.uk

Ages: 4–13 (boarding from year 4)
Pupils: 366
Boarders: 18 boys/7 girls full, 105 weekly/flexi
Day: £9,510 – £18,345 pa
Boarding: £23,190 – £24,990 pa

Headmaster: Since September 2013, Mr Alex Osiatynski (30s), previously director of music of the Loughborough Endowed Schools foundation. Educated at Dulwich College and Oxford; PGCE at Roehampton. Has also taught music at Gresham's, The British School in the Netherlands, Smithdon High and Oakham. Married to Freya, with two young sons.

Entrance: Non-selective but placement test and interview for candidates – academic potential looked for (aim is to find something at which each child can excel). When spaces available children can enter at any time. Typically two form entry in pre-prep and three forms in older years, roughly 60:40 boys to girls.

Exit: Majority to senior boarding schools. Popular destinations include: Rugby, Uppingham, Repton, Oakham, Princethorpe and Oundle, with typically 10 scholarships a year, including Foundation ones to nearby Rugby School. Odd grumble that school is not well disposed to those who flee Bilton at 11; school's defence is that early leavers miss out on

scholarships, responsibilities and the excitement of the final year, including cementing life-long friendships. Plus side is that occasional places appear for those from schools that finish at 11.

Remarks: Main school, decorated and extended by Pugin in the 1840s, consists of an elegant mansion complete with grand entrance bordered on two sides by high red-brick walls, stunning Pugin chapel used almost daily (all children, irrespective of faith, expected to attend) and superb, uninterrupted views across the Warwickshire countryside. Inside, the trappings of 21st century classrooms and teaching blend seamlessly with classic wood panelled halls (teeming at break-times with earnest youngsters playing chess and snooker), acres of windows, tiled floors and creaking floorboards.

Looks, feels and is a traditional 24/7 country prep, with good old-fashioned values, frequent assemblies and, in line with its boarding ethos, full Saturdays (from Y4). Pitches, playing fields, a nine-hole golf course, large sports hall and well-maintained swimming pool make this a haven for the sporty, yet even the most studious child

929

would be hard-pressed to dismiss the Bilton out-doors. Intrepid explorers are free to investigate the 100 acres of grounds and woods, grow their own veg in the organic garden, participate in outdoor crafts or toast marshmallows on the fire pit – even an outdoor classroom complete with log benches and swings – all duly risk-assessed.

Sport and the open air are a major constituent of school life, but the arty are abundantly catered for. The director of music is boosting quality and quantity of music (most play at least one instrument but aim is to involve all) – choirs, concerts, bands and orchestras perform regularly; drama is consistently strong and popular, with the creative arts and DT abiding favourites. Activity weeks are emphatic highlights of the school year; our guides jabbered enthusiastically about the posse of dare-devil activities – climbing, canoeing, 24-hour survival – and jolly japes: mud diving, arm joust-ing and mandatory dorm raids.

The work hard, play hard ethos is tangible, but pressure isn't. Even in the final year prep is com-pleted in school, a conscious move by the school to keep a lid on what can be a difficult and demand-ing time. Small classes, some setting in prep and wide curriculum for all – even tinies are treated to drama, dance, ICT and French. All try Latin. No weak lessons. RE popular (do ask about WOW), maths divides, reading is ably supported by good teaching, knowledgeable librarian and well-stocked library. We were treated to two science lessons (loved the lively informative posters, the work of artistic scientists, adorning the modern labs), a lively whizz and bang session and a traditional chalk and talk, perhaps typifying the breadth of approaches and styles. Indeed, we were reliably informed, by our young tour guide, 'Teachers look at the type of learner you are such as audio [sic], visual etc and try to teach you in that way'.

BG children are easily identified by their impeccable manners: they shake your hand and look you in the eye

No BG mould – former pupils include humorist Miles Kington, actor Alexander Hanson, composer Sir Arthur Bliss (organ on which he learned to play fully restored and in regular use) and film star Rupert Evans, but BG children are easily identi-fied by their impeccable manners: they ask to be excused from the table, shake your hand, look you in the eye ('We practise that,' say staff), stand when an adult enters the room and speak with confidence, interest and knowledge but no tinge of arrogance. Universally good rapport between staff and pupils; school exudes warmth. It's a lovely, cosy

Former pupils include humorist Miles Kington and composer Sir Arthur Bliss (organ on which he learned to play fully restored and in regular use)

environment to grow and be a child in and, 'regard-less of ability, they get best out of them,' say parents.

Can cater for a range of needs, particularly the dys-strata and ADD, but nothing heavyweight – 'My child is dyslexic but I always felt they were delighted to have him, no sense they were doing us a favour'. Takes a genuinely broad church, cel-ebrates diversity, welcomes and looks after all. 'Learning support staff are so fab, so lovely and so helpful,' said one delightful, delighted youngster, but odd parental mumble that knowledge of SEN across core teaching staff is patchy.

Parents praise pastoral care, 'Staff are good at setting boundaries and stamping on transgres-sions before they become serious'. Boarding houses are light, bright and comfortable. Communal areas offer TV, gaming, board games and jigsaws. Facilities and rooms (up to nine per dorm) clean and cosy but not clinical (encourages youngsters to decorate with posters and teddies). Atmosphere in boys a little formal, more relaxed in girls. Mixed reports in recent times about both quantity and quality of girls' boarding (do ask how many full, 11+ girl boarders), but new housemistress a unanimous hit. 'She has transformed things for the girls. I try to persuade my daughter to come home during the week but she never does'.

Eclectic parent body – new money, old and those with very little who work long and hard to pay the fees. Plenty happening socially and just as friendly, inclusive and welcoming to parents as they are to pupils – even a Saturday parental networking break-fast complete with bacon butties and croissants.

Aims to offer a truly rounded education where all are encouraged to try out new things, have a go, take part. Staff say, 'We let children explore the ox-bow, not just row down the river. We want them to take a risk, make mistakes, work out the rules.' Parents agree, 'BG children are enthused by life and learning.' One added, 'Thanks to Bilton, my daughter has had two extra years of childhood and a relatively untroubled path to adolescence – that's worth thousands to us.'

A breath of fresh air – a welcoming prep that builds confidence in the shy, empowers the gifted and is equally ideal for the imaginative, rumbustious child who can turn a tree into their castle. A tad boys' own (precious children would hate it), but those who are happy to join in, with a little rough-and-tumble along the way, should have the time of their lives.

Bromsgrove School

Worcester Road, Bromsgrove, Worcestershire B61 7DU

01527 579679
admissions@bromsgrove-school.co.uk
www.bromsgrove-school.co.uk
C of E

Ages: 13–18
Pupils: 940; sixth form: 425
Boarders: 365 full, 60 weekly
Day: £6,735 – £14,820 pa
Boarding: £15,570 – £32,430 pa

Headmaster: Since September 2014, Peter Clague, previously principal of Kristin School in Auckland, New Zealand. He grew up in South Auckland, spent his first teaching years there and has been at Kristin School for 15 years. He has a BA from Auckland University and an MBA from Massey University.

Academic matters: Small classes, outstanding teachers and high expectations produce some very impressive results. Prides itself on value added – not least because it competes for pupils with the King Edward VI foundation schools in Birmingham. Not highly selective on intake but makes a very good showing at GCSE – 61 per cent A*/A grades in 2015.

Facilities for all subjects are very good, in many subjects outstanding. An impressive library, careers and IT complex with lots of well-lit desks and plenty of natural light and space. Range of modern foreign languages available, including Italian and Russian. Latin and classics on offer. All pupils take IGCSEs in English, maths and sciences. Most take 11 subjects at GCSE.

Of the 900+ pupils, over 400 are in the sixth form. Offers both A levels and the IB. A level results are excellent across the board with 85 per cent A*-B grades and 61 per cent A*/A in 2015, and particularly strong results in economics, maths, languages and biology. A wide range of subjects available, including politics, drama and design technology. The IB is a relatively recent introduction (the first cohort completed it in 2011) and the head and staff are passionate about it. At present about 20 per cent of the sixth form take the IB. Initial results were somewhat disappointing, but the 2015 cohort averaged an impressive 39 points. Whether parents will catch the enthusiasm of the staff remains to be seen.

While not by any means a hothouse, pupils need to be up to the mark and ready to push themselves to make the most of what it offers. Possibly not a school for the very timid, children battling with dyslexia or those with other less 'mainstream' learning profiles.

Games, options, the arts: Outstanding standard and range of sports. For a start it has fantastic facilities – 25m swimming pool, two Astroturfs, dance studios, gym, new sports arena and lots of playing fields, netball and tennis courts. It also has excellent coaching – recent coaches have included the England under-18 rugby coach, and an international hockey player. Three Bromsgrovians in current England rugby squad. Cricket has had its share of caps; also a large number of students who play representative sport in hockey (Bromsgrovians represented Great Britain and Germany at the 2012 Olympics), netball, swimming, fencing and show jumping. Plays to win. That said, you don't have to be a sporting demigod to represent the school – A to D teams for most sports and development squads, so enthusiasm and application all it takes to get stuck in.

A wide range of activities on offer from jewellery making to RADA classes, film club and debating. The CCF is strong – a proud history of achievement in the Services (five VCs are commemorated in the school chapel). D of E Award is very popular and other forms of community service are strongly encouraged.

Unique Saturday morning programme – optional for most pupils (compulsory for staff). Offers a vast array of intellectual, cultural and physical activities, from Oxbridge extension lessons to ethics, first aid and table tennis. According to pupils, 'Everyone comes in,' and staff reckon take up of even fairly esoteric activities is very high.

After some time in the shadows, music is now coming on in leaps and bounds – more than 30 a year now take it at GCSE. Lots of opportunities to play in orchestras, informal concerts, chamber and chapel choirs, pop, and jazz ensemble etc. The school choir has recently performed in St Paul's Cathedral and St John the Divine in New York. A new music block is next on the wish list.

Gorgeous DT/art block with excellent woodwork and metalwork facilities, beautiful light studios. Great textile work and paintings on display.

Boarding: One mixed, two girls' and three boys' boarding houses, each with own parents' association. Staffed by resident houseparents (all academic teachers), resident assistant houseparent and team of tutors who share day and evening duties. Sixth form boarders can eat in at Housman Hall in the evening but it's communal meals otherwise.

Whether the passion is for sport, aviation, engineering or music, pupils are encouraged to be their best and given the resources they need

Activities range from theatre trips to London and Stratford and concerts to paintballing and go-karting (aim, says school is to 'inform, entertain and, occasionally, thrill'). Enough full boarders (there are no exeats) to avoid ghost town atmosphere. School 'nourishes boarders without forcefeeding').

Background and atmosphere: Founded as a charity school in the 15th century, re-founded in the reign of Edward VI and substantially reinvigorated in the 17th century (some lovely original buildings still extant). The 100-acre campus is situated in the centre of Bromsgrove but has no feel of a town centre school – very spacious, landscaped and looked after with great care. Despite the enormous building activity (including the rebuild of the off-campus sixth form boarding house) and the very significant increase in pupil numbers in recent years, does not feel overcrowded. The house system seems to prevent pupils from feeling swamped.

Very happy buzz, well ordered, with polite and focused pupils. Puts great emphasis on pupils being themselves and not trying to fit into a particular Bromsgrove 'shape'. Whether the passion is for sport, aviation, engineering or music, pupils are encouraged to be their best and given the resources they need to try out their ideas. 'We do what we think is right for the pupils regardless,' say staff. The school tradition is middle-of-the-road Anglican – twice weekly chapel is compulsory but with the emphasis on ethos not denomination. All faiths and none are welcomed.

No bells between lessons and although the atmosphere is relaxed, uniforms and bedrooms have to be kept neat and tidy – spot checks carried out. Staff wear gowns to chapel and detentions are held in a panelled 17th century hall, where wrongdoers have to explain themselves to staff in front of the head boy and girl, so in some respects quite a traditional feel. Day and boarding pupils pretty equally split – good balance between the two. Day pupils participate enthusiastically in weekend activities.

Pastoral care, well-being and discipline: All pupils are divided into houses – houseparents and their tutor teams (roughly one tutor to 10 pupils) provide daily input, support and oversight. 'We can tell from the way they walk in whether they're looking forward to the day or not,' say staff. Houses are furnished and designed with great attention to detail, have a home from home feel and very good boarding facilities.

School has team of trained student listeners and pupil-led anti bullying policy. Pupils say bullying not an issue, all staff are approachable and that any issue would be 'picked up straight away'. Parents praise the school for its 'positive input and affirmation of the children', excellent communications and ethos. 'It's about creativity, not ego,' one told us. 'The school delivers good citizens. No one gets pushed into a mould.'

No second chances for pupils who break the rules on sex or drugs – very few do. 'We have an ethos of responsibility and good behaviour,' say staff. 'The pupils are very good at self policing.'

Pupils and parents: Pupils are a delight – happy, enthusiastic, unpretentious and genuinely keen to take on responsibilities and contribute to the school and the wider community. Optional Saturday classes are full, huge enthusiasm for the vast array of extracurricular activities. A large local catchment from Worcestershire, Shropshire, Warwickshire and Birmingham, and boarders from all over – Italy, Germany, Russia and China. Most UK parents are professionals, middle class and Midlands-based. A significant number of Forces families. Staff say parents are very collaborative and supportive. Not many landed gentry – and this is not a school where a title would cut much ice.

Entrance: For the senior school entry is via the school's own test or CE. The largest cohort come from Bromsgrove's own large prep (700 strong), whose pupils are assessed informally and most of whom progress to the senior school. Others come from local schools. Entry to the sixth form is massively oversubscribed – GCSEs at B or above essential.

Exit: Few leave after GCSEs. Virtually all sixth formers to university, with three-quarters gaining places at top universities – Durham, UCL and Exeter particularly popular. Two to Oxbridge in 2015.

Money matters: Scholarships, though available, are nominal and carry kudos, not cash. However bursaries, strictly means-tested and worth up to 100 per cent of fees, are available to the right candidates. Serious about enabling access for those who would benefit from what it has to offer.

Remarks: A remarkably impressive and exciting school. Produces engaged, friendly, unstuffy and highly successful pupils who thrive within an excellent academic and pastoral environment, with national standard sports. 'We are free to do what we think best because we're under the radar,' says the school. We don't think they will stay under the radar for long.

Christ College, Brecon

Brecon, Powys LD3 8AF

01874 615440
enquiries@christcollegebrecon.com
www.christcollegebrecon.com

Ages: 11–18 (boarding from year 5)
Pupils: 376; sixth form: 130
Boarders: 168 full, 10 flexi
Day: £8,295 – £16,791 pa
Boarding: £19,392 – £25,944 pa

The Head: Since 2007, Mrs Emma Taylor MA (40s). Educated at St Antony's Leweston and Canford. Exhibitioner at New College Oxford (PPE). Previously philosophy, religious studies and economics teacher Stowe; housemistress Canford; deputy head Dean Close. Seriously bright, wears it lightly but it shows in both what she writes and in what you see going on here, for this, you will find, is a school with a curving bow wave. Unstuffy, capable, effective. Shrewd in her strategic vision: understands her market and dreams not of bigger but better. Has already topped the school up and lifted exam results. Does not shy away from decisions which, in a school which venerates tradition, can elicit dismay – an example: school colours are no longer the exclusive reward for good sports but are now conferred – following a painstaking justification process – on high achievers in anything.

A terrifically good sport in her own right, an indefatigable supporter of absolutely everything that goes on: 'She's everywhere!' Widely liked and admired. Has fostered links with the local community. Likes to know what parents think and, as one avowedly difficult mother told us, usually responds to an email within the hour. Her husband is a modern linguist, currently a house husband. Two daughters, one at the school.

Academic matters: For reasons of geography and demographics CCB – as they call it – is very much its own place. Small schools are normally for children who aren't terribly good at school, need to 'develop at their own pace'. If that's what you're after, don't shortlist this one. Intake is unusually comprehensive, always will be, and the sixth form is annually boosted by switchers from other schools, state and independent, and overseas students – the lack of a good local sixth form college is a great help here. The top end is seriously bright – handful to Oxbridge annually – with those not so bright not so very far behind. Results, hitherto thoroughly respectable, are on the up, seriously good by any standards. Good crop of A*/A grades at A level (55 per cent in 2015, with 74 per cent A*-B`). At GCSE, 45 per cent A*/A. Mrs Taylor has managed to lure some really good teachers here.

Small class sizes, even for an independent school – in the sixth form some are minuscule, possibly a little too much so. Meticulous monitoring. Academic pressure is insistent, but 'the teachers aren't on your case the whole time'. A 'per ardua

A marvellous sense of community – even inscrutable strangers like this reviewer are enfolded from the word go

ad astra' culture pervades all areas of life here and, in the classroom, they seem to be getting it about right – cheerfully perspiring students are the ones who work best; parents are more than happy with the bottom line.

Subjects studied all untrendily academic, plus Cymraeg. For any school this is a good range, with no concessions to soft options. Can be the usual small-school timetabling snags, though. Exceedingly strong maths, good science, superb art and photography – no weak areas. Modern languages in stormingly good shape under the influence of marvellous head of department. Classrooms are bright and, given the school's income stream, commendably well equipped. The new science block is a class act as is their new Centre for the Creative Arts – simply stunning.

SENs mild to moderate mostly – you must be able to work independently; anything more severe only if allied with high intelligence. One SEN teacher, a full-time, unusually well qualified member of staff whom the mother of a dyslexic boy instructed us in a manner not to be contravened to praise to the skies. Her classroom is not a self-pity inducing ICU – more a pit stop. Highly flexible, she can see any student as and when for as

long as necessary – a reminder that remedial intervention is more about the interaction of two people than the administration of clinical nostrums. Sixth formers, particularly, like to use her for study skills support. And what about this – no extra charge for her services.

Games, options, the arts: To wake up and gaze at the new day here is to lift your eyes unto the hills (it's probably raining again), for, verily, they are all around. If that makes you quail, go some place else – fresh air is what these boys and girls gulp much of. And here we come to another peculiar quality of the school: when there's anything to be done, it's all hands to the pump, your school needs you – it's a small school thing. Opportunities are more plentiful, necessity for involvement more urgent, which could be a recipe for desperate, heroic failure if results didn't prove otherwise. As the boys and girls like to say here, they punch above their weight, an assertion borne out by a rugby victory just before our visit over a school three times its size. The heritage sport is rugby, unsurprise unsurprise, and it's well coached. 'There are three of us who've played to a fairly decent level,' explained a former Ireland international. For those who do not get off on rough-housing it in mud opportunities as diverse as fencing and riding. 'Whatever you're good at they really get behind you,' said one boy.

Rugby remains pre-eminent, but only just – other sports are coming up fast. Are girls playing a demure second fiddle? No way – their achievements actually place them at a higher level than the boys. Hockey (recent Welsh champions at U18s, U14s and U12s) and netball are outstanding, and it doesn't stop there – students are to be found doing all sorts at county and international level. You've got to be impressed, you really have.

No school for a laidback child – masses on offer outside the classroom and plenty of expectation to do it. A school this size is especially sensitive to the enthusiasms of its teachers, so kayaking is strong, as is mountain biking. As are all manner of outdoor pursuits activities, and D of E. With its army links – Brecon is HQ of the army in Wales and some parents are based at, er-hem, Hereford – the CCF is taken massively seriously.

On the culture front, music is top notch, with eight choirs (eight, for heaven's sake), and the singing in chapel has to be heard to be believed. Lots of ensembles, Thursday lunchtime concerts, links with Welsh National Opera, Welsh Symphonia and Brecon Cathedral, plus a fiercely contested inter-house competition in which all take part (a competitive element to most things here). Drama is well done. Art is incredibly strong, photography a glory. Best of all, boys and girls get to do all sorts of things they normally wouldn't – your country needs you, you see. Look, there's the captain of the XV in a surplice.

Any school community stands in danger of being inward looking. They counteract that by inviting the local community to use the school's facilities (charity commissioners well pleased), cultural exchanges with China and Japan and school trips to all corners in the holidays.

Boarding: Boarding remains strong, always will – Forces families particularly want it and numbers are trend-buckingly high. It accounts for the social tenor of the school. Boarding done badly is the stuff of fag-roasts; done well it is what you see here: warm relationships between pupils of all ages and between pupils and staff. It's a marvellous sense of community, it really is – even inscrutable strangers like this reviewer are enfolded from the word go. Add to that a strong responsibility felt by older pupils to give something back, testament to a regime of vigilant, humane supervision.

A school this size is especially dependent on the enthusiasms of its teachers. Kayaking and mountain biking are strong, as are all manner of outdoor pursuits

The school's small size is just one factor, and it enables a brand new year 7 away from home for the first time to feel comfy at once. They have their own house, the year 7s and 8s, a jolly, caring place run by husband and wife houseparents, with occasional reinforcement by specially assigned senior boys and girls, for whom it is a proud duty. Everyone here is known by everybody else. One parent lauded the inability of her spotlight-averse son to elude attention. Parents and pupils alike agree that pastoral care really is very good. A most touching and illustrative emblem of social health here is the custom of pupils leading most morning chapel services, where they often share highly sensitive personal experiences – you wouldn't do that if you didn't feel you were among friends. Accommodation is adequate and up to date, with room sharing up to the end of year 11, and single study bedrooms for almost all thereafter. Food meets general approval.

Background and atmosphere: Founded in 1541 by Henry VIII on the site of the sacked and wracked Black Friars' church, victim of the Dissolution. The choir of the original chapel survives – well, some of it: it's been Gilbert Scott-ed – and the splendid refectory. Students are touchingly proud of this ancientness, as of the crowned 'h' tag, which is the school's logo, and of the fact that the chapel where they meet every morning has been worshipped in continuously since around 1250. The ancient buildings are architecturally charming, the rest of the campus unremarkable but easy enough on the eye. The 19th century big school is now the library. The new science block, with its dry-stone outer wall, is undeniably handsome. A campus feel. It's not at all a swanky place – the Welsh don't do grandeur; its appeal is its human scale. And its ravishing setting, of course, bang in the middle of the attractive market town of Brecon, washed on its eastern fringe by the excitable river Usk.

Recently awarded the best possible inspection grades in all three areas examined by Estyn, the office of Her Majesty's chief inspector of education and training in Wales.

Opened a junior school for 7 – 11 year olds, St Nicholas House, in 2014.

Pastoral care, well-being and discipline: This is the sort of school which embraces differentness only so long as it's allied to a strong dynamic. Rebels, hangers back and bunkers off do not find a social niche – discipline is observable and bought into. They're a bit square, that's one way of looking at it. Or are they? One parent with current experience of a big, smart school, reflecting on this, was inclined to wish for more dabblers in radicalism, more what you might call racy sophistication and worldly wiseness. Then she reflected on the grottiness of teen nihilism and all the perils inherent – and came down firmly in favour of Christ College. What best equips your child for the world as it is? That is the question. Well, these boys and girls are far too busy and sunny-minded for substance abuse for sure. Damn it, the highest estimate of cigarette smoking we could elicit from the pupils was two per cent. Heavy-handed discipline is rendered unnecessary by a strong, consensual sense of purpose. Buck that, though, and you're out.

Students are touchingly proud of the fact that the chapel where they meet every morning has been worshipped in since 1250

Pupils and parents: Most from within 50 miles, from primaries and preps in Wales, the English marches and further east. Parents are businesspeople, professionals, farmers and army officers. Some expats. Around 17 per cent of pupils actively recruited from abroad, especially Japan, China, Hong Kong and other Asian and European countries. A steady annual inflow of sixth formers from Germany – they come for a term, that's what they intend, then stay on for the year, even two years. Also a little contingent of Nepalis, sons and daughters of Gurkhas.

So it's a pretty good multicultural mix, but how English, how Welsh? A strong Welsh flavour, as you might expect – some pupils come from Welsh-speaking homes and a lilt in the voices of many of the teachers. Also a significant English presence. The head, English as can be, puts it this way: she wants everyone to be imbued with 'a sense of place, a sense of history', while a Welsh parent pronounced the school 'sufficiently Welsh'. In truth, they all rub along perfectly happily – simply not an issue. All nationalities well integrated – we were impressed by the number of Chinese boys, customarily prone to solitariness, who play rugby. And, gosh, they do all love to get together to sing those Welsh hymns.

Former pupils include Tori James, polar explorer and adventurer; Peter Watkins, film director; Simon Hughes, Lib Dem; and Jonathan Smith, playwright and author of The Learning Game – a book you should read.

Entrance: Three entry major points: around 30 arrive at year 7, 20 at year 9 and 30 at year 12. At years 7 and 9 an entry exam: English, maths and an IQ test. At year 12 you need six GCSEs at C minimum. Taster days in addition to open days, overnight if you wish. Greater pressure for places now than has been – a broad church, for sure, ability wise, but no pushover. Parents say the school is very good at assigning boys and girls to the right house.

Exit: Some 15 per cent leave after GCSEs. At 18, more or less all to university to study subjects such as architecture, medicine (four in 2015), music, engineering at eg Cardiff, Exeter, Manchester and UWE.

Money matters: Scholarships and bursaries for the able and deserving needy. The full fee is astonishingly good value, a tribute to astute management

– around 25 per cent less than flagship competitors and, what's more, no inescapable extras. This does emphatically not make it a poor relation.

Remarks: A damn fine little school with a well-satisfied core constituency, by which it is well known. Lacks cachet? If that's what gives bang to your buck, you'll look elsewhere. If it's first-class boarding you're after, you ought to have at least one small school on your shortlist and this is an excellent candidate, reached by roads more rapid than you'd think, through ravishing countryside. Here's a school which inspires affection and admiration in both equal measure and in spades.

Concord College

Acton Burnell Hall, Shrewsbury, Shropshire SY5 7PF

01694 731631
admissions@concordcollege.org.uk
www.concordcollegeuk.com

Ages: 13–18
Pupils: 515; sixth form: 340
Boarders: 435 full
Day: £12,810 pa
Boarding: £34,200 pa

Principal: Since 2005, Mr Neil Hawkins MA (40s). An experienced schoolmaster, whose former jobs include head of history at Sevenoaks, where he also coached cricket. Immediately before joining Concord he was director of studies at The Leys School, Cambridge. A graduate of the university there, he read history and, even more importantly, 'saw this lovely lady during the first lecture I attended and invited her back to my rooms for tea afterwards'. The lovely lady, Vanessa, now Mrs Hawkins, keeps an eye on the girls' welfare and teaches geography. Students we spoke to described her in the same words as her husband had used.

Engaging, warm and welcoming, with a bubbling sense of humour and an air of inner calm, Mr

Hawkins clearly delights in being at Concord – 'As a historian, it is wonderful. Look out there. Over to the right the castle and to the left the Parliamentary Barn'. As principal, he talks with infectious enthusiasm about the students, the staff and the whole set up, cheerfully and convincingly dealing with common misconceptions of the college.

'He really cares about us,' said a student. 'He knows our names, comes into lunch every day and asks us how we're getting on and he listens to our answers. That is why so many student-led initiatives are implemented.' 'He certainly has his finger on the pulse,' said one parent. The right man for the job, and during his reign the college has gone from strength to strength.

Academic matters: The very smart coffee table pro-spectus – brochure might be a better word – has eye-watering pictures of the beauty of the setting, the excellent facilities and, prominently, masses of statistics. So, too, does the website, so rather than make this entry read like a company report, we highlight unique features. The impressive statistics are freely available elsewhere.

To an extent the school owes its continuing success to statistics. It is, after all, an international school. Parents and children living abroad and searching for the 'best schools' are bound to look closely at league tables and take note. Older, more distinguished, schools may rely on their historical reputation and the perceived social advantages that go with them, but affluent parents from abroad – and 85 per cent of the students are from overseas – are pragmatic in their approach and will go for what appears in those ghastly league tables. Above all, they want to see results, and where better than in those league tables? Concord, not surprisingly, trumpets theirs. In terms of results they are hugely successful, regularly up in the top five of co-educational schools, out-punching many public schools in Shropshire and beyond. 'But,' says the principal, 'I always tell prospective parents and pupils we're not a crammer. We offer so much more.'

And here's the interesting thing about Concord's success compared with so many traditional schools jostling for position in the market place. It uses its results (78 per cent A*/A grades at A level in 2015, and 79 per cent A*/A at GCSE) as an

initial attraction and then displays its full range of wares; many other schools display their wares first and then speak quietly, sometimes rather defensively, about their results. Both approaches can stimulate doubts. Visitors to Concord may have them allayed.

Academic study is unashamedly the most important aspect of the college. Every Saturday morning students in year 10 and above sit internal tests to prepare them for public examinations

In the sixth form students choose to study either three or four subjects to A level plus one or two subjects to AS level. Unsurprisingly, maths and sciences are the most popular subjects, but the principal has been keen to broaden the academic scope to include European languages, history and geography. He cites two Oxford PPE students and a Cambridge historian in recent years, along with other Oxbridge successes. Clearly such possibilities exist, though the humanities at A level are unlikely outstrip maths and the sciences.

The lower school has expanded to over 150 pupils, including a number of local day pupils, some of them from nearby prep schools. The parent of a local girl, who had turned down the offer of a scholarship from a nearby public school, told us that her daughter was ecstatically happy and had grown immeasurably in confidence. 'The best thing we ever did was to send our daughter to Concord, the first school she has ever attended where she has been really happy.' One prep school head we spoke to was full of the praise for Concord's 'delightful' pupils and the amazing facilities.

We had a fascinating series of tours into specific areas of the school, all conducted by different groups of students from the junior to those in their last years. So we were able to talk in depth with some 16 students. They were uniformly open and fresh in their enthusiasm for talking about their school and clearly immensely happy. Not the faintest whiff of arrogance, cynicism or world weariness. Impossible to winkle out a serious complaint and no, the principal had not bribed them. What emerged, with a strength which might surprise some, is that it is 'cool to be clever and to work hard'. Nothing conceited about this, no smugness about recognising they had academic talents, no hint of intellectual superciliousness. They just seemed to delight in their talents and the opportunities to exercise them.

Just as well – academic study is unashamedly and vigorously promoted as the most important

aspect of the college. Every Saturday morning students in year 10 and above sit internal tests to give them as much preparation as possible for the public examinations. Some may gasp in horror, muttering 'crammer, crammer', but it does not seem to the students to be force-feeding. One very impressive girl told us it was just to ensure they were 'conceptually sound' – a memorable phrase. This was the same girl, incidentally, who told us, 'I chose to come to Concord because my school in Singapore was too relentlessly academic.' We asked about the pressure to perform well in these and the public exams. 'The pressure does not come so much from the teachers', we were told. 'We are disappointed with ourselves if we do badly.' So is it self-imposed pressure? The boy we asked just chuckled – it was obviously a silly question.

It is sometimes suggested, and some league tables seem to confirm it, that confronted with bright, dedicated girls, boys tend to shrug their shoulders and switch off. Not so here, it would seem. The boys we met and witnessed were perfectly happy to admit how keen they were to do well. It is interesting to note that the boys sometimes outperform the girls.

Games, options, the arts: One of the frequently repeated criticisms that circulate in Shropshire and beyond is that Concord has impressive facilities for sport but no-one uses them. The few football teams perform reasonably well in local leagues; rugby is on the decline. Sport is offered as a recreation, not a religion. That's not to say no interest. One boy told us that when a football match is on the television in the senior school common room (the West End), a visitor might think that Concord was a girls' school – not a boy to be seen (all watching the game). Squash and basketball flourish – we were shown the results of a three-figure thrashing the latter team dished out to a famous local public school; archery, badminton, tennis, athletics, water-polo, fencing, riding, climbing and mountain biking are on offer, with some county players. A huge and impressive sports hall, but really enthusiastic games players should look elsewhere. Lower sixth form students must now attend some physical fitness sessions – mens sana in corpore sano is not completely ignored.

Over the years the school has spread out to include some or much of the village of Acton Burnell, and there in the attractive village is one of the jewels in the Concord crown: the art building. This has no architectural merit at all beyond being functional – the jewels are kept inside, where we saw some inspirational work completed and in progress. Evidence of much imaginative and creative work in textiles, ceramics, photography, painting and graphics. Art is increasingly popular, partly because 'It uses another part of your brain and needs a different sort of concentration', partly

because an increasing number of students want to go on to study architecture and, every bit as popular a reason, because it is fun.

Unique feature is that overseas pupils can stay on during part of the Christmas and all of the Easter holidays, as well as half terms, at no extra expense

Wonderful, wonderful music school, with as good a concert hall as any we have seen. Now well over 100 students take music lessons and more than 60 sing in the choir. A student recently won the Shropshire Concerto competition and for the last two years over 200 students have been involved in charitable fundraising concerts. We were lucky enough to attend an evening concert, which was memorable not just for the high standard of the singing and playing (by all ages), but also for the obvious enjoyment shared by participants and audience alike. A short and entertaining play followed, written and produced by a student. We've seen slicker productions, but it was performed with huge intelligence and zest.

The philosophy club is hugely popular, as are Scrabble, bridge, international societies, charity club, Outreach (voluntary work) and the choir. One

Eastern European boy told us, 'In my country, if something is voluntary we run out of the door and into the street. Here I am interested and I go, perhaps because it is voluntary.'

Boarding: The 17 boarding houses, some in the village just beyond the school gates, are comfortable and well laid out; the houseparents are warmly appreciated. The superbly roomy and comfortable common room, the West End, is a popular rendezvous, encouraging school rather than cliquey house friendships and contributing to the sense of community. The food is astonishingly good and in generous proportions and variety – we know of no other school where the dining room is thickly carpeted.

A unique feature of the school is that overseas pupils can – and up to 250 do – stay on during part of the Christmas and all of the Easter holidays, as well as half term holidays, at no extra expense.

Background and atmosphere: As the principal observed, he has a beautiful view from the window of his study in the handsome 18th century building at the heart of the school campus. It is also of historical significance, since the 13th century ruined barn housed what is often referred to as the first meeting of a parliament where the Commons was seriously represented, summoned by Edward I. It gave the principal the opportunity to write that the Princess Royal in 2010 may have been the first member of the royal family to visit since 1283. T S Eliot would have delighted in the Elizabethan tomb in the parish church erected, to Sir Richard Lee, an ancestor of Robert E Lee – here, the intersection of the timeless moment.

Over the years, a village of new buildings has grown up, nearly all of them in keeping with their surroundings. The overall effect is aesthetically pleasing – no battle here between beauty and utility

The main house, which appears magically out of nowhere as you approach through the lanes of very rural Shropshire, was built in 1814 by a prominent Catholic family who, during the Napoleonic war, gave sanctuary to the Benedictine monks who later went on to found Ampleforth, Downside and Stoneyhurst.

Do the students know about all this history? Well, clearly they know some. Telling us about the excitement and beauty of the fireworks display on

The food is astonishingly good and in generous proportions and variety – we know of no other school where the dining room is thickly carpeted

the recent 5 November, one of them pointed to the ruined walls of the Parliament Barn and said, 'We succeeded this year.' Others volunteered how much they liked the beauty of the surroundings and the elegance of the main building – 'It does make a difference'.

Over the years, a village of new buildings has grown up around the campus, nearly all of them in keeping with their surroundings. The overall effect is aesthetically pleasing, blending in with the glorious wooded hills that back on to the house – no battle here between beauty and utility. The new, bright, fascinatingly-designed library is a necessary enlargement to the wonderful early 19th century gothic chapel which used to house the books, but now offers comfortable chairs and computers in its new role as a common room. In a room off the chapel (firmly locked) we were told there was a ghost – that is unconfirmed

The school was founded in Sussex in 1949. Nearly 25 years later it moved to its present site and four years later the college accepted girls for the first time. In 1983 it became a charitable trust with a board of trustees, and in order to attract the most able students a substantial scholarship programme was introduced. So nothing hasty about the way in which the school has evolved – no shoring up, no swift changes of direction, just steady building, in every sense.

It is an obviously happy school. Staff and students greet one with a smile of welcome and reveal themselves as friendly, easy conversationalists. Like puppies, if the analogy may be excused, they seem to know no fear but greet with an open freshness, expecting the same in return. This is clearly the result of mutual respect and affection between students and staff, where an impressive mixture of long-serving teachers and young risers. Students obviously cherish the strong sense of community. They had touching stories to tell about the warmth of the welcome they experienced on arrival for the first time – 'I was very anxious as the taxi drew up, but everyone was so kind when I went inside the building that after 10 minutes I suddenly remembered my parents were still in the car'. Another younger girl felt that their shared learning of English drew together students from varied backgrounds and languages.

They showed mutual physical respect – no jostling and shoving, no groups of no-good boyos huddling in the corner planning their next escapade, no boisterous calls, but plenty of vivacity and liveliness, natural courtesy without enforced restriction, boys and girls walking freely together.

Pastoral care, well-being and discipline: The high profile staff involvement is benign rather than military, with a lack of silly idiosyncratic school rules. None of the 20 or so students we asked could come up with any obvious bone of contention. They feel they are listened to and, in return, accept what has been arrived at, often through mutual consent. Trust is at the heart of it all. Smoking and drinking can lead to rustication and eventually expulsion; involvement with drugs leads to instant dismissal.

Pupils and parents: Past pupils remain deeply loyal to their school and frequently send their children to follow in their footsteps. Around 84 per cent of boarders are from overseas. Asians predominate, but a strong African contingent and a burgeoning number from Eastern Europe – in fact about 40 nationalities. A number of local day pupils from a variety of backgrounds has further increased the diversity.

Entrance: Day and boarding applications welcome for year 9, year 10 or year 12. The school is unashamedly selective, especially for year 12 candidates.

Exit: An impressive array of top universities. In 2015, 19 to Oxbridge; the London universities next along the list, alongside Warwick, Durham, Bristol and York.

Money matters: The school is generous, though not profligate, with scholarships. Details on the website.

Remarks: Those who prefer the chapel and team games approach of the traditional public school won't wish to consider Concord, as in many ways it is the antithesis. Students who seek an excellent academic grounding particularly, but not quite exclusively, in the sciences might be attracted. Those who see the future as global rather than merely western should be interested: international friendships are there for the making. A school where intellect and academia are celebrated, but not at the expense of personal happiness. It really is more than an exam factory – it could be the start of a great adventure.

The Downs Malvern

Brockhill Road, Malvern, Worcestershire WR13 6EY

01684 544100
registrar@thedowns.malcol.org
www.thedownsmalvern.org.uk
C of E

Ages: 2–13 (boarders from year 3)
Pupils: 223 (two-thirds boys)
Boarders: 43
Day: £6,576 – £15,795 pa
Boarding: £11,916 – £20,907 pa

Linked school: Malvern College

Head: Since 2009, Alastair (known to everyone as Sam) Cook. Previously head of Pembroke House in Gilgil, Kenya, he is a graduate from Westminster College, Oxford. There is something of the old London gentleman's club about his study. The comfortable chairs, leather, old school photos, stirring mountain landscapes speak of a man and school at ease with the world. Alastair Cook certainly is that and much more. He has energetically meshed three schools (The Downs merged with Malvern College Prep in 2008) together into a now seamless unit, worked on relationships with Malvern College to mutual benefit and made himself much respected and loved by parents and the children whom he places firmly at the centre of everything.

He teaches, does sport with the pre-preps and runs a swimming club. 'He is always around when the children arrive, there with his dog, at matches, just all the time', said one parent. He knows all the children, even those who have just arrived. 'You would never worry about approaching him over anything', said a mother.

Entrance: Entrance is non-selective – can support all but those with serious learning difficulties. Informal observations and interviews on taster days, combined with discussions with parents, lead to offers. Depending on the age of the child, may also request information from the current school.

Exit: More or less all take the common entrance and about 90 per cent go onto Malvern College – there is a strong flow through in curriculum terms. A smattering goes to other local schools or further flung public schools. If there is a problem academically, parents are told at an early stage and alternative plans discussed.

Remarks: The Downs has the feel of a much-loved school with the bucket-loads of unspoilt charm that you find in the very best rural prep schools. It spreads over the Malvern Hills, and the only downside we could see were the narrow roads and precipitous bends on the way there. There is a flexibility and breadth about everything. Pick-up times are to suit parents not the school, boarding can be when families need it – it is all about individuals growing up in a community that cares, and for which families too care and show respect. The curriculum has all the academic rigour combined with creativity that you would hope for – strong science in suitably equipped labs ('We get to use proper chemicals,' one 10 year old was bursting to tell us), French is all the way through with Spanish or German in years 7 and 8, Latin from year 6, art has its own kiln and there is masses of music.

There are fun and cosily low key events organised at weekends for boarders – a visit to the circus, theme parks, ice skating, Christmas shopping

All of this spills out of the classroom into the rich extracurricular programme that runs at lunchtimes, after school and on Saturday mornings (not compulsory but much loved by parents.) There is sport galore (including girls' soccer), gardening, chess, Chinese, pottery, cookery, world history, computer coding, current affairs, science in the news, touch-typing, debating, Scrabble, endless drama and music and so it goes on. Perhaps what best sums up the timeless charm is the little steam train that runs through the school grounds. The oldest miniature light railway in the world, this is a serious educational tool. The children learn to drive and maintain it. The wholesome environment too is fully utilised – the children are outside as much as possible, soaking in subliminally, we would like to think, the awe-inspiring rolling landscape, but also using it for serious geographical and scientific measurements and as inspiration for their artwork, which is of a seriously high standard.

There are plenty of links with the world outside the school. Its own first rate facilities are

The little steam train that runs through the school grounds is the oldest miniature light railway in the world. The children learn to drive and maintain it

supplemented by some use of Malvern College – its theatre, chapel, swimming pool, for instance. The choir sings locally and the school hosts national music and art events for other schools. About three-quarters of the boarders are from overseas (11 different countries when we visited) and parents commented on how well the school integrates the day pupils and the boarders. The school offers excellent preparation to overseas boarders wanting to brush up their English and understand British values ready for senior school. There are fun and cosily low key events organised at weekends for boarders – a visit to the circus, theme parks, ice skating, Christmas shopping. The flexi-boarding is popular with parents who want to give their children a taste of boarding before the full immersion as they move on to Malvern College. The boarding accommodation is in The Warren – rightly named as it rambles round the centre of the original school buildings, not smart but very homely.

Parents say the teachers are very quick to pick up on any individual needs and that they take huge pride in the children's small achievements. 'Go to Friday assemblies', parents urged us. 'Everyone is invited and we really get a sense of how much the school praises the children, how the discipline works in practice, the clear moral message the school is getting across, and we can see the opportunities all the children get for developing confidence through public speaking.'

The head told us, 'Care comes first and then education'. Parents and children praised the flexibility and common sense – no rigid rules that stunt children. Fairness is the basis of the approach to discipline. Teachers want to find out what the situation actually is by spending time talking to children involved in any difficulties – and then it is a quiet word and a real attempt to equip the children with the skills to move forward.

'So what do you give school out of 10?', we asked one boy. 'Ten+++', he said with a big grin.

Elmhurst School for Dance

249 Bristol Road, Edgbaston, Birmingham B5 7UH

0121 472 6655
enquiries@elmhurstdance.co.uk
www.elmhurstdance.co.uk

Ages: 11–19
Pupils: 173: (113 girls, 60 boys); sixth form: 69
Boarders: 163 full
Day: £18,378 – £19,047 pa
Boarding: £23,556 – £25,395 pa

Principal: Since 2010, Jessica Wheeler BA NPQH, (30s). There can't be many people in the world, never mind the UK, who combine professional dance experience with top notch educational management expertise. But Elmhurst has found it. Laban trained, she then became resident with the Laban dance company. Moved into teaching as freelance and guest teacher. Tough London comprehensive that employed her to teach dance spotted the charisma, energy and determination and she was fast-tracked to assistant headship before moving with a team of super fixers to work magic in one of the worst schools in London.

Aspirations since arriving at Elmhurst are to make it the dance school of choice in the UK and beyond. Her vision is a holistic one – to ensure talented dancers are also healthy and wise – and this is being realised through detailed, methodical planning, management and monitoring. She is stunning in every sense, and warm with it.

Brilliantly supported by artistic director Robert Parker, the driving force behind the increasingly world-class dance side of the school. He had a meteoric career through the Royal Ballet School, into the company and to Birmingham Royal Ballet as principal dancer. He knows the industry inside out and inspires huge respect in the young dancers. Coming from a Billy Elliot background, he is driven and self disciplined but also hugely charming, brimming with enthusiasm and cares passionately about the experience Elmhurst gives its young dancers. And he has collected a commercial pilot's licence along the way.

Sarah Evans is acting principal until April 2016 while Jessica Wheeler is on maternity leave.

Academic matters: Given that admission is entirely done on dance potential, results are good and the principal and new deputy are determined to continue the upward trajectory for GCSE and A level results. Just under 73 per cent of pupils gained five or more A*-C grades at GCSE including maths and English in 2015 (24 per cent A*/A). At A level, 22 per cent of grades at A*/A in 2015, 43 per cent at A*/B.

Academic staff are up against students who say all they want to do is dance, but while they might be guided by their hearts, they are surrounded by adults who know you can't dance for ever, however talented you are.

Principal and her team have brought in changes to ensure any dip in academic performance is picked up and acted upon swiftly. She is building a curriculum that will play to the strengths of young dancers who are increasingly getting their five A*-Cs at GCSE. Baseline testing for children coming in to allow individual target setting and tracking of progress year on year. Most importantly, there is now transparency for students and parents about where things are heading.

School is rightly proud of its serious A level programme – dance, music, art, English and maths are on offer – and hopes to introduce geography and biology. Most dance schools give up on academic side at 16 but there is a philosophical commitment here to the value of an academic training, heavily underpinned by the practical consideration that a student who is seriously injured at 17 or has simply grown a bit too tall must have alternatives to a dance career.

Classes are around 20 – smaller once options are chosen. A real strength, parents tell us. Some streaming for EAL students and English exams are very careful chosen to meet the individual's best needs. Teachers all comment that the discipline and focus of the dance studio infuses academic lessons. The issue is sometimes getting the students to speak at all (they are so used to the silence of dance class). Teachers are very conscious that many of the students are kinaesthetic learners and match their teaching styles to maximise this.

This a rigorous training for the most gifted and resilient. The artistic and dance side of the

curriculum takes up about a third of the students' time up to 16. Then, as they head towards their three-year National Diploma in Professional Dance, it takes up two-thirds. Training is in classical ballet but there is also a strong emphasis on jazz, contemporary and other supporting dance styles. There is an assessing out process in year 9 and year 11, when students who have not developed as dancers as expected are asked to leave. Process is done as compassionately as possible and warning given in good time for families to find an alternative. About eight per cent of the cohort assessed out across these two key stages.

Teachers comment that the discipline and focus of the dance studio infuses academic lessons. The issue can be getting students to speak after the silence of dance class

Recent major review of the programme drew on the views of the professional dance companies, ensuring students are prepared for the demands of the dance industry today. Increasing number and diversity of visiting artists, directors and choreographers, running workshops, masterclasses and lecturing to enrich the students' experience.

Partnership with Birmingham Royal Ballet (reason why Elmhurst moved to Edgbaston 10 years ago) is the icing on the cake for the artistic side of the school. It means getting top quality dance teachers is much easier than anywhere else outside London and students get the chance to perform regularly with the company. Even the youngest can audition for children's parts in productions like The Nutcracker. Also allows for easy professional exchanges.

Games, options, the arts: Dancers simply don't do risky contact sports but Elmhurst is keen for them to try everything else and takes its responsibility for overall fitness very seriously. Attractive fitness suite has been created and staff and students are encouraged to use it. They also share sports facilities and coaches with a nearby mainstream school.

With no sports fields, there are no obvious spaces for younger children to run around but school's pretty, landscaped grounds give a sense of openness to the site.

Friday afternoons have been developed as an off-timetable fun time for learning new skills and offering enrichment and students love it. Sport, art and craft, academic clubs, drama, student-led choreography projects and yoga. Keen to showcase the students' talents outside dance, the school takes part in a host of national competitions – poetry and

short story writing, for example, have seen recent successes.

Heart of the school is the excellent 250-seater theatre where the many performances take place, culminating in the outstanding end of year productions.

Boarding: Accommodation for the vast majority who board (just under nine per cent from overseas) is excellent, with many single and double rooms. When we visited the girls had set up their own beauty studio for pamper time with the help of a beauty-trained member of the house staff.

Sixth form accommodation has now moved into a purpose-built space nearer the main campus. This better links the sixth form experience and the rest of the school. Prior to this, one parent felt that when the children were younger they were in a very protected, small environment and then at 16 were suddenly launched into independent living. Students and parents commented on the recent increase in weekend activities, making the most of Birmingham, once Saturday classes have finished.

Background and atmosphere: The moment you walk into Elmhurst, you arrive in a huge dance studio, where there is invariably a class going on. From that point, you are in the ballet world. Students move around the corridors as though they are still on stage. They are graceful, hold themselves beautifully and even when they are chatting outside a maths classroom manage to group themselves as though in a corps de ballet. Most of the time they are either in dancewear or track suits in which they naturally look elegant and purposeful.

Students' health and well-being is at the core of everything and systems are in place that recognise the unique nature of vocational ballet training

Staff comment on the maturity with which students relate to adults. Students we spoke to were articulate, able to express themselves confidently and had plenty to say. No bells and the atmosphere is calm and quiet. Something about the absolute dedication to a highly disciplined vocation infuses the whole place. Drive is there in academic as well as artistic classes. 'I have never been in classes with fewer discipline problems,' one teacher told us. 'The children succeed more than they would in other schools because all the time they are asking "how can I improve?" They do that in their ballet and they have that attitude to their GCSEs too.'

School's recently developed 'live, dance, learn' slogan captures the holistic approach to dance education. This is also underlined by 'the Elmhurst way', four statements posted all over the school to remind students and staff what it is all about – choose the right attitude, be there, make someone's day and have fun. We like the sentiments – they give an adventurous and humane dimension to the gruelling discipline of the ballet world.

Pastoral care, well-being and discipline: There has been a huge amount of heartbreak over the years about 'assessing out,' the process at the end of years 9 and 11 when students are told if they are good enough at dance to carry on. Elmhurst has done much soul searching as to how they can make this stressful time as bearable as possible for everyone concerned. They have introduced pre-assessment, which allows teachers to give early indication to both students and parents if things are not looking good. In some cases it can be turned around and every opportunity is given, but sometimes, no matter how much they work, it just can't. At least everyone knows sooner rather than later and the school support swings into action, looking for other alternatives (of which there actually are a lot). Pupils may not end up as Giselle at the Bolshoi but they could still have a career in the dance industry.

Overall, Elmhurst has moved way beyond the usual pastoral care. Students' health and well-being is at the core of everything and systems are in place that recognise the unique nature of vocational ballet training. Dedicated medical centre, with qualified nursing staff, on-site GP appointments, physiotherapy services, dance psychology, dance nutritionist, sports massage and chiropractor.

The school is ahead of the game – linking with university researchers to ensure pre-emptive strategies are in place to keep the students dancing at their peak. More in the pipeline – working with international researchers to develop motivational programmes based on the psychology of success. Probably because of the emphasis on well-being, there are virtually no cases of anorexia. Principal told us that during her time at the school there have only been two diagnoses (both of which had positive outcomes) and that this is proportionately far fewer than at her last school (a large comprehensive).

Everyone stressed the very special friendships made. 'I have become a different person,' said one girl. 'I am independent and confident now that I am doing what I love.'

The school holds student inset days, much like those for staff. Outside agencies come in to run workshops and talks on subjects like e-safety, cancer, injury prevention and choreography. Staff make every effort to ensure that parents have the same information to complete the circle and ensure maximum input for the students.

'The children are simply in love with what they are doing,' one houseparent told us in an attempt to explain the enthusiasm and buzz about the boarding experience.

Pupils and parents: Most are encouraged to apply by their ballet teachers and all are there because they want to dance. There is a real warmth in relations between staff and students and between the students themselves. One boy told us: 'I have finally got friends who have the same interests as me.' Everyone we spoke to stressed the very special people here and the friendships made. 'I have become a different person,' said one girl. 'I am independent and confident now that I am doing what I love.' Parents commented on the way the school by its very nature encouraged independence. 'Our son is noticeably more mature and independent that his contemporaries at other independent boarding schools,' observed one father.

Not surprisingly, parents are quite intense. They are acutely aware of both the dangers and the strengths of opting for a specialist vocational education at 11. A number choose the school because they can see that it tries very hard to keep the academic doors open.

Parents are more obviously desperate for their children to succeed than those in other schools (although given the limited employment opportunities with the world top ballet companies, they know that not many can). This gives an edge to how they relate to the school and one or two thought some parents were reluctant sometimes to approach the school with criticisms. The last thing they want is for their child to be asked to leave. Those with children about to start auditioning for their first jobs were unsure if the school was doing enough to support them, although they recognised it did as much or more than other dance schools. A parent whose child had just had a minor injury wanted to see even more physiotherapy and counselling support. But even the most anxious parents agreed that their child couldn't be happier.

Former pupils (known as Old Elms) include actresses Helen Baxendale, Hayley Mills, Juliet Mills, Jenny Agutter and Joanna David, singer Sarah Brightman and ballet dancers Dame Merle Park, Diana Fox and Isabel McMeekan.

Entrance: Entrance is entirely on artistic merit. Auditions are held at various times in the year in the UK and overseas, although the overseas auditions are increasingly conducted via DVD submissions and then by Elmhurst staff travelling to host auditions overseas. Children will have had ballet lessons before they come and the school has links with some of the best local ballet teachers around the country. The school also runs its own associate classes for the under 11s in Birmingham, Sunderland, Manchester and Plymouth as outreach. Also visits some very challenged primary schools to talent spot. Students are re-auditioned at the end of the third year (year 9) and fifth year (year 11) and places are either confirmed or not.

Exit: More than 80 per cent of graduates enter dance related employment within six months of graduating – increasingly to join internationally prestigious companies. Ninety per cent of year 11 leavers go on to further dance training (up to 40 per cent leave after GCSEs). A graduate placement scheme has been introduce to allow students who don't gain immediate employment to stay at the school to sustain audition-ready fitness. The odd student for whom the idea of a ballet career has palled by the time they are 19 head to university. When we visited one had just got an offer from York to read English.

Money matters: Given that the fees include all the specialist ballet tuition, they are reasonable. Many UK families are able to take advantage of two government funded, means-tested, bursary/scholarship schemes. Music and dance scheme (MDS) for those aged 11 to 16 and dance and drama awards (DaDa) for the sixth form. Awards are highly competitive but all credit to the government for ensuring highly talented children can get the specialist training they need, regardless of parental income.

Remarks: The only purpose-built ballet school in the country, this is the ballet school to watch. Elmhurst isn't afraid to look beyond the intense and sometimes claustrophobic ballet world. It challenges the conventional thinking that young dancers must be silent sponges soaking up the technical knowledge of their teachers. With the school's rising academic profile and development of pupil voice, the dancers coming out of Elmhurst are critical learners ready to take ownership of their own careers.

Elmhurst is not the Royal Ballet School and in that sense it has to fight really hard to prove itself. There are no laurels to rest on here. It reinvented itself when it moved to Birmingham and it has the drive and energy of a young institution hungry for success. The Royal Ballet School is still the first choice for the majority of families but Elmhurst is biting at its heels, offering something new and very special.

The Elms School

Colwall, Malvern, Worcestershire WR13 6EF

01684 540344
office@elmsschool.co.uk
www.elmsschool.co.uk
C of E

Ages: 3–13 (boarders from 8)
Pupils: 138
Boarders: 55 full, 15 weekly
Day: £7,680 – £19,650 pa
Boarding: £22,065 pa

Head: Since September 2010, Mr Alastair J L Thomas. Mid-30s and married with two young daughters, the eldest of whom is in the early years department at the school. A degree in French from Kings' College, London was followed by a brief stint at John Lewis before he joined Kingshott Prep School, where he became head of French. Moved to The Downs School nearby as head of French and Latin before becoming deputy head at Lambrook in Ascot.

A very social animal, approachable and full of energy, very keen on sports and music, eager to update the facilities of the school while retaining its ethos of fresh air, muddy knees, and plenty of independence. Staff say he is 'making things

947

happen' and in particular cite his improvements in the profile of drama and music. He says the perception of the school is that the academics need to be strengthened – something he feels is unjustified, although he accepts that facilities need to be modernised. Teaches study skills and eats breakfast and lunch in hall with the children.

Wife, Hannah, throws herself into the life at the school, especially in the gardens, which she has transformed.

Entrance: Entrance into pre-prep as early as 3, regular intake at 7 and 8. Most children from Herefordshire, Gloucestershire, Worcestershire, Monmouthshire and Powys. A few Forces families and a handful from overseas. Entry is by assessment rather than selection, and children who are intending to board can stay the night to test the waters. No scholarships but means-tested bursaries of up to 100 per cent for those 'who could benefit from what we offer'. 'We can and do get our children into leading public schools but we also support children who struggle'.

Exit: A few girls still leave at 11 but most stay on to 13. On exit the children go to a variety of schools: Malvern College, Cheltenham College, Bryanston, Radley, Heathfield, Eton, Rugby, Winchester, Wellington, Harrow, Milton Abbey, Oundle, lots to Shrewsbury. The school achieves a good collection of scholarships including a number for art and sport. A bright child could do very well here but it is not primarily an academic school.

School farm – rural studies compulsory up to year 7– boasts a prize Hereford bull as well as Gloucester Old Spots, walked by the children round the grounds

Remarks: The oldest prep school in England, founded by Humphry Walwyn in 1614. Facing away from what passes for the main road in the village of Colwall, near Malvern, it opens out onto a site of 150 acres full of lovely green spaces and beautiful gardens. The school itself has rather the feeling of a collection of period houses that have grown together, sometimes in a slightly idiosyncratic manner. However, the school is much more than its academic buildings. For a start it has enviable sports facilities – including Astroturf, games field, swimming pool, a large sports hall, a stables of about 15-20 ponies (boarders can also bring their own) and a new outdoor riding arena. Sport obviously important – riding and shooting particularly

Boys wear cord shorts and tweed blazers, girls wear kilts and jumpers, the children go out for a walk before breakfast

so; the school has its own pistol and rifle shooting clubs. Then there is the school farm – rural studies compulsory up to and including year 7– which boasts a prize Hereford bull as well as Gloucester Old Spots, walked by the children round the grounds, a large flock of hens and a rather lovely vegetable garden. Each year group has a plot in which it is expected to grow its own vegetables. The children clearly love their involvement in the farm and take pleasure and pride in it. And they all speak very highly of the food – beef, pork and eggs come from the farm when available.

Boarding and teaching accommodation require some modernisation. The boarding facilities are a little overcrowded, although homely and tidy. Every child in the prep school (not pre-prep) has a designated bed; there are rest periods after lunch every day. This means that day children can board when they want. New science facility under construction.

The children are genuinely charming – friendly, respectful but responsive, confident and very happy indeed; well motivated and thoroughly self disciplined – we saw groups working on their art, music and sports during break, all purposeful, focussed and notably unsupervised, teachers within range if needed but leaving them to their own devices if not. There is an impressive new auditorium/theatre with some good music practice spaces, a beautiful new grand piano, and good sized music classroom attached at the back. A good art room too – full of innovative, varied and careful work. Parents say their children are very happy and they are keen on the head, whom they perceive as raising the academic standard of the school while retaining its ethos.They appreciate the variety of activities offered and the freedom of each child to 'be a little bit eccentric' if they want to.

Relatively high fees fund a staff:pupil ratio of about 1:7. Academically sound with many long-serving staff who say relationships with children are excellent, respectful but friendly and that parents are extremely supportive. Two ICT rooms, a pleasant library, not much prep as Saturday school is compulsory, and most reinforcement/prep style work is done within the classroom. Traditional curriculum includes a strong classics department. Follows a policy of moving children through classes as the need appears – the school calls this the ladder system – which can mean that the brighter sparks might spend the last two years in the top class. However, it is clear that the school is sensitive to parental concerns and in reality the majority of pupils are taught within a cohort of their own age. Groups are very small and no class is larger than 13; the smallest we saw was seven. The teaching model seems to work well and certainly destinations on exit don't point to any major hiccups.

On the whole a very traditional feel – there is something of the flavour of the Famous Five about the place – which may raise the hackles of some potential parents. Boys wear cord shorts and tweed blazers, girls wear kilts and jumpers, the children go out for a walk before breakfast and have outdoor activities every afternoon. There are no mobile phones, no cash, no sweets and no straying out of the school grounds. Chapel four times a week with visits from the local vicar and Catholic pupils taken to mass once a week. There are proper napkins at mealtimes, and grace is said. Some staff keep dogs in their classrooms and there is a 'pet palace' for the children's own rabbits and other small animals. Some parents may think it too sheltered by far, others will breathe a sigh of relief when they find it.

Weekend activities range from The Elms Tetrathlon to bugboarding to Nerf Gun War. children might also go off geocaching in the Malvern Hills, paintballing or ice skating, or on a shopping trip to Cheltenham.

A school which wears its differences from the mainstream with pride but which is now also taking seriously the need for some changes. With its farm, fields and outdoor ethos this is a glorious place to get muddy while you learn – and somehow it manages to preserve childhood while fostering independence.

Foremarke Hall (Repton Preparatory School)

Milton, Derby DE65 6EJ

01283 707100
registrar@foremarke.org.uk
www.foremarke.org.uk

Ages: 3–13 (boarding from 7)
Pupils: 523
Boarders: 66 full, 52 weekly/flexi (two thirds boys)
Day: £9,000 – £18,387 pa
Boarding: £23,815 pa

Linked school: Repton School

Headmaster: Since 2011, Mr Richard Merriman, previously headmaster of Birchfield School, co-ed prep near Wolverhampton, for 12 years, and before that head for a year of Wolborough Hill School in Devon. BSc in PE and sports science with education from Loughborough; MA in English local history from Leicester. Began his career teaching PE in Canterbury before moving to Clayesmore School as head of boys' PE and housemaster, then to Kimbolton School as director of sport. Has played cricket and hockey at county level.

Entrance: Youngest need only enrol for pre-prep and attend for day visit before starting. Virtually all pre-prep children progress through to prep. From age of 7, prospective pupils are assessed in English and maths. School takes 'broad range of ability', although keeps sights on Repton's academic requirements. When it comes to special educational needs, school says it takes a 'thoughtful and sensitive approach' and each case is decided on individual basis.

Exit: At 13 around 90 per cent go on to Repton. Others leave for schools like Denstone College, Radley, Rugby, Eton, Oundle, Abbotsholme and Cheltenham Ladies'. Foremarke is officially Repton's prep school, but pupils bound for Repton must still take common entrance or scholarship exams to get there – level playing field for all. Brightest children go into scholarship class for more intense tuition and school regularly wins a clutch of awards.

Remarks: Foremarke Hall's setting has the real 'wow' factor, with long drive sweeping up to stunning 18th Century Palladian mansion in the wilds of Derbyshire. Once a grand country house, it later became a WW1 hospital, then a WW2 cadet training unit and finally, in 1947, a school. Grounds stretch as far as the eye can see (55 acres in all) and are a fabulous mix of woodlands, walks, sports pitches and even a lake. Plenty of room, as we said last time, to stretch legs, lungs and imagination. Head of history told us that when he arrived for his interview he gazed in wonder at the grounds and thought 'can I really be this lucky?' He certainly could.

High proportion of staff live on school site. Major £6 million building programme (following close consultation with English Heritage) has seen revamped music facilities, new classrooms and new art and DT block. Aside from the main house, a very mixed bag of buildings, from ancient to modern. One of the newest is the light and airy pre-prep. Facilities include library, computer room and ultra-posh cloakrooms that have lights and water activated by sensor – so no floods! Pre-prep very keen on forest school approach, with all children spending an hour and a half in the woods every other week, building dens, counting leaves etc. Nursery children eat lunch in pre-prep hall but reception classes, year 1s and year 2s walk across to prep's dining hall with their teachers. Whilst pre-prep day finishes at 3.45pm children can enrol for activities till 6pm. Staying for pre-prep activities costs extra but it's a boon for working parents.

The school is busy, busy, busy. The school day consists of 12 25-minute lessons, with one of the loudest bells we've heard in a long time signalling the end of each class. From year 3, day pupils can either go home at 4pm or stay on till 5pm or 6pm for activities, tea and supervised prep. School offers French from year 1 and Latin from year 5. Setting by ability for maths, English and French from year 5. Pupils in upper school (years 5 to 8) taught by subject specialists. One-to-one and group support is available for those who need it. Three learning support teachers on prep staff and four learning support assistants.

Lower school (years 3 and 4) and upper school are in own self-contained areas. Average class sizes of around 16 and none larger than 20. Saturday school for year 5s upwards but year 3s and 4s can sign up for Foremarke Plus, a Saturday morning activity programme with pursuits like film-making, swimming, football, hockey on offer. Large, well-stocked library, both print and electronic. All computers on school network for security. Children's work (academic and art) on display everywhere you look.

Members of school's engineering club design and build their own electric cars and Foremarke's Racing F-24 team (supported by parents) competes all the over country

The 180-seat theatre, with fold-back seating and large stage, in constant use for music and drama. Music is key to Foremarke life, with loads of concerts, competitions and choir trips. Several current pupils are members of the National Children's Orchestra or National Youth Choir. When we arrived a visiting string quartet was encouraging young violinists in grand, high-ceilinged entrance hall.

Foremarke is a very sporty school and teachers reckon sport is 'an integral part' of the school. In recent years, pupils have won national football, hockey and rounders trophies, and cricket, netball,

swimming and fencing are all strong too. Large sports hall, football and hockey pitches, Astro, hard courts and 25m indoor swimming pool used all year round. Sport for all philosophy, with dedicated games staff supplemented by academic teachers. Extras include sailing, canoeing, horse riding, dance and golf.

School also rightfully proud of its Greenpower programme – run by the go-ahead DT department, year 7 and 8 members of school's engineering club design and build their own electric cars and Foremarke's Racing F-24 team (supported by parents) competes all over country in them. Autumn term starts with outdoor pursuits trips for years 5 to 8 – camping, team-building exercises etc. Outdoor pursuits instructors on most recent trip so impressed by the children's energy and enthusiasm that one said, 'I've never seen a group of children who are so up for it.' To which a Foremarke teacher replied: 'What do you expect? They're Foremarke, for goodness sake!'

Around 60 per cent boys, 40 per cent girls. Day pupils come from 20 mile radius (one or two from as far as Solihull and Sutton Coldfield – quite a trek). Parents a mix of local business people, farmers and some from county set too. A few boarders from abroad (some 20 per cent), including three Russian orphans who come to Foremarke for a year, financed by the Foremarke Trust (set up by former head Richard Theobald).

Loads of organised activities for boarders – swimming, dodgeball, craft, gardening etc, but in summer they're off riding bikes and playing in the woods

Boarders live in one of four boarding houses – two for boys, one for girls and one for flexi boarders, who can book in for certain days every term or on an ad hoc basis. Some even do 'home and away' boarding, going home on Wednesday nights but boarding the rest of the week. The boys' boarding houses and flexi boarding house are all part of the main school building but the girls are housed in a converted stable block. Dorms range from two to eight pupils and houses are run by houseparents, mostly with young children of their own. Family atmosphere, with houseparents testing children on Latin vocab and serving 'M-n-B' (milk and biscuits) before lights out. Youngest in bed by 8pm, then quiet reading for 20 minutes, year 8s in bed by 9.10pm and lights out at 9.30pm. Loads of organised activities for boarders – swimming, dodgeball, craft, gardening etc, but in summer they're off

riding bikes and playing in the woods. Weekends a whirl of action too – anything from 30 to 50 boarders most Saturday and Sunday nights.

Pastoral care excellent. Anti-bullying policy clearly stated in school's invaluable 'blue book', which lists everything from Foremarke's sports code for pupils (and parents!) to the school's daily routine. Assemblies held three mornings a week and a weekend service for boarders at nearby St Saviour's Church or in school. Day pupils aren't allowed to bring in electronic games, but boarders can use iPods and mobiles (no internet-enabled phones, though) in their free time. Games rooms for boarders equipped with Wii, table football etc and computers for boarders to email home. Overseas boarders are now allowed to use Skype to talk to their families (a suggestion made by the boarders' council and agreed by staff).

No prefects or head boy/head girl system. Instead children apply for and are interviewed for specific roles – pre-prep, assembly, music helpers etc. Badges for academic excellence awarded too.

Parents kept informed of children's progress with face-to-face meetings and termly reports giving grades for effort and attainment. Weekly Foremarke Flyer newsletter keeps parents updated on everything from drama productions to sports results. Parents' group, Friends of Foremarke, runs regular social get-togethers.

Foremarke allows pupils the time (and space – acres of it) to grow up in their own time. Pupils are encouraged to have a go at the myriad of activities on offer, whilst being supported and nurtured throughout. As the head of boarding told us: 'It's a great place for children who like doing things and being busy'.

Haberdashers' Monmouth School For Girls

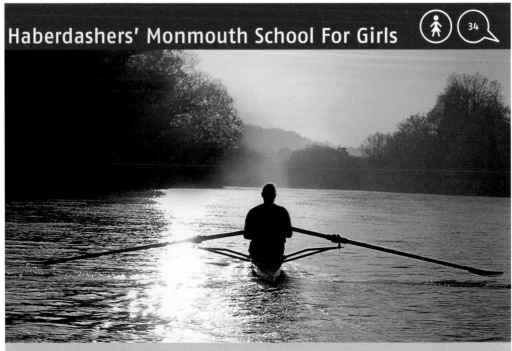

Hereford Road, Monmouth NP25 5XT

01600 711100
admissions@hmsg.co.uk
www.habs-monmouth.org

Ages: 11–18
Pupils: 478; sixth form: 136
Boarders: 137
Day: £13,524 pa
Boarding: £26,223 – £27,801 pa

Headmistress: Since April 2014, Mrs Caroline Pascoe (40s), previously head of Truro High School for Girls. Microbiology degree from Bristol, member of GB rowing squad at 1992 Barcelona Olympics, still adores sport. An officer in the RAF Volunteer Reserve. Worked in Himalayas and continues to lead high altitude trekking expeditions. Married to a very supportive husband, with a son at Monmouth School, and very involved as a family, in town and county life. Much admired and respected by the girls. She knows everyone's names and it is widely held that she 'walks the talk'. As far as encouraging girls to take risks is concerned, in addition to joining them on outdoor pursuits adventures, she learnt a One Direction tune on the recorder and played it in assembly. We were impressed, and so were her pupils. She has developed a Confidence for Life programme which is all about moving outside your comfort zone. She has also encouraged a higher profile for the creative arts on a regular basis – assemblies have been transformed and are much anticipated, being regularly used to showcase dance and music.

Her appointment of an assistant head to lead co-curricular activities is part of her drive to give breadth, as is her development of the expeditions programme. She is creating a generation of proactive girls with high levels of resilience – no worrying about a glass ceiling here. Breadth isn't just about trips to India; Caroline also wants to keep raising academic horizons – 'Girls don't read enough after year 10, ' she tells us. 'We want to see a continuing love of learning here'. She is also committed to building the boarding, which has grown since her arrival.

A can-do, action head, Caroline leads from the front and her constant presence round school, from eating with the girls to supporting everything they are involved in, creates a buzz around the place. The energy and pace you feel everywhere here is coming from the top. Parents find her very approachable and feel she has ambition for the school to drive it forward to greater things.

Academic matters: The results at GCSE and A level are very good and the school says it achieves this without putting the girls under too much pressure. In 2015, 74 per cent A*/A grades at GCSE and 53 per cent at A level. Art, modern languages, maths and science are popular choices. At sixth form level,

Monmouth School for boys and the girls' school come together, allowing 30 subjects to be on offer across both schools, which ensures virtually everyone gets the combination of subjects they want. It means some girls will be taught in some subjects at the boys' school and boys at the girls'. This works well. The girls say they like the different perspective the boys bring to subjects and comment on an often-repeated observation that it is noticeably that the girls think before they speak, unlike the boys.

The girls really struggled to think of naughty things that anyone did. The worst seems to be not doing your kitchen duty or being late to breakfast

Parents say that the school doesn't heap unreasonable amounts of pressure on the girls, but that doesn't mean that HMSG has any lower expectations that the big London day schools, with which parents were often comparing it. Learning support is available on an individual/shared basis from suitably qualified staff. The girls say teachers will always make time for them if they need a bit of extra help on a less formal basis. Most departments run surgeries for individual help, too.

Links with outside organisations enhance the academic work. Renishaw plc sponsored a STEM competition last year that led to further work supported by the school staff, which led in turn to two girls exhibiting their invention at the NEC, pitching it on Dragons' Den and selling to national retailers.

Games, options, the arts: The school has a deserved reputation for being very sporty, and clearly even the girls who aren't games mad are very proud of the reputation. Those girls told us that respect and resources are given to the arts as well and there is a policy of introducing girls to different sports to help them all find some physical activity that appeals. Girls regularly represent the region and Wales in a variety of sports. One parent told us that her daughters had asked the PE staff if they could start a gym club. Within a few months they had it – well resourced and competing nationally.

Drama and dance are popular, with excellent facilities shared with the local community. Music is strong with 50 per cent taking some additional music lessons. The annual interhouse Eisteddfod gives an extra frisson to these activities. The glass atrium is hung with house flags on such occasions. Art is popular and high quality – lots is displayed around the school. Parents praise the standard of the drama productions.

At senior level, most of the extracurricular performing arts are done with the boys' school along with CCF, shared visiting speakers and a number of societies. It would be nice to have even more, the girls tell us. D of E and other local community service opportunities as well as fundraising for overseas projects. Girls are committed to these ventures both for their own personal development but also, we felt, out of a genuine desire to serve others.

Boarding: The boarding houses are on the school site and are purpose built. They are strikingly attractive and friendly in feel. From year 11 up, girls have rooms of their own. Below that they share in twos or threes. There is a lot organised for the boarders outside lesson time, some trips including the boys' school. Much sport goes on at weekends and in the evenings. There is shopping, cinema trips, salsa evenings, BBQs and generally a purposeful but relaxed atmosphere, which is very appealing and might account for the very low incidence of illness, despite the attractions of the medical facilities – there are soft toys on every bed. It might also account for the equally low level of law breaking. The girls really struggled to think of naughty things that anyone did. The worst seems to be not doing your kitchen duty or being late to breakfast (punishment – go in early the next day).

Boarding is flexible but that hasn't meant the school opts out of providing after-school and weekend activities. This is an active school with high energy pursuits on offer throughout the days and weekends. The meal menu is wide and quality good with meals served in an attractive extended dining room.

Background and atmosphere: Founded in 1892, to offer girls the opportunities that Monmouth School

had provided since 1614, the Girls' School was funded by the original bequest of a local man, William Jones, a member of the Haberdashers' Company who made his fortune in Russian. The livery company is responsible for the school and provides financial support and stability, which reassures staff and has allowed for continual development of facilities. Although the boys' school is not far away, the girls' school has its own extracurricular facilities such as an Astroturf and swimming pool. The original Victorian buildings have been enhanced by imaginative, modern expansions such as a glass atrium and sixth form centre.

The school works hard at being a part of the Monmouth community and from those we spoke to, it is liked and respected. We arrived in the middle of the Monmouth Literary Festival – Carol Ann Duffy had been speaking the night before – which is organised entirely by the sixth forms of the three Monmouth secondary schools, the two Habs schools and Monmouth comprehensive. A remarkable achievement involving contacting agents, organising programmes, ticket sales and so on. There is another serious collaboration through the Monmouth Science Initiative, where state and independent schools work together with Cardiff University to bridge the gap between A level science and university science.

There is a lovely sixth form centre with study areas and a cool common room café – 'The boys love it', the girls tell us. 'We have to remind them that they are here for lessons not to drink hot chocolate all day'. Sixth formers still wear a uniform, suits, and tell us that they like it as they don't want to feel separate from the rest of the school. The drop-out rate between year 11 and the sixth form is quite small – girls can't wait to wear suits and go to the café, we are told.

The location is very inspiring. You feel the fresh, clear air from the Welsh hills permeates the whole ethos

Pastoral care, well-being and discipline: The atmosphere is one of calm and sunny good manners. The relationships between the girls and staff are universally praised and we saw lots of warm and relaxed exchanges. 'They are interested in you and what you want to make of your life', sixth formers say. We heard about the much-anticipated annual satirical review put on by staff as part of the sixth form Christmas entertainments, a good indication of strong relationships. There are anti-bullying ambassadors and a buddy scheme working between year 7 and year 13. The girls tell us they would like even more integration between year groups. Prefects apply for their role and are eager for an opportunity to give back to the school. 'It is the school empowering us to experience responsibility', we were told by a successful applicant. The head has opened up the subject of social media and bullying and the girls are aware of the effects this can have and are being helped to combat it. The school is less focused on punishment and more concerned that the girls understand the dangers and causes.

A coloured card system operates for minor disciplinary infringements throughout the school – three yellow cards for something like late homeworks leads to a detention. 'It is really to help us get caught up,' the girls say. There are orange cards for uniform matters – zero tolerance for nail varnish: it gets that naughty. Parents say problems are nipped in the bud early and the staff are open and honest in their communications on pastoral issues. Pastoral care is outstanding, we were told.

Pupils and parents: Pupils come from a wide local area. There are buses coming from Cardiff, the north Bristol area, the Monmouthshire border, Hereford, Newport and the Ledbury area. The calendars for both day and boarding pupils are coordinated across the five Haberdashers' Monmouth schools, which is clearly a huge advantage for parents.

The bursary scheme ensures a good social mix. There are émigrés from the home counties, old Monmouth families, families with very little in the way of income and lots with both parents working hard to afford the fees. Staff commented to us that you find none of the sense of entitlement that some schools engender – pupils seem grateful to be at the school.

The head takes parents' surveys very seriously and we were impressed by how positive she was about parental criticisms. She wants the school to be on a constant improvement journey and uses parental feedback to keep raising the game. School council is valued by her as well as by the girls. This is an example of a school that pays more than lip service to parent and pupil voices. Parents complimented the school on its proactive approach to keeping them aware of current problem issues such as e-safety. 'They are taking care of my education as a parent,' one mother told us. Parents' view of the HMSG 'product' is one of engaging, confident, interesting girls who are keen to try new things, unaffected and enthusiastic. We would agree.

Former pupils include Lisa Rogers, Sandra Huggett and Jackie Ballard MP.

Entrance: About a third from their own prep school, Inglefield House, a third from other independent schools and a third from maintained schools. Entry is by entrance exam, interview and junior school report. At 13+ by own exam or common entrance. Some join at sixth form following an interview and good GCSE results.

Exit: There is less of the problem than some girls' schools face with large numbers of year 11 leaving for mixed schools. A few will go for financial reasons or because A levels really aren't for them, but most stay on for the final two years. Sixth formers and parents say the school prepares girls very well for university and beyond. There are lots of links with old girls – staff meet up semi-formally with those who are London-based very regularly. There are plenty of opportunities to visit universities and the girls are starting to think about the possibility of apprenticeships. At the moment virtually everyone goes to university – two to Cambridge in 2015, the majority to Russell Group universities and others to do niche high quality courses such as stage management and technical theatre, agri-food marketing, anthropology and media. A number study science,

including medicine and engineering. A few go overseas – University of Hong Kong, Yale, École Hotelière de Lausanne, Maastricht in recent years.

Money matters: One in five are receiving financial assistance through a means-tested scheme that reassesses every year from endowment income.

Remarks: Habs has been in Monmouth for 400 years and reinvented itself over that time. The current structure is a selling point, so parents tell us. They like the all through concept with co-ed for the little ones in Agincourt and at sixth form level. Parents frequently used the word 'honest' when describing the school. You feel the fresh, clear air from the Welsh hills permeates the whole ethos. The location is very inspiring. From the sports fields you look out along the Wye Valley and from anywhere in the school you have views down to the rest of Monmouth and beyond. It is a lovely place to live – for the boarders, but also for staff and for families moving into the area.

We wondered if it was all a rather awful shock when girls had to move outside the Monmouth bubble, but we were assured that the school was anything but parochial. There are lots of visits to far-flung parts of the globe and the head's background in overseas work has re-emphasised the idea of a global village. Having said that, there is no doubt that Monmouth feels a very long way from Cardiff or Bristol, where a number of day girls live – no doubt part of its appeal for many families. It has the ambitious feel of a big city school without any of the traffic jams and tower blocks.

One parent summed up the feel of the school well: 'HMGS may lack a little of the pomp, ceremony and glitz of some public schools, but what you get is genuine care and a commitment to help your child reach her potential, whatever that may be.'

Lincoln Minster School

The Prior Building, Lincoln LN2 5RW

01522 551300
senior@lincolnminsterschool.co.uk
www.lincolnminsterschool.co.uk

Ages: 11–18 (junior boarding from year 3)
Pupils: 366; sixth form: 121
Boarders: 66
Day: £12,651 pa
Boarding: £23,133 – £29,856 pa

Principal: Since September 2015, Mark Wallace, previously principal deputy head at Kingston Grammar. Studied maths with computer science at Queen's Belfast; began his teaching career at Cambridge House Boys' Grammar before joining

Caterham School, where he spent 14 years. Has played hockey at national level; coaches this and cricket as well as playing golf, enjoying TT racing and gardening. Three children.

Academic matters: Spacious, airy classrooms and eight impressive labs in the new build, some with far-reaching views across the Trent plain. All very well-equipped with state-of-the-art IT equipment creating an environment that's clearly serious about teaching and learning. There is a real pride about the place with plenty of quality work on display and a general sense of order and rigour, all wrapped up with warmth and bonhomie. Wide corridors with carpets and plenty of natural light create an almost corporate feel – more businesslike and less school-like than the norm. Parents recognise the importance of the huge value added by this mixed ability school – seems it is down to strong pupil/teacher relationships and lots of individual support and attention as and when required. In 2015, 38 per cent A*/A grades at GCSE, and 64 per cent A*-B and 36 per cent A*/A grades at A level. The three sciences are taught in rotation at key stage 3, then separately and fully beyond that, leading to plenty of As and A*s in triple sciences.

French and Spanish taught, other languages occasionally on demand as extracurricular options. Basic range of subjects on offer at GCSE with most studying 8 or 10 subjects. Wider range of subjects at AS and A2, all the usual trad subjects plus a few less common ones such as graphics, psychology, sociology and travel and tourism.

Average class size 17, max 24. Pupils say teachers have 'an infectious passion for their subject'; typical is the Earl Grey Society – other teas (and biscuits) are available – an extracurricular activity run by the English dept offering university seminar-type sessions to discuss a shared love of literature and broaden both reading and horizons. There is a clear work ethic; teachers look busy and focused, as do pupils, but no sense of hothousing. A chilled-out common room for sixth form sits alongside a silent study area, with a teacher on duty and plenty of uni prospectuses and careers advice around to guide and inspire.

Choir rehearsals take place on four weekday mornings and weekends are carefully balanced with 'a busy one followed by a lighter one' to allow for a life outside school

Easy access to the local university brings additional academic range and scope; use of their library for sixth form extended projects, masterclasses and an introduction to engineering are all there to be experienced and enjoyed. Mild and moderate learning difficulties catered for; around 80 identified as SEN, a handful have statements, rest mainly dyslexia, dyspraxia, occasionally ASD. No extra charge for specialist support.

Games, options, the arts: Music plays a very large part in the school's curriculum with its close relationship to the cathedral – they say you don't have to be musical to come here but it 'still touches you'. The director of music's role is (uniquely) divided between the cathedral and school, which provides 40 choristers (20 boys and 20 girls), so standards are incredibly high, with a number of orchestras,

bands and groups making for a busy concert programme and occasional radio and TV appearances. Cathedral choristers enjoy a busy life and can be day or boarding; choral scholarships available, normally 50 per cent off full fees (boarding and tuition). Choir rehearsals take place on four weekday mornings and weekends are carefully balanced with 'a busy one followed by a lighter one' to allow for a life outside school. Chamber choir performed on Howard Goodall's chart-topping album Inspired.

GCSE express music course for year 9 pupils allows them to complete the full course two years early. Cookery is an adventurous experience here: teacher is ex-military so only for the brave. Butcher a chicken? 'Why not? After all, it's cheaper than buying chicken portions so great prep for uni,' say grinning pupils. Wealth of extracurricular choices in addition to the music options; all the usual plus rarer alternatives such as rowing and remote-control car club. 'Flamboyant' head of art so plenty of wow factor in that department, stunning work on display. Drama is thriving and all year groups are encouraged to take part; it's 'taken seriously here,' say staff, and taught to A level.

Sports field is a short walk away in Lincoln's conservation area and the newish sports hall and new Astroturf have fuelled the school's already high standard of team and individual performance. Rugby and hockey are king, but football, netball, basketball and tennis also popular. Plenty of recent success in rugby 7s as county plate winners in three age groups and county champions in U15 girls' cricket. Also has riding teams who compete regularly at events across the country and, just to prove this really isn't an unsophisticated backwater at all, polo now on offer and growing in popularity, with parents too, who particularly enjoy the après polo activities. Sailing offered as an extracurricular activity; a high level of involvement in the Duke of Edinburgh Award scheme and a very full outdoor and adventurous programme; Young Enterprise regional finalists.

Small-ish city but school has big ideas and knows that there is a big world out there, so no sense of isolation. Rugby tours to Italy, geography trips to Iceland and Switzerland, annual ski trips and more besides extend opportunities to explore and learn about the world beyond – but these are grounded young people; fundraising to cover their own costs is not unusual here and is to be admired. Project India is a venture close to their hearts, working to provide essential aid in Southern India. Sixth formers visit for up to three weeks at a time to create buildings for the deaf, community cafés, clearing land for fruit farms and teaching English, with the occasional cricket match thrown in just for fun.

Boarding: As part of United Learning (formerly UCST), it now houses boarders – most seniors, just four junior pupils – on four sites, three on school campus. Latest, The Mount, for years 3-8, including choristers, opened May 2015. Bucking the trend with boarding on the increase, a few Forces children remain; boarders are a 50/50 home-grown and overseas mix; full, weekly or flexi boarding all available. Plenty of investment in boarding; it's holding its own in a dwindling local market and recent investment is paying off as boarding houses are revamped and refurbed on a rolling programme; big expenditure on girls' boarding over last few years. Serious funding in this area indicates a real commitment to boarding into the future. Weekends for boarders involve cinema, theatre, 10-pin bowling trips, barbecues on sunny evenings and the annual summer camp is a real highlight; midweek there are plenty of opportunities to join a smorgasbord of school activities, go swimming, learn karate or join the Guides or Scouts.

Background and atmosphere: Formed in 1996 through a merger of the Cathedral School for Boys, St Joseph's School for Girls and Stonefield House School. In 2011, St Mary's Preparatory School merged to form the new preparatory school.

Polo now on offer and growing in popularity – with parents too – who particularly enjoy the après polo activities. Sailing offered as an extracurricular activity

Christian-based but attracts all faiths and none. Religious services (including communion) held at the Minster, but not an issue, nobody pulls out. Five school houses, named after cathedral cities, attract fierce loyalty and healthy competition between pupils of all ages. A mix of building styles and eras, some rented from the Dean and Chapter; hugely attractive and spacious new buildings sit cheek by jowl with the old; a converted Victorian school building is wonderful for drama with its bell tower, leaded windows and brick arches and sits alongside a stunning contemporary £10m music school, recital hall and sports hall. It is hard to tell which are school buildings and which are not: they all seem to intermingle across this concentrated historic quarter of the city, which includes the Minster and, interestingly, a school-owned pub. The profits from the pub provide useful additional funds for scholarships; anxious parents need not worry, it's not a place for pupils, but thirsty locals can enjoy a drink here, safe in the knowledge that they are supporting a good cause.

Unsurprisingly in this somewhat ancient and crowded setting, car parking is extremely limited.

Apart from special occasions and evening events, when the playground can be used, it's street parking for all. Sixth-formers bemoan the lack of parking (and the army of zealous local traffic wardens), wise parents manage it by avoiding the journey altogether and sensibly taking advantage of the school transport: 12 buses carry pupils on from all directions, as far afield as Nottingham.

School buildings are in the historic quarter of the city, which includes the Minster and, interestingly, a school-owned pub whose profits go towards scholarships

Pupils (unprompted) tell us that 'the food here is very good' – huge spacious dining room, part of which becomes a café at break time, all very civilised. Themed lunches are popular, especially Italian day.

Pastoral care, well-being and discipline: Good manners are important, as is respect; 'Bullying, incorrect uniform and chewing gum are big no-nos,' say pupils. All seems quite low key but take it as read that anything more serious than that is prohibited and brings severe reprimands. Tutors are always on hand to help pupils and answer parents' concerns. A pupil mentoring system works well and means that prefects, too, are approachable, even by the younger members of the school.

'Business wear' is the order of the day for sixth form and they are an unusually smart lot. Below sixth form it's a uniform with an attractive and

distinctive striped blazer (a view not necessarily shared by pupils) for both boys and girls. Good to see so many sixth formers in school during our summer term visit – it's unusual during what is normally regarded as a term of study leave by most schools. It's a healthy sign when pupils are offered taught revision classes and extra individual tuition right through and up to exams, and wisely they grab it with both hands – they simply want to be here.

Pupils and parents: Large number of first time buyers with a mix of professionals and business-people – farmers, hospital and university staff, Siemens employees – most working locally, plus a fair-sized commuter set heading to London and other cities beyond the county borders.

Parents tell us that they like the fact that this is a 'through school', ie 3-18, and are also fans of the school's commitment to 'old-fashioned principles of respect, discipline, manners, consideration of others and kindness – right from the earliest stages'. Parentmail system keeps them up-to-date with info and news.

Thoroughly charming yet sensibly grounded pupils, hard working and ambitious, unafraid to look you in the eye and chat easily. Notable former pupils include: Jack Harvey (motor racing), Lizzie Simmonds (Olympic swimmer), Alice Ross (pastry chef at Michel Roux's Le Gavroche), Sophie Allport (renowned ceramic designer and businesswoman), John Scarborough (education officer, Cameron Mackintosh).

Entrance: The majority of pupils come from the Minster's own prep school; other popular sources include St Hugh's Prep, Woodhall Spa and Highfield's Prep, Newark, plus a myriad of other prep and junior schools. External applicants attend a personal assessment day in January, the intention being to indicate and understand the breadth of ability or potential, although entrance is not based purely on ability.

Exit: Over 80 per cent go through to sixth form. Wide variety of university destinations: in 2015, nearly 30 per cent to Russell Group including two to Oxbridge. Award-winning virtual careers library, which can be accessed from computers outside the school, is a tremendous resource for leavers.

Money matters: Well-endowed under the auspices of United Learning. Scholarships for academic, art, music and sport. Means-tested United Learning assisted places.

Remarks: Forget preconceptions of Lincolnshire being a flat and remote county: you can commute to London from here without too much difficulty, indeed many do; and the school occupies a magnificent setting high on a hill overlooking the rooftops of the historic quarter of the city with views of the Minster from (almost) every window. A happy and successful product of a four-way merger, no doubt tricky at the time but thriving now that the dust has well and truly settled, and the place ticks like a well-oiled machine.

Loughborough Grammar School

Burton Walks, Loughborough, Leicestershire LE11 2DU

01509 233233
registrar@lesgrammar.org
www.lesgrammar.org

Ages: 10–18
Pupils: 1,005; sixth form: 300
Boarders: 70 full
Day: £11,433 pa
Boarding: £24,786 pa

Headmaster: Since 1998, Mr Paul Fisher MA (mid-50s). Came via Prior Park College in Bath and Marlborough College before becoming headmaster of Mount St Mary's College and thence to Loughborough. Married to Helen, who teaches Spanish and French in the school, with two boys. Read classics at Christ Church, Oxford, where he won a cricket blue, played for the university second XV and ended up as president of Vincent's, the élite sporting club of the university. Later he played cricket for Middlesex and Worcestershire. Has run the London and Paris marathons.

A naturally modest man – we had to prise his sporting triumphs out of him – he is not a red-faced hearty nor the lapel-tugging, bullfrog sort of headmaster who booms out educational edicts from Olympus. The word 'fun' appears more often than 'leagues' in his vocabulary. Thoughtful and quietly spoken, his main concern seemed to be how, with so many boys in the school and such a compact day, he can get to know them better. He lunches with them as often as time allows, seeking 'ground level information' and 'taking the temperature of the day'; he teaches RE to year 10 pupils, 'Islam and philosophical things, such as free will', and 'wanders around a lot,' as one boy put it. 'An excellent listener,' one parent told us; 'surprisingly accessible,' said another.

The day we visited, the A level candidates were attending their last day of lessons before retreating for study leave. An ideal opportunity, one would have thought, for hearing the truth about the headmaster and the school. Without a flicker of hesitation, all the boys we approached spoke glowingly of the whole set up, including the headmaster. 'Lightness of touch', 'good sense of humour,' 'is interested in us' were the sort of comments which cropped up over and over again. Judging by the easy banter that staff and head were indulging in over the very good lunch we had in the

boys' refectory, relations with staff are good, too. It certainly feels a very happy school.

Academic matters: As with much we encountered at Loughborough, the academic programme is carefully thought out. For the first three years the emphasis seems to be on learning for pleasure – or the pleasure of learning. Breadth rather than an exclusive drive towards good grades is the aim; a genuine wish to stimulate a sense of enquiry and wonder as well as accumulating knowledge. Clubs and societies outside the classroom seek to support that – see the list of clubs and activities below. 'We aim to eliminate any barriers surrounding the classroom,' one member of staff told us. All boys take nine GCSEs in addition to a further programme of religion and philosophy, PHSE and outside activities. Some Latin and less Greek is taken at GCSE and Latin is on offer at A level.

Breadth of choice is encouraged and if there are difficulties matching a pupil's choice of subjects, the school will seek to accommodate them. There's a genuine wish to stimulate a sense of enquiry

The excellent website and prospectus give generous information about the academic side of the school. Those who thrive on statistics can positively gorge themselves, revelling in small percentage differences between the popularity of subjects from year to year and the percentage of A and B grades. They will see that, in general, the sciences, maths, politics and economics seem the most popular, but they will also note that 28 A level subjects are on offer and they do not include raffia dolly making or flower arranging. Breadth of choice is encouraged and where difficulties matching a pupil's choice of subjects, the school will seek to accommodate. For those who still insist on reading league tables, Loughborough scores well. In 2015, 61 per cent A*/A grades at GCSE and 45 per cent at A level. Facilities in support of their enlightened approach are excellent, with a delightful and much-used library – not quite as big as it looks in the pictures – a superb language laboratory and a state-of-the-art new science complex; new maths building under construction.

Games, options, the arts: Plenty of sport and healthily enjoyed, 'though you don't have to be good at sports to make friends,' a youngish boy told us. Rugby probably the most popular game but has also had some notable successes at football, both locally and at international level, cricket, cross-country, basketball and tennis. In addition to pitches close to the school buildings, about 40 acres of specially-levelled games pitches, a cross-country course and a grass athletics track near Quorn, about four miles away. Pupils are driven there and back. The scene from the superb pavilion is most impressive.

Debating, chess and bridge are highly popular; bridge players have been particularly successful, winning honours in national and international competitions

Extracurricular activities include a thriving CCF section, the popular D of E award scheme, debating, chess and bridge, the last three obviously helping to break down any barriers that might surround the classroom. Bridge, in particular, popular and successful, with players moving on to national and international honours. We were assured 300 chess players – amongst other things, a thinking school.

An excellent drama studio, of which the school is justifiably proud, leads on to 'stunning productions' in conjunction with the girls' High School. The new music school, run by a wildly enthusiastic head of music, has seen more and more people learn instruments (year 6 pupils all do). Singing is increasingly popular and the choirs and orchestras go out and about nationwide and overseas.

Boarding: Two separate boarding houses run by housemasters with their own families, both in the heart of the school. School House, for senior pupils, has room for over 30, of whom about 65 per cent

Family feel further enhanced by the cleaning ladies (some see their posts as hereditary) who obviously care about the boys and know them well

are from at least five different countries. The rest tend to be Forces children. Housed in a delightfully quirky, mid-19th century listed building, it was the headmaster's house, as witness the mosaic floor in the hallway and the welcoming Latin message over what was originally the front door – ask the housemaster to translate, if you can't: he is primed. No longer a green baize door – he and his wife (a teacher) live cheek by jowl with their extended family. The boys' accommodation is approached via an amusing rabbit warren of stairs and passageways and comprises shared bedsits before seniors gravitate to rooms of their own. Pleasant recreational facilities as well as kitchen and laundry. A resident house tutor. The genuine family feel is further enhanced by the cleaning ladies, some of whom see their posts as hereditary, obviously care about the boys and know them well – another example of that community feeling.

Denton House for juniors (10–13 years) takes up to 18 boarders and is decorated cheerfully and imaginatively in a building which was once a private house and still retains that feeling. In addition to full boarding, flexi and weekly boarding are welcomed when space is available. Lots of weekend activities on offer. Occasionally boys choose to do a stint of boarding in order to help them feel even more at home in the school. Pupils from abroad receive support and encouragement from the housemaster's wife, a trained EAL teacher. Cautious noises about increasing the amount of boarding and both buildings are in line for refurbishment.

Background and atmosphere: Founded in 1495, moved up to its present site in 1850 and now part of Loughborough Endowed Schools, sharing the delightfully spacious and leafy campus with Loughborough High School for girls and Fairfield School, the co-educational prep. Though independent of each other, the three schools share the same governing body and a number of facilities.

For those parents who cannot decide between co-ed or single sex, Loughborough could be the answer. The main quad with its Tennysonian Tower and cherry trees is a delightful fusion of old and new buildings blending in sensitively across the centuries. In fact, the whole campus feels more like a university, an impression confirmed by the school's approach to the pupils, who are treated as burgeoning adults. Sixth formers, currently having their designated centre upgraded, may have lunch in the school refectory or in town and the house system is designed to be 'healthily competitive and fun' (that word again).

Boys come from a wide variety of ethnic backgrounds, but diversity seems genuinely celebrated and seen as an opportunity to enlarge mutual understanding. Boys look you in the eyes and smile. They seem very much at ease with each other and the staff – that includes non-teaching staff as well. The departure of the head groundsman after nearly 40 years of loyal service was marked by a ceremony at the top of the tower while below the entire school gathered to cheer him – a real community.

Pastoral care, well-being and discipline: 'I think the best thing about this school is that they trust you,' a leaver told us. Another said, 'I'll be a bit sad to leave but I'm ready now. I think they've prepared me well.' He then added wryly, 'Well, I hope they have.' Small tutor groups, not selected on purely academic grounds, help form friendships and understanding not only between pupils but also with staff who seem, in general, much appreciated – 'They always seem to have time to help, even the weird ones'. A good anti-bullying policy in place, but all the boys we spoke to said that it really wasn't an issue and that they felt supported and understood. One or two offered the theory that going home in the evenings helped diffuse any tensions. All sixth form boys are made prefects, giving them a sense of responsibility and belonging; senior prefects are elected by the boys concerned – a system which seems to work well and is another example of the important part trust plays in the running of the school.

One boy told us, 'I'll be a bit sad to leave but I'm ready now. I think they've prepared me well.' He then added wryly, 'Well, I hope they have'

Pupils and parents: Not a school for toffs; one which absorbs about 25 per cent of boys from ethnic minority backgrounds and a wide cross-section of parents. The ones we spoke to felt involved and part of the community. Buses come in daily from a radius of about 20 miles as well as the local area. Boys return home at 4pm unless they are staying on for extra-mural activities. Approx 35 boys from Hong Kong and mainland China as well as other parts of the world. An impressive variety of famous Old Boys testifies to the feeling that Loughborough does not do pigeon-holing eg Shiv Thakor, cricketer, Amit Guptor, film director, Felix Buxton, dancer, and Ben Hammersley, journalist.

Entrance: By own examination at 10, 11 and 13 or CE at 13. Selective, more on the grounds of suitability than academic ability. It does not set out to be a specialist school for learning difficulties but all boys are screened for dyslexia on entry and help is available from learning support. About 50 per cent of pupils come from Fairfield, Loughborough's prep school, and the rest from primaries and other preps. Caters for pupils who transfer at age 10 by having a year 6 class which is integrated into the senior school to prepare them socially and academically for continuing into year 7.

Sixth form entry is based on GCSE results. Conditional offers made after interview with the headmaster, report from present school and predicted GCSE grades. Overseas pupils are required to sit examinations in those subjects they wish to study at A level.

Exit: About 10 to 15 per cent leave after GCSE, usually in pursuit of courses not available at Loughborough. Virtually all sixth formers go on to university: two to Oxbridge in 2015 (archaeology and anthropology and medicine) and nine other medics. London unis, Durham, Exeter, Birmingham, Bath and Newcastle popular. No outstanding subjects, but a greater proportion reading for science-based degrees than the humanities.

Money matters: A number of scholarships at different levels are available – don't be afraid to ask. A 25 per cent boarding fee remission for Forces children.

Remarks: A civilised school at ease with itself but constantly looking to improve. Ask to see a copy of the regular newsletter from governors to parents and guardians, a document which aims to keep the whole community aware of the thinking behind decisions and aspirations – not many schools do that. A happy school where boys are encouraged to pursue worthwhile individual goals, while having fun. Highly regarded locally and by connoisseurs further afield. A special community preparing boys sensitively and intelligently for university and beyond.

Maidwell Hall

Maidwell, Northampton NN6 9JG

01604 686234
headmaster@maidwellhall.co.uk
www.maidwellhall.co.uk

Ages: 7–13
Pupils: 124
Boarders: 108 full, 2 flexi
Day: £15,600 pa
Boarding: £24,600 pa

Headmaster: Since 2001, Mr Robert Lankester MA PGCE (50s). Educated at Elstree School, Charterhouse and Selwyn College, Cambridge, where he read history. Worked as city stockbroker for seven years before deciding he wanted to teach – 'the best decision I ever made.' After PGCE at Durham, he spent 13 years at Uppingham, 10 as a housemaster. Enthusiastic and focused, with firm, no-nonsense approach. School has thrived under his leadership and introduction of girls in 2010 – 'a very exciting development,' he says – has gone smoothly. Head says girl numbers won't go above 50 at the very most. He's adamant that Maidwell will remain a small, full boarding school but transitional boarding for two or three nights has recently been introduced as an option for local day children. Loves teaching and still manages to fit six periods of geography for CE pupils into his busy week. 'He is an exceptional headmaster,' one parent told us. 'He believes in bringing the best out of every child.' Married, with two grown-up children. Carey, his charming Montessori-trained wife, is very involved

in school life. She is in charge of the girls (housemistress will be appointed once the new girls' house opens), head of swimming, teaches drama and does a host of boarding duties (boys and girls). Family lives in leafy wing of the main school.

Entrance: 'We have a very broad intake,' says the head. 'Our target is to get the pupils into their first choice of school at 13 and we've succeeded in that for the last 13 years.' Boys and girls arrive from pre-preps and state primaries and visit a year prior to entry for informal assessment – maths, reading, spelling, non-verbal reasoning and relaxed 10 minute chat with head. Smattering of scholarships and bursaries available – though 'there isn't a bottomless pit of gold.' Head keen to dispel the notion that pupils have to be extrovert, outdoorsy types. 'Any child would thrive here and it's unusual for me to say no,' he says, while his wife comments that the pupils are 'nurtured and looked out for.' All have a 24-hour boarding trial the summer before they start, 'just to get them

(and their mothers) used to the idea.' Most pupils live up to two hours away and are from rural areas (Lincs, Notts, Rutland, Leics, Cambs, East Anglia etc) but a few come from London area. Handful (under 10 per cent) from abroad, including Spain, Japan, China, Thailand and Russia. Some children of Old Maidwellians. Old boys include Earl Spencer and former poet laureate Sir Andrew Motion.

Exit: Boys progress to a wide variety of senior schools, including Uppingham (most popular), Eton, Radley and Stowe. School reckons girls are likely to choose co-ed schools like Stowe and Oundle, or single-sex Queen Margaret's, York and Tudor Hall. Two or three scholarships a year.

Remarks: Eleven miles north of Northampton, in a pretty country village. School was founded in 1913 and moved to present 44-acre site in 1933. Main building is an imposing 17th century turreted mansion overlooking its own lake (pupils must pass swimming test before they are allowed anywhere near it). Spacious grounds mean children can build camps, climb trees (the favourite tree is called Radar) and play hide and seek and British Bulldog in their spare time. We visited on Shrove Tuesday and arrived in the middle of the annual (and hotly-contested) house pancake race. Lots of debate about how high the pancakes must be tossed, with welly-clad director of studies joking 'there may have to be a stewards' inquiry.'

Food gets the thumbs–up – tradition of one boiled sweet after lunch still firmly in place (plastic tub solemnly passed from pupil to pupil) and £1 of tuck on Sundays

Classes are small. Maximum 15, but more likely to be around 12. Two streams in each year group (maths setted separately) and lessons taught by subject specialists. Traditional curriculum (including French and Latin, and Greek for senior pupils). Extra one-to-one SEN provision (from three-strong SEN team) at extra cost for those with mild dyslexia and dyspraxia. Despite gloomy headlines about reluctant readers, most pupils read avidly. They all have 20-minute reading period every day after lunch, either in dorms or outside on sunny days. Current favourite authors, the children informed us, include Michelle Paver, Conn Iggulden and (still) JK Rowling. All do ICT and touch-typing. School assembly each morning, with prayers read by a pupil and thought for the day from a member of staff, plus a service at the church in the school

grounds on Sunday mornings (lots of parents attend too). Relatively young teaching staff – 19 full-time, two part-time. Head and his wife, director of boarding, two matrons and three gap students live on-site.

Sports-wise, the school punches above its weight. Head is particularly proud that Maidwell recently won the national under-13 cross-country championship – quite a feat when they're up against far larger schools. Pupils play sport six days a week – boys do rugby, hockey, football and cricket, while girls do hockey, netball and rounders. Sports hall with cricket nets, climbing wall and squash court. Rowing on the lake in the summer and weekly swimming for all in school's own indoor pool. Loads of activities during break-times, evenings and at weekends, including crafts, carpentry, textiles, school magazine, gardening, clay shooting and outdoor pursuits trips. When we asked two boys whether they ever got bored, they looked puzzled. 'Of course not,' they told us. Music, drama and art good. Two-thirds of pupils learn musical instruments and music practice is timetabled. Two major concerts a year and choir sings an anthem in the church every Sunday. Art is very popular – everything from surrealism to gargoyles – and on the drama front, there are lots of plays, musicals and public speaking events.

All meals are cooked in-house. Lunch is a formal affair, in a light, airy dining room with long, narrow tables. Grace is said at the start and finish and a member of staff sits at each end to serve food, encourage good table manners and chat to boys and girls. Tradition of one boiled sweet after lunch still firmly in place (plastic tub solemnly passed from pupil to pupil) and £1 of tuck on Sundays. When we visited, a group of jolly 12-year-olds tucked into a lunch of beef pie and pancakes (stylishly served with slices of lemon) and chatted enthusiastically about the school. Food gets the thumbs-up from pupils. As head says: 'We're aiming for the good bits of Jamie Oliver but we still have fish and chips on Fridays.' Breakfast and supper are more informal. House system in place, with head boy/girl, prefects and four house captains. House competitions range from rugby and cross-country to water polo and conkers, with points scored for the annual house cup. 'It's taken very seriously,' the head boy told us.

Boarding is at the very heart of the school. Lots of parental access (church, matches etc) but boarders must stay at school at weekends. Leave-out weekends (from lunch on Friday till Monday evening) every second or third weekend. Pupils can be weekly boarders during their first year but most opt for full boarding from the start. Boy boarders are housed on first floor while girls get the self-contained top floor of the school. Boys' dorms (up to six per room) are wholesome and shipshape while girls' dorms (three to six per room) are decorated with jolly bunting, Keep Calm and Carry On posters and lots of Cath Kidston (there are plans for them to move to a purpose-built house of their own in due course). Older girls' bathroom looks straight out of an interiors magazine – chic circular basins, tongue and groove and laminate flooring.

Pupils are courteous, well-behaved and good company. When benefactor Oliver Wyatt was once asked about the ideal Maidwell pupil, he described him/her as the sort of child who 'was invited to someone's house and invited back again.' His view still holds true, with Maidwell putting an emphasis on being kind, well-mannered and tidy. Boys look smart in navy cords, striped or check shirts, ties and tweed jackets while girls wear corduroy culottes, blouses and smart jackets. Perhaps unusually in this day and age (but very popular with parents), mobile phones, PSPs and iPods are banned (although final year pupils can listen to iPods in their dorms). Boys and girls are allowed to watch key sports matches and a film on Saturday nights, while older pupils see the nightly TV news, but no TV apart from that. Boyfriend/girlfriend relationships actively discouraged. 'We are resistant to the idea of girls and boys "going out",' says the head. 'We talk it through with the pupils and I am very clear that we are not having it.' All pupils write a weekly letter home – 'we emphasise how much it means to parents,' he says.

Discipline isn't an issue here. 'It's because we're a small school and everybody looks out for each other,' say staff. 'You don't get division or ganging up because it's so close-knit.' Parents agree. 'We love the fact that because it's slightly smaller it has a real family atmosphere,' one mother told us. 'It gives children the opportunity to shine. Everyone gets to play in a team and everyone is in the school play.' Meanwhile a father commented: 'I'm delighted with all aspects of the school. The teaching staff are great and the boarding care is just superb.' Head is adamant that it isn't a 'snobby' place either. 'Privilege has no place in this school,' he says. 'Everyone is equal here.'

Maidwell Hall remains a traditional, full-boarding prep school that has stuck to its full boarding guns and held its own in a declining market. Small enough for everyone to know each other but big enough to offer a first-rate, all-round education, it encourages pupils to work hard, get lots of fresh air and have fun along the way.

Malvern College

College Road, Malvern, Worcestershire WR14 3DF

01684 581500
enquiries@malcol.org
www.malverncollege.org.uk

Ages: 13–18
Pupils: 670; sixth form: 330
Boarders: 530 full
Day: £23,241 pa
Boarding: £35,061 – £36,288 pa

Linked school: The Downs Malvern

Headmaster: Since 2008, Antony Clark MA HDE (50s). Widely regarded as a safe anchor for the school, he has been at Malvern long enough to make his own significant mark. He brought all his experience of being head at two schools in South Africa, and Gresham's for six years, to Malvern. He has focused on growing the school (it is now up to capacity, he tells us) and on developing the academic culture within the school, and is overseeing the three international school offshoots in China

and Egypt. His wife is a lecturer in law and enjoys being involved in the school as much as she can. Antony is seen by the pupils and parents as a measured and balanced head, a bit distant, but the pupils feel he does know them and they respect the aura of authority that exudes from him. He sets clear boundaries and parents as well as pupils know just where they stand with him.

Academic matters: The school offers an interesting academic dynamic. On the one hand, there are super bright European students who are there for the IB and do very well indeed. About half of those taking IB achieve 40+ points. Then there are the home grown pupils who are much more mixed ability. The common entrance pass mark is a relatively modest 50, and about 20 per cent of those coming in at year 9 receive some level of learning support. Given that, GCSE results are very good – 60 per cent per cent A* and A grades in 2015, with A levels at 72 per cent A*-B grades. The school says that it wants to be open to as wide an ability range as it can, partly because it is interested in a broad range of talents and partly because the it wants all the family to come, not just the bright one of the clan.

Parents rave about the level of academic support. There are carefully tailored individual programmes, and whatever their level, pupils say their teachers really know their strengths and weaknesses. Pupils are highly encouraged to focus hard on their academic work. Some parents feel there is rather too much pressure and the school is expecting pupils to spin an awful lot of plates, but others recognise that this is what gets the results that would not have been forthcoming in a school

with less resources to put into teaching and learning. Parents are full of praise for the availability of teachers and the tight level of communication between staff that ensures each pupil is getting the academic support and challenge they need.

Sport is outstanding – and there is a lot of it. We spoke to parents who had specifically chosen the college for its sporting excellence and were delighted with how it had delivered

The head has upped the academic profile in the school by very visibly encouraging intellectual societies to flourish, with a range of top quality outside speakers as well as opportunities for sixth formers to present papers reflecting their own intellectual interests. Here is the stretch and challenge that the bright sixth formers need. The head has also been keen to develop ideas about teaching and learning among his staff, has established a staff group to move ideas forward and initiated peer to peer observations to help share the very best practice.

In terms of subjects, the range is much what you would expect in a well-resourced school catering for a mixed ability range where the sixth form is split more or less exactly in half between IB and A level. Parents talk about how strong history, economics, English, maths, classics and modern languages are. Sixth formers also enthuse about politics and business studies. Science is about to

965

have a real boost with the opening of a modern science centre named after a past pupil, the current prime minister of Malaysia, Najib Razak. Teachers and parents told us that there is a lot of effort put into constructing sixth form timetables that will really play to the strengths of the pupils, resulting in some strong results and a thoroughly valuable sixth form experience for those of fairly modest academic ability as well as the high flyers.

Academic facilities are strikingly good across the board. The internet access has just been speeded up, much to everyone's satisfaction. Not every department has the spanking new facilities of the sciences, but music, which is housed in one of the older buildings, shows that energy, enthusiasm and high achievement are certainly not dependent on buildings alone. The library has all the aura of an ancient seat of learning with the buzz of a 21st century learning resource centre. Pupils commented on the helpful library opening hours.

Games, options, the arts: Sport is outstanding – and there is a lot of it. The sports facilities are excellent, with a splendid new sports centre that incorporates a generous function room for lectures and dinners, all of which are available for community use on occasion. We were pleased to hear of the girls' football teams' successes. There are special programmes for the elite sports players with high quality coaches and professional contacts, but everyone is expected to participate in games at some level. We spoke to parents who had specifically chosen the college for its sporting excellence and were delighted with how it had delivered, but also to one or two with unsporty children who resented the amount of time they had to spend on games, especially if they had really strong other passions – such as music – that required a big time commitment. We would recommend a parent whose 13 year old is clearly not sporty to think hard about whether the other, considerable, attractions, outweigh all that compulsory games.

The college's music helps to foster links with the local community – the brass band played at the switching on of the Malvern town Christmas lights

The other attractions certainly are there. The art is phenomenal and spreads way beyond the art building itself. The whole school is enhanced with a great deal of the pupils' artwork in a brilliant variety of media. It was wonderful to see pupils encouraged to work on a large scale, with great big canvases giving the senior art areas the feel of an art school. Pupils told us that they are invited to use the art building outside of lesson time and it is clear that there is much enthusiasm for doing this. DT is another strength, and both boys and girls spoke passionately about projects they were undertaking there. Drama is housed in a well-adapted old gymnasium, and again there is masses going on, both within the houses and at school level. Thespians benefit from the very close proximity of Malvern Theatre, which has a number of pre-West End runs, and there are house trips to see various productions. Music is very strong too, particularly choral and chapel singing, but there is a huge range of ensembles and orchestras. Every year 9 learns a musical instrument. Those looking for choral scholarships at Oxbridge are well prepared, and the school has had success here. The music offers welcome links with the local community – the brass band played at the switching on of the Malvern town Christmas lights, and the choir were doing three carol services in the town during the week we visited.

Most of the school is involved in CCF at some stage and D of E is also offered. The school makes the most of the wonderful Malvern Hills, with various hill runs being an important part of the annual school calendar. Both IB and D of E candidates involved community service, and the school has links with a local school for blind children.

'It offers all a great school should – and more', one parent told us.

Boarding: Eighty per cent of the school are full boarders. There is no flexi-boarding (though day pupils can stay the occasional night for official school events) but there are two compulsory week-ends out of school each half term. Day pupils are incorporated into the boarding houses and have the same study space as the boarders. Pupils eat in the houses and house staff make the most of this opportunity to understand exactly what is going on in the daily life of their charges. Non-house staff and other visitors eat with the pupils at lunchtimes too, and the atmosphere is warm, stimulating and highly conducive to developing the best social manners. Pupils and parents say they know the house staff are there for them and will give unstintingly of their time to offer support.

The school suits high energy all rounders and there is a tremendous amount on offer round the clock. One or two parents felt the demands on the pupils were almost too great, with very little down time, but the pupils we met absolutely thrived on the high octane atmosphere and recognised the diversity of gifts that make up a flourishing and healthy community.

Background and atmosphere: The school is very cosmopolitan in feel and outlook – about 35 per cent are from overseas, and there are about 40 different nationalities represented at the moment. This global feel is grounded in the quintessentially British landscape of the Malvern Hills. The site is stunning, set on the side of the Malverns with spectacular views. There are 11 houses (six boys' and five girls') around the 250 acre site – many in huge 19th century villas that could well have been the houses of the successful financiers of the Empire who made their home in this health resort for the Victorian rich. Malvern is a delightful and slightly quirky town to wander around – staff and parents can feel as relaxed as they could anywhere in permitting pupils to go out to do a bit of shopping or have a coffee.

The Victorian foundation of the school, 1865, with that glorious mid 19th century architecture that exudes confidence in Church and Country, is an essential part of the school's feel today. Everyone goes to the chapel four times a week for a broadly Church of England service, where hymns are still sung and prayers said although the emphasis is on wise words that will speak to those of all persuasions. There are non-Christians in the school – dietary and other religious observations are happily accommodated – but this is a Church of England foundation and you do feel that is a living

reality. The head tells us that past pupils really value the regular worship as they move out into the wider world.

Pastoral care, well-being and discipline: Everyone to whom we spoke valued the pastoral care highly, even parents who had other grumbles. The emphasis is on the individual needs – there is no one-size-fits-all here. One parent told us how accommodating everyone was when her daughter suffered a bad sports injury, and pupils spoke about the staff with genuine warmth. Staff, too, showed a strong sense of loyalty to pupils who had come up through the school, wanting to ensure they had the smoothest possibly transition to the next stage and making it clear each pupil was valued for themselves not just for their A* exam results. The atmosphere felt well-disciplined without being too formal. The rules are clear and everyone recognises a no-nonsense approach to any transgressions, but it is rewards rather than punishments that reinforce the school's strong moral values.

Pupils and parents: Among the alumni of the college are at least two Commonwealth prime ministers, two Nobel prize winners, an Olympic gold medallist and many other notables from the worlds of science, law, the military, business, politics, sports and literature – including CS Lewis. The school produces an eclectic range that bears out its claims to suit the all rounders.

There are a lot of wealthy families forming the backbone of the school. Bursary help is available and we heard of families who were pooling generational resources to send children to the college, but one or two parents speculated that this might not be a comfortable school for a child whose parents were really having to push the boat out financially to pay the fees. The international clientèle rubs shoulders with the children of successful Hereford farming families, of London commuters, and of the technological elite who can choose to live in such a delightful part of the country.

The school has been co-educational for about 20 years and there are now more-or-less half boys and girls. Some said that the families put children under some pressure to look good as well as do well, and we certainly saw none of the much publicised childhood obesity here. Housemistresses are aware of teenage girls' desire to look slim and beautiful and on the alert for any obsession, but the girls we met relished the outdoorsy, sporty opportunities of the school and didn't appear to be under pressure to present as cover girls. Both boys and girls appeared pleasingly extrovert and outward-looking. Perhaps not a school for the very quiet and reflective who need a lot of time to themselves.

Entrance: Most families start looking two or three years before entry and some houses fill up faster than others. There are open days, but most families have personalised tours. In some cases there is pre-testing, but the main admission is through common entrance at 13+, or for those coming from non-common entrance schools, the school's own tests in maths, English and science. About 50 join the sixth form each year and they normally do tests in the subjects they want to study at A level or IB, including an English and maths paper as appropriate. The interviews are important too, as are school reports.

Exit: Almost all the sixth form going on to higher education. Those staying in the UK are attracted to campus and collegiate universities like Durham

and Exeter or the big Russell Group names; six to Oxbridge and two to Harvard in 2015. About a third go on to US, Canada and mainland Europe top institutions, and may put in UK applications as well to see what comes up. This group is aiming high – one boy had an interview at Trinity, Cambridge the week after we met him, but it was sixth on his list behind US and Canadian top universities.

Money matters: This sort of education, staffing level, facilities, opportunities and general ambiance does not come cheap. There are means-tested bursaries and scholarships for a wide range of talents. Pupils can accumulate these but learning support and EAL tuition come as extras.

Remarks: This is a school for the international set, and those who come from the local area, or even 'over the hill' – as the other side of the Malverns is described – undoubtedly benefit by having their horizons expanded beyond the comfortable values of the English shires. There are huge opportunities for pupils to learn from different cultures here and the college does well to work on its links with the local community, so it is not just the moneyed international culture that pupils assimilate, delightfully appealing though that is. There is a wholesomeness about Malvern for those who lift their eyes to the hills that can balance the daily busyness. The offshoots in China and Egypt will add to the global dimension and set everyone looking to the far horizons – not just at the opportunities but also, we hope, at the challenges. This is a school deeply bedded in the British public school tradition but with its sights now set across the globe to prepare the pupils for world citizenship.

Malvern St James Girls' School

15 Avenue Road, Great Malvern, Worcestershire WR14 3BA

01684 584624
admissions@malvernstjames.co.uk
www.malvernstjames.co.uk
C of E

Ages: 11–18 (boarding from 7)
Pupils: 445; sixth form: 125
Boarders: 183 full, 49 weekly/flexi
Day: £7,980 – £18,465 pa
Boarding: £19,980 – £33,150 pa

Headmistress: Since 2010, Mrs Patricia Woodhouse BMus. After studying music at London University, started professional life as a freelance musician, composing, singing and conducting, before moving via a brief period in the City to the world of education. Has been involved in 'all sorts' of schools over the past 20 years. Director of music at Wimbledon High School, sixth form housemistress at Queenswood,

deputy headmistress at St Mary's Wantage and formerly headmistress at Abbots Bromley School for Girls. A governor of Bloxham School, and an ISI Inspector. Very enthusiastic, passionate about the school and the girls: 'The school serves the girls, not the other way around', 'we're equipping them for life after university', and loving being where she is: 'I've found my school – I'm so lucky'.

Leaving in July 2016. Her successor will be Mrs Olivera Raraty BA PGCE, currently deputy head academic at Notting Hill and Ealing High. History degree from Leeds and PGCE from London University; began her teaching career at Francis Holland NW1. Has taught history and politics at both day and boarding schools, including a long stint at Wycombe Abbey, where her posts included head of department, head of year and assistant director of studies. Married with two daughters; enjoys baking and hill walking.

Academic matters: Good results both at GCSE and A level. At A level in 2015, 79 per cent A*-B and 56 per cent A*/A. At GCSE, 60 per cent A*/A. Most girls take 10 or 11 GCSEs. Many sixth formers also take SATs for the US universities. An increasing use of IGCSEs to stretch the girls and increase flexibility. The head is 'not tempted' by the IB but promotes the school's education enrichment programme, running alongside the A level curriculum, which has been designed to give the girls the opportunities, especially in terms of creative thinking and learning resilience, to glean many benefits traditionally seen as an 'IB preserve'. The school also offers critical thinking for years 10 to 13.

Lovely facilities – an excellent purpose-built science block, beautiful and spacious art block, good drama studio and plenty of computers for girls to use in class and for prep. Virtual learning environment allows submission of work online to teachers. Small class sizes – never more than 18. Well organised and supported prep time at the end of each school day.

Teaching is highly responsive to the needs of individual girls – the school has an excellent reputation locally for untangling able girls whose dyslexia/dyspraxia has been a stumbling block to them elsewhere, and learning support is woven into the school structure. 'We welcome the full spectrum of learning profiles.' One-to-one support is available for dyslexia, dyspraxia and EAL at extra cost.

Many outdoor pursuits making good use of the Malvern Hills. School is developing its equestrian team, making use of the facilities at Hartpury Equine College

A good choice of modern foreign languages at GCSE and A level, and a modern language at GCSE is 'as close to compulsory as it can be'. French, Spanish, German, Chinese, Russian and Latin taught. A well-stocked and well-set-out library with specific areas set aside for sixth formers. Academic reports are termly, with progress checks every half term.

Games, options, the arts: Fantastic sports facilities – newish and splendid sports hall – and plenty of opportunities to make use of them. Where girls show exceptional promise and talent in sports (currently national representatives in lacrosse and golf) their curriculum commitments will be adjusted to allow them to flourish on the sports field. Growing an equestrian team which makes use of the facilities at Hartpury Equine College. Many outdoor pursuits also supported – not least by virtue of being at the foot of the Malvern Hills. Lots of girls involved in Duke of Edinburgh too.

There are plenty of opportunities to get involved with music groups or to take individual lessons. Very good drama facilities, and for those interested in life a step beyond there are debating societies, involvement in Model UN, volunteering opportunities at local schools, fundraising for local charities and so on.

The lovely artwork on display around the school deserves a mention, and the textiles department produces some breathtaking pieces. Girls who want a go at pottery, painting, stitching or drawing will have a ball here.

Boarding: Boarding is done by age group with a prep house, two houses for years 9 – 11 and two sixth form houses. Boarding houses are well set up and comfortable, with plenty of space and privacy for older girls, and nice common rooms. Sixth form boarding life aims to ease transition between school and university – girls are supervised but encouraged to take responsibility for establishing good habits of independent study, dealing with their own finances, travel arrangements – and laundry. Sixth formers may also go into Worcester or Birmingham at the weekend as long as they are in a group.

Day girls are well integrated with boarders – each day girl assigned to a boarding house and many using flexi-boarding either regularly or occasionally. There is no Saturday school but plenty to keep girls busy at the weekends including croquet, reeling, discos and barbecues plus trips into nearby Worcester and Birmingham. Reciprocal social arrangements with nearby boys' school.

Background and atmosphere: The school is well situated in the centre of Malvern, directly opposite the train station, in the building which was once the Imperial Hotel. Founded in 1893 as Malvern Girls' College, it was renamed Malvern St James following a merger in 2006 with St James' School in West Malvern. The surroundings are lovely, with the hills stretching up behind the town, and the buildings feature lots of high ceilings, generous rooms and well-lit spaces. Younger girls seen skipping about chatting and hopping, older girls seem calm and happy. 'We'd notice someone walking round with her head down (or her nose up) straight away.'

The atmosphere is calm and relaxed but with

No Saturday school but plenty to keep girls busy at the weekends including croquet, reeling, discos and barbecues plus trips into nearby Worcester and Birmingham

an underlying energy and a sense of fingers on the pulse. Small enough for the headmistress to know every girl by name. The school has a full-time chaplain and there is a sense of respect for and interest in a diverse collection of girls from varied backgrounds. A mixture of UK and overseas students, although the head has now capped the number of international students. Pupils come from the very local to the far-flung – Thailand, Brunei, Russia and Nigeria amongst others.

Food is good – recently brought back in house to improve standards and, according to our sources, successfully so. There are always halal and vegetarian options available and the staff eat with the girls.

A strong commitment to sharing facilities with the local community. The school is well liked by the locals, who say the pupils are polite and never give any trouble. Few rules, relatively late curfews by comparison with other local boarding schools – the girls are given a lot of responsibility, self-discipline is encouraged and the girls respond positively. A family atmosphere – 'the school is all about good relationships'.

Pastoral care, well-being and discipline: Pastoral care permeates the structure of the school, with school staff and older pupils committed to maintaining the highest standards. Prefects are trained as 'sixth form listeners' by Childline and know exactly what to do and when to pass concerns on to staff. Prefects are elected by a combination of sixth form and staff votes. Zero tolerance of drugs – but head has 'never had to deal' with drugs at the

school. Sixth formers are encouraged to attend and host dinner parties with members of other nearby schools. Alcohol consumption is restricted to two glasses of wine on such occasions, but not allowed on school premises otherwise, though 18 years olds are allowed to go to local pubs.

Prefects, head and parents all say that bullying 'does not happen'. Girls are allocated to small tutor groups of about 12 and each form also has a prefect. The head says, 'There is nowhere to hide', and the combination of house staff, peer support, small classes and an open door policy 'from the head down' mean the girls always have someone to talk to. 'We train the girls to manage themselves and the girls are comfortable being themselves.'

Girls of all ages mix well and the head makes time to have teas and dinners with small groups of them so that she can get to know them better.

Pupils and parents: Pupils and parents come from all over the place. Day girls live up to an hour away (minibuses from very nearby and also from Hereford and Ross-on-Wye). Some boarders are local too; about a quarter of pupils are from overseas. The girls we met were cheerful, polite, welcoming and thoroughly enjoy being at the school. Parents say, 'It's lovely, friendly and happy – and every teacher is up to speed'.

Clara Furse, the first woman chief executive of the London Stock Exchange, the late HRH Princess Alice, Duchess of Gloucester and the childcare expert Penelope Leach are former pupils of St James's School, while Malvern Girls' alumnae include the writer Aminatta Forna. More recent former pupils include BBC correspondent Hannah Hennessy, journalist Elizabeth Day, surgeon Abbie Franklin and city high flyers Helen Freer and Elizabeth Sharpe.

Entrance: Prospective pupils are interviewed by the head – via Skype if need be – and all face formal assessment tests. Formal interviews and often quite a long 'courtship' including taster days etc. Prep department provides a growing number into year 7, with others coming from local primaries and prep schools (boarding and day) like Hatherop Castle, The Elms, Abberley Hall, Godstowe and The Croft. At 11, girls sit cognitive ability and comprehension tests, while others do common entrance at 13. Main entry points are years 7, 9 and sixth form. Girls looking to enter sixth form must take a written paper in one of the subjects they wish to study at A level and a general essay paper. All international students must take an EAL test. Not highly selective, but girls 'must be intellectually curious, with a good IQ' and 'able to benefit from what we offer'.

Exit: Around two-thirds stay on after GCSEs. Virtually all sixth form leavers to university. A handful to Oxbridge (one in 2015) and a good number to Russell Group destinations. Recent destinations include many to London: LSE, UCL, King's, Queen Mary, Royal Holloway and Imperial; medicine, music and mathematics amongst the courses chosen.

Money matters: The school offers a number of academic, music, sport, art and drama scholarships, which are worth between 10 and 20 per cent of fees. Bursaries are also available and may be combined with scholarships. The maximum bursary/scholarship combination available is 40 per cent of fees.

Remarks: A school that is different, 'not tethered to league tables', with a lovely relaxed atmosphere, yielding impressive results in the classroom and on the sports field. Happy, confident girls and staff.

Monmouth School

Almshouse Street, Monmouth NP25 3XP

01600 713143
admissions@monmouthschool.org
www.habs-monmouth.org

Ages: 11–18 (boarding from 9)
Pupils: 521; sixth form: 210
Boarders: 150 full
Day: £14,472 pa
Boarding: £26,223 – £27,801 pa

Headmaster: Since September 2015, Dr Andrew Daniel, previously senior deputy head at Wellington School, Somerset. A former pupil of Atlantic College, Dr Daniel graduated with a starred first in geophysical sciences from the University of East Anglia and University of Washington, Seattle. He was awarded his doctorate from Liverpool University on the mathematical modelling of plate tectonics in Patagonia. He was head of mathematics at Taunton School and responsible for the academic life of Aiglon College in Switzerland before joining Wellington.

Married to Alison, an oceanographer; they have a young daughter and son. His interests include mountaineering, hill walking, cycling, coaching squash and the French horn.

Academic matters: Good performance at both GCSE and A level over the last five years, with consistently impressive grades for high fliers – though whole year averages fluctuate a bit. In 2015, 45 per cent A*/A at A level. More telling is that between 20 and 35 out of around 85 candidates regularly get three or more A*/As. There is a small tail of C, D, E grades which probably reflects the school policy of allowing enthusiastic hard workers to 'have a go' (they only need five B grades at GCSE to join sixth form).

At GCSE results are consistent, with 63 per cent A*/A grades in 2015. English, maths and science (now IGCSE 'because it's more rigorous') have a pretty impressive clutch of top grades and minimal below C. All take core subjects of English, maths, three separate sciences (a few do double award) plus a modern language (French, Spanish, German, Russian or Mandarin – Welsh can be arranged as an extra). Latin (good take-up) and Greek (a few) right up to A level. Lots of A level choice – around 30 options in conjunction with Haberdashers' Monmouth School for Girls. Arrangement gives flexibility amounting to virtual freedom of choice as well as spin-off benefits of mixing with girls for curricular and extracurricular stuff.

The Monmouth Science Initiative gives boys the chance to work alongside scientific development at Cardiff University and is extended not only to the girls' school but also to local state schools, with clear feedback that it is making a significant difference to potential science high fliers. Learning support on an individual/shared basis from qualified staff, although additional charges apply for numeracy and literacy support.

Monmouth (comparatively small) has consistently challenged the giants of school sport in rugby, rowing, soccer and cricket. Rugby is top dog

Parents say individual teaching staff are exceptionally encouraging to enthusiastic pupils, though one commented that you have to push quite hard to do more than the statutory 10 GCSEs. 'The school could vaunt its academic image more but likes to be seen as inclusive,' said another. Lessons in study skills for all and sixth formers are encouraged to tailor choice towards career. Lots of additional help from local experts in minority subjects.

Games, options, the arts: Sport is tip-top here and Monmouth (comparatively small) has consistently challenged the giants of school sport in rugby, rowing, soccer and cricket. Rugby is top dog, though parents say other sports have had more of a look in recently. Not content with schoolboy competition, pupils have played for the Newport Gwent Dragons, Junior Welsh and other professional and

semi-professional teams. Recent head boy is combining medicine at Cardiff with his professional Welsh Rugby commitments. This, and the fact that former Wales and Lions player John Bevan is a teacher first and rugby coach second, typifies the school's approach to sport as something to be done alongside life rather than an end in itself, though it doesn't stop them taking some significant trophies. As well as coaching the 1st XV he takes the younger boys on tours to Blackpool, Ireland and Italy.

Rowing, not surprisingly as the Wye surges right past the games pitches, has a strong though small take-up. It's in the tent-and-sandwiches league rather than turreted-pavilion-and-champagne at the posh school competitions, but still manages to sweep the board. Tennis, cross-country, squash, golf and sailing all flourish. Several teams in each year group – gives more boys a chance to represent the school and helps identify potential.

A bewildering range of activities available – artistic, intellectual, sporting, and practical. Juniors (11 to 13-year-olds) must do two a week and everyone does either CCF or some form of community service. In A-Z terms astronomy to water polo (no zoology) gives a flavour of what's on and it's

Lovely mansion and gardens of Chapel House are bursting with happy junior boarders; maths department is housed in a former pub

good to see literature and poetry enjoyed by boys (something the head sees as too easily excluded by gender stereotyping in co-ed schools).

Perhaps the music school looks a little elderly in comparison with the jazzier modern developments, but it is comprehensive and bursting with energetic activity. Around 40 per cent play instruments and enjoy a plethora of groups, choirs, bands and orchestras. A recent deputation from the Haberdashers' Company was staggered to find themselves entertained by a full scale performance of Carmina Burana, involving the second year en masse. A good record of music college entry (recent leaver offered four scholarships to different academies) and parents feel the school gives boys a musical resource for life. The usual gamut of school visits, choir trips and exchanges.

Drama studio and new 500-seat theatre (as well as being used by the school it hosts a programme of public performance art, including ballet and world cinema). Quality art – the venerable but well-equipped art block full of boys working in a wide range of media.

Boarding: Over a quarter of the senior school boards (full or flexi). Around a third overseas. By sixth form, ratio of day to boarding is 60:40. Still has Saturday morning school for all but the sixth form – not universally popular with parents, but how else would the school have time to run outside all those activities? Plans afoot to increase boarding capacity. Five boarding houses have sensible rather than luxurious accommodation for boarders though the old Grange (prep school) buildings make a shamelessly luxurious sixth form house.

Background and atmosphere: Founded in 1614 as a local 'fre schole' by William Jones, a member of the Haberdashers' Company (one of the oldest Livery Companies in London), it became a 'public' school in the 19th century to expand its boarding beyond the locality and was a direct grant school until 1975. Part of the Haberdashers' family of Monmouth schools, which includes Agincourt (pre-prep), the Grange (boys' prep), Inglefield (girls' prep) and Haberdashers' Monmouth Girls'.

Rebuilt in the 1880s, with a magnificent Jacobean-style main building, it occupies and gives character to a significant part of Monmouth. Sensitive restorations, acquisitions such as the lovely mansion and gardens of Chapel House, bursting with happy junior boarders, the ex-pub housing the maths department and rows of almshouses (now staff offices) complement the new buildings that house the prep school and swimming pool. The William Jones building provides new classrooms, meeting space and admin centre. Pleasant grassy areas break up the hotch-potch of main buildings but it's something of a maze. Gorgeous playing fields bordering the Wye are reached by a pedestrian tunnel under the busy A40.

Uniform is plain navy blazer and grey trousers, replaced in the sixth form by a 'smart' business dress code. Food, boys say, is pretty good at lunchtime and OK-ish in the evening.

Pastoral care, well-being and discipline: Tutors are the focal point for monitoring academic performance, while housemasters look after pastoral well-being. One parent commented that no trouble is spared to find specialist help where needed and to support boys in difficulties. School rules are sensible and concentrate on the standard of behaviour expected, rather than a prescriptive list of dos and don'ts. Relations between staff and boys appear relaxed, but are formal enough to engender respect. Clear policies on drinking, smoking and drugs – not considered a problem, but boys are made aware of the damage they could do to themselves.

Pupils and parents: School attracts boys from south west England and south Wales, plus a few from Hong Kong etc, but is spreading the net wider and is popular with Forces families and expats. Definitely unstuffy and produces confident but considerate young men who are open and independent. Notable old boys include Christopher Herbert, the Bishop of St Albans, David Broome, Eddie Butler, Major Dick Hern, Lord Moynihan, Lord Ezra, Steve James, Keith Jarrett, Tony Jordan, Victor Spinetti and recent silver medallist Olympic rower Tom Lucy.

Entrance: Three-form entry at 11, from its own prep department and local primary schools. Both groups sit the school's own entrance exam, with scholarships awarded on that performance alone – no supplementary papers. School at pains to stress that there is no pass mark, but looking for potential – great store put on interviews. A further one-form entry at 13 from a growing list of prep schools – based on CE. Foundation scholarship exam or an entrance exam for those at state schools.

Exit: A dribble (some 10 per cent) leave post-GCSE. Majority to sound universities – Swansea, Bristol, Cardiff, Exeter etc – with engineering, business and economics very popular. Quite a few gap years. Ten to Oxbridge in 2015.

Money matters: About a third of the government assisted places now replaced by the school's own scheme and this offers a number of scholarships and bursaries. One in three get means-tested help with fees in the senior school. Day fees about what you'd expect from similar schools but boarding is exceptionally good value.

Remarks: A school that sets out to serve its community and has now been discovered by the wider world, with high quality education and a real flair for sport and the more aesthetic life skills.

Moor Park School

Moor Park, Ludlow, Shropshire SY8 4DZ

01584 876061
head@moorpark.org.uk
www.moorpark.org.uk
RC

Ages: 2.5–13 (boarders from year 3)
Pupils: 232
Boarders: 14 full,125 weekly/flexi
Day: £6,930 – £15,465 pa
Boarding: £18,990 – £22,785 pa

Headmaster: Since September 2015, Charlie Minogue, previously deputy head at Aldwickbury school in Hertfordshire, where he worked for nine years. Educated at Perrott Hill and Wellington College. Degree in biology from Newcastle, PGCE from York. Taught science to GCSE at Heywood Community High School then moved onto St Paul's Cathedral School in London as head of science. Currently studying for a masters in educational leadership. Keen musician, sportsman and mountaineer. Wife, Rebecca, is a chartered surveyor; they have two children.

Entrance: Broadly speaking, four starting blocks from which to start the Moor Park adventure. Those 'rising 3' may continue through the nursery and kindergarten to the transition stage, aged 7, then on to the senior school. (School will take new pupils into any year group, providing room.) Potential pupils come for a taster day and sit a relaxed assessment. Pupils aged 4 are screened for learning difficulties and offered help, if appropriate. Children come from a broadish cross-section of society: old money in crumbling houses; new money from escaped Londoners; farmers, who

cannot escape; Catholics and Protestants – all drawn by the country feel of the school, with its delight in muddy boots and bright-eyed pupils. The catchment area has increased significantly as boarding has become ever more popular.

Wonderful grounds complete with fishing lake and distant views of Housman's 'blue remembered hills'

Exit: To an increasingly varied number of schools. An eclectic range of destinations: Eton, Harrow, Radley, Shrewsbury, St Mary's Calne, Westonbirt, Moreton Hall, Stowe, Monmouth, Hereford Cathedral and Bedstone.

Remarks: Founded in 1964 as a Roman Catholic school and housed in an elegant Queen Anne mansion surrounded by wonderful grounds, complete with lake, old trees, a winding drive with a lodge at the foot and distant views of Housman's 'blue remembered hills': a paradise for children. Work on the banks of the lake has restored vegetation, improved fishing and introduced some boating. Nearby, a classroom has been constructed for outdoor studies and the estate management regularly checks the trees, so that this is one of those increasingly rare schools where children may climb trees. Also a boilersuit school where, we were told with great delight, 'the children often come to lessons covered with mud'. Yes, it's all a long way from

the Thames Valley, but that shouldn't detract from the underlying seriousness of academic endeavour. This is not a play school – rather a school which believes that encouraging all round happiness leads to self-realisation and success. Most schools trumpet that belief – this one fulfils it.

The main entrance of the house is warm and inviting with a roaring log fire in the winter, an impressive staircase and remarkable tooled leather wallpaper. Old photographs dotted around remind us that this is an old country house; splendid artwork reminds us that this is a lively and creative school. How well the two blend together. Within the house are the various dining rooms (food excellent, as we can testify), the bright and generously proportioned dormitories, with custom made bunks ('Super!' enthused a guide) and home to 12 members of staff, some married with children. This arrangement must be one of the reasons why there's such a tangible family atmosphere – really a happy overlap between staff and pupils. The fine library and the chapel, which has adapted effortlessly from being a spectacular ballroom, are uplifting features. Chapel is held on a daily basis and much appreciated by those to whom we spoke. 'I'm not a Roman Catholic,' said one mother, 'but I like the feel it gives. I'm glad it's around.'

The youngest adventurers start off in the old clock house and are referred to as the Tick Tocks. Thereafter, nearly all classrooms built within the past few years. Even the one remaining old style Portakabin is brightly done up and ideal for the purpose. Wonderful art block with paint-daubed atelier for senior artists, who are allowed to work up there unsupervised, another example of the mantra of trust. Lively and spirited art teaching. Fizzing DT with basic carpentry taught to all before moving on to more modern techniques of creation. New computer block. All these marvellous facilities on offer and enthusiastically taken up during after-school clubs and any free time that is available. Art and DT are timetabled in and remain part of the core curriculum; intelligent use of computers means they play an integral part in the whole learning process. We've seen smarter, slicker buildings but none where the teaching was any better as a result. This is a school where teaching really matters and where those with learning difficulties are well looked after.

Boarding – mostly flexi – is on the increase – partly as a result of the hugely popular weekend activities, partly because of the enthusiasm and involvement of the staff, but mostly through word of mouth. It clearly is fun – 'My child nagged and nagged us to let him board,' said one delighted parent. In celebration of the increase in boarding numbers and as an example of putting into practice what is being taught, has recently built a low cost sustainable house for young boarders. Not only is it an absolutely fascinating example of eco-building with its larch exteriors and oak interiors brought in from Wales, it is also a trend-setting design for comfortable and practical boarding. Some 24 boys and girls now live in magical surroundings with houseparents, a resident matron, a dog, kitchens for snacks and rooms for chilling out.

Not long ago it was described as a 'gem' – the word remains appropriate. Forty-four activities, hobbies and sports on offer, from Swahili to origami, jewellery making to bushcraft. 'Fun' is the buzz word – and how the staff throw themselves at it. A number are ex-pupils drawn, they say, by the magical surroundings and their happy memories. All of them appear cheerful and involved. A wonderful place in which to grow up: particularly in these exciting times.

Moreton Hall School

Weston Rhyn, Oswestry, Shropshire SY11 3EW

01691 773671
registrar@moretonhall.com
www.moretonhall.org

Ages: 11–18 (boarders from 7)
Pupils: 328; sixth form: 120
Boarders: 201 full (including junior)
Day: £8,880 – £25,950 pa
Boarding: £20,460 – £31,500 pa

Principal: Since 1992, Jonathan Forster BA PGCE (50s) who still 'just loves every day at Moreton Hall'. His daughters have been through the school and he and his wife, who's heavily involved in school life, can testify as parents to what a wonderful place it is bring up children. Jonathan – who has a degree from Leeds and was previously housemaster and English teacher at Strathallan – rescued the school from imminent closure, and he has continued to drive it at a pace that speaks of a life-long mission and endless creative energy. He is always ahead of the game, ensuring the school leads not follows market demands. He has kept true to the liberal educational vision of its founders and provided that liberalism with a modern twist, to give Moreton Hall girls the edge when they enter the adult world of work. Jonathan says he has been empowered by the environment, and it must be mutual, because his entrepreneurial spirit, his thinking outside the box, shows in the girls and in the whole ethos of the place. He has done remarkable things and when he eventually does leave, it will take someone very special to take his place.

Academic matters: Academic results are strong (though 2015 A levels a disappointing 36 per cent at A*/A; GCSEs more encouraging 72 per cent A*/A) and the value-added scores at both GCSE and A level are usually huge. Its increasing success draws in star teachers and bright girls, so it's all on an upward trajectory. With lots of living accommodation on site, the job becomes a lifestyle choice for teachers as well as families. There is no deadening insistence on the latest Department for Education pedagogy here. The principal is far more interested in bringing in people who have done things – the English department boasts a writer, the art department has practising artists and the girls told us that their chemistry teacher had been testing perfumes before joining Moreton Hall. There is a strong science drive in the school (innovative science centre includes medical science facility – the first for any UK school) and well over half are taking at least one science A level. Close links to Keele University and the orthopaedic hospital at nearby Gobowen.

Though edging up all the time, the ability is quite wide on entry, which makes the results

particularly encouraging. It's down to excellent teachers as well as small class sizes. The girls describe their teachers as 'passionate and enthusiastic' and are very aware that they are there literally all the time. 'They give you as much extra as you need,' says one sixth former who told us that when she was working late on a piece of work, she had emailed her teacher with a query at 11pm and had a reply.

There is no extra charge for learning support, whether it is Oxbridge preparation or getting through GCSE maths. Teachers are there for the girls whatever their needs – no sense of children having to fit into rigid school systems here. One parent commented on the flexibility the school offered in terms of curriculum – girls can study more or less any combination of subjects they want at GCSE and A level.

Games, options, the arts: It's in this side of school life where its radical and constantly progressing nature really shines. In sport it embraces that most traditional of girls' sports, lacrosse, where the Moreton Hall teams win everything this side of London and a fair bit nationally as well, but there are masses of other successes and opportunities with the fabulous sports facilities on site – a nine hole golf course and grounds that mean cross-country really is cross country.

Lots of music goes on, classical and popular, with girls performing regularly to both large and small audiences. Drama is hugely popular and professional. 'Musical theatre can consume everything', said one non-thespian parent, worrying about exam results, but the girls are queuing up to take part.

All this is nothing like enough for Moreton Hall. The school is strong on connections and is extraordinarily well linked with a network of influential men and women whom Jonathan brings into the school for inspirational talks. Outside London this is not easy, and you would never guess this school was in the depth of gorgeous Shropshire. Dame Jocelyn Bell Burnett, world famous astrophysicist, had just been when we visited, and strong links with Keele University produce a steady flow of high-powered visitors. These not only enhance academic lessons but often come to speak at one of the many societies to which parents also drop in. There is wine-tasting, a feminist society, a medical science group, share dealing and so it goes on, reflecting the scope of opportunities for young women in the 21st century world.

Head organises lively programme of inspirational outside speakers. Dame Jocelyn Bell Burnett, the world famous astrophysicist, was a recent visitor

All the girls get involved in the English Speaking Board to enhance confidence, presentation skills and the ability to think on their feet. One parent said, 'Everyone gets a 2.1 from Bristol or wherever these days, but Jonathan Forster really understands that the girls will need a lot more than that – he is giving them the life skills to succeed.'

Moreton Enterprises is part of this – a unique business venture consisting of a shopping mall run entirely by the girls. There is a branch of Ryman's stationery, Barclays Bank and home grown shops. The girls have business mentors, but basically the lower sixth operates as a small business turning over £50,000 a year. It is seriously impressive.

Boarding: About 90 per cent are boarders, and there is Saturday morning school, but apart from that, it is pretty flexible. One parent felt that girls new to boarding could be unsettled by friends coming and going, but we didn't find any girls who worried about this. The school wants girls to love boarding there and they do, partly because of the very special staff and partly because there is so much going on. 'It's like a long sleep-over but with loads to do as well,' said an enamoured 13 year old who had started as a day girl and then converted to boarding after a few taster nights.

We asked the sixth formers whether they felt a long way from all the city lights and boys, but were assured they saw quite as much as they wanted to of Shrewsbury School boys and often stayed Saturday night with friends in Manchester or Birmingham if they could fit it in between rehearsals, choir, talks. 'But it is just so lovely to come back,' they said with heartfelt sincerity.

Senior boarding accommodation is single or double (very popular in holidays with overseas adults as well as children), adding to the home from home feel. Junior girls and boys, often boarding one or two nights a week, have their own cheerful dormitories.

Background and atmosphere: As you would expect from girls who run a business at the age of 16, they are confident and at ease with themselves. They work and play hard, but there is something in the rural Shropshire surroundings (the school is set in 100 acres of parkland) that takes any unattractive edge off the ambition and drive. We felt that every girl in England should have at least a term in this environment.

The school was started by women educationalists 100 years ago, and Jonathan holds firm to their liberal view of education. He has used the school's centenary year to ensure the girls know about the strong female role models in the school's past. 'It was never meant to be like other schools,' he tells us. 'The Lloyd Williams family wanted a school where girls could enjoy the country and experience a rounded education that would set them up for life and all the different people they would meet'.

> *When asked why he had chosen Moreton Hall for his daughters, one parent looked rather bemused and said, 'Well, why wouldn't you?' We agree*

The very English country landscape and original school building, a moated Tudor house with the current façade dating from William and Mary, are balanced by new state-of-the-art purpose built areas. There is a stunning new science block planned in a collaboration with Keele University and local state schools. The facilities are used by the university to run science taster session for local students with a particular emphasis on medical careers. The library is both welcoming and very modern. One girl talked about working in the library before her GCSEs and being able to take her kettle, mug and biscuits in there for a real go at her revision – good for the librarian.

Pastoral care, well-being and discipline: The principal wants the girls to love Moreton Hall as they would love their home, and to care for the school and each other in the same way. From what we saw, they do. There was a genuine warmth between the older and younger girls and a sincere appreciation for their surroundings and the attention they receive from teachers and boarding staff. Given the entrepreneurial energy about the place, the girls are amazingly relaxed. One member of staff said, 'They have time and space here so you don't get a frenetic atmosphere building up where no one has room for anyone except themselves'. These are not privileged princesses who think the world owes them. They are self-disciplined young women who have learnt in school that you can make a difference and live happily together. The centenary pageant included everyone who is a part of the school – not just teachers and girls. It's an inclusive place. Discipline was not a word we heard mentioned, and for a school that can happily host tribute bands in the outdoor amphitheatre on the last night of the summer term without a qualm – who needs lots of rules and punishment?

Pupils and parents: Some 80 per cent of the boarders are from the UK, a deliberate policy, and about 90 per cent of those girls are from within one to two hours travel. The school caters for business, diplomatic and professional families where often both parents are working and see the boarding option as a lifestyle choice, with the girls having endless activities and friends on tap. Communication, both formal and informal, works very effectively. Overseas parents tell us the school makes brilliant use of modern technology and emails are responded to very quickly by both the head and staff. Parents are supportive both in terms of social events and also by acting as mentors for the business enterprises. They can drop in to more or less any event going on, and the division between home and school seems very fluid compared with many schools. One parent said, 'There are very traditional families who find it all rather liberal, but the principal soon shows them it works'. The principal and staff are well known for their assiduous attendance at school events and their detailed knowledge of the girls and their families.

There is a separate study centre for overseas students and multi-activity holidays for children and their parents.

Entrance: Many of 11+ entrants from co-ed junior school, Moreton First. Then further entry points at 13 and 16 into the sixth form. Number from overseas capped at 10 per cent. Test, interview and school report to determine entry. Oversubscribed at various points, particularly in sixth form. Once girls are there, the school sticks with them and very few leave – including hardly any year 11 leavers (some 10 per cent).

Exit: Almost all to university including two to Oxford in 2015. Leeds very popular (including for physics and biology), then Bath, Exeter, Liverpool and Oxford Brookes. Not surprisingly, given their experience in school, a remarkable number of Old Moretonians are running successful businesses.

Money matters: The school has worked hard to increase means-tested bursaries, particularly to allow local girls from state schools to join the sixth form. Everyone pays something, but the aim is to give girls who would otherwise not have the opportunity a chance to experience the high-powered, aspirational world of Moreton Hall.

Remarks: It is outside the radar of parents who don't look beyond the home counties but more fool them – they are the ones missing out here. When asked why he had chosen Moreton Hall for his daughters, one parent looked vaguely bemused and said, 'Well, why wouldn't you?' We agree. This is a school with a difference, rigour in everything but going about it in a way that shows girls they can lead the world in a new way. And they will.

Oakham School

Chapel Close, Oakham, Rutland LE15 6DT

01572 758758
admissions@oakham.rutland.sch.uk
www.oakham.rutland.sch.uk
C of E

Ages: 10–18
Pupils: 1,043; sixth form: 405
Boarders: 544 full/flexi
Day: £16,650 to £18,780 pa
Boarding: £19,950 – £31,110 pa

Headmaster: Since 2009, Mr Nigel Lashbrook BA (late 40s). Educated at King's Heath Boys' Technical School (he was one of the last grammar school intake) and Hertford College, Oxford, where he read chemistry, played in the university's 2nd cricket XI and captained his college rugby side. Stayed on at Oxford to train as a teacher and began teaching career at Manchester Grammar School, where he taught science and coached rugby and cricket teams. After eight years moved south to Tonbridge School as head of science and chemistry. Later became a housemaster and, at the age of 40, second master. Jumped at the opportunity to become acting head for a term while head was on sabbatical – he did so well that returning head predicted, 'I don't think you'll be here for long'. Sure enough, he was appointed head of King's Bruton soon after and spent five years at the helm there before moving to Oakham.

Approachable, affable and ambitious, he took to Oakham like a duck to water. Married to Jill, a geography and economics teacher. They live on site and have two grown up sons and daughter at Oakham.

A firm believer in education not just being about what happens in the classroom, he is proud of the fact that Oakham manages to be a 'happy and successful' school 'without being a hothouse in any shape or form'. He's determined, too, to open Oakham's doors to pupils who would thrive at the school but whose parents can't afford to send them, and is busy developing stronger links with local state schools, especially the 11-16 academy. Proud of Oakham's sense of community – the school has a lively volunteering programme and the school's musicians give free (and very well attended) concerts for the town at All Saints' Church every Wednesday.

Academic matters: Results commendable. In 2015, 34 per cent of A level grades were A*/A grades whilst 68 per cent were A*/B. Twenty-six subjects on offer at AS/A2 – all the usual ones, plus business studies, classical civilisation, economics, PE and sport studies and politics. Prides itself on being an innovative school and has offered the IB since 2000. In 2015, average IB points score was 36. School helps pupils decide between IB and A levels. Deputy head reckons it's a myth that the IB is only for the brightest – 'It depends on the breadth of pupils' academic interest,' he says, 'but it's quite transformative in developing a much broader approach to their work'.

At GCSE, 65 per cent of grades were A*/A in 2015. All core subjects (maths, English, modern languages and the sciences) are now examined through the more academically rigorous IGCSE. Unlike some comparable schools, Oakham still submits its results for listing in the league tables. 'But,' says the head, 'it's just a snapshot. There is far more to what we offer than the league tables show.'

Impressive computerised language labs where pupils learn French from year 7. German and

Loads of top sportsmen and women started at Oakham – GB Olympic bronze hockey medallist Crista Cullen, cricketer Stuart Broad and several rugby internationals

Spanish on offer from year 8. Everyone takes at least one language at GCSE, but most take two. Setting for all in maths, French and science from year 9. Up until GCSE, maximum class size is 24, though often much smaller, whilst A level and IB classes tend to have 10 pupils or fewer. SEN supported by team of four learning support teachers. School prefers to give in-class support rather than take pupils out of class – no charge made for this.

Games, options, the arts: School talks a lot about the 'total curriculum' and the importance of pupils achieving their full potential in every sense. With this in mind, opportunities galore in sport and the arts. By any measure, a very sporty school – independent school of the year in the Daily Telegraph Sport Matters Awards a few years ago, 1st XV rugby side reached the final of the Daily Mail U19 national schools' rugby cup recently. Loads of top sportsmen and women started at Oakham – GB Olympic bronze hockey medallist Crista Cullen, cricketer Stuart Broad and rugby internationals Lewis Moody, Alex Goode and Tom Croft, to name a few. School has more than 40 acres of games pitches (pretty much the summer home of ECB age

group county cricket), sports centre, 25m indoor pool, two all-weather pitches, squash courts and a fitness centre. Around 30 sports on offer, including cycling, golf and sailing (on nearby Rutland Water), but main sports are rugby, hockey, cricket and athletics for boys and hockey, netball, tennis and athletics for girls. Seven hundred pupils take part in competitive sport, from 1st XV rugby to polo. Some weekends the school fields six rugby or hockey teams per year group. Over 60 staff involved in sports coaching – 12 full-timers, 20 visiting coaches and some 30 teachers from the common room.

Drama is an integral part of the school. Two hundred and fifty-seat Queen Elizabeth Theatre, recently refurbished, hosts four main school productions a year (rehearsals for Little Shop of Horrors in full swing when we visited), along with shows by touring companies. Each house competes for the MacFadyen Shield, given to the school by Pride and Prejudice actor Matthew MacFadyen, a former pupil. Music just keeps expanding, with 600 instrumental lessons a week (some of the instrumental teachers travel from as far afield as London and Manchester). Around 80 concerts a year. A quarter of pupils sing in a choir and for the past four years pupils have won the competition to compose a fanfare for the Royal Opera House. The go-ahead music department is the first in the school to offer the subject as a Cambridge Pre-U qualification (alternative to A level.)

> *Each house competes for the MacFadyen Shield, a drama prize given to the school by Pride and Prejudice actor Matthew MacFadyen, a former pupil*

Art is amazing – everything from life drawing, abstracts and sculpture to textiles and jewellery – with new Wheelhouse Gallery for exhibitions. Has been offering critical and contextual studies (a modern form of art history) at A level for three years and has won The Good Schools Guide's award for the best results by independent school girls in the subject two years running. DT department rightfully proud of the brand new Jerwoods School of Design, which cost £2m and is equipped with state-of-the-art technology. Third formers (year 8s) get off to a productive start by making their own USB sticks, whilst an enterprising former pupil recently set up his own business selling the gun box he designed for his DT A level.

On two afternoons a week everyone does activities, trying their hand at everything from aerobics and film production to stone carving and yoga. From year 10 onwards pupils can opt for Duke of Edinburgh Award scheme (school was first to achieve 1,000 D of E golds), CCF or community service.

Boarding: No weekly boarding – very much a full boarding school, with so much going on at weekends that day pupils often pitch up to join in activities on Sundays. Also offers transition boarding, of two to four nights a week, in the lower school (10-13 year olds) and day boarding, of three nights a week, in the middle and upper schools. Transition boarding is a great way for youngsters to try boarding life and see if they like it. As well as half term, two 'leave-out' weekends every term when boarders can go home.

Houses all have common rooms, quiet rooms and games rooms. One housemaster, aware that it would be all too easy for boarders to live in 'this little Oakham bubble', gets his GCSE boys to lead a debate every week – everything discussed, from politics to the Pope's visit to ideas for house trips. Sixth formers get rooms of their own, with younger years usually two, three or four to a room. Parents can express preferences for boarding houses but school has final say.

Background and atmosphere: Founded in 1584, sits in the centre of the prosperous market town of Oakham, surrounded by the rolling Rutland countryside. The main parts have the feel of a Cambridge college – quiet quads, old stone buildings overlooking immaculate lawns and flower beds. Much is owed to pioneering former head, John Buchanan, whose tenure from 1958 to 1977 oversaw the school's move to full independence and co-education, as well as the landscaped garden feel of the whole site.

Lessons take place in two to four-storey purpose-built blocks. Superb Smallbone Library is a match for public library standards – spacious, well-stocked, computerised, it boasts a careers room, first floor for silent individual study and is open every day. New science faculty brings biology, chemistry, physics and sports science under one roof and there's a new auditorium that provides much-needed lecture space. Chapel twice a week and all meals eaten in school's light, airy dining hall.

Pastoral care, well-being and discipline: Sixteen houses, scattered across the large campus: four junior houses (two day and two boarding), 10 houses for 13-17 year olds (five for boys and five for girls) and two upper sixth houses (one for boys, one for girls). Comfortable, well-kept houses are run by staff, who have teaching responsibilities too. Useful 'settling in' guide for new pupils, with wise advice from prefects, like 'Don't be shy or afraid to get involved' and 'Give everything a go'.

'It's hard to stereotype an Oakhamian,' said the head boy. 'There is so much on offer here for everyone and it's given me the chance to try so many new things'

Rules clearly spelled out in Oakham's 'red book'. Anyone who tests positive for drugs or admits to drug misuse faces suspension or expulsion. Any pupil who supplies or brings drugs into the school is out straight away. One youngster expelled for drugs in last five years. Rules on alcohol and smoking crystal clear too. Head boy and head girl appointed every year, along with 22 school prefects (known as The Decem, because used to be 10 of them).

Plenty of sympathetic ears for pupils in need of advice and help – housemasters/mistresses, tutors, matrons, chaplains, medical centre and school counsellor. New pupils given mentors to guide them through their early weeks. Uniform is compulsory and pupils look well turned out as they hurry between lessons. Business suits for sixth formers, while boys wear blazers and ties and girls are clad in black and white tartan skirts and blazers. 'We want them to look smart,' says head. 'They are ambassadors for the school.'

Pupils and parents: Outgoing, enthusiastic bunch, determined to make the most of every second at Oakham. 'It's hard to stereotype an Oakhamian,'

the head boy told us. 'There is so much on offer here for everyone and it's given me the chance to have a go at so many new things.' Most come from one to three hours' drive away. Around 10 per cent from overseas. Past pupils (known as OOs) are an eclectic lot – they include actors Matthew MacFadyen and Greg Hicks, director Katie Mitchell and international sports stars Lewis Moody, Stuart Broad, Lucy Pearson and Crista Cullen. Parents are a supportive crew – director of sport reckons 60 per cent regularly turn out to cheer teams on.

Entrance: More and more competitive to get in. Pupils come from all over the shop – 30+ different preps. At 10 and 11, intake is mostly youngsters from local primary schools and preps, while 13+ entrants tend to be mostly boarders. Entrance exams at 10+ and 11+ in maths, English and verbal reasoning. At 13+ CE mark of 55 per cent needed or, for those coming from schools which don't do CE, school's own exams in English, maths, French and science. Lower school pupils don't need to take exam to progress into middle school. Around 40 to 50 new pupils enter the sixth form each year – they need seven Bs at GCSE, with a minimum of Bs in the subjects to be studied in the sixth form.

Exit: A handful leave after GCSEs, mainly to take vocational courses or subjects Oakham doesn't offer (like law, psychology or the dreaded media studies). At 18 virtually all progress to higher education – popular destinations include Birmingham, Bristol, Cambridge, Durham, Exeter, Leeds, Manchester, Newcastle, Nottingham and UCL, as well as across the world (USA, Canada, Germany, Italy and Switzerland). Ten Oxbridge places in 2015 and 13 medical offers; popular courses include business management, economics, the sciences, engineering, maths, medicine, art and history.

Money matters: Variety of scholarships on offer – academic and music at 11, academic, music, art, DT, sport and all-rounder at 13. More available at 16, including the recent introduction of science and engineering scholarships for pupils to join the sixth form from a state school. Oakham scholarships offer five to 10 per cent off the fees, but the school says greater financial assistance may be available (in cases of proven need, this can be up to 100 per cent).

Remarks: A friendly, unpretentious and forward-thinking school that achieves impressive academic results. Far from being an academic hothouse, has high expectations and achievements across the board. For all-rounders who like rolling their sleeves up and throwing themselves into a staggering range of activities it's a very exciting place to be.

Oundle School

Great Hall, Oundle, Peterborough, Northamptonshire PE8 4GH

01832 277125
admissions@oundleschool.org.uk
www.oundleschool.org.uk
C of E

Ages: 11–19
Pupils: 1,103; sixth form: 400
Boarders: 852 full
Day: £16,230 – £21,345 pa
Boarding: £25,320 – £33,300 pa

Headmaster: Since September 2015, Mrs Sarah Kerr-Dineen, previously warden of Forest School. Read English at Cambridge followed by postgraduate study at Oxford and NPQH. Taught at Open University, Kelly College (now Mount Kelly), Oxford High School (where she was an acting subject head) and St Edward's Oxford (for 13 years – she was boarding housemistress and responsible for the pastoral care of 80 girls, then director of studies). She is married with four adult children and her interests include reading, walking, theatre and music.

Academic matters: Possibly the most academically selective of all the co-ed full-boarding schools. Results are good – 85 per cent A/A* at GCSE/IGCSE and 64 per cent A*/A at A level in 2015. Many end up with a mix of qualifications, depending on the subjects taken: Pre-U (linear, no modules), a more rigorous alternative to A level, is the only option in eight subjects: chemistry, English lit, history, history of art, German, Italian, Chinese and physics. No weak spots but Latin and chemistry perceived

to be especially strong. Staff teach beyond the curriculum, investigate, explore and extend. All sixth-formers follow a non-examined general studies course which includes weekly lectures, discussions, debate and more.

It's not only cool to work but to do so with pace and purpose. Staff say pupils are a delight: 'Teaching is a serious business but students help make it fun, they have a good sense of humour, you can let your guard down a bit.' Not all are angels all of the time: 'My child had a problem concentrating and was allowed to change groups to get away from another child who was messing around'. We dropped in on a couple of lessons to find pupils engaged and on task, aided by some inspirational teaching. Parents happy with school but not gushingly so; they choose Oundle because their baseline is excellence and, for almost all, Oundle delivers. Very few parental moans: ad-hoc report times irritate some; girls, top students and strugglers (ie borderline B/C grade at A level) do well but feel some middling boys could do better; parent portal on wish list, but appreciative of extensive use of email.

School will support and encourage those with mild SEN, mainly specific learning difficulties but Asperger's and other SEN considered, so long as child is good university fodder. Parents say approach is matter of fact, no pandering: 'This is what we have, this is what we will do.' Help given with study skills plus whatever is identified in ed psych report. Minimal one-to-one help available but support for all (SEN or not) from individual departments. Pacey, demanding curriculum means EAL students need excellent English prior to arrival.

Good and ever improving facilities; latest jewel is the SciTec block with 16 well-designed labs. Whizzy new Adamson Centre languages block has state-of-the-art everything including an 'international suite' which 'provides a perfect venue for language conferences, films, lectures from visiting speakers and competitions'. The super 20,000 volume library stays open late and offers a book-ordering service. Flagship, innovative DT (BBC B computer started life here) – a veritable hive of activity and inspiration when we visited – continues to thrive. Industrious atmosphere, wonderful, woody workshops with casting, lasers, wind tunnels, micro-electronics and CAD all adding to the scintillating sensory experience. Mr Bean's car may have vamoosed but others remain, in various glorious states of build and disrepair.

Music department has formed partnership with the Royal College of Music, a huge nod to the very high standard of musicianship

Games, options, the arts: All major sports pursued including rugby, football, hockey, netball, squash, fives, water polo, rowing, athletics, aerobics, cross-country, golf. Recently became a Marylebone Cricket Club Foundation Hub, working to improve coaching for local state school children. Good facilities include a multi-sports complex with sports shop, pool, an outdoor synthetic athletics track, rifle range etc. Generally hold their own, win some, lose some, with a few key successes along the way including notable individual honours and national team selection – not bad considering sports schols only recently introduced. Parents say, 'Not all coaches are equally capable and enthusiastic; lower teams very much at mercy of master in charge but genuine sport for all – if they can put a team out, they will'.

For the stage-struck the charming Stahl Theatre, enjoyed by school and locals alike, provides a professional venue for touring companies as well as for esteemed pupil productions. Busy music department has recently formed a partnership with the Royal College of Music, a huge nod to the very high standard of musicianship. Two-thirds learn an instrument though far fewer perform. Music and drama lean towards the exclusive, pupils and parents grumble that those whose trumpet blowing is enthusiastic rather than virtuoso, or who hide their dramatic light under a bushel, are unlikely to be placed centre-stage or even on-stage, making it difficult for late developers to get a look in.

Art popular and prolific. We saw superb sculptures and castings, plus exquisite fine art. Yarrow Gallery regularly hosts visiting exhibitions as well as pupils' own masterpieces. Millennium marked by pupil-design inspired, vibrantly coloured stained-glass windows made for the school chapel, a lively foil to John Piper's sedately beautiful east windows.

Field trips, exchanges, tours and expeditions galore to the near, the exotic and the remote. Extraordinarily varied list of activities known as 'voluntaries' are, paradoxically, compulsory for younger students; courses range from knitting, bee-keeping and bridge through to junior economics, dance and DT. Virtually all do D of E. CCF compulsory in the fourth form, remains a popular choice thereafter. Optional fifth and sixth form community action programme recognised as a class-leader, not just holding hands with the elderly or cleaning out chicken sheds but tough stuff too, including street sleeping to help understand the harsher side of life and instil a 'give-back' culture. A busy school with little let-up, though all get chance to let their hair down via active social programme now enhanced by transformation of old fives courts into social centres.

Boarding: The 13 self-contained, well-maintained boarding houses have unique personalities; according to 'Oundelian', the school's own rather chic publication, Sanderson is 'intimidating', Laundimer 'friendly'. In reality school mixes pupils to ensure no cliques, or types ('the Scottish house' notwithstanding) – apply early if you yearn for a particular house. Compulsory chapel on Sunday plus two other weekly slots.

Background and atmosphere: Situated in the delightful market town of Oundle, with its gentle, honey-toned Cotswold stone, the school was founded in 1556 as the local grammar. In 1876 the school split into Laxton, for the sons of tradesmen and local farmers, and Oundle, for the sons of gentlemen. Full co-education came in the early 1990s and Laxton was brought back into the fold as a day house in 2000. Today it's hard to distinguish the extensive school campus and its 1,100 pupils from the eponymous town. Size matters; fortunately house loyalty endures.

Activities known as 'voluntaries' are, paradoxically, compulsory for younger students; courses include beekeeping, bridge, knitting, dance and junior economics

Pastoral care, well-being and discipline: No time for prolonged hand holding – pupils heed the emphasis on self-reliance – but HMs and personal tutors help and support. 'Most youngsters get something wrong at some point. We keep our ear to the ground and lines of communication open. We watch them try and sometimes fail, try again. We pick them up, dust them down, help them move on.' Parents say some HMs are excellent, stress there are no weak ones, but caution that HMs vary in outlook, attitude, expectations and communications. All dine in-house which means a careful eye can be kept on eating issues, friendships et al. Odd comment from parents of girls that house system is more geared up for boys, citing fewer events with parents, and more fall-outs between girls (no more than anywhere else, we suspect); certainly the girls we met were friendly, articulate and clearly had a sense of community. Parents of boys praise the range of house activities, camaraderie, and parental involvement; 'We appreciate the even-handedness of staff in dealing with issues'. Parents who live afar are especially praiseworthy of helpful, prompt and detailed home-school comms and of school's honesty about 'incidents'.

All incidences of bullying taken seriously, work done with victims and perpetrators. On the very rare occasion when things don't work out, students may be sent home to rethink, or supported in their quest to find something that suits better. 'Sometimes a fresh start elsewhere is all that is needed. All will make fantastic adults, we simply have to help them through the stupidity of adolescence.' Pupils at ease with each other and with staff, though some older students confess to feeling a little stifled by rules and ready for the freedom of life after school. Rules are fair and the school, perceived to be 'very, very strict', upholds the policy re drugs and sex – instant out. Those aged 18 allowed controlled access to pub and alcohol (understandably strict – a former student once tried unsuccessfully to sue school after a drunken fall several years earlier left her permanently disabled). Hot on electronic footprint, work hard to ensure youngsters understand cyber dangers.

Pupils and parents: From all over UK, including strong Scottish contingent, currently over 120 prep schools represented. Close family ties, some 12 percent are offspring of OOs. Twelve per cent from continental Europe or the Pacific Rim. Parents range from the professional to farming folk – open minded, ambitious. Not an obvious choice for first-time buyers but those who opt in are justifiably proud of their acquisition. School says London parents are the trickiest; 'They want the Oundle experience but on weekly boarding terms' – little chance of that, we suspect. Social credentials abound but social club this isn't, some parents keen to be more involved and for greater social interaction and parental events but a tricky feat for what is a genuine boarding school with a global community. Exeats a rarity; officially one per annum but flexibility when essential.

Pupils are bright, friendly, articulate and courteous. Uniform adhered to, girls look glam in their swishing culottes, boys business-like in dark suit and tie. OOs include Arthur Marshall, Cecil Lewis (aviator), Peter Scott (ornithologist), A Alvarez, Anthony Holden (royal biographer), Richard Dawkins, Professor Sir Alan Budd, Charles Crichton (film director), Bruce Dickinson (lead singer of Iron Maiden – allegedly expelled following a rock-star style prank).

Entrance: Rigorous at 11+, 13+ and 16+. Waiting list (up to two years) with sibling preference (a third have a brother or sister in the school). Feeder schools are well primed and start preparation early. The registrar makes it his business to ensure only those who will succeed are entered. Minimum CE requirement of 55 per cent in English, maths, French and sciences but in reality those accepted typically average 70 per cent (scholars do even better). Officially no pre-testing but runs practice CE day in November, 'to avoid disappointment'; those not following CE are assessed early via assortment of tests. Sixth form entry requires minimum three As and three Bs in GCSEs but competition for handful of places at 16+ means successful external applicants typically have fistfuls of A and A* grades. As with many popular, larger schools, when visiting you are unlikely to meet with the head (unless specifically requested); potential Oundelians are left in the very capable hands of trusty registrar.

Exit: Nearly all move on to the sixth form and thence to university. Mainly traditional courses at traditional universities – with Newcastle, Bristol, Exeter, Durham, UCL, Nottingham and Edinburgh favoured destinations. Forty per cent take arts degrees with the rest split between social sciences and sciences; history, economics and engineering the most popular subjects. Plenty of extra help for those wishing to apply to Oxbridge – 26 successful candidates in 2015, though school says it is sometimes surprised by who is accepted and saddened that some outstanding students are turned away. Increasing numbers head across the pond thanks, in part, to well-versed influence of US staff.

Money matters: Range of scholarships awarded at 11+, 13+ and 16+, most limited to 10 per cent of fees. Bursaries as high as 100 per cent available in cases of proven need; apply at least two years prior to entry for help, expect to fill in extensive forms designed to unearth every last sou. No automatic sibling or forces discounts but Old Oundelian bursaries for the sons and daughters of OOs.

Remarks: A very busy school, ideal for the resilient, confident, energetic, academic child, who thrives in a large, pacey setting, rejoices in a heavy, focussed workload and delights in an abundance of extracurricular activities. Average all-rounders should head elsewhere, stragglers will struggle, strugglers will likely be lost in the milieu. For those who can, Oundle does. Anyone considering a full-boarding education for their motivated, able offspring should short-list Oundle.

Packwood Haugh School

Ruyton XI Towns, Shrewsbury, Shropshire SY4 1HX

01939 260217
headmaster@packwood-haugh.co.uk
www.packwood-haugh.co.uk
C of E

Ages: 4–13 (boarders from 7)
Pupils: 240
Boarders: 91 full, 53 flexi (two thirds boys)
Day: £7,710 – £16,680 pa
Boarding: £20,970 pa

Headmaster: Since September 2012, Mr Clive Smith-Langridge, previously deputy head at Hordle Walhampton (now Walhampton). A maths and sports specialist, he qualified as a teacher whilst teaching games at Cumnor House in Sussex after a business career. He is married with two daughters.

Entrance: Not selective. Short informal assessment – maths and English – for entry to prep. Scholarships awarded: academic, sporting, music, art, all-rounder. Means-tested bursaries and bursaries for Forces families. Children come from Shropshire, Cheshire, Wales, Staffordshire, London. Handful of overseas students, particularly from Spain, Japan, China and Thailand.

Exit: Typically 15+ different schools every year. The most popular destination for boys and girls is Shrewsbury (where rumour mill has it that Packwood children are noted for an ability to get on with others); steady numbers to Rugby, Malvern, Eton, Rugby, Oundle, Moreton Hall, Sedbergh, Stowe, Tonbridge, Uppingham, Warwick; Concord College.

Remarks: Traditional country prep school, a 'proper' boarding school. Head is committed to boarding, now with some flexibility including transitional boarding, occasional nights and optional weekends. Boarding numbers are holding up well – resists pressure for more day school places.

Academic but unpressurised. Careful streaming. Has gained more scholarships in recent years, and strong common entrance results; parents like the broad range of abilities: 'They look after the quirky child, and work hard to find what makes

each child tick,' said one. 'A goodish number' of children (around 60) have varied SEN, some physical. Good learning support department. Prides itself on being inclusive and does seem so – one boy in a wheelchair was getting stuck into a vigorous playtime ball game. A recent leaver, born with hemiplaegia, played an active part in the school's sporting and musical life, winning the coveted Character cup.

Good place for children who like the great outdoors. Strong sports – competes successfully at football, cricket, netball, hockey, punches above its weight for lacrosse, and is regarded highly for its rugby. Regularly sends out third and fourth teams. Winter sports programme recently changed so can play bigger schools: 'More travelling, but more – and tougher – matches'. Competitions between houses (known as 'Sixes'). Fantastic new sports hall. Judo and fencing particularly popular. Over 80 children signed up for summer Duel in the Sun fencing competition and several rated nationally. Riding is big – has a cross-country course, runs its own gymkhana and hosts a series of horsey events, show jumpers placed third at National Schools Equestrian Competition recently. Sympathy for the non-sporting, who might do other activities – 'My son hates all sport, but found his niche in a very sporty school,' says one parent. Another avowedly non-sporting boy became a whizz at stage-lighting.

Strong music – 75 per cent of pupils learn an instrument and 70+ take music exams. A recent development has been to introduce more ensembles. Art is good and popular – fantastic new facilities have meant greater scope for adventurous projects. A corridor of computers links the art studio and DT room, where shutters close off the scariest equipment so children can work there in free time. Big year-based drama productions. One parent felt that drama wasn't the strongest point but school says new head of drama has invigorated the department – drama lessons for all in years 3-6, lots of class open assemblies and drama activities.

Strong common entrance results; parents like the broad range of abilities: 'They look after the quirky, and work hard to find what makes each child tick'

Large majority of boarders in school at weekends. Three levels of boarding: occasional (up to three nights on regular basis); a year's transitional, giving children an option of going home at weekends; and full boarding with a few optional weekends. Boys' dormitories are over four landings in main school supported by kind matrons. Rolling programme of refurbishment is updating all boys' dormitories, and new bedrooms are very comfortable; boys like the prospect of being in Crocodile Swamp or Snake Pit and love the appropriately themed murals. A move to add bunks has created more floor-space. The recently redecorated girls' dormitories (in a separate building, Park House) look very welcoming.

Main building comprises original sandstone house and farm buildings dotted with additions – some unlovely 1960/70s, with nicer newer ones, including great theatre. Grounds roll away from the buildings like a green sea. Space (66 acres) is its luxury and it makes the most of it. Lovely grass tennis courts. A big draw is The Spinney, a wooded area with an intricate den system where boys and girls go on Wednesday and weekend afternoons and where pre-prep pupils (Packwood Acorns) have their forest school.

Lots going on at weekends. 'Be aware if you have day children, you will come under huge pressure from your children to let them board,' warned one mother. Clubs range from the outdoorsy – clay pigeon and rifle-shooting, fly-fishing and fly-tying – to chess and jewellery making. No association, but gets a lot of support from parents, who help run events like the popular biannual Dog Show (black labs in abundance). Winter match teas in front of a roaring fire are popular – a sociable place. Lots of traditional country families.

Maybe it's all that fresh air and space, but children seem a particularly cheerful, unprecious bunch, happy to chatter away to adults, and feel no 'them and us' between boarders and day pupils.

Repton School

Repton, Derby DE65 6FH

01283 559222
registrar@repton.org.uk
www.repton.org.uk
C of E

Ages: 13–18
Pupils: 648; sixth form: 310
Boarders: 443 full
Day: £24,531 pa
Boarding: £33,066 pa

Linked school: Foremarke Hall (Repton Preparatory School)

Head: The new head from April 2016 will be Alastair Land, currently deputy head at Harrow School. First class honours in natural sciences from Cambridge; taught biology at Eton, where he also ran the CCF. Moved to Winchester as master in college and senior housemaster before joining Harrow in 2012. As well as involvement in CCF, he has directed house plays, organised and competed in endurance challenges and chaired an adventurous training committee. His wife, Madeleine, is currently head of maths at North London Collegiate; they have a young son.

Sarah Tennant, deputy head, took over as acting head in December 2014 when Robert Holroyd stood down due to ill health.

Academic matters: In the past Repton produced sound but unexceptional exam grades, but these have been well and truly been put in the shade by recent results. In 2015, 56 per cent A*/A, 81 per cent A*-B grades at A level. GCSEs strong too – 61 per cent A*/A grades. Lots of maths and French GCSEs taken a year early. Most subjects setted according to ability. Traditional teaching methods, with all pupils allocated an academic tutor to monitor progress. Year groups of 110 to 120 in years 9, 10 and 11 (or B block, A block and O block, as they're known here) and up to 150 in both lower sixth and upper sixth. Class sizes are 15 on average.

Wide choice of subjects on offer, including business studies, PE, drama and politics. Everyone does French, and keen linguists can take Spanish or German from year 9 too. Youngest also take either Latin or classical civilisation. Pupils very much encouraged to read for pleasure. Year 9s have graded reading scheme, with target to read three books of a certain level every term. Appointment of academic 'tsar' has seen more outside involvement in school curriculum, with well-known names invited to lecture students. Guests have included BBC foreign correspondent David Loyn, Holocaust survivor Freddie Knoller and diplomat and environmentalist Sir Crispin Tickell. Academic deputy has also introduced electronic reporting on pupils' progress. Teachers' reports on academic work (effort and achievement) emailed to parents every four or five weeks, plus usual end-of-term reports too.

Learning support available in small groups or one-to-one and individual education plans for each pupil to monitor progress. Relevant information and strategies passed to subject teachers to ensure support continues in class. Head full of praise for his team and pupils agree that teachers go the extra mile to help them. Teachers we met seemed to have boundless energy and enthusiasm. Prep from 7 to 9pm on weekday nights (all day pupils stay till 9pm too). Youngest supervised, the rest work independently in their houses.

Games, options, the arts: Sport goes from strength to strength. Boys play football, hockey and cricket, girls hockey, netball, tennis. At the time of our visit the boys had recently won the national U18 hockey championships for the first time, whilst the girls had clinched the national U18 title for the sixth year in a row. Not only that, a trio of old girls are in the current England ladies' hockey squad. Football is pretty impressive too – indeed a sixth form boy already has four full Northern Ireland caps to his name. Cricket, tennis, athletics, fencing report similar triumphs. Clutch of county and test cricketers

regularly produced. When it comes to principal sports, school regularly fields three teams per year group, sometimes five. Impressive sports facilities, including sports complex, large indoor pool, water-based and sand-based Astros, 16 outdoor tennis courts, two indoor tennis courts, squash and fives courts. CCF compulsory for youngest pupils and then can opt to continue or choose D of E or community service.

Weekend activities or SLOPs (Sunday leisure options) as they are known include cycling in the Peak District, paintballing, trips to Clothes Show Live etc

Unusually for a school, has three art galleries in the village, exhibiting the work of pupils as well as resident and visiting artists. Artwork on display everywhere throughout school – a huge abstract painted by former pupil Matthew Drage hangs in pride of place in the headmaster's hall and particularly caught our eye. Money made from hiring out school artwork to local businesses goes into pot to fund foreign trips for art students – very entrepreneurial.

Music is huge, with around 250 individual instrument lessons a week. Stunning newly refurbished music school in former san, with 200-seat recital hall, recording studio, 16 practice rooms. Vast array of orchestras, choirs, jazz bands, string quartets etc, annual musician of the year prize and RockIt competition for budding young rock bands. Series of subscription concerts held throughout year for school and community attracts musicians of international renown. Everyone does term of drama in year 9 and some go on to take it at GCSE and A level. Plethora of productions, will now take place in the newly renovated auditorium, throughout school year, including house plays, lower school production and charity cabaret.

Boarding: School prides itself on being a 'seven-days-a-week boarding school' – no exeats, but each pupil allowed three Saturday nights of own choice a term at home ('privilege weekends'). This helps to ensure that the school 'doesn't empty at weekends,' says a member of staff. Weekend activities on offer, or SLOPs as they are known (Sunday leisure options) include cycling in the Peak District, paintballing, trips to Clothes Show Live etc.

The house system is integral to the school. Each house (four girls' and six boys') has resident house-parent and prides itself on having 'family atmosphere'. All pupils eat breakfast, lunch and supper in their houses. Food cooked in-house and every pupil we talked to claimed the food in their house was the best. We were invited to lunch in a girls' house and it was one of the most delicious school lunches we've had in a long time – chicken pasta, homemade focaccia and excellent chocolate brownies. Vegetarian and gluten-free options always available too. Lunch is the most formal meal of the day, often attended by guests from within school and outside, and students are encouraged to chat and be sociable. Mealtimes also give houseparents the chance to keep an eye on whether pupils are eating enough. Youngest pupils tend to be in dorms of four, sixth formers have their own study bedrooms with wash basins. Houses also have quiet rooms for working, kitchens to make toast and pasta and mixed-age common rooms, where pupils from other houses can visit at specified times.

Background and atmosphere: On the banks of the River Trent (the head's study is in a free-standing medieval tower overlooking the river), the school is absorbed into the village of Repton rather than dominating it. Pupils are kept fit as they hurry between boarding houses up leafy lanes and classrooms, sports centre, games pitches etc. With a busy B road running through the village, Repton is by no means a sleepy idyll, but the school lends the place a certain vitality. The central part of the school is based around a 12th century Augustan priory. School founded under the will of Sir John Port, who died in 1557. It celebrated 450th anniversary of its creation in 2007 with a son et lumière production.

Good blend of ancient and modern architecture. Two-floor library in old priory building is breathtaking. National Literacy Trust has recently published report saying a third of today's students don't use their school library, but this isn't the case

here. When we visited a happy group of year 9s were reading (everything from Bill Bryson to Conan Doyle) in comfy leather armchairs. Library criticised by inspectors in past but latest inspection said situation had been 'amply addressed,' with first-ever full-time librarian brought in and million-pound make-over. Recent building developments include 400 theatre as well as the spectacular multi-million pound Science Priory, complete with animal centre, observatory and ecological research centre and a modern, high-tech and fully equipped ICT centre.

We were invited to lunch in a girls' house and it was one of the most delicious school lunches we've had in a long time, especially the homemade focaccia and chocolate brownies

---

Once boys only but fully co-ed since 1991 – boy/girl ratio roughly 55/45. School is big enough to create a 'buzz' and maintain standards of real quality but is small enough for everyone to know each other. Pupils and parents say it's a very friendly place and the latest ISI report specifically commented on the school's 'sense of community'.

Pastoral care, well-being and discipline: House system underpins everything at Repton. As one housemistress says: 'We are here 24/7 and I see each one of my girls every day.' Plenty of people for pupils to talk to if they need a sympathetic ear – including house prefects, matrons, houseparents, house tutors, school counsellor and chaplain. Head boy and girl plus heads of houses and raft of prefects. New pupils given a mentor, someone who has been at school for at least a year, to guide them through the early weeks. Mobile phones allowed but only at certain times of day and youngest must hand them in to prefects at night. All pupils attend chapel twice a week.

Clear school rules, with written tasks for minor breaches and detentions for more serious lapses. Meanwhile policies on drugs, drink and smoking are unambiguous. Zero tolerance on drugs – as deputy head for pastoral side of school says, 'Repton isn't a second-chance school'. Drinking and smoking both yellow-card offences. Sixth formers allowed two alcoholic drinks with a meal at JCR on Saturday nights. Smoking is a 'minimal' problem, but if pupils are found smoking they incur loss of privileges (or 'lopping', as it's known in Reptonese).

Uniform is compulsory and looks very smart. Dark suits for sixth formers, while boys wear

blazers and ties and girls are clad in grey skirts, blazers and a V neck jumper of their own choice in a 'quiet' tone – pale pink, mauve and grey from Zara seem to be the current favourites. No nail varnish and minimum make-up.

Pupils and parents: A very down-to-earth, straightforward lot – polite, ultra-proud of their school and appreciative of the opportunities it gives them. Pupils come from all over – north, south and everywhere in between. Around 10 per cent from overseas. Past pupils of school include writers Christopher Isherwood and Roald Dahl and Top Gear supremo Jeremy Clarkson.

Entrance: Students arrive at Repton from a large number of schools. Roughly half from Repton's own prep up the road, Foremarke Hall, other half from prep schools like S Anselm's, Terra Nova, Terrington Hall, Malsis, Orwell Park and Swanbourne House. Not overly selective – director of admissions says the school doesn't state common entrance pass mark required, but in previous years it has been 50 per cent. About 30 new teenagers into sixth form each year – they need minimum of five Bs at GCSE,

but preferably As in chosen A level subjects. School takes pupils with special educational needs who can cope with the curriculum – every case considered on individual merit.

Exit: Nearly all go through to sixth form. Most sixth formers to top universities; 12 to Oxbridge in 2015, including four off to Cambridge to study medicine. Others to eg Durham, Edinburgh, St Andrews, UCL, Warwick and York.

Money matters: Range of scholarships on offer – academic, music, art, DT, drama, ICT, sport and all-rounder. Also Foremarke scholarships, given to children who want to transfer to Foremarke Hall for years 7 and 8 and then on to Repton.

Remarks: Repton is definitely on a roll. A happy school that offers an all-round education in the wilds of Derbyshire. It gives students time to be themselves, whilst opening their minds and nurturing their interests and enthusiasms. As the head girl told us: 'I'll be very sad to leave here. It's a special place.'

Rugby School

Rugby, Warwickshire CV22 5EH

01788 556216
enquiries@rugbyschool.co.uk
www.rugbyschool.co.uk
C of E

Ages: 11–18 (boarding from 13)
Pupils: 815; sixth form: 360
Boarders: 650
Day: £20,697 pa
Boarding: £32,985 pa

Headmaster: Since 2014, Peter Green MA PGCE (early 50s), previously head of Ardingly. Educated at St Joseph's College, Dumfries, then University of Edinburgh, where he read geography. Although he comes from a family of lawyers and judges he always wanted to be a teacher. Studied for Cert Ed in religious studies and PGCE at St Andrew's Foundation for Catholic Teacher Education (now part of the University of Glasgow). First job was at an inner-city comprehensive in the Gorbals. He taught at St Olave's Grammar in Orpington and then Strathallan before moving to Uppingham, where he was head of geography, a housemaster and introduced all-rounder scholarships. Spent five years as lay second master of Ampleforth, followed by seven years as head of Ardingly College, where numbers rose from 720 to 950 under his watch.

A vastly experienced and engaging head (wearing fetching bright pink socks when we visited),

he talks fast, sensibly and enthusiastically and is full of good tales and ideas. He says 'the whole person is the whole point of education at Rugby', and while this isn't a unique declaration for a head he believes Rugby is 'uniquely placed to make the claim.' Doesn't teach these days – 'I'd sack myself,' he jokes – but spends as much time as he can talking to pupils and staff and observing lessons. On the day we met he arrived hotfoot from discussing Lake District geomorphology with the youngest pupils in the school.

He's enjoying his job at Rugby – 'we have fantastic children here and it's a wonderful environment to work in,' he says. He finds the school's history a huge inspiration but emphasises that while Rugby is 'traditional,' it isn't 'traditionalist.' Delights in the fact that he's sitting in Dr Thomas Arnold's study – with a portrait of the great man, Arnold's own (surprisingly small) desk, a hidden key rack above the fireplace and the spiral staircase in the corner that pupils used if they wanted to talk to him privately.

The head says that Rugby is 'phenomenally strong' but is always looking for ways to improve – whether it's blended learning, flipped classrooms, character development, teaching tolerance and respect or engaging pupils in STEAM (science, technology, engineering, arts and maths) subjects. He's particularly proud of the fact that there isn't a Rugby type. 'The duckbilled platypus and the behemoth can be equally at home at Rugby School,' he says. Like his predecessor (Westminster head Patrick Derham), he wants Rugby to remain as inclusive as possible. The Arnold Foundation offers 100 per cent funded boarding places to pupils whose parents are unable to afford the fees and since 2003 well over 100 youngsters have benefited from the scheme.

Wife Brenda is an English and learning support teacher at Rugby. They have two children, a son who has just finished university and a daughter who has just started. In his spare time he enjoys reading, opera and the opportunity 'to pray and be silent.'

Academic matters: Rugby has a tradition of innovation – it was, for instance, the first school in the country to teach science as part of the school curriculum in the 1850s – and this continues apace. The school offers the IGCSE in most subjects and A levels in 29 subjects (plus the Pre-U in physics, chemistry, biology and art and design). Around 50 students a year take the Extended Project Qualification (EPQ), which was developed at Rugby via a pilot qualification called Perspectives in Science and involves an

Lewis Gallery, a light, airy space cleverly converted from old squash courts, hosts exhibitions by pupils and outside artists

extended piece of research on a topic they choose themselves.

In 2015 more than 60 per cent A*/A grades at A level/Pre-U. More than 50 per cent A* and more than 79 per cent A*/A at GCSE. 'The head is definitely on an academic mission,' a parent told us. French, German and Spanish offered at GCSE and A level, with exchange trips to Montpellier, Vienna, Madrid. Wonderful new language block, with 11 classrooms, two language labs and computers and software in every language. Sixth formers can study an ab initio language, such as Russian or Japanese. Pupils also write, edit and code their own online magazine, Page Polyglotte.

Most do three separate sciences at GCSE. The sciences are housed in an imaginatively refurbished Victorian building, with lecture theatre, seminar rooms and labs. Learning development department offers support for those who need it (for EAL as well as specific learning difficulties), either one-to-one or in small groups. Enrichment programme for all pupils, with additional weekly sessions for academic scholars (140 currently). All pupils have their own laptops, supplied by school and charged to parents.

Teachers are skilled and experienced. Many pursue their own academic research and the school is producing its own document on approaches to teaching and learning at Rugby. School runs parallel sets (including two top sets) in English, maths and the sciences.

Games, options, the arts: Rugby has overseen a huge investment in sports facilities in recent years. It has the only listed gym in the world and, of course, the famous School Close, where William Webb Ellis first ran with the ball in 1823 and invented the game of rugby football. Members of the 1st XV are very proud to play on it, along with leading players and teams who visit from all over the world. More than 200 TV crews pitched up to film at Rugby ahead of the 2015 World Cup and the school featured in the opening ceremony (Prince Harry and Jonny Wilkinson had cameo roles in a video shot at the school). Immaculately maintained playing fields, with 13 rugby pitches and five cricket squares. Locals use school's three Astroturfs, tennis courts and 25-metre indoor pool.

Sports centre, with squash courts, polo pitches and fitness centre. Boys play rugby, hockey, soccer, cricket, tennis and athletics while girls' main sports are hockey, netball, tennis, rounders and athletics. Other sports include badminton, fives, rackets, basketball, fencing, gymnastics, tai chi, pilates, dance, aerobics, riding, polo, clay pigeon shooting, sailing and triathlon. One girl is the current under-19 British champion in wakeboarding. Huge number of sports tours – recent expeditions include hockey and netball to Australia and Singapore, rugby to Japan and Canada and cricket to Sri Lanka and Dubai.

Music department has more than 40 practice rooms, a recording studio and small concert hall. Music is magical, with masses of orchestras, choirs, ensembles and rock bands. Total of 600 music lessons a week. An impressive variety of drama productions at school's fully equipped theatre. Pupils stage a major school play and musical every year, plus a house drama season and annual arts festival. Art, design and photography flourishing and a third of sixth formers study related subjects at art school or university. Lewis Gallery, a light, airy space cleverly converted from old squash courts, runs programme of exhibitions by pupils and outside artists.

Boarding: Sixteen houses in total – eight for boys, seven for girls, plus Marshall House, a co-ed house for year 7 and 8 boys and girls (all day pupils). Each boarding house has up to 60 pupils and the furthest is no more is than a 10-minute walk from the heart of the school. We visited soon after the school's annual pushcart race, hotly contested by all. The victorious house had a jaunty skull and crossbones flag fluttering from a top window.

Pupils eat breakfast, lunch and supper in their own houses – 'it encourages a real sense of community,' a parent told us. Food gets the thumbs up and there's plenty of it, including snacks in morning and afternoon breaks and in the evening. In a recent move, all but the sixth formers hand in their phones, tablets and laptops before bed each night. The new rule has brought a few grumbles from pupils, 'but nothing but parental support,' said a housemaster.

Head is particularly proud of the fact that there isn't a Rugby type. 'The duckbilled platypus and the behemoth can be equally at home at Rugby School'

Houses are very wholesome. The boys' houses used to be less ritzy but are in the process of being upgraded. A house we visited boasted a cinema room, neat as a pin laundry, tuck shop (the 'stodge' in Rugby-speak) and individual studies for all. Each year group has their own common room and dorms vary from singles for sixth-formers to dorms of four to six for younger pupils. 'Your house is your home,' one boy declared.

Housemasters and housemistresses all live in (many with their own families) and see pupils as they come and go during the day. Youngest have to be back in houses by 9.30pm (lights out half an hour later), while sixth-formers return by 10.15pm (they don't have to be in their rooms till 11pm, though). Tutors are house-based and see their tutees formally at least twice a week, as well as when they're on duty.

Background and atmosphere: Founded as a grammar school in 1567 by Lawrence Sheriff, purveyor of spices to Elizabeth I. Moved to its present site in the centre of Rugby 200 years later. Home of the famous Dr Arnold and immortalised in Tom Brown's Schooldays. With its red-brick, Victorian schoolhouses the site feels rather like north Oxford. Pupils like being based in a town, close to shops and cafés. One told us: 'You get a sense of the real world. We aren't in a bubble.'

Glorious Victorian library, the Temple Reading Room, provides a quiet, inspiring place to work. Pupils attend chapel three mornings a week and on Sundays. Chapel – Thomas Arnold is buried beneath chancel steps – is majestic and awe-inspiring, with walls adorned with tablets in memory of famous Rugbeian writers like Lewis Carroll and Rupert Brooke. School chaplain describes the chapel as 'the base' of the school and pupils say it's a place where the whole school sings its heart out.

School went fully co-ed in 1993 and boy/girl ratio is now 55/45. All wear smart uniform for lessons. Girls sport distinctive ankle-length grey skirts, now redesigned so they can run in them. Girls say they really like their skirts – they suit everyone and you can wear woolly tights and leggings underneath to keep warm in winter, they told us. The only gripe from boys is that their tweed jackets get 'a bit smelly' in the rain. Prefects – or levée as they are known – wear different ties and gold buttons on dark blazers. Four buttons for heads of school (boy and girl), three for heads of house and two for school prefects – a simple and subtle way to work out exactly who's who.

All wear smart uniform for lessons. Girls sport distinctive ankle-length grey skirts, now redesigned so they can run in them

The sixth form has impressive new Collingwood Centre, housed in a former Catholic secondary school on the edge of the site. Careers, economics, philosophy, business studies, art history, PE and politics departments are based there (politics classroom is set up as a mock House of Commons, even down to the green leather seats) and centre is used for studying, socialising and school events. There's also the Saturday evening Crescent Club, where sixth formers are allowed a maximum of two drinks (wine or beer) with food.

Pastoral care, well-being and discipline: School has put an enormous amount of time and effort into its pastoral care. It is also one of 10 schools across the UK chosen to work with the PSHE Association on the development of a new character curriculum, which aims to develop skills and attributes like motivation and resilience.

Each pupil is given a copy of the school's Guidelines for Life, which covers everything from its anti-bullying policy to relationships and where and when boys and girls can be in their free time. Policies on smoking, alcohol and drugs all clearly laid out. Expulsions are few and far between – two in the last five years. Public displays of affection (PDAs) between pupils banned – 'couples must behave in a way which would be appropriate if a member of staff were in the room,' says the school.

A host of opportunities for pupils to make sure their views are heard. 'Councils are huge here,' declared the head boy. He's right – there's a social council, music council, academic council, sports council and changes council. School is good at picking up on problems before they escalate. 'There are lots of people looking out for them,' a teacher told us. Cleaners spot things and chefs notice if a pupil hasn't eaten much at lunch.

Pupils and parents: Pupils come from all over, many from London, Oxford or locations within two hours' driving distance. Around 10 per cent international students. Parents are very supportive of the school. Many are sons and daughters of Rugby alumni and one described pupils as 'unpretentious, natural, spontaneous, courteous, tolerant and unstuffy.' Illustrious former pupils include Rupert Brooke (a girls' house is named after him), Lewis Carroll, Robert Hardy, Tom King, Salman Rushdie,

AN Wilson and Anthony Horowitz. Not forgetting, of course, Harry Flashman and Tom Brown.

Entrance: Admission at 11 is open only to day pupils from local state schools or independent schools finishing at 11. Entrance exam consists of computerised test, interview and report from current school. Pupils starting at 13 sit aptitude pre-test and interview in year 7. CE pass mark is 55 per cent but average is higher. Boys and girls come from more than 300 feeder schools across the country, including The Dragon, Bilton Grange, Packwood Haugh and S Anselm's.

Around 40 new pupils (mostly girls, but some boys) join in the sixth form. UK candidates need at least three As and three Bs at GCSE. They sit sixth form entrance exams and have a house interview. Potential scholars are invited back at a later date for scholarship interviews. Keen competition for sixth form places.

Exit: Virtually all to university – around 94 per cent head to Russell Group universities most years. Bath, Bristol, Durham, Edinburgh, Leeds, Manchester, Newcastle and UCL are popular choices. On average, 10 to 15 Oxbridge places a year but a disappointing five in 2015, although eight candidates were reapplying at the time of our visit. Gap years 'less fashionable' than previously and interest in US universities is growing.

Money matters: Complex range of bursaries and awards. School offers academic, music, drama, art, DT, computing and sport scholarships – it led the way in 2003 by limiting scholarships to 10 per cent of the school fees, although this can be augmented to 100 per cent if family need can be shown through a means test. Bursaries of up to 100 per cent of the fees, depending on parental means.

Remarks: This famous public school takes huge pride in its history and traditions – and quite right too – but it is genuinely innovative and forward thinking, especially when it comes to academic matters. Boarding houses have a real sense of community, pupils are welcoming and unpretentious and facilities are second to none.

S. Anselm's School

S. Anselm's Preparatory School, Bakewell, Derbyshire DE45 1DP

01629 812734
headmaster@anselms.co.uk
www.sanselms.co.uk

Ages: 3–13 (boarders from year 3)
Pupils: 200
Boarders: 31 full, 34 weekly/flexi
Day: £9,150 – £17,400 pa
Boarding: £21,600 pa

Headmaster: Since September 2012, Mr Peter Phillips. Head of Cundall Manor in Yorkshire for 13 years; built up school from around 80 to some 400 pupils. Started as a surveyor before seeing the light and becoming an English teacher. Head of English at Yardley Court and Dulwich College then director of studies at Cargilfield in Edinburgh.

A tall man, by any standards, he does not belong to the pinstriped, lapel-tugging, bullfrog school of heads. He is a thinker, a man of intelligence and vision, of great kindness, strong-minded and determined, and not easily swayed. Above all, he is dedicated to the welfare of the pupils. He does not like being pushed about by autocracy, but will listen for hours to children's worries and concerns. Some parents have complained that he is something of a recluse, that he doesn't come out to see them. The pupils we met – and they were marvellously forthcoming and natural – said how much they like him because he takes such a keen interest in them, makes a fuss of them when they are sent by their teachers to show him a good piece of work, and so obviously cares about them.

Though he denies being a Luddite, he knows nothing of computers and announced early on in his time at S Anselm's that he did not do emails but was always willing to talk. All emails go through his wife, Sarah, who has a delightfully zany sense of humour and helps look after the girls in the evening. He teaches 18 lessons a week and referees some matches. Pupils enjoy his lessons and he enjoys the contact.

He has encouraged some of the older staff to leave, causing some disquiet among a few parents and indignation from those staff. The overall feeling amongst the parents we talked to was a sadness that even teachers have to move on, but an acceptance of the inevitability. This has not been a St Bartholomew's Day Massacre of the not-so-innocent over-50s: he has displayed considerable wisdom in retaining some of the finest teachers on merit, reputation and – importantly – a willingness to accept his enlarged expectations. One experienced teacher said that due to the new demands of helping at weekends she now knew the pupils better.

Many young, talented and dedicated staff. Parents queued up to tell us of the new buzz in the school, the energy and drive, the sense of purpose and fun, the fresh air

Perhaps most exciting has been the arrival of a cohort of young, lively, talented and dedicated staff. Many of them followed Mr Phillips, along with children and families, from Cundal Manor. Their arrival caused much excitement among the parents and children, and they are a most delightful and engaging group. Parents queued up to tell us of the new buzz in the school, the energy and drive, the sense of purpose and fun, the fresh air. Even we could feel it. When we wandered out during break and saw the running, the chasing, the laughter, the sense of timeless delight, it felt as if we had taken a detour with Thomas Traherne: 'Boys and girls tumbling in the street, and playing, were moving jewels. I knew not that they were born or should die; but all things abided eternally as they were in their proper places.'

Mr Phillips has given up the rather grand and slightly intimidating study of his predecessors, and now inhabits a smaller but delightful room overlooking the beautiful gardens. As the visitor glances around he sees a rugby ball in the (unlit) fireplace, a set of bagpipes on a table, a model steam train made by one of the science masters (an inspirational teacher whose lesson we had observed earlier), and a pile of papers. No badges or hints of office, no pomposity or sense of importance. The same is true of the website. Search as you may, you will not find one of those proprietorial messages from a head looking like a stockbroker or as if they were fresh from a stylish garden party, urging you with false modesty and marketing acumen to come and visit. With a dash of daring, S Anselm's has done away with all mentions of the head and doesn't have a prospectus. 'The school belongs to, and exists for, the children.' You'll only find the head's name on the copy of the recent inspection report, and pretty good it was. He doesn't do swank nor is he interested in suits and tailors. He greeted us in bright, pinky-red trousers and sweater.

Entrance: Mostly into the nursery and pre-prep, which is superbly run with first class teaching, according to happy parents. The overall head of the pre-prep is 'wonderful' and children in the prep look back with fondness and an early whiff of nostalgia. But anyone may apply at any stage if there is room. One parent told us with huge appreciation of how her son, joining as a boarder a little later than the main group when the family moved up from London, had been welcomed with kindness and consideration by boys and housemaster, and had settled in very quickly.

Exit: The school has an excellent reputation for scholarships, achieved through excellent free-range teaching rather than force-feeding. Parents talk of the way teachers assess their pupils realistically and sensitively. A few parents, of course, have unrealistic demands and expectations, but the head is good at nudging them towards greater reality, even though that doesn't always endear him. Public school heads said they appreciate the lively, inquisitive approach of Anselmians, their willingness to get stuck in and their articulate courtesy and friendliness. Varying numbers to Eton, Harrow, Shrewsbury, Oundle, Fettes, Uppingham, Winchester, Downe House, Repton and Malvern.

School has expanded to secondary level: S Anselm's College (day only) opened with year 9 in September 2015 on the same site.

Remarks: The school has been through a turbulent period over the last five years. Numbers dropped, and morale amongst many parents and staff dipped, and they told us that a few years ago they were very worried. With the arrival of fresh blood and new energies, numbers and morale are looking up, with a doubling of intake into reception and increased numbers in the main school.

Boarding is becoming ever more popular. Weekends are action packed and hugely enjoyed. 'He doesn't want to come home,' one parent told us

Mr Phillips has restructured the timetable in the junior prep. English and maths is the staple diet in the morning, 'when the children are at their most alert', with other subjects in the afternoon. We listened to an exciting and challenging science lesson. When asked to describe their teacher, pupils said, 'distinctive, epic, fun, super, funny and heroic.' They were still yelling out adjectives as we left the room. Art teacher wearing spectacularly bright trousers; 'I love getting messy in art,' said one enthusiastic painter with rainbow coloured hands and face. Excellent artwork everywhere, not just in the large-windowed studio. We saw groups of young Romans planning a three course dinner which included stuffed doormice. They were off to Chester soon to explore all things Roman there. 'Don't mess with this man,' said our guides as we entered the classroom of a gentle-looking man. 'He teaches karate.' A woman was teaching the value of a sensible diet in a brilliant lesson incorporating geography, chemistry, history, common sense and health.

Another of the head's ideas is for the whole school to share a topic and approach it from all angles. When we visited it was lighthouses, so there were pictures of lighthouses everywhere, calculations of light travelling, weather maps etc. Teachers described the excitement of approaching a topic right across the school from the youngest to the oldest, the way that seems to unite the pupils in a common aim, enabling them to share and exchange knowledge. A visit to a Northumberland lighthouse involved camping: the buzz, the fun and the almost unnoticed accumulation of knowledge.

Saturday mornings are voluntary up to year 6, but the take-up is enthusiastic. There is the excitement of starting to learn Spanish, and Latin and Greek are, in the words of one distinguished exponent, 'full on'.

Terrific facilities include a well-designed music block where we watched children rehearsing for an arts evening. About 90 per cent of them learn an instrument. The wonderful sports hall is, perhaps, even slightly improved following the recent fire during the winter holidays. The library is being extended and improved, a proud 10 year old librarian told us. Now there are plans for a real farm with real animals and the real hard work that goes with it, and a domestic science building.

Boarding facilities are excellent and improving all the time. In fact, under the new 'amazing and seriously mad' master in charge of boarding, according to parents and children, it is becoming ever more popular. Weekends are action packed and hugely enjoyed. 'He doesn't want to come home,' one parent told us, and talking of home, not long ago a group went up to Sheffield to help with the Archer Project. On that occasion it took the form of sleeping on cardboard on the streets in the rain with some young homeless people and some hardy members of staff. A thought-provoking experience. 'Boarding is just the greatest fun!' children said to us over and over again.

These feelings of excitement, pleasure and happiness seem to permeate right through the school – including the gardeners and maintenance staff and the charming and friendly cooks. (We had the most delicious lunch of roast pork and all the trimmings.) All of them are, of course, vitally important contributors to the overall happiness and smooth running of the school.

No doubt the excellent food contributes to the success of S Anselm's sport, which is taken seriously and played with zest and skill. County players abound in all areas, and there is huge excitement, though not at the expense of academic work. Or so they say.

S Anselm's celebrated its 125th anniversary with an elegantly produced book, with a forward signed by The Duchess of Devonshire. In it the writer comments on the founder's choice of motto : 'Esse Quam Videri......to be and not to seem to be'. It's a wonderful motto extolling the virtues of honesty and, to use that overworked word, transparency. Several people have suggested to us that Mr Phillips fits the message behind that motto. He may not be universally popular – people who need to make changes rarely are – but he is now presiding over a deeply happy school with parents falling over themselves to tell us how pleased they are with the current set up. Such bubbling enthusiasm is rare.

St David's College

Llandudno, Conwy LL30 1RD

01492 875974
hmsec@stdavidscollege.co.uk
www.stdavidscollege.co.uk

Ages: 9–19
Pupils: 240: (169 boys, 71 girls); sixth form: 75
Boarders: 100
Day £6,600 – £16,230 pa; SEN £9,600 – £19,620 pa
Boarding: £15,900 – £30,090 pa; SEN £18,900 – £33,090 pa

Head: Since 2008, Mr Stuart Hay BEng PGCE (early 40s). Joined as deputy head from Warminster School, where he was head of electronics and product design. After gaining his electronic engineering degree and PGCE at Bath University, he taught in both independent and maintained sectors.

He is married to Lucy and they have three children, Ben, Milly and Thomas. Ben, the eldest, attends the school and appeared to be loving it when we came across him in a lively reading class. Mr Hay's main interests are mountaineering, road cycling, mountain biking, racquet sports and St David's. Parents speak very highly of Mr and Mrs Hay. 'It may sound corny,' said one parent we spoke to, 'but their happy family really seems to include all the pupils, whether it's Mrs Hay's cooking activity or Mr Hay sea kayaking round Anglesey.' All the parents we spoke to, and they were queuing up to do so, spoke of the open and natural friendliness of Mr and Mrs Hay and their involvement around the school. 'Mrs Hay is really super,' said a number of children, who assured us she was not their mum. Mr Hay is much admired for the sensitive, generous minded and understanding way he encounters pupils, staff and parents. 'He's astonishingly energetic,' an admiring mum told us.

Mr Hay took a lot of persuading to become headmaster. He was reluctant to lose the close contact with the pupils and the opportunities to teach them and to share in their activities, especially the outdoor pursuits he likes so much and which he believes are so important for the development of the pupils. He most emphatically does not belong to the pompous bullfrog style of head: he is a listener who really does seem to put the welfare of his pupils first. 'He's no softy,' said a father to us. 'He's good at judging pupils' abilities and how far he can encourage them without expecting too much. He'll push if he feels that is necessary, but essentially he does that through encouragement, because he knows them.' We found him extremely thoughtful and pleasantly modest, warm in manner, wholly committed and with what seemed an inner calm. He is completely genuine and, incidentally, very good company.

Academic matters: What a joy it was not to have examination results and league tables thrust under our noses. There is a belief in some quarters that education is dead and has been replaced by a slavish seeking after grade levels and that dreaded, often misused, word 'targets'. At St David's there are individual goals for each pupil but they are personal rather than political. Education at its best is very much alive and shining at St David's. The reticence they have in not trumpeting their grade results is for no reason other than the firmly held conviction that grades are not the most important aspect of life at this school.

Parents couldn't speak highly enough of Mr and Mrs Hay. 'It may sound corny,' said one parent, 'but their happy family really seems to include all the pupils'

Average class sizes are 10 and every teacher is a qualified dyslexia teacher. An infinitely better system than that where a pupil is given one session of help a week and then goes back to a class where the teacher is making no allowances at all. That happens in a number of schools. This school was one of the first to adopt a multi-sensory teaching policy and we witnessed some marvellously lively, creative and stimulating teaching from a staff who seem universally dedicated and fun. None more so than those we met in the Cadogen Centre, a specialised building where each pupil enjoys one-on-one teaching with a programme individually planned for them after careful discussion with their class teachers.

The facilities for IT are excellent and we had a wonderful time with some very bright sixth form pupils who were about to go off for an exhibition. Not only was the work they were doing as part of NVQs in CAD outstandingly good, but so were the fluent and perceptive comments which accompanied the work. 'Dyslexics often think out of the box,' a teacher told us. Recently a young man from St David's, who while there had attended one-on-one lessons, graduated in architecture at Manchester University. Another is reading nuclear physics. There are so many success stories.

Games, options, the arts: To gaze down from the beautiful terrace in front of the house is to marvel at the immaculate state of the games pitches, the superb Astroturf and the lure of mountains beyond. Virtually every game you can think of is on offer, and other schools talk of the verve and energy with which St David's teams perform. In addition there is a shooting range, an indoor climbing hall and vast amounts of equipment for outdoor activities, one of the distinctive features of the school. The excellent prospectus and online introduction to the school reveal the depth and breadth of the activities on offer. There is an activity, an expedition, a challenging outing once a week, but lest anyone think this is an attractive offer replacing academic pursuits, think again. The school academic day continues until 5pm Monday to Friday and there are additional lessons, activities and games sessions timetabled on Saturday mornings. When questioned about Saturday morning lessons, 'Fair enough,' said the boy we asked. Sixth formers can take a BTec in sports (traditional or outdoor ed).

A particularly popular activity is 4x4 off road driving in a spectacularly battered and mud caked old Land Rover. The school really is a paradise of activity, challenge, determination, broadening horizons and going beyond the syllabus.

Very lively art in an old building where budding artists can express themselves without worrying about spilling paint. Those are often the best buildings for producing the exciting art work. There was plenty here and in the photographic section adjoining. Such creativity and such joy, delight and encouragement.

Boarding: The boarding houses (three for boys and one for girls) are bright, airy and friendly; the house teams dedicated and involved. Boarding seems to work well, which is probably one reason why pupils come from so far afield from throughout the UK. Huge variety of indoor and especially outdoor activities available at weekends.

The reticence they have in not trumpeting their exam results is for no reason other than the firmly held conviction that grades are not the most important aspect of life at this school

Background and atmosphere: In 1965 a deputy head from Cheshire, John Mayor, upset by the way boys and girls with learning difficulties were smothered, if not dismissed, because they were seen as lazy or stupid, decided to found a school where their needs were addressed. It was founded on three main principals: a determination to respect, understand and help the pupils; adventurous outdoor activities where the young could experience freedom and excitement; and all this within a gentle Christian ethos. Fifty years later the school largely continues to follow those guidelines. And it shows. We met happy pupils who spoke confidently and unselfconsciously about how miserable they had been on arrival, with a bleak and cheerless outlook on life and no self-esteem at all. For some,

St David's was last chance saloon, and some of them were far from home. They spoke of the warmth of the welcome they received from the whole community.

A particularly popular activity is 4x4 off road driving in a spectacularly battered and mud caked old Land Rover. The school really is a paradise of activity, challenge and determination

'Community' is a word which sits easily on the lips of pupils eager to talk about their school. And that's not a cliché either: they really do feel as if the school belongs to them and they to the school. There's a very real closeness. They talk of the increasing delight they derived from their lessons; the love and interest shown by the teachers; the friendliness of their contemporaries. 'It's just everything,' said a young boy, struggling to articulate the indefinable. 'Surely there must be some things you don't like?' we pressed. 'Of course,' came the reply, 'but there's far less to worry about than there was at my previous school. It could be very depressing there and a bit scary on occasions.' What they all agreed on was the 'overall atmosphere'. They looked surprised when we suggested that that came from them. These young have not been stuffed with cheesy old clichés raked off that useful pile plundered by professional prospectus writers or that irritating band of media trained heads. These are real people making real discoveries about themselves. Perhaps it is not a coincidence to have a parent describing the head as a real person.

Pastoral care, well-being and discipline: Within the academic, as well as the sporting and sporty side of life at the school, there are practical and generous ways in which pupils help each other. This is manifest by the way in which older pupils help younger pupils with academic subjects as well as more personal, private anxieties. The people we spoke with were unanimous in the feeling that there was always someone there to help. A word they were fond of evoking is 'banter.' Affectionate teasing. One of the most moving moments of our tour was when our guides pointed out the Prayer Garden, 'or whatever you like to call it. You can approach it in any way you like, but it's essentially a place for reflection. You can take it or leave it.' It's a lovely touch, and the statue in front, created by Nick Elphick, an old boy of the school, is a thought-provoking addition. This is not a threatening environment. Discipline is sensible, thoughtful, considerate. It seemed as natural as breathing.

Pupils and parents: From a wide range of primary and prep schools. Day pupils from across the whole of North Wales. Boarders from all over the UK, a small number from overseas. Inclusive entry helped by quite a number of pupils being funded by their local education authorities. Apart from those with special educational needs, many parents choose the school because of its broad all-round education and its small class sizes. Recent extension to boarding provision due to increase in pupil numbers.

Entrance: The majority enter aged at about 10 after an interview and a report from their school. A large number come from local primary schools, but others come from far afield. We heard how sensitively the business of arrivals is handled. Always a sign of a happy school. A few leave and a number come into the sixth form, attracted by the reputation of the teaching and the breadth of subjects on offer. The sixth form handbook says that the most important qualities for entry into the school are commitment and enthusiasm. That handbook is, incidentally, one of the best of its kind we have ever seen.

Exit: Around 15-25 per cent leave at 16. The school goes to tremendous lengths to help the boys and girls choose the courses that match interests and abilities. The vast majority do go on to further or higher education. Technical subjects seem the most popular, but not exclusively so.

Money matters: The school works hard to keep the costs down. The wonderful expeditions are very carefully budgeted. No swanky hotels. Parents we spoke to said that they felt the school was very thoughtful about money matters and we got the impression that those who ran into severe financial difficulties would be carefully listened to.

Remarks: This is a very special school, almost a magical place. Pupils develop in an unsentimental atmosphere of love and generosity. The staff are almost as amazing as the pupils and, yes, there is plenty of banter along with the seriousness. Over the years a strong bond has matured with Kampala. Pupils and gap year students are deeply and genuinely involved. 'The projects we are involved in come from the dreams of our own pupils,' says that handbook. The same could be said about the school as a whole.

St Hugh's School (Woodhall Spa)

Cromwell Avenue, Woodhall Spa, Lincolnshire LN10 6TQ

01526 352169
office@st-hughs.lincs.sch.uk
www.st-hughs.lincs.sch.uk
C of E

Ages: 2–13
Pupils: 181
Boarders: 10 full, 60 flexi
Day: £7,917 – £13,797 pa
Boarding: £19,527 pa

Headmaster: Since September 2013, Chris Ward BEd, late 30s; first headship, previously deputy head of Worksop College Prep. He spent several years as director of music at St John's-on-the-Hill School in Monmouthshire, though now does some science teaching. Approachable, visible and welcoming to pupils and parents. A keen and competitive rugby player, spends Wednesday and Saturday afternoons refereeing matches or supporting from the pavilion, mingling with parents over a cup of tea.

Believes that St Hugh's is unique in Lincolnshire, as a stand alone co-educational prep school, providing all round care and catering for everyone. Is proud that 'when St Hugh's pupils leave they are able to stand on their own'. Parents feel that he has given the school 'a new lease of life' which they hope will continue.

Recognising the shift in the demands of modern parents for flexible boarding, he is transforming boarding under newly appointed houseparents and UK gappies to a more cosy, warm and family experience. Keen to build and strengthen the nursery provision to provide sustained growth in pupil numbers over the years and enhance the structure and shape of the school day.

Married to Angharad, who has traditional prep head's spouse's role, with three children, all pupils at the school.

Entrance: Majority of the children rise through the ranks of the school's nursery and pre-prep with some recruitment in year 3 and 4. Prospective pupils spend a day at the school for assessment. A web of school minibus routes brings children from a wide area.

Exit: Seventy-five per cent go on to independent senior schools in Lincolnshire and the A1 corridor, Uppingham, Oundle, Oakham, Repton, Stamford. Further afield Sedbergh and Barnard Castle. The remaining 25 per cent get places at local grammar schools, usually at 11.

Remarks: Located in the attractive, former Victorian spa resort of Woodhall Spa, in the midst of what was RAF heartland, St Hugh's is situated in a leafy avenue of traditional, Edwardian villas. Founded by the Forbes family in 1925 as a boys' boarding school, loyalty to the school has been strong and successive generations of often farming families continue to be educated here. A charitable trust since 1962 and co-educational since 1981.

Everyone (children, teachers and parents) agrees that the food is 'fantastic', with plenty of choice. The place is absolutely spotless throughout

Whilst first impressions are of a modest establishment, once through the door the extent of the buildings and facilities become immediately apparent and the newly-acquired playing field now allows the grounds to be described as extensive for a school of this size. Currently building an Astroturf; this addition to the functional yet well-maintained sport shall and swimming pool will provide a sporting facility gold, particularly for the hockey players. An adventure playground and nature pond – increasing use of the natural environment, staff undertaking forest school training, part of a green school kitemark. Boarding facilities in the upper echelons of the main school house, well away from classrooms.

Nursery and pre-prep classrooms flow through a building across the playground from the older children. Bright, well-resourced and full of colourful displays, features common across the school. Corridors adorned with interesting displays and children's work provide a sense of pride and commitment from staff. Good specialist facilities for science, music, art and DT with whiteboards in each classroom, a dedicated ICT suite and wireless connectivity throughout the school.

St Hugh's pupils have been successful in achieving scholarships, particularly in sports, music and arts, and it is the head's plan to strengthen further the number of academic and all-rounder awards. In the early years foundation stage the new department head has developed numeracy work, and investigational skills in mathematics is a focus of teaching and learning. Specialist French starts in nursery, increasing across subjects so that by year 5 all teaching is by specialists, with German and Latin being introduced and setting for mathematics and science. Classes are grouped according to ability from year 5 with an average of 14 in a class. Whilst teaching broadly follows the national curriculum, there is a weekly session for senior pupils to enhance independent learning. Ten per cent SEN, mainly dyslexia and dyspraxia though several children with statements/EHC plans. Personalised learning plans, good coordinated strategies between SENCo and teachers, with one-on-one support where required.

Everyone is given the opportunity to contribute to the school, either on the games field, musically or in drama, but it's sport that rules the roost. Focus on traditional team sports and swimming, and everyone encouraged to play in a team. Good fixture list mainly against local independents but outlying location involves lengthy travelling times. It really is 'sport for all' – no one is left out. Hosts an annual netball tournament using boarding accommodation for teams from far afield.

Music flourishes with three-quarters of pupils from year 3 playing an instrument up to grade 8. Plenty of performance opportunity with termly concerts and musicals, and public recitals for the two choirs; two orchestras with seniors scaling symphonic heights; string and wind ensembles. Joint production with drama each year – recently the Wizard of Oz and Bugsy Malone – though plays, sketches and nativities, as well as assembly presentations, give lots of scope for budding lovies. Elocution competitions too.

Expressive arts thrive in well-equipped, dedicated rooms with specialist art, pottery and design technology workshops and weekly scholarship classes. Textiles and cookery are included throughout the curriculum.

St Hugh's pupils get out and about on numerous curriculum enriching visits and outings. Years 5 and 7 have residential French trips and year 8 a week's outdoor pursuits experience. Biennial hockey and rugby tours to Dublin and South Africa.

Positive reinforcement is key to rewards and sanctions with gold points accumulating for the benefit of the pupil and their house. Not just academic achievement: effort, good behaviour and citizenship are all equally recognised. We were wowed by the Wow board where individual exceptional achievements are displayed. When needed, clearly defined sanctions escalating through report cards to detentions. Parents feel very well informed about their children's progress through teacher emails and regular reports.

Pupils and staff are polite, friendly and welcoming; evidence of real rapport between teachers and pupils, anecdotal comments tinged with humour and respect; no doubt that every child is known well here. Citizenship prized – and awards presented at weekly assemblies. St Hugh's Award for actions above and beyond – recently presented to one of the house captains who went home for a night to bake a cake to cheer up a young house member who had sustained a complicated broken femur on the rugby pitch. Strong house structure (named for three previous heads) with sporting, general knowledge and arts competitions and fundraising activities. Peer mentors in years 7 and 8; worry boxes discretely placed for confidential concerns.

Attuned to changing needs (and a declining number of Forces' children), the metamorphosis of boarding has seen a rise in the number of children deciding for themselves to board weekly or occasionally. A programme of investment has provided houseparent accommodation and upgraded bathrooms, and will create common rooms available to all and improve storage space, much needed as the bedrooms accommodating up to nine children are not large – though not always full. Friday nights are the most popular – great fun, and for the price of a babysitter, no early morning rising for parents

to make Saturday school. There is a small number of full-time boarders, who are well looked after at weekends and kept busy. Everyone (children, teachers and parents) agrees that the food is 'fantastic', with plenty of choice. The place is absolutely spotless throughout the boarding and school sides.

Parents tell us that they 'love the wonderful family atmosphere' and that the children 'mix throughout the year groups and are very supportive and encouraging of each other'. One parent told us, 'I have seen older year groups, unprompted, clapping and encouraging the little ones as they walk through the dining hall to go to perform in a play, which gave them such a boost'.

St Hugh's turns out well-rounded children who are polite and self-confident. Happy children – and parents.

St Richard's School

Brendenbury Court, Bromyard, Herefordshire HR7 4TD

01885 482491
schooloffice@st-richards.org.uk
www.st-richards.org.uk
RC

Ages: 3–13 (boarders from 7)
Pupils: 106
Boarders: 49
Day: £5,220 – £13,890 pa
Boarding: £19,140 – £20,640 pa

Head: Since January 2014, Mr Fred de Falbe, previously deputy head at Knightsbridge School. Began his teaching career aged 18 in Honduras, before gaining a BA in theology at Manchester University

and joining the film business, later going back to teaching after a year in Australia. Since then he has worked in state secondary schools in London and Devon and also started and managed a residential property company. Married to Juliet; they have three teenage children.

Entrance: Most pupils arrive in the prep school via the nursery and pre-prep, but others are welcome to apply at any time. The school is non-selective, but likes to meet parents and potential pupils. Minibuses for day children run from Leominster, Hereford and Worcester. Boarders tend to come from further afield, but the opportunity for flexi-boarding sometimes lures those living nearby into full-time boarding in preparation for secondary school.

Exit: To a wide range of schools, though fewer these days to the distant Catholic schools of Ampleforth, Downside and Stonyhurst. Christ's College Brecon, Malvern College, Malvern St James and Hereford Cathedral the most popular recently: it's horses for courses (literally, sometimes), and a number of senior school heads and registrars commented on the reliability and open friendliness of children from St Richard's. Fifteen scholarships in 2015 – music, sports, academic, drama and all-rounder.

Remarks: Anyone who fails to respond to the beautiful setting should perhaps be looking elsewhere, since the building and its 35 acres of Herefordshire countryside play a crucial part in the ethos of the place. Ofsted, which would probably describe the Taj Mahal as a pretty nifty tomb, commented that 'the grounds..are developed extremely well to provide for outstanding outdoor learning and recreation.' In this lovely Fern Hill setting, children disport themselves 'in the sun that is young once only.' They have a lot of fun. That's the word.

Good boarding routine in place: supper followed by supervised prep for older children, games or reading for younger ones, plus well-structured weekend activities

The main building was erected in 1876 by a young army officer who had received the whole village of Bredenbury as a wedding present. Later it was bought by a profligate land owner, who spent most of his time in Kenya's Happy Valley, though records relate that both the vastness of his girth and his addiction to alcohol prevented his being a full party member. Of course no whiffs of his lifestyle permeate the building, apart from his additions of a ballroom (now the assembly hall) and a lovely vaulted dining room (now the chapel). St Richard's School moved into the house in 1968 and

the last squire-head, who retired in 2005, turned it into a charitable trust.

Darcy the dog wandering around the dining room during lunch; beautiful pictures everywhere; a polar bear; chickens, horses and a shy terrapin

The school has moved into the 21st century without eradicating its gentlemanly feel of tweeds, eccentricity and individuality. The very wide and detailed list of school policies appears on the website, a wise precaution appreciated by parents. 'You know where you stand,' said one. The children can feel safe and secure in their activities, but the school has retained a sense of proportion. The delightful forest school offers opportunities for adventure and discovery. The pre-prep prospectus even has a wonderful picture on the front of a young boy climbing up a gnarled old tree with the legend, 'Exercising young Minds!'

One distinguished, not as young as he used to be, former pupil told us that his parents had chosen to send him to St Richard's because during their initial tour they had been taken into the kitchen (how many schools would do that?) where they had found a pony tethered to the Aga. You're unlikely to find that these days, but ponies have been known to look in at the windows of classrooms. Like so much at St Richard's, there's a lot of fun to be had, but it is a serious business, whether it's preparing for dressage competitions or hunter trials. And, most importantly, those horses need to be looked after. And if you don't own a horse and keep it at school? In truth, most of the children don't. There's no sense of a social divide here; no snobbery, no world-weary sophistication.

Lessons seem lively and fun; bright and airy classrooms lead off rabbit warrens of corridors in a building that is comforting rather than snazzy. We were delighted to see old-style desks with lids and inkwells; teaching facilities are good (newly refurbished art room, imaginatively laid out French rooms, book-filled English room) without being flashy. The children reported that 'some teachers are very funny'. Intentionally or not? We didn't discover, but clearly there exist excellent relations between staff and pupils from the tinies to the prefects. The school usually wins an impressive fistful of scholarships.

Bedrooms are genuinely homely and inviting. Many new and junior children begin flexi-boarding one or two nights a week and build up from there. A number of day pupils choose to board eventually because it is such obviously good fun and because of the friendships it develops and confirms. There is a good routine in place: supper followed by supervised prep for the older children, games or reading upstairs for the younger ones, plus a well-structured weekend activity programme. Boarders, who have a large, airy sitting room with comfy chairs, sofas and a television, spoke highly of the matrons and many staff who live in the main house and get involved in activities.

Some schools embarking on the great facilities race seem to have lost sight of the basic fact that they exist for children, not for impressing parents. We've seen sports halls so clean you wonder whether anyone ever uses them, and with such sophisticated equipment that they can only be used by children when supervised by highly trained certificated adults who have been on endless courses. St Richard's sports hall is really a barn, named after a certain Sergeant Major Hirons, who taught PE at St Richard's between 1920 and 1983. The school has launched an appeal for a new sports hall, but it will not be 'a place where you have to remove your shoes before you go in. Children must be allowed to horse around. During break, this is their market place.' The same is true of their climbing wall, which is far wider than high. The result is that children can use it without sending for a mountain guide.

Although it is a Catholic school, around two-thirds of pupils are not Catholics. However, mass is celebrated on Saturday mornings, presided over by a real live monk, and at other assemblies those attending are invited to reflect. Reflect on their own behaviour, how they treat others, how they might have done better in certain circumstances. It's good to 'pause awhile from letters to be wise', and it surely contributes to the overall happiness of the school.

The setting is like a country house where the owner rather eccentrically has lots of children to stay, including a conservatory with an enormous fig tree growing through it; a magnificent staircase; Darcy the dog wandering around the dining room during lunch; beautiful pictures everywhere; a polar bear; chickens, horses and a shy terrapin. There are lakes for canoeing; grounds for camping in and learning about survival; horses grazing alongside jumps in a nearby field; and everywhere, as far as the eye can see, luscious Herefordshire countryside with a distant hint of neighbouring Elgar.

There is, undeniably, an old-fashioned feel to this country prep school. The school's insistence on good manners and courtesy might seem so. But we saw nothing false about the children's open friendliness and willingness to engage. They wore their manners as easily as an old pair of brogues, happy, bouncy and natural in a school which does what it says on the label. It prepares the young for adulthood.

School is closing in July 2016.

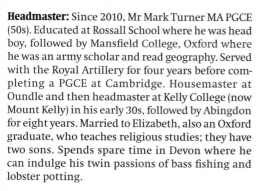

Shrewsbury School

The Schools, Shrewsbury, Shropshire SY3 7BA

01743 280552
admissions@shrewsbury.org.uk
www.shrewsbury.org.uk
C of E

Ages: 13–18
Pupils: 775 (597 boys, 178 girls); sixth form: 360
Boarders: 612 full
Day: £22,980 pa
Boarding: £32,820 pa

Headmaster: Since 2010, Mr Mark Turner MA PGCE (50s). Educated at Rossall School where he was head boy, followed by Mansfield College, Oxford where he was an army scholar and read geography. Served with the Royal Artillery for four years before completing a PGCE at Cambridge. Housemaster at Oundle and then headmaster at Kelly College (now Mount Kelly) in his early 30s, followed by Abingdon for eight years. Married to Elizabeth, also an Oxford graduate, who teaches religious studies; they have two sons. Spends spare time in Devon where he can indulge his twin passions of bass fishing and lobster potting.

A 'crisp and keen administrator' who wants to 'retain the best of the past with the cutting edge technology of the future' and to up the academic ante. Having a close look at teaching styles and practice and work ethic, but does not want the school to become overly selective – believing in rigour rather than elitism. Cuts a slightly remote figure; parents and boys still feel that they hardly know him. Abingdon parents felt that Mr Turner's military demeanour and focused approach was just what that school needed – and we agree – but while many Shrewsbury parents feel that discipline did need tightening up, some are concerned that he is bearing down on eccentricities and traditions, and is too pernickety and keen on process. Capable and ambitious.

Academic matters: In 2015, 86 per cent A*/B at A level/Pre-U but also a few lower grades – a comforting indication that this is a school that does not chuck out kids at 16. Particularly good showing at maths and further maths. Sixty-four per cent A*/A in IGCSE (most subjects) and GCSE in 2015. Wide choice at A level/Pre-U – usual academic subjects plus ceramics, photography, computing, design, theatre studies, PE and most combinations can be accommodated. 'Clinics' offer support for anyone who is struggling. Vibrant academic life outside main curriculum – voluntary complementary study programme in sixth form, some examined and some not eg global perspectives Pre-U, BTec in public services, extended project, sports leadership programme, Russian, Arabic, law and book-keeping for beginners as well as debating societies and Model United Nations. Range of academic societies with presentations by pupils and visitors. School hosted the International Young Physicists tournament and received a gold medal in the British Biology Olympiad.

About 130 pupils with SEN – mainly mild dyslexia. One full- and five part-time members of staff provide support. EAL offered but pupils must be able to follow the curriculum. Plenty of careers and university advice includes help finding work experience and talks on what employers are looking for. The school offers tuition for SATs (American university entrance exams) and is a registered SAT centre. Lectures from universities, agricultural and art colleges and the world of work plus lower sixth talks

Witty and irreverent school magazine follows in satirical tradition of the Old Salopian founders of Private Eye

on interview technique and an interview coaching course (charged for).

Low turnover of staff – loyal band, some were at Shrewsbury themselves. Increasing number of NQTs but most changes come from retirements. Hugely supportive staff who 'bring out the best in everyone and take children as far as they want to go academically'. One parent told us, 'The school has brought out things in my son that none of us knew he had'.

Games, options, the arts: Sport taken seriously here both at house and school level but still with an emphasis on 'fun, friendship and fitness', as the school puts it. Wide range of sports; big on rowing, girls are now also afloat in numbers – lots of national competitions, significant presence at Henley and many Shrewsbury boys have represented their country on the water. Newish Yale boathouse with training room and indoor rowing tank. New head of rowing is from Abingdon – so interesting times ahead on the river. The elite can take it as a major sport for all three terms, the rest compete at house level. A leading fives school (Eton variety) with 14 courts – a recent pupil was one of the first girls to be awarded a half blue at Oxford.

Venerable cross-country running club known as The Hunt is prominent on national circuit. Stunning cricket pitches described by Sir Neville Cardus as 'the most beautiful playing fields in the world'. Top class indoor cricket centre also used by local and regional clubs, funded by the Foundation. Recent winners of the national boys' cricket 20:20 championships.

Masses of non-team sports including canoeing, kayaking, climbing, mountain biking, and sub-aqua club. Outdoor pursuits and hill walking weekends to Tally, the school's own cottage in Snowdonia, with the aim of having 'serious fun'. Thriving CCF and Duke of Edinburgh up to gold.

Rich and impressive musical tradition with numerous ensembles and choirs (places in the chapel choir particularly sought after), annual house singing competition. Pupils often take productions to the Edinburgh Fringe and perform concerts in London and Birmingham. All new pupils offered a free lesson on an instrument of their choice and there are several Steinways and an organ to practice on. Two major drama productions a year a well as house plays.

Buzzing art department with mezzanine art gallery where upper sixth students can hold solo art exhibitions – particularly strong ceramics. A number go on to art school each year.

Dozens of societies, both academic and not so academic, from millinery and wine tasting to beekeeping and the green power electric car racing team. Witty and irreverent school magazine follows in the satirical tradition of the Old Salopian founders of Private Eye.

Community service popular, but not compulsory; involves work in old people's homes, schools, charity shops etc – oh, and a trip to Malawi. School has close links with Shrewsbury House community centre in Liverpool, known as The Shewsy; sixth formers can spend a week there and see another side of life and children come back for a return match to Shrewsbury.

Boarding: Eight boys' boarding houses, of about 60 beds, two day boys' houses and three girls' houses – mixed day and boarding. Housemaster or mistress, matron and team of four or five tutors in each house. Boys' houses scruffy and comfortable – girls' houses newly built or refurbished with en suite bathrooms – some harrumphing from the boys about this but their houses next on the list for refurbishment. Boys start off in dorms and then graduate to study bedrooms as they move up the school.

Background and atmosphere: Founded in 1552 by Edward VI, the school throve, faltered and then revived in 1882 when it moved across the river into the old workhouse-cum-lunatic-asylum. It was named as one of the 'great' public schools by the Clarendon Commission in 1886 along with Eton, Harrow et al. Set in 100 acres high above the river Severn with distant views to the Malvern hills. Sir Arthur Blomfield's chapel was one of the first buildings to be built and is very much the centre of the community, with its vibrant red and blue interior, striking modern ceramics and pew runners representing the River Severn. Not everyone can fit in the chapel so houses take it in turns to have a Sunday lie-in.

Elegant Edwardian houses cluster round the cricket pitch connected by immaculate lawns and fine avenues of trees. Programme of refurbishment under way and new buildings (more to come) blend into the landscape overseen by imposing statues of famous old boys Charles Darwin and the warrior poet Sir Philip Sydney.

Dozens of societies, both academic and not so academic, from millinery and wine tasting to beekeeping and the green power electric car racing team

The ancient Chained Library, open on Sunday mornings, contains some remarkable books including John Gower's Confessio Amantis, printed by Caxton in 1483, and Newton's Principia, which the school bought on publication in 1687, as well as books, manuscripts and letters of Charles Darwin.

The first girls joined sixth form in 2008 and school started taking in girls at 13+ and 14+ in 2014, aiming for 65:35 ratio with scope for numbers to increase to 780. Parents divided on this change between the huffers and puffers and those who felt it was a bit of a pity but probably inevitable. The blow softened by the evident high quality of the current sixth form girls, and the long lead time that means that all who joined for a boys' school with girls in the sixth will get just that. In our view Shrewsbury boys will adapt well to co-ed – a civilised and courteous lot.

Pastoral care, well-being and discipline: Strong sense of community and a family atmosphere with many staff living on site. 'Staff totally committed and often find it difficult to leave' but still a healthy number of young teachers. Comfortable relationships between staff and pupils who are still expected to call teachers 'Sir'.

The house system 'preserves the innocence of school days but makes sure children are ready for the next stage,' said one happy mother. Children not allowed out on Saturday night without good reason (granny's birthday dinner likely to be as exciting as it gets) and they mostly keep to their side of the river anyway. It is too far away to 'bunk off to the King's Road on a Saturday night', said another. Strong house loyalty with lots of inter-house competitions in music, drama and sport. Enormous dining room where everyone can eat together – pupils sit in house groups with tutors. Food much improved in recent years – lots of choice, praised by children.

Sixth form common room, known as Quod (no one knows why) with separate social and study areas and a shop, is run by a committee of sixth formers who organise talks, lectures, film nights and socials. Sixth formers choose their own tutor and anyone who wants to be a prefect, known as a praeposter, has to write a letter of application to the headmaster.

A school with a genuine sense of individuality, 'where you can really be yourself and everyone's personality has a place'

The chapel is central to school life but Catholics can attend services at the cathedral across the river and other faiths are accommodated. Whole school policy on bullying is underpinned by extreme vigilance from housemasters (a comfortable and friendly crew): none of the parents we talked to mentioned bullying as a concern, and we heard no grisly stories from the boys either. If there is clear evidence of drug taking a pupil will be asked to leave, if it is unclear they have to comply with a testing regime. When asked about drinking, children said there was 'no point as you would only get caught', and there is no doubt in their minds as to how Mr T would react.

Pupils and parents: An eclectic mix of landed gentry, City money, local farmers and intellectuals, all happy to keep their children away from the rat race of the south east. From all over the country including London but most live within a couple of hours of the school. About 10 per cent from overseas. Fleet of coaches ferries children home for exeats – as one father said, 'the school has something special and it is worth the long journey'. Lots of children of Old Salopians, sometimes fourth or fifth generation.

A school with a genuine sense of individuality, 'where you can really be yourself and where everyone's personality has a place,' according to one sixth form girl. Described by a parent as 'interesting, interested and able to get on with people from all backgrounds'. Lovely quirky Salopian sense of humour can be seen in the Blue Chair Charity set up some years ago to raise money for leukaemia research. Old Salopians take two blue chairs with them on their gap year and photograph them in unusual places – they have been spotted outside the Blue Mosque in Istanbul, and at the Taj Mahal; one fell down a ravine and had to be rescued and another is being held hostage on the Somali border and an £8,000 ransom has been demanded. The 8,000 members of the old Salopian Club have a great bond and sense of community. Most famous old Salopian of all is Charles Darwin, who was at the school from 1818-1825. Others include Sir Martin Rees, cosmologist and astrophysicist, Richard Ingrams, Willie Rushton and Christopher Booker, who cut their satirical teeth on the school magazine The Public Nose and went on to found

Private Eye, and Paul Foot, who was a major contributor; also Michaels Palin and Heseltine.

Entrance: Fairly broad church and also looking for potential. Most come from about 12 preps within about two hours of the school. Entry mainly via CE (55 per cent required) or academic scholarship (held in the May before entry). School's own tests in English and maths for those at non-CE schools. A few join in the fourth form (year 10) if things have not worked out elsewhere but must be able to 'hit the ground running' some 25 boys and 50 girls join for sixth form – a number of boys come from local state schools.

At sixth form entry they are looking for candidates who will make a contribution to school life – sport, music academic, drama. Assessment weekend in Nov prior to entry – candidates can choose three or four subjects in which to be assessed, plus a reference from current school, interview and personal statement.

Exit: About 50 per cent take a gap year – Shrewsbury International School in Bangkok useful source of employment for gappies; travel scholarships available for interesting and challenging gap years. About 98 per cent to university, 12 in 2015 to Oxbridge; otherwise mainly Russell Group – Bristol, Newcastle, Leeds, Edinburgh. Anyone who does not achieve at least five Bs at GCSE will be asked to leave – parents get plenty of warning if this is likely to happen.

Money matters: Scholarships and bursaries a tradition since the school was founded. Not a rich school but very supportive Old Salopians and parents put their hands in their pockets for the annual Foundation appeal, a telephone campaign staffed by sixth formers and recent leavers. Range of Foundation awards and scholarships worth up to 50 per cent can be topped up with a bursary – testing, interviews and consultation with prep schools (and some primary schools) for talented children who can't afford fees. Academic, sports, all-rounder, drama, music, DT and arts awards offered. Sixth form Margaret Cassidy Sports Scholarship worth up to full fees for talented footballer, cricketer or oarsman, and Alex Wilson day boy scholarship also worth up to full fees, for academic and sporting excellence (we assume girls not eligible for these).

Remarks: A school where individuals and individual talent are truly celebrated and where there is a 'breadth of opportunity without pressure cooker atmosphere'. Produces people with a wonderful and quirky sense of humour who are not afraid to be different.

Stamford High School

St Martin's, Stamford, Lincolnshire PE9 2LL

01780 484200
headshs@ses.lincs.sch.uk
www.ses.lincs.sch.uk
C of E

Ages: 11–18 (junior boarding from 8)
Pupils: 574; joint sixth form: 200
Boarders: 38 full, 21 weekly/flexi
Day: £13,917 pa
Boarding: £19,533 – £25,782 pa

Linked school: Stamford School

Head: Since September 2015, Mrs Vicky Buckman, previously deputy head at City of London Freeman's School. Leeds University graduate; spent 15 years as housemistress at Christ's Hospital. She is an ISI inspector, has been involved in sport and D of E, and is a qualified scuba diver.

Principal: Stephen Roberts oversees all three Stamford Endowed Schools and is very clear that modern schools benefit from this sort of leadership structure. 'No one person can do everything that is now expected of a head', he tells us, and we would expect to see more schools in the independent sector examining this model in the future.

His team work very well together, and he supports each school at events and through the wider implementation of the strategy. He was head at Felsted before coming to Stamford, and is an ideas man, but not burdened with a huge ego that would make his type of job impossible. The girls like him and many got to know him well when they were at the junior school.

He is retiring in July 2016. Will Phelan, currently head of Stamford School, will take over as principal of the three schools.

Academic matters: The Stamford Endowed Schools have a diamond structure. Girls and boys are taught together in the junior school, separately from 11 to 16, then come together again for sixth form.

Although the school is increasingly selective as girls go through, entry from the junior school to the senior is virtually automatic, so there is a wider ability range than you might find in some other selective schools. Having said that, the school does reasonably well in external exams. In 2015, 34 per cent of A level grades were A*/A in the joint sixth form, as were 60 per cent of GCSEs (a dip over the past couple of years). The joint sixth form allows for a really good range of subjects. There is music technology, design technology, food, politics, performance studies and theatre studies, textiles and Russian as well as Spanish, French and German. Philosophy and psychology are popular at A level and the school rightly prides itself on being strong all round with no weak departments.

Girls coming up from co-ed junior schools remark approvingly on the calmer class room and single sex atmosphere. A very few are statemented and there is a SENCo across the three schools who has assistants to support those with milder learning difficulties. Much of this support is included in the fees. It is only when long term, intensive intervention is needed that parents are charged extra, and even then it is heavily subsidised. Parents report a high degree of satisfaction with the learning support. They say communication between staff is excellent and the school really does deliver individually tailored programmes.

Lots of additional help is on offer particularly around exam time, when there are voluntary Saturday morning classes and revision sessions during exam leave. Girls report that staff are endlessly willing to give individual help. There is an overarching powerful strategy of 'independent learning and intellectual curiosity' which is embedded in all curriculum areas. Girls are encouraged to enquire 'What questions must I ask to learn more about this?' The aim is that girls will find their own passions to drive them through life. No sitting back and giving up on difficulties allowed here.

Co-ed junior boarding house in the grounds of the junior school, with climbing frame, rabbits and chickens in the garden. Boarders come from a range of backgrounds

Games, options, the arts: Games are strong. The school sends out an impressive number of teams and we sensed that virtually everyone who wants to play for a team gets a chance. When asked what was the best thing about the school, sport figured highly. There are lovely outdoor facilities a short walk from the school on the edge of the town. A few commented that it would be good to have sports fields actually on site, but this would never be possible given the town site, and the walk is very pleasant – at least when we visited on a sunny summer day. There is trampoline, fitness and zumba on offer and the girls play football, row and run with enthusiasm.

The quality of the big public music and drama occasions is very high, drawing on all three schools. Budding thespians are attracted to the school for the drama opportunities, which have gone up a notch with the opening of the new joint performing arts centre.

CCF is popular and strongly supported by the head. One family said they had chosen the school because in their first interview with the head, she was resplendent in her CCF uniform.

The school celebrates girls' out-of-school successes as well as school achievements – we like this and so do parents. There are regular trips, some with the boys' school, including language and sports tours, and adventure activities include D of E and rock climbing. The girls are encouraged to be feisty and physically confident.

Boarding: Boarding is small, in two separate town houses (one for 11-16s and one for sixth formers) very close to school. It is all centre of town, so security is tight but unobtrusively managed. Both houses are a delight, with the least institutional feel that we have ever met. The sixth form house feels like a very well-loved student hall of residence with some 'flats' that allow for considerable independence. Co-ed junior boarding house in the grounds of the junior school, with climbing frame, rabbits and chickens in the garden. Boarders come from a range of backgrounds – some Forces families, some local and a smattering of international students. There are weekend trips to London, to local attractions, to the cinema, plus other organised activities.

Background and atmosphere: Set on the High Street, the school seems infused with the calm and dignity of the quintessentially English 18th and 19th century buildings all around, much loved by film producers of costume dramas. It must be one of the most gorgeous English towns in which to educate children. Something of a period feel is continued inside the school, with the girls up to sixth form wearing very long skirts. Sixth formers are allowed knee length school skirts. No-one seemed to mind.

The school is very clear about the advantages of the diamond structure. The high school doesn't feel like a closeted girls' school because there are boys about – going to A level lessons, play or music rehearsals, club meetings or just socialising in the sixth form common room. The single sex years from 11 to 16 are used to build confidence in this can-do community, where girls 'lean in', understanding the importance of high levels of aspiration, determination and ambition. There is a High School spirit of rolling your sleeves up and getting on with it. Girls are not precious princesses. They know life has rocks as well as roses and that you just have to pick yourself up and carry on. There is a breezy wholesomeness about the atmosphere.

Pastoral care, well-being and discipline: Although as a whole the Stamford Endowed Schools educate around 1,600 children, the way they are divided up gives a sense at the High School that you are part of a close community. There is calmness about it and a friendliness recognised by girls and parents.

Pastoral concerns are picked up quickly and the run-of-the-mill late homework is headed off by a quiet word. The preventative approach carries through to actively managing relations with parents. A series of talks – Teenage Challenge – mirrors PHSE sessions with the girls, and topics such as online safety are chosen as a result of parental anxieties. Stretched but not stressed is the strapline that sums up the approach to ensuring girls have a balanced approached to life.

Sixth form is seen as excitingly different enough to make everyone want to stay on. It must be those knee length skirts. 'My daughter made so many new friends'

The school structures try to ensure girls mix with everyone. The form groups and form teachers change every year, and those coming in at year 9, 10 or into the sixth form tell us they found it easy to integrate in the absence of any long-established cliques being allowed to form. A few parents who had approached the school about pastoral concerns had felt very well supported – lots of unobtrusive intervention and good advice.

Health problems are very well addressed as are major family problems such as bereavement

– again, this seems a result of excellent communication between staff and between staff and families. As you might expect in a school that encourages the girls to take responsibility seriously, externally imposed discipline feels light touch. There is a hugely orderly and purposeful feel about the school. When someone fails to live up to the high expectations, the first response is one of mild surprise and disappointment. That usually works, according to staff. If not, there is the normal range of sanctions. Parents are very supportive of discipline issues. The head senses that they are usually at a loss themselves and only too keen to stand shoulder to shoulder with the school.

'Daughters of the Empire' is a phrase that comes to mind when you meet the girls. They have an uncomplicated, determined outlook on life

The girls say you know where you stand, you know the consequences of misbehaviour but it is not 'scary strict'. They describe their relations with teachers as relaxed. Sixth formers notice the difference in the atmosphere at the boys' school, commenting on the sharp banter that is the male conversational norm.

Pupils and parents: The Stamford Endowed Schools have acted as the local grammar school for a long time and the county scholarship scheme is only just being phased out. The governors are determined to keep the genuine social inclusivity and have a large bursary fund to make this a reality. However, it is not unrealistic to suppose the intake will in the future be a little more well-heeled. But regardless of the financial situation, parents see this as a local school, genuinely embedded in the community.

We met a number of girls whose parents had themselves been to nearby big, traditional boarding schools and who had clearly been delighted to find a school for their daughters with an ethos they recognised that didn't involve boarding, Saturday school and the consequent high fees.

Staff said girls come from hard working families and the girls knew how fortunate they were to be somewhere like Stamford. We found them unpretentious, straightforward and open. Teachers felt they could experiment and take risks in a way not possible in other schools with less engaged students. Stamford itself as well as the school has a safe, middle class enclave feel about it – and parents love it exactly for that.

Parents are sold on the diamond structure. 'It's the best of both worlds,' we heard a number of times, and very few pull girls out after year 11 unless they are really pressed financially, because the sixth form is seen as excitingly different enough to make everyone want to stay on. It must be those knee length skirts. 'My daughter made so many new friends when she went into the sixth form and noticeably matured,' said one delighted mother.

Parents universally told us that they had chosen the school because of the all-round quality and they have not been disappointed.

Entrance: The Endowed Schools have their own entrance exam at 11+. It is the same for the boys and girls and involves maths, English and reasoning. Progression from the junior school is almost automatic. At 13+ by CE. For sixth form entry, generally at least five B grades at GCSE, including in all A level subjects.

Exit: Around 20 per cent leave after GCSEs. Nearly all into higher education, with a sprinkling to Oxbridge (four in 2015), a few medics, some gap years and art foundation courses. There is a careers programme from year 7 to year 13. It's overarching and age appropriate, with careers talks and an annual careers convention for year 10 and above. Much appreciated higher education advice and preparation operates across the two schools.

Money matters: The loss of the county grammar school places will be felt by financially strapped parents in the future, but the school is working hard on its bursary fundraising to compensate in part for the loss. The success of this is going to be important not least because a number of parents spoke about the attractions of the social mix that the free places currently assure. All parents to whom we spoke mentioned value for money. It is of course in a market place with pricey boarding schools, and there is a section of parents who are escapees from London day schools. They can't quite believe just what they are getting for a relatively modest outlay.

Remarks: 'Daughters of the Empire' is a phrase that comes to mind when you meet the girls. They have an uncomplicated, determined outlook on life that makes you feel this England of ours will be safe in their hands. The school encourages them to live life to the full, explore all their talents and put them to the use of others. If you want to temper the self-obsessed, neurotic trends in contemporary teenage culture, this is the place to send your daughter.

Stamford School

Southfields House, Stamford, Lincolnshire PE9 2BQ

01780 750300	**Ages:** 11–18 (junior boarding from 8)
headss@ses.lincs.sch.uk	**Pupils:** 668; joint sixth form: 210
www.ses.lincs.sch.uk	**Boarders:** 41 full, 46 weekly/flexi
C of E	**Day:** £13,917 pa
	Boarding: £19,533 – £25,782 pa

Linked school: Stamford High School

Head: Since 2011, Will Phelan (40s). Read medieval and modern history at Royal Holloway, followed by PGCE at Reading and MBA in education management. Formerly deputy head at Warwick, head of sixth form and director of rugby at Abingdon School, and head of year at Royal Grammar School, High Wycombe. A dedicated head, he can be found at most matches and concerts. He still teaches history to the year 7s. Considered a career as a professional rugby player until injury forced a different direction.

Originally planned to study economics and 'make money' but didn't quite make the grade, so headed to Australia to consider his future. 'Not getting my first choice turned out to be the making of me,' he says. A year as a boarding master in Australia, where he also coached rugby and cricket, made the decision for him. 'I loved being at the school coaching and being with the boys, so decided that I wanted to teach. I've spent 20 years

with boys and I know what makes them tick. The boys from Stamford are some of the nicest boys I've met. The school is spread out over a large site, which is perfect, as I don't think boys should be on top of each other, they need room. A Stamford boy is a tryer – he's stretched, but not stressed. I want the school to be the best all-round boys' school in the country.'

He is charismatic, very well liked and respected by boys and parents alike (we're sure the mothers love him). Married with three children (two daughters at Stamford Junior School, Freddie still in a pushchair). A huge man, he towers over the tallest of boys (well, he was going to be a rugby player). In July 2016 he moves onward and upward to take over as principal of the three schools.

Principal: Stephen Roberts oversees all three Stamford Endowed Schools and is very clear that modern schools benefit from this sort of leadership structure. 'No one person can do everything that is

now expected of a head', he tells us, and we would expect to see more schools in the independent sector examining this model in the future. His team work very well together, and he supports each school at events and through the wider implementation of the strategy. He was head at Felsted before coming to Stamford, and is an ideas man, but not burdened with a huge ego that would make his type of job impossible.

Retiring in July 2016; Will Phelan will take over as principal.

Academic matters: Consistent, solid results. In 2015, 52 per cent A*/A at GCSE, and 34 per cent A*/A at A level (65 per cent A*/B) – results for joint sixth form (Stamford High School and Stamford School). Most boys take 10 GCSEs in a wide range of subjects. French, German, Spanish, Russian and Latin are language options. DT is strong (the workshops and work produced are impressive; two self-propelled vehicles built by the boys caught our eye). Twenty-eight subjects offered in the sixth form that is joined with the High School, most popular being maths and the sciences, with economics and business studies rising fast. Philosophy and ethics rated highly throughout the three schools.

The lessons we observed showed involved, enthusiastic boys. The year 8 Latin scholars were wriggling in their seats, they were so keen – well

disciplined, though. Lots of arm raising in the year 11 philosophy and ethics debate and diligent studying in year 9 maths. All boys leapt to their feet when we entered the classrooms. The year 13 lessons had a very different atmosphere. Much less formal but strongly focused pupils. Determined and interested, these boys had their eye on the end game. You could feel expectations of the staff and boys were high.

Learning support is available for boys who need it. Around 80 boys with SEN and 40 or so get learning support. One boy has a statement of special educational needs. Extra support also offered to invited boys on Saturday mornings.

Games, options, the arts: Sport features highly – even the non-sporty boy is encouraged to have a go. A strength of the school is the number of teams in different sports, so even the boy who is 'rubbish' (our words, not theirs) gets to play. But don't be fooled. Stamford's 1st XV was unbeaten last year and are formidable opponents. Eye-catching rugby kit, but one unimpressed mother wanted to know 'why do they make the sixth form play in white shorts? I just can't get them clean'.

Some of these boys are playing at county level, others selected by local premiership sides, and the captain was invited to represent England in the U18 squad, while a previous captain is now playing professionally. The cricket team is largely unbeaten (ex-England international Dean Headley coaches), the squash squad has been unbeaten for three years, and the basketball team (including another national player) too. They're pretty good at hockey and swimming as well. Their first year with a triathlon team resulted in a GB squad selection (and the school had to teach the boy in question to swim).

A parent told us that if a boy was yellow carded in any sport at the weekend he was up in front of the headmaster on Monday morning to explain himself. Excellent. Parents are happy and trust the school. The odd grouse about sporting stars possibly being cut more slack (sour grapes maybe?) but every parent we spoke to was happy and 'hugely impressed.'

The new £6.1 million sports centre dominates the skyline, looking out over the rugby pitches, and offers gym facilities as well as a 25m pool (pity they don't brush the walkways more often) and is well used by all the school.

Music and art are equally strong. SES is the largest independent centre for LAMDA exams in the country and six boys recently opted for music or music tech at university. A visit to the music department revealed a stash of new Macs for composing and music tech as well as the usual instruments.

The combined productions with fellow endowed school, Stamford High School (girls), are very popular (can't imagine why): recent production of Les

Combined productions with fellow endowed school, Stamford High School (girls), are very popular (can't imagine why)

Misérables involving all three schools was a sell out. Thriving choirs, bands and orchestras, ranging from big band and jazz to full orchestra. House singing and music competitions are hotly contested. A new drama and music block opened in 2014.

Artwork is displayed throughout the school. Portraits seemed to be popular, albeit mainly from the upper school, in the more prominent spots. Arty boys are encouraged to spend time in the studio.

CCF section is one of the largest in the country (combined with the girls' school from year 10 up), with opportunities to go flying if you're in the RAF section. The shooting team is good (they have their own range), winning the Bermuda Cup at Bisley and Country Life competitions. Lots of silver in the cabinet.

World Challenge trips to Peru, India, Madagascar, Patagonia and Borneo. D of E popular; 18 boys left recently having already completed their gold award.

Boarding: Although Stamford is predominantly a day school,15 per cent of the pupils board. Most are weekly or three night boarders who live within 100 miles of the school. There are also boys from China, Poland, Holland and Russia. The boarders are divided into two houses – years 7-10 (Byard House) and years 11-13 (Browne). More boys board in the latter years and most have single rooms. Facilities recently updated – new furniture, lots of snooker and table tennis tables, all clean, bright and tidy, with posters on the walls (nothing inappropriate though). The older boarders must be the fittest around as the gym is a regular haunt in the evenings after prep. Co-ed junior boarding house in the grounds of the junior school, with climbing frame, rabbits and chickens in the garden.

We were shown every nook and cranny by the younger boys, who enthusiastically told us about boarders' outings to the cinema, Alton Towers, paintballing, go karting and local Leicester Tigers' matches, as well as table tennis tournaments. All age groups said how like home it is – boys change their own sheets and can bring their own duvet covers – and how much they like the boarding staff. There are televisions, but they don't get used a lot. More time is spent on Xbox and table tennis, after two hours of supervised prep every night. Boarders eat together in the main dining hall and seem happy and relaxed with each other.

Background and atmosphere: Founded in 1532, Stamford School still operates from its original site in the middle of the town (recently voted the best place to live by The Sunday Times). The school chapel, surrounded by its immaculate lawns, is at the heart of the school. Stamford School is part of the Stamford Endowed Schools (includes Stamford Junior School and Stamford High School). Each school is run separately – with its own head but a common principal. Teaching at the Stamford Endowed Schools is via the diamond structure – mixed junior and sixth forms, single sex 11-16 – which seems very successful and strongly supported by the parents. 'Lots of info on drugs, drink, driving and sex, which the boys seem to find easier to take in a single sex environment,' one parent told us. A year 8 parent commented: 'My son is just hitting adolescence and they know exactly how to handle him. The single sex education is a godsend.'

Sixth form teaching is split between the two schools, so there's a 10 minute walk across town if there is a site change in the timetable. This gives the school a collegiate feel and allows the sixth form boys a certain degree of independence. There's a lot of trust involved but it doesn't seem to be abused. Because of this constant walking – great in the summer, not so good in the winter – the boys are highly visible in the town. The local shops can no doubt set their clocks by hordes of hungry boys dashing in for sustenance for the 'long walk' through the beautiful town. (The school food used to be awful, now greatly improved, we're told). No driving is allowed between sites. Woe betide any boy who is caught doing so. We understand keys have been confiscated on occasion. There is also the 'six-inch rule' to be considered. Six inches must be kept between a boy and a girl at all times...

Sixth formers often have to cross town between lessons. Local shops no doubt set their clocks by hordes of hungry boys dashing in for sustenance for the 'long walk' between sites

Boys are very involved with the wider community and help out with many of the local charities. The Evergreen Trust in Stamford and Help for Heroes get lots of support. Year 7 boys took part in the Sleep for Shelter Night, spending a night in a cardboard box in the school grounds.

School site is spread over a large area, giving the boys plenty of room. Part of the site features beautiful, honey-coloured stone Georgian and older buildings with beautiful gardens. Perhaps one of the most iconic features of the school (probably to their disappointment) is the incredibly ugly foot-bridge that connects two parts split by a very busy road. We were told that plans are afoot to improve it.

Pastoral care, well-being and discipline: Discipline is hot and any problems nipped in the bud quickly. School doesn't deny bullying exists, hooray, but it's dealt with promptly, quite often by the boys themselves. Mentoring system means older boys mentor the younger ones (years 7-11) and there is a one-to-one mentoring system between year 10 and year 12 boys. Lots of banter, but lines aren't crossed. The atmosphere is friendly and happy – these boys seem to like each other. Quite how the introvert sitting in the corner fares we're not so sure, but we were assured by a parent that 'the school knows their boys.'

'Support is there if you need it; you just have to ask,' a pupil told us. A younger boy's mother said: 'Parent mail is a fairly new system. We can access the school portal and see what and when homework is due. We are very quickly told if deadlines are missed, so my son knows he is being watched very closely by us all and knuckles down and gets on with it. A great improvement.'

Parents say that 'communication is very strong both ways.' One told us: 'We have needed pastoral help and the school has been very supportive and dealt with matters calmly, effectively and efficiently.'

Pupils and parents: Boys mainly from a 30-mile radius, slightly further afield in the sixth form. Mostly from professional families who value the all-round education of their sons rather than a well-known name. Boys we met were confident, courteous, friendly and grounded. In school's own words,

a 'Stamford boy is well rounded and up for anything.' Boys are encouraged to get involved and say that if you get stuck in (and everyone does) 'you fit in.'

Every parent we spoke to gave glowing references: 'Excellent, I would recommend it every time; they turn out grounded, confident boys,' said one. 'My son loved being there so much he says he will send his own son, if he has one,' said another. A third told us: 'They take in boys and send out confident young men, and they guide them through really well.' A few parents felt Stamford was undersold, but they're working on that, and a couple felt communication between the two schools in the sixth form could be improved.

Old boys include General Sir Mike Jackson, former Chief of the General Staff, Nick Anstee, former Lord Mayor of the City of London, Colin Dexter (Inspector Morse), Iwan Thomas (Olympic athlete), golfer Mark James, conductor Sir Malcolm Sargent and Simon Hodgkinson (England rugby international).

Entrance: Entry is mainly at year 7, based on an entrance exam covering maths, English and verbal reasoning. The main feeder is Stamford Junior School, just under 50 per cent, with an automatic transfer; the remainder come from local primaries and preps. Forces families are well represented, as are farming families.

There's a smaller intake in year 9, based on performance or CE, and in the sixth form five GCSEs at grade B or higher (internal and external) are required.

Exit: A handful leave after GCSEs – a couple to other sixth forms, usually boarding, a few to the local college for vocational courses. Most boys head to a Russell Group or redbrick universities. Popular are Durham, Newcastle, Loughborough, Leeds and Sheffield. Engineering, business and sciences slightly favoured but too many choices to judge. A handful of Oxbridge entries – four in 2015, plus several to the US and two to Sciences Po (university for social science in Paris and Reims). One or two into the Forces, the odd boy straight into employment, eg an engineering apprenticeship with Audi, another spending his gap year as a Deloitte scholar.

Money matters: Means-tested bursaries (up to full fees) and academic, sports and music scholarships, all funded by the school. A Stamford School boy could have a parent who is CEO of a multi-national company or be a postman in the town, a huge strength of the school. Many boys are second or even third generation pupils.

Remarks: Stamford is surrounded by some very big hitters – Uppingham, Oundle and Oakham spring to mind – so can be overlooked, as it doesn't seem to have the same kudos. But Stamford more than holds its own, academically and sportswise. It's a hidden gem but we doubt it's going to be hidden for much longer. It shouldn't be. Prosecco rather than champagne, but better value for money and preferred by many.

Uppingham School

High Street West, Uppingham, Rutland LE15 9QE

01572 822216
admissions@uppingham.co.uk
www.uppingham.co.uk
C of E

Ages: 13–18
Pupils: 790; sixth form: 345
Boarders: nearly all full
Day: £23,799 pa
Boarding: £33,999 pa

Headmaster: Since 2006, Richard Harman MA PGCE. He was educated at The King's School, Worcester, and Trinity College, Cambridge, where he read English. Having spent two years working for an academic publisher, he decided his real vocation was in teaching. After five years at Marlborough College teaching English and drama, he went to Eastbourne College, head of English, housemaster of a sixth form girls' boarding house and member of the senior management team. He then became headmaster of Aldenham in 2000, and thence to Uppingham in 2006.

When we met Richard Harman, he had just begun his year as chairman of HMC. The last headmaster of Uppingham to hold this illustrious post was the Reverend Edward Thring, who presided over the inaugural meeting of the Headmasters' Conference at Uppingham in 1869. Richard says, 'Edward Thring believed that the purpose of education was to find out what a child could do, and then he encouraged his pupils to do it to the best of their ability. He also understood the importance of the pastoral development of children. His legacy remains at Uppingham.'

His robust HMC chairman's speech, lashing out at those who make independent schools a scapegoat for lack of social mobility, caused a stir in the political establishment, but he told us that Uppingham parents have welcomed his place on the national stage, and enjoy swopping ideas about the state of the nation's education on the touch line, where he is a regular spectator. Parents say he has considerable presence but is also highly approachable. He articulates passionately the importance of a liberal, holistic education and is on a mission to inspire young people to become confident, self-reliant global citizens.

He is married, with one daughter, and has a keen interest in sport, music and theatre.

Leaving in July 2016. His successor will be Dr Richard Maloney MA (theology at St Andrew's) PGCE (Cantab), early 40s, currently head of Bede's Senior School. An alumnus of Latymer Upper School, Dr Maloney began his career in West Yorkshire. In 1997, he became head of RS and, later, head of sixth, at Chigwell School, during which period he completed an MA at King's College, London. In 2006, he was appointed deputy headmaster of Sutton Valence. During his tenure there he became a PhD but left after three years to take up the Bede's headship – whilst still in his 30s. We described him at Bede's as 'A man of palpable energy – physical and intellectual – complemented by equal measures of compassion, dedication, ambition and vision'. He has transformed that school and become hot educational property.

He is married to Tracey, who runs an educational consultancy, and they have two children.

Academic matters: Although the emphasis is on holistic education, academic matters do not suffer. It was obvious from talking to pupils that teachers relish challenging the most able to get as far as they can. All abilities are making excellent progress and exam results are strong, but parents hastened to inform us that Uppingham is no academic hothouse, and compared the approach to education very favourably to what they see as the stressful academic day schools of Cambridge and London. In 2015, 49 per cent of A levels were at A or A* and 76 per cent were at A* to B. At GCSE, over 70 per cent A*/A grades in 2015; this stays fairly steadily in the high 60s, low 70s year on year.

There are separate girls' and boys' boarding houses spread over the small market town. Most are vertical – pupils from every age group

The school considers all subjects to be strong, pointing to outstanding results and large numbers taking both science and arts subjects at A level. Pupils enthuse about the history, religious studies and politics, but also approve of the various innovations that the stunning new science block has inspired, including the outdoor science classroom. The new labs are designed with one half for practical work and the other half for the theory – a great improvement to the traditional labs where students make notes between the gas taps and Bunsen burners. With 29 A level subjects on offer, there is a superb range. The head is keeping the post-16 curriculum under close review but thinks that a combination of A levels, Pre-U, and the Extended Project will offer lots of stimulus for all in the sixth form. Average class size is 16, and nine in the sixth form. There is support for those with mild learning difficulties and those who need help with English language (at extra cost).

Games, options, the arts: You would expect a school that prides itself on its holistic education to provide a rich extracurricular offer and Uppingham doesn't disappoint. Facilities, which are also used by the local community, are outstanding – the biggest stage, the pupils informed us, of any school they had heard of, and drama is supported by fantastic teachers and professional technicians. Endless sports on offer and, pupils assure us, it is for everyone, not just the elite. One year 13 boy spoke with considerable enthusiasm about his engagement with a lowly rugby team. As well as 'major' sports there is a plethora of others – just as well, given that it is compulsory to do something.

Music is outstanding – one parent said that all independent schools say their music is good, but at Uppingham it is really good. Everyone mentions whole school congregational singing in chapel. There are House Shouts in which everyone seems to get involved, and then highly selective choirs and orchestras for the specialists. These groups tour in the UK and overseas as well as having endless performance opportunities in school. Masterclasses given by eminent musicians are regular features. Recording studios, a radio station and music technology encourage those who aspire to find renown in more celebrity spheres, honing their acts along the way in the school Battle of the Bands.

Everyone does CCF, though there is an opt-out for older pupils, who can get involved in community service. Some help in local primary schools, including teaching a Latin programme; others visit elderly people, ride with disabled people or take part in various overseas aid projects.

The art is vibrant and diverse – taking place in the Leonardo Centre, named after the Renaissance Man, the ultimate model for the Uppingham student.

Boarding: All but a tiny handful board. Everyone says it is a school for children who really want the full boarding experience – no flexi approach countenanced here to ease the way for those valuing their own 'me time'. There are separate girls' and boys' boarding houses spread over the small market town. Most are vertical – pupils from every age group – but there is also a sixth form girls' house, as more girls join the school at sixth form level. Some houses are in the centre, having the advantage of being minutes away from teaching areas, others are further out and have the advantage of more space – one boasting its own swimming pool. Prospective

Recording studios, a radio station and music technology for those who aspire to find renown in celebrity spheres

families are normally taken to see just a few of the houses, though you can see all 15 if you really want.

Boys' houses have around 50 pupils and girls about 60. Each has a housemaster or mistress living there with their own family. There are resident tutors and a team of non-resident tutors attached to each house. Meals are taken in the house and house staff share the tables with the pupils. There is a rota of other staff circulating around the houses, so the students are very used to visitors.

Background and atmosphere: Uppingham is a boarding school with no half measures. Only a handful of pupils go home for the night – it is a school for those who want people around all the time and masses to do. 'Much too much, really,' said one boy who knew his AS results could have been a bit better if there weren't just such a brilliant amount going on all the time. However, one mother who spoke to us said that the housemasters have a close grip on this sort of problem and can usually sort things out early on.

When we dined at one house, the boys were completely charming – enthusiastic about everything at school and genuinely interested in their visitors. These are young people whose emotional intelligence is being unobtrusively developed on a daily basis. Separate girls' and boys' houses add to the individual flavour of each house. They can come to breakfast in their pyjamas and experience single sex norms as well as the hurly burly of co-ed in the classroom. Parents who had visited a number of houses before the children joined Uppingham said that every houseparent they met had credibility, and had proved to be inspirational.

With all the high quality activity on offer both in regulated and not regulated time, you would have to work very hard at being bored round here. Sixth formers have their own social centre, which is open once a term to other years, but most pupils are dashing from sports fields to drama studios to art rooms to music rehearsals, getting the most out of every minute.

Pastoral care, well-being and discipline: A lot of thought goes into settling in new pupils. They have a mentor in the year above and a sixth form mentor in their house. House staff make sure there is plenty going on at the weekends, so new pupils are quickly immersed in the busy life of the school.

We got the sense that the staff all loved communal life, and their enthusiasm is infectious. Pupils all talked about their close friendships – 'My friends are always there for me and probably always will be,' said one year 13, starting to contemplate life beyond Uppingham.

There are school counsellors and a school psychotherapist, and all the pupils we spoke to felt there were plenty of staff to whom they could take any concerns. As part of the curriculum, there is health and social education that supports the usual areas of teenage angst, with self-help techniques as well as information and advice. Sixth formers are trained to support the younger pupils.

There are very firm rules and sanctions about bullying, drugs, smoking and alcohol use. Spirits are taken more seriously than wine. Everyone knows the score, and where a pupil has fallen foul of the sanctions, parents have accepted the firm and clear way the school has dealt with the matter.

Pupils and parents: The large map in the registrar's office with its pins indicating where in the UK families come from shows, not surprisingly, a preponderance from the wealthy parts of the country – largely home counties, but there are plenty from the midlands and the north too. Parents are mostly from the professional and business classes. A steady 12 to 15 per cent of boarders are from overseas. Parents like the real mix of nationalities. They also like the school's approach to the family. 'The school gives you the sense that it is the whole family joining the school; they really want us to get involved too'.

The pupils are fully aware of the preconceptions that others have of them. 'But we are not arrogant,' they assure us. 'The school actively teaches us humility. We are confident, but when you are living with lots of different people and learning how to get on

together, it tends to make you confident.' Parents say they are delighted with how Uppingham pupils turn out – they are engaging, personable, gregarious and go out into the world with enthusiasm and interest in other people.

Entrance: As you would expect, the admissions process is a very well-oiled machine. Many families start the process three years before the actually date of entry. It is all very welcoming and informative. Most join at 13+, but there is also a significant entry at 16+, particularly from girls who have been in a single sex environment. Most of these girls (typically 25-30 a year) are housed in the sixth form girls' house, The Lodge.

There is a pre-testing round at 11 (year 7) with papers in maths and English, an interview and references from current school. Places are then conditional on further tests in year 8, when pupils can sit common entrance (55 per cent average pass mark) or the school's own exam, consisting of maths and English with a further interview.

At sixth form level, there is a six GCSE at B grade minimum requirement for everyone, but virtually all existing pupils get those. For those coming in from outside, there are also sixth form scholarship and non-scholarship exams, plus two interviews – a house one and an academic one.

Exit: Very few leave after GCSEs. In 2015, six to Oxbridge; Bristol, Newcastle, Oxford Brookes, Edinburgh, Durham and Exeter also popular. There is a good range of subjects, business, history, sciences, politics and international relations coming out top. The careers advice and particularly support with UCAS applications are highly regarded, with subject staff and house staff all contributing.

Money matters: A serious number of scholarships are awarded at both 13+ and 16+: music, art, DT, sport and all-rounder as well as academic. There is also a new sixth form science scholarship. Typically, in a year group of about 150, there will be 35 scholarships awarded.

There is also some means-tested bursary support available – the registrar says the approach is flexible to respond to the very individual needs of a family.

Remarks: Even though it is big and spreads throughout the small market town of Uppingham, everyone tells us the school has a homely feel. We know just what they mean – though it is probably Home and Gardens homely rather than the average urban semi. It is a rather wonderful bubble, and feels a world away from the relatively close midlands cities. Uppingham is charming English small market town, with its own theatres (owned and run by the school) and its own cafés and shops that the pupils wonder round relatively freely. Parents and pupils love it.

We had some sense that by the time the pupils leave the school, they are hungry for the wider world, but that is a good thing. A sixth former who wanted to party hard might start to find it restricting, but the community feel is energising enough for most. The pupils are aware of how fortunate they are. They are not taking all this for granted, and the ones we spoke to were determined to make the most of all their wonderful opportunities. They were enthusiastic, curious and positive – as one would hope for from a liberal, holistic education. Will they change the world, lead the revolution? Probably not. Will they spread sweetness and light wherever they go? We think probably yes. Will they be responsible citizens of the world? Another yes.

UWC Atlantic College

St Donat's Castle, Llantwit Major, Vale of Glamorgan CF61 1WF

01446 799000
jan.bishop@atlanticcollege.org
www.atlanticcollege.org

Ages: 15–19
Pupils: 367
Boarders: all full
Boarding: £28,106 pa

Principal: Since 2011, Mr John Walmsley BSc PGCE. Previously head of Sidcot School; before that, assistant head at Simon Langton Girls' Grammar School in Canterbury, preceded by department head posts at Budmouth School in Weymouth, Greengates School in Mexico City and Churchill School in Somerset. Educated at one of the first comprehensives in East Yorkshire, his first love and degree subject (at Leeds) was geology, though niche standing on the curriculum meant he tended to teach sciences and, at one point, geography. ICT also featured for years in his job title after IT course gave him sought-after expertise amongst schools

desperate to get to grips with high tech delights coming their way.

Tall and engaging, with dry humour (Albariño, he thought, rather than amontillado, our suggestion) he has a committee-friendly voice – whether natural or honed by years of meetings, it's hard to tell – betraying little in the way of emotion beyond occasional fleeting pained expression.

Headship at Sidcot, due to end when he reached 60 was, he'd thought, last hurrah before sashay into gentle retirement. Then came discreet call from headhunter and realisation that he wasn't yet ready to spend more quality time with his family (second wife Barbara is a former English teacher and burgeoning stonemason) and children (six in total aged mid-30s to early teens) or fishing boat in Ireland.

He's now completely hooked on what, if not the most interesting school leadership post in the country, must come close. Goals, structure and curriculum set it apart from just about everywhere else in the UK. Even hard-bitten officials, including inspectors, get all shook up by philosophy that trains up pupils as emissaries for a better world – many, embedded in powerful institutions, endeavouring to inspire change from within.

Like many a minority movement not totally understood by outsiders, college radiates a certain cult-like fervour. Principal was slightly discombobulated by references to The Mission when he first arrived. 'I thought, "Oh, no, what have I got myself into?"' Any resemblance to a niche religion is, however, entirely coincidental, with worshippers of every description catered for with multi-denominational prayer room as well as delightful church.

Considerable values overlap with Society of Friends makes this a sort of spiritual home from home, thinks principal. And though occupies its own quadrant in the educational universe, has kissing cousins, notably Gordonstoun (which shares the same founding father – German educationalist Kurt Hahn – as well as large chunks of the philosophy). Perhaps oddly, the two currently have no contact to speak of, something Mr Walmsley plans to rectify with a family get-together. The success of this remains to be seen.

College newsletter praised students' freedom to 'chase academic hares into the undergrowth of learning ... keeping an eye on the syllabus and sometimes even a blind eye'

With everything else on his plate, retirement could be some way down the agenda. While many pupils come from settled homes round the globe, college is in effect an international rescue centre for others escaping conflict, poverty or the potentially life-threatening consequences of standing up to extremism, and requiring not just an education but a place of refuge. Often comes about following intervention of high profile celebrities and politicians – principal, a frequent flyer, meets the lot.

There's also a fair amount of missing organisational nuts and bolts business that needs sorting out. Sense of purpose might be rock solid, financial underpinning rather less so, spending having exceeded income for a number of years. Bureaucratic slippage meant that college wasn't even registered as a school and drifted off the inspection radar. First 'for about 20 years' happened in 2012, scoring, to principal's delight (and slight surprise), an all-categories 'outstanding', despite unfenced swimming pool. 'I prepared them by saying the pool is unfenced – and so is the sea', he says.

Nuts and bolts paperwork was similarly lacking with few policies (now coming on stream). Tighter grip on the money side has resulted in a bit of natural wastage (departing staff weren't replaced) and temporary reduction on scholarships. Numbers now back in the black – essential when wooing potential sponsors (for donations) and bank manager (for loans).

Principal's first task on arrival was to write a formal strategic plan (and, no, there wasn't one of those, either). Biggest change is addition of pre-IB year for 25 students (probably in year 11 or 12) not yet ready for the full on two-year experience. They lead largely separate lives, with own boarding house and co-curriculum, and the best are invited to stay on. Many students aren't keen, seeing it as dilution, if not betrayal of the two-year education that they believe should define the UWC experience. Mr Walmsley, who is presumably getting used to having just about every decision challenged, remains courteous but unmoved. 'It's controversial but unnecessarily so', he says. 'Some students think it will change everything. I don't think it will'.

On top of this, there are crumbling teaching blocks to be replaced and extras added, notably a big new sports hall. That, too, has been met with some opposition, this time from staff who see the mountains and sea as offering all the gym you'll ever need. Principal's view is that when there's a force nine blowing and it's dark, even the most rugged of spirits might prefer to commune with weights rather than nature in the raw.

It's education the immersive way, students picking a theme that interests them and following its thread through their studies – real world, practical studies

Greatest ire has been reserved for alarms now fitted to dorm front doors. Though Ofsted and Welsh equivalent boarding school regulations non-negotiable, it's gone down extremely badly with anonymous notes, bannered-up protests and, months on, a still flickering flame of resentment amongst students.

Mr Walmsley is regarded as a slightly unknown quantity (discernible in pupils' quick, appraising glances when asked for their thoughts in his presence). Though does his bit with enthusiasm (was star turn at pupil fashion show, where his snappy outfit was so enthusiastically received 'that I couldn't hear the backing music') some would like more informal chatting time to share views.

When we visited, a book of Quaker values had pride of place on his desk. Given fabulous but exhausting feistiness of colleagues and pupils, wouldn't be surprising if he opened the covers and inhaled a big lungful every morning, along with the bracing sea air. He must need every last drop he can get.

Academic matters: Education starts with the IB but, like the battery-powered toy bunnies in those long ago TV ads, keeps on going long after other schools have ground to a halt, courtesy of the Atlantic College Diploma, the compulsory, wrap-around co-curricular programme introduced in 2012.

Diploma extras take up a good 30 per cent of pupils' time, 'and probably more,' thinks principal, requiring the academic component of the IB (no picnic at the best of times) to be breezed through in just five mornings plus an afternoon in the classroom each week. Pupils choose one of four 'experiential' faculties, each big on the redemptive powers of active, selfless participation (very Kurt Hahn), that add to the IB's magnificent seven and tick off its creativity, action and service component en route.

There's outdoor (focus on those in peril on the seas – past pupil and teacher developed now best-selling RIB boat, then, combining brilliance and philanthropy in equal measure, selflessly

donated patent to the RNLI); social justice (first hand encounters of a robust kind, including work with refugees and prisoners' families); global (everything from organising peace events to sharing a dorm with traditional enemies); and environmental, where commitment to sustainability is no light matter (students, who recycle everything, deeply miffed by college's failure to consult over green disposal of fittings following boarding house refurb).

It's education the immersive way, students picking a theme that interests them and following its thread through their studies – real world, practical applications dovetailing with academic side. Someone with an interest in Middle East might study Arabic, prepare an extended essay in world studies, help set up a project week in Jordan and, through this, 'understand the UWC mission in the way they choose to develop their strengths,' says head of curriculum.

At its best (which is much of the time) diploma activities feed back into lessons, making for a buzzy classroom atmosphere where passionate debate is a way of life. There's nothing like hearing about refugees' experiences then discussing them back at base to add bite to economics or geography lessons, says principal. 'Makes it much more interesting and stimulating. I think it affects their exam grades, too'. Worked wonders on inspectors too, who assumed students leading lessons (spreading the word to peers in other diploma facilities is part of the syllabus) were teachers and had graded them outstanding before misunderstanding pointed out.

Structure won't be for everyone, particularly those with league-leaping performance as sole aspiration. Principal holds trenchant views on results, which are 'meaningless after a few years. It's the outcome that is important. We measure the success in the effect our students have on the world'.

Despite this, college has earned itself plenty of bragging rights, with average IB score of 35 in 2015, including a good proportion of bilingual diplomas. If not at the very top of the tree, it's well ahead of the world average (around 30) and not to be sniffed at, particularly as for some students, who are selected on potential rather than educational back story, this may be their first ever brush with formal schooling.

Hot spots include spectacular languages (nine mother tongue or foreign options and a further 21, including Khmer, Mongolian and Welsh, as self-taught subjects). Maths and science are also very strong, say students – big clue to expectations the vast university physics textbook toted with pride by first year student.

With run of the mill IB students elsewhere already reckoned to be worked more intensively than A level counterparts, it's useful to arrive with work ethic fully formed and be good with stress,

say students, who rapidly acquire super-efficient learning techniques.

In the main, it's attitude of mind that determines student suitability. 'Not for the weak-hearted,' thought one. Just as true for teachers, many with similar international background. Total conversion to college philosophy the norm and few move back to conventional posts afterwards. Once recruited, becomes a forever post, others paling into comparison. 'You're spoiled for life', thought one, while college newsletter praised students' freedom to 'chase academic hares into the undergrowth of learning [...] keeping an eye on the syllabus and sometimes even a blind eye'.

Generous with their time (lots of impromptu one-to-one sessions were under way in final run up to IB exams), teachers praised for effective problem-spotting system that kicks in early, tutors the first point of call, subject specialists alerted and involved as necessary.

Hot spots include spectacular languages: nine mother tongue or foreign options and a further 21, including Khmer, Mongolian and Welsh

Other areas (notably EAL, learning needs, gifted and talented), formerly a bit piecemeal but are having policies written and in some cases coordinators, including SENCo, appointed. Essential, given some pupils' patchy educational history and/or imperfect grasp of English (no minimum language requirement for EU students). Lack of screening during committee-based recruitment system also means learning needs (mostly mild Asperger's, SpLD and ADHD) will only be picked up on arrival, though good to see real commitment to disabled access. Wheelchair access determinedly provided wherever possible, whole classes relocated if necessary when it isn't.

Overall, exceptionally demanding curriculum covers emotional, intellectual and practical terrain that many adults would find hard going. Though something you'd hesitate to impose elsewhere, impressively mature bunch here take it in their stride. Only student doubt was perception that college is putting greater focus on IB scores. Principal is adamant this isn't the case. Teachers 'would not have the faintest idea of college's ranking', he says. We assume he approves.

Games, options, the arts: Whichever diploma faculty they choose, students are unlikely to spend much time sitting on their hands, all areas being long on activity. Derring-do comes with the territory no matter what the gradient, acquisition of skills in graceful failure as important as trappings of success (fallibility reckoned by Kurt Hahn to be essential part of the learning process). As a result, there isn't much pupils here would say no to, from consorting with top scientists and politicians at climate change summit in Fiji to qualifying as a music therapist.

Outdoor faculty is the most obviously action-packed of the bunch. Students join either aquatic water activities team (kayaking and surfing on offer but highlight lifeboat training at college's own RNLI station) or sign up to Terra Firma, which features mountain walking, navigation, emergency first aid and climbing (Brecon Beacons, a few miles inland, the venue for unlimited yomping).

While physical activity is compulsory, organised sport isn't. Stems from character building the Kurt Hahn way, which almost heretically relegates organised games to an 'important but not predominant' position in the hierarchy.

What happens and whether it happens at all is largely down to pupils. Though specialist coaches visit (pupils seemed slightly hazy about the details), there's no head of sport and activities vary from year to year depending on each cohort's enthusiasms. As a result, vast games field is intermittently used. Only sound on a fine spring afternoon was the bleating of newborn lambs from on-site farm. Anyone expecting pitches groaning with glory-seeking team endeavours may well be in for a bit of a shock.

Similarly, though IB studies are efficiently catered for with public showcases including drama reviews and weekly music recitals, there's not much in the way of large scale musical or dramatic endeavours.

Boarding: Seven boarding houses. Their distinctive characters, reflected in not always flattering secret student nicknames (we know what they are, too, but had to promise not to tell), are home to just under 50 pupils each. Pastoral care efficiently provided by brace of well-liked houseparents. Facilities are 'simple', says college, and they're not wrong. Perfectly acceptable though, with extensive communal drying rooms and welly racks (essential given climate) and enough single showers to ensure sufficient privacy for those who find communal versions problematic.

There's the odd idiosyncrasy when it comes to equipment – irons are allowed in dorms, kettles are not (one boarding house has just been rebuilt following a fire). But this is outweighed by impressive, all-round sensitivity, subtle pooling of kitchen equipment in mixed common rooms avoiding distinctions between haves and have-nots, daily deliveries of communal food essentials.

Setting – in 800-year-old castle by the sea – is out of this world and frequently used by production companies (has featured in Dr Who)

Background and atmosphere: For mood and idealism, think educational version of Star Trek, the crew's goal less about finding 'strange new worlds' than improving the one they're in, one dilithium crystal at a time. While hippies might give peace a chance by putting flowers in gun barrels, Hahn's solution to unify Cold War ridden world of the 1960s and ward off what he saw as the physical and moral decline of the young was to found a school (two, if you count Gordonstoun, many more if you allow Round Square schools).

Here, the aim was to create a harmonious blend of nations and cultures, pairing opposites of every sort, oppressors and oppressed, poor and rich, who by living and studying together would develop shared outlook and common purpose (though took until 1967 before they got round to adding girls).

College remains a one-off in the UK and was the first of what is now 12-strong United World Colleges international movement. Its niche status and relatively low profile (even amongst heads, let alone the average parent) is, however, in inverse proportion to behind the scenes clout. Former students are embedded in some of the most powerful organisations and political administrations in the world, from the Chinese and US governments to top banks, providing under the radar alternative to conventional old boys' (and girls') network and one with huge clout.

Setting – in 800-year-old castle by the sea – is out of this world and much appreciated by production companies (has featured in Dr Who). In addition to as many corkscrewing staircases as you can shake a medieval flail at, castle interior features terrific library, galleried and home to municipal quantities of books including Harry Potter (a college favourite) in assorted translations.

Appearances are slightly deceptive. Assorted chunks of apparently authentic gorgeousness such as stone entrance to dining hall pillaged wholesale from Boston Church in Lincolnshire by former owner, the newspaper magnate William Randolph Hearst. His wholesale salvage sweep also included the carved heads adorning the breakfast room ceiling – Lewis Carroll's inspiration, apparently, for Tweedledum and Tweedledee.

Lessons in many cases a perfect match for surroundings. History lessons compete with hard to improve vistas through arrow slits to wooded hill beyond, art and music located in nicely converted stable block. Other subjects are taught in three 1970s teaching blocks (science and maths, perhaps appropriately, in crumbliest and flakiest), all apparently constructed, together with admin centre, by embittered town planner having a bad day and featuring urban-style mini-underpass.

With just one communal TV to its name, a climate that's far from tropical and the nearest cinema nine miles away by land (or 13 if teamed with a bracing swim across the Bristol Channel), this is a place that needs decent social events more than most. Until recently, though, it wasn't getting them, felt pupil. Far better now, with weekly disco (noise levels bravely borne by principal, who lives opposite), boarding houses charged with weekend event organisation, and much more to do.

The sense of being a body apart is reinforced by two-term structure that follows the beat of the IB drum – with the result that pupils only have four days off between January and May and are then off on holiday until early August when second year pupils arrive back for a week's bonding before new intake turns up.

Physical apartness makes it something of unknown quantity within the local community. 'Out of my league,' thought one local. 'Feels exclusive – if you can afford for your kids to go there, you're doing well'. No wonder the principal is contemplating a hearts, minds and meters job to get locals, starting with taxi drivers, who are probably the college's most frequent visitors, on side.

Pastoral care, well-being and discipline: New arrivals are paired with 'excellent' buddies, big on tea and sympathy (favour returned when it comes to exam time). Their first task is probably to settle nerves after meeting and greeting ceremony, where they're drummed in with chorus of pots and pans pillaged from common rooms by second years ('it leaves terrible dents', said one pupil, who as kitchen monitor was charged with subsequent search and rescue mission).

With full boarding the only option (though parents can come and stay nearby at beginning and ends of term), inner core of steel probably helps, given policy of picking room-mates for differences, the more apparently irreconcilable the better. 'We would always put Israelis and Palestinians together', says principal, who is spearheading drive to recruit Syrians from both sides of current conflict.

Pupils aren't just in favour of approach but drawn to college because of it. Beliefs that elsewhere would be on collision course (there's a strong GLBT movement, for example) spark enduring friendships and sometimes more, with potential for heartache when relationships breach cultural barriers.

Whether deliberately or by chance, student bonds are well and truly cemented by decision to involve them in the nuts and bolts of college operations. Open book policy on everything from finances to rebuilding ensures that student voice isn't merely heard but is a force to be reckoned with, from spontaneous orations in assembly on whatever issues take their fancy, college-related or otherwise (polemic following death of Mrs Thatcher made for edgy listening) to indignation over any perceived high-handedness. 'If they give us a voice, that's what they have to expect', said one.

So while there's considerable disquiet over new pre-IB year, it's as nothing compared with fury, manifested in banners and even anonymous notes, following introduction of boarding house locks (sadly an inspection non-negotiable). It's just as well college pre-empted decades of conflict by ditching uniform in the 1970s. 'Pupils fear change', thought principal. Might be right at that, what with tolerance for far more obtrusive but longer-standing security measures such as airport-style library security gate and 11 separate entry codes (a school record, we reckon) covering everything from Mac lab to harp storage. No wonder one pupil adopts low-tech approach of banging on the window to attract attention instead.

Impressive maturity means that nobody sweats the small stuff. Courtesy on both sides is a given, teachers generally liked (only one got thumbs down) and while big issues go to the wire, there are minimal rules elsewhere, nous and good sense taken as read. 'We don't need a rule about using phones in lessons when it would clearly be rude', a pupil told us.

Pupils and parents: Easy to gush over pupils' self-assurance and intelligence which carries all before it (just one non-show in recent memory, pupil so

overcome with nerves that unable to board the plane). A sassy bunch, it's no surprise that many have persuaded their parents that this is the place to be and in one case at least secured the sponsorship to pay the fees.

Vocal and passionate espousal of college and ideals often continues for life, endorsements from everyone including Nelson Mandela and Queen Noor of Jordan

Though fees are 'low compared to other top boarding schools', says college, they are still high enough to skew social mix towards luxury ingredients rather than salt of the earth. Or in UWC words, 'similar people simply born in different places'. A pupil says that this 'isn't the place for the materialistic or those who believe the world can get better with money alone'. Parent philanthropy is a way of life, one family funding not only their own child but three others, too. Similar acts of generosity both widespread and long term.

Five-strong development department works with alumni who include King of the Netherlands, chairman of Shell and vice-president of European Bank to get that giving feeling early. And give they do. Vocal and passionate espousal of college and ideals often continues for life, endorsements from everyone from Nelson Mandela to Queen Noor of Jordan setting the tone. It's resulting in growing numbers from the poorest and most war-torn regions of earth.

Some local recruitment, extending to deprived Liverpool, Birmingham and Valleys schools, requires a bit of careful eggshell treading to avoid Orphan Annie connotations, college raising grateful poor to a life of privilege. So far so good.

Entrance: 'The world is our catchment area', says college (90 nationalities currently). Makes a refreshing change from same old distance from home criteria, but downside is labyrinthine admissions process requiring minotaur-seeking levels of persistence (though no string). Think Oxbridge inter-college pupil swapsies at admissions time, add international dimension requiring agreement between parents, students and UWC staff who may all be on different continents, and it's not surprising that entrance process is officially badged as 'extremely complicated'. On the surface it's highly competitive, too, with nearly 100 nations jostling for places, just 20 available for UK nationals and a further 17 places in other UWC colleges.

Would-be pupils submit applications either to one of 140 UWC national committees, often staffed by alumni, or direct to colleges – specific requirements as individual as they are. Though they can express college preferences, they're assumed to be signing up to UWC aims rather than a location, and so could end up being offered a place somewhere completely different. Loving care is advised to ensure that focus on community work and support for UWC ideals shine through. Also useful to ensure academic endorsement (no GCSE minimum grades specified, every application considered on merit) is from teacher '... who supports the idea of you going to a UWC'. (Our tip: use the word 'mission' at least once).

Shortlisted UK candidates have an overnight stay at the castle, followed by informal 20-minute interview with committee members, alumni and, unusually, former rather than current teachers. Final decision communicated around three weeks later (though can take longer). Whole process is an excellent Kurt Hahn-style challenge and, if you meet the age criteria (students normally start aged 16 or 17, though there's some flexibility), there's the chance to do it all over again the following year.

Exit: It's off to better things not just for pupils, but with 70 per cent ultimately ending up in humanitarian-linked careers, for the world as a whole. While US admissions tutors zoom in early, like dealers at a jumble sale before the doors open to the general punters, other top unis aren't far behind.

US is the most popular university destination overall with close to 40 per cent of places (college doesn't train students to take SATs, but is a test centre), followed by UK (28 per cent – vast majority to Russell/1994 group members, including two to Oxbridge in 2015) then Canada and Europe, with a few to Asia. Recent destinations include Harvard, Cambridge, Brown, MIT, Yale, Princeton, UCL, Sherbrooke and Cornell.

Around 16 per cent take a gap year. Courses many and various. A pupil we spoke to hoped to major in physics with laudable aim of investigating travel across vacuums in outer space.

Money matters: Admissions process supported by large fundraising and development department working overtime to bring in the dosh. Latest initiative themed to college's 50th anniversary (think of a number, any number, with a 50 in it and hand it over) is generating over £2 million a year, almost all used to fund scholarships. Other countries chip in, too (Norwegian government funds 10 of its own students, for example). In all, over 55 per cent of students have some sort of financial support.

Remarks: Once a glorious experiment, still out on a limb (and, we suspect, in no hurry to shed iconoclastic status), Atlantic College provides an education as remarkable as the feisty, impassioned students it attracts. The ticking of admin boxes may annoy, but it's a necessary evil that parents will welcome. Its location may be isolated but its perspective, genuinely global, is anything but. Just don't expect a picnic by the sea.

Warwick School

Myton Road, Warwick CV34 6PP

01926 776400
enquiries@warwickschool.org
www.warwickschool.org

Ages: 11–18
Pupils: 1,235; sixth form: 290
Boarders: 56 full
Day: £9,285 – £11,829 pa
Boarding: £13,800 pa

Head Master: Since September 2013, Mr Augustus (Gus) Lock, MA Oxon (late 30s). Educated at Haberdashers' Aske's School, Elstree, he read ancient and modern history at Oxford. First teaching post was at The Manchester Grammar School, thence to Merchant Taylors' School in Northwood, where he became head of middle school and met and married Alison (a French and Italian teacher). Mr Lock then moved to Warwick School, where he served as deputy head before taking on the headship. Gus and Alison have three young children, two of whom attend Warwick Prep School.

Academic matters: It is clear that academic work is a top priority and taken seriously by most of the boys. The pace is vigorous and demanding – for pupils and staff alike – and the overall results are impressive. When we asked if there was any truth in the rumour that Warwick was an exam factory, one boy replied, 'Well, if it is, I haven't noticed it. There is lots of work but you expect that. You just get on with it.' One ex-teacher at Warwick confirmed that the pace was demanding. That word 'pace' crops up a lot – Warwick is a very busy school with lots to offer. It may be a day school but, in the words of another boy, 'it never seems to close. With all the extracurricular activities on offer, a 12 hour day starting at 7.30am is not that unusual.' League table junkies can pore over the statistics, salivating at the various permutations, but here's a quick fix: of the 27 subjects on offer for A level, maths, economics, physics, chemistry, biology and politics account for some 250 entries; English, history, French and Spanish, 50. Just an observation but it

does reveal the breadth of subjects on offer and the strengths of scientific subjects in the sixth form. How well they do overall is confirmed by the consistently high percentage of A*-B at A level (81 per cent in 2015, and 53 per cent A*/A). GCSE results from 28 subjects are impressive too. A*-B grades have not dropped below 91 per cent in the last seven years and in 2015, 78 per cent of papers were graded A*/A. This is clearly not a school where boys spend time during their first few years 'settling down and making friends' before starting to work seriously.

The facilities for teaching and learning are impressive. Foremost is the new science building of which the school is justifiably proud. Like most of the new buildings at Warwick, it is superbly designed, both aesthetically and functionally. From the moment you enter the large bright foyer, decorated with a fascinating creation stretching up through two floors like a curling spine, you are in a genuinely stimulating building. In this instance it is all about experiment, discovery and excitement. Each of the three floors is allocated to a science, with spacious laboratories designed in consultation with the teachers themselves. All the latest gizmos and terrific teaching to go with them. One huge laboratory is used for extended projects where budding Nobel laureates are joined by the no less budding girls from King's High and students from other local schools. Certainly no sign of science declining in popularity here – many boys go on to university to read science-based subjects. How some of them must pine for the excellence of the facilities at Warwick. But it's not just the scientists who are well served; we hear many reports of excellent teaching in other subjects too. The delightfully designed lecture theatre hosts talks embracing all disciplines from within and beyond the curriculum.

The superb Bridge House Theatre is kitted out to professional standards. A number of boys have taken small parts at the RSC; recently a year 9 pupil played Gershom, first born son of Moses, in Exodus

If the heartbeat of real education is a library, Warwick is very healthy. The library is housed in The Masefield Centre, named after an old boy, charmingly described to us by a current pupil as 'some kind of a poet, I believe.' A superb set-up with over 20,000 books, it is an invaluable centre for reference resources and information files as well as CDs, DVDs and now e-books. The school even has e-readers to lend out. The wonderfully enthusiastic librarian told us that the issue of books had recently risen by 30 per cent, and inviting pamphlets, one with an encouraging foreword from the headmaster, explain and exhort. Those pupils we spoke to genuinely appreciated the facility.

Everyone entering the school is screened for dyslexia and those with learning difficulties receive help from the 'very good' learning support team. Curriculum support is also available to those who encounter academic difficulties.

Games, options, the arts: Naturally sport plays an important part. However, this is not a hearty school where prizes and recognition are given only to games players. Colours are awarded for music and drama, for instance, and one boy we spoke to, a confessed non-sportsman, said he didn't feel an outcast in any way. 'There are plenty of opportunities for taking exercise. In fact I'm almost spoilt for choice.' Nevertheless, the ethos that permeates the school – 'if you're going to do something, do it to the best of your ability' – is much in evidence on the games field. In the winter term, for example, over 20 rugby teams could be turning out on a Saturday afternoon. The 1st XV has a very strong fixture list and is renowned for its prowess, but the great thing is that everyone who wants to has a good chance of playing in a team. However, 'it's not all about rugby,' as somebody once said. In addition there is hockey, cricket, swimming, tennis, cross-country, athletics, rowing, canoeing, clay pigeon shooting: you name it. No wonder the boy who didn't like rugby didn't feel left out. Facilities are excellent with a top rate swimming pool (they have been national schools water polo champions more than once), squash courts, tennis courts, a superb sports hall, including an indoor hockey pitch, and games fields that seem to stretch on for ever. A recent cricket tour to

Sri Lanka, golf to Spain and rugby to Ireland are just some of the opportunities to play abroad; boys who cannot afford to go are supported financially.

Music is excellent (ask for a copy of their DVD) and generally regarded as cool. Harmony maintained by a charismatic director with a wonderful team of teachers, most of whom are concert players themselves. In a recent and highly successful initiative, new boys were lent an instrument of their choice and given free tuition for a year; the enthusiastic take-up means the music department now has 720 lessons a week to organise. Five orchestras, three wind bands, three jazz bands, rock groups, quartets and much more. Huge programme of concerts and the chapel choir sings every Sunday morning during term; local parents, old boys, friends of the school and boarders attend. The musicians perform all over Europe (as with sports tours, financial support given if necessary) and recently four bands were awarded platinum, two golds and a silver at the National Concert Band Finals – the Little Big Band got a platinum award for the third consecutive year and as a result was presented with a consistent achievement certificate.

Proximity to Stratford may account for the school's high achievements in drama. The superb Bridge House Theatre is kitted out to professional standards with proper lighting and sound equipment, adjustable stage and seating arrangements for 300 people and musicians; it is used by community theatre groups as well as for school productions. A number of boys have taken small parts at the RSC; recently a year 9 pupil played Gershom, first born son of Moses, in Exodus, and a few go on to take theatre studies at A level. One ecstatic mother told us of the huge encouragement given to her young son when he was given a demanding role. 'It boosted his confidence right across the board,' she said. Warwick productions have won awards at the National Student Drama Festival, the only school to have done so. There are large scale drama productions every term as well as pupil led plays, many shared with girls from King's High.

Art and DT very good. All pupils have a double period of art and design a week for their first three years and can then go on to GCSE and beyond.

Astonishing range of clubs and societies to try – debating, scuba diving, robotics (UK champions several years running). Boys can also sign up for D of E, Young Enterprise and CCF. Wonderful opportunities enthusiastically seized. Exam factory, forsooth.

Boarding: Upstairs from chapel in the old building is a little corner of Asia where the 50+ Chinese boys in the sixth form live with the housemaster, a resident tutor and a matron. Boarding is available from year 9. Warwick has been taking Chinese

students for many years now and those we chatted to seemed very happy and proud to be there. Activities sensitively arranged to reflect both boys' cultural background and traditional British life – there's Autumn Moon Festival and bonfire night; Christmas and Chinese New Year. Trips, many suggested by boarders' council, include photographers' visit to London and football-themed visit to Manchester, taking in United game.

Background and atmosphere: The gates to the main entrance hint at the tradition of the school. In addition to the Tudor Rose and the school's coat of arms depicting, significantly, the Warwickshire bear without chains, you can read the dates 914, 1545 and 1958. These refer to the traditional dates for the founding of the school by Edward the Confessor, its reinstatement by Henry VIII and the visit of the Queen Mother when the school was once more in the ascendant after a period in the doldrums. From a succession of sites in the town the school moved out to its present position beside the Avon in 1879. The neo-Tudor building with lovely oriel windows is typical of 19th century public school architecture, though to some, apparently, the colour of the brick is reminiscent of a hospital. A fascinating archive room with old photographs of school groups and haunting pictures of teams from 1914, testifies to the pride the school takes in its past. After all, isn't this one of the oldest boys' schools in the country, nay, the world?

The current site is a mixture of old and new buildings, increasingly dominated by the new, close but not jostling. Always an interesting insight into a school is to ask for directions and note the response; those boys we asked were uniformly helpful and charming, courtesy and good manners are the norm here. One new boy told us not to worry; 'Just ask,' he said, 'you can't go far wrong.' He spoke with feeling of the help he had received on arrival. All schools trumpet 'the excellent relationships between pupils and staff'; unobtrusively and naturally, this school demonstrates it. We witnessed a number of conversations between staff and boys and were struck by the obvious mutual respect and friendliness between them.

Activities reflect both boys' cultural backgrounds and traditional British life – Autumn Moon Festival, bonfire night; Christmas and Chinese New Year

The school's aims may be serious and pursued with determination but there is an underlying sense of well-being and community which extends to the town; the civilised behaviour of the boys was acknowledged by the residents to whom we spoke. Sixth formers are allowed, with permission, to have lunch in town; so are senior girls from King's High. 'What we almost take for granted,' said one elderly resident, 'is that there is no arrogance about them. No swaggering and showing off. Not like those public school kids.' An interesting observation. Much is done for charity, an excellent way of combining community spirit and awareness of those less fortunate. Along with girls from King's High, teams have twice swum the Channel. According to the records the boys' team was the 50th ever two-way swim; the 13th ever successful swim by any UK team and the first by a boys' school team.

Impressive chapel with college seating where services take place most days of the week.

Pastoral care, well-being and discipline: Typical of the caring efficiency of the school is the trouble it takes to welcome new boys and blend them in. There are unobtrusive but clearly delineated policies to ensure 'there is always someone to pick us up' and the welcome package, is helpful, informative and encouraging. The effortlessly friendly atmosphere that pervades is, perhaps, because boys know where they stand (a phrase oft repeated when we asked). Prefects, selected by peers and staff, regard it as one of their prime functions to ensure boys are happily integrated and that consideration for others is maintained. Rules and guidelines are clear and thorough, even down to expectations of behaviour in the classroom; uniforms are smartly worn. One parent, talking about a boy who had been excluded – a rare event by all accounts – spoke of the trouble the school had gone to ensure the boy was well established in his next school. 'They really do care about the individual, but however friendly, they are strict about implementing the rules.' 'We know what is required of us. Mostly it's common sense,' a senior boy told us. 'Firm but fair.' No-one – boys or staff – claimed that bullying could never happen here, but parents we spoke to said it was quickly and sensitively dealt with. 'Staff are very approachable and understandable,' more than one boy told us.

Pupils and parents: Warwick has a large catchment area, a result not only of its excellent transport links but also the determination of parents and boys to make the effort. By bus, by train, by car, they come; from as far afield as Oxfordshire and Northamptonshire. Just under half the year's intake comes from the junior school and others from local primary schools and nearby prep schools. This is not a toff school; parents come from a broad cross-section of society, mostly professional middle classes, and thanks to the availability of bursaries many who might otherwise not be able to afford it do send their boys. The head and governors plan to raise funds and offer more.

Eclectic is the word that springs to mind when considering notable old boys. Currently there are two MPs, Iain Pears the novelist; Marc Elliott of East Enders; Christian Horner, Red Bull motor racing; Michael Billington, theatre critic; an Italian rugby international, an Australian rugby international, an England Sevens player and, from the ranks of the departed, the poet John Masefield. More evidence of breadth.

Entrance: The school is selective and competition is strong. It's not just the strongest academics who are awarded places; lively, quirky boys who can keep pace and bring with them special talents will be given consideration. Entry points are 11 and 13. Details of the examinations are on the website and follow the usual pattern. For entry to sixth form at least five B grades with A grades needed in some subjects to be studied at AS level.

Exit: Most – about 85 per cent – of boys stay on to do their A levels and nearly all go on to university. As well as purely academic subjects eg maths, classics, English, history, PPE, recent leavers have gone on to read marine vertebrate zoology, management with entrepreneurship, forensic science and architecture. Twelve to Oxbridge in 2015. Popular destinations include Birmingham, Durham, Leeds, Nottingham, UCL and Loughborough.

Money matters: The school is fortunate in benefiting from a number of ancient charities, some specifically aimed at boys living in the town of Warwick. Scholarships are offered in music and academics but not for sport. About a quarter of boys in the school are assisted financially.

Remarks: This is a winning school and achieves success right across the board. 'I don't know how we do it,' a boy told us in genuine amazement; 'there must be some reason for it.' There are plenty of reasons why this is such an excellent school although, like all good schools, it won't suit everyone. But for those seeking a day school that offers more excellent facilities and opportunities than many boarding schools; for those who are possessed of energy, stamina and self-discipline; above all, for those who can match the pace and plunge in, this might very well be the school. Not a school for drifting in, a school for striking out through the waves. Even across the Channel.

Winchester House School

44 High Street, Brackley, Northamptonshire NN13 7AZ

01280 702483
registrar@winchester-house.org
www.winchester-house.org

Ages: 3–13 (boarders from year 3)
Pupils: 315
Boarders: 95 weekly/flexi
Day: £8,010 – £17,760 pa
Boarding: £22,485 pa

Head: Since 2014, Emma Goldsmith (40s). Born and educated in Durham before reading English at Manchester. Landed first teaching job at Oakham where she threw herself into coaching netball, D of E: 'The last thing in the world I wanted to be was a teacher,' she says, 'but from that point on, I was committed to boarding schools.' Later recruited to help set up sixth form girls' boarding at Rugby and whilst there visited Bloxham School for a sports fixture. She loved it and was recruited to introduce girls and to manage the transition to co-ed, including setting up the first girls' boarding house, rising to deputy head.

Both of her children attended Winchester House, and she was asked to join the board of governors, so approached the headship 'from a unique position.' 'Bowled over by the quality of teaching and level of dedication and commitment of staff.' Focuses on every child leaving with a 'tool kit' for success in their future school. Parents approve, and describe her as the kind of person they would want running their business, as their best friend or their sister: 'She's fantastic,' they say. 'She is everywhere and has time for everyone...which has stopped all the tittle tattle because you can ask her anything.'

Warm and attractive, 'a brilliant communicator,' in the words of one happy parent, with a gentle humour (happily swapped places with a pupil for Comic Relief day) – and the chicest office we've ever seen. Still teaches year 7 English and 'occasionally' umpires netball matches, reads stories in pre-prep and occasionally serves lunch. Children attend Bloxham, where husband is a teacher.

Entrance: Non-selective into pre-prep with automatic entry to prep. All assessed prior to entry into year 3 and above to identify learning needs.

There's a secret garden tucked through a tiny archway, where year 8s are allowed to 'hang out'

Pupils mainly local (within 10 miles) with those joining after pre-prep mainly either from families moving out of London or from local state primaries and pre-preps. Strong old school, rather than aspirational bias. Lots of former pupils in parent cohort. Some year groups oversubscribed.

Exit: Some 85 per cent to boarding schools – school prides itself on sending its pupils on to a broad range of destinations, usually around 13 or 14 different schools in any given year. Oundle, Rugby, Radley, Tudor Hall, Uppingham and St Edwards, to name but a few current favourites. Popular day choices are MCS, Warwick and Headington. Scholarships for over half of 2015 leavers across the board – academic, sport, DT and art. Hardly any leavers at 11+.

Strong focus on 'right school, right child'. Conversations regarding moving on start in year 5, with 100 per cent heading off to their first choice school.

Remarks: Set in a former hunting lodge approached directly from the charming village high street through grand wrought iron gates, opening into a Tardis-like 18 acre campus, school sits astride a small country road which separates the pre-prep from the main prep school. Delightful pre-prep setting where classes are taught in large, bright classrooms with every possible millimetre of space adorned with creative offerings and the ceilings festooned with bunting and mobiles. Seamless transition for the youngest from on-site nursery, housed in a light and spacious recent extension. Years 3 and 4 housed in own building, with much evidence of the 'creative curriculum' followed on display.

Good facilities across the board – many secondary schools would envy the enormous sports hall and new full-sized Astroturf. A lovely outdoor pool (although parents would like it used more) and cricket nets sit amongst the manicured lawns of the walled garden with the main playing fields across the road. Each year group has its own play area – some with super modern equipment and all with new, rainbow striped 'buddy benches.' The real magic of Winchester House, however, is in its enchanting and unique features: a secret garden tucked through a tiny archway, where year 8s are allowed to 'hang out' and lower years tend allotments and sit around camp fires; a beautifully panelled dining room where lunch is served family-style by teaching staff; tongue in cheek rules on the walls of the girls' boarding house (our favourites: no whining, laugh a lot and break the rules...sometimes) and vibrant works of art created collectively by visiting artists and pupils.

Staff bury artefacts to be found by pupils with metal detectors; children arrive at school to find snowy footsteps leading to their classrooms

Fully co-educational (girls first introduced in the 80s), with a charming cohort of pupils who mix easily together and come across as children enjoying being just that – no ties, lots of untucked shirts and not a hiked up skirt or gelled quiff in sight. Our lunchtime hosts were bright-eyed, chatty and full of the joys of boarding – quite something for 11 year old boys. A traditional vibe prevails and school makes no bones about its boarding culture and preparation for public school, but it's by no means stuck in the dark ages. Technology, whilst not cutting edge, is up to date and the curriculum strikes an excellent balance of remaining traditional whilst moving with the times. The innovative 'creative curriculum' followed in the lower part of the school is well established and revered by staff and pupils alike – head speaks passionately about its execution: staff burying artefacts to be found by

children with metal detectors (Romans) and children arriving at school to find snowy footsteps leading to their classrooms which were draped in fur throws (Frozen Worlds).

Science a huge strength with all three sciences taught separately by specialist teaching staff through 'as much practical work as we can manage,' according to the physics teacher. Outstanding computing, too – our year 8 guide lost us totally in a conversation about coding, but her enthusiasm and knowledge was clear to see. Pupils we spoke to unanimously voted history their favourite subject, thanks to the inspirational young teacher. French from reception by native speakers ('they only talk to children in French,' says head), Spanish from year 5, Latin from year 6 and Greek from year 7. Setting from year 3 in maths and English, when pupils start to move between teachers, leading to entirely specialist teaching from year 5.

All screened on arrival for SEN to identify areas for either support or extension. Dedicated SENCo 'aims for as little withdrawal from the classroom as possible,' with small groups to 'boost' performance where needed, although those with greatest need withdrawn from Latin to receive extra support. Can accommodate mild to moderate dyslexia and dyscalculia and mild ASD.

Boarders describe food as 'amazing' – having sampled the roast beef and banoffee pie we agree

A school alive with the sound of music – 'we're very much a singing school,' says head and parents concur, describing the termly concerts in glowing terms. With around three-quarters of all pupils playing an instrument, it's music for all with choirs (both auditioned and otherwise), bands and ensembles aplenty for musicians of all levels. Performance is 'one of the key aspects of the school,' says head, but 'you don't have to be brilliant to perform – we're building pupils' confidence all the time.' Specialist taught drama on curriculum to year 8 and around 60 per cent take LAMDA activity, although parents would like to see more productions. Strong art department focuses on 'much more than just drawing,' says head, with visiting artists offering masterclasses on disciplines from woodcarving to animation.

Head says sports department is 'successful and ambitious,' but also clear to point out that they are keen their charges 'learn to fail.' Inclusive approach with everyone getting the opportunity to represent the school – sometimes with up to 10 teams each for boys and girls representing the school each

week. Recent introduction of graduate gap year coaches keeps things lively for the children.

Pupils able to board from year 3, and some do, in one of two single sex boarding houses – boys upstairs in the main school building, girls in a purpose built block. Unsurprisingly, the girls' house with its cosy dorms, sleeping up to 10, has a homelier feel than the boys', although both are spacious and comfortable, with plenty of spaces for down time. Head says boarding 'really takes off' in years 7 and 8, with an 'all or nothing' approach for the oldest pupils who are required to board all week rather than occasionally as is allowed lower down the school, although there's no boarding on Saturday nights and Saturday school has now been abolished altogether for years 4 and below. Prep kept quite light and boarders have their own schedule of after-school activities, with all catering for both sexes. Boarders describe food as 'amazing' – and having sampled the kitchen's roast beef followed by banoffee pie, we can't disagree.

Awareness of pupils' pastoral needs dramatically stepped up under newish head. School's unique 'Learn to Lead' programme encourages pupils to take risks and approach failure with a sense of humour to build emotional resilience, through expeditions and on-site activities. Recent appointment of retired staff member as 'well-being mentor' ensures pupils – who are well informed on the 'circle of support' within the school – have someone to turn to if things go wrong. Head's visibility and approachability also seen as having 'made school a friendlier place', particularly in keeping 'alpha' parents in check. Pupils in year 3 and above are each assigned a tutor who keeps a beady eye on their pastoral and academic well-being, stepping in to help them handle heavy workloads around exam time or making sure they keep up their sporting commitments when academics threaten to take over.

New, open approach to extracurricular (welcomed by parents, who say it was previously a bit 'cloak and dagger'), focuses on three pillars – creative, enriching and physical – to give balance and breadth. Importantly, activities on offer are now communicated clearly to parents. Many, such as squash, chess, gymnastics and debating are included in fees, with those such as skiing (at Milton Keynes) and golf charged as extra. For working parents, children are able to arrive at school from 8.10am with pre-prep children cared for until 4.45pm and from year 3 onwards until 6.30pm, when they can be collected having done activities, prep and eaten supper. Daily minibus services bring children to school from locations including Chipping Norton, Bloxham and South Newington.

With a fresh face at its helm, Winchester House is one to watch. In the words of one year 8 parent: 'I wish my children were starting from the beginning now. In a few years' time, Winchester House will be one of the top preps in the country.'

Witham Hall Preparatory School

Witham-on-the-Hill, Bourne, Lincolnshire PE10 0JJ

01778 590222
secretary@withamhall.com
www.withamhall.com

Ages: 4–13 (boarders from 8)
Pupils: 249
Boarders: 122 weekly/flexi
Day: £8,670 – £14,475 pa
Boarding: £19,410 pa

Headmaster: Since 2009, Mr Charles Welch (40s) BEd. Educated at Oakham and Exeter University. Previous schools include Rishworth, West Yorks and Oakham School, where he was first director of sport and then foundation director for a year before his appointment to Witham Hall. Considers the pastoral system at Witham is its core strength, giving the pupils the confidence and happiness necessary to succeed academically. Married to Jo, who teaches part-time and is closely involved with the running of the boarding houses. They have two young children of their own.

Entrance: The majority of pupils join the school at the pre-prep stage and this is non-selective. From year 4 onwards prospective pupils are assessed

Strong parental support at matches contributes to the ease and friendliness of relations between parents and the school

using standardised tests to ensure they will be able to cope with common entrance. A number join from other schools in year 7 specifically to prepare for the exam.

Exit: Majority to the 'local' schools eg Oakham, Oundle, Uppingham and Stamford. A clutch go further afield – Eton, Rugby, Repton, Stowe. Excellent scholarship track record with over half of pupils achieving awards of various kinds, academic, sporting and arts.

Remarks: A school of outstanding quality both academically and pastorally. The school's profile is discreet – there is no open day, for example – and pupils are attracted by word of mouth recommendation in the main. Numbers are steadily increasing and families are drawn from a radius of 40 miles. Weekly boarding is a popular option, with flexi boarding also available. Day pupils are very well integrated but boarding becomes increasingly the norm in the higher forms; by year 7 virtually all pupils are boarders.

Previous heads undertook a major building programme and the school benefits from excellent facilities for drama, music and sport plus new science and resource centre. Boarding is in the original Queen Anne house, and whilst dormitories are pleasant enough there is a slightly transient feeling

– possibly due to piles of suitcases on the landing awaiting Saturday collection.

Academically the school is on top form. Average class size in the pre-prep is 15, and 16 in the prep school. Around 40 pupils benefit from the Supported Learning programme and parents are encouraged to discuss worries about progress with the staff – 'nothing is too much trouble'. SEN department has three members of staff. Referrals are made by individual staff or parents and support is targeted at enabling pupils to remain in the class rather than being 'withdrawn'. Parents are confident about seeking help, 'Got my son through maths at common entrance and he has just passed GSCE'. One pupil has a statement of special educational need.

Successful at scholarship level, particularly art, sport and all-rounder. Inspirational art teaching produces astonishingly good work including large sculptures and murals. Music and drama are also popular throughout. A sport-for-all policy and the standard is high with teams reaching national finals in rugby, hockey, netball, cricket and rounders. Strong support from parents at matches and this contributes to the ease and friendliness of relations between parents and the school.

Underpinning the academic and sporting success is excellent pastoral care. The head and his wife take this seriously and are personally involved at all levels. High standard of behaviour; pupils show both friendliness and courtesy (holding doors, standing up for visitors) but atmosphere is relaxed not stiff and starchy. Pupils understand the reasons for rules such as no sweets and no mobiles. The food is spoken highly of.

This is 'a good school becoming a great school'; strong foundations and real warmth.

Northern England and Scotland

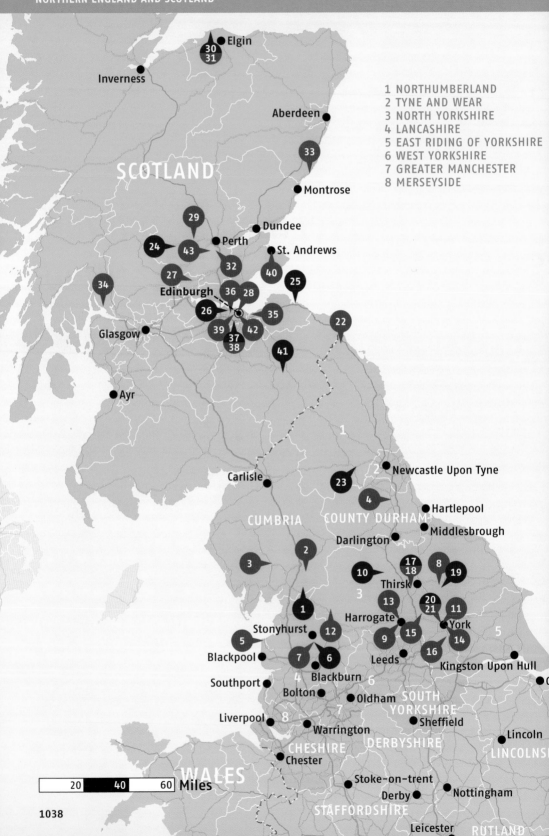

1 NORTHUMBERLAND
2 TYNE AND WEAR
3 NORTH YORKSHIRE
4 LANCASHIRE
5 EAST RIDING OF YORKSHIRE
6 WEST YORKSHIRE
7 GREATER MANCHESTER
8 MERSEYSIDE

NORTHERN ENGLAND AND SCOTLAND

CUMBRIA

1. Casterton, Sedbergh Preparatory School, Carnforth 1059
2. Sedbergh School 1148
3. Windermere School 1161

COUNTY DURHAM

4. Durham School 1064

LANCASHIRE

5. Rossall School, Fleetwood 1124
6. St Mary's Hall, Stonyhurst 1139
7. Stonyhurst College, Clitheroe 1153

NORTH YORKSHIRE

8. Ampleforth College, York 1041
9. Ashville College, Harrogate 1046
10. Aysgarth School, Bedale 1048
11. Bootham School, York 1053
12. Giggleswick School, Settle 1070
13. Harrogate Ladies' College 1083
14. The Mount School, York 1108
15. Queen Ethelburga's College, York 1113
16. Queen Margaret's School, York 1116
17. Queen Mary's School (Junior department), Thirsk 1119
18. Queen Mary's School, Thirsk 1120
19. St Martin's Ampleforth, York 1137
20. St Olave's School, York 1142
21. St Peter's School, York 1144

NORTHUMBERLAND

22. Longridge Towers School, Berwick-upon-Tweed 1093
23. Mowden Hall School, Stocksfield 1111

SCOTLAND

24. Ardvreck School, Crieff 1044
25. Belhaven Hill School, Dunbar 1051
26. Cargilfield School, Edinburgh 1057
27. Dollar Academy 1060
28. Fettes College, Edinburgh 1068
29. Glenalmond College, Perth 1074
30. Gordonstoun Junior School, Elgin 1078
31. Gordonstoun School, Elgin 1079
32. Kilgraston School, Bridge Of Earn 1085
33. Lathallan School, Johnshaven 1088
34. Lomond School, Helensburgh 1091
35. Loretto School, Musselburgh 1096
36. The Mary Erskine School, Edinburgh 1099
37. Merchiston Juniors (aka Pringle), Edinburgh 1103
38. Merchiston Castle School, Edinburgh 1104
39. St George's School (Edinburgh) 1128
40. St Leonards School, St Andrews 1132
41. St Mary's School (Melrose) 1141
42. Stewart's Melville College, Edinburgh 1150
43. Strathallan School, Perth 1157

Ampleforth College

Ampleforth, York, North Yorkshire YO62 4ER

01439 766000
admissions@ampleforth.org.uk
www.college.ampleforth.org.uk
RC

Ages: 13–18
Pupils: 607; sixth form: 270
Boarders: 367 boys/144 girls full
Day: £22,548 pa
Boarding: £22,085 – £32,733 pa

Linked school: St Martin's Ampleforth

Headmaster: Since September 2014, David Lambon (40s), the school's first lay head. Previously principal of St Malachy's College in Belfast, he is a trained engineer and mathematician, with an MBA in school leadership and management. He worked as an engineer in France and Germany before becoming a teacher. He is a keen triathlete. His wife, Sasha, is also a teacher and they have two grown up sons.

Academic matters: Top of the Catholic league but proud of non-elitist intake – from A stream scholars to IQs around 100, who get extra help with English and maths. Ninety per cent of the slowest workers get three A levels, which bears out the college's mission statement – an extract from the Rule of St Benedict: 'the strong should have something to strive for and the weak nothing to run from'. Determined to stress academic rigour and unashamedly and successfully pushing up A and B grades at A level (2015: 43 per cent A*/A), 'though these are not laurels on which we are proposing to

rest'; still aiming higher and the value-added score increases all the time, especially at A level. GCSE: 52 per cent A*/A.

'They never discard,' says a parent. 'The pupils gain self-respect, the staff have an ability to unlock potential.' School prudently adds that sometimes pupils cannot or will not cope: 'We try to reach an agreement with parents about them leaving'. Overall aim is for everyone to fulfil, and preferably exceed, their academic ability. The most able are challenged by membership of an unashamedly intellectual discussion club.

Core curriculum plus Christian theology throughout, Latin and Greek too. Half GCSE year takes separate sciences, half (of all abilities) double award. English department now doing IGCSE. Humanities traditionally have more takers and the edge at A level, but maths and science continue to strengthen. English very strong (most get A or B); history and Christian theology regularly successful and enormously popular.

Dyslexics taught 'for the most part' in main stream; additional specialist one-to-one teaching available. EAL provision for pupils whose first language isn't English.

Games, options, the arts: Traditionally powerful games school. Strong first XV, respected throughout the North. Hockey exceptionally strong for boys and girls, netball, lacrosse, athletics (own track), squash, golf (own nine-hole course), fly-fishing, renowned independently-owned beagle pack, shooting (brace of pheasants recently spotted hanging on coathanger outside boarding cubicle). Phenomenal 20 rugby sides – 'We want wide participation in school teams', 10 cricket sides, eight tennis teams, and so on. Sports hall, Astroturf, 25-metre pool. DT and art (centre includes photography and electronics). Very successful voluntary CCF and it has been known for the girls' platoon to teach the boys a tough lesson by winning the CCF challenge. Flourishing D of E.

Music outstanding – Schola Cantorum choir tours regularly, singing in Catholic and Anglican cathedrals, also impressive girls' Schola Puellarum. Talented chamber music group and the biggest school pipe band south of the border, with own Ampleforth kilts. Enthusiastic singing by whole school in the abbey church, though sometimes, by their own admission, 'more Twickenham than heavenly hosts'.

Art is a real strength of the school, hugely impressive work on display – a direct result they say of 'an interaction between inspirational teaching and the environment'. Performing arts theatre (two productions per term) and also smaller studio theatre, popular with pupils, who would like to do even more. Annual pilgrimage for seniors to Lourdes. Own charity, run by students, raised funds to build school in Nepal and to sponsor East European students in school's sixth form. Also several other eye-openingly worthwhile international projects.

They usually win the regional school shooting range challenge, 'though not quite sure where that fits with the Benedictine philosophy.' Apparently 'being busy makes you happy'

A new staff appointment has strengthened careers advice, including preparation for university and after. It's a work in progress but a deliberate and concerted change – 'it's a meritocratic world and our students need to be prepared'. Long list of extracurricular activities, including some rarer options such as croquet; also the opportunity to strip down and build a Land Rover. And they usually win the regional school shooting range challenge, 'though not quite sure where that fits with the Benedictine philosophy.' Activities are compulsory between 5-7 pm and though a small number wriggle and squirm, most are happy to take part because apparently 'being busy makes you happy'. This is definitely a busy school – boarding philosophy through and through and even day pupils do everything (except sleep) here.

Boarding: Houses vary considerably in character, with deliberate spread of ability – seven for boys and three for girls. Charming and articulate boys and girls rub very comfortably alongside each other, the girls raising the bar in a number of areas and the boys raising their game in response. Rolling programme of improvement in boarding houses; 'I have a power shower!' exclaimed one girl proudly. Home from home, clearly, and it matters, especially to the girls. Some girls' houses have nominated 'guardian angels' as peer mentors; varying approach across individual houses, boys tend and befriend as necessary, usually without being asked. A real plus with the boys is that 'this is a place where you don't have to choose between singing in the choir and playing rugby' – it's acceptable, even cool possibly, to do both. Lunch with houseparents each day, central dining room and cafeteria system in use for other meals. Apparently (according to pupils) 'the food is good – for school food', a guarded mix of fierce loyalty and sensitive disclaimer.

Background and atmosphere: Founded 1802. Girls originally in sixth form only but co-education introduced elsewhere in 2010 and now growing throughout school. Magnificent setting in 3,000 acres of stunning countryside, very calming to

the soul with the Abbey as its central focus, physically and spiritually. Though fairly remote, 'in fact easy to reach – with some determination – from all parts of the country and world'. Beautiful Victorian gothic main wing plus Giles Gilbert Scott's huge abbey church and school buildings (1930s), with late 1980s and more recent additions.

School keeps in touch with outside world through excellent lecture programme and far-away projects, eg Chile and E Europe. No exeats except for two in winter term, otherwise half-terms. Handy list of local hotels, restaurants and B&Bs sent to parents in very comprehensive booklet, Your Questions Answered. Not unknown for parents to rent a local cottage during their child's time at Ampleforth. Warmth of hospitality legendary, 'Part of the Rule of St Benedict is to welcome guests as Christ welcomed his'.

Pastoral care, well-being and discipline: A key change in recent times is that of the deployment of monastic personnel: there are fewer monks and they no longer perform the role of housemasters. This role has been taken over by families who serve as houseparents – 'very civilising' was the comment. Monks now act as chaplains to the school houses, 10 chaplains for 10 houses and parents and pupils commend them for being both priests and friends.

Consciences worked on rather than harsh restrictions imposed, all with the aim of turning students into responsible adults. It appears relaxed on the surface; essentially you are 'allowed it until you misuse it'. Fair enough. At the same time, 'this means clear structure and boundaries; St Benedict was not lax'.

Rolling programme of improvement in boarding houses; 'I have a power shower!' exclaimed one girl proudly

Tough on bullying – those directly implicated and also bystanders – no one ever implicated in bullying can reach the position of monitor at the top of the school; 'a moment of madness can cost you dear.'

No uniform as such, but dress code in place.

Pupils and parents: Numbers close to full and consistently so. Pupils from all over the UK and beyond, 30 per cent Yorkshire families, 40 per cent elsewhere UK (often with OA connections), remaining 30 per cent from overseas. Five per cent of overseas pupils are expats, rest mainly European mix of French, German, Swiss, Spanish. The recession has gently pushed up overseas numbers and reduced the number from the rest of the UK. 'We're a long

way from London and you have to pass a lot of good schools to get here'. That said, many do, the main attractions being the Catholic Benedictine tradition and – bucking the trend here – full boarding provision; 'the school doesn't empty at weekends'. Scions of top and middle Catholic families (80 per cent); the rest mainly Anglican, but special welcome for orthodox.

There's a sense of comfortable ease between parents and school – 'if you want to be involved and constantly in touch, that's possible, If you want to take a more relaxed approach, then that is fine too'. Former pupils include Rupert Everett, Hugo Young, Lord Tugendhat, Lord Nolan, Sir Anthony Bamford (JCB), Michael Ancram, Sir Anthony Gormley, Lawrence Dallaglio, Joe Simpson.

Entrance: From a plethora of prep schools, most notably its own – St Martin's Ampleforth. Common entrance (50 per cent), or school test, and interview. Exceptions 'for faith or family', but no one admitted if he or she won't be able to cope with curriculum – even from St Martin's (rare). Sixth form entry: at least five GCSEs at B or above. Non-Catholics expected to take full part in school's religious life.

Exit: Hardly any leave after GCSEs. In 2015, four to Oxbridge; Edinburgh and Bristol also popular. Overseas destinations include Stanford University in California, McGill University in Montreal, the University of British Columbia in Vancouver and Trinity College, Dublin.

Money matters: Generous financial help. Academic, music and all-rounder scholarships. Nearly 13 per cent receive means-tested bursary help. In last two years some pupils have attained scholar status after entry.

Remarks: It has been said that people who leave Ampleforth take with them a 'compass for life', a spiritual direction finder, which allows them to hold on to their moral bearings. Three fundamental college aims underpin the thinking and approach here: for parents to call up and say their son/daughter is 'having a whale of a time', to succeed academically and finally, while 'not all super pious', to 'treasure a place in their hearts for the spiritual side of life'. The pupils we met confidently achieved all three.

Parents like and appreciate the 'strong moral feel' of the school 'encompassing faith and learning, as well as 'the welcoming atmosphere'. They describe it as 'surely one of the most beautiful places to go to school', hoping (and praying) that it can 'live up to the challenge and expectations in coming years', that particular challenge being one of 'raising the bar academically with first rate and inspiring teachers'. School is listening and has taken note.

Ardvreck School

Gwydyr Road, Crieff, Perthshire PH7 4EX

01764 653112
admissions@ardvreck.org.uk
www.ardvreckschool.co.uk

Ages: 3–13 (boarding from 7)
Pupils: 100
Boarders: 43 full
Day: £13,494 pa
Boarding: £20,280 pa

Headmaster: Since September 2015, Dan Davey, previously head of Bramcote Junior School in Yorkshire. An experienced head – this is his third headship – he is married to Nichola, who teaches modern languages and helps on the pastoral side. They have three sons.

Entrance: Via pre-prep but most come at 8. Boarding in the last year no longer compulsory but great majority do. Prospective pupils visit school, meet head and get a pupil tour, then spend a taster day in school (or overnight if boarding) wearing school uniform 'so they don't stick out'. Each child is issued with a 'school brother or sister'. They arrive at 10.30am and leave after lunch the following day. Head reports back to parents after feedback from staff.

Exit: Over the past five years senior school destinations have included Ampleforth, Bryanston, Eton, Fettes, Glenalmond, Gordonstoun, Harrow, Marlborough, Merchiston, Millfield, Oundle, Radley, Rugby, Sherborne, Stowe, St Mary's Calne, Strathallan and Uppingham.

Remarks: Jolly popular. School founded in 1883 by former housemaster from nearby Glenalmond. Purpose-built with swimming pool (rather grand but in a polythene tent nonetheless) and a fairly ad hoc collection of classrooms (some a lot better than others) perched on 42 hilly acres (woods etc) – we had 75 acres previously, wonder what happened to them? Littlest Ardvreckers all together at one end of the hog's back – rows of green wellies. Currently slightly boy heavy, not many in nursery (Morrisons down the road slightly cheaper), down in boarding numbers.

Younger boarders live in main house (boys and girls on different floors) in a motley collection of cosy rooms; top two years live in his'n'hers chalets 'to prepare them for public school'. Common rooms tarted up after our previous comments,

selected television only, no Wiis for the younger boarders, whose mobiles are handed out when needed. Skype on offer. Older girls can do their own washing, stay abed late on Sundays – boys apparently watch Match of the Day at 8am. Dorms filled with climbing boots and rucksacks, school does three mini Barvicks (expeditions) each summer term. Fixed exeat every third weekend, Friday noon to 10.15am on Mondays now in summer term only, otherwise back to base by 6pm Sundays (but school 'not inflexible' to requests). Parents particularly pleased that this is a proper boarding school and not a day school with weekly sleepovers, consequently popular with the army and diplomatic corps as well as traditional parents. Day pupils stay till 6pm and usually try to board eventually (their choice). NB: School won Tatler Award for Best School Food a few years back (signature dish home made chicken pie).

We spent 20 rainy minutes in mid-March hearing notices, observing the flag being raised and listening to the junior pipe band play Highland Cathedral, following by croissants, choccy spread and coffee

Impressive weekend programme (parents and pupils confirm 'no time to get bored'); bonfire building practice the Sunday before our previous visit, which coincided with grandparent day (a tough, fairly toffish lot, some of whom fill in for expat parents). We spent 20 rainy minutes in mid-March hearing notices, observing the flag being raised and listening to the junior pipe band (senior boys on a rugby toot to Oundle) play Highland Cathedral followed by croissants, choccy spread and coffee. Pupils were in (their family) kilts and green jerseys. Not really a first-time buyer school, popular with quite grand Scots, many of whom aim to send their young South. Parents 'a close-knit group of families', with pupils 'tending to remain friends well into middle age' and beyond.

A splendid child-orientated school, though becoming 'seriously academic'. Class sizes 15/16, no streaming, but maths taught in sets. Two parallel CE classes in sixth, plus scholarship class. Lots of scholarships and awards, but no honours board ('The only honours board we have is our war memorial'). Percentage-wise, Ardvreck topped the Scottish League Table (not that we think there is such a thing) in scholarships recently with a whopping 18 to schools all over, in almost every discipline (three academic).

Head of learning support plus three pick up both the bright and those with dyslexia et al, three student teachers help in class. One hour at one-to-one, plus one hour group sessions are free, thereafter £20 per hour. All assessed on arrival for maths, English and spelling age. Handwriting important, and lousy writers (like this editor) referred to handwriting clinic. Keyboarding skills important, computers much used for teaching maths and English as well as more trad stuff; French from 4, lyrical art room (buzzy new art teacher). Two retirements shortly in the modern lang dept, replacements being actively sought; policy change in the offing: possibly more Spanish and a smattering of German. Watch this space. Revamp on the cards for the IT department.

'School has begun an enrichment programme in which leading educationalists are invited to the school in order to engage with the children about interesting topics' is how the school puts it, we say fantastic selection of really interesting speakers, with talks open both to day parents and local state children. Think International Relations, Young Engineers' Science Workshop, Expeditions in the Arctic or the History of the Plague (bubonic, pneumonic and septicemic) with pupils given envelopes containing their possible immortality. Magic. If not Faustian.

New expressive arts centre opened by Turner shortlisted Scottish artist Nathan Coley. Fab orchestra – 40 play at assembly each Friday – with trips both for the choir and the orchestras in the offing. Singing and drama outstanding – school regularly features in the ribbons at the Perth Festival, orchestra plays on Thursday assembly. Popular pipe band played at St Giles Cathedral for Prince William's inauguration as a Knight of the Thistle, at The Old Course, St Andrews, and St Ninian's Cathedral in Perth and on telly… trips too, to Edinburgh, the zoo, the botanic garden and Glasgow for the Burrell, as well as toots to Normandy, and Berlin (with pipes and drums).

Outstanding on the games front – all sports, all comers, though parents from other schools have been heard to mutter about trying too hard (still). Trips all over the shop, both sports and subject based. New sports inclusion policy introduced and going down well – 'School continues to thrive on games field but not at the expense of sports for all'. Games pitches fairly well scattered on the flatter areas. New combo-hall, with carpentry below, all singing and dancing above, cunningly perched on really quite a steep slope. Four tennis courts, three netball courts, hockey pitch, Astroturf and shooting range. Serious rugby coaching camp during summer hols with top Scots and English players (Lewis Moody et al).

Ashville College

9

Green Lane, Harrogate HG2 9JP

01423 566358
ashville@ashville.co.uk
www.ashville.co.uk

Ages: 11–18 (junior boarding from year 5)
Pupils: 530; sixth form: 107
Boarders: 110
Day: £12,950 – £13,225 pa
Boarding: + £7,200 – £13,350 pa

Headmaster: Since 2010 Mr Mark Lauder MA (mid 40s), educated at Hermitage Academy, Helensburgh, did an MA in English literature and history at the University of Aberdeen, spending his junior honours year at the University of Oregon, Eugene, USA. After graduating he embarked on research at St Edmund Hall, Oxford, where as well as winning a graduate scholarship, he achieved two half blues in rowing. Previously deputy head of Felsted School, Essex, head of history and then housemaster at St Edward's School, Oxford, and before that head of history and master in charge of rowing at Shiplake College, Henley-on-Thames.

Married to peripatetic piano teacher, Caroline, with two sons, both at Ashville College, in junior school. Pupils describe the head as 'having an open door, listening to pupils and making change happen'. Change not so evident to the parents we spoke to – maybe as his approach is 'evolutionary not revolutionary'.

Interests include rowing, rugby, politics and restoring a 17th century Yorkshire parsonage, in between long walks in the Dales and all things Scottish. Believes in whole child development, 'the individual of infinite worth, the social creed of Methodism being the foundation and teacher/pupil relationship the cornerstone'.

Academic matters: Good value-added, especially at GCSE – 45 per cent A*/A in 2015. Science, mathematics, economics and PE all very popular at A level (34 per cent A*/A grades in 2015). Not a shining star in the league tables but most pupils exceed predicted potential and very able pupils do particularly well. Good choice of subjects at GCSE; A level offering includes history of art and government and politics.

Average class size 16, max 22, dropping to 10, max 16, in the sixth form. Years 7–9 follow broad curriculum including at least two modern foreign languages; set for mathematics and languages. For GCSE years, pupils split into ability bands A and B; A are taught Latin and B do extra lessons in English, geography and ICT. Majority take three separate sciences, a few dual award, all at least one modern foreign language.

All year 7 pupils (and year 3 in the junior school) are screened for dyslexia, with further testing and screening as necessary. No pupil has a statement of special educational need/EHC plan, but over 130 pupils receive some additional help for 'mild dyslexic tendencies' – individual support if deemed necessary. Those with dyslexia thrive thanks to the kindly environment and carefully planned programmes of study; indeed in recent years few haven't get the benchmark five A*-Cs at GCSE, and most gain at least a B in English.

Believes in whole child development, 'the individual of infinite worth, the social creed of Methodism being the foundation and the teacher/pupil relationship the cornerstone'

Over 60 international students require English as an additional language, mostly taught alongside mainstream English. Target is Cambridge FCE by year 11 and all sixth form sit Cambridge IELTS in year 13.

Games, options, the arts: Facilities – two gyms, 30m swimming pool, fabulous climbing wall, squash courts, fitness room and ample pitches, including a new all weather surface pitch – show importance of sport. Teams and fixtures galore in traditional team sports. All usual suspects on offer plus American influenced disc golf – something for everyone. Director of activities recently appointed to provide even more challenging outdoor opportunities.

Well-resourced and well-used music centre – a third take individual instrumental or singing lessons. An array of choirs and bands, from chamber to soul and jazz to strings. Talented musicians play in the National Children's and National Youth Orchestras, but plenty of playing and performing opportunities for those just starting out too: Verdi Requiem in Leeds Town Hall, Messiah from Scratch for charity.

Dedicated art studios and drama facilities always busy. Unusually for a boarding school, a 4pm finish and no Saturday school, but plenty of choice of after-school activities and clubs and supervised prep until 5.30pm; D of E from year 10. Trip for older students to Malawi ties in with charity fundraising to support the Open Arms Orphanage, which has close links with the school.

Boarding: School viewed as a day school with boarding – under 20 per cent board, and half of these are sixth form; firmly in the head's sights to improve these statistics. Three senior boarding houses, two boys' and one girls', are comfortably furnished with usual facilities: kitchens, common rooms, games areas and computers. Co-ed junior and girls' boarding houses recently upgraded.

Approximately one-third of boarders are from South East Asia – this has reduced in recent years. More emphasis on weekly/flexi boarding and more recruitment from the Forces. Girls and boys encouraged to socialise, with trips regularly organised at weekends and half-termly theme evenings. Plenty of activities on offer after school but all optional. Cultural differences mean not much integration with day pupils after school hours.

Background and atmosphere: Founded in 1877 by the Methodist Church as a senior boys' boarding school, co-ed since 1984. Pleasant, well-maintained site is in a leafy residential area, with a swathe of pitches and playing fields fringed by the trinity of schools (college, junior and pre-prep), sports centre and boarding houses. Evacuated to Windermere during the war as the premises were requisitioned for the war effort and used by Air Ministry.

Plenty of well-kept facilities – atmospheric Memorial Hall is home to lectures, meetings and some concerts, with larger gatherings filling the school hall. Recent, much-needed, extensive refurbishment programme to most classrooms, with the library now excellent. Investment in ICT infrastructure and hardware and more planned. New head of sixth form and review of academic offering, pupil monitoring and facilities in sixth form centre.

Plenty of performing opportunities for those just starting out too: Messiah from Scratch for charity

Underpinned by Methodist tradition, a positive, supportive family ethos where pupils feel valued and their voices heard. A genuine sense of community that keeps ex-pupils in contact long after they have left the school gates.

Pastoral care, well-being and discipline: Excellent individual pastoral care continues to be a real strength of the school. Head believes in picking up problems quickly to 'fix it small' and then 'partnership between school and parents'. This is recognised by parents, who said that the school 'tried very hard to get it right'.

All year 7 are taken to the Lake District for a bonding weekend early in the autumn term; this receives rave reviews not only from the new pupils but also from sixth formers, who work as liaison prefects and, if assigned to year 7, go too.

Fines if caught smoking, with possibility of exclusion for repeated offences. Drugs: out for supplying or intending to – no issues in recent times.

Pupils and parents: Mainly from local professional and business families, extending from Ripon to north Leeds and surrounding villages. Quite a few first time buyers; Americans from nearby Menwith Hill military base add an interesting dimension. For about 10 per cent of pupils English is not a first language and overall approximately 14 per cent come from a variety of minority ethnic backgrounds, mainly Chinese, Nigerian and European. Thriving Friends of Ashville runs regular, well-supported activities.

Old boys: Ian Dodds (designer of the Moon Buggy), Commander Ian Grieve (head of anti-terrorism Scotland Yard), Jim Carter (Downton Abbey actor), Simon Theakston (director of Theakston's Brewery and chairman of the Yorkshire Agricultural Show) and Peter McCormick (lawyer to the Football Association).

Entrance: For year 7, a day in January with English, mathematics and non-verbal reasoning papers followed by practical activities, plus a report from previous head. Usually a three form entry of 60 pupils, though recent demand has increased this to four forms.

Majority of pupils come from own junior school and nearby preps: Belmont Grosvenor and Brackenfield in Harrogate, Richmond House, Moorlands and Frobelian in Leeds, plus local state primary schools. Six bus routes in operation starting in Leeds, Thorner, Addingham, Ripon and Bramham.

Sixth form entry is via interview and satisfactory reference; five grade Cs with minimum grade Bs in subjects to be studied. Exams, interview and reference are norm for entry at other times.

Exit: Around 30 per cent leave at the end of year 11. Majority of sixth formers go on to higher education, generally a couple to Oxbridge (two to Cambridge in 2015), rest to a wide range of Russell Group/redbrick universities.

Money matters: Academic, music, sports, art and drama scholarships are available in the senior school. Scholarships are awarded on entry into year 7, year 10 and sixth form and are reviewed at key stages. Means-tested bursaries of up to 100 per cent of fees are available either in conjunction with scholarships or on a stand-alone basis. Additional discounts are awarded to the children of Methodist ministers and parents in the Forces.

Remarks: A successful all-round day school with a boarding ethos. Plenty of happy pupils in a caring and supportive environment. Academics and teaching being strengthened. Offers a trinity of schools providing seamless transition through each stage of education, obviously popular with many parents and pupils.

Aysgarth School

Newton-le-Willows, Bedale, North Yorkshire DL8 1TF

01677 450240
enquiries@aysgarthschool.co.uk
www.aysgarthschool.com

Ages: boys 3-13, girls 3-8 (boarding from 8)
Pupils: 227
Boarders: 89 full, 48 weekly
Day: £9,510 – £17,595 pa
Boarding: £22,905 pa

Headmaster: Since September 2015, Rob Morse, previously head of Perrot Hill, with his wife Lottie and their children, Daisy and Harry, and black labrador, Nel. Moved from Somerset, though no newcomer to the north as former deputy head at S Anselm's in Derbyshire. Summary view of parents who have met him is 'that he will serve Aysgarth very well and with his wife will build on the successes of the [previous head and family] Goddards'.

Head of co-ed pre-prep since 2014, Mrs Susie Drake BEd primary education, Liverpool University (early 40s). Has over 20 years', predominantly state school experience, most recently as a primary school adviser for 17 schools in North Yorkshire. Previous roles include early years consultant, deputy headteacher at a Skipton primary school and leading teacher for IT. Interested in educational research, always searching for 'what is right for the children at Aysgarth, rather than being driven purely by the current political agenda'.

Warm, intuitive and wholeheartedly believes in children progressing at their own pace to prevent storing problems for the future and opening the wider school curriculum beyond the classroom

door. 'Every moment matters' is her personal mantra and she believes in gently challenging children to be the best they possibly can.

Speaks proudly and in detail of the individual strengths of her teaching team. Feels that she's inherited a happy, steady ship and will build on that. Forging stronger links with local independents and state primaries a focus, mindful of easing the transition to new schools for the girls at 8. Parents very positive about her appointment, one saying that their 'children positively adore her'.

Entrance: Non-selective, but for prep an interview and assessment (no exam) to look for boys with a 'willingness to get stuck in', 'We try not to turn anyone away'. A few scholarships of between 10 – 25 per cent and some bursary help, which can be up to 100 per cent. Siblings and Forces discounts available.

Exit: Excellent record to public schools: Harrow, Eton, Ampleforth, Uppingham, Radley, Sedbergh, Shrewsbury, Stowe, Fettes and Winchester. Good sprinkling of academic, music and sports scholarships.

Heads and senior staff of senior schools spend one weekend a year at Aysgarth meeting boys and parents after chapel and at social events.

Remarks: Quiet, rural setting with glorious views in 50 acres of parkland, feels remote but only a short distance from the A1. Approached through a sleepy village, purposely anonymous except for landmark of the splendid school tower on the

horizon. A grand, purpose-built, 19th century school building, including a gem of a chapel, complemented by modern facilities. As you journey from the entrance your eye is caught by the profusion of discarded balls in the grounds, underlying a parent's description of 'a place where boys can be boys', though girls are welcomed into pre-prep.

The game of COW – cricket off the wall – is a love of Aysgarthians old and new, the real challenge being to hit the ball from the playground into the head's garden

Pre-prep established in 1993 in Oak House, a gentle amble from the prep school. Well adapted with well-equipped, secure, outdoor play area running along the front of the attractive building. The curriculum is traditional and broadly based on the national curriculum, though French is introduced in reception.

The weekly early years' newsletter helps parents understand the real learning outcomes from the play-based activity in EYFS, nursery and reception. This becomes more formal in year 1 with specialist teaching beginning to be introduced for French, PE and music. In year 2 concepts are developed through creative topic work. Transition is high on the agenda in year 3, with boys preparing for the prep school and girls for their next step at another school. House captain and other responsibilities allow the children to develop confidence. Golden time in assemblies celebrates rewards for academic achievement and good deeds, focussing on a difference aspect each week.

The rural setting provides the natural habitat for the forest school in 'Mr McGregor's garden' and the woodland areas. All the usual opportunities for music, drama and sport, with fixtures from year 3 and swimming for all. Good range of extracurricular clubs on offer, sport and choir with cookery, forest school and multi-activity acorn club – ballet at an additional charge. Pre- and after-school care is on offer from 8.00am – 6.00pm and there is school transport from Ripon and Asenby, all at extra cost.

In the prep school, small class sizes (max 16) with traditional and demanding curriculum; setting and streaming from year 5. Extraordinary continuity over the years in gaining places at top public schools. Challenge is to keep abreast of 'subtle shifts' in senior schools and 'keep improving in every sense' as the bar gets higher to top schools. SEN provision improving all the time as the school becomes an even more 'broader and kinder place'.

Top notch sports facilities, especially cricket field, swimming pool and newly built sports hall. The Aysgarth game of COW – cricket off the wall – is a love of Aysgarthians old and new, the real challenge being to hit the ball from the playground into the head's garden. Sport is high profile and

They can play anything here, including bagpipes if they so wish, and the choir is 'as cool as being in the first XV' and a joy to hear

they play to win, while still managing a well done and a slap on the back for the chap who comes last. Rugby, football, shooting, fishing, sailing, riding, golf and climbing all on offer. Won Rosslyn Park National Sevens Rugby tournament recently.

Art is strong and design technology is popular in well-equipped rooms where the boys can get their hands on serious equipment and tools. Four classrooms which provide light, stimulating spaces for the first year of the prep school. Music is outstanding with over 70 per cent of the pupils singing or playing an instrument. Boys – both the very musical and the less so – can be seen enthusiastically practising their musical instruments in dorms and classrooms at reserved times. They can play anything here, including bagpipes if they so wish, and the choir is 'as cool as being in the first XV' and a joy to hear. Drama lessons and lots of performance opportunities in newly built 200 seat theatre. Good to see boys enjoying reading sessions in the library after lunch.

Many of the boys look as though they are about to take Eton in their stride – happy, confident and courteous, without being arrogant, they are both charming and endearing but clearly relish this boy-friendly atmosphere where you can 'be your own man'.

Staff know the boys well and, although the phrase is often over used, there is really a 'family feel' about this place, thanks chiefly to great enthusiasm and care from the top. Very much focused on full boarding – in fact, north of Oxford, it's the only all boys' boarding prep in England and parents come from both north and south of the border and say, 'It's worth the journey'. Day boys are welcomed, though certainly in the minority, and they follow the boarding routine.

Boarding accommodation on the top three floors of the school, includes serried ranks of sinks, where boys have to be reminded to wash occasionally. Cheerful dorms, a mix of beds and bunks, yet mainly unadorned walls, where caring staff keep a close eye, tidying up after them and providing a homely feel. Delightful to see much-loved soft toys adorning many a bed – in the senior dorms as well.

Common rooms on ground floor showing signs of good wear and tear. Extensive after-hours activities for boarders include both pillow and water fights (though not at the same time) and it's fine to get down and dirty and build dens in the grounds as well as engaging in debating. Full boarding with diverse range of weekend activities and breaks at exeats only.

Food is ample, prepared in-house using fresh ingredients and 'not bad for school food' (though the boys did say they would like a little more salmon and duck on the menu, please), served in a pleasant if slightly old fashioned style dining room, long tables and benches, where good old fashioned courtesy and table manners count.

Clientèle mainly solid (upper) middle class from the North and Midlands, with a few Forces families from Catterick. Strong full boarding ethos attracts families from further away, Scotland and Northern Ireland, with 10 per cent international

boarders from Europe, Middle East and Russia. Families are a mix of old school and new, many first time into boarding, including some who, interestingly, say they had previously neither considered boarding nor single sex. Initially a little reluctant to let go, these parents place huge value on all that Aysgarth has to offer, both in and out of the classroom, the end result being that their sons are well prepared for the next school, commenting that 'Aysgarth boys are both in demand and popular'.

Governors very active and close to headmaster. There's a lively Old Aysgarthian association. Old boys include Sir Matthew Pinsent and Robert Swan OBE, whose achievements espouse the Aysgarth ethos.

Belhaven Hill School

Dunbar, East Lothian EH42 1NN

01368 862785
headmaster@belhavenhill.com
www.belhavenhill.com

Ages: 7–13
Pupils: 127
Boarders: 79
Day: £10,530 – £15,150 pa
Boarding: £21,750 pa

Head: Since 2009, Mr Innes MacAskill BEd (late 50s), previously head of Beeston Hall School, Norfolk, having spent 17 years at Caldicott, where he became deputy head. Educated at Bedford Modern; his wife, Sandy, is much involved in school life (though this ed still has not met her). They have three grown

up daughters. A hands-on head who believes that school has to be 'homely and comfortable', and described by his peers as 'having all the best bits of headmastering under his belt and actually likes the children' – not a universal characteristic. We thought him splendid, avuncular and confident.

School, and MacAskill, have weathered both the recession and a couple of years of mega staff retirals : those staff whom we met were young and buzzy. (Particularly the classics master, who made a point of finding us to confirm that during his time at the school, pupils had gone to some 27 different schools – now that is dedication). Pensions on the horizon; the MacAskills have a retirement home in the Cotswolds, so don't expect him to last the stay of next year's newbies. He is retiring in July 2016.

Entrance: No test, but register as soon as possible. Children spend a day at Belhaven the term before they come. Informal test when they come in but no official screening until age 9 – 'when we don't often find any surprises'.

Exit: Oundle, Rugby, Glenalmond, Queen Margaret's, Fettes, Radley, Ampleforth, Eton and Harrow, Wycombe Abbey, St Mary's Calne, plus all the big Scottish schools. Thereafter, anywhere.

Remarks: Numbers still high; full for the next few years: number of day children, many of whom convert to boarding. Brilliant house staff, matrons (and talkative cooking squad – but no requirement for kosher or halal; ditto cleaners – all natty in blue tabliers). Brace of learning support staff. Ed psych comes in to meet head of LS. The learning support base, aka The Hut, has been revamped (to the envy of some non-learning support pupils). Withdrawn from class, one-to-one, small groups, dual teaching – all disciplines covered, at no extra cost; though if a child has severe and particular difficulties school is relaxed about parents employing additional help.

Young encouraged to have their own chunk of the head's walled garden in which they take great pride

Still perceived as Scotland's school for the occasional toff which specialises in sending the little darlings to public school in the south, but now with a much broader base. School went co-ed in 1995, and thereafter welcomed the day squad. Boys based in late 18th century sandstone house with tower and imaginative additions: fairly pedestrian rumpus room; rules for backgammon laid out on the table but apparently no board. Dorms recently revamped with carpets and pin boards, alas bunks now a thing of the past (and round the world ditto): collection of tartan curtains, desks rather than bedside cabinets for older pupils. The snazzy girls' house has a spit new circular Rosy room, with plasma television and brightly coloured beanbags,

though we doubt whether 32 young ladies could all watch telly together.

No books or newspapers spotted in either the boys' or the girls' common rooms; head assured us there were books and papers aplenty in the reconfigured library just steps away. We are delighted that there are books and magazines in the library but this ed wants to see them everywhere on tables/chairs any place that children might find them-

---

A hands-on head described by his peers as 'having all the best bits of headmastering under his belt and actually likes the children' – not a universal characteristic

selves waiting. Daily papers visible in girls' house kitchen (The Times and Scotsman, since you ask); we were told that pupils could 'come and get them at bedtime'; heck, daily papers should be on every coffee table and flat surface, ditto magazines: Reader's Digest was perfect, but New Scientist will do just as well for interesting titbits. Bored children are good at instant literary grazing. But perhaps it was too early in the term.

Eight new classrooms, most grouped cloister-like round the lily pond – Jeremy Fisher, where art thou? – fab double and a half decker music school, but still a bit of a rabbit warren. All pupils online, two computer rooms. Own laptops not a problem. Pupils set in core subjects – maths, English, science and languages – throughout, but lots of to-ing and fro-ing. Science from age 8 and dedicated science, as in physics, chemistry and biology, from age 10. No setting for music, art and PE (friendships important). Tutors for top two years, otherwise classroom based, with form teachers and class sizes to 10/14. No scholarship stream as such, but more a case 'of children extended through setting and provided with opportunities for further support in activities and prep' (quite, scholarship stream in all but name). Clinic (aka drop in centre on Fridays) where lesser performers can seek help, and high flyers challenge. Vast choice of extracurricular activities; bright creatures steered towards the more intellectually challenging.

Latin, as you might expect, and Greek on offer (but on rather an ad hoc basis post CE, that sort of thing). Drama and dance increasingly popular, and wow, the costumes – masterminded by head's wife, who often dragoons parents onto their sewing machines. Inspired art, ceramics and design, with climbing wall on the outside of this converted squash court – sand below, not high, hats not de rigueur. Slightly tired, if functional, sports hall which adapts for school plays, has ping pong tables aloft and new cricket nets. Secured open swimming pool.

Piping much encouraged with FPs core of pipe bands in English public schools and in demand at weddings and funerals; or getting their tuppence worth on the corner of Princes Street to garner for gap years. Manicured grounds including two cricket pitches, six tennis courts, masses of Astroturf, a putting course and an 18-hole golf course 'over the wall'. Head plays too, though claims 'to be getting worse'. Bracing sea air. Streams of unbeaten teams in almost every discipline. Regular trips to Hillend artificial ski slope. Young encouraged to have their own chunk of the head's walled garden in which they take great pride: fierce competition for annual trophies. One member of staff, along with the children, uses all the apples from the orchard to make one big brew of apple juice for the children and staff to drink (head suspects this has something to do with cider making) but expect home-made apple pies, dumplings and crumbles. Grub for all in the dining room – benches and tables – with quartered oranges on offer during our visit.

Happy children when we visited, racing round lily pond – 'how many more times?'; relaxed uniform, ties and grown up stuff (long trousers, white shirts) only in last two years. Social parents and children, with masses of input from locals – tranches of farmers/Charlotte Rangers from East Lothian, plus the usual quota of quite grand children from the north and an increasing gang from south of the border, usually with Scottish connections. Girls fully absorbed. Grandparents and parents ('wish I'd been there,' said one prosperous Edinburgh property developer, who was educated within the city limits) have nothing but praise. Daily assembly, but don't expect surprises, charming little prayer book just printed for newbies ('put their name in it, it has to last three years'); God important, ditto values, bullying or aggravated teasing kept firmly under control, 'girls worse than boys'.

Sadness earlier this year that the annual rounders match between girls who had just left and those in their final year mid-summer term was a damp squib – not many leavers could make the match. With few participants and decided lack of tea ('used to make the best sandwiches in East Lothian,' said our informant; 'all I got was one lousy biscuit'. Head reassured us that the barbeque did go ahead; parents usually pick up afterwards.) That notwithstanding, the school is flourishing. Can't fault it.

Bootham School

51 Bootham, York, North Yorkshire YO30 7BU

01904 623261
admissions@boothamschool.com
www.boothamschool.com

Ages: 11–18
Pupils: 445; sixth form: 175
Boarders: 52 boys/36 girls full, 38 weekly/flexi
Day: £15,435 – £17,010 pa
Boarding: £17,445 – £29,625 pa

Head: Since 2004, Mr Jonathan Taylor BA (50s). Read English at Lincoln College, Oxford and has MEd from Sussex. Previously deputy head (eight years) and acting head (for four terms) at Bedales. Not a Quaker but clearly in tune with Friends' ideals; quick-thinking, articulate, unstuffy, approachable and clear-sighted about his vision for Bootham. He describes Bootham as his 'ideal headship' and appears very much at home. His devolved leadership style suits the place – a collaborative and cohesive way of working ('always consider you might be mistaken') encouraging healthy discussion and debate.

Married to Nicola and his interests include the arts, gardening and the outdoor life. Fascinating and engaging in conversation, he displays a real understanding of pedagogy coupled with an endearing ability to put people quickly at ease. He might just be the only member of staff you meet wearing a neck tie, possibly a reassuring touch for new parents, though his brightly coloured striped socks reveal a slight sense of the maverick within and he is all the more likeable for it.

Retiring in July 2016. His successor will be Christopher Jeffrey BA (50s), currently head of The Grange School, Cheshire. Read history at York. Previously deputy head at The Perse School, Cambridge. His wife is a nurse; three children. Very involved in the local church, plays the piano and guitar and composes music in his spare time. Fast talking and energetic.

Academic matters: In recent years the school has transformed itself from middle-of-the-road into a Yorkshire leader. Staff aren't exactly sure how this has happened but point to an infectious work ethic ('it's OK to achieve'), backed up by individual attention (Quaker maxim is 'seek that of God in everyone') and powerful sense of community. Academic achievement is 'not the be-all and end-all', say parents, but 'results are good nevertheless'. In 2015, 64 per cent A*/A at GCSE, 41 per cent A*/A grades and 72 per cent A*-B at A level. Sees itself as a 'premier science school', and results back this up. English and history popular, excellent art and maths. Class sizes throughout emphatically on the small side. Staff aim to fit A and AS combinations round pupils' choices, quite a feat in a smallish school. The approach is 'give them room and they'll deliver', which applies equally to staff and pupils. Staff are an engaged and creative bunch. They have room to breathe here and pupils feel the benefit. 'It's just good practice', says the head modestly.

Specialist science facilities, new arts centre for music, art and performance, design studios and an IT centre. Wireless network to help laptop users. Excellent John Bright library much used, recent addition of mezzanine floor adding an attractive additional workspace. Teaching lively and interactive; common claim that pupils take responsibility for their own learning and interrogate their teachers carries more weight here than in many schools – an aspect, perhaps, of the Quaker principle of 'speaking truth to authority' (ie don't take it lying down). Has opened its doors by offering masterclasses and summer schools for pupils from other schools, bringing much needed openness across the school community locally and no real surprise that Bootham should drive this. Currently a

He might just be the only member of staff you meet wearing a neck tie, though his brightly coloured striped socks reveal a slight sense of the maverick within

waiting list for Latin GCSE class for external pupils, all the more impressive as it is run after school.

Wide range of special needs catered for. School goes out of its way to help – ground floor biology lab created to enable pupil with a motor disability to learn alongside her peers.

Games, options, the arts: School encourages sport 'as a healthy part of life that hopefully will be continued'. Sport is played by all for enjoyment, but new director of sport has brought more training rigour, which had been demanded by some parents. Tennis and football traditionally popular, swimming (own pool), sports hall with climbing wall, no rugby; teams in all sports accommodate everyone, not just the talented. Despite – or because of – this, plenty of creditable achievement all round; basketball team has been district champion, as too were the U18 football team, and individual successes include an international fencer, Olympic swimmer, county netball, hockey and cricket squad members and Leeds academy footballers. Playground cricket is the stuff of legend here and a fiercely guarded

tradition – one former pupil went on to become a member of the Hong Kong women's cricket team.

Outstanding design work has received national critical acclaim. Vibrant art department, now housed in new arts centre, with wonderfully creative pupils' work led by practising and exhibiting artists. Music a major strength. Twenty different ensembles and over 60 per cent learn a musical instrument – mainly for enjoyment but many get to grade 8 and beyond, as well as scholarships to London music colleges. Regular buffet concerts held in main hall. Drama also strong; LAMDA on offer.

Expeditions to exotic places like Bolivia, Peru and Iceland and regular exchanges with France and Germany. School has its own well-used observatory (original William Cooke telescope and lovely polished brass fittings) and boasts oldest natural history society in the country.

A school with a conscience, it's no surprise that Bootham is a Fairtrade school and has been named as an Oxfam World Shaper School. It has the highly-regarded Eco-Schools' Ambassador Status Green Flag and can proudly boast that it sends no waste to landfill. BEAST (nickname for Bootham Environment and Sustainability Team) leads the way in reducing the school's carbon footprint, beginning (naturally) in the junior school with mini-BEAST; awarded Eco-Schools Ambassador status – one of only 11 schools in the country – for education leadership in eco matters.

Boarding: Good standard of boarding accommodation – possibly better for girls than for boys, but that's not unusual and it bothers the boys less. Flat-sharing for the sixth form (college) girls, which they love and seems sensible in terms of preparation for the future. Good wholesome food, plenty of choice. Day pupils can try boarding in one of many flexible options.

Hard to be bored here – plenty to do, huge range of extracurricular activities after school from bell ringing to water polo; lessons on Saturday morning and fixtures in the afternoon, with evening activities organised by the boarding house teams. Sundays relaxed and informal.

Background and atmosphere: Founded in 1823 on liberal, intellectual, tolerant principles. No need to belong to Society of Friends, or even be Christian, but non-credal umbrella, underlined by regular, silent Meetings, does seem to work a kind of magic, and parents willingly buy into it.

Originally for boys only, became co-ed in 1983. Within shouting distance of the Minster and city walls but the only visible part of the school is the fine Georgian terrace and passers-by would be surprised to learn that the site covers nine acres. From the busy main road, look out for the clearly

identifiable Bootham blue-green doors, behind which lie a spacious and tranquil campus, with additional buildings gradually edging alongside. The fact that much of the school is hidden from view adds to an air of mystery about the place, yet the irony is that these buildings house some of the most open-minded people you could ever meet. Original buildings are undergoing a cycle of cosmetic updates and more radical facelifts; new arts centre has greatly boosted arts and music provision and freed up useful space elsewhere.

Teaching lively and interactive; common claim that pupils take responsibility for their own learning and interrogate their teachers carries more weight here

This is a largely non-hierarchical place and not rigidly conformist. Relationships between pupils and staff clearly very good – mutual respect is the order of the day. New pupils surprised and impressed by the fact the 'the head will open a door for you'. Parents comment on friendliness of receptionist, catering and ground staff as well as teaching staff. Younger pupils wear a kind of uniform. A dress code for older ones, though it's not immediately obvious, but an impressive alumni list suggests that perhaps it really doesn't matter as clearly clothes do not necessarily maketh the man. Self-run school council is more than a talking shop and can subject authority to awkward questions about how the school is run. 'Not snobby' say parents, who welcome the fact that pupils are 'encouraged to think about wider social concerns and global issues'.

Slight whinge from some pupils about Saturday morning school, but the upside is that the school is in town and so you can make a quick escape to the shops when lessons are over.

Pastoral care, well-being and discipline: Given the emphasis on a warm, family-type atmosphere, it would be easy to assume a laid-back, rule-less school short on structure and discipline. Not so. Expected standards of behaviour are clear and 'all the usual systems are in place'. No alcohol allowed on premises, suspicion of drug taking renders a pupil liable to random testing, drug peddling leads to expulsion. The key difference is that pupils here are encouraged to consider the effect of their actions on others and that in itself acts as an effective mechanism for self-control, most of the time. In line with the Quaker ethos, pupils say 'school comes down hard on bullying'.

Pupils and parents: Pupils look like your average floppy-haired teenagers but these are a happy, confident, savvy bunch, probably more comfortable in their own skin than most. A combination of clear yet equitable guidelines and being accepted for what and who you are makes a big difference in these impressionable years. Prospective parents who found themselves being asked a host of questions by their 'delightfully curious' pupil guides signed up immediately – because 'these were the kind of young people we want our children to be'.

School has its own well-used observatory (original William Cooke telescope and lovely polished brass fittings) and boasts oldest natural history society in the country

No real parent 'type' – more an attitude. Many children of university teachers and medics, plus a raft of curious first time buyers. Once you've had the conversation and removed any preconceived notions, the Quaker reference point makes lots of sense and clearly appeals. Active parents' association holds regular coffee mornings, walks, lectures and a grandparents' day. Weekly recitals – music, poetry-readings and the like – open to all. Regular Saturday morning gatherings with coffee and croissants at no charge – head and deputy often pop in so can be useful for a catch-up. Some even stay for lunch.

Parents say Bootham is 'addictive' and that 'it gets under your skin'. They appreciate the 'open access to teachers via email, enabling parents to discuss any concerns they may have'. Time and time again it's the 'beyond the academic' bit that parents rave about here. Not that there is any lack of academic rigour, there isn't. It's simply that there is something else, not quite tangible and not appearing in league tables, but you can feel it in your bones.

Day pupils mainly from York and up to 25-mile radius of school. Around a quarter of pupils are boarders, nearly 60 per cent from overseas. Of these, 40 per cent are from Hong Kong and 17 per cent from China, with increasing numbers from Nigeria and Russia. They are all English-speaking or near-fluent if not.

Notable former pupils: include AJP Taylor, Brian Rix, Philip Noel Baker (Nobel prizewinner and Olympic medallist), John Bright (parliamentarian), Stuart Rose (former boss of Marks & Spencer), Silvanus Thompson (physicist), plus 16 more fellows of the Royal Society.

Entrance: A third of the entry at 11 comes from Bootham Junior School, the rest from schools far and wide. Entrants at 11 have an assessment day, at 13 a more traditional exam. For sixth form entry a minimum of seven Cs or six Bs at GCSE required, which must include maths and English. Head interviews all applicants and asks for report from previous school.

Exit: Some 20 per cent leave post-GCSE, mainly to local sixth form college, either for vocational courses or to avoid Saturday school. Many take gap years. Newcastle popular as well as Durham, Warwick and Exeter. A number to art courses in 2015: Camberwell, Chelsea & Wimbledon, Leeds College of Art, Manchester School of Art. Psychology a popular course but also engineering and marine biology.

Money matters: Not a rich school: most income generated through fees and fundraising. Some academic scholarships (means-tested), music scholarships (not means-tested) and some special provision for Quaker families.

Remarks: School does well by all and parents say 'differences are celebrated, not shunned or ridiculed'. But don't expect to find a community of meek souls. Far from it. Bootham helps pupils to develop into bright, articulate and considerate individuals. Pupils admit it 'may not suit the highly competitive or the attention-seeker', but having said that, they are quick to add that 'we'd help them to get over themselves..'

Cargilfield School

45 Gamekeeper's Road, Edinburgh EH4 6HU

01313 362207
admin@cargilfield.com
www.cargilfield.com

Ages: 3–13; boarding from 8
Pupils: 325
Boarders: 8 full, 47 weekly/flexi
Day: £9,525 – £14,820 pa
Boarding: £18,195 pa

Headmaster: Since September 2014, Rob Taylor, previously registrar at Harrow School. He has also been head of Ashdown Prep School in Sussex. He is married to Sarah, and they have three children. Took over from acting head following the abrupt departure in October 2013 of previous head and his wife.

Entrance: Nursery and pre-prep popular; upper school numbers have grown enormously; places pretty well guaranteed through pre-prep but tests if learning difficulties suspected. Wannabes assessed: occasional places may occur throughout the school – logistics.

Exit: All the Scottish public schools – Glenalmond and Fettes head the list, but also Merchiston, Kilgraston, fewer to Gordonstoun, almost none to Loretto, much as you would expect. Huge cohort – around half – head south of the border: Eton (biggest feeder north of Oxford). In the past pupils have won scholarships to Winchester, also Harrow, Downe House etc etc, you name it. More scholarships than you can shake a stick at – 50+ last three

or four years: 'genuine academic awards'. Top award to Fettes regularly and top classics to all.

Pipe band is second to none, practising on the games pitch as we left, some interesting baton chucking

Remarks: Cargilfield had a bad case of wobbles with rapid head turn-over. We arrived to find the school covered in scaffolding and wondered about a new, new-build, but no, just roof repairs. (The £1.2 million games changing rooms are up and running). This former parent of the pre-prep (still brill) regrets the reduction of play area (previously 23 acres now 15: posho pads equal new builds); the sports hall (a 21st century prerequisite) impinges on the games pitch, alongside a couple of cedar-clad (rather grand inside) huts, which blend well, but look like early huts for battery hens (or photographs of Bletchley Park), and provide a new teaching centre plus a 10-room (soundproof) music school with a mini-concert rehearsal room, used for drama too. A stonking 80 per cent take extra music. Strong choir, which tours 'down south', and terrific strings ensemble: 'our top area and they have won major awards at the Edinburgh Music Festival'; pop group. Pipe band is second to none, taster sessions for all in pre-prep, they were practising on the games pitch as we left, certain amount of interesting baton chucking.

Impressive two-storey classroom block for English, ICT and history, with colonnades, cloisters and walkways. Certain amount of internal restructuring, with dorms becoming classrooms (and vice versa).

Pupils setted and streamed, maths from age 8. Most year groups divided into three: scholarship stream (currently boasting some 14 pupils) for the last three or four years plus two mixed-ability classes. French from nursery, Latin from 9 or 10; ancient Greek at 11, classical civilisation, Spanish for the last two years. (German and Mandarin clubs). Fantastic learning support (known as learning development) all assessed on entry; head of learning support plus two and a half staff. One of the best departments in Scotland, combining individual and co-teaching: max 5.5 hours per week. Currently has a parent-underwritten (ie they pay school fees and for a dedicated teacher) unit for two pupils who have very special needs, (previous) head hesitated for a moment, but agreed this was still in place 'an unusual arrangement'. But isn't this what the independent sector is about? School can no longer accommodate many of the weaker brethren, unless they are, in fact, brethren. Jolly Phonics and any 'other combination that works' on the reading front.

Mega weekend activities, no Saturday school ('children more relaxed and less tired on Mondays'). Nine year olds camping in the Highlands, 12/13 year olds at Hadrian's Wall

Founded in 1873, the school moved to its purpose-built site in 1890. Girls' boarding house is full, difficult to find space for flexis. Jolly sitting-rooms on ground floor (along with showers etc) and some of the prettiest dorms we have seen in a long time. Odd space in boys' dorms: trad old school dorms, huge, with sofas and games tucked into corners – given the choice, chaps preferred more mates to smaller bedrooms. Chaps in bunks, girls have drawers below beds, total replacement of furniture and fittings factored in every three years. Two-weekly boarding for all (max 74 boarders at any one time, 35 weekly, 15 full time). Day pupils regularly join boarders for a huge variety of weekend activities (though all must stay for three nights and can't just pick and choose). Mega weekend activities, no Saturday school ('children more relaxed and less tired on Mondays'). Nine year olds camping in the Highlands, 12/13 year olds at Hadrian's Wall.

Odd space in boys' dorms: trad old school dorms, huge, with sofas and games tucked into corners – given the choice, chaps preferred more mates to smaller bedrooms

Deep complaints from parents whose young played Cargilfield girls' netball squad at the recent Belhaven tournament. Cargilfield wore sponsored hoodies, with Cargilfield First Netball Team on the back, and 'Imagine having Strutt & Parker on your bosom,' said one irate papa.

Kayaking, shooting, international coaching in fishing, fencing, judo, hockey, skiing both at Hillend and the real thing. Two small Astroturfs. Eighty clubs on offer – chess champions with boards set up all over the place (and visiting chess master). Trips all over, both at weekends and longer ones abroad to Rome and France. Much use made of resources in grand Scots cities. New website.

Discounts for MoD children (handy for Scottish Command). Hundred per cent bursaries on offer: means-tested – five or six pupils on this kind of bursary (but not necessarily every year), graduated sibling discount. Mixed bunch of parents, grander than previously, FWAGS now thinner on the ground, one or two proper foreigners, tiny ethnic mix. Boarders from Yorkshire, the Borders, West Coast, Aberdeenshire, Angus and Perthshire. Bus on Sundays from Angus, and daily from Saxe Coburg Place in Edinburgh and Fife but, as children often stay until after 8pm, parents must collect them themselves.

Pre-prep and nursery based in stunning £3.5m building with cherished (quite small) Astroturf and enclosed play area, share big school facilities. School not keen on folk using the nursery as a spring-board for a couple of years and then heading off elsewhere (like this editor!).

Casterton, Sedbergh Preparatory School

Kirkby Lonsdale, via Carnforth, Lancashire LA6 2SG

01524 279200
ajm@sedberghprep.org
www.sedberghprep.org

Ages: 6m–13
Pupils: 200
Boarders: 60
Day: £7,476 – £14,580 pa
Boarding: £17,493 – £22,008 pa

Linked school: Sedbergh School

Headmaster: Since 2013, Mr Scott Carnochan (40s), previously head of Sedbergh Junior, now head of the newish joint school. Educated at Dollar Academy, BEd from Herriott-Watt Edinburgh, former Scottish U18 rugby cap. Married to Kate, they have two young children; Mrs Carnochan also works in the school, doubling up on the key roles of headmaster's wife and head of marketing. They are a strong, capable and immensely likeable team and parents are huge fans.

Entrance: Assessment by head's interview and previous school report for younger children; English, maths and cognitive ability tests for year 4 upwards.

Exit: Nearly all to Sedbergh senior school.

Remarks: Eggs, 'laid with love' (says the sign) from the free range chickens here, plus the goats and the rabbits bring out the 'softer side of a prep school,' says the head. The children, while not quite 'free range' (tiger mothers and helicopter parents need not worry), have an abundance of outdoor space

and room to breathe. They mostly ignore the glorious views and the weather that changes almost hourly; they are too busy enjoying their childhood.

Housed in a range of buildings, with plenty to spare; specialist science labs, inspirational art studios, music and superb sports facilities, these prep and pre-prep children are enjoying all the benefits of this former senior school. With reference to the relatively recent merger, parents say, 'it was the best thing that could have happened' – Casterton parents with older girls may disagree somewhat, but undoubtedly the feel-good factor is back and they are bucking the trend in this northern demographic with excellent post-merger recruitment figures and a good solid number of boarders. This is no mean feat in a school tucked away with no passing traffic; you have to seek it out, but advice from parents is 'if you are at all unsure, go and take a look – and take your children with you, that'll do it'. Most of us have at some point seen teary parents and weeping children at school gates at some point – well, here the children were weeping

because they'd been for a taster morning and didn't want to leave..

Variously described as a 'broad church' and 'a good all-round education', the facilities are matchless for a prep school, having originally been designed for pupils up to A level. Note the six full size science labs, massive sports hall with cricket nets and a bowling machine, swimming pool, Astroturf, music practice rooms and much more besides, and they make full use of every bit of it. Nothing precious about it; parents say the children 'live in it' rather than 'just exist', and whilst they are quick to add that 'it's the people who really make the place', they also tell us they feel as though they have 'hit the jackpot here'.

You can bring your bike, you can also bring your horse – though not essential if you have a love of riding, as the school has 10 ponies that they happily loan. Work hard and play hard could be the school's motto, though presumably only if translated into Latin; the energy is astounding, before, during and after school. Rugby, hockey, cricket, netball and much more besides mean that there is no lack of fresh air and exercise. For obvious reasons, the location means that boarding makes sense, and it also allows you to join in with activities ranging from a parachute regiment leadership day to abseiling, bouldering, go-karting, clay pigeon shooting, bushcraft and (for the gentler soul) cheese-tasting; essentially, you just 'don't stay in'.

The pupils are a refreshing and captivating blend of childlike naivety and honesty alongside a wisdom that belies their years. Shoe-polishing night for boarders, fastening your top shirt button and a ban on chewing gum are happily tolerated by pupils, but, for them, the deal-breaker would be bullying, 'a real no-no', as is anything which essentially 'makes the atmosphere less friendly'. All meals are prepared in-house from, as far as possible, local produce; adults sit with the children in mixed age groups and apparently the curry is legendary.

Boarding accommodation, in rooms with views to die for, is spacious and homely; there are kitchens for extra toast-making and generally hanging out, plus a sitting room with TV and games for the boys; similar though slightly smaller and prettier accommodation for the girls with the obligatory One Direction posters. It's so quiet here that one boarder told us he falls asleep each night to the sound of the birds singing outside, and then they wake him up again in the morning.

Parents are a mix of medics from Lancaster, local business owners and landed gentry; tweed is somewhat de rigueur – practical and stylish, as befits the place. It's only a 15 minute drive to the senior school from here so parents and staff can and do manage both. Parents say it 'doesn't matter what car you drive, or even if you land your helicopter on the back field, you're made very welcome here'. House staff use Twitter to keep parents of boarders up-to-date, regular photos home of joyful, smiling children.

Clearly the merger and change of status required careful handling, but thanks to good management and huge parental advocacy, they've not only survived but thrived. A portrait of old girl Charlotte Brontë still hangs in the sitting room, and although it's still slightly old school here (and all the better for that – good manners and etiquette still count), she'd hardly recognise the warm and happy place it is today.

Dollar Academy

Dollar, Clackmannanshire FK14 7DU

01259 742511
rector@dollaracademy.org.uk
www.dollaracademy.org

Ages: 11–18
Pupils: 1,220; sixth form: 152
Boarders: 83
Day: £8,703 – £11,637 pa
Boarding: £22,527 – £26,928 pa

Rector: Since September 2010, Mr David Knapman BA (maths) MPhil (40s), previously deputy head of Hampton School in London, where he still has a foot on the property ladder. At Hampton he established a non-nonsense reputation but was also notable for his work with charities and the local community. Educated at Morrisons, 'doon the road', followed by Sheffield and Exeter. Married to Brigitte with two sons (younger one in the school). His mother lives in Dunblane and 'is my fiercest critic; she keeps her ear to the ground'. Plays tennis regularly and enjoys 'playing the piano badly'. Wife also a teacher, came from a country background and is 'pleased to be in Scotland', they like walking the hills and are planning to tackle Ben Lomond this summer (Munro bashing very popular around here).

They live in a stunning Georgian street which houses a collection of school buildings – much in demand by film crews no doubt – we yomped to the burn to see Mylne Bridge (built and named for the local minister and first rector, who opened the school in 1818, to give him a short cut to the kirk) and were told that if it 'weren't for that pine tree, we could see Castle Campbell' (we googled it – it is pretty impressive).

Has a dry sense of humour: when asked how his son felt about moving to Scotland he explained that the bribe of a new puppy had been more than sufficient, though he is coy about the exact species (we suspect a spot of Mr Heinz 57). Hugely enthusiastic and 'very popular – going down well' and 'doing just fine,' say our spies. Sits in on classes, walks round every day and never misses a match, concert or play. Boarding numbers going up and examination results at a record high last year.

He was mentored by Dr Ken Greig, rector of Hutchesons Grammar in Glasgow (we hadn't realised that heads had mentors too) who seems to have grown a beard in solidarity. Certain number of staff changes; new assistant rector, 12 new staff, including Rob Moffat to coach PE (previously coach to the Edinburgh rugby squad, he was dismissed in 2011 'as the team failed to progress up the league table' – doubt if Dollar is quite in that league, but rugby here has a long tradition – three former pupils currently members of the Scotland squad), a mixture of young and old teachers, housing not cheap in the Dollar area but it is the perfect place for families.

Academic matters: Strong academic tradition, particularly science with a compressed science option on offer for 14-16 year olds and large numbers for medical school; English and mod langs good too, German and French more popular than Spanish; Latin, Greek and classical studies (heroes for zeros) all on offer and four dedicated classics teachers. All three langs from junior school plus some Japanese, Russian, Italian, philosophy, car mechanics and other jolly options. Broad streaming for English (with EFL if needed), tight setting for maths and mixed ability in most subjects, plus. Large business department offering economics, business management, finance and accountancy.

Rumours abound whether the monies came from slavery or piracy but they were certainly augmented by bribes from ship owners eager to be first

Rector and/or senior staff have a 20 minute meeting with every pupil (and their parents, who usually keep stumm during the interview) to discuss their personal subject choice. Pupils choose the subjects they want to study and classes are worked round them, rather than the trad system of block choice. There is a distinct emphasis on the academic rather than the vocational.

School follows a mixed bag of courses: National 4 and 5, Intermediate I and II; Highers, Advanced Highers and the Scottish baccalaureate – which doesn't seem to have many followers outside Dollar.

In 2015, 59 per cent of Highers and 48 per cent of Advanced Highers were A grade.

Classes of 6-24. Efficient support for learning in place; one-to-one, small groups and support learning in class all on offer. School has a positive approach to those with ADHD: pupils can drop into the dyslexia centre at any time. Serious homework, carefully spelt out in a smart little green book full of info for parents which interestingly persists in referring to the school as the Academy. 'Whatever else, we expect that all pupils in the Academy should have enough work to occupy their evenings and any child who indicates otherwise misunderstands.' Not quite all singing and dancing new computer system (school report says 'could do better'), touch-typing for all, strong on techy subjects – most to Advanced Higher level.

Games, options, the arts: No sport is compulsory. That said, boasts a first XV rugby team unbeaten for the first seven years of this century. Regular tours to Europe and further afield: Canada, Japan, Italy et al. Shooting 'phenomenal'; always a strong showing at Bisley. Hockey hot stuff. Numerous individual county reps in major and minor sports – golf, skiing and badminton, as well as more esoteric activities such as shotput, curling, table tennis, equestrian vaulting (gymnastics on horseback) and triathlon (NB Clackmannanshire ain't that big). mass of

games fields, 63 acres of school grounds, much-used hall and swimming pool. Amazing circular Maguire Building – sports, arts, drama – million pound bequest from FP Brian Maguire; formidable school art on display and used for external exhibitions too – even the Scottish Examinations Authority asked for a painting for their new premises. Second bequest from the Price family resulted in a new 5.3 metre inflatable for the navy section. All weather surface was opened by Linda Clement, Scottish Ladies' hockey captain. Presumably by bullying off.

Strong volunteer CCF – good following, not just because of the trips to Canada. Three pipe bands, who all sport the Campbell tartan; the B band was third in the national CCF championships this year. Two orchestras, jazz bands, oodles of choirs; the annual Christmas concert in the Usher Hall was a sell-out with almost 2,000 in the auditorium. Drama timetabled with masses of productions – the rector believes that 'pupils gain confidence through performance'; lots of smaller concerts – 'six performers, 30 in the audience'; that sort of thing. Hot on debating, all sorts of trophies as well as representation in the winning Scotland team at recent world champs in South Africa – a tour de force. Ballroom dancing on Fridays; participants learn Latin American and rock 'n' roll, Japanese dancing the latest wheeze but no medals for this nor for Scottish country dancing. Prize winners sport their bronze, silver, gold or Scottish Awards proudly on their blazers thereafter.

Munro bashing, D of E, exchange and trips, work experience at home and abroad, go-kart racing at Knockhill, skiing, motor mechanics, surfing, falconry. Clubs for everything, usually post school, late buses nightly. Fabric technology timetabled. Over 70 options in total; terrific facilities; powerful charities committee (15 mile sponsored walk raised over £50,000, staff, parents and doggies all included).

Boarding: The boarding houses are small, two with up to 24 girls in each, one for boys that takes up to 49; all three have had recent million pound facelifts, stunning. Usual range of after-school and weekend activities – cooking to sub aqua.

Background and atmosphere: Captain John McNabb, a former herd boy who rose to become a ship's captain and, latterly, a ship husband – literally looking after ships in port – died in 1802, leaving half his fortune, £55,000, to found a school to educate children of 'the parish wheir I was born'. Rumours abound whether the monies came from slavery or piracy but they were certainly augmented by bribes from ship owners eager to be first past the post. After much shilly shallying, the Rev Andrew Mylne, a trustee, commissioned Playfair to build a 'hospital' which finally opened in 1818. The first

Botanical garden boasting some of the rarest trees in the country – certainly the most northerly tulip tree, as well as a Corsican pine

co-ed in Scotland. McNabb's corpse was rediscovered in the 1930s and proudly brought back to Scotland, and cremated. Gruesome or what. His ashes are entombed in the wall above the main Bronze Doors; this has to be the only school in the land where pupils pass under the founder every day. By 1830, the grounds at Dollar had become an Oeconomical and Botanical garden, boasting some of the rarest trees in the country – certainly the most northerly tulip tree, as well as a Corsican pine, and specimen sequoias. Pupils originally had their own plot of garden, though we are not sure whether this was for ornamental purposes or whether they were expected to augment the school kitchen. The interior of Playfair's original building was gutted by fire in 1961, which allowed a certain amount of internal rearrangement. Zinging concert hall (the Gibson Building), improved science block. Current wish-list includes a new technology, engineering science and earth science building – to be built out of 'funds'. The grounds are open to the public daily. And the library is no longer lollipop pink.

Formerly a direct grant school, Dollar became independent in 1974 – a day school, with an international boarding element. Easily accessible from most of Scotland and just a short hop from the Forth Road Bridge and Edinburgh Airport. Wet weather a feature of the place and masses of matches are rained (or snowed) off (school says very rarely due to new all-weather Astroturf courts and pitches). NB The school uniform includes beanies (first time ever for us on a clothes' list) and macs with fleecy linings. Rector says he doesn't mind what they wear on their heads, as long as they are warm.

Pastoral care, well-being and discipline: Automatic out for drugs. Lousy work equals detentions post-school or early morning – dead unpopular with parents, plus out if 'The pupil is not deriving benefit from being at the school or indicates by his/her conduct that he/she does not accept the rules of the Academy.' Pupils not particularly streetwise – 'Pupils have a reasonable amount of self-knowledge but on the whole they are not young people obsessively interested in the major interests of the day; it is no bad thing for them to remain children for a little longer'. Victorian values, with clear rules; many of the petty restrictions have been done away with, and the kilt may be worn by chaps at almost any time, though most prefer to be 'breeched', except for dances or reels.

Pupils and parents: The vast majority comes from within a 30 mile radius – impressive number of buses, plus Forces children and a contingent from the Scottish diaspora worldwide. Dollar itself has the reputation of having the highest percentage of graduates of any town in the country. School has a long tradition of looking after the children of tea-planters, missionaries and engineers – still. Perhaps a tad parochial and 'mercifully' free of Sloanes. Exceptionally strong and active FP network, including Sir Frank Swettenham, the first Governor of Malaysia, Sir James Dewar, the inventor of the vacuum flask, and the sculptor, George Paulin. The governing body is mostly FPs, which ensures that the place has freedom to develop but an awareness of its history shapes the thinking – no bad thing.

Entrance: Usually at 11 or 12, by examination, which is quite selective. Generally over-subscribed for entry at fifth and sixth forms; each case individually considered; good GCSE or National/Intermediate grades required plus good refs and an ability to put something into the school. No open days as such – parents and prospective pupils are welcome to visit at any point of the year, which gives the opportunity to see the school in action.

Exit: A handful to Oxbridge each year (one to Cambridge in 2015). Otherwise most students head for the Scottish universities: Edinburgh, St Andrews, Glasgow, Aberdeen, with under a quarter going south or abroad. Low gap year take up: either a reflection of the recession or the 'get on with it' mentality. The chairman of governors and his wife have set up a trust with more than £1 million to encourage the youngsters to take up challenges involving travel. If that doesn't persuade entrepreneurs overseas.

Money matters: Collection of means tested-academic bursaries at 11 and 12, plus ESU, Forces and boarding bursaries (usually means-tested, with tuition not covered). Fees very reasonable; governors tough on non-payers.

Remarks: Very sound – this large, solid, co-ed school provides education in the best Scottish 'get on with it' tradition, facing the 21st century with the expectations and values of an earlier age, mercifully free of most of the excesses of the 60s. 'Robust teaching and meritocracy' are important here. Up there with the best of the merchant schools, though possibly 'not quite so trendy'.

Durham School

Quarry Heads Lane, Durham DH1 4SZ

01913 864783
enquiries@durhamschool.co.uk
www.durhamschool.co.uk
C of E

Ages: 11–18
Pupils: 445: 300 boys/145 girls; sixth form: 165
Boarders: 110
Day: £13,512 – £16,236 pa
Boarding: £19,995 – £28,500 pa

Headmaster: Since September 2014, Kieran McLaughlin (early 40s), previously deputy head (academic) at Rugby. Studied natural sciences at Cambridge, specialising in physics and theoretical physics. Has been head of science and technology at Sevenoaks and head of physics at City of London Girls. Attended selective boys' school St Edward's College in Liverpool, having won an assisted place. In the past was the bass player in an obscure Liverpudlian rock band, as well as pursuing the ancient martial art of jiu-jitsu to black belt level. Married with three young children.

Feels that after some change the school needs time to consolidate. He brings experience of a variety of schools (Durham is his sixth): single sex, co-ed, city day, day and boarding, traditional boarding. Although only 15 per cent of pupils are regular boarders (27 per cent when occasional/flexi boarders are included), he says, 'The school feels like a boarding school', and we would agree.

His focus has been on delivering the school's message in the city and beyond. He believes that 'the school is much better than is generally perceived at delivering its core purpose'. Emphasis is on holistic educational experience, evidenced by the value added at A level being in the top 10 per cent of independent schools. Reminders, too, about academic success, and work is in progress to drive standards higher without being 'an academic hothouse'. Durham is a city where education really does matter and word of mouth really does count. One parent we spoke told us that they had researched in depth seven schools before selecting Durham School.

Has a collegiate management style; teaches physics to year 12. Has an easy manner, and when walking around the school it is obvious he is a visible head to his pupils. Very strong vote of confidence from parents, with one summing up the tenor of the parents we spoke to: 'He is an asset to the school and clearly has a firm grasp on the challenges within education and the strategic development needed to stay ahead and maintain standards of excellence'.

Currently not too distracted by the Durham International Schools initiative – a franchising joint venture with Indian company Infinity, looking to clone Durham ethos in the UAE.

Academic matters: A level nearly 37 per cent A*/A, 63 per cent A*-B in 2015, consistent with 2014 and an improvement on 2013. Probably why school is working to develop academic aspects of the sixth form ('more rigour', a study centre, supervised study time, more intellectual societies). Wide choice of subjects includes economics, politics, psychology, philosophy and ethics, government and politics, classical civilisation, photography, theatre and business studies. EPQ now available together with an enrichment programme which includes a lecture series and five societies, supervised by staff but run by students: Academic, Politic, Heretics, Tristam (scientists) and Medsoc (would-be medics). Very good support with university applications and Oxbridge/elite university preparation.

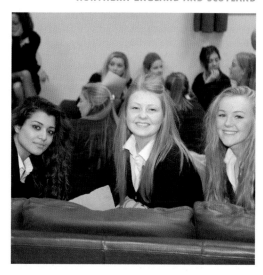

GCSE results 43 per cent A*/A in 2015. Mathematics, two English, separate sciences or dual award and a modern language compulsory. Option choice includes Latin, classical civilisation, ethics and drama, music, PE, DT graphic products and Greek, off timetable. German or Spanish added to French in year 9 (can also do Latin) and language awareness days, with themed meals. Most recent inspection praised pupil-staff relationships, teaching and use of monitoring, but commented on some marking inconsistency, which school is addressing.

Classrooms tend to be traditional, with just one computer plus projector (only a few interactive whiteboards), some darkish, but also some new ones and some modern ICT facilities with a stock of iPads though probably 'bring your own device' the way forward. Wifi connectivity has improved and a VLE to be launched shortly.

Strong learning support department – well qualified, flexible, sensitive; can cope with most needs apart from severe behavioural problems. The spread out nature of the campus could be a problem for anyone with major physical disabilities. Screens all new entrants for dyslexia and ESL, if from overseas (extra charge for ESL – full-time specialist – and learning support sessions); trains other staff. Thorough-going gifted and talented policy – systematic identification and monitoring, early maths GCSE, fourth A level and extra, challenging activities.

Games, options, the arts: Astroturf, functional swimming pool, sports hall, playing fields, very good rowing facilities and access to top flight coaching. Individuals and teams successful at regional, county and national levels with rugby first XV reaching the Natwest Trophy semi finals and the hockey teams getting to the National Schools Regional Finals in 2014.

One of the oldest rowing clubs in the country (dates from 1847) – the whole 1970 crew represented GB and has current international stars. Water polo taking off in a big way, ski team reached finals of English Schools' Championships, a GB fencer; also cross-country, golf, squash, boxing, rifle shooting, wind surfing and climbing. All pupils participate in 4.5 hours of sport and physical activity per week, still partly compulsory in the sixth form. Girls have more chance of being in teams through being in a minority.

On Remembrance Day the whole school lines the stairs at twilight, holding candles, while a wreath is laid on the memorial plaque, which must be very moving

Very accomplished choral singing – TV appearances, radio broadcasts, including Radio 4's Sunday Worship and a number of CDs. All Steinway school so plenty of pianists. Orchestras, jazz band, rock group; performance opportunities abound with concerts at The Sage, Gateshead and Durham Cathedral plus foreign tours.

Plenty of opportunity to showcase their dramatic talents in a variety of genres and settings – big musicals like Les Misérables in Durham's Gala Theatre or plays like The Great Gatsby in the school's own performance space, The Luce. Also more informal performances take place in the school's modern studio theatre.

Inter-house competition is rife with the show-stopping annual music competition (staged alternate years in the Sage and the Chapel) top of the bill. Sporting and drama events are staged throughout the year with much-coveted trophies for the winners.

Wide choice of activities from creative writing to computer programming, peer support to the languages film club. D of E and CCF (all three sections). School participates in BBC School Report (writing news bulletins and reports) and the lively and entertaining school newspaper, The Durham Eye, printed in house, has reached the finals of a national schools media competition. Careers education now expanding using network of Old Dunelmians.

Lots of fundraising for charity and foreign trips – staff and pupils seem to have bags of energy and enterprise; Chinese Exchange Visit to Chengdu; World Challenge to Borneo, Africa, Ecuador, Vietnam or India, cricket tour to Antigua, hockey tour to Portugal, rowing camps in Belgium and Norway, winter walking in Scotland, ski trip to the Alps – plenty of opportunities to do good and see the world.

Boarding: With boarding all is possible – full (starts in year 9), weekly and part time. Four of the five houses include day and boarding pupils – three for boys and one for girls. The majority of boarders are from overseas (plus Forces children) – most from Hong Kong, mainland China and Germany – and room allocations mix nationalities. Each house, located along a street outside the main campus, has studies (shared or single), common rooms, kitchen and leisure facilities, and have had some refurbishment. The boarding provision was graded good in the last inspection – a relaxed atmosphere, flexible eating arrangements on Sundays, plenty of activities. Good range of food (we can recommend the

In the past the bass player in an obscure Liverpudlian rock band, as well as pursuing the ancient martial art of jiu–jitsu to black belt level

home-made veg soup), but boarders we met wanted a more substantial meal later in the evening, after their sports training.

Background and atmosphere: One of oldest schools in the country – goes back to Cardinal Langley's re-founding of Durham Cathedral in 1414; at the end of the last century became more or less independent of the dean and chapter. Originally situated on Palace Green, next to the cathedral; moved to present site on other side of River Wear, 1844, only five minutes' walk from city centre.

The entrance to the school provides an attractive glimpse of the site – though there is no time to enjoy it if arriving at break times. Hordes of pupils stream across the car park on the way to their houses, seemingly oblivious to any car navigating its way to the tightly packed parking bays.

Once stationary, just enjoy the view; mellow sandstone buildings flank grassy lawns leading to the hill that ascends to the chapel. The 98 steps all commemorate old boys who died in the two world wars. On Remembrance Day the whole school lines the stairs at twilight, holding candles, while a wreath is laid on the memorial plaque, which must be very moving. Stunning view of viaduct, cathedral and school from the top. The 1926 traditional chapel has pews etched with the names of all leavers.

Further up is the Astroturf and beyond, up again, are rugby pitches. You need to be pretty fit just to get to them, let alone train and play. The sports hall and sixth form centre can be found in this vicinity after passing the quirky classics building.

There is a real feel of a traditional rural boarding school, with lovely views of sports fields and gardens containing many mature trees. Although the majority of the pupils don't board (day ends at 6pm), each has a house where they have common rooms and their own space to retreat to before and after school and during breaks in the day. Registration is held here each morning with the houseparent and there are strong bonds between fellow house members.

Girls were introduced into the sixth form in 1985 and Durham became fully co-educational in 1998. Girls feel that there has been a move in recent years to fully integrate them in what is now a true co-educational setting. They are outnumbered 2:1 by the boys, but feel 'very comfortable with the balance,' having single sex houses.

There is a strong sense of community and leadership opportunities with house captains and monitors (prefects) who are now selected through written application and interview.

Chapel plays a central role in school life with three assemblies a week. There are also strong links to the cathedral with services and concerts held there. Various school councils and pupils told us that they feel their voices are heard. A parent told us that 'The school finds where the individual can develop and works with it'. Not only discovering academic, sporting or musical latent talent but 'developing confident individuals with great self belief'. Parents like the house system, providing 'ever greater maturity and acceptance of responsibility' to pupils – and the competition too, 'They all get very involved'.

Pastoral care, well-being and discipline: Pastoral care centred on form tutor and house staff, plus chaplain – rated outstanding by inspection, which glowed about relationships in general and moral and social development. Bullying not seen as a problem – pupils we met felt should it occur, it would be dealt with quickly and effectively (school would exclude if necessary), anti-cyber-bullying policy devised by staff and pupils. There is a clear escalation of staff to speak to about any problems, academic or pastoral. Pupils we met told us that they knew who they were and would be happy to talk to a number.

There is a real feel of a traditional rural boarding school, with lovely views of sports fields and gardens. Majority don't board, but each has a house with their own space

Senior prefects and school and house monitors support younger pupils – 'It's a very caring environment: the house system works very well'. A sixth former who joined in year 12 from a state school spoke of how quickly he had been integrated into friendship groups 'who conducted themselves so differently' from his previous school.

New children have an acquaintance day in the summer term before entry, an induction day just before term starts and a 'buddy' in their house when they arrive. Prep school pupils will also have used the senior school facilities regularly and visited for a day in year 5.

Pupils and parents: At 11, about half from prep school, most of rest from state primaries; at 13 and 16 from a range of state and independent schools. Many of day and weekly boarding pupils from within or close to Durham, others from as far as Sunderland, Newcastle or Darlington. A range of ethnic and financial backgrounds but mostly professional or self-employed.

Plenty of contact with generally satisfied parents – weekly e-letter, website, academic diaries, meetings, a parents' forum. Forthcoming, well-mannered, confident pupils. Proud of their school and appreciative of what they have gained; one boy told us, 'I often wonder what person I would be now if I hadn't been at Durham'. Certainly, new sixth formers joining from local secondaries are bowled over by the collegiality, welcome and attitude to learning.

Entrance: At 11+: short tests in English, mathematics and VR; 13+: all have to take tests in English and mathematics plus short interview. Above average ability but a wide range. Sixth form entrants need five GCSEs at B or above with a minimum C in mathematics and English; also by interview and school report.

If overseas applicants can't sit the entrance exam, they can get in with a school reference, but need a good level of English – for sixth form need level 5.5 IELTS. Some stay in sixth for three years – special programme for first year. Has top rated tier 4 boarding sponsors' licence.

Exit: A small number leaves at the end of year 11 for vocational courses or jobs and a few at the end of year 12, after some more maturing. Northern redbrick and 'new' universities favourite, north and south of the border: Newcastle, and Northumbria top choices, Edinburgh, St Andrews, Sheffield, York, Liverpool and Durham popular. A few to Oxbridge – three in 2015 – and US universities sneaking in. Wide range of subjects: civil and chemical engineering popular choices as well, as business, biomedical sciences and psychology, plus a few medics and lawyers.

Money matters: Various academic, music, drama, art and sports awards, at 11+ and 13+, with organ scholarship and Burkitt scholarships and exhibitions added on at 16+. Sibling, Forces and clergy discounts. About 150 pupils have means-tested assistance and 105 non-means-tested admissions scholarships of a maximum of £1,000.

Remarks: A sense of community and history binds the pupils together, underpinned by the strong house system for day and boarding pupils alike. Work in progress on the academic front, but produces well-rounded, confident young people, who have opportunities to develop a wide range of talents to a high level in a supportive, peaceful and very attractive environment.

Fettes College

Carrington Road, Edinburgh EH4 1QX

01313 116744
admissions@fettes.com
www.fettes.com

Ages: 13–18 (junior boarding from 7)
Pupils: 561; sixth form: 258
Boarders: 422 full (plus 53 in prep)
Day: £24,375 pa
Boarding: £31,245 pa

Headmaster: Since 1998, Mr Michael C B Spens MA (60s), educated at Marlborough and Selwyn College Cambridge, where he read natural sciences. Came to Fettes after five years as head of Caldicott, having previously spent 20 years at Radley, where he was housemaster and taught geology, after a short spell in business. The transition between junior and senior schools is always an interesting one, but Mr Spens has weathered his double change with charm and élan – one might say nonchalance, but that would be harsh, and misleading; quarter is not easily found here: there is a tightly-wound spring beneath the cultivated appearance of charm and relaxation. Expect zero tolerance on the drugs front, 'The students don't want it around', and the Fettesian druggy alcy image no longer makes headlines in the Scottish press. Fettes is challenging all-comers as Scotland's school of choice, surprisingly, even on the day front, 'And we're more expensive than the others,' says the head – but then we are talking Edinburgh (think mink and nae knickers). Married to Debbie, they have three young children (one at Fettes, one on a gap year and one at university) and a much-loved labrador ('Kiwi,

because she's all black'). Charismatic, vibrant, fun. Fettes and Mr Spens are zinging. Currently forefront of the campaign to keep Scottish independent schools' charitable status and all over the Sunday papers.

Leaving in July 2017.

Academic matters: Almost all heads of departments have changed during the past few years – 'new young staff', 'very good', 'strong', 'Edinburgh is a strong draw'; and, having played the Scottish versus the English system along with all the other big players, added the IB in 2006. Pupils can choose whether they want to specialise, therefore do A levels (2015: 77 per cent A*-B, 45 per cent A*/A) – or take the broader IB syllabus: excellent results – average score 39. At GCSE, 70 per cent A*/A grades.

Three sciences on offer throughout, plus trad French, German and Spanish, as well as Mandarin (available for beginners as well as for native speakers). No particular bias – physics, chemistry, history and geography outstanding at GCSE level, maths and English almost equally strong; results in all disciplines equally impressive at A level. Art results outstanding throughout the school. Tranche of outstanding French GCSEs taken early. Strong tradition of classics; government and politics and history of art available at A level. Broad range of subjects, but not the biggest take up at A level in langs, classics or further maths.

Foreign pupils with minimal English are no longer accepted willy-nilly, unless they happen to be particularly bright or have siblings in the school. EFL is on hand, but pupils who don't have 'a pretty good working knowledge of English' are encouraged to do an English lang course before they arrive (Edinburgh School of English is popular).

Has weathered his double change with charm and élan – one might say nonchalance, but that would be harsh, and misleading; quarter is not easily found here

Good staff:pupil ratio. 'Computers zooming ahead' – wireless networked throughout, with all senior school students having their own laptop.

Games, options, the arts: Wide range of opportunity for games. 'Rugby is strong, though no longer a religion' (73 blues to date). Needle matches with Glenalmond and Merchiston on the rugby field and Strathallan in hockey. Lacrosse impressive, girls play hockey and netball as well; sixth form not forced to play team games at all – 20+ other sports including swimming and aerobics also available. Big sports centre and swimming pool providing a wide range of other sports, old pool now an exam hall/ceilidh and disco area.

Music 'a huge strength' with loads of bands, orchestras, three choirs and a string quartet etc etc, two popular concerts in spring and autumn plus carol service all in aid of charity. Keen drama with imaginative productions, pupils often perform at the Edinburgh Festival (and win awards). Frankenstein the most recent production with over 100 pupils involved. New art centre in pipeline (still) and 'very inspirational head of art' (another one, if you follow) recently appointed. Pipe band popular. CCF, community service, D of E etc. Masses of trips, everywhere, for everything.

Boarding: Two prep school and eight senior school houses, all single sex, for day and boarding pupils, with tutors attached. New posho boarding house – Craigleith, dead modern – to accommodate the expanded sixth form, which is due to increase by 25 per cent. The sixth form centre houses 125 upper sixth pupils in two identical wings (surely

this should be 126 or 124?) each with their own individual room and provides a transition between the disciplines of school and uni with pupils being able to cook their own meals if they want to.

Background and atmosphere: William Fettes (later Sir William), the son of an Edinburgh grocer, made his fortune during the Napoleonic Wars when 'he became Scotland's leading contractor for provisions for the army'; his only son died in 1815, and William in 1836. Whilst he had originally intended to found a hospital, he later 'decided to create a school for orphans and the needy'; and – after prudent investment – the trustees decided that with £166,000 in the kitty, there were enough funds to acquire land, and both build and endow a school: Fettes opened in 1870 with 200 boys.

Vast Grimms' fairy tale of a building, turreted and with acres of wood panelling and shiny black floors (are they granite or stone flag underneath the tarry surface?) purpose-built in 1870 by Bryce. Part of the main building still has the original steam-driven heating which starts up twice a day with alarming groans and wheezes – ripe for the engineering museum, methinks.

Various Victorian edifices scattered about the school's wonderful 90 acre grounds plonk in the middle of Edinburgh. 'School uses Edinburgh much more now,' says the head. Spectacular development after school sold 'redundant' acres to build Fettes Village, a collection of neat little boxes which splits the games field and provided the cash for much-needed expansion. The collection of new and converted buildings that house the new prep department are much bigger than they look from the outside, an example of space well used, and about to be extended. Currently in process of building Fettes North – new block that will house 25

classrooms plus music school, art school, history of art building and sixth form studio and workshop.

The school has gradually metamorphosed from famous trad boys' school to genuinely co-ed. The flavour has changed from home-grown Scots to more exotic (school says '75 per cent UK, 15 per cent British expats, 10 per cent foreign nationals with over 40 countries represented in this').

Pastoral care, well-being and discipline: Despite colourful stories in the Edinburgh press in past years – drugs, booze, etc, grossly overstated, says the head – there is a clear framework of discipline that is well understood by all. This is a school with a zero tolerance policy on drugs. Edinburgh is the drugs capital of the north and running a school in the middle of it is no joke. Under-age drinking is an acknowledged problem. Three tier system on the discipline side: housemaster/deputy head/head = rustication/formal warning and suspension or expulsion. Ditto smoking. Very clear house-visiting rules – no overt demonstrations of affection; bonking equals out. And yes, they do lose the occasional pupil for all these misdemeanours, ditto bullying. Strong anti-bullying ethos. Prefects very responsible – imaginative anti-bullying code involves culprits writing down what they must or must not do and signing it. Expulsion is always an option.

Pupils and parents: School topped up with many non-Brits in the bad old days, now the mix is veering more towards the British norm but still collections of exotic foreigners – Russians, Chinese, Japanese, Americans, Ukrainians, but fewer Bulgarians than previously. Increasing numbers of locals and Scots from all over. 'Pupils from 40 different countries, East European connection sadly dropping off.' Very strong old Fettesian stream, plus loads of first-time buyers, intellectuals etc etc. Good vibrant mix. Old Fettesians include John de Chastelaine, Ian McLeod, James Bond, Tilda Swinton, Lord Woolf and Tony Blair – remembered fondly for 'his acting ability'!

Entrance: CE or school's own exam for those not coming from UK preps. Approx 40 students a year join the sixth form after GCSE elsewhere, currently much sought after as pupils pile in from other, mainly Scottish, schools.

Exit: Hardly any leave post-GCSE. Most to university – Aberdeen, Durham, Edinburgh, Exeter, Glasgow, King's College London, Manchester, Newcastle, St Andrews, Warwick (seven Oxbridge places) to study eg engineering, English, maths or law.

Money matters: Well-endowed with scholarships including academic, music, sports, all-rounder, piping, art, up to 10 per cent of fees. Also means-tested bursaries: 'The level of these awards depend upon parents' financial means and can cover up to the full value of the fees'.

Special (Todd) bursaries for Old Fettesians, 12.5 per cent discount for Forces (not so many of these around). However risks being stripped of charitable status by the Scottish Charity Regulator if it does not make fees more affordable for lower income families.

Remarks: Undoubtedly the strongest school in Edinburgh – possibly riding too high? To quote one governor, 'It is better to have a challenge, otherwise we become complacent'. Head adds, 'No danger of becoming complacent; the most dangerous thing in a school is to stand still.' Exciting cosmopolitan mix in an exciting city.

Giggleswick School

Giggleswick, Settle, North Yorkshire BD24 0DE

01729 893000
enquiries@giggleswick.org.uk
www.giggleswick.org.uk
C of E

Ages: 11–18 (junior boarding from 7)
Pupils: 385; sixth form: 135
Boarders: 100 boys/66 girls full, 67 flexi; 10 full junior
Day: £17,313 – £21,321 pa
Boarding: £20,229 – £31,134 pa

Headmaster: Since September 2014, Mark Turnbull MA, previously deputy head of Eastbourne College. Studied geography at Liverpool University and did an MA in London; taught geography at Sevenoaks, where he was also head of department, housemaster and head of boarding. An active hockey, cricket and rugby coach, he has led charity and international projects. Married with three children.

Academic matters: In 2015, 49 per cent A*/A grades at GCSE and 34 per cent at A level (60 per cent A*/B). Improved academic standards 'spectacular with the same intake', due to personalised learning, with setting in French, maths, science and humanities, focused learning support and 'aspire' programme for gifted and talented. Combined with individual monthly assessment of effort and attainment measured against targets, with tutor sessions to motivate further improvement. All available online to pupil and parents, together with full reports three times a year. Success breeds success and has allowed the school to turn down the odd pupil.

Broad curriculum with separate sciences and a taste of three modern foreign languages and Latin in year 7, reducing to two language subjects by year 9. Choice of 19 GCSE subjects – usually nine or 10 taken. Committed staff, a blend of age and experience who 'provide inspiration to the pupils and are very positive and caring'. 'A pretty impressive bunch' a general view from parents, articulated by one. Small class sizes, less than 20, and significantly smaller groups, down to four pupils, study a selection of the 22 A level courses offered. Sixth form enrichment through the EPQ plus Open University YASS modules – offered alongside A levels for those who require stretch and challenge. Most interests and abilities catered for though those wanting to pursue purely vocational courses are directed elsewhere at 16. No massaging of results here – if you study for a subject you sit the exam. 'Failure not necessarily a bad thing,' says school. 'Sometimes it can provide a much needed wake-up call.'

Special educational needs support tailored to individual need and provided through support in the classroom on the whole. Full time special educational needs co-ordinator and successful buddy system where older children with experience of a learning difficulty mentor younger ones. EFL provided (two to four lessons a week), one-to-one, in study periods, but anyone arriving from abroad must have a basic level of English.

No massaging of results here – if you study for a subject you sit the exam. 'Failure is not necessarily a bad thing. Sometimes it can provide a much-needed wake-up call'

Lots of computers, including some in each boarding house; every pupil has email and a computer link in their study bedroom.

Games, options, the arts: Rugby, cricket, cross-country and hockey loom large in the (very full) fixture list. International coaching over the past few years has led to such success that the school has had to drop traditional fixtures in search of more competition. With impressive investment in indoor and outdoor sports facilities almost any and every sporting interest is covered. Seven hard and three grass courts, together with the opportunity to train in Portugal, ensure continued popularity of tennis.

Keen drama started by Russell Harty – several OGs and some pupils active in the profession, but luvvies and their tantrums not tolerated. The

Richard Whiteley Theatre, named after the late TV presenter, who was an old boy and governor, provides a suitable and flexible venue for such recent diverse productions as We Will Rock You and Alice in Wonderland.

Art and design taken seriously – a real strength with good facilities across the disciplines, resident artist changing annually, impressively ambitious design work allowing some pupils to skip university foundation courses.

A third of pupils learn an instrument (some play professionally), heavenly chapel choir and lots of bands regularly tour home and abroad. Plenty of opportunity to perform in front of a home crowd with a programme including recitals, concerts and annual rock concert, not to mention the fiercely contested 'themed' inter-house Singing and Speaking competition.

CCF compulsory in year 10, those that carry on can gain silver and gold D of E awards and earn an additional four A/A* GCSEs through the CVQO Public Services BTec scheme, in addition to military qualifications. Making the most of its glorious Dales location, outdoor pursuits activities abound; conservation projects and all the usual opportunities too.

Boarding: Seven houses – four boys', two girls', one junior (years 7 and 8 together with junior school boarders). Different character to each of the boys' houses (not surprising with 500 years of history), not so for the girls. All pupils allocated a bed, room mates usually a mix of day and boarding. Small dorms for years 7 and 8, study bedrooms for years 9 and up, shared until year 11 (boys) or sixth form (girls). Senior house staff tutor years 7-10, with pupils choosing their tutors from year 11. Exeats – four a term.

The boarding houses we visited were comfortably furnished and in good order though the boys'

Attractive buildings overlook Giggleswick village beneath the fabulously restored chapel, complete with landmark copper dome, a fitting reward for the walk

evidenced more wear and tear. Rooms were reassuringly 'lived in', personalised with posters, photos, soft toys and general clutter. 'Keep calm and carry on' seems to be the universal mantra. Sixth formers play an important role in the smooth running of the house and are rewarded with single rooms. Year 9 prep is done in separate study areas and monitored by sixth formers. Common rooms, displaying fine examples of residents' art, are filled with squashy sofas, board games, puzzles, a Wii, DVDs and music. Strict rules on TV watersheds but Saturday night is film night.

Background and atmosphere: Set in the western margins of the magnificent Yorkshire Dales beneath an imposing limestone escarpment, 60 minutes' drive north of Manchester and Leeds (so the brochure says). Founded in 1512, moved to present site in 1869. Attractive buildings overlook Giggleswick village beneath the fabulously restored chapel, complete with landmark copper dome, a fitting reward for the walk up the steep hill.

Immaculate and comfortably sized school campus (big enough to be roomy, small enough to retain a real sense of community) with a calming oasis of lawn in its midst. Happy, relaxed but purposeful atmosphere, knots of pupils engaged in conversation amongst themselves or with staff. Polite and smiling welcome from everyone; a real sense of community.

Promotes a real 'can do' philosophy, encouragement and support for pupils to have a go at anything and everything. Evening prep, activities, clubs, house events, rehearsals and sports practices mean it's a 12 hour school day, with little respite on Saturdays. All the pupils we spoke to seemed to thrive on it, though Sunday evening chapel was popular for the lie in it provided. Not surprisingly, day pupils opt to use their bed in their boarding house on occasions – for a fee.

Recent sympathetic development has included the Richard Whitely theatre, sports halls, all weather pitch, upgrade to classroom facilities and at the heart of the school, the wonderful Sharpe library, where there's always a buzz of activity. IT suite and internet café are popular venues for nightly prep.

All meals eaten in the modern dining hall (cafeteria system, separate sittings, lots of choice and pupil endorsement that the food is good). Boarders can supplement with toast, hot drinks and other snacks they prepare in the house kitchenettes (girls' facilities more extensive than boys' – surprise, surprise).

Sixth form centre with bar on the edge of the main campus– current cohort trying to find ways to make it more 'happening'. Alcohol allowed at weekends but consumption strictly monitored.

Pastoral care, well-being and discipline: Parents see pastoral care supported by medical centre, school doctor and chaplain as a major strength. They describe pastoral care as 'fantastic', 'the staff are dedicated and genuinely care about the children'. Correspondingly, there are no significant pupil behaviour problems, though lack of accessibility to temptation in this rural location may help. Chapel is an integral and important part of the school but faith more important than denomination and appreciated by a number of parents who believe 'it adds a special personal spiritual experience'.

Thorough drugs checks (this is no-nonsense Yorkshire) – sniffer dogs brought in termly; compulsory drugs testing used on known and suspected offenders and anyone dealing faces immediate expulsion. Smokers required to attend cessation clinics.

More traffic from boys to girls' houses, visits welcomed but permission must be sought to move away from public areas. Behaviour between sexes 'should not cause embarrassment to anyone'. Staff vigilant for anorexia and similar – system in place to check on pupils suspected of skipping meals, including height/weight monitoring and meal attendance cards.

Art and design taken seriously – a real strength with good facilities across the disciplines, resident artist changing annually, impressively ambitious design work

School engenders a non-bullying culture and staff vigilant for anything that may make a child feel isolated. Sixth formers charged to look out for anyone feeling wobbly. House masters maintain good communication links with parents.

Pupils and parents: Some 55 per cent fully board, the rest are local children from a large catchment area; school transport system. Numbers stable though reduction in boarding. Recession has seen families release property equity by moving to the area – children remain as day pupils; parent commutes to work. Healthy 60:40 ratio boys to girls. School fully

co-ed since 1983. Seventeen per cent overseas, 16 per cent expats and Forces – popular with all these. Parents in business and the professions. OGs: James Agate; Richard Whiteley; William Gaunt; Sarah Fox. OG society well established on the internet.

Rooms were reassuringly lived in, personalised with posters, photos, soft toys and general clutter. 'Keep calm and carry on' seems to be the universal mantra

Entrance: Not a great problem – at age 11 Giggleswick entrance exam, at age 13 normally CE together with interview and previous school's report. Entrance into sixth form is by a minimum of five GCSEs at grade B; around 35 new sixth form entrants per year. Giggleswick Junior School, the main feeder for Giggleswick at age 11, shares campus.

Exit: Around 15 per cent leave after GCSEs. Sixth formers to a range of mostly northern universities; three to Oxford in 2015. Others to eg Bath, LSE, St Andrews, York, Leeds, Manchester, Newcastle, Durham, Edinburgh, Warwick, Central St Martins.

Money matters: Scholarships and exhibitions for academic, all round achievement, sport and music are awarded at 11+, 13+ and sixth form, with art at 13+ and sixth form and sixth form only design, drama. There are 15-20 awards annually, ranging in value from 10-50 per cent of fees a year, the majority for 20-25 per cent. Means-tested bursaries can increase fee reduction to 75 per cent for scholars who could not otherwise take up an offered place. School has benefited from large gifts from OG Norman Sharpe and more recently Graham Watson (late governor).

Remarks: An 'all round' education with support and encouragement across a spectrum of academic and extracurricular activity, for any willing to take on the challenge. It is a warm and welcoming school with no sign of snobbishness (as you would expect in Yorkshire); secure in its strong moral foundations. As one of our guides said, 'you just have to be prepared to give everything a try, and if you fall out of line there's always someone to help pick you up.'

Glenalmond College

Glenalmond, Perth PH1 3RY

01738 842000
registrar@glenalmondcollege.co.uk
www.glenalmondcollege.co.uk

Ages: 12–18
Pupils: 388; sixth form: 164
Boarders: 180 boys/134 girls full
Day: £15,990 – £21,315 pa
Boarding: £23,445 – £31,290 pa

Warden: Since September 2015, Ms Elaine Logan, previously deputy head at Loretto. Born in Perth; read English at Edinburgh; spent 14 years at Dollar Academy before moving to Loretto, where taught English, drama and PSHCE, was a housemistress and recently child protection officer and acting head. A trained singer with a wide range of musical interests and experiences including solo singing in jazz and dance bands, she has three children.

Academic matters: Follows the English system. Only. An astonishing 24 subjects on offer at A level, including ancient history, DT and PE. No current Greek scholars; but Latin-ists, Russian and Dutch candidates. A few of musicians, and, as ever, one taking music technology (one – 'one of the relatively few schools to offer this as an examined subject'). Several presentations in French. Pleasing number of candidates in the usual suspects – maths, English, history, and geography the strongest both in candidates and success, though the odd D creeps in. Economics popular, government and politics available. Science strong – science and maths block is awkwardly placed on the slope

to the north of the main complex and connected at various levels, the traditional build-it-by-numbers confection we see so often, with tubular rails and bog standard three-level classrooms. Some excellent science results, but school still leans towards the arts; religious studies A level equals philosophy and ethics. DT rather the poor relation. Suspect the syllabus may be in a state of change – it can't make sense to present so few candidates in so many subjects in not a very large school, which is what we said last time too. In 2015, 31 per cent A*/A grades at A level and 53 per cent at GCSE.

Setting in the third year – core subjects still set individually, four sets. Loads of class related trips. Recent timetable revision resulted in longer lessons and a fortnightly rotation.

New heads of art, chemistry, English, lang, maths, geography, biology, history of art and learning support; collection of buzzy young staff around, though still one or two who reckon that teaching at Glenalmond is 'a way of life'. Contractually, staff must live on site (now allowed to live off site for three years before retiring), which makes it more difficult to get part-timers.

Two computer suites tick the boxes; internet access in houses (nannynet, intranet, wireless), 10-fold increase in broadband speed. Fibre optics, JANET, two networks throughout school, Apple and PCs, computers in classrooms. Laptops all over the place. Software used to detect fraud with pupils downloading coursework from elsewhere (does it work, we wonder?).

All screened on entry. Dyslexia support represented at meetings of heads of departments. Certified ed psych's report needed for extra time in exams; SENCo and three fully trained dyslexia staff, plus classroom assistant – 'strategies for life as well as time management'; can deal with most of the dys-strata – 'loads of one-to-one lessons', dedicated learning support room. Prep club more or less acts as a drop-in centre for instant help, from prefects as well as contactable tutors ('we can knock on most doors at any time' said one sixth former.)

Originally dubbed the scholars club, exclusively for scholars and exhibitioners, the William Bright Society (WBS) runs both a lecture series (open to all including parents) and a thinking series – variety of erudite texts: this year by Hobbes, Locke, JJ Rousseau, Paine, Declaration of Independence etc: read, digest, discuss. WBS now attracts a wider base, with nominees from form takers/housemasters (this editor was flattered to be asked but wasn't quite sure she was up for 'induction and pseudoscience'). Additional programmes include long term academic planning, Oxbridge prep, and research programmes with local unis.

Most of the male chauvinists are now a thing of the past (we hope).

Games, options, the arts: Half term letter summer a couple of years back announced that because of 'ealth and safety considerations, needle rugby matches with Strath and the like were to be abandoned (well, school had lost comprehensively that year 79-0 to Strath, 52-7 to Loretto, and 67-0 to George Watsons). Certain amount of grief amongst the rugger bugger fathers: relief for mothers. We understood, from a prep source, that the aforementioned schools had been known to 'educate' hefty chaps from the southern hemisphere during the rugby months in the northern hemisphere and vice versa; and that the Strath team weighed more than the Scottish one. Watch this space.

Boys' hockey coming up fast, girls' hockey and lacrosse strong, ditto tennis and netball. Sports are a key part of life here and daily participation is compulsory (the constitutionally disinclined can get by with a spot of umpiring), regular interruption by vile weather. Rich in all-weather, spectacularly floodlit pitches. School majors in outdoor pursuits activities and uses its site to good advantage – all sorts of activities: conservation projects, Munro Club, full-bore shooting as well as clays, indoor and outdoor .22 range, Scottish Islands Peaks Race, skiing with regular trips to freezing Glenshee (a number of past and current members of Scottish ski teams – own artificial ski slope was 'ealth and safety-ed), curling a not too surprising newcomer, own nine hole golf course at Cairnies (golf scholarship), sailing. Several gold D of E assessors on staff – hugely popular option, with trips to Norway and the more rugged parts of the USA. Fishing (on the River Almond).

Sports are a key part of life here and daily participation is compulsory (the constitutionally disinclined can get by with a spot of umpiring), regular interruption by vile weather

Terrific CCF (Coll has strong army links) – fifth form CCF (both sexes) now an option but compulsory in fourth form, regular camps throughout term popular ('important to be serious about it,' said our 15 year old guide; 'looks good on your CV, and helps with your D of E'). Oy? We think skool should be fun. Strong emphasis on leadership training: more cadets for officer training from Glenalmond than any other school in Scotland. Granny bashing, or community service, for non-militant sixths. mass of add-ons: chainsaw course, first aid at work; food hygiene course (essential if you want to work in food industry in the hols). Masses of charitable fundraising: 100 mile sponsored walks. That sort of thing.

New head of art has two splendid pics of his own on the wall. Ok, early in the year, but we were less

than convinced by either the layout of the department, nor the pupil work. Some ceramics to die for. Computer links with the outside world. Life class.

Imaginative drama with musicals top of the pops. Recent refurbishment and remodelling of the theatre. Costa coffee shop in theatre foyer (and jolly good it was too).

Strong music assisted by new chapel organ: we just missed choir practice. Resident vicar looks strangely '70s and could do with a haircut. Two pipe bands, which hotshot on the charity front: played at Lords for England/Australia International.

Boarding: This proper boys' boarding school took girls at sixth form in 1990 (last ditch saloon) went 'all the way' in 1995; admissions now running 50/50. Currently five boys' boarding houses and three for girls (45 per cent girls).

New boys' boarding house, Skrines (old one has been converted into learning support centre), one of the smartest houses we have seen in a long time – 'the largest single investment in the school's history' – providing bedroom and communal accommodation that the school claims is 'comparable with the best in Britain' (which has to be QE). Decent-sized single rooms and huge four bedrooms for the youngest with good wide corridors – still blighted by the site of the garage: according to the bursar at the time, housemasters wanted garages close to the house: sure, but housemasters' wives would prefer a view from the kitchen.

Architect obviously took his eye off the ball – the showers – nasty plastic sort of triangular things – are rapidly showing signs of wear (well, boys will swing from the shower rails). Ditto the silly islands in the Brew rooms – most now gone. The lighting in the Brew rooms is sensor controlled, which makes television viewing and film nights a health and

Prep club acts as drop-in centre for instant help, from prefects as well as contactable tutors ('we can knock on most doors at any time')

safety hazard. (Ladders required to baffle the sensors – geddit? Ladder climbing not allowed.)

Fifth form girls (ie GCSE year) move to a previous boys' house, Cairnies (now upgraded), quite distant from the main campus, adjacent to the golf course – same architect. The aforementioned showers, whilst in better heart, are too small for girls to wash their hair in (think about it); they much prefer to use the old fashioned (which school thought had been abandoned) five bath, power shower room in the basement instead.

The double bedrooms are smaller than cabins in steerage on a not very good shipping line – not enough space for a rabbit to work, far less girls studying for their GCSEs, though, in mitigation, it has one of the best common rooms we have seen. We await developments with interest. This had to be the worst million pounds spent anywhere. School maintained 'this is an unreasonable remark, as the overwhelming reaction from girls and their parents to the accommodation in Cairnies' (no bedrooms on the ground floor, bars on ground floor windows, deserted at night! Scary stuff) 'has been wholly positive.' Not from my contacts it ain't, and if it is so powerfully appreciated, why are there plans to turn it vertical?

Boys and girls mix socially during the day and after prep in school, but not in each others' houses, although moves are afoot for each house to have a co-ed common room for limited access. Sixth form bar on Saturdays; Scotland is unique in that sixth formers are allowed access to booze plus grub under 'well monitored circumstances'.

Glenalmond is remote – (school sez 'only an hour from the centre of Edinburgh': this ex-racing driver-trained ed has never done it in that time) and rather set apart from the world – you can't just wander round at will. Shopping bus to Perth twice a week, in house tuck shops, with variable hours. Fixed exeats on either side of half term – 'Parents have free and welcome access to their children at any time and can take them out on Saturdays and Sundays (after chapel)'.

We toured Goodacre's. Pupils graduate from individual tables in prep room – overseen by prefect – to desks in their dorms, and one lucky fourth form dorm had four beds, two showers, two basins and a loo – how's that for ensuite? At age 14? Pupils can use the clothes washing machines when matron doesn't need them (sock bags). Good games/

telly room, book case in corner bung full of books, DVDs, games. Housemaster, previously in the real world with Price Waterhouse, has written the seminal IB text book on business and economics, professional tutor with the uni of Buckingham, laments the little uptake he has from pupils who want to study economics and business studies. This is a waste of opportunity and yet school/GSG website indicates that many current students are indeed going down that line.

Background and atmosphere: Known to the pupils as Coll. Founded in 1847 by Prime Minister Gladstone, Scotland's oldest, most elegant school. Spectacular self-contained quad with cloisters, centred on the chapel (with its surprising spiral staircase) set in immaculate 300 acre estate surrounded by some of the smartest grouse shooting in Scotland. Several modern additions stuck round the back, including Basil Spence music block, science and maths block. Gorgeous library (chapel of learning, 'natch), well stocked (real old collection as well as lots of modern stuff) inviting armchairs; media area downstairs. Jemma Pearson bronze of Gladstone. The mixed sixth form common room was crowded, noisy and relaxed.

Spectacular self-contained quad with cloisters, set in immaculate 300 acre estate, surrounded by some of the smartest grouse shooting in Scotland

Informative school prospectus (an earlier prospectus could have been a VisitScotland guide to Perthshire, not at all the sort of thing to impress grannies, who might well end up footing the bill); jolly handy supplement goes into enormous detail. Weekends said to be more organised. Boy and girl joint heads of college, which scares the pants off OGs.

Magical dining room with good buffet hot/cold – we had a delightful chicken tikka. Interestingly, there is a hospital-type antiseptic hand wipe machine at the exit to the dining room; most used it, but shouldn't it have been at the entrance? Apparently there are 'also three at the entrance to the dining hall'; we must have missed them.

Pastoral care, well-being and discipline: Previous high jinks some time ago have resulted in a massively impressive, tightly worded code of behaviour which covers everything from cycling without a helmet to public displays of affection between pupils, as well as extensive drugs etc document – 'Smoking is a major social gateway to the smoking of illegal drugs. The

College may regard persistent tobacco smoking as a reason for asking parents and pupils to agree to future drug testing'. These documents are unique in our experience and we are slightly concerned that sometimes alleged offences may be judged in black and white – the HMI boarding report was rather fazed by it too. Pupils and parents 'receive a copy of the Code of Behaviour Expectations, Encouragement and Sanctions'. We didn't.

Basically: random drugs testing on suspicion, out if positive; smoking equals house gating, warden's gating and letters home, followed by suspension. Smoking in a building equals suspension even for the first time. Drinking to excess in permitted zones equals warden's gating, followed by bans and possible suspension, no spirits allowed in the (local) recognized pubs and watering holes. No bringing alcohol back to school under any circumstances. Local keepers still complain about empties and other detritus on the neighbouring grouse moor. (We like a tad of spirit!)

No reported bullying – head of boarding both neutral and approachable. Anorexia said to be less of a problem – couple of girls under watchful eye, but nothing serious. Jury still out on how to deal with cyberbullying (trolling).

Pupils and parents: Scotland's school for toffs – 'Jolly nice parents' says the school. Traditionally, Scottish upper middle and middle class, army, Highland families. About 20 per cent locals and 21 per cent foreigners from all over, plus seven per cent expats. All real foreigners must have guardians, via parents or contacts, or school will fix 'em up with guardianship agencies 'with whom we have worked successfully in the past'. EAL in place. Number of first time buyers, though trad parents are coming back in handfuls. Girls float daily in tweed jackets and black skirts, and long tartan kiltettes for best; chaps have moved from grey shirts to white, and look a tad like refugees from the local state school with their often outgrown grey bags and blazers. Tweed coats for sixth form only. Full kilt with short tweed jacket for best. Second hand shop.

This is seven day a week boarding; the 50 day boys and girls stay to 6pm most nights and 9pm on Wednesdays, Saturday morning school with match play if required in the afternoons; odd bed available – up to 15 a term at 20 quid a night. More ecumenical than an Episcopalian foundation might imply – 20 per cent Catholic, who are prepared for confirmation, plus Church of Scotland.

FPs (known as OGs) a generous bunch, include Sandy Gall, Robbie Coltrane, Miles Kington, Allan Massie, David Sole and Andrew MacDonald (Trainspotting fame), Adair Turner (former chairman of FSA) Charlie (Lord) Falconer, erstwhile flatmate of Tony Blair – who was at arch-rival school: Fettes.

Entrance: Own entrance exam at 12, most at 13+ via CE, oodles from Belhaven, Ardvreck, Craigclowan, St Mary's Melrose, Malsis and Aysgarth, with a clutch from Cargilfield, Mowden etc, as well as state primaries or overseas. Entrance not a difficult hurdle at the moment ('academic threshold 50 per cent'). Department heads visit primaries/preps and do 'fun experiments' pour encourager.

Sixth form intake need six passes at national five or GCSE or entrance test and previous school's recommendation; a number from Germany.

Exit: Hardly any leave post GCSEs. School has been assiduous in filling in our bits and bobs online, a great help, and unusual. Majority to university or some form of higher education – Glasgow, Edinburgh, Exeter and Newcastle popular, ditto Forces. Three to Oxbridge in 2015.

Money matters: Discounts for siblings of 25 per cent, a whopping 50 per cent for fourth child, 10 per cent for children whose parents are in the Forces and Fil Cler bursaries for offspring of the clergy. Otherwise myriads of bursaries, means-tested, from five to 100 per cent. Music (including piping), art, sport, plus all round scholarships. Latest wheeze is for individuals to sponsor deserving but needy pupils by direct giving (anonymously).

Remarks: This editor christened Glenalmond 'the Eton of the North' in our first edition: serious glitch caused downturn in numbers, girls were introduced and Glenalmond started regaining momentum. Girls now more confident (complete with rash of pearl earrings and sophisticated make-up) and altogether more girl-like – rather than honorary boys as previously. School says: 'In last HMI inspection, we were rated as excellent for improvements in performance.' Well it would, wouldn't it? We wonder why it took 10 years to turn Glenalmond back into the sort of place non-first time buyers are prepared to boast about.

Gordonstoun Junior School

Gordonstoun School, Elgin, Moray IV30 5RF

01343 837829
admissions@gordonstoun.org.uk
www.gordonstoun.org.uk

Ages: 7–13
Pupils: 92
Boarders: 31 full, 7 weekly
Day: £13,176 pa
Boarding: £21,429 pa

Linked school: Gordonstoun School

Head of the Junior School: Mr Robert McVean, BSc (40s), taught science at Aberlour House (as the junior school is called) from 2000, became head in 2003. Educated at Hurstpierpoint College, he read environmental biology at Swansea, thence five years in the state sector, followed by Edinburgh Academy. Married to Laura (bubbly and fun; she helps with SEN), two children in the school ('all been huge fun, wouldn't have changed a thing'). Looking down from our common room eyrie at children returning from games, this editor commented that a certain young man looked a tad sad – he was on his own, munching a fairy cake – 'he gets overwrought,' was the instant reply, 'he is just a little ADHD'. School wanted to remove this last comment, we prefer it remain to show just how on top of things the McVeans are.

Entrance: By assessment and interview plus report from previous school.

Dedicated scholarships for juniors, who will lose them if they don't keep up to snuff.

Exit: Nearly all to senior school.

Remarks: When we first visited this rather jolly purpose-built junior school in the grounds of Gordonstoun with self-contained classrooms and dorms all in the same building, the dorms, strategically placed on the second floor, with glorious views, were filled (and we mean over-filled) with somewhat incongruous work-station type beds. The school opened two weeks late, all the young having been sent camping for a fortnight. The demand for places exceeded expectations and four young were farmed out. Aberlour has been a runaway success, an extension was built to cope with demand for boarding places, including extra classrooms, common rooms, a large assembly hall and house-parents' accommodation. The expanded boarding

spaces are nearly full again – though in truth there is loads of room for extra beds.

Siblings of children already in the school are flocking in, often from abroad. EAL costs extra. Gordonstoun funds its own guardianship service. Parents appreciate the convenience of having all their young in the same place. Flexi and weekly boarding recently introduced. There are 100 pupils with an average of 35 or so in each weekend, which is jam-packed with activities. School day starts 8.20am, with brekky before that for day children if they turn up on time; ends at 5.35pm when day

children can go home, having done their homework. Children use senior school facilities: fleet of minibuses to main school for music, drama, games, gym, pool, which is quite a hike for small legs. 'Lab in a Lorry' parked outside when we visited to stimulate would-be scientists.

Playing fields to the west (new all-weather playing field), protected by banking from north winds, provide a haven with child-inspired woods, and customised climbing frame (and another one beside the main games pitch further east).

Gordonstoun School

Elgin, Moray IV30 5RF

01343 837837
admissions@gordonstoun.org.uk
www.gordonstoun.org.uk

Ages: 13–18
Pupils: 575; sixth form: 250
Boarders: 458 full
Day: £13,176 – £26,022 pa
Boarding: £21,492 – £35,160 pa

Linked school: Gordonstoun Junior School

Principal: Since 2011, Mr Simon Reid BA (50s), a South African who read English at the University of Witwatersrand. Came to Britain in 1985 because he 'wanted to teach English literature in the country where it was written'. Comes from Worksop College where he was deputy head, having started his UK teaching career at Brentwood School, thence Stowe, and Christ's Hospital (housemaster for six years). His wife, Michele, is French, the family bi-lingual. Two young, one at uni and t'other in sixth form at Gordonstoun.

Enthusiastic about the Round Square ethos, Reid upbraided us when we spouted our usual mantra: please could we have results by subject by number of pupils by results... with a sharp, 'for some pupils a B or a C in any subject is a triumph in itself.' We know, we know academia is not what Gordonstoun is about, but we like to trace trends. By the time they leave, 'Gordonstoun pupils should know about service, face up to challenge, be capable of leading, globally aware, resilient not arrogant', which is fine and dandy as far as it goes. Focus is useful. Perhaps it should be adopted as the sixth Gordonstoun commandment? We reiterate our editor's brief, why should anyone send a child to any school when they have no idea about the academic strengths and weaknesses of the place?

Academic matters: 'Students are here for the whole broad experience'; 'The balance is important'. Huge range of ability, from those 'at the lower end of the academic scale', to all A* candidates. 'School getting more academic', says the head. In 2015, 26 per cent A*/A grades at GCSE, 47 per cent A*-B and 24 per cent A*/A at A level. 'What is worth noticing this year is that the highest number of students achieving above their predictions, whether that is at A* level or below. This is far more important than detailed examination results and highlights the distinctiveness of our broad curriculum and ethos'. Native speakers can do A levels in their own langs. Classes setted for maths and English from 13. Networked computers throughout, wireless connection in all boarding houses. Bespoke international

School has its own 80 foot sail-training yacht, timetabled sailing weeks (when weather can be 'pretty wild', according to the skippers)

citizenship course new kid on the block, Reid takes it at top end: not PSHE or RS but 'examining real problems against a global background'. Good remedial support – all pupils screened on arrival. Will scribe for exams. EAL available at all levels.

Games, options, the arts: Community service is important at Gordonstoun. All do service training aged 16 and choose which discipline to follow: the fire brigade (the most popular), mountain rescue, coastguards, canoe life guards, ski patrol, first aid, technical, marine training and rescue, conservation, pool life guards. Number of exchanges with other Round Square schools – Canada, Germany, Australia. Local projects and joint international expeditions to India, Sinai, Thailand, Kenya, Honduras to work on conservation/ecological schemes. The latter are expensive – students are encouraged to fundraise to meet own costs. Outdoor pursuits expeditions, sleeping in snow holes, add a whole new dimension.

School has its own 80 foot sail-training yacht, Ocean Spirit of Moray, timetabled sailing weeks (when the weather can be 'pretty wild', according to the skippers, ditto the crew). Tall Ships' race a regular feature; school has a new 28 foot training

cutter and a rash of new Lasers (which could make for interesting sailing).

Mainstream games on course but long distances to other schools for matches cause problems. Reid says 'school plays locals and rugby league'. New sports hall opened in 2013 by Olympians Heather Stanning and Zara Tindall. Those over 16 can be in charge of swimming pool and do lifeguard training. Outstanding Ogston theatre, new extension, performing arts studio with sprung dance floor. Newest drama studios look stunning. We were shown the previous green room, now a storage area of monumental proportions, in detail; how anyone finds anything in the place goodness only knows. Par hazard, our guide was the daughter of a long time friend; our other guide was a most charming clever-clogs about to hit global mathematical hotspots (from Norfolk, full blown scholarship). A level pupils lead dance workshops in local primaries. Each year group has 'headmaster's reels' of a Saturday, with a caller. Head not yet been known to wear the kilt.

Trips all over – Europe, Australasia, points west. Magnificent art, lots of disciplines, graphic design impressive. Particularly strong DT with pupils learning not only to make lights but also cost them effectively.

Boarding: Houses spread all over, some quite a hike from the main school (you would never guess they were originally army huts). Recent HMI/Care Commission inspection awarded 'excellent' for two out of the five categories and 'very good' in the remaining three. Minimal exeats – distances are huge (even more so for 30 per cent overseas boarders), but pupils often do not want to go home, regular socials (by block on Saturdays), films and formal dinners. This is a school that has to make its own entertainment. Shopping bus to Elgin on Friday, but only the upper sixth can visit on Saturdays and can 'have meals out in the evening'. Head removed our previous comment that Elgin can be pretty rough and has had a serious, and we mean serious, drug problem in the not too recent past.

Certain amount of re-jigging houses; girls' houses bung full, but some boys' houses (sixth form particularly) could be busier. The lease on Duffus House at the entrance to the school will be given up within the next five years. Prospectus lists nearby hotels, B&Bs (with prices) and ways of getting to school (a good four hours from Edinburgh but less than that flying from London). Non-stop social life which swings right through the holidays – caveat for Southerners.

Background and atmosphere: Founded in 1934 by the German educationalist, Kurt Hahn, Jewish refugee, founder of Salem School in Baden-Württemberg and believer in educating and developing all aspects

of children, not just the academic. Grounds and setting lovely – half a mile from the Moray Firth with cliffs and beaches nearby, and not as cold as one might think (Gulf Stream). Gordonstoun House is a former residence of Gordon-Cumming of card-cheating fame. Beautiful circular stable block (hence Round Square) houses the library and boys' house. Cunning music rooms round exotic chapel (shaped like an open book – magnificent, but repairs to the pews are sadly botched).

Grounds and setting are lovely – half a mile from the Moray Firth with cliffs and beaches nearby, and not as cold as one might think (Gulf Stream)

Head is masterminding a £10.5 million (apparently no problem getting dosh) 'refurbishment' of the Round Square boarding house and making the old building above accessible to all 'by creating a curriculum centre for international and spiritual citizenship'.

NB planes from nearby Lossiemouth (currently under reprieve) 'the largest and busiest fast-jet base in the Royal Air Force'. Low flying planes screech overhead about every three minutes (strangely, and this editor has visited Gordonstoun five or six times, this is not a memory we have of previous visits). The young say you get used to them after a while. Reid says: 'This is not accurate. They are not allowed to fly directly over the school and only take off over the nearby runway two or three times a day unless they are on a major exercise'. Okay, but they seemed to be only hundreds of feet above the games field nearest to the swimming pool every couple of minutes.

Pastoral care, well-being and discipline: Occasional problems with drugs, smoking and alcohol (not to mention the P word) – 'not totally whiter than white'. No automatic expulsions; pupils get alcohol or smoking points, and head negotiates with the parents. 'Not accurate, head manages according to Gordonstoun code of conduct', according to Reid. 'The Code of Conduct is not on our website but is posted to every parent before their child joins the school and is re-sent if there are any changes', in other words, the goal posts have changed. Drugs: straight to the head, usually straight out. Will take pupils who have had to leave other schools: contract in place. Head tough on perpetual offenders, particularly bullies – 'Children have eventually had to leave the school as a result', said the previous head. Commendably clear rules. Girls and boys can visit each others' houses but only allowed in the opposite sex's 'mixed common room' (sounds a blast) and nowhere else. Each pupil has an academic tutor, boarders have houseparents and assistant houseparents in every house. God worshipped in a Christian fashion, more than lip-service to other faiths. Local minister can prepare for confirmation. (Principal would prefer we changed this to 'prepares for confirmation'.)

Bespoke international citizenship course new kid on the block; Reid takes it at top end: not PHSE or RS but 'examining real problems against a global background'

Pupils and parents: A third English, a third Scottish and a third from the rest of the world – wide diversity of students, some deeply rich, some less so, with the less so benefiting from serious scholarships. Numbers of first time buyers. Parents dropping off their young have been known to stay 'for a few days'. FPs include royals; William Boyd; Eddie Shah; the composer of The Flower of Scotland – Roy Williamson; Martin Shea; Alan Shiach; Lara Croft; Sophie Morgan, who commentated for Channel 4 for the Paralympics; 2012 Olympian gold medal winner, rower Heather Stanning. Numbers currently (Reid changed this to 'marginally') down, particularly boarding boys and day pupils (60 in senior school).

Entrance: Pupils come up through the junior school, Aberlour (usually automatically, at 11), Ardvreck,

Cargilfield, Belhaven (under the new management) and prep schools south of the border. Assessment for those joining at year 10 (about 10 each year) and influx to sixth form. Pupils are assessed both academically and for personality. Odd places sometimes available for pupils, 'at any level of the school for short periods – although not normally less than one term'. Keen to keep up its intake from outside Scotland – may pay travel/hotel bills for prospective parents. Gordonstoun challenge – usually in June – invites UK prep schools to send teams of four or five, all expenses paid for a three day jamboree at Gordonstoun. The idea, of course, being that the little darlings will be so impressed, that whatever school they had previously considered will be cast aside. (NB in previous times Gordonstoun gave scholarships to all prep heads' children regardless).

Exit: 'Non-stimulated young' and even some less academic young have been known to leave Gordonstoun at sixth form level to study A levels elsewhere, either at other schools or crammers. Around 15 per cent don't aim for university but for family business (fair number of local farmers – as opposed to landowners), vocational training, though not, we think, the Forces. Otherwise to universities all over: Oxford Brookes, UCL, Exeter, Glasgow, St Andrews, MIT (Massachusetts Institute of Technology, USA). Courses range from aeronautical engineering, Japanese studies, music and agriculture to law.

Money matters: Set fee; parents can 'opt above', and some do, 'notably so'. Scholarships and bursaries awarded after means-testing. Hardship fund. Success of flourishing international summer school helps with dosh. Fundraising doesn't seem that difficult. Stunning new bursaries for children of fisherfolk. Second hand clothes shop. Picked up the tab when Aberlour House was closed in 2004 (it was losing money); the buildings were sold and funds realised more or less paid for the stunning new build, Aberlour, in the grounds.

Remarks: Children and parents appear happy. Fashionable, co-ed outdoor pursuit-ish boarding school with vast range of pupil backgrounds, not overtly academic, though current head vows it is getting more so. Increasingly popular, Aberlour prep school in the grounds has been an enormous addition. Budget airline flights to nearest airports popular with southern-based families as well as those further afield. Regular direct links from Inverness to Amsterdam: Aberdeen to Frankfurt, and thence to points global. It is still a long drive from Edinburgh and Glasgow.

Harrogate Ladies' College

Clarence Drive, Harrogate HG1 2QG

01423 537045
admissions@hlc.org.uk
www.hlc.org.uk

Ages: 11–18
Pupils: 320; sixth form: 125
Boarders: 130 full plus some weekly and flexi
Day: £15,255 – £21,225 pa
Boarding: £26,625 – £33,375 pa

Principal: Since 2013, Mrs Sylvia Brett BA MA (40s). Read theology at Durham, followed by masters in philosophy and religion. Taught RS and was sixth form housemistress at Royal Masonic School, then became lay chaplain and head of RS at Caldicott Boys Preparatory School. Head of lower school, RS teacher and year 7 housemistress at Downe House before being appointed as sole deputy at Roedean.

Married to Justin, a classics teacher, and has one daughter. Her interests include music (singing and piano), art, swimming, family and friends.

Academic matters: In 2015, 29 per cent A*/A grades at A level and 54 per cent A*/A at GCSE. Strength is with mathematics and sciences (especially physics), a particular bias in the sixth form, but modern languages are fine – normally only the odd D at GCSE, otherwise all A*-C. Only a handful (three or four per language) opt for modern languages at A level but achieve good results. Over the past four years, 32 per cent of girls have pursued a business-related degree course. Launched 2010 in purpose built business suite, the Business School has increased business-related subjects to include accounting, business studies, economics and psychology. Wider purpose to promote enterprise and entrepreneurship throughout the school. Extended Project Qualification introduced for older pupils.

After-school group delighting in dismembering an old moped for spare parts for their go-kart

Teaching is generally very good – friendly good-humoured staff and girls feel both known and supported. As one parent said, 'My daughter has loved every minute – the environment, the work ethic and the dedication of the teachers.' Practical subjects good too – impressive art throughout the school and girls using a wide range of complex design and technology equipment, with an

after-school group delighting in dismembering an old moped for spare parts for their go-kart. Well-equipped food technology room used up to GCSE – A2 available if demand. Enrichment programme for first year GCSE and sixth form to widen horizons in preparation for higher education. Plenty of IT facilities and ICT available as GCSE. Class size maximum 20, average 12. Reports always discussed with head or tutor prior to being sent home. Displays everywhere – a striking balance of pupil work and thought-provoking material, alongside posters from house captains rallying the troops.

Overseas students encouraged to sit exams in their native language, additional English language tuition available (and certainly encouraged) at no extra charge. EAL students used to sit IELTS rather than GCSE English, but pilot study of integration with mainstream English classes in years 10 and 11 has proved highly successful and will be the way forward. Some SEN, usually mild to moderate dyslexia, catered for out of the classroom on an individual basis by specialist teachers.

Games, options, the arts: Sport, the life-blood of the school, is keenly pursued by all. Lacrosse ('lackie') is king – current holders of northern schools' lacrosse title with good representation at county and regional level. Tennis – under 13s Yorkshire schools' champions. Good, much-used, sports facilities include plenty of tennis and badminton courts, multi-gym, 25-metre pool and an enormous indoor general-purpose sports hall which doubles up as a venue for social events, speech day etc.

Friendly, comfortable feel, not snobbish or overtly feminine; girls mix well with the sense of a supportive sisterhood. Encouraged to mix across the ages

An extensive extracurricular menu embraces golf, sailing and ski trips as well as keen D of E and masses of charity and community work. Interesting business breakfast club and model United Nations. Burgeoning participation and success in Leeds Young Enterprise. Also boasts a flourishing ham radio station (call sign GX0HCA) – historic triumph was a hook-up with the Mir space station and the International space station.

Dedicated music house accommodates ensembles galore, from samba to string. Music is a real strength and majority of girls learn an instrument or two. Choir ran away with prizes at the Harrogate Festival, features on BBC Radio, at cathedral services across the land and on tours, Eastern Europe

Also boasts a flourishing ham radio station – historic triumph was a hook-up with the Mir space station and the International Space Station

being a favoured destination. AS and A level theatre studies on offer, with plays and productions acted out in the suitably-equipped drama studio. Curriculum supported by regular trips to concerts, theatre and cinema. Many girls take LAMDA lessons (honours and distinctions the norm). Careers education taken seriously – two weeks' work experience for all followed by presentation and lunch.

Boarding: Four well-presented boarding houses each have generously-sized attractive study bedrooms, a common room centred on the TV, kitchen and games room. Up to four share a room in lower school, but most sixth formers have their own room with internet access for all in studies and bedrooms. Friendly, comfortable feel, not snobbish or overtly feminine, girls mix well with the sense of a supportive sisterhood. Girls are encouraged to mix across the ages with a buddy system operating for new pupils. Flexi and weekly boarding as well as day and full boarding, weekends brimming with trips and activities.

Upper sixth housed in Tower – a half way house between school and university where pupils prepare and eat breakfast and a couple of evening meals in house and have greater freedom than lower down the school (team building exercises at start of upper sixth aid the bonding process). At 16+ girls are allowed out one night a week.

Background and atmosphere: School founded in 1893 on a nearby site and is one of the Allied Schools. Within walking distance of the busy town centre, in the heart of Harrogate's leafy prime real estate, originally part of the Duchy of Lancaster. The pleasant Victorian mock-Tudor buildings with sympathetic additions blend gently with the locality. C of E (own chapel, resounding hymns et al) in small doses for all without exception. New assembly hall officially opened in 2013 to mark school's 120 year anniversary. Separate sixth form centre in main school complete with common rooms, study centre, kitchens, AV room etc with use of business school café. Unique sixth form studies valued by girls as their space and used for personal study until 9.00pm each evening. Food is now provided by external catering company, which has seen a marked improvement in the choice and quality of meals available; recently refurbished dining room.

Staff and girls dine together in main dining room, self-service with occasional formal dining.

School council meets regularly, though girls would like it to be less of a talking shop and to exert more power. A new uniform (predominantly navy) has been introduced throughout the school whilst keeping the traditional green cloak. Dress code for sixth form – business wear, recently more rigorously enforced.

Pastoral care, well-being and discipline: Manners strictly monitored. Occasional links with other schools, but not into creating artificial exposure to boys. Drugs and similar problems uncommon and treated with firmness – head retains discretion, expulsions rare. Health centre, specialist counsellor, tutors and staff all on hand to help if things go wrong.

Pupils and parents: Mostly from Harrogate and the environs. Number of boarders from overseas, especially high number in the sixth form, though work in progress to widen intake and balance ratio. Hong Kong, USA, China, Thailand, Spain, Brunei, Germany, France and Baltic Republic currently being marketed.

Parents predominantly from the usual professions, many Harrogate notables, also self-employed and some farming families, popular with the Forces. Turns out informed, assured, polite and articulate girls, cooperative rather than competitive. Strong OG network, including Baroness McIntosh; Jenny Savill, author; Juliet Bremner; Claire King; Henrietta Butler and most recently Laura Winwood, former president of the Oxford Union. Working hard to encourage more recent leavers to stay in touch.

Entrance: Own entrance test (maths, English, verbal reasoning) taken on assessment day, together with reports from previous school. Main entry points are 11, 13 and 16 but school flexible. Highfield Prep is the linked feeder school. Minimum five GCSEs at grade C or above required for entry to sixth form, international pupils tested in English and appropriate subjects. Scholarship assessment programme.

Exit: Historically largeish numbers – some 15 per cent – at 16 leave for local state or independents and there's an influx of international pupils. Recent culture shift – majority of day pupils staying and wider range of international boarders.

Sixth formers leave for a widespread selection of universities, including London colleges, Exeter and Bath, though northern locations preferred, eg Durham, Edinburgh and Manchester. Occasional one to Oxbridge. Courses include international relations and politics, 3D design and architecture, medicine, PPE, engineering with management and entrepreneurship, maths and law.

Money matters: Academic scholarships of up to 25 per cent of fees. Armed forces scholarships of up to 15 per cent. Music (in form of lessons) and honorary scholarships in art, sport, drama and all-rounder also awarded. Bursaries up to 100 per cent at governors' discretion.

Remarks: An 'in-town' girls boarding/day school that shouts 'girl-centred' education, is proud of it and walks the talk. A new whole school approach aims to provide a 'traditionally modern' experience for its pupils. A convincing start to re-balancing the school, with sixth form retention and diversifying overseas pupils. One to keep on the radar.

Kilgraston School

Bridge Of Earn, Perthshire PH2 9BQ

01738 812257
headoffice@kilgraston.com
www.kilgraston.com
RC

Ages: 11–18 (junior boarding from 8)
Pupils: 310 girls; sixth form: 40
Boarders: 126 full
Day: £8,985 – £16,305 pa
Boarding: £21,285 – £27,855 pa

Principal: Since April 2015, Mrs Dorothy MacGinty, previously head of St Francis' College in Hertfordshire, where she has also been head of biology, head of games, boarding housemistress and deputy head. She is married to Frank and they have three children; the youngest has joined Kilgraston.

Academic matters: Eighteen month year group; individual classes can accommodate all sorts and sizes. Scottish system has changed, Standard grades have been replaced by National 4s and 5s; warmly embraced by most schools as 'they blend seamlessly into Highers and Advanced Highers in sixth form'.

We have no idea of how subject results bear out; school only provides basic exam results (A-C percentage), and nothing at all at subject level. We reckon it is unacceptable to ask parents to commit to a school without seeing full exam information. French and English used to be good. Pupils say science on the up with new head of physics, stunning recently completed science block, complete with shower and disabled loo. In 2015, 67 per cent A grades at Higher level and 30 per cent at Advanced Higher.

Efficient remedial unit (CReSTeD WS); specialist teachers for dyslexia and dyspraxia – one-to-one teaching, small groups. School has completed our SEN questionnaire, but would not expand on exactly how inclusive Kilgraston was. Well nigh impossible for the physically challenged, stairs all over the place.

Lang labs popular, EFL offered. Many exchanges, French, German and Spanish (both pupils and staff), via Sacred Heart network.

Games, options, the arts: Impressive 25m swimming pool complex, sports hall (fitness suite and climbing wall) faced in sandstone, with niches echoing those in the stable building (well-converted into prep school with attached nursery) – historic Scotland at its best. Wide choice of sports. Eight floodlit tennis courts, international-sized, all-weather, floodlit hockey pitch and specialist academy coaching (costs extra). Some golf. Touch rugby. Netball popular, girls play local Bridge of Earn club, good for community spirit. Dedicated director of weekend and outdoor activities encourages all sorts of

Oodles of clubs. The only school in Scotland with equestrian facilities on campus – double size dressage arena, floodlit manège and livery. Coaching by Olympians and internationalists

co-curricular options such as whitewater rafting, canoeing, sailing. Oodles of clubs.

The only school in Scotland with equestrian facilities on campus – 60m x 40m (double size dressage arena, how does that work, we wonder?) floodlit manège and livery. Coaching by Olympians and internationalists. The horse mad can graduate with an SVQII in basic horse care (worming and the like), which, as far as we can work out is the equivalent of Pony Club B or the lowest qualification to start on a BHS certification course. Seems potty not to offer the BHSAI. That having been said, one or two equestriennes have done commendably well in local competitions with Kilgraston sponsoring a show at Gleneagles Hotel.

The art department overlooks the Rotunda and boasts an enormous computer-linked loom. Exciting ceramics, regular master classes. D of E, debating, leadership courses. Strong drama. Music centre in the attics, with keyboards and 14 individual sound-proofed study rooms; guitars and stringed instruments everywhere (and hanging from the walls); sound recording studio, music

lessons (cost extra). Writers' group. Debating. Cooking: tantalising smells in the kitchens. Girls no longer make their own ball gowns for the annual Merchiston hoolie, just fabric design, some of which was to die for but ain't quite so good for the pocket. Sewing machine time is spent altering their purchases to fit.

Boarding: Bedsits from third year, tinies' dorms divided into individual cabins. Moderated Wifi access and single rooms with washing facilities for girls from age 12.

School stops at 4.10pm on Fridays for day and weekly boarders, but masses of alternative activities for those who stay. Computers, games hall/ tennis courts, art, music and sewing rooms open throughout the weekend. Charming and well-used chapel: God important here – most attend assembly and mass on Sundays, feast days still special. Lady Day a blast.

Background and atmosphere: Founded in 1920 – one of 200 networked schools and colleges of the Society of the Sacred Heart. Moved to the handsome red Adamesque sandstone house in 1930, set in 54 acres of parkland (though to be brutally honest it does look a bit like a grand pony club camp when you go down the drive); masses of extensions including Barat wing: huge wide passages filled with pupil art. Splendid new science block. Library off the rotunda has had a face lift.

Moved to handsome red Adamesque sandstone house in 1930, set in 54 acres of parkland; masses of extensions; huge, wide passages filled with pupil art

New sixth form centre carved out of former labs give every girl 'a private study space': presumably for the 35/40 day pupils in the sixth. Boarders have their own bedrooms and work stations. Bit sheep and goats-ish?

No books or newspapers to be seen in existing sixth form centre; we were told that 'books were in the careers centre' (a hop skip and a jump away) and so they were, but we do like to see something/ anything to read whenever the young are in limbo/ waiting for a chum.

Pastoral care, well-being and discipline: Sacred Heart ethos prevails – staff enormously caring, 'will go the extra mile'. Pastoral conferences every week, independent counsellor on tap, bullying handled by BFG. 'Educate on cyber-bullying' from early. We think the dangers of trolling are not yet fully expounded. Disciplinary committee, gatings, suspensions, fatigues round school for smoking. Drinkers are suspended and a not-so-recent problem was 'nipped in the bud'. Will test areas, not girls, if drugs suspected. Charming little handbook for new pupils full of helpful advice. Problems like anorexia not discussed as openly as in some schools.

Girls not as streetwise as they think they are – tendency to cover woolly pullies and blazers with badges: bosoms and badges are strange bedfellows. New blue jacket for lower sixth changes to tweed jacket for upper sixth (quelle expense). All covered in badges. Could have been the 50s (though oddly enuff, make up quite common).

Pupils and parents: Trad boarders from all over Scotland and beyond (London and overseas – about 20 per cent of boarders). Day children from Fife, Dundee and Perthshire Stirling. Buses. Tranches of first time buyers: 'useful little school, just south of Perth.' RC but plenty of non-Catholics, including Muslims.

Entrance: Not that difficult, numbers down, though not consistently throughout. Space available both for day and boarders. Scholarship exams in February. Junior school entrants do CE. Otherwise 11+ from primary schools and 12+ from prep schools. Pupils can come whenever, half term/next week if space available. Sixth form entry: school report and exams to date; pupils from overseas or local state schools and are steered to 'appropriate' levels of study.

Exit: One or two leave before sixth form. Most to uni, most choose Scotland, huge variety: from Chinese studies to fashion and accountancy. The odd gapper.

Money matters: Up to 10 academic, art and music scholarships. Also riding, tennis and sporting scholarships. Almost one-third receive assistance of some sort. School is 'good at finding trust funding' for those who have fallen on hard times.

Remarks: The only all-girls' boarding school in Scotland. Small, not overtly Catholic, splendid facilities. Popular prep; day pupils at both. A gentling school which majors on horse activities and superb sports; that having been said, leavers' destinations are wide and far reaching in every possible discipline. Numbers steady, confident about next academic year.

Lathallan School

Brotherton Castle, Johnshaven, Angus DD10 0HN

01561 362220
admissions@lathallan.org.uk
www.lathallan.org.uk

Ages: 6m–18 (boarding from 10)
Pupils: 227; sixth form: 33
Boarders: 11 full, 21 weekly/flexi
Day: £15,930 – £17,325 pa
Boarding: £22,356 – £23,751 pa

Headmaster: Since 2009, Mr Richard Toley BA MPhil PGCE (40s) who joined Lathallan in 2006 as director of co-curriculum from nearby High School of Dundee. Educated at The Merchant Taylor's School, Liverpool, followed by St David's Lampeter MPhil at St Andrews and PGCE at Strathclyde. He and his wife live on site, with their young now in school.

Six years down the road (Toley was catapulted into headship after an 18 month apprenticeship) he is comfortably confident in his role. (We usually pop in for a quick check on our way down from Aberdeen, though alas this time we were both caught in traffic and had to do some crisis management, so missed our meet). School moved from being 'just' a prep school with a hugely popular and often over-subscribed nursery in 2006, to building up a senior base year by year.

A historian, charming and relaxed, Toley teaches classics (as in classical studies) and history 12 periods a week in the senior school, and runs school with senior school head, Mr Duncan Lyall BSc PGCE (40s), an Edinburgh lad, and Mr James Ferrier BA (Cantab) PGCE (50s), head of junior school since 2011, having first come to school in 2001 from Moor Park in Shropshire. Lyall, who read mechanical engineering at Edinburgh, is married with a brace of young, and came to Lathallan from Peebles High, having previously taught in both the borders and Aberdeen.

Ferrier lives on campus with his wife, was educated at Hardyes School, Dorset, read humanities of Christ Church, followed by PGCE at the University of Kent, and runs his part of the Lathallan empire with gentle humour.

Impressive collection of uber-powerful governors plus parent governors, 'tremendous backing'.

Academic matters: Scottish curriculum: 17+ subject options at all levels. Recent results encouraging, good scattering of As across the board in 2015 in both Highers (40 per cent) and Advanced Highers (69 per cent) As ever, we ask for individual results per subject, with number of candidates in each subject and results (as in 12 did English Higher, two got A, four B, five C – that sort of thing). Whilst school 'does hold such results, it does not divulge them'. So now you know. Interesting results we did get: of the 17 candidates presenting for Nat 5s (118 exams) a mere 57 scored A, with four candidates being D(oomed) and 10 unplaced. S5s do a combo of Nat

5s and Highers, which is unusual. Several unplaced in both disciplines, but 40 per cent A pass rate over all (though we have no idea in which subjects) and 69 per cent A at Higher level is encouraging, though number of presentees unplaced; school is non-selective and for some a C or a D may be a real achievement. The staff whom we have met over the years have been bubbly and enthusiastic.

Variety pack of langs on offer – Mandarin – whenever (number of native speakers in school) plus French (from P1) and Spanish (S1) (native speakers). Not a lot of take-up in the former, though occasional outstanding results at all levels. Pupils study both French and Spanish throughout S2 before opting for one or t'other for Nat 5s.

Latin from aged 11 (classical studies at Higher and Advanced Higher), crash course in Italian (ab initio) – offered at Higher level, but no take-up – plus the usual suspects: maths, English, three sciences, history, geography (pleasing and popular), business and classical studies, art, PE and drama, and managing environmental resources (MER). This is penny number stuff, occasional glitch.

Civilianship the latest addition – ie how to open doors, ladies first, that sort of thing; school is talking to exam boards as to how they could make this an examinable subject. Think finishing schools, think nanny, think how clever.

All assessed for dyslexia et al on arrival. Two dedicated learning support staff, one-to-one, clusters, or co-teaching, throughout school. Costs the same as a piano lesson. Back-up for the bored and the brightest. Class sizes around 13 (max 16), pupils streamed for maths and English both taught in refurb'ed classrooms in the castle, interactive whiteboards all over.

IT impressive – Dell computers plus Apple Macs in senior school. iPads for all seems to be the current flavour of the month (last time we did a round up it was the 'virtual learning experience'). Only for those in the dyslexia stream at Lathallan. We were told that Toley 'was not convinced' by rolling 'em out across the board.

Science still in a hotch-potch of temporary buildings beside the nursery complex: but zinging new science centre more than a couple of metres off the ground (as ever, near the nursery complex). We have a natty brochure with pics, showing three dedicated science labs plus one for environmental study and junior science lab. Plus accessible loos, shower – got to have 'em now and pupil inspired 'treehouse' (to enhance outdoor learning experiences). Natty brochure has fundraising options, so we hope there is enough dosh to complete the project. Impressive sounding new head of science Ian Smith comes from Cults Academy where he was head principal teacher of chemistry.

Staff whom we have met are young, enthusiastic and fun. Twenty-six on the books and six part-timers. Peris pulled in for the more esoteric subjects (or instruments). No apparent problem in attracting staff, particularly in the current financial climate, when property prices have in some quarters reached basement level. The Aberdeen catchment area was pricey.

Games, options, the arts: Music everywhere – bagpipe boxes all over the porch and hall, both girls and boys in pipe bands much in demand for charities and have entertained Princess Anne of late, played in the Angus show, the Glamis gathering, the Scottish parliament etc. Pipes and drums played at the battlefields in Belgium during the Great War memorial year and compete in the Royal Pipe Band competitions with success. Scottish country dancing no longer has parental input; marvellous photographs in the porch of a junior Scottish country dancing lesson – note the kilt loops and the ecstasy on the faces of the young. Strong drama: new head of music previously with Aberdeen Youth Theatre; no orchestra per se (yet) but wind and ceilidh bands.

Marvellous photographs in the porch of a junior Scottish country dancing lesson – note the kilt loops and the ecstasy on the faces of the young

Toley has introduced a new formal school-wide traditional PE programme, which 'through age-appropriate indoor exercises aims to improve co-ordination and mental agility both in and outside the academic classroom' (sounds a tad Steiner-ish). School thinks this sounds harsh. 'We have a real focus on sports/PE and outdoor education but this sounds almost military'. 'We realise the importance of exercise.' 'We want our pupils to be well-rounded by participating in PE/sports and outdoor ed.'

Thrashing all comers in under-16 rugby 7s, new games pavilion (board member head of SRU); 7s rugby team toot to Dubai on the cards, but 'mainly it is regional' with all points south of Gordonstoun. All 7+ year olds play sport daily, tennis courts double up for netball (Astroturf), 10 acres of playing field overlooking the North Sea and own beach (bracing), plus refurbished gym. Lots of jolly rugby trips and netball tours. Sea at the bottom of the garden, but no sea sports – too rough. Impressive games area adjacent to junior/baby school. Astro: tennis: you name it; plus dedicated gym (though hall in main school building equally adaptable).

Head of outdoor education is Monro-potty, 'probably climbed them all three times,' says Toley.

D of E timetabled and huge numbers – school claims 'highest percentage of participation in the D of E scheme in all of the country (Scotland)'.

First two years of senior school spend six days in the mountains, mountain rescue, navigation (shades of Round Square). Skiing, both at home and abroad for all. Huge emphasis on outdoor education, self-resilience, and leadership training. New 50 foot long zip wire in the wood (100 foot drop). Scary. Six pupils and guides did an unsupported, exploratory exped to Eastern Greenland last August. (Scary again). Recent trip to Iceland has even more scary photos. SCIS sponsored Outdoor Education Conference planned for 2016.

ISCO (careers guidance) enrollment (as ever) and ongoing advice as to 'what happens next'.

Boarding: Influx of foreign boarders since full boarding reopened: 30 boarders housed in separate wings of the castle (previous staff quarters), co-ed boarding tidily arranged, mainly oily children, from Thailand, China, Spain, Nigeria, Russia. Scottish Guardian Overseas Association oversees them (and individual guardians have to pick up the flack if their charges are sent 'home', ie gated). Some locals, bed and breakfasting available. ESOL on hand to help with language glitches. Interesting to see whether boarding numbers hold up during current oil turn-down.

Background and atmosphere: Founded in the imposing Victorian Brotherton Castle (1867) in the early 1930s. Originally trad boys' boarding prep school, set in 62 acres of woodland which catered for 'the folk over the hill'; now a thriving nursery (handful of real babes being pushed out in three prams when we visited; good North Sea air) through to Advanced Highers co-ed offering full, weekly or flexi-boarding (from age 10).

Civilianship the latest addition – how to open doors, ladies first, that sort of thing; school is talking to exam boards about making this an examinable subject

Regular exchange programmes with 'small-ish' schools in Canada, Switzerland and Australia; the latter were enjoying their six weeks in Angus during a previous visit. More than 25 clubs; 'we rotate them,' says Toley.

William Bruce house-lets (which pre-date the castle) guard corners of the long abandoned formal garden which makes a splendid play area. Library and resource centre in main building with classrooms and nursery in bright converted stable block with massive additions (and home to new science build but see above). Some lessons in temporary classrooms. Irritating steps both too shallow and too wide link the two sites. Nursery/junior wing surrounded by play/games areas, stunning nursery playground. Collection of toddler sized loos and mini basins: one wonders how they cope at home.

Newly refurb'ed common room for senior school pupils. School uniform provided in house, with jolly fleecy waterproof jackets which staff wear too. Staff all have to take the minibus test.

Pastoral care, well-being and discipline: School small enough for every child to be known (cherished is a word that comes to mind if it didn't sound so soppy), strong anti-bullying policy. Occasional gatings for wickedness, no child yet asked to leave. School is 'bespoke, focused'.

Pupils and parents: Increasing number of first time buyers. FPs supportive, strong parental input, parents will drive many miles out of their way to drop off their tinies in the nursery. Return buses for older children from Stonehaven, Edzell and Aberdeen with coaches from Brechin, Forfar and Montrose.

Aberdeen business community plus local farmers, commuters, usually from within 90 minute radius (which takes you to Dundee). Rob

Wainwright an old boy (and does the odd spot of coaching), ditto Ian Lang (Lord Lang of Monkton).

Niche school: perfect for the occasional non-performing refugee from bigger trad schools: Fettes, Merchiston, Robert Gordons. Children thrive in the smaller environment. 'We care'. (Those parents to whom we spoke fell into the latter category. Their relief was palpable.)

Entrance: Springboard Nursery: from six weeks, 80 tinies registered but no more than 49 at any one time. Entrance to junior school seamless from nursery test-ette for problems and 'nearly all go' (95 per cent). Juniors are checked 'carefully' and if problems obvious, they get a 'proper test'.

Entry to senior school at any time to any year group if places available, many come via junior school. Otherwise form 5 (P7: 11, 12 year olds). Taster day. Informal tests in English, maths and verbal reasoning, but not a selective school. Numbers up from prep school, 10/12 a year. Currently full first three years of senior school (and nursery and pre-junior school ie ages 5 and 6).

Exit: Tiny trickle leave for trad independents age 13, occasional departure age 8, otherwise the odd relocation. Sixth formers head in the main to the Scottish unis: St Andrews, Edinburgh, Aberdeen, Heriot Watt, Stirling and Glasgow.

Money matters: Money matters 'under control', up to 100 per cent bursaries (and extra help if necessary): huge raft: academic, sports, rugby 7s, netball, music and pipes and drums. Sibling discount. Secondhand clothes shop. Will keep child if parents fall on hard times with the usual caveat of being up front about the problem.

Springboard Nursery in partnership with Aberdeen County council (discounts). Hours roughly 7.30am to 6pm but check fee structure, deeply expensive if child not collected by designated time (emergency cover and charged by the quarter hour). This is a 50 week nursery with two weeks off for Christmas.

Remarks: This is the tail that wagged the dog. We have visited Lathallan over the past 20 odd years: six headmasters. This was a school which had – quite frankly – been toiling. Sometimes it had a nursery which took babes from 2 months, sometimes from 3 years. In any case it was a boys' boarding prep school with an increasingly dismal roll call (even after they took girls and day pupils) and a glorious view. Two (or was it three?) heads ago, the brave decision (we thought nuts) was made to expand, on a year by year basis, to become a fully fledged school, with

Highers and Advanced Highers and all. We were wrong. Very wrong (and we won't rehearse further the various decisions down the line). Remarkable success story which keeps on growing.

Lomond School

10 Stafford Street, Helensburgh, Argyll and Bute G84 9JX

01436 672476
admissions@lomondschool.com
www.lomondschool.com

Ages: 3–18 (boarding from 10)
Pupils: 389; sixth form: 103
Boarders: 52
Day: £7,710 – £10,725 pa
Boarding: £24,390 pa

Headmaster: Since September 2014, Mrs Johanna Urquhart, previously depute head (academic) at George Watson's College. She has a degree in maths and statistics and a masters in education, specialising in leadership and management. She has also been depute head at Breadalbane Academy.

Academic matters: Setted in English, French and maths at the age of 12, French taught from age five, German from 11. Huge range of subjects on offer, including such esoteric ones as graphic communication, modern studies and business management, as well as French, German and Spanish. Three sciences. Latin GCSE taught by video conference

link and distance learning. In 2015, 46 per cent A grades in Advanced Highers, 44 per cent A grades in Highers and 61 per cent A grades in National 5.

Maximum class size 20. Sixth form were working supervised (which is unheard of at that age) in the library when we visited. Homework very important – children keep a diary and expect to do at least two and a half hours each night in their National grade year. Has strong links with private schools in China, Germany and US. Computers everywhere, networked, and all have access to the internet; keyboarding skills for all, electronic interactive whiteboard presentations for all by all. Tutors for all. Good learning support (and provision for those with dyslexia, ADD or ADHD). English as a second language on hand.

Games, options, the arts: Huge playing field just along the (tree-lined) road. Full-sized floodlit Astroturf hockey pitch. Rugby and hockey the two main winter games, with tennis, cricket and athletics in the summer and oodles of add-ons. Swimming in the local pool, option of squash, riding and badminton. Inter-house matches popular. mass of lunch time clubs, D of E popular and, of course, sailing, The Scottish Islands Peaks Race, Lomond Challenge (a beastly tough triathlon) – not a school for sissies. New games hall, adjacent to the Astroturf, includes badminton courts, climbing wall, dance studio, fitness suite and indoor cricket lanes. Further development to include another smaller Astroturf.

Tremendous enthusiasm here – enchanting flower costume, made for last summer's play, on show

Traditional Scottish music important – clarsach players, fiddlers, pipers and singers are in regular demand. Strong music, based in the old stables – one wall entirely covered with guitars, not just for decoration, judging by the enthusiasm the guitar teacher generated. Recording facilities in place. Big bands and chamber orchestras, over 20 instruments on curriculum with some 150 individual lessons. Sparkling art department, with old school desks press-ganged into use. Huge variety of disciplines – photography with spit-new kit, magical screen printing, jewellery making, as well as the more prosaic (which it wasn't) sculpture, painting and etching. Tremendous enthusiasm here – enchanting flower costume, complete with design, basque and wings, made for last summer's play, on show. Strong drama.

Boarding: Burnbrae now the most modern boarding house in Scotland – boys and girls (boarders from age 10) share the same building but are separated by a state-of-the-art security system using biometric readers.

Background and atmosphere: Based on the northern edge of the posh, sleepy, seaside town of Helensburgh, originally housed in a series of Victorian villas. Present school is an amalgam of Larchfield, founded in 1845, and the girls' school, St Bride's, founded in 1895. The schools combined in 1977; later a stunning rebuild. The resulting school is a curious combination of old and new, with three floors replacing the original two and subject rooms being grouped in series. Most impressive – massive amount of

glass, super new dining hall, good gym and terrific entrance hall with glorious views out over the Clyde. All pupils wear uniform (kilts for females) – neat and tidy with ties and a thoroughly purposeful air.

Pastoral care, well-being and discipline: Strong anti-bullying procedure in place – the 'no blame' circle appears to be the most effective. Confidential suggestion boxes all over the school are really part of the anti-bullying programme. Good PSD programme. CCTV cameras throughout. Children not 'given a lot of rope', eg any substance abuse leads to suspension, 'pending a discussion of their school future'. Dealing equals straight out. Smoking is apparently 'not happening just now', but smoking in uniform is 'not on'.

Pupils and parents: An upmarket lot – solid middle class, from the surrounding area (they organise the buses), some from as far away as Glasgow. Number of Forces families (Faslane naval base next door) and some from further 'round the bay' send their children here (the local state school thought to be too state). A few mainland Chinese usually come for most of their secondary schooling, plus connection with Germany, whence the occasional pupil comes for a year or a term – not much take-up of Scots going to Germany in exchange.

Bonar Law was educated at Larchfield, as well as John Logie Baird – his school report, displayed in the dining room, apart from showing that he was 14th out of 14 in maths, expresses the hope that he will eventually 'go on and do something with his life'!

Entrance: Either up via nursery or from local state primaries.

Exit: Usual dribble away after National grades and could fill up the resulting places several times over, trickle leaves after Highers; some, eg those going south to university, tend to stay and do their Advanced Highers. Most will end up at university – destinations include Glasgow, Strathclyde, Highlands & Islands, Paisley, Glasgow Caledonia, Edinburgh, Dundee, Heriot Watt and Aberdeen. Usually two or three to Oxbridge.

Money matters: Not a rich school. Will support pupils in financial difficulties; an increasing number of means-tested bursaries (up to 100 per cent) available at the age of 10 and 11 and post-National grades.

Remarks: A jolly, busy school, perfect for those who want to keep their children at home without the hassle of going daily to Glasgow.

Longridge Towers School

Berwick-upon-Tweed, Northumberland TD15 2XQ

01289 307584
pupilsadmissions@lts.org.uk
www.lts.org.uk

Ages: 3–18
Pupils: 200; sixth form: 44
Boarders: 42
Day: £7,896 – £12,336 pa
Boarding: £18,153 – £25,128 pa

Headmaster: Since 2009, Mr Tim Manning BA (50s), a Londoner who chose to study maths at Bangor and liked it so much that he did a PGCE in order to stay on for an extra year, and 'found when I got up in front of a class I just loved it'. Then King Williams College on the Isle of Man was looking for a rugby playing maths teacher. He joined Longridge as head of maths in 1993, became deputy head in 1995 and was appointed head in 2009 on the sudden departure of his predecessor. A keen rugby player (played for his uni and looks the part) and golfer, he has encouraged excellent sport with remarkable success. Highly complimentary recent Independent Schools Inspectorate report praised academic achievement and the activities programme, commenting on his outstanding leadership and the provision for personal development. He firmly attributes success to his strong management and pastoral care teams but has clearly worked wonders himself. Living within walking distance on what was once the Longridge estate, both his children went right through the school from early years to university.

Retiring in July 2016.

Academic matters: All-through school from 3-18, with French started at 7 and German at 11. Spanish, Italian and Latin as extracurricular but can be taken at GCSE, as can Chinese. Wide range of GCSE subjects with flexible time timetabling based on the needs of each particular year group so that 95 per cent get to take what they want. English, Eng lit and maths for all plus six other options (can include three – or two – separate sciences or science and additional science.) Usual subjects plus ICT, CDT (done in a well-equipped but basic hut in the grounds), sports studies, drama and music. Consistently sound record with a good sprinkling of A and A* in biology and maths and a few in Eng lit and elsewhere. Almost everyone takes drama and IT, both with solid results and no significant weaknesses, though art a bit up and down. In 2015, nearly 30 per cent of GCSEs were A*/A.

At A level, 21 per cent A*/A in 2015. Choice includes the usual subjects plus economics with business studies, sports science and further maths; general studies AS for all now replaced by critical thinking after rather iffy results; while psychology can be taken at AS over two years. Dusting of A*/As across most subjects and a consistently solid 'pass' rate but also quite a smattering of C/D. Inevitably small groups – will put on a mainstream subject for one pupil in sixth form. Anyone with 5+ Cs can take A/AS though B preferred in subject concerned.

SEN support offered mostly by individual withdrawal with personal education plans used to keep teachers aware of needs. English help for pupils from China etc and efforts to provide extra stimulus for the very bright.

Juniors start from early years foundation stage (tiny classes of five to 10 only) on Oxford Reading Tree, supplemented by lots of Jolly Phonics and Ginn letters and sounds.

Classrooms pretty modern with a few interactive whiteboards and computer projectors, lots of IT including laptop trolleys for use in amazingly antiquated though very adequately equipped labs. The smartest lab is in the junior school building for 7–11s. Called Stobo after a benefactor, the junior school is still clean and new looking with state of art (though cheerfully decorated) classrooms, cloakrooms and hall etc. Early years to junior 3 have humbler but thoroughly refurbished quarters absolutely brimming with colour, imaginative stimulus material and even recorded birdsong. A pleasant fenced outdoor area for tinies and some smashing all weather play equipment, in enthusiastic use.

Games, options, the arts: Sport flourishes with highly successful seven-a-side rugby reaching finals in county tournaments – they struggle to produce a top-level full teams from a small co-ed school but are outstanding in sevens. Recent leaver runs at Scottish, English and Great Britain under 20 championship level, soccer just starting, lots of hockey for girls with several county players, a school champion skier and masses of opportunity for basketball,

volleyball, badminton, cricket, tennis, curling (Scottish school finalists) etc. Spacious sports hall (takes a marquee inside for prize days and dances,) defunct swimming pool left by previous convent school so minibuses take them to Eyemouth pool but grounds lend themselves to hosting local cross country etc. Pipedream of a new Astroturf hockey pitch is still pretty distant.

Falconry clearly the latest craze – the juniors couldn't stop talking about it – but also the tip of an impressive iceberg: archery, wildlife gardening (with good muddy pond)

Lots of choir, orchestra, jazz groups etc with star pupil in Northern Youth Orchestra but little take up of academic music beyond GCSE. Informal lunchtime concerts much enjoyed by all. Special centre for peripatetic music in a pretty gothic house in the grounds which the previous head rejected as a home. Drama in the round in strange theatre converted from former convent chapel, with jazzy lighting, provided by the enterprising parents' 'school development association'. Recent production is Billy Liar. Art seems a bit marginalised in a building seven minutes walk from main school but is looking to a new art teacher to hot it up next year. Head's ambition is to reincorporate this in a new sciences and practical subjects building. The school is now full and seemingly growing, so he hopes to revamp abandoned plans for new labs into a more inclusive facility.

Boundless activities! Almost all day pupils including juniors stay till 4.40pm for an hour of activity which can include supervised study, tutorials, extra coursework or teaching. Falconry is clearly the latest craze – the juniors couldn't stop talking about it – but also the tip of an impressive iceberg: archery, athletics, lacrosse and other sports, debating, wildlife gardening (with a good muddy pond), Yoga, a new Radio Longridge, science and engineering clubs, cheerleading, war games and lashings of other things. Head comments that having rearranged activity times, to suit staff and pupils better, the staff can do what they really like. Bags of trips: German exchange, sport to Canada, South Africa, Iceland etc. Charitable links with Borneo and others. D of E for seniors and Adventure Service challenge for juniors.

Boarding: Boarding on two floors (girls above, boys below) has spacious mostly two-bedded rooms, some with en suite showers. Their height makes them a little stark though inmates are allowed locked doors and a free-ish hand with posters and personal paraphernalia. Pleasant and well-planned recreation room, with spotless kitchenette and generous supplies of luscious fruit.

Background and atmosphere: The extraordinary Victorian Tudor extravaganza built of sandstone ashlar in 1880s for Sir Hubert Jerningham, a liberal MP, on the estate inherited by his wife Annie, Liddell was designed to impress (it does!) by the Buckleys who redid Arundel Castle. It features battlemented stone chimneys, magnificent great hall, now for concerts, with hammer-beams sporting snarling monsters with grotesquely bared teeth, an imperial staircase and an elaborate portico added to shelter the Prince of Wales' carriage (though history is silent over whether he actually arrived to use it) all making Longridge the grandest house in the area. Set in 80 acres of parkland, it became a hotel, then in 1949 an Ursuline Convent school. In 1983 it was re-structured as the co-educational Longridge Towers School.

In a fantastic rural setting with imaginative use of the castellated grand areas, the school also has the problem of making stone staircases, high ceilings and a warren corridors of work for 21st century education. The original library had a cunning makeover with a gallery providing working space and banishing the previous nightmare scenario of children on ladders to glass (non-safety) fronted bookcases. There's lots of help on hand and an ambitious programmes of visiting authors etc. 'Service wings' house boarders, dining rooms and kitchens – some tasty dishes (pupils actually like it on the whole) made on site with a few home-grown veg. All obviously well used and well cared for but lots of echoey passages and stairwells, improved by pupil artwork (not always the right way up, though it's hard to tell!) Most noticeably some stunning Aboriginal hangings done for a drama performance liven one of the central stairways. Everything clean and mainly litter free, well used and not unnaturally tidy.

Pastoral care, well-being and discipline: Independent Schools Inspectorate really praised pastoral care. Qualified nurse in boarding and system of tutors and year heads (form teachers for juniors) and three school houses which run vertically through juniors to senior school. Pupils respect and value system and genuine interest of staff, so problems are picked up quickly and children tend to monitor and report issues like bullying before they become serious. New junior school council is prized by pupils. Plentiful contact between all ages with seniors helping with reading and games. Unusually friendships across year groups are not uncommon, especially valuable in such a small and variable boarding situation.

Strong sense of community enhanced by boarding and also by the school's involvement with its neighbourhood. Activities provided supplement rather than compete with local amenities such as junior golf. Pupils are ready to take responsibility as elected prefects etc within and without school. One sixth former even combines his school duties with being chief coastguard for Lindisfarne.

Pupils and parents: Masses of bus routes bring pupils coming from a scattered area which includes not only Berwick-upon-Tweed, the surrounding border country in both England and Scotland, but also the Holy Island (Lindisfarne) population, whose children need to board on days when the tide cuts off their journey to or from school. Hence boarding has a special wing for them where siblings can be together and the provision has a more temporary feel than the full termly boarding, though they share its amenities and supervision. So boarding at Longridge is more 'flexi' than most and the population fluctuates. Boarding seems to be on the increase with about 32 current maximum and applications going up. A few boarders from abroad, mainly China, otherwise a largely British intake.

Uniform is in a state of flux though everyone looks quite smart. New blue blazers, white shirts, grey trousers and knee straight skirts with prominent kick pleats in blue, white and grey tartan look neat and innocuous, while tinies wear blue and white cotton summer dresses.

Scattered area includes not only border country but also the Holy Island (Lindisfarne), whose children need to board on days when the tide cuts off their journey

Parents run a dynamic programme of events and raise significant amounts for equipment etc. Governors take an active interest in the school and the local worthies, whose families give the names to houses etc, support it with visits and interest.

Entrance: By assessment at all levels but school will take anyone capable of benefiting from what's on offer. Since Longridge pupils come from Scotland and England with different systems involving changes of school at 7, 11, 12, 14 and even different age cut off points, September for England but February for Scotland, need careful induction and class sizes are unpredictable. Now started a class for 3 year olds in response to local demand.

Exit: Some leave from juniors at either 11 and 12 (English and Scottish systems!) mainly to independent, Ampleforth, Merchiston Castle etc, though not usually to local state schools. There is more than a trickle (around 45 per cent) after GCSE to local and Newcastle sixth forms and a few to independent boarding. Those who stay to upper sixth go mostly to uni, a few to blue chip and a surprising quota of sports degrees. Some to academic courses too. Popular destinations include Newcastle, King's College London, Leeds Beckett (vocational courses), York, Edinburgh, Northumbria, Central Lancashire.

Money matters: Not a rich school but awards available for academic (up to 50 per cent), sporting (up to 10 per cent) or musical (free tuition) excellence are offered to those qualifying by exam, achieving county sports honours or by audition. Pupils from Holy Island are sponsored by the local authority, which would otherwise be unable to provide adequate hostel accommodation.

Remarks: Small, with all the advantages of good supervision, care, close-knit community and friendliness a small school can give. Copes very well with the disadvantages of scale, so pupils do not lose out on activities, subjects etc. Berwick-upon-Tweed is jolly lucky to have this alternative at hand.

Loretto School

1–7 Linkfield Road, Musselburgh, East Lothian EH21 7RE

01316 534444
admissions@loretto.com
www.loretto.com

Ages: 12–18 (junior boarding from 11)
Pupils: 619; sixth form: 150
Boarders: 179 full, 77 flexi
Day: £8,220 – £20,850 pa
Boarding: £16,920 – £30,600 pa

Headmaster: Since September 2014, Dr Graham Hawley BSc PhD PGCE, previously head of Kelly College, Tavistock; has also taught at Ardingly and Warwick School. Educated at Mill Hill School, followed by Durham and Exeter. Not a pinstripe suited, hands on lapels, sound bite delivering headmaster of the bullfrog sort – a modest and gently amusing conversationalist who listens sensitively. Dr Hawley's first class hons in natural sciences and his doctorate have taken him to solitary places: the west coast of Scotland, Devon, Cornwall, India, Bangladesh and Sumatra. Do not think Gussie Fink-Nottle – think someone who is highly intelligent and articulate, with a close eye for detail and the willing ability to notice and pay attention to everyone. Married to Rachel; two children.

Academic matters: Monthly tutorial assessments are 'minuted and followed through' with pupils and parents, but watch this space. School follows the English system – GCSEs and A levels for all. In 2015, 38 per cent A*/A grades at A level and 50 per cent at GCSE. No (current) thoughts of moving to the IB, but goodness knows what is going to happen in the world of academe over the next few years. Classics back on stream but not – currently – offered at A level. Goodly selection of top end passes; maths, physics strong as ever, but Eng lit and art in the ribbons; v strong German – native speakers perhaps? Music a tad sad exam-wise in the last few years, and not many sporting heroes...

Traditionally strong on science and engineering, humanities, government and politics (number in both cabinets recently); business studies creeping up the ladder, plus economics, French and Spanish. Boy/girl ratio pretty even across the field, Russian and Mandarin available at all levels, native speakers encouraged to sit for qualifications in their own langs, tutors can be pulled on if necessary. Three sciences standard at GCSE, though one can be dropped for art.

Setting in English, maths and languages, most subjects from third form. School recently became an Associate school of the Royal Society, which sounds pretty grand but only lasts two years. Apparently girls no longer set the academic bar, 'it depends on the year group'. The staff we met were all bright, bubbly and enthusiastic. ESL (extra cost) and learning support available throughout. Drop in centres, 'staff very helpful' said head boy. Special societies for clever clogs. Smartboards in classrooms and networked computers everywhere, including study-bedrooms. Eighty pupils each year in sixth form. Impressive visiting lecturer programme, usually one per week, members of upper sixth regularly give lectures too; interview practice for all.

Games, options, the arts: Singing as ever good and keen: the whole school sings in the war memorial chapel choir and performs at the Schools Proms at the Royal Albert Hall. Music improving in leaps and bounds, with orchestra and jazz band, most of the second form (ie 12 year olds) study one or more instruments. The pipe band performed with Sir Paul McCartney in Liverpool recently. Wow! Claims to have been the first all-Steinway independent school in Europe – Steinways throughout campus. Drama on the up – theatre studies taken at all exam levels (sprinking of As at A), school is a registered LAMDA centre. Art scholars do life classes, screen printing and textiles. Campus and online Loretto radio station as well as all singing and dancing recording studio.

PE is an examinable subject, strong sport – girls' athletics and lacrosse do well; the appointment of a head of girls' games has given it a real impetus. Impressive string of wins on the rugby pitch over the last few years has put 1st XV firmly back in the top league. Fine all-weather court, new Olympic blue Astroturf at Pinkie (pretty garish), and acres of playing fields. Canoeing in the Musselburgh lagoons, but not a lot of use made of the sea itself (enthusiasts sail in North Berwick).

The golf academy is flourishing, currently number one in Europe (school has a long tradition of senior golfing FPs), and golf is professionally coached throughout the school, with all pupils using top class practice facilities on campus, including a nine-hole Huxley all-weather putting green. Rounds are played at the local Craigielaw, and Archerfield down the firth. Rash of success over the years, older pupils' lessons re-jigged to accommodate coaching; three golf scholarships to leading American universities to date; wins in many county championships. Summer residential golf camps are run to encourage new golfers to apply (ie as pupils at the school). Variety of trips and exchanges, for pupils, and for staff.

Do not think Gussie Fink-Nottle – think someone who is highly intelligent and articulate, with a close eye for detail and the ability to notice and pay attention to everyone

Boarding: Current prospectus (not enuff words, too many pics for grandparents – who like more words if they are to pay the bill, and many do) about to be replaced by zinging new edition with proper words and descriptions. If one is brutally honest, whilst the CD and memory stick are super, in the real world of marketing grandparents/parents, particularly first time buyers, like to leave the prospectus lying around – it sure beats ducks on the wall! Very jolly map at back is spoiled by beastly black arrows to Pinkie House and Junior School and there is, as yet, no mention of the new Eleanora Almond girls' house – arranged by apartments – which was due to open on the High Street the day after our visit (it had been ready for months, but the Care Commission had been a little tardy in inspections). Holm House (with lift for disabled access) and Balcarres, for girls, are adjacent to the (small) sports centre, junior girls' house and girls' sixth form house. Study bedrooms in sixth form house. Senior common rooms for sixth form with a certain amount of male access; barbecues are popular at the girls' houses and attended by all. Girls' boarding bung full, certain availability for chaps (but not dead empty you understand). The Yard (under staff supervision) is the new social centre for sixth form weekend shenanigans.

The golf academy is flourishing, currently number one in Europe, and golf is professionally coached throughout the school, with all pupils using top class facilities on campus

Full boarding, weekly boarding, flexi-boarding plus day pupils, the latter particularly well integrated. Sixth form boarders can get permission to go into Edinburgh on any night of the week 'providing that their work is in order'. They can go to a film, the theatre, concerts (rock or otherwise), and the upper sixth can go racing in Musselburgh, all of 10 yards from main school entrance. The young told this editor that they take taxis home after partying in Edinburgh and charge it to their parents' bill, this has been kyboshed by the school and buses are gaining in popularity. Younger boarders take the school bus of a weekend to Kinaird Park, which houses a collection of utterly desirable shops – a great improvement on Musselburgh. This is a chilly corner of East Lothian and the east wind whistling across the racecourse from the North Sea is an almost permanent feature (school is not so sure, and boasts of the Musselburgh micro-climate).

Background and atmosphere: Founded in 1827 in the 'honest toun' (which is why Pinkie House had the first electronic gates in Scotland), and bought by Hely Hutchison Almond in 1862 (a distinguished scholar of unconventional convictions – Scotland's answer to Dr Arnold). Loretto went fully co-ed in 1995. The traditional East Lothian ochre-coloured buildings straddle the A1; on occasion, the tunnel below is used for sailing boats...don't ask, it needs to be flooded first. Slightly disjointed campus with various outbuildings, including The Nippers and a wodge of playing fields north of the river Esk. Rolling plan of refurbishing houses and a certain amount of tinkering location-wise. School House has become the day centre. Pinkie House, with its important painted ceiling in the gallery under the roof, has a particularly gruesome extension and is home to some of the sixth form boys who have obviously driven out the ghost of the first Lady Seaton, Green Jean, wife of Alexander, who jumped from the gallery (there is a most unflattering portrait of her on the main staircase). The gallery itself, dissed by Historic Scotland as a dorm (too much sweating) is now a function room (roof repaired, £45k worth of fire alarms and sprinklers, bank of loos), licensed for 120, temporary kitchen available – that sort of thing. Lesser rooms converted into rather grand exam centre and extra lecture rooms. Linkfield, previously a pupil-led bar (ah, those were the days), now houses the CCF and outdoor centre etc. CCF for all, navy and army only.

Kilts on Sundays – some remnants of the traditional uniform remain. Red jackets the norm for all, with navy collars distinguishing sixth form: 'just get it sewn on, no need for new blazer'. Still no ties for daily dress. An absolute ban on any form of platform heels – no more 'tottering on the asphalt'. Second hand shop.

'The CRC (communication and resource centre) now houses a modern sixth form centre – designated areas for independent academic study, university admissions, individual tutoring and socializing'. Quite. This was formerly a disaster area with unusable polychrome covered computers on the first floor, it's now a jolly library with all sorts of nooks and crannies in the midst of the main school campus, useful when time is too short to get back to study bedrooms, and a good resource centre. Must have had more money thrown at it than you would believe, and finally, it works! 'The aim is to create an ambience more like a university's and provide good opportunities to develop leadership skills'. Yah.

Pastoral care, well-being and discipline: Zero tolerance for drugs no longer the norm – pupils are not

automatically out for being caught actively using any drug; though they are for dealing. 'Each case treated on its merits'. No random testing unless pupil has been suspended and is back on probation. The GSG wonders about 'legal spikes'. School is tough on persistent bullying ('We spend hours on it – please don't use the word "tough" '), cyber bullying the next kid on the block. Recognised ladder for punishments, no longer entirely in the houseparents' domain: breathalyser, gatings, rustications and out for alcohol; gatings and letters home for smoking. NB pupils can be expelled both for their own misdemeanours or if their parents have 'treated the school or members of its staff unreasonably.'

Pupils and parents: Usual Scottish collection. Not a lot of foreigners; representatives from 21 countries currently (penny numbers); large number of OLs' sons, daughters and grandchildren, some of whom join for the sixth form only. Numbers of first time buyers, particularly amongst the day crew, who see Musselburgh as a viable alternative to going all the way into town. Buses from all over: East Lothian, central Edinburgh, the Borders and more in the pipeline. School operates a six morning, three afternoon schedule; day pupils can and do go home during the week at 4.30pm if they have no further activities (otherwise it is 6.30/8.30pm).

Not really a Sloane/Charlotte Ranger school. OLs include a gang of MPs, Lord Lamont, Lord (Hector) Laing, Andrew Marr and Alastair Darling.

Entrance: Own entrance exam or CE from Scottish and northern prep schools; 20 per cent of pupils come up from The Nippers en masse. Special exam and interview for those from the state sector or from overseas. Around 50 per cent now day, outstanding 20 per cent increase in boarders during the last few years, with more boys coming in sixth. Six GCSEs at C and above for entry into sixth form, with As in subjects to be taken at A level. Scholarships and bursaries are available.

Exit: Vast majority (85 per cent or so) stay on to sixth form. Edinburgh and Edinburgh Napier universities popular as well as Lancaster and Newcastle. Sporadic Oxbridge trickle (four in 2015) and a few to study overseas eg golf in USA and economics in Mengenegro, as well as one to Glasgow Conservatoire.

Money matters: Scholarships for academics, musicians, drama, art, sport, golf, plus scholarships for those from the state sector and for those coming up from The Nippers etc etc. Bursaries rigorously means tested (private detectives, that sort of thing) but the fiercely academic Almond Scholarship, worth 100 per cent plus is income blind. Sixth form scholarships and bursaries awarded to those 'who have deserved well of Loretto'.

Remarks: Famous Scottish co-ed public school that has embraced day pupils to combine the best of both worlds: trad boarding with robust day option. Small enough to gentle those in need of nurturing and big enough to compete with the rest of the Scottish pack. And with an almost unbeaten XV...

The Mary Erskine School

Ravelston, Edinburgh EH4 3NT

01313 475700
admissions@esms.org.uk
www.esms.org.uk

Ages: 12–18
Pupils: 733; joint sixth form: 250
Boarders: 17 full, 3 weekly/flexi
Day: £10,548 pa
Boarding: £20,634 – £21,162 pa

Linked school: Stewart's Melville College

Principal: Since 2000, Mr David Gray BA PGCE (50s), who was educated at Fettes, and read English at Bristol, where he did his PGCE. Taught English in a Bristol comprehensive, before moving to a language school in Greece, then taught English and modern Greek at Dulwich College and was head of English at Leeds Grammar, before heading Pocklington School in East Yorkshire, for eight years. Since the Erskine Stewart's Melville vast conglomerate forms the largest independent school in Europe, it is not surprising he feels he is in a position here 'to give something back to Scotland, having been away for almost a quarter of a century'. Brought up in Inverness, he is proud of his Scottish roots and sees himself and Stewart's Melville/Mary Erskine as at the 'most exciting cutting edge of Scottish education', and stresses that he's the first overall principal who is actually Scottish. Mr Gray spends part of the week in each school. We visited him at his base in Mary Erskine, where he was busily involved in compiling a history of the school for his teaching contact with the girls.

Very much a hands-on head, the principal reckons to keep sane (and fit) by swimming and jogging at 7am each morning, and is a familiar sight as he cycles between the two campuses. He also 'works the room' quite beautifully – 'We all think we know him well and that he knows our children almost as well as we do,' said one father (a gift no doubt inherited from his politician father?) Keen on promoting self-confidence in his pupils, he sees himself as an 'educator' and is teaching English and coaching cricket at Stewart's Melville. After 14 years he feels pleased that the school has 'become a gentler place' and that the 'children are wedded to our values of reasonable, sensible behaviour'. No need for draconian action on the discipline side recently – when silliness occurs, 'the student body can be very conservative on behaviour,' while parents 'don't want to be ashamed of the school'.

Mr Gray runs the twin senior schools with two deputy heads and the head of the co-ed junior school, Bryan Lewis, who is also vice principal. Mrs Linda Moule took over as deputy head of The Mary Erskine School in August 2009; she was previously vice principal of New Hall School, Chelmsford. Mr Neal Clark, deputy head of Stewart's Melville for

The principal reckons to keep sane (and fit) by swimming and jogging at 7am each morning, and is a familiar sight cycling between the campuses

the last 10 years, describes himself as a 'grammar school boy, in tune with Scottish social culture'. Significant developments in recent years, including refurbishment on the main hall/theatre at MES and construction of six new tennis courts.

Academic matters: The principal and three heads have agonised together over the pros and cons of single-sex v co-ed. All four speak with the same passion – and often the same phrasing – of their 'best of both worlds' system. Boys and girls educated together at junior school, separately from age 12-17 – gains for girls (being able to get on with learning) and boys (feeling free to talk about poetry etc); then the social etc gains of co-education for the sixth year and all activities. 'Not a highly selective school' – however described by an educationalist as a 'grade one academic machine'. Classes of up to 25 (20 for practical classes) setted, with groups subdivided to extend the most able.

School has embraced the new Advanced Highers in depth – greater analysis, independent study, projects and dissertation. Mr Clark – glad that so many students do three Advanced Highers with considerable success – notes that, in recent years, as admission to Scottish universities has

become very competitive, there remains a strong desire to undertake further Highers. Recent results show a pleasing number of As and Bs across the board in both schools, with some outstanding successes in history, sciences and maths. Advanced Higher results in 2015: 58 per cent A. Higher results also impressive (63 per cent A in 2015), particularly at MES 'on the languages front' and for SMC in history and geography. French, German, Spanish and Latin on offer to Advanced Higher grade.

Standard grades phased out (except drama) in favour of Intermediate 2 (which is based on the same assessment pattern as Highers) and the new National 5. Results pretty impressive here too – 76 per cent A grades.

Very good links (still) with the Merchant Company, which provides masses of business breakfasts and connections with professional firms around Edinburgh. Single IT network across all three schools with 'massive schools' intranet', interactive whiteboards galore and close on 1000 computers. Biology department links with the horticultural department of the world famous Edinburgh Botanic Gardens. Impressive careers structure across both schools and excellent library facilities. Pupils can sign in for private study.

Schools combine for sixth form, most extras and pastoral structure. In the interests of integration, sixth formers have to take academic courses from both schools – a feat resulting in limitless (almost) variety of course permutations, miraculous timetabling and quite a few bus journeys. Outstanding back up for those with learning difficulties – school uses its own educational psychologist and counsellor; 'will never abandon anyone'.

Games, options, the arts: Big is beautiful, providing a list of over 75 different clubs for all, from allotment club to Greek, costume design to curling and cross-country, lunchtime and post-school – popular. Major sports have separate clubs for ages/stages and 27 rugby teams. Good at football too. Girls prefer hockey and basketball, still better at shooting than boys, and both sexes join the voluntary CCF (trillions of girls, over 400 members in all). Two super floodlit Astroturfs at MES, 'so everyone gets a chance'; dramatic wavy roofed swimming pool (at Stewart's Melville) with co-ed sixth form slump-out room adjacent, new gym (at MES), cricket pavilion (MES again). FPs and current pupils share sporting facilities at MES; extra games pitches and Astroturf at Inverleith. Needle matches in almost all disciplines, with FPs representing both county and country across the board.

Incredibly strong drama – regular performances at the Edinburgh Festival and throughout the year at the Playhouse etc. Masses of every sort of orchestra. New £2.5m performing arts centre's opening splash was Snowman composer, Howard Blake, and Scottish Chamber Orchestra. Centre took 12 years in the planning – seats 800 with a 'retractable' stage and dividing walls, replacing the old assembly hall, which was huge and impressive, and jolly nice in its way. Pupils can learn to fly and ski (Hillend and the real thing: the Alps, Canada). Brilliant debating team – regularly the Scottish Debating Champions and European Youth Parliament winners; SMC has represented Great Britain abroad all over the shop. Good home economics. Art spectacular – dramatic art room atop MES (with adjoining pottery and greenhouse).

> *Very good links (still) with the Merchant Company, which provides masses of business breakfasts and connections with professional firms around Edinburgh*

Boarding: Two boarding houses, Dean Park House (boys) and Erskine House (girls), furnished like large (and very well-equipped) family houses and based on the edge of the Stewart's Melville campus. Tremendous family feel – boarders are encouraged to invite friends home, caring house parents, only 56 boarding places.

Background and atmosphere: Stewart's Melville campus is based round the magnificent David Rhind-designed Daniel Stewart's Hospital, which opened in 1885 and merged with Melville College in 1972. Fairy-tale Victorian gothic with a cluster of necessary modern additions, surrounded by ever-decreasing games pitches and car parks. The old chapel is now a library, complete with organ and stained-glass windows. Stewart's Melville is also home to the senior department of the junior school.

Mary Erskine was founded in 1694, as the Merchant Maiden Hospital, moved to Ravelston in 1966, changing its name to The Mary Erskine School, and amalgamated with the boys' school in 1978 (girls wear charming Mary Erskine tartan kilts). MES clusters in decidedly 1960s architecture – with now quite a lot of more modern extensions, round the pretty but sadly overwhelmed Ravelston House (1791): swimming pool, tennis courts, games pitches, Astroturfs etc, the last much used by FPs. The nursery department and the youngest classes of the junior school are also based here.

Smart dining room complex serves all juniors and 80 per cent of seniors opt in. Sixth form coffee bars with stunning overview of school and pitches.

Regular buses from East and West Lothian and Fife service both schools, which operate as one, under the auspices of Erskine Stewart's Melville Governing Council. Each school, though, is fiercely proud of its individual heritage.

Girls prefer hockey and basketball, still better at shooting than boys, and both sexes join the voluntary CCF (trillions of girls, over 400 members in all)

Pastoral care, well-being and discipline: Both schools (which are linked and have a joint sixth form) have a tutorial system for the first year, followed by house system in upper schools. Houses are common to both schools and house competitions have mixed sex teams. Good links with parents. Brief is that 'all children have a right to be happy here'. Code of conduct established by consulting pupils so 'they know exactly where they stand'. Excellent anti-bullying policy: wary pastoral staff and peer-support group 'with professional training' stop 'children slipping through the net'. Sophisticated PSE programme right up the school, including study skills. Buddy system for those coming up from junior schools.

Automatic expulsion – 'zero-tolerance' – for those bringing in illicit substances – 'Those on the periphery of the same incident will not necessarily be excluded, but can come back in as long as they agree to random testing'. Smoking 'unacceptable and pupils suspended'. Alcohol 'not an issue in school'.

Brief is that 'all children have a right to be happy here'. Code of conduct established by consulting pupils so 'they know exactly where they stand'. Excellent anti–bullying policy

Pupils and parents: Edinburgh hotch-potch of New Town and suburbs, with many first-time buyers and lots up from England. Siblings and FPs' children. Taking over a third of Edinburgh's independent secondary pupils, it's less élitist and perhaps less dusty than some city schools. Children living far out can spend the night when doing evening activities. Parent-teacher group ('the red socks brigade') slightly better organised into a Friends of the School group – fundraising, ceilidhs, 'good cash cow'.

Entrance: At 11,12, 13 or sixth form – otherwise 'by default'. Automatic from junior school. Entrance assessments held in January but can be arranged at any time. Waiting lists for some stages but just go on trying. Entrance to upper school is by entrance exam, plus school report plus GCSEs/National 5s. Numbers up overall.

Exit: Minimal leakage pre Highers; most sixth year (96 per cent) go on to university (gap years, still an option for some), most opt for Scottish universities – Aberdeen, Edinburgh, Dundee, Glasgow, St Andrews and Strathclyde popular – but a number apply to English universities including one or two to Oxbridge (three in 2015). SATs (for American colleges) not a problem; some go to European universities. Art college, music/drama are popular alternatives.

Money matters: Scholarships/bursaries available, some linked to the Merchant Company, others sibling directed. 'No child will be left wanting in a (financial) crisis.'

Remarks: A glance at the school mags, Merchant Maiden and The Collegian, sums it up: multiple hockey, rugby and cricket teams, Oxbridge places, fabulous art, photos and writing, plus fascinating glimpses from boys and girls reporting on the same activities with subtly different views.

An outstanding school: happy pupils, happy staff – focused on self-development with impressive results.

Merchiston Juniors (aka Pringle)

Colinton Road, Edinburgh EH13 0PU

01313 122200
admissions@merchiston.co.uk
www.merchiston.co.uk

Ages: 7-13
Pupils: 104
Boarders: 26 full and 7 step-up (flexi) boarders
Day: £13,620 – £15,390 pa
Boarding: £19,035 – £22,125 pa

Linked school: Merchiston Castle School

Head: Mr Andrew Hunter BA (see senior school)
Head of junior school: Since 2012, Mrs Niamh Waldron (40s); came to the school in 2005 and was previously head of The Pringle Centre.

Entrance: Most join at 7, via maths and English tests, informal interview and report from current school.

Exit: Unless intellectual impairment intervenes, or logistics apply, all move on to senior school (around 40 a year).

Remarks: Merchiston Juniors, aka Pringle, is tucked tidily into the south west corner of the school grounds, though pupils have access to, and use of, the entire campus eg swimming pool, gym, games fields.

Traditionally a boarding school, both Pringle (Merchiston Juniors) and Merchiston itself now boast a fair number of day boys, many of whom sleep over on occasion, often boarding full time by their last year in Pringle. Known to the rest of us as flexi-boarding, Merchiston prefers the term 'step-up' (softly softly catchee monkey). Pringle House can sleep max 46 boys at any one time. Enclosed in its own private (secret) garden; boys can climb the one tree as far as the white mark and do all the things that little boys like doing without being made to feel silly. Book-inspired day room, plus obligatory television and rather complicated game of Diplomacy up on the wall. School in good heart, well used, nothing flash but no signs of real distress either. Huge amount of dosh spent recently on mega-revamp including loos and individual showers.

Junior school has its own director of studies, tinies taught in the starkly modern Pringle Centre classrooms – we enjoyed a treatise on tropical fish from the youngest year group; computers in every classroom and a bank of laptops for class use. Langs from the start. Specialist teachers for science, maths, the arts. Learning support teacher dedicated to the juniors, who heads a team of one full-timer and roughly three part-timers. No pupil accepted who can't 'access mainstream education' (min 100 IQ). All pupils assessed on entry on a whole year group basis for reading, writing and 'rithmetic. Support is individually tailored to each pupil's profile. Plus cluster groups for foreign languages and Latin (age 11): as much to get boys up to speed as for actual diagnosable problems. In-class support too, plus 'concentrated units' for spelling, reading and individual subjects. Maths on the whole catered for by the maths department, whilst the SEN specialists provide support lower down the school – sometimes withdrawn and sometimes in class.

Chaps take lessons in main school aged 10, are set aged 11, and follow three individual sciences aged 12, moving seamlessly up to senior school (without common entrance) at the age of 13 or thereabouts.

Ten years in the same campus could be a daunting experience. Moving from one building to another within that complex might be the answer. Colinton is hardly Edinburgh City Centre, but the school itself is a bare five minutes' drive from the Edinburgh bypass, which might tick all the boxes for some.

Merchiston Castle School

294 Colinton Road, Edinburgh EH13 0PU

01313 122200
registrar@merchiston.co.uk
www.merchiston.co.uk

Ages: 13–18
Pupils: 460; sixth form: 160
Boarders: 297 full
Day: £13,620 – £21,945 pa
Boarding: £19,035 – £29,700 pa

Linked school: Merchiston Juniors (aka Pringle)

Headmaster: Since 1998, Mr Andrew Hunter BA PGCE, educated at Aldenham and Manchester University, where he read combined studies: English, theology and biblical studies. Came to Merchiston after eight years at Bradfield, where he ended as housemaster of Army House and, before that, eight years at Worksop, housemaster of Pelham House. Trails of glory on games fields: ex-county hockey, squash and tennis player (school has tennis academy in partnership with Tennis Scotland). An expat, he was brought up on a Kenyan coffee farm and started school at Kenton College, Nairobi. Married to the glamorous Barbara, who teaches art and design. Three children – one son a Merchistonian now at university, one son at college and a daughter also now at university. Keen on the arts, theatre, wine tasting.

He goes from strength to strength – spot of tinkering with the syllabus, trawling all over the UK, Europe, and the world on behalf of school, plus a dabble into building. A purpose-built sixth form house opened after an £8 million fundraiser. Excellent Hunter-inspired 45 page information booklet that is undoubtedly the best guide to any school we have ever seen, plus a really comprehensive leaflet on exam results, including a rather complicated value-added section – other schools please note.

Academic matters: School continues to ply the mainly English system, though a few sit a combination of AS and Scottish Highers over two years. In 2015, 40 per cent A*/A grades at A level; 70 per cent A*/A grades at GCSE. Thirty-seven percent of Highers, and 100 of advanced Highers, A grades. All boys must do two separate sciences at GCSE and a large proportion go on to study science at A level. Maths, English and science results very good; humanities good, too, and increasingly popular. A level critical thinking, economics and classical civilisation and junior school Mandarin added recently. Excellent showing in out-of-school activities, maths, physics and chemistry Olympiads and the like.

Recent investments include Mount Olympus – a suite of classrooms for classics, economics and geography, and the Masterchef kitchen, in which senior pupils complete a practical course and gain

knowledge of nutrition, food hygiene and healthy eating. The Balfour Paul science laboratory was opened by Air Marshall Sir John Baird, Merchistonian (1951-55), primarily for use by junior pupils. The labs have all been refurbished – interesting design, repeated throughout the school: a mixture of trad tables and octagonal plinths. Interactive whiteboards and projectors in many classrooms – increasing use of computers as teaching tools; pupils from age 12 upwards are required to have their own laptop. Also a good IT suite plus more computers in the magical, double-decker Spawforth Library, but prep is not necessarily done online. Pupils must score 100 in IQ assessments to follow main curriculum and do the standard eight or nine GCSEs.

All pupils are assessed on entry on a whole year group basis for their reading, writing and maths. Support is specially geared for each pupil – all have individually tailored profiles. Timetabled support varies from year to year, with small groups for foreign languages and Latin, as much to get boys up to speed as for actual diagnosable problems. In-class support too, plus 'concentrated units' for spelling, reading and individual subjects. Maths on the whole catered for by the maths department, whilst the SEN specialists provide support lower down the school – sometimes via withdrawal, sometimes in class. Support for the gifted too. SENCo appears to be a one woman, 24 hour, referral unit – boys can and do come at all times. Complex problems need more info and background than she feels the SEN department can give.

All the dys-stream catered for, plus two or three currently with 'mild Asperger's' diagnosed in-school; ADHD not a problem, physical disability not 'a real problem': classes are relocated if access complicated; profoundly deaf boy recently went through the school with a (free) monitor paid for by West Lothian authority – wow! Can scribe in exams and pupils get extra time both in school and public exams. Really quite a large number of boys 'in the system'. Laptops not provided by the school, but masses in the special needs department, all on the school network, and parents often buy their own.

Fantastic pipe band, sounding good during our visit, with some of the smallest pipers looking like embryo masons, lugging their bagpipe cases with grave determination

Games, options, the arts: Rugby popular, cricket, athletics, curling back in favour, hockey growing, skiing, sailing. Well-used sports hall, very well-used swimming pool, weights room replaced by fitness centre. Merchiston Golf Academy based at nearby Kings Acre golf club. Tennis academy run jointly with St George's and Tennis Scotland – serious ambitions.

Wide variety of activities and successes in many areas. Popular CCF – community service and work in special schools a viable alternative, rifle range built into school wall. The head and the dean of sixth form extremely keen on outreach, so the latest initiative is a group of lower sixth formers mentoring in several Edinburgh primary schools. Masses of trips all over the place in every discipline.

Fantastic pipe band, sounding good during our visit, with some of the smallest pipers looking like embryo masons, lugging their oblong bagpipe cases with grave determination. Strong choral tradition, including close harmony group, and a number of orchestras and bands. Super art department, with terrific paintings both in the department and displayed all over the school. DT uses Cad Cam – good juxtaposition with computer suite and music hall, open till late.

Boarding: Boys work in their dorm space and day boys have desks in the same area – superb posters. Sixth formers are billeted to each house for the year to act as monitors and have attractive kitchens to make their tasks less onerous. Cooking the flavour of the month – stunning pupil-inspired kitchens. 'Steaks would be good,' said our guide and housemaster. Impressive sixth form boarding house, Laidlaw House – 126 ensuite bedrooms, modern kitchens, a café area, multi-gym and open plan social spaces with stunning views of Edinburgh.

Just under a quarter of boarders are overseas. Flexi-boarding from age 7, also an option for senior boys though at the housemaster's discretion and dependent on availability, without charge if they are about official business – 'debates, plays and the like', or for £45 a night if for 'parental convenience'.

Background and atmosphere: Founded in 1833 by scientist Charles Chalmers, moved from Merchiston Castle (now owned by Napier University) to the rather gaunt, purpose-built Colinton House in 1930 (ruins of Colinton Castle in grounds). Set in 100 acres of park-like playing fields, with stunning views to the north.

Sick bay with visiting sports physiotherapists, own ultrasound machine and delightful bubblegum pink isolation room (which would put any boy off thoughts of malingering)

School in good heart, well used, nothing flash here but no signs of real distress either. Huge amount of cash recently spent on revamping loos and individual showers and refurbishing various boarding houses.

Sick bay with visiting sports physiotherapists, own ultrasound machine and a delightful bubblegum pink isolation room (which would put any self-respecting boy off thoughts of malingering). Dining hall with servery and buffet service. Food very good – soup, meat and veg, acres of bread and rice pudding when we visited, impressive salad bar for a boys' school too. Boys praise the new arrangement: 'The food is still good at the end of term' – when the budget is low.

First floor Memorial Hall doubles as a chapel (service inter-denominational) and dance hall and boasts Cameron tartan cushions on removable pews, with an impressive tartan stair carpet up to the entrance. Girls are regularly corralled in from (primarily) St George's, but also Kilgraston and St Margaret's, for reel parties, with lots of practice before the real thing – Merchiston boys are regularly voted the best dancing partners in Scotland. Visiting girls 'not a problem' – they come and go at weekends and can join the boys in the sixth form club. Vast number of trips and options for boarders – day pupils can join if space available.

Pastoral care, well-being and discipline: Good rapport between pupils and staff. The horizontal house system is said to have made bullying practically 'non-existent' and 'Anyway, physical bullying has been superseded by text bullying from mobile phones'. Head will and has asked pupils to leave. Believes in tough love, though a couple of prefects to whom we spoke obviously hadn't needed to hear the phrase before. Mr Hunter is keen on parent/

pupil/school partnership; will take in boys who have been excluded elsewhere – both boy and parent sign a contract and the boy will be subject to very stringent and regular drugs testing routine. Expect to be drugs tested if either caught or suspected of dealing or dabbling, followed by (but nothing in black and white) temporary or permanent exclusion.

Ordinary misdemeanours (alcohol, smoking etc) are treated on their own demerits. No longer cool to smoke. Discipline seminars. Jolly school policies booklet, reprinted every year, of which head is justifiably proud, lists all the dos and don'ts of the place. Purchase of cigarettes or alcohol on or off the campus and dealings with betting shops are no-go areas. Betting is a new one to the GSG, but perhaps other schools aren't as clear-cut in their expectations.

Low grade rumours persist about charges of historic abuse: the school 'has been made aware of allegations concerning a former member of staff. We have passed this information to the police and we understand they are currently making enquiries' (latest update – no case to answer – no complaint has been made). 'We have also notified the Care Inspectorate, Education Scotland, the Registrar of Independent Schools and the General Teaching Council for Scotland'. Recent Care Inspectorate reports have been fairly sniffy about 'the quality of child protection practice': a couple of former teachers were charged previously, with an even earlier incident resulting in suicide. As the current case involves a female member of staff having 'inappropriate relationships' with pupils at this all boys' school, the outcome should be intriguing.

Girls are regularly corralled in for reel parties, with lots of practice before the real thing – Merchiston boys are regularly voted the best dancing partners in Scotland

Pupils and parents: 'A down to earth school, rooted in values,' says the head. The only all-boys boarding school in Scotland. Strong middle class ethos, good values – no change here. Record number of pupils in the school. Around five per cent are expats. Real foreigners come from all over – Japan, Hong Kong and mainland China as well as the States, Mexico, plus a number from Europe, usually for the sixth form. Germany popular at present. Head keen not to lose the boarding ethos and littlies at Pringle are encouraged to flexi-board. Day officially ends at 4.10pm, but pupils can stay till after supper if they want to – must be the cheapest babysitting

service in the country. Boys open, friendly and well-mannered.

Sixth formers have attractive kitchens to make their tasks less onerous. Cooking the flavour of the month. 'Steaks would be good,' said our guide and housemaster

Entrance: At 13 and 16, always via exams – own entrance exam, scholarship exam or CE – 55 per cent pass mark; boys come from own junior school and from prep schools all over Scotland and the north of England. Entry to sixth form automatic from inside school, others need a satisfactory report from previous school. Range of scholarships and means-tested bursaries.

Exit: Refer again to the useful little booklet for details of the favoured universities – two to Oxbridge in 2015, three to US and one to Hong Kong, and over half to Russell Group universities. Durham, Bristol, London, Newcastle, Edinburgh, Glasgow, St Andrews, Aberdeen all popular. Science, engineering, economics, management/business and languages/classics/English the favoured subjects. Pupils go on to be fully paid up members of the Edinburgh mafia – law lords etc.

Money matters: Myriads of scholarships and bursaries for almost everything but all are now means-tested – scholarships awarded for the honour alone. Sibling discounts with Kilgraston, Casterton and Queen Margaret's York. New Laidlaw scholarships donated by Merchistonian to pay full fees for several boys each year – targeting 'talented individuals whose financial circumstances would not otherwise allow them to attend Merchiston'.

Remarks: No change. Still the top boys' school in Scotland (indeed, the only boys-only boarding school north of the home counties, which extraordinary position achieved through defection to co-education by the rest) and on the way up anyway. Charismatic head; boys are encouraged to 'try their hardest, make the most of their talents and look after each other'. 'No thoughts of going co-ed,' say head, staff and boys – the latter positively shuddered at the idea.

The Mount School

Dalton Terrace, York, North Yorkshire YO24 4DD

01904 667500
registrar@mountschoolyork.co.uk
www.mountschoolyork.co.uk

Ages: 11–18
Pupils: 220; sixth form: 80
Boarders: 84
Day: £6,900 – £17,205 pa
Boarding: £18,945 – £27,225 pa

Principal: Since January 2016, Adrienne Richmond, previously deputy head at Durham High School for Girls. She has also been director of studies at Newcastle Central High. She studied maths at Newcastle and trained as a maths teacher at Manchester. She is an ISI inspector and a D of E award leader, enjoying hill walking and camping.

Academic matters: A level results 49 per cent A*/A in 2015, A*/B 75 per cent. Traditional A levels with biggest uptake in maths and sciences (perhaps due to recent recruitment of more international students to sixth form) though class size remains small 'with nowhere to hide,' said one sixth former, smiling ruefully. PE, theatre studies, psychology and business studies on offer too. Ever-expanding enrichment programme with weekly lectures, community and global focus. Strong uptake of EPQ – now extended down to GCSE years.

At GCSE, 58 per cent A*/A in 2015. Good choice of options, 10 subjects standard, MFL either French or German (Spanish GCSE on offer in sixth form). Maths setted in year 7 onwards, English in year 9 onwards. Good IT provision – Wifi and iPads

throughout, interactive whiteboards in most classrooms and two modern computer suites plus dedicated department clusters; qualifications including vocational OCR Nationals taken in middle school and sixth form.

Pupils and parents alike comment on the quality and commitment of teachers; girls enjoy lessons. 'They are kind, supportive, encouraging, nurturing as well as being fantastic teachers': one pupil voice spoke for many. A parent told us, 'When she has had a wobble, the teachers have been there supporting her; her form teacher understood and knew my daughter straight away'.

York used for local cross-curricular and thinking skills work via 'Investigating York' in year 7; archaeology is part of history in younger years; links with university. Elements of the Peacejam programme, devised by Nobel Peace Laureates, introduced to the sixth form, form part of a weekly enrichment carousel of activities within the curriculum for whole school.

Selective, though does well with all abilities including EAL – support available. Specialist learning support teaching provided in and out of classroom dependent on need.

Very good careers education, skills-based in year 10, work experience post-GCSE in year 11. Focus in sixth form is university preparation, particularly for medicine and Oxbridge, some jointly with co-educational Quaker school Bootham.

Games, options, the arts: Beautifully kept grounds with grass and hard tennis/netball courts, sports fields for hockey and athletics, an indoor pool and sports hall including a fitness suite. Successful at traditional competitive team sports and offers non-competitive options such as rock climbing, dance and outdoor pursuits. Has players at county and country level in several disciplines.

A parent told us, 'When she has had a wobble, the teachers have been there supporting her; her form teacher understood and knew my daughter straight away'

Very strong and varied musical life, from classical to rock; all abilities participate in Christmas concert; regular concerts with other Quaker schools. Almost half of pupils learn instruments at school. Regular speech and drama successes, regional winners of Poetry by Heart, best delegate at Model United Nations conference and regional team finalists in Rotary Youth Speaks. Annual school production, most recently The Witches; sixth form play produced entirely by pupils. Very impressive artwork throughout the school encompassing ceramics, photography, sculpture, textiles and graphics. Design and technology studied up to A level – no cooking, except for fun; sixth form university preparation.

Huge range of after-school activities, eg jewellery making, photography, ultimate Frisbee – a non-combat, self-refereed game originating in the US; all take part. D of E popular – strong tradition of community involvement. Emphasis on understanding the wider world and global issues is important – Peacejam, Ibba school in Southern Sudan, electronic links to Quaker schools in Palestine and Lebanon.

Boarding: Sixth form boarding is across the road from the main school building with younger boarding in the upper echelons of the main school building. Accommodation is comfortable and homely, recently refurbished. Three to four to a bedroom still the norm – no single rooms in sixth form.

Whilst 75 per cent of boarders are in school at weekends, the high number of sixth form boarders with right to opt out of activities means smallish numbers and a wide age range. Regular organised off-site activities and freedom for unescorted paired trips to the city centre from year 9.

Background and atmosphere: Origins go back to 18th century; present building, close to the centre of York, has a very fine 1857 façade with modern additions. Approached through iron gate from the car park, it's like entering the Secret Garden, though beautifully maintained, stretching beyond the eye to green fields – an unseen total of 16 acres. The girls make the most of the outdoor space, some practising their tennis strokes, others deep in conversation, and even 12 year olds are not too cool to race to the garden swing at break times.

Classrooms are a mix of old and new, very traditional library, which the girls enjoy, and a spacious and light dining room, serving excellent fare, decorated with posters to inspire the girls to reduce food wastage. Attractive and well-designed new sixth form study centre has revitalised the top end of the school, giving private study areas as well as allowing extra activities such as cookery and social gatherings.

Though only a small percentage of staff and girls are Quakers, the ethos is at the heart of the school, manifest in respect for everyone in the community, a high degree of tolerance of differences, caring for others and democratic practices. 'It provides girls with a moral compass,' says the principal. 'They are valued for who they are'. 'Very little herd mentality,' say parents; pupils are demonstrably happy to be themselves. The head girl is appointed by the school, as the 'girls have a strong sense of fairness and justice'; the school council,

conducted on Quaker business meeting lines, discusses internal affairs and, unlike most, really does have a voice. Morning Meetings include a period of silent reflection. Widespread involvement rather than bald achievement is regarded highly, and girls view additional activities, such as lectures from visiting speakers, as 'opportunities not to be missed'.

Pastoral care, well-being and discipline: Considered very important – an absolute strength of the school. Girls feel they have an identity, are known and receive a lot of individual attention. Size helps, and activities transcending year groups with good integration of international boarders promote cohesiveness from sixth form down, resulting in the friendly and happy environment. There is a lot of social interaction between year groups, observed in mixed ages, day pupils and boarders all round the same table at lunchtime. Peer mentoring from sixth form for younger pupils.

Non-confrontational approach to discipline, huge amount of trust around the place, which girls appreciate with a typical common sense approach. 'If you mess up, you mess it up for everyone'. Time is given to listen to pupils and they are encouraged to speak and have a voice – in a respectful manner.

Exclusion only for persistent offences or major breach of rules, though the current management has not had to deal with incidents involving drugs or alcohol. Even more extraordinary, there is no litter and no evidence of chewing gum. School puts this down to 'pupils having a strong culture of ownership of their school'.

Emphasis on understanding the wider world and global issues is important – Peacejam, electronic links to Quaker schools in Palestine and Lebanon

Plenty of contact with parents – school website, weekly newsletter. Termly forum where parent representatives meet the senior leadership team to discuss topics of mutual interest.

Pupils and parents: Not just those with Quaker connection (it's the only all-girls Quaker school in England) – large number of local parents, often without an independent school background; not a county set school but local family loyalty over several generations. Wide range of religions or none. Over 60 per cent of senior school board – half are in the sixth form; the majority are full boarders from Pacific Rim, South America, USA and a variety of other countries, though 'not too many from

Non-confrontational approach to discipline, huge amount of trust around the place, which girls appreciate with a typical common sense approach

any one language group'. Some European, mainly German Dresden Scholarship pupils plus several MOD funded. Girls wear white shirt, tartan skirt and blue jumper; no uniform for sixth form – 'relaxed' dress code. Famous old girls include Dame Judi Dench, Margaret Drabble, Antonia Byatt, Mary Ure, Kate Bellingham, Laura Sayers.

Entrance: Assessments for years 7-10 entry in English, maths and verbal reasoning plus interview with principal, who looks for 'spark – interesting girls with wide interests'. School report also important. Average and above average abilities catered for. Six GCSEs A*-C and interview for sixth form.

Exit: A very small number leave post-GCSE, most for local sixth form college. Otherwise to a variety of universities, predominantly Russell Group – Exeter, Nottingham and Bath currently popular. One to Cambridge in 2015 (medieval and modern languages), three to Central St Martins and two lawyers.

Money matters: Year 7 academic and music scholarships; year 9 academic, art and design, sport, music and drama; lower sixth (College) academic, art, sport, drama and music – all give five per cent remission of fees, to which a means-tested bursary of up to 100 per cent can be added. Music and drama scholars get free lessons. Separate bursary fund for Quaker children.

Remarks: True to its Quaker ethos, evident in the school's caring and cohesive community of multi-faith and international students. Girls are highly motivated self-starters, with teachers who prepare them well for life outside the school gates. Articulate, mature, collaborative rather than competitive, but nevertheless driven by a determination to do as well as they can.

Mowden Hall School

Newton, Stocksfield, Northumberland NE43 7TP

01661 842147
info@mowdenhall.co.uk
www.mowdenhall.co.uk
C of E

Ages: 3-13 years (boarders from year 4)
Pupils: 140 (83 girls, 57 boys)
Boarders: 37 full, 64 weekly/flexi
Day: £8,550 – £17,160 pa
Boarding: £22,230 pa

Headmaster: Since September 2014, Mr Neal Bailey BA PGCE (30s), previously directeur of Sauveterre, the French school which hosts the year 7 Mowden children for a term each year. He has also taught at Cothill. Educated at Eton and Newcastle University (international business management), and worked in the City before turning to education. He teaches French and maths and is a talented sportsman, particularly keen on football, running and tennis, plus skiing, surfing, camping and bushcraft.

His wife, Nici, is also a qualified teacher, specialising in individual SEN support, and is head of pastoral care. They have two young sons who have joined the school.

Entrance: Wide ability range – non-selective, informal assessment and interview with head. Majority of pre-prep transfer to prep. Pupils come from local or prep schools all over the north of England and southern Scotland – Northumberland, Yorkshire, Cumbria, Dumfries and Galloway, Scottish Borders.

Exit: Oundle, Uppingham, Shrewsbury, Newcastle High and Ampleforth most popular this year, though Eton, Harrow, Downe House, Rugby, Millfield, Queen Margaret's, Sedbergh, Glenalmond and Fettes feature. Some 40 awards in last five years. Few leave at 11.

Remarks: Splendid setting, on a 50 acre site with fine views, reached via a sweeping drive, dodging wildlife, sleeping policemen and miscreants ignoring the one way system through the estate. Far less isolated and much more accessible (just off the A69 and 10 miles from Newcastle) than its setting would suggest. Though unusual for the times, no mobiles, no iPods or electronic devices allowed. Pupils communicate with their parents by the old fashioned means of weekly letters, email (access after supper) or use of the two payphones. Neither pupils nor parents had any complaints.

Impressive sports fields abound (games every afternoon) and woodland provides a muddy but exciting landscape for den-building competitions

and a BMX trail. Also the much anticipated 'gappy games' which involve an energetic 'hare and hounds' pursuit through natural terrain led by the gap students. Indoor heated swimming pool, but sadly no Astroturf.

The heart of the school is the main house, the Victorian Newton Hall, which houses the head's family, common rooms, library and dining rooms on the ground floor and boarding accommodation on first and second floors. Many additions and conversions, including a gym and theatre. Prep classrooms are housed in estate buildings around the former stable yard. Light bright classrooms with plenty of work on display and heaps of encouragement on hand. Cleverly converted science, art and technology centre in the stable yard (very busy at club time in evenings and over weekends) and super art. Amazingly detailed plaster casts of hands on display after weekend master class run by Oundle head of art.

Prep children are set for English and mathematics for years 4 and 5, then streamed from year 6. The top class studies Greek and a number will sit scholarships (good track record). Maximum class size 16; French for all from nursery; Latin from year 5. Good and imaginative teaching at all levels. 'Our teachers make learning exciting', said one pupil to a chorus of nodding heads. SENCo with specialist dyslexia qualification provides support throughout the school and EAL qualified teacher works with small number, primarily Spanish children.

Woodland provides muddy but exciting landscape for den-building. Much anticipated 'gappy games' involve an energetic pursuit through natural terrain

Focus on CE kicks off in year 7 after the unique experience of 'entente cordiale', a term spent at Château de Sauveterre near Toulouse, immersed in French and the French way of life. This experience is reinforced on their return through weekly lunches with French speaking staff. Children also spend a week in summer term in year 7 at Tree School in Dorset, a centre for natural sciences. Assisting scientists from the Natural History Museum, children extract DNA from trees and plants for an international project to barcode Britain's plant life.

The next step is a big one and the school has close links with the head and senior staff at a number of senior boarding schools. Choices helped by regular reporting through prep years; effort and attainment grades every three weeks; full written report each term. Pupils de-stress after

CE with a diverse and challenging three week leavers' programme.

The first step can be nursery from the age of 3 and the unstreamed pre-prep, popular with local families, though small numbers. Accommodated in attractive building with years 1 and 2, separated from main house by the netball courts; year 3 providing well-prepared transition to prep school, housed separately in adjoining building. Nursery and reception linked through sliding doors and direct access to outdoors play on its way. Own secure playground. Specialist music, French, IT and swimming; drama from year 2. No iPads here, weekly IT lesson in IT suite from reception; a PC in each classroom. Range of clubs and activities; after-school care until 6pm is an extra.

Keenly sporting – particularly successful at rugby, netball and girls' hockey, with soccer, swimming and tennis also popular. Sport (activities on Tuesdays, ranging from first aid to woodwork) timetabled for an hour each day and all of Wednesday afternoons, from year 3. Evening clubs (priority for boarders) offer usuals plus fencing, cookery and Scalextrix. Healthy number of musicians; choir and music ensembles from orchestra to rock and blues; music workshop three times a term and as one mum puts it, 'a child who has just started the violin will play a tentative piece on the stage followed by a grade 6 trumpet player, and no one turns a hair'. Big Christmas production; most recent was Joseph, involving cast of over 100.

Stars for academic work, house points for good behaviour – these far outweigh debits, which require some form of community service and can accumulate to Wednesday afternoon detention. Children are allocated to one of four houses, named after illustrious northerners, and sit with their house chums at lunch. Plenty of healthy, inter-house rivalry.

Relaxed but cheerful, busy and purposeful atmosphere, a family school with a healthy balance of discipline and freedom. Endorsed by parents, who 'love the family atmosphere', and 'believe that if their children are really happy they will flourish'. Pupils encouraged to have a 'broad outlook', be open-minded and prepared to 'have a go', otherwise they may struggle here, at least initially. Good food in agreeable dining room with staff seated at each table, children on rotas to clear plates. Healthy eating is a focus in accordance with the school's enthusiasm for sport, fitness and general well-being; add to that the recently ordained school chaplain and this should ensure that both body and soul remain in good shape.

Boarding numbers are growing. All children (however local) encouraged to board early and particularly for their final three years. Response to current market means that flexi-boarding remains an option, although the emphasis is on full boarding. Separate accommodation for girls and boys under the daily operation of the much-loved matron (Matey Ellie) and her team. Tidy dorms, though not excessively so; plenty of personalised walls to make them feel homely. Storage space limited and in corridors for most; year 8 have modern high sleeper beds.

Weekend life is kept busy and full, with Saturday school, lots of expeditions, outdoor pursuits of all kinds (madly popular), plenty of staff on hand. Deputy head ensures that Saturday evenings have a clear focus (themed suppers – Mexican night, Harry Potter evening etc) and that Sundays are structured. Many boarders opt to stay in for the weekend – four exeats in autumn and two in spring and summer. Children work hard and play hard and when asked what they do at home replied, 'have a rest'.

Parents a mix of long-established Tyne Valley residents, Newcastle professionals, Forces, north Cumbrian and Yorkshire county set, Borders and Scottish landowners and the occasional country squire. Fair percentage of first-time buyers opting for boarding as a lifestyle choice rather than because of any long-standing family traditions. Parents we spoke to see it as a 'go-ahead school on the up'.

Good traditional prep school with lots going on, exuding energy from the top down. Concentrates on developing well-rounded individuals whilst still aiming for those highly competitive top scholarships. Very positive comments from parents.

Queen Ethelburga's College

Thorpe Underwood Hall, York, North Yorkshire YO26 9SS

01423 333330
qeoffice@qe.org
www.qe.org

Ages: 14–20 (junior boarding from 6)
Pupils: 476; sixth form: 210
Boarders: 404 full
Day: £14,085 – £14,985 pa
Boarding: £32,835 – £34,434 pa, International Boarding £40,236 – £42,471 pa

Principal: Since 2006, Mr Steven Jandrell BA (50s), married to Margaret, with a young son at home. Warm, friendly, genuine and approachable, he understands education and enjoys discussing it. Well-respected and liked by staff and pupils, he's part of the furniture, having been here for many years as head of music and deputy head. Long-standing parents describe him as 'the best head so far'; 'He's a good listener who doesn't bat you away with standard answers'. A successor to more commercial heads here, he's a breath of fresh air.

Academic matters: Small classes, unashamedly setted, with regular testing for all – pupils say 'it's good for us'. Sixteen maximum per class for A levels. Choice of 20 A levels, with BTecs for those with less academic bent. French, Spanish and German for all, Russian and Chinese all on offer. No classics. Single science available – and fab modern labs with spectacular views. High percentage of overseas students means that science and maths are a strength. In 2015, 70 per cent A*/A grades at GCSE; 81 per cent A*/A grades at A level.

Dyslexia help available. All children tested on arrival in the prep school during the first half term, ed psych's report if necessary, usually individual lessons for free twice a week, if more needed then extra charge. Three specialist teachers of specific learning difficulties. EFL free throughout the school.

Very happy to be judged by its positioning within school league tables. However, this is achieved largely by separating off from year 10 upwards in the Faculty, a school-within-a-school offering an alternative less academic but more creative and vocational option. Although this is on the same site and with the same uniform, its results are supplied – and judged – separately. In 2015, 30 per cent A*/A and 61 per cent A*-B grades at GCSE

A classy medical centre that resembles a private hospital and oodles of huge common rooms – all with leather sofas, toasters and TVs

contrasts with 81 per cent A*/A at A level (many take BTecs and A levels in their native language). About 60 per cent of Faculty students are from abroad. NB overseas parents in particular should note that the fees – including the astonishingly high international ones – are the same for both schools, and ensure they know which they are paying for.

Games, options, the arts: Music (for all) on the up under 'fantastic' head of music, with frequent opportunities for performance. The old refectory (now the Phoenix Centre) contains no fewer than four practice drama and dance studios and a dedicated theatre. Art good and strong, with sewing machines in the art department. Enthusiastic home economics and Leith's food and wine course for sixth formers (no more than two sets of eight per year group), with the smashing kitchen used for grown-up classes in the holidays.

Ten acres of floodlit pitches for hockey, soccer, rugby, high jump, volleyball etc and four new Astroturfs. CCF popular, clubs for IT, archery, fencing, golf. A new swimming pool has just opened as part of the giant sports centre. D of E with plenty of gold participants. Lots of extracurricular activities – the list is (almost) endless, but some are costly.

Boarding: From age 6 (at Chapter House). International students from 61 counties make up about two-thirds of boarding community. Modern boarding accommodation consists of smart and well-equipped bedrooms, the majority now with private bathrooms, all with flat screen TVs (in fact two TVs in some twin rooms – just in case these lucky pupils wish to watch different programmes..), DVD players, telephones with voice mail, fridges, electric kettles, microwaves, air conditioning, trouser presses, room safes and ice-makers – pretty much everything except a mini-bar in fact. Great attention to detail and, it would appear, no expense spared – new boarding houses have fantastic limed oak doors, skirting boards et al. A classy medical centre that resembles a private hospital and oodles of huge common rooms – all with leather sofas, toasters and TVs. Houses for the younger ones surrounded by squidgy playgrounds filled with serious kit. Boys' and girls' accommodation is separate. Day pupil centre for day children plus B&B available if needed. The campus has a strong mobile signal.

Houseparents occasionally express concern that individual facilities are so good that pupils, particularly senior (Chinese) boys, are loath to leave their bed/study rooms and join in communal activities. No Saturday school, but full range of activities on offer during weekends – trips to Whitby, the latest cinema preview. After their first term sixth formers can nip into York or Leeds on a Saturday night, but must meet the pickup by 10pm at the local station (or be in by 10.30pm if they miss the train).

Background and atmosphere: Founded in 1912, was the intellectual doyenne of the Northern Circuit, rivalled only by St Leonard's in Scotland. However falling numbers and threatened closure precipitated the move to Thorpe Underwood, conveniently situated 25 minutes from York and Harrogate and a 10 minute drive from the A1. Owned by the Martin family (who still live on site), Thorpe Underwood dates back to the Domesday Book, where it is described as Chirchie, Usebrana and Useburn, before becoming part of the monastery of Fountains Abbey in 1292. (The stew pond used by the monks to supply food for the passing travellers has been meticulously restored, though it now boasts a fountain, which might surprise earlier travellers, and has been reinforced with trim stones round the edges.) The hall itself was rebuilt in 1902 in best Edwardian Tudor style and the extensions have been sympathetically carried out with leaded paned windows to match the original. The place is a complex mix of old and new – in style and attitude – and full of surprises. Modern facilities sit comfortably alongside a trad country house setting, and modern teaching sits (less comfortably) alongside old-fashioned notions of a 'no trousers' policy for female students and staff.

Became part of the monastery of Fountains Abbey in 1292. (The stew pond used by the monks to supply food for the passing travellers has been meticulously restored)

Impressive newer office facilities include a vast dining room (The Undercroft) that doubles as an assembly hall – though the acoustics are pretty grim and mealtimes can be a deafening experience, say some staff. Huge solid oak tables fill the room with comfortable seating on the balcony above, alongside exciting sculptures courtesy of Mr Martin's brother. Fruit available at all times with good salad bar, home-cooked food with a veggie option. Self-service queuing system moves around barriers like a busy post office. A lift has

been installed for wheelchair users, a stair lift is also available. A popular activity centre has now been established on the perimeter of the campus.

The original Hall – previously the home of the Martin family – houses a traditional library and the Phoenix Centre. Some of the classrooms and corridors are a tad surprising, not least the excess of taxidermy and hunting trophies around the place – look out for the crouching tigers, which might upset small children or those of a sensitive nature (though they remain one of the most photographed parts of the school).

Leased for a peppercorn from a charitable foundation (originally the brain child of Brian Martin), has benefited from millions of pounds' worth of investment. Good, if not lavishly stocked, library, banks of computers, teletext business info displayed around the school, free internet available to all boarding houses, with Wifi covering the whole 100 acre estate as well. Regular formal dinner parties with silver service and speaker for sixth form 'to give them practice in the real world'. Almost 50/50 boy/girl mix, boarding numbers up, though still relying heavily on the overseas market (61 different countries represented here), and a clever move some years ago in reducing day fees has brought a considerable rise in day pupils too.

A car park for which most schools (and parents) would give their right arm, an apparently endless building programme and growing numbers – all in a quiet little backwater between York and Harrogate. Describes itself as a 'broad church' – and it's certainly that, though all faiths and none are welcome. In fact anyone who can afford it is welcome really – with little academic selection and a determination to meet all needs, the place could be in danger of becoming a jack of all trades, but its current level of success in doubling pupil numbers in six years is due, they say, to 'painstaking and careful design' and they are enormously proud of their 'very real and rapid progress'.

Pastoral care, well-being and discipline: According to one parent, the pastoral care here is really good – 'Can't plug it enough'. Tutorial system – tutors change yearly, no more than 20 tutees to each. Discipline is described as 'sensible' – exclusion for violence and selling drugs, possibly also for taking drugs, 'depending on what it is'. Reserves the right to search boarders' rooms and to test for drugs and alcohol – and does. Charming 'leavers' letter' inviting any former pupil (until they 'leave university, or their 21st birthday, whichever is the later') to contact the college – reverse charge – at any time, if they have got into a scrape and need help or (free) legal advice (a GSG first). 'One or two take up the offer,' says Mr Jandrell.

At time of writing, there was much comment in the press following a critical report from the

Independent Schools Inspectorate on the efficacy of QE's child safeguarding systems, including a network of CCTV cameras. ISI is due to review the school's action plan, which the school says covers all the points raised in the report, soon.

Brian Martin has stepped aside from his day-to-day involvement with the school while a police investigation is carried out into an allegation of a historic sexual offence. His daughter has taken over as provost.

Pupils and parents: No longer so fiercely middle class – lots of first time buyers, pupils come to board from all over: Scotland, Wales as well as East Anglia and locally on daily basis. Expect a mass of regional accents, as well as students from abroad – Chinese, Germans, Russians, Scandinavians, with a number just coming for the sixth form. Nine buses collect day pupils from all over Yorkshire (not cheap – one parent said it was less expensive to call a cab), buses collect from local station. Parents talk of 'exponential growth' at the school with a mix of pride and delight at being part of that success and the improved facilities, and some regret at both the loss of the small-time old school and the change in student profile.

Entrance: Many via Chapter House, but generally aged 14; As and Bs at GCSE for potential A level candidates at sixth form. External candidates come from other independents, local state schools or out of the area. Pupils below year 10 accepted at any time during the school year 'if places available'. Promotes itself heavily locally, nationally and internationally – regular pop-outs from Good Housekeeping and the like. Informative DVD which plays in Chinese Simplified and Traditional, English, German, Japanese and Russian. The heaviest prospectus bundle that we have ever

encountered, though fear not, it is fairly repetitive. Entry to College sixth form requires at least four As and 2B grades at GCSE; entry to The Faculty is four C grade GCSEs – more a matter of state of mind and wallet than qualifications.

Exit: Around 30 per cent of pupils leave after GCSEs. About fifty per cent of sixth formers to top universities; three to Oxbridge from the College in 2015.

Money matters: Ex-provost Brian Martin FCMI, FFA, FinstD, executive trustee of the QE Charitable Foundation, hasn't lost his Midas touch. A true businessman, he masterminds the marketing of the school and drives the development of the site. The school is well underpinned financially but quite expensive and 'you pay for absolutely everything,' say parents. Countered a little by masses of scholarships, plenty of awards, 30 per cent corporate body awards (boarding fees only), rebate if you move to QE from another independent school; 20 per cent discount for Forces, diplomats and professional bodies. Add to that list sports, art and music scholarships and many, many more. 'You can also pay by Barclaycard or Amex' – but it costs extra to spread the payment over several months. Very streetwise management and 'all awards granted will be repayable in full, if the school fees bill is not paid seven days prior to the commencement of each term, and, or, if a pupil does not complete their education with us for any reason, regardless of commencement age, until the completion of the end of year 13...' etc etc. Read the small print very carefully.

Remarks: Has come a long way, not just in its facilities but also in its academic provision.

However, in view of events that were still unfolding as we went to press, you may want to check the current state of affairs on our website.

Queen Margaret's School

Escrick Park, York, North Yorkshire YO19 6EU

01904 727600
admissions@queenmargarets.com
queenmargarets.com
C of E

Ages: 11–18
Pupils: 334; sixth form: 130
Boarders: 250 full
Day: £18,990 pa
Boarding: £29,250 pa

Head: Since April 2015, Mrs Jessica Miles MA PGCE. Prior to this was deputy head of Leweston School in Dorset for seven years. After graduating from Oriel College, Oxford with a degree in modern languages, she worked for short time in public relations and

arts administration, then did PGCE at King's College, London. First teaching post was at Dulwich College, where she became head of Spanish, deputy head of upper school and director of rowing. After a move to Dorset and a year teaching Spanish and

French at Sherborne School, she moved to Leweston. Married to Paul, with two sons.

Academic matters: Although entry is not particularly selective, academic success matters. Fine GCSE results: 59 per cent A*/A grades in 2015. At A level, mathematics, English, physics, chemistry, geography, art and French popular, but no weaknesses. Overall performance fine – 55 per cent A*/A grades in 2015. Pupil support department (three full-time) and two teachers for EFL.

Games, options, the arts: Lots of healthy outdoor life – an hour a day of sport for all. Highly successful sports department with games keenly played in glorious surroundings and stunning facilities: lacrosse (long journeys for fixtures), hockey (floodlit all-weather pitch), two swimming pools (one indoor, one outdoor), sports hall, tennis courts, dance studio, new sixth form cardio suite etc – hard to find something they don't have. Riding popular (private riding school on campus); some girls bring ponies, school keeps 15. Good art, but not an 'arty' school. Home economics for all. Strong choral music, and lots of drama in wonderful theatre. Stunning modern chapel, Catholics go to nearby Thicket Priory for mass; half-termly vigil masses in school; annual Anglican and RC confirmations. Extracurricular activities too numerous to mention but include clay pigeon shooting, driving remote control cars and climbing walls.

Boarding: Welcoming, homey boarding house for 11 year olds with a Cath Kidston inspired kitchen for tea, toast and home comforts around the Aga. Girls live in year groups all the way through – 'Prevents them from growing up too fast,' observed one pleased parent. School claims the strong vertical house system, house supper nights on Fridays and an assortment of trips and visits encourage girls of different ages to mix, new social mixing areas encouraging and supporting this. Year 5 has a boarding house named after old girl, Winifred Holtby; lower sixth boarders are housed nearby and enjoy sitting and walking on the Cloisters lawn – they do because they can. Their accommodation recently refurbished with rooms 'designed on American student loft living' – including drawers which are also steps up to their beds. Upper sixth formers have increased independence in attractively converted cottages on site; head girl has the first pick of houses; all have large kitchens, 'great for entertaining', and communal sitting rooms; cottage life has the feel of a college campus.

Background and atmosphere: Founded in Scarborough in 1901, moved to this fine Palladian house (by John Carr), with later 'rustic timber' purpose-built classrooms, in 1949. Glorious sweeping drive, set amongst 60 plus acres of North Yorkshire loveliness, the flag is flying proudly from the rooftop. A school where girls have big hair and even bigger ideas – aspirations and expectations, of self and others, are high. Confident yet not brash, articulate and considered, girls are fiercely loyal, hard working and committed. New social areas where girls of all ages meet together and the use of in-school mentors have brought increased opportunities for greater independence and respon-sibility. Girls now feel they have a voice and, being girls, they use it. The school earns many approving noises from parents as well as envious glances over the wall from its competitors, with good reason.

It's been top notch academically for quite a while now, but is cultivating a purposeful nurtur-ing side without losing any of its academic rigour. Has a large yet tight and cohesive campus with a number of Victorian additions, clever conver-sions, award-winning centenary theatre, chapel and indoor swimming pool. Superb library – wood panelling everywhere, open fire, huge windows looking out on to lawns – but not too precious to be used, the range of reference books is impressive; also smaller but well-stocked fiction library with the relaxed feel of a welcoming bookshop.

Circular dining hall (once an indoor lunging school), with somewhat noisy acoustics. Food much improved in recent years, say parents and girls, with school rarities such as a cappuccino machine and balsamic vinegar; younger girls envious of the privilege of pain au chocolat delivered to sixth form houses for breakfast, all very civilised. Breaktime snacks provided, excellent cakes and fruit, girls on school council keep a watchful eye over food provision and choice.

Girls now feel they have a voice and, being girls, they use it. The school earns many approving noises from parents as well as envious glances over the wall from competitors

Recent changes include an alteration to prep time; once timetabled and closely monitored – now girls choose where and when they do their prep, and, if need be, learn by getting it wrong. All part of the independence = taking responsibility phi-losophy. And it's working. However girls are kept 'pretty busy' all the time – new girls are monitored to check they aren't overdoing it and taking on too much in the early days. Uniform is an attractive tartan and charcoal; own clothes worn after tea – don't provide anything that you wouldn't want boil-washed. Smart dress code rather than uniform for sixth form, jackets required.

Pastoral care, well-being and discipline: The pace of life in this rural idyll is anything but slow and a there's a noticeable air of protectiveness towards the girls. 'There are no silly rules,' say parents and girls, but it is by no means light on discipline – 'We are pretty old fashioned about smoking and drink-ing'. Parents speak with great enthusiasm about the

Younger girls envious of the privilege of pain au chocolat delivered to sixth form houses for breakfast, all very civilised

life skills provided by being part of a boarding com-munity, citing 'independence, knowing how to get on with people, young and old, and standing up and being counted' as so very important. All girls have a personal tutor, around eight girls per staff member (including the head), and run on a three year cycle. Add to this a mentor for sixth formers who acts as a guide in their subject of choice to provide extra reading, advice and support university applications.

A café, assortment of TV rooms with games (including Wii), a room for Skype-ing home (priority given to overseas boarders) and new ICT rooms have really given the place a lift and provided the girls with much-needed places to go. Quiet work rooms for those who need or want it, and other rooms where girls can work or chat, computers arranged in pods and some even blissfully Facebook-free for those serious about working. Sixth formers also have their own socialising area known as the 'cel-lars' – once used for keeping wine cool, now a cool place for maturing girls to hang out with friends before, during and after school and to bring guests (boys even) at weekends.

Apart from school, not a great deal to do around here, so a trip to the village shop is an excit-ing treat – a shock for girls with serious shopping habits. Sixth formers can go into York during free time on Wednesdays and Saturdays; they are usu-ally careful not to abuse this freedom.

Pupils and parents: Friendly pupils, happy to chat and proud of their school, clearly enjoying the many benefits of living and learning in such a lovely environment. No lack of ambition – even younger girls talk about going to university as though it is a self-evident truth: 'You'd be hard-pressed to find someone who is not heading for uni,' they tell us. Parents mainly upper and middle class: landown-ers, farmers, professionals; boarders – some 20 per cent from overseas – span 13 nations and four continents, many from Scotland ('It's the first real boarding school you hit driving south'), Cumbria, East Anglia, and of course Yorkshire. Essentially the main catchment is the east coast train line. OGs include Winifred Holtby (author), Ann Jellicoe (playwright), Sarah Connolly (opera singer), Dame Justice Eleanor King (High Court judge).

Entrance: Own exam at 11, 12 and 13. Additional intake into sixth form: minimum eight GCSEs, including English, mathematics and a science, with at least two As and three Bs.

Exit: Virtually all sixth formers to higher education nationwide – Bristol, Exeter, Durham and London universities popular; two to Oxbridge in 2015. Courses include engineering, art foundation, history, actuarial accounting, music management and law. Small trickle post-16 to co-ed sixth form, a few girls becoming restless each year, though many go and look elsewhere before then deciding to stay put.

Money matters: Scholarships at 11, 12, 13 and sixth form; academic, art, choral, dance, drama, music and sport scholarships. Means-tested bursaries.

Remarks: According to one parent, with three daughters at the school, 'Whether your daughter is tall or short, academic or sporty, shy or confident, it works for them all – and that's the beauty of it'.

Queen Mary's School (Junior department)

17

Baldersby Park, Thirsk, North Yorkshire YO7 3BZ

01845 575000
m.chapman@queenmarys.org
www.queenmarys.org
C of E

Ages: Girls 2-11; boys 2-8 (boarders from 7)
Pupils: 96
Boarders: 2 full, 20 weekly/flexi
Day: £6,945 – £13,770 pa
Boarding: £18,660 pa

Linked school: Queen Mary's School

Head: Since September 2015, Mrs Carole Cameron, previously deputy and acting head at Queen Margaret's School in York.

Entrance: Non-selective.

Exit: Majority to senior school.

Remarks: Tucked round the corner from the Palladian mansion is the pastoral setting for the single storey timber classrooms that cosily house early years to year 2. They open out into a secure and spacious play area, and the boys and girls also have use of the main school facilities. Pre-prep is currently a girls' only zone; children receive a lot of individual attention and the department has been awarded the local authority's gold award for quality assurance.

Play-based learning and participation in department productions builds confidence in nursery, with care available until 4.10pm each day and flexibility in the number of sessions. From reception, core learning is in numeracy and literacy, with specialist teaching in games, swimming and music – and tinies have computers too. Emphasis is learning through fun, creativity and exploration. Each reception child can take the lead and organise a school trip for their class to enjoy – helps too if parents are farmers. Very small numbers allow interaction with older children at meals, playtimes and in celebrating special events.

Unique to years 1 and 2 are Thrilling Thursdays, when the day is spent out of school in a new experience, or in school with a special visitor. Specialist teaching extended to French and IT; cross-curricular projects using art and IT. Ballet, tennis, horse riding and gymnastics all available as extracurricular options, at a charge.

Girls in prep, years 3 to 6, are accommodated in the main school building and are taught in small, mixed-ability classes for all subjects. Fun, cross-curricular learning such as when an English lesson in invitation writing blossomed into a full-blown tea party for parents. A request to let them make cake – and they did.

Opportunities for performance; instrumental group and orchestra, theatre and music in and out of school. Full range of lunchtime and after-school activities, from God squad and confirmation to solar engineering and film making – clay pigeon shooting at extra charge. Lots of interface with senior girls, who help with clubs and in the production of performances, from choreography to stage management.

Secret missions, overnight camps and canoe expeditions – led by outdoor teacher Miss Charmer, Queen Mary's version of Lara Croft – lay the foundation for what's in store in senior school.

Girls encouraged to flexi-board from year 4 and sleep in designated three and four bedded dorms in the mansion's upper echelons. Often younger sisters of senior girls, their family home usually within 60 mile radius of the school. Some Forces' families, though declining, no international boarders. Very small number of junior boarders stay in school at the weekend, those that do enjoy outdoor activities, local attractions and have 'fun on a shoestring' with their older counterparts.

A warm, friendly and fun family atmosphere. Children thrive and develop in the small, secure and supportive environment with their horizons widened by outdoor pursuits and adventures. Parents like the 'relaxed approach that produces motivation without pressure'.

Queen Mary's School

Baldersby Park, Thirsk, North Yorkshire YO7 3BZ

01845 575000
admin@queenmarys.org
www.queenmarys.org
C of E

Ages: 11–16
Pupils: 232
Boarders: 24 full, 80 weekly/flexi
Day: £6,945 – £16,935 pa
Boarding: £18,660 – £22,020 pa

Linked school: Queen Mary's School (Junior department)

Head: Since September 2015, Mrs Carole Cameron, previously acting head at Queen Margaret's School in York. Geography degree and MA in education management; she has also been head of Highfield, the Harrogate Ladies' College prep school. She worked in schools in Nottinghamshire, London and Leeds before spending 10 exciting years in international schools in the Caribbean while her family lived in Grenada and the Cayman Islands. She has two grown up daughters.

Academic matters: Pleasing GCSE results in 2015 with 41 per cent A*/A grades. A very mixed ability school, non-selective intake – all take English, maths, dual sciences, religious studies; nearly all take French as well. Two sets of French in year 7; top set add German and bottom Spanish in year 8. Lots of role-play, telephone conversation and presentation work in lessons. 'Amusing yet educational,' seems to be the general opinion of the pupils. No exchanges but Spanish and French pupils regularly spend one term here. Classics and Latin on timetable and available as GCSE options, bringing GCSE

subject choice to 17 – pretty good for a school this size. German and music results consistently good and the humanities well represented.

Introduction of bespoke challenge curriculum, on timetable and led by outdoor adventure instructor, to develop 'collaborative working, leadership, problem solving and resilience alongside presentational skills, ability to research and evaluate'.

Very small tutor groups and tiny classes, setted and streamed. Lunch with form tutor; termly target setting with 'grades, a trigger for conversation'. Saturday morning school followed by drama rehearsals, choir practice and matches. Staff/pupil relationship exemplary – seems that school never closes and girls can be found wandering around in the Easter holidays having been 'doing extra workshops' with dedicated staff, who never seem to take holidays either. Parents also say staff very good at motivating their daughters without them feeling under pressure.

Good and sensitive SEN, most commonly dyslexia help; either two sessions of one-on-one or shared in a small group. Library used extensively, reading encouraged through wide selection of fiction.

Recent improvements in IT network, high level security where every device in school logged, necessary when lots of own devices; iPads provided in library and dedicated IT suite. Specialist teaching from year 1 with focus on upskilling rather than software package training; programming, network design and logic with project work cross-curricular – though not available as GCSE option.

Prepared for life post-16 through life skills curriculum alongside GCSE – first aid, cooking, managing finances etc. Good careers library, Cambridge profiling, interview training and work experience organised.

Games, options, the arts: Traditional sports, daily, full fixture list with lacrosse, athletics and tennis teams all doing well. Own tennis courts, all-weather pitches and small indoor swimming pool. Outdoor adventure is where the school comes into its own – from adjacent River Swale, popular for canoeing and the occasional swim (hardy girls up north), wild running assault course (aptly named WOLF), and even a 160 feet bungee jump as a special treat. No wonder the girls say, 'You learn to face your fears'.

Aerial performance at Christmas concert by outdoor education teacher to Walking in the Air

Music is very important and the place hums with junior and senior choirs and delicious concerts open to the general public as well as for inmates – impressive for a school of this size. Chapel choristers wear much-coveted green sweatshirts and give regular performances both home and away. Lots of opportunity for instrumentalists – classical focus though annual battle of the bands competition.

Bright, colourful art in the attics including creative textiles, ceramics; sewing machines in the DT room. Drama good and well supported, musicals popular, though lacking good performance facilities. Cooking timetabled and enjoyed by all.

Superb equestrian facilities; children can and do bring their own ponies and ride daily, girls enjoy mucking in – and out – in the stables at weekends, after lessons and occasionally before breakfast. Outdoor manège of Olympian size, as well as rides across the local landowner's fields, school in constant negotiation with neighbours to increase riders' scope, cross-country course on site. Tadcaster polo club is nearby and looks like becoming the next horsey activity.

Wide range of after-school clubs including the unusual pheasant plucking club, with fruits of their labours enjoyed at a dinner with invited guests. Superb selection of residentials, expeditions for all, plus D of E.

House activity – usual sport and performing arts plus boundary run and Wolf assault course. Fundraising for local and international charities – adopted school in Madagascar, support for child in Sherpa school in Kathmandu.

Boarding: Girls have a sense of ownership of their mansion – no showpiece, consequently shows signs of being well-used, a little shabby in places.

Staff and girls are happy with the relaxed atmosphere – like an extended family (all ages mix) with a mass of sisterly teasing

Boarding in top echelons; girls 'like sleeping in stately home'. Rash of good-sized dorms, three to five to a room; top bunks for flexi-boarders used only up to year 8. Bathrooms receiving a timely refurbishment; furniture tired in places, some with limited storage, though additional lockers on ground floor. Common rooms small and underwhelming, though totally underutilised, according to head of boarding. 'The girls have such a busy life there's no time for TV,' she said. Dorms on the balcony over the Great Hall are a rite of passage for those in their last year.

Background and atmosphere: Founded in 1925, moved from Duncombe Park to its present rural setting Baldersby Park in 1983. Said to be the first Palladian mansion built in Britain by Colen Campbell, 1721, and Jacobethanised following a fire in 1902. Impressive approach, long curving driveway bordered by pastures – like stepping into a Gainsborough landscape.

Well-proportioned, former drawing room now a head's study to die for. Glorious main hall used for daily service, with the girls sitting on the carpet, head sitting in front of the stairs, the choir ranged behind in serried ranks. When it is not being used for formal occasions, and even sometimes when it is (aerial performance at Christmas concert by pyjama clad outdoor education teacher to accompanied singing Walking in the Air), girls can be seen walking the trapeze from balcony to balcony high above the main hall, wisely harnessed; not a rite of passage but, as with most things here, girls encouraged to 'have a go'.

Beyond, leading off narrow corridors, a warren of classrooms, a number displaying 'dogs in residence' signs on their door. Home from home applies to staff canine pets as well as pupils. Girls like it and say they find a pooch pat mid lesson beneficial. Classrooms in the main building and converted outhouses; science department boasts a greenhouse and freshwater pond for hands-on experience.

School uniform evolves over the years with girls graduating from beige to green jerseys and royal hunting Stewart tartan kilts. Some rationalisation taken place; senior summer dresses culled.

School food is good quality, wholesome home cooking and girls' earlier wish for 'a visit from Jamie Oliver' to liven things up has almost been granted with appointment of a chef manager who trained in one of his restaurants.

Charming chapel, a peaceful haven for all; school has its own chaplain; school is keen that religion should be 'part of the school routine' but not rammed down the throat. Staff and girls are happy with the relaxed atmosphere – like an extended family (all ages mix) with a mass of sisterly teasing. Younger girls like to play and build dens in the woods, 'benign supervision' allowing a sense of freedom with a nod to health and safety. The early assumption of seniority (at 16 rather than 18) gives girls confidence and maturity – a great balance with the younger girls happily staying young and the older girls demonstrating early maturity and the ability to take on responsibilities.

They love 'the opportunity to try lots of different things' and the 'enduring friendships' they feel they are making, but some feel rural isolation and would welcome more social interface with other schools – work in progress.

Pastoral care, well-being and discipline: Like home. No petty rules and others which are bendable, but an underlying sense of organisation. Definitely carrot not stick, detentions rare; house points with head's awards for a tally of five; woman of the week award – much wider than academic achievement. Badges pepper senior pupils' uniforms – awarded for contribution and achievement across a wide range. Prefects elected by head, staff and year 10 ballot.

Outdoor adventure is where the school comes into its own – wild running assault course and even a 160 feet bungee jump as a special treat. 'You learn to face your fears'

Parents' requests granted when reasonable. Not a sophisticated place, no obvious sin, just an occasional ticking off for a girl wearing make-up, but it's few and far between.

Most board – flexi-boarding popular from year 4, building to weekly and termly boarding by year 10. Boarding staff and NZ gappies organise 'fun on a shoe string' weekend activities for around 15 to 25 girls; seniors don't have to join in. Boarding notice boards display weekly winners of 'good egg' and 'make a smile' awards.

Very few have never boarded and who can blame them, with pillow fights, mattress surfing down the great hall staircase and abseiling over the banisters as boarder activities. Discos, film nights and socials with Aysgarth boys (strong sibling links) for the younger pupils.

Pupils and parents: Local as opposed to county school – combination of first time buyers, local farmers, landowners and professionals – 'not as Tatler and Vogue as some of its competitors'. Relaxed 7.30am drop off time for working parents. Quite a lot of army families though number reducing – Catterick is just up the road – some of whom pop their daughters into the school 'while they are based in Yorkshire' and are so pleased with the place that they leave their daughters there, younger sisters often joining them, when they are posted elsewhere.

Offers six routes on school minibuses – encompassing Aysgarth, Masham, Helmsley, Ripon and Wetherby.

Parents and pupils can use school facilities in the holidays. No real overseas presence, one or two expats, a couple of Spanish and French for a term, but boarding holding up and no wish to change its nature.

Entrance: At any time, middle of term if needed. At all ages. Entry test but, places permitting, only those with special needs beyond the school's capability are liable to be turned away. Feeders local prep schools and primaries.

Exit: At all ages. Some take common entrance at 11, and a small number at 13. Girls have previously mainly gone to Queen Margaret's Eskrick, with one or two to Tudor Hall, Heathfield or co-eds, Uppingham, Millfield, Rugby. Senior girls go on to do A levels at Ampleforth, St Aidan's, Ripon Grammar, Sedbergh, St Peter's, Uppingham etc etc. Good collection of scholarships – music predominates, plus academic and sports.

Money matters: Not a rich school and not endowed, though has benefited recently from generous donations. Scholarships for academics, music, art and sport, plus discount for clergy daughters, sisters and Forces.

Remarks: Girls' – predominantly weekly – boarding school without a sixth form or international pupils. Queen Mary's is a very jolly place, a home from home, with muddy wellies on the doorstep, smiling cheery girls and teachers; a predominance of four-wheeled drives in the car park and very dog-friendly.

It provides a good solid education focusing on creating girls with confidence, a 'have a go' mentality and freedom to grow into their own skin. Fierce competition locally, shows in numbers lower down the school. It's possibly too small for those at the sharp end – but many would thrive here and the girls say they 'wouldn't change a thing'.

Rossall School

Broadway, Fleetwood, Lancashire FY7 8JW

01253 774201
enquiries@rossall.org.uk
www.rossallschool.org.uk
C of E

Ages: 11–18 (junior boarders from 7)
Pupils: 638; sixth form: 195
Boarders: 270 full, 12 weekly
Day: £10,200 – £12,450 pa
Boarding: £16,500 – £35,550 pa

Head: Since September 2013, Ms Elaine Purves BA PGCE (mid-40s). Brought up and state educated in Scotland and then in Nottinghamshire, Studied English and German at Hull University. On graduation she worked briefly for agricultural manufacturer John Deere in Germany before going to Durham to do her PGCE. She nearly returned to East Germany to teach English at Leipzig University, but after the Berlin Wall came down everything became uncertain and she ended up taking her first teaching post in the UK – at Oakham School in Rutland – and she has worked in the independent sector ever since. From Oakham she went to The Royal High School, progressing through the ranks from head of languages eventually to deputy head. After 13 years in Bath, in 2006 she became head of Ipswich High School for Girls, where she stayed for seven years before moving her whole family from Suffolk to Lancashire to take the job at Rossall.

One aspect of Rossall that attracted her was its international intake (50 per cent of pupils come from abroad, and that figure rises to 60-65 per cent by the sixth form). She says: 'Another reason why I wanted to come and work in a school like this was for my children. I wanted them to have that global perspective'. She and her husband have a son and a daughter who are both pupils at Rossall. She says 'they've really thrown themselves into it' here. Her husband was born in Preston, so the family did already have some ties to the north west. The excellent local golf facilities seem to have been a draw for him. And now they live in the head's house on site. She says it's a 'nice thing' to live on site and, although she acknowledges that she pretty much is on call 24-hours a day, she doesn't seem to mind in the slightest.

The first female head at Rossall, Ms Purves still likes to get into the classroom teaching languages and, although she comes across as approachable and softly spoken, we had no doubts that she could command both a class and a workforce. Parents say she's 'fantastic', 'hands-on' and 'approachable'. Several parents said how impressed they were with the way she listens both to parents and to pupils, and they also note approvingly that she turns up to every rugby match.

Academic matters: Rossall provides an all-round education – aiming to meet the needs of every pupil within its broad intake. Classes are small – usually 18-20 in years 7-11 (an absolute maximum of 22) and a maximum of 18 in the sixth form. The head identifies maths, the sciences, English, technology and art as departments that are doing particularly well. Food studies, Mandarin and drama recently added to curriculum. Parents we met were very happy with their children's attainment. One mother told us how impressed she'd been that the school offered to take her bilingual children, raised until recently in France, out of mainstream French lessons to teach them separately so that they could continue to study French as a first language. But there's a comprehensive and inclusive ethos here. Parents felt that the school was about much more than academia and that it doesn't focus resources and attention on high flyers at the expense of those in the middle or who are struggling. 'They don't single out the star pupils,' said one parent. 'They give praise subtly and they don't make a big song and dance of it.' 'Mine are never made to feel inferior,' said another mum. 'They do their best and they get praise for that.' There's no streaming but there is setting in some subjects. Parents said that sets were constantly under review and so 'you're not stuck in your set'.

Examples include astrophysics (the school boasts a space science centre – complete with planetarium, Victorian observatory and telescope – and a resident astronomer)

Results reflect the broad intake. In 2015, 34 per cent of GCSEs entered were awarded A*-A and at A level that figure was 27 per cent. Roughly a third of sixth formers choose to do the International Baccalaureate rather than A levels and in 2015 they achieved an average of 30 IB points per pupil. The school languishes in the bottom quartile of the independent schools league tables but, unlike the high-flyers in the league tables, Rossall is not a selective school. It's also one of the most international schools in the UK, meaning that a large proportion of the children sitting those GCSE, A level and IB exams (about 60 per cent of them) don't have English as a first language.

International students can enter the main school if their English is already close to fluent. Those whose level of English would hold them back from achieving their potential academically are placed in the International Study Centre. This isn't as separate as it sounds; it's really a stream within the main school where pupils receive intensive English language support. Some pupils only stay in the ISC for a term or two, others stay for a year or more and some complete an intensive one-year iGCSE course there to prepare them for entering the sixth form in the main school.

The school supports pupils with a range of special educational needs. A new full-time SEN support teacher has just joined the school. There may be an additional charge to parents of children with SEN if a very high level of support is required.

Games, options, the arts: This is a very sporty school. Ian Botham sent his son, Liam, here and many alumni have gone on to play rugby, hockey or cricket professionally. More than a dozen pupils – male and female – currently play hockey for Lancashire. And there are countless sports options beyond the more obvious team games: pupils can also play basketball, squash or badminton, or lift weights, climb, dance or shoot. As you'd expect, there is an extensive range of top quality pitches, playing fields, squash courts and the like on campus; almost all sports offered have on-site facilities apart from horse-riding, ice-skating and golf. The 25-metre indoor swimming pool looked particularly inviting – although we didn't jump in – and we weren't surprised to see a large bank of seats on the poolside for crowds of supportive pupils to cheer on their peers. Sport is a unifying force at Rossall: one day the children might be competing fiercely in one of the many inter-house tournaments and the next day they'd be whooping with pride when another pupil scores a winning goal or try against a rival school. Rossall sport is steeped in tradition; 'Ross-Hockey' is a unique game – a hockey-rugby hybrid played only on the beach next to the school; and the school regularly competes in rugby fives tournaments at prestigious public schools as well as hosting its own national 'Rossall Fives' tournament each October.

One pupil we spoke to hinted, diplomatically, that the school could maybe invest a little more in girls' sport – particularly hockey. A couple of mums agreed. One said that the school hadn't traditionally pushed girls' hockey as much as the boys' game, but that she felt things are now improving and that the school has been responsive to criticism. But another mum said there was still some underinvestment in the girls' game. She said that her daughter recently went to training, only four girls turned up and there was no coach. 'It's demoralising,' she said, 'because the ones that do want to play are a bit ignored... and I can see my daughter's face – you know: "Why am I here marking four players on my own?"'

Beyond sport the extracurricular opportunities are seemingly endless – with a particularly wide range of opportunities for arty and musical children and for outdoorsy types. Some more unusual examples include stage set design, costume making, film making, cryptography, psychology, jazz band, knitting, Warhammer and astrophysics (the school boasts a space science centre – complete with a planetarium, Victorian observatory and a telescope – and a resident astronomer). And this is just the tip of the iceberg. Many students are working towards their Duke of Edinburgh Award and pupils from year 9 and above can join the CCF.

Rossall has a diverse tradition in the arts. Choral music is strong here – closely bound in with the life of the historic chapel – but students play different types of music in various performances and concerts throughout the year; and they can learn instruments at school with visiting tutors – for an extra fee. There is also a literary society, which meets regularly to discuss poetry, books and culture. The school puts on two plays a year in one of two well-equipped performance spaces. The drama department also has links with a local theatre school and casting agency, which has enabled some pupils to appear in national radio and television productions. Keen artists are allowed to use the well-stocked workshops and studios every day after school. Each year in the Lent term Rossall devotes a week solely to art, music and drama and parents told us that even the highest performing sports players would never be discouraged to getting involved in the school play or any other creative endeavour.

Boarding: Pupils can board just five days a week or at weekends too. If day pupils want to flexi-board – which they often do – then they always stay in spare beds within their own house. Flexi-boarding allows day pupils to stay at the school for a night or longer – for pretty much any reason. Parents love

Even on a grey, murky day the space is picturesque and peaceful. 'Yes, it's a bubble,' said one mum, 'but it's a lovely bubble to be in'

it because it gives them a night off (or a weekend in Paris...) but, more importantly, the kids can't get enough of it. They typically flexi-board on a Friday night if they have to be at school early the next morning for a match or on a Saturday night if they want to tag along on the boarding house's Sunday outing.

Although there are no classes on a Saturday, it tends to be a busy day with sports practices and fixtures. Every Sunday boarders can, at no extra cost, go on an outing – examples include bowling or crazy golf activities or trips to Alton Towers or the Manchester Christmas markets. Just over 42 per cent of boarders are international and these will be met at and delivered back to Manchester Airport by a representative of the school at the start and end of term. They don't have an option to stay in school during the holidays, though. If they can't fly home then they'll need to have a UK guardian to look after them.

The boarding houses are very homely – softer and more cosy than a typical university hall of residence. The boarding houses are a home from home where any pupil can come to relax and socialise during lunchtimes – and consequently there's lots of scope for different age-groups and both local and international pupils to mix. There are some single rooms available and a few are en-suite, but the majority of boarders share with one or two other pupils and share a bathroom on the corridor. Each pupil has a desk in their room and the freedom to put up pictures and customise their living space. Each house has a pair of live-in houseparents – who are either teachers or support staff. The houseparents we met were warm and affectionate – they seemed to love the job and that was reflected in the way the children spoke about them: 'yeah, they're very supportive,' said one sixth former and another added 'they look out for you and you can talk to them about anything'.

Background and atmosphere: An aerial photo in the school's prospectus shows the campus green, soft red and light blue. It is expansive and grassy; the buildings red-brick, grand and turreted; and beyond them stretches a thin strip of pale yellow beach before the misty sea. Even on a grey, murky day the space is picturesque and peaceful. 'Yes, it's a bubble,' one mum said to us, 'but it's a lovely bubble to be in.' This is one of the happiest schools that this reviewer has visited: pupils raved – with no hint of cynicism – about their friends and teachers, the school's traditions and jolly japes in the boarding houses.

The fact that it's a boarding school – and a very international one – is integral to Rossall life. The house system connects boarders with day pupils: all day pupils are assigned to a boarding house and from year 9 onwards they meet there, in cosy common rooms, each morning for registration. Even if they're not staying for a sleepover, this is a school where older pupils in particular just don't want to go home. They can stay late for prep (with teachers on hand to help) and have their tea at school. There's even a licensed bar and café on site, open to sixth formers three nights a week. One dad told us how pleased he was that when his nearly 17-year-old son stays out late, he doesn't need to wonder where he is or what he's up to because he knows he's safe and happy with his friends at school.

Tradition is very big here. Every year during Christmas dinner in the imposing, oak-panelled dining hall, the pupils sing The Twelve Days of Christmas – each house taking a different verse. No-one tells them to do it, the pupils explain, 'it just sort of happens, spontaneously'. It gets quite competitive – each house singing more boisterously than the last. One pupil told me this tradition summed up what's special about Rossall. Might some prospective parents baulk at the hearty traditions, the special public-schooly Rossall sports, the sense that this could be the setting for an undiscovered Enid Blyton saga? Certainly we found no hint of social snobbery – we simply saw young people having a deliciously happy time at school. If grand old traditions make you cringe then Rossall may not be the perfect fit for you as a parent – when it comes to the pupils, though, the school is so warm and good-humoured, and there is such opportunity and encouragement to become the person you want to be, that we felt even if your teenager is something of a non-conformist he or she would still stand a good chance of finding a niche here.

Pastoral care, well-being and discipline: Several parents identified the quality of pastoral care as the single thing they most appreciated about Rossall. They raved about how well their children are known by staff. One dad was full of praise for a teacher who stayed in regular contact with him, by text, to keep him updated on a particularly protracted UCAS application process. 'Teachers always remember what's going on with your child,' said another parent. 'It's just great that there's always that concern... and so I don't worry about my children here at all because I know the staff are really looking out for them.'

All children in the seniors eat in the dining hall. We didn't find a child who complained about the food. Most parents said their children enjoyed the food and the one mum who said hers didn't conceded they were very fussy! We thought the food was very good with plenty of choice.

Religion is significant in school life: there's a full-time Church of England school chaplain and the whole school attends chapel every Friday. But, particularly with the diverse, international intake, the school takes care to ensure that worship is inclusive and that other faiths get a look in too.

Discipline is firm here. Serious breaches of the rules would be dealt with case-by-case but expulsion is a possibility. If you're caught smoking three times, you're out. (Although pupils told us that some of the German boarders are stalwart smokers so, presumably, they're good at not getting caught.) Pupils couldn't think of any instances of bullying in their experience and they spoke with real conviction about how caring an environment this is. They said that pupils wouldn't tolerate bullying – that they would tell a teacher and offer support to the victim. Parents knew of no bullying either. Like most schools, Rossall has a stringent anti-bullying policy. We were impressed that parents told us that they knew of several pupils at the school who had come out as gay – with minimal fuss or drama and complete acceptance from their peers. Parents felt the school was very accepting of difference – perhaps also because of the diversity that the international students bring to the community.

Pupils and parents: The parents are a mixed bunch. A good few are alumni of Rossall but many others were state educated. Some get help with fees from grandparents or from the school's own means-tested bursary scheme. The kids are also diverse.

Across the school, 50 per cent are international – coming from a very wide spread of countries and cultures. Further up the school, more than 60 per cent are international. But there are far more British children than those of any other single nationality. The pupils seem inclusive and grounded. And they were positive and polite.

Alumni include Booker-Prize-winning novelist JG Farrell; Father Thomas RD Byles, the Catholic priest who refused to leave the Titanic so that he could help other passengers; eminent figures in the world of sport, music and industry; and a few bastions of the Establishment: a governor of a couple of colonies; a private secretary to Queen Victoria; and the magnificently-named Sir Walton Clopton Wingfield, who patented the game of lawn tennis.

Entrance: The school takes pupils with a broad range of abilities, including some with special educational needs. There are entrance tests in English, maths and non-verbal reasoning but it is rare to say no to a prospective pupil: this would normally only be done if the school couldn't meet his/her needs. Pupils in the junior school have an automatic passport to entry to the seniors – although they still sit the tests which are used as a baseline.

For international students, the admissions procedure is largely a question of assessing their English. The school has a Skype conversation with every student before a place is offered. They must have at least some English: if they can't hold a Skype conversation they can't come here. If their English is already good enough that it won't hold them back academically then they can go straight into the main school. If not, then they may need to first of all come to the International Study Centre (see above in Academic for more information.)

All pupils need to achieve five GCSEs at grade A* to C to enter the sixth form. If they don't they can either repeat the year or leave.

Exit: Most pupils go on to UK universities with about 10 per cent going to university abroad. Economics and business studies are particularly popular courses but there's a real spread across arts, sciences and humanities. Popular universities are Edinburgh, Lancaster, Manchester, Leeds and York; one to Oxbridge in 2015.

Money matters: The school has been in very good financial health for a number of years – the influx of international students has really turned its fortunes around. About six per cent of pupils in the senior school receive significant means-tested bursaries (a 50 per cent reduction of fees or more). There are also some scholarships available for high performers in sport, music, drama or academia.

Remarks: This is a very happy school. Its population is so diverse, there's no one type of child who would fit in better than another. But we did feel the school would particularly appeal to busy parents who perhaps don't have a lot of support locally or who find domestic life to be somewhat relentless – because the school offers a round-the-clock home-from-home programme of activities which could ease the pressure on families at times of stress. It's no academic pressure-cooker and less able pupils will be praised for their efforts just as much as the high flyers but there are excellent teachers, facilities and opportunities that should give the brightest pupils every chance to excel. Overall, Rossall is a warm, inclusive and remarkably happy place to be. Staff and pupils seem to genuinely love it here – and there's not much higher praise you can offer than that.

St George's School (Edinburgh)

Garscube Terrace, Edinburgh EH12 6BG

01313 118000
admissions@stge.org.uk
www.stge.org.uk

Ages: 10–18
Pupils: 825; sixth form: 185
Boarders: 50 full/flexi
Day: £7,785 – £12,645 pa
Boarding: £23,835 – £26,430 pa

Head: Since 2010, Mrs Anne Everest BA (50s). A classicist, Yorkshire born and bred, who has lived in Scotland for 30 years. Formerly deputy head of Robert Gordon's College, Aberdeen and head of St Margaret's School, Aberdeen. Educated at St Mary's Grammar School and University of Hull.

Taught classics and ancient history, lectured in ancient history, Latin and New Testament Greek at her alma mater. Married 'very early' to an oily husband, she 'had three babies instead of finishing her PhD', resuming her career in 1991 when she was appointed acting head of classics at St Margaret's,

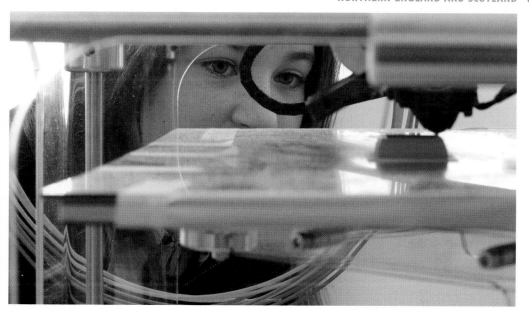

Aberdeen and, subsequently, head. Oily wives must follow the drum. The head runs the school with a senior management team, including the heads of both junior and lower school, and a clutch of deputies.

Everest lives in Edinburgh with her (now retired) husband, is about to sell up in Aberdeen, and regularly hosts visits from foreign academics, head teachers, and probationers. No mega staff changes, 'teachers replaced as retirement happened'. A delegator, when this editor asked for detailed exam results, and offered her card, she was told to 'email the request, and she would pass it on'. (We might have delegated someone to remove the security fencing). Interestingly, during our 25+ years with the GSG, we have seen many heads pick up detritus in the school grounds and drop it in the nearest bin; encountering a pair of socks by the side of the path, Everest merely kicked one to the side and continued talking to the new Mandarin teacher (it was left to my companion to collect them both).

Academic matters: School no longer narrowly academic; girls follow English or Scottish system as best fits the bill. League tables are meaningless in this school, given that two systems are followed. Current exam boards' status on either side of the border is nothing short of chaotic, St G's timetabling both systems must be a nightmare. 'Absolutely no thought of moving to the IB'. Some impressive results in both disciplines, though rather more glitches than we have seen previously, and quite a number of soft subjects with tiny numbers: early education and childcare, media studies, travel and tourism, all at Higher level. We have no difficulty with penny numbers doing langs, but to have one each taking graphic communication, information systems and computing, and two doing modern studies cannot make economic sense. Results include those from the Royal Environmental Health Institute of Scotland: number of pupils have achieved introductory (two hour course) or elementary certificates in food hygiene (six hour course) though we couldn't find any hospitality exams higher than Intermediate 2.

Drop-in centre for instant problem solving, 'weekly support sessions in every subject, plus subject clinics in break, before school or by email'. This is what we like to hear

Possibly more followers of the Scottish system, physics and geography strong (oil?). As ever the English system popular for art and design, religious moral and philosophical studies, hefty showing in Highers. 'Lots of flexibility' in course selection (this editor reckons too much; but no doubt horses for courses). School employs VLE – Virtual Learning Environment; students can access/collect coursework, or refer to staff notes online. Claims to be the 'top school in Scotland for A levels and Advanced Highers'. As do many others, though perhaps not both at the same time. In 2015, 47 per cent A grades at Higher level and 66 per cent at Advanced Higher;

34 per cent A*/A at A level. At GCSE, 48 per cent A*/A grades. No particular bias: English, maths, langs; French, German, Spanish, Latin and classical Greek. Latin for all in L4 (top end of the junior school), thereafter girls must choose from a 'revolving carousel' of double period tasters in Spanish, German, Mandarin. The latter popular with both pupils and parents in the school's Chinese centre. Thirty-six native speakers in school, many pupils host sessions in their native languages: Russian, Chinese, Gaelic; and can study for individual A levels (or whatever) in those langs. School will arrange specialist tutors. Rate my teachers makes interesting reading, the head does not feature. Four or five parallel classes in the upper school, max class size 21 and down.

Much to-ing and fro-ing with local unis, pupils and staff combine on various projects, 'and take part in an impressive outreach programme which encompasses both the academic and the appreciation of the wider world'. 'Joint seminars in a plethora of subjects with an eclectic collection of schools, the state sector as well as other independents (in all disciplines: sport and music as well as academia)', according to the school. Good general studies, curriculum choice support and careers advice (careers breakfasts), 500 options in careers dept.

Comprehensive learning support, pick up early, can deal with most of the dys-strata and ADHD; laptops encouraged. SENCo on site, four specialist teachers plus rash of assistants. Small ESOL department to help non-nationals (charge). Drop-in centre for instant problem solving, 'weekly support sessions in every subject, plus subject clinics at lunch time, in break, before school or by email in the evening' (so presumably pupils have access to staff emails). This is what we like to hear. Buddy system: older girls help tinies with reading and much else besides.

'Joint seminars in a plethora of subjects with an eclectic collection of schools, the state sector as well'

School split into three distinct departments – junior, which encompasses the nursery, lower and upper (senior in GSG speak). Everest has offices in both lower and upper. School not totally wheelchair friendly but will make allowances and change classrooms if necessary (lift in junior school new build), chairlift in the main building; no problem with boarding houses. Hearing loops.

Games, options, the arts: Fabulous centenary sports hall with viewing area over hall and squash courts; much-used lacrosse pitches, floodlit all-weather pitch. Trad games played with a vengeance: lacrosse tours, hockey tours, swimming, judo, cycling. Local sports clubs use facilities: Grange Junior Hockey Club et al. Robertson Music Centre houses untold numbers of choirs, ensembles, three orchestras, over 600 musicians (can be hired for functions, popular with Alex McCall Smith's Really Terrible Orchestra, as well as National Youth Choir of Scotland, Edinburgh Youth Orchestra and Waddell School of Music). Impressive collection of music results. Vibrant art department, pottery, textiles, sculpture et al. Drama and theatre good, timetabled, not much pursued at higher level.

Oodles of D of E, dozens of bronze but tails off somewhat as girls grow older. CCF, Outreach outdoor education from age 10. Sixth formers join forces with Merchiston for dances, sport, art, music, drama etc. Zillions of after-school clubs that offer everything from keyboarding to extra IT. Hot on exchanges: girls as young as 12 whizz off to spend a month or so in Canada, Hong Kong, Australasia, Chile, wherever.

Boarding: Boarders, from 11, 50 per cent overseas, live in a couple of converted Edwardian villas behind the tennis courts in an uninspiring road full of equally dreary (if upwardly mobile) villas. Hardly swinging Edinburgh. Purpose-built bungalow for sixth formers, singles or twins, all very jolly, lots of extra activities, but perhaps not very stimulating. Serious revamp recently; re-wired,

new heating. Mixture of real foreigners and long distance Scots who can have friends to stay (charge). Flexi and weekly boarding option.

Background and atmosphere: St George's High School for Girls, a member of the Girls' School Association, founded in 1886 as a training school for women teachers, transmogrified into St G's in 1888. The purpose-built, colonial neo-Georgian 1914 complex by A F Balfour-Paul is pure Jean Brodie, and sits uneasily with inspiring new additions. Lower school in converted former boarding house (plus ugly add-on); magical extension for junior school, complete with dance studio (that hall again) and dedicated nursery area has a cantilevered first floor over a bungee surface popular with senior pupils as well as a strategic undercover play area for tinies. Stunning dining hall (exit bridge known as Bridget), entertainment area below has released valuable space for extra libraries and study. Parents can (and do) use the dining centre as a coffee shop.

New uniform compulsory for all within the year, certain leeway in upper sixth. Kilts for all from lower sixth down, in St G's ancient red millennium tartan, with optional trimmed fitted jackets, 'kilts not more than six cm above the knee' (most appeared much longer). Otherwise pretty standard, check dresses, blue gym tunics, navy tights, red or blue wellies. No problems with headscarves (number of Muslims in the school), presumably like the hair bands they will need to be in school colours. Sibling-led house system.

Latest wheeze was to approach posh Edinburgh restaurants for their chef's fave recipes, publish them in a book and charge the restaurants to advertise

Long-running romance with the Edinburgh Academy fractured by EA's decision to go co-ed, though they still share the same bus routes. St Gs tells us that links with Merchiston Castle are very much alive; the Edinburgh rumour mill, not to mention the local education rumour mill, assured this editor that St Gs had made an approach to Merchiston to link up on a more formal footing some time ago. Everest dissed this as a canard, but numbers are less buoyant than previously, particularly lower down the school (despite St Margaret's untimely demise).

Student council includes both juniors and seniors, terrific charity input/output; latest wheeze was to approach posh Edinburgh restaurants for their chef's fave recipes, publish them in a book and charge the restaurants to advertise. Help with City Mission. YPI with the (oily Sir Ian) Wood Foundation gives girls practice in marshalling arguments and persuading fund to dosh out for good causes. God followed broadly via Christian principles, regular assemblies, PSE cross year on Fridays, business on Mondays, year groups Thursdays and Fridays. Local minister for high days and holidays. Loads of staff jollies: keep fit, choir, and dedicated welfare programme.

IT (mostly wireless) and for tinies and in the boarding houses. School website dominated by downmarket woman's magazine type romantic fuzzy pic of Balfour-Paul's garden side. Website should be a window into the school; St G's is full of head's previous speeches but pretty low on content: collection of badly written (and often incomprehensible) mission statements but no staff list with email addresses, list of governors, senior management team – info that could be useful. For an academic school to live or die by something out of People's Friend is incomprehensible.

Pastoral care, well-being and discipline: Miscreants are given heavy hints that they should 'move elsewhere' (and sometimes they do). 'No need to break out; this is a liberal environment.' 'No sniff of drugs.' Good PSE, positive behaviour policy which incorporates 'the best of human rights legislation'.

Pupils and parents: The Edinbourgeousie: middle class Scots, professionals, incomers, wannabes and first time buyers. Boarders from the Highlands and Islands, the Borders and the Scottish diaspora abroad (alma mater stuff). Handful of real foreigners. Skype useful. Global links and exchanges. Trad. Lots of parent/pupil forums on every subject under the sun; Friends of St George's for social events. Quick poll round parents (in address book) produced no surprises: non-stimulated girls were bored at the top end, parents were fed up at having to buy a new uniform for such a short time (not in secondhand shop yet), sixth formers seemed to be working (and playing) hard. Particularly the latter. School shouldn't be so petty about make up. Not really a sophisticated bunch, and probably not yummy mummys' school of choice.

Entrance: 'Unashamedly academic in outlook' was how we previously described this school, indeed there was a time when wannabe parents coached their 5 year olds pre school interview. Everest maintains, 'not so strict an entrance test; important that we can meet a child's needs'. Will welcome a girl who is able to keep up with the pace of academic life but who seems set for Bs and Cs rather than A*s. Assessment, school report and interview. Entry to sixth form is more or less automatic for home-grown pupils; external pupils by interview and school report. Demands for sixth form places heavy. 'Skype handy for interviewing girls from abroad'.

Exit: Some leave after GCSE/Standard grade to go co-ed; otherwise gap, uni, and higher education of all sorts – Scots law popular, as are the sciences, medicine and business management. Around 60 per cent opt for Scottish universities, eg Aberdeen, St Andrew's, Edinburgh and Glasgow. Two to Oxbridge in 2015; Bristol, Durham, York and London unis also popular; odd bods to US, France, Hong Kong, Thailand.

Money matters: Means-tested bursary scheme now replaces assisted places; 'mustn't let the really bright down'. Full bursaries available, plus help with school uniform. Will keep child if parents fall on hard times, as long as bursar is kept in the loop. Sibling discounts. Joint discount with Merchiston Castle School. After being told to provide more help for pupils from low income families, school passed the charity test in 2013 and has maintained its charitable status.

Remarks: The top girls' school in Scotland (pace chaps in nursery); more liberal than previously. Tatler calls it the 'St Paul's of the north', but with only four girls' schools in Scotland (two of which are overgrown dame schools and one of which takes boarders and ponies) there's not much competition.

At regular intervals this editor is asked for advice by parents who have had their little darlings at St George's since they were in nappies and are looking for a change of scene in sixth form (teenagers being what they are and Edinburgh being what it is). We have to say that, in all honesty, if it is a challenge they need then they must go South, for there is nowhere in Scotland that can hold a candle to St George's, be it in the realm of academe or of global awareness.

St Leonards School

South Street, St Andrews, Fife KY16 9QJ

01334 472126
info@stleonards-fife.org
www.stleonards-fife.org

Ages: 4–19 (boarding from 12)
Pupils: 515 ; sixth form: 145
Boarders: 127 full
Day: £9,297 – £12,693 pa
Boarding: £30,957 pa

Headmaster: Since 2008, Dr Michael (Mike) Carslaw BSc MBA PhD (early 50s), educated at Merchiston, read zoology at Newcastle, spent three years doing VSO in Ghana ('discovered I loved teaching') followed by PGCE at Exeter ('where I met my wife'); comes to St Leonards via City of London Freemen's and Ardingly (responsible for more heads than you can shake a stick at). A Scot and a weedgie (as is this editor: work it out) he is a shoo-in and won The Tatler public school head of the year a couple of years back (he would have won ours too, but we don't do that sort of thing). St Leonards now has a head with vision, common sense and ambition, this is real CEO stuff; school is back on track, after suffering a variety of slings and arrows from a previous collection of headless chickens.

Once Scotland's girls' academic (boarding) school of choice, St Leonards has weathered the storm caused by so-called brother schools opening their doors to the fairer sex to counteract (their) falling numbers (NB: fairer sex originally chosen on looks, rather than academic ability – how's that for daft?). School more or less went into free fall. Day girls were welcomed. Chaps were encouraged into the sixth form (for free – all two of them). A sixth form stand-alone college was trialled. Junior school (aka St Kats, St Katharine's) dissed boarders. Certain amount of family silver was sold.

St Leonards now has a head with vision, common sense and ambition; this is real CEO stuff; school is back on track, after suffering a variety of slings and arrows

The breakthrough came when junior school absorbed local co-ed prep, New Park in 2005: chunk of New Park Educational Trust kicks in (took a wee while: rest of this moderately rich trust is devoted to 'providing equipment, project costs and bursaries', 'primarily in North East Fife – occasional individual bursary': so now you have chapter and verse). Boys and girls work their way up the school in true co-ed fashion: roughly 50/50.

In 2006, St Leonards adopted the two year IB as standard for all in sixth form. Brave stuff: going IB all the way is expensive; staff need to be trained, with mandatory follow-up courses both in and out of house. Fees need to be paid, by staff and pupil alike.

Carslaw an IB enthusiast, 'better to have scientists who can write essays'; the IB is popular with international pupils, of whom, as we write, there are over 30 different nationalities; and is 'still delighted to be part of such a vibrant school community with so much going on.' Obvious good rapport with both staff and pupil: fun; our canter round the school was a delight.

Having moulded the three parts of the school into a cohesive unit, with sixth formers having more-or-less university privileges – tickets to the uni-library, can use uni gym and go 'by arrangement to lectures of interest', relaxed trips to approved cafes – that sort of thing; Carslaw now has a double edged mission. The university town of St Andrews is a great draw, as is (whisper it soft) the golf; but school could still do with more punters. Both Carslaw and his marketing manager make global trips to far flung places pour encourager international students to both enjoy the St Leonards and the St Andrews experience. They also employ agents. Dividends are paying off. Numbers are up: particularly on the boarding side, where the elegant Edwardian houses no longer quite resemble the Marie Celeste. Head adds 'for boarding in 2015 we are full.'

An ongoing rolling programme of up-grading starts soon (where £2.5 million is a sum regularly bandied about). The external fabric is in need of serious help (sea breezes are hell on paintwork): windows and sills are flaking, though much has been done within the neglected exteriors. A full time painter has been employed – think Forth Road Bridge and multiply him by 10 and they would still be toiling.

Academic matters: School prides itself on 'high quality education right from the preparatory school through to the senior school.' Scotland's only all-IB sixth form – focuses 100 per cent on the IB (average 33 points in 2015, with more than half gaining bilingual diplomas). 'We haven't taken any half measures with the qualification by offering alternative post-16 options, we have dedicated ourselves to it and we believe that's to the great benefit of our students.' Sixth formers help out in junior school as part of the charitable leg of the IB (CAS) with up to 50 hours' assistance 'reading, 'riting, 'rithmetic sort of thing.

Most pupils take GCSES/iGCSES in the normal way (43 per cent A*/A grades in 2015), before seamlessly switching disciplines. A one year pre-IB course ticks all the boxes for those joining school age 15 (often refugees from state systems) as well as international students who sit fewer IGCSE/GCSEs, and, if needed, get up to speed in English (about a fifth of non-native English speakers need some EAL help, and must pass a written proficiency test – ESOL). St Andrews Uni fields a raft of international speakers, St Leonards boasts help in 'a wide range of native langs in all year groups'...'be aware that some of this tuition may be subject to an additional charge', 'dependent on number of students and lang'.

When we visited (the week before summer half term) those taking the diploma were done and dusted: exams over, pupils were now home (think pay for six terms, school for five and a half: though, to be honest, 'yearly fees are divided, for the convenience of parents into three equal instalments'.. 'students can, and do, remain in school after their IB exams if that is easier for them, until prize-giving and leavers' ball'). IB schools no longer mark in house, but pupils know their results by first week in July; expensive exam-wise too, current cost some £554 per pupil. (Expect GCSE exams to run around – currently – max 30-40 quid per subject). These costs are, of course, unilateral, but this ed thinks it is the first time she has seen prices laid out (in the splendid handbook – slightly strange page layout at odd moments) with quite such brutality. Extra charges too, for some of the more esoteric subject choices.

Nearby well-equipped BHS riding centre with hot horse shower (wow!) offers a variety of options, from bringing your own nag to renting one of theirs

Head says, 'The IB is probably the least tinkered about with qualification in the world – its basic philosophy of keeping a breadth of subjects going into the sixth form but also studying three to a level comparable to Advanced Higher or A level has remained.' 'Native lang' for IB may be English, Russian, German, French, Mandarin (currently on offer) or whatever, while Latin qualifies as a foreign language, as well as French, Spanish, German, Italian (ab initio). UCAS gives points for individual subjects studied under the IB system which means that non-linguists/mathematicians, previously disadvantaged in the overall IB grading, now get full credit for their strong subjects.

Most study two or three langs, with all doing French from year 1 (think junior school: ie 5 year olds) and Spanish and /or German/Latin aged 10/11. Max class size 20, smaller for practical or specialist subjects.

School appoints a St Leonards Associate Researcher or two, often a PhD student at St Andrews, to liaise with pupils and point them at the joys of research – or, as we said previously, 'helping them to develop an appreciation and knowledge of research'. Quite. Senior pupils have access to the university library and regularly attend lectures. (Lots of profs' children and consequently no dearth of academic governors or visiting speakers.)

Dyslexia/dyspraxia support – 'no statemented pupils accepted' – mostly provided for 'a small proportion of pupils' in mainstream teaching, but a good programme both withdrawal, group sessions and one-to-one if necessary (stunning, said one thrilled parent – 'saved our lives') at extra cost. School tests if they reckon extra help needed; specialist staff of four straddle both senior and junior schools.

IT still a tad in the wings, but on being asked about mandatory keyboarding skills for all, this ed was told that 'there were a couple of recommended courses for pupils to follow' – the implication being

that these were mainly of use to those in the SEN stream. Pschaw. Head adds 'now linked to university network with campus-wide Wifi.

Games, options, the arts: Proper matches for chaps as well as chapesses. Think Edinburgh Schools, Robert Gordon's... Full range of sporting options – rugby, lacrosse, hockey against Glenalmond, Strath and Dundee High: the hallowed main school site (birth of lacrosse in the UK) now boasts rugby matches et al (roll over Dame Louisa). Girls' sports still strong, with usual mass of international lax players. Practice matches held on beach if games pitches frozen.

Loads of individual sports and international coaches – needle chaps' tennis match in progress during our canter: judo, trampoline, skiing, badminton, swimming – university uses pool for water polo; snowboarding and surfing; rock-climbing as well as expeditions to the Alps. Annual skiing trips both at home and abroad; sailing now thoroughly embraced, ditto windsurfing and all 'local water sports activities' – and about time too. Local (and not so local) race-horse trainers use beach for exercise, as does the Scots Guards polo team, now based at Leuchars and St Andrews uni polo team. It being St Andrews, golf reigns supreme with about a third of the school playing; all lucky boarders can and do become youth members of the St Andrews Links Trust (as residents in St Andrews) so they can play the Old Course. £1350 to enrol in the elite programme and currently £48 to allow pupils to play on Old and Castle courses (though as playing on the Old Course has been subject to a lottery, one wonders whether St Leonards' pupils will get a bye and not have to take their chances behind a novice foursome).

Individual sports and international coaches – needle chaps' tennis match in progress during our canter

Nearby well-equipped BHS riding centre (moderately expensive, but not over the top) with a hot horse shower (wow!) offers a variety of options, from bringing your own nag to renting one of theirs. Strangely enough, pic of girl on horse featured fairly hefty bitting arrangement plus martingale, and brushing boots. Odd combo. This ed has been riding since age 3 and cannot, in all honesty, think of any discipline the rider pictured could have been tacked up for, unless her steed was unstoppable and she fancied a bash at the brush (for the uninitiated – hurdles). 'Weekly lessons available for keen able riders'.

Great new all-weather pitch, despite prolonged problems with Historic Scotland about floodlights, 'which would damage the fabric of the city wall':

v expensive telescopic solution finally arrived at. Currently fundraising for new sports hall development.

Outstanding art department, attracting pupils outside normal lessons as well as curricular – huge range of alternative media, dark rooms, textiles etc. Current craze is for zig-zag (as in card zig-zagging) art work. Fun, but difficult to live with, perhaps.

Head of art was hanging fiendish model birds from the ceiling during our visit – complete with two elderly black labs – preparatory to the next biannual art show – open to the public. Artists in residence. Regularly in the ribbons for local photography prize – the Kodak Cup – 10 times since 2002.

Music strong in fabulous Bob Steedman (husband of four heads ago, who, alas, died recently) designed centre. St Leonards Junior School pupils sang in front of the cameras at the televised St Andrews Royal Wedding Breakfast celebrations. Rash of bands/orchestras, 'choir for every day of the week', ambitious singing programmes. Pipe band; we were treated to a brilliant rendition by an 11 year old, who warned us that his favourite piece was 14 minutes long. We heard about four (though it seemed to take him longer to find his pipes).

Drama on the up; school performs twice a year in the revamped nearby Byre theatre in St Andrews (popular with both school and public) students must study history of theatre as well as pounding boards. Drama types take shows to Ed Festival and go on mega drama-fest to Broadway every other year. Trips (one per subject per year) planned on a two-year cycle. D of E of course. Youth Enterprise with goodies often sold in aid of local school-adopted fav charity TICCL.

Boarding: Weekly and termly boarding: emphasis is on day. Fairly harem scarum boarding houses, passages littered with rather grand bookcases and rows of servant's bells – relics of a former age. Day pupils in the sixth form included in house system with 'day rooms' in boarding houses. Couple of small dorms, mostly single rooms, usual teenage tip sort of thing, but they were in the midst of revising. Stunning shower: (and this was in a house about to be done up!). £2.5 million refurb of all three boarding houses started recently.

No Saturday lessons. We were concerned at possible lack of organised activities for boarders at weekend, but were assured, several times, 'that they were too busy with their various IB projects'. Various jaunts to Edinburgh and Dundee were mooted but we are still a tad concerned. Head adds 'Boarders generally are taken up with sport on Saturdays, there is a boarders' outing every Sunday, the last few have been Elie (sic) (Ely?) Watersports, beach kite buggies on west sands, go karting, bubble football etc etc.'

Off duty gear as you might expect. School praised for high standard of pastoral care for boarders by the Care Inspectors.

Background and atmosphere: Founded by dons and wives of St Andrews's profs for their daughters in 1877 in what was once a medieval priory, backing on to the sea wall, the sprawling hotch-potch collection of impressive-looking granite has neither form nor symmetry: think Topsy. Dame Louisa Lumsden was first head (Dame Frances Dove, who succeeded her many years later, founded Wycombe Abbey in 1896).

Curious combo of gracious living: elegant house drawing rooms reminiscent of Country Life plus lawned courts nestling among old stone building in dreaming spires style, combined with faintly scruffy corridors, classrooms, common rooms. (Bursar/cabinet maker needs to be shot: steel screws: Georgian half moon inlaid card table – pschaw).

St Leonards inhabits a notoriously windswept corner of Fife, on the sea, bracing air, bone-chilling easterly gales, tracksuits popular for games. Nay, essential.

Golf, riding and the beach all great draws, as well as trips up town and forays to the surrounding countryside. Castle and cathedral a couple of minutes away. Mega library and selection of 'Maryana' in Queen Mary's House (oddly flanked by a boys' loo). Library much in use by those in sixth form, but available to all.

Mary Queen of Scots and King Charles II reputed to have stayed at Queen Mary's Library when it was a private house, but not, of course, at the same time.

Splendid menu posted online: lunch we had was sumptuous and imaginative. All food scourced 'locally' (ie within 100 miles). International students can and do cook their own dishes. Veggie option, naturally, and fresh fruit available

whenever. Central dining room recently given an internal overhaul: outside still pretty rank.

Comprehensive buses for day pupils: Dundee, Kirkcaldy, (Auchter)muchty, Perth, the East Neuk, and presumably special pick up at Leuchars following deployment of Scots Guards. Juniors can be dropped off early (8am) and collected late (5.30pm). (This represents a reduced school day but incorporates time for activities, which has 'settled down well and parents appreciate it'). Otherwise return journey leaves 5.40 pm.

Founded by dons and wives of St Andrew's profs for their daughters in 1877 in what was once a medieval priory. Curious combo of gracious living with faintly scruffy corridors

Sixth formers wear suits (or a fair approximation thereof) during the working day. Boys rather tidier than some we have seen at that age; girls less so: sixth formers adopt a theme (or two) in black – quite short shorts and thick tights apparently ok (skool says quite short skirts...). Machine washable blazers and blue tartan kilts for girls, grey breeks for chaps are senior/junior school uniform with blue woolly pullies. Ah but we hanker for the cloaks of yesteryear. Second hand shop run by the 'bullish' PA which also organises family fun tennis etc.

School is proud of its Scottish heritage and tradition – Burns Day celebrated though Scottish Country Dancing is apparently only taught in the junior school.

Pastoral care, well-being and discipline: School rules feature punctuality, security and civilised behaviour; the student handbook has a rash of rules, most of which are sheer common sense: L-drivers may not drive other pupils and the like. But members of the sixth form have a mass of privileges – can visit some (some definitely out of bounds) local pubs if aged 18 and over, smoke off-campus – je m'en doute in these days of stalag Scotland ('but not if I feel they are bringing the school into disrepute and are identifiable as St Leonards pupils,' says head) and are generally expected to behave like grown-ups. No smoking on campus, no under-age drinking and absolute zero tolerance of drugs. Parents like the drugs policy – random drugs testing and testing on suspicion, out for pushing, forfeit right to remain in school for using – depends on individual and other factors and for how long, and pupils may be allowed back under fairly arduous conditions. Suspension for continued failure to observe the booze rules. Police are called for theft.

No chaplain but team of local ministers who regularly preach. Plenty of fundraising for good causes.

Pupils and parents: No boarding in junior school, hence strong Scots contingent in senior school; small number of UK boarders but most from abroad, particularly at sixth form level, when incomers swell the ranks to follow the IB course – a boon. Those pupils whom we met (either IB or newbies) were a more sophisticated bunch – particularly the former – than we would normally expect in a school which is so geographically challenged...with sea on three sides!

Eclectic mix of international and first time buyers: Fifers see school as a viable option. Think butcher, baker, candlestick maker, farmer, landed estate owner and very senior CEOs. Think oligarchs, think wannabe Donald Trumps. No longer does this ed hear from mates that 'we put Amelia/Georgina/Freddie into St Leonards, but really it didn't take'. Parents, both past, and present are now positive about the place.

St Leonards has a strong old girls' network and many at the school are offspring or grand offspring of Seniors; Seniors must now be referred to as FPs. Some concern previously from Seniors about school's new direction though others welcomed its new impetus. Famous Seniors include Betty Harvey Anderson, Dame Kathleen Ollerenshaw (previous president of St Leonards) past head Mary James, Gillian Glover of the Scotsman (who didn't last the course), Stella Tennant (ditto), Baroness Byford and Anji Hunter.

Entrance: At any time. Mid-term ok. Accepts CE, but usually own (written) entrance assessment (English and maths) or scholarship exam. Seamless transition from juniors to seniors. Six GCSEs or equivalent for sixth with As and Bs in subjects to be studied at higher level in the IB. 'We usually pick up 15/20 at sixth from entry' for IB. School prefers to meet with international applicants but, if pushed, will Skype.

Exit: 'Minimum' drop out at transition from juniors to seniors and some (15 per cent or so) depart post-GCSE (only accept good English speakers to sixth form). Around 90 per cent to universities – mostly Scottish and northern English destinations eg Durham, Leeds, Warwick, around a third abroad (including in 2015: Harvard, Brown, Princeton and McGill). Subjects range from law to medicine to aviation management to music. Many do a gap year, armed with addresses of welcoming Seniors throughout the world (a boon for worried parents).

Money matters: A means-tested, assisted places scheme in operation; open to application from existing parents in financial difficulties: sibling discount. Raft of scholarships: though only of nominal monetary value, and usually only lasting a couple of years – ranging from academic through music, drama and sport – golf scholarships very popular (as you might imagine).

Remarks: The IB is a winner. Dr Carslaw has the world in his hands: St Leonards runs seamlessly from age five to 18.. the IB niche gives it an academic edge with an international flavour. All he needs is more punters, though currently boarding is full, with waiting lists in some years.

St Martin's Ampleforth

Gilling Castle, York, North Yorkshire YO62 4HP

01439 766600
headmaster@stmartins.ampleforth.org.uk
www.stmartins.ampleforth.org.uk
RC

Ages: 3-13
Pupils: 150
Boarders: 30 full, some flexi
Day: £7,920 – £14,679 pa
Boarding: £22,083 pa

Linked school: Ampleforth College

Headmaster: Since September 2014, Mark O'Donnell, previously head of Alleyn's Junior School in south London. Educated at Stonyhurst and St Ignatius College, New South Wales, he has a masters in education from Harvard and a postgraduate diploma in education from Oxford. He is a Fellow of the Royal College of Arts, a Duke of Edinburgh assessor and an alpine ski leader. He is married with three sons.

Off in July 2016 to head Westminster Under School.

Entrance: By interview, assessment, and report from current school. All entrants encouraged to come for taster day.

Exit: Nearly all go on to Ampleforth College. A few students return to their home countries for secondary education. Though linked closely with Ampleforth, it is 'a prep school in its own right'.

Remarks: Prep school of Ampleforth, founded in 1929, merged with St Martin's RC prep in 2001. Main building is imposing Gilling Castle – grade 1 listed – glorious but also gloriously expensive to maintain. Unbelievable 16th century Great Chamber, probably the finest Tudor interior in England (don't miss the ceiling and stained glass); the children eat there, though are more interested in checking out the sausages and rarely look up. The castle was the inspiration for Hogwarts in the Harry Potter films, according to JK Rowling's cousin, who went to the college – though site not used for filming. Three miles from the senior school, with all the freedom of its 3,000 acres; tree-climbing, den-building, bike rides through the woods all allowed and indeed encouraged, despite risk assessments, and thankfully deemed infinitely preferable to Playstations, iPods and PSPs. Hazy sunny days of children rolling down grassy banks, making daisy chains, playing on all-weather skateboards, practising in the cricket nets..it's all about space, freedom and spontaneity.

Boarding is important, and growing; quite a few persuade parents to let them convert from day. The integrity of a boarding mix is guarded fiercely here to create a real sense of school community.

Southern pupils catch a Hogwarts Express at the beginning of term: it is (just) possible to enjoy breakfast in London and lunch in school

School day ends at 5.35pm for all; a longish day but includes prep time and plenty of extracurricular activities. Boarders come from all over UK; southern pupils catch a Hogwarts Express at the beginning of term: it is (just) possible to enjoy breakfast in London and lunch in school. Day pupils from Yorkshire; parents a genuine mix of local aristocracy, a few military, professional and non-professional. Open days and school events bring a range of shabby chic Citroens, Land Rovers and Rolls Royces bearing Fortnum and Masons hampers. A good sprinkling from abroad, mainly Europe plus a few South Americans, increasingly popular as education abroad becomes more secular.

Catholics make up 70 per cent; (40 per cent in pre-prep); other denominations are clearly happy to be there, 'being educated in the life of the Christian faith', as the school puts it. Like its Benedictine big brother, it 'asks much from the children's strengths and supports their weaknesses'. Pastoral care very good (chaplain Father John is a friend to all and mainstay of the school); children are confident, courteous and seem happy in their extended school family. Benedictine sense of togetherness and 'anti-me' culture encourages compassion and understanding. Lovely chapel, pretty almost, ideal

for this age group, fewer bells and smells than the senior school but full of character nonetheless and the gospel message filters through.

Average class size of 15; standard curriculum up to common entrance, pupils also tested at key stage 1 and 2. Five new classrooms focus on the teaching of languages (and English), French, Latin, Greek all taught; Spanish, Mandarin, German and Italian also on offer as extracurricular activities. Gifted and talented pupils recognised and supported, though children 'not deemed less worthy if less academic or less sporty'. Large well-stocked library is popular. The school is now 40 per cent girls, a sparky and capable bunch; their advent knocked down barriers, opened up the curriculum and raised the game for everyone.

Games predictably important and takes place every afternoon – hence extended teaching day. Rugby and cricket for boys; hockey, netball, rounders for girls. The overseas pupils quickly catch on to the idea of picking up a ball and running with it and the first XV rugby team almost looks like an outing from the UN. Athletics, swimming, cross-country also on offer. School has a floodlit Astroturf pitch. Golf increasingly popular, own golf course, though challenging with much of it on a slope. Plenty of activities, including fishing, riding and shooting; a modern pentathlon team competes nationally.

Music superb, based in fine performing arts block. ISI noted 'high level of musicianship, inspirational teaching'. Schola (choir) sings with senior school, tours across Europe. Over 80 per cent of pupils learn instruments; years 3 and 4 all play the violin, cello, double bass or oboe, with varying degrees of success, but a great opportunity to give it a try.

St Mary's Hall

Stonyhurst, Lancashire BB7 9PU

01254 826242
admissions@stonyhurst.ac.uk
www.stonyhurst.ac.uk
RC

Ages: 3–13 (boarders from year 5)
Pupils: 257
Boarders: 43
Day: £8,013 – £14,907 pa
Boarding: £19,449 – £22,950 pa

Linked school: Stonyhurst College

Headmaster: Since September 2014, Ian Murphy, previously head of All Hallows prep school in Somerset for nine years. He was educated at Jesuit school Wimbledon College and is married to Rachel, also a teacher. They have two children.

Entrance: Pupils enter all years but most commonly at age 3 and 11; boarding from year 5. Admission to nursery and reception via interview with the head and head of pre-prep; older children admitted following an interview and on receipt of a school report. Ages 10-12 require additional tests in maths, English and verbal reasoning.

Two academic scholarships and one for music awarded for entry at 11 worth between 10–50 per cent of fees. St Francis Xavier awards of 20 per cent of fees are also available to those who 'are most likely to benefit from and contribute to life as full boarders in a Catholic boarding school'. All can be topped up with a means-tested bursary – capped at a maximum of 70 per cent for St Francis Xavier award.

Exit: Straight on to Stonyhurst College. It is rare for a pupil to stray elsewhere, however school will advise appropriately if it feels Stonyhurst would be unsuitable.

Remarks: Set in glorious countryside amongst rolling fields, just a walk through the woods from college. Housed in a Victorian former priests' seminary overlooking verdant grass, junior rugby pitches, and, on a clear day, Pendle Hill. Tucked behind, sits modern yet sympathetic, purpose-built pre-prep Hodder House, with delightful teaching areas, indoors and outside, to facilitate the EYFS multi-sensory approach to learning. The complementary and contrasting nature of the buildings reflect the education here, steeped in Jesuit traditions and beliefs yet forward-thinking with the creative curriculum (gradually making its way up the school), modelled on the International Primary Curriculum, but 'retaining our Ignatian language'.

So be prepared to learn a whole new vocabulary to enter the world of a Jesuit school. For starters, 'lines' are school houses, 'playrooms' are year groups, 'playroom masters' are housemasters and as for the school year groups – Elements, lower and upper, Figures and Rudiments. And then there's the Latin..

Yet the school is forward-thinking enough to pick up on the whims of modern children, issuing a 'credit card' for consistent good work that allows you to jump the lunch queue, MSN offering an active forum for after-school chat and the top year producing its own web page. Whiteboards abound and the ICT centre is open after hours. Traditional in that a scholarship programme is in place to 'push' the brightest; French taught from 3 and Spanish, from 7, Mandarin after-school and Russian on the director of studies' radar. From 11+ common entrance curriculum followed with specialist teaching.Tutor system looks after the development of the 'whole child'.

The complementary and contrasting nature of the buildings reflect the education here, steeped in Jesuit traditions and beliefs yet forward-thinking with the creative curriculum

Project week embraces whole school in early June, from residential trips such as the battlefields for older pupils to celebration of the school's history and famous alumni for the younger. Provides learning opportunities and life skills beyond the confines of the classroom.

Ignatian values and Jesuit traditions underpin all aspects of school life; everyone's contribution is valued and giving of their best an expectation. As one parent commented, 'a heart of faith communicated through everything they do'. 'Everyone helps you out,' said one pupil. 'It's a really good school. Coming here changes your character, pushes you to aspire to make the change, so you can make a difference'. Staff feel that talent is not enough without the confidence to say 'this is what I've got, this is what I can give'. A quiet centre for reflective thought and the beautiful chapel in the heart of the school are open for those that need a peaceful moment.

A music gallery at top of school resounds with chamber choir, brass and strings – lots of uptake, though some pressure applied to join and stay according to parents; with composition on the curriculum at an early age school. Art similarly located up in the 'gods' providing a light and airy environment for some colourful and creative work. Performances are enjoyed in the theatre; one annual school production for leavers (and pre-prep nativity) though plenty of drama and performance opportunity through assemblies before then. After a previous school experience one parent was grateful that curriculum time was not lost 'in constant rehearsals honing a production to perfection'. Sport is popular with excellent coaching and facilities for traditional games, resulting in good representation at area and regional level. Usual carousel of after-school activities, with something to suit all interests.

The prep school pupils live and learn under one roof in the rambling and much-loved Victorian building. First floor classrooms are sandwiched between the age-appropriate, well-equipped ground floor playrooms and dining room on the ground floor and the upper echelons of boys' boarding accommodation on the third floor and girls' on fourth. Strong full or weekly boarding ethos: 'flexible boarding unsettling for all' says director of boarding. Over half from overseas, predominantly Spanish and Mexican, but with a league of nations from Nigeria to Korea. Parents like the diversity of pupils (and staff), a global dimension in this rural retreat. Unlike college, all ages up to 13 board together in comfortable, well-sized rooms shared by four or five, though with far less artwork on the walls usually so conspicuous in boarding houses. Where were all those 'Keep calm and carry on' posters?

Boarding maxim 'tolerance, empathy and independence' emphasises ethos and without doubt, this underpins daily life. Pupils kept busy on a schedule of activity from waking to mid-evening, though daily access to mobile phones allows for regular 'phone homes'. Weekly photo e-newsletter sent to parents by director of boarding very nice touch. Plenty of gappies ensure smooth running operationally and immersed in boarding life providing pastoral support too. Formally addressed by pupils, as 'children get confused with the blur'. Round the clock access to medical professionals, merit system determining amount of weekly tuck, rota of weekend activities, clear rules and systems neatly displayed on central notice boards – it certainly feels like a well-oiled machine.

Pupil voice is heard through the school council and boarding committee and pupils feel engaged with the way their school is run. Charitable giving is important; the school has its own charity and a link with a school near Harare supporting the culture of 'men and women for others'.

Parents are a mixed bag of former pupils and local professionals; 70 per cent Catholic, other denominations accepting the liturgy also welcome. Pupils are hugely loyal, and though well prepared, sad to leave the security of these warm and supportive surroundings.

St Mary's School (Melrose)

Abbey Park, Melrose TD6 9LN

01896 822517
office@stmarysmelrose.org.uk
www.stmarysmelrose.org.uk

Ages: 2–13 (boarders from 7)
Pupils: 185
Boarders: up to 30 flexi
Day: £11,841 – £14,691 pa
Boarding: £17,091 pa

Headmaster: Since 2010, Mr William (Liam) Harvey BEd (40s). The son of a local doc, and an FP, he went on to George Watson's followed by a BEd in PE at Liverpool John Moores University. Taught PE to A level in the state secondary sector before moving to Belhaven as housemaster and head of history and PE.

We met Harvey's Canadian wife, Marnia, efficiently organising the mysteries of the gap student's computer. Their daughters are in the school.

Entrance: All things to all men. The only independent school in the borders; children come from within a 50 mile radius, can come mid-term at any time if space available, otherwise automatically up from kindergarten. The odd state child has been known simply to come for an '18-month blast' before going back into the maintained sector, but this is rarer and rarer and none this year. Some come at 11 to do CE.

Exit: 'Most but not all' stay on until they go to their senior school at 11, 12, or 13 (the occasional toff pops off to Belhaven, Aysgarth, but none so far under the new regime), preferred secondary schools used to be Glenalmond, Fettes, Merchiston, Loretto, St George's in Edinburgh or Longridge Towers in Berwick, Queen Margaret's York and whilst these did indeed feature in our random poll, increasingly numbers are more likely to be turning south, Sedbergh gaining in popularity, Ampleforth and even Harrow. Winchester, Eton next?

Remarks: WOW. Didn't recognise the place. Totally transformed since our last visit and some of the most exciting (and cleverly sited to act as a windbreak) skool buildings we have ever seen. The Hamilton building opened in 2010 was funded by a gift from 'an anonymous benefactor'. Guestimate cost? A million near as dammit. Named after John Hamilton who founded the school in 1895 (good, if somewhat belated, way to celebrate a centenary).

Two non-parallel buildings with terrific reception area, full of photographs – though a tad Nuffield in aspect (think neutral carpets and comfy seating). Only thing missing is the coffee machine,

although we were topped up with copious amounts – the head had his own insulated mug. Reception area littered with prospectuses of senior schools – not, as previously, concentrating on the Scottish mafia, but Shrewsbury, Uppingham, Cheltenham and Harrow. Quite a change, though those whom we asked mainly seemed to be heading North. Wide corridors – one outside the art dept was recently turned into a drawing 'road' where parents and pupils depicted the best aspects of their childhood (and jolly good some of them were too – we particularly liked the footballer). Photographs everywhere in main building, the art building – with yet more light, airy, and huge classrooms has walls filled with pupil offerings and classrooms for younger pupils.

Chef comes complete with starched hat and sparkling white uniform. Cor. He also makes scrumptious millionaire's shortbread for the head's guests

We previously described St Mary's as a 'Jolly useful little school, incredibly flexible, with flexi, weekly and day pupils; one or two toffs, but mostly farmers and local professionals who stay to the bitter end, plus 'masses of' first time buyers.' But gosh. Still tiny classes, max 18 but usually much less, only one stream, scholars will be 'hived off' and set at 10 if necessary and 'provided with evening tutorials with subject teachers'. Latin from 8, languages from 5, taster term of French, then specialists in French for common entrance. Fantastic and envy-making French trips when the entire form decamp to a monastery for a week. Science taught separately for the last four years, and pupils move round the staff (from age 9 – a transition class).

'Strong' dyslexia department, all singing and dancing and recently reorganised, oversees regular testing, and support for the very bright. Withdrawn help and support staff (masses of 'em, chaps as well as chapesses) go into class too – 'pretty flexible' (might be the school motto). Keen on handwriting. Interactive whiteboards abound, all classrooms are computered to the hilt, state of the art. Loads of staff changes since head's arrival (but see below), certain number of redundancies, and terrific young buzzy staff abound (think policemen). School now boasts 'a strong academic team'.

Drama strong and timetabled, the school has links with local borders youth theatre. Good music, rehearsals and lessons in functional school hall, whilst pre-prep has own gym, with Noah and his ark drawn by the young. The somewhat surprising cloistered classroom corridor (the 'veranda classrooms') have been relegated to music, a theatre store room, boarders' activity room, music and a thrift shop.

Day children can stay from 7.30am (and breakfast in school) right through to 7.30pm, by which time they will have done their prep and had supper, kindergarten can stay till 4pm. Tinies wear delightful green and white check tabliers and girls evolve from gym slips to proper kilts; we checked, most were eight pleats thick. Dining room with weekly menu, over-high benches for littlies to sit at table. Brown bread only and lots of sugar-free puds, mainly organic as far as possible. Robert

the chef comes complete with starched chef's hat and sparkling white uniform. Cor. He also makes scrumptious millionaire's shortbread for the head's guests – not sugar-free at all, and has lost a mega amount of weight since we last saw him... now deeply into marathons. One is always told to beware the skinny chef, but he is still triumphant, and gives the boarders special cooking lessons (it was Burns night/lunch during our visit, and the haggis was piped in with aplomb). Pheasant (plucking lessons and all) on the menu next.

The Harveys live in the main school house, with dorms above, separate corridors for boys and for girls – room for up to 30 flexi boarders. The girls live in somewhat cramped conditions in a conversion of what used to be the main drawing room – fantastic ceiling, but divided into three – with what must be one of the grandest ceiling-ed bathrooms ever. Jolly dorms upstairs, all brightly painted with splendid stripy duvet covers. Very homey; bunks, the odd poster, random teddy bears. B&B charged per night.

Squads and teams triumph all over the place. Swimming off-site in Gala(shiels) and main games pitches just across some National Trust land. Smashing little school.

St Olave's School

Queen Anne's Road, York, North Yorkshire YO30 7WA

01904 527416
enquiries@stolavesyork.org.uk
www.st-peters.york.sch.uk
C of E

Ages: 8–13
Pupils: 355
Boarders: 25 full/flexi
Day: £11,325 – £13,695 pa
Boarding: £21,120 – £23,295 pa

Linked school: St Peter's School, York

Master: Since 2005, Mr Andy Falconer MBA BA (40s). An ISI inspector, recent chair of IAPS as well as a Walter Hines Page Scholar. Previously deputy head at Chafyn Grove School and before that was head of geography at Craigclowan School. Married to Lesley, a nurse, with three young daughters. Enjoys skiing, grew up near a Scottish ski resort and is a qualified instructor, former travel writer and currently into marathon running, otherwise free time is family time. Kind, charming, with a soft Scottish lilt and a delightful manner. Chats very comfortably with pupils, knows who they are and equally they know him – pupils tuck their shirts in when they see him coming. He misses nothing, touring school with a watchful eye, even turning off lights in empty rooms – 'a Scotsman in Yorkshire,' he

grins. Hugely knowledgeable about and committed to the education of children, up to speed on all the latest developments, cherry picking the best and applying them with skill and understanding to enhance the learning experience. Parents and children trust him implicitly, never doubting that he has the children's best interests at heart. A rock solid practitioner.

Entrance: Automatic from Clifton Pre-Preparatory (takes ages 3-8), otherwise selective but not massively so, looking for cognitive ability scores of 100+. All entrants are tested in maths, English, reading, spelling, and reasoning. Entrance examinations end of January.

Exit: Almost all to St Peter's School, York. A few to Queen Margaret's, Bootham, Queen Ethelburga's and local state schools.

Remarks: Sited in the former Queen Anne's grammar school buildings – a number of mums are old girls. The buildings have been adapted, extended and improved to create a more welcoming space for children and their parents. It's a very grounded school, not stuffy in any sense. Footbridge to senior school makes it easy to get from one campus to the other, 'distinct and separate, yet linked' (is the official line, and it seems to work).

Staff encouraged to 'share the learning journey' – the head is learning to play the drums (and gives the children regular updates on his progress in assembly)

Good facilities, shares Astroturf and indoor pool with senior school, but has own sports hall with indoor nets; music block; science lab; language rooms; DT; cookery, not as a discrete subject but linked eg to maths, DT, languages (recipes in French); art and ceramic studios; dining hall, Shepherd Hall for assemblies and regular productions, medical room and veg garden.

Parents delight in the school's 'responsiveness', answering questions, dealing with any concerns and, importantly, 'never underestimating children'. Stretch and challenge include sparky discussions on current events in assembly that then continue over supper at home and the ability of staff to 'see qualities in children that others might overlook'. PTA members are busy with social and fundraising events twice a term varying from murder mystery nights to wine-tasting and a denim and diamante evening.

Invariably over-subscribed at 11+, year on year; some leakage of girls at year 6 to girls' schools, but only a handful and they are 'easily replaced' we are told. Equal numbers of boys/girls, 25 full/flexi boarders. About a fifth of boarders are from overseas, third armed forces, the rest from across the UK or even local – one boarder lives close enough to kick a rugby ball into his own garden. Saturday morning school for everyone, 'allows a broader curriculum and more time spent with your mates', says school, 'great fun but requires stamina,' say parents. Parents of day pupils (that's most of them) pass the time having coffee or shopping, almost 50 take to school rowing boats on the river, it's all part of the service. Day pupils travel from as far afield as Scarborough, Harrogate, Selby and Wetherby – short cut to the railway station makes it possible. The train is a good idea because parking is tricky – has to be a quick drop off in the mornings though the playground is opened up so that you can 'park and pick up' after school.

No common entrance or national curriculum testing here yet plenty of rigour. For those heading for public schools beyond York school organises own testing/entrance procedures and supports accordingly. Healthy outlook on education, 'you've got to play the long game' says the head, 'it's more about learning and thinking and less about testing', quoting that old Chinese proverb about 'not fattening a pig by weighing it'. Doing something right as the library bucks the trend by being packed with boys at breaktime (clever librarian – great choice of 'boy' books) and academic standards, across the board, are high. Average class size 18 with maximum usually 20. Chapel twice a week, traditional C of E service. No issue with bright dyslexics, have strategies to help, specialist tutors, extra lessons and extra time for those who need them.

Staff are encouraged to 'share the learning journey' – the head is learning to play the drums (and gives the children regular updates on his progress in assembly); others offer four week courses to their colleagues (teaching and non-teaching) in a range of subjects, skills and challenges. Years 6 to 8 have all their lessons with subject specialists, younger children gradually work towards this. There is setting throughout for maths and for French and Latin in the top two years. Carousel for French/Spanish/German/Latin in years 4 and 5, pupils choose post year 7.

Music is high profile, a school concert sees two-thirds of pupils taking part. Years 4 and 5 have three class lessons of music each week; add to that the usual choirs, brass groups, sax and clarinet groups, recorder, woodwind and cello groups – plus the school rock band 'Stereo Flair'. Some phenomenal art on display, 'talent is recognised and nurtured' say parents.

Sport is impressive here, plenty of teams and older pupils competing at national level. Bigger schools such as RGS Newcastle and QEGS Wakefield provide serious challenge; smaller preps may struggle to compete with the first team here. Sporting successes include four times winners of the National Rugby Sevens Tournament; winners of national JET Cup cricket; national finals for hockey, soccer and cricket. Outward bound, yacht sailing with Ocean Youth Trust and rowing (school has rowing machines as well as river access and own rowing club) plus an Easter ski trip and sports tours (years 5 and 8) keep pupils busy and active all year round.

Lots of extracurricular choice including enterprising young apprentice-type challenges and history model-making club, which essentially means making weapons from wood. Pupils also enjoy charity days and fundraising, pink day for breast cancer, organised by pupils, and green day in support of NSPCC, among recent events. Wide range of after-school clubs and activities, including prep clubs for day children of working parents.

Pupils eat and register in their mixed age houses,' helping everyone to, 'know the school vertically and horizontally'. Strong house identity (that children describe as 'Harry Potter-esque'), linked to pastoral care. A teacher/mentor follows through with groups of children year on year, a type of wraparound care valued hugely by parent body. Homemade lunches prepared by chef, the legendary Dave.

Smart (ish) navy uniform, different from and more appealing than the brown of the senior school; sports kit is linked across the schools.

St Peter's School, York

Clifton, York, North Yorkshire YO30 6AB

01904 527300
g.daniells@stpetersyork.org.uk
www.stpetersyork.org.uk
C of E

Ages: 13–18 (boarding from 10)
Pupils: 548; sixth form: 250
Boarders: 142
Day: £7,890 – £16,560 pa
Boarding: £21,120 – £27,375 pa

Linked school: St Olave's School

Head Master: Since 2010, Mr Leo Winkley MA MEd (40s), previously managing head at Bedales. Read theology at Lady Margaret Hall, Oxford. Taught at Ardingly College and The Cheltenham Ladies' College as head of religious studies. Still teaches religious studies and contributes to the global perspectives programme for sixth form: he enjoys teaching – 'it keeps you honest'. A keen runner and follower of sport. Married to medical oncologist Jules; they have three young children. Committed to the breadth and all-round nature of independent education as lessons for life – says 'school should be serious fun', currently encouraging all parties to 'think big'. Pupils tell us he has 'smartened things

up a bit and increased pupil involvement', parents say he is a 'fine chap' and has 'got the bit between his teeth'. You get a very warm welcome from this clear-sighted, ambitious strategist; he was born into the world of independent education, son of a headmaster, so knows the perils, pitfalls and joys, though it is different up north and it will be interesting to see how the school develops under his leadership.

Academic matters: Consistent achiever, sets the bar high in a robust local market. Strong work ethos with plenty of stretch and challenge, normal to try hard but fine-tuning from the top is pushing to 'broaden the pupil experience' ie accumulation of exam certificates is great but balance is also important.

Takes the academic rigour for granted; bright pupils will always do well, but hard workers also do well here, hence the very positive value-added. Believes good results are down to having really good teachers as well as selective but not highly selective intake; no weak subject areas; staff know what is expected and are multi-talented and self-driven. 'Learn Something New' is a St Peter's initiative that persuades staff to share interests and learn from each other with a range of activities across the school(s) encouraging staff to try out and learn new skills – 'learning teachers teach better' is the head's strapline.

Class size averages 18 in the middle school (maximum 24) and 12 in the sixth form. The occasional D or E grade creeps in at GCSE, but 73 per cent of passes A*/A in 2015. IGCSEs being taken in maths, science and languages. Equally impressive performance at A level where 56 per cent of grades were A*/A and a very commendable 81 per cent of all entries graded A*-B.

Some support for the handful with mild dyslexia – must be bright and able to cope. Part-time dyslexia specialist. Approximately 10 per cent have an ed psych report; five per cent qualify for extra time in exams. Third modern language replaced by extra English and study skills for some. Gifted and talented programme in place but don't target top 10 per cent. 'All the children here are bright; it would be wrong to concentrate on a handful.' Olympiads and similar challenges stretch those with real talent. Global Perspectives an additional course for sixth form with Horizons introduced for middle school. Does not allow students to take any GCSE early and moving towards more challenging IGCSEs.

A surprising amount of outdoor space; you'd never guess it is so close to the city. Nearest to the school is the hallowed ground of the first XV rugby pitch

Careers advice and support flagged up by parents as something to be worked on and improved, especially important for boarders whose parents are not around to have those all-important conversations. They are getting pupils into good and great universities, but what next? Both pupils and parents feel they would like more guidance and direction as life beyond university becomes tougher and more competitive. The school has responded swiftly by bringing in a second careers advisor and opening up careers events, visits, conferences plus 'exploration week' for the lower sixth – 'life after St Peter's' is a drum they will keep on banging.

Games, options, the arts: A surprising amount of outdoor space; you'd never guess it is so close to the city. Nearest to the school is the hallowed ground of the first XV rugby pitch, but there are plenty of others beyond. Sport is compulsory for all. Facilities include two sports centres, one with super climbing wall, multi-surface pitch, fitness centre, indoor swimming pool, extensive well-kept playing fields, boathouse and tennis and squash courts. Rugby popular and strong, rowing crews regularly pick up national honours and awards, boast 20 international rowers in the last eight years. Hockey, rowing and netball are the most popular girls' sports but tennis, athletics, squash, swimming and usual suspects on offer for all. Generally put best coaches with best teams but playing opportunities for all via B teams and house competitions. Competitiveness and fair play are a prominent feature of the school and success is universally applauded at weekly assembly. D of E and CCF flourishing. Plenty of trips including expeditions to Morocco, sports tours to New Zealand and South Africa, language holidays and music tours to the USA, Prague, Italy as well as singing in York Minster.

Very good art facilities, including super gallery. Art department appears in the Guinness Book of Records for a remarkable 100 per cent A*/A grade pass rate achieved four years running, though recent years have seen lower grades creep in – 'we were pleased, it took the pressure off, allowed the pupils to experiment, be more creative rather than formulaic,' said one art master. Many learn

Says 'school should be serious fun', currently encouraging all parties to 'think big'. Pupils tell us he has 'smartened things up a bit'

a musical instrument or two, 300 individual lessons each week with professional specialist music staff, 160 strong choir and plenty of opportunities to perform; director of music described as 'inspirational'. Each boarding house has a practice room with piano. Over 100 pupils involved with Community Action projects and all participate in charity fundraising.

Boarding: Around a quarter of pupils board, of whom 30 per cent are from overseas. Most are full boarders but a few stay on a flexi/weekly basis. Boarding received an Outstanding rating in last Ofsted inspection. Six day and four boarding houses, the latter well equipped with a selection of common rooms, games rooms and a kitchen for snacks (all eat in school dining hall). Pupils and staff strike a good balance between amity and mutual respect. Houses are headed by husband and wife teams and supported by resident and non-resident assistants. Good pastoral care, 'just wonderful,' say parents. They describe house parents as 'something out of the ordinary', creating boarding houses that are 'home from home' with all the care and support that may be needed and equally 'a kick up the jacksy as required'. Staff vigilant – invariably have one or two they're watching for eating problems etc.

Background and atmosphere: The school was founded in 627 AD by Paulinus, first Archbishop of York, and is one of the world's oldest schools, 'only two older', we are told. In 1844 it was established on its present, impressive, green, grade 2 listed site in Clifton, with 47 acres, river access and all within walking distance of York Minster, the city centre and station.

Beyond the imposing main building, others are a mix of ancient and modern. Some classrooms and corridors are a bit tatty round the edges; we get the sense that it's not a priority – it's a workhorse, not a show pony. Good range of facilities, with all angles covered, though pupils tell us they are pestering the head for a new sports hall; 'it could be so much better'. It's one of the head boy's pet projects, though not on the agenda (yet) – might have to settle for a new boathouse instead. Pupils rave about the new swimming pool, opened by Olympic diver Tom Daley. Other recent additions include four bright biology labs, a sixth form microbiology lab, chemistry lab and design and technology room with Cad Cam technology. Three computer rooms are complemented by clusters of computers throughout the school and houses – virtual learning environment with Wifi throughout the campus.

Pastoral care, well-being and discipline: Advice, help and support may be sought from tutors, house staff, resident health centre staff or the school chaplain. Pupils tell us that the unforgivables are drugs and bullying; if caught smoking it's three strikes and you're out.

Pupils are allowed to visit town twice a week (more in older years) and for younger ones a timetable of supervised events is on offer. All eat in the modern dining hall. Menus offer a wide choice with mixture of typical school meal fare, continental options, salad bar, sandwiches, fruit and healthy eating options. Pupils say food is 'great', with 'boy-sized portions'; Sunday brunch is legendary.

Pupil voice has grown and developed through a pupil symposium. Head's question time is chaired by the head boy or girl – 'direct government-type stuff' – raising all kinds of ideas and questions from the downright silly to the well-considered and serious.

If it were a car, we'd probably describe it as a Volvo, albeit a top of the range high performance 4WD version with sporty extras such as a ski rack and maybe a tow bar

Middle school uniform uninspiring, disliked, yet (bizarrely) defended, by pupils – when push comes to shove there's nothing more conservative or radically opposed to change than your average 15 year old: brown blazer, grey trousers for boys, and brown checked skirt for girls. Apparently the current line is 'brown is good'. Sixth form (boys and girls) wear dark business suits.

Strong Christian ethos; pupils meet thrice weekly for collective act of worship in school chapel – the new chaplain has 'livened things up a bit,' pupils tell us with a grin; assemblies at other times.

Pupils and parents: Day pupils mainly from North Yorkshire, Harrogate, Leeds conurbation, York, and surrounding villages. Majority of boarders live within an hour's drive but others from wide area in the UK. Parents in business and the professions, a popular choice for Forces families, minority from overseas – 'it's a world view we need to develop,' says the head. Mix of Hong Kong, China, Russia, one or two others – about 25 per cent overall.

'Parents,' say school, 'are interested – but not helicopters', ambitious and driven; quite a few first time buyers here but also dynasties with names all over the honours boards.

Old Peterites include Guy Fawkes, Alcuin (eighth century scholar), Greg Wise, John Barry, Laurence Eusden (poet laureate), Harry Gration (journalist, TV presenter), C Northcote Parkinson (inventor of Parkinson's Law) and Clare Wise (director of the British Film Commission).

Entrance: Automatic entry from Clifton Pre-prep to St Olave's (St Peter's junior school) and then from St Olave's to St Peter's. Seventy per cent follow this route, rest by CE and school's own entrance test at any age including 13 or 16 (minimum six GCSE grade B passes). Assessment and filtering does take place in prep and pre-prep to weed out those who won't cope with the demands of St Peter's, but it is rare. Generally entry to St Olave's requires a child to have a reading age at least a year ahead of chronological age (sympathetic to siblings). Will take pupils who pass exam at any time provided a place is available. Other main feeder schools: Terrington Hall, Cundall Manor and Aysgarth, some state schools also.

Exit: Around 10 per cent leave at the end of year 11. Of those leaving after A levels, 95 per cent go directly to university, vast majority selecting Russell Group. Eight to Oxbridge in 2015 (though UCL and Imperial often favoured by high fliers). Edinburgh, Newcastle, Birmingham and Sheffield also popular; some 15 per cent applying next year; a few to employment.

Money matters: Not a rich school but has increased bursary funding considerably over the past few years. Means-tested bursaries available at 11, 13 and at sixth form regardless of previous school. Qualification criteria for bursaries on a sliding scale from 10 to 100 per cent based on need, and typically if household income is less than £45,000. Honorary (ie no dosh) subject scholarships are awarded; music awards, including fee remission, available for tuition and instruments.

Remarks: Very much the big brother of the 3-18 triumvirate of St Peter's schools, encompassing Clifton Pre-Prep and St Olave's junior school ('continuity, but difference' is the mantra here) and you get the impression that this is where it all becomes rather serious. If it were a car, we'd probably describe it as a Volvo, albeit a top of the range high performance 4WD version with sporty extras such as a ski rack and maybe a tow bar. It can accommodate the whole family and you can't doubt the quality, reliability and solidity of the product it delivers, pretty much unfailingly, in all areas.

Sedbergh School

Malim Lodge, Sedbergh, Cumbria LA10 5HG

01539 620535
enquiries@sedberghschool.org
www.sedberghschool.org
C of E

Ages: 13–18
Pupils: 512 (319 boys, 193 girls); sixth form: 205
Boarders: 500
Day: £22,950 pa
Boarding: £31,146 pa

Linked school: Casterton, Sedbergh Preparatory School

Head Master: Since 2010, Mr Andrew Fleck MA (late 40s), educated at Marlborough College, read geology at Nottingham and has an MA in education from Sussex. Member of HMC Professional Development Committee, a governor of Westville House Preparatory School and a fellow of the Royal Geographical Society.

Urbane, charming and appears, as one parent put it, 'very comfortable in his own skin'. Committed to the Sedbergh values of a 'properly balanced education', providing pupils with the 'vision, aspirations and leadership skills to succeed in a global labour market' and determined to dispel the public perception that only sports rule here.

Married to Anne, who runs a software development company working primarily in agro-technology and with whom he cycled the deserts of central Iceland and the northern Sahara on a tandem. Interests include sailing, canoeing and cycling – canoed around Ireland, Newfoundland, Japan and Arctic Norway to the Russian border

and cycled the east/west European border. Has twin daughters, both at Sedbergh.

Academic matters: In 2015, 63 per cent A*/B grades and nearly 33 per cent A*/A at A level, and 39 per cent A*/A grades at GCSE. Not bad for a school with a comprehensive intake, that welcomes all to stay for sixth form and a policy of entering all pupils for exams; very good value-added. Pupils and parents speak of 'caring, dedicated and helpful staff, committed to the children'. Gifted and talented are stretched and learning support (primarily for dyslexia) is provided in the classroom or by individual tuition in a separate building known as The Shack. Head admits more to do in this provision and it is 'work in progress'.

Broad curriculum, French plus German or Spanish on offer for year 9 (overseas visits but no exchange programme). Drama recently introduced at GCSE and jewellery design at GCSE and AS level. Has launched a new BTec subsidiary diploma in agriculture, a joint venture with Newton Rigg College in Penrith and the equivalent of one A level. Also offers EPQ.

Many classrooms, language labs and laboratories have been given a facelift, extensive art facilities and good DT workshops, embracing new IT investment. Well-stocked departmental libraries and shelves of fiction in the boarding houses – does this deter pupils from making the main library a centre of learning and research? Housed in a super conversion of Georgian building on the site of Lupton's original school, the library has been revamped recently, but its primary use seems as a venue for debate, lectures and academic house competitions.

Games, options, the arts: Renowned for its sporting prowess (34 sporting activities on offer) with many pupils winning representative honours, especially in rugby and shooting. Sport is timetabled five times a week, adjusted winter and summer to make best use of daylight. All you would expect in facilities and more (even a heated cricket square) set in idyllic surroundings. Plenty of opportunities to canoe and cave, orienteer and rock climb. Also famous for its Wilson Run – a 10-mile fell race open to ages 16+. All pupils participate in CCF in year 9 but involvement is optional after that, though many continue.

All you would expect in facilities and more (even a heated cricket square) set in idyllic surroundings. Plenty of opportunities to canoe and cave, orienteer and rock climb

The hills here are certainly alive with the sound of music. Some 350 pupils take individual lessons up to grade 8 and diploma, with representation in national ensembles. Fizzing director has developed choral singing to a crescendo, together with classic chamber groups and orchestra, swing, jazz, rock and CCF bands. Excellent, spacious and recently updated music school with composing and recording facilities, plus the Thornely Studio, a £1 million performance hall with sprung floors.

Lots of performance opportunities for music and drama at home and away with regular trips and tours abroad. Range of clubs and societies available, from mountain biking to debating and specialist lectures in science, medicine and music. Flourishing D of E award scheme. House competitions for everything from singing to chess.

Boarding: The nine boarding houses (six for boys and three for girls) widely dispersed through campus and town, giving pupils plenty of daily

exercise as they move through the school day. No wonder a bicycle for transit around campus is a prefect privilege.

Pivotal to the success of the school are the keen house loyalty (quickly assumed by new entrants) and the level of care pupils receive there. Each pupil is assigned to a house where they live, eat all meals, including lunch, collectively, when manners and conversation are nurtured. Excellent food, lots of choice, special diets catered for. Girls' boarding houses are bright, modern and well furnished; all the boys' boarding houses have been refurbished in recent years. One parent commented that her son 'enjoys it so much he never wants to come home'.

Background and atmosphere: Founded in 1525 by Roger Lupton, a provost of Eton. School lies in the centre of a small, picturesque town surrounded by magnificent fells, in the heart of the splendid (if often wet and cold) Yorkshire Dales National Park but only a short drive from the M6. Departments housed in a number of well-spaced, separate buildings.

Girls arrived in 2001 and with the opening of a third girls' boarding house in 2013 they now account for nearly 40 per cent of the school population. They have made their mark as a significant, vibrant and impressive part of the school. Few shrinking violets here, matching the boys for healthy inter-house rivalry, success in extracurricular, whilst helping the academic results along the way. Make sure to check out The Sedberghian, the school magazine, for information on every facet of the place and the pupils who populate it.

Sedburgh merged with Casterton School in 2013. The merged junior school has moved to the Casterton site (and is now known as Casterton, Sedbergh Preparatory School), whilst the merged senior school, named Sedbergh School, remains on this site.

Pastoral care, well-being and discipline: Very effective house system with strong, popular and caring housemasters and mistresses heading up dedicated teams who have good relationships with the pupils. Teachers also attached to houses. Rules recognised by pupils and parents as firm but fair, well thought out and communicated clearly. Structured and well-thought-out sanctions and rewards system. Bullying is rare – the ethos in houses militates against it.

Pupils given freedom around town, a safe bet when you consider you're never far from someone connected to the school. Bar available at weekends to sixth formers; school encourages a sensible attitude to alcohol. Controlled access between boys' and girls' houses but over-familiar relationships between boys and girls discouraged.

Pupils and parents: A complete mix – mostly northern professionals but increasingly from Scotland

and the South. Traditionally a school for land-owners, industrialists and farmers' sons (Wordsworth was a parent), but now an eclectic mix including Forces, expats and a few foreigners. Pupils are confident, sparky and generally, though not universally, sporty, very grounded, have a practical approach and are not afraid to get their hands dirty. Willingness to help others, loyalty and compassion are values universally to the fore. A very happy school – lots of laughter in and out of lessons. Still not a place for the timid or loner but anyone else, especially those who appreciate the fantastic surroundings and teamwork, will love it here.

Old boys include Simon Beaufoy (Full Monty); Wills Carling and Greenwood; Lord Bingham (Lord Chief Justice); James Wilby; Sir Jock Slater (First Sea Lord); Sir Christopher Bland (chairman BT); Robert Napier (chief exec of Met Office, ex chief exec WWF and chairman of governors).

Entrance: For most, CE is the normal route, others applying in years 9-11 sit exams in English and maths. A current school report is required. Sixth form requires a minimum of five GCSEs at C or above. Main feeder is Casterton, Sedbergh Preparatory School, but significant proportion come from prep schools across the north of England and beyond.

Exit: Mostly to university – northern popular, a number of Scottish; degree choice spread across science, business and arts. Steady trickle to Oxbridge (traditionally strong links with Cambridge – one place in 2015). Several opt for a gap year having secured their university place. Handful embark on vocational courses or careers at 18, trickle (around 10-15 per cent) leave at 16.

Money matters: A number of scholarships for entry at years 9, 10 and 12: academic, all-round, art, DT, music sport and drama. Awards vary but may be up to half fees. Index-linked major scholarships – in exceptional circumstances. Exhibitions and bursaries also available.

Remarks: Has retained its traditional values and ethos (and market) while responding to the demands of the 21st century. Renowned as a formidable force on the sports field, it seeks to embed that gold standard throughout the school. Pupils, whether sporty, academic, musical or arty, are well catered for and seem to love it, although a love of fresh air and the great outdoors is a distinct advantage. Opportunities are provided in a happy and caring environment to create a 'can do' philosophy in pupils. Numbers suggest that pupils and their parents very much approve. We watch with interest the results of its merger with Casterton School.

Stewart's Melville College

Queensferry Road, Edinburgh EH4 3EZ

01313 111000
admissions@esms.org.uk
www.esms.org.uk

Ages: 12–18
Pupils: 756; joint sixth form: 250
Boarders: 20 full, 1 flexi
Day: £10,548 pa
Boarding: £20,634 – £21,162 pa

Linked school: The Mary Erskine School

Principal: Since 2000, Mr David Gray BA PGCE (50s), who was educated at Fettes, read English at Bristol, where he did his PGCE. Taught English in a Bristol comprehensive, before moving to a language school in Greece, then taught English and modern Greek at Dulwich and was head of English at Leeds Grammar, before heading Pocklington School in East Yorkshire for eight years. Since the Erskine Stewart's Melville vast conglomerate forms the largest independent school in Europe, it is not surprising he feels he is in a position here 'to give something back to Scotland having been away for

almost a quarter of a century'. Brought up in Inverness, he is proud of his Scottish roots and sees himself and Stewart's Melville/Mary Erskine as at the 'most exciting cutting-edge of Scottish education' and stresses that he's the first overall principal who is actually Scottish. Mr Gray spends part of the week in each school. We visited him at his base in Mary Erskine, where he was busily involved in compiling a history of the school for his teaching contact with the girls.

Very much a hands-on head, the principal reckons to keep sane (and fit) by swimming and jogging

Sixth formers have to take academic courses from both schools – a feat resulting in an endless (almost) variety of course permutations

at 7am each morning, and is a familiar sight as he cycles between the two campuses. He also 'works the room' quite beautifully, 'we all think we know him well and that he knows our children almost as well as we do,' said one father (a gift no doubt inherited from his politician father?). Keen on promoting self-confidence in his pupils, he sees himself as an 'educator', and teaches English and coaches cricket at Stewart's Melville. After 15 years he feels pleased that the school has 'become a gentler place' and that the 'children are wedded to our ethos of reasonable, sensible behaviour'. No need for draconian action on the discipline side recently and, when there is silliness, 'the student body can be very conservative on behaviour,' while parents 'don't want to be ashamed of the school.'

Mr Gray runs the twin senior schools with two deputy heads, and the head of the co-ed junior school, Bryan Lewis, who is also vice principal. Mrs Linda Moule took over as deputy head of The Mary Erskine School in August 2009; she was previously vice principal of New Hall School in Chelmsford. Mr Neal Clark, depute head of Stewart's Melville for the last 15 years describes himself as a 'grammar school boy, in tune with Scottish social culture.' All school facilities have been upgraded in the last 10 years 'so future plans are for maintenance rather than development.'

Academic matters: The principal and three heads have agonised together over the pros and cons of single-sex v co-ed. All four speak with the same passion – and often the same phrasing – of their 'best of both worlds' system. Boys and girls educated together at junior school, separately from age 12-17 – gains for girls (being able to get on with learning) and boys (feeling free to talk about poetry etc) – then the social etc plus factors of co-ed for sixth year and all activities. 'Not a highly selective school,' however, described by an educationalist as a 'grade one academic machine.' Classes of up to 25 (20 for practical classes) setted, with groups subdivided to extend the most able. School has embraced the new Advanced Higher in depth – greater analysis, independent study, projects and dissertation. Mr Clark – glad that so many students do three Advanced Highers with considerable success – notes that, in recent years, as admission to Scottish universities has become very competitive, there remains a strong desire to undertake further Highers. Recent results show a pleasing number of As and Bs across the board (51 per cent of Advanced Highers graded A in 2015 at Stewart's Melville College) in both schools, with some outstanding successes in history, sciences and maths. Higher results impressive (59 per cent A in 2015), particularly at MES 'on the languages front' and for SMC in history, English and science. French, German, Spanish and Latin on offer to Advanced Higher Grade.

Standard Grades phased out (except drama) in favour of Intermediate 2 (which is based on the

same assessment pattern as Highers) and now the National 5. Results pretty impressive here too (77 per cent As in 2015).

Very good links (still) with the Merchant Company which does masses of business breakfasts and links with professional firms around Edinburgh. Single IT network across all three schools with 'massive schools' intranet', interactive whiteboards galore and close on 1000 computers. Biology dept links with the horticultural dept of the world-famous Edinburgh Botanic Gardens. Impressive careers structure across both schools and excellent library facilities. Pupils can sign in for private study.

Schools combine for sixth form, most extras, and pastoral structure. In the interests of integration sixth formers have to take academic courses from both schools – a feat resulting in limitless (almost) variety of course permutations, miraculous timetabling and a quite a few bus journeys. Outstanding back-up for those with learning difficulties; school uses its own educational psychologist; 'will never abandon anyone.'

Games, options, the arts: Big is beautiful; providing a list of over 75 different clubs for all – from goldsmithing to Greek, costume design to curling and cross-country – lunch time and post school. Popular. Major sports have separate clubs for ages/stages and 27 rugby teams. Good at football too. Girls prefer hockey and basketball, still better at shooting than boys and both sexes join the voluntary CCF (trillions of girls, over 400 members in all). A second super new floodlit Astroturf at MES, 'so everyone gets a chance,' dramatic wavy roofed swimming pool (at Stewart's Melville) with co-ed sixth form slump-out room adjacent, new gym (at MES), cricket pavilion (MES again). FPs and current pupils share sporting facilities at MES; extra games pitches at Inverleith. Needle matches in almost all disciplines, with FPs

representing both county and country across the board. Smart dining room complex serves all juniors and 80 per cent seniors opt in. Sixth form coffee bars with stunning overview of school and pitches.

No need for draconian action on the discipline side; 'student body can be very conservative on behaviour'

Incredibly strong drama – regular performances at the Edinburgh Festival and throughout the year at the Playhouse etc. Masses of every sort of orchestras. Pupils can learn to fly, ski (Hillend and the real thing, the Alps, Canada); brilliant debating team (regularly the Scottish Debating Champions, European Youth Parliament finalists) and SMC has represented Great Britain abroad all over the shop. Good home economics. Arts spectacular. Dramatic art room atop MES (with adjoining pottery and greenhouse). £3.5m performing arts centre's opening splash was Snowman composer, Howard Blake and Scottish Chamber Orchestra. Centre took 12 years in the planning – seats 800 with a retractable stage and dividing walls, replacing the old assembly hall – which was huge and impressive – and jolly nice in its way.

Boarding: Two boarding houses, Dean Park House and Erskine House, furnished like large (and very well-equipped) family houses and based on the edge of the Stewart's Melville campus. Tremendous family feel, boarders are encouraged to invite friends home, caring house parents and only 60 boarding places. Boarders organise most of their own out-of-school activities eg quiz nights, weekend outings, summer barbecues.

Background and atmosphere: Stewart's Melville campus is based round the magnificent David Rhind-designed Daniel Stewart's Hospital which opened in 1885 and merged with Melville College in 1972. Fairy-tale Victorian gothic with a cluster of necessary modern additions surrounded by ever-decreasing games pitches and car parks. The old chapel is now a library complete with organ and stained glass windows. Stewart's Melville is also home to the senior department of the junior school – see separate entry.

Mary Erskine was founded in 1694, as the Merchant Maiden Hospital, moved to Ravelston in 1966, changing its name to The Mary Erskine School, and amalgamated with the boys' school in 1978. (Girls wear charming Mary Erskine tartan kilts.) MES clusters in decidedly 1960s architecture with, now, quite a lot of more modern extensions, round the pretty but sadly overwhelmed Ravelston House (1791): swimming pool, tennis courts, games pitches,

Astroturfs etc. The last much used by FPs. The nursery department and the youngest classes of the junior school are also based here – see separate entry.

Regular buses from East and West Lothian and Fife service both schools, which operate as one, under the auspices of Erskine Stewart's Melville Governing Council. Each school, though, is fiercely proud of its individual heritage.

Pastoral care, well-being and discipline: Both schools have a tutorial system for the first year, followed by house system in upper schools. Houses are common to both schools and house competitions have mixed sex teams. Good links with parents. Brief is that 'all children have a right to be happy here.' Code of conduct established by consulting pupils so 'they know exactly where they stand.' Excellent anti-bullying policy: wary pastoral staff and peer-support group 'with professional training' stop 'children slipping through the net.' Sophisticated PSE programme right up the school, including study skills. Buddy system for those coming up from junior schools. Automatic expulsion, 'zero-tolerance,' for those bringing in illicit substances – 'those on the periphery of the same incident will not necessarily be excluded but can come back in as long as they agree to random testing'. Fags 'unacceptable and pupils suspended'. Booze 'not an issue in school'.

Pupils and parents: Edinburgh hotch-potch of New Town and suburbs, with many first-time buyers and lots up from England. Siblings and FPs' children. Taking over a third of Edinburgh's independent secondary pupils, it's less elitist and perhaps less dusty than some city schools. Children living far out can spend the night when doing evening activities.

Parent-teacher group ('the red socks brigade') slightly better organised into a Friends of the School group, fundraising, ceilidhs, 'good cash cow.'

Entrance: At 11, 12, 13 or sixth form – otherwise 'by default.' Automatic from junior school. Entrance assessments held in January but can be arranged at any time. Waiting lists for some stages but just go on trying. Entrance to upper school is by interview, plus school report plus GCSEs/National grades (five credit passes for S5 entry.) Numbers up overall.

Exit: Minimal leakage pre-Highers, most sixth year go on to university (gap years growing in popularity, especially for girls), most opt for Scottish universities but a few go to Oxbridge (five to Cambridge in 2015), London, Bristol etc. SATs (for American colleges) not a problem; some students also go to European universities. Art college, music/drama are popular alternatives.

Money matters: Scholarships/bursaries available, some linked to the Merchant Company, others sibling directed. 'No child will be left wanting in a (financial) crisis.'

Remarks: A glance at the school mags, Merchant Maiden and The Collegian, sums it up: bags of boys' poetry, multiple hockey, rugby and cricket teams, several Oxbridge places, fabulous art, photos and writing plus fascinating glimpses from boys and girls reporting on the same activities with subtly different views.

An outstanding school; happy pupils, happy staff – focused on self-development with impressive results.

Stonyhurst College

Stonyhurst, Clitheroe, Lancashire BB7 9PZ

01254 827073
admissions@stonyhurst.ac.uk
www.stonyhurst.ac.uk
RC

Ages: 13–18
Pupils: 465; sixth form: 250
Boarders: 325
Day: £17,814 pa
Boarding: £26,661 – £31,989 pa

Linked school: St Mary's Hall

Headmaster: Since 2006, Mr Andrew Johnson BA (40s), former deputy head of Birkdale School. Previously at Winchester College for 10 years, head of modern languages for final four years. Educated at the Skinners' School, Tunbridge Wells, read

French and Spanish at Bristol University, followed by postgraduate diploma in education management from Portsmouth University. Catholic, clear sighted, energetic, confident yet approachable; married to Dawn, sixth form tutor, member of the marketing team and musician who teaches piano, with two sons approaching GCSEs – all at the college; quite a family affair. Interests are walking, cinema, music and drama – when time allows. Loves his job '90 per cent of the time' and sees his role to develop young people 'to be as good as they can be in the areas where they have talents' and 'to be comfortable in their own skins'.

Moving on in July 2016 to head St Benedict's School in London.

Academic matters: Good value-added, especially at GCSE; in 2015, 51 per cent of all passes were A*/A. Seventy-one per cent of A level passes were graded A*-B, 41 per cent A*/A. Maths consistently popular at A level, achieving good results. Introduced IB in 2013 – 'fits approach to learning in a Jesuit school,' says the head, who believes success in IB lies in being 'organised, hard-working, academically able but not necessarily super bright'. First results in 2015 saw an average of 32 points.

Broad curriculum including French, Spanish and German, together with Greek and Latin. Average class size 18, 10 in the sixth form. Compulsory RE to GCSE, non-examined theology/ethics in sixth form. Four classes set according to ability at entrance. In recent years influx of new teaching staff who 'provide a good balance'; much investment in sharing good practice, training and development. Head sees his appointment 'to focus on academics' – and he has.

Pupils are assigned a personal tutor whom they meet weekly to discuss all-round progress. Stays with them through their school career, just one aspect of the Jesuit ethos of individual care. Broad ability intake and thus not the academic powerhouse of city day schools. Genuine desire for each pupil to fulfill their potential – many pupils exceed this and very able pupils do particularly well.

Twenty per cent of pupils have EAL support provided in discrete lessons and within mainstream lessons. Special needs (mainly dyslexic and dyspraxic) similarly provided under supervision of specialist SEN teacher. Learning mentor helps with organisation and study skills.

Much of the school is truly splendid: huge staircases, wood panelling, polished stone, works of art, brimming with history and tradition. Some formerly hidden treasures

Plenty of computers around linked up to the school's intranet and all pupils have their own email address. Pupils timetabled IT to year 9, then GCSE option. Laptop internet connections in sixth form study bedrooms; PCs at study work places for younger pupils.

Games, options, the arts: A 'sport for all' policy encompasses both pupils and wealth of activities on offer. Compulsory sport throughout the school, achieving notable success in rugby, golf, hockey and netball. Super indoor swimming pool and all-weather pitch.

Music is highly valued; extensive music department in the basement complete with high tech soundproof pods for practice and lessons. The proud owner of three grand pianos, a Steinway, a Bosendorfer and a Bechstein. College's orchestras, ensembles and choirs thrive – pupils win places with regional orchestras too. Opportunities near and far – most recently the Big Band Belgian Tour.

Good DT department with plenty of scope for those artistically inclined. Strong drama – recent big musical productions emulate West End success in Les Mis, Sweeney Todd and the Sound of Music. Excellent performance space provided by newly upgraded Academy Room. With 'horizontal boarding' pupils divided vertically into four 'lines' for competitions, aka inter-line. More recent emphasis with appointment of a master in charge – now compete across sporting disciplines, and interestingly, share dealing.

Outdoor pursuits in abundance – fishing, canoeing, sailing, fell walking and clay pigeon shooting. Hugely proud of VCs awarded to seven OS; not surprising CCF (compulsory in year 10) thriving. Further afield pupils participate in world challenge trips, pilgrimages to Lourdes, D of E expeditions, to name but a few.

Service to the community and charity – writ large. Arrupe Programme – sixth form pupils give a period of voluntary service each week in the local community, sixth form holiday week for disabled children and a mentor scheme and swap visits with Catholic primary in Liverpool plus support for partner school in Zimbabwe.

Boarding: Boarding accommodation mostly situated in the upper reaches of the historic buildings. Boys board in playrooms but there is separate accommodation for the girls, in two linked houses, one for sixth form. Each playroom has its own common room and boarding facilities, cared for by a married couple; girls are looked after by a housemistress. On entry it's four or five to a room but this reduces, so by the sixth form single study/bedrooms are the norm. Well-presented, spacious with adequate storage, the standard of facilities is only surpassed by the care each pupil receives, rated outstanding in all respects by a recent Ofsted inspection.

This is essentially a full-time boarding school, 'no mass exodus at weekends', but exeats are readily approved, according to pupils. Long and busy school day, Sunday afternoon appreciated by some as their only free time to do as they please. Much of the weekend is consumed by prep, sports, excursions and church though activities available on a Sunday afternoon should the pupil choose.

Background and atmosphere: Founded by the Jesuits at St Omer, in what is now northern France,

for English families forced to pursue a Catholic education abroad. After a succession of moves the school was given refuge at its present site in the Catholic part of Lancashire by Thomas Weld, who later donated the property to the school. The buildings are magnificent, though perhaps don't quite live up to the idyllic photography in the glossy marketing materials. No doubting the majesty of the architecture, and with its own observatory and nine hole golf course, set in a 2,500-acre estate, most of which is farmed. 'I arrive each morning and cannot believe that this is my school,' commented one pupil.

Much of the school is truly splendid; huge staircases, wood panelling, polished stone, works of art, brimming with history and tradition. Some formerly hidden treasures and the Waterton Collection are now exhibited in the Long Gallery for all to enjoy. The Collections Group, under the auspices of the curator, is allowed access to the treasures in the Square Library. Recent developments include a sympathetically refurbished and equipped library and study centre in the heart of the school. New refectory and sixth form boarding house with en-suite facilities has taken the standard of accommodation up a notch.

Be prepared to learn a whole new vocabulary to enter the world of a Jesuit school. For starters 'lines' are school houses, 'playrooms' are year groups, 'playroom masters' are housemasters and as for the school year groups – Lower Grammar, Grammar, Syntax, Poetry and Rhetoric. Religion is taken seriously but is not oppressive. Co-ed for more than 10 years, feels as if it has always been so. Girls 'have improved communication at all levels'.

A few years ago Stonyhurst hit the tabloids twice but parents we spoke to showed overwhelming support for the way the issues were dealt with.

'Open and honest communication, the school showed compassion while taking a firm line': one parent's words encapsulated the opinion of others.

Pastoral care, well-being and discipline: Spirituality is at the heart of the school, promoting a 'caring, supportive and prayerful community', providing a safe environment that allows 'pupils to feel safe in doing their own thing without fear of ridicule'. Tolerance and respect of each other's differences, collaboration when working together. Demonstrated by the non-sporty keen photographer, whose talents were spotted, and is now the official chronicler for the first XV rugby team, accompanying them on tours and at matches.

Body of prefects called Committee, selected through interview process and votes from staff and lower sixth. Duties include affiliation to a particular playroom. Girl and boy head of Committee chosen from the group of 13.

Demonstrated by the non-sporty keen photographer, whose talents were spotted, and is now the official chronicler for the first XV rugby team, accompanying them on tours

Pupils 'are given quite a lot of freedom based on the mutual confidence and trust that exists between pupils and staff' according to one parent. A Family Handbook sets out clear expectations of conduct and behaviour; rules are few, clear and enforced; 'we expect them to get it right,' says the head. A review of sanctions has introduced a more incremental scale of chastisement. Rewards success celebrated through playroom and headmaster award ceremonies. A 'line' card accumulates debits and credits for academic and social performance which then contribute to the relevant 'line' grand total.

Cases of bullying are rare, dealt with by playroom staff and the pupil-run playroom committees. A few suspensions in the past for soft drug offences, but not a drugs school and no regular random testing. Alcohol restricted to one drink on a Saturday evening under supervision for year 12. Saturday evening access allowed to village pub for year 13 until 10.15pm. Suspension for those bringing alcohol on the premises. Discipline not a big issue here.

Pupils and parents: Diverse – more socially mixed than equivalent schools, with 65 per cent Catholic faith. Southern parents like school's lack of consumerism and social competitiveness. Rich mix of accents – regional and international; 40 per cent of boarders are non-Brits, with small numbers from 28 nations, predominantly Spanish and Mexican, but with a league of nations from Nigeria to Korea. International links are highly valued and there has 'never been a problem with racism'.

Confident, articulate and mature pupils praise the community feel of the school and are rightfully proud of its heritage. Day pupils are encouraged to stay after school for studies and activities – a facility valued by parents – and may feel left out if they choose not to do so.

Alumni include 12 martyrs and seven VCs. Also Arthur Conan Doyle, Charles Laughton, General Walters, Paul Johnson, Peter Moorhouse, Bishop Hollis, Bishop Hines, Charles Sturridge, Hugh Woolridge, Jonathon Plowright, Bill Cash MP, Bruce Kent, Mark Thompson, Lords Chitnis and Talbot, Kyran Bracken and Robert Brinkley.

Entrance: Day pupils from local Lancashire schools, day and boarding from own prep (St Mary's Hall), boarding from St John's Beaumont and a variety of other schools, both here and abroad. Particularly strong links with Spain. Broad ability intake – 'for some, six GCSEs will be an achievement'. Academic entrance exam but other factors taken into account, particularly family connections with the school. Five GCSE passes at C and above, plus interview, for entry into sixth form though many AS subject choices require a minimum grade B. Those unable to attend for interview eg overseas pupils, write a 500 word essay explaining why they wish to come to Stonyhurst.

Exit: Wide range of English universities, Russell Group and redbrick, London popular, and Edinburgh. Numbers vary to Oxbridge – three places in 2015. Breadth of degree courses from medical to media arts, engineering to economics with 'ologies' as well. Plenty of international links and scope for travel through the Jesuit community with many students taking a gap year.

Money matters: A variety of scholarships awarded at entry 13+ and sixth form; academic, music and art and design, as well as all-rounder awards, ranging from 10 per cent to a maximum of 50 per cent of fees. St Francis Xavier awards of 20 per cent of fees are also available to those who 'are most likely to benefit from and contribute to life as full boarders in a Catholic boarding school'. All can be topped up with a means-tested bursary.

Remarks: Jesuit values permeate every aspect of this distinguished boarding school, steeped in history and set in beautiful surroundings. A genuine concern for the individual ensures that each pupil is given every opportunity to fulfill the school motto 'Quant Je Pius' – all that I can.

Strathallan School

Forgandenny, Perth, Perthshire PH2 9EG

01738 812546
admissions@strathallan.co.uk
www.strathallan.co.uk

Ages: 9–18
Pupils: 551; sixth form: 200
Boarders: 331 full
Day: £13,446 – £20,499 pa
Boarding: £21,546 – £30,210 pa

Headmaster: Since 2000, Mr Bruce Thompson MA (Oxon) (mid 50s), educated at Newcastle High, thence New College where he read literae humaniores (classics to the rest of us) and came to Strathallan via Cheltenham College, where he was head of classics, and Dollar Academy – he wanted to 'try the Scottish system'. 'Loves Scotland, and loves Strathallan,' as does his wife, Fabienne (French: teaches at local prep school, worked in travel and tourism, expert skier – coaches it and most likely to be found whizzing round the campus on her bike). Two daughters, now up and running.

Thompson's initial reaction when we quizzed him about moving on was an emphatic no, though he subsequently seemed to wobble a bit about his future plans... Teaches Latin, coaches rugby ('a man for all seasons' then) and looks not a scrap older than when we first met him 15 years ago and talks almost as fast as this ed. Pupils enjoy finding him practising weights alongside them. Head has a reputation for calling into houses – unannounced as far as pupils are concerned – for the odd chat on

their own ground and has lots of informal brainstorming sessions in the evenings. ('Great fun, got to kick 'em out'.) Though increased responsibility (HMC Sports Committee, Scottish Rugby Council, New Park Charitable Trustee, etc. etc.) makes it 'harder and harder' to find enough time for pupil contact: this is still his raison d'être.

Academic matters: Not tremendously academic (school says 'strong academic record' – umm: 2015 A level results showed 48 per cent A*/As; GCSEs 38 per cent A*/As). Splendid mega million quid (expandable) computer suite, where 'the young are given screwdrivers to dismantle the things and sixth formers then expected to fix 'em', to quote the charming hands on head of computing. 'Problem solving skills' more important than rote. Three network engineers on site. Intranet access all over. Mandatory keyboarding in first form, then 'can catch up online'.

Strath not following blindly (as have so many others) into the Virtual Learning Experience where

pupils are expected to work exclusively online (with teachers correcting and parents informed – online). We were enchanted to find a history teacher carefully hand marking (slightly scruffy) handwritten exam papers. Trips to battlefields, and re-enactments the norm.

Strong on langs – particularly Chinese (Chinese counsellor on staff), Spanish and German – native speakers perhaps? – French a poor relation. On our delightful trip round the school in blazing sunshine (groups of ad hoc revision classes squatted on the grass: tieless teachers and pupils – this was shirtsleeve order stuff) we met the head of foreign langs, who was introduced as 'teaching Russian'. Confusion reigned: Russian is not an offered option, though native Russian speakers may get tuition to get them up to speed for A levels ('can do public exams'). Ditto any native speaker. Classical civilisation (aka Heroes for Zeros – head doesn't like that sobriquet). Latin still in the frame.

Class size around 20: usual thing, smaller for practical stuff and as pupil specialisation kicks in. GCSE for all, 'no Scottish qualifications below age 16,' said the head. Nine or 10 GCSEs the norm; all do each science, although around a third take the dual award.

Twenty assorted A levels on offer: school plays the system, both Scottish and English – AS/A levels. Seventy-five per cent follow the A level route; others opt for Highers over two years. School tries to please parents but the choice between A levels and Highers is always contentious. Highers are particularly popular for wannabe medics as school is one of the few to offer human biology.

State-of-the art school with marvellous light and inspired work – current conundrum is how to retrieve two ginormous feet, finalists in Saachi Schools competition

Mixed age common room: discrimination 'even to raise the subject of age.' Staff live on campus with their families, a boon for younger staff who might otherwise be reluctant to commit to somewhere with no nearby university for PhDs or MBAs (think Open University). Finding a new head of physics proved a (finally solvable) nightmare. Head of academics, a recent appointment, comes from Dean Close: good to get fresh and experienced blood in the place.

School has always had a welcome reputation for supporting weaker brethren (siblings in particular) and has a small but effective learning support system which had a smashing HMI report

with talk of 'systematic identification', 'sensitive support', 'informative advice' (yawn yawn). All pupils screened on entry with ed psychs brought in where necessary. One-to-one, small groups, plus after-school clinics in various disciplines which act as drop-in centres. Two full-time trained staff, plus ancillaries, cover entire age range. Extra time for exams. Regular assessment orders for all. 'Rarely costs extra.' School can cope with mild Asperger's/autism and the dys-stream: if SEN is on your radar, check out its comprehensive 'can-do' list below: physical infirmity not a problem, most classrooms on ground floor and lifts whizz you up to top floor of all new builds complete with disabled bathrooms in head of house. Massive EFL input for those who do not have English as their mother tongue: 'normally no extra charge for this.'

Tutors per year group, meet weekly, max 10 per tutor. Strong features of support for learning include: systematic identification of pupils with specific learning difficulties and sensitive support for individual pupils; well-planned arrangements for pupils requiring special assistance with examinations; informative advice to teachers on the learning needs of pupils requiring support; an appropriate range of programmes for pupils for whom English was an additional language; effective use of the expertise of external specialists such as educational psychologists; and after-school 'clinics' run by a number of subject departments. The priority is to provide long term support for individuals and groups of pupils and to respond positively to the needs of pupils referred from individual departments. Teachers have been provided with briefings on issues such as dyslexia and the focus in the last year has been on helping departments adapt approaches and materials to pupils' different needs. The department consists of two full-time members of staff with the help of three other teachers.

Games, options, the arts: Plaudits fail. We are gobsmacked. School has county, national, international, Commonwealth and Olympic presence across the board and at all ages: from rugby, footie, tennis, hockey, netball; fantastic swimming (speedos, goggles and shaven chests); silver at recent Commonwealth Games. Team and individual. Shooting: clay and small bore (plus popular CCF – boys and girls, voluntary) fencing, own golf course, sailing.

School mag and termly news catch up bung full of smiling prize winners/competitors (mebbe this ed is blind/stupid, but couldn't find an essay, poem, trip description anywhere). Head says, 10 pages of art and DT work in centre of skool mag: this ed was hoping for an essay or a poem.

Think Millfield of the North. Rugby squad thrashes all comers, beat Glenalmond 79-4. Coll now refuses to play them, abandoned rugby and gave out that Strath were importing South Africans and Kiwis to boost their front line. Fact: only one South African (son of a Strathallian) has played for the XV, his little bro comes shortly. South African exchange students come in the hockey term. Tennis academy triumphed in all three of the UK senior finals recently. Serious and successful skiing. County/national/international coaches in most disciplines. The list of sporting achievements is endless and impressive.

School has county, national, international, Commonwealth and Olympic presence across the board and at all ages: from rugby, footie, tennis, hockey, netball

To celebrate its centenary, school has given itself a fitness/weight-training centre (open at night), dance and drama practice area and possibly the most enormous covered sports area this ed has ever seen to complement the 70s sports hall (complete with climbing wall) and utterly delicious 20s gym. Think snow. Think footie, think tennis, think space age.

State-of-the art school over three floors with marvellous light and inspired work (we said that last time but it is still top of the pops) – current conundrum is how to retrieve two ginormous feet which were finalists in the Saatchi Schools competition. Enthusiastic head of art opens art rooms whenever: 'can always work on my own projects'; always open three nights a week. Unusual screen printing/photography combination involving rough-hewn branches and strange frame: eye-catching and imaginative (but one rather wonders.). Darkroom, pottery, kiln, very much in use, fabric design and inspired corsets on display (for outside rather than inside wear, you understand) some slightly uninspired work in progress.

Art/history combined field trips to Venice, Prague and the like.

Good music. Stop here. Stupendous music. Enormous diversification. Pipe major plays with Red Hot Chilli Pipers (as do many of his pupils). Seventy-strong boys' choirs for house music competition blow the roof off, choristers at St Ninians in Perth get paid a less than living wage – choral scholarships on offer, church music popular 'and fun,' said our guide. Headmaster's Music (freebie) in Perth Concert Hall (which holds 1,000 and is always full) has musicians (often the same musician) swapping seamlessly from complicated classical concertos to self-composed electronic dance music and rock. Several of the young have professional contracts under their belts. This is exciting stuff.

Loads of drama: small theatre, previously the dining hall, insides scooped out (which doubles as exam hall).

mass of charity work: mega Kenyan input. Help in charity shop. D of E. (Granny bashing apparently a thing of the past: pupils used to give them computer lessons... times change).

Boarding: Houses new and newish, boys and girls have own study bedrooms for their last four years, lots of kitchens and common room areas on each floor. New girls' house completed with an increase in girls. Heads of girls' houses have disabled type loos (lifts): an interesting juxtaposition.

Random books (which is what we like to see) in common rooms, plus mandatory CDs. And tuck shop – seemed to be over-full of cereal packs.

Much general to-ing and fro-ing, but co-ed works well here; girls' houses out of bounds to boys on Sunday mornings so that girls 'can laze around in their dressing gowns if they want.' PR whizzo disputed this: silly PR guru: our guide confirmed it as 'brilliant' (school says 'still not the case').

Chapel every other Sunday, new chaplain in the wings (ex RAF, natch). School facilities much used by groups during holiday period. New girls' house the furthest away, but otherwise houses fairly cloistered.

Background and atmosphere: School founded in 1913 by Harry Riley, based in 19th century red sandstone country house with masses of sympathetic additions, set in 153 beautifully manicured acres. Couple of double-deck libraries, one with the carpet reflecting the plaster work in the ceiling; adjacent media rooms – cosy and useful. Fairly utilitarian chapel (children quite rude about it) and refurbished dining room, million quid – ceiling dropped, new floor – though not sure it is that good for dancing. Main classrooms 150 yards away beyond the old stable building which has been transformed into junior house, Riley, boasting an atrium plus library and music practice rooms etc. (But see separate entry).

All eat in dining room, with younger pupils getting a head start – think that means they eat first – rather than pigging all the grapes.

Classroom blocks clustered and cloistered on t'other side of the valley now refurbed, latest improvements include three state-of-the-art chemistry labs, 'nother new lab this summer. Not an overwhelming school, beautifully landscaped, though some of the signs – to car park et al – are out of kilter. School council operates under aegis of head girl and boy. House council meetings plus international council.

Reel parties by year group and Scottish country dancing an essential. Raft of hobbies: bee-keeping current craze (head disputed this: but apiarist on staff, and senior girls love it: suspect they may get some honey). Trippettes to Perth and Edinburgh at weekend, riding nearby (sleek collection of bays in neighbouring field). Girls have a dressmaking enthusiast on tap and one of 'em made her own ball gown last year – to the amazement of her peers. (Leavers' Ball a wow).

Pastoral care, well-being and discipline: Seven houses in senior school, four for boys and three for girls. Houseparents live on site with two staff on duty in each house every night. B&B in senior school only. Academic tutor attached to each pupil and tutorial team in every house. Tutors often using the time available for informal chats.

Thompson 'aware that things happen' and talks of rustication and drugs testing 'in case of suspicion'. Automatically suspends for drugs and contact police. Tiny glitch recently, all aware of legal highs 'always a concern'. Random tests on suspicion.

Musicians swapping seamlessly from complicated classical concertos to self-composed electronic dance music and rock

Head works hard on bullying awareness, lots of briefing – expectations, ownership, relationships, 'be reasonable'. 'Like running a huge great family,' with a 'good cross age group.' Boy/girl relationship 'works well'. Punishment system for misdemeanours of 'fatigues' – jobs around the buildings and grounds – 'no shortage of them'.

Assemblies on Fridays. Loads of medals and congratulations all round. Oodles of trips, both fun and cultural – skiing much enjoyed. Prague, Vienna, battlefields of France and concentration camps in Germany ('eerie,' said our guide).

Food said to be 'excellent'; 'fresh bread and milk every day'. Fruit everywhere.

Pupils and parents: A quarter of the pupils from overseas, mostly expats, plus 80-odd foreign pupils from Spain, Russia, Africa, China, Eastern Europe, Hong Kong, Germany currently 23 different nationalities. No exeats, guardians needed for half terms (our guide seemed to think that there 'was always a house available for those who prefer to stay in school'; 'not so', said the school). Popular with Scots (regional accents of all kinds), well-placed, an hour from both Edinburgh and Glasgow, plus a small contingent from south of the border. (School claims it is 'two hours from London Heathrow': three from Heathrow or Gatwick more like.)

Day pupils allocated to one of the houses; daily buses to and from Perth, Kinross, Auchterarder, Stirling, Crieff and Dundee. About a third or more come daily, with younger day children converting to boarders on going to senior school age 13.

FPs Dominic Diamond (computer games whizzo), Colin Montgomerie (golfer), Sir Jack Shaw, (Bank of Scotland), John Gray (former chairman of the Hong Kong and Shanghai Bank). Not a toffs' school, despite brief showing in the fashion stakes when David Pighills took the school co-ed. 'Very good relationship with parents,' says the head. Grandparents, whom we met couple of days ago were over the moon: granddaughter just left, 'loved it to bits' (and thought head a star): grandson ('deeply difficult') 'doing well at uni'. Couldn't praise the place high enough.

We only saw pupils in shirt sleeves or sports kit. Girls wear elegant (washable) tartan skirts which make the most of the strangest of shapes, long kilts on Wednesdays – seems a funny way to predict a cold spell.

Entrance: At 9, 10, 11 or 12 for the junior house (entry day and aptitude report/tests) then automatic entry, otherwise by CE. Not a high bar. Later entry by report and interview if space available.

All pupils screened for learning difficulties on entry and IEPs plus ed psychs rolled on if necessary but see above.

Excellent route map for parents unfamiliar with public school entry procedures.

Exit: More than 95 per cent to range of universities (Edinburgh, Aberdeen, Newcastle, Glasgow and Durham are popular but also Kent, Bath, Bristol, London, Brighton). Trickle to Oxbridge ('where they often get firsts') – three in 2015. Forces popular. Odd gap year.

Money matters: School financially strong. Mega centenary appeal 'helped the most recent developments'.

Junior scholarships, open scholarships and sixth form scholarship plus academic, all-rounder, sport, music, cathedral and art scholarships. Parents can apply for means-tested help with fees – 'moving towards bursaries' for all.

Many parents in oil industry: school had downturn last time oil went belly up but appears to be weathering this current hiccup: industry covers school fees when parents based abroad, but not when either in Europe or the UK.

Remarks: Outstanding head – tops in Scotland. The school is in fantastic heart and at ease in the local community. Not for the would be Brideshead contingent. Can't fault it.

Windermere School

Browhead, Windermere, Cumbria LA23 1NW

01539 446164
admissions@windermereschool.co.uk
www.windermereschool.co.uk
C of E

Ages: 11–18 (junior boarders from 8)
Pupils: 257; sixth form: 80
Boarders: 122 full (two thirds boys), 23 weely/flexi
Day: £14,589 – £16,785 pa
Boarding: £23,400 – £29,970 pa

Headmaster: Since 2009, Mr Ian Lavender MA (Oxon) NPQH. Has a strong background in independent secondary school education, boarding and the Round Square ethos, having been a housemaster at Gordonstoun School for 11 years and before that a chemistry teacher at Cranleigh School and Eton College. He also has broad experience that extends well beyond teaching, including an early career in management consulting and service with the Territorial Army. His wife is a GP and they have three children.

A quietly spoken, measured and thoughtful man, parents say 'he cares deeply about the students...and is an impressive headmaster'. Now in his sixth year at the school, he is beginning to 'see things more clearly'; there is no lack of ambition: his vision is that Windermere becomes 'the best small school in the country'.

Academic matters: Windermere pupils might not be dancing right at the top of the league tables but they appear hard-working and happy. Due in part to the broad intake, the results at GCSE, whilst undoubtedly solid (39 per cent A*/A in 2015), can't compete with bigger, more selective schools so it focuses on its considerable international appeal. Crucially, however, it is the highest performing independent school in Cumbria post 16, not least because there is no A level on offer here; it's the rigour of IB or a small choice of BTecs, and that's it. Exams and the choice of exams are a natural sieving process and the school's choice of the IB route means the game is raised considerably in sixth form; average IB point score 31 in 2015. With small classes (around 12), teaching is up close and personal, there's nowhere to hide, and pupil-teacher relationships appear warm and relaxed. Personal academic tutors guide and, if necessary, handhold, helping students in their choice of subjects and mentoring them along the way. Parents tell us 'there are many inspirational teachers here', with a number of them prepared to offer extra tutorials on request at lunchtime or after school.

French, German, Italian and Spanish are all taught in this language-rich environment, with Latin and Greek being offered off-timetable as

1161

extras, classes running every Thursday evening. Outside of class, eager young linguists who keep their ears open can experience over 20 languages being spoken around school. Students are given the opportunity to participate in worldwide exchanges by spending up to a term in another Round Square school. There are also annual language trips to France and Spain and Germany.

Full-time head of learning support, dyslexia specialist and two part-time assistants; it's a strong department. Parents are charged for the support according to whether it's in-class or on an individual basis.

Games, options, the arts: Built on a slope; the site brings its own challenges and there aren't acres of pitches here; the biggest area of flat ground is the lake, so that's where most activities take place. Better suited to small team sports, and there are probably more expeditions than fixtures, but they do have an Astroturf and a sports hall for year-round play. Whilst they can't compete with the big boys at team sports, they take it seriously and offer the full range of usual school sports and others besides, including equestrianism, sailing and kayaking. Hodge Howe, the school's own watersports centre and the only school centre in the country to hold RYA champion club status, has two boathouses, a private beach and a pavilion with a classroom (also available for wedding receptions..) and a fleet of sailing boats and kayaks. Other outdoor activities include camping trips, fell walking, ghyll scrambling, orienteering, caving and climbing, so if you are the adventurous type and not joined at the hip to your hair straighteners or worried by a patchy mobile phone signal, there's plenty here for you. All students in years 7, 8 and 9 complete the Windermere Adventure Award. They

The only school centre in the country to hold RYA champion club status, has two boathouses, a private beach and a pavilion

also spend one morning a fortnight outside school doing anything from mountain biking to conservation and environmental work.

Art takes place in the old stables; super natural light and plenty of Apple Macs for those with a penchant for design and design technology, and kilns for keen potters; it's an appropriately messy yet inspirational space. Drama is popular; it's a small school so very inclusive, and everyone who wants to take part can do, whether centre stage or behind the scenes.

Lots of individual tuition in music and the Holst Room, a space designed for its acoustics, is a valuable teaching and performance space. It's not the strongest subject, here according to parents, so a particularly musical child may not be able to shine, but there is undoubtedly a 'have a go' attitude to the subject, as with everything else.

The school supports community projects in South Africa; each year students help out with resources and provide physical help to a project with Tiger Kloof School – in fact just mentioning the name of the school brings a warm smile and glow of pride to the faces of the older students, who view it as an extension of their school life at Windermere.

A highly rated international summer school is proving increasingly popular and has effectively added a fourth term to the school year.

Boarding: Despite the national park location, it's only 90 minutes to either Manchester or Liverpool airports (outside London considered a safer option by some nervous parents), three hours to London by train and the school has a fleet of shuttle buses catering for students' many and varied travel needs.

Word of mouth is the biggest factor in attracting parents, both locally and overseas. There are a few expat Forces parents who love the leadership challenges here, and whilst more than half of the students are from within the UK, the rest represent around 24 different countries far and wide, including China, Germany, Hong Kong, Lithuania, Poland, Romania, Ukraine, Spain and Russia.

Customary dorms in single sex houses on site for boarders aged 8-16; there are a few single rooms but not many choose them, most preferring to share. Each house has a staff house 'family', comfortable shared common rooms with views across the lake and well-equipped kitchens for snacking

and, in the girls' house at least, baking seems popular with Mary Berry cake recipes much in evidence. Well-behaved sixth formers earn the right to have more space and freedom in self-contained flats in a co-educational house on site, still supervised, of course, but a step along the road to preparation for life beyond school. A sixth form bar allows (with parental permission) two drinks with dinner on a Saturday night; younger pupils love the occasional takeaway, shared with friends in the boarding house. If that sounds a little tame, there's not much else you can get up to here (a definite plus for many parents), but cinema visits and occasional weekend trips to the Trafford Centre in Manchester or Alton Towers keep restless adolescents happy. They are also very busy after school, so much so that a parent of a day boy told us they relocated to be on the school's doorstep simply because their son was 'reluctant to go home after school – way too much going on'.

Background and atmosphere: On this site since 1924 and co-ed since 1999, there is a good mix of boys and girls here. Extensive additional building took place in the '70s and '80s, but the national park setting places real limitations on new building – essentially it's all about how the place looks from the lake. Some attractive newer and recently refurbed buildings are scattered around the grounds of the Victorian mansion of the original Browhead estate, some boarding facilities, others classrooms and labs. Highlights are the Jenkins Centre for music, performing arts, languages and a superb dining room and Crampton Hall – a spacious auditorium for theatrical and musical productions.

Round Square is a worldwide association of schools that is all about the whole person – the Kurt Hahn view that says students can only understand life by experiencing it in exciting and challenging ways. Opportunities for travel and exchanges to other Round Square schools bring extra opportunities, and they welcome international students who wish to experience British culture whilst bringing with them their own perspective and world view. There is a real sense that, although surrounded by mountains here, their hearts and heads go way beyond the valley and into the wider world beyond. The core of the IB diploma programme encompasses many of the Round Square principles, making the curriculum ideal here. Daily reflection is an important start to the day and something valued hugely by the students themselves. 'It lifts you up,' they tell us; 'you're in school, lessons haven't started yet but you're saying hello to everyone'; 'it's a nice place to be' and it is often, apparently, like a mini TED talk to start your day, food for thought and a valued and laudable touchstone. Outside speakers

are welcomed as regular visitors and students also attend conferences and exchanges worldwide.

Pastoral care, well-being and discipline: Many parents are attracted by the fact that the school isn't especially selective – telling us they didn't want their offspring to be a 'public school product' but rather they 'wanted their individuality to be valued'. They appreciate the weekly online newsletter and feel that they 'could walk into the school at any time if they had any concerns at all'. Also of great value to parents is the way in which 'teachers respond very promptly to even the smallest queries...pastoral care is excellent,' they say. Overseas parents enjoy a 'close relationship' with the staff and love the fact that their offspring often enjoy tea or dinner with the head and his wife.

Staff do, of course, keep a careful watching brief, but essentially Windermere pupils are encouraged to be self-disciplined. Problems are rare, as older and younger students jog along happily in the knowledge that they want for nothing (except perhaps a Starbucks) in this sprawling, healthy and supportive environment. Strong views from the sixth formers themselves on smoking – 'why would you?' It seems there's a degree of

> *There is a real sense that, although surrounded by mountains here, their hearts and heads go way beyond the valley and into the wider world beyond*

self-policing going on.

Students appear comfortable and relaxed but with an uncommon sense of responsibility too; they recently 'simply couldn't stand back and do nothing' following the recent earthquakes in Nepal, and within hours were actively fundraising within the local community in support of the victims. Charity fundraising such as this, alongside work in a soup kitchen and orphanage, affords them a 'very different reality,' say parents – 'one which puts their very privileged life into sharp focus'.

Pupils and parents: Any passing traffic is likely to be either hikers or tourists, so recruitment is a challenge, though undoubtedly helped in the overseas market by the Beatrix Potter and Peter Rabbit connection. It's a lifestyle choice living here in the Lake District, and some parents have huge commutes to city offices, whilst others are simply escaping the city altogether.

High on the list of attractions for many is the extensive programme of adventurous outdoor activities – something the pupils coming through from the school's own prep department have already enjoyed in abundance. It seems to result not only in hardy pupils but also in a 'can do' attitude, parents buying in to the opportunities for growth and independence in a safe environment. The words 'warmth' and 'friendliness' are oft repeated by parents when talking about the staff; they are aware that this is more typical of a small school and for them, it's a valid and valuable trade off for bigger and better facilities.

Entrance: Most pupils enter from the school's own prep. The school likes to look for 'potential' rather than performance and 'well-rounded students with a genuine interest in education in the broadest sense of the word,' say staff. Candidates for entry (below 16+) sit papers in English, mathematics and non-verbal reasoning. Year 12 places conditional on a minimum of five GCSEs at grade C or above.

Exit: Most leavers continue in higher education at home or overseas, some via gap years. In 2015, to a range from Edinburgh to SOAS to Hammond Chester Dance and Drama School to the University of British Columbia. A handful have gone on to key musical success. Notable former pupils include dressage Olympian Emma Hindle and internationally respected soprano Claire Booth.

Money matters: Non means-tested scholarships are available in performing arts, visual arts, general academic subjects and sport. There are some means-tested bursaries available.

Remarks: The photograph on the cover of the school's prospectus looks like an oil painting – and yes, that really is the view from the school. A glorious backdrop in which to learn and grow, and the school makes full use of it. It's not the ideal destination for the child without a cagoule or for whom manicured lawns and extensive sporting facilities are key, but you do have all the amenities of the Lake District at your disposal, so give even those indoor types a month or so and they'll be away from their Playstations and kayaking with the best of them.

On a sunny day you can see for miles. On other days you can't see your hand in front of your face. The weather can change in an instant, but no one allows that fact to get in the way of an existence where hard work, good friends, rosy cheeks and fresh air in your lungs are all part of the package. The introduction of the International Baccalaureate has upped the game academically at the top end and also encouraged a more diverse intake, with pupils introduced to a wider range of subjects with exceptional extracurricular enhancements.

State boarding schools

STATE

Adams' Grammar School

High Street, Newport, Shropshire TF10 7BD

01952 386300
TAW705Enquiries@taw.org.uk
www.adamsgs.org.uk

Ages: 11–18 boys
Pupils: 842; sixth form: 300 (including 60 girls)
Boarders: 95
Day: free (day boarding £2,890 pa)
Boarding: £10,640 – £12,170 pa

Headmaster: Since January 2015, Gary Hickey, previously deputy head. Degree in music and drama from Manchester Met and a PGCE from Birmingham City, and has been awarded a Teacher Fellowship by Cambridge University. Gary is a man of many talents: he scooped a special commendation for 'extraordinary work in drama' in the 2000 National Teaching Awards, and lectures globally on raising the achievement of boys. He is also an award-winning theatre director and a professional musician. He joined Adams in 2009, understands it through and through and knows just what potential he has been handed.

Academic matters: Strong results, as you would expect in a selective school boosted by girls coming into the sixth form. A levels were 74 per cent A*-B grades in 2015 and 49 per cent A*/A. GCSEs were 64 per cent A*/A grades. Value added is great too. There is a real ethos of hard work from the word go. Staff know students well enough to stop the sort of coasting you can often find with boys after the first year or so. Form teachers are known to email parents after just one late homework and parents

find that reassuring. Chemistry and physics results are particularly good – but so is English. Class sizes up to 30 at the lower end of the school but much smaller groups in the sixth form.

Curriculum is a traditional grammar school one – except there is no classics other than Latin, which is offered along with Mandarin and Polish as an after-school or lunchtime class. Though music and art are encouraged, the numbers taking them at A level are small. One or two slightly unusual A levels such as geology, government and politics and PE. DT popular, has just embraced a Life Bike Design project where the boys are enthusiastically rising to the challenge of building their own bikes.

Very few statemented children and a small number with milder learning difficulties, all of which are broadly dealt with in the classroom, though a part time SENCo has just started. Students testify to plenty of support from staff if things get tough. There is peer support and sixth form mentoring for younger boys.

Games, options, the arts: A long-serving member of staff told us that the school used to be known as the rugby school that did maths and science very well. Things move on. The science is still excellent, and rugby is thriving, but you are as likely to find the students throwing themselves into music and drama as much as into games. Sport itself has expanded, and although we heard one request for girls' rugby, the sporting offer is considered wide enough to suit most tastes. Even football has been controversially introduced, and students say they love their sport, whatever the weather. House sports competitions include cross-country in the beautiful grounds of the junior boarding house, to get even the less athletically inclined involved, and the emphasis is on inclusion, not solely on the gifted few. But those with the expertise are encouraged to play at regional and national level as well as for the school. Biannual rugby, hockey and netball tours abroad for senior teams.

Performing arts, which also blossomed under the previous head, looks set to continue to grow under the current one, with his degree in music and drama. The tremendously popular house drama and music events draw the whole school into the arts. There are opportunities for the very best actors, actresses and singers in the big school productions – The Crucible, Les Mis, Romeo and Juliet and Grease in recent years. A refurbished art space, although not enormous, stimulates some pretty sensational artwork that is seen around the school.

CCF is very strong and many ex-students join Sandhurst, the Royal Air Force College or Royal Naval College. There are plenty of Easter and summer camps on offer, and boys can join the CCF marching band. There is a good range of clubs and societies. A poet in residence brings in the culture that is not as readily available in the heart of Shropshire as it would be in a big city.

Curriculum is traditional grammar school – except there is no classics other than Latin, which is offered along with Mandarin and Polish as an after-school or lunchtime class

Boarding: The senior boarding house is one of a group of Georgian town houses along the Newport High Street; parts of it are decidedly tatty. Junior boarding is idyllically housed about a mile away in a gorgeous Georgian mansion. 'Grade 2 listed buildings cost'; school has clearly spent money on the interior here. There are 100 acres of land attached to the house, used by the whole school for various sporting activities. Boys are bussed to and from the main school. The number of boarders about at weekends varies but there are always full boarders there. Activities centre round games, with some visits and other offerings depending on numbers and popularity. Day boarding – an optional extra for year 7-9 – includes tea, after-school activities and supervised prep, with a 7.30pm pick up.

Background and atmosphere: The school dates back to 1656 – it was founded by haberdasher William Adams – and is one of the Haberdashers' group of schools. Behind the senior boarding house is a series of more modern and imaginatively refurbished specialist teaching areas; the new music block is in a converted coach house. The new areas such as the sixth form centre are impressive but there is further to go on refurbishment.

Everyone talks about the house system. The school has managed to generate house energy and vitality without losing a basic allegiance to the school. 'It's not nasty competitiveness', said one boy, 'it's nice tribalism', and we heard about one excellent dancer teaching those in rival houses how to move. The various house competitions encourage everyone to try new areas and the strong narrative is that everyone has a contribution to make. 'It is a great day whoever wins,' one boy told us. 'You have the freedom to choose whether to take part, but everyone wants to because you would be letting the house down if you don't.' There are school and house traditions that apparently take a bit of getting used to but are much loved.

It is unusual to find a predominantly boys' school tackle headlong and consistently the prejudices that can plague all male institutions, so Adams' very active and visible commitment to celebrating diversity is hugely refreshing. What used to be casually swept aside as male 'banter' is now no longer acceptable and is rigorously scrutinised for racist, sexist or homophobic overtones by the boys themselves. One of the heads of house who pioneered the work told us that initially there was a raised eyebrow or two amongst colleagues, but soon everyone was behind the work. Relevant news articles are routinely circulated, there is a dedicated school noticeboard and dedicated tutor time. The governors have had a presentation and such matters are the standard fare in school assemblies. Girls coming into the sixth form still report a certain amount of 'laddishness' at first, but 'we roll our eyes, get on with our work and they soon get over it.' Students spoke easily about such matters as respect, community and equality, and see a major strength of the school as encouraging everyone to be themselves.

Staff say it's a lovely place and all want their children to come. 'Every year someone's child doesn't get through the exam and it is a real sadness for everyone'. Parents say it is warm and friendly and has the intimate feel of a small school. Pupils spontaneously want to share not only personal news but also what they have been reading or hearing. There is an informality about the relationships and a sense of mutual respect. The occasional child who doesn't flourish is probably the one who doesn't talk to staff or take opportunities.

Pastoral care, well-being and discipline: The school rightly prides itself on its pastoral care and we got a strong sense that not only were all the staff alert to individual needs but the students looked out for each other. There is close communication between the boarding house staff and those running the whole school house system, where pastoral responsibility securely sits. Misdemeanours are dealt with very promptly using a traditional range of sanctions. We were pleased to note frontline staff reported full support from parents. 'We know they will back the school to the hilt when it comes to having to punish someone'. None of the 'my child right or wrong' attitude increasingly common in fee-paying schools. Counsellors attend regularly and the school is very well staffed in non-lesson time.

There is a zero tolerance approach to drugs, parents told us. Other offences are firmly stamped on and the boys know from the start that the school will take any deviation from their high standards very seriously. However, the nurturing goes hand in hand with this and the comment from all the parents we spoke to was that discipline and pastoral care were spot on.

Pupils and parents: The boys are unselfconscious and articulate. They look smart, and the accolade of having won a place at Adams' acts as a real boost to the less confident. The majority of day boys come from a 20 mile radius of the school, which includes Wolverhampton and Telford, so there is more racial and social diversity than you would expect from a

school that draws on the Shrewsbury set and is in deep Shropshire countryside. The school does some work with local primaries to try to widen access, but the overall impression is that most students come from middle class professional backgrounds.

Boarders come from across the country and the world (some eight per cent from overseas). If parents are looking for budget boarding with excellent exam results, this is hard to beat. Adams' is one of only a very few academically selective state UK boarding schools.

Everyone talks about the house system. The school has managed to generate house energy and vitality without losing a basic allegiance to the school. 'It's not nasty competitiveness', said one boy, 'it's nice tribalism'

The school has taken girls into the sixth form since 1993. They are still in the minority, about 70 in a sixth form of 300, which means, according to one girl, that they form a very close community. The type of girl who does well (and, probably, who applies in the first place) is likely to be feisty and willing to speak her mind – 'just like the women who work here,' said one male teacher somewhat ruefully.

The only kind of child who might not thrive here, one parent speculated, is the one who has been heavily coached for the entrance exam. 'The boys put themselves under pressure: they are all very ambitious and only one can be top,' another parent said.

Old Boys include Blue Peter presenter Radzi Chinyanganya, disc jockey Simon Bates, Labour leader Jeremy Corbyn and England rugby player Graham Kitchener.

Entrance: About four or five applicants for every place. The exam is one used by other selective state Midlands schools and is administered centrally, away from the school. It aims to be something which it's hard to coach for and includes reading comprehension, maths and non-verbal reasoning. For sixth form entry there is an expectation of at least five Bs at GCSE, but most have much higher results.

Exit: At the end of year 11 a few go to sixth forms that have a wider range of subjects. Vast majority go to university – four to Oxbridge 2015; Birmingham and Cardiff currently the most popular destinations.

Money matters: Tuition is free. The only charge is for boarding – currently £10,640 a year for most and £12,171 for overseas pupils. There is an optional day boarder fee of £2890 a year and an overnight stay rate of £50 a night. Lots of flexibility.

Remarks: Amazing value for money as far as boarding is concerned – exam results, academic rigour combined with the community boarding ethos. But this being a state school you are exposed to the vagaries of the political climate and funding constraints of a particular government.

As good as it gets for boys in a single sex school in its determination to prepare them for a world where white patriarchy is no longer the default model. It is a particular type of girl who blossoms in a predominantly male environment – those who do, no doubt have brilliant advantage when they move on.

There is a charm about Adams' that is part to do with its rural catchment, part with an unaffected enthusiasm and part a thoughtfulness – not a combination that is easy to find.

Beechen Cliff School

Alexandra Park, Bath, Somerset BA2 4RE

01225 480466
headmaster@beechencliff.org.uk
www.beechencliff.org.uk

Ages: 11–18
Pupils: 1,216; sixth form: 352 (including 110 girls)
Boarders: 25 full, 8 weekly (boys only)
Day: free
Boarding: weekly £6,840 pa, full £9,600 pa

Headmaster: Since 2005, Mr Andrew Davies, (40s), history graduate of University of Sussex. Married to Anne, an assistant head, with two teenage children, one at his school, one at local girls' independent. Career has followed normal trajectory (teaching, head of dept, head of humanities, deputy head) in five local authorities, plus a spell in the commercial sector as principal of Kings International College in Surrey. Has worked in the most and least desirable bits of SW England, so no airs and graces. Direct, engaging and warm, he is passionate about providing his flock with all manner of opportunity to extend and test themselves.

Refreshingly liberated, too, from some spectres of state education: 'We are not slaves to Ofsted', he says, but with a major success story on his hands, he can afford not to be. Still teaches – he offers GCSE in humanities to year 9 boys in their own time: take-up and results are good. Keen shot, cricketer (coaches both) and general outdoor type who involves himself in school endeavours, such as the Centurion Challenge, 100 mile slog in 48 hours as a Roman foot soldier. Proud of his school, and encourages his pupils to be the same. Well liked and respected by parents, who reckon he's 'good at dragging the goods out of the non-academic' as well as the academic.

Academic matters: Completely non-selective on entry but tends to get more able boys by default. All year 7s assessed with cognitive ability tests on entry to enable better setting than Sats scores provide. Results at GCSE and A level have crept up over last

few years and academic aspiration encouraged. In 2015, 70 per cent got at least five grades A*-C at GCSE including maths and English (29 per cent of grades A*/A) with 62 per cent A*-B, 28 per cent A*/A at A level.

Refreshingly liberated, too, from some spectres of state education: 'We are not slaves to Ofsted', he says, but with a major success story on his hands, he can afford not to be

Has specialist technology college status and is a founder member of Bath Educational Trust set up in 2009, a collaboration between Hayesfield School (sister school), Bath University, City of Bath College and global engineering firm Rotork, headquartered in Bath, which aims to 'to provide a better experience for children'. In fact it provides a lot of good practical stuff too, such as far more options post-16, resources and economies of scale in terms of buying power, as well as a smart minibus to shuttle pupils between sites. BET will evaluate its efforts by tracking pupils' early careers until the age of 25.

Thriving and oversubscribed sixth form where IB was offered since 2009 jointly with Hayesfield: those who teach and learn unequivocal in their praise, however suspended for the moment because of modest take-up. However, EPQ offered.

A level choices still extensive at 27 subjects, with the possibility of more at Hayesfield or Bath College. Others can choose Route 2, where they spend a year doing more vocational things at Bath College, along with retakes of English and/or maths GCSE.

Enthusiastic and proactive head of sixth form has gone down well with pupils and their parents. The academically precocious are encouraged to push on and take GCSEs early or AS in year 11; maths and further maths are taught within the same timetable. Most pupils start a second foreign language in year 8 (German, Spanish, Italian) and classics on offer after school. Clearly the message is that pupils will be given extra chances to get ahead, but the onus rests firmly on them. Nonetheless, a few parents worry that a good work ethic is not sufficiently instilled in the boys, and that to be labelled a 'keener' is social death; it is fair to add that the school comes down hard on this. Less able pupils taught in smaller sets and emphasis placed on extracurricular opportunities and successes for those in the bottom set for everything.

Busy SEN department caters for most needs one would expect to find in mainstream, the difference perhaps being that, in tune with the school's general ethos, pupils are expected to take responsibility for their own learning – 'I can't be doing with this excuse culture in education,' states the head. Lessons seem a good blend of purpose and fun, with lots of participation, and hi tech infrastructure to support them. Significant amounts of homework from year 7 compensate for short day – school ends at 3.40pm.

Games, options, the arts: Simply masses on offer, particularly for a state school, due in part to the all-hours culture where so much happens after the school day and at weekends; indeed it is the only comprehensive in Bath to take on the independents at Saturday fixtures. Impressive array of sporting successes in rugby, football, hockey, cricket and shooting borne out by the honours board in the entrance hall, where Amy Williams (GB's only gold medallist in the 2010 winter Olympics) appears, along with fellow Olympian Jason Gardener – and Roger Bannister. Competitive sport taken pretty seriously and winning is encouraged; some parents feel that the school's rugby and cricket coaches select more top players from city clubs than those outside Bath, but the school strenuously asserts that team selection done strictly on merit. Amazing results emanate from facilities which recently received massive investment, including the all-important all-weather pitch. Tennis and athletics in summer. Super sports hall has exterior climbing wall on one end, funded through parental gift aid. Strong links with top notch facilities (such as a 50m pool) and expertise at nearby Bath University too. Enough choice for sixth form girls, including

Amazing results from facilities which recently received massive investment, including the all important all-weather pitch. Tennis and athletics in summer. Super sports hall has exterior climbing wall, funded through parental gift aid

rugby, but they say they are not compelled to do anything in the sporting line.

Art and DT have their own well-equipped if dilapidated block – and a committed following producing high quality work. Provision in photography hugely enhanced by the arrival of an industrial printer, bid for by the head of art, who has other grand plans (eg gallery space), if only funds would permit. Music, now housed in a splendid new block with a recording studio alongside more traditional teaching and practice rooms, attracts fewer takers, despite avoiding the trap of being a girls' preserve below sixth form, but there's a good range from brass to folk, and they do compete and succeed in the Mid-Somerset Festival, and tour Europe. School recently held its first internal young musician competition. Some plays done in collaboration with the (all female) Royal High; choices like Tartuffe and A Midsummer Night's Dream suggest no lack of ambition. Beechen Cliff also makes its mark locally at Model UN and debating with other schools. Much 'boys' own' stuff goes on in terms of outdoor activities aside from team games: Ten Tors race, Centurion Challenge, D of E and all the opportunities offered at Tir-y-Cwm, the school's cottage in the Brecons, a gem of an asset. All of year 7 go for a weekend's bonding near the start of their first term; thence participation in orienteering, climbing and caving is voluntary. Trips on offer compare well with far better resourced schools, and go beyond the confines of Europe, to Africa for charity work and Canada for skiing.

Boarding: Since 2013, 26 boarding places on offer for boys whose family circumstances mean they would benefit from the stability of a boarding education, or for whom proximity to Bath University's facilities and coaching programmes would enable them to exploit their sporting gifts and potential fully. Accommodation is more Travelodge than Sheraton: rooms are neat, clean, all en-suite and wireless.

Background and atmosphere: Feels and looks like a boys' grammar (which of course it was). It became a comprehensive in 1972, after amalgamating with the then boys' secondary modern, and takes its name from the hill on which its 1930s buildings stand. Its future was touch-and-go in 1990, but its head and governors mounted a huge campaign ending in the High Court to get it grant maintained status, and keep it open. Beechen remains prominent on the Bath scene in every way, and in recent years has upgraded its infrastructure to give its sixth formers, sportsmen and musicians what they deserve. One parent left a recent open evening wondering why he had shelled out so much money on independent education for his children, when he could have had so much of it for free at Beechen. Definitely a sense of tradition about the place (boys are addressed as 'gentlemen', 'gents' or 'chaps'), but it's not oppressive: all seem to absorb the values of discipline, courtesy, academic confidence and pride the school promotes, not least in its year book, The Gryphon. Loyalty and considerable affection from its old boys/girls (Old Sulians), and former members of staff come in to teach extra sessions – for love.

'Middle class and aspirant, reflecting Bath as a whole', according to the head, who woos newcomers, parents that is, with Pimms and lemonade

The head has beefed up the house system, renaming them after illustrious authors, after whom local roads are also named (this part of Bath is known as poets' corner); introducing a house tie and vertical tutor groups within houses to engender a spot of house loyalty. He's hot on uniform too: boys are picked up on untucked shirts and half-mast ties even outside school, no trainers or wild hair either. Some feel, however, that sixth form girls get away with murder as far as dress is concerned. Food is terrific too: Beechen's departed award-winning chef leaves much broader gastronomic horizons and a take-up for school meals much higher than average behind him – a new kitchen and dining hall are on the horizon. There's a real effort to source food locally – indeed, some of the salad and veg are grown on site by students. Popular snack bar forms part of a gorgeous new sixth form centre, with views over Bath and a sunny terrace with café tables. Some parents worry that they are given too much leeway by being allowed off site in free periods – 'they are still at school after all' – and that staff do not crack the whip sufficiently over punctuality or wasting time in free periods.

Pastoral care, well-being and discipline: Undoubted reward culture for all achievement is balanced by traditional sanctions for those who play fast and loose with expected standards, academic or otherwise. Anyone re-interpreting the uniform can expect to receive 250 lines on the vice of scruffiness, slackers get academic detentions on Saturdays. 'Pupils need to see consequences for their actions', as the head says. Parents report good relationships within school and quick response times from staff; the school takes concerns seriously. Sixth formers provide pastoral input to junior boys within tutor groups, in class on occasion and as directors in music and drama. Expectations of them are laid out in the sixth form code they sign before entry. No-one mentioned smoking, drink or drugs – possibly because they are strictly extracurricular?

Pupils and parents: 'Middle class and aspirant, reflecting Bath as a whole', according to the head, who woos newcomers, parents that is, with Pimms and lemonade. Mostly white and very local: the catchment area is strictly drawn. Some 20 per cent of boarders from overseas. Much emphasis put on the partnership between parents and the school, and it is the sense of shared values, rather than class or money, which unites them. The vast majority are totally supportive – 'it really wouldn't suit non-conformists or anyone with authority issues,' said one mother. Strong family connections too. Active PTA runs a gift-aid scheme, whose funds are doled out to successful bidders from amongst the staff or pupils for extras that wealthier schools would take for granted – a climbing wall and better stage lighting, for example. Old Sulians include several sporting greats (see above), as well as Arnold Ridley (Private Godfrey in Dad's Army), Andrew Lincoln (Drop the Dead Donkey, This Life, Love Actually), Curt Smith (Tears for Fears), research scientist, Nobel prize winner and generous benefactor Sir Richard Roberts and the current head of MI6, Sir John Sawers.

Entrance: There are 192 places on offer at 11, 'without reference to ability or aptitude', to boys living within the Greater Bath Consortium. When it's oversubscribed, precedence is given to normal state sector criteria of boys in care, followed by siblings. Applications taken in October for the following September. Admissions policy below sixth form is rigid – worth scrutinising the local authority website, especially as they prefer applications online. In practice, boys come from nearly 20 different primary schools – and the odd prep. Sixth form entry – boys and girls – by interview, but conditional on five GCSE passes, ideally with B or above for subjects chosen for A level. At least 20 places for outsiders at this stage.

Exit: A third or so leave after GCSEs. Some 50-60 per cent of upper sixth leavers to universities all over the country to pursue a diversity of courses. Four to Oxbridge in 2015 (experimental psychology, medicine, engineering and natural sciences); Exeter popular recently; also eg Cardiff, Southampton and Sheffield; subjects range from Abrahamic religions to aeronautics and astronautics. Plaudits from work experience placements indicate that those who start work straight from school are well equipped to do so.

Money matters: Well-supported by fundraising and parental contributions, which are, shall we say, greatly encouraged by the school, and bring in some £90K per annum. Less advantaged pupils are able to take part in trips and music lessons by means of a special school fund. Staff keep a sharp eye out for opportunities to bid for or win equipment there is no school budget for; an entrepreneurial culture prevails. Boarding fees are met by parents and are roughly a third cheaper than the boarding component of independent school fees.

Remarks: A Bath institution and good counterweight to local independents, in that it manages to offer much of what they do for free, but for boys only below sixth form. An outstanding non-selective choice for almost any boy, or sixth form girl, now with 26 boarding places for boys.

Brymore Academy

Cannington, Bridgwater, Somerset TA5 2NB

01278 652369
office@brymore.somerset.sch.uk
www.brymoreacademy.co.uk

Ages: 11–17
Pupils: 250; sixth form: 3, tuition at Bridgwater College
Boarders: 150
Day: free
Boarding: £9,550 pa

Head: Since 2011, Mr Mark Thomas (acting head since September 2010). Originally from Cornwall, Mr Thomas came to Brymore from Courtfields School, Wellington where he had been deputy and acting head. Previously deputy head at Brittons Academy in Rainham, his early teaching career was mainly in London. Down to earth, no-nonsense and determined, he is married with one 3 year old son – 'too young to think about Brymore yet!' – and his wife teaches locally. He spends several nights each week in his school house in the grounds. Sport is both his subject and his hobby though he says, cheerfully, that he hasn't had time for anything except Brymore since his appointment. Determined to 'keep the unique identity and nature of Brymore but create a truly secure atmosphere while raising academic expectations and achievement'. The pride of boys and teachers in their achievements, their interest in academic as well as practical work, as well as the national 'Raise Online' statistics, give strong witness to how much he has achieved in four years. Parents were a little apprehensive about changes, particularly the number of new staff and higher academic expectations, but now feel 'it has all come together'.

Academic matters: Since Mr Thomas' appointment there have been huge changes, with nearly three-quarters of current teaching staff appointed since 2011. Five of these are Brymore alumni, so tradition has certainly not gone out with the bathwater.

The farm and gardens are the heart of learning at Brymore. Practical hands-on farm work: tractor driving (from 13), milking, winter and summer feeding of cattle, pigs and poultry, calving and lambing, cultivation of vegetables and maintenance of the grounds. Getting up at 6am, come rain, come shine, come snow and ice, for seven days a week, making and maintaining heavy equipment, means learning to keep yourself fit and disciplined enough to do it all. If, in the past, the academic curriculum has taken second place, this balance is being altered in a major curriculum overhaul.

From year 10 up boys are now in sets (so a boy may be in a fast set for one subject and a more supportive group for another according to individual need) and years 7 to 9 are three streamed groups. A six day timetable gives 30 one hour lessons (doubles for practical subjects). Much more flexible options now with horticulture and agriculture compulsory for first three years but for not for exam years (10 and 11). This makes room for choice and art, modern foreign languages, history and geography, though there is still huge and successful take up in practical land-based subjects. Sadly for Brymore, these subject results won't register in the new league tables, though Mr Thomas is fighting the cause! Modern foreign languages haven't worked though to results yet, but there is a big take up of French in the lower school. Engineering can be taken to 'Industry standard' and DT is a core subject. Academic expectations are high. One boy aiming at an engineering career told us he hoped to go on to grammar school to study maths, higher maths and economics A Level, while another, readily admitting to struggling with English, relished his reading and was an exceptionally articulate living proof of success. In 2015, 34.7 per cent got 5+ A*-C GCSE grades including maths and English (100 per cent pass rate in BTecs).

Classes average 16, though there are much smaller groups for boys needing more help and every boy has an individual learning plan. Mentors regularly discuss progress, both academic and personal, and help boys to set and achieve appropriate targets. Very comprehensive learning support is managed by a SENCo with a team of 10 full time, qualified learning support assistants. Most are subject specialists working in their subject area, and the others plug gaps. Resourceful staff are dedicated to improving achievement, and initiatives such as reading nights – just being read to – for younger boys, house points for reading journals, triple input marking, which encourages boys to correct and learn from their own and others' work, are clearly having an impact. Statistics for improvement in maths are not quite as impressive as in English, where the school is in the top three per cent in national stats for improvement, but are OK, and the maths department is still developing new strategies.

Games, options, the arts: Brymore is a sporty school with good rugby, doing respectably at district level – no mean achievement with year groups of under 30 in competition with year groups bigger than the whole Brymore population. Hockey, mountain biking, with an exciting new track and bikes sponsored by Sport England, daily training on the MUGA (multi usage games area), a small Astroturf area, and above all, the Chad Hill daily run: three and a half miles of cross-country which is all but compulsory ('expected' is official terminology).

Sport and activities are partly in curriculum, partly after school, but central to everything is the agricultural and horticultural practice and theory. Taught elements are in the teaching day but in addition every boy has to take his turn in the routine of the farm, boarding for a seven day week in order to be up 6am and be permanently on hand for emergencies. DT and engineering centres round farming. One boy explained that a few days fencing showed him the need for an efficient trailer for fencing materials. Brymore's metal and wood workshops, including smithy and foundry, enable really professional work, from handy little metal hammers made by beginners to roadworthy trailers and specialist tractor accessories – things with real practical value on the farm.

The farm and gardens are the heart of learning. Practical hands–on farm work: tractor driving (from 13), milking, winter and summer feeding of cattle, pigs and poultry, calving and lambing, cultivation of vegetables and maintenance of the grounds

There is a farm manager and a head groundsman, but all the work on the farm and maintaining the grounds and gardens is done by boys. There is nothing to make you understand better why people shouldn't trample across a perfect lawn than mowing it yourself! Horticultural minded boys can have personal plots in the walled garden and use of the potting and tool sheds to grow their own crops – Brymore 's kitchens happily buy salad, potatoes and veg from them. Art and music are newly available as options. Languages and other options may be taught outside the main school day.

Boarding: Since a major refurbish, boarding is comfortable and clean, the slightly institutional layout softened by posters of giant tractors, 'great big combine harvesters', animals and sport and no institutional smell. Bins outside the doors of the two newish boarding houses take muddy farm clothes and sports gear. Dorms sleep four, except in the main house, where it's up to six. Very tidy – a few unwashed coffee mugs in the boys' kitchen sink confirmed that it is actually lived in. Each house has its own houseparents and relief team for continuity.

Background and atmosphere: Brymore was founded as a School of Rural Technology in 1952 for sons of Somerset farmers on an impressive 60-acre farm on the edge of Cannington, between the Quantocks and Bristol Channel. Half a mile of tree-lined drive ends in a cluster of farm buildings which surround the original 13th century house, much added to over the centuries, and once owned by the Cromwell's financier John Pym. Exceptionally loyal ex-pupils meet and encourage the current generation at the annual, misleadingly named, Pym's Night. Boys really seem to value the traditional standards of Brymore and are proud of taking part in the local church festivals – harvest especially – and of their reputation among local farmers: Brymore boys are useful on the farm. Shoes are miraculously clean despite farmyard mud, smart black uniform sports the Brymore spur and motto Diligentia et Labore on the pocket. It is also emblazoned on the walls in each boarding house, as the boys' chosen decoration. Parents and staff praise Brymore as 'feeling more like an independent school'. 'The noise of 180 boys singing out at full volume nearly knocks you out,' a proud parent commented after her first carol service.

Pastoral care, well-being and discipline: Brymore had a reputation as a pretty tough place in the past, but its toughness now focuses on the personal resilience and responsibility of the boys rather than rough and tumble rivalries. 'Resilience, Responsibility and Resourcefulness' is used as a strap-line by staff and pupils alike and there is no doubt constant reference to it has rubbed off on the boys' approach to academic and farm work. Day and boarding pupils mix in the three houses (not to be confused with the boarding houses), with house masters and tutors, who meet them weekly. Vertical tutor groups means the oldest mentor the year 7s and get to know all age groups. Year 11 boys take the usual prefect duties (hotly contested) and supervise younger ones for milking and feeding duties. Currently, they are very keen on creating an anti-bullying atmosphere, and are super-watchful over the newly-admitted first years. Down to earth matron on duty all day and liked by boys. Food said to be 'better than it was' but still a cause of some contention.

Pupils and parents: The farming community both local and much further flung (boarders from Hong Kong, France, Norway and midlands) definitely dominates, but boys and parents are beginning to demand a wider outlook and academic curriculum. Past pupils visit frequently and are still part of school life. One, teaching blacksmithing at Brymore alongside his own small business, makes an excellent role model. Others include MEP Neil Parish, Mark Irish, England U21 rugby player, Alex Wright, British race walking champion, and Robert

Watts, Brymore's head of boarding. Both alumni and parents fundraise enthusiastically.

Entrance: About 50 pupils, 28 boarders and 22 day boys, admitted to year 7. Currently there is a similar intake to year 9, though this will inevitably diminish once the early years are full. Now oversubscribed. Day places on the usual Somerset criteria, a combination of first come first served and distance from the school. Boarding places also now oversubscribed, open to any boy qualifying for UK schooling and 'suitability for boarding'. Brymore is good with boys who haven't thrived in mainstream, but increased demand has meant that the academic profile of the school is now higher that previously.

Exit: A few boarders stay on to year 12 but attend all courses at Bridgewater College. A large contingent to agricultural colleges, Kingston Maurward, Duchy College Cornwall, Bridgwater College (Cannington Centre) and all over the country. 'Brymore boys often get fast tracked at college,' said one farmer dad. A significant interest in engineering, and some boys go on to do A levels with a view to uni places. Lack of modern foreign language teaching has been a bit of a barrier with local sixth form college, so it's as well it's now on offer. Many to apprenticeships and a significant number end up running their own businesses.

Money matters: Fees only for boarding, not tuition, so miles cheaper than the independent sector, despite recent fee rises. Some pupils obtain educational grants from home LAs. All day boys, known as 'out boarders', have to board and pay for the weeks they are on farm duties, though some have found educational grants for this..

Remarks: There are still too few schools like Brymore and, though more are being established, it will be hard to rival its atmosphere and achievement. Articulate, friendly boys are not afraid of the pressures and daily grind of farm work. If this is what hands on experience and responsibility gives to children, schools could do with more of it. No hayseeds at Brymore – more business aware agriculturalists who understand the need to supply food and respect the land that grows it. Parents appreciate that every member of staff is there to give the very best possible education to their children.

Burford School

Cheltenham Road, Burford, Oxfordshire OX18 4PL

01993 823303
head.4040@burford.oxon.sch.uk
www.burford.oxon.sch.uk

Ages: 11–18
Pupils: 1,140; sixth form: 220
Boarders: 90
Day: free
Boarding: £9,900 pa

Headteacher: Since 2008, Mrs Kathy Haig BA MEd (40s). Educated at Burford School herself (her family lived at nearby Shipton-under-Wychwood), followed by Leeds University, where she studied food science and nutrition. Taught at schools in Hull, Keighley and Preston before moving to Ellesmere Port Catholic High School in Cheshire. Spent 12 years there, rising to be deputy head. Made a point of focusing on teaching and learning from the minute she arrived at Burford. When it comes to making decisions she always asks 'does it improve the teaching and learning?' If it doesn't, the school doesn't do it. Her approach has paid dividends. GCSE and A level results have risen year on year over the last seven years and the school received a letter of congratulations from the schools minister on being in the top 90 secondary schools in England for sustained improvement.

Outgoing, full of ideas and a good listener, she says that 'the culture of inclusivity and mutual respect' is key to the school's ethos. Parents told us that she is 'very down-to-earth,' 'easy to approach' and knows every pupil by name (no mean feat in a school this size). Her open-door policy means that if her door is open pupils can stop by and chat. When a group of boys mentioned that they'd like to play chess at lunchtimes she immediately put the idea into action. Now there's a chess league four times a week and Burford competes against other schools.

Head still teaches five hours a fortnight (child development GCSE to year 11 pupils). 'I love teaching and I think that it does the staff good to see that the head still has to do reports,' she says. Married to management consultant and has two teenage children, both at Burford.

'We loved the feel of the place from the start. There's no keeping up with the Joneses. It's very diverse and there are people from all walks of life'

Academic matters: A large, rural comprehensive that takes boarders (it's one of only 30 or so state boarding schools in the country). Offers wide range of subjects to wide ability intake but expects everyone to work hard and fulfil their potential – in line with head's belief that if you have high expectations then 'children will live up to what you expect of them.' Curriculum is mainly academic, with a small number of vocational qualifications. Most pupils take nine or 10 GCSEs and homework plays integral part, with parents asked to sign children's student record books once a week up to GCSE.

Exam results are very good – 61 per cent of pupils gained at least five GCSEs at grades A*-C including English and maths in 2015, with 21 per cent at A*/A grades. At A level, 25.3 per cent at A*/A and 51 per cent A*-B. Thirty A level and BTec subjects on offer at A level – all the usual, plus economics, psychology, media studies and photography. EPQ and AS critical thinking also available.

Lessons are largely taught in form groups, apart from maths and French, which are set according to ability. Class sizes of 26 up to GCSE (20 for practical subjects) and average of 12 to 14 in the sixth form. Languages compulsory at key stage 3. All students do French in years 7 to 9 and can add a second language in years 8 and 9.

Learning support is housed in own block – The Learning Zone – and deals with a wide range of needs, including speech, language and communication difficulties, autistic spectrum conditions, dyslexia, dyspraxia and dyscalculia and social, emotional and mental health needs. Help given to children who arrive with lower than average literacy and numeracy as well as those with EAL requirements and the gifted and talented. There's also an inclusion room called The Bridge for students who temporarily need to study away from the main classroom. A mother whose daughter had to undergo spinal surgery was full of praise for it. 'Lessons were brought to her there,' she said. 'Potentially she could have had four months being home-schooled but thanks to The Bridge she only missed two or three weeks of school.'

In keeping with its rural setting, school has an outdoor classroom called The Acre. As well as being a base for GCSE course in environmental land based studies it has chickens, ducks, rabbits, two miniature donkeys and a vegetable patch.

Games, options, the arts: With acres of green space for pupils to run around in, Burford is very sporty. PE and games are compulsory – sports offered include hockey, football, rugby, netball, tennis, athletics, keep fit and dance. As well as games fields (including a cricket square and pavilion), school has a gym and sports hall, netball and tennis courts. Loads of matches with local state and independent schools (rugby, hockey and netball teams particularly successful). Burford also hosts schools from Argentina and Australia every year for rugby, hockey, netball and cricket. School has its own equestrian team and runs an inter-house riding competition in the grounds every summer – everything from best turned-out pony to show-jumping and dressage. If there's a sport pupils want to do, 'we will try and put it on,' says the deputy head, citing girls' cricket and volleyball as recent examples.

Music is fantastic. Around 300 pupils have instrumental lessons – 'you name it, we play it,' said one of our sixth form guides. Wide range of orchestras, string ensemble, wind band, jazz band and rock school plus a music residential for 100 pupils in North Wales in the summer. School hopes to build its own concert hall and recently became music hub for the area, offering workshops by visiting specialists, the chance to play in professional concerts and master classes at St Anne's College, Oxford. School stages musical every two years – they'd just done Sunshine on Leith when we visited – and a drama production in the intervening years. 'We try and involve everyone,' said the assistant head.

Well equipped art block, with different areas for art, design, photography, textiles, plus computers, scanners, colour printers and digital cameras that professional studios would give their eye-teeth for. Loads of voluntary extracurricular activities – during lunch breaks and after school on Monday, Tuesday and Thursday (late buses put on so everyone can attend).

D of E and Young Enterprise on offer and lots of trips to foreign climes. The school is rightfully proud of its 20-year tie with a school in Uganda. The first group visited Uganda in 1995 and since then an annual exchange has taken place. Burford pupils visit partner students in Uganda one year, then host them in Burford the next. Along the way Burford has raised money for everything from a library and computer room for its partner school to two cows.

Boarding: The head says she could fill boarding places twice over and we're not in the least surprised. Parents pay for children's accommodation but their education is free. 'State boarding schools show that you can have it all, but at a fraction of the price of independent schools,' the mother of a sixth form boarder told us. 'We loved the feel of the place from the start. There's no keeping up with the Joneses. It's very diverse and there are people from all walks of life.'

The 90 boarders (half of them boys, half girls) live in Lenthall House, a listed building in Burford itself and a ten-minute walk from the main school (uphill on the way there, downhill on the way back). As we said last time, it's a bit of a Tardis – a maze of interconnecting buildings with bright, newly refurbished rooms and excellent facilities. This year the school has created a flat within the boarding house for five sixth form girls – to help them prepare for the university years. Boarders come from all over, from down the road in Oxfordshire to Hong Kong and China. Most are full boarders (a couple of weekly boarders when we visited) and staff put on loads of evening and weekend activities. Everything from go karting and ice skating to theatre trips and craft sessions. Supervised prep every night and in-house structured revision during GCSE and A level study leave.

School still maintains many old grammar school traditions, including house system, prefects and smart uniform (blazer and house tie) for all but the sixth form

Pupils eat breakfast (full English on Saturdays and croissants on Sundays) and tea at the boarding house – food cooked by own catering staff – and lunch at the main school. Boarders can invite day pupils to tea and there's a formal dinner at Christmas, plus monthly lunches for local OAPs. Six live-in staff, including head of boarding and his wife. Boarding head moved to Burford from the independent sector and says: 'There is more drive and purpose among the boarders here. They are keener to do well and to take advantage of all the opportunities we offer.'

Application form on school website for boarding places. School asks for reference from children's current school and prospective pupils are invited to attend a taster day during term time. Students from overseas (30 per cent of total number of boarders) welcome as long as they have a relative or host family living in the UK.

Background and atmosphere: Founded as a grammar school for boys by charter in 1571 and still celebrates Charter Day in October each year. Main school is situated on the busy A40 on edge of beautiful Cotswold town of Burford (just over an hour away from London in reasonable traffic). Moved to its present 36-acre site in 1960, with boarders moving into the original grammar school at the bottom of the high street. An academy since 2012.

School still maintains many old grammar school traditions, including house system, prefects and smart uniform (blazer and house tie) for all but the sixth form (who wear their own clothes but are expected to dress appropriately – no ripped jeans or Ugg boots). This year's first XV rugby team have opted to wear smart suits when they travel to matches – a custom they reckon will continue.

Sixth formers have their own block, with common room, study area and more freedom. Year 13s are allowed off-site at lunchtime and if they don't have lessons. Some drive to school. 'We get treated like grown-ups,' an appreciative youngster told us. The only grumble we heard was that they'd like more parking places. Students keen to be head girl or head boy write their own manifestos, take part in hustings and are voted for by staff and fellow sixth formers.

Like the pupils themselves, the atmosphere here is busy and purposeful. Ofsted's 2014 report judged students' behaviour to be outstanding and when we visited we were impressed by pupils' politeness, charm and enthusiasm for the school.

Pastoral care, well-being and discipline: Well-defined rules set out in excellent student record book – smart hardback given to each pupil at the start of the year, with ruler and whiteboard they can hold up for plenary sessions in class. Contains everything from equipment needed for school to spelling lists and what to do if the school bus is late.

School's core tenet is that 'everyone will act with care and consideration to others at all times,' and it clearly works. School governor told us that Burford is 'very caring' and 'takes great pride in how we look after our youngsters.' There's a strong Team Burford ethos, with students keeping in touch for years after they leave.

Excellent induction programme for new pupils. Year 7s are mentored by trained year 13s and also get a three-day residential trip early in first term to help them settle in. Year groups are divided into seven or eight forms, each with own tutor, who's also responsible for registration and PHSE. All pupils belong to one of four houses named after school founders and benefactors – Falkland, Heylin, Warwick and Wysdom. Houses are fiercely competitive, with lots of competitions, from rugby and netball to art and even forensics. School council with four reps from each year group. Pupils have assembly twice a week – once for the whole school and once for their year group.

Pupils say the food has improved a lot and offers a daily choice of hot meals, pasta, salad bar, vegetarian options and baguettes. Cashless canteen – biometric system reads students' thumbprints.

Pupils and parents: A real mix. Pupils come from a wide variety of backgrounds, from disadvantaged to quite posh. Some have lived in the area for years, others have parents who commute to Oxford or London every day. Relatively few from the town of Burford itself – steep house prices mean properties tend to be owned by older residents and second-homers. School gives financial support 'very discreetly' to pupils whose families can't afford to pay for school trips.

Old pupils include Gilbert Jessop (cricketer), Simon West (film director) and Alice Freeman (rower).

Entrance: Children living in the catchment area and attending one of Burford's nine partner schools are virtually guaranteed a place. Thirty-five to 40 per cent of pupils come from outside the catchment area, from as far afield as Hook Norton, Faringdon and Bourton-on-the-Water, with priority given to those with siblings already at the school. Additional pupils arrive in year 9, including up to 30 a year from local private schools. 'We've had to put in an extra year 9 form,' says the head.

Up to 20 new pupils a year join the 220-strong sixth form (minimum of two Bs and four Cs at GCSE required by all, plus some subject-specific requirements).

Exit: Around 40 per cent leave after GCSE – for vocational courses at local FE colleges (including Cirencester, Abingdon and Witney and City of Oxford), apprenticeships and employment.

Three-quarters head to university after A levels – to study everything from biomedical science to fine art. Universities in the south west and Wales including Bristol, Reading, Plymouth and UWE all popular destinations in 2015. School has a full-time careers adviser – professionally qualified and very experienced – who organises higher education and apprenticeships evenings, mock interviews, a careers convention and work experience (for year 10s and year 12s) and sees students one-to-one. School is creating strong links with local businesses too.

Remarks: A happy and successful comprehensive school with an impressive 'can-do' attitude. Pupils are keen to succeed and rise to the challenge admirably.

Colchester Royal Grammar School

6 Lexden Road, Colchester, Essex CO3 3ND

01206 509100
info@crgs.co.uk
www.crgs.co.uk

Ages: 11–18
Pupils: 850; sixth form: 350 (including 80 girls)
Boarders: 30 (sixth form boys only)
Day: free
Boarding: £8,100 – £11,400 pa

Headmaster: Since September 2015, Mr John Russell, previously deputy head of Cranbrook School. Physics degree from Imperial College; first job in a Loughton comprehensive school before becoming head of physics at Ilford County High. Wife, Michelle, is a chemistry teacher, and they have three children. Describes himself as an enthusiastic sportsman if not a very accomplished one.

Academic matters: Extremely high academic standards. No setting in years 7 or 8, French and maths setted from year 9 – 'But this is only a question of pace,' says school. 'Set 4 pupils will still be expected to achieve A* at GCSE.' French and Latin in year 7, choice of German or Greek in year 8. One of the very few state schools to offer Greek to A level – for a state school, an above average number go on to study classics at university. Fantastic results at GCSE and A level – in 2015, 84 per cent A*/A grades at GCSE and 89 per cent A*-B at A level.

Occasional SEN pupil with physical disabilities or Asperger's; any EAL pupil will have had a high enough standard of English to pass the selection tests.

Games, options, the arts: Cricket and rugby particularly strong. Regular fixtures against state and independent schools. Netball, and now rugby, as well as racket sports and fencing for the sixth form girls. Many other sports available as extracurricular activities including athletics, sailing and weight-training. Also plenty of non-sporting activities. Great music department with loads of opportunities for any pupil with any musical ambitions.

Boarding:Two boarding houses with a mixture of single and double bedrooms; family-style facilities, five resident staff members for the 30 boarders. Boarders – all sixth form boys – mainly those who would have too far to travel to school each day and pupils from abroad; very popular in Hong Kong – a member of staff visits the country each year to interview potential sixth formers. They can use school sports and music facilities during evenings and weekends. Good cultural mix.

Background and atmosphere: Directly descended from a Colchester town school that existed in 1206 and was granted royal charters by Henry VIII in 1539 and Elizabeth I in 1584. Set in an affluent residential area of Colchester, the main buildings date back to the late 19th century. Latest additions, which include new blocks for history, classics and art and renovated music and drama facilities, fit well with the attractive old school buildings. The new George Young Building serves as a concert hall, performance studio and lecture theatre. Lovely, well-tended gardens of a standard unusual in a state school, featuring quiet and private sitting areas for pupils. Extensive playing fields five minutes' walk from the main school and a heated outdoor swimming pool. The uniform includes a vivid purple blazer not very popular with the boys (school begs to differ); no uniform for sixth formers but smart dress required.

Pastoral care, well-being and discipline: Generally very high standard of conduct and not many discipline problems. Punishments include loss of privileges and lunchtime and after school detentions. Few expulsions in the head's time at the school. Zero tolerance of drugs – possession leads to expulsion.

Pupils and parents: Years 7-11 mainly from Colchester and surrounding area, but pupils travel

Set in an affluent residential area of Colchester, the main buildings date back to the late 19th century. Latest additions include new blocks for history, classics and art and renovated music and drama facilities

up to an hour each way each day, sixth formers (including girls) from further afield. Very active parents' association raising funds for the school.

Old Boys include Telegraph columnist Giles Smith, economics commentator Tim Congdon, costume designer and double Oscar winner Jim Acheson, founder of Freeserve, John Pluthero and former BBC education correspondent Mike Baker.

Entrance: Highly competitive 11+ exam – 50 per cent verbal reasoning, 25 per cent English and 25 per cent maths. 'Places will be awarded in rank order to the top 96 boys in the order of merit who have named Colchester Royal Grammar School as a preference.' The exam is set by the consortium of selective schools in Essex, which has 12 members, and is held in November at the school. Candidates do not have to live in Essex. Four places available for entry to the school in year 9, but the competition is stiff – report, plus tests in maths, English, science and a modern language.

Minimum of four A and two B grade GCSEs for entry into sixth form for internal and external candidates. The 80 or so external entrants (half of them girls) also require a school report and must satisfy the school's academic requirements. Candidates for sixth form boarding places must meet the academic requirements first. Overseas boarders must be British or EU passport holders.

Exit: Hardly any leave post-GCSEs. Sixth formers virtually all to university; 30+ to Oxbridge most years (three Oxbridge medics in 2015) and 20+ to medical school. Very high percentage of Russell Group places.

Remarks: One of the country's top selective boys' state schools, rivals many independents. Any academically able and hard-working boy (and sixth form girl) should thrive here.

Cranbrook School

Waterloo Road, Cranbrook, Kent TN17 3JD

01580 711804
registrar@cranbrook.kent.sch.uk
www.cranbrookschool.co.uk

Ages: 13–18
Pupils: 745: 410 boys, 335 girls; sixth form 290
Boarders: 290
Day: free
Boarding: £11,655 – £13,983 pa

Headmaster: Since 2012, Dr John Weeds MA MPhil EdD (50s). Read classics at Pembroke College, Cambridge and his academic studies have long been part of his life. He jokes that he didn't want to be outdone by his talented micro-biologist wife, but the letters after his name attest to a driven and committed educationalist.

His most recent thesis was on the subject of the gifted and talented, which will come in useful here. But having consciously chosen to work in the state sector, he is very concerned with equality of opportunity too. He has an eye on re-balancing Cranbrook's increasingly independent school intake; he has ensured there are some less financially demanding school trips and wants to see the girls at Cranbrook given more of a voice too.

We visited a year after his arrival, following what has been described to us by the tactful as 'a difficult period of adjustment' and by the more forthright as a 'baptism of fire.' The head heartily agrees with the latter, clearly enjoying the calm for now – although the thought of having to tackle performance related pay next makes his hair stand on end.

He found the school somewhat laid back, and hasn't been afraid to grapple with it – 'some traditions I'm prepared to take on,' he told us. One of the contentious changes was suits for sixth formers five days a week. 'It's created a different feel – more business-like and focused,' he says. Understanding that parents 'really do want best grades,' he aims to deliver consistency of performance and to retain the focus on the academic. 'I don't want to lose sight of the diverse extracurricular offer, but we need more balance,' he says.

The parents we spoke to are right behind him. One told us: 'He is not a slick performer but the benefit is that I believe he listens and engages with both students and parents.' Another said: 'I feel his quest to raise results is to be praised and supported.'

He has three university-age sons.

Academic matters: A level results on upward curve in 2015 – 46 per cent A*/A grades. There have been tweaks all round, including a new approach to mock exams. Pupils know what is expected of them and are fired up to achieve it.

Some subjects notably out-perform others by a mile, namely the large cohort of talented mathematicians. The school has been a specialist science school for years and has a new observatory equipped with telescopes. A third of pupils take science A levels, with chemistry particularly popular with the girls, and almost all taking single sciences at GCSE. Strong humanities, but English seems to be a weak spot. Head says the new assessment framework is challenging. Numbers taking languages fall off at A level, to only 10 per cent. Most seem pretty focused on traditional curriculum subjects but a sixth form enrichment programme offers additional choices such as astronomy, sports leadership and psychology.

At GCSE in 2015, 64 per cent A*/A grades. Pupils study 11 or more (mainly academic) subjects at GCSE, excelling at maths, physics, Latin, IT, French and art. Maths and RE are out of the way a year early. A third of maths whizzes currently take home an IGCSE too, with year 9 and 10 students winning a clutch of gold medals in national maths challenges. Languages on offer are French and Spanish, with Chinese for native speakers.

More than a third of teachers have been at the school for longer than 10 years. The head assured us that only two staff left last year but parents are less concerned about turnover. They approve of the new focus on performance and are keen on removing the few 'dead wood.' One told us: 'There are a handful of teachers who struggle to control the class and some who could explain their teaching and homework better.' Other teachers singled out as inspirational. The pupils we spoke to said teachers will stay behind to explain things if they don't understand something, while RS and physics teachers were praised for their revision guides and pre-university preparation. The brilliance of the maths results is due quite simply, says the head, to 'the best maths teacher in Kent.'

Parents seem split between those who think the amount of homework is about right and those who think there should be more, particularly in the holidays. A pupil said: 'Teachers will always give you more if you ask for it' – clearly a loophole for the less inclined, but there don't seem to be many of those here. The online parent portal keeps parents up-to-date with progress and there are half-termly assessment records for effort and attainment.

Two full-time student support assistants offer additional support for specific difficulties (outside the classroom). SENCo is a dyslexia specialist and admin assistant is also listed as having mentoring skills. Between 10 or 20 pupils each year with special educational needs (whether or not recorded by the local authority as such).

Pupils won't slip under the radar here, he said, and added: 'We will pick up those who can become hard on themselves and down, and won't forget others who can achieve great things'

Head told us with feeling: 'We're very committed to supporting those with particular needs. We will do just about everything we can.' If pupils need a laptop they don't necessarily need to bring one – the school will find one. Pupils won't slip under the radar here, he said, and added: 'We will pick up those who can become hard on themselves and down, and won't forget other children who can achieve great things.' A handful with EAL needs – EAL tuition is offered free of charge for anyone who needs it.

Some pretty glamorous sporting tours – South Africa for cricket, Fiji and New Zealand for rugby. A team of under-15 girls recently became British fencing champions

Games, options, the arts: School has a strong sports tradition. Fifty acres of sports fields and everyone participates. High-calibre cricket and rugby teams, with a growing fixtures list. One pupil told us he'd left a prestigious local grammar specifically to join the Cranbrook rugby first XV (he'd played against the team and admired it). Some pretty glamorous sporting tours – South Africa for cricket, Fiji and New Zealand for rugby. A team of under-15 girls recently became British fencing champions. Facilities include an outdoor heated pool, squash courts, Astroturf, plus sports hall with dance studio (currently offering Bollywood classes), climbing wall and gym (popular in the evenings with sporty boys).

Not much consensus about music here. Head claims it's the 'story of the year' but some parents not so ecstatic. One told us: 'One concern is that the extracurricular music programme is not as strong as it could be. There are great facilities and talent but this is not always harnessed effectively.' It's certainly a well-resourced and vibrant part of school life, with several choirs, an orchestra, jazz and rock bands, folk, string, sax and brass groups, charity concerts and community carol services. Total of 150 students take individual instrument lessons, with many learning more than one and working on higher grades. Lots of pupils trying an instrument for the first time. Live music at every assembly and whilst pupils still seemed a little wrapped up in their early morning fugs we saw teachers toe-tapping along to a jazz band which could easily take a turn at Ronnie Scott's.

The more artistic may be in the minority – a lone music A level student most recently and a handful taking art A level. Having tackled exam performance as her first priority, art teacher is encouraging boys into the classroom (now one third of pupils). Art room is open all hours and cool graffiti art pop-ups grab the attention of everyone as they move around the school. Large, well-used facilities for DT and food technology.

The Queen's Hall is the home of the drama department and is a fully equipped and recently refurbished theatre – largely run by the pupils, but also used by outside touring companies. Annual house plays as well as junior, senior and whole school productions.

What Cranbrook does well is encourage pupils to be self-reliant and take responsibility, whether that is through CCF or D of E, fundraising for the charities they care passionately about – no standard Sports Relief here – or being given the freedom to set up any clubs they're interested in (40 at the last count, including curling club which promptly won a county-wide competition).

Annual trip to Tanzania to work on health and education projects is a stand-out opportunity. Pupils compete for a place and work hard to raise the money themselves. 'It was the best thing I have done in my life,' said the head girl. There's also an exchange partnership with a school in Kerala for two weeks at the end of the autumn term. All richly eye-opening, and no doubt contributed to the school's International Schools Award from the British Council.

Enrichment programme for years 9 and 10 means pupils go off timetable for two weeks. 'We take them out of their comfort zone,' said the head. 'They have to research and do presentations on what they've learned. This year they met everyone from a policeman to a prisoner. It gets youngsters who are bright to think.'

Boarding: Boarding houses are a bit of a lottery architecturally – some old, some modern. The year 10 dorms we visited in one house were more like tiny ships' cabins, with multi-tasking bunk-beds/desks, but as pupils get older they often get more space. There's a rolling programme of new carpets, curtains and bathrooms and we were impressed by the accommodation – squishy sofas, polished wood, no institutional paint colours (tasteful greys). Washing gets turned around in 24 hours – setting the bar quite high for when pupils return home – and there wasn't the slightest whiff of a less than fresh sock. Boarding pupils can invite day pupils over after school and it's easy to see how self-sufficient youngsters can be here, without the need of the rural parental taxi service.

Background and atmosphere: Founded in 1518 and given a Royal Charter by Elizabeth I in 1574. School's buildings straddle the main road into the pretty Kent town of Cranbrook and are a jumble of every architectural style, from 1970s accommodation blocks to a fine Georgian mansion. Local church of St Dunstan's is in the middle of the campus – very much part of the community.

The fact that Cranbrook is a selective state school with a large boarding contingent gives the place a unique feel. The alumni society is awash with hugging groups from reunited houses. Total of 12 houses – seven for boys and five for girls. Day pupils are grouped geographically to start with to help out of school socialising.

A parent told us that the school offers 'a balance of high academic achievement and extracurricular activities that is the equal to many public schools.' Another described Cranbrook as 'a very intriguing mix of competitive and laid-back.' They added that 'it places responsibility on the students rather than spoon-feeding them, which means that students need to step up.' Pupils want to go places here – it's not uncool to be clever.

Pastoral care, well-being and discipline: Pastoral care is highly praised. On arrival each child is allocated a tutor who will monitor their academic and activities programme, social progress and work with their head of house. As one parent pointed out, the houses and tutor groups are something of a haven. Pupils return to their houses regularly throughout the day – which helps to prevent the build-up of any bullying.

Mentoring is a word that crops up a lot (peer to peer, sixth form to younger pupils, staff to pupils). There is a smart new medical centre (like a mini hospital, with beds for sick boarding pupils), and counsellors offer appointments four times a week. Head has tightened up on discipline and believes the behaviour of pupils is now excellent (a view backed up by parents). Good liaison with parents, plus contracts for good behaviour.

Parents reckon school is ideal for self-motivated, well-rounded pupils who have capabilities beyond the academic

Pupils and parents: Head says that youngsters who are 'particularly interested in learning' and have 'a real spirit of enterprise and adventure' will thrive here. Parents reckon school is ideal for self-motivated, well-rounded pupils who have capabilities beyond the academic, and are organised, not overly sensitive or under confident – or 'the engaged, interested and aspirational'. The place 'may not be suited to students expecting to be hand held,' although quieter children have found their niche too. Independence is held in exceptionally high esteem.

Parents tend to be less the super-rich and more middle class professionals with increasingly high expectations. Definitely a varied bunch, suggesting there's a good chance of finding like minds. Some parents are reputedly stirred up and vocal about the recent changes, whilst every other parent we spoke to was quick to say they liked to be 'hands off.' Head cites strong relationships with parents and a tradition for supportive involvement, particularly with careers teaching.

Notable alumni include Es Devlin, superstar stage and costume designer of the 2012 Olympic closing ceremony, Tim Smit, founder of the Eden Project, astronaut Dr Piers Sellers, comedian Harry Hill, designer Ptolemy Mann, journalist Sir Charles Wheeler and sports commentators Peter West, Brian Moore and Barry Davis, plus many high up in the Forces.

Entrance: Selective entrance at 13+, catering for the top 20-25 per cent of the academic ability range, but head is committed to introducing the 11+ as the main mode of entry in the very near future.

A total of 150 places on offer, including 52 boarders. There is an 8.5 km preferred catchment, pushing up house prices even further nearby (inaccurate addresses taken very seriously). Applicants previously often came from the Cranbrook state secondary, The High Weald Academy. Now the competition has shifted up a gear – a strong intake from prep schools such as Marlborough House, Dulwich Prep and St Ronan's. Boarders mostly come from just outside the catchment area – most within 40 miles, including London and the home counties. About one third are based overseas – they must hold a UK or EU passport.

Applications via local authority website, with annual deadline in October, or January for the sixth form. Autumn open days, plus summer 'school in action' day, to see school during a normal working day. Boarding tours available all year.

Entrance exam (day pupils in January, boarders in November) is a three-hour, multiple-choice verbal reasoning test, plus the school's own papers in maths and English. As for some other Kent selectives, now a more rigorous English entrance exam, including 20 minutes of free writing, looking for flair beyond the basics. The maths test is based on the national curriculum, but designed to root out those performing at the higher and lower ends.

Only room for a few new entrants into the sixth form – 16 or so day students and a few new boarders. They require 11 points at GCSE (or equivalent) with A*=4, A=3 and B=1 point, but given lack of spaces, likely to be far more demanding in reality. Anyone who does not achieve the 11 points at GCSE is asked to leave.

Exit: Around 20 per cent a year exit at year 11. Parents and pupils feel the school prepares well for university, and helps with gap years too. Around 95 per cent of sixth formers head to university. Five to Oxbridge in 2015, plus a large contingent to Russell Group. Popular destinations include Bristol, Nottingham, Leeds, UCL, Warwick, Exeter and Birmingham. Many traditionally academic subjects, but also Asian studies, criminology, anthropology, product design and psychology.

Money matters: New academic scholarships for year 9 entry – 'identifying those who are not just just strong at their subject, but passionate as well'. Small financial reward but inclusion in high achievers' scheme.

Remarks: Recent changes have definitely left everyone a little shaken and stirred, but if the school's recent results are anything to go by Cranbrook is raising its game nicely. As an alternative to the high pressure Kent grammars, with the facilities and atmosphere of many private schools and the fun of boarding too, it's an excitingly different proposition for the adventurous young teen.

De Aston School

Willingham Road, Market Rasen, Lincolnshire LN8 3RF

01673 843415
enquiries@de-aston.lincs.sch.uk
www.de-aston.lincs.sch.uk

Ages: 11–18
Pupils: 908; sixth form: 167
Boarders: 68
Day: free
Boarding: £9,300 pa

Head: Since 2006, Ellenor Beighton (50s). A Scot, with an English and politics degree from Dundee. Never taught in Scotland but headed south to Lincolnshire to teach English after doing her PGCE in Sheffield. Head of sixth form at Priory in Lincoln before coming to De Aston as deputy, followed by appointment as head two years later. Husband also a head; three sons, youngest one in his final year at school, but not at de Aston.

Likeable, elegant and immaculately turned out. Looks like an executive and acts like one. 'Runs a tight ship,' was said more than once. 'She maintains her distance, which is a good thing,' said one wise mother. 'She has a very good management team and uses them well.' Every parent said she knew

their children. Well respected by children and parents alike. 'She knows exactly where she wants the school to be going.' Our guides said they didn't see a great deal of her, but added, 'She spends a lot of time with year 11 English and is always at the door of the hall offering moral support on exam days.'

Very aware of what this expanding school should be offering the community and knows the community well. 'Lincolnshire is a very rural county and pupils come from far and wide. We are non-selective, rightly so, as where else would these pupils go?'

Academic matters: In 2015, 62 per cent of pupils achieved five or more passes at GCSE A*- C with English and maths. At A level, 37 per cent A*-B grades. They are on top of the pupils, offering support for all. Gifted and talented spotted in year 7 and nurtured throughout their time at the school. Lunch time sessions offered to explore subjects in more detail, plus a broader church such as chess, discussion and quizzes. G&Ts also help with the younger years with learning support. The less able are monitored constantly and 'pulled along,' to quote one parent. Learning support very effective, with lots of extra tutoring available. We spotted quite a few one-on-one lessons on our tour of the school. 'My child is dyslexic and got tremendous support in the early years. Less so further up the school but, to be fair, he hasn't needed it as much. I know he is being constantly monitored though and they will step in if necessary.' EAL unit quite large, 59 students, effective and proactive. Many of these students are the boarders who pick up the language impressively quickly.

The main subjects are set early on. French for all up to GCSE, German on offer if enough takers. Lots of impressive artwork on show. DT room had a lovely smell of varnish and very well equipped. All parents were happy that the teachers knew their children well. The head is very proud of the school's value added record. Class sizes average 24, but can go up to 34. All pupils well behaved and attentive. A couple in isolation: obviously Monday morning not going well for some. But all was dealt with calmly and effectively. Some year 13s helping out with the year 7s; looks good on their UCAS forms. Many long-serving staff and many more are ex-pupils.

> *Gifted and talented nurtured throughout their time at the school. Lunch time sessions offered to explore subjects in more detail, plus chess, discussion and quizzes*

Sixth form block fairly new and well equipped. Large common room and lots of IT rooms being well used. Quite amusing to see that the 'unsupervised' room had a CCTV camera in it so the teacher in the 'supervised' room could keep an eye on them, including what was on their computers. Pleased to note that all was well. Lots of A level choices on offer, all the usual academic plus 'softer' subjects such as media studies and photography. English and history seem to be strong contenders. BTecs also available. Lots of careers advice, encouragingly, university not being the only option. School recently awarded Careers Mark accreditation.

Games, options, the arts: A sporty school with loads of pitches and facilities. No swimming pool but Astroturf and courts as well as a large dance studio and fitness suite. Massive sports hall. Plenty of silverware on show in reception area. Pleased to note that there is sport for all; the enthusiastic but less talented get chance to play in teams as well. Lots of lunch time practice sessions. Rugby dominant but girls' hockey and netball strong. Enthusiastic director of sport offering vocational training for sixth formers to help younger years including junior schools. Competitive inter-house sports day every year.

Instruments taught within school but not a huge take up. Opportunity for pupils to show their talents in many shows and end of term performances. Plenty of rooms available for practice. No school orchestra and very few bands, but choir sessions for all.

Drama popular with whole school involved in annual production. More than one drama studio, all well used. D of E up to silver on offer and becoming more popular. Plenty of theatre visits and school trips including World Challenge.

Boarding: One of only 34 state boarding schools. Has always been a boarding school, originally to

One of the tidiest, best-kept schools we have visited. Immaculate paintwork throughout; they must have a tremendous caretaker

accommodate pupils from the far flung corners of rural Lincolnshire. Boarders are virtually all foreign students, but with the right to be educated in the UK. Most from Europe, particularly Spain, and a large contingent from Hong Kong. The occasional child with parents in the Forces. Many of the foreign students dip into the school for a couple of years to perfect their English.

Attractive large Victorian boarding house. Dated but spotlessly clean. Maximum of three to a room, most in pairs with the odd single room. Nice to see the rooms were slightly messy – teenagers allowed to be teenagers. Plenty of room available for more boarders, but 'we have as many as we want.' Virtually all are full boarders. Large communal areas, including a room with piano. The sixth formers are able to use their own common room in the school (accessed through a door from the boarding house). Plenty of trips. Friday night is cinema night. Saturdays spent in Lincoln or further afield at theme parks, shopping, sports venues or theatres. Well-liked housemaster incumbent since 1994. Plenty of outside space. Visitors welcome and friends allowed to stay. Tea and toast making facilities for all. Lots of prep sessions and a roll call at 10.30pm to ensure all sixth formers are back. Pretty relaxed about phones. An independent lot, but they know their parameters. 'We aren't allowed to go to parties,' our guide told us. 'It's annoying, as we'd like to go, but we accept it.' Very strong friendships forged within the house.

Background and atmosphere: Opened in 1863, it recently celebrated its 150th anniversary. Initially a boys' grammar school with boarding facilities for the farmers' and workers' sons who were too far away to travel daily. Still housed on the original site on the edge of Market Rasen, a pretty, small town well known for its racecourse. It has been extended extensively. A massive site with lots of land around it, including numerous sports pitches. A veritable rabbit warren. 'We get given maps in year 7 and it took me about two weeks to find my way around,' commented our guide. One of the tidiest, best-kept schools we have visited. Immaculate paintwork throughout; they must have a tremendous caretaker. A very nondescript black uniform, but all students are smart and polite. Lots of 'sirring' going on, surprisingly even from the staff member who accompanied us. Interesting to note that we were not allowed to tour the school with our guides unaccompanied by an adult – not that they had anything to hide, far from it, just school policy. We weren't sure whether to be insulted or reassured, but it's the school's safeguarding policy. Sixth form wear their own clothes but 'no jeans or bare shoulders.' Very much more relaxed relationship between sixth form and staff. It's a large school, particularly so for the county, but the bedding in period seems to stand them in great stead. 'When my daughter started she struggled at first, but was helped along her way and given huge encouragement.'

Pastoral care, well-being and discipline: Discipline is hot. They don't stand for any nonsense here. Pupils isolated if need be, often for the whole day. We were openly shown the list of detentions for that day. Most misdemeanours involved rudeness or insolence, the odd uniform malfunction. The school has very clear rules that the pupils are expected to follow. 'Most pupils accept that they are in the wrong, take the detention and see the error of their ways.' A very proactive intervention teacher who understands teenagers. 'We offer a safe secure spot where they can come and have a chat.' Sympathetic but firm, working closely with educational support department. Counsellors readily available if need be. 'Refreshingly, the school acknowledges bullying happens,' said one parent. 'The protagonists are brought together by the head of year and it's usually sorted out without parental involvement.' Pleased to hear that one child was moved into a different group with members of that form asked to help out and offer support. Sixth formers trained to spot bullying and how to handle it. Parents and pupils know who to turn to for advice. Active school council that meets every half term. School open to suggestions from members.

Pupils and parents: A true comprehensive. Parents can be local professionals or on the minimum wage.

All are supportive and back the school wholeheartedly. Pupils can travel a long way, up to an hour, but mainly from the northern half of Lincolnshire. Some 80 per cent of them are bussed in. A long list of primaries, up to 30, sending pupils, many just the one child. Many children are third, fourth or fifth generation to attend. And then there's the boarding contingent.

Entrance: First are siblings, then local children from a wide area. The boarding is open to all who qualify ie British citizens, EU passport holders and those who have the right of UK residence. Most boarders are interviewed and references asked for before being offered a place. Entry to the sixth form requires 5+ GCSEs at A*-C or higher depending on subjects studied. The school is expanding, so very unusual to not get a place.

Exit: Around 50 per cent leave after GCSEs, most to vocational courses locally. Between 15 and 20 join the sixth form from other local schools. A large handful leave after year 12, mainly to apprenticeships. 'Employment prospects aren't good for young people in this area so if an opportunity comes up it is hard to turn down,' said the head. The majority, up to 70 per cent, leave in year 13 and go on to university, many to local ones such as Lincoln. None to Oxbridge recently, but historically one or so each year. Interesting to note that almost 20 per cent go straight into employment or apprenticeships at this age. Gap years taken by very few.

Remarks: Quite an unusual place, with the boarding contingent adding a cosmopolitan flavour to a conservative community – good to see. A truly comprehensive establishment, open to all and serving the community well.

Gordon's School

West End, Woking, Surrey GU24 9PT

01276 858084
registrar@gordons.surrey.sch.uk
www.gordons.surrey.sch.uk

Ages: 11–18
Pupils: 735; sixth form: 165
Boarders: 128 full, 74 weekly
Day: free (day boarding £6,867 pa)
Boarding: £14,553 – £15,546 pa

Head Teacher: Since September 2010, Mr Andrew Moss BA MEd NPQH (40s). Started teaching in 1992 and has worked in a variety of boarding and day schools, including most recently a headship in a Cognita independent school. Before that he was a deputy head in Hampshire, and deputy, director of studies and housemaster at Wymondham College (also a state boarding school). 'He's a breath of fresh air,' said one in the know, 'bringing the school forward, without losing the best parts.'

He's less of a father figure than his predecessor, who transformed Gordon's from plodding to premier league, but is equally enthusiastic about this rather unusual school. 'I'm in the best of both worlds,' he says. 'We have the sort of heritage and behaviour you'll typically see in an independent, but with more grounded, authentic people around, people from all walks of life.'

Every parent we spoke to described him as 'professional', then variously as 'dynamic', 'pleasant' and 'ambitious', although some admitted they did not know him very well yet. 'He speaks well at meetings, seems a good manager and has a very business-like manner,' said one, 'but he hasn't put himself out to get to know people'. Yet all agree he has a good handle on the school and is well-respected by pupils, from whom he'll take no nonsense. 'If he told my children to jump, they would simply ask "How high, Sir?"' said one. Interviewed by pupils in the school magazine, they said of him, 'His signature stern, tough chapel talks have become synonymous with his presence itself'.

He's undoubtedly got strong ideas, but does use staff and parents as a sounding board and talks about 'empowering people' and 'decentralisation'. 'You can't build capacity all by yourself,' he says. 'You need good people to get involved and play a role in ideas and delivery'. Wasted no time in making his presence felt – investing in several projects including building new and revamping existing facilities, improving reporting systems and assessment methods and sorting out better communications with parents.

Keeps a finger on the pulse by taking PSHE lessons on economics and finance once a week. Has two children of his own (both at the school) and is a keen skier in his spare time.

Academic matters: Among the very best state offerings in the country, with an academically rigorous curriculum. It is an all-ability school, for which pupils are not selected via entrance exams, yet its results are top notch. In 2015, 89 per cent of pupils achieved five or more GCSE A*-C grades, including English and maths, with 40 per cent A*/A grades. At A level in 2015, 42 per cent A*/A and 76 per cent A*-B grades.

Its secret? Head puts it down to school's balance of traditional and modern methods – everything from reading out loud and spelling tests, through to use of peer assessment and mini whiteboards. Parents like its size (small), the emphasis on setting (rather than mixed-ability teaching) and its boarding school ethos.

Although two-thirds of its pupils live at home, the school is structured as a boarding school, with these 'day boarders' (as they are known) organised the same way as the wholly residential boarders in an extended school day. So everyone is in a house, with house parents, and following the same programme, including supervised homework, until 7.30pm.

Everyone is set for English, maths and science (out of four) and also for languages in years 7 and 8 – a language is compulsory at GCSE; either German, French or Spanish. Lowish requirements for additional support; some seven per cent have one-to-one EAL help and four per cent have statements/EHC plans, led by full-time SENCo and delivered in small groups and individually. 'Although it's a regimented place, the school does adapt well to

individuals', said one mother. 'They are very good at saying, this person has issues, let's sort him out – and I've seen some children really blossom here'.

They plough through the work, books filled at a pace, and there are plenty of practice papers and timed tests to make sure everyone is well prepared for GCSE. 'The new linear exams will suit us,' says AM. 'In fact we will gain as our work ethic is all about keeping it together to the end'. School has never been keen on the 'retakes' culture which fuelled much of the GCSE discontent.

Among the very best state offerings in the country, with an academically rigorous curriculum. It is an all-ability school yet its results are top notch

Parents praise a strong and disciplined teaching team with high expectations that pupils will be self-disciplined to work hard and be courteous at all times. Good systems in place ensure that nobody slips through the net. 'Monitoring is really good', said one parent. 'If someone isn't working at the expected level they will be pulled into a clinic to get them up to scratch'. One of AM's tasks has been to improve the process still further, with more informative, more frequent reporting, particularly for key stage 4/5. On top of an effort grade, pupils now receive target and working grades and every half term they receive significant feedback on what they need to do next. Lessons are fairly formal, there's an atmosphere of calm, but pupils are fully involved. Word on the street is that supply teachers find covering lessons at Gordon's a pleasure – they do not get ripped to shreds as in some state schools.

Homework is 'reasonable' – homework diaries are an important part of keeping on top of everything, really well used, signed every week by parents and school. 'They have to have it with them at all times and it's great for day to day communications, gets them organised and responsible,' said a parent. 'It's almost like the children are on report at all times,' said another. 'But it's for good comments too – they can get a stamp (like a gold star) and sometimes we'll get a note from a head of department or a house master if they've done something wonderful'. Evidently the regime can be stressful for some. 'My son cried for half an hour when he lost his homework once,' one mother said.

Around 180 at sixth form take 'facilitating' A levels (serious subjects that will win students places at Russell Group and other leading universities). No vocational qualifications on offer. 'We retain those for whom the sixth form is suitable,' says AM. Parents like it that sixth formers are not allowed off-site during teaching hours, so are more likely to work during their free periods – school calls them 'study periods, there are no frees'.

Ofsted rated school as 'outstanding'; its glowing report is littered with superlatives like 'exceptional' and 'beyond excellent'.

Games, options, the arts: It's all going on, both during the school day and as extracurricular options. After what would be the end of the school day at most state schools, the extended day here begins with 'period 6' – anything from sport to cooking, calligraphy to mountain biking or ultimate Frisbee. It's compulsory, and costs some £6867 a year, although if pupils have a bona fide after hours activity not available at the school there will be a dispensation.

Masses of sport on offer, with good facilities on site – more than 40 acres of playing fields, and all the usual football, rugby and hockey pitches, to the less usual (for a state school) shooting range, Astroturf and indoor heated swimming pool. Gordon's teams are happy to take on the toughest opponents and often play independent schools. Next on AM's wish list is a new sports hall – you don't doubt he will get one. 'Sport is a great release for everyone here,' said one mother. 'There's so much for them to do so that it's not all about pure academia. It's more of a lifestyle, there's a total mix of ages on the parade square after school and always someone around to kick a ball with'. 'I love that my son's outside instead of on his Xbox,' said another. 'The amount of physical activity is great.'

There's a huge emphasis on Duke of Edinburgh, with some 90 pupils achieving awards every year and lots of it at the much tougher gold end of things. 'Bronze is one thing, but getting stuck into a trip to Borneo is quite different from working in a charity shop for an hour a week,' said AM. 'It's quite striking how many golds we get, in fact we have organised 40 overseas trips in the past 10 years'. And all three Forces are represented in Gordon's combined cadet force – quite a feat to manage a naval unit in landlocked Surrey.

Great tradition of hard-fought inter-house competition gets everyone involved, regardless of ability; not just in sport but also in art, music and drama, with specialist facilities for all – an outdoor theatre is the latest addition. There are two annual art exhibitions and two full scale productions every year. Music very big, as well as an orchestra, choir and concert band, there's a pipe and drum band which, together with marching practice, is a major focus of the school.

Boarding: There are five day houses and four residential houses – all well used by both day and full boarders, who mix well. Boys and girls are allowed freely in each other's houses, but no boy is allowed upstairs in the girls' boarding houses and vice versa. Boys' houses with pool and table tennis tables, girls' centred more around comfy sofas and bean bags. Full boarding houses include common rooms, study areas and dormitories with study/bed units – all homely and understandably more relaxed and not as tidy and regimented as other parts of the school. Ofsted's inspection of boarding facilities pronounced them 'outstanding' in every respect. One boarder said that he doesn't 'go home' in the holidays, saying that he and his parents considered the school to be his main home.

Background and atmosphere: Ceremony and discipline is in the DNA of Gordon's, which was founded in 1885, at the behest of Queen Victoria, as a national memorial to General Gordon who was killed at Khartoum. The reigning monarch has been the school's patron ever since.

Every pupil learns to march and takes part in every one of the eight parades and chapel services held each year, accompanied by the previously mentioned pipes and drums marching band. There is marching practice every Friday, and once a year pupils go to London and literally stop the traffic when they march down Whitehall to the Cenotaph, ending up at the bronze statue of General Gordon on the Embankment. Although right up the street of the keen musicians in the band, it can be rather a chore for the others. 'I wouldn't say the marching is universally popular, but they get used to it – it's just what they do, everybody does it, it's part of Gordon's,' said a parent. 'And in fact after they have left school I think that trip along Whitehall will be a really special memory for them.'

Day to day things are rather less regimented, but all very orderly – AM likes to describe the

Classrooms are light and spacious, in both the older and newer buildings, and well resourced. Stunning chapel, built in 1894, which houses numerous school treasures

atmosphere as 'purposeful calm'. The school is built around a large quadrangle, quite bare and military in feel, with the odd bench here and there, where the students hang out during break and lunch if they are not in their houses. Alongside the original Victorian buildings are some less pretty 1960s additions, and (much better) 21st century facilities, including the new music and drama centre, science block and sixth form centre. Classrooms are large, light and spacious, in both the older and newer buildings, and well resourced. Stunning chapel, built in 1894, which houses numerous school treasures, including a book which lists the names of all the Gordon's boys killed in the two world wars. Pupils are never for a moment in any doubt about their school's heritage.

Pastoral care, well-being and discipline: A very disciplined place; 'Without good order there can be no learning in the classroom,' says school. Generally not much allowance for anyone stepping out of line, but for those obedient souls happy to stay within the set boundaries there are plenty of rewards and responsibilities on offer. Pupils quickly pick up on what's expected of them at Gordon's – they get it and are generally hardworking and appreciative of what's on offer. 'It's brilliant fun' and 'not one horrible teacher', our tour guides told us. They don't even seem to mind their 'boarders' duties' – vacuuming and emptying the bins.

School terribly keen on simple good manners, insists that pupils are courteous and considerate of others. Similarly picky about uniform. If a girl's skirt is deemed too short (and we didn't see any) she will be given a week's grace to get a new one. Everyone attends the chapel twice a week. Very close companionship among pupils who say they trust each other. New peer mentoring system working well. Need we mention zero tolerance of bullying, alcohol, drugs and associated misdemeanours? Strong culture of 'telling' to house parents and tutors is encouraged from the off. One longstanding parent convinced it's the combined support from house parents, tutors and teachers that underpins the academic success here.

Pupils and parents: Although it's a state school, most parents have money, certainly parents of boarders who have to cover the boarding fees. Parents of day boarders must be able to afford the £6800+ day boarding fees and will be in a certain socio-economic demographic to live in the catchment; of necessity they must live practically next door and some will move house to get this education for their children. 'We may have spent time and effort moving so close, but we saved on tutoring for entrance to a selective school and are continuing to save a fortune in comparison to the level of fees we'd pay for an independent school now,' said one. Aside from these locals, parents are a huge mix of professional, diplomatic and Forces. Weekly boarders typically live within an hour's drive, full boarders come from all over the UK, with about 15 per cent from overseas.

Pupils seem friendly, happy and very proud of their school; all regular young people, not quiet and cowed by the rules and regulations, but confident and ambitious types who seem to thrive in the order of everything.

Parent/school communications have improved – still a way to go, but would have been more of a criticism a few years ago. Text messaging system, emails, more frequent newsletters and bulletins are all AM innovations and remodelling of website is next on his 'to do' list.

Entrance: Tough. There are typically 400 applications for the 108 year 7 places on offer (76 day boarders – around 300 applicants – and 32 full/weekly boarders) and around half of these are generally swallowed up by siblings. Non-selective, so no entrance exams. Full or weekly boarder places prioritised by 'need to board'. This usually means children from Forces families from the UK and overseas – the school foresees increasing numbers of such children following recent changes to legislation.

Once a year pupils go to London and literally stop the traffic when they march down Whitehall to the Cenotaph, ending up at the bronze statue of General Gordon

For admission as a 'day boarder' think purely of location. Catchment varies but typically you'll need to live no further than 600m from the school. Mother of a baby was enquiring when we visited and local estate agents are well used to dealing with desperate parents who've left it rather later, but want to move next door. A small number of places allocated each year to children with statements of special educational needs.

Some additional places are available for the sixth form, where the entry requirement for both existing and new pupils is five GCSEs A*-C (including English and maths) with Bs for subjects to be taken at A level.

Exit: Around 40 per cent leave after GCSEs, some to more vocational courses at nearby Brooklands College. Most sixth formers on to university; around half to Russell Group.

Money matters: The education is free, but parents pay for the boarding, and even parents of day pupils (called 'day boarders') must pay for the compulsory post 3.30pm element of the day, house system, Saturday school, lunches and teas. Some bursaries available.

Remarks: A very different state offering – more like a private school without the price tag and elitism. Committed to traditional values, high standards, good discipline – doesn't share its 'semper fidelis' motto with the US marine corps for nothing. Those happy with the 'heads down and work' ethos are rewarded with an all-round, top notch education, pastoral care par excellence and enviable opportunities for sport. Suits focused, self-directed types, rather than a rebel who would be exhausted by the discipline. It's a school for achievers – a child with no oomph or aspirations would be lost among these go-getters.

Hockerill Anglo-European College

Dunmow Road, Bishop's Stortford, Hertfordshire CM23 5HX

01279 658451
admin@hockeril.com
www.hockerill.herts.sch.uk

Ages: 11–19
Pupils: 865; sixth form: 260
Boarders: 179 full, 17 weekly
Day: free (day boarding £6,036 pa)
Boarding: £11,331 – £15,330 pa

Principal: Since September 2013, Mr Richard Markham MA. An Oxford historian and former international hockey player who represented Wales, he began his teaching career at Marlborough College in 1994, where a variety of roles (including teacher of history and history of art, deputy housemaster, master in charge of hockey and IB coordinator) culminated in director of studies for his last four years. Insists the differences between Marlborough and Hockerill are 'not as pronounced as most people think', with key similarities including boarding and academic rigour. Whilst he inherited a school that was by no means complacent about its continued success, staff and students agree that he has pushed for a rounder education than his predecessor, believing that 'exam results are important, but a good education is about so much more.'

Relaxed but self-assured, he manages that winning headteacher combo of putting people immediately at ease, whilst still retaining a clear air of leadership. Staff clearly feel valued, able to explore innovative teaching techniques, and are never micromanaged, but woe betide any who go to him with a problem rather than a solution. Regularly dines with groups of students to seek their feedback, pointing out that with 92 per cent of day students eating lunch on site, the refectory is 'a good place to keep your finger on the pulse.' Meanwhile, year 12 students in his history class are taught at the conference table in his magnificent, spacious office.

Married with two children, he lives on site; interests include reading history, as well as playing and watching most sports, notably cycling, golf and hockey, the latter of which he coaches at Hockerill. Favours the term principal over head.

Academic matters: One of the most successful comprehensives in the country. In 2015, 47 per cent A*/A grades at GCSE and 91 per cent of pupils got 5+ A*-C grades including maths and English. Also top non-selective state school post-16, with an average IB point core of 36 in 2015 (and 25 per cent obtained 40 plus points) – excellent by any standard.

Part of the DNA of the school is to bookend GCSEs with the IB, with an IB middle years programme that means all pupils continue with a language, arts and technology. Class sizes average around 24, dropping to 18 at sixth form. Setting in English and maths from year 7 and science from year 9. Students expect to (and largely do) work hard and study hard, with Saturday morning school compulsory and plenty of prep (two hours a night by year 10). But this isn't just a school for the academically gifted; it has a wide mix of ability. 'You're not pressurised to get good grades, but you are expected to do your best,' said one student. Another, who has now left to study A levels at an independent school, said, 'Unlike my current school, which is all about teaching you how to get top marks, learning exam techniques, and basically being an alpha student, Hockerill's ethos is that education should be much broader, and I love that I left with so much more than a bunch of qualifications.'

Head claims the biggest change for him was 'coming to a school with a curriculum model I had not seen anywhere else.' Indeed, even in the gilded private sector, you'll be hard pushed to find a school where years 8, 9 and 10 are taught geography and history in either French or German – a programme with 80 per cent participation and which really sets the pace for this truly international school, where languages are genuinely embedded in the curriculum. Seven languages as separate subjects also currently on offer, including Japanese and Mandarin, with less than a handful of students doing fewer than two languages.

Popular orchestras and choirs, with a good balance of classical and modern, of which one parent said: 'You go away with goosebumps because they're just so good'

Truth be told, nothing here is taught in siloes, with students expected to link humanities with languages, languages with art etc. Lots of self-appraisals of work are encouraged throughout the school, especially at sixth form, and teachers are particularly praised for making subjects exciting and offering careers support in their topic area. 'There's a real passion among teachers about preparing us for both university and life beyond university,' said one student.

The college had 15 children with a statement of SEN when we visited, including one wheelchair user, extreme dyslexia and Asperger's, all of whom are dealt with by the SEN co-ordinator, both in and outside the classroom. 'The transition in year 7 was faultless, with the school knowing all about our daughter and her needs before she'd even started,' said one parent, who added, 'The reviews are excellent, the head of SEN is accessible and there's a great emphasis on any extra help being made to be enjoyable.' Meanwhile, the EAL co-ordinator helps the international students who need assistance with language and settling into a different way of teaching. 'We keep abreast of teaching styles in the countries these students come from,' explains head.

Games, options, the arts: The IB requires a mood of involvement and pupils here lap this up, with over 70 popular clubs which run on weekdays from 4-5pm, including fencing, public speaking, knitting and dance. 'Younger students really get stuck in, trying new things out before they find where their interests lie,' said one student. Sport is strong, with girls playing mainly hockey, netball, rounders and athletics, whilst boys are largely drawn to rugby, cricket and football. Fixtures against both state and private schools in all these sports, with the school pulling above its weight, and there's some exceptional individual talent too, with national champions in golf and karate, among others. Facilities are good, with two outdoor courts, a full-size Astroturf pitch, two rugby pitches, two training pitches and a rather tired indoor hall (although there are plans in motion for a new sports hall).

Music, drama and art part of the curriculum until year 10, with music including music technology, and 388 individual musical instrument lessons a week, including the organ (the director of music is an organ scholar). Regular performances from the popular orchestras and choirs, with a good balance of classical and modern, of which one parent said: 'You always go away with goosebumps because they're just so good.' There's a rotating pattern for drama performances – one year, there's a whole school production; the next, there's a dance show; and the next there's an art-based competition. Art and DT boast good facilities and interlinked rooms.

Given the global theme of the school, it will come as no surprise that there are some impressive international trips, including to India and Uganda, as well as language exchanges in years 8, 9, 10 and 12, whilst in school pastimes include Amnesty International and Model United Nations.

Boarding: There are 296 residential boarders, of whom 17 are weekly (from Monday morning to Saturday lunchtimes) and 179 are full-time (seven days a week). Also on offer is a day boarding pupil option, which enables pupils to be dropped off at 7.15am and picked up post-prep at 9pm, a great asset for those living a distance away or working long hours. 'You do everything the boarders do, except actually sleep here,' explained one student.

Year 7s start off in Winchester (girls) and Canterbury (boys). At 13, boys move onto Durham, and at 15, girls move onto Rochester. Rochester takes girls aged 15-16, whilst Roding is for girls aged 15-18 and then there's the pupils' favourite boarding house, Thames, for boys aged 15-18. All the boarding houses (where the teachers also have flats) are world class – bright, well-maintained and welcoming, with all pupils having a study bedroom, sharing until year 12, then winning their own private space in their final year. Regular room inspections ensure pupils keep their belongings tidy, with downstairs reception rooms in Thames boasting polished floors, leather Chesterfields, beautiful fireplaces and large windows, whilst the other more modern boarding houses including comfortable and homely reception rooms.

All boarders are cared for in relaxed manner by housemaster (male or female), some with own family. All meals are in the refectory. Supervised prep sessions for all boarders, as well as plenty of opportunities for clubs and organised activities, events and trips. In fact, boarders enjoy the vibrant lifestyle so much that many choose to hang around even on exeat weekends. School prides itself on constantly evolving its boarding offering according to student feedback, and there are several forums (eg entertainment committee and food committee). Pastoral care praised. 'My eldest was horrendously homesick for a very long time, and the school was brilliant,' said

Given the global theme of the school, it will come as no surprise that there are some impressive international trips, including to India and Uganda, as well as language exchanges

one parent. 'They make sure there's a real sense of community among the boarders,' said another.

Background and atmosphere: Compact and leafy site close to Bishop's Stortford town centre with an attractive mix of arts and crafts, 1930s and contemporary buildings, including a new boarding house. Boarding schools are a relatively rarity in the state system, but this is very much first and foremost a boarding school, with two large senior boarding houses pre-GCSE and another for those entering the sixth form. (Teachers have flats within the boarding houses.) The school's calendar is similar to a conventional independent boarding school, with longer holidays to allow boarders to return home for two weeks at October half term, three weeks at Christmas and nine weeks in the summer. Pupils make good use of the extra time – 'It allowed me to go to China,' said one. Boarding houses are bright and well maintained and all pupils have a study bedroom, sharing till year 12, then winning their own private space in their final year. Classrooms are quiet, teachers politely addressed. Very strong community feel, with everyone getting involved. 'Not just a place to be – a place where you grow up,' said one remarkably mature young man. Strong sense of mutual respect between teachers and pupils: 'Teachers give a lot. We want the knowledge and the teachers help us to learn'.

Pastoral care, well-being and discipline: A traditional but non-denominational school, where teachers are called Sir or Ma'am and everyone has sensible haircuts and wears uniform (blue in the lower school, black and white in the sixth form). Not excessive on school rules, though, with more of an emphasis on expectations of politeness, kindness and punctuality. 'If you set the right tone, you avoid major issues,' says the head, with low level prep-related detentions about as harsh as it has to get on the discipline front. Attendance problems and defiance non-existent, which students attribute to being well aware there are 10 applications for every place. 'There's an ethos that we are fortunate, and with that comes responsibility,' explained one. Incidents of bullying extremely rare, with incidents of unkindness dealt with quickly. Pastoral care is praised.

Pupils and parents: The latest school photo shows mainly white faces, but by no means exclusively, and even those are by no means all English. Indeed, 40 per cent of boarders (who are required to hold an EU passport) come from overseas, with significant numbers from mainland Europe eg Spain, Germany, Italy and France. Twenty-four nationalities altogether. Weekly boarders generally from 1.5 hours travelling radius, whilst day students tend to be local families. Pupils are articulate, mature, friendly and confident, appearing genuinely to enjoy interaction with adults. 'I walk into school, knowing I'll be stopped and asked how I am and that they really mean it,' says head. Certainly no signs of teenage diffidence, where students avoid eye contact. Parents are grateful. Hockerill Parents and Friends Association, which includes both current and former parents, is an active fundraising and social community responsible for changes such as refurbishment of the library and chapel, and which runs staff bids in the summer term which have resulted in eg 3D printers and a camera for sixth form.

Entrance: Eight hundred plus applications from over 60 primary schools for 120 places in year 7. Hertfordshire residents are allowed four choices at year 7, and you can use two of these to apply for both a day and boarding place. Places are allocated on the basis of siblings, language and music aptitude tests, children of staff and distance. For boarders, priority is given to Forces and diplomatic personnel plus future boarding need. Those looking to board are interviewed – away from their parents – to assess how well they would adapt to life away from home. Boarders pay for board and lodgings, but all academic provision is covered by the government. About half of the 130 year 12 places are reserved for boarders.

Exit: Around 40 per cent leave post GCSE, some because they prefer A levels, some because they don't meet the entrance criteria and some because they fancy moving to a sixth form college or other local school. Post IB, over 90 per cent get first choice of university, with around three-quarters to Russell Group universities (Nottingham, Exeter, Edinburgh and Trinity are particularly popular) including six to Oxbridge in 2015. A few to European universities, including Bologna, Bocconi, The Hague, Milan and Rome. 'We get lots of help to apply for universities, both here and overseas,' said one student. Very wide range of subjects – languages, humanities and medics (disproving the myth that IB makes it harder to get into medical school). Pupils would like to see more alumni involvement, and the school and sixth form are working on it.

Money matters: Boarding fees far cheaper than a conventional independent boarding school, stretching from £11,331 per year for weekly boarders (£14,400 in sixth form) to £12,231 for full boarders (£15,330 in sixth form). Day boarding option is £6,036 per year.

Remarks: 'There is no such thing as a typical Hockerill student,' the head girl wrote in a speech she was about to deliver when we visited, and you really do feel variety is the spice of life at this extremely well-run school, where students are encouraged to gain a genuinely holistic education, but with enough opportunity to follow real passions. For students who are willing to knuckle down (and this doesn't necessarily mean they have to be highly academic), this is an exciting and dynamic place to learn and grow up, knocking the socks off many fee-paying schools.

Keswick School

Vicarage Hill, Keswick, Cumbria CA12 5QB

01768 772605
admin@keswick.cumbria.sch.uk
www.keswick.cumbria.sch.uk

Ages: 11–18
Pupils: 1,185; sixth form: 300
Boarders: 48 full, 5 weekly
Day: free
Boarding: £9,576 pa

Headmaster: Since September 2012, Mr Simon Jackson MA (Oxon) MEd FRSA (30s), previously deputy head, only the eighth head in the last 115 years. Educated at the Royal Latin Grammar School in Buckingham and St Catherine's College, Oxford, where he studied biological sciences. Did his PGCE at Wolfson College, Oxford and MEd at University of Gloucestershire. Married with a young family, he is youthful, well-respected, hugely bright and enthusiastic; 'We plough our own furrow here'. He clearly enjoys the freedoms academy status brings and doubtless wouldn't have it any other way. A scientist and outdoorsy type, he commands respect from all and sundry and you can see why – he has a real presence about the place and wraps enormous charm and an intelligent approach to education around it.

Academic matters: Results at GCSE and A level remarkable across the board in view of non-selective comprehensive entry. At GCSE 74 per cent of pupils got 5+ A*-C grades including English and maths in 2015; 25 per cent A*/A grades; English, maths and science do especially well. Unusually, separate sciences taught by specialists to almost all pupils – school has been awarded science specialist status and was rated outstanding in every respect in a recent science survey inspection. Setting in most subjects from year 8, working towards 10 GCSEs as the expected norm. French or German taught in year 7, two languages (or more) for most after that. In 2015, a disappointing 19 per cent A*/A grades at A level, though 60 per cent A*-B. New buildings opened in 2014 allow an increase in the range of A levels on offer. Leadership and volunteering opportunities are encouraged and welcomed to add breadth. A useful Parents' Guide to Home Learning (aka homework) is on the website. Some provision in small department for SEN – other local schools specialise more in this area.

Teaching styles lean towards the traditional. Staff are an interesting bunch ('inspiring people create aspiration,' says head); an unusually high number have had previous professional lives (a doctor, a lawyer, an engineer and a journalist to name but a few) and came to teaching via a road to Damascus moment. Most stay forever – and not just

The jazz band is heading for commercial success; you can even hire them for your wedding. Drama popular, school works closely with the Theatre by the Lake

for the stunning view from the staffroom window. Parents and pupils appreciate staff commitment and teaching quality; school has leading edge status and is a hub for teacher training, attracting interest (and admiration) from far and wide.

Games, options, the arts: Regular successes in sport at county level; all the usual sports on offer, played at a seriously competitive level; 'See you later Sir, we're off to win,' say girls to the head as they set off for a hockey match. Sports fields overlook Derwentwater; large sports hall on site and lots of tennis/netball courts. No swimming pool; the outdoor pool was closed a long time ago due to health and safety legislation, but open water swimming in the lake is surprisingly popular, and for those unafraid of heights, the school even has its own dry ski slope. Professional coaching via links with local sports clubs has enabled talented pupils to excel even further, with former pupils (male and female) now competing successfully at national level.

Music thrives – much instrumental and singing tuition, very successful choir and orchestra and various other ensembles. When we visited school was about to purchase a baby grand piano

for the main entrance for passing pupils to enjoy during break. The jazz band is heading for commercial success; you can even hire them for your wedding. Drama popular, school works closely with the Theatre by the Lake and a week-long 'iPerform festival' is a whole school treat each July.

The John Muir award for conservation is undertaken by everyone; beyond that the surrounding mountains and lakes create a whole realm of opportunities to get seriously wet and/or muddy with canoeing, raft-building, orienteering, sailing, rock-climbing, fell-running, horse-riding, mountain biking and skiing all on offer.

Interestingly, many of the extracurricular clubs and activities are organised and run by the pupils themselves – they can suggest, manage and become the budget holder for clubs should they so wish. One boy is already proving himself to be commercially astute, making money from an app business he runs alongside the computer programming club and his school work. The theatre group and astronomy club allow pupils to experience a world far beyond the Lakes, as do numerous overseas trips and an annual German exchange.

Boarding: Even though the boarders are a small percentage of the whole, it adds a sense of all-round care and helps to shape the ethos; Ofsted recently rated boarding school outcomes and boarding provision as outstanding. Boys and girls occupy separate floors in a shared boarding house; rooms are two, three or four bed and equipped with all the basics, there is a shared common room for younger pupils and a separate one for sixth form. Plenty for boarders to do; there is evening prep with tutors in school followed by a raft of optional activities, trips to the cinema and theatre and organised outings every weekend.

Clearly lots of fun to be had outdoors, but they mean business inside the classroom and pupils get the message early on. Mobile phones are not allowed, unusual but sensible – that said, nobody checks

Originally intended to accommodate children from remote settlements and the Forces, the boarding list is now made up of UK and EU passport holders from all over the world. More boarding provision would be welcomed by both the school and those on the waiting list for places: they could easily triple the size of the boarding house and then fill it overnight.

Background and atmosphere: As old as Cambridge University, though considerably less well known to all but the locally wise, this school has evolved through the centuries to become one of the top comprehensives in the country. Now, as an academy, it is essentially independent in all but name (and fees); the views alone from this place are worth more than any pupil premium. Originally founded mid 14th century by a local vicar, the boarders still attend the church where it all began. Re-founded in 1898 by Victorian pioneer Cecil Grant, who surprised everyone by creating a coeducational school and also opening a sister school in Harpenden. The Queen has visited three times to date; this is a place that attracts much admiration from interested academics and inspectors alike, and is running out of shelf and wall space for the number of cups and national awards it has won over the years.

On the present site since 1996 on the outskirts of town, it is a mix of buildings, old and new, with more planned and approved for the near future – so the builders are a regular feature here. This is an ambitious place; it has so much, yet wants more. Recent additions include new drama theatre, dance studio, recording studio, expansion to sixth form centre, suite of geography classrooms, media suite and additional science laboratory.

Despite the size and space needed to accommodate 1,120 pupils, the teaching site is compact, the music house and sports fields are just a short walk away. Plenty of IT provision; pupils scan in for registration and use of biometrics allows school to be a cash free zone, with lunch and any equipment extras payable directly with parents able to top up from home. Classrooms are attractive and well-resourced and mostly more attractive in than out; the weather can be bleak here and external decor can and does take a hammering. Impressive art and design on display in circulation areas.

The school motto – 'Levavi Oculus – I Lift My Eyes Up' – is taken very literally in your first year here. Part of the induction for the year 7 intake is to climb Skiddaw, which at 932 metres above sea level and the fourth highest mountain in England, is no mean feat. Surely after that nothing at school will ever feel daunting again, but that's the point, school is proud and defiant in its claim that the pupils here 'are not risk-averse'.

Plenty of civic pride about, big on community spirit and strong sense of identity. Locals benefit from a shared use of (some of) the facilities and this, alongside neighbours in close proximity, keeps the school ever mindful of its public image locally, which is no bad thing.

Pastoral care, well-being and discipline: School majors in its 'sense of community' mantra. Lots of talk of 'partnership'; high expectations are made clear from the outset and pupils play ball. It's a large school yet manages a small school feel – you are known here. School claims pupils are self-disciplined but, realistically, they are teenagers and there is a real sense that someone is always watching. Clearly lots of fun to be had outdoors, but they mean business inside the classroom and pupils get the message early on. Mobile phones are not allowed, unusual but sensible – that said, nobody checks, the need to do so hasn't arisen, yet. The pastoral system is straightforward, clear, and appears to work.

Distinctive and traditional green and maroon uniform for all, including sixth form. Smart crested blazer worn proudly by younger pupils, a few shirts hanging out further up the school but most look smart.

No room for complaints about the food; school boasts the national catering manager of the year and lays claim to the best puddings in the country. They also cater for local primaries as well as running four food outlets on site ('it's a bit like M&S,' said one boy).

Pupils and parents: A whole fleet of school buses, plus excellent local transport (Keswick is a good transport hub and therefore more accessible than you might have thought), helps to attract pupils from a very wide area. This brings an unusually broad social intake from right across the Lake District and out to the industrial belt of west Cumbria and beyond. Although most travel by bus, some parents are prepared to drive many miles a day to get here. 'We had a school just down the road,' says one parent, 'but our daughter visited here as a Brownie, remembered it well and knew instantly it was the place for her..and no regrets, it's well worth the drive'.

Pupils are a busy and breezy bunch – focused academically yet still finding the energy to go above and beyond. They might be surrounded by sheep, but no sheep-like behaviour here – there is a big world out there and they aim to play their part and make the most of it. Some three-quarters of the small boarding contingent are from overseas.

Old Keswickians act as mentors to older pupils, providing advice on university and career pathways and bringing a welcome voice of experience to teenage ambitions and aspirations.

Entrance: No entry tests, though asks for recent report from current school, for information but not selection. Preference given to siblings and prospective boarders – who must have an EU/UK passport; preference to Forces families and others living or travelling abroad frequently. Out of catchment day applicants considered on strict basis of distance from school. Many of the feeder primaries are remote village settings and the school works hard on induction days to make new pupils feel welcome – especially important if you are the only one from your school. Further intake into sixth form, minimum requirement of five A*-C grades, including English and maths, with entry requirement of B grades in maths and sciences.

Exit: About 25 per cent leave after GCSE and a further 10-15 after year 12. Ninety per cent of year 13 leavers go on to university, including a handful each year to Oxbridge (five places in 2015); others to eg Durham, Northumbria, Edinburgh, Leeds, Manchester Met, Newcastle and St Andrews.

Money matters: Interestingly, and unusually, scholarships available in biology, geography, music and drama, so do ask.

Remarks: It's an ambitious place – you can take the academics as read, but the adventurous, creative and often entrepreneurial spirit is what gives it the edge. Think of it as Richard Branson meets Bear Grylls with Stephen Hawking thrown in for good luck, and you are some way to finding the heart of the place. And of course, that goes for the female equivalent of those guys too – there's no shortage of female high-flyers, from the girls' rugby team yet to concede a point to a UK champion downhill skier and mountain biker – plenty of impressive girls feature here.

Lancaster Royal Grammar School

East Road, Lancaster, LA1 3EF

01524 580600
theaton@lrgs.org.uk
www.lrgs.org.uk

Ages: 11–18
Pupils: 1,024; sixth form: 310
Boarders: 64 full, 103 weekly
Day: free
Boarding: £9,765 – £10,740 pa

Headmaster: Since 2012, Dr Christopher Pyle MA (Cantab), PhD (Cantab), NPQH (mid 40s). Previously a deputy head at Perse School, Cambridge and before that head of geography there, particular interest glaciers, hydrology and climate change. Briefly a manager at Anglian Water before taking up teaching. Married to Sally, a mathematics teacher at a local school, with three young sons, two of them pupils at the school. Headed north back to roots in the Lakes and lured to LRGS as 'the nearest thing to an independent school'. Parents and pupils comment positively on the visibility of the Head.

He has been churchwarden and PCC member of a large Anglican church. A keen runner, he has also completed the Devizes to Westminster canoe race for charity, and is a fan of the Lakeland fells.

Academic matters: Superb tradition – regularly in top 100 schools nationally at A level; consistently near top of regional table at GCSE; strong value-added results. Perhaps explains why Ofsted data dashboard not a focus for head. Aiming high taken

for granted, as is 'getting stuck in' to support it. In 2015, 48 per cent of A level grades A*/A; 62 per cent of GCSE grades A*/A. Very much the traditional grammar school ethos, challenging boys to fulfil their potential in a competitive environment. Mathematics outstanding, stronger classics than a lot of independents.

Wide choice of subjects at A level and Cambridge Pre-U including classics and philosophy – a third do four A levels, a quarter add on EPQ. An expectation to lead and be involved with the wide range of extracurricular; sport top of the league; CCF and D of E, volunteering – home and away with InspirUS (LRGS outreach gifted and talented programme) and the Erasmus programme.

GCSE: exceptional mathematics results and strong science as might be expected. HPQ (stepping stone to EPQ) recently introduced. Narrow ability range, setting in mathematics, English and French up to GCSE; class size averages 28. Ten GCSEs the norm; all do technology up to GCSE – school historically had technology, languages, mathematics and

computing specialisms. French, German (with annual exchange) and Spanish timetabled, twilight sessions of Mandarin Chinese on offer. Sciences taught separately up to GCSE and all three are popular sixth form options – seen as a 'sciencey' school, says head. Special needs (eg dyslexia, Asperger's) looked after in-house. The especially gifted are stretched by further enhancement schemes and wide-ranging extracurricular provision.

Librarian works closely with English department to encourage reading – using an accelerated reading programme in years 7 and 8, collecting points per book with results published in a league table. IT infrastructure investment so Wifi throughout school but hardware lacking; some netbooks, but BYO not discouraged.

Games, options, the arts: Team games rather than individual sports dominate though increasing opportunity for minority interests that will last a lifetime. Strong rugby and cricket, taken seriously – they beat most independents. Frequent tours – Hong Kong, Australia, Japan and the 'Windies'. An impressive list of other sports, plenty of outdoor pursuits in nearby Lake District and rowing on the Lune leading to some successful pairs at Henley. Much encouragement to join in – no place for couch potatoes.

Music popular; 10 per cent take individual lessons in school practice rooms in the boarding houses. No need for Gareth Malone – choirs popular and everything instrumental from blues to philharmonic on tap. Annual musical drama production in city theatre (often with Lancaster sister school). Very good art and design results.

Frequent tours – Hong Kong, Australia, Japan and the 'Windies'. Plenty of outdoor pursuits in nearby Lake District and rowing on the Lune leading to some success at Henley

An extensive and eclectic range of extra curricular, humorously titled to suit all tastes or none (Texas Hold'em Society?) from Bad Boyz Bakin through Doctor Who Catch Up to PhilThy. These are on top of all the expected sport and fitness, debating, D of E, CCF, expressive and performing arts.

Boarding: Boarding gives the school an edge and identity and attractive facilities have understandably brought a resurgence of interest from 'first generation' boarders, often from the Lakeland valleys. Some 10-12 per cent of boarders in years 7-9, increasing to 20 per cent in year 10; few international boarders. Weekly boarders are the majority but about 60, mainly older boys, are full boarders. Fees for weekly or full boarding are the same so boys have flexibility to stay weekends, often influenced by sports fixtures.

Junior boys have a splendid boarding house with views to die for and a back garden of immaculate cricket pitches with the stunning backdrop of the Ashton Memorial. Dorms are bunk-bedded, cheery, comfortable and well-furnished, with sitting rooms and homely kitchens for tea and toast after school. Seniors have a choice of two houses, School House and Ashton House, each with different character and design. School House is an attractive and well-designed conference centre-style building adjoining a Victorian villa, with some comfortable ensuite single studies alongside relaxed sitting rooms and a modern kitchen, allowing the boys both privacy and companionship as and when required. Ashton House is more traditional, with bigger rooms of up to four beds, but similar recreational spaces and kitchen facilities. The houses exude family atmosphere (with gardens, tree planting and chickens) and the boys speak warmly of collegiality and that this really is 'home from home'.

All the house staff have an academic role and there are now communal study areas in each of the houses for homework, as well as a desk in each of the dorms. Boys are given some freedom (Lancaster is a small city) and there are organised activities most Sundays, whilst Saturdays are taken up with prep and sports fixtures for many.

Catering is considered 'acceptable', no complaints so must be a positive. Dining room has had a recent cosmetic makeover with the addition of rainbow coloured chairs. New Grab and Go café in award nominated new City View building voted a great success by all.

Background and atmosphere: An ancient foundation, in existence by 1235 and endowed in 1472. Moved to its current location in 1852 when Queen Victoria donated £100, hence its 'Royal' tag – and the school still receives the same amount (sadly not index-linked) annually from the Duchy. Took the decision to become an academy in 2011, to provide greater autonomy.

An extensive though fragmented site skirting either side of hilly East Road around a busy crossroad – pedestrian and vehicular. Building styles change from gothic to modern from the lower to upper site, and timetabling can mean crossing two roads between lessons, but boys take it in their stride and 20mph speed limits are enforced. Mixture of Victorian houses and purpose-built blocks in traditional style, leading to newer additions (science and business/design centres, new boarding houses). Parking is tricky but most walk or use public transport.

Though there is some resemblance to its independent competitors, lack of funding is evident in some parts of the school. It doesn't necessarily matter, as the school's focus is rightly on excellent teaching and positive learning outcomes, but it does mean the place can look a touch untidy at the edges. Extensive areas of the Old School House have been de-commissioned but, at last, it seems priority school funding is coming to the rescue, and the head certainly has grand designs for the building.

The houses exude family atmosphere (gardens, tree planting, chickens). Boys speak warmly of collegiality and say that this really is 'home from home'

Real sense of history and tradition about the place: 'Best of the old and the new' is the head's mantra. Boys bustle purposefully between classrooms that range from tired-looking utilitarian to smartly refurbished. Older parents will be reminded of the grammar school of their youth

– 'no-nonsense, no-frills,' says one successful and grateful old boy. An ambitious and exciting 50-year master plan is attracting support from old boys and five years in, there is evidence of some success in the green shoots of improvements.

Pastoral care, well-being and discipline: Boys respond to the no-nonsense direct approach of staff in a school that thoroughly understands them. The school looks to recruit 'schoolmasters' (of either sex) rather than 'teachers'. Thorough care systems for both boarding and day work well – pastoral staff heavily committed to pupils' welfare and relations between boys and teachers admired by parents and inspectors. High personal standards expected. Not much evidence of real wickedness; school suspends for possession and would expel for dealing – and the boys know it.

Boys and parents very proud of school. As one boy put it, 'LRGS is an awesome place to be'. Parents comment that their sons are thriving academically and relishing boarding life

---

Thriving mentor scheme where senior boys spend time with junior boys with similar interests and prefects have weekly tutor time with year 7 helping with pastoral and organisational issues. All the pupils (and parents) we spoke to commented on the sense of community and excellent staff/pupil relationships.

Pupils and parents: Lancaster is a city with a small town feel – boys come from every walk of life and are a very genuine mix. Head says the school is not about one size fits all. 'We take quirky characters who are valued in school and can say that there will be clubs for you'. Still 'the school on the hill' to some, yet no wish for this to become a middle class enclave – rather it is open to any boy, from any street, who can cope with living and working alongside a future Oxbridge don. Local day boys given preference; about 40 places go to those further afield. Boarders come from all over but must be a UK subject or have an EEA passport and a UK guardian (some 18 per cent overseas boarders from 10 countries).

Boys and parents very proud of school and its regional standing. As one boy put it, 'LRGS is an awesome place to be'. Parents comment that their sons are thriving academically and relishing life as a boarder. Old boys include Prof T Hugh

Pennington, microbiologist; Kevin Roberts CNZM, CEO Worldwide Saatchi and Saatchi (retains the link with six summer internships for U6 boys each year); Jason Queally, Olympic cycling champion; Brigadier Alex Birtwistle, foot and mouth star; Tom Sutcliffe, journalist and Sir Richard Owen, dinosaur man.

Entrance: By oversubscribed competitive exam at 11 (English/maths/reasoning). Three strands of entry: local day, regional day, boarding. Boarders considered separately but all 'must be of an aptitude and ability suited to an academic curriculum'. All leave at 16 and then reapply for sixth form places: 'Tell us why we should give you a place here' – great practice for university UCAS or even the real world. Regularly increasing intake at 16 and growing interest from independents for sixth form places – grab a boarding place whilst you still can.

Exit: A few leave after GCSE; vast majority to good universities, mainly in the Midlands and North, eg Durham, Edinburgh, Manchester, Newcastle, Warwick and York, though some dipping a toe into southern universities such as Bristol and Bath. In 2015, eight to Oxbridge – fewer than in recent years.

Remarks: Vibrant, selective grammar school with big reputation in the region; chiefly a day school but also offers excellent boarding provision. Has managed to retain marked degree of independence as an academy, offering a curriculum above and beyond the norm, including classics.

Unashamedly academic but takes all-round education seriously and delivers – recognised by pupils and parents alike. LRGS is a fabulous school which offers a wealth of opportunities to all boys. Besides academic progress, skills and interests are nurtured and developed which adds to the confidence of pupils.

Peter Symonds College

Owens Road, Winchester, Hampshire SO22 6RX

01962 852764	**Ages:** 16–18
psc@psc.ac.uk	**Pupils:** 3,861
www.psc.ac.uk	**Boarders:** 67 full
	Day: free
	Boarding: £12,675 – £13,620 pa

Principal: Since 2013, Mr Stephen Carville. Joined Peter Symonds in 2002 as assistant principal and was promoted to vice principal two years later. Prior to joining Symonds he was an HMI inspector for Ofsted, leading college and area inspections nationally and before that, worked at Barton Peveril College as curriculum manager for business, economics and modern languages. He has been a manager and teacher in other sixth form, tertiary and general FE colleges.

Academic matters: Everything is here, both in terms of subject matter and the full range of human ability, from the star student who became head of the Cambridge Union last year to those who bump along at the bottom with a string of Ds and Es. A level performance on a mega-roll, improving year after year. Exam results outshine many independent schools – 'and we send more students to Oxbridge!' In 2015, 62 per cent A*/B grades and 50 per cent A*/As. The usual wide array of courses one finds at sixth form colleges, includes, eg, photography, film studies and environmental science.

Everyone takes general studies ('It strengthens university applications') and quite a few go for other non-subjects like critical thinking (very good results) and citizenship. A few subjects beam particularly brightly: maths, art, textiles, music, media studies. Some courses are 'victims of their own success' and students have reported that they could not study their first choices. Candidates may have to audition for dance or performing arts.

Numbers are huge – 21 sets for biology. No streaming. Largish class sizes with 15-19 average – sounds overwhelming in theory but seems to work in practice. Less academic students (about 100 of the total) can pursue vocational courses – level 2 BTecs or OCR Nationals in, eg, health and social care or business and finance: 'Much more useful than resitting GCSEs and struggling with A levels'. A few GCSEs on offer for retakes, and good linguists may pick up Italian or Spanish from scratch, taking GCSE on the way to A level in just two years. Those aiming for Oxbridge or competitive courses such as medicine or vet science get additional guidance (with governors roped in to provide interview practice).

Fifteen per cent benefit from some form of learning support including essay planning and self-organisation. Wheelchair access to much of the site ('We don't do badly for a sloping site'). Corridor to learning support centre lined with pictures of successful and famous dyslexics. Lunchtime workshops for those needing extra tuition – at both the top and the bottom ends of the achievement spectrum. Students report all the help they need if they ask for it – but they have to ask for it. Organisational ability is important here – 'it's like going to uni,' said a girl – and indeed PS has now been authorised to offer university courses for those who cannot tear themselves away from the place.

Latest Ofsted report gushingly rated Symonds 'outstanding' across the board.

Games, options, the arts: Strong teams because of its size. Sports hall funded by 'Mercers' money' (loosely part of the Mercers 'cluster' alongside, eg, St Paul's and Abingdon). Lots of grass about the place but the principal dreams of an Astro; however, new sports pavilion now open. Drama strong and an A level in performing arts is offered. A performing arts centre also on the principal's wish list. Brilliant results in art – course said to be very broad: 'almost like a foundation course'. Former fives court enjoying a second life as a photo studio. DT wedged into one large workshop. Students take part in an extracurricular programme (two hours a week) with activities chosen from long list (50+) ranging from Amnesty International to creating the high quality American-style yearbook; knitting particularly hot at the mo. Some of these are accredited, such as the Community Sports Leader award and the Duke of Edinburgh award. Lots of fundraising and local community work.

Fabulous, unique Hampshire specialist music course curiously low profile. Around 12 students a year are selected and study two instruments (free of charge) to a high standard, alongside academic music and two or three further A levels. 'Costs a fortune – we spend three times as much on the music specialists as we do on the other students,' says Mr Hopkins. The course gives the college a solid core of talent, but music spills out over its edges: 140 students are studying music and/or music technology A level. Other music students receive free tuition on their main instrument and can play in a variety of bands, orchestras and choirs.

Boarding: Two boarding houses (girls one floor, boys the other, electric door between). School House is a handsome Victorian building in which students share two to four bedded rooms. Falkland Lodge was opened in 1998: single or twin rooms, all en suite, but it costs more. Feel almost, but not quite, like university halls of residence, with an air of independence, eg boarders do their own laundry,

aside from bedding. Boarding inspection reports rated it 'outstanding'.

Boarders (from 16) may use college's LRC until 8.30pm and the sports facilities are also open three evenings a week. Boarding 'events' take place once every half term but there's not a huge programme of activities. Boarders are given quite a bit of freedom to manage their own time but are expected to be back in their rooms by 10.20pm (11pm weekends); they may stay with friends or have people to stay by prior arrangement.

Background and atmosphere: Peter Symonds founded Christes Hospital (no relation to the Horsham school – it was a 'trendy name' at the time) in the 17th century to look after aged brethren, assist two divinity students and educate four poor boys. Sale of land during the expansion of the railways enabled a boys' grammar school to be built on the current site in 1897, operating first as a boys' independent, then a grammar and finally becoming a co-ed sixth form college in the early 70s. Heads arrive and proceed to make the place their life's work: only six since 1897.

Students socialise in giant departure lounge style common room and sunbathe like seals on Hopkin's Hump, a little knoll named after former head, Neil Hopkins

An intense conurbation perched on a hilly spot overlooking the suburbs of Winchester. Original late Victorian building now completely surrounded by dedicated buildings purpose-built in the last 10 years, including newish cavernous learning and resources centre (library plus). Everything being used to full capacity – jam-packed with strapping youths. Students socialise in giant departure lounge style common-room and sunbathe like seals on Hopkin's Hump, a little knoll named after former head, Neil Hopkins. Large canteen plus satellites provide cheap and plentiful food. No uniform (style leans to grungy rather than trendy), teachers called by their first names, 55 minute lessons, no bells: really a halfway house between school and university.

Pastoral care, well-being and discipline: Sanctions minimal, although a zero tolerance policy on drugs and alcohol on site and smoking is not permitted except in one small fenced off area outdoors. 'Six or seven' students expelled most years – more common for them to leave 'by mutual consent'. Most common reason is 'laziness'; the occasional drugs bust. Full time counsellors available for personal matters.

Pupils and parents: Fifty per cent from the three Winchester 11-16 schools – Kings, Westgate and Henry Beaufort. Perins in Alresford tops the long list of other feeder schools. A further 15-20 per cent from independent schools and the rest from far and wide – Reading, Salisbury and the Isle of Wight included. Student social profile directly reflects Winchester skew towards ambitious middle classes – one teacher remarked, 'Nothing as formidable as a Winchester mother protecting her young'. Former pupils include comedian Jack Dee, Olympic gold medallists Ben Ainsley and Iain Percy, Coldplay drummer William Champion, 'Page 3 girl' Lucy Pinder.

Entrance: 1,600 pupils pile into the school at 16. Deadline for application is December. Non-selective, but requirement for A level courses is at least five grade Cs at GCSE level, 'ideally' including maths and English. Maths and science are exceptions – you need a B. Every applicant is interviewed. Vastly oversubscribed – local pupils automatically get in; beyond that pupils are accepted geographically in concentric circles radiating out from Winchester. Exceptions made for musicians, boarders and students from a windswept corner of the South Atlantic (has the honour of being the official sixth form of the Falkland Islands – construction of Falkland Lodge boarding house was partly funded by the Falklands government). Candidates for the Hampshire specialist music course audition in February/March on two instruments, one of which should be at grade 7/8 standard.

Exit: Some 85 per cent to universities of all descriptions. Forty-one to Oxbridge in 2015 and over a third to Russell Group. Students on the music course frequently move on to the top music colleges.

Invited by Cambridge University to act as a regional hub as part of its HE+ initiative. This involves providing extension classes for its own and other local sixth formers and helping with applications to the most selective universities.

Money matters: Sixth form colleges receive less money per pupil than normal schools so the management employs meticulous budgeting, plus a dash of sorcery, to keep the whole shebang on the road. Hardship fund available. Students compete for several bursaries each year for gap year projects.

Remarks: A huge, friendly metropolis which falls neatly between school and university in approach. Most people would be happy here, but not those who need spoon-feeding.

Polam Hall School

Grange Road, Darlington, County Durham DL1 5PA

01325 463383
information@polamhall.com
www.polamhall.com

Ages: 11–19
Pupils: 150: 95 girls/55 boys; sixth form: 27
Boarders: 43
Day: free
Boarding: £10,200 pa

Headmaster: Since 2011, Mr J R Moreland MA (Oxon) PGCE NPQH (50s). Educated at Huddersfield New College (then grammar school) and then modern history degree from St Edmund Hall, Oxford. Previously headmaster of Bury Lawn School, Milton Keynes; housemaster, head of history and assistant head Rugby School; taught history at Epsom College, started teaching life with history, geography and politics at Watford Boys' Grammar.

Played rugby, basketball and athletics at school and university (a double Oxford Blue). Holds Northern Ireland record for the discus and now competes in masters championships, currently British champion. Teaches history, coaches and huge supporter of school sport. Believes in leading by example – for Sport Relief competed again a relay of pupils running a mile by throwing a combo of discus and wellies the equivalent distance – and won! Fifty-one times in 4 minutes 10 seconds – for the record.

His wife, Alison, is a teacher and they have one adult son. Enjoys walking, reading, cinema. Keen to see 'pupils add to their skills and competencies, build on their talents and exploit opportunities in preparation for careers that currently do not exist'. Introducing challenge-based learning experiences; problem-solving in teams to find collaborative learning solutions. A brave new world for the seniors.

Also developing ICT in the school – encouraging pupils to make the most of personally owned smart phones and other mobile devices. Seeking to increase the number of boys and widen the international flavour in boarding as school grows to fully co-educational model – 'a 10 year plan'.

Academic matters: Non-selective intake – diagnostic tests to assess level of attainment for setting purposes only. Some 20 per cent of pupils on SEN register. In that context A level and GCSE results good, with 22 per cent A*/A and 51 per cent A*-B at A level in 2015, and 32 per cent A*/A at GCSE; 67 per cent of pupils got 5+ A*-C GCSE grades including English and maths.

Pupils expected to work hard, with non-high flyers achieving beyond expectations in all areas; art, music and drama vibrant and popular; physics and chemistry labs fully refurbished; ICT much in evidence; comprehensive range of A level subjects for size of school.

Broad curriculum with French from year 7 and opportunities for German and Spanish from year 8. Sciences taught separately and with specialists from year 9. Mathematics and French set from year 7, science and English from year 10. IGCSE English. Small groups at A level, average five per subject; some one-to-one, thus losing group dynamic.

New emphasis on developing pupils' skills and competencies needed 'to think outside the box'. Introducing 'Kangaroo Days' of problem-solving, team-building and challenge-based learning. Big push with ICT, embracing mobile technology and encouraging pupils to use free online software to hone their research and presentation skills. Students incentivised by collaborative learning competition which involves whole school community, pupils, staff and parents, in professionally-run training sessions.

Accommodation homely, clean and comfortable with three and four bedded rooms the norm and shared rooms even in sixth form. Warm and caring house staff

Very modest about their SEN provision, saying, 'We strive to support effectively our pupils with special needs, but we do not wish to present ourselves as experts in the field'. Difficulties range from dyslexia, dyspraxia and dysgraphia to Asperger's and autism. Support is provided using a range of educational programmes, one-to-one teaching, assistants to support in class, reduced timetables, focused study support, mentoring, differentiation in class and bringing in outside specialists.

Games, options, the arts: Netball, swimming, cross-country, tennis, athletics all popular. Cricket, football and rugby (emerging) for the boys and mixed hockey. Fixtures against local schools and independent schools further afield. Good level of sports for the boys but would suggest not enough yet for those sports-driven and hyper-competitive.

Attractive playing fields, courts, new dance studio and sports hall on school premises; range of indoor sports activities and clubs; a national swimmer and a member of the England equestrian team. Recent major sports tours to Canada and Gibraltar.

Music through to A level; 30 per cent play a musical instrument; plenty of opportunities to perform from termly music concerts; intimate 'coffee' concerts held in the music centre to showcase developing talent. Purpose-built theatre with big summer production eg West Side Story. Curriculum drama through to A level.

Duke of Edinburgh Award operating with sustained success at all levels. Fledgling CCF – in early stages. Extended view of the world encouraged with inspirational speakers, annual overseas visits, World Challenge to Malawi. Orienteering – pre-drive schemes and Young Enterprise for sixth formers.

Boarding: Boarding facilities upgraded a few years ago. Accommodation homely, clean and comfortable with three and four bedded rooms the norm and shared rooms even in sixth form. Warm and caring house staff; boarders have freedom of grounds for relaxation with limited access off-site (depending on age), logging themselves in and out. Regular organised activities at weekends.

Boarders elect a leadership team of head boarder, assistant head boarder(s) and two heads of house who work closely with the staff to ensure the smooth running of the boarding community. Good preparation for life after school. The boarding council has representatives of all age groups and meets regularly. An Independent Listener is available to all boarding students.

Background and atmosphere: Founded in 1848 by Quakers sisters for young Quaker ladies paying 50 guineas a year. In 1854 school moved to Polam

Hall, a Georgian mansion set in 19 acres of parkland, close to the town centre, with a history of sharing its grounds with the people of Darlington. Descendants of founding families still represented on governing body and school remains true to its Quaker roots. The sense of a shared, warm, caring community is evident throughout the school.

Tight, cohesive site including main school, junior school and boarding houses, with a number of newer additions to original school house. Residential on three sides, attractive open parkland adjoining school grounds on other side lends a feeling of open space.

Pupils take responsibility as form representatives or house captains. House system with competitions in music, drama, sport and orienteering. Before and after-school care, and homework clubs

Recent changes to main entrance hall replaced museum pieces of school history with brightly lit display cabinets of pupils' work and an arresting contemporary wall hanging above the main staircase, symbolising changes afoot at this school.

Boys in school since 2010 with closure of boys' school Hurworth House. Brief flirtation with diamond model but since 2012 fully co-educational. Parents we spoke to were fully supportive of the change and 'feel the school is moving in the right direction', though some have been lured by all girls' offering in Durham or good, local state co-educational. Now a free school, charging only for boarding.

Core of long-established, experienced teachers with more recent injection of new blood; average age 48. Mutually supportive, spirit of goodwill – 'working together for the good of the whole' encouraged by collaborative leadership style.

Pastoral care, well-being and discipline: Few formal rules but very clear guidelines as to sanctions; high standards of courtesy and behaviour expected and delivered, based on respect for self and others. Strong anti-bullying policy; serious misconduct extremely rare. Head says, 'staff care about school' and 'work closely with pupils to provide support for them'. Peer mentoring recently introduced though size of school enables friendships across age groups.

Regular assemblies ('Readings') reflecting Quaker foundations; awareness of the wider world and strong spirit of generosity. Successful

and enthusiastic fundraising for charities, in conjunction with Interact, Junior Rotary. Active school council produces manifestos and contributes to relevant decision-making throughout school.

Pupils willing to take responsibility as form representatives or house captains. House system with inter-house competition in music, drama, sport and orienteering. Before and after-school care, and homework clubs. Pupils can arrive at school at 8am, breakfast in the dining room and stay up to 7pm in the evening, with tea.

Pupils and parents: A broad cross-section of abilities, backgrounds and cultures here in a community that welcomes diversity. A changing profile with 25 per cent (and increasing) of pupils from overseas, mainly from year 10 onwards. A number of Forces boarders too. Pupils are friendly, remarkably modest about their achievements and down to earth, reflecting the honest, unpretentious character of this northern school.

Parents a mixture of urban and rural, first-time buyers and second and third generation Polamites. Strong Parents' Association organising free events for parent body. Parents' focus group presents views/perspectives to head. Notable old girls Nadine Bell, NASA scientist; Ruth Gemmell, actress.

Entrance: For day children, preference to those with an EHC plan naming the school, then looked after children. Then 20 per cent of places to pupil premium and Forces children. After that, 60 per cent to those living in DL1 or DL3 postcodes, remainder to those living outside these areas.

Boarding places offered after interview to ascertain suitability to board. Preference, again, to those with an EHC plan and looked after children, Forces children and then with a 'boarding need' eg parents living overseas or in a remote rural location, or difficult home circumstances.

For sixth form, everyone – internal and external – must have at least six GCSEs at C+, including English and maths, and generally at least B in A level subjects.

Exit: Varying numbers depart post-GCSE (half in 2015) – to local sixth form college or co-ed boarding schools. Students go on to a wide range of universities and courses; small number to Oxbridge. Destinations in 2015 included Newcastle, Southampton, Lancaster, Derby and King's College London.

Money matters: Now a state day and boarding school, with fees only for boarding.

Remarks: Warm, welcoming atmosphere emanates from busy pupils at work and play, supported and encouraged to do well by their teachers. Intent on providing pupils with skills, competencies and technological knowledge to 'future proof' them for life in 21st century. Winds of change blowing over Polam Hall as it becomes a free school, but still remaining true to its Quaker roots.

Queen Victoria School

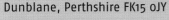

Dunblane, Perthshire FK15 0JY

01786 822288
enquiries@qvs.org.uk
www.qvs.org.uk

Ages: 10–18
Pupils: 265; sixth form: 30
Boarders: all full from Forces families
Boarding: Funded by the MOD but a parental contribution is expected for some expenses.

Head: Since 2007, Mrs Wendy Bellars MA PGCE (late 40s), born and educated in Glasgow. With an English mother and Scottish father, holidays with relatives in Somerset and Thurso were the norm, so it was only when she moved to England (for work) and north Wales (to live) in 1988 that the real cultural differences dawned on her.

She taught English in Renfrew High School for two years, then moved to Gordonstoun. Since then she has taught in virtually every type of school – day, boarding, independent, state, mixed and single sex (both girls and boys) in a variety of roles, including a spell as head of St Leonards in Fife when it was undergoing cataclysmic change, and as a housemistress at Cheltenham Ladies' College. She returned to Scotland in 2004/5 and worked for the Open University, developing the then new to Scotland OU PGCE etc.

She has been involved with ATC and CCF cadets and held a 10-year Volunteer Reserve Commission in the Royal Air Force. Theatre, reading and walking two large pupil-friendly dogs – sweeping long-skirted with an elegant greyhound reminiscent of 19th century paintings – occupy her leisure.

As an enthusiast for both playing and listening to music, one of her dreams for the school is to extend its fantastic tradition in military music to a wider field and to establish a full orchestra. She and QV seem to be on duck and water terms: she exudes deep and knowledgeable concern about the minutest aspect of school life, bringing a wealth of relevant and well-balanced experience.

Academic matters: A very firmly Scottish school using only the Scottish curriculum. Forces children often find themselves moving from school to school – the known record is 11 and the average four or five – so P7 (approximately half way between top primary and first year secondary in English terms) is used to assess and consolidate. The very occasional pupil may have to repeat a year at this stage. After the entry year spent consolidating in three streams (red, green and blue) carefully not labelled by ability, pupils are setted (by ability) for maths, English and sciences. Curriculum is trad but flexible, classes not more than 20. Down to earth labs (new ones on the way as part of a complete classroom rebuild planned by the MoD for the middle term future) and lots of computers in class and available in houses at night, including impressive Macs for the enterprising art department (better for photography and image manipulation).

Learning support flexible and pupils say 'really supportive', with in-class help, withdrawal, extra tuition in groups or one-to-one etc as appropriate. Good rapport between SEN and teachers. School prides itself on 'holistic' education but results hard to obtain. Though wholly MoD funded, QV competes and compares with independent rather than state schools in style (both academic and pastoral).

Pipe band has played for every home rugby international since 1922, until last year's ban (health and safety). QV pipes, drums and dancers renowned throughout Scotland and perform in Edinburgh military tattoo and all over the world

Games, options, the arts: Games staff assert proudly that as a small school QV 'punches above its weight' in both girls' and boys' sports. Football, rugby, hockey, netball and athletics strong, tennis less so. Spacious terraced pitches, huge multi-purpose sports hall with free access to smashing fitness training for older pupils and ancient but serviceable swimming pool often on loan to neighbouring primaries.

Military music is king of the activities curriculum. The pipe band has played for every home rugby international since 1922, until last year's ban on health and safety grounds. QV pipes, drums and dancers (PDD) are renowned throughout Scotland and perform in the Edinburgh military tattoo and all over the world. Every pupil must learn one PDD skill. Marching is also compulsory and during our visit pupils joining after S2 (year 10) were doing

daily catch up marching practice. The head girl reckoned that her brother's role of drum major was as iconic as her own. Pupils said that almost everyone enjoyed and felt a sense of pride in the military identity the school gives them. Masses of tours abroad, mainly with band but also recently to Malawi on a school building project.

Pupils choose own charities and recently raised £1,700 for Help for Heroes, as well as doing a sponsored walk to help themselves (the school development fund). About 80 clubs in all, ranging from skiing to jewellery making and some participation is compulsory. CCF plays a strong part with units for all three forces – myriad activities extending into holiday time and D of E is much in evidence. The friendly dogginess of school, spearheaded by Mrs Bellars' Dash and Ginger, is highlighted by girls doing D of E service at a stray dogs' home and completed by Molly, the IT department dog.

Boarding: Full boarding, seven days a week for all, though weekend leave is allowed, except for parade days. The more recent boarding accommodation is well thought out and comfortable. Two houses for boys and one for girls, plus one co-ed junior house (Trenchard). A particularly telling touch there – the common room with clocks showing the time in Afghanistan and Iraq. Older pupils volunteer to spend a term or so in Trenchard to act as mentors for new arrivals. Sixteen and over can visit cinemas etc in relatively sleepy Dunblane.

Background and atmosphere: With a mission 'to provide stable and uninterrupted education for the children of Scottish service personnel', has to balance an imposing site steeped in military history with the need for a 'home from home' environment for children with parents on inaccessible active service. Founded by public subscription as a memorial to Scots who fell in the South African wars, has been co-ed since 1996. The magnificent chapel is dedicated to Queen Victoria and its splendour, enhanced by modern audiovisual equipment and comfy seats, typifies emphasis placed on service to queen and country. Pupils confirmed that this gives most of them a sense of purpose and identity. The school chaplain cares for all denominations though children can go to Dunblane for mass etc.

The granite cliff of a main building, opened by Edward VII in 1908, is maintained, like everything else on site, by the MoD – hence the brilliantly polished but battered floors, doors etc. Public gifts from, for example the MacRobert Trust, have provided a smashing and recently refurbished, up to date and very fully used library, plus (much earlier) pool and sports hall. The accretion of buildings,

each in the style of the current MoD (War Office), has made a hotchpotch of buildings over the years.

The development fund has taken over from the centenary appeal. Its planned new theatre/auditorium had to be abandoned because MoD requirements were escalating the expense. Priority is now a major upgrade of the existing theatre, still hidden under wraps/tin hats.

The friendly dogginess of school, spearheaded by Mrs Bellars' Dash and Ginger, is highlighted by girls doing D of E service at a stray dogs' home and completed by Molly, the IT department dog

The san, shiny with new pastel paint and a 'chill out area' complete with relaxation tapes, candles and every kind of health information leaflet, retains its 'hospital ward' since QV, unlike other boarding schools, cannot ship pupils home at the first sign of an epidemic. Efficient looking bedsteads sport teddies and pretty bedspreads. Someone was in for a bit of space and motherly care on the day we visited.

One of the few schools where pupils really do look smart and seem to enjoy it. Formal dress is real military red, high collared jackets, with hunting Stewart kilts and Lovat tweed for everyday, plus some fantastic ceremonial gear – nylon bearskins and the like. MoD supplies, so cost not a problem.

Food looks good; no one complained though not all were entirely complimentary.

Pastoral care, well-being and discipline: Not many real problems bar the occasional smoker and, 'surprisingly', no drugs. Very structured disciplinary system including categories of offences, a behaviour management group and punishments such as litter picking days or clearing tables. Strong PSE and careful discussion of problems – medical services much involved here. Observable loving attention to the real underlying needs of children away from home underpins pastoral care – impressive. Pupils claimed to like the training of a military style discipline ('teaches you how to manage your things') but evidently also enjoyed a bit of teenage squalor in their bedrooms without undue interference.

Pupils and parents: By definition, parents are serving members of Scottish Forces or are/have been stationed in Scotland (eg Ghurkas in Glasgow). Founded for NCOs, but officers' children are eligible, so a real mixed bag. Oddly the MoD don't fund a past pupils' database but voluntary help is starting this – with a huge reservoir of Scottish history to tap. Strong parent network and generations of same families. Liaison group welcomes new families and supports children. No guardian system needed because most have relatives or close colleagues ready to help.

Entrance: Applications deadline 15 January and admissions board sits in Feb/March. School is full but tries to keep a few places for emergency postings/compassionate need etc. Purpose is to take orphans and needy (in that order) and parents meet the high powered, but 'not too scary', admissions panel, while children are assessed for academic and emotional suitability. Mrs Bellars wonders if info on the school actually reaches those who most need it.

Exit: Increasing percentage to university (now about 50 per cent) though still low in view of its academic record. A few go straight into the Forces. Others to local colleges or nursing. Most have a gap year. No notice required since MoD posts are instantaneous.

Money matters: Places are funded by the MOD if you meet the eligibility criteria, but a 'parental contribution' is expected (to cover cost of travel, activities etc). Details of the parental contribution are available from the admissions secretary.

Remarks: Thriving – an amazing opportunity for those who qualify.

Ripon Grammar School

Clotherholme Road, Ripon, North Yorkshire HG4 2DG

01765 602647
admin@ripongrammar.co.uk
www.ripongrammar.co.uk

Ages: 11–18
Pupils: 860; sixth form: 260
Boarders: 70, nearly all weekly
Day: free
Boarding: £9,300 – £10,745 pa

Headmaster: Since 2004, Mr Martin Pearman (pronounced Pierman) MA (mid 50s). Read chemistry at Oxford, taught previously at Bristol GS, Merchiston Castle, Stamford and Woodhouse Grove, where he was deputy head. Three sons, all attended his school. Staff positive about their head and his method of gradual, thoughtful change. 'It's the atmosphere in this school which sets it apart', he told us. 'The quality of relationships between staff and students is better than in any school I've worked in'. Parents like that the head is very evident in school and approachable – some sixth form chemistry teaching.

A very approachable, unpretentious man, who brings a wide experience of schools and a clear vision of his school's purpose which is 'to serve the local community with a high quality education,

increasing the life chances of ordinary boys and girls'. Believes passionately that 'pieces of paper are only part of what makes you' and that time at school is for learning to deal with failure as well as success.

Keen sportsman – cricket, five-a-side and half marathons. Inspired to run London Marathon for a charity that provides outdoor activities for people with disabilities, after a pupil broke her back in a cycling accident. Wife, Fiona, very involved with PTA.

Academic matters: Exam results consistently very good – 74 per cent A*-B at A level in 2015, 48 per cent A*/A grades, with girls just outperforming boys, though boys pipped them with A* grades. STEM subjects unsurprisingly strong – roughly equal numbers of girls and boys take chemistry

Big band performs frequently in Ripon Cathedral, even entertained the Queen. Vocalists can join one of three choirs. Annual drama production and joint musical production on alternate years

and mathematics, though physics remains a male stronghold with school working hard to change this.

Some 30 per cent take up of EPQ; good range of enrichment and community activities; pupil-led societies with weekly guest speakers. Well-drilled programme of support and encouragement for Oxbridge candidates. Strong careers and higher education advice with a week's work experience for all in year 12.

Elsewhere some evidence of girl-dominated subjects – for example in art (turning STEM to STEAM), English literature and French, compulsory at GCSE. Latin, classics, psychology, PE also available. German, though declining in many schools, still on offer, and Latin, originally started as a twilight subject, appearing by popular demand at GCSE and A level. Ancient Greek offered as an extracurricular subject at GCSE.

Sixty-three per cent A/A* at GCSE; mirroring national trend girls outperformed boys at these top grades and, better still, matched boys in mathematics. Engineering specialism has brought astronomy,

statistics and product design into the GCSE curriculum. Complete lab refurbishment in recent years.

Only setting in mathematics and French from year 8. Cross-curricular themed challenge days, off-timetable, set for years 7, 8 and 9 provide opportunities for leadership, teamwork and problem-solving, working with external advisers. Lays the groundwork for later success as regional finalists in Young Enterprise and Prince's Trust competitions.

School does a very fine job over value-added; near the top of the tree nationally. RGS is not as highly selective as some grammar schools in, for instance, Kent and Essex, being unable to draw pupils in great numbers from outside its defined catchment area.

SEN support very good – oversees provision for, eg, visual and hearing impairment and a range of special needs. In addition learning resource manager works with SENCo on intervention strategies. Paired reading with sixth formers in assembly time set up for those identified by on-line literacy assessment.

Games, options, the arts: Compulsory sport: rugby and cricket mainstay for boys, hockey for girls. Football popular for both sexes – girls have been Yorkshire junior champions – also mixed hockey, badminton, rock climbing, dance and swimming in newly refurbished swimming pool. Good representation at area and regional level in range of sports, including national U14 netball finalists. Excellent facilities, new Astroturf and sports hall paid for by independent fundraising campaign, available for local use too.

Music block plus performing arts facility in the new sixth form centre. Lots of enthusiastic musicians – over 100 receive tuition in school. Big band performs frequently in Ripon Cathedral, even entertained the Queen. Vocalists encouraged to join one of the three choirs. Annual drama production and joint musical production on alternate years.

Superb art on display. Visiting artists augment strong teaching team, most recently famous comic strip illustrator.

Lots of out of the classroom experiences to be had. Duke of Edinburgh, biennial World Challenge, revived music tour in Belgium, Barcelona trip for Spanish speakers, art trips to London and Paris, as well as the more local curriculum enriching visits.

Over 90 different clubs and activities on offer, ranging from the Greenpower electric car, Pageturner bookclub to philosophy – something for even the most reluctant sportsman or woman to get involved in. Pupils encouraged to take the initiative to set up and run activities and clubs. Annual charity week is just one example, sixth form led it encompasses a diverse number of activities raising money for the school's chosen charities.

Boarding: Boys' boarding house, School, is integral and has had a makeover in recent years, met with considerable approval by boarders. Light and spacious rooms, beds not bunks, a relaxed and positive environment for down time and study. Bit of a maze but the character of the building endears itself to its occupants. Johnson, girls' boarding house, recently expanded, with single rooms for some sixth formers – long overdue, by some accounts.

This is a day school with boarding, predominantly weekly boarding; pupils come from North Yorkshire and beyond, a minority from India, Africa, Caribbean and China. Boarders (room for

This is a can do, will do school – pupils talk of friendly rivalry, pushing each other to achieve. Strong protestations from both girls and boys on question of true equality: 'not an issue here'

100 out of 800+) do well academically and the very few in residence over the weekends are well catered for. Good relationships with day pupils extend into informal joint weekend activities and membership of local groups and clubs. Demand for boarding places (14 available a year) outstrips supply, especially post-GCSE, with lots of interest in girls' boarding.

Boarders have a personal tutor and are in mixed age tutor groups. As majority of boarding staff are teachers, 'boarders are very well known as individuals'. Slightly at odds, the head of boarding (also deputy head) does not sleep over, maybe losing an opportunity to feel the vibes from the girls in Johnson.

Background and atmosphere: Long pedigree; there's been a grammar school in Ripon since Anglo Saxon times. School originally housed in city centre and current foundation granted a royal charter by Queen Mary in 1555. Moved to present green and pleasant 23-acre site in 1874, gift from Marquess of Ripon. Original Victorian buildings added to over the years, not always sympathetically, but more recent additions: sports hall, sixth form centre, mathematics and engineering block, state-of-the-art music facilities, observatory and girls' boarding house bring more gravitas to the school façade. The most recent addition, a humanities and modern languages block, opened in 2014.

School has remained true to North Yorkshire LA and eschewed academy status.

There is an air of purposefulness in the school; a quiet hum from classrooms and sensible movement between lessons. High profile house system in the day school involves all pupils and offers leadership opportunities. Competition in sport, rock climbing, debating, Masterchef, University Challenge and house drama competition.

Pastoral care, well-being and discipline: Very good pastoral system in operation; in addition, pupils look after each other, 'very collegiate', as one parent put it. Sixth formers are trained as peer listeners and teams of form tutors ably support heads of school. Newcomers to sixth form are 'buddied' with existing pupils to ease integration.

School says pupils interact well and both poor behaviour and exclusions are rare. At worst, usually sorted by after school detention. Genuinely good relations between staff and students throughout the school; friendly and compassionate house staff create a relaxed boarding environment. Pupils and parents cannot speak highly enough of staff, their commitment and willingness to go 'above and beyond'.

Any bullying 'stamped on' and internet safety policy written by pupils, wired into PCSHE and teaching programmes.

Pupils and parents: Boarders from abroad, Yorkshire Dales and London, some from Forces, day pupils from Ripon and around. Wide range of parental backgrounds and wealth (or lack of it) though only a handful eligible for free school meals, with significant effect on pupil annual grant income. Parents feel well informed on their child's progress with regular reports three times a year and an annual parents' evening. School contact is primarily email and parents like that the termly newsletter and new sports magazine have content provided by the pupils. Very supportive PTA.

Pupils friendly, courteous, articulate and insightful; confident not arrogant, with a real pride in their school. Lots of heads up, eye contact and smiles as you walk around. This is a can do, will do school – pupils talk of friendly rivalry, pushing each other to achieve. Strong protestations from both girls and boys on question of true equality: 'not an issue here'. On election of school officers, 'it's the best person for the job every time'.

Former pupils include fashion designer Bruce Oldfield, rugby international Peter Squires, William Hague MP, David Curry MP, Guardian editor Katharine Viner, TV presenter Richard Hammond.

Entrance: Mainly from local primaries but a smattering from prep schools, about 40 schools in total. Heavily oversubscribed at 11+. Selection by verbal and non-verbal reasoning tests administered by local authority; school takes top 28 per cent of cohort.

Sixth form – around 140 external applicants for approximately 30 places for students from other schools. Numbers applying increasing. Sixth form requires minimum six B grades at GCSE but vast majority comfortably exceed this, achieving mainly A*/A grades.

Exit: About 15 per cent leavers at 16+. At 18 most progress to university – many to Russell Group or 1994 Group and some to Oxbridge (six in 2015). Medicine, sciences, engineering popular, also art, law and economics. University destinations include Newcastle, Manchester, Edinburgh, Sheffield, Durham and a number lured to London. Excellent careers advice has meant leading apprenticeships for students considering alternatives to university.

Money matters: Yorkshire's only state boarding school, free for day pupils, charge for boarding, but still much cheaper than independent alternatives.

Remarks: High achieving without being highly pressurised, with learning and life skill opportunities going beyond exam syllabuses. Aims to provide a blend of tradition – academic rigour and high expectations – with innovation – up-to-date technology and opportunities for the development of the whole person – and does it well. Parents have utter confidence that whatever their child's talents the school will help them to make the best of them. Keen to serve its community and clearly valued by the people of Ripon.

The Royal Grammar School, High Wycombe

Amersham Road, High Wycombe, Buckinghamshire HP13 6QT

01494 524955
admin@rgshw.com
www.rgshw.com

Ages: 11–18
Pupils: 1,370; sixth form: 400
Boarders: 14 full, 40 weekly
Day: free (day boarding £4,500 pa)
Boarding: £12,450 – £14,031 pa

Headmaster: Since September 2015, Philip Wayne, previously head of Chesham Grammar. He studied at Manchester University and the Royal Northern College of Music. Following a number of years as a freelance organist, pianist, conductor and lecturer, he qualified as a teacher and held several leadership posts in the Midlands. He moved to Buckinghamshire in 2004 as deputy head of John Hampden Grammar and became head of CGS in 2007. He is married with twins.

Academic matters: Consistently delivers a good showing in national league tables for academics, although still snaps at the heels of the area's top performing grammar when it comes to hard exam data. Local competition is very stiff but school proves itself a real all-rounder at GCSE with 68 per cent of GCSEs graded A/A* in 2015. Seventy-eight per cent of A levels achieved grades A*-B and 51 per cent A*/A in 2015.

Boys take an average of 10 or 11 GCSEs, with about 60 per cent taking four subjects at A2 level. Brainboxes can take more (one boy took seven a few years ago, achieving A* in all of them) but the school only encourages this in exceptional circumstances. Good range of subjects on offer at GCSE,

---

'Stunning' performance of Les Misérables with local girls' schools. Check it out on YouTube for instant goosebumps

---

including Latin and Greek, with French compulsory and a large take-up of geography, history, Spanish and German. Sciences, economics and maths highly popular at A level. Languages 'really excellent' according to pupils and parents, with Italian, Mandarin and Japanese all available either on or off curriculum.

Six classes of 32 in each year group with setting in maths and French starting from year 9. School 'goes in heavy with homework from the word go',

according to parents, with at least three 30 minute pieces per night, but boys seem to take this in their stride – as they do the rigorous tests they take after every topic. The minority of pupils joining from prep schools (about 25 per cent) 'can coast a bit' in year 7 say parents, and the uplift in recent years in children from non-English speaking homes presents some challenges for teachers initially, but by the time the heat is turned up in year 10 things are reportedly pretty equal across the board.

Cutting edge technology not widely used across the board of subjects, although iPads are starting to creep in, but parents say the VLE is 'great – and genuinely useful', particularly when it comes to revision. Geography department is trialling virtual lessons to be taken at home over the VLE then followed up with practical discussion and development in class.

Games, options, the arts: Sport, sport and more sport for those so inclined, with rugby leading the charge as a year-round occupation. When the rugby league season finishes, top players continue to play rugby union – and to a very high standard, with the under 12 rugby league team going to Wembley to compete in the finals of the Carnegie Champion Schools tournament recently. No football ('we get used to it quickly', say boys), but hockey and cricket are main sports and taught to a high standard by the 'inspirational' games teachers, although a few parents grumble they don't get the same quality fixtures or kudos as the rugby teams. Sighs of relief from some non-rugby parents though as it's a 'major commitment' with training five times a week and fixtures most weekends in season.

A-D teams in junior school take on – and frequently beat – schools such as Wellington, Marlborough and Harrow as well as their local grammar peers and recently vanquished Charterhouse at Eton fives, despite only having played the sport for two years. Although parents consistently equate sports here with rugby, there really is something for everyone, whether it's rowing, fencing, swimming or tennis. Just don't expect the same hero status in the playground.

Thursday afternoon activities (TAA) allow boys to choose from a vast array of sporting or academic enrichment activities ranging from Japanese or Mandarin to eco army. This is in addition to after-school activities and indulges boys' passions for more marginal activities like climbing (the school boasts an impressive 40ft climbing wall in main sports hall) and astronomy or endeavours like the 'Caterham project', which sees year 13s building a car from scratch. CCF is also extremely popular from year 10 and 'offers huge leadership opportunities', says head.

Music 'really, really strong', according to parents. A quarter of boys learn one or more instruments – 'they all play about three these days', according to head – and about 180 turning up on a weekly basis to participate in various choirs, bands and orchestras. The school's big band is currently run by the BBC big band leader and the director of music is 'highly charismatic', say parents. The performing arts community is also thriving with high quality productions put on annually, most recently a 'stunning' performance of Les Misérables in conjunction with local girls' schools. Check it out on YouTube for instant goosebumps. Plenty of opportunities to get involved for non-performers too, with the school's stage lighting and sound team proving hugely popular.

Trips, tours and exchanges galore. World Challenge scheme starts in year 7 then branches out globally higher up the school, with destinations in recent years including China, Vietnam and Belize. Lots of other opportunities for boys to get out and about to enhance the curriculum, enrich their cultural experience or just for fun.

Boarding: The bright, modern boarding house (1999) sits in the heart of the school campus and is home to some 54 boarders, albeit 'an important 54,' insists school. Boarding offers great value for money, with full boarding costing less than most day school fees. Boarders say they 'feel really at home' and the boarding house has a relaxed, happy feel, partly dictated by the energetic and approachable head of boarding who seems almost like one of the boys, and partly by the way older boys mentor the younger ones. Each academic subject has a pupil champion that younger boys can approach if they need guidance with any part of their studies

and the pupil food and boarding council electorate voices collective opinions about how the boarding house is run.

Younger boys are housed in spacious four-man dorms, decorated with personal effects to varying degrees. Years 12 and 13 are in cabin-like single rooms with en-suite shower rooms and the communal areas are peppered with boy toys like pool tables, table tennis and air hockey tables and flat screen TVs. No wonder most years are oversubscribed.

Boys return to the boarding house after school to get the blood sugar levels back up with a snack then participate in organised group activities on two or three afternoons a week. All meals are taken in the boarders' own canteen ('better food than in the main school', agree pupils) and prep takes place after supper from 7.30 to 9pm. Major advantages according to boarders' parents are that 'masters are on tap' to help with tricky homework and they have the 'luxury of not wasting time commuting to school', instead playing touch rugby or football with friends while others sit on the bus for up to 45 minutes each way. Some 10 or so 'day boarders' come for breakfast and stay for supper and prep each day at a cost of £4,500 pa.

The majority go home at weekends, with around 15 – mainly international pupils – staying. The schedule at the weekend is 'pretty relaxed' and boys are allowed into town in groups of two or three. There is a major trip organised every half term – paintballing and Thorpe Park recent highlights. Mobile phones are allowed until bedtime when prefects collect them from the younger boys. Older boarders are given lots of responsibility to mentor and guide their younger housemates, with one describing the self-discipline and independence he has gained during his time at the school as 'great preparation for uni'.

Background and atmosphere: Founded in the 12th century and given a royal charter in 1562. Centred round an attractive red-brick Queen Anne style building, with the usual ubiquitous additions bolted on from the 60s onwards. An interesting mix of ancient (the oldest classrooms are just approaching their 100th birthdays) and modern, the school has recently been the beneficiary of large grants from the Academies Capital Maintenance Fund and now boasts gleaming new facilities including a bright, modern canteen, cookery suite (all boys do one term of cooking 'to prepare them for real life'), multi gym plus outdoor terrace with panoramic views of the sports fields and new changing facilities for the sports hall and swimming pool. There's also a lovely pool with retractable roof which, despite its 40-year vintage, still knocks spots off many we've seen, three lofty art rooms displaying an array of boys' superb work (pity some of this hasn't made its way into the rest of the school, though) and a large, airy library with plenty of space for quiet study. Sixth formers lack a common room, although measures in place to fundraise for one, but do have two study mezzanines to cram for those all-important exams in free periods. Size of the vast music block gives away the school's collective passion for music, driven by the 'inspirational' director of music, and is home to a drumming suite ('as far away from head's office as possible', say staff) and a music technology centre.

Overall vibe of the school is traditional with a modern, multi-cultural twist. Despite its mixed socio-demographic and ethnic profile, with its boarding house, chaplain and expectation for formal manners (all staff are 'sir' or 'ma'am' to boys) place feels like a 'natural step from prep school' and, say parents, 'offers the roundedness of public school'. The majority join from state primaries, however, and all are polite, fun and talk with genuine enthusiasm about their school. A true camaraderie between year groups is immediately visible in the playground and boarding house.

Pastoral care, well-being and discipline: School 'doesn't put up with any rubbish,' according to parents and pulls boys back into line quick smart if they step out. Few major disciplinary issues, but severe punishments administered for smoking, although 'apparently all the sixth form do,' sighed one parent. Boys dismissive of bullying question and it's clearly not a regular feature of school life here, with reports of just occasional issues in the Twittersphere. School is active in social media and carries out periodic checks to ensure no pupils are breaching the online code of conduct – acting swiftly if they do. Full care for boarders from matron, housemasters and tutors.

Pupils and parents: Diversity at its best with all-comers ranging from those hailing from leafy south Bucks villages to boys from the less affluent local towns. Ethnic mix changing rapidly and school is now about 30 per cent non-Caucasian (higher in lower years), reflecting the local community. Intellect is the common denominator and school sees social mix as 'one of our great strengths; if we're preparing future leaders of the world, we have to be fully appreciative of other backgrounds and races'. Parents of boarders lean towards the middle classes, often professional dual income families, and internationals. About half a dozen girls join for specific lessons (Greek, classics) in year 13.

A plethora of high profile alumni from the sporting, political and showbiz worlds England rugby players Matt Dawson, Nick Beal and Tom Rees; GB hockey captain and Olympian Jonathan Wyatt; professional golfer Luke Donald and, representing the artsy crowd, pop stars Howard Jones and the late Ian Dury and comedian Jimmy Carr.

Entrance: Ferocious competition for places. Selection subject to success at 11+ exam and Buckinghamshire criteria, including the ever-moveable feast of catchment. School's own procedure adopted as and when places become available higher up the school. Some places available in year 10 when a few boys each year choose to move, largely to independent schools, and again in year 12 when around 25 new places are up for grabs, about half of these in the boarding house.

Worth considering boarding at 11 if a day place looks unlikely and candidate has a high 11+ score. Forces families and boys in care are prioritised and these are mixed with some overseas pupils (although they must have a British passport) and locals keen for the boarding experience.

Exit: Some 90 per cent stay on to sixth form. Majority straight into higher education with between 10 and 20 into Oxbridge most years – 16 in 2015 – and strong numbers to other top universities – Durham, Exeter, Birmingham and Southampton popular. Good university advisory provision in place, with specialist support for those hoping for entry to international universities.

Money matters: Rolling renovation plan funded by a number of external sources. Ongoing fundraising by highly active parents' association who run well-attended events, including family quiz nights, wine-tasting (parents only!) and good old-fashioned school discos. Old boys also generous donors and current parents are asked to make annual voluntary contributions to be channelled towards music, transport, the school as a whole or all of the above – and many do.

Remarks: Don't believe the hype pitching The Royal Grammar School as a hotbed of rugger boys. Yes, they play rugby (and 18 other sports from Eton fives and racketball to fencing) to an exceptionally high level, but there's also outstanding music, drama and academics all wrapped up in a supportive, friendly package. Parents at other local grammars might consider it 'a bit God and country' but the traditional values that have the school competing ably with its independent and state maintained neighbours – and thrashing many top public schools on the sports field – mean boys (and their parents) benefit from a private school ethos without the hefty price tag.

St George's School (Harpenden)

Sun Lane, Harpenden, Hertfordshire AL5 4EY

01582 765477
admin@stgeorges.herts.sch.uk
www.stgeorges.herts.sch.uk

Ages: 11–18
Pupils: 1,140; sixth form: 384
Boarders: 110 full
Day: free
Boarding: £11,175 pa

Headmaster: Since 2013, Raymond McGovern MA (early 50s). Educated at St Thomas Aquinas School, Glasgow. Came to teaching via, in his words, 'a circumvented route.' Left school at 16 to take up engineering apprenticeship at British Leyland, then fulfilled his childhood dream, born from his time in the ATC whilst at school ('it gave me a real sense of community') of joining the RAF where he spent nine years, including a stint in Germany. In his early 30s, landed role as lecturer in engineering and aerospace technology at HE college in Hounslow before undertaking two years' training whilst teaching DT at Charles Darwin School in Kent. Promoted to deputy head of sixth form before moving on to Christ's College, Brecon as head of DT then boarding housemaster. Bitten hard by boarding bug, moved to state boarding school, Sexey's School, firstly to run boarding and pastoral care, rising to head after seven years.

Inherited school in top five per cent of non-selective schools nationally, so clear vision to 'ensure quality remains stable.' Team comprises many 'very professional', longstanding teaching staff who, despite tenure, were 'hungry for change' in some areas of school. Reporting systems previously paper based and overly bureaucratic so major

investment in bringing them up to date – now all done online. Head's vision is to make school 'as paperless as possible', as well as enabling parents to access information 'as and when they need it rather than when we choose to release it.'

Likeable, sincere and grounded, head has the aura of a vocational teacher and leader. Senior pupils reminisce about looking up at vaulted chapel ceiling with McGovern when they joined and him pointing out 'it's like a boat, and we're in all in it together.' Not all parents have met him, but describe his weekly newsletter as 'informative and amusing' and uniformly seem impressed, albeit sometimes from afar. Lives locally with wife Rachel and three children – two boys in their 20s who are working and at university respectively and a daughter who is at St George's.

Academic matters: As a totally non-selective school regularly delivering high results, parents can bank on St George's knocking it out of the park when it comes to value-added, with a vast majority of students (91 per cent in 2015) leaving with at least five A*- C grades at GCSE; 38 per cent of grades A*/A. Head is clear to point out, however, that this is not just in the realm of academia, but also in 'confidence, values and esprit de corps' that his students outperform expectations, acclaiming his staff's 'ability to instil a sense of can-do' in its charges. Top A level grades are similarly commonplace. In 2015, nearly 73 per cent A*-B, 43 per A*/A at A level.

Ten to 11 GCSEs are the norm, with compulsory RE amongst them, leading, unusually, to a full class at A level. Parents appreciate flexible approach to timetabling at GCSE. Maths, 'without reservation,' says head, is the jewel in St George's crown and the most popular A level choice by both sexes – 'it's phenomenal to see how much they enjoy it.' Art also outstanding with school boasting the highest percentage of top grades in county at both art GCSE and A level. Setting in maths and science from end of year 7, with English set for GCSE.

Certainly wins prize for smartest comprehensive school uniform with its green Harris Tweed blazers for boys and pleated kilts for girls

French from year 7, German and Spanish from year 8 and all on offer at GCSE but, disappointingly, only French at A level. Mandarin available to all, although not examined, and school is one of just 45 'Confucius Classrooms' across the UK, meaning that it has Chinese firmly embedded in its own curriculum and strong links with China, including a popular exchange programme. Also has International School status.

Maths, 'without reservation,' says head, is the jewel in St George's crown

SEN all in a day's work for the full time SENCo and seven teaching assistants on staff. Plenty of experience dealing with statemented children, and learning support ranges from helping with a few extra spellings to an individually planned timetable. Large percentage of cohort identified as gifted and talented, with extension work provided accordingly both on and off curriculum with Science Olympiads and Maths Challenges.

Games, options, the arts: Sport taken seriously but 'not elitist', according to head, with all abilities trained together. Rugby and cricket are main boys' sports, with A-C teams playing competitive fixtures most weeks in all year groups. It's lacrosse for the girls – St George's is the only state maintained school in the south of England to play, so all fixtures are against independents, hence often at weekends. Other popular options are netball, rounders, basketball, tennis, athletics and, to a limited extent, dance. Compulsory participation to year 13, with more casual mixed classes in sixth form that encompass table tennis, badminton and trampolining. Indoor games take place in the impressive newish sports centre, also home to an attractive and well-equipped gym and weights room.

Possibly the best art department of any school for miles around – 'the pride of the school,' say pupils. Every inch of the art corridor walls and ceilings festooned with breathtakingly creative and technically exemplary work also spilling over to cover most walls throughout school. Huge (four foot) three dimensional papier mâché masks welcome visitors into this showcase area, and from that point on it's hard to know where to look, as outstanding paintings, drawings, sculptures and installations – no two the same – assault the senses. Creative facilities also superb, with three huge DT labs – again with some wonderfully turned work on display – and two huge art rooms provide yet more exhibition space for pupils' superb creative endeavours. Textiles, photography, sculpture and graphic design all on offer.

Music provides St George's heartbeat. Choirs, orchestras and bands galore and so much talent to display that annual house music competition now takes place in Watford Colosseum. One major annual drama production – Scrooge, Fame and

Hairspray in recent years – in which all year groups can participate as well as smaller shows throughout the year.

Plenty of extracurricular activities from sewing and gardening to chess or curriculum based classes take place before and after school – excellent for boarders and day pupils alike. Well-attended ATC as well as World Challenge expeditions to far flung destinations from Argentina to Mongolia. School's connection with Gansu Province, China, has yielded exchange trips and a small team led by head to lecture at University of Beijing. Other trips include educational expeditions to Washington (politics), Space Camp (maths) and a popular biennial ski trip.

Boarding: Despite the small number of boarders (maximum capacity 135, with anything between five and 15 each of boys and girls in any given year group), they are very well integrated into the school. Friendships between day and boarding pupils flourish and visits to day pupils' homes encouraged. Far from feeling like a minority group, boarders take pride in their status to the point of having requested their own, slightly different, tie. Relationships between year groups are forged through fun activities such as 'speed dating' – an in house way of getting to know newcomers.

Boarding houses have friendly family feel, thanks in no small part to the young (40s), bubbly director of boarding who lives on campus and oversees the pastoral welfare of her charges full time. 'She really understands what makes teenagers tick,' said one happy parent. Girls from years 7 to 12 are housed in the old school building – safely tucked away up what seems like 15 flights of stairs – in dorms which sleep anything from two to six: 'we tailor it according to intake from year to year and girls' individual needs,' says director of boarding. Year 13 girls have the run of a swish new house with single rooms and en suite bathrooms. Boys are in a stand-alone block with a less cosy, more practical feel – though we are assured that the sparse decorations in dorms and common room are purely by choice ('it's not cool to have posters up,' said one of our guides). Both houses have tons of communal space – massive common rooms furnished with plenty of squashy sofas and other nooks and crannies around the house with beanbags, armchairs and computers for boys and girls to congregate outside of school hours. Both houses have well-equipped kitchen areas for boarders to make themselves snacks – and there are baskets of goodies out to keep them going after school.

Boys and girls are allowed to visit each other but only in common rooms – although apparently romantic liaisons are incredibly rare: 'There is a strong sibling-like feel amongst the boarders,' say pupils. The terms 'flexi' and 'weekly' are not used

and, although some boarders go home more frequently than others, all pay the same fees (less by some stretch than most private day schools) and have the same status. Around half stay for weekends (more boys than girls), with all meals apart from weekend breakfasts taken in the main school dining room. Pupils from year 9 allowed into Harpenden with permission in twos and many attend classes such as yoga or dance in the village. Pupils grumble that school is too strict about them leaving the premises – parents breathe secret sighs of relief.

Channels of communication to home left wide open with boarders allowed phones, handed in at bedtime, although they are trusted to keep iPads and laptops 'to keep it as much like home life as possible.' Weekends bring Friday night football club, competitive matches for many on Saturdays, cinema trips and one big trip each term (paintballing, Thorpe Park, Brighton have featured recently). Boarders also have their own formal dinner or ball each term, organised by senior pupils. Younger pupils have a fixed programme of after school activities including boarding skills – learning how cook, do their laundry, make jam etc.

Background and atmosphere: Feels more like a private school than some private schools we know – and certainly wins the prize for smartest

comprehensive school uniform with its green Harris Tweed blazers for the boys and new pleated kilts for the girls. Situated a stone's throw from Harpenden High Street, school was founded in 1907 by the Rev Cecil Grant as a non-denominational Christian foundation with its own Anglican chaplain and weekly Sunday chapel service, which occasionally hosts up to 400 members of the school community and their families. One of the longest established fully co-educational boarding schools in England, the school retains many of its historic traditions, with pupils taking great pride in their house competitions, formality of chapel, speech days and all the different ties awarded.

The original Victorian gothic-style building still provides the heart of the school – and girls' boarding house – with various additions and extensions which run the full gauntlet from occasionally gleaming (sports hall, language block) to downright shabby (most of the rest). Despite its somewhat down at heel sum of the parts, however, the whole hangs together with a feel of purposefulness and functionality and is actually part of the school's overall charm. Sixth form common room and study areas in dire need of a refurb, but nobody seems to mind – the overall feel of the school is welcoming and contented – 'children can grow up at their own pace,' say parents. A new link with nearby Batchwood Tennis Academy hopes to attract talented players from all over the country to boarding houses.

Pastoral care, well-being and discipline: Very little need for strong discipline – hard to believe that 'chewing gum' is the worst that happens but that was all our guides would confess to. Occasionally pupils 'don't work out' on the boarding side but in the main 'they feel very lucky to be here – there's no sense of entitlement,' says director of boarding. 'Traditional values and caring ethos,' makes school tick, according to head with strong support from parents. Pupils rewarded for demonstrating school's core values of courtesy, integrity, manners and discipline. Head has passport sized photo of every child in school on his study wall – split by the four houses that give school its shape. Houses presided over by a head of house, assistant and team of tutors. The arrangement of tutor groups gives pupils very little room for manoeuvre when it comes to bad behaviour. An 'excellent' student services department supports children with welfare or emotional needs with its qualified counsellor, to whom pupils can self-refer, and a pastoral support worker.

Pupils and parents: Affluent Harpenden and its surrounding villages provide the vast majority of day pupils with boarders coming mainly from further afield, and around 55 per cent of these from overseas. Cohort is hence naturally inclined towards hard work and success upon which school can build. A highly involved and vocal parent body turns out in droves for matches, concerts and shows and the Sunday service in chapel is very well attended. Alumni include philosopher and political theorist Michael Oakeshott, classicist and writer Rex Warner, actress Laura Haddock and rugby player Owen Farrell.

Entrance: The most oversubscribed of Harpenden's three secondary schools, with a complex admissions process run by school. No academic selection but a series of priorities including catchment (currently extending to around 800 metres from school), regular church attendance for at least two years (minister's letter required), and siblings receiving priority. Genuine devoutness not put to the test – local parents can cynically choose to pray rather than pay as long as they think ahead and accept that their child will have to attend chapel at school on at least three Sundays a term. A handful each year from local prep schools join in year 7.

Boarders must be EU resident or hold British passport and are interviewed by head and director of boarding to assess suitability, as well as provide a good reference from their previous school. 'Need' also comes into play – for example children with both parents working or in the Forces, with occasional children switching from day to boarding places to save time on the daily commute. Applications should be in a year in advance, although boarding places not currently oversubscribed. Very occasional charitable places but no bursaries offered.

Exit: Just under three quarters stayed on into sixth form after GCSEs – leavers generally move to other schools and colleges. In 2015, 56 per cent after A level to Russell Group universities with a good handful each year to Oxbridge – eight offers in 2015.

Money matters: As a voluntary aided school, St George's buildings are owned by the school's Foundation, which has to find 10 per cent of the cost of all capital projects and on-going building maintenance from very limited funds. 'There is a lot of do-it-yourself work here'; school enlists the assistance of its active parents' association for fundraising support throughout the year.

Remarks: A real gem of a local secondary school with plenty to offer pupils whether they want to paint, study or play their way to success. Riding high as one of the top non-selective state schools in the country, St George's can boast a secure, Christian community as well as top notch results.

Sexey's School

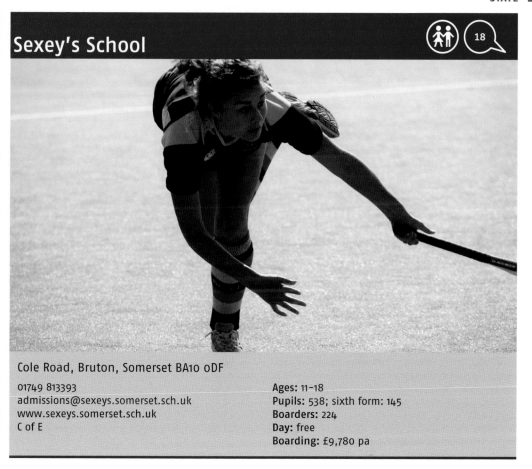

Cole Road, Bruton, Somerset BA10 0DF

01749 813393
admissions@sexeys.somerset.sch.uk
www.sexeys.somerset.sch.uk
C of E

Ages: 11–18
Pupils: 538; sixth form: 145
Boarders: 224
Day: free
Boarding: £9,780 pa

Head Master: Since 2013, Irfan Latif BSc (40s). Educated at Emanuel School – as a sixth former he helped to rescue injured people from the 1988 Clapham rail disaster. Read chemistry at King's College London, followed by a PGCE. First teaching post was at Kidbrooke School in Greenwich (where Jamie's School Dinners began). Taught at several independent schools, including Haberdashers' Aske's Boys', Whitgift and St Benedict's in Ealing, where he was head of chemistry and director of science. He was previously deputy head (academic) at Bedford School and says Bedford's then head John Moule (now warden of Radley) was a huge inspiration to him.

Describes his appointment to run Sexey's as 'serendipity.' With boarding fees at independent schools on an upward trajectory, he feels that state boarding is the future. 'We are like Essential Waitrose,' he jokes. He has kept the traditional aspects of Sexey's (which celebrates its 125th anniversary in 2016) while ensuring that it is cutting edge when it comes to teaching and technology. He has used his knowledge of the independent sector to good effect, changing the school's house system,

academic structure and governance, taking a close look at feedback, assessment and pupils' progression and introducing far more sports fixtures. Firmly believes in giving a wealth of opportunities to all and encourages students to work hard and flourish. 'We're in the business of transforming lives here,' he says. 'But it's not a holiday camp. They are here to work.'

Won two national awards for being in top 10 per cent of schools for progress between key stage 2 results and GCSE; in the top 10 per cent nationally for high attainment

Head knows every pupil by name. He has an open door policy for students, writes a comment on every child's report and is much in evidence around the school. Still teaches six periods of chemistry per 10-day teaching cycle – to GCSE pupils last year and AS students this year. 'I arrange my meetings around my teaching, not the other way round,' he says. Lectures at the Royal Institution of Great Britain, is a fellow of the Royal Society of Chemistry and is also a magistrate. 'He never sleeps,' jokes a colleague. Head puts it differently. 'There's no point sitting around,' he says. 'If a parent has entrusted me with their most precious commodity then I have to deliver on all fronts.' His teacher wife Jocelyn is very involved in the school, including organising fundraising events for Macmillan Cancer Support (founder Douglas Macmillan was a pupil at Sexey's). They and their two young daughters live in a house on the school site.

Academic matters: Results are consistently good. At GCSE, 81 per cent A*-C including English and maths in 2015, with 33 per cent of grades A*/A, and at A level, 34 per cent A*/A grades, 65 per cent A*-B. The Department for Education recently named Sexey's as the best performing state school in Somerset and Dorset for GCSE. Most pupils take 10 subjects at GCSE, with around 38 per cent doing triple science.

New deputy head (academic) has launched major focus on teaching and 'supporting students to be successful' and school continually looks at how pupils can improve. Strategy has paid dividends – school recently won two national awards for being in the top 10 per cent of schools for progress made by pupils between key stage 2 results and GCSE and in the top 10 per cent nationally for high attainment. Year 7 to 9 pupils are set for maths, science and languages (French and German). Average class sizes are 22 at key stage 3, fewer at key stage 4 and 10 to 12 in the sixth form. Good SEN provision – SENCo and her five-strong team offer literacy and numeracy support in small groups to pupils who meet county criteria. One boy increased his spelling age by 22 months after 10 weeks of specialist literacy classes.

At A level, all the usual subjects, plus business, government and politics, media studies, photography, psychology and sociology. Sport and exercise science is the only BTec available. School is continuing with AS levels and pupils must achieve three Ds in year 12 to continue into year 13. One or two opt to retake their AS exams each year. Impressive head of sixth form keeps a weather eye on all and advises on higher education and career choices. A third of sixth formers do the EPQ and all year 12s do work experience.

Extracurricular activities include circuit training, creative writing, radio club and Warhammer. Two boys who are gardening enthusiasts are developing the school's centenary garden

School is forward thinking when it comes to technology. Prep diaries have been dispensed with and students use the Show My Homework app – so pupils and parents alike can see the prep that has been set and when it's due in. School has introduced philosophy as a discrete lesson for year 7 to 9 pupils and Mandarin as an after-school enrichment subject. Younger pupils do food technology for three years (everything from nutrition and healthy eating to cooking and food safety) and the subject is offered at GCSE and A level too.

Games, options, the arts: Sport has progressed in leaps and bounds in recent years. School now plays loads of matches against independent and state schools (including two Saturday fixtures a term, one for boys, one for girls) and holds its own against the likes of Millfield and Dauntsey's. Parents contribute to a voluntary sports subs fund to help cover transport costs to matches – but there's no compulsion. When we visited, the under-15 girls' cricket team had just beaten their rivals at Millfield and King Edward's, Bath respectively. All age groups do at least two hours of sport each week. Rugby, hockey, netball, cricket, football, equestrian pursuits, sailing – you name it, they do it. Sports hall with weights room and gym, 18m heated indoor pool, good pitches and five hard tennis courts that double up for netball and five-a-side football. Emphasis is on healthy, active lifestyles and sixth formers can also choose activities like yoga, keep fit and Pilates. Dynamic new director of sport says her aim is to broaden the PE curriculum for all – 'the

girls want to do football and rugby and the boys want to do basketball and hockey,' she says.

Loads of music, drama and dance on offer. Around 130 pupils play instruments (lessons are rotated so pupils don't miss the same lessons each week). Music department is housed in former head's house and includes large classroom, recording studio and practice rooms. Reasonable numbers take music at GCSE but the subject isn't offered at A level. Performance groups include choir, wind band and folk group. Yearly drama production (Little Shop of Horrors in 2015) – studio space for smaller productions and traditional hall for major performances. Drama and theatre studies available at GCSE and A level. Art is breathtaking. We were particularly impressed by a montage of year 10 kaleidoscope paintings inspired by artist Brian Moss. The school has wisely formed close links with Hauser & Wirth Somerset, the stunning contemporary art gallery just a mile up the road.

A plethora of extracurricular activities – including circuit training, creative writing, radio club and Warhammer. Two boys who are gardening enthusiasts are developing the school's centenary garden. D of E, plus Army Cadet Force and Air Training Corps (at nearby Castle Cary). Pupils produce their own termly school magazine – recent issue included an insightful advice column on coping with exams.

Boarding: Boarders (weekly and full boarding available) account for nearly half of the school roll. They occupy three vertical, mixed boarding houses – Coombe, Lisbury and the newest, Macmillan, which opened in 2011. Boarders' dorms are mainly for two or three pupils. All well-kept and wholesome. Each house has its own houseparents, most of whom have teaching or support roles too. After-school activities between 3.40pm and 5pm every day, then boarding team takes over. Two hours of prep a night for most – year 7 to 9 boarders are supervised, older pupils can work in their rooms.

Loads of weekend activities – everything from foraging to theatre trips. Younger pupils are allowed (with permission) to visit Bruton once a week, older pupils twice a week. The mother of a year 7 boarder told us that she likes being able to drop her son off on Monday morning and pick him up on Friday afternoon. 'I feel we get the best of both worlds,' she said. 'There is no Saturday school so we get a proper family weekend.'

Background and atmosphere: School is named after Hugh Sexey, the son of poor parents who rose to become royal auditor to Elizabeth I and James I. After his death in 1619 the trustees of his will established Sexey's Hospital, which still provides care for the elderly today. The trustees later established a school for apprentices within the school grounds

but it closed 200 years later. The current school was founded in 1891 and was the inspiration of East Somerset MP Hugh Hobhouse, who drafted the 1902 Education Act (his great, great grandson is a boarder at Sexey's). School later became a grammar school and then metamorphosed through voluntary controlled, grant maintained to voluntary aided. Went co-ed in 1977 and expanded its boarding provision in the 1980s to become one of the largest state boarding schools in the country. State boarding schools provide free education but charge fees for boarding.

The school's expansion over the years has resulted in a hotchpotch of architectural styles (some new, some old) squeezed into a narrow, 30-acre site, with a main road on one side and a picturesque valley on the other. Some areas of the school are slightly tired looking but the glorious countryside that bounds it on three sides more than makes up for it. In recent years Bruton, with its ancient streets of stone and stucco houses, has become one of the most sought-after places to live in the country. So many showbiz and fashion names have houses in the area – Cameron Mackintosh, Dominic West, Rhys Ifans, Sam Taylor-Wood and Mariella Frostrup to name but a few – that it's been dubbed 'the new Notting Hill' and the opening of Hauser & Wirth has added to the cachet. Mariella Frostrup was the guest of honour at the school's 2015 speech day, cautioning students about the power of social media.

Year 7 to 11 pupils wear blazer and tie uniform (burgundy polo shirts in summer). Head recently changed dress code for sixth formers – they now wear business suits. Most like this, a few don't. 'I'd been waiting for five years to wear my own clothes,' a year 12 girl told us. Sixth form has its own common room with views over the Somerset landscape and a pervading air of studiousness when we visited at exam time. Sixth formers who have passed their driving tests are allowed to drive to school. We asked a year 12 group what they'd miss about the school when they left and they unanimously said 'Squares' – a playground game invented by Sexey's pupils. Parents praise the school's sense of community and family atmosphere and say that its size means that teachers know every child. 'Children feel proud to say they are at Sexey's,' the mother of a year 11 told us.

The current school was the inspiration of East Somerset MP Hugh Hobhouse, who drafted the 1902 Education Act (his great, great grandson is a boarder)

Food is excellent. Most have school dinners, with only a tiny handful bringing packed lunches. Everything is cooked in-house by talented chef (a former chef de partie at Heathrow) and his 20-strong team. Six hundred lunches served every day. Food is locally sourced where possible and halal, vegetarian and gluten-free options are available. Bustling canteen, with pupils allowed to sit where they want.

Pastoral care, well-being and discipline: Every pupil (day and boarding) belongs to one of four houses, each of which has a head of house and team of tutors. Lots of healthy inter-house rivalry – houses compete in sport, music, drama, enterprise, poetry and more to win the annual Bint Shield. Vertical tutor groups, with 15 minutes of tutor time every morning. School takes a huge amount of care in helping pupils' transition from primary school. Pupils due to board in year 7 come and stay for a boarding weekend in the July before they start. 'It means they're not sitting at home worrying over the summer holidays,' explains the head.

School is very keen on creating a culture of well-being and happiness. The key words at Sexey's are tolerance, respect and kindness and with that in mind the school has created The Sanctuary, a quiet place for children to go and reflect or chat about anything that's bothering them. 'The pastoral care is second to none,' a mother told us. 'The communication between teachers and parents is good too. They seem to take pride in going that extra mile.' As a C of E school, it prides itself on its close links with Diocese of Bath and Wells and St Mary's Church in Bruton (boarders regularly attend Sunday services there). School san, staffed by rotating team of three nurses, is open 24/7 for boarders.

Active school council, plus head boy, head girl and raft of prefects.

Pupils and parents: A real mix. School prides itself on its diversity and pupils come from a wide variety of backgrounds – from horsey types who compete in the school equestrian team to youngsters with 'chaotic' home lives. Boarders come from all over (from Spain to Hong Kong) but must be UK nationals, hold an EU passport or be domiciled in the UK. Quite a few boarders are from army families, others from RNAS base at Yeovilton. The students we met were friendly, enthusiastic, down to earth and unpretentious. A sixth former reckoned she might have been a 'bit of a brat' if she'd gone to an independent school but said no one was like that at Sexey's.

Parents are very involved – thriving parent and staff association, with spring ball hosted in the school hall every year. Former pupils include the late Ned Sherrin, Million Dollar website creator Alex Tew and BBC wildlife film-maker James Brickell.

Entrance: Demand for day places is intense. Day admissions are handled by Somerset County Council but there's virtually no chance of a day place in years 7 to 10 unless you live within two kilometres of the school. Boarding numbers are increasing so boarding places are easier to come by. Main intakes are year 7, year 9 and sixth form. Head and head of boarding interview prospective boarders and reference from previous school required.

No new pupils admitted in year 11 and no catchment area rules for day pupils in the sixth form. Around 60 new pupils join the sixth form each year. Minimum of five GCSEs at A*–C needed, plus some subject-specific requirements.

Exit: Up to 50 per cent leave after GCSE, mainly to take vocational courses at FE colleges in Street and Yeovil. Some to do apprenticeships.

After A level 96 per cent go to university. A wide variety of courses – from physics and biomedical science to law and history. Universities in the south west are perennially popular – Exeter, Bath, Falmouth and Plymouth – but an increasing number are going further afield, to places like Durham, Leeds, Manchester and Southampton. A few do art foundation courses and one or two go to Oxbridge most years.

Remarks: If you want your child to be a day pupil and you're lucky enough to live in the (tiny) catchment area then applying here is a no-brainer. If you want your child to board then Sexey's offers all the advantages of boarding in a small school – but without the enormous price tag or social pretentiousness.

Sir Roger Manwood's School

Manwood Road, Sandwich, Kent CT13 9JX

01304 613286
info@srms.kent.sch.uk
www.srms.kent.sch.uk

Ages: 11–18
Pupils: 952; sixth form: 260
Boarders: 47
Day: free
Boarding: £10,734 pa

Headteacher: Since September 2013, Mr Lee Hunter, previously deputy head of Tiffin Girls' Grammar School in Surrey. A biochemist (read natural sciences at Cambridge), he first joined Tiffin Girls' as head of science in 1997. His career also includes stints as a science teacher at the Royal Grammar School in High Wycombe, the Sir James Henderson British School of Milan and Framwellgate Moor School in Durham.

Some of Mr Hunter's proudest school moments have included leading expeditions to the Indian Himalayas and introducing the Duke of Edinburgh award. Living on the Kent coast enables him to enjoy his hobbies of running, walking and cycling, as well as travelling frequently to France.

Academic matters: In 2015, 27 per cent A*/A and 64 per cent A*/B at A level and 43 per cent A/A* at GCSE. A quarter take history to A level. Maths is also a popular choice with more than a third of students taking A level and others taking further maths. The school has a resident maths genius who competed last year in the International Mathematics Olympiad and was placed 30th out of 548 of the world's best mathematicians. All three sciences also strongly represented at A level. The school is designated a high performing language college, and languages offered include French, German, Spanish and Mandarin Chinese, plus Italian as a sixth form option.

If there's a weak department, it would appear to be ICT. Given that the school has computing as a specialism, it's surprising that very few candidates take it to A level. 'It's the way the lessons are taught, it needs changing,' complain sixth-formers. This cohort were among the first to take a compulsory GCSE in business and communications systems, which has appeared to turn many off computing (although it may well be a qualification they appreciate more when they are drawing up CVs). There are plans to introduce ICT courses which students will find more stimulating and relevant, following a government review of the ICT curriculum. Student requests led to A levels being introduced in film studies, psychology and sports studies, although head says that some universities'

preference for traditional academic subjects seems to be turning the tide away from these newcomers.

Pupils feel they are largely taught well, 'There are one or two teachers I wouldn't employ myself, but many are the best you could get,' said one student. It's a competitive environment, but not harshly so. 'People who arrive here for the sixth form say they are pushed harder here than at other schools, but teachers work with you, they help people who are not doing so well,' one student said.

Rooms look like every teenage girl's bedroom with mates' pictures on the walls and hair straighteners lying across the beds. The housemates are 'like a family', said a boarder

In the sixth form group, the brainy boy off to do medicine at Cambridge comes in for as much gentle joshing as the one who has found the going harder and will be reading sports sciences. 'I was one of the people who got extra help, but it didn't make me feel that everyone else was better than me,' says the latter. Another related how effective the teaching support was. 'It was spotted that I was weak at French and I got extra help. Well, then I got an A* in my French GCSE,' he said.

SEN department caters for students with dyspraxia, dyslexia and autism and provides individual support for a pupil with visual impairment.

Games, options, the arts: Sporting whizzes will be right at home here. The head reels off a long list of current and former pupils who are competing at the highest levels. 'We're very good at tennis, we've got the under-14 number two in the country. We've allowed him to reduce his timetable and take time off school. One girl is representing the country in the under-19 MCC ladies' cricket team. Two girls represent England in the ISF World Cross Country Under-18 championship. One girl competed in the National Youth Swimming championships, and the school has produced an international hockey player who has represented GB at two Olympic games, and a member of the England ladies' cricket team.' Such high levels of sporting success gave one parent of a boy out of this league cause for concern, but she said, 'He is not sporty and I worried about him fitting in, but he quickly found friends through the CCF and music groups.'

About 120 pupils get involved with the CCF, going on annual camps, shooting days and field weekends, and D of E awards are also popular. One parent wished there was more kudos for the musicians. 'Music is tiny within the life of the school, sports and languages get much more attention,' she said. However, the school counters that music has a very high profile with lots of students learning to play an instrument, and many opportunities to play music in the orchestra, various bands, choirs and concerts. Orchestral tours have recently taken pupils to Sicily and Istanbul, and the school is 'very good for musicals' according to the sixth formers. The annual big production is open to all. 'Obviously some singers are better than others, but you can still get a part if you're mediocre,' said a student.

An internationalist approach is a big part of the school's ethos, and this sees children offered exchange visits to China, India and Germany. There are language tours to Barcelona, Madrid, Paris and Berlin, a politics trip to Washington, and a visit to the Gambia every Easter, where sixth formers work at the village school.

It was founded 450 years ago by Sir Roger Manwood to bring learning to the townspeople of Sandwich. Academy status has given the school more autonomy and extra funding

Boarding: It's a spacious campus with lots of green space and the two boarding houses are a stone's throw from the teaching blocks. Boys have the grander accommodation with oak floors, ornate staircases and mullioned windows (33 spaces). The girls' house (23 spaces) is nondescript but cosy. All but two bedrooms are shared. Rooms have high sleepers with desks underneath and look like every teenage girls' bedroom with mates' pictures on the walls and hair straighteners lying across the beds. The housemates are 'like a family', said a boarder. The menu pinned up featured school meal standards – the food is 'bad', lamented a boarder, although the school argues that it has been rated good by Ofsted.

Boarders' weekends are filled with a mixture of organised outings and pursuing individual

Orchestral tours recently to Sicily and Istanbul, and the school is 'very good for musicals' according to sixth formers

interests – students can, for example, take riding lessons or go for sleepovers at friends' houses. More staff are now on duty at weekends to organise a wider range of activities for the increasing numbers of younger boarders.

Background and atmosphere: Tucked down a quiet and leafy residential street, the school is an appealing jumble of historic buildings with modern day additions such as an IT resource centre, science blocks and Astroturf. It was founded 450 years ago by Sir Roger Manwood to bring learning to the townspeople of Sandwich. Academy status has given the school more autonomy and extra funding which has so far financed building refurbishments and an extension to the sixth form common room.

Pastoral care, well-being and discipline: Asked who is most approachable on the staff, the students rattle off a long list of names – clearly it's the majority rather than the odd one. Relationships with the staff seem unusually warm. 'The teachers are friendly, they really care and they know you on a personal level,' said one pupil. 'They care about us so much, and help us so much,' echoed another. And it would seem that treating students with kindness and respect filters down through the school. The sixth formers looked genuinely surprised when we asked about any tendency for the big kids to put the younger ones in their place, and said that would never happen. A parent concurred: 'There is no rough and tumble, there's no bullying, our child has been happy all the way through'. Another parent was worried about her child making the transition from a small independent school, but she said: 'He fitted into a family incredibly quickly.'

Pupils and parents: There's an uncommon gentleness about the school, which makes it an absolute find for parents who are concerned about how their child will deal with the hurly-burly of secondary school. A few minutes in the company of these young people is all it takes for pro-single sex school arguments to crumble. There's a warmth and naturalness between the students – no macho posturing from the boys or cliquey ring-fencing from the girls. 'Our year gets on really well,' the year 13s agree.

Sandwich regarded as posher than many of its neighbouring towns on the depressed East Kent coast and free school meal numbers lower than at nearby schools. Recently the town has been hit hard by the withdrawal of pharmaceutical giant Pfizer and the loss of 2,500 jobs, although the local council is offering enticements to businesses with the aim of creating a life sciences hub on the site. The commute to London is a slow trundle stopping at all stations; parents tend to be employed locally or stay in town for the working week.

Around half of boarders are from overseas; pupils from Nigeria, Nepal, Hong Kong, Estonia and Germany bring a healthy melée of cultures and backgrounds to the pupil mix.

Entrance: Pupils must pass the local 11+, the Kent test. Children with British or EU passports are entitled to a free education here. Out of 120 places in year 7, six are reserved for boarders. The boarding places are not usually over-subscribed, but day places are. Each year around 30 cases go to appeal, with around a further six places being awarded after appeals.

Pupils come from more than 30 feeder primary schools and the catchment is just below five miles, with the majority of pupils living in Deal, Walmer and Sandwich.

Entrance from year 8 onwards via a test administered by the school. Vast majority stays on for the sixth form; new pupils need six GCSEs at A* to C, and at least a B grade in chosen subjects.

Exit: A handful – around 20 per cent – leaves after GCSEs, either for college or apprenticeships. Three to Oxbridge in 2015, others to the old guard of eg Imperial, UCL, Durham and Bristol. Creative types headed for courses in advertising, footwear design, sports journalism, dance, and musical theatre. Each year a few go on to study medicine, encouraged by the Claringbold scholarship from an old Manwoodian which provides an income of £1,000 per year during their studies.

Remarks: If you're seeking a school to move house for, this should be on your list. With a full hand of grade 1s from Ofsted it's unquestionably a good school, and the town of Sandwich offers a gorgeous beach, a golf course which regularly plays host to the Open Championship, creekside walks, and some of the best preserved mediaeval architecture in the country. Plus, unusually, it's a mixed sex grammar, so you can educate sons and daughters together.

If you don't want to move house, there's also the option of boarding at state school prices. Parents fighting whitened tooth and manicured nail over places in the West Kent grammars may be missing a trick here. You can get a top flight education paying only the boarding fee, a snip compared to independent day school prices in the south east.

Steyning Grammar School

Shooting Field, Steyning, West Sussex BN44 3RX

01903 814555
sgs@sgs.uk.net
www.sgs.uk.net
C of E

Ages: 11–18
Pupils: 2,100; sixth form: 500
Boarders: 125 full
Day: free
Boarding: £9,060 – £10,575 pa

Head: Since 2013, the energetic and insightful Nick Wergan (40s). He began his career in investment banking before retraining as an English teacher in 2004; then rose rapidly after being dubbed Outstanding New Teacher of the Year (2007) by the National Teaching Awards, through posts as head of English (Sackville School, East Grinstead) and deputy head (Blatchington Mill, Hove). He's resourceful and decisive, empowers his teaching team to lead and role model leadership for the pupils, and this delegation means he can also turn his powerful brain to looking at business partnerships to help with the funding crisis that dogs state schools, no matter which party sits in power in Westminster.

He has a house on site in the Elizabethan part of the school, but also owns and lives on a vineyard nearby with his family – producing award-winning sparkling wine. This pragmatic mix of localism and global business is at the heart of his tenure. He looks to local secondaries (through Challenge Partners network) to keep Steyning Grammar striving to be its best, trumpets the school's 400 year tradition to make new legacy connections, has a conference phone on the table in one of his two offices to enable frequent management communication across two sites, and tweets and blogs avidly. He teaches English to year 7 once a week, and students say he pops in and out of classes, corridors and the canteen, working closely with the head boys and girls to take the temperature of the school too.

Academic matters: Reflections on learning are intrinsic to the school success – whether that is implicit in weekly year group assemblies (hall only holds 350); explicit in the title of the school's newsletter; or sustained through what has been created through the IB learner profile, even after the qualification is no longer on offer here. (Few state schools in the UK can afford it financially at present because of the change to formula funding means only 4.5 A levels are funded and IB is worth 6.5). The size of the school means that over 30 A levels and just as many GCSEs are on offer, class sizes normally 24 with 16 (restriction in practical subjects) to 20 at A level. In 2015, nearly 30 per cent A*/A at GCSE and 63 per cent got 5+ A*-C including English and maths. At A level, over a quarter A*/A and 51 per cent A*-B. The final IB cohort averaged 35 points.

Years 7 and 8 are in the Church Street site, so their atmospheric classrooms have parquet floors and a maze of doorways leading to subject-based areas. Learning is far from low tech, though; there are banks of computers and we saw a fizzy drink can that had been rigged to record sound. At the other end of the tech spectrum, a class loved building the rock cycle using plasticine. The library was buzzy with authors visiting and pupil volunteers, and an enterprise day involved a pitch to businessman Lord Sugar. However, by the time they have made their GCSE choices pupils are panting to get the open corridors and swell of new students in the Shooting Fields Site. The latter is dominated by the huge and successful A level specialist sixth form, which feels more like a college but with the pastoral support of a school – a real draw for the third of students who join for GCSE.

The library was buzzy with authors visiting and pupil volunteers, and an enterprise day involved a pitch to businessman Lord Sugar

---

Tutorials are one-to-one and a curriculum reform back in 2013 means pupils now do fewer topics but more richly. Project-based learning is electric here; the pupils love it and the opportunities it provides to anchor their academic subjects in the practical and take the experience back into the classroom: a trip to the European Organization for Nuclear Research in Cern; Kimmeridge for biology and geology; the Globe Theatre; Oviedo for Spanish.

The learning resource centre is not just about books – a remote access system means students can log on at home and avoid emailing documents back and forth. The mezzanine level is the sixth form domain and students congregate here even in break time, a sure sign of their commitment to learning – they also gather in the canteen and a learning zone behind that.

A trial period of the 'show my homework' app pleases parents as well; they like to log in and see what needs to/has been done and by when. Kahoot gamifies learning in conjuction with an interactive whiteboard; apparently a warm up to a class can get pretty heated.

Engaging teachers make for the most popular A level subjects, maths, politics and chemistry at present – science labs have loads of space for practicals, which might have 16 in each class compared to 20 in extended subjects. The school is a member of 250 Challenge Partners, in a hub with three Brighton secondaries sharing constructive collaboration and challenge to improve practice and so the education of their children – the leadership team finds it a really valuable to have such critical friends. During the GCSE years the pupils become responsible for booking their parents' appointments and act as their guides on the parents' evening itself – family feedback is that this independence works well.

The Cuthman Centre is a separate building that acts as a haven for the more vulnerable students (category 3 SEN), eight at present with specific learning difficulties; they have roll-call or more casual tea and toast there when needed, and there are NHS nurses, a counselling programme funding by pupil premium and enabled by GP referrals. In-class SEN support with learning support mentors is targeted and the impact evaluated: it ranges from laptops in exams for those with illegible writing to an SEN passport created with parent and carers. The gifted and talented (now More Able) are supported outside lesson time with book clubs and an Oxbridge programme.

Games, options, the arts: Competitive sports are netball, rugby, football, rounders and cricket, with fixtures against both independent and state schools across the county – and the Marylebone Cricket Club. The site itself has two rugby pitches and a football one hidden behind a line of trees, while sixth formers have free access to the town leisure centre adjoining the school – they can use facilities such as the pool, squash courts and dance studio (external reputation for good boys' dance). They also love the chaos of the sixth form sports day with its wheelbarrow races and Fairy Liquid slide. The equestrian team (pupil-owned horses) trains at Hickstead. We saw a game of rounders being planned using the computer suite below the boarding house – a wet weather PE lesson. If PE is not a GCSE choice, then pupils have non-competitive sport a couple of times a week.

The music department is thriving with ticketed performances each season and 20 A level students, but would love more space (who wouldn't). Logic is used for composition on Macs, there are opportunities for mixing with the use of the live room. Plenty of individual practitioners eg a boy playing the violin, guitar, piano; a ukulele and keyboard in a shared room in the boarding house.

Pupils share rooms in the younger years and are joyful about the different cultural traditions that they get to experience, from jollof rice on Nigerian Independence Day to Chinese New Year

Art and technology is exhibited throughout the halls of the school – and the drama hall is open to the public. The whole school competition is Steyning's Got Talent – some kids think it is profoundly uncool, others use it as a springboard to more public performances across the county. Full school performances such as The Wedding Singer might involve 300 people in the six-night production – set, backstage, make-up as well as performers.

The 50th school anniversary trip to the Norfolk Broads had just passed when we visited and all were proud that they are the only school still doing it, despite Health and Safety hobbling. Jailbreak is another riot of a challenge where the whole of year 13 is locked up and has to escape from the science department windows, source vehicles, collect permits and get to Horsham for their recapture. This, and other initiatives such as Macmillan coffee mornings, Pink Day, Comic and Sport Relief, all add up to raising around £15,000 each year for charity.

Wilton Park is nearby, the only branch of the Foreign Office outside London, and interns from there come to work with the More Able – this gives rise to a foreign affairs discussion group, tackling topics such as Syria and Ebola. For prospective medics and vets there are established links with Brighton University and timetabled prep. There are opportunities for students to become equalities, digital or eco-commissioners, do Duke of Edinburgh award and Young Enterprise, as well as lunchtime enrichment activities and independent learning working across year groups.

Boarding: On the State Boarding Schools Association committee and in the second tier of state boarding in terms of numbers. The first state boarding school to be judged outstanding by Ofsted under the new framework – in every category, with no recommendations to make. Since the school cannot make a profit, there is a limited return to invest in the boarding; the major advantage of the provision is the diversity of students. The boarders take enormous joy in their international mix, while grounding themselves by earning money on shifts in the canteen and volunteering.

Four boarding houses, two adapted and two purpose built, all with live-in houseparents. The pupils share rooms in the younger years, and are really joyful about the different cultural traditions that they get to experience, from jollof rice on Nigerian Independence Day to Chinese New Year; they promote their differences yet all order takeaways together. In the most modern house the year 13 pupils have a wet-room shower/toilet ensuite; they prop their doors open to their shared corridors and apparently are very responsive when told to turn their music down – 10.30pm curfew in the week and 11pm at weekends. The (mostly) boys watch the Premier League on their laptops; they have an ironing board and a kettle in their shared kitchen; when fending for themselves they eat toasties and pizza since Health and Safety dictates there is no proper oven. The houseparents lend their kitchen when a bake-a-thon is organised for charity and a list of suppliers is amended weekly to taste eg Marmite, jam, squash, milk, biscuits, bread.

The girls have photos as well as their names up on their doors – the images are taken by a photography student, whose work also features on the achievement board; this is the most obvious sign of a real sense of supportive celebration of peers. One girls' common room is huge and more homely, with desks for quiet study places too, since this is a realistic experience away from home, with scheduled time for work, although laundry returned to your cubby within a day would be unusual at home...

Facebook photos posted (eg rocket club with powder paint ejected from a parachute) and well dones handed out by the houseparents for being tidy and general good, with prizes drawn at the end of term – once it was a helicopter ride! There is chance to pitch to a 'houseparents' dragon's den' for a new piece of equipment, whether a freezer or a pool table. As elsewhere, technology is used to facilitate rather than trumpeted for its own sake: Skype interviews for prospective boarders; applications scanned and emailed in; Wifi or ethernet with hotspots means that Skyping home via an iPad is easy; WhatsApp is used to tackle awkward time differences.

Background and atmosphere: Founded in 1614, turned co-ed in 1953 and now spread over two sites in the small Sussex town of Steyning with architectural styles ranging from chocolate box Elizabethan black and white, through classic 50s secondary modern school architecture, to the super functional and crisp boarding house, not yet a decade old. It was boys only before the turn of the millennium; now it is equally co-ed and non-selective (apart from the 125 boarders), and the leading school in the country on character-based learning. The latter is now at the centre of the curriculum – teaching, assessing and reporting home on learning characteristics like grit, growth mindset, curiosity and zest.

The 'Steyning family' children are encouraged to take risks so that they are not afraid of failure; staff are set on preparing the next generation to take over – 'the sooner the better!' says head

The 'Steyning family' is made up of children who are encouraged to take risks so that they are not afraid of failure, and staff who are set on preparing the next generation to take over – 'the sooner the better!' says the head. The ethos of the school is printed large on boards in both sites, and the children are resilient and well-supported through exam and everyday academic pressure. The infrastructure for boarding, with the 125 teaching staff and 150 support staff, helps to produce excellent outcomes for disadvantaged students in particular. The staff tenure is traditionally long (30 years is not that unusual), since it is a big school with plenty of space to develop and enough room for children to escape a parent/teacher's shadow. The results are above national average, so it is really the staff's continuing challenge to find the hook to secure each student into a love of learning, demonstrate stickiness in all relationships and make sure they discover how to apply all this both in and outside the exam hall.

There are plenty of huts that deal with the overflow of lessons from this huge school; however, the head is collaborating with local industry to scratch backs and improve the school's facilities, and make those research links even stronger – funding has just been won to demolish the huts and replace them with a new classroom block.

Pupils bus in from local villages (two-thirds), are dropped off by their parents, or walk if they are lucky enough to live that close. Far from an inner city urban intake, but everyone is aware of where they stand in the wider society – boarders from the Caribbean come across occasional piercings and extensive LGBT support, the local village kids

taste cultures from Barbados to Spain, and parents say, 'it opens up everyone's minds'.

Busy, big and teeming with children at break time – especially in wet weather, when they head to the gym, eat lunch in the classrooms or the school canteen. No hall large enough for a whole school gathering, but the split site means that the pupils have a real sense of progression and responsibility, from getting a key to their own locker in year 7 to wearing their own clothes in the sixth form, and using the canteen as a study space as well as one to eat in. Those with food intolerances struggle to enjoy mass meals produced within a tight budget, and the low maintenance cashless system means some parents worry about students selecting from a tempting array of sugary snacks instead of some of the healthier fruit.

Independence is highly valued here, and pupils often ask teachers for help on what suits them best in terms of learning as an individual. The staff are committed and respond swiftly and with initiative; the 400 year heritage adds gravitas when looking for aspirational connections. Ofsted, the State Boarding School Association and C of E status are all three seen as important benchmarks, but by no means the most important measure of the school's success.

Pastoral care, well-being and discipline: Both school and year councils provide feedback on issues such as uniform, the colour of leavers' hoodies, the learning resource centre, internet access to YouTube research etc. Prospective head boys and girls write a letter of application, then the school participates in an online survey, meaning year 13s get some input even though they are leaving – then they must pitch with a speech to the whole of the boarding cohort.

Horizontal pastoral system through year head and form tutor; the tutors have 12 students each and the learning mentors 10. Their aim is to personalise the school – whether that is via checking in at the Cuthman Centre and munching a piece of toast or through Pizza and Paragraphs for English Support. Growing confidence is vital, and the classes of 24 are a practical maximum to enable that.

More casually, there is supported (by the heads of year) revision in the dual purpose school canteen – peer mentors enable paired reading and might meet for breakfast in Boltons (one of the boarding houses).

No truancy, no smoking on site and no drinking. If a kid impacts the learning in a classroom then they are removed from that classroom. The student could end up in the Cuthman Centre, then a follow up and re-integration. Blazers must be worn in the corridors and using of phones in classes is at teacher discretion. The range and policy of sanctions is reportedly reassuring for kids who have been beating at the boundaries at other schools; 'It's different here, you know what to expect'. The documentation and communication of the next steps is vital for everyone involved. Academic, social or emotional barriers are identified and everyone gets analysing, understanding and working together – parents and grandparents included – with reflection and using principles of restorative justice. Head says, 'we see the best of the students' behaviour at school...'

Pupils and parents: Local, rural and coastal catchment area encompasses a huge range of parental employment – multinational companies, small business owners, teachers; families will relocate and buy within the area to ensure they can get access to such a good state secondary education. A state boarding school that offered IB was a niche choice for many students – from Northern Ireland, Antigua, Denmark, to name just three.

The live Twitter feed on school trips is much more reassuring for smartphone equipped parents than interesting for the pupils back at school – likewise the Facebook page. Pupils arrange their own social lives, which is part of the independence that the school aims to build, and since so many walk, ride or bus into the school there is very little chance to of casual school gate friendships between parents.

Entrance: Strong relationships with primary schools such as Steyning Primary, Upper Beeding, Ashurst, Jolesfield in Horsham, Henfield. Catchment is 200 square kilometres encompassing Henfield to Rydon, from schools such as The Towers Covent, Shoreham College, St Andrew's High School, and Durrington High School. The local authority handle the year 7 and year 9 intake. Only boarding is selective, and that is about balancing fit and gender in a year group, aiming for 50 per cent of each sex. The sixth form is amongst the largest in the south east of England and only started marketing in 2013; before that it was just word of mouth. As a level 3 course provider (A level and equivalents), the admission is usually a B or above in the subject of choice.

Exit: After the leavers' celebration – they get into limos and head off to a club in Worthing, thrilled there is no room on site for something more low key – 70 per cent head off to higher education. Destinations and subjects range from Guildford School of Acting to history at Exeter; one to Oxbridge in 2015 and four to study medicine; others attracted to the reduced fees in Holland or by the established link with Harvard in the US.

Money matters: No fees for tuition, £125 donation to school fund on acceptance of a sixth form place. Bus passes approximately £100 per term, travel and meals bursaries available for household incomes under £16,190. Boarding (from year 9) £8,790-10,410, discounts available for up to three siblings.

Remarks: A grammar school by name only, non-selective with a huge sixth form and all the curriculum choices that size enables. Diversity of boarding provision enables the broadening of everyone's minds – from Sussex villagers to Caribbean islanders.

Welbeck, the Defence Sixth Form College

Forest Road, Woodhouse, Loughborough, Leicestershire LE12 8WD

01509 891712
pa@dsfc.ac.uk
www.dsfc.ac.uk/

Ages: 16–18
Pupils: 328: 241 boys/87 girls
Boarders: all full
Boarding: £0 – £18,000 pa

Principal: Since September 2013, Mr Peter Middleton MA. Previously deputy head at Clifton College, Mr Middleton was born in Somerset and educated at Radley before reading chemistry at Oriel College, Oxford. He began his teaching career at Cheltenham College, where he was a deputy housemaster, master in charge of rowing and first VIII coach, and an officer in the army section of the CCF. Not difficult to see the direction he was taking, confirmed by his next move, which was back to Oxford, to St Edward's, where he was a housemaster, re-formed the royal navy section, was master i/c rowing and, by now, an international rowing coach. It wasn't altogether surprising to hear that at Welbeck he likes wearing military uniform occasionally and exchanging the occasional salute. Any whisper of Apthorpe is irrelevant. Married to Clare, an educational psychologist. They have three children.

Clearly he is an ambitious man, and those who know him well speak of his drive, energy and desire to be a head. Not a ruthless man, he struck us as being like a schoolboy with a new train set. He is clearly very excited about running the school, and in his desire to share his excitement we hardly had time to exchange opening civilities before he was gesticulating wildly with something in his hand which, we realised, was being pointed at a screen nearby. The powerpoint presentation had begun. Very informative it was, and most of what he said as introduction can be found in the prospectus bundle which will arrive when asked for.

In the course of conversations with pupils, staff and parents, it became obvious that his experience as a boarding housemaster has stood him in good stead. We heard how, shortly after his arrival, he had asked pupils to tell him how they thought the overall structure and living arrangements could be improved. As a result he has, we are told, made the boarding houses kinder establishments: they were never foot stamping, command bellowing places, but now housemasters – who, incidentally, seemed a delightful bunch – have more support, so that boys and girls have a wider range of people to whom they can talk, gain wisdom and encouragement, seek advice and just 'chill out together.' Those connected with the boarding came over as enthusiastic and affectionate about the pupils.

Academic matters: The Defence Sixth Form College is unique. It is, as the prospectus states, a fully co-educational sixth form boarding school. Every year 175 young men and women join the college. All are destined for the military and are required to choose

This is a fully co-educational sixth form boarding school. Every year 175 young men and women join the college and all are destined for the military

one from the Royal Navy, the Army, the Royal Air Force and the DESG (Defence Engineering and Science Group). Papers accompanying the prospectus tell you which grades you must have at GCSE and which subjects you have to take at A level. Always the inevitable emphasis on maths and science – everyone studies maths and the vast majority physics. Fitness tests, interviews and school reports form the basis of acceptance. They are all important. English language and the subjects required are governed by whichever branch of the military you wish to pursue. There are then lists of universities which offer places for what you wish to learn. This is where aspirants must be sure they really want to pursue these routes. Boats could be burned sooner than expected. Under good king Middleton academic aspirations have risen, but there is a limit to the breadth of A levels available. Foreign languages are taught only as enrichment AS options; for instance no Greek or Latin, no art or music A levels. Alongside maths, sciences, technology and computing you can study geography, politics or business studies, but no other humanities. In 2015. 31 per cent A*/A grades 59 per cent A*-B. Fine for many, but be aware. This school, with all its

excellence, is geared towards a specific area: engineering or technical careers in the armed forces or as a civilian within the MOD. Of course a government paid bursary of £4,000pa would be most welcome, but there are stipulations. The school is scrupulously honest and helpful about the various permutations.

Games, options, the arts: One of the most delightful incidents of our tour was witnessing what is locally referred to as the dash for cash. This refers to the possibility of winning a bursary for university, providing your grades reach the requirements and that you are sufficiently fit to be accepted. Hence dash for cash. We watched a boy who was not, on his own admission, a natural athlete driving himself to achieve the required time. The PE staff were cheering him on, shouting encouragement, and some running with him. Passers by paused to cheer him on. It seemed the world had stopped but for those runners. And he did it by about five seconds. So he'll get his bursary. It was, he said, between gasps, 'the happiest day of my life, not so much for the bursary but because I can now go to the university of my choice.' The end of his time at Welbeck is the start of his new life.

In 1913 Archduke Franz Ferdinand of Austria visited the Duke of Portland at Welbeck Abbey, and was involved in a very serious shooting accident

As might be imagined there is a wide variety of activities and sport is hugely popular. All pupils are required to join the CCF for varied activities designed to prepare for different challenges and to encourage leadership.

We did hear talk of music and art but didn't see or hear any.

Boarding: That the general atmosphere throughout the school seems very happy must owe something to the quality and lay-out of the boarding accommodation. Everyone boards and the facilities are genuinely homely and in, the words of one of our guides, 'great places to live.' Those in their second and final year live, for the most part, in single ensuite bedsits; those in their first year share three in a room with ensuites. Initially we were a little surprised by having three in a room – two's company etc – but our guides assured us it worked.

Background and atmosphere: Anyone coming across the name Welbeck and thinking it sounds familiar

may be thinking of Welbeck Abbey, destroyed by Henry VIII's thugs, and later adapted over the years into a huge house in Nottinghamshire in the midst of vast estates. From 1953, the year of its foundation, the college was housed in the building until 2000 when, despite its ducal associations and grandeur, it was deemed unsuitable and impractical. One snippet of history which might send a frisson of interest through the most dozy readers is that in 1913 Archduke Franz Ferdinand of Austria visited the Duke of Portland at Welbeck Abbey, and was involved in a very serious shooting accident which very nearly caused his death.

The college retains the name of Welbeck, and the specially designed and constructed buildings are excellent. Designed and built by the architectural firm HLM, the buildings are grouped in an enveloping, friendly way which creates a sense of team effort and space, housing very well laid out rooms.

Pastoral care, well-being and discipline: All the pupils we met spoke with appreciative warmth of the staff who were looking after them. They did not seem to possess any of the casual arrogance one sometimes detects in public school pupils. They were open, trusting, forthcoming and friendly. Discipline seemed easy as a result. A good touch is the presence of three serving officers and the college sergeant major, who mingle with pupils and the staff, forging useful links and running the mandatory CCF. One told us how much he was learning by being there, listening and partaking.

Pupils and parents: Pupils and parents come from all over the country and from all walks of life. Most had never boarded before but they were keen to tell us of the benefits they feel they have enjoyed during this two year spell. In amongst the literature sent in reply to parental enquiries there is a pie chart highlighting the types of feeder schools. Most come from other state schools and few from abroad. Not surprising. This is, rightly, perceived as a special school offering specific targets. Not many schools can include in their packet the near certainty of going on to university to read a subject of their choice and with such financial aid. Parents we spoke to were grateful for what the school was doing; some expressed amazed delight.

Entrance: These differ slightly according to which branch of the Forces you are aiming at, but basically include at least an A and a B in maths and physics plus a C in English GCSE. RAF and DESG must have at least 45 and army and navy at least 40 GCSE points from their best seven subjects (at 8 for A*, 7 for A etc). You must also be medically fit and a British, Commonwealth or Irish citizen.

Exit: All those who go to university on the Defence Technical Undergraduate Scheme (DTUS) must go to one of nine universities – Aston, Birmingham, Cambridge, Loughborough, Newcastle, Northumbria, Oxford, Southampton or Strathclyde – to do an approved DTUS course. These are mostly engineering and science based, with a few management degrees. In 2015, Northumbria, Loughborough, Portsmouth and Newcastle were the most popular. The majority do go on to join a branch of the armed forces. They almost have to. The prospectus papers contain some delightful articles from pupils who have gone on to work with the military, taking with them the benefits they so readily acknowledge.

Money matters: The school has lots to say about money matters and offers many forms to fill in if, as is the case most of the time, parents require assistance. No one need be shy. After all, the intention of Welbeck is to help with means-testing when required and to make the seemingly impossible possible. The government, it seems, is poised to help.

Remarks: In view of the Duke of Edinburgh's connexions with Welbeck it is, perhaps, neither too fanciful nor (just) too silly to compare the school with a Battenberg cake. Both the cake and the school have different layers contributing to the whole. A number of parents and friends of the school commented on the difficulty of balancing the various facets of the school. There are the military aspects: going out on exercise, parades, map reading; the academic side: the need to work at the A level subjects in order to get to university and thence to the job; personal fitness to a pretty high standard. No doubt all these activities and the pressure they bring are perceived by many as standard. This school with its serious extras represents a very high standard and many pupils have put all their eggs in one basket. One high-ranking military man we know described Welbeck as the finest preparation not just for the armed forces but for any job in the world. But... it's not for everyone. A commitment to this excellent establishment needs careful thought and dedication.

Wymondham College

Golf Links Road, Wymondham, Norfolk NR18 9SZ

01953 609000
admissions@wymondhamcollege.org
www.wymondhamcollege.org

Ages: 11–18
Pupils: 1,308; sixth form: 437
Boarders: 640 mostly weekly
Day: free (day boarding £1,968 –£5,175 pa)
Boarding: £9,750 – £10,398 pa

Principal: Since September 2014, Mr Jonathan Taylor, formerly principal at Torch Academy Gateway Trust, Nottinghamshire. Educated at The Leys school, Cambridge, then read theology at Oxford before returning to Cambridge for a PGCE year. First teaching post in nearby Cottenham, followed by assistant head at De Aston school, Market Rasen, then deputy head of Toot Hill, Nottinghamshire, before a move to the Torch Academy. A swift progress, leaving outstanding Ofsted reports in his wake. Thoughtful and immensely hard working – breakfast meetings at 7am a regular fixture with key staff- yet he hasn't disappeared in a cloud of management initiatives, preferring lots of contact with pupils and staff and teaching classes of his own. This is going down well – 'It's early days, but he seems to want to know us,' we were told.

In a big school, he is aware of danger of becoming out of touch and sets store by personal example.

He greeted every single GCSE pupil outside the exam hall on the day of their first exam this summer to wish them luck and gets occasionally frustrated by the isolated position of his office complex – a new build under the previous principal. He is seen about the campus a lot, often accompanied by his dog, Bertie, who is, needless to say, immensely popular with pupils. Believes there is a special quality about Wymondham college, and 'the common purpose of learning for its own sake'. From personal experience he knows about boarding and understands that there is 'a lot more to a successful state boarding school than tacking a Travellodge onto a comprehensive', as has been suggested in certain quarters. Encourages pupils to contact him directly, email or in person, should they wish to, and some do. Determined to encourage the special qualities of Wymondham college and to raise standards even further – staff have fortnightly personal development sessions and are paired with a senior colleague to help share best practice and provide support.

Lives on the site and is married to Julie, herself a senior education adviser.

Academic matters: Though strictly speaking non-selective, the varied intake (50 per cent boarding) plus provision of music and sports places – and a perception in the area that 'It's for bright children' – means pupils appreciate their good fortune in being there and are motivated to work hard. Parents are a strong support and the school's results reflect all round achievement. In 2015, 40 per cent GCSE grades at A*/A. Modern languages are compulsory to GCSE level (Spanish most popular).

Close to 80 per cent take religious studies at GCSE – interesting for a non-faith school.

Sixth form definitely academic – despite a low bar of three Bs and four Cs required at GCSE for entry, most do well and higher grades are often needed for external applicants. Only four vocational courses offered in the long list of subjects to be studied, with maths taken by over half the cohort. Sciences also have a high take up. Headmaster feels this may reflect current anxieties about the need to take degrees that help lead to good jobs, but 'we are holding the line that subjects should also be studied for their own sake'. In 2015, 35 per cent A*/A grades at A level.

Some of the newer buildings are interesting and well designed, but most interesting of all is the single remaining Nissen hut, now listed and used as the chapel

As the school is regarded as 'being for bright children', there are relatively few pupils, around 12 per cent, requiring learning support, and these are milder cases of dyslexia/dyspraxia/dyscalculia, with only a small number of statemented/EHC plan pupils. Well resourced and a positive attitude about extra support. There are also breakfast and catch-up clubs run by individual departments for those needing an extra boost. All year 7s are tested on entry to the school. There is also a structured programme for teaching EFL. School has a well-established system for identifying the very bright ('gifted and talented, in the jargon) early on and they spend an extra two periods a week, plus own time on an extension programme comprising a research project and an extra course chosen from space science, Russian, Latin, literature and ideas and government and politics. The presence of post-graduate fellows in the sixth form and some also resident in the houses help pupils learn good work habits – we saw a light-hearted revision session in action during GCSE study leave – and give sixth formers insider guidance with UCAS and Oxbridge entrance. A programme of visiting speakers and workshops are led by local university staff, notably from UEA and Cambridge.

Games, options, the arts: If sporty, there is plenty on offer. Usual team games – rugby included, and an extensive match schedule for the most competent though fewer games for those lower down the rankings. Games are compulsory up to sixth form, when they become optional.Pupils themselves run the five-a-side football league that operates at lunchtimes. Good facilities including swimming pool, gigantic sports hall which doubles for assemblies/concerts, Astroturf, pitches and courts galore. Keen involvement in D of E (the college runs the county scheme) and CCF also offered, though involvement in this is a voluntary activity and not timetabled.

Music important. The annual Mair cup is an opportunity for all pupils to perform in a competition between houses and is extremely popular. Over 250 have individual instrumental lessons and there are choirs and excellent jazz and concert bands that perform at events locally- including the Royal Norfolk Show. A string group has been recently established.

Flourishing art and textiles, which are taught in the Tech block, a light and airy building designed around a central atrium with good provision for display of finished efforts. Good take-up at GCSE and A level and significant numbers go on to study at degree level.

Boarding: The five boarding houses for the main school are drearily functional, though homelike enough upstairs in the dormitories. Houses are all mixed, though girls and boys have separate floors for sleeping, and day pupils as well as boarders return to houses at break and lunchtimes. Plenty of staff, matrons and resident fellows around, and pupils are cheerful and well-behaved.

A few struggle with homesickness at the beginning. Flexi or part boarding is not on offer and swapping from boarding to day is impossible, so a decision to board, taken at aged 10, has to be considered carefully. 'It's not for everyone and this is why we interview all potential boarders', we were told. Those joining in year 9 generally have fewer problems settling. The houses provide something of a refuge at break and lunchtimes when most return to base, although 'It is annoying if your friends are in another house', said one pupil. House staff around at all key times, and matrons remain on the premises at night. The majority go home at weekends but plenty remain and outings/activities are planned throughout the term. Exeats once each side of half term.

Background and atmosphere: Founded in 1951, the brainchild of Sir Lincoln Ralphs, then chief education officer for Norwich. It is the largest state boarding school in the country. The site is a former US military hospital and, despite the utilitarian nature of the buildings, it is very peaceful and in the middle of nowhere (Wymondham itself is several miles off). Some of the newer buildings – modern languages, for example – are interesting and well designed, but the most interesting of all is the single remaining Nissen hut, now listed and used, rather effectively, as the chapel. The college has a strong Christian ethos, but this is non-denominational. There is great pride in the school's history and traditions, with a memorial garden and key anniversaries celebrated regularly. Striking new sixth form centre, set around a courtyard, with boarding facilities in individual rooms with en-suite bathrooms, a refectory, working and computer areas.

Traditional uniform (including ties for girls) compulsory up to year 11, but it is the cheap and cheerful sort – no Harris tweed or boaters. Pupils don't mind the slightly bleak boarding houses: 'You get used to it so quickly, and anyway, we like the people', we were told by one pupil, with nods and agreement from others. The old system of year 7s being kept in their own separate house has been

Pupils don't mind the slightly bleak boarding houses: 'You get used to it so quickly, and anyway, we like the people', we were told

discontinued and everyone is mixed up from the start. Saturday morning school for all (though not sixth form) accepted readily enough – holidays slightly longer than usual in state schools to compensate. One of the virtues of the site is that there is lots of 'promenade' time out in fresh air between lessons, and this seems to contribute to the calm and disciplined atmosphere of the school.

Pastoral care, well-being and discipline: House-based tutor groups with tutors overseeing academic and extracurricular activities from year 7 to 11. Emphasis is on good relationships. 'Work hard, be kind' is the phrase coined and we heard it quoted by year 11s quite cheerfully, if slightly tongue-in-cheek. The presence of resident fellows in the houses help with friendship and other difficulties and in addition to house staff, the school also has two counsellors and a chaplain, so there is a network of support. Looking out for younger pupils is encouraged and there is very little evidence of bad behaviour or bullying, though school is ever alert and anti-bullying strategies are in place. The parent liaison office helps to smooth communications between home and school, especially for parents of boarders.

Pupils and parents: Pupils come from Norfolk in the main (including boarders), though an increasing number are from further afield thanks, in part, to the improvements to the A11. Over 20 per cent are from overseas, a mixture of Europeans and Chinese mostly, plus those with parents working abroad. Fewer Forces families than formerly; the majority of parents are professional or managerial. 'It's an unpretentious place, not for show-offs, and we like that,' said a parent, and that is the common view. Quite a few have chosen the school because it is a state funded one and without the perceptions of privilege that independent boarding schools may possess. Pupils regard themselves as fortunate and appear straightforward and hard working.

Entrance: Main intake at 11+ but places are available at 13 (boarding only) and again in the sixth form. Day and boarding places are split roughly

50:50. Day places very oversubscribed and awarded according to the LA criteria of looked after children, siblings and distance from school. Once other categories have been dealt with, the distance from the school can be as little as 0.6 mile, though commonly up to two miles. Check carefully – despite the name, the town of Wymondham itself is not in the catchment. Eight musical aptitude and eight sporting aptitude places – four day and four boarding for each. Competition for such places is fierce.

All potential boarders are interviewed by the house heads to check that pupils are prepared for all that boarding entails (a hard call in a 10 minute chat). Places are less competitive, but still oversubscribed. It is perhaps worth adding that although you can apply for both day and boarding places, you must list them in order of preference, and if allocated a boarding place you cannot make a crafty switch to day later on. The number of places in each category is fixed.

Most remain for the sixth form, assuming they meet baseline attainment of four Cs and three Bs at GCSE. Not a high bar, but as numbers applying from outside exceed places available, admission is, effectively, dependant on rank order of results at GCSE for those applying from elsewhere.

Exit: Majority – some 75 per cent – move on to higher education. Wide range of degree subjects studied though a definite bias towards the sciences, maths, computing and business. Almost half to Russell group institutions with seven to Oxbridge in 2015. The resident Lincoln Fellow in the sixth form is an Oxbridge graduate with a brief to dispel myths about the application process and help pupils with UCAS generally.

Money matters: Tuition is free; fees are payable for boarding provision only. Fees compare favourably with the cost of a local day independent schools. Day boarding and enhanced day boarding, for relatively modest fees, are popular option (they include meals and various after-school activities) but there are no flexible boarding arrangements.

At least one sixth form boarding scholarship a year, worth 100 per cent of fees, for a student with exceptional academic, music or sporting potential.

Remarks: Has a well deserved reputation locally, and increasingly nationally as a leading state boarding school. It is a bargain for parents who want a boarding education for their children, but without the associations of privilege or having to fork out fortunes in school fees. It is a big school and hard-working, socially outgoing types do best.

Why choose boarding for the SEN child?

A perhaps surprising number of pupils with SEN will board for at least some of their schooldays. For those with very complex or profound difficulties who require intensive support, residential care can be the best way of providing this. For other families, it's down to logistics. If the perfect specialist education is on one side of the country and work or other family commitments on the other, boarding is often the only realistic solution. But boarding can also be an important, and valuable, part of the therapeutic process for children whose needs go beyond classroom support.

From making friends to changing duvet covers, planning and cooking meals to operating a washing machine, boarding can be an invaluable way for pupils learn the social and organisational skills that will one day allow them to lead independent lives. It's the reason that many schools encourage pupils, even those living very close to a school, to start spending nights away. Surrounded by people who know how they tick, when to step in – and when to step back – it can be a happy, confidence-inspiring experience for both parents and children.

What to look out for

Boarding for the first time can be unsettling for any child. For those with SEN, the uncertainties and worries are often magnified. Here are some questions parents could have in mind when looking round an SEN boarding school.

- How good is the school at working with parents to prepare children for this new experience? Are there online or visual guides that show clearly how it works and what pupils are expected to do? What personal possessions are they able to take (pictures, duvet covers, even pets) so their room becomes their own?
- Does the school's approach get the official stamp of approval? Ofsted carries out separate accommodation

inspections. What is the school's rating? (They can drop or rise rapidly)

- How is unstructured free time after school and at weekends organised? It may be the highlight of the week for most boarders, but unsettling to those with social or communication difficulties – so is someone there to help pupils plan their time? Is there a quiet place they can retreat to if they need time out?
- An action-packed programme for boarders can sound amazing, but does it include activities your child enjoys, and are staff on hand to encourage (and keep on encouraging) pupils to try something new? If your child has a niche interest (wind turbines and George VI are two examples recently encountered) will the school be right behind them?
- How good are the staff – subject teachers, matrons, therapists – at talking to each other? If a child is sleeping badly, has lost a prized possession or had a meltdown in a lesson, will there be a bit of unobtrusive extra support to get them through a bad time?
- What's the boarding accommodation like? Slightly scruffy isn't necessarily an issue as long as it's clean, tidy, secure and well supervised and organised, with instructions and visual timetables to make the routine easy to understand.
- Bullying happens even in the best schools but children with SEN frequently won't report it, so how is it spotted and dealt with, particularly if it happens in free time?

And finally, do boarding staff 'get' your child, understand and empathise with their quirks? Does their experience extend to pupils with similar difficulties and how have they been supported?

Are they kind, empathetic and welcoming when you visit? If a boarding school makes parents feel at home, children, whatever their learning needs, are far more likely to feel the same way.

SEN boarding schools

These are shortened versions of some of our reviews. Full reviews of these and other schools can be found on our website: www.goodschoolsguide.co.uk

Appleford School, Wiltshire, SP3 4HL
www.appleford.wilts.sch.uk
126 boys and girls aged 7-18, day and boarding

Long-established all-through co-ed day and boarding school for dyslexic pupils set in lovely countryside near Stonehenge. First cohort took GCSEs in 2015, everyone achieving at least one pass (G or above) but an A* in there as well. Courses for school's new sixth form (currently all boys) include BTecs and life skills qualifications (AQA and Asdan) as well as GCSE retakes. Tiny classes, encouraging atmosphere (pupils choose colours and paint dorms) and host of learning support specialists achieve marvels of confidence building while dynamic head instils sense of corporate pride in accomplishments (teachers encouraged to wear academic gowns). Much endorsed by celebrities (Zoë Wanamaker is patron).

Breckenbrough School, North Yorkshire YO7 4EN
www.breckenbrough.org.uk
50 boys aged 9-19, day and boarding

UK's only Quaker residential special school, operating with often challenging pupils (all statemented and LEA funded) who have complex learning and emotional needs including ASD and ADHD. Need to be academically able though won't necessarily be reflected in previous academic results. Calm, peaceful environment often transformative, one boy, previously labeled 'unteachable' going on to gain pilot's licence. Boarding sensibly tailored to needs – the 20 boarders (full and weekly) can seek refuge in rooms before and after lessons, for example. Qualifications include GCSEs and A levels with maths and sciences a particular strength, as are fab activities, ranging from leadership to motorbike maintenance.

Bruern Abbey School, Oxfordshire, OX26 1UY
www.bruernabbey.org
110 boys aged 7-13, day and boarding

Top class senior school destinations reflect exceptionally hard work put in by staff (some with SpLD themselves) to give bright but often very dyslexic pupils skills they need to succeed in common entrance. Some have additional needs (Asperger's, ADHD) – quirkiness a common feature. All trad subjects covered though English and maths dominate curriculum, taking up half the timetable. Dorms are large, airy, clean and tidy but in need of smartening, though bathrooms are newly kitted out. Spare cash ploughed into teaching resources, though parents show appreciation for often stellar progress made by their sons with tireless fundraising.

Centre Academy East Anglia, Suffolk IP7 7QR
www.centreacademy.net
50 pupils aged 4-19, day and boarding

Homely buildings with attractive grounds including duck pond are home for country offshoot of popular special day school in Clapham. Good range of facilities (some courtesy of nearby sympathetic prep school) and some unusual (own fleet of fire engines, for example). Weekly and flexi boarding, juniors in main building, seniors in coach house. Cheerful rooms, boarders able to bring small pet and bike from home. Pupils, some LEA funded, have range of needs including dyslexia, ADD, dyspraxia and the milder autistic spectrum disorders, are taught in small classes selected by ability rather than age. Some return to mainstream schools, others complete US high school diploma which has proved successful springboard to university.

Frewen College, East Sussex, TN31 6NL
www.frewencollege.co.uk
100 pupils aged 7-18, day and boarding

Special school for dyslexic pupils (some with additional needs including Asperger's) with very small classes throughout, SEN-trained staff, well-planned teaching (classes include whole-school literacy session) and range of therapists (OT, sensory integration and psychotherapists among them). Flexible boarding, no extra charge for weekend stays, from age 9, girls and boys with separate quarters and common rooms but meeting for meals. Many of juniors go through to senior school though some take and pass competitive entrance exams to mainstream senior schools. Goal for seniors is at least five GCSEs, achieved by 50 per cent in 2015 with grades A*-G; a third gained at least five A*-C grades. Sixth form officially open to those achieving four GCSEs at C grade or better but open to discussion, with most BTecs and A levels provided through school's partnership with local colleges (Bexhill, Plumpton and Great Dixter Gardens).

Limpsfield Grange, Surrey, RH8 0RZ
www.limpsfield-grange.surrey.sch.uk
70 girls aged 11-16, day and boarding

Rarity in sea of boys' only or boy-dominated schools – a maintained special school for girls with communication

difficulties including ASD and Asperger's, some too
emotionally vulnerable to cope in mainstream education.
Boarding time includes life skills and independence training,
lessons also used to explore emotions, traditional elements
(desks in rows) combined with encouragement for girls
to find own ways to cope (one brings hot water bottle into
class). Lack of therapy only major downside. Dogs a soothing
presence (one hears readers). Most pupils will go on to take
up to eight GCSEs, less academic studying for vocational
qualifications. In 2015, 31 per cent of year 11 students
achieved at least one GCSE with grades A*-C; 94 per cent
with minimum of one GCSE at A*-G. All achieved entry level
certificates in maths.

Mark College, Somerset, TA9 4NP
www.priorygroup.com/markcollege
77 pupils aged 10 to 19, day and boarding

Engaging curriculum, individually tailored and effectively
delivered is hallmark of residential school (flexi, weekly and
full boarding) that supports pupils with specific learning
difficulties but also helps overcome behavioural issues that
can result from plummeting self-esteem after miserable
experiences in mainstream education. Dog-friendly school
in lovely (Georgian) building, founded in 1980s, now part of
Priory Group, nurtures and has extensive extracurricular
activities as well as high academic expectations. Pupils are
able to take up to eight GCSEs before moving into sixth form
in partnership with Strode and Weston Colleges, school
providing extra backup for pupils.

Mary Hare School, Berkshire, RG14 3BQ

www.maryhare.org.uk

240 pupils aged 11-19, day and boarding

School for the profoundly and severely hearing impaired which uses language acquisition to give best chance in later life – uses advanced amplification system, developed by on-site firm. Academically successful, with 61 per cent of GCSEs and BTecs at grades A*-C in 2015. A levels (20 subjects) and BTecs offered in sixth form (98 per cent A* to E grades in 2015, 73 per cent of grades A* to C). Huge grounds (150 acres) brilliant for mountain biking. Other sports – basketball and volleyball – also flourish, as does performing arts with plenty of soloists and groups, including school orchestra. Boarding (flexi, weekly, termly) praised for caring staff and well-implemented rewards and sanctions. Only niggle girls' accommodation – slightly less good than boys'. Sixth formers graduate to university-style accommodation.

Moon Hall School, Surrey, RH5 6LQ

www.moonhallschool.co.uk

46 pupils aged 7-12, day and boarding

Weekly and flexi-boarding for dyslexic pupils in Surrey in grounds of mainstream prep, allowing considerable sharing of resources, from uniforms to team sport. Run by highly regarded head, school is staffed by SpLD specialists with full quota of therapists and follows national curriculum, though with extra literacy and maths and no MFL. Meticulously planned multi-sensory teaching in small groups means engaged pupils – Sats results in year 6 often very impressive with many pupils moving to mainstream senior schools in year 7 and coping well there.

More House School (Farnham) Surrey, GU10 3AP
www.morehouseschool.co.uk
440 boys aged 8-18, day and boarding

Caring but no nonsense admissions process (SpLD must
be primary diagnosis, no to behavioural difficulties unless
secondary and definitely under control with medication)
ensures focus on what school does best – supporting able
boys whose dyslexia has held them back. Far-flung families
make boarding a necessity. Most flexi, minority full, some
reluctant. School does its best – a tad more cosiness would
make it even better. Education starts with confidence
building – erratic spelling no bar to success. Support –
extensive – is timetabled. Though results can fluctuate wildly,
2015 was bumper year, with 82 per cent of GCSEs graded A*-C
and IGCSE and 41 per cent of A levels at A*-B.

Northease Manor School, East Sussex, BN7 3EY
www.northease.co.uk
90 pupils aged 10-17, day and boarding

Attractive school in picturesque courtyard setting with
cosy boarding (flexi and weekly). Girls' rooms in particular
impressively decorated, staff happy to dispense 2am
reassurance if homesickness kicks in. Small classes and
enthusiastic staff, many home grown (school runs own
training courses) contribute to academic results. A quarter
gained at least five A*-C GCSEs including maths and English
in 2015, several subjects beating national averages –
impressive for SpLD pupils who, though all of at least average
ability, find learning a challenge. No plans for sixth form
though works closely with local sixth form colleges Sussex
Downs, Varndean, Ringmer, Plumpton, in some cases pushing
to get pupils on desired courses.

Nunnykirk Centre for Dyslexia, Northumberland NE61 4PB

www.nunnykirk.co.uk
26 pupils aged 9-18, eight weekly boarders

Small, successful dyslexia specialist school in rural location (red squirrel territory) with pupils both LEA and privately funded. Much support provided in classes of eight max, one-to-one help if necessary. Follows national curriculum with all pupils sitting GCSEs – entry level qualifications also offered – and school scoring in top five per cent for value added. Plenty of vigorous activities (fishing and swimming in river). Flexible range of A levels include art and photography. Academic rigour is de rigueur – two former pupils recently received first class honours degrees at good universities. Weekly boarders from wide area (Birmingham to Edinburgh) have rooms (two beds maximum) in warren upstairs, unfussed by well-worn accommodation. High supervision levels, evenings busy and day pupils welcome to stay on for activities.

Oversands School, Cumbria LA11 6SD

www.witherslackgroup.co.uk
47 boys (though co-ed since 2013) aged 8-19, day and boarding

Pupils are all LEA referred, some with very complex needs which range from ASD to emotional and social difficulties. Admitted if school in ultra-out of town setting (mains water only since 2007) feels can make a difference. School radiates stability with plenty of encouragement to try new things. Tailored therapeutic support within what school describes as '24-hour curriculum' that extends from GCSE options (currently 12 subjects with half of pupils gaining at least five or more GCSEs in 2015) to practical lessons in independent living, older pupils learning to manage for themselves in cottages in the woods. High standard of boarding accommodation, children, who normally go home every two weeks, choosing bedding from Argos catalogue so ready and waiting when they arrive.

Shapwick School, Somerset, TA7 9NJ
www.shapwickschool.com
155 pupils aged 8-19, 90 boarders

Located in beautiful Tudor manor close to sleepy village and a sanctuary for dyslexic pupils, (who need to be of at least average ability) with small classes, tailored curriculum and staff who 'get' them. Children sit eight GCSEs, 38 per cent gaining at least five GCSEs from A*-C in 2015, down from last year, English the big area where children struggle. About two-thirds are full boarders, trad model with Saturday school and two formal exeats per term, also weekly and flex boarders, all from year 6. Boarding recently criticised by Ofsted but since improved and, while adequate rather than luxurious, praised by parents for caring staff.

Slindon College, West Sussex, BN18 0RH
www.slindoncollege.co.uk
85 boys aged 8-18, 38 boarders

Touch of the Hogwarts popular, as are views of Isle of Wight on good day, but it's happy blend of robust but caring staff that really counts. Staff receive extra training to support increasing numbers of boys with ASD (also ADHD though not behavioural problems). Small classes (12 max) allow differentiated teaching plus plenty of one-to-one where needed. Goal for most is GCSEs with core subjects (English, maths, science, IT) taken – usually with at least some success – by all. In 2015, 50 per cent achieved five or more

A*-C grades, while at A level/BTec, 72 per cent of grades at A-C grade, 100 per cent A to E. Vocational courses include horticulture with 'farm tech' the latest innovation (there are on-site donkeys, alpacas, pigs and chickens). Boarding scruffy in places but being refurbished – appealing family room for staff and pupils does wonders for building social skills with board games, conversation and lively table football sessions – cash prizes funded by tuck shop takings.

Swalcliffe Park, Oxfordshire, OX15 5EP
www.swalcliffepark.oxon.sch.uk
47 boys aged 11-19, 36 boarders

Special and outstanding school in tucked away tranquil setting complete with Georgian mansion. Learning approach makes much use of 'The Four Whys' – communication, independence, self-management and achievement, to help convert troubled autistic boys into confident achievers (some excluded from previous schools). Good GCSEs no use to pupils unable to leave bedroom. Tiny class sizes with primary school environment for younger pupils – teachers come to them – pupils moving around for most lessons only in KS4. Six boarding houses, all deliberately similar, the focus for life skill acquisition and practice, from planning and shopping to cooking and clearing meals for mixed age boarding families, while individual bedrooms have en suite shower room and personal touches (including a gecko).

Sunnydown School, Surrey, CR3 5ED
www.sunnydown.surrey.sch.uk
80 boys aged 11-16, 40 weekly boarders

Supports severely dyslexic pupils, some with behavioural and communication difficulties, in small classes that combine discipline with attention-grabbing techniques including laughter and peer evaluation to banish fear of failure. Mainstream curriculum from year 7, good range of GCSEs as well as Entry Level Certificates – everyone leaves with a qualification – 25 per cent with five GCSEs at grades A*-C, including English and maths, in 2015. Big emphasis on sport, basketball particularly popular, with many other activities suggested by the pupils. Boarding rates Ofsted outstanding (as does rest of school) and pupils 'delight in it'. Two areas, juniors in main building, and notable for levels of trust – mobile phones left around with impunity.

A word on child protection

Any parent preparing to entrust their child to a school –
whether day or boarding – will rightly expect that child's
safety and well-being to be a priority at all times. Such
expectations are nearly always fulfilled but in a sad minority
of cases that is not what happens.

We have all read news reports of bullying and abuse and
shuddered to imagine the horror felt by the children and
families involved. A flood of historical allegations against
schools and subsequent court cases, not to mention mobile
phones, flexi-boarding, more parental involvement and
heightened awareness have together helped usher in some
sunlight and fresh air.

Child protection policies, found on every school website,
now make explicit reference to the possibility of abuse at
schools – something rarely contemplated a generation ago.

Boarding schools in particular can be very closed worlds
but abuse can occur at any school, anywhere. Fame is no
protection, and nor is obscurity. Some kinds of school,
though, need to take particular care – and how they do
this should be obvious to you when you visit. International
schools have transient pupil populations, and teachers whose
histories may be overseas and hard to research. Specialist
music teaching necessarily involves a good deal of physical
contact with the teacher and the pupil alone in a closed
room. Religious schools may have a system of authority that
serves to keep abuse concealed. Special schools may have to
deal with a large range of communication and emotional
difficulties.

What can you do?
Parents should talk to their children – gently but seriously –
about the dangers, however remote these may be. It is worth
pointing out that abuse can come from anyone – including
a teacher or an adult they know well, or from another child

at the school. Having this discussion will make it easier for a child to come to you with anything they're worried about.

When visiting a school, inquire about the steps taken to safeguard children in the same way you might ask about bullying or learning support. As always, much can be gleaned from the head's attitude when questions about child protection are asked. Is he or she ill at ease or happy to engage and proud of the steps their school has taken? Openness is what you're looking for.

You could also ask about how a child or parent would go about reporting an incident. Schools make this possible in a variety of ways; what matters is that passing on concerns is a routine thing (children and parents do it about lots of things all the time), and is welcomed by the school. Doing this should be low-stakes, in other words the person registering the concern knows that they are not putting their relationships within the school at risk, let alone threatening someone's place in the school. That may seem an odd thing to say, but if you fear to report, say, careless management of a museum trip because it could harm an otherwise much-loved teacher, you might choose to keep quiet. An environment that seems hostile to raising such concerns may mean you never pass on those troubling observations that may be the outward indication of serious problems. To be safe, schools need to hear the little voices, not just the shouting.

And finally, do not think less of a school because a case of abuse has been brought to light there. Tabloid coverage can be the price the school has to pay for handling a case of abuse or bullying openly. It is inevitable that abuse will occur somewhere. What matters is how well the school deals with it, how well it performs in bringing the abuse to light and how open it is on the subject with current and future parents.

You may also like to read....

The Good Schools Guide 20th edition
Features independent and unbiased views of over 1,200 state and independent schools throughout Britain, written by parents for parents.

The Good Schools Guide London North
We have plundered the knowledge and experience of our North London based writers and advisers to provide not just the opinionated and unbiased school reviews for which The Good Schools Guide is renowned, but also fascinating pen portraits of the capital's diverse areas. An invaluable guide for any family considering education in the capital.

The Good Schools Guide London South
Packed with local South London knowledge, candid reviews and parent comments, not to mention a full run-down of how the English education system works.

The Good Schools Guide online subscription
Read all our reviews plus exam data, catchment maps, university entrance information, and advice on choosing a school, tutors, SEN, talented children and much more.

Uni in the USA
Written by students who have been through the US system, features in-depth descriptions of 65 US universities, plus the inside track on getting in and preparing for life across the pond.

Uni in the USA and Beyond online subscription and ebook
Also includes unis in Europe and the East, from Alberta to Abu Dhabi, and advice from SATS to visas.

The Good Schools Guide International online subscription
The one-stop educational shop for ex-pats, it reviews the best state and independent schools round the globe, plus insider knowledge on life overseas.

All available via http://www.goodschoolsguide.co.uk/shop-online

Need more info?
Visit us online...

The Good Schools Guide website, now available on all digital devices. Access exam data, catchment area maps, special needs specifics and the latest news and opinion at home or on the go.

Visit www.goodschoolsguide.co.uk and try our interactive school search today

Boarding schools index

School	Region	Page

List of advertisers

House Ads